1987 CATHOLIC ALMANAC

Felician A. Foy, O.F.M.
EDITOR

Rose M. Avato
ASSOCIATE EDITOR

Our Sunday Visitor Publishing Division
Our Sunday Visitor, Inc.
HUNTINGTON • INDIANA

ACKNOWLEDGMENTS: NC News Service, for
coverage of news and documentary texts; *The
Documents of Vatican II,* ed. W. M. Abbott
(Herder and Herder, America Press: New York
1966), for quotations of Council documents;
Annuario Pontificio (1986); *Statistical Yearbook
of the Church* (1983); *The Official Catholic
Directory* (P. J. Kenedy & Sons, 1986); *The Papal
Encyclicals,* 5 vols., ed. C. Carlen (McGrath
Publishing: Wilmington, NC 1981); The United
States Catholic Mission Assoc. (1233 Lawrence
St. N.E., Washington, D.C. 20017), for U.S.
foreign-mission compilations and statistics;
Catholic Press Directory (1986); *Annuaire/Directory
1986* (copyright© Concacan Inc., 1986; reproduced
with permission of the Canadian Conference
of Catholic Bishops) for Canadian Catholic
statistics; Rev. Thomas J. Reese, S.J., associate
editor of *America,* for names of dioceses for
which U.S. bishops were ordained; other
sources as credited in particular entries.

1987 Catholic Almanac

Copyright © Our Sunday Visitor Publishing Division,
Our Sunday Visitor, Inc., 1986
Published annually, with ecclesiastical
permission, by Our Sunday Visitor Publishing Division,
Our Sunday Visitor, Inc.,
200 Noll Plaza, Huntington, Indiana 46750.
Address inquiries to the Publisher.

ISBN 0-87973-257-1
Library of Congress Catalog Card No. 73-641001
International Standard Serial Number (ISSN) 0069-1208

TABLE OF CONTENTS

Index 4-31
Special Reports 32-60
  Pope John Paul in India 32-35
  Pope John Paul's Visit to Colombia
    and Saint Lucia 35-37
  Pope John Paul at the
    Synagogue of Rome 37-39
  The Holy Spirit in the Church and the
    World: Encyclical Letter 39-43
  Synod of Bishops: Extraordinary
    Assembly, 1985 43-45
  Abortion-Related Court Decisions ... 45-47
  The Curran Controversy 47-51
  Life and Death Questions 51-53
  The Nuclear Crisis and a Just Peace:
    A Methodist Pastoral Letter 53-54
  Sects: Vatican Report 54-56
  Liberation Theology II: Christian
    Freedom and Liberation 56-60
News Events
  (October 1985 to September 1986) ... 61-106
Pope John Paul II 107-09
Dates, Events in Church History 110-20
Ecumenical Councils 120-22
Popes 123-33
  Popes of the 20th Century 128-33
Canonizations 133-35
Encyclicals 135-40
Hierarchy of the Catholic Church 141-44
  Synod of Bishops 143-44
Roman Curia 144-51
Cardinals 151-67
Representatives of the Holy See 167-70
Diplomats at the Vatican 170-71
  U.S.-Vatican Relations 171-72
Vatican City 173-75
Doctrine of the Catholic Church 176-204
  Constitution on the Church 176-79
  The Pope, Teaching Authority,
    Collegiality 179-80
  Constitution on Revelation 180-83
  The Bible 183-93
  Apostles and Evangelists 193-95
  Fathers and Doctors 195-97
  Social Doctrine 199-204
The Challenge of Peace 204-06
Liturgy 207-20
  The Mass 210-13
  Liturgical Developments 215-20
Sacraments 221-35
  Permanent Diaconate 228
  Marriage Doctrine 229-32
Church Calendar 236-48
Saints 248-58
The Mother of Jesus 258-61
Apparitions of Mary 262
Eastern Catholic Churches 263-70
Separated Eastern Churches 271-72
Eastern Ecumenism 272
Protestant Churches 273-78
Ecumenism 278-90
  Ecumenical Dialogues 281-87

Ecumenical Reports 287-90
Judaism 290-91
Catholic-Jewish Relations 291-93
Islam 293-94
Non-Abrahamic Religions 294
Glossary 295-331
The Church in Countries 332-65
Catholic World Statistics 365-66
The Church in Troubled Areas 366
Episcopal Conferences 367-69
International Catholic Organizations .. 370-72
The Catholic Church in Canada 373-83
Missionaries to the Americas 384-86
History, Chronology of
  the Church in the U.S. 387-405
Church-State Supreme Court
  Decisions 405-10
U.S. Hierarchy, Jurisdictions 410-20
Catholic Population of U.S.,
  Other Statistics 421-30
Cathedrals, Minor Basilicas,
  Chancery Offices 430-35
National Conference of Catholic
  Bishops, U.S. Catholic Conference .. 435-38
State Catholic Conferences 438-39
Biographies of American Bishops 439-64
American Bishops of the Past 465-80
Black Catholics 480-81
Hispanics 481-82
Religious, Men and Women 483-510
Organizations of Religious 510-11
Secular Institutes 511-13
Secular Orders 514
Missionary Activity of the Church 514-18
Catholic Education, U.S. 518-31
  Statistics 519-23
  Colleges and Universities 524-28
  Diocesan and Interdiocesan
    Seminaries 529-31
Pontifical Universities, Institutes 531-34
Pontifical Academy of Sciences 534-35
Social Services 535-52
  Facilities for Retired and Aged 536-44
  Facilities for Handicapped 545-50
Retreats, Renewal Programs 552-58
Lay Persons and Their Apostolate 559-70
  Special Apostolates 560-63
  Associations, Movements,
    Societies 563-70
Communications 571-92
  Catholic Periodicals in U.S. 571-81
  Foreign Catholic Periodicals 581-82
  Catholic Writers' Market 582-85
  Radio, Television, Theatre 586-87
  Communications Offices 587-91
  Publishers 591-92
Shrines and Places of
  Historical Interest 592-95
Honors and Awards 595-99
  American Catholic Awards 596-99
Deaths 599-600

A

Abbacies, 142
  World Statistics, 365
Abbacy, 295
Abbess, 295
Abbey (Monastery), 318
Abbot, 295
Abelard, Peter (1140), 114
Abington v. Schempp (Prayer in Public Schools), 407
Abjuration, 295
Ablution, 295
Abortion (Moral Principles), 295
  Church Teaching and Dissent, 63, 82
Abortion, Death Sentence of, 73
  Demographic Suicide, 61
  Italy, 64, 76, 104
  Singapore, 79
  Spain, 68
  Third World, 80
Abortion, U.S., Developments, 45-7, 62, 63, 66, 70, 71, 75, 82, 87, 94, 95, 102
  Ad Signers, 63, 82
  Clinic Bombings, 71
  Court Rulings, 62, 70, 87
  Hyde Amendment, 46
  March for Life, 75
  Statistics, 46-7
  Supreme Court Decisions, 45-7, 87
Abramowicz, Alfred L., Bp., 439
Absolution, 225, 295
  See also Penance (Penitential Celebrations).
Absolution, General, 225-26
Absolution, General (Blessing), 295
Abstinence, Days of, 237
Acacius, Patriarch (484), 111
Academy of American Franciscan History, 563
Acadians, **see** Canada, Church in
Accessory to Sin, 295
Accommodated Senses (Bible), 192
Acerra, Angelo Thomas, O.S.B., Bp., 439
Achille Lauro Hijacking, 62
Ackerman, Richard, C.S.Sp., Bp., 439
Acolyte, 227
Act of Supremacy (1533), 115
Acta Apostolicae Sedis, 174
Acta Sanctae Sedis, 174
Actors' Guild, Catholic, 587
Acts of the Apostles, 190
Actual Grace, 311
Actual Sin, 327
Ad Gentes (Mission Decree), 122
Ad Limina Visit, 142
Addresses of John Paul II, **see** John Paul II
Adjutor, St., 248
Adoptionism, 119
Adoration, 295
Adorno Fathers (Clerics Regular Minor), 485
Adultery, 295
Advent, 236
Advent, First Sunday, Dates (1987-2010), 244
Advent Wreath, 296
Adventists, 295-96
Afghanistan, 332
Africa
  American Missionary Bishops, 420
  Cardinals, 166
  Catholic Statistics, 365-66
  Eastern Rite Jurisdictions, 267
  Episcopal Conferences, 369
  Plea for Children, 89
  Polygamous Families, 91-2
Africa, Missionaries of, 483
Africa, Missionary Sisters of Our Lady, 493
African Missions, Society of, 483

Agape, 296
Agatha, St., 248
Agca, Mehmet Ali, 109
Age of Reason, 296
Aged, Eucharistic Fast, 309
Aged, Facilities for (U.S.), 536-44
  World, 365
Aggiornamento, 296
Agnes, St., 248
  Feast Day Presentation, 74
Agnes, Sisters of St., 493
Agnosticism, 296
Agnus Dei, 296
Agrimissio, 386
Aguilar v. Felton (Remedial Classes Decision), 87, 94, 409
Ahern, Patrick V., Bp., 439
Ahr, George William, Bp., 439
Aid to Churches in Distress, 92
AIDS, Care for Victims, 62, 71, 79, 98
Alabama, 390, 423, 426, 428, 521, 536, 546, 549, 553, 587, 592
Alaska, 390, 425, 427, 429, 523, 553, 587
Alb, 212
Albania, 332
  Persecution in, 85
Albanian Byzantines, 265
Albanian Catholic Information Center, 563
Albert the Great, St., 195
Albigensianism, 120
Alcoholics, Social Services, 551
Alcoholism, National Catholic Clergy Conference, 568
Alexandrian Rite, 264
Alexian Brothers, 490
Alfrink, Bernard Jan, Card., 152, 165, 166
Algeria, 332
Alhambra, Order of, 568
Aliens, Undocumented (Illegal), **see** Sanctuary Movement
All Saints, 245
All Souls, 245
Alleluia, 296
Allocution, 296
Allouez, Claude, 384
Alms, 296
Alonso, Rodriguez, Bl., 385
Aloysius Gonzaga, St., 248
Alpha and Omega, 296
Alpha Sigma Nu, 563
Alphonsa, Sister, Beatificaton, 34
Alphonsus Liguori, St., 195
Altar, 213, 214
  Dedication, New Rites, 218
  Relics, 212
Altar Cloth, 213
Altham, John, 384
Amand, St., 248
Ambo (Pulpit), 214
Ambrose, St., 195
Ambrosian Rite (Rites), 209
Ambrozic, Aloysius, Bp., 378
Ambry, 214
Amen, 296
America, **see** United States
American Benedictine Academy, 563
  Catholic Correctional Chaplains Association, 563
  Catholic Historical Association, 563
  Catholic Philosophical Association, 563
  Committee on Italian Migration, 564
  Friends of the Vatican Library, 564
American College, Louvain, 72, 122
American Heresy, 388-89
American Lutheran Church, **see** Lutheran Churches
Amice, 212
Amos, 189
Anabaptism, 273

Anagni, Italy, Papal Visit, 101
Analogy of Faith, 182
Anaphora (Canons, Eucharistic Prayers), 299
Anathema, 296
Anchieta, Jose de, Bl., 384
Anchorite, 296
Ancient Order of Hibernians in America, 564
Anderson, Moses B., S.S.E., Bp., 439
Anderson, Paul F., Bp., 439
Andorra, 332
Andre Bessette, Bl., 248
  St. Joseph's Oratory, 372
Andre Grasset, Bl., 248
Andreis, Felix, 384
"Andres Bello" Catholic Univ. (Venezuela), 532
Andrew, St. (Apostle), 193
Andrew Corsini, St., 248
Andrew Fournet, St., 248
Andrew Kim, Paul Chong and Companions, Sts., 248
Angela Merici, St., 249
Angelic Salutation (Hail Mary), 311
Angelica, Mother, 586
Angelico, Fra (Bl. Angelico), 249
Angelicum, 533
Angell, Kenneth A., Bp., 439
Angels, 296
  Existence and Role (John Paul II), 97
Angels, Guardian, 246
Angelus, 296-97
Anger, 297
Anglican Communion, 274
  Ecumenical Reports, 288, 289
  Ordination of Women, 68, 100
  See also Episcopal Church, U.S.
Anglican Orders, 297
Anglican-Roman Catholic Consultation U.S. (Episcopal), Dialogues, Statements, 282-83
Anglican-Roman Catholic International Commission, 289
Angola, 332, 367
Anguilla, 332
Ann (Anne), St., 247
Ann, Sisters of St., 493
Anne, Sisters of St., 493
Anne de Beaupre, St., Shrine, 372
Anne Mary Javouhey, Bl., 249
Annuario Pontificio, 174
Annulment, 233-34, 235
Annunciation, 245
Anointing of the Sick, 221, 226
Anselm, St., 195
  Pontifical Athenaeum, 533
Ansgar, St., 249
Ansgar's Scandinavian Catholic League, St., 569
Anthony, St. (Abbot), 249
Anthony, St. (of Padua), 195
Anthony, St., Missionary Servants of, 493
Anthony Daniel, St., 384
Anthony House, 551
Anthony Mary Claret, St., 249
Anthony Mary Zaccaria, St., 249
Anti-Catholic Booklets, 86
Anti-Defamation League Award, 66
Antichrist, 297
Anticlericalism (Clericalism), 302
Antigua, 332
Antilles, Episcopal Conference, 367
Antilles, Netherlands, 352
Antimension, 270
Antiochene Rite, 264-65
  in United States, 268
Antiphon, 297
Antipopes, 126-27
Anti-Semitism, 291
Anti-Semitism of Louis Farrakhan, 63

4

Antonelli, Ferdinando G., O.F.M., Card., 152, 165, 166
Antonianum, Pontifical Athenaeum, 533
Aparicio, Sebastian, Bl., 384
Apartheid (South Africa), 68, 76, 81
  Mass for Victims, 76
  Pastoral Letter on, 68
  See also South Africa
Apocalyptic Book, New Testament (Revelation), 191
Apocrypha, 185
Apollonia, St., 249
Apologetics, 297
Aponte Martinez, Luis, Card., 152, 165, 166
Apostasy (Apostate), 297
Apostles, 193-94
Apostles' Creed, 197
Apostleship of Prayer, 564
  Prayer Intentions (1987), 238-43
Apostleship of the Sea, 560
Apostolate, 297
  See also Laity; Lay Apostolate
Apostolate, Sisters Auxiliaries of the, 493
  Society of the Catholic, see Pallottines
Apostolate for Family Consecration, 564
Apostolates, Special, 560-62
Apostolic
  Administrator, 142
  Chamber, 149
  Constitution, 303
  Delegates, 167, 168-70
  Fathers, 195
  Nuncios, Pro-Nuncios, 167, 168-70
  Penitentiary, 147
  Signatura, 147
Apostolic Life, Societies, 483
Apostolic See (Holy See), 311
Apostolic Succession, 297
Apostolicae Curae, see Anglican Orders
Apostolicam Actuositatem (Lay Apostolate Decree), 122
Apostolos, 269
Appalachia, Catholic Committee, 518
Apparitions of the BVM, 262
  Yugoslavia, 127
Apuron, Anthony Sablan, O.F.M. Cap., Abp., 94, 439-40
Aquinas, Thomas, St., see Thomas Aquinas, St.
Aquinas Medal, 596
Aquino, Corazon, Pres. (Philippines), 80
Arab Countries, Episcopal Conference, 367
Arabian Peninsula, 332
Arabic and Islamic Studies, Pontifical Institute, 534
Aramburu, Juan Carlos, Card., 152, 165, 166
Archangel, 297-98
Archangels (Michael, Gabriel, Raphael), Feast, 247
Archbishop, 298
  ad Personam, 142
  Titular, 142
Archbishops, 142
  Canada, 374
  United States, 412-20
  World Statistics, 365
Archconfraternity of Christian Mothers, 564
  Holy Ghost, 564
  Our Lady of Perpetual Help, 564
Archdiocese, 298
Archdioceses
  Canada, 374
  United States, 412-20
  World Statistics, 365
Arche (L') Communities, 370
Archeology, Pontifical Commission, 149
  Pontifical Institute, 533

Archimandrite, 295
Architecture, see Church Building
Archives, 298
Archives, Ecclesiastical, Italy, Commission, 149
Archives, Vatican II, 150
Archivists, Association of Catholic Diocesan, 564
Archpriest, 298
Argentina, 333, 367
Arianism, 119
Arias, David, O.A.R., Bp., 440
Arinze, Francis A., Card., 152, 166
Arizona, 390, 424, 427, 429, 438, 522, 536, 553, 587, 592
  Sanctuary Workers, 66-7
Ark of the Covenant, 298
Arkansas, 390-91, 424, 427, 429, 522, 536, 553, 587
Arkfeld, Leo, S.V.D., Abp., 440
Arliss, Reginald, C.P., Bp., 440
Armenian Rite, 265
  in United States, 268
Arminianism, 273
Arms Race, 204, 205
  See also Methodist Pastoral Letter; Nuclear Weapons
Arns, Paulo E., O.F.M., Card., 152, 165, 166
Art, Byzantine, 269
Art, Liturgical (Sacred), 209
Arzube, Juan A., Bp., 440
Ascension (May 28, 1987), 240, 245
  Dates (1987-2010), 244
Asceticism, 298
Ash Wednesday (Mar. 4, 1987), 239, 245
  Dates (1987-2010), 244
Ashes, 298
Asia
  American Missionary Bishops, 420
  Cardinals, 166
  Catholic Statistics, 365-66
  Christian Conference of, 71
  Eastern Rite Jurisdictions, 266-67
  Federation of Bishops' Conferences (FABC), 369
  Meeting of Religious Women, 68
Asmara University (Ethiopia), 532
Aspergillum, 298
Aspersory, 298
Aspiration, 298
Assisi, Interfaith Day of Prayer for Peace, 73, 80, 85
Associates of Ven. Maria Teresa of Savoy, 89
Association
  for Religious and Value Issues in Counseling, 564
  for Social Economics, 564
  of Catholic Diocesan Archivists, 564
  of Catholic Trade Unionists, 564
  of Contemplative Sisters, 511
  of Marian Helpers, 564
  of Permanent Diaconate Directors, 228
  of Romanian Catholics, 564
Associations, Catholic, U.S., 563-70
Assumption, 245
  John Paul II on, 101
Assumption, Augustinians of, 483
  Little Sisters of, 493
  of Blessed Virgin, Sisters of, 493
  Religious of, 493
Assumptionists, 483
Asteriskos, 270
Athanasian Creed, 198
Athanasius, St., 195
Atheism, 298
  See also Non-Believers, Secretariat
Atonement, 298
Atonement, Day of (Yom Kippur), 291
Atonement, Franciscan Friars of, 483
Attila (452), 111
Attributes of God, 298
Attrition, see Contrition
Audet, Lionel, Bp., 378

Audet, Rene, Bp., 378
Audiences, Papal, 174
  See also John Paul II
Augsburg, Peace of (1555), 115
Augsburg Confession (1530), 115
Augustine, Order of St., 483
Augustine, Third Order of St., 514
Augustine of Canterbury, St., 249
Augustine of Hippo, St., 195
  Anniversary of Conversion, 87
  Apostolic Letter, 102
Augustinian Cloistered Nuns, 493
Augustinian Recollects, 483
Augustinian Sisters, Servants of Jesus and Mary, 493
Augustinian Volunteers, 560
Augustinians, 483
Auschwitz, Carmelite Convent, 76
Australia, 333, 367
  Land Rights of Aborigines, 72
Austria, 333, 367
Authority
  Encyclicals, 135
  of Councils, 120
  Papal, 179-80
Authority, Teaching, of Church (Magisterium), 179-80, 181
  Curran Controversy, 47-51
Autograph Letter (Chirograph), 302
Auxiliaries of Our Lady of the Cenacle, 560
Auxiliary (Titular) Bishop, 142
Avarice, 298
Ave Maria (Hail Mary), 311
Avignon Residency of Papacy, 127
Awards, Catholic, 597-99
Azores, 333
  Diocesan Anniversary, 68

B

Badin, Stephen, 384
Baby Doe Legislation, 94
Bafile, Corrado, Card., 152, 162
Baggio, Sebastiano, Card., 152, 165, 166
Bahamas, 333
Bahrain, 333
Baldachino, 298
Balduino, Tomas, Bp., 68
Balearic Islands, 333
Balke, Victor, Bp., 440
Ballestrero, Anastasio Alberto, O.C.D., Card., 152-53, 165, 166
Baltakis, Paul Antanas, O.F.M., Bp., 440
Baltimore, Plenary Councils, 388
Bangladesh, 333, 367
Banks, Robert J., Bp., 440
Banneaux, 262
Baptism, 221, 222-23
  Rite of Initiation of Adults, 217, 222-23
Baptism of the Lord, Feast (Jan. 11, 1987), 238, 245
Baptisms, Catholic, U.S., 427-29
  World, 365
  See also Individual Countries
Baptistery, 214
Baptists, 274
  Churches, U.S., 274
  Ecumenical Dialogues, 281-82
  International Catholic-Baptist Colloquium, 289
Baraga, Frederic, 384
Barbados, 333
Barbuda, 333
Barnabas, St., 193
Barnabites, 483
Barrera Case, see Wheeler v. Barrera
Bartholomew, St., 193
Baruch, 188
Basel, Council of (1431-1449), 115
Basic Communities, 57
Basil, St., Congregation of Priests, 483-84
Basil the Great, St., 195-96
Basil the Great, St., Order, 483

Basil the Great, Srs. of the Order of St., 493
Basilian Fathers, 483-84
Basilian Order of St. Josaphat, 483
Basilian Salvatorian Fathers, 484
Basilica, 432
  St. John Lateran, 173, 245
  St. Mary Major, 246
  St. Mary of the Angels, Assisi, 72
  St. Peter. 173
Basilicas, Minor, U.S. and Canada, 432-33
Baudoux, Maurice, Abp., 378
Baum, William W., Card., 43, 153, 165, 166, 167
Bayside Shrine, N.Y., Warning, 70
Beahen, John, Bp., 378
Beatific Vision, 298
Beatification, 298
Beatifications (1985), 61, 65
Beatifications (1986), 34
Beatitude, 299
Beauraing, 262
Bede the Venerable, St., 196
Begley, Michael J., Bp., 440
Belgium, 333-34, 367
Belief, Catholic, see Doctrine, Catholic
Belisle, Gilles, Bp., 378
Belize, 334
Bellarmine, Robert, St., 197
Bellarmine Medal, 596
Beltran, Eusebius J., Bp., 440
Benedict, St. (of Nursia), 249
Benedict, St., Order of, 484
Benedict, St., Sisters of Order of, 493
Benedict XIV, Pope, Encyclicals, 135
Benedict XV, Pope, 129
  Canonizations, 133
  Encyclicals, 138
Benedict the Black (il Moro), St., 249
Benedictine Congregation of Solesmes, 493
Benedictine Monks, 484
Benedictine Nuns of Primitive Observance. 493
Benedictine Sisters, 493-94
Benedictines, Olivetan, 484
Benedictines, Sylvestrine, 484
Benediction of Blessed Sacrament, 308
Benedictus, 299
Benemerenti Medal, 596
Benin, 334, 367
Benincasa, Pius A., Bp. (Death), 599
Benjamin, Raymond, Bp., 72
Berakah Award, 596
Beran, Josef, Abp., see Czechoslovakia
Beras Rojas, Octavio, Card., 153, 165, 166
Berengarian Heresy, 119
Berlin Wall Anniversary, 101
Bermuda, 334
Bernadette Soubirous, St., 249
  Lourdes Apparitions, 262
Bernard of Clairvaux, St., 196
Bernard of Montjoux (or Menthon), St., 249
Bernardin, Joseph L., Card., 63, 66, 86, 99, 153, 165, 166, 167
Bernardine of Feltre, Bl., 249
Bernardine of Siena, St., 249
Bernardine Sisters, 499
Bernarding, George, S.V.D., Abp., 440
Bertoli, Paolo, Card., 153, 165, 166
Bertran, Louis, St., 384
Betancur, Pedro de San Jose, Bl., 384
Bessette, Andre, Bl., 248, 372
Bethany, Brothers of, 490
Bethany, Sisters of, 494
Bethlehem Missionaries, Society of, 484
Bethlemita Sisters, 494
Better World Movement, 562
Bevilacqua, Anthony J., Bp., 78, 440
Bhutan, 334

Bible, 183-93
  Canons, 183-84
  Federation, 185
  First Printed (c. 1456), 115
  Inerrancy, 182
  Interpretation, 181-82, 191-93
  Pontifical Commission, 150-51
  Studies, 183, 192-93
  Vatican II Constitution, 180-83
  See also Tradition
Bible, Mary in, 258
Bible Reading in Public Schools, see Church-State Decisions
Biblical Apostolate, World Federation, 185, 189
Biblical Commission, Pontifical, 150-51
Biblical Institute, Pontifical, 533
Biblical Studies, 183, 192-93
  Warning Against Fundamentalism, 189
Biffi, Giacomo, Card., 153, 166
Biglietto, 299
Bilock, John M., Bp., 440
Bination, 212, 216-17
Bioethics, and Patient Care (John Paul II), 101
Book, England, Imprimatur Removed, 103-04
  Life and Death Questions, 51-3
Biographies
  Apostles, Evangelists, 193-94
  Bishops (Canadian), 378-83
  Bishops (U.S.), 439-64
  Bishops (U.S.), of Past, 465-80
  Cardinals, 152-65
  Fathers and Doctors, Church, 195-97
  John Paul II, 107-09
    See also John Paul II
  Missionaries to the Americas, 384-86
  Popes, Twentieth Century, 128-33
  Saints, 248-54
Biretta, 299
Birth Control, Catholic Teaching (Humanae Vitae), 230-31
  John Paul II on, 231-32
  See also Contraception
Birth Control Clinics in Schools, 99
Birthright, 429
Bishops, 142, 226-27
  and Ecumenical Councils, 120
  Collegiality, 180, 302-03
  Conferences, 367-69
  Congregation, 146
  First, see Apostles
  Nomination, 142
  Statistics, World, 365
  Synod, 43-5, 143-44
  See also Synod of Bishops
  Titular, 142
Bishops, Canadian, 374-75, 378-83
  Conference, 378
Bishops, U.S., 412-20, 439-64, 465-80
  Black, 480-81
  Blood Brothers, 464
  "The Challenge of Peace: God's Promise and Our Response," 204-06
  Collegeville Meeting, 438
  Committees, 435-36
  Conferences, 435-38
  Conferences, Court Case, 82, 90
  Critique of Uniform Rights of Terminally Ill Act (Life and Death Questions), 51-3
  Economy Letter, Third Draft, 206, 437
  Ecumenical Affairs Committee, 280
  Guidelines for Legislation for Life-Sustaining Treatment (Life and Death Questions), 51-3
  Hispanic, 481
  Meeting (1985), 67, 437-38
  of the Past, 465-80
  Opposition to Contra Aid, 95, 102
  Report on CRS, 437
  Retired. 464-65

Bishops
  Secretariat, Catholic-Jewish Relations, 291-92
  Serving Overseas. 420-21. 464
  War and Peace Pastoral, 204-06
Black Catholics, U.S., 480-81
  National Office for, 480
  Sisters Conference, 511
  Statistics, 480
  Unity Needed, 78-9
Black Death (1347-1350), 114
Black History Month, 78
Blais, Leo, Bp., 378-79
Blanchet, Bertrand, Bp., 379
Blase, St., 249
Blasphemy, 299
Blasphemy of the Spirit, 42, 299
  See also Holy Spirit in the Church and World (Encyclical Letter)
Blessed Sacrament, see Eucharist, Holy
Blessed Sacrament, Exposition, 220, 308
Blessed Sacrament (Religious)
  and Our Lady, Religious of the Order of, 509
  Congregation of, 484
  Missionary Sisters of Most, 508
  Nuns of Perpetual Adoration, 508
  Oblate Sisters of, 508
  Religious Sisters of, 508
  Servants of, 508
  Srs. of, for Indians and Colored People, 508-09
  Srs. of Incarnate Word, 503
  Srs. Servants of, 509
Blessed Virgin Mary, 258-61
  Annunciation, 245
  Apparitions, 262
  Assumption, 245
  Birth, 245
  First Saturday Devotion, 309
  Immaculate Conception, 246
  Immaculate Heart, 247
  Joys (Franciscan Crown), 309
  Purification (Presentation of the Lord), 247
  Queenship, 247-48
  Rosary (Devotion), 324
  Rosary (Feast), 247
  Solemnity, 248
  Sorrows (Feast), 247
  Visitation, 247
  See also Mary
Blessed Virgin Mary (Religious)
  Institute of, 494
  Sisters of Charity, 496
  Sisters of Presentation of, 508
Blessing, 299
Blind, Catholic Facilities, Organizations, 549, 550
Blind, International Federation for Catholic Associations, 371
Blue Army, 564
  Shrine, 564
Boat, 299
Boccella, John H., T.O.R., Abp., 440
Boff, Leonardo, O.F.M., 82
Boland, Ernest B., O.P., Bp., 440
Bolivarian Pontifical University (Colombia), 531-32
Bolivia, 334, 367
Bollandists (1643), 116
Bon Secours, Sisters of, 494
Bonaventure, St., 196
Bonaventure, St., Pontifical Theological Faculty, 533
Boniface, St., 249
Book Clubs, Catholic, 581
Book of Common Prayer (1549), 115
Book of Kells, 112
Books, 581
  Awards (1986), 599
  Censorship, 301
  Index of Prohibited, 313
  Liturgical, see Lectionary; Sacramentary
Books of the Bible, 185-91

Booths, Festival, 290
Borders, William D., Abp., 440
Borecky, Isidore, Bp., 379
Borromeo, Charles, St., 249
Borromeo Award, 596
Bosco, Anthony G., Bp., 440
Bosco, John, St. (Don Bosco), 252
Bossilkoff, Eugene, Bp., **see** Bulgaria
Botswana, 334
Boudreaux, Warren L., Bp., 440-41
Bourgeoys, Marguerite, St., 384
Boy Scouts, 562
Boyle, Cornelia, O.S.B., Sr. (Death), 599
Boys Town (Nebraska), 546
Braga Rite, (Rites), 209
Brandao Vilela, Avelar, Card., 153, 165, 166
Brandsma, Titus, Beatification, 65
Brazil, 334-35, 367
 Bishops' Assembly, 88
 Land Reform, 96
 Papal Concerns, 81
 Sacraments Denied Officials, 92
Brebeuf, John de, St., 384
Breitenbeck, Joseph M., Bp., 441
Brendan, St., 249
Brennan, Francis (U.S. Cardinals), 167, 466
Brennan, Peter J. (Catholics in Presidents' Cabinets), 404
Brennan, William (Catholics in Supreme Court), 405
Brent Award, 596
Breviary, 208
Bridget (Birgitta), St. (of Sweden), 249
Bridget (Brigid), St. (of Ireland), 249
Brief, Apostolic, 299
Brigid, Congregation of St., 494
Brigittine Monks, 484
Brigittine Sisters, 494
British Honduras, **see** Belize
Brizgys, Vincas, Bp., 441
Broadcasting Union, European, 61
Broderick, Edwin B., Bp., 441
Brom, Robert H., Bp., 441
Brothers, 483
 Recruitment, 73
 World Statistics, 365
Brothers, U.S., 490-91
 National Assembly, 511
 Statistics, 421-25
Brown, Charles A., M.M., Bp., 441
Brunei, 335
Brunini, Joseph B., Bp., 441
Bruno, St., 249
Brust, Leo J., Bp., 441
Brzana, Stanislaus, Bp., 441
Buddhism, 294
Bueno y Monreal, Jose Maria, Card., 153, 165, 166
Bulgaria, 335, 367
Bulgarian Catholics (Byzantine Rite), 265
Bulgarians, Papal Plot Decision, 81
Bull, Bulla, Bullarium, 299
Bull of Demarcation (1493), 115
Bullock, William H., Bp., 441
Bureau of Catholic Indian Missions, 517-18
Burial, Ecclesiastical, 299
 See also Funeral Rites
Burke, Austin-Emile, Bp., 379
Burke, James C., O.P., Bp., 441
Burkina Faso (Upper Volta), 335, 367
Burma, 335, 367
Burse, 213
Burundi, 335, 367
 Harassment, Restriction of Church, 64, 71-2, 79
Buswell, Charles A., Bp., 441
Butler, Pierce (Catholics in Supreme Court), 405
Byelorussians, 265, 268
Byrne, James J., Abp., 441
Byzantine Rite (Catholic), 265-66
 in U.S., 267-68

Byzantine
 Liturgy, Calendar, Features, Vestments, 268-70

C

Cabrini, Mother (St. Frances Xavier Cabrini), 251
Cabrini Sisters, (Sacred Heart Missionary Sisters), 509
Caesar, Raymond R., S.V.D., Bp., 441
Cagney, James (Death), 599
Cajetan, St., 249
Calendar, Church, 236-44
 Byzantine, 268-69
 Gregorian (1582), 115
Califano, Joseph A. (Catholics in Presidents' Cabinets), 404
California, 391, 424-25, 427, 429, 438, 522-23, 529, 536, 545, 547, 553, 587-88, 592-93
 Burial of Fetuses, 62
 Excommunications, San Jose Diocese, 102
Calix Society, 564
Callistus I, St., 249
Calumny, 299
Calvary, 299
Calvin, John, 273
Camacho, Tomas Aguon, Bp., 441
Camaldolese Congregation, 484
Camaldolese Hermits, 484
Cambodia (Kampuchea), 335-36
Camerlengo, **see** Chamberlain
Cameroon, 336, 367
 Natural Gas Disaster, 101
Camillian Fathers and Brothers, 484
Camillus de Lellis, St., 249
Camp Fire, Inc., 562
Campaign for Human Development, 67, 272
Campbell, James (Catholics in Presidents' Cabinets), 404
Campinas, University of (Brazil), 531
Campion, Edmund, St., 250
Campion Award, 596
Campus Ministry, 529
Canada, 336, 373-83
 Abortion and Human Life, 63
 Basilicas, 432-33
 Bishops (Biographies,) 378-83
 Bishops' Conference, Statements, 378
 Catholic Publications, 383
 Eastern Rite Catholics, 377
 Shrines, 372
 Statistics, 336, 376-77, 378
 Support for Fur Trappers, 87, 104
 Universities, Catholic, 531
Canadian Conference of Catholic Bishops, 378
Canary Islands, 336
Cancer de Barbastro, Louis, 384
Cancer Homes and Hospitals, 550-51
Candle, Paschal, 320
Candlemas Day (Presentation), 247
Candles, 214
Canon, 299
 of Bible, 183-84, 299
 of Mass, (Eucharistic Prayer), 211, 216, 299
Canon Law, Code of, 299
 Authentic Interpretation, Commission, 148
 Marriage Annulments, 85
Canon Law, Oriental Code, Commission for Revision, 148
Canon Law Society of America, 564
Canonization, 299-300
 Francesco Antonio Fasani, 85
Canonizations (Leo XIII to Present), 133-35
Canons Regular of Holy Cross (Crosier Fathers), 485
Canons Regular of Premontre (Premonstratensians), 489
Canticle, 300
Canuto, Vittorio, 64
Cap-de-la-Madeleine, Shrine, 372

Cape Verde, 336
Capital Punishment, 300
Capital Sins, 300
Cappa Magna, 213
Caprio, Giuseppe, Card., 153, 166
Capuchins, 486
CARA, 560-61
Carberry, John, Card., 91, 153, 165, 166, 167
Cardinal, 151-52
 Bishops, 151, 165
 Deacons, 151, 166
 in Pectore (Petto), 152
 Patriarchs, 151, 165
 Priests, 151, 165-66
Cardinal Gibbons Award, 596
Cardinal Mindszenty Foundation, 564
Cardinal Spellman Award, 596
Cardinal Virtues, 300
Cardinal Wright Award, 596
Cardinals, 151-66
 American, 167
 Biographies, 152-65
 Categories, 151, 165-66
 Chamberlain, 301
 College, 151-52
 Council of, 66, 149
 Dean, 151
 Geographical Distribution, 166
 Meeting (1985), 66
 Retirement Age, 152
 Seniority (Categories), 165-66
 Voting Eligibility, 166
Carew, William A., Abp., 379
Caritas, 513
Caritas Christi, 512
Caritas Internationalis, 65-6, 370
Carlson, Robert J., Bp., 441
Carmel, **see** Mt. Carmel
Carmel Community, 494
Carmelite Missionaries of St. Theresa, 494
Carmelite Nuns, Byzantine, 494
Carmelite Nuns, Discalced, 494-95
Carmelite Nuns of Ancient Observance, 495
Carmelite Sisters, 495
 for Aged and Infirm, 495
 of Charity, 495
 of Corpus Christi, 495
 of St. Therese of the Infant Jesus, 495
 of the Divine Heart of Jesus, 495
 of the Sacred Heart, 495
Carmelites (Men), 484-85
Carmelites, Secular Orders, 514
Carney, James F., Abp., 379
Carolines and Marshalls, The, 336
Carpatho-Russians (Ruthenians), 265, 267-68
Carpino, Francesco, Card., 153, 165, 166
Carroll, Charles, 387
Carroll, John, Bp., 387, 467
Carroll, Mark K., Bp., 467
Carroll Center for the Blind, 550
Carter, Alexander, Bp., 379
Carter, Gerald Emmett, Card., 153-54, 165, 166
Carthusians, Order of, 485
Casaroli, Agostino, Card., 154, 165, 166
 Support for UN, 62-3
Casey, James V., Abp. (Death), 599
Casey, Luis Morgan, Bp., 441
Casimir, St., 249
Casimir, Sisters of St., 495
Casoria, Giuseppe, Card., 154, 166
Cassata, John J. Bp., 441
Cassian, St., 249
Cassock, 213
Castel Gandolfo, 173
Castillo, John de, Bl., 384
Castillo Lara, Rosalio Jose, Card., 154, 166
Castro, Fidel, **see** Cuba
Catacombs, 300
Catala, Magin, 384
Catechesis, 300

Catechism, 300
Catechism, Universal, 94
  Commission of Cardinals, 149
Catechumen, 300
  See also Baptism
Catechumenate, 222
Catechumens, Mass, 210
Catechumens, Oil of, 319
Catharism, 120
Cathedra, 300
  See also Ex Cathedra
Cathedral, 430
Cathedrals, U.S., 430-32
Cathedraticum, 300
Catherine Laboure, St., 249
  Miraculous Medal, 262
Catherine of Bologna, St., 249
Catherine of Siena, St., 196
Catholic, 300
  Action, **see** Lay Apostolate
  Actors' Guild of America, 587
  Aid Association, 564
  Alumni Clubs International, 564
  Associations, 563-70
  Awards, 597-99
  Baptisms, **see** Baptisms
  Belief, **see** Doctrine, Catholic
  Biblical Assn. of America, 564
  Central Union, 560
  Charities, USA, 75, 535
  Chronology in U.S., 390-404
  Church Extension Society, 63, 518, 597
  Colleges, U.S., 523-28
  Commission on Intellectual and Cultural Affairs, 564
  Communications Foundation, 587
  Conferences, State, 438-39
  Conferences, U.S., 435-36
  Converts, American, **see** Converts
  Daughters of the Americas, 564
  Daughters of the Americas, Junior, 563
  Dictionary, **see** Glossary
  Doctrine, **see** Doctrine, Catholic
  Eastern Churches, 263-70
  Education, **see** Education, Catholic
  Family Life Insurance, 564
  Forester Youth Program, 562
  Fraternity for Sick and Handicapped, 370
  Golden Age, 564
  Guardian Society, 564
  Health Association, 535
  Hierarchy, **see** Hierarchy
  History in the U.S., 387-404
  Home Bureau for Dependent Children, 564
  Hospitals, **see** Hospitals, Catholic
  Interracial Council of New York, 564
  Knights of America, 564
  Knights of Ohio, 564
  Kolping Society, 564
  Laity, National Council, 559
  League, 564-65
  League for Religious and Civil Rights, 552
  Library Association, 565
  Medical Mission Board, 82, 560
  Men, National Council of, 559
  Missions, 514-18
  Near East Welfare Association, 565
  Negro-American Mission Board, 518
  News Agencies, 582
  One Parent Organization, 565
  Order of Foresters, 565
  Organizations (U.S.), 563-70
  Organizations, International, 370-72
  Pamphlet Society, 565
  Peace Fellowship, 565
  Periodicals, Foreign, 581-82
  Periodicals, U.S., 571-81
  Population, **see** Statistics, Catholic
  Press, **see** Press, Catholic
  Press Association, 565, 598-99
  Radio Programs, U.S., 586

Catholic
  Relief Services, 64, 67, 70, 76, 79, 98, 437, 559-60
  Schools, **see** Schools, Catholic
  Social Doctrine, 199-204
  Social Services, 535-52
  Societies in U.S., 563-70
  Statistics, **see** Statistics, Catholic
  Supreme Court Justices, 405
  Telecommunications Network of America, 587
  Television Network, 587
  Television Programs, 586, 587
  Theatre, U.S., 587
  Theological Society of America, 565
  Universities, Pontifical, 531-32
  Universities, U.S., 523-28
  University of America, 524, 532, 596
    See also, Curran Controversy
  War Veterans, 565
  Women, National Council of, 559
  Worker Movement, 565
  Workman, 565
  Writers' Market, 582-85
  Youth Organization (CYO), 562
  Youth Organizations, 562-63
    See also Church, Catholic
Catholic-Jewish Relations, 291-93
  Commission, 149
  John Paul II at Rome Synagogue, 37-9
  Latin America, 67
Catholic-Moslem Relations, 293-94
  Commission, 149
Catholic-Orthodox Dialogues, 285-86, 287, 288
  Declarations of Popes, Other Prelates, 287, 288
  International Theological Commission, 290
    See also Orthodox Churches, Eastern
Catholics
  in Presidents' Cabinets, U.S., 404
  in Supreme Court, U.S., 405
  in Statuary Hall, 404-05
  Statistics, **see** Statistics
Catholics United for Spiritual Action, 565
Catholics United for the Faith, 565
Causality, **see** Existence of God
Causes of Saints, Congregation, 146
Cayenne, **see** French Guiana
Cayman Islands, 336
Cè, Marco, Card., 154, 165, 166
Cecilia, St., 249
Cecilia Medal, 596
CELAM (Latin American Bishops' Conference), 369
Celebret, 300
Celebrezze, Anthony (Catholics in Presidents' Cabinets), 404
Celibacy, 300
  John Paul II on, 89
Cenacle, 301
Cenacle, Congregation of Our Lady of Retreat in the, 495
Cenobitic Life (318), 111
Censer, 301
Censorship of Books, 301
Censures, 301
Center for Applied Research in the Apostolate, (CARA), 560-61
Center of Concern, 562
Central African Republic, 336, 367
Central America
  American Missionary Bishops, 421
  Cardinals, 166
  Episcopal Conferences, 369
  Refugees in U.S., Status, 70, 74
    See also El Salvador; Guatemala; Nicaragua
Central Association of the Miraculous Medal, 565
Central Statistics Office, 150
Ceremonies, Master of, 301
Cerularius, Michael (1043-1059), 113
Ceuta, 336

Ceylon, **see** Sri Lanka
Chabanel, Noel, St., 384
Chad, 336, 367
Chair of Peter (Feast), 245
Chalcedon, Council of, 121
Chaldean Rite, 266
  in U.S., 268
Chalice, 213
"The Challenge of Peace: God's Promise and Our Response" (U.S. Bishops' Pastoral), 204-06
Challenger Space Shuttle Disaster, 74, 75
Chamber, Apostolic, 149
Chamberlain, 301
Chancellor, 301
Chancery, 301
Chancery Offices, U.S., 433-35
Chant, Gregorian, 208-09
Chapel, 301
Chaplain, 301
Chaplains, Military, Role (John Paul II), 81
Chaplains, National Association of Catholic, 536
Chaplains Aid Association, 565
Chaplet, 301
Chapter, 301
Charbonneau, Paul E., Bp., 379
Charismatic Renewal, Catholic, 140
Charisms, 301-02
Charities, Catholic, National Conference, **see** Charities USA, Catholic
Charities, Pontifical Council, Cor Unum, 158
Charities USA, Catholic, 75, 535
Charity, 302
  Heroic Act, 311
Charity, Brothers of, 490
  Institute of (Rosminians), 489
  Servants of, 485
Charity, Daughters of, Divine, 495
Charity, Sisters of (List), 495-96
Charles, Missionaries of St., Congregation, 488
Charles Borromeo, St., 249
Charles Borromeo, St., Missionary Sisters of, 496
Charles Garnier, St., 384
Charles Lwanga and Comps., Sts. (Uganda Martyrs), 95, 249
Chastity, 302
Chasuble, 212
Chasuble-Alb, 212
Chaumonot, Pierre J., 384
Chavara, Kuriokose Elias, Beatification, 34
Chavez, Gilbert, Bp., 441-42
Chedid, John, Bp., 442
Chernobyl Nuclear Accident (USSR), 85, 90
Cherubim (Angels), 296
Chiasson, Donat, Abp., 379
Chick Publications, 86
Child Jesus, Sisters of the Poor, 496
Children, Mass for, 217
Chile, 76, 84, 336, 367
  Bishops Statements, 84, 100
Chimy, Jerome, Bp., 379
China, 65, 72, 75, 96, 337
  Churches Reopened, 72
  Hope for Union (John Paul II), 65
  Religious Breakthrough Speculation, 75, 96
Chinese Rites (1704), 116
Chirograph, 302
Choirs of Angels (Angels), 296
Chretienne, Sisters of Ste., 497
Chrism, **see** Oils, Holy
Christ, 302
  Annunciation, 245
  Ascension, 245
  Baptism, 245
  Circumcision (Solemnity of Mary), 248
  Epiphany (Theophany), 246
  in Gospels, 190

Christ
Kingship, 245
Mystical Body, 176-77
Nativity (Christmas), 245
Passion, 247
See Stations of the Cross
Presentation, 247
Resurrection (Easter), 246
Sacred Heart, 248
Seven Last Words, 326
Transfiguration, 248
Virgin Birth, 259
Christ, Adorers of Blood of, 497
Christ, Society of, 485
Christ, United Church of, 277
Christ Child Society, National, 563
Christ the King (Feast) (Nov. 22, 1987), 243, 245
Christ the King, Rural Parish Workers, 512
Christ the King, Sister Servants, 497
Christ the King, Sisters of St. Francis, 501
Christian, see Christians
Christian Brothers, 590
Christian Charity, Franciscan Sisters of, 500
Sisters of, 496
Christian Church, U.S. (Disciples of Christ), 277
Ecumenical Dialogues, 282, 289
Christian Conference of Asia, 71
Christian Culture Award, 597
Christian Doctrine, Confraternity, 559
Christian Doctrine, Sisters of Our Lady, 497
Christian Education, Religious of, 497
Christian Family Movement, 561
Christian Initiation (Baptism), 222-23
Christian Instruction, Brothers of, 590
Christian-Jewish Relations, National Workshop, 91
Christian Life Communities, 561
Christian-Marxist Dialogue, Budapest, 85
Christian Schools, Brothers, 590
Christian Science, 302
Christian Students, Young, 563
Christian Unity, Week of Prayer for, 73, 331
See also Ecumenism
Christian Unity Secretariat, 147
Christian Witness, 331
Christianity, 302
Christianity and Social Progress (Social Doctrine), 199
Christians, 302
Christians, Baptized, Reception into Church, 223
Christmas, 245
Message, John Paul II, 69
Christmas Nativity Scenes, see Church-State Decisions
Christmas Season, 236
Christopher, St., 250
Christopher Movement, 565
Awards, 599
Radio-TV Work, 586
Christos (Christ), 302
Christus Dominus, 122
Chronicles (Books of Bible), 186
Chronology
Church History, 110-18
Church in U.S., 390-404
Ecumenical Councils, 120-22
Old Testament, 189
Popes, 123-26
U.S. Episcopates, 412-20
Chrysostom, John, St., 196
Church, 302
Church (Catholic), 176-79
and Unity, see Ecumenism
and World Council of Churches, 280, 289
Apostolic Succession, 297
Authority, (Magisterium), 179-80, 181
Belief, see Doctrine

Church (Catholic)
Constitution on (Vatican II), 120, 176-80, 210, 221-22, 301-02, 325
Creeds, 197-98
Doctrine, 176-204
Eastern, 263-68
Hierarchy, 141-42
History, Dates, 110-18
Holy Spirit in (Encyclical), 39-43
in Canada, 373-83
in Countries of the World, 332-66
See also Individual Countries
in Modern World, Constitution (Vatican II), 199-201, 203-04, 229-30
in U.S., 387 ff
Infallibility, 179
Languages, 316
Liberating Mission of, 56
Liturgy, see Liturgy
Marriage Doctrine, Laws, see Marriage
Ministries, 227
Moral Obligations, 198-99
Mystery of, 176-77
Precepts, 199
Prophetic Office, 177-78
Relations with Other Churches, see Ecumenism;   Catholic-Jewish Relations
Rites, 209-10, 264-67
Sacraments, 221-30
Salvation, 325
Social Doctrine, 199-204
Statistics, see Statistics
Treasury, 330
Year (Calendar), 236-44
Church, Daughters of the, 497
Church and State (U.S.)
Court Decisions, 405-10
Legal Status of Catholic Education, 518-19
Wall of Separation, 410
Church Building, 214-15
Church Membership, 95
Churches, Eastern, 271-72
Churches, National Council, 281
Churches, Orthodox, 271
Churches, Protestant, in U.S., 274-78
Churches, World Council, see World Council of Churches
Ciappi, Mario Luigi, O.P., Card., 154, 166
Ciborium, 213
Cimichella, Andre, O.S.M., Bp., 379
Cincture, 212
Circumcision, 302
Feast, see Solemnity of Mary
Circumincession, 302
Cistercian Nuns, 497
Cistercian Nuns of Strict Observance, 497
Cistercians, Order of (Men), 485
Cistercians of the Strict Observance (Trappists), 485
Citizens for Educational Freedom, 565
Civardi, Ernesto, Card., 154, 166
Civil Rights League, Catholic, 552
Civiletti, Benjamin (Catholics in Presidents' Cabinets), 404
Clairvaux Abbey (1115), 114
Clare, St., 250
Clare, St., Order of, see Poor Clare Nuns, Franciscan
Clare, St., Sisters of, 497
Claretians, 485
Clark, Mark, Gen.(U.S.-Vatican Relations), 172
Clark, Matthew H., Bp., 442
Claver, Peter, St., 384
Clement I, St., 250
Clement XIII, Pope, Encyclicals, 135
Clement XIV, Pope, Encyclicals, 135
Clements, George, Rev., 98
Clergy, 302
Congregation, 146
Clergy, Byzantine, 270

Clergy, Congr. of Our Lady Help of the, 497
Clergy, Servants of Our Lady Queen of, 497
Clericalism, 302
Clerics of St. Viator, 490
Clerics Regular, Congregation of (Theatines), 490
Clerics Regular Minor, 485
Clerics Regular of St. Paul (Barnabites), 479
Clinch, Harry A., Bp., 442
Clinchy, Everett R. (Death), 599
Cloister, 302
Clown Ministry, 220
Clune, Robert B., Bp., 379
Cluny Abbey (910), 113
Coadjutor Bishop, 142
Code, 302
See also Canon Law
Coderre, Gerard M., Bp., 379
Cohill, John E., S.V.D., Bp., 442
Coins, Vatican, 174
College of Cardinals, 151-52
Colleges, Catholic, U.S., 523-28
Colleges and Universities, Catholic, Proposed Rules, 83
Collegiality, 180, 302-03
See also Synod of Bishops
Collegian Award, 597
Collettines (Franciscan Poor Clare Nuns), 500
Colombia, 97, 337, 367
Papal Visit, 35-6, 98
Colombo, Giovanni, Card., 154, 165, 166
Colorado, 391, 424, 427, 429, 438, 522, 529, 536, 545, 553, 588
Colors, Liturgical, 212-13
Colossians, 191
Columba, St., 250
Columban, St., 250
Columban, St., Missionary Sisters, 497
Columban, St., Society of, 485
Columbian Squires, 562
Columbus, Knights of, see Knights of Columbus
Comber, John W., M.M., Bp., 442
Comboni Missionaries of the Sacred Heart (Verona Fathers), 485
Comboni Missionary Sisters (Missionary Srs. of Verona), 497
Comillas, Pontifical Univ. (Spain), 532
Commandments of God, 198
Commissariat of the Holy Land, 303
Commission for Catholic Missions among Colored and Indians, 517
Commissions, Roman Curia, 148-49
Common of Mass, 211
Communications, U.S., 571-92
See also Press, Catholic
Communications Commission, Papal, 148
Communications Offices, U.S., 587-91
Communion, Holy (Holy Eucharist), 221, 223-25
Fast before Reception, 309
First, and First Confession, 224
Hosts, 218
In-Hand Reception, 218-19
Intinction, 315
Ministers, Special, 217
Reception Outside of Mass, 224
Reception Twice a Day, 224
under Forms of Bread and Wine, 219, 224
Viaticum, 330
See also Eucharist, Holy
Communion of Mass, 211
Communion of Saints, 303
Communion of the Faithful, 303
"Communione   e   Liberazione" Fraternity, 370
Communism, 491
Ostpolitik, 88, 319
"Communist Manifesto" (1848), 117

Community (Social Doctrine), 199-201
Comoros, 337
Company of Mary, 505
Company of Mary, Little, 505
Company of St. Paul, 512
Company of St. Ursula, 512
Compostela Award, 597
Concelebration, 303
   Inter-Ritual, 217
Conciliarists (Council of Florence), 121
Conclave (Papal Election), 320
Concord, Formula of (1577), 115
Concordance, Biblical, 203
Concordat, 303
   of Worms (1122), 114
Concordat, Vatican-Italy, 175
Concupiscence, 303
Conewega Chapel (Penn., 1741), 401
Confalonieri, Carlo, Card. (Death), 599
Conference on Lay Ministry, 95
Conference of Major Superiors of Men in U.S., 510
Confession (Penance), 217, 221, 225-26, 303
   First, and First Communion, 224
   Frequent, 226
   Individual, after General Absolution, 226
   Revised Rite, 217, 225-26
   Seal, 326
   Synod of Bishops' Theme, 143
   See also General Absolution; Penance
Confessional, 214-15
Confessor, 303
Confirmation, 217, 221, 223
   Sponsor, 223
Confraternity, 303
   of the Immaculate Conception, 565
Confraternity of Catholic Clergy, 565
Confraternity of Christian Doctrine, 559
Confucianism, 294
Congo, 337-38, 367
Congregationalists, 274
Congregations, Curial, 145-47
Congresses, Eucharistic, 82, 307-08
Connare, William G., Bp., 442
Connecticut, 391, 421, 425, 427, 438, 519, 529, 536-37, 545, 547, 554, 588, 593
Connolly, James L., Bp., **442**
   Death, 599
Connolly, Thomas A., Abp., 442
Connolly, Thomas J., Bp., 442
Connor, John (Catholics in Presidents' Cabinets), 404
Connors, Ronald G., C.SS.R., Bp., 442
Conscience, 303
   Examination of, 303
   John Paul II on, 61
Conscientious Objectors, 203
Consecrated Life, Institutes, 483
Consecration (Dedication) of Church, 305
Consecration of the Mass, 211
Consistory, 303
Consolata Missionary Sisters, 497
Consolata Society for Foreign Missions, 485
Consortium Perfectae Caritatis, 511
Constance, Council, 121
Constantinople, Councils of, 121
Constantinople, Fall of (1453), 115
Constitution, 303
Consubstantiation, 303
Consultation on Church Union, 281
Contardo Ferrini, Bl., 250
Contemplative Institutes (Religious), 483
Contraception, 303
   John Paul II on, 69
   See also *Humanae Vitae*
Contrition, 303-04
Contumely, 304
Conventuals (Franciscans), 486

Conversion of St. Paul (Feast), 245
Convert Movement Our Apostolate, 565
Converts (Rite of Christian Initiation), 222-23
Converts (U.S.), 427-29
Cook Islands, 338
Cooke, Terence J. (U. S. Cardinals), 167, 467
Cooney, Patrick R., Bp., 442
Cooray, Thomas B., O.M.I., Card., 154, 165, 166
Cope, 213
Coptic Orthodox Pope Shenouda III — Paul VI Declaration, 288
Copts, Catholic, 264
Cor Unum, 148
Cordeiro, Joseph, Card., 154, 165, 166
Corinthians, 190-91
Cornelius, St., 250
Corporal, 213
Corporal Works of Mercy, 304
Corporate Responsibility, Interfaith Center, 74
Corpus Christi (June 21, 1987), 240, 245
   John Paul II Observance, 89
Corrada del Rio, Alvaro, S.J., Bp., 442
Corripio Ahumada, Ernesto, Card., 155, 165, 166
Coscia, Benedict D., O.F.M., Bp., 442
Cosgrove, William M., Bp., 442
Cosmas and Damian, Sts., 250
Cossiga, Francesco, Pres. (Italy), 61
Costa Rica, 338, 367
Costello, Thomas J., Bp., 442
Cotey, Arnold R., S.D.S., Bp., 442
Couderc, St. Therese, 254
Council, Second Vatican, 122
   and Mary, 258
   Evaluation (Synod of Bishops), 43-5
   Excerpts from Documents, 120, 176-80, 180-83, 199-201, 203-04, 207-08, 210, 221-22, 229-30, 236, 263-64, 272, 278-79, 291, 293-94, 301-02, 305, 309-10, 325, 511-12
Council of European Bishops, 369
Councils of the Church (Catholic), 304
   Ecumenical, 120-22
   Plenary, 304
   Plenary, Baltimore, 388
   Provincial, 304
Counsels, Evangelical, 304
Counter-Reformation, 304
Countries, Church in, 332-66
Countries, Patrons, 256-57
Court, Supreme, **see** Supreme Court, U.S.
Cousins, William E., Abp., 442
Couture, Jean-Guy, Bp., 379
Couture, Maurice, R.S.V., Bp., 379
Couturier, Gerard, Bp., 379
Covenant, 304
Covenant, Old, **see** Revelation, Constitution
Covenant House, 551
Covetousness (Avarice), 298
Creation, 304
Creator, 304
Creature, 304
Creed of the Mass (Nicene), 197-98, 211
Creeds of the Church, 197-98
Cremation, 304
Crete, **see** Greece
Crib, 304
Crime and Pornography, 75
Crispin and Crispinian, Sts., 250
Crispin of Viterbo, St., 250
Criticism, Biblical, 192
Croatians (Byzantine Rite), 266
Cromwell, Oliver (1649), 116
Cronin, Daniel A., Bp., 442
Crosier, 304
Crosier Fathers, 485
Cross
   Pectoral, 321
   Sign of the, 327

Cross
   Stations of the, 328
   Triumph (Exaltation), 248
Cross, Canons Regular of Holy, 485
   Congregation of Holy (Brothers), 490
   Congregation of Holy (Priests), 485
   Daughters of, 497
   Sisters, Lovers of the Holy, 497
   Sisters of the Holy, 497
Cross and Passion, Sisters of the, 497
"Crossroads," 586
Croteau, Denis, O.M.I., Bp., 379
Crowley, Jim (Death), 599
Crowley, Joseph R., Bp., 442-43
Crowley, Leonard P., Bp., 379
Crown, Franciscan, 309
Crowned Shrine, 326
Crucifix, 215
Crucifix, Stations (Stations of the Cross), 328
Cruets, 215
Crusades (1097-1099), 113
Crypt, 304
Cuba, 96, 338, 367
   Encuentro, 80
   National Meeting of Catholics, 77
Cult of Saints, 325
Cults, Education Needed, 66
Cults, Vatican Report, 54-6
Culture, Pontifical Council, 148
   Papal Address, 73
Cum Gravissima, **see** Cardinals, College
Cummins, John S., Bp., 443
Cura Animarum, 304
Curacao, **see** Netherlands Antilles
Curia, 304
Curia, Roman, 144-50
   Disciplinary Commission, 149
   Reform Commission, 150
Curran, Charles E., Rev. **see** Curran Controversy
Curran Controversy, 47-51, 83, 103
Cursillo Movement, 561
Curtis, Walter W., Bp., 443
Curtiss, Elden F., Bp., 443
Cushing, Richard J. (U.S. Cardinals), 167, 468
Custos, 304
Cyprian, St., 250
Cyprus, 338
Cyril and Methodius, Sts., 250
   See also Czechoslovakia
Cyril and Methodius, Srs. of Sts., 497
Cyril of Alexandria, 196
Cyril of Jerusalem, St., 196
Czech Catholic Union of Texas, 565
Czechoslovakia, 338-39
   Catholic Strength, 88
   Political Clergy Organizations, 84
Czestochowa, Our Lady of, Shrine, 594

D

Daciuk, Myron, O.S.B.M., Bp., 379
Dadaglio, Luigi, Card., 155, 166
Dahomey, **see** Benin
Daily, Thomas V., Bp., 443
Dalmatic, 212
Daly, James, Bp., 443
Damasus I, St., 250
Damian, St. (Sts. Cosmas and Damian), 250
Damien, Father (Joseph de Veuster) (Hawaii, 1873), 393
Damien-Dutton Society, 565
   Award, 597
Danglmayr, Augustine, Bp., 443
Daniel, 188
Daniel, Anthony, St., 384
Danneels, Godfried, Card., 155, 165, 166
D'Antonio, Nicholas, O.F.M., Bp., 443
D'Arcy, John M., Bp., 443
Darmojuwono, Justin, Card., 155, 165, 166
Darwin, Charles (1882), **117**
Das Kapital (1867), **117**

Dates, see Chronology
Daughters of Isabella, 565
Daughters of Our Lady of Fatima, 513
Daughters of St. Paul, 507
David, see Historical Books of Bible
David, St., 250
Davis, James P., Abp., 443
Davis, Thurston N., S.J. (Death), 585
Day of Atonement, 291
Dazzi, Bernard, O.F.M. (Death), 599
Deacon, 227
Deaconess, 305
Deacons, 227
Deacons, First Seven, 227
Deacons, Permanent, 227, 228
   United States, 228, 421-25
   World Statistics, 365
Dead, Masses for, 212, 213
Dead Sea Scrolls, 185
Deaf, 550
   Facilities for, 545
Dean, 305
Dean of Sacred College, 151, 305
De Araujo Sales, Eugenio, Card., 155, 165, 166
Dearden, John F., Card., 155, 165, 166, 167
Death (Life and Death Questions), 51-3
   Definition of, 52
Death of God, see Atheism
Death Penalty, see Capital Punishment
Deaths (September, 1985 to September, 1986), 585, 599-600
Decalogue (Ten Commandments), 198
Decision, Apostolic, 305
Declaration, 305
"Declaration of Solidarity Ad," 82
Decosse, Aime, Bp., 379
Decourtray, Albert Card., 155, 166
Decree, 305
Decree of Nullity (Annulment), 233-34, 235
Decretals, False (847-852), 113
Dedication of a Church, 305
Dedication of Basilica of St. Mary Major, 246
   of Lateran Basilica, 245
Defensor Pacis (1324), 114
De Furstenberg, Maximilien, Card., 155, 165, 166
Dei Verbum (Divine Revelation Constitution), 44, 122, 180-83, 330
Deism, 305
Deksnys, Antanas L., Bp., 443
Delaquis, Noel, Bp., 379
Delaney, Joseph P., Bp., 443
De La Salle Medal, Manhattan, 597
Delaware, 391-92, 422, 426, 428, 520, 537, 545, 554, 588
De La Torre, Edicio, Rev., 84
Delegates, Apostolic, see Apostolic Delegates
Delta Epsilon Sigma, 563
De Lubac, Henri, J., S.J., Card., 155, 166
Dempsey, Michael J., O.P., Bp., 443
Denis, St., 250
Denmark, 339
Denning, Joseph P., Bp., 443
De Palma, Joseph A., S.C.J., Bp., 443
De Paoli, Ambrose, Abp., 443
De Paul University, 86, 524
De Porres, Martin, St., 385
De Roo, Remi J., Bp., 379
DeSales, Francis, St., 196
DeSales Secular Institute, 512
D'Escoto, Miguel, M.M., 84
De Simone, Louis, A., Bp., 443
Deskur, Andrzej Marie, Card., 155, 166
De Smet, Pierre, 384
Despair, 305
Despatie, Roger A., Bp., 379
Detachment, 305
Detraction, 305

Deusto, Catholic University (Spain), 532
Deuterocanonical Books, 184
Deutero-Isaiah (Isaiah), 188
Deutero-Zechariah (Zechariah), 189
Deuteronomy, 186
Development, Human, see Campaign for Human Development
Development of Peoples, see Social Doctrine
Developmentally Handicapped, Catholic Facilities, 546-49
Devil, 101, 305
Devotion, 305
Devotion, Eucharistic, 224
Devotions, 305-06
Diabolical Obsession, 319
Diabolical Possession, 322
Diaconate, see Deacons, Permanent
Dialogues, Ecumenical, 281-87
Dictionary, see Glossary
Didache (Second Century), 111
Didymus (Thomas), 194
Diego, Juan (Guadalupe Apparition), 262
Diego Luis de San Vitores, Beatification, 61
Dies Natalis, 237
Dignitatis Humanae (Religious Freedom Declaration), 122, 309-10
Dimino, Joseph T. Bp., 443
Dimmerling, Harold J., Bp., 443-44
Dingman, Maurice J., Bp., 444
Diocesan Laborer Priests, 512
Diocese, 306
   Curia, 304
   Synod, 329
Dioceses, Canadian, 374-75
Dioceses, U.S., 412-20
   Chancery Office Addresses, 433-35
   Communications Offices, 587-91
   Eastern Rite, 267-68
   with Interstate Lines, 425
Dioceses, World, 365
Diocletian (292, 303), 111
Dion, Georges E., O.M.I., Bp., 444
Dionne, Gerard, Bp., 379
Dionysius Exiguus (c. 545), 112
Diplomacy, Papal, 167
Diplomacy, Role of Church, 86-7
Diplomats at Vatican, 170-71
   Dean, 171
   New Ambassadors, 69
Disabled, Facilities, Organizations for, 545-52
Disarmament, 204, 205
Disasters, 62, 63, 75, 90, 101
Discalced, 306
Discalced Carmelites (Nuns), 494-95
   Carmelites, Order of (Men), 484-85
Disciple, 306
Disciples of Christ (Christian Church), 277, 282, 289
Disciples of the Divine Master, Sister, 497
Disciplina Arcani, 306
Diskos, 270
Dismas, St., 250
Dispensation, 306
District of Columbia, 392, 422, 426, 428, 520, 529, 537, 547, 554, 588, 593
Divination, 306
Divine Compassion, Sisters, 497
Divine Love, Oblates to, 497
Divine Office, see Liturgy of the Hours
Divine Positive Law, see Law
Divine Praises, 306
Divine Redeemer, Sisters, 508
Divine Revelation, Constitution, 44, 122, 180-83, 330
Divine Savior, Sisters, 509
Divine Spirit, Congregation, 497
Divine Word, Society of, 485
Divine Worship, Congregation, 146
Divino Afflante Spiritu (Biblical Studies), 193

Divorce, 233
Divorce Referendum, Ireland, 92, 96
Divorced and Remarried Catholics, Ministry for, 234-35
   Good Conscience Procedure, 235
   See also Marriage
Djibouti, 339
Docetism, 119
Doctors, Church, 195-97
Doctrine, Catholic, 176-204
   Development, 181
   Marian, 258-61
   Marriage, 229-32
   Social, 199-204
Doctrine of the Faith, Congregation, 145
   Extremist Influence Denied, 97
   Letter to Father Curran, 47-8
   Liberation Theology (Second Document) 56-60
   Masonic Membership Ruling, 310
Doherty, Catherine de Hueck (Death), 599
Dolinay, Thomas V., Bp., 444
Dolors, see Sorrows of BVM
Dominations (Angels), 296
Dominic, St., 250
Dominic, St., Sisters of, 498
   See also Dominicans
Dominic Savio, St., 250
Dominic Savio Club, St., 563
Dominica, 339
Dominican Laity, 514
Dominican Nuns, 497-98
Dominican Republic, 339-40, 367
Dominicans (Men), 485-86
Dominicans (Women), 497-98
Dominum et Vivificantem (Encyclical on the Holy Spirit in the Church), 39-43, 90
Don Bosco Volunteers, 512
Donaghy, Frederick, M.M., Bp., 444
Do Nascimento, Alexandre, Card., 155-56, 165, 166
Donation of Pepin (754), 112
Donatism, 119
Donnellan, Thomas A., Abp., 444
Donnelly, Robert William, Bp., 444
Donoghue, John D., 599
Donoghue, John F., Bp., 444
Donohoe, Hugh A., Bp., 444
Donovan, Jean, 71
Donovan, John A., Bp., 444
Donovan, Paul V., Bp., 444
Donovan, Raymond J., (Catholics in Presidents' Cabinets), 404
Dorothy, Institute of Sisters of St., 498
Dorsey, Norbert M., C.P., Bp., 444
Douay-Rheims Bible, 184
Double Effect Principle, 306
Dougherty, Dennis (U.S. Cardinals), 167, 468
Dougherty, John J., Bp. (Death), 599
Douville, Arthur, Bp., 379
Downey, Morton (Death), 599
Doxology, 306
   Mass, 211, 218
Doyle, James L., Bp., 379
Doyle, W. Emmett, Bp., 379
Dozier, Carroll T., Bp. (Death), 599
Drainville, Gerard, Bp., 379
Drug Abuse, Rehabilitation Centers, 551
Drug Addiction, John Paul II on, 93
Drury, Thomas, Bp., 444
Duchesne, Rose Philippine, Bl., 384
Dudick, Michael J., Bp., 444
Dudley, Paul, Bp., 444
Duhart, Clarence J., C.SS.R., Bp., 444
Dulia, 306
Du Maine, Roland Pierre, Bp., 444
Dumouchel, Paul, O.M.I., Abp., 379
Dunn, Francis J., Bp., 444
Dunstan, St., 250
Durick, Joseph A., Bp., 444
Durning, Dennis, C.S.Sp., Bp., 445
Durocher, Marie Rose, Bl., 250
Dutch Guiana, see Suriname

Duty, Easter, 306
Duval, Leon-Etienne, Card., 156, 165, 166
Duvalier, Jean Claude, 77, 79, 92
Dymphna, St., 250

E

East Germany, 343, 344
Easter, 246
  Controversy, 306-07
  Dates (1987-2010), 244
  Duty, 307
  Season, 236
  Time, **see** Easter Duty
  Triduum, 236
  Vigil, 246
  Water, 307
Easter Message (John Paul II), 82
Eastern Churches, Catholic, 263-70
  Celibacy, 300
  Clergy, 270
  Decree (Vatican II), 122, 263-64, 272
  Inter-Ritual Concelebrations, 217
  Jurisdictions, 266-67
  Liturgy, Byzantine Rite, 268
  Marriage Laws, 234
  Patriarchs, 263
  Rites and Faithful, 264-66
  Sacraments, 263-64
  Sacred Congregation, 145-46
  Statistics, Canada, 377
  Statistics, U.S., 267-68, 425, 429, 523
  Synods, Assemblies, 267
  Worship, 264
    See also Byzantine Rite
Eastern Churches, Separated, 271-72
  Intercommunion, 225
    See also Ecumenism; Orthodox Churches, Eastern; Orthodox Church, Oriental
Eastern Ecumenism, 272
  Catholic-Oriental Church Dialogue, 286
    See also Ecumenical Reports
Eastern Rite Information Service, 582
Ebacher, Roger, Bp., 379
Ecclesiastes, 187
Ecclesiastical
  Burial, 299
  Calendar, 236-44
  Honors, 595-96
  Jurisdictions, World (Statistics), 365-66
  Provinces, Canada, 374
  Provinces, U.S., 411-12
Ecclesiasticus, **see** Sirach
Ecclesiology, 307
Economic Affairs, Prefecture, 149
Economy, Letter on (U.S. Bishops), 206
Ecstasy, 307
Ecthesis (649), 112
Ecuador, 340, 367
  Catholic University, 532
  Training Center, 100
Ecumenical Councils, 120-22
    See also Council, Second Vatican
Ecumenical Reports, 287-90
Ecumenism, 272, 278-90, 307
  Agencies, 279-81
  and Intercommunion, 81, 225, 314
  and Mary, 261
  and Separated Eastern Christians, 272
  Declarations of Popes, Other Prelates, 287-88
  Decree on, 281-87
  Developments in Scotland, 80
  Dialogues, U.S., 281-87
  Eastern, 272
  Interfaith Prayer Service, Washington, D.C., 66
  International Consultations, 288-89
  International Bilateral Commissions, 289-90
  John Paul II on, 73, 81
  Participation in Worship, 279
  Reports, International, 287-90

Ecumenism
  Vatican Secretariat, 147, 278
  Week of Prayer for Christian Unity, 73, 331
  World Council of Churches 280, 289
    See also Catholic-Jewish Relations; Catholic-Moslem Relations
Eddy, Mary Baker (Christian Science), 302
Edict of Milan (313), 111
Edith Stein Guild, 566
  Award, 597
Edmund, Society of St., 486
Edmund Campion, St., 250
Education, Catholic, Congregation, 146
Education, Catholic, U.S., 518-31
  Campus Ministry, 529
  Facilities for Handicapped, 545-50
  Legal Status, 518-19
    See also Church-State Decisions
  Seminaries, 529-31
  Statistics, 519-23
  Universities and Colleges, 524-28
    See also Schools, Catholic; Seminaries
Education, Religious, 561
  Pupils Receiving Instruction, 523
Educational Association, National Catholic, 87, 523
Edwin Vincent O'Hara Institute (Rural Ministry Institute), 518
Egan, Edward M., Bp., 445
Egypt, 340
Eileton, 270
Eire, **see** Ireland
Ekandem, Dominic, Card., 156, 165, 166
Elections, Papal, 320
  Eligibility of Cardinals, 166
Elevation, 307
Eligius, St., 250
Elijah (Kings), 186
Elisha (Kings), 186
Elizabeth of Hungary, St., 250
Elizabeth of Portugal, St., 250
Elizabeth Seton, St., 250
Elko, Nicholas T., Abp., 445
El Paso Diocesan Synod, 91
El Salvador, 340, 367
  Government Bombings, 76
  Refugees in U.S., 70
Elvira, Council (306), 111
Elya, John A., B.S.O., Bp., 445
Ember Days, 237
Emblems of Saints, 257-58
Embolism (Prayer for Deliverance), 211
Emmanuel D'Alzon Medal, 597
Emotionally Maladjusted, Catholic Facilities, 545-46
Encuentro, Cuba, 80
Encuentro, Third National, 102
    See also Hispanics
Encyclicals, 135
  Authority, 135
  "Holy Spirit in the Church and the World," 39-43
  List, Benedict XIV to John Paul II, 135-40
  Social, 199, 201-03
End Justifies the Means, 307
Engaged Encounter, 313
England, 340-41, 367
  Catholic Relief Act (1926), 118
  Church of England Synod, 68, 100
  Imprimatur Removed from Bioethics Book, 103-04
  Popish Plot (1678), 116
  Test Act (1673), 116
Enlightenment, Age, 116
Enrique y Tarancon, Vicente, Card., 156, 165, 166
Enthronement of the Sacred Heart, 566
Environment, Protection of, 85
Envy, 307

Eparch, 142
Ephesians, 191
Ephesus, Council, 121
Ephesus, "Robber" Council (449), 111
Ephraem, St., 196
Epikeia, 307
Epimanikia, 270
Epiphany, 246
Episcopal Church, **see** Anglican Communion; Anglicans
Episcopal Church in U.S., 276-77
  Ecumenical Dialogues, Statements, 282-83
    See also Ecumenism
Episcopal Conferences, 367-69
Episcopal Vicar, 142
Episcopate, 307
Epistles (Letters), 190-91
Epitrachelion, 270
Equality (Social Doctrine), 200
Equatorial Guinea, 341, 367
Equivocation, 307
Erasmus, St., 250
Eritrea, **see** Ethiopia
Eschatology, 307
Escriva de Balaguer, Jose Maria (Opus Dei), 319
Esseff, John A., Msgr., 75-6
Essenes, **see** Dead Sea Scrolls
Esther, 187
Estonia, 341
Etchegaray, Roger, Card., 72, 156, 165, 166
Eternal Word Network, 586
Eternity, 307
Ethelbert, St., 250
Ethics, 307
  Situational, 327-28
Ethiopia, 341, 367
  Relief, 76, 79
Ethiopian Rite Catholics, 264
Etteldorf, Raymond P., Abp. (Death), 599
Euangelion (Gospel), 190
Eucharist (Holy), 217, 221, 223-25
  Administration to Non-Catholics, 225
  Devotion Outside of Mass, 224
  Exposition, 220, 308
  Fast, 309
  Hosts, 218
  Ministers, Special, 217
  Reservation of, **see** Tabernacle
  Sacrifice, **see** Mass
  Worship, 218
    See also Communion, Holy; Transubstantiation
Eucharist, Religious of, 498
Eucharistic Congresses, 307-08
  44th International, 82
Eucharistic Guard for Nocturnal Adoration, 566
Eucharistic Liturgy, 211
Eucharistic Missionary Sisters, 499
Eucharistic Prayers (Mass), 211, 216
Eudes, John, St., 252
Eudists (Congregation of Jesus and Mary), 486
Eugenics, 308
Euphrasia Pelletier, St., 250
Europe
  Bishops' Conference, 369
  Cardinals, 166
  Catholic Statistics, 365-66
  Eastern Rite Jurisdictions, 266
  Symposium of Bishops, 64
Europe, Abortion Results, 61
Eusebius of Vercelli, St., 251
Euthanasia, 308
  John Paul II Address, 65
    See also Life and Death Questions
Euthanasia, Netherlands, 88, 93
Eutychianism, 119
Evangelical Counsels, 304
Evangelicalism, 277-78
Evangelion, 269
Evangelists, 190, 193-94

Evangelization, 44, 56, 69, 70, 73, 89
Events (1985), 69
John Paul II on, 73, 89
Evangelization of Peoples, Congregation of, 147
Evans, George R., Bp., 469
Everson v. Board of Education (Bus Transportation), 406
Evolution, 308
John Paul II on, 85
Ex Cathedra, 179
See also Infallibility
Exaltation (Triumph) of the Holy Cross, 248
Examen, Particular (Examination of Conscience), 303
Exarch, 142
Exceptional Children, see Handicapped, Facilities for
Excommunication, 308
Excommunication, Rhode Island, Planned Parenthood Executive, 75
Excommunications, San Jose Diocese, 102
Exegesis, 191-92
Existentialism, 308
Exner, Adam, O.M.I., Abp., 379
Exodus, 186
Exorcism, 101, 308
by Priests and Bishops Only, 77
Exorcist, 227
Exposition of the Blessed Sacrament, 308
Extended Periods of Time, 220
Extension Society, 63, 518, 597
External Forum, 309
Extreme Unction, see Anointing of the Sick
Eymard League, 566
Ezekiel, 188
Ezra, 186-87

F

Fabian, St., 251
Fabian, Arpad, Bp. (Death), 599
Faculties, 308-09
of Ecclesiastical Studies, 532-33
Faith, 309
Congregation for Doctrine of, 47-8, 56-60, 145
Congregation for Propagation of, 147
Mysteries, 318
Privilege of (Petrine Privilege), Promoter of, 322
Rule of, 309
Society for Propagation of, 569
See also Creed; Doctrine
Faithful, Communion of, 303
Faithful, Mass of, 210
Faithful, Prayer of the, 211
Falkland Islands, 341
False Decretals (847-852), 113
Families for Christ, 566
Families for Prayer, 566
Family, Council for, 148
Family, Holy (Feast), 246
Family Movement, Christian, 561
Family Rosary, Inc., 566
Family Theater, Father Peyton's, 586
Farley, James A. (Catholics in Presidents' Cabinets), 404
Farley, John (U.S. Cardinals), 167, 469
Farmer, Ferdinand, 384
Farm Crisis, Response, 70-1, 75
Faroe Islands, 341
Farrakhan, Louis, 63
Fasani, Francesco, Canonization, 85
Fast, Eucharistic, 309
Fast Days, 237
Father, 309
Father Flanagan's Boys Town, 546
Father McKenna Award, 597
Fathers, Church, 195
Fathers of Mercy, 488
Fatima, 262

Favalora, John C., Bp., 445
Fear, 309
Feast Days, 237, 245-48
Feast of Weeks, 291
Feasts, Movable, 237, 244
Febres Cordero, Miguel, St., 253
Febronianism (1764), 116
Federal, Joseph L., Bp., 445
Federal Aid to Education, 518-19
See also Church-State Decisions
Federation of Diocesan Liturgical Commissions, 566
Feeley, Maura, Sr., 99
F.E.L. Suit, Ruling, 62
Felice, John, O.F.M., 103
Felician Sisters (Sisters of St. Felix), 499
Felicity, St. (Perpetua and Felicity, Sts.), 253
Fellowship of Catholic Scholars, 566
Ferdinand III, St., 251
Fernando Po, see Equatorial Guinea
Ferrario, Joseph A., Bp., 445
Festival of Lights (Hanukkah), 299
Fetus, Minnesota Ruling, 70
Fetuses, Burial, 62
Fiacra, St., 251
Fidelis of Sigmaringen, St., 251
Fidelitas Medal, 597
Fides (Mission News Service), 582
Fiji, 341
Filevich, Basil (Wasyl), Bp., 379
Filippini, Religious Teachers, 499
Film Awards, 599
Films, Catholic, see Television
Finger Towel, 213
Finland, 341
Finnis, John, 98
Fiorenza, Joseph A., Bp., 445
First Amendment (Wall of Separation), 410
See also Church-State Decisions
First Catholic Slovak Ladies Association, 566
First Catholic Slovak Union (Jednota), 566
First Friday, 309
First Saturday, 309
Fisher, Eugene, Dr., see Catholic-Jewish Relations
Fisher, John, St., 252
Fisherman's Ring, 309
Fitzpatrick, John J., Bp., 445
Fitzsimons, George K., Bp., 445
FitzSimons, Thomas, 387
Flag, Papal, 173
Flaget, Benedict, 384
Flahiff, George B., C.S.B., Card., 156, 165, 166
Flanagan, Bernard J., Bp., 445
Flanagan, Edward J., Rev. (Boys' Town), Commemorative Stamp, 99
Flavin, Glennon P., Bp., 445
Fliss, Raphael M., Bp., 445
Florence, Council, 121
Flores, Felixberto, Abp. (Death), 599
Flores, Patrick, Abp., 445
Florida, 392, 422, 426, 428, 438, 520, 529, 537, 547, 554, 588, 593
"Health Centers," in Schools, 86
Religious Bias, Prisons, 86
Florit, Ermenegildo, Card. (Death), 600
Floyd, John B. (Catholics in Presidents' Cabinets), 404
Flynn, Harry J., Bp., 445
Focolare Movement, 513
Foi et Lumiere, 370
Foley, David E., Bp., 445
Foley, John Patrick, Abp., 43, 91, 96, 445-46
Responsibility of Catholic Newspapers, 96
Foreign Mission Society of America, Catholic (Maryknoll), 488
Foreign Missions, U.S. Personnel, 514-16

Foreign Missions, U.S. Personnel
American Bishops, 420-21
Foreign Missions, Consolata Society for, 485
St. Joseph's Society for (Mill Hill Missionaries), 488
Forester Youth Program, 562
Foresters, Catholic Order of, 565
Forgiveness of Sin, 309
See also Confession; Penance
Formosa, see Taiwan
Forst, Marion F., Bp., 446
Fortier, Jean-Marie, Abp., 380
Fortitude, 309
Fortune Telling, 309
Forty Hours Devotion, 309
Forum, 309
Foster Homes, Children in, 430
Four Books of Sentences (1160), 114
Fox, Matthew, O.P., 62
France, 341-42, 367
Catholicism in, 88
Nuclear Deterrence Stand of Bishops, 84
Religious Sanctions (1901), 117
Revolution (1789), 116
Frances of Rome, St., 251
Frances Xavier Cabrini, St., 251
Francis, Joseph A., S.V.D., Bp., 446
Francis, St., Assisi, 251
See also Crib; Portiuncula
Francis, St. (Religious)
Brothers of the Poor, 490
Little Brothers of, 491
Secular Order, 514
Sisters of (List), 499-502
Third Order Regular (Men), 486
See also Franciscans; Friars Minor
Francis Association for Catholic Evangelism, St., 586
Francis Borgia, St., 251
Francis de Sales, St., 196
Francis de Sales, St. (Religious)
Oblate Sisters, 499
Oblates of, 486
Society of (Salesians), 489
Francis de Sales, St., Award (CPA), 598
Francis of Paola, St., 251
Francis Solanus, St., 386
Francis Xavier, St., 251
Brothers of, 491
Catholic Mission Sisters, 510
Franciscan Advertising and Media Enterprises, 586
Franciscan Brothers of Brooklyn, 491
Franciscan Brothers of Christ the King, 491
Franciscan Brothers of the Good News, 491
Franciscan Brothers of the Holy Cross, 491
Franciscan Communications, 586
Franciscan Crown, 309
Franciscan Friars of the Atonement, 483
Franciscan International Award, 597
Franciscan Missionary Brothers, 491
Franciscan Missions (California), 386
Franciscan Sisters (List), 499-502
Franciscans (Friars Minor), 486
Franciscans, Capuchins, 486
Conventuals, 486
Third Order Regular, 486
Franco, Francisco (1936), 118
Franz, John B., Bp., 446
Franzetta, Benedict C., Bp., 446
Frassinetti, Paola, St., 253
Free Will, 310
Freedom, Religious, 309-10
Freeman, James D., Card., 156, 165, 166
Freemasons, 310
Freking, Frederick W., Bp., 446
French Guiana, 344
French Polynesia, 355

Fresno Larrain, Juan Francisco, Card., 156, 166
Frey, Gerard L., Bp., 446
Friar, 310
Friars Minor, Order of (Franciscans), 486
Friars Preachers, Order of (Dominicans), 485
Friend, William B., Bp., 446
Friendship House, 566
Frontier Apostolate, 561
Frosi, Angelo, S.X., Bp., 446
Fruits of the Holy Spirit, 310
Fruits of the Mass, 212
Fu Jen University (Taiwan), 532
Fulda, Monastery (744), 112
Fulton, Thomas B., Bp., 380
Fundamentalism and Biblical Study, 189
Fundamentalists, 278
Funeral Mass, Rites, Vestments, 212, 213
Fur Trappers, Canada, 87, 104
Furlong, Philip J., Bp., 446
Futuna Islands, 363

G

Gabon, 342, 367
Gabriel (Archangel), 247
Gabriel Lalemant, St., 385
Gabriel of the Sorrowful Mother, St., 251
Gabriel Richard Institute, 566
Gagnon, Edouard, P.S.S., Card., 156, 166
Galatians, 191
Galician Ruthenian Catholics, 265
Galilei, Galileo (1642), 116
Gallagher, Raymond J., Bp., 446
Gallegos, Alphonse, O.A.R., Bp., 446
Gallican Declaration (1682), 116
Gallitzin, Demetrius, 384
Gambia, The, 342, 367
Gambling, 310
Ganter, Bernard J., Bp., 446
Gantin, Bernardin, Card., 156, 165, 166
Garate, Francisco, Beatification, 61
Garland, James H., Bp., 446
Garmendia, Francisco, Bp., 446
Garmo, George, Abp., 446
Garner, Robert F., Bp., 446
Garnier, Charles, St., 384
Garrone, Gabriel, Card., 156, 165, 166
Gaston, William (North Carolina), 399
Gaudete Sunday, Vestments, **see** Liturgical Colors
Gaudium et Spes (Church in Modern World), 44, 122, 199-201, 203-04, 229-30
Gaughan, Norbert F., Bp., 446
Gaumond, Andre, Bp., 380
Gehenna (Gehinnom), 310
Gelasian Guild, 566
Gelasius I, Pope, St. (494), 111
Gelineau, Louis E., Bp., 446
Gemayel, Amin, Pres., 77-8
Gendron, Odore, Bp., 446-47
General Absolution, 225-26
John Paul II on, 85
Genesis (Bible), 185-86
Genesius, St., 251
Genevieve, St., 251
Genocide Ban Treaty, 79
Genuflection, 310
George, St., 251
George M. Cohan Award, 597
Georgetown University, 387, 525, 532
Georgia, 392-93, 422, 426, 428, 438, 520, 545, 554, 588
Franciscan Martyrs, (Georgia, 1597), 392
Georgian Byzantine Rite, 265
Gerard Majella, St., 251
Gerber, Eugene, Bp., 447
Gerbermann, Hugo, M.M., Bp., 447
Gerety, Peter L., Abp., 447
People of Hope Conflict, 67, 90

Gerhardinger, Maria Teresa, Beatification, 65
Germany, 342-43, 367
Kulturkampf (1871), 117
Gerrard, James J., Bp., 447
Gerry, Joseph, O.S.B., Bp., 447
Gertrude, St., 251
Gervais, Marcel A., Bp., 380
Gethsemani, 310
Ghana, 343, 367
Catholic Newspaper Banned, 76
Ghandi, Mahatma, Papal Tribute, 32, 34
Gibault, Pierre, 384
Gibbons, James (Catholic History of U.S.), 388, 470
Gibraltar, 343
Gifts, Preternatural, 322
Gifts of the Holy Spirit, 310
Gilbert, Arthur J., Bp., 380
Gilbert Islands (Kiribati), 348
Girl Scouts, Catholic, 563
Glemp, Jozef, Card., 87-8, 156-57, 165, 166
See also Poland
Glenmary Missioners, 486, 517
Sisters (Home Mission Sisters of America), 503
See also Home Missions
Glenn, Laurence A., Bp., 447
Glennie, Ignatius, S.J., Bp., 447
Glennon, John (U.S. Cardinals), 167, 470
Glory to God (Mass), 210
Glossary, 295-331
Gluttony, 310
Gnosticism, 119
God, 310-11
Attributes, 298
Commandments, 198
Godparents, 222
God-Spell (Gospel), 190
Golden Bull (1338), 114
Golden Spur, Order of, 595
Goncalves Kamtedza, Joao de Deus, Rev., 65
Gonzalez Martin, Marcelo, Card., 157, 165, 166
Gonzalez, Roch, Bl., 384
"Good Conscience" Procedures (Marriage), 235
Good Friday (Apr. 17, 1987), 239, 246
Good Samaritan Award, 597
Good Shepherd Sisters, 502
Good Shepherd, Society of Brothers, 491
Gorbachev, Mikhail, Appeal to, 65
Gospel, 190
Gospel (Mass), **see** Readings
Gospel Message and Social Life, 57
Gospels, 182-83, 190
Synoptic, 190
Gossman, F. Joseph, Bp., 447
Gottwald, George J., Bp., 447
Goupil, Rene, St., 384
Gouyon, Paul, Card., 157, 165, 166
Government, Church, 142-43
See also Roman Curia
Grace, 311
at Meals, 311
Gracida, Rene H., Bp., 74, 447
Grady, Thomas J., Bp., 447
Graham, John J., Bp., 447
Grahmann, Charles V., Bp., 447
Grail, 561
Grasset de Saint Sauveur, Andre, Bl., 248
Gratian (1160), 114
Gratton, Jean, Bp., 380
Graves, Lawrence P., Bp., 447
Gravier, Jacques, 384
Gravissimum Educationis, 122
Gray, Gordon J., Card., 157, 165, 166
Graymoor Institute, 591
Graymoor Sisters (Franciscan Srs. of the Atonement), 500
Graziano, Lawrence, O.F.M., Bp., 447
Greco, Charles P., Bp., 447

Great Britain
Episcopal Conferences, 367-68
See also England, Scotland, Wales
Greece, 343, 368
Greek Byzantine Rite Catholics, 265
Greek Melkites, 265
in U.S., 268
Green, Francis J., Bp., 447
Greene, Richard, Rev., 103
Greenland, 343
Gregoire, Paul, Abp., 380
Gregorian Calendar (1582), 115
Gregorian Chant, 208-09
Gregorian Masses, 212
Gregorian University, Pontifical, 533
New Rector, 92
Gregory, Wilton D., Bp., 447
Gregory Nazianzen, St., 196
Gregory I, the Great, St., 196
Gregory VII, St. (Hildebrand), 251
Gregory XVI, Pope, Encyclicals, 136
Gregory the Great, Order of St., 595
Gregory the Illuminator, St., 251
Grellinger, John B., Bp., 470
Grenada, 343
Greschuk, Michael, Bp., 380
Greteman, Frank, Bp., 447-48
Grey Nuns, **see** Charity, Sisters of
Grey Nuns of the Sacred Heart, 502
Griffin, James A., Bp., 448
Gronouski, John (Catholics in Presidents' Cabinets), 404
Groppi, James E. (Death), 600
Grutka, Andrew G., Bp., 448
Guadalupe, Our Lady of, 262
Guadalupe, Sisters of, 502
Guadeloupe, 343
Guam, 343-44
Guard of Honor of the Immaculate Heart, 566
Guardian Angels, 246
Guardian Angels, Sisters of Holy, 502
Guatemala, 344, 368
Guerri, Sergio, Card., 157, 165, 166
Guiana, Dutch, **see** Suriname
Guiana, French, 344
"Guideline," 586
Guild of Our Lady of Ransom, 566
of St. Paul, 566
Guilfoyle, George H., Bp., 448
Guinea, 344, 368
Guinea, Equatorial, 341, 367
Guinea-Bissau, 344
Gulbinowicz, Henryk, Card., 157, 166
Gumbleton, Thomas J., Bp., 448
Gunpowder Plot (1605), 115
Gutenberg, Johann (c. 1456), 115
Gutierrez, Gustavo, Rev., 80
Guyana, 344
Hostile Government Actions, 72
Guyot, Louis J., Card., 157, 165, 166

H

Habakkuk, 189
Habit, 311
Habit, Religious, 213
Habitual Grace, 311
Hacault, Antoine, Bp., 380
Hacker, Hilary B., Bp., 448
Hackett, John F., Bp., 448
Hagarty, Paul, O.S.B., Bp., 470-71
Haggai, 189
Hagiography, 311
Haig, Alexander M. (Catholics in Presidents' Cabinets), 404
Hail Mary, 311
Hains, Gaston, Bp., 380
Haiti, 344, 368
Ouster of Duvalier, 77, 79
Political Freedom, 92
Hakim, Michel, Abp., 380
Halpin, Charles A., Abp., 380
Ham, J. Richard, M.M., Bp., 448
Hamelin, Jean-Guy, Bp., 380
Hamer, Jean Jerome, Card., 157, 166
Hammes, George A., Bp., 448

Handicapped, Catholic Facilities, Organizations, 545-51
Handicapped Needs and the Churches, 79
Handmaids of Divine Mercy, 512
of Mary Immaculate, 502
of the Precious Blood, 502
"Hands across America," 94
Handschlegel, Arsenius, C.M.M., Bro. (Death), 600
Hanifen, Richard C., Bp., 448
Hannan, Philip M., Abp., 448
Hannegan, Robert E. (Catholics in Presidents' Cabinets), 404
Hanukkah, 290
Harper, Edward, C.SS.R., Bp., 448
Harrington, Timothy J., Bp., 78, 448
Harris, Vincent M., Bp., 448
Harrison, Francis J., Bp., 448
Diocesan Tridentine Masses Halted, 74
Hart, Daniel A., Bp., 448
Hart, Joseph, Bp., 448
Hartke, Gilbert, O.P. (Death), 600
Hastrich, Jerome J., Bp., 448-49
Hawaii, 393, 425, 427, 429, 523, 588
Hayes, James M., Abp., 380
Hayes, Nevin W., O.Carm., Bp., 449
Head, Edward D., Bp., 449
Health Association, Catholic, 535-36
Health Care Facilities (Aged), 536-44
Health Care Workers, Pontifical Commission, 148
"Health Centers" in Public Schools, 86
Healy, James A. (Maine, 1875), 395, 471
Heart of Jesus, Institute, 512
Heart of Mary, Daughters of, 505
Heaven, 311
Hebrews (Letter), 191
Heckler, Margaret (Catholics in Presidents' Cabinets), 404
Hedwig, St., 251
Hegira (622), 112
Hegumen (Abbot), 295
Helena, St., 251
Hell, 311
Helmsing, Charles H., Bp., 449
Helpers, Society of, 502
Helpless, Mothers of the, 501
Hennepin, Louis, 384
Henoticon (484), 111
Henry, Frederick, Bp., 380
Henry, St., 251
Henry VIII, King (1533), 115
Heresies, 118-20
Heresy, Heretic, 118
Hermanas Catequistas Guadalupanas, 502
Hermanas Josefinas, 502
Hermaniuk, Maxim, C.SS.R., Abp., 380
Hermeneutics, 191-92
Hermit (Anchorite), 296
Hermit Sisters of Christ in Solitude, 502
Heroic Act of Charity, 311
Herrmann, Edward J., Bp., 449
Hesburgh, Theodore, Rev., 63
Heterodoxy, 311
Hettinger, Edward G., Bp., 449
Hickey, Dennis W., Bp., 449
Hickey, James A., Abp., 449
Statement on Father Curran, 48-9
Hierarchy, 141-42
Hierarchy, Canadian, **see** Bishops, Canadian
Hierarchy, U.S., **see** Bishops, U.S.
High Schools, Catholic, U.S. (Statistics), 519-23
Higi, William L., Bp., 449
Hilary, St., 196
Hildebrand, (Gregory VII, St.), 251
Hill, Morton A., S.J. (Death), 600
Hinduism, 294
Hines, Vincent J., Bp., 449
Hippolytus, St., 251

Hispanic Telecommunications Network, 586
Hispanics, U.S., 481-82
Pastoral Plan, Los Angeles, 95
Religious Commitment, 78
Ministry to, 481-82
Third National Encuentro, 102
Historical Association, American Catholic, 563
Historical Books of the Bible, 186-87
Historical Sciences, Commission, 149
History
Catholic, Canada, 373
Catholic, U.S., 387-404
Church, Significant Dates, 110-18
Hitler, Adolf (1933), 118
See also Germany
Hoch, Lambert A., Bp., 449
Hodapp, Robert, S.J., Bp., 449
Hodges, Joseph J., Bp., 471
Hoeffner, Joseph, Card., 68, 157, 165, 166
Hoey Awards, 597
Hoffman, James R., Bp., 449
Hofstee, Leo Anthony, O.P. (Death), 600
Hogan, James J., Bp., 449
Hogan, Joseph L., Bp., 449
Holiness Sects, 278
Holocaust, John Paul II on, 37
Holocaust Memorial Day, 291
Holy Child Jesus, Society, 502
Holy Childhood Association, 562
Holy Communion, **see** Communion, Holy; Eucharist
Holy Days, 237, 245-48
Byzantine Rite, 269
Holy Eucharist, **see** Eucharist, Holy
Holy Eucharist, Brothers of, 491
Holy Faith, Sisters of the, 502-03
Holy Family (Feast), 246
Holy Family (Religious)
Congregation of Missionaries of, 486
Congregation of Sisters of, 499
Little Sisters of, 499
of Nazareth, Sisters of, 499
Sisters of, 499
Sons, 487
Holy Father, **see** Pope
Holy Ghost, **see** Holy Spirit
Holy Ghost Fathers, 487
Holy Heart of Mary, Servants, 503
Holy Innocents, 246
Holy Land, Commissariat, 303
Holy Name Society, 566
Holy Name Society, Natl. Assn., 566
Holy Names of Jesus and Mary, Srs. of, 503
Holy Office, **see** Doctrine of the Faith, Congregation
Holy Oils, 218, 319
Holy Orders, 217, 221, 226-27
Holy Saturday, 246
Holy See, 311
Publications, 174-75
Representatives, 167-70, 175
See also Vatican
Holy Sepulchre, Order of, 595
Holy Spirit, 311
Blasphemy of, 299
Fruits of, 310
Gifts of, 310
Sins Against, 327
"Holy Spirit in the Church and the World," Encyclical Letter, 39-43
Holy Spirit (Religious)
and Mary Immaculate, Sister Servants of, 503
Community of, 503
Daughters of, 503
Mission Sisters, 503
Missionaries of, 487
Missionary Sisters, Servants, 503
Sisters of, 503
Holy Spirit of Perpetual Adoration, Sister Servants of, 503
Holy Thursday, 246
Papal Letter to Priests, 81

Holy Trinity, 248
Holy Trinity, Missionary Servants of the Most, 490
Order of Most, 490
Sisters of Most, 509-10
Holy Water, 311
Holy Week, 218
Holy Year, 311-12
Home Mission Sisters (Glenmary), 503
Home Missioners of America, 486, 517
Home (Rural) Missions, U.S., 517-18
See also Hispanics
Home Visitors of Mary, 503
Homeless, Temporary Shelters, 551-52
Homes for Aged and Retired, 536-44
Homily, 211
Homosexual Rights Bills, Opposition, 78, 99
Homosexual Seminars, 62
Homosexuality, 312
Homosexuals, Ministry to, 83
Honduras, 344-45, 368
Hong Kong, 345
Honor et Veritas Award, 597
Hope, 312
Hosanna, 312
Hosea, 188
Hospitaller Order of St. John of God, 491
Hospitals, Catholic, U.S., 535-36
See also Cancer Homes, Hospitals; Health Care Facilities
Host, Sacred, 312
See also Communion, Holy
Hosts, Eucharistic, 218
Houck, William Russell, Bp., 75, 449
Hours, Liturgy of, 208, 218
Howard R. Marraro Prize, 597
Howze, Joseph Lawson, Bp., 449
Hoye, Daniel F., Msgr., 82
Hubbard, Howard J., Bp., 449
Hubert, Bernard, Bp., 380
Hubert, St., 251
Hugh of Cluny, St., 251
Hughes, Alfred C., Bp., 449
Hughes, Edward T., Bp., 449-50
Hughes, William A., Bp., 450
Hugo, John J., Rev. (Death), 600
Human Development Campaign, 67, 272
Human Rights, **see** Various Countries
Humanae Vitae, 230-31
Humani Generis (Authority of Encyclicals), 135
Hume, George Basil, O.S.B., Card., 64, 88, 157, 165, 166
Humeral Veil, 213
Humility, 312
Humility of Mary, Congregation of, 503
Sisters of, 503
Hungarian Byzantine Catholics, 265
Hungarian Catholic League of America, 566
Hungary, 345, 368
Hunger, U.S., 62
Hunger, World, 64
Hunthausen, Raymond G., Abp., 87, 91, 450
Apostolic Visitator's Report, 67
Authority Curbed, 105-06
Hurley, Francis T., Abp., 450
Hurley, Mark J., Bp., 450
Hus, John, 273
Hyde Amendment, 46
Hyperdulia, 312
Hypnosis, 312
Hypostatic Union, 312

I

Ibrahim, Ibrahim N., Bp., 450
Iceland, 345
Iconoclasm, 119
Iconostas, 270
Icons, 312
Idaho, 393, 424, 427, 429, 522, 554, 588

Idolatry, 312
Ignatius of Antioch, St., 251
Ignatius of Loyola, St., 251
IHS, 312
Illegal Aliens, see Sanctuary Movement
Illinois, 393, 422, 426, 428, 438, 520, 529, 537, 545, 547, 549, 554, 588, 593
  Abortion Law Ruling, Supreme Court, 87
Imesch, Joseph L., Bp., 450
Immaculate Conception, 246, 260
Immaculate Conception (Religious)
  Little Servant Sisters, 503
  Missionary Sisters, 501
  of BVM, Sisters, 503
  Sisters of, 503
Immaculate Conception Shrine, 220
Immaculate Heart of Mary, 247
Immaculate Heart of Mary, (Religious)
  Brothers, 491
  Congregation of (Missionhurst), 488
  Missionary Sisters, 503
  Missionary Sons (Claretians), 485
  Sisters, 503
  Sisters, Servants, 503
Immersion, see Baptism
Immortality, 312
Impanation, (Consubstantiation), 303
Impediments, Matrimonial, 233
Imprimatur, 301
  Removed from Bioethics Book, 103-04
Impurity, 312
In Pectore, see Cardinal in Pectore
In Sin, 314
Incardination, 312
Incarnate Word and Blessed Sacrament, Cong., 503
Incarnation, 312
Incense, 312
Incest, 312
Inculturation, 312-13
Index of Prohibited Books, 313
India, 345-46, 368
  Beatifications of First Two Native Indians, 34
  Caste Discrimination, 64
  Inter-Ritual Collaboration, 69
  Papal Visit, 32-5
Indiana, 394, 422, 426, 428, 438, 520, 529, 537-38, 545, 547, 554, 588, 593
Indians (Native Americans), Organizations, 517-18
  Statistics, 518
  See also Pelotte, Donald E., Bp.
Indifferentism, 313
Indonesia, 346, 368
  Bishops' Aims, 75
Indulgence, 97-8, 313, 570
Indulgence, Portiuncula, 321-22
Indult, 313
Inerrancy of the Bible, 182
Infallibility, 179-80
Infant Jesus, Congregation of the, 503
Infant Jesus of Prague, 313
Information Office, National Catholic, 591
Infused Virtues, 313
Infusion, see Baptism
Innocent III, Pope (1198-1216), 114
Innocenti, Antonio, Card., 157, 166
Inquisition, 314
Inquisition, Spanish, 314
INRI, 314
Insemination, Artificial, 314
Insignis Medal, 597
Inspiration, Biblical, 181-82
Institute of Apostolic Oblates, 513
Institute of Blessed Virgin Mary, 494
Institute of Charity (Rosminians), 489
Institute of Secular Missionaries, 512
Institute of the Heart of Jesus, 512
Institute on Religious Life, 511
Institutes, Secular, 511-13
Institutes and Universities, Pontifical, 533-34

Institutes of Consecrated Life, 483
Institutes of the Christian Religion (1536), 115
Institutions, Catholic, see Social Services, Catholic
Instruction, Apostolic, 314
Inter-American Conference on Religious Life, 67
Intercommunion, 225, 314
Interdict, 314
Interfaith Center on Corporate Responsibility, 74
Interfaith Prayer Service, Washington, D.C., 66
Interfaith Reports, 287-90
Inter Mirifica (Communications Document), 122
Internal Forum, 309
International
  Catholic Deaf Association, 550
  Catholic-Jewish Liaison Committee, 293
  Catholic Migration Commission, 371
  Catholic Union of the Press, 371
  Eucharistic Congresses, 82, 307-08
  Federation of Catholic Medical Associations, 101, 371
  Institute of the Heart of Jesus, 566
  Liaison, 561
  Organizations, Catholic, 370-72
  Organizations, Vatican Representatives, 175
  Theological Commission, 150
  Union of Superiors General, 89, 511
Internuncio, see Representatives, Vatican
Interpretation, Biblical, 181-82, 191-92
  Teaching Authority of Church, 181
Interracial Council, Catholic, 564
Interracial Justice, National Catholic Conference, 568
Interregnum, 314
Intinction, 315
Iowa, 394, 423, 426, 428, 433, 521, 529, 538, 554, 588, 593
Iran, 346
Iranyi, Ladislaus A., Sch. P., Bp., 450
Iraq, 346
Ireland, 346-47, 368
  Anglo-Irish Agreement, 66
  Divorce Referendum, 92, 96
  Partitioning (1922), 118
  See also North Ireland
Irenaeus of Lyons, St., 251
Irenicism, 315
Irregularity, 315
Isaac Jogues, St., 385
Isaiah, 188
Iscariot (Judas), 194-95
Isidore of Seville, St., 196
Isidore the Farmer, St., 251
Islam, 293-94
  Catholic-Moslem Relations Commission, 149
Israel, 347
Italian Catholic Federation of California, 566
Italo-Albanians, 265
Italy, 347, 368
  Abortion, 64, 76, 104
  Church-State Independence, 61
  Concordat with Vatican, 175
  Optional Religious Instruction, 72
  Papal Visit to Romagna Region, 89
Itinerarium, 315
Ivory Coast, 347, 368

J

Jamaica, 347-48
James the Greater, St., 193
James the Less, St., 193-94
  Letter, 191
Jane Frances de Chantal, St., 251
Jansenism, 315
Januarius, St., 251
Japan, 348, 368
Japanese Martyrs, see Paul Miki, St.

Jaricot, Pauline (1822), 117
Jeanne d'Arc, Sisters of St., 503
Jeanne Jugan, Bl., 252
Jehovah's Witnesses, 315
Jenco, Lawrence, Rev., 67, 75, 98-9, 101
  Release of, 98-9
Jeremiah, 188
Jerome, St., 196
Jerome Emiliani, St., 251
Jerusalem, 348
Jerusalem Bible, 185
Jerusalem Council (51), 111
Jesuit North American Martyrs, 384
  Shrine at Auriesville, 594
Jesuit Martyrs' Shrine (Canada), 372
Jesuit Volunteer Corps, 561
Jesuits, 487
  Increase in Third World, 68
  Suppression (1773), 116
Jesus, 315
  See also Christ
Jesus, Daughters of, 503
  Daughters (Filles de Jesus), 503-04
  Little Brothers of, 491
  Little Sisters of, 504
  Servants of, 504
  Society of, see Jesuits
  Society of Sisters, Faithful Companions, 504
Jesus Caritas — Fraternity of Priests, 513
Jesus Crucified, Congregation of, 504
  and Sorrowful Mother, Poor Sisters, 504
Jesus-Mary, Religious of, 504
Jesus, Mary and Joseph, Missionaries of, 504
Jesus Prayer, 315
Jette, Edouard, Bp., 380
Jews
  Canon of Scripture, 184
  Judaism, 290-91
  Persecution, Germany (1933), 118
  Relations with Catholics, 37-9, 291-93
  See also Anti-Semitism; Israel
Joachim, St., 247
Joan Antida, Sisters of Charity of St., 496
Joan of Arc, St., 251-52
Job (Bible), 187
Joel, 189
Jogues, Isaac, St., 385
John, St. (Apostle), 194
  Gospel, 190
  Letters, 191
John Baptist de la Salle, St., 252
John Berchmans, St., 252
John Bosco, St., 252
John Bosco, Salesians of St., 489
John Capistran, St., 252
John Carroll Society, 566
John Chrysostom, St., 196
John Courtney Murray Award, 597
John Damascene, St., 196
John de Brebeuf, St. 384
John de Castillo, Bl., 384
John de Massias, (Macias), St., 385
John Eudes, St., 252
John Fisher, St., 252
John Gilmary Shea Prize, 597
John Kanty, St., 252
John LaFarge Memorial Award, 597
John Lalande, St., 385
John Lateran Basilica, St., 173
  Feast of Dedication, 245-46
John Leonardi, St., 252
John Nepomucene, St., 252
John Neumann, St., 252
John of God, St., 252
John of God, St., Hospitaller Order of, 491
John of the Cross, St., 197
John I, St., 252
John Paul I, Pope, 133
John Paul II, 32-43, 45, 61-2, 65-6, 69-70, 73-4, 77-8, 81-2, 85-6, 89-90, 93-4,

John Paul II
  97-8, 101-02, 105, 107-09, 201-03, 231-32, 292-93
  Assisi Interfaith World Day of Prayer for Peace, 73, 80, 85
  at Synagogue in Rome, 37-9
  Beatifications (1985, 1986), 34, 61, 65
  Biography, 107-09
  Canonization (1986), 85
  Canonizations, 134
  Colombia and Saint Lucia Visits, 35-7
  Ecumenical Statements, 288
  Encyclicals, 39-43, 140, 201-03
  "The Holy Spirit in the Church and the World," Encyclical Letter, 39-43
  India Visit, 32-5
  Laborem Exercens Excerpts, 201-03
  Statements on Humanae Vitae, 231-32
  Statements on Relations with Jews, 293-94
  Visits in Italy, 61, 89, 101
  World Day of Peace Message, 74
John the Baptist, St., 247
John the Baptist, St., Sisters of, 504
John XXIII, Pope
  Biography, 131-32
  Canonizations, 134
  Encyclicals, 140
  Relations with Jews, 37
  Second Vatican Council, 122, 131
  Social Encyclicals, 199
John Vianney, St., 252
Johnson, Harvey (Death), 600
Johnson, William R., Bp. (Death), 600
Jonah, 189
Jordan, 348
Josaphat, Sts., 252
Jose Maria Rubio y Peralto, Beatification, 61
Joseph, St., 247
Joseph the Worker, St., 89
Joseph, St. (Religious)
  Congregation of, 487
  Missionary Servants of, 504
  Oblates of, 487
  Poor Sisters of, 504
  Religious Daughters of, 504
  Religious Hospitallers, 504
  Sisters of (List), 504
  Society for Foreign Missions (Mill Hill Missionaries), 488
  Society of the Sacred Heart (Josephites), 487
Joseph Benedict Cottolengo, St., 252
Joseph Cafasso, St., 252
Joseph Calasanz, St., 252
Joseph of Cupertino, St., 252
Josephinism (1760s), 116
Josephites (Baltimore), 487
  Pastoral Center, 481
Josephites (California), 487
Joshua, 186
Journalists, Religious Training, 91
Joyce, Robert F., Bp., 450
Joys of the Blessed Virgin Mary (Franciscan Crown), 309
Jubany Arnau, Narciso, Card., 157, 165, 166
Judaism, 290-91
Judaizers, 118-19
Judas, 194-95
Jude Thaddeus, St., 194
  Letter, 191
Judean Society, 566
Judges, 186
Judgment, Last and Particular, 315
  Rash, 323
Judith, 187
Jugan, Jeanne Bl., 252
Julian the Apostate (361-363), 111
Junior Catholic Daughters of the Americas, 563
Jurisdiction, 315
Justice, 315

Justice, Church Involvement in, 58-9
Justice and Peace Commission, 148
Justification, 315
Justin, St., 252

K

Kaffer, Roger L., Bp., 450
Kalisz, Raymond P., S.V.D., Bp., 450
Kampuchea (Cambodia), 335-36
Kaniecki, Michael Joseph, S.J., Bp., 450
Kansas, 394, 423, 427, 439, 521, 529, 538, 547, 554-55, 588
  Archdiocesan Aid for Retired Nuns, 98
Kappa Gamma Pi, 563
Karma, see Buddhism
Kashmitter, William A., M.M. (Death), 600
Kateri Tekakwitha, Bl., 252
  Shrine, 594
Katholicos, 141
Kazel, Dorothy, O.S.U., Sr., 71
Keating, John Richard, Bp., 450
Keeler, William H., Bp., 450
Keleher, James P., Bp., 450
Kellenberg, Walter P., Bp. (Death), 600
Kells, Book of, 112
Kelly, George A., Msgr., 83
Kelly, Thomas, O.P., Abp., 450
Kennedy, John F. (Catholic History in U.S.), 388
Kennedy, Robert F. (Catholics in Presidents' Cabinets), 404
Kenney, Lawrence J., Bp., 450
Kenny, Michael H., Bp., 450-51
Kentucky, 394, 423, 426, 428, 439, 521, 529, 538, 545, 547, 555, 588-89
Kenya, 348, 368
Kerygma, 315
Keys, Power of, 315
Khmer Refugees, 91
Khoraiche, Antoine Pierre, Card., 157-58, 165, 166
Kim, Stephen Sou Hwan, Card., 72, 158, 165, 166
King, Martin Luther, Jr., Federal Holiday, 74-5
King Award, 597
King James Bible, 185
Kingdom of God, 176
Kingdom of Heaven (God), 311
Kings, Books of, 186
Kingship of Christ, Missionaries, 512
Kinney, John, Bp., 451
Kino, Eusebio, 385
Kiribati (Gilbert Islands), 348
Kitbunchu, Michael Michai, Card., 158, 165, 166
Kmiec, Edward U., Bp., 451
Knights of Columbus, 570
  Charities, 94-5
Knights of Lithuania, 567
Knights (Order) of Malta, 595-96
Knights of Peter Claver, 566
Knights of St. Gregory, 595
Knights of St. John, 566
Knights of the Altar, 563
Knights of the Immaculata, 566
Kocisko, Stephen, Abp., 43, 451
Koenig, Franz, Card., 88, 158, 165, 166
Koenigsknecht, Albert I., M.M., Msgr. (Death), 600
Koester, Charles R., Bp., 451
Kolbe, Maximilian, St., 253
Kolping Society, Catholic, 564
Korea, 348, 368
Korea, South, 72, 75
Korean Martyrs (Sts. Andrew Kim and Comps.), 256
Krawczak, Arthur H., Bp., 451
Krohn, Juan Fernandez, 68
Krol, John J., Card., 43, 74, 158, 165, 166
Kucera, Daniel, O.S.B., Bp., 451
Kuharic, Franjo, Card., 158, 165, 166

Kulturkampf (1871), 117
Kung, Hans, 68
Kung Pin-Mei, Ignatius, Bp., see China
Kupfer, William, M.M., Bp., 451
Kuwait, 348

L

Labor Day Statement, 102
Laborem Exercens, 201-03
Labrie, Jean-Paul, Bp., 380
Lacey, Michael Pearse, Bp., 380
Lacroix, Fernand, C.J.M., Bp., 380
Ladies of Charity, Pittsburgh, 63
Ladies of Charity in the U.S., 567
Ladislaus, St., 252
Laetare Medal, 83, 597
Laghi, Pio, Abp., 67, 170
  See also U.S.-Vatican Relations
Lahey, Raymond, Bp., 380
Laicization, 315-16
Laity
  Council for, 148
  East Asian Meeting, 91
  in Foreign Missions, 515, 516
  Mobilization of, 65
  National Center for, 568
  National Council of (U.S.), 559
  Priesthood of, 322
  Role of, 59, 70
  Special Ministers (Eucharist), 217
Lalande, John, St., 385
Lalemant, Gabriel, St., 385
Lamb of God (Mass), 211
Lamb of God, Sisters of, 504
Lambert, Francis, S.M., Bp., 451
LaMennais Brothers (Bros. of Christian Instruction), 490
Lamentations, 188
Lamy, Jean (John) Baptiste, 385
Landazuri Ricketts, Juan, O.F.M., Card., 158, 165, 166
Landers, Dorothy, O.P., Sr., 72
Landriault, Jacques, Bp., 380
Landrieu, Moon (Catholics in Presidents' Cabinets), 404
Langevin, Louis-de-Ganzague, Bp., 380
Languages, Liturgical, 316
  Spanish, U.S., 219
Languages of the Bible, 184
Laos, 348-49, 368
Lapsi (249-251), 110
Larkin, W. Thomas, Bp., 451
LaRocque, Eugene, Bp., 380
LaSalette, Missionaries of, 487
LaSalette, Our Lady of, 262
Las Casas, Bartolome, 385
Las Hermanas, 567
Last Judgment, 315
Lateran, Canons Regular of, 487
Lateran Agreement (Roman Question), 130, 170
  1985 Concordat, 175
Lateran Councils, 121, 122
Lateran University, 533
Latin (Languages of Church), 316
  Mass in, 217
  See also Tridentine Mass
Latin America
  Bishops' Conference (CELAM), 369
  Catholic-Jewish Relations, 67
  Confederation of Religious, 511
  Liberation Theology, Errant Forms, 63-4
  Pontifical Commission, 148
  See also Individual Countries
Latin Liturgy Association, 567
Latin (Roman) Rite, 209
Latria, see Adoration
Latvia, 349, 368
  Anniversary, 93
  Catholics Praised, 101
Laval, Francoise de Montmorency, Bl., 385
Laval University (Canada), 531
Lavery, Charles J., C.S.B. (Death), 600

Lavery, Emmet (Death), 600
Lavigerie, Charles (Missionaries of Africa), 483
Law, 316
Law, Bernard F., Card., 43, 158, 166, 167
Law, Canon, see Canon Law
Law, Civil, 316
Law, Divine, 316
Law, Natural, 316
Lawlor, Kevin, O.F.M., Bro., 96
Lawrence, St., 252
Lawrence of Brindisi, St., 197
Lay Apostolate (Organizations), 559-70
Lay Brothers, see Brothers
Lay Carmelites, 514
Lay Institutes of Men, 483
Lay Ministry, Conference on, 95
Lay Mission-Helpers, 561
Lazarists (Vincentians), 490
Leadership Conference of Women Religious, 510-11
Lebanon, 349
Christians, 71, 100
Hostages, 67
Problems of Homeless, 75-6
Le Bar, James, Rev., 66
Lebel, Robert, Bp., 380
LeBlanc, Camille A., Bp., 380
Lebrun Maratinos, Jose Ali, Card., 158, 165, 166
Leclerc, Marc, Bp., 380
Lectionary, 216
Lector, 227
Leech, George L., Bp., 473
Lefebvre, Marcel, Archbishop, 104
Legare, Henri, O.M.I., Abp., 380-81
Legates, Papal, see Representatives, Vatican
Leger, Paul Emile, S.S., Card., 158, 165, 166
Legion of Mary, 561
Legionaries of Christ, 487
Leguerrier, Jules, O.M.I., Bp., 381
Leibrecht, John J., Bp., 451
Lekai, Laszlo, Card. (Death), 600
Lemieux, Marie Joseph, O.P., Abp., 381
Lent, 236
Byzantine Rite, 269
John Paul II on, 77
Observances, 78
Leo I, the Great, St., 197
Leo III, the Isaurian (726), 112
Leo IX, St. (1049-54), 113
Leo XII, Pope, Encyclicals, 136
Leo XIII, Pope (1878), 117, 128
Canonizations, 133
Document on Anglican Orders, 297
Encyclicals, 137-38
Social Teachings, 128, 199
Leonard, Vincent M., Bp., 451
Leonard of Port Maurice, St., 252
Leopold Mandic, St., 252
Lepanto (1571), 115
Lessard, Raymond W., Bp., 451
Lesotho, 349, 368
Letters (Epistles), 190-91
Letters, Papal, see Encyclicals
Levada, William J., Abp., 451
Levesque, Louis, Abp., 381
Leviticus, 186
Liberalism, 316
Liberation Theology, 56-60, 63-4, 73, 85
Doctrinal Congregation (Second Document), 56-60
Errant Versions, Latin America, 63-4
Liberia, 349, 368
Liberty Weekend Celebration, 98
Libya, 349
Libya, U.S. Bombing, Reactions, 85, 86, 88
Lichten, Joseph, 103
Liechtenstein, 349
Life, Dignity of, 93
Life, March for, 75
Life in Outer Space, 316

Life and Death Questions, 51-3
Lille, Catholic University (France), 532
Limbo, 316
Linens, Altar, 213
Linscott, Mary, Sr., 61
Lipscomb, Oscar H., Abp., 451
Litany, 316
Literary Criticism, Bible, 192
Literary Forms of Bible, 182
Lithuania, 84, 94, 100, 101, 349-50, 368
Anniversary of Christianity, 84
Ordination Anniversary of Bishop Steponavicius, 94
Lithuanian Catholic Alliance, 567
Lithuanian Catholic Federation Ateitis, 567
Lithuanian Catholic Religious Aid, 108, 567
Lithuanian Roman Catholic Federation, 567
Lithuanian Roman Catholic Priests' League, 567
Little, Thomas F., Msgr. (Death), 600
Little Brothers of Jesus, 491
Little Brothers of St. Francis, 491
Little Flower, see Therese of Lisieux, St.
Little Flower Mission League, 567
Little Flower Society, 567
Little Sisters of Jesus, 504
Little Sisters of the Holy Family, 499
Little Sisters of the Poor, 507
Liturgical
Art, 209
Colors, 212-13
Conference, 567
Developments, 215-20
Formation and Inculturation, 219-20
Music, 208, 218
Year (Church Calendar), 236-37
Liturgy, 207-20
Adaptation, 220
Clown Ministry, 220
Constitution, 122, 207-09, 210, 236, 305
Dancing and Worship, 219
Developments, 215-20
Eastern Churches, 268
Eucharistic, 211
Popular Piety, 220
See also Mass
Liturgy of the Hours, 208, 218
Liturgy of the Word, 210-11
Living Will Legislation, 79
Life and Death Questions, 51-3
Living Word, Sisters of, 504
Lodge, Henry Cabot, 172
Lohmuller, Martin J., Bp., 451
Lombard, Peter (1160), 114
Lopez Trujillo, Alfonso, Card., 158, 165, 166
Lord's Prayer, 211
Loreto, House of, 316
Loretto at the Foot of the Cross, Sisters, 504
Lorscheider, Aloisio, O.F.M., Card., 158, 165, 166
Lorscheiter, Jose Ivo, Bp., 88
L'Osservatore Romano, 174
Losten Basil, Bp., 451
Lotocky, Innocent Hilarius, O.S.B.M., Bp., 451
Louis, Congregation of Sisters of St., 504
Louis Bertran, St., 384
Louis de Montfort, St., 252
Louis IX of France, St., 252
Louise de Marillac, St., 252
Louisiana, 394-95, 424, 429, 439, 522, 530, 538, 545, 547, 555, 589, 593
Lourdes Apparition, Shrine, 262
Lourdusamy, D. Simon, Card., 158-59, 166
Louvain, University, 531
American College, 72, 122
Loyal Christian Benefit Association, 567

Lubachivsky, Myroslav J., Card., 43, 100, 159, 166
Lubich, Chiara, see Focolare Movement
Lublin, Catholic University (Poland), 532
Luciani, Albino, see John Paul I, Pope
Lucker, Raymond A., Bp., 451
Lucy, St., 252
Luke, St., 194
Acts of the Apostles, 190
Gospel, 190
Lumen Christi Award, 597
Lumen Gentium, see Church, Constitution
Lumen Vitae Center, 371
Luna (Lunette, Lunula), 213
Lussier, Philippe, C.SS.R., Bp., 381
Lust, 316
Lustiger, Jean-Marie, Card., 88, 103, 159, 165, 166
Luther, Martin, 273
Lutheran-Catholic Dialogue, U.S., 283-84
Lutheran-Roman Catholic Commission, 289
Lutheran Churches, U.S., 275-76
Merger, 103
Lutheran World Federation, 289
Luxembourg, 350
Lyke, James P., O.F.M., Bp., 452
Lynch, George E., Bp., 452
Lyne, Timothy J., Bp., 452
Lyon, Catholic Faculties, 532
Lyonnaise Rite, see Rites
Lyons, Councils, 121
Lyons, Thomas W., Bp., 452

M

Macau (Macao), 350
McAuliffe, Christa, 75
McAuliffe, Michael F., Bp., 452
Maccabees, 187
McCann, Owen, Card., 159, 165, 166
McCarrick, Theodore E., Abp., 94, 452
McCarthy, Edward A., Abp., 452
McCarthy, John E., 83
McCarthy, John E., Bp., 452
McCarthy, Thomas J., Bp., 381
McCloskey, John (U.S. Cardinals), 167, 473
McCollum v. Board of Education (Released Time), 406
McCord, James I., Dr., 79
McCormick, J. Carroll, Bp., 452
McDonald, Andrew J., Bp., 452
MacDonald, James H., C.S.C., Bp., 381
MacDonald, Joseph F., Bp., 381
Apartheid Report, 80
McDonald, William J., Bp., 452
McDonough, Thomas J., Abp., 452
McDowell, John B., Bp., 452
Macedonianism, 119
McEleney, John J., S.J., Abp., 452
McFarland, Norman F., Bp., 452
McGann, John R., Bp., 71, 452-53
McGarry, Urban, T.O.R., Bp., 453
McGivney, Michael J., see Knights of Columbus
McGranery, James P. (Catholics in Presidents' Cabinets), 404
McGrath, J. Howard (Catholics in Presidents' Cabinets), 404
McGrath, Richard T., Bp., 381
Macharski, Franciszek, Card., 159, 165, 166
McIntyre, James F., Card. (U.S. Cardinals), 167, 474
McKenna, Joseph (Catholics in Presidents' Cabinets), 404
McKinney, Joseph C., Bp., 453
McLaughlin, Bernard J., Bp., 453
McManus, William E., Bp., 453
McNabb, John C., O.S.A., Bp., 453
McNamara, John R., Msgr., 63
McNamara, Lawrence J., Bp., 453

McNamee. Catherine T., Sr., 71
McNaughton, William, M.M., Bp., 453
MacNeil. Joseph N., Abp., 381
McRaith. John Jeremiah, Bp., 453
McShea. Joseph M., Bp., 453
McVean, John. O.F.M., 103
Madagascar, 350, 368
Madeira Islands, 350
Madera, Joseph J., M.Sp.S., Bp., 453
Madonna House Apostolate, 513
Magazine Awards, CPA, 598-99
Magazines, Catholic, Canada, 383
Magazines, Catholic, Foreign, 581-82
Magazines, Catholic, U.S., 575-81
Magi, 316
Magisterium (Teaching Authority),
    179-80
  and Interpretation of Bible, 181
  Ordinary, Authority of, 47-8
Magnificat, 316
Maguire, John J., Abp., 453
Maguire, Joseph F., Bp., 453
Maguire, Marjorie, 78
Maher, Leo T., Bp., 86, 99, 453
Mahoney, James Bp. (Canada), 381
Mahoney, James P., Bp. (U.S.), 453
Mahony, Roger M., Abp., 79, 86, 94,
    95, 99, 453
  Plea for Central American Refu-
    gees, 74
Maida, Adam J., Bp., 453
Maine, 395, 421, 425, 427, 519, 538-39,
    549, 555, 589
Mainz Council (848), 113
Major Orders, see Holy Orders
Malabar Rite, see Chaldean Rite
Malachi, 189
Malachy, St., Prophecies, 323
Malagasy Republic, see Madagascar
Malankarese (Malankara Rite), 265
Malawi, 350, 368
Malaysia, 350, 368
  Islamic State Plan, 103
Maldives, 350
Mali, 350, 368
Malone, James W., Bp., 43, 75, 82, 453
Maloney, Charles G., Bp., 453
Maloney, David, Bp., 453
Malta, 350, 368
  School Agreement, 100
Malta, Order of, 595-96
Malula, Joseph, Card., 159, 165, 166
Malvinas, see Falkland Islands
Manchuria, see China
Mandic, Leopold, St., 252
Manning, Thomas R., O.F.M., Bp.,
    454
Manning, Timothy, Card., 159, 165, 166
Manogue, Patrick, 385
Marathonians, 119
Marcellinus and Peter, Sts., 252
March for Life, 75
Marcinkus, Paul C., Abp., 454
Marcionism, 119
Marconi, Dominic A., Bp., 454
Marcos, Ferdinand, 80
  See also Philippines
Marcus Aurelius (161-180), 110
Margaret Clitherow, St., 252
Margaret Mary Alacoque, St., 252-53
  Promises of the Sacred Heart, 324
Margaret of Scotland, St., 253
Margil, Antonio, 385
Marguerite Bourgeoys, St., 384
Maria Goretti, St., 253
Marialis Cultus, 258
Marian Devotion, 258-61
Marian Fathers and Brothers, 487
Marian Library Medal, 597
Marian Movement of Priests, 567
Marian Sisters of Diocese of Lincoln,
    505
Marian Society of Dominican Cate-
    chists, 505
Marian Union of Beauraing, 262
Mariana Paredes of Jesus, St., 253
Marianas, The, 350-51
Marianist Award, 597

Marianists (Priests), 487
Marianites of the Holy Cross, Sisters,
    505
Mariannhill Missionaries, 487
Marianum Theological Faculty, 534
Marie-Leonie Paradis, Bl., 253
Marie of the Incarnation, Bl., 385
Marino, Eugene A., S.S.J., Bp., 78, 454
Mariological Society of America, 567
Mariology, see Mary
Maris, Roger E. (Death), 600
Marist Brothers, 491
  Anniversary, 103
Marist Fathers, 487
Marist Sisters, 505
Mark, St., 194
  Gospel, 190
Markiewicz, Alfred J., Bp., 454
Maronite Antonine Sisters, 505
Maronite Hermits of St. Francis, 487
Maronites, 265
  in U.S. (Antiochene Rite), 268
  Patriarch, 88
Marquard, Philip, O.F.M. (Death),
    600
Marquesas Islands (French Polyne-
    sia), 355
Marquette, Jacques, 385
Marquette University, Suit Against,
    78
Marriage (Matrimony), 221-22, 229-35
  Annulments, 73
  Doctrine on, 229-32
  Laws of the Church, 232-34
  Mixed, 234
Marriage Encounter, 331
Marriages, Invalid, and Sacraments,
    234-35
Marriages, Catholic Statistics (U.S.),
    430
  World, 365
Marshall, John A., Bp., 454
Marsilius of Padua (1324), 114
Martha, St., 253
Marthe, Sisters of Sainte, 505
Martin, Albertus, Bp., 381
Martin de Porres, St., 385
Martin Luther King Holiday, 74-5
Martin of Tours, St., 253
Martin I, St., 253
Martini, Carlo Maria, S.J., Card., 159,
    165, 166
Martinique, 351
Marty, François, Card., 159, 165, 166
Martyr, 316
Martyrology, 316
Marxism, 42
  See also Communism
Mary
  Catholic Teaching, 258-61
    See also Blessed Virgin Mary
Mary (Religious)
  Company of, 505
  Daughters of Heart of, 505
  Little Company of, 505
  Missionaries of Company (Montfort
    Missionaries), 498
  Missionary Sisters of Society, 505
  Missionary Sons of Immaculate
    Heart (Claretians), 485
  Servants of, 505
  Sisters of St., 505
  Sisters, Servants of, 505
  Society, 487
  Third Order Secular, 514
Mary, Legion of, 561-62
Mary and Joseph, Daughters, 505
Mary Aquinas, Sr. (Death), 600
Mary Help of Christians, Daughters,
    505
Mary Immaculate (Religious)
  Daughters, 505
  Missionary Oblates of, 488
  Religious, 505
  Sisters, Servants, 505
Mary Magdalene, St., 253
Mary Magdalene de Pazzi, St., 253

Mary Major, Basilica of St., Dedi-
    cation, 246
Mary of Immaculate Conception,
    Daughters, 505
Mary of Namur, Sisters of St., 505
Mary of Providence, Daughters of St.,
    505
Mary Productions, 586
Mary Reparatrix, Society of, 505
Maryheart Crusaders, 567
Maryknoll, 488
  Anniversary, 95
Maryknoll Sisters, 498
Maryland, 395, 422, 426, 428, 439, 520,
    530, 539, 545, 547-48, 555, 589, 593
Masons (Freemasons), 310
Mass, The, 210-12, 216-17, 218
  Byzantine Rite, 268
  Canon, 211, 216, 299
  Changes, 216-17
  Children's, 218
  Clown Ministry, 220
  Concelebration, 303
  Dancing and Worship, 219
  Doxology, 211, 218
  Eucharistic Prayers, 216, 299
  for Deceased Non-Catholics, 219
  for People, 316-17
  Inter-Ritual Concelebration, 217
  Home (Mass for Special Groups),
    216
  Hosts, 218
  Latin, 217
  Lectionary, 216
  Missal (Sacramentary), 216
  Nuptial, and Blessing, 212
  Places and Altars, 212
  Saturday Evening, 216
  Stipends, 328-29
  Study, 218
  Tridentine, 219
  Trination, 216
  Vestments, Vessels, 212
Massachusetts, 395-96, 421, 425, 427,
    439, 519, 530, 539, 545, 548, 555, 589,
    593
Massias (Macias), John de, St., 385
Master of Ceremonies, 301
Master of Novices, 317
Mater et Magistra Award, 597
Materialism, 42, 317
Matrimony, see Marriage
Matthew, St., 194
  Gospel, 190
Matthias, St., 194
Matthiesen, Leroy T., Bp., 454
Maundy Thursday, see Holy Thursday
Maurer, Jose Clemente, C.SS.R.,
    Card., 159, 165, 166
Mauritania, 351
Mauritius, 351
Maximilian Kolbe, St., 253
May, John L., Abp., 78, 454
May, William, 98
May Laws, see Kulturkampf
Mayer, Augustin, O.S.B., Card., 159,
    166
Mayotte, 351
Mazzuchelli, Samuel C., 385
Medal, Miraculous, 262
Medal, Scapular, 325
Medals, Papal, 596
Medals, Catholic, 596-99
Medeiros, Humberto (U.S. Cardi-
    nals), 167, 474
Media, Good-Evil Potential, 61
Medical Mission Sisters, 505
Medical Missionaries of Mary, 505
Medical Sisters of St. Joseph, 506
Medicus Mundi Internationalis, 371
Meditation, 317
Medjugorje, Yugoslavia, Apparition,
    127
Meek v. Pittenger (Auxiliary Ser-
    vices, Schools), 408
Meeking, Basil, Msgr., 78
Meisner, Joachim, Card., 159-60, 165,
    166

Mekhitarist Order of Vienna, 488
Melczek, Dale J., Bp., 454
Melilla, 351
Melkite Byzantine Rite, 265
Melkites, U.S., 268
Membre, Zenobius, 385
Men, Conference of Major Superiors, 510
Men, Religious Institutes, Membership, 492-93
Men, Religious Institutes, U.S., 483-91
Men of the Sacred Hearts, 567
Menaion, 269
Mendel Medal, 597
Mendez, Alfred, C.S.C., Bp., 454
Mendicants, 317
Mennonites, see Anabaptism
Menologion, 269
Mentally Retarded Persons, National Apostolate with, 550
Mentally Retarded, Sacramental Guidelines, Chicago, 66
Mentally Retarded, Schools for, 546-49
Mercedarian Missionaries of Berriz, 506
Mercedarian Third Order, 514
Mercedarians, 488
Mercy
    Corporal Works, 304
    Divine, 317
    Spiritual Works, 328
Mercy (Religious)
    Brothers of, 491
    Daughters of Our Lady of, 506
    Fathers of, 488
    Missionary Sisters of Our Lady of, 506
    Order of Our Lady of, 488
    Sisters of, 506
    Sisters of, of the Union, 98, 506
Merit, 317
Messiah, see Christ
Mestice, Anthony F., Bp., 454
Metempsychosis, 317
Methodist Churches, U.S., 275
    Dialogues, 285
Methodist Pastoral Letter, 53-4, 87
Methodist-Roman Catholic Commission, 289-90
Methodists, 274
Methodius, St. (Cyril and Methodius, Sts.), 250
    See also Czechoslovakia
Metropolitan, 142
Metzger, Sidney M., Bp. (Death), 600
Mexican Americans, 481-82
    Mexican American Cultural Center, 482
    PADRES, 482
    See also Hispanics
Mexico, 351, 368
    Drug Traffic, 104
    Earthquake, 63
    Political Activism Needed, 67
    Warning Against Consumerism, 72
Mexico, Twelve Apostles, 386
Meyer, Albert (U.S. Cardinals), 167, 474
Micah, 189
Michael, Archangel, 247
Michaels, James E., S.S.C., Bp., 454
Michigan, 396, 423, 426, 428, 439, 521, 530, 539, 545-46, 548, 555, 589
Middle East, 100
Mieszko (966), 112
Migrant Workers, U.S., see Hispanics
Migration, Pontifical Commission, 148
Migration Week, National, 74
Miguel Febres Cordero, St., 253
Milan, Edict (313), 111
Military Archdiocese, U.S., 74, 420
Military Vicariates, World Statistics, 365
Military Service, 203
Militia of Our Lord Jesus Christ, 595
Mill Hill Missionaries, 488

Millennium, 317
Milone, Anthony, Bp., 454
Minder, John, O.S.F.S., Bp., 454
Mindszenty, Jozsef, Card. (Hungary), 345
Minim, Sisters of Mary Immaculate, 506
Ministries of the Church, 227
Minnesota, 396-97, 423, 426, 428, 439, 521, 530, 539-40, 546, 548, 555-56, 589
    Fetus Ruling, 70
Minorities (U.S.), see Blacks; Hispanics
Minton, Sherman (Justices of the Supreme Court), 405
Miracles, 317
Miraculous Medal, 262
Miranda y Gomez, Miguel Dario, Card. (Death), 600
Mirari Vos (1832), 117
Misericordia Sisters, 506
Missal, 216, 317
Missiology, 317
Mission, 317
Mission, Congregation of (Vincentians), 490
Mission Association, U.S., 516-17
Mission Contributions, U.S., 86
Mission Doctors Association, 561
Mission Helpers of the Sacred Heart, 506
Missionaries, American, 514-18
    Bishops, 420-21
    in Foreign Countries, 514-16
    in Home Missions, 517
Missionaries of Charity, 495
Missionaries of Sacred Heart, 489
Missionaries of St. Charles, 488
Missionaries of the Holy Apostles, 488
Missionary Association of Catholic Women, 567
Missionary Catechists of the Sacred Hearts of Jesus and Mary, 506
Missionary Cenacle Apostolate, 567
Missionary Sisters of the Catholic Apostolate, 506
Missionary Union in the U.S., Pontifical, 569
Missionary Vehicle Association, 567
Missionhurst, 488
Missions, Catholic (U.S.), 517
    See also Hispanics
Mississippi, 397, 423, 426, 428, 521, 540, 589
Missouri, 397, 423, 426, 428, 439, 521, 530, 540, 545, 546, 548, 556, 589, 593
Mitchell, James P. (Catholics in Presidents' Cabinets), 404
Mitre, 213
Mixed Marriages, 234
Modalism, 119
Modern World, Constitution (Vatican II), 44, 122, 199-201, 203-04, 229-30
Modernism, 318
    Syllabus of St. Pius X, 129, 329
Mogrovejo, Turibius de, St., 386
Mohammed (622), 112
Monaco, 351
Monarchianism, 119
Monastery, 318
Monasticism (Sixth Century), 112
Mongolia, 351
Monica, St., 253
Monk, 318
Monophysite Churches, 271
Monophysitism, 119
Monotheism, 318
Monothelitism, 119
Monsignor (Honorary Prelate), 142
Monstrance, 213
Montana, 397, 424, 427, 429, 439, 522, 530, 540, 556, 589, 593-94
Montanism, 119
Monte Cassino (c. 529), 112
Montfort Missionaries, 488
Montrose, Donald, Bp., 454
Montserrat, 351

Moore, Emerson John, Bp., 74-5, 454
Mooney, Edward (U.S. Cardinals), 167, 475
Moral Obligations, 198-99
Morality, 318
Morality in Media, Inc., 567
Moran, Patrick R. (Death), 600
Moran, William J., Bp., 454
Morand, Blaise, Bp., 381
Moravian Church, see Hus, John
More, Thomas, St., 254
Moreno, Manuel D., Bp., 454
Morin, Laurent, Bp., 381
Morkovsky, John Louis, Bp., 454-55
Mormons, 318
Morneau, Robert F., Bp., 455
Morocco, 351
Morrow, Louis, S.D.B., Bp., 455
Mortal Sin, 327
Mortification, 318
Moskal, Robert, Bp., 455
Moslems (Muslims), 293-94
    Dialogue, 93-4
Mother Co-Redemptrix, Congregation of, 488
Mother of God, see Mary, Catholic Teaching
Mother of God, Missionary Sisters, 506
Mother of God, Sisters, Poor Servants, 506
Mother Teresa, 64, 91, 100
Motu Proprio, 318
Mount Carmel, BVM of (July 16), 241
Mount Carmel (Religious)
    Congregation of Our Lady of, 494
    Institute of Our Lady of, 494
    Order of Our Lady, 484
    See also Carmelites
Movement for a Better World, 562
Movimiento Familiar Cristiano USA, 562
Mozambique, 103, 351-52, 368
    Jesuit Missionaries Killed, 65
Mozarabic Rite (Rites), 209
Muench, Aloysius (U.S. Cardinals), 167, 475
Mugavero, Francis J., Bp., 78, 455
Mulcahy, John J., Bp., 455
Mulrooney, Charles R., Bp., 455
Mulvee, Robert, Bp., 455
Mundelein, George (U.S. Cardinals), 167, 475
Mundo, Michael P., Bp., 455
Munoz Duque, Anibal, Card., 160, 165, 166
Munoz Vega, Pablo, S.J., Card., 160, 165, 166
Muratorian Fragment, 183
Murphy, Frank (Catholics in Presidents' Cabinets), 404
Murphy, Michael J., Bp., 455
Murphy, Philip F., Bp., 455
Murphy, T. Austin, Bp., 455
Murphy, Thomas J., Bp., 455
Murphy, Thomas W., C.SS.R., Bp., 455
Muscat, see Arabian Peninsula
Music, Sacred, 208-09, 218
    Pontifical Institute, 533
Muskie, Edmund S. (Catholics in Presidents' Cabinets), 404
Muslims, see Moslems
Mysteries of Faith, 318
Mysteries of Rosary, see Rosary
Mysterii Paschalis (Calendar), 236
Mysterium Fidei, see Transubstantiation
Mystery of Church, 176
Mystery of Eucharist, see Mass
Mystical Body, 176-77

N

Nahum, 189
Namibia (South West Africa), 352
Napoleon (1789, 1809), 116
Nasalli Rocca di Corneliano, Mario, Card., 160, 165, 166

Nathaniel (Bartholomew), 193
National
  Apostolate with Mentally Retarded Persons, 550
  Assembly of Religious Brothers, 511
  Assembly of Religious Women, 567
  Association of Boards of Education, 523
  Association of Catholic Chaplains, 536
  Association of Church Personnel Administrators, 567
  Association of Diocesan Ecumenical Officers, 567
  Association of Pastoral Musicians, 567
  Association of Permanent Diaconate Directors, 228
  Association of Priest Pilots, 567
  Black Sisters Conference, 511
  Catholic Bandmasters' Association, 567
  Catholic Cemetery Conference, 568
  Catholic Conference for Interracial Justice, 568
  Catholic Conference for Seafarers, 560
  Catholic Development Conference, 568
  Catholic Disaster Relief Committee, 568
  Catholic Educational Association, 87, 523
  Catholic Forensic League, 563
  Catholic Office for Information, 591
  Catholic Office for Persons with Disabilities, 550
  Catholic Office for the Deaf, 550
  Catholic Pharmacists Guild, 567
  Catholic Rural Life Conference, 559
  Catholic Society of Foresters, 568
  Catholic Stewardship Council, 568
  Catholic Vocation Council, 511
  Catholic Women's Union, 568
  Catholic Young Adult Ministry Association, 563
  Center for Urban Ethnic Affairs, 568
  Center for the Laity, 568
  Christ Child Society, 563
  Clergy Conference on Alcoholism and Related Drug Problems, 568
  Coalition of American Nuns, 511
  Conference of Catholic Bishops, 82, 90, 435-38
    See also Bishops (U.S.)
  Conference of Catholic Charities, 75
  Conference of Diocesan Directors of Religious Education, 568
  Conference of Diocesan Vocation Directors, 568
  Conference of Religious Vocations Directors, 568
  Conference of Vicars for Religious, 511
  Council of Catholic Laity, 559
  Council of Catholic Men, 559
  Council of Catholic Women, 63, 559
  Council of Churches of Christ, 281
  Federation for Catholic Youth Ministry, 563
  Federation of Catholic Physicians Guilds, 568
  Federation of Priests' Councils, 87, 513
  Federation of Spiritual Directors, 568
  Forum of Catholic Parent Organizations, 528
  Guild of Catholic Psychiatrists, 568
  Office for Black Catholics, **see** Black Catholics
  Organization for Continuing Education of Roman Catholic Clergy, 568
  Sisters Vocation Conference, 511
  Youth Pro-Life Coalition, 71

NC News Service, 582
Native Americans, **see** Indians
Nativity, Blessed Virgin Mary, 245
Nativity, Christ (Christmas), 245
Nativity, St. John the Baptist, 247
Natural Law, 316
Natural Virtue, **see** Virtue
Nauru, 352
Navarra, Catholic University (Spain), 532
Nazareth, Poor Sisters of, 506
Nebraska, 397, 423, 427, 429, 439, 521, 540-41, 546, 548, 556, 589
Necromancy, 318
Nehemiah, 186-87
Nelson, Knute, O.S.B., Bp., 455
Nepal, 352
  New Ambassador, 69
Nereus and Achilleus, Sts., 253
Nerinckx, Charles, 385
Nero (64), 111
Nestorian Churches, 271
Nestorianism, 119
Netherlands, 352, 368
  Euthanasia, 88, 93
  Roman Catholic University, 532
Netherlands Antilles, 352
Network, 568
Neumann, John, St., 252
Nevada, 398, 424, 427, 429, 522, 546, 589
Nevin, John (Death), 600
Nevins, John J., Bp., 455
New American Bible, 184-85
New Caledonia, 352
New English Bible, 185
New Guinea, **see** Papua New Guinea
New Hampshire, 398, 421, 425, 427, 519, 556, 589
New Hebrides (Vanuatu), 362
New Jersey, 398, 422, 426, 428, 439, 520, 530, 541, 548, 549, 556, 589, 594
  People of Hope, Berkeley Heights, 67, 90
New Mexico, 398, 424, 427, 429, 522, 530, 541, 548, 556, 589, 594
New Testament, 182-83, 190-91
New York, 398-99, 421, 425, 428, 439, 519, 530-31, 541, 545, 546, 548, 549, 556-57, 589-90, 594
  Medicaid Programs, 95
  Tridentine Masses Halted, Syracuse, 74
New Zealand, 352, 368
Newell, Hubert M., Bp., 455
Newman, John H. (1833), 117
Newman, William C., Bp., 455
News Agencies, Catholic, 582
News Events (1985-1986), 61-106
News Services, U.S., 582
News Stories, Top (1985), 71
Newspaper Awards, CPA, 598
Newspapers, Catholic, U.S., 571-75
  Reports on Church Dissent, 96
Neylon, Martin J., S.J., Bp., 455-56
Niagara Univ. (U.S.), 526, 532
Nicaea, Councils of, 121
Nicaragua, 64, 69, 76, 80, 82-3, 84, 88, 92, 96, 99, 100, 102, 352-53, 368
  Persecution, Harassment of Church, 64, 69, 76, 82-3
  Popular Church, 80, 88
Nicene Creed, 197-98
Nicholas, St., 253
Nicholas of Tolentine, St., 253
Niedergeses, James D., Bp., 456
Niger, 353, 368
Nigeria, 68, 87, 91, 353, 368
  Church Concerns, 68, 87
Nihil Obstat (Censorship of Books), 301
Niue, 353
Noble Guards, 173
Nobrega, Manoel, 385
Nocturnal Adoration Society of U.S., 568
Noel, Laurent, Bp., 381
Noel Chabanel, St., 384
Nolker, Bernard C., C.SS.R., Bp., 456

Non-Abrahamic Religions, 294
Non-Believers, Secretariat, 148
Non-Christian Religions, Declaration (Vatican II), 37-8, 122, 291, 293-94
Non-Christians, Secretariat, 148
Non-Expedit, 318
Norbert, St., 253
Norbert, Third Order of St., 514
Norbertines (Premonstratensians), 489
North America, Cardinals, 166
North American Academy of Liturgy, 568
North American College, 261
North American Martyrs, Jesuit, 384
North Carolina, 399, 422, 426, 428, 520, 542, 549, 557, 590
North Dakota, 400, 423, 426, 428, 439, 521, 531, 542, 546, 557, 590
North Ireland, 80, 347
  Anglo-Irish Agreement, 66
  See also Ireland
Northeast Pastoral Center for Hispanics, 482
Norway, 353
Nostra Aetate (Non-Christian Religions Declaration), 122, 291, 293-04
  Relations with Jews, 37-8
Notre Dame (Religious)
  de Namur, Srs. of, 506-07
  de Sion, Congregation, 507
  School Sisters, 506
  Sisters, 506
  Sisters of Congregation, 506
Notre Dame University, 71, 526
  South Africa Divestment, 63
Novak, Alfred, C.SS.R., Bp., 456
Novalis Marriage Preparation Center, 371
Novatianism, 119
Novena, 318
Novice, 318
Novices, Master, 317
Novitiate, **see** Novice
Nsubuga, Emmanuel, Card., 160, 165, 166
Nuclear Accident, Chernobyl, 85, 90
Nuclear Crisis, Methodist Pastoral Letter, 53-4
Nuclear Deterrence, French Bishops, 84
Nuclear War (U.S. Bishops Pastoral), 204-05
Nulla Celebrior, **see** Patriarchs
Nullity Decree (Annulment), 233, 235
Numbers, 186
Nun, 318
Nuns, Role of, 66
Nunc Dimittis, 318
Nuncios, 167, 168-70
Nuptial Mass, Blessing, 212
Nurses' Schools, Catholic, 430

O

O Salutaris Hostia, 319
Oath, 318
Oath of Succession (1563), 115
Obadiah, 189
Obando Bravo, Miguel, Card., 92, 160, 166
  Appeal to UN, 76
  Solidarity with, 82-3
Obedience, 318
Obedience of Faith, 309
Oblate Missionaries of Mary Immaculate, 512
Oblate Sisters of
  Blessed Sacrament, 508
  Providence, 508
  St. Francis de Sales, 499
Oblates of
  Mary Immaculate, 488
  Most Holy Redeemer, 508
  St. Francis de Sales, 508
Obligations, Moral, 198-99
O'Boyle, Patrick A., Card., 160, 165, 166, 167

O'Brien, Lawrence (Catholics in Presidents' Cabinets), 404
O'Brien, Thomas Joseph, Bp., 456
Obsession, Diabolical, 319
O'Byrne, Paul J., Bp., 381
Occasions of Sin, 327
Occultism, 319
Oceania
  American Bishops, 421
  Cardinals, 166
  Catholic Statistics, 365-66
  Eastern Rite Jurisdictions, 267
O'Connell, William (U.S. Cardinals), 167, 475
O'Connor, Hubert P., O.M.I., Bp., 381
O'Connor, John J., Card., 62, 63, 66, 78, 79, 94, 160, 166, 167
O'Connor, Martin J., Abp., 456
Octave, 319
Octave of Birth of Our Lord (Solemnity of Mary), 248
Oddi, Silvio, Card., 160, 165, 166
Odilia, St., 253
O'Donnell, Cletus F., Bp., 456
O'Donnell, Edward J., Bp., 456
O'Donnell, Edward J.,S.J. (Death), 600
Of Human Life (Humanae Vitae), 230-31
Offertory, 211
Office, Divine (Liturgy of the Hours), 208, 218
Offices of the Roman Curia, 149-50
O'Fiaich, Tomas, Card., 160, 165, 166
O'Grady, John F., O.M.I., Bp., 381
O'Hair, Madalyn Murray, 91
O'Hara, John F. (U.S. Cardinals), 167, 476
Ohio, 400, 422, 426, 428, 439, 520, 531, 542, 545, 546, 549, 557, 590, 594
  Living Will Legislation, 79
Oil of Catechumens, 319
Oil of the Sick, 319
Oils, Holy, 218, 319
O'Keefe, Gerald, Bp., 456
O'Keefe, Joseph Thomas, Bp., 456
Oklahoma, 400, 424, 427, 429, 522, 542, 557, 590, 594
Oktoechos, 269
Old Catholics, 319
Old Testament, 182, 183, 185-89
  See also Bible
O'Leary, Edward C., Bp., 456
Olga, St. (955), 113
Oliver Plunket, St., 253
Olivetan Benedictine Sisters, 493
O'Malley, Sean, O.F.M. Cap., Bp., 456
Oman, 353
O'Mara, John A., Bp., 381
O'Meara, Edward T., Abp., 66, 456
"On this Rock," 586
One Church, One Child Program, 98
O'Neil, Leo E., Bp., 456
O'Neill, Arthur J., Bp., 456
O'Neill D'Amour Award, 597-98
Optatam Totius, 122
Opus Dei, 319
Oratorians, 488
Oratory, 319
Oratory of St. Philip Neri, 488
Order of the Alhambra, 568
Orders, Anglican, **see** Anglican Orders
Orders, Holy, **see** Holy Orders
Orders, Religious, 483
Orders of Knighthood, 593
Ordinariate, 319
Ordinary, 142
Ordination, 319
  See also Deacons, Permanent; Holy Orders
Ordo Paenitentiae, **see** Penance
Oregon, 400-01, 424, 427, 429, 439, 522, 531, 542, 546, 549, 557, 590, 594
O'Reilly-Conway Medal, 598
Organ Transplants, 52, 319
Organizations, Catholic, 563-70

Oriental Church, Orthodox, Dialogues, 286
Oriental Churches, Sacred Congregation, 145
Oriental Studies, Pontifical Institute, 533
Orientalium Ecclesiarum, 122
  See also Eastern Churches, Catholic
Original Sin, 319
O'Riordan, Dick, Rev., 80
O'Rourke, Edward W., Bp., 456
Ortega, Daniel, Pres. (Nicaragua), 76, 99
Orthodox Churches, Eastern, 271
  Catholic-Orthodox Theological Commission, 290
  Conference of Bishops, 272
  Dialogues, 285-86
  Ecumenical Statements, 287, 288
  Ecumenism, 272, 290
  Jurisdictions, 271
Orthodox Churches, Oriental, 271
  Dialogues, 286
Osservatore Romano (L'), 174
Ostensorium, 213
Ostpolitik, 88, 319
Ott, Stanley J., Bp., 456
Ottenweller, Albert H., Bp., 456
Otto I (962), 113
Otunga, Maurice, Card., 160, 165, 166
Ouellet, Gilles, P.M.E., Abp., 381
Ouellette, Andre, Bp., 381
Our Father (Lord's Prayer), 211
Our Lady, **see** Apparitions of BVM; Blessed Virgin Mary
Our Lady of Charity, North American Srs. of Union of, 507
Our Lady of LaSalette, Missionaries, 487
Our Lady of Mercy, Missionary Sisters, 506
Our Lady of Roses Shrine, Bayside, Warning about, 70
Our Lady of Sorrows, Sisters, 507
Our Lady of the Garden, Sisters, 507
Our Lady of the Way, Society, 513
Our Lady of Victory Missionary Sisters, 507
Oxford Movement, 319-20
Ozanam, Frederic (St. Vincent de Paul Society), 535

P

Pacem in Terris, **see** Social Doctrine
Pachomius, St. (318), 111
Pactum Callixtinum (1122), 114
Padilla, Juan de, 385
PADRES, 482
Paenitemini, **see** Penance (Penitence)
Paganism, 320
Pakistan, 353, 368
  Prejudice Against Christians, 71
Palaeologus, Michael (1281), 114
Palatine Guard of Honor, 173
Palazzini, Pietro, Card., 160, 165, 166
Palestinian Homeland, 94
Pall, 213
Pallium, 213
Pallottine Sisters, 507
Pallottines, 488
Palm Sunday (Sunday of the Passion), 247
Palms, 320
Palou, Francisco, 385
Panama, 353, 368
Pancras, St., 253
Pange Lingua, 320
Pantheism, 320
Paola Frassinetti, St., 253
Papacy, **see** Pope
Papal
  Addresses, **see** John Paul II
  Audience, 174
    See also Vatican in News Events
  Election, 320

Papal
  Flag, 173
  Medals, 596
  Representatives, 167-70, 175
  Secretariat of State, 145
  States (1870), 117, 173
    See also Apostolic; Pontifical; Pope; Vatican
Papal Plot Decision, 81
Pappalardo, Salvatore, Card., 161, 165, 166
Pappin, Bernard F., Bp., 381
Papua New Guinea, 353, 368
Paraclete, 320
Paraclete, Servants of the Holy, 488
Paraguay, 354, 368
  Abuse of Rights, 92
  Priest Refused Reentry, 99, 100
Paraliturgical Services, **see** Devotions
Pare, Marius, Bp., 381
Parecattil, Joseph, Card., 161, 165, 166
Paredes of Jesus, St. Mariana, 253
Parente, Pietro, Card., 161, 165, 166
Parents, Duties, 320
Paris, Catholic Institute, 532
Paris Foreign Mission Society, 488
Pariseau, Mother Joseph, 385
Parish, 320
Parish Visitors of Mary Immaculate, 507
Parishes (Statistics), U.S., 421-25
  World, 365
Parker, Matthew, **see** Anglican Orders
Parochial Schools, **see** Schools, Catholic
Parousia, 320
Particular Examen, **see** Conscience, Examination of
Paschal Baylon, St., 253
Paschal Candle, 320
Paschal Precept, 320
Paschal Season (Easter Season), 236
Paschal Vigil (Easter Vigil), 246
Paschang, John L., Bp., 456-57
Passion, Congregation of, 488
Passion of Christ, 320
Passion (Palm) Sunday, 247
Passionist Communication Service, 586
Passionist Nuns, 507
Passionist Sisters, 497
Passionists, 488
Passover, 291
Pastor, 320
Pastor Aeternus (Primacy of Pope), 179
Pataki, Andrew, Bp., 457
Paten, 213
Pater Noster, 320
Patriarchates, Catholic, 141-42, 264
Patriarchates, Orthodox, 271
Patriarchs, Catholic, 141-42, 263
  Cardinals, 151
  Eastern, 263
  Synods, 267
Patrick, St., 253
Patrick, St., Brothers of (Patrician Brothers), 491
Patrick's Missionary Society, St., 488
Patrimony of the Holy See, 149
Patripassianism, 119
Patron Saints, 254-57
Paul, John J., Bp., 457
Paul, St. (Apostle), 194
  Feast, Conversion, 245
  Feast (Peter and Paul), 247
  Letters (Epistles), 190-91
Paul, St. (Religious)
  Angelic Sisters of, 507
  Daughters of, 507
  for Apostolate of Communications, Society of, 488
  of Chartres, Sisters of, 507
  the Apostle, Missionary Society of, 488-89
  the First Hermit, Order of, 488

Paul Miki and Companions, Sts., 253
Paul of the Cross, St., 253
Paul VI, Pope
  Biography, 132-33
  Canonizations, 134
  Ecumenical Meetings, 288, 289
  Encyclicals, 140, 230-31
Pauline Fathers (Doylestown), 488
Pauline Fathers and Brothers, 488
Pauline Letters, 190-91
Pauline Privilege, 233
Paulinus of Nola, St., 253
Paulist Award for Lay Evangelization, 598
Paulist Communications Services, 586
Paulist League, 568
Paulist National Catholic Evangelization Association, 568
Paulist Productions, 586
Paulists, 488-89
Paupini, Giuseppe, Card., 161, 165, 166
Pavan, Pietro, Card., 161, 166
Pax Christi International, 371, 562
Pax Christi USA, 562
Pax Christi (Pious Association), 513
Pax Christi Award, 598
Pax Romana, 371-72
Pax Romana, U.S., 562
Peace, 203-06
  Assisi Interfaith World Day of Prayer, 73, 80, 85
  Commission for, 148
  Methodist Bishops' Pastoral, 53-4
  World Peace Day Message (John Paul II), 74
  U.S. Bishops' Pastoral, 204-06
Peace, Sign of (Mass), 320-21
Peace Award, 598
Peace Prayer, Mass, 211
Pearce, George H., S.M., Abp., 457
Pechillo, Jerome, T.O.R., Bp., 457
Pectoral Cross, 321
Pednault, Roch, Bp., 381
Pelagianism, 119
Pelland, Gilles, S.J., 92
Pellegrino, Michele, Card., 161, 165, 166
Pelletier, Georges, Bp., 381
Pelotte, Donald E., S.S.S., Bp., 457
  Appointment, Ordination, 78, 90
Pena, Raymundo J., Bp., 91, 457
Penance (Penitence), 321
Penance (Sacrament), 217, 221, 225-26
  First, and First Communion, 224
  Norms on General Absolution, 226
  Penitential Celebrations, 226
Penitential Rite, Mass, 210
Penitentiary, Apostolic, 147
Penney, Alphonsus L., Abp., 381
Pennsylvania, 401, 422, 426, 428, 439, 520, 531, 542-43, 545, 546, 549, 557-58, 590, 594
Pentateuch, 185-86
Pentecost, 247
  Dates (1987-2010), 244
Pentecost (Jewish Festival), 291
Pentecostal Churches, 278
Pentecostal-Roman Catholic Consultation, 290
Pentecostarian, 269
People of God, 177
People of Hope, Berkeley, N.J., 67, 90
Pepin (754), 112
Peregrine, St., 253
Perfect Contrition, 303
Perfectae Caritatis, 122
  See also Religious Life
Perfection, Christian Life, 198
Perfectionist Churches, 278
Periodicals, Catholic, 571-81
Perjury, 321
Permanent Diaconate, 227, 228
Pernicone, Joseph M., Bp., 476
Perpetua and Felicity, Sts., 253
Perry, Harold R., S.V.D., Bp., 457
Persecution, Religious, 321
Personal Prelature, 321
  Opus Dei, 319

Persia, **see** Iran
Peru, 354, 368
  Papal Appeal for Reconciliation, 97
Peter, St. (Apostle), 194
  Feast (Chair of St. Peter), 245
  Letters, 191
Peter and Paul, Sts. (Feast), 247
Peter Canisius, St., 197
Peter Chanel, St., 253
Peter Chrysologus, St., 197
Peter Claver, St., 384
Peter Claver, St., Missionary Sisters, 507
Peter Damian, St., 197
Peter Gonzalez, St., 253
Peter Guilday Prize, 598
Peter of Alcantara, St., 253
Peter of Ghent, 385
Peter's Pence, 321
Petition, 321
Petrine Privilege, 233
Pevec, A. Edward, Bp., 457
Pews, 214
Pfeifer, Michael, O.M.I., Bp., 457
Phantasiasm, 119
Pharisees, 321
Phelonian, 270
Phi Kappa Theta Fraternity, 563
Philangeli, 568
Philemon, 191
Philip, St. (Apostle), 194
Philip Neri, St., 253
Philip Neri, St., Congregation of Oratory of, 488
  Missionary Teachers, Sisters, 501
Philip of Jesus, St., 253
Philippians, 191
Philippines, 68, 76, 80, 83-4, 87, 97, 104, 354, 368
  Election, 80
  Influence of Church, 83-4, 87, 97
Philosophical Association, American Catholic, 563
Phoebe (Deaconess), 305
Photius (857), 113
Piarists, 489
Picachy, Lawrence Trevor, S.J., Card., 161, 165, 166
Piche, Paul, O.M.I., Bp., 381
Picpus Fathers (Sacred Hearts Fathers), 489
Pierce v. Society of Sisters, 405, 518
Pilarczyk, Daniel E., Abp., 457
Pilgrimages, Papal, **see** John Paul II
Pilla, Anthony M., Bp., 457
Pinger, Henry A., O.F.M., Bp., 457
Pious Fund, 321
Pious Schools, Order of, 489
Pious Schools, Sisters of, 507
Pious Union
  of Holy Spirit, 569
  of Prayer, 568
Piovanelli, Silvano, Card., 161, 166
Pironio, Eduardo, Card., 161, 166
Pisa, Council (1409), 114
Pius IV, Creed, 198
Pius V, St., 253
Pius VI, Encyclicals, 135
Pius VII (1809), 116
  Encyclical, 136
Pius VIII, Encyclical, 136
Pius IX (1864, 1870), 117
  Encyclicals, 136
  Order of, 595
  Syllabus, 329
Pius X, St. (1903), 117
  Biography, 128-29
  Canonizations, 133
  Encyclicals, 138
  Liturgical Movement, 215
  Syllabus (*Lamentabili*), 129, 329
Pius X, St., Brothers of, 491
  Secular Institute of, 513
Pius XI (1922), 118
  Biography, 129-30
  Canonizations, 133
  Encyclicals, 138-39
Pius XII, Pope

Pius XII, Pope
  Biography, 130-31
  Canonizations, 133-34
  Encyclicals, 139-40
  Liturgical Movement and, 130-31, 215
Pius XII Marian Award, 598
Planned Parenthood Executive, Rhode Island, 75
Plenary Councils, 304
Plenary Councils, Baltimore, 388
Pliny the Younger (112), 110
Plourde, Joseph A., Abp., 381
Plunket, Oliver, St., 253
Pneumatomachists, 119
Poggi, Luigi, Abp., 62
Poland, 64, 69, 84, 87-8, 92, 96, 104, 354-55, 368
  Atheism in Schools, 94
  Church-State Dialogue Hindered, 87-8
Poletti, Ugo, Card., 161, 165, 166
Polish National Catholic Church, Dialogue, 286
Polycarp, St., 253
Polygamy, Africa, 91-2
Polyglot Press, Vatican, 294
Polynesia, French, 355
Polytheism, 321
Poma, Antonio, Card. (Death), 600
Pompei, Loreto and Bari, Sanctuaries, Comm. for, 149
Pontian, St., 253
Pontiff **see** Pope
Pontifical
  Academy of Sciences, 74, 93, 534-35
    See also Life and Death Questions
  Assn. of the Holy Childhood, 562
  Biblical Commission, 150
  College Josephinum, 533
  Commissions, 148-49
  Ecclesiastical Faculties, 532-33
  Household, Prefecture, 149
  Institute for Foreign Missions, 489
  Letters, **see** Encyclicals
  Mission for Palestine, 75-6, 569
  Missionary Union, 569
  Orders of Knighthood, 595
  Universities, 531-32, 533-34
    See also Papal
Poor, Little Sisters of, 507
Poor, Option for, 57
Poor, U.S., Increase, 83
Poor Box, 321
Poor Clare Missionary Sisters, 507
Poor Clare Nuns, 500
Poor Clares of Perpetual Adoration, 501
Poor Handmaids of Jesus Christ, 507
Pope, 141
  Authority, Infallibility, Primacy, 179-80
  Election, 320
    See also John Paul II
Pope Joan, 321
Pope John XXIII International Peace Prize, 85
Popes (List), 123-36
Popes, Encyclicals (List), 135-40
Popes, False (Antipopes), 126-27
Popes, Twentieth Century, 128-33
Popieluszko, Jerzy, Rev., Anniversary, 64
"Popish Plot" (1678), 117
Popp, Bernard, Bp., 457
Popular Church, Nicaragua, 80, 88
Population, Catholic
  Canada, 336, 376-77, 378
  Countries of World, 332-65
  United States, 421-30
  World Totals, 365-66
Pornography, 67
Pornography and Crime, 75
Porres, Martin de, St., 385
Porter, 227
Portiuncula, 321-22
Portugal, 355-56, 368

Portuguese Guinea, **see** Guinea-Bissau
Portuguese Timor, **see** Timor, Eastern
Possession, Diabolical, 322
Postulant, 322
Poterion, 270
Poupard, Paul, Card., 161-62, 166
Poverello Medal, 598
Poverty, 322
Povish, Kenneth J., Bp., 457
Power, Cornelius M., Abp., 457
Power, William E., Bp., 381
Power of the Keys, 315
　　See also Infallibility; Primacy
Powers (Angels), 296
Pragmatic Sanction (1438), 115
Pragmatism, 322
Prague, Infant Jesus of, 313
Praises, Divine, 306
Prayer, 322
Prayer, Religious and, 89
Prayer Intentions, Monthly, **see** Calendar, 1987
Prayer of the Faithful, 211
Prayer over the Gifts, 211
Precept, Paschal, 320
Precepts, 322
Precepts of the Church, 199
Precious Blood (Religious)
　　Daughters of Charity of the Most, 507
　　Missionary Sisters, 507
　　Sisters Adorers, 507
　　Sisters of Most, 507
　　Society of, 489
Predestination, **see** Calvin, John
Preface, 211
Prefect Apostolic, 142
Premontre, Order of Canons Regular (Premonstratensians), 489
Presbyterian Churches, U.S., 276
Presbyterians, 274
Presbyterians, Reformed, Dialogue, 287
Presbyterium Ordinis, 122
Presence of God, 322
Presentation (Feast), 247
Presentation (Religious)
　　Brothers of Mary, 491
　　of Mary, Sisters, 507
　　of the BVM, Sisters, 508
Press, Catholic, U.S., 571-81
　　Statistics, 571
Press, International Catholic Union, 371
Press, Vatican, 174-75
Press Association, Catholic, 565
　　St. Francis de Sales Award, 598
Press Office, Vatican, 174
Presumption, 322
Preternatural Gifts, 322
Pride, 322
Prie-Dieu, 322
Priest, 227
Priesthood (Synod of Bishops), 143
Priesthood of the Laity, 322
Priests
　　Holy Thursday Letter (John Paul II), 81
　　World Support Group, 102
Priests, Canada (Statistics), 376-77
Priests, U.S. (Statistics), 421-25
　　in Foreign Missions, 515-16
Priests, World (Statistics), 365
Priests' Councils, National Federation (U.S.), 87, 513
Priests' Eucharistic League, 569
Primacy of Pope, 141, 179
Primary Option, 322
Primate, 142
Primatesta, Raul Francisco, Card., 162, 165, 166
Primeau, Ernest, Bp., 457
Principalities (Angels), 296
Prior, 322
Priscillianism, 119

Prisons, Florida, Religious Bias, 86
Privilege, 322
Privilege of Faith (Petrine Privilege), 233
Probabilism, 322
Pro-Cathedral, 322
Pro Comperte Sane, **see** Roman Curia
Pro Ecclesia et Pontifice Medal, 596
Pro Ecclesia Foundation, 569
Pro Fidelitate et Virtute Award, 91
Pro-Life Efforts, 81
Pro-Life Violence Denounced, 98
Pro Maria Committee, 569
Promoter of the Faith, 322
Pro-Nuncio, 167
Propagation of the Faith, Cong. of, 147
　　Society of, 569
Proper of the Mass, 211
Prophecies of St. Malachy, 323
Prophecy, 323
Prophets, 188-89
Pro Sanctity Movement, 372, 569
Prost, Jude, O.F.M., Bp., 457
Protestant
　　Canon of the Bible, 184
　　Churches in the U.S., Major, 274-77
　　See also Ecumenism
Protestants and Intercommunion, 225
Protocanonical Books (Canons of Bible), 184
Proulx, Adolph E., Bp., 382
Proulx, Amedee W., Bp., 457-58
Proverbs, 187
Providence (Sisters)
　　Daughters of Divine, 508
　　Missionary Catechists, 508
　　Oblate Sisters of, 508
　　Sisters of, 508
　　Sisters of Divine, 508
Providence, Sons of Divine, 489
Providence Association of Ukrainian Catholics, 569
Province, 323
Provinces, Ecclesiastical, Canada, 374
　　United States, 411-12
Provincial Councils, 304
Providentissimus Deus, 193
Prudence, 323
Psalms, 187
Pseudepigrapha, 185
Public Affairs of Church, Council for, 145
Public Schools
　　"Health, Centers," 86
　　Released Time, 519
Publications, Vatican, 174-75
Publishers, 591-92
Puerto Rico, 356, 368
　　Dates in Catholic History, 403-04
　　Episcopal Conference, 368
　　Minor Basilica, 432
Puerto Rican Catholics in U.S., **see** Hispanics
Pulpit, 214
Punishment Due for Sin, 323
Purgatory, 323
Purification (Presentation of the Lord), 247
Purificator, 213
Purim, 291
Puritans, 274
Pursley, Leo A., Bp., 458
Puscas, Louis, Bp., 458
Pyx, 213

Q

Qatar, 356
Quakers, 274
Quam Singulari, **see** Communion, First and First Confession
Quanta Cura (1864), 117
Quartodecimans (Easter Controversy), 306
Queenship of Mary, 247-48
Quinlan, Karen Ann, 51

Quinn, Alexander James, Bp., 458
Quinn, Bernard, C.M., 71
Quinn, Francis A., Bp., 458
Quinn, John R., Abp., 61, 458
Quiroga, Vasco de, 385
Qumran Scrolls (Dead Sea Scrolls), 185

R

Racism, 323
Radio, Catholic, U.S., 586
　　Diocesan Communications Directors, 587-91
Radio, Vatican, 173-74
Ramirez, Ricardo, C.S.B., Bp., 458
Raphael, Archangel, 247
Rash Judgment, 323
Raskob Foundation, 569
Rationalism, 323
Ratzinger, Joseph, Card., 47-51, 97, 162, 165, 166
　　See also Doctrine of the Faith, Congregation
Ravalli, Antonio, 385
Raya, Joseph M., Abp., 458
Raymbaut, Charles, 385
Raymond Nonnatus, St., 253
Raymond of Penyafort, St., 253-54
Razafimahatratra, Victor, S.J., Card., 162, 165, 166
Reader (Lector), 227
Readings, Mass, 210
Readings, Office of (Liturgy of Hours), 208
Reagan, Ronald, Pres., Papal Message to, 65
Reason, Age of, 296
Rebaptism Controversy, 119
Recollection, 323
Recollects, Augustinian, 483
Reconciliation Room, 214-15
Red Elk, Steven (Death), 600
Redeemer, Divine, Sisters of the, 508
Redeemer, Holy (Religious)
　　Congregation of the Most, 489
　　Oblates of the Most, 508
　　Order of the Most, 508
　　Sisters of the, 508
Redemptorists, 489
Reformation (1517), 115
　　Men, Doctrines, Churches, 273-74
Reformed Churches-Roman Catholic Conversations, 290
Refuge, Sisters of Our Lady of Charity, 507
Refugees, Central American, U.S., 70, 74
Refugees, Khmer, 91
Regan, Joseph, M.M., Bp., 458
Regimini Ecclesiae Universae (Roman Curia), 144
Regina Caeli (Angelus), 297
Regina Medal, 598
Regis College Lay Apostolate, 562
Regular Clergy, 302
Reh, Francis, Bp., 458
Reilly, Daniel P., Bp., 458
Reilly, Thomas F., C.SS.R., Bp., 458
Reiss, John C., Bp., 458
Relativism, 323
Released Time, 519
　　See also Church-State Decisions
Relics, 323-24
Relief Services, Catholic, 64, 67, 70, 76, 79, 437, 559-60
　　U.S. Bishops Report, 437
Religion, 324
Religions, Non-Abrahamic, 294
Religious, 483
　　and Prayer (John Paul II), 89
　　Congregation for, 146
　　Latin American Confederation, 511
　　Retired, Needs of, 91, 98
　　Superiors, Internatl. Union, 511
　　U.S., Papal Commission Report, 79
　　Vicars of, 511
　　Vocation of, 81
Religious, Men, 483

Religious, Men
  Brothers National Assembly, 511
  Brothers in World, 365
  Conference of Major Superiors, U.S., 510
  in U.S. (List), 483-91
  in U.S. (Statistics), 421-25
  Priests in the World, 365
  World Membership, 492-93
Religious, Women, U.S., 493-510
  Meeting with Vatican Officials, 82
  Organizations, 510, 511
  Statistics, 421-25
  Teachers, Catholic Schools, 523
Religious, Women, World, 365
Religious Education (John Paul II), 73
Religious Education, U.S., 559
  Pupils Receiving Instruction, 523
Religious Formation Conference, 511
Religious Freedom, 309-10
Religious Life, Institute on, 511
Religious News Service, 582
Reliquary, 324
Remedial Education Classes (Aguilar v. Felton), 87, 94, 409
Rene Goupil, St., 384
Reparation, 324
  of Congregation of Mary, Sisters of, 508
  Society of the Immaculate Heart of Mary, 569
Representatives, Vatican, 167-70, 175
Requiem Mass, 212
Rescript, 324
Reserved Case, 324
Restitution, 324
Resurrection (Easter), 246
Resurrection, Congregation, 489
Resurrection, Sisters of, 508
Retarded, Facilities for, 546-49
Retired, Facilities for, 536-44
Retired Religious, Needs, 91, 98
Retreat Houses, U.S., 553-58
Retreats International, 552
Reunion, 356
Revelation (Dogmatic Constitution), 180-83, 330
  See also Bible
Revelation, Book of, 191
Revised Standard Version (Bible), 185
Revolution, American, **see** Catholic History of U.S.
Rheims, Synod (1148), 114
Rhode Island, 401, 421, 425, 427, 519, 531, 543, 558, 590
Rhodes, 356
Rhodesia, **see** Zimbabwe
Ribeiro, Antonio, Card., 162, 165, 166
Ricard, John, S.S.J., Bp., 458
Ricci, Matteo (1610), 116
  See also China
Rice, Nick, Rev., 67
Richard, Arsène, Bp., 382
Richard, Gabriel, 385
Rigali, Justin, Abp., 458
Righi-Lambertini, Egano, Card., 162, 166
Right to Life Federation, International, 80, 81
Riley, Lawrence J., Bp., 458
Ring, 324
  Fisherman's, 309
Ring, William (Death), 600
Rio de Janeiro, University, 531
Rio Grande do Sul, University, 531
Rita, St., Sisters of, 508
Rita of Cascia, St., 254
Rites, 209-10
Rites, Eastern, 264-66
Ritter, Bruce, O.F.M. Conv., Rev., 75
Ritter, Joseph (U.S. Cardinals), 165, 477
Ritual, 324
Rivera Damas, Arturo, Abp. (San Salvador), 70, 76
Roach, John R., Abp., 458

Robert Bellarmine, St., 197
Robert Southwell, St., 254
Robidoux, Omer, O.M.I., Bp., 87, 382
  Fur Trappers Rights, 87
Roch, St., 254
Roch Gonzalez, Bl., 384
Rochet, 213
Rodimer, Frank J., Bp., 459
Rodriguez, Alonso, Bl., 385
Rodriguez, Miguel, C.S.S.R., Bp., 459
Rodriguez, Placido, C.M.F., Bp., 459
Roe v. Wade, 45
Rogation Days, 237
Rogationist Fathers, 489
Rogito, 324
Role of Law Award, 598
Roman, Agustin, Bp., 459
Roman Catholic Church, **see** Church
Roman Curia, **see** Curia, Roman
Roman Martyrology, 316
Roman Missal (Sacramentary), 216, 317
Roman Pontiffs, **see** Popes
Roman Question, **see** Lateran Agreement
Roman Rite, 209
Romania, 356
Romanian Byzantine Rite, 265
  in the United States, 268
Romaniello, John, M.M., Msgr., 600
Romans, 190
Romero, Oscar, Abp., Anniversary of Assassination, 84
Romuald, St., 254
Roque, Francis, Bp., 459
Rosary, 324
  Feast, 247
  Franciscan Crown, 309
Rosary, Family, 566
Rosary, Holy, Brothers of the, 491
  Congregation of Our Lady of the, 508
  Missionary Sisters of Our Lady of the, 508
Rosary, Our Lady of, Shrine (Colombia), 35
Rosary Altar Society, 569
Rosary League, 569
Rosati, Joseph, 385
Rosazza, Peter A., Bp., 459
Rose, Robert John, Bp., 459
Rose of Lima, St., 254
Rosminians (Institute of Charity), 489
Rosh Hashana, 291
Rossi, Agnelo, Card., 162, 165, 166
Rossi, Opilio, Card., 162, 166
Rota, Roman, 147
Routhier, Henri, O.M.I., Abp., 382
Roy, Maurice, Card. (Death), 600
Roy, Raymond, Bp., 383
Rubin, Wladyslaw, Card., 162, 166
Rubrics, Mass, 216
Rudin, John J., M.M., Bp., 459
Rugambwa, Laurean, Card., 162-63, 165, 166
Rule of Faith, 309
Runcie, Robert, Abp. (Anglican), 68, 288
Rural Life Conference, 559
Rural Ministry Institute, 518
Rural Parish Workers of Christ the King, 512
Rusnak, Michael, C.S.S.R., Bp., 382
Russell, John J., Bp., 459
Russia, **see** Union of Soviet Socialist Republics
Russian Byzantine Rite, 265
  in the United States, 268
Ruth, 186
Ruthenian Byzantine Rite, 265
  in the United States, 267-68
Rwanda, 356-57
Ryan, Daniel L., Bp., 459
Ryan, Gerald, Bp., 477
Ryan, James C., O.F.M., Bp., 459
Ryan, Joseph F., Bp., 382
Ryan, Joseph T., Abp., 459

S

Sabatini, Lawrence, C.S., Bp., 382
Sabattani, Aurelio, Card., 163, 166
Sabbath, 324
Sabbath (Jewish), 290
Sabellianism, 119
Sacerdotal Fraternity, Congregation of, 489
Sacrament, Blessed, **see** Blessed Sacrament
Sacrament, Sisters of Most Holy, 509
Sacramental Forum, **see** Forum
Sacramentals, 207-08
Sacramentary, 216, 324
Sacramentine Nuns, 509
Sacraments, 221-31
  Congregation, 146
  Eastern Churches, 263
  Grace, 311
  Liturgical Developments, 217
Sacraments for Mentally Retarded, Guidelines, 66
Sacrarium, 324
Sacred Heart (June 26, 1987), 248
  Enthronement, 324
  Promises, 324
Sacred Heart (Religious)
  Brothers, 491
  Daughters of Our Lady, 509
  Mission Helpers, 506
  Missionaries, 489
  Missionary Sisters, 509
  Religious of the Apostolate of, 509
  Society Devoted to, 509
  Society of, 509
Sacred Heart Catholic Univ. (Italy), 532
Sacred Heart League, 569
Sacred Heart of Jesus (Religious)
  and of Poor, Servants, 509
  Apostles of, 509
  Congregation of, 489
  for Reparation, Cong. of Handmaids, 509
  Franciscan Missionary Brothers, 491
  Handmaids, 509
  Missionary Sisters of Most, 509
  Oblate Sisters of, 509
  Servants of Most, 509
  Sisters of, 509
Sacred Heart of Mary, Religious, 509
Sacred Heart Program, 586
Sacred Hearts, Fathers of, 489
Sacred Hearts, Religious of Holy Union of, 509
Sacred Hearts and of Perpetual Adoration, Sisters, 509
Sacred Hearts of Jesus and Mary, Missionaries of, 489
  Sisters of, 509
Sacred Scripture, **see** Bible
Sacrifice of Mass, **see** Mass
Sacrilege, 324-25
Sacristy, 325
Sacrosanctum Concilium, 44, 122
  See also Liturgy Constitution
Sacrum Diaconatus Ordinem, **see** Deacon, Permanent
Sadducees, 325
Sahagun, Bernardino de, 386
Saint
  Anne de Beaupre, Shrine, 372
  Ann's Church, Vatican City, 173
  Ansgar's Scandinavian Catholic League, 569
  Anthony's Guild, 569
  Bonaventure University Medal, 598
  Christopher (St. Kitts) and Nevis, 357
  Francis de Sales Award, 598
  Francis Xavier Medal, 598
  Joan's International Alliance, 372
  Joseph's Oratory Shrine, 372
  Joseph's University of Beirut, 532
  Jude League, 569
  Lucia, 357

Saint
Lucia, Papal Visit, 36-7, 98
Margaret of Scotland Guild, 569
Martin de Porres Guild, 569
Patrick's College, Maynooth (Ireland), 532
Paul's University, Ottawa, 531
Pierre and Miquelon, 357
Susanna Church, Rome, 175
Thomas Aquinas Foundation, 569
Thomas of Villanueva Univ. (Cuba), 532
Vincent and Grenadines, (West Indies), 357
Vincent de Paul Medal, 598
Vincent de Paul Society, 535
Saint-Antoine, Jude, Bp., 382
Saint-Gelais, Raymond, Bp., 382
Saints, 325
Biographical Sketches, 248-54
Canonization, 299-300
Canonization (1986), 85
Canonized since Leo XIII, 133-35
Commemorations in Calendar, 236-37, 238-43
Communion of, 303
Congregation for Causes of, 146
Cult, 325
Emblems, 257-58
Patrons, 254-57
Veneration, 325
See also Proper Names of Individual Saints
Salamanca, University of (Spain), 532
Salatka, Charles, Abp., 459
Salazar Lopez, Jose, Card., 163, 165, 166
Sales, Eugenio de Araujo, Card., 155, 165, 166
Salesian Cooperators, 372
Salesian Sisters (Daughters of Mary Help of Christians), 505
Salesians of St. John Bosco, 489
Letter of Major Superior, 64
Salesianum, Pontifical University, 533
Salvation, 325
Salvation History, 325
Salvation outside the Church, 325
Salvatorian Fathers, Basilian, 484
Salvatorians, 489
Samoa, American, 357
Samoa, Western, 357
Samuel, 186
San Marino, 357
Sanchez, Robert, Abp., 459
Sanctifying Grace, 311
See also Sacraments
Sanctuary, 214
Sanctuary Lamp, 215
Sanctuary Movement, 66-7, 74, 80
Sandinistas, see Nicaragua
San Pedro, Enrique, S.J., Bp., 459
Sanschagrin, Albert, O.M.I., Bp., 382
Santo Tomas University (Philippines), 532
Sao Paulo University (Brazil), 531
Sao Tome and Principe, 357
Sardinia, Papal Visit, 61
Satan (Devil), 305
John Paul II on, 101
Satanism, 325
Satowaki, Joseph Asajiro, Card., 163, 165, 166
Saudi Arabia, 357
Saul (Historical Books of the Bible), 186
Savior, see Jesus
Savior, Company of, 509
Order of Most Holy (Brigittine Sisters), 494
Sisters of Divine, 509
Society of Divine, 489
Scalia, Antonin, 94, 405
Scandal, 325
Scandinavia, Episcopal Conference, 368-69
Scanlan, John J., Bp., 459

Scapular, 325
Medal, 325
Promise, 325-26
Scarpone, Gerald, O.F.M., Bp., 459
Schad, James L., Bp., 459
Scherer, Alfred Vicente, Card., 163, 165, 166
Scheut Fathers, see Immaculate Heart Missioners
Schierhoff, Andrew B., Bp., 459-60
Schism, Schismatic, 326
Schism, Western, 127
Schladweiler, Alphonse, Bp., 460
Schlaefer Berg, Salvator, O.F.M. Cap., Bp., 460
Schlarman, Stanley G., Bp., 460
Schlotterback, Edward, O.S.F.S., Bp., 460
Schmidt, Firmin M., O.F.M. Cap., Bp., 460
Schmidt, Mathias, O.S.B., Bp., 460
Schmitt, Mark, Bp., 460
Schmitz, Paul, O.F.M. Cap., Bp., 460
Schoenherr, Walter J., Bp., 460
Schoenstatt Sisters of Mary, 513
Scholastica, St., 254
Scholasticism, 326
Schools, Malta, see Malta
Schools, Catholic (U.S.), 518-22
Aid, 518-19
Colleges and Universities, 519-23
for Handicapped, 545-50
Legal Status, 518-19
Honor for, 95
Religious Identity (John Paul II), 65
Remedial Education, 78, 87, 94, 409
See also Church-State Decisions of Supreme Court
NCEA, 87, 523
Shared Time, 519
Statistics, 519-23
See also Religious Education; Seminaries
Schools, Public, see Public Schools
Schroeder, William (Death), 600
Schuck, James A., O.F.M., Bp., 460
Schulte, Francis B., Bp., 460
Schuster, Eldon, Bp., 460
Sciences, Pontifical Academy, 74, 93, 534-35
Scotland, 357-58, 368
Church of Scotland, 92
South African Boycott Proposed, 72
Scribes, 326
Scripture, see Bible
Scruple, 326
Sea, Apostleship of, 560
Seal of Confession, 326
Seasons, Church, 236
Sebastian, St., 254
Sebastian Aparicio, Bl., 384
Second Vatican Council, see Council, Second Vatican
Secretariat of State, Vatican, 145
Secretariats (Roman Curia), 147-48
Sects, Vatican Report, 54-6
Secular (Diocesan) Clergy, 302
Statistics (World), 365
See also Individual Countries
Secular Institutes, 511-13
Congregation, 146
Secular (Third) Orders, 514
Secularism, 326
Sede Vacante, see Interregnum
See, 326
Seelos, Francis X., 386
Seghers, Charles J., 386
Semi-Arians, 119
Seminarians
Countries of the World, 332-65
United States, 530
World (Summary), 365
Seminaries, U.S., 529-31
Seminary, 326
Semi-Pelagianism, 119
Sendero Luminoso Movement, Peru, 97
Senegal, 358, 369

Senses of the Bible (Interpretation), 192
Sensi, Giuseppe Maria, Card., 163, 166
Separated and Divorced Catholics, Pastoral Ministry, 234-35
Separation, Marriage, 233
Septuagint Bible, 184
Seraphim (Angels), 296
Serbs (Byzantine Rite), 266
Sermon on the Mount, 326
Serra, Junipero, 386
Serra Award of the Americas, 598
Serra International, 569
Convention, 95
Servants of Mary, Order of Friar (Servites), 489
Servants of Mary, Sisters, 505
Servite Sisters, 505
Servites, 489
Servitium Christi Secular Institute, 513
Setian, Nerses Mikail, Bp., 460
Seton, Elizabeth Bayley, St., 250
Seven Holy Founders, 254
Seven Joys of the Blessed Virgin Mary, see Franciscan Crown
Seven Last Words of Christ, 326
Seventh Day Adventists (Adventists), 295-96
Sex and Crime, 75
Seychelles, 358
Sfeir, Nasrallah, Patriarch (Maronites), 88
Shaheen, Elias, Bp., 382
Shea, Francis R., Bp., 460
Sheehan, Daniel E., Abp., 460
Sheehan, Michael J., Bp., 460
Shehan, Lawrence J., Card. (U.S. Cardinals), 167, 478
Sheldon, Gilbert I., Bp., 460
Shenouda III, Pope (Coptic Orthodox), 288
Sherbrooke University (Canada), 531
Sherlock, John M., Bp., 382
Shrine, Bayside, N.Y., Warning about, 70
Shrine, Crowned, 326
Shrine, Immaculate Conception, 220
Shrines, Canada, 372
Shrines, U.S., 592-95
Shroud of Turin, 326-27
Shubsda, Thaddeus A., Bp., 460
Sick, Anointing of, see Anointing of Sick
Sick, Eucharistic Fast, 309
Sick, Oil of, 319
Sick Calls, 327
Sidarouss, Stephanos I, C.M., Patriarch, Card., 163, 165, 166
Sierra Leone, 358, 369
Sign of Cross, 327
Signatura, Apostolic, 147
Signs of the Times, 327
Signum Fidei Medal, 598
Silva Henriquez, Raul, S.D.B., Card., 163, 165, 166
Simon, St. (Apostle), 194
Simon, William (Catholics in Presidents' Cabinets), 404
Simonis, Adrianus J., Card., 163, 166
Simony, 327
Sin, 327
Accessory to, 295
John Paul II on, 101
Original, 319
Punishment, 323
Righteousness and Judgment (Holy Spirit Encyclical), 41-2
Social, 58
Sin, Jaime L., Card., 83-4, 163, 165, 166
See also Philippines
Singapore, 358, 368
Abortion, Contraception, 79
Sins
against Holy Spirit, 42, 327
Capital, 300
Forgiveness, 309
See also Penance (Sacrament)

Sins
  Occasions, 327
  That Cry to Heaven for Vengeance, 327
Sirach, 188
Siri, Giuseppe, Card., 163, 165, 166
Sister, 327
Sisterhood, 327
Sisters, United States, 493-510
  Retired, 91, 98
  Statistics, 421-25
  See also Religious, Women
Situation Ethics, 327-28
Sixtus II, St., 254
Skinner, Patrick J., C.J.M., Abp., 382
Sklba, Richard J., Bp., 460
Skylstad, William, Bp., 460-61
Slander, 328
Sloth, 328
Slovak Byzantine Catholics, 265
Slovak Catholic Federation of America, 87, 569
Slovak Catholic Sokol, 569
Slovakia, Persecution (Czechoslovakia), 338-39
Smeal, Eleanor, 75, 86
Smith, Alfred E. (Catholic History in U.S., Bigotry), 387-88
Smith, Kate (Death), 600
Smith, Philip M., O.M.I., Abp., 461
Smith, William J., Bp., 382
Snyder, John J., Bp., 461
Social Communications Commission, 148
  See also Communications
Social Doctrine of the Church, 199-204
Social Service, Sisters of, 509
Social Services, Catholic, U.S., 535-52
Social Sin, 58
Social Teaching, (Liberation Theology II), 56-60
Socially Maladjusted, Facilities for, 545-46
Societies, Catholic, in U.S., 563-70
Societies, Religious, **see** Religious, Men, Women, in U.S.
Society for the Propagation of the Faith, 569
  U.S. Contributions, 86
Society of St. Paul, 488
Society of St. Peter the Apostle, 569
Society of St. Vincent de Paul, 535
Sodality of Our Lady, **see** Christian Life Communities
SODEPAX (Society for Development and Peace), 280
Soenneker, Henry J., Bp., 461
Soens, Lawrence D., Bp., 461
Solanus, Francis, St., 386
Solemnity of Mary, 248
Solidarity, **see** Poland
Sollicitudo Omnium Ecclesiarum (Representatives of the Holy See), 167
Solomon (Kings 1 and 2), 186
Solomon Islands, 358
Somalia, 358
Somascan Fathers, 489
Song of Songs (Bible), 187
Sons of Mary Missionary Society, 489
Sophia, Catholic University (Japan), 532
Sorcery, 328
Sorin, Edward F., 386
Sorrentino, Mary Ann, 75
Sorrows (Dolors) of the Blessed Virgin Mary, 247
Soteriological Award, 598
Soteriology, 328
Souls, Holy, **see** All Souls
South Africa, 61, 63, 68, 72, 76, 80, 84, 90-1, 92, 96, 104, 358, 367
  Church in, 358
South America
  Cardinals, 166
  Catholic Statistics, 365-66
  Eastern Rite Jurisdictions, 267
  Episcopal Conferences, 369

South America
  Missionary Bishops, 421
South Carolina, 401, 422, 426, 428, 520, 543, 558, 590
  Living Will Legislation, 79
South Dakota, 402, 423, 426, 429, 521, 543, 558, 590
South Korea, 72, 75, 348
Southern Baptist Convention, 274
Southwell, Robert, St., 254
Southwest Volunteer Apostolate, 562
Sowada, Alphonse, O.S.C., Bp., 461
Soweto, Commemoration Banned, 96
Space, Peaceful Uses, 93
Spain, 358-59, 369
  Abortion, 68
  Civil War (1936), 118
  Inquisition, 314
  Persecution (1931), 118
Spanish Sahara, **see** Western Sahara
Spanish-Speaking in U.S., **see** Hispanics
Species, Sacred, 328
Spellman, Francis J. (U.S. Cardinals), 167, 478
Speltz, George H., Bp., 461
Spence, Francis J., Abp., 382
Speyrer, Jude, Bp., 461
Spiritism, 328
Spiritual Life Institute of America, 569
Spiritual Works of Mercy, 328
Sponsor, **see** Confirmation
Spoon, 270
Sri Lanka, 359, 369
  Reconciliation Plea, 75
Stafford, James F., Abp., 75, 94, 461
Stamps, Vatican, 174
Stanislaus, St., 254
State and Church, **see** Church-State
State Catholic Conferences, 438-39
State of Grace, **see** Grace
Stational Churches, Days, 328
Stations of the Cross, 328
Statistics, Catholic
  Canada, 336, 376-77, 378
  Countries of World, 332-65
  Men Religious, 492-93
  United States, **see** Statistics, Catholic, U.S.
  World (Summary), 365-66
Statistics, Catholic, United States
  Baptisms, 427-29
  Black Catholics, 480
  Brothers, 421-25, 430
  Converts, 427-29, 430
  Eastern Rite, 267-68, 425, 429, 523
  Missionary Personnel Abroad, 514-16
  Permanent Deacons, 228, 421-25, 430
  Population, 421-25, 430
  Press, 571
  Priests, 421-25, 430
  Schools and Students, 519-23
  Seminarians, 530
  Sisters, 421-25, 430
  Summary, 430
Statistics Office, Central, 150
Statuary Hall, U.S., Catholics in, 404-05
Statue of Liberty Anniversary, 98
Statues, 214
Statutes, 328
Steib, J. (James) Terry, S.V.D., Bp., 461
Steinbock, John T., Bp., 461
Steiner, Kenneth D., Bp., 461
Stephen, St. (Deacon), 254
Stephen, St. (King), 254
Stepinac, Aloysius (Yugoslavia), 364
Stewardship Council, National Catholic, 568
Sticharion, 270
Stigmata, 328
Stigmata, Congregation of Sacred (Stigmatine Fathers and Brothers), 490

Stipend, Mass, 328
Stockholder Resolutions, 74
Stole, 212
Stole, Use of, Confirmation, 217
Stole Fee, 329
Stoup, 329
Straling, Phillip F., Bp., 79, 461
Stickler, Alfons, S.D.B., Card., 163, 166
Strecker, Ignatius, Abp., 461
Stritch, Samuel (Cardinals in U.S.), 167, 478
Students, Catholic
  United States, 519-23
  University, College, U.S., 524-28
  World (Catholic World Statistics), 365-66
Subdeacon, 227
Subordinationism, 119
Sudan, 88, 92, 96, 359, 369
Suenens, Leo J., Card., 80, 163, 165, 166
Suffering, Redemptive Value, 93
Suffragan See, 329
Suicide, 329
Sullivan, James S., Bp., 461
Sullivan, John J., Bp., 461
Sullivan, Joseph M., Bp., 461
Sullivan, Walter F., Bp., 461
Sulpice, Society of Priests of St. (Sulpicians), 490
Sulyk, Stephen, Abp., 43, 461
Sunday, 237
Sunday Mass on Saturday, 216
Supererogation, 329
Superiors (Religious), Organizations of, 510-11
Supernatural, 329
Supernatural Virtue, 331
Superstition, 329
Supremacy, Act of (1533), 115
Supreme Court, U.S.
  Abortion Rulings, 45-7
  Church-State Decisions, 405-10
  Decisions and Actions (1985, 1986), 78, 83, 87, 94, 95, 409, 410
  Hostility to Religion, 74
  Scalia Appointment, 94, 405
Supreme Court, U.S., Catholics in, 405
Supreme Order of Christ, 595
Suquia Goicoechea, Angel, Card., 164, 166
Suriname, 359
Surplice, 213
Suspension, 329
Sutton, Peter A., O.M.I., Bp., 382
Swaggart, Jimmy, 103
Swanstrom, Edward W., Bp., 478
Swaziland, 359
Swearing, 329
Sweden, 359-60
Swedenborgianism, 329
Sweeney, Terrance, S.J., 103
Swiss Guards, 173
  New Recruits, 89
Switzerland, 360, 369
Sword of Loyola Award, 598
Syllabus, 329
Sylvester, Order of St., 595
Sylvester I, St., 254
Sylvestrine Benedictines, 484
Symbols, **see** Emblems of Saints
Symons, J. Keith, Bp., 461
Synaxis, 269
Synod, Diocesan, 329
Synod of Bishops, 143-44
Synod of Bishops, Extraordinary Assembly (1985), 43-5, 70
  Final Report, 44-5
Synod of Whitby (664), 113, 307
Synods, Patriarchal, 267
Synoptic Gospels, 190
Syria, 360
Syrian Orthodox-Catholic Joint Statement, 288
Syrian Rite Catholics 265
Syro-Malabar Rite Catholics, 266
Szoka, Edmund C., Abp., 461-62

T

Tabernacle, 214
Tabernacles, Festival, 290
Tafoya, Arthur N., Bp., 462
Tahiti, (French Polynesia), 355
Taiwan, 360, 367
    Bishops Meeting with Pope, 65
    First Native Bishop, 72
Taney, Roger Brooke (Catholic Justice, Supreme Court), 405
Tanner, Paul F., Bp., 462
Tanzania, 360, 369
Taofinu'u, Pio, S.M., Card., 164, 165, 166
Tarasevitch, Vladimir, O.S.B. (Death), 600
Tarcisius, St., 254
Tawil, Joseph, Abp., 462
Tax Exemption, Churches, 90, 409-10
Taylor, Myron C., 172
Te Deum, 329
Teachers, Lay, Catholic Schools, 523
Teachers, Religious, Catholic Schools, 523
Teaching Authority of the Church (Magisterium), 179-80
    and Interpretation of Bible, 181
Technology, Moral Guidance Needed, 93
Tekakwitha, Kateri, Bl., 252
Tekakwitha Conference, 518
Telecommunications Network, Catholic, 587
Television, 586
    Diocesan Offices, Directors, 587-91
Television Network, Catholic, 587
Temperance, 329
Templeton Foundation Prize, 79
Temporal Punishment, 323
Temptation, 329
Ten Commandments, 198
Tennessee, 402, 423, 426, 428, 521, 543, 546, 549, 558, 590
Teresa, Mother, (of Calcutta), see Mother Teresa
Teresa (Theresa) of Jesus (Avila), St., 197
Teresa of Jesus, Society of St., 509
Teresian Institute, 513
Terrorism, John Paul II on, 69, 73
Tertullian (206), 111
    See also Montanism
Tessier, Maxime, Bp., 382
Testament, Old and New, see Bible
Texas, 87, 402, 424, 427, 429, 439, 522, 531, 543-44, 546, 549, 559, 590-91, 594
    El Paso Synod, 91
Textbook Loans, see Schools, Catholic, Aid
Thaddeus, Jude, St., 194
Thailand, 80, 94, 95-6, 360-1, 369
    Catholic Office for Emergency Relief, 94
Thanksgiving, 329
That's the Spirit Productions, 587
Theatines, 490
Theatre, Catholic, 587
Theism, 329
Theodosian Code (438), 111
Theologians and Dissent, (John Paul II), 86
    See also Curran Controversy
Theological Commission, International, 150
    Deaconess Statement, 305
Theological Virtues, 330
Theology, 330
Theology of Liberation, see Liberation Theology
Theophany, see Epiphany
Therese Couderc, St., 254
Therese of Lisieux, St., 254
Theresians of America, 570
Thessalonians, 191
Thiandoum, Hyacinthe, Card., 164, 165, 166

Third Order Regular of St. Francis, 486
Third Orders (Secular Orders), 514
Third World, Abortion, 80
Third World, Aid for, 68
Thirty-Nine Articles (1563), 115
Thirty Years' War (1648), 116
Thomas, St. (Apostle), 194
    See also India
Thomas Aquinas, St., 197
    Pontifical University (Angelicum), 533
Thomas Becket, St., 254
Thomas Christians, see Syro-Malabar Catholics
Thomas More, St., 254
Thomas of Villanova, St., Congregation of Srs., 509
Thrones (Angels), 296
Thurible, see Censer
Timlin, James C., Bp., 462
Timor, Eastern, 361
Timothy, St., 254
    Letter, 191
Tiso, Joseph, Msgr. (Czechoslovakia), 338-39
Tithing, 330
Titular Archbishop, Bishop, 142
Titular Sees, 330
Titus, St., 254
    Letter, 191
Titus Brandsma, Beatification, 65
Toaff, Elio, Chief Rabbi (Rome), 37
Tobago, 361
Tobin, Maurice J. (Catholics in Presidents' Cabinets), 404
Tobit, 187
Todadilla, Anthony de, 386
Togo, 361, 369
Tokelau, 361
Toleration Act, England (1689), 116
Tomasek, Frantisek, Card., 84, 164, 165, 166
Tomasi, Silvano, Rev., 74
Tomko, Jozef, Card., 62, 87, 164, 166
Tonga, 361
Tonnos, Anthony, Bp., 382
Tonsure, see Holy Orders
Topel, Bernard J., Bp., 462
Torres Oliver, John, Bp., 43
Toulouse, Catholic Institute, 532
Tourism, Commission, 148
Tradition, 181
Transfiguration, 248
Transfinalization, 330
Transignification, 330
Transkei, see South Africa
Translations, Bible, 184-85
Transplants, Organ, 319
    See also Life and Death Questions
Transubstantiation, 330
    See also Miracles
Trappists, 485
Trautman, Donald W., Bp., 462
Traxler, Margret Ellen, Sr., 66
Treasury of the Church, 330
Treinen, Sylvester, Bp., 462
Tremblay, Gerard, P.S.S., Bp., 382
Trent, Council of, 122
    and Canon of Bible, 183-84, 193
    and Celibacy, 300
    Doctrine on Mass, 210
Tribunals of Roman Curia, 147
Tridentine Mass, 219
    Halted, Syracuse Diocese, 74
Triduum, 330
Trination, 216-17
Trinh van-Can, Joseph-Marie, Card., 164, 165, 166
Trinidad, 361
Trinitarians, 490
Trinity, Blessed, Missionary Servants of Most, 509
Trinity, Holy, 248
Trinity, Holy (Religious)
    Missionary Servants of Most, 490
    Order of Most, 490
    Sisters of Most, 509-10

Trinity, Holy
    Third Order Secular of Most, 514
Trinity Missions, 490
Triodion, 269
Triumph of the Cross, 248
Troy, J. Edward, Bp., 382
Truce of God (1027), 113
Truman, Pres. Harry S., 172
Tschoepe, Thomas, Bp., 462
Tuite, Marjorie, O.P., Sr. (Death), 600
Tunisia, 361
Turcotte, Jean-Claude, Bp., 382
Turibius de Mogrovejo, St., 386
Turin, Shroud of, 326-27
Turkey, 361, 369
Turks and Caicos Islands, 361
Tuvalu (Ellice Islands), 361-62
Twelve Apostles of Mexico, 386
"Type" (649), 112
Typical Sense (Bible), 192
Tzadua, Paulus, Card., 164, 166

U

Uchida, Sonoo, Ambassador, 61
Uganda, 362, 269
Uganda Martyrs (Sts. Charles Lwanga, Companions), 249
    Centennial of, 93, 95
Ukrainian Byzantine Rite Catholics, 265-66
    Persecution (Ukraine), 61
    in the United States, 267
Unam Sanctam (1302), 114
Unbaptized, 178
Unda-USA, 587
    General Assembly, 70
Unemployment, 81
Union of Soviet Socialist Republics, 362
    Chernobyl Nuclear Accident, 85, 90
Union of European Conferences of Major Superiors, 511
Union of Superiors General, 511
Unitarianism, 274
Unitatis Redintegratio, 122
    See also Ecumenism Decree
United Arab Emirates, 362
United Brethren Church (John Hus), 273
United Church of Christ, 277
United Methodist Church, 275
    Dialogues, 285
    Pastoral Letter, 53-4, 87
United Nations, 61, 62-3, 64
    Fortieth Anniversary, 61
    Mother Teresa Honored, 64
UNESCO, Vatican Support, 62
United Societies of U.S.A., 570
United States
    Apostolic Delegates, 170
    Bishops, see Bishops, U.S.
    Catholic Historical Society, 570
    Catholic Population, 421-27
    Eastern Rite Catholics, 267-68, 425, 429, 523
    Ecumenical Dialogues, 281-87
    History, Catholic, 387-405
    Jurisdictions, Hierarchy, 412-20, 439-64
    Liturgical Developments, 215-20
    Missionaries, 420-21, 514-16
    Pontifical Ecclesiastical Faculties, 533
    Pontifical Universities, 532
    Protestant Churches, Major, 274-77
    Religious Practice, 103
    Social Services, Catholic, 535-52
    Statistics, Catholic, see Statistics
    Supreme Court, see Supreme Court
    Universities and Colleges, 524-28
    Vatican Relations, 171-72
U.S. Catholic Award, 598
United States Catholic Conference, 436-38
    Secretariat for Hispanic Affairs, 481-82

United States Catholic Mission Association, 516-17
United States-Vatican Diplomatic Relations, 171-72
Unity, Christian, **see** Ecumenism
Universalism, 274
Universities, Pontifical, 531-32
Unmarried Couples (John Paul II), 89
Untener, Kenneth E., Bp., 462
Unterkoefler, Ernest L., Bp., 79, 462
Upper Volta (Burkina Fasso), 335
Ursi, Corrado, Card., 164, 165, 166
Ursula, Company of St., 512
Ursula of the Blessed Virgin Mary, Society of Srs., 510
Ursuline Nuns, 510
Ursuline Sisters, 510
Uruguay, 362, 369
Ustrzycki, Matthew, Bp., 382
Usury, 330
Utah, 402, 424, 427, 429, 522, 544, 559, 591

V

Vachon, Louis-Albert, Card., 164, 166
Vaivods, Julijans, Card., 164, 165, 166
Valdivia, Luis de, 386
Valentine, St., 254
Valero, Rene A., Bp., 462
Valois, Charles, Bp., 382
Valparaiso, Pontifical University (Chile), 531
Vanuatu (New Hebrides), 362
Vasques de Espinosa, Antonio, 386
Vath, Joseph G., Bp., 462
Vatican City, 173-75
    Commission, 149
    Diplomacy, Purpose, 86-7
    Diplomats at, 170-71
    Italian Concordat, 175
    Library, 173
    Office for U.S. Visitors, 174
    Press Office, 174
    Radio, 173-74
    Representatives, 167, 168-70, 175
    Secretariat of State, 145
    Television, 174
Vatican Council I, 122
Vatican Council II, **see** Council, Second Vatican
Vaughan, Austin B., Bp., 462
Veeck, William (Death), 600
Vega, Pablo Antonio, Bp., **see** Nicaragua
Veigle, Adrian, T.O.R., Bp., 462
Veil, 213, 270
Veil, Humeral, 213
Venerini Sisters, 510
Venezuela, 362-63, 369
Venial Sin, 327
Vercelli Medal, 598
Vermont, 402-03, 421, 425, 427, 519, 544, 591, 594
Verona, Missionary Sisters of (Comboni Missionary Srs.), 497
Verona Fathers (Comboni Missionaries), 485
Veronica, 386
Vessels, Sacred, 213
Vestments, 212-13
    Byzantine, 270
Viaticum, 330
Viator, Clerics of St., 490
Vicar Apostolic, 142
Vicar General, 330
Vicariates Apostolic, World, 365
Victor Emmanuel II (1870), 117
Victory, Missionary Sisters of Our Lady of, 507
Vidal, Ricardo, Card., 164, 166
Vienne, Council, 121
Vieira, Antonio, 386
Vietnam, 62, 363, 369
    Government Control of Seminaries, 84
    Problems Facing Bishops (John Paul II), 65

Vietnamese Congregation of the Mother Co-Redemptrix, 488
Vigano, Egidio, S.D.B., 64
Vigil, Easter, 246
Vilela, Avelar Brandao, Card., 153, 165, 166
Vincent, St., 254
Vincent de Paul, St., 254
Vincent de Paul, St. (Religious)
    Daughters of Charity, 496
    Sisters of Charity of, 496
Vincent de Paul, St., Society, 535
Vincent Ferrer, St., 254
Vincentian Sisters of Charity, 496
Vincentians, 490
Violence, 93
Violence, Different Views, 72
Virgin Birth of Christ, 259
Virgin Islands, 363
Virgin Islands, British, 363
Virginia, 403, 422, 426, 428, 520, 544, 549, 559, 591
    Church of Blessed Vietnamese Martyrs, 63
Virginity, 330-31
Virtue, 331
Virtues (Angels), 296
Virtues, Cardinal, 300
Virtues, Infused, 313-14
Virtues, Theological, 330
Visitation, 248
Visitation Nuns, 510
Visitation Sisters, 510
Vlazny, John G., Bp., 462
Vocation, 331
Vocation Conference, National Sisters, 511
Vocation Council, National, 511
Vocationist Fathers, 490
Vocationist Sisters, 510
Vocations (John Paul II), 77, 85, 93
Vocations and Wealth, 100
Volk, Hermann, Card., 164, 165, 166
Volpe, John (Catholics in Presidents' Cabinets), 404
Voluntas Dei; 513
Vonesh, Raymond J., Bp., 462
Votive Mass, 212
Vow, 331
Vulgate Bible, 184
    Commission for Revision, 149

W

Wagner, Robert E., 172
Waldensianism, 120
Waldschmidt, Paul E., C.S.C., Bp., 462
Wales, 363
Walker, Frank (Catholics in Presidents' Cabinets), 404
Wall, Leonard J., Bp., 382
Wall of Separation (First Amendment), 410
Wallis and Futuna Islands, 363
Walsh, Daniel F., Bp., 462-63
Walsh, Nicolas E., Bp., 463
Walter, Joseph J., S.J., 82
Walters, David, 172
Walz v. Tax Commission of New York, 407, 409-10
Wanderer Forum, 63
War
    Church Teaching (Vatican II), 203-04
    U.S. Bishops Pastoral, 204-06
Ward, John J., Bp., 463
Washington, 403, 424, 427, 429, 439, 522, 531, 544, 546, 549, 559, 591
Water, Easter, 307
Water, Holy, 311
Watson, Alfred M., Bp., 463
Watters, Loras J., Bp., 463
Watty Urquidi, Ricardo, M.Sp.S., Bp., 463
Way of the Cross (Stations of the Cross), 328
Weakland, Rembert, O.S.B., Abp., 98, 463

Weber, Jerome, O.S.B., Abbot, 382
Week of Prayer for Christian Unity, 73, 331
Weekdays (Church Calendar), 237
Weigand, William K., Bp., 463
Weitzel, John Quinn, M.M., Bp., 463
Welch, David P., Msgr. (Death), 600
Welsh, Lawrence H., Bp., 463
Welsh, Thomas J., Bp., 463
Welzbacher, Robert (Death), 600
Wenceslaus, St., 254
Wesley, John, 274
West, Catholic University of (France), 532
West Virginia, 403, 422, 426, 428, 520, 531, 544, 559, 591
Western Catholic Union, 570
Western Sahara, 363-64
Western Samoa, 357
Western Schism, 127
Westphalia Peace (1648), 116
Wetter, Friedrich, Card., 164-65, 166
Whealon, John F., Abp., 463
Wheeler v. Barrera (Student Aid), 407
Whelan, Robert L., S.J., Bp., 463
Whitby, Synod (664), 112, 307
White, Andrew, 386
White, Edward Douglass (Catholic Justices of Supreme Court), 405
White Fathers (Missionaries of Africa), 483
White Russian Byzantines, 265
Whitsunday (Pentecost), 247
Wildermuth, Augustine F., S.J., Bp., 463
Wilhelm, Joseph L., Abp., 382
Will, Free, 310
Willebrands, Johannes, Card., 165, 166
Williams, James Kendrick, Bp., 463
Williams, Thomas Stafford, Card., 165, 166
Willke, John, Dr., 80
Wilson, William A., 171
    Resignation, 90, 91
Wimmer, Boniface, 386
Windle, Joseph R., Bp., 383
Wirz, George O., Bp., 463
Wisconsin, 403, 423, 426, 428, 439, 521, 531, 544, 559, 591, 595
Wisdom, Daughters of, 510
Wisdom Books (Bible), 187-88
Wiseman, Nicholas (1850), 117
Witness, Christian, 331
Witnesses, Jehovah's, 315
Wojtyla, Karol, **see** John Paul II, Pope
Wolman v. Walter (Textbook Loans), 408
Women, Ordination, Church of England, 100
Women for Faith and Family, 63, 570
Women's Organizations, Catholic, World Union, 372
Word, Liturgy of, 210-11
Word of God Institute, 570
Work, Encyclical on (*Laborem Exercens*), 201-03
Workers, Church's Concern for, 33
World Conference of Secular Institutes, 511
World Council of Churches, 289, 511
World Day of Peace, 74
World Lutheran Federation, Interfaith Statements, 289
World Statistics, Catholic, 365-66
    Men Religious, 492-93
Worldwide Marriage Encounter, 98, 331
Worms, Concordat (1122), 114
Worship, **see** Adoration
Worship, Divine, Congregation, 146
Worship, Eastern Rite, 264
Worship, Liturgical, **see** Liturgy
Wright, John J. (U.S. Cardinals), 167, 479
Writers' Market, Catholic, 582-85
Wuerl, Donald, Bp., 73, 105-06, 463
Wycislo, Aloysius J., Bp., 463

Wycliff, John, 273
Wynne, Gerard R. (Death), 600
Wyoming, 403, 424, 427, 429, 522, 546, 591
Wyszynski, Stefan, Card. (Poland), 354-55

X

Xaverian Brothers, 491
Xaverian Missionary Fathers, 490
Xaverian Missionary Society of Mary, 510
Xavier Mission Sisters, 510
Xavier Society of the Blind, 550

Y

Yago, Bernard, Card., 165, 166
Year, Church (Calendar), 236-37
Yemen, North, 364
Yemen, South, 364

Yom HaShoah, 291
Yom Kippur, 291
Young Christian Students, 563
Young Ladies' Institute, 570
Young Men's Institute, 570
Youth, (John Paul II), 81
Youth Organizations, 562-63
Youville, Marie D', Bl., 386
Yuan, Paul, S.V.D. (Death), 600
Yugoslav Byzantines, 266
Yugoslavia, 69, 364, 369
    Apparitions at Medjugorje, 127
    Religious Freedom Report, 83

Z

Zaire, 364, 369
Zakka I, Syrian Orthodox Patriarch, and John Paul II, Joint Statement, 288

Zambia, 364, 369
Zanzibar (Tanzania), 360, 369
Zayek, Francis, Abp., 463
Zdebekis, Juozas, Rev. (Death), 600
Zechariah, 189
Zechariah, Canticle (Benedictus), 299
Zeitler, Englebert, Rev., 84
Zephaniah, 189
Zimbabwe (Rhodesia), 69, 364-65, 369
Zita, St., 254
Zorach v. Clauson (Released Time), 406
Zone, 270
Zoungrana, Paul, Card., 165, 166
Zucchetto, 213
Zumarraga, Juan de, O.F.M., 386
Zuroweste, Albert R., Bp., 463-64
Zwingli, Ulrich, 273

ST. AUGUSTINE: APOSTOLIC LETTER

Following are excerpts from Pope John Paul's apostolic letter commemorating the 16th centenary of the conversion of St. Augustine, Bishop and Doctor of the Church. The letter was dated Aug. 28, 1986. These excerpts are from the text published in the Sept. 15 English edition of L'Osservatore Romano. Subheads have been added.

One may rightly say that the summit of the theological thinking of the Bishop of Hippo is Christ and the Church; indeed, one could add that this is the summit of his philosophy too, in that he rebukes the philosophers for having done philosophy "without the Man Christ." The Church is inseparable from Christ. From the time of his conversion onwards, he recognized and accepted with joy and gratitude the law of Providence which has established in Christ and in the Church "the entire summit of authority and the light of reason in that one saving name and in his own Church, re-creating and reforming the human race."

Christ, Sole Mediator and Head of the Church

Christ, the Man-God, is the sole mediator between the righteous and immortal God and mortal and sinful human beings, because he is at once mortal and righteous. It follows that he is the universal way of liberty and salvation; outside this way, "which has never been lacking for the human race, no one has been set free, no one is set free, no one will be set free."

Because Christ, the only mediator and redeemer of men, is head of the Church, Christ and the Church are one single mystical person, the total Christ. He writes with force: "We have become Christ. Just as he is the head, we are the members; the whole man is he and ourselves." This doctrine of the total Christ is one of the teachings that mattered most to the Bishop of Hippo, and one of the most fruitful themes of his ecclesiology.

Holy Spirit, Soul of the Church

Another fundamental theme is that of the Holy Spirit as the soul of the mystical body: "What the soul is to the body of a man, the Holy Spirit is for the body of Christ, which is the Church."

The Holy Spirit is also the principle of community by which the faithful are united to one another and to the Trinity itself. "By means of what is common to the Father and the Son, they willed that we should have communion both among ourselves and with them. They willed to gather us together, through that gift, into that one thing which both have in common; that is, by means of God the Holy Spirit and the gift of God."

He therefore says in the same text: "The fellowship of unity of the Church of God, outside of which there is no remission of sins, is properly the work of the Holy Spirit, of course with the cooperation of the Father and the Son, because the Holy Spirit himself is in a certain manner the fellowship of the Father and the Son."

The Church Is Communion

Contemplating the Church as the body of Christ, given life by the Holy Spirit who is the Spirit of Christ, Augustine gave varied development to a concept which was also emphasized in a special way by the recent (Second Vatican) Council: that of the Church as communion. He speaks in three different but converging ways: first, the communion of the sacraments, or the institutional reality founded by Christ on the foundation of the apostles. He discusses this at length in the Donatist controversy, defending the unity, universality, apostolicity and sanctity of the Church, and showing that she has as her center the See of Peter, "in which the primacy of the apostolic see has always been in force." Second, he speaks of the communion of the saints, or the spiritual reality that unites all the righteous from Abel until the end of the ages. Third, he speaks of the communion of the blessed, or the eschatological reality that gathers in all those who have attained salvation; that is, the Church "without spot or wrinkle."

The Church Is Mother and Teacher

Another theme dear to Augustine's ecclesiology was that of the Church as mother and teacher, a theme on which he wrote profound and moving pages, because it had a close connection to his experience as convert and to his teaching as theologian. While he was on the path back to faith, he met the Church, no longer opposed to Christ as he had been made to believe, but rather as the manifestation of Christ, "most true mother of Christians" and authority for the revealed truth.

The Church is the mother who gives birth to Christians: "Two parents have given us the birth that leads to death, two parents have given us the birth that leads to life. The parents who gave us birth for death are Adam and Eve; the parents who gave us birth for life are Christ and the Church." The Church is a mother who suffers on account of those who have departed from righteousness, especially those who destroy her unity; she is the dove who moans and calls all to return or draw near to her wings; she is the manifestation of God's universal fatherhood, by means of the charity which "is mild for some, severe for others; an enemy to none, but mother for all."

She is a mother, but also, like Mary, a virgin: mother by the ardor of charity, virgin by the integrity of the faith that she guards, defends and teaches. This virginal motherhood is linked to her task of teacher, a task which the Church carries out in obedience to Christ. For this reason, Augustine looks to the Church as guarantor of the Scriptures, and attests that he will remain secure in her, whatever difficulties arise for him, urgently exhorting others to do the same: "Thus, as I have often said and impress upon you with vehemence, whatever we are, you are secure if you have God as your Father and his Church as your mother."

Love for God and the Church

From this firm conviction is born his passionate exhortation that one should love God and the Church — God as Father and the Church as Mother. Perhaps no one else has spoken of the Church with such great affection and passion as Augustine.

I have pointed out a few of his statements in the hope that these are sufficient to show the depth and the beauty of a teaching that will never be studied sufficiently, especially from the point of view of the love that animates the Church as the effect of the Holy Spirit's presence within her. He writes: "We have the Holy Spirit if we love the Church; we love the Church if we remain in her unity and charity."

Legacy to Theologians

Augustine's legacy to theologians, whose meritorious task is to study more deeply the contents of the faith, is the immense patrimony of his thought, which is as a whole valid even now; above all, his legacy is the theological method to which he remained absolutely faithful. We know that this method implied full adherence to the authority of the faith, which is one in its origin — the authority of Christ — and is revealed through Scripture, Tradition and the Church. His legacy includes:

• the ardent desire to understand his own faith: "Be a great lover indeed of understanding," is his command to others, which he applies to himself also.

• likewise, the profound sense of mystery: "For it is better," he exclaims, "to have a faithful ignorance than a presumptuous knowledge."

• likewise, the sure conviction that Christian doctrine comes from God and thus has its own original source which must not only be preserved in its integrity — this is the "virginity" of the faith, of which he spoke — but must also serve as a measure to judge the philosophies that conform to it or diverge from it.

• Augustine reads Scripture in the Church, taking account of Tradition, the nature and obligatory force of which he forcefully underlines. He made the celebrated statement: "I should not believe the Gospel unless I were moved to do so by the authority of the Catholic Church."

ORDINATION OF WOMEN: AN ECUMENICAL OBSTACLE

The Vatican released June 30, 1986, letters exchanged among Pope John Paul, Anglican Archbishop Robert Runcie and Cardinal Johannes Willebrands concerning the effect on Catholic-Anglican relations of the ordination of women to the priesthood in some provinces of the Anglican Communion.

• In a letter addressed Dec. 20, 1984, to Archbishop Runcie, the Pope said: "The increase in the number of Anglican churches which admit, or are preparing to admit, women to priestly ordination constitutes, in the eyes of the Catholic Church, an increasingly serious obstacle" to ecumenical progress.

• Archbishop Runcie, after consultation with leaders of the Anglican Communion, replied to the Pope's letter Nov. 22, 1985: "On the Anglican side (despite internal division on the matter), there has been a growing conviction that there exist in Scripture and tradition no fundamental objections to the ordination of women to the ministerial priesthood. . . . The humanity taken by the Word, and now the risen and ascended humanity of the Lord of all creation, must be a humanity inclusive of women, if half the human race is to share in the redemption he won for us on the cross. . . . Because the humanity of Christ our high priest includes male and female, it is thus urged that the ministerial priesthood should now be opened to women the more perfectly to represent Christ's inclusive high priesthood."

• Cardinal Willebrands replied to Archbishop Runcie June 17, 1986: "A development like the ordination of women does nothing to deepen the communion between us and weakens the communion that currently exists. . . . The ordination only of men to the presbyterate and episcopate is the unbroken tradition of the Catholic and Orthodox Churches. Neither Church understands itself to be competent to alter this tradition." The Catholic position is that "we can never ignore the fact that Christ is a man. His male identity is an inherent feature of the economy of salvation. . . . The priest represents Christ in his saving relationship with his body, the Church. He does not primarily represent the priesthood of the whole people of God. . . . It must be clearly stated that this is a theological issue and cannot be resolved on sociological or cultural grounds. . . . The question of the rights of women to hold secular office is a quite separate matter and should not be connected or paralleled with the question of women's ordination."

POPE JOHN PAUL IN INDIA

Pope John Paul, on the 29th foreign pastoral pilgrimage of his pontificate, visited 14 cities of India Feb. 1 to 10, 1986.

He made the tour at the invitation of Indian President Zail Singh and the nation's episcopal conference.

Despite several demonstrations of protest and the minority status of Catholics (12 million in a total population of 762.5 million), his reception was generally cordial and occasionally — especially in the South — enthusiastic. The size of crowds at various functions ranged from tens of thousands to several hundred thousands.

While straightforward in his statements of Catholic doctrine in about 30 addresses, the Pontiff was respectful of Indian sensibilities and spiritual traditions, with which he was deeply impressed. In response to a question by a journalist, he said: "I was not there to criticize. I was there to evangelize. Exactly that. I have evangelized the Indian people through the words of Mahatma Ghandi."

FEBRUARY 1

New Delhi

On arrival at the New Delhi Airport, Pope John Paul told government officials: "I come to India as a servant of unity and peace. I come in friendship, with a deep desire to pay honor to all your people and to your different cultures," and to draw attention to "what we have in common."

Ghandi Tribute: The Pope paid tribute to Mahatma Ghandi at the Raj Ghat monument to the great spiritual and political leader of the country.

"Mahatma Ghandi taught that, if all men and women, whatever the differences between them, cling to the truth with respect for the unique dignity of every human being, a new world order — a civilization of love — can be achieved."

Citing resemblances between the Beatitudes of Jesus and the "deep thoughts of (Ghandi's) heart," the Holy Father also said: "I wish to express to the people of India and of the world my profound conviction that the peace and justice of which contemporary society has such great need will only be achieved along the path which was at the core of (Ghandi's) teaching: the supremacy of the spirit and Satyagraha, the 'truth force' which conquers without violence by the dynamism intrinsic to just action."

"May Ghandi live forever. He who lived by nonviolence appeared to be defeated by violence (assassination in 1948). For a brief moment, the light seemed to have gone out. Yet, his teachings and the example of his life live on in the minds of millions of men and women."

Spiritual Traditions of India: The Pope celebrated Mass at the Indira Ghandi Stadium before a gathering of 25,000 people. He spoke about the spiritual traditions of India in a homily.

"As man on this earth passes from birth to death, he is aware of being a pilgrim of the Abso-

lute. . . . Here in India, this consciousness is very deep. Your ancient sages have expressed the anguished cry of the soul for the Absolute. In India, this quest for God and this expression of him have been accompanied by great simplicity, asceticism and renunciation. All of this renders great honor to India as a religious nation."

Speaking of the Christian's spiritual quest, he said: "Man no longer has to search all alone for God. In partnership with Christ, man discovers God."

Various Themes: Several themes of papal remarks during the visit were summed up by the Pope in an address to bishops.

• Liberation: "The Church endeavors to ensure the true development and liberation of millions of human beings. . . . The proclamation of the new commandment of love can never be separated from efforts to promote the integral advancement of man in justice and peace."

• Interreligious Dialogue: It represents a serious phase of the bishops' ministry.

• Inculturation: "Reflection and study are necessary (regarding liturgy). . . . It is important that doctrinal verification and pastoral preparation of the faithful should always precede the implementation of liturgical norms." Efforts for liturgical inculturation must be carried out with pastoral charity and understanding."

• Church Unity: He noted the importance of "close collaboration between the different rites of the Church so that, in their relationships, the churches may live according to the will of Christ."

FEBRUARY 2

New Delhi

Spiritual and Material Liberation: This was a principal theme of the Pope's homily during his second Mass at Ghandi Stadium.

The freedom from sin and death which Christ won for all people through his death and resurrection "is so fundamental and all-embracing that it calls for freedom from all other forms of slavery which are linked to the introduction of sin into the world. . . . This liberation calls for a struggle against poverty. And it requires all who belong to Christ to engage in persevering efforts to relieve the suffering of the poor."

He praised Christians and non-Christians whose "efforts aimed at fostering social liberation and integral human development are in accord with the spirit of the Gospel."

Problems: "So many problems of social life in India and throughout the world need refinement and purification. Individuals and groups need healing and reconciliation. Ignorance and prejudice must be replaced by tolerance and understanding. Indifference and class struggle must be turned into brotherhood and committed service. Discrimination based on race, color, creed, sex or ethnic origin must be rejected as totally incompatible with human dignity."

Spiritual Vision: "India's greatest contribution to the world can be to offer it a spiritual vision of man." The wisdom of the country shows that "increased possession is not the ultimate goal of life. . . . This is the humanism that unites us today." So stated the Pope at a gathering of cultural and religious leaders at Ghandi Stadium. Among those who attended were Hindus, Sikhs, Buddhists, Moslems, Jains, Parsees and Zoroastrians.

During the day, the Pope met, for the third time in his pontificate, with the Dalai Lama, the exiled leader of Tibetan Buddhists.

FEBRUARY 3

Ranchi — Calcutta

In Ranchi, en route to Calcutta, the Pope celebrated Mass at an industrial site and delivered a homily before a large gathering of workers.

Church Concern for Workers: "The Church, seeking to be faithful to the example and witness of Christ, has a very special concern for the welfare of workers."

In view of the value and dignity of work, he repeated a theme of many previous addresses: "No one should be used as a mere instrument of production, as though the person were a machine or a beast of burden. . . . The Church rejects any social or economic system that leads to the depersonalization of workers."

He cited an urgent need "to take fresh initiatives to solve the grave problem" of unemployment which gives "rise to frustration and a feeling of uselessness, and causes disharmony in the family."

He had particular sympathy for "the many unemployed who want to work but are unable to find suitable employment, at times because of discrimination based on religion, caste, community or language."

Proper working conditions and just wages were among other subjects mentioned by the Pope.

Nirmal Hriday: In Calcutta, the Holy Father visited Nirmal Hriday, the house founded and maintained by Mother Teresa and her Missionaries of Charity for the dying, elderly poorest of the poor. The Pope was deeply moved at his personal contact with the 86 residents, the latest of more than 22,000 for whom the Sisters had cared since 1952. He called the hospice a place of "anguish and pain," but also "a house built of courage and faith."

At an evening meeting with Catholic and non-Catholic religious and academic leaders, the Pope spoke about the "intense" suffering of people on the fringe of society, mentioning in particular the "growing inequality between developed areas and those which are increasingly dependent."

He told Christians in the gathering that the quest for religious unity was a "pastoral priority" for Catholics.

FEBRUARY 4

Shillong — Calcutta

At Shillong in remote northeastern India, the Pope celebrated an outdoor Mass before about 150,000 tribal peoples. He told them that Christianity had been "incarnated in (their) cultures without doing violence to them," and that the proclamation of the Gospel was being carried out "in harmonious dialogue" with their traditions.

Back in Calcutta, the Holy Father celebrated a second Mass at the Brigade Parade Ground and delivered a homily before about 200,000 people, most of whom were non-Catholic.

Mission of the Church: "It is the fundamental mission of the Church to proclaim to the world the good news of the redemption. And this is why I have come to you: to celebrate with you, especially in the Eucharist, the redemptive mystery of the passion and resurrection of Christ, and to encourage you in your efforts to bear witness to this mystery before the world."

"While esteeming the value of these (India's) religions and seeing in them at times the action of the Holy Spirit, . . . the Church remains convinced of the need for her to fulfill her task of offering to the world the fullness of revealed truth, the truth of the redemption in Jesus Christ."

Appeal for the Poor: The Pope voiced an appeal for the poor and for justice. Citing the example of Mother Teresa and her Missionaries of Charity in their care for the poorest-of-the-poor, he said: "Such charity and self-sacrifice, done out of love for Christ, challenges the world . . . which is all too familiar with selfishness and hedonism, with greed for money, prestige and power."

"Do nothing to perpetuate hatred, injustice or suffering! Do nothing in favor of the arms race! Do nothing to promote the oppression of people and nations! Do nothing (that is) inspired by hypocritical forms of imperialism or inhuman ideologies!"

FEBRUARY 5

Madras

At the southeastern coastal city of Madras, the Pope visited and prayed at the site where, it is believed, St. Thomas the Apostle was martyred about the year 72. He is regarded as the first preacher of the Gospel in the region and as the spiritual father of Thomas Christians.

Dialogue and the Right to Evangelize: These were among the subjects mentioned by the Pope at a meeting with 250 non-Christian religious leaders.

"Dialogue between members of different religions increases and deepens mutual respect and paves the way for relationships that are crucial in solving the problems of human suffering. Dialogue which proceeds from the 'internal drive of charity' is a powerful means of collaboration between people in eradicating evil from human life and from the life of the community, in establishing right order in human society and thus contributing to the common good."

The Holy Father coupled his remarks about dialogue with a reference to the provision of the Indian constitution which "specifically includes the right to profess, practice and propagate religion." He called for support of "this precious principle" against a background of anti-conversion current in the country.

He also said that the Church's idea of religious freedom precludes "coercion on the part of individuals or social groups or any human power."

Appeal to Lay Persons: In a homily delivered during a Mass celebrated before 500,000 people at Marina Beach along the Bay of Bengal, the Pope called on lay persons to play an active role in society. He said: "The Church's task of proclaiming the Gospel and of being at the service of society is supremely important in India today."

FEBRUARY 6

Goa — Mangalore

Divisions and Conflicts: The Pope spoke about divisive social factors in a homily during a Mass celebrated at the Campal Grounds.

"Within the borders of India . . . can be found opposing groups and factions, rivalries arising from prejudice and ideologies, from historical stereotypes and ethnic barriers." Catholics should seek to heal such divisions by seeing "every person as a child of God, as a brother or sister of equal dignity, regardless of his or her social status."

Divisions among Christians, he said, are a "scandal" to non-Christians and a "serious obstacle" to evangelization.

The Task of Priests: The Pontiff met with 700 priests and seminarians at the Basilica of Bom Jesus, the burial place of St. Francis Xavier, the great missionary of the region.

He compared priests with gurus, "spiritual teachers," saying: "How much more zealously should priests fulfill their mission as spiritual guides to the people entrusted to their care?" He urged them to meditate on Scripture and church teaching, and added: "Fidelity to the teaching authority of the Church will be a guarantee of the real effectiveness of . . . priestly ministry." Their task is to help build "a new human community where brother does not exploit brother, but where hearts are united in peace."

The Holy Father was greeted by a crowd of 300,000 people at the Mangalore airport, on the Malabar Coast. He conducted a service of the word and prayed especially for the victims of the Bhopal disaster in which about 2,000 died of toxic fumes from a Union Carbide chemical plant.

FEBRUARY 7

Trichur — Cochin

The Pope began the first of two days in the State of Kerala, the cradle of Catholicism in India, at a paraliturgical service in Trichur where he addressed and gave his blessing to 300 newlyweds.

Later in the day at an industrial site in Cochin, he celebrated a Mass attended by prelates of the three rites — Syro-Malabar, Syro-Malankara and Latin — with members in the area first evangelized, according to tradition, by St. Thomas the Apostle shortly after the middle of the first Christian century. The attendance of these prelates at the Mass, together with papal visits to churches of the various rites, symbolized the unity as well as the diversity of the Church.

FEBRUARY 8

Kottayam — Trivandrum

Beatifications: In Kottayam, during a Mass celebrated in the Syro-Malabar Rite, Pope John Paul proclaimed the beatification of two native Indians who, he said, exemplified the "beauty and greatness of the religious vocation." The first-ever Indian Blesseds named were: Sister Alphonsa Mattathupadathu of the Immaculate Conception, who died in 1946 at the age of 36, a victim of serious and prolonged illness; and Father Kuriakose Elias Chavara, founder in the 19th century of a Carmelite religious institute.

Social Justice: At a prayer service in Trivandrum, the Holy Father spoke about social justice. He said material development often makes existing economic and social inequalities harder for the poor to bear. He added an often-mentioned theme: Technological development must be placed at the service of "every man, woman and child," without "intolerable forms of discrimination."

FEBRUARY 9

Vasai — Bombay

The Pope conducted a prayer service at Vasai before proceeding to Bombay where he celebrated Mass at Shivaji Park before a large gathering and entrusted the people of India to the intercession of Mary.

The Family and Peace: With this theme in mind, the Holy Father said: "Peace in the world has its roots in the human heart, in the conscience of each man and woman. Peace can only be the fruit of a spiritual change, beginning in the heart of every human being and spreading throughout communities. The first of these communities is the family. It is the family that is the first community to be called to peace and the first community to call for peace — peace and fellowship between individuals and peoples."

"It is our hope that a great cry for peace and fellowship will rise from this smallest and most basic cell of society. This cry must reach all groups; it must reach the family of each nation and, finally, the vast family of all the nations of the world."

"Here may the voice of India and the voice of the Church be joined in unison."

Responsible Parenthood: "We see in the statement of Mahatma Ghandi certain similarities (with the teaching of the Church on this subject). While he asserted that 'the act of generation should be controlled for the ordered growth of the world,' he asked the question: 'How is the suspension of procreation to be brought about?' And he answered: 'Not by immoral and artificial checks . . . but by a life of discipline and self-control.' And he added: 'Moral results can only be produced by moral restraints.' This, dear brothers and sisters, is the Church's profound conviction.

"Furthermore, it is the role of the family everywhere and of all society to proclaim that all human life is sacred from the moment of conception. It is the task of all mankind to reject whatever wounds, weakens or destroys human life — whatever offends the dignity of any human being."

Concern of the Church for the Family: "The well-known opposition of the Church to the moral evils that affect the family and married life is due to her profound conviction that such evils are contrary to God's plan for humanity and that they violate the sacredness of marriage and the values of human life. The Church has a responsibility to defend the rights of the family and the total well-being of humanity, and it is for this reason that she renews her commitment to proclaiming the full truth about man."

Also in Bombay, the Pope met for 30 minutes or more with Anglican Archbishop Robert Runcie of Canterbury.

FEBRUARY 10
Poona — Bombay

In Poona, the spiritual and educational center of the Bombay region as well as the stronghold of Hindu radicalism, the Pope celebrated Mass outdoors before 50,000 people on the grounds of the pontifical university.

Priests: Speaking of them again as spiritual leaders, he said: "The Church's ministers are not called to play leadership roles in the secular spheres of society. India has many competent lay men and women to attend to these matters." Priests themselves should realize the "precious value" of their own specific vocation.

Back in Bombay, before departing for Rome in the evening, the Pope met with Religious at Goregoan Seminary and with young people at Shivaji Park.

Because of a snowstorm in Italy, the last leg of the Pope's trip home Feb. 11 was by train from Naples.

POPE JOHN PAUL'S VISIT TO COLOMBIA AND SAINT LUCIA

Pope John Paul, on the 30th foreign pastoral mission of his pontificate July 1 to 7, 1986, visited 11 cities of Colombia and the small island nation of Saint Lucia. His itinerary included 35 meetings, Masses and other ceremonial events. One of the special events was his consecration of the people of Colombia to Our Lady of the Rosary at the national shrine at Chinquinquirá.

Following is an account of the trip given by the Pope during a general audience July 16, 1986, and carried in the July 21 English edition of *L'Osservatore Romano*.

On the Paths of Colombia

"With the peace of Christ on the paths of Colombia": These words expressed the principal theme on which the Colombian bishops planned the Pope's pilgrimage in their country.

I wish cordially to thank that episcopate for the invitation to make this visit, which I was able to carry out in the early days of July.

At the same time I thank the civil authorities, and particularly President Betancur, both for the invitation and for the various facilities provided during this pastoral ministry "on the paths of Colombia."

Geography of the Visit

These "paths" set out in relief, first of all, the geography of the visit.

Colombia is a large country (more than a million square kilometers). The greater part of it, toward the southeast, is covered by equatorial forest and is sparsely inhabited. But the Pacific coast, where the inhabitants are mainly Afro-American, is more densely populated. However, the predominant part of the Colombian population is centered in the central region between the high mountain chains of the Andes and, on the Atlantic coast, the Caribbean zone.

This also explains the itinerary of the visit. Beginning from the capital, Bogotá, the path first led south: Cali — Tumaco (Pacific coast) — Popayan, and then north to Pereira — Medellin — Bucaramanga, and finally to the Atlantic coast, to Cartagena and Barranquilla.

The Historical Dimension

In this outline of the geography of the visit there is inscribed also the historical dimension: The country's history advances *pari passu* with the history of evangelization.

We are approaching the 500th anniversary of the discovery of America and also of the beginning of evangelization in that continent. For Colombia, this beginning is linked with the 400th anniversary of the miraculous renewal of the image of Our Lady of the Rosary at Chinquinquirá. Colombia is celebrating a National Marian Year in honor of this anniversary.

The Pope's pilgrimage was also directed to this Shrine on 3 July, to thank the Lord and the Most Blessed Virgin for the great gift of faith and to pray that it may bear ever more abundant fruits.

The beginnings of evangelization call to mind those to whom this work owed so much during the course of the generations: the priests, religious institutes, the laity, recalling especially the celebrated figures of St. Louis Bertran and St. Peter Claver.

Many Concerns

Unfortunately, Colombia — a beautiful and rich country — is often the victim of natural disasters. In 1983 a terrible earthquake devastated the city of Popayan; and then in November, 1985, the eruption of the Nevado del Ruiz volcano caused immense damage and numerous human victims.

The pilgrimage along the "paths of Colombia" has therefore led also to these places of destruction and suffering: Popayan, Chinchiná, Armero, Lérida, where I paused in prayer and where I exhorted all to confidence in God and to fraternal solidarity.

Evangelization of the Continent

In inviting the Pope on these paths of Colombia in the spirit of the peace of Christ, the pastors of the Church had before their eyes, especially, the universal work of evangelization. In fact, the aim of evangelization is to make Christ our peace and our reconciliation with God and with mankind.

The episcopate of Colombia and likewise the

bishops of the whole of Latin America have this conviction and nourish this hope. The meeting on 2 July, with the Colombian Episcopal Conference and with the Latin American Episcopal Council offered a propitious occasion to re-launch to the whole of Latin America an appeal to peace in Christ, reconciliation, social justice and solidarity.

From this derives the special concern for vocations to the priesthood and religious life, a concern that was solemnly underlined with the ceremony of priestly ordinations at Medellín (5 July) and in the meeting with women Religious (5 July) and with the directors of the Latin American Confederation of Religious (2 July).

Lay Apostolate

Together with the concern for priests and consecrated persons, there is also the reawakening of the awareness of the apostolate of the laity. This theme, of such importance for the Church and present-day society, was dealt with particularly during the Holy Mass at Bucaramanga (6 July), with the participation of representatives of lay movements and organizations.

There was a special word on the family during the Eucharistic Celebration at Cali (4 July), on youth during the great meeting at Bogotá (2 July), on children and missionary movements also at Cali (4 July), on intellectuals at Medellín (5 July), and finally on the world of labor in industry and especially in agriculture.

The Colombian Church is conscious of being always missionary, but not only in Colombia; inded, in the whole of Latin America there are territories which require a missionary apostolate (a subject addressed at Tumaco, 4 July).

Social Tasks

This awareness is linked with the necessity of also assuming tasks of a social nature in regard to indigenous groups such as the Indios, (Popayan, 4 July), as also in the case of the Afro-Americans, descendants of those whom the colonizers of those times transported there as slaves (discourse, Tumaco, 4 July, and later at Cartagena, 6 July), as well as in regard to socially depressed groups, as witnessed to in the meeting with the inhabitants of the shanty-towns at Bogotá (3 July) and at Medellín (5 July).

In order that the peace that Christ brings may prevail on the paths of Colombia, it is necessary to have a complete and coordinated evangelization in the spirit of the Church's social doctrine, committed to a multiple activity in favor of social justice, the safeguarding and promotion of the rights of the person, of the family and of human communities, so as to create a more balanced equality between the evident contrasts of a very rich world and another too poor.

Expression was given to all this on different occasions during the pilgrimage on the paths of Colombia (e.g., the discourses to managerial groups, 1 July, or the concluding one at Barranquilla, 7 July). Reflecting on the life work of St. Peter Claver, it can be said that this heroic missionary

figure is a sign of the authentic theology of liberation.

Deeply Christian Nation

In the course of this pilgrimage — of which I preserve in my heart a profound remembrance — I met a deeply Christian nation, full of hope and loving peace. Alas, this nation is disturbed by the sad phenomenon of guerrilla warfare, which is the cause of so much suffering and bloodshed. From the city of Bogotá I issued an appeal that those who have embarked on this road "should direct their energies — inspired perhaps by ideals of justice — to constructive actions which will truly contribute to the progress of the country." The grave social inequalities should be overcome by dialogue between the parties: this is the path which the Church for some time has been indicating as the one to follow.

In Colombia I met a good people, desirous to fight against the slavery of drug-abuse, a commerce of death carried on by a group of people who do not reflect the soul and authentic countenance of the nation.

Vitality of Lay Persons

The vitality of the Catholic laity offers great hope for the future of that beloved nation. They are becoming progressively aware of their role in the Church and of their responsibilities in social commitment enlightened by the Gospel. They are harvesting encouraging fruits in the field of the family apostolate. Young men and women are responding in an ever increasing number with the total gift of self to Christ's invitation, and they are undertaking to follow him without reserve, placing their energies at the service of the Kingdom. This enables the Church in Colombia to be of assistance to other Churches with her own priests and Religious.

Saint Lucia

The apostolic journey in Colombia was concluded with a pastoral visit to the island of Saint Lucia. It was a brief visit of a few hours, but warm and intense. I vividly recall the Eucharistic Celebration at Reduit Park in Castries, where I mentioned that faith is a precious gift, that it has formed the culture and history of that island. I then met in the cathedral the sick, the disabled and the elderly, bringing to them a word of comfort.

To all, I renew the exhortation to fervent perseverance in the Christian faith with consistency of life and commitment in charity.

I wish to thank the Governor General, Sir Allen Montgomery Lewis, the Archbishop of Castries, Mons. Kelvin Edward Felix, all the civil and religious authorities, and the dear population, so profoundly Christian.

At the end of this exacting apostolic journey, I express heartfelt thanks to all those who prayed with a lively faith and accompanied me with their affection. I have carried out, in God's name, an ecclesial service. To all classes of persons I expounded the word of Christ, which enlightens and saves. To all, the lowly and the great, the poor and the rich, the healthy and the sick, the little ones and adults, I left a message of love and encouragement. I appealed for justice, concord and an ordered progress for all.

With all my heart, I wish for the multitudes of Colombia and for the dear faithful of Saint Lucia the peace of Christ, in a faith more ardent and fervent, in a charity ever more dynamic and committed, in a brotherhood ever more sensitive and cordial.

POPE JOHN PAUL AT THE SYNAGOGUE OF ROME

Pope John Paul visited the main synagogue of Rome Apr. 13, 1986, at the invitation of its Chief Rabbi, Elio Toaff, and the Jewish community of the city. During an 80-minute service of prayer and song, the Rabbi and the Pope addressed the gathering of some 1,000 persons.

The following excerpts of the Pope's address are from the Vatican's English-language text circulated by the NC Documentary Service, Origins, Apr. 24, 1986 (Vol. 15, No. 45).

Significance of the Visit

I would like us to reflect together in the presence of the Holy One — May he be blessed! (as your liturgy says) — on the fact and the significance of this meeting between the Bishop of Rome, the Pope, and the Jewish community that lives and works in this city which is so dear to you and to me.

I had been thinking of this visit for a long time. In fact, the Chief Rabbi was kind enough to come and see me in February, 1981, when I paid a pastoral visit to the nearby parish of San Carlo ai Catenari. In addition, a number of you have been more than once to the Vatican on the occasion of the numerous audiences that I have been able to have with representatives of Italian and world Jewry, and still earlier, in the time of my predecessors Paul VI, John XXIII and Pius XII. I am likewise well aware that the Chief Rabbi, on the night before the death of Pope John, did not hesitate to go to St. Peter's Square and, accompanied by members of the Jewish faithful, he mingled with the crowd of Catholics and other Christians in order to pray and keep vigil, as it were bearing witness in a silent but very effective way to the greatness of soul of that Pontiff, who was open to all people without distinction and in particular to the Jewish brethren.

Heritage of Pope John

The heritage that I would now like to take up is precisely that of Pope John, who on one occasion as he passed by here — as the Chief Rabbi has just mentioned — stopped the car so that he could bless the crowd of Jews coming out of this very temple. And I would like to take up his heritage at this very moment when I find myself not just outside but, thanks to your generous hospitality, inside the Synagogue of Rome.

This gathering in a way brings to a close, after the pontificate of John XXIII and the Second Vatican Council, a long period which we must not tire of reflecting upon in order to draw from it the appropriate lessons. Certianly we cannot and should not forget that the historical circumstances of the past were very different from those that have laboriously matured over the centuries. The general acceptance of a legitimate plurality on the social, civil and religious levels has been arrived at with great difficulty. Nevertheless, a consideration of centuries-long cultural conditioning could not prevent us from recognizing that the acts of discrimination, unjustified limitation of religious freedom, oppression also on the level of civil freedom in regard to the Jews were, from an objective point of view, gravely deplorable manifestations. Yes, once again, through myself, the Church, in the words of the well-known declaration, *Nostra Aetate* ("Declaration on the Relationship of the Church to Non-Christian Religions," No. 4), "deplores the hatred, persecutions and displays of anti-Semitism directed against the Jews at any time and by anyone." I repeat, "By anyone."

The Holocaust

I would like once more to expess a word of abhorrence for the genocide decreed against the Jewish people during the last war, which led to the holocaust of millions of innocent victims.

When I visited on June 7, 1979, the concentration camp at Auschwitz and prayed for the many victims from various nations, I paused in particular before the memorial stone with the inscription in Hebrew and thus manifested the sentiments of my heart:

"This inscription stirs the memory of the people whose sons and daughters were destined to total extermination. This people has its origin in Abraham, who is our Father in faith (cf. Rom. 4:12), as Paul of Tarsus expressed it. Precisely this people, which received from God the commandment: 'Thou shalt not kill,' has experienced in itself to a particular degree what killing means. Before this inscription it is not permissible for anyone to pass by with indifference" (*Insegnamenti,* 1979, p. 1484).

The Jewish community of Rome too paid a high price in blood.

And it was surely a significant gesture that in those dark years of racial persecution the doors of our religious houses, of our churches, of the Roman seminary, of buildings belonging to the Holy See and of Vatican City itself were thrown open to offer refuge and safety to so many Jews of Rome being hunted by their persecutors.

Nostra Aetate, Turning Point

Today's visit is meant to make a decisive contribution to the consolidation of the good relations between our two communities in imitation of the example of so many men and women who have worked and who are still working today on both sides to overcome old prejudices and to secure ever wider and fuller recognition of that "bond" and that "common spiritual patrimony" that exists between Jews and Christians.

This is the hope expressed in the fourth paragraph of the Council's declaration, *Nostra Aetate,* which I have just mentioned, on the "Relationship of the Church to Non-Christian Religions." The decisive turning point in relations between the Catholic Church and Judaism, and with individual Jews, was occasioned by this brief but incisive paragraph.

Three Key Points

We are all aware that, among the riches of this paragraph No. 4 of *Nostra Aetate,* three points are especially relevant. I would like to underline them here before you in this truly unique circumstance.

• The first is that the Church of Christ discovers her "bond" with Judaism by "searching into her own mystery" (cf. *Nostra Aetate,* ibid.). The Jewish religion is not "extrinsic" to us, but in a certain way is "intrinsic" to our own religion. With Judaism therefore we have a relationship which we do not have with any other religion. You are our dearly beloved brothers, and in a certain way it could be said that you are our elder brothers.

• The second point noted by the Council is that no ancestral or collective blame can be imputed to the Jews as a people for "what happened in Christ's passion" (cf. *Nostrae Aetate,* ibid.). Not indiscriminately to the Jews of that time nor to those who came afterward nor to those of today. So, any alleged theological justification for discriminatory measures or, worse still, for acts of persection is unfounded. The Lord will judge each one "according to his own works," Jews and Christians alike (cf. Rom. 2:6).

• The third point that I would like to emphasize in the Council's declaration is a consequence of the second. Notwithstanding the Church's awareness of her own identity, it is not lawful to say that Jews are "repudiated or cursed," as if this were taught or could be deduced from the Sacred Scriptures of the Old or the New Testament (cf. *Nostra Aetate,* ibid.). Indeed, the Council had already said in this same text of *Nostra Aetate,* but also in the dogmatic constitution *Lumen Gentium* ("Dogmatic Constitution on the Church," No. 16), referring to St. Paul in the Letter to the Romans (11:28-29), that the Jews are beloved of God, who has called them with an irrevocable calling.

On these convictions rest our present relations. On the occasion of this visit to your Synagogue, I wish to reaffirm them and to proclaim them in their perennial value.

For this is the meaning which is to be attributed to my visit to you, to the Jews of Rome.

It is not, of course, because the differences between us have now been overcome that I have come among you. We know well that this is not so.

Respect for Identity

First of all, each of our religions, in the full awareness of the many bonds which unite them to each other and in the first place that "bond" which the Council spoke of, wishes to be recognized and respected in its own identity, beyond any syncretism and any ambiguous appropriation.

Furthermore, it is necessary to say that the path undertaken is still at the beginning, and therefore a considerable amount of time will still be needed, notwithstanding the great efforts already made on both sides to remove all forms of prejudice, even subtle ones, to readjust every manner of self-expression and therefore to present always and everywhere to ourselves and to others the true face of the Jews and of Judaism, as likewise of Christians and of Christianity, and this at every level of outlook, teaching and communication.

Guidelines

In this regard, I would like to remind my brothers and sisters of the Catholic Church, also those living in Rome, of the fact that the guidelines for implementing the Council in this precise field are already available to everyone in the two documents published respectively in 1974 and in 1985 by the Holy See's Commission for Religious Relations with Judaism. It is only a question of studying them carefully, of immersing oneself in their teachings and of putting them into practice.

Perhaps there still remain between us difficulties of the practical order waiting to be overcome on the level of fraternal relations. These are the results of centuries of mutual misunderstanding and also of different positions and attitudes, not easily settled, in complex and important matters.

Difficulties, Differences

No one is unaware that the fundamental difference from the very beginning has been the attachment of us Catholics to the person and teaching of Jesus of Nazareth, a son of your people . . . , from which were also born the Virign Mary, the apostles who were the "foundations and pillars of the Church" and the greater part of the first Christian community. But this attachment is located in the order of faith, that is to say, in the free assent of the mind and heart guided by the Spirit, and it can never be the object of exterior pressure in one sense or the other. This is the reason why we wish to deepen dialogue in loyalty and friendship, in respect for one another's intimate convictions, taking as a fundamental basis the elements of the revelation which we have in common as a "great spiritual patrimony" (cf. *Nostra Aetate,* 4).

Collaboration for Man

It must be said, then, that the ways opened for our collaboration in the light of our common heritage drawn from the law and the prophets are various and important. We wish to recall, first of all, a collaboration in favor of man, his life from conception until natural death, his dignity, his freedom, his rights, his self-development, in a society which is not hostile but friendly and favorable, where justice reigns and where, in this nation, on the various continents and throughout the world, it is peace that rules, the *shalom* hoped for by the lawmakers, prophets and wise men of Israel.

Morality

More in general, there is the problem of morality, the great field of individual and social ethics. We are all aware of how acute the crisis is on this point in the age in which we are living. In a society which is often lost in agnosticism and individualism and which is suffering the bitter consequences of selfishness and violence, Jews and Christians are the trustees and witnesses of an ethic marked by the Ten Commandments, in the observance of which man finds his truth and freedom. To promote a common reflection and collaboraton on this point is one of the great duties of the hour.

And, finally, I wish to address a thought to this city in which there live side by side the Catholic community with its Bishop and the Jewish community with its authorities and its Chief Rabbi.

Community, Not Coexistence

Let this not be a mere "coexistence," a kind of juxtaposition interspersed with limited and occasional meetings but let it be animated by fraternal love.

The problems of Rome are many. You know this well. Each one of us, in the light of that blessed heritage to which I alluded earlier, is conscious of an obligation to work together, at least to some degree, for their solution. Let us seek, as far as possible, to do so together. From this visit of mine and from the harmony and serenity which we have attained may there flow forth a fresh and health-giving spring like the river that Ezekiel saw gushing from the eastern gate of the Temple of Jerusalem (cf. Ez. 47:1ff.), which will help to heal the wounds from which Rome is suffering.

In doing this, I venture to say, we shall each be faithful to our most sacred commitments and also to that which most profoundly unites and gathers us together: faith in the one God who "loves strangers" and "renders justice to the orphan and the widow" (cf. Dt. 10:18), commanding us too to love and help them (cf. ibid., and Lv. 19:18-34). Christians have learned this desire of the Lord from the Torah, which you here venerate, and from Jesus, who took to its extreme consequences the love demanded by the Torah.

THE HOLY SPIRIT IN THE CHURCH AND THE WORLD: ENCYCLICAL LETTER

Dominum et Vivificantem ("Lord and Giver of Life") is the title of Pope John Paul's fifth encyclical letter, dated May 18 and released on the Solemnity of Pentecost, May 30, 1986. The letter was issued in anticipation of the forthcoming celebration of the 2000th anniversary of the birth of Christ and of the role of the Holy Spirit in the mystery of the Incarnation and the work of Redemption.

The following excerpts are from the Vatican's English-language version of the letter, circulated by the NC Documentary Service, Origins, June 12, 1986 (Vol. 16, No. 4).

INTRODUCTION

The Church, . . . , instructed by the words of Christ and drawing on the experience of Pentecost and her own apostolic history, has proclaimed since the earliest centuries her faith in the Holy Spirit as the giver of life, the one in whom the inscrutable triune God communicates himself to human beings, constituting in them the source of eternal life.

This faith, uninterruptedly professed by the Church, needs to be constantly reawakened and deepened in the consciousness of the people of God.

In our own age, then, we are called anew by the ever ancient and ever new faith of the Church to draw near to the Holy Spirit as the giver of life. In this we are helped and stimulated . . . by the heritage we share with the Eastern Churches, which have jealously guarded the extraordinary riches of the teachings of the Fathers on the Holy Spirit.

My previous encyclicals, *Redemptor Hominis* and *Dives in Misericordia,* (celebrate) the event of our salvation accomplished in the Son. . . . Now comes the present encyclical on the Holy Spirit, who proceeds from the Father and the Son, with the Father and the Son he is adored and glorified: a divine person, he is at the center of the Christian

faith and is the source and dynamic power of the Church's renewal. The encyclical has been drawn from the heart of the heritage of the (Second Vatican) Council.

The considerations that follow do not aim to explore exhaustively the extremely rich doctrine on the Holy Spirit nor to favor any particular solution of questions which are still open. Their main purpose is to develop in the Church the awareness that "she is compelled by the Holy Spirit to do her part toward the full realization of the will of God, who has established Christ as the source of salvation for the whole world."

PART 1

THE SPIRIT OF THE FATHER AND THE SON GIVEN TO THE CHURCH

Promise and Revelation at the Last Supper: When the time for Jesus to leave this world had almost come, he told the apostles of "another Counselor . . . I will pray the Father, and he will give you another Counselor, to be with you forever, even the Spirit of truth."

It is precisely this Spirit of truth whom Jesus calls the Paraclete, (meaning) Counselor and also Intercessor or Advocate. And he says that the Paraclete is "another" Counselor, the second one, since he, Jesus himself, is the first Counselor, being the first bearer and giver of the good news. The Holy Spirit comes after him and because of him, in order to continue in the world, through the Church, the work of the good news of salvation.

A little while after the prediction just mentioned, Jesus adds: "But the Counselor, the Holy Spirit, whom the Father will send in my name, he will reach you all things, and bring to your remembrance all that I have said to you." The Holy Spirit will be the Counselor of the apostles and the Church, always present in their midst — even though invisible — as the teacher of the same good news that Christ proclaimed. He will help people to understand the correct meaning of the content of Christ's message. He will ensure continuity and identity of understanding in the midst of changing conditions and circumstances. The Holy Spirit . . . will ensure that in the Church there will always continue the same truth which the apostles heard from their master.

Association of the Apostles with the Holy Spirit: In transmitting the good news, the apostles will be in a special way associated with the Holy Spirit. This is how Jesus goes on: "When the Counselor comes, whom I shall send to you from the Father, even the Spirit of truth, who proceeds from the Father, he will bear witness to me; and you also are witnesses, because you have been with me from the beginning."

The supreme and most complete revelation of God to humanity is Jesus Christ himself, and the witness of the Spirit inspires, guarantees and convalidates the faithful transmission of this revelation in the preaching and writing of the apostles, while the witness of the apostles ensures its human expression in the Church and in the history of humanity.

Between the Holy Spirit and Christ there thus subsists, in the economy of salvation, an intimate bond whereby the Spirit works in human history as "another Counselor," permanently ensuring the transmission and spreading of the good news revealed by Jesus of Nazareth. Thus, in the Holy Spirit-Paraclete, who in the mystery and action of the Church unceasingly continues the historical presence on earth of the Redeemer and his saving work, the glory of Christ shines forth.

Father, Son and Holy Spirit: It is a characteristic of the text of the Gospel of John that the Father, the Son and the Holy Spirit are clearly called persons, the first distinct from the second and the third, and each of them from one another. . . . Thus "the Holy Spirit . . . proceeds from the Father" and the Father "gives" the Spirit. The Father "sends" the Spirit in the name of the Son, the Spirit "bears witness" to the Son. The Son asks the Father to send the Spirit-Counselor, but likewise affirms and promises in relation to his own "departure" through the cross: "If I go, I will send him to you." Thus the Father sends the Holy Spirit in the power of his fatherhood, as he has sent the Son; but at the same time he sends him in the power of the redemption accomplished by Christ — and in this sense the Holy Spirit is sent also by the Son: "I will send him to you."

Here it should be noted that, while all the other promises made in the Upper Room foretold the coming of the Holy Spirit after Christ's departure, the one contained in the text of John 16:7ff also includes and clearly emphasizes that the Holy Spirit will come not only afterward, but because of, the redemption accomplished by Christ, through the will and action of the Father.

The Holy Spirit, being consubstantial with the Father and the Son in divinity, is love and uncreated gift from which derives as from its source (*fons vivus*) all giving of gifts vis-a-vis creatures (created gift): the gift of existence to all things through creation; the gift of grace to human beings through the whole economy of salvation.

The Salvific Self-Giving of God in the Holy Spirit: The original beginning of God's salvific self-giving . . . is identified with the mystery of creation itself. The biblical concept of creation includes not only the call to existence of the very being of the cosmos, that is to say, the giving of existence, but also the presence of the Spirit of God in creation; that is to say, the beginning of God's salvific self-communication to the things he creates.

Christ links the new beginning of God's salvific self-communication in the Holy Spirit with the mystery of the redemption. It is a new beginning, first of all because, between the first beginning and the whole of human history — from the original fall onward — sin has intervened, sin which is in contradiction to the presence of the Spirit of God in creation and which is above all in contradiction to God's salvific self-communication to man.

Therefore, Jesus Christ says in the Upper Room: "It is to your advantage I go away; . . . If I go, I will send him to you." The "departure" of Christ through the cross has the power of the redemption — and this also means a new presence of the Spirit of God in creation: the new beginning of God's self-communication to man in the Holy Spirit.

At the price of the cross which brings about the redemption, in the power of the whole paschal mystery of Jesus Christ, the Holy Spirit comes in order to remain from the day of Pentecost onward with the apostles, to remain with the Church and in the Church, and through her in the world.

In this way there is definitively brought about that new beginning of the self-communication of the triune God in the Holy Spirit through the work of Jesus Christ, the redeemer of man and of the world.

The Risen Christ Says: "Receive the Holy Spirit": Thus there is established a close link between the sending of the Son and the sending of Holy Spirit. There is no sending of the Holy Spirit (after original sin) without the cross and the resurrection: "If I do not go away, the Counselor will not come to you." There is also established a close link between the mission of the Holy Spirit and that of the Son in the redemption. The mission of the Son, in a certain sense, finds its "fulfillment" in the redemption. The mission of the Holy Spirit "draws from" the redemption: "He will take what is mine and declare it to you." The redemption is totally carried out by the Son as the Anointed One, who came and acted in the power of the Holy Spirit, offering himself finally in sacrifice on the wood of the cross. And this redemption is, at the same time, constantly carried out in human hearts and minds — in the history of the world — by the Holy Spirit, who is the "other Counselor."

The Holy Spirit and the Era of the Church: "Having accomplished the work that the Father had entrusted to the Son on earth (cf. Jn. 17:4), on the day of Pentecost the Holy Spirit was sent to sanctify the Church forever, so that believers might have access to the Father through Christ in one Spirit (cf. Eph. 2:18). He is the Spirit of life, the fountain of water springing up to eternal life (cf. Jn. 4:14; 7:38ff), the one through whom the Father restores life to those who are dead through sin, until one day he will raise in Christ their mortal bodies (cf. Rom. 8:10ff)."

The era of the Church began with the "coming," that is to say, with the descent of the Holy Spirit on the apostles gathered in the Upper Room in Jerusalem, together with Mary, the Lord's mother. The time of the Church began at the moment when the promises and predictions that so explicitly referred to the Counselor, the Spirit of truth, began to be fulfilled in complete power and clarity upon the apostles, thus determining the birth of the Church.

Transmission of the Grace of the Holy Spirit: For the grace of the Holy Spirit, which the apostles gave to their collaborators through the imposition of hands, continues to be transmitted in episcopal ordination. The bishops, in turn, by the sacrament of orders render the sacred ministers sharers in this spiritual gift and, through the sacrament of confirmation, ensure that all who are reborn of water and the Holy Spirit are strengthened by this gift. And thus, in a certain way, the grace of Pentecost is perpetuated in the Church.

As the Council writes, "The Spirit dwells in the Church and in the hearts of the faithful as in a temple (cf. 1 Cor. 3:16; 6:19). In them he prays and bears witness to the fact that they are adopted sons (cf. Gal. 4:6; Rom. 8:15-16, 26). The Spirit guides the Church into the fullness of truth (cf. Jn. 16:13) and gives her a unity of fellowship and service. He furnishes and directs her with various gifts, both hierarchical and charismatic, and adorns her with the fruits of his grace (cf. Eph. 4:11-12; 1 Cor. 12:4; Gal. 5:22). By the power of the Gospel, he makes the Church grow, perpetually renews her and leads her to perfect union with her spouse."

The era of the Church began with the coming of the Holy Spirit. . . . This era, the era of the Church, continues. It continues down the centuries and generations. In our own century when humanity is already close to the end of the second millennium after Christ, this era of the Church expressed itself in a special way through the Second Vatican Council, as the Council of our century. For we know that it was in a special way an "ecclesiological" Council: a Council on the theme of the Church. At the same time, the teaching of this Council is essentially "pneumatological": it is permeated by the truth about the Holy Spirit, as the soul of the Church. We can say that in its rich variety of teaching the Second Vatican Council contains precisely all that "the Spirit says to the churches" with regard to the present phase of the history of salvation.

PART 2

THE SPIRIT WHO CONVINCES THE WORLD CONCERNING SIN

Sin, Righteousness and Judgment: When Jesus during the discourse in the Upper Room foretells the coming of the Holy Spirit "at the price of" his own departure and promises, "I will send him to you," in the very same context he adds, "And when he comes, he will convince the world concerning sin and righteousness and judgment."

Sin, in this passage, means the incredulity that Jesus encountered among "his own," beginning with the people of his own town of Nazareth. Sin means the rejection of his mission, a rejection that will cause people to condemn him to death. When he speaks next of *righteousness,* Jesus seems to have in mind that definitive justice which the Father will restore to him when he grants him the glory of the resurrection and ascension into heaven: "I go to the Father." In its turn and in the context of sin and righteousness thus understood, *judgment* means that the Spirit of truth will show the guilt of the "world" in condemning Jesus to death on the cross.

The Witness concerning the Beginning: The Original Reality of Sin: Sin in its original reality takes place in man's will — and conscience — first of all as "disobedience," that is, as opposition of the will of man to the will of God. This original disobedience presupposes a rejection or at least a turning away from the truth contained in the word of God, who creates the world.

The ultimate roots of this disobedience are to be sought in the whole real situation of man. Having been called into existence, the human being — man and woman — is a creature. In his existence and essence he depends on the Creator. According to the Book of Genesis, "the tree of the knowledge of good and evil" was to express and constantly remind man of the "limit" impassable for a created being.

"Disobedience" means precisely going beyond that limit, which remains impassable to the will and the freedom of man as a created being. For God the Creator is the one definitive source of the moral order in the world created by him. Man cannot decide by himself what is good and what is evil.

In the created world God indeed remains the first and sovereign source for deciding about good and evil through the intimate truth of being, which is the reflection of the Word, the eternal Son, consubstantial with the Father. To man, created to the image of God, the Holy Spirit gives the gift of conscience so that in this conscience the image may faithfully reflect its model, which is both wisdom and eternal law, the source of the moral order in man and in the world. "Disobedience," as the original dimension of sin, means the rejection of this source through man's claim to become an independent and exclusive source for deciding about good and evil.

Turning Away From God: Man's disobedience . . . always means a turning away from God and in a certain sense the closing up of human freedom in his regard. It also means a certain opening of this freedom — of the human mind and will — to the one who is the "father of lies."

The analysis of sin in its original dimension indicates that, through the influence of the "father of lies," throughout the history of humanity there will be a constant pressure on man to reject God, even to the point of hating him.

We see this confirmed in the modern age, when the atheistic ideologies seek to root out religion on the grounds that religion causes the radical "alienation" of man, as if man were dispossessed of his own humanity when, accepting the ideas of God, he attributes to God what belongs to man and exclusively to man! Hence a process of thought and historico-sociological practice in which the rejection of God has reached the point of declaring his "death." An absurdity, both in concept and expression! But the ideology of the "death of God" is more a threat to man, as the Second Vatican Council indicates when it analyzes the question of the "independence of earthly affairs" and writes: "For without the Creator the creature would disappear. . . . When God is forgotten the creature itself grows unintelligible." The ideology of the "death of God" easily demonstrates in its effects that on the "theoretical and practical" levels it is the ideology of the "death of man."

The Sin against the Holy Spirit: Blasphemy against the Holy Spirit consists precisely in the radical refusal to accept . . . forgiveness, of which he is the intimate giver and which presupposes the genuine conversion which he brings about in the conscience. If Jesus says that blasphemy against the Holy Spirit cannot be forgiven either in this life or in the next, it is because this "non-forgiveness" is linked, as to its cause, to "non-repentance," in other words, to the radical refusal to be converted.

The action of the Spirit of truth, which works toward the salvific "convincing concerning sin," encounters in a person in this condition an interior resistance, as it were an impenetrability of conscience, a state of mind which could be described as fixed by reason of a free choice. That is what Sacred Scripture usually calls "hardness of heart." In our own time this attitude of mind and heart is perhaps reflected in the loss of the sense of sin. Pope Pius XII had already declared that "the sin of the century is the loss of the sense of sin," and this loss goes hand in hand with the "loss of the sense of God."

PART 3

THE SPIRIT WHO GIVES LIFE

Man's Inner Conflict: Resistance to the Holy Spirit finds in every period of history and especially in the modern era its external dimension, which takes concrete form as the content of culture and civilization, as a philosophical system, an ideology, a program for action and for the shaping of human behavior. It reaches its clearest expression in materialism, both in its theoretical form as a system of thought, and in its practical form as a method of interpreting and evaluating facts, and likewise as a program of corresponding conduct. The system which has developed most and carried to extreme practical consequences this form of thought, ideology and praxis is dialectical and historical materialism, which is still recognized as the essential core of Marxism.

In principle and in fact, materialism radically excludes the presence and action of God. Fundamentally this is because it does not accept God's existence, being a system that is essentially and systematically atheistic. This is the striking phenomenon of our time: atheism.

It follows that religion can only be understood as a kind of "idealistic illusion" to be fought with the most suitable means and methods according to circumstances of time and place, in order to eliminate it from society and from man's very heart.

The Pauline contrast between the "Spirit" and the "flesh" includes the contrast between "life" and "death." This is a serious problem, and concerning it one must say at once that materialism, as a system of thought, in all its forms, means the acceptance of death as the definitive end of human existence.

Signs and Symptoms of Death: It must be added that on the horizon of contemporary civilization — especially in the form that is most developed in the technical and scientific sense — the signs and symptoms of death have become particularly present and frequent. One has only to think of the arms race and of its inherent danger of nuclear self-destruction. Moreover, everyone has become more and more aware of the grave situation of vast areas of our planet marked by death-dealing poverty and famine. It is a question of problems that are not only economic but also and above all ethical.

But on the horizon of our era there are gathering ever darker "signs of death": a custom has become widely established — in some places it threatens to become almost an institution — of taking the lives of human beings even before they are born or before they reach the natural point of death. Furthermore, despite many noble efforts for peace, new wars have broken out and are taking place, wars which destroy the lives or the health of hundreds of thousands of people. And how can one fail to mention the attacks against human life by terrorism, organized even on an international scale?

Certain Hope: At any rate, even independently of the measure of human hopes or despairs, and of the illusions or deceptions deriving from the development of materialistic systems of thought and life, there remains the Christian certainty that the Spirit blows where he wills and that we possess "the first fruits of the Spirit," and that therefore, even though we may be subjected to the sufferings of time that passes away, "we groan inwardly as we wait for . . . the redemption of our bodies" or of all our human essence, which is bodily and spiritual.

Yes, we groan, but in an expectation filled with unflagging hope, because it is precisely this human being that God has drawn near to, God who is Spirit, God the Father, "sending his own Son in the likeness of sinful flesh and for sin, he condemned sin in the flesh." At the culmination of the paschal mystery, the Son of God, made man and crucified for the sins of the world, appeared in the midst of his apostles after the resurrection, breathed on them and said: "Receive the Holy Spirit." This "breath" continues forever, for "the Spirit helps us in our weakness."

The Holy Spirit Strengthens the Inner Man: Christian Anthropology: If man is the way of the Church, this way passes through the whole mystery of Christ as man's divine model. Along this way the Holy Spirit, strengthening in each of us "the inner man," enables man ever more "fully to find himself through a sincere gift of self." These words of the pastoral constitution of the Council can be said to sum up the whole of Christian anthropology: that theory and practice, based on the Gospel, in which man discovers himself as belonging to Christ and discovers that in Christ he is raised to the status of a child of God, and so understands better his own dignity as man, precisely because he is the subject of God's approach and prsence, the subject of the divine condescension, which contains the prospect and the very root of definitive glorification. Thus it can truly be said that "the glory of God is the living man, yet man's life is the vision of God": Man, living a divine life, is the glory of God, and the Holy Spirit is the hidden dispenser of this life and this glory.

SYNOD OF BISHOPS: EXTRAORDINARY ASSEMBLY, 1985

(See separate entry for background information on the Synod of Bishops.)

The second Extraordinary Assembly of the Synod of Bishops was convened by Pope John Paul Nov. 24 to Dec. 8, 1985.

Its purposes were to: (1) recall the Second Vatican Council; (2) evaluate the implementation of its enactments during the 20 years since its conclusion; (3) seek ways and means of promoting renewal in the Church in accordance with the spirit and letter of the council.

The agenda of the synod was developed by its secretariat and council after consultation with episcopal conferences throughout the world.

Fathers of the Synod

Many of the 164 members of the synod were presidents of episcopal conferences in: Africa (34), Central and South America (22), the United States and Canada (2), Asia (17), Europe (24), Oceania (4). Others were Eastern-Rite patriarchs and lower-rank prelates, officials of the Roman Curia, 3 representatives of men Religious, and 20 papal appointees. One hundred and three members were from the Third World; 65 had attended at least one session of the Second vatican Council.

Presidential delegates of the synod were Cardinals John Krol, archbishop of Philadelphia, Joseph Malula, archbishop of Kinshasa, and Johannes Willebrands, president of the Secretariat for Promoting Christian Unity.

Other officers were Cardinal Godfried Danneels, archbishop of Malines-Brussels, recording secretary, and special secretary Father Walter Kasper, member of the International Theological Commission.

U.S. Members

U.S. members of the synod were: Bishop James W. Malone, president of the National Conference of Catholic Bishops; Cardinal Myroslav T. Lubachivsky, head of the Ukrainian Archdiocese of Lvov, former head of the Ukrainian Archdiocese of Philadelphia; Ruthenian Archbishop Stephen Kocisko of Pittsburgh; Ukrainian Archbishop Stephen Sulyk of Philadelphia; Cardinal William W. Baum, prefect of the Congregation for Catholic Education; Archbishop John P. Foley, president of the Pontifical Commission for Social Communications; Bishop John Torres Oliver, president of the Puerto Rican Bishops' Conference. Two U.S. members were papal appointees: Cardinals John J. Krol and Bernard F. Law of Boston.

Other Attendants

Other attendants at the synod included 51 papal appointees, among whom were nine or 10 representatives of Christian bodies in dialogue with the Catholic Church. Twelve theologians served as advisers to the secretariat and members of the synod.

Sessions and Results

A Mass concelebrated with the Pope marked the opening of the synod Nov. 24. Work on the agenda began the following day and continued for a week of plenary meetings, most of another week of meetings of five language groups, and a final series of plenary gatherings for discussion and voting on recommendations. The Holy Father addressed the assembly Dec. 7. The synod was adjourned the following day after its members had approved "A Message to the People of God" and "The Final Report" on their deliberations.

Excerpts from both statements, below, are from the Vatican's English translations distributed by the NC Documentary Service, Origins, Dec. 19, 1985 (Vol. 15, No. 27).

A MESSAGE TO THE PEOPLE OF GOD

The Holy Father invited us during these days to recall with him the Second Vatican Council, to evaluate its implementation, to promote it in the Church in such a way that it might be fully lived.

All of us . . . have shared unanimously in . . . the conviction that the Second Vatican Council is a gift of God to the Church and to the world. In full adherence to the council, we see in it a wellspring offered by the Holy Spirit to the Church, for the present and the future. We do not fix upon the errors, confusions and defects which, because of sin and human weakness, have been the occasion of suffering in the midst of the people of God. We firmly believe and we see that the Church finds today in the council the light and strength that Christ has promised to give to his followers in each period of history.

Mystery of the Church

Through the Church which is his body, Christ is ever present in the midst of humanity. We are all called to live fully communion with God. Inasmuch as she is communion with the living God, Father, Son and Holy Spirit, the Church is, in Christ, the 'mystery' of the love of God present in the history of mankind. The council has powerfully recalled this, and we adhere to it in faith.

It is ... necessary to understand the profound reality of the Church and, consequently, to avoid false sociological or political interpretations of the nature of the Church.

Key Conciliar Documents

We invite you to know better and more fully the Second Vatican Council, to intensify its deepened study, to understand better the unity and richness of all the constitutions, decrees and declarations. It is also a question of putting them (especially the four constitutions) more deeply into practice: in communion with Christ present in the Church *(Lumen Gentium)*, in listening to the word of God *(Dei Verbum)*, in the holy liturgy *(Sacrosanctum Concilium)*, in the service of mankind, especially of the poor *(Gaudium et Spes)*. The message of Vatican II . . . cannot bring forth its fruits except through a sustained and persevering effort.

Every baptized man and woman, according to his or her state in life and in the Church, receives the mission to proclaim the good news of salvation for man in Jesus Christ. Each is therefore called to exercise his or her particular responsibility. Likewise, every community is called to deeply study the concrete exigencies of the mystery of the Church and of her communion. . . . The courage and discernment required today for the evangelization of the world can draw their light and dynamism from the Second Vatican Council.

Renewal for Evangelization

The council, in effect, was convoked in order to promote the renewal of the Church with a view to evangelizing a radically changed world. Today we feel impelled toward a deeper understanding of the true significance of Vatican II, in order to respond to the world's new challenges and to those which Christ ever addreses to the world. And this, whether it be a question of challenges of the social, economic or political order, or those related to lack of respect for human life, the suppression of civil and religious liberties, contempt for the rights of families, racial discrimination, economic imbalance, insurmountable debts and the problems of international security, and the race for more powerful and terrible arms.

THE FINAL REPORT

The first portion of the "Final Report," excerpted below, consisted of general observations regarding the purpose of the synod, along with positive and negative developments since the Second Vatican Council.

The report also covered many of the subjects discussed during the assembly, including: the mystery of the Church, the universal vocation to holiness, evangelization, collegiality, the role of episcopal conferences, the relationship of bishops and theologians, unity and pluralism, the integral relationship between doctrine and pastoral activity, ecumenical dialogue, inculturation and the preferential (but not exclusive) option for the poor.

This was the first publicly released final report of the deliberations and recommendations of an assembly of the Synod of Bishops.

Aims of the Synod

The end for which this synod was convoked was the celebration, verification and promotion of Vatican Council II. With grateful hearts, we feel that we have truly obtained this fruit, with God's assistance. Unanimously, we have celebrated the Second Vatican Council as a grace of God and a gift of the Holy Spirit, from which have come forth many spiritual fruits for the universal Church and the particular churches, as well as for the men of our time. Unanimously and joyfully, we also verify that the council is a legitimate and valid expression and interpretation of the Deposit of Faith as it is found in sacred Scripture and in the living tradition of the Church. Therefore, we are determined to progress further along the path indicated to us by the council. There has been full consensus among us regarding the need to further promote the knowledge and application of the council, both in its letter and in its spirit. In this way new progress will be achieved in the reception of the council, that is, in its spiritual interiorization and practical application.

Lights and Shadows

The large majority of the faithful received the Second Vatican Council with zeal; a few, here and there, showed resistance to it.

Nonetheless, although great fruits have been obtained from the council, we have at the same time recognized, with great sincerity, deficiencies and difficulties in the acceptance of the council. In truth, there certainly have also been shadows in the postconciliar period, in part due to an incomplete understanding and application of the council, in part to other causes. However, in no way can it be affirmed that everything which took place after the council was caused by the council.

In a particular way, the question must be posed as to why in the so-called "First World," following a doctrine of the Church which has been so extensively and profoundly explained, quite often a certain estrangement is manifested toward the Church, even though in this area of the world the fruits of the council abound. Instead, where the Church is oppressed by totalitarian ideologies or where the Church raises her voice against social injustices, she seems to be accepted in a more positive way. Yet, it cannot be denied that even in such places not all the faithful fully and totally identify with the Church and her primary mission.

Internal Causes of Difficulties

Among the internal causes (of difficulties since the council) there must be noted a partial and selective reading of the council, as well as a superficial interpretation of its doctrine in one sense or another. On the one hand, there have been disappointments because we have been too hesitant in the application of the true doctrine of the council. On the other hand, because of a partial reading of the council, a unilateral presentation of the Church as a purely institutional structure devoid of her mystery has been made. We are probably not immune from all responsibility for the fact that especially the young critically consider the Church a pure institution. Have we not perhaps favored this opinion in them by speaking too much of the renewal of the Church's external structures and too little of God and of Christ? From time to time, there has also been a lack of the discernment of spirits, with the failure to correctly distinguish between a legitimate openness of the council to the world and the acceptance of a secularized world's mentality and order of values.

These and other deficiencies show the need for a deeper reception of the council. And this requires four successive phases: a deeper and more extensive knowledge of the council, its interior assimilation, its loving reaffirmation and its implementation. Only interior assimilation and practical implementation can make the conciliar documents alive and life-giving.

The theological interpretation of the conciliar doctrine must show attention to all the documents, in themselves and in their close interrelationship, in such a way that the integral meaning of the council's affirmations — often very complex — might be understood and expressed. Special attention must be paid to the four major constitutions of the council, which contain the interpretative key for the other decrees and declarations. It is not licit to separate the pastoral character from the doctrinal vigor of the documents. In the same way, it is not legitimate to separate the spirit and the letter of the council. Moreover, the council must be understood in continuity with the great tradition of the Church, and at the same time we must receive light from the council's own doctrine for today's Church and the men of our time. The Church is one and the same throughout all the councils.

Pastoral Suggestions

It is suggested that a pastoral program be implemented in the particular churches for the years to come, having as its objective a new, more extensive and deeper knowledge and reception of the council. This can be attained above all through a new diffusion of the documents themselves, through the publication of studies that explain the documents and bring them closer to the understanding of the faithful. The conciliar doctrine must be proposed in a suitable and continued way by means of conferences and courses in the permanent formation of priests and seminarians, in the formation of men and women religious, and also in the catechesis of adults. Diocesan synods and other ecclesial conferences can be very useful for the application of the council. The opportune use of the means of social communication (mass media) is recommended. For a correct understanding and implementation of the council's doctrine, great help will be had from the reading and the practical implementation of what is found in the various apostolic exhortations, which are, as it were, the fruit of the ordinary synods held beginning in 1969.

REMARKS OF POPE JOHN PAUL

"Twenty years after the conclusion of the council, this common assembly appeared necessary, indeed absolutely demanded, after the great and vast heritage of the Ecumenical Council of Vatican II," Pope John Paul said Dec. 7 in an address to members of the synod.

"It was necessary that at this moment, above all, those who were called to take part in it express their judgment on Vatican II in order to avoid divergent interpretations."

The assembly served "to present, at least in some manner, the experience of those years between 1962 and 1965, and in a particular way to take up the task of realizing more fully the Second Vatican Council."

"It is now your task to ensure that the great force and awareness of the importance of the council penetrate deeply into the universal Church, into your particular churches and into the various communities."

ABORTION-RELATED COURT DECISIONS

Following is a chronological list of abortion-related decisions handed down by the U.S. Supreme Court and other courts since Jan. 22, 1973.

• In Roe v. Wade, the Court ruled, 7 to 2, Jan. 22, 1973: (1) During the first three months of pregnancy a woman's right to privacy is paramount. Accordingly, she has an unrestricted right to abortion with the consent and cooperation of a physician. (2) In the second trimester, the principle controlling legislation on abortion is the health or welfare of the mother, understood in the widest possible sense. (3) In the "state subsequent to viability," the controlling principles are the State's "interest in the potentiality of human life" and "the preservation of the life or health of the mother." These rulings canonized the absolutely private right of a woman to have an abortion and denied to the unborn the right to life.

• In Dole v. Bolton, also decided Jan. 22, 1973, the Court ruled, 7 to 2, against restrictions on facilities that could be used in performing abortions.

• In Danforth v. Planned Parenthood, the Court ruled, 6 to 3, July 1, 1976, against the constitutionality of state laws requiring spousal (in the case of a married woman) or parental (in the case of a minor) consent for an abortion.

Restrictive Amendment

• (The first of several versions of the Hyde Amendment was adopted by Congress Sept. 30, 1976, in an appropriations measure for the Department of Labor and the Department of Health, Education and Welfare. The amendment provided for limiting federal funding of abortions under Medicaid to cases of danger to the life of a mother and to cases of rape or incest reported in a required manner. See below.)

• An injunction against the amendment was issued Oct. 22, 1976, by U.S. District Court Judge John F. Dooling Jr., in a suit originally filed by Cora McRae.

• In Maher v. Roe, the Court ruled, 6 to 3, June 20, 1977, that the Constitution does not require states to pay for non-therapeutic (elective) abortions and does not require public hospitals to provide them.

• The Court set aside June 19, 1977, Judge Dooling's injunction against the Hyde Amendment and ordered him to restudy his ruling of the previous October in the light of its decision in Maher v. Roe.

• Funding restrictions of the Hyde Amendment went into effect Aug. 4, 1977, and the McRae case went back to the Dooling courtroom.

• The Court ruled, 6 to 3, Jan. 9, 1979, in Colautti v. Franklin against the constitutionality of a 1974 Pennsylvania law because of its vagueness about the timing of fetal viability. The decision had the effect of meaning that a woman exercising a legal right to have an abortion had the right to a dead fetus and that the doctor performing the abortion could not be charged civilly or criminally for the death of the fetus.

• In Bellotti v. Baird, the Court ruled, 8 to 1, July 2, 1979, against the constitutionality of a Massachusetts law requiring a minor to consult with her parents before having an abortion. In the absence of parental consent (which the Court ruled in 1976 was not required) or parental consultation (not required either), a court could clear the way for the abortion of a minor judged to be mature enough to have one.

• Judge Dooling ruled Jan. 15, 1980, against the constitutionality of the Hyde Amendment but stayed enforcement of his decision to permit an appeal to the Supreme Court.

• The Court responded Feb. 19, 1980, to Judge Dooling's action with a one-sentence order requiring federal and state governments to provide Medicaid funding for abortions deemed "medically necessary." The Court also agreed to rule on the constitutionality of the Hyde Amendment, in connection with another case (Williams v. Zbaraz) that originated in Illinois.

Hyde Amendment Constitutional

• In Harris v. McRae, the Court, with a 5-to-4 decision June 30, 1980, upheld the constitutionality of the Hyde Amendment and its restrictions on Medicaid abortion funding. The decision overturned the Dooling ruling, of Jan. 15, 1980.

While deciding that neither the federal government nor state governments are required to provide funding for "medically necessary" abortions, the Court noted that "abortion is inherently different from other medical procedures because no other medical procedure involves the purposeful termination of a potential life."

The Hyde Amendment provided: "None of the funds provided for in this paragraph shall be used to perform abortions except where the life of the mother would be endangered if the fetus were carried to term; or except for such medical procedures necessary for the victims of rape or incest, where such rape or incest has been reported promptly to a law enforcement agency or public health service."

About two-thirds of the states dropped elective abortion funding from their Medicaid programs after the 1977 decision of the Supreme Court. As of January, 1986, 14 states permitted the use of Medicaid funds to subsidize abortions.

Additional Decisions

• The Supreme Court, by a 6-to-3 vote in H.L. v. Matheson, upheld Mar. 23, 1981, the constitutionality of a Utah law requiring physicians to notify the parents of an unmarried, immature minor daughter seeking an abortion.

• With another 6-to-3 vote in Gary-Northwest Indiana Woman v. Orr, the Court ruled Apr. 27, 1981, that states may outlaw the performance of abortions outside of hospitals for women more than three months pregnant.

• The Court struck down, 6 to 3, June 15, 1983, major provisions of a Dayton, O., ordinance regulating the practice of abortion; in so doing, it reaffirmed its key decisions of 1973 against any such constraints.

The Court also struck down a Missouri law requiring that abortions after 12 weeks of pregnancy be performed in hospitals.

At the same time, the Court upheld two Missouri laws: one requiring the presence of a second physician during abortions after viability, the other requiring a pathology report for each abortion performed.

• The Pennsylvania Commonwealth Court ruled Mar. 9, 1984, that a 1980 state law prohibiting public funding of abortion violated the equal protection clause of the state's constitution and equal rights amendment.

• The 3rd U.S. Circuit Court of Appeals struck down May 31, 1984, some regulatory provisions of Pennsylvania's Abortion Control Act, but upheld the requirement that a child born alive through abortion be protected.

In Thornburgh v. American Society of Obstetricians and Gynecologists, the Court ruled 5 to 4 against the constitutionality of the Pennsylvania Abortion Control Act of 1982. Among provisions of the act were requirements that information be provided women seeking abortions with respect to various aspects of abortion, the development of the fetus, and agencies offering alternatives to abortion. The act also required that doctors make relevant reports and provide due care for viable aborted fetuses.

The five-Justice majority contended that requirements of the Pennsylvania law violated the Constitution because they posed an "unacceptable danger" of deterring women from choosing an abortion. Chief Justice Warren Burger said in dissent: "The Court astonishingly goes so far as to say that the state may not even require that a woman contemplating an abortion be provided with accurate medical information concerning the risks." He also said: "The Court's astonishing rationale . . . is that such information might have the effect of 'discouraging abortion,' as though abortion is something to be advocated and encouraged."

Statistics on legal abortions performed in the U.S. each year from 1972 to 1979 provide reliable indices of the magnitude of the challenge facing right-to-life proponents. The rising numbers of abortions and years, as reported by the Center for Disease Control, U.S. Department of Health and Human Services, were: 586,760 (1972), 615,831 (1973), 763,476 (1974), 854,853 (1975), 988,267 (1976), 1,079,430 (1977), 1,157,776 (1978), 1,251,921 (1979), 1,297,606 (1980). Another source reported 1,573,800 abortions in 1982. It was estimated that 17 million abortions were performed between 1973 and 1986.

The total number of abortions performed annually worldwide is estimated in the range of 30 to 35 million.

Charges Against the Church

The Catholic Church is the largest and strongest institutional opponent of abortion, because of its firm teaching and practice on the subject, and also because of the number of its members who are against it.

Because this is so in a cultural climate favoring abortion and moral liberalism, the Church has been accused and charged with:

• dominating the pro-life movement;

• trying to force its views on others who do not share its faith;

• violating a peculiar interpretation of the principle of separation of Church and state.

These accusations have been implicit and explicit in reporting of the abortion controversy ever since it began.

The Church insists, however, on its right to speak and act on moral issues on an equal basis with others who claim rights of conscience and freedom to influence others in a society which is subject not only to the laws of man but, above all, to universal moral law.

THE CURRAN CONTROVERSY

Following are the texts of three documents dealing with the substance of controversy concerning Father Charles E. Curran's views in dissent from church teaching:

• a letter to Father Curran from the Congregation for the Doctrine of the Faith, dated July 25, 1986, signed by Cardinal Joseph Ratzinger, prefect, and issued with the approval of Pope John Paul;

• a statement by Archbishop James A. Hickey of

Washington, chancellor of The Catholic University of America, dated Aug. 18;

• a statement given by Father Curran at a news conference Aug. 20 in response to the congregation's declaration that he "is not suitable nor eligible to teach Catholic theology."

These texts were circulated by the NC Documentary Service, Origins, Aug. 28, 1986 (Vol. 16, No. 11). Subheads and lead lines have been added.

LETTER TO FATHER CURRAN FROM THE DOCTRINAL CONGREGATION

This congregation wishes to acknowledge receipt of your letter of Apr. 1, 1986, with which you enclosed your definitive reply to its critical observations on various positions you have taken in your published work. You note that you "remain convinced of the truthfulness of these positions at the present time." You reiterate as well a proposal which you have called a "compromise" according to which you would continue to teach moral theology but not in the field of sexual ethics.

The purpose of this letter is to inform you that the congregation has confirmed its position that one who dissents from the magisterium as you do is not suitable nor eligible to teach Catholic theology. Consequently, it declines your compromise solution because of the organic unity of authentic Catholic theology, a unity which in its content and method is intimately bound to fidelity to the Church's magisterium.

Dissenting Positions

The several dissenting positions which this congregation contested — namely, on a right to public dissent from the ordinary magisterium, the indissolubility of consummated sacramental marriage, abortion, euthanasia, masturbation, artificial contraception, premarital intercourse and homosexual acts — were listed carefully enough in the above-mentioned observations in July of 1983 and have since been published. There is no point in entering into any detail concerning the fact that you do indeed dissent on these issues.

There is, however, one concern which must be brought out. Your basic assertion has been that, since your positions are convincing to you and diverge only from the "non-infallible" teaching of the Church, they constitute "responsible" dissent and should therefore be allowed by the Church. In this regard, the following considerations seem to be in order.

Authority of Ordinary Magisterium

First of all, one must remember the teaching of the Second Vatican Council, which clearly does not confine the infallible magisterium purely to matters of faith nor to solemn definitions. *Lumen Gentium* "Dogmatic Constitution on the Church", No. 25, states: "When, however, they (the bishops), even though spread throughout the world, but still maintaining the bond of communion between themselves and with the successor of Peter, and authentically teaching on matters of faith or morals, are in agreement that a particular position ought to be held as definitive, then they are teaching the doctrine of Christ in an infallible manner." Besides this, the Church does not build its life upon its infallible magisterium alone but on the teaching of its authentic, ordinary magisterium as well.

In light of these considerations, it is clear that you have not taken into adequate account, for example, that the Church's position on the indissolubility of sacramental and consummated marriage, which you claim ought to be changed, was in fact defined at the Council of Trent and so belongs to the patrimony of the faith. You likewise do not give sufficient weight to the teaching of the Second Vatican Council when, in full continuity with the tradition of the Church, it condemned abortion, calling it an "unspeakable crime." In any case, the faithful must accept not only the infallible magisterium. They are to give the religious submission of intellect and will to the teaching which the Supreme Pontiff or the college of bishops enunciate on faith or morals when they exercise the authentic magisterium, even if they do not intend to proclaim it with a definitive act. This you have continued to refuse to do.

Inquiry Based on His Works

There are, moreover, two related matters which have become widely misunderstood in the course of the congregation's inquiry into your work, especially in the past few months, and which should be noted. First, you publicly claimed that you were never told who your "accusers" were. The congregation based its inquiry exclusively on your published works and on your personal responses to its observations. In effect, then, your own works have been your "accusers" and they alone.

You further claimed that you were never given the opportunity of counsel. Since the inquiry was conducted on a documentary basis, you had every opportunity to take any type of counsel you wished. Moreover, it is clear that you did so. When you replied to the congregation's observations with your letter of Aug. 24, 1984, you stated that you had taken the positions you have "with a great deal . . . of consultation"; and in the congregation's letter of Sept. 17, 1985, you were actually urged to continue the use of that very means so that an acceptable resolution of the differences between you and

the teaching of the Church could be attained. Finally, at your own request, when you came for our meeting on Mar. 8, 1986, you were accompanied by a theologian of your own choosing and confidence.

Verdict: Not Suitable

In conclusion, this congregation calls attention to the fact that you have taken your dissenting positions as a professor of theology in an ecclesiastical faculty at a pontifical university. In its letter of Sept. 17, 1985, to you, it was noted that "the authorities of the Church cannot allow the present situation to continue in which the inherent contradiction is prolonged that one who is to teach in the name of the Church in fact denies her teaching." In light of your repeated refusal to accept what the Church teaches and in light of its mandate to promote and safeguard the Church's teaching on faith and morals throughout the Catholic world, this congregation, in agreement with the Congregation for Catholic Education, sees no alternative now but to advise the Most Reverend Chancellor that you will no longer be considered suitable nor eligible to exercise the function of a professor of Catholic theology.

This decision was presented to His Holiness in an audience granted to the undersigned prefect on the 10th of July of this year, and he approved both its content and the procedure followed.

This dicastery also wishes to inform you that this decision will be published as soon as it is communicated to you.

May I finally express the sincere hope that this regrettable, but necessary, outcome to the congregation's study might move you to reconsider your dissenting positions and to accept in its fullness the teaching of the Catholic Church.

STATEMENT BY ARCHBISHOP HICKEY

Today I am authorized to release a letter from the Congregation for the Doctrine of the Faith conveying its final decision concerning the case of Father Charles E. Curran, professor of moral theology at The Catholic University of America. The congregation found that a number of Father Curran's writings are in serious conflict with the authentic teaching of the Catholic Church. For that reason the CDF declared that Father Curran "will no longer be considered suitable nor eligible to exercise the function of a professor of Catholic theology." This judgment has been approved by the Holy Father, Pope John Paul II.

Withdrawal of License To Teach

I fully support this judgment of the Holy See. The Holy Father and the bishops have the right and the duty to ensure that what is taught in the name of the Church be completely faithful to its full and authentic teaching. The faithful have a right to sound teaching, and the Church's officially commissioned teachers have a particular responsibility to honor that right. In view of the Holy See's declaration and in accordance with the statutes of Catholic University, I have initited the withdrawal of Father Curran's ecclesiastical license to teach Catholic theology. Father Curran will enjoy the

right to the procedures of due process set forth in the statutes.

The declaration of the Holy See follows a lengthy correspondence which the CDF initiated with Father Curran in 1979 regarding certain errors and ambiguities in his published writings on moral theology. The congregation asked Father Curran to respond to its observations and later asked him to reconsider his positions which dissent from the authentic teaching of the Church. Father Curran released this correspondence to the press several months ago.

In 1980, when I was appointed the archbishop of Washington and ex officio the chancellor of Catholic University, exchanges between the CDF and Father Curran were already under way. As chancellor, I sought to facilitate that process. As occasion demanded, I met with Father Curran and with officials of the university and the Holy See. This past year, when the case reached its final phase, Cardinal (Joseph) Bernardin, chairman of the board of Catholic University and I met with Father Curran four times to discuss his dissenting opinions in light of his official license to teach Catholic theology.

In the letter to Father Curran, the congregation points out that the authentic teachings of the

Church, enunciated by the Holy Father and the bishops in communion with him, although not solemnly defined, require a religious submission of intellect and will. The infallible teachings of the Church do not stand alone; they are intimately related to all official Church teachings and, together, form an organic unity of faith.

While this decision is surely difficult for Father Curran, it is my hope that his love for the Church will prompt him to reconsider his dissenting opinions and to accept the guidance of the magisterium. So also I pray that all of us will grow in an appreciation of that truth and power of the Gospel with which the Lord has endowed his Church.

FATHER CURRAN'S RESPONSE

From the very beginning of the public discussion of my dispute with the Vatican's Congregation for the Doctrine of the Faith, I insisted on making this a teaching moment.

On Monday, Aug. 18, at a 4 p.m. meeting, Archbishop James A. Hickey, the chancellor of The Catholic University of America, handed me a letter addressed to me by Cardinal Joseph Ratzinger, the prefect of the Congregation for the Doctrine of the Faith. Ratzinger informed me that I "will no longer be suitable nor eligible to exercise the function of a professor of Catholic theology." The archbishop informed me that this letter had at that time been released to the press.

The Chancellor's Letter

In addition, Archbishop Hickey gave me his own letter in which, as chancellor of The Catholic University of America, he initiated the withdrawal of the canonical mission which permits me to teach theology at this university. The letter also reminded me of my right to request the procedures found in the canonical statutes of the ecclesiastical faculties. If I do not exercise that right by Sept. 1, he will notify the president of the university that the canonical mission has been withdrawn. In addition, he gave me his press release. He also said that he could give me no answer as to whether or not I would still be allowed to teach at the university in some faculty other than the faculty of theology. That answer, according to Archbishop Hickey, could only be given by the board of trustees.

Three Issues

In keeping with my aim of making this a teaching moment, I want, first, to address the issues involved in Cardinal Ratzinger's July 25 letter to me and then to raise further issues not discussed in that letter. The issues involved in Cardinal Ratzinger's July 25 letter to me are basically three: the moral theological positions I have taken, the legitimacy of my theological dissent and my criticisms of the process.

Moral Theological Positions: First, the letter of Cardinal Ratzinger gives the impression that, on the specific moral issues involved in the dispute, the official teaching is opposed to such actions and I am in favor of them. That is not the case. I have always developed my moral theology in the light of accepted Catholic principles. My positions on the particular issues involved are always carefully nuanced and often in fundamental agreement with the existing hierarchical teaching. Yes, occasionally I have dissented from the official teaching on some aspects of specific issues, but this is within a more general and prevailing context of assent.

Dissent: Second, the issue of dissent. The July 25 letter refers to both the infallible and non-infallible magisterium. However, in all the correspondence before 1985 the Congregation for the Doctrine of the Faith recognized that the issue was public dissent from the non-infallible hierarchical magisterium as is spelled out in the very first sentence of the "observations" sent to me in April, 1983. In reality, the July 25 letter refers only to the indissolubility of marriage as defined at the Council of Trent and belonging to the patrimony of faith. However, all Catholic theologians recognize the teaching of the Council of Trent does not exclude as contrary to faith the practice of *economia* in the Greek church. I have maintained that the position I propose on the indissolubility of marriage is in keeping with this tradition.

Thus, we are dealing with the non-infallible hierarchical teaching. Here too, in my writing and recent public statements, I have not proposed the possibility and legitimacy of dissent from all non-infallible teaching. In moral matters, all Christians must recognize that the follower of Jesus should be loving, caring, just and faithful. My disagreements are on the level of complex, specific actions which involve many conflicting circumstances and situations. By their very nature these specific, concrete questions are far removed from the core of faith. Recall that official hierarchical teaching does not condemn all sterilization but recognizes that in some situations indirect sterilization is permitted. The 1968 statement of the Canadian bishops about Catholics who cannot accept the teaching of *Humanae Vitae* absolutely condemning artificial contraception for spouses is most pertinent. "Since they are not denying any point in divine and Catholic faith nor rejecting the teaching authority of the Church, these Catholics should not be considered or consider themselves shut off from the body of the faithful."

In short, I have defended my dissent as being in accord with the norms laid down by the U.S. bishops in their 1968 pastoral letter "Human Life in Our Day." The congregation still must answer the questions I have been asking for six years. Does the congregation agree with the teaching proposed on dissent by the U.S. bishops or are they claiming that such teaching is wrong?

Criticism of the Process: Third, the process. Most legal systems in the contemporary world recognize that the defendant has a right to the record of the trial, including the right to know who are the accusers. No such record has ever been made available to me. The process itself does not allow the individual involved to have counsel in any official meeting with the congregation or its officials. Cardinal Ratzinger himself maintained that my meeting with the officials of the congregation was a non-official meeting. Ratzinger himself admitted in 1984 that the congregation had decided to revise its present procedures, but workload and time constraints have not allowed this to take place. In this context, I should also point out that I have been given a copy of a letter from a cardinal member of the congregation dated July 11, 1986, in which this cardinal voting member says he has never received any dossier on my case.

Additional Issues

Now I want to raise three issues that are not found in the July 25, 1986, letter of Cardinal Ratzinger.

Right To Dissent? First, the right of the faithful to dissent in practice from some of the non-infallible teachings with which I disagree. Do the faithful have such a right? What is the ecclesial status of those who so dissent? What does their practice say about the present teaching of the Church?

Support for Positions: Second, the theological community. The evidence in the last few months has clearly supported my contention that I am a theological moderate and that a strong majority of Catholic theologians support the legitimacy of my position. Over 750 theologians in North America have signed a theological statement of support for me.

This present support from the theological community is in continuity with the support shown for my theological endeavors over the last 25 years, most of which have been spent here at The Catholic University of America. The theological community has been in critical dialogue with my positions, but in the eyes of my peers I have been recognized as a significant Catholic moral theologian. My colleagues have elected me president of the Catholic Theological Society of America and of the Society of Christian Ethics. I was the first recipient of the John Courtney Murray Award of the Catholic Theological Society of America for outstanding achievement in theology.

What does this split between theologians and pastors say? This is a pressing problem for the Roman Catholic Church, which has always given great weight and importance to the theological community. What action, if any, will be taken against people holding positions similar to mine? Are all those who maintain the possibility of legitimate theological dissent from some non-infallible teaching not suitable or eligible to exercise the function of a professor of Catholic theology?

Academic Freedom: Third, academic freedom in Catholic institutions. The vast majority of leaders of Catholic higher education in the United States, including William J. Byron, the president of this university, have claimed that the ability of a church authority to intervene in the hiring, promotion and terminating of faculty is a violation of academic freedom. Such procedures in Catholic institutions, according to these educational leaders, jeopardize the very nature of a university or college. Such interventionist procedures are now possible in accord with the statutes for the ecclesiastical faculties of The Catholic University. However, the present universal law of the Church already enshrines the same legislation for all Catholic institutions of higher learning. In addition, proposed legislation for Catholic institutions of higher learning spells this out in greater detail.

The Matter of Appeal

Before concluding, some other issues must be addressed. My colleagues have urged me to go through the process provided by the statutes of the ecclesiastical faculties if I have the physical and spiritual strength to do so. I would like to honor their request, but there are some problems that must first be clarified. I have written that the existing canonical statutes are themselves a violation of academic freedom. Also, in 1982 I wrote an official letter to the university asserting that these statutes do not apply to me since my tenured contract with the university predates these statutes and the university cannot unilaterally add anything to my contractual obligations. Only after receiving academic and legal counsel on these points can I make a final decision about the process.

No Change of Position: In conclusion, I am conscious of my own limitations and my own failures. I am aware of the consequences of what is involved. But I can only repeat what I wrote Cardinal Ratzinger in my final response of April 1, 1986: "In conscience at the present time, I cannot and do not change the theological positions I have taken." In my own judgment and in the judgment of the majority of my peers I have been and am suitable and eligible to exercise the function of a professor of Catholic theology.

Conviction about Right To Dissent: I remain convinced that the hierarchical teaching office in the Roman Catholic Church must allow dissent on these issues and ultimately should change its teaching. My conviction in this matter is supported by a number of factors. First, the overwhelming support of my theological colleagues has buoyed me personally and strengthened my own hope for the ultimate acceptance of these convictions. Second, the best and the mainstream of the Catholic theological tradition support my basic approach. According to Catholic theological tradition, the word and work of Jesus must always be made present and meaningful in the contemporary historical and cultural circumstances. The Catholic tradition also insists on the transcendence of faith and the principle that faith and reason can never contradict one another. In addition, Catholic ethics has insisted on an intrinsic morality. Something is commanded because it is good and not the other way around. Authority must conform to the truth.

Finally, some historical examples give me hope. Theologians who have been condemned have at later times been vindicated and their teachings have been accepted. The experience of the Second Vatican Council illustrates this fact.

From a personal perspective, I have been comforted and strengthened by the support of so many. I remain a loyal and committed Roman Catholic. I pray daily that I might continue to love and serve the Church without bitterness and anger.

I will continue to work for the legitimacy of some theological and practical dissent, the need to change some official hierarchical church teachings, the importance of academic freedom for Catholic theology, and the need for just structures to deal with the inevitable tensions that from time to time will exist between theologians and pastors. I believe these are all for the good of the Roman Catholic Church — my church.

LIFE AND DEATH QUESTIONS

Questions concerning the treatment of terminally ill persons have increased in number and intensity since 1975 when Karen Ann Quinlan became comatose and her parents sought court authorization to remove her from a life-supporting respirator. Authorization was given by the New Jersey Supreme Court Mar. 31, 1976, and the apparatus was detached from the young woman. Artificially fed and hydrated, she lived until June 11, 1985.

New Jersey Superior Court ruled Apr. 23, 1986, that a nasogastric tube, for artificial feeding and hydration, could be removed from irreversibly comatose Nancy Ellen Jobes. Another New Jersey court authorized the removal of Kathleen Farrell from a respirator; she died June 29, 1986, while an appeal was pending. In California, an appeals court authorized Apr. 16, 1986, Elizabeth Bouvia's refusal of artificial feeding.

Court decisions on these and other cases have been based on grounds related to quality-of-life criteria and the supremacy of the right of privacy over the state's interest in preserving life. These, however, are not the only norms of judgment.

Relevant moral principles were the subject of a document issued by the Committee for Pro-Life Activities, National Conference of Catholic Bishops, Nov. 10, 1984: "Guidelines for Legislation on Life-Sustaining Treatment." The text was circulated by the NC Documentary Service, Origins. The guidelines stated, in part, as follows.

MORAL PRINCIPLES

Our Judeo-Christian heritage celebrates life as the gift of a loving God, and respects the life of each human being because each is made in the image and likeness of God. As Christians, we also celebrate the fact that we are redeemed by Christ and called to share eternal life with him. From these roots the Roman Catholic tradition has devleoped a distinctive approach to fostering and sustaining human life. Our tradition not only condemns direct attacks on innocent life, but also promotes a general view of life as a sacred trust over which we can claim stewardship but not absolute dominion. As conscientious stewards, we see a duty to preserve life while recognizing certain limit to that duty, as was reiterated in the Vatican "Declaration on Euthanasia." This and other documents have set forth the following moral principles defining a "stewardship of life" ethic.

1. The Second Vatican Council condemned crimes against life, including "euthansia or willful suicide." Grounded as it is in respect for the dignity and fundamental rights of the human person, this teaching cannot be rejected on grounds of political pluralism or religious freedom.

2. As human life is the basis and necessary condition for all other human goods, it has a special value and significance; both murder and suicide are violations of human life.

3. "Euthanasia" is "an action or an omission which of itself or by intention causes death, in order that all suffering may in this way be eliminated" ("Declaration on Euthanasia"). It is an attack on human life which no one has a right to make or request. Although individual guilt may be reduced or absent because of suffering or emotional factors which cloud the conscience, this does not change the objective wrong of the act. It should also be recognized that an apparent plea for death may really be a plea for help and love.

4. Suffering is a fact of human life and has special significance for the Christian as an opportunity to share in Christ's redemptive suffering. Nevertheless, there is nothing wrong in trying to relieve someone's suffering as long as this does not interfere with other moral and religious duties. For example, it is permissible in the case of terminal illness to use painkillers which carry the risk of shortening life, so long as the intent is to relieve pain effectively rather than to cause death.

5. Everyone has the duty to care for his or her own health and to seek necessary medical care from others, but this does not mean that all possible remedies must be used in all circumstances. One is not obliged to use "extraordinary" means — that is, means which offer no reasonable hope of benefit or which involve excessive hardship.

Although these principles have grown out of a specific religious tradition, they appeal to a common respect for the dignity of the human person rather than to any specific denominational stance. We offer them without hesitation to the consideration of men and women of good will, and commend them to the attention of legislators and other policy-makers. We see them as especially appropriate to a society which, whatever its moral and political pluralism, was founded on the belief that all human beings are created equal as bearers of the inalienable right to life.

Recommendations

The committee made the following recommendations concerning legislation on life-sustaining treatment.

• Presuppose the fundamental right to life of every human being, including the disabled, the elderly and the terminally ill. In general, phrases which seem to romanticize death, such as 'right to die' or 'death with dignity,' should be avoided.

• Recognize that the right to refuse medical treatment is not an independent right, but is a corollary to the patient's right and moral responsibility to request reasonable treatment.

• Place the patient's right to determine medical care within the context of other factors which limit the exercise of that right — e.g., the state's interest in protecting innocent third parties, preventing homicide and suicide, and maintaining good ethical standards in the health-care profession. Policy statements which define the right to refuse treatment in terms of the patient's constitutional rights (e.g., a "right of privacy") tend to inhibit the careful balancing of all the interests that should be considered in such cases.

• Avoid granting unlimited power to a document (living will) or proxy decision-maker to make health-care decisions on a patient's behalf. The right to make such decisions on one's own behalf is itself not absolute and, in any event, cannot be fully exercised when a patient has had no opportunity to assess the burdens and benefits of treatment in a specific situation. Laws which allow a decision to be made on behalf of a mentally incompetent patient must include safeguards to ensure that the decision adequately represents the patient's wishes or best interests and is in accord with responsible medical practice.

• Reaffirm public policies against homicide and assisted suicide. Medical-treatment legislation may clarify procedures for discontinuing treatment which only secures a precarious and burdensome prolongation of life for the terminally ill patient, but should not condone or authorize any deliberate act or omission designed to cause a patient's death.

• Recognize the presumption that certain basic measures such as nursing care, hydration, nourishment and the like must be maintained out of respect for the human dignity of every patient.

• Protect the interests of innocent parties who are not competent to make treatment decisions on their own behalf. Life-sustaining treatment should not be discriminatorily withheld or withdrawn from mentally incompetent or retarded patients.

• Provide that life-sustaining treatment should not be withdrawn from a pregnant woman if continued treatment may benefit her unborn child.

PONTIFICAL ACADEMY DECLARATION

Ethical, medical and legal questions on the artificial prolongation of life were the subject of a declaration issued by members of the Pontifical Academy of Sciences and published in the English edition of L'Osservatore Romano.

On the invitation of the Pontifical Academy of Sciences, a study group met on 10, 19 and 21 October 1985 to study the "artificial prolongation of life and the exact determination of the moment of death."

After having noted the recent progress of the techniques of resuscitation and the immediate and long-term effects of brain damange, the study group discussed the objective criteria of death and of the rules of conduct in the face of a persistent state of apparent death. On the one hand, experiments carried out reveal that brain resistance to the absence of cerebral circulation can permit recoveries otherwise deemed impossible.

On the other hand, it as been found that when the entire brain has suffered irreversible damage (cerebral death), all possibility of sensitive and cognitive life is definitively ruled out, while a brief vegetative survival can be maintained by artificial prolongation of respiration and circulation.

Definition of Death

A person is dead when he has irreversibly lost all capacity to integrate and coordinate the physical and mental functions of the body.

Death occurs when:

a) the spontaneous cardiac and respiratory functions have definitively ceased, or

b) if an irreversible cessation of every brain function is verified.

From the debate, it emerged that cerebral death is the true criterion of death, since the definitive arrest of the cardio-respiratory functions leads very quickly to cerebral death.

The group then analyzed the different clinical and instrumental methods that enable one to ascertain the irreversible arrest of cerebral functions. To be certain — by means of the electroencephalogram — that the brain has become flat, that is to say, that it no longer displays electric activity, it is necessary that the examination be carried out at least twice at a six-hour interval.

Medical Guidelines

By the term treatment, the group understands all those medical interventions available and appropriate in a specific case, whatever the complexity of the techniques involved.

If the patient is in a permanent, irreversible coma, as far as can be foreseen, treatment is not required, but all care should be lavished on him, including feeding (and hydration).

If it is clinically established that there is a possibility of recovery, treatment is required.

If treatment is of no benefit to the patient, it may be interrupted, while continuing with the care of the patient.

By the term care, the group understands ordinary help due to sick patients, such as (nutrition and hydration), compassion and spiritual and affective support due to every human being in danger.

Artificial Prolongation of Vegetative Functions

In the case of cerebral death, artificial respiration can prolong the cardiac function for a limited time. This induced survival of the organs is indicated in the case of a foreseen removal of organs for a transplant.

This eventuality is possible only in the case of total and irreversible brain damage occurring in a young person, essentially as a result of a very severe injury.

Taking into consideration the important advances made in surgical techniques and in the means to increase tolerance to transplants, the group holds that transplants deserve the support of the medical profession, of the law and of people in general.

The donation of organs should, in all circumstances, respect the last will of the donor, or the consent of the family if present.

CRITIQUE OF PROPOSED UNIFORM ACT

The U.S. Bishops' Committee on Pro-Life Activities declared July 2, 1986, that a proposal to eliminate disparities among state laws on treatment for the terminally ill raised "new and significant moral problems," and called for "serious debate." The committee said "The Uniform Rights of the Terminally Ill Act.," proposed by the National Conference on Uniform State Laws, could lead to unethical legislation which would further compromise "the right to life and respect for life in American society."

Like "living will laws" enacted in most states in the previous decades, the Uniform Act was intended to authorize the withdrawal of life-sustaining treatment from patients in the final stage of a terminal condition. The Pro-Life Committee was critical of the proposal, noting three key points.

Objections

• "The ambiguity of terms in the 'definitions' section creates the potential for a much broader application." The proposal could be read as authorizing withdrawal of life-sustaining treatment in cases where the patient could live a long time with treatment but would die quickly without it. "Thus, the potential for abuse is greater here than in laws whose scope is clearly limited to patients in the final stage of a terminal condition."

• The proposal said it would not affect any existing responsibility to provide measures such as nutrition and hydration. The committee called that approach "a serious lapse" because "the law should establish a strong presumption in favor of their use. .... Food and water are necessities of life for all human beings, and can generally be provided without the risks and burdens of more aggressive means for sustaining life."

• Regarding pregnant women: "The Uniform Act explicitly allows a pregnant woman to refuse treatment that could save the life of her unborn child whenever she fulfills the conditions of the Uniform Act." This provision goes beyond the U.S. Supreme Court's 1973 decision legalizing abortion.

The committee also objected to immunities provided for in the proposal, saying they were so broad that they reinforced the act's "bias" in favor of withdrawal of treatment.

THE NUCLEAR CRISIS AND A JUST PEACE: A METHODIST PASTORAL LETTER

Following is the text of a pastoral letter entitled "In Defense of Creation: The Nuclear Crisis and a Just Peace," approved Apr. 29, 1986, by the bishops of the United Methodist Church. Briefly, the letter states one of the principal theses of a longer foundation document: "We say a clear and unconditioned 'no' to nuclear war and to any use of nuclear weapons. We conclude that nuclear deterrence is a position which cannot receive the church's blessing."

(For coverage of the U.S. bishops' pastoral letter on these and related subjects, see "The Challenge of Peace: God's Promise and Our Response.")

The text of the pastoral letter was circulated by the NC Documentary Service, Origins, May 29, 1986 (Vol. 16, No. 2).

From your brothers and sisters in Christ Jesus, the Council of Bishops, to all those people called United Methodist in every land: Grace to you and peace in the name of our Lord Jesus Christ.

With hearts and minds open to Christ, who is our peace; in obedience to his call to be peacemakers; and in response to the biblical vision of a holistic peace, *shalom*, revealed in Scripture to be God's will and purpose for all of creation: We, the Bishops of the United Methodist Church, have been moved by the spirit of Jesus to send you a message, which we have titled "In Defense of Creation: The Nuclear Crisis and a Just Peace," a message we believe to be of utmost urgency in our time.

Serious Concerns

This message has been prepared over a span of two years, during which time we have earnestly sought to hear the word of God through the Scriptures. At the same time, we have prayerfully and penitently reflected on the continuing buildup of nuclear arsenals by some of the nations. We have become increasingly aware of the devastation that such weapons can inflict on planet Earth. We have watched and agonized over the increase in hostile rhetoric and hate among nations. We have seen the threat of a nuclear confrontation increasing in our world. We have been motivated by our own sense of Christian responsibility and stewardship for the world God created.

This brief pastoral letter is an introduction to a substantial foundation document which we have produced as the major portion of our message to the church. In our foundation document, we have attempted to state with clarity the biblical basis for our concerns and our conclusions about the issue we are addressing. We have set forth a theology for peace with justice in our time which reflects our understanding of the mind and will of Jesus Christ. This theology for a just peace reflects also our understanding of those insights of both pacifism and just-war theory which speak with relevance to the issues of the present nuclear crisis.

No to Nuclear War, Deterrence

We write in defense of creation. We do so because the creation itself is under attack. Air and water, trees and fruits and flowers, birds and fish and cattle, all children and youth, women and men live under the darkening shadows of a threatening nuclear winter. We call the United Methodist Church to more faithful witness and action in the face of this worsening nuclear crisis. It is a crisis that threatens to assault not only the whole human family but planet Earth itself, even while the arms race itself cruelly destroys millions of lives in conventional wars, repressive violence and massive poverty.

Therefore, we say a clear and unconditioned no

to nuclear war and to any use of nuclear weapons. We conclude that nuclear deterrence is a position which cannot receive the church's blessing. We state our complete lack of confidence in proposed "defenses" against nuclear attack and are convinced that the enormous cost of developing such defenses is one more witness to the obvious fact that the arms race is a social justice issue, not only a war and peace issue.

Our document sets forth a number of policies for a just peace, including such disarmament proposals as a comprehensive test ban, a multi-lateral and mutually verifiable nuclear-weapons freeze and the ultimate dismantling of all such weapons, and bans on all space weapons. However, the nuclear crisis is not primarily a matter of technology: It is a crisis of human community. We encourge independent U.S. and Soviet initiatives to foster a political climate conducive to negotiations. We urge a renewed commitment to building the institutional foundations of common security, economic justice, human rights and environmental conservation. And we make appeal for peace research, studies and training at all levels of education.

A Pastoral and Prophetic Word

This message, which we are sending to United Methodist people, is not meant to be a consensus opinion of our church or a policy statement of our denomination on the nuclear crisis and the pursuit of peace. It is given from the bishops to the church as a pastoral and a prophetic word. It is pastoral in that we as bishops will seek to lead the church in study, prayer and action related to this issue and this theme, using this document as a basic resource and guide. It is prophetic in that this document is our response to the word of God. It faithfully states our understanding of that word to our world at this moment in history.

Our message is the result of many months of prayerful study, research and reflection. It is not given to the church with any feeling that it should be the final word on this issue or with the hope that it will silence all contrary opinions; but rather, we are sending this statement to the church seeking the fullest and fairest possible discussion of our understandings and convictions, together with an honest consideration of different and critical opinions.

SECTS: VATICAN REPORT

Sects, cults and new religious movements were the subjects of a Vatican report issued May 4, 1986, based on the findings of a survey of episcopal conferences throughout the world. The survey was conducted between February, 1984, and October, 1985, under the auspices of the Secretariat for Promoting Christian Unity, the Secretariat for Non-Christians, the Secretariat for Non-Believers, and the Pontifical Council for Culture.

The following excerpts are from the text circulated by the NC Documentary Service, Origins, May 22, 1986 (Vol. 16, No. 1).

Working Definition

For practical reasons, a cult or sect is sometimes defined as "any religious group with a distinctive world view of its own derived from, but not identical with, the teachings of a major world religion." . . . Cults have also been characterized as possessing a number of distinctive features. These often are that they are authoritarian in structure, that they exercise forms of brain washing and mind control, that they cultivate group pressure and instill feelings of guilt and fear, etc.

Pastoral Problems

Almost all the local churches see the emergence and rapid proliferation of all kinds of "new" religious or pseudoreligious movements, groups and practices. The phenomenon is considered by almost all the respondents as a serious matter; by some, as an alarming matter.

In some cases, the phenomenon appears within the mainline churches themselves (sectarian attitudes). In other cases, it occurs outside the churches (independent or free churches, messianic or prophetic movements) or against the churches (sects, cults), often establishing for themselves churchlike patterns. However, not all

are religious in their real content or ultimate purpose.

The phenomenon develops fast, and often quite successfully, and poses pastoral problems.

Those Most Affected

(Those most affected by sects appear to be young people and, in various degrees, middle-aged, well-to-do and highly educated persons.) Mention must be made of university campuses, which are often favorable breeding grounds for sects or places of recruitment. Moreover, difficult relations with the clergy or an irregular marriage situation can lead one to break with the Church and join a new group.

Very few people seem to join a sect for evil reasons. Perhaps the greatest opportunity of the sects is to attract good people and good motivation in those people. In fact, they usually succeed best when society or church has failed to touch this good motivation.

The reasons for success among Catholics . . . are primarily related to the needs and aspirations which are seemingly not being met in the mainline churches. They are also related to the recruitment and training techniques of the sects. They can be external either to the mainline churches or to the new groups: economic advantages, political interest or pressure, mere curiosity, etc.

Response to Crisis Situations

The phenomenon seems to be symptomatic of the depersonalizing structures of contemporary society . . . which create multiple crisis situations on the individual as well as on the social level. These crisis situations reveal various needs, aspirations and questions which, in turn, call for psychological and spiritual responses. The sects claim to have and to give these responses. They do this on both the affective and cognitive level, often responding to the affective needs in a way that deadens the cognitive faculties.

Aspirations and Motivations

Crisis situations or general vulnerability can reveal and/or produce needs and aspirations which become basic motivations for turning to the sects. . . . These needs and aspirations can be grouped under nine major (and sometimes overlapping) headings.

1. Quest for Belonging (Sense of Community): The sects apper to offer: human warmth, care and support in small and close-knit communities; sharing of purpose and fellowship; attention for the individual; protection and security, especially in crisis situations; resocialization of marginalized individuals (for instance, the divorced and immigrants); the sect often does the thinking for the individual.

2. Search for Answers: The sects appear to offer: simple and ready-made answers to complicated questions and situations; simplified and partial versions of traditional truths and values; a pragmatic theology, a theology of success, a syncretistic theology proposed as 'new revelation'; 'new truth' to people who often have little of the 'old truth'; clear-cut directives; a claim to moral superiority; proofs from 'supernatural' elements; glossolalia, trance, mediumship, prophecies, possession, etc.

3. Search for Wholeness (Holism): The sects appear to offer: a gratifying religious experience — being saved, conversion; room for feelings, emotions, spontaneity (e.g., in religious celebrations); bodily and spiritual healing; help with drug or drink problems; relevance to the life situation.

4. Search for Cultural Identity: The sects appear to offer: plenty of room for traditional cultural/religious heritage, creativity, spontaneity, participation, a style of prayer and preaching closer to the cultural traits and aspirations of the people.

5. Need To Be Recognized, To Be Special: "The sects appear to offer: concern for the individual; equal opportunities for ministry and leadership, for participation, for witnessing, for expression; awakening to one's own potential, the chance to be part of an elite group.

6. Search for Transcendence: The sects appear to offer: the Bible and Bible education; a sense of salvation; gifts of the Spirit; meditation; spiritual achievement.

7. Need of Spiritual Guidance: The sects appear to offer: guidance and orientation through strong, charismatic leadership. The person of the master, leader, guru, plays an important role in binding the disciples. At times there is not only submission but emotional surrender and even an almost hysterical devotion to a strong spiritual leader (messiah, prophet, guru).

8. Need of Vision: The sects appear to offer: a 'new vision' of oneself, of humanity, of history, of the cosmos. They promise the beginning of a new age, a new era.

9. Need of Participation and Involvement: The sects appear to offer: a concrete mission for a better world, a call for total dedication, participation on most levels.

Recruitment and Training Techniques

Although all this (above) mostly accounts for the success of the cults, other reasons also exist, such as the recruitment and training techniques and indoctrination procedures used by certain sects.

These techniques proceed from a positive approach but gradually achieve a type of mind control through the use of abusive behavior-modification techniques:

• Subtle process of introduction of the convert and his gradual discovery of the real hosts.

• Overpowering techniques: love-bombing, offering "a free meal at an international center for friends," "flirting fishing" technique (prostitution as a method of recruitment).

• Ready-made answers and decisions are being almost forced upon the recruits.

• Flattery.

• Distribution of money, medicine.

• Requirement of unconditional surrender to the initiator, leader.

• Isolation: control of the rational thinking process, elimination of outside information and influence (family, friends, newspapers, magazines, television, radio, medical treatment, etc.) which might break the spell of involvement and the process of absorption of feelings and attitudes and patterns of behavior.

• Processing recruits away from their past lives; focusing on past deviant behavior such as drug use, sexual misdeeds; playing upon psychological hang-ups, poor social relationships, etc.

• Consciousness-altering methods leading to cognitive disturbances (intellectual bombardment); use of thought-stopping cliches; closed system of logic; restriction of reflective thinking.

• Keeping the recruits constantly busy and never alone; continual exhortation and training in order to arrive at an exalted spiritual status, altered consciousness, automatic submission to directives; stifling resistance and negativity; response to fear in a way that greater fear is often aroused.

• Strong focus on the leader; some groups may even downgrade the role of Christ in favor of the founder (in the case of some "Christian sects").

We cannot simply be satisfied with condemning and combatting the sects, with seeing them perhaps outlawed or expelled and individuals "deprogrammed" against their will. The "challenge" of the new religious movements is to stimulate our own renewal for a greater pastoral efficacy.

(Summarily, positive pastoral approaches to problems posed by sects include: development of the sense of community in the Church; emphasis on evangelization, catechesis and ongoing biblical, theological and ecumenical formation; adoption of a personal, holistic approach to the needs of individuals; adaptation between faith and culture [inculturation]; ways and means of prayer and worship; opportunities for participation and leadership in the Catholic community.)

TWO VIEWS

Father James LeBar, a New York priest and chaplain at the Hudson River Psychiatric Institute, Poughkeepsie, called the Vatican report "a primer, a basic education book on cults and a basic resource for pastoral action."

He said key cult movements in the U.S. include the Rev. Sun Myung Moon's Unification Church, the Children of God, the Way International (The Way) and the Shepherding-Discipleship Movement.

Cults were the subject of a 1985 address by Cardinal Franz Koenig, former president of the Secretariat for Non-Believers. He said, in part:

"A special difficulty for the Church . . . is constituted by the growing number of particular communities or sects. These fuse elements of the Christian religions with a number of syncretistic ideas, often with economic interests as well. They have strong group communities. Their almost innumerable tendencies and titles may be grouped under three heads:

• "Communities oriented to the end of time . . .
• "The second group fuses elements of Christianity with esoteric-occult sciences . . .
• "A third group: Non-Christian elements predominate here. Economic and political ends fuse with pseudoreligious purposes. To this group belong missions coming from the Far East, with yoga and Zen schools. Buddhist and Hindu concepts play quite an important part here.

"Among the neo-Islamic missions are to be found the Baha'i, who aim at attaining the unity of all religions. There are a great number of 'new age' and psychic cults. They do a lot of propaganda with the spoken and written word, for a new era."

LIBERATION THEOLOGY II: CHRISTIAN FREEDOM AND LIBERATION

A second document on liberation theology, entitled "Instruction on Christian Freedom and Liberation," was issued by the Congregation for the Doctrine of the Faith Apr. 5, 1986, with the approval of Pope John Paul. It complements the critical "Instruction on Certain Aspects of 'Liberation Theology'" released by the same congregation Sept. 4, 1984.

Under five chapter headings, the "Instruction on Christian Freedom and Liberation" treats subjects related to: the state of freedom in the world today, man's vocation to freedom and the tragedy fo sin, liberation and Christian freedom, the liberating mission of the Church, and the social doctrine of the Church for a Christian practice of liberation.

The following excerpts from the last two chapters are from the Vatican's English translation of the text, circulated by the NC Documentary Service, Origins, Apr. 17, 1986 (Vol. 15, No. 44).

The Liberating Mission of the Church

The Church is firmly determined to respond to the anxiety of contemporary man as he endures oppression and yearns for freedom. The political and economic running of society is not a direct part of her mission, but the Lord Jesus has entrusted to her the word of truth which is capable of enlightening consciences.

The Proclamation of Salvation: The Church's essential mission, following that of Christ, is a mission of evangelization and salvation. She draws her zeal from the divine love. Evangelization is the proclamation of salvation, which is a gift of God. Through the word of God and the sacraments, man is freed in the first place from the power of sin and the power of the Evil One which oppress him; and he is brought into a communion of love with God. Following her Lord, who "came into the world to save sinners" (1 Tm. 1:15), the Church desires the salvation of all people.

In this mission, the Church teaches the way which man must follow in this world in order to enter the kingdom of God. Her teaching therefore extends to the whole moral order, and notably to the justice which must regulate human relations. This is part of the preaching of the Gospel.

But the love which impels the Church to communicate to all people a sharing in the grace of divine life also causes her, through the effective action of her members, to pursue people's true temporal good, help them in their needs, provide for their education and promote an integral liberation from everything that hinders the development of individuals. The Church desires the good of man in all his dimensions: first of all, as a member of the City of God, and then as a member of the earthly city.

Evangelization and the Promotion of Justice: Therefore, when the Church speaks about the promotion of justice in human societies, or when she urges the faithful laity to work in this sphere according to their own vocation, she is not going beyond her mission. She is, however, concerned that this mission should not be absorbed by preoccupations concerning the temporal order or reduced to such preoccupations. Hence, she takes great care to maintain clearly and firmly both the unity and the distinction between evangelization and human promotion: unity, because she seeks the good of the whole person; distinction, because these two tasks enter, in different ways, into her mission.

The Gospel and Earthly Realities: It is thus by pursuing her own finality that the Church sheds the light of the Gospel on earthly realities in order that human beings may be healed of their miseries and raised in dignity. The cohesion of society in accordance with justice and peace is thereby promoted and strengthened. Thus, the Church is being faithful to her mission when she condemns the forms of deviation, slavery and oppression of which people are victims.

She is being faithful to her mission when she opposes attempts to set up a form of social life from which God is absent, whether by deliberate opposition or by culpable negligence.

She is likewise being faithful to her mission when she exercises her judgment regarding political movements which seek to fight poverty and oppression according to theories or methods of action which are contrary to the Gospel and opposed to man himself.

It is, of course, true that, with the energy of grace, evangelical morality brings man new perspectives and new duties. But its purpose is to perfect and elevate a moral dimension which already belongs to human nature and with which the Church concerns herself in the knowledge that this is a heritage belonging to all people by their very nature.

Love of Preference for the Poor: In its various forms — material deprivation, unjust oppression, physical and psychological illnesses, and finally death — human misery is the obvious sign of the natural condition of weakness in which man finds himself since original sin and the sign of his need for salvation. Hence, it drew the compassion of Christ the Savior to take it upon himself and to be identified with the least of his brethren (cf. Mt. 25:40, 45). Hence also, those who are oppressed by poverty are the object of a love of preference on the part of the Church which, since her origin and in spite of the failings of many of her members, has not ceased to work for their relief, defense and liberation. She has done this through numberless works of charity which remain always and everywhere indispensable. In addition, through her social doctrine which she strives to apply, she has sought to promote structural changes in society so as to secure conditions of life worthy of the human person.

In loving the poor, the Church also witnesses to man's dignity. She clearly affirms that man is worth more for what he is than for what he has. She bears witness to the fact that this dignity cannot be destroyed, whatever the situation of poverty, scorn, rejection or powerlessness to which a human being has been reduced. She shows her solidarity with those who do not count in a society by which they are rejected spiritually and sometimes even physically. She is particularly drawn with maternal affection toward those children who, through human wickedness, will never be brought forth from the womb to the light of day, as also for the elderly, alone and abandoned.

The special option for the poor, far from being a sign of particularism or sectarianism, manifests the universality of the Church's being and mission. This option excludes no one.

This is the reason why the Church cannot express this option by means of reductive sociological and ideological categories which would make this preference a partisan choice and a source of conflict.

Basic Communities and Other Christian Groups: The new basic communities or other groups of Christians which have arisen to be witnesses to this evangelical love are a source of great hope for the Church. If they really live in unity with the local church and the universal Church, they will be a real expression of communion and a means of constructing a still deeper communion. Their fidelity to their mission will depend on how careful they are to educate their members in the fullness of the Christian faith through listening to the word of God and through fidelity to the teaching of the magisterium, to the hierarchical order of the Church and to the sacramental life. If this condition is fulfilled, their experience, rooted in a commitment to the complete liberation of man, becomes a treasure for the whole Church.

Theological Reflections: Similarly, a theological reflection developed from a particular experience can constitute a very positive contribution, inasmuch as it makes possible a highlighting of aspects of the word of God, the richness of which has not yet been fully grasped. But, in order that this reflection may be truly a reading of the Scripture and not a projection on to the word of God of a meaning which it does not contain, the tholoegian will be careful to interpret the experience from which he begins in the light of the experience of the Church herself. This experience of the Church shines with a singular brightness and in all its purity in the lives of the saints. It pertains to the pastors of the Church, in communion with the successor of Peter, to discern its authenticity.

The Christian Practice of Liberation

The salvific dimension of liberation cannot be reduced to the socio-ethical dimension, which is a consequence of it. By restoring man's true freedom, the radical liberation brought about by Christ assigns to him a task: Christian practice, which is the putting into practice of the great commandment of love. The latter is the supreme principle of Christian social morality, founded upon the Gospel and the whole of tradition since apostolic times and the age of the fathers of the Church up to and including the recent statements of the magisterium.

The considerable challenges of our time constitute an urgent appeal to put into practice this teaching on how to act.

The Gospel Message and Social Life: The Church's social teaching is born of the encounter of the Gospel message and of its demands summarized in the supreme commandment of love of God and neighbor in justice with the problems emanating from the life of society. This social teaching has established itself as a doctrine by using the resources of human wisdom and the sciences. It concerns the ethical aspect of life. It takes into account the technical aspects of problems but always in order to judge them from the moral point of view.

Being essentially oriented toward action, this teaching develops in accordance with the changing circumstances of history. This is why, together with principles that are always valid, it also involves contingent judgments. Far from constituting a closed system, it remains constantly open to the new questions which continually arise; it requires the contribution on all charisms, experiences and skills.

Fundamental Principles: The supreme commandment of love leads to the full recognition of the dignity of each individual, created in God's image. From this dignity flow natural rights and duties. In the light of the image of God, freedom, which is the essential prerogative of the human person, is manifested in all its depth. Persons are the active and responsible subjects of social life.

Intimately linked to the foundation, which is man's dignity, are the principle of solidarity and the principle of subsidarity.

By virtue of the first, man with his brothers is obliged to contribute to the common good of society at all its levels. Hence, the Church's doctrine is opposed to all the forms of social or political individualism.

By virtue of the second, neither the state nor any society must ever substitute itself for the initiative and responsibility of individuals and of intermediate communities at the level on which they can function, nor must they take away the room necessary for their freedom. Hence the Church's social doctrine is opposed to all forms of collectivism.

Criteria for Judgment: These principles are the basis of criteria for making judgments on social situations, structures and systems.

Thus, the Church does not hesitate to condemn situations of life which are injurious to man's dignity and freedom.

These criteria also make it possible to judge the value of structures. These are the sets of institutions and practices which people find already existing or which they create, on the national and international level, and which orientate or organize economic, social and political life. Being necessary in themselves, they often tend to become fixed and fossilized as mechanisms relatively independent of the human will, thereby paralyzing or distorting social development and causing injustice. However, they always depend on the responsibility of man, who can alter them, and not upon an alleged determinism of history.

Institutions and laws, when they are in conformity with the natural law and ordered to the common good, are the guarantees of people's freedom and of the promotion of that freedom. One cannot condemn all the constraining aspects of law, nor the stability of a lawful state worthy of the name. One can therefore speak of structures marked by sin, but one cannot condemn structures as such.

The criteria for judgment also concern economic, social and political systems. The social doctrine of the Church does not propose any particular system; but, in the light of other fundamental principles, she makes it possible at once to see to what extent existing systems conform or do not conform to the demands of human dignity.

Primacy of Persons over Structures: The Church is, of course, aware of the complexity of the problems confronting society and of the difficulties in finding adequate solutions to them. Nevertheless, she considers that the first thing to be done is to appeal to the spiritual and moral capacities of the individual and to the permanent need for inner conversion, if one is to achieve the economic and social changes that will truly be at the service of man.

The priority given to structures and technical organization over the person and the requirements of his dignity is the expression of a materialistic anthropology and is contrary to the construction of a just social order.

On the other hand, the recognized priority of freedom and of conversion of heart in no way eliminates the need for unjust structures to be changed. It is therefore perfectly legitimate that those who suffer oppression on the part of the wealthy or the politically powerful should take action, through morally licit means, in order to secure structures and institutions in which their rights will be truly respected.

Restrictive Meaning of Social Sin: It remains true, however, that structures established for people's good are of themselves incapable of securing and guaranteeing that good. The corruption which in certain countries affects the leaders and the state bureaucracy, and which destroys all honest social life, is a proof of this. Moral integrity is a necessary condition for the health of society. It is therefore necessary to work simultaneously for the conversion of hearts and for the improvement of structures. For the sin which is at the root of unjust situations is, in a true and immediate sense, a voluntary act which has its source in the freedom of individuals. Only in a derived and secondary sense is it applicable to structures, and only in this sense can one speak of "social sin".

Moreover, in the process of liberation, one cannot abstract from the historical situation of the nation or attack the cultural identity of the people. Consequently, one cannot passively accept, still less actively support, groups which by force or by the manipulation of public opinion take over the state apparatus and unjustly impose on the collectivity an imported ideology contrary to the culture of the people. In this respect, mention should be made of the serious moral and political responsibility of intellectuals.

Guidelines for Action: Basic principles and criteria for judgment inspire guidelines for action. Since the common good of human society is at the service of people, the means of action must be in conformity with human dignity and facilitate education for freedom. A safe criterion for judgment and action is this: There can be no true liberation if, from the very beginning, the rights of freedom are not respected.

Systematic recourse to violence put forward as the necessary path to liberation has to be condemned as a destructive illusion and one that opens the way to new forms of servitude. One must condemn with equal vigor violence exercised by the powerful against the poor, arbitrary action by the police, and any form of violence established as a system of government. In these areas one must learn the lessons of tragic experiences which the history of the present century has known and continues to know. Nor can one accept the culpable passivity of the public powers in those democracies where the social situation of a large number of men and women is far from corresponding to the demands of constitutionally guaranteed individual and social rights.

The Struggle for Justice: When the Church encourages the creation and activity of associations such as trade unions which fight for the defense of the rights and legitimate interests of the workers and for social justice, she does not thereby admit that theory that sees in the class struggle the structural dynamism of social life. The action which she sanctions is not the struggle of one class against another in order to eliminate the foe. She does not proceed from a mistaken acceptance of an alleged law of history. This action is rather a noble and reasoned struggle for justice and social solidarity. The Christian will always prefer the path of dialogue and joint action.

Christ has commanded us to love our enemies. Liberation in the spirit of the Gospel is therefore incompatible with hatred of others, taken individually or collectively; and this includes hatred of one's enemy.

The Myth of Revolution: Situations of grave injustice require the courage to make far-reaching reforms and to suppress unjustifiable privileges. But those who discredit the path of reform and favor the myth of revolution not only foster the illusion that the abolition of an evil situation is in itself sufficient to create a more humane society; they also encourage the setting up of totalitarian regimes. The fight against injustice is meaningless unless it is waged with a view to establishing a new social and political order in conformity with the demands of justice. Justice must already mark each stage of the establishment of this new order. There is a morality of means.

A Last Resort: These principles must be especially applied in the extreme case where there is recourse to armed struggle, which the Church's magisterium admits as a last resort to put an end to an obvious and prolonged tyranny which is gravely damaging the fundamental rights of individuals and the common good. Nevertheless, the concrete application of this means cannot be contemplated until there has been a very rigorous analysis of the situation. Indeed, because of the continual development of the technology of violence and the increasingly serious dangers implied in its recourse, that which today is termed "passive resistance" shows a way more conformable to moral principles and having no less prospects for success. One can never approve, whether perpetrated by established power or insurgents, crimes such as reprisals against the general population, torture, or methods of terrorism and deliberate provocation aimed at causing deaths during popular demonstrations. Equally unacceptable are detestable smear campaigns capable of destroying a person psychologically or morally.

The Role of the Laity: It is not for the pastors of the Church to intervene directly in the political construction and organization of social life. This task forms part of the vocation of the laity acting on their own initiative with their fellow citizens. They must fulfill this task conscious of the fact that the purpose of the Church is to spread the kingdom of Christ so that all men may be saved and that, through them, the world may be effectively ordered to Christ. The work of salvation is thus seen to be indissolubly linked to the task of improving and raising the conditions of human life in this world.

The distinction between the supernatural order of salvation and the temporal order of human life must be seen in the context of God's singular plan to recapitulate all things in Christ. Hence, in each of these spheres the lay person, who is at one and the same time a member of the Church and a citizen of his country, must allow himself to be constantly guided by his Christian conscience.

Social action, which can involve a number of concrete means, will always be exercised for the common good and in conformity with the Gospel message and the teaching of the Church. It must be ensured that the variety of options does not harm a sense of collaboration, or lead to a paralysis of efforts, or produce confusion among Christian people.

The orientation received from the social doctrine of the Church should stimulate an acquisition of the essential technical and scientific skills. The social doctrine of the Church will also stimulate the seeking of moral formaton of character and a deepening of the spiritual life. While it offers principles and wise counsels, this doctrine does not dispense from education in the political prudence needed for guiding and running human affairs.

Need for a Cultural Transformation: Christians working to bring about that "civilization of love," which will include the entire ethical and social heritage of the Gospel, are today faced with an unprecedented challenge. This task calls for renewed reflecton on what constitutes the relationship between the supreme commandment of love and the social order considered in all its complexity.

The immediate aim of this in-depth reflection is to work out and set in motion ambitious programs aimed at the socio-economic liberation of millions of men and women caught in an intolerable situation of economic, social and political oppression.

This action must begin with an immense effort at education: education for the civlization of work, education for solidarity, access to culture for all.

The Gospel of Work: The life of Jesus of Nazareth, a real "Gospel at work," offers us the living example and principle of the radical cultural transformation which is essential for solving the grave problems which must be faced by the age in which we live. He who, though he was God, became like us in all things, devoted the greater part of his earthly life to manual labor. The culture which our age awaits will be marked by the full recognition of the dignity of human work, which appears in all its nobility and fruitfulness in the light of the mysteries of creation and redemption. Recognized as a form of the person, work becomes a source of creative meaning and effort.

A True Civilization of Work: Thus, the solution of most of the serious problems related to poverty is to be found in the promotion of a true civilization of work. In a sense, work is the key to the whole social question.

It is therefore in the domain of work that priority must be given to the action of liberation in freedom. Because the relationship btween the human person and work is radical and vital, the forms and models according to which this relationship is regulated will exercise a positive influence for the solution of a whole series of social and political problems facing each people. Just work relationships will be a necessary precondition for a system of political community capable of favoring the integral development of every individual.

If the system of labor relations put into effect by those directly involved, the workers and employers, with the essential support of the public powers succeeds in bringing into existence a civilization of work, then there will take place a profound and peaceful revolution in people's outlooks and in institutional and political structures.

National and International Common Good: A work culture such as this will necessarily presuppose and put into effect a certain number of essential values. It will acknowledge that the person of the worker is the principle, subject and purpose of work. It will affirm the priority of work over capital, and the fact that material goods are meant for all. It will be animated by a sense of solidarity involving not only rights to be defended but also duties to be performed. It will involve participation aimed at promoting the national and international common good and not just defending individual or corporate interests. It will assimilate the methods of confrontation and of frank and vigorous dialogue.

As a result, the political authorities will become more capable of acting with respect for the legitimate freedoms of individuals, families and subsidiary groups; and they will thus create the conditions necessary for man to be able to achieve his authentic and integral welfare, including his spiritual goal.

The Value of Human Work: A culture which recognizes the eminent dignity of the worker will emphasize the subjective dimension of work.

The value of any human work does not depend on the kind of work done; it is based on the fact that the one who does it is a person. There we have an ethical criterion whose implications cannot be overlooked.

Thus, every person has a right to work, and this right must be recognized in a practical way by an effective commitment to resolving the tragic problem of unemployment. The fact that unemployment keeps large sectors of the population, and notably the young, in a situation of marginalization is intolerable. For this reason the creation of jobs is a primary social task facing individuals and private enterprise, as well as the state. As a general rule, in this as in other matters, the state has a subsidiary function; but often it can be called upon to intervene directly, as in the case of international agreements between different states. Such agreements must respect the rights of immigrants and their families.

Promoting Participation: Wages, which cannot be considered as a mere commodity, must enable the worker and his family to have access to a truly human standard of living in the material, social, cultural and spiritual orders. It is the dignity of the person which constitutes the criterion for judging

work, not the other way round. Whatever the type of work, the worker must be able to perform it as an expression of his personality. There follows from this the necessity of a participation which, over and above a sharing in the fruits of work, should involve a truly communitarian dimension at the level of projects, undertakings and responsibilities.

Priority of Work over Capital: The priority of work over capital places an obligation in justice upon employers to consider the welfare of the workers before the increase of profits. They have a moral obligation not to keep capital unproductive and, in making investments, to think first of the common good. The latter requires a prior effort to consolidate jobs or create new ones in the production of goods that are really useful.

The right to private property is inconceivable without responsibilities to the common good. It is subordinated to the higher principle which states that goods are meant for all.

In-Depth Reforms: This teaching must inspire reforms before it is too late. Access for everyone to the goods needed for a human, personal and family life worthy of the name is a primary demand of social justice. It requires application in the sphere of industrial work and in a particular way in the area of agricultural work. Indeed, rural peoples, especially in the Third World, make up the vast majority of the poor.

Promotion of Solidarity

A New Solidarity: Solidarity is a direct requirement of human and supernatural brotherhood. The serious socio-economic problems which occur today cannot be solved unless new fronts of solidarity are created: solidarity of the poor among themselves, solidarity with the poor to which the rich are called, solidarity among the workers and with the workers. Institutions and social organizations at different levels, as well as the state, must share in a general movement of solidarity. When the Church appeals for such solidarity, she is aware that she herself is concerned in a quite special way.

Goods Are Meant for All: The principle that goods are meant for all, together with the principle of human and supernatural brotherhood, express the responsibilities of the richer countries toward the poorer ones. These responsibilities include solidarity in aiding the developing countries, social justice through a revision in correct terms of commercial relationships between North and South, the promotion of a more human world for all, a world in which each individual can give and receive, and in which the progress of some will no longer be an obstacle to the development of others, nor a pretext for their enslavement.

Aid for Development: International solidarity is a necessity of the moral order. It is essential not only in cases of extreme urgency but also for aiding true development. This is a shared task, which requires a concerted and constant effort to find concrete technical solutions and also to create a new mentality among our contemporaries. World peace depends on this to a great extent.

OCTOBER 1985

VATICAN

Media Potential for Good and Evil — "The tremendous potential for good" of radio and television "is constantly increasing," but "I am aware that the opposite possibility is also there, the ever greater capacity for evil, because of the temptation to use these sophisticated means of social communication in ways that distort the truth or which offend the dignity and freedom of the human person." So stated the Pope Oct. 3 in an address to participants in the 21st Administrative Symposium of the European Broadcasting Union.

Independence of Church and State — The independence of Church and state in Italy must be recognized by everyone "despite their different religious and ideological convictions," the Pope told President Francesco Cossiga Oct. 4. At the same time, both should be "at the service of the personal and social vocation of the human person. . . . The Church does not intend to request privileges" from the state, but "offers and requests cooperation" of the state in its social work.

Ukrainians Persecuted — While addressing 17 Ukrainian bishops Oct. 5, the Pope said he shared their pain and sorrow over religious persecution in their homeland, with its estimated 4.5 million Catholics. He said that he and Vatican diplomats had repeatedly urged that Catholics in the Ukraine be permitted to practice their faith freely, in accordance with provisions of the 1975 Helsinki agreements on human rights. He called on the Ukrainian faithful to "show courageous witness to your faith in front of all those who attempt, in any way, to weaken it." The bishops were in Rome for a synod of their own, with primary focus on the ongoing revision of the Code of Canon Law for Eastern Churches.

Beatifications — The Holy Father beatified three Spanish Jesuits Oct. 6: Father Diego Luis de San Vitores (1627-72), the first martyr of Guam, where he established the first permanent mission; Father Jose Maria Rubio y Peralta (1864-1929), who ministered to the poor in Madrid; Brother Francisco Garate (1857-1929), who the Pope said was an "evangelizing force" through his "humble and silent service" as a university doorkeeper in Bilbao.

Demographic Suicide — Pope John Paul told European bishops Oct. 11 that widespread legalized abortion was contributing to "demographic suicide" on the Continent. He said demographic forecasts predicted that Europeans would represent only five percent of world population by the middle of the 21st century. The move to legalize abortion, he said, was spurred by "a subjectivism and individualism which seeks only one's own egotistical self-realization. . . . The introduction of permissive legislation on abortion has been considered an affirmation of the principle of freedom." Instead, it is "the triumph of the principle of well-being and egoism over the more sacred value of human life."

Seventh Anniversary — Seven years after his election to the papacy, Pope John Paul was cited by *L'Osservatore Romano* Oct. 16 for his efforts for peace, his care for local churches and his doctrinal concerns. One writer noted the significance of his pastoral visits — 53 to places in Italy and to 56 nations on 28 trips abroad.

Visit to Sardinia — Pope John Paul, visiting Sardinia Oct. 18 to 20, called for action against unemployment, made an impromptu show of support for Solidarity, the outlawed Polish labor union, and repeated earlier condemnations of racial discrimination in South Africa. In an address to 4,000 miners, he said: "With ever-rising percentages, the phenomenon of unemployment castigates today nearly all the more industrialized countries. . . . The phenomenon can be resolved satisfactorily only by international treaties and cooperation agreements." The trip was the Pope's 54th to a place in Italy beyond the immediate vicinity of Rome.

Advice for Future Priests — The years of seminary study and formation should help students develop virtues that are indispensable in the personal and pastoral life of priests, said the Pope Oct. 22 during a meeting with a group of Roman seminarians. "The vocation to priesthood does not change human nature and does not eliminate the attraction of the world. Therefore, you need to develop self-control, personal discipline, mortification, a sense of humility and obedience."

Conscience — "Faced with studies, inventions and technical exploits that men are developing in all domains, it is urgent to develop at the same time a heightened conscience, through a sharpened sense of good and evil, a respect for creation, and an absolute respect for man who transcends all things." So stated the Pope Oct. 28 as he accepted the credentials of Japanese Ambassador Uchida.

The Pope Also:

• Gave the title of office head at the Congregation for Religious and Secular Institutes to Sister Linscott, the highest-ranking nun at the Vatican.

• Met Oct. 10 with Archbishop John R. Quinn of San Francisco and other members of a special commission studying the life of Religious in the U.S.

• Decried violations of human rights, urged efforts for peace and pleaded the case of indebted Third World countries, in a message Oct. 18 marking the 40th anniversary of the United Nations.

• Condemned Oct. 20 the execution of South African black poet Benjamin Moloise and called racial discrimination in South Africa "a persistent situation of objective injustice."

• Told a group of priests Oct. 24: "Children and young people need a concrete model more than a theoretical presentation of a style of life" in order "to discover the ideals of the Christian message with all its demands."

• Appealed for emergency relief aid to Vietnam Oct. 30, citing the "devastation" of the central region of the country by a violent typhoon Oct. 15 and 16.

Vatican Briefs:

• Archbishop Luigi Poggi, staff member of the Council for the Public Affairs of the Church, pledged Oct. 11 continued Vatican support of the overall goals of UNESCO, but urged member states to end "vain confrontations" which harm the agency's work.

• *L'Osservatore Romano,* in its Oct. 13 edition, called the hijacking of the Italian cruise ship, Achille Lauro, "an infamous and shameful act."

• Cardinal Jozef Tomko, prefect of the Congregation for the Evangelization of Peoples, appealed Oct. 17 for more missionary vocations: "In almost all Christian countries, the numbers of missionaries are diminishing, and at the frontiers of Christianity the announcement of Jesus Christ is in crisis."

• The Congregation for the Doctrine of the Faith was reviewing an evaluation by U.S. Dominicans of writings of Dominican Father Matthew Fox, director of the Institute of Culture and Creation Spirituality.

Liberation, Unity, Political Involvement

These were among subjects mentioned by the Pope at three meetings with bishops from the Philippines.

• He criticized promotion of a "merely temporal" liberation Oct. 12. The Gospel cannot be placed "at the service of any objective other than the fullness of life and love. . . . This love is incompatible with the use of division, opposition, hatred or violence as a program of Christian life or of progress in justice. Time and again, you have to proclaim that no merely temporal and imminent liberation can be the object of the Church's evangelical mission."

• On Oct. 17, he said: "We have a fundamental obligation to defend and strengthen the unity of the one Church of Christ." Backgrounding the remark was awareness of an unacceptable "concept of a church 'of the people' falsely contrasted with the concept of the 'institutional' Church."

• Speaking Oct. 25 about priests and Religious engaged in social work, he said: They "certainly proclaim the Gospel message of liberation. But they must be careful not to subvert the message by imposing on it a reductive interpretation, or by putting it at the service of a particular form of political involvement, or by taking part in activities that do not appear in consonance with their ecclesial status."

NATIONAL

Total Care for AIDS Victims — Cardinal John J. O'Connor stood by his statement in the Sept. 19 edition of *Catholic New York,* that the archdiocese was committed to a "total care system" for victims of AIDS, including educational opportunities for children afflicted with the disease (Acquired Immune Deficiency Syndrome). He called on people not to retreat from AIDS victims in fear, confusion and ignorance, and said the archdiocese "is committed to do its best to minister to every person who is ill, of whatever disorder, because of our commitment to the belief that every person is made in the image and likeness of God." The cardinal noted that the archdiocese had begun a year earlier to provide financial assistance to AIDS victims, and that St. Vincent's Hospital had already provided free care valued at more than $1 million.

Fetuses Buried — Sixteen thousand, 433 aborted fetuses found three years earlier in a disposal container in Santa Monica, California, were buried Oct. 6 at Odd Fellows Cemetery in East Los Angeles. Burial followed protracted legal proceedings which ended with a decision of the Los Angeles County Board of Supervisors to allow the burial to take place.

Ruling against Chicago Archdiocese — The U.S. Supreme Court let stand Oct. 7 a copyright award in a suit against the Archdiocese of Chicago by F.E.L. Publications, Ltd. At issue in the case were illegal reproduction of F.E.L. copyrighted music and interference with sales operations of the firm.

Hunger in the United States — "There are still too many hungry people in our communities," and Congress and the White House are to blame, according to "Unfed America 1985," a report released Oct. 8 by Bread for the World. The report contained details of findings from surveys conducted by the Hunger Watch USA program in 36 communities across the nation. The report said "our churches are being called upon to feed and assist growing numbers of needy individuals and families," and that "the severe crisis of the early 1980s has become a stubborn problem that refuses to go away. Congress has not restored federal public assistance programs to their pre-1982 levels, and the impact of food stamp program cuts continues to be felt." The report noted also that the Reagan administration was recommending further cuts in the food stamp program. Researchers reported that "every survey uncovered unmet hunger needs in their community and barriers to participation in programs meant to help hungry people."

Homosexual Seminars Barred — Three bishops in Minnesota and one in Wisconsin barred the Catholic Coalition for Gay Civil Rights from holding seminars in Catholic facilities. Bishop John Paul of La Crosse explained in a newspaper article Oct. 10: "The theological and pastoral positions of the coalition are not fully coherent with the teaching and pastoral practice of the Roman Catholic Church, a teaching which does not condemn the homosexual but compassionately invites and assists the homosexual, as it does all believers, to lead a chaste life."

United Nations a Special Place — Four days before the 40th anniversary of the founding of the U.N., Cardinal Agostino Casaroli said that, despite the organization's "inadequacies," it remained "a special place" for working to build a peaceful world. Speaking at a Mass in New York's St. Patrick's Cathedral Oct. 20, the Vatican secretary of state said: "There are two extremes to be avoided

— a blind optimism and an unenlightened but certainly not Christian pessimism. . . . I would dare to say that the present situation of the world, with all its negative and frighteningly dangerous aspects, can and must be transformed into a providential opportunity" for peace making. "The enterprise is historically gigantic, but not beyond the capacity of humanity."

Extension Society Anniversary — The Catholic Church Extension Society marked its 80th anniversary Oct. 18, nearly three weeks after the celebration of a commemorative Mass in a train chapel car in Nevada City, Mont. The car was one of three Pullman-style "chapels on wheels" used by the society between 1907 and the 1930s to make the sacraments and pastoral services of the Church available to people in poor and rural areas without priests.

NCCW Convention — Evangelization, family life and world peace were the focus of attention during the Oct. 20-to-25 convention of the National Council of Catholic Women in Orlando, Fla. "Our sense of mission," said keynoter Susan Blum, "is the result of our faith in Jesus Christ. . . . We are instructed to come and follow Jesus, and we are instructed to go and minister in his name." Archbishop Edward A. McCarthy of Miami told 1,700 delegates that the highest priority should be given to proclaiming the Catholic faith from the pulpit, at school and home, in liturgies and even through the media and art." He called on the delegates "to transform the world" by evangelizing people inside as well as outside the Church. Toni Bischoff was elected president during the convention.

Notre Dame Not Divesting — Father Theodore Hesburgh, president, announced Oct. 25 that the University of Notre Dame was not divesting itself of stock in some 30 U.S. companies doing business in South Africa. He said "divestment would be a nice symbolic gesture; but, the day you do that, your influence (with the companies) ends." He added that, while the university board voted to retain its stock for the present, criteria had been strengthened for holding such stock and for future investment in other U.S. companies doing business in South Africa.

National Briefs:
• Vietnamese refugee parishioners burned the mortgage on their Church of the Blessed Vietnamese Martyrs in Annandale, Va., six years after 20 of their number obtained a loan of $135,000 to buy an abandoned building for use as a church.

• Msgr. John R. McNamara of the Boston Archdiocese was appointed Navy Chief of Chaplains and director of religious ministries, with the rank of rear admiral.

• In a *Catholic New York* column Oct. 3, Cardinal John J. O'Connor said he was "certain that Catholics and many others will make clear that they can in no way support the anti-Semitic and racist statements attributed to Minister (Louis) Farrakhan."

• The Association of Ladies of Charity in the Pittsburgh Diocese raised more than $250,000 for the aged poor in nine years.

• Women for Faith and Family held its first national conference Oct. 4 to 6 in St. Louis. In June, the organization issued a statement with 10,000 signatures entitled "Affirmation for Catholic Women," expressing loyalty to the Church and unity with the pope.

• St. Patrick's Cathedral, New York, was one of many sites of anti-apartheid protests Oct. 5, the National Day of Mourning for Victims of Violence in the Republic of South Africa.

• Approximately 350 persons attended the 18th annual Wanderer Forum Oct. 18 and 19 in Washington; secular humanism was a leading subject of discussion.

Several Abortion Ad Signers Cleared

Four Sisters of Charity of St. Elizabeth who signed an October 7, 1984, *New York Times* ad asserting that there is more than one "legitimate Catholic position" on the morality of abortion, were cleared of disciplinary action by the Vatican. So reported Sister Ellen Joyce, general superior of the institute, Oct. 29. Their clearance brought to six the number of sisters who no longer faced possible dismissal from their communities. Unreported was the status of 18 other nuns who signed the ad.

In a statement issued Oct. 2, a few days before the observance of Respect Life Sunday, Cardinal Joseph L. Bernardin said on behalf of the U.S. bishops: "The Church's teaching in this matter is binding not only because the Church says so, but because this teaching expresses the objective demands placed on all of us by the inherent dignity of human life. . . . A Catholic who chooses to dissent from this teaching, or to support dissent from it, is dissenting not only from church law but from a higher law which the Church seeks to observe and teach. Such dissent can in no way be seen as legitimate alternative teaching."

INTERNATIONAL

Abortion Is the Taking of Human Life — So stated Ontario Provincial Court Judge A.K. Meen in a statement contained in an 11-page judgment issued in the trial of 14 persons charged with trespassing at an abortion clinic. "Considerable evidence (was presented) by the defense with respect to the point at which life begins, and there appears to be no disagreement with the concept that human life begins at the moment of conception, with the fetus having from that time forward a separate genetic existence, distinct from that of its mother. It follows logically, therefore, that abortion deals with the taking of human life."

Earthquake Recovery in Mexico — Father Enrique Gonzalez Torres, executive secretary of the Mexican bishops' Commission on Social Work, reported early in the month that the bishops had established housing and employment cooperatives for victims of the earthquakes which devastated Mexico City Sept. 19 and 20. He also said that the Catholic Assistance Fund established by the bishops had received more than $1 million in contributions from Mexican and international sources (much of it from the U.S.).

Errant Liberation Theology — Versions of liberation theology out of line with Vatican guidelines were being disseminated in Latin America in numerous books, essays and articles, according to a document signed by four Latin American bishops, 20 priests and lay persons involved in pastoral programs. Such versions "demand an essentially political rereading of the word of God, which leads to interpreting the entire Christian existence, faith and theology according to a political formula." The document, drafted at a July 24-to-28 meeting of pastoral workers in Los Andes, Chile, was published in the Oct. 11 edition of *L'Osservatore Romano.*

Criticism of the Pope Is Disastrous — Those who "dissent from or pay no attention to pastoral guidelines of the Pope contribute to the weakening among people of his charism of ecclesial direction," said the major superior of the Salesians in a letter to the 17,000 members of the order. "At the present day, we are witnessing disastrous consequences of criticism of the Pope" and dissent from his teachings, especially concerning moral values. Because of such criticism, "one sees public opinion getting even further away from the very foundations of Christian morality, to such an extent that the ethical criterion is no longer the Gospel but statistics, the civil law, or manners of behavior accepted by society. . . . The harm caused to people, and especially to young people, by pastoral workers and professors who oppose, undervalue or mock the pastoral direction of the present successor of Peter, is serious from a pastoral point of view." He called on Salesians not to have an "anti-Roman complex" and not to be parties to "a growing animosity to this Pope of the present day." Father Vigano's letter, dated Sept. 3, was reported Oct. 11.

Caste Discrimination — Bishop Joseph S. Thumma, secretary general of the Indian Bishops' Conference, called on the government of the State of Andhra Pradesh to take "positive steps" in response to discrimination against untouchable-class converts to Christianity. He made the request in a letter of protest against an attack the previous July 16 and 17 on a community of converts in the Diocese of Nellore in which six persons were killed.

Protest in Nicaragua — The bishops of Nicaragua released a statement Oct. 20 in which they protested against government treatment of the Church and the latest restrictions on religious freedom and other civil rights. Specifically, the bishops meant "intimidation of priests, break-ins and raiding of church property," together with violations of respect for freedom of conscience and religious expression.

Courage Needed in Burundi — In a pastoral letter dated Aug. 20, the bishops of Burundi called on Catholics in the country to face government restrictions on the Church with enlightenment and courage. "We need enlightenment to know how to work without denying our identity as children of God. We need the courage to act with truth and justice."

Silence Decried by Italian Bishops — "We denounce the silence which continues to grow in Ital-

ian society and public opinion about abortion and divorce," said the Permanent Council of the Italian Bishops' Conference at the conclusion of a meeting Oct. 21 to 24. "Abortion is not a way, euthanasia is not a way," declared the bishops as they reaffirmed the value of human life along with the unity and permanence of marriage and the sacred value of the family.

Hunger — People are morally bound to change the "crazy and deadly situation" of a world in which at least 750 million people went hungry in 1984 while millions of tons of food were wasted, Cardinal George Basil Hume of Westminster told members of British aid agencies Oct. 22. He said 30 million Africans were near starvation while enough food was produced in the world to give everyone three meals a day with plenty to spare.

Mother Teresa Honored — *New York Times* writer James Brooke said "the warmest ovation of the United Nations' 40th anniversary observances" was for Mother Teresa of Calcutta, foundress of the Missionaries of Charity. The occasion for her appearance at the U.N. was the screening of a film, "Mother Teresa," depicting the work of the missionaries among the poorest of the poor in 60 countries. She spoke Oct. 26 about abortion and AIDS before an assembly of 1,000 dignitaries.

International Briefs:

• Catholic Relief Services reported it was providing $113,250 for the funding of a vocational program for a drug rehabilitation center at a Buddhist temple in Thailand.

• Cardinal Agostino Casaroli, Vatican secretary of state, conferred the knighthood of the Order of St. Gregory the Great on Vittorio Canuto Oct. 17. Canuto, a member of the Vatican delegation to the United Nations General Assembly, was honored for his contributions to the work of the Pontifical Academy of Sciences.

• Thousands of Poles flocked to the grave of Father Jerzy Popieluszko in Warsaw the weekend of Oct. 18 to 20, marking the first anniversary of the kidnapping and murder of the supporter of the outlawed Solidarity labor union.

Symposium of European Bishops

"The Challenges to Evangelization in Europe's Secularized Societies" was the theme of the Symposium of European Bishops Oct. 7 to 11 in Rome. Some of the critical challenges highlighted during the meeting of 73 bishops from 20 or more countries were the following:

• neglect of Sunday Mass participation as an important criterion of active membership in the Church;

• selective adherence to church doctrine;

• rejection of moral norms, especially with respect to marriage and sexual behavior;

• the erosive effect of individualistic and subjectivist philosophies on the conscience and practice of many Catholics;

• various values of contemporary culture which might be viewed as opportunities for evangelization.

NOVEMBER 1985

VATICAN

Beatifications — The Pope beatified four servants of God during the month:
• Dutch Carmelite Father Titus Brandsma (1881-1942), university professor and journalist, martyred at the Dachau concentration camp, Nov. 3;
• Mother Maria Teresa Gerhardinger (1796-1879), foundress of the School Sisters of Notre Dame; Passionist Brother Pio di San Luigi Campidelli (1868-89), a student for the priesthood; Sister Rafka Al-Rayes (1832-1914), of the Lebanese Maronite Order of St. Anthony — all on Nov. 17.

Religious Identity of Catholic Schools — "I insist on the upholding of Christian catechesis in Catholic schools, of its carefully adapted presentation, its doctrinal correctness, and its great respect for the mystery of God," said the Holy Father Nov. 5 during an audience with the International Association of Catholic Educators. He also called attention to the fact that in some cases "the emphasis given to the transmission of the faith, witness and celebration has been thoughtlessly reduced."

Jesuit Missionaries Killed — The killing of two Jesuit missionaries in Mozambique was a "savage crime" which illustrated the risks faced by missionaries, the Pope said Nov. 6 during a general audience. Fathers Ira Moreira and Joao de Deus Goncalves Kamtedza were killed Oct. 30 near their mission at Lifidzi in the northern region of the country. There were reports that the murders were committed by members of the Mozambique National Resistance, a rebel group which also claimed responsibility for the kidnapping in June and July of five women Religious, two novices and a Jesuit priest.

Hope for Union with Catholics in China — At a meeting Nov. 8 with bishops from Taiwan, the Pope expressed hope that obstacles to the union of (mainland) Chinese Catholics with the universal Church might be overcome. "I daily beseech the Spirit that the day may soon come when, after the obstacles of various kinds have been removed, there will come the desired moment of communion fully lived, expressed and enjoyed. . . . It is a question of a bond which joins every local church with the Pope and with the Catholic communities of all other countries, and which is essential for the faith of Catholics." The obstacles included the Chinese government's objection to Vatican relations with Taiwan and government sponsorship of the Patriotic Association of Chinese Catholics opposed to union with the Pope.

Help for the Hungry and Needy — In an address Nov. 9 to members of the Pontifical Commission for Justice and Peace, the Pope said they should "never tire" of promoting world peace and economic justice. On the following day, he told representatives of the 40-year-old U.N. Food and Agriculture Organization that it was "urgently necessary" for wealthier nations to make more joint commitments to help the needy.

Euthanasia an Offense to Human Dignity — In an address Nov. 15 to medical personnel attending a conference on leukemia, the Pope said: "The practice of euthanasia, more or less openly proclaimed, marks a moment of regression and of abdication by science. . . . (It) is an offense against the dignity of the dying person." At the same time, he encouraged the use of experimental medicine, even when such therapy might involve "a high percentage of risk"; he cautioned, however, that such treatment could be used only with the patient's permission and in the absence of a safer alternative. He also said the use of experimental medicine must include "guarantees that risks will be toned down" for the patient, and that experimenters will not become "carried away with the desire for experimentation to the bitter end."

Appeal to Reagan and Gorbachev — Shortly before the Nov. 19 and 20 meeting of President Reagan and Soviet leader Mikhail Gorbachev in Geneva, the Pope said Nov. 17 that he had sent "a personal message to the two personalities, expressing hope that from their talks will come the basis for the development of a dialogue which overcomes distrust, banishes the risk of war and favors peace, in a context of fairness and justice."

Mobilization of Lay Persons — Pope John Paul called for a "mobilization of the laity" before the 1987 assembly of the Synod of Bishops, voicing "great hope" for "collaboration between the lively forces of the laity" and the bishops. He urged the Pontifical Council for the Laity to "stimulate" efforts for that purpose, in an address Nov. 18 at a plenary session of the council.

Avoidance of Collective Egoism — Pope John Paul, while citing the duty of wealthy nations to aid poor ones, said developing nations should not be forced to adopt the economic or social models of the nations which help them. Industrial nations risk falling into a "collective egoism" if they regard developing countries in purely economic terms, he said Nov. 22 in an address to participants in a symposium on "The Church and the Economic World."

Problems of Vietnamese Bishops — The Pope, citing "protracted and increasing" problems facing the bishops in Vietnam, expressed disappointment that most of them had not been permitted by the government to make their consultative (*ad limina*) visits to the Vatican during the year. He did so in a Nov. 24 letter marking the 25th anniversary of the establishment of the hierarchy in that country. He told the bishops: "Despite the geographic distance which separates us, I know well your religious sentiments, the pride you have in belonging to the Catholic Church, and the courage with which you testify to your faith in the midst of difficulties that are protracted and increasing." The difficulties were not spelled out, but the hostile attitude of the Vietnamese government toward the Church was well known.

The Pope Also:
• Said Nov. 13 that the "contribution which *Caritas* is making in the Church today . . . is a vital part of the Church's mission of proclaiming the

Gospel." *(Caritas Internationalis* coordinated the efforts of 117 national relief organizations.)

• Called Nov. 14 the problems of hundreds of thousands of refugees in Southeast Asia "an immense human tragedy" in need of "increased international attention."

• Spoke to a group of Indian bishops Nov. 22 about the "great need for a sustained effort to evangelize and catechize the faithful, especially the young," in their country.

Spiritual Maternity of Nuns — "The religious women who desire and look for the realization of their vocation in the Church in the exercise of ministerial priesthood misconstrue the proper and inalienable role that is reserved to them." Their role is to provide "a spiritual maternity which, transmitted through the Spirit and virginity of heart, generates and sustains the priestly ministry." There are different roles in the Church, and "they do not give rise to the superiority of one over the other. . . . It would be an error to consider access to the priestly ministry as a 'right' given to men and denied to women." So stated Cardinal Jean Jerome Hamer, prefect of the Congregation for Religious and Secular Institutes, in an interview published in the November edition of *30 Giorni,* an Italian monthly magazine.

Vatican Briefs:

• Nations should guarantee the cultural rights of believers, including freedom of religious education and expression. So stated a Vatican delegation Nov. 15 during a meeting on human rights in Budapest.

• An Anglo-Irish agreement signed Nov. 15 was called a "truly positive development" ` by *L'Osservatore Romano* in its edition of Nov. 16. The agreement provided for consultation by the government of the Republic of Ireland with the British government on matters pertaining to Northern Ireland.

• The Vatican reported an estimated operating budget shortfall of $50.2 million for 1985.

Meetings of Cardinals

Two meetings of cardinals were held at the Vatican shortly before the opening Nov. 24 of the extraordinary assembly of the Synod of Bishops.

• A 15-member special council appointed by the Pope met Nov. 19 and 20 for the purpose of framing proposals for reform of the Roman Curia, the complex of the central administrative offices of the Church.

• One hundred and 22 cardinals attending a second meeting Nov. 21 to 23 voiced "substantial approval" of proposals for clarifying the responsibilities of the Curia and its relations with bishops and their conferences.

The Pope told cardinals Nov. 21 that the Curia acts with authority given it by the Pope. He said it "should meet all the obligations of the Church in our time, as they have gradually become evident in the light of Vatican II." He also criticized "those concepts which try to oppose the Curia to the Pope as if it were a parallel power" or a barrier "which blocks or filters the pastoral solicitudes of the Pope."

NATIONAL

Sacramental Guidelines for Mentally Retarded — Guidelines for sacramental ministry to mentally retarded persons were issued Nov. 1 by Caridnal Joseph L. Bernardin of Chicago. Of the mentally retarded, he said: "These people have a right to live in and be welcomed into all areas of life. Especially, they have the right to be baptized and welcomed into the liturgical life of God's people." He told them: "I want you to know that you have a place at the table of the Lord." The guidelines were entitled, "Access to the Sacraments of Initiation and Reconciliation for Developmentally Disabled Persons."

Criticism of Pro-Choice Nun — Archbishop Edward T. O'Meara said Sister Margaret Ellen Traxler committed a "serious ecclesial impropriety" in giving a keynote speech at a pro-choice rally in the Archdiocese of Indianapolis Nov. 2. "Her often-stated position on abortion is not reconcilable with the clearly and frequently stated position of the Catholic Church," he said.

Cult Education Needed — Two priests and a Christian Brother, in an interview published in *The Texas Catholic,* said the Church needed to "inoculate" young people at the high school and college levels against the lure of cults. One of the priests, Father James LeBar of the Archdiocese of New York, called attention to five characteristics of cults:

• a charismatic leader who directs attention to himself or herself rather than to God;

• deceptive techniques in recruiting;

• a tunnel-vision approach to teaching about themselves;

• the use of excessive guilt, fear and other factors to keep members;

• how the group uses money, much of which "seems to go to the benefit of the cult leader."

Cardinal O'Connor Honored — Cardinal John J. O'Connor received the first Cardinal Bea Interfaith Award from the Anti-Defamation League of B'nai B'rith Nov. 6 at a fund-raising dinner in New York. During the affair, he declined a public appeal by Edgar Bronfman, president of the World Jewish Congress, to get involved in the issue of diplomatic relations between the Vatican and Israel. The cardinal said the question was "the kind of thing I would have to leave completely to the judgment of the Holy See."

Interfaith Prayer Service — About 70 Catholic bishops, Lutheran bishops, clergy and more than 200 other persons attended a joint worship service Nov. 14 at the Lutheran Church of the Reformation on Capitol Hill in Washington. The service, during which a rite newly approved by a group of Catholic and Lutheran bishops was used, marked what was called "a historical moment."

Sanctuary Workers on Trial — Eleven persons, including two priests and a nun, were on trial in Tucson, charged with conspiracy to smuggle, transport and harbor illegal aliens from El Salvador and Guatemala. They were forbidden by Federal District Judge Earl Carroll from presenting defense testimony regarding their religious or humanitarian motivations, conditions in Central America, or U.S. policy in the region.

Trouble in Berkeley Heights, New Jersey — Conflict between members of a charismatic group called The People of Hope and other members of Little Flower Parish was the subject of a report, based on a six-month-long study, being readied for review by authorities of the Archdiocese of Newark. Among issues in dispute were separatist tendencies of The People, administration of the parochial school, and the role of the pastor.

Cultural Exorcist of Pornography — "The Church has a proper role as a 'cultural exorcist' because pornography ridicules women, children and the Judeo-Christian principles of sexual behavior." So stated Father Nick Rice, communications director of the Louisville Archdiocese, in an address to leaders of 60 Knights of Columbus councils in Kentucky. Also reported was a statewide action plan of the Knights which included:

• requesting a letter from the state's bishops in support of their anti-pornography effort;

• providing information about pornography to their 8,000 members in the state;

• urging councils to stage pornography awareness programs in their localities;

• making effective use of local media in stimulating concern about pornography.

Coincidentally with the talk by Father Rice, death came Nov. 6 to Jesuit Father Morton A. Hill, president of Morality in Media, a Manhattan-based anti-pornography group.

Investigation of Archbishop Ended — Archbishop Pio Laghi, papal nuncio to the U.S., in a letter released Nov. 27, announced the end of a two-year investigation of the pastoral leadership of Archbishop Raymond Hunthausen of Seattle. The letter praised various aspects of the prelate's leadership, citing his "Gospel values," "apostolic zeal," "concern for peace and justice," "clear . . . loyalty to the Church," and "devotion and obedience to our Holy Father." At the same time, the letter called on the archbishop to "bring into clear focus" doctrines about Christ and the Church, the teaching authority of the Church and the role of conscience. It warned against liturgical abuses, with specific reference to the practice of general absolution, the proper first confession-first Communion sequence, and "routine intercommunion" at weddings and funerals. Other problem areas noted were marriage tribunal practice, the continuing education of priests, and the selection and formation of candidates for the priesthood.

NCCB-USCC Meeting

About 300 bishops attended the annual meeting of the National Conference of Catholic Bishops and the U.S. Catholic Conference Nov. 11 to 15 in Washington. The bishops:

• reviewed trends in the Church since the Second Vatican Council;

• received reports on a variety of subjects;

• authorized statements on evangelization and matters related to ministry among black people;

• issued a pastoral letter on campus ministry;

• approved a 1986 budget of $26.9 million.

National Briefs:

• Catholic Relief Services appealed again Nov. 8 for the release of Servite Father Lawrence M. Jenco and his fellow American hostages in Lebanon.

• Some 75 members of religious orders discussed their ministry to the poor and oppressed at the fifth Inter-American Conference on Religious Life in the Western Hemisphere, Nov. 17 to 22 at Marriottsville, Md.

• Farm-related projects were reported to be major targets of funding by the Campaign for Human Development.

• Catholic Relief Services delivered 50,000 pounds of medicine, blankets, bedding and clothing to an estimated 5,500 survivors of volcanic eruptions Nov. 13 in west-central Colombia; the supplies were valued at $79,000.

• Honored: Drs. James Muller and John Pastore, Nobel laureates for their efforts to prevent nuclear war, with the Rev. John J. Cavanaugh Award of the Notre Dame Alumni Association; comedian Danny Thomas, with Loyola University's Sword of Loyola Award, for his "untiring and successful efforts on behalf of scientific research and health care for children," in connection with his support of the St. Jude Children's Hospital in Memphis.

INTERNATIONAL

Political Activism — Christians should strive to change unjust socio-economic conditions through political activism "on behalf of our brothers in society," said Mexican Bishop Samuel Ruiz of San Cristobal de las Casas in a pastoral letter reported early in the month. He encouraged persons working for social justice to maintain unity and to pursue non-violent tactics "even when other interests introduce divisions and provoke the use of unjust methods."

Catholic-Jewish Relations in Latin America — Participants in a two-day conference on Catholic-Jewish relations in Latin America said they hoped the meeting would spark continuing dialogue. Bishop Antonio Quarracino of Avellaneda, Argentina, said there was progress toward better relations after a slow start. Rabbi Henry I. Sobel of San Paolo, an organizer of the conference, said: "In Brazil, interfaith dialogue and interfaith action are a reality. . . . The Brazilian bishops are the most progressive bishops that I know." The conference was sponsored by the Brazilian Bishops' Conference, the American Jewish Committee and the Latin American Jewish Congress.

Seduction of Irish Politicians — Early in the month, Bishop Jeremiah Newman of Limerick said Irish government officials had been "seduced into the new religion of politics prevailing in other countries," and were separating their religious from their political principles. Supporters of traditional Irish Catholic values were upset by what they considered the zeal with which some politicians had advocated a referendum to legalize divorce. Bishop Newman said the most serious danger was the insistence by party leaders that members of Parliament support the party line even if they were against it on moral grounds.

Abortion in Spain — Protests by bishops, pro-life groups and many doctors continued against abortion legislation in effect since Aug. 3, permitting abortion in cases of rape, fetal malformation and danger to the life of a mother. Feminists, on the other hand, demonstrated in support of abortion without any limitations.

Apartheid Is Unacceptable — Using force to repress the violence sweeping South Africa without redressing the cause was like trying in vain to hold back the flood waters of a river, said Archbishop Stephen Naidoo of Cape Town. In a pastoral letter read in churches of the archdiocese Nov. 10, he said: "Apartheid is totally unacceptable. It is sinful, because it is a denial of the God-given value of a human being. Far from accepting it, a Christian true to his name must condemn it (and) the present state of emergency."

Church Concerns in Nigeria — In a pastoral letter marking the 25th anniversary of their nation's independence from Great Britain, the bishops of Nigeria:
• called for restoration of the Church's role in education, which was curtailed in the 1960s with nationalization of church-run schools;
• cited the need for more aid to the poor, especially in rural areas:
• were critical of tribalism, nepotism in public office, excessive government control, religious and social discrimination.

Anglicans Need Stronger Links — The worldwide Anglican Communion may need "more effective links" among its autonomous member churches to deal with common issues, said Archbishop Robert Runcie of Canterbury during the Church of England's fourth General Synod Nov. 19 to 22 in London. He said that, if Anglicans "possessed a stronger sense of communion, expressed in a more structured affection just a few years ago, it is arguable that we might have handled the question of the ordination of women in a more satisfactory way." (Some Anglican provinces, including those in the U.S. and Canada, ordain women to the priesthood, but the Church of England does not.) It was also reported that Archbishop Runcie and the Anglican archbishop of York had initiated a study of the theological implications of women as bishops.

Third World Aid — Christians should support land reform, arms cuts and increased development as a sign of solidarity with hungry nations of the Third World. So declared West German Cardinal Joseph Hoffner during a Nov. 21-to-24 symposium in Rome on "The Church and the Economic World." He recommended:
• expansion of trade between rich nations and developing countries;
• abolition of economic protectionism;
• drastic reduction of arms to free funds for international aid;
• an increase of arable land in developing countries;
• small-scale, labor-intensive aid programs rather than "prestigious large-scale projects."

Increase in Number of Third World Jesuits — The latest statistics on members of the Society of Jesus reflected a significant increase in the number of those from the Third World between 1945 and Jan. 1, 1985. "In 1945, about 90 percent of the Jesuits lived in Europe, the United States or Canada," according to Father Johannes G. Gerhartz, secretary of the society. "Today, only 60 percent of the membership lives in Europe, the United States and Canada." Twenty percent were in Asia, 14 percent in Latin America, and four percent in Africa. The total number of Jesuits, as of Jan. 1, 1985, was 25,549 in 110 countries; there were 18,455 priests, 3,684 students for the priesthood, and 3,140 brothers. Father Gerhartz said the Jesuits were "moving away from being a European- and North American-centered organization."

Hans Kung a Liberal Protestant — In an article appearing in West German and Italian newspapers during the month, Father Hans Urs von Balthasar described Father Hans Kung as "the guide of that which can be called the liberal Protestant party of the Catholic Church." Father von Balthasar, a widely known author of more than 50 books on theological and other subjects, was called "one of the great contemporary theologians," by Pope John Paul in 1979.

International Briefs:
• The 450th anniversary of the establishment of the Diocese of Angra in the Azores was observed Nov. 3.
• Cardinal Stephen Kim of Seoul urged women Religious to "struggle" for the physical and spiritual liberation of Asian women, according to a delayed report of an address he delivered in October at the seventh Asian Meeting of Religious Women, held in Seoul.
• Bishop Tomas Balduino of Goias, Brazil, said in an interview published in *Latinamerica Press* that missionaries should "immerse themselves not only in the language, culture and customs of a people, but also in their religious experience."
• The bishops of England and Wales reaffirmed their condemnation of apartheid in South Africa.
• Ontario Catholics were asked by their bishops to provide volunteer help to thousands of psychiatric patients and developmentally handicapped people released from institutions in recent years.
• Juan Fernandez Krohn, an illicitly ordained priest who attempted to kill Pope John Paul in 1982 at Fatima, Portugal, was released from prison after serving half of his six-and-a-half-year sentence.

Fear in the Philippines

Missionaries on Mindanao said they believed government forces were trying to repress the Church by killing local leaders. Several priests said they thought the military was responsible for the killing of 18 of 19 local church leaders, including a priest, between April and July. One said that church activities had been curtailed because people were "afraid of the military." Parishioners in one area were told by members of the paramilitary Civilian Home Defense Force that membership in the Catholic Church was tantamount to subversion, and that military forces would continue a campaign against "subversives."

DECEMBER 1985

VATICAN

Church Harassment in Nicaragua — In a letter released Dec. 7, the Pope appealed for an end to government harassment of the Church in Nicaragua, seconded the bishops' offer to mediate between the government and U.S.-supported contras, and expressed hope that mediation might produce "fruits of concord and brotherly love" in the beleaguered country. The letter was addressed to the bishops in the wake of a recent increase in "distinct forms of intimidations and tauntings of ordained ministers and Catholic faithful. ... I cherish the firm hope that existing problems can be solved quickly in a satisfactory manner," the Pope said. One of the problems was the threat of expulsion of foreign missionaries.

Contraception — The Pope strongly defended the Church's teaching against contraceptive birth control Dec. 13 in an address at a plenary meeting of the Pontifical Council for the Family. While stating that conscience "can deceive itself by orienting itself toward something that reasonably seems to be a good thing," he said: "The faithful have the right to receive from the magisterium (the official teaching authority of the Church) the teaching on moral truths. One cannot say that the Church's magisterium is opposed to 'rights of conscience.'"

Inter-Ritual Collaboration — The Pope told several Syro-Malabar and Syro-Malankara bishops of India Dec. 19 that they should collaborate with Latin-Rite bishops in resolving problems related to evangelization and pastoral jurisdiction. He observed that problems encountered by Eastern-Rite faithful living under the care of Latin-Rite bishops had "not yet found a satisfactory solution." He said: "The Holy See desires that these faithful residing outside Eastern-Rite circumscriptions be offered all the facilities of pastoral care and catechetical formation in their own tradition. ... I trust that the inter-ritual problems can be solved before long" in a manner "fully befitting the Church's maternal and pastoral solicitude."

Evangelization Events — In a traditional year-end address Dec. 20 to cardinals, personnel of the Roman Curia and staff members of the papal household, the Pope cited three key evangelization events of 1985:

• the extraordinary assembly of the Synod of Bishops, for discussions concerning the effects of the Second Vatican Council.

• International Youth Year, initiated by the United Nations and celebrated by the Vatican with a special meeting of young people and with publication of a papal message to youth of the world;

• the encyclical *Slavorum Apostoli,* commemorating missionary work among the Slavs by Sts. Cyril and Methodius.

Christmas Message — The Holy Father, calling himself "defenseless in the midst of a world that is armed and too often defeated by the temptation of arrogant power and oppression," asked Christians to unite to make Christ's message of love and justice a reality in the world. Christians, who "should

be zealous for good deeds," must combat massive starvation, violations of human rights and a type of material progress which "is indifferent to moral values," he said during his *Urbi et Orbi* — "To the City (of Rome) and the World" — Christmas message. Christians must be "a people that knows how to be sober with regard to the resources of the universe and wise in the use of the energies of its own mind." They must "resist the false image of a progress that is indifferent to moral values and looks only to the immediate and material advantage." They should be a people "inspired by justice in their thoughts, resolutions and deeds." The Pope spoke from the central balcony of St. Peter's Basilica after celebrating the third Mass of Christmas before a congregation of 10,000 people. Thirty-thousand people in St. Peter's Square witnessed delivery of the message, which was transmitted by radio and television to 22 countries. The Pope extended Christmas greetings worldwide in 51 languages.

Needed: United Effort Against Terrorism — Speaking four days after an attack by Palestinian terrorists, in which nearly 70 persons were killed and more than 700 wounded, the Pope said Dec. 31: "It is necessary to unite efforts in order to break this spiral of senseless violence and in order to heal at the roots these manifestations of criminality and terrorism, which disfigure the face of our age." Earlier, the Holy Father said: "There are no words strong enough to deplore such criminal misdeeds which cause horror to the conscience of every civilized person."

Meetings with Diplomats — The Pope received the credentials of three new ambassadors to the Vatican during the month:

• Simha Pratap Shah of Nepal, Dec. 9, to whom he said: "The Holy See hopes that the voice of Nepal will be raised in the international arena in support of a vision of humanity that respects the deepest aspirations of the human heart to peace and goodness."

• Ben Kufakunesu Jambga of Zimbabwe, Dec. 11, to whom he expressed hope that citizens of his country would achieve "genuine liberation" and peace with their neighbors. He said the Church tries to help "create a climate in which individuals and families can fulfill their duties and safeguard their rights."

• Stefan Cigoj of Yugoslavia, Dec. 19, before whom he emphasized the theme of religious freedom, stating: "Believers who are respected in all their rights and are therefore treated with fairness and benevolence, are so much better disposed to be loyal and courageous citizens."

The Pope Also:

• Against the background of a government crackdown on dissent in Polish universities, said Dec. 4 that professors there, acting "according to their consciences," had a dignity not recognized by "outside authorities."

• Said Dec. 14 that Catholic businessmen must develop ways and means of protecting the dignity of workers in the rapidly changing world of technology.

• Told a general audience Dec. 18 that the pursuit of holiness involves a "radical refusal" of sin.

• Prayed Dec. 26 for "victims of violence which sweeps the face of the earth with dramatic intensity."

• Told a group of U.S. seminarians that their study of Scripture was a "priceless" preparation for the priesthood.

Vatican Briefs:

• The travel and accommodation expenses of some participants in the extraordinary Synod of Bishops were paid for by the Vatican.

• An article in the Dec. 15 edition of *L'Osservatore Romano* by Father Gino Concetti criticized the Dec. 6 decision of the Minnesota Supreme Court that a fetus is not a human being.

• French Cardinal Roger Etchegaray left Rome Dec. 30 to visit, as a papal envoy, Iranian prisoners in Iraq.

Extraordinary Synod of Bishops

An extraordinary assembly of the Synod of Bishops in progress since Nov. 24 ended Dec. 8, two decades after the conclusion of the Second Vatican Council. It was convoked by Pope John Paul "to recall . . . the Second Vatican Council, to evaluate its implementation, to promote it in the Church in such a way that it might be fully lived."

(See separate entry.)

NATIONAL

Plea for Salvadoran Refugees — In letters released by the U.S. Catholic Conference Dec. 2, Archbishop Arturo Rivera Damas of San Salvador urged members of Congress to pass legislation that would allow Salvadoran refugees to remain temporarily in the U.S. instead of being deported and subjected to persecution in El Salvador. He wrote: "I . . . ask each and every one of you . . . that you open your arms, your hearts and your Christian charity to my suffering people, and that you double your efforts against the deportation of Salvadoran refugees and in support of measures . . . which in some way will contribute to a temporary solution to the agony of my flock in search of refuge." The Reagan administration was opposed to the granting of extended departure status to Salvadorans, claiming that they were seeking economic gain in the U.S. rather than safety or freedom from repression in El Salvador.

Emphasis on Development — Terry Martin, Catholic Relief Services director for Latin America, said in an interview Dec. 2 that the agency would continue to carry out welfare projects where needed, but would increase its emphasis on programs to help people become self-supporting. CRS was conducting programs in 17 countries in Latin America.

Money for Building — Three Franciscan priests were awarded $1.32 million by New York City to buy a rundown building for renovation into a shelter for homeless, mentally-ill persons. The money came from a settlement by the city of a $2 million claim against real-estate developer Harry Macklowe. The building to be purchased and refurbished would be the third of its kind run by the priests.

Fetus Ruled Not Human — The Minnesota Supreme Court ruled 6-to-1 Dec. 6 that a fetus is not a human being under state law. The decision meant that a man accused of killing an eight-and-a-half-month-old fetus in a 1984 automobile accident could not be charged in the death. An official of the U.S. bishops' pro-life office said the decision "boggles the mind."

Evangelization by Lay Persons — In a pastoral letter released Dec. 8, the bishops of Florida acknowledged "gratefully the commitment to the Gospel of so many men and women who continuously labored to build up the kingdom in our region. In reflecting over the past 20 years, we salute you, the laity of Florida, for your continuously increasing contributions as you serve in so many different roles in our parishes, apostolic movements and organizations."

Media Meeting — Catholics around the world need to learn how the media can "work in their favor . . . for development of the whole person," said Father C. Murphy, general secretary, at the 14th annual general assembly of Unda-USA, Dec. 10 to 13 in San Antonio. Another speaker at the meeting of Catholic communicators, Father Edward K. Braxton, said they can play a key role in educating black Catholics and the general Catholic community about church teaching on racism. Father Richard McBrien, chairman of the Department of Theology of Notre Dame University, told the communicators that they faced the challenge of merging new technology with the Gospel message.

Warning about Bayside Shrine — Archbishop Edward A. McCarthy of Miami warned Florida Catholics that advertisements promoting Our Lady of the Roses shrine in Bayside, N.Y., might mislead people into believing in apparitions disclaimed by church authorities. He said the shrine was "not affiliated with the Roman Catholic Church," and that on "May 8, 1985, in fact, it was reported that 'the Vatican Congregation for the Doctrine of the Faith has said there is nothing supernatural at Bayside.' " He also noted that the office of the chancellor of the Brooklyn Diocese, in which the shrine was located, said in a statement Apr. 11, 1984, that "a thorough investigation was made and the conclusion was reached that there is no doubt that the alleged 'apparitions' lacked complete authenticity. . . . No credibility can be given to the so-called 'vision' of Bayside."

Farm Crisis Response — Dioceses in Wisconsin were reported to be increasing their efforts to assist family farmers in crisis situations. The state's Catholic conference, in conjunction with the Wisconsin Conference of Churches, was supporting establishment of a Farm Crisis Response Network, to promote awareness of farm problems, provide support for farm families, and help people generate the power necessary to change institutions affecting their life and work. In another development, Catholic and Lutheran bishops in Minnesota told their U.S. senators in November that the federal government should replace its "immoral" farm policy with a plan that would protect the land and ensure opportunities for farmers. They said, in criticism: "Presently, our federal government is fostering an agricultural policy which effectively promotes the erosion of farming, both as a way of life and as a viable opportunity for employment and human development."

Euthanasia — "All of us stand under the threat of being made victims of the sentimental murder movement that is now sweeping our nation," Dominican Father Robert Barry told participants in the National Youth Pro-Life Coalition convention in Pittsburgh near the end of the month. "Euthanasia will become the abortion issue of the 1980s and, as such, it demands our fullest attention," he said. He urged young people to organize "in behalf of life" because "the mercy killing movement" was seeking to gain legal endorsement through legislation for "suicide, assisted suicide and mercy killing." Mary Jo Cooley of Ft. Madison, Ia., was elected president of the coalition.

Abortion Developments — Bishop John R. McGann of Rockville Centre was joined by nearly 3,000 people in a silent march on an abortion clinic in Hempstead, N.Y., late in the month. "I think the walk proclaimed very strongly people's support of a consistent life ethic," said the bishop after the peaceful march. At an hour-long prayer service before the march, he told some 1,400 people that the "evil of abortion" is a core issue "in the whole panorama of the disrespect for life we witness each day."

• Five pro-life groups offered a $5,000 reward for information leading to the apprehension and conviction of those responsible for the bombing of a New York City abortion clinic Dec. 10.

• The New York State Court of Appeals, reversing two lower-court decisions, ruled unanimously Dec. 17 that the state government had followed proper procedures in granting permits for the opening of two abortion clinics, one in Albany and the other in Hudson. The Albany Diocese had initiated a suit to prevent opening of the clinics.

National Briefs:
• A low-key commemoration marked the fifth anniversary Dec. 2 of the murders of Ursuline Sister Dorothy Kazel and lay missionary Jean Donovan, two of four missionary workers killed in El Salvador.

• Sister Catherine T. McNamee, dean of Dexter Hanley College, University of Scranton, was elected the first female president of the National Catholic Educational Association.

• The University of Notre Dame was given $6 million by Joan B. Kroc, widow of the founder of the McDonald restaurant chain, to establish an institute for peace studies.

• Three convicts terminally ill with AIDS were released to the care of Mother Teresa of Calcutta as she opened a New York residence for victims of the disease on Christmas Eve.

Leading 1985 News Stories

Thirty-five Catholic editors responding to an NC News poll rated the following as the 10 leading religious news stories of the year.

1. The extraordinary assembly of the Synod of Bishops, for review of the effects of the Second Vatican Council on the Church.

2. Continuing discussion of the U.S. bishops' proposed pastoral letter on the economy.

3. Famine in Ethiopia and aid response thereto.

4. The decision by the U.S. Supreme Court against the constitutionality of publicly-funded remedial programs in church-related schools.

5. Crisis in family farming.

6. Abortion-related developments.

7. Escalating Church-state tension in Nicaragua.

8. Anti-apartheid developments in South Africa.

9. U.S. government action against the sanctuary movement, with convictions in Texas and indictments in Arizona.

10. Tragedies in Mexico (earthquakes) and Colombia (volcanic eruption), and aid to the victims.

INTERNATIONAL

Cooperation in Asia — The general committee of the Christian Conference of Asia, a voluntary fellowship of 110 Protestant churches in 16 nations, approved the formation of a Protestant-Catholic working group to foster interreligious cooperation. On approval by the Asian bishops, the group would coordinate joint Catholic and Protestant work in various areas of mutual interest and concern.

Support for Christians in Lebanon — Cardinals and bishops of Western Europe formed a committee to show solidarity and support for Lebanese Christians in their "dramatic situation" of "conquering hate and violence." They said in a statement issued Dec. 5: "We wish to stand at your side in the midst of your great trial." Among the 16 signers from 13 countries were Cardinals George Basil Hume of Westminster, Jean-Marie Lustiger of Paris, Tomas O'Fiaich of Armagh and Ugo Poletti, papal vicar for the Diocese of Rome. The prelates hoped that "the personal relations of friendship, prayer and mutual assistance which exist between your parishes and ours, your schools and ours, might receive a new and powerful impulse in the months to come."

Prejudice against Christians in Pakistan — Life for practicing Christians in Moslem Pakistan can be difficult, especially in rural villages, according to Father Emmanuel Asi, rector of the Catholic National Theological Institute in Karachi. He said that Christian evangelizing is almost impossible because of social pressures, and that most evangelization is accomplished through the work of catechists.

Harassment in Burundi — The government of Burundi was cracking down on church activities out of fear "it will lose its credibility with the people." So stated Vincentian Father Bernard Quinn, a veteran U.S. missionary who left the country after his request for visa renewal was turned down. Jealousy of the Church's ability to assemble people for Mass and meetings, which the government could not do for political rallies, and of church development projects financed by outside funds, had fueled the attempt to weaken the influence of the

Church. "They feel they are not in control and regard the Church as a threat to the party's power," said Father Quinn.

Optional Religious Instruction — Church and state officials agreed Dec. 14 that Catholic instruction in Italian public schools would become a matter of choice for individual students and their parents, beginning in 1986. The agreement, signed by Cardinal Ugo Poletti, papal vicar of Rome, and Italian Education Minister Franca Falcucci, followed guidelines established by the 1984 concordat governing relations between the Vatican and Italy.

South African Boycott Wanted — The bishops of Scotland announced support of a call from their justice and peace commission for Catholics to boycott South African goods, discourage emigration to South Africa, and question personal financial investment in the country. "This is an act of solidarity with the mainly black Roman Catholic Church in South Africa and a sign of our opposition to the policy of apartheid," said a commission spokesman. "We must speak for those who have no voice. And we must match our words with sacrifices in solidarity with those who are already giving up their lives for the sake of freedom of their people."

For Democracy in South Korea — In a Christmas message dated Dec. 18, Cardinal Stephen Kim of Seoul appealed for authentic democracy in South Korea, saying: "The will of the people is to see all political leaders cooperate in a drive for the realization of genuine democracy in the country. Democratization which respects human rights and guarantees decent living is the only way to surmount the current difficult situations" in politics and economics.

Reopened Churches in China — A Vatican source said Dec. 19 that China had agreed to reopen the largest Catholic church in Beijing and to turn it over to the government-sponsored Patriotic Association of Chinese Catholics. The Church of the Savior thus became the third church reopened in the capital city. An observer familiar with the status of Vatican-Chinese relations said the move represented a continuation of China's so-called liberalization policy regarding religion. On Dec. 17, Vatican Radio reported that, according to the Chinese Communist Party's *People's Daily*, 51 churches were reopened in November in one southern province. The report did not say to which religions the churches belonged.

Land Rights of Aborigines — Bishop Raymond Benjamin of Townsville, interviewed during a meeting of the Australian Bishops' Conference, said the issues of aboriginal land rights were not "about mining or money or property," but "about life. . . . Aboriginal people feel that they are not living unless they have land which is theirs. Otherwise, they remain refugees — strangers and prisoners within their own country." White Australians "can no longer look upon land rights as some kind of modern fad Aborigines have just thought up." They must develop a "theology, a philosophy and an attitude toward the Aborigines which takes account of the permanence of their presence as fellow Australians."

Hostile Action in Guyana — A background paper issued Dec. 18 expressed concern about increased harassment of the Church under President Desmond Hoyte. "Although the government under (the late President) Forbes Burnham brought systematic pressure to bear on the Catholic Church . . . the present campaign surpasses in its vindictiveness, passion and scope anything experienced to date," said church leaders. The most recent incidents included searches of the homes of several religious leaders and an order to expel a British Jesuit who had worked in the country for 21 years. Those whose homes were searched included Bishop Benedict Singh of Georgetown, the Rev. George Richmond, head of the Moravian Church in Guyana and chairman of the Guyana Council of Churches, and the Rev. Oswald Best, head of the Guyanese Presbyterians.

Mexicans Warned against Consumerism — Retired Mexican Bishop Sergio Mendez Arceo said in a newspaper interview late in the month that the "fascination" of many Latin Americans with U.S. affluence opened the region to "the importation of a foreign lifestyle with distinct values and the difficulty of integrating those values into our system. . . . Not all aspirations to a higher standard of living are Christian, if its achievement accepts the domination of one man by another and produces inequality."

International Briefs:
• Dominican Sister Dorothy Landers, the first woman appointed to the staff of the university's school of theology, was named associate director of pastoral formation at the American College of Louvain University.
• The Basilica of St. Mary of the Angels, site of the death of St. Francis of Assisi, was slightly damaged by a small pipe bomb Dec. 11.
Pontifical Commission for Justice and Peace, was awarded the first Ladislau Laszt Prize at the Ben Gurion University in Beersheba, Israel, for his contribution to mutual understanding among Christians, Moslems and Jews.
• The first Taiwan-born bishop Most Rev. Jose Lin Tien-chu of Chiayi, was appointed to a diocese in his own country.

Different Views of Violence

Blacks in South Africa do not see violence in the same way as whites, according to Father Buti Tlhagale, a black South African theologian. In an article in the Dec. 22 edition of Cape Town's *The Southern Cross,* he said that, when black people resort to violence as a means of "redressing the wrongs of an intrinsically violent political system, they perceive this not only as a right to resist in the name of elementary justice, but as a duty to check the repression of the racist regime."

"What the white community perceives as savagery . . . blacks interpret differently. . . . So desperate have large sections of the people become, that they are determined that the present system can no longer continue, unless over their dead bodies. . . . The present violence is therefore understood as an act of self-defense."

JANUARY 1986

VATICAN

Religious Education — In a letter made public Jan. 7, the Pope said: "Religious education, besides culturally enriching students, helps them find answers to basic questions that emerge in the human soul, especially among youth: What is the meaning of life? What are the moral laws of the conscience and society? What are the real values?" He added that, in cultures like that of Italy, a person could not study history without referring to the significant role played by religion throughout the centuries. "Catholicism, in fact, is deeply rooted in the history and life of the Italian people," he said.

Terrorism and Terrorists — Pope John Paul, in an annual address Jan. 11 to diplomats of 117 countries accredited to the Vatican, condemned terrorism and armed reprisals against terrorists which kill innocent people. He repeated a call for governments to unite against terrorism and its "massacres of innocents to plead a cause," but condemned armed reprisals "which also indiscriminately reach innocent people and continue the spiral of violence."

Evangelization Needed — The Holy Father voiced concern about the "confused" state of contemporary society and called for the integration of Gospel values with contemporary culture, in a speech Jan. 13 to the Pontifical Council for Culture. He challenged the council to promote "an ethical and spiritual vision" in the world, while stating that "minds and hearts are in search of a light which clarifies and a love which gives them warmth again." In a letter to European bishops, released Jan. 16, the Pope said they must unite to re-evangelize the Continent, threatened by an "atheism (which) has spread in an impressive way . . . , especially in the forms of scientific atheism and humanistic atheism. . . . Contemporary Europe needs to be given a soul and a new self-awareness. . . . The profound and complex cultural, political, ethical and spiritual transformations that have given a new face to the fabric of European society must be matched by a new quality of evangelization."

Liberation Theology — The Pope warned a group of Brazilian bishops Jan. 17 that some theologies of liberation contained "grave deviations" that were incompatible with the faith. In its work for the poor, he said, the Church cannot be reduced to a "socio-political" role. Its special and primary commitment to the poor is to bring them the "message of full (spiritual) liberation."

Ecumenism — In the 20 years since the end of the Second Vatican Council, "ecumenism has become inscribed deeply and indelibly in the Church's consciousness," the Pope said at a general audience Jan. 22. He prayed that Christians would "unite to achieve justice and peace in the world." Speaking about the deeper bond among Christians during the Week of Prayer for Christian Unity (Jan. 18 to 25), he said: "It is our faith in Jesus Christ, together with our common baptism, that is the basis of our prayer for one another as brothers and sisters, longing for unity. Common baptism constitutes a sacramental bond of unity among us, and thus is the point of departure in our search for unity."

Recruitment and Role of Brothers — "All pastors of the Church" should encourage men to become Brothers, said the Pope Jan. 24 in a talk to members of the Congregation for Religious and Secular Institutes. He also said that Brothers, together with priests in their orders, should do "all they can to favor the vitality of their institutes. . . . The Code of Canon Law opens to them many possibilities for participation in the life and mission of their religious families," except those aspects that depend strictly on priestly ordination. He added that "the more precise study and application of these possibilities" should be determined by their respective general chapters.

Prayer for Peace — Pope John Paul invited world religious leaders to join him for a day of prayer for world peace at Assisi, the birthplace of St. Francis, who "transformed the place into a center of universal fraternity." Speaking Jan. 25 at an ecumenical prayer service at the Basilica of St. Paul Outside the Walls, he said he had begun consulting with leaders of Christian and other religions "in order to promote with them a special encounter of prayers for peace." The Pope noted that 1986 had been designated by the United Nations as the International Year of World Peace.

The Death Sentence of Abortion — Governments that allow abortion participate in the "execution of a death sentence" for innocent human beings, the Pope told leaders of the Italian Movement for Life Jan. 25. He said that laws that legalize abortion are based on "inconsistent and insidious" arguments. "In reality, abortion is a grave defeat for man and for civilized society. With it, the life of a human being is sacrificed to lower values, with motives often inspired by lack of courage and lack of trust in life, and sometimes by the desire for a misunderstood well-being."

Marriage Annulments — In an address Jan. 30 to members of the Roman Rota, the highest appeals court for judgments regarding the validity of marriages, the Holy Father urged them to commit themselves "to the maximum so that (marriage cases) might be concluded with the solicitude that the good of souls requires and which the new Code of Canon Law prescribes. . . . May no member of the faithful be able to use the excessive length of the ecclesiastical process as a reason for refusing to propose a cause or for giving up on it, choosing (instead) solutions (to marriage problems) in clear contrast to Catholic doctrine."

The Pope Also:

• Ordained Auxiliary Bishop Donald Wuerl of Seattle and six other bishops, Jan. 6.

• At a general audience Jan. 8, said: "Many scientists have assumed an attitude of increasing respect for the Christian view of creation, which allows for the possibility of fruitful dialogue concerning the different ways of approaching the reality of the world and the human person."

• Was presented Jan. 21, the feast of St. Agnes, with two lambs whose wool was destined for use in making the pallium, a distinctive vestment of metropolitan archbishops.

• Donated $10,000 for relief work among Ugandan civilians displaced by civil war in their country.

• Expressed his sympathy for the families of the five men and two women killed in the explosion Jan. 28 of the Challenger space shuttle, in a message to President Reagan.

Vatican Briefs:

• Carlo Rubbia, 1984 Nobel laureate in physics and professor of physics at Harvard University, was one of six scientists named to the Pontifical Academy of Sciences.

• Catholic communicators should fill a current "video void" by developing quality programs explaining the faith, said Archbishop John Foley, head of the Commission for Social Communications, Jan. 27.

Day of Peace Message

Pope John Paul pledged support Jan. 1 for the United Nations in its efforts for peace and in its designation of 1986 as the International Peace Year.

In a message delivered before 10,000 persons in St. Peter's Square on the 19th annual World Day of Peace, he also called for a "new solidarity" of the human family to replace the "way of thinking that leads to divisions and exploitation." Christians, motivated by the desire for peace, must "overcome the barriers of ideologies and systems in order to enter into dialogue with all people of good will," he said.

NATIONAL

Migration Week — The observance of National Migration Week, Jan. 6 to 11, provided "an opportunity to become aware of and to treasure our roots, our heritage and our gifts," said Bishop Anthony J. Bevilacqua, chairman of the U.S. bishops' Migration and Tourism Committee.

In other comments about the observance:

• Father Silvano M. Tomasi, director of pastoral care of migrants and refugees for the U.S. bishops, said the Church's commitment to help refugees remained firm.

• Archbishop Roger Mahony of Los Angeles, in a pastoral letter, called for "extended voluntary departure status for Central American refugees fleeing violence," and for a fair immigration policy that would provide legal status to aliens "who are a countributing part of our society."

• Bishop Rene H. Gracida of Corpus Christi appealed to "all priests to help meet the corporal and spiritual needs of our immigrants as they pass through our communities seeking to better themselves."

Judicial Hostility to Religion — Cardinal John J. Krol said in a homily Jan. 11 that the U.S. Supreme Court had departed in some of its decisions from the constitutional provisions regarding the establishment of religion and, instead, had expressed "judicial hostility to all religion." He also said

that Catholics, in addition to criticizing the influence of secular humanism on the court, should examine their own consciences as to whether or not they have been sufficiently alert in claiming their rights. The cardinal spoke during a Mass for the New York chapter of the Catholic League for Religious and Civil Rights.

Military Archdiocese — The Archdiocese for the Military Services, United States of America — formerly the U.S. Military Vicariate — opened new offices Jan. 13 at 962 Wayne Ave., Silver Spring, Md. 20910, under the direction of Archbishop Joseph T. Ryan. The archdiocese serves personnel in the five U.S. military services, their families at home or abroad, persons in Veteran Administration hospitals, and U.S. government overseas personnel and their families.

Sanctuary Suit — The Presbyterian Church (U.S.A.), the American Lutheran Church and four Arizona congregations filed suit against the U.S. government Jan. 13, charging that it violated constitutional guarantees of religious freedom, protection against unreasonable search and seizure, and due process in legal proceedings when it authorized infiltration of congregations and secret tape recordings of church services for the purpose of obtaining evidence against persons aiding undocumented aliens. The suit was filed in U.S. District Court in Phoenix.

Tridentine Masses Halted — *The Catholic Sun* of the Diocese of Syracuse reported Jan. 15 that Bishop Frank J. Harrison had halted an experiment with the Tridentine Mass, saying that celebrations of it the previous fall had been used as occasions for "attacks on the integrity of church officials and on the orthodoxy of church teaching pertaining to the Mass of Pope Paul VI." (A new Order of the Mass, taking the place of the one authorized by the Council of Trent in the 16th century, was approved by Paul VI in 1969. Limited use of the Tridentine Mass was authorized by Pope John Paul II in 1984.)

Stockholder Resolutions — The Interfaith Center on Corporate Responsibility reported that church-related groups had submitted 84 resolutions to 68 companies for consideration at 1986 stockholder meetings. The resolutions had reference to a number of issues, including investment in South Africa, military production, environmental protection, international debt, infant formula, and discrimination against women and minority groups. The interfaith center was related to the National Council of Churches and provided staff services for a dozen Protestant denominations and about 220 Catholic organizations, *Church Proxy Resolutions* was the title of the center's 1986 compilation.

King Holiday — Catholics joined the general chorus of tribute to the Rev. Dr. Martin Luther King, Jr., on Jan. 20, the first federal holiday commemorating the birthday (Jan. 15) of the civil rights leader who was murdered Apr. 4, 1968.

• Auxiliary Bishop Emerson Moore of New York, one of the nation's 10 black Catholic bishops, said he was, "most of all, a minister of the Gospel who could not remain silent in the face of injustice.

... We have in him the challenge to love, to be non-violent and to overcome our powerlessness."

• "Now, more than ever, we need to hear his message of peace and social change through non-violence," said Bishop J. Francis Stafford of Memphis.

• Bishop William R. Houck of Jackson prayed at a prayer service Jan. 15 that the observance would "motivate all of us in Mississippi to re-dedicate ourselves to eradicating the evil of racism wherever it exists."

Catholic Charities USA — Members of the National Conference of Catholic Charities approved a name change for their organization, to Catholic Charities USA. The new name, effective Jan. 20, "bridges the gap" between local and national human-services offices of the Church, according to Father Thomas Harvey, executive director. "It indicates greater emphasis on what unites us — service to people — and less emphasis on our structural relationship."

Planned Parenthood Executive Excommunicated — Mary Ann Sorrentino, director of Planned Parenthood of Rhode Island, "excommunicated herself by her very own choice to be director of Planned Parenthood. . . . Her excommunication (of which she was notified in June, 1985) is self-inflicted and is a logical consequence of her position." So stated Father Salvatore Matano, co-chancellor of the Diocese of Providence, Jan. 23. The reason for the excommunication (specified in Canon 1398 of the Code of Canon Law) was her involvement as accessory in abortion-related activities of Planned Parenthood.

Sex and Crime — Franciscan Father Bruce Ritter, founder of Covenant House and a member of the U.S. Attorney General's Commission on Pornography, said in an interview Jan. 24: "My problem is this: We have a pornography industry and a drug industry taking in billions and billions of dollars a year with tens of millions of customers. To go to a peep show or to snort some coke is a moral decision, and tens of millions of good Americans, God-fearing Americans, do that. Nobody wants to accept the reality that they make themselves part of a murderous process, a situation that leads to thousands of murders and suicides, that brings enormous police and judicial corruption, that destroys thousands of families."

Challenger Disaster — Bishop James W. Malone, president of the National Conference of Catholic Bishops, expressed "sorrow at the tragedy" of the explosion of the Challenger space shuttle Jan. 28, in which five men and two women lost their lives. Cardinal Bernard F. Law celebrated a Mass the evening of the disaster for Mrs. Christa McAuliffe at her parish of St. Jeremiah in Framingham, Mass.

National Briefs:

• Family members, fellow priests and a former hostage attended Mass Jan. 8 marking the first anniversary of the kidnapping of Father Lawrence M. Jenco in Lebanon.

• Parishes in the Archdiocese of Milwaukee gave $20,000 to aid Wisconsin farmers within the first three weeks of the archdiocesan Project Isidore campaign.

• A spokesman for The Catholic University of America announced Jan. 30 that Eleanor Smeal, a pro-choice advocate of abortion and president of the National Organization for Women, would not be permitted to deliver a public address on the university campus.

March for Life

Nearly 40,000 persons converged on Washington Jan. 22 to take part in the 13th annual March for Life in protest against the pro-abortion decisions (Roe v. Wade, Dole v. Bolton) handed down by the U.S. Supreme Court in 1973. Related events in the capital city and demonstrations in other places across the country also marked the anniversary. President Reagan told those in Washington that he was in support of their "long march for the right to life."

It was estimated that 17 million abortions were performed in the U.S. since 1973.

(See separate entry, Abortion.)

INTERNATIONAL

Religious Breakthrough in China? — There was speculation that visits in 1985 of officials of the government-sponsored Association of Patriotic Chinese Catholics with Catholic bishops and other persons in union with the Pope might represent a breakthrough in Catholic-China relations. Another sign regarded as significant was the release by the government July 3, 1985, of Bishop Ignatius Kung Pin-Mei after he had spent nearly 30 years in prison.

Violation of Rights in South Korea — The Korean Catholic Justice and Peace Committee said in a statement that abuses of human rights had increased in South Korea in recent years. Referring to daily searches, arrests and seizures on the streets, the bishops said: "When we see such severe human-rights problems, we cannot but question deeply where it is all going. . . . The dignity of the human person is rooted in the image of God. Accordingly, to improve human rights is the demand of the gospel and the summons of the Church for those who suffer from injustice. When the function of power is exercised wholly or mainly in the form of intimidation, the common good can never be promoted."

Aim of Indonesian Bishops — John Riberu, head of the documentation and information service of the bishops of Indonesia, said the prelates wanted the Church to become more involved in the country's economic and cultural life in 1986 while trying at the same time to avoid the full effects of a government regulation requiring organizations to adopt a national philosophy as their guiding principle. He said the bishops wanted to promote better understanding among Indonesian Catholics, the government and the general society.

Homeless in Lebanon — Msgr. John Esseff, director of the Pontifical Mission for Palestine, said that a decade of Christian-Moslem civil war had created "one huge problem" of homelessness in Lebanon. It was estimated that about 500,000 of the nation's 2.5 million people were homeless and were living wherever they could find shelter. The priest said there were "probably as many displaced and homeless Lebanese as there once were displaced and homeless Palestinians." The pontifical mission, which provided social services and development aid in Lebanon, was using 40 percent of its budget to help displaced persons.

Ghanaian Paper Shut Down — The publishing permit of *The Catholic Standard,* Ghana's Catholic weekly newspaper, was canceled by the nation's information ministry for allegedly being "unpatriotic and determined to use its pages to undermine the noble cause" of recovery from economic hardship and political turmoil. A report in the Nairobi-based All Africa Press Service said the ban was issued in December by Undersecretary of Information Kofi Totobu Quakyi, who said the paper had jeopardized the nation's interests. According to some observers, the crackdown was ordered because of the paper's coverage of violations of human rights.

Ethiopia Still Needs Help — Catholic Relief Services official Terrence Kirch said in an interview Jan. 7 that the food situation in Ethiopia had improved considerably since October, 1984, but that more aid was still needed. Although some drought areas got rains in 1985, harvests nationwide were still 20 percent below the levels of 1980-83, and 1.2 million metric tons of food from outside the country were needed for 1986. "We're afraid people will assume the situation has resolved itself," said Kirch. "It hasn't. There has been tremendous improvement but, if we don't keep the resources coming, we'll see serious famine problems again and undo a lot of the good that has been done."

Abortions in Italy — The bishops of Italy expressed "horror and dismay" at the number of abortions — more than 1.5 million, according to official statistics — performed in the previous eight years. Italian law, adopted against the will of the bishops, provides state-paid abortions for adult women virtually on demand in the first three months of pregnancy. In a message made public Jan. 21, the bishops said: "We ask everyone to consider the serious consequences of the legislation that permits this."

Mass for Apartheid Victims — South African and foreign bishops concelebrated Mass Jan. 26 in a black township near Pretoria in what they said was a demonstration "in solidarity with the victims of apartheid." The event commemorated, especially, the 13 people who died in riots Nov. 13, 1985, in Mamelodi. In another development, the Southern African Catholic Bishops' Conference said in a letter that a proposed boycott of schools by black students could lead to new forms of "slavery" in the future. They asked persons making decisions about the "year of no school" not to "jeopardize the (limited but real) opportunity of primary school children to obtain that basic education so essential for their human dignity."

Repression in Haiti — Bishop Francois Gayot of Cap Haitien condemned Haitian armed forces for "brutal and blind repression" after three "young innocent people" were killed in anti-government demonstrations Jan. 27. "We protest strongly against this brutal and blind repression that was carried out against the population of Cap Haitien, particularly its young people," he said in a radio address Jan. 28.

Objections to a Convent near Auschwitz — Some Jewish groups in the United States and Western Europe expressed dismay at the location of a convent near the Auschwitz death camp, calling it an affront to the memory of Jews who were killed there by the Nazis. *The New York Times* reported Jan. 28 that the presence of the convent was apparently not widely known until a Catholic group began a campaign to raise funds for renovating the building in which Carmelite nuns were living. Israel Singer, secretary general of the World Jewish Congress, said: "We are not asking a confrontation with the Church. We have no objection to a convent a mile or so from the camp. But we don't want it right there very close and visible. Auschwitz was mainly a Jewish death camp." About 2 million to 2.25 million Jews and 1.25 to 1.5 million non-Jews, mostly Polish Catholics, died at Auschwitz, according to a spokesman for the Simon Wiesenthal Center.

International Briefs:

• In a statement read in his name Jan. 12, Archbishop Arturo Rivera Damas condemned the Salvadoran government for indiscriminate bombing of civilians and the destruction of homes and crops in rebel areas.

• Filipino bishops issued a pastoral letter urging voters to fight against a "conspiracy of evil" threatening the Feb. 7 presidential election.

• The bishops of Chile asked the military regime Jan. 15 to open talks with civilian politicians about a return to government by popularly elected officials.

Persecution in Nicaragua

Cardinal Miguel Obando Bravo of Managua appealed to U.N. Secretary General Javier Perez de Cuellar Jan. 21 for help in dealing with "persecution" of the Church by the Sandinista government of Nicaragua. He said the bishops wanted a "constructive dialogue with the government," and thought the U.N. might help to arrange it.

The cardinal quoted a letter from the bishops to President Daniel Ortega, dated Dec. 6, 1985, and stating: "There is a general cry from the faithful in the country and the city . . . that the whole nation is concerned, even to the point of thinking, in many cases, that we are in a state of persecution." Among "attacks on the Catholic Church," the letter listed:

• threats against foreign priests;

• interrogation of priests by security and police personnel;

• pressures on lay persons to make them "collaborate as informers" against the Church;

• "harassment of church institutions";

• forcing Catholics to "sign documents containing falsehoods and calumnies against the honor of church persons";

• "harsh censorship."

FEBRUARY 1986

VATICAN

Be Present to Those Who Suffer — Christians should be "present in the world, and especially in the world of suffering," declared the Pope in an annual Lenten message made public Feb. 6. "At this beginning of Lent (on Ash Wednesday, Feb. 12), the season of penance, reflection and generosity, Christ appeals to all of you once more (to) . . . save bodies and bring fresh life to souls" so that "the expression, 'civilization of love,' will no longer be devoid of meaning." "Make Charity Your Aim" was the theme of the message, in which the Holy Father asked: "Can we refuse to be disturbed, bothered, put out or jostled by these millions of (suffering) human beings? How can we remain indifferent before those children with their despairing faces and skeleton-like bodies?" Of charity, he said: "It rids us of our selfishness; it breaks down the walls of our isolation; it opens our eyes to our neighbor, . . . Charity is demanding but it is also heartening, for it is the carrying out of our basic Christian vocation and makes us sharers in the Lord's love."

Historic Moment for Haitians — Five days after President-for-Life Jean-Claude Duvalier fled the country, the Pope said Feb. 12 that Haitians were experiencing "an important and delicate moment in their history," as they aspired to "humane and just living conditons, freeing themselves from sufferings and privations which (were) among the worst in the world and (had) lasted too long." After widespread violence forced Duvalier into exile, the Pontiff joined Haitian bishops in calling for reconstruction of the country "through fraternity, solidarity and union."

Coordination of Relief Efforts — Pope John Paul called on national and international groups to coordinate their efforts to relieve the needs of the hungry, during a meeting Feb. 13 with participants in a conference on food and disarmament. He said there were "numerous and generous initiatives of solidarity with the hungry," and added that such initiatives needed "to be coordinated and made more effective in order to avoid either duplication or dissipation of efforts."

Church Renewal in Cuba — The Holy Father expressed hope Feb. 18 that the first national meeting of Catholics in Cuba since Fidel Castro took control of the country in 1959 would contribute to renewal of the Church. In a message to the Feb. 17-to-22 meeting of 200 Catholics — bishops, priests and lay persons — he said: "I am convinced that in your example of faith, of service to charity, and of your edifying ecclesial communion, you will find inspiration toward your goals." Archbishop Patrick F. Flores of San Antonio was an observer at the meeting in Havana.

Vocations to the Priesthood and Religious Life — In a message issued Feb. 20 for the observance of the 23rd World Day of Prayer for Vocations, the Pope said: "Christians cannot accept with passivity and indifference the decline in vocations. Vocations are the future of the Church. The community which is poor in vocations impoverishes the whole Church; but a community which is rich in vocations enriches the whole Church."

Jerusalem, a Symbol of Peace — "Jerusalem, the city of David, the place of the death and resurrection of Jesus, the site of Mohammed's night journey to God: this city must be a living symbol that God's will for us is to live in peace and mutual respect." So stated the Pope Feb. 26 in an address to participants in a seminar on the quest for reconciliation among people of the three great religions of the world. "New solutions," he said, needed to be found "to the political, racial and confessional conflicts which have plagued the human family throughout history."

Support for Ministry in Italy — Pope John Paul told the bishops of Italy Feb. 26 that he hoped a new formula for payment of the clergy would free priests from the need to seek outside employment for their support. Such freedom would permit them to devote themselves to full-time ministry. Under a church-state agreement to be put into effect gradually by 1990, the Church would lose state subsidies to the clergy, amounting to about $200 million a year. The bishops hoped to replace that amount by a system of tax checkoffs, deductions, and contributions by the faithful. The Pope said the plan should cover the necessities of life for each priest, "so that he won't have to seek his own sustenance in other activities." He added: "Full-time dedication to the ministry is particularly urgent today."

Unity in the Philippines — The Pope prayed for unity in the Philippines Feb. 26, a day after former President Ferdinand Marcos left the country because of popular rejection of his claim to victory in the elections of Feb. 7. As the administration of President Corazon Aquino went into operation, the Pope said: "I want to repeat to these people that I continue to be close to them in affection, and I hope that everyone can rediscover unity of heart in pursuing the true good of the country." He also voiced support for the bishops' call for "a non-violent struggle for justice" in the Philippines.

Media Responsibility — In an address Feb. 27 before 35 members of the Pontifical Commission for Social Communications, the Pope said Catholic communicators should help develop "a public moral consensus" favorable to religious values. They should focus on people who are good role models, report on restrictions of religious and other human rights, and stress personal responsibility toward others. He said special emphasis should be directed toward the development of personal responsibility for protecting "the unborn, who are the weakest and most defenseless members of human society."

The Pope Also:

• Urged the Catholics of Brazil Feb. 13 to help overcome their country's problems of unemployment, housing, hunger and illiteracy.

• Told a group of Iraqi bishops Feb. 14 that he was continuing to pray for an end to the "ruinous conflict" between their country and Iran.

• Interrupted his annual Lenten retreat Feb. 19

to meet with embattled Lebanese President Amin Gemayel.

Vatican Briefs:
• Duly appointed priests and bishops, not lay persons, may perform exorcisms, stated a letter sent to dioceses throughout the world by Cardinal Joseph Ratzinger, prefect of the Congregation for the Doctrine of the Faith. The letter, dated Sept. 29, 1985, was not reported until this month.

• Msgr. Basil Meeking, undersecretary of the Secretariat for Promoting Christian Unity, said Feb. 10 that plans were being made to revise the *Directory on Ecumenism,* issued by the secretariat in 1967 and revised for the first time in 1970.

Trip to India

Pope John Paul, on the 29th foreign pastoral trip of his pontificate, visited 14 cities in India Feb. 1 to 10. In scores of addresses, he encouraged Catholics in the practice of their faith and declared his respect for the religious traditions of India. En route back to Rome, he told journalists: "I have evangelized the Indian people through the words of Mahatma Ghandi." (See separate entry.)

National

Limited Resumption of Remedial Classes — Catholic educators in Pennsylvania welcomed a Feb. 5 federal court ruling permitting the resumption of federal remedial education programs for the rest of the school term for some 13,000 parochial school students in six districts — Philadelphia, Pittsburgh, Erie, Harrisburg, Allentown and Johnstown. The ruling provided temporary relief from the effects of the U.S. Supreme Court's 1985 decision which barred public school teachers from conducting remedial classes in parochial schools (Grand Rapids v. Ball, Aguilar v. Felton).

Homosexual Bill Opposed — A proposed homosexual rights bill for New York City drew the united opposition of Cardinal John J. O'Connor of New York and Bishop Francis J. Mugavero of Brooklyn. In a joint statement Feb. 6, they said the bill carried a "potential for grave harm to all society," and added that the dioceses opposed it "for compelling moral and social reasons. . . . From the history of this bill and similar legislative proposals, we believe it is clear that what the bill primarily and ultimately seeks to achieve is the legal approval of homosexual conduct and activity, something that the Catholic Church, and indeed other religious faiths, consider to be morally wrong." They said their concern was heightened by the "common perception of the public that whatever is declared legal, by that very fact, becomes morally right."

Permanent Deacons — The National Conference of Catholic Bishops reported 1984-to-1985 increases in the numbers of permanent deacons (7,102 to 7,425) and candidates for the permanent diaconate (2,114 to 2,263).

Religious Commitment of Hispanics — A national survey, reported Feb. 7, found that the traditional religious commitment of Hispanic Catholics was strong, but less so among those born in the United States, and those who were younger, better educated and more affluent. Also indicated were a low level of involvement in parish activities and little knowledge of recent developments in the Church. The survey was carried out by Franciscan Father Roberto O. Gonzalez, research director of the New York Hispanic center; it consisted of telephone interviews of 1,010 randomly selected persons in the 40 U.S. metropolitan areas with more than 50,000 Hispanics.

Maguire Suit Dismissed — Marjorie Reiley Maguire's suit to force her employment in the theology department of Marquette University was dismissed Feb. 12 by U.S. District Judge John W. Reynolds of the Eastern District of Wisconsin. He said in a summary decision that a court order requiring her employment "would necessarily violate the free exercise clause of the First Amendment and impermissibly entangle government with religion." The university claimed the right to reject her application "because of her perceived hostility to the institutional Church and its teachings, and to the goals and mission of Marquette University."

Lenten Themes — The traditional themes of prayer, fasting and works of charity were among those in pastoral messages issued by U.S. bishops for Lent.

• Bishop Timothy J. Harrington of Worcester: " 'The old' practices of fasting, almsgiving and prayer are still in vogue."

• Archbishop John May of St. Louis: "Lent is a time to make sure we are nourishing our souls (with prayer), as we need to nourish our bodies with wholesome food and exercise."

• Bishop Anthony Bevilacqua of Pittsburgh: "In prayer, we discover God's will and the strength we need to do all that he asks of us. (Lent) helps us remember that no activity is more powerful or rewarding for the Christian than that of prayer."

Black and Indian Mission Collection — Catholics contributed nearly $5.2 million in 1985 in the annual Black and Indian Mission Collection, breaking the $5 million mark for the first time. The highest per capita contributions came from largely rural dioceses with some of the smallest Catholic populations.

First Native Indian Bishop — Father Donald Pelotte, provincial superior of the Blessed Sacrament Fathers, was appointed Feb. 24 coadjutor bishop of Gallup. He was the first American Indian named a bishop. Native Americans "have longed for this moment for many years," said Msgr. Paul Lenz, executive director of the Bureau of Catholic Indian Missions. "There is no group of people in the world more supportive of the Holy Father and more dedicated to the Catholic Church than the Native Peoples," he added.

Black Unity — Blacks must not let major differences in religion or minor differences in style divide them when they have mutual problems to solve, Auxiliary Bishop Eugene A. Marino of Washington said at a conference commemorating February as Black History Month. At the "One in Spirit" annual liturgical conference, held in Fort Walton Beach, Fla., he called on black people to remember the pain of their heritage and to work together to overcome social problems confronting them. Legitimate differences should not lead to competition, he said: "We have neither the time nor the energy to fight each other."

Aid for Victims of AIDS — A number of dioceses reported efforts to aid victims of AIDS.

• Archbishop Roger Mahony of Los Angeles promised to work for the establishment of a hospice.

• Bishop Phillip F. Straling authorized a task force to help victims in the Diocese of San Bernardino.

• Plans called for the opening in the summer of Michigan's first residence for persons dying of AIDS, with approval and financial grants from the Archdiocese of Detroit and the Oblates of St. Francis de Sales.

National Briefs:

• Cardinal John J. O'Connor told a forum on Religion and Rehabilitation Feb. 13 in New York that "profound ignorance" regarding the handicapped pervaded the Church as well as the rest of society. Such ignorance, rather than deliberate callousness, explained why so few churches were (physically) accessible to the disabled and why ministries to meet their special needs were lacking.

• After 37 years of sporadic debate, the Senate ratified, by a vote of 83 to 11, an international treaty banning genocide. The U.S. Catholic Conference called the ratification "long overdue."

• The U.S. government asked countries supplying food relief to Ethiopia to send those supplies to Catholic Relief Services rather than to the Marxist government of the country. Bart Kull, a spokesman for the U.S. Agency for International Development, said it was "no secret" that the agency was opposed to direct shipments of food to the Marxist regime.

• Members of a papal commission and experts studying the life of religious men and women in the U.S. agreed that religious life "is in a generally healthy state and has a promising future in the Church, even though the numbers may be down." The commission, meeting Feb. 21 to 23 in San Francisco, was chaired by Archbishop John R. Quinn.

• Thousands of applications for American Express-sponsored community service grants proved the existence of many unmet needs in the country, said Father Thomas J. Harvey, director of Catholic Charities USA, Feb. 26 at a press conference in New York. With the Reagan administration "down on" social welfare programs, he said the private sector had to find new ways of serving the poor.

• Dr. James I. McCord, president of the Princeton Theological Seminary from 1959 to 1982, was named Feb. 26 the 1986 winner of the Templeton Prize for Progress in Religion, worth $250,000. The 66-year-old Presbyterian was chosen because of his work as an educator, and particularly for his founding of the Center of Theological Inquiry at Princeton.

Living Will Legislation Opposed

Bishops in two states voiced oppositon to "living will" proposals.

• The Catholic Conference of Ohio called a bill pending in the state Senate "bad legislation" which posed "a critical challenge to the Catholic population" of the state.

• In South Carolina, Bishop Ernest Unterkoefler of Charleston asked Gov. Richard Riley to veto a bill, while questioning whether legislators had understood "the moral and legal implications of their action" in sending the measure along for his signature. The bishop also complained that the South Carolina Society for the Right to Die had been making "highly misleading and completely false" assertions that provisions of the bill were in accord with Catholic moral teaching.

Church teaching allows refusal of extraordinary medical treatment to sustain or prolong life; it also allows reasonable treatment for comfort or the alleviation of pain, even when such treatment might shorten life. Church teaching, however, does not allow the withdrawal of ordinary medical treatment, the denial of necessary sustenance of food and water, or any positive intervention to cause or to hasten death.

(See separate article.)

INTERNATIONAL

Abortion and Contraception in Singapore — More than 200,000 abortions were performed in Singapore since the practice was legalized in 1970, said Archbishop Gregory Yong Sooi Nghean in a homily reported Feb. 6. "Unborn babies have been butchered, slaughtered, murdered," he declared, while stating that "no power on earth, no parents, no mother has the right to destroy the life of an innocent, defenseless human being." Speaking of contraception, he said: "It is a delusion to think we can create a loving, unselfish and peaceful society with a contraceptive mentality . . . a package deal consisting of contraceptives, sterilization, abortion, euthanasia . . . a sex explosion" producing increasing divorce, adultery and teen-age pregnancies.

Priest and Lay Persons Jailed — All Africa Press reported that a priest and eight lay persons received sentences of one week to five years early in the month for writing and distributing a document criticizing Burundi's ban on religious activities on weekdays. The government accused the Church of interfering with economic development by holding weekday services which, it was said, conflicted with working hours. Government hostility toward the Church had already been evident in its record of expulsions of missionaries, more than 200 since 1972.

Duvalier Out, Violence In — Two days after the flight Feb. 7 of President Jean-Claude Duvalier, Archbishop Francois-Wolff Ligonde of Port-au-Prince called on Haitians to put an end to violence related to the celebration of his ouster. The archbishop, in a letter read in churches, said: "We must not let our passions lead us to violence. . . . We do not have the right to hate anyone, even those people we call our enemies or the enemies of our nation. . . . As human beings, as Christians, we must pardon the outrages, forget the insults and love one another." He called the end of 29 years of

Duvalier rule a "victory of truth, justice, prayer and love."

Apartheid Enslavement — "The systematic repression of all social, economic and political rights for black South Africans, and the repression and imprisonment of other non-white opposition groups and individuals, is reprehensible," according to Bishop Joseph Faber MacDonald of Grand Falls, Newfoundland. Speaking at a press conference on his return from a 12-day visit to South Africa, he said the trip was an experience of the "devastation that has been brought to millions of black citizens, the poverty and the squalor that the system has created, and the brutality with which the military and police are responding to the widespread non-violent opposition on the part of African and Indian and Colored People."

Lithuanians Jailed — Two men were jailed and three others were given suspended sentences following their conviction for running an illegal religious printing operation, according to the Brooklyn-based Lithuanian Information Center. A Soviet publication reported in January that the men had operated the press for seven years, producing a variety of religious items including cards, calendars and prayer books.

Popular Church — Nicaragua's "popular church" — of Catholics organized in support of the Sandinista government — was not necessarily a good expression of liberation theology, said Peruvian Father Gustavo Gutierrez, one of Latin America's leading liberation theologians. "I do not doubt that the theology of liberation could have contributed to making Christians in Nicaragua feel more clearly the need to commit themselves to the fight for the liberation of their people. But, I do not think it can be maintained that that which came afterwards in Nicaragua is the result of the theology of liberation." The priest's views were stated in an interview published in the February edtion of the Italian monthly *30 Giorni*.

Seminary Rector Deported — Father Dick O'Riordan, rector of the Zingisa Seminary in Umtata, was deported from the South African tribal homeland of Transkei to Ireland Feb. 21. No official reason was given for the deportation, but Father O'Riordan believed the action was taken by the government in retaliation against him for winning a court case involving the killing of a rights activist by police.

Ecumenism in Scotland — In a decision called unprecedented by the Rev. Robin Barbour, a leading Protestant churchman, Catholics of Scotland joined nationwide discussions with members of mainstream Protestant churches on the fundamentals of Christian belief. The project was regarded as significant because it was nationwide, comprehensive and involved parishioners rather than official delegates and theologians alone. Participants included Catholics, Baptists, Methodists, Anglicans, Quakers and members of the Salvation Army.

Encuentro in Cuba — Cuban Catholics "desire to become an evangelizing church . . . assuming with serenity and courage the risks that might arise from being faithful to the mission of announcing in good and bad times the Gospel of Jesus Christ." So stated 181 delegates to the first national meeting of bishops, priests and lay persons in more than 25 years. More than 5,000 people attended the Mass in Havana which marked the conclusion of the seven-day encuentro on Feb. 23. Msgr. Carlos Manuel de Cespedes, secretary of the bishops' conference, said at a press conference that the Church "must be present to (the reality of Cuba), not from outside but from within. It must do so in the image of Jesus' parable, like yeast in the midst of a mass of dough, the whole of which will become impregnated with the yeast."

Abortion in the Third World — The International Right to Life Federation targeted the Third World for special attention in its anti-abortion campaign; the group also expressed concern about infanticide and euthanasia. President Dr. John Willke said late in the month that the federation would "work throughout the Third World to help developing countries fight against manipulation of their peoples by use of abortion to cut their numbers." He also reported that one country of concern was Kenya, where "people are being strongly pressured by international business consortiums and many in their governments into cutting the size of their families by various means, including abortion."

International Briefs:

• Militant Protestants in Belfast heckled Cardinal Leo Suenens as he tried to deliver a sermon during an ecumenical service Jan. 29 in an Anglican cathedral in the city, according to a delayed report.

• Catholic officials in Thailand denied allegations by Buddhist monks that Thais were being paid to become Christian converts.

• Pope John Paul's call for religious leaders to meet for a day of prayer for peace at Assisi was welcomed by the Rev. Gunner Staalsett, general secretary of the Lutheran World Federation, and Anglican Archbishop Robert Runcie of Canterbury.

Aquino In, Marcos Out

Corazon Aquino assumed office as President of the Philippines Feb. 25 after more than two weeks of mass demonstrations of protest against the claim of Ferdinand Marcos that he had won the election Feb. 7. Factors leading to his downfall included popular discontent with his dictatorial regime, obvious electoral fraud, and the moral and practical influence of the Church through the bishops, priests, religious, lay persons, and the communications media.

The bishops issued a key statement a week after the election in which they said "the polls were unparalleled in the fraudulence of their conduct. And we condemn especially the following modes of fraudulence and irregularities: (1) the systematic disenfranchisement of voters . . . (2) the widespread and massive vote-buying . . . (3) the deliberate tampering with the election returns . . . (4) intimidation, harassment, terrorism and murder."

MARCH 1986

VATICAN

Pro-Life Efforts — The Church encourages efforts against trends favoring "the evils of abortion, infanticide, euthanasia and contraception," the Pope declared Mar. 1 in an address to participants in a seminar sponsored by the International Right to Life Federation. "What is needed," he said, "is the courage to speak the truth clearly, candidly and boldly, but never with hatred or disrespect for persons. . . . You know the necessity of focusing on specific problems which demand urgent attention and action, such as the evils of abortion, infanticide, euthanasia and contraception."

Defense of Peace, Ministry of Chaplains — Promoting the cause of peace can include using force to defend it, declared the Pope Mar. 10 in an address to 300 Italian military chaplains. "One does not help the cause of peace (by) negating the possibility and the duty to defend it." Speaking of the mission of chaplains, he said: "It would not be wise for the Church to miss the precious opportunity of encounter and dialogue which is tied to the period of military service. . . . Where there is a man, there is room for the priest — so much the more when there are hundreds of thousands of men."

Response to Spiritual Hunger — The Pope told 90 vicars for Religious from the U.S. Mar. 10 that men and women Religious should respond appropriately to society's "new hunger for the transcendent and divine." He said they were in a favorable position to meet this challenge because their commitment "bears witness before the world of the value of living for God alone, especially when" their lives "are marked by joyful trust and generous service." He also said Religious should have an "informed and zealous love for the Church . . . by reason of the public nature of their vocation."

Decision-Making by Youths — In an address Mar. 12 to several thousands of young people, the Pope said: "Life is opening up for you in immense richness, with many prospects and boundless possibilities. What will become of you tomorrow? Which is the way to take? What future should you prepare for? . . . In the end, the decisive response must come from you, and you alone, in obedience, of course, to the will of God. . . . Our human dignity lets us know that no one can decide for us."

Concerns regarding Brazil — The Pope capped three days of discussions with 21 senior Brazilian bishops Mar. 15 with an address in which he dealt with a number of sensitive pastoral issues in their country.

• He praised the bishops for their efforts to deal with specific socio-economic problems, such as the widening gap between rich and poor, unemployment, housing, widespread poverty, illiteracy and hunger. Efforts should be based on Catholic doctrine "without ambiguities or deformations." He said that liberation theology, purified of alien elements — "is not only orthodox but necessary." He noted that the Church needs a theological reflection on liberation which attempts "to give an answer to the grave questions regarding social justice; equality in personal, national and international relations; peace and disarmament, and fundamental human rights."

• Bishops must remember, however, that their primary mission is a spiritual one. They "should not identify with nor substitute themselves for politicians, economists, sociologists, intellectuals or labor leaders."

The Pontiff's remarks were prompted by reported differences of opinion and friction between Vatican officials and Brazilian prelates on the substance and manner of pastoral response to needs of the Church in Brazil.

Plague of Unemployment — The Pope, on a one-day trip to Prato Mar. 19, called unemployment "a plague" that had developed into "a story of crises and of moral and psychological devastation." On the feast of St. Joseph, patron of workers, he emphasized the dignity of man over machines in an address to the unemployed and workers at the textile industrial center near Florence.

Interfaith Problems — Pope John Paul told a group of Dutch Protestant leaders Mar. 21 that the Church could not permit interfaith Communion in the absence of agreement on the nature of the Church and on the priesthood. "For Catholics, the problem of Eucharistic sharing cannot be resolved in isolation from our understanding of the mystery of the Church and of the ministry which serves unity." The Pope made his remarks in response to criticism of the stance of the Church with respect to intercommunion, intermarriage and the ordination of women to the priesthood. While insisting "again that ecumenism is a pastoral priority in the Catholic Church and for all Christians," he also said: "Pastoral problems can never be resolved surely or fully if we gloss over the differences in faith of which those pastoral problems are the fruit."

Apartheid Condemned — "We strongly condemn the inhumanity of apartheid and express solidarity with the victims of the violence it generates," said the Pope Mar. 24. He called the South African policy a "deplorable system."

Letter to Priests — In a Holy Thursday letter addressed to priests throughout the world, the Holy Father warned them against overemphasis on the "social aspect" of their ministry to the neglect of spiritual discipline. Priests should be models of prayer, obedience and renunciation, he said, and added: "It is essential to the Church that the identity of the priest be safeguarded. . . . It is not the world which determines his status as though it depended on changing needs or ideas about social roles. The priest is marked with the seal of the priesthood of Christ, in order to share his function as the one mediator and redeemer."

Papal Plot Decision — An Italian court released three Bulgarians and three Turks accused of complicity in the 1981 shooting of Pope John Paul, saying there was "insufficient proof" of their involvement. The Mar. 29 verdict of "not proven" left some doubt as to whether or not there had been an international plot to shoot the Holy Father.

The Pope Also:

• In a message to educators meeting in Bangalore, India, said believers of every religion should work for everyone's right "to full growth in culture, in harmony with human dignity, without distinction of race, sex, nation, religion or social circumstance."

• Met Mar. 7 with six cardinals commissioned to develop plans for reform of the Roman Curia.

• Condemned euthanasia and society's "mentality of death," Mar. 16.

• Told Polish judges and legal experts Mar. 20 that the defense of human rights was a fundamental part of their profession.

Vatican Briefs:

• Representatives of U.S. women Religious concluded meetings with Vatican officials Mar. 1 regarding social ministry and the relationship of the Leadership Conference of Women Religious with church officials and groups.

• Seoul, South Korea, was announced Mar. 14 as the site of the 44th International Eucharistic Congress, to be held in 1989.

• An 11-month-old disciplinary period of "respectful silence" for "serious reflection" — and restraint from lecturing and writing on theology — came to an end late in the month for Father Leonardo Boff, O.F.M. He had been disciplined for his radical and undermining critique of doctrine concerning the structure of the Church, the abiding truth of dogmatic formulas, the exercise of sacred power, and the nature and relation of the charism of prophecy and the authority of the hierarchy. His views were contained in the book, *Church: Charisma and Power.*

Easter Message

Pope John Paul concluded his Easter message *Urbi et Orbi* ("To the City and the World") as follows.

"Christ rose at a particular moment of history, but he is still waiting to rise in the history of innumerable men and women, in the history of individuals and the history of peoples. This is a resurrection that presupposes the cooperation of man, of all people. But it is a resurrection in which there is always seen a stream of that life that burst forth from the tomb on an Easter morning so many centuries ago. Wherever a heart, overcoming selfishness, violence and hate, turns in a gesture of love toward someone in need, there Christ rises again today. Wherever in active commitment for justice a true desire for peace emerges, there death gives way and the life of Christ is affirmed. Wherever there dies someone who has lived in faith, love and suffering, there the resurrection of Christ celebrates its final victory.

"The last word of God on the human condition is not death, but life; not despair, but hope. To this hope the Church invites the men and women of today as well. She repeats to them the incredible but true proclamation: Christ is risen! Let the whole world rise with him! Alleluia!"

After delivering the message before 200,000 people in St. Peter's Square, the Holy Father extended Easter greetings in 49 languages to people throughout the world.

NATIONAL

"Declaration of Solidarity" — This was the heading of an advertisement in the Mar. 2 edition of *The New York Times,* in which dissenters from church teaching sought to shift attention from abortion itself to authority and free speech in the Church. More than 900 Catholics subscribed to the ad in support of 97 Catholics who had sponsored an earlier ad — in the Oct. 7, 1984, edition of The Times — asserting that there is more than one "legitimate Catholic position on the morality of direct abortion. In response, Bishop James W. Malone, president of the National Conference of Catholic Bishops, declared Mar. 7: "There is no such thing as legitimate dissent by a Catholic from the proposition that, to seek or perform a direct abortion is, objectively considered, a grave moral evil." Archbishop Roger Mahony of Los Angeles called it "misleading and wrong to describe a situation of dissent . . . from authentic church teaching as if it were only a matter of diversity or plurality of opinions in the Church." Archbishop John L. May of St. Louis told reporters "there is absolutely no room for a pro-choice position in the Catholic Church."

Medicine for the Poor — The Catholic Medical Mission Board shipped more than $13.5 million worth of medicine to the poor in 1985, reported Jesuit Father Joseph J. Walter, director. Nearly $5 million went to 961 missions in 18 African countries; $2.6 million went to 391 missions in eight Central American countries. The board also placed 39 medical volunteers (doctors, dentists, nurses, other personnel) in eight countries, for periods of service ranging from a month to a year or more.

Won't Comply with Subpoena — The National Conference of Catholic Bishops announced in a letter Mar. 7 that it would accept a contempt-of-court citation rather than turn over documents subpoenaed by Abortion Rights Mobilization in an effort to have the Church's tax exempt status revoked because of alleged illegal political activity. Such a stance appeared to be the only way to bring issues of the suit to the attention of a federal appeals court. Msgr. Daniel F. Hoye, general secretary of the conference, said the subpoena raised "the prospect of the court's and ARM's involvement in the internal affairs of the Church and, consequently, of a potential infringement of (conference) rights under the religious clauses of the First Amendment."

Solidarity with Nicaraguan Cardinal — Noting that he had been "subjected to a barrage of distortions, slanderous insults and innuendos at home and by some representatives of the government abroad," Cardinals John J. O'Connor of New York and Bernard F. Law of Boston told Cardinal Miguel Obando Bravo of Nicaragua of their "solidarity" with him during a time of trial for the Church in his country. They also said: "We have taken the extraordinary step of making this letter (of Mar. 14) public so that the faithful in our archdioceses and as many as possible in our country will know what is actually happening to their brothers and sisters in Nicaragua." The letter cited such happenings as "physical harassment, crude attempts at intimidation, censorship, expulsion of priests, raiding of archdiocesan offices, confiscation of a church publication and closing of the Catholic radio station.

Refugees — The Office of Migration and Refugee Services, U.S. Catholic Conference, helped resettle 25,890 refugees in 1985, according to a report issued in the middle of the month. "Over the years," said Bishop Anthony J. Bevilacqua of Pittsburgh, "the church network has welcomed more than two million stateless strangers" to the United States. The bishop also said that an estimated 10 to 12 million people — most of them running from violence, poverty and persecution — "wander homeless" in the world.

Rules for Colleges and Universities — Proposed Vatican rules for Catholic colleges and universities posed a threat to academic freedom and to government funding, and should be substantially revised, if not scrapped altogether, the heads of 110 Catholic institutions of higher learning told the Vatican. Their views were contained in a synthesis of responses to norms written and distributed in 1985 by the Congregation for Catholic Education. The "real crux" of the norms, the report said, was "perceived by many to be the assertion of a power on the part of the (appropriate) bishop to control theologians . . . and to assure 'orthodoxy' in their teaching." The head of the Fellowship of Catholic Scholars said his organization, made up primarily of Catholics working in higher education, supported the norms. Msgr. George A. Kelly of St. John's University, Jamaica, N.Y., told an audience at The Catholic University of America in mid-March that it was "inconceivable that a school at any stage of education can call itself Catholic without simultaneously relating itself to the teaching authority of the Church."

Increase in Number of Poor People — The Campaign for Human Development, in a booklet entitled *Poverty Profile USA: In the 80s,* reported that the number of poor Americans increased faster than the general population in the previous 10 years, from 24.3 million in 1975 to 33.7 million in 1985. Factors contributing to the increase were said to be the government's "conservative pursuit" of social welfare policies, chronic unemployment and changes in economic structures and development in this country and others. In another development, the Administrative Board of the U.S. Catholic Conference said in a statement Mar. 24 that budget questions involved moral as well as financial issues. The board said federal budget policies should protect the poor while cutting defense and domestic spending.

Ministry to Homosexuals — Baptized Catholics who are homosexuals have an "equal claim" on the Church for pastoral care, stated guidelines issued by the Diocese of San Jose. Such ministry, it was said, requires persons with "special understanding, sensitivity and skill." Noting that sexual orientation in itself is not sinful, the guidelines were based on the "perennial teaching of the Cath-

olic Church on sexual morality, conscience and personal sin."

Court Decisions — In decisions handed up Mar. 25, the U.S. Supreme Court:
• Let stand a federal court decision permitting a public high school Bible study group to have the same "equal access" to school facilities as other extracurricular clubs (Bender v. Williamsport Area School District);
• Ruled that the military forces may properly ban the wearing of such religious apparel as the yarmulke, or Jewish skull cap, by military personnel.
The 3rd U.S. Circuit Court of Appeals dismissed Mar. 21 efforts to force the U.S. government to end diplomatic relations with the Holy See.

National Briefs:
• John E. McCarthy, president of the International Catholic Migration Commission and former director of Migration and Refugee Services, U.S. Catholic Conference, was named a Knight of St. Gregory.
• Thomas P. Carney, chairman of the Notre Dame University board of trustees, and his wife, Mary Elizabeth, were named the 1986 recipients of the university's Laetare Medal.
• The National Conference of Catholic Bishops announced Mar. 27 that one of its committees had begun writing the first draft of a "pastoral response" to the concerns of Catholic women; completion of the statement was expected in 1988.

Father Curran's Refusal To Retract

Father Charles E. Curran, a professor of moral theology at The Catholic University of America, announced Mar. 11 that he had refused to retract dissenting views in moral theology and that he could face the loss of his right to teach at the university. At issue, stated the Congregation for the Doctrine of the Faith in a letter dated Sept. 17, 1985, were his views in dissent from church teaching on artificial contraception, direct sterilization, abortion, euthanasia, masturbation, premarital intercourse, homosexual acts, and the indissolubility of sacramental and consummated marriage. The letter informed Father Curran that the congregation, which had reviewed his writings over a period of several years, was "in a position to bring this inquiry to its conclusion." (See separate article.)

INTERNATIONAL

Religious Freedom with Restrictions — An interfaith delegation that visited Yugoslavia in February reported it had found more religious freedom there than in other Communist countries of Eastern Europe. It was also reported that government authorities in Yugoslavia were appreciative of religion's positive contribution to social stability. At the same time, delegation members said the government continued to impose many restrictions on religion, and that believers could not expect to advance in professions or government leadership on an equal basis with Marxists. The delegation was sponsored by the New York-based Appeal to Conscience Foundation.

Church Influence in the Philippines — Church

involvement in the post-election crisis in the Philippines prevented bloodshed, said Cardinal Jaime Sin of Manila. "I think there could have been violence, the shedding of blood, and maybe the Communists could have taken over," if it had not been for the influence of the bishops and the Church, he said Mar. 5 during a press conference at a Rome airport.

Funeral in South Africa — Father Smangaliso Mkhatshwa, general, secretary of the Southern African Catholic Bishops' Conference, led some 60,000 people in a funeral procession Mar. 5 for 17 black victims of political violence in Johannesburg's Alexandria Township. In comment after the funeral, he said: "The international visitors to the occasion can have been left in no doubt that the country is in a state of war and that the people do not believe the government is serious about change or the need to talk to them."

Lithuanian Celebration — As Lithuanians continued preparations for the celebration in 1987 of the 600th anniversary of Christianity in their country, the bishops said in a pastoral letter: "Today, the catechism and the prayer book are the only sources of religious truths available to you, so they are all the more to be studied." The letter, dated Nov. 11, 1985, was published during the month in the West.

Atheism in Poland's Schools — In a statement sharply critical of government schools, the bishops of Poland said Mar. 13 that a campaign of "intense atheistic propaganda" was being aimed at Catholic schoolchildren. "Unfortunately, the school is becoming, under the motto of secularism, the terrain of a more intense atheistic propaganda," the prelates said. "Polish families are overwhelmingly Christian, and cannot accept that outside their domestic walls their children are educated in a climate hostile to the Church and to religion." The statement also expressed "esteem" for teachers who, "despite pressures, remain loyal to their own convictions and respect the convictions of parents and young believers."

Government Control of Seminarians — The training of priests in Vietnam is a government-controlled activity, according to letters from and visitors to the country. Sources said candidates for the priesthood are chosen by provincial authorities and managed by the Religious Affairs Department, which controls all aspects of their lives, including registration of their personal identity.

Nuclear Deterrence Criticized — Five French bishops challenged their own episcopal conference's defense of nuclear deterrence. In a document entitled "Peace in Another Way: Self-Defense without Betrayal," they said: "A nation does not have the right to threaten to do something which it does not have the right to do. It does not have the right to possess arms which it will never have the right to use." At the same time, they said they rejected the "temptations of pacifism," because "that is to resign oneself to injustice and enslavement." The dissenting bishops called for a reduction of nuclear arms production, leading to a nuclear freeze. They also endorsed the creation of nuclear-free zones and "non-violent civil dissuasion."

Criticism of D'Escoto — The bishops of Nicaragua accused the nation's foreign minister, suspended Maryknoll Father Miguel D'Escoto, of heading a campaign to incite Catholics to rebel against the Pope and the hierarchy. In a statement issued Mar. 21, they criticized him for saying, among other things, that bishops opposed to the government should leave the country. In another development, *L'Osservatore Romano* charged in its Mar. 2 edition that Father D'Escoto was using the Way of the Cross devotion as a "demagogic manipulaton" to get Catholics to support the Sandinista regime.

Priests Should Avoid Political Clergy Organizations — Cardinal Frantisek Tomasek called on priests in Czechoslovakia to "devote themselves to their work" and avoid involvement in political clergy organizations. Speaking in the Prague cathedral on Holy Thursday, he urged priests to resist government pressure to join communist-backed groups such as Pacem in Terris and the Priests' Movement for Peace. "Priests must devote themsleves to their work," he said. "In some cases they are not doing this.

International Briefs:

• Filipino Father Edicio de la Torre, a political prisoner of the Marcos regime, was released Mar. 2 after spending nine years in detention.

• Father Engelbert Zeitler, a missionary to India since 1954 and former secretary of the Asian Bishops' Conference, was refused readmission to India after spending seven months in West Germany for medical treatment.

• Nichiko Niwano, president-designate of a six-million-member Buddhist association, was awarded an honorary doctorate by Rome's Salesian University Mar. 20.

• About 2,000 demonstrators marched through the streets of San Salvador Mar. 24 to commemorate the sixth anniversary of the assassination of Archbishop Oscar Romero.

• Father Zithulele Patrick Mvemve, a native of South Africa's Transvaal Province, was named auxiliary bishop of Johannesburg Mar. 29.

Citizens' Rights in Chile

The bishops of Chile, in a statement entitled "Without Fear and Full of Hope" and issued Mar. 11, said the people had a "right" and a "duty" to express their political opinions, and that the government had "the duty to listen" to them. They also stated: "An important part of the Chilean people asks for change in politics and government. It must be achieved through legitimate and peaceful means. . . . The immense hope of men in this century (is) to be able to establish a world in which all men can live in dignity and mutual respect, free and united, equal in their diversity and open to the values of faith and culture, with more than just the basic necessities evenly distributed." The nation had been plagued by violence since 1973 when the government of Gen. Augusto Pinochet came into power in a bloody coup in which Marxist President Salvador Allende was killed.

APRIL 1986

VATICAN

Prayer for Peace at Assisi — The Holy Father announced Apr. 6 that leaders of Christian and non-Christians faiths would meet Oct. 27 in Assisi to pray for world peace. "The meeting," he said, "should constitute a coming together of a vast movement of reflection and prayer, in which followers of every religious faith should feel themselves involved." Among those expected to take part in the meeting were Anglican Archbishop Robert Runcie, representatives of the World Council of Churches, and the Dalai Lama, the exiled head of Tibetan Buddhists.

Synagogue Visit — The Holy Father paid a historic visit Apr. 13 to the main synagogue of Rome where he joined Chief Rabbi Elio Toaff in addressing a gathering of about 1,000 persons during an 80-minute service of prayer and song. The visit was the first by a Pope to a synagogue since apostolic times. (See separate entry.)

Canonization — The Pope canonized Franciscan Father Francesco Antonio Fasani (1681 to 1742) Apr. 13. He called the "Apostle of the Italian South" a perfect model for priestly ministry, especially in service to the poor and the imprisoned.

Bombing of Libya — At a weekly general audience Apr. 16, the Pope expressed "anguish and intense worry" over the U.S. bombing of targets in Libya the previous day. While condemning terrorism and its "massacres of innocents to plead a cause," he called on nations to take "concrete and firm action to banish terrorism from human affairs." He also said that armed reprisals "continue the spiral of violence."

Evolution — Catholics can accept the theory of evolution of the human body but not of the human soul, declared the Pope at a general audience Apr. 16. "The soul of every man and woman is created directly by God and could never evolve from other living things" or from matter, he said.

General Absolution, First Confession — The Pope said Apr. 17 that conferences of bishops should make it clear to their people that general absolution without individual confession of sins is reserved for cases of grave necessity, duly noted in official directives. Pastors must make a special effort, he stated, "to make the faithful understand the reasons which justify the need for the individual confession of serious sins . . . even after one has been absolved" through general absolution. The Holy Father also, speaking to personnel of the Congregation for the Sacraments, criticized the practice of postponing first confession until after first Communion. He questioned: "How can one not see the great help which the appropriate administration of this sacrament (of penance) can be, even for children, in the progressive and harmonious development of conscience and self-control."

Day of Prayer for Vocations — "The fostering of vocations (to the priesthood) cannot be considered a marginal activity, but must be incorporated into the life and activity of the community," said the Pope in a message marking the World Day of Prayer for Vocations, Apr. 20. "The Church has an urgent need of priests. This is one of the most crucial problems facing Christian communities," he said. "Christians cannot accept with passivity and indifference the decline in vocations. Vocations are the future of the Church. Jesus did not wish for a Church without priests. If priests are lacking, then Jesus is lacking in the world."

Praise for the Church in Southeast Asia — The Pope praised the Church in Brunei, Burma, Malaysia and Singapore Apr. 27, saying: "Their Christian community is small, but uniquely alive. They are immersed in a population which is almost totally Buddhist or Moslem, but the work of their catechists is intense, and their commitment to charitable works and human promotion is fervent."

Persecution in Albania — Pope John Paul decried religious persecution in Albania Apr. 27 during a meeting with a group of Catholics from that country. Religious freedom, he said, is one of man's "fundamental rights, recognized internationally" — but not in Albania, which was officially declared in 1967 to be an atheist state.

The Pope Also:

• Said Apr. 2 that protecting the environment is necessary, and that those who damage it show contempt for the divine order of creation.

• Urged a group of European bishops and priests Apr. 10 to teach young people "to love the Church as the sign and instrument of the grace of Christ."

• Called on members of Italy's largest Catholic lay organization Apr. 25 to mobilize a "courageous (Christian) presence" in society.

• Was deeply concerned about the fact and victims of the Chernobyl (U.S.S.R.) nuclear power plant accident, according to a statement issued Apr. 30.

Liberation Theology — With the approval of Pope John Paul, the Congregation for the Doctrine of the Faith issued Apr. 5 a second, 16,000-word document on the subject, entitled "Instruction on Christian Freedom and Liberation." (See separate entry.)

Vatican Briefs:

• The Secretariat for Non-Believers and the Hungarian Academy of Sciences announced plans Apr. 21 to co-sponsor a Christian-Marxist dialogue on society and moral values, to be held in the fall in Budapest.

• Two Cardinals, Francis Arinze and Johannes Willebrands, praised the Rev. Philip Potter, former secretary general of the World Council of Churches, who was honored Apr. 22 with the peace prize of the Buddhist Niwano Peace Foundation in Tokyo for his efforts for unity among Christians.

• Joined the World Council of Churches in a statement Apr. 15, that South African apartheid is "incompatible with the Christian faith."

• The Catholic Organization for Emergency Relief to Refugees, sponsored by the bishops' conference of Thailand, was named to receive the Pope John XXIII International Peace Prize, according to a report in the Apr. 12 edition of *L'Osservatore Romano.*

Theological Dissent

The Pope said Apr. 10 that theologians who teach dissenting views on moral issues risk violating the "fundamental right" of Catholics to learn church doctrine instead of "the opinions of theological schools."

Addressing a congress of some 200 moral theologians, he stated that "the Catholic theologian owes obedience" to the official teaching authority of the Church, and that the Church has the duty to "unmask" theological error. . . . To appeal to a 'faith of the Church' to oppose the moral magisterium of the Church, is equivalent to denying the Catholic conception of revelation. Not only that; one can even go so far as to violate the fundamental right of the faithful to have, from whoever teaches theology with a canonical mission, the doctrine of the Church and not the opinions of theological schools. . . . Error must be unmasked and judged. The love that the Church has for man obligates it to say how and when its truth is denied, its goodness not recognized, its dignity violated, and its values not adequately appreciated."

NATIONAL

Mission Contributions — U.S. Catholics contributed more than $46.5 million to the general fund of the Society for the Propagation of the Faith in 1985, a 6.7 percent increase over the amount given in 1984. The society also reported that an additional $2.6 million was given for the support of mission seminarians and Religious through the Society of St. Peter the Apostle, another mission-aid society.

Comments on Bombing of Libya — While a number of bishops commented on the U.S. bombing of Libyan targets Apr. 15, most of them, as well as their national conference, declined to do so. The Reagan administration said the action was in self-defense and was carried out in a discriminating manner as a last resort and proportionate response to terrorism. Among comments by bishops were the following.

• "Information currently available indicates that the administration sought to make what it judged a proportionate response to Libyan-sponsored terrorism, focusing on military-related targets. . . . My prayer . . . is that current tensions and hostile acts will not escalate into further violence, destruction and death" (Cardinal Joseph L. Bernardin).

• "I seriously question whether proportionality was respected" (Archbishop John R. Roach of St. Paul-Minneapolis).

• "There are better ways" to deal with terrorism than by "increased confrontation" (Archbishop Raymond G. Hunthausen of Seattle).

• "The whole thing seems to me to be too macho and too vindictive and, pragmatically, of not much use" (Auxiliary Bishop Thomas J. Gumbleton of Detroit).

Smeal Speech Cancelled — DePaul University cancelled a May speech by Eleanor Smeal, president of the National Organization for Women. James R. Doyle, university vice president for student affairs, said Apr. 17 that one of two reasons for the cancellation "was purely her position and working aggressively for (pro-choice) abortion legislation." The other reason was a structural problem with the committee which extended the invitation for her appearance.

Anti-Catholic Booklets — The Charlotte Area Clergy Association adopted a resolution saying that anti-Catholic booklets published by Chick Publications of Chino, Calif., and distributed in the area were "offensive to all people of good will and character." The association called on people to "disassociate themselves from this and all forms of prejudice," and urged book sellers to "use good judgment and scrutiny in the selection of . . . material for public consumption." *The Charlotte Observer* denounced the literature as "sick stuff" and "garbage."

Religious Bias in Florida Prisons — The bishops of Florida and the American Jewish Congress called for an independent investigation of alleged discrimination against Catholics and Jews in state prisons. For one thing, they said, the state had never hired a full-time Catholic or Jewish chaplain. Sister Hannah Daly, engaged in prison ministry in the northern part of the state since 1980, said in a report that religious intolerance against Catholics in the prison system ranged from fundamentalist Protestant proselytism to the exclusion of Catholic volunteer workers, from the removal of Catholic reading materials to wide distribution of anti-Catholic literature. Sister Hannah's findings were supported by Rabbi Dennis Ward, a part-time chaplain at two state prisons.

"Health Centers" in Schools — The bishops of Florida, in a letter issued Apr. 24, opposed proposals in the state legislature and Dade County that would permit the establishment of health clinics and the distribution of contraceptives on public school premises. They said sex education programs like those envisioned in the proposals are ineffective because:

• "They do not adequately respect the rights and obligations of parents or the conscience of the young people.

• "They do not represent the ethical-moral dimension of human sexuality.

• "They do not integrate sexual development into total personal development.

• "They are the expression of a secular philosophy which, in effect, becomes a sectarian religion."

In California, Bishop Leo T. Maher of San Diego said in a letter to people of the diocese that the placement of health centers in public high schools seemed to be a disguised way of providing contraceptives and abortion counseling for students.

Diplomacy and the Church — "If diplomacy is the art of making peace, then it certainly belongs logically and naturally to the Church." So stated Archbishop Giovanni Cheli, the Vatican's permanent observer to the United Nations, Apr. 28 at Seton Hall University. The influence exerted by the Holy See is "essentially moral," he said, adding: "Moral values are not only useful, they are indispensable for the very survival of the international order. In their absence, nations cannot be guided by justice, reason and law, but fall victims to the force of arrogance and the tyranny of might."

Aftermath of Aguilar v. Felton — The U.S. Supreme Court's 1985 decision in Aguilar v. Felton — that it was unconstitutional for public school teachers to conduct remedial classes on the premises of church-related schools — fueled tension between the two sectors, according to educators attending a conference Apr. 29 in Arlington, Va. The first year after the ruling "has been a total disaster," said Richard Duffy, a representative of the U.S. Catholic Conference. He called it ironic that the decision came just months after the 20th anniversary of the Elementary and Secondary Education Act of 1965, which mandated services for poor, disadvantaged students in both public and private schools. Duffy said a survey of 174 dioceses found that "30 to 50 percent of non-public school students" were not receiving prescribed services.

Nuclear Rejection — By unanimous vote Apr. 29, the bishops of the United Methodist Church issued a pastoral letter rejecting any use of nuclear weapons and the entire concept of nuclear deterrence. The letter was entitled "In Defense of Creation: The Nuclear Crisis and a Just Peace." (See separate entry.)

Illinois Abortion Law — With a 9-to-0 ruling on procedural grounds, the U.S. Supreme Court dismissed Apr. 30 an Illinois statute requiring doctors to use abortion methods most likely to save the life of the child and to tell women that certain birth control items are abortifacients.

National Briefs:
• With a Mass, pageant and related observances Apr. 6 in San Antonio, Catholics in Texas celebrated the accomplishments of the Church in the state since, and before, it became independent of Mexico in 1836.
• Cardinal Jozef Tomko, prefect of the Congregation for the Evangelization of Peoples, celebrated Mass Apr. 20 in Wilkes Barre, Pa., to commemorate the 75th anniversary of the Slovak Catholic Federation.
• The role of the Church was one of the focal points of discussion at the Apr. 20-to-24 convention of the National Federation of Priests' Councils in Salt Lake City. Archbishop Raymond G. Hunthausen of Seattle was the recipient of the federation's 1986 President's Award.
• Nine hundred Catholics from the Midwest attended the Heartland Conference on ministry Apr. 22 to 24 in Kansas City, Mo.
• Augustinians began Apr. 24 a year-long Centenary 16 celebration of the 1,600th anniversary of the conversion of St. Augustine.

NCEA Convention

About 15,000 teachers, administrators and other personnel attended the 83rd convention of the National Catholic Educational Association May 31 to Apr. 3 in Anaheim, Calif. The theme of the meeting was "Mission and Ministries — A Celebration."

The celebration was about the accomplishments of Catholic education, especially on the elementary and secondary levels, during the previous 15 or more difficult years. The real focus, however, was on the future and work to be done for:
• quality education keyed to faith and committed to the service of peace and justice;
• intellectual leadership;
• education of the poor and minorities, as well as an increasing number of non-Catholic students;
• a counter-cultural mentality to counteract un-Christian values and to leaven society with the Gospel.
Serious consideration, of course, was given to problems related to finances and enrollments.

INTERNATIONAL

Silent Bishops — News reports indicated that, in contrast to their outspoken leadership during the revolution that ousted Ferdinand Marcos, most bishops in the Philippines had been virtually silent on political matters since the government of Corazon Aquino took office Feb. 25. It was also noted that prelates had expressed a lack of ease with the degree of political power they had been able to wield in events leading to the overthrow of the Marcos government. Cardinal Jaime Sin, when questioned about the silence, said: "It is the duty of lay people to restore the temporal order. The Church steps in only if lay people are unwilling, or unable, to do so."

Rights To Hunt and Trap Animals — Bishop Omer Robidoux of Churchill-Hudson Bay, Manitoba, urged special consideration for Canadian Indians suffering economic hardship because of a European ban on the import of Canadian seal furs. He said the economic and cultural survival of native Canadians was threatened by anti-fur trade and anti-trapping lobbyists, whose efforts had seriously reduced the international market for fur products. It is important to express "solidarity with those active hunters and trappers and all those working to maintain a way of life which promotes Christian stewardship of northern lands," he said Apr. 2.

Appeal of Nigerian Bishops — The bishops' conference of Nigeria called on the government to withdraw from the Organization of the Islamic Conference, with a membership of 40 Moslem countries and a base in Jidda, Saudi Arabia. In a delayed report of a statement published Mar. 2, the bishops said: "With its religious pluralism, Nigeria cannot as a state become a member of an international body whose objectives are essentially the promotion of one particular religion. . . . To elevate one religion to the status of a state religion, is clearly against our constitution."

Dialogue Hampered in Poland — Cardinal Jozef Glemp said Apr. 7 that a recent statement by government spokesman Jerzy Urban hindered the development of church-state dialogue. His reference was to a denunciation of priests who were critical of government officials. He also said that criticism of the Church was common "at various (Communist) ideological meetings." Earlier disruptions of dialogue for better church-state relations were the crucifix war of 1984 and the murder in October of that year of solidarity supporter Father Jerzy Popieluszko by policemen of the Interior Ministry.

Euthanasia — Public opinion polls revealed that pressure was continuing to increase in The Netherlands for the legalization of active euthanasia, despite opposition of the hierarchy. One bill would permit doctors to kill a patient who claimed "unbearable sufferings" or whose situation was deemed hopeless and who asked that his life be ended. Another bill proposed legalized euthanasia only in the case of imminent death. Action on both bills was postponed by the government. The bishops had stated church teaching on euthanasia in a pastoral letter issued in 1985.

New Epoch in Vatican Relations — Two hundred and 60 bishops of Brazil ended their 24th annual assembly, Apr. 9 to 18, with a prediction of a "new epoch" in relations with the Vatican. Bishop Jose Ivo Lorscheiter, chairman of the bishops' conference, cited several reasons for the bishops' optimism:

• the positive atmosphere of a meeting between representatives of the hierarchy and Vatican officials in March;

• publication by the Vatican during the month of a second document on liberation theology, entitled "Instruction on Christian Freedom and Liberation" (see separate entry);

• presence at the assembly of Cardinal Bernardin Gantin, prefect of the Congregation for Bishops and president of the Pontifical Commission for Latin America;

• a special message from the Pope to the bishops, calling for a liberation theology, based on church teaching, to deal with social problems.

Ostpolitik — The Vatican policy of negotiation rather than confrontation with Communist regimes — known as Ostpolitik — is part of a long-range strategy to obtain religious freedom. So stated Cardinal Franz Konig, former head of the Secretariat for Non-Believers, Apr. 10 in an address at The Catholic University of America. The Vatican "proceeds with small steps and there are temporary reverses, but it never loses sight of the goal . . . to enlarge and safeguard the sphere in which believers may move with freedom," he said. The first aim "is always the installaton of diocesan bishops," because the bishop is the outward sign of the unity of the Church. In Eastern Europe, he also said, "the Church is subject to an administrative persecution which is invisible and noiseless but nevertheless very effective."

New Maronite Patriarch — Maronite bishops meeeting in Lebanon Apr. 19 elected Bishop Nasrallah Sfeir as the new Patriarch of Maronite Catholics; ratification of the election by the Pope was pending. Msgr. Mario Rizzi, undersecretary of the Congregation for the Oriental Churches, said in comment about the election: "I think he has all the qualities for productive dialogue in Lebanon. He is a man of dialogue and peace. I don't think he will create problems between Lebanese communities. He will be appreciated by Moslems as a man who really wants to save the country."

Jesuits May Stay — Five Jesuit missionaries were granted permission by their provincial superior to remain at their mission in southern Sudan despite the threat of major military action by Libyan-backed government forces and Ethiopian-supplied rebels. Father Howard Gray said late in the month that the situation continued to be "touchy," but the men wanted to stay "for the maintenance of the school and for the support of the people." One of the missionaries, Brother Joseph Shubitowski, said the situation was not as bad as reported, and added: "All church property and personnel in Wau have been treated with respect."

- **Worry over Catholic Strength in Czechoslovakia** — The underground monthly, *Information on the Church,* reported that Communist authorities were concerned about the continuing influence of the Church in areas where it had strong traditional roots. In 1984: in Slovakia, 72 percent of newborns were baptized, and 53 percent of weddings and 80 percent of funerals were performed in church ceremonies; in another republic, 31 percent of newborns were baptized, and 16 percent of weddings and 51 percent of funerals took place in church. Meanwhile, religious life and regular parish activity remained restricted, and 10 of the nation's 13 dioceses were without resident bishops.

International Briefs:

• Cardinal George Basil Hume of Westminster said he shared "the profound disquiet and moral outrage of many" in reaction to the U.S. bombing of Libya. In an article in the Apr. 20 edition of *The Observer* of London, he stated: "I fear that we may be entering a jungle of repeated violence and use of force. And Britain is walking with an uneasy conscience in American footsteps."

• Cardinal Jean-Marie Lustiger of Paris, in an interview Apr. 26, said he was worried about the state of Catholicism in France. With the lowest number of churchgoers in Western Europe, "France has been submitted to the most serious and deepest religious crisis" on the Continent, he declared.

Nicaragua's "Popular Church"

The bishops of Nicaragua criticized the country's so-called "popular church," accusing activist priests and Religious of manipulating the Gospel "for their own ends." In a statement issued Apr. 7, they said: "A belligerent group of priests, religious workers and lay people of various nationalities, who say they belong to the Catholic Church, are in reality working actively to undermine the Church. . . . They manipulate the fundamental truths of our faith, taking upon themselves the right to reinterpret and even to rewrite the word of God, in order to make it fit their own ideology and use it for their own ends."

This was not the first criticism of the popular church by the bishops; they had already said it was an effort to form a pro-government church. The Pope had criticized it for not accepting the authority of the bishops. It was estimated that perhaps from 20 to 100 priests, as well as numbers of Religious, were involved in the popular church movement.

MAY 1986

VATICAN

Unmarried Couples — The Pope asked 16 Italian bishops May 2 to be "patient and loving" in attitude toward couples not married in the Church. "Even though it is impossible to admit them to Eucharistic Communion, they are not excluded from our affection, benevolence and prayer," he said. "Approach people living together with discretion and respect, and strive through patient and loving action to remove the impediments and smooth the road toward regularizing the situation." He also said the living together of unmarried couples is one of the principal social conditions causing the "disintegration of the family."

Visit to Red Romagna — "I come to you on a pastoral pilgrimage . . . to advance the eminently spiritual mission of the Church," said the Pope in Forli on May 8, the first day of a four-day tour of seven cities in a region known for its excessive anti-clericalism. The Holy Father was well received everywhere. During the tour, he baptized seven infants in Forli; administered the sacraments of the Eucharist in Cesena, confirmation in Imola and matrimony in Faenza; and met with candidates for the priesthood in Ravenna. The visit was the Pope's 56th outside Rome since the beginning of his pontificate.

Evangelization — The Pope told participants in the general assembly of pontifical mission-aid societies May 13 that, along with the need to evangelize new places, the Church has to keep in mind the "duty to re-evangelize" Christian countries. "In the modern age, which boasts of being the society of information, millions of human beings are yearning for salvation, yet know little or nothing about the Savior of the world, Jesus Christ. . . . Moreover, in the Old World, raised for centuries in the school of Christian faith, such powerful forms of ideological materialism exist that there is fear that entire regions may fall under the shadows of atheism. . . . Today, as never before, the world needs to be saved, and men need to be renewed by the Gospel."

Avoid Superficial Theology — "Grow in your knowledge and love of the great mystery of the Church" and be aware that "not just any knowledge of the Church, the Bride of Christ, will do." So stated the Pope before a group of New York priests and students for the priesthood. Priests must not have "the mere knowledge based on partial and contingent sociological conceptions." They should seek, rather, "a profound spiritual and theological understanding of the mystery of salvation at work in the lives of people through the ministry of the Church." At a meeting with 37 U.S. priests May 15, he said: "Administering the sacrament of penance can be one of the most consoling and uplifting parts of our ministry."

Plea for African Children — On UNICEF's World Children's Day, May 19, Pope John Paul made a plea for children in drought- and poverty-stricken countries of Africa. "The urgency of immediate aid to those in the greatest need, to the populations and, in particular, to the children of African nations, needs to be felt by all. . . . No one can ignore the children who are suffering today and dying today."

Schools of Prayer — The Pope, addressing the general assembly of the International Union of Superiors General (of women) May 22, said that religious communities should be "veritable schools of prayer." He called special attention to the need for communities to ground new members in prayer, and said: "The candidates who present themselves to your religious families need to find there a climate marked by contemplation, silence, and a simple and poor lifestyle conducive to the giving of oneself in joy and self-discipline." The Holy Father also praised the nuns for their "remarkable and laudable efforts to improve the quality of liturgical life" in their communities.

Celibacy of Priests — Priestly celibacy is a "gift of the Spirit" whose "discipline the Church is resolved to protect as a treasure," said the Pope at a meeting May 23 with a group of bishops from Angola. He called celibacy a sign of the priest's "undivided and liberated heart" which is dedicated to "the service of God and men, . . . an eminently spiritual service which is not comparable to the exercise of a learned profession. It is mission, the mission of the Church."

Corpus Christi Procession — The Pope marked the solemnity of Corpus Christi May 29 by carrying the Eucharist in a mile-long evening procession from the Basilica of St. John Lateran to the Basilica of St. Mary Major. "The Church desires to go into the streets, announcing to the whole world" that Christ is present in the Eucharist, he said in a homily before the beginning of the procession.

Church and Scripture — "Only the official teaching authority of the Church authentically interprets and transmits" Scripture, said the Pope May 30 in a brief address to members of the Italian Associates of the Venerable Maria Teresa of Savoy. "Because of this, awareness of the documents of the Church is indispensable." He urged the associates to make Jesus known, "above all, among those who, through ignorance, live in religious indifference."

The Pope Also:

• Expressed concern for unemployment May 1, the feast of St. Joseph the Worker, Labor Day in many countries.

• Told representatives of the Belgian Christian Center for Forestry and Construction Workers May 2: The Christian "does not become concerned with promoting class struggle, a struggle against others, because hatred of class is not compatible with Christian sentiments."

• Welcomed 31 recruits into the Swiss Guard May 6 at induction ceremonies marking the anniversary of the sack of Rome in 1527 when 147 Swiss Guards lost their lives defending Pope Clement VII.

• Commended the educational work of the Christian Brothers and urged them to maintain its high quality, especially in catechetics.

• At a meeting with several Gypsy leaders May

16, offered his moral support in their struggle against discrimination.

• Celebrated his 66th birthday May 18.

• Ordained 74 priests, including nine from the U.S., May 25.

Vatican Briefs:

• "Sects or New Religious Movements: Pastoral Challenge," is the title of a report issued May 4 by the Secretariat for Promoting Christian Unity (see separate entry).

• William A. Wilson, the first U.S. ambassador to the Vatican, announced May 21 that he was resigning the post in order to return to private life.

Dominum et Vivificantem

The Holy Spirit, "Lord and Giver of Life," is the subject of Pope John Paul's fifth encyclical letter, dated May 18 and released 12 days later. It is a detailed treatment of the theology of the Holy Spirit and of the role of the Holy Spirit in the life of the Church, its members and the world. It completes a "trinitarian trilogy" of encyclical letters whose other two parts are *Redemptor Hominis* ("On Redemption and the Dignity of the Human Race") and *Dives in Misericordia* ("On the Mercy of God"). (See separate entry for excerpts.)

NATIONAL

Sanctuary Workers Convicted — Eight church workers, including two priests and a nun, were found guilty May 1 on charges of conspiracy, smuggling, transporting and harboring undocumented aliens from Guatemala and El Salvador. Most of those found guilty were subsequently (in July) given suspended sentences and placed on probation. During the course of the trial, the sanctuary workers were not permitted to present arguments that the persons they aided were political refugees in fear of their personal safety if forced to return to their homelands. While the National Conference of Catholic Bishops had no stated official position on the sanctuary movement, the three bishops of Arizona said in a statement May 1: "The help offered refugees by the sanctuary workers continues to deserve our respect, as flowing from valid religious, humanitarian motives and beliefs, and is consistent with the ideals upon which our country was founded." The sanctuary movement had the endorsement of about 300 churches, approximately 20 U.S. cities and the State of New Mexico.

First Indian Bishop — In a liturgy filled with the sights and sounds of American Indian culture, Bishop Donald R. Pelotte, the first Native American elevated to the episcopate, was ordained May 6 as coadjutor bishop of Gallup. Archbishop Robert F. Sanchez of Santa Fe, in the homily at the ordination Mass, acknowledged his special mission to serve the Indian population of the diocese while reminding him also of his mission to serve all people of the Church.

Tax Exemption Case — U.S. District Judge Robert Carter found the National Conference of Catholic Bishops and the U.S. Catholic Conference in contempt of court May 8 for refusing to turn over thousands of subpoenaed documents on their pro-

life activities, and imposed fines of $50,000 a day on each conference. The documents were sought in the course of a legal battle which began in 1980 when Abortion Rights Mobilization sued the Internal Revenue Service and the U.S. Treasury Department in order to force the government to revoke the tax exempt status of the Church. The pro-abortion group charged that Catholic officials and agencies had violated norms for tax exemption because of their anti-abortion activities. Attorneys for the conferences, in appealing for dismissal of subpoena orders, argued that:

• "The contempt citation . . . must be reversed because the district court erred in ruling that plaintiffs have standing to challenge the exempt status" of the conferences.

• "Permitting cases like this to go forward could involve courts on a massive scale in overseeing" tax exemption decisions of the IRS.

• If such suits are allowed, "those who wish to quiet the voice of any religious group on a controversial public issue" could use the courts to "chill the legitimate exercise of First Amendment rights."

• "The plaintiffs fail to meet" legal tests required to give them standing to sue.

A federal appeals court set aside the contempt-of-court fines, pending further action on the case.

Aid in Wake of the Chernobyl Accident — Following widespread contamination in Eastern Europe by the Soviet nuclear accident at Chernobyl, Catholic Relief Services announced May 8 that it was committing $100,000 in aid for the purchase of powdered milk at the request of the bishops of Poland. It was thought CRS might eventually provide up to $6 million worth of aid for 2.1 million endangered Polish children.

Archbishop vs. People of Hope — The authority of Archbishop Peter L. Gerety of Newark over a controversial charismatic group in his archdiocese was supported by the Vatican. In a letter read to members of the People of Hope May 9, Cardinal Johannes Willebrands, head of the Secretariat for Promoting Christian Unity, affirmed the archbishop's authority "in matters concerning teaching, evangelization, spiritual formation and ecumenism" in his archdiocese. The group in Berkeley Heights, N.J., had contested the archbishop's authority with the support of Sword of the Spirit, an international ecumenical evangelical movement which had no standing as a Catholic organization or movement. People of Hope had also been criticized for elitism and disruption in the Little Flower Parish.

South African Divestment — The Archdiocese of Milwaukee announced it was divesting itself of holdings valued at $700,000 in four U.S. companies that had not signed the Sullivan Principles, a set of standards for companies operating in South Africa. The companies were: Perkin Elmer Corp. of Norwalk, Conn.; Air Products and Chemicals, Inc., of Allentown, Pa.; GTE Corp. of Stamford, Conn., and Ogilvy Group of New York.

• Archbishop William D. Borders of Baltimore approved a policy of responsible investing that could be applied to firms dealing with South

Africa. The policy states that the archdiocese "has a duty to use responsibly the resources at its disposal to serve others: to promote social justice, to address structures that oppress people, and to be consistent with the mission of Jesus Christ and the Church's own mission."

Dialogue between Christians and Jews — Christian-Jewish dialogue has to involve more lay people if their attitudes of "bias, suspicion, stereotyping and misunderstanding" are to change, said speakers at the ninth National Workshop on Christian-Jewish relations. Scholars, members of the clergy and interfaith leaders were among the 900 participants in the workshop May 13 to 16 in Baltimore. The theme of discussions was "Coming to Grips with Our Past: Forging Our Future."

Charities Projects — The Emergency Food and Shelter National Board announced May 15 that projects under the auspices of Catholic Charities organizations nationwide had received $13,859,966 since 1983 for the care of hungry and homeless persons. The Society of St. Vincent de Paul received $2,683,380 for the same purposes.

El Paso Synod — About 45,000 Catholics attended May 18 ceremonies marking the conclusion of a three-year diocesan synod in El Paso's Sun Bowl Stadium. Bishop Raymundo J. Pena said in an address that the final synod document, approved the day before, contained three stand-out items which would enhance lay involvement: the integral evangelization of all Catholics, establishment of an adult formation and ministry training institute, and the development of parish and diocesan pastoral councils. Among other recommendations, the document called for the establishment of two bodies: a pastoral planning committee to "give emphasis to the pastoral care of .. alienated Catholics, the elderly, physically challenged, unwed teen-age parents, the sick, divorced and separated persons, substance abusers and their families; and a border commission to assist parishes in the care of migrants, immigrants, and undocumented aliens from Mexico.

Vatican Ambassador To Resign — William A. Wilson, the first U.S. ambassador to the Vatican, announced May 21 that he intended to resign from the post. He denied allegations that he was being pressured to quit and refused to give details about a January trip to Libya for which he was reprimanded by Secretary of State George Shultz.

Plea for Resettlement of Refugees — The U.S. Catholic Conference urged the U.S. government to take steps to reunite with relatives in the U.S. homeless Khmer refugees trapped along the Thailand-Cambodia border. An estimated 10,000 to 20,000 of the refugees had close ties to family members in this country. A letter addressed to President Reagan asked for help in reuniting families "rent by decades of persecution, conflict and war."

National Briefs:

• Archbishop John P. Foley, president of the Pontifical Commission for Social Communications, called May 2 in New York for greater attention to religion in the training of journalists: "The education of any contemporary journalist is sorely lacking if it does not include a study of and an attempt to understand religion."

• Atheist Madalyn Murray O'Hair, who once described herself as "the most hated woman in America," handed over leadership of the American Atheist Center to her son, Jon Garth Murray, according to an announcement May 1.

• Honored: Archbishop Raymond G. Hunthausen of Seattle, with the first Peacemaker of the Year Award of the Portland, Ore., Catholic Peace Ministry; Cardinal John Carberry, retired archbishop of St. Louis, with the first Pro Fidelitate et Virtute Award of the Institute on Religious Life.

Retirement Needs of Religious

Three major Catholic agencies announced May 30 in Washington a new two-year project to help religious orders deal with the increasing financial burdens of retirement. They also released a study — "Retirement Needs Survey of United States Religious" — showing that, although male and female religious institutes were increasing efforts to fund their retirement needs, the debt for such costs amounted to about $2.5 billion. The reporting agencies were the National Conference of Catholic Bishops, the Conference of Major Superiors of Men and the Leadership Conference of Women Religious. Congregations of Sisters were the hardest hit by the crisis.

In 1985, the Archdiocese of Cincinnati made the final payment on a pledge made in the mid-1970s — to contribute $3 million to 19 orders toward the retirement of nuns who had worked in schools, parishes and other institutions of the archdiocese.

INTERNATIONAL

Recommendations of Lay Persons — Forty-three East Asian lay persons attending an April meeting in Taipei said in a statement that "the Church should become more aware of the needs of laborers and low-income groups, and should reach out to them more effectively." They also cited as priorities for lay persons spiritual formation, participation in decision-making, the establishment of Christian communities, attention to inculturation and recognition of the role of women in the Church and society.

Social Activism Not for Mother Teresa — Mother Teresa, interviewed at the motherhouse of the Missionaries of Charity in Calcutta, said she and her 3,000 sisters did not feel called to direct activism in politics or for social justice. "That's not our charism. . . . (We are) not social workers, but contemplatives in action, sisters leading consecrated lives," she said. "It's better that each follow the way God has given them," she stated while acknowledging that others have different charisms and forms of apostolic action.

Missionaries Refused Entry — "Catholic priests invited to work in Nigeria by local bishops are being refused permission to enter the country," according to a report in the May 7 edition of *Fides,* the publication service of the Congregation for the Evangelization of Peoples.

Concern for Polygamous Families — All Africa Press Service reported May 12 that an assembly of

African bishops had called for studies that might help to incorporate polygamous families into Christian communities, declaring: "With the good of these families at heart, we recommend that a religious teaching be developed in the hope of integrating them into the Christian communities and gradually leading them to fulfill freely the conditions required for full participation in the life of the Church." The prelates also spoke in a closing statement against the widespread practice of trial marriage, saying it negated biblical teachings on love and commitment.

Manipulation of Bishops' Statements — While strongly criticizing Sandinista efforts to censor or "manipulate" the statements of Nicaraguan bishops, Cardinal Miguel Obando Bravo called again for government and rebel forces to reach "reconciliation through dialogue." Writing in the May 12 edition of *The Washington Post,* he also reiterated previous statements that the bishops opposed "any outside interference, whether by the United States or the Soviet Union," in Nicaragua.

Divorce Referendum in Ireland — The bishops of Ireland issued a pastoral letter critical of the government's plan for a referendum on legalizing divorce as Parliament began debate on the matter May 14. The letter said divorce defines all marriages as candidates for breakup, rather than lasting for life. "It is not true that a divorce law would affect only the minority of marriages which break down irretrievably. Divorce introduces a quite radical change in society's legal understanding of marriage."

Protest in Paraguay — During Independence Day celebrations May 18, Archbishop Ismael Blas Rolon Silvero of Asuncion canceled a traditional Mass in his cathedral and spoke in criticism of violence by police and others, as well as of violations of human rights by the military regime of Gen. Alfredo Stroessner. Two and a half weeks earlier, police beat May Day demonstrators marching from Mass to take part in a rally in a city square in Asuncion. The incident occurred amid a series of strikes and demonstrations against the 31-year-long repressive rule of Gen. Stroessner.

Brazilian Officials Forbidden the Sacraments — The 11 bishops of the State of Maranhao declared May 21 that the governor, the police chief and directors of the Democratic Rural Union "exclude themselves from the church community" through "calumnious statements and their anti-evangelical behavior. . . . 'It makes no sense for them to continue to receive the sacraments offered by the Church until they show public signs of conversion to evangelical wisdom." The bishops said in a letter that the authorities — who were not excommunicated — owed "explanations to the population on land-grabbing, the impunity of those who have murdered peasant workers and destroyed their villages, and many violations of the law and of human rights."

Help for Haitians — Bishop Emmanuel Constant of Les Gonaives, speaking in New York, said the bishops in Haiti were determined to help their people keep their newly found political freedom, following the ouster of President Jean-Claude

Duvalier Feb. 7, and would "speak out for the poor, no matter what it might cost." "From the day he left the country," the bishop said, "we called for reconciliation. But, when things cooled, we also called for justice, since there is no true reconciliation without justice." Bishop Constant said the bishops had issued a demand for land reform and greater employment opportunities, and had organized literacy and related educational programs to enable the people to "make good political decisions."

Worry about Missionaries in Sudan — Officials of four religious orders reported May 28 worry about the status and conditions of their missionaries in southern Sudan. They said they had had little or no contact in recent weeks with their missions in areas of worsening guerrilla combat. Some missionaries had moved from outlying towns to larger cities for protection, but others had stayed behind and had been cut off because of increased fighting. All of them, including 11 American Jesuits, were committed to stay and work in the predominantly Moslem country.

International Briefs:
- "Without full respect for human rights, social groups and labor unions, the economic problems now facing Poland cannot be resolved," stated the bishops during a plenary meeting early in the month. They also called for "prompt repeal" of the 1956 law which legalized abortion.
- French-Canadian Jesuit Father Gilles Pelland was named rector of the Pontifical Gregorian University.
- The General Assembly of the Church of Scotland voted overwhelmingly May 21 to repudiate anti-Catholic statements in the Westminster Confession, the 1647 statement of faith for Presbyterianism.
- Churches in Eastern Europe received nearly $13 million in donations in 1985 from Aid to the Church in Distress, an international Catholic fundraising group. Nearly $10 million went to the Church in Latin America and about $8 million to the Church in Africa.

South African Bishops Back Economic Pressure

The South African bishops became the first governing body of a church in South Africa to support economic attack on apartheid. They gave their qualified support to "economic pressure for justice" May 2 at the end of a three-day special meeting in Durban. In a pastoral letter, they said they took their stand because of "the unprecedented seriousness of our present crisis, the enormity of the present suffering of the oppressed people of South Africa, and the horrifying specter of escalating violence." Economic pressure, they said, seemed to be the most effective of the non-violent forms of pressure available.

In their decision, the bishops stated, they were "deeply concerned about the additional suffering that some form of economic pressure might cause," but against this was balanced "the enormity of the present suffering and rate of unemployment, and the prospects for the future if the system of apartheid is not dismantled soon."

JUNE 1986

VATICAN

Challenge to Ugandans — In a message, released June 4, marking the 100th anniversary of the Martyrs of Uganda, the Pope challenged people of the troubled nation to build "a new Uganda on the foundation of love, reconciliation and true justice. ... Take up your responsibilities," he said, "for upon you depends the future of your country." He told them to place their hope in Christ, who "will enable you to bear your responsibilities for shaping a better world, one free of violence, discrimination and injustice."

Dignity of Life — Pope John Paul defended the dignity of life in comments to Baron Seger Jan Joseph van Voorst, The Netherlands' new ambassador to the Holy See. "In regard to respect for life from conception and during times of grave illness or old age," he said June 5, "the Church, without ceasing, challenges consciences to arouse them morally." Action on the issue of euthanasia was pending in the Dutch Parliament, which had already studied and debated the matter of allowing doctors to kill patients who claim "unbearable sufferings" or who ask for an end to life when their situation is deemed hopeless.

Suffering Can Be Redemptive — To understand the problem of evil in the world, one must consider the redemptive suffering of Christ, said the Pope June 11 during a general audience. "To the question, 'How can evil and suffering . . . be reconciled with the truth of divine Providence?' one cannot give a definitive response without making reference to Christ," he said. Faced with the age-old question, "the individual might not find an immediate answer, especially if he does not possess the living faith in the paschal mystery of Jesus Christ. . . . Gradually, however, and with the help of faith nourished by prayer, the true sense of suffering is discovered." The crucifixion of Christ gave all suffering "a redemptive purpose and value."

Vocations to the Priesthood and Religious Life — In a letter addressed to the U.S. bishops' meeting at Collegeville, Minn., the Holy Father said: "There is a very special need in the Church today to promote vocations to the priesthood and religious life." The Church does so because it is "God's will to maintain both the hierarchical structure of his Church and the state of religious life. . . . The Church cannot exempt herself from utilizing every worthy means to attract vocations, including proper publicity and personal example." The Pontiff also said: "An integral part of Christian family life is the inculcation in its members of an appreciation of the priesthood and religious life."

Scientists Appointed to Academy — Two U.S. cancer researchers, both women, were among nine new members of the Pontifical Academy of Sciences whose appointments were announced June 12: Beatrice Mintz, head researcher at the Institute for Cancer Research, Philadelphia, and Maxine Singer, a laboratory director at the National Cancer Institute, Bethesda, Md.

Plea against Violence — As a government-declared state of emergency continued in South Africa. The Pope urged those who joined him for recitation of the Angelus June 15: "I ask you to unite your prayer to those of our brothers in southern Africa. Together with them, we ask the Lord to enlighten the minds and sustain the work of those who intend to work for justice and peace, respecting the rights of the human person and, in a spirit of true unity, avoid the temptation of hatred and violence."

Technology Needs Moral Guidance — This was one of the subjects of the Pope's address at a general audience June 18. He said: "The more progress we make in mastering the forces of nature, the easier it is for us to think we do not need God. This false pretense of self-sufficiency, if not corrected by the moral law, results in the most disastrous consequences." He encouraged technological development; by it, people continue "the Creator's work" and contribute to "realization in history of the divine plan."

Use of Space for Peace — Pope John Paul appealed to nations to develop "joint agreements" for the development of "peaceful uses of space resources" to unite the human family "in justice and peace." He did so in an address June 20 to a study group of the Pontifical Academy of Sciences that was exploring "remote sensing and its impact on developing countries." He said that remote sensing, which makes possible satellite-surveying of huge expanses of the earth, could lead to increased food production. He urged scientists to use remote sensing for "the improvement of soil conditions, forecasting and increasing the development of crop harvesting, and the introduction of new crops."

Resurrection from Drugs — The Pope called victory over drug addiction a form of resurrection and asked for greater public awareness about the harmful effects of narcotics. "Is it not perhaps a resurrection to have known how to conquer the slavery of drug addiction?" he asked June 21 during ceremonies inaugurating a church-sponsored drug rehabilitation center in Rome. For people trying to overcome addiction, "to carry the cross," means to exit from isolation" and once again to "become part of the family of redemption."

Latvian Anniversary — At an ecumenical service commemorating the 800th anniversary of Christianity in Latvia, the Pope said June 26: "The name of Christ should not be erased from the hearts of the younger generation which, all over the world, is threatened by atheistic ideologies and materialistic attitudes." Three hundred and 50 persons of Latvian descent attended the anniversary celebration.

Moslem-Christian Dialogue — "Today, dialogue between Christians and Moslems is more necessary than ever. ... The Catholic Church teaches that all men and women must respect one another, rise above all discrimination and serve the universal brotherhood." So stated the Pope June 27 as he accepted the credentials of Wissam

Chawkat al-Zawahi, Iraq's new ambassador to the Holy See.

The Pope Also:

• Awarded the Pope John XXIII International Peace Prize June 3 to Thailand's Catholic Office for Emergency Relief and Refugees.

• Called June 4 for an end to environmental policies that ignore human needs.

• Expressed concern June 18 for political prisoners in Poland, saying their plight was a question of fundamental human rights.

• Met June 19 in private audience with Nicaraguan Vice President Sergio Ramirez Mercado.

• Sent a message June 21 to Lithuanian Bishop Julijonas Steponavicius, under house arrest for 25 years, to commemorate the 50th anniversary of his ordination to the priesthood.

• Presented a pallium (see separate entry) June 29 to 19 archbishops, including Roger Mahony of Los Angeles, James F. Stafford of Denver, Theodore McCarrick of Newark and Anthony Sablan Apuron of Agana, Guam.

Vatican Briefs:

• *L'Osservatore Romano* front-paged June 1 an editorial in praise of "hands across America," calling it a U.S. response "to the needs of others."

• The Pontifical Commission for Justice and Peace announced it had compiled 19 papal World Day of Peace messages in *Ways of Peace,* a book marking the International Year of Peace proclaimed by the United Nations for 1986.

A Universal Catechism

A universal catechism, for use as a reference for locally produced catechisms, could end instructions and interpretations opposed to church teaching, the Pope said June 28. The development of such a catechism was recommended by the 1985 extraordinary assembly of the Synod of Bishops, because, the Pope noted, of the "demand currently felt in the Church for greater clarity and doctrinal security to put an end to teachings or interpretations of faith and morals which disagree among themselves or are opposed to the universal teaching authority of the Church." On June 12 the Vatican announced that a 12-member commission had been formed to prepare the proposed catechism; Cardinal Joseph Ratzinger, prefect of the Congregation for the Doctrine of the Faith, was named head of the commission; American members were Cardinals William Baum and Bernard F. Law.

The Pope also announced June 28 that a Synod-recommended study would be made of the theological and doctrinal nature of episcopal conferences; Cardinal Bernardin Gantin, prefect of the Congregation for Bishops, was placed in charge of the project.

NATIONAL

Baby Doe Regulations Invalidated — The U.S. Supreme Court ruled 5 to 3 June 9 against regulations requiring federal intervention to assure medical treatment for severely handicapped infants. At issue in the case was whether the regulations were justified by congressional passage in 1973 of Section 504 of the Rehabilitation Act, which says that a handicapped person cannot be discriminated against by a federally assisted agency "solely by reasons of his handicap." The Court distinguished between overt discrimination — denial of treatment — by hospitals because a person is handicapped, and decisions made by parents to refuse forms of medical care to their handicapped babies. The Court said the record used by the Secretary of Health and Human Services to justify the regulations "contains no evidence that hospitals have ever refused treatment authorized by parents or by court order." The regulations in question were developed after the death in 1982 of an infant — called Baby Doe — born with Down's syndrome whose unidentified parents denied permission for surgery to open his blocked esophagus.

Father Edward M. Bryce, director of the Office for Pro-Life Activities, National Conference of Catholic Bishops, said the ruling denied the federal government an important "regulatory lever" in dealing with the treatment of handicapped newborns. The "sharply divided" Court invalidated an initiative designed to protect handicapped infants from "lethal neglect."

Remedial Educational Services — The U.S. Department of Education issued guidelines June 17 outlining ways of providing remedial educational services for more of the 200,000 disadvantaged students in Catholic elementary and secondary schools. An estimated 30 to 50 percent of such students had not received any remedial services since the U.S. Supreme Court ruled in July, 1985, that public school teachers may not provide the services on the premises of church-related schools (Grand Rapids v. Ball, Aguilar v. Felton). The guidelines focused mainly on conditions the department believed necessary for the constitutional use of vans as classrooms. The department believed vans would be permissible if they were "free of religious symbols," were at a "sufficient distance" from school buildings, and were not used for other purposes. By the time the guidelines were issued, the practice of using vans was already under legal challenge.

Scalia Named to Supreme Court — Antonin Scalia, 50, a Catholic known in judicial circles as a conservative, was nominated to the U.S. Supreme Court by President Reagan June 17, to replace Justice William Rehnquist who was named to succeed Warren Burger as chief justice.

Palestinian Homeland — Diplomatic recognition of Israel by the Vatican would not help to bring peace to the Middle East unless it was tied to a comprehensive package which included the establishment of a Palestinian homeland and the assurance of protection for the millions of Christians in the region, said Cardinal John J. O'Connor. He also defended Israel's right to exist and said June 19 that founding a Palestinian homeland should involve "nothing adverse to Israel."

K of C Charities — In 1985, members of the Knights of Columbus donated more than $66 million and logged more than 23 million hours in volunteer service, according to a survey conducted by their headquarters. Among the principal donations were: $16 million to the sick, needy, disabled and handicapped; $9.3 million for church and community activities; $9.2 million to churches, homes for the aged, orphanages and hospitals; $6.9 million for welfare organizations, community projects, scouting and other funds; $5.7 million for scholarships, schools, libraries and other educational purposes.

Catholic Schools Honored — Thirty-four Catholic schools were reported among the 270 outstanding elementary schools on the 1985-86 honor roll of the U.S. Department of Education. The schools were honored because of their special emphasis on student achievement in reading and mathematics, and for their success in "overcoming obstacles and sustaining progress."

Church Membership in 1984 — Two hundred and 24 religious denominations in the U.S. reported a collective membership in 1984 of 142,172,138, an increase of 1,355,753 over the figure reported for 1983. *The Yearbook of American and Canadian Churches* reported that in 1984 there were 78,701,677 Protestants, 52,286,043 Catholics, 5,817,000 Jews, 4,052,668 Eastern Christians.

Maryknoll Anniversary — Maryknoll Missioners from far and near converged June 29 on their headquarters at Ossining, N.Y., to celebrate the 75th anniversary of their foundation as the first American foreign missionary society. The society, which sent its first missionaries to China in 1911, had members in 30 countries in Africa, Asia and Latin America.

U.S. Supreme Court Decisions — The Court, declaring that "not all burdens on religion are unconstitutional," rejected on an 8-to-1 vote an American Indian's claim that use of a Social Security number hinders religious belief.

On June 30, the Court, in a 5-to-4 decision in Bowers v. Hardwick, upheld a Georgia law forbidding sodomy. "The dividing line between private morality and public morality" was the key issue before the Court, according to Father Thomas Gannon, S.J., director of the Woodstock Theological Center at Georgetown University.

Meetings — Meetings during the month included those of:

• The National Conference on the Charismatic Renewal in the Catholic Church, attended by 8,000 persons May 30 to June 1 at the University of Notre Dame; "Proclaim the Gospel with Power" was the theme.

• The Catholic Health Assembly, June 1 to 4 in San Diego; discussions centered around prophet and profit in health care.

• Conference on Lay Ministry, attended by 350 lay ministers June 3 to 6 in St. Paul; "Birthing: Delivering the Minister in Every Christian" was the theme.

• The Catholic Press Association, June 4 to 7 in Columbus. (For CPA Awards, see separate entry.)

• The National Conference of Catholic Bishops, June 9 to 16 at St. John's University, Collegeville, Minn.

• Serra International, attended by 1,400 persons June 23 to 25 in Milwaukee; delegates voted to admit women to membership.

National Briefs:

• Archbishop Roger Mahony of Los Angeles urged Gov. George Deukmejian June 22 to delete from the California state budget all funding for abortion and contraceptive programs.

• The U.S. Catholic Conference, in a letter to the House of Representatives, again voiced opposition June 25 to U.S. military aid to the contras in Nicaragua.

• New York state's Medicaid program should permit pregnant, middle-class teen-agers to get prenatal care but should not allow funds provided "on behalf of the unborn child" to be used for abortions, said the New York State Catholic Conference.

Pastoral Plan for Hispanics

Before a throng of 50,000 persons in Dodger Stadium June 1, Archbishop Roger Mahony of Los Angeles unveiled a pastoral plan for Hispanics designed to promote vocations to the priesthood and religious life, halt gang violence, help immigrants, and make sure that every Hispanic feels welcome in the archdiocese, the largest in the U.S. The plan, he said, focused on family life, education, youth, and preserving the "close link between faith and Hispanic culture." A key element in the plan was a visitation program aimed at every Spanish-speaking person in the archdiocese. "The goal must be nothing less than a one-to-one visitation contact . . . in order to communicate a personal message of welcome from their local Catholic community," the archbishop stated.

INTERNATIONAL

Centennial of Uganda Martyrs — Ceremonies marking the 100th anniversary of the Ugandan Martyrs were attended June 3 by Cardinal Jozef Tomko, prefect of the Congregation for the Evangelization of Peoples, and thousands of the faithful. The celebrations in Kampala honored St. Charles Lwanga and 12 other Catholics who were killed in 1886 by King Mwanga of Buganda for voicing disapproval of immorality and refusing to renounce their faith and the practice of Christian virtue. At a Mass of thanksgiving, the cardinal declared that there is no contradiction between being a good Christian and a good citizen.

Reconciliation Plea in Sri Lanka — The bishops and superiors of men Religious in Sri Lanka issued a plea April 14 for reconciliation and peace to end ethnic tensions between Tamils and Sinhalese. They said "racism and hatred" kept increasing in the nation, and that an "outburst of rhetoric on all sides" had taken the place "of serious, practical, political negotiations." The churchmen's action was reported by the *Fides* mission news agency.

Fewer Missionaries for Thailand — The Thai government hoped to reduce the number of missionaries in the country by 10 percent annually until a "necessary level" is reached, according to Deputy Education Minister Sampan Thongsamak. He said the increasing number of missionaries was making it difficult for government officials to monitor the activities of foreigners. Catholic leaders had already been informed of the policy, said

Father Chamnian Kitcharoen, secretary to Cardinal Kitbunchu of Bangkok.

Nicaraguan Developments — In a statement released June 9, the bishops were critical of parts of a proposed new constitution, with respect to such provisions as:

• "The right of Nicaraguans to build a family is recognized. This may be accomplished through marriage or through cohabitation."

• "No one should use the invocation of religious beliefs or disciplines to elude the fulfillment of the laws or to impede others (in) the exercise of their duties." The bishops said this section was open to "misunderstandings and abuses."

On June 19, after eight months of occupation, the government returned to the Church stripped offices of the Catholic social agency in Managua.

Toward the end of the month, the government barred return to the country by Msgr. Bismarck Carballo, spokesman for the Archdiocese of Managua.

Soweto Commemoration Banned — South Africa's ban on public meetings to commemorate June 16 the 10th anniversary of the Soweto uprising in which about 700 people were killed, was called a "recipe for disaster" and "the latest government blunder," by Father Smangaliso Mkhatshwa, as violence continued in the country.

In other developments:

• More than 500 black refugees from violence in the Crossroads squatter camp were being housed by Catholic institutions, reported Archbishop Stephen Naidoo of Cape Town.

• Archbishop Denis Hurley of Durban, speaking June 13 in Washington, said South Africa's declaration of a state of emergency and the hundreds of arrests and searches that followed "constitute one further stage in the long, unwinding tale of conflict between apartheid and liberation.'

Conflicts in Sudan — The president of the Sudanese Bishops' Conference sharply criticized divisions in Sudan which had led to civil war and had caused Christians, blacks and the poor to be treated as "second-class citizens." Archbishop Gabriel Zubeir Wako of Khartoum scored attempts of government authorities at "forced uniformity," including the imposition of Islamic law for all citizens. He said the Sudanese lacked freedom of expression and suffered from distorted information from government sources. The archbishop made these and other remarks in a speech reported in the June 17 edition of *L'Osservatore Romano*.

Vatican-China Difficulties — Chinese Communist Party Secretary Hu Yaobang, at a news conference June 21 in Rome, said that China was willing to discuss church-state relations with the Vatican "after we have overcome some difficulties." On the Chinese side, the difficulties seemed to be headed by Vatican diplomatic relations with Taiwan. On the Vatican side, difficulties included the imprisonment of numerous priests and government support for the National Association of Patriotic Catholics which rejects relations with the Holy See.

Divorce Voted Down in Ireland — Contrary to public opinion poll predictions, Irish voters downed June 26 a referendum proposal for the legalization of divorce. Bishop Joseph Cassidy of Clonfert, commenting on the outcome of the election, said it meant that the Church must have an "increased understanding of marriage problems and a willingness to respond to them. . . . On behalf of the Catholic Church, I can promise continued expansion and improvement of our service to marriage, especially to those in difficulty. While the Church already commits substantial human and financial resources to the support of marriage and the family, we must intensify our efforts in the years ahead."

Land Reform in Brazil — A special meeting on land reform between President Jose Sarney and the head of the Brazilian Bishops' Conference apparently satisfied demonstrators camped in front of the presidential palace in Brasilia. Sarney had refused to meet with more than 300 rural workers pressing for reforms, but Bishop Jose Ivo Lorschieter of Santa Maria presented their demands to the president on June 26. The bishop said Sarney listened attentively and promised action on their requests in his program for land reform. Many of the protesters were former parishioners of Father Josino Moraes Tavares, who was murdered in May shortly before he was due to become head of a pastoral land commission. Government statistics showed that 1.2 percent of the farmers controlled 45.8 percent of the arable land in Brazil; 50 percent of the farmers worked only 2.4 percent of the land.

International Briefs:

• The bishops of Cuba appealed to the Reagan administration to permit U.S. entry for 75 prisoners whose release had been offered by the Cuban government.

• New Zealand Brother Kevin Lawlor, O.F.M., 31, on his first missionary assignment, was shot and killed in Uganda late in the month.

• The bishops of Poland challenged the government to declare jailed dissidents and banned Solidarity activists as political prisoners, saying June 30: "Social and legal measures must be introduced which prevent political discrimination and bring about a lasting solution to the problem of (300) political prisoners."

Report Dissent in Context

As Father Charles E. Curran's dissent from church teaching was making headlines in the U.S., the head of the Pontifical Commission for Social Communications declared that Catholic newspapers must report on dissent in the Church, but should always do so within "the context of what Catholic teaching truly is. . . . "Dissent must be reported," said Archbishop John P. Foley. "Not to do so would be a failure to recognize reality and could possibly undermine the credibility of the (diocesan) newspaper." At the same time, "Catholic newspapers should defend the teaching of the Church and should place reports in the context of what official Catholic teaching truly is." Archbishop Foley spoke June 20 at a meeting of the Italian Federation of Catholic Weekly Newspapers.

JULY 1986

VATICAN

Angels — The existence and role of angels in salvation history were subjects of the Pope's address at a general audience July 9. He stated: "All of the Church's tradition is unanimous in affirming that they do exist. One would have to alter Sacred Scripture itself if one wished to eliminate this teaching." Although angels are not the heart of revelation — "that is, the truth about God and about the salvation of all men and women" — the truth about them is "inseparable" from this revelation. He said that "at certain points in salvation history angels have had a fundamental role to play in the unfolding of human events."

In recapitulating major points of belief about angels, the Holy Father said July 23: "The angels are purely spiritual beings, created by God and given intelligence and free will. Through an immediate intuition of the truth, their intelligence grasps its object in a way that is much more complete than is possible for man. . . . The world of the pure spirits is divided into good angels and bad ones. And this division has happened precisely as a result of their freedom to choose. God was present to their intelligence and free will as the supreme good. He also wished to give them, through grace, a share in the mystery of his divinity. The good angels have chosen God. But the others . . . have turned against God and the revelation of his grace. Their decision was inspired by a false sense of self-sufficiency, and it emerges as hatred and rebellion against God."

Avoid Partisan Politics — "The Church is not called to take positions of a political character or to take part in partisan conflicts," Pope John Paul told bishops of the Philippines in a letter released July 14. He said: "The Church in the Philippines cannot forget that a large portion of the population finds itself living in economic and social conditions that are extremely difficult and at times unbearable. . . . Preferential love for the poor . . . must be one of the principal lines of action." But this ministry must "be in conformity with the nature of the mission of the Church, which is not of the temporal but of the spiritual order; not of the social, political or economic order, but of the religious one." The Pontiff encouraged the bishops "to stimulate the preparation of lay persons to assume their responsibilities . . . in the political construction and organization of social life."

Social Doctrine and Evangelization — The Pope urged Colombians to put the Church's social doctrine into effect in the work of evangelizing their country. For Christ's message of peace to prevail, he said at a general audience July 16, "a complete and coordinated evangelization in the spirit of the social doctrine of the Church is necessary." Such evangelization should involve activities in support of social justice, the safeguarding of personal, family and community rights, and a better balance between the rich and the poor. "The most obvious of (Colombia's) problems are the great contrast between rich and poor, and the scourge of the drug traffic, a death-dealing business in the hands of people who do not reflect the true soul of the people." He also condemned the "deplorable phenomenon of the guerrilla war, which is the source of much suffering and of much bloodshed."

Appeal for Reconciliation — The Pope supported July 16 a call by the bishops of Peru for dialogue and national reconciliation after 250 convicts were killed by government troops putting down riots in three prisons; most of the dead belonged to *Sendero Luminoso,* the Shining Path guerrilla organization. He called the incidents "a brusque and sudden aggravation" of existing problems, causing an "intensification of political and social tensions." He also said: "It is important that the institutions entrusted with guarding public order and the administration of justice, the mission of which is the defense of life and of the legal system, should succeed in inspiring the confidence of the population." Christians recognize the need to fight for social justice, but to do so "through understanding, dialogue, effective and generous work, and social harmony — excluding solutions by means of hate and death."

The Pope Also:
- Said dialogue is the only true alternative to violence and war, in a message to an international conference July 2 to 4 in Rome.
- Appealed for the safe return of 10 cloistered Carmelite nuns who were kidnapped by armed men July 11 in the Philippines.
- Said Religious who overwork themselves in pastoral tasks run the risk of becoming spiritually empty, in an address to the Brazilian Conference of Religious, meeting July 21 to 26 in Sao Paolo.
- Condemned bombings in Madrid, July 14, and Beirut, July 28 and 29, in which nearly 70 people were killed and more than 210 wounded.

Extremist Influence Denied — Cardinal Joseph Ratzinger, addressing the bishops of Peru July 22 in Lima, denied that the Congregation for the Doctrine of the Faith was "excessively influenced" by extremists. Rather, he said, the congregation's "reliable sources of information are the bishops, the nunciatures and published works." He explained: "Often it is said that the congregation lets itself be excessively influenced by anonymous denunciations or by groups which are more or less extremist. . . . The congregation never takes an initiative based solely on confirmed private information." Procedures are geared toward "sufficient control so as to eliminate everything which is purely subjective and private, and so that partisan tendencies of one side or the other are not favored." He also said: "It is our desire that, when possible, problems be resolved in the local church." The Vatican becomes involved, however, when issues "go beyond the limit of a determined geographical or cultural area and, as a result, cannot be treated solely by a bishop or by a single bishops' conference."

Vatican Briefs:
- Publication was announced July 15 of a new,

simplified third edition of *Enchiridion Indulgentiarum* ("Manual of Indulgences").

• An article by *Fides* criticized political instability and international pricing systems as major contributing factors in widespread famine in Africa.

• *L'Osservatore Romano* strongly condemned July 20 a resurgence of terrorism in Europe, calling it a product of "ideological hallucination."

• A front-page editorial in the July 27 edition of *L'Osservatore Romano* said that calling abortion a matter of women's rights was "adolescent confusion" resulting from a "pseudo-liberated" mentality.

Visit to Colombia and Saint Lucia

Pope John Paul, on the 30th foreign pastoral tour of his pontificate July 1 to 7, visited 11 cities of Colombia and the island nation of Saint Lucia. His itinerary included 35 meetings, Masses and other ceremonial events. One of the special events was his consecration of the people of Colombia to Our Lady of the Rosary at the national shrine at Chinquinquirá. (See separate entry.)

NATIONAL

Liberty Weekend — Early events of Liberty Weekend took place July 3 at St. Patrick's Cathedral, New York, with the celebration of Mass, the ringing of a replica of the Liberty Bell and the playing of a videotaped message from Pope John Paul. During the observance of the 100th anniversary of the Statue of Liberty, the Holy Father said: "My prayer today is that the Statue of Liberty, that gift from the people of France to the people of the United States, may continue to serve not only as a symbol of hope but also as a symbol of faith."

Appointee to Theological Commission — William May, a professor of theology at The Catholic University of America, was named by Pope John Paul a member of the International Theological Commission. He and British theologian John Finnis became the first two laymen on the commission.

Pro-Life Violence Denounced — Archbishop Rembert G. Weakland of Milwaukee denounced anti-abortion protests involving violence and the destruction of property as "morally unacceptable," and termed "inappropriate" the picketing of the homes of doctors who perform abortions. Writing in the July 10 edition of the archdiocesan newspaper, *The Catholic Herald,* he said it should be clear that he opposed abortion, and added: "The question is not about the morality of the issue, but about what kind of public protests or gestures can help alter our present legal situation."

Retirement Aid for Nuns — Archbishop Ignatius J. Strecker announced July 11 that the Archdiocese of Kansas City, Kan., would provide $5.2 million to help meet the retirement costs of nuns serving the archdiocese. He said the congregations of nuns would share $1,273,654 in immediate relief and another $4 million over 10 years, for a total of $5,273,654.

Mercy Sisters' Decisions — Delegates to a general chapter of the Sisters of Mercy of the Union approved Core Constitutions proposed as the basis for uniting the Sisters of Mercy of the Union and 17 other Mercy congregations in the Western Hemisphere. They also reaffirmed commitment to political ministry, which had led to departure from the order of three of their members in recent years: Arlene Violet, attorney general of Rhode Island; Elizabeth Morancy, four-term member of the Rhode Island Legislature, and Agnes Mansour, director of the Michigan Department of Social Services. The general chapter was held July 22 to 27 in Baltimore.

One Church, One Child — Through the One Church, One Child program he started less than six years earlier, Father George Clements, a Chicago inner-city pastor, was credited with being instrumental in bringing about at least 5,000 adoptions of black children in 23 states.

WME Convention — More than 1,700 couples and their nearly 2,300 children were joined by 150 priests and eight bishops at the Mass which concluded the national convention of Worldwide Marriage Encounter July 18 to 20 in Tampa. Pope John Paul, in a special message, expressed appreciation for the efforts of WME and similar movements "to inspire married couples with a true Christian vision of their vocation to marriage and family life." He contrasted such efforts with those of "the materialistic and consumerist civilization which strips marital and family love of its deepest human and divine content." He said the vocation of married persons is a call to holiness which must include "an ethic of conjugal and family life" as "an essential element."

Aid for AIDS Sufferers — Catholic attention to the AIDS crisis and church programs to help its victims were on the increase, with the development of educational and service programs in places including California (Los Angeles, San Diego, San Bernardino, San Francisco), Kentucky, Cleveland, Detroit, Washington, D.C., and New York. As of July 14, the federal Centers for Disease Control in Atlanta reported 22,635 AIDS sufferers since the start of data collection in 1981; 12,422 of them had died.

CRS Activity the Most Ever — Response to drought in Ethiopia and other parts of Africa brought activity of Catholic Relief Services to the highest level ever in 1985, according to a report issued July 23. It reported total income of $499 million and total disbursements of $471 million. Reported disbursements included: $258 million for development, $125 million for emergency relief, $60 million for general welfare and $15 million for refugee work. Although Ethiopia and Africa generally were a major focus of activity in 1985, CRS responded to needs in other areas as well; for example, to Mexico City, shattered by earthquake, and Colombia where mudslides destroyed whole villages.

Father Jenco Freed — Father Lawrence M. Jenco, kidnapped and held hostage for almost 19 months by Shiite Moslems, was released by his captors July 26 and flown from Lebanon to the U.S.

Air Force hospital at Wiesbaden, West Germany, where he underwent a physical examination and was reunited with members of his family. He spent the first six months of his captivity chained to a wall, in solitary confinement; the rest of the time, he was with several other American hostages. After being released, he expressed gratitude to God and those who had worked to gain his freedom. He was happy to learn that Catholic Relief Services, of which he was a staff member, was continuing its operations in Lebanon. Within a week of his release, he met with Pope John Paul, Anglican Archbishop Robert Runcie and President Reagan. He was welcomed home to Joliet, Ill., Aug. 2 and 3.

Sexual Orientation Bill Rejected — The Chicago City Council July 29 voted down a proposal which would have changed civil rights law to forbid discrimination because of "sexual orientation." The 30-to-18 defeat of "sexual orientation" amendments came after a three-week delay in voting which Cardinal Joseph L. Bernardin provoked when he issued a public statement on the proposal July 8. He said he backed civil rights for homosexuals and could support legislation in line with criteria spelled out by his fellow bishops of Illinois. He could not back the proposal as it was written, however, because it was too vague and did not clearly protect the right of the Church to "present and practice its moral teaching" on homosexuality. "The term 'sexual orientation' is not defined in the amendments and, therefore, may be interpreted to imply acceptance or approval of homosexual activity or of a homosexual lifestyle," he said.

Bishops Refuse Meeting with Ortega — Officials of the U.S. Catholic Conference refused to meet with Nicaraguan President Daniel Ortega during his visit to the United Nations late in the month. Spokesman Russell Shaw said their decision "was based on concern" over the "unresolved" situation of Bishop Pablo Antonio Vega and Msgr. Bismarck Carballo, both of whom were in effect exiled from Nicaragua.

National Briefs:

• Sister of Mercy Maura Feeley was named chancellor of the Diocese of San Bernardino; she was the fifth woman to become a diocesan chancellor in California.

• Sixteen hundred Sisters of St. Joseph, representing more than 13,000 others, took part in a variety of ceremonies late in June in St. Louis to mark the 150th anniversary of the arrival of the first members of their community in St. Louis from France, according to a delayed report.

• Daniel J. Kane, former director of communications for the Archdiocese of Cincinnati, was the recipient of the first Religious Communications Award of the University of Dayton.

• A four-cent postage stamp commemorating the centennial of the birth of Father Edward J. Flanagan was issued July 14 at Boys Town, which he founded.

• One priest offering spiritual guidance and service to illegal aliens and another offering them legal assistance were overwhelmed by the needs of inmates at an isolated, controversial detention center in rural Louisiana.

Birth Control Clinics in Schools

Efforts nationwide to increase the number of school health clinics distributing birth control information or contraceptives were being opposed by church leaders and pro-life groups. Attempts were under way to multiply the three to four dozen clinics in U.S. high schools which already included sex education and contraceptives among their services, according to Richard Doerflinger, assistant director of the bishops' Committee for Pro-Life Activites. In Florida, Illinois and California, however, clinic proposals were reported halted, at least temporarily.

• Bishops in Florida said in a pastoral letter that public school programs on sexuality had failed to stem "the high incidence of teen-age pregnancies, premarital sex and promiscuity, venereal disease, abortion and the rising rate of sex-oriented crimes. . . . Instead of developing a sense of moral and personal control, (clinics) offer contraceptives, information on birth control and referral for abortion."

• In Illinois, Cardinal Joseph L. Bernardin said he opposed providing contraceptives to teen-agers not only on moral grounds, but also because "it simply doesn't work. . . . There is no reason to think more and better contraception will help teenagers grow up as sexually mature adults. It is a cheap solution that will not work and that, if it did work, would not meet the real developmental needs of teen-agers searching for their sexual identity."

• In San Diego, where the school board discontinued further study of school-based clinics, Bishop Leo T. Maher praised the many citizens "who expressed so vocally their opinion that these . . . clinics undermine parental authority and religious values."

INTERNATIONAL

Religion, Opium of the People — "Religion is (still) the opium of the people," according to the ideology of the Chinese Communist Party, declared Jiang Ping, vice director of the State Council's United Front Department. Writing in the party's theoretical journal, *Hongqi,* he said: "The men of the Communist Party are atheists. They . . . firmly believe that religion will eventually wither away. . . . We do not agree with the view that 'religion's being the opium of the people' is now obsolete. Nor do we approve, on the one hand, of using Marxism to study religion while, on the other hand, obstinately wanting to use Marxism to adapt to and satisfy the faith of religious believers." It appeared that Ping's article was written in response to a challenge made against the classical Marxist position on religion at the 1985 meeting of the Chinese People's Political Consultative Committee.

No Reentry for Priest — The government of Paraguay announced July 3 that it had forbidden reentry to Spanish Franciscan Father Javier Arancon, director of Radio Charitas in Asuncion. Guillermo Yaluf, a spokesman for the station, said the staff believed the move against the priest stemmed from the station's coverage of political and labor unrest in April and May. "(Father) Arancon and I received anonymous death threats, warning us to stop reporting these events," Yaluf said. "(Father) Arancon refused, preventing any censorship, and that is why we think they will not let him enter now." A politician opposed to the regime of President Alfredo Stroessner said Father Arancon's banishment was "a demonstration that more than just press freedom is missing in Paraguay; the government also does not respect fundamental human rights."

Lithuanian Priest Murdered — The underground *Chronicle of the Catholic Church in Lithuania* reported that the automobile accident in which Father Juozas Zdebskis was killed Feb. 5 was "a carefully planned and executed act of violence." He had been under surveillane by secret police for more than 20 years and had been repeatedly threatened during that time. He was pastor of Holy Trinity Church in Rudamina and a founding member of the banned Catholic Committee for the Defense of Believers' Rights. He was imprisoned in 1971 to 1972 for teaching religion to children.

Action Delayed on Ordination of Women — The 574-member General Synod of the Church of England decided July 8 to postpone for six months action on the ordination of women. There was fear that approval of ordination might split the church. About 750 women had been ordained in various provinces of the Anglican Communion, but none by the mother Church of England.

End Sought to Military Government — The bishops of Chile, at the conclusion of a meeting July 11 and 12, asked for an end to the military government of Gen. Pinochet and expressed support for 15 jailed opposition leaders. The bishops said "the militarization of national civic life is not suited to the nation." They added that a return to civilian government could bring an end to current violence in the country.

Wealth and Vocations — Cardinal Myroslav Ivan Lubachivsky, speaking in Toronto early in the month, said that vocations had declined in North America because its people had become "too rich." North Americans "prefer the easy, pleasurable life" over the sacrifice and restraint that vocations to the priesthood require. He added that young men would be more willing to respond to a call to the priesthood if their parents gave witness to a dynamic Christian life and implanted the same conviction in their hearts. The cardinal cited a study released in April by the Vatican's Central Office of Church Statistics which indicated that the smallest increase of major seminarians was reported in the United States, Canada and Western Europe.

Religious Intolerance — Angelo d'Almeida Ribeiro, a special investigator of the United Nations, said in a Vatican Radio interview July 17 that religious intolerance was a fact in a number of countries, including Northern Ireland, Iran, Lebanon, India and countries of Eastern Europe.

Seventh Sandinist Anniversary — As the Sandinist government of Nicaragua celebrated July 19 the seventh anniversary of the overthrow of the regime of Gen. Anastasio Somoza, pressure against the Church was reported on the increase. It included the deportation of priests, the muzzling of church communications, efforts to alienate the people from the bishops, and the recent exiling of Msgr. Bismarck Carballo (in the U.S.) and Bishop Pablo Antonio Vega (in Honduras). The worst of the human toll of the revolution was the number of victims of continuing civil war — some 13,000 dead and other thousands wounded and injured.

Training Center in Quito — The purpose of the Working Boys' Center in Quito is to counteract a "general trend" in impoverished Ecuador and other Latin American countries "toward a gradual conversion of working boys into non-working aliens from their own family groups and from society." So stated Jesuit Father John J. Halligan, director for 22 years of a program of vocational and social development for the urban poor of Quito.

School Agreement in Malta — A church-state agreement signed July 31 guaranteed 50 percent state financing of Cathoic high schools for the 1985-86 and following school years. The temporary accord eased economic pressure on the nation's Catholic high schools whose maintenance and operation had been threatened because of a 1984 legal prohibition against charging tuition. In the new accord, the government also agreed to amend the education law so that licenses to operate schools would be issued for an indefinite period instead of one year.

International Briefs:

• Mother Teresa announced July 8 in Havana that Fidel Castro had agreed to permit the Missionaries of Charity to establish a mission in Cuba.

• Bishop George Phimphisan of Udon Thani said that thousands of Indochinese refugees remained in Thailand with no hope of resettlement in other countries. "We must continue to care for them," he said.

• The bishops of Mozambique called for an immediate cease-fire in the country's 11-year civil war, and appealed to East and West bloc powers to stop supplying military aid in the country.

• Six days after being kidnapped July 11 on Minodanao, 10 Carmelite nuns were released by their Moslem captors.

Threat to Christianity in Middle East

"All of Christianity is threatened in Lebanon. If we don't do something, Christ will disappear from the Middle East." So stated Father John D. Faris, chancellor of the Diocese of St. Maron, during the annual convention of the National Apostolate of Maronite Catholics July 23 to 27 in Philadelphia. "For 11 years Lebanese Christians have fought to maintain their independenence; and yet, in the world's eyes, they have not died as heroes," said Msgr. John Esseff, former director of the Pontifical Mission in Lebanon. "The world is well informed about the Holocaust of six million Jews during the Third Reich. The world is thoroughly informed about the plight of the Palestinian refugees that came about after the establishment of Israel. . . . The world knows little or nothing of the suffering of Christians in Lebanon."

AUGUST 1986

VATICAN

Praise for Baltic Catholics — On separate occasions, the Pope praised Catholics in Latvia and Lithuania.

• In a letter Aug. 6 marking the introduction of Christianity in Latvia, he expressed his "communion in spirit" with the Church there in "this time of grace. He specifically praised catechetical efforts "aimed at awakening and reinvigorating that faith that you have inherited from your ancestors and which everyone is called to live and to transmit to future generations." He also praised the people for remaining "firm in the faith, courageous in hope and ardent in charity," despite "the difficulties" they have encountered.

• At Castel Gandolfo Aug. 31, the Pope lauded the "strong faith" of Lithuanian Catholics and urged parents to keep Christianity alive among the young. Whie observing that Lithuanians were celebrating the 600th anniversary of Christianity in their country, he said the people had maintained the faith despite "painful moments" in their history.

Bioethics and Patient Care — These were the subjects of a letter from the Pope to the president of the Pontifical Commission for Health Care Workers, in connection with the 16th World Congress of the International Federation of Catholic Medical Associations which met Aug. 8 to 12 in Buenos Aires. He said the federation brings about "an ever more effective Catholic involvement in health care and an ever more consistent witness of Catholic doctors with regard to today's extremely delicate challenges in the area of biomedical ethics." He cited an "impelling need" to ensure that human dignity and the sacredness of human life "are reaffirmed as the very center of health care and as the indispensable condition for progress in medicine." Because health care is becoming a major economic factor in many countries, the letter added that Catholic doctors should help make the full health of the person rather than financial considerations "the criterion by which progress in medicine is to be measured."

Concern for Imprisoned South African Priest — The Pope joined other Catholic leaders in expressing concern for an imprisoned black South African priest, and criticized "violence and abuse of power" in South Africa. The Pontiff said he was "deeply saddened at news of the detention and mistreatment of Father Smangaliso Mkhatshwa, secretary general of the Southern African Catholic Bishops' Conference." The priest had been held by the government since his arrest June 12. According to testimony given in court, he endured 30 hours of interrogation and torture during detention. The Pope also said in the message sent late in the month to the bishops' conference that it was his "fervent hope that the present violence and abuse of power will cease and that respect for personal dignity and legal guarantees will be ensured for all."

Mary's Assumption — By her assumption into heaven, Mary, who had an "extraordinary mission in the history of salvation," became a "great sign" of the covenant of salvation between God and mankind, said the Holy Father in a homily on the feast, Aug. 15.

Satan and Exorcism — The Pope concluded a series of talks Aug. 20 on "God, Creator of visible and invisible things," in which he referred to, among other things, the devil, good and bad angels, and their relationship to good and evil in Christian life. Satan's power is "not infinite," he said, but nevertheless it causes serious damage and in some cases might require exorcism. "The existence of bad angels requires of us a sense of vigilance, so we will not give in to their flattery." The devil, as "head of the demons," is a real power but has been "dethroned" by Christ with the assurance that good will triumph over evil. Christ "gave his disciples the power to cast out demons, . . . and the Church uses such victorious power through faith in Christ and through prayer, which in specific cases can assume the form of exorcism."

Sin and Salvation — One must understand the reality of sin in order to understand the true meaning of salvation, said the Pope during a general audience Aug. 27. Since salvation is primarily "liberation from sin," the truth about sin must be included in the "nucleus of the Christian faith." Sin must be viewed in the light of divine Providence, he said, adding: "Where sin increased, grace abounded all the more," in redemption through the death and resurrection of Christ. "The reality of sin becomes, in the light of redemption, the occasion for a more profound knowledge of the mystery of God. who is love."

Visit to Anagni — The Pope visited Anagni in southern Italy Aug. 31. During a Mass outside the city's 11th-century cathedral, he said that Christianity requires an "unselfish and concrete charity" of all its members. Christ demonstrated his "preference for the suffering," and "charity is still necessary, because the one who suffers is still among us." Christians have a special duty to help "all the humble of the world, the poor, the hungry, and the marginalized." Charity should be both a personal and social matter. Christians should be able to say at the end of each day that they have practiced charity in a definite way. Thousands of people cheered the Pope as he rode through the winding streets of the town, where Pope Boniface VIII in 1303 was humiliated by emissaries of King Philip the Fair when he was slapped across the face and held prisoner for three days.

The Pope Also:

• Said Aug. 3: "Let's thank the Lord for the liberation of Father Jenco (from Moslem hostages in Lebanon) and ask with trust that all the kidnapped may soon be released."

• Noted Aug. 13 the 25th anniversary of the construction of the Berlin Wall by commemorating its "victims."

• Expressed his sympathy for victims of the natural gas disaster Aug. 22 in Cameroon.

Said in a letter released Aug. 22: The Church has "prophetically warned against the dangers of an excessive concentration of political planning and economic interests in urban-industrial sectors, while rural areas remain unattended or action is delayed."

Vatican Briefs:

• A Vatican diplomat familiar with developments in Lebanon said the Pope had not authorized Terry Waite, an aide to Anglican Archbishop Robert Runcie, to speak for him regarding hostages in Lebanon.

• A 40 percent decline in the number of visitors to Vatican museums was attributed to fears of terrorism which deterred American and other tourists from traveling to Europe and, specifically, in Italy.

Apostolic Letter on St. Augustine

St. Augustine's fidelity to the doctrine of the Church is a model for 20th century theologians, said the Holy Father in an apostolic letter made public Aug. 26, two days before the feast of the great Father and Doctor of the Church. "We know," said the Pope, "that (his) method (in theology) included full adherence to the authority of the faith which, in its origin — the authority of Christ — is manifested through Scripture, tradition and the Church."

He noted that the fact St. Augustine lost his faith before struggling to rediscover it, makes his life an even more valuable lesson for people today. From early "errors" he progressed in faith and spiritual perfection to become one of the greatest theologians in the history of the Church.

NATIONAL

Labor Day Statement — "U.S. labor and welfare policies, along with employer practices, must meet the needs of the nation's changing labor force," said a Labor Day statement from the U.S. Catholic Conference. It said that a major item, among many others, on the public policy agenda is welfare reform, in which the family "must be at the center of discussion." The statement outlined five criteria for welfare reform that would protect human and family dignity: promotion of family stability, adequate levels of assistance, opportunity for healthy child development, support for eventual self-sufficiency and humane administration.

Worldwide Priests' Group — In line with a plan which emerged from a meeting Aug. 4 to 8 in Chicago, priests from many nations launched a movement for the establishment of an international support and liaison group that will foster a sense of brotherhood and develop their awareness of issues of worldwide significance. Sponsoring organizations included the National Federation of Priests' Councils, the National Conference of Priests of England, the National Federation of Councils of Priests of Canada, and the National Council of Priests of Australia.

Hispanic Ministry — Pablo Sedillo, executive director of the bishops' Secretariat for Hispanic Affairs, said Aug. 5 that the 1985 Third National Hispanic Pastoral Encuentro was succeeding in bringing diverse Hispanic groups together to face common problems and by making the Church more aware of the need to include Hispanics in all areas of ministry. He also reported progress in the development of a national ministry program to be voted on by the National Conference of Catholic Bishops in November.

Opposition to Contra Aid — The general secretary of the U.S. Catholic Conference urged the Senate to reject a proposed $70 million in U.S. military aid to anti-government guerrillas in Nicaragua. "We deplore the recent vote in the House of Representatives approving such aid, and urge that the Senate exhibit the superior wisdom of rejecting it," said Msgr. Daniel F. Hoye in a letter Aug. 7. (The Senate subsequently voted in favor of the aid.)

In New York, Cardinal John J. O'Connor said Aug. 4 that the U.S. bishops were denouncing oppression in Nicaragua with "much stronger statements" than before. He also said their position would reflect the Nicaraguan bishops' statement of Aug. 6, which said: "It is our judgment that any kind of help, whatever the source, that leads to the destruction, sorrow and death of our families, to hatred and division between Nicaraguans, is to be condemned."

Abortion Funding — The Senate Appropriations Committee, proposing a change in a five-year-old federal policy on abortion funding (danger of maternal death cases only) voted 13 to 12 Aug. 15 to allow funding in cases of rape and incest. Such funding had been cut off by Congress since adoption of the Hyde Amendment in 1981 and subsequent years. The committee action was called "a great disappointment" by Father Edward M. Bryce, director of the bishops' Office for Pro-Life Activities. He said "the committee's 'rape-incest' amendment was worded to create a vast loophole in abortion funding policy — providing, for example, free abortions for whatever reason to young teenagers in every state with a 'statutory rape' law (affecting sexual relations with a girl below the age of consent).

In other developments:

• Cardinal Joseph L. Bernardin urged the Senate to reject support for contraceptive research and for high school programs that "enforce use" of contraceptives.

• The federal Agency for International Development decided to cut off all U.S. funding of the U.N. Fund for Population Activities because it condoned China's alleged practice of forced abortion.

Excommunication of Two Vietnamese — Bishop Pierre DuMaine of San Jose excommunicated two Vietnamese men, saying their leadership of a group opposed to the status of their mission and its new pastor had spread dissension and division in the Vietnamese community. The men headed a group seeking to establish a "personal parish" determined by ethnic identity rather than geographical boundaries in place of the year-old Vietnamese Catholic Mission. They also rejected the bishop's appointment of a new pastor. In letters to Bai An Tran and Thien Cong Tran Aug. 18, the bishop said: Because of "your continued incitement of our confused and suffering Vietnamese Catholics, to the point of invading our cathedral church, interfering with the celebration of Mass and depriving our people of the Eucharist, . . . I consider that you have separated yourselves from the Catholic family." He said he would lift the penalty if the two men would publicly acknowledge Father Paul Duong as pastor and would "cease obstructing his ministry and inciting our people against him."

Jimmy Swaggart: Anti-Catholic — In a series of 17 weekly columns appearing in Lafayette (La.)-area newspapers during the summer, Father Richard Greene called fundamentalist evangelist the Rev. Jimmy Swaggart "today's most anti-Catholic TV personality" and a preacher who "deliberately distorts" Catholic teaching and "bears false witness" against the Catholic Church. Father Greene, a doctor of theology and campus minister at the University of Southwestern Louisiana, focused his criticisms on an eight-part series of articles by Mr. Swaggart published between July, 1985, and February, 1986, in his nationally circulated magazine, *The Evangelist.* In the series, Mr. Swaggart falsely accused Catholics of worshiping Mary, saints and images, and of blocking God's word by establishing such things as the Eucharist, the confessional, the papacy, the priesthood and a "two-source" theory of revelation.

Lutheran Merger — Three Lutheran churches voted overwhelmingly Aug. 29 to merge into a single, more diverse and more effective denomination of 5.3 million members. The merging churches were the Lutheran Church in America, the American Lutheran Church and the Association of Evangelical Lutheran Churches. The name of the new denomination, to begin functioning Jan. 1, 1988, is the Evangelical Lutheran Church in America.

Meetings — Meetings during the month included those of the following organizations.

• The Knights of Columbus, Aug. 5 to 7 in Chicago.

• The Conference of Major Superiors of Men, Aug. 10 to 14 in St. Louis.

• Pax Christi USA, Aug. 15 to 17 in Boston.

• The Leadership Conference of Women Religious, Aug. 24 to 26 in Milwaukee.

National Briefs:

• In New York, Franciscan Fathers John Felice and John McVean took legal possession Aug. 7 of a rundown building to be renovated and operated as a 90-room shelter for homeless, mentally ill persons.

• An intensive effort to unite New Yorkers in a campaign against drugs was launched by Cardinal John J. O'Connor Aug. 7 with an evening prayer vigil and rally in front of St. Patrick's Cathedral.

• Joseph Lichten, a representative of the Anti-Defamation League of B'nai B'rith in Rome since 1971, was named by Pope John Paul a Knight Commander of the Order of St. Gregory the Great.

• In Miami, St. Thomas University established a Center for Catholic Evangelism as part of its graduate program in pastoral ministries.

• Jesuit Father Terrance A. Sweeney signed a formal decree of dismissal from the order Aug. 15

in Los Angeles rather than comply with an order to destroy findings of his survey of the views of Catholic bishops on priestly celibacy and the ordination of women to the priesthood.

• Cardinal Joseph L. Bernardin called the Marist Brothers "a precious gift" to the Church as they celebrated the 100th anniversary of their educational work in the U.S., Aug. 15 to 18 in Poughkeepsie, N.Y.

No Curran Retraction

After being informed by the Congregation for the Doctrine of the Faith that he would "no longer be considered suitable nor eligible to exercise the function of a professor of Catholic theology," Father Charles E. Curran said in a statement Aug. 20: "In conscience at the present time, I cannot and do not change the theological positions I have taken. In my own judgment and in the judgment of a majority of my peers, I have been and am suitable and eligible to exercise the function of a professor of Catholic theology." (See separate entry, The Curran Controversy.)

INTERNATIONAL

Missionaries Freed — Missionary superiors reported Aug. 6 that three nuns, held by anti-government guerrillas for several months in Mozambique, had been released unharmed. Two other nuns, Americans, were released by Sudanese guerrillas July 24. The Comboni missionaries reported that two of their priests were released Aug. 15 by anti-government rebels in Sudan.

Unacceptable Plan for an Islamic State — The Pan-Malayan Islamic Party's plan to make Malaysia an Islamic state was called unacceptable by a coalition of non-Moslem groups. Jesuit Father Paul Tan, honorary secretary of the Malaysian Consultative Council for Buddhism, Christianity, Hinduism and Sikhism, said that, as religious leaders upholding "parliamentary democracy as enshrined in our constitution," the group's members were "against any attempt to set up an Islamic state." Buddhist Rev. Seet Kim Beng, chairman of the Moslem Council, said it would be unjust to force all parties to uphold Islam as the true way of life. Bishop James Chan Soon Cheong of Malaka-Johore said: "An Islamic state means that only Moslems can be trusted. It is a postion which only Moslems can accept. There is no fairness in this."

Impressive U.S. Religious Practice — Cardinal Jean-Marie Lustiger of Paris, writing about his visit to the United States Apr. 26 to May 10, said U.S. Catholics have "an impressive rate of religious practice" and are "in the front line" facing the challenges confronting American society. "Today, of all Western societies, it seems to me that the United States is the most religious. I say, 'the most religious.' I do not say, 'the most faithful to the demands of Christianity.' "

Imprimatur Removed from Bioethics Book — The Archdiocese of Westminster announced it had withdrawn the imprimatur from a book on bioethics written by one of Great Britain's leading moral theologians, Jesuit Father John Mahoney. People "from various quarters" told archdiocesan officials that *Bioethics and Belief,* published in 1984, contained material contrary to church teaching, according to a statement issued by Father Mahoney and Msgr. Ralph Brown, vicar general of the archdiocese. The material at issue was at variance with church teaching on abortion and experimentation on human embryos. Withdrawal of the imprimature left firm Father Mahoney's attitude "of deep respect for the teaching of the Church and its authority."

Concern for the Poor — Concern for the poor was the reason for gains of the Catholic Church in Indonesia during the previous two decades, according to the country's largest Islamic magazine, *Panji Masyarakat.* The magazine also said that, unless Moslems paid more attention to poverty, unemployment and injustice, the Church would become more influential and convert many poor people.

Support for Canadian Fur Trappers — Catholic and Anglican bishops in northern Canada announced their support of Indian fur trappers against campaigns threatening their livelihood. They urged the government to expand domestic and international fur markets and to press the European Economic Community to lift its ban on seal products. The anti-fur campaign in Europe and elsewhere, they said, "poses a direct threat to aboriginal peoples and their way of life in the North. . . . Contrary to charges made by campaign activists, aboriginal peoples are not out to destroy the animal population." The statement was signed by Archbishop Peter Sutton of Keewatin-LePas and Bishop Jack Sperry, chairman of the Anglican Council of the North.

Drug Traffic in Mexico — Bishops in southern Mexico charged federal officials with "complicity" in a sophisticated system of illegal cultivation of and traffic in narcotics. The nine bishops of Chiapas and Oaxaca also warned in a pastoral letter, their fourth on the subject, that the traffic "could lead us in no time toward a generalized social disaster, given that each day the amount of arable land dedicated to cultivating drugs is increasing." In the letter, entitled "Narcotics Trafficking, A Pastoral Concern," they said drug traffickers in southern Mexico had a network for providing seed, credit, fertilizers and transport "which would be impossible without the complicity of high state and federal officials."

Irresponsible Accusations — Lebanon's Maronite patriarchate issued a statement during the month in response to accusations by Nabih Berri, head of the Shiite Moslem militia, that the Vatican had been responsible for delaying efforts to end the Lebanese civil war. The statement said the patriarchate did not want "to get involved in a polemic" with Berri, but told him "he had better prove his accusations with facts and review the Vatican's documents, read them deeply and understand their content, before he launches fancy accusations." The statement also noted that Pope John Paul had addressed messages and appeals for peace and reconciliation to all Christians and to all Lebanese, as well as Maronites.

100 Days of Prayer — The bishops of the Philip-

pines endorsed a call by Cardinal Jaime Sin for 100 days of prayer for reconciliation and unity in the country. Their action was prompted by a pastoral letter of July 1 in which the cardinal urged such an observance by the people of the Archdiocese of Manila. The period of prayer was set for Aug. 22 to Nov. 27. Prayer intentions noted by the cardinal were that: the nation's constitution would be wise and just; local and national elections would be held soon to confirm the legitimacy of the Aquino government; churches will work together and with the government to confront and respond positively to problems of the country.

Protest against Torture of Priest — The reported torture of a prominent black South African priest drew international Catholic protest and intensified efforts by the bishops' conference there to gain his release from detention. The government promised a Pretoria appeals court Aug. 28 that it would not torture Father Smangaliso Mkhatshwa, secretary general of the bishops' conference, but would not admit that he had been abused. The bishops planned to ask the court for the priest's release, arguing that his detention was illegal because he was tortured. Meanwhile, protests against the treatment of the priest were registered in the United States, England and Scotland.

International Briefs:

• A recent poll found that support for abortion in Italy was declining, although a large majority remained in favor of legalized abortion in some cases.

• More than 100 church leaders and missionaries endorsed a letter calling for an end to U.S. military aid to the Philippines. In a letter of concern, they said: "Though cloaked in terms of promotion of democracy for Filipinos, policies aimed at preserving American military bases and commercial interests in the Philippines have actually been detrimental to the Philippines and its peoples."

• The sixth anniversary of Solidarity, the banned labor union movement in Poland, was observed at the end of the month.

Lefebvre Seminary in France

Dissident Archbishop Marcel Lefebvre planned to open a major seminary in southern France at Flavigny-sur-Ozerain Oct. 5 during Pope John Paul's visit to the neighboring towns of Paray-le-Monial and Taize, according to Father Jean Coache, administrator of the school. He said the seminary would accommodate 120 students and that the first 40 would be from France, Australia, white South Africa and Zimbabwe. Archbishop Lefebvre was suspended from the exercise of holy orders in 1976 for the unauthorized ordination of priests; since that time, he has rejected enactments of the Second Vatican Council and flaunted the authority of the Pope. He was the founder of the dissident Priestly Society of St. Pius X.

In a related development, Vatican Radio reported Aug. 23 the return to "full communion" with the Church of a French Benedictine community which had been associated with Archbishop Lefebvre and his rejection of Vatican II.

SEPTEMBER 1986

VATICAN

The Challenge of Science — "The contemporary vision of the cosmos, the conception of time and space, the abundant discoveries in physics, chemistry and biology, call for a new formulation of Christian anthropology and a renewal of philosophical thought among Christians." So stated the Holy Father at a meeting Sept. 5 with theologians, philosophers and scientists at Castel Gandolfo. He added that sometimes the scientific method and Christian belief are "difficult to harmonize." He offered the Bible as an example, but said its theological lessons "teach us less the 'how' of things than the 'why.'" For Christians, the "why" includes providential design, grace and redemption.

Mountain Weekend — The Pope spoke about a variety of subjects during the Sept. 6 and 7 weekend in northern Italy.

• Terrorism: He condemned the hijacking Sept. 5 of a Pan American airliner in Karachi, which resulted in the deaths of 18 persons and the wounding of more than 200, and the murder Sept. 6 of 21 worshippers at a synagogue in Istanbul.

• Spiritual Heritage of Europe: Europeans must "overcome anachronistic tensions and old-fashioned conceptions" to rediscover "the values which have made their history great." The future of Europe is to develop "the best classical humanism, elevated and enriched by Christian revelation. . . . Europe is a family of peoples united by ties of a common religious heritage."

• Priests and Religious: He urged them to study daily, "taking into account the official documents of the Church's teaching authority."

• Army Officers: "Your primary responsibility is called a commitment to peace. . . . Military life has its moral foundation in the demand to defend the spiritual and material goods of the national community. . . . This defense . . . is a prerequisite for peace and concord among nations."

Disobedience, the Model of All Sin — This was the subject of the Pope's remarks during a general audience Sept. 10. "We continue our reflection on how sin entered human history, as described in the third chapter of Genesis. We take into account the literary form of the text, but we cannot deny that it describes an event or action which happened at the very beginning of history. As a consquence of this original act of sin, there has been a fundamental change in the human condition. Our relationships with God, with ourselves and with others are marked by an inclination to sin. Following divine revelation, the Church teaches that our first parents enjoyed a privileged friendship with God which was meant not only for themselves but for the whole human race. But, when they disobeyed God, they were deprived of this sanctifying grace, and so were all their descendants.

"We see in Genesis how the woman talks with the tempter who is presented as a serpent, although in fact he belongs to the world of invisible spiritual beings. Later, in the Book of Revelation, he will be described as 'the great dragon, the ancient serpent, who is called the devil or Satan, the deceiver of the whole world.' He persuades the woman to eat of the fruit of the tree of the knowledge of good and evil, and says: 'You will not die. For God knows when you eat of it your eyes will be opened, and you will be like God, knowing good and evil.'

"This temptation expresses well the basic problem of our desire to be 'like God, knowing good and evil.' But this problem is linked with our condition of being limited creatures. God alone is the eternal lawgiver from whom every law and in particular the natural law derives. We cannot claim to decide for ourselves what is good and what is evil.

"With St. Paul we can say that the first sin of our race consisted in disobedience to God. And this first sin of humanity is the original 'model' of every sin."

Need for Re-Evangelization — "A new evangelization is necessary, above all in countries that have a long Christian cultural tradition," said the Pope in a message to German Catholics taking part in the *Katholikentag* Sept. 10 to 14 in Aachen. In the message, he said the conference theme, "Your Kingdom Come," suggested the coming of the kingdom of God. He continued: In this century many ideologies have promised perfect happiness and peace, but "the consequences were blood and tears, conflicts and death." The pursuit of human omnipotence in today's highly industrialized world has resulted in a widespread sense of "resignation and a bitter negation of the future." The only alternative to the delusion of human omnipotence is "hope in the future of God, in his kingdom that will come.'

He also said there was a growing gap in Christian countries between the Christian message and the behavior of Christians. Specific signs of the need for re-evangelization include immoral behavior, decreasing participation in the sacraments, the lack of vocations to the priesthood, and the failure of Catholic families to pass on the faith to the next generation. The Pope expressed hope that the conference would "be the impulse for a new evangelization."

NATIONAL

Archbishop's Authority Curbed — Archbishop Raymond Hunthausen of Seattle announced Sept. 4 that, at the request of the Holy See, he was delegating to Auxiliary Bishop Donald Wuerl complete, final authority over archdiocesan matters in the areas of liturgy, the tribunal, formation of seminarians and priests, laicized priests, and moral issues of health care and ministry to homosexuals. Following is the text of Archbishop Hunthausen's statement.

"I am aware that for quite some time speculation has taken place, both in printed form and in less formal ways, regarding the roles and responsibilities of Bishop Donald Wuerl. His appointment here shortly after the formal conclusion of the apostolic visitation (1983 to 1985) made it inevitable that people would wonder whether, in appointing him as my auxiliary, the Holy See had not also intended for him to have some specific additional responsibilities with reference to the findings and conclusions of the visitation. As a matter of fact, it did; but, at the time of his appointment, both Bishop Wuerl and I, along with the apostolic pronuncio, judged it best to make no public announcement to that effect. The importance of making Bishop Wuerl's transition to the archdiocese as smooth as possible and of assuring him of the best possible climate for beginning his ministry among us seemed to outweigh any possible good that might have been realized by giving a full public acknowledgment of all the specifications surrounding his appointment as auxiliary bishop. However, at the time of his appointment, I did not understand the nature and extent of Bishop Wuerl's role. After considerable discussion with the Holy See, it was confirmed that it was the understanding of the Holy See in December, 1985, when appointing Bishop Wuerl that he not only assist me by assuming a general oversight and responsibility for these five areas (identified in the apostolic visitation), but that he actually be delegated by me to have complete and final decision-making power over them. The clarification of his decision took place in June at the Collegeville (Minn.) meeting of bishops where I met with the apostolic pronuncio. It was subsequently confirmed to me in a letter dated July 1, 1986.

"Once I received this clarification, I not only took steps to carry out the wishes of the Holy See, but also arrived at the conclusion that it was important for me to share these matters with my close collaborators in the ministry and administration of the archdiocese."

Priests and others in the archdiocese expressed "confusion" and "pain" over the Vatican order. At the same time, the priests made it clear they wanted Bishop Wuerl to continue as the auxiliary but recommended a return to "normalcy" — a development to be hoped for. Msgr. Marcello Costalunga, undersecretary of the Congregation for Bishops, said the Vatican's action was meant to correct an extraordinary situation. He added that the measures would not necessarily be permanent, and that "one hopes everything will eventually return to normal."

Honors — Fellow bishops, black Catholics and others gathered in New Orleans Sept. 4 to celebrate with Auxiliary Bishop Harold R. Perry the 20th anniversary of his ordination as the first black bishop in the U.S. in the 20th century.

The Catholic University of America announced that the Cardinal Gibbons Medal would be awarded Oct. 11 to Nancy Reagan for her anti-drug activities.

Divestment in South Africa — The Administrative Board of the U.S. Catholic Conference called for divestment of stocks in firms doing business in South Africa if the government there fails "to undertake significant progress" toward ending apartheid by May 15, 1987. Meeting in Washington Sept. 9 to 11, the 46-member board urged dioceses

and other Catholic institutions to "give consideration to" divestment and shareholder stock actions to oppose apartheid.

Death of Father Young — Paulist Father James Young, 46, nationally known for his ministry of reconciliation among separated and divorced Catholics, died Sept. 12 at Georgetown Hospital, Washington, D.C. The cause of death may have been related to a recurring respiratory problem.

International

Fund for Polish Farmers Abandoned — The bishops of Poland said Sept. 3 they were abandoning plans for an independent agricultural fund because the government sought to control it. Cardinal Jozef Glemp called unacceptable the government's demand that the agriculture minister have veto power over the fund's programs in order to "correlate" them with government programs. Such a veto would "contradict the basic concepts of the foundation, especially its autonomy," the caridnal's statement said. The fund had been planned to provide farmers, with church and foreign financing, with the means for purchasing supplies and equipment for the modernization of agriculture in Poland.

Three Priests Expelled, Chile under Siege — The Chilean government expelled three French priests Sept. 11 despite a warning from Cardinal Juan Francisco Fresno Larrain of Santiago that "their expulsion will make the search for peace even more difficult." The missionaries were arrested during a widespread police crackdown on opposition activists following an unsuccessful attempt on the life of President Augusto Pinochet by unknown assailants Sept. 7. Also detained, but released Sept. 8, were American Maryknoll Fathers Thomas Henehan and Terrence Cambias.

Church in Vietnam — Despite government efforts to eliminate the Church, there was "terrific Mass attendance" along with conversions, according to Jesuit Father Henri Forest, undersecretary of the Pontifical Council Cor Unum. Available information indicated the government would like to "choke off the Church completely." Father Forest said the regime controlled the choice and education of candidates for the priesthood, and had established a controlled organization of patriotic Catholics analogous to a similar "church" in China.

Wanted: Religious Education — More than 40 percent of parents in the region around Zagreb, Yugoslavia, said they would like to see religion taught in state schools, according to a survey published in *Borba*, a publication of the Yugoslavian Communist League. The teaching of religion was allowed only in places of worship.

Anti-Apartheid Pressure — The South African Council of Priests passed a resolution supporting economic pressure to end the nation's system of apartheid. The resolution gave formal support to the stand of the Southern African Catholic Bishops' Conference with respect to economic pressure against the government, as outlined in a pastoral letter issued in May.

(See many related entries under John Paul II in the Index.)

Cardinal-Archbishop Karol Wojtyla of Cracow was elected Bishop of Rome Oct. 16, 1978, on the seventh or eighth ballot cast on the second day of voting at a conclave of 111 cardinals. He chose the name John Paul II and was invested with the pallium, the symbol of his papal office, Oct. 22 in ceremonies attended by more than 250,000 persons in St. Peter's Square.

The 263rd successor of St. Peter as Bishop of Rome and Supreme Pastor of the Universal Church, he is the first non-Italian Pope since Adrian VI (1522-23), the first Polish Pope in the history of the Church, and the youngest at the time of his election since Pius IX (1846-78).

Early Career

Karol Wojtyla was born May 18, 1920, in Wadowice, Poland.

He began higher studies at the age of 18, with major interests in poetry and theater arts. Forced to suspend university courses because of the outbreak of World War II, he went to work in a stone quarry and a chemical plant, thereby earning the later designation of himself as the "Worker Cardinal."

He started studies for the priesthood in 1942 in the underground seminary of Cracow, whose operations had been banned after the Nazi invasion of Poland.

Ordained to the priesthood Nov. 1, 1946, he was immediately sent to Rome for studies at the Angelicum University, where he earned a doctorate in ethics.

Back home in Poland, he worked as an assistant pastor in a village parish and as a chaplain to university students while continuing studies at the Catholic University of Lublin. He was awarded another doctorate there, in moral theology.

He began writing about this time, and eventually produced more than 100 articles and several books on ethical and other themes. Phenomenology was one of his fields of expertise.

University teaching came next, in 1953, with appointment in 1954 to the position of lecturer and later to the chair of ethics at the Catholic University of Lublin, the most prestigious institute of higher learning in Poland.

Bishop and Cardinal

He was ordained Auxiliary Bishop of Cracow Sept. 28, 1958, became vicar capitular in 1962 after the death of Apostolic Administrator Eugeniusz Baziak, and was appointed Archbishop Jan. 13, 1964. He was the first residential head of the see since the death of Cardinal Adam Sapieha in 1951. Between then and 1964 the archdiocese was run by administrators because the communist government refused to permit the appointment and ministry of a residential bishop.

Archbishop Wojtyla attended all sessions of the Second Vatican Council from 1962 to 1965, and was one of the writers of the *Pastoral Constitution on the Church in the Modern World.* He also contributed input to the *Declaration on Religious Freedom* and the *Decree on the Instruments of Social Communication.*

His efforts to put into effect the directives of the council induced him to write a book, *Foundations of Renewal,* in 1972 and to start that same year an archdiocesan synod he saw concluded as Pope during his visit to Poland in 1979.

He was inducted into the College of Cardinals June 26, 1967, as one of the younger members, and subsequently served actively in the Congregation for the Sacraments and Divine Worship, the Congregation for the Clergy, and the Congregation for Catholic Education.

He also served as a theological consultant to Pope Paul VI.

He attended assemblies of the Synod of Bishops as a representative of the Polish Bishops' Conference and was a member of the Synod's permanent council.

From the beginning of his priestly career, and especially during his episcopate, the Cardinal was vigorous in the defense of human and religious rights, the rights of workers, and rights to religious education.

Close to Cardinal Wyszynski and in company with his fellow bishops, he negotiated the tightrope of Catholic survival in a country under communist control. With them, and as their spokesman at times, he was stalwart in resisting efforts of the regime to impose atheism, materialism and secularism on the people and culture of Poland.

Active Pope

Since the beginning of his pontificate, John Paul has been active as Bishop of Rome, with frequent visits to parishes and institutions of the diocese for the celebration of Mass and participation in other events. During these visits, as well as others to places of pilgrimage and historic significance in Italy, he has had perhaps more personal contact with the faithful than any other Pope. The number of attendants at weekly general audiences at the Vatican and Castel Gandolfo has been unprecedented.

Extensive Travels

By the end of September, 1986, the Pope had made 30 pastoral trips to foreign countries.

• The Pope made four trips in 1979, to: the Dominican Republic and Mexico, Jan. 5 to Feb. 1; Poland, June 2 to 10; Ireland and the United States, Sept. 29 to Oct. 7; Turkey, Nov. 28 to 30.

In Turkey, he met with Orthodox Ecumenical Patriarch Dimitrios I and, with him, announced the establishment of a commission of theologians to begin formal dialogue in quest of the union of the Roman Catholic and Orthodox Churches.

• There were four trips in 1980, to: Africa (Zaire, Congo Republic, Kenya, Ghana, Upper Volta, Ivory Coast), May 2 to 12; France, May 30 to June 2; Brazil (13 cities), June 30 to July 12; West Germany, Nov. 15 to 19.

In Africa, he spoke about the Africanization of the Church, the cultural values of Africans, and the independence they should have from alien influences of other countries and cultures.

In France, before the United Nations Educational, Scientific and Cultural Organization, he delineated with great clarity the stance of the Church on a wide variety of subjects, with special emphasis on its role in a secularized state, society and culture.

In Brazil, he declared that the Church is on the side of poor, appealed for across-the-board respect for human rights by governments and people of influence, called for measures of economic and social reform, and indicated approval of non-violent activism for the good of all peoples. He attended a plenary assembly of the bishops of the country and took part in opening ceremonies of a national Eucharistic Congress.

• In 1981, he made only one trip, to the Philippines, Guam and Japan, with stopovers in Pakistan and Alaska, Feb. 16 to 27.

Plans for additional trips in 1981 — to Lourdes, for the 42nd International Eucharistic Congress, and to Switzerland — had to be cancelled because of the attack on the Pope's life in May.

• He made seven trips in 1982, to: Africa (Nigeria, Benin, Gabon, Equatorial Guinea), Feb. 12 to 19; Portugal, May 12 to 15; Great Britain, May 28 to June 2; Argentina, June 11 and 12; Switzerland, June 15; San Marino, Aug. 29; Spain, Oct. 31 to Nov. 9.

In Portugal, at the Marian shrine at Fatima, he consecrated the world to the Blessed Virgin Mary.

• On four trips in 1983, the Pope visited: Central America (Costa Rica, Nicaragua, Panama, El Salvador, Guatemala, Belize, Honduras) and Haiti, Mar. 2 to 10; Poland, June 16 to 23; Lourdes, France, Aug. 14 and 15; Austria, Sept. 10 to 13.

• The Pope made four trips in 1984, to: South Korea, Papua New Guinea, Solomon Islands, Thailand, May 2 to 12; Switzerland, June 12 to 17; Canada, Sept. 9 to 20; Spain, Dominican Republic and Puerto Rico, Oct. 10 to 12.

• The Pope made four trips in 1985 by the middle of September, to: Venezuela, Ecuador, Peru, Trinidad and Tobago, Jan. 26 to Feb. 6; Belgium, The Netherlands and Luxembourg, May 11 to 21; Africa (Togo, Ivory Coast, Cameroon, Central African Republic, Zaire, Kenya and Morocco), Aug. 8 to 19; Liechtenstein, Sept. 8.

• In 1986, he visited India Feb. 1 to 10, Colombia-St. Lucia July 1 to 7 (see separate entries).

Plans were being made in 1986 for a visit to Southern and Western U.S. in September, 1987.

Key Writings

Encyclicals: The homilies and addresses delivered by the Pope on these trips were the equivalent of doctrinal, pastoral and social encyclical letters on a wide variety of subjects, all related to the key document of the first year of his pontificate. That was the formal encyclical, *Redemptor Hominis,* a treatise on Christian an-

thropology dealing with the divine and human aspects of redemption and the mission of the Church to carry on a dialogue of salvation with all peoples.

Two other encyclicals published within less than a year of each other were *Dives in Misericordia* ("On the Mercy of God") in 1980 and *Laborem Exercens* ("On Human Work") in 1981. *Slavorum Apostoli* in 1985 honored Sts. Cyril and Methodius, apostles of the Slavic peoples. *Dominum et Vivificantem* ("Lord and Giver of life") was published in 1986 (see separate entry for excerpts).

Other Writings: The Pope published a lengthy exhortation on the family, *Familiaris Consortio,* in December, 1981. It is an extensive synthesis of the theology of the family based not only on traditional doctrinal background but also on recommendations that emanated from the 1980 assembly of the Synod of Bishops.

Writings published in 1984 included two apostolic letters — on suffering, *Salvifici Doloris,* and on Jerusalem; an apostolic exhortation, *Redemptionis Donum,* addressed to and about Religious; a "Charter of the Rights of the Family"; and an apostolic exhortation, "Reconciliation and Penance in the Ministry of the Church." In 1986, he issued an apostolic letter on the 1600th anniversary of the conversion of St. Augustine.

Various Items

Doctrinal Concern: In December, 1980, the Pope directly confronted the controversial writings of Father Hans Kung by giving his approval to a declaration by the Congregation for the Doctrine of the Faith that he could not be regarded as a Catholic theologian.

On Aug. 6, 1983, he authorized release by the Doctrinal Congregation of a letter to bishops throughout the world in refutation of unorthodox views — especially those of Father Edward Schillebeeckx, O.P. — concerning "The Minister of the Eucharist."

The Holy Father regarded as extremely important a series of talks begun at general audiences in the summer of 1984 on marriage and sexual morality, explaining and firmly supporting traditional doctrine, with emphasis on teaching contained in the encyclical letter, *Humanae Vitae,* by Pope Paul VI.

He approved instructions on liberation theology issued by the Congregation for the Doctrine of the Faith in 1984 and 1986. (See separate entry for excerpts from the 1986 instruction.)

He approved the 1986 declaration of the Congregation for the Doctrine of the Faith that U.S. theologian Father Charles E. Curran is not eligible to function as a Catholic theologian. (See separate entry, The Curran Controversy.)

These actions, along with various other statements and indications of attitude, mark John Paul as a pastor of decisive leadership for doctrinal orthodoxy and church discipline.

Canon Law: The Pope was deeply involved in the work of completing the revision of the Code of Canon Law, which he ordered into effect as of Nov.

27, 1983. He called it, in effect, the final act of the Second Vatican Council. He emphasized its innovative force in an address Jan. 26, 1984, to personnel of the Sacred Roman Rota.

Causes of Saints: In 1984, the Pope canonized St. Paola Frassinetti, foundress of the Sisters of St. Dorothy, and 103 Korean martyrs who were killed during persecutions in the mid-1800s. He beatified 99 persons who were martyred for their faith during the French Revolution. At Rome and while en route on several pastoral trips, he has beatified numerous servants of God. In 1986, he canonized Franciscan Father Francesco Fasani.

Synods: The Holy Father convoked three of them in 1980.

With the Dutch bishops at the Vatican for a particular synod in January, he called for measures to cope with differences among the prelates, polarization among the people and action to remedy doctrinal and disciplinary irregularities. Later reports indicated that results of the synod were less than satisfactory.

Meeting with Ukrainian bishops in March, he named a successor to Cardinal Josyf Slipyi as the ranking Ukrainian bishop and turned down demands of some Ukrainians for a patriarchate.

With more than 200 delegates from episcopal conferences around the world, he held the fifth ordinary assembly of the Synod of Bishops.

He convoked another ordinary assembly of the Synod in 1983 and an extraordinary one that was held Nov. 25 to Dec. 8, 1985. The purpose of the 1985 assembly was to evaluate the effects and implementation of the enactments of the Second Vatican Council, on the occasion of the 20th anniversary of its conclusion. (See separate entries, Synod of Bishops.)

Holy Year: The Holy Father proclaimed a Jubilee celebration of the 1950th anniversary of the Redemption from the Solemnity of the Annunciation of the Lord Mar. 25, 1983, to Easter Sunday, Apr. 22, 1984.

Cardinals: In June, 1979, the Holy Father inducted 14 new cardinals into the Sacred College, raising its membership at that time to 135. A second group was inducted into the Sacred College Feb. 3, 1983, at which time the total membership was 138. Twenty-eight new members inducted into the College May 25, 1985, brought the membership to an all-time high of 152.

Meetings with Bishops: In relations with the hierarchy since becoming Pope, John Paul has met with groups of bishops making required *ad limina* visits to the Vatican, for first-hand reports and admonitions regarding conditions in dioceses all over the world. He has also met with assemblies of bishops in the countries he has visited.

Ecumenism: He met with Anglican Archbishop Robert Runcie at the Canterbury Cathedral during his visit to Great Britain in May, 1982. The two prelates prayed together, renewed their baptismal promises and issued a joint statement in which they announced the formation of a new joint Catholic-Anglican theological commission for a second phase of interfaith dialogue.

Ever since the beginning of his pontificate, the Pope has maintained contact with Orthodox leaders and officials of other churches and religious bodies.

While visiting the headquarters of the World Council of Churches in Geneva June 12, 1984, the Pope said the Church's engagement in the quest for religious unity is irreversible. At the same time, he mentioned two points of extreme significance in Catholic doctrine and practice.

The Church, he said, "entered on the hard ecumenical task bringing with it a conviction" about the role of the bishop of Rome. "It is convinced that in the ministry of the bishop of Rome it has preserved the visible pole and guarantee of unity in full fidelity to the apostolic tradition and to the faith of the Fathers."

He also reiterated doctrinal opposition to sharing the Eucharist until full unity is achieved. "It is not yet possible for us to celebrate the Eucharist together and communicate at the same table."

Nevertheless, he placed emphasis on things Christians have in common, among them, baptism, reverence for Scripture, prayer, a rediscovery of the "whole role of the Holy Spirit," and cooperation in work for social justice and human rights.

A significant interfaith event of 1986 was the papal visit to the Synagogue of Rome. (See entry.)

Audiences and Addresses: The Pope has delivered hundreds of addresses at general and private audiences and on special occasions. All of them have characteristically been grounded in doctrinal essentials coupled with relevance to the people being addressed or the events being commemorated.

World Affairs: In 1984, the Pope agreed to a new concordat with Italy, regulating church-state relations. He agreed also to the establishment of diplomatic relations with the United States. One hundred and 16 nations maintained diplomatic relations with the Vatican as of Sept. 30, 1986.

On his travels as well as at the Vatican, the Pope has been an outstanding advocate of human rights and dignity, of respect for life, of peace, of nuclear and conventional disarmament, of reconciliation among nations, of aid and relief for distressed peoples and nations, of people first and things second in all areas of life.

Near Tragedy: The Pope narrowly escaped death May 13, 1981, when he was fired upon at close range by Mehmet Ali Agca as he entered St. Peter's Square to address a general audience. Wounded more seriously than realized at first, he underwent emergency surgery and remained in Gemelli Polyclinic Hospital until June 3. On release, he stayed at the Vatican until June 20 when he was hospitalized a second time, until Aug. 14.

Agca told reporters July 8, 1983, that the Bulgarian secret service and the KGB were involved in his attempt on the life of the Pope, but hard and convincing evidence appeared to be missing, despite exhaustive investigation by Italian authorities. Results of the conspiracy trial were inconclusive.

As the trial began, the Vatican announced it was not involved in the proceedings.

FIRST CENTURY

Early 30's: First Christian Pentecost: gathering together of the Christian community, outpouring of the Holy Spirit, preaching of St. Peter to Jews in Jerusalem, baptism and aggregation of some 3,000 persons to the Christian community.

St. Stephen, deacon, was stoned to death at Jerusalem; he is venerated as the first Christian martyr.

34: St. Paul, formerly Saul the persecutor of Christians, was converted, baptized and joined to the college of Apostles. After three major missionary journeys, he was martyred in 64 or 67 at Rome.

39: The Gentile Cornelius and his family were baptized by St. Peter.

42: Persecution of Christians in Palestine broke out during the rule of Herod Agrippa; St. James the Greater, the first Apostle to die, was beheaded in 44; St. Peter was imprisoned for a short time; many Christians fled to Antioch and elsewhere.

At Antioch, the followers of Christ were first called Christians.

49: Christians at Rome, who were considered members of a Jewish sect, were adversely affected by a decree of Claudius which forbade Jewish worship there.

51: The Council of Jerusalem, in which all the Apostles participated under the presidency of St. Peter, decreed that circumcision, dietary regulations, and various other prescriptions of Mosaic Law were not obligatory for Gentile converts to the Christian community. The decree was issued in opposition to Judaizers who contended that observance of the Mosaic Law in its entirety was necessary for salvation.

64: Persecution under Nero. The emperor, accusing Christians of starting a fire which destroyed half of Rome, inaugurated the era of major Roman persecutions.

64 or 67: Martyrdom of St. Peter at Rome during the Neronian persecution. He established his see and spent his last years there after preaching in and around Jerusalem, establishing a see at Antioch, and presiding at the Council of Jerusalem.

70: Destruction of Jerusalem by Titus.

88-97: Pontificate of St. Clement I, third successor of St. Peter as bishop of Rome, one of the Apostolic Fathers. The *First Epistle of Clement to the Corinthians,* with which he has been identified, was addressed by the Church of Rome to the Church at Corinth, the scene of irregularities and divisions in the Christian community.

95: Domitian persecuted Christians, principally at Rome.

c. 100: Death of St. John, Apostle and Evangelist, marking the end of the Age of the Apostles and the first generation of the Church.

SECOND CENTURY

c. 107: St. Ignatius of Antioch was martyred at Rome. He was the first writer to use the expression, "the Catholic Church."

112: Emperor Trajan, in a rescript to Pliny the Younger, governor of Bithynia, instructed him not to search out Christians but to punish them if they were publicly denounced and refused to do homage to the Roman gods. This rescript set a pattern for Roman magistrates in dealing with Christians.

117-138: Persecution under Hadrian. Many *Acts of Martyrs* date from this period.

c. 125: Spread of Gnosticism.

c. 155: St. Polycarp, bishop of Smyrna and disciple of St. John the Evangelist, was martyred.

c. 156: Beginning of Montanism.

161-180: Reign of Marcus Aurelius. His persecution, launched in the wake of natural disasters, was more violent than those of his predecessors.

165: St. Justin, an important early Christian writer, was martyred at Rome.

c. 180: St. Irenaeus, bishop of Lyons and one of the great early theologians, wrote *Adversus Haereses.* He stated that the teaching and tradition of the Roman See was the standard for belief.

196: Easter Controversy.

The *Didache,* written in the second century, was an important record of Christian belief, practice and government in the first century.

Latin was introduced in the West as a liturgical language.

The Catechetical School of Alexandria, founded about the middle of the century, increased in importance.

THIRD CENTURY

202: Persecution under Septimius Severus, who wanted to establish one common religion in the Empire.

206: Tertullian, a convert since 197 and the first great ecclesiastical writer in Latin, joined the heretical Montanists. He died in 230.

215: Death of Clement of Alexandria, teacher of Origen and a founding father of the School of Alexandria.

217-235: St. Hippolytus, the first antipope. He was reconciled to the Church while in prison during persecution in 235.

232-254: Origen established the School of Caesarea after being deposed in 231 as head of the School of Alexandria; he died in 254. A scholar and voluminous writer, he was one of the founders of systematic theology and exerted wide influence for many years.

c. 242: Manichaeism originated in Persia.

249-251: Persecution under Decius. Many of those who denied the faith *(lapsi)* sought readmission to the Church at the end of the persecution in 251. Pope St. Cornelius had correspondence with St. Cyprian on the subject and ordered that *lapsi* were to be readmitted after suitable penance.

250-300: Neo-Platonism of Plotinus and Porphyry gained followers.

251: Novatian, an antipope, was condemned at Rome.

256: Pope St. Stephen I upheld the validity of

baptism administered by heretics, in the Rebaptism Controversy.

257: Persecution under Valerian, who attempted to destroy the Church as a social structure.

258: St. Cyprian, bishop of Carthage, was martyred.

c. 260: St. Lucian founded the exegetical School of Antioch.

Pope St. Dionysius condemned teachings of Sabellius and the Marcionites.

St. Paul of Thebes became a hermit.

261: Gallienus issued an edict of toleration which ended general persecution for nearly 40 years.

c. 266: Sabellianism was condemned and Paul of Samosata deposed.

c. 292: Diocletian divided the Roman Empire into East and West. The division emphasized political, cultural and other differences between the two parts of the Empire and influenced the Church in the East and West. The prestige of Rome began to decline.

FOURTH CENTURY

303: Persecution broke out under Diocletian. It ended in the West in 306 but continued for 10 years in the East; it was particularly violent in 304.

305: St. Anthony of Heracles established a foundation for hermits near the Red Sea in Egypt.

c. 306: The first local legislation on clerical celibacy was enacted by a council held at Elvira, Spain; bishops, priests, deacons and other ministers were forbidden to have wives.

310: St. Hilarion established a foundation for hermits in Palestine.

311: An edict of toleration issued by Galerius at the urging of Constantine and Licinius officially ended persecution in the West; some persecution continued in the East.

313: The *Edict of Milan* issued by Constantine and Licinius recognized Christianity as a lawful religion and the legal freedom of all religions in the Roman Empire.

314: The Council of Arles condemned Donatism in Africa and declared that baptism by heretics was valid.

318: St. Pachomius established the first foundation of the cenobitic (common) life, as compared with the solitary life of hermits in Upper Egypt.

325: The Ecumenical Council of Nicaea (I), first of its kind in the history of the Church, condemned Arianism; see separate entry.

326: Discovery of the True Cross on which Christ was crucified.

337: Baptism and death of Constantine.

c. 342: Beginning of a 40-year persecution in Persia.

343-344: A local Council of Sardica reaffirmed doctrine formulated by Nicaea I and declared that bishops had the right of appeal to the pope as the highest authority in the Church.

361-363: Julian the Apostate waged an unsuccessful campaign against the Church in an attempt to restore paganism as the religion in the Empire.

c. 365: Persecution under Valens in the East.

c. 376: Beginning of the barbarian invasion in the West.

379: Death of St. Basil, the Father of Monasticism in the East. His writings contributed greatly to the development of rules for the religious life.

381: The Ecumenical Council of Constantinople (I); see separate entry.

382: The *Decree of Pope St. Damasus* listed the Canon of Sacred Scripture.

382-c. 406: St. Jerome translated the Old and New Testaments into Latin. His work is called the Vulgate Version of the Bible.

396: St. Augustine became bishop of Hippo in North Africa.

397: A local Council of Carthage published the Canon of Sacred Scripture.

FIFTH CENTURY

410: Visigoths sacked Rome.

411: Donatism was condemned by a council at Carthage.

430: St. Augustine, bishop of Hippo for 35 years, died. He was a strong defender of orthodox doctrine against Manichaeism, Donatism and Pelagianism. The depth and range of his writings made him a dominant influence in Christian thought for many centuries.

431: The Ecumenical Council of Ephesus; see separate entry.

432: St. Patrick arrived in Ireland. By the time of his death in 461 most of the country had been converted, monasteries founded and the hierarchy established.

438: The *Theodosian Code,* a compilation of decrees for the Empire, was issued by Theodosius II. It had great influence on subsequent civil and ecclesiastical law.

449: The Robber Council of Ephesus, which did not have ecclesiastical sanction, declared itself in favor of the opinions of Eutyches who contended that Christ had only one nature.

451: The Ecumenical Council of Chalcedon; see separate entry.

452: Pope St. Leo the Great persuaded Attila the Hun to spare Rome.

455: Vandals sacked Rome. The decline of imperial Rome dates approximately from this time.

484: Patriarch Acacius of Constantinople was excommunicated for signing the *Henoticon,* a unity law published by Emperor Zeno in 482 to end the turmoil associated with the Monophysite heresy. The document capitulated to the heresy. The excommunication triggered a 35-year-long schism.

494: Pope St. Gelasius I declared in a letter to Emperor Anastasius that the pope had power and authority over the emperor in spiritual matters.

496: Clovis, King of the Franks, was converted and became the defender of Christianity in the West. The Franks became a Catholic people.

SIXTH CENTURY

520 and later: Irish monasteries flourished as centers for spiritual life, missionary training and scholarly activity.

529: The Second Council of Orange condemned Semi-Pelagianism.

c. 529: St. Benedict founded the Monte Cassino Abbey. Some years before his death in 543 he wrote a monastic rule which exercised tremendous influence on the form and style of religious life. He is called the Father of Monasticism in the West.

533: John II became the first pope to change his name. The practice did not become general until the time of Sergius IV (1009).

533-534: Emperor Justinian promulgated the *Corpus Juris Civilis* for the Roman world. Like the *Theodosian Code,* it influenced subsequent civil and ecclesiastical law.

c. 545: Death of Dionysius Exiguus who was the first to date history from the birth of Christ, a practice which resulted in use of the B.C. and A.D. abbreviations. His calculations were at least four years late.

553: The Ecumenical Council of Constantinople (II); see separate entry.

585: St. Columban founded an influential monastic school at Luxeuil. He died in 615.

589: The most important of several councils of Toledo was held. The Visigoths renounced Arianism, and St. Leander began the organization of the Church in Spain.

590-604: Pontificate of Pope St. Gregory I the Great. He set the form and style of the papacy which prevailed throughout the Middle Ages; exerted great influence on doctrine and liturgy; was strong in support of monastic discipline and clerical celibacy; authored writings on many subjects. Gregorian Chant is named in his honor.

596: Pope St. Gregory I the Great sent St. Augustine of Canterbury and 40 monks to do missionary work in England.

597: St. Columba died. He founded an important monastery at Iona, established schools and did notable missionary work in Scotland.

By the end of the century, monasteries of nuns were common; Western monasticism was flourishing; monasticism in the East, under the influence of Monophysitism and other factors, was losing its vigor.

SEVENTH CENTURY

613: St. Columban established the influential monastery of Bobbio in northern Italy.

622: The Hegira (flight) of Mohammed from Mecca to Medina signalled the beginning of Islam, which, by the end of the century, claimed almost all of the southern Mediterranean area.

629: Emperor Heraclius recovered the True Cross from the Persians.

649: A Lateran Council condemned two erroneous formulas *(Ecthesis* and *Type)* issued by emperors Heraclius and Constans II as means of reconciling Monophysites with the Church.

664: Actions of the Synod of Whitby advanced the adoption of Roman usages in England, especially regarding the date for the observance of Easter. (See Easter Controversy.)

680-681: The Ecumenical Council of Constantinople (III); see separate entry.

692: Trullan Synod. Eastern-Church discipline on clerical celibacy was settled, permitting marriage before ordination to the diaconate and continuation in marriage afterwards, but prohibiting marriage following the death of the wife thereafter. Anti-Roman canons contributed to East-West alienation.

During the century, the monastic influence of Ireland and England increased in Western Europe; schools and learning declined; regulations regarding clerical celibacy became more strict in the East.

EIGHTH CENTURY

711: Moslems began the conquest of Spain.

726: Emperor Leo III, the Isaurian, launched a campaign against the veneration of sacred images and relics; called Iconoclasm (image-breaking), it caused turmoil in the East until about 843.

731: Pope Gregory III and a synod at Rome condemned Iconoclasm, with a declaration that the veneration of sacred images was in accord with Catholic tradition.

Venerable Bede issued his *Ecclesiastical History of the English People.*

732: Charles Martel defeated the Moslems at Poitiers, halting advance by them in the West.

744: The Monastery of Fulda was established by St. Sturmi, a disciple of St. Boniface.

754: A council of more than 300 Byzantine bishops endorsed Iconoclast errors. This council and its actions were condemned by the Lateran Synod of 769.

Stephen II (III) crowned Pepin ruler of the Franks. Pepin twice invaded Italy, in 754 and 756, to defend the pope against the Lombards. His land grants to the papacy, called the Donation of Pepin, were later extended by Charlemagne (773) and formed part of the States of the Church.

c. 755: St. Boniface (Winfrid) was martyred. He was called the Apostle of Germany for his missionary work and organization of the hierarchy there.

781: Alcuin was chosen by Charlemagne to organize a Palace School, which became a center of intellectual leadership.

787: The Ecumenical Council of Nicaea (II); see separate entry.

792: A council at Ratisbon condemned Adoptionism.

The famous *Book of Kells* ("The Great Gospel of Columcille") dates from the early eighth or late seventh century.

NINTH CENTURY

800: Charlemagne was crowned Emperor by Pope Leo III on Christmas Day.

Egbert became king of West Saxons. He unified England and strengthened the See of Canterbury.

813: Emperor Leo V, the Armenian, revived Iconoclasm, which persisted until about 843.

814: Charlemagne died.

843: The Treaty of Verdun split the Frankish kingdom among Charlemagne's three grandsons.

844: A Eucharistic controversy involving the writings of St. Paschasius Radbertus, Ratramnus and Rabanus Maurus occasioned the development of terminology regarding the doctrine of the Real Presence.

846: The Moslems invaded Italy and attacked Rome.

847-852: Period of composition of the *False Decretals,* a collection of forged documents attributed to popes from St. Clement (88-97) to Gregory II (715-731). The *Decretals,* which strongly supported the autonomy and rights of bishops, were suspect for a long time before being repudiated entirely about 1628.

848: The Council of Mainz condemned Gottschalk for heretical teaching regarding predestination. He was also condemned by the Council of Quierzy in 853.

857: Photius displaced Ignatius as patriarch of Constantinople. This marked the beginning of the Photian Schism, a confused state of East-West relations which has not yet been cleared up by historical research. Photius, a man of exceptional ability, died in 891.

865: St. Ansgar, Apostle of Scandinavia, died.

869: St. Cyril died and his brother, St. Methodius (d. 885), was ordained a bishop. The Apostles of the Slavs devised an alphabet and translated the Gospels and liturgy into the Slavonic language.

869: The Ecumenical Council of Constantinople (IV); see separate entry.

871-c. 900: Reign of Alfred the Great, the only English king ever anointed by a pope at Rome.

TENTH CENTURY

910: William, Duke of Aquitaine, founded the Benedictine Abbey of Cluny, which became a center of monastic and ecclesiastical reform.

915: Pope John X played a leading role in the expulsion of Saracens from central and southern Italy.

955: St. Olga, of the Russian royal family, was baptized.

962: Otto I, the Great, crowned by Pope John XII, revived Charlemagne's kingdom, which became the Holy Roman Empire.

966: Mieszko, first of a royal line in Poland, was baptized; he brought Latin Christianity to Poland.

989: Vladimir, ruler of Russia, was baptized. Russia was subsequently Christianized by Greek missionaries.

993: John XV was the first pope to decree the official canonization of a saint (Ulrich) for the universal Church.

997: St. Stephen became ruler of Hungary. He assisted in organizing the hierarchy and establishing Latin Christianity in that country.

999-1003: Pontificate of Sylvester II (Gerbert of Aquitaine), a Benedictine monk and the first French pope.

ELEVENTH CENTURY

1009: Beginning of lasting East-West schism in the Church, marked by dropping of the name of Pope Sergius IV from the Byzantine diptychs (the listing of persons prayed for during the liturgy). The deletion was made by Patriarch Sergius II of Constantinople.

1012: St. Romuald founded the Camaldolese Hermits.

1025: The Council of Arras, and other councils later, condemned the Cathari (Neo-Manichaeans, Albigenses).

1027: The Council of Elne proclaimed the Truce of God as a means of stemming violence. The truce involved armistice periods of varying length, which were later extended.

1038: St. John Gualbert founded the Vallombrosians.

1043-1059: Constantinople patriarchate of Michael Cerularius, the key figure in a controversy concerning the primacy of the papacy. His and the Byzantine synod's refusal to acknowledge this primacy in 1054 widened and hardened the East-West schism in the Church.

1047: Pope Clement II died. He was the only pope ever buried in Germany.

1049-54: Pontificate of St. Leo IX, who inaugurated a movement of papal, diocesan, monastic and clerical reform.

1055: Condemnation of the Eucharistic doctrine of Berengarius.

1059: A Lateran Council issued new legislation regarding papal elections. Voting power was entrusted to the Roman cardinals.

1066: Death of St. Edward the Confessor, King of England from 1042 and restorer of Westminster Abbey.

Defeat, at Hastings, of Harold by William I, who subsequently exerted strong influence on the life style of the Church in England.

1073-1085: Pontificate of St. Gregory VII (Hildebrand). A strong pope, he carried forward programs of clerical and general ecclesiastical reform and struggled against Henry IV and other rulers to end the evils of lay investiture. He introduced the Latin liturgy in Spain and set definite dates for the observance of ember days.

1077: Henry IV, excommunicated and suspended from the exercise of imperial powers by Gregory VII, sought absolution from the Pope at Canossa. Henry later repudiated this action and in 1084 forced Gregory to leave Rome.

1079: The Council of Rome condemned Eucharistic errors of Berengarius, who retracted.

1084: St. Bruno founded the Carthusians.

1097-1099: The first of several Crusades undertaken between this time and 1265. Recovery of the Holy Places and gaining free access to them for Christians were the original purposes, but these were diverted to less worthy objectives in various ways. Results included: a Latin Kingdom of Jerusalem, 1099-1187; a military and political misadventure in the form of a Latin Empire of Constantino-ple, 1204-1261; acquisition, by treaties, of visiting rights for Christians in the Holy Land. East-West economic and cultural relationships increased during the period. In the religious sphere, actions of the Crusaders had the effect of increasing the alienation of the East from the West.

1098: St. Robert founded the Cistercians.

TWELFTH CENTURY

1108: Beginnings of the influential Abbey and School of St. Victor.

1115: St. Bernard established the Abbey of Clairvaux and inaugurated the Cistercian Reform.

1118: Christian forces captured Saragossa, Spain; the beginning of the Moslem decline in that country.

1121: St. Norbert established the original monastery of the Praemonstratensians near Laon, France.

1122: The Concordat of Worms (Pactum Callixtinum) was formulated and approved by Pope Callistus II and Emperor Henry V to settle controversy concerning the investiture of prelates. The concordat provided that the emperor could invest prelates with symbols of temporal authority but had no right to invest them with spiritual authority, which came from the Church alone, and that the emperor was not to interfere in papal elections. This was the first concordat in history.

1123: The Ecumenical Council of the Lateran (I), the first of its kind in the West; see separate entry.

1139: The Ecumenical Council of the Lateran (II); see separate entry.

1140: St. Bernard met Abelard in debate at the Council of Sens. Abelard, whose rationalism in theology was condemned for the first time in 1121, died in 1142 at Cluny.

1148: The Synod of Rheims enacted strict disciplinary decrees for communities of women religious.

1152: The Synod of Kells reorganized the Church in Ireland.

1160: Gratian, whose *Decretum* became a basic text of canon law, died.

Peter Lombard, compiler of the *Four Books of Sentences,* a standard theology text for nearly 200 years, died.

1170: St. Thomas Becket, archbishop of Canterbury, who clashed with Henry II over Church-state relations, was murdered in his cathedral.

1171: Pope Alexander III reserved the process of canonization of saints to the Holy See.

1179: The Ecumenical Council of the Lateran (III); see separate entry.

1184: Waldenses and other heretics were excommunicated by Pope Lucius III.

THIRTEENTH CENTURY

1198-1216: Pontificate of Innocent III, during which the papacy reached its medieval peak of authority, influence and prestige in the Church and in relations with civil rulers.

1208: Innocent III called for a crusade, the first in Christendom itself, against the Albigensians.

1209: Verbal approval was given by Innocent III to a rule of life for the Order of Friars Minor, started by St. Francis of Assisi.

1212: The Second Order of Franciscans, the Poor Clares, was founded.

1215: The Ecumenical Council of the Lateran (IV); see separate entry.

1216: Formal papal approval was given to a rule of life for the Order of Preachers, started by St. Dominic.

The Portiuncula Indulgence was granted by the Holy See at the request of St. Francis of Assisi.

1221: The Third Order of St. Francis for lay persons was founded.

1226: Death of St. Francis of Assisi.

1245: The Ecumenical Council of Lyons (I); see separate entry.

1247: Preliminary approval was given by the Holy See to a Carmelite rule of life.

1270: St. Louis IX, king of France, died. Beginning of papal decline.

1274: The Ecumenical Council of Lyons (II); see separate entry.

Death of St. Thomas Aquinas, Doctor of the Church, of lasting influence; see separate entry.

1280: Pope Nicholas III, who made the *Breviary* the official prayer book for clergy of the Roman Church, died.

1281: The excommunication of Michael Palaeologus by Pope Martin IV ruptured the union effected with the Eastern Church in 1274.

FOURTEENTH CENTURY

1302: Pope Boniface VIII issued the bull *Unam Sanctam,* concerning the unity of the Church and the temporal power of princes, against the background of a struggle with Philip IV of France; it was the most famous medieval document on the subject.

1308-1378: For a period of approximately 70 years, seven popes resided at Avignon because of unsettled conditions in Rome and other reasons; see separate entry.

1311-1312: The Ecumenical Council of Vienne; see separate entry.

1321: Dante Alighieri died a year after completing the *Divine Comedy.*

1324: Marsilius of Padua completed *Defensor Pacis,* a work condemned by Pope John XXII as heretical because of its denial of papal primacy and the hierarchical structure of the Church, and for other reasons. It was a charter for conciliarism.

1337-1453: Period of the Hundred Years' War, a dynastic struggle between France and England.

1338: Four years after the death of Pope John XXII, who had opposed Louis IV of Bavaria in a years-long controversy, electoral princes declared at the Diet of Rhense that the emperor did not need papal confirmation of his title and right to rule. Charles IV later (1356) said the same thing in a *Golden Bull,* eliminating papal rights in the election of emperors.

1347-1350: The Black Death swept across Europe, killing perhaps one-fourth to one-third of the total population; an estimated 40 per cent of the clergy succumbed.

1374: Petrarch, poet and humanist, died.

1378: Return of the papacy from Avignon to Rome.

Beginning of the Western Schism; see separate entry.

FIFTEENTH CENTURY

1409: The Council of Pisa, without canonical authority, tried to end the Western Schism but succeeded only in complicating it by electing a third claimant to the papacy; see Western Schism.

1414-1418: The Ecumenical Council of Constance ended the Western Schism; see separate entry.

1431: St. Joan of Arc was burned at the stake.

1431-1449: The Council of Basel, which began with convocation by Pope Martin V in 1431, turned into an anti-papal forum of conciliarists seeking to subject the primacy and authority of the pope to the overriding authority of an assembly of bishops. It was not an ecumenical council.

1438: The Pragmatic Sanction of Bourges was enacted by Charles VIII and the French parliament to curtail papal authority over the Church in France, in the spirit of conciliarism. It found expression in Gallicanism and had effects lasting at least until the French Revolution.

1438-1443: The Ecumenical Council of Florence affirmed the primacy of the pope in opposition to conciliarism and effected a measure of union with separated Eastern Christians; see separate entry.

1453: The fall of Constantinople to the Turks.

c. 1456: Gutenberg issued the first edition of the Bible printed from movable type, at Mainz, Germany.

1476: Pope Sixtus IV ordered observance of the feast of the Immaculate Conception on Dec. 8 throughout the Church.

1492: Columbus discovered the Americas.

1493: Pope Alexander VI issued a *Bull of Demarcation* which determined spheres of influence for the Spanish and Portuguese in the Americas.

The Renaissance, a humanistic movement which originated in Italy in the 14th century, spread to France, Germany, the Low Countries and England. A transitional period between the medieval world and the modern secular world, it introduced profound changes which affected literature and the other arts, general culture, politics and religion.

SIXTEENTH CENTURY

1512-1517: The Ecumenical Council of the Lateran (V); see separate entry.

1517: Martin Luther signalled the beginning of the Reformation by posting 95 theses at Wittenberg. Subsequently, he broke completely from doctrinal orthodoxy in discourses and three published works (1519 and 1520); was excommunicated on more than 40 charges of heresy (1521); remained the dominant figure in the Reformation in Germany until his death in 1546.

1519: Zwingli triggered the Reformation in Zurich and became its leading proponent there until his death in combat in 1531.

1524: Luther's encouragement of German princes in putting down the two-year Peasants' Revolt gained political support for his cause.

1528: The Order of Friars Minor Capuchin was approved as an autonomous division of the Franciscan Order; like the Jesuits, the Capuchins became leaders in the Counter-Reformation.

1530: The *Augsburg Confession* of Lutheran faith was issued; it was later supplemented by the *Smalcald Articles* approved in 1537.

1533: Henry VIII divorced Catherine of Aragon,

married Anne Boleyn, was excommunicated. In 1534 he decreed the Act of Supremacy, making the sovereign the head of the Church in England, under which Sts. John Fisher and Thomas More were executed in 1535. Despite his rejection of papal primacy and actions against monastic life in England, he generally maintained doctrinal orthodoxy until his death in 1547.

1536: John Calvin, leader of the Reformation in Switzerland until his death in 1564, issued the first edition of *Institutes of the Christian Religion,* which became the classical text of Reformed (non-Lutheran) theology.

1540: The constitutions of the Society of Jesus (Jesuits), founded by St. Ignatius of Loyola, were approved.

1541: Start of the 11-year career of St. Francis Xavier as a missionary to the East Indies and Japan.

1545-1563: The Ecumenical Council of Trent formulated statements of Catholic doctrine under attack by the Reformers and mobilized the Counter-Reformation; see separate entry.

1549: The first *Book of Common Prayer* was issued by Edward VI. Revised editions were published in 1552, 1559 and 1662 and later.

1553: Start of the five-year reign of Mary Tudor who tried to counteract actions of Henry VIII against the Roman Church.

1555: Enactment of the Peace of Augsburg, an arrangement of religious territorialism rather than toleration, which recognized the existence of Catholicism and Lutheranism in the German Empire and provided that citizens should adopt the religion of their respective rulers.

1558: Beginning of the reign of Elizabeth I, during which the Church of England took on its definitive form.

1559: Establishment of the hierarchy of the Church of England, with the consecration of Matthew Parker as archbishop of Canterbury.

1563: The first text of the *39 Articles* of the Church of England was issued. Also enacted were a new Act of Supremacy and Oath of Succession to the English throne.

1570: Elizabeth I was excommunicated. Penal measures against Catholics subsequently became more severe.

1571: Defeat of the Turkish armada at Lepanto staved off the invasion of Eastern Europe.

1577: The *Formula of Concord,* the classical statement of Lutheran faith, was issued; it was, generally, a Lutheran counterpart of the canons of the Council of Trent. In 1580, along with other formulas of doctrine, it was included in the *Book of Concord.*

1582: The Gregorian Calendar, named for Pope Gregory XIII, was put into effect and was eventually adopted in most countries: England delayed adoption until 1752.

SEVENTEENTH CENTURY

1605: The Gunpowder Plot, an attempt by Catholic fanatics to blow up James I of England and the houses of Parliament, resulted in an anti-Catholic

Oath of Allegiance; the Oath was condemned by Pope Paul V in 1606.

1610: Death of Matteo Ricci, outstanding Jesuit missionary to China, pioneer in cultural relations between China and Europe.

Founding of the first community of Visitation Nuns by Sts. Francis de Sales and Jane de Chantal.

1611: Founding of the Oratorians.

1613: Catholics were banned from Scandinavia.

1625: Founding of the Congregation of the Mission (Vincentians) by St. Vincent de Paul. He founded the Sisters of Charity in 1633.

1642: Death of Galileo, scientist, who was censured by the Congregation of the Holy Office for supporting the Copernican theory of the sun-centered planetary system.

Founding of the Sulpicians by Jacques Olier.

1643: Start of publication of the Bollandist *Acta Sanctorum,* a critical work on lives of the saints.

1648: Provisions in the Peace of Westphalia, ending the Thirty Years' War, extended terms of the Peace of Augsburg (1555) to Calvinists and gave equality to Catholics and Protestants in the 300 states of the Holy Roman Empire.

1649: Oliver Cromwell invaded Ireland and began a severe persecution of the Church there.

1653: Pope Innocent X condemned five propositions of Jansenism, a complex theory which distorted doctrine concerning the relations between divine grace and human freedom. Jansenism was also a rigoristic movement which seriously disturbed the Church in France, the Low Countries and Italy in this and the 18th century.

1673: The Test Act in England barred from public office Catholics who would not deny the doctrine of transubstantiation and receive Communion in the Church of England.

1678: Many English Catholics suffered death as a consequence of the Popish Plot, a false allegation by Titus Oates that Catholics planned to assassinate Charles II, land a French army in the country, burn London, and turn over the government to the Jesuits.

1682: The four articles of the *Gallican Declaration,* drawn up by Bossuet, asserted political and ecclesiastical immunities of France from papal control. The articles, which rejected the primacy of the pope, were condemned in 1690.

1689: The Toleration Act granted a measure of freedom of worship to other English dissenters but not to Catholics.

EIGHTEENTH CENTURY

1704: Chinese Rites — involving the Christian adaptation of elements of Confucianism, veneration of ancestors and Chinese terminology in religion — were condemned by Clement XI. An earlier ban was issued in 1645; a later one, in 172.

1720: The Passionists were founded by St. Paul of the Cross.

1724: Persecution in China.

1732: The Redemptorists were founded by St. Alphonsus Liguori.

1738: Freemasonry was condemned by Clement XII and Catholics were forbidden to join, under penalty of excommunication; the prohibition was repeated by Benedict XIV in 1751 and by later popes.

1760's: Josephinism, a theory and system of state control of the Church, was initiated in Austria; it remained in force until about 1850.

1764: Febronianism, an unorthodox theory and practice regarding the constitution of the Church and relations between Church and state, was condemned for the first of several times. Proposed by an auxiliary bishop of Trier using the pseudonym Justinus Febronius, it had the effects of minimizing the office of the pope and supporting national churches under state control.

1773: Clement XIV issued a brief of suppression against the Jesuits, following their expulsion from Portugal in 1759, from France in 1764 and from Spain in 1767. Political intrigue and unsubstantiated accusations were principal factors in these developments. The ban, which crippled the Society, contained no condemnation of the Jesuit constitutions, particular Jesuits or Jesuit teaching. The Society was restored in 1814.

1778: Catholics in England were relieved of some civil disabilities dating back to the time of Henry VIII, by an act which permitted them to acquire, own and inherit property. Additional liberties were restored by the Roman Catholic Relief Act of 1791 and subsequent enactments of Parliament.

1789: Religious freedom in the United States was guaranteed under the First Amendment to the Constitution.

Beginning of the French Revolution which resulted in: the secularization of church property and the Civil Constitution of the Clergy in 1790; the persecution of priests, religious and lay persons loyal to papal authority; invasion of the Papal States by Napoleon in 1796; renewal of persecution from 1797-1799; attempts to dechristianize France and establish a new religion; the occupation of Rome by French troops and the forced removal of Pius VI to France in 1798.

This century is called the age of Enlightenment or Reason because of the predominating rational and scientific approach of its leading philosophers, scientists and writers with respect to religion, ethics and natural law. This approach downgraded the fact and significance of revealed religion. Also characteristic of the Enlightenment were subjectivism, secularism and optimism regarding human perfectibility.

NINETEENTH CENTURY

1809: Pope Pius VII was made a captive by Napoleon and deported to France where he remained in exile until 1814. During this time he refused to cooperate with Napoleon who sought to bring the Church in France under his own control.

The turbulence in church-state relations in France at the beginning of the century recurred in connection with the Bourbon Restoration, the July Revolution, the second and third Republics, the Second Empire and the Dreyfus case.

1814: The Society of Jesus, suppressed since 1773, was restored.

1817: Reestablishment of the Congregation for the Propagation of the Faith (Propaganda) by Pius VII was an important factor in increasing missionary activity during the century.

1820: Years-long persecution, during which thousands died for the faith, ended in China. Thereafter, communication with the West remained cut off until about 1834. Vigorous missionary work got under way in 1842.

1822: The Pontifical Society for the Propagation of the Faith, inaugurated in France by Pauline Jaricot for the support of missionary activity, was established.

1829: The Catholic Emancipation Act relieved Catholics in England and Ireland of most of the civil disabilities to which they had been subject from the time of Henry VIII.

1832: Gregory XVI, in the encyclical *Mirari Vos,* condemned indifferentism, one of the many ideologies at odds with Christian doctrine which were proposed during the century.

1833: Start of the Oxford Movement which affected the Church of England and resulted in some notable conversions, including that of John Henry Newman in 1845, to the Catholic Church.

Frederic Ozanam founded the Society of St. Vincent de Paul in France. The society, whose objective was works of charity, became worldwide.

1848: The *Communist Manifesto,* a revolutionary document symptomatic of socio-economic crisis, was issued.

1850: The hierarchy was reestablished in England and Nicholas Wiseman made the first archbishop of Westminster. He was succeeded in 1865 by Henry Manning, an Oxford convert and proponent of the rights of labor.

1853: The Catholic hierarchy was reestablished in Holland.

1854: Pius IX proclaimed the dogma of the Immaculate Conception in the bull *Ineffabilis Deus.*

1858: The Blessed Virgin Mary appeared to St. Bernadette at Lourdes, France; see separate entry.

1864: Pius IX issued the encyclical *Quanta Cura* and the *Syllabus of Errors* in condemnation of some 80 propositions derived from the scientific mentality and rationalism of the century. The subjects in question had deep ramifications in many areas of thought and human endeavor; in religion, they explicitly and/or implicitly rejected divine revelation and the supernatural order.

1867: The first volume of *Das Kapital* was published. Together with the Communist First International, formed in the same year, it had great influence on the subsequent development of Communism and Socialism.

1869: The Anglican Church was disestablished in Ireland.

1869-1870: The First Vatican Council; see separate entry.

1870-1871: Victor Emmanuel II of Sardinia, crowned king of Italy after defeating Austrian and papal forces, marched into Rome in 1870 and expropriated the Papal States after a plebiscite in which Catholics, at the order of Pius IX, did not vote. In 1871, Pius IX refused to accept a Law of Guarantees. Confiscation of church property and hindrance of ecclesiastical administration by the regime followed.

1871: The German Empire, a confederation of 26 states, was formed. Government policy launched a Kulturkampf whose May Laws of 1873 were designed to annul papal jurisdiction in Prussia and other states and to place the Church under imperial control. Resistance to the enactments and the persecution they legalized forced the government to modify its anti-Church policy by 1887.

1878: Beginning of the pontificate of Leo XIII, who was pope until his death in 1903. Leo is best known for the encyclical *Rerum Novarum,* which greatly influenced the course of Christian social thought and the labor movement. His other accomplishments included promotion of a revival of Scholastic philosophy and the impetus he gave to scriptural studies.

1881: The first International Eucharistic Congress was held in Lille, France.

Alexander II of Russia died. His policies of Russification — as well as those of his two predecessors and a successor during the century — caused great suffering to Catholics, Jews and Protestants in Poland, Lithuania, the Ukraine and Bessarabia.

1882: Charles Darwin died. His theory of evolution by natural selection, one of several scientific highlights of the century, had extensive repercussions in the faith-and-science controversy.

1889: The Catholic University of America was founded in Washington, D.C.

1893: The U.S. apostolic delegation was set up in Washington, D.C.

TWENTIETH CENTURY

1901: Restrictive measures in France forced the Jesuits, Benedictines, Carmelites and other religious orders to leave the country. Subsequently, 14,000 schools were suppressed; religious orders and congregations were expelled; the concordat was renounced in 1905; church property was confiscated in 1906. For some years the Holy See, refusing to comply with government demands for the control of bishops' appointments, left some ecclesiastical offices vacant.

1903: Start of the 11-year pontificate of St. Pius X. He initiated the codification of canon law, 1904; removed the ban against participation by Catholics in Italian national elections, 1905; issued decrees calling upon the faithful to receive Holy Communion frequently and daily, and stating that children should begin receiving the Eucharist at the age of seven, 1905 and 1910, respectively; ordered the establishment of the Confraternity of Christian Doctrine in all parishes throughout the world, 1905; condemned Modernism in the decree *Lamentabili* and the encyclical *Pascendi,* 1907.

1908: The United States and England, long under the jurisdiction of the Congregation for the Propagation of the Faith as mission territories, were removed from its control and placed under the common law of the Church.

1910: Laws of separation were enacted in Portugal, marking a point of departure in church-state relations.

1911: The Catholic Foreign Mission Society of America — Maryknoll, the first U.S.-founded society of its type — was established.

1914: Start of World War I, which lasted until 1918.

Start of the eight-year pontificate of Benedict XV. Much of his pontificate was devoted to seeking ways and means of minimizing the material and spiritual havoc of World War I. In 1917 he offered his services as a mediator to the belligerent nations, but his pleas for settlement of the conflict went unheeded.

1917: The Blessed Virgin Mary appeared to three children at Fatima, Portugal; see separate entry.

A new constitution, embodying repressive laws against the Church, was enacted in Mexico. Its implementation resulted in persecution in the 1920's and 1930's.

Bolsheviks seized power in Russia and set up a communist dictatorship. The event marked the rise of Communism in Russian and world affairs. One of its immediate, and lasting, results was persecution of the Church, Jews and other segments of the population.

1918: The *Code of Canon Law,* in preparation for more than 10 years, went into effect in the Western Church.

1919: Benedict XV stimulated missionary work through the decree *Maximum Illud,* in which he urged the recruiting and training of native clergy in places where the Church was not firmly established.

1922: Beginning of the 17-year pontificate of Pius XI. He subscribed to the Lateran Treaty, 1929, which settled the Roman Question created by the confiscation of the Papal States in 1871; issued the encyclical *Casti Connubii,* 1930, an authoritative statement on Christian marriage; resisted the efforts of Benito Mussolini to control Catholic Action and the Church, in the encyclical *Non Abbiamo Bisogno,* 1931; opposed various Fascist policies; issued the encyclicals *Quadragesimo Anno,* 1931, developing the social doctrine of Leo XIII's *Rerum Novarum,* and *Divini Redemptoris,* 1937, calling for social justice and condemning atheistic Communism; condemned anti-Semitism, 1937.

Ireland was partitioned. All but two of the predominantly Catholic counties were included in the southern part of the country, which eventually attained the status of an independent republic in 1949.

1926: The Catholic Relief Act repealed virtually all legal disabilities of Catholics in England.

1931: Leftists proclaimed Spain a republic and proceeded to disestablish the Church, confiscate church property, deny salaries to the clergy, expel the Jesuits and ban teaching of the Catholic faith. These actions were preludes to the civil war of 1936-1939.

1933: Emergence of Adolf Hitler to power in Germany. By 1935 two of his aims were clear, the elimination of the Jews and control of a single na-

tional church. Persecution decimated the Jews over a period of years. The Church was subject to repressive measures, which Pius XI protested futilely in the encyclical *Mit Brennender Sorge* in 1937.

1936: A three-year civil war broke out in Spain between the leftist Loyalists and forces led by Francisco Franco. The Loyalists were defeated and one-man, one-party rule was established. A number of priests, religious and lay persons fell victims to Loyalist persecution.

1939: Start of World War II, which lasted until 1945.

Start of the 19-year pontificate of Pius XII; see separate entry.

1940: Start of a decade of communist conquest in more than 13 countries, resulting in conditions of persecution for a minimum of 60 million Catholics as well as members of other faiths; see various countries.

Persecution diminished in Mexico through non-enforcement of anti-religious laws still on record.

1950: Pius XII proclaimed the dogma of the Assumption of the Blessed Virgin Mary.

1954: St. Pius X was canonized.

1957: The communist regime of China attempted to start a national schismatic church.

1958: Beginning of the five-year pontificate of John XXIII; see separate entry.

1962: The Second Vatican Council began the first of four sessions; see separate entry.

1963: Beginning of 15-year pontificate of Paul VI; see separate entry.

1978: Thirty-four-day pontificate of John Paul I; see separate entry.

Beginning of pontificate of John Paul II; see separate entry.

1983: The revised *Code of Canon Law* was promulgated and placed in effect.

HERESIES

Heresy is the formal and obstinate denial or doubt by a baptized person, who remains a nominal Christian, of any truth which must be believed as a matter of divine and Catholic faith. Formal heresy involves deliberate resistance to the authority of God who communicates revelation through Scripture and tradition and the teaching authority of the Church. Obstinate refusal to accept the infallible teaching of the Church constitutes the canonical crime of heresy.

Formal heretics automatically incur the penalty of excommunication (Canon 1364 of the Code of Canon Law). Material heretics are those who, in good faith and without formal obstinacy, do not accept articles or matters of divine and Catholic faith.

Heresies have been significant not only as disruptions of unity of faith but also as occasions for the clarification and development of doctrine.

Heresies from the beginning of the Church to the 13th century are listed below.

Judaizers: Early converts from Judaism who claimed that members of the Church had to observe all the requirements of Mosaic Law as well as the obligations of Christian faith. This view was condemned by the Council of Jerusalem held in 51 under the presidency of St. Peter (Acts 15:28).

Gnosticism: A combination of elements of Platonic philosophy and Eastern mystery religions which claimed that its secret-knowledge principle gave its adherents a deeper insight into Christian doctrine than divine revelation and faith. One Gnostic thesis denied the divinity of Christ; others denied the reality of his humanity, calling it mere appearance (**Docetism, Phantasiasm**).

Modalism: A general term covering propositions (**Monarchianism, Patripassianism, Sabellianism**) that the Father, Son and Holy Spirit are not really distinct divine Persons but are only three different modes of being and self-manifestation of the one God. Various forms of Modalism, which appeared in the East in the second century and spread westward, were all condemned.

Marcionism: A Gnostic creation named for its author, who claimed there was total opposition and no connection at all between the Old Testament and the New Testament, between the God of the Jews and the God of the Christians; and that the canon of Scripture consisted only of portions of Luke's Gospel and 10 epistles of Paul. Marcion was excommunicated in 144 at Rome, and his tenets were condemned again by a Roman council about 260. The heresy was checked at Rome by 200 but persisted for several centuries in the East and had some adherents as late as the Middle Ages.

Montanism: A form of extremism preached about 170 by Montanus of Phrygia, Asia Minor. Its principal tenets were: an imminent second coming of Christ, denial of the divine nature of the Church and its power to forgive sin, excessively rigorous morality. The heresy was condemned by Pope St. Zephyrinus (199-217). Tertullian was one of its victims.

Novatianism: A heresy of excessive rigorism named for its author, a priest of Rome and antipope. Its principal tenet was that persons who fell away from the Church under persecution and or those guilty of serious sin after baptism could not be absolved and readmitted to communion with the Church. The heresy, condemned by a Roman synod in 251, slowly subsided in the West and died in the East by the end of the seventh century.

Subordinationism, Adoptionism: Christological errors and logical antecedents of Arianism. The key tenet was that Christ, while the most excellent of creatures, was subordinate to God whose Son he was by adoption rather than by nature. First proposed at Rome late in the second century, it was condemned by Pope St. Victor in 190 and again in the following century, in 785 by Pope Adrian I, in 794 by a council of Frankfurt, and in 1177 by Pope Alexander III.

Arianism: Denial of the divinity of Christ, the most devastating of the early heresies, authored by Arius of Alexandria, a priest, and condemned by the Council of Nicaea I in 325. Arians and several kinds of **Semi-Arians** propagandized their tenets widely, raised havoc in the Church for several centuries, and established their own hierarchies and churches.

Macedonianism: Denial of the divinity of the Holy Spirit, who was said to be a creature of the Son. Condemned by the Council of Constantinople I in 381. Macedonians were also called **Pneumatomachists**, enemies of the Spirit; and **Marathonians**, after the name of one of their leaders, a bishop of Nicomedia.

Nestorianism: Denial of the real unity of divine and human natures in the single divine Person of Christ, proposed by Nestorius, patriarch of Constantinople. He also held that Mary could not be called the Mother of God (*Theotokos*); that is, of the Second Person of the Trinity made Man. Condemned by the councils of Ephesus in 431 and Chalcedon in 451.

Monophysitism: Denial of Christ's human nature; also called **Eutychianism**, after the name of one of its leading advocates. The heresy was condemned by the Council of Chalcedon in 451.

Monothelitism: Denial of the human will of Christ. Severus of Antioch and Sergius, patriarch of Constantinople, were leading advocates of the heresy, which was condemned by the Council of Constantinople III in 681.

Priscillianism: A fourth century amalgamation of elements from various sources — Sabellianism, Arianism, Docetism, Pantheism, belief in the diabolical nature of marriage, corruption of Scripture. The heresy was condemned by a council of Braga in 563 on 17 different counts.

Donatism: A development of the error at the heart of the third century **Rebaptism Controversy** (baptism conferred by heretics is invalid because persons deprived of grace are incapable of being ministers of grace to others). Followers of Donatus the Great asserted throughout the fourth century that sacraments administered by sinners were invalid. Condemnation of the heresy is traced to Pope St. Stephen I (254-257) and the principle that sacraments have their efficacy from Christ, not from their human ministers.

Pelagianism: Denial of the supernatural order of things, proposed by Pelagius (360-420), a Breton monk. Proceeding from the assumption that Adam had a natural right to supernatural life, the theory held that man could attain salvation through the efforts of his own free will and natural powers. The theory involved errors concerning the nature of original sin, the meaning of grace and other matters. St. Augustine opposed the heresy, which was condemned by the Council of Ephesus in 431. **Semi-Pelagianism** was condemned by a council of Orange in 529.

Iconoclasm: An image-breaking campaign which resulted from an edict issued by Eastern Emperor Leo the Isaurian in 726, that the veneration of images, pictures and relics was idolatrous. The theoretical basis of the heresy was the Monophysite error which denied the humanity of Christ. It was denounced several times before its condemnation by the Council of Nicaea II in 787.

Berengarian Heresy: Denial of the Real Presence of Christ under the appearances of bread and wine, the first clear-cut Eucharistic heresy; proposed by Berengarius of Tours (c. 1000-1088). The heresy was condemned by various synods and finally by a council held at Rome in 1079.

Waldensianism: Claimed by Peter Waldo, a merchant of Lyons, to be a return to pure Christianity, the heresy rejected the hierarchical structure of the Church, the sacramental system and other doctrines. Its adherents were excommunicated in 1184 and their tenets were condemned several times thereafter.

Albigensianism, Catharism: Related errors based on the old **Manichaean** assumption that two supreme principles of good and evil were operative in creation and life, and that the supreme objective of human endeavor was liberation from evil (matter). The heresy denied the humanity of Christ, the sacramental system and the authority of the Church (and state), and endorsed a moral code which threatened seriously the fabric of social life in southern France and northern Italy in the 12th and 13th centuries. The heresy was condemned by councils of the Lateran III and Lateran IV in 1179 and 1215.

ECUMENICAL COUNCILS

An ecumenical council is an assembly of the college of bishops, with and under the presidency of the pope, which has supreme authority over the Church in matters pertaining to faith, morals, worship and discipline.

The Second Vatican Council stated: "The supreme authority with which this college (of bishops) is empowered over the whole Church is exercised in a solemn way through an ecumenical council. A council is never ecumenical unless it is confirmed or at least accepted as such by the successor of Peter. It is the prerogative of the Roman Pontiff to convoke these councils, to preside over them, and to confirm them" (*Dogmatic Constitution on the Church,* No. 22).

Pope Presides

The pope is the head of an ecumenical council; he presides over it either personally or through legates. Conciliar decrees and other actions have binding force only when confirmed and promulgated by him. If a pope dies during a council, it is suspended until reconvened by another pope. An ecumenical council is not superior to a pope; hence, there is no appeal from a pope to a council.

Collectively, the bishops with the pope represent the whole Church. They do this not as democratic representatives of the faithful in a kind of church parliament, but as the successors of the Apostles with divinely given authority, care and responsibility over the whole Church.

Council participants with a deliberative vote are: cardinals, including those who are retired; residential patriarchs, primates, archbishops and bishops, even if they are not yet consecrated; abbots and certain other prelates, an abbot primate, abbot superiors of monastic congregations and heads of exempt clerical religious; titular bishops, on invitation. Experts in theology and canon law may be given a consultative vote. Others, including lay persons, may address a council or observe its actions, but may not vote.

Basic legislation concerning ecumenical councils is contained in the Code of Canon Law. Basic doctrinal considerations were stated by the Second Vatican Council in the *Dogmatic Constitution on the Church.*

Background

Ecumenical councils had their prototype in the Council of Jerusalem in 51, at which the Apostles under the leadership of St. Peter decided that converts to the Christian faith were not obliged to observe all the prescriptions of Old Testament law (Acts 15). As early as the second century, bishops got together in regional meetings, synods or councils to take common action for the doctrinal and pastoral good of their communities of faithful. The expansion of such limited assemblies to ecumenical councils was a logical and historical evolution, given the nature and needs of the Church.

Emperors were active in summoning or convoking the first eight councils, especially the first five and the eighth. Among reasons for intervention of this kind were the facts that the emperors regarded themselves as guardians of the faith; that the settlement of religious controversies, which had repercussions in political and social turmoil, served the cause of peace in the state; and that the emperors had at their disposal ways and means of facilitating gatherings of bishops. Imperial actions, however, did not account for the formally ecumenical nature of the councils.

Some councils were attended by relatively few bishops, and the ecumenical character of several was open to question for a time. However, confirmation and de facto recognition of their actions by popes and subsequent councils established them as ecumenical.

Role in History

The councils have played a highly significant role in the history of the Church by witnessing to and defining truths of revelation, by shaping forms of worship and discipline, and by promoting measures for the ever-necessary reform and renewal of Catholic life. In general, they have represented attempts of the Church to mobilize itself in times of crisis for self-preservation, self-purification and growth.

The first eight ecumenical councils were held in the East; the other 13, in the West. The majority of separated Eastern Churches — e.g., the Orthodox — recognize the ecumenical character of the first seven councils, which formulated a great deal of basic doctrine. Nestorians, however, acknowledge only the first two councils; the Monophysite Armenians, Syrians, and Copts acknowledge the first three.

The 21 Councils

The 21 ecumenical councils in the history of the Church are listed below, with indication of their names or titles (taken from the names of the places where they were held); the dates; the reigning and/or approving popes; the emperors who were instrumental in convoking the eight councils in the East; the number of bishops who attended, when available; the number of sessions; the most significant actions.

1. Nicaea I, 325: St. Sylvester I (Emperor Constantine I); attended by approximately 300 bishops; sessions held between May 20 or June 19 to near the end of August. Condemned Arianism, which denied the divinity of Christ; contributed to formulation of the Nicene Creed; fixed the date of Easter; passed regulations concerning clerical discipline; adopted the civil division of the Empire as the model for the organization of the Church.

2. Constantinople I, 381: St. Damasus I (Emperor Theodosius I); attended by approximately 150 bishops; sessions held from May to July. Condemned various brands of Arianism, and Macedonianism which denied the divinity of the Holy Spirit; contributed to formulation of the Nicene Creed; approved a canon which made the bishop of Constantinople the ranking prelate in the East, with primacy next to that of the pope. Doubt about the ecumenical character of this council was resolved by the ratification of its acts by popes and the Council of Chalcedon.

3. Ephesus, 431: St. Celestine I (Emperor Theodosius II); attended by 150 to 200 bishops; five sessions held between June 22 and July 17. Condemned Nestorianism, which denied the real unity of the divine and human natures in the Person of Christ; defined *Theotokos* ("Bearer of God") as the title of Mary, Mother of the Son of God made Man; condemned Pelagianism, which reduced the supernatural to the natural order of things.

4. Chalcedon, 451: St. Leo I (Emperor Marcian); attended by approximately 600 bishops; 17 sessions held between Oct. 8 and Nov. 1. Condemned: Monophysitism, also called Eutychianism, which denied the humanity of Christ by holding that he had only one, the divine, nature; and the Monophysite Robber Synod of Ephesus, of 449.

5. Constantinople II, 553: Vigilius (Emperor Justinian I); attended by 165 bishops; eight sessions held between May 5 and June 2. Condemned the *Three Chapters,* Nestorian-tainted writings of Theodore of Mopsuestia, Theodoret of Cyrus and Ibas of Edessa.

6. Constantinople III, 680-681; St. Agatho, St. Leo II (Emperor Constantine IV); attended by approximately 170 bishops; 16 sessions held between Nov. 7, 680, and Sept. 16, 681. Condemned Monothelitism, which held that there was only one will, the divine, in Christ; censured Pope Honorius I for a letter to Sergius, bishop of Constantinople, in which he made an ambiguous but not infallible statement about the unity of will and/or operation in Christ. Constantinople III is also called the Trullan Council because its sessions were held in the domed hall, Trullos, of the imperial palace.

7. Nicaea II, 787: Adrian I (Empress Irene); attended by approximately 300 bishops: eight sessions held between Sept. 24 and Oct. 23. Condemned: Iconoclasm, which held that the use of images was idolatry; and Adoptionism, which claimed that Christ was not the Son of God by nature but only by adoption. This was the last council regarded as ecumenical by Orthodox Churches.

8. Constantinople IV, 869-870: Adrian II (Emperor Basil I); attended by 102 bishops; six sessions held between Oct. 5, 869, and Feb. 28, 870. Condemned Iconoclasm; condemned and deposed Photius as patriarch of Constantinople; restored Ignatius to the patriarchate. This was the last ecumenical council held in the East. It was first called ecumenical by canonists toward the end of the 11th century.

9. Lateran I, 1123: Callistus II; attended by approximately 300 bishops; sessions held between Mar. 18 and Apr. 6. Endorsed provisions of the Concordat of Worms concerning the investiture of prelates: approved reform measures in 25 canons.

10. Lateran II, 1139: Innocent II; attended by 900 to 1,000 bishops and abbots; three sessions held in April. Adopted measures against a schism organized by antipope Anacletus; approved 30 disciplinary measures and canons, one of which stated that holy orders is an invalidating impediment to marriage.

11. Lateran III, 1179: Alexander III; attended by at least 300 bishops; three sessions held between Mar. 5 and 19. Enacted measures against the Waldenses and Albigensians; approved reform decrees in 27 canons; provided that popes be elected by two-thirds vote of the cardinals.

12. Lateran IV, 1215: Innocent III; sessions held between Nov. 11 and 30. Ordered annual confession and Communion; defined and made first official use of the term "transubstantiation"; adopted measures to counteract the Cathari and Albigensians; approved 70 canons.

13. Lyons I, 1245: Innocent IV; attended by approximately 150 bishops; three sessions held between June 28 and July 17. Confirmed the deposition of Emperor Frederick II; approved 22 canons.

14. Lyons II, 1274: Gregory X; attended by approximately 500 bishops; six sessions held between May 7 and July 17. Accomplished a temporary reunion of separated Eastern Churches with the Roman Church; issued regulations concerning conclaves for papal elections; approved 31 canons.

15. Vienne, 1311-1312: Clement V; attended by 132 bishops; three sessions held between Oct. 16, 1311, and May 6, 1312. Suppressed the Knights Templar; enacted a number of reform decrees.

16. Constance, 1414-1418: Gregory XII, Martin V; attended by nearly 200 bishops, plus other prelates and many experts; 45 sessions held between Nov. 5, 1414, and Apr. 22, 1418. Took successful action to end the Western Schism; rejected the teachings of Wycliff; condemned Hus as a heretic. One decree, passed in the earlier stages of the council, asserted the superiority of an ecumenical council over the pope; this was later rejected.

17. Florence (also called Basel-Ferrara-Florence), 1438-1445: Eugene IV; attended by many Latin-Rite and Eastern-Rite bishops; preliminary sessions were held at Basel and Ferrara before definitive work was accomplished at Florence. Reaffirmed the primacy of the pope against the claims of Conciliarists that an ecumenical council is superior to the pope; formulated and approved decrees of union — with the Greeks, July 6, 1439; with the Armenians, Nov. 22, 1439; with the Jacobites, Feb. 4, 1442. These decrees failed to gain general or lasting acceptance in the East.

18. Lateran V, 1512-1517: Julius II, Leo X; 12 sessions held between May 3, 1512, and Mar. 16, 1517. Stated the relation and position of the pope with respect to an ecumenical council; acted to counteract the Pragmatic Sanction of Bourges and exaggerated claims of liberty by the French Church; condemned erroneous teachings concerning the nature of the human soul; stated doctrine concerning indulgences. The council reflected concern for abuses in the Church and the need for reforms but failed to take decisive action in the years immediately preceding the Reformation.

19. Trent, 1545-1563: Paul III, Julius III, Pius IV; 25 sessions held between Dec. 13, 1545, and Dec. 4, 1563. Issued a great number of decrees concerning doctrinal matters opposed by the Reformers, and mobilized the Counter-Reformation. Definitions covered the rule of faith, the nature of justification, grace, faith, original sin and its effects, the seven sacraments, the sacrificial nature of the Mass, the veneration of saints, use of sacred images, belief in purgatory, the doctrine of indulgences, the jurisdiction of the pope over the whole Church. Initiated many reforms for renewal in the liturgy and general discipline in the Church, the promotion of religious instruction, the education of the clergy through the foundation of seminaries, etc. Trent ranks with Vatican II as the greatest ecumenical council held in the West.

20. Vatican I, 1869-1870: Pius IX; attended by approximately 800 bishops and other prelates; four public sessions and 89 general meetings held between Dec. 8, 1869, and July 7, 1870. Defined papal primacy and infallibility in a dogmatic constitution on the Church; covered natural religion, revelation, faith, and the relations between faith and reason in a dogmatic constitution on the Catholic faith. The council suspended sessions Sept. 1 and was adjourned Oct. 20, 1870.

Vatican II

The Second Vatican Council, which was forecast by Pope John XXIII Jan. 25, 1959, was held in four sessions in St. Peter's Basilica.

Pope John convoked it and opened the first session, which ran from Oct. 11 to Dec. 8, 1962. Following John's death June 3, 1963, Pope Paul VI reconvened the council for the other three sessions which ran from Sept. 29 to Dec. 4, 1963; Sept. 14 to Nov. 21, 1964; Sept. 14 to Dec. 8, 1965.

A total of 2,860 Fathers participated in council proceedings, and attendance at meetings varied between 2,000 and 2,500. For various reasons, including the denial of exit from Communist-domi-

nated countries, 274 Fathers could not attend.

The council formulated and promulgated 16 documents — two dogmatic and two pastoral constitutions, nine decrees and three declarations — all of which reflect its basic pastoral orientation toward renewal and reform in the Church. Given below are the Latin and English titles of the documents and their dates of promulgation.

• *Lumen Gentium* (Dogmatic Constitution on the Church), Nov. 21, 1964.

• *Dei Verbum* (Dogmatic Constitution on Divine Revelation), Nov. 18, 1965.

• *Sacrosanctum Concilium* (Constitution on the Sacred Liturgy), Dec. 4, 1963.

• *Gaudium et Spes* (Pastoral Constitution on the Church in the Modern World), Dec. 7, 1965.

• *Christus Dominus* (Decree on the Bishops' Pastoral Office in the Church), Oct. 28, 1965.

• *Ad Gentes* (Decree on the Church's Missionary Activity), Dec. 7, 1965.

• *Unitatis Redintegratio* (Decree on Ecumenism), Nov. 21, 1964.

• *Orientalium Ecclesiarum* (Decree on Eastern Catholic Churches), Nov. 21, 1964.

• *Presbyterorum Ordinis* (Decree on the Ministry and Life of Priests), Dec. 7, 1965.

• *Optatam Totius* (Decree on Priestly Formation), Oct. 28, 1965.

• *Perfectae Caritatis* (Decree on the Appropriate Renewal of the Religious Life), Oct. 28, 1965.

• *Apostolicam Actuositatem* (Decree on the Apostolate of the Laity), Nov. 18, 1965.

• *Inter Mirifica* (Decree on the Instruments of Social Communication), Dec. 4, 1963.

• *Dignitatis Humanae* (Declaration on Religious Freedom), Dec. 7, 1965.

• *Nostra Aetate* (Declaration on the Relationship of the Church to Non-Christian Religions), Oct. 28, 1965.

• *Gravissimum Educationis* (Declaration on Christian Education), Oct. 28, 1965.

The key documents were the four constitutions, which set the ideological basis for all the others. To date, the documents with the most visible effects are those on the liturgy, the Church, the Church in the world, ecumenism, the renewal of religious life, the life and ministry of priests, the lay apostolate.

The main business of the council was to explore and make explicit dimensions of doctrine and Christian life requiring emphasis for the full development of the Church and the better accomplishment of its mission in the contemporary world.

THE AMERICAN COLLEGE, LOUVAIN

The American College was founded by the bishops of the United States in 1857 as a house of formation for U.S. seminarians and as a residence for graduate priest students pursuing courses in theology and related subjects at The Catholic Universities of Leuven and Louvain-la-Neuve (dating from 1425) in Belgium.

The college is administered by an American rector and staff, and operates under the auspices of a special committee of the National Conference of

Catholic Bishops. Bishop Eusebius J. Beltran of Tulsa is chairman of the committee. The present rector, the 11th, is Father John J. Costanzo of Pueblo, Colo. The address is: The American College, University of Louvain, Naamsestraat 100, 3000 Leuven, Belgium.

The current enrollment of The American College includes students from more than 40 dioceses in the U.S., Canada, Europe and the Third World countries.

Information includes the name of the pope, in many cases his name before becoming pope, his birthplace or country of origin, the date of accession to the papacy, and the date of the end of reign which, in all but a few cases, was the date of death. Double dates indicate times of election and coronation.

Source: "Annuario Pontificio."

St. Peter (Simon Bar-Jona): Bethsaida in Galilee; d. c. 64 or 67.

St. Linus: Tuscany; 67-76.

St. Anacletus (Cletus): Rome; 76-88.

St. Clement: Rome; 88-97.

St. Evaristus: Greece; 97-105.

St. Alexander I: Rome; 105-115.

St. Sixtus I: Rome; 115-125.

St. Telesphorus: Greece; 125-136.

St. Hyginus: Greece; 136-140.

St. Pius I: Aquileia; 140-155.

St. Anicetus: Syria; 155-166.

St. Soter: Campania; 166-175.

St. Eleutherius: Nicopolis in Epirus; 175-189.

Up to the time of St. Eleutherius, the years indicated for the beginning and end of pontificates are not absolutely certain. Also, up to the middle of the 11th century, there are some doubts about the exact days and months given in chronological tables.

St. Victor I: Africa; 189-199.

St. Zephyrinus: Rome; 199-217.

St. Callistus I: Rome; 217-222.

St. Urban I: Rome; 222-230.

St. Pontian: Rome; July 21, 230, to Sept. 28, 235.

St. Anterus: Greece; Nov. 21, 235, to Jan. 3, 236.

St. Fabian: Rome; Jan. 10, 236, to Jan. 20, 250.

St. Cornelius: Rome; Mar., 251, to June, 253.

St. Lucius I: Rome; June 25, 253, to Mar. 5, 254.

St. Stephen I: Rome; May 12, 254, to Aug. 2, 257.

St. Sixtus II: Greece; Aug. 30, 257, to Aug. 6, 258.

St. Dionysius: July 22, 259, to Dec. 26, 268.

St. Felix I: Rome; Jan. 5, 269, to Dec. 30, 274.

St. Eutychian: Luni; Jan. 4, 275, to Dec. 7, 283.

St. Caius: Dalmatia; Dec. 17, 283, to Apr. 22, 296.

St. Marcellinus: Rome; June 30, 296, to Oct. 25, 304.

St. Marcellus I: Rome; May 27, 308, or June 26, 308, to Jan. 16, 309.

St. Eusebius: Greece; Apr. 18, 309 or 310, to Aug. 17, 309 or 310.

St. Melchiades (Miltiades): Africa; July 2, 311, to Jan. 11, 314.

St. Sylvester I: Rome; Jan. 31, 314, to Dec. 31, 335. (Most of the popes before St. Sylvester I were martyrs.)

St. Marcus: Rome; Jan. 18, 336, to Oct. 7, 336.

St. Julius I: Rome; Feb. 6, 337, to Apr. 12, 352.

Liberius: Rome; May 17, 352, to Sept. 24, 366.

St. Damasus I: Spain; Oct. 1, 366, to Dec. 11, 384.

St. Siricius: Rome; Dec. 15, or 22 or 29, 384, to Nov. 26, 399.

St. Anastasius I: Rome; Nov. 27, 399, to Dec. 19, 401.

St. Innocent I: Albano; Dec. 22, 401, to Mar. 12, 417.

St. Zosimus: Greece; Mar. 18, 417, to Dec. 26, 418.

St. Boniface I: Rome; Dec. 28 or 29, 418, to Sept. 4, 422.

St. Celestine I: Campania; Sept. 10, 422, to July 27, 432.

St. Sixtus III: Rome; July 31, 432, to Aug. 19, 440.

St. Leo I (the Great): Tuscany; Sept. 29, 440, to Nov. 10, 461.

St. Hilary: Sardinia; Nov. 19, 461, to Feb. 29, 468.

St. Simplicius: Tivoli; Mar. 3, 468, to Mar. 10, 483.

St. Felix III (II): Rome; Mar. 13, 483, to Mar. 1, 492.

He should be called Felix II, and his successors of the same name should be numbered accordingly. The discrepancy in the numerical designation of popes named Felix was caused by the erroneous insertion in some lists of the name of St. Felix of Rome, a martyr.

St. Gelasius I: Africa; Mar. 1, 492, to Nov. 21, 496.

Anastasius II: Rome; Nov. 24, 496, to Nov. 19, 498.

St. Symmachus: Sardinia; Nov. 22, 498, to July 19, 514.

St. Hormisdas: Frosinone; July 20, 514, to Aug. 6, 523.

St. John I, Martyr: Tuscany; Aug. 13, 523, to May 18, 526.

St. Felix IV (III): Samnium; July 12, 526, to Sept. 22, 530.

Boniface II: Rome; Sept. 22, 530, to Oct. 17, 532.

John II: Rome; Jan. 2, 533, to May 8, 535.

John II was the first pope to change his name. His given name was Mercury.

St. Agapitus I: Rome; May 13, 535, to Apr. 22, 536.

St. Silverius, Martyr: Campania; June 1 or 8, 536, to Nov. 11, 537 (d. Dec. 2, 537).

St. Silverius was violently deposed in March, 537, and abdicated Nov. 11, 537. His successor, Vigilius, was not recognized as pope by all the Roman clergy until his abdication.

Vigilius: Rome; Mar. 29, 537, to June 7, 555.

Pelagius I: Rome; Apr. 16, 556, to Mar. 4, 561.

John III: Rome; July 17, 561, to July 13, 574.

Benedict I: Rome; June 2, 575, to July 30, 579.

Pelagius II: Rome; Nov. 26, 579, to Feb. 7, 590.

St. Gregory I (the Great): Rome; Sept. 3, 590, to Mar. 12, 604.

Sabinian: Blera in Tuscany; Sept. 13, 604, to Feb. 22, 606.

Boniface III: Rome; Feb. 19, 607, to Nov. 12, 607.

St. Boniface IV: Abruzzi; Aug. 25, 608, to May 8, 615.

St. Deusdedit (Adeodatus I): Rome; Oct. 19, 615, to Nov. 8, 618.

Boniface V: Naples; Dec. 23, 619, to Oct. 25, 625.

Honorius I: Campania; Oct. 27, 625, to Oct. 12, 638.

Severinus: Rome; May 28, 640, to Aug. 2, 640.

John IV: Dalmatia; Dec. 24, 640, to Oct. 12, 642.

Theodore I: Greece; Nov. 24, 642, to May 14, 649.

St. Martin I, Martyr: Todi; July, 649, to Sept. 16, 655 (in exile from June 17, 653).

St. Eugene I: Rome; Aug. 10, 654, to June 2, 657.

St. Eugene I was elected during the exile of St. Martin I, who is believed to have endorsed him as pope.

St. Vitalian: Segni; July 30, 657, to Jan. 27, 672.

Adeodatus II: Rome; Apr. 11, 672, to June 17, 676.

Donus: Rome; Nov. 2, 676, to Apr. 11, 678.

St. Agatho: Sicily; June 27, 678, to Jan. 10, 681.

St. Leo II: Sicily; Aug. 17, 682, to July 3, 683.

St. Benedict II: Rome; June 26, 684, to May 8, 685.

John V: Syria; July 23, 685, to Aug. 2, 686.

Conon: birthplace unknown; Oct. 21, 686, to Sept. 21, 687.

St. Sergius I: Syria; Dec. 15, 687, to Sept. 8, 701.

John VI: Greece; Oct. 30, 701, to Jan. 11, 705.

John VII: Greece; Mar. 1, 705, to Oct. 18, 707.

Sisinnius: Syria; Jan. 15, 708, to Feb. 4, 708.

Constantine: Syria; Mar. 25, 708, to Apr. 9, 715.

St. Gregory II: Rome; May 19, 715, to Feb. 11, 731.

St. Gregory III: Syria; Mar. 18, 731, to Nov., 741.

St. Zachary: Greece; Dec. 10, 741, to Mar. 22, 752.

Stephen II (III): Rome; Mar. 26, 752, to Apr. 26, 757.

After the death of St. Zachary, a Roman priest named Stephen was elected but died (four days later) before his consecration as bishop of Rome, which would have marked the beginning of his pontificate. Another Stephen was elected to succeed Zachary as Stephen II. (The first pope with this name was St. Stephen I, 254-57.) The ordinal III appears in parentheses after the name of Stephen II because the name of the earlier elected but deceased priest was included in some lists. Other Stephens have double numbers.

St. Paul I: Rome; Apr. (May 29), 757, to June 28, 767.

Stephen III (IV): Sicily; Aug. 1 (7), 768, to Jan. 24, 772.

Adrian I: Rome; Feb. 1 (9), 772, to Dec. 25, 795.

St. Leo III: Rome; Dec. 26 (27), 795, to June 12, 816.

Stephen IV (V): Rome; June 22, 816, to Jan. 24, 817.

St. Paschal I: Rome; Jan. 25, 817, to Feb. 11, 824.

Eugene II: Rome; Feb. (May), 824, to Aug., 827.

Valentine: Rome; Aug. 827, to Sept., 827.

Gregory IV: Rome; 827, to Jan., 844.

Sergius II: Rome; Jan., 844 to Jan. 27, 847.

St. Leo IV: Rome; Jan. (Apr. 10), 847, to July 17, 855.

Benedict III: Rome; July (Sept. 29), 855, to Apr. 17, 858.

St. Nicholas I (the Great): Rome; Apr. 24, 858, to Nov. 13, 867.

Adrian II: Rome; Dec. 14, 867, to Dec. 14, 872.

John VIII: Rome; Dec. 14, 872, to Dec. 16, 882.

Marinus I: Gallese; Dec. 16, 882, to May 15, 884.

St. Adrian III: Rome; May 17, 884, to Sept., 885. Cult confirmed June 2, 1891.

Stephen V (VI): Rome; Sept., 885, to Sept. 14, 891.

Formosus: Portus; Oct. 6, 891, to Apr. 4, 896.

Boniface VI: Rome; Apr., 896, to Apr., 896.

Stephen VI (VII): Rome; May, 896, to Aug., 897.

Romanus: Gallese; Aug., 897, to Nov., 897.

Theodore II: Rome; Dec., 897, to Dec., 897.

John IX: Tivoli; Jan., 898, to Jan., 900.

Benedict IV: Rome; Jan. (Feb.), 900, to July, 903.

Leo V: Ardea; July, 903, to Sept., 903.

Sergius III: Rome; Jan. 29, 904, to Apr. 14, 911.

Anastasius III: Rome; Apr., 911, to June, 913.

Landus: Sabina; July, 913, to Feb., 914.

John X: Tossignano (Imola); Mar., 914, to May, 928.

Leo VI: Rome; May, 928, to Dec., 928.

Stephen VII (VIII): Rome; Dec., 928, to Feb., 931.

John XI: Rome; Feb. (Mar.), 931, to Dec., 935.

Leo VII: Rome; Jan. 3, 936, to July 13, 939.

Stephen VIII (IX): Rome; July 14, 939, to Oct., 942.

Marinus II: Rome; Oct. 30, 942, to May, 946.

Agapitus II: Rome; May 10, 946, to Dec., 955.

John XII (Octavius): Tusculum; Dec. 16, 955, to May 14, 964 (date of his death).

Leo VIII: Rome; Dec. 4 (6), 963, to Mar. 1, 965.

Benedict V: Rome; May 22, 964, to July 4, 966.

Confusion exists concerning the legitimacy of claims to the pontificate by Leo VIII and Benedict V. John XII was deposed Dec. 4, 963, by a Roman council. If this deposition was invalid, Leo was an antipope. If the deposition of John was valid, Leo was the legitimate pope and Benedict was an antipope.

John XIII: Rome; Oct. 1, 965, to Sept. 6, 972.

Benedict VI: Rome; Jan. 19, 973, to June, 974.

Benedict VII: Rome; Oct. 974, to July 10, 983.

John XIV (Peter Campenora): Pavia; Dec., 983, to Aug. 20, 984.

John XV: Rome; Aug., 985, to Mar., 996.

Gregory V (Bruno of Carinthia): Saxony; May 3, 996, to Feb. 18, 999.

Sylvester II (Gerbert): Auvergne; Apr. 2, 999, to May 12, 1003.

John XVII (Siccone): Rome; June, 1003, to Dec., 1003.

John XVIII (Phasianus): Rome; Jan., 1004, to July, 1009.

Sergius IV (Peter): Rome; July 31, 1009, to May 12, 1012.

The custom of changing one's name on election to the papacy is generally considered to date from the time of Sergius IV. Before his time, several popes had changed their names. After his time, this became a regular practice, with few exceptions; e.g., Adrian VI and Marcellus II.

Benedict VIII (Theophylactus): Tusculum; May 18, 1012, to Apr. 9, 1024.

John XIX (Romanus): Tusculum; Apr. (May), 1024, to 1032.

Benedict IX (Theophylactus): Tusculum; 1032, to 1044.

Sylvester III (John): Rome; Jan. 20, 1045, to Feb. 10, 1045.

Sylvester III was an antipope if the forcible removal of Benedict IX in 1044 was not legitimate.

Benedict IX (second time): Apr. 10, 1045, to May 1, 1045.

Gregory VI (John Gratian): Rome; May 5, 1045, to Dec. 20, 1046.

Clement II (Suitger, Lord of Morsleben and Hornburg): Saxony; Dec. 24 (25), 1046, to Oct. 9, 1047.

If the resignation of Benedict IX in 1045 and his removal at the December, 1046, synod were not legitimate, Gregory VI and Clement II were antipopes.

Benedict IX (third time): Nov. 8, 1047, to July 17, 1048 (d. c. 1055).

Damasus II (Poppo): Bavaria; July 17, 1048, to Aug. 9, 1048.

St. Leo IX (Bruno): Alsace; Feb. 12, 1049, to Apr. 19, 1054.

Victor II (Gebhard): Swabia; Apr. 16, 1055, to July 28, 1057.

Stephen IX (X) (Frederick): Lorraine; Aug. 3, 1057, to Mar. 29, 1058.

Nicholas II (Gerard): Burgundy; Jan. 24, 1059, to July 27, 1061.

Alexander II (Anselmo da Baggio): Milan; Oct. 1, 1061, to Apr. 21, 1073.

St. Gregory VII (Hildebrand): Tuscany; Apr. 22 (June 30), 1073, to May 25, 1085.

Bl. Victor III (Dauferius; Desiderius): Benevento; May 24, 1086, to Sept. 16, 1087. Cult confirmed July 23, 1887.

Bl. Urban II (Otto di Lagery): France; Mar. 12, 1088, to July 29, 1099. Cult confirmed July 14, 1881.

Paschal II (Raniero): Ravenna; Aug. 13 (14), 1099, to Jan. 21, 1118.

Gelasius II (Giovanni Caetani): Gaeta; Jan. 24 (Mar. 10), 1118, to Jan. 28, 1119.

Callistus II (Guido of Burgundy): Burgundy; Feb. 2 (9), 1119, to Dec. 13, 1124.

Honorius II (Lamberto): Fiagnano (Imola); Dec. 15 (21), 1124, to Feb. 13, 1130.

Innocent II (Gregorio Papareschi): Rome; Feb. 14 (23), 1130, to Sept. 24, 1143.

Celestine II (Guido): Citta di Castello; Sept. 26 (Oct. 3), 1143, to Mar. 8, 1144.

Lucius II (Gerardo Caccianemici): Bologna: Mar. 12, 1144, to Feb. 15, 1145.

Bl. Eugene III (Bernardo Paganelli di Montemagno): Pisa; Feb. 15 (18), 1145, to July 8, 1153. Cult confirmed Oct. 3, 1872.

Anastasius IV (Corrado): Rome; July 12, 1153, to Dec, 3, 1154.

Adrian IV (Nicholas Breakspear): England; Dec. 4 (5), 1154, to Sept. 1, 1159.

Alexander III (Rolando Bandinelli): Siena; Sept. 7 (20), 1159, to Aug. 30, 1181.

Lucius III (Ubaldo Allucingoli): Lucca; Sept. 1 (6), 1181, to Sept. 25, 1185.

Urban III (Uberto Crivelli): Milan; Nov. 25 (Dec. 1), 1185, to Oct. 20, 1187.

Gregory VIII (Alberto de Morra): Benevento; Oct. 21 (25), 1187, to Dec. 17, 1187.

Clement III (Paolo Scolari): Rome; Dec. 19 (20), 1187, to Mar., 1191.

Celestine III (Giacinto Bobone): Rome; Mar. 30 (Apr. 14), 1191, to Jan. 8, 1198.

Innocent III (Lotario dei Conti di Segni); Anagni; Jan. 8 (Feb. 22), 1198, to July 16, 1216.

Honorius III (Cencio Savelli): Rome; July 18 (24), 1216, to Mar. 18, 1227.

Gregory IX (Ugolino, Count of Segni): Anagni; Mar. 19 (21), 1227, to Aug. 22, 1241.

Celestine IV (Goffredo Castiglioni): Milan; Oct. 25 (28), 1241, to Nov. 10, 1241.

Innocent IV (Sinibaldo Fieschi): Genoa; June 25 (28), 1243, to Dec. 7, 1254.

Alexander IV (Rinaldo, Count of Segni): Anagni; Dec. 12 (20), 1254, to May 25, 1261.

Urban IV (Jacques Pantaléon): Troyes; Aug. 29 (Sept. 4), 1261, to Oct. 2, 1264.

Clement IV (Guy Foulques or Guido le Gros): France; Feb. 5 (15), 1265, to Nov. 29, 1268.

Bl. Gregory X (Teobaldo Visconti): Piacenza; Sept. 1, 1271 (Mar. 27, 1272), to Jan. 10, 1276. Cult confirmed Sept. 12, 1713.

Bl. Innocent V (Peter of Tarentaise): Savoy; Jan. 21 (Feb. 22), 1276, to June 22, 1276. Cult confirmed Mar. 13, 1898.

Adrian V (Ottobono Fieschi): Genoa: July 11, 1276, to Aug. 18, 1276.

John XXI (Petrus Juliani or Petrus Hispanus): Portugal; Sept. 8 (20), 1276, to May 20, 1277.

Elimination was made of the name of John XX in an effort to rectify the numerical designation of popes named John. The error dates back to the time of John XV.

Nicholas III (Giovanni Gaetano Orsini): Rome; Nov. 25 (Dec. 26), 1277, to Aug. 22, 1280.

Martin IV (Simon de Brie): France; Feb. 22 (Mar. 23), 1281, to Mar. 28, 1285.

The names of Marinus 1 (882-84) and Marinus II (942-46) were construed as Martin. In view of these two pontificates and the earlier reign of St. Martin I (649-55), this pope was called Martin IV.

Honorius IV (Giacomo Savelli): Rome; Apr. 2 (May 20), 1285, to Apr. 3, 1287.

Nicholas IV (Girolamo Masci): Ascoli; Feb. 22, 1288, to Apr. 4, 1292.

St. Celestine V (Pietro del Murrone): Isernia; July 5 (Aug. 29), 1294, to Dec. 13, 1294; d. 1296. Canonized May 5, 1313.

Boniface VIII (Benedetto Caetani): Anagni; Dec. 24, 1294 (Jan. 23, 1295), to Oct. 11, 1303.

Bl. Benedict XI (Niccolo Boccasini): Treviso; Oct. 22 (27), 1303, to July 7, 1304. Cult confirmed Apr. 24, 1736.

Clement V (Bertrand de Got): France; June 5 (Nov. 14), 1305, to Apr. 20, 1314. (First of Avignon popes.)

John XXII (Jacques d'Euse): Cahors; Aug. 7 (Sept. 5), 1316, to Dec. 4, 1334.

Benedict XII (Jacques Fournier): France; Dec. 20, 1334 (Jan. 8, 1335), to Apr. 25, 1342.

Clement VI (Pierre Roger): France; May 7 (19), 1342, to Dec. 6, 1352.

Innocent VI (Etienne Aubert): France; Dec. 18 (30), 1352, to Sept. 12, 1362.

Bl. Urban V (Guillaume de Grimoard): France; Sept. 28 (Nov. 6), 1362, to Dec. 19, 1370. Cult confirmed Mar. 10, 1870.

Gregory XI (Pierre Roger de Beaufort): France; Dec. 30, 1370 (Jan. 5, 1371), to Mar. 26, 1378. (Last of Avignon popes.)

Urban VI (Bartolomeo Prignano): Naples; Apr. 8 (18), 1378, to Oct. 15, 1389.

Boniface IX (Pietro Tomacelli): Naples; Nov. 2 (9), 1389, to Oct. 1, 1404.

Innocent VII (Cosma Migliorati): Sulmona; Oct. 17 (Nov. 11), 1404, to Nov. 6, 1406.

Gregory XII (Angelo Correr): Venice; Nov. 30 (Dec. 19), 1406, to July 4, 1415, when he voluntarily resigned from the papacy to permit the election of his successor. He died Oct. 18, 1417. (See The Western Schism.)

Martin V (Oddone Colonna): Rome; Nov. 11 (21), 1417, to Feb. 20, 1431.

Eugene IV (Gabriele Condulmer): Venice; Mar. 3 (11), 1431, to Feb. 23, 1447.

Nicholas V (Tommaso Parentucelli): Sarzana; Mar. 6 (19), 1447, to Mar. 24, 1455.

Callistus III (Alfonso Borgia): Jativa (Valencia); Apr. 8 (20), 1455, to Aug. 6, 1458.

Pius II (Enea Silvio Piccolomini): Siena; Aug. 19 (Sept. 3), 1458, to Aug. 15, 1464.

Paul II (Pietro Barbo): Venice; Aug. 30 (Sept. 16), 1464, to July 26, 1471.

Sixtus IV (Francesco della Rovere): Savona; Aug. 9 (25), 1471, to Aug. 12, 1484.

Innocent VIII (Giovanni Battista Cibo): Genoa; Aug. 29 (Sept. 12), 1484, to July 25, 1492.

Alexander VI (Rodrigo Borgia): Jativa (Valencia); Aug. 11 (26), 1492, to Aug. 18, 1503.

Pius III (Francesco Todeschini-Piccolomini): Siena; Sept. 22 (Oct. 1, 8), 1503, to Oct. 18, 1503.

Julius II (Giuliano della Rovere): Savona; Oct. 31 (Nov. 26), 1503, to Feb. 21, 1513.

Leo X (Giovanni de' Medici): Florence; Mar. 9 (19), 1513, to Dec. 1, 1521.

Adrian VI (Adrian Florensz): Utrecht; Jan. 9 (Aug. 31), 1522, to Sept. 14, 1523.

Clement VII (Giulio de' Medici): Florence; Nov. 19 (26), 1523, to Sept. 25, 1534.

Paul III (Alessandro Farnese): Rome; Oct. 13 (Nov. 3), 1534, to Nov. 10, 1549.

Julius III (Giovanni Maria Ciocchi del Monte): Rome; Feb. 7 (22), 1550, to Mar. 23, 1555.

Marcellus II (Marcello Cervini): Montepulciano; Apr. 9 (10), 1555, to May 1, 1555.

Paul IV (Gian Pietro Carafa): Naples; May 23 (26), 1555, to Aug. 18, 1559.

Pius IV (Giovan Angelo de' Medici): Milan; Dec. 25, 1559 (Jan. 6, 1560), to Dec. 9, 1565.

St. Pius V (Antonio-Michele Ghislieri): Bosco (Alexandria); Jan. 7 (17), 1566, to May 1, 1572. Canonized May 22, 1712.

Gregory XIII (Ugo Buoncompagni): Bologna; May 13 (25), 1572, to Apr. 10, 1585.

Sixtus V (Felice Peretti): Grottammare (Ripatransone); Apr. 24 (May 1), 1585, to Aug. 27, 1590.

Urban VII (Giovanni Battista Castagna): Rome; Sept. 15, 1590, to Sept. 27, 1590.

Gregory XIV (Niccolo Sfondrati): Cremona; Dec. 5 (8), 1590, to Oct. 16, 1591.

Innocent IX (Giovanni Antonio Facchinetti): Bologna; Oct. 29 (Nov. 3), 1591, to Dec. 30, 1591.

Clement VIII (Ippolito Aldobrandini): Florence; Jan. 30 (Feb. 9), 1592, to Mar. 3, 1605.

Leo XI (Alessandro de' Medici): Florence; Apr. 1 (10), 1605, to Apr. 27, 1605.

Paul V (Camillo Borghese): Rome; May 16 (29), 1605, to Jan. 28, 1621.

Gregory XV (Alessandro Ludovisi): Bologna; Feb. 9 (14), 1621, to July 8, 1623.

Urban VIII (Maffeo Barberini): Florence; Aug. 6 (Sept. 29), 1623, to July 29, 1644.

Innocent X (Giovanni Battista Pamfili): Rome; Sept. 15 (Oct. 4), 1644, to Jan. 7, 1655.

Alexander VII (Fabio Chigi): Siena; Apr. 7 (18), 1655, to May 22, 1667.

Clement IX (Giulio Rospigliosi): Pistoia; June 20 (26), 1667, to Dec. 9, 1669.

Clement X (Emilio Altieri): Rome; Apr. 29 (May 11), 1670, to July 22, 1676.

Bl. Innocent XI (Benedetto Odescalchi): Como; Sept. 21 (Oct. 4), 1676, to Aug. 12, 1689.

Alexander VIII (Pietro Ottoboni): Venice; Oct. 6 (16), 1689, to Feb. 1, 1691.

Innocent XII (Antonio Pignatelli): Spinazzola; July 12 (15), 1691, to Sept. 27, 1700.

Clement XI (Giovanni Francesco Albani): Urbino; Nov. 23, 30 (Dec. 8), 1700, to Mar. 19, 1721.

Innocent XIII (Michelangelo dei Conti): Rome; May 8 (18), 1721, to Mar. 7, 1724.

Benedict XIII (Pietro Francesco — Vincenzo Maria — Orsini): Gravina (Bari); May 29 (June 4), 1724, to Feb. 21, 1730.

Clement XII (Lorenzo Corsini): Florence; July 12 (16), 1730, to Feb. 6, 1740.

Benedict XIV (Prospero Lambertini): Bologna; Aug. 17 (22), 1740, to May 3, 1758.

Clement XIII (Carlo Rezzonico): Venice; July 6 (16), 1758, to Feb. 2, 1769.

Clement XIV (Giovanni Vincenzo Antonio — Lorenzo — Ganganelli): Rimini; May 19, 28 (June 4), 1769, to Sept. 22, 1774.

Pius VI (Giovanni Angelo Braschi): Cesena; Feb. 15 (22), 1775, to Aug. 29, 1799.

Pius VII (Barnaba — Gregorio — Chiaramonti): Cesena; Mar. 14 (21), 1800, to Aug. 20, 1823.

Leo XII (Annibale della Genga): Genga (Fabriano); Sept. 28 (Oct. 5), 1823, to Feb. 10, 1829.

Pius VIII (Francesco Saverio Castiglioni): Cingoli; Mar. 31 (Apr. 5), 1829, to Nov. 30, 1830.

Gregory XVI (Bartolomeo Alberto — Mauro — Cappellari): Belluno; Feb. 2 (6), 1831, to June 1, 1846.

Pius IX (Giovanni M. Mastai Ferretti): Senigallia; June 16 (21), 1846, to Feb. 7, 1878.

Leo XIII (Gioacchino Pecci): Carpineto (Anagni); Feb. 20 (Mar. 3), 1878, to July 20, 1903.

St. Pius X (Giuseppe Sarto): Riese (Treviso); Aug. 4 (9), 1903, to Aug. 20, 1914. Canonized May 29, 1954.

Benedict XV (Giacomo della Chiesa): Genoa; Sept. 3 (6), 1914, to Jan. 22, 1922.

Pius XI (Achille Ratti): Desio (Milan); Feb. 6 (12), 1922, to Feb. 10, 1939.

Pius XII (Eugenio Pacelli): Rome; Mar. 2 (12), 1939, to Oct. 9, 1958.

John XXIII (Angelo Giuseppe Roncalli): Sotto il Monte (Bergamo); Oct. 28 (Nov. 4). 1958, to June 3, 1963.

Paul VI (Giovanni Battista Montini): Concessio (Brescia); June 21 (June 30), 1963, to Aug. 6, 1978.

John Paul I (Albino Luciani): Forno di Canale (Belluno); Aug. 26 (Sept. 3), 1978, to Sept. 28, 1978.

John Paul II (Karol Wojtyla): Wadowice, Poland; Oct. 16 (22), 1978.

ANTIPOPES

This list of men who claimed or exercised the papal office in an uncanonical manner includes names, birthplaces and dates of alleged reigns.

Source: "Annuario Pontificio."

St. Hippolytus: Rome; 217-235; was reconciled before his death.

Novatian: Rome; 251.

Felix II: Rome; 355 to Nov. 22, 365.

Ursinus: 366-367.

Eulalius: Dec. 27 or 29, 418, to 419.

Lawrence: 498; 501-505.

Dioscorus: Alexandria; Sept. 22, 530, to Oct. 14, 530.

Theodore: ended alleged reign, 687.

Paschal: ended alleged reign, 687.

Constantine: Nepi; June 28 (July 5), 767, to 769.

Philip: July 31, 768; retired to his monastery on the same day.

John: ended alleged reign, Jan., 844.

Anastasius: Aug., 855, to Sept., 855; d. 880.

Christopher: Rome; July or Sept., 903, to Jan., 904.

Boniface VII: Rome; June, 974, to July, 974; Aug., 984, to July, 985.

John XVI: Rossano; Apr., 997, to Feb., 998.

Gregory: ended alleged reign, 1012.

Benedict X: Rome; Apr. 5, 1058, to Jan. 24, 1059.

Honorius II: Verona; Oct. 28, 1061, to 1072.

Clement III: Parma; June 25, 1080 (Mar. 24, 1084), to Sept. 8, 1100.

Theodoric: ended alleged reign, 1100; d. 1102.

Albert: ended alleged reign, 1102.

Sylvester IV: Rome; Nov. 18, 1105, to 1111.

Gregory VIII: France; Mar. 8, 1118, to 1121.

Celestine II: Rome; ended alleged reign, Dec., 1124.

Anacletus II: Rome; Feb. 14 (23), 1130, to Jan. 25, 1138.

Victor IV: Mar., 1138, to May 29, 1138; submitted to Pope Innocent II.

Victor IV: Montecelio; Sept. 7 (Oct. 4), 1159, to Apr. 20, 1164; he did not recognize his predecessor (Victor IV, above).

Paschal III: Apr. 22 (26), 1164, to Sept. 20, 1168.

Callistus III: Arezzo; Sept., 1168, to Aug. 29, 1178; submitted to Pope Alexander III.

Innocent III: Sezze; Sept. 29, 1179, to 1180.

Nicholas V: Corvaro (Rieti); May 12 (22), 1328, to Aug. 25, 1330; d. Oct. 16, 1333.

Four antipopes of the Western Schism:

Clement VII: Sept. 20 (Oct. 31), 1378, to Sept. 16, 1394.

Benedict XIII: Aragon; Sept. 28 (Oct. 11), 1394, to May 23, 1423.

Alexander V: Crete; June 26 (July 7), 1409, to May 3, 1410.

John XXIII: Naples; May 17 (25), 1410, to May 29, 1415.

Felix V: Savoy; Nov. 5, 1439 (July 24, 1440), to April 7, 1449; d. 1451.

AVIGNON PAPACY

Avignon was the residence of a series of French popes from Clement V to Gregory XI (1309-77). Prominent in the period were power struggles over the mixed interests of Church and state with the rulers of France (Philip IV, John II), Bavaria (Lewis IV), England (Edward III); factionalism of French and Italian churchmen; political as well as ecclesiastical turmoil in Italy, a factor of significance in prolonging the stay of popes in Avignon. Despite some positive achievements, the Avignon papacy was a prologue to the Western Schism which began in 1378.

WESTERN SCHISM

The Western Schism was a confused state of affairs which divided Christendom into two and then three papal obediences from 1378 to 1417.

It occurred some 50 years after Marsilius theorized that a general (not ecumenical) council of bishops and other persons was superior to a pope and nearly 30 years before the Council of Florence stated definitively that no kind of council had such authority.

It was a period of disaster preceding the even more disastrous period of the Reformation.

Urban VI, following transfer to Rome of the 70-year papal residence at Avignon, was elected pope Apr. 8, 1378, and reigned until his death in 1389. He was succeeded by Boniface IX (1389-1404), Innocent VII (1404-1406) and Gregory XII (1406-1415). These four are considered the legitimate popes of the period.

Some of the cardinals who chose Urban pope, dissatisfied with his conduct of the office, declared that his election was invalid. They proceeded to elect Clement VII, who claimed the papacy from 1378 to 1394. He was succeeded by Benedict XIII.

Prelates seeking to end the state of divided papal loyalties convoked the Council of Pisa which, without authority, found Gregory XII and Benedict XIII, in absentia, guilty on 30-odd charges of schism and heresy, deposed them, and elected a third claimant to the papacy, Alexander V (1409-1410). He was succeeded by John XXIII (1410-1415).

The schism was ended by the Council of Constance (1414-1418). This council, although originally called into session in an irregular manner, acquired authority after being convoked by Gregory XII in 1415. In its early irregular phase, it deposed John XXIII whose election to the papacy was uncanonical anyway. After being formally convoked, it accepted the abdication of Gregory in 1415 and dismissed the claims of Benedict XIII two years later, thus clearing the way for the election of Martin V on Nov. 11, 1417. The Council of Constance also rejected the theories of John Wycliff and condemned John Hus as a heretic.

APPARITIONS AT MEDJUGORJE?

Apparitions of Mary to six young people at Medjugorje, Yugoslavia, have been the center of controversy since they were first reported in 1981, initially in a neighboring field and later at a small chapel in the village. Reports say the young people continue to see, hear and touch Mary during visions, and that they have been given secret "messages" foretelling great world events and urging a quest for peace through the conversion of people.

An investigative commission appointed by Bishop Pavao Zanic of Mostar-Duvno reported in March, 1984, that the authenticity of the apparitions had not been established and that cases of healings had not been verified. He called the apparitions a case of "collective hallucination" exploited by local Franciscan priests at odds with him over control of a parish.

Archbishop Frane Franic of Split-Makarska, on the other hand, said in December, 1985: "Speaking as a believer and not as a bishop, my personal conviction is that the events at Medjugorje are of supernatural inspiration." He based his conviction on prayer, penitence and conversion related to the apparitions.

TWENTIETH CENTURY POPES

LEO XIII

Leo XIII (Gioacchino Vincenzo Pecci) was born May 2, 1810, in Carpineto, Italy. Although all but three years of his life and pontificate were of the 19th century, his influence extended well into the 20th century.

He was educated at the Jesuit college in Viterbo, the Roman College, the Academy of Noble Ecclesiastics, and the University of the Sapienza. He was ordained to the priesthood in 1837.

He served as an apostolic delegate to two States of the Church, Benevento from 1838 to 1841 and Perugia in 1841 and 1842. Ordained titular archbishop of Damietta, he was papal nuncio to Belgium from January, 1843, until May, 1846; in the post, he had controversial relations with the government over education issues and acquired his first significant experience of industrialized society.

He was archbishop of Perugia from 1846 to 1878. He became a cardinal in 1853 and chamberlain of the Roman Curia in 1877. He was elected to the papacy Feb. 20, 1878. He died July 20, 1903.

Canonizations: He canonized 18 saints and beatified a group of English martyrs.

Church Administration: He established 300 new dioceses and vicariates; restored the hierarchy in Scotland, set up an English, as contrasted with the Portuguese, hierarchy in India; approved the action of the Congregation for the Propagation of the Faith in reorganizing missions in China.

Encyclicals: He issued 86 encyclicals, on subjects ranging from devotional to social. In the former category were *Annum Sacrum,* on the Sacred Heart, in 1899, and 11 letters on Mary and the Rosary.

Interfaith Relations: He was unsuccessful in unity overtures made to Orthodox and Slavic Churches. He declared Anglican orders invalid in the apostolic bull *Apostolicae Curae* Sept. 13, 1896.

International Relations: Leo was frustrated in seeking solutions to the Roman Question arising from the seizure of church lands by the Kingdom of Italy in 1870. He also faced anticlerical situations in Belgium and France and in the Kulturkampf policies of Bismarck in Germany.

Social Questions: Much of Leo's influence stemmed from social doctrine stated in numerous encyclicals, concerning liberalism, liberty, the divine origin of authority; socialism, in *Quod Apostolici Muneris,* 1878; the Christian concept of the family, in *Arcanum,* 1880; socialism and economic liberalism, relations between capital and labor, in *Rerum Novarum,* 1891. Two of his social encyclicals were against the African slave trade.

Studies: In the encyclical *Aeterni Patris* of Aug. 4, 1879, he ordered a renewal of philosophical and theological studies in seminaries along scholastic, and especially Thomistic, lines, to counteract influential trends of liberalism and Modernism. He issued guidelines for biblical exegesis in *Providentissimus Deus* Nov. 18, 1893, and established the Pontifical Biblical Commission in 1902.

In other actions affecting scholarship and study, he opened the Vatican Archives to scholars in 1883 and established the Vatican Observatory.

United States: He authorized establishment of the apostolic delegation in Washington, D.C. Jan. 24, 1893. He refused to issue a condemnation of the Knights of Labor. With a document entitled *Testem Benevolentiae,* he eased resolution of questions concerning what was called an American heresy in 1899.

ST. PIUS X

St. Pius X (Giuseppe Melchiorre Sarto) was born in 1835 in Riese, Italy.

Educated at the college of Castelfranco and the seminary at Padua, he was ordained to the priesthood Sept. 18, 1858. He served as a curate in Trombolo for nine years before beginning an eight-year pastorate at Salzano. He was chancellor of the Treviso diocese from November, 1875, and bishop of Mantua from 1884 until 1893. He was cardinal-patriarch of Venice from that year until his election to the papacy by the conclave held from July 31 to Aug. 4, 1903.

Aims: Pius' principal objectives as pope were "to restore all things in Christ, in order that Christ may be all and in all," and "to teach (and defend) Christian truth and law."

Canonizations, Encyclicals: He canonized four saints and issued 16 encyclicals. One of the encyclicals was issued in commemoration of the 50th anniversary of the proclamation of the dogma of the Immaculate Conception of Mary.

Catechetics: He introduced a whole new era of religious instruction and formation with the encyclical *Acerbo Nimis* of Apr. 15, 1905, in which he called for vigor in establishing and conducting parochial programs of the Confraternity of Christian Doctrine.

Catholic Action: He outlined the role of official Catholic Action in two encyclicals in 1905 and 1906. Favoring organized action by Catholics themselves, he had serious reservations about interconfessional collaboration.

He stoutly maintained claims to papal rights in the anticlerical climate of Italy. He authorized bishops to relax prohibitions against participation by Catholics in some Italian elections.

Church Administration: With the motu proprio *Arduum Sane* of Mar. 19, 1904, he inaugurated the work which resulted in the Code of Canon Law; the code was completed in 1917 and went into effect in the following year. He reorganized and strengthened the Roman Curia with the apostolic constitution *Sapienti Consilio* of June 29, 1908. While promoting the expansion of missionary work, he removed from the jurisdiction of the Congregation for the Propagation of the Faith the Church in the United States, Canada, Newfoundland, England, Ireland, Holland and Luxembourg.

International Relations: He ended traditional

prerogatives of Catholic governments with respect to papal elections, in 1904. He opposed anti-Church and anticlerical actions in several countries: Bolivia in 1905, because of anti-religious legislation; France in 1906, for its 1901 action in annulling its concordat with the Holy See, and for the 1905 Law of Separation by which it decreed separation of Church and state, ordered the confiscation of church property, and blocked religious education and the activities of religious orders; Portugal in 1911, for the separation of Church and state and repressive measures which resulted in persecution later.

In 1912 he called on the bishops of Brazil to work for the improvement of conditions among Indians.

Liturgy: "The Pope of the Eucharist," he strongly recommended the frequent reception of Holy Communion in a decree dated Dec. 20, 1905; in another decree, *Quam Singulari*, of Aug. 8, 1910, he called for the early reception of the sacrament by children. He initiated measures for liturgical reform with new norms for sacred music and the start of work on revision of the *Breviary* for recitation of the Divine Office.

Modernism: Pius was a vigorous opponent of "the synthesis of all heresies," which threatened the integrity of doctrine through its influence in philosophy, theology and biblical exegesis. In opposition, he condemned 65 of its propositions as erroneous in the decree *Lamentabili* July 3, 1907; issued the encyclical *Pascendi* in the same vein Sept. 8, 1907; backed both of these with censures; and published the Oath against Modernism in September, 1910, to be taken by all the clergy. Ecclesiastical studies suffered to some extent from these actions, necessary as they were at the time.

Pius followed the lead of Leo XIII in promoting the study of scholastic philosophy. He established the Pontifical Biblical Institute May 7, 1909.

His death, Aug. 20, 1914, was hastened by the outbreak of World War I. He was beatified in 1951 and canonized May 29, 1954. His feast is observed Aug. 21.

BENEDICT XV

Benedict XV (Giacomo della Chiesa) was born Nov. 21, 1854, in Pegli, Italy.

He was educated at the Royal University of Genoa and Gregorian University in Rome. He was ordained to the priesthood Dec. 21, 1878.

He served in the papal diplomatic corps from 1882 to 1907; as secretary to the nuncio to Spain from 1882 to 1887, as secretary to the papal secretary of state from 1887, and as undersecretary from 1901.

He was ordained archbishop of Bologna Dec. 22, 1907, and spent four years completing a pastoral visitation there. He was made a cardinal just three months before being elected to the papacy Sept. 3, 1914. He died Jan. 22, 1922. Two key efforts of his pontificate were for peace and the relief of human suffering caused by World War I.

Canonizations: Benedict canonized three saints; one of them was Joan of Arc.

Canon Law: He published the Code of Canon Law, developed by the commission set up by St.

Pius X, May 27, 1917; it went into effect the following year.

Curia: He made great changes in the personnel of the Curia. He established the Congregation for the Oriental Churches May 1, 1917, and founded the Pontifical Oriental Institute in Rome later in the year.

Encyclicals: He issued 12 encyclicals. Peace was the theme of three of them. In another, published two years after the cessation of hostilities, he wrote about child victims of the war. He followed the lead of Leo XIII in *Spiritus Paraclitus*, Sept. 15, 1920, on biblical studies.

International Relations: He was largely frustrated on the international level because of the events and attitudes of the war period, but the number of diplomats accredited to the Vatican nearly doubled, from 14 to 26, between the time of his accession to the papacy and his death.

Peace Efforts: Benedict's stance in the war was one of absolute impartiality but not of uninterested neutrality. Because he would not take sides, he was suspected by both sides and the seven-point peace plan he offered to all belligerents Aug. 1, 1917, was turned down. The points of the plan were: recognition of the moral force of right; disarmament; acceptance of arbitration in cases of dispute; guarantee of freedom of the seas; renunciation of war indemnities; evacuation and restoration of occupied territories; examination of territorial claims in dispute.

Relief Efforts: Benedict assumed personal charge of Vatican relief efforts during the war. He set up an international missing persons bureau for contacts between prisoners and their families, but was forced to close it because of the suspicion of warring nations that it was a front for espionage operations. He persuaded the Swiss government to admit into the country military victims of tuberculosis.

Roman Question: Benedict prepared the way for the meetings and negotiations which led to settlement of the question in 1929.

PIUS XI

Pius XI (Ambrogio Damiano Achille Ratti) was born May 31, 1857, in Desio, Italy.

Educated at seminaries in Seviso and Milan, and at the Lombard College, Gregorian University and Academy of St. Thomas in Rome, he was ordained to the priesthood in 1879.

He taught at the major seminary of Milan from 1882 to 1888. Appointed to the staff of the Ambrosian Library in 1888, he remained there until 1911, acquiring a reputation for publishing works on palaeography and serving as director from 1907 to 1911. He then moved to the Vatican Library, of which he was prefect from 1914 to 1918. In 1919, he was named apostolic visitor to Poland in April, nuncio in June, and was made titular archbishop of Lepanto Oct. 28. He was made archbishop of Milan and cardinal June 13, 1921, before being elected to the papacy Feb. 6, 1922. He died Feb. 10, 1939.

Aim: The objective of his pontificate, as stated in the encyclical *Ubi Arcano*, Dec. 23, 1922, was to establish the reign and peace of Christ in society.

Canonizations: He canonized 34 saints, including the Jesuit Martyrs of North America, and conferred the title of Doctor of the Church on Sts. Peter Canisius, John of the Cross, Robert Bellarmine and Albertus Magnus.

Eastern Churches: He called for better understanding of the Eastern Churches in the encyclical *Rerum Orientalium* of Sept. 8, 1928, and developed facilities for the training of Eastern-Rite priests. He inaugurated steps for the codification of Eastern-Church law in 1929. In 1935 he made Syrian Patriarch Tappouni a cardinal.

Encyclicals: His first encyclical, *Ubi Arcano*, in addition to stating the aims of his pontificate, blueprinted Catholic Action and called for its development throughout the Church. In *Quas Primas*, Dec. 11, 1925, he established the feast of Christ the King for universal observance. Subjects of some of his other encyclicals were: Christian education, in *Rappresentanti in Terra*, Dec. 31, 1929; Christian marriage, in *Casti Connubii*, Dec. 31, 1930; social conditions and pressure for social change in line with the teaching in *Rerum Novarum*, in *Quadragesimo Anno*, May 15, 1931; atheistic Communism, in *Divini Redemptoris*, Mar. 19, 1937; the priesthood, in *Ad Catholici Sacerdotii*, Dec. 20, 1935.

Missions: Following the lead of Benedict XV, Pius called for the training of native clergy in the pattern of their own respective cultures, and promoted missionary developments in various ways. He ordained six native bishops for China in 1926, one for Japan in 1927, and others for regions of Asia, China and India in 1933. He placed the first 40 mission dioceses under native bishops, saw the number of native priests increase from about 2,600 to more than 7,000 and the number of Catholics in missionary areas more than double from nine million.

In the apostolic constitution *Deus Scientiarum Dominus* of May 24, 1931, he ordered the introduction of missiology into theology courses.

Interfaith Relations: Pius was negative to the ecumenical movement among Protestants but approved the Malines Conversations, 1921 to 1926, between Anglicans and Catholics.

International Relations: Relations with the Mussolini government deteriorated from 1931 on, as indicated in the encyclical *Non Abbiamo Bisogno*, when the regime took steps to curb liberties and activities of the Church; they turned critical in 1938 with the emergence of racist policies. Relations deteriorated also in Germany from 1933 on, resulting finally in condemnation of the Nazis in the encyclical *Mit Brennender Sorge*, March, 1937. Pius sparked a revival of the Church in France by encouraging Catholics to work within the democratic framework of the Republic rather than foment trouble over restoration of a monarchy. Pius was powerless to influence developments related to the civil war which erupted in Spain in July, 1936, sporadic persecution and repression by the Calles regime in Mexico, and systematic persecution of the Church in the Soviet

Union. Many of the 10 concordats and two agreements reached with European countries after World War I became casualties of World War II.

Roman Question: Pius negotiated for two and one-half years with the Italian government to settle the Roman Question by means of the Lateran Agreement of 1929. The agreement provided independent status for the State of Vatican City; made Catholicism the official religion of Italy, with pastoral and educational freedom and state recognition of Catholic marriages, religious orders and societies; and provided a financial payment to the Vatican for expropriation of the former States of the Church.

PIUS XII

Pius XII (Eugenio Maria Giovanni Pacelli) was born Mar. 2, 1876, in Rome.

Educated at the Gregorian University and the Lateran University, in Rome, he was ordained to the priesthood Apr. 2, 1899.

He entered the Vatican diplomatic service in 1901, worked on the codification of canon law, and was appointed secretary of the Congregation for Ecclesiastical Affairs in 1914. Three years later he was ordained titular archbishop of Sardis and made apostolic nuncio to Bavaria. He was nuncio to Germany from 1920 to 1929, when he was made a cardinal, and took office as papal secretary of state in the following year. His diplomatic negotiations resulted in concordats between the Vatican and Bavaria (1924), Prussia (1929), Baden (1932), Austria and the German Republic (1933). He took part in negotiations which led to settlement of the Roman Question in 1929.

He was elected to the papacy Mar. 2, 1939. He died Oct. 9, 1958, at Castel Gandolfo after the 12th longest pontificate in history.

Canonizations: He canonized 34 saints, including Mother Frances X. Cabrini, the first U.S. citizen-Saint.

Cardinals: He raised 56 prelates to the rank of cardinal in two consistories held in 1946 and 1953. There were 57 cardinals at the time of his death.

Church Organization and Missions: He increased the number of dioceses from 1,696 to 2,048. He established native hierarchies in China (1946), Burma (1955) and parts of Africa, and extended the native structure of the Church in India. He ordained the first black bishop for Africa.

Communism: In addition to opposing and condemning Communism on numerous occasions, he decreed in 1949 the penalty of excommunication for all Catholics holding formal and willing allegiance to the Communist Party and its policies. During his reign the Church was persecuted in some 15 countries which fell under communist domination.

Doctrine and Liturgy: He proclaimed the dogma of the Assumption of the Blessed Virgin Mary Nov. 1, 1950 (apostolic constitution, *Munificentissimus Deus*.)

In various encyclicals and other enactments, he provided background for the *aggiornamento* introduced by his successor, John XXIII: by his formulations of doctrine and practice regarding the

Mystical Body of Christ, the liturgy, sacred music and biblical studies; by the revision of the Rites of Holy Week; by initiation of the work which led to the calendar-missal-breviary reform ordered into effect Jan. 1, 1961; by the first of several modifications of the Eucharistic fast; by extending the time of Mass to the evening. He instituted the feasts of Mary, Queen, and of St. Joseph the Worker, and clarified teaching concerning devotion to the Sacred Heart.

His 41 encyclicals and nearly 1,000 public addresses made Pius one of the greatest teaching popes. His concern in all his communications was to deal with specific points at issue and/or to bring Christian principles to bear on contemporary world problems.

Peace Efforts: Before the start of World War II, he tried unsuccessfully to get the contending nations — Germany and Poland, France and Italy — to settle their differences peaceably. During the war, he offered his services to mediate the widened conflict, spoke out against the horrors of war and the suffering it caused, mobilized relief work for its victims, proposed a five-point program for peace in Christmas messages from 1939 to 1942, and secured a generally open status for the city of Rome. After the war, he endorsed the principles and intent of the United Nations and continued efforts for peace.

United States: Pius appointed more than 200 of the 265 American bishops resident in the U.S. and abroad in 1958, erected 27 dioceses in this country, and raised seven dioceses to archiepiscopal rank.

JOHN XXIII

John XXIII (Angelo Roncalli) was born Nov. 25, 1881, at Sotte il Monte, Italy.

He was educated at the seminary of the Bergamo diocese and the Pontifical Seminary in Rome, where he was ordained to the priesthood Aug. 10, 1904.

He spent the first nine or 10 years of his priesthood as secretary to the bishop of Bergamo and as an instructor in the seminary there. He served as a medic and chaplain in the Italian army during World War I. Afterwards, he resumed duties in his own diocese until he was called to Rome in 1921 for work with the Society for the Propagation of the Faith.

He began diplomatic service in 1925 as titular archbishop of Areopolis and apostolic visitor to Bulgaria. A succession of offices followed: apostolic delegate to Bulgaria (1931-1935); titular archbishop of Mesembria, apostolic delegate to Turkey and Greece, administrator of the Latin vicariate apostolic of Istanbul (1935-1944); apostolic nuncio to France (1944-1953). On these missions, he was engaged in delicate negotiations involving Roman, Eastern-Rite and Orthodox relations; the needs of people suffering from the consequences of World War II; and unsettling suspicions arising from wartime conditions.

He was made a cardinal Jan. 12, 1953, and three days later was appointed patriarch of Venice, the position he held until his election to the papacy

Oct. 28, 1958. He died of stomach cancer June 3, 1963.

John was a strong and vigorous pope whose influence far outmeasured both his age and the shortness of his time in the papacy.

Second Vatican Council: John announced Jan. 25, 1959, his intention of convoking the 21st ecumenical council in history to renew life in the Church, to reform its structures and institutions, and to explore ways and means of promoting unity among Christians. Through the council, which completed its work two and one-half years after his death, he ushered in a new era in the history of the Church.

Canon Law: He established a commission Mar. 28, 1963, for revision of the Code of Canon Law. The revised Code was promulgated in 1983.

Canonizations: He canonized 10 saints and beatified Mother Elizabeth Ann Seton, the first native of the U.S. ever so honored. He named St. Lawrence of Brindisi a Doctor of the Church.

Cardinals: He created 52 cardinals in five consistories, raising membership of the College of Cardinals above the traditional number of 70; at one time in 1962, the membership was 87. He made the college more international in representation than it had ever been, appointing the first cardinals from the Philippines, Japan and Africa. He ordered episcopal ordination for all cardinals. He relieved the suburban bishops of Rome of ordinary jurisdiction over their dioceses so they might devote all their time to business of the Roman Curia.

Eastern Rites: He made all Eastern-Rite patriarchs members of the Congregation for the Oriental Churches.

Ecumenism: He assigned to the Second Vatican Council the task of finding ways and means of promoting unity among Christians. He established the Vatican Secretariat for Promoting Christian Unity June 5, 1960. He showed his desire for more cordial relations with the Orthodox by sending personal representatives to visit Patriarch Athenagoras I June 27, 1961; approved a mission of five delegates to the General Assembly of the World Council of Churches which met in New Delhi, India, in November, 1961; removed a number of pejorative references to Jews in the Roman-Rite liturgy for Good Friday.

Encyclicals: Of the eight encyclicals he issued, the two outstanding ones were *Mater et Magistra* ("Christianity and Social Progress"), in which he recapitulated, updated and extended the social doctrine stated earlier by Leo XIII and Pius XI; and *Pacem in Terris* ("Peace on Earth"), the first encyclical ever addressed to all men of good will as well as to Catholics, on the natural-law principles of peace.

Liturgy: In forwarding liturgical reforms already begun by Pius XII, he ordered a calendar-missal-breviary reform into effect Jan. 1, 1961. He authorized the use of vernacular languages in the administration of the sacraments and approved giving Holy Communion to the sick in afternoon hours. He selected the liturgy as the first topic of major discussion by the Second Vatican Council.

Missions: He issued an encyclical on the missionary activity of the Church; established native hierarchies in Indonesia, Vietnam and Korea; and called on North American superiors of religious institutes to have one-tenth of their members assigned to work in Latin America by 1971.

Peace: John spoke and used his moral influence for peace in 1961 when tension developed over Berlin, in 1962 during the Algerian revolt from France, and later the same year in the Cuban missile crisis. His efforts were singled out for honor by the Balzan Peace Foundation. In 1963, he was posthumously awarded the U.S. Presidential Medal of Freedom.

PAUL VI

Paul VI (Giovanni Battista Montini) was born Sept. 26, 1897, at Concesio in northern Italy.

Educated at Brescia, he was ordained to the priesthood May 29, 1920. He pursued additional studies at the Pontifical Academy for Noble Ecclesiastics and the Pontifical Gregorian University. In 1924 he began 30 years of service in the Secretariat of State; as undersecretary from 1937 until 1954, he was closely associated with Pius XII and was heavily engaged in organizing informational and relief services during and after World War II.

He was ordained archbishop of Milan Dec. 12, 1954, and was inducted into the College of Cardinals Dec. 15, 1958. He was elected to the papacy June 21, 1963, two days after the conclave began. He died of a heart attack Aug. 6, 1978.

Second Vatican Council: He reconvened the Second Vatican Council after the death of John XXIII, presided over its second, third and fourth sessions, formally promulgated the 16 documents it produced, and devoted the whole of his pontificate to the task of putting them into effect throughout the Church. The main thrust of his pontificate — in a milieu of cultural and other changes in the Church and the world — was toward institutionalization and control of the authentic trends articulated and set in motion by the council.

Canonizations: He canonized more saints, 84, than any other pope. They included groups of 22 Ugandan martyrs and 40 martyrs of England and Wales, as well as two Americans — Elizabeth Ann Bayley Seton and John Nepomucene Neumann.

Cardinals: He created 144 cardinals, and gave the Sacred College a more international complexion than it ever had before. He limited participation in papal elections to 120 cardinals under the age of 80.

Collegiality: He established the Synod of Bishops in 1965 and called it into session five times. He stimulated the formation and operation of regional conferences of bishops, and of consultative bodies on other levels.

Creed and Holy Year: On June 30, 1968, he issued a Creed of the People of God in conjunction with the celebration of a Year of Faith. He proclaimed and led the observance of a Holy Year from Christmas Eve of 1974 to Christmas Eve of 1975.

Diplomacy: He met with many world leaders, including Soviet President Nikolai Podgorny in

1967, Marshal Tito of Yugoslavia in 1971 and President Nicolas Ceausescu of Rumania in 1973. He worked constantly to reduce tension between the Church and the intransigent regimes of Eastern European countries by means of a detente type of policy called Ostpolitik. He agreed to significant revisions of the Vatican's concordat with Spain and initiated efforts to revise the concordat with Italy. More then 40 countries established diplomatic relations with the Vatican during his pontificate.

Encyclicals: He issued seven encyclicals, three of which are the best known. In *Populorum Progressio* ("Development of Peoples") he appealed to wealthy countries to take "concrete action" to promote human development and to remedy imbalances between richer and poorer nations; this encyclical, coupled with other documents and related actions, launched the Church into a new depth of involvement as a public advocate for human rights and for humanizing social, political and economic policies. In *Sacerdotalis Caelibatus* ("Priestly Celibacy") he reaffirmed the strict observance of priestly celibacy throughout the Western Church. In *Humanae Vitae* ("Of Human Life") he condemned abortion, sterilization and artificial birth control, in line with traditional teaching and in "defense of life, the gift of God, the glory of the family, the strength of the people."

Interfaith Relations: He initiated formal consultation and informal dialogue on international and national levels between Catholics and non-Catholics — Orthodox, Anglicans, Protestants, Jews, Moslems, Buddhists, Hindus, and unbelievers. He and Greek Orthodox Patriarch Athenagoras I of Constantinople nullified in 1965 the mutual excommunications imposed by their respective churches in 1054.

Liturgy: He carried out the most extensive liturgical reform in history, involving a new Order of the Mass effective in 1969, a revised church calendar in 1970, revisions and translations into vernacular languages of all sacramental rites and other liturgical texts.

Ministries: He authorized the restoration of the permanent diaconate in the Roman Rite and the establishment of new ministries of lay persons.

Peace: In 1968, he instituted the annual observance of a World Day of Peace on New Year's Day as a means of addressing a message of peace to all the world's political leaders and the peoples of all nations. The most dramatic of his many appeals for peace and efforts to ease international tensions was his plea for "No more war!" before the United Nations Oct. 4, 1965.

Pilgrimages: A "Pilgrim Pope," he made pastoral visits to the Holy Land and India in 1964, the United Nations and New York City in 1965, Portugal and Turkey in 1967, Colombia in 1968, Switzerland and Uganda in 1969, and Asia, Pacific islands and Australia in 1970. While in Manila in 1970, he was stabbed by a Bolivian artist who made an attempt on his life.

Roman Curia: He reorganized the central administrative organs of the Church in line with provisions of the apostolic constitution, *Regimini*

Ecclesiae Universae, streamlining procedures for more effective service and giving the agencies a more international perspective by drawing officials and consultors from all over the world. He also instituted a number of new commissions and other bodies. Coupled with curial reorganization was a simplification of papal ceremonies.

JOHN PAUL I

John Paul I (Albino Luciani) was born Oct. 17, 1912, in Forno di Canale (now Canale d'Agordo) in northern Italy.

Educated at the minor seminary in Feltre and the major seminary of the Diocese of Belluno, he was ordained to the priesthood July 7, 1935. He pursued further studies at the Pontifical Gregorian University in Rome and was awarded a doctorate in theology. From 1937 to 1947 he was vice rector of the Belluno seminary, where he taught dogmatic and moral theology, canon law and sacred art. He was appointed vicar general of his diocese in 1947 and served as director of catechetics.

Ordained bishop of Vittorio Veneto Dec. 27, 1958, he attended all sessions of the Second Vatican Council, participated in three assemblies of the Synod of Bishops (1971, 1974 and 1977), and was vice president of the Italian Bishops' Conference from 1972 to 1975.

He was appointed archbishop and patriarch of Venice Dec. 15, 1969, and was inducted into the College of Cardinals Mar. 5, 1973.

He was elected to the papacy Aug. 26, 1978, on the fourth ballot cast by the 111 cardinals participating in the largest and one of the shortest conclaves in history. The quickness of his election was matched by the brevity of his pontificate of 33 days, during which he delivered 19 addresses. He died of a heart attack Sept. 28, 1978.

JOHN PAUL II

See separate entry.

CANONIZATIONS BY LEO XIII AND HIS SUCCESSORS

Canonization is an infallible declaration by the pope that a person who suffered martyrdom and/or practiced Christian virtue to a heroic degree is in glory with God in heaven and is worthy of public honor by the universal Church and of imitation by the faithful.

(See Canonization entry in Glossary.)

Leo XIII
(1878-1903)

1881: Clare of Montefalco, virgin (d. 1308); John Baptist de Rossi, priest (1698-1764); Lawrence of Brindisi, doctor (d. 1619).

1883: Benedict J. Labre (1748-1783).

1888: Seven Holy Founders of the Servite Order; Peter Claver, priest (1581-1654); John Berchmans (1599-1621); Alphonsus Rodriguez, lay brother (1531-1617).

1897: Anthony M. Zaccaria, founder of Barnabites (1502-1539); Peter Fourier, co-founder of Augustinian Canonesses of Our Lady (1565-1640).

1900: John Baptist de La Salle, founder of Christian Brothers (1651-1719); Rita of Cascia (1381-1457).

St. Pius X
(1903-1914)

1904: Alexander Sauli, bishop (1534-1593); Gerard Majella, lay brother (1725-1755).

1909: Joseph Oriol, priest (1650-1702); Clement M. Hofbauer, priest (1751-1820).

Benedict XV
(1914-1922)

1920: Gabriel of the Sorrowful Mother (1838-1862); Margaret Mary Alacoque, virgin (1647-1690); Joan of Arc, virgin (1412-1431).

Pius XI
(1922-1939)

1925: Therese of Lisieux, virgin (1873-1897); Peter Canisius, doctor (1521-1597); Mary Magdalen Postel, foundress of Sisterhood of Christian Schools (1756-1846); Mary Magdalen Sophie Barat, foundress of Society of the Sacred Heart (1779-1865); John Eudes, founder of Eudist Fathers (1601-1680); John Baptist Vianney (Curé of Ars), priest (1786-1859).

1930: Lucy Filippini, virgin (1672-1732); Catherine Thomas, virgin (1533-1574); Jesuit North American Martyrs (see Index); Robert Bellarmine, bishop-doctor (1542-1621); Theophilus of Corte, priest (1676-1740).

1931: Albert the Great, bishop-doctor (1206-1280) (equivalent canonization).

1933: Andrew Fournet, priest (1752-1834); Bernadette Soubirous, virgin (1844-1879).

1934: Joan Antida Thouret, foundress of Sisters of Charity of St. Joan Antida (1765-1826); Mary Michaeli, foundress of Institute of Handmaids of the Blessed Sacrament (1809-1865); Louise de Marillac, foundress of Sisters of Charity (1591-1660); Joseph Benedict Cottolengo, priest (1786-1842); Pompilius M. Pirotti, priest (1710-1756); Teresa Margaret Redi, virgin (1747-1770); John Bosco, founder of Salesians (1815-1888); Conrad of Parzham, lay brother (1818-1894).

1935: John Fisher, bishop-martyr (1469-1535); Thomas More, martyr (1478-1535).

1938: Andrew Bobola, martyr (1592-1657); John Leonardi, founder of Clerics Regular of the Mother of God (c. 1550-1609); Salvatore of Horta, lay brother (1520-1567).

Pius XII
(1939-1958)

1940: Gemma Galgani, virgin (1878-1903); Mary Euphrasia Pelletier, foundress of Good Shepherd Sisters (1796-1868).

1943: Margaret of Hungary, virgin (d. 1270) (equivalent canonization).

1946: Frances Xavier Cabrini, foundress of Missionary Sisters of the Sacred Heart (1850-1917).

1947: Nicholas of Flue, hermit (1417-1487); John of Britto, martyr (1647-1693); Bernard Realini, priest (1530-1616); Joseph Cafasso, priest (1811-1860); Michael Garicoits, founder of Auxiliary Priests of the Sacred Heart (1797-1863); Jeanne Elizabeth des Ages, cofoundress of Daughters of the Cross (1773-1838); Louis Marie Grignon de Montfort, founder of Montfort Fathers (1673-1716); Catherine Laboure, virgin (1806-1876).

1949: Jeanne de Lestonnac, foundress of Religious of Notre Dame of Bordeaux (1556-1640); Maria Josepha Rossello, foundress of Daughters of Our Lady of Pity (1811-1880).

1950: Emily de Rodat, foundress of Congregation of the Holy Family of Villefranche (1787-1852); Anthony Mary Claret, bishop, founder of Claretians (1807-1870); Bartolomea Capitanio (1807-1833) and Vincenza Gerosa (1784-1847), foundresses of Sisters of Charity of Lovere; Jeanne de Valois, foundress of Annonciades of Bourges (1461-1504); Vincenzo M. Strambi, bishop (1745-1824); Maria Goretti, virgin-martyr (1890-1902); Mariana Paredes of Jesus, virgin (1618-1645).

1951: Maria Domenica Mazzarello, co-foundress of Daughters of Our Lady Help of Christians (1837-1881); Emilie de Vialar, foundress of Sisters of St. Joseph "of the Apparition" (1797-1856); Anthony M. Gianelli, bishop (1789-1846); Ignatius of Laconi, lay brother (1701-1781); Francis Xavier Bianchi, priest (1743-1815).

1954: Pius X, pope (1835-1914); Dominic Savio (1842-1857); Maria Crocifissa di Rosa, foundress of Handmaids of Charity of Brescia (1813-1855); Peter Chanel, priest-martyr (1803-1841); Gaspar del Bufalo, founder of Missioners of the Most Precious Blood (1786-1837); Joseph M. Pignatelli, priest (1737-1811).

1958: Herman Joseph, O. Praem., priest (1150-1241) (equivalent canonization).

John XXIII
(1958-1963)

1959: Joaquina de Vedruna de Mas, foundress of Carmelite Sisters of Charity (1783-1854); Charles of Sezze, lay brother (1613-1670).

1960: Gregory Barbarigo, bishop (1625-1697) (equivalent canonization); John de Ribera, bishop (1532-1611).

1961: Bertilla Boscardin, virgin (1888-1922).

1962: Martin de Porres, lay brother (1579-1639); Peter Julian Eymard, founder of Blessed Sacrament Fathers (1811-1868); Anthony Pucci, priest (1819-1892); Francis Mary of Camporosso, lay brother (1804-1866).

1963: Vincent Pallotti, founder of Pallottine Fathers (1795-1850).

Paul VI
(1963-1978)

1964: Charles Lwanga and Twenty-One Companions, Martyrs of Uganda (d. between 1885-1887).

1967: Benilde Romancon, Christian Brother (1805-1862).

1969: Julia Billiart, foundress of Sisters of Notre Dame de Namur (1751-1816).

1970: Maria Della Dolorato Torres Acosta, foundress of Servants Sisters of Mary (1826-1887); Leonard Murialdo, priest, founder of Congregation of St. Joseph (1828-1900); Therese Couderc, foundress of Congregation of Our Lady of the Cenacle (1805-1885); John of Avila, preacher and spiritual director (1499-1569); Nicholas Tavelic, Deodatus of Aquitaine, Peter of Narbonne and Stephen of Cuneo, martyrs (d. 1391); Forty English and Welsh Martyrs (d. 16th cent.).

1974: Teresa of Jesus Jornet Ibars, foundress of Little Sisters of Abandoned Aged (1843-1897).

1975: Vicenta Maria Lopez y Vicuna, foundress of Institute of Daughters of Mary Immaculate (1847-1890); Elizabeth Bayley Seton, foundress of Sisters of Charity in the U.S. (1774-1821); John Masias, Dominican brother-missionary (1585-1645); Oliver Plunket, archbishop-martyr (1629-1681); Justin de Jacobis, missionary bishop (1800-1860); John Baptist of the Conception, priest, reformer of the Order of the Most Holy Trinity (1561-1613).

1976: Beatrice da Silva, foundress of Congregation of the Immaculate Conception of the BVM (1424 or 1426-1490); John Ogilvie, Scottish Jesuit martyr (1579-1615).

1977: Rafaela Maria Porras y Ayllon, foundress of Handmaids of the Sacred Heart (1850-1925); John Nepomucene Neumann, bishop (1811-1860); Sharbel Makhlouf, Maronite Rite monk (1828-1898).

John Paul II
(1978-   )

1982: Crispin of Viterbo, Capuchin brother (1668-1750); Maximilian Kolbe, Conventual Franciscan priest (1894-1941); Marguerite Bourgeoys, foundress of Congregation of Notre Dame (1620-1700); Jeanne Delanoue, foundress of Sisters of St. Anne of Providence of Saumur, France (1666-1736).

1983: Leopold Mandic, Capuchin priest (1866-1942).

1984: Paola Frassinetti, foundress of Sisters of St. Dorothy (1809-1892); 103 Korean Martyrs (d. between 1839-1867); Miguel Febres Cordero, of the Brothers of the Christian Schools (1854-1910).

1986: Francis Anthony Fasani, Franciscan priest (1681-1742).

English and Welsh Martyrs

Forty Martyrs of England and Wales, victims of persecution from 1535 to 1671, were canonized by Pope Paul Oct. 25, 1970.

The martyrs were prosecuted and executed as traitors for refusal to comply with laws enacted by Henry VIII and Elizabeth I regarding supremacy (the sovereign was proclaimed the highest authority of the Church in England, acknowledgment of papal primacy was forbidden), succession and the prohibition of native-born to study for the priesthood abroad and return to England for practice of the ministry.

John Houghton, prior of the London Charterhouse, was the first of his group to die (1535) for opposing Henry's Acts of Supremacy and Succession. Cuthbert Mayne (d. 1577) was the protomartyr of the English seminary at Douay. Margaret Clitherow (d. 1586) and Swithun Wells (d.

1591) were executed for sheltering priests. Richard Gwyn (d. 1584), poet, was the protomartyr of Wales.

Others in the group were:

John Almond, Edmund Arrowsmith, Ambrose Barlow, John Boste, Alexander Briant, Edmund Campion, Philip Evans, Thomas Garnet, Edmund Gennings;

Philip Howard, John Jones, John Kemble, Luke Kirby, Robert Lawrence, David Lewis, Ann Line, John Lloyd;

Henry Morse, Nicholas Owen, John Paine, Polydore Plasden, John Plessington, Richard Reynolds, John Rigby, John Roberts;

Alban Roe, Ralph Sherwin, Robert Southwell, John Southworth, John Stone, John Wall, Henry Walpole, Margaret Ward, Augustine Webster and Eustace White.

PAPAL ENCYCLICALS — BENEDICT XIV (1740) TO JOHN PAUL II

(Source: *The Papal Encyclicals* (5 vols.), Claudia Carlen, I.H.M.; a Consortium Book, © McGrath Publishing Co., Wilmington, N.C. Used with permission.)

An encyclical letter is a pastoral letter addressed by a pope to the whole Church. In general, it concerns matters of doctrine, morals or discipline. Its formal title consists of the first few words of the official text. A few encyclicals, notably *Pacem in terris* by John XXIII and *Ecclesiam Suam* by Paul VI, have been addressed to "all men of good will" as well as to bishops and the faithful in communion with the Church.

An encyclical epistle, which is like an encyclical letter in many respects, is addressed to part of the Church, that is, to the bishops and faithful of a particular country or area. Its contents may concern other than doctrinal, moral or disciplinary matters of universal significance; for example, the commemoration of historical events, conditions in a certain country.

The authority of encyclicals was stated by Pius XII in the encyclical *Humani generis* Aug. 12, 1950.

"Nor must it be thought that what is contained in encyclical letters does not of itself demand assent, on the pretext that the popes do not exercise in them the supreme power of their teaching authority. Rather, such teachings belong to the ordinary magisterium, of which it is true to say: 'He who hears you, hears me' (Lk. 10:16); for the most part, too, what is expounded and inculcated in encyclical letters already appertains to Catholic doctrine for other reasons. But if the supreme pontiffs in their official documents purposely pass judgment on a matter debated until then, it is obvious to all that the matter, according to the mind and will of the same pontiffs, cannot be considered any longer a question open for discussion among theologians."

The following list contains the titles and indicates the subject matter of encyclical letters and epistles. The latter are generally distinguishable by the limited scope of their titles or contents.

Benedict XIV
(1740-1758)

1740: *Ubi primum* (On the duties of bishops), Dec. 3.

1741: *Quanta cura* (Forbidding traffic in alms), June 30.

1743: *Nimiam licentiam* (To the bishops of Poland: on validity of marriages), May 18.

1745: *Vix pervenit* (To the bishops of Italy: on usury and other dishonest profit), Nov. 1.

1748: *Magnae Nobis* To the bishops of Poland: on marriage impediments and dispensations), June 29.

1749: *Peregrinantes* (To all the faithful: proclaiming a Holy Year for 1750), May 5.

Apostolica Constitutio (On preparation for the Holy Year), June 26.

1751: *A quo primum* (To the bishops of Poland: on Jews and Christians living in the same place), June 14.

1754: *Cum Religiosi* (To the bishops of the States of the Church: on catechesis), June 26.

Quod Provinciale (To the bishops of Albania: on Christians using Mohammedan names), Aug. 1.

1755: *Allatae sunt* (To missionaries of the Orient: on the observance of Oriental rites), July 26.

1756: *Ex quo primum* (To bishops of the Greek rite: on the Euchologion), Mar. 1.

Ex omnibus (To the bishops of France: on the apostolic constitution, *Unigenitus*), Oct. 16.

Clement XIII
(1758-1769)

1758: *A quo die* (Unity among Christians), Sept. 13.

1759: *Cum primum* (On observing canonical sanctions), Sept. 17.

Appetente Sacro (On the spiritual advantages of fasting), Dec. 20.

1761: *In Dominico agro* (On instruction in the faith), June 14.

1766: *Christianae reipublicae* (On the dangers of anti-Christian writings), Nov. 25.

1768: *Summa quae* (To the bishops of Poland: on the Church in Poland), Jan. 6.

Clement XIV
(1769-1774)

1769: *Decet quam maxime* (To the bishops of Sardinia: on abuses in taxes and benefices), Sept. 21.

Inscrutabili divinae sapientiae (To all Christians: proclaiming a universal jubilee), Dec. 12.

Cum summi (Proclaiming a universal jubilee), Dec. 12.

1774: *Salutis nostrae* (To all Christians: proclaiming a universal jubilee), Apr. 30.

Pius VI
(1775-1799)

1775: *Inscrutabile* (On the problems of the pontificate), Dec. 25.

1791: *Charitas* (To the bishops of France: on the civil oath in France), Apr. 13.

Pius VII
(1800-1823)

1800: *Diu satis* (To the bishops of France: on a return to Gospel principles), May 15.

Leo XII
(1823-1829)

1824: *Ubi primum* (To all bishops: on Leo XII's assuming the pontificate), May 5.

Quod hoc ineunte (Proclaiming a universal jubilee), May 24.

1825: *Charitate Christi* (Extending jubilee to the entire Church), Dec. 25.

Pius VIII
(1829-1830)

1829: *Traditi humilitati* (On Pius VIII's program for the pontificate), May 24.

Gregory XVI
(1831-1846)

1832: *Summo iugiter studio* (To the bishops of Bavaria: on mixed marriages), May 27.

Cum primum (To the bishops of Poland: on civil obedience), June 9.

Mirari vos (On liberalism and religious indifferentism), Aug. 15.

1833: *Quo graviora* (To the bishops of the Rhineland: on the "pragmatic Constitution"), Oct. 4.

1834: *Singulari Nos* (On the errors of Lammenais), June 25.

1835: *Commissum divinitus* (To clergy of Switzerland: on Church and State), May 17.

1840: *Probe nostis* (On the Propagation of the Faith), Sept. 18.

1841: *Quas vestro* (To the bishops of Hungary: on mixed marriages), Apr. 30.

1844: *Inter praecipuas* (On biblical societies), May 8.

Pius IX
(1846-1878)

1846: *Qui pluribus* (On faith and religion), Nov. 9.

1847: *Praedecessores Nostros* (On aid for Ireland), Mar. 25.

Ubi primum (To religious superiors: on discipline for religious), June 17.

1849: *Ubi primum* (On the Immaculate Conception), Feb. 2.

Nostis et Nobiscum (To the bishops of Italy: on the Church in the Pontifical States), Dec. 8.

1851: *Exultavit cor Nostrum* (On the effects of jubilee), Nov. 21.

1852: *Nemo certe ignorat* (To the bishops of Ireland: on the discipline for clergy), Mar. 25.

Probe noscitis Venerabiles (To the bishops of Spain: on the discipline for clergy), May 17.

1853: *Inter multiplices* (To the bishops of France: pleading for unity of spirit), Mar. 21.

1854: *Neminem vestrum* (To clergy and faithful of Constantinople: on the persecution of Armenians), Feb. 2.

Optime noscitis (To the bishops of Ireland: on the proposed Catholic university for Ireland), Mar. 20.

Apostolicae Nostrae caritatis (Urging prayers for peace), Aug. 1.

1855: *Optime noscitis* (To the bishops of Austria: on episcopal meetings), Nov. 5.

1856: *Singulari quidem* (To the bishops of Austria: on the Church in Austria), Mar. 17.

1858: *Cum nuper* (To the bishops of the Kingdom of the Two Sicilies: on care for clerics), Jan. 20.

Amantissimi Redemptoris (On priests and the care of souls), May 3.

1859: *Cum sancta mater Ecclesia* (Pleading for public prayer), Apr. 27.

Qui nuper (On Pontifical States), June 18.

1860: *Nullis certe verbis* (On the need for civil sovereignty), Jan. 19.

1862: *Amantissimus* (To bishops of the Oriental rite: on the care of the churches), Apr. 8.

1863: *Quanto conficiamur moerore* (To the bishops of Italy: on promotion of false doctrines), Aug. 10.

Incredibili (To the bishops of Bogota: on persecution in New Granada), Sept. 17.

1864: *Maximae quidem* (To the bishops of Bavaria: on the Church in Bavaria), Aug. 18.

Quanta cura (Condemning current errors), Dec. 8.

1865: *Meridionali Americae* (To the bishops of South America: on the seminary for native clergy), Sept. 30.

1867: *Levate* (On the afflictions of the Church), Oct. 27.

1870: *Respicientes* (Protesting the taking of the Pontifical States), Nov. 1.

1871: *Ubi Nos* (To all bishops: on Pontifical States), May 15.

Beneficia Dei (On the twenty-fifth anniversary of his pontificate), June 4.

Saepe Venerabiles Fratres (On thanksgiving for twenty-five years of pontificate), Aug. 5.

1872: *Quae in Patriarchatu* (To bishops and people of Chaldea: on the Church in Chaldea), Nov. 16.

1873: *Quartus supra* (To bishops and people of the Armenian rite: on the Church in Armenia), Jan. 6.

Etsi multa (On the Church in Italy, Germany and Switzerland), Nov. 21.

1874: *Vix dum a Nobis* (To the bishops of Austria: on the Church in Austria), Mar. 7.

Omnem sollicitudinem (To the bishops of the Ruthenian rite: on the Greek-Ruthenian rite), May 13.

Gravibus Ecclesiae (To all bishops and faithful: proclaiming a jubilee for 1875), Dec. 24.

1875: *Quod nunquam* (To the bishops of Prussia: on the Church in Prussia), Feb. 5.

Graves ac diuturnae (To the bishops of Switzerland: on the Church in Switzerland), Mar. 23.

Leo XIII
(1878-1903)

1878: *Inscrutabili Dei consilio* (On the evils of society), Apr. 21.

Quod Apostolici muneris (On socialism), Dec. 28.

1879: *Aeterni Patris* (On the restoration of Christian philosophy), Aug. 4.

1880: *Arcanum* (On Christian marriage), Feb. 10.

Grande munus (On Sts. Cyril and Methodius), Sept. 30.

Sancta Dei civitas (On mission societies), Dec. 3.

1881: *Diuturnum* (On the origin of civil power), June 29.

Licet multa (To the bishops of Belgium: on Catholics in Belgium), Aug. 3.

1882: *Etsi Nos* (To the bishops of Italy: on conditions in Italy), Feb. 15.

Auspicato concessum (On St. Francis of Assisi), Sept. 17.

Cum multa (To the bishops of Spain: on conditions in Spain), Dec. 8.

1883: *Supremi Apostolatus officio* (On devotion to the Rosary), Sept. 1.

1884: *Nobilissima Gallorum gens* (To the bishops of France: on the religious question), Feb. 8.

Humanum genus (On Freemasonry), Apr. 20.

Superiore anno (On the recitation of the Rosary), Aug. 30.

1885: *Immortale Dei* (On the Christian constitution of states), Nov. 1.

Spectata fides (To the bishops of England: on Christian education), Nov. 27.

Quod auctoritate (Proclamation of extraordinary Jubilee), Dec. 22.

1886: *Iampridem* (To the bishops of Prussia: on Catholicism in Germany), Jan. 6.

Quod multum (To the bishops of Hungary: on the liberty of the Church), Aug. 22.

Pergrata (To the bishops of Portugal: on the Church in Portugal), Sept. 14.

1887: *Vi e ben noto* (To the bishops of Italy: on the Rosary and public life), Sept. 20.

Officio sanctissimo (To the bishops of Bavaria: on the Church in Bavaria), Dec. 22.

1888: *Quod anniversarius* (On his sacerdotal jubilee), Apr. 1.

In plurimis (To the bishops of Brazil: on the abolition of slavery), May 5.

Libertas (On the nature of human liberty), June 20.

Saepe Nos (To the bishops of Ireland: on boycotting in Ireland), June 24.

Paterna caritas (To the Patriarch of Cilicia and the archbishops and bishops of the Armenian people: on reunion with Rome), July 25.

Quam aerumnosa (To the bishops of America: on Italian immigrants), Dec. 10.

Etsi cunctas (To the bishops of Ireland: on the Church in Ireland), Dec. 21.

Exeunte iam anno (On the right ordering of Christian life), Dec. 25.

1889: *Magni Nobis* (To the bishops of the United States: on the Catholic University of America), Mar. 7.

Quamquam pluries (On devotion to St. Joseph), Aug. 15.

1890: *Sapientiae Christianae* (On Christians as citizens), Jan. 10.

Dall'alto Dell'Apostolico seggio (To the bishops and people of Italy: on Freemasonry in Italy), Oct. 15.

Catholicae Ecclesiae (On slavery in the missions), Nov. 20.

1891: *In ipso* (To the bishops of Austria: on episcopal reunions in Austria), Mar. 3.

Rerum novarum (On capital and labor), May 15.

Pastoralis (To the bishops of Portugal: on religious union), June 25.

Pastoralis officii (To the bishops of Germany and Austria: on the morality of dueling), Sept. 12.

Octobri mense (On the Rosary), Sept. 22.

1892: *Au milieu des sollicitudes* (To the bishops, clergy and faithful of France: on the Church and State in France), Feb. 16.

Quarto abeunte saeculo (To the bishops of Spain, Italy, and the two Americas: on the Columbus quadricentennial), July 16.

Magnae Dei Matris (On the Rosary), Sept. 8.

Inimica vis (To the bishops of Italy: on Freemasonry), Dec. 8.

Custodi di quella fede (To the Italian people: on Freemasonry), Dec. 8.

1893: *Ad extremas* (On seminaries for native clergy), June 24.

Constanti Hungarorum (To the bishops of Hungary: on the Church in Hungary), Sept. 2.

Laetitiae sanctae (Commending devotion to the Rosary), Sept. 8.

Non mediocri (To the bishops of Spain: on the Spanish College in Rome), Oct. 25.

Providentissimus Deus (On the study of Holy Scripture), Nov. 18.

1894: *Caritatis* (To the bishops of Poland: on the Church in Poland), Mar. 19.

Inter graves (To the bishops of Peru: on the Church in Peru), May 1.

Litteras a vobis (To the bishops of Brazil: on the clergy in Brazil), July 2.

Iucunda semper expectatione (On the Rosary), Sept. 8.

Christi nomen (On the propagation of the Faith and Eastern churches), Dec. 24.

1895: *Longinqua* (To the bishops of the United States: on Catholicism in the United States), Jan. 6.

Permoti Nos (To the bishops of Belgium: on social conditions in Belgium), July 10.

Adiutricem (On the Rosary), Sept. 5.

1896: *Insignes* (To the bishops of Hungary: on the Hungarian millennium), May 1.

Satis cognitum (On the unity of the Church), June 29.

Fidentem piumque animum (On the Rosary), Sept. 20.

1897: *Divinum illud munus* (On the Holy Spirit), May 9.

Militantis Ecclesiae (To the bishops of Austria, Germany, and Switzerland: on St. Peter Canisius), Aug. 1.

Augustissimae Virginis Mariae (On the Confraternity of the Holy Rosary), Sept. 12.

Affari vos (To the bishops of Canada: on the Manitoba school question), Dec. 8.

1898: *Caritatis studium* (To the bishops of Scotland: on the Church in Scotland), July 25.

Spesse volte (To the bishops, priests, and people of Italy: on the suppression of Catholic institutions), Aug. 5.

Quam religiosa (To the bishops of Peru: on civil marriage law), Aug. 16.

Diuturni temporis (On the Rosary), Sept. 5.

Quum diuturnum (To the bishops of Latin America: on Latin American bishops' plenary council), Dec. 25.

1899: *Annum Sacrum* (On consecration to the Sacred Heart), May 25.

Depuis le jour (To the archbishops, bishops, and clergy of France: on the education of the clergy), Sept. 8.

Paternae (To the bishops of Brazil: on the education of the clergy), Sept. 18.

1900: *Omnibus compertum* (To the Patriarch and bishops of the Greek-Melkite rite: on unity among the Greek Melkites), July 21.

Tametsi futura prospicientibus (On Jesus Christ the Redeemer), Nov. 1.

1901: *Graves de communi re* (On Christian democracy), Jan. 18.

Gravissimas (To the bishops of Portugal: on religious orders in Portugal), May 16.

Reputantibus (To the bishops of Bohemia and Moravia: on the language question in Bohemia), Aug. 20.

Urbanitatis Veteris (To the bishops of the Latin church in Greece: on the foundation of a seminary in Athens), Nov. 20.

1902: *In amplissimo* (To the bishops of the United States: on the Church in the United States), Apr. 15.

Quod votis (To the bishops of Austria: on the proposed Catholic University), Apr. 30.

Mirae caritatis (On the Holy Eucharist), May 28.

Quae ad Nos (To the bishops of Bohemia and Moravia: on the Church in Bohemia and Moravia), Nov. 22

Fin dal principio (To the bishops of Italy: on the education of the clergy), Dec. 8.

Dum multa (To the bishops of Ecuador: on marriage legislation), Dec. 24.

Saint Pius X ·
(1903-1914) *

1903: *E supremi* (On the restoration of all things in Christ), Oct. 4.

1904: *Ad diem illum laetissimum* (On the Immaculate Conception), Feb. 2.

Iucunda sane (On Pope Gregory the Great), Mar. 12.

1905: *Acerbo nimis* (On teaching Christian doctrine), Apr. 15.

Il fermo proposito (To the bishops of Italy: on Catholic Action in Italy), June 11.

1906: *Vehementer Nos* (To the bishops, clergy, and people of France: on the French Law of Separation), Feb. 11.

Tribus circiter (On the Mariavites or Mystic Priests of Poland), Apr. 5.

Pieni l'animo (To the bishops of Italy: on the clergy in Italy), July 28.

Gravissimo officio munere (To the bishops of France: on French associations of worship), Aug. 10.

1907: *Une fois encore* (To the bishops, clergy, and people of France: on the separation of Church and State), Jan. 6.

Pascendi dominici gregis (On the doctrines of the Modernists), Sept. 8.

1909: *Communium rerum* (On St. Anselm of Aosta), Apr. 21.

1910: *Editae saepe* (On St. Charles Borromeo), May 26.

1911: *Iamdudum* (On the Law of Separation in Portugal), May 24.

1912: *Lacrimabili statu* (To the bishops of Latin America: on the Indians of South America), June 7.

Singulari quadam (To the bishops of Germany: on labor organizations), Sept. 24.

Benedict XV
(1914-1922)

1914: *Ad beatissimi Apostolorum* (Appeal for peace), Nov. 1.

1917: *Humani generis Redemptionem* (On preaching the Word of God), June 15.

1918: *Quod iam diu* (On the future peace conference), Dec. 1.

1919: *In hac tanta* (To the bishops of Germany: on St. Boniface), May 14.

Paterno iam diu (On children of central Europe), Nov. 24.

1920: *Pacem, Dei munus pulcherrimum* (On peace and Christian reconciliation), May 23.

Spiritus Paraclitus (On St. Jerome), Sept. 15.

Principi Apostolorum Petro (On St. Ephrem the Syrian), Oct. 5.

Annus iam plenus (On children of central Europe), Dec. 1.

1921: *Sacra propediem* (On the Third Order of St. Francis), Jan. 6.

In praeclara summorum (To professors and students of fine arts in Catholic institutions of learning: on Dante), Apr. 30.

Fausto appetente die (On St. Dominic), June 29.

Pius XI
(1922-1939)

1922: *Ubi arcano Dei consilio* (On the peace of Christ in the Kingdom of Christ), Dec. 23.

1923: *Rerum omnium perturbationem* (On St. Francis de Sales), Jan. 26.

Studiorum Ducem (On St. Thomas Aquinas), June 29.

Ecclesiam Dei (On St. Josaphat), Nov. 12.

1924: *Maximam gravissimamque* (To the

bishops, clergy, and people of France: on French diocesan associations), Jan. 18.

1925: *Quas primas* (On the feast of Christ the King), Dec. 11.

1926: *Rerum Ecclesiae* (On Catholic missions), Feb. 28.

Rite expiatis (On St. Francis of Assisi), Apr. 30.

Iniquis afflictisque (On the persecution of the Church in Mexico), Nov. 18.

1928: *Mortalium animos* (On religious unity), Jan. 6.

Miserentissimus Redemptor (On reparation to the Sacred Heart), May 8.

Rerum Orientalium (On the promotion of Oriental studies), Sept. 8.

1929: *Mens Nostra* (On the promotion of Spiritual Exercises), Dec. 20.

Quinquagesimo ante (On his sacerdotal jubilee), Dec. 23.

Rappresentanti in terra (On Christian education), Dec. 31. [Latin text, *Divini illius magistri,* published several months later with minor changes.]

1930: *Ad salutem* (On St. Augustine), Apr. 20.

Casti connubii (On Christian marriage), Dec. 31.

1931: *Quadragesimo anno* (Commemorating the fortieth anniversary of Leo XIII's *Rerum novarum:* on reconstruction of the social order), May 15.

Non abbiamo bisogno (On Catholic Action in Italy), June 29.

Nova impendet (On the economic crisis), Oct. 2.

Lux veritatis (On the Council of Ephesus), Dec. 25.

1932: *Caritate Christi compulsi* (On the Sacred Heart), May 3.

Acerba animi (To the bishops of Mexico: on persecution of the Church in Mexico), Sept. 29.

1933: *Dilectissima Nobis* (To the bishops, clergy, and people of Spain: on oppression of the Church in Spain), June 3.

1935: *Ad Catholici sacerdotii* (On the Catholic priesthood), Dec. 20.

1936: *Vigilanti cura* (To the bishops of the United States: on motion pictures), June 29.

1937: *Mit brennender Sorge* (To the bishops of Germany: on the Church and the German Reich), Mar. 14.

Divini Redemptoris (On atheistic communism), Mar. 19.

Nos es muy conocida (To the bishops of Mexico: on the religious situation in Mexico), Mar. 28.

Ingravescentibus malis (On the Rosary) Sept. 29.

Pius XII
(1939-1958)

1939: *Summi Pontificatus* (On the unity of human society), Oct. 20.

Sertum laetitiae (To the bishops of the United States: on the 150th anniversary of the estab-

lishment of the hierarchy in the United States), Nov. 1.

1940: *Saeculo exeunte octavo* (To the bishops of Portugal and its colonies: on the eighth centenary of the independence of Portugal), June 13.

1943: *Mystici Corporis Christi* (On the Mystical Body of Christ), June 29.

Divino afflante Spiritu (On promoting biblical studies, commemorating the fiftieth anniversary of *Providentissimus Deus),* Sept. 30.

1944: *Orientalis Ecclesiae* (On St. Cyril, Patriarch of Alexandria), Apr. 9.

1945: *Communium interpretes dolorum* (To the bishops of the world: appealing for prayers for peace during May), Apr. 15.

Orientales omnes Ecclesias (On the 350th anniversary of the reunion of the Ruthenian Church with the Apostolic See), Dec. 23.

1946: *Quemadmodum* (Pleading for the care of the world's destitute children), Jan. 6.

Deiparae Virginis Mariae (To all bishops: on the possibility of defining the Assumption of the Blessed Virgin Mary as a dogma of faith), May 1.

1947: *Fulgens radiatur* (On St. Benedict), Mar. 21.

Mediator Dei (On the sacred liturgy), Nov. 20.

Optatissima pax (Prescribing public prayers for social and world peace), Dec. 18.

1948: *Auspicia quaedam* (On public prayers for world peace and solution of the problem of Palestine), May 1.

In multiplicibus curis (On prayers for peace in Palestine), Oct. 24.

1949: *Redemptoris nostri cruciatus* (On the holy places in Palestine), Apr. 15.

1950: *Anni Sacri* (On the program for combatting atheistic propaganda throughout the world), Mar. 12.

Summi maeroris (On public prayers for peace), July 19.

Humani generis (Concerning some false opinions threatening to undermine the foundations of Catholic doctrine), Aug. 12.

Mirabile illud (On the crusade of prayers for peace), Dec. 6.

1951: *Evangelii praecones* (On the promotion of Catholic missions), June 2.

Sempiternus Rex Christus (On the Council of Chalcedon), Sept. 8.

Ingruentium malorum (On reciting the Rosary), Sept. 15.

1952: *Orientales Ecclesias* (On the persecuted Eastern Church), Dec. 15.

1953: *Doctor Mellifluus* (On St. Bernard of Clairvaux, the last of the fathers), May 24.

Fulgens corona (Proclaiming a Marian Year to commemorate the centenary of the definition of the dogma of the Immaculate Conception), Sept. 8.

1954: *Sacra virginitas* (On consecrated virginity), Mar. 25.

Ecclesiae fastos (To the bishops of Great Britain, Germany, Austria, France, Belgium, and Holland: on St. Boniface), June 5.

Ad Sinarum gentem (To the bishops, clergy, and people of China: on the supranationality of the Church), Oct. 7.

Ad Caeli Reginam (Proclaiming the Queenship of Mary), Oct. 11.

1955: *Musicae sacrae* (On sacred music), Dec. 25.

1956: *Haurietis aquas* (On devotion to the Sacred Heart), May 15.

Luctuosissimi eventus (Urging public prayers for peace and freedom for the people of Hungary), Oct. 28.

Laetamur admodum (Renewing exhortation for prayers for peace for Poland, Hungary, and especially for the Middle East), Nov. 1.

Datis nuperrime (Lamenting the sorrowful events in Hungary and condemning the ruthless use of force), Nov. 5.

1957: *Fidei donum* (On the present condition of the Catholic missions, especially in Africa), Apr. 21.

Invicti athletae (On St. Andrew Bobola), May 16.

Le pelerinage de Lourdes (Warning against materialism on the centenary of the apparitions at Lourdes), July 2.

Miranda prorsus (On the communications field: motion picture, radio, television), Sept. 8.

1958: *Ad Apostolorum Principis* (To the bishops of China; on Communism and the Church in China), June 29.

Meminisse iuvat (On prayers for persecuted Church), July 14.

John XXIII
(1958-1963)

1959: *Ad Petri Cathedram* (On truth, unity, and peace, in a spirit of charity), June 29.

Sacerdotii Nostri primordia (On St. John Vianney), Aug. 1.

Grata recordatio (On the Rosary: prayer for

the Church, missions, international and social problems), Sept. 26.

Princeps Pastorum (On the missions, native clergy, lay participation), Nov. 28.

1961: *Mater et Magistra* (On Christianity and social progress), May 15.

Aeterna Dei sapientia (On fifteenth centenary of the death of Pope St. Leo I: the see of Peter as the center of Christian unity), Nov. 11.

1962: *Paenitentiam agere* (On the need for the practice of interior and exterior penance), July 1.

1963: *Pacem in terris* (On establishing universal peace in truth, justice, charity, and liberty), Apr. 11.

Paul VI
(1963-1978)

1964: *Ecclesiam Suam* (On the Church), Aug. 6.

1965: *Mense maio* (On prayers during May for the preservation of peace), Apr. 29.

Mysterium Fidei (On the Holy Eucharist), Sept. 3.

1966: *Christi Matri* (On prayers for peace during October), Sept. 15.

1967: *Populorum progressio* (On the development of peoples), Mar. 26.

Sacerdotalis caelibatus (On the celibacy of the priest), June 24.

1968: *Humanae vitae* (On the regulation of birth), July 25.

John Paul II
(1978-   )

1979: *Redemptor hominis* (On redemption and the dignity of the human race), Mar. 4.

1980: *Dives in misericordia* (On the mercy of God), Nov. 30.

1981: *Laborem exercens* (On human work), Sept. 14.

1985: *Slavorum Apostoli* (Commemorating Sts. Cyril and Methodius, on the eleventh centenary of the death of St. Methodius), June 2.

1986: *Dominum et Vivificantem* (On the Holy Spirit in the Life of the Church and the World), May 18.

CHARISMATIC RENEWAL

(Written with the assistance of the staff of the national office of the Catholic Charismatic Renewal of the U.S.)

The movement originated with a handful of Duquesne University students and faculty members in the 1966-67 academic year and spread from there to Notre Dame, Michigan State University, the University of Michigan and to other campuses.

The movement is strong in the U.S., Canada and some 120 other countries, probably involving more than a million participants.

Scriptural keys to the renewal are:

• Christ's promise to send the Holy Spirit upon the Apostles;

• the description, in the Acts of the Apostles, of the effects of the coming of the Holy Spirit upon the Apostles on Pentecost;

• St. Paul's explanation, in the Letters to the Co-

rinthians and Romans, of the charismatic gifts (for the good of the Church and persons) the Holy Spirit would bestow on Christians;

• New Testament evidence concerning the effects of charismatic gifts in and through the early Church.

The personal key to the renewal is a personal relationship to Jesus as Lord and Savior, and prayer for release of the Holy Spirit involving the personally experienced actualization of grace already sacramentally received.

Among the movement's strongest points of emphasis are prayer, openness to the Holy Spirit, community experience and the sharing of spiritual gifts.

William J. Beatty is executive director of Chariscenter USA, 237 N. Michigan St., South Bend, Ind. 46601.

HIERARCHY OF THE CATHOLIC CHURCH

ORGANIZATION AND GOVERNMENT

As a structured society, the Catholic Church is organized and governed along lines corresponding mainly to the jurisdictions of the pope and bishops.

The pope is the supreme head of the Church. He has primacy of jurisdiction as well as honor over the entire Church.

Bishops, in union with and in subordination to the pope, are the successors of the Apostles for care of the Church and for the continuation of Christ's mission in the world. They serve the people of their own dioceses, or particular churches, with ordinary authority and jurisdiction. They also share, with the pope and each other, in common concern and effort for the general welfare of the whole Church.

Bishops of exceptional status are Eastern-Rite patriarchs who, subject only to the pope, are heads of the faithful belonging to their rites throughout the world.

Subject to the Holy Father and directly responsible to him for the exercise of their ministry of service to people in various jurisdictions or divisions of the Church throughout the world are: resident archbishops and metropolitans (heads of archdioceses), diocesan bishops, vicars and prefects apostolic (heads of vicariates apostolic and prefectures apostolic), certain abbots and prelates, apostolic administrators. Each of these, within his respective territory and according to the provisions of canon law, has ordinary jurisdiction over pastors (who are responsible for the administration of parishes), priests, Religious and lay persons.

Also subject to the Holy Father are titular archbishops and bishops, religious orders and congregations of pontifical right, pontifical institutes and faculties, papal nuncios and apostolic delegates.

Assisting the pope and acting in his name in the central government and administration of the Church are cardinals and other officials of the Roman Curia.

THE HIERARCHY

The ministerial hierarchy is the orderly arrangement of the ranks and orders of the clergy to provide for the spiritual care of the faithful, the government of the Church, and the accomplishment of the Church's total mission in the world. Persons belong to this hierarchy by virtue of ordination and canonical mission.

The term hierarchy is also used to designate an entire body or group of bishops; for example, the hierarchy of the Church, the hierarchy of the United States.

Hierarchy of Order: Consists of the pope, bishops, priests and deacons. Their purpose, for which they are ordained to holy orders, is to carry out the sacramental and pastoral ministry of the Church.

Hierarchy of Jurisdiction: Consists of the pope and bishops by divine institution, and other church officials by ecclesiastical institution and mandate, who have authority to govern and direct the faithful for spiritual ends.

The Pope

His Holiness the Pope is the Bishop of Rome, the Vicar of Jesus Christ, the successor of St. Peter, Prince of the Apostles, the Supreme Pontiff who has the primacy of jurisdiction and not merely of honor over the universal Church, the Patriarch of the West, the Primate of Italy, the Archbishop and Metropolitan of the Roman Province, the Sovereign of the State of Vatican City, Servant of the Servants of God.

Cardinals

(See Index)

Patriarchs

Patriarch, a term which had its origin in the Eastern Church, is the title of a bishop who, second only to the pope, has the highest rank in the hierarchy of jurisdiction. He is the incumbent of one of the sees listed below. Subject only to the pope, an Eastern-Rite patriarch is the head of the faithful belonging to his rite throughout the world. The patriarchal sees are so called because of their special status and dignity in the history of the Church.

The Council of Nicaea (325) recognized three patriarchs — the bishops of Alexandria and Antioch in the East, and of Rome in the West. The First Council of Constantinople (381) added the bishop of Constantinople to the list of patriarchs and gave him rank second only to that of the pope, the bishop of Rome and patriarch of the West; this action was seconded by the Council of Chalcedon (451) and was given full recognition by the Fourth Lateran Council (1215). The Council of Chalcedon also acknowledged patriarchal rights of the bishop of Jerusalem.

Eastern Rite patriarchs are as follows: one of Alexandria, for the Copts; three of Antioch, one each for the Syrians, Maronites and Greek Melkites (the latter also has the personal title of Greek Melkite patriarch of Alexandria and of Jerusalem). The patriarch of Babylonia, for the Chaldeans, and the patriarch of Sis, or Cilicia, for the Armenians, should be called, more properly, *Katholikos* — that is, a prelate delegated for a universality of causes. These patriarchs are elected by bishops of their rites: they receive approval and the pallium, symbolic of their office, from the pope.

Latin Rite patriarchates were established for Antioch, Jerusalem, Alexandria and Constantinople during the Crusades; afterwards, they became patriarchates in name only. Jerusalem, however, was reconstituted as a patriarchate by Pius IX, in virtue of the bull *Nulla Celebrior* of July 23, 1847. In 1964, the Latin titular patriarchates of Constantinople, Alexandria and Antioch, long a bone of contention in relations with Eastern Rites, were abolished.

As of July 15, 1986, the patriarchs in the Church were:

The Pope, Bishop of Rome, Patriarch of the West; Stephanos II (Andraos) Ghattas, C.M., of Alexandria, for the Copts; Ignace Antoine II Hayek, of Antioch, for the Syrians; Maximos V Hakim, of Antioch, for the Greek Melkites (he also has the titles of Alexandria and Jerusalem for the Greek Melkites); Nasrallah Pierre Sfeir, of Antioch, for the Maronites; Giacomo Beltritti, of Jerusalem, for the Latin Rite; Paul II Cheikho, of Babylon, for the Chaldeans; Jean Pierre XVIII Kasparian, of Cilicia, for the Armenians.

The titular patriarchs (in name only) of the Latin Rite were: Cardinal Antonio Ribeiro, of Lisbon; Cardinal Marco Cé of Venice and Archbishop Raul Nicolau Goncalves of the East Indies (Archbishop of Goa and Daman, India). The patriarchate of the West Indies has been vacant since 1963.

Archbishops, Metropolitans

Archbishop: A bishop with the title of an archdiocese.

Metropolitan: Archbishop of the principal see, an archdiocese, in an ecclesiastical province consisting of several dioceses. He has the full powers of bishop in his own archdiocese and limited supervisory jurisdiction and influence over the other (suffragan) dioceses in the province. The pallium, conferred by the pope, is the symbol of his status as a metropolitan.

Titular Archbishop: Has the title of an archdiocese which formerly existed in fact but now exists in title only. He does not have ordinary jurisdiction over an archdiocese. Examples are archbishops in the Roman Curia, papal nuncios, apostolic delegates.

Archbishop ad personam: A title of personal honor and distinction granted to some bishops. They do not have ordinary jurisdiction over an archdiocese.

Primate: A title of honor given to the ranking prelate of some countries or regions.

Bishops

Diocesan Bishop: A bishop in charge of a diocese.

Coadjutor Bishop: An assistant (auxiliary) bishop to a diocesan bishop, with right of succession to the see.

Titular Bishops: A bishop with the title of a diocese which formerly existed in fact but now exists in title only; an assistant (auxiliary) bishop to a diocesan bishop.

Episcopal Vicar: An assistant, who may or may not be a bishop, appointed by a residential bishop as his deputy for a certain part of a diocese, a determined type of apostolic work, or the faithful of a certain rite.

Eparch, Exarch: Titles of bishops of Eastern-Rite churches.

Nomination of Bishops: Nominees for episcopal ordination are selected in several ways. Final appointment and/or approval in all cases is subject to decision by the pope.

In the U.S., bishops periodically submit the names of candidates to the archbishop of their province. The names are then considered at a meeting of the bishops of the province, and those receiving a favorable vote are forwarded to the pro-nuncio for transmission to the Holy See. Bishops are free to seek the counsel of priests, religious and lay persons with respect to nominees.

Eastern-Rite churches have their own procedures and synodal regulations for nominating and making final selection of candidates for episcopal ordination. Such selection is subject to approval by the pope.

The Code of Canon Law concedes no rights or privileges to civil authorities with respect to the election, nomination, presentation or designation of candidates for the episcopate.

Ad Limina Visit: Diocesan bishops and apostolic vicars are obliged to make an *ad limina* visit ("to the threshold" of the Apostles) every five years to the tombs of Sts. Peter and Paul, have audience with the Holy Father, consult with appropriate Vatican officials and present a written report on conditions in their jurisdictions. The most recent regulations concerning the formalities and scheduling of visits by bishops from various countries, generally every five years, were issued by the Congregation for Bishops in a decree dated Nov. 27, 1975.

Others with Ordinary Jurisdiction

Ordinary: One who has the jurisdiction of an office: the pope, diocesan bishops, vicars general, prelates of missionary territories, vicars apostolic prefects apostolic, vicars capitular during the vacancy of a see, superiors general, abbots primate and other major superiors of men Religious.

Some prelates and abbots, with jurisdiction like that of diocesan bishops, are pastors of the people of God in territories (prelatures and abbacies) not under the jurisdiction of diocesan bishops.

Vicar Apostolic: Usually a titular bishop who has ordinary jurisdiction over a mission territory.

Prefect Apostolic: Has ordinary jurisdiction over a mission territory.

Apostolic Administrator: Usually a bishop appointed to administer an ecclesiastical jurisdiction temporarily. Administrators of lesser rank are also appointed for special and more restricted supervisory duties.

Vicar General: A bishop's deputy for the administration of a diocese. Such a vicar does not have to be a bishop.

Honorary Prelates

Honorary prelates belonging to the Pontifical Household are: Apostolic Prothonotaries, Honorary Prelates of His Holiness, and Chaplains of His Holiness. Their title is Reverend Monsignor.

SYNOD OF BISHOPS

The Synod of Bishops was chartered by Pope Paul VI Sept. 15, 1965, in a document he issued on his own initiative under the title, *Apostolica Sollicitudo*. Provisions of this *motu proprio* are contained in Canons 342 to 348 of the Code of Canon Law. According to major provisions of the Synod charter:

• The purposes of the Synod are: "to encourage close union and valued assistance between the Sovereign Pontiff and the bishops of the entire world; to insure that direct and real information is provided on questions and situations touching upon the internal action of the Church and its necessary activity in the world of today; to facilitate agreement on essential points of doctrine and on methods of procedure in the life of the Church."

• The Synod is a central ecclesiastical institution, permanent by nature.

• The Synod is directly and immediately subject to the Pope, who has authority to assign its agenda, to call it into session, and to give its members deliberative as well as advisory authority.

• In addition to a limited number of ex officio members and a few heads of male religious institutes, the majority of the members are elected by and representative of national or regional episcopal conferences. The Pope reserved the right to appoint the general secretary, special secretaries and no more than 15 per cent of the total membership.

The Pope is president of the Synod.

The secretary general is Archbishop Jan Schotte of Belgium.

An advisory council of 15 members (12 elected, three appointed by the pope) provides the secretariat with adequate staff for carrying on liaison with episcopal conferences and for preparing the agenda of synodal assemblies.

Assemblies

1. The first assembly was held from Sept. 29 to Oct. 29, 1967. Its objectives, as stated by Pope Paul VI, were "the preservation and strengthening of the Catholic faith, its integrity, its force, its development, its doctrinal and historical coherence." One result was a recommendation for the establishment of an international commission of theologians to assist the Congregation for the Doctrine of the Faith and to broaden approaches to theological research. Pope Paul set up the commission in 1969.

2. The second assembly, held Oct. 11 to 28, 1969, was extraordinary in character. It opened the way toward greater participation by bishops with the pope and each other in the governance of the Church. Proceedings were oriented to three main points: (1) the nature and implications of collegiality; (2) the relationship of bishops and their conferences to the pope; (3) the relationships of bishops and their conferences to each other.

3. The ministerial priesthood and justice in the world were the principal topics under discussion at the second ordinary assembly, Sept. 30 to Nov. 6, 1971. In one report, the Synod emphasized the primary and permanent dedication of priests in the

Church to the ministry of word, sacrament and pastoral service as a full-time vocation. In another report, the assembly stated: "Action on behalf of justice and participation in the transformation of the world fully appear to us as a constitutive dimension of the preaching of the Gospel; or, in other words, of the Church's mission for the redemption of the human race and its liberation from every oppressive situation."

4. The assembly of Sept. 27 to Oct. 26, 1974, produced a general statement on evangelization of the modern world, covering the need for it and its relationship to efforts for total human liberation from personal and social evil. The assembly observed: "The Church does not remain within merely political, social and economic limits (elements which she must certainly take into account) but leads towards freedom under all its forms — liberation from sin, from individual or collective selfishness — and to full communion with God and with men who are like brothers. In this way the Church, in her evangelical way, promotes the true and complete liberation of all men, groups and peoples."

5. The fourth ordinary assembly, Sept. 30 to Oct. 29, 1977, focused attention on catechetics, with special reference to children and young people. The participants issued a "Message to the People of God," the first synodal statement issued since inception of the body, and also presented to Pope Paul VI a set of 34 related propositions and a number of suggestions.

6. "A Message to Christian Families in the Modern World" and a proposal for a "Charter of Family Rights" were produced by the assembly held Sept. 26 to Oct. 25, 1980. The assembly reaffirmed the indissolubility of marriage and the contents of the encyclical letter *Humanae Vitae* (see separate entry), and urged married couples who find it hard to live up to "the difficult but loving demands" of Christ not to be discouraged but to avail themselves of the aid of divine grace. In response to synodal recommendation, Pope John Paul issued a charter of family rights late in 1983.

7. Penance and reconciliation in the mission of the Church was the theme of the assembly held Sept. 29 to Oct. 29, 1983. Sixty-three propositions related to this theme were formulated on a wide variety of subjects, including: personal sin and so-called systemic or institutional sin; the nature of serious sin; the diminished sense of sin and of the need of redemption, related to decline in the administration and reception of the sacrament of penance; general absolution; individual and social reconciliation; violence and violations of human rights; reconciliation as the basis of peace and justice in society. In a statement issued Oct. 27, the Synod stressed the need of the world to become, increasingly, "a reconciled community of peoples," and said that "the Church, as sacrament of reconciliation to the world, has to be an effective sign of God's mercy."

8. The second extraordinary assembly was convened Nov. 24 to Dec. 8, 1985, for the purposes of:

(1) recalling the Second Vatican Council; (2) evaluating the implementation of its enactments during the 20 years since its conclusion; (3) seeking ways and means of promoting renewal in the Church in accordance with the spirit and letter of the council. (See separate entry, Synod of Bishops: Extraordinary Assembly, 1985.)

9. An ordinary assembly of the Synod in 1986 was postponed until 1987. Its stated topic: "The Vocation and Mission of the Laity in the World."

ROMAN CURIA

The Roman Curia consists of the Secretariat of State, the Council for the Public Affairs of the Church, congregations, tribunals, secretariats, and a complex of commissions, councils and offices which administer church affairs at the highest level, with authority granted by the pope.

Background

The Curia evolved gradually from advisory assemblies or synods of the Roman clergy with whose assistance the popes directed church affairs during the first 11 centuries. Its original office was the Apostolic Chancery, established in the fourth century to transmit documents. The antecedents of its permanently functioning agencies and offices were special commissions of cardinals and prelates. Its establishment in a form resembling what it is now dates from the second half of the 16th century.

Pope Paul initiated a four-year reorganization study in 1963 which resulted in the constitution *Regimini Ecclesiae Universae*. The document was published Aug. 18, 1967, and went into full effect in March, 1968.

While the study was under way, the Pope took preliminary steps toward curial reorganization by reorienting and changing the title of the Sacred Congregation of the Holy Office (to the Sacred Congregation for the Doctrine of the Faith) and by appointing a number of non-Italians to key curial positions.

The stated purposes of the reorganization were to increase the efficiency of the Curia and to make it more responsive to the needs and concerns of the Universal Church. The pursuit of these objectives involved various modifications.

Curial Departments

• The Office of the Pope, including the Papal Secretariat or Secretariat of State and the Council for the Public Affairs of the Church.

• Nine congregations, instead of twelve as formerly. The functions of the Congregation of Ceremonies were transferred to the Prefecture of the Pontifical Household; the duties of the Congregation for Extraordinary Ecclesiastical Affairs were taken over by the Council for the Public Affairs of the Church; the Congregation of the Basilica of St. Peter was reduced in rank. In 1969, the Congregation of Rites was phased out of existence and its functions were assigned to the Congregation for the Causes of Saints and the Congregation for Divine Worship.

The Congregation for the Sacraments and Divine Worship, established in 1975 to replace the Congregation for the Discipline of the Sacraments and the Congregation for Divine Worship, was made two separate congregations in 1984.

• Three secretariats, the Council of the Laity and the Pontifical Commission on Justice and Peace.

• Three tribunals.

• Six offices, including the former Apostolic Chancery (abolished in 1973) and Apostolic Chamber, and the newly constituted Prefecture of Economic Affairs, Prefecture of the Pontifical Household, Administration of the Patrimony of the Apostolic See, and Central Statistics Office. Functions of the former Apostolic Datary and the Secretariats of State, of Briefs to Princes, and of Latin Letters were transferred to the Secretariat of State.

Operational Procedures

• The papal secretary or secretary of state has authority to take initiative in coordinating and expediting business through meetings and other cooperative procedures.

• Officials of departments have five-year terms of office, which may be renewed. Terms end automatically on the death of a pope. The five-year terms of consultors are renewable.

• Diocesan bishops as well as full-time curial personnel have membership in curial departments, in accordance with provisions of the decree *Pro Comperto Sane* of Aug. 6, 1967. Three general superiors of male religious institutes hold membership in the Congregation for Religious and Secular Institutes.

• Lay persons are eligible to serve as consultors to curial departments.

• Close liaison with episcopal conferences is required.

• Matters in which the competence of two or more departments is involved are handled on a cooperative basis, with mutual consultation and decision.

• Although Latin remains the official language of the Curia, communication in any of the widely known modern languages is acceptable.

• Authority to act and decide on many matters belongs to departmental officials in virtue of delegation from the pope. Some matters, however, have to be referred to the pope for final decision.

Internationalization

As of July 15, 1986, principal officials of the Roman Curia (cardinals unless indicated otherwise) were from the following countries: Italy (Baggio, Caprio, Casaroli, Dadaglio, Innocenti, Palazzini, Opilio Rossi, Sabattani, Abps. Angelini, Bovone, Fagiolo, Noe, Silvestrini, Verolino, Msgr. Fiore); France (Etchegaray, Poupard, Abp. Martin); Germany (Mayer, Ratzinger, Bp. Cordes); Spain (Abps. Javierre Ortas, Martinez Somalo, Romero de Lema); United States (Baum, Abps. Foley, Marcinkus); Brazil (Agnelo Rossi, Abp. Moreira Neves); India (Lourdusamy, Parecattil); Poland

(Abp. Grocholewski); Argentina (Pironio); Belgium (Hamer); Benin (Gantin); Canada (Gagnon); Czechoslovakia (Tomko); Hungary (Abp. Kada); Netherlands (Willebrands); Nigeria (Arinze); Philippines (Abp. Sanchez); Romania (Abp. Crisan); Ukraine (Abp. Marusyn); Venezuela (Castillo Lara).

DEPARTMENTS

Secretariat of State: Provides the pope with the closest possible assistance in the care of the universal Church and in dealings with all departments of the Curia.

The cardinal secretary is the key coordinator of curial operations. He has authority to call meetings of the prefects of all departments for expediting the conduct of business, for consultation and intercommunication. He handles: any and all matters entrusted to him by the pope, and ordinary matters which are not within the competence of other departments; some relations with bishops; relations with representatives of the Holy See, civil governments and their representatives, without prejudice to the competence of the Council for the Public Affairs of the Church.

The secretariat has two offices for preparing and writing letters for the pope and a Central Statistics Office. It handles work formerly done by the Apostolic Datary and the Apostolic Chancery, (care of the pope's leaden seal and the Fisherman's Ring). It has supervisory duties over the Commission for the Instruments of Social Communication, two Vatican publications, *Acta Apostolicae Sedis* and *Annuario Pontificio*, and the Vatican Personnel Office. The Prefecture of Vatican City is answerable to the secretary of state.

OFFICIALS: Cardinal Agostino Casaroli, secretary of state; Most Rev. Eduardo Martinez Somalo, undersecretary and secretary of the Cifra.

Council for the Public Affairs of the Church: Handles diplomatic and other relations with civil governments. With the Secretariat of State, it supervises matters concerning nunciatures and apostolic delegations. It also has supervision of the Pontifical Commission for Russia.

OFFICIALS: Cardinal Agostino Casaroli, prefect, secretary of state; Most Rev. Achille Silvestrini, secretary.

BACKGROUND: Originated by Pius VI in 1793 as the Congregation for Extraordinary Affairs from the Kingdom of the Gauls; given wider scope by Pius VII, July 19, 1814; formerly called the Sacred Congregation for Extraordinary Ecclesiastical Affairs.

CONGREGATIONS

Congregation for the Doctrine of the Faith: Has responsibility to safeguard the doctrine of faith and morals. Accordingly, it examines doctrinal questions; promotes studies thereon; evaluates theological opinions and, when necessary and after prior consultation with concerned bishops, reproves those regarded as opposed to principles of the faith; examines books on doctrinal matters and can reprove such works, if the con-

tents so warrant, after giving authors the opportunity to defend themselves. It examines matters pertaining to the Privilege of Faith (Petrine Privilege) in marriage cases, and safeguards the dignity of the sacrament of penance. It has working relations with the Pontifical Biblical Commission and the Theological Commission

OFFICIALS: Cardinal Joseph Ratzinger, prefect; Most Rev. Alberto Bovone, secretary.

BACKGROUND: At the beginning of the 13th century, legates of Innocent III were commissioned as the Holy Office of the Inquisition to combat heresy; the same task was entrusted to the Dominican Order by Gregory IX in 1231 and to the Friars Minor by Innocent IV from 1243 to 1254. On July 21, 1542 (apostolic constitution *Licet*), Paul III instituted a permanent congregation of cardinals with supreme and universal competence over matters concerning heretics and those suspected of heresy. Pius IV, St. Pius V and Sixtus V further defined the work of the congregation. St. Pius X changed its name to the Congregation of the Holy Office.

Paul VI, in virtue of the motu proprio *Integrae Servandae* of Dec. 7, 1965, began reorganization of the Curia with this body, to which he gave the new title, Congregation for the Doctrine of the Faith. Its orientation is not merely negative, in the condemnation of error, but positive, in the promotion of orthodox doctrine. The right of appeal, judicial representation, and the consultation of their proper regional conference of bishops, are assured to persons accused of unorthodox doctrine. The office for the censorship of books and the Roman Index of Prohibited Books were abolished.

Congregation for the Oriental Churches: Has competence in matters concerning the persons and discipline of Eastern-Rite Churches. It has jurisdiction over territories in which the majority of Christians belong to Oriental Rites (i.e., Egypt, the Sinai Peninsula, Eritrea, Northern Ethiopia, Southern Albania, Bulgaria, Cyprus, Greece, Iran, Iraq, Lebanon, Palestine, Syria, Jordan, Turkey, Afghanistan, the part of Thrace subject to Turkey); also, over minority communities of Orientals no matter where they live. It is under mandate to consult with the Secretariat for Promoting Christian Unity on questions concerning separated Oriental Churches, and with the Secretariat for Non-Christians, especially in relations with Moslems. It has a special commission on the liturgy and an Oriental Church Information Service.

OFFICIALS: Cardinal D. Simon Lourdusamy, prefect; Most Rev. Miroslav Stefan Marusyn, secretary.

Members include all Eastern Rite patriarchs and the president of the Secretariat for Promoting Christian Unity. Consultors include the secretary of the same secretariat.

BACKGROUND: Special congregations for the affairs of the Greek and other Oriental Churches were founded long before this body was created by Pius IX Jan. 6, 1862 (apostolic constitution *Romani Pontifices*), and united with the Congregation for the Propagation of the Faith. The congregation was made autonomous by Benedict XV May 1, 1917 (motu proprio *Dei Providentis*), and given wider authority by Pius XI Mar. 25, 1938 (motu proprio *Sancta Dei Ecclesia*). John XXIII appointed six patriarchs, five of Eastern Rites and one of the Roman Rite, to the congregation.

Congregation for Bishops, formerly called the Consistorial Congregation, has functions related in one way or another to bishops and the jurisdictions in which they serve. Its concerns are: the establishment and changing of dioceses, provinces, military vicariates and other jurisdictions; providing for the naming of bishops and other prelates; studying things concerning the persons, work and pastoral activity of bishops; providing for the care of bishops when they leave office; receiving and studying reports on the conditions of dioceses; general supervision of the holding and recognition of particular councils and conferences of bishops; publishing and circulating pastoral norms and guidelines through conferences of bishops. It supervises the Pontifical Commission for Latin America and the Pontifical Commission for Migration and Tourism.

OFFICIALS: Cardinal Bernardin Gantin, prefect; Most Rev. Lucas Moreira Neves, O.P., secretary.

Ex officio members are the prefects of the Council for the Public Affairs of the Church, and of the Congregations for the Doctrine of the Faith, for the Clergy, and for Catholic Education. The substitute secretaries and undersecretaries of these curial departments are ex officio consultors.

BACKGROUND: Established by Sixtus V Jan. 22, 1588 (apostolic constitution *Immensa*); given an extension of powers by St. Pius X June 20, 1908, and Pius XII Aug. 1, 1952 (apostolic constitution *Exsul Familia*).

Congregation for the Sacraments: Supervises the discipline of the sacraments without prejudice to the competencies of the Congregation for the Doctrine of the Faith and other curial departments.

OFFICIALS: Cardinal Paul Augustin Mayer, O.S.B., prefect; Most Rev. Lajos Kada, secretary.

BACKGROUND: Instituted by St. Pius X, June 29, 1908, as the Congregation for the Discipline of the Sacraments; replaced by the Congregation for the Sacraments and Divine Worship by Paul VI (apostolic constitution, *Constans novis studium*, July 11, 1975); reestablished as a separate congregation by John Paul II in an autograph letter dated April 5, 1984.

Congregation for Divine Worship: Has general competence over the ritual and pastoral aspects of divine worship in the Roman and other Western rites.

OFFICIALS: Cardinal Paul Augustin Mayer, O.S.B., prefect; Most Rev. Virgilio Noe, secretary.

BACKGROUND: Established by Paul VI, May 8, 1969, to replace the Congregation of Rites instituted by Pope Sixtus V in 1588; united with Congregation for the Discipline of the Sacraments by Paul VI in 1975; reestablished as a separate congregation by John Paul II in an autograph letter dated Apr. 5, 1984.

Congregation for the Causes of Saints: Handles matters connected with beatification and canonization causes (in accordance with revised procedures decreed in 1983), and the preservation of relics.

OFFICIALS: Cardinal Pietro Palazzini, prefect; Most Rev. Traian Crisan, secretary.

BACKGROUND: Established by Sixtus V in 1588 as the Congregation of Rites; affected by legislation of Pius XI in 1930; title changed and functions defined by Paul VI, 1969 (apostolic constitution *Sacra Rituum Congregatio*). It was restructured and canonization procedures were revised by John Paul II in 1983 (apostolic constitution *Divinus Perfectionis Magister*).

Congregation for the Clergy, formerly called the Congregation of the Council, handles matters concerning the persons, work and pastoral ministry of clerics and Religious who exercise their apostolate in a diocese.

OFFICIALS: Cardinal Antonio Innocenti, prefect; Most Rev. Maximino Romero de Lema, secretary.

BACKGROUND: Established by Pius IV Aug. 2, 1564 (apostolic constitution *Alias Nos*), under the title, Congregation of the Cardinals Interpreters of the Council of Trent; affected by legislation of Gregory XIII and Sixtus V.

Congregation for Religious and Secular Institutes, formerly known as the Congregation of Religious or for the Affairs of Religious, has competence over institutes of Religious, societies of the apostolic life, third orders and secular institutes. With two sections, the congregation has authority in matters related to the establishment, general direction and suppression of the various institutes; general discipline in line with their rules and constitutions; the movement toward renewal and adaptation of institutes in contemporary circumstances; the setting up and encouragement of councils and conferences of major religious superiors for intercommunication and other purposes.

OFFICIALS: Cardinal Jean Jerome Hamer, O.P. prefect; Most. Rev. Vincenzo Fagiolo, secretary.

BACKGROUND: Founded by Sixtus V May 27, 1586, with the title, Congregation for Consultations of Regulars (apostolic constitution *Romanus Pontifex*); confirmed by the apostolic constitution *Immensa* Jan. 22, 1588; made part of the Congregation for Consultations of Bishops and other Prelates in 1601; made autonomous by St. Pius X in 1908.

Congregation for Catholic Education, formerly known as the Congregation of Seminaries and Universities, has supervisory competence over institutions and works of Catholic education. It carries on its work through three offices. One office handles matters connected with the direction, discipline and temporal administration of seminaries, and with the education of diocesan clergy, religious and members of secular institutes. A second office oversees Catholic universities, faculties of study and other institutions of higher learning inasmuch as they depend on the authority of the Church; encourages cooperation and mutual assistance among Catholic institutions, and the establishment of Catholic hospices and centers on campuses of non-Catholic institutions. A third office is concerned in various ways with all Catholic schools below the college-university level, with general questions concerning education and studies, and with the cooperation of conferences of bishops and civil authorities in educational matters. The congregation supervises Pontifical Works for Priestly Vocations.

OFFICIALS: *Cardinal William Wakefield Baum, prefect; Most Rev. Antonio M. Javierre Ortas, S.D.B., secretary.*

BACKGROUND: The title and functions of the congregation were defined by Benedict XV Nov. 4, 1915; Pius XI, in 1931 and 1932, and Pius XII, in 1941 and 1949, extended its functions. Its work had previously been carried on by two other congregations erected by Sixtus V in 1588 and Leo XII in 1824.

Congregation for the Evangelization of Peoples or the Propagation of the Faith: Directs and coordinates missionary work throughout the world. Accordingly, it has competence over those matters which concern all the missions established for the spread of Christ's kingdom. These include: fostering missionary vocations; providing for the training of missionaries in seminaries; assigning missionaries to fields of work; establishing ecclesiastical jurisdictions and proposing candidates to serve them as bishops and in other capacities; encouraging the recruitment and development of indigenous clergy; mobilizing spiritual and financial support for missionary activity. In general, the varied competence of the congregation extends to most persons and affairs of the Church in areas classified as mission territories.

To promote missionary cooperation, the congregation has a Supreme Council for the Direction of Pontifical Missionary Works. Subject to this council are the general councils of the Missionary Union of the Clergy, the Society for the Propagation of the Faith, the Society of St. Peter the Apostle for Native Clergy, the Society of the Holy Childhood, the International Center of Missionary Animation and the *Fides* news agency.

OFFICIALS: *Cardinal Jozef Tomko, prefect; Most Rev. Jose T. Sanchez, secretary.*

The heads of the Secretariats for Promoting Christian Unity, for Non-Christians, and for Non-Believers are ex officio members of the congregation.

BACKGROUND: Originated as a commission of cardinals by Gregory XIII and modified by Clement VIII to promote the reconciliation of separated Eastern Christians; erected as a stable congregation by Gregory XV June 22, 1622 (apostolic constitution *Inscrutabili*).

The Pontifical Commission for Health Care published in April, 1986, the first census of more than 12,000 church-related health care agencies.

TRIBUNALS

Apostolic Penitentiary: Has jurisdiction for the internal forum only (sacramental and non-sacramental). It issues decisions on questions of conscience; grants absolutions, dispensations, commutations, sanations and condonations; has charge of non-doctrinal matters pertaining to indulgences.

OFFICIALS: *Cardinal Luigi Dadaglio, major penitentiary; Msgr. Luigi de Magistris, regent.*

BACKGROUND: Origin dates back to the 12th century; affected by the legislation of many popes; radically reorganized by St. Pius V in 1569; jurisdiction limited to the internal forum by St. Pius X; Benedict XV annexed the Office of Indulgences to it Mar. 25, 1917.

Apostolic Signatura: The principal concerns of this supreme court of the Church are to resolve questions concerning juridical procedure and to supervise the observance of laws and rights at the highest level. It decides the jurisdictional competence of lower courts and has jurisdiction in cases involving personnel and decisions of the Rota. It is the supreme court of the State of Vatican City.

OFFICIALS: *Cardinal Aurelio Sabattani, prefect; Most Rev. Zenon Grocholewski, secretary.*

BACKGROUND: A permanent office of the Signatura has existed since the time of Eugene IV in the 15th century; affected by the legislation of many popes; reorganized by St. Pius X in 1908 and made the supreme tribunal of the Church.

Roman Rota: The ordinary court of appeal for cases appealed to the Holy See. It is best known for its competence and decisions in cases concerning the validity of marriage.

OFFICIAL: *Msgr. Ernesto Fiore, dean.*

BACKGROUND: Originated in the Apostolic Chancery; affected by the legislation of many popes; reorganized by St. Pius X in 1908 and further revised by Pius XI in 1934.

SECRETARIATS

Secretariat for Promoting Christian Unity: Handles relations with members of other Christian ecclesial communities; deals with the correct interpretation and execution of the principles of ecumenism; initiates or promotes Catholic ecumenical groups and coordinates on national and international levels the efforts of those promoting Christian unity; undertakes dialogue regarding ecumenical questions and activities with churches and ecclesial communities separated from the Apostolic See; sends Catholic observer-representatives to Christian gatherings, and invites to Catholic gatherings observers of other churches; orders into execution conciliar decrees dealing with ecumenical affairs.

The Commission for Catholic-Jewish Relations is attached to the secretariat.

It has two offices, for the West and for the East. Each office is under the immediate direction of a delegate.

The prefects of the Congregation for the Oriental Churches and of the Congregation for the Evangelization of Peoples are ex officio members of the secretariat. Consultors include the secretaries of these two departments.

OFFICIALS: *Cardinal Johannes Willebrands, president; Very Rev. Pierre Duprey, P.A., secretary.*

BACKGROUND: Established by John XXIII June 5, 1960, as a preparatory secretariat of the Second Vatican Council; raised to commission status during the first session of the council in the fall of 1962; this status confirmed Jan. 3, 1966.

Secretariat for Non-Christians: Is concerned with persons who are not Christians but profess some kind of religious faith. Its function is to promote studies and dialogue for the purpose of increasing mutual understanding and respect between Christians and non-Christians.

The Commission for Catholic-Moslem Relations is attached to the secretariat.

The prefect of the Congregation for the Evangelization of Peoples is an ex officio member of the secretariat.

OFFICIALS: *Cardinal Francis Arinze, president; Very Rev. Marcello Zago, O.M.I., secretary.*

BACKGROUND: Established by Paul VI May 19, 1964.

Secretariat for Non-Believers: Studies the background and philosophy of atheism, and initiates and carries on dialogue with non-believers.

OFFICIALS: *Cardinal Paul Poupard, president; Very Rev. Jordan Gallego Salvadores, secretary.*

BACKGROUND: Established by Paul VI Apr. 9, 1965.

COUNCILS, COMMISSIONS, COMMITTEES

Laity, Pontifical Council for: Instituted on an experimental basis by Paul VI Jan. 6, 1967; given permanent status Dec. 10, 1976 (motu proprio *Apostolatus Peragendi*); its competence covers the apostolate of the laity in the Church and the discipline of the laity as such. Members are mostly lay people from different parts of the world and involved in different apostolates. The council is headed by a cardinal. The Council for the Family is attached to the Council while retaining its own identity. Cardinal Eduardo Pironio, president.

Justice and Peace, Pontifical Commission: Instituted by Paul VI Jan. 6, 1967, on an experimental basis; reconstituted and made a permanent body Dec. 10, 1976 (motu proprio *Iustitiam et Pacem*). Holy See's organization for examining and studying (from the point of view of doctrine, pastoral practice and the apostolate) problems connected with justice and peace and awakening the sensitivity of the people of God to their responsibility in these areas. Cardinal Roger Etchegaray, president.

Authentic Interpretation of the Code of Canon Law, Pontifical Commission: Established by John Paul II (motu proprio, *Recognito iuris canonici codice*, Jan. 2, 1984) to interpret canons of the revised Code of Canon Law and other universal laws

of the Church. Cardinal Rosalio Jose Castillo Lara, S.D.B., president.

Revision of the Code of Oriental Canon Law: Reconstituted by Paul VI in 1972 to replace a former commission dating from July 17, 1935, "to prepare . . . the reform of the Code of Oriental Canon Law, both in the sections already published by . . . four motu proprios" (1,950 canons concerning marriage; processes; religious, church property and terminology; Eastern Rites and persons), "and in the remaining sections which have been completed but not published" (the balance of a total of 2,666 canons); Cardinal Joseph Parecattil, president.

Social Communications Commission: Instituted on an experimental basis by Pius XII in 1948; reorganized three times in the 1950s; made permanent commission by John XXIII Feb. 22, 1959; name changed to present title Apr. 11, 1964; authorized to implement the *Decree on the Instruments of Social Communication* promulgated by the Second Vatican Council; under supervision of the Secretariat of State and the Council for the Public Affairs of the Church; Most Rev. John P. Foley, president; Most Rev. Martin J. O'Connor and Cardinal Andrzej M. Deskur, presidents emeriti.

Latin America, Commission: Instituted by Pius XII Apr. 19, 1958; placed under supervision of the Congregation for Bishops July, 1969; Cardinal Bernardin Gantin, president.

Migration and Tourism, Commission: Instituted by Paul VI Mar. 19, 1970, for pastoral assistance to migrants, nomads, tourists, sea and air travelers; placed under the general supervision and direction of the Congregation for Bishops; Cardinal Bernardin Gantin, president.

Cor Unum, Council: Instituted by Paul VI July 15, 1971, to provide informational and coordinating services for Catholic aid and human development organizations and projects on a worldwide scale; Cardinal Roger Etchegaray, president.

Family, Pontifical Council: Instituted by John Paul II May 9, 1981, replacing the Committee for the Family established Jan. 11, 1973, for "promoting the pastoral care of the family . . . by putting into effect the teachings and directives of the ecclesiastical magisterium, so that Christian families may carry out the educative, evangelizing and apostolic mission to which they have been called"; has special relations with the Pontifical Council for the Laity. Cardinal Edouard Gagnon, P.S.S., president.

Culture, Pontifical Council: Established in 1982 by Pope John Paul II to facilitate contacts between the saving message of the Gospel and the plurality of cultures. Cardinal Gabriel-Marie Garrone, head of presidential committee; Cardinal Paul Poupard, president of executive committee.

Health Care Workers, Pontifical Commission for Apostolate of: Established in 1985 by Pope John Paul II to stimulate and foster the work of formation, study and action carried out by various international Catholic organizations in the health care field; attached to the Council for the Laity.

Cardinal Eduardo Pironio, president; Most Rev. Fiorenzo Angelini, pro-president.

Roman Curia, Disciplinary Commission: Cardinal Rosalio Jose Castillo Lara, S.D.B., president.

Council of Cardinals for Study of Organizational and Economic Problems of the Holy See: Council established in 1981 by Pope John Paul II; composed of 15 cardinals — residential archbishops — from countries outside of Italy.

Theological Commission: Instituted by Paul VI Apr. 11, 1969, as an advisory adjunct of no more than 30 theologians to the Congregation for the Doctrine of the Faith; Cardinal Joseph Ratzinger, president. (See separate entry.)

Biblical Commission: Instituted by Leo XIII Oct. 30, 1902; completely restructured by Paul VI June 27, 1971; Cardinal Joseph Ratzinger, president. (See separate entry.)

Revision and Emendation of the Vulgate, Pontifical Commission: Established in 1983 by John Paul II to replace the Abbey of St. Jerome instituted by Pius XI in 1933; Rev. Jean Gribomont, O.S.B., director.

Sacred Archeology, Commission: Instituted by Pius IX Jan, 6, 1852; Most Rev. Gennaro Verolino, president.

Historical Sciences, Committee: Instituted by Pius XII Apr. 7, 1954, as a continuation of a commission dating from 1883; Msgr. Michele Maccarrone, president.

Ecclesiastical Archives of Italy, Commission: Instituted by Pius XII Apr. 5, 1955; Rev. Joseph Metzler, O.M.I., president.

Sacred Art in Italy, Commission: Instituted by Pius XI Sept. 1, 1924. Cardinal Egano Righi-Lambertini, honorary president.

Sanctuaries of Pompei, Loreto and Bari, Cardinalatial Commission: Originated by Leo XIII for Sanctuary of Pompei, Loreto placed under commission in 1965, St. Nicholas of Bari, 1980; under supervision of the Congregation for the Clergy; Cardinal Opilio Rossi, president.

Russia, Commission: Instituted by Pius XI Apr. 6, 1930, to handle all ecclesiastical affairs of the country; placed under supervision of the Congregation for Extraordinary Ecclesiastical Affairs (now the Council for the Public Affairs of the Church) in 1934, with jurisdiction limited to clergy and faithful of the Roman Rite; under supervision of the Council for the Public Affairs of the Church; Most Rev. Achille Silvestrini, president.

Catholic-Jewish Relations, Commission: Instituted by Paul VI, Oct. 22, 1974, to promote and foster relations of a religious nature between Jews and Christians; attached to the Secretariat for Christian Unity; Cardinal Johannes Willebrands, president.

Catholic-Moslem Relations, Commission: Instituted by Paul VI, Oct. 22, 1974, to promote, regulate and interpret relations between Catholics and Moslems; attached to the Secretariat for Non-Christians; Cardinal Francis Arinze, president.

State of Vatican City, Commission: Cardinal Sebastiano Baggio, president; Most Rev. Paul Marcinkus, pro-president.

Protection of the Historical and Artistic Monuments of the Holy See, Commission: Instituted by Pius XI in 1923, reorganized by Paul VI in 1963.

Preservation of the Faith, Erection of New Churches in Rome: Instituted by Pius XI Aug. 5, 1930, to replace a commission dating from 1902; Cardinal Ugo Poletti, president.

Works of Religion, Commission: Instituted by Pius XII June 27, 1942, to bank and administer funds for works of religion; replaced an earlier administration established by Leo XIII in 1887; Most Rev. Paul C. Marcinkus, president.

Catechism Commission: Established by John Paul II, June 10, 1986, to draw up a draft catechism on which bishops of the whole church will be invited to express their views. Its work must be finished by the 1990 ordinary assembly of the Synod of Bishops. Composed of 12 cardinals and bishops. Cardinal Joseph Ratzinger, president.

OFFICES

Apostolic Chamber: Administers the temporal goods and rights of the Holy See between the death of one pope and the election of another, in accordance with special laws.

OFFICIALS: *Cardinal Sebastiano Baggio, chamberlain of the Holy Roman Church; Most Rev. Ettore Cunial, vice-chamberlain.*

BACKGROUND: Originated in the 11th century; reorganized by Pius XI in 1914.

Prefecture of the Economic Affairs of the Holy See: A financial office which coordinates and supervises administration of the temporalities of the Holy See.

OFFICIAL: *Cardinal Giuseppe Caprio, president.*

BACKGROUND: Established by Paul VI Aug. 15, 1967.

Administration of the Patrimony of the Apostolic See: Handles the estate of the Apostolic See under the direction of papal delegates acting with ordinary or extraordinary authorization.

OFFICIALS: *Cardinal Agnelo Rossi, president; Most Rev. Lorenzo Antonetti, secretary.*

BACKGROUND: Some of its functions date back to 1878; established by Paul VI Aug. 15, 1967.

Prefecture of the Pontifical Household: Oversees the papal chapel — which is at the service of the pope in his capacity as spiritual head of the Church — and the pontifical family — which is at the service of the pope as a sovereign. It arranges papal audiences, has charge of preparing non-liturgical elements of papal ceremonies, makes all necessary arrangements for papal visits and trips outside the Vatican, and settles questions of protocol connected with papal audiences and other formalities.

OFFICIALS: *Most Rev. Jacques Martin, prefect; Msgr. Dino Monduzzi, secretary.*

BACKGROUND: Established by Paul VI Aug. 15, 1967, under the title, Prefecture of the Apostolic Palace; it supplanted the Sacred Congregation for Ceremonies founded by Sixtus V Jan. 22, 1588. The office was updated and reorganized under the present title by Paul VI, Mar. 28, 1968.

Central Statistics Office: Compiles. systematizes and analyzes information on the status and condition of the Church and the needs of its pastoral ministry, from parish to top levels.

The office is one of the organs of the Secretariat of State.

BACKGROUND: Established by Paul VI Aug. 15, 1967.

Aid Office: Distributes alms and aid to the aged, sick, handicapped and other persons in need.

OFFICIAL: Most Rev. Antonio M. Travia, director.

BACKGROUND: The office originated as a charitable office in the time of Bl. Gregory X (1271-1276).

Vatican II Archives: Preserves the acts and other documents of the Second Vatican Council.

CURIA REFORM

Cardinal Sebastiano Baggio was named by Pope John Paul in March, 1986, head of a commission of cardinals responsible for final recommendations regarding reform of the various agencies of the Roman Curia, with a special view, in the words of the Pope, toward forging "tight connection between the Curia and conferences of bishops."

THEOLOGICAL COMMISSION

Establishment with experimental status of a Theological Commission as an adjunct to the Congregation for the Doctrine of the Faith was announced by Pope Paul VI Apr. 28, 1969. The move had been recommended by the Second Vatican Council and was proposed by the Synod of Bishops in 1967. The commission was removed from experimental status in virtue of a *motu proprio* of John Paul II dated Aug. 6, 1982, and effective the following Oct. 1.

The purpose of the commission is to provide the Doctrinal Congregation with the consultative and advisory services of theologians and scriptural and liturgical experts representative of various schools of thought. The international membership is restricted to 30, and the ordinary term of membership is five years (renewable).

Membership

The commission is headed by Cardinal Joseph Ratzinger, prefect of the Doctrinal Congregation.

Thirteen former members (auxiliary bishops, priests) were reappointed to five-year terms in July, 1986: Msgr. Philippe Delhaye, secretary (Belgium), Hans Urs von Balthasar (Switzerland, systematic theology), Msgr. Carlo Caffara (Italy, moral theology), Msgr. Giuseppe Colombo (Italy, systematic theology), Msgr. Wilhelm Ernst (East Germany, moral theology), Walter Kasper (West Germany, systematic theology), Bishop Carlos Jose Boaventura Kloppenburg (Brazil, systematic theology), Michael Ledwith (Ireland, systematic theology), Auxiliary Bishop Jorge Medina Estevez (Chile, systematic theology), Carl J. Peter (U.S., systematic theology), Candido Pozo, S.J. (Spain, systematic theology), Christophe von Schonborn,

O.P. (Switzerland, systematic theology), Jan Walgrave, O.P. (Belgium, systematic theology).

Seventeen new members appointed in July, 1986, included two laymen — John Finnis (Great Britain, moral theology) and William E. May (U.S., moral theology) — and 15 priests: Barthelemy Adoukonou (Benin, systematic theology), Jan Ambaum (The Netherlands, systematic theology), Jean Louis Bruges, O.P. (France, moral theology), Melkite Jean Corbon (Lebanon, oriental theology), Georges Cottier, O.P. (Switzerland, moral theology), Joachim Gnilka (West Germany, Scripture), Gilles Langevin, S.J. (Canada, moral theology), Jose M. Ibanez Langlois (Chile, moral theology), Peter Miyakawa (Japan, moral theology), Francis Moloney, S.D.B. (Australia, Scripture), Stanislaw Nagy, S.C.J. (Poland, systematic theology), Henrique de Noronha Galvao (Portugal, systematic theology), James Okoye, C.S.Sp. (Nigeria, Scripture), Franc Perko (Yugoslavia, oriental theology), Felix Wilfred (India, systematic theology).

Meetings and Studies

Since its establishment in 1969, the commission has held plenary meetings every year escept 1978. Products of its work have been research and reports on a wide variety of subjects, some of which have been on the agenda of the Synod of Bishops. Subjects have included penance and reconciliation, the priesthood, pluralism in theology, collegiality, apostolic succession and ordination, Christian morality, evangelization and liberation, the teaching authority of the Church, and Christian marriage.

BIBLICAL COMMISSION

The Pontifical Biblical Commission, was established by Leo XIII Oct. 30, 1902, with the apostolic letter *Vigilantiae Studiique,* at a time when biblical studies were open to great promise as well as to the serious threat of Modernism.

The commission was ordered to promote biblical studies; to safeguard the correct interpretation of Scripture, in the pattern of the rule of faith and against the background of sound scholarship; to state positions which had to be held by Catholics on biblical questions; to indicate questions requiring further study and/or those which were open to the judgment of competent scholars. The commission was also authorized — by St. Pius X in 1904, Pius XI in 1924 and 1931, and Pius XII in 1942 — to set up standards for biblical studies and to grant degrees in Sacred Scripture. It was reorganized June 27, 1971, in line with directives issued by Paul VI on his own initiative under the title *Sedula Cura,* and was linked with the Congregation for the Doctrine of the Faith.

The commission issued 23 decrees or decisions between 1905 and 1953; letters on the scientific study of the Bible (1941) and the Pentateuch (1948); instructions on teaching Scripture in seminaries (1950), biblical associations (1955), and the historical truth of the Gospels (1964).

Pope St. Pius X stated the authority of decisions of the commission in the letter *Illibatae,* which he issued June 29, 1910, on his own initiative:

"All are bound in conscience to submit to the decisions of the Pontifical Biblical Commission pertaining to doctrine, whether already issued or to be issued in the future, in the same way as to the decrees of the Sacred Congregations (of the Roman Curia) approved by the Pontiff; nor can they avoid the stigma both of disobedience and temerity or be free from grave sin who by any spoken or written words impugn these decisions."

Decisions of the commission regarding points of doctrine are not infallible of themselves. They require religious assent, however, so long as there is no positive evidence that they are wrong. They do not close the door to continuing investigation and study.

Members and Studies

Members listed in the 1986 edition of *Annuario Pontifico* were: Cardinal Joseph Ratzinger, president; Bishop Pasinya Monsengwo; Jean-Dominique Barthelemy, O.P., Pierre Benoit, O.P., Marcel Dumais, O.M.I., Jacques Dupont, O.S.B., Joseph Fitzmyer, S.J. (U.S.), Joachim Gnilka, Pierre Grelot, Jacques Guillet, S.J., Augustyn Jankowski, O.S.B., Jan Lambrecht, S.J., Joao Evangelista Martins Terra, S.J., John F. McHugh, Antonio Moreno Casamitjana, Domingo Munoz Leon, Joseph Pathrapankal, C.M.I., Gianfranco Ravasi, Msgr. Josef Schreiner, Giuseppe Segalia, Albert Vanhoye, S.J.

In recent years, the commission has focused its attention on various subjects, including Christology and inculturation.

The purpose of the latter study, as stated by Pope John Paul, has been "to establish the distinction" between what is culturally conditioned (language, manner of expression, historical circumstances) "and what must always retain its value" (truth relating to salvation) in the words and events used to communicate divine revelation in the Bible.

COLLEGE OF CARDINALS

Cardinals are chosen by the pope to serve as his principal assistants and advisers in the central administration of church affairs. Collectively, they form the Sacred College of Cardinals. Provisions regarding their selection, rank, roles and prerogatives are detailed in Canons 349 to 359 of the Code of Canon Law.

History of the College

The Sacred College of Cardinals was constituted in its present form and categories of membership in the 12th century. Before that time the pope had a body of advisers selected from among the bishops of dioceses neighboring Rome, priests and deacons of Rome. The college was given definite form in 1150, and in 1179 the selection of cardinals was reserved exclusively to the pope. Sixtus V fixed the number at 70, in 1586. John XXIII set aside this rule when he increased membership at the 1959 and subsequent consistories. The number was subsequently raised to 145 by Paul VI in 1973 and to 152 by John Paul II in 1985. The number of cardinals entitled to participate in papal elections was limited to 120.

In 1567 the title of cardinal was reserved to members of the college; previously it had been used by priests attached to parish churches of Rome and by the leading clergy of other notable churches. The Code of Canon Law promulgated in 1918 decreed that all cardinals must be priests. Previously there had been cardinals who were not priests (e.g., Cardinal Giacomo Antonelli, d. 1876, Secretary of State to Pius IX, was a deacon). John XXIII provided in the motu proprio *Cum Gravissima* Apr. 15, 1962, that cardinals would henceforth be bishops; this provision is included in the revised Code of Canon Law.

Pope Paul VI placed age limits on the functions of cardinals in the apostolic letter *Ingravescentem Aetatem,* dated Nov. 21, 1970, and effective as of Jan. 1, 1971. At 80, they cease to be members of curial departments and offices, and become ineligible to take part in papal elections. They retain membership in the College of Cardinals, however, with relevant rights and privileges.

Three Categories

All cardinals except Eastern patriarchs are aggregated to the clergy of Rome. This aggregation is signified by the assignment to each cardinal, except the patriarchs, of a titular church in Rome.

The three categories of members of the college are cardinal bishops, cardinal priests and cardinal deacons.

Cardinal bishops include the six titular bishops of the suburban sees of Rome and Eastern patriarchs.

First in rank are the titular bishops of the suburban sees, neighboring Rome: Ostia, Palestrina, Porto and Santa Rufina, Albano, Velletri, Frascati, Sabina and Poggio Mirteto. The dean of the college holds the title of the See of Ostia as well as his other suburban see. These cardinal bishops are engaged in full-time service in the central administration of church affairs in departments of the Roman Curia.

Full recognition is given in the revised Code of Canon Law to the position of Eastern patriarchs as the heads of sees of apostolic origin with ancient liturgies. They are assigned rank among the cardinals in order of seniority, following the suburban titleholders.

Cardinal priests, who were formerly in charge of leading churches in Rome, are bishops whose dioceses are outside Rome.

Cardinal deacons, who were formerly chosen according to regional divisions of Rome, are titular bishops assigned to full-time service in the Roman Curia.

The dean and sub-dean of the college are elected by the cardinal bishops — subject to approval by the pope — from among their number. The dean, or the sub-dean in his absence, presides over the college as the first among equals.

Selection and Duties

Cardinals are selected by the pope and are inducted into the college in appropriate ceremonies.

Cardinals under the age of 80: elect the pope when the Holy See becomes vacant (See Papal Election; in 1059 cardinals were given the exclusive right to elect the pope.) and are major administrators of church affairs, serving in one or more departments of the Roman Curia. Cardinals in charge of agencies of the Roman Curia and Vatican City are asked to submit their resignation from office to the pope on reaching the age of 75.

All cardinals enjoy a number of special rights and privileges. Their title, while symbolic of high honor, does not signify any extension of the powers of holy orders. They are called princes of the Church.

A **cardinal in pectore (petto)** is one whose selection has been made by the pope but whose name has not been disclosed; he has no title, rights or duties until such disclosure is made, at which time he takes precedence from the time of the secret selection.

BIOGRAPHIES OF CARDINALS

Biographies of the cardinals, as of Aug. 15, 1986, are given below in alphabetical order. For historical notes, order of seniority and geographical distribution of cardinals, see separate entries.

An asterisk indicates cardinals ineligible to take part in papal elections.

Alfrink,* Bernard Jan: b. July 5, 1900, Nijkerk, Netherlands; ord. priest Aug. 15, 1924; professor of Sacred Scripture at Utrecht major seminary, 1933; consultor to Pontifical Biblical Commission, Rome, 1944; professor at Catholic University of Nijmegen, 1945; ord. titular archbishop of Tiana and coadjutor archbishop of Utrecht, July 17, 1951; archbishop of Utrecht, 1955-75; cardinal Mar. 28, 1960; titular church, St. Joachim. Archbishop emeritus of Utrecht.

Antonelli,* Ferdinando Giuseppe, O.F.M.: b. July 14, 1896, Subbiano, Italy; solemnly professed in Order of Friars Minor, Apr. 7, 1914; ord. priest July 25, 1922; taught church history, 1928-32, and Christian archeology, 1932-65, at Antonianum; rector magnificus of Antonianum, 1937-43, 1953-59; definitor general of Friars Minor, 1939-45; held various offices in Roman Curia; secretary of Congregation of Rites, 1965-69, and Congregation for Causes of Saints, 1969-73; ord. titular archbishop of Idicra, Mar. 19, 1966; cardinal Mar. 5, 1973; titular church, San Sebastian (on the Palatine).

Aponte Martinez, Luis: b. Aug. 4, 1922, Lajas, Puerto Rico; ord. priest Apr. 10, 1950; parish priest at Ponce; ord. titular bishop of Lares and auxiliary of Ponce, Oct. 12, 1960; bishop of Ponce, 1963-64; archbishop of San Juan, Nov. 4, 1964; cardinal Mar. 5, 1973; titular church, St. Mary Mother of Providence (in Monteverde). Archbishop of San Juan. Curial membership:

Causes of Saints (congregation).

Aramburu, Juan Carlos: b. Feb. 11, 1912, Reduccion, Argentina; ord. priest in Rome, Oct. 28, 1934; ord. titular bishop of Plataea and auxiliary of Tucuman, Argentina, Dec. 15, 1946; bishop, 1953, and first archbishop, 1957, of Tucuman; titular archbishop of Torri di Bizacena and coadjutor archbishop of Buenos Aires, June 14, 1967; archbishop of Buenos Aires, Apr. 22, 1975; cardinal May 24, 1976; titular church, St. John Baptist of the Florentines. Archbishop of Buenos Aires, ordinary for Eastern Rite Catholics in Argentina without ordinaries of their own rites. Curial membership:

Oriental Churches, Divine Worship, Catholic Education (congregations); Economic Affairs (office).

Arinze, Francis A.: b. Nov. 1, 1932, Eziowelle, Nigeria; ord. priest Nov. 23, 1958; ord. titular bish-

op of Fissiana and auxiliary of Onitsha, Aug. 29, 1965; archbishop of Onitsha, 1967-84; pro-president of Secretariat for Non-Christians, 1984; cardinal May 25, 1985; deacon, St. John (della Pigna). President of Secretariat for Non-Christians, 1985. Curial membership:

Evangelization of Peoples, Causes of Saints (congregations); Christian Unity, Non-Believers (secretariats); Justice and Peace (commission).

Arns, Paulo Evaristo, O.F.M.: b. Sept. 14, 1921, Forquilhinha, Brazil; ord. priest Nov. 30, 1945; held various teaching posts; director of *Sponsa Christi*, monthly review for religious, and of the Franciscan publication center in Brazil; ord. titular bishop of Respetta and auxiliary of Sao Paulo, July 3, 1966; archbishop of Sao Paulo, Oct. 22, 1970; cardinal Mar. 5, 1973; titular church, St. Anthony of Padua (in Via Tuscolana). Archbishop of Sao Paulo. Curial membership:

Sacraments (congregation).

Bafile,* Corrado: b. July 4, 1903, L'Aquila, Italy; practiced law in Rome for six years before beginning studies for priesthood; ord. priest Apr. 11, 1936; served in Vatican secretariat of state, 1939-59; ord. titular archbishop of Antiochia in Pisidia, Mar. 19, 1960; apostolic nuncio to Germany, 1960-75; pro-prefect of Congregation for Causes of Saints, July 18, 1975; cardinal May 24, 1976; deacon, S. Maria (in Portico); prefect of Congregation for Causes of Saints, 1976-80.

Baggio, Sebastiano: b. May 16, 1913, Rosa, Italy; ord. priest Dec. 21, 1935; ord. titular archbishop of Ephesus, July 26, 1953; served in Vatican diplomatic corps, 1953-69; nuncio to Chile, apostolic delegate to Canada, nuncio to Brazil; cardinal Apr. 28, 1969; archbishop of Cagliari, 1969-73; entered order of cardinal bishops as titular bishop of Velletri, Dec. 12, 1974; prefect of Congregation for Bishops, 1973-84. President of Pontifical Commission for Vatican City, 1984; Chamberlain (Camerlengo) of Holy Roman Church, 1985; Sub-Dean of the College of Cardinals, 1986. Curial membership:

Doctrine of the Faith, Religious and Secular Institutes, Catholic Education, Evangelization of Peoples (congregations); Authentic Interpretation of Code of Canon Law, Latin America (commissions); Patrimony of Holy See (office).

Ballestrero, Anastasio Alberto, O.C.D.: b. Oct. 3, 1913, Genoa, Italy; professed in Order of Discalced Carmelites, 1929; ord. priest June 6, 1936; provincial, 1942-48, and superior general, 1955-67, of Carmelites; author of many books on Christian life; ord. archbishop of Bari, Feb. 2, 1974; archbishop of Turin, Aug. 1, 1977; cardinal June 30,

1979; titular church, S. Maria (sopra Minerva). Archbishop of Turin. Curial membership:

Council for Public Affairs of the Church; Bishops, Religious and Secular Institutes (congregations).

Baum, William Wakefield: b. Nov. 21, 1926, Dallas, Tex.; moved to Kansas City, Mo., at an early age; ord. priest (Kansas City-St. Joseph diocese) May 12, 1951; executive director of U.S. bishops commission for ecumenical and interreligious affairs, 1964-69; attended Second Vatican Council as *peritus* (expert adviser); ord. bishop of Springfield-Cape Girardeau, Mo., Apr. 6, 1970; archbishop of Washington, D.C., 1973-80; cardinal May 24, 1976; titular church, Holy Cross (on the Via Flaminia). Prefect of Congregation for Catholic Education, 1980 (reappointed 1985); grand chancellor of Pontifical Gregorian University. Curial membership:

Council for Public Affairs of the Church; Doctrine of the Faith, Bishops, Oriental Churches, Religious and Secular Institutes, Evangelization of Peoples (congregations); Non-Believers (secretariat); Council for Laity, Authentic Interpretation of Code of Canon Law (commissions); Patrimony of Holy See (office).

Beras Rojas, Octavio Antonio: b. Nov. 16, 1906, Seibo, Dominican Republic; ord. priest Aug. 13, 1933; founded national Catholic youth movement; ord. titular archbishop of Euchaitae and coadjutor archbishop of Santo Domingo, Aug. 12, 1945; archbishop of Santo Domingo, 1961-81; cardinal May 24, 1976; titular church, San Sisto. Archbishop emeritus of Santo Domingo.

Bernardin, Joseph L.: b. Apr. 2, 1928, Columbia, S.C.; ord. priest (Charleston diocese) Apr. 26, 1952; ord. titular bishop of Lugara and auxiliary bishop of Atlanta, Ga., Apr. 26, 1966; general secretary, 1968-72, and president, 1974-77, of NCCB/USCC; archbishop of Cincinnati, 1972-82; archbishop of Chicago, July 10, 1982, installed Aug. 25, 1982; cardinal Feb. 2, 1983; titular church, Jesus the Divine Worker. Archbishop of Chicago. Curial membership:

Divine Worship, Evangelization of Peoples (congregations); Christian Unity (secretariat).

Bertoli, Paolo: b. Feb. 1, 1908, Poggio Garfagnana, Italy; ord. priest Aug. 15, 1930; entered diplomatic service of the Holy See, serving in nunciatures in Yugoslavia, France, Haiti and Switzerland; ord. titular archbishop of Nicomedia, May 11, 1952; apostolic delegate to Turkey (1952-53), nuncio to Colombia (1953-59), Lebanon (1959-60), France (1960-69); cardinal Apr. 28, 1969; prefect of Congregation for Causes of Saints, 1969-73; entered order of cardinal bishops as titular bishop of Frascati, June 30, 1979; Chamberlain (Camerlengo) of Holy Roman Church, 1979-85.

Biffi, Giacomo: b. June 13, 1928, Milan, Italy; ord. priest June 3, 1950; ord. titular bishop of Fidene and auxiliary of Milan, Jan. 11, 1976; archbishop of Bologna, Apr. 19, 1984; cardinal May 25, 1985; titular church, Sts. John the Evangelist and Petronio. Archbishop of Bologna. Curial membership:

Divine Worship, Clergy (congregations); Apostolic Signatura (tribunal).

Brandao Vilela, Avelar: b. June 13, 1912, Vicosa, Brazil; ord. priest Oct. 27, 1935; professor and spiritual director at diocesan seminary at Aracaju; ord. bishop of Petrolina, Oct. 27, 1946; archbishop of Teresina, Nov. 5, 1955; established 20 social centers and a radio station; introduced agrarian reform of church properties; erected the Institute of Catechetics: archbishop of Sao Salvador da Bahia, Mar. 25, 1971; president of CELAM, 1967-72; co-president of Medellin Conference, 1968; cardinal Mar. 5, 1973; titular church, Sts. Boniface and Alexius. Archbishop of Sao Salvador da Bahia. Curial membership:

Causes of Saints (congregation); Latin America (commission).

Bueno y Monreal,* Jose Maria: b. Sept. 11, 1904, Zaragoza, Spain; ord. priest Mar. 19, 1927; ord. bishop of Jaca, Mar. 19, 1946; bishop of Vitoria, 1950-54; titular archbishop of Antioch in Pisidia and coadjutor archbishop of Seville, Oct. 27, 1954; archbishop of Seville, 1957-82; cardinal Dec. 15, 1958; titular church, Sts. Vitus, Modestus and Crescentia. Archbishop emeritus of Seville.

Caprio, Giuseppe: b. Nov. 15, 1914, Lapio, Italy; ord. priest Dec. 17, 1938; served in diplomatic missions in China (1947-51, when Vatican diplomats were expelled by communists), Belgium (1951-54), and South Vietnam (1954-56); internuncio in China with residence at Taiwan, 1959-67; ord. titular archbishop of Apollonia, Dec. 17, 1961; pro-nuncio in India, 1967-69; secretary, 1969-77, and president, 1979-81, of Administration of Patrimony of Holy See; substitute secretary of state, 1977-79; cardinal June 30, 1979; deacon, St. Mary Auxiliatrix in Via Tuscolana. President of Prefecture of Economic Affairs of the Holy See, 1981. Curial membership:

Council for Public Affairs of Church; Bishops, Oriental Churches, Causes of Saints, Evangelization of Peoples (congregations).

Carberry,* John J.: b. July 31, 1904, Brooklyn, N.Y.; ord. priest (Brooklyn diocese) July 28, 1929; ord. titular bishop of Elis and coadjutor bishop of Lafayette, Ind., July 25, 1956; bishop of Lafayette, Nov. 20, 1957; bishop of Columbus, Ohio, Jan. 16, 1965; archbishop of St. Louis, Mo., 1968-79; cardinal Apr. 28, 1969; titular church, St. John Baptist de Rossi (Via Latina). Archbishop emeritus of St. Louis.

Carpino,* Francesco: b. May 18, 1905, Palazzolo Acreide, Italy; ord. priest Aug. 14, 1927; ord. titular archbishop of Nicomedia and coadjutor archbishop of Monreale, Apr. 8, 1951; archbishop of Monreale, 1951-61; titular archbishop of Sardica, Jan. 19, 1961; assessor of Consistorial Congregation, 1961; pro-prefect of Congregation of the Council, Apr. 7, 1967; cardinal June 26, 1967; archbishop of Palermo, 1967-70; entered order of cardinal bishops as titular bishop of Albano, Jan. 27, 1978.

Carter, Gerald Emmett: b. Mar. 1, 1912, Montreal, Canada; ord. priest May 22, 1937; engaged in pastoral and teaching ministry in Montreal; founder and president of St. Joseph Teachers' College and co-founder and director of Thomas More Institute for adult education; ord. titular bishop of Altiburo and auxiliary bishop of London, Ont., Feb. 2, 1962; bishop of London, Ont., 1964-78; vice president, 1971-73, and president, 1975-77, of Canadian Conference of Catholic Bishops; archbishop of Toronto, Apr. 27, 1978; cardinal June 30, 1979; titular church, St. Mary (in Traspontina). Archbishop of Toronto. Curial membership:

Evangelization of Peoples (congregation); Christian Unity, Non-Christians (secretariats).

Casaroli, Agostino: b. Nov. 24, 1914, Castel San Giovanni, Italy; ord. priest May 27, 1937; entered service of Vatican secretariat of state, 1940; undersecretary, 1961-67, of the Congregation for Extraordinary Ecclesiastical Affairs, and secretary, 1967-79, of its successor the Council for Public Affairs of the Church; ord. titular archbishop of Cartagina, July 16, 1967; chief negotiator for the Vatican with East European communist governments; missions included visits to Hungary, Yugoslavia, Poland, Czechoslovakia, Bulgaria; headed Vatican delegations to several UN conferences and the Helsinki Conference (1975); Pro-Secretary of State and Pro-Prefect of Council for Public Affairs of the Church, Apr. 28, 1979; cardinal June 30, 1979; titular church, the Twelve Apostles; president, 1981-84, of Administration of Patrimony of Holy See and Pontifical Commission for Vatican City; entered order of cardinal bishops as titular bishop of Porto and Santa Rufina, May 25, 1985. Secretary of State and prefect of Council for Public Affairs of the Church, July 1, 1979 (given increased responsibility in government of Vatican City State, 1984). Curial membership:

Doctrine of the Faith, Bishops (congregations); Non-Believers (secretariat); Authentic Interpretation of Code of Canon Law, Revision of Oriental Code of Canon Law, Institute for Works of Religion (commissions).

Casoria, Giuseppe: b. Oct. 1, 1908, Acerra, Italy; ord. priest Dec. 21, 1930; jurist; Roman Curia official from 1937; under-secretary, 1959-69, and secretary, 1969-73, of Congregation for Sacraments and Divine Worship; secretary of Congregation for Causes of Saints, 1973-81; ord. titular archbishop of Vescovia, Feb. 13, 1972; pro-prefect of Congregation for Sacraments and Divine Worship, 1981-83; cardinal Feb. 2, 1983; deacon, St. Joseph on Via Trionfale. Prefect of Congregation for Sacraments and Divine Worship, 1983-84. Curial membership:

Doctrine of the Faith, Sacraments, Oriental Churches, Causes of Saints (congregations); Authentic Interpretation of Code of Canon Law (commission).

Castillo Lara, Rosalio Jose, S.D.B.: b. Sept. 4, 1922, San Casimiro, Venezuela; ord. priest Sept. 4, 1949; ord. coadjutor bishop of Trujillo, May 24, 1973; archbishop of titular see of Precausa, May 26, 1982; pro-president of Pontifical Commission for Revision of Code of Canon Law, 1982-84; pro-president of Commission for Authentic Interpretation of Code of Canon Law, 1984-85; cardinal May 25, 1985; deacon, Our Lady of Coromoto (in St. John of God). President of: Pontifical Commission for Authentic Interpretation of Code of Canon Law,

1985; Disciplinary Commission of Roman Curia, 1981. Curial membership:

Catholic Education (congregation); Christian Unity (secretariat); State of Vatican City (commission).

Cé, Marco: b. July 8, 1925, Izano, Italy; ord. priest Mar. 27, 1948; taught sacred scripture and dogmatic theology at seminary in his home diocese of Crema; rector of seminary, 1957; presided over diocesan liturgical commission, preached youth retreats; ord. titular bishop of Vulturia, May 17, 1970; auxiliary bishop of Bologna, 1970-76; general ecclesiastical assistant of Italian Catholic Action, 1976-78; patriarch of Venice, Dec. 7, 1978; cardinal June 30, 1979; titular church, St. Mark. Patriarch of Venice. Curial membership:

Divine Worship, Clergy, Catholic Education (congregations).

Ciappi, Mario Luigi, O.P.: b. Oct. 6, 1909, Florence, Italy; ord. priest Mar. 26, 1932; papal theologian from 1955, serving Pius XII, John XXIII and Paul VI; ord. titular bishop of Misenum June 18, 1977; cardinal June 27, 1977; deacon, Our Lady of the Sacred Heart. Pro-theologian of pontifical household. Curial membership:

Causes of Saints (congregation); Apostolic Signatura (tribunal).

Civardi, Ernesto: b. Oct. 21, 1906, Fossarmato, Italy; ord. priest June 29, 1930; assistant rector of Pontifical Lombard Seminary in Rome; held various curial offices; undersecretary, 1953-67, and secretary, 1967-79, of the Congregation for Bishops (known as the Consistorial Congregation until 1967); ord. titular archbishop of Sardica, July 16, 1967; secretary of College of Cardinals, 1967-79; filled office of secretary at 1978 conclaves which elected Popes John Paul I and John Paul II; cardinal June 30, 1979; deacon, St. Theodore. Curial membership:

Causes of Saints, Evangelization of Peoples (congregations); Apostolic Signatura (tribunal).

Colombo,* Giovanni: b. Dec. 6, 1902, Caronno, Italy; ord. priest May 29, 1926; rector of Milan Seminary, 1953; ord. titular bishop of Filippopoli and auxiliary bishop of Milan, Dec. 7, 1960; archbishop of Milan, 1963-79; cardinal Feb. 22, 1965; titular church, Sts. Sylvester and Martin. Archbishop emeritus of Milan.

Cooray,* Thomas B., O.M.I.: b. Dec. 28, 1901, Periyamulla Negombo, Ceylon (now Sri Lanka); ord. priest June 23, 1929; ord. titular archbishop of Preslavo, Mar. 7, 1946; coadjutor archbishop of Colombo, Sri Lanka, 1946-47; succeeded as archbishop of Colombo, July 26, 1947 (retired 1976); cardinal Feb. 22, 1965; titular church, Sts. Nereus and Achilleus. Archbishop emeritus of Colombo, Sri Lanka.

Cordeiro, Joseph: b. Jan. 19, 1918, Bombay, India; ord. priest Aug. 24, 1946; served in educational and other diocesan posts at Karachi, Pakistan; ord. archbishop of Karachi, Aug. 24, 1958, the first native-born prelate in that see; cardinal Mar. 5, 1973; titular church, St. Andrew Apostle. Archbishop of Karachi. Curial membership:

Religious and Secular Institutes (congregation); Non-Christians (secretariat).

Corripio Ahumada, Ernesto: b. June 29, 1919, Tampico, Mexico; ord. priest Oct. 25, 1942, in Rome, where he remained until almost the end of World War II; taught and held various positions in local seminary of Tampico, 1945-50; ord. titular bishop of Zapara and auxiliary bishop of Tampico, Mar. 19, 1953; bishop of Tampico, 1956-67; archbishop of Antequera, 1967-76; archbishop of Puebla de los Angeles, 1976-77; archbishop of Mexico City and primate of Mexico, July 19, 1977; cardinal June 30, 1979; titular church, Mary Immaculate al Tiburtino. Archbishop of Mexico City. Curial membership:

Divine Worship, Clergy, Catholic Education (congregations); Latin America (commission).

Dadaglio, Luigi: b. Sept. 28, 1914, Sezzadio, Italy; ord. priest May 22, 1937; entered diplomatic service of Holy See in 1940s; served in Haiti, the U.S., Canada, Australia, New Zealand and Colombia; ord. titular archbishop of Lero, Dec. 8, 1961; nuncio to Venezuela 1961-67; nuncio to Spain, 1967-80; secretary of Congregation for Sacraments and Divine Worship, 1980-84; pro-Major Penitentiary, 1984-85; cardinal May 25, 1985; deacon, St. Pius V. Major Penitentiary, 1985. Curial membership:

Council for Public Affairs of the Church; Bishops, Sacraments, Evangelization of Peoples (congregations); State of Vatican City (commission).

Danneels, Godfried: b. June 4, 1933, Kanegem, Belgium; ord. priest Aug. 17, 1957; professor of liturgy and sacramental theology at Catholic University of Louvain, 1969-77; ord. bishop of Antwerp Dec. 18, 1977; app. archbishop of Mechelen-Brussel, Dec. 19, 1979; installed Jan. 4, 1980; elected member of general secretariat of Synod of Bishops, 1981; cardinal Feb. 2, 1983; titular church, St. Anastasia. Archbishop of Mechelen-Brussel, military vicar of Belgium. Curial membership:

Council for Public Affairs of the Church; Doctrine of the Faith, Bishops, Divine Worship, Evangelization of Peoples, Catholic Education (congregations); Non-Believers (secretariat).

Darmojuwono, Justin: b. Nov. 2, 1914, Godean, Indonesia; ord. priest May 25, 1947; ord. archbishop of Semarang, Apr. 6, 1964 (resigned July 3, 1981, for health reasons); cardinal June 26, 1967; titular church, Most Holy Names of Jesus and Mary. Archbishop emeritus of Semarang. Curial membership:

Sacraments (congregation).

De Araujo Sales, Eugenio: b. Nov. 8, 1920, Acari, Brazil; ord. priest Nov. 21, 1943; ord. titular bishop of Tibica and auxiliary bishop of Natal, Aug. 15, 1954; archbishop of Sao Salvador, 1968-71; cardinal Apr. 28, 1969; titular church, St. Gregory VII. Archbishop of Rio de Janeiro (1971), ordinary for Eastern Rite Catholics in Brazil without ordinaries of their own rites. Curial membership:

Council for Public Affairs of the Church; Bishops, Oriental Churches, Divine Worship, Clergy, Evangelization of Peoples, Catholic Education (congregations); Social Communications (commission); Culture (council).

Dearden, John Francis.: b. Oct. 15, 1907, Valley Falls, R. I.; ord. priest (Cleveland diocese) Dec. 8, 1932; ord. titular bishop of Sarepta and coadjutor bishop of Pittsburgh, May 18, 1948; bishop of Pittsburgh, Dec. 22, 1950; archbishop of Detroit, 1958-80; first president of the National Conference of Catholic Bishops and the United States Catholic Conference, 1966-71; cardinal Apr. 28, 1969; titular church, St. Pius X (alla Balduina). Archbishop emeritus of Detroit. Curial membership:

Sacraments (congregation).

Decourtray, Albert: b. Apr. 9, 1923, Wattignies, France; ord. priest June 29, 1947; ord. titular bishop of Ippona Zarito and auxiliary of Dijon, July 3, 1971; bishop of Dijon, 1974-81; archbishop of Lyon, Oct. 29, 1981; prelate of Mission of France, 1982; cardinal May 25, 1985; titular church, Most Holy Trinity (al Monte Pincio). Archbishop of Lyon, Prelate of Mission of France. Curial membership:

Christian Unity, Non-Believers (secretariats).

De Furstenberg,* Maximilien: b. Oct. 23, 1904, Heerlen, Netherlands; ord. priest Aug. 9, 1931; ord. titular archbishop of Palto and apostolic delegate to Japan, Apr. 25, 1949; internuncio, 1952, when Japan established diplomatic relations with the Vatican; apostolic delegate to Australia, New Zealand and Oceania, Feb. 11, 1960; nuncio to Portugal, 1962-67; cardinal June 26, 1967; titular church, Most Sacred Heart of Jesus (a Castro Pretorio); prefect of the Congregation for the Oriental Churches, 1969-73. Grand Master of Equestrian Order of Holy Sepulchre of Jerusalem. Curial membership:

Institute for Works of Religion (commission).

De Lubac,* Henri, S.J.: b. Feb. 20, 1896, Cambrai, France; entered Society of Jesus, October, 1913; ord. priest Aug. 22, 1927; taught fundamental theology and history of religions at the Theology Faculty of Lyons from 1929 to the early 1950s when he was dismissed because of misunderstanding of his book *The Supernatural,* intended to re-emphasize the doctrine on supernatural destiny; reinstated to his teaching post by Pope John XXIII; chief consultor of preparatory theological commission for Vatican II and *peritus* for Council itself; appointed member of International Theological Commission (1969-74) by Paul VI; cardinal Feb. 2, 1983, with permission to decline episcopal ordination; deacon, St. Mary in Domnica.

Deskur, Andrzej Marie: b. Feb. 29, 1924, Sancygniow, Poland; ord. priest Aug. 20, 1950, in France; assigned to Vatican secretariat of state, 1952; undersecretary and later secretary of Pontifical Commission for Film, Radio and TV (Social Communications), 1954-73; ord. titular bishop of Tene, June 30, 1974; archbishop, 1980; president of Pontifical Commission for Social Communications, 1974-84; cardinal May 25, 1985; deacon, St. Cesario (in Palatio). President emeritus of Pontifical Commission for Social Communications. Curial membership:

Causes of Saints (congregation); State of Vatican City, Health Care Workers (commissions).

do Nascimento, Alexandre: b. Mar. 1, 1925, Malanje, Angola; ord. priest Dec. 20, 1952, in Rome; professor of dogmatic theology in major seminary of Luanda, Angola; editor of *O Apostolada,* Catholic newspaper; forced into exile in Lisbon, Portugal, 1961-71; returned to Angola, 1971; active with student and refugee groups; professor at Pius XII Institute of Social Sciences; ord. bishop of Malanje, Aug. 31, 1975; archbishop of Lubango and apostolic administrator of Onjiva, 1977-86; held hostage by Angolan guerrillas, Oct. 15 to Nov. 16, 1982; cardinal Feb. 2, 1983; titular church, St. Mark in Agro Laurentino. Archbishop of Luanda, 1986. Curial membership: Divine Worship, Evangelization of Peoples (congregations).

Duval,* Leon-Etienne: b. Nov. 9, 1903, Chenex, France; ord. priest Dec. 18, 1926; ord. bishop of Constantine, Algeria, Feb. 11, 1947; archbishop of Algiers, Feb. 3, 1954; cardinal Feb. 22, 1965; titular church, St. Balbina. Archbishop of Algiers.

Ekandem, Dominic Ignatius: b. 1917, Obio Ibiono, Nigeria; ord. priest Dec. 7, 1947; ord. titular bishop of Gerapoli di Isauri and auxiliary bishop of Calabar, Feb. 7, 1954, the first Nigerian to become a bishop; first bishop of Ikot Ekpene, Mar. 1, 1963; cardinal May 24, 1976; titular church, San Marcello. Bishop of Ikot Ekpene, superior of mission "sui juris" of Abuja. Curial membership: Evangelization of Peoples (congregation).

Enrique y Tarancon, Vicente: b. May 14, 1907, Burriana, Spain; ord. priest Nov. 1, 1929; ord. bishop of Solsona, Mar. 24, 1946; bishop of Oviedo, Apr. 12, 1964; archbishop of Toledo, 1969-71; cardinal Apr. 28, 1969; titular church, St. John Chrysostom; archbishop of Madrid, 1971-83. Archbishop emeritus of Madrid.

Etchegaray, Roger: b. Sept. 25, 1922, Espelette, France; ord. priest July 13, 1947; deputy director, 1961-66, and secretary general, 1966-70, of French Episcopal Conference; ord. titular bishop of Gemelle di Numidia and auxiliary of Paris, May 27, 1969; archbishop of Marseilles, 1970-84; president of Mission de France, 1975-82; president of French Episcopal Conference, 1979-81; cardinal June 30, 1979; titular church, St. Leo I. President, 1984, of Pontifical Commission for Justice and Peace and the Pontifical Council *Cor Unum.* Curial membership: Evangelization of Peoples, Catholic Education (congregations); Christian Unity (secretariat).

Flahiff,* George B., C.S.B.: b. Oct. 26, 1905, Paris, Ont., Canada; ord. priest Aug. 17, 1930; professor of medieval history at the University of Toronto and Pontifical Institute of Medieval Studies in Toronto, 1934-54; superior general of Basilian Fathers, 1954; ord. archbishop of Winnipeg, May 31, 1961 (retired 1982); president of Canadian Conference of Bishops, 1963-65; cardinal Apr. 28, 1969; titular church, St. Mary della Salute (Primavalle). Archbishop emeritus of Winnipeg.

Freeman, James Darcy: b. Nov. 19, 1907, Sydney, Australia; ord. priest July 13, 1930; ord. titular bishop of Ermopoli minore and auxiliary of Sydney, Jan. 24, 1957; bishop of Armidale, 1968-71; archbishop of Sydney, 1971-83; cardinal Mar. 5, 1973; titular church, St. Mary Queen of Peace. (in Ostia Mare). Archbishop emeritus of Sydney.

Fresno Larrain, Juan Francisco: b. July 26, 1914, Santiago, Chile; ord. priest Dec. 18, 1937; ord. bishop of Copiapo, Aug. 15, 1958; archbishop of La Serena, 1967-83; archbishop of Santiago, May 3, 1983; cardinal May 25, 1985; titular church, St. Mary Immaculate of Lourdes (a Boccea). Archbishop of Santiago. Curial membership: Catholic Education (congregation).

Gagnon, Edouard, P.S.S.: b. Jan. 15, 1918, Port Daniel, Que., Canada; ord. priest Aug. 15, 1940; ord. bishop of St. Paul in Alberta Mar. 25, 1969 (resigned May 3, 1972); rector of Canadian College in Rome, 1972-77; vice president-secretary of Vatican Committee for the Family, 1973-80; titular archbishop of Giustiniana Prima, July 7, 1983; pro-president of Pontifical Council for the Family, 1983; cardinal May 25, 1985; deacon, St. Elena (fuori Porta Prenestina). President of Pontifical Council for the Family, 1985. Curial membership: Sacraments, Causes of Saints (congregations).

Gantin, Bernardin: b. May 8, 1922, Toffo, Dahomey (now Benin): ord. priest Jan. 14, 1951; ord. titular bishop of Tipasa di Mauritania and auxiliary bishop of Cotonou, Feb. 3, 1957; archbishop of Cotonou, 1960-71; associate secretary (1971-73) and secretary (1973-75) of Congregation for Evangelization of Peoples; vice-president (1975) and president (1976-84) ot Pontifical Commission for Justice and Peace; cardinal June 27, 1977; deacon; transferred to order of priests June 25, 1984; titular church, Sacred Heart of Christ the King. Prefect of Congregation for Bishops, 1984; president of commissions for Latin America and Migration and Tourism. Curial membership: Council for Public Affairs of the Church; Doctrine of the Faith, Sacraments, Divine Worship, Causes of Saints, Evangelization of Peoples, Oriental Churches, Religious and Secular Institutes, Catholic Education (congregations); Apostolic Signatura (tribunal); Non-Believers, Non-Christians (secretariats); Social Communications, Institute for Works of Religion, Sanctuaries of Pompei, Loreto and Bari (commissions).

Garrone,* Gabriel-Marie: b. Oct. 12, 1901, Aix-les-Bains, France; ord. priest Apr. 11, 1925; captain during World War II, cited for bravery, taken prisoner; rector of major seminary of Chambery, 1947; ord. titular archbishop of Lemno and coadjutor of Toulouse, June 24, 1947; archbishop of Toulouse, 1956-66; titular archbishop of Torri di Numidia and pro-prefect of Congregation of Seminaries and Universities, Mar. 24, 1966; cardinal June 26, 1967; titular church, St. Sabina; prefect of Congregation for Catholic Education, 1968-80. Head of presidential committee of Pontifical Council for Culture.

Glemp, Jozef: b. Dec. 18, 1928, Inowroclaw, Poland; assigned to forced labor on German farm in Rycerzow during Nazi occupation; ord. priest May 25, 1956; studied in Rome, 1958-64, receiving degree in Roman and canon law from Pontifical Lateran University; secretary of primatial major seminary at Gniezno on his return to Poland, 1964; spokesman for secretariat of primate of Poland and chaplain of primate for archdiocese of Gniezno, 1967; ord. bishop of Warmia, Apr. 21, 1979; archbishop of Gniezno, July 7, 1981, with title of archbishop of Warsaw and primate of Poland; cardinal Feb. 2, 1983; titular church, St. Mary in

Trastevere. Archbishop of Gniezno and Warsaw, primate of Poland, ordinary for faithful of Greek Catholic and Armenian rites in Poland. Curial membership:

Oriental Churches (congregation).

Gonzalez Martin, Marcelo: b. Jan. 16, 1918, Villanubla, Spain; ord. priest June 29, 1941; taught theology and sociology at Valladolid diocesan seminary; founded organization for construction of houses for poor; ord. bishop of Astorga, Mar. 5, 1961; titular archbishop of Case Mediane and coadjutor of Barcelona, Feb. 21, 1966; archbishop of Barcelona, 1967-71; archbishop of Toledo, Dec. 3, 1971; cardinal Mar. 5, 1973; titular church, St. Augustine. Archbishop of Toledo. Curial membership:

Clergy, Evangelization of Peoples (congregations).

Gouyon, Paul: b. Oct. 24, 1910, Bordeaux, France; ord. priest Mar. 13, 1937; ord. bishop of Bayonne, Oct. 7, 1957; titular archbishop of Pessinonte and coadjutor archbishop of Rennes, Sept. 6, 1963; archbishop of Rennes, Sept. 4, 1964 (resigned Oct. 15, 1985); cardinal Apr. 28, 1969; titular church, Nativity of Our Lord Jesus Christ (Via Gallia). Archbishop emeritus of Rennes. Curial membership:

Causes of Saints (congregation).

Gray, Gordon Joseph: b. Aug. 10, 1910, Edinburgh, Scotland; ord. priest June 15, 1935; ord. archbishop of Saint Andrews and Edinburgh, Sept. 21, 1951 (resigned May 30, 1985); chairman of International Committee for English in the Liturgy; cardinal Apr. 28, 1969; titular church, St. Clare. Archbishop emeritus of Saint Andrews and Edinburgh. Curial membership:

Sacraments, Clergy, Evangelization of Peoples, (congregations).

Guerri,* Sergio: b. Dec. 25, 1905, Tarquinia, Italy; ord. priest Mar. 30, 1929; ord. titular archbishop of Trevi, Apr. 27, 1969; cardinal Apr. 28, 1969; titular church, Most Holy Name of Mary; pro-president of Pontifical Commission for State of Vatican City, 1968-81.

Gulbinowicz, Henryk Roman: b. Oct. 17, 1928, Szukiszk, Poland; ord. priest June 18, 1960; ord. titular bishop of Acci and apostolic administrator of Polish territory in Lithuanian archdiocese of Vilnius (Vilna), Feb. 8, 1970; archbishop of Wroclaw, Poland, Jan. 3, 1976; cardinal May 25, 1985; titular church, Immaculate Conception of Mary (a Grottarosa). Archbishop of Wroclaw. Curial membership:

Oriental Churches, Clergy (congregations).

Guyot,* Jean: b. July 7, 1905, Bordeaux, France; ord. priest June 29, 1932; held various offices in Bordeaux diocese; ord. titular bishop of Helenopolis and coadjutor of Coutances, May 4, 1949; bishop of Coutances, 1950-66; archbishop of Toulouse, 1966-78; invested with Legion of Honor by French government; cardinal Mar. 5, 1973; titular church, Saint Agnes Outside the Walls. Archbishop emeritus of Toulouse.

Hamer, Jean Jerome, O.P.: b. June 1, 1916, Brussels, Belgium; ord. priest Aug. 3, 1941; taught dogmatic and fundamental theology and ec-

clesiology in France and Rome, 1944-62; author of several works; secretary of Christian Unity Secretariat, 1969-73; ord. titular bishop of Lorium June 29, 1973; archbishop; secretary of Congregation for Doctrine of the Faith, 1973-84; pro-prefect of Congregation for Religious and Secular Institutes, 1984; cardinal May 25, 1985; deacon, St. Saba (al Aventino). Prefect of Congregation for Religious and Secular Institutes, 1985. Curial membership:

Council for Public Affairs of the Church; Doctrine of the Faith, Bishops, Catholic Education (congregations); Authentic Interpretation of the Code of Canon Law (commission).

Hoeffner, Joseph: b. Dec. 24, 1906, Horhausen, Germany; ord. priest Oct. 30, 1932; ord. bishop of Munster, Sept. 14, 1962; titular archbishop of Aquileia and coadjutor archbishop of Cologne, Jan. 6, 1969; archbishop of Cologne, Feb. 23, 1969; cardinal Apr. 28, 1969; titular church, St. Andrew of the Valley. Archbishop of Cologne. Curial membership:

Religious and Secular Institutes, Evangelization of Peoples, Catholic Education (congregations); Economic Affairs (office).

Hume, George Basil, O.S.B.: b. Mar. 2, 1923, Newcastle-upon-Tyne, England; began monastic studies at Benedictine Abbey of St. Laurence at Ampleforth, 1941; made solemn perpetual vows as Benedictine, 1945; ord. priest July 23, 1950; abbot of Ampleforth, 1963-76; ord. archbishop of Westminster, Mar. 25, 1976; cardinal May 24, 1976; titular church, St. Silvestro (in Capite). Archbishop of Westminster. Curial membership:

Religious and Secular Institutes (congregation); Christian Unity (secretariat); Health Care Workers (commission).

Innocenti, Antonio: b. Aug. 23, 1915, Poppi, Italy; ord. priest July 17, 1938; held curial and diplomatic positions; ord. titular archbishop of Eclano, Feb. 18, 1967; nuncio to Paraguay, 1967-73; secretary of Congregation for Causes of Saints, 1973-75; secretary of Congregation for Sacraments and Divine Worship, 1975-80; nuncio to Spain, 1980-85; cardinal May 25, 1985; deacon, St. Marie (in Aquiro). Prefect of Congregation for the Clergy, 1986. Curial membership:

Council for Public Affairs of the Church; Bishops, Sacraments, Causes of Saints (congregations); State of Vatican City; Sanctuaries of Pompei, Loreto and Bari (commissions).

Jubany Arnau, Narciso: b. Aug. 12, 1913, Santa Coloma de Farnes, Spain; ord. priest July 30, 1939; professor of law at Barcelona seminary; served on ecclesiastical tribunal; ord. titular bishop of Ortosia and auxiliary of Barcelona, Jan. 22, 1956; bishop of Gerona, 1964-71; archbishop of Barcelona, Dec. 3, 1971; cardinal Mar. 5, 1973; titular church, San Lorenzo (in Damaso). Archbishop of Barcelona. Curial membership:

Sacraments, Divine Worship, Religious and Secular Institutes (congregations).

Khoraiche, Antoine Pierre: b. Sept. 20, 1907, Ain-Ebel, Lebanon; ord. priest Apr. 12, 1930; ord. titular bishop of Tarsus and auxiliary bishop of Sidon of the Maronites, Oct. 15, 1950; bishop of Sidon, Nov. 25, 1957; elected patriarch of Antioch for Maronites. Feb. 3, 1975, granted ecclesial communion by Paul VI, Feb. 15, 1975 (resigned May, 1986); advocate of reconciliation among various Lebanese ethnic and religious groups and withdrawal of foreign troops from country; cardinal Feb. 2, 1983. Patriarch emeritus of Antioch for Maronites. Curial membership:

Oriental Churches (congregation); Revision of Code of Oriental Canon Law (commission).

Kim, Stephan Sou Hwan: b. May 8, 1922, Tae Gu, Korea; ord. priest Sept. 15, 1951; ord. bishop of Masan, May 31, 1966; archbishop of Seoul, Apr. 9, 1968; cardinal Apr. 28, 1969; titular church, St. Felix of Cantalice (Centocelle). Archbishop of Seoul, apostolic administrator of Pyeong Yang. Curial membership:

Evangelization of Peoples (congregation); Non-Christians (secretariat).

Kitbunchu, Michael Michai: b. Jan. 25, 1929, Samphran, Thailand; ord. priest Dec. 20, 1959, in Rome; rector of metropolitan seminary in Bangkok, 1965-72; ord. archbishop of Bangkok, June 3, 1973; cardinal Feb. 2, 1983, the first from Thailand; titular church, St. Laurence in Panisperna. Archbishop of Bangkok. Curial membership:

Evangelization of Peoples (congregation).

Koenig,* Franz: b. Aug. 3, 1905, Rabenstein, Lower Austria; ord. priest Oct. 29, 1933; ord. titular bishop of Livias and coadjutor bishop of Sankt Poelten, Aug. 31, 1952; archbishop of Vienna, May 10, 1956 (resigned Sept. 16, 1985); cardinal Dec. 15, 1958; titular church, St. Eusebius; president of Secretariat for Non-Believers, 1965-80. Archbishop emeritus of Vienna.

Krol, John Joseph: b. Oct. 26, 1910, Cleveland, Ohio; ord. priest (Cleveland diocese) Feb. 20, 1937; ord. titular bishop of Cadi and auxiliary bishop of Cleveland, Sept. 2, 1953; archbishop of Philadelphia, Feb. 11, 1961, installed Mar. 22, 1961; cardinal June 26, 1967; titular church, St. Mary (della Merced) and St. Adrian Martyr; vice-president, 1966-72, and president, 1972-74, of NCCB/USCC. Archbishop of Philadelphia. Curial membership:

Oriental Churches, Clergy (congregations); Economic Affairs (office).

Kuharic, Franjo: b. Apr. 15, 1919, Pribic, Yugoslavia; ord. priest July 15, 1945; ord. titular bishop of Meta and auxiliary bishop of Zagreb, May 3, 1964; apostolic administrator of archdiocese of Zagreb, 1968-70; archbishop of Zagreb, June 16, 1970; cardinal Feb. 2, 1983; titular church, St. Jerome of the Croats. Archbishop of Zagreb. Curial membership:

Council for Public Affairs of the Church; Bishops, Divine Worship, Clergy (congregations); Non-Believers (secretariat).

Landazuri Ricketts, Juan, O.F.M: b. Dec. 19, 1913, Arequipa, Peru; entered Franciscans, 1933; ord. priest Apr. 16, 1939; ord. titular archbishop of Roina and coadjutor archbishop of Lima, Aug. 24, 1952; archbishop of Lima, May 2, 1955; cardinal Mar. 19, 1962; titular church, St. Mary (in Aracoeli). Archbishop of Lima. Curial membership:

Clergy, Religious and Secular Institutes (congregations).

Law, Bernard F.: b. Nov. 4, 1931, Torreon, Mexico, the son of U.S. Air Force colonel; ord. priest (Jackson diocese) May 21, 1961; editor of Natchez-Jackson, Miss., diocesan paper, 1963-68; director of NCCB Committee on Ecumenical and Interreligious Affairs, 1968-71; ord. bishop of Springfield-Cape Girardeau, Mo., Dec. 5, 1973; archbishop of Boston, 1984; cardinal May 25, 1985; titular church, St. Susanna. Archbishop of Boston. Curial membership:

Religious and Secular Institutes, Evangelization of Peoples (congregations).

Lebrun Moratinos, Jose Ali: b. Mar. 19, 1919, Puerto Cabello, Venezuela; ord. priest Dec. 19, 1943; ord. titular bishop of Arado and auxiliary bishop of Maracaibo, Sept. 2, 1956; first bishop of Maracay, 1958-62; bishop of Valencia, 1962-72; titular archbishop of Voncaria and coadjutor archbishop of Caracas, Sept. 21, 1972; archbishop of Caracas, May 24, 1980; cardinal Feb. 2, 1983; titular church, St. Pancratius. Archbishop of Caracas. Curial membership:

Council for Public Affairs of Church; Bishops, Catholic Education (congregations).

Leger,* Paul Emile, S.S.: b. Apr. 26, 1904, Valleyfield, Quebec, Canada; ord. priest May 25, 1929; rector Canadian College, Rome, 1947; ord. archbishop of Montreal, Apr. 26, 1950; cardinal Jan. 12, 1953; titular church, St. Mary (of the Angels); resigned as archbishop of Montreal (Apr. 20, 1968) to become missionary to lepers, retired 1979. Archbishop emeritus of Montreal.

Lopez Trujillo, Alfonso: b. Nov. 8, 1935, Villahermosa, Colombia; ord. priest Nov. 13, 1960, in Rome; returned to Colombia, 1963; taught at major seminary; was pastoral coordinator for 1968 International Eucharistic Congress in Bogota; vicar general of Bogota, 1970-72; ord. titular bishop of Boseta (with personal title of archbishop), Mar. 25, 1971; auxiliary bishop of Bogota, 1971-72; secretary-general of CELAM, 1972-78; helped organize 1979 Puebla Conference in which Pope John Paul II participated; app. coadjutor archbishop of Medellin, 1978; archbishop of Medellin, Jan. 2, 1979; president of CELAM, 1979-83; cardinal Feb. 2, 1983; titular church, St. Prisca. Archbishop of Medellin. Curial membership:

Doctrine of the Faith, Divine Worship, Evangelization of Peoples (congregations); Social Communications, Latin America (commissions).

Lorscheider, Aloisio, O.F.M.: b. Oct. 8, 1924, Linha Geraldo, Brazil; received in Franciscan Order, Feb. 1, 1942; ord. priest Aug. 22, 1948; professor of theology at the Antonianum, Rome, and director of Franciscan international house of studies; ord. bishop of Santo Angelo, Brazil, May 20, 1962; archbishop of Fortaleza, Mar. 26, 1973; president of CELAM, 1975-79; cardinal May 24, 1976; titular church, S. Pietro (in Montorio). Archbishop of Fortaleza. Curial membership:

Religious and Secular Institutes (congregation); Non-Christians, Non-Believers (secretariats).

Lourdusamy, D. Simon: b. Feb. 5, 1924, Kalleri, India; ord. priest Dec. 21, 1951; ord. titular bishop of Sozusa and auxiliary of Bangalore, Aug. 22, 1962; titular archbishop of Filippi and coadjutor archbishop of Bangalore, Nov. 9, 1964; archbishop of Bangalore, 1968-71; associate secretary, 1971-73, and secretary, 1973-85, of Congregation for Evangelization of Peoples; cardinal May 25, 1985; deacon, St. Mary of Grace. Prefect of Congregation for Oriental Churches, 1985. Curial membership:

Evangelization of Peoples, Causes of Saints (congregations); Non-Christians (secretariat); Revision of Oriental Code of Canon Law, Family (commissions).

Lubachivsky, Myroslav Ivan: b. June 24, 1914, Dolynian, Ukraine; ord. priest Sept. 21, 1938; began pastoral work in U.S., 1947; became U.S. citizen, 1952; ord. archbishop of Ukrainian-rite archeparchy of Philadelphia, Nov. 13, 1979; coadjutor archbishop of Lwow of the Ukrainians, Mar. 27, 1980; archbishop of Lwow and major archbishop of Ukrainians, Sept. 7, 1984; cardinal May 25, 1985; titular church, St. Sofia (a Via Boccea). Archbishop of Lwow, major archbishop of the Ukrainians (resides in Rome). Curial membership:

Oriental Churches (congregation); Non-Believers (secretariat); Revision of Oriental Code of Canon Law (commission).

Lustiger, Jean-Marie: b. Sept. 16, 1926, Paris, France, of Polish-Jewish parents who emigrated to France after World War I; taken in by Catholic family in Orleans when his parents were deported during Nazi occupation (his mother died in 1943 at Auschwitz); convert to Catholicism, baptized Aug. 25, 1940; active in Young Christian Students during university days; ord. priest Apr. 17, 1954; ord. bishop of Orleans, Dec. 8, 1979; archbishop of Paris, Jan. 31, 1981; cardinal Feb. 2, 1983; titular church, Sts. Marcellinus and Peter. Archbishop of Paris, ordinary for Eastern-Rite faithful without ordinaries of their own. Curial membership:

Council for Public Affairs of Church; Sacraments, Divine Worship, Bishops, Oriental Churches, Clergy, Religious and Secular Institutes (congregations).

McCann, Owen: b. June 29, 1907, Woodstock, South Africa; ord. priest Dec. 21, 1935; ord. titular bishop of Stettorio and vicar apostolic of Cape Town, May 18, 1950; first archbishop of Cape Town, Jan. 11, 1951 (retired Oct. 20, 1984); opponent of apartheid policy; cardinal Feb. 22, 1965; titular church, St. Praxedes. Archbishop emeritus of Cape Town. Curial membership:

Evangelization of Peoples (congregation).

Macharski, Franciszek: b. May 20, 1927, Cracow, Poland; ord. priest Apr. 2, 1950; engaged in pastoral work, 1950-56; continued theological studies in Fribourg, Switzerland, 1956-60; taught pastoral theology at the Faculty of Theology in Cracow; app. rector of archdiocesan seminary in Cracow, 1970; ord. archbishop of Cracow, Jan. 6, 1979, by Pope John Paul II; cardinal June 30, 1979; titular church, St. John at the Latin Gate. Archbishop of Cracow. Curial membership:

Council for Public Affairs of Church; Bishops, Clergy, Catholic Education (congregations); Non-Believers (secretariat).

Malula, Joseph: b. Dec. 17, 1917, Kinshasa, Zaire; ord. priest June 9, 1946; ord. titular bishop of Attanaso and auxiliary bishop of Kinshasa, Sept.

20, 1959; archbishop of Kinshasa. July 7, 1964; cardinal Apr. 28, 1969; titular church, Ss. Protomartyrs (Via Aurelia Antica). Archbishop of Kinshasa.

Manning, Timothy: b. Nov. 15, 1909, Ballingeary, Ireland; completed studies for the priesthood at St. Patrick's Seminary, Menlo Park, Calif.; ord. priest (Los Angeles archdiocese) June 16, 1934; became American citizen, Jan. 14, 1944; ord. titular bishop of Lesvi and auxiliary of Los Angeles, Oct. 15, 1946; first bishop of Fresno, 1967-69; titular archbishop of Capri and coadjutor of Los Angeles, May 26, 1969; archbishop of Los Angeles, 1970-85; cardinal Mar. 5, 1973; titular church, Santa Lucia. Archbishop emeritus of Los Angeles. Curial membership:

Religious and Secular Institutes (congregation).

Martini, Carlo Maria, S.J.: b. Feb. 15, 1927, Turin, Italy; entered Jesuits Sept. 25, 1944; ord. priest July 13, 1952, at the age of 25; biblical scholar; seminary professor, Chieti, Italy, 1958-61; professor and later rector, 1969-78, of Pontifical Biblical Institute; rector of Pontifical Gregorian University, 1978-79; author of theological, biblical and spiritual works; ord. archbishop of Milan, Jan. 6, 1980, by Pope John Paul II; cardinal Feb. 2, 1983; titular church, St. Cecilia. Archbishop of Milan. Curial membership:

Council for Public Affairs of the Church; Doctrine of the Faith, Bishops, Sacraments, Catholic Education, Religious and Secular Institutes, Evangelization of Peoples (congregations).

Marty,* Francois: b. May 18, 1904, Pachins, France; ord. priest June 28, 1930; ord. bishop of Saint-Flour, May 1, 1952; titular archbishop of Emesa and coadjutor archbishop of Rheims, Dec. 14, 1959; archbishop of Rheims, May 9, 1960; archbishop of Paris, 1968-81; cardinal Apr. 28, 1969; titular church, St. Louis of France. Archbishop emeritus of Paris.

Maurer,* Jose Clemente, C.SS.R.: b. Mar. 13, 1900, Puttlingen, Germany; ord. priest Sept. 19, 1925; assigned to Bolivian missions, 1926; became a Bolivian citizen; ord. titular bishop of Cea and auxiliary bishop of La Paz, Apr. 16, 1950; archbishop of Sucre, 1951-83; cardinal June 26, 1967; titular church, Most Holy Redeemer and St. Alphonsus. Archbishop emeritus of Sucre.

Mayer, Paul Augustin, O.S.B.: b. May 23, 1911, Altotting, West Germany; ord. priest Aug. 25, 1935; rector of St. Anselm's Univ., Rome, 1949-66; secretary of Congregation for Religious and Secular Institutes, 1972-84; ord. titular archbishop of Satriano, Feb. 13, 1972; pro-prefect of Congregations for Sacraments and Divine Worship, 1984; cardinal May 25, 1985; deacon, St. Anselm. Prefect of Congregations for Sacraments and Divine Worship, 1985. Curial membership:

Council for Public Affairs of the Church; Doctrine of the Faith, Religious and Secular Institutes (congregations); Authentic Interpretation of the Code of Canon Law (commission).

Meisner, Joachim: b. Dec. 25, 1933, Breslau, Silesia, Germany (present-day Wroclaw, Poland); ord. priest Dec. 22, 1962; regional director of Caritas; ord. titular bishop of Vina and auxiliary of apostolic administration of Erfurt-Meiningen, E. Germany, May 17, 1975; app. bishop of Berlin, Apr. 22, 1980, installed May 17, 1980 (resides in East Berlin); cardinal Feb. 2, 1983; titular church, St. Prudenziana. Bishop of Berlin. Curial membership:

Sacraments, Divine Worship, Catholic Education (congregations); Non-Believers (secretariat); Justice and Peace (commission).

Munoz Duque, Anibal: b. Oct. 3, 1908, Santa Rosa de Osos, Colombia; ord. priest Nov. 19, 1933; ord. bishop of Soccoro y San Gil, May 27, 1951; bishop of Bucaramango, 1952-59; archbishop of Nueva Pamplona, 1959-68; titular archbishop of Cariana and coadjutor archbishop of Bogota, 1968; archbishop of Bogota and military vicar, 1972-84; cardinal Mar. 5, 1973; titular church, St. Bartholomew. Archbishop emeritus of Bogota. Curial membership:

Catholic Education (congregation).

Munoz Vega,* Pablo, S. J.: b. May 23, 1903, Mira, Ecuador; ord. priest Apr. 15, 1933; ord. titular bishop of Ceramo and auxiliary bishop of Quito, Mar. 19, 1964; archbishop of Quito, 1967-85; cardinal Apr. 28, 1969; titular church, St. Robert Bellarmine. Archbishop emeritus of Quito.

Nasalli Rocca di Corneliano,* Mario: b. Aug. 12, 1903, Piacenza, Italy; ord. priest Apr. 9, 1927; ord. titular archbishop of Anzio, Apr. 20, 1969; cardinal Apr. 28, 1969; titular church, St. John the Baptist.

Nsubuga, Emmanuel: b. Nov. 5, 1914, Kisule, Uganda; ord. priest Dec. 15, 1946; ord. bishop of Kampala, Oct. 30, 1966; cardinal May 24, 1976; titular church, S. Maria Nuova. Archbishop of Kampala. Curial membership:

Evangelization of Peoples (congregation).

Obando Bravo, Miguel, S.D.B.: b. Feb. 2, 1926, La Libertad, Nicaragua; ord. priest Aug. 10, 1958; ord. titular bishop of Puzia di Bizavena and auxiliary of Matagalpa, Mar. 31, 1968; archbishop of Managua, Feb. 16, 1970; cardinal May 25, 1985; titular church, St. John the Evangelist (a Spinaceta). Archbishop of Managua. Curial membership:

Clergy (congregation).

O'Boyle,* Patrick A.: b. July 18, 1896, Scranton, Pa.; ord. priest (New York archdiocese) May 21, 1921; executive director of War Relief Services, NCWC, 1943; ord. archbishop of Washington, Jan. 14, 1948 (retired, 1973); cardinal June 26, 1967; titular church, St. Nicholas (in Carcere). Archbishop emeritus of Washington.

O'Connor, John J.: b. Jan. 15, 1920, Philadelphia, Pa.; ord. priest (Philadelphia archdiocese) Dec. 15, 1945; joined U.S. Navy and Marine Corps as a chaplain, 1952; overseas posts included service in South Korea and Vietnam; U.S. Navy chief of chaplains, 1975; retired from Navy June 1, 1979, with rank of rear admiral; ord. titular bishop of Curzola and auxiliary of military vicariate, May 27, 1979; bishop of Scranton, May 6, 1983; archbishop of New York, Jan. 26, 1984; cardinal May 25, 1985; titular church, Sts. John and Paul. Archbishop of New York. Curial membership:

Council for Public Affairs of the Church; Bish-

ops (congregation); Social Communications, Institute for Works of Religion, Health Care Workers (commissions).

Oddi, Silvio: b. Nov. 14, 1910, Morfasso, Italy; ord. priest May 21, 1933; ord. titular archbishop of Mesembria, Sept. 27, 1953; served in Vatican diplomatic corps, 1953-69; apostolic delegate to Jerusalem, Palestine, Jordan and Cyprus, internuncio to the United Arab Republic, and nuncio to Belgium and Luxembourg; cardinal Apr. 28, 1969; titular church, St. Agatha of the Goths. Pontifical legate for Patriarchal Basilica of St. Francis of Assisi; prefect of Sacred Congregation for the Clergy, 1979-86. Curial membership:

Council for Public Affairs of Church; Bishops, Oriental Churches, Causes of Saints, Evangelization of Peoples (congregations); Apostolic Signatura (tribunal); Authentic Interpretation of Code of Canon Law (commission); Patrimony of the Holy See (office).

O'Fiaich, Tomas: b. Nov. 3, 1923, Crossmaglen, Ireland; ord. priest July 6, 1948; lecturer, 1953, and professor, 1959, of modern history at Maynooth College; vice president, 1970, and president, 1974, of Maynooth; prolific author of scholarly works; recognized authority on early Irish Christianity; ord. archbishop of Armagh and primate of All Ireland, Oct. 2, 1977; pledged to work for the cause of peace in Northern Ireland; outspoken in his condemnation of violence; cardinal June 30, 1979; titular church, St. Patrick. Archbishop of Armagh, primate of All Ireland. Curial membership:

Council for Public Affairs of Church; Bishops, Clergy, Catholic Education, Evangelization of Peoples (congregations); Christian Unity (secretariat).

Otunga, Maurice: b. January, 1923, Chebukwa, Kenya; son of pagan tribal chief; baptized 1935, at age of 12; ord. priest Oct. 3, 1950, at Rome; taught at Kisumu major seminary for three years; attaché in apostolic delegation at Mombasa, 1953-56; ord. titular bishop of Tacape and auxiliary of Kisumu, Feb. 25, 1957; bishop of Kisii, 1960-69; titular archbishop of Bomarzo and coadjutor of Nairobi, Nov. 15, 1969; archbishop of Nairobi, Oct. 24, 1971; cardinal Mar. 5, 1973; titular church, St. Gregory Barbarigo. Archbishop of Nairobi, military vicar of Kenya, 1981. Curial membership:

Sacraments, Religious and Secular Institutes, Evangelization of Peoples, Catholic Education (congregations).

Palazzini, Pietro: b. May 19, 1912, Piobbico, Pesaro, Italy; ord. priest Dec. 6, 1934; assistant vice-rector of Pontifical Major Roman Seminary and vice-rector and bursar of Pontifical Roman Seminary for Juridical Studies; professor of moral theology at Lateran University; held various offices in Roman Curia; secretary of Congregation of Council (now Clergy), 1958-73; ord. titular archbishop of Caesarea in Cappadocia, Sept. 21, 1962; author of numerous works on moral theology and law; cardinal Mar. 5, 1973; titular church, St. Jerome. Prefect of Congregation for Causes of Saints, 1980. Curial membership:

Oriental Churches, Sacraments, Clergy (congregations); Apostolic Signatura (tribunal); Authentic Interpretation of Code of Canon Law (commission).

Pappalardo, Salvatore: b. Sept. 23, 1918, Villafranca Sicula, Sicily; ord. priest Apr. 12, 1941; entered diplomatic service of secretariat of state, 1947; ord. titular archbishop of Miletus, Jan. 16, 1966; pro-nuncio in Indonesia, 1966-69; president of Pontifical Ecclesiastical Academy, 1969-70; archbishop of Palermo, Oct. 17, 1970; cardinal Mar. 5, 1973; titular church, St. Mary Odigitria of the Sicilians.· Archbishop of Palermo. Curial membership:

Council for Public Affairs of Church; Bishops, Oriental Churches, Clergy, Catholic Education (congregations).

Parecattil, Joseph: b. Apr. 1, 1912, Kidangoor, India; ord. priest Aug. 24, 1939; ord. titular bishop of Aretusa for Syrians and auxiliary bishop of Ernakulam, Nov. 30, 1953; archbishop of Ernakulam (Syro-Malabar Rite), 1956-84; appointed one of seven members of Pope Paul VI's advisory council for Eastern Rite churches, 1968; cardinal Apr. 28, 1969; titular church, Our Lady Queen of Peace (Monte Verde). Archbishop emeritus of Ernakulam of the Syro-Malabar Rite. President of Commission for Revision of Oriental Code of Canon Law, 1972. Curial membership:

Oriental Churches (congregation); Non-Christians (secretariat).

Parente,* Pietro: b. Feb. 16, 1891, Casalnuovo, Monterotaro, Italy; ord. priest Mar. 18, 1916; director of Archiepiscopal Seminary at Naples, 1916-26; rector of Pontifical Urban College of Propagation of the Faith, 1934-38; Consultor of the Congregations of the Holy Office, Council, Propagation of the Faith, and Seminaries and Universities; ord. archbishop of Perugia, Oct. 23, 1955; titular archbishop of Tolemaide di Tebaide, Oct. 23, 1959; assessor (1959-65) and secretary (1965-67) of Congregation of Holy Office (now Doctrinal Congregation); cardinal June 26, 1967; titular church, St. Lawrence (in Lucina).

Paupini, Giuseppe: b. Feb. 25, 1907, Mondavio, Italy; ord. priest Mar. 19, 1930; ord. titular archbishop of Sebastopolis in Abasgia, Feb. 26, 1956; served in Vatican diplomatic corps, 1956-69; internuncio to Iran, 1956-57; nuncio to Guatemala and El Salvador, 1957-58, nuncio to Colombia, 1959-69; cardinal Apr. 28, 1969; titular church, All Saints Church; major penitentiary 1973-84. Chamberlain of the College of Cardinals, 1986. Curial membership:

Causes of Saints (congregation).

Pavan,* Pietro: b. Aug. 30, 1903, Povegliano, Italy; ord. priest July 8, 1928, expert at Vatican Council II; rector of Lateran University, 1969-74; chief contributor to drafting of encyclicals *Mater et Magistra* and *Pacem in Terris:* cardinal May 25, 1985, without episcopal ordination; deacon, St. Francis of Paola (ai Monti).

Pellegrino,* Michele: b. Apr. 25, 1903, Centallo, Italy; ord. priest Sept. 19, 1925; ord. archbishop of Turin, Oct. 17, 1965 (resigned 1977); cardinal June 26, 1967; titular church, Most Holy Name of Jesus. Archbishop emeritus of Turin.

Picachy, Lawrence Trevor, S.J.: b. Aug. 7, 1916, Lebong, India; ord. priest Nov. 21, 1947; dean, 1950-54, and then rector, 1954-60, of St. Francis Xavier University College, Calcutta; ord. bishop of Jamshedpur, Sept. 9, 1962; archbishop of Calcutta, May 29, 1969 (resigned 1986); cardinal May 24, 1976; titular church, Sacred Heart of Mary. Archbishop emeritus of Calcutta. Curial membership: Divine Worship (congregation).

Piovanelli, Silvano: b. Feb. 21, 1924, Ronta di Mugello, Italy; ord. priest July 13, 1947; ord. titular bishop of Tubune di Numidia and auxiliary of Florence, June 24, 1982; archbishop of Florence, Mar. 18, 1983; cardinal May 25, 1985; titular church, St. Mary of Graces (Via Trionfale). Archbishop of Florence. Curial membership:

Catholic Education (congregation); Non-Believers (secretariat).

Pironio, Eduardo: b. Dec. 3, 1920, Nueve de Julio, Argentina; ord. priest Dec. 5, 1943; taught theology at Pius XII Seminary of Mercedes diocese, 1944-59; vicar general of diocese 1958-60; attended Second Vatican Council as *peritus*; ord. titular bishop of Ceciri, May 31, 1964; apostolic administrator of diocese of Avellaneda, 1967-72; secretary general, 1967-72, and president, 1973-75, of CELAM; bishop of Mar del Plata, 1972-75; titular archbishop of Thiges and pro-prefect of Congregation for Religious and Secular Institutes, Sept. 20, 1975; cardinal May 24, 1976; deacon, Sts. Cosmas and Damian. Prefect of the Congregation for Religious and Secular Institutes, 1976-84. President of Pontifical Council for the Laity, 1984, and Commission for Apostolate of Health Care Workers, 1985. Curial membership:

Council for Public Affairs of the Church; Bishops, Divine Worship, Catholic Education, Oriental Churches (congregations); Latin America, Authentic Interpretation of Code of Canon Law (commissions).

Poletti, Ugo: b. Apr. 19, 1914, Omegna, Italy; ord. priest June 29, 1938; served in various diocesan offices at Novara; ord. titular bishop of Medeli and auxiliary of Novaro, Sept. 14, 1958; president of Pontifical Mission Aid Society for Italy, 1964-67; archbishop of Spoleto, 1967-69; titular archbishop of Cittanova, 1969; served as second viceregent of Rome, 1969-72; pro-vicar general of Rome, 1972; cardinal Mar. 5, 1973; titular church, Sts. Ambrose and Charles. Vicar general of Rome, 1973; archpriest of Patriarchal Lateran Archbasilica, 1973; grand chancellor of Lateran University. Curial membership:

Council for Public Affairs of the Church; Bishops, Clergy, Divine Worship, Oriental Churches, Religious and Secular Institutes (congregations); Laity (council).

Poupard, Paul: b. Aug. 30, 1930, Bouzille, France; ord. priest Dec. 18, 1954; scholar; author of a number of works; ord. titular bishop of Usula and auxiliary of Paris, Apr. 6, 1979; archbishop and pro-president of the Secretariat for Non-Believers, 1980; cardinal May 25, 1985; deacon, St. Eugene. President of Secretariat for Non-Believers, 1985; president of executive committee of

Pontifical Council for Culture, 1982. Curial membership:

Divine Worship, Evangelization of Peoples, Catholic Education (congregations); Non-Christians (secretariat).

Primatesta, Raul Francisco: b. Apr. 14, 1919, Capilla del Senor, Argentina; ord. priest Oct. 25, 1942, at Rome; taught at minor and major seminaries of La Plata; contributed to several theology reviews; ord. titular bishop of Tanais and auxiliary of La Plata, Aug. 15, 1957; bishop of San Rafael, 1961-65; archbishop of Cordoba, Feb. 16, 1965; cardinal Mar. 5, 1973; titular church, St. Mary Sorrowful Virgin. Archbishop of Cordoba, Argentina. Curial membership:

Clergy, Religious and Secular Institutes, Sacraments, Evangelization of Peoples (congregations).

Ratzinger, Joseph: b. Apr. 16, 1927, Marktl am Inn, Germany; ord. priest June 29, 1951; professor of dogmatic theology at University of Regensburg, 1969-77; member of International Theological Commission, 1969-80; ord. archbishop of Munich-Freising, May 28, 1977 (resigned Feb. 15, 1982); cardinal June 27, 1977; titular church, St. Mary of Consolation (in Tiburtina). Prefect of Congregation for Doctrine of the Faith, 1981; president of Biblical and Theological Commissions. Curial membership:

Council for Public Affairs of the Church; Bishops, Divine Worship, Oriental Churches, Clergy, Evangelization of Peoples, Causes of Saints, Catholic Education (congregations); Apostolic Signatura (tribunal); Christian Unity (secretariat); Authentic Interpretation of Code of Canon Law, Revision of Oriental Code of Canon Law (commissions).

Razafimahatratra, Victor, S.J.: b. Sept. 8, 1921, Ambanitsilena-Ranomasina, Madagascar; entered Society of Jesus, 1945; ord. priest July 28, 1956; rector of Fianarantsoa Minor Seminary, 1960-63; superior of Jesuit residence at Ambositra, 1963-69; rector of Tananarive Major Seminary, 1969-71; ord. bishop of Farafangana, Apr. 18, 1971; archbishop of Tananarive, Apr. 10, 1976; cardinal May 24, 1976; titular church, Holy Cross in Jerusalem. Archbishop of Tananarive. Curial membership:

Evangelization of Peoples (congregation).

Ribeiro, Antonio: b. May 21, 1928, Gandarela di Basto, Portugal; ord. priest July 5, 1953; professor of fundamental theology at major seminary at Braga; ord. titular bishop of Tigillava and auxiliary of Braga, Sept. 17, 1967; patriarch of Lisbon, May 10, 1971; cardinal Mar. 5, 1973; titular church, St. Anthony of Padua (in Rome). Patriarch of Lisbon, military vicar. Curial membership:

Clergy, Catholic Education (congregations); Social Communications (commission).

Righi-Lambertini,* Egano: b. Feb. 22, 1906, Casalecchio di Reno, Italy; ord. priest May 25, 1929; entered service of secretariat of state, 1939; served in diplomatic missions in France (1949-54), Costa Rica (1955), England (1955-57); first apostolic delegate to Korea, 1957-60; ord. titular archbishop of Doclea, Oct. 28, 1960; apostolic nuncio in Lebanon, 1960-63, Chile, 1963-67, Italy, 1967-69; France, 1969-79; while nuncio in France he also served as special envoy at the Council of Europe, 1974-79; cardinal June 30, 1979; deacon, St. John Bosco in Via Tuscolana. Honorary president of Commission on Sacred Art in Italy. Curial membership:

Council for Public Affairs of the Church; Bishops, Causes of Saints (congregations); Non-Christians (secretariat); Patrimony of Holy See (office).

Rossi, Agnelo: b. May 4, 1913, Joaquim Egidio, Brazil; ord. priest Mar. 27, 1937; ord. bishop of Barra do Pirai, Apr. 15, 1956; archbishop of Ribeirao Preto, 1962-64; archbishop of Sao Paulo, 1964-70; cardinal Feb. 22, 1965; titular church, Mother of God; entered order of cardinal bishops as titular bishop of Sabina and Poggia Mirteto June 25, 1984; prefect of Congregation for Evangelization of Peoples, 1970-84. President of Administration of Patrimony of the Holy See, 1984. Curial membership:

Council for Public Affairs of Church; Clergy, Doctrine of Faith, Bishops, Oriental Churches, Causes of Saints, Religious and Secular Institutes, Catholic Education (congregations); Institute for Works of Religion (commission).

Rossi, Opilio: b. May 14, 1910, New York, N.Y.; holds Italian citizenship; ord. priest for diocese of Piacenza, Italy, Mar. 11, 1933; served in nunciatures in Belgium, The Netherlands and Germany, 1938-53; ord. titular archbishop of Ancyra, Dec. 27, 1953; nuncio in Ecuador, 1953-59, Chile, 1959-61, Austria, 1961-76; cardinal May 24, 1976; deacon, S. Maria Liberatrice (on the Monte Testaccio). President of: Commission for the Sanctuaries of Pompeii, Loreto and Bari, 1984; Permanent Committee for International Eucharistic Congresses, 1983. Curial membership:

Council for Public Affairs of the Church; Bishops, Oriental Churches, Sacraments, Religious and Secular Institutes, Clergy, Causes of Saints, Evangelization of Peoples (congregations); Apostolic Signatura (tribunal); Authentic Interpretation of Code of Canon Law (commission); Laity (council).

Rubin, Wladyslaw: b. Sept. 20, 1917, Toki, Poland; seminary studies interrupted during World War II when he was arrested and deported to labor camp; completed studies at St. Joseph's University in Beirut; ord. priest in Beirut June 30, 1946, and served Polish community there; sent to Rome for further studies, 1949; chaplain for Polish refugees in Italy, 1953-58; rector of Polish College in Rome, 1959-64; ord. titular bishop of Serta, primate of Poland's delegate for emigration and auxiliary of Gniezno, Nov. 29, 1964; established contact with Polish emigrants throughout the world; secretary general of Synod of Bishops, 1967-79; cardinal June 30, 1979; deacon, St. Mary in Via Lata. Prefect of Congregation for Oriental Churches, 1980-85.

Rugambwa, Laurean: b. July 12, 1912, Bukongo, Tanzania; ord. priest Dec. 12, 1943; ord. titular bishop of Febiano and vicar apostolic of Lower Kagera, Feb. 10, 1952; bishop of Rutabo, Mar. 25, 1953; cardinal Mar. 28, 1960; titular church, St. Francis of Assisi (a Ripa Grande); bishop of

Bukoba, 1960-68. Archbishop of Dar-es-Salaam, 1968. Curial membership:
Causes of Saints (congregation).

Sabattani, Aurelio: b. Oct. 18, 1912, Casal Fiumanese, Italy; ord. priest July 26, 1935; jurist; served in various assignments in his native diocese of Imola and as judge and later an official of the regional ecclesiastical tribunal of Bologna; called to Rome in 1955 as prelate auditor of the Roman Rota; ord. titular archbishop of Justinian Prima, July 25, 1965; prelate of Loreto, 1965-71; secretary of Supreme Tribunal of Apostolic Signatura and consultor of Secretariat of State, 1971; pro-prefect of Apostolic Signatura, 1982-83; cardinal Feb. 2, 1983; deacon, St. Apollinaris. Prefect of Apostolic Signatura, 1983, archpriest of St. Peter's Basilica, 1983. Curial membership:
Council for Public Affairs of the Church; Bishops, Oriental Churches (congregations); Authentic Interpretation of Code of Canon Law (commission).

Salazar Lopez, Jose: b. Jan. 12, 1910, Ameca, Mexico; ord. priest May 26, 1934, in Rome; instrumental in building of new seminary at Guadalajara, the largest in Mexico; vice-rector and later rector of seminary; ord. titular bishop of Prusiade and coadjutor bishop of Zamora, Aug. 20, 1961; bishop of Zamora, 1967-70; archbishop of Guadalajara, Feb. 21, 1970; cardinal Mar. 5, 1973; titular church, Santa Emerentia. Archbishop of Guadalajara. Curial membership:
Sacraments (congregation).

Satowaki,* Joseph Asajiro: b. Feb. 1, 1904, Shittsu, Japan; ord. priest Dec. 17, 1932; served in various pastoral capacities in Nagasaki archdiocese after his ordination; apostolic administrator of Taiwan (then a Japanese possession), 1941-45; director of Nagasaki minor seminary, 1945-57; vicar general of Nagasaki, 1945; ord. first bishop of Kagoshima, May 3, 1955; archbishop of Nagasaki, Dec. 19, 1968; cardinal June 30, 1979; titular church, St. Mary of Peace. Archbishop of Nagasaki.

Scherer,* Alfred Vicente: b. Feb. 5, 1903, Bom Principio, Brazil; ord. priest Apr. 3, 1926; ord. archbishop of Porto Alegre, Feb. 23, 1947 (retired Aug. 29, 1981); cardinal Apr. 28, 1969; titular church, Our Lady of La Salette. Archbishop emeritus of Porto Alegre, Brazil.

Sensi, Giuseppe Maria: b. May 27, 1907, Cosenza, Italy; ord. priest Dec. 21, 1929; entered Vatican diplomatic service; served in nunciatures in Hungary, Switzerland, Belgium and Czechoslovakia, 1934-49; ord. titular archbishop of Sardes, July 24, 1955; apostolic nuncio to Costa Rica, 1955; apostolic delegate to Jerusalem, 1956-62; nuncio to Ireland, 1962-67, and Portugal, 1967-76; cardinal May 24, 1976; deacon, SS. Biagio e Carlo (ai Catinari). Curial membership:
State of Vatican City (commission).

Sidarouss,* Stephanos I, C.M.: b. Feb. 22, 1904, Cairo, Egypt; ord. priest July 2, 1939; ord. titular bishop of Sais, Jan. 25, 1948; auxiliary to the patriarch of Alexandria for the Copts, 1948-58; patriarch of Alexandria, May 10, 1958 (resigned May,

1986); cardinal Feb. 22, 1965. Patriarch emeritus of Alexandria for the Copts. Curial membership:
Revision of Code of Oriental Canon Law (commission).

Silva Henriquez, Raul, S.D.B.: b. Sept. 27, 1907, Talca, Chile; ord. priest July 3, 1938; ord. bishop of Valparaiso, Nov. 29, 1959; archbishop of Santiago de Chile, 1961-83; cardinal Mar. 19, 1962; titular church, St. Bernard (alle Terme). Archbishop emeritus of Santiago de Chile.

Simonis, Adrianus J.: b. Nov. 26, 1931, Lisse, Netherlands; ord. priest June 15, 1957; ord. bishop of Rotterdam, Mar. 20, 1971; coadjutor archbishop of Utrecht, July 8, 1983; archbishop of Utrecht, Dec. 3, 1983; cardinal May 25, 1985; titular church, St. Clement. Archbishop of Utrecht. Curial membership:
Sacraments (congregation); Christian Unity (secretariat).

Sin, Jaime L.: b. Aug. 31, 1928, New Washington, Philippines; ord. priest Apr. 3, 1954; diocesan missionary in Capiz, 1954-57; app. first rector of the St. Pius X Seminary, Roxas City, 1957; ord. titular bishop of Obba and auxiliary bishop of Jaro, Mar. 18, 1967; apostolic administrator of archdiocese of Jaro, June 20, 1970; titular archbishop of Massa Lubrense and coadjutor archbishop of Jaro, Jan. 15, 1972; archbishop of Jaro, Oct. 8, 1972; archbishop of Manila, Jan. 21, 1974; cardinal May 24, 1976; titular church, S. Maria (ai Monti). Archbishop of Manila. Curial membership:
Council for Public Affairs of the Church; Bishops, Sacraments, Divine Worship, Clergy, Evangelization of Peoples, Catholic Education (congregations); Non-Christians (secretariat); Social Communications (commission); Economic Affairs (office).

Siri,* Giuseppe: b. May 20, 1906, Genoa, Italy; ord. priest Sept. 22, 1928; ord. titular bishop of Liviade and auxiliary bishop of Genoa, May 7, 1944; archbishop of Genoa, May 14, 1946; cardinal Jan. 12, 1953; titular church, St. Mary (della Vittoria). Archbishop of Genoa, apostolic administrator of Bobbio. Curial membership:
Clergy, Catholic Education (congregations).

Stickler, Alfons, S.D.B.: b. Aug. 23, 1910, Neunkirchen, Austria; ord. priest Mar. 27, 1937; director of the Vatican Library, 1971; ord. titular bishop of Bolsena, Nov. 1, 1983; archbishop; Pro-Librarian and Pro-Archivist, 1984; cardinal May 25, 1985; deacon, St. George (in Valabro). Librarian and Archivist of the Holy Roman Church, 1985. Curial membership:
Religious and Secular Institutes, Causes of Saints (congregations); Apostolic Signatura (tribunal); Authentic Interpretation of Code of Canon Law, Social Communications (commissions); Patrimony of the Holy See (office).

Suenens,* Leo Josef: b. July 16, 1904, Brussels, Belgium; ord. priest Sept. 4, 1927; ord. titular bishop of Isinda, Dec. 16, 1945; auxiliary bishop of Mechelen, 1945-61; archbishop of Mechelen-Brussels, 1961-79; cardinal Mar. 19, 1962; titular church, St. Peter in Chains. Archbishop emeritus of Mechelen-Brussels.

Suquia Goicoechea, Angel: b. Oct. 2, 1916, Zaldivia, Spain; ord. priest July 7, 1940; ord. bishop of Almeria, July 16, 1966; bishop of Malaga, 1969-73; archbishop of Santiago de Compostela, 1973-83; archbishop of Madrid, Apr. 12, 1983; cardinal May 25, 1985; titular church, Great Mother of God. Archbishop of Madrid. Curial membership:
Council for Public Affairs of the Church; Bishops, Catholic Education (congregations).

Taofinu'u, Pio, S.M.: b. Dec. 9, 1923, Falealupo, W. Samoa; ord. priest Dec. 8, 1954; joined Society of Mary, 1955; ord. bishop of Apia (Samoa and Tokelau), May 29, 1968, the first Polynesian bishop; cardinal Mar. 5, 1973; titular church, St. Humphrey. Archbishop of Samoa-Apia and Tokelau (Sept. 10, 1982). Curial membership:
Causes of Saints (congregation).

Thiandoum, Hyacinthe: b. Feb. 2, 1921, Poponguine, Senegal; ord. priest Apr. 18, 1949; studied at Gregorian University, Rome, 1951-53; returned to Senegal, 1953; ord. archbishop of Dakar, May 20, 1962; cardinal May 24, 1976; titular church, S. Maria (del Popolo). Archbishop of Dakar. Curial membership:
Clergy, Religious and Secular Institutes (congregations); Social Communications (commission).

Tomasek,* Frantisek: b. June 30, 1899, Studenka, Moravia, Czechoslovakia; ord. priest July 5, 1922; professor of pedagogy and catechetics at the theology faculty of Olomouc, 1934-39; resumed academic activity after liberation in 1945; author, *Catechism of the Catholic Religion;* ord. titular bishop of Butus and auxiliary of Olomouc, Oct. 13, 1949; only Czech bishop to attend Second Vatican Council; apostolic administrator of Prague, Feb. 18, 1965; cardinal May 24, 1976 (*in pectore*); solemnly proclaimed at June 27, 1977, consistory; titular church, Sts. Vitalis, Valeria, Gervase and Protase. Archbishop of Prague, 1978. Curial membership:
Clergy (congregation).

Tomko, Jozef: b. Mar. 11, 1924, Udavake, Slovakia; ord. priest Mar. 12, 1949; ord. titular archbishop of Doclea, Sept, 15, 1979; secretary-general of the Synod of Bishops, 1979-85; cardinal May 25, 1985; deacon, Jesus the Good Shepherd (alla Montagnola). Prefect of the Congregation for the Evangelization of Peoples, 1985. Curial membership:
Council for Public Affairs of the Church; Bishops, Religious and Secular Institutes, Catholic Education (congregations); Christian Unity, Non-Christians, Non-Believers (secretariats); Authentic Interpretation of Code of Canon Law, State of Vatican City (commissions).

Trinh van-Can, Joseph-Marie: b. Mar. 19, 1921, Trac But, Vietnam; ord. priest Dec. 3, 1949; held various offices in Hanoi archdiocese; ord. titular bishop of Ela (with personal title of archbishop) and coadjutor archbishop of Hanoi, June 2, 1963; archbishop of Hanoi, Nov. 27, 1978; cardinal June 30, 1979; titular church, St. Mary in Via. Archbishop of Hanoi. Curial membership:
Evangelization of Peoples (congregation).

Tzadua, Paulos: b. Aug. 25, 1921, Addifini, Ethiopia; ord. priest Mar. 12, 1944; ord. titular bishop of Abila di Palestina and auxiliary of Addis Ababa, May 20, 1973; archbishop of Addis Ababa, Feb. 24, 1977; cardinal May 25, 1985; titular church, Most Holy Name of Mary (a Via Latina). Archbishop of Addis Ababa. Curial membership:
Oriental Churches (congregation); Non-Christians (secretariat); Revision of Oriental Code of Canon Law (commission).

Ursi, Corrado: b. July 26, 1908, Andria, Italy; ord. priest July 25, 1931; vice-rector and later rector of the Pontifical Regional Seminary of Molfetta, 1931-51; ord. bishop of Nardo, Sept. 30, 1951; archbishop of Acerenza, Nov. 30, 1961; archbishop of Naples, May 23, 1966; cardinal June 26, 1967; titular church, St. Callistus. Archbishop of Naples. Curial membership:
Catholic Education (congregation).

Vachon, Louis-Albert; b. Feb. 4, 1912, Saint-Frederic, Que., Canada; ord. p.·iest June 11, 1938; ord. titular bishop of Mesarfelta and auxiliary of Quebec, May 14, 1977; archbishop of Quebec, Mar. 20, 1981; cardinal May 25, 1985; titular church, St. Paul of the Cross (a Corviale). Archbishop of Quebec. Curial membership:
Clergy (congregation).

Vaivods,* Julijans: b. Aug. 18, 1895, Vorkova, Latvia; ord. priest Apr. 7, 1918; chaplain of various schools, 1918-23; wrote and published catechetical books and theatrical works for youth; vicar general of Liepaja, 1944; apostolic activity curtailed by political situation, he resumed writing; publications denounced as hostile to regime, he was tried and sentenced to two years' exile, 1958-60; released early but not permitted to exercise his priestly ministry for a time; vicar general of Riga, 1962; attended Vatican II, 1964; ord. titular bishop of Macriana Maior and apostolic administrator of archdiocese of Riga and diocese of Liepaja, Nov. 18, 1964, in Rome; cardinal Feb. 2, 1983; titular church, SS. Quattro Coronati. Apostolic administrator of Riga and Liepaja.

Vidal, Ricardo J.: b. Feb. 6, 1931, Magpoc, Philippines; ord. priest Mar. 17, 1956; ord. titular bishop of Claterna and coadjutor of Melalos, Nov. 30, 1971; archbishop of Lipa, 1973; coadjutor archbishop of Cebu, Apr. 13, 1981; archbishop of Cebu, Aug. 24, 1982; cardinal May 25, 1985; titular church, Sts. Peter and Paul (in Via Ostiensi). Archbishop of Cebu. Curial membership:
Divine Worship (congregation); Health Care Workers (commission).

Volk,* Hermann: b. Dec. 27, 1903, Steinheim, Germany; ord. priest Apr. 2, 1927; professor of dogmatic theology at University of Muenster; ord. bishop of Mainz, June 5, 1962 (retired Dec. 27, 1982); cardinal Mar. 5, 1973; titular church, Saints Fabian and Venanzio (at Villa Fiorelli). Archbishop emeritus of Mainz.

Wetter, Friedrich: b. Feb. 20, 1928, Landau, West Germany; ord. priest Oct. 10, 1953; ord. bishop of Speyer, June 29, 1968; archbishop of Munich and Freising, Oct. 28, 1982; cardinal May 25, 1985; titular church, St. Stephen (al Monte Celio). Archbishop of Munich and Freising. Curial membership:

Evangelization of Peoples (congregation); Non-Christians (secretariat).

Willebrands, Johannes: b. Sept. 4, 1909, Bovenkarspel, The Netherlands; ord. priest May 26, 1934; ord. titular bishop of Mauriana, June 28, 1964; secretary of Secretariat for Christian Unity, 1960-69; cardinal Apr. 28, 1969; titular church, St. Sebastian (alle Catacombe); archbishop of Utrecht, 1975-83. President of Secretariat for Christian Unity. Curial membership:

Doctrine of Faith, Sacraments, Oriental Churches, Catholic Education, Evangelization of Peoples (congregations), Revision of Oriental Code of Canon Law (commission).

Williams, Thomas Stafford: b. Mar. 20, 1930, Wellington, New Zealand; ord. priest Dec. 20, 1959, in Rome; studied in Ireland after ordination, receiving degree in social sciences; served in various pastoral assignments on his return to New Zealand; missionary in Western Samoa to 1976; ord. archbishop of Wellington, New Zealand, Dec. 20, 1979; cardinal Feb. 2, 1983; titular church, Jesus the Divine Teacher at Pineda Sacchetti. Archbishop of Wellington. Curial membership:

Divine Worship, Evangelization of Peoples (congregations); Non-Christians (secretariat).

Yago, Bernard: b. July, 1916, Pass, Ivory Coast; ord. priest May 1, 1947; ord. archbishop of Abidjan, May 8, 1960, by Pope John XXIII in St. Peter's Basilica, becoming the first native member of the hierarchy of Ivory Coast; cardinal Feb. 2, 1983; titular church, St. Chrysogonus. Archbishop of Abidjan. Curial membership:

Evangelization of Peoples (congregation); Christian Unity (secretariat).

Zoungrana, Paul, P.A.: b. Sept. 3, 1917, Ouagadougou, Upper Volta (now Burkina Faso); ord. priest May 2, 1942, in the Missionaries of Africa; ord. archbishop of Ouagadougou at St. Peter's Basilica by John XXIII, May 8, 1960; cardinal Feb. 22, 1965; titular church, St. Camillus de Lellis. Archbishop of Ouagadougou. Curial membership:

Divine Worship, Religious and Secular Institutes, Evangelization of Peoples (congregations); Health Care Workers (commission).

CATEGORIES OF CARDINALS
(As of Aug. 15, 1986.)

Information below includes categories of cardinals and dates of consistories at which they were created. Seniority or precedence usually depends on order of elevation.

Two of these cardinals were named by Pius XII (consistory of Jan. 12, 1953); 7 by John XXIII (consistories of Dec. 15, 1958, Mar. 28, 1960, and Mar. 19, 1962); 77 by Paul VI (consistories of Feb. 22, 1965, June 26, 1967, Apr. 28, 1969, Mar. 5, 1973, May 24, 1976, and June 27, 1977); 60 by John Paul II (consistories of June 30, 1979, Feb. 2, 1983, May 25, 1985).

Order of Bishops

Titular Bishops of Suburban Sees: Agnelo Rossi (Feb. 22, 1965); Francesco Carpino (June 26, 1967); Paolo Bertoli (Apr. 28, 1969); Sebastiano Baggio (Apr. 28, 1969); Agostino Casaroli (June 30, 1979).

Eastern Rite Patriarchs: Stephanos I Sidarouss, C.M. (Feb. 22, 1965); Antoine Pierre Khoraiche (Feb. 2, 1983).

Order of Priests

1953 (Jan. 12): Giuseppe Siri, Paul Emile Leger, S.S.

1958 (Dec. 15): Jose M. Bueno y Monreal, Franz Koenig.

1960 (Mar. 28): Bernard Jan Alfrink, Laurean Rugambwa.

1962 (Mar. 19): Juan Landazuri Ricketts, O.F.M., Raul Silva Henriquez, S.D.B., Leo Josef Suenens.

1965 (Feb. 22): Thomas B. Cooray, Owen McCann, Leon-Etienne Duval, Paul Zoungrana, Giovanni Colombo.

1967 (June 26): Gabriel Garrone, Patrick O'Boyle, Maximilien de Furstenberg, Jose Clemente Maurer, C.SS.R., Pietro Parente, John J. Krol, Corrado Ursi, Justin Darmojuwono, Michele Pellegrino.

1969 (Apr. 28): Alfredo Vicente Scherer, Gordon J. Gray, Silvio Oddi, Giuseppe Paupini, Joseph Parecattil, John F. Dearden, Francois Marty;

George Flahiff, Paul Gouyon, Vicente Enrique y Tarancon, Joseph Malula, Pablo Muñoz Vega, S.J.;

John J. Carberry, Stephan Sou Hwan Kim, Eugenio de Araujo Sales, Joseph Hoeffner, Johannes Willebrands, Mario Nasalli Rocca di Corneliano, Sergio Guerri.

1973 (Mar. 5): Antonio Ribeiro, Avelar Brandao Vilela, Joseph Cordeiro, Anibal Muñoz Duque, Pietro Palazzini, Luis Aponte Martinez, Raul Francisco Primatesta, Salvatore Pappalardo, Ferdinando Giuseppe Antonelli, Marcelo Gonzalez Martin, Louis Jean Guyot, Ugo Poletti, Timothy Manning, Maurice Otunga, Jose Salazar Lopez, Paulo Evaristo Arns, James Darcy Freeman, Narciso Jubany Arnau, Hermann Volk, Pio Taofinu'u.

1976 (May 24): Octavio Beras Rojas, Juan Carlos Aramburu, Hyacinthe Thiandoum, Emmanuel Nsubuga, Lawrence Trevor Picachy, Jaime L. Sin, William W. Baum, Aloisio Lorscheider, George Basil Hume, O.S.B., Victor Razafimahatratra, Frantisek Tomasek, Dominic Ekandem.

1977 (June 27): Bernardin Gantin, Joseph Ratzinger.

1979 (June 30): Marco Ce, Joseph-Marie Trinh van-Can, Ernesto Corripio Ahumada, Joseph Asajiro Satowaki, Roger Etchegaray, Anastasio Alberto Ballestrero, O.C.D., Tomas O'Fiaich, Gerald Emmett Carter, Franciszek Macharski.

1983 (Feb. 2): Bernard Yago, Franjo Kuharic, Jose Ali Lebrun Moratinos, Joseph L. Bernardin, Michael Michai Kitbunchu, Alexandre do Nascimento, Alfonso Lopez Trujillo, Godfried Danneels, Thomas Stafford Williams, Carlo Maria Martini, Jean-Marie Lustiger, Jozef Glemp, Julijans Vaivods, Joachim Meisner.

1985 (May 25): Juan Francisco Fresno Larrain, Miguel Obando Bravo, Angel Suquia Goicoechea, Ricardo Vidal, Henryk Roman Gulbinowicz, Paulus Tzadua, Myroslav Ivan Lubachivsky, Louis-Albert Vachon, Albert Decourtray, Friedrich Wetter, Silvano Piovanelli, Adrianus J. Simonis, Bernard F. Law, John J. O'Connor, Giacomo Biffi.

Order of Deacons

1976 (May 24): Opilio Rossi, Giuseppe Maria Sensi, Corrado Bafile, Eduardo Pironio.

1977 (June 27): Luigi Ciappi.

1979 (June 30): Giuseppe Caprio, Egano Righi-Lambertini, Ernesto Civardi, Wladyslaw Rubin.

1983 (Feb. 2): Aurelio Sabattani, Giuseppe Casoria, Henri de Lubac.

1985 (May 25): Luigi Dadaglio, Simon D. Lourdusamy, Francis A. Arinze, Antonio Innocenti, Paul Augustin Mayer, Jean Jerome Hamer, Jozef Tomko, Andrzej Maria Deskur, Paul Poupard, Rosalio Jose Castillo Lara, Edouard Gagnon, Alfons Stickler, S.D.B., Pietro Pavan.

Ineligible To Vote

As of Aug. 15, 1986, 34 of the 146 cardinals were ineligible to take part in a papal election in line with the apostolic letter *Ingravescentem Aetatem* effective Jan. 1, 1971, which limited the functions of cardinals after completion of their 80th year.

Cardinals affected were: Alfrink, Antonelli, Bafile, Bueno y Monreal, Carberry, Carpino, Colombo, Cooray, De Furstenberg, de Lubac, Duval, Flahiff, Garrone, Guerri, Guyot, Koenig, Leger, Marty, Maurer, Munoz Vega, Nasalli Rocca di Corneliano, O'Boyle, Parente, Pavan, Pellegrino, Righi-Lambertini, Satowaki, Scherer, Sidarouss, Siri, Suenens, Tomasek, Vaivods, Volk.

Three more cardinals were due to become ineligible to vote by the end of 1986: Ernesto Civardi, after Oct. 21; Octavio Antonio Beras Rojas, after Nov. 16; Joseph Hoeffner, after Dec. 24.

Cardinals completing their 80th year in 1987: Giuseppe Paupini, Feb. 25; Vicente Enrique y Taracon, May 14; Giuseppe Sensi, May 27; Owen McCann, June 29; Antoine Pierre Khoraiche, Sept. 20; Raul Silva Henriquez, S.D.B., Sept. 27; John F. Dearden, Oct. 15; James D. Freeman, Nov. 19.

DISTRIBUTION OF CARDINALS

As of Aug. 15, 1986, there were 146 cardinals from more than 50 countries or areas. Listed below are areas, countries, number and last names.

Europe — 76

Italy (34): Antonelli, Bafile, Baggio, Ballestrero, Bertoli, Biffi, Caprio, Carpino, Casaroli, Casoria, Cé, Ciappi, Civardi, Colombo, Dadaglio, Guerri, Innocenti, Martini, Nasalli Rocca di Corneliano, Oddi, Palazzini, Pappalardo, Parente, Paupini, Pavan, Pellegrino, Piovanelli, Poletti, Righi-Lambertini, Rossi, Sabattani, Sensi, Siri, Ursi.

France (9): Decourtray, De Lubac, Etchegaray, Garrone, Gouyon, Guyot, Lustiger, Marty, Poupard.

Germany (6): Hoeffner, Mayer, Meisner, Ratzinger, Volk, Wetter.

Poland (5): Deskur, Glemp, Gulbinowicz, Macharski, Rubin.

Spain (5): Bueno y Monreal, Enrique y Tarancon, Gonzalez Martin, Jubany Arnau, Suquia Goicoechea.

Netherlands (4): Alfrink, De Furstenberg, Simonis, Willebrands.

Belgium (3): Danneels, Hamer, Suenens.

Austria (2): Koenig, Stickler.

Czechoslovakia (2): Tomasek, Tomko (Slovakia).

One from each of the following countries: England, Hume; Ireland, O'Fiaich; Latvia (USSR), Vaivods; Portugal, Ribeiro; Scotland, Gray; Yugoslavia, Kuharic.

Asia — 13

India (3): Lourdusamy, Parecattil, Picachy.

Philippines (2): Sin, Vidal.

One from each of the following countries: Indonesia, Darmojuwono; Japan, Satowaki; Korea, Kim; Lebanon, Khoraiche; Pakistan, Cordeiro; Sri Lanka, Cooray; Thailand, Kitbunchu, Vietnam, Trinh van-Can.

Oceania — 3

Australia, Freeman; New Zealand, Williams; Pacific Islands (Samoa), Taofinu'u.

Africa — 16

Nigeria (2): Arinze, Ekandem.

One from each of the following countries: Algeria, Duval; Angola, do Nascimento; Benin, Gantin; Burkina Faso, Zoungrana; Egypt, Sidarouss; Ethiopia, Tzadua; Ivory Coast, Yago; Kenya, Otunga; Madagascar, Razafimahatratra; Senegal, Thiandoum; South Africa, McCann; Tanzania, Rugambwa; Uganda, Nsubuga; Zaire, Malula.

North America — 18

United States (10): Baum, Bernardin, Carberry, Dearden, Krol, Law, Lubachivsky (head of Lwow archdiocese in Ukraine), Manning, O'Boyle, O'Connor.

Canada (5): Carter, Flahiff, Gagnon, Leger, Vachon.

Mexico (2): Corripio Ahumada, Salazar Lopez.

Puerto Rico (1): Aponte Martinez.

Central and South America — 20

Brazil (6): Arns, Brandao Vilela, De Araujo Sales, Lorscheider, Rossi, Scherer.

Argentina (3): Aramburu, Pironio, Primatesta.

Chile (2): Fresno Larrain, Silva Henriquez.

Colombia (2): Lopez Trujillo, Munoz Duque.

Venezuela (2): Castillo Lara, Lebrun Moratinos.

One from each of the following countries: Bolivia, Maurer; Dominican Republic, Beras Rojas; Ecuador, Munoz Vega, S.J.; Nicaragua, Obando Bravo; Peru, Landazuri Ricketts.

Cardinals of U.S.

As of Aug. 15, 1986, U.S. cardinals, years of elevation and sees.

Patrick A. O'Boyle, 1967, Washington (retired 1973); John J. Krol, 1967, Philadelphia; John F. Dearden, 1969, Detroit (retired 1980); John J. Carberry, 1969, St. Louis (retired 1979); Timothy Manning, 1973, Los Angeles (retired 1985); William W. Baum, 1976, Washington, D.C. (1973-80); prefect of Congregation for Catholic Education, 1980; Joseph L. Bernardin, 1983, Chicago; Myroslav Lubachivsky, 1985, Lwow of the Ukrainians; Bernard F. Law, 1985, Boston; John J. O'Connor, 1985, New York.

Deceased cardinals of the United States,. Data: years of elevation, sees, years of birth and death.

John McCloskey, 1875, New York, 1810-1885; James Gibbons, 1886, Baltimore, 1834-1921; John Farley, 1911, New York, 1842-1918; William O'Connell, 1911, Boston, 1859-1944; Dennis Dougherty, 1921, Philadelphia, 1865-1951; Patrick Hayes, 1924, New York, 1867-1938; George Mundelein, 1924, Chicago, 1872-1939; John Glennon, 1946, St. Louis, 1862-1946; Edward Mooney, 1946, Detroit, 1882-1958;

Francis Spellman, 1946, New York, 1889-1967; Samuel Stritch, 1946, Chicago, 1887-1958; James F. McIntyre, 1953, Los Angeles, 1886-1979; John O'Hara, C.S.C., 1958, Philadelphia, 1888-1960; Richard Cushing, 1958, Boston, 1895-1970; Albert Meyer, 1959, Chicago, 1903-1965; Aloysius Muench, 1959, Fargo (and papal nuncio), 1889-1962; Joseph Ritter, 1961, St. Louis, 1892-1967; Francis Brennan, 1967, official of Roman Curia, 1894-1968; John P. Cody, 1967, Chicago 1907-1982; John J. Wright, 1969, prefect of Congregation for Clergy, 1909-1979; Humberto S. Medeiros, 1973, Boston, 1915-1983; Terence J. Cooke, 1969, New York, 1921-1983; Lawrence J. Shehan, 1965, Baltimore, 1898-1984.

REPRESENTATIVES OF THE HOLY SEE

Papal representatives and their functions were the subject of a document entitled *Sollicitudo Omnium Ecclesiarum* which Pope Paul VI issued on his own initiative under the date of June 24, 1969.

Delegates and Nuncios

Papal representatives "receive from the Roman Pontiff the charge of representing him in a fixed way in the various nations or regions of the world.

"When their legation is only to local churches, they are known as apostolic delegates. When to this legation, of a religious and ecclesial nature, there is added diplomatic legation to states and governments, they receive the title of nuncio, pronuncio, and internuncio."

[An apostolic nuncio has the diplomatic rank of ambassador extraordinary and plenipotentiary. Traditionally, because the Vatican diplomatic service has the longest uninterrupted history in the world, a nuncio has precedence among diplomats in the country to which he is accredited and serves as dean of the diplomatic corps on state occasions. Since 1965 pro-nuncios, also of ambassadorial rank, have been assigned to countries in which this prerogative is not recognized.]

(Other representatives, who are covered in the Almanac article, Vatican Representatives to International Organizations, are clerics and lay persons "who form . . . part of a pontifical mission attached to international organizations or take part in conferences and congresses." They are variously called delegates or observers.)

"The primary and specific purpose of the mission of a papal representative is to render ever closer and more operative the ties that bind the Apostolic See and the local churches.

"The ordinary function of a pontifical representative is to keep the Holy See regularly and objectively informed about the conditions of the ecclesial community to which he has been sent, and about what may affect the life of the Church and the good of souls.

"On the one hand, he makes known to the Holy See the thinking of the bishops, clergy, religious and faithful of the territory where he carries out his mandate, and forwards to Rome their proposals and their requests; on the other hand, he makes himself the interpreter, with those concerned, of the acts, documents, information and instructions emanating from the Holy See."

Service and Liaison

Representatives, while carrying out their general and special duties, are bound to respect the autonomy of local churches and bishops. Their service and liaison responsibilities include the following:

• **Nomination of Bishops:** To play a key role in compiling, with the advice of ecclesiastics and lay persons, and submitting lists of names of likely candidates to the Holy See with their own recommendations.

• **Bishops:** To aid and counsel local bishops without interfering in the affairs of their jurisdictions.

• **Episcopal Conferences:** To maintain close relations with them and to assist them in every possible way. (Papal representatives do not belong to these conferences.)

• **Religious Communities of Pontifical Rank:** To advise and assist major superiors for the purpose of promoting and consolidating conferences of men and women religious and to coordinate their apostolic activities.

• **Church-State Relations:** The thrust in this area is toward the development of sound relations with civil governments and collaboration in work for peace and the total good of the whole human family.

The mission of a papal representative begins with appointment and assignment by the pope and continues until termination of his mandate. He acts "under the guidance and according to the instructions of the cardinal secretary of state and prefect of the Council for the Public Affairs of the Church, to whom he is directly responsible for the execution of the mandate entrusted to him by the Supreme Pontiff." Normally, representatives are required to retire at the age of 75.

NUNCIOS AND DELEGATES

(Sources: *Annuario Pontificio, L'Osservatore Romano, Acta Apostolicae Sedis,* NC News Service.)

Data, as of July 15, 1986, country, rank of legation (corresponding to rank of legate unless otherwise noted), name of legate (archbishop unless otherwise noted) as available.

Delegate for Papal Representatives: Archbishop Giovanni Coppa. The post was established in 1973 to coordinate papal diplomatic efforts throughout the world. The office entails responsibility for "following more closely through timely visits the activities of papal representatives . . . and encouraging their rapport with the central offices" of the Secretariat of State and the Council for the Public Affairs of the Church.

Africa, Southern (Botswana, South Africa, Namibia, Swaziland): Pretoria, South Africa, Apostolic Delegation; Joseph Mees (also Pro-Nuncio to Lesotho).

Algeria: Algiers, Nunciature; Pro-Nuncio (He is also Pro-Nuncio to Tunisia and Apostolic Delegate to Libya.)

Angola: Luanda, Apostolic Delegation; Fortunato Baldelli (also Pro-Nuncio to Sao Tome and Principe).

Antilles: Apostolic Delegation; Manuel Monteiro de Castro (resides in Port of Spain, Trinidad).

Argentina: Buenos Aires, Nunciature; Ubaldo Calabresi.

Australia: Canberra, Nunciature; Franco Brambilla, Pro-Nuncio.

Austria: Vienna, Nunciature; Michele Cecchini.

Bahamas: Nunciature; Manuel Monteiro de Castro. Pro-Nuncio (resides in Port of Spain, Trinidad).

Bangladesh: Dacca, Nunciature; Luigi Accogli, Pro-Nuncio (also serves as Apostolic Delegate to Burma.)

Barbados: Nunciature; Manuel Monteiro de Castro. Pro-Nuncio (resides in Port of Spain, Trinidad).

Belgium: Brussels, Nunciature; Angelo Pedroni (also Nuncio to Luxembourg and European Community).

Belize: Nunciature; Manuel Monteiro de Castro, Pro-Nuncio (resides in Port-of-Spain, Trinidad).

Benin (formerly Dahomey): Nunciature; Ivan Dias, Pro-Nuncio (resides in Accra, Ghana).

Bolivia: La Paz, Nunciature; Santos Abril y Castello.

Botswana: See Africa, Southern.

Brazil: Brasilia, Nunciature; Carlo Furno.

Brunei: See Malaysia and Brunei.

Burkina Faso: Ouagadougou, Nunciature; Antonio Mattiazzo, Pro-Nuncio (resides in Abidjan, Ivory Coast).

Burma: See Bangladesh.

Burundi: Bujumbura, Nunciature; Pietro Sambi, Pro-Nuncio.

Cameroon: Yaounde, Nunciature; Donato Squicciarino, Pro-Nuncio (also Pro-Nuncio to Gabon and Equatorial Guinea).

Canada: Ottawa, Nunciature; Angelo Palmas, Pro-Nuncio.

Cape Verde, Republic of: Nunciature; Pablo Puente, Pro-Nuncio (resides in Dakar, Senegal).

Central African Republic: Bangui, Nunciature; Giovanni Bulaitis, Pro-Nuncio (also Pro-Nuncio to Congo and Apostolic Delegate to Chad).

Chad: Apostolic Delegation; Giovanni Bulaitis (resides in Bangui, Central African Republic).

Chile: Santiago, Nunciature; Angelo Sodano.

China: Taipei (Taiwan), Nunciature.

Colombia: Bogota, Nunciature; Angelo Acerbi.

Congo: Brazzaville, Nunciature; Giovanni Bulaitis, Pro-Nuncio (resides in Bangui, Central African Republic).

Costa Rica: San Jose, Nunciature; Pier Giacomo de Nicolo.

Cuba: Havana, Nunciature; Giulio Einaudi, Pro-Nuncio.

Cyprus: Nicosia, Nunciature; Carlo Curis, Pro-Nuncio (also Apostolic Delegate to Jerusalem).

Denmark: Copenhagen, Nunciature; Henri Lemaitre, Pro-Nuncio (also Pro-Nuncio to Finland, Iceland, Norway and Sweden).

Djibouti: See Red Sea Region.

Dominica: Nunciature; Manuel Monteiro de Castro, Pro-Nuncio (resides in Port-of-Spain, Trinidad).

Dominican Republic: Santo Domingo, Nunciature; Blasco Francisco Collaco (also Apostolic Delegate to Puerto Rico).

Ecuador: Quito, Nunciature; Vincenzo Farano.

Egypt: Cairo, Nunciature; Giovanni Moretti, Pro-Nuncio.

El Salvador: San Salvador, Nunciature; Francesco De Nittis.

Equatorial Guinea: Santa Isabel, Nunciature; Donato Squicciarino, Pro-Nuncio (resides in Yaounde, Cameroon).

Ethiopia: Addis Ababa, Nunciature; Thomas White, Pro-Nuncio.

Fiji: Nunciature; Antonio Magnoni, Pro-Nuncio (resides in New Zealand).

Finland: Helsinki, Nunciature; Henri Lemaitre, Pro-Nuncio (resides in Denmark).

France: Paris, Nunciature; Angelo Felici.

Gabon: Libreville, Nunciature; Donato Squicciarino, Pro-Nuncio (resides in Yaounde, Cameroon).

Gambia: Nunciature; Romeo Panciroli, Pro-Nuncio (resides in Monrovia, Liberia).

Germany: Bonn, Nunciature; Giuseppe Uhac.

Ghana: Accra, Nunciature; Ivan Dias, Pro-Nuncio (also Pro-Nuncio to Benin and Togo).

Great Britain: London, Nunciature; Luigi Barbarito, Pro-Nuncio (also papal representative to Gibraltar).

Greece: Athens, Nunciature; Giovanni Mariani, Pro-Nuncio.

Grenada: Nunciature; Manuel Monteiro de

Castro, Pro-Nuncio (resides in Port of Spain, Trinidad).

Guatemala: Guatemala City, Nunciature; Oriano Quilici.

Guinea: Conakry, Nunciature (1986); Romeo Panciroli, Pro-Nuncio (resides in Monrovia, Liberia).

Guinea-Bissau: Nunciature (1986); Pablo Puente, Pro-Nuncio (resides at Dakar, Senegal).

Haiti: Port-au-Prince, Nunciature; Paolo Romeo.

Honduras: Tegucigalpa, Nunciature; Francesco De Nittis (also Nuncio to El Salvador).

Iceland: Nunciature; Henri Lemaitre, Pro-Nuncio (resides in Denmark).

India: New Delhi, Nunciature; Agostino Caccavillan, Pro-Nuncio.

Indonesia: Jakarta, Nunciature; Francesco Canolini, Pro-Nuncio.

Iran: Teheran, Nunciature; Giovanni De Andrea, Pro-Nuncio.

Iraq: Baghdad, Nunciature; Luigi Conti, Pro-Nuncio (also Pro-Nuncio to Kuwait).

Ireland: Dublin, Nunciature; Gaetano Alibrandi.

Italy: Rome, Nunciature; Luigi Poggi.

Ivory Coast: Abidjan, Nunciature; Antonio Mattiazzo, Pro-Nuncio (also Pro-Nuncio to Niger and Burkina Faso).

Jamaica: Nunciature; Manuel Monteiro de Castro, Pro-Nuncio (resides in Port of Spain, Trinidad).

Japan: Tokyo, Nunciature; William A. Carew, Pro-Nuncio.

Jerusalem, Palestine, Jordan, Israel: Jerusalem, Apostolic Delegation; Carlo Curis (also Pro-Nuncio to Cyprus).

Kenya: Nairobi, Nunciature; Clemente Faccani, Pro-Nuncio.

Korea: Seoul, Nunciature; Francesco Monterisi, Pro-Nuncio.

Kuwait: Al Kuwait, Nunciature; Luigi Conti, Pro-Nuncio (resides in Baghdad, Iraq).

Laos: Apostolic Delegation; Renato Raffaele Martino (resides in Bangkok, Thailand).

Lebanon: Beirut, Nunciature; Luciano Angeloni.

Lesotho: Maseru, Nunciature; Joseph Mees, Pro-Nuncio (resides in Pretoria, S. Africa).

Liberia: Monrovia, Nunciature; Romeo Panciroli, Pro-Nuncio (also Pro-Nuncio to Gambia and Guinea and Apostolic Delegate to Sierra Leone).

Libya: Apostolic Delegation; (resides in Algiers, Algeria).

Luxembourg: Nunciature; Angelo Pedroni (resides in Brussels, Belgium).

Madagascar: Tananarive, Nunciature; Agostino Marchetto, Pro-Nuncio (also Pro-Nuncio to Mauritius and Apostolic Delegate to Reunion).

Malawi: Lilongwe, Nunciature; Eugenio Sbarbaro, Pro-Nuncio (resides in Zambia).

Malaysia and Brunei: Apostolic Delegation; Renato Raffaele Martino (resides in Bangkok, Thailand).

Mali: Nunciature; Pablo Puente, Pro-Nuncio (resides in Dakar, Senegal).

Malta: La Valletta, Nunciature; Pier Luigi Celata.

Mauritania: Nouakchott, Apostolic Delegation; Pablo Puente (resides in Dakar, Senegal).

Mauritius: Port Louis, Nunciature; Agostino Marchetto, Pro-Nuncio (resides in Tananarive, Madagascar).

Mexico: Mexico City, Apostolic Delegation; Girolamo Prigione.

Morocco: Rabat, Nunciature; Bernard Jacqueline, Pro-Nuncio.

Mozambique: Maputo, Apostolic Delegation; Patrick Coveney (also Pro-Nuncio to Zimbabwe).

Namibia: See Africa, Southern.

Nepal: Nunciature; Agostino Cacciavillan, Pro-Nuncio.

Netherlands: The Hague, Nunciature; Edward Cassidy, Pro-Nuncio.

New Zealand: Wellington, Nunciature; Antonio Magnoni, Pro-Nuncio. (He is also Pro-Nuncio to Fiji and Apostolic Delegate to Pacific Islands).

Nicaragua: Managua, Nunciature; Paolo Giglio.

Niger: Niamey, Nunciature; Antonio Mattiazzo, Pro-Nuncio (resides in Abidjan, Ivory Coast).

Nigeria: Lagos, Nunciature; Paul Fouad Tabet, Pro-Nuncio.

Norway: Nunciature; Henri Lemaitre, Pro-Nuncio (resides in Denmark).

Pacific Islands: Apostolic Delegation; Antonio Magnoni (resides in New Zealand).

Pakistan: Islamabad, Nunciature; Emanuele Gerada, Pro-Nuncio.

Panama: Panama, Nunciature; Jose Sebastian Laboa.

Papua New Guinea: Port Moresby; Nunciature; Antonio Maria Veglio, Pro-Nuncio. (He is also Pro-Nuncio to western and southern Solomon Islands.)

Paraguay: Asuncion, Nunciature; Georg Zur.

Peru: Lima, Nunciature; Luigi Dossena.

Philippines: Manila, Nunciature; Bruno Torpigliani.

Poland: Francesco Colasuonno, head of Holy See's delegation for permanent working contacts with the government of the People's Republic of Poland.

Portugal: Lisbon, Nunciature; Salvatore Asta.

Puerto Rico: See Dominican Republic.

Red Sea Region (Somalia, Djibouti, part of Arabian Peninsula): Apostolic Delegation; Luis Robles Diaz, (resides in Khartoum, Sudan).

Reunion: See Madagascar.

Rhodesia: See Zimbabwe.

Rwanda: Kigali, Nunciature. Giovanni Battista Morandini, Pro-Nuncio.

Saint Lucia: Nunciature; Manuel Monteiro de Castro, Pro-Nuncio (resides in Port of Spain, Trinidad).

Sao Tome and Principe: Nunciature; Fortunato Baldelli, Pro-Nuncio (also apostolic delegate to Angola).

Senegal: Dakar, Nunciature; Pablo Puente, Pro-Nuncio (also Pro-Nuncio to Cape Verde,

Guinea-Bissau and Mali; Apostolic Delegate to Mauritania.)

Seychelles Islands: Nunciature; Clemente Faccani, Pro-Nuncio (resides in Nairobi, Kenya).

Sierra Leone: Apostolic Delegation; Romeo Panciroli (resides in Monrovia, Liberia).

Singapore: Nunciature; Renato Raffaele Martino, Pro-Nuncio (resides in Bangkok, Thailand).

Solomon Islands: Nunciature, Antonio Maria Veglio, Pro-Nuncio (resides in Port Moresby, Papua New Guinea).

Somalia: See Red Sea Region.

South Africa: See Africa, Southern.

Spain: Madrid, Nunciature; Mario Tagliaferri.

Sri Lanka: Colombo, Nunciature; Ambrose De Paoli, Pro-Nuncio.

Sudan: Khartoum, Nunciature; Luis Robles Diaz, Pro-Nuncio (also Apostolic Delegate to Red Sea Region).

Swaziland: See Africa, Southern.

Sweden: Nunciature; Henri Lemaitre, Pro-Nuncio (resides in Denmark).

Switzerland: Bern, Nunciature; Eduardo Rovida.

Syria (Syrian Arab Republic): Damascus, Nunciature; Nicola Rotunno, Pro-Nuncio.

Tanzania: Dar-es-Salaam, Nunciature; Gian Vincenzo Moreni, Pro-Nuncio.

Thailand: Bangkok, Nunciature; Renato Raffaelo Martino, Pro-Nuncio (also Pro-Nuncio to Singapore and Apostolic Delegate to Laos, Malaysia and Brunei).

Togo: Lome, Nunciature; Ivan Dias, Pro-Nuncio (resides in Accra, Ghana).

Trinidad and Tobago: Port of Spain, Trinidad, Nunciature; Manuel Monteiro de Castro, Pro-Nuncio (also Pro-Nuncio to Bahamas, Barbados, Belize, Dominica, Grenada, Jamaica, Saint Lucia and Apostolic Delegate to Antilles).

Tunisia: Tunis, Nunciature; Pro-Nuncio (resides in Algiers, Algeria).

Turkey: Ankara, Nunciature; Sergio Sebastiani, Pro-Nuncio.

Uganda: Kampala, Nunciature; Karl Joseph Rauber, Pro-Nuncio.

United States of America: Washington, D.C., Nunciature; Pio Laghi, Pro-Nuncio.

Uruguay: Montevideo, Nunciature; Andrea Cordero Lanza di Montezemolo.

Venezuela: Caracas, Nunciature; Luciano Storero.

Vietnam and Cambodia: Apostolic Delegation.

Yugoslavia: Belgrade, Nunciature; Gabriel Montalvo, Pro-Nuncio.

Zaire: Kinshasa-Gombe, Nunciature; Alfio Rapisarda, Pro-Nuncio.

Zambia: Lusaka, Nunciature; Eugenio Sbarbaro, Pro-Nuncio (also Pro-Nuncio to Malawi).

Zimbabwe: Nunciature; Patrick Coveney, Pro-Nuncio (is also Apostolic Delegate to Mozambique).

European Community: Brussels, Belgium, Nunciature; Angelo Pedroni, Nuncio.

Pro-Nuncio to U.S.

The representative of the Pope to the Church in the United States is Archbishop Pio Laghi, pro-nuncio. Archbishop Laghi was born May 21, 1922, in Castiglione, Italy. Ordained to the priesthood Apr. 20, 1946, he entered the Vatican diplomatic service in 1952. He served in Nicaragua, the U.S. (as secretary of the apostolic delegation, 1954-61) and India. He was recalled to Rome and served on the Council for the Public Affairs of the Church. He was appointed to the titular see of Mauriana and received episcopal ordination June 22, 1969. He was apostolic delegate to Jerusalem and Palestine, 1969-74, and apostolic nuncio to Argentina, 1974-80. On Dec. 10, 1980, he was appointed apostolic delegate to the United States and permanent observer to the Organization of American States.

He was named first pro-nuncio in 1984 when the U.S. and the Vatican reestablished diplomatic relations (See Index: U.S.-Vatican Relations).

The U.S. Apostolic Nunciature is located at 3339 Massachusetts Ave. N.W., Washington, D.C. 20008.

From 1893 to 1984, papal representatives to the Church in the U.S. were apostolic delegates (all archbishops): Francesco Satolli (1893-1896), Sebastiano Martinelli, O.S.A. (1896-1902), Diomede Falconio, O.F.M. (1902-1911), Giovanni Bonzano (1911-1922), Pietro Fumasoni-Biondi (1922-1933), Amleto Cicognani (1933-1958), Egidio Vagnozzi (1958-1967); Luigi Raimondi (1967-1973); Jean Jadot (1973-1980); Pio Laghi (1980-84).

DIPLOMATS AT VATICAN

(Sources: *Annuario Pontificio, L'Osservatore Romano, Acta Apostolicae Sedis*).

Listed below are countries maintaining diplomatic relations with the Vatican, dates of establishment (in some cases) and names of Ambassadors (as of July, 1986). Leaders (. . . . .) indicate the post was vacant.

The dean of the diplomatic corps at the Vatican is Ambassador Joseph Amichia of Ivory Coast (from 1971) who succeeded to the post in 1983.

Algeria (1972): Abdelmalek Benhabyles.
Argentina: Santiago Manuel de Estrado.
Australia (1973): Sir Peter Lawler.
Austria: Hans Pasch.
Bahamas (1979): . . . .
Bangladesh (1972): Ataul Karim.
Barbados (1979): Harold McDonald Forde.
Belgium (1835): Baron Alexandre Paternotte de La Vaille.
Belize (1983): . . . .
Benin (formerly Dahomey): Saliou Aboudou.
Bolivia: Carlos Romero Alvarez Garcia.
Brazil: Affonso Arinos de Mello-Franco.
Burkina Faso (1973): . . . .
Burundi: . . . .
Cameroon: Jean Melaga.
Canada (1969): Eldon Pattyson Black.
Cape Verde (1976): . . . .
Central African Republic (1975): Albert Sato.
Chile: Hector Riesle Contreras.
China (Taiwan): Chow Shu-Kai.

Colombia: Bernardo Gaitan Machecha.
Congo (1977): Jean-Marie Ewengue.
Costa Rica: Carlos Melendez Chaverri.
Cuba: Manuel Estevez Perez.
Cyprus (1973): Polys Modinos.
Denmark (1982): Troels Munk.
Dominica (1981): . . . . ,
Dominican Republic: Antonio Zaglul.
Ecuador: Francisco Alfredo Salazar Alvarado.
Egypt: Ahmed Ibrahim Adel.
El Salvador: Prudencio Llach Schonenberg.
Equatorial Guinea (1981): . . . .
Ethiopia: Gatechew Kebreth.
Fiji (1978): Sailosi Wai Kepa.
Finland: Kaarlo Yrjo-Koskinen.
France: Bertrand Dufourcq.
Gabon: . . . .
Gambia, The (1978): Samuel Jonathan Okikiola Sarr.
Germany: Peter Hermes.
Ghana: Mrs. Therese Striggner Scott.
Great Britain (1982): David Neil Lane.
Greece (1980): Christos Rokofyllis.
Grenada (1979): . . . .
Guatemala: Jose Alejandro Deutschmann Miron.
Guinea (1986): . . . .
Guinea-Bissau (1986): . . . .
Haiti: Pierre Pompee.
Honduras: Oscar Acosta.
Iceland: Niels P. Sigurdsson.
India: Ashoke Sen Chib.
Indonesia: Hardinan Sastrapoespita.
Iran: Seyed Hadi Khosrovshahian.
Iraq: Wassam Chawkat Al-Zawahi.
Ireland: . . . .
Italy: Andrea Cagiata.
Ivory Coast: Joseph Amichia.
Jamaica (1979): Glaister G. Duncan.
Japan: Sonoo Uchida.
Kenya: . . . .
Korea: Young Hoon Kang.
Kuwait: Essa Ahmad Al-Hamad.
Lebanon: Gazi Chidiac.
Lesotho: Reginald Mokheseng Tekateka.
Liberia: . . . .
Liechtenstein (1985) . . . .
Lithuania: Stasys Lozoraitis, Jr., first secretary.
Luxembourg: Jean Wagner.
Madagascar: . . . .
Malawi: Linnaeus Stephen Kauta Msiska.

Mali (1979): Yaya Diarra.
Malta: Paolo Farrugia.
Mauritius: Dhurma Gian Nath.
Monaco: Cesar Charles Solamito.
Morocco: Youssef Ben Abbes.
Nepal (1983):Simha Pratap Shah.
Netherlands: Seger Jan Joseph Van Voorst tot Voorst.
New Zealand (1973): John G. McArthur.
Nicaragua: Ricardo Agustin Peter Silva.
Niger (1971): . . . .
Nigeria: Edwin Morvan Ihama.
Norway (1982): Ketil Börde.
Order of Malta (see Index): Christophe de Kallay.
Pakistan: Saidulla Khan Dehlavi.
Panama: Jaime Ingram Jaen.
Papua New Guinea (1977): Peter Ipu Peipul.
Paraguay: Juan Livieres Argana.
Peru: Hugo de Zela Hurtado.
Philippines: . . . .
Portugal: João de sa Coutinho
Rwanda: Ildephonse Munyesayaka.
San Marino (1986): Dr. Giovanni Galassi.
Saint Lucia (1984): Francis J. Carasco.
Sao Tome and Principe (1984): . . . .
Senegal (1971): Andre Coulbray.
Seychelles (1984): . . . .
Singapore (1981): Chiang Hai Ding.
Solomon Islands (1984): . . . .
Spain: Don Gonzalo Puente Ojea.
Sri Lanka: Daluwatumulle Gamage Bandusena de Silva.
Sudan (1972): Sayed Yousif Mukhtar Yousif.
Sweden (1982): Gunnar Johan Ljungdahl.
Syria (Arab Republic): Adib Daoudy.
Tanzania: Ahmed Diria Hassan.
Thailand: Montri Jalichandra.
Togo (1981): . . . .
Trinidad and Tobago (1978): Maurice Oscar St. John.
Tunisia (1972): Abdelmadjid Chaker.
Turkey: Sulhi Dislioglu.
Uganda (1966): James Nagai Obua-Otoa.
United States (1984): . . . .
Uruguay: Alejandro Zorrilla de San Martin.
Venezuela: Reinaldo Leandro Rodriguez.
Yugoslavia: Stefan Cigoj.
Zaire: Atembina-te-Bombo.
Zambia: Peter Dingiswayo Zuze.
Zimbabwe (1980): Ben Kufakunesu Jambga.

U.S. — VATICAN RELATIONS

The United States and the Vatican announced Jan. 10, 1984, the establishment of full diplomatic relations, thus ending a gap of 117 years in their relations. The announcement followed action by the Congress in November, 1983, to end a prohibition on diplomatic relations enacted in 1867.

William A. Wilson, a Catholic and President Ronald Reagan's personal representative to the Vatican since February, 1981, was confirmed as the U.S. ambassador by the Senate on Mar. 7, 1984; he presented his credentials to Pope John Paul on Apr. 9, 1984. He resigned in May, 1986. As of Aug. 25, 1986, the post was vacant.

Archbishop Pio Laghi, apostolic delegate to the U.S. since 1980, was named pro-nuncio by the Pope on Mar. 26, 1984.

Nature of Relations

The nature of relations was described in nearly identical statements by John Hughes, a State Department spokesman, and the Vatican.

Hughes said: "The United States of America and the Holy See, in the desire to further promote the existing mutual friendly relations, have decided by common agreement to establish diplomatic relations between them at the level of embassy on the part of the United States of America, and nunciature on the part of the Holy See, as of today, Jan. 10, 1984."

The Vatican statement said: "The Holy See and the United States of America, desiring to develop the mutual friendly relations already existing, have decided by common accord to establish diplomatic relations at the level of apostolic nunciature on the side of the Holy See and of embassy on the side of the United States beginning today, Jan. 10, 1984."

The establishment of relations was criticized as a violation of the separation-of-church-and-state principle by spokesmen for the National Council of Churches, the National Association of Evangelicals, the Baptist Joint Committee on Public Affairs, Seventh Day Adventists, Americans United for Separation of Church and State, and the American Jewish Congress.

U.S. District Judge John P. Fullam, ruling May 7, 1985, in Philadelphia, dismissed a legal challenge to U.S.-Vatican relations brought by Americans United for Separation of Church and State. He stated that Americans United and its allies in the challenge lacked legal standing to sue, and that the courts did not have jurisdiction to intervene in foreign policy decisions of the executive branch of the U.S. government. Parties to the suit brought by Americans United were the National Association of Laity, the National Coalition of American Nuns and several Protestant church organizations.

Not a Religious Issue

Bishop James W. Malone, president of the U.S. Catholic Conference, said in a statement: "This matter has been discussed at length for many years. It is not a religious issue but a public policy question which, happily, has now been settled in this context."

Russell Shaw, a conference spokesman, said the decision to send an ambassador to the Vatican was not a church-state issue and "confers no special privilege or status on the Church."

Earlier Relations

Official relations for trade and diplomatic purposes were maintained by the United States and the Papal States while the latter had the character of and acted like other sovereign powers in the international community.

Consular relations developed in the wake of an announcement, made by the papal nuncio in Paris to the American mission there Dec. 15, 1784, that the Papal States had agreed to open several Mediterranean ports to U.S. shipping.

U.S. consular representation in the Papal States began with the appointment of John B. Sartori, a native of Rome, in June, 1797. Sartori's successors as consuls were: Felix Cicognani, also a Roman, and Americans George W. Greene, Nicholas Browne, William C. Sanders, Daniel LeRoy, Horatio V. Glentworth, W.J. Stillman, Edwin C. Cushman, David M. Armstrong.

Consular officials of the Papal States who served in the U.S. were: Count Ferdinand Lucchesi, 1826 to 1829, who resided in Washington; John B. Sartori, 1829 to 1841, who resided in Trenton, N.J.; Daniel J. Desmond, 1841 to 1850, who resided in

Philadelphia; Louis B. Binsse, 1850 to 1895, who resided in New York.

U.S. recognition of the consul of the Papal States did not cease when the states were absorbed into the Kingdom of Italy in 1871, despite pressure from Baron Blanc, the Italian minister. Binsse held the title until his death Mar. 28, 1895. No one was appointed to succeed him.

Diplomatic Relations

The U.S. Senate approved a recommendation, made by President James K. Polk in December, 1847, for the establishment of a diplomatic post in the Papal States. Jacob L. Martin, the first charge d'affaires, arrived in Rome Aug. 2, 1848, and presented his credentials to Pius IX Aug. 19. Martin, who died within a month, was succeeded by Lewis Cass, Jr. Cass became minister resident in 1854 and served in that capacity until his retirement in 1858.

John P. Stockton, who later became a U.S. Senator from New Jersey, was minister resident from 1858 to 1861. Rufus King was named to succeed him but, instead, accepted a commission as a brigadier general in the Army. Alexander W. Randall of Wisconsin took the appointment. He was succeeded in August, 1862, by Richard M. Blatchford who served until the following year. King was again nominated minister resident and served in that capacity until 1867 when the ministry was ended because of objections from some quarters in the U.S. and failure to appropriate funds for its continuation. J. C. Hooker, a secretary, remained in the Papal States until the end of March, 1868, closing the ministry and performing functions of courtesy.

Personal Envoys

Myron C. Taylor was appointed by President Franklin D. Roosevelt in 1939 to serve as his personal representative to Pope Pius XII and continued serving in that capacity during the presidency of Harry S. Truman until 1951. Henry Cabot Lodge was named to the post by President Richard M. Nixon in 1970, served also during the presidency of Gerald Ford, and represented President Carter at the canonization of St. John Neumann in 1977. Neither Taylor nor Lodge had diplomatic status.

Miami attorney David Walters, a Catholic, served as the personal envoy of President Jimmy Carter to the Pope from July, 1977, until his resignation Aug. 16, 1978. He was succeeded by Robert F. Wagner, also a Catholic and former mayor of New York, who served from October, 1978, to the end of the Carter presidency in January, 1981. William A. Wilson, a California businessman and Catholic, was appointed by President Ronald Reagan in February, 1981, to serve as his personal envoy to the Pope.

None of the personal envoys had diplomatic status.

President Harry S. Truman nominated Gen. Mark Clark to be ambassador to the Vatican in 1951, but withdrew the nomination at Clark's request because of controversy over the appointment.

VATICAN CITY

The State of Vatican City (Stato della Citta del Vaticano) is the territorial seat of the papacy. The smallest sovereign state in the world, it is situated within the city of Rome, embraces an area of 108.7 acres, and includes within its limits the Vatican Palace, museums, art galleries, gardens, libraries, radio station, post office, bank, astronomical observatory, offices, apartments, service facilities, St. Peter's Basilica, and neighboring buildings between the Basilica and Viale Vaticano.

The extraterritorial rights of Vatican City extend to more than 10 buildings in Rome, including the major basilicas and office buildings of various congregations of the Roman Curia, and to the **Villa of Castel Gandolfo** 15 miles southeast of the City of Rome. Castel Gandolfo is the summer residence of the Holy Father.

The government of Vatican City is in the hands of the reigning pope, who has full executive, legislative and judicial power. The administration of affairs, however, is handled by the Pontifical Commission for the State of Vatican City. The legal system is based on Canon Law; in cases where this code does not obtain, the laws of the City of Rome apply. The City is an absolutely neutral state and enjoys all the rights and privileges of a sovereign power. The Secretariat of State (Papal Secretariat) maintains diplomatic relations with other nations. The citizens of Vatican City, and they alone, owe allegiance to the pope as a temporal head of state.

Cardinals of the Roman Curia residing outside Vatican City enjoy the privileges of extraterritoriality.

The normal population is approximately 1,000. While the greater percentage is made up of priests and religious, there are several hundred lay persons living in Vatican City. They are housed in their own apartments in the City and are engaged in secretarial, domestic, trade and service occupations. About 4,000 persons are employed by the Vatican.

Services of honor and order are performed by the Swiss Guards, who have been charged with responsibility for the personal safety of popes since 1506. Additional police and ceremonial functions are under the supervision of a special office. These functions were formerly handled by the Papal Gendarmes, the Palatine Guard of Honor, and the Guard of Honor of the Pope (Pontifical Noble Guard) which Pope Paul disbanded Sept. 14, 1970.

The **Basilica of St. Peter,** built between 1506 and 1626, is the largest church in Christendom and the site of most papal ceremonies. The pope's own patriarchal basilica, however, is **St. John Lateran,** whose origins date back to 324.

St. Ann's is the parish church of Vatican City.

The vicar general of the pope for Vatican City, which is part of the diocese of Rome, is Most Rev. Peter Canisius Van Lierde, O.S.A., titular bishop of Porfireone.

The **Vatican Library,** one of five in the City, has among its holdings 70,000 manuscripts, 770,000 printed books, and 7,500 incunabula.

The independent temporal power of the pope, which is limited to the confines of Vatican City and small areas outside, was for many centuries more extensive than it is now. As late as the nineteenth century, the pope ruled 16,000 square miles of Papal States across the middle of Italy, with a population of over 3,000,000. In 1870 forces of the Kingdom of Italy occupied these lands which, with the exception of the small areas surrounding the Vatican and Lateran in Rome and the Villa of Castel Gandolfo, became part of the Kingdom by the Italian law of May 13, 1871.

The **Roman Question,** occasioned by this seizure and the voluntary confinement of the pope to the Vatican, was settled with ratification of the Lateran Agreement June 7, 1929, by the Italian government and Vatican City. The agreement recognized Catholicism as the religion of Italy and provided, among other things, a financial indemnity to the Vatican in return for the former Papal States; it became Article 7 of the Italian Constitution Mar. 26, 1947.

The Lateran Agreement was superseded by a new concordat given final approval by the Italian Chamber of Deputies Mar. 20 and formally ratified June 3, 1985.

Papal Flag

The papal flag consists of two equal vertical stripes of yellow and white, charged with the insignia of the papacy on the white stripe — a triple crown or tiara over two crossed keys, one of gold and one of silver, tied with a red cord and two tassels. The divisions of the crown represent the teaching, sanctifying and ruling offices of the pope. The keys symbolize his jurisdictional authority.

The papal flag is a national flag inasmuch as it is the standard of the Supreme Pontiff as the sovereign of the state of Vatican City. It is also universally accepted by the faithful as a symbol of the supreme spiritual authority of the Holy Father.

Vatican Radio

The declared purpose of Vatican Radio Station HVJ is "that the voice of the Supreme Pastor may be heard throughout the world by means of the ether waves, for the glory of Christ and the salvation of souls." Designed by Guglielmo Marconi, the inventor of radio, and supervised by him until his death, the station was inaugurated by Pope Pius XI in 1931. The original purpose has been extended to a wide variety of programming.

Vatican Radio operates on international wave lengths, transmits programs in 35 languages, and serves as a channel of communication between the Vatican, church officials and listeners in general in many parts of the world. The station broadcasts about 280 hours a week throughout the world. The daily English-language program for North America is broadcast on 6030 kilohertz.

The staff of 350 broadcasters and technicians includes 35 Jesuits. Studios and offices are at Palazzo Pio, Piazza Pia, 3, 00193 Rome. The transmitters are situated at Santa Maria di Galeria, a short distance north of Rome.

1986 Vatican Stamps and Coins

The Vatican Philatelic Office issued the following stamps and stationery, as of June 30, 1986:

• Series commemorating Vatican City State in world patrimony; issued Apr. 14, 1986, in six-stamp set (350 lire each).

• Series commemorating 1986 International Year of Peace; issued Apr. 14, 1986, in five values (50, 350, 450, 650 and 2,000 lire) on five subjects.

• Series commemorating the centenary of the proclamation of St. Camillus de Lellis and St. John of God as patrons of hospitals and all the sick in the world; issued June 12, 1986, in two values (two 700 and one 2,000 lire) on three subjects.

• Airletter (aerogramme). Issued June 12, 1986.

The Vatican Numismatics Office issued a series of coins Feb. 24, 1986, for the seventh year of the pontificate of Pope John Paul II. The set consisted of seven coins (10, 20, 50, 100, 200, 500 and 1,000 lire).

Papal Audiences

General audiences are scheduled weekly, on Wednesday.

In Vatican City, they are held in the Audience Hall on the south side of St. Peter's Basilica or, weather permitting, in St. Peter's Square. The hall, which was opened in 1971, has a seating capacity of 6,800 and a total capacity of 12,000.

Audiences are also held during the summer at Castel Gandolfo when the pope is there on a working vacation.

General audiences last from about 60 to 90 minutes, during which the pope gives a talk and his blessing. A résumé of the talk, which is usually in Italian, is given in several languages.

Arrangements for papal audiences are handled by an office of the Prefecture of the Apostolic Household.

American visitors can obtain passes for general audiences by applying to the Bishops' Office for United States Visitors to the Vatican, Casa Santa Maria, Via dell'Umilita, 30, 00187 Rome.

Private and group audiences are reserved for dignitaries of various categories and for special occasions.

Publications

Acta Apostolicae Sedis: The only "official commentary" of the Holy See, was established in 1908 for the publication of activities of the Holy See, laws, decrees and acts of congregations and tribunals of the Roman Curia. The first edition was published in January, 1909.

St. Pius X made *AAS* an official organ in 1908. Laws promulgated for the Church ordinarily take effect three months after the date of their publication in this commentary.

The publication, mostly in Latin, is printed by the Vatican Polyglot Press.

The immediate predecessor of this organ was *Acta Sanctae Sedis,* founded in 1865 and given of-

ficial status by the Congregation for the Propagation of the Faith in 1904.

Annuario Pontificio: The yearbook of the Holy See. It is edited by the Central Statistics Office of the Church and is printed in Italian, with some portions in other languages, by the Vatican Polyglot Press. It covers the worldwide organization of the Church, lists members of the hierarchy, and includes a wide range of statistical information.

The publication of a statistical yearbook of the Holy See dates back to 1716, when a volume called *Notizie* appeared. Publication under the present title began in 1860, was suspended in 1870, and resumed again in 1872 under the title *Catholic Hierarchy.* This volume was printed privately at first, but has been issued by the Vatican Press since 1885. The title *Annuario Pontificio* was restored in 1912, and the yearbook was called an "official publication" until 1924.

L'Osservatore Romano: The daily newspaper of the Holy See. It began publication July 1, 1861, as an independent enterprise under the ownership and direction of four Catholic laymen headed by Marcantonio Pacelli, vice minister of the interior under Pope Pius IX and a grandfather of the late Pius XII. Leo XIII bought the publication in 1890, making it the "pope's" own newspaper.

The only official material in *L'Osservatore Romano* is that which appears under the heading, "Nostre Informazioni." This includes notices of appointments by the Holy See, the texts of papal encyclicals and addresses by the Holy Father and others, various types of documents, accounts of decisions and rulings of administrative bodies, and similar items. Additional material includes news and comment on developments in the Church and the world. Italian is the language most used.

The editorial board is directed by Prof. Mario Agnes. A staff of about 15 reporters covers Rome news sources. A corps of correspondents provides foreign coverage.

A weekly roundup edition in English was inaugurated in 1968. Other weekly editions are printed in French, Spanish, Portuguese, German and Polish. *L'Osservatore della Domenica* is published weekly as a supplement to the Sunday issue of the daily edition.

Vatican Press Office: The establishment of a single Vatican Press Office was announced Feb. 29, 1968, to replace service agencies formerly operated by *L'Osservatore Romano* and an office created for press coverage of the Second Vatican Council. Joaquin Navarro-Valls is the director.

Television: *Centro Televisivo Vaticano* was instituted by John Paul II Oct. 23, 1983, with the rescript, *Ex Audentia.* Archbishop John P. Foley is president of the administrative council.

Vatican Polyglot Press: The official printing plant of the Vatican.

The Vatican press was conceived by Marcellus II and Pius IV but was actually founded by Sixtus V on Apr. 27, 1587, to print the Vulgate and the writings of the Fathers of the Church and other authors. A Polyglot Press was established in 1626 by the Congregation for the Propagation of the Faith to serve the needs of the Oriental Church. St. Pius X merged both presses under this title.

The plant has facilities for the printing of a wide variety of material in about 30 languages.

Activities of the Holy See: An annual documentary volume covering the activities of the pope — his daily work, general and special audiences, discourses and messages on special occasions, visits outside the Vatican, missionary and charitable endeavors, meetings with diplomats, heads of state and others — and activities of the congregations, commissions, tribunals and offices of the Roman Curia.

Statistical Yearbook of the Church: Issued by the Central Statistics Office of the Church, it contains principal data concerning the presence and work of the Church in the world. The first issue was published in 1972 under the title *Collection of Statistical Tables, 1969.* It is printed in corresponding columns of Italian and Latin. Some of the introductory material is printed in other languages.

VATICAN REPRESENTATIVES

(Sources: *Annuario Pontificio;* NC News Service.)

The Vatican has representatives to a number of quasi-governmental and international organizations.

Governmental Organizations: United Nations (Abp. Giovanni Cheli, permanent observer); UN Office in Geneva and Specialized Institutes (Abp. Justo Mullor Garcia, permanent observer); International Atomic Energy Agency (Msgr. Giovanni Ceirano, permanent representative); UN Organization for Industrial Development (Msgr. Giovanni Ceirano, permanent observer); UN Food and Agriculture Organization (Bp. Agostino Ferrari-Toniolo, permanent observer); UN Educational, Scientific and Cultural Organization (Msgr. Renzo Frana, permanent observer);

Council of Europe (Msgr. Luigi Bressan, special envoy with function of permanent observer); Council for Cultural Cooperation of the Council of Europe (Msgr. Luigi Bressan, delegate); Organization of American States (Abp. Pio Laghi, permanent observer, Msgr. Alberto Bottari de Castello, alternate); International Institute for the Unification of Private Law (Prof. Pio Ciprotti, delegate); International Committee of Military Medicine and Pharmacy (Adolphe Vander Perre, delegate), World Organization of Tourism (Rev. Giovanni Arrighi, O.P., permanent observer).

Universal Postal Union; International Telecommunications Union; International Council on Grain; World Organization of Intellectual Property; International Union for the Protection of Literary and Artistic Works; International Union for the Protection of Industrial Property; International Organization of Telecommunication via Satellite (Intelsat); European Conference of Postal and Telecommunication Administration (CEPT).

Non-Governmental Organizations: International Committee of Historical Sciences (Msgr. Michele Maccarrone); International Committee of Paleography (Msgr. Jose Ruysschaert, delegate); International Committee of the History of Art (Prof. Carlo Pietrangeli, delegate); International Committee of Anthropological and Ethnological Sciences;

International Committee for the Neutrality of Medicine (Rev. Michel Riquet, S.J., permanent observer); International Center of Study for the Preservation and Restoration of Cultural Goods (Prof. Carlo Pietrangeli, permanent observer); International Council of Monuments and Sites (Prof. Carlo Pietrangeli, delegate); International Alliance on Tourism; International Astronomical Union; International Institute of Administrative Sciences; International Technical Committee for Prevention and Extinction of Fires; World Medical Association.

AMERICAN CHURCH

The Church of Santa Susanna was established as the national church for Americans in Rome Feb. 28, 1922, and entrusted to the Paulist Fathers who have served there continuously since then except for several years during World War II.

VATICAN-ITALIAN CONCORDAT

A new concordat on relations between the Vatican and Italy, designed to replace the one in effect since 1929, was formally ratified June 3, 1985. It bears the title, "An Agreement on the Revision of the Lateran Concordat."

The 14-article agreement ended the privileged status of the Catholic Church as the official religion of Italy. It refers, not to "the sacred character of the Eternal City of Rome," but to the "particular significance of Rome for Catholicism." It provides that Catholic religious teaching in state schools shall be optional, and makes marriage annulments by church tribunals subject to civil review before ratification by the state.

The treaty guarantees the rights of the Church to: perform its pastoral mission; oversee dioceses, other institutions, and priests; establish schools; minister in public institutions.

It recognizes Sundays as holidays, along with Catholic religious feast days to be agreed upon. It provides for the protection of church buildings, and calls on Church and state to safeguard the country's historical and artistic treasures. The concordat provides also for the continuing exemption of priests, deacons and members of religious orders from military service, but requires them to perform some kind of civil service instead.

It was expected that the tax-exempt status of church organizations outside the Vatican would continue in effect.

Government subsidies to the Church and related financial issues not covered in the earlier text were the subjects of agreement reached Aug. 2, 1984, in the Italian Parliament. Substantially, the arrangement envisaged the end of subsidies in 1990, coupled with provisions for tax deductible contributions for support of the personnel and institutions of the Church.

DOCTRINE OF THE CATHOLIC CHURCH

Following are excerpts from the first two chapters of the "Dogmatic Constitution on the Church" promulgated by the Second Vatican Council. They describe the relation of the Catholic Church to the Kingdom of God, the nature and foundation of the Church, the People of God, the necessity of membership and participation in the Church for salvation.

Additional subjects in the constitution are treated in other Almanac entries.

I. MYSTERY OF THE CHURCH

By her relationship with Christ, the Church is a kind of sacrament or sign of intimate union with God, and of the unity of all mankind (No. 1).

He (the eternal Father) planned to assemble in the holy Church all those who would believe in Christ. Already from the beginning of the world the foreshadowing of the Church took place. She was prepared for in a remarkable way throughout the history of the people of Israel and by means of the Old Covenant. Established in the present era of time, the Church was made manifest by the outpouring of the Spirit. At the end of time she will achieve her glorious fulfillment. Then . . . all just men from the time of Adam, "from Abel, the just one, to the last of the elect," will be gathered together with the Father in the universal Church (No. 2).

When the work which the Father had given the Son to do on earth (cf. Jn. 17:4) was accomplished, the Holy Spirit was sent on the day of Pentecost in order that he might forever sanctify the Church, and thus all believers would have access to the Father through Christ in the one Spirit (cf. Eph. 2:18).

The Spirit dwells in the Church and in the hearts of the faithful as in a temple (cf. 1 Cor. 3:16; 6:19). . . . The Spirit guides the Church into the fullness of truth (cf. Jn. 16:13) and gives her a unity of fellowship and service. He furnishes and directs her with various gifts, both hierarchical and charismatic, and adorns her with the fruits of His grace (cf. Eph. 4:11-12; 1 Cor. 12:4; Gal. 5:22). By the power of the Gospel he makes the Church grow, perpetually renews her, and leads her to perfect union with her Spouse (No. 4).

Foundation of the Church

The mystery of the holy Church is manifest in her very foundation, for the Lord Jesus inaugurated her by preaching the Good News, that is, the coming of God's Kingdom, which, for centuries, had been promised in the Scriptures. . . . In Christ's word, in his works, and in his presence this Kingdom reveals itself to men.

The miracles of Jesus also confirm that the Kingdom has already arrived on earth.

Before all things, however, the Kingdom is clearly visible in the very Person of Christ, Son of God and Son of Man.

When Jesus rose up again after suffering death on the cross for mankind, he manifested that he had been appointed Lord, Messiah, and Priest for-

ever (cf. Acts 2:36; Heb. 5:6; 7:17-21), and he poured out on his disciples the Spirit promised by the Father (cf. Acts 2:33). The Church, consequently, equipped with the gifts of her Founder and faithfully guarding her precepts . . . receives the mission to proclaim and to establish among all peoples the Kingdom of Christ and of God. She becomes on earth the initial budding forth of that Kingdom. While she slowly grows, the Church strains toward the consummation of the Kingdom and, with all her strength, hopes and desires to be united in glory with her King (No. 5).

Figures of the Church

In the Old Testament the revelation of the Kingdom had often been conveyed by figures of speech. In the same way the inner nature of the Church was now to be made known to us through various images.

The Church is a sheepfold . . . a flock . . . a tract of land to be cultivated, the field of God . . . his choice vineyard . . . the true vine is Christ . . . the edifice of God . . . the house of God . . . the holy temple (whose members are) . . . living stones . . . this holy city . . . a bride . . . our Mother . . . the spotless spouse of the spotless Lamb . . . an exile (No. 6).

In the human nature which he united to himself, the Son of God redeemed man and transformed him into a new creation (cf. Gal. 6:15; 2 Cor. 5:17) by overcoming death through his own death and resurrection. By communicating his Spirit to his brothers, called together from all peoples, Christ made them mystically into his own body.

In that body, the life of Christ is poured into the believers, who, through the sacraments, are united in a hidden and real way to Christ who suffered and was glorified. Through baptism we are formed in the likeness of Christ.

Truly partaking of the body of the Lord in the breaking of the eucharistic bread, we are taken up into communion with him and with one another (No. 7).

One Body in Christ

As all the members of the human body, though they are many, form one body, so also are the faithful in Christ (cf. 1 Cor. 12:12). Also, in the building up of Christ's body there is a flourishing variety of members and functions. There is only one Spirit who . . . distributes his different gifts for the welfare of the Church (cf. 1 Cor. 12:1-11). Among these gifts stands out the grace given to the apostles. To their authority, the Spirit himself subjected even those who were endowed with charisms (cf. 1 Cor. 14).

The head of this body is Christ (No. 7).

Mystical Body of Christ

Christ, the one Mediator, established and ceaselessly sustains here on earth his holy Church, the community of faith, hope, and charity, as a visible structure. Through her he communicates truth and grace to all. But the society furnished with hierarchical agencies and the Mystical Body of Christ are not to be considered as two realities, nor are the visible assembly and the spiritual community, nor the earthly Church and the Church enriched with heavenly things. Rather they form one interlocked reality which is comprised of a divine and a human element. For this reason . . . this reality is compared to the mystery of the incarnate Word. Just as the assumed nature inseparably united to the divine Word serves him as a living instrument of salvation, so, in a similar way, does the communal structure of the Church serve Christ's Spirit, who vivifies it by way of building up the body (cf. Eph. 4:16).

This is the unique Church of Christ which in the Creed we avow as one, holy, catholic, and apostolic. After his Resurrection our Savior handed her over to Peter to be shepherded (Jn. 21:17), commissioning him and the other apostles to propagate and govern her (cf. Mt. 28:18, ff.). Her he erected for all ages as "the pillar and mainstay of the truth" (1 Tm. 3:15). This Church, constituted and organized in the world as a society, subsists in the Catholic Church, which is governed by the successor of Peter and by the bishops in union with that successor, although many elements of sanctification and of truth can be found outside of her visible structure. These elements, however, as gifts properly belonging to the Church of Christ, possess an inner dynamism toward Catholic unity.

The Church, embracing sinners in her bosom, is at the same time holy and always in need of being purified, and incessantly pursues the path of penance and renewal.

The Church, "like a pilgrim in a foreign land, presses forward . . ." announcing the cross and death of the Lord until he comes (cf. 1 Cor. 11:26) (No. 8).

II. THE PEOPLE OF GOD

At all times and among every people, God has given welcome to whosoever fears him and does what is right (cf. Acts 10:35). It has pleased God, however, to make men holy and save them not merely as individuals without any mutual bonds, but by making them into a single people, a people which acknowledges him in truth and serves him in holiness. He therefore chose the race of Israel as a people unto himself. With it he set up a covenant. Step by step he taught this people by manifesting in its history both himself and the decree of his will, and by making it holy unto himself. All these things, however, were done by way of preparation and as a figure of that new and perfect covenant which was to be ratified in Christ.

Christ instituted this New Covenant, that is to say, the New Testament, in his blood (cf. 1 Cor. 11:25), by calling together a people made up of Jew and Gentile, making them one, not according to the flesh but in the Spirit.

This was to be the new People of God . . . reborn . . . through the Word of the living God (cf. 1 Pt. 1:23) . . . from water and the Holy Spirit (cf. Jn. 3:5-6) . . . "a chosen race, a royal priesthood, a holy nation, a purchased people. . . . You who in times past were not a people, but are now the People of God" (1 Pt. 2:9-10).

That messianic people has for its head Christ. . . . Its law is the new commandment to love as Christ loved us (cf. Jn. 13:34). Its goal is the Kingdom of God, which has been begun by God himself on earth, and which is to be further extended until it is brought to perfection by him at the end of time.

This messianic people, although it does not actually include all men, and may more than once look like a small flock, is nonetheless a lasting and sure seed of unity, hope, and salvation for the whole human race. Established by Christ as a fellowship of life, charity, and truth, it is also used by him as an instrument for the redemption of all, and is sent forth into the whole world as the light of the world and the salt of the earth (cf. Mt. 5:13-16).

Israel according to the flesh . . . was already called the Church of God (Neh. 13:1; cf. Nm. 20:4; Dt. 23:1, ff.). Likewise the new Israel . . . is also called the Church of Christ (cf. Mt. 16:18). For he has bought it for himself with his blood (cf. Acts 20:28), has filled it with his Spirit, and provided it with those means which befit it as a visible and social unity. God has gathered together as one all those who in faith look upon Jesus as the author of salvation and the source of unity and peace, and has established them as the Church, that for each and all she may be the visible sacrament of this saving unity (No. 9).

Priesthood

The baptized, by regeneration and the anointing of the Holy Spirit, are consecrated into . . . a holy priesthood.

[All members of the Church participate in the priesthood of Christ, through the common priesthood of the faithful. See Priesthood of the Laity.]

Though they differ from one another in essence and not only in degree, the common priesthood of the faithful and the ministerial or hierarchical priesthood are nonetheless interrelated. Each of them in its own special way is a participation in the one priesthood of Christ (No. 10).

It is through the sacraments and the exercise of the virtues that the sacred nature and organic structure of the priestly community is brought into operation (No. 11). (See Role of the Sacraments.)

Prophetic Office

The holy People of God shares also in Christ's prophetic office. It spreads abroad a living witness to him, especially by means of a life of faith and charity and by offering to God a sacrifice of praise. . . . The body of the faithful as a whole, anointed as they are by the Holy One (cf. Jn. 2:20, 27), cannot err in matters of belief. Thanks to a supernatural sense of faith which characterizes the People as a whole, it manifests this unerring quality when, "from the bishops down to the last member of the laity," it shows universal agreement in matters of faith and morals.

God's People accepts not the word of men but the very Word of God (cf. 1 Thes. 2:13). It clings without fail to the faith once delivered to the saints (cf. Jude 3), penetrates it more deeply by accurate insights, and applies it more thoroughly to life. All this it does under the lead of a sacred teaching authority to which it loyally defers.

It is not only through the sacraments and Church ministries that the same Holy Spirit sanctifies and leads the People of God. . . . He distributes special graces among the faithful of every rank. By these gifts he makes them fit and ready to undertake the various tasks or offices advantageous for the renewal and upbuilding of the Church. . . . These charismatic gifts . . . are to be received with thanksgiving and consolation, for they are exceedingly suitable and useful for the needs of the Church.

Judgment as to their genuineness and proper use belongs to those who preside over the Church, and to whose special competence it belongs . . . to test all things and hold fast to that which is good (cf. 1 Thes. 5:12; 19-21) (No. 12).

All Are Called

All men are called to belong to the new People of God. Wherefore this People, while remaining one and unique, is to be spread throughout the whole world and must exist in all ages, so that the purpose of God's will may be fulfilled. In the beginning God made human nature one. After his children were scattered, he decreed that they should at length be united again (cf. Jn. 11:52). It was for this reason that God sent his Son . . . that he might be Teacher, King, and Priest of all, the Head of the new and universal People of the sons of God. For this God finally sent his Son's Spirit as Lord and Lifegiver. He it is who, on behalf of the whole Church and each and every one of those who believe, is the principle of their coming together and remaining together in the teaching of the apostles and in fellowship, in the breaking of bread and in prayers (cf. Acts 2:42) (No. 13).

One People of God

It follows that among all the nations of earth there is but one People of God, which takes its citizens from every race, making them citizens of a Kingdom which is of a heavenly and not an earthly nature. For all the faithful scattered throughout the world are in communion with each other in the Holy Spirit. . . . the Church or People of God . . . foster(s) and take(s) to herself, insofar as they are good, the ability, resources and customs of each people. Taking them to herself, she purifies, strengthens, and ennobles them . . . This characteristic of universality which adorns the People of God is a gift from the Lord himself. By reason of it, the Catholic Church strives energetically and constantly to bring all humanity with all its riches back to Christ its Head in the unity of his Spirit.

In virtue of this catholicity each individual part of the Church contributes through its special gifts to the good of the other parts and of the whole Church. Thus through the common sharing of gifts . . . the whole and each of the parts receive increase.

All men are called to be part of this catholic unity of the People of God. . . . And there belong to it or are related to it in various ways, the Catholic faithful as well as all who believe in Christ, and indeed the whole of mankind. For all men are called to salvation by the grace of God (No. 13).

The Catholic Church

This sacred Synod turns its attention first to the Catholic faithful. Basing itself upon sacred Scripture and tradition, it teaches that the Church . . . is necessary for salvation. For Christ, made present to us in his Body, which is the Church, is the one Mediator and the unique Way of salvation. In explicit terms he himself affirmed the necessity of faith and baptism (cf. Mk. 16:16; Jn. 3:5) and thereby affirmed also the necessity of the Church, for through baptism as through a door men enter the Church. Whosoever, therefore, knowing that the Catholic Church was made necessary by God through Jesus Christ, would refuse to enter her or to remain in her could not be saved.

They are fully incorporated into the society Church who, possessing the Spirit of Christ, accept her entire system and all the means of salvation given to her, and through union with her visible structure are joined to Christ, who rules her through the Supreme Pontiff and the bishops. This joining is effected by the bonds of professed faith, of the sacraments, of ecclesiastical government, and of communion. He is not saved, however, who, though he is part of the body of the Church, does not persevere in charity. He remains indeed in the bosom of the Church, but . . . only in a "bodily" manner and not "in his heart."

Catechumens who, moved by the Holy Spirit, seek with explicit intention to be incorporated into the Church, are by that very intention joined to her. . . . Mother Church already embraces them as her own (No. 14).

Other Christians, The Unbaptized

The Church recognizes that in many ways she is linked with those who, being baptized, are honored with the name of Christian, though they do not profess the faith in its entirety or do not preserve unity of communion with the successor of Peter.

We can say that in some real way they are joined with us in the Holy Spirit, for to them also he gives his gifts and graces, and is thereby operative among them with his sanctifying power (No. 15).

Finally, those who have not yet received the Gospel are related in various ways to the People of God. In the first place there is the people to whom the covenants and the promises were given and from whom Christ was born according to the flesh (cf. Rom. 9:4-5). On account of their fathers, this people remains most dear to God, for God does not repent of the gifts he makes nor of the calls he issues (cf. Rom. 11:28-29).

But the plan of salvation also includes those who acknowledge the Creator. In the first place among these are the Moslems. . . . Nor is God himself far distant from those who in shadows and images seek the unknown God.

Those also can attain to everlasting salvation

who through no fault of their own do not know the Gospel of Christ or his Church, yet sincerely seek God and, moved by grace, strive by their deeds to do his will as it is known to them through the dictates of conscience. Nor does divine Providence deny the help necessary for salvation to those who, without blame on their part, have not yet arrived at an explicit knowledge of God, but who strive to live a good life, thanks to his grace. Whatever goodness or truth is found among them is looked upon by the Church as a preparation for the Gospel. She regards such qualities as given by him who enlightens all men so that they may finally have life (No. 16).

THE POPE, TEACHING AUTHORITY, COLLEGIALITY

The Roman Pontiff — the successor of St. Peter as the Vicar of Christ and head of the Church on earth — has full and supreme authority over the universal Church in matters pertaining to faith and morals (teaching authority), discipline and government (jurisdictional authority).

The primacy of the pope is real and supreme power. It is not merely a prerogative of honor — that is, of his being regarded as the first among equals. Neither does primacy imply that the pope is just the presiding officer of the collective body of bishops. The pope is the head of the Church.

Catholic belief in the primacy of the pope was stated in detail in the dogmatic constitution on the Church, *Pastor Aeternus,* approved in 1870 by the fourth session of the First Vatican Council. Some elaboration of the doctrine was made in the *Dogmatic Constitution on the Church* which was approved and promulgated by the Second Vatican Council Nov. 21, 1964. The entire body of teaching on the subject is based on Scripture and tradition and the centuries-long experience of the Church.

Infallibility

The essential points of doctrine concerning infallibility in the Church and the infallibility of the pope were stated by the Second Vatican Council in the *Dogmatic Constitution on the Church,* as follows:

"This infallibility with which the divine Redeemer willed his Church to be endowed in defining a doctrine of faith and morals extends as far as extends the deposit of divine revelation, which must be religiously guarded and faithfully expounded. This is the infallibility which the Roman Pontiff, the head of the college of bishops, enjoys in virtue of his office, when, as the supreme shepherd and teacher of all the faithful who confirms his brethren in their faith (cf. Lk. 22:32), he proclaims by a definitive act some doctrine of faith or morals. Therefore his definitions, of themselves, and not from the consent of the Church, are justly styled irreformable, for they are pronounced with the assistance of the Holy Spirit, an assistance promised to him in blessed Peter. Therefore they need no approval of others, nor do they allow an appeal to any other judgment. For then the Roman Pontiff is not pronouncing judgment as a private person. Rather, as the supreme teacher of the universal Church, as one in whom the charism of the infallibility of the Church herself is individually present, he is expounding or defending a doctrine of Catholic faith.

"The infallibility promised to the Church resides also in the body of bishops when that body exercises supreme teaching authority with the successor of Peter. To the resultant definitions the assent of the Church can never be wanting, on account of the activity of that same Holy Spirit, whereby the whole flock of Christ is preserved and progresses in unity of faith.

"But when either the Roman Pontiff or the body of bishops together with him defines a judgment, they pronounce it in accord with revelation itself. All are obliged to maintain and be ruled by this revelation, which, as written or preserved by tradition, is transmitted in its entirety through the legitimate succession of bishops and especially through the care of the Roman Pontiff himself.

"Under the guiding light of the Spirit of truth, revelation is thus religiously preserved and faithfully expounded in the Church. The Roman Pontiff and the bishops, in view of their office and of the importance of the matter, strive painstakingly and by appropriate means to inquire properly into that revelation and to give apt expression to its contents. But they do not allow that there could be any new public revelation pertaining to the divine deposit of faith" (No. 25).

Authentic Teaching

The pope rarely speaks *ex cathedra* — that is, "from the chair" of St. Peter, for the purpose of making an infallible pronouncement. More often and in various ways he states authentic teaching in line with Scripture, tradition, the living experience of the Church, and the whole analogy of faith. Of such teaching, the Second Vatican Council said in its *Dogmatic Constitution on the Church* (No. 25):

"Religious submission of will and of mind must be shown in a special way to the authentic teaching authority of the Roman Pontiff, even when he is not speaking *ex cathedra.* That is, it must be shown in such a way that his supreme magisterium is acknowledged with reverence, the judgments made by him are sincerely adhered to, according to his manifest mind and will. His mind and will in the matter may be known chiefly either from the character of the documents, from his frequent repetition of the same doctrine, or from his manner of speaking."

With respect to bishops, the constitution states: "They are authentic teachers, that is, teachers endowed with the authority of Christ, who preach to the people committed to them the faith they must believe and put into practice. By the light of the Holy Spirit, they make that faith clear, bringing forth from the treasury of revelation new things and old (cf. Mt. 13:52), making faith bear fruit and vigilantly warding off any errors which threaten their flock (cf. 2 Tm. 4:1-4).

"Bishops, teaching in communion with the Roman Pontiff, are to be respected by all as witnesses to divine and Catholic truth. In matters of faith and morals, the bishops speak in the name of Christ and the faithful are to accept their teaching and adhere to it with a religious assent of soul."

Magisterium—Teaching Authority

Responsibility for teaching doctrine and judging orthodoxy belongs to the official teaching authority of the Church.

This authority is personalized in the pope, the successor of St. Peter as head of the Church, and in the bishops together and in union with the pope, as it was originally committed to Peter and to the whole college of apostles under his leadership. They are the official teachers of the Church.

Others have auxiliary relationships with the magisterium: theologians, in the study and clarification of doctrine; teachers — priests, religious, lay persons — who cooperate with the pope and bishops in spreading knowledge of religious truth; the faithful, who by their sense of faith and personal witness contribute to the development of doctrine and the establishment of its relevance to life in the Church and the world.

The magisterium, Pope Paul VI noted in an address at a general audience Jan. 11, 1967, "is a subordinate and faithful echo and secure interpreter of the divine word." It does not reveal new truths, "nor is it superior to sacred Scripture." Its competence extends to the limits of divine revelation manifested in Scripture and tradition and the living experience of the Church, with respect to matters of faith and morals and related subjects.

Official teaching in these areas is infallible when it is formally defined, for belief and acceptance by all members of the Church, by the pope, acting in the capacity of supreme shepherd of the flock of Christ; also, when doctrine is proposed and taught with moral unanimity of bishops with the pope in a solemn collegial manner, as in an ecumenical council, and/or in the ordinary course of events. Even when not infallibly defined, official teaching in the areas of faith and morals is authoritative and requires religious assent.

The teachings of the magisterium have been documented in creeds, formulas of faith, decrees and enactments of ecumenical and particular councils, various kinds of doctrinal statements, encyclical letters and other teaching instruments. They have also been incorporated into the liturgy, with the result that the law of prayer is said to be a law of belief.

Collegiality

The bishops of the Church, in union with the pope, have supreme teaching and pastoral authority over the whole Church in addition to the authority of office they have for their own dioceses.

This collegial authority is exercised in a solemn manner in an ecumenical council and can be exercised in other ways as well, "provided that the head of the college calls them to collegiate action, or at least so approves or freely accepts the united action of the dispersed bishops that it is made a true collegiate act."

This doctrine is grounded on the fact that: "Just as, by the Lord's will, St. Peter and the other apostles constituted one apostolic college, so in a similar way the Roman Pontiff as the successor of Peter, and the bishops as the successors of the apostles are joined together."

Doctrine on collegiality was stated by the Second Vatican Council in the *Dogmatic Constitution on the Church* (Nos. 22 and 23).

REVELATION

Following are excerpts from the "Constitution on Revelation" promulgated by the Second Vatican Council. They describe the nature and process of divine revelation, inspiration and interpretation of Scripture, the Old and New Testaments, and the role of Scripture in the life of the Church.

I. REVELATION ITSELF

God chose to reveal himself and to make known to us the hidden purpose of his will (cf. Eph. 1:9) by which through Christ, the Word made flesh, man has access to the Father in the Holy Spirit and comes to share in the divine nature (cf. Eph. 2:18; 2 Pt. 1:4). Through this revelation, therefore, the invisible God (cf. Col. 1:15; 1 Tm. 1:17) . . . speaks to men as friends (cf. Ex. 33:11; Jn. 15:14-15) and lives among them (cf. Bar. 3:38) so that he may invite and take them into fellowship with himself. This plan of revelation is realized by deeds and words having an inner unity: the deeds wrought by God in the history of salvation manifest and confirm the teaching and realities signified by the words, while the words proclaim the deeds and clarify the mystery contained in them. By this revelation then, the deepest truth about God and the salvation of man is made clear to us in Christ, who is the Mediator and at the same time the fullness of all revelation (No. 2).

God . . . from the start manifested himself to our first parents. Then after their fall his promise of redemption aroused in them the hope of being saved (cf. Gn. 3:15), and from that time on he ceaselessly kept the human race in his care, in order to give eternal life to those who perseveringly do good in search of salvation (cf. Rom. 2:6-7). . . . He called Abraham in order to make of him a great nation (cf. Gn. 12:2). Through the patriarchs, and after them through Moses and the prophets, he taught this nation to acknowledge himself as the one living and true God . . . and to wait for the Savior promised by him. In this manner he prepared the way for the Gospel down through the centuries (No. 3).

Revelation in Christ

Then, after speaking in many places and varied ways through the prophets, God "last of all in these days has spoken to us by his Son" (Heb. 1:1-2). . . . Jesus perfected revelation by fulfilling it through his whole work of making himself present and manifesting himself: through his words and deeds, his signs and wonders, but especially through his death and glorious resurrection from the dead and final sending of the Spirit of truth. Moreover, he confirmed with divine testimony what revelation proclaimed: that God is with us to free us from the darkness of sin and death, and to raise us up to life eternal.

The Christian dispensation, therefore, as the new and definitive covenant, will never pass away, and we now await no further new public revelation before the glorious manifestation of our Lord Jesus Christ (cf. 1 Tm. 6:14; Ti. 2:13) (No. 4).

II. TRANSMISSION OF REVELATION

God has seen to it that what he had revealed for the salvation of all nations would abide perpetually in its full integrity and be handed on to all generations. Therefore Christ the Lord, in whom the full revelation of the supreme God is brought to completion (cf. 2 Cor. 1:20; 3:16; 4:6), commissioned the apostles to preach to all men that Gospel which is the source of all saving truth and moral teaching, and thus to impart to them divine gifts. This Gospel had been promised in former times through the prophets, and Christ himself fulfilled it and promulgated it with his own lips. This commission was faithfully fulfilled by the apostles who, by their oral preaching, by example, and by ordinances, handed on what they had received from . . . Christ . . . or what they had learned through the prompting of the Holy Spirit. The commission was fulfilled, too, by those apostles and apostolic men who under the inspiration of the same Holy Spirit committed the message of salvation to writing (No. 7).

Tradition

But in order to keep the Gospel forever whole and alive within the Church, the apostles left bishops as their successors, "handing over their own teaching role" to them. This sacred tradition, therefore, and sacred Scripture of both the Old and the New Testament are like a mirror in which the pilgrim Church on earth looks at God (No. 7).

The apostolic preaching, which is expressed in a special way in the inspired books, was to be preserved by a continuous succession of preachers until the end of time. Therefore the apostles, handing on what they themselves had received, warn the faithful to hold fast to the traditions which they have learned. . . . Now what was handed on by the apostles includes everything which contributes to the holiness of life, and the increase in faith of the People of God; and so the Church, in her teaching, life, and worship, perpetuates and hands on to all generations all that she herself is, all that she believes (No. 8).

Development of Doctrine

This tradition which comes from the apostles develops in the Church with the help of the Holy Spirit. For there is a growth in the understanding of the realities and the words which have been handed down. This happens through the contemplation and study made by believers . . . through the intimate understanding of spiritual things they experience, and through the preaching of those who have received through episcopal succession the sure gift of truth. For, as the centuries succeed one another, the Church constantly moves forward toward the fullness of divine truth until the words of God reach their complete fulfillment in her.

The words of the holy Fathers witness to the living presence of this tradition, whose wealth is poured into the practice and life of the believing and praying Church. Through the same tradition the Church's full canon of the sacred books is known, and the sacred writings themselves are more profoundly understood and unceasingly made active in her; . . . and the Holy Spirit, through whom the living voice of the Gospel resounds in the Church, and through her, in the world, leads unto all truth those who believe and makes the word of Christ dwell abundantly in them (cf. Col. 3:16) (No. 8).

Tradition and Scripture

Hence there exist a close connection and communication between sacred tradition and sacred Scripture. For both of them, flowing from the same divine wellspring, in a certain way merge into a unity and tend toward the same end. For sacred Scripture is the word of God inasmuch as it is consigned to writing under the inspiration of the divine Spirit. To the successors of the apostles, sacred tradition hands on in its full purity God's word, which was entrusted to the apostles by Christ the Lord and the Holy Spirit. Thus, led by the light of the Spirit of truth, these successors can in their preaching preserve this word of God faithfully, explain it, and make it more widely known. Consequently, it is not from sacred Scripture alone that the Church draws her certainty about everything which has been revealed. Therefore both sacred tradition and sacred Scripture are to be accepted and venerated with the same sense of devotion and reverence (No. 9).

Sacred tradition and sacred Scripture form one sacred deposit of the word of God, which is committed to the Church (No. 10).

Teaching Authority of Church

The task of authentically interpreting the word of God, whether written or handed on, has been entrusted exclusively to the living teaching office of the Church, whose authority is exercised in the name of Jesus Christ. This teaching office is not above the word of God, but serves it, teaching only what has been handed on . . . it draws from this one deposit of faith everything which it presents for belief as divinely revealed.

It is clear, therefore, that sacred tradition, sacred Scripture, and the teaching authority of the Church . . . are so linked and joined together that one cannot stand without the others, and that all together and each in its own way under the action of the one Holy Spirit contribute effectively to the salvation of souls (No. 10).

III. INSPIRATION, INTERPRETATION

Those . . . revealed realities . . . contained and presented in sacred Scripture have been committed to writing under the inspiration of the Holy

Spirit. Holy Mother Church, relying on the belief of the apostles, holds that the books of both the Old and New Testament in their entirety, with all their parts, are sacred and canonical because, having been written under the inspiration of the Holy Spirit (cf. Jn. 20:31; 2 Tm. 3:16; 2 Pt. 1:19-21; 3:15-16) they have God as their author and have been handed on as such to the Church herself. In composing the sacred books, God chose men and, while employed by him, they made use of their powers and abilities, so that, with him acting in them and through them, they, as true authors, consigned to writing everything and only those things which he wanted (No. 11).

Inerrancy

Therefore, since everything asserted by the inspired authors or sacred writers must be held to be asserted by the Holy Spirit, it follows that the books of Scripture must be acknowledged as teaching firmly, faithfully, and without error that truth which God wanted put into the sacred writings for the sake of our salvation. Therefore "all Scripture is inspired by God and useful for teaching, for reproving, for correcting, for instruction in justice; that the man of God may be perfect, equipped for every good work" (2 Tm. 3:16-17) (No. 11).

Literary Forms

However, since God speaks in sacred Scripture through men in human fashion, the interpreter of sacred Scripture, in order to see clearly what God wanted to communicate to us, should carefully investigate what meaning the sacred writers really intended, and what God wanted to mainfest by means of their words.

The interpreter must investigate what meaning the sacred writer intended to express and actually expressed in particular circumstances as he used contemporary literary forms in accordance with the situation of his own time and culture. For the correct understanding of what the sacred author wanted to assert, due attention must be paid to the customary and characteristic styles of perceiving, speaking, and narrating which prevailed at the time of the sacred writer, and to the customs men normally followed at that period in their everyday dealings with one another (No. 12).

Analogy of Faith

No less serious attention must be given to the content and unity of the whole of Scripture, if the meaning of the sacred texts is to be correctly brought to light. The living tradition of the whole Church must be taken into account along with the harmony which exists between elements of the faith. . . . All of what has been said about the way of interpreting Scripture is subject finally to the judgment of the Church, which carries out the divine commission and ministry of guarding and interpreting the word of God (No. 12).

IV. THE OLD TESTAMENT

In carefully planning and preparing the salvation of the whole human race, the God of supreme love,

by a special dispensation, chose for himself a people to whom he might entrust his promises. First he entered into a covenant with Abraham (cf. Gn. 15:18) and, through Moses, with the people of Israel (cf. Ex. 24:8). To this people which he had acquired for himself, he so manifested himself through words and deeds as the one true and living God that Israel came to know by experience the ways of God with men. . . . The plan of salvation, foretold by the sacred authors, recounted and explained by them, is found as the true word of God in the books of the Old Testament: these books, therefore, written under divine inspiration, remain permanently valuable (No. 14).

Principal Purpose

The principal purpose to which the plan of the Old Covenant was directed was to prepare for the coming both of Christ, the universal Redeemer, and of the messianic Kingdom. . . . Now the books of the Old Testament, in accordance with the state of mankind before the time of salvation established by Christ, reveal to all men the knowledge of God and of man and the ways in which God . . . deals with men. These books . . . show us true divine pedagogy (No. 15).

The books of the Old Testament with all their parts, caught up into the proclamation of the Gospel, acquire and show forth their full meaning in the New Testament (cf. Mt. 5:17; Lk. 24:27; Rom. 16:25-26; 2 Cor. 3:14-16) and in turn shed light on it and explain it (No. 16).

V. THE NEW TESTAMENT

The word of God . . . is set forth and shows its power in a most excellent way in the writings of the New Testament. For when the fullness of time arrived (cf. Gal. 4:4), the Word was made flesh and dwelt among us in the fullness of grace and truth (cf. Jn. 1:14). Christ established the Kingdom of God on earth, manifested his Father and himself by deeds and words, and completed his work by his death, resurrection, and glorious ascension and by the sending of the Holy Spirit. Having been lifted up from the earth, he draws all men to himself (cf. Jn. 12:32). . . . This mystery had not been manifested to other generations as it was now revealed to his holy apostles and prophets in the Holy Spirit (cf. Eph. 3:4-6), so that they might preach the Gospel, stir up faith in Jesus, Christ and Lord, and gather the Church together. To these realities, the writings of the New Testament stand as a perpetual and divine witness (No. 17).

The Gospels and Other Writings

The Gospels have a special preeminence . . . for they are the principal witness of the life and teaching of the incarnate Word, our Savior.

The Church has always and everywhere held and continues to hold that the four Gospels are of apostolic origin. For what the apostles preached . . . afterwards they themselves and apostolic men, under the inspiration of the divine Spirit, handed on to us in writing: the foundation of faith, namely, the fourfold Gospel, according to Matthew, Mark, Luke, and John (No. 18).

The four Gospels, . . . whose historical character the Church unhesitatingly asserts, faithfully hand on what Jesus Christ, while living among men, really did and taught for their eternal salvation until the day he was taken up into heaven (see Acts 1:1-2). Indeed, after the ascension of the Lord the apostles handed on to their hearers what he had said and done. . . . The sacred authors wrote the four Gospels, selecting some things from the many which had been handed on by word of mouth or in writing, reducing some of them to a synthesis, explicating some things in view of the situation of their churches, and preserving the form of proclamation but always in such fashion that they told us the honest truth about Jesus. For their intention in writing was that . . . we might know "the truth" concerning those matters about which we have been instructed (cf. Lk. 1:2-4) (No. 19).

Besides the four Gospels, the canon of the New Testament also contains the Epistles of St. Paul and other apostolic writings, composed under the inspiration of the Holy Spirit. In these writings . . . those matters which concern Christ the Lord are confirmed, his true teaching is more and more fully stated, the saving power of the divine work of Christ is preached, the story is told of the beginnings of the Church and her marvelous growth, and her glorious fulfillment is foretold (No. 20).

VI. SCRIPTURE IN CHURCH LIFE

The Church has always venerated the divine Scriptures just as she venerates the body of the Lord. . . . She has always regarded the Scriptures together with sacred tradition as the supreme rule of faith, and will ever do so. For, inspired by God and committed once and for all to writing, they impart the word of God himself without change, and make the voice of the Holy Spirit resound in the words of the prophets and apostles. Therefore, like the Christian religion itself, all the preaching of the Church must be nourished and ruled by sacred Scripture (No. 21).

Easy access to sacred Scripture should be provided for all the Christian faithful. That is why the Church from the very beginning accepted as her own that very ancient Greek translation of the Old Testament which is named after seventy men (the Septuagint); and she has always given a place of honor to other translations, Eastern and Latin, especially the one known as the Vulgate. But since the word of God should be available at all times, the Church with maternal concern sees to it that suitable and correct translations are made into different languages, especially from the original texts of the sacred books. And if, given the opportunity and the approval of Church authority, these translations are produced in cooperation with the separated brethren as well, all Christians will be able to use them (No. 22).

Biblical Studies, Theology

The constitution encouraged the development and progress of biblical studies "under the watchful care of the sacred teaching office of the Church."

It noted also: "Sacred theology rests on the written word of God, together with sacred tradition, as its primary and perpetual foundation," and that "the study of the sacred page is, as it were, the soul of sacred theology" (Nos. 23, 24).

THE BIBLE

The Canon of the Bible is the Church's official list of sacred writings. These works, written by men under the inspiration of the Holy Spirit, contain divine revelation and, in conjunction with the tradition and teaching authority of the Church, constitute the rule of Catholic faith. The Canon was fixed and determined by the tradition and teaching authority of the Church.

The Catholic Canon

The Old Testament Canon of 45 books is as follows.

• **The Pentateuch,** the first five books: Genesis (Gn.), Exodus (Ex.), Leviticus (Lv.), Numbers (Nm.), Deuteronomy (Dt.).

• **Historical Books:** Joshua (Jos.), Judges (Jgs.), Ruth (Ru.) 1 and 2 Samuel (Sm.), 1 and 2 Kings (Kgs.), 1 and 2 Chronicles (Chr.), Ezra (Ezr.), Nehemiah (Neh.), Tobit (Tb.), Judith (Jdt.), Esther (Est.), 1 and 2 Maccabees (Mc.).

• **Wisdom Books:** Job (Jb.), Psalms (Ps.), Proverbs (Prv.), Ecclesiastes (Eccl.), Song of Songs (Song), Wisdom (Wis.), Sirach (Sir.).

• **The Prophets:** Isaiah (Is.), Jeremiah (Jer.), Lamentations (Lam.), Baruch (Bar.), Ezechiel (Ez.), Daniel (Dn.), Hosea (Hos.), Joel (Jl.), Amos (Am.), Obadiah (Ob.), Jonah (Jon.), Micah (Mi.), Nahum (Na.), Habakkuk (Hb.), Zephaniah

(Zep.), Haggai (Hg.), Zechariah (Zec.) Malachi (Mal.).

The New Testament Canon of 27 books is as follows.

• **The Gospels** of Matthew (Mt.), Mark (Mk.), Luke (Lk.), John (Jn.)

• **The Acts of the Apostles** (Acts).

• **The Pauline Letters** — Romans (Rom.), 1 and 2 Corinthians (Cor.), Galatians (Gal.), Ephesians (Eph.), Philippians (Phil.), Colossians (Col.), 1 and 2 Thessalonians (Thes.) 1 and 2 Timothy (Tm.), Titus (Ti.), Philemon (Phlm.), Hebrews (Heb.).

• **The Catholic Letters** — James (Jas.), 1 and 2 Peter (Pt.), 1, 2 and 3 John (Jn.), Jude (Jude).

• **Revelation** (Rv.).

Developments

The Canon of the Old Testament was firm by the fifth century despite some questioning by scholars. It was stated by a council held at Rome in 382, by African councils held in Hippo in 393 and in Carthage in 397 and 419, and by Innocent I in 405.

All of the New Testament books were generally known and most of them were acknowledged as inspired by the end of the second century. The Muratorian Fragment, dating from about 200, listed most of the books recognized as canonical in later decrees. Prior to the end of the fourth century, however, there was controversy over the inspired character of several works — the Letter to the Hebrews, James, Jude, 2 Peter, 2 and 3 John and Revelation. Controversy ended in the fourth century and these books, along with those about which there was no dispute, were enumerated in the canon stated by the councils of Hippo and Carthage and affirmed by Innocent I in 405.

The Canon of the Bible was solemnly defined by the Council of Trent in the dogmatic decree *De Canonicis Scripturis,* Apr. 8, 1546.

Hebrew and Other Canons

The Hebrew Canon of sacred writings was fixed by tradition and the consensus of rabbis, probably by about 100 A.D. by the Synod or Council of Jamnia and certainly by the end of the second or early in the third century. It consists of the following works in three categories.

• **The Law (Torah),** the five books of Moses: Genesis, Exodus, Leviticus, Numbers, Deuteronomy.

• **The Prophets:** former prophets — Joshua, Judges, 1 and 2 Samuel, 1 and 2 Kings; latter prophets — Isaiah, Jeremiah, Ezekiel, and 12 minor prophets (Hosea, Joel, Amos, Obadiah, Jonah, Micah, Nahum, Habakkuk, Zephaniah, Haggai, Zechariah, Malachi).

• **The Writings:** 1 and 2 Chronicles, Ezra, Nehemiah, Job, Psalms, Proverbs, Ecclesiastes, Song of Songs, Ruth, Esther, Daniel.

This Canon, embodying the tradition and practice of the Palestine community, did not include a number of works contained in the Alexandrian version of sacred writings translated into Greek between 250 and 100 B.C. and in use by Greek-speaking Jews of the Dispersion (outside Palestine). The rejected works, called apocrypha and not regarded as sacred, are: Tobit, Judith, Wisdom, Sirach, Baruch, 1 and 2 Maccabees, the last six chapters of Esther and three passages of Daniel (3:24-90; 13; 14). These books have also been rejected from the Protestant Canon, although they are included in bibles under the heading, Apocrypha.

The aforementioned books are held to be inspired and sacred by the Catholic Church. In Catholic usage, they are called deuterocanonical because they were under discussion for some time before questions about their canonicity were settled. Books regarded as canonical with little or no debate were called protocanonical. The status of both categories of books is the same in the Catholic Bible.

The Protestant Canon of the Old Testament is the same as the Hebrew.

The Old Testament Canon of some separated Eastern churches differs from the Catholic Canon.

Christians are in agreement on the Canon of the New Testament.

Languages

Hebrew, Aramaic and Greek were the original languages of the Bible. Most of the Old Testament books were written in Hebrew. Portions of Daniel, Ezra, Jeremiah, Esther, and probably the books of Tobit and Judith were written in Aramaic. The Book of Wisdom, 2 Maccabees and all the books of the New Testament were written in Greek.

Manuscripts and Versions

The original writings of the inspired authors have been lost. The Bible has been transmitted through ancient copies called manuscripts and through translations or versions.

Authoritative Greek manuscripts include the Sinaitic and Vatican manuscripts of the fourth century and the Alexandrine of the fifth century A.D.

The Septuagint and Vulgate translations are in a class by themselves.

The Septuagint version, a Greek translation of the Old Testament for Greek-speaking Jews, was begun about 250 and completed about 100 B.C. The work of several Jewish translators at Alexandria, it differed from the Hebrew Bible in the arrangement of books and included several, later called deuterocanonical, which were not acknowledged as sacred by the community in Palestine.

The Vulgate was a Latin version of the Old and New Testaments produced from the original languages by St. Jerome from about 383 to 404. It became the most widely used Latin text for centuries and was regarded as basic long before the Council of Trent designated it as authentic and suitable for use in public reading, controversy, preaching and teaching. Because of its authoritative character, it became the basis for many translations into other languages. A critical revision was completed by a pontifical commission in 1977.

Hebrew and Aramaic manuscripts of great antiquity and value have figured more significantly than before in recent scriptural work by Catholic scholars, especially since their use was strongly encouraged, if not mandated, in 1943 by Pius XII in the encyclical *Divino Afflante Spiritu.*

The English translation of the Bible in general use among Catholics until well into the 20th century was the *Douay-Rheims,* so called because of the places where it was prepared and published, the New Testament at Rheims in 1582 and the Old Testament at Douay in 1609. The translation was made from the Vulgate text. As revised and issued by Bishop Richard Challoner in 1749 and 1750, it became the standard Catholic English version for about 200 years.

A revision of the Challoner New Testament, made on the basis of the Vulgate text by scholars of the Catholic Biblical Association of America, was published in 1941 in the United States under the sponsorship of the Episcopal Committee of the Confraternity of Christian Doctrine.

New American Bible

A new translation of the entire Bible, the first ever made directly into English from the original languages under Catholic auspices, was projected in 1944 and completed in the fall of 1970 with publication of the *New American Bible.* The Episcopal Committee of the Confraternity of Christian Doctrine sponsored the NAB. The translators were members of the Catholic Biblical Association of America and several fellow scholars of other faiths. The typical edition was produced by St. Anthony Guild Press, Paterson, N.J.

Old Testament portions of the NAB were published in separate volumes before undergoing final revision and being bound in one cover. Genesis and Psalms were issued in 1948 and 1950; Genesis to Ruth, in 1952; Job to Sirach, in 1955; the Prophets, in 1961; Samuel to the Maccabees, in 1969. The new translation of the New Testament was issued for the first time in 1970.

The *Jerusalem Bible* is an English translation of a French version based on the original languages. It was published by Doubleday & Co., Inc., which is also working toward completion of the *Anchor Bible*.

The Protestant counterpart of the *Douay-Rheims Bible* was the *King James Bible*, called the *Authorized Version* in England. Originally published in 1611, it was in general use for more than three centuries. Its modern revisions include the *English Revised Version*, published between 1881 and 1885; the *American Revised Version*, 1901, and revisions of the New Testament (1946) and the Old Testament (1952) published in 1957 in the United States as the *Revised Standard Version*. The latest revision, a translation in the language of the present day made from Greek and Hebrew sources, is the *New English Bible*, published Mar. 16, 1970. Its New Testament portion was originally published in 1961.

Biblical Federation

In November, 1966, Pope Paul commissioned the Secretariat for Promoting Christian Unity to start work for the widest possible distribution of the Bible and to coordinate endeavors toward the production of Catholic-Protestant Bibles in all languages.

The World Catholic Federation for the Biblical Apostolate, established in 1969, sponsors a program designed to create greater awareness among Catholics of the Bible and its use in everyday life.

The U. S. Center for the Catholic Biblical Apostolate, under the direction of Father Stephen Hartdegen, O.F.M., is related to the Department of Education, U.S. Catholic Conference. Address: 1312 Massachusetts Ave. N.W., Washington, D.C. 20005.

APOCRYPHA

In Catholic usage, Apocrypha are books which have some resemblance to the canonical books in subject matter and title but which have not been recognized as canonical by the Church. They are characterized by a false claim to divine authority; extravagant accounts of events and miracles alleged to be supplemental revelation; material favoring heresy (especially in "New Testament" apocrypha); minimal, if any, historical value.

Among examples of this type of literature itemized by J. McKenzie, S.J., in *Dictionary of the Bible* are: *the Books of Adam and Eve, Martyrdom of Isaiah, Testament of the Patriarchs, Assumption of Moses, Sibylline Oracles; Gospel of James, Gospel of Thomas, Arabic Gospel of the Infancy, History of Joseph the Carpenter; Acts of John, Acts of Paul, Acts of Peter, Acts of Andrew*, and numerous epistles.

Books of this type are called pseudepigrapha by Protestants.

In Protestant usage, some books of the Catholic Bible (deuterocanonical) are called apocrypha because their inspired character is rejected.

DEAD SEA SCROLLS

The Qumran Scrolls, popularly called the Dead Sea Scrolls, are a collection of manuscripts, all but one of them in Hebrew, found since 1947 in caves in the Desert of Juda west of the Dead Sea.

Among the findings were a complete text of Isaiah dating from the second century, B.C., more or less extensive fragments of other Old Testament texts (including the deuterocanonical Tobit), and a commentary on Habakkuk. Until the discovery of these materials, the oldest known Hebrew manuscripts were from the 10th century, A.D.

Also found were messianic and apocalyptic texts, and other writings describing the beliefs and practices of the Essenes, a rigoristic Jewish sect.

The scrolls, dating from about the first century before and after Christ, are important sources of information about Hebrew literature, Jewish history during the period between the Old and New Testaments, and the history of Old Testament texts. They established the fact that the Hebrew text of the Old Testament was fixed before the beginning of the Christian era and have had definite effects in recent critical studies and translations of the Old Testament. Together with other scrolls found at Masada, they are still the subject of intensive study.

BOOKS OF THE BIBLE

OLD TESTAMENT
(Dates are before Christ.)

Pentateuch

The Pentateuch is the collective title of the first five books of the Bible. Substantially, they identify the Israelites as Yahweh's Chosen People, cover their history from Egypt to the threshold of the Promised Land, contain the Mosaic Law and Covenant, and disclose the promise of salvation to come. Principal themes concern the divine promise of salvation, Yahweh's fidelity and the Covenant. Work on the composition of the Pentateuch was completed in the sixth century.

Genesis: The book of origins, according to its title in the Septuagint. In two parts, covers: religious prehistory, including accounts of the origin of the world and man, the original state of innocence and the fall, the promise of salvation, patriarchs before and after the Deluge, the Tower of Babel narrative, genealogies (first 11 chapters);

the Covenant with Abraham and patriarchal history from Abraham to Joseph (balance of the 50 chapters). Significant are the themes of Yahweh's universal sovereignty and mercy.

Exodus: Named with the Greek word for departure, is a religious epic which describes the oppression of the 12 tribes in Egypt and their departure, liberation or passover therefrom under the leadership of Moses; Yahweh's establishment of the Covenant with them, making them his Chosen People, through the mediation of Moses at Mt. Sinai; instructions concerning the tabernacle, the sanctuary and Ark of the Covenant; the institution of the priesthood. The book is significant because of its theology of liberation and redemption. In Christian interpretation, the Exodus is a figure of baptism.

Leviticus: Mainly legislative in theme and purpose, contains laws regarding sacrifices, ceremonies of ordination and the priesthood of Aaron, legal purity, the holiness code, atonement, the redemption of offerings and other subjects. Summarily, Levitical laws provided directives for all aspects of religious observance and for the manner in which the Israelites were to conduct themselves with respect to Yahweh and each other. Leviticus was the liturgical handbook of the priesthood.

Numbers: Taking its name from censuses recounted at the beginning and near the end, is a continuation of Exodus. It combines narrative of the Israelites' desert pilgrimage from Sinai to the border of Canaan with laws related to and expansive of those in Leviticus.

Deuteronomy: The concluding book of the Pentateuch, recapitulates, in the form of a testament of Moses, the Law and much of the desert history of the Israelites; enjoins fidelity to the Law as the key to good or bad fortune for the people; gives an account of the commissioning of Joshua as the successor of Moses. Notable themes concern the election of Israel by Yahweh, observance of the Law, prohibitions against the worship of foreign gods, worship of and confidence in Yahweh, the power of Yahweh in nature. The Deuteronomic Code or motif, embodying all of these elements, was the norm for interpreting Israelite history.

Joshua, Judges, Ruth

Joshua: Records the fulfillment of Yahweh's promise to the Israelites in their conquest, occupation and division of Canaan under the leadership of Joshua. It also contains an account of the return of Transjordanian Israelites and of a renewal of the Covenant. It was redacted in final form probably in the sixth century or later.

Judges: Records the actions of charismatic leaders, called judges, of the tribes of Israel between the death of Joshua and the time of Samuel, and a crisis of idolatry among the people. The basic themes are sin and punishment, repentance and deliverance; its purpose was in line with the Deuteronomic motif, that the fortunes of the Israelites were related to their observance or non-observance of the Law and the Covenant. It was redacted in final form probably in the sixth century.

Ruth: Named for the Gentile (Moabite) woman who, through marriage with Boaz, became an Israelite and an ancestress of David (her son, Obed, became his grandfather). Themes are filial piety, faith and trust in Yahweh, the universality of messianic salvation. Dates ranging from c. 950 to the seventh century have been assigned to the origin of the book, whose author is unknown.

Historical Books

These books, while they contain a great deal of factual material, are unique in their preoccupation with presenting and interpreting it, in the Deuteronomic manner, in primary relation to the Covenant on which the nation of Israel was founded and in accordance with which community and personal life were judged.

The books are: Samuel 1 and 2, from the end of Judges (c. 1020) to the end of David's reign (c. 961); Kings 1 and 2, from the last days of David to the start of the Babylonian Exile and the destruction of the Temple (587); Chronicles 1 and 2, from the reign of Saul (c. 1020-1000) to the return of the people from the Exile (538); Ezra and Nehemiah, covering the reorganization of the Jewish community after the Exile (458-397); Maccabees 1 and 2, recounting the struggle against attempted suppression of Judaism (168-142).

Three of the books listed below — Tobit, Judith and Esther — are categorized as religious novels.

Samuel 1 and 2: A single work in concept and contents, containing episodic history of the last two Judges, Eli and Samuel, the establishment and rule of the monarchy under Saul and David, and the political consequences of David's rule. The royal messianic dynasty of David was the subject of Nathan's oracle in 2 Sm. 7. The books were edited in final form probably late in the seventh century or during the Exile.

Kings 1 and 2: Cover the last days of David and the career of Solomon, including the building of the Temple and the history of the kingdom during his reign; stories of the prophets Elijah and Elisha; the history of the divided kingdom to the fall of Israel in the North (721) and the fall of Judah in the South (587), the destruction of Jerusalem and the Temple. They reflect the Deuteronomic motif in attributing the downfall of the people to corruption of belief and practice in public and private life. They were completed probably in the sixth century.

Chronicles 1 and 2: A collection of historical traditions interpreted in such a way as to present an ideal picture of one people governed by divine law and united in one Temple worship of the one true God. Contents include genealogical tables from Adam to David, the careers of David and Solomon, coverage of the kingdom of Judah to the Exile, and the decree of Cyrus permitting the return of the people and rebuilding of Jerusalem. Both are related to and were written about 400 by the same author, the Chronicler, who composed Ezra and Nehemiah.

Ezra and Nehemiah: A running account of the return of the people to their homeland after the Exile and of practical efforts, under the leadership of Ezra and Nehemiah, to restore and reorganize the religious and political community on the basis of Israelite traditions, divine worship and observance of the Law. Events of great significance were the building of the second Temple, the building of a wall around Jerusalem and the proclamation of the Law by Ezra. This restored community was the start of Judaism. Both are related to and were written about 400 by the same author, the Chronicler, who composed Chronicles 1 and 2.

Tobit: Written in the literary form of a novel and having greater resemblance to wisdom than to historical literature, narrates the personal history of Tobit, a devout and charitable Jew in exile, and persons connected with him, viz., his son Tobiah, his kinsman Raguel and Raguel's daughter Sarah. Its purpose was to teach people how to be good Jews. One of its principal themes is patience under trial, with trust in divine Providence which is symbolized by the presence and action of the angel Raphael. It was written about 200.

Judith: Recounts, in the literary form of a historical novel or romance, the preservation of the Israelites from conquest and ruin through the action of Judith. The essential themes are trust in God for deliverance from danger and emphasis on observance of the Law. It was written probably during the Maccabean period.

Esther: Relates, in the literary form of a historical novel or romance, the manner in which Jews in Persia were saved from annihilation through the central role played by Esther, the Jewish wife of Ahasuerus; a fact commemorated by the Jewish feast of Purim. Like Judith, it has trust in divine Providence as its theme and indicates that God's saving will is sometimes realized by persons acting in unlikely ways. It may have been written near the end of the fourth century.

Maccabees 1 and 2: While related to some extent because of common subject matter, are quite different from each other.

The first book recounts the background and events of the 40-year (175-135) struggle for religious and political freedom led by Judas Maccabaeus and his brothers against the Hellenist Seleucid kings and some Hellenophiles among the Jews. Victory was symbolized by the rededication of the Temple. Against the background of opposition between Jews and Gentiles, the author equated the survival of belief in the one true God with survival of the Jewish people, thus identifying religion with patriotism. It was written probably near the year 100.

The second book supplements the first to some extent, covering and giving a theological interpretation to events from 180 to 162. It explains the feast of the Dedication of the Temple, a key event in the survival of Judaism which is commemorated in the feast of Hanukkah; stresses the primacy of God's action in the struggle for survival; and indicates belief in an afterlife and the resurrection of the body. It was completed probably about 124.

Wisdom Books

With the exceptions of Psalms and the Song of Songs, the titles listed under this heading are called wisdom books because their purpose was to formulate the fruits of human experience in the context of meditation on sacred Scripture and to present them as an aid toward understanding the problems of life. Hebrew wisdom literature was distinctive from pagan literature of the same type, but it had limitations; these were overcome in the New Testament, which added the dimensions of the New Covenant to those of the Old. Solomon was regarded as the archtype of the wise man.

Job: A dramatic, didactic poem consisting mainly of several dialogues between Job and his friends concerning the mystery involved in the coexistence of the just God, evil and the suffering of the just. It describes an innocent man's experience of suffering and conveys the truth that faith in and submission to God rather than complete understanding, which is impossible, make the experience bearable; also, that the justice of God cannot be defended by affirming that it is realized in this world. Of unknown authorship, it was composed between the seventh and fifth centuries.

Psalms: A collection of 150 religious songs or lyrics reflecting Israelite belief and piety dating from the time of the monarchy to the post-Exilic period, a span of well over 500 years. The psalms, which are a compendium of Old Testament theology, were used in the temple liturgy and for other occasions. They were of several types suitable for the king, hymns, lamentations, expressions of confidence and thanksgiving, prophecy, historical meditation and reflection, and the statement of wisdom. About one-half of them are attributed to David; many were composed by unknown authors.

Proverbs: The oldest book of the wisdom type in the Bible, consisting of collections of sayings attributed to Solomon and other persons regarding a wide variety of subjects including wisdom and its nature, rules of conduct, duties with respect to one's neighbor, the conduct of daily affairs. It reveals many details of Hebrew life. Its nucleus dates from the period before the Exile. The extant form of the book dates probably from the end of the fifth century.

Ecclesiastes: A treatise about many subjects whose unifying theme is the vanity of strictly human efforts and accomplishments with respect to the achievement of lasting happiness; the only things which are not vain are fear of the Lord and observance of his commandments. The pessimistic tone of the book is due to the absence of a concept of afterlife. It was written by an unknown author probably in the third century.

Song of Songs: A collection of love lyrics reflecting various themes, including the love of God for Israel and the celebration of ideal love and fidelity between man and woman. It was written by an unknown author after the Exile.

Wisdom: Deals with many subjects including the reward of justice; praise of wisdom, a gift of Yahweh proceeding from belief in him and the practice of his Law; the part played by him in the history of his people, especially in their liberation from Egypt; the folly and shame of idolatry. Its contents are taken from the whole sacred literature of the Jews and represent a distillation of its wisdom based on the law, beliefs and traditions of Israel. The last of the Old Testament books, it was written in the early part of the first century before Christ by a member of the Jewish community at Alexandria.

Sirach: Resembling Proverbs, is a collection of sayings handed on by a grandfather to his grandson. It contains a variety of moral instruction and eulogies of patriarchs and other figures in Israelite history. Its moral maxims apply to individuals, the family and community, relations with God, friendship, education, wealth, the Law, divine worship. Its theme is that true wisdom consists in the Law. (It was formerly called Ecclesiasticus, the Church Book, because of its extensive use by the Church for moral instruction.) It was written in Hebrew between 200 and 175, during a period of strong Hellenistic influence, and was translated into Greek after 132.

The Prophets

These books and the prophecies they contain "express judgments of the people's moral conduct, on the basis of the Mosaic alliance between God and Israel. They teach sublime truths and lofty morals. They contain exhortations, threats, announcements of punishment, promises of deliverance. . . . In the affairs of men, their prime concern is the interests of God, especially in what pertains to the Chosen People through whom the Messiah is to come; hence their denunciations of idolatry and of that externalism in worship which exclude the interior spirit of religion. They are concerned also with the universal nature of the moral law, with personal responsibility, with the person and office of the Messiah, and with the conduct of foreign nations" (*The Holy Bible,* Prophetic Books, CCD Edition, 1961; Preface). There are four major (Isaiah, Jeremiah, Ezekiel, Daniel) and 12 minor prophets (distinguished by the length of books), Lamentations and Baruch. Earlier prophets, mentioned in historical books, include Samuel, Gad, Nathan, Elijah and Elisha.

Before the Exile, prophets were the intermediaries through whom God communicated revelation to the people. Afterwards, prophecy lapsed and the written word of the Law served this purpose.

Isaiah: Named for the greatest of the prophets whose career spanned the reigns of three Hebrew kings from 742 to the beginning of the seventh century, in a period of moral breakdown in Judah and threats of invasion by foreign enemies. It is an anthology of poems and oracles credited to him and a number of followers deeply influenced by him. Of special importance are the prophecies concerning Immanuel (6 to 12), including the prophecy of the virgin birth (7:14). Chapters 40 to 55, called Deutero-Isaiah, are attributed to an anonymous poet toward the end of the Exile; this portion contains the Songs of the Servant. The concluding part of the book (56-66) contains oracles by later disciples. One of many themes in Isaiah concerned the saving mission of the remnant of Israel in the divine plan of salvation.

Jeremiah: Combines history, biography and prophecy in a setting of crisis caused by internal and external factors, viz., idolatry and general infidelity to the Law among the Israelites and external threats from the Assyrians, Egyptians and Babylonians. Jeremiah prophesied the promise of a new covenant as well as the destruction of Jerusalem and the Temple. His career began in 626 and ended some years after the beginning of the Exile. The book, the longest in the Bible, was edited in final form after the Exile.

Lamentations: A collection of five laments or elegies over the fall of Jerusalem and the fate of the people in Exile, written by an unknown eyewitness. They convey the message that Yahweh struck the people because of their sins and reflect confidence in his love and power to restore his converted people.

Baruch: Against the background of the already begun Exile, it consists of an introduction and several parts: an exile's prayer of confession and petition for forgiveness and the restoration of Israel; a poem praising wisdom and the Law of Moses; a lament in which Jerusalem, personified, bewails the fate of her people and consoles them with the hope of blessings to come; and a polemic against idolatry. Although ascribed to Baruch, Jeremiah's secretary, it was written by several authors probably in the second century.

Ezekiel: Named for the priest-prophet who prophesied in Babylon from 593 to 571, during the first phase of the Exile. To prepare his fellow early exiles for the impending fall of Jerusalem, he reproached the Israelites for past sins and predicted woes to come upon them. After the destruction of the city, the burden of his message was hope and promise of restoration. Ezekiel had great influence on the religion of Israel after the Exile.

Daniel: The protagonist is a young Jew, taken early to Babylon where he lived until about 538, who figured in a series of edifying stories which originated in Israelite tradition. The stories, whose characters are not purely legendary but rest on historical tradition, recount the trials and triumphs of Daniel and his three companions, and other episodes including those concerning Susannah, Bel, and the Dragon. The book is more apocalyptic than prophetic: it envisions Israel in glory to come and conveys the message that men of faith can resist temptation and overcome adversity. It states the prophetic themes of right conduct, divine control of men and events, and the final triumph of the kingdom. It was written by an unknown author in the 160's to give moral support to Jews during the persecutions of the Maccabean period.

Hosea: Consists of a prophetic parallel between Hosea's marriage and Yahweh's relations with his people. As the prophet was married to a faithless wife whom he would not give up, Yahweh was bound in Covenant with an idolatrous and unjust Israel whom he would not desert but would chastise for purification. Hosea belonged to the Northern Kingdom of Israel and began his career about the middle of the eighth century. He inaugurated the tradition of describing Yahweh's relation to Israel in terms of marriage.

Joel: Is apocalyptic and eschatological regarding divine judgment, the Day of the Lord, which is symbolized by a ravaging invasion of locusts, the judgment of the nations in the Valley of Josaphat and the outpouring of the Spirit in the messianic era to come. Its message is that God will vindicate and save Israel, in view of the prayer and repentance of the people, and will punish their enemies. It was composed about 400.

Amos: Consists of an indictment against foreign enemies of Israel; a strong denunciation of the people of Israel, whose infidelity, idolatry and injustice made them subject to divine judgment and punishment; and a messianic oracle regarding Israel's restoration. Amos prophesied in the Northern Kingdom of Israel, at Bethel, in the first half of the eighth century; chronologically, he was the first of the canonical prophets.

Obadiah: A 21-verse prophecy, the shortest and one of the sternest in the Bible, against the Edomites, invaders of southern Judah and enemies of those returning from the Exile to their homeland. It was probably composed in the fifth century.

Jonah: A parable of divine mercy with the theme that Yahweh wills the salvation of all, not just a few, men who respond to his call. Its protagonist is a disobedient prophet; forced by circumstances beyond his control to preach penance among Gentiles, he is highly successful in his mission but baffled by the divine concern for those who do not belong to the Chosen People. It was written after the Exile, probably in the fifth century.

Micah: Attacks the injustice and corruption of priests, false prophets, officials and people; announces judgment and punishment to come; foretells the restoration of Israel; refers to the saving remnant of Israel. Micah was a contemporary of Isaiah.

Nahum: Concerns the destruction of Nineveh in 612 and the overthrow of the Assyrian Empire by the Babylonians.

Habakkuk: Dating from about 605-597, concerns sufferings to be inflicted by oppressors on the people of Judah because of their infidelity to the Lord. It also sounds a note of confidence in the Lord, the Savior, and declares that the just will not perish.

Zephaniah: Exercising his ministry in the second half of the seventh century, during a time of widespread idolatry, superstition and religious degradation, he prophesied impending judgment and punishment for Jerusalem and its people. He prophesied too that a holy remnant of the people (*anawim*, mentioned also by Amos) would be spared. Zephaniah was a forerunner of Jeremiah.

Haggai: One of the first prophets after the Exile, Haggai in 520 encouraged the returning exiles to reestablish their community and to complete the second Temple (dedicated in 515), for which he envisioned greater glory, in a messianic sense, than that enjoyed by the original Temple of Solomon.

Zechariah: A contemporary of Haggai, he prophesied in the same vein. A second part of the book, called Deutero-Zechariah and composed by one or more unknown authors, relates a vision of the coming of the Prince of Peace, the Messiah of the Poor.

Malachi: Written by an anonymous author, presents a picture of life in the post-Exilic community between 516 and the initiation of reforms by Ezra and Nehemiah about 432. Blame for the troubles of the community is placed mainly on priests for failure to carry out ritual worship and to instruct the people in the proper manner; other factors were religious indifference and the influence of doubters who were scandalized at the prosperity of the wicked. The vision of a universal sacrifice to be offered to Yahweh (1:11) is interpreted in Catholic theology as a prophecy of the sacrifice of the Mass. Malachi was the last of the minor prophets.

OLD TESTAMENT DATES

c. 1800 — c. 1600: Period of the patriarchs (Abraham, Isaac, Jacob).

c. 1600: Israelites in Egypt.

c. 1250: Exodus of Israelites from Egypt.

c. 1210: Entrance of Israelites into Canaan.

c. 1210 — c. 1020: Period of the Judges.

c. 1020 — c. 1000: Reign of Saul, first king.

c. 1000 — c. 961: Reign of David.

c. 961 — 922: Reign of Solomon. Temple built during his reign.

922: Division of the Kingdom into Israel (North) and Judah (South).

721: Conquest of Israel by Assyrians.

587-538: Conquest of Judah by Babylonians. Babylonian Captivity and Exile. Destruction of Jerusalem and the Temple, 587. Captivity ended with the return of exiles, following the decree of Cyrus permitting the rebuilding of Jerusalem.

515: Dedication of the Second Temple.

458-397: Restoration and reform of the Jewish religious and political community; building of the Jerusalem wall, 439. Leaders in the movement were Ezra and Nehemiah.

168-142: Period of the Maccabees; war against Syrians.

142: Independence granted to Jews by Demetrius II of Syria.

135-37: Period of the Hasmonean dynasty.

63: Beginning of Roman rule.

37-4: Period of Herod the Great.

WARNING AGAINST BIBLICAL FUNDAMENTALISM

In an address to members of the World Catholic Federation for the Biblical Apostolate, Pope John Paul warned against "narrow fundamentalism" in biblical study, interpretation and teaching. "Attention must be given," he said Apr. 7, 1986, "to the literary forms of the various biblical books.

... And it is most helpful ... to be aware of the personal situation of the biblical writer, to the circumstances of culture, time, language, etc., which influenced the way the message was presented." And, the Bible should be approached in line with "the living tradition of the Church."

NEW TESTAMENT BOOKS

Gospels

The term Gospel is derived from the Anglo-Saxon *god-spell* and the Greek *euangelion*, meaning good news, good tidings. In Christian use, it means the good news of salvation proclaimed by Christ and the Church, and handed on in written form in the Gospels of Matthew, Mark, Luke and John.

The initial proclamation of the coming of the kingdom of God was made by Jesus in and through his Person, teachings and actions, and especially through his Passion, death and resurrection. This proclamation became the center of Christian faith and the core of the oral Gospel tradition with which the Church spread the good news by apostolic preaching for some 30 years before it was committed to writing by the Evangelists.

Nature of the Gospels

The historical truth of the Gospels was the subject of an instruction issued by the Pontifical Commission for Biblical Studies Apr. 21, 1964.

• The sacred writers selected from the material at their disposal (the oral Gospel tradition, some written collections of sayings and deeds of Jesus, eyewitness accounts) those things which were particularly suitable to the various conditions (liturgical, catechetical, missionary) of the faithful and the aims they had in mind, and they narrated these things in such a way as to correspond with those circumstances and their aims.

• The life and teaching of Jesus were not simply reported in a biographical manner for the purpose of preserving their memory but were "preached" so as to offer the Church the basis of doctrine concerning faith and morals.

• In their works, the Evangelists presented the true sayings of Jesus and the events of his life in the light of the better understanding they had following their enlightenment by the Holy Spirit. They did not transform Christ into a "mythical" Person, nor did they distort his teaching.

Passion narratives are the core of all the Gospels, covering the suffering, death and resurrection of Jesus as central events in bringing about and establishing the New Covenant. Leading up to them are accounts of the mission of John the Baptizer and the ministry of Jesus, especially in Galilee and finally in Jerusalem before the Passion. The infancy of Jesus is covered by Luke and Matthew with narratives inspired in part by appropriate Old Testament citations.

Matthew, Mark and Luke, while different in various respects, have so many similarities that they are called Synoptic; their relationships are the subject of the Synoptic Problem.

Matthew: Written probably between 80 and 100 for Jewish Christians, with clear reference to Jewish background and identification of Jesus as the divine Messiah, the fulfillment of the Old Testament. Distinctive are the use of Old Testament citations regarding the Person, activity and teaching of Jesus, and the presentation of doctrine in sermons and discourses.

Mark: The first of the Gospels, dating from about 70. Written for Gentile Christians, it is noted for the realism and wealth of concrete details with which it reveals Jesus as Son of God and Savior more by his actions and miracles than by his discourses. Theologically, it is less refined than the other Gospels.

Luke: Written about 75 for Gentile Christians. It is noted for the universality of its address, the insight it provides into the Christian way of life, the place it gives to women, the manner in which it emphasizes Jesus' friendship with sinners and compassion for the suffering.

John: Edited and arranged in final form probably between 90 and 100, is the most sublime and theological of the Gospels, and is different from the Synoptics in plan and treatment. Combining accounts of signs with longer discourses and reflections, it progressively reveals the Person and mission of Jesus — as Word, Way, Truth, Life, Light — in line with the purpose, "to help you believe that Jesus is the Messiah, the Son of God, so that through this faith you may have life in his name" (Jn. 20:31). There are questions about the authorship but no doubt about the Johannine authority and tradition behind the Gospel.

Acts of the Apostles

Acts of the Apostles: Written by Luke about 75 as a supplement to his Gospel. It describes the origin and spread of Christian communities through the action of the Holy Spirit from the resurrection of Christ to the time when Paul was placed in custody in Rome in the early 60's.

Letters (Epistles)

These letters, many of which antedated the Gospels, were written in response to existential needs of the early Christian communities for doctrinal and moral instruction, disciplinary action, practical advice, and exhortation to true Christian living.

Pauline Letters

These letters, which comprise approximately one-fourth of the New Testament, are primary and monumental sources of the development of Christian theology. Several of them may not have had Paul as their actual author, but evidence of the Pauline tradition behind them is strong. The letters to the Colossians, Philippians, Ephesians and Philemon have been called the "Captivity Letters" because of a tradition that they were written while Paul was under house arrest or another form of detention.

Romans: Written about 57 probably from Corinth on the central significance of Christ and faith in him for salvation, and the relationship of Christianity to Judaism; the condition of mankind without Christ; justification and the Christian life; duties of Christians.

Corinthians 1: Written near the beginning of 57 from Ephesus to counteract factionalism and disorders, it covers community dissensions, moral irregularities, marriage and celibacy, conduct at religious gatherings, the Eucharist, spiritual gifts (charisms) and their function in the Church, charity, the resurrection of the body.

Corinthians 2: Written later in the same year as 1 Cor., concerning Paul's defense of his apostolic life and ministry, and an appeal for a collection to aid poor Christians in Jerusalem.

Galatians: Written probably between 54 and 55 to counteract Judaizing opinions and efforts to undermine his authority, it asserts the divine origin of Paul's authority and doctrine, states that justification is not through Mosaic Law but through faith in Christ, insists on the practice of evangelical virtues, especially charity.

Ephesians: Written probably between 61 and 63, mainly on the Church as the Mystical Body of Christ.

Philippians: Written between 56 and 57 or 61 and 63 to warn the Philippians against enemies of their faith, to urge them to be faithful to their vocation and unity of belief, and to thank them for their kindness to him while he was being held in detention.

Colossians: Written probably while he was under house arrest in Rome from 61 to 63, to counteract the influence of self-appointed teachers who were watering down doctrine concerning Christ. It includes two highly important Christological passages, a warning against false teachers, and an instruction on the ideal Christian life.

Thessalonians 1 and 2: Written within a short time of each other probably in 51 from Corinth, mainly on doctrine concerning the Parousia, the second coming of Christ.

Timothy 1 and 2, Titus: Written between 65 and 67, or perhaps in the 70's, giving pastoral counsels to Timothy and Titus who were in charge of churches in Ephesus and Crete, respectively. 1 Tm. emphasizes pastoral responsibility for preserving unity of doctrine; 2 Tm. describes Paul's imprisonment in Rome.

Philemon: A private letter written between 61 and 63 to a wealthy Colossian concerning a slave, Onesimus, who had escaped from him; Paul appealed for kind treatment of the man.

Hebrews: Dating from sometime between 70 and 96, a complex theological treatise on Christology, the priesthood and sacrifice of Christ, the New Covenant, and the pattern for Christian living. Critical opinion is divided as to whether it was addressed to Judaeo or Gentile Christians.

Catholic Letters, Revelation

These seven letters have been called "catholic" because it was thought for some time, not altogether correctly, that they were not addressed to particular communities.

James: Written sometime before 62 in the spirit of Hebrew wisdom literature and the moralism of Tobit. An exhortation to practical Christian living, it is also noteworthy for the doctrine it states on good works and its citation regarding anointing of the sick.

Peter 1 and 2: The first letter may have been written between 64 and 67 or between 90 and 95; the second may date from 100 to 125. Addressed to Christians in Asia Minor, both are exhortations to perseverance in the life of faith despite trials and difficulties arising from pagan influences, isolation from other Christians and false teaching.

John 1: Written sometime in the 90's and addressed to Asian churches, its message is that God is made known to us in the Son and that fellowship with the Father is attained by living in the light, justice and love of the Son.

John 2: Written sometime in the 90's and addressed to a church in Asia, it commends the people for standing firm in the faith and urges them to perseverance.

John 3: Written sometime in the 90's, it appears to represent an effort to settle a jurisdictional dispute in one of the churches.

Jude: Written probably about 80, it is a brief treatise against erroneous teachings and practices opposed to law, authority and true Christian freedom.

Revelation: Written in the 90's along the lines of Johannine thought, it is a symbolic and apocalyptic treatment of things to come and of the struggle between the Church and evil combined with warning but hope and assurance to the Church regarding the coming of the Lord in glory.

INTERPRETATION OF THE BIBLE

According to the *Constitution on Revelation* issued by the Second Vatican Council, "the interpreter of Sacred Scripture, in order to see clearly what God wanted to communicate to us, should carefully investigate what meaning the sacred writers really intended, and what God wanted to manifest by means of their words" (No. 12).

Hermeneutics, Exegesis

This careful investigation proceeds in accordance with the rules of hermeneutics, the normative science of biblical interpretation and explanation. Hermeneutics in practice is called exegesis.

The principles of hermeneutics are derived from various disciplines and many factors which have to be considered in explaining the Bible and its parts.

These include: the original languages and languages of translation of the sacred texts, through philology and linguistics; the quality of texts, through textual criticism; literary forms and genres, through literary and form criticism; cultural, historical, geographical and other conditions which influenced the writers, through related studies; facts and truths of salvation history; the truths and analogy of faith.

Distinctive to biblical hermeneutics, which differs in important respects from literary interpretation in general, is the premise that the Bible, though written by human authors, is the work of divine inspiration in which God reveals his plan for the salvation of men through historical events and persons, and especially through the Person and mission of Christ.

Textual, Form Criticism

Textual criticism is the study of biblical texts, which have been transmitted in copies several times removed from the original manuscripts, for the purpose of establishing the real state of the original texts. This purpose is served by comparison of existing copies; by application to the texts of the disciplines of philology and linguistics; by examination of related works of antiquity; by study of biblical citations in works of the Fathers of the Church and other authors; and by other means of literary study.

Since about 1920, the sayings of Christ have been a particular object of New Testament study, the purpose being to analyze the forms of expression used by the Evangelists in order to ascertain the words actually spoken by him.

Literary Criticism

Literary criticism aims to determine the origin and kinds of literary composition, called forms or genres, employed by the inspired authors. Such determinations are necessary for decision regarding the nature and purpose and, consequently, the meaning of biblical passages. Underlying these studies is the principle that the manner of writing was conditioned by the intention of the authors, the meaning they wanted to convey, and the then-contemporary literary style, mode or medium best adapted to carry their message — e.g., true history, quasi-historical narrative, poems, prayers, hymns, psalms, aphorisms, allegories, discourses. Understanding these media is necessary for the valid interpretation of their message.

Literal Sense

The key to all valid interpretation is the literal sense of biblical passages. Regarding this matter and the relevance to it of the studies and procedures described above, Pius XII wrote the following in the encyclical *Divino Afflante Spiritu.*

"What the literal sense of a passage is, is not always as obvious in the speeches and writings of ancient authors of the East as it is in the works of our own time. For what they wished to express is not to be determined by the rules of grammar and philology alone nor solely by the context; the interpreter must, as it were, go back wholly in spirit to those remote centuries of the East and with the aid of history, archeology, ethnology, and other sciences accurately determine what modes of writing, so to speak, the authors of that ancient period would be likely to use and in fact did use. . . . In explaining the Sacred Scripture and in demonstrating and proving its immunity from all error (the Catholic interpreter) should make a prudent use of this means, determine to what extent the manner of expression or literary mode adopted by the sacred writer may lead to a correct and genuine interpretation; and let him be convinced that this part of his office cannot be neglected without serious detriment to Catholic exegesis."

The literal sense of the Bible is the meaning in the mind of and intended by the inspired writer of a book or passage of the Bible. This is determined by the application to texts of the rules of hermeneutics. It is not to be confused with word-for-word literalism.

Typical Sense

The typical sense is the meaning which a passage has not only in itself but also in reference to something else of which it is a type or foreshadowing. A clear example is the account of the Exodus of the Israelites: in its literal sense, it narrates the liberation of the Israelites from death and oppression in Egypt; in its typical sense, it foreshadowed the liberation of men from sin through the redemptive death and resurrection of Christ. The typical sense of this and other passages emerged in the working out of God's plan of salvation history. It did not have to be in the mind of the author of the original passage.

Accommodated Senses

Accommodated, allegorical and consequent senses are figurative and adaptive meanings given to books and passages of the Bible for moral and other purposes. Such interpretations involve the danger of stretching the literal sense beyond proper proportions. Hermeneutical principles require that interpretations like these respect the integrity of the literal sense of the passages in question.

In the Catholic view, the final word on questions of biblical interpretation belongs to the teaching authority of the Church. In other views, generally derived from basic principles stated by Martin Luther, John Calvin and other reformers, the primacy belongs to individual judgment acting in response to the inner testimony of the Holy Spirit, the edifying nature of biblical subject matter, the sublimity and simplicity of the message of salvation, the intensity with which Christ is proclaimed.

Biblical Studies

The first center for biblical studies, in some strict sense of the term, was the School of Alexandria, founded in the latter half of the second century. It was noted for allegorical exegesis. Literal interpretation was a hallmark of the School of Antioch.

St. Jerome, who produced the Vulgate, and St. Augustine, author of numerous commentaries, were the most important figures in biblical studies during the patristic period. By the time of the latter's death, the Old and New Testament canons had been stabilized. For some centuries afterwards, there was little or no progress in scriptural studies, although commentaries were written, collections were made of scriptural excerpts from the writings of the Fathers of the Church, and the systematic reading of Scripture became established as a feature of monastic life.

Advances were made in the 12th and 13th centuries with the introduction of new principles and methods of scriptural analysis stemming from renewed interest in Hebraic studies and the application of dialectics.

By the time of the Reformation, the Bible had become the first book set in movable type, and more than 100 vernacular editions were in use throughout Europe.

The Council of Trent

In the wake of the Reformation, the Council of Trent formally defined the Canon of the Bible; it also reasserted the authoritative role of tradition and the teaching authority of the Church as well as Scripture with respect to the rule of faith. In the heated atmosphere of the 16th and 17th centuries, the Bible was turned into a polemical weapon; Protestants used it to defend their doctrines, and Catholics countered with citations in support of the dogmas of the Church. One result of this state of affairs was a lack of substantial progress in biblical studies during the period.

Rationalists from the 18th century on and later Modernists denied the reality of the supernatural and doctrine concerning inspiration of the Bible, which they generally regarded as a strictly human production expressive of the religious sense and experience of mankind. In their hands, the tools of positive critical research became weapons for biblical subversion. The defensive Catholic reaction to their work had the temporary effect of alienating scholars of the Church from solid advances in archeology, philology, history, textual and literary criticism.

Catholic Developments

Major influences in bringing about a change in Catholic attitude toward use of these disciplines in biblical studies were two papal encyclicals and two institutes of special study, the Ecole Biblique, founded in Jerusalem in 1890, and the Pontifical Biblical Institute established in Rome in 1909. The encyclical *Providentissimus Deus,* issued by Leo XIII in 1893, marked an important breakthrough; in addition to defending the concept of divine inspiration and the formal inspiration of the Scriptures, it encouraged the study of allied and ancillary sciences and techniques for a more fruitful understanding of the sacred writings. The encyclical *Divino Afflante Spiritu,* 50 years later, gave encouragement for the use of various forms of criticism as tools of biblical research. The documents encouraged the work of scholars and stimulated wide communication of the fruits of their study.

Great changes in the climate and direction of biblical studies have occurred in recent years. One of them has been an increase in cooperative effort among Catholic, Protestant, Orthodox and Jewish scholars. Their common investigation of the Dead Sea Scrolls is well known. Also productive has been the collaboration of Catholics and Protestants in turning out various editions of the Bible.

The development and results of biblical studies in this century have directly and significantly affected all phases of the contemporary renewal movement in the Church. Their influence on theology, liturgy, catechetics, and preaching indicate the importance of their function in the life of the Church.

APOSTLES AND EVANGELISTS

The Apostles were the men selected, trained and commissioned by Christ to preach the Gospel, to baptize, to establish, direct and care for his Church as servants of God and stewards of his mysteries. They were the first bishops of the Church.

St. Matthew's Gospel lists the Apostles in this order: Peter, Andrew, James the Greater, John, Philip, Bartholomew, Thomas, Matthew, James the Less, Jude, Simon and Judas Iscariot. Matthias was elected to fill the place of Judas. Paul became an Apostle by a special call from Christ. Barnabas was called an Apostle.

Two of the Evangelists, John and Matthew, were Apostles. The other two, Luke and Mark, were closely associated with the apostolic college.

Andrew: Born in Bethsaida, brother of Peter, disciple of John the Baptist, a fisherman, the first Apostle called; according to legend, preached the Gospel in northern Greece, Epirus and Scythia, and was martyred at Patras about 70; in art, is represented with an x-shaped cross, called St. Andrew's Cross; feast, Nov. 30; is honored as the patron of Russia and Scotland.

Barnabas: Originally called Joseph but named Barnabas by the Apostles, among whom he is ranked because of his collaboration with Paul; a Jew of the Diaspora, born in Cyprus; a cousin of Mark and member of the Christian community at Jerusalem, influenced the Apostles to accept Paul, with whom he became a pioneer missionary outside Palestine and Syria, to Antioch, Cyprus and southern Asia Minor; legend says he was martyred in Cyprus during the Neronian persecution; feast, June 11.

Bartholomew (Nathaniel): A friend of Philip; according to various traditions, preached the Gospel in Ethiopia, India, Persia and Armenia, where he was martyred by being flayed and beheaded; in art, is depicted holding a knife, an instrument of his death; feast, Aug. 24 in the Roman Rite, Aug. 25 in the Byzantine Rite.

James the Greater: A Galilean, son of Zebedee, brother of John (with whom he was called a "Son of Thunder"), a fisherman; with Peter and John, witnessed the raising of Jairus' daughter to life, the transfiguration, the agony of Jesus in the Garden of Gethsemani; first of the Apostles to die, by the sword in 44 during the rule of Herod Agrippa; there is doubt about a journey legend says he made to Spain and also about the authenticity of relics said to be his at Santiago de Compostela; in art, is depicted carrying a pilgrim's bell; feast, July 25 in the Roman Rite, Apr. 30 in the Byzantine Rite.

James the Less: Son of Alphaeus, called "Less" because he was younger in age or shorter in stature than James the Greater; one of the Catholic Epistles bears his name; was stoned to death in 62 or thrown from the top of the temple in Jerusalem and clubbed to death in 66; in art, is depicted with a club or heavy staff; feast, May 3 in the Roman Rite, Oct. 9 in the Byzantine Rite.

John: A Galilean, son of Zebedee, brother of James the Greater (with whom he was called a "Son of Thunder"), a fisherman, probably a disciple of John the Baptist, one of the Evangelists, called the "Beloved Disciple"; with Peter and James the Greater, witnessed the raising of Jairus' daughter to life, the transfiguration, the agony of Jesus in the Garden of Gethsemani; Mary was commended to his special care by Christ; the fourth Gospel, three Catholic Epistles and Revelation bear his name; according to various accounts, lived at Ephesus in Asia Minor for some time and died a natural death about 100; in art, is represented by an eagle, symbolic of the sublimity of the contents of his Gospel; feast, Dec. 27 in the Roman Rite, May 8 in the Byzantine Rite.

Jude Thaddeus: One of the Catholic Epistles, the shortest, bears his name; various traditions say he preached the Gospel in Mesopotamia, Persia and elsewhere, and was martyred; in art, is depicted with a halberd, the instrument of his death; feast, Oct. 28 in the Roman Rite, June 19 in the Byzantine Rite.

Luke: A Greek convert to the Christian community, called "our most dear physician" by Paul, of whom he was a missionary companion; author of the third Gospel and Acts of the Apostles; the place — Achaia, Bithynia, Egypt — and circumstances of his death are not certain; in art, is depicted as a man, a writer, or an ox (because his Gospel starts at the scene of temple sacrifice); feast, Oct. 18.

Mark: A cousin of Barnabas and member of the first Christian community at Jerusalem; a missionary companion of Paul and Barnabas, then of Peter; author of the Gospel which bears his name; according to legend, founded the Church at Alexandria, was bishop there and was martyred in the streets of the city; in art, is depicted with his Gospel and a winged lion, symbolic of the voice of John the Baptist crying in the wilderness, at the beginning of his Gospel; feast, Apr. 25.

Matthew: A Galilean, called Levi by Luke and John and the son of Alphaeus by Mark, a tax collector, one of the Evangelists; according to various accounts, preached the Gospel in Judea, Ethiopia, Persia and Parthia, and was martyred; in art, is depicted with a spear, the instrument of his death, and as a winged man in his role as Evangelist; feast, Sept. 21 in the Roman Rite, Nov. 16 in the Byzantine Rite.

Matthias: A disciple of Jesus whom the faithful 11 Apostles chose to replace Judas before the Resurrection; uncertain traditions report that he preached the Gospel in Palestine, Cappadocia or Ethiopia; in art, is represented with a cross and a halberd, the instruments of his death as a martyr; feast, May 14 in the Roman Rite, Aug. 9 in the Byzantine Rite.

Paul: Born at Tarsus, of the tribe of Benjamin, a Roman citizen; participated in the persecution of Christians until the time of his miraculous conversion on the way to Damascus; called by Christ, who revealed himself to him in a special way; became the Apostle of the Gentiles, among whom he did most of his preaching in the course of three major missionary journeys through areas north of Palestine, Cyprus, Asia Minor and Greece; 14 epistles bear his name; two years of imprisonment at Rome, following initial arrest in Jerusalem and confinement at Caesarea, ended with martyrdom, by beheading, outside the walls of the city in 64 or 67 during the Neronian persecution; in art, is depicted in various ways with St. Peter, with a sword, in the scene of his conversion; feasts, June 29, Jan. 25 (Roman Rite).

Peter: Simon, son of Jona, born in Bethsaida, brother of Andrew, a fisherman; called Cephas or Peter by Christ who made him the chief of the Apostles and head of the Church as his vicar; named first in the listings of Apostles in the Synoptic Gospels and the Acts of the Apostles; with James the Greater and John, witnessed the raising of Jairus' daughter to life, the transfiguration, the agony of Jesus in the Garden of Gethsemani; was the first to preach the Gospel in and around Jerusalem and was the leader of the first Christian community there; established a local church in Antioch; presided over the Council of Jerusalem in 51; wrote two Catholic Epistles to the Christians in Asia Minor; established his see in Rome where he spent his last years and was martyred by crucifixion in 64 or 65 during the Neronian persecution; in art, is depicted carrying two keys, symbolic of his primacy in the Church; feasts, June 29, Feb. 22 (Roman Rite).

Philip: Born in Bethsaida; according to legend, preached the Gospel in Phrygia where he suffered martyrdom by crucifixion; feast, May 3 in the Roman Rite, Nov. 14 in the Byzantine Rite.

Simon: Called the Cananean or the Zealot; according to legend, preached in various places in the Middle East and suffered martyrdom by being sawed in two; in art, is depicted with a saw, the instrument of his death, or a book, symbolic of his zeal for the Law; feast, Oct. 28 in the Roman Rite, May 10 in the Byzantine Rite.

Thomas (Didymus): Notable for his initial incredulity regarding the Resurrection and his subsequent forthright confession of the divinity of Christ risen from the dead; according to legend, preached the Gospel in places from the Caspian Sea to the Persian Gulf and eventually reached India where he was martyred near Madras; Thomas Christians trace their origin to him; in art, is depicted kneeling before the risen Christ, or with a carpenter's rule and square; feast, July 3 in the Roman Rite, Oct. 6 in the Byzantine Rite.

Judas

The Gospels record only a few facts about Judas, the Apostle who betrayed Christ.

The only non-Galilean among the Apostles, he was from Carioth, a town in southern Judah. He was keeper of the purse in the apostolic band. He was called a petty thief by John. He voiced dismay at the waste of money, which he said might have been spent for the poor, in connection with the anointing incident at Bethany. He took the initiative in arranging the betrayal of Christ. Afterwards, he confessed that he had betrayed an innocent man and cast into the Temple the money he had received for that action. Of his death, Matthew says that he hanged himself; the Acts of the Apostles states that he swelled up and burst open; both reports deal more with the meaning than the manner of his death — the misery of the death of a sinner.

The consensus of speculation over the reason why Judas acted as he did in betraying Christ focuses on disillusionment and unwillingness to accept the concept of a suffering Messiah and personal suffering of his own as an Apostle.

APOSTOLIC FATHERS, FATHERS, DOCTORS OF THE CHURCH

The writers listed below were outstanding and authoritative witnesses to authentic Christian belief and practice, and played significant roles in giving them expression.

Apostolic Fathers

The Apostolic Fathers were Christian writers of the first and second centuries whose writings echo genuine apostolic teaching.

Chief in importance are: St. Clement (d.c. 97), bishop of Rome and third successor of St. Peter in the papacy; St. Ignatius (50-c. 107), bishop of Antioch and second successor of St. Peter in that see, reputed to be a disciple of St. John; St. Polycarp (69-155), bishop of Smyrna and a disciple of St. John. The authors of the *Didache* and the *Epistle of Barnabas* are also numbered among the Apostolic Fathers.

Other early ecclesiastical writers included: St. Justin, martyr (100-165), of Asia Minor and Rome, a layman and apologist; St. Irenaeus (130-202), bishop of Lyons, who opposed Gnosticism; and St. Cyprian (210-258), bishop of Carthage, who opposed Novatianism.

Fathers and Doctors

The Fathers of the Church were theologians and writers of the first eight centuries who were outstanding for sanctity and learning. They were such authoritative witnesses to the belief and teaching of the Church that their unanimous acceptance of doctrines as divinely revealed has been regarded as evidence that such doctrines were so received by the Church in line with apostolic tradition and Sacred Scripture. Their unanimous rejection of doctrines branded them as heretical. Their writings, however, were not necessarily free of error in all respects.

The greatest of these Fathers were: Sts. Ambrose, Augustine, Jerome and Gregory the Great in the West; Sts. John Chrysostom, Basil the Great, Gregory of Nazianzen and Athanasius in the East.

The Doctors of the Church were ecclesiastical writers of eminent learning and sanctity who have been given this title because of the great advantage the Church has derived from their work. Their writings, however, were not necessarily free of error in all respects.

Albert the Great, St. (c. 1200-1280): Born in Swabia, Germany; Dominican; bishop of Regensburg (1260-1262); wrote extensively on logic, natural sciences, ethics, metaphysics, Scripture, systematic theology; contributed to development of Scholasticism; teacher of St. Thomas Aquinas; canonized and proclaimed doctor, 1931; named patron of natural scientists, 1941; called Doctor Universalis, Doctor Expertus; feast, Nov. 15.

Alphonsus Liguori, St. (1696-1787): Born near Naples, Italy; bishop of Saint Agatha of the Goths (1762-1775); founder of the Redemptorists; in addition to his principal work, *Theologiae Moralis,* wrote on prayer, the spiritual life and doctrinal subjects in response to controversy; canonized, 1839; proclaimed doctor, 1871; named patron of confessors and moralists, 1950; feast, Aug. 1.

Ambrose, St. (c. 340-397): Born in Trier, Germany; bishop of Milan (374-397); one of the strongest opponents of Arianism in the West; his homilies and other writings — on faith, the Holy Spirit, the Incarnation, the sacraments and other subjects — were pastoral and practical; influenced the development of a liturgy at Milan which was named for him; Father and Doctor of the Church; feast, Dec. 7.

Anselm, St. (1033-1109): Born in Aosta, Piedmont, Italy; Benedictine; archbishop of Canterbury (1093-1109); in addition to his principal work, *Cur Deus Homo,* on the atonement and reconciliation of man with God through Christ, wrote about the existence and attributes of God and defended the *Filioque* explanation of the procession of the Holy Spirit from the Father and the Son; proclaimed doctor, 1720; called Father of Scholasticism; feast, Apr. 21.

Anthony of Padua, St. (1195-1231): Born in Lisbon, Portugal; first theologian of the Franciscan Order; preacher; canonized, 1232; proclaimed doctor, 1946; called Evangelical Doctor; feast, June 13.

Athanasius, St. (c. 297-373): Born in Alexandria, Egypt; bishop of Alexandria (328-373); participant in the Council of Nicaea I while still a deacon; dominant opponent of Arians whose errors regarding Christ he refuted in *Apology against the Arians, Discourses against the Arians* and other works; Father and Doctor of the Church; called Father of Orthodoxy; feast, May 2.

Augustine, St. (354-430): Born in Tagaste, North Africa; bishop of Hippo (395-430) after conversion from Manichaeism; works include the autobiographical and mystical *Confessions, City of God,* treatises on the Trinity, grace, passages of the Bible and doctrines called into question and denied by Manichaeans, Pelagians and Donatists; had strong and lasting influence on Christian theology and philosophy; Father and Doctor of the Church; called Doctor of Grace; feast, Aug. 28.

Basil the Great, St. (c. 329-379): Born in Caesarea, Cappadocia, Asia Minor; bishop of Caesarea (370-379); wrote three books *Contra Eunomium* in refutation of Arian errors, a treatise on the Holy Spirit, many homilies and several rules for monastic life, on which he had lasting influence; Father and Doctor of the Church; called Father of Monasticism in the East; feast, Jan. 2.

Bede the Venerable, St. (c. 673-735): Born in Northumberland, England; Benedictine; in addition to his principal work, *Ecclesiastical History of the English Nation* (covering the period 597-731), wrote scriptural commentaries; regarded as probably the most learned man in Western Europe of his time; called Father of English History; feast, May 25.

Bernard of Clairvaux, St. (c. 1090-1153): Born near Dijon, France; abbot; monastic reformer, called the second founder of the Cistercian Order; mystical theologian with great influence on devotional life; opponent of the rationalism brought forward by Abelard and others; canonized, 1174; proclaimed doctor, 1830; called Mellifluous Doctor because of his eloquence; feast, Aug. 20.

Bonaventuré, St. (c. 1217-1274): Born near Viterbo, Italy; Franciscan; bishop of Albano (1273-1274); cardinal; wrote *Itinerarium Mentis in Deum, De Reductione Artium ad Theologiam, Breviloquium,* scriptural commentaries, additional mystical works affecting devotional life and a life of St. Francis of Assisi; canonized, 1482; proclaimed doctor, 1588; called Seraphic Doctor; feast, July 15.

Catherine of Siena, St. (c. 1347-1380): Born in Siena, Italy; member of the Third Order of St. Dominic; mystic; authored a long series of letters, mainly concerning spiritual instruction and encouragement, to associates, and *Dialogue,* a spiritual testament in four treatises; was active in support of a crusade against the Turks and efforts to end war between papal forces and the Florentine allies; had great influence in inducing Gregory XI to return himself and the Curia to Rome in 1376, to end the Avignon period of the papacy; canonized, 1461; proclaimed the second woman doctor, Oct. 4, 1970; feast, Apr. 29.

Cyril of Alexandria, St. (c. 376-444): Born in Egypt; bishop of Alexandria (412-444); wrote treatises on the Trinity, the Incarnation and other subjects, mostly in refutation of Nestorian errors; made key contributions to the development of Christology; presided at the Council of Ephesus, 431; proclaimed doctor, 1882; feast, June 27.

Cyril of Jerusalem, St. (c. 315-386): Bishop of Jerusalem from 350; vigorous opponent of Arianism; principal work, *Catecheses,* a pre-baptismal explanation of the creed of Jerusalem; proclaimed doctor, 1882; feast, Mar. 18.

Ephraem, St. (c. 306-373): Born in Nisibis, Mesopotamia; counteracted the spread of Gnostic and Arian errors with poems and hymns of his own composition; wrote also on the Eucharist and Mary; proclaimed doctor, 1920; called Deacon of Edessa and Harp of the Holy Spirit; feast, June 9.

Francis de Sales, St. (1567-1622): Born in Savoy; bishop of Geneva (1602-1622); spiritual writer with strong influence on devotional life through treatises such as *Introduction to a Devout Life,* and *The Love of God;* canonized, 1665; pro-

claimed doctor, 1877; patron of Catholic writers and the Catholic press; feast, Jan. 24.

Gregory Nazianzen, St. (c. 330-c. 390): Born in Arianzus, Cappadocia, Asia Minor; bishop of Constantinople (381-390); vigorous opponent of Arianism; in addition to five theological discourses on the Nicene Creed and the Trinity for which he is best known, wrote letters and poetry; Father and Doctor of the Church; called the Christian Demosthenes because of his eloquence and, in the Eastern Church, The Theologian; feast, Jan. 2.

Gregory I, the Great, St. (c. 540-604): Born in Rome; pope (590-604): wrote many scriptural commentaries, a compendium of theology in the *Book of Morals* based on Job, *Dialogues* concerning the lives of saints, the immortality of the soul, death, purgatory, heaven and hell, and 14 books of letters; enforced papal supremacy and established the position of the pope vis-a-vis the emperor; worked for clerical and monastic reform and the observance of clerical celibacy; Father and Doctor of the Church; feast, Sept. 3.

Hilary of Poitiers, St. (c. 315-368): Born in Poitiers, France; bishop of Poitiers (c. 353-368); wrote *De Synodis,* with the Arian controversy in mind, and *De Trinitate,* the first lengthy study of the doctrine in Latin; introduced Eastern theology to the West; contributed to the development of hymnology; proclaimed doctor, 1851; called the Athanasius of the West because of his vigorous defense of the divinity of Christ against Arians; feast, Jan. 13.

Isidore of Seville, St. (c. 560-636): Born in Cartagena, Spain; bishop of Seville (c. 600-636); in addition to his principal work, *Etymologiae,* an encyclopedia of the knowledge of his day, wrote on theological and historical subjects; regarded as the most learned man of his time; proclaimed doctor, 1722; feast, Apr. 4.

Jerome, St. (c. 343-420): Born in Stridon, Dalmatia; translated the Old Testament from Hebrew into Latin and revised the existing Latin translation of the New Testament to produce the Vulgate version of the Bible; wrote scriptural commentaries and treatises on matters of controversy; regarded as Father and Doctor of the Church from the eighth century; called Father of Biblical Science; feast, Sept. 30.

John Chrysostom, St. (c. 347-407): Born in Antioch, Asia Minor; archbishop of Constantinople (398-407); wrote homilies, scriptural commentaries and letters of wide influence in addition to a classical treatise on the priesthood; proclaimed doctor by the Council of Chalcedon, 451; called the greatest of the Greek Fathers; named patron of preachers, 1909; called Golden-Mouthed because of his eloquence; feast, Sept. 13.

John Damascene, St. (c. 675-c. 749): Born in Damascus, Syria; monk; wrote *Fountain of Wisdom,* a three-part work including a history of heresies and an exposition of the Christian faith, three *Discourses against the Iconoclasts,* homilies on Mary, biblical commentaries and treatises on moral subjects; proclaimed doctor, 1890; called Golden Speaker because of his eloquence; feast, Dec. 4.

John of the Cross, St. (1542-1591): Born in Old Castile, Spain; Carmelite; founder of Discalced Carmelites; one of the greatest mystical theologians, wrote *The Ascent of Mt. Carmel — The Dark Night, The Spiritual Canticle, The Living Flame of Love;* canonized, 1726; proclaimed doctor, 1926; called Doctor of Mystical Theology; feast, Dec. 14.

Lawrence of Brindisi, St. (1559-1619): Born in Brindisi, Italy; Franciscan (Capuchin); vigorous preacher of strong influence in the post-Reformation period; 15 tomes of collected works include scriptural commentaries, sermons, homilies and doctrinal writings; canonized, 1881; proclaimed doctor, 1959; feast, July 21.

Leo I, the Great, St. (c. 400-461): Born in Tuscany, Italy; pope (440-461); wrote the *Tome of Leo,* to explain doctrine concerning the two natures and one Person of Christ, against the background of the Nestorian and Monophysite heresies; other works included sermons, letters and writings against the errors of Manichaeism and Pelagianism; was instrumental in dissuading Attila from sacking Rome in 452; proclaimed doctor, 1574; feast, Nov. 10.

Peter Canisius, St. (1521-1597): Born in Nijmegen, Holland; Jesuit; wrote popular expositions of the Catholic faith in several catechisms which were widely circulated in 20 editions in his lifetime alone; was one of the moving figures in the Counter-Reformation period, especially in southern and western Germany; canonized and proclaimed doctor, 1925; feast, Dec. 21.

Peter Chrysologus, St. (c. 400-450): Born in Imola, Italy; served as archbishop of Ravenna (c. 433-450); his sermons and writings, many of which were designed to counteract Monophysitism, were pastoral and practical; proclaimed doctor, 1729; feast, July 30.

Peter Damian, St. (1007-1072): Born in Ravenna, Italy; Benedictine; cardinal; his writings and sermons, many of which concerned ecclesiastical and clerical reform, were pastoral and practical; proclaimed doctor, 1828; feast, Feb. 21.

Robert Bellarmine, St. (1542-1621): Born in Tuscany, Italy; Jesuit; archbishop of Capua (1602-1605); wrote *Controversies,* a three-volume exposition of doctrine under attack during and after the Reformation, two catechisms and the spiritual work, *The Art of Dying Well;* was an authority on ecclesiology and Church-state relations; canonized, 1930; proclaimed doctor, 1931; feast, Sept. 17.

Teresa of Jesus (Avila), St. (1515-1582): Born in Avila, Spain; entered the Carmelite Order, 1535; in the early 1560's, initiated a primitive Carmelite, discalced-Alcantarine reform which greatly influenced men and women religious, especially in Spain; wrote extensively on spiritual and mystical subjects; principal works included her *Autobiography, Way of Perfection, The Interior Castle, Meditations on the Canticle, The Foundations, Visitation of the Discalced Nuns;* canonized, 1622; proclaimed first woman doctor, Sept. 27, 1970; feast, Oct. 15.

Thomas Aquinas, St. (1225-1274): Born near Naples, Italy; Dominican; teacher and writer on virtually the whole range of philosophy and theology; principal works were *Summa contra Gentiles,* a manual and systematic defense of Christian doctrine, and *Summa Theologiae,* a new (at that time) exposition of theology on philosophical principles; canonized, 1323; proclaimed doctor, 1567; called Doctor Communis, Doctor Angelicus, the Great Synthesizer because of the way in which he related faith and reason, theology and philosophy (especially that of Aristotle), and systematized the presentation of Christian doctrine; named patron of Catholic schools and education, 1880; feast, Jan. 28.

CREEDS

Creeds are formal and official statements of Christian doctrine. As summaries of the principal truths of faith, they are standards of orthodoxy and are useful for instructional purposes, for actual profession of the faith and for expression of the faith in the liturgy.

The classical creeds are the Apostles' Creed and the Creed of Nicaea-Constantinople. Two others are the Athanasian Creed and the Creed of Pius IV.

Apostles' Creed

Text: I believe in God, the Father almighty, Creator of heaven and earth.

And in Jesus Christ, his only Son, our Lord; who was conceived by the Holy Spirit, born of the Virgin Mary, suffered under Pontius Pilate, was crucified, died, and was buried. He descended into hell; the third day he arose again from the dead; he ascended into heaven, sits at the right hand of God, the Father almighty; from thence he shall come to judge the living and the dead.

I believe in the Holy Spirit, the holy Catholic Church, the communion of saints, the forgiveness of sins, the resurrection of the body, and life everlasting. Amen.

Background: The Apostles' Creed reflects the teaching of the Apostles but is not of apostolic origin. It probably originated in the second century as a rudimentary formula of faith professed by catechumens before the reception of baptism. Baptismal creeds in fourth-century use at Rome and elsewhere in the West closely resembled the present text, which was quoted in a handbook of Christian doctrine written between 710 and 724. This text was in wide use throughout the West by the ninth century. The Apostles' Creed is common to all Christian confessional churches in the West, but is not used in Eastern Churches.

Nicene Creed

The following translation of the Latin text of the creed was prepared by the International Committee on English in the Liturgy.

Text: We believe in one God, the Father, the Almighty, maker of heaven and earth, of all that is seen and unseen.

We believe in one Lord, Jesus Christ, the only

Son of God, eternally begotten of the Father, God from God, Light from Light, true God from true God, begotten, not made, one in Being with the Father. Through him all things were made. For us men and for our salvation he came down from heaven: by the power of the Holy Spirit he was born of the Virgin Mary, and became man. For our sake he was crucified under Pontius Pilate; he suffered, died, and was buried. On the third day he rose again in fulfillment of the Scriptures; he ascended into heaven and is seated at the right hand of the Father. He will come again in glory to judge the living and the dead, and his kingdom will have no end.

We believe in the Holy Spirit, the Lord, the giver of life, who proceeds from the Father and the Son. With the Father and the Son he is worshiped and glorified. He has spoken through the prophets.

We believe in one holy catholic and apostolic Church. We acknowledge one baptism for the forgiveness of sins. We look for the resurrection of the dead, and the life of the world to come. Amen.

Background: The Nicene Creed (Creed of Nicaea-Constantinople) consists of elements of doctrine contained in an early baptismal creed of Jerusalem and enactments of the Council of Nicaea (325) and the Council of Constantinople (381). Its strong trinitarian content reflects the doctrinal errors, especially of Arianism, it served

to counteract. Theologically, it is much more sophisticated than the Apostles' Creed. Since late in the fifth century, the Nicene Creed has been the only creed in liturgical use in the Eastern Churches. The Western Church adopted it for liturgical use by the end of the eighth century.

The Athanasian Creed

The Athanasian Creed, which has a unique structure, is a two-part summary of doctrine concerning the Trinity and the Incarnation-Redemption bracketed at the beginning and end with the statement that belief in the cited truths is necessary for salvation; it also contains a number of anathemas or condemnatory clauses regarding doctrinal errors. Although attributed to St. Athanasius, it was probably written after his death, between 381 and 428, and may have been authored by St. Ambrose. It is not accepted in the East; in the West, it formerly had place in the Roman-Rite Liturgy of the Hours and in the liturgy for the Solemnity of the Holy Trinity.

Creed of Pius IV

The Creed of Pius IV, also called the Profession of Faith of the Council of Trent, was promulgated in the bull *Injunctum Nobis,* Nov. 13, 1564. It is a summary of doctrine defined by the council·

MORAL OBLIGATIONS

The basic norm of Christian morality is life in Christ. This involves, among other things, the observance of the Ten Commandments, their fulfillment in the twofold law of love of God and neighbor, the implications of the Sermon on the Mount and the whole New Testament, and membership in the Church established by Christ.

The Ten Commandments

The Ten Commandments, the Decalogue, were given by God through Moses to his Chosen People for the guidance of their moral conduct in accord with the demands of the Covenant he established with them as a divine gift.

In the traditional Catholic enumeration and according to Dt. 5:6-21, the Commandments are:

1. "I, the Lord, am your God . . . You shall not have other gods besides me. You shall not carve idols. . . ."
2. "You shall not take the name of the Lord, your God, in vain. . . ."
3. "Take care to keep holy the Sabbath day. . . ."
4. "Honor your father and your mother. . . ."
5. "You shall not kill."
6. "You shall not commit adultery."
7. "You shall not steal."
8. "You shall not bear dishonest witness against your neighbor."
9. "You shall not covet your neighbor's wife."
10. "You shall not desire your neighbor's house or field, nor his male or female slave, nor his ox or ass, nor anything that belongs to him" (summarily, his goods).

Another version of the Commandments, substantially the same, is given in Ex. 20:1-17.

The traditional enumeration of the Commandments in Protestant usage differs from the above. Thus: two commandments are made of the first, as above; the third and fourth are equivalent to the second and third, as above, and so on; and the 10th includes the ninth and 10th, as above.

Love of God and Neighbor

The first three of the commandments deal directly with man's relations with God, viz.: acknowledgment of one true God and the rejection of false gods and idols; honor due to God and his name; observance of the Sabbath as the Lord's day.

The rest cover interpersonal relationships, viz.: the obedience due to parents and, logically, to other persons in authority, and the obligations of parents to children and of persons in authority to those under their care; respect for life and physical integrity; fidelity in marriage, and chastity; justice and rights; truth; internal respect for faithfulness in marriage, chastity, and the goods of others.

Perfection in Christian Life

The moral obligations of the Ten Commandments are complemented by others flowing from the twofold law of love, the whole substance and pattern of Christ's teaching, and everything implied in full and active membership and participation in the community of salvation formed by Christ in his Church. Some of these matters are covered in other sections of the Almanac under appropriate headings.

Precepts of the Church

These are moral precepts binding Roman Catholics in conscience. They originated in the Middle Ages; five of them were mentioned in the writings of St. Peter Canisius and St. Robert Bellarmine in the second half of the 16th century.

1. Assist at Mass on Sundays and holy days of obligation. (Also, to avoid work and involvement in business which impede participation in divine worship and enjoyment of rest and relaxation from unnecessary servile work on these days.)

2. Fast and abstain on the days appointed. (The fasting obligation binds persons from the 18th until the 59th birthday; the days of fast are Ash Wednesday and Good Friday. The abstinence obligation binds from the 14th birthday on these days, and is obligatory for all Fridays in Lent in the U.S.) These regulations, which have been modified in recent years, are penitential in purpose but do not exhaust the obligations of penance. Other ways of doing penance are left to personal option.

3. Confess their sins at least once a year.

4. Receive Holy Communion during the Easter season.

5. Contribute to the support of the Church.

6. Observe the laws of the Church concerning marriage.

SOCIAL DOCTRINE

Since the end of the last century, Catholic social doctrine has been formulated in a progressive manner in a number of authoritative documents. Outstanding examples are the encyclicals: *Rerum Novarum*, issued by Leo XIII in 1891; *Quadragesimo Anno*, by Pius XI in 1931; *Mater et Magistra* ("Christianity and Social Progress") and *Pacem in Terris* ("Peace on Earth"), by John XXIII in 1961 and 1963, respectively; *Populorum Progressio* ("Development of Peoples"), by Paul VI in 1967; and *Laborem Exercens* ("On Human Work"), by John Paul II in 1981. Pius XII, among other accomplishments of ideological importance in the social field, made a distinctive contribution with his formulation of a plan for world peace and order in Christmas messages from 1939 to 1941, and in other documents.

These documents represent the most serious attempts in modern times to systematize the social implications of the Gospel and the rest of divine revelation as well as the socially relevant writings of the Fathers and Doctors of the Church. Their contents are theological penetrations into social life, with particular reference to human rights, the needs of the poor and those in underdeveloped countries, and humane conditions of life, freedom, justice and peace. In some respects, they read like juridical documents; underneath, however, they are Gospel-oriented and pastoral in intention.

Nature of the Doctrine

Pope John XXIII, writing in *Christianity and Social Progress,* made the following statement about the nature and scope of the doctrine stated in the encyclicals in particular and related writings in general.

"What the Catholic Church teaches and declares regarding the social life and relationships of men is beyond question for all time valid.

"The cardinal point of this teaching is that individual men are necessarily the foundation, cause, and end of all social institutions . . . insofar as they are social by nature, and raised to an order of existence that transcends and subdues nature.

"Beginning with this very basic principle whereby the dignity of the human person is affirmed and defended, Holy Church — especially during the last century and with the assistance of learned priests and laymen, specialists in the field — has arrived at clear social teachings whereby the mutual relationships of men are ordered. Taking general norms into account, these principles are in accord with the nature of things and the changed conditions of man's social life, or with the special genius of our day. Moreover, these norms can be approved by all."

The Church in the World

Even more Gospel-oriented and pastoral in a distinctive way is the *Pastoral Constitution on the Church in the Modern World* promulgated by the Second Vatican Council in 1965.

Its purpose is to search out the signs of God's presence and meaning in and through the events of this time in human history. Accordingly, it deals with the situation of men in present circumstances of profound change, challenge and crisis on all levels of life.

The first part of the constitution develops the theme of the Church and man's calling, and focuses attention on the dignity of the human person, the problem of atheism, the community of mankind, man's activity throughout the world, and the serving and saving role of the Church in the world. This portion of the document, it has been said, represents the first presentation by the Church in an official text of an organized Christian view of man and society.

The second part of the document considers several problems of special urgency: fostering the nobility of marriage and the family (see Marriage Doctrine), the proper development of culture, socio-economic life, the life of the political community, the fostering of peace (see Peace and War), and the promotion of a community of nations.

In conclusion, the constitution calls for action to implement doctrine regarding the role and work of the Church for the total good of mankind.

Excerpts

Following are a number of key excerpts from the ideological heart of the constitution.

One Human Family and Community: God, who has fatherly concern for everyone, has willed that all men should constitute one family and treat one another in a spirit of brotherhood.

For this reason, love for God and neighbor is the first and greatest commandment. Sacred Scripture . . . teaches us that the love of God cannot be separated from love of neighbor. . . . To men growing daily more dependent on one another, and to a world becoming more unified every day, this truth proves to be of paramount importance (No. 24).

Human Person Is Central: Man's social nature makes it evident that the progress of the human person and the advance of society itself hinge on each other. For the beginning, the subject and the goal of all social institutions is and must be the human person, which for its part and by its very nature stands completely in need of social life. This social life is not something added on to man. Hence, through his dealings with others, through reciprocal duties and through fraternal dialogue, he develops all his gifts and is able to rise to his destiny.

Influence of Social Circumstances: But if by this social life the human person is greatly aided in responding to his destiny, even in its religious dimensions, it cannot be denied that men are often diverted from doing good and spurred toward evil by the social circumstances in which they live and are immersed from their birth. To be sure, the disturbances which so frequently occur in the social order result in part from the natural tensions of economic, political and social forms. But at a deeper level they flow from man's pride and selfishness, which contaminate even the social sphere. When the structure of affairs is flawed by the consequences of sin, man, already born with a bent toward evil, finds there new inducements to sin which cannot be overcome without strenuous efforts and the assistance of grace (No. 25).

Human Necessities: Every social group must take account of the needs and legitimate aspirations of other groups, and even of the general welfare of the entire human family.

At the same time, however, there is a growing awareness of the exalted dignity proper to the human person, since he stands above all things and his rights and duties are universal and inviolable. Therefore, there must be made available to all men everything necessary for leading a life truly human, such as food, clothing, and shelter; the right to choose a state of life freely and to found a family; the right to education, to employment, to a good reputation, to respect, to appropriate information, to activity in accord with the upright norm of one's own conscience, to protection of privacy and to rightful freedom in matters religious too.

Hence, the social order and its development must unceasingly work to the benefit of the human person if the disposition of affairs is to be subordinate to the personal realm and not contrariwise, as the Lord indicated when he said that the Sabbath was made for man, and not man for the Sabbath.

Improvement of Social Order: This social order requires constant improvement. It must be founded on truth, built on justice and animated by love; in freedom it should grow every day toward a more humane balance. An improvement in attitudes and widespread changes in society will have to take place if these objectives are to be gained.

God's Spirit, who with a marvelous providence directs the unfolding of time and renews the face of the earth, is not absent from this development. The ferment of the Gospel, too, has aroused and continues to arouse in man's heart the irresistible requirements of his dignity (No. 26).

Regard for Neighbor as Another Self: Coming down to practical and particularly urgent consequences, this Council lays stress on reverence for man; everyone must consider his every neighbor without exception as another self, taking into account first of all his life and the means necessary to living it with dignity.

In our times a special obligation binds us to make ourselves the neighbor of absolutely every person and to actively help him when he comes across our path.

Inhuman Evils: . . . Whatever is opposed to life itself, such as any type of murder, genocide, abortion, euthanasia, or willful self-destruction; whatever violates the integrity of the human person, such as mutilation, torments inflicted on body or mind, attempts to coerce the will itself; whatever insults human dignity, such as subhuman living conditions, arbitrary imprisonment, deportation, slavery, prostitution, the selling of women and children; as well as disgraceful working conditions, where men are treated as mere tools for profit rather than as free and responsible persons: all these things and others of their like are infamies indeed. They poison human society, but they do more harm to those who practice them than those who suffer from the injury. Moreover, they are a supreme dishonor to the Creator (No. 27).

Respect for Those Who Are Different: Respect and love ought to be extended also to those who think or act differently than we do in social, political and religious matters. In fact, the more deeply we come to understand their ways of thinking through such courtesy and love, the more easily will we be able to enter into dialogue with them.

Distinction between Error and Persons in Error: This love and good will, to be sure, must in no way render us indifferent to truth and goodness. Indeed, love itself impels the disciples of Christ to speak the saving truth to all men. But it is necessary to distinguish between error, which always merits repudiation, and the person in error, who never loses the dignity of being a person, even when he is flawed by false or inadequate religious notions. God alone is the judge and searcher of hearts; for that reason he forbids us to make judgments about the internal guilt of anyone.

The teaching of Christ even requires that we forgive injuries, and extends the law of love to include every enemy (No. 28).

Men Are Equal but Different: Since all men possess a rational soul and are created in God's likeness; since they have the same nature and origin, have been redeemed by Christ, and enjoy the same divine calling and destiny: the basic equality of all must receive increasingly greater recognition.

True, all men are not alike from the point of view of varying physical power and the diversity of intellectual and moral resources. Nevertheless, with respect to the fundamental rights of the person, every type of discrimination, whether social or cultural, whether based on sex, race, color, social condition, language or religion, is to be overcome and eradicated as contrary to God's intent.

Humane Conditions for All: Although rightful differences exist between men, the equal dignity of persons demands that a more humane and just condition of life be brought about. For excessive economic and social differences between the members of the one human family . . . cause scandal and militate against social justice, equity and the dignity of the human person as well as social and international peace.

Human institutions, both private and public, must labor to minister to the dignity and purpose of man. At the same time, let them put up a stubborn fight against any kind of slavery, whether social or political, and safeguard the basic rights of man under every political system. Indeed, human institutions themselves must be accommodated by degrees to the highest of all realities, spiritual ones, even though, meanwhile, a long enough time will be required before they arrive at the desired goal (No. 29).

Profound and rapid changes make it particularly urgent that no one, ignoring the trend of events or drugged by laziness, content himself with a merely individualistic morality. It grows increasingly true that the obligations of justice and love are fulfilled only if each person, contributing to the common good according to his own abilities and the needs of others, also promotes and assists the public and private institutions dedicated to bettering the conditions of human life.

Social Necessities Are Prime Duties: Let everyone consider it his sacred obligation to count social necessities among the primary duties of modern man and to pay heed to them. For the more unified the world becomes, the more plainly do the offices of men extend beyond particular groups and spread by degrees to the whole world. But this challenge cannot be met unless individual men and their associations cultivate in themselves the moral and social virtues and promote them in society. Thus, with the needed help of divine grace, men who are truly new and artisans of a new humanity can be forthcoming (No. 30).

In order for individual men to discharge with greater exactness the obligations of their conscience toward themselves and the various groups to which they belong, they must be carefully educated to a higher degree of culture through the use of the immense resources available today to the human race.

Living Conditions and Freedom: A man can scarcely arrive at the needed sense of responsibility unless his living conditions allow him to become conscious of his dignity and to rise to his destiny by spending himself for God and for others. But human freedom is often crippled when a man falls into extreme poverty, just as it withers when he indulges in too many of life's comforts and imprisons himself in a kind of splendid isolation. Freedom acquires new strength, by contrast, when a man consents to the unavoidable requirements of social life, takes on the manifold demands of human partnership and commits himself to the service of the human community.

Hence, the will to play one's role in common endeavors should be everywhere encouraged (No. 31).

Communitarian Character of Life: God did not create man for life in isolation but for the formation of social unity. So also "it has pleased God to make men holy and save them not merely as individuals, without any mutual bonds, but by making them into a single people, a people which acknowledges him in truth and serves him in holiness" (*Dogmatic Constitution on the Church,* No. 9). So from the beginning of salvation history he has chosen men not just as individuals but as members of a certain community. Revealing his mind to them, God called these chosen ones "his people" (Ex. 3:7-12) and, furthermore, made a covenant with them on Sinai.

This communitarian character is developed and consummated in the work of Jesus Christ. For the very Word made flesh willed to share in the human fellowship. He was present at the wedding of Cana, visited the house of Zaccheaus, ate with publicans and sinners. He revealed the love of the Father and the sublime vocation of man in terms of the most common social realities and by making use of the speech and the imagery of plain everyday life. Willingly obeying the laws of his country, he sanctified those human ties, especially family ones, from which social relationships arise. He chose to lead the life proper to an artisan of his time and place.

In his preaching he clearly taught the sons of God to treat one another as brothers. In his prayers he pleaded that all his disciples might be "one." Indeed, as the Redeemer of all, he offered himself for all even to the point of death. He commanded his Apostles to preach to all peoples the Gospel message so that the human race might become the Family of God, in which the fullness of the Law would be love.

The Community Founded by Christ: As the first-born of many brethren and through the gift of his Spirit, he founded after his death and resurrection a new brotherly community composed of all those who receive him in faith and in love. This he did through his Body, which is the Church. There everyone, as members one of the other, would render mutual service according to the different gifts bestowed on each.

This solidarity must be constantly increased until that day on which it is brought to perfection. Then, saved by grace, men will offer flawless glory to God as a family beloved of God and of Christ their Brother (No. 32).

WORK

The nature of work, its relation to social issues and its significance, along with prayer, as the "way of sanctification," are among key subjects treated in Pope John Paul's third encyclical letter, *Laborem Exercens.* Following are several paragraphs from the encyclical delineating a definition of work together with capsule coverge of a number of salient points in the letter.

Definition

"Through work man must earn his daily bread and contribute to the continual advance of science and technology and, above all, to elevating unceasingly the cultural and moral level of the society within which he lives in community with those who belong to the same family.

"And work means any activity by man, whether manual or intellectual, whatever its nature or circumstances; it means any human activity that can and must be recognized as work, in the midst of all the many activities of which man is capable and to which he is predisposed by his very nature, by virtue of humanity itself.

"Man is made to be in the visible universe an image and likeness of God himself, and he is placed in it in order to subdue the earth. From the beginning, therefore, he is called to work.

"Work is one of the characteristics that distinguish man from the rest of creatures, whose activity for sustaining their lives cannot be called work. Only man is capable of work and only man works, at the same time by work occupying his existence on earth. Thus, work bears a particular mark of man and of humanity, the mark of a person operating within a community of persons. And this mark decides its interior characteristics; in a sense, it constitutes its very nature."

Salient Points

Fundamental Criterion of Economics: "Respect for the objective rights of the worker . . . must constitute the adequate and fundamental criterion for shaping the whole economy, both on the level of the individual society and state and within the whole of the world economic policy as well as the systems of international relationships that derive from it."

Work and Family: "Work constitutes a foundation of the formation of family life" by providing the economic means necessary to maintain a family.

Just Wage: "A just wage is the concrete means of verifying the justice of the whole socio-economic system and, in any case, of checking that it is functioning justly."

Family Wage: A "family wage" is needed, "a single salary given to the head of the family for his work, sufficient for the needs of the family without the other spouse having to take up gainful employment outside the home," or without the need of recourse to other social provisions for aid.

Women: Women who work "should be able to fulfill their tasks in accordance with their own nature without being discriminated against and without being excluded from jobs for which they are capable." Respect is due "for their family aspirations and for their specific role in contributing, together with men, to the good of society."

Mothers: Provisions should be made for "measures such as family allowances or grants to mothers devoting themselves exclusively to their families."

Unions: Workers have the right to form a union to protect their vital interests and to be "a mouthpiece for the struggle for social justice."

"Union activity undoubtedly enters the field of politics, understood as prudent concern for the common good." But unions should not engage in partisan politics; otherwise, "they become an instrument used for other purposes."

Strike: Workers should be assured the right to strike without being subject to personal sanctions, but have the responsibility of not striking if a strike "is contrary to requirements of the common good."

Unemployment Benefits: "The obligation to provide unemployment benefits . . . is a duty springing from the fundamental principle of the common use of goods or, to put it in another way, the right to life and subsistence."

Disabled Persons: Society should provide work for disabled persons in keeping with their physical disabilities. Failure to do so means "a serious form of discrimination, that of the strong and healthy against the weak and sick."

Health Care: "The expenses involved in health care, especially in the case of accidents at work, demand that medical assistance should be easily available for workers."

Technology: It is meant to be the worker's ally but can become his enemy when mechanization supplants him or takes away "all personal satisfaction and the incentive to creativity and responsibility," thus reducing "man to the status of slave."

Haves and Have-Nots: "A disconcerting fact of immense proportions" occurs on the world scene. "While conspicuous natural resources remain unused, there are huge numbers of people who are unemployed or underemployed, and countless multitudes of people suffering from hunger." This means that there is "something wrong with the organization of work and employment" on national and international levels.

Foreign Workers: People have a right to emigrate in search of work. "The person working away from his native land, whether as a permanent emigrant or as a seasonal worker, should not be placed at a disadvantage in comparison with the workers in that society in the matter of working rights. Emigration in search of work must in no way become an opportunity for financial or social exploitation."

Marxism: Catholic social teaching "diverges radically from the program of collectivism proclaimed by Marxism and put into practice in various countries."

Private Property and Capitalism: "Christian tradition has never upheld" the right to private property "as absolute and untouchable. On the contrary, it has always understood this right common to all to use the goods of the whole creation."

"Deeply desired reforms" of capitalism "cannot be achieved by an *a priori* elimination of private ownership of the means of production." This is not sufficient to insure "satisfactory socialization" because new managers form another special group "from the fact of exercising power in society. This group . . . may carry out this task badly by claiming for itself a monopoly of the administration and disposal of the means of production and not refraining even from offending basic human rights."

Exploitation by Multinationals: "The highly industrialized countries, and even more so the businesses that direct on a large scale the means of industrial production, fix the highest possible prices for their products while trying at the same time to fix the lowest possible prices for raw materials or semi-manufactured goods."

PEACE AND WAR

The following excerpts, stating principles and objectives of social doctrine concerning peace and war, are from the "Pastoral Constitution on the Church in the Modern World" (Nos. 77 to 82) promulgated by the Second Vatican Council.

(See also: "The Challenge of Peace: God's Promise and Our Purpose.")

Call to Peace: This Council fervently desires to summon Christians to cooperate with all men in making secure among themselves a peace based on justice and love, and in setting up agencies of peace. This Christians should do with the help of Christ, the Author of peace (No. 77).

Conditions for Peace: Peace is not merely the absence of war. Nor can it be reduced solely to the maintenance of a balance of power between enemies. Nor is it brought about by dictatorship. Instead, it is rightly and appropriately called "an enterprise of justice" (Is. 32:7). Peace results from that harmony built into human society by its divine Founder and actualized by men as they thirst after ever greater justice.

The common good of men is in its basic sense determined by the eternal law. Still the concrete demands of this common good are constantly changing as time goes on. Hence peace is never attained once and for all, but must be built up ceaselessly. Moreover, since the human will is unsteady and wounded by sin, the achievement of peace requires that everyone constantly master his passions and that lawful authority keep vigilant.

But such is not enough. This peace cannot be obtained on earth unless personal values are safeguarded and men freely and trustingly share with one another the riches of their inner spirits and their talents. A firm determination to respect other men and peoples and their dignity, as well as the studied practice of brotherhood, are absolutely necessary for the establishment of peace. Hence peace is likewise the fruit of love, which goes beyond what justice can provide.

Renunciation of Violence: We cannot fail to praise those who renounce the use of violence in the vindication of their rights and who resort to methods of defense which are otherwise available to weaker parties too, provided that this can be done without injury to the rights and duties of others or of the community itself (No. 78).

Mass Extermination: The Council wishes to recall first of all the permanent binding force of universal natural law and its all-embracing principles. Man's conscience itself gives ever more emphatic voice to these principles. Therefore, actions which deliberately conflict with these same principles, as well as orders commanding such actions, are criminal. Blind obedience cannot excuse those who yield to them. Among such must first be counted those actions designed for the methodical extermination of an entire people, nation, or ethnic minority. These actions must be vehemently condemned as horrendous crimes. The courage of those who openly and fearlessly resist men who issue such commands merits supreme commendation.

International Agreements: On the subject of war, quite a large number of nations have subscribed to various international agreements aimed at making military activity and its consequences less inhuman. Such are conventions concerning the handling of wounded or captured soldiers, and various similar agreements. Agreements of this sort must be honored. They should be improved upon.

Conscientious Objectors: It seems right that laws make humane provisions for the case of those who for reasons of conscience refuse to bear arms, provided, however, that they accept some other form of service to the human community.

Legitimate Defense: Certainly, war has not been rooted out of human affairs. As long as the danger of war remains and there is no competent and sufficiently powerful authority at the international level, governments cannot be denied the right to legitimate defense once every means of peaceful settlement has been exhausted. Therefore, government authorities and others who share public responsibility have the duty to protect the welfare of the people entrusted to their care and to conduct such grave matters soberly.

But it is one thing to undertake military action for the just defense of the people, and something else again to seek the subjugation of other nations. Nor does the possession of war potential make every military or political use of it lawful. Neither does the mere fact that war has unhappily begun mean that all is fair between the warring parties.

Nature of Military Service: Those who are pledged to the service of their country as members of its armed forces should regard themselves as agents of security and freedom on behalf of their people. As long as they fulfill this role properly, they are making a genuine contribution to the establishment of peace (No. 79).

Total War Condemned: This most holy Synod makes its own the condemnations of total war already pronounced by recent popes, and issues the following declaration:

Any act of war aimed indiscriminately at the destruction of entire cities or of extensive areas along with their population is a crime against God and man himself. It merits unequivocal and unhesitating condemnation.

The unique hazard of modern warfare consists in this: it provides those who possess modern scientific weapons with a kind of occasion for perpetrating just such abominations. Moreover, through a certain inexorable chain of events, it can urge men on to the most atrocious decisions. That such in fact may never happen in the future, the bishops of the whole world, in unity assembled, beg all men, especially government officials and military leaders, to give unremitting thought to the awesome responsibility which is theirs before God and the entire human race (No. 80).

Retaliation and Deterrence: Scientific weapons, to be sure, are not amassed solely for use in war. The defensive strength of any nation is considered to be dependent upon its capacity for immediate retaliation against an adversary. Hence this accumulation of arms, which increases each year, also serves, in a way heretofore unknown, as a deterrent to possible enemy attack. Many regard this state of affairs as the most effective way by which peace of a sort can be maintained between nations at the present time.

Arms Race: Whatever be the case with this method of deterrence, men should be convinced that the arms race in which so many countries are engaged is not a safe way to preserve a steady peace. Nor is the so-called balance resulting from this race a sure and authentic peace. Rather than being eliminated thereby, the causes of war threaten to grow gradually stronger.

While extravagant sums are being spent for the furnishing of ever new weapons, an adequate remedy cannot be provided for the multiple miseries afflicting the whole modern world. Disagreements between nations are not really and radically healed. On the contrary, other parts of the world are infected with them. New approaches initiated by reformed attitudes must be adopted to remove this trap and to restore genuine peace by emancipating the world from its crushing anxiety.

Therefore, it must be said again: the arms race is an utterly treacherous trap for humanity, and one which injures the poor to an intolerable degree. It is much to be feared that, if this race persists, it will eventually spawn all the lethal ruin whose path it is now making ready (No. 81).

Outlaw War: It is our clear duty, then, to strain every muscle as we work for the time when all war can be completely outlawed by international consent. This goal undoubtedly requires the establishment of some universal public authority acknowledged as such by all, and endowed with effective power to safeguard, on behalf of all, security, regard for justice, and respect for rights.

Multilateral and Controlled Disarmament: But before this hoped-for authority can be set up, the highest existing international centers must devote themselves vigorously to the pursuit of better means for obtaining common security. Peace must be born of mutual trust between nations rather than imposed on them through fear of one another's weapons. Hence everyone must labor to put an end at last to the arms race, and to make a true beginning of disarmament, not indeed a unilateral disarmament, but one proceeding at an equal pace according to agreement, and backed up by authentic and workable safeguards.

In the meantime, efforts which have already been made and are still under way to eliminate the danger of war are not to be underrated. On the contrary, support should be given to the good will of the very many leaders who work hard to do away with war, which they abominate.

Public Opinion: Men should take heed not to entrust themselves only to the efforts of others, while remaining careless about their own attitudes. For government officials, who must simultaneously guarantee the good of their own people and promote the universal good, depend on public opinion and feeling to the greatest possible extent. It does them no good to work at building peace so long as feelings of hostility, contempt, and distrust, as well as racial hatred and unbending ideologies, continue to divide men and place them in opposing camps.

Hence arises a surpassing need for renewed education of attitudes and for new inspiration in the area of public opinion. Those who are dedicated to the work of education . . . should regard as their most weighty task the effort to instruct all in fresh sentiments of peace (No. 82).

THE CHALLENGE OF PEACE:
GOD'S PROMISE AND OUR RESPONSE

Following is an excerpt from a summary of the pastoral letter, "The Challenge of Peace: God's Promise and Our Response," copyright ©1983 by the United States Catholic Conference, all rights reserved. A copy of the complete text can be ordered from the Office of Publishing Services, USCC, 1312 Massachusetts Ave. N.W., Washington, D.C. 20005.

The letter was approved by a vote of 238 to 9 at a special meeting of U.S. bishops May 2 and 3, 1983, in Chicago.

I. SOME PRINCIPLES, NORMS AND PREMISES OF CATHOLIC TEACHING

A. On War

1. Catholic teaching begins in every case with a presumption against war and for peaceful settlement of disputes. In exceptional cases, determined by the moral principles of the just-war tradition, some uses of force are permitted.

2. Every nation has a right and duty to defend itself against unjust aggression.

3. Offensive war of any kind is not morally justifiable.

4. It is never permitted to direct nuclear or conventional weapons to "the indiscriminate destruction of whole cities or vast areas with their populations. . . ." (*Pastoral Constitution on the Church in the Modern World*, No. 80.) The intentional killing of innocent civilians or non-combatants is always wrong.

5. Even defensive response to unjust attack can cause destruction which violates the principle of proportionality, going far beyond the limits of legitimate defense. This judgment is particularly important when assessing planned use of nuclear weapons. No defensive strategy, nuclear or con-

ventional, which exceeds the limits of proportionality is morally permissible.

B. On Deterrence

1. "In current conditions 'deterrence' based on balance, certainly not as an end in itself but as a step on the way toward a progressive disarmament, may still be judged morally acceptable. Nonetheless, in order to ensure peace, it is indispensable not to be satisfied with this minimum which is always susceptible to the real danger of explosion." (Pope John Paul II, Message to U.N. Special Session on Disarmament, No. 8, June, 1982.)

2. No *use* of nuclear weapons which would violate the principles of discrimination or proportionality may be *intended* in a strategy of deterrence. The moral demands of Catholic teaching require resolute willingness not to intend or to do moral evil even to save our own lives or the lives of those we love.

3. Deterrence is not an adequate strategy as a long-term basis for peace; it is a transitional strategy justifiable only in conjunction with resolute determination to pursue arms control and disarmament. We are convinced that "the fundamental principle on which our present peace depends must be replaced by another, which declares that the true and solid peace of nations consists not in equality of arms but in mutual trust alone." (Pope John XXIII, Encyclical *Peace on Earth*, No. 113.)

C. The Arms Race and Disarmament

1. The arms race is one of the greatest curses on the human race; it is to be condemned as a danger, an act of aggression against the poor, and a folly which does not provide the security it promises. (Cf. *Pastoral Constitution*, No. 81; Statement of the Holy See to the United Nations, 1976.)

2. Negotiations must be pursued in every reasonable form possible; they should be governed by the "demand that the arms race should cease; that the stockpiles which exist in various countries should be reduced equally and simultaneously by the parties concerned; that nuclear weapons should be banned; and that a general agreement should eventually be reached about progressive disarmament and an effective method of control." (Pope John XXIII, *Peace on Earth*, No. 112.)

D. On Personal Conscience

1. *Military Service:* "All those who enter the military service in loyalty to their country should look upon themselves as the custodians of the security and freedom of their fellow countrymen; and when they carry out their duty properly, they are contributing to the maintenance of peace." (*Pastoral Constitution*, No. 79.)

2. *Conscientious Objection:* "Moreover, it seems just that laws should make humane provision for the case of conscientious objectors who refuse to carry arms, provided they accept some other form of community service." (*Pastoral Constitution*, No. 79.)

3. *Non-violence:* "In this same spirit we cannot but express our admiration for all who forego the use of violence to vindicate their rights and resort to other means of defense which are available to weaker parties, provided it can be done without harm to the rights and duties of others and of the community." (*Pastoral Constitution*, No. 78.)

4. *Citizens and Conscience:* "Once again we deem it opportune to remind our children of their duty to take an active part in public life, and to contribute towards the attainment of the common good of the entire human family as well as to that of their own political community. . . . In other words, it is necessary that human beings, in the intimacy of their own consciences, should so live and act in their temporal lives as to create a synthesis between scientific, technical and professional elements on the one hand, and spiritual values on the other." (Pope John XXIII, *Peace on Earth*, Nos. 146, 150.)

II. MORAL PRINCIPLES AND POLICY CHOICES

As bishops in the United States, assessing the concrete circumstances of our society, we have made a number of observations and recommendations in the process of applying moral principles to specific policy choices.

A. On the Use of Nuclear Weapons

1. *Counter Population Use:* Under no circumstances may nuclear weapons or other instruments of mass slaughter be used for the purpose of destroying population centers or other predominantly civilian targets. Retaliatory action which would indiscriminately and disproportionately take many wholly innocent lives, lives of people who are in no way responsible for reckless actions of their government, must also be condemned.

2. *The Initiation of Nuclear War:* We do not perceive any situation in which the deliberate initiation of nuclear war, on however restricted a scale, can be morally justified. Non-nuclear attacks by another state must be resisted by other than nuclear means. Therefore, a serious moral obligation exists to develop non-nuclear defensive strategies as rapidly as possible. In this letter we urge NATO to move rapidly toward the adoption of a "no first use" policy, but we recognize this will take time to implement and will require the development of an adequate alternative defense posture.

3. *Limited Nuclear War:* Our examination of the various arguments on this question makes us highly skeptical about the real meaning of "limited." One of the criteria of the just-war teaching is that there must be a reasonable hope of success in bringing about justice and peace. We must ask whether such a reasonable hope can exist once nuclear weapons have been exchanged. The burden of proof remains on those who assert that meaningful limitation is possible. In our view the first imperative is to prevent any use of nuclear weapons and we hope that leaders will resist the notion that nuclear conflict can be limited, contained or won in any traditional sense.

B. On Deterrence

In concert with the evaluation provided by Pope John Paul II, we have arrived at a strictly conditional moral acceptance of deterrence. In this letter we have outlined criteria and recommendations which indicate the meaning of conditional acceptance of deterrence policy. We cannot consider such a policy adequate as a long-term basis for peace.

C. On Promoting Peace

1. We support immediate, bilateral, verifiable agreements to halt the testing, production and deployment of new nuclear weapons systems. This recommendation is not to be identified with any specific political initiative.
2. We support efforts to achieve deep cuts in the arsenals of both superpowers; efforts should concentrate first on systems which threaten the retaliatory forces of either major power.
3. We support early and successful conclusion of negotiations of a comprehensive test ban treaty.
4. We urge new efforts to prevent the spread of nuclear weapons in the world, and to control the conventional arms race, particularly the conventional arms trade.
5. We support, in an increasingly interdependent world, political and economic policies designed to protect human dignity and to promote the human rights of every person, especially the least among us. In this regard, we call for the establishment of some form of global authority adequate to the needs of the international common good.

This letter includes many judgments from the perspective of ethics, politics and strategy needed to speak concretely and correctly to the "moment of supreme crisis" identified by Vatican II. We stress again that readers should be aware, as we have been, of the distinction between our statement of moral principles and of official Church teaching and our application of these to concrete issues. We urge that special care be taken not to use passages out of context; neither should brief portions of this document be cited to support positions it does not intend to convey or which are not truly in accord with the spirit of its teaching.

ECONOMIC JUSTICE FOR ALL

(Based on an article by Jerry Filteau, NC News.)

Following are a number of policy statements and recommendations contained in the third draft of a proposed pastoral letter of the bishops of the United States entitled, "Economic Justice for All." Voting for adoption of the letter was scheduled to be held during the November, 1986, meeting of the National Conference of Catholic Bishops and the U.S. Catholic Conference.

General Principles: The basic questions about economic life are, what it does to people and for people, and how they participate in it. All people have a God-given right to basic economic necessities; so, "fulfillment of the basic needs of the poor is of the highest priority" in any economy.

• A "preferential option for the poor" is a matter of social justice, not charity. In any society, the "litmus test of its justice or injustice" is how it treats its poor and powerless.

• Because "the family is the most basic form of human community," economic policies must be "continually evaluated in light of their impact on the strength and stability of family life."

• Recognition and fulfillment of the economic rights of all is "the unfinished business of the American experiment," calling for "the development of a new cultural consensus."

Employment: "Full employment is the foundation of a just economy," and the creation of new jobs is the nation's "most urgent priority for domestic economic policy."

• Job discrimination against women and racial and ethnic minorities is a major concern. Huge expenditures on the arms race cost jobs and "create a massive drain" on America's financial and human resources.

Poverty: "Dealing with poverty is not a luxury.

... Rather, it is an imperative of the highest order." More than 33 million Americans are in poverty. It falls hardest on women, children, Hispanics, Blacks and Native Americans.

• The disparities are not only in income and wealth, but also reflect "the uneven distribution of power in our society" and the inability of many to have a real part in U.S. political and social life.

Food and Agriculture: U.S. public policies have played a major role in creating the conditions that have led to the current farm crisis, and public policy must play a positive role in solving the crisis.

• The economic viability of family farms should be preserved, and agricultural policy should view the stewardship of American natural resources as a "central consideration."

Global Economy: As with domestic policy, "the preferential option for the poor is the central priority" that ought to guide U.S. dealings with poorer nations.

• The U.S. tendency in recent years to make "national security the central policy issue ... must be resisted." Militarization and politicization of development aid are "a grave distortion" of the way that aid should be handled.

Public-Private Partnerships: A "new American experiment" in economic rights requires cooperation and partnership in business, government, churches, unions, other social organizations and individuals at all levels. This must include national economic planning, policies and priorities, although economic justice for all is the cooperative task of all elements of society, not just the government.

• The new American experiment should extend beyond national borders to U.S. leadership in global economic cooperation and partnership. International solidarity is a form of enlightened self-interest, since "the cause of democracy is closely tied to the cause of economic justice."

The nature and purpose of the liturgy, along with norms for its revision, were the subject matter of the "Constitution on the Sacred Liturgy" promulgated by the Second Vatican Council. The principles and guidelines stated in this document, the first issued by the Council, are summarized here and/or are incorporated in other Almanac entries on liturgical subjects.

Nature and Purpose of Liturgy

The paragraphs under this and the following subhead are quoted directly from the "Constitution on the Sacred Liturgy."

"It is through the liturgy, especially the divine Eucharistic Sacrifice, that 'the work of our redemption is exercised.' The liturgy is thus the outstanding means by which the faithful can express in their lives, and manifest to others, the mystery of Christ and the real nature of the true Church . . ." (No. 2).

"The liturgy is considered as an exercise of the priestly office of Jesus Christ. In the liturgy the sanctification of man is manifested by signs perceptible to the senses, and is effected in a way which is proper to each of these signs; in the liturgy full public worship is performed by the Mystical Body of Jesus Christ, that is, by the Head and his members.

"From this it follows that every liturgical celebration, because it is an action of Christ the priest and of his Body the Church, is a sacred action surpassing all others. No other action of the Church can match its claim to efficacy, nor equal the degree of it" (No. 7).

"The liturgy is the summit toward which the activity of the Church is directed; at the same time it is the fountain from which all her power flows. For the goal of apostolic works is that all who are made sons of God by faith and baptism should come together to praise God in the midst of his Church, to take part in her sacrifice, and to eat the Lord's Supper.

". . . From the liturgy, therefore, and especially from the Eucharist, as from a fountain, grace is channeled into us; and the sanctification of men in Christ and the glorification of God, to which all other activities of the Church are directed as toward their goal, are most powerfully achieved" (No. 10).

Full Participation

"Mother Church earnestly desires that all the faithful be led to that full, conscious, and active participation in liturgical celebrations which is demanded by the very nature of the liturgy. Such participation by the Christian people as 'a chosen race, a royal priesthood, a holy nation, a purchased people' (1 Pt. 2:9; cf. 2:4-5), is their right and duty by reason of their baptism.

"In the restoration and promotion of the sacred liturgy, this full and active participation by all the people is the aim to be considered before all else; for it is the primary and indispensable source from which the faithful are to derive the true Christian spirit . . ." (No. 14).

"In order that the Christian people may more securely derive an abundance of graces from the sacred liturgy, holy Mother Church desires to undertake with great care a general restoration of the liturgy itself. For the liturgy is made up of unchangeable elements divinely instituted, and elements subject to change. The latter not only may but ought to be changed with the passing of time if features have by chance crept in which are less harmonious with the intimate nature of the liturgy, or if existing elements have grown less functional.

"In this restoration, both texts and rites should be drawn up so that they express more clearly the holy things which they signify. Christian people, as far as possible, should be able to understand them with ease and to take part in them fully, actively, and as befits a community . . ." (No. 21).

Norms

Norms regarding the reforms concern the greater use of Scripture; emphasis on the importance of the sermon or homily on biblical and liturgical subjects; use of vernacular languages for prayers of the Mass and for administration of the sacraments; provision for adaptation of rites to cultural patterns.

Approval for reforms of various kinds — in liturgical texts, rites, etc. — depends on the Holy See, regional conferences of bishops and individual bishops, according to provisions of law. No priest has authority to initiate reforms on his own. Reforms may not be introduced just for the sake of innovation, and any that are introduced in the light of present-day circumstances should embody sound tradition.

To assure the desired effect of liturgical reforms, training and instruction are necessary for the clergy, religious and the laity. The functions of diocesan and regional commissions for liturgy, music and art are to set standards and provide leadership for instruction and practical programs in their respective fields.

Most of the constitution's provisions regarding liturgical reforms have to do with the Roman Rite. The document clearly respects the equal dignity of all rites, leaving to the Eastern Churches control over their ancient liturgies.

(For coverage of the **Mystery of the Eucharist,** see The Mass; **Other Sacraments,** see separate entries.)

Sacramentals

Sacramentals, instituted by the Church, "are sacred signs which bear a resemblance to the sacraments: they signify effects, particularly of a spiritual kind, which are obtained through the Church's intercession. By them men are disposed to receive the chief effect of the sacraments, and various occasions in life are rendered holy" (No. 60).

"Thus, for well-disposed members of the faithful, the liturgy of the sacraments and sacramentals sanctifies almost every event in their lives; they are given access to the stream of divine grace which flows from the paschal mystery of the passion, death, and resurrection of Christ, the fountain from which all sacraments and sacramentals draw their power. There is hardly any proper use of material things which cannot thus be directed toward the sanctification of men and the praise of God'' (No. 61).

Some common sacramentals are priestly blessings, blessed palm, candles, holy water, medals, scapulars, prayers and ceremonies of the Roman Ritual.

Liturgy of the Hours

The Liturgy of the Hours (Divine Office) is the public prayer of the Church for praising God and sanctifying the day. Its daily celebration is required as a sacred obligation by men in holy orders and by men and women religious who have professed solemn vows. Its celebration by others is highly commended and is to be encouraged in the community of the faithful.

"By tradition going back to early Christian times, the Divine Office is arranged so that the whole course of the day and night is made holy by the praises of God. Therefore, when this wonderful song of praise is worthily rendered by priests and others who are deputed for this purpose by Church ordinance, or by the faithful praying together with the priest in an approved form, then it is truly the voice of the bride addressing her bridegroom; it is the very prayer which Christ himself, together with his Body, addresses to the Father'' (No. 84).

"Hence all who perform this service are not only fulfilling a duty of the Church, but also are sharing in the greatest honor accorded to Christ's spouse, for by offering these praises to God they are standing before God's throne in the name of the Church their Mother'' (No. 85).

The Liturgy of the Hours, revised since 1965, was the subject of Pope Paul VI's apostolic constitution *Laudis Canticum,* dated Nov. 1, 1970. The master Latin text was published in 1971; its four volumes have been published in authorized English translation since May, 1975.

One-volume, partial editions of the Liturgy of the Hours containing Morning and Evening Prayer and other elements, have been published in approved English translation.

The revised Liturgy of the Hours consists of:

• Office of Readings, for reflection on the word of God. The principal parts are three psalms, biblical and non-biblical readings.

• Morning and Evening Prayer, called the "hinges" of the Liturgy of the Hours. The principal parts are a hymn, two psalms, an Old or New Testament canticle, a brief biblical reading, Zechariah's canticle (the *Benedictus,* morning) or Mary's canticle (the *Magnificat,* evening), responsories, intercessions and a concluding prayer.

• Daytime Prayer. The principal parts are a hymn, three psalms, a brief biblical reading and one of three concluding prayers corresponding to the time at which the prayer is offered (midmorning, midday, midafternoon).

• Night Prayer: The principal parts are one or two psalms, a brief biblical reading, Simeon's canticle *(Nunc Dimittis),* a concluding prayer and an antiphon in honor of Mary.

In the revised Liturgy of the Hours, the hours are shorter than they had been, with greater textual variety, meditation aids, and provision for intervals of silence and meditation. The psalms are distributed over a four-week period instead of a week; some psalms, entirely or in part, are not included. Additional canticles from the Old and New Testaments are assigned for Morning and Evening Prayer. Additional scriptural texts have been added and variously arranged for greater internal unity, correspondence to readings at Mass, and relevance to events and themes of salvation history. Readings include some of the best material from the Fathers of the Church and other authors, and improved selections on the lives of saints.

The book used for recitation of the Office is the **Breviary.**

For coverage of the **Liturgical Year,** see Church Calendar.

Sacred Music

"The musical tradition of the universal Church is a treasure of immeasurable value, greater even than that of any other art. The main reason for this pre-eminence is that, as sacred melody united to words, it forms a necessary or integral part of the solemn liturgy.

"... Sacred music increases in holiness to the degree that it is intimately linked with liturgical action, winningly expresses prayerfulness, promotes solidarity, and enriches sacred rites with heightened solemnity. The Church indeed approves of all forms of true art, and admits them into divine worship when they show appropriate qualities'' (No. 112).

The constitution decreed:

• Vernacular languages for the people's parts of the liturgy, as well as Latin, may be used.

• Participation in sacred song by the whole body of the faithful, and not just by choirs, is to be encouraged and brought about.

• Provisions should be made for proper musical training for clergy, religious and lay persons.

• While Gregorian Chant has a unique dignity and relationship to the Latin liturgy, other kinds of music are acceptable.

• Native musical traditions should be used, especially in mission areas.

• Various instruments compatible with the dignity of worship may be used.

Gregorian Chant: A form and style of chant called Gregorian was the basis and most highly regarded standard of liturgical music for centuries. It originated probably during the formative period of the Roman liturgy and developed in conjunction with Gallican and other forms of chant. Gregory the Great's connection with it is not clear, although it is known that he had great concern for and interest in church music. The earliest extant written versions of Gregorian Chant date from the ninth century. A thousand years later, the Benedictines of Solesmes, France, initiated a revival of chant which gave impetus to the modern liturgical movement.

Sacred Art and Furnishings

"Very rightly the fine arts are considered to rank among the noblest expressions of human genius. This judgment applies especially to religious art and to its highest achievement, which is sacred art. By their very nature both of the latter are related to God's boundless beauty, for this is the reality which these human efforts are trying to express in some way. To the extent that these works aim exclusively at turning men's thoughts to God persuasively and devoutly, they are dedicated to God and to the cause of his greater honor and glory" (No. 122).

The objective of sacred art is "that all things set apart for use in divine worship should be truly worthy, becoming, and beautiful, signs and symbols of heavenly realities. . . . The Church has . . . always reserved to herself the right to pass judgment upon the arts, deciding which of the works of artists are in accordance with faith, piety, and cherished traditional laws, and thereby suited to sacred purposes.

". . . Sacred furnishings should worthily and beautifully serve the dignity of worship . . ." (No. 122).

According to the constitution:

• Contemporary art, as well as that of the past, shall "be given free scope in the Church, provided that it adorns the sacred buildings and holy rites with due honor and reverence . . ." (No. 123).

• Noble beauty, not sumptuous display, should be sought in art, sacred vestments and ornaments.

• "Let bishops carefully exclude from the house of God and from other sacred places those works of artists which are repugnant to faith, morals, and Christian piety, and which offend true religious sense either by their distortion of forms or by lack of artistic worth, by mediocrity or by pretense.

• "When churches are to be built, let great care be taken that they be suitable for the celebration of liturgical services and for the active participation of the faithful" (No. 124).

• "The practice of placing sacred images in churches so that they may be venerated by the faithful is to be firmly maintained. Nevertheless, their number should be moderate and their relative location should reflect right order. Otherwise they may create confusion among the Christian people and promote a faulty sense of devotion" (No. 125).

• Artists should be trained and inspired in the spirit and for the purposes of the liturgy.

• The norms of sacred art should be revised. "These laws refer especially to the worthy and well-planned construction of sacred buildings, the shape and construction of altars, the nobility, location, and security of the Eucharistic tabernacle, the suitability and dignity of the baptistery, the proper use of sacred images, embellishments, and vestments . . ." (No. 128).

RITES

Rites are the forms and ceremonial observances of liturgical worship coupled with the total expression of the theological, spiritual and disciplinary heritages of particular churches of the East and the West.

Different rites have evolved in the course of church history, giving to liturgical worship and church life in general forms and usages peculiar and proper to the nature of worship and the culture of the faithful in various circumstances of time and place. Thus, there has been development since apostolic times in the prayers and ceremonies of the Mass, in the celebration of the sacraments, sacramentals and the Liturgy of the Hours, and in observances of the liturgical calendar. The principal sources of rites in present use were practices within the patriarchates of Rome (for the West) and Antioch, Alexandria and Constantinople (for the East). Rites are identified as Eastern or Western on the basis of their geographical area of origin in the Roman Empire.

Eastern and Roman

Eastern Rites are proper to Eastern Catholic Churches (see separate entry). The principal rites are Byzantine, Alexandrian, Antiochene, Armenian and Chaldean.

The Latin or Roman Rite prevails in the Western Church. It was derived from Roman practices and the use of Latin from the third century onward, and has been the rite in general use in the West since the eighth century. Other rites in limited use in the Western Church have been the Ambrosian (in the Archdiocese of Milan), the Mozarabic (in the Archdiocese of Toledo), the Lyonnais, the Braga, and rites peculiar to some religious orders like the Dominicans, Carmelites and Carthusians.

The purpose of the revision of rites in progress since the Second Vatican Council is to renew them, not to eliminate the rites of particular churches or to reduce all rites to uniformity. The Council reaffirmed the equal dignity and preservation of rites as follows.

"It is the mind of the Catholic Church that each individual church or rite retain its traditions whole and entire, while adjusting its way of life to various needs of time and place. Such individual churches, whether of the East or the West, although they differ somewhat among themselves in what are called rites (that is, in liturgy, ecclesiastical discipline and spiritual heritage), are, nevertheless, equally entrusted to the pastoral guidance of the Roman Pontiff, the divinely appointed successor of St. Peter in supreme government over the universal Church. They are, consequently, of equal dignity, so that none of them is superior to the others by reason of rite."

Determination of Rite

Determination of a person's rite is regulated by church law. Through baptism, a child becomes a member of the rite of his or her parents. If the parents are of different rites, the child's rite is decided by mutual consent of the parents; if there is lack of mutual consent, the child is baptized in the rite of the father. A candidate for baptism over the age of 14 can choose to be baptized in any approved rite. Catholics baptized in one rite may receive the sacraments in any of the approved ritual churches; they may transfer to another rite only with the permission of the Holy See and in accordance with other provisions of the Code of Canon Law.

MASS, EUCHARISTIC SACRIFICE AND BANQUET

Declarations of Vatican II

The Second Vatican Council made the following declarations, among others, with respect to the Mass.

"At the Last Supper, on the night when he was betrayed, our Savior instituted the Eucharistic Sacrifice of his Body and Blood. He did this in order to perpetuate the Sacrifice of the Cross throughout the centuries until he should come again, and so to entrust to his beloved spouse, the Church, a memorial of his death and resurrection: a sacrament of love, a sign of unity, a bond of charity, a paschal banquet in which Christ is consumed, the mind is filled with grace, and a pledge of future glory is given to us" (*Constitution on the Sacred Liturgy,* No. 47).

". . . As often as the Sacrifice of the Cross in which 'Christ, our Passover, has been sacrificed' (1 Cor. 5:7) is celebrated on an altar, the work of our redemption is carried on. At the same time, in the sacrament of the Eucharistic bread the unity of all believers who form one body in Christ (cf. 1 Cor. 10:17) is both expressed and brought about. All men are called to this union with Christ . . ." (*Dogmatic Constitution on the Church.* No 3).

". . . The ministerial priest, by the sacred power he enjoys, molds and rules the priestly people. Acting in the person of Christ, he brings about the Eucharistic Sacrifice, and offers it to God in the name of all the people. For their part, the faithful join in the offering of the Eucharist by virtue of their royal priesthood . . ." (*Ibid.,* No. 10).

Declarations of Trent

Among its decrees on the Holy Eucharist, the Council of Trent stated the following points of doctrine on the Mass.

1. There is in the Catholic Church a true Sacrifice, the Mass instituted by Jesus Christ. It is the Sacrifice of his Body and Blood, Soul and Divinity, himself, under the appearances of bread and wine.

2. This Sacrifice is identical with the Sacrifice of the Cross, inasmuch as Christ is the Priest and Victim in both. A difference lies in the manner of offering, which was bloody upon the Cross and is bloodless on the altar.

3. The Mass is a propitiatory Sacrifice, atoning for sins of the living and dead for whom it is offered.

4. The efficacy of the Mass is derived from the Sacrifice of the Cross, whose superabundant merits it applies to men.

5. Although the Mass is offered to God alone, it may be celebrated in honor and memory of the saints.

6. Christ instituted the Mass at the Last Supper.

7. Christ ordained the Apostles priests, giving them power and the command to consecrate his Body and Blood to perpetuate and renew the Sacrifice.

ORDER OF MASS

The Mass consists of two principal divisions called the **Liturgy of the Word,** which features the proclamation of the Word of God, and the **Eucharistic Liturgy,** which focuses on the central act of sacrifice in the Consecration and on the Eucharistic Banquet in Holy Communion. (Formerly, these divisions were called, respectively, the **Mass of the Catechumens** and the **Mass of the Faithful.**) In addition to these principal divisions, there are ancillary introductory and concluding rites.

The following description covers the Mass as celebrated with participation by the people. This Order of the Mass was approved by Pope Paul VI in the apostolic constitution *Missale Romanum* dated Apr. 3, 1969, and promulgated in a decree issued Apr. 6, 1969, by the Congregation for Divine Worship. The assigned effective date was Nov. 30, 1969.

Introductory Rites

Entrance: The introductory rites begin with the singing or recitation of an entrance song consisting of one or more scriptural verses stating the theme of the mystery, season or feast commemorated in the Mass.

Greeting: The priest and people make the Sign of the Cross together. The priest then greets them in one of several alternative ways and they reply in a corresponding manner.

Introductory Remarks: At this point, the priest or another of the ministers may introduce the theme of the Mass.

Penitential Rite: The priest and people together acknowledge their sins as a preliminary step toward worthy celebration of the sacred mysteries. This rite includes a brief examination of conscience, a general confession of sin and plea for divine mercy in one of several ways, and a prayer for forgiveness by the priest.

Glory to God: A doxology, a hymn of praise to God, sung or said on festive occasions.

Opening Prayer: A prayer of petition offered by the priest on behalf of the worshipping community.

I. Liturgy of the Word

Readings: The featured elements of this liturgy are readings of passages from the Bible. If three readings are in order, the first is usually from the Old Testament, the second from the New Testament (Letters, Acts, Revelation), and the third from one of the Gospels; the final reading is always a selection from a Gospel. The first reading(s) is concluded with the formula, "This is the Word of the Lord," to which the people respond, "Thanks be to God." The Gospel reading is concluded with the formula, "This is the Gospel of the Lord," to which the people respond, "Praise to you, Lord Jesus Christ." Between the readings, psalm verses are sung or recited. A Gospel acclamation is either sung or omitted.

Homily: Sermon on a scriptural or liturgical subject; ideally, it should be related to the liturgical service in progress.

Creed: The Nicene profession of faith, by priest and people, on certain occasions.

Prayer of the Faithful: Litany-type prayers of petition, with participation by the people. Called general intercessions, they concern needs of the Church, the salvation of the world, public authorities, persons in need, the local community.

II. Eucharistic Liturgy

Offertory Song: Scriptural verses related to the theme of the Mass, or a suitable hymn, may be sung or said while things are prepared at the altar for the Eucharistic Liturgy and while the offerings of bread and wine are brought to the altar.

Offertory Procession: Presentation to the priest of the gifts of bread and wine, principally, by participating members of the congregation.

Offering of and Prayer over the Gifts: Consists of the prayers and ceremonies with which the priest offers bread and wine as the elements of the sacrifice to take place during the Eucharistic Prayer and of the Lord's Supper to be shared in Holy Communion.

Washing of Hands: After offering the bread and wine, the priest cleanses his fingers with water in a brief ceremony of purification.

Pray, Brethren: Prayer that the sacrifice to take place will be acceptable to God. The first part of the prayer is said by the priest; the second, by the people.

Prayer over the Gifts: A prayer of petition offered by the priest on behalf of the worshipping community.

Eucharistic Prayer

Preface: A hymn of praise, introducing the Eucharistic Prayer or Canon, sung or said by the priest following responses by the people. The Order of the Mass contains a variety of prefaces, for use on different occasions.

Holy, Holy, Holy; Blessed Is He: Divine praises sung or said by the priest and people.

Canon: The Eucharistic Prayer of the Mass whose central portion is the Consecration, when the essential act of sacrificial offering takes place with the changing of bread and wine into the Body and Blood of Christ. The prayers of the Canon, which are said by the celebrant only, commemorate principal mysteries of salvation history and include petitions for the Church, the living and dead, and remembrances of saints. There are four Eucharistic Prayers, for use on various occasions and at the option of the priest. (Additional Canons

for Masses with children and for reconciliation were approved in 1975.)

Doxology: A formula of divine praise sung or said by the priest while he holds aloft the chalice containing the consecrated wine in one hand and the paten containing the consecrated host in the other.

Communion Rite

Lord's Prayer: Sung or said by the priest and people.

Prayer for Deliverance from evil: Called an **embolism** because it is a development of the final petition of the Lord's Prayer; said by the priest. It concludes with a memorial of the return of the Lord to which the people respond, "For the kingdom, the power, and the glory are yours, now and forever."

Prayer for Peace: Said by the priest, with corresponding responses by the people. The priest can, in accord with local custom, bid the people to exchange a greeting of peace with each other.

Lamb of God (*Agnus Dei*): A prayer for divine mercy sung or said while the priest breaks the consecrated host and places a piece of it into the consecrated wine in the chalice.

Communion: The priest, after saying a preparatory prayer, administers Holy Communion to himself and then to the people, thus completing the sacrifice-banquet of the Mass. (This completion is realized even if the celebrant alone receives the Eucharist.) On giving the Eucharist to the people, the priest says, "The Body of Christ," to each recipient; the customary response is "Amen." If the Eucharist is administered under the forms of bread and wine, the priest says, "The Body and Blood of Christ."

Communion Song: Scriptural verses or a suitable hymn sung or said during the distribution of Holy Communion. After Holy Communion is received, some moments may be spent in silent meditation or in the chanting of a psalm or hymn of praise.

Prayer after Communion: A prayer of petition offered by the priest on behalf of the worshipping community.

Concluding Rite

Announcements: Brief announcements to the people are in order at this time.

Dismissal: Consists of a final greeting by the priest, a blessing, and a formula of dismissal. This rite is omitted if another liturgical action immediately follows the Mass; e.g., a procession, the blessing of the body during a funeral rite.

Some parts of the Mass are changeable with the liturgical season or feast, and are called the **proper** of the Mass. Other parts are said to be **common** because they always remain the same.

Additional Mass Notes

Catholics are seriously obliged to attend Mass in a worthy manner on Sundays and holy days of obligation. Failure to do so without a proportionately serious reason is gravely wrong.

It is the custom for priests to celebrate Mass

daily whenever possible. To satisfy the needs of the faithful on Sundays and holy days of obligation, they are authorized to say Mass twice (**bination**) or even three times (**trination**). Bination is also permissible on weekdays. On Christmas and All Souls' Day every priest may say three Masses.

The **fruits of the Mass**, which in itself is of infinite value, are: **general**, for all the faithful; **special (ministerial)**, for the intentions or persons specifically intended by the celebrant; **most special (personal)**, for the celebrant himself. On Sundays and certain other days pastors are obliged to offer Mass for their parishioners, or to have another priest do so. If a priest accepts a stipend or offering for a Mass, he is obliged in justice to apply the Mass for the designated intention. Mass may be applied for the living and the dead, or for any good intention.

Mass can be celebrated in several ways: e.g., with people present, without their presence (privately), with two or more priests as co-celebrants (concelebration), with greater or less solemnity.

Some of the various types of Masses are: **for the dead** (Funeral Mass or Mass of Christian Burial, Mass for the Dead — formerly called Requiem Mass); **ritual**, in connection with celebration of the sacraments, religious profession, etc.; **nuptial**, for married couples, with or after the wedding ceremony; **votive**, to honor a Person of the Trinity, a saint, or for some special intention. **Gregorian Masses** are a series of 30 Masses celebrated on 30 consecutive days for a deceased person.

On Good Friday instead of Mass, there is a celebration of the Lord's Passion consisting of a Liturgy of the Word, Veneration of the Cross and Holy Communion.

Places, Altars for Mass

The ordinary place for celebrating the Eucharist is a church or other sacred place, at a fixed or movable altar.

The altar is a table at which the Eucharistic Sacrifice is celebrated.

A *fixed altar* is attached to the floor of the church. It should be of stone, preferably, and should be consecrated. The Code of Canon Law orders observance of the custom of placing under a fixed altar relics of martyrs or other saints.

A *movable altar* can be made of any solid and suitable material, and should be blessed or consecrated.

Outside of a sacred place, Mass may be celebrated in an appropriate place at a suitable table covered with a linen cloth and corporal. An altar stone containing the relics of saints, which was formerly prescribed, is not required by regulations in effect since the promulgation Apr. 6, 1969, of *Institutio Generalis Missalis Romani.*

Spanish Lectionary

The U.S. Bishops' Committee on the Liturgy, in collaboration with its Hispanic counterparts in the U.S. and Latin America, was working in 1986 on the selection of a single Spanish lectionary to take the place of several in use in this country.

LITURGICAL VESTMENTS

In the early years of the Church, vestments worn by the ministers at liturgical functions were the same as the garments in ordinary popular use. They became distinctive when their form was not altered to correspond with later variations in popular style. Liturgical vestments are symbolic of the sacred ministry and add appropriate decorum to divine worship.

Mass Vestments

Alb: A body-length tunic of white fabric; a vestment common to all ministers of divine worship.

Amice: A rectangular piece of white cloth worn about the neck, tucked into the collar and falling over the shoulders; prescribed for use when the alb does not completely cover the ordinary clothing at the neck.

Chasuble: Originally, a large mantle or cloak covering the body, it is the outer vestment of a priest celebrating Mass or carrying out other sacred actions connected with the Mass.

Cincture: A cord which serves the purpose of a belt, holding the alb close to the body.

Dalmatic: The outer vestment worn by a deacon in place of a chasuble.

Stole: A long, band-like vestment worn about the neck and falling to about the knees. (A stole is used for other functions also.)

The material, form and ornamentation of the aforementioned and other vestments are subject to variation and adaptation, according to norms and decisions of the Holy See and concerned conferences of bishops. The overriding norm is that they should be appropriate for use in divine worship. The customary ornamented vestments are the chasuble, dalmatic and stole.

The minimal vestments required for a priest celebrating Mass are the alb, stole and chasuble.

Chasuble-Alb: A vestment combining the features of the chasuble and alb; for use with a stole by concelebrants and, by way of exception, by celebrants in certain circumstances.

Liturgical Colors

The colors of outer vestments vary with liturgical seasons, feasts and other circumstances. The colors and their use are:

Green: For the season of Ordinary Time; symbolic of hope and the vitality of the life of faith.

Purple: For Advent and Lent; may also be used in Masses for the dead; symbolic of penance.

Red: For the Sunday of the Passion, Good Friday, Pentecost; feasts of the Passion of Our Lord, the Apostles and Evangelists, martyrs; symbolic of the supreme sacrifice of life for the love of God.

Rose: May be used in place of purple on the Third Sunday of Advent (Gaudete Sunday) and the Fourth Sunday of Lent (Laetare Sunday); symbolic of anticipatory joy during a time of penance.

White: For the seasons of Christmas and Easter; feasts and commemorations of Our Lord, except those of the Passion; feasts and commemorations of the Blessed Virgin Mary, angels, saints who are not martyrs, All Saints (Nov. 1), St. John the Baptist (June 24), St. John the Evangelist (Dec. 27), the Chair of St. Peter (Feb. 22), the Conversion of St. Paul (Jan. 25). White, symbolic of purity and integrity of the life of faith, may generally be substituted for other colors, and can be used for funeral and other Masses for the dead.

Options are provided regarding the color of vestments used in offices and Masses for the dead. The newsletter of the U.S. Bishops' Committee on the Liturgy, in line with No. 308 of the General Instruction of the Roman Missal, announced in July, 1970: "In the dioceses of the United States, white vestments may be used, in addition to violet (purple) and black, in offices and Masses for the dead."

On more solemn occasions, better than ordinary vestments may be used, even though their color (e.g., gold) does not match the requirements of the day.

Other Vestments

Cappa Magna: Flowing vestment with a train, worn by bishops and cardinals.

Cassock: A non-liturgical, full-length, close-fitting robe for use by priests and other clerics under liturgical vestments and in ordinary use; usually black for priests, purple for bishops and other prelates, red for cardinals, white for the pope. In place of a cassock, priests belonging to religious institutes wear the habit proper to their institute.

Cope: A mantle-like vestment open in front and fastened across the chest; worn by sacred ministers in processions and other ceremonies, as prescribed by appropriate directives.

Habit: The ordinary (non-liturgical) garb of members of religious institutes, analogous to the cassock of diocesan priests; the form of habits varies from institute to institute.

Humeral Veil: A rectangular vestment worn about the shoulders by a deacon. or priest in Eucharistic processions and for other prescribed liturgical ceremonies.

Mitre: A headdress worn at some liturgical functions by bishops, abbots and, in certain cases, other ecclesiastics.

Pallium: A circular band of white wool about two inches wide, with front and back pendants, marked with six crosses, worn about the neck. It is a symbol of the fullness of the episcopal office. Pope Paul VI, in a document issued July 20, 1978, on his own initiative and entitled *Inter Eximia Episcopalis,* restricted its use to the pope and archbishops of metropolitan sees. In 1984, Pope John Paul II decreed that the pallium would ordinarily be conferred on metropolitans by the pope on the solemnity of Sts. Peter and Paul, June 29. The pallium is made from the wool of lambs blessed by the pope on the feast of St. Agnes (Jan. 21).

Rochet: A knee-length, white linen-lace garment of prelates worn under outer vestments.

Surplice: A loose, flowing vestment of white fabric with wide sleeves. For some functions, it is interchangeable with an alb.

Zucchetto: A skullcap worn by bishops and other prelates.

SACRED VESSELS, LINENS

Vessels

Chalice and Paten: The principal sacred vessels required for the celebration of Mass are the chalice (cup) and paten (plate) in which wine and bread, respectively, are offered, consecrated and consumed. Both should be made of solid and noble material which is not easily breakable or corruptible. Gold coating is required of the interior parts of sacred vessels subject to rust. The cup of a chalice should be made of non-absorbent material.

Vessels for containing consecrated hosts (see below) can be made of material other than solid and noble metal — e.g., ivory, more durable woods — provided the substitute material is locally regarded as noble or rather precious and is suitable for sacred use.

Sacred vessels should be blessed, according to prescribed requirements.

Vessels, in addition to the paten, for containing consecrated hosts are:

Ciborium: Used to hold hosts for distribution to the faithful and for reservation in the tabernacle.

Luna, Lunula, Lunette: A small receptacle which holds the sacred host in an upright position in the monstrance.

Monstrance, Ostensorium: A portable receptacle so made that the sacred host, when enclosed therein, may be clearly seen, as at Benediction or during extended exposition of the Blessed Sacrament.

Pyx: A watch-shaped vessel used in carrying the Eucharist to the sick.

Linens

Altar Cloth: A white cloth, usually of linen, covering the table of an altar. One cloth is sufficient. Three were used according to former requirements.

Burse: A square, stiff flat case, open at one end, in which the folded corporal can be placed; the outside is covered with material of the same kind and color as the outer vestments of the celebrant.

Corporal: A square piece of white linen spread on the altar cloth, on which rest the vessels holding the Sacred Species — the consecrated host(s) and wine — during the Eucharistic Liturgy. The corporal is similarly used whenever the Blessed Sacrament is removed from the tabernacle; e.g., during Benediction the vessel containing the Blessed Sacrament rests on a corporal.

Finger Towel: A white rectangular napkin used by the priest to dry his fingers after cleansing them following the offering of gifts at Mass.

Pall: A square piece of stiff material, usually covered with linen, which can be used to cover the chalice at Mass.

Purificator: A white rectangular napkin used for cleansing sacred vessels after the reception of Communion at Mass.

Veil: The chalice intended for use at Mass can be covered with a veil made of the same material as the outer vestments of the celebrant.

THE CHURCH BUILDING

A church is a building set aside and dedicated for purposes of divine worship, the place of assembly for a worshiping community.

A Catholic church is the ordinary place in which the faithful assemble for participation in the Eucharistic Liturgy and other forms of divine worship.

In the early years of Christianity, the first places of assembly for the Eucharistic Liturgy were private homes (Acts 2:46; Rom. 16:5; 1 Cor. 16:5; Col. 4:15) and, sometimes, catacombs. Church building began in the latter half of the second century during lulls in persecution and became widespread after enactment of the Edict of Milan in 313, when it finally became possible for the Church to emerge completely from the underground. The oldest and basic norms regarding church buildings date from about that time.

The essential principle underlying all norms for church building was reformulated by the Second Vatican Council, as follows: "When churches are to be built, let great care be taken that they be suitable for the celebration of liturgical services and for the active participation of the faithful" (Constitution on the Sacred Liturgy, No. 124).

This principle was subsequently elaborated in detail by the Congregation for Divine Worship in a document entitled Institutio Generalis Missalis Romani, which was approved by Paul VI Apr. 3 and promulgated by a decree of the congregation dated Apr. 6, 1969. Coverage of the following items reflects the norms stated in Chapter V of this document.

Main Features

Sanctuary: The part of the church where the altar of sacrifice is located, the place where the ministers of the liturgy lead the people in prayer, proclaim the word of God and celebrate the Eucharist. It is set off from the body of the church by a distinctive structural feature — e.g., elevation above the main floor — or by ornamentation. (The traditional communion rail, removed in recent years in many churches, served this purpose of demarcation.) The customary location of the sanctuary is at the front of the church; it may, however, be centrally located.

Altar: The main altar of sacrifice and table of the Lord is the focal feature of the sanctuary and entire church. It stands by itself, so that the ministers can move about it freely, and is so situated that they face the people during the liturgical action. In addition to this main altar, there may also be others; in new churches, these are ideally situated in side chapels or alcoves removed to some degree from the body of the church.

Adornment of the Altar: The altar table is covered with a suitable linen cloth. Required candelabra and a cross are placed upon or near the altar in plain sight of the people and are so arranged that they do not obscure their view of the liturgical action.

Seats of the Ministers: The seat of the celebrant, corresponding with his role as the presiding minister of the assembly, is best located behind the altar and facing the people; it is raised a bit above the level of the altar but must not have the appearance of a throne. The seats of other ministers are also located in the sanctuary.

Ambo, Pulpit, Lectern: The stand at which scriptural lessons and psalm responses are read, the word of God preached, and the prayer of the faithful offered. It is so placed that the ministers can be easily seen and heard by the people.

Places for the People: Seats and kneeling benches (pews) and other accommodations for the people are so arranged that they can participate in the most appropriate way in the liturgical action and have freedom of movement for the reception of Holy Communion. Reserved seats are out of order.

Place for the Choir: Where it is located depends on the most suitable arrangement for maintaining the unity of the choir with the congregation and for providing its members maximum opportunity for carrying out their proper function and participating fully in the Mass.

Tabernacle: The best place for reserving the Blessed Sacrament is in a chapel suitable for the private devotion of the people. If this is not possible, reservation should be at a side altar or other appropriately adorned place. In either case, the Blessed Sacrament should be kept in a tabernacle, i.e., a safe-like, secure receptacle.

Statues: Images of the Lord, the Blessed Virgin Mary and the saints are legitimately proposed for the veneration of the faithful in churches. Their number and arrangement, however, should be ordered in such a way that they do not distract the people from the central celebration of the Eucharistic Liturgy. There should be only one statue of one and the same saint in a church.

General Adornment and Arrangement of Churches: Churches should be so adorned and fitted out that they serve the direct requirements of divine worship and the needs and reasonable convenience of the people.

Other Items

Ambry: A box containing the holy oils, attached to the wall of the sanctuary in some churches.

Baptistery: The place for administering baptism. Some churches have baptisteries adjoining or near the entrance, a position symbolizing the fact that persons are initiated in the Church and incorporated in Christ through this sacrament. Contemporary liturgical practice favors placement of the baptistery near the sanctuary and altar, or the use of a portable font in the same position, to emphasize the relationship of baptism to the Eucharist, the celebration in sacrifice and banquet of the death and resurrection of Christ.

Candles: Used more for symbolical than illuminative purposes, they represent Christ, the light and life of grace, at liturgical functions. They are made of beeswax. (See Index: Paschal Candle.)

Confessional, Reconciliation Room: A booth-like structure for the hearing of confessions, with separate compartments for the priest and penitents and a grating or screen between them. The use of confessionals became general in the Roman Rite after the Council of Trent. Since the Second Vatican Council, there has been a trend in the U.S. to replace or supplement confessionals with small reconciliation rooms so arranged that priest and penitent can converse face-to-face.

Crucifix: A cross bearing the figure of the body of Christ, representative of the Sacrifice of the Cross.

Cruets: Vessels containing the wine and water used at Mass. They are placed on a credence table in the sanctuary.

Holy Water Fonts: Receptacles containing holy water, usually at church entrances, for the use of the faithful.

Sanctuary Lamp: A lamp which is kept burning continuously before a tabernacle in which the Blessed Sacrament is reserved, as a sign of the Real Presence of Christ.

LITURGICAL DEVELOPMENTS

The principal developments covered in this article are enactments of the Holy See and actions related to their implementation in the United States.

Modern Movement

Origins of the modern movement for renewal in the liturgy date back to the 19th century. The key contributing factor was a revival of liturgical and scriptural studies. Of special significance was the work of the Benedictine monks of Solesmes, France, who aroused great interest in the liturgy through the restoration of Gregorian Chant. St. Pius X approved their work in a motu proprio of 1903 and gave additional encouragement to liturgical study and development.

St. Pius X did more than any other single pope to promote early first Communion and the practice of frequent Communion, started the research behind a revised breviary, and appointed a group to investigate possible revisions in the Mass.

The movement attracted some attention in the 1920's and 30's but made little progress.

Significant pioneering developments in the U.S. during the 20's, however, were the establishment of the Liturgical Press, the beginning of publication of *Orate Fratres* (now *Worship*), and the inauguration of the League of the Divine Office by the Benedictines at St. John's Abbey, Collegeville, Minn. Later events of influence were the establishment of the Pius X School of Liturgical Music at Manhattanville College of the Sacred Heart and the organization of a summer school of liturgical music at Mary Manse College by the Gregorian Institute of America. The turning point toward real renewal was reached during and after World War II.

Pius XII gave it impetus and direction, principally through the background teaching in his encyclicals on the *Mystical Body* (1943), *Sacred Liturgy* (1947), and the *Discipline of Sacred Music* (1955), and by means of specific measures affecting the liturgy itself. His work was continued during the pontificates of John XXIII and Paul VI. The Second Vatican Council, in virtue of its *Constitution on the Sacred Liturgy,* inaugurated changes of the greatest significance.

Before and After Vatican II

The most significant liturgical changes made in the years immediately preceding the Second Vatican Council were the following:

(1) Revision of the Rites of Holy Week, for universal observance from 1956.

(2) Modification of the Eucharistic fast and permission for afternoon and evening Mass, in effect from 1953 and extended in 1957.

(3) The Dialogue Mass, introduced in 1958.

(4) Use of popular languages in administration of the sacraments.

(5) Calendar-missal-breviary reform, in effect from Jan. 1, 1961.

(6) Seven-step administration of baptism for adults, approved in 1962.

The *Constitution on the Sacred Liturgy* approved (2,174 to 4) and promulgated by the Second Vatican Council Dec. 4, 1963, marked the beginning of a profound renewal in the Church's corporate worship. Implementation of some of its measures was ordered by Paul VI Jan. 25, 1964, in the motu proprio *Sacram Liturgiam*. On Feb. 29, a special commission, the Consilium for Implementing the Constitution on the Sacred Liturgy, was formed to supervise the execution of the entire program of liturgical reform. Implementation of the program on local and regional levels was left to bishops acting through their own liturgical commissions and in concert with their fellow bishops in national conferences.

Liturgical reform in the United States has been carried out under the direction of the Liturgy Committee, National Conference of Catholic Bishops. Its secretariat, established early in 1965, is located at 1312 Massachusetts Ave. N.W., Washington, D.C. 20005.

Stages of Development

Liturgical development after the Second Vatican Council proceeded in several stages. It started with the formulation of guidelines and directives, and with the translation into vernacular languages of virtually unchanged Latin ritual texts. Then came structural changes in the Mass, the sacraments, the calendar, the Divine Office and other phases of the liturgy. These revisions were just about completed with the publication of a new order for the sacrament of penance in February, 1974. A continuing phase of development, in progress from the beginning, involves efforts to deepen the liturgical sense of the faithful, to increase their participation in worship and to relate it to full Christian life.

The master texts of all documents on liturgical reform are in Latin. Effective dates of their implementation have depended on the completion and approval of appropriate translations into vernacular languages. English translations were made by the International Committee for English in the Liturgy.

The principal features of liturgical changes and the effective dates of their introduction in the United States are covered below under topical headings. (For expanded coverage of various items, especially the sacraments, see additional entries.)

The Mass

A new Order of the Mass, supplanting the one authorized by the Council of Trent in the 16th century, was introduced in the U.S. Mar. 22, 1970. It had been approved by Paul VI in the apostolic constitution *Missale Romanum,* dated Apr. 3, 1969.

Preliminary and related to it were the following developments.

Mass in English: Introduced Nov. 29, 1964. In the same year, Psalm 42 was eliminated from the prayers at the foot of the altar.

Incidental Changes: The last Gospel (prologue of John) and vernacular prayers following Mass were eliminated Mar. 7, 1965. At the same time, provision was made for the celebrant to say aloud some prayers formerly said silently.

Rubrics: An instruction entitled *Tres Abhinc Annos,* dated May 4 and effective June 29, 1967, simplified directives for the celebration of Mass, approved the practice of saying the canon aloud, altered the Communion and dismissal rites, permitted purple instead of black vestments in Masses for the dead, discontinued wearing of the maniple, and approved in principle the use of vernacular languages for the canon, ordination rites, and lessons of the Divine Office when read in choir.

Canons or Eucharistic Prayers: Three additional Eucharistic prayers authorized May 23, 1968, were approved for use in vernacular translation the following Aug. 15. They have the same basic structure as the traditional Roman Canon, whose use in English was introduced Oct. 22, 1967.

The customary Roman Canon, which dates at least from the beginning of the fifth century and has remained substantially unchanged since the seventh century, is the first in the order of listing of the Eucharistic prayers. It can be used at any time, but is the one of choice for most Sundays, some special feasts like Easter and Pentecost, and for feasts of the Apostles and other saints who are commemorated in the canon. Any preface can be used with it.

The second Eucharistic prayer, the shortest and simplest of all, is best suited for use on weekdays and various special circumstances. It has a preface of its own, but others may be used with it. This canon bears a close resemblance to the one framed by St. Hippolytus about 215.

The third Eucharistic prayer is suitable for use on Sundays and feasts as an alternative to the Roman Canon. It can be used with any preface and has a special formula for remembrance of the dead.

The fourth Eucharistic prayer, the most sophisticated of them all, presents a broad synthesis of salvation history. Based on the Eastern tradition of Antioch, it is best suited for use at Masses attended by persons versed in Sacred Scripture. It has an unchangeable preface.

Five additional Eucharistic prayers — three for Masses with children and two for Masses of reconciliation — were approved in 1974 and 1975, respectively, by the Congregation for the Sacraments and Divine Worship. The original approval for a limited period of experimentation was extended indefinitely, until further notice, according to a letter issued by the congregation Dec. 15, 1980.

Lectionary: A new compilation of scriptural readings and psalm responsories for Mass was published in 1969. The *Lectionary* contains a three-year cycle of readings for Sundays and solemn feasts, a two-year weekday cycle, and a one-year cycle for the feasts of saints, in addition to readings for a great variety of Masses, ritual Masses and Masses for various needs. There are also responsorial psalms to follow the first readings, and gospel or alleluia versicles to follow the second readings.

A second edition of the *Lectionary,* substantially the same as the first, was published in 1981. New features included an expanded introduction, extensive scriptural references and additional readings for a number of solemnities and feasts.

Sacramentary (Missal): The Vatican Polyglot Press began distribution in June, 1970, of the Latin text of a new *Roman Missal,* the first revision published in 400 years. The English translation was authorized for optional use beginning July 1, 1974; the mandatory date for use was Dec. 1, 1974.

The missal is the celebrant's book of prayers and sacramental formulas and does not include the readings of the Mass, such as the Gospel and the Epistle. It contains the texts of entrance songs, prefaces and other prayers of the Mass. The number of prefaces is four times greater than it had been. There are 10 commons (or sets of Mass prayers) of martyrs, two of doctors of the Church, and a dozen for saints or groups of saints of various kinds, such as religious, educators and mothers of families. There are Masses during which certain sacraments are administered and others for religious profession, the Church, the pope, priests, Christian unity, the evangelization of nations, persecuted Christians, and other intentions.

Mass for Special Groups: Reasons and norms for the celebration of Mass at special gatherings of the faithful were the subject of an instruction issued May 15, 1969. Two years earlier, the U.S. Bishops' Liturgy Committee went on record in support of the celebration of Mass in private homes.

Sunday Mass on Saturday: The Congregation for the Clergy, under date of Jan. 10, 1970, granted the request that the faithful, where bishops consider it pastorally necessary or useful, may satisfy the precept of participating in Mass in the late afternoon or evening hours of Saturdays and the days before holy days of obligation.

Bination and Trination: Canon 905 of the Code of

Canon Law provides that local ordinaries may permit priests to celebrate Mass twice a day (bination), for a just cause; in cases of pastoral need, they may permit priests to celebrate Mass three times a day (trination) on Sundays and holy days of obligation.

Mass in Latin: According to notices issued by the Congregation for Divine Worship June 1, 1971, and Oct. 28, 1974: (1) Bishops may permit the celebration of Mass in Latin for mixed-language groups. (2) Bishops may permit the celebration of one or two Masses in Latin on weekdays or Sundays in any church, irrespective of mixed-language groups involved (1971). (3) Priests may celebrate Mass in Latin when people are not present. (4) The approved revised Order of the Mass is to be used in Latin as well as vernacular languages . (5) By way of exception, bishops may permit older and handicapped priests to use the Council of Trent's Order of the Mass in private celebration of the holy Sacrifice. (See Permission for Tridentine Mass.)

Inter-Ritual Concelebration: The Apostolic Delegation in Washington, D.C., announced in June, 1971, that it had received authorization to permit priests of Roman and Eastern rites to celebrate Mass together in the rite of the host church. It was understood that the inter-ritual concelebrations would always be "a manifestation of the unity of the Church and of communion among particular churches."

Ordo of the Sung Mass: In a decree dated June 24 and made public Aug. 24, 1972, the Congregation for Divine Worship issued a new *Ordo of the Sung Mass* — containing Gregorian chants in Latin — to replace the *Graduale Romanum*.

Mass for Children: Late in 1973, the Congregation for Divine Worship issued special guidelines for children's Masses, providing accommodations to the mentality and spiritual growth of pre-adolescents while retaining the principal parts and structures of the Mass. The *Directory for Masses with Children* was approved by Paul VI Oct. 22 and was dated Nov. 1, 1973. Three Eucharistic prayers for Masses with children were approved by the congregation in 1974; English versions were approved June 5, 1975. Their use, authorized originally for a limited period of experimentation, was extended indefinitely Dec. 15, 1980.

Sacraments

The general use of English in administration of the sacraments was approved for the U.S. Sept. 14, 1964. Structural changes of the rites were subsequently made and introduced in the U.S. as follows.

Pastoral Care of the Sick: Revised rites, covering also administration of the Eucharist to sick persons, were approved Nov. 30,. 1972, and published Jan. 18, 1973. The effective date for use of the provisional English prayer formula was Dec. 1, 1974. The mandatory effective date for use of the ritual, Pastoral Care of the Sick in English, was Nov. 27, 1983.

Baptism: New rites for the baptism of infants, approved Mar. 19, 1969, were introduced June 1, 1970.

Christian Initiation of Adults: Revised rites were issued Jan. 6, 1972, for the Christian initiation of adults — affecting preparation for and reception of baptism, the Eucharist and confirmation; also, the reception of already baptized adults into full communion with the Church. These rites, which were introduced in the U.S. on the completion of English translation, nullified a seven-step baptismal process approved in 1962.

Confirmation: Revised rites, issued Aug. 15, 1971, became mandatory in the U.S. Jan. 1, 1973. The use of a stole by persons being confirmed should be avoided, according to an item in the December, 1984, edition of the *Newsletter* of the Bishops' Committee on the Liturgy. The item said: "The distinction between the universal priesthood of all the baptized and the ministerial priesthood of the ordained is blurred when the distinctive garb (the stole) of ordained ministers is used in this manner."

Special Ministers of the Eucharist: The designation of lay men and women to serve as special ministers of the Eucharist was authorized by Paul VI in an "Instruction on Facilitating Communion in Particular Circumstances" *(Immensae Caritatis)*, dated Jan. 29 and published by the Congregation for Divine Worship Mar. 29, 1973. Provisions concerning them are contained in Canons 230 and 910 of the Code of Canon Law.

Qualified lay persons may serve as special ministers for specific occasions or for extended periods in the absence of a sufficient number of priests and deacons to provide reasonable and appropriate service in the distribution of Holy Communion, during Mass and outside of Mass (to the sick and shut-ins). Appointments of ministers are made by priests with the approval of the appropriate bishop.

Holy Orders: Revised ordination rites for deacons, priests and bishops, validated by prior experimental use, were approved in 1970. The sacrament of holy orders underwent further revision in 1972 with the elimination of the Church-instituted orders of porter, reader, exorcist, acolyte and sub-deacon, and of the tonsure ceremony symbolic of entrance into the clerical state. The former minor orders of reader and acolyte were changed from orders to ministries.

Matrimony: New rites, issued Mar. 19, 1969, were introduced June 1, 1970. Minor revisions had been made in 1964 in conjunction with a directive for imparting the nuptial blessing at all weddings.

Penance: Ritual revision of the sacraments was completed with the approval by Paul VI Dec. 2, 1973, of new directives for the sacrament of penance or reconciliation. The U.S. Bishops' Committee on the Liturgy set Feb. 27, 1977, as the mandatory date for use of the new rite. The committee also declared that it could be used from Mar. 7, 1976, after adequate preparation of priests and people. Earlier, authorization was given by the Holy See in 1968 for the omission of any reference to excommunication or other censures in the formula of absolution unless there was some indication that a censure had actually been incurred by a penitent.

Additional Developments

Calendar: A revised liturgical calendar, approved by Paul VI Feb. 14 and made public May 9, 1969, went into effect in the U.S. in 1972.

Funeral Rites: The Order of Christian Funerals, a revision of the 1970 Rite of Funerals, was approved for use in U.S. dioceses by the National Conference of Catholic Bishops Nov. 14, 1985.

Holy Week: The English version of revised Holy Week rites went into effect in 1971. They introduced concelebration of Mass, placed new emphasis on commemorating the institution of the priesthood on Holy Thursday, and modified Good Friday prayers for other Christians, Jews and other non-Christians.

Liturgy of the Hours: The background, contents, scope and purposes of the revised Divine Office, called the Liturgy of the Hours, were described by Paul VI in the apostolic constitution *Laudis Canticum,* dated Nov. 1, 1970. A provisional English version, incorporating basic features of the master Latin text, was published in 1971. The four complete volumes of the Hours in English have been published since May, 1975. One-volume, partial editions, intended for use by Religious and lay persons not bound to pray the Liturgy of the Hours, have also been published in approved form. Nov. 27, 1977, was set by the Congregation for Divine Worship and the National Conference of Catholic Bishops as the effective date for exclusive use in liturgical worship of the translation of the Latin text of the Office approved by the International Committee on English in the Liturgy.

Music: An *Instruction on Music in the Liturgy,* dated Mar. 5 and effective May 14, 1967, encouraged congregational singing during liturgical celebrations and attempted to clarify the role of choirs and trained singers. More significantly, the instruction indicated that a major development under way in the liturgy was a gradual erasure of the distinctive lines traditionally drawn between the sung liturgy and the spoken liturgy, between what had been called the high Mass and the low Mass.

In the same year, the U.S. Bishops' Liturgy Committee approved the use of contemporary music, as well as guitars and other suitable instruments, in the liturgy. The Holy See authorized in 1968 the use of musical instruments other than the organ in liturgical services, "provided they are played in a manner suitable to worship."

Oils: The Congregation for Divine Worship issued a directive in 1971 permitting the use of other oils — from plants, seeds or coconuts — instead of the traditional olive oil in administering some of the sacraments. The directive also provided that oils could be blessed at other times than at the usual Mass of Chrism on Holy Thursday, and authorized bishops' conferences to permit priests to bless oils in cases of necessity.

Environment and Art in Catholic Worship: A booklet with this title was issued by the U.S. Bishops' Committee on the Liturgy in March, 1978.

Doxology: The bishops' committee called attention in August, 1978, to the directive that the Doxology concluding the Eucharistic Prayer is said or sung by the celebrant (concelebrants) alone, to which the people respond, "Amen."

Churches, Altars, Chalices: The *Newsletter* of the U.S. Bishops' Committee on the Liturgy reported in November, 1978, that the Congregation for Divine Worship had given provisional approval of a new English translation for the rite of dedicating churches and altars, and of a new form for the blessing of chalices.

Study of the Mass: The Bishops' Committee on the Liturgy, following approval of the project by the National Conference of Catholic Bishops in May, 1979, began a study of the function and position of some elements of the Mass, including the Gloria, the sign of peace, the penitential rite and the readings. Completion of the first phase of the study was reported in July, 1980; its product was a 175-page study document. The second phase of the project got under way in the spring of 1981 with publication of a work book entitled *The Mystery of Faith: A Study of the Structural Elements of the Order of Mass.* Another draft of the study was circulated late in 1983, for recommendations and final proposals.

Eucharistic Hosts: Father Thomas Krosnicki, a staff member of the Bishops' Committee on the Liturgy, reported in July, 1979, that the committee was preparing new guidelines on the preparation of hosts, in compliance with a request from the Congregation for the Doctrine of the Faith. He said the congregation had "questioned the contents of some of the recipes" used in this country. Cardinal Franjo Seper, prefect of the congregation, stressed the importance of carefully observing traditional theological principles relating to the making of hosts — which should be of wheat, unleavened, with the appearance of food, and capable of being broken and distributed to communicants. In 1980, the congregation ruled definitely against changes in the preparation of hosts, and so informed the bishops' committee. The same prohibition was stated in the "Instruction on Certain Norms concerning Worship of the Eucharistic Mystery" approved by the Pope Apr. 17, and released May 23, 1980.

Eucharistic Worship: This was the subject of two documents issued in 1980. *Dominicae Coenae* was a letter addressed by Pope John Paul to bishops throughout the world in connection with the celebration of Holy Thursday; it was dated Feb. 24 and released Mar. 18. It was more doctrinal in content than the "Instruction on Certain Norms concerning Worship of the Eucharistic Mystery" (*Inaestimabile Donum,* "The Priceless Gift"), which was approved by the Pope Apr. 17 and published by the Congregation for the Sacraments and Divine Worship May 23. Its stated purpose was to reaffirm and clarify teaching on liturgical renewal contained in enactments of the Second Vatican Council and in several related implementing documents.

Communion in Hand: Since 1969, the Holy See has approved the practice of in-hand reception of the Eucharist in regions and countries where it had the approval of the appropriate episcopal conferences. The first grant of approval was to Belgium, in May, 1969. Approval was granted the United States in June, 1977.

Mass for Deceased Non-Catholic Christians: The Congregaton for the Doctrine of the Faith released a decree June 11, 1976, authorizing the celebration of public Mass for deceased non-Catholic Christians under certain conditions: "(1) The public celebraton of the Masses must be explicitly requested by the relatives, friends, or subjects of the deceased person for a genuine religious motive. (2) In the ordinary's judgment, there must be no scandal for the faithful."

"In these cases public Mass may be celebrated, provided, however, that the name of the deceased is not mentioned in the Eucharistic Prayer, since that mention presupposes full communion with the Catholic Church."

Book of Worship: The Congregation for Divine Worship confirmed by a decree dated Sept. 20, 1984, the approval and authorization by the U.S. bishops of a *Book of Divine Worship* for temporary and exclusive use by communities of former members of the Episcopal Church who had been received into the full communion of the Catholic Church.

Spanish, a Liturgical Language: The Congregation for Divine Worship, in a letter dated Jan. 19, 1985, confirmed a decision of the U.S. bishops approving Spanish as a liturgical language in the United States.

SUNDAY COMMUNION

More than two-thirds of the U.S. bishops voted (187 to 82) during the general meeting of their national conference in November, 1978, or afterwards for allowing the administration of Holy Communion under the forms of bread and wine on Sundays and holy days — subject to the options of bishops of dioceses, priests celebrating Mass and persons receiving the Eucharist. (Reception of Communion in this manner on certain occasions was already provided for in directives of the Congregation for Divine Worship, but Sundays and holy days were not mentioned.) The Congregation for Divine Worship subsequently approved the practice.

DANCING AND WORSHIP

Dancing and worship was the subject of an essay which appeared in a 1975 edition of Notitiae (11, pp. 202-205), the official journal of the Congregation for the Sacraments and Divine Worship. The article was called a "qualified and authoritative sketch," and should be considered "an authoritative point of reference for every discussion of the matter."

The principal points of the essay were:

• "The dance has never been made an integral part of the official worship of the Latin Church."

• "If the proposal of the religious dance in the West is really to be made welcome, care will have to be taken that in its regard a place be found outside of the liturgy, in assembly areas which are not strictly liturgical. Moreover, the priests must always be excluded from the dance."

PERMISSION FOR TRIDENTINE MASS

The celebration of Mass according to the last pre-Vatican II revision of the Roman Missal approved by Pope Paul VI in 1962 (the so-called Tridentine Mass), was authorized under certain conditions by Pope John Paul. The Congregation for Divine Worship announced this authorization in a letter dated Oct. 3 and released Oct. 15, 1984.

The letter said the Pope wished "to be responsive to priests and faithful who remained attached to the so-called Tridentine Rite." Accordingly, "he grants to diocesan bishops the faculty of using an indult on behalf of such priests and faithful. The diocesan bishop may allow those who are explicitly named in a petition submitted to him to celebrate Mass by use of the 1962 *editio typica* (typical, master, edition) of the Roman Missal. The following norms must be observed.

"A. There must be unequivocal, even public, evidence that the priest and people petitioning have no ties with those who impugn the lawfulness and doctrinal soundness of the Roman Missal promulgated in 1970 by Pope Paul VI.

"B. The celebration of Mass in question must take place exclusively for the benefit of those who petition it; the celebration must be a church or oratory designated by the diocesan bishop (but not in parish churches unless, in extraordinary instances, the bishop allows this); the celebration may take place only on those days and in those circumstances approved by the bishop, whether for an individual instance or as a regular occurrence.

"C. The celebration is to follow the Roman Missal of 1962 and must be in Latin.

"D. In the celebration there is to be no intermingling of the rites or texts of the two missals.

"E. Each bishop is to inform this congregation of the concessions he grants and, one year from the date of the present indult, of the outcome of its use.

"The Pope, who is the Father of the entire Church, grants this indult as a sign of his concern for all his children. The indult is to be used without prejudice to the liturgical reform that is to be observed in the life of each ecclesial community."

LITURGICAL FORMATION, INCULTURATION

These were the subjects of remarks by Pope John Paul Oct. 17, 1985, at a meeting with members of the Congregation for Divine Worship. He said, in part:

"Obvious progress (in liturgical renewal and practice) has been achieved on many planes with the clergy as well as with the faithful. But it must be stated that, mixed in with this progress, lamentable defects are sometimes to be seen which must be corrected. For example, too personal a style, illicit omissions or additions, rites which are contrived outside the established norms, attitudes which do not foster a sense of the sacred, of beauty and of recollection. We deplore all these weaknesses, which must be corrected since they cause a delay and a deviation injurious to the life of prayer in the Church.

"The first task, then, is to assure a solid formation for the clergy, who will pass it on to the faithful."

ADAPTATION

"A second important point . . . is that of the adaptation of the liturgy to different cultures."

"An important work is under way, but one must be attentive to the legitimacy of the various adaptations. Many are necessary or simply useful. Certain ones, nevertheless, would appear useless or dangerous, especially if they bear the imprint of pagan or superstitious beliefs. That is to say that the necessary adaptation must, above all, preserve the substantial unity of the Roman liturgy, and must therefore be the fruit of a superior competence and of solid studies in liturgy, theology, law, history, sociology and the languages of the different ethnic groups. The adaptation must take into account the fact that in the liturgy, especially the liturgy of the sacraments, there is an unchangeable part of which the Church is the guardian, and a part which is not unchangeable and which she has the power — and sometimes even the duty — to adapt to the cultures of recently evangelized peoples. Once again, this requires a serious formation and a longer and more delicate effort than that required for changing from one language to another."

CLOWN MINISTRY IS NOT LITURGY

Clown ministry was the subject of a statement (excerpted below) issued by the Secretariat of the U.S. Bishops' Committee on the Liturgy and made public in the November, 1985, edition of the committee's *Newsletter*.

In recent years new and old art forms have come into the service of worship in the Church in the United States. Among these has been what has come to be known as "clown ministry." The sincerity of those involved in "clown ministry" is not to be questioned, but it must be made clear that they have no liturgical function. While the clown has a place in the world of entertainment, or may be involved in works of charity such as visiting the sick in hospitals or those confined to nursing homes or homes for the elderly, or as a pedagogic aid in schools or in the religious education of children, or even in certain traditions of Christological reflection, the clown as such is not to be understood as a liturgical minister. While special pastoral reasons may sometimes suggest the use of clowns or mimes in certain celebrations for small children, it is not normally appropriate for clowns to function in any way in celebration of the Mass or in other liturgical rites.

The use of clowns during the liturgy personalizes the liturgy too much and detracts from that prayerful atmosphere necessary for the good order of a community's sense of the transcendent in worship.

POPULAR PIETY AND LITURGY

The relation of popular piety to the liturgy was the subject of remarks by Pope John Paul at a meeting with a group of Italian bishops Apr. 24, 1986. He said, in part:

"It could be affirmed that in the lives of the faithful and of the Christian communities there is and there should be a place for forms of piety that do not strictly come under the category of liturgical celebration. This implies a requirement: these forms of piety should not be superimposed on the times for liturgical celebration; they should not be allowed to compete with the most important solemnities of the liturgical year. If there is a devotion that has a value superior to al' the others, it is the devotion of the Church, namely, the cult it renders to God, its liturgical life, in the mysteries and in the seasons which follow each other in succession in the course of the year of the Lord."

"An authentic liturgical ministry will never be able to neglect the riches of popular piety, the values proper to the culture of a people, so that such riches might be illuminated, purified and introduced into the liturgy as an offering of the people."

EXTENDED EUCHARISTIC EXPOSITION

In response to queries, the Secretariat of the U.S. Bishops' Committee on the Liturgy issued an advisory stating that, in the following two cases only, liturgical law permits and encourages in parish churches:

- a. exposition of the Blessed Sacrament for an extended period of time once a year, with the consent of the local Ordinary and only if suitable numbers of the faithful are expected to be present;
- b. exposition ordered by the local Ordinary, for a grave and general necessity, for a more extended period of supplication when the faithful assemble in large numbers.

With regard to perpetual exposition, this form is permitted only in the case of those religious communities of men or women who have the general practice of perpetual Eucharistic adoration or adoration over extended periods of time.

The Secretariat's advisory appeared in the June-July, 1986, edition of the *Newsletter* of the Bishops' Committee on the Liturgy.

NATIONAL SHRINE

The National Shrine of the Immaculate Conception is dedicated to the honor of the Blessed Virgin Mary, who was declared patroness of the United States in 1846.

The shrine is the seventh largest religious building in the world and the largest Catholic church in the Western Hemisphere, with normal seating and standing accommodations for 6,000 persons. The shrine contains some of the largest mosaics in the world.

Approximately one million persons visit the shrine each year. Open daily, it is located adjacent to the Catholic University of America, Michigan Ave. and Fourth St. N.E., Washington, D.C., 20017.

The sacraments are actions of Christ and his Church (itself a kind of sacrament) which signify grace, cause it in the act of signifying it, and confer it upon persons properly disposed to receive it. They perpetuate the redemptive activity of Christ, making it present and effective. They infallibly communicate the fruit of that activity — namely grace — to responsive persons with faith. Sacramental actions consist of the union of sensible signs (matter of the sacraments) with the words of the minister (form of the sacraments).

Christ himself instituted the seven sacraments of the New Law by determining their essence and the efficacy of their signs to produce the grace they signify.

Christ is the principal priest or minister of every sacrament; human agents — an ordained priest, baptized persons contracting marriage with each other, any person conferring emergency baptism in a proper manner — are secondary ministers. Sacraments have efficacy from Christ, not from the personal dispositions of their human ministers.

Each sacrament confers sanctifying grace for the special purpose of the sacrament; this is, accordingly, called sacramental grace. It involves a right to actual graces corresponding to the purposes of the respective sacraments.

While sacraments infallibly produce the grace they signify, recipients benefit from them in proportion to their personal dispositions. One of these is the intention to receive sacraments as sacred signs of God's saving and grace-giving action. The state of grace is also necessary for fruitful reception of the Holy Eucharist, confirmation, matrimony, holy orders and anointing of the sick. Baptism is the sacrament in which grace is given in the first instance and original sin is remitted. Penance is the secondary sacrament of reconciliation, in which persons guilty of serious sin after baptism are reconciled with God and the Church, and in which persons already in the state of grace are strengthened in that state.

Role of Sacraments

The Second Vatican Council prefaced a description of the role of the sacraments with the following statement concerning participation by all the faithful in the priesthood of Christ and the exercise of that priesthood by receiving the sacraments (*Dogmatic Constitution on the Church,* Nos. 10 and 11).

"The baptized by regeneration and the anointing of the Holy Spirit are consecrated into a spiritual house and a holy priesthood. Thus through all those works befitting Christian men they can offer spiritual sacrifice and proclaim the power of him who has called them out of darkness into his marvelous light (cf. 1 Pt. 2:4-10)."

"Though they differ from one another in essence and not only in degree, the common priesthood of the faithful and the ministerial or hierarchical priesthood (of those ordained to holy orders) are nonetheless interrelated. Each of them in its own special way is a participation in the one priesthood of Christ. The ministerial priest, by the sacred power he enjoys, molds and rules the priestly people. Acting in the Person of Christ, he brings about the Eucharistic Sacrifice, and offers it to God in the name of all the people. For their part, the faithful join in the offering of the Eucharist by virtue of their royal priesthood. They likewise exercise that priesthood by receiving the sacraments, by prayer and thanksgiving, by the witness of a holy life, and by self-denial and active charity."

"It is through the sacraments and the exercise of the virtues that the sacred nature and organic structure of the priestly community is brought into operation."

Baptism: "Incorporated into the Church through baptism, the faithful are consecrated by the baptismal character to the exercise of the cult of the Christian religion. Reborn as sons of God, they must confess before men the faith which they have received from God through the Church."

Confirmation: "Bound more intimately to the Church by the sacrament of confirmation, they are endowed by the Holy Spirit with special strength. Hence they are more strictly obliged to spread and defend the faith both by word and by deed as true witnesses of Christ."

Eucharist: "Taking part in the Eucharistic Sacrifice, which is the fount and apex of the whole Christian life, they offer the divine Victim to God, and offer themselves along with It. Thus, both by the act of oblation and through holy Communion, all perform their proper part in this liturgical service, not, indeed, all in the same way but each in that way which is appropriate to himself. Strengthened anew at the holy table by the Body of Christ, they manifest in a practical way that unity of God's People which is suitably signified and wondrously brought about by this most awesome sacrament."

Penance: "Those who approach the sacrament of penance obtain pardon from the mercy of God for offenses committed against him. They are at the same time reconciled with the Church, which they have wounded by their sins, and which by charity, example, and prayer seeks their conversion."

Anointing of the Sick: "By the sacred anointing of the sick and the prayer of her priests, the whole Church commends those who are ill to the suffering and glorified Lord, asking that he may lighten their suffering and save them (cf. Jas. 5:14-16). She exhorts them, moreover, to contribute to the welfare of the whole People of God by associating themselves freely with the passion and death of Christ (cf. Rom. 8:17; Col. 1:24; 2 Tm. 2:11-12; 1 Pt. 4:13)."

Holy Orders: "Those of the faithful who are consecrated by holy orders are appointed to feed the Church in Christ's name with the Word and the grace of God."

Matrimony: "Christian spouses, in virtue of the sacrament of matrimony, signify and partake of the mystery of that unity and fruitful love which exists between Christ and his Church (cf. Eph. 5:32). The spouses thereby help each other to attain to holiness in their married life and by the rearing and education of their children. And so, in their state and way of life, they have their own special gift among the People of God (cf. 1 Cor. 7:7).

"For from the wedlock of Christians there comes the family, in which new citizens of human society are born. By the grace of the Holy Spirit received in baptism these are made children of God, thus perpetuating the People of God through the centuries. The family is, so to speak, the domestic Church. In it parents should, by their word and example, be the first preachers of the faith to their children. They should encourage them in the vocation which is proper to each of them, fostering with special care any religious vocation."

"Fortified by so many and such powerful means of salvation, all the faithful, whatever their condition or state, are called by the Lord, each in his own way, to that perfect holiness whereby the Father himself is perfect."

Baptism

Baptism is the sacrament of spiritual regeneration by which a person is incorporated in Christ and made a member of his Mystical Body, given grace, and cleansed of original sin. Actual sins and the punishment due for them are remitted also if the person baptized was guilty of such sins (e.g., in the case of a person baptized after reaching the age of reason). The theological virtues of faith, hope and charity are given with grace. The sacrament confers a character on the soul and can be received only once.

The matter is the pouring of water. The form is: "I baptize you in the name of the Father and of the Son and of the Holy Spirit."

The minister of solemn baptism is a bishop, priest or deacon, but in case of emergency anyone, including a non-Catholic, can validly baptize. The minister pours water on the forehead of the person being baptized and says the words of the form while the water is flowing. The water used in solemn baptism is blessed during the rite.

Baptism is conferred in the Roman Rite by immersion or infusion (pouring of water), depending on the directive of the appropriate conference of bishops, according to the Code of Canon Law. The Church recognizes as valid baptisms properly performed by non-Catholic ministers. The baptism of infants has always been considered valid and the general practice of infant baptism was well established by the fifth century. Baptism is conferred conditionally when there is doubt about the validity of a previous baptism.

Baptism is necessary for salvation. If a person cannot receive the baptism of water described above, this can be supplied by baptism of blood (martyrdom suffered for the Catholic faith or some Christian virtue) or by baptism of desire (perfect contrition joined with at least the implicit intention of doing whatever God wills that men should do for salvation).

A sponsor is required for the person being baptized. (See Godparents, below).

A person must be validly baptized before he can receive any of the other sacraments.

Christian Initiation of Infants: Infants should be solemnly baptized as soon after birth as conveniently possible. In danger of death, anyone may baptize an infant. If the child survives, the ceremonies of solemn baptism should be supplied.

The sacrament is ordinarily conferred by a priest or deacon of the parents' parish.

Catholics 16 years of age and over who have received the sacraments of confirmation and the Eucharist and are practicing their faith are eligible to be sponsors or godparents. Only one is required. Two, one of each sex, are permitted. A non-Catholic Christian cannot be a godparent for a Catholic child, but may serve as a witness to the baptism. A Catholic may not be a godparent for a child baptized in a non-Catholic religion, but may be a witness.

The role of godparents in baptismal ceremonies is secondary to the role of the parents. They serve as representatives of the community of faith and with the parents request baptism for the child and perform other ritual functions. Their function after baptism is to serve as proxies for the parents if the parents should be unable or fail to provide for the religious training of the child.

At baptism every child should be given a name with Christian significance, usually the name of a saint, to symbolize newness of life in Christ.

Christian Initiation of Adults: According to the *Ordo Initiationis Christianae Adultorum* ("Rite of the Christian Initiation of Adults") issued by the Congregation for Divine Worship under date of Jan. 6, 1972, adults are prepared for baptism and reception into the Church in several stages:

• An initial period of inquiry, instruction and evangelization.

• The catechumenate, a period of formal instruction and progressive formation in and familiarity with Christian life. It starts with a statement of purpose and includes a rite in which the catechumen is signed with the cross, blessings, exorcisms, and introduction into church for celebration of the word of God.

• Immediate preparation, called a period of purification and enlightenment, from the beginning of Lent to reception of the sacraments of initiation — baptism, confirmation, Holy Eucharist — at Easter. The period is marked by scrutinies, formal giving of the creed and the Lord's Prayer, the choice of a Christian name, and a final statement of intention.

• A final phase whose objective is greater familiarity with Christian life in the Church through observances of the Easter season and association with the community of the faithful.

The priest who baptizes a catechumen can also administer the sacrament of confirmation.

A sponsor is required for the person being baptized.

The *Ordo* also provides a simple rite of initiation for adults in danger of death and for cases in which all stages of the initiation process are not necessary, and guidelines for: (1) the preparation of adults for the sacraments of confirmation and Holy Eucharist in cases where they have been baptized but have not received further formation in the Christian life; (2) for the formation and initiation of children of catechetical age.

The Church recognizes the right of anyone over the age of seven to request baptism and to receive the sacrament after completing a course of instruction and giving evidence of good will. Practically, in the case of minors in a non-Catholic family or environment, the Church accepts them when other circumstances favor their ability to practice the faith — e.g., well-disposed family situation, the presence of another or several Catholics in the family. Those who are not in such favorable circumstances are prudently advised to defer reception of the sacrament until they attain the maturity necessary for independent practice of the faith.

Reception of Baptized Christians: Procedure for the reception of already baptized Christians into full communion with the Catholic Church is distinguished from the catechumenate, since they have received some Christian formation. Instruction and formation are provided as necessary, however; and conditional baptism is administered if there is reasonable doubt about the validity of the person's previous baptism.

In the rite of reception, the person is invited to join the community of the Church in professing the Nicene Creed and is asked to state: "I believe and profess all that the holy Catholic Church believes, teaches, and proclaims as revealed by God." The priest places his hand on the head of the person, states the formula of admission to full communion, confirms (in the absence of a bishop), gives a sign of peace, and administers Holy Communion during a Eucharistic Liturgy.

Confirmation

Confirmation is the sacrament by which a baptized person, through anointing with chrism and the imposition of hands, is endowed with the gifts and special strength of the Holy Spirit for mature Christian living. The sacrament, which completes the Christian initiation begun with baptism, confers a character on the soul and can be received only once.

According to the apostolic constitution *Divinae Consortium Naturae* dated Aug. 15, 1971, in conjunction with the *Ordo Confirmationis* ("Rite of Confirmation"): "The sacrament of confirmation is conferred through the anointing with chrism on the forehead, which is done by the imposition of the hand (matter of the sacrament), and through the words: 'N . . . ., receive the seal of the Holy Spirit, the Gift of the Father' " (form of the sacrament). On May 5, 1975, bishops' conferences in English-speaking countries were informed by the Congregation for Divine Worship that Pope Paul had approved this English version of the form of the sacrament: "Be sealed with the gift of the Holy Spirit."

The ordinary minister of confirmation in the Roman Rite is a bishop. Priests may be delegated for the purpose. A pastor can confirm a parishioner in danger of death, and a priest can confirm in ceremonies of Christian initiation and at the reception of a baptized Christian into union with the Church.

Ideally, the sacrament is conferred during the Eucharistic Liturgy. Elements of the rite include renewal of the promises of baptism, which confirmation ratifies and completes, and the laying on of hands by the confirming bishop and priests participating in the ceremony.

"The entire rite," according to the *Ordo;* "has a twofold meaning. The laying of hands upon the candidates, done by the bishop and the concelebrating priests, expresses the biblical gesture by which the gift of the Holy Spirit is invoked. . . . The anointing with chrism and the accompanying words clearly signify the effect of the Holy Spirit. Signed with the perfumed oil by the bishop's hand, the baptized person receives the indelible character, the seal of the Lord, together with the Spirit who is given and who conforms the person more perfectly to Christ and gives him the grace of spreading the Lord's presence among men."

A sponsor is required for the person being confirmed. Eligible is any Catholic 16 years of age or older who has received the sacraments of confirmation and the Eucharist and is practicing the faith. The baptismal sponsor, preferably, can also be the sponsor for confirmation. Parents may present their children for confirmation but cannot be sponsors.

In the Roman Rite, it has been customary for children to receive confirmation within a reasonable time after first Communion and confession. There is a developing trend, however, to defer confirmation until later when its significance for mature Christian living becomes more evident. In the Eastern Rites, confirmation is administered at the same time as baptism.

Eucharist

The Holy Eucharist is a sacrifice (see The Mass) and the sacrament in which Christ is present and is received under the appearances of bread and wine.

The matter is bread of wheat, unleavened in the Roman Rite and leavened in the Eastern Rites, and wine of grape. The form consists of the words of consecration said by the priest at Mass: "This is my body. . . . This is the cup of my blood" (according to the traditional usage of the Roman Rite).

Only a priest can consecrate bread and wine so they become the body and blood of Christ. After consecration, however, the Eucharist can be administered by deacons and, for various reasons, by religious and lay persons.

Priests celebrating Mass receive the Eucharist under the appearances of bread and wine. In the Roman Rite, others receive under the appearances of bread only, i.e., the consecrated host, or in some circumstances they may receive under the appearances of both bread and wine. In Eastern-Rite practice, the faithful generally receive a piece of consecrated leavened bread which has been dipped into consecrated wine (i.e., by intinction).

Conditions for receiving the Eucharist, commonly called Holy Communion, are the state of grace, the right intention and observance of the Eucharistic fast.

The faithful of Roman Rite are required by a precept of the Church to receive the Eucharist at least once a year, ordinarily during the Easter time.

(See Eucharistic Fast, Mass, Transubstantiation, Viaticum.)

First Communion and Confession: Children are to be prepared for and given opportunity for receiving both sacraments (Eucharist and reconciliation, or penance) on reaching the age of discretion, at which time they become subject to general norms concerning confession and Communion. This, together with a stated preference for first confession before first Communion, was the central theme of a document entitled *Sanctus Pontifex* and published May 24, 1973, by the Congregation for the Discipline of the Sacraments and the Congregation for the Clergy, with the approval of Pope Paul VI .

What the document prescribed was the observance of practices ordered by St. Pius X in the decree *Quam Singulari* of Aug. 8, 1910. Its purpose was to counteract pastoral and catechetical experiments virtually denying children the opportunity of receiving both sacraments at the same time. Termination of such experiments was ordered by the end of the 1972-73 school year.

At the time the document was issued, two- or three-year experiments of this kind — routinely deferring reception of the sacrament of penance until after the first reception of Holy Communion — were in effect in more than half of the dioceses of the U.S. They have remained in effect in many places, despite the advisory from the Vatican.

One reason stated in support of such experiments is the view that children are not capable of serious sin at the age of seven or eight, when Communion is generally received for the first time, and therefore prior reception of the sacrament of penance is not necessary. Another reason is the purpose of making the distinctive nature of the two sacraments clearer to children.

The Vatican view reflected convictions that the principle and practice of devotional reception of penance are as valid for children as they are for adults, and that sound catechetical programs can avoid misconceptions about the two sacraments.

A second letter on the same subject and in the same vein was released May 19, 1977, by the aforementioned congregations. It was issued in response to the question:

" 'Whether it is allowed after the declaration of May 24, 1973, to continue to have, as a general rule, the reception of first Communion precede the reception of the sacrament of penance in those parishes in which this practice developed in the past few years.'

"The Sacred Congregations for the Sacraments and Divine Worship and for the Clergy, with the approval of the Supreme Pontiff, reply: Negative, and according to the mind of the declaration.

"The mind of the declaration is that one year after the promulgation of the same declaration, all experiments of receiving first Communion without the sacrament of penance should cease so that the discipline of the Church might be restored, in the spirit of the decree, *Quam Singulari.*"

The two letters from the Vatican congregations have not produced uniformity of practice in this country. Simultaneous preparation for both sacraments is provided in some dioceses where a child has the option of receiving either sacrament first, with the counsel of parents, priests and teachers. Programs in other dioceses are geared first to reception of Communion and later to reception of the sacrament of reconciliation.

Commentators on the letters note that: they are disciplinary rather than doctrinal in content; they are subject to pastoral interpretation by bishops; they cannot be interpreted to mean that a person who is not guilty of serious sin must be required to receive the sacrament of penance before (even first) Communion.

Canon 914 of the Code of Canon Law states that sacramental confession should precede first Communion.

Holy Communion under the Forms of Bread and Wine (by separate taking of the consecrated bread and wine or by intinction, the reception of the host dipped in the wine): Such reception is permitted under conditions stated in instructions issued by the Congregation for Divine Worship (May 25, 1967; June 29, 1970), the *General Instruction on the Roman Missal* (No. 242), and directives of bishops' conferences and individual bishops.

Accordingly, Communion can be administered in this way to: persons being baptized, received into communion with the Church, confirmed, receiving anointing of the sick; couples at their wedding or jubilee; religious at profession or renewal of profession; lay persons receiving an ecclesiastical assignment (e.g., lay missionaries); participants at concelebrated Masses, retreats, pastoral commission meetings, daily Masses and, in the U.S., Masses on Sundays and holy days of obligation.

A communicant has the option of receiving the Eucharist under the form of bread alone or under the forms of bread and wine.

Holy Communion Twice a Day: The reception of Holy Communion at Mass a second time on the same day is permitted. A person in danger of death is urged to receive Communion a second time, even outside of Mass.

Holy Communion and Eucharistic Devotion outside of Mass: These were the subjects of an instruction (*De Sacra Communione et de Cultu Mysterii Eucharistici extra Missam*) dated June 21 and made public Oct. 18, 1973, by the Congregation for Divine Worship.

Holy Communion can be given outside of Mass to persons unable for a reasonable cause to receive it during Mass on a given day. The ceremonial rite is modeled on the structure of the Mass, consisting of a penitential act, a scriptural reading, the Lord's Prayer, a sign or gesture of peace, giving of the Eucharist, prayer and final blessing. Viaticum and Communion to the sick can be given by extraordinary ministers (authorized lay persons) with appropriate rites.

Forms of devotion outside of Mass are exposition of the Blessed Sacrament (by men or women religious, especially, or lay persons in the absence of a priest; but only a priest can give the blessing), processions and congresses with appropriate rites.

Intercommunion: Church policy on intercommunion was stated in an "Instruction on the Admission of Other Christians to the Eucharist," dated June 1 and made public July 8, 1972, against the background of the *Decree on Ecumenism* approved by the Second Vatican Council, and the *Directory on Ecumenism* issued by the Secretariat for Promoting Christian Unity in 1967.

Basic principles related to intercommunion are:

• "There is an indissoluble link between the mystery of the Church and the mystery of the Eucharist, or between ecclesial and Eucharistic communion; the celebration of the Eucharist of itself signifies the fullness of profession of faith and ecclesial communion" (1972 Instruction).

• "Eucharistic communion practiced by those who are not in full ecclesial communion with each other cannot be the expression of that full unity which the Eucharist of its nature signifies and which in this case does not exist; for this reason such communion cannot be regarded as a means to be used to lead to full ecclesial communion" (1972 Instruction).

• The question of reciprocity "arises only with those churches which have preserved the substance of the Eucharist, the sacrament of orders and apostolic succession" (1967 Directory).

• "A Catholic cannot ask for the Eucharist except from a minister who has been validly ordained" (1967 Directory).

The policy distinguishes between separated Eastern Christians and other Christians.

With Separated Eastern Christians (e.g., Orthodox): These may be given the Eucharist (as well as penance and anointing of the sick) at their request. Catholics may receive these same sacraments from priests of separated Eastern churches if they experience genuine spiritual necessity, seek spiritual benefit, and access to a Catholic priest is morally or physically impossible. This policy (of reciprocity) derives from the facts that the separated Eastern churches have apostolic succession through their bishops, valid priests, and sacramental beliefs and practices in accord with those of the Catholic Church .

With Other Christians (e.g., members of Reformation-related churches, others): Admission to the Eucharist in the Catholic Church, according to the *Directory on Ecumenism,* "is confined to particular cases of those Christians who have a faith in the sacrament in conformity with that of the Church, who experience a serious spiritual need for the Eucharistic sustenance, who for a prolonged period are unable to have recourse to a minister of their own community and who ask for the sacrament of their own accord; all this provided that they have proper dispositions and lead lives worthy of a Christian." The spiritual need is defined as "a need for an increase in spiritual life and a need for a deeper involvement in the mystery of the Church and of its unity."

Circumstances under which Communion may be given to other properly disposed Christians are danger of death, imprisonment, persecution, grave spiritual necessity coupled with no chance of recourse to a minister of their own community.

Catholics cannot ask for the Eucharist from ministers of other Christian churches who have not been validly ordained to the priesthood.

Penance

Penance is the sacrament by which sins committed after baptism are forgiven and a person is reconciled with God and the Church.

Individual and integral confession and absolution are the only ordinary means for the forgiveness of serious sin and for reconciliation with God and the Church.

(Other than ordinary means are perfect contrition and general absolution without prior confession, both of which require the intention of subsequent confession and absolution.)

A revised ritual for the sacrament — *Ordo Paenitentiae,* published by the Congregation of Divine Worship Feb. 7, 1974, and made mandatory in the U.S. from the first Sunday of Lent, 1977 — reiterates standard doctrine concerning the sacrament; emphasizes the social (communal and ecclesial) aspects of sin and conversion, with due regard for personal aspects and individual reception of the sacrament; prescribes three forms for celebration of the sacrament; and presents models for community penitential services.

The basic elements of the sacrament are sorrow for sin because of a supernatural motive, confession (of previously unconfessed mortal or grave sins, required; of venial sins also, but not of necessity), and reparation (by means of prayer or other act enjoined by the confessor), all of which comprise the matter of the sacrament; and absolution, which is the form of the sacrament.

The traditional words of absolution — "I absolve you from your sins in the name of the Father, and of the Son, and of the Holy Spirit" — remain unchanged at the conclusion of a petition in the new rite that God may grant pardon and peace through the ministry of the Church.

The minister of the sacrament is an authorized priest — i.e., one who, besides having the power of orders to forgive sins, also has faculties of jurisdiction granted by an ecclesiastical superior and/or by canon law.

The sacrament can be celebrated in three ways.

• For individuals: The traditional manner remains acceptable but is enriched with additional elements including: reception of the penitent and making of the Sign of the Cross; an exhortation by the confessor to trust in God; a reading from Scripture; confession of sins; manifestation of repentance; petition for God's forgiveness through the ministry of the Church and the absolution of the priest; praise of God's mercy, and dismissal in peace. Some of these elements are optional.

• For several penitents, in the course of a community celebration including a Liturgy of the Word of God and prayers, individual confession and absolution, and an act of thanksgiving.

• For several penitents, in the course of a community celebration, with general confession and general absolution. In extraordinary cases, reconciliation may be attained by general absolution without prior individual confession as, for example, under these circumstances: (1) danger of death, when there is neither time nor priests available for hearing confessions; (2) grave necessity of a number of penitents who, because of a shortage of confessors, would be deprived of sacramental grace or Communion for a lengthy period of time through no fault of their own. Persons receiving general absolution are obliged to be properly disposed and resolved to make an individual confession of the grave sins from which they have been absolved; this confession should be made as soon as the opportunity to confess presents itself and before any second reception of general absolution.

Norms regarding general absolution, issued by the Congregation for the Doctrine of the Faith in 1972, are not intended to provide a basis for convoking large gatherings of the faithful for the purpose of imparting general absolution, in the absence of extraordinary circumstances. Judgment about circumstances that warrant general absolution belongs principally to the bishop of the place, with due regard for related decisions of appropriate episcopal conferences.

Communal celebrations of the sacrament are not held in connection with Mass.

The place of individual confession, as determined by episcopal conferences in accordance with given norms, can be the traditional confessional or another appropriate setting.

A precept of the Church obliges the faithful guilty of grave sin to confess at least once a year.

The Church favors more frequent reception of the sacrament not only for the reconciliation of persons guilty of serious sins but also for reasons of devotion. Devotional confession — in which venial sins or previously forgiven sins are confessed — serves the purpose of confirming persons in penance and conversion.

Penitential Celebrations: Communal penitential celebrations are designed to emphasize the social dimensions of Christian life — the community aspects and significance of penance and reconciliation.

Elements of such celebrations are community prayer, hymns and songs, scriptural and other readings, examination of conscience, general confession and expression of sorrow for sin, acts of penance and reconciliation, and a form of non-sacramental absolution resembling the one in the penitential rite of the Mass.

If the sacrament is celebrated during the service, there must be individual confession and absolution of sin.

(See Absolution, Confession, Confessional, Confessor, Contrition, Faculties, Forgiveness of Sin, Power of the Keys, Seal of Confession, Sin. Reconciliation and Penance: Apostolic Exhortation.)

Anointing of the Sick

This sacrament, promulgated by St. James the Apostle (Jas. 5:13-15), can be administered to the faithful after reaching the age of reason who begin to be in danger because of illness or old age. By the anointing with blessed oil and the prayer of a priest, the sacrament confers on the person comforting grace; the remission of venial sins and inculpably unconfessed mortal sins, together with at least some of the temporal punishment due for sins; and, sometimes, results in an improved state of health.

The matter of this sacrament is the anointing with blessed oil (of the sick — olive oil, or vegetable oil if necessary) of the forehead and hands; in cases of necessity, a single anointing of another portion of the body suffices. The form is: "Through this holy anointing and his most loving mercy, may the Lord assist you by the grace of the Holy Spirit so that, when you have been freed from your sins, he may save you and in his goodness raise you up."

Anointing of the sick, formerly called extreme unction, may be received more than once, e.g., in new or continuing stages of serious illness. Ideally, the sacrament should be administered while the recipient is conscious and in conjunction with the sacraments of penance and the Eucharist. It should be administered in cases of doubt as to whether the person has reached the age of reason, is dangerously ill or dead.

The sacrament can be administered during a communal celebration in some circumstances, as in a home for the aged.

Matrimony

Coverage of the sacrament of matrimony is given in the articles, Marriage Doctrine, *Humanae Vitae*, Marriage Laws, Pastoral Ministry for Divorced and Remarried.

Holy Orders

Holy orders is the sacrament by which spiritual power and grace are given to constitute and enable an ordained minister to consecrate the Eucharist, forgive sins, perform other pastoral and ecclesiastical functions, and form the community of the People of God. Holy orders confers a character on the soul and can be received only once. The minister of the sacrament is a bishop.

Holy orders, like matrimony but in a different way, is a social sacrament. As the Second Vatican Council declared in the *Dogmatic Constitution on the Church:*

'For the nurturing and constant growth of the People of God, Christ the Lord instituted in his Church a variety of ministries, which work for the good of the whole body. For those ministers who are endowed with sacred power are servants of their brethren, so that all who are of the People of God, and therefore enjoy a true Christian dignity, can work toward a common goal freely and in an orderly way, and arrive at salvation'' (No. 18).

Bishop: The fullness of the priesthood belongs to those who have received the order of bishop. Bishops, in hierarchical union with the pope and their fellow bishops, are the successors of the Apostles as pastors of the Church: they have individual responsibility for the care of the local churches they serve and collegial responsibility for the care of the universal Church (see Collegiality). In the ordination or consecration of bishops, the essential form is the imposition of hands by the consecrator(s) and the assigned prayer in the preface of the rite of ordination.

"With their helpers, the priests and deacons, bishops have . . . taken up the service of the community presiding in place of God over the flock whose shepherds they are, as teachers of doctrine, priests of sacred worship, and officers of good order" (No. 20).

Priests: A priest is an ordained minister with the power to celebrate Mass, administer the sacraments, preach and teach the word of God, impart blessings, and perform additional pastoral functions, according to the mandate of his ecclesiastical superior.

Concerning priests, the Second Vatican Council stated in the *Dogmatic Constitution on the Church* (No. 28):

"The divinely established ecclesiastical ministry is exercised on different levels by those who from antiquity have been called bishops, priests, and deacons. Although priests do not possess the highest degree of the priesthood, and although they are dependent on the bishops in the exercise of their power, they are nevertheless united with the bishops in sacerdotal dignity. By the power of the sacrament of orders, and in the image of Christ the eternal High Priest (Hb. 5:1-10; 7:24; 9:11-28), they are consecrated to preach the Gospel, shepherd the faithful, and celebrate divine worship as true priests of the New Testament. . . .

"Priests, prudent cooperators with the episcopal order as well as its aides and instruments, are called to serve the People of God. They constitute one priesthood with their bishop, although that priesthood is comprised of different functions."

In the ordination of a priest of Roman Rite, the essential matter is the imposition of hands on the heads of those being ordained by the ordaining bishop. The essential form is the accompanying prayer in the preface of the ordination ceremony. Other elements in the rite are the presentation of the implements of sacrifice — the chalice containing wine and the paten containing a host — with accompanying prayers.

Deacon: There are two kinds of deacons: those who receive the order and remain in it permanently, and those who receive the order while advancing to ordination to the priesthood. The following quotation — from Vatican II's *Dogmatic Constitution on the Church* (No. 29) — describes the nature and role of the diaconate, with emphasis on the permanent diaconate.

"At a lower level of the hierarchy are deacons, upon whom hands are imposed 'not unto the priesthood, but unto a ministry of service.' For strengthened by sacramental grace, in communion with the bishop and his group of priests, they serve the People of God in the ministry of the liturgy, of the word, and of charity. It is the duty of the deacon, to the extent that he has been authorized by competent authority, to administer baptism solemnly, to be custodian and dispenser of the Eucharist, to assist at and bless marriages in the name of the Church, to bring Viaticum to the dying, to read the sacred Scripture to the faithful, to instruct and exhort the people, to preside at the worship and prayer of the faithful, to administer sacramentals, and to officiate at funeral and burial services. (Deacons are) dedicated to duties of charity and administration."

"The diaconate can in the future be restored as a proper and permanent rank of the hierarchy. It pertains to the competent territorial bodies of bishops, of one kind or another, to decide, with the approval of the Supreme Pontiff, whether and where it is opportune for such deacons to be appointed for the care of souls. With the consent of the Roman Pontiff, this diaconate will be able to be conferred upon men of more mature age, even upon those living in the married state. It may also be conferred upon suitable young men. For them, however, the law of celibacy must remain intact" (No. 29).

The Apostles ordained the first seven deacons (Acts 6:1-6): Stephen, Philip, Prochorus, Nicanor, Timon, Parmenas, Nicholas.

Other Ministries: The Church later assigned ministerial duties to men in several other orders, as:

Subdeacon, with specific duties in liturgical worship, especially at Mass. The order, whose first extant mention dates from about the middle of the third century, was regarded as minor until the 13th century; afterwards, it was called a major order in the West but not in the East.

Acolyte, to serve in minor capacities in liturgical worship.

Exorcist, to perform services of exorcism for expelling evil spirits; a function which came to be reserved to specially delegated priests.

Lector, to read scriptural and other passages during liturgical worship.

Porter, to guard the entrance to an assembly of Christians and to ward off undesirables who tried to gain admittance; an order of early origin and utility but of present insignificance.

Long after it became evident that these positions and functions had fallen into general disuse or did not require clerical ordination, the Holy See started a revision of the orders in 1971. By an indult of Oct. 5, the bishops of the United States were permitted to omit ordaining porters and exorcists. Another indult, dated three days later, permitted the use of revised rites for ordaining acolytes and lectors, and authorized the use of a service celebrating admission to the clerical state in place of the ceremony of tonsure which had previously served this purpose.

To complete the revision, Pope Paul VI abolished Sept. 14, 1972, the orders of porter, exorcist and subdeacon; decreed that laymen, as well as candidates for the diaconate and priesthood, can be installed (rather than ordained) in the ministries (rather than orders) of acolyte and lector; reconfirmed the suppression of tonsure and its replacement with a service of dedication to God and the Church; and stated that a man enters the clerical state on ordination to the diaconate.

PERMANENT DIACONATE

Authorization for restoration of the permanent diaconate in the Roman Rite — making it possible for men to become deacons permanently, without going on to the priesthood — was promulgated by Pope Paul VI June 18, 1967, in a document entitled *Sacrum Diaconatus Ordinem* ("Sacred Order of the Diaconate").

The Pope's action implemented the desire expressed by the Second Vatican Council for reestablishment of the diaconate as an independent order in its own right not only to supply ministers for carrying on the work of the Church but also to complete the hierarchical structure of the Church of Roman Rite.

Permanent deacons have been traditional in the Eastern Church. The Western Church, however, since the fourth or fifth century, generally followed the practice of conferring the diaconate only as a sacred order preliminary to the priesthood, and of restricting the ministry of deacons to liturgical functions.

The Pope's document, issued on his own initiative, provided:

• Qualified unmarried men 25 years of age or older may be ordained permanent deacons. They cannot marry after ordination.

• Qualified married men 35 years of age or older may be ordained permanent deacons. The consent of the wife of a prospective deacon is required. A married deacon cannot remarry after the death of his wife.

• Preparation for the diaconate includes a course of study and formation over a period of at least three years.

• Candidates who are not Religious must be affiliated with a diocese. Reestablishment of the permanent diaconate among Religious is reserved to the Holy See.

• Deacons will practice their ministry under the direction of a bishop and with the priests with whom they will be associated. (For functions, see also the description of deacon, under Holy Orders.)

Restoration of the permanent diaconate in the United States was approved by the Holy See in October, 1968. Shortly afterwards the U.S. bishops established a committee of the same name, which is chaired by Bishop John F. Kinney of Bismarck. The committee operates through a secretariat, with offices at 1312 Massachusetts Ave. N. W., Washington, D.C. 20005. Samuel M. Taub, permanent deacon, is executive director.

Status and Functions

Reports filed by 134 program directors in response to an October, 1985, questionnaire indicated that there were in the U.S. 7,425 permanent deacons (323 more than in 1984) and 2,263 candidates (149 more than in 1984). The increase in the number of candidates reverses a five-year trend of declining numbers. Hispanic deacons numbered 978 (13 percent of the total). Sixty-two percent of the

deacons had a college education, 17 percent of whom had advance degrees.

Seventeen dioceses had 100 or more deacons; the leaders were Chicago with 494 and Hartford with 249. Forty deacons and five candidates were members of religious communities.

Training programs of spiritual, doctrinal and pastoral formation are based on guidelines emanating from the National Conference of Catholic Bishops.

Deacons have various functions, depending on the nature of their assignments. Liturgically, they can officiate at baptisms, weddings, wake services and funerals, can preach and distribute Holy Communion. Some are engaged in religious education work. All are intended to carry out works of charity and pastoral service of one kind or another.

The majority of permanent deacons, 93 per cent of whom are married, continue in their secular work. Their ministry of service is developing in three dimensions: of liturgy, of the word, and of charity. Depending on the individual deacon's abilities and preference, he is assigned by his bishop to either a parochial ministry or to one particular field of service. The latter is the most challenging ministry to develop. Deacons are active in a variety of ministries including those to prison inmates and their families, the sick in hospitals, nursing homes and homes for the aged, alienated youth, the elderly and the poor, and in various areas of legal service to the indigent, of education and campus ministry. Sixty-nine deacons (28 more than last year) have been assigned as administrators of parishes. The possibilities for diaconal ministry are under realistic assessment in a number of dioceses.

In the conclusion of recently revised guidelines the bishops said: "The diaconate is a ministry through which the needs of the world are brought to the Church, and the gifts the Church has to offer are brought to the world. This mediating role can be made visible in particularly powerful ways by the manner in which the deacon fulfils his secular occupation and his civic and public responsibilities. In turn, deacons should be able to bring to the Church the appreciation of the meaning and value of the Gospel that derives from their regular and deep involvement in the world, bearing as they do both the questions the world has to pose and the unique insights secular activity can provide."

National Association of Permanent Diaconate Directors: Membership organization of directors, vicars and other staff personnel of permanent diaconate programs. Established in 1977 to promote effective communication and facilitate the exchange of information and resources of members; to develop professional expertise and promote research, training and self evaluation; to foster accountability and seek ways to promote means of implementing solutions to problems. NAPDD is governed by an executive board of elected officers. President for the 1986-87 term: Rev. Arthur W. Bastress, 320 Cathedral St., Baltimore, Md. 21201.

MARRIAGE DOCTRINE

The following excerpts, stating key points of doctrine on marriage, are from the "Pastoral Constitution on the Church in the Modern World" (Nos. 48 to 51) promulgated by the Second Vatican Council.

Conjugal Covenant

The intimate partnership of married life and love has been established by the Creator and qualified by his laws. It is rooted in the conjugal covenant of irrevocable personal consent.

God himself is the author of matrimony, endowed as it is with various benefits and purposes. All of these have a very decisive bearing on the continuation of the human race, on the personal development and eternal destiny of the individual members of a family, and on the dignity, stability, peace, and prosperity of the family itself and of human society as a whole. By their very nature, the institution of matrimony itself and conjugal love are ordained for the procreation and education of children, and find in them their ultimate crown.

Thus a man and a woman . . . render mutual help and service to each other through an intimate union of their persons and of their actions. Through this union they experience the meaning of their oneness and attain to it with growing perfection day by day. As a mutual gift of two persons, this intimate union, as well as the good of the children, imposes total fidelity on the spouses and argues for an unbreakable oneness between them (No. 48).

Sacrament of Matrimony

Christ the Lord abundantly blessed this many-faceted love. . . . The Savior of men and the Spouse of the Church comes into the lives of married Christians through the sacrament of matrimony. He abides with them thereafter so that, just as he loved the Church and handed himself over on her behalf, the spouses may love each other with perpetual fidelity through mutual self-bestowal.

Graced with the dignity and office of fatherhood and motherhood, parents will energetically acquit themselves of a duty which devolves primarily on them; namely, education, and especially religious education.

The Christian family, which springs from marriage as a reflection of the loving covenant uniting Christ with the Church, and as a participation in that covenant, will manifest to all men the Savior's living presence in the world, and the genuine nature of the Church (No. 48).

Conjugal Love

The biblical Word of God several times urges the betrothed and the married to nourish and develop their wedlock by pure conjugal love and undivided affection.

This love is an eminently human one since it is directed from one person to another through an affection of the will. It involves the good of the whole person. Therefore it can enrich the expressions of body and mind with a unique dignity, ennobling these expressions as special ingredients and signs of the friendship distinctive of marriage. This love the Lord has judged worthy of special gifts, healing, perfecting, and exalting gifts of grace and of charity.

Such love, merging the human with the divine, leads the spouses to a free and mutual gift of themselves, a gift proving itself by gentle affection and by deed. Such love pervades the whole of their lives. Indeed, by its generous activity it grows better and grows greater. Therefore it far excels mere erotic inclination, which, selfishly pursued, soon enough fades wretchedly away.

This love is uniquely expressed and perfected through the marital act. The actions within marriage by which the couple are united intimately and chastely are noble and worthy ones. Expressed in a manner which is truly human, these actions signify and promote that mutual self-giving by which spouses enrich each other with a joyful and a thankful will.

Sealed by mutual faithfulness and hallowed above all by Christ's sacrament, this love remains steadfastly true in body and in mind, in bright days or dark. It will never be profaned by adultery or divorce. Firmly established by the Lord, the unity of marriage will radiate from the equal personal dignity of wife and husband, a dignity acknowledged by mutual and total love.

The steady fulfillment of the duties of this Christian vocation demands notable virtue. For this reason, strengthened by grace for holiness of life, the couple will painstakingly cultivate and pray for constancy of love, largeheartedness, and the spirit of sacrifice (No. 49).

Fruitfulness of Marriage

Marriage and conjugal love are by their nature ordained toward the begetting and educating of children. Children are really the supreme gift of marriage and contribute very substantially to the welfare of their parents. . . . God himself . . . wished to share with man a certain special participation in his own creative work. Thus he blessed male and female, saying: "Increase and multiply" (Gn. 1:28).

Hence, while not making the other purposes of matrimony of less account, the true practice of conjugal love, and the whole meaning of the family life which results from it, have this aim: that the couple be ready with stout hearts to cooperate with the love of the Creator and the Savior, who through them will enlarge and enrich his own family day by day.

Parents should regard as their proper mission the task of transmitting human life and educating those to whom it has been transmitted. They should realize that they are thereby cooperators with the love of God the Creator, and are, so to speak, the interpreters of that love. Thus they will fulfill their task with human and Christian responsibility (No. 50).

Norms of Judgment

They will thoughtfully take into account both their own welfare and that of their children, those already born and those who may be foreseen. For this accounting they will reckon with both the material and the spiritual conditions of the times as well as of their state in life. Finally, they will consult the interests of the family group, of temporal society, and of the Church herself.

The parents themselves should ultimately make this judgment in the sight of God. But in their manner of acting, spouses should be aware that they cannot proceed arbitrarily. They must always be governed according to a conscience dutifully conformed to the divine law itself, and should be submissive toward the Church's teaching office, which authentically interprets that law in the light of the Gospel. That divine law reveals and protects the integral meaning of conjugal love, and impels it toward a truly human fulfillment.

Marriage, to be sure, is not instituted solely for procreation. Rather, its very nature as an unbreakable compact between persons, and the welfare of the children, both demand that the mutual love of the spouses, too, be embodied in a rightly ordered manner, that it grow and ripen. Therefore, marriage persists as a whole manner and communion of life, and maintains its value and indissolubility, even when offspring are lacking — despite, rather often, the very intense desire of the couple (No. 50).

Love and Life

This Council realizes that certain modern conditions often keep couples from arranging their married lives harmoniously, and that they find themselves in circumstances where at least temporarily the size of their families should not be increased. As a result, the faithful exercise of love and the full intimacy of their lives are hard to maintain. But where the intimacy of married life is broken off, it is not rare for its faithfulness to be imperiled and its quality of fruitfulness ruined. For then the upbringing of the children and the courage to accept new ones are both endangered.

To these problems there are those who presume to offer dishonorable solutions. Indeed, they do not recoil from the taking of life. But the Church issues the reminder that a true contradiction cannot exist between the divine laws pertaining to the transmission of life and those pertaining to the fostering of authentic conjugal love.

For God, the Lord of Life, has conferred on men the surpassing ministry of safeguarding life — a ministry which must be fulfilled in a manner which is worthy of men. Therefore from the moment of its conception life must be guarded with the greatest care, while abortion and infanticide are unspeakable crimes. The sexual characteristics of man and the human faculty of reproduction wonderfully exceed the dispositions of lower forms of life. Hence the acts themselves which are proper to conjugal love and which are exercised in accord with genuine human dignity must be honored with great reverence (No. 51).

Church Teaching

Therefore when there is question of harmonizing conjugal love with the responsible transmission of life, the moral aspect of any procedure does not depend solely on the sincere intentions or on an evaluation of motives. It must be determined by objective standards. These, based on the nature of the human person and his acts, preserve the full sense of mutual self-giving and human procreation in the context of true love. Such a goal cannot be achieved unless the virtue of conjugal chastity is sincerely practiced. Relying on these principles, sons of the Church may not undertake methods of regulating procreation which are found blameworthy by the teaching authority of the Church in its unfolding of the divine law.

Everyone should be persuaded that human life and the task of transmitting it are not realities bound up with this world alone. Hence they cannot be measured or perceived only in terms of it, but always have a bearing on the eternal destiny of men (No. 51).

HUMANAE VITAE

Marriage doctrine and morality were the subjects of the encyclical "Humanae Vitae" ("Of Human Life") issued by Pope Paul, July 29, 1968. Following are a number of key excerpts from the document, which was framed in the pattern of traditional teaching and statements by the Second Vatican Council.

Each and every marriage act ("quilibet matrimonii usus") must remain open to the transmission of life (No. 11).

Indeed, by its intimate structure, the conjugal act, while most closely uniting husband and wife, capacitates them for the generation of new lives, according to laws inscribed in the very being of man and of woman. By safeguarding both these essential aspects, the unitive and the procreative, the conjugal act preserves in its fullness the sense of true mutual love and its ordination toward man's most high calling to parenthood (No. 12).

It is, in fact, justly observed that a conjugal act imposed upon one's partner without regard for his or her condition and lawful desires is not a true act of love, and therefore denies an exigency of right moral order in the relationships between husband and wife. Hence, one who reflects well must also recognize that a reciprocal act of love which jeopardizes the responsibility to transmit life — which God the Creator, according to particular laws, inserted therein — is in contradiction with the design constitutive of marriage and with the will of the Author of life. To use this divine gift, destroying, even if only partially, its meaning and its purpose, is to contradict the nature both of man and of woman and of their most intimate relationship, and therefore it is to contradict also the plan of God and his will (No. 13).

Forbidden Actions

The direct interruption of the generative process already begun, and, above all, directly willed and procured abortion, even if for therapeutic reasons, are to be absolutely excluded as licit means of regulating birth.

Equally to be excluded . . . is direct sterilization, whether perpetual or temporary, whether of the man or of the woman. Similarly excluded is every action which, either in anticipation of the conjugal act, or in its accomplishment, or in the development of its natural consequences, proposes, whether as an end or as a means, to render procreation impossible.

Inadmissible Principles

To justify conjugal acts made intentionally infecund, one cannot invoke as valid reasons the lesser evil, or the fact that such acts would constitute a whole together with the fecund acts already performed or to follow later and hence would share in one and the same moral goodness. In truth, if it is sometimes licit to tolerate a lesser evil in order to avoid a greater evil or to promote a greater good, it is not licit, even for the gravest reasons, to do evil so that good may follow therefrom; that is, to make into the object of a positive act of the will something which is intrinsically disorder, and hence unworthy of the human person, even when the intention is to safeguard or promote individual, family or social well-being.

Consequently, it is an error to think that a conjugal act which is deliberately made infecund, and so is intrinsically dishonest, could be made honest and right by the ensemble of a fecund conjugal life (No. 14).

Family Planning

If, then, there are serious motives to space out births, which derive from the physical or psychological conditions of husband and wife, or from external conditions, the Church teaches that it is then licit to take into account the natural rhythms immanent in the generative functions, for the use of marriage in the infecund periods only, and in this way to regulate birth without offending earlier stated principles (No. 16).

Pastoral Concern

We do not at all intend to hide the sometimes serious difficulties inherent in the life of Christian married persons; for them, as for everyone else, "the gate is narrow and the way is hard that leads to life." But the hope of that life must illuminate their way, as with courage they strive to live with wisdom, justice and piety in this present time, knowing that the figure of this world passes away.

Let married couples, then, face up to the efforts needed, supported by the faith and hope which "do not disappoint . . . because God's love has been poured into our hearts through the Holy Spirit, who has been given to us." Let them implore divine assistance by persevering prayer; above all, let them draw from the source of grace and charity in the Eucharist. And, if sin should still keep its hold over them, let them not be discouraged but rather have recourse with humble perseverance to the mercy of God, which is poured forth in the sacrament of penance (No. 25).

STATEMENTS OF POPE JOHN PAUL

Teaching enunciated by Pope Paul VI in *Humanae Vitae* and by the Second Vatican Council in the *Pastoral Constitution on the Church in the Modern World* has been reaffirmed time after time by Pope John Paul since the beginning of his pontificate. Following are several of his statements.

Objectively Wrong

Addressing 50 priests attending a seminar on responsible procreation Sept. 17, 1983, he said: "Contraception is to be judged objectively so profoundly illicit that it can never, for any reason, be justified. To think, or to say, anything to the contrary is tantamount to saying that in human life there can be situations where it is legitimate not to recognize God as God."

Users of contraception "attribute to themselves a power that belongs only to God; the power to decide in the final instance the coming into existence of a human being."

The Pope also said that the sexual act should symbolize in marriage the complete donation of the essential beings of two persons to each other. But: "The contraceptive act introduces a substantial limitation . . . of this reciprocal donation and expresses an objective refusal to give to the other all the good of femininity or masculinity."

Encyclical and Council

In one of a series of about a dozen talks on *Humanae Vitae* at general audiences during the summer of 1984, Pope John Paul said July 11 that in the encyclical letter "we are reminded of the Church's teaching that each marriage act must remain open to the transmission of life.

"The inseparable connection between the unitive and procreative aspects of marriage is founded on the intimate structure of the conjugal act itself, which enables husband and wife to generate new life, according to laws inscribed in the very being of man and of woman. By safeguarding both of these essential aspects, the conjugal act preserves in its fullness the sense of true mutual love. At the same time, it remains faithful to God's design for the purposes of marriage in directing husband and wife toward their high calling of parenthood."

On July 25, the Holy Father continued: "Today we continue our reflection on the ethical dimension of conjugal love by linking the teaching of the encyclical *Humanae Vitae* to our whole treatment of the theology of the body. The encyclical serves as a complement to the doctrine expressed in the pastoral constitution *Gaudium et Spes* of the Second Vatican Council. We find clear emphasis on the importance of harmonizing human love with a respect for life. The Church teaches that there can be no conflict between the divine laws which govern the transmission of life and which foster authentic married love.

"The council document and the encyclical of Pope Paul VI have the same aim, namely, to respond to the moral questions of the people of our time. Both documents seek to show the Church's great pastoral concern for the welfare of contemporary man and woman. To many people, the Church's teaching on the regulation of birth will appear difficult to put into practice. Indeed, its observance would not be possible without the help of God, who upholds and strengthens the human will. Yet, to anyone who reflects well, it will be very clear that efforts to put this teaching into practice make the human person more noble and are truly beneficial to the human community.

"Our biblical theology of the body provides a key to understanding the basis of the Church's pastoral concern for the true good of the human person, and for the defense and promotion of authentic human values. Here we come to understand that the only true good of the human person consists in discovering ever more clearly God's plan concerning human love and putting this divine plan into practice, as God has willed it."

Authoritative Teaching

Once again, on Aug. 1, the conciliar and papal documents keyed the Pontiff's remarks.

"The council document reminds us that, when it is a question of harmonizing married love with the responsible transmission of life, it is not enough to take into account one's own good intention and motivations. Objective criteria must be used, criteria drawn from the nature of the human person and human action, criteria which respect the total

meaning of self-giving and human procreation in the context of true love. All this is possible only if the virtue of married chastity is seriously practiced. ... Members of the Church cannot use methods of birth control which are disapproved of by the Church's teaching authority.

"Responsible parenthood, according to the Second Vatican Council and the encyclical *Humanae Vitae,* calls for a careful reflection on the physical, psychological, economic and social conditions whereby the good of the individual, the good of the children already born or yet to come, as well as the good of the family, of society and of the Church, are properly taken into account. However, married people are called to realize that in their consideration of all these factors they must arrive at a judgment before God. In their behavior they must be ruled by conscience, that is, they must make their decisions in the light of the teaching authority of the Church, which is the authentic interpreter of divine law. For the divine law throws light on the meaning of married love, protects it and leads it to truly human fulfillment.

"In this way, the married couple remains faithful to the fundamental principle of the inseparable connection between the unitive and procreative meanings of the marriage act, a connection which conforms to the intimate structure of conjugal love as willed by God in his plan for the human race."

MARRIAGE LAWS

The Catholic Church claims jurisdiction over its members in matters pertaining to marriage, which is a sacrament. Church legislation on the subject is stated principally in 111 canons of the Code of Canon Law.

Marriage laws of the Church provide juridical norms in support of the marriage covenant. In 10 chapters, the revised Code covers: pastoral directives for preparing men and women for marriage; impediments in general and in particular; matrimonial consent; form for the celebration of marriage; mixed marriages; secret celebration of marriage; effects of marriage; separation of spouses, and convalidation of marriage.

Catholics are bound by all marriage laws of the Church. Non-Catholics, whether baptized or not, are not considered bound by these ecclesiastical laws except in cases of marriage with a Catholic. Certain natural laws, in the Catholic view, bind all men and women, irrespective of their religious beliefs; accordingly, marriage is prohibited before the time of puberty, without knowledge and free mutual consent, in the case of an already existing valid marriage bond, in the case of antecedent and perpetual impotence.

Formalities

These include, in addition to arrangements for the time and place of the marriage ceremony, doctrinal and moral instruction concerning marriage and the recording of data which verifies in documentary form the eligibility and freedom of the persons to marry. Records of this kind, which are confidential, are preserved in the archives of

the church where the marriage takes place.

Premarital instructions are the subject matter of Pre-Cana Conferences.

Marital Consent

The exchange of consent to the marriage covenant, which is essential for valid marriage, must be rational, free, true and mutual.

Matrimonial consent can be invalidated by an essential defect, substantial error, the strong influence of force and fear, the presence of a condition or intention against the nature of marriage.

Form of Marriage

A Catholic is required, for validity and lawfulness, to contract marriage — with another Catholic or with a non-Catholic — in the presence of a competent priest or deacon and two witnesses.

There are two exceptions to this law. A Roman Rite Catholic (since Mar. 25, 1967) or an Eastern Rite Catholic (since Nov. 21, 1964) can contract marriage validly in the presence of a priest of a separated Eastern Rite Church, provided other requirements of law are complied with. With permission of the competent Roman-Rite or Eastern-Rite bishop, this form of marriage is lawful, as well as valid. (See Eastern Rite Laws, below.)

With these two exceptions, and aside from cases covered by special permission, the Church does not regard as valid any marriages involving Catholics which take place before non-Catholic ministers of religion or civil officials.

(An excommunication formerly in force against Catholics who celebrated marriage before a non-

Catholic minister was abrogated in a decree issued by the Sacred Congregation for the Doctrine of the Faith on Mar. 18, 1966.)

The ordinary place of marriage is the parish of either Catholic party or of the Catholic party in case of a mixed marriage.

Church law regarding the form of marriage does not affect non-Catholics in marriages among themselves. The Church recognizes as valid the marriages of non-Catholics before ministers of religion and civil officials, unless they are rendered null and void on other grounds.

The canonical form is not to be observed in the case of a marriage between a non-Catholic and a baptized Catholic who has left the Church by a formal act.

Impediments

Diriment Impediments to marriage are factors which render a marriage invalid.

• age, which obtains before completion of the 14th year for a woman and the 16th year for a man;

• impotency, if it is antecedent to the marriage and permanent (this differs from sterility, which is not an impediment);

• the bond of an existing valid marriage;

• disparity of worship, which obtains when one party is a Catholic and the other party is unbaptized;

• sacred orders;

• religious profession of the perpetual vow of chastity;

• abduction, which impedes the freedom of the person abducted;

• crime, variously involving elements of adultery, promise or attempt to marry, conspiracy to murder a husband or wife;

• blood relationship in the direct line (father-daughter, mother-son, etc.) and to the fourth degree inclusive of the collateral line (brother-sister, first, second and third cousins);

• affinity, or relationship resulting from a valid marriage, in any degree of the direct line;

• public honesty, arising from an invalid marriage or from public or notorious concubinage; it renders either party incapable of marrying blood relatives of the other in the first degree of the direct line.

• legal relationship arising from adoption; it renders either party incapable of marrying relatives of the other in the direct line or in the second degree of the collateral line.

Dispensations from Impediments: Persons hindered by impediments either may not or cannot marry unless they are dispensed therefrom in view of reasons recognized in canon law. Local bishops can dispense from the impediments most often encountered (e.g., disparity of worship) as well as others.

Decision regarding some dispensations is reserved to the Holy See.

Separation

A valid and consummated marriage of baptized persons cannot be dissolved by any human authority or any cause other than the death of one of the persons.

In other circumstances:

• 1. A valid but unconsummated marriage of baptized persons, or of a baptized and an unbaptized person, can be dissolved:

a. by the solemn religious profession of one of the persons, made with permission of the pope. In such a case, the bond is dissolved at the time of profession, and the other person is free to marry again;

b. by dispensation from the pope, requested for a grave reason by one or both of the persons. If the dispensation is granted, both persons are free to marry again.

Dispensations in these cases are granted for reasons connected with the spiritual welfare of the concerned persons.

• 2. A legitimate marriage, even consummated, of unbaptized persons can be dissolved in favor of one of them who subsequently receives the sacrament of baptism. This is the Pauline Privilege, so called because it was promulgated by St. Paul (1 Cor. 7:12-15) as a means of protecting the faith of converts. Requisites for granting the privilege are:

a. marriage prior to the baptism of either person;

b. reception of baptism by one person;

c. refusal of the unbaptized person to live in peace with the baptized person and without interfering with his or her freedom to practice the Christian faith. The privilege does not apply if the unbaptized person agrees to these conditions.

• 3. A legitimate and consummated marriage of a baptized and an unbaptized person can be dissolved by the pope in virtue of the Privilege of Faith, also called the Petrine Privilege.

Civil Divorce

Because of the unity and the indissolubility of marriage, the Church denies that civil divorce can break the bond of a valid marriage, whether the marriage involves two Catholics, a Catholic and a non-Catholic, or non-Catholics with each other.

In view of serious circumstances of marital distress, the Church permits an innocent and aggrieved party, whether wife or husband, to seek and obtain a civil divorce for the purpose of acquiring title and right to the civil effects of divorce, such as separate habitation and maintenance, and the custody of children. Permission for this kind of action should be obtained from proper church authority. The divorce, if obtained, does not break the bond of a valid marriage.

Under other circumstances — as would obtain if a marriage was invalid (see Annulment, below) — civil divorce is permitted for civil effects and as a civil ratification of the fact that the marriage bond really does not exist.

Annulment

This is a decision by a competent church authority — e.g., a bishop, a diocesan marriage tribunal, the Roman Rota — that an apparently valid marriage was actually invalid from the beginning because of the unknown or concealed existence, from the beginning, of a diriment impediment, an essential defect in consent, radical incapability for marriage, or a condition placed by one or both of the parties against the very nature of marriage.

Eastern Rite Laws

Marriage laws of the Eastern Church differ in several respects from the legislation of the Roman Rite. The regulations in effect since May 2, 1949, were contained in the motu proprio *Crebre Allatae* issued by Pius XII the previous February.

According to both the Roman Code of Canon Law and the Oriental Code, marriages between Roman Rite Catholics and Eastern Rite Catholics ordinarily take place in the rite of the groom and have canonical effects in that rite.

Regarding the form for the celebration of marriages between Eastern Catholics and baptized Eastern non-Catholics, the Second Vatican Council declared:

"By way of preventing invalid marriages between Eastern Catholics and baptized Eastern non-Catholics, and in the interests of the permanence and sanctity of marriage and of domestic harmony, this sacred Synod decrees that the canonical 'form' for the celebration of such marriages obliges only for lawfulness. For their validity, the presence of a sacred minister suffices, as long as the other requirements of law are honored" (*Decree on Eastern Catholic Churches,* No. 18).

Marriages taking place in this manner are lawful, as well as valid, with permission of a competent Eastern Rite bishop.

The Rota

The Roman Rota is the ordinary court of appeal for marriage, and some other cases, which are appealed to the Holy See from lower church courts. Appeals are made to the Rota if decisions by diocesan and archdiocesan courts fail to settle the matter in dispute.

MIXED MARRIAGES

"Mixed Marriages" (*Matrimonia Mixta*) was the subject of: (1) a letter issued under this title by Pope Paul VI Mar. 31, 1970, and (2) a statement, *Implementation of the Apostolic Letter on Mixed Marriages,* approved by the National Conference of Catholic Bishops Nov. 16, 1970.

One of the key points in the bishops' statement referred to the need for mutual pastoral care by ministers of different faiths for the sacredness of marriage and for appropriate preparation and continuing support of parties to a mixed marriage.

Pastoral experience, which the Catholic Church shares with other religious bodies, confirms the fact that marriages of persons of different beliefs involve special problems related to the continuing religious practice of the concerned persons and to the religious education and formation of their children.

Pastoral measures to minimize these problems include instruction of a non-Catholic party in essentials of the Catholic faith for purposes of understanding. Desirably, some instruction should also be given the Catholic party regarding his or her partner's beliefs.

Requirements

The Catholic party to a mixed marriage is required to declare his (her) intention of continuing practice of the Catholic faith and to promise to do all in his (her) power to share his (her) faith with children born of the marriage by having them baptized and raised as Catholics. No declarations or promises are required of the non-Catholic party, but he (she) must be informed of the declaration and promise made by the Catholic.

Notice of the Catholic's declaration and promise is an essential part of the application made to a bishop for (1) permission to marry a baptized non-Catholic, or (2) a dispensation to marry an unbaptized non-Catholic.

A mixed marriage can take place with a Nuptial Mass. (The bishops' statement added this caution: "To the extent that Eucharistic sharing is not permitted by the general discipline of the Church, this is to be considered when plans are being made to have the mixed marriage at Mass or not.")

The ordinary minister at a mixed marriage is an authorized priest, and the ordinary place is the parish church of the Catholic party. A non-Catholic minister may not only attend the marriage ceremony but may also address, pray with and bless the couple.

For appropriate pastoral reasons, a bishop can grant a dispensation from the Catholic form of marriage and can permit the marriage to take place in a non-Catholic Church with a non-Catholic minister as the officiating minister. A priest may not only attend such a ceremony but may also address, pray with and bless the couple.

"It is not permitted," however, the bishops' statement declared, "to have two religious services or to have a single service in which both the Catholic marriage ritual and a non-Catholic marriage ritual are celebrated jointly or successively."

PASTORAL MINISTRY FOR DIVORCED AND REMARRIED

Ministry to divorced and remarried Catholics is a difficult field of pastoral endeavor, situated as it is in circumstances tantamount to the horns of a dilemma.

At Issue

On the one side is firm church teaching on the permanence of marriage and norms against reception of the Eucharist and full participation in the life of the Church by Catholics in irregular unions.

On the other side are men and women with broken unions followed by second and perhaps happier attempts at marriage which the Church does not recognize as valid and which may not be capable of being validated because of the existence of an earlier marriage bond.

The forces at work in these circumstances are those of the Church, upholding its doctrine and practice regarding the permanence of marriage, and those of many men and women in irregular second marriages who desire full participation in the life of the Church.

Sacramental participation is not possible for those whose first marriage was valid, although there is no bar to their attendance at Mass, to sharing in other activities of the Church, or to their efforts to have children baptized and raised in the Catholic faith.

An exception to this rule is the condition of a divorced and remarried couple living in a brother-sister relationship.

There is no ban against sacramental participation by separated or divorced persons who have not attempted a second marriage.

Unverified estimates of the number of U.S. Catholics who are divorced and remarried vary between six and eight million.

Tribunal Action

What can the Church do for them and with them in pastoral ministry, is an old question charged with new urgency because of the rising number of divorced and remarried Catholics.

One way to help is through the agency of marriage tribunals charged with responsibility for investigating and settling questions concerning the validity or invalidity of a prior marriage. There are reasons in canon law justifying the Church in declaring a particular marriage null and void from the beginning, despite the short- or long-term existence of an apparently valid union.

Decrees of nullity (annulments) are not new in the history of the Church. If such a decree is issued, a man or woman is free to validate a second marriage and live in complete union with the Church.

U.S. tribunals issued 450 annulments in 1968 and approximnately 48,000 in 1981. The increase was a result not just of new tribunal procedures but, more significantly, of judgments regarding the radical incapability of persons to contract valid marriage in the first place.

Reasons behind Decrees

Pastoral experience reveals that some married persons, a short or long time after contracting an apparently valid marriage, exhibit signs that point back to the existence, at the time of marriage, of latent and serious personal deficiencies which made them incapable of valid consent and sacramental commitment.

Such deficiencies might include gross immaturity and those affecting in a serious way the capacity to love, to have a true interpersonal and conjugal relationship, to fulfill marital obligations, to accept the faith aspect of marriage.

Psychological and behavioral factors like these have been given greater attention by tribunals in recent years and have provided grounds for numerous decrees of nullity.

Decisions of this type do not indicate any softening of the Church's attitude regarding the permanence of marriage. They affirm, rather, that some persons who have married were really not capable of doing so.

Serious deficiencies in the capacity for real interpersonal relationship in marriage were the reasons behind a landmark decree of nullity issued in 1973 by the Roman Rota, the Vatican high court of appeals in marriage cases. Pope John Paul referred to such deficiencies — the "grave lack of discretionary judgment," incapability of assuming "essential matrimonial rights and obligations," for example — in an address Jan. 26, 1984, to personnel of the Rota.

The tribunal way to a decree of nullity regarding a previous marriage, however, is not open to many persons in second marriages — because grounds are either lacking or, if present, cannot be verified in tribunal process.

One unacceptable solution of the problem, called "good conscience procedure," involves administration of the sacraments of penance and the Eucharist to divorced and remarried Catholics unable to obtain a decree of nullity for a first marriage who are living in a subsequent marriage "in good faith."

This procedure, despite the fact that it has no standing or recognition in church law, is being advocated and practiced by some priests and remarried Catholics.

Pastoral Concern

Pastoral concern for divorced and remarried persons was cited by Pope John Paul in his apostolic exhortation on the family, *Familiaris Consortium.* He called upon pastors and all members of the Church:

"Help the divorced with solicitous care to make sure that they do not consider themselves as separated from the Church, for as baptized persons they can and indeed must share in her life. They should be encouraged to listen to the word of God, to attend the Sacrifice of the Mass, to persevere in prayer, to contribute to works of charity and to community efforts of justice, to bring up their children in the Christian faith, to cultivate the spirit and practice of penance and thus implore, day by day, God's grace."

This concern is shared by hosts of priests, Religious and lay persons, as well as by numerous apostolates and support groups like the Judeans, founded in 1952, and the North American Conference of Separated and Divorced Catholics, founded in 1972.

Statistics compiled and circulated in November, 1985, by the conference indicated that 80 percent of U.S. dioceses formally included ministry to divorced persons in their family-life apostolates; 30 percent of the diocese had full-time, salaried personnel in the ministry; 25 percent of U.S. parishes had support groups for divorced persons.

Ms. K. L. Kircher is executive director of the North American Conference of Separated and Divorced Catholics. The mailing address is: 3015 Fourth St. N.E., Washington, D.C. 20017.

THE CHURCH CALENDAR

The calendar of the Roman Church consists of an arrangement throughout the year of a series of liturgical seasons, commemorations of divine mysteries and commemorations of saints for purposes of worship.

The purposes of this calendar were outlined in the "Constitution on the Sacred Liturgy" (Nos. 102-105) promulgated by the Second Vatican Council.

Within the cycle of a year . . . (the Church) unfolds the whole mystery of Christ, not only from his incarnation and birth until his ascension, but also as reflected in the day of Pentecost, and the expectation of a blessed, hoped-for return of the Lord.

Recalling thus the mysteries of redemption, the Church opens to the faithful the riches of her Lord's powers and merits, so that these are in some way made present at all times, and the faithful are enabled to lay hold of them and become filled with saving grace (No. 102).

In celebrating this annual cycle of Christ's mysteries, holy Church honors with special love the Blessed Mary, Mother of God (No. 103).

The Church has also included in the annual cycle days devoted to the memory of the martyrs and the other saints. . . . (who) sing God's perfect praise in heaven and offer prayers for us. By celebrating the passage of these saints from earth to heaven the Church proclaims the paschal mystery as achieved in the saints who have suffered and been glorified with Christ; she proposes them to the faithful as examples who draw all to the Father through Christ, and through their merits she pleads for God's favors (No. 104).

In the various seasons of the year and according to her traditional discipline, the Church completes the formation of the faithful by means of pious practices for soul and body, by instruction, prayer, and works of penance and mercy (No. 105).

THE ROMAN CALENDAR

Norms for a revised calendar for the Western Church as decreed by the Second Vatican Council were approved by Paul VI in the motu proprio Mysterii Paschalis dated Feb. 14, 1969. The revised calendar was promulgated a month later by a decree of the Congregation for Divine Worship and went into effect Jan. 1, 1970, with provisional modifications. Full implementation of all its parts was delayed in 1970 and 1971, pending the completion of work on related liturgical texts. The U.S. bishops ordered the calendar into effect for 1972.

The Seasons

Advent: The liturgical year begins with the first Sunday of Advent, which introduces a season of four weeks or slightly less duration with the theme of expectation of the coming of Christ. During the first two weeks, the final coming of Christ as Lord and Judge at the end of the world is the focus of attention. From Dec. 17 to 24, the emphasis shifts to anticipation of the celebration of his Nativity on the solemnity of Christmas.

Advent has four Sundays. Since the 10th century, the first Sunday has marked the beginning of the liturgical year in the Western Church. In the Middle Ages, a kind of pre-Christmas fast was in vogue during the season.

Christmas Season: The Christmas season begins with the vigil of Christmas and lasts until the Sunday after January 6, inclusive.

The period between the end of the Christmas season and the beginning of Lent belongs to the Ordinary Time of the year. Of variable length, the pre-Lenten phase of this season includes what were formerly called the Sundays after Epiphany and the suppressed Sundays of Septuagesima, Sexagesima and Quinquagesima.

Lent: The penitential season of Lent begins on Ash Wednesday, which occurs between Feb. 4 and Mar. 11, depending on the date of Easter, and lasts until the Mass of the Lord's Supper (Holy Thursday). It has six Sundays. The sixth Sunday marks the beginning of Holy Week and is known as Passion (formerly called Palm) Sunday.

The origin of Lenten observances dates back to the fourth century or earlier.

Easter Triduum: The Easter Triduum begins with evening Mass of the Lord's Supper and ends with Evening Prayer on Easter Sunday.

Easter Season: The Easter season whose theme is resurrection from sin to the life of grace, lasts for 50 days, from Easter to Pentecost. Easter, the first Sunday following the vernal equinox, occurs between Mar. 22 and Apr. 25. The terminal phase of the Easter season, between the solemnities of the Ascension of the Lord and Pentecost, stresses anticipation of the coming and action of the Holy Spirit.

Ordinary Time: The season of Ordinary Time begins on the Monday after the Sunday following January 6 and continues until the day before Ash Wednesday, inclusive. It begins again on the Monday after Pentecost and ends on the Saturday before the first Sunday of Advent. It consists of 33 or 34 weeks. The last Sunday is celebrated as the Solemnity of Christ the King. The overall purpose of the season is to elaborate the themes of salvation history.

The various liturgical seasons are characterized in part by the scriptural readings and Mass prayers assigned to each of them. During Advent, for example, the readings are messianic; during the Easter season, from the Acts of the Apostles, chronicling the Resurrection and the original proclamation of Christ by the Apostles, and from the Gospel of John; during Lent, baptismal and penitential passages. Mass prayers reflect the meaning and purpose of the various seasons.

Commemorations of Saints

The commemorations of saints are celebrated concurrently with the liturgical seasons and feasts

---

The general and mission prayer intentions given for each month of 1987 have been recommended to all the faithful by Pope John Paul.

236

of our Lord. Their purpose is to illustrate the paschal mysteries as reflected in the lives of saints, to honor them as heroes of holiness, and to appeal for their intercession.

In line with revised regulations, some former feasts were either abolished or relegated to observance in particular places by local option for one of two reasons: (1) lack of sufficient historical evidence for observance of the feasts; (2) lack of universal significance.

The commemoration of a saint, as a general rule, is observed on the day of death (*dies natalis*, day of birth to glory with God in heaven). Exceptions to this rule include the feasts of St. John the Baptist, who is honored on the day of his birth; Sts. Basil the Great and Gregory Nazianzen, and the brother Saints, Cyril and Methodius, who are commemorated in joint feasts.

Sundays and Other Holy Days

Sunday is the original Christian feast day and holy day of obligation because of the unusually significant events of salvation history which took place and are commemorated on the first day of the week — viz., the Resurrection of Christ, the key event of his life and the fundamental fact of Christianity; and the descent of the Holy Spirit upon the Apostles on Pentecost, the birthday of the Church. The transfer of observance of the Lord's Day from the Sabbath to Sunday was made in apostolic times. The Mass and Liturgy of the Hours (Divine Office) of each Sunday reflect the themes and set the tones of the various liturgical seasons.

Holy days of obligation are special occasions on which Catholics who have reached the age of reason are seriously obliged, as on Sundays, to assist at Mass: they are also to refrain from work and involvement with business which impede participation in divine worship and the enjoyment of appropriate rest and relaxation.

The holy days of obligation observed in the United States are: Christmas, the Nativity of Jesus, Dec. 25; Solemnity of Mary the Mother of God, Jan. 1; Ascension of the Lord; Assumption of Blessed Mary the Virgin, Aug. 15; All Saints' Day, Nov. 1; Immaculate Conception of Blessed Mary the Virgin, Dec. 8.

In addition to these, there are four other holy days of obligation prescribed in the general law of the Church which are not so observed in the U.S.: Epiphany, Jan. 6; St. Joseph, Mar. 19; Corpus Christi; Sts. Peter and Paul, June 29. The solemnities of Epiphany and Corpus Christi are transferred to a Sunday in countries where they are not observed as holy days of obligation.

Categories of observances according to dignity and manner of observance are: solemnity (highest, corresponding to former first-class feasts); feast (corresponding to former second-class feasts); memorial (corresponding to former third-class feasts); optional memorial (observable by choice). Observances of the first three categories are universal in the Roman Rite.

Fixed observances are those which are regularly celebrated on the same calendar day each year.

Movable observances are those which are not observed on the same calendar day each year. Examples of these are Easter (the first Sunday after the first full moon following the vernal equinox), Ascension (40 days after Easter), Pentecost (50 days after Easter).

Weekdays are those on which no proper feast or vigil is celebrated in the Mass or Liturgy of the Hours (Divine Office). On such days, the Mass may be that of the preceding Sunday, which expresses the liturgical spirit of the season, an optional memorial, a votive Mass, or a Mass for the dead. Weekdays of Advent and Lent are in a special category of their own.

Days of Prayer: Dioceses, at times to be designated by local bishops, should observe "days or periods of prayer for the fruits of the earth, prayer for human rights and equality, prayer for world justice and peace, and penitential observance outside of Lent." So stated the *Instruction on Particular Calendars* (No. 331) issued by the Congregation for the Sacraments and Divine Worship June 24, 1970.

These days are contemporary equivalents of what were formerly called ember and rogation days.

Ember days originated at Rome about the fifth century, probably as Christian replacements for seasonal festivals of agrarian cults. They were observances of penance, thanksgiving, and petition for divine blessing on the various seasons; they also were occasions of special prayer for clergy to be ordained. These days were observed four times a year.

Rogation days originated in France about the fifth century. They were penitential in character and also occasions of prayer for a bountiful harvest and protection against evil.

Days of Penance

The Code of Canon Law states that all the Christian faithful are bound by divine law to do penance, and prescribes times for the common observance of penance. These times are Fridays throughout the year and the season of Lent.

Abstinence from meat or another kind of food is to be observed on all Fridays except those on which a solemnity (e.g., Christmas) is celebrated, subject to directives from an appropriate conference of bishops. Whether or not such abstinence is ordered by a conference, the obligation to do penance still binds and can be discharged by alternative works of penance, like voluntary abstinence, prayer, self-denial, works of charity.

Ash Wednesday and Good Friday are days of fast and abstinence.

In the United States, in accord with provisions of the Code and decisions of the National Conference of Catholic Bishops, Ash Wednesday and Good Friday are days of fast and abstinence, and all Fridays of Lent are days of abstinence.

The obligation to abstain from meat binds Catholics from the age of 14 throughout life. The obligation to fast, limiting onself to one full meal and two lighter meals in the course of a day, binds adults (from 18 in the U.S.) to the beginning of their 60th year.

JANUARY 1987

1—Thurs. Solemnity of Mary, Mother of God. Holy day of obligation. (Nm. 6:22-27; Gal. 4:4-7; Lk. 2:16-21.)

2—Fri. Sts. Basil the Great and Gregory Nazianzen, bishops-doctors; memorial.

3—Sat. Weekday. BVM on Saturday; optional memorial.

4—Sun. Epiphany of the Lord (in U.S.); solemnity. (Is. 60:1-6; Eph. 3:2-3a, 5-6; Mt. 2:1-12.) [St. Elizabeth Ann Seton; memorial in U.S.]

5—Mon. St. John Neumann, bishop; memorial (in U.S.).

6—Tues. Weekday. Bl. Andre Bessette, religious; optional memorial (in U.S.). [Epiphany is celebrated on a Sunday between Jan. 2 and Jan. 8 in the United States.]

7—Wed. Weekday. St. Raymond of Penyafort, priest; optional memorial.

8—Thurs. Weekday.

9—Fri. Weekday.

10—Sat. Weekday. BVM on Saturday; optional memorial.

11—Sun. Baptism of the Lord; feast. (Is. 42:1-4, 6-7; Acts. 10:34-38; Mt. 3:13-27.)

12—Mon. Weekday. (First Week of the Year.)

13—Tues. Weekday. St. Hilary, bishop-doctor; optional memorial.

14—Wed. Weekday.

15—Thurs. Weekday.

16—Fri. Weekday.

17—Sat. St. Anthony, abbot; memorial.

18—Second Sunday of the Year. (Is. 49:3,5-6; 1 Cor. 1:1-3; Jn. 1:29-34.)

19—Mon. Weekday.

20—Tues. Weekday. St. Fabian, pope-martyr, or St. Sebastian, martyr; optional memorials.

21—Wed. St. Agnes, virgin-martyr; memorial.

22—Thurs. Weekday. St. Vincent, deacon-martyr; optional memorial.

23—Fri. Weekday.

24—Sat. St. Francis de Sales, bishop-doctor; memorial.

25—Third Sunday of the Year. (Is. 8:23b to 9:3; 1 Cor. 1:10-13, 17; Mt. 4:12-23) [Conversion of St. Paul, apostle; feast.]

26—Mon. Sts. Timothy and Titus, bishops; memorial.

27—Tues. Weekday. St. Angela Merici, virgin; optional memorial.

28—Wed. St. Thomas Aquinas, priest-doctor; memorial.

29—Thurs. Weekday.

30—Fri. Weekday.

31—Sat. St. John Bosco, priest; memorial.

GENERAL PRAYER INTENTION: Unity in Christ's Church. "Reconciled in Christ" is the theme of the Week of Prayer for Christian Unity, Jan. 18 to 25.

MISSION PRAYER INTENTION: Religious liberty in countries where laws and governments seriously restrict human activities, especially with respect to religion.

FEBRUARY 1987

1—Fourth Sunday of the Year. (Zep. 2:3 and 3:12-13; 1 Cor. 1:26-31; Mt. 5:1-12a).

2—Mon. Presentation of the Lord; feast.

3—Tues. Weekday. St. Blase, bishop-martyr, or St. Ansgar, bishop; optional memorials.

4—Wed. Weekday.

5—Thurs. St. Agatha, virgin-martyr; memorial.

6—Fri. Sts. Paul Miki and Companions, martyrs; memorial.

7—Sat. Weekday. BVM on Saturday; optional memorial.

8—Fifth Sunday of the Year. (Is. 58:7-10; 1 Cor. 2:1-5; Mt. 5:13-16). [St. Jerome Emiliani; optional memorial.]

9—Mon. Weekday.

10—Tues. St. Scholastica, virgin; memorial.

11—Wed. Weekday. Our Lady of Lourdes; optional memorial.

12—Thurs. Weekday.

13—Fri. Weekday.

14—Sat. Sts. Cyril, monk, and Methodius, bishop; memorial.

15—Sixth Sunday of the Year. (Sir. 15:15-20; 1 Cor. 2:6-10; Mt. 5:17-37.)

16—Mon. Weekday.

17—Tues. Weekday. Seven Holy Founders of the Servite Order; optional memorial.

18—Wed. Weekday.

19—Thurs. Weekday.

20—Fri. Weekday.

21—Sat. Weekday. St. Peter Damien, bishop-doctor, or BVM on Saturday; optional memorials.

22—Seventh Sunday of the Year. (Lv. 19:1-2, 17-18; 1 Cor. 3:16-23; Mt. 5:38-48.) [Chair of Peter, apostle; feast.]

23—Mon. St. Polycarp, bishop-martyr; memorial.

24—Tues. Weekday.

25—Wed. Weekday.

26—Thurs. Weekday.

27—Fri. Weekday.

28—Sat. Weekday. BVM on Saturday; optional memorial.

GENERAL PRAYER INTENTION: The pilgrim Church in Brazil. The Church faces many problems in the country: poverty, lack of development, need for land reform, in the general area of society; internally, there have been difficulties arising from different interpretations of liberation theology, sometimes disruptive influence of basic Christian communities, and other matters of concern discussed by the Pope with bishops of the country during the past year. The Church is indeed a pilgrim on the way, through trials, to renewal in the spirit of the Second Vatican Council.

MISSION PRAYER INTENTION: Harmony among the people of Southern Africa. Efforts from within the country as well as from outside have hardly cracked the iron hold of apartheid on the predominantly black population of the region.

MARCH 1987

1—Eighth Sunday of the Year. (Is. 49:14-15; 1 Cor. 4:1-5; Mt. 6:24-34.)

2—Mon. Weekday.

3—Tues. Weekday.

4—Ash Wednesday. Beginning of Lent. *Fast and abstinence.* Ashes are blessed on this day and imposed on the forehead of the faithful to remind them of their obligation to do penance for sin and to seek spiritual renewal by means of prayer, fasting, good works, and by bearing with patience and for God's purposes the trials and difficulties of everyday life. [St. Casimir; optional memorial.]

5—Thurs. Weekday of Lent.

6—Fri. Weekday of Lent. *Abstinence.*

7—Sat. Weekday of Lent. [Sts. Perpetua and Felicity, martyrs; memorial.]

8—First Sunday of Lent. (Gn. 2:7-9 and 3:1-7; Rom. 5:12-19; Mt. 4:1-11.) [St. John of God, religious; optional memorial.]

9—Mon. Weekday of Lent. [St. Frances of Rome, religious; optional memorial.]

10—Tues. Weekday of Lent.

11—Wed. Weekday of Lent.

12—Thurs. Weekday of Lent.

13—Fri. Weekday of Lent. *Abstinence.*

14—Sat. Weekday of Lent.

15—Second Sunday of Lent. (Gn. 12:1-4a; 2 Tm. 1:8b-10; Mt. 17:1-9.)

16—Mon. Weekday of Lent.

17—Tues. Weekday of Lent. [St. Patrick, bishop; optional memorial.]

18—Wed. Weekday of Lent. [St. Cyril of Jerusalem, bishop-doctor; optional memorial.]

19—Thurs. St. Joseph; solemnity. Weekday of Lent.

20—Fri. Weekday of Lent. *Abstinence.*

21—Sat. Weekday of Lent.

22—Third Sunday of Lent. (Ex. 17:3-7. Rom. 5:1-2, 5-8; Jn. 4:5-42.)

23—Mon. Weekday of Lent. [St. Turibius, bishop; optional memorial.]

24—Tues. Weekday of Lent.

25—Wed. Annunciation of the Lord; solemnity. Weekday of Lent.

26—Thurs. Weekday of Lent.

27—Fri. Weekday of Lent. *Abstinence.*

28—Sat. Weekday of Lent.

29—Fourth Sunday of Lent. (1 Sm. 16:1b, 6-7, 10-13a; Eph. 5:8-14; Jn. 9:1-41.)

30—Mon. Weekday of Lent.

31—Tues. Weekday of Lent.

GENERAL PRAYER INTENTION: Those who work for the homeless. Thousands of homeless people are in need of shelter in this country, along with many thousands more in other countries, especially in the underdeveloped Third World.

MISSION PRAYER INTENTION: Communications media as instruments of evangelization. Pope John Paul has spoken often about use of the media to proclaim the Gospel in an effective and direct way.

APRIL 1987

1—Wed. Weekday of Lent.

2—Thurs. Weekday of Lent. [St. Francis of Paola, hermit; optional memorial.]

3—Fri. Weekday of Lent. *Abstinence.*

4—Sat. Weekday of Lent. [St. Isidore of Seville, bishop-doctor; optional memorial.]

5—Fifth Sunday of Lent. (Ez. 37:12-14; Rom. 8:8-11; Jn. 11:1-45.) [St. Vincent Ferrer, priest; optional memorial.]

6—Mon. Weekday of Lent.

7—Tues. Weekday of Lent. [St. John Baptist de la Salle, priest; memorial.]

8—Wed. Weekday of Lent.

9—Thurs. Weekday of Lent.

10—Fri. Weekday of Lent. *Abstinence.*

11—Sat. Weekday of Lent. [St. Stanislaus, bishop-martyr; memorial.]

12—Sunday of the Passion (Palm Sunday). (Procession — Mt. 21:1-11. Mass — Is. 50:4-7; Phil. 2:6-11; Mt. 26:14 to 27:66.)

13—Monday of Holy Week. [St. Martin I, pope-martyr; optional memorial.]

14—Tuesday of Holy Week.

15—Wednesday of Holy Week.

16—Thursday of Holy Week. Holy Thursday. The Paschal Triduum begins with evening Mass of the Supper of the Lord.

17—Friday of the Passion of the Lord. Good Friday. *Fast and abstinence.*

18—Holy Saturday. The Easter Vigil.

19—Easter Sunday; solemnity. (Acts 10:34a, 37-43; Col. 3:1-4 or 1 Cor. 5:6b-8; Jn. 20:1-9 or Mt. 28:1-10 or (Evening) Lk. 24:13-35.)

20—Monday of Easter Octave.

21—Tuesday of Easter Octave. [St. Anselm, bishop-doctor; optional memorial.]

22—Wednesday of Easter Octave.

23—Thursday of Easter Octave. [St. George, martyr; optional memorial.]

24—Friday of Easter Octave. [St. Fidelis of Sigmaringen, priest-martyr; optional memorial.]

25—Saturday of Easter Octave. [St. Mark, evangelist; feast.]

26—Second Sunday of Easter. (Acts 2:42-47; 1 Pt. 1:3-9; Jn. 20:19-31.)

27—Mon. Weekday.

28—Tues. Weekday. St. Peter Chanel, priest-martyr; optional memorial.

29—Wed. St. Catherine of Siena, virgin-doctor; memorial.

30—Thurs. Weekday. St. Pius V, pope; optional memorial.

GENERAL PRAYER INTENTION: The preparation of young people for their future responsibilities. Such responsibilities are those of citizens of the world and of members of the Body of Christ.

MISSION PRAYER INTENTION: The Pontifical Society of St. Peter the Apostle and the formation of native clergy — for indigenization of the Church in mission areas.

MAY 1987

1—Fri. Weekday. St. Joseph the Worker; optional memorial.

2—Sat. St. Athanasius, bishop-doctor; memorial.

3—Third Sunday of Easter. (Acts. 2:14, 22-28; 1 Pt. 1:17-21; Lk. 24:13-35.) [Sts. Philip and James, apostles; feast.]

4—Mon. Weekday.

5—Tues. Weekday.

6—Wed. Weekday.

7—Thurs. Weekday.

8—Fri. Weekday.

9—Sat. Weekday.

10—Fourth Sunday of Easter. (Acts 2:14a, 36-41; 1 Pt. 2:20b-25; Jn. 10:1-10.)

11—Mon. Weekday.

12—Tues. Weekday. Sts. Nereus and Achilleus, martyrs, or St. Pancras, martyr; optional memorials.

13—Wed. Weekday.

14—Thurs. St. Matthias, apostle; feast.

15—Fri. Weekday.

16—Sat. Weekday.

17—Fifth Sunday of Easter. (Acts 6:1-7; 1 Pt. 2:4-9; Jn. 14:1-12.)

18—Mon. Weekday. St. John I, pope-martyr; optional memorial.

19—Tues. Weekday.

20—Wed. Weekday. St. Bernardine of Siena, priest; optional memorial.

21—Thurs. Weekday.

22—Fri. Weekday.

23—Sat. Weekday.

24—Sixth Sunday of Easter. (Acts 8:5-8, 14-17; 1 Pt. 3:15-18; Jn. 14: 15-21.)

25—Mon. Weekday. St. Bede the Venerable, priest-doctor, or St. Gregory VII, pope, or St. Mary Magdalene de Pazzi, virgin; optional memorials.

26—Tues. St. Philip Neri, priest; memorial.

27—Wed. Weekday. St. Augustine of Canterbury, bishop; optional memorial.

28—Thurs. Ascension of the Lord; solemnity. Holy day of obligation. (Acts 1:1-11; Eph. 1:17-23; Mt. 28:16-20.)

29—Fri. Weekday.

30—Sat. Weekday.

31—Seventh Sunday of Easter. (Acts 1:12-14; 1 Pt. 4:13-16; Jn. 17:1-11a.) [Visitation of Blessed Mary the Virgin; feast.]

GENERAL PRAYER INTENTION: The ongoing application of the Second Vatican Council, through the intercession of Mary, Mother of the Church. The need for integral implementation of the enactments of the Council, in the true spirit of the Council, has been a constant theme of concern since the Council ended in 1965.

MISSION PRAYER INTENTION: The Church in Cambodia and Laos. In addition to problems with governments, the Church has the need to provide care for thousands of refugees with little hope of resettlement.

JUNE 1987

1—Mon. St. Justin, martyr; memorial.

2—Tues. Weekday. Sts. Marcellinus and Peter, martyrs; optional memorial.

3—Wed. Sts. Charles Lwanga and Companions, martyrs; memorial.

4—Thurs. Weekday.

5—Fri. St. Boniface, bishop-martyr; memorial.

6—Sat. Weekday. St. Norbert, bishop; optional memorial.

7—Sun. Pentecost; solemnity. (Acts 2:1-11; 1 Cor. 12:3b-7, 12-13; Jn. 20:19-23.)

8—Mon. Weekday. (Tenth Week of the Year.)

9—Tues. Weekday. St. Ephraem, deacon-doctor; optional memorial.

10—Wed. Weekday.

11—Thurs. St. Barnabas, apostle; memorial.

12—Fri. Weekday.

13—Sat. St. Anthony of Padua, priest-doctor; memorial.

14—Trinity Sunday; solemnity. (Ex. 34:4b-6, 8-9; 2 Cor. 13:11-13; Jn. 3:16-18.)

15—Mon. Weekday. (Eleventh Week of the Year.)

16—Tues. Weekday.

17—Wed. Weekday.

18—Thurs. Weekday.

19—Fri. Weekday. St. Romuald, abbot; optional memorial.

20—Sat. Weekday. BVM on Saturday; optional memorial.

21—Sun. Corpus Christi (in U.S.); solemnity. Dt. 8:2-3, 14b-16a; 1 Cor. 10:16-17; Jn. 6:51-58.) [St. Aloysius Gonzaga, religious; memorial.]

22—Mon. Weekday. St. Paulinus of Nola, bishop, or Sts. John Fisher, bishop-martyr, and Thomas More, martyr; optional memorials.] (Twelfth Week of the Year.)

23—Tues. Weekday.

24—Wed. Birth of St. John the Baptist; solemnity.

25—Thurs. Weekday.

26—Fri. Sacred Heart of Jesus; solemnity.

27—Sat. Weekday. Immaculate Heart of Mary or St. Cyril of Alexandria, bishop-doctor; optional memorials.

28—Thirteenth Sunday of the Year. (2 Kgs. 4:8-11, 14-16a; Rom. 6:3-4, 8-11; Mt. 10:37-42.) [St. Irenaeus, bishop-martyr; memorial.]

29—Mon. Sts. Peter and Paul, apostles; solemnity.

30—Tues. Weekday. First Martyrs of the Roman Church; optional memorial.

GENERAL PRAYER INTENTION: Spreading the spirit of the Redemption. The communication of the gift, the spirit and the truth of Redemption is the responsibility of the baptized who participate in the threefold redemptive mission of Christ, to worship, bear witness to the faith and build the kingdom of God in the world of men.

MISSION PRAYER INTENTION: The Church in India and its mission of world evangelization. The special evangelizing thrust of the Church in India is toward the people of Asian, non-Abrahamic, religions.

JULY 1987

1—Wed. Weekday.

2—Thurs. Weekday.

3—Fri. St. Thomas, apostle; feast.

4—Sat. Weekday. St. Elizabeth of Portugal, or BVM on Saturday, optional memorials. Independence Day Votive Mass (permitted in U.S.).

5—**Fourteenth Sunday of the Year.** (Zec. 9:9-10; Rom. 8:9, 11-13; Mt. 11:25-30.) [St. Anthony Zaccaria, priest; optional memorial.]

6—Mon. Weekday. St. Maria Goretti, virgin-martyr; optional memorial.

7—Tues. Weekday.

8—Wed. Weekday.

9—Thurs. Weekday.

10—Fri. Weekday.

11—Sat. St. Benedict, abbot; memorial.

12—**Fifteenth Sunday of the Year.** (Is. 55:10-11; Rom. 8:18-23; Mt. 13:1-23.)

13—Mon. Weekday. St. Henry; optional memorial.

14—Tues. Bl. Kateri Tekakwitha, virgin; memorial (in U.S.). Weekday. St. Camillus de Lellis, priest; optional memorial.

15—Wed. St. Bonaventure, bishop-doctor; memorial.

16—Thurs. Weekday. Our Lady of Mt. Carmel; optional memorial.

17—Fri. Weekday.

18—Sat. Weekday. BVM on Saturday; optional memorial.

19—**Sixteenth Sunday of the Year.** (Wis. 12:13, 16-19; Rom. 8:26-27; Mt. 13:24-43.)

20—Mon. Weekday.

21—Tues. Weekday. St. Lawrence of Brindisi, priest-doctor; optional memorial.

22—Wed. St. Mary Magdalene; memorial.

23—Thurs. Weekday. St. Bridget, religious; optional memorial.

24—Fri. Weekday.

25—Sat. St. James, apostle; feast.

26—**Seventeenth Sunday of the Year.** (1 Kgs. 3:5, 7-12; Rom. 8:28-30; Mt. 13:44-52.) [Sts. Joachim and Anne, parents of Blessed Mary the Virgin; memorial.]

27—Mon. Weekday.

28—Tues. Weekday.

29—Wed. St. Martha; memorial.

30—Thurs. Weekday. St. Peter Chrysologus, bishop-doctor; optional memorial.

31—Fri. St. Ignatius of Loyola, priest; memorial.

GENERAL PRAYER INTENTION: Respect for human rights everywhere. These rights are under attack and siege in many countries. Appeals for their recognition and protection have been voiced and supported by popes and other churchmen, together with world leaders and rights activists, for years. Of special concern is the often denied right of religious freedom.

MISSION PRAYER INTENTION: The new bishops' conference of the southwest Indian Ocean region, for collegial action.

AUGUST 1987

1—Sat. St. Alphonsus Liguori, bishop-doctor; memorial.

2—**Eighteenth Sunday of the Year.** (Is. 55:1-3; Rom. 8:35, 37-39; Mt. 14:13-21.) [St. Eusebius of Vercelli, bishop; optional memorial.]

3—Mon. Weekday.

4—Tues. St. John Vianney, priest; memorial.

5—Wed. Weekday. Dedication of St. Mary Major Basilica; optional memorial.

6—Thurs. Transfiguration of the Lord; feast.

7—Fri. Weekday. Sts. Sixtus II, pope, and companions, martyrs; or St. Cajetan, priest; optional memorials.

8—Sat. St. Dominic, priest; memorial.

9—**Nineteenth Sunday of the Year.** (1 Kgs. 19:9a, 11-13a; Rom. 9:1-5; Mt. 14:22-23.)

10—Mon. St. Lawrence, deacon-martyr; feast.

11—Tues. St. Clare, virgin; memorial.

12—Wed. Weekday.

13—Thurs. Weekday. Sts. Pontian, pope, and Hippolytus, priest, martyrs; optional memorial.

14—Fri. St. Maximilian Kolbe, priest-martyr; memorial.

15—**Sat. Assumption of Blessed Mary the Virgin; solemnity. Holy day of obligation.** (Rv. 11:19a and 12:1-6a, 10ab; 1 Cor. 15:20-26; Lk. 1:39-56.)

16—**Twentieth Sunday of the Year.** (Is. 56:1, 6-7; Rom. 11:13-15, 29-32; Mt. 15:21-28.) [St. Stephen of Hungary; optional memorial.]

17—Mon. Weekday.

18—Tues. Weekday.

19—Wed. Weekday. St. John Eudes, priest; optional memorial.

20—Thurs. St. Bernard of Clairvaux, abbot-doctor; memorial.

21—Fri. St. Pius X, pope; memorial.

22—Sat. Queenship of Mary; memorial.

23—**Twenty-First Sunday of the Year.** (Is. 22:19-23; Rom. 11:33-36; Mt. 16:13-20.) [St. Rose of Lima, virgin; optional memorial.]

24—Mon. St. Bartholomew, apostle; feast.

25—Tues. Weekday. St. Louis, or St. Joseph Calasanz, priest; optional memorials.

26—Wed. Weekday.

27—Thurs. St. Monica; memorial.

28—Fri. St. Augustine, bishop-doctor; memorial.

29—Sat. Beheading of St. John the Baptist; memorial.

30—**Twenty-Second Sunday of the Year.** (Jer. 20:7-9; Rom. 12:1-2; Mt. 16:21-27.)

31—Mon. Weekday.

GENERAL PRAYER INTENTION: Faith and right reason in family life. These are basic elements of the family as the "domestic church" in which parents with their children grow in grace and wisdom as members of the Church which is the Body of Christ.

MISSION PRAYER INTENTION: The Church in Japan. The Nagasaki Martyrs, victims of persecution in 1597, have been, like other martyrs, the seed of the Church.

SEPTEMBER 1987

1—Tues. Weekday.

2—Wed. Weekday.

3—Thurs. St. Gregory the Great, pope-doctor; memorial.

4—Fri. Weekday.

5—Sat. Weekday. BVM on Saturday; optional memorial.

6—Twenty-Third Sunday of the Year. (Ez. 33:7-9; Rom. 13:8-10; Mt. 18:15-20.)

7—Mon. Labor Day Votive Mass (prescribed in U.S.).

8—Tues. Birth of Mary; feast.

9—Wed. St. Peter Claver, priest; memorial (in U.S.). Weekday.

10—Thurs. Weekday.

11—Fri. Weekday.

12—Sat. Weekday. BVM on Saturday; optional memorial.

13—Twenty-Fourth Sunday of the Year. (Sir. 27:30 to 28:7; Rom. 14:7-8; Mt. 18:21-35.) [St. John Chrysostom, bishop-doctor; memorial.]

14—Mon. Triumph of the Cross; feast.

15—Tues. Our Lady of Sorrows; memorial.

16—Wed. Sts. Cornelius, pope, and Cyprian, bishop, martyrs; memorial.

17—Thurs. Weekday. St. Robert Bellarmine, bishop-doctor; optional memorial.

18—Fri. Weekday.

19—Sat. Weekday. St. Januarius, bishop-martyr, or BVM on Saturday; optional memorials.

20—Twenty-Fifth Sunday of the Year. (Is. 55:6-9; Phil. 1:20c-24, 27a; Mt. 20:1-16a.) [Sts. Andrew Kim, priest, Paul Chong, lay apostle, and Companions, martyrs of Korea; memorial.]

21—Mon. St. Matthew, apostle-evangelist; feast.

22—Tues. Weekday.

23—Wed. Weekday.

24—Thurs. Weekday.

25—Fri. Weekday.

26—Sat. Weekday. Sts. Cosmas and Damian, martyrs, or BVM on Saturday; optional memorials.

27—Twenty-Sixth Sunday of the Year. (Ez. 18:25-28; Phil. 2:1-11; Mt. 21:28-32.) [St. Vincent de Paul, priest; memorial.]

28—Mon. Weekday. St. Wenceslaus, martyr; optional memorial.

29—Tues. Sts. Michael, Gabriel and Raphael, archangels; feast.

30—Wed. St. Jerome, priest-doctor; memorial.

GENERAL PRAYER INTENTION: The successful rehabilitation of drug abusers. Elements of rehabilitation are physical and psychological therapy, "straight" peer pressure, change of lifestyle, conversion of values, community support, conviction that drug use is not only destructive but also morally evil, spiritual inspiration and strength from prayer, the sacraments and observance of the Commandments.

MISSION PRAYER INTENTION: Cooperation of young Christians and Moslems.

OCTOBER 1987

1—Thurs. St. Therese of the Child Jesus, virgin; memorial.

2—Fri. Guardian Angels; memorial.

3—Sat. Weekday. BVM on Saturday; optional memorial.

4—Twenty-Seventh Sunday of the Year. (Is. 5:1-7; Phil. 4:6-9; Mt. 21:33-43.) [St. Francis of Assisi; memorial.]

5—Mon. Weekday.

6—Tues. Weekday. Bl. Marie-Rose Durocher, virgin; optional memorial (in U.S.); St. Bruno, priest; optional memorial.

7—Wed. Our Lady of the Rosary; memorial.

8—Thurs. Weekday.

9—Fri. Weekday. Sts. Denis, bishop, and Companions, martyrs; or St. John Leonard, priest; optional memorials.

10—Sat. Weekday. BVM on Saturday; optional memorial.

11—Twenty-Eighth Sunday of the Year. (Is. 25:6-10a; Phil. 4:12-14, 19 20; Mt. 22:1-14.)

12—Mon. Weekday.

13—Tues. Weekday.

14—Wed. Weekday. St. Callistus I, pope-martyr; optional memorial.

15—Thurs. St. Teresa of Jesus (Avila), virgin-doctor; memorial.

16—Fri. Weekday. St. Hedwig, religious, or St. Margaret Mary Alacoque, virgin; optional memorials.

17—Sat. St. Ignatius of Antioch, bishop-martyr; memorial.

18—Twenty-Ninth Sunday of the Year. (Is. 45:1, 4-6; 1 Thes. 1:1-5b; Mt. 22:15-21. [St. Luke, evangelist; feast.]

19—Mon. Sts. Isaac Jogues, John de Brebeuf, priests, and Companions, martyrs; memorial (in U.S.). Weekday. St. Paul of the Cross; optional memorial.

20—Tues. Weekday.

21—Wed. Weekday.

22—Thurs. Weekday.

23—Fri. Weekday. St. John of Capistrano, priest; optional memorial.

24—Sat. Weekday. St. Anthony Mary Claret, bishop, or BVM on Saturday; optional memorials.

25—Thirtieth Sunday of the Year. (Ex. 22:20-26; 1 Thes. 1:5c-10; Mt. 22:34-40.)

26—Mon. Weekday.

27—Tues. Weekday.

28—Wed. Sts. Simon and Jude, apostles; feast.

29—Thurs. Weekday.

30—Fri. Weekday.

31—Sat. Weekday. BVM on Saturday; optional memorial.

GENERAL PRAYER INTENTION: That the 1987 assembly of the Synod of Bishops may provide an apostolic impetus for lay persons. Lay persons in the Church and the world is the theme of the assembly.

MISSION PRAYER INTENTION: Participation of the faithful in World Mission Month.

NOVEMBER 1987

1—Sun. All Saints; solemnity. (Rv. 7:2-4, 9-14; 1 Jn. 3:1-3; Mt. 5:1-12a.)

2—Mon. Commemoration of All the Faithful Departed (All Souls' Day). (Thirty-First Week of the Year.)

3—Tues. Weekday. St. Martin de Porres, religious; optional memorial.

4—Wed. St. Charles Borromeo, bishop; memorial.

5—Thurs. Weekday.

6—Fri. Weekday.

7—Sat. Weekday. BVM on Saturday; optional memorial.

8—Thirty-Second Sunday of the Year. (Wis. 6:12-16; 1 Thes. 4:13-18; Mt. 25:1-13.)

9—Mon. Dedication of St. John Lateran (Archbasilica of Most Holy Savior); feast.

10—Tues. St. Leo the Great, pope-doctor; memorial.

11—Wed. St. Martin of Tours, bishop; memorial.

12—Thurs. St. Josaphat, bishop-martyr; memorial.

13—Fri. St. Frances Xavier Cabrini, virgin; memorial (in U.S.).

14—Sat. Weekday. BVM on Saturday; optional memorial.

15—Thirty-Third Sunday of the Year. (Prv. 31:10-13, 19-20, 30-31; 1 Thes. 5:1-6; Mt. 25:14-30.) [St. Albert the Great, bishop-doctor; optional memorial.]

16—Mon. Weekday. St. Margaret of Scotland, or St. Gertrude, virgin; optional memorials.

17—Tues. St. Elizabeth of Hungary, religious; memorial.

18—Wed. Weekday. Dedication of Basilicas of Sts. Peter and Paul, apostles; optional memorial.

19—Thurs. Weekday.

20—Fri. Weekday.

21—Sat. Presentation of Blessed Mary the Virgin; memorial.

22—Sun. Christ the King; solemnity. (Ez. 34:11-12, 15-17; 1 Cor. 15:20-26, 28; Mt. 25:31-46.) [St. Cecilia, virgin-martyr; memorial.]

23—Mon. Weekday. St. Clement I, pope-martyr, or St. Columban, abbot; optional memorials. (Thirty-Fourth [Last] Week of the Year.)

24—Tues. Weekday.

25—Wed. Weekday.

26—Thurs. Weekday. Thanksgiving Day Votive Mass (prescribed in U.S.).

27—Fri. Weekday.

28—Sat. Weekday. BVM on Saturday; optional memorial.

29—First Sunday of Advent. (Is. 63:16b-17, 19b and 64:2b-7; 1 Cor. 1:3-9; Mk. 13:33-37.) [Start of the 1988 liturgical year.]

30—Mon. St. Andrew, apostle; feast.

GENERAL PRAYER INTENTION: Prayer for all who have died in the peace of Christ.

MISSION PRAYER INTENTION: Christians living in China, where a government-supported church opposes the Church

DECEMBER 1987

1—Tues. Weekday of Advent.

2—Wed. Weekday of Advent.

3—Thurs. St. Francis Xavier, priest; memorial.

4—Fri. Weekday of Advent. St. John Damascene, priest-doctor; optional memorial.

5—Sat. Weekday of Advent.

6—Second Sunday of Advent. (Is. 40:1-5, 9-11; 2 Pt. 3:8-14; Mk. 1:1-8.) [St. Nicholas, bishop; optional memorial.]

7—Mon. St. Ambrose, bishop-doctor; memorial.

8—Tues. Immaculate Conception of Blessed Mary the Virgin; solemnity. Holy day of obligation. (Gn. 3:9-15, 20; Eph. 1:3-6, 11-12; Lk. 1:26-38.)

9—Wed. Weekday of Advent.

10—Thurs. Weekday of Advent.

11—Fri. Weekday of Advent. St. Damasus I, pope; optional memorial.

12—Sat. Our Lady of Guadalupe; memorial (in U.S.). Weekday of Advent. St. Jane Frances de Chantal, religious; optional memorial.

13—Third Sunday of Advent. (Is. 61:1-2a, 10-11; 1 Thes. 5:16-24; Jn. 1:6-8, 19-28.) [St. Lucy, virgin-martyr; memorial.]

14—Mon. St. John of the Cross, priest-doctor; memorial.

15—Tues. Weekday of Advent.

16—Wed. Weekday of Advent.

17—Thurs. Weekday of Advent.

18—Fri. Weekday of Advent.

19—Sat. Weekday of Advent.

20—Fourth Sunday of Advent. (2 Sm. 7:1-5, 8b-11, 16; Rom. 16:25-27; Lk. 1:26-38.)

21—Mon. Weekday of Advent. St. Peter Canisius, priest-doctor; optional memorial.

22—Tues. Weekday of Advent.

23—Wed. Weekday of Advent. St. John of Kanty, priest; optional memorial.

24—Thurs. Weekday of Advent.

25—Fri. Christmas. Birth of the Lord; solemnity. Holy day of obligation. (Vigil — Is. 62:1-5; Acts 13:16-17, 22-25; Mt. 1:1-25. Midnight—Is. 9:1-6; Ti. 2:11-14; Lk. 2:1-14. Dawn—Is. 62:11-12; Ti. 3:4-7; Lk. 2:15-20. During the Day—Is. 52:7-10; Heb. 1:1-6; Jn. 1:1-18.)

26—Sat. St. Stephen, first martyr; feast.

27—Sun. Holy Family; feast. (Sir. 3:2-6, 12-14; Col. 3:12-21; Lk. 2:22-40.) [St. John, apostle-evangelist; feast.]

28—Mon. Holy Innocents, martyrs; feast.

29—Tues. Fifth Day of Christmas Octave. St. Thomas Becket, bishop-martyr; optional memorial.

30—Wed. Sixth Day of Christmas Octave.

31—Thurs. Seventh Day of Christmas Octave. St. Sylvester I, pope; optional memorial.

GENERAL PRAYER INTENTION: Renewal of evangelization in Europe. Several times in 1986, Pope John Paul called for the re-evangelization of the Christian nations of Europe and other parts of the world.

MISSION PRAYER INTENTION: Peace among all peoples, in the spirit of Christmas.

TABLE OF MOVABLE FEASTS

Year	Ash Wednesday	Easter	Ascension	Pentecost	Week	Ends	Week	Begins	First Sunday of Advent
					Before Lent		After Pent.		
1987	Mar. 4	Apr. 19	May 28	June 7	8	Mar. 3	10	June 8	Nov. 29
1988	Feb. 17	Apr. 3	May 12	May 22	6	Feb. 16	8	May 23	Nov. 27
1989	Feb. 8	Mar. 26	May 4	May 14	5	Feb. 7	6	May 15	Dec. 3
1990	Feb. 28	Apr. 15	May 24	June 3	8	Feb. 27	9	June 4	Dec. 2
1991	Feb. 13	Mar. 31	May 9	May 19	5	Feb. 12	7	May 20	Dec. 1
1992	Mar. 4	Apr. 19	May 28	June 7	8	Mar. 3	10	June 8	Nov. 29
1993	Feb. 24	Apr. 11	May 20	May 30	7	Feb. 23	9	May 31	Nov. 28
1994	Feb. 16	Apr. 3	May 12	May 22	6	Feb. 15	8	May 23	Nov. 27
1995	Mar. 1	Apr. 16	May 25	June 4	8	Feb. 28	9	June 5	Dec. 3
1996	Feb. 21	Apr. 7	May 16	May 26	7	Feb. 20	8	May 27	Dec. 1
1997	Feb. 12	Mar. 30	May 8	May 18	5	Feb. 11	7	May 19	Nov. 30
1998	Feb. 25	Apr. 12	May 21	May 31	7	Feb. 24	9	June 1	Nov. 29
1999	Feb. 17	Apr. 4	May 13	May 23	6	Feb. 16	8	May 24	Nov. 28
2000	Mar. 8	Apr. 23	June 1	June 11	9	Mar. 7	10	June 12	Dec. 3
2001	Feb. 28	Apr. 15	May 24	June 3	8	Feb. 27	9	June 4	Dec. 2
2002	Feb. 13	Mar. 31	May 9	May 19	5	Feb. 12	7	May 20	Dec. 1
2003	Mar. 5	Apr. 20	May 29	June 8	8	Mar. 4	10	June 9	Nov. 30
2004	Feb. 25	Apr. 11	May 20	May 30	7	Feb. 24	9	May 31	Nov. 28
2005	Feb. 9	Mar. 27	May 5	May 15	5	Feb. 8	7	May 16	Nov. 27
2006	Mar. 1	Apr. 16	May 25	June 4	8	Feb. 28	9	June 5	Dec. 3
2007	Feb. 21	Apr. 8	May 17	May 27	7	Feb. 20	8	May 28	Dec. 2
2008	Feb. 6	Mar. 23	May 1	May 11	4	Feb. 5	6	May 12	Nov. 30
2009	Feb. 25	Apr. 12	May 21	May 31	7	Feb. 24	9	June 1	Nov. 29
2010	Feb. 17	Apr. 4	May 13	May 23	6	Feb. 16	8	May 24	Nov. 28

Season of Ordinary Time

Weeks between the end of the Christmas season and the beginning of Lent, and from the day after Pentecost to the last Sunday of the liturgical year, belong to the season of Ordinary Time. The table indicates the number and terminal date of the week ending the first part, and the number and starting date of the week beginning the second part, of this season. In some years, a week of this season is eliminated because of calendar conditions.

Holiday Masses

Liturgical experiments in recent years have led to the development of votive Masses for national holidays, like those introduced in the U.S. for Thanksgiving Day in 1969 and July 4 in 1972. This development is in line with a custom whereby "from the earliest times the Church has crowned many non-Christian feasts with Christian fulfillment by instituting its own liturgical festivals" to coincide with them.

Labor Day, in lieu of a special votive Mass, may be observed with celebration of the Mass of St. Joseph the Worker.

Readings at Mass

The texts of scriptural readings for Mass on Sundays, holy days and some other days are indicated under the respective dates. The first (A) cycle of readings in the Lectionary is prescribed for the 1987 liturgical year (Nov. 30, 1986, to Nov. 28, 1987); the second (B) cycle is prescribed for the 1988 liturgical year which begins with the first Sunday of Advent, Nov. 29, 1987.

Weekday cycles of readings are the first and second, respectively, for liturgical years 1987 and 1988.

Monthly Prayer Intentions

General and mission intentions chosen and recommended by Pope John Paul II to the prayers of the Apostles of Prayer are given under each month of the calendar. He has expressed his desire that all Catholics make these intentions their own "in the certainty of being united with the Holy Father and praying according to his intentions and desires." These intentions represent the worldwide needs of the Church and its missions as seen through the eyes of the Pope.

HOLY DAYS AND OTHER FEASTS

The following list includes the six holy days of obligation observed in the United States and additional observances of devotional and historical significance. The dignity or rank of observances is indicated by the terms: **solemnity** (highest in rank); **feast; memorial** (for universal observance); **optional memorial** (for celebration by choice).

All Saints, Nov. 1, holy day of obligation, solemnity. Commemorates all the blessed in heaven, and is intended particularly to honor the blessed who have no special feasts. The background of the feast dates to the fourth century when groups of martyrs, and later other saints, were honored on a common day in various places. In 609 or 610, the Pantheon, a pagan temple at Rome, was consecrated as a Christian church for the honor of Our Lady and the martyrs (later all saints). In 835, Gregory IV fixed Nov. 1 as the date of observance.

All Souls, Commemoration of the Faithful Departed, Nov. 2. The dead were prayed for from the earliest days of Christianity. By the sixth century it was customary in Benedictine monasteries to hold a commemoration of deceased members of the order at Pentecost. A common commemoration of all the faithful departed on the day after All Saints was instituted in 998 by St. Odilo, of the Abbey of Cluny, and an observance of this kind was accepted in Rome in the 14th century. In 1915, Benedict XV granted priests throughout the world permission to celebrate three Masses for this commemoration. He also granted a special indulgence for the occasion.

Annunciation of the Lord (formerly, Annunciation of the Blessed Virgin Mary), Mar. 25, solemnity. A feast of the Incarnation which commemorates the announcement by the Archangel Gabriel to the Virgin Mary that she was to become the Mother of Christ (Lk. 1:26-38), and the miraculous conception of Christ by her. The feast was instituted about 430 in the East. The Roman observance dates from the seventh century, when celebration was said to be universal.

Ascension of the Lord, movable observance held 40 days after Easter, holy day of obligation, solemnity. Commemorates the Ascension of Christ into heaven 40 days after his Resurrection from the dead (Mk. 16:19; Lk. 24:51; Acts 1:2). The feast recalls the completion of Christ's mission on earth for the salvation of all people and his entry into heaven with glorified human nature. The Ascension is a pledge of the final glorification of all who achieve salvation. Documentary evidence of the feast dates from early in the fifth century, but it was observed long before that time in connection with Pentecost and Easter.

Ash Wednesday, movable observance, six and one-half weeks before Easter. It was set as the first day of Lent by Pope St. Gregory the Great (590-604) with the extension of an earlier and shorter penitential season to a total period including 40 weekdays of fasting before Easter. It is a day of fast and abstinence. Ashes, symbolic of penance, are blessed and distributed among the faithful during the day. They are used to mark the forehead with the Sign of the Cross, with the reminder: "Remember, man, that you are dust, and unto dust you shall return," or: "Repent, and believe the Good News."

Assumption Aug. 15, holy day of obligation, solemnity. Commemorates the taking into heaven of Mary, soul and body, at the end of her life on earth, a truth of faith that was proclaimed a dogma by Pius XII on Nov. 1, 1950. One of the oldest and most solemn feasts of Mary, it has a history dating back to at least the seventh century when its celebration was already established at Jerusalem and Rome.

Baptism of the Lord, movable, usually celebrated on the Sunday after January 6, feast. Recalls the baptism of Christ by John the Baptist (Mk. 1:9-11), an event associated with the liturgy of the Epiphany. This baptism was the occasion for Christ's manifestation of himself at the beginning of his public life.

Birth of Mary, Sept. 8, feast. This is a very old feast which originated in the East and found place in the Roman liturgy in the seventh century.

Candlemas Day, Feb. 2. See Presentation of the Lord.

Chair of Peter, The feast, which has been in the Roman calendar since 336, is a liturgical expression of belief in the episcopacy and hierarchy of the Church.

Christmas, Birth of Our Lord Jesus Christ, Dec. 25, holy day of obligation, solemnity. Commemorates the birth of Christ (Lk. 2:1-20). This event was originally commemorated in the East on the feast of Epiphany or Theophany. The Christmas feast itself originated in the West; by 354 it was certainly kept on Dec. 25. This date may have been set for the observance to offset pagan ceremonies held at about the same time to commemorate the birth of the sun at the winter solstice. There are texts for three Christmas Masses — at midnight, dawn and during the day.

Christ the King, movable, celebrated on the last Sunday of the liturgical year, solemnity. Commemorates the royal prerogatives of Christ and is equivalent to a declaration of his rights to the homage, service and fidelity of men in all phases of individual and social life. Pius XI instituted the feast Dec. 11, 1925.

Conversion of St. Paul, Jan. 25, feast. An observance mentioned in some calendars from the 8th and 9th centuries. Pope Innocent III (1198-1216) ordered its observance with great solemnity.

Corpus Christi, movable, celebrated on the Thursday (or Sunday, as in the U.S.) following Trinity Sunday, solemnity. Commemorates the institution of the Holy Eucharist (Mt. 26:26-28). The feast originated at Liege in 1246 and was extended throughout the Church in the West by Urban IV in 1264. St. Thomas Aquinas composed the Liturgy of the Hours for the feast.

Dedication of St. John Lateran, Nov. 9, feast. Commemorates the first public consecration of a church, that of the Basilica of the Most Holy Savior by Pope St. Sylvester Nov. 9, 324. The church, as well as the Lateran Palace, was the gift of Emperor Constantine. Since the 12th century it has been known as St. John Lateran, in honor of John the Baptist after whom the adjoining baptistery was named. It was rebuilt by Innocent X (1644-55), reconsecrated by Benedict XIII in 1726, and enlarged by Leo XIII (1878-1903). This basilica is regarded as the church of highest dignity in Rome and throughout the Roman Rite.

Dedication of St. Mary Major, Aug. 5, optional memorial. Commemorates the rebuilding and dedication by Pope Sixtus III (432-40) of a church in honor of Blessed Mary the Virgin. This is the Basilica of St. Mary Major on the Esquiline Hill in Rome. An earlier building was erected during the pontificate of Liberius (352-66); according to legend, it was located on a site covered by a miraculous fall of snow seen by a nobleman favored with a vision of Mary.

Easter, movable celebration held on the first Sunday after the full moon following the vernal equinox (between Mar. 22 and Apr. 25), solemnity with an octave. Commemorates the Resurrection of Christ from the dead (Mk. 16:1-7). The observance of this mystery, kept since the first days of the Church, extends throughout the Easter season which lasts until the feast of Pentecost, a period of 50 days. Every Sunday in the year is regarded as a "little" Easter. The date of Easter determines the dates of movable feasts, such as Ascension and Pentecost, and the number of weeks before Lent and after Pentecost.

Easter Vigil, called by St. Augustine the "Mother of All Vigils," the night before Easter. Ceremonies are all related to the Resurrection and renewal-in-grace theme of Easter: blessing of the new fire, procession with the Easter Candle, singing of the Easter Proclamation (Exsultet), Liturgy of the Word with at least three Old Testament readings, the Litany of Saints, blessing of water, baptism of converts and infants, renewal of baptismal promises, Liturgy of the Eucharist. The vigil ceremonies are held after sundown.

Epiphany of Our Lord, Jan. 6 or (in the U.S.) a Sunday between Jan. 2 and 8, solemnity. Commemorates the manifestations of the divinity of Christ. It is one of the oldest Christian feasts, with an Eastern origin traceable to the beginning of the third century and antedating the Western feast of Christmas. Originally, it commemorated the manifestations of Christ's divinity — or Theophany — in his birth, the homage of the Magi, and baptism by John the Baptist. Later, the first two of these commemorations were transferred to Christmas when the Eastern Church adopted that feast between 380 and 430. The central feature of the Eastern observance now is the manifestation or declaration of Christ's divinity in his baptism and at the beginning of his public life. The Epiphany was adopted by the Western Church during the same period in which the Eastern Church accepted Christmas. In the Roman Rite, commemoration is made in the Mass of the homage of the wise men from the East (Mt. 2:1-12).

Good Friday, the Friday before Easter, the second day of the Easter Triduum. Liturgical elements of the observance are commemoration of the Passion and Death of Christ in the reading of the Passion (according to John), special prayers for the Church and people of all ranks, the veneration of the Cross, and a Communion service. The celebration takes place in the afternoon, preferably at 3:00 p.m.

Guardian Angels, Oct. 2, memorial. Commemorates the angels who protect people from spiritual and physical dangers and assist them in doing good. A feast in their honor celebrated in Spain in the 16th century was extended to the whole Church by Paul V in 1608. In 1670, Clement X set Oct. 2 as the date of observance. Earlier, guardian angels were honored liturgically in conjunction with the feast of St. Michael.

Holy Family, movable observance on the Sunday after Christmas, feast. Commemorates the Holy Family of Jesus, Mary and Joseph as the model of domestic society, holiness and virtue. The devotional background of the feast was very strong in the 17th century. In the 18th century, in prayers composed for a special Mass, a Canadian bishop likened the Christian family to the Holy Family. Leo XIII consecrated families to the Holy Family. In 1921, Benedict XV extended the Divine Office and Mass of the feast to the whole Church.

Holy Innocents, Dec. 28, feast. Commemorates the infants who suffered death at the hands of Herod's soldiers seeking to kill the child Jesus (Mt. 2:13-18). A feast in their honor has been observed since the fifth century.

Holy Saturday, the day before Easter. The Sacrifice of the Mass is not celebrated, and Holy Communion may be given only as Viaticum. If possible the Easter fast should be observed until the Easter Vigil.

Holy Thursday, the Thursday before Easter. Commemorates the institution of the sacraments of the Eucharist and holy orders, and the washing of the feet of the Apostles by Jesus at the Last Supper. The Mass of the Lord's Supper in the evening marks the beginning of the Easter Triduum. Following the Mass, there is a procession of the Blessed Sacrament to a place of reposition for adoration by the faithful. At an earlier Mass of Chrism, bishops bless oils (of catechumens, chrism, the sick) for use during the year. (For pastoral reasons, diocesan bishops may permit additional Masses, but these should not overshadow the principal Mass of the Lord's Supper.)

Immaculate Conception, Dec. 8, holy day of obligation, solemnity. Commemorates the fact that Mary, in view of her calling to be the Mother of Christ and in virtue of his merits, was preserved from the first moment of her conception from original sin and was filled with grace from the very beginning of her life. She was the only person so preserved from original sin. The present form of the feast dates from Dec. 8, 1854, when Pius IX defined the dogma of the Immaculate Conception. An earlier feast of the Conception, which testified to long-existing belief in this truth, was observed in the East by the eighth century, in Ireland in the ninth, and subsequently in European countries. In 1846, Mary was proclaimed patroness of the U.S. under this title.

Immaculate Heart of Mary, Saturday following the second Sunday after Pentecost, optional memorial. On May 4, 1944, Pius XII ordered this feast observed throughout the Church in order to obtain Mary's intercession for "peace among nations, freedom for the Church, the conversion of sinners, the love of purity and the practice of virtue." Two years earlier, he consecrated the entire human race to Mary under this title. Devotion to Mary under the title of her Most Pure Heart originated during the Middle Ages. It was given great impetus in the 17th century by the preaching of St. John Eudes, who was the first to celebrate a Mass and Divine Office of Mary under this title. A feast, celebrated in various places and on different dates, was authorized in 1799.

Joachim and Ann, July 26, memorial. Commemorates the parents of Mary. A joint feast, celebrated Sept. 9, originated in the East near the end of the sixth century. Devotion to Ann, introduced in the eighth century at Rome, became widespread in Europe in the 14th century; her feast was extended throughout the Latin Church in 1584. A feast of Joachim was introduced in the West in the 15th century.

John the Baptist, Birth, June 24, solemnity. The precursor of Christ, whose cousin he was, was commemorated universally in the liturgy by the fourth century. He is the only saint, except the Blessed Virgin Mary, whose birthday is observed as a feast. Another feast, on Aug. 29, commemorates his passion and death at the order of Herod (Mk. 6:14-29).

Joseph, Mar. 19, solemnity. Joseph is honored as the husband of the Blessed Virgin Mary, the patron and protector of the universal Church and workman. Devotion to him already existed in the eighth century in the East, and in the 11th in the West. Various feasts were celebrated before the 15th century when Mar. 19 was fixed for his commemoration; this feast was extended to the whole Church in 1621 by Gregory XV. In 1955, Pius XII instituted the feast of St. Joseph the Workman for observance May 1; this feast, which may be celebrated by local option, supplanted the Solemnity or Patronage of St. Joseph formerly observed on the third Wednesday after Easter. St. Joseph was proclaimed protector and patron of the universal Church in 1870 by Pius IX.

Michael, Gabriel and Raphael, Archangels, Sept. 29, feast. A feast bearing the title of Dedication of St. Michael the Archangel formerly commemorated on this date the consecration in 530 of a church near Rome in honor of Michael, the first angel given a liturgical feast. For a while, this feast was combined with a commemoration of the Guardian Angels. The separate feasts of Gabriel (Mar. 24) and Raphael (Oct. 24) were suppressed by the calendar in effect since 1970 and this joint feast of the three archangels was instituted.

Octave of Christmas, Jan. 1. See Solemnity of Mary, Mother of God.

Our Lady of Sorrows, Sept. 15, memorial. Recalls the sorrows experienced by Mary in her association with Christ: the prophecy of Simeon (Lk. 2:34-35), the flight into Egypt (Mt. 2:13-21), the three-day separation from Jesus (Lk. 2:41-50), and four incidents connected with the Passion: her meeting with Christ on the way to Calvary, the crucifixion, the removal of Christ's body from the cross, and his burial (Mt. 27:31-61; Mk. 15:20-47; Lk. 23:26-56; Jn. 19:17-42). A Mass and Divine Office of the feast were celebrated by the Servites, especially, in the 17th century, and in 1817 Pius VII extended the observance to the whole Church.

Our Lady of the Rosary, Oct. 7, memorial. Commemorates the Virgin Mary through recall of the mysteries of the Rosary which recapitulate events in her life and the life of Christ. The feast was instituted to commemorate a Christian victory over invading Mohammedan forces at Lepanto on Oct. 7, 1571, and was extended throughout the Church by Clement XI in 1716.

Passion Sunday (formerly called **Palm Sunday**), the Sunday before Easter. Marks the start of Holy Week by recalling the triumphal entry of Christ into Jerusalem at the beginning of the last week of his life (Mt. 21:1-9). A procession and other ceremonies commemorating this event were held in Jerusalem from very early Christian times and were adopted in Rome by the ninth century, when the blessing of palm for the occasion was introduced. Full liturgical observance includes the blessing of palm and a procession before the principal Mass of the day. The Passion, by Matthew, Mark or Luke, is read during the Mass.

Pentecost, also called **Whitsunday,** movable celebration held 50 days after Easter, solemnity. Commemorates the descent of the Holy Spirit upon the Apostles, the preaching of Peter and the other Apostles to Jews in Jerusalem, the baptism and aggregation of some 3,000 persons to the Christian community (Acts 2:1-41). It is regarded as the birthday of the Catholic Church. The original observance of the feast antedated the earliest extant documentary evidence from the third century.

Peter and Paul, Sts., June 29, solemnity. Commemorates the martyrdoms of Peter by crucifixion and Paul by beheading during the Neronian persecution. This joint commemoration of the chief Apostles dates at least from 258 at Rome.

Presentation of the Lord (formerly called Purification of the Blessed Virgin Mary, also Candlemas), Feb. 2, feast. Commemorates the presentation of Jesus in the Temple — according to prescriptions of Mosaic Law (Lv. 12:2-8; Ex. 13:2; Lk. 2:22-32) — and the purification of Mary 40 days after his birth. In the East, where the feast antedated fourth century testimony regarding its existence, it was observed primarily as a feast of Our Lord; in the West, where it was adopted later, it was regarded more as a feast of Mary until the calendar in effect since 1970. Its date was set for Feb. 2 after the celebration of Christmas was fixed for Dec. 25, late in the fourth century. The blessing of candles, probably in commemoration of Christ who was the Light to enlighten the Gentiles, became common about the 11th century and gave the feast the secondary name of Candlemas.

Queenship of Mary, Aug. 22, memorial. Commemorates the high dignity of Mary as Queen of heaven, angels and men. Universal observance of the memorial was ordered by Pius XII in the encyclical *Ad Caeli Reginam*, Oct. 11, 1954, near the close of a Marian Year observed in connection with the centenary of the proclamation of the dogma of the Immaculate Conception and four years after the proclamation of the dogma of the Assumption. The original date of the memorial was May 31.

Resurrection. See Easter.

Sacred Heart of Jesus, movable observance held on the Friday after the second Sunday after Pentecost (Corpus Christi, in the U.S.), solemnity. The object of the devotion is the divine Person of Christ, whose heart is the symbol of his love for men — for whom he accomplished the work of Redemption. The Mass and Office now used on the feast were prescribed by Pius XI in 1929. Devotion to the Sacred Heart was introduced into the liturgy in the 17th century through the efforts of St. John Eudes who composed an Office and Mass for the feast. It was furthered as the result of the revelations of St. Margaret Mary Alacoque after 1675 and by the work of Claude de la Colombiere, S.J. In 1765, Clement XIII approved a Mass and Office for the feast, and in 1856 Pius IX extended the observance throughout the Roman Rite.

Solemnity of Mary, Mother of God, Jan. 1, holy day of obligation, solemnity. The calendar in effect since 1970, in accord with Eastern tradition, reinstated the Marian character of this commemoration on the octave day of Christmas. The former feast of the Circumcision, dating at least from the first half of the sixth century, marked the initiation of Jesus (Lk. 2:21) in Judaism and by analogy focused attention on the initiation of persons in the Christian religion and their incorporation in Christ through baptism. The feast of the Solemnity supplants the former feast of the Maternity of Mary observed on Oct. 11.

Transfiguration of the Lord, Aug. 6, feast. Commemorates the revelation of his divinity by Christ to Peter, James and John on Mt. Tabor (Mt. 17:1-9). The feast, which is very old, was extended throughout the universal Church in 1457 by Callistus III.

Trinity, Most Holy, movable observance held on the Sunday after Pentecost, solemnity. Commemorates the most sublime mystery of the Christian faith, i.e., that there are Three Divine Persons — Father, Son and Holy Spirit — in one God (Mt. 28:18-20). A votive Mass of the Most Holy Trinity dates from the seventh century; an Office was composed in the 10th century; in 1334, John XXII extended the feast to the universal Church.

Triumph of the Cross, Sept. 14, feast. Commemorates the finding of the cross on which Christ was crucified, in 326 through the efforts of St. Helena, mother of Constantine; the consecration of the Basilica of the Holy Sepulchre nearly 10 years later: and the recovery in 628 or 629 by Emperor Heraclius of a major portion of the cross which had been removed by the Persians from its place of veneration at Jerusalem. The feast originated in Jerusalem and spread through the East before being adopted in the West. General adoption followed the building at Rome of the Basilica of the Holy Cross "in Jerusalem," so called because it was the place of enshrinement of a major portion of the cross of crucifixion.

Visitation, May 31, feast. Commemorates Mary's visit to her cousin Elizabeth after the Annunciation and before the birth of John the Baptist, the precursor of Christ (Lk. 1:39-47). The feast had a medieval origin and was observed in the Franciscan Order before being extended throughout the Church by Urban VI in 1389. It is one of the feasts of the Incarnation and is notable for its recall of the Magnificat, one of the few New Testament canticles, which acknowledges the unique gifts of God to Mary because of her role in the redemptive work of Christ. The canticle is recited at Evening Prayer in the Liturgy of the Hours.

SAINTS

Biographical sketches of additional saints are under other Almanac titles. See Index.

An asterisk with a feast date indicates that a memorial or feast is observed according to the general Roman-Rite calendars.

Adjutor, St. (d. 1131): Norman knight; fought in First Crusade; monk-recluse after his return; legendary accounts of incidents on journey to Crusade probably account for his patronage of yachtsmen; Apr. 30.

Agatha, St. (d. c. 250): Sicilian virgin-martyr; her intercession credited in Sicily with stopping eruptions of Mt. Etna; patron of nurses; Feb. 5*.

Agnes, St. (d. c. 304): Roman virgin-martyr; martyred at age of 10 or 12; patron of young girls; Jan. 21*.

Aloysius Gonzaga, St. (1568-1591): Italian Jesuit; died while nursing plague-stricken; canonized 1726; patron of youth; June 21*.

Amand, St. (d. c. 676): Apostle of Belgium; b. France; established monasteries throughout Belgium; Feb. 6.

Andre Bessette, Bl. (Bro. Andre) (1845-1937): Canadian Holy Cross Brother; prime mover in building of St. Joseph's Oratory, Montreal; beatified May 23, 1982; Jan. 6* (U.S.).

Andre Grasset de Saint Sauveur, Bl. (1758-1792): Canadian priest; martyred in France, Sept. 2, 1792, during the Revolution; one of a group called the Martyrs of Paris who were beatified in 1926; Sept. 2.

Andrew Corsini, St. (1302-1373): Italian Carmelite; bishop of Fiesoli; mediator between quarrelsome Italian states; canonized 1629; Feb. 4.

Andrew Fournet, St. (1752-1834): French priest; co-founder with St. Jeanne Elizabeth des Anges of the Congregation of Daughters of the Cross; canonized 1933; May 13.

Andrew Kim, Paul Chong and Companions, Sts. (d. between 1839-1867): Korean martyrs (103) killed in persecutions of 1839, 1846, 1866, and 1867; among them were Andrew Kim, the first Korean priest, and Paul Chong, lay apostle; canonized May 6, 1984, during Pope John Paul II's visit to Korea; entered into General Roman Calendar, 1985, as a memorial. Sept. 20*.

Angela Merici, St. (1474-1540): Italian nun; foundress of Institute of St. Ursula, 1535, the first teaching order of nuns in the Church; canonized 1807; Jan. 27*.

Angelico, Bl. (Fra Angelico; John of Faesulis) (1378-1455): Dominican; Florentine painter of early Renaissance proclaimed blessed by John Paul II, 1983; patron of artists; Feb. 18.

Anne Mary Javouhey, Bl. (1779-1851): French virgin; foundress of Institute of St. Joseph of Cluny, 1812; beatified 1950; July 15.

Ansgar, St. (801-865): Bishop, Benedictine monk; b. near Amiens; missionary in Denmark, Sweden, Norway and Northern Germany; apostle of Denmark; Feb. 3*.

Anthony Abbot, St. (c. 251-c. 354): Egyptian hermit; patriarch of all monks; established communities for hermits which became models for monastic life, especially in the East; friend and supporter of St. Athanasius in the latter's struggle with the Arians; Jan. 17*.

Anthony Mary Claret, St. (1807-1870): Spanish priest; founder of Missionary Sons of the Immaculate Heart of Mary (Claretians), 1849; archbishop of Santiago, Cuba, 1851-57; canonized 1950; Oct. 24*.

Anthony Mary Zaccaria, St. (1502-1539): Italian priest; founder of Barnabites (Clerks Regular of St. Paul), 1530; canonized 1897; July 5*.

Apollonia, St. (d. 249): Deaconess of Alexandria; martyred during persecution of Decius; her patronage of dentists probably rests on tradition that her teeth were broken by pincers by her persecutors; Feb. 9.

Augustine of Canterbury, St. (d. 604 or 605): Italian missionary; apostle of the English; sent by Pope Gregory I with 40 monks to evangelize England; arrived there 597; first archbishop of Canterbury; May 27*.

Benedict of Nursia, St. (c. 480-547): Abbot; founder of monasticism in Western Europe; established monastery at Monte Cassino; proclaimed patron of Europe by Paul VI in 1964; July 11*.

Benedict the Black (il Moro), St. (1526-1589): Sicilian Franciscan; born a slave; joined Franciscans as lay brother; appointed guardian and novice master; canonized 1807; Apr. 4.

Bernadette Soubirous, St. (1844-1879): French peasant girl favored with series of visions of Blessed Virgin Mary at Lourdes (see Lourdes Apparitions); joined Institute of Sisters of Notre Dame at Nevers, 1866; canonized 1933; Apr. 16.

Bernard of Montjoux (or Menthon), St. (d. 1081): Italian priest; founded Alpine hospices near the two passes named for him; patron of mountaineers; May 28.

Bernardine of Feltre, Bl. (1439-1494): Italian Franciscan preacher; a founder of montes pietatis; Sept. 28.

Bernardine of Siena, St. (1380-1444): Italian Franciscan; noted preacher and missioner; spread of devotion to Holy Name is attributed to him; represented in art holding to his breast the monogram IHS; canonized 1450; May 20*.

Blase, St. (d. c. 316): Armenian bishop; martyr; the blessing of throats on his feast day derives from tradition that he miraculously saved the life of a boy who had half-swallowed a fish bone; Feb. 3*.

Boniface (Winfrid), St. (d. 754): English Benedictine; bishop, martyr; apostle of Germany; established monastery at Fulda which became center of German missionary work; archbishop of Mainz; martyred near Dukkum in Holland; June 5*.

Brendan, St. (c. 489-583): Irish abbot; founded monasteries; his patronage of sailors probably rests on tradition that he made a seven-year voyage in search of a fabled paradise; called Brendan the Navigator; May 16.

Bridget (Brigid), St. (c. 450-525): Irish nun; founded nunnery at Kildare, the first erected on Irish soil; patron, with Sts. Patrick and Columba, of Ireland; Feb. 1.

Bridget (Birgitta), St. (c. 1303-1373): Swedish mystic; widow; foundress of Order of Our Savior (Brigittines); canonized 1391; wrote *Revelationes,* accounts of her visions; patroness of Sweden; July 23*.

Bruno, St. (1030-1101): German monk; founded Carthusians, 1084, in France; Oct. 6*.

Cabrini, Mother: See Frances Xavier Cabrini.

Cajetan of Thiene, St. (1480-1547): Italian lawyer; religious reformer; a founder of Oratory of Divine Love, forerunner of the Theatines; canonized 1671; Aug. 7*.

Callistus I, St. (d. 222): Pope, 217-222; martyr; condemned Sabellianism and other heresies; advocated a policy of mercy toward repentant sinners; Oct. 14*.

Camillus de Lellis, St. (1550-1614): Italian priest; founder of Camillians (Ministers of the Sick); canonized 1746; patron of the sick and of nurses; July 14*.

Casimir, St. (1458-1484): Polish prince; grand duke of Lithuania; noted for his piety; buried at cathedral in Vilna, Lithuania; canonized 1521; patron of Poland and Lithuania; Mar. 4*.

Cassian, St. (d. 298): Roman martyr; an official court stenographer who declared himself a Christian; patron of stenographers; Dec. 3.

Catherine Laboure, St. (1806-1876): French nun; favored with series of visions; first Miraculous Medal (see Index) struck as the result of one of the visions; canonized 1947; Nov. 28.

Catherine of Bologna, St. (1413-1463): Italian Poor Clare; mystic, writer, artist; canonized 1712; patron of artists; May 9.

Cecilia, St. (2nd-3rd century): Roman virgin-martyr; traditional patron of musicians; Nov. 22*.

Charles Borromeo, St. (1538-1584): Italian cardinal; nephew of Pope Pius IV; cardinal bishop of Milan; influential figure in Church reform in Italy; promoted education of clergy; canonized 1610; Nov. 4*.

Charles Lwanga and Companions, Sts. (d. 1886 and 1887): Martyrs of Uganda; pages of King Mwanga of Uganda; Charles Lwanga and 12 companions were martyred near Rubaga, June 3, 1886; the other nine were martyred between May 26, 1886, and Jan. 27, 1887; canonized 1964; first martyrs of black Africa; June 3*.

Christopher, St. (3rd cent.): Early Christian martyr inscribed in Roman calendar about 1550; feast relegated to particular calendars because of legendary nature of accounts of his life; traditional patron of travelers; July 25.

Clare, St. (1194-1253): Foundress of Poor Clares; b. at Assisi; later joined in religious life by her sisters Agnes and Beatrice, and her mother Ortolana; canonized 1255; patroness of television; Aug. 11*.

Clement I, St. (d. c. 100): Pope, 88-97; third successor of St. Peter; wrote important letter to Church in Corinth settling disputes there; venerated as a martyr; Nov. 23*.

Columba, St. (521-597): Irish monk; founded monasteries in Ireland; missionary in Scotland; established monastery at Iona which became the center for conversion of Picts, Scots, and Northern English; Scotland's most famous saint; June 9.

Columban, St. (545-615): Irish monk; scholar; founded monasteries in England and Brittany (famous abbey of Luxeuil), forced into exile because of his criticism of Frankish court; spent last years in northern Italy where he founded abbey at Bobbio; Nov. 23*.

Contardo Ferrini, Bl. (1859-1902): Italian secular Franciscan; model of the Catholic professor; beatified 1947; patron of universities; Oct. 20.

Cornelius, St. (d. 253): Pope, 251-253; promoted a policy of mercy with respect to readmission of repentant Christians who had fallen away during the persecution of Decius *(lapsi)*; banished from Rome during persecution of Gallus; regarded as a martyr; Sept. 16 (with Cyprian)*.

Cosmas and Damian, Sts. (d. c. 303): Arabian twin brothers; physicians who were martyred during Diocletian persecution; patrons of physicians; Sept. 26*.

Crispin and Crispinian, Sts. (3rd cent.): Early Christian martyrs; said to have met their deaths in Gaul; patrons of shoemakers, a trade they pursued; Oct. 25.

Crispin of Viterbo, St. (1668-1750): Capuchin brother; beatified 1806; canonized June 20, 1982; May 21.

Cyprian, St. (d. 258): Early ecclesiastical writer; b. Africa; bishop of Carthage, 249-258; supported Pope St. Cornelius concerning the readmission of Christians who had apostasized in time of persecution; erred in his teaching that baptism administered by heretics and schismatics was invalid; wrote *De Unitate*; Sept. 16 (with St. Cornelius)*.

Cyril and Methodius, Sts.: Greek missionaries; brothers venerated as apostles of the Slavs; Cyril (d. 869) and Methodius (d. 885) began their missionary work in Moravia in 863; developed a Slavonic alphabet; eventually their use of the vernacular in the liturgy was approved; declared patrons of Europe with St. Benedict, Dec. 31, 1980; Feb. 14*.

Damasus I, St. (d. 384): Pope, 366-384; opposed Arians and Apollinarians; commissioned St. Jerome to work on Bible translation; developed Roman liturgy; Dec. 11*.

Damian, St.: See Cosmas and Damian, Sts.

David, St. (5th-6th cent.): Welsh monk; founded monastery at Menevia; patron saint of Wales; Mar. 1.

Denis and Companions, Sts. (d. 3rd cent.): Denis, bishop of Paris, and two companions identified by early writers as Rusticus, a priest, and Eleutherius, a deacon; martyred near Paris; Denis is popularly regarded as apostle of France; Oct. 9*.

Dismas, St. (1st cent.): Name given to repentant thief (Good Thief) to whom Jesus promised salvation; regarded as patron of prisoners; Mar. 25.

Dominic, St. (Dominic de Guzman) (1170-1221): Spanish priest; founder of Dominican Order (Friars Preachers), 1215; preached against the Albigensian heresy; a contemporary of St. Francis of Assisi; canonized 1234; Aug. 8*.

Dominic Savio, St. (1842-1857): Italian youth; pupil of St. John Bosco; died before his 15th birthday; canonized 1954; patron of choir boys; May 6.

Dunstan, St. (c. 910-988): English monk; archbishop of Canterbury; initiated reforms in religious life; royal counselor to several kings; considered one of greatest Anglo-Saxon saints; patron of armorers, goldsmiths, locksmiths, jewelers; May 17.

Durocher, Marie-Rose, Bl. (1811-1849): Canadian religious; foundress of Sisters of Holy Names of Jesus and Mary; beatified May 23, 1982; Oct. 6* (in U.S.).

Dymphna, St. (dates uncertain): Nothing certain known of her life; presumably she was an Irish maiden whose relics were discovered at Gheel near Antwerp, Belgium, in the 13th century; since that time many cases of mental illness and epilepsy have been cured at her shrine; patron of those suffering from mental illness; May 15.

Edmund Campion, St. (1540-1581): English Jesuit; convert 1573; martyred at Tyburn; canonized 1970, one of the Forty English and Welsh Martyrs; Dec. 1.

Eligius, St. (c. 590-660): Born in Gaul; founded monasteries and convents; bishop of Noyon and Tournai; famous worker in gold and silver; Dec. 1.

Elizabeth Bayley Seton, St. (1774-1821): American foundress; convert, 1805; founded Sisters of Charity in the U.S.; beatified 1963; canonized Sept. 14, 1975; the first American-born saint; Jan. 4 (U.S.)*.

Elizabeth of Hungary, St. (1207-1231): Became secular Franciscan after death of her husband in 1227; devoted life to poor and destitute; a patron of the Secular Franciscan Order; Nov. 17*.

Elizabeth of Portugal, St. (1271-1336): Queen of Portugal; b. Spain; retired to Poor Clare convent as a secular Franciscan after the death of her husband; July 4*.

Erasmus, St. (d. 303): Life surrounded by legend; martyred during Diocletian persecution; patron of sailors; June 2.

Ethelbert, St. (552-676): King of Kent; baptized by St. Augustine 597; issued legal code; furthered spread of Christianity; Feb. 26.

Euphrasia Pelletier, St. (1796-1868): French nun; founded Sisters of the Good Shepherd at Angers, 1829; canonized 1940; Apr. 24.

Eusebius of Vercelli, St. (283-370): Italian bishop; exiled from his see for a time because of his opposition to Arianism; considered a martyr because of sufferings he endured; Aug. 2*.

Fabian, St. (d. 250): Pope, 236-250; martyred under Decius; Jan. 20*.

Felicity, St.: See Perpetua and Felicity, Sts.

Ferdinand III, St. (1198-1252): King of Castile and Leon; waged successful crusade against Mohammedans in Spain; founded university at Salamanca; canonized 1671; May 30.

Fiacre, St. (d. c. 670): Irish hermit; patron of gardeners; Aug. 30.

Fidelis of Sigmaringen, St. (Mark Rey) (1577-1622): German Capuchin; lawyer before he joined the Capuchins; missionary to Swiss Protestants; stabbed to death by peasants who were told he was agent of Austrian emperor; Apr. 24*.

Frances of Rome, St. (1384-1440): Italian model for housewives and widows; happily married for 40 years; after death of her husband in 1436 joined community of Benedictine Oblates she had founded; canonized 1608; patron of motorists; Mar. 9*.

Frances Xavier Cabrini, St. (Mother Cabrini) (1850-1917): American foundress; b. Italy; foundress of Missionary Sisters of the Sacred Heart, 1877; settled in the U.S. 1889; became an American citizen at Seattle 1909; worked among Italian immigrants; canonized 1946, the first American citizen so honored; Nov. 13 (U.S.)*.

Francis Borgia, St. (1510-1572): Spanish Jesuit; joined Jesuits after death of his wife in 1546; became general of the Order, 1565; Oct. 10.

Francis of Assisi, St. (Giovanni di Bernardone) (1182-1226): Founder of the Franciscans, 1209; received stigmata 1224; canonized 1228; one of best known and best loved saints; patron of Italy, Catholic Action and ecologists; Oct. 4*.

Francis of Paola, St. (1416-1507): Italian hermit; founder of Minim Friars; Apr. 2*.

Francis Xavier, St. (1506-1552): Spanish Jesuit; missionary to Far East; canonized 1602; patron of foreign missions; considered one of greatest Christian missionaries; Dec. 3*.

Gabriel of the Sorrowful Mother, St. (Francis Possenti) (1838-1862): Italian Passionist; died while a scholastic; canonized 1920; Feb. 27.

Genesius, St. (d. c. 300): Roman actor; according to legend, was converted while performing a burlesque of Christian baptism and was subsequently martyred; patron of actors; Aug. 25.

Genevieve, St. (422-500): French nun; a patroness and protectress of Paris; events of her life not authenticated; Jan. 3.

George, St. (d. c. 300): Martyr, probably during Diocletian persecution in Palestine; all other incidents of his life, including story of the dragon, are legendary; patron of England; Apr. 23*.

Gerard Majella, St. (1725-1755): Italian Redemptorist lay brother; noted for supernatural occurrences in his life including bilocation and reading of consciences; canonized 1904; patron of mothers; Oct. 16.

Gertrude, St. (1256-1302): German mystic; writer; helped spread devotion to the Sacred Heart; Nov. 16*.

Gregory VII (Hildebrand), St. (1020?-1085): Pope, 1075-1085; Benedictine monk; adviser to several popes; as pope, strengthened interior life of Church and fought against lay investiture; driven from Rome by Henry IV; died in exile; May 25*.

Gregory the Illuminator, St. (257-332): Martyr; bishop; apostle and patron saint of Armenia; helped free Armenia from the Persians; Sept. 30.

Hedwig, St. (1174-1243): Moravian noblewoman; married duke of Silesia, head of Polish royal family; fostered religious life in country; canonized 1266; Oct. 16*.

Helena, St. (250-330): Empress; mother of Constantine the Great; associated with discovery of the True Cross; Aug. 18.

Henry, St. (972-1024): Bavarian emperor; cooperated with Benedictine abbeys in restoration of ecclesiastical and social discipline; canonized 1146; July 13*.

Hippolytus, St. (d. c. 236): Roman priest; opposed Pope St. Callistus I in his teaching about the readmission of Christians who had apostasized during time of persecution; elected antipope; reconciled before his martyrdom; important ecclesiastical writer; Aug. 13*.

Hubert, St. (d. 727): Bishop; his patronage of hunters is based on legend that he was converted while hunting; Nov. 3.

Hugh of Cluny (the Great), St. (1024-1109): Abbot of Benedictine foundation at Cluny; supported popes in efforts to reform ecclesiastical abuses; canonized 1120; Apr. 29.

Ignatius of Antioch, St. (d. c. 107): Early ecclesiastical writer; martyr; bishop of Antioch in Syria for 40 years; Oct. 17*.

Ignatius of Loyola, St. (1491-1556): Spanish soldier; renounced military career after recovering from wounds received at siege of Pampeluna (Pamplona) in 1521; founded Society of Jesus (Jesuits), 1534, at Paris; canonized 1622; author *The Book of Spiritual Exercises;* July 31*.

Irenaeus of Lyons, St. (130-202): Early ecclesiastical writer; opposed Gnosticism; bishop of Lyons; traditionally regarded as a martyr; June 28*.

Isidore the Farmer, St. (d. 1170): Spanish layman; farmer; canonized 1622; patron of farmers; May 15 (U.S.).*

Jane Frances de Chantal, St. (1572-1641): French widow; foundress, under guidance of St. Francis de Sales, of Order of the Visitation; canonized 1767; Dec. 12*.

Januarius (Gennaro), St. (d. 304): Bishop of Benevento; martyred during Diocletian persecution; fame rests on liquefaction of some of his blood preserved in a phial at Naples, an unexplained phenomenon which has occurred regularly several times each year for over 400 years; declared patron of Campania region around Naples, 1980; Sept. 19*.

Jerome Emiliani, St. (1481-1537): Venetian priest; founded Somascan Fathers, 1532, for care of orphans; canonized 1767; patron of orphans and abandoned children; Feb. 8*.

Joan of Arc, St. (1412-1431): French heroine, called The Maid of Orleans, La Pucelle; led

French army against English invaders; captured by Burgundians, turned over to ecclesiastical court on charge of heresy, found guilty and burned at the stake; her innocence was declared in 1456; canonized 1920; patroness of France; May 30.

John I, St. (d. 526): Pope, 523-526; martyr; May 18*.

John Baptist de la Salle, St. (1651-1719): French priest; founder of Brothers of the Christian Schools, 1680; canonized 1900; Apr. 7*.

John Berchmans, St. (1599-1621): Belgian Jesuit scholastic; patron of Mass servers; canonized 1888; Aug. 13.

John Bosco, St. (1815-1888): Italian priest; founded Salesians, 1859, for education of boys and cofounded the Daughters of Mary Help of Christians for education of girls; canonized 1934; Jan. 31*.

John Capistran, St. (1386-1456): Italian Franciscan; preacher; papal diplomat; canonized 1690; declared patron of military chaplains, Feb. 10, 1984. Oct. 23*.

John Eudes, St. (1601-1680): French priest; founder of Sisters of Our Lady of Charity of Refuge, 1642, and Congregation of Jesus-Mary (Eudists), 1643; canonized 1925; Aug. 19*.

John Fisher, St. (1469-1535): English prelate; theologian; martyr; bishop of Rochester, cardinal; refused to recognize validity of Henry VIII's marriage to Anne Boleyn; upheld supremacy of the pope; beheaded for refusing to acknowledge Henry as head of the Church; canonized 1935; June 22 (with St. Thomas More)*.

John Kanty (Cantius), St. (1395-1473): Polish theologian; canonized 1767; Dec. 23*.

John Leonardi, St. (1550-1609): Italian priest; worked among prisoners and the sick; founded Clerics Regular of the Mother of God; canonized 1938; Oct. 9*.

John Nepomucene, St. (1345-1393): Bohemian priest; regarded as a martyr; canonized 1729; patron of Czechoslovakia; May 16.

John Nepomucene Neumann, St. (1811-1860): American prelate; b. Bohemia; ordained in New York 1836; missionary among Germans near Niagara Falls before joining Redemptorists, 1840; bishop of Philadelphia, 1852; first bishop in U.S. to prescribe Forty Hours devotion in his diocese; beatified 1963; canonized June 19, 1977; Jan. 5 (U.S.)*.

John of God, St. (1495-1550): Portuguese founder; his work among the sick poor led to foundation of Brothers Hospitallers of St. John of God, 1540, in Spain; canonized 1690; patron of sick, hospitals, nurses; Mar. 8*.

John Vianney (Cure of Ars), St. (1786-1859): French parish priest; noted confessor, spent 16 to 18 hours a day in confessional; canonized 1925; patron of parish priests; Aug. 4*.

Josaphat Kuncevyc, St. (1584-1623): Basilian monk; b. Poland; archbishop of Polotsk, Lithuania; worked for reunion of separated Easterners; martyred by mob of schismatics; canonized 1867; Nov. 12*.

Joseph Benedict Cottolengo, St. (1786-1842): Italian priest; established Little Houses of Divine Providence (Piccolo Casa) for care of orphans and the sick; canonized 1934; Apr. 30.

Joseph Cafasso, St. (1811-1860): Italian priest; renowned confessor; promoted devotion to Blessed Sacrament; canonized 1947; June 23.

Joseph Calasanz, St. (1556-1648): Spanish priest; founder of Piarists (Order of Pious Schools); canonized 1767; Aug. 25*.

Joseph of Cupertino, St. (1603-1663): Italian Franciscan; noted for remarkable incidents of levitation; canonized 1767; Sept. 18.

Jugan, Jeanne Bl. (1792-1879): French religious; foundress of Little Sisters of the Poor; beatified Oct. 5, 1982; Aug. 30.

Justin Martyr, St. (100-165): Early ecclesiastical writer; *Apologies for the Christian Religion, Dialog with the Jew Tryphon;* martyred at Rome; June 1*.

Kateri Tekakwitha, Bl. (1656-1680): "Lily of the Mohawks." Indian maiden born at Ossernenon (Auriesville), N.Y.; baptized Christian, Easter, 1676, by Jesuit missionary Father Jacques de Lambertville; lived life devoted to prayer, penitential practices and care of sick and aged in Christian village near Montreal; buried at Caughnawaga, Ont.; beatified June 22, 1980; July 14* (in U.S.).

Ladislaus, Saint (1040-1095): King of Hungary; supported Pope Gregory VII against Henry IV; canonized 1192; June 27.

Lawrence, St. (d. 258): Widely venerated martyr who suffered death, according to a long-standing but unverifiable legend, by being roasted alive on a gridiron; Aug. 10*.

Leonard of Port Maurice, St. (1676-1751): Italian Franciscan; ascetical writer; preached missions throughout Italy; canonized 1867; patron of parish missions; Nov. 26.

Leopold Mandic, St. (1866-1942): Croatian-born Franciscan priest, noted confessor; spent most of his priestly life in Padua, Italy; canonized, 1983, July 30.

Louis IX, St. (1215-1270): King of France, 1226-1270; participated in Sixth Crusade; patron of Secular Franciscan Order; canonized 1297; Aug. 25*.

Louis de Montfort, St. (1673-1716): French priest; founder of Sisters of Divine Wisdom, 1703, and Missionaries of Company of Mary, 1715; wrote *True Devotion to the Blessed Virgin;* canonized 1947; Apr. 28.

Louise de Marillac, St. (1591-1660): French foundress, with St. Vincent de Paul, of the Sisters of Charity; canonized 1934; Mar. 15.

Lucy, St. (d. 304): Sicilian maiden; martyred during Diocletian persecution; one of most widely venerated early virgin-martyrs; patron of Syracuse, Sicily; invoked by those suffering from eye diseases (based on legend that she offered her eyes to a suitor who admired them); Dec. 13*.

Marcellinus and Peter, Sts. (d.c. 304): Early Roman martyrs; June 2*.

Margaret Clitherow, St. (1556-1586): English martyr; convert shortly after her marriage; one of Forty Martyrs of England and Wales; canonized 1970; Mar. 25.

Margaret Mary Alacoque, St. (1647-1690):

French nun; spread devotion to Sacred Heart in accordance with revelations made to her in 1675 (see Sacred Heart); canonized 1920; Oct. 16*.

Margaret of Scotland, St. (1050-1093): Queen of Scotland; noted for solicitude for the poor and promotion of justice; canonized 1251; Nov. 16*.

Maria Goretti, St. (1890-1902): Italian virgin-martyr; a model of purity; canonized 1950; July 6*.

Mariana Paredes of Jesus, St. (1618-1645): South American recluse; Lily of Quito; canonized 1950; May 26.

Marie-Leonie Paradis, Bl. (1840-1912): Canadian religious; founded Little Sisters of the Holy Family, 1880; beatified 1984; May 4.

Martha, St. (1st cent.): Sister of Lazarus and Mary of Bethany; Gospel accounts record her concern for homely details; patron of cooks; July 29*.

Martin I, St. (d. 655): Pope, 649-55; banished from Rome by emperor in 653 because of his condemnation of Monothelites; considered a martyr; Apr. 13*.

Martin of Tours, St. (316-397): Bishop of Tours; opposed Arianism and Priscillianism; pioneer of Western monasticism, before St. Benedict; Nov. 11*.

Mary Magdalene, St. (1st cent.): Gospels record her as devoted follower of Christ to whom he appeared after the Resurrection; her identification with Mary of Bethany (sister of Martha and Lazarus) and the woman sinner (Lk 7:36-50) has been questioned; July 22*.

Mary Magdalene de Pazzi, St. (1566-1607): Italian Carmelite nun; recipient of mystical experiences; canonized 1669; May 25*.

Maximilian Kolbe, St. (1894-1941): Polish Conventual Franciscan; prisoner at Auschwitz who heroically offered his life in place of a fellow prisoner; beatified 1971, canonized 1982; Aug. 14*.

Methodius, St.: See Index.

Miguel Febres Cordero, St. (1854-1910): Ecuadorian Christian Brother; educator; canonized 1984; Feb. 9.

Monica, St. (332-387): Mother of St. Augustine; model of a patient mother; her feast is observed in the Roman calendar the day before her son's; Aug. 27*.

Nereus and Achilleus, Sts. (d. c. 100): Early Christian martyrs; soldiers who, according to legend, were baptized by St. Peter; May 12*.

Nicholas of Myra, St. (4th cent.): Bishop of Myra in Asia Minor; one of most popular saints in both East and West; most of the incidents of his life are based on legend; patron of Russia; Dec. 6*.

Nicholas of Tolentino, St. (1245-1305): Italian hermit; famed preacher; canonized 1446; Sept. 10.

Norbert, St. (1080-1134): German bishop; founder of Norbertines or Premonstratensians, 1120; promoted reform of the clergy, devotion to Blessed Sacrament; canonized 1582; June 6*.

Odilia, St. (d. c. 720): Benedictine abbess; according to legend she was born blind, abandoned by her family and adopted by a convent of nuns where her sight was miraculously restored; patron of blind; Dec. 13.

Oliver Plunket, St. (1629-1681): Irish martyr;

theologian; archbishop of Armagh and primate of Ireland; beatified 1920; canonized, 1975; July 1.

Pancras, St. (d. c. 304): Roman martyr; May 12*.

Paola Frassinetti, St. (1809-1882): Italian nun; foundress, 1834, of Sisters of St. Dorothy; canonized 1984; June 11.

Paschal Baylon, St. (1540-1592): Spanish Franciscan lay brother; spent life as door-keeper in various Franciscan friaries; defended doctrine of Real Presence in Blessed Sacrament; canonized 1690; patron of all Eucharistic confraternities and congresses, 1897; May 17.

Patrick, St. (389-461): Famous missionary of Ireland; began missionary work in Ireland about 432; organized the Church there and established it on a lasting foundation; patron of Ireland, with Sts. Bridget and Columba; Mar. 17*.

Paul Miki and Companions, Sts. (d. 1597): Martyrs of Japan; Paul Miki, Jesuit, and twenty-five other priests and laymen were martyred at Nagasaki; canonized 1862, the first canonized martyrs of the Far East; Feb. 6*.

Paul of the Cross, St. (1694-1775): Italian religious; founder of the Passionists; canonized 1867; Oct. 19*.

Paulinus of Nola, St. (d. 451): Bishop of Nola (Spain); writer; June 22*.

Peregrine, St. (1260-1347): Italian Servite; invoked against cancer (he was miraculously cured of cancer of the foot after a vision); canonized 1726; May 1.

Perpetua and Felicity, Sts. (d. 203): Martyrs; Mar. 7*.

Peter Chanel, St. (1803-1841): French Marist; missionary to Oceania, where he was martyred; canonized 1954; Apr. 28*.

Peter Gonzalez, St. (1190-1246): Spanish Dominican; worked among sailors; court chaplain and confessor of King St. Ferdinand of Castile; patron of sailors; Apr. 14.

Peter of Alcantara, St. (1499-1562): Spanish Franciscan; mystic; initiated Franciscan reform; confessor of St. Teresa of Avila; canonized 1669; Oct. 19.

Philip Neri, St. (1515-1595): Italian religious; founded Congregation of the Oratory; considered a second apostle of Rome because of his mission activities there; canonized 1622; May 26*.

Philip of Jesus, St. (1571-1597): Mexican Franciscan; martyred at Nagasaki, Japan; canonized 1862; patron of Mexico City; Feb. 6*.

Pius V, St. (1504-1572): Pope, 1566-1572; enforced decrees of Council of Trent; organized expedition against Turks resulting in victory at Lepanto; canonized 1712; Apr. 30*.

Polycarp, St. (2nd cent.): Bishop of Smyrna; ecclesiastical writer; martyr; Feb. 23*.

Pontian, St. (d. c. 235): Pope, 230-235; exiled to Sardinia by the emperor; regarded as a martyr; Aug. 13 (with Hippolytus)*.

Raymond Nonnatus, St. (d. 1240): Spanish Mercedarian; cardinal; devoted his life to ransoming captives from the Moors; Aug. 31.

Raymond of Penyafort, St. (1175-1275): Spanish Dominican; confessor of Gregory IX; systematized and codified canon law, in effect until 1917; master general of Dominicans, 1238; canonized 1601; Jan. 7*.

Rita of Cascia, St. (1381-1457): Widow; cloistered Augustinian religious of Umbria; invoked in impossible and desperate cases; May 22.

Robert Southwell, St. (1561-1595): English Jesuit; poet; martyred at Tyburn; canonized 1970, one of the Forty English and Welsh Martyrs; Feb. 21.

Roch, St. (1350-1379): French layman; pilgrim; devoted life to care of plague-stricken; widely venerated; invoked against pestilence; Aug. 17.

Romuald, St. (951-1027): Italian monk; founded Camaldolese Benedictines; June 19*.

Rose of Lima, St. (1586-1617): Peruvian Dominican tertiary; first native-born saint of the New World; canonized 1671; Aug. 23*.

Scholastica, St. (d. c. 559): Sister of St. Benedict; regarded as first nun of the Benedictine Order; Feb. 10*.

Sebastian, St. (3rd cent.): Roman martyr; traditionally pictured as a handsome youth with arrows; martyred; patron of athletes, archers; Jan. 20*.

Seven Holy Founders of the Servants of Mary (Buonfiglio Monaldo, Alexis Falconieri, Benedict dell'Antello, Bartholomew Amidei, Ricovero Uguccione, Gerardino Sostegni, John Buonagiunta Monetti): Florentine youths who founded Servites, 1233, in obedience to a vision; canonized 1888; Feb. 17*.

Sixtus II and Companions, Sts. (d. 258): Sixtus, pope 257-258, and four deacons, martyrs; Aug. 7*.

Stanislaus, St. (1030-1079): Polish bishop; martyr; canonized 1253; Apr. 11*.

Stephen, St. (d. c. 33): First Christian martyr; chosen by the Apostles as the first of the seven deacons; stoned to death; Dec. 26*.

Stephen, St. (975-1038): King; apostle of Hungary; welded Magyars into national unity; canonized 1083; Aug. 16*.

Sylvester I, St. (d. 335): Pope 314-335; first ecumenical council held at Nicaea during his pontificate; Dec. 31*.

Tarcisius, St. (d. 3rd cent.): Early martyr; according to tradition, was martyred while carrying the Blessed Sacrament to some Christians in prison; patron of first communicants; Aug. 15.

Therese Couderc, St. (1805-1885): French religious; foundress of the Religious of Our Lady of the Retreat in the Cenacle, 1827; canonized 1970; Sept. 26.

Therese of Lisieux, St. (1873-1897): French Carmelite nun; b. Therese Martin; allowed to enter Carmel at 15, died nine years later of tuberculosis; her "little way" of spiritual perfection became widely known through her spiritual autobiography; despite her obscure life, became one of the most popular saints; canonized 1925; patron of foreign missions; Oct. 1*.

Thomas Becket, St. (1118-1170): English martyr; archbishop of Canterbury; chancellor under Henry II; murdered for upholding rights of the Church; canonized 1173; Dec. 29*.

Thomas More, St. (1478-1535): English martyr; statesman, chancellor under Henry VIII; author of *Utopia;* opposed Henry's divorce, refused to renounce authority of the papacy; beheaded; canonized 1935; June 22 (with St. John Fisher)*.

Timothy, St. (d. c. 97): Bishop of Ephesus; disciple and companion of St. Paul; martyr; Jan. 26*.

Titus, St. (d. c. 96): Bishop; companion of St. Paul; recipient of one of Paul's epistles; Jan. 26*.

Valentine, St. (d. 269): Priest, physician; martyred at Rome; legendary patron of lovers; Feb. 14.

Vincent, St. (d. 304): Spanish deacon; martyr; Jan. 22*.

Vincent de Paul, St. (1581?-1660): French priest; founder of Congregation of the Mission (Vincentians, Lazarists) and co-founder of Sisters of Charity; declared patron of all charitable organizations and works by Leo XIII; canonized 1737; Sept. 27*.

Vincent Ferrer, St. (1350-1418): Spanish Dominican; famed preacher; Apr. 5*.

Wenceslaus, St. (d. 935): Duke of Bohemia; martyr; patron of Bohemia; Sept. 28*.

Zita, St. (1218-1278): Italian maid; noted for charity to poor; patron of domestics; Apr. 27.

SAINTS—PATRONS AND INTERCESSORS

A patron is a saint who is venerated as a special intercessor before God. Most patrons have been so designated as the result of popular devotion and long-standing custom. In many cases, the fact of existing patronal devotion is clear despite historical obscurity regarding its origin. The Church has made official designation of relatively few patrons; in such cases, the dates of designation are given in the list below. The theological background of the patronage of saints includes the dogmas of the Mystical Body of Christ and the Communion of Saints.

Listed below are patron saints of occupations and professions, and saints whose intercession is sought for special needs.

Accountants: Matthew.
Actors: Genesius.

Advertisers: Bernardine of Siena (May 20, 1960).
Alpinists: Bernard of Montjoux (or Menthon) (Aug. 20, 1923).
Altar boys: John Berchmans.
Anesthetists: Rene Goupil.
Animals: Francis of Assisi.
Archers: Sebastian.
Architects: Thomas, Apostle.
Armorers: Dunstan.
Art: Catherine of Bologna.
Artists: Luke, Catherine of Bologna, Bl. Angelico (Feb. 21, 1984).
Astronomers: Dominic.
Athletes: Sebastian.
Authors: Francis de Sales.
Aviators: Our Lady of Loreto (1920), Therese of Lisieux, Joseph of Cupertino.
Bakers: Elizabeth of Hungary, Nicholas.

Bankers: Matthew.

Barbers: Cosmas and Damian, Louis.

Barren women: Anthony of Padua, Felicity.

Basket-makers: Anthony, Abbot.

Beggars: Martin of Tours.

Blacksmiths: Dunstan.

Blind: Odilia, Raphael.

Blood banks: Januarius.

Bodily ills: Our Lady of Lourdes.

Bookbinders: Peter Celestine.

Bookkeepers: Matthew.

Booksellers: John of God.

Boy Scouts: George.

Brewers: Augustine of Hippo, Luke, Nicholas of Myra.

Bricklayers: Stephen.

Brides: Nicholas of Myra.

Brushmakers: Anthony, Abbot.

Builders: Vincent Ferrer.

Butchers: Anthony (Abbot), Luke.

Cabdrivers: Fiacre.

Cabinetmakers: Anne.

Cancer patients: Peregrine.

Canonists: Raymond of Peñafort.

Carpenters: Joseph.

Catechists: Viator, Charles Borromeo, Robert Bellarmine.

Catholic Action: Francis of Assisi (1916).

Chandlers: Ambrose, Bernard of Clairvaux.

Charitable societies: Vincent de Paul (May 12, 1885).

Children: Nicholas of Myra.

Children of Mary: Agnes, Maria Goretti.

Choirboys: Dominic Savio (June 8, 1956), Holy Innocents.

Church: Joseph (Dec. 8, 1870).

Clerics: Gabriel of the Sorrowful Mother.

Communications personnel: Bernardine.

Confessors: Alphonsus Liguori (Apr. 26, 1950), John Nepomucene.

Convulsive children: Scholastica.

Cooks: Lawrence, Martha.

Coopers: Nicholas of Myra.

Coppersmiths: Maurus.

Dairy workers: Brigid.

Deaf: Francis de Sales.

Dentists: Apollonia.

Desperate situations: Gregory of Neocaesarea, Jude Thaddeus, Rita of Cascia.

Dietitians (in hospitals): Martha.

Dyers: Maurice, Lydia.

Dying: Joseph.

Ecologists: Francis of Assisi (Nov. 29, 1979).

Editors: John Bosco.

Emigrants: Frances Xavier Cabrini (Sept. 8, 1950).

Engineers: Ferdinand III.

Epilepsy, Motor Diseases: Vitus, Willibrord.

Eucharistic congresses and societies: Paschal Baylon (Nov. 28, 1897).

Expectant mothers: Raymund Nonnatus, Gerard Majella.

Eye diseases: Lucy.

Falsely accused: Raymund Nonnatus.

Farmers: George, Isidore.

Farriers: John the Baptist.

Firemen: Florian.

Fire prevention: Catherine of Siena.

First communicants: Tarcisius.

Fishermen: Andrew.

Florists: Therese of Lisieux.

Forest workers: John Gualbert.

Foundlings: Holy Innocents.

Fullers: Anastasius the Fuller, James the Less.

Funeral directors: Joseph of Arimathea, Dismas.

Gardeners: Adelard, Tryphon, Fiacre, Phocas.

Glassworkers: Luke.

Goldsmiths: Dunstan, Anastasius.

Gravediggers: Anthony, Abbot.

Greetings: Valentine.

Grocers: Michael.

Hairdressers: Martin de Porres.

Happy meetings: Raphael.

Hatters: Severus of Ravenna, James the Less.

Headache sufferers: Teresa of Jesus (Avila).

Heart patients: John of God.

Hospital administrators: Basil the Great, Frances X. Cabrini.

Hospitals: Camillus de Lellis and John of God (June 22, 1886), Jude Thaddeus.

Housewives: Anne.

Hunters: Hubert, Eustachius.

Infantrymen: Maurice.

Innkeepers: Amand, Martha.

Invalids: Roch.

Jewelers: Eligius, Dunstan.

Journalists: Francis de Sales (Apr. 26, 1923).

Jurists: John Capistran.

Laborers: Isidore, James, John Bosco.

Lawyers: Ivo (Yves Helory), Genesius, Thomas More.

Learning: Ambrose.

Librarians: Jerome.

Lighthouse keepers: Venerius.

Locksmiths: Dunstan.

Maids: Zita.

Marble workers: Clement I.

Mariners: Michael, Nicholas of Tolentino.

Medical record librarians: Raymond of Peñafort.

Medical social workers: John Regis.

Medical technicians: Albert the Great.

Mentally ill: Dymphna.

Merchants: Francis of Assisi, Nicholas of Myra.

Messengers: Gabriel.

Metal workers: Eligius.

Military chaplains: John Capistran (Feb. 10, 1984).

Millers: Arnulph, Victor.

Missions, Foreign: Francis Xavier (Mar. 25, 1904), Therese of Lisieux (Dec. 14, 1927).

Missions, Black: Peter Claver (1896, Leo XIII), Benedict the Black.

Missions, Parish: Leonard of Port Maurice (Mar. 17, 1923).

Mothers: Monica.

Motorcyclists: Our Lady of Grace.

Motorists: Christopher, Frances of Rome.

Mountaineers: Bernard of Montjoux (or Menthon).

Musicians: Gregory the Great, Cecilia, Dunstan.

Notaries: Luke, Mark.

Nurses: Camillus de Lellis and John of God (1930, Pius XI), Agatha, Raphael.

Nursing and nursing service: Elizabeth of Hungary, Catherine of Siena.

Orators: John Chrysostom (July 8, 1908).

Organ builders: Cecilia.

Orphans: Jerome Emiliani.

Painters: Luke.

Paratroopers: Michael.

Pawnbrokers: Nicholas.

Pharmacists: Cosmas and Damian, James the Greater.

Pharmacists (in hospitals): Gemma Galgani.

Philosophers: Justin.

Physicians: Pantaleon, Cosmas and Damian, Luke, Raphael.

Pilgrims: James the Greater.

Plasterers: Bartholomew.

Poets: David, Cecilia.

Poison sufferers: Benedict.

Policemen: Michael.

Poor: Lawrence, Anthony of Padua.

Poor souls: Nicholas of Tolentino.

Porters: Christopher.

Possessed: Bruno, Denis.

Postal employees: Gabriel.

Priests: Jean-Baptiste Vianney (Apr. 23, 1929).

Printers: John of God, Augustine of Hippo, Genesius.

Prisoners: Dismas, Joseph Cafasso.

Protector of crops: Ansovinus.

Public relations: Bernardine of Siena (May 20, 1960).

Public relations (of hospitals): Paul, Apostle.

Radiologists: Michael (Jan. 15, 1941).

Radio workers: Gabriel.

Retreats: Ignatius Loyola (July 25, 1922).

Rheumatism: James the Greater.

Saddlers: Crispin and Crispinian.

Sailors: Cuthbert, Brendan, Eulalia, Christopher, Peter Gonzales, Erasmus, Nicholas.

Scholars: Brigid.

Schools, Catholic: Thomas Aquinas (Aug. 4, 1880), Joseph Calasanz (Aug. 13, 1948).

Scientists: Albert (Aug. 13, 1948).

Sculptors: Claude.

Seamen: Francis of Paola.

Searchers of lost articles: Anthony of Padua.

Secretaries: Genesius.

Seminarians: Charles Borromeo.

Servants: Martha, Zita.

Shoemakers: Crispin and Crispinian.

Sick: Michael, John of God and Camillus de Lellis (June 22, 1886).

Silversmiths: Andronicus.

Singers: Gregory, Cecilia.

Skaters: Lidwina.

Skiers: Bernard of Montjoux (or Menthon).

Social workers: Louise de Marillac (Feb. 12, 1960).

Soldiers: Hadrian, George, Ignatius, Sebastian, Martin of Tours, Joan of Arc.

Speleologists: Benedict.

Stenographers: Genesius, Cassian.

Stonecutters: Clement.

Stonemasons: Stephen.

Students: Thomas Aquinas.

Surgeons: Cosmas and Damian, Luke.

Swordsmiths: Maurice.

Tailors: Homobonus.

Tanners: Crispin and Crispinian, Simon.

Tax collectors: Matthew.

Teachers: Gregory the Great, John Baptist de la Salle (May 15, 1950).

Telecommunications workers: Gabriel (Jan. 12, 1951).

Television: Clare of Assisi (Feb. 14, 1958).

Television workers: Gabriel.

Tertiaries (Secular Franciscans): Louis of France, Elizabeth of Hungary.

Theologians: Augustine, Alphonsus Liguori.

Throat ailments: Blase.

Travelers: Anthony of Padua, Nicholas of Myra, Christopher, Raphael.

Travel hostesses: Bona (Mar. 2, 1962).

Universities: Blessed Contardo Ferrini.

Vocations: Alphonsus.

Watchmen: Peter of Alcantara.

Weavers: Paul the Hermit, Anastasius the Fuller, Anastasia.

Wine merchants: Amand.

Women in labor: Anne.

Women's Army Corps: Genevieve.

Workingmen: Joseph.

Writers: Francis de Sales (Apr. 26, 1923), Lucy.

Yachtsmen: Adjutor.

Young girls: Agnes.

Youth: Aloysius Gonzaga (1729, Benedict XIII; 1926, Pius XI), John Berchmans, Gabriel of the Sorrowful Mother.

Patron Saints of Places

Alsace: Odilia.

Americas: Our Lady of Guadalupe, Rose of Lima.

Angola: Immaculate Heart of Mary (Nov. 21, 1984).

Argentina: Our Lady of Lujan.

Armenia: Gregory Illuminator.

Asia Minor: John, Evangelist.

Australia: Our Lady Help of Christians.

Belgium: Joseph.

Bohemia: Wenceslaus, Ludmilla.

Borneo: Francis Xavier.

Brazil: Nossa Senhora de Aparecida, Immaculate Conception, Peter of Alcantara.

Canada: Joseph, Anne.

Chile: James the Greater, Our Lady of Mt. Carmel.

China: Joseph.

Colombia: Peter Claver, Louis Bertran.

Corsica: Immaculate Conception.

Czechoslovakia: Wenceslaus, John Nepomucene, Procopius.

Denmark: Ansgar, Canute.

Dominican Republic: Our Lady of High Grace, Dominic.

East Indies: Thomas, Apostle.

Ecuador: Sacred Heart.

El Salvador: Our Lady of Peace (Oct. 10, 1966).

England: George.

Europe: Benedict (1964), Cyril and Methodius, co-patrons (Dec. 31, 1980).

Finland: Henry.

France: Our Lady of the Assumption, Joan of Arc, Therese (May 3, 1944).

Germany: Boniface, Michael.

Gibraltar: Blessed Virgin Mary under title, "Our Lady of Europe" (May 31, 1979).

Greece: Nicholas, Andrew.

Holland: Willibrord.

Hungary: Blessed Virgin, "Great Lady of Hungary," Stephen, King.

Iceland: Thorlac (Jan. 14, 1984).

India: Our Lady of Assumption.

Ireland: Patrick, Brigid and Columba.

Italy: Francis of Assisi, Catherine of Siena.

Japan: Peter Baptist.

Korea: Joseph and Mary, Mother of the Church.

Lesotho: Immaculate Heart of Mary.

Lithuania: Casimir, Bl. Cunegunda.

Luxembourg: Willibrord.

Malta: Paul, Our Lady of the Assumption.

Mexico: Our Lady of Guadalupe.

Monaco: Devota.

Moravia: Cyril and Methodius.

New Zealand: Our Lady Help of Christians.

Norway: Olaf.

Papua New Guinea (including northern Solomon Islands): Michael the Archangel (May 31, 1979).

Paraguay: Our Lady of Assumption (July 13, 1951).

Peru: Joseph (Mar. 19, 1957).

Philippines: Sacred Heart of Mary.

Poland: Casimir, Bl. Cunegunda, Stanislaus of Cracow, Our Lady of Czestochowa.

Portugal: Immaculate Conception, Francis Borgia, Anthony of Padua, Vincent of Saragossa, George.

Russia: Andrew, Nicholas of Myra, Therese of Lisieux.

Scandinavia: Ansgar.

Scotland: Andrew, Columba.

Silesia: Hedwig.

Slovakia: Our Lady of Sorrows.

South Africa: Our Lady of Assumption (Mar. 15, 1952).

South America: Rose of Lima.

Spain: James the Greater, Teresa.

Sri Lanka (Ceylon): Lawrence.

Sweden: Bridget, Eric.

Tanzania: Immaculate Conception (Dec. 8, 1984).

United States: Immaculate Conception (1846).

Uruguay: Blessed Virgin Mary under title "La Virgen de los Treinte y Tres" (Nov. 21, 1963).

Venezuela: Our Lady of Coromoto.

Wales: David.

West Indies: Gertrude.

Emblems, Portrayals of Saints

Agatha: Tongs, veil.

Agnes: Lamb.

Ambrose: Bees, dove, ox, pen.

Andrew: Transverse cross.

Anne, Mother of the Blessed Virgin: Door.

Anthony, Abbot: Bell, hog.

Anthony of Padua: Infant Jesus, bread, book, lily.

Augustine of Hippo: Dove, child, shell, pen.

Barnabas: Stones, ax, lance.

Bartholomew: Knife, flayed and holding his skin.

Benedict: Broken cup, raven, bell, crosier, bush.

Bernard of Clairvaux: Pen, bees, instruments of the Passion.

Bernardine of Siena: Tablet or sun inscribed with IHS.

Blase: Wax, taper, iron comb.

Bonaventure: Communion, ciborium, cardinal's hat.

Boniface: Oak, ax, book, fox, scourge, fountain, raven, sword.

Bridget of Sweden: Book, pilgrim's staff.

Bridget of Kildare: Cross, flame over her head, candle.

Catherine of Ricci: Ring, crown, crucifix.

Catherine of Siena: Stigmata, cross, ring, lily.

Cecilia: Organ.

Charles Borromeo: Communion, coat of arms with word *Humilitas*.

Christopher: Giant, torrent, tree, Child Jesus on his shoulders.

Clare of Assisi: Monstrance.

Cosmas and Damian: A phial, box of ointment.

Cyril of Alexandria: Blessed Virgin holding the Child Jesus, pen.

Cyril of Jerusalem: Purse, book.

Dominic: Rosary, star.

Edmund the Martyr: Arrow, sword.

Elizabeth of Hungary: Alms, flowers, bread, the poor, a pitcher.

Francis of Assisi: Wolf, birds, fish, skull, the Stigmata.

Francis Xavier: Crucifix, bell, vessel.

Genevieve: Bread, keys, herd, candle.

George: Dragon.

Gertrude: Crown, taper, lily.

Gervase and Protase: Scourge, club, sword.

Gregory I (the Great): Tiara, crosier, dove.

Helena: Cross.

Hilary: Stick, pen, child.

Ignatius of Loyola: Communion, chasuble, book, apparition of Our Lord.

Isidore: Bees, pen.

James the Greater: Pilgrim's staff, shell, key, sword.

James the Less: Square rule, halberd, club.

Jerome: Lion.

John Berchmans: Rule of St. Ignatius, cross, rosary.

John Chrysostom: Bees, dove, pen.

John of God: Alms, a heart, crown of thorns.

John the Baptist: Lamb, head cut off on platter, skin of an animal.

John the Evangelist: Eagle, chalice, kettle, armor.

Josaphat Kuncevyc: Chalice, crown, winged deacon.

Joseph, Spouse of the Blessed Virgin: Infant Jesus, lily, rod, plane, carpenter's square.

Jude: Sword, square rule, club.

Justin Martyr: Ax, sword.

Lawrence: Cross, book of the Gospels, gridiron.

Leander of Seville: A pen.

Liborius: Pebbles, peacock.

Longinus: In arms at foot of the cross.

Louis IX of France: Crown of thorns, nails.

Lucy: Cord, eyes on a dish.

Luke: Ox, book, brush, palette.

Mark: Lion, book.
Martha: Holy water sprinkler, dragon.
Mary Magdalene: Alabaster box of ointment.
Matilda: Purse, alms.
Matthew: Winged man, purse, lance.
Matthias: Lance.
Maurus: Scales, spade, crutch.
Meinrad: Two ravens.
Michael: Scales, banner, sword, dragon.
Monica: Girdle, tears.
Nicholas: Three purses or balls, anchor or boat, child.
Patrick: Cross, harp, serpent, baptismal font, demons, shamrock.
Paul: Sword, book or scroll.
Peter: Keys, boat, cock.

Philip, Apostle: Column.
Philip Neri: Altar, chasuble, vial.
Rita of Cascia: Rose, crucifix, thorn.
Roch: Angel, dog, bread.
Rose of Lima: Crown of thorns, anchor, city.
Sebastian: Arrows, crown.
Simon Stock: Scapular.
Teresa of Jesus (Avila): Heart, arrow, book.
Therese of Lisieux: Roses entwining a crucifix.
Thomas, Apostle: Lance, ax.
Thomas Aquinas: Chalice, monstrance, dove, ox, person trampled under foot.
Vincent (Deacon): Gridiron, boat.
Vincent de Paul: Children.
Vincent Ferrer: Pulpit, cardinal's hat, trumpet, captives.

THE MOTHER OF JESUS IN CATHOLIC UNDERSTANDING

This article was written by the Rev. Eamon R. Carroll, O. Carm., member of the theological faculty of Loyola University, Chicago; author of "Understanding the Mother of Jesus" (published by M. Glazier, Wilmington, Del.; 1979).

Documents of the Second Vatican Council have provided the charter for current Catholic understanding of the Virgin Mary, Mother of Jesus. This conciliar teaching was expanded and applied in the pastoral letter, "Behold Your Mother: Woman of Faith," issued by the U.S. bishops Nov. 21, 1973. Pope Paul VI added guidelines for devotion, in the revised liturgy and with respect to the Rosary, in the letter *Marialis Cultus* ("To Honor Mary"), dated Feb. 2, 1974.

Conciliar Documents

The first conciliar document, the *Constitution on the Sacred Liturgy*, linked Mary with the life, death and exaltation of Jesus, stating: "In celebrating this annual cycle of Christ's mysteries, holy Church honors with special love blessed Mary, Mother of God, who is joined by an inseparable bond to the saving work of her Son. In her the Church holds up and admires the most excellent fruit of the redemption, and joyfully contemplates, as in a faultless manner, that which she herself wholly desires and hopes to be" (No. 103).

The eighth and final chapter of the *Dogmatic Constitution on the Church* is entitled "The Blessed Virgin Mary, Mother of God, in the Mystery of Christ and the Church." The seventh chapter deals with the communion of saints, the bond between the pilgrim Church on earth and the blessed joined to the risen Christ — what John deSatgé, an English Anglican, describes as the "mutual sharing and caring in Christ for one another." At the Eucharist, above all, "in union with the whole Church we honor Mary, the ever-Virgin Mother of Jesus Christ our Lord and God" (First Eucharistic Prayer; cf. *Constitution on the Church*, No. 50).

What Catholics believe about the Mother of Jesus is the basis for her place in their prayer life, both in the liturgy and particularly the Eucharist, and in other forms of piety, especially the Rosary.

The Church's growth in insight about the Blessed Virgin comes about as Christians ponder the meaning of Mary in prayer as well as in study. The Church has come to know Mary's role by experience and by contemplation of her hidden holiness (*Constitution on the Church*, No. 64). The tradition about Mary has been transmitted by doctrinal teaching and also by life and worship, even as in her own life Mary treasured in her heart God's words and deeds (*Dogmatic Constitution on Divine Revelation*, No. 8).

Mary in the Bible

The possibility of consensus on the Virgin Mary in the Bible was the theme of a book published in 1978, entitled *Mary in the New Testament* (edited by R. E. Brown, J. A. Fitzmyer, J. Reumann and K. P. Donfried). Limiting their study to the New Testament and using critical techniques of interpretation, a team of 12 authors — Catholics, Lutherans, Anglicans and others — agreed on a biblical portrait of Mary the Virgin as the great gospel model of faith commitment.

One valuable insight centers on the "true kinsmen" incident (Mk. 3:31-35; Mt. 12:46-50; Lk. 8:19-21). One day while Jesus was preaching, word was sent to him that his "mother and brethren" wished to see him. In St. Mark, the oldest account, there is a sharp distinction between the circle of the hearers of Jesus, who were "inside" and counted as his "true family," and the relatives "outside," who failed to understand him. St. Mark does not clearly place Mary among the outsiders, but neither does he carefully distinguish her from the other relatives who did not esteem Jesus. St. Luke shifts the focus completely, placing the relatives, especially the Mother of Jesus, among the true followers, as he does also in the Acts of the Apostles by mentioning them in the Upper Room before Pentecost.

St. Luke is fond of speaking of the "word of God." At the Annunciation, Mary consented with the statement, "Be it done to me according to your word" (Lk. 1:26-38), and "the Word was made flesh" (Jn. 1:14). Jesus said in reply to the message about his visitors, "My mother and my brothers are those who hear the word of God and do it"

(Lk. 8:21). St. Luke relates this event just after the parables of the sower and the seed and the lamp on the lampstand. Consistent with his high praise of the Virgin Mary in the infancy chapters, he regards Mary as the rich soil — she heard the word and brought forth fruit in abundance, the Holy One who is the Son of God. She is the pure light, rekindled by the coming of the Redeemer; she is the "woman clothed with the sun" (Rv. 12:1), for Jesus is the "sun of justice."

St. Luke alone saved one other mention of Mary during the public ministry of Jesus, in the story of the "enthusiastic woman" (Lk. 11:27-28). One day while Jesus was preaching, a woman cried out, "Blessed is the womb that bore you and the breasts that nursed you." He replied, "Still more blessed are those who hear the word of God and keep it." The obedient Mary, handmaid of the Lord, brought together opposed beatitudes — the anonymous woman's praise of her motherhood and Jesus' tribute to her faith.

In the opening chapter of St. Luke, Elizabeth did the same when, filled with the Holy Spirit, she returned Mary's greeting with the loud cry, "Of all women you are the most blessed, and blessed is the fruit of your womb." Continuing in praise of her young cousin's faith, she added: "Yes, blessed is she who has believed, for the things promised her by the Lord will be fulfilled" (Lk. 1:39-45).

Mary the Virgin

Both St. Luke and St. Matthew, whose infancy narratives differ so much otherwise, agree that Mary conceived Jesus virginally, that her Son had no human father. The Creed affirms that Jesus was "conceived of the Virgin Mary by the power of the Holy Spirit."

St. Luke writes of the virginal conception of Jesus from the standpoint of Mary. To her question, "How can this be since I know not man?" the angel replied by appealing to God's power.

St. Matthew's viewpoint is that of Joseph, who was informed in a dream-vision that Mary's child was of no human father. God accomplishes his saving purposes without dependence on the will of the flesh and the will of man (Jn. 1:13). God shows his favor where he chooses — whether for the barren Sara, wife of Abraham, or aged Elizabeth, the wife of Zechariah, or the Virgin Mary. In the words of the promise to Abraham, repeated by Gabriel to Mary, "Nothing is impossible to God" (Lk. 1:37; Gn. 18:14).

Mary and Joseph accepted as God's will the virginal conception, an unprecedented event, the sign of God sending his Son to be the Savior. Their lives were henceforth totally dedicated to the service of Jesus.

As various forms of Christian witness developed in the Church, the conviction that Mary remains always a virgin came to be held as Catholic doctrine. The Gospels leave undecided the identity of the "brethren" of Jesus. From lived experience, by the fourth century the Church had come to see Mary's life-long virginity as part of her commitment to her Son and his mission. Such "development of doctrine" remains a point of difference between Catholics and Protestants, although the great Reformers — Luther, Calvin and later John Wesley — all held that Mary was ever-Virgin.

St. Luke and St. John on Mary

Along with the role of Mary in the childhood of Jesus, St. Luke sees her as part of the fulfillment of messianic prophecy. The Second Vatican Council spoke of "the exalted daughter of Zion in whom the times are fulfilled after the long waiting for the promise, and the new economy inaugurated when the Son of God takes on human nature from her in order to free men from sin by the mysteries of his flesh." The expectations of Israel for the Messiah reach their peak in Mary of Nazareth: "She stands out among the Lord's lowly and poor who confidently look for salvation from him" (*Constitution on the Church*, No. 55).

The Gospel of St. John introduces Mary at the opening and closing of her Son's ministry, which began with the first of his signs at Cana (Jn. 2:1-11) and ended on Calvary (Jn. 19). Both scenes deal with a "third day," both turn on the "hour," not yet come at Cana but achieved in the decisive event of Calvary. In both, Jesus addresses his Mother with the unaccustomed title, "Woman." The request of Mary at Cana is for more than wine to save the wedding feast. She stands for Israel of old, symbolized by the water pots required for religious purifications; Mary stands also for the new Israel, the Church, the bride of Christ, symbolized by the abundant choice wine of the messianic banquet. The marriage feast looks forward to the hour when Christ, the bridegroom, will lay down his life in love for his bride, the Church.

When Jesus spoke from the cross to his Mother and the beloved disciple, "Woman, behold your son," and "Behold your Mother," more was meant than that the disciple should provide for Mary's care (Jn. 19:26-27). In his farewell discourse at the Last Supper, Jesus spoke of the woman in agony because her hour had come. "But when she has borne her child, she no longer remembers her pain for joy that a man has been born into the world" (Jn. 16:21). The longing of Israel for the coming of the Messiah was sometimes compared to labor pains. The "daughter of Zion" had been promised she would become the mother of all races and all nations. The words of Jesus on Calvary announced the fulfillment of that promise; Mary stands for the "woman" who is mother Church, new Israel, new People of God.

In St. John's Gospel, it is only after his words to his Mother and the disciple that Jesus, knowing "that everything was now finished," said, "I am thirsty," and then, "Now it is finished." "Then he bowed his head and delivered over his spirit" (Jn. 19:28-29).

The giving up of the spirit means both the expiring of Jesus and the giving of the Holy Spirit to the Church. The wine Mary requested at Cana was the wine of the Spirit, to be poured out at the messianic banquet. The prayer for the wine of the Spirit is answered through the self-surrender of Jesus on the cross. The triumphant Christ "gives up his spirit," and the Church comes into being. The Acts of the Apostles describes the effects of the outpouring of the Spirit at Pentecost and afterwards. What Mary requested at Cana, what she prayed for in agony at the cross of Jesus, what she sought before Pentecost in union with the Apostles and relatives and the women — all "with one accord devoted to prayer" — is the gift of the Spirit. At Nazareth Mary conceived her Son, and God became man by the power of the Holy Spirit; in the Upper Room she prayed for the Spirit that Jesus be born again in the members of his Church (*Constitution on the Church,* No. 59).

The New Eve

To the titles of Mary already familiar from the Gospels — "the Virgin," "Favored One," "Mother of Jesus," "Mother of my Lord" (Elizabeth's greeting, meaning "Mother of the Messianic King") — the early Church added other descriptions. By the mid-second century Mary was being compared to Eve. Eve was deceived by the word of the evil angel and by disobedience brought death; Mary, the obedient Virgin, heeded the message of the good angel and by her consent brought Life to the world. The title of "New Eve" became common for Mary. By the time of St. Jerome (d. 419), it was proverbial to say, "Death through Eve, life through Mary."

Immaculate Conception

Reflecting on the Blessed Virgin, Christians pondered various aspects of her holiness. The question arose of her freedom from original sin, God's gift of grace that came to be called her Immaculate Conception (not to be confused with the virginal conception of Jesus, for Mary was the child of the father and mother recalled as Joachim and Anne). It took centuries of development before the Immaculate Conception was held to be revealed by God and defined as dogma by Pius IX in 1854. The absence of clear scriptural evidence was one delaying factor; another was lack of clarity about the meaning of original sin; and most cogent was the requirement that Mary be beneficiary of the saving work of Christ. As the English Anglican John deSatgé expresses it, "Mary, who rejoiced in her Savior, was the last person to have no need of one." The Franciscan John Duns Scotus (d. 1308) suggested that Mary was kept free of original sin by a "preservative redemption" — in anticipation of the foreseen merits of Jesus Christ — the explanation eventually recognized as revealed truth.

The Assumption

The final facet of Mary's holiness is the Assumption, her union body and soul with the risen Christ in the glory of heaven, defined as dogma by Pope Pius XII in 1950. By the sixth century the feast of the Assumption was being celebrated in the East, a development from a still earlier August 15 feast that had been known as the Memory of Mary (like the birthdays into heaven of the martyrs), as the Passing of Mary, and as the Dormition or Falling Asleep of the Mother of God. There is no compelling biblical testimony; the appeal is to the concordant faith of the Church, convinced that the promise of the resurrection of the flesh in union with the risen Savior has already been fulfilled for the Mother of the Lord, who gave him human birth in her pure body and was his loyal disciple unto the end.

Model of the Church

All beliefs about the Blessed Virgin lead to Christ. God kept her free from original sin for the sake of Jesus, that she might give herself wholeheartedly to his life and work (*Constitution on the Church,* No. 56), and in consideration of his redemptive mission. Mary's Assumption is her reunion with her Son in the power of his resurrection. The Marian privileges of the Immaculate Conception and the Assumption enrich also the self-understanding of the Church, for she is the "most excellent fruit of the redemption, the spotless model of the Church," the one in whom Christians admire God's plan for his Church. "In the most holy Virgin the Church has already reached that perfection whereby she exists without spot or wrinkle (Eph. 5:27)" (*Constitution on the Church,* No. 65).

Mary Immaculate is a sign of the love of Christ for his bride, the Church; the bridegroom purifies her by his blood to make her all-holy. The preface for the Solemnity of the Immaculate Conception (December 8) addresses the Father: "You allowed no stain of sin to touch the Virgin Mary. Full of grace, she was to be a worthy Mother of your Son, your sign of favor to the Church at its beginning, and the promise of its perfection as the bride of Christ, radiantly beautiful."

Faithful to his promise, Christ has prepared a place for his bride, the Church. In Mary, daughter of the Church, now joined to Christ body and soul in glory, the pilgrim Church sees the successful completion of its own journey. The resurrection of Jesus is the central truth; the Assumption of Mary is the living sign of the Church's call to glory, to loving union with the victorious Redeemer. The preface at Mass for August 15 reads: "Today the Virgin Mother of God was taken up into heaven to be the beginning and the pattern of the Church in its perfection, and a sign of sure hope and comfort for your pilgrim people. You would not allow decay to touch her body, for she had given birth in the glory of the Incarnation to your Son, the Lord of all life." (Cf. also *Constitution on the Church,* No. 68.)

Mother of God

In 325 the first ecumenical council, at Nicaea, proclaimed that Jesus is truly Son of God. Defenders of the faith there were the first to call Mary "Mother of God." At the third ecumenical council, Ephesus, in 431, it was solemnly established that the Virgin Mary is indeed "Mother of God," for the Son to whom she gave birth is the pre-existent Second Person of the Blessed Trinity. "Mother of God" had already been used as a popular title in some parts of the Church, and after Ephesus it was adopted in the prayers of the Mass, as is still the practice in the Catholic Church and all Eastern Churches. For example, the current third Eucharistic Prayer reads: "May he (the Holy Spirit) make us an everlasting gift to you (the Father) and enable us to share in the inheritance of your saints, with Mary, the Virgin Mother of God."

Mother of the Church

When the Church began to celebrate the Assumption of Mary, it did so in the conviction Mary did not leave the members of the Church orphans when her days on earth were ended. She continues her interest for them in union with her Son, the supreme intercessor. By the time of the Council of Ephesus in 431, authors of both the East and West — like St. Ephrem of Syria (d. 373) and St. Ambrose of Italy (d. 397) — proposed Mary as the model of Christian life, and the practice of asking her to pray for her clients on earth began to appear. The feasts of the Nativity of Mary (September 8), the Annunciation (March 25) and the Presentation of Jesus (February 2, also known as the Purification of Mary or Candlemas) have been kept from the sixth and seventh centuries.

When the words of Gabriel and Elizabeth from St. Luke's infancy narrative became part of prayer, the first part of the Hail Mary, their use led to deeper awareness of Mary's holiness as well as to counting on her heavenly help — well expressed in the second part of the Hail Mary — "Holy Mary, Mother of God, pray for us sinners now and at the hour of our death," which reached its fixed form only in the fifteenth century. Mary's place in liturgical prayer and in private prayer reflected and strengthened the sense of her continuing role as loving friend in heaven of the Church on earth. People asked Mary's prayers on their behalf, recalling Mary's own "pilgrimage of faith" and trusting in her abiding maternal care.

Greek homilists like St. John of Damascus (d. ca. 749), St. Andrew of Crete (d. 740) and St. Germanus of Constantinople (d. ca. 733) sang Mary's praises and urged confidence in her loving intercession with Christ. In the West, after the upsurge of the Carolingian times (about 800), remembered for the origin of the Saturday observance in honor of Mary, came the flowering of medieval piety, as evidenced in the writings of St. Anselm (d. 1109), St. Bernard (d. 1153) and his fellow Cistercians, and the great scholastic doctors like St. Thomas Aquinas (d. 1274) and St. Bonaventure (d. 1274). The medieval authors described Mary as Mediatrix of grace, Dispensatrix of grace, spiritual Mother. Blessed Guerric, the Cistercian abbot of Igny (France, d. 1157), emphasized the maternal role of Mary in the formation of Christ in the faithful: "Like the Church of which she is a figure, Mary is Mother of all who are born to life."

Christian Unity and Mary

At the Reformation, in reaction to abuses, the invocation of the saints was rejected as harmful to confidence in Christ, the unique Mediator. Since the sixteenth century Western Christians have been sharply divided in their understanding of the communion of saints and the legitimacy of "praying to Mary." Recent events, however, hold out hope for a meeting of minds and hearts even in this sensitive area. The Second Vatican Council offered a biblical portrait of Mary without neglecting later developments in doctrine and devotion. The council described the place of Mary in words designed to meet Protestant difficulties; e.g., the much misunderstood word, Mediatrix, was used once only and was explained as completely dependent on the unique mediatorship of Christ (*Constitution on the Church*, Nos. 67, 69).

The conciliar *Decree on Ecumenism*, issued Nov. 21, 1964, spoke of the "order" or "hierarchy of truths" among Catholic doctrines, which differ in their relationship to the foundation of the faith (No. 11). The foundation is Jesus Christ, and here all Christians share a common profession of faith. The document mentioned realistically some differences that still divide Catholics and other Christians, in this "order of truths': the meaning of the Incarnation and Redemption, the mystery and ministry of the Church, and the role of Mary in the work of salvation (No. 20). The decree also said in this context: "We rejoice to see our separated brethren looking to Christ as the source and center of ecclesiastical communion. Inspired by longing for union with Christ, they feel compelled to search for unity ever more ardently, and to bear witness to their faith among all the peoples of the earth."

The formation of the Ecumenical Society of the Blessed Virgin Mary in England in 1967, and of the American branch in 1976, is an encouraging sign. The American bishops' pastoral, *"Behold Your Mother,"* appealed to the "basic reverence" of all Christians for Mary, "a veneration deeper than doctrinal differences and theological disputes" (Nos. 101-112). Pope Paul VI's major document, *Marialis Cultus*, contains an appeal to other Christians (Nos. 32 and 33). With Christians of the East, said Pope Paul, Catholics honor the Mother of God as "hope of Christians." Catholics join with Anglicans and Protestants in common praise of God, using the Virgin's own words (Lk. 1:46-55).

It may well be that the growing interest in the bonds between the Blessed Virgin and the Holy Spirit will help Christians together. The Spirit of unity inspired Mary's prophecy: "All generations will call me blessed, because he who is mighty has done great things for me" (Lk. 1:48-49).

NORTH AMERICAN COLLEGE

The North American College was founded by the bishops of the United States in 1859 as a residence and house of formation for U.S. seminarians and graduate students in Rome. The first ordination of an alumnus took place June 14, 1862. Pontifical status was granted the college by Leo XIII Oct. 25, 1884. Students living at the college study theology and related subjects in the various pontifical universities and institutes in Rome, principally at the Pontifical Gregorian University.

The college is directed by an American rector (Msgr. Lawrence Purcell of San Diego) and staff, and operates under the auspices of a U.S. bishops' committee which was set up in 1924.

APPARITIONS OF THE BLESSED VIRGIN MARY

Only seven of the best known apparitions of the Blessed Virgin Mary are described briefly below.

The sites of the following apparitions have become shrines and centers of pilgrimage. Miracles of the moral and physical orders have been reported as occurring at these places and/or in connection with related practices of prayer and penance.

Banneux, near Liege, Belgium: Mary appeared eight times between Jan. 15 and Mar. 2, 1933, to an 11-year-old peasant girl, Mariette Beco, in a garden behind the family cottage in Banneux, near Liege. She called herself the Virgin of the Poor, and has since been venerated as Our Lady of the Poor, the Sick, and the Indifferent. A small chapel was built by a spring near the site of the apparitions and was blessed Aug. 15, 1933. Approval of devotion to Our Lady of Banneux was given in 1949 by Bishop Louis J. Kerkhofs of Liege, and a statue of that title was solemnly crowned in 1956.

Over 100 sanctuaries throughout the world are dedicated to the honor of Our Lady of Banneux.

Beauraing, Belgium: Mary appeared 33 times between Nov. 29, 1932, and Jan. 3, 1933, to five children in the garden of a convent school in Beauraing. A chapel, which became a pilgrimage center, was erected on the spot. Reserved approval of devotion to Our Lady of Beauraing was given Feb. 2, 1943, and final approbation July 2, 1949, by Bishop Charue of Namur.

The **Marian Union of Beauraing,** a prayer association for the conversion of sinners, has thousands of members throughout the world (see Pro Maria Committee).

Fatima, Portugal: Mary appeared six times between May 13 and Oct. 13, 1917, to three children in a field called Cova da Iria near Fatima, north of Lisbon. She recommended frequent recitation of the Rosary; urged works of mortification for the conversion of sinners; called for devotion to herself under the title of her Immaculate Heart; asked that the people of Russia be consecrated to her under this title, and that the faithful make a Communion of reparation on the first Saturday of each month.

The apparitions were declared worthy of belief in October, 1930, after a seven-year canonical investigation, and devotion to Our Lady of Fatima was authorized under the title of Our Lady of the Rosary. In October, 1942, Pius XII consecrated the world to Mary under the title of her Immaculate Heart. Ten years later, in the first apostolic letter addressed directly to the peoples of Russia, he consecrated them in a special manner to Mary.

Fatima, with its sanctuary and basilica, ranks with Lourdes as the greatest of modern Marian shrines.

(See First Saturday Devotion.)

Guadalupe, Mexico: Mary appeared four times in 1531 to an Indian, Juan Diego, on Tepeyac hill outside of Mexico City, and instructed him to tell Bishop Zumarraga of her wish that a church be built there. The bishop complied with the request about two years later after being convinced of the genuineness of the apparition by the evidence of a miraculously painted life-size figure of the Virgin on the mantle of the Indian. The mantle bearing the picture has been preserved and is enshrined in the Basilica of Our Lady of Guadalupe, which has a long history as a center of devotion and pilgrimage in Mexico. The shrine church, originally dedicated in 1709 and subsequently enlarged, has the title of basilica.

Benedict XIV, in a decree issued in 1754, authorized a Mass and Office under the title of Our Lady of Guadalupe for celebration on Dec. 12, and named Mary the patroness of New Spain. Our Lady of Guadalupe was designated patroness of Latin America by St. Pius X in 1910 and patroness of the Americas by Pius XII in 1945.

La Salette, France: Mary appeared as a sorrowing and weeping figure Sept. 19, 1846, to two peasant children, Melanie Matthieu, 15, and Maximin Giraud, 11, at La Salette in southern France. The message she confided to them, regarding the necessity of penance, was communicated to Pius IX in 1851 and has since been known at the "secret" of La Salette. Bishop de Bruillard of Grenoble declared in 1851 that the apparition was credible, and devotion to Mary under the title of Our Lady of La Salette was authorized. The devotion has been confirmed by popes since the time of Pius IX, and a Mass and Office with this title were authorized in 1942. The shrine church was given the title of minor basilica in 1879.

Lourdes, France: Mary, identifying herself as the Immaculate Conception, appeared 18 times between Feb. 11 and July 16, 1858, to 14-year-old Bernadette Soubirous at the grotto of Massabielle near Lourdes in southern France. Her message concerned the necessity of prayer and penance for the conversion of peoples. Mary's request that a chapel be built at the grotto and spring was fulfilled in 1862 after four years of rigid examination established the credibility of the apparitions. Devotion under the title of Our Lady of Lourdes was authorized later, and a Feb. 11 feast commemorating the apparitions was instituted by Leo XIII. St. Pius X extended this feast throughout the Church in 1907.

The Church of Notre Dame was made a basilica in 1870, and the Church of the Rosary was built later. The underground Church of St. Pius X, consecrated Mar. 25, 1958, is the second largest church in the world, with a capacity of 20,000 persons.

Our Lady of the Miraculous Medal, France: Mary appeared three times in 1830 to Catherine Laboure in the chapel of the motherhouse of the Daughters of Charity of St. Vincent de Paul, Rue de Bac, Paris. She commissioned Catherine to have made the medal of the Immaculate Conception, now known as the Miraculous Medal, and to spread devotion to her under this title. In 1832, the medal was struck according to the model revealed to Catherine.

The Second Vatican Council, in its "Decree on Eastern Catholic Churches", stated the following points. regarding Eastern heritage, patriarchs, sacraments and worship.

The Catholic Church holds in high esteem the institutions of the Eastern Churches, their liturgical rites, ecclesiastical traditions, and Christian way of life. For, distinguished as they are by their venerable antiquity, they are bright with that tradition which was handed down from the Apostles through the Fathers, and which forms part of the divinely revealed and undivided heritage of the universal Church (No. 1).

That Church, Holy and Catholic, which is the Mystical Body of Christ, is made up of the faithful who are organically united in the Holy Spirit through the same faith, the same sacraments, and the same government and who, combining into various groups held together by a hierarchy, form separate Churches or rites. . . . It is the mind of the Catholic Church that each individual Church or rite retain its traditions whole and entire, while adjusting its way of life to the various needs of time and place (No. 2).

Such individual Churches, whether of the East or of the West, although they differ somewhat among themselves in what are called rites (that is, in liturgy, ecclesiastical discipline, and spiritual heritage) are, nevertheless, equally entrusted to the pastoral guidance of the Roman Pontiff, the divinely appointed successor of St. Peter in supreme government over the universal Church. They are consequently of equal dignity, so that none of them is superior to the others by reason of rite (No. 3).

Eastern Heritage: Each and every Catholic, as also the baptized . . . of every non-Catholic Church or community who enters into the fullness of Catholic communion, should everywhere retain his proper rite, cherish it, and observe it to the best of his ability (No. 4).

The Churches of the East, as much as those of the West, fully enjoy the right, and are in duty bound, to rule themselves. Each should do so according to its proper and individual procedures (No. 5).

All Eastern rite members should know and be convinced that they can and should always preserve their lawful liturgical rites and their established way of life, and that these should not be altered except by way of an appropriate and organic development (No. 6)

Patriarchs: The institution of the patriarchate has existed in the Church from the earliest times and was recognized by the first ecumenical Synods.

By the name Eastern Patriarch is meant the bishop who has jurisdiction over all bishops (including metropolitans), clergy, and people of his own territory or rite, in accordance with the norms of law and without prejudice to the primacy of the Roman Pontiff (No. 7).

Though some of the patriarchates of the Eastern Churches are of later origin than others, all are equal in patriarchal dignity. Still the honorary and lawfully established order of precedence among them is to be preserved (No. 8).

In keeping with the most ancient tradition of the Church, the Patriarchs of the Eastern Churches are to be accorded exceptional respect, since each presides over his patriarchate as father and head.

This sacred Synod, therefore, decrees that their rights and privileges should be re-established in accord with the ancient traditions of each Church and the decrees of the ecumenical Synods.

The rights and privileges in question are those which flourished when East and West were in union, though they should be somewhat adapted to modern conditions.

The Patriarchs with their synods constitute the superior authority for all affairs of the patriarchate, including the right to establish new eparchies and to nominate bishops of their rite within the territorial bounds of the patriarchate, without prejudice to the inalienable right of the Roman Pontiff to intervene in individual cases (No. 9).

What has been said of Patriarchs applies as well, under the norm of law, to major archbishops, who preside over the whole of some individual Church or rite (No. 10).

Sacraments: This sacred Ecumenical Synod endorses and lauds the ancient discipline of the sacraments existing in the Eastern Churches, as also the practices connected with their celebration and administration (No. 12).

With respect to the minister of holy chrism (confirmation), let that practice be fully restored which existed among Easterners in most ancient times. Priests, therefore, can validly confer this sacrament, provided they use chrism blessed by a Patriarch or bishop (No. 13).

In conjunction with baptism or otherwise, all Eastern-Rite priests can confer this sacrament validly on all the faithful of any rite, including the Latin; licitly, however, only if the regulations of both common and particular law are observed. Priests of the Latin rite, to the extent of the faculties they enjoy for administering this sacrament, can confer it also on the faithful of Eastern Churches, without prejudice to rite. They do so licitly if the regulations of both common and particular law are observed (No. 14).

The faithful are bound on Sundays and feast days to attend the divine liturgy or, according to the regulations or custom of their own rite, the celebration of the Divine Praises. That the faithful may be able to satisfy their obligation more easily, it is decreed that this obligation can be fulfilled from the Vespers of the vigil to the end of the Sunday or the feast day (No. 15).

Because of the everyday intermingling of the communicants of diverse Eastern Churches in the same Eastern region or territory, the faculty for hearing confession, duly and unrestrictedly granted by his proper bishop to a priest of any rite, is applicable to the entire territory of the grantor, also to the places and the faithful belonging to any other rite in the same territory, unless an Ordinary of the place explicitly decides otherwise with respect to the places pertaining to his rite (No. 16).

This sacred Synod ardently desires that where it has fallen into disuse the office of the permanent diaconate be restored. The legislative authority of each individual church should decide about the subdiaconate and the minor orders (No. 17).

By way of preventing invalid marriages between Eastern Catholics and baptized Eastern non-Catholics, and in the interests of the permanence and sanctity of marriage and of domestic harmony, this sacred Synod decrees that the canonical 'form' for the celebration of such marriages obliges only for lawfulness. For their validity, the presence of a sacred minister suffices, as long as the other requirements of law are honored (No. 18).

Worship: Henceforth, it will be the exclusive right of an ecumenical Synod or the Apostolic See to establish, transfer, or suppress feast days common to all the Eastern Churches. To establish, transfer, or suppress feast days for any of the individual Churches is within the competence not only of the Apostolic See but also of a patriarchal or archiepiscopal synod, provided due consideration is given to the entire region and to other individual Churches (No. 19).

Until such time as all Christians desirably concur on a fixed day for the celebration of Easter, and with a view meantime to promoting unity among the Christians of a given area or nation, it is left to the Patriarchs or supreme authorities of a place to reach a unanimous agreement, after ascertaining the views of all concerned, on a single Sunday for the observance of Easter (No. 20).

With respect to rules concerning sacred seasons, individual faithful dwelling outside the area or territory of their own rite may conform completely to the established custom of the place where they live. When members of a family belong to different rites, they are all permitted to observe sacred seasons according to the rules of any one of these rites (No. 21).

From ancient times the Divine Praises have been held in high esteem among all Eastern Churches. Eastern clerics and religious should celebrate these Praises as the laws and customs of their own traditions require. To the extent they can, the faithful too should follow the example of their forebears by assisting devoutly at the Divine Praises (No. 22).

Origin

The Church had its beginnings in Palestine, whence it spread to other regions of the world. As it spread, certain cities or jurisdictions became key centers of Christian life and missionary endeavor — notably, Jerusalem, Alexandria, Antioch and Constantinople in the East, and Rome in the West — with the result that their practices became diffused throughout their spheres of influence. Various rites originated from these practices which, although rooted in the essentials of Christian faith, were different in significant respects because of their relationships to particular cultural patterns.

Patriarchal Jurisdictions

The main lines of Eastern Church organization and liturgy were drawn before the Roman Empire was separated into Eastern and Western divisions in 292. It was originally co-extensive with the boundaries of the Eastern Empire. Its jurisdictions were those of the patriarchates of Alexandria and Antioch (recognized as such by the Council of Nicaea in 325), and of Jerusalem and Constantinople (given similar recognition by the Council of Chalcedon in 451). These were the major parent bodies of the Eastern Rite Churches which for centuries were identifiable only with limited numbers of nationality and language groups in Eastern Europe, the Middle East and parts of Asia and Africa. Their members are now scattered throughout the world.

RITES AND FAITHFUL OF EASTERN CHURCHES

(Principal source of statistics: *Annuario Pontificio*. The statistics are for Eastern-Rite jurisdictions only, and do not include Eastern-Rite Catholics under the jurisdiction of Roman-Rite bishops. Some of the figures reported are only approximate. Some of the jurisdictions listed may be inactive because of government suppression.)

The Byzantine, Alexandrian, Antiochene, Armenian and Chaldean are the five principal rites used in their entirety or in modified form by the various Eastern churches. The number of Eastern Catholics throughout the world is more than 12 million.

Alexandrian Rite

Called the Liturgy of St. Mark, the Alexandrian Rite was modified by the Copts and Melkites, and contains elements of the Byzantine Rite of St. Basil and the liturgies of Sts. Mark, Cyril and Gregory of Nazianzen. The liturgy is substantially that of the Coptic Church, which is divided into two branches — the Coptic or Egyptian, and the Ethio-

pian or Abyssinian. The faithful of this rite are:

COPTS: Resumed communion with Rome about 1741; situated in Egypt, the Near East; liturgical languages are Coptic, Arabic. Jurisdictions (located in Egypt): patriarchate of Alexandria, five dioceses; 150,178.

ETHIOPIANS: Resumed comunion with Rome in 1846: situated in Ethiopia, Jerusalem, Somalia; liturgical language is Geez. Jurisdictions (located in Ethiopia): one archdiocese, two dioceses; 111,862.

Antiochene Rite

This is the source of more derived rites than any of the other parent rites. Its origin can be traced to the Eighth Book of the *Apostolic Constitutions* and to the Liturgy of St. James of Jerusalem, which ultimately spread throughout the whole patriarchate and displaced older forms based on the *Apostolic Constitutions*. The faithful of this rite are:

MALANKARESE: Resumed communion with Rome in 1930; situated in India; liturgical languages are Syriac, Malayalam. Jurisdictions (located in India): one archdiocese, two dioceses; 265,406.

MARONITES: United to the Holy See since the time of their founder, St. Maron; have no counterparts among the separated Eastern Christians: situated throughout the world: liturgical languages are Syriac, Arabic. Jurisdictions (located in Lebanon, Cyprus, Egypt, Syria, U.S., Brazil, Australia, Canada): patriarchate of Antioch, 17 archdioceses and dioceses, one patriarchal vicariate; 1,754,613. Where no special jurisdictions exist, they are under jurisdiction of local Roman-Rite bishops.

SYRIANS: Resumed communion with Rome in 1781; situated in Asia, Africa, the Americas, Australia; liturgical languages are Syriac, Arabic. Jurisdictions (located in Lebanon, Iraq, Egypt and Syria): patriarchate of Antioch, seven archdioceses and dioceses, three patriarchal vicariates; 96,132.

Armenian Rite

Substantially, although using a different language, this is the Greek Liturgy of St. Basil; it is considered an older form of the Byzantine Rite, and incorporates some modifications from the Antiochene Rite. The faithful of this rite are:

ARMENIANS, exclusively: Resumed communion with Rome during the time of the Crusades; situated in the Near East, Europe, Africa, the Americas, Australasia: liturgical language is Classical Armenian. Jurisdictions (located in Lebanon, Iran, Iraq, Egypt, Syria, Turkey, Poland, France, Greece, Rumania, Argentina (for Latin America, including Mexico), and the United States (for Canada and the U.S.): patriarchate of Cilicia, nine archdioceses and dioceses, two patriarchal vicariates, two exarchates, two ordinariates; 152,104.

Byzantine Rite

Based on the Rite of St. James of Jerusalem and the churches of Antioch, and reformed by Sts. Basil and John Chrysostom, the Byzantine Rite is proper to the Church of Constantinople. (The city was called Byzantium before Constantine changed its name; the modern name is Istanbul.) It is now used by the majority of Eastern Catholics and by the Eastern Orthodox Church (which is not in union with Rome). It is, after the Roman, the most widely used rite. The faithful of this rite are:

ALBANIANS: Resumed communion with Rome about 1628; situated in Albania; liturgical language is Albanian. Jurisdiction (located in Albania): one apostolic administration.

BULGARIANS: Resumed communion with Rome about 1861; situated in Bulgaria; liturgical language is Old Slavonic. Jurisdiction (located in Bulgaria): one apostolic exarchate.

BYELORUSSIANS, also known as WHITE RUSSIANS: Resumed communion with Rome in the 17th century; situated in Europe, the Americas, Australia; liturgical language is Old Slavonic. They have an apostolic visitator.

GEORGIANS: Resumed communion with Rome in 1861; situated in Georgia (Southern Russia), France; liturgical language is Georgian. They have an apostolic administrator.

GREEKS: Resumed communion with Rome in 1829; situated in Greece, Asia Minor, Europe; liturgical language is Greek. Jurisdictions (located in Greece and Turkey): two exarchates; 2,360.

HUNGARIANS: Descendants of Ruthenians who resumed communion with Rome in 1646; situated in Hungary, the rest of Europe, the Americas; liturgical languages are Greek, Hungarian, English. Jurisdictions (located in Hungary): one diocese and one exarchate: 272,800.

ITALO-ALBANIANS: Have never been separated from Rome; situated in Italy, Sicily, the Americas; liturgical languages are Greek, Italo-Albanian. Jurisdictions (located in Italy): two dioceses, one abbacy; 69,109.

MELKITES (GREEK CATHOLICS-MELKITES): Resumed communion with Rome during the time of the Crusades, but definitive reunion did not take place until early in the 18th century; situated in the Middle East, Asia, Africa, Europe, the Americas, Australia; liturgical languages are Greek, Arabic, English, Portuguese, Spanish. Jurisdictions (located in Syria, Lebanon, Jordan, Israel, U.S., Brazil, Canada): patriarchate of Antioch (with patriarchal vicariates in Egypt, Sudan, Jerusalem, Iraq and Kuwait), 17 archdioceses and dioceses; 970,003.

ROMANIANS: Resumed communion with Rome in 1697; situated in Romania, the rest of Europe, the Americas; liturgical language is Modern Romanian. Jurisdictions (located in Romania and U.S.): one archdiocese, four dioceses, one exarchate. There were 1.5 million members in 1948 when they were forcibly incorporated into the Romanian Orthodox Church. They have an apostolic exarchate in the U.S.

RUSSIANS: Resumed communion with Rome about 1905; situated in Europe, the Americas, Australia, China; liturgical language is Old Slavonic. Jurisdictions (located in Russia and China): two exarchates.

RUTHENIANS, or CARPATHO-RUSSIANS (Rusins): Resumed communion with Rome in the Union of Brest-Litovek, 1596, and the Union of Uzhorod, Apr. 24, 1646; situated in Hungary, Czechoslovakia, elsewhere in Europe, the Americas, Australia; liturgical languages are Old Slavonic, English. Jurisdictions (located in Russia and the U.S.): one archdiocese, four dioceses.

SLOVAKS: Jurisdictions (located in Czechoslovakia and Canada): two dioceses 386,648.

UKRAINIANS, or GALICIAN RUTHENIANS: Resumed communion with Rome about 1595; situated in Europe, the Americas, Australasia; liturgical languages are Old Slavonic and Ukrainian. Jurisdictions (located in Russian Galicia, Poland, the U.S., Canada, England, Australia, Germany, France, Brazil, Argentina): major archdiocese of Lwow, two archdioceses, 12 dioceses, four apostolic exarchates: 4.3 million. This total includes the 1943 figure of 3.5 million Ukrainian Catholics in jurisdictions subsequently forced into the Russian Orthodox Church.

YUGOSLAVS, SERBS and CROATIANS: Resumed communion with Rome in 1611; situated in Yugoslavia, the Americas; liturgical language is Old Slavonic. Jurisdiction (located in Yugoslavia): one diocese (which also has jurisdiction over all Byzantine-Rite faithful in Yugoslavia); 48,822. They are under the jurisdiction of Ruthenian bishops elsewhere.

Chaldean Rite

This rite, listed as separate and distinct by the Congregation for the Oriental Churches, was derived from the Antiochene Rite. The faithful of this rite are:

CHALDEANS: Descendants of the Nestorians, resumed communion with Rome in 1692; situated throughout the Middle East, in Europe, Africa, the Americas; liturgical languages are Syriac, Arabic. Jurisdictions (located in Egypt, Iraq, Iran, Lebanon, Syria, Turkey, U.S.); patriarchate of Babylonia, 21 archdioceses and dioceses; 409,894. There is a patriarchal vicar for Jordan.

SYRO-MALABARESE: Descended from the St. Thomas Christians of India; situated mostly in the Malabar region of India; they use a Westernized and Latinized form of the Chaldean Rite in Syriac and Malayalam. Jurisdictions (located in India): two archdioceses, 18 dioceses; 2,625,411.

EASTERN JURISDICTIONS

For centuries Eastern-Rite Catholics were identifiable with a limited number of nationality and language groups in certain countries of the Middle East, Eastern Europe, Asia and Africa. The persecution of religion in the Soviet Union since 1917 and in communist-controlled countries since World War II, however — in addition to decimating and destroying the Church in those places — has resulted in the emigration of many Eastern-Rite Catholics from their homelands. This forced emigration, together with voluntary emigration, has led to the spread of Eastern Rites and their faithful to many other countries.

Europe

(Bishop Vasile Cristea, A.A., is apostolic visitor for Romanian Byzantine Rite Catholics in Europe.)

ALBANIA: Byzantine Rite, apostolic administration.

AUSTRIA: Byzantine Rite, ordinariate.

BULGARIA: Byzantine Rite (Bulgarians), apostolic exarchate.

CZECHOSLOVAKIA: Byzantine Rite (Slovakians and other Byzantine-Rite Catholics), eparchy.

FRANCE: Byzantine Rite (Ukrainians), apostolic exarchate.

Armenian Rite, eparchy (1986).

Ordinariate for all other Eastern-Rite Catholics.

GERMANY: Byzantine Rite (Ukrainians), apostolic exarchate.

GREAT BRITAIN: Byzantine Rite (Ukrainians), apostolic exarchate.

GREECE: Byzantine Rite, apostolic exarchate.

Armenian Rite, ordinariate.

HUNGARY: Byzantine Rite (Hungarians), eparchy, apostolic exarchate.

ITALY: Byzantine Rite (Italo-Albanians), two eparchies, one abbacy.

POLAND: Byzantine Rite (Ukrainian), apostolic exarchate.

Armenian Rite, archeparchy.

RUMANIA: Byzantine Rite (Romanians), metropolitan, four eparchies.

Armenian Rite, ordinariate.

RUSSIA: Byzantine Rite (Russians), apostolic exarchate; (Ruthenians), eparchy; (Ukrainians), major archeparchy, two eparchies.

YUGOSLAVIA: Byzantine Rite (Yugoslav and other Byzantine-Rite Catholics), eparchy.

Asia

CHINA: Byzantine Rite (Russians), apostolic exarchate.

CYPRUS: Antiochene Rite (Maronites), archeparchy.

INDIA: Antiochene Rite (Malankarese), metropolitan see, two eparchies.

Chaldean Rite (Syro-Malabarese), two metropolitan sees, 18 eparchies.

IRAN: Chaldean Rite (Chaldeans), two metropolitan sees, one archeparchy, one eparchy.

Armenian Rite, eparchy.

IRAQ: Antiochene Rite (Syrians), two archeparchies.

Byzantine Rite (Greek-Melkites), patriarchal vicariate.

Chaldean Rite (Chaldeans), patriarchate, two metropolitan sees, eight archeparchies and eparchies.

Armenian Rite, archeparchy.

ISRAEL (includes Jerusalem): Antiochene Rite (Syrians), patriarchal vicariate; (Maronites), patriarchal vicariate.

Byzantine Rite (Greek-Melkites), archeparchy, patriarchal vicariate.

Chaldean Rite (Chaldeans), patriarchal vicariate.

Armenian Rite, patriarchal vicariate.

JORDAN: Byzantine Rite (Greek-Melkites), archeparchy.

KUWAIT: Byzantine Rite (Greek-Melkites), patriarchal vicariate.

LEBANON: Antiochene Rite (Maronites), patriarchate, eight archeparchies and eparchies; (Syrians), patriarchate.

Byzantine Rite (Greek-Melkites), seven metropolitan and archeparchal sees.

Chaldean Rite (Chaldeans), eparchy.

Armenian Rite, patriarchate, eparchy.

SYRIAN ARAB REPUBLIC: Antiochene Rite (Maronites), two archeparchies, one eparchy; (Syrians), four archeparchies.

Byzantine Rite (Greek-Melkites), patriarchate, four metropolitan sees, one archeparchy.

Chaldean Rite (Chaldeans), eparchy.

Armenian Rite, archeparchy, eparchy, patriarchal vicariate.

TURKEY (Europe and Asia): Antiochene Rite (Syrians), patriarchal vicariate.

Byzantine Rite (Greeks), apostolic exarchate.

Chaldean Rite (Chaldeans), one archeparchy, two eparchies.

Armenian Rite, archeparchy.

Oceania

AUSTRALIA: Byzantine Rite (Ukrainians), eparchy.

Antiochene Rite (Maronites), eparchy.

Africa

EGYPT, ARAB REPUBLIC OF: Alexandrian Rite (Copts), patriarchate, five eparchies.

Antiochene Rite (Maronites), eparchy; (Syrians), eparchy.

Byzantine Rite (Greek-Melkites), patriarchal vicariate.

Chaldean Rite (Chaldeans), eparchy.

Armenian Rite, eparchy.

ETHIOPIA: Alexandrian Rite (Ethiopians), metropolitan see, two eparchies.

SUDAN: Byzantine Rite (Greek-Melkites), patriarchal vicariate.

North America

CANADA: Byzantine Rite (Ukrainians), one metropolitan, four eparchies; (Slovaks), eparchy; (Greek-Melkites), eparchy.

Armenian Rite, apostolic exarchate for Canada and the U.S. (New York is see city).

Antiochene Rite (Maronites), eparchy.

UNITED STATES: Antiochene Rite (Maronites), eparchy.

Byzantine Rite (Ukrainians), one metropolitan see, three eparchies; (Ruthenians), one metropolitan see, three eparchies; (Greek-Melkites), eparchy; (Romanians), apostolic exarchate; (Byelorussians), apostolic visitator.

Armenian Rite, apostolic exarchate for Canada and U.S. (New York is see city).

Chaldean Rite, eparchy.

Other Eastern-Rite Catholics are under the jurisdiction of local Roman-Rite bishops. (See Eastern-Rite Catholics in the United States.)

South America

Armenian-Rite Catholics in Latin America (including Mexico) are under the jurisdiction of an apostolic exarchate (see city, Buenos Aires, Argentina).

ARGENTINA: Byzantine Rite (Ukrainians), eparchy.

Armenian Rite, apostolic exarchate (for Latin America)

Ordinariate for all other Eastern-Rite Catholics.

BRAZIL: Antiochene Rite (Maronites), eparchy.

Byzantine Rite (Greek-Melkites), eparchy; (Ukrainians), eparchy.

Ordinariate for all other Eastern-Rite Catholics.

A Ukrainian liturgy celebrated Dec. 1, 1985, in Detroit marked the 100th anniversary of Ukrainian Christianity in the United States.

SYNODS, ASSEMBLIES

These assemblies are collegial bodies which have pastoral authority over members of the Eastern Rite Churches.

Patriarchal Synods: Maronites: Nasrallah Sfeir, patriarch of Antioch of the Maronites.

Melkites: Maximos V Hakim, patriarch of Antioch of the Greek Catholics-Melkites.

Chaldeans: Paul II Cheikho, patriarch of Babylonia of the Chaldeans.

Copts: Andraos Ghattas, C.M., patriarch of Alexandria of the Copts.

Syrians: Ignace Antoine II Hayek, patriarch of Antioch of the Syrians.

Armenians: Jean Pierre XVIII Kasparian, patriarch of Cilicia of the Armenians.

Non-Patriarchal Synod: The Synod of the Ukrainian Catholic Hierarchy is an extraterritorial synod convoked with the assent of the Pope. Cardinal Myroslav Ivan Lubachivsky, major archbishop of Lwow of the Ukrainians, is president.

Assemblies: Assembly of Ordinaries of the Arab Republic of Egypt: Andraos Ghattas, C.M., patriarch of Alexandria of the Copts, president.

Assembly of Catholic Patriarchs and Bishops of Lebanon.

Assembly of Ordinaries of the Syrian Arab Republic: Maximos V Hakim, patriarch of Antioch of the Greek Catholics-Melkites, president.

Interritual Union of the Bishops of Iraq: Paul II Cheikho, patriarch of Babylonia of the Chaldeans, president.

Syro-Malabarese Episcopal Conference (June 4, 1970): Most Rev. Anthony Padiyara, archbishop of Ernakulam, president.

Iranian Episcopal Conference (Aug. 11, 1977): Most Rev. Youhannan Semaan Issayi, metropolitan of Teheran of the Chaldeans, president.

Of the collegial bodies listed above, the patriarchal synods have the most authority. In addition to other prerogatives, they have the right to elect bishops and regulate discipline for their respective rites.

EASTERN RITES IN U.S.

(Statistics, from the *Official Catholic Directory*, are membership figures reported by Eastern-Rite jurisdictions. Additional Eastern-Rite Catholics are included in statistics for Roman-Rite dioceses.)

Byzantine Rite

Ukrainians: There were 156,674 reported in four jurisdictions in the U.S.: the metropolitan see of Philadelphia (1924, metropolitan 1958) and the suffragan sees of Stamford, Conn. (1956), St. Nicholas of Chicago (1961) and St. Josaphat in Parma (1983).

Ruthenians: There were 281,449 reported in four jurisdictions in the U.S.: the metropolitan see of Pittsburgh (est. 1924 at Pittsburgh; metropolitan and transferred to Munhall, 1969; transferred to Pittsburgh, 1977) and the suffragan sees of Passaic, N.J. (1963), Parma, Ohio (1969) and Van

Nuys, Calif. (1981). Hungarian and Croatian Byzantine Catholics in the U.S. are also under the jurisdiction of Ruthenian-Rite bishops.

Melkites (Greek Catholics-Melkites): In 1986, 24,218 were reported under the jurisdiction of the Melkite eparchy of Newton, Mass. (established as an exarchate, 1965; eparchy, 1976).

Romanians: There were 3,400 reported in 16 Romanian Catholic Byzantine Rite parishes in the U.S., under the jurisdiction of an apostolic exarchate established in 1982 (see city, Canton, Ohio).

Byelorussians: Have one parish in the U.S. — Christ the Redeemer, Chicago, Ill.

Russians: Have parishes in California (St. Andrew, El Segundo, and Our Lady of Fatima Center, San Francisco); Massachusetts (Our Lady of Kazan, Boston); New York (St. Michael's Chapel of St. Patrick's Old Cathedral). They are under the jurisdiction of local Roman-Rite bishops.

Antiochene Rite

In 1986, 50,893 Maronites were reported under the jurisdiction of the eparchy of St. Maron, Brooklyn (established at Detroit as an exarchate, 1966; eparchy, 1972; transferred to Brooklyn, 1977).

Armenian Rite

An apostolic exarchate for Canada and the United States (see city, New York) was established July 3, 1981; 32,000 in both countries (*Annuario Pontificio*).

Chaldean Rite

In 1986, 42,000 were reported under the jurisdiction of the eparchy of St. Thomas Apostle of Detroit (established as an exarchate, 1982; eparchy, 1986).

BYZANTINE DIVINE LITURGY

The Divine Liturgy in all rites is based on the consecration of bread and wine by the narration-reactualization of the actions of Christ at the Last Supper. Aside from this fundamental usage, there are differences between the Roman (Latin) Rite and Eastern Rites, and among the Eastern Rites themselves. Following is a general description of the Byzantine Divine Liturgy which is in widest use in the Eastern-Rite Churches.

In the Byzantine, as in all Eastern Rites, the bread and wine are prepared at the start of the Liturgy. The priest does this in a little niche or at a table in the sanctuary. Taking a round loaf of leavened bread stamped with religious symbols, he cuts out a square host and other particles while reciting verses expressing the symbolism of the action. When the bread and wine are ready, he says a prayer of offering and incenses the oblations, the altar, the icons and people.

Liturgy of the Catechumens: At the altar a litany for all classes of people is sung by the priest. The congregation answers, "Lord, have mercy."

The Little Entrance comes next. In procession, the priest leaves the sanctuary carrying the Book of the Gospels, and then returns. He sings prayers especially selected for the day and the feast. These are followed by the solemn singing of the prayer, "Holy God, Holy Mighty One, Holy Immortal One."

The Epistle follows. The Gospel is sung or read by the priest facing the people at the middle door of the sanctuary.

An interruption after the Liturgy of the Catechumens, formerly an instructional period for those learning the faith, is clearly marked. Catechumens, if present, are dismissed with a prayer. Following this are a prayer and litany for the faithful.

Great Entrance: The Great Entrance or solemn Offertory Procession then takes place. The priest first says a long silent prayer for himself, in preparation for the great act to come. Again he incenses the oblations, the altar, the icons and people. He goes to the table on the gospel side for the veil-covered paten and chalice. When he arrives back at the sanctuary door, he announces the intention of the Mass in the prayer: "May the Lord God remember all of you in his kingdom, now and forever."

After another litany, the congregation recites the Nicene Creed.

Consecration: The most solemn portion of the sacrifice is introduced by the preface, which is very much like the preface of the Roman Rite. At the beginning of the last phrase, the priest raises his voice to introduce the singing of the Sanctus. During the singing he reads the introduction to the words of consecration.

The words of consecration are sung aloud, and the people sing "Amen" to both consecrations. As the priest raises the Sacred Species in solemn offering, he sings: "Thine of Thine Own we offer unto Thee in behalf of all and for all."

A prayer to the Holy Spirit is followed by the commemorations, in which special mention is made of the all-holy, most blessed and glorious Lady, the Mother of God and ever-Virgin Mary. The dead are remembered and then the living.

Holy Communion: A final litany for spiritual gifts precedes the Our Father. The Sacred Body and Blood are elevated with the words, "Holy Things for the Holy." The Host is then broken and commingled with the Precious Blood. The priest recites preparatory prayers for Holy Communion, consumes the Sacred Species, and distributes Holy Communion to the people under the forms of both bread and wine. During this time a communion verse is sung by the choir or congregation.

The Liturgy closes quickly after this. The consecrated Species of bread and wine are removed to the side table to be consumed later by the priest. A prayer of thanksgiving is recited, a prayer for all the people is said in front of the icon of Christ, a blessing is invoked upon all, and the people are dismissed.

BYZANTINE CALENDAR

The Byzantine-Rite calendar has many distinctive features of its own, although it shares common elements with the Roman-Rite calendar

— e.g., general purpose, commemoration of the mysteries of faith and of the saints, identical dates for some feasts. Among the distinctive things are the following.

The liturgical year begins on Sept. 1, the **Day of Indiction,** in contrast with the Latin or Roman start on the First Sunday of Advent late in November or early in December. The Advent season begins on Dec. 10.

Cycles of the Year

As in the Roman usage, the dating of feasts follows the Gregorian Calendar. Formerly, until well into this century, the Julian Calendar was used. (The Julian Calendar, which is now about 13 days late, is still used by some Eastern-Rite Churches.)

The year has several cycles, which include proper seasons, the feasts of saints, and series of New Testament readings. All of these elements of worship are contained in liturgical books of the rite.

The ecclesiastical calendar, called the **Menologion,** explains the nature of feasts, other observances and matters pertaining to the liturgy for each day of the year. In some cases, its contents include the lives of saints and the history and meaning of feasts.

The Divine Liturgy (Mass) and Divine Office for the proper of the saints, fixed feasts, and the Christmas season are contained in the **Menaion.** The **Triodion** covers the pre-Lenten season of preparation for Easter; Lent begins two days before the Ash Wednesday observance of the Roman Rite. The **Pentecostarion** contains the liturgical services from Easter to the Sunday of All Saints, the first after Pentecost. The **Evangelion** and **Apostolos** are books in which the Gospels, and Acts of the Apostles and the Epistles, respectively, are arranged according to the order of their reading in the Divine Liturgy and Divine Office throughout the year.

The cyclic progression of liturgical music throughout the year, in successive and repetitive periods of eight weeks, is governed by the **Oktoechos,** the Book of Eight Tones.

Sunday Names

Many Sundays are named after the subject of the Gospel read in the Mass of the day or after the name of a feast falling on the day — e.g., Sunday of the Publican and Pharisee, of the Prodigal Son, of the Samaritan Woman, of St. Thomas the Apostle, of the Fore-Fathers (Old Testament Patriarchs). Other Sundays are named in the same manner as in the Roman calendar — e.g., numbered Sundays of Lent and after Pentecost.

Holy Days

The calendar lists about 28 holy days. Many of the major holy days coincide with those of the Roman calendar, but the feast of the Immaculate Conception is observed on Dec. 9 instead of Dec. 8, and the feast of All Saints falls on the Sunday after Pentecost rather than on Nov. 1. Instead of a single All Souls' Day, there are five All Souls' Saturdays.

According to regulations in effect in the Byzantine-Rite (Ruthenian) Archeparchy of Pittsburgh

and its suffragan sees of Passaic, Parma and Van Nuys, holy days are obligatory, solemn and simple, and attendance at the Divine Liturgy is required on five obligatory days — the feasts of the Epiphany, the Ascension, Sts. Peter and Paul, the Assumption of the Blessed Virgin Mary, and Christmas. Although attendance at the liturgy is not obligatory on 15 solemn and seven simple holy days, it is recommended.

In the Byzantine-Rite (Ukrainian) Archeparchy of Philadelphia and its suffragan sees of St. Josaphat in Parma, St. Nicholas (Chicago) and Stamford, the obligatory feasts are the Circumcision, Epiphany, Annunciation, Easter, Ascension, Pentecost, Dormition (Assumption of Mary), Immaculate Conception and Christmas.

Lent

The first day of Lent — the Monday before Ash Wednesday of the Roman Rite — and Good Friday are days of strict abstinence for persons in the age bracket of obligation. No meat, eggs, or dairy products may be eaten on these days.

All persons over the age of 14 must abstain from meat on Fridays during Lent, Holy Saturday, and the vigils of the feasts of Christmas and Epiphany; abstinence is urged, but is not obligatory, on Wednesdays of Lent. The abstinence obligation is not in force on certain "free" or "privileged" Fridays.

Synaxis

An observance without a counterpart in the Roman calendar is the synaxis. This is a commemoration, on the day following a feast, of persons involved with the occasion for the feast — e.g., Sept. 9, the day following the feast of the Nativity of the Blessed Virgin Mary, is the Synaxis of Joachim and Anna, her parents.

Holy Week

In the Byzantine Rite, Lent is liturgically concluded with the Saturday of Lazarus, the day before Palm Sunday, which commemorates the raising of Lazarus from the dead.

On the following Monday, Tuesday and Wednesday, the Liturgy of the Presanctified is prescribed.

On Holy Thursday, the Liturgy of St. Basil the Great is celebrated together with Vespers.

The Divine Liturgy is not celebrated on Good Friday.

On Holy Saturday, the Liturgy of St. Basil the Great is celebrated along with Vespers.

BYZANTINE FEATURES

Art: Named for the empire in which it developed, Byzantine art is a unique blend of imperial Roman and classic Hellenic culture with Christian inspiration. The art of the Greek Middle Ages, it reached a peak of development in the 10th or 11th century. Characteristic of its products, particularly in mosaic and painting, are majesty, dignity, refinement and grace. Its sacred paintings, called icons, are reverenced highly in all Eastern Rites.

Church Building: The classical model of Byzantine church architecture is the Church of the Holy Wisdom (Hagia Sophia), built in Constantinople in the first half of the sixth century and still standing. The square structure, extended in some cases in the form of a cross, is topped by a distinctive onion-shaped dome and surmounted by a triple-bar cross. The altar is at the eastern end of building, where the wall bellies out to form an apse. The altar and sanctuary are separated from the body of the church by a fixed or movable screen, the iconostas, to which icons or sacred pictures are attached (see below).

Clergy: The Byzantine Rite has married as well as celibate priests. In places other than the US, where married candidates have not been accepted for ordination since about 1929, men already married can be ordained to the diaconate and priesthood and can continue in marriage after ordination. Celibate deacons and priests cannot marry after ordination; neither can a married priest remarry after the death of his wife. Bishops must be unmarried.

Iconostas: A large screen decorated with sacred pictures or icons which separates the sanctuary from the nave of a church; its equivalent in the Roman Rite, for thus separating the sanctuary from the nave, is an altar rail.

An iconostas has three doors through which the sacred ministers enter the sanctuary during the Divine Liturgy: smaller (north and south) Deacons' Doors and a large central Royal Door.

The Deacons' Doors usually feature the icons of Sts. Gabriel and Michael; the Royal Door, the icons of the Evangelists — Matthew, Mark, Luke and John. To the right and left of the Royal Door are the icons of Christ the Teacher and of the Blessed Virgin Mary with the Infant Jesus. To the extreme right and left are the icons of the patron of the church and St. John the Baptist (or St. Nicholas of Myra).

Immediately above the Royal Door is a picture of the Last Supper. To the right are six icons depicting the major feasts of Christ, and to the left are six icons portraying the major feasts of the Blessed Virgin Mary. Above the picture of the Last Supper is a large icon of Christ the King.

Some icon screens also have pictures of the 12 Apostles and the major Old Testament prophets surmounted by a crucifixion scene.

Liturgical Language: In line with Eastern tradition, Byzantine practice has favored the use of the language of the people in the liturgy. Two great advocates of the practice were Sts. Cyril and Methodius, apostles of the Slavs, who devised the Cyrillic alphabet and pioneered the adoption of Slavonic in the liturgy.

Sacraments: Baptism is administered by immersion, and confirmation is conferred at the same time. The Eucharist is administered by intinction, i.e., by giving the communicant a piece of consecrated leavened bread which has been dipped into the consecrated wine. When giving absolution in the sacrament of penance, the priest holds his stole over the head of the penitent. Distinctive marriage ceremonies include the crowning of the bride and groom. Ceremonies for anointing the sick closely resemble those of the Roman Rite. Holy orders are conferred by a bishop.

Sign of the Cross: Eastern-Rite Catholics have a distinctive way of making it (see entry in the Glossary). The sign of the cross in conjunction with a deep bow, instead of a genuflection, expresses reverence for the presence of Christ in the Blessed Sacrament.

VESTMENTS, APPURTENANCES

Sticharion: A long white garment of linen or silk with wide sleeves and decorated with embroidery; formerly the vestment for clerics in minor orders, acolytes, lectors, chanters, and subdeacons; symbolic of purity.

Epitrachelion: A stole with ends sewn together, having a loop through which the head is passed; its several crosses symbolize priestly duties.

Zone: A narrow clasped belt made of the same material as the epitrachelion; symbolic of the wisdom of the priest, his strength against enemies of the Church and his willingness to perform holy duties.

Epimanikia: Ornamental cuffs; the right cuff symbolizing strength, the left, patience and good will.

Phelonion: An ample cape, long in the back and sides and cut away in front; symbolic of the higher gifts of the Holy Spirit.

Antimension: A silk or linen cloth laid on the altar for the Liturgy; it may be decorated with a picture of the burial of Christ and the instruments of his passion; the relics of martyrs are sewn into the front border.

Eileton: A linen cloth which corresponds to the Roman-Rite corporal.

Poterion: A chalice or cup which holds the wine and Precious Blood.

Diskos: A shallow plate, which may be elevated on a small stand, corresponding to the Roman-Rite paten.

Asteriskos: Made of two curved bands of gold or silver which cross each other to form a double arch; a star depends from the junction, which forms a cross; it is placed over the diskos holding the consecrated bread and is covered with a veil.

Veils: Three are used, one to cover the poterion, the second to cover the diskos, and the third to cover both.

Spoon: Used in administering Holy Communion by intinction; consecrated leavened bread is dipped into consecrated wine and spooned onto the tongue of the communicant.

All Rites Equal

The Second Vatican Council's *Decree on Eastern Catholic Churches* declared that the Latin Rite and the Eastern Rites are all "of equal dignity," and "that none of them is superior to the others by reason of rite." The decree also challenged Eastern Churches to recover their authentic liturgical, legal and spiritual traditions, and to play "a special role . . . in promoting the unity of all Christians, particularly Easterners."

SEPARATED EASTERN CHURCHES

Orthodox

Orthodox Churches, the largest and most widespread of the separated Eastern Churches, have much in common with their Eastern Catholic counterparts, including many matters of faith and morals, general discipline, valid orders and sacraments, and liturgy. One important difference is their acceptance of only the first seven ecumenical councils. Another is their rejection of any single supreme head of the Church. They do not acknowledge and hold communion with the pope.

Like their Catholic counterparts, Orthodox Churches are organized in jurisdictions under patriarchs. The patriarchs are the heads of approximately 15 autocephalic and several other autonomous jurisdictions organized along lines of nationality and/or language.

The Ecumenical Patriarch of Constantinople, Dimitrios I, has the primacy of honor among his equal patriarchs but his actual jurisdiction is limited to his own patriarchate. As the spiritual head of worldwide Orthodoxy, he keeps the book of the Holy Canons of the Autocephalous Churches, in which recognized Orthodox Churches are registered, and has the right to call Pan-Orthodox assemblies.

The definitive Orthodox break with Rome dates from 1054.

Top-level relations between the Churches have improved in recent years through the efforts of former Ecumenical Patriarch Athenagoras I, John XXIII, Paul VI and Patriarch Dimitrios I. Pope Paul met with Athenagoras three times before the latter's death in 1972. The most significant action of both spiritual leaders was their mutual nullification of excommunications imposed by the two Churches on each other in 1054.

The largest Orthodox body in the western hemisphere is the Greek Orthodox Archdiocese of North and South America consisting of the Archdiocese of New York, nine dioceses in the U.S., and one diocese each in Canada and South America; it is headed by Archbishop Iakovos and has an estimated membership of 1.9 million. The second largest is the Orthodox Church in America, with approximately one million members; it was given independent status by the Patriarchate of Moscow May 18, 1970, against the will of Athenagoras I who refused to register it in the book of the Holy Canons of Autocephalous Churches. An additional 650,000 or more Orthodox belong to smaller national and language jurisdictions.

Heads of Orthodox jurisdictions in this hemisphere hold membership in the Standing Conference of Canonical Orthodox Bishops in the Americas.

Jurisdictions

The principal jurisdictions of the Greek, Russian and other Orthodox Churches are as follows.

Greek: Patriarchate of Constantinople, with jurisdiction in Turkey, Crete, the Dodecanese, Western Europe, the Americas, Australia; Dimitrios I is Ecumenical Patriarch.

Patriarchate of Alexandria, with jurisdiction in Egypt and the rest of Africa; there is also a native African Orthodox Church in Kenya and Uganda.

Patriarchate of Antioch (Melkites or Syrian Orthodox), with jurisdiction in Syria, Lebanon, Iraq, Australasia, the Americas; Syrian or Arabic, in place of Greek, is the liturgical language.

Patriarchate of Jerusalem, with jurisdiction in Israel and Jordan.

Churches of Greece, Cyprus and Sinai are autocephalic but maintain relations with their fellow Orthodox.

Russian: Patriarchate of Moscow with jurisdiction centered in the Soviet Union.

Other: Patriarchate of Serbia, with jurisdiction in Yugoslavia, Western Europe, the Americas, Australasia.

Patriarchates of Rumania and Bulgaria.

Katholikate of Georgia, the Soviet Union.

Byelorussians and Ukrainian Byzantines.

Churches of Albania, China, Czechoslovakia, Estonia, Finland, Hungary, Japan, Latvia, Lithuania, Poland.

Other minor communities in various places; e.g., Korea, the U.S., Carpatho-Russia.

The Division of Archives and Statistics of the Eastern Orthodox World Foundation reported a 1970 estimate of more than 200 million Orthodox Church members throughout the world. Other sources estimate the total to be approximately 125 million.

Nestorians, Monophysites

Unlike the majority of Eastern Christian Churches, several bodies do not acknowledge all of the first seven ecumenical councils. Nestorians acknowledge only the first two councils; they do not accept the doctrinal definition of the Council of Ephesus concerning Mary as the Mother of God. Monophysite Armenians, Syrians, Copts, Ethiopians and Jacobites acknowledge only the first three councils; they do not accept the doctrinal definition of the Council of Chalcedon concerning the two natures in Christ.

The Armenian Church has communicants in the Soviet Union, the Middle and Far East, the Americas.

The Coptic Church has communicants in Egypt and elsewhere.

The Ethiopian or Abyssinian Church has communicants in Africa, the Middle East, the Americas, India.

The Jacobite Church (West Syrians) has communicants in the Middle East, the Americas, India.

Nestorians (Assyrians) are scattered throughout the world.

It is estimated that there are approximately 10 million or more members of these other Eastern Churches throughout the world. For various reasons, a more accurate determination is not possible.

Conference of Orthodox Bishops

The Standing Conference of Canonical Orthodox Bishops in the Americas was established in 1960 to achieve cooperation among the various Orthodox jurisdictions in the Americas. Office: 8-10 East 79th St., New York, N.Y. 10021.

Member churches of the conference are the: Albanian Orthodox Diocese of America (Ecumenical Patriarchate), American Carpatho-Russian Orthodox Greek Catholic Diocese in the U.S.A. (Ecumenical Patriarchate), Antiochian Orthodox Christian Archdiocese of North America, Bulgarian Eastern Orthodox Church, Greek Orthodox Archdiocese of North and South America (Ecumenical Patriarchate), Orthodox Church in America, Romanian Orthodox Missionary Archdiocese in America and Canada, Serbian Orthodox Church in the United States of America and Canada, Ukrainian Orthodox Church in America (Ecumenical Patriarchate).

EASTERN ECUMENISM

The Second Vatican Council, in the "Decree on Eastern Catholic Churches," pointed out the special role they have to play "in promoting the unity of all Christians, particularly Easterners." The document also stated in part as follows.

The Eastern Churches in communion with the Apostolic See of Rome have a special role to play in promoting the unity of all Christians, particularly Easterners, according to the principles of this sacred Synod's *Decree on Ecumenism* first of all by prayer, then by the example of their lives, by religious fidelity to ancient Eastern traditions, by greater mutual knowledge, by collaboration, and by a brotherly regard for objects and attitudes (No. 24).

If any separated Eastern Christian should, under the guidance of grace of the Holy Spirit, join himself to Catholic unity, no more should be required of him than what a simple profession of the Catholic faith demands. A valid priesthood is preserved among Eastern clerics. Hence, upon joining themselves to the unity of the Catholic Church, Eastern clerics are permitted to exercise the orders they possess, in accordance with the regulations established by the competent authority (No. 25).

Divine Law forbids any common worship (*communicatio in sacris*) which would damage the unity of the Church, or involve formal acceptance of falsehood or the danger of deviation in the faith, of scandal, or of indifferentism. At the same time, pastoral experience clearly shows that with respect to our Eastern brethren there should and can be taken into consideration various circumstances affecting individuals, wherein the unity of the Church is not jeopardized nor are intolerable risks involved, but in which salvation itself and the spiritual profit of souls are urgently at issue.

Hence, in view of special circumstances of time, place, and personage, the Catholic Church has often adopted and now adopts a milder policy, offering to all the means of salvation and an example of charity among Christians through participation in the sacraments and in other sacred functions and objects. With these considerations in mind, and "lest because of the harshness of our judgment we prove an obstacle to those seeking salvation," and in order to promote closer union with the Eastern Churches separated from us, this sacred Synod lays down the following policy:

In view of the principles recalled above, Eastern Christians who are separated in good faith from the Catholic Church, if they ask of their own accord and have the right dispositions, may be granted the sacraments of penance, the Eucharist, and the anointing of the sick. Furthermore, Catholics may ask for these same sacraments from those non-Catholic ministers whose Churches possess valid sacraments, as often as necessity or a genuine spiritual benefit recommends such a course of action, and when access to a Catholic priest is physically or morally impossible (Nos. 26, 27).

Again, in view of these very same principles, Catholics may for a just cause join with their separated Eastern brethren in sacred functions, things, and places (No. 28).

This more lenient policy with regard to common worship involving Catholics and their brethren of the separated Eastern Churches is entrusted to the care and execution of the local Ordinaries so that, by taking counsel among themselves and, if circumstances warrant, after consultation also with the Ordinaries of the separated Churches, they may govern relations between Christians by timely and effective rules and regulations (No. 29).

HUMAN DEVELOPMENT CAMPAIGN

The Campaign for Human Development was inaugurated by the U.S. Catholic Conference in November, 1969, to combat injustice, oppression, alienation and poverty in this country by funding self-help programs begun and carried out by the poor or by the poor and non-poor working together, and by seeking a re-evaluation of the priorities of individuals, families, the Church and the civic community with respect to the stewardship of God-given goods.

The campaign got under way with a collection taken up in all parishes throughout the country on Nov. 22, 1970. Seventy-five per cent of the money contributed in this and subsequent annual collections was placed in a national fund principally for funding self-help projects and also for educational purposes; 25 per cent remained in the dioceses where it was collected.

From 1970 to 1985, the campaign raised more than $120 million in contributions from U.S. Catholics, and approximately $88 million was disbursed by the national office for the funding of some 2,500 projects.

The national office is located at 1312 Massachusetts Ave. N.W., Washington, D.C. 20005.

MEN, DOCTRINES, CHURCHES OF THE REFORMATION

Some of the leading figures, doctrines and churches of the Reformation are covered below. A companion article covers Major Protestant Churches in the United States.

John Wycliff (c. 1320-1384): English priest and scholar who advanced one of the leading Reformation ideas nearly 200 years before Martin Luther — that the Bible alone is the sufficient rule of faith — but had only an indirect influence on the 16th century Reformers. Supporting belief in an inward and practical religion, he denied the divinely commissioned authority of the pope and bishops of the Church; he also denied the Real Presence of Christ in the Holy Eucharist, and wrote against the sacrament of penance and the doctrine of indulgences. Nearly 20 of his propositions were condemned by Gregory XI in 1377; his writings were proscribed more extensively by the Council of Constance in 1415. His influence was strongest in Bohemia and Central Europe.

John Hus (c. 1369-1415): A Bohemian priest and preacher of reform who authored 30 propositions condemned by the Council of Constance. Excommunicated in 1411 or 1412, he was burned at the stake in 1415. His principal errors concerned the nature of the Church and the origin of papal authority. He spread some of the ideas of Wycliff but did not subscribe to his views regarding faith alone as the condition for justification and salvation, the sole sufficiency of Scripture as the rule of faith, the Real Presence of Christ in the Eucharist, and the sacramental system. In 1457 some of his followers founded the Church of the Brotherhood which later became known as the United Brethren or Moravian Church and is considered the earliest independent Protestant body.

Martin Luther (1483-1546): An Augustinian friar, priest and doctor of theology, the key figure in the Reformation. In 1517, as a special indulgence was being preached in Germany, and in view of needed reforms within the Church, he published at Wittenberg 95 theses concerning matters of Catholic belief and practice. Leo X condemned 41 statements from Luther's writings in 1520. Luther, refusing to recant, was excommunicated the following year. His teachings strongly influenced subsequent Lutheran theology; its statements of faith are found in the Book of Concord (1580).

Luther's doctrine included the following: The sin of Adam, which corrupted human nature radically (but not substantially), has affected every aspect of man's being. Justification, understood as the forgiveness of sins and the state of righteousness, is by grace for Christ's sake through faith. Faith involves not merely intellectual assent but an act of confidence by the will. Good works are indispensably necessary concomitants of faith, but do not merit salvation. Of the sacraments, Luther retained baptism, penance and the Holy Communion as effective vehicles of the grace of the Holy Spirit; he held that in the Holy Communion the consecrated bread and wine are the Body and Blood of Christ. The rule of faith is the divine revelation in the Sacred Scriptures. He rejected purgatory, indulgences and the invocation of the saints, and held that prayers for the dead have no efficacy. Lutheran tenets not in agreement with Catholic doctrine were condemned by the Council of Trent.

Anabaptism: Originated in Saxony in the first quarter of the 16th century and spread rapidly through southern Germany. Its doctrine included several key Lutheran tenets but was not regarded with favor by Luther, Calvin or Zwingli. Anabaptists believed that baptism is for adults only and that infant baptism is invalid. Their doctrine of the Inner Light, concerning the direct influence of the Holy Spirit on the believer, implied rejection of Catholic doctrine concerning the sacraments and the nature of the Church. Eighteen articles of faith were formulated in 1632 in Holland. Mennonites are Anabaptists.

Ulrich Zwingli (1484-1531): A priest who triggered the Reformation in Switzerland with a series of New Testament lectures in 1519, later disputations and by other actions. He held the Gospel to be the only basis of truth; rejected the Mass (which he suppressed in 1525 at Zurich), penance and other sacraments; denied papal primacy and doctrine concerning purgatory and the invocation of saints; rejected celibacy, monasticism and many traditional practices of piety. His symbolic view of the Eucharist, which was at odds with Catholic doctrine, caused an irreconcilable controversy with Luther and his followers. Zwingli was killed in a battle between the forces of Protestant and Catholic cantons in Switzerland.

John Calvin (1509-1564): French leader of the Reformation in Switzerland, whose key tenet was absolute predestination of some persons to heaven and others to hell. He rejected Catholic doctrine in 1533 after becoming convinced of a personal mission to reform the Church. In 1536 he published the first edition of *Institutes of the Christian Religion,* a systematic exposition of his doctrine which became the classic textbook of Reformed — as distinguished from Lutheran — theology. To Luther's principal theses — regarding Scripture as the sole rule of faith, the radical corruption of human nature, and justification by faith alone — he added absolute predestination, certitude of salvation for the elect, and the incapability of the elect to lose grace. His Eucharistic theory, which failed to mediate the Zwingli-Luther controversy, was at odds with Catholic doctrine. From 1555 until his death Calvin was the virtual dictator of Geneva, the capital of the non-Lutheran Reformation in Europe.

Arminianism: A modification of the rigid predestinationism of Calvin, set forth by Jacob Arminius (1560-1609) and formally stated in the *Remonstrance* of 1610. Arminianism influenced some Calvinist bodies.

Unitarianism: A 16th century doctrine which rejected the Trinity and the divinity of Christ in favor of a uni-personal God. It claimed scriptural support for a long time but became generally rationalistic with respect to "revealed" doctrine as well as in ethics and its world-view. One of its principal early proponents was Faustus Socinus (1539-1604), a leader of the Polish Brethren.

A variety of communions developed in England in the Reformation and post-Reformation periods.

Puritans: Extremists who sought church reform along Calvinist lines in severe simplicity. (Use of the term was generally discontinued after 1660.)

Presbyterians: Basically Calvinistic, called Presbyterian because church polity centers around assemblies of presbyters or elders. John Knox (c. 1513-1572) established the church in Scotland.

Congregationalists: Evangelical in spirit and seeking a return to forms of the primitive church, they uphold individual freedom in religious matters, do not require the acceptance of a creed as a condition for communion, and regard each congregation as autonomous. Robert Browne influenced the beginnings of Congregationalism.

Quakers: Their key belief is in internal divine illumination, the inner light of the living Christ, as the only source of truth and inspiration. George Fox (1624-1691) was one of their leaders in England. Called the Society of Friends, the Quakers are noted for their pacificism.

Baptists: So called because of their doctrine concerning baptism. They reject infant baptism and consider only baptism by immersion as valid.

Leaders in the formation of the church were John Smyth (d. 1612) in England and Roger Williams (d. 1683) in America.

Methodists: A group who broke away from the Anglican Communion under the leadership of John Wesley (1703-1791), although some Anglican beliefs were retained. Doctrines include the witness of the Spirit to the individual and personal assurance of salvation. Wesleyan Methodists do not subscribe to some of the more rigid Calvinistic tenets held by other Methodists.

Universalism: A product of 18th-century liberal Protestantism in England. The doctrine is not Trinitarian and includes a tenet that all men will ultimately be saved.

ANGLICAN COMMUNION

This communion, which regards itself as the same apostolic Church as that which was established by early Christians in England, derived not from Reformation influences but from the renunciation of papal jurisdiction by Henry VIII (1491-1547). His Act of Supremacy in 1534 called Christ's Church an assembly of local churches subject to the prince, who was vested with fullness of authority and jurisdiction. In spite of Henry's denial of papal authority, this Act did not reject substantially other principal articles of faith. Notable changes, proposed and adopted for the reformation of the church, took place in the subsequent reigns of James VI and Elizabeth, with respect to such matters as Scripture as the rule of faith, the sacraments, the nature of the Mass, and the constitution of the hierarchy. (See Episcopal Church, Anglican Orders.)

MAJOR PROTESTANT CHURCHES IN THE UNITED STATES

There are more than 250 Protestant church bodies in the United States.

The majority of U.S. Protestants belong to the following denominations: Baptist, Methodist, Lutheran, Presbyterian, Protestant Episcopal, the United Church of Christ, the Christian Church (Disciples of Christ), Holiness Sects.

See Ecumenical Dialogues, Briefs and related entries for coverage of relations between the Catholic Church and other Christian churches.

Baptist Churches

(Courtesy of the Office of Communication, American Baptist Churches in the U.S.A.)

Baptist churches, comprising the largest of all American Protestant denominations, were first established by John Smyth near the beginning of the 17th century in England. The first Baptist church in America was founded at Providence by Roger Williams in 1639.

Largest of the nearly 30 Baptist bodies in the U.S. are:

The Southern Baptist Convention, 460 James Robertson Parkway, Nashville, Tenn. 37219, with 14.1 million members;

The National Baptist Convention, U.S.A., Inc., 915 Spain St., Baton Rouge, La. 70802, with 7.35 million members;

The National Baptist Convention of America, 954 Kings Rd., Jacksonville, Fla. 32204, with 2.6 million members.

The American Baptist Churches in the U.S.A., P.O. Box 851, Valley Forge, Pa. 19482, with 1.5 million members.

The total number of U.S. Baptists is more than 29 million. The world total is 33 million.

Proper to Baptists is their doctrine on baptism. Called an "ordinance" rather than a sacrament, baptism by immersion is a sign that one has experienced and decided in favor of the salvation offered by Christ. It is administered only to persons who are able to make a responsible decision. Baptism is not administered to infants.

Baptists do not have a formal creed but generally subscribe to two professions of faith formulated in 1689 and 1832 and are in general agreement with classical Protestant theology regarding Scripture as the sole rule of faith, original sin, justification through faith in Christ, and the nature of the Church. Their local churches are autonomous.

Worship services differ in form from one congregation to another. Usual elements are the reading of Scripture, a sermon, hymns, vocal and silent prayer. The Lord's Supper, called an "ordinance," is celebrated at various intervals.

Methodist Churches

(Courtesy of Joe Hale, General Secretary of the World Methodist Council.)

John Wesley (1703-1791), an Anglican clergyman, was the founder of Methodism. In 1738, following a period of missionary work in America and strongly influenced by the Moravians, he experienced a new conversion to Christ and shortly thereafter became a leader in a religious awakening in England. By the end of the 18th century, Methodism was strongly rooted also in America.

The United Methodist Church, formed in 1968 by a merger of the Methodist Church and the Evangelical United Brethren Church, is the second largest Protestant denomination in the U.S., with nine million members; its principal agencies are located in New York, Evanston, Ill., Nashville, Tenn., Washington, D.C., Dayton, O., and Lake Junaluska, N.C. (World Methodist Council, P.O. Box 518. 28745). The second largest body, with more than two million communicants, is the African Methodist Episcopal Church. Four other major churches in the U.S. are the African Methodist Episcopal Zion, Christian Methodist Episcopal, Free Methodist Church and the Wesleyan Church. The total Methodist membership in the U.S. is about 14 million.

Worldwide, there are more than 64 autonomous Methodist/Wesleyan churches in 90 countries, with a membership of more than 23 million. All of them participate in the World Methodist Council, which gives global unity to the witness of Methodist communicants.

Methodism, although it has a base in Calvinistic theology, rejects absolute predestination and maintains that Christ offers grace freely to all men, not just to a select elite. Wesley's distinctive doctrine was the "witness of the Spirit" to the individual soul and personal assurance of salvation. He also emphasized the central themes of conversion and holiness. Methodists are in general agreement with classical Protestant theology regarding Scripture as the sole rule of faith, original sin, justification through faith in Christ, the nature of the Church, and the sacraments of baptism and the Lord's Supper. Church polity is structured along episcopal lines in America, with ministers being appointed to local churches by a bishop; churches stemming from British Methodism do not have bishops but vest appointive powers within an appropriate conference. Congregations are free to choose various forms of worship services; typical elements are readings from Scripture, sermons, hymns and prayers.

Lutheran Churches

(Courtesy of Thomas Hartley Dorris, editor of Ecumenical Press Service, Box 66, CH-1211 Geneva 20, Switzerland.)

The origin of Lutheranism is generally traced to Oct. 31, 1517, when Martin Luther — Augustinian friar, priest, doctor of theology — tacked "95 Theses" to the door of the castle church in Wittenberg, Germany. This call to debate on the subject of indulgences and related concerns has come to symbolize the beginning of the Reformation. Luther and his supporters intended to reform the Church they knew. Though Lutheranism has come to be visible in separate denominations and national churches, at its heart it professes itself to be a confessional movement within the one, holy, catholic and apostolic Church.

The world's 70 million Lutherans form the third largest grouping of Christians, following Roman Catholics and Eastern Orthodox. About 54 million belong to churches which make up the Lutheran World Federation, headquartered in Geneva.

Numbering about 9 million, Lutherans are the fourth largest grouping of North American Christians, exceeded by Roman Catholics, Baptists and Methodists. About 95 per cent of them belong to one of three denominations: Lutheran Church in America, three million members, 231 Madison Avenue, New York, N.Y 10016; Lutheran Church-Missouri Synod, 2.7 million, 1333 S. Kirkwood Rd., St. Louis, Mo. 63122; American Lutheran Church, 2.3 million, 422 S. Fifth St., Minneapolis, Minn. 55415. Canadian Lutherans belong to the Evangelical Lutheran Church of Canada, the Lutheran Church in America, or the Lutheran Church-Missouri Synod. There are about a dozen other smaller Lutheran denominations in North America.

The Lutheran Church in America, the Lutheran Church-Missouri Synod and the American Lutheran Church, together with the Association of Evangelical Lutheran Churches and the Latvian Evangelical Church in America, form the Lutheran Council in the U.S.A., a cooperative agency for work in several fields. The council's main offices are at 360 Park Ave. South, New York, N.Y. 10010.

The Lutheran Church in America, the American Lutheran Church and the Association of Evangelical Lutheran Churches also form Lutheran World Ministries, (the U.S. agency of the Lutheran World Federation), headquartered at 360 Park Ave. South, New York, N.Y. 10010.

The statements of faith which have shaped the confessional life of Lutheranism are found in the *Book of Concord*. This 1580 collection includes the three ancient ecumenical creeds (Apostles', Nicene and Athanasian), Luther's *Large and Small Catechisms* (1529), the *Augsburg Confession* (1530) and the *Apology* in defense of it (1531), the *Smalcald Articles* (including the "Treatise on the Power and Primacy of the Pope") (1537), and the *Formula of Concord* (1577).

The central Lutheran doctrinal proposition is that Christians "receive forgiveness of sins and become righteous before God by grace, for Christ's sake."

Baptism and the Lord's Supper (Holy Communion, the Eucharist) are universally celebrated among Lutherans as sacramental means of grace in which the Word and promise of God are made visible by being bound to earthly elements — water, bread and wine. In baptism, a person is reborn and by God's gracious action is made a member of the Church catholic. Likewise, the Eucharist celebrates and re-presents God's gracious action. With the body and blood of Christ — "in, with, and under" the bread and wine — come the gifts of life, salvation, forgiveness.

Lutherans also treasure the Word proclaimed in the reading of the Scriptures, preaching from the pulpit, and pronouncement of absolution. The Word read and preached is always part of the Eucharist. Absolution is usually imparted generally, but it may also be given individually in connection with private confession.

Although it was not the wish of the early Lutherans to deny the bishop's place as the ordinary minister of ordination, the general unwillingness of 16th century bishops to ordain Lutheran pastors led to the usual Lutheran system of presbyteral rather than episcopal ordination. Lutherans are concerned to preserve apostolic succession in life and doctrine, and generally concede the value, though not the necessity, of ordination by bishops.

Confirmation among Lutherans has been generally connected with first communion, though recent years have seen a tendency to separate the two. In the U.S., the tendency is to have first communion around grade-five age, though infant communion is not unknown. Confirmation, sometimes called affirmation of the baptismal covenant, generally occurs during the junior high school years, slightly younger than in European practice.

Lutheran jurisdictions corresponding to dioceses are called districts or synods in North America. There are more than 100 of them on the continent.

A visitor to a North American Lutheran parish would generally find adornments, vestments, church calendars and an order of service similar to that of Episcopal or Roman Catholic congregations. Weekly celebration of the Eucharist is increasingly common and is generally stressed as the desired practice by Lutheran liturgical and sacramental theologians. Lutherans generally like to sing in worship, and successive generations have built up a rich tradition of church music and hymnody.

Presbyterian Churches

(Courtesy of Gerald W. Gillette, United Presbyterian Church in the U.S.A.; and Office of the General Assembly, Presbyterian Church in the United States.)

Presbyterians are so called because of their tradition of governing the church through a system of representative bodies composed of elders (presbyters).

Presbyterianism is a part of the Reformed Family of Churches that grew out of the theological work of John Calvin following the Lutheran Reformation, to which it is heavily indebted. Countries in which it acquired early strength and influence were Switzerland, France, Holland, Scotland and England.

Presbyterianism spread widely in this country in the latter part of the 18th century and afterwards. Presently, it has approximately 4.5 million communicants in nine bodies.

The two largest Presbyterian bodies in the country — the United Presbyterian Church in the U.S.A. and the Presbyterian Church in the United States — were reunited in June, 1983, to form the Presbyterian Church (U.S.A.), with a membership of 3.3 million.

The United Presbyterian Church in the U.S.A., with a membership of 2.5 million, was headquartered at 475 Riverside Drive, New York, N.Y. 10027. It was formed May 28, 1958, by a merger of the Presbyterian Church in the U.S.A. and the United Presbyterian Church of North America.

The Presbyterian Church in the United States, with 815,000 members, had headquarters at 341 Ponce de Leon Avenue N.E., Atlanta, Ga. 30308.

These churches, now merged, are closely allied with the Reformed Church in America, the United Church of Christ, the Cumberland Presbyterian Churches and the Associate Reformed Presbyterian Church.

In Presbyterian doctrine, baptism and the Lord's Supper, viewed as seals of the covenant of grace, are regarded as sacraments. Baptism, which is not necessary for salvation, is conferred on infants and adults The Lord's Supper is celebrated as a covenant of the Sacrifice of Christ. In both sacraments, a doctrine of the real presence of Christ is considered the central theological principle.

The Church is twofold, being invisible and also visible; it consists of all of the elect and all those Christians who are united in Christ as their immediate head.

Presbyterians are in general agreement with classical Protestant theology regarding Scripture as the sole rule of faith and practice, salvation by grace, and justification through faith in Christ.

Presbyterian congregations are governed by a session composed of elders (presbyters) elected by the communicant membership. On higher levels there are presbyteries, synods and a general assembly with various degrees of authority over local bodies; all such representative bodies are composed of elected elders and ministers in approximately equal numbers.

Worship services, simple and dignified, include sermons, prayer, reading of the Scriptures and hymns. The Lord's Supper is celebrated at intervals.

Doctrinal developments of the past several years included approval in May, 1967, by the General Assembly of the United Presbyterian Church of a contemporary confession of faith to supplement the historic Westminster Confession. The new confession emphasizes the commitment of the Church and its members to reconciliatory and apostolic works in society. A statement entitled "The Declaration of Faith" was approved in 1977 by the Presbyterian Church in the U.S. for teaching and liturgical use.

Episcopal Church

(Courtesy of The Episcopal Church Center, Office of Communication.)

The Episcopal Church, which includes dioceses in the United States, Central and South America, and elsewhere overseas, regards itself as part of the same apostolic church which was established by early Christians in England. Established in this country during the colonial period, it became independent of the jurisdiction of the Church of England when a new constitution and Prayer Book were adopted at a general convention held in 1789. It has approximately 3 million members worldwide.

Offices of the presiding bishop and the executive council are located at 815 Second Ave., New York, N.Y. 10017.

The presiding bishop is chief pastor and primate; he is elected by the House of Bishops and confirmed by the House of Deputies.

The Episcopal Church, which belongs to the Anglican Communion, accepts the Archbishop of Canterbury as the "First among Equals."

The Anglican Communion, worldwide, has 70 million members in 27 self-governing churches.

Official statements of belief and practice are found in the Book of Common Prayer. Scripture has primary importance with respect to the rule of faith, and some authority is attached to tradition.

An episcopal system of church government prevails, but presbyters, deacons and lay persons also have an active voice in church affairs. The levels of government are the general convention, the executive council, territorial provinces and dioceses, and local parishes. At the parish level, the congregation has the right to select its own rector, with the consent of the bishop.

Liturgical worship is according to the Book of Common Prayer as adopted in 1979, but details of ceremonial practice vary from one congregation to another.

United Church of Christ

(Courtesy of the Rev. Carol Joyce Brun, secretary of the United Church of Christ.)

The 1,684,777-member United Church of Christ was formed in 1957 by a union of the Congregational Christian and the Evangelical and Reformed Churches. The former was originally established by the Pilgrims and the Puritans of the Massachusetts Bay Colony, while the latter was founded in Pennsylvania in the early 1700's by settlers from Central Europe. The denomination has 6,419 congregations throughout the United States.

It considers itself "a united and uniting church" and keeps itself open to all ecumenical options.

Its headquarters are located at 105 Madison Ave., New York, N.Y. 10016.

Its statement of faith recognizes Jesus Christ as "our crucified and risen Lord (who) shared our common lot, conquering sin and death and reconciling the world to himself." It believes in the life after death, and the fact that God "judges men and nations by his righteous will declared through prophets and apostles."

The United Church further believes that Christ calls its members to share in his baptism "and eat at his table, to join him in his passion and victory." Ideally, according to its Lord's Day Service, Communion is to be celebrated weekly. Like other Calvinistic bodies, it believes that Christ is spiritually present in the sacrament.

The United Church is governed along congregational lines, and each local church is autonomous. However, the actions of its biennial General Synod are taken with great seriousness by congregations. Between synods, a 43-member executive council oversees the work of the church.

Christian Church (Disciples of Christ)

(Courtesy of Robert L. Friedly, Vice President for Communication.)

The Christian Church (Disciples of Christ) originated early in the 1800's from two movements against rigid denominationalism led by Presbyterians Thomas and Alexander Campbell in western Pennsylvania and Barton W. Stone in Kentucky. The two movements developed separately for about 25 years before being merged in 1832.

The church, which identifies itself with the Protestant mainstream, now has approximately 1.2 million members in the U.S. and Canada. The greatest concentration of members in the U.S. is located roughly along the old frontier line, in an arc sweeping from Ohio and Kentucky through the Midwest and down into Oklahoma and Texas.

The general offices of the church are located at 222 South Downey Ave., Box 1986, Indianapolis, Ind. 46206.

The church's persistent concern for Christian unity is based on a conviction expressed in a basic document, *Declaration and Address,* dating from its founding. The document states: "The church of Christ upon earth is essentially, intentionally and constitutionally one."

The Disciples have no official doctrine or dogma. Their worship practices vary widely from more common informal services to what could almost be described as "high church" services. Membership is granted after a simple statement of belief in Jesus Christ and baptism by immersion; most congregations admit un-immersed transfers from other denominations. The Lord's Supper, generally called Communion, is always open to Christians of all persuasions. Lay men and women routinely preside over the Lord's Supper, which is celebrated each Sunday; they often preach and perform other pastoral functions as well. Distinction between ordained and non-ordained members is blurred somewhat because of the Disciples' emphasis on all members of the church as ministers.

The Christian Church is oriented to congregational government, and has a unique structure in which three levels of polity (general, regional and congregational) operate as equals rather than in a pyramid of authority. At the national or international level, it is governed by a general assembly which has voting representation direct from congregations and regions as well as all ordained clergy.

Evangelicalism

Evangelicalism, dating from 1735 in England (the Evangelical Revival) and after 1740 in the United States (the Great Awakening), has had and continues to have widespread influence in Protestant churches. It has been estimated that about 45 millon American Protestants — communicants of both large denominations and small bodies — are evangelicals.

The Bible is their rule of faith and religious practice. Being born again in a life-changing experience through faith in Christ is the promise of salvation. Missionary work for the spread of the Gospel is a normal and necessary activity. Additional matters of belief and practice are generally of a conservative character.

Fundamentalists, numbering perhaps 4.5 million, comprise an extreme right-wing subculture of evangelicalism.They are distinguished mainly by militant biblicism, belief in the absolute inerrancy of the Bible and emphasis on the Second Coming of Christ. Fundamentalism developed early in the 20th century in reaction against liberal theology and secularizing trends in mainstream and other Protestant denominations.

The Holiness or Perfectionist wing of evangelicalism evolved from Methodist efforts to preserve, against a contrary trend, the personal-piety and inner-religion concepts of John Wesley. There are at least 30 Holiness bodies in the U.S.

Pentecostals, probably the most demonstrative of evangelicals, are noted for speaking in tongues and the stress they place on healing, prophecy and personal testimony to the practice and power of evangelical faith.

ECUMENISM

The modern ecumenical movement, which started about 1910 among Protestants and led to formation of the World Council of Churches in 1948, developed outside the mainstream of Catholic interest for many years. It has now become for Catholics as well one of the great religious facts of our time.

The magna charta of ecumenism for Catholics is a complex of several documents which include, in the first place, the *Decree on Ecumenism* promulgated by the Second Vatican Council Nov. 21, 1964. Other enactments underlying and expanding this decree are the *Dogmatic Constitution on the Church*, the *Decree on Eastern Catholic Churches*, and the *Pastoral Constitution on the Church in the Modern World*.

VATICAN II DECREE

The following excerpts from the "Decree on Ecumenism" cover the broad theological background and principles and indicate the thrust of the Church's commitment to ecumenism, under the subheads: Elements Common to Christians, Unity Lacking, What the Movement Involves, Primary Duty of Catholics.

Men who believe in Christ and have been properly baptized are brought into a certain, though imperfect, communion with the Catholic Church. Undoubtedly, the differences that exist in varying degrees between them and the Catholic Church — whether in doctrine and sometimes in discipline, or concerning the structure of the Church — do indeed create many and sometimes serious obstacles to full ecclesiastical communion. These the ecumenical movement is striving to overcome (No. 3).

Elements Common to Christians

Moreover some, even very many, of the most significant elements or endowments which together go to build up and give life to the Church herself can exist outside the visible boundaries of the Catholic Church: the written word of God; the life of grace; faith, hope, and charity, along with other interior gifts of the Holy Spirit and visible elements. All of these, which come from Christ and lead back to Him, belong by right to the one Church of Christ (No. 3).

[In a later passage, the decree singled out a number of elements which the Catholic Church and other churches have in common but not in complete agreement: confession of Christ as Lord and God and as mediator between God and man; belief in the Trinity; reverence for Scripture as the revealed word of God; baptism and the Lord's Supper; Christian life and worship; faith in action; concern with moral questions.]

The brethren divided from us also carry out many of the sacred actions of the Christian religion. Undoubtedly, in ways that vary according to the condition of each church or community, these actions can truly engender a life of grace, and can be rightly described as capable of providing access to the community of salvation.

It follows that these separated Churches and Communities, though we believe they suffer from defects already mentioned, have by no means been deprived of significance and importance in the mystery of salvation. For the Spirit of Christ has not refrained from using them as means of salvation which derive their efficacy from the very fullness of grace and truth entrusted to the Catholic Church (No. 3).

Unity Lacking

Nevertheless, our separated brethren, whether considered as individuals or as Communities and Churches, are not blessed with that unity which Jesus Christ wished to bestow on all those whom he has regenerated and vivified into one body and newness of life — that unity which the holy Scriptures and the revered tradition of the Church proclaim. For it is through Christ's Catholic Church alone, which is the all-embracing means of salvation, that the fullness of the means of salvation can be obtained. It was to the apostolic college alone, of which Peter is the head, that we believe our Lord entrusted all the blessings of the New Covenant, in order to establish on earth the one Body of Christ into which all those should be fully incorporated who already belong in any way to God's People (No. 3).

What the Movement Involves

Today, in many parts of the world, under the inspiring grace of the Holy Spirit, multiple efforts are being expended through prayer, word, and action to attain that fullness of unity which Jesus Christ desires. This sacred Synod, therefore, exhorts all the Catholic faithful to recognize the signs of the times and to participate skillfully in the work of ecumenism.

The "ecumenical movement" means those activities and enterprises which, according to various needs of the Church and opportune occasions, are started and organized for the fostering of unity among Christians. These are:

• First, every effort to eliminate words, judgments, and actions which do not respond to the condition of separated brethren with truth and fairness and so make mutual relations between them more difficult.

• Then, "dialogue" between competent experts from different Churches and Communities [scholarly ecumenism].

• In addition, these Communions cooperate more closely in whatever projects a Christian conscience demands for the common good [social ecumenism].

• They also come together for common prayer, where this is permitted [spiritual ecumenism].

• Finally, all are led to examine their own faithfulness to Christ's will for the Church and, wherever necessary, undertake with vigor the task of renewal and reform.

It is evident that the work of preparing and reconciling those individuals who wish for full Catholic communion is of its nature distinct from ecumenical action. But there is no opposition between the two, since both proceed from the wondrous providence of God (No. 4).

Primary Duty of Catholics

In ecumenical work, Catholics must assuredly be concerned for their separated brethren, praying for them, keeping them informed about the Church, making the first approaches toward them. But their primary duty is to make an honest and careful appraisal of whatever needs to be renewed and achieved in the Catholic household itself, in order that its life may bear witness more loyally and luminously to the teachings and ordinances which have been handed down from Christ through the Apostles.

Every Catholic must . . . aim at Christian perfection (cf. Jas. 1:4; Rom. 12:1-2) and, each according to his station, play his part so that the Church . . . may daily be more purified and renewed, against the day when Christ will present her to himself in all her glory, without spot or wrinkle (cf. Eph. 5:27).

Catholics must joyfully acknowledge and esteem the truly Christian endowments from our common heritage which are to be found among our separated brethren.

Nor should we forget that whatever is wrought by the grace of the Holy Spirit in the hearts of our separated brethren can contribute to our own edification. Whatever is truly Christian never conflicts with the genuine interests of the faith; indeed, it can always result in a more ample realization of the very mystery of Christ and the Church (No. 4).

Participation in Worship

Norms concerning participation by Catholics in the worship of other Christian Churches were sketched in this conciliar decree and elaborated in a number of other documents such as: the *Decree on Eastern Catholic Churches,* promulgated by the Second Vatican Council in 1964; *Interim Guidelines for Prayer in Common,* issued June 18, 1965, by the U.S. Bishops' Committee for Ecumenical and Inter-Religious Affairs; a *Directory on Ecumenism,* published in 1967 by the Vatican Secretariat for Promoting Christian Unity; additional communications from the U.S. Bishops' Committee, and numerous sets of guidelines issued locally by and for dioceses throughout the U.S.

The norms encourage common prayer services for Christian unity and other intentions. Beyond that, they draw a distinction between separated churches of the Reformation tradition and of the Anglican Communion and separated Eastern churches, in view of doctrine and practice the Catholic Church has in common with the latter concerning the apostolic succession of bishops, holy orders, liturgy, and other credal matters.

Full participation by Catholics in official Protestant liturgies is prohibited, because it implies profession of the faith expressed in the liturgy. Intercommunion by Catholics at Protestant liturgies is prohibited. Under certain conditions, Protestants may be given Holy Communion in the Catholic Church (see Intercommunion). A Catholic may stand as a witness, but not as a sponsor, in baptism, and as a witness in the marriage of separated Christians. Similarly, a Protestant may stand as a witness, but not as a sponsor, in a Catholic baptism, and as a witness in the marriage of Catholics.

Separated Eastern Churches

The principal norms regarding liturgical participation with separated Eastern Christians are included under Eastern Ecumenism.

ECUMENICAL AGENCIES

Vatican Secretariat

The top-level agency for Catholic ecumenical efforts is the Vatican Secretariat for Promoting Christian Unity, which originated in 1960 as a preparatory commission for the Second Vatican Council. Its purposes are to provide guidance and, where necessary, coordination for ecumenical endeavor by Catholics, and to establish and maintain relations with representatives of other Christian Churches for ecumenical dialogue and action.

The secretariat, first under the direction of Cardinal Augustin Bea, S. J., and now of Cardinal Johannes Willebrands, has established firm working relations with representative agencies of other churches and the World Council of Churches. It has joined in dialogue with Orthodox Churches, the Anglican Communion, the Lutheran World Federation, the World Alliance of Reformed Churches, the World Methodist Council and other religious bodies. In the past several years, staff members and representatives of the secretariat have been involved in one way or another in nearly every significant ecumenical enterprise and meeting held throughout the world.

While the secretariat and its counterparts in other churches have focused primary attention on theological and other related problems of Christian unity, they have also begun, and in increasing measure, to emphasize the responsibilities of the churches for greater unity of witness and effort in areas of humanitarian need.

Bishops' Committee

The U.S. Bishops' Committee for Ecumenical and Interreligious Affairs was established by the American hierarchy in 1964. Its purposes are to maintain relationships with other Christian churches and other religious communities at the national level, to advise and assist dioceses in developing and applying ecumenical policies, and to maintain liaison with corresponding Vatican offices — the Secretariats for Christian Unity and Non-Christian Religions.

This standing committee of the National Conference of Catholic Bishops is chaired by Bishop William H. Keeler of Harrisburg. Operationally, the committee is assisted by the Rev. John F. Hotchkin, director; the Rev. Joseph W. Witmer, associate director; Dr. Eugene J. Fisher, executive secretary of the Secretariat for Catholic-Jewish Relations.

The committee co-sponsors several national consultations with other churches and confessional families. These bring together on a regular basis Catholic representatives and their counterparts from the Episcopal Church, the Lutheran World Federation (U.S. Committee), the United Methodist Church, the Orthodox Churches, the Oriental Orthodox Churches, the Alliance of Reformed Churches (North American area), the Interfaith Witness Department of the Home Mission Board of the Southern Baptist Convention. (See Ecumenical Dialogues.)

The committee relates with the National Council of Churches of Christ, through membership in the Faith and Order Commission and through observer relationship with the Commission on Regional and Local Ecumenism, and has sponsored a joint study committee investigating the possibility of Roman Catholic membership in that body.

Advisory and other services are provided by the committee to ecumenical commissions and agencies in dioceses throughout the country.

Through the Secretariat for Catholic-Jewish Relations, the committee is in contact with several national Jewish agencies and bodies. Issues of mutual interest and shared concern are reviewed for the purpose of furthering deeper understanding between the Catholic and Jewish communities.

Through the Secretariat for Non-Christians, the committee promotes activity in wider areas of dialogue. The Rev. John F. Hotchkin serves as executive secretary for this secretariat.

Offices of the committee are located at 1312 Massachusetts Ave. N.W., Washington, D.C. 20005.

World Council

The World Council of Churches is a fellowship of churches which acknowledge "Jesus Christ as Lord and Savior." It is a permanent organization providing constituent members — 301 churches with some 450 million communicants in 100 countries — with opportunities for meeting, consultation and cooperative action with respect to doctrine, worship, practice, social mission, evangelism and missionary work, and other matters of mutual concern.

The WCC was formally established Aug. 23, 1948, in Amsterdam with ratification of a constitution by 147 communions. This action merged two previously existing movements — Life and Work (social mission), Faith and Order (doctrine) — which had initiated practical steps toward founding a fellowship of Christian churches at meetings held in Oxford, Edinburgh and Utrecht in 1937 and 1938. A third movement for cooperative missionary work, which originated about 1910 and, remotely, led to formation of the WCC, was incorporated into the council in 1971 under the title of the International Missionary Council (now the Commission for World Mission and Evangelism).

Additional general assemblies of the council have been held since the charter meeting of 1948: in Evanston, Ill. (1954), New Delhi, India (1961), Uppsala, Sweden (1968), Nairobi, Kenya (1975) and Vancouver, British Columbia, Canada (1983).

Between assemblies, the council operates through a central committee which meets every 12 or 18 months, and an executive committee which meets every six months.

The council continues the work of the International Missionary Council, the Commission on Faith and Order, and the Commission on Church and Society. The structure of the council has three program units: Faith and Witness, Justice and Service, Education and Communication.

Liaison between the council and the Vatican has been maintained since 1966 through a joint working group. Roman Catholic membership in the WCC is a question officially on the agenda of this body. The Joint Commission on Society, Development and Peace (SODEPAX) was an agency of the council and the Pontifical Commission for Justice and Peace from 1968 to Dec. 31, 1980, after which another working group was formed. Roman Catholics serve individually as full members of the Commission on Faith and Order and in various capacities on other program committees of the council.

WCC headquarters are located in Geneva, Switzerland. The United States Conference for the World Council of Churches at 475 Riverside Drive, Room 1062, New York, N.Y. 10115, provides liaison between the U.S. churches and Geneva. The WCC also maintains fraternal relations with regional, national and local councils of churches throughout the world.

The Rev. Dr. Emilio Castro, a Methodist from Uruguay, was elected secretary general in July, 1984.

WCC presidents are: Dame R. Nita Barrow, Barbados; Dr. Marga Buehrig, Switzerland; H. E. Metropolitan Gregorios, India; Bishop Dr. Johannes W. Hempel, German Democratic Republic; His Beatitude Ignatios IV, Lebanon; Most Rev. W.P.K. Makhulu, Botswana; Very Rev. Dr. Lois Wilson, Canada.

National Council of Churches

The National Council of the Churches of Christ in the U.S.A., the largest ecumenical body in the United States, is a cooperative organization of 31 Protestant, Orthodox and Anglican church bodies having about 40 million members.

The NCCC, established by the churches in 1950, was structured through the merger of 12 separate cooperative agencies. Presently, through four main program divisions and six commissions, the NCCC carries on work in behalf of member churches in home and overseas missions, Christian education, communications, disaster relief and rehabilitation, family life, stewardship, regional and local ecumenism, international affairs and other areas.

Policies of the NCCC are determined by a governing board of approximately 260 members appointed by the constituent churches. The governing board meets twice a year.

The NCCC's 1985 budget was $46 million, about 80 per cent of which is devoted to compassionate ministries of aid and relief to victims of disasters and endemic poverty in lands overseas.

The president and general secretary, respectively, are Bishop Philip R. Cousin and the Rev. Dr. Arie Brouwer.

NCCC headquarters are located at 475 Riverside Drive, New York, N.Y. 10115.

Consultation on Church Union

The Consultation on Church Union, officially begun in 1962, is a venture of American churches seeking a united church "truly catholic, truly evangelical, and truly reformed." The churches engaged in this process, representing 25 million Christians, are the African Methodist Episcopal Church, the African Methodist Episcopal Zion Church, the Christian Church (Disciples of Christ), the Christian Methodist Episcopal Church, the Episcopal Church, the Presbyterian Church (U.S.A); the United Church of Christ, and the United Methodist Church. The International Council of Community Churches is also a member of COCU.

Representatives of these denominations, at a plenary session of COCU in November, 1984, approved a statement designed to serve as a theological basis for union. The 48,000-word document expressed agreement on such subjects as baptism, forms of ministry, creeds and worship. The statement was submitted to members for two years of study before further action by the plenary session of 1988.

The Rev. George Pike, a pastor of the Presbyterian Church (U.S.A.), was elected COCU president in 1984. The Rev. Gerald F. Moede is general secretary.

Offices are located at 151 Wall St., Princeton, N.J. 08540.

Graymoor Institute

The Graymoor Ecumenical Institute provides informational services concerning ecumenism and interfaith developments. One of its publications is *Ecumenical Trends*. The main office is located at the Interchurch Center, 475 Riverside Drive, New York, N.Y. 10115.

ECUMENICAL DIALOGUES

(Source: Bishops' Committee for Ecumenical and Interreligious Affairs, National Conference of Catholic Bishops.)

Following is a list of principal consultations, from Mar. 16, 1965, involving representatives of the U.S. Catholic Bishops' Committee for Ecumenical and Interreligious Affairs and representatives of other Christian Churches, with names of the churches, places and dates of meetings, and the subject matter of discussions.

Baptist Convention, American (Division of Cooperative Christianity): (1) De Witt, Mich., Apr. 3, 1967 — American Baptist and Roman Catholic dialogue; a Baptist view of areas of theological agreement. (2) Green Lake, Wis., Apr. 29, 1968 — Baptism and confirmation; Christian freedom and ecclesiastical authority. (3) Schiller Park, Ill., Apr. 28, 1969 — Nature and communication of grace; Christian freedom and ecclesiastical authority; baptism and confirmation.

(4) Atchison, Kan., Apr. 17, 1970 — Role of the Church, resume of years past and the future; Roman Catholic-American Baptist dialogues; observations concerning bilateral ecumenical conversations and the future course of American Baptist-Roman Catholic conversations.

(5) Detroit, Mich., Apr. 23 to 24, 1971 — Theological perspective on clergy and lay issues and relations; theology of the local church; growth in understanding. (6) Liberty, Mo., Apr. 14 to 15, 1972 — Relationships between Church and State.

Baptists, Southern (Ecumenical Institute, Wake Forest University, and, since the 11th meeting, the Interfaith Witness Dept., Home Mission Board, Southern Baptist Convention): (1) Winston-Salem, N.C., May 8, 1969 — Impact of biblical criticism on Roman Catholicism and contemporary Christianity in general; holy use of the world; creeds and the Faith; liturgy and spontaneity in worship; retreat, revival and monasticism; world view of ecumenism.

(2) St. Benedict, La., Feb. 4, 1970 — Liturgy and spontaneity in worship; perspectives on Baptist views on Scripture and tradition; the priesthood of all Christians; authority of the Old Testament; Baptist concepts of the Church; retreat, revival and monasticism. (3) Louisville, Ky., May 13, 1970 — The priesthood of all Christians; the ecumenical

tide — a pastoral perspective; the enduring meaning of the Old Testament; retreat, revival and monasticism.

(4) Daytona Beach, Fla., Feb. 1 to 3, 1971 — Issues and answers, prepared by the Interfaith Witness Department of the Home Mission Board, Southern Baptist Convention. (5) Houston, Tex., Oct. 16 to 18, 1972 — Second regional conference planned in conjunction with the Interfaith Witness Department.

(6) Marriottsville, Md., Feb. 4 to 6, 1974 — Third regional conference, planned in conjunction with the Interfaith and Witness Department, concerning different types of reform and their appropriateness at different levels of church life. (7) Menlo Park, Calif., Oct. 27 to 29, 1975 — Fourth regional conference. The theme: "Conversion to Christ and Life-Long Growth in the Spirit."

(8) Winston-Salem, N.C., Nov. 10-12, 1975 — Fraternal dialogue, planned in conjunction with the Ecumenical Institute of Wake Forest University and Belmont Abbey College, on the abortion issue in Christian perspective, with publication of a statement and proceedings.

(9) Winston-Salem, N.C., Nov. 3-5, 1976 — Dialogue, planned as above, on Church-state issues, with publication of a statement and proceedings.

(10) Kansas City, Mo., Nov. 28 to 30, 1977 — Fifth regional conference on the theology and experience of worship. (11) Cincinnati, O., Apr. 28 to 30, 1978 — Inauguration of a scholars' dialogue, with presentation of papers on the Church in the New Testament and the experience of God in the Church.

(12) Cincinnati, O., Nov. 3 to 5, 1978 — Roman Catholicism in the U.S.A., an historical perspective; Southern Baptist experience in America; overviews of each tradition by the other; the local congregation or church. (13) St. Louis, Mo., Apr. 20 to 22, 1979 — Salvation as understood and taught in both traditions.

(14) Cincinnati, O., Nov. 9 to 11, 1979 — The authority of Scripture from Southern Baptist and Roman Catholic viewpoints. (15) Conyers, Ga., Apr. 11 to 13, 1980 — Spirituality as understood in each tradition, including sacraments, saints and social justice; Roman Catholic teaching on ministry from the Scriptures and the Fathers of the Church.

(16) Kerrville, Tex., Nov. 21 to 23, 1980 — Mission and social action in Southern Baptist life; eschatology; review of previous papers toward publication. (17) Cincinnati, O., Apr. 16 to 18, 1982 — Initial meeting of second round of dialogue, on the life of grace within us.

(18) Atlanta, Ga., Nov. 12 to 14, 1982 — The life of grace within us, continued. (19) Browns, Summit, N.C., Apr. 22 to 24, 1983 — The life of grace within us, continued. (20) Belmont, N.C., Nov. 18 to 20, 1983 — The life of grace within us, continued.

(21) Belmont, N.C., Mar. 30 to Apr. 1, 1984 — Discipleship and the life of grace, the communion of saints. (22) Kerrville, Tex., Nov. 30 to Dec. 2, 1984 — Development of summary statement (for publication) on the second round of dialogue.

(23) Conyers, Ga., Sept. 13 to 16, 1985 — First meeting of third round of dialogue, focusing on the

practice of mission in the respective traditions. (24) Fort Worth, Tex., Feb. 28 to Mar. 2, 1986 — Biblical foundations for mission. (25) Washington, D.C., Oct. 17 to 19, 1986 — Images of mission.

Christian Church, Disciples of Christ (Council on Christian Unity): (1) Indianapolis, Ind., Mar. 16, 1967 — A look at Disciples for Catholics. (2) Kansas City, Mo., Sept. 25, 1967 — Roman Catholic view of the nature of unity being sought; opportunities in the contemporary ecumenical movement. (3) St. Louis, Mo., Apr. 29, 1968 — Eucharistic sharing.

(4) Washington, D.C., Oct. 16, 1968 — Disciple of Christ inquiry regarding the sacramentality of marriage; pastoral reflections on mixed marriage. (5) New York, N.Y., Apr. 25, 1969 — Recognition and reconciliation of ministries; theological presuppositions concerning ministry among the Disciples; role of the priest in the Catholic community.

(6) Columbus, O., Nov. 3 to 5, 1970 — The parish concept in a plan of union (Consultation on Church Union); directions emerging in Catholic parish life. (7) New York, N.Y., June 8 to 10, 1971 — Disciples' theology of baptism; meaning of baptism as liberation, incorporation, empowerment.

(8) Indianapolis, Ind., Mar. 8 to 10, 1972 — Ministry of healing and reconciliation as practiced in the two communities. (9) Madison, Wis., June 26 to 28, 1972 — Review and summary of five years of dialogue; planning for future themes.

(10) Pleasant Hill, Shaker Town, Ky., May 22 to 24, 1973 — The Church in the New Testament.

(11) Indianapolis, Ind., Jan. 5-6, 1977 — Planning session, with the Council on Christian Unity of the Christian Church and the International Disciples Ecumenical Consultative Council, for a five-year consultation on apostolicity and catholicity in the visible unity of the church.

(12) Indianapolis, Ind., Sept. 22 to 27, 1977 — First session of a new and international consultation on the nature of the Church and elements of unity relating to it from New Testament and historical perspectives.

(13) Rome, Italy, Dec. 9 to 14, 1978 — Baptism, gift and call in the search for unity; study of various modes of baptism.

(14) Annapolis, Md., Sept. 7 to 12, 1979 — The faith of the individual and the faith of the Church; tradition and the faith of the Church; an agreed account on both subjects.

(15) New Orleans, La., Dec. 5 to 10, 1980 — Unity as gift and call; dynamics of division of the church. (16) Ardfert, Kerry, Ireland, Sept. 10 to 17, 1981 — Completion of final report of this round, "Apostolicity and Catholicity in the Visible Unity of the Church," published June 1, 1982.

Episcopal (The Anglican-Roman Catholic Consultation, Standing Commission on Ecumenical Relations): (1) Washington, D.C., June 22, 1965 — Preliminary discussions. (2) Kansas City, Mo., Feb. 2, 1966 — Eucharist as source or expression of community; Eucharist as sign and cause of unity, and the Church as a Eucharistic fellowship.

(3) Providence, R.I., Oct. 10, 1966 — Function of the minister in Eucharistic celebration; minister of the Eucharist. (4) Milwaukee, Wis., May 2, 1967 — Eucharist. (5) Jackson, Miss., Jan. 5, 1968 — Various aspects of the ministerial priesthood and the priesthood of the faithful in Eucharistic celebration; the priest's place and function in the Church's mission of service; the laity in Episcopal Church government.

(6) Liberty, Mo., Dec. 2, 1968 — Directions of the ecumenical movement; episcopal symbol of unity in the Christian community; collegiality; Citizens for Educational Freedom; a layman's view of jurisdictional and cultural factors in division; Church and society in contemporary America.

(7) Boynton Beach, Fla., Dec. 8, 1969 — All in each place; toward the reconciliation of the Roman Catholic Church and Churches of the Anglican Communion; an approach to designing a Roman Catholic-Episcopal parish; preparation of joint statement on the meeting. (8) Green Bay, Wis., June 17, 1970 — Is the (COCU — Consultation on Church Union) plan of union truly Catholic, with special reference to the priest and the episcopacy; Anglican-Roman Catholic dialogue — achievement and prognostication.

(9) St. Benedict, La., Jan. 26 to 29, 1971 — The primacy of jurisdiction of the Roman Pontiff according to the First Vatican Council; the teaching of the Second Vatican Council concerning the hierarchy of truths; analysis of the ground of "Church Elements: An Ecclesiological Investigation."

(10) Liberty, Mo., June 20 to 23, 1971 — Gift of infallibility; sharing in the teaching authority of the Church; official view of episcopacy in the Episcopal Church in the USA; symposium on Hans Kung's *Infallibility? An Inquiry*; dogma as an ecumenical problem; Revelation and statement in Anglicanism; revised working paper on theological truth, propositions and Christian unity; reflections on the teaching ministry of the Church.

(11) New York, N.Y., Jan 20 to 24, 1972 — Theological truth, propositions and Christian unity; the Protestant Episcopal Church's view of authority, tradition and the Bible; a comment on the Windsor "Statement of Eucharistic Agreement" issued by the International Anglican-Roman Catholic Consultation.

(12) Cincinnati, O., June 12 to 15, 1972 — The notion of *typos* and *typoi* as applied to the forms of the Christian Church; correspondences and differences in the Anglican and Roman Catholic understanding and exercise of teaching authority.

(13) Cincinnati, O., Mar. 18 to 22, 1973 — Formulation of a preliminary draft on the purpose of the Church. (14) Vicksburg, Miss., Jan. 6 to 10, 1974 — Formulation of a response to the "Canterbury Statement" of the International Anglican-Roman Catholic Consultation on ministry and ordination; discussion and amendment of a draft on the purpose of the Church; other subjects in a continuing dialogue on the mission of the Church.

(15) Cincinnati, O., Nov. 10 to 13, 1974 — Discussion on the nature of authority in Anglicanism and Roman Catholicism. Report prepared on the purpose of the Church. (16) Cincinnati, O., June 22 to

25, 1975 — Special ad hoc consultation on women and orders.

(17) Erlanger, Ky., Oct. 21-24, 1975 — Continuation of discussion on women and orders, with release of joint statement on the ordination of women. (18) Overland Park, Kan., Mar. 10-13, 1976 — Continuation of discussion on authority in the Church.

(19) New Orleans, La., Jan. 19-22, 1977 — Presentation and discussion of a paper entitled "Some Implications of a 'Communio Ecclesiology' for the Authority Question"; formulation of an initial response to the "Venice Statement" (see separate entry); near completion of a 12-year report on the consultation.

(20) Cincinnati, O., Aug. 9 to 12, 1977 — Preparation of a second response to the Venice Statement, "Authority in the Church," and of a 12-year report, "Where We Are: A Challenge for the Future" (planned for publication). (21) Savannah, Ga., Mar. 7 to 10, 1978 — Christian anthropology and discussion of issues raised by the topic of the 12-year report in dialogue.

(22) Cincinnati, O., Jan. 3 to 6, 1979 — Christian anthropology in the patristic period and documents of the Second Vatican Council on the subject; New Testament arguments for and against the ordination of women.

(23) Cincinnati, O., Oct. 29 to Nov. 1, 1979 — Christian anthropology from the viewpoints of biotechnology/bodiliness, and Mariology. (24) Cincinnati, O., June 17 to 20, 1980 — Maleness and femaleness in Christian anthropology.

(25) Cincinnati, O., Mar. 10 to 13, 1981 — Human sexuality in relation to Christology; ordination of women; homosexuality.

(26) Cincinnati, O., Dec. 8 to 11, 1981 — Work on the first draft of a document on Christian anthropology. (27) Savannah, Ga., June 7 to 10, 1982 — additional work on the aforementioned document. (28) Columbus, O., Feb. 22 to 25, 1983 — Completion of final report, "Images of God: Reflections on Christian Anthropology."

(29) Cincinnati, O; Jan. 23 to 26, 1984 — Consideration of the ARCIC-II agenda. (30) New York, N.Y., Dec. 10 to 13, 1984 — Discussion of ways of expressing unity now possible with respect to sharing in worship and the question of the validity of Anglican orders.

(31) New York, N.Y., Oct. 13 to 16, 1985 — Apostolic succession, the sacrificial nature of the Eucharist. (32) Albany, N.Y., June 16 to 19, 1986 — Teaching authority in the church; orders.

Lutheran, U.S.A. (Lutheran World Ministries): (1) Baltimore, Md., Mar. 16, 1965 — Exploratory discussion. (2) Baltimore, Md., July 6, 1965 — Nicene Creed as dogma of the Church. (3) Chicago, Ill., Feb. 10, 1966 — Baptism, in the context of the New Testament; Lutheran understanding; teaching of the Council of Trent.

(4) Washington, D.C., Sept. 22, 1966 — Eucharist as sacrifice, in traditional and contemporary Catholic and Lutheran contexts. (5) New York, N.Y., Apr 7, 1967 — Propitiation and five presentations on various aspects of the Eucharist. (6) St. Louis,

Mo.. Sept. 29, 1967 — Eucharist. (7) New York, Mar. 8, 1968 — Intercommunion, with respect to Catholic discipline, Lutheran practice, and theological reflections.

(8) Williamsburg, Va., Sept. 27, 1968 — Ministry; the competent minister of the Eucharist; scriptural foundations of diakonia (ministry of service). (9) San Francisco, Calif., Feb. 21, 1969 — Apostolic succession in the patristic era and in a contemporary view; Lutheran view of the validity of Lutheran orders; Christian priesthood in the light of documents of the Second Vatican Council.

(10) Baltimore, Md., Sept. 26, 1969 — The minister of the Eucharist, according to the Council of Trent; the use of "church" as applied to Protestant denominations in the documents of Vatican II; Lutheran doctrine of the ministry — Catholic and Reformed; the ordained minister and layman in Lutheranism. (11) St. George, Bermuda, Feb. 19, 1970 — Preparation of joint statement on the ministry.

(12) New York, N.Y., May, 1970. (13) Chicago, Ill., Oct. 30 to Nov. 1, 1970. (14) Miami, Fla., Feb. 19 to 22, 1971 — Peter and the New Testament; the papacy in the late patristic era, Middle Ages, Renaissance; text of the *Dogmatic Constitution on the Church* (Vatican II) with respect to the papacy and infallibility.

(15) Seabury, Conn., Sept. 24 to 27, 1971 — An investigation of the concept of divine right *(jus divinum)*; teaching of the First Vatican Council on primacy and infallibility; a Lutheran understanding of what papal primacy in the Church might mean.

(16) New Orleans, La., Feb. 18 to 21, 1972 — Further discussion of the concept of divine right; ecumenical projections concerning the Petrine office; teaching authority in the Lutheran Church. (17) Minneapolis, Minn., Sept. 22 to 25, 1972 — Further investigation of the Petrine function; councils and conciliarism.

(18) San Antonio, Tex., Feb. 16 to 19, 1973 — Discussion of work and papers of the Petrine panel concerning ministry and the Church universal, Catholic and Lutheran interpretive statements; work on papal primacy papers. (19) Allentown, Pa., Sept. 21 to 24, 1973 — Work on a joint statement concerning ministry and the Church universal, the concluding session on this topic; selection of infallibility as the next topic for consideration. (20) Marriottsville, Md., Feb. 15 to 17, 1974 — Start of discussion on infallibility; commissioning of 16 future research papers.

(21) Princeton, N.J., Sept. 19 to 22, 1974 — Scriptural studies re infallibility, inquiries into the teachings of early Lutheranism. (22) St. Louis, Mo., Jan. 30 to Feb. 2, 1975 — Historical and systematic studies of the teaching of infallibility. (23) Washington, D.C., Apr. 2 to 3, 1975 — Special meeting of several Lutheran presidents and Catholic bishops to review the work of the scholars' consultation and propose future directions. Press report issued.

(24) Washington, D.C. Sept. 17 to 21, 1975 — Further historical and case studies re infallibility: ecumenical councils and Marian definitions. (25)

Scottsdale, Ariz., Feb. 19 to 22, 1976 — Infallibility discussion continued.

(26) Washington, D.C., Apr. 2-3, 1975 — Meeting of Lutheran presidents and Catholic bishops to evaluate the direction and progress of Lutheran-Catholic dialogue in the U.S., with release of a joint statement. (27) Washington, D.C., Feb. 4-5, 1976 — Continuation of discussion concerning the direction and progress of dialogue.

(28) Gettysburg, Pa., Sept. 15-18, 1976 — Presentation of papers entitled: "Draft I — Authority and Doctrine," "The Roman View of the Petrine Office in the Church 366-461," "The Status of the Nicene Creed as Dogma in the Church," "Ecumenical Methodology — Report of Task Force."

(29) Washington, D.C., Feb. 16-20, 1977 — Discussion of the second draft of a common statement; presentation of a "Note on the Papacy as an Object of Faith."

(30) Columbia, S.C., Sept. 14 to 18, 1977 — Continued discussion of the common statement, "Infallibility and Teaching Authority in the Church." (31) Lantana, Fla., Feb. 15 to 19, 1978 — Discussion on the fourth draft of a comon statement reporting the findings of dialogue on infallibility.

(32) Minneapolis, Minn., Sept. 13 to 17, 1978 — Statement on infallibility produced. (33) Cincinnati, O., Feb. 14 to 18, 1979 — Beginning of study of justification. (34) Princeton, N.J., Sept. 13 to 16, 1979 — Further study of justification.

(35) Atlanta, Ga., Mar. 5 to 9, 1980 — Justification by faith, in the Bible and the teaching of the Council of Trent.

(36) Gettysburg, Pa., Sept. 18 to 21, 1980 — Justification by faith, patristic and medieval views. (37) Cincinnati, O., Feb. 19 to 22, 1981 — Merit and reward language; additional biblical material on justification by faith.

(38) Paoli, Pa., Sept. 23 to 27, 1981 — Drafting session on document on justification by faith. (39) Biloxi, Miss., Feb. 18 to 21, 1982 — Drafting session. (40) New York, N.Y., Sept. 23 to 26, 1982 — Drafting session. (41) Belmont, N.C., Feb. 17 to 20, 1983 — Drafting session. (42) Milwaukee, Wis., Sept. 15 to 18, 1983 — Final report, "Justification by Faith."

(43) Sequin, Tex., Feb. 23 to 26, 1984 — Initial discussion concerning Mary and the communion of saints. (44) Cincinnati, O., Sept. 20 to 23, 1984 — Mary in Patristics; Catholic Marian documents since Vatican II; contemporary Catholic Marian devotion; Luther and the veneration of Mary.

(45) Marriottsville, Md., Feb. 21 to 24, 1985 — Mediation of saints; saints in glory; saints and angels; Mary and the saints in Lutheran confessions and contemporary Lutheran worship; biblical data on the veneration of holy people. (46) Techny, Ill., Sept. 19 to 22, 1985 — Mary in the liturgy; medieval Marian piety.

(47) Burlingame, Calif., Feb. 20 to 23, 1986 — Pre-Constantinian origins of the veneration of saints; Aquinas, Bonaventure and Scotus on Marian doctrine; liturgical forms of Marian devotion through the ages. (48) Wheeling, W. Va., Sept. 18 to 21, 1986 — Questions and answers in writing and discussion.

Methodist (United Methodist Church): (1) Chicago, Ill., June 28, 1966 — Methodists and Roman Catholics: comments for Catholic-Methodist conversation. (2) Chicago, Ill., Dec. 18, 1966 — Salvation, faith and good works; Catholic Church and faith. (3) Lake Junaluska, N.C., June 28, 1967 — Roman Catholic position regarding the Spirit in the Church; mission of the Holy Spirit, in the light of the Second Vatican Council's *Dogmatic Constitution on the Church* and the writings of John Wesley.

(4) New York, N.Y., Dec. 17, 1967 — Three generations of Church-State argumentation. (5) San Antonio, Tex., Sept. 30, 1968 — Shared convictions about education. (6) Delaware, O., Oct. 9, 1969 — Major Methodist ecumenical documents; an appraisal of some documents of Vatican II; racial confrontation in Roman Catholicism, Methodism and the National Council of Churches. (7) Chicago, Ill., Jan. 30, 1970 — Review and planning.

(8) Washington, D.C., Dec. 16, 1970 — Completion of a statement of shared convictions about education. Task force meetings during 1971. (9) Cincinnati, O., Feb. 25 to 26, 1972 — Ministry in the United Methodist Church and the spirituality of the ordained ministry; problems of ministry. (10) Dayton, O., Oct. 13 to 14, 1972 — Dialogue on the holiness of the Church and Christian holiness.

(11) Washington, D.C., Mar. 9 to 10, 1973 — Spirituality of the ministry. (12) Washington, D.C., Nov. 1 to 2, 1973 — Start of preparatory work on a consensus statement on spirituality of the ministry.

(13) Washington, D.C., Jan. 30 to Feb. 2, 1975 — Report prepared on Catholic and United Methodist understandings of holiness and spirituality in the ordained ministry; statement on holiness and spirituality of the ordained ministry released in January, 1976.

(14) Washington, D.C., May 16, 1977 — Planning session for the next round of dialogue.

(15) Washington, D.C., Dec. 4 to 6, 1977 — New phase of dialogue on the Eucharist in both traditions. (16) Marriottsville, Md., Apr. 16 to 18, 1978 — Continuing research on Eucharistic theology as developed in the two churches.

(17) Washington, D.C., Oct. 12 to 14, 1978 — Eucharistic practice in both traditions. (18) Marriottsville, Md., May 17 to 19, 1979 — The Eucharist; contemporary Eucharistic devotional practices of both traditions.

(19) Washington, D.C., Nov. 4 to 6, 1979 — The presence of Christ in the word, related to Eucharistic presence; the notion of sacrifice in the Eucharist. (20) Washington, D.C., May 4 to 6, 1980 — Comparison of liturgical texts of Methodists and Catholics; further exploration of the relationship of word and sacrament.

(21) Erlanger, Ky., Dec. 6 to 8, 1981 — Completion of statement, "Eucharistic Celebration: Converging Theology — Divergent Practice." (22) Columbus, O., Sept. 11 to 14, 1986 — First meeting for new round of talks, on ethical issues related to dying.

Orthodox (Standing Conference of Canonical Orthodox Bishops of America): (1) Worcester, Mass., Sept. 5, 1965 — Preliminary discussions. (2) New York, N.Y., Sept. 29, 1966 — Consultation led to appointment of task forces to investigate differences in theological methods, questions of sacramental sharing, possible cooperation in theological education and the formation of seminarians. (3) Worcester, Mass., May 5 to 6, 1967 — Theological diversity and unity; intercommunion; common witness in theological education. (4) Maryknoll, N.Y., Dec. 6 to 7, 1968 — Eucharist and Church; indissolubility of marriage; cooperation in theological education.

(5) Worcester, Mass., Dec. 12 to 13, 1969 — Orthodox and Catholic views of the Eucharist and membership in the Church; an agreed statement on the Eucharist. (6) New York, N.Y., May 19 to 20, 1970 — New Order of the Mass; membership of schismatics and heretics in the ancient Church; current legislation of the Catholic Church and current practices of the Greek Orthodox Church concerning common worship; current legislation of the Catholic Church concerning mixed marriages; Orthodox view of mixed marriages; an agreed statement on mixed marriages.

(7) Brookline, Mass., Dec. 4 to 5, 1970 — Ministers, doctrine and practice of matrimony in Eastern and Western traditions. (8) Barlin Acres, Mass., Nov. 3 to 4, 1971 — Ethical issues relating to marriage; revision of an agreed statement on mixed marriages; the primacy of Rome as seen by the Eastern Church.

(9) New York, N.Y., Dec. 6, 1973 — Study of a draft statement on the sanctity of marriage. (10) Washington, D.C., May 23 to 24, 1974 — Dialogical process; witness of the Church on the American scene; approval of an agreed statement on respect for life; Orthodox and Catholic views of contemporary Orthodoxy and Catholicism.

(11) New York, N.Y., Dec. 9 to 10, 1974 — Prepared and issued an agreed statement on the Church. (12) Washington, D.C., May 19 to 20, 1975 — Dialogue on the local church and on the theology of priesthood. (13) New York, N.Y., Jan. 23 to 24, 1976 — Further dialogue on the theology of priesthood, et al.

(14) Washington, D.C., May 18-19, 1976 — Additional discussion of theology of the priesthood, and ecumenical councils; release of joint statements entitled "The Principle of Economy" and "The Pastoral Office."

(15) Brookline, Mass., Jan. 13-14, 1977 — Presentations on "Orthodox/Roman Catholic Marriages Revisited" and of two reports on the first pre-synodal Pan-Orthodox Conference in preparation for the coming Great and Holy Council.

(16) Washington, D.C., Sept. 28 to 29, 1977 — Presentation and discussion of papers concerning the agenda of the forthcoming Great and Holy Council of the Orthodox Church, the theology of marriage and Orthodox-Roman Catholic marriages.

(17) New York, N.Y., Jan. 24 to 25, 1978 — Preparation of a common statement on the sanctity of

marriage, authorization for writing a history of the Orthodox-Roman Catholic Consultation.

(18) Washington, D.C., May 15 to 16, 1978 — Additional work on a common statement on the sanctity of marriage, and initial discussion concerning the religious upbringing of children in Orthodox-Catholic marriages.

(19) Garrison, N.Y., Dec. 7 to 8, 1978 — Study of the religious formation of children of marriages between Eastern Orthodox and Roman Catholics; release of "An Agreed Statement on the Sanctity of Marriage."

(20) Washington, D.C., Mar. 15 to 16, 1979 — Continued study of a draft entitled "Joint Recommendations on the Spiritual Formation of Children of Marriages between Orthodox and Roman Catholics."

(21) Pittsburgh, Pa., Nov. 2 to 3, 1979 — Additional work on a document, "Spiritual Formation of Children"; study of early Christian commissioning rites.

(22) New York, N.Y., Oct. 10 to 11, 1980 — Study of the theology of ordained ministry; approval of "Joint Recommendations on the Spiritual Formation of Children of Marriages between Orthodox and Roman Catholics."

(23) Garrison, N.Y., Oct. 1 to 3, 1981 — Papers on "The Priest as Icon of Christ" and "The Sacramental Life of the Church in Light of Trinitarian Ecclesiology." (24) Milwaukee, Wis., May 27 to 29, 1982 — Papers on "Aspects of the Theme: Spirit and Sacrament," and "The Theological and Canonical Traditions of Marriage in the Orthodox and Roman Catholic Traditions."

(25) Pittsburgh, Pa., Nov. 18 to 20, 1982 — "Pneumatology and Sacramentology: A View of Systematic Theology"; an analysis of the most recent statement issued by the Anglican-Roman Catholic International Commission.

(26) New York, N.Y., May 23 to 25, 1983 — Beginning of a theological statement on the relationship of the Holy Spirit to Christ, especially in the Eucharist; publication of an official reaction to "The Mystery of the Church and of the Eucharist in Light of the Mystery of the Holy Trinity," a statement issued by the Joint International Commission for Theological Dialogue between the Roman Catholic Church and the Orthodox Church.

(27) Milwaukee, Wis., Oct. 27 to 29, 1983 — Sacraments of initiation.

(28) Crestwood, N.Y., June 4 to 6, 1984 — Joint reflection on baptism, Eucharist and ministry.

(29) Douglaston, N.Y., Oct. 25 to 27, 1984 — Final development of an agreed statement on the Lima Document — "Baptism, Eucharist and Ministry" — of the Faith and Order Commission, World Council of Churches.

(30) Brookline, Mass., June 3 to 5, 1985 — Initial discussion of the sacrament of order in the sacramental structure of the Church.

(31) Douglaston, N.Y., Oct. 30 to Nov. 2, 1985 — The people of God as bearers of the apostolicity of the Church; apostolicity, apostolic sees and primacy; marriage and priestly office in East and West. (32) Crestwood, N.Y., June 2 to 4, 1986 — Papal primacy as understood in contemporary Catholic and Orthodox theology; revision of a draft statement on the Church's experience of apostolicity.

Orthodox, Oriental (Armenian, Coptic, Ethiopian, Indian Malabar and Syrian Orthodox Churches): (1) New York N.Y., Jan. 27, 1978 — Start of a new consultation, with initial consideration of a historical study of Oriental Orthodoxy.

(2) New York, N.Y., May 26 to 27, 1978 — Purpose and method of dialogue; histories of Oriental Orthodox Churches. (3) Washington, D.C., Dec. 1 to 2, 1978 — Presentation of papers on the Council of Chalcedon, Christology and the Church today, concluding that ancient controversy over Christology does not seem to apply at the present time.

(4) New York, N.Y., May 25 to 26, 1979 — Roman Catholic Christology; Eucharistic Liturgy of the Syrian Orthodox Church.

(5) New York, N.Y., Dec. 27 to 28, 1979 — Paper on Byzantine liturgical commentary; reflection on joint statements of Paul VI with Vasken I, Ignatius Jacoub III and Amba Shenouda III. (6) New York, N.Y., Apr. 18 to 19, 1980 — Paper on Coptic Orthodox Divine Liturgy followed by that Eucharistic Liturgy.

(7) Jamaica, N.Y., Nov. 14 to 15, 1980 — Adoption of a statement on the purpose, scope and method of the dialogue between the Oriental Orthodox and Roman Catholic Churches, and a paper on celebration of the Eucharistic liturgy of the Roman Catholic Church.

(8) New York, N.Y., Dec. 3 and 4, 1981 — Papers on the role of Christ and the Spirit in the Divine Liturgies of each tradition, and on the development of the Public Office in the Armenian Church.

(9) New York, N.Y., Sept. 9 to 11, 1982 — Draft of "An Agreed Statement on the Church Crises in Egypt and Lebanon."

(10) New York, N.Y., June 8 to 10, 1983 — Official release of the aforementioned agreed statement and also of an "Agreed Statement on the Eucharist"; discussion of history of the churches' views on mixed marriages, and of the Armenian liturgy.

(11) Plymouth, Mich., Jan. 12 to 14, 1984 — Discussion of pastoral practice concerning mixed marriages; theological reflection on the Eucharist as Sacrifice. (12) New York, N.Y., Dec. 13 and 14, 1984 — Orthodox perception of the establishment of Eastern Catholic exarchates in the U.S. (13) New York, N.Y., Dec. 17 to 19, 1985 — Chrismation/Confirmation in the churches.

Polish National Catholic Church: (1) Passaic, N.J., Oct. 23, 1984 — Review of elements common to the life of the two churches. (2) New York, N.Y., May 7, 1985 — Eucharistic devotions and penitential practices of the two churches. (3) Scranton, Pa., Nov. 5, 1985 — Apostolic succession and the ordained ministry.

(4) Philadelphia, Pa., May 6, 1986 — Sacramentality and permanence of marriage; matrimonial tribunals; mixed marriages. (5) Buffalo, N.Y., Nov. 6, 1986 — Forms and structures for oversight and collegiality.

Presbyterian and Reformed (The Roman Catholic-Presbyterian Consultation Group, North American Area Council of the World Alliance of Reformed Churches): (1) Washington, D.C., July 27, 1965 — Exploratory discussions. (2) Philadelphia, Pa., Nov. 26, 1965 — Role of the Holy Spirit in renewal and reform of the Church. (3) New York, May 12, 1966 — Roman Catholic view of Scripture and tradition; apostolic and ecclesiastical tradition.

(4) Chicago, Ill., Oct. 27, 1966 — Development of doctrine; dialogue, a program of peace, prayer and study for Roman Catholics and Protestants. (5) Collegeville, Minn., Apr. 26, 1967 — Order and ministry in the Reformed tradition; validity of orders; changes in mixed marriage. (6) Lancaster, Pa., Oct. 26, 1967 — Work was begun on a joint statement on ministry. (7) Bristow, Va., May 9, 1968 — Structures and ministries. (8) Allen Park, Mich., Oct. 24, 1968 — Marriage. (9) Charleston, S.C., May 21, 1969 — Validation of ministries and ministry; theological view of marriage.

(10) Macatawa, Mich., Oct. 30, 1969 — Apostles and apostolic succession in the patristic era; report concerning office; divorce and remarriage as understood in the United Presbyterian Church in the USA; the Church and second marriage; recommendations for changes regarding inter-Christian marriages. (11) Morristown, N.J., May 13, 1970 — Joint statements on ministry in the Church and women in Church and society.

(12) Princeton, N.J., Oct. 29 to 30, 1970 — Episcopal presbyteral polity; episcopacy. (13) Columbus, O., May 13 to 15, 1971 — Ministry in the Church; man-woman relationships; the future of the Church. (14) Richmond, Va., Oct. 28 to 30, 1971 — Reports finalized on women in the Church and ministry in the Church. (15) Oct. 26 to 29, 1972 — The shape of the unity we seek.

(16) Columbus, O., May 30 to June 2, 1973 — Theological and sociological views of the shape of unity we seek. (17) Columbus, O., Oct. 24 to 27, 1973 — Renewed discussion of the previous topic. (18) Columbus, O., May 8 to 11, 1974 — Further discussion of the previous topic in the light of Scripture, tradition, theology and reflection on the total Christian experience; worship and belief; discussion of plans for publication of a book on progress of the dialogue.

(17) Cincinnati, O., Oct. 24 to 26, 1974 — Dialogue on the unity we seek in worship and in structures. (18) Washington, D.C., May 22 to 24, 1975 — Report prepared on the mission and nature of the one Church of Christ, with attention to the unity sought in worship, in structure and in common faith.

(19) Princeton, N.J., Oct. 20-23, 1976 — Presentation of: an overview of the history of the consultation; a paper covering a Roman Catholic summary of the diversity and unity of current Christian responses to moral issues facing the Church; a paper on ethics and ethos in the Reformed/Presbyterian tradition.

(20) Washington, D.C., May 25 to 27, 1977 — Human rights, distributive justice and the abortion issue as faced by the churches. (21) Princeton, N.J., Oct. 6 to 7, 1977 — Discussion of racism in South Africa and continuation of a study on human rights.

(22) Washington, D.C., May 30 to June 1, 1978 — Study of the problem of unwanted pregnancies; preparation of statements on abortion and human rights. (23) Washington, D.C., Mar. 4 to 6, 1979 — Re-drafting of proposed statements on abortion and human rights.

(24) Washington, D.C., Sept. 27 to 29, 1979 — Statements on abortion and human rights approved along with commentaries, and an interpretative report. (25) Princeton, N.J., May 19 to 21, 1982 — Beginning of the fourth round of dialogue, on the theme, "Church, Society and Kingdom of God," related to the theme of international bilateral dialogue.

(26) Washington, D.C., Nov. 17 to 19, 1982 — Papers on "Church, Society and Kingdom in the Roman Catholic and Reformed Traditions."

(27) Princeton, N.J., Mar. 24 to 26, 1983 — Paper on the Church and society from a political-science point of view; case-study analysis of respective statements on nuclear arms.

(28) Washington, D.C., Oct. 20 to 22, 1983 — Papers on Church-State issues; discussion of initial drafts of statements on "Church, State, Kingdom," and "Convergences and Divergences in Approaches to Nuclear Arms."

(29) Princeton, N.J., May 16 to 18, 1984 — Initial discussion of church-state issues, aid to private education and support of public schools. (30) Charleston, S.C., Oct. 17 to 19, 1984 — Case studies, theological framework, ecumenical conclusions.

(31) Princeton, N.J., May 8 to 10, 1985 — Approval of joint statement, "Partners in Peace and Education: The Roman Catholic/Presbyterian Reformed Consultation." (32) Washington, D.C., Dec. 9, 1985 — Planning for a fifth round of talks, on the role of the laity.

ECUMENICAL REPORTS

(Source: Rev. John F. Hotchkin, Executive Director, Bishops' Committee for Ecumenical and Interreligious Affairs, National Conference of Catholic Bishops.)

DECLARATIONS OF POPES, OTHER PRELATES

The following ecumenical statements, issued by several popes and prelates of other Christian churches, carry the authority given them by their signators.

Paul VI and Orthodox Ecumenical Patriarch Athenagoras I, First Common Declaration, Dec. 7, 1965: They expressed their regret for offenses the churches caused each other in the past and stated their intent to "erase from memory and the midst of the Church the sentences of excommunication which followed them." Through "this reciprocal act of justice and mutual forgiveness," they hoped the differences between the churches would be overcome, with the help of the Holy Spirit, and that their "full communion of faith, brotherly concord and sacramental life" would be restored.

Paul VI and Anglican Archbishop Michael Ramsey of Canterbury, Mar. 24, 1966: They wished "to leave in the hands of the God of mercy all that in the past has been opposed to the precept of charity." They stated their intention "to inaugurate between the Roman Catholic Church and the Anglican Communion a serious dialogue which, founded on the Gospels and on the ancient common traditions, may lead to that unity in truth for which Christ prayed."

Paul VI and Patriarch Athenagoras I, Second Common Declaration, Oct. 27, 1967: They wished "to emphasize their conviction that the restoration of full communion (between the churches) . . . is to be found within the framework of the renewal of the Church and of Christians in fidelity to the traditions of the Fathers and to the inspirations of the Holy Spirit who remains always with the Church." To this end, they called for a "dialogue of charity" at many levels between Orthodox and Catholics.

Paul VI and Vasken I, Orthodox Catholicos-Patriarch of All Armenians, May 12, 1970: They invited the people of their churches "to respond with greater fidelity to the call of the Holy Spirit stimulating them to a more profound unity," asked everyone to strive to know one another, and called for closer collaboration "in all domains of Christian life. . . . This collaboration must be based on the mutual recognition of the common Christian faith and the sacramental life, on the mutual respect of persons and their churches."

Paul VI and Mar Ignatius Jacob III, Syrian Orthodox Patriarch of Antioch, Oct. 27, 1971: They declared themselves to be "in agreement that there is no difference in the faith they profess concerning the mystery of the Word of God made flesh and become really man, even if over the centuries difficulties have arisen out of the different theological expressions by which this faith was expressed. They therefore encourage the clergy and faithful of their churches to even greater endeavors at removing the obstacles which still prevent complete communion among them."

Paul VI and Shenouda III, Coptic Orthodox Pope of Alexandria, May 10, 1973: Their common declaration recalls the common elements of the Catholic and Coptic Orthodox faith in the Trinity, the divinity and humanity of Christ, the seven sacraments, the Virgin Mary, the Church founded upon the Apostles, and the Second Coming of Christ. It recognizes that the two churches "are not able to give more perfect witness to this new life in Christ because of existing divisions which have behind them centuries of difficult history" dating back to the year 451 A.D. In spite of these difficulties, they expressed "determination and confidence in the Lord to achieve the fullness and perfection of that unity which is his gift." To that end, they announced their intention to set up a joint commission "whose function will be to guide common study in the fields of church tradition, patristics, liturgy, theology, history and practical problems." They rejected "all forms of proselytism" which disturb their respective churches.

Paul VI and Anglican Archbishop Donald Coggan of Canterbury, Apr. 29, 1977: They stated many points on which Anglicans and Roman Catholics hold the faith in common and called for greater cooperation between Anglicans and Roman Catholics. Such cooperation "is the true setting for continued dialogue and for the general extension and appreciation of its fruits, and for progress toward that goal which is Christ's will — the restoration of complete communion in faith and scramental life."

John Paul II and Orthodox Ecumenical Patriarch Dimitrios I, Nov. 30, 1979: They expressed gratitude to their predecessors "for everything they did to reconcile our churches and cause them progress in unity," and stated: "Purification of the collective memory of our churches is an important fruit of the dialogue of charity and an indispensable condition of future progress." They announced the establishment of the Catholic-Orthodox Theological Commission, an international body, responsible for theological dialogue between the churches.

John Paul II and Anglican Archbishop Robert Runcie of Canterbury, May 29, 1982: They stated their agreement to establish a new Anglican-Roman Catholic commission with the task of continuing work already begun toward the eventual resolution of doctrinal differences. The new commission was also charged with the task of studying "all that hinders the mutual recognition of the ministries of our communions, and to recommend what practical steps will be necessary when, on the basis of our unity in faith, we are able to proceed toward the restoration of full communion."

John Paul II and Ignatius Zakka I, Syrian Orthodox Patriarch of Antioch, June 23, 1984: They recalled and solemnly reaffirmed the common profession of faith made by their predecessors, Paul VI and Mar Ignatius Jacob III, in 1971. They said: "The confusions and the schisms that occurred between the churches . . . , they realize today, in no way affect or touch the substance of their faith, since these arose only because of differences in terminology and culture, and in the various formulae adopted by different theological schools to express the same matter. Accordingly, we find today no real basis for the sad divisions which arose between us concerning the doctrine of the Incarnation." On the pastoral level, they declared: "It is not rare . . . for our faithful to find access to a priest of their own church materially or morally impossible. Anxious to meet their needs and with their spiritual benefit in mind, we authorize them in such cases to ask for the sacraments of penance, Eucharist and anointing of the sick from lawful priests of either of our two sister churches, when they need them."

INTERNATIONAL CONSULTATIONS

International interfaith consultations involving Roman Catholics (through official appointment by the Secretariat for Promoting Christian Unity) and representatives of other Christian churches have issued a great number and wide variety of reports since 1965. The statements presented here reflect the findings of the respective dialogue participants. They do not carry the formal ecclesiastical authority of the various churches; rather, they have been submitted to the churches for review and such action or response as they deem appropriate.

World Council of Churches-Vatican: The Joint Working Group established by the WCC and the Holy See in 1965 has issued five official reports, in 1965, 1967, 1969, 1975 and 1983.

The group also prepared studies on the following subjects between 1965 and 1982: joint worship at ecumenical gatherings, ecumenical dialogue, common witness and proselytism, catholicity and apostolicity, a fixed date for Easter, patterns of relationships between the Roman Catholic Church and the World Council of Churches, toward a confession of common faith, common witness, the significance and contribution of councils of churches in the ecumenical movement.

• The WCC Faith and Order Commission (with Catholics in full membership since 1968) issued the final text of a Baptism-Eucharist-Ministry statement at a meeting held in 1982 in Lima, Peru; the document represents theological convergence achieved through decades of dialogue.

INTERNATIONAL BILATERAL COMMISSIONS

Anglican-Roman Catholic International Commission, sponsored by the Unity Secretariat and the Lambeth Conference, held 13 sessions during the first phase of its work, from January, 1970, to September, 1981. Its final report, published in 1982, contains statements of agreement on Eucharistic doctrine, ministry-ordination and authority in the church, plus elucidations in response to comments made by others on the work of the commission. The report is under study by provinces of the Anglican Communion and episcopal conferences of the Roman Catholic Church.

• An Anglican-Roman Catholic Preparatory Commission held three sessions in 1967 and published its Malta Report Jan. 2, 1968. Its recommendations — regarding increasing contact in prayer, worship, dialogue and mission — were endorsed in substance by Cardinal Augustin Bea, president of the Unity Secretariat, and the Lambeth Conference.

• The Anglican-Roman Catholic Commission on the Theology of Marriage and Its Application to Mixed Marriages held six sessions between April, 1968, and June, 1975. Its report contains reflections on: the theology of marriage, defective marital situations, canonical legislation regarding mixed marriages of Anglicans and Roman Catholics, the Roman Catholic requirement of the canonical form of marriage, the promise concerning the baptism and rearing of children (and a possible alternative to the promise), and pastoral care of mixed-marriage households.

• A Feb. 27 to Mar. 3, 1978, consultation co-sponsored by the Unity Secretariat and the Anglican Consultative Council issued a report on the ordination of women, named for the place of the meeting, Versailles.

The International Theological Colloquium between Baptists and Catholics was established by the Unity Secretariat and the Commission for Faith and Interchurch Cooperation of the Baptist World Alliance. The first two sessions were held in 1984 and 1985. The topic of the 1986 meeting was "The Church as the Koinonia (Fellowship) of the Spirit."

The Disciples of Christ-Roman Catholic Dialogue was organized by the Council of Christian Unity of the Christian Church (Disciples of Christ) and the U.S. Bishops' Committee for Ecumenical and Interreligious Affairs, along with participation by the Disciples' Ecumenical Consultative Council and the Unity Secretariat. Agreed accounts of five annual meetings from 1977 to 1981 cover a number of themes including the nature of the Church, unity under various aspects, faith and tradition, apostolicity and catholicity.

The Evangelical-Roman Catholic Dialogue on Mission, organized by Evangelicals and the Unity Secretariat, held three sessions from 1977 to 1984, and published a report in 1986 covering the nature of mission, response in the Holy Spirit and other subjects.

The Joint Lutheran-Roman Catholic Study Commission, established by the Unity Secretariat and the Lutheran World Federation, met five times between 1967 and 1971 and made public in 1972 a report entitled, "The Gospel and the Church" (Malta Report). Its four chapters cover the Gospel in relation to tradition, the world, the office of ministry in the Church and unity of the Church.

• The subsequently established Lutheran-Roman Catholic Joint Commission held 10 sessions during the first period of its work, from 1973 to 1984. The titles of its reports are: "The Eucharist" (1978/79); "Ways to Community" (1980/81); "All Under One Christ," marking the 450th anniversary of the Augsburg Confession (1980); "The Ministry in the Church" (1981/82); "Martin Luther: Witness to Jesus Christ," marking the 500th anniversary of the birth of Luther (1983); "Facing Unity: Models, Forms and Phases of Catholic-Lutheran Church Fellowship" (1985).

• The Roman Catholic-Lutheran-Reformed Study Commission on the Theology of Marriage and the Problem of Mixed Marriages was established by the Unity Secretariat, the Lutheran World Federation and the World Alliance of Reformed Churches in 1971. In 1976, it issued a final report on the proceedings of five sessions.

The Joint Methodist-Roman Catholic Commission was inaugurated by the Unity Secretariat and the World Methodist Council in 1966. It has sponsored a series of four continuing dialogues and has prepared four reports named for the places of meetings.

• The Denver Report (1971) covers Christianity and the contemporary world, spirituality, Christian home and family, the Eucharist, ministry and authority.

• The Dublin Report (1976) includes such topics as common witness and salvation, inter-church marriages, euthanasia and other moral questions.

• The Honolulu Report (1981) covers a variety of subjects related to the general theme of an agreed statement on the Holy Spirit.

• The Nairobi Report (1986) deals with the concept of primacy and the subject of infallibility.

The International Catholic-Orthodox Theological Commission, established by the Holy See and 14 autocephalous Orthodox Churches, began its work at a first session held at Patmos/Rhodes in 1980. Subsequent sessions have been held at Munich (1982), Crete (1984) and Bari (1986). The commission's first report, "The Mystery of the Church and the Eucharist in the Light of the Most Holy Trinity," was published in 1982.

Pentecostal-Roman Catholic Conversations have been held in two series, the first of which was conducted from 1966 to 1976. A final report on this series, issued in 1976, deals with baptism in the Holy Spirit, Christian initiation and the gifts, public worship and the gifts, prayer and praise. A final report on the second series of talks, between 1977 and 1982, was published in 1984, covering speaking in tongues, faith and experience, perspectives on Mary, recognition of ministries and other subjects.

The Reformed-Roman Catholic Conversations, after preliminary meetings in 1968 and 1969, were inaugurated in 1970 by the Unity Secretariat and the World Alliance of Reformed Churches. Subjects covered in five full sessions were summarized in a final report, "The Presence of Christ in Church and World," issued in 1977. The subjects were: Christ's relationship to the Church (1970), the teaching authority of the Church (1971), the presence of Christ in the world (1972), the Eucharist (1974) and ministry (1975).

JUDAISM

Judaism is the religion of the Old Testament and of contemporary Jews. Divinely revealed and with a patriarchal background (Abraham, Isaac, Jacob), it originated with the Mosaic Covenant, was identified with the Israelites, and achieved distinctive form and character as the religion of The Law from this Covenant and reforms initiated by Ezra and Nehemiah after the Babylonian Exile.

Judaism does not have a formal creed but its principal points of belief are clear. Basic is belief in one transcendent God who reveals himself through The Law, the prophets, the life of his people and events of history. The fatherhood of God involves the brotherhood of men. Religious faith and practice are equated with just living according to The Law. Moral conviction and practice are regarded as more important than precise doctrinal formulation and profession. Formal worship, whose principal act was sacrifice from Canaanite times to 70 A.D., is by prayer, reading and meditating upon the sacred writings, and observance of the Sabbath and festivals.

Judaism has messianic expectations of the complete fulfillment of the Covenant, the coming of God's kingdom, the ingathering of his people, final judgment and retribution for all men. Views differ regarding the manner in which these expectations will be realized — through a person, the community of God's people, an evolution of historical events, an eschatological act of God himself. Individual salvation expectations also differ, depending on views about the nature of immortality, punishment and reward, and related matters.

Sacred Books

The sacred books are the 24 books of the Masoretic Hebrew Text of The Law, the Prophets and the Writings (see The Bible). Together, they contain the basic instruction or norms for just living. In some contexts, the term Law or Torah refers only to the Pentateuch (Genesis, Exodus, Leviticus, Numbers, Deuteronomy); in others, it denotes all the sacred books and/or the whole complex of written and oral tradition.

Also of great authority are two Talmuds which were composed in Palestine and Babylon in the fourth and fifth centuries A.D., respectively. They consist of the Mishna, a compilation of oral laws, and the Gemara, a collection of rabbinical commentary on the Mishna. Midrash are collections of scriptural comments and moral counsels.

Priests were the principal official ministers during the period of sacrificial and temple worship. Rabbis were, and continue to be, teachers and leaders of prayer. The synagogue is the place of community worship. The family and home are focal points of many aspects of Jewish worship and practice.

Of the various categories of Jews, Orthodox are the most conservative in adherence to strict religious traditions. Others — Reformed, Conservative, Reconstructionist — are liberal in comparison with the Orthodox. They favor greater or less modification of religious practices in accommodation to contemporary culture and living conditions.

Principal events in Jewish life include the circumcision of males, according to prescriptions of the Covenant; the bar mitzvah which marks the coming-of-age of boys in Judaism at the age of 13; marriage; and observance of the Sabbath and festivals.

Sabbath and Festivals

Observances of the Sabbath and festivals begin at sundown of the previous calendar day and continue until the following sundown.

Sabbath: Saturday, the weekly day of rest prescribed in the Decalogue.

Booths (Tabernacles): A seven-to-nine-day festival in the month of Tishri (Sept.-Oct.), marked by some Jews with Covenant-renewal and reading of The Law. It originated as an agricultural feast at the end of the harvest and got its name from the temporary shelters used by workers in the fields.

Hanukkah (The Festival of Lights, the Feast of Consecration and of the Maccabees): Commemorates the dedication of the new altar in the Temple at Jerusalem by Judas Maccabeus in 165 B.C. The eight-day festival, during which candles in an eight-branch candelabra are lighted in succession, one each day, occurs near the winter solstice, close to Christmas time.

Passover: A seven-day festival commemorating the liberation of the Israelites from Egypt. The narrative of the Exodus, the Haggadah, is read at ceremonial Seder meals on the first and second days of the festival, which begins on the 14th day of Nisan (Mar.-Apr.).

Pentecost (Feast of Weeks): Observed 50 days after Passover. Some Jews regard it as commemorative of the anniversary of the revelation of The Law to Moses.

Purim: A joyous festival observed on the 14th day of Adar (Feb.-Mar.), commemorating the rescue of the Israelites from massacre by the Persians through the intervention of Esther. The festival is preceded by a day of fasting. A gift- and alms-giving custom became associated with it in medieval times.

Rosh Hashana (Feast of the Trumpets, New Year): Observed on the first day of Tishri (Sept.-Oct.), the festival focuses attention on the day of judgment and is marked with meditation on the ways of life and the ways of death. It is second in importance only to the most solemn observance of Yom Kippur, which is celebrated 10 days later.

Yom Kippur (Day of Atonement): The highest holy day, observed with strict fasting. It occurs 10 days after Rosh Hashana.

Yom HaShoah (Holocaust Memorial Day): Observed in the week after Passover; increasingly observed with joint Christian-Jewish services of remembrance.

CATHOLIC-JEWISH RELATIONS

The Second Vatican Council, in addition to the "Decree on Ecumenism" concerning the movement for unity among Christians, stated the mind of the Church on a similar matter in a "Declaration on the Relationship of the Church to Non-Christian Religions." This document, as the following excerpts indicate, backgrounds the reasons and directions of the Church's regard for the Jews. (Other portions of the document, not cited here, refer to Hindus, Buddhists and Moslems.)

Spiritual Bond

As this sacred Synod searches into the mystery of the Church, it recalls the spiritual bond linking the people of the New Covenant with Abraham's stock.

For the Church of Christ acknowledges that, according to the mystery of God's saving design, the beginnings of her faith and her election are already found among the patriarchs, Moses, and the prophets. She professes that all who believe in Christ, Abraham's sons according to faith (cf. Gal. 3:7), are included in the same patriarch's call, and likewise that the salvation of the Church was mystically foreshadowed by the Chosen People's exodus from the land of bondage.

The Church, therefore, cannot forget that she received the revelation of the Old Testament through the people with whom God in his inexpressible mercy deigned to establish the Ancient Covenant. Nor can she forget that she draws sustenance from the root of that good olive tree onto which have been grafted the wild olive branches of the Gentiles (cf. Rom.11:17-24). Indeed, the Church believes that by his cross Christ, our Peace, reconciled Jew and Gentile, making them both one in himself (cf. Eph. 2:14-16).

The Jews still remain most dear to God because of their fathers, for he does not repent of the gifts he makes nor of the calls he issues (cf. Rom. 11:28-29). In company with the prophets and the same Apostle (Paul), the Church awaits that day, known to God alone, on which all peoples will address the Lord in a single voice and "serve him with one accord" (Zeph. 3:9; Cf. Is. 66:23; Ps. 65:4; Rom. 11:11-32).

Since the spiritual patrimony common to Christians and Jews is thus so great, this sacred Synod wishes to foster and recommend that mutual understanding and respect which is the fruit above all of biblical and theological studies, and of brotherly dialogues.

No Anti-Semitism

True, authorities of the Jews and those who followed their lead pressed for the death of Christ (cf. Jn. 19:6); still, what happened in his passion cannot be blamed upon all the Jews then living, without distinction, nor upon the Jews of today. Although the Church is the new People of God, the Jews should not be presented as repudiated or cursed by God, as if such views followed from the holy Scriptures. All should take pains, then, lest in catechetical instruction and in the preaching of God's Word they teach anything out of harmony with the truth of the Gospel and the spirit of Christ.

The Church repudiates all persecutions against any man. Moreover, mindful of her common patrimony with the Jews, and motivated by the Gospel's spiritual love and by no political considerations, she deplores the hatred, persecutions, and displays of anti-Semitism directed against the Jews at any time and from any source. (No. 4).

The Church rejects, as foreign to the mind of Christ, any discrimination against men or harassment of them because of their race, color, condition of life, or religion. (No. 5).

Bishops' Secretariat

The American hierarchy's first move toward implementation of the Vatican II *Declaration on the Relationship of the Church to Non-Christian Religions (Nostra Aetate)* was to establish, in 1965, a Subcommission for Catholic-Jewish Relations in the framework of its Commission for Ecumenical and Interreligious Affairs. This subcommission was reconstituted and given the title of secretariat in September, 1967. Its moderator is Bishop Francis J. Mugavero of Brooklyn. The Secretariat for Catholic-Jewish Relations is located at 1312 Massachusetts Ave. N.W., Washington, D.C. 20005. The executive director is Dr. Eugene J. Fisher.

According to the key norm of a set of guidelines issued by the secretariat Mar. 16, 1967 and updated Apr. 9, 1985: "The general aim of all Catholic-Jewish meetings (and relations) is to increase our understanding both of Judaism and the Catholic faith, to eliminate sources of tension and misunderstanding, to initiate dialogue or conversations on different levels, to multiply intergroup meetings between Catholics and Jews, and to promote cooperative social action."

Vatican Guidelines

In a document issued Jan. 3, 1975, the Vatican Commission for Religious Relations with the Jews offered a number of suggestions and guidelines for implementing the Christian-Jewish portion of the Second Vatican Council's *Declaration on Relations with Non-Christian Religions*.

Among "suggestions from experience" were those concerning dialogue, liturgical links between Christian and Jewish worship, the interpretation of biblical texts, teaching and education for the purpose of increasing mutual understanding, and joint social action.

The document concluded with the statement:

"On Oct. 22, 1974, the Holy Father instituted for the universal Church this Commission for Religious Relations with the Jews, joined to the Secretariat for Promoting Christian Unity. This special commission, created to encourage and foster religious relations between Jews and Catholics — and to do so in collaboration with other Christians — will be, within the limits of its competence, at the service of all interested organizations, providing information for them and helping them to pursue their task in conformity with the instructions of the Holy See.

"The commission wishes to develop this collaboration in order to implement, correctly and effectively, the express intentions of the (Second Vatican) Council."

On June 24, 1985, the Vatican Commission for Religious Relations with the Jews promulgated its "Notes on the Correct Way to Present Jews and Judaism in Preaching and Catechesis in the Roman Catholic Church," with the intent of providing "a helpful frame of reference for those who are called upon in the course of their teaching assignments to speak about Jews and Judaism and who wish to do so in keeping with the current teaching of the Church in this area."

The document states emphatically that, since the relationship between the Church and the Jewish people is one "founded on the design of the God of the Covenant," Judaism does not occupy "an occasional and marginal place in catechesis," but an "essential" one that "should be organically integrated" throughout the curriculum on all levels of Catholic education.

The Notes discuss the relationship between the Hebrew Scriptures and the New Testament, focusing especially on typology,' which is called "the sign of a problem unresolved." Underlined is the "eschatological dimension," that "the people of God of the Old and the New Testament are tending toward a like end in the future: the coming or re-

turn of the Messiah." Jewish witness to God's Kingdom, the Notes declare, challenges Christians to "accept our responsibility to prepare the world for the coming of the Messiah by working together for social justice . . . and reconciliation."

The Notes emphasize the Jewishness of Jesus' teaching, correct misunderstandings concerning the portrayal of Jews in the New Testament and describe the Jewish origins of Christian liturgy. One section addresses the "spiritual fecundity" of Judaism to the present, its continuing "witness — often heroic — of its fidelity to the one God," and mandates the development of Holocaust curricula and a positive approach in Catholic education to the "religious attachment which finds its roots in biblical tradition" between the Jewish people and the Land of Israel, affirming the "existence of the State of Israel" on the basis of "the common principles of international law."

Papal Statements

(Courtesy of Dr. Eugene Fisher, executive director of the Secretariat for Catholic-Jewish Relations, National Conference of Catholic Bishops; consultor to the Vatican Commission for Religious Relations with the Jews; member of the International Catholic-Jewish Liaison Committee.)

Pope John Paul, in a remarkable series of addresses beginning in 1979, has sought to promote and give shape to the development of dialogue between Catholics and Jews.

In a homily delivered June 7, 1979, at Auschwitz, which he called the "Golgotha of the Modern World," he prayed movingly for "the memory of the people whose sons and daughters were intended for total extermination."

In a key address delivered Nov. 17, 1980, to the Jewish community in Mainz, the Pope articulated his vision of the three "dimensions" of the dialogue: (1) "the meeting between the people of God of the Old Covenant . . . and the people of the New Covenant"; (2) the encounter of "mutual esteem between today's Christian churches and today's people of the Covenant concluded with Moses"; (3) the "holy duty" of witnessing to the one God in the world and "jointly to work for peace and justice."

In addressing representatives of episcopal conferences gathered in Rome by the Vatican Commission from around the world, the Pope again stressed Mar. 6, 1982, the continuing validity of God's covenant with the Jewish people. In his 1982 address, the Pope called especially for a renewal of catechesis that "will not only present Jews and Judaism in an honest and objective manner, but will also do so with a lively awareness" of "our common spiritual heritage . . . taking into account the faith and religious life of the Jewish people as professed and lived now as well." The delegates to the meeting began the process of considering the biblical, theological, and contemporary dynamics of such a catechesis, a process which culminated in the issuance, mentioned above, of the 1985 Notes on preaching and catechesis.

On Mar. 22, 1984, at an audience with members

of the Anti-Defamation League of B'nai B'rith, the Pope commented on "the mysterious spiritual link which brings us close together, in Abraham and through Abraham, in God who chose Israel and brought forth the Church from Israel." He urged joint social action on "the great task of promoting justice and peace, the sign of the messianic age in both the Jewish and the Christian tradition, grounded in its turn in the great prophetic heritage."

In receiving a delegation of the American Jewish Committee Feb. 14, 1985, the Holy Father confirmed that *Nostra Aetate* "remains always for us . . . a teaching which is necessary to accept not merely as something fitting, but much more as an expression of the faith, as an inspiration of the Holy Spirit, as a word of the divine wisdom."

During his historic visit to the Great Synagogue in Rome Apr. 13, 1986 (see separate entry), the Pope listened attentively to the reading in Hebrew and Italian of Gen. 15:1-7 and Micah 4:1-5, and also to the Chief Rabbi's interpretation of the meaning of these key texts. In his turn, the Holy Father affirmed that God's covenant with the Jewish people is "irrevocable," and stated: "The Jewish religion is not 'extrinsic' to us, but in a certain way is 'intrinsic' to our own religion. With Judaism, therefore, we have a relationship which we do not have with any other religion."

International Liaison Committee

The International Catholic-Jewish Liaison Committee was formed in 1971 and is the official link between the Commission for Religious Relations with the Jewish People and the International Jewish Committee for Interreligious Consultations. The committee, which meets every 18 months to examine matters of common interest, devoted its meeting of Oct. 28 to 30, 1985, to a study of the Notes on preaching and catechesis.

Previous meetings discussed such topics as mission and witness (Venice, 1977), religious education (Madrid, 1978), religious liberty and pluralism (Regensburg, 1979), religious commitment (London, 1981), the sanctity of human life in an age of violence (Milan, 1982), youth and faith (Amsterdam, 1984).

The Holy See appointed Dr. Eugene Fisher a member of the Liaison Committee Apr. 1, 1984. He is the only lay person and the only American on the eight-member committee.

U.S. Dialogue

National Workshops on Christian-Jewish Relations, an increasingly important forum for dialogue, have been held since 1975 in several U.S. cities.

A continuing dialogue on religious tradition and social policy — sponsored by the Synagogue Council of America and the NCCB Secretariat for Catholic-Jewish Relations — has been held annually since 1979.

Ongoing relationships are also maintained by the NCCB Secretariat with other Jewish agencies, such as the American Jewish Committee, the Anti-Defamation League of B'nai B'rith, the Union of American Hebrew Congregations and the American Jewish Congress.

In 1984, major inter-seminary programs were held in Dallas, Los Angeles, Chicago and Boston. In 1985, these and some two dozen other dioceses joined with Jewish agencies to sponsor programs celebrating the 25th anniversary of *Nostra Aetate;* Seton Hall University, St. Mary's Seminary and University in Baltimore and the University of Notre Dame were among academic institutions sponsoring reflective celebrations of the Declaration.

In 1986, the NCCB Secretariat for Catholic-Jewish Relations and the American Jewish Committee were collaborating on a three-year project to develop curriculum and homiletic guidelines and models to implement the Notes (noted above).

ISLAM

Islam is the religion of Mohammed and his followers, called Moslems, or Muslims. Islam, meaning submission to God, originated with Mohammed (570-632), an Arabian, who taught that he had received divine revelation and was the last and greatest of the prophets.

Moslems believe in one God. There were six great prophets—Adam, Noah, Abraham, Moses, Jesus and Mohammed—and Mohammed was the greatest. The creed states: "There is no God but Allah and Mohammed is the prophet of Allah."

The principal duties of Moslems are to: profess the faith by daily recitation of the creed; pray five times a day facing in the direction of the holy city of Mecca; give alms; fast daily from dawn to dusk during the month of Ramadan; make a pilgrimage to Mecca once if possible.

Moslems believe in a final judgment, heaven and hell. Polygamy is practiced. Some dietary regulations are in effect. The weekly day of worship is Friday, and the principal service is at noon in a mosque. Moslems do not have an ordained minis-

try. The general themes of their prayer are adoration and thanksgiving.

The basis of Islamic belief is the Koran, the created word of God revealed to Mohammed by the angel Gabriel over a period of 20 years. The contents of this sacred book are complemented by the Sunna, a collection of sacred traditions, and reinforced by Ijma, the consensus of Moslems which guarantees them against error in matters of belief and practice.

There are several sects of Moslems.

Conciliar Statement

The attitude of the Church toward Islam was stated as follows in the Second Vatican Council's *Declaration on the Relationship of the Church to Non-Christian Religions* (No. 3).

"Upon the Moslems, too, the Church looks with esteem. They adore one God, living and enduring, merciful and all-powerful, Maker of heaven and earth and Speaker to men. They strive to submit wholeheartedly even to his inscrutable decrees, just as did Abraham, with whom the Islamic faith is pleased to associate itself. Though they do not acknowledge Jesus as God, they revere him as a prophet. They also honor Mary, his virgin mother; at times they call on her, too, with devotion. In addition they await the day of judgment when God will give each man his due after raising him up. Consequently, they prize the moral life, and give worship to God especially through prayer, alms-giving and fasting.

"Although in the course of the centuries many quarrels and hostilities have arisen between Christians and Moslems, this most sacred Synod urges all to forget the past and to strive sincerely for mutual understanding. On behalf of all mankind, let them make common cause of safeguarding and fostering social justice, moral values, peace and freedom."

NON-ABRAHAMIC RELIGIONS

Hinduism, Buddhism, Confucianism and some other religions can be called non-Abrahamic because — unlike Judaism, Christianity and Islam — they do not recognize Abraham as their father in faith.

Hinduism

Hinduism is the traditional religion of India with origins dating to about 5,000 B.C. Its history is complex, including original Vedic Hinduism, with a sacred literature (Veda) of hymns, incantations and other elements, and with numerous nature gods; Brahmanism, with emphasis on ceremonialism and its power over the gods; philosophical speculation, reflected in the Upanishads, with development of ideas concerning Karma, reincarnation, Brahman, and the manner of achieving salvation; the cults of Vishnu, Shiva and other deities; reforms in Hinduism and in relation to Islam and Christianity.

The principal tenets of Hinduism are open to various interpretations. Karma is the law of the deed, of sowing and reaping, of retribution. It determines the progress of a person toward liberation from the cycle of rebirths necessary for salvation. Liberation is accomplished in stages, through successive reincarnations which indicate the previous as well as the existing state of a person. The means of liberation are the practice of ceremonialism and asceticism; faith in, devotion to and worship of the gods Vishnu and Shiva in their several incarnations; and/or knowledge attained through disciplined meditation called Yoga. Salvation, according to philosophical Hinduism, consists in absorption in Brahman, the neuter world-soul. Vishnu, the sun-god, and Shiva, the destroyer or generative force of the universe, are the principal popular deities. Ancient belief in nature gods (pantheism) is reflected in sacred respect for some animals. The concept of reincarnation underlies the caste system in Indian society.

There are many sects in Hinduism, which does not have a definite creed. It lends itself easily to syncretism or amalgamation with other beliefs, as evidenced in the 15th century Sikh movement which adopted the monotheism and militancy of Islam. Hindu rituals are various and elaborate, with respect to foods, festivals, pilgrimages, marriage and other life-events.

Buddhism

Buddhism originated in the sixth century B.C. in reaction to formalism, pantheism and other trends in Hinduism. The Buddha, the Enlightened One, was Sidartha Gautama, an Indian prince, who sought to explain human suffering and evil and to find a middle way between the extremes of austerity and sensuality.

The four noble truths of Buddhism are: (1) existence involves suffering or pain; (2) suffering comes from craving: (3) craving can be overcome; (4) the way to overcome craving is to follow the "noble eightfold path" of right views, right intention, right speech, right action, right livelihood, right effort, right mindfulness and right concentration.

Karma, the deed-principle of judgment and retribution, and reincarnation are elements of Buddhism. The ultimate objective of life is Nirvana — the absorption of a person in the absolute — which ends the cycles of rebirth.

Buddhism is essentially atheistic and more of a moral philosophy and ethical system than a religion. It has a cultic element in veneration for Buddha. Monasteries, temples and shrines are places of contemplation and ritualistic observance. There are several categories of Buddhist monks and nuns.

Buddhism has many sects. Mahayana Buddhism, with an elaborate ideology, is strong in China, Korea and Japan. Hinayana Buddhism is common in Southeast Asia. Zen Buddhism is highly contemplative. Lamaism in Tibet is a combination of Buddhism and local demonolatry.

Confucianism

Confucianism is an ethical system based on the teachings of Confucius (c. 551-479 B.C.). It is oriented toward the moral perfection of individuals and society, the attainment of the harmony of individual and social life with the harmony of the universe, through conduct governed by the relationships of humanity, justice, ritual and courtesy, wisdom, and fidelity. Originally and basically humanistic, Confucianism was eventually mingled with elements of Chinese religion. It exerted a strong influence on national life in China from 125 to the beginning of the 20th century, despite some periods of decline.

Relations with Non-Christians

Archbishop Jean Jadot described Mar. 16, 1984, the goals of the Vatican Secretariat for Non-Christians: "to see that Catholics living among non-Christians have better objective knowledge of non-Christian religions"; "to share in social action and cultural activities as far as possible"; "to work together against moral and cultural problems."

"Religious groups have to work together, to help people to be concerned about spiritual values and to see people as human beings."

A

Abbacy: A non-diocesan territory whose people are under the pastoral care of an abbot acting in general in the manner of a bishop.

Abbess: The female superior of a monastic community of nuns; e.g., Benedictines, Poor Clares, some others. Elected by members of the community, an abbess has general authority over her community but no sacramental jurisdiction.

Abbey: See Monastery.

Abbot: The male superior of a monastic community of men religious; e.g., Benedictines, Cistercians, some others. Elected by members of the community, an abbot has ordinary jurisdiction and general authority over his community. Eastern-Rite equivalents of an abbot are a *hegumen* and an *archimandrite*. A regular abbot is the head of an abbey or monastery. An abbot general or archabbot is the head of a congregation consisting of several monasteries. An abbot primate is the head of the modern Benedictine Confederation.

Abjuration: Renunciation of apostasy, heresy or schism by a solemn oath.

Ablution: A term derived from Latin, meaning washing or cleansing, and referring to the cleansing of the hands of a priest celebrating Mass, after the offering of gifts; and to the cleansing of the chalice with water and wine after Communion.

Abortion: The expulsion of a nonviable human fetus from the womb of the mother, with moral implications stemming from the humanity of the fetus from the moment of conception and its consequent right to life. Accidental expulsion, as in cases of miscarriage, is without moral fault. Direct abortion, in which a fetus is intentionally removed from the womb, constitutes a direct attack on an innocent human being, a violation of the Fifth Commandment. A person who procures an abortion is automatically excommunicated (Canon 1398 of the Code of Canon Law). Direct abortion is not justifiable for any reason, e.g.: therapeutic, for the physical and/or psychological welfare of the mother; preventive, to avoid the birth of a defective or unwanted child; social, in the interests of family and/or community. Indirect abortion, which occurs when a fetus is expelled during medical or other treatment of the mother for a reason other than procuring expulsion, is permissible under the principle of double effect for a proportionately serious reason; e.g., when a medical or surgical procedure is necessary to save the life of the mother.

Absolution: The act by which an authorized priest, acting as the agent of Christ and minister of the Church, grants forgiveness of sins in the sacrament of penance. The essential formula of absolution is: "I absolve you from your sins; in the name of the Father, and of the Son, and of the Holy Spirit. Amen." Priests receive the power to absolve in virtue of their ordination and the right to exercise this power in virtue of faculties of jurisdiction given them by their bishop, their religious superior, or by canon law. The faculties of jurisdiction can be limited or restricted regarding certain sins and penalties or censures. In cases of necessity, and also in cases of the absence of their own confessors, Eastern- and Roman-Rite Catholics may ask for and receive sacramental absolution from a priest of a separated Eastern Church. Separated Eastern Christians may similarly ask for and receive sacramental absolution from an Eastern- or Roman-Rite priest. Any priest can absolve a person in danger of death; in the absence of a priest with the usual faculties, this includes a laicized priest or a priest under censure. (See additional entry under Sacraments.)

Absolution, General: A blessing of the Church to which a plenary indulgence is attached, given at the hour of death, and at stated times to members of religious institutes and secular (third) orders. (See also under Penance, Sacrament.)

Accessory to Another's Sin: One who culpably assists another in the performance of an evil action. This may be done by counsel, command, provocation, consent, praise, flattery, concealment, participation, silence, defense of the evil done.

Adoration: The highest act and purpose of religious worship, which is directed in love and reverence to God alone in acknowledgment of his infinite perfection and goodness, and of his total dominion over creatures. Adoration, which is also called *latria*, consists of internal and external elements, private and social prayer, liturgical acts and ceremonies, and especially sacrifice.

Adultery: (1) Sexual intercourse between a married person and another to whom one is not married; a violation of the obligations of chastity and justice. The Sixth Commandment prohibition against adultery also prohibits all external sins of a sexual nature. (2) Any sin of impurity (thought, desire, word, action) involving a married person who is not one's husband or wife has the nature of adultery.

Adventists: Members of several Christian sects whose doctrines are dominated by belief in a more or less imminent second advent or coming of Christ upon earth for a glorious 1,000-year reign of righteousness. This reign, following victory by the forces of good over evil in a final Battle of Armageddon, will begin with the resurrection of the chosen and will end with the resurrection of all others and the annihilation of the wicked. Thereafter, the just will live forever in a renewed heaven and earth. A sleep of the soul takes place between the time of death and the day of judgment. There is no hell. The Bible, in fundamentalist interpretation, is regarded as the only rule of faith and practice. About six sects have developed in the course of the Adventist movement which originated with William Miller (1782-1849) in the United States. Miller, on the basis of calculations made from the Book of Daniel, predicted that the second advent of Christ would occur between 1843 and 1844. After the prophecy went unfulfilled, divisions occurred in the movement and the Seventh Day

Adventists, whose actual formation dates from 1860, emerged as the largest single body. The observance of Saturday instead of Sunday as the Lord's Day dates from 1844.

Advent Wreath: A wreath of laurel, spruce, or similar foliage with four candles which are lighted successively in the weeks of Advent to symbolize the approaching celebration of the birth of Christ, the Light of the World, at Christmas. The wreath originated among German Protestants.

Agape: A Greek word, meaning love, love feast, designating the meal of fellowship eaten at some gatherings of early Christians. Although held in some places in connection with the Mass, the agape was not part of the Mass, nor was it of universal institution and observance. It was infrequently observed by the fifth century and disappeared altogether between the sixth and eighth centuries.

Age of Reason: (1) The time of life when one begins to distinguish between right and wrong, to understand an obligation and take on moral responsibility; seven years of age is the presumption in church law. (2) Historically, the 18th century period of Enlightenment in England and France, the age of the Encyclopedists and Deists. According to a basic thesis of the Enlightenment, human experience and reason are the only sources of certain knowledge of truth; consequently, faith and revelation are discounted as valid sources of knowledge, and the reality of supernatural truth is called into doubt and/or denied.

Aggiornamento: An Italian word having the general meaning of bringing up to date, renewal, revitalization, descriptive of the processes of spiritual renewal and institutional reform and change in the Church; fostered by the Second Vatican Council.

Agnosticism: A theory which holds that a person cannot have certain knowledge of immaterial reality, especially the existence of God and things pertaining to him. Immanuel Kant, one of the philosophical fathers of agnosticism, stood for the position that God, as well as the human soul, is unknowable on speculative grounds; nevertheless, he found practical imperatives for acknowledging God's existence, a view shared by many agnostics. The First Vatican Council declared that the existence of God and some of his attributes can be known with certainty by human reason, even without divine revelation. The word agnosticism was first used, in the sense given here, by T. H. Huxley in 1869.

Agnus Dei: A Latin phrase, meaning Lamb of God. (1) A title given to Christ, the Lamb (victim) of the Sacrifice of the New Law (on Calvary and in Mass). (2) A prayer said at Mass before the reception of Holy Communion. (3) A sacramental. It is a round paschal-candle fragment blessed by the pope. On one side it bears the impression of a lamb, symbolic of Christ. On the reverse side, there may be any one of a number of impressions; e.g., the figure of a saint, the name and coat of arms of the reigning pope. The *agnus dei* may have originated at Rome in the fifth century. The first definite mention of it dates from about 820.

Alleluia: An exclamation of joy derived from Hebrew, All hail to him who is, praise God, with various use in the liturgy and other expressions of worship.

Allocution: A formal type of papal address, as distinguished from an ordinary sermon or statement of views.

Alms: An act, gift or service of compassion, motivated by love of God and neighbor, for the help of persons in need; an obligation of charity, which is measurable by the ability of one person to give assistance and by the degree of another's need. Almsgiving, along with prayer and fasting, is regarded as a work of penance as well as an exercise of charity. (See Corporal and Spiritual Works of Mercy.)

Alpha and Omega: The first and last letters of the Greek alphabet, used to symbolize the eternity of God (Rv. 1:8) and the divinity and eternity of Christ, the beginning and end of all things (Rv. 21:6; 22:13). Use of the letters as a monogram of Christ originated in the fourth century or earlier.

Amen: A Hebrew word meaning truly, it is true. In the Gospels, Christ used the word to add a note of authority to his statements. In other New Testament writings, as in Hebrew usage, it was the concluding word to doxologies. As the concluding word of prayers, it expresses assent to and acceptance of God's will.

Anathema: A Greek word with the root meaning of cursed or separated and the adapted meaning of excommunication, used in church documents, especially the canons of ecumenical councils, for the condemnation of heretical doctrines and of practices opposed to proper discipline.

Anchorite: A kind of hermit living in complete isolation and devoting himself exclusively to exercises of religion and severe penance according to a rule and way of life of his own devising. In early Christian times, anchorites were the forerunners of the monastic life. The closest contemporary approach to the life of an anchorite is that of Carthusian and Camaldolese hermits.

Angels: Purely spiritual beings with intelligence and free will, whose name indicates their mission as ministers of God and ministering spirits to men. They were created before the creation of the visible universe; the devil and bad angels, who were created good, fell from glory through their own fault. In addition to these essentials of defined doctrine, it is held that angels are personal beings; they can intercede for persons; fallen angels were banished from God's glory in heaven to hell; bad angels can tempt persons to commit sin. The doctrine of guardian angels, although not explicitly defined as a matter of faith, is rooted in long-standing tradition. No authoritative declaration has ever been issued regarding choirs or various categories of angels: according to theorists, there are nine choirs, consisting of seraphim, cherubim, thrones, dominations, principalities, powers, virtues, archangels and angels. In line with scriptural usage, only three angels can be named—Michael, Raphael and Gabriel.

Angelus: A devotion which commemorates the Incarnation of Christ. It consists of three versicles, three Hail Marys and a special prayer, and recalls the announcement to Mary by the Archangel Gabriel that she was chosen to be the Mother of Christ, her acceptance of the divine will, and the Incarnation (Lk. 1:26-38). The Angelus is recited in the morning, at noon and in the evening. The practice of reciting the Hail Mary in honor of the Incarnation was introduced by the Franciscans in 1263. The *Regina Caeli,* commemorating the joy of Mary at Christ's Resurrection, replaces the Angelus during the Easter season.

Anger: Passionate displeasure arising from some kind of offense suffered at the hands of another person, frustration or other cause, combined with a tendency to strike back at the cause of the displeasure; a violation of the Fifth Commandment and one of the capital sins if the displeasure is out of proportion to the cause and or if the retaliation is unjust.

Anglican Orders: Holy orders conferred according to the rite of the Anglican Church, which Leo XIII declared null and void in the bull *Apostolicae Curae,* Sept. 13, 1896. The orders were declared null because they were conferred according to a rite that was substantially defective in form and intent, and because of a break in apostolic succession that occurred when Matthew Parker became head of the Anglican hierarchy in 1559. In making his declaration, Pope Leo cited earlier arguments against validity made by Julius III in 1553 and 1554 and by Paul IV in 1555. He also noted related directives requiring absolute ordination, according to the Catholic ritual, of convert ministers who had been ordained according to the Anglican Ordinal.

Antichrist: The man of sin, the lawless and wicked antagonist of Christ and the work of God; a mysterious figure of prophecy mentioned in the New Testament. Supported by Satan, submitting to no moral restraints, and armed with tremendous power, Antichrist will set himself up in opposition to God, work false miracles, persecute the People of God, and employ unimaginable means to lead people into error and evil during a period of widespread defection from the Christian faith before the end of time; he will be overcome by Christ. Catholic thinkers have regarded Antichrist as a person, a caricature of Christ, who will lead a final violent struggle against God and his people; they have also applied the title to personal and impersonal forces in history hostile to God and the Church. Official teaching has said little about Antichrist. In 1318, it labeled as partly heretical, senseless, and fanciful the assertions made by the Fraticelli about his coming; in 1415, the Council of Constance condemned the Wycliff thesis that excommunications made by the pope and other prelates were the actions of Antichrist.

Antiphon: (1) A short verse or text, generally from Scripture, recited in the Liturgy of the Hours before and after psalms and canticles. (2) Any verse sung or recited by one part of a choir or congregation in response to the other part, as in antiphonal or alternate chanting.

Apologetics: The science and art of developing and presenting the case for the reasonableness of the Christian faith, by a wide variety of means including facts of experience, history, science, philosophy. The constant objective of apologetics, as well as of the total process of pre-evangelization, is preparation for response to God in faith; its ways and means, however, are subject to change in accordance with the various needs of people and different sets of circumstances.

Apostasy: (1) The total and obstinate repudiation of the Christian faith. An apostate automatically incurs a penalty of excommunication. (2) Apostasy from orders is the unlawful withdrawal from or rejection of the obligations of the clerical state by a man who has received major orders. An apostate from orders is subject to a canonical penalty. (3) Apostasy from the religious life occurs when a Religious with perpetual vows unlawfully leaves the community with the intention of not returning, or actually remains outside the community without permission. An apostate from religious life is subject to a canonical penalty.

Apostolate: The ministry or work of an apostle. In Catholic usage, the word is an umbrella-like term covering all kinds and areas of work and endeavor for the service of God and the Church and the good of people. Thus, the apostolate of bishops is to carry on the mission of the Apostles as pastors of the People of God: of priests, to preach the word of God and to carry out the sacramental and pastoral ministry for which they are ordained; of religious, to follow and do the work of Christ in conformity with the evangelical counsels and their rule of life; of lay persons, as individuals and/or in groups, to give witness to Christ and build up the kingdom of God through practice of their faith, professional competence and the performance of good works in the concrete circumstances of daily life. Apostolic works are not limited to those done within the Church or by specifically Catholic groups, although some apostolates are officially assigned to certain persons or groups and are under the direction of church authorities. Apostolate derives from the commitment and obligation of baptism, confirmation, holy orders, matrimony, the duties of one's state in life, etc.

Apostolic Succession: Bishops of the Church, who form a collective body or college, are successors to the Apostles by ordination and divine right; as such they carry on the mission entrusted by Christ to the Apostles as guardians and teachers of the deposit of faith, principal pastors and spiritual authorities of the faithful. The doctrine of apostolic succession is based on New Testament evidence and the constant teaching of the Church, reflected as early as the end of the first century in a letter of Pope St. Clement to the Corinthians. A significant facet of the doctrine is the role of the pope as the successor of St. Peter, the vicar of Christ and head of the college of bishops. The doctrine of apostolic succession means more than continuity of apostolic faith and doctrine; its basic requisite is ordination by the laying on of hands in apostolic succession.

Archangel: An angel who carries out special missions for God in his dealings with persons.

Three of them are named in the Bible: Michael, leader of the angelic host and protector of the synagogue; Raphael, guide of Tobiah and healer of his father, who is regarded as the patron of travelers; Gabriel, called the angel of the Incarnation because of his announcement to Mary that she was to be the Mother of Christ.

Archdiocese: An ecclesiastical jurisdiction headed by an archbishop. An archdiocese is usually a metropolitan see, i.e., the principal one of a group of dioceses comprising a province; the other dioceses in the province are suffragan sees.

Archives: Documentary records, and the place where they are kept, of the spiritual and temporal government and affairs of the Church, a diocese, church agencies like the departments of the Roman Curia, bodies like religious institutes, and individual parishes. The collection, cataloguing, preserving, and use of these records are governed by norms stated in canon law and particular regulations. The strictest secrecy is always in effect for confidential records concerning matters of conscience, and documents of this kind are destroyed as soon as circumstances permit.

Archpriest: For some time, before and during the Middle Ages, a priest who took the place of a bishop at liturgical worship. In Europe, the term is sometimes used as an honorary title. It is also an honorary title in Eastern-Rite Churches.

Ark of the Covenant: The sacred chest of the Israelites in which were placed and carried the tablets of stone inscribed with the Ten Commandments, the basic moral precepts of the Old Covenant (Ex. 25: 10-22; 37:1-9). The Ark was also a symbol of God's presence. The Ark was probably destroyed with the Temple in 587 B.C.

Asceticism: The practice of self-discipline. In the spiritual life, asceticism — by personal prayer, meditation, self-denial, works of mortification, and outgoing interpersonal works — is motivated by love of God and contributes to growth in holiness.

Ashes: Religious significance has been associated with their use as symbolic of penance since Old Testament times. Thus, ashes of palm blessed on the previous Sunday of the Passion are placed on the foreheads of the faithful on Ash Wednesday to remind them to do works of penance, especially during the season of Lent, and that they are dust and unto dust will return. Ashes are a sacramental.

Aspergillum: A vessel or device used for sprinkling holy water. The ordinary type is a metallic rod with a bulbous tip which absorbs the water and discharges it at the motion of the user's hand.

Aspersory: A portable metallic vessel, similar to a pail, for carrying holy water.

Aspiration: Short exclamatory prayer; e.g., My Jesus, mercy.

Atheism: Denial of the existence of God, finding expression in a system of thought (speculative atheism) or a manner of acting (practical atheism) as though there were no God. The Second Vatican Council, in its *Pastoral Constitution on the Church in the Modern World* (Nos. 19 to 21), noted that a profession of atheism may represent an explicit denial of God, the rejection of a wrong notion of God, an affirmation of man rather than of God, an extreme protest against evil. It said that such a profession might result from acceptance of such propositions as: there is no absolute truth; man can assert nothing, absolutely nothing, about God; everything can be explained by scientific reasoning alone; the whole question of God is devoid of meaning. The constitution also cited two opinions of influence in atheistic thought. One of them regards recognition of dependence on God as incompatible with human freedom and independence. The other views belief in God and religion as a kind of opiate which sedates man on earth, reconciling him to the acceptance of suffering, injustice, shortcomings, etc., because of hope for greater things after death, and thereby hindering him from seeking and working for improvement and change for the better here and now. All of these views, in one way or another, have been involved in the No-God and Death-of-God schools of thought in recent and remote history.

Atonement: The redemptive activity of Christ, who reconciled man with God through his Incarnation and entire life, and especially by his suffering and Resurrection. The word also applies to prayer and good works by which persons join themselves with and take part in Christ's work of reconciliation and reparation for sin.

Attributes of God: Perfections of God. God possesses — and is — all the perfections of being, without limitation. Because he is infinite, all of these perfections are one, perfectly united in him. Man, however, because of the limited power of understanding, views these perfections separately, as distinct characteristics — even though they are not actually distinct in God. God is: almighty, eternal, holy, immortal, immense, immutable, incomprehensible, ineffable, infinite, invisible, just, loving, merciful, most high, most wise, omnipotent, omniscient, omnipresent, patient, perfect, provident, supreme, true.

Avarice (Covetousness): A disorderly and unreasonable attachment to and desire for material things; called a capital sin because it involves preoccupation with material things to the neglect of spiritual goods and obligations of justice and charity.

Ave Maria: See Hail Mary.

B

Baldachino: A canopy over an altar.

Beatification: A preliminary step toward canonization of a saint. It begins with an investigation of the candidate's life, writings and heroic practice of virtue, and the certification of at least two miracles worked by God through his intercession. If the findings of the investigation so indicate, the pope decrees that the Servant of God may be called *Blessed* and may be honored locally or in a limited way in the liturgy. Additional procedures lead to canonization (see separate entry).

Beatific Vision: The intuitive, immediate and direct vision and experience of God enjoyed in the light of glory by all the blessed in heaven. The vision is a supernatural mystery.

Beatitude: A literary form of the Old and New Testaments in which blessings are promised to persons for various reasons. Beatitudes are mentioned 26 times in the Psalms, and in other books of the Old Testament. The best known beatitudes — identifying blessedness with participation in the kingdom of God and his righteousness, and descriptive of the qualities of Christian perfection — are those recounted in Mt. 5:3-11 and Lk. 6:20-22.

Benedictus: The canticle or hymn of Zechariah at the circumcision of St. John the Baptist (Lk. 1:68-79). It is an expression of praise and thanks to God for sending John as a precursor of the Messiah. The *Benedictus* is recited in the Liturgy of the Hours as part of the Morning Prayer.

Biglietto: A papal document of notification of appointment to the cardinalate.

Biretta: A stiff, square hat with three ridges on top worn by clerics in church and on other occasions.

Blasphemy: Any expression of insult or contempt with respect to God, principally, and to holy persons and things, secondarily; a violation of the honor due to God in the context of the First and Second Commandments.

Blasphemy of the Spirit: Deliberate resistance to the Holy Spirit, called the unforgivable sin (Mt. 12:31) because it makes his saving action impossible. Thus, the only unforgivable sin is the one for which a person will not seek pardon from God.

Blessing: Invocation of God's favor, by official ministers of the Church or by private individuals. Blessings are recounted in the Old and New Testaments, and are common in the Christian tradition. Many types of blessings are listed in the *Roman Ritual*. Private blessings, as well as those of an official kind, are efficacious. Blessings are imparted with the Sign of the Cross and appropriate prayer.

Boat: A small vessel used to hold incense which is to be placed in the censer.

Brief, Apostolic: A papal letter, less formal than a bull, signed for the pope by a secretary and impressed with the seal of the Fisherman's Ring. Simple apostolic letters of this kind are issued for beatifications and with respect to other matters.

Bull, Apostolic: The most solemn form of papal document, beginning with the name and title of the pope (e.g., John Paul II, Servant of the Servants of God), dealing with an important subject, and having attached to it either a leaden seal called a *bulla* or a red ink imprint of the device on the seal. Bulls are issued to confer the titles of bishops and cardinals, to promulgate canonizations, and for other purposes. A collection of bulls is called a *bullarium*.

Burial, Ecclesiastical: Interment with ecclesiastical rites, a right of the Christian faithful. The Church recommends burial of the bodies of the dead, but cremation is permissible if it does not involve reasons against church teaching. Ecclesiastical burial is in order for catechumens; for unbaptized children whose parents intended to have them baptized before death; and even — in the absence of their own ministers — for baptized non-Catholics unless it would be considered against their will.

C

Calumny: Harming the name and good reputation of a person by lies; a violation of obligations of justice and truth. Restitution is due for calumny.

Calvary: A knoll about 15 feet high just outside the western wall of Jerusalem where Christ was crucified, so called from the Latin *calvaria* (skull) which described its shape.

Canon: A Greek word meaning rule, norm, standard, measure. (1) The word designates the Canon of Sacred Scripture, which is the list of books recognized by the Church as inspired by the Holy Spirit. (2) In the sense of regulating norms, the word designates the Code of Canon Law enacted and promulgated by ecclesiastical authority for the orderly and pastoral administration and government of the Church. A revised Code, effective Nov. 27, 1983, consists of 1,752 canons in seven books under the titles of general norms, the people of God, the teaching mission of the Church, the sanctifying mission of the Church, temporal goods of the Church, penal law and procedural law. The antecedent of this Code was promulgated in 1917 and became effective in 1918; it consisted of 2,414 canons in five books covering general rules, ecclesiastical persons, sacred things, trials, crimes and punishments. Eastern-Rite Churches have their own canon law. (3) The term also designates the canons (Eucharistic Prayers, anaphoras) of the Mass, the core of the liturgy. (4) Certain dignitaries of the Church have the title of Canon, and some Religious are known as Canons.

Canonization: An infallible declaration by the pope that a person, who died as a martyr and/or practiced Christian virtue to a heroic degree, is now in heaven and is worthy of honor and imitation by all the faithful. Such a declaration is preceded by the process of beatification and another detailed investigation concerning the person's reputation for holiness, writings, and (except in the case of martyrs) miracles ascribed to his or her intercession after death. Miracles are not required for martyrs. The pope can dispense from some of the formalities ordinarily required in canonization procedures (equivalent canonization), as Pope John XXIII did in the canonization of St. Gregory Barbarigo on May 26, 1960. A saint is worthy of honor in liturgical worship throughout the universal Church. From its earliest years the Church has venerated saints. Public official honor always required the approval of the bishop of the place. Martyrs were the first to be honored. St. Martin of Tours, who died in 397, was an early non-martyr venerated as a saint. The first official canonization by a pope for the universal Church was that of St. Ulrich by John XV in 993. Alexander III reserved the process of canonization to the Holy See in 1171. In 1588 Sixtus V established the Sacred Congregation of Rites for the principal purpose of handling causes for beatification and canonization: this function is now the work of the Congregation for the Causes of Saints. The official listing of saints and blessed is contained in the *Roman Martyr-*

ology and related decrees issued after its last publication. Butler's unofficial *Lives of the Saints* (1956) contains 2,565 entries. The Church regards all persons in heaven as saints, not just those who have been officially canonized. (See Beatification, Saints, Canonizations by Leo XIII and His Successors.)

Canticle: A scriptural chant or prayer differing from the psalms. Three of the canticles prescribed for use in the Liturgy of the Hours are: the *Magnificat* (Lk. 1:46-55), the *Benedictus* (Lk. 1:68-79), and the *Nunc Dimittis* (Lk. 2:29-32).

Capital Punishment: Punishment for crime by means of the death penalty. The political community, which has authority to provide for the common good, has the right to defend itself and its members against unjust aggression and may in extreme cases punish with the death penalty persons found guilty before the law of serious crimes against individuals and a just social order. Such punishment is essentially vindictive. Its value as a crime deterrent is a matter of perennial debate. The prudential judgment as to whether or not there should be capital punishment belongs to the civic community. The U.S. Supreme Court, in a series of decisions dating from June 29, 1972, ruled against the constitutionality of statutes on capital punishment except in specific cases and with appropriate consideration, with respect to sentence, of mitigating circumstances of the crime. Capital punishment was the subject of a statement issued Mar. 1, 1978, by the Committee on Social Development and World Peace, U.S. Catholic Conference. The statement said, in part: "The use of the death penalty involves deep moral and religious questions as well as political and legal issues. In 1974, out of a commitment to the value and dignity of human life, the Catholic bishops of the United States declared their opposition to capital punishment. We continue to support this position, in the belief that a return to the use of the death penalty can only lead to the further erosion of respect for life in our society." Additional statements against capital punishment have been issued by Pope John Paul II, numerous bishops and other sources.

Capital Sins: Moral faults which, if habitual, give rise to many more sins. They are pride, covetousness, lust, anger, gluttony, envy, sloth. The opposite virtues are: humility, liberality, chastity, meekness, temperance, brotherly love, diligence.

Cardinal Virtues: The four principal moral virtues are prudence, justice, temperance and fortitude.

Catacombs: Underground Christian cemeteries in various cities of the Roman Empire and Italy, especially in the vicinity of Rome; the burial sites of many martyrs and other Christians.

Catechesis: Religious instruction and formation not only for persons preparing for baptism but also for the faithful in various stages of their spiritual development.

Catechism: A summary of Christian doctrine in question and answer form, used for purposes of instruction.

Catechumen: A person preparing in a program of instruction and spiritual formation for baptism and reception into the Church. The Church has a special relationship with catechumens. It invites them to lead the life of the Gospel, introduces them to the celebration of the sacred rites, and grants them various prerogatives that are proper to the faithful (one of which is the right to ecclesiastical burial).

Cathedra: A Greek word for chair, designating the chair or seat of a bishop in the principal church of his diocese, which is therefore called a cathedral (see separate entry).

Cathedraticum: The tax paid to a bishop by all churches and benefices subject to him for the support of episcopal administration and for works of charity.

Catholic: A Greek word, meaning universal, first used in the title Catholic Church in a letter written by St. Ignatius of Antioch about 107 to the Christians of Smyrna.

Celebret: A Latin word, meaning Let him celebrate, the name of a letter of recommendation issued by a bishop or other superior stating that a priest is in good standing and therefore eligible to celebrate Mass or perform other priestly functions.

Celibacy: The unmarried state of life, required in the Roman Church of candidates for holy orders and of men already ordained to holy orders, for the practice of perfect chastity and total dedication to the service of people in the ministry of the Church. Celibacy is enjoined as a condition for ordination by church discipline and law, not by dogmatic necessity. In the Roman Church, a consensus in favor of celibacy developed in the early centuries while the clergy included both celibates and men who had been married once. The first local legislation on the subject was enacted by a local council held in Elvira, Spain, about 306; it forbade bishops, priests, deacons and other ministers to have wives. Similar enactments were passed by other local councils from that time on, and by the 12th century particular laws regarded marriage by clerics in major orders to be not only unlawful but also null and void. The latter view was translated by the Second Lateran Council in 1139 into what seems to be the first written universal law making holy orders an invalidating impediment to marriage. In 1563 the Council of Trent ruled definitely on the matter and established the discipline in force in the Roman Church. Some exceptions to this discipline have been made in recent years. Several married Protestant and Episcopalian (Anglican) clergymen who became converts and were subsequently ordained to the priesthood have been permitted to continue in marriage. Married men over the age of 35 can be ordained to the permanent diaconate. Eastern Church discipline on celibacy differs from that of the Roman Church. In line with legislation enacted by the Synod of Trullo in 692 and still in force, candidates for holy orders may marry before becoming deacons and may continue in marriage thereafter, but marriage after ordination is forbidden. Eastern-Rite bishops in the U.S., however, do not ordain married candidates for the priesthood. Eastern-Rite bishops are unmarried.

Cenacle: The upper room in Jerusalem where Christ ate the Last Supper with his Apostles.

Censer: A metal vessel with a perforated cover and suspended by chains, in which incense is burned. It is used at some Masses, Benediction of the Blessed Sacrament and other liturgical functions.

Censorship of Books: An exercise of vigilance by the Church for safeguarding authentic religious teaching. Pertinent legislation in a decree issued by the Congregation for the Doctrine of the Faith Apr. 9, 1975, is embodied in the Code of Canon Law (Book III, Title IV). (1) Pre-publication clearance is required for: editions of Sacred Scripture, liturgical texts and books of private devotion, catechisms and other writings relating to catechetical instruction. Books dealing with Scripture, theology, canon law, church history and religious or moral disciplines may not be used as basic texts in educational institutions (from elementary to university levels) unless they have been published with the approval of competent church authority. (2) Pre-publication clearance is recommended for all books on the aforementioned subjects, even though they are not used as basic texts in teaching. (3) Books or other writings dealing with religion or morals may not be displayed, sold or given out in churches or oratories unless published with the approval of competent ecclesiastical authority. (4) Except for a just and reasonable cause, Catholics should not write for newspapers, magazines or periodicals which regularly and openly prove to be inimical to the Catholic religion and good morals. The approval of the local bishop is required before clerics or members of religious institutes (who also need the approval of their superior) may write for such publications. Permission to publish works of a religious character, together with the apparatus of reviewing them beforehand, falls under the authority of the bishop of the place where the writer lives or where the works are published. Clearance for publication is usually indicated by the terms *Nihil obstat* (Nothing stands in the way) issued by the censor and *Imprimatur* (Let it be printed) authorized by the bishop; an equivalent statement is, Published with ecclesiastical permission. The clearing of works for publication does not necessarily imply approval of an author's viewpoint or his manner of handling a subject.

Censures: Spiritual penalties inflicted by the Church on baptized persons for committing certain serious offenses and for being or remaining obstinate therein: excommunication (exclusion from the community of the faithful, barring a person from sacramental and other participation in the goods and offices of the community of the Church), suspension (prohibition of a cleric to exercise orders) and interdict (deprivation of the sacraments and liturgical activities). Their intended purposes are to deter persons from committing sins which, more seriously and openly than others, threaten the common good of the Church and its members; to punish and correct offenders; and to provide for the making of reparation for harm done to the community of the Church. Censures may be in-

curred automatically (*ipso facto*) on the commission of certain offenses for which fixed penalties have been laid down in church law (*latae sententiae*); or they may be inflicted by sentence of a judge (*ferendae sententiae*). Automatic excommunication is incurred for the offenses of abortion, apostasy, heresy and schism. Obstinacy in crime — also called contumacy, disregard of a penalty, defiance of church authority — is presumed by law in the commission of offenses for which automatic censures are decreed. The presence and degree of contumacy in other cases, for which judicial sentence is required, is subject to determination by a judge. Absolution can be obtained from any censure, provided the person repents and desists from obstinacy. Absolution may be reserved to the pope, the bishop of a place, or the major superior of an exempt clerical religious institute. In danger of death, any priest can absolve from all censures; in other cases, faculties to absolve from reserved censures can be exercised by competent authorities or given to other priests. The penal law of the Church is contained in Book VI of the Code of Canon Law.

Ceremonies, Master of: One who directs the proceedings of a rite or ceremony during the function.

Chamberlain: (1) The Chamberlain of the Holy Roman Church is a cardinal who administers the property and revenues of the Holy See. On the death of the pope he becomes head of the College of Cardinals and summons and directs the conclave until a new pope is elected. (2) The Chamberlain of the Sacred College of Cardinals has charge of the property and revenues of the College and keeps the record of business transacted in consistories. (3) The Chamberlain of the Roman Clergy is the president of the secular clergy of Rome.

Chancellor: Notary of a diocese, who draws up written documents in the government of the diocese; takes care of, arranges and indexes diocesan archives, records of dispensations and ecclesiastical trials.

Chancery (1) A branch of church administration that handles written documents used in the government of a diocese. (2) The administrative office of a diocese, a bishop's office.

Chapel: A building or part of another building used for divine worship; a portion of a church set aside for the celebration of Mass or for some special devotion.

Chaplain: A priest appointed for the pastoral service of any division of the armed forces, religious communities, institutions, various groups of the faithful.

Chaplet: A term, meaning little crown, applied to a rosary or, more commonly, to a small string of beads used for devotional purposes; e.g., the Infant of Prague chaplet.

Chapter: A general meeting of delegates of religious orders for elections and the handling of other important affairs of their communities.

Charisms: Gifts or graces given by God to persons for the good of others and the Church. Examples are special gifts for apostolic work, prophecy, healing, discernment of spirits, the life of evangelical poverty, here-and-now witness to faith in various circumstances of life. The Second Vatican Council made the following statement about charisms in the *Dogmatic Constitution on the Church* (No. 12): "It is not only through the sacraments and Church ministries that the same Holy Spirit sanctifies and leads the People of God and enriches it with virtues. Allotting his gifts 'to everyone according as he will' (1 Cor. 12:11), he distributes special graces among the faithful of every rank. By these gifts he makes them fit and ready to undertake the various tasks or offices advantageous for the renewal and upbuilding of the Church, according to the words of the Apostle: 'The manifestation of the Spirit is given to everyone for profit' (1 Cor. 12:7). These charismatic gifts, whether they be the most outstanding or the more simple and widely diffused, are to be received with thanksgiving and consolation, for they are exceedingly suitable and useful for the needs of the Church. "Still, extraordinary gifts are not to be rashly sought after, nor are the fruits of apostolic labor to be presumptuously expected from them. In any case, judgment as to their genuineness and proper use belongs to those who preside over the Church, and to whose special competence it belongs, not indeed to extinguish the Spirit, but to test all things and hold fast to that which is good" (cf. 1 Thes. 5:12; 19-21).

Charity: Love of God above all things for his own sake, and love of one's neighbor as oneself because and as an expression of one's love for God; the greatest of the three theological virtues. The term is sometimes also used to designate sanctifying grace.

Chastity: Properly ordered behavior with respect to sex. In marriage, the exercise of the procreative power is integrated with the norms and purposes of marriage. Outside of marriage, the rule is self-denial of the voluntary exercise and enjoyment of the procreative faculty in thought, word or action. The vow of chastity, which reinforces the virtue of chastity with the virtue of religion, is an evangelical counsel and one of the three vows professed by Religious.

Chirograph or Autograph Letter: A letter written by a pope himself, in his own handwriting.

Christ: The title of Jesus, derived from the Greek translation *Christos* of the Hebrew term *Messiah,* meaning the Anointed of God, the Savior and Deliverer of his people. Christian use of the title is a confession of belief that Jesus is the Savior.

Christianity: The sum total of things related to belief in Christ — the Christian religion, Christian churches, Christians themselves, society based on and expressive of Christian beliefs, culture reflecting Christian values.

Christians: The name first applied about the year 43 to followers of Christ at Antioch, the capital of Syria. It was used by the pagans as a contemptuous term. The word applies to persons who profess belief in the divinity and teachings of Christ and who give witness to him in life.

Christian Science: A religious doctrine consisting of Mary Baker Eddy's interpretation and formulation of the actions and teachings of Christ. Its basic tenets reflect Mrs. Eddy's ideas regarding the reality of spirit and its control and domination of what is not spirit. The basic statement of the doctrine is contained in *Science and Health, with Key to the Scriptures,* which she first published in 1875, nine years after being saved from death and healed on reading the New Testament. Mary Baker Eddy (1821-1910) established the church in 1879, and in 1892 founded at Boston the First Church of Christ, Scientist, of which all other Christian Science churches are branches. The individual churches are self-governing and self-supporting under the general supervision of a board of directors. Services consist of readings of portions of Scripture and *Science and Health.* One of the church's publications, *The Christian Science Monitor,* has a worldwide reputation as a journal of news and opinion.

Church: (1) See several entries under Church, Catholic. The universal Church is the Church spread throughout the world. The local Church is the Church in a particular locality; e.g., a diocese. The Church embraces all of its members — on earth, in heaven, in purgatory. (2) In general, any religious body. (3) A building set aside and dedicated for divine worship.

Circumcision: A ceremonial practice symbolic of initiation and participation in the covenant between God and Abraham.

Circumincession: The indwelling of each divine Person of the Holy Trinity in the others.

Clergy: Men commissioned for sacred ministries and assigned to pastoral and other duties for the service of the people and the Church. (1) Diocesan or secular clergy are committed to pastoral ministry in parishes and in other capacities in a particular church (diocese) under the direction of their bishop, to whom they are bound by a promise of obedience. (2) Regular clergy belong to religious institutes (orders, congregations, societies — institutes of consecrated life) and are so called because they observe the rule (*regula,* in Latin) of their respective institutes. They are committed to the ways of life and apostolates of their institutes. In ordinary pastoral ministry, they are under the direction of local bishops as well as their own superiors.

Clericalism: A term generally used in a derogatory sense to mean action, influence and interference by the Church and the clergy in matters with which they allegedly should not be concerned. Anticlericalism is a reaction of antipathy, hostility, distrust and opposition to the Church and clergy arising from real and/or alleged faults of the clergy, overextension of the role of the laity, or for other reasons.

Cloister: Part of a monastery, convent or other house of religious reserved for use by members of the institute. Houses of contemplative Religious have a strict enclosure.

Code: A digest of rules or regulations, such as the Code of Canon Law.

Collegiality: The bishops of the Church, in union with and subordinate to the pope — who has full, supreme and universal power over the Church which he can always exercise independently — have supreme teaching and pastoral authority over the whole Church. In addition to their proper authority of office for the good of the faithful in their respective dioceses or other jurisdictions, the bishops have authority to act for the good of the universal Church. This collegial authority is exercised in a solemn manner in an ecumenical council and can also be exercised in other ways sanctioned by the pope. Doctrine on collegiality was set forth by the Second Vatican Council in the *Dogmatic Constitution on the Church.* (See separate entry.) By extension, the concept of collegiality is applied to other forms of participation and co-responsibility by members of a community.

Commissariat of the Holy Land: A special jurisdiction within the Order of Friars Minor, whose main purposes are the collecting of alms for support of the Holy Places in Palestine and staffing of the Holy Places and missions in the Middle East with priests and brothers. There are about 70 such commissariats in more than 30 countries. One of them has headquarters at Mt. St. Sepulchre, Washington, D.C. Franciscans have had custody of the Holy Places since 1342.

Communion of Faithful, Saints: The communion of all the People of God — on earth, in heavenly glory, in purgatory — with Christ and each other in faith, grace, prayer and good works.

Concelebration: The liturgical act in which several priests, led by one member of the group, offer Mass together, all consecrating the bread and wine. Concelebration has always been common in churches of Eastern Rite. In the Roman Rite, it was long restricted, taking place only at the ordination of bishops and the ordination of priests. The *Constitution on the Sacred Liturgy* issued by the Second Vatican Council set new norms for concelebration, which is now relatively common in the Roman Rite.

Concordance, Biblical: An alphabetical verbal index enabling a user knowing one or more words of a scriptural passage to locate the entire text.

Concordat: A church-state treaty with the force of law concerning matters of mutual concern — e.g., rights of the Church, arrangement of ecclesiastical jurisdictions, marriage laws, education. Approximately 150 agreements of this kind have been negotiated since the Concordat of Worms in 1122.

Concupiscence: Any tendency of the sensitive appetite. The term is most frequently used in reference to desires and tendencies for sinful sense pleasure.

Confession: Sacramental confession is the act by which a person tells or confesses his sins to a priest who is authorized to give absolution in the sacrament of penance.

Confessor: A priest who administers the sacrament of penance. The title of confessor, formerly given to a category of male saints, was suppressed with publication of the calendar reform of 1969.

Confraternity: An association whose members practice a particular form of religious devotion and/or are engaged in some kind of apostolic work.

Conscience: Practical judgment concerning the moral goodness or sinfulness of an action. In the Catholic view, this judgment is made by reference of the action, its attendant circumstances and the intentions of the person to the requirements of moral law as expressed in the Ten Commandments, the summary law of love for God and neighbor, the life and teaching of Christ, and the authoritative teaching and practice of the Church with respect to the total demands of divine Revelation. A person is obliged: (1) to obey a certain and correct conscience; (2) to obey a certain conscience even if it is inculpably erroneous; (3) not to obey, but to correct, a conscience known to be erroneous or lax; (4) to rectify a scrupulous conscience by following the advice of a confessor and by other measures; (5) to resolve doubts of conscience before acting. It is legitimate to act for solid and probable reasons when a question of moral responsibility admits of argument (see Probabilism).

Conscience, Examination of: Self-examination to determine one's spiritual state before God, regarding one's sins and faults. It is recommended as a regular practice and is practically necessary in preparing for the sacrament of penance. The *particular examen* is a regular examination to assist in overcoming specific faults and imperfections.

Consistory: An assembly of cardinals presided over by the pope.

Constitution: (1) An apostolic or papal constitution is a document in which a pope enacts and promulgates law. (2) A formal and solemn document issued by an ecumenical council on a doctrinal or pastoral subject, with binding force in the whole Church; e.g., the four constitutions issued by the Second Vatican Council on the Church, liturgy, Revelation, and the Church in the modern world. (3) The constitutions of institutes of consecrated life and societies of apostolic life spell out details of and norms drawn from the various rules for the guidance and direction of the life and work of their members.

Consubstantiation: A theory which holds that the Body and Blood of Christ coexist with the substance of bread and wine in the Holy Eucharist. This theory, also called *impanation,* is incompatible with the doctrine of transubstantiation.

Contraception: Anything done by positive interference to prevent sexual intercourse from resulting in conception. Direct contraception is against the order of nature. Indirect contraception — as a secondary effect of medical treatment or other action having a necessary, good, non-contraceptive purpose — is permissible under the principle of the double effect. The practice of periodic continence is not contraception because it does not involve positive interference with the order of nature.

Contrition: Sorrow for sin coupled with a purpose of amendment. Contrition arising from a supernatural motive is necessary for the forgiveness of sin. (1) Perfect contrition is total sorrow for and renunciation of attachment to sin, arising from the motive of pure love of God. Perfect contrition, which implies the intention of doing all God wants done for the forgiveness of sin (including confession in a reasonable period of time), is sufficient for the forgiveness of serious sin and the remission of all temporal punishment due for sin. (The intention to receive the sacrament of penance is implicit — even if unrealized, as in the case of some persons — in perfect contrition.) (2) Imperfect contrition or attrition is sorrow arising from a quasi-selfish supernatural motive; e.g., the fear of losing heaven, suffering the pains of hell, etc. Imperfect contrition is sufficient for the forgiveness of serious sin when joined with absolution in confession, and sufficient for the forgiveness of venial sin even outside of confession.

Contumely: Personal insult, reviling a person in his presence by accusation of moral faults, by refusal of recognition or due respect; a violation of obligations of justice and charity.

Corporal Works of Mercy: Feeding the hungry, giving drink to the thirsty, clothing the naked, visiting the imprisoned, sheltering the homeless, visiting the sick, burying the dead.

Council, Plenary: A council held for the particular churches belonging to the same episcopal conference. Such a council can be convoked to take action related to the pastoral activity and mission of the Church in the territory. The membership of such councils is fixed by canon law; their decrees, when approved by the Holy See, are binding in the territory (see Index, Plenary Councils of Baltimore).

Councils: Bodies representative of various categories of members of the Church which participate with bishops and other church authorities in making decisions and carrying out action programs for the good of the Church and the accomplishment of its mission to its own members and society in general. Examples are priests' senates or councils, councils of Religious and lay persons, parish councils, diocesan pastoral councils.

Councils, Provincial: Meetings of the bishops of a province. The metropolitan, or ranking archbishop, of an ecclesiastical province convenes and presides over such councils in a manner prescribed by canon law to take action related to the life and mission of the Church in the province. Acts and decrees must be approved by the Holy See before being promulgated.

Counsels, Evangelical: Gospel counsels of perfection, especially voluntary poverty, perfect chastity and obedience, which were recommended by Christ to those who would devote themselves exclusively and completely to the immediate service of God. Religious (members of institutes of consecrated life) bind themselves by public vows to observe these counsels in a life of total consecration to God and service to people through various kinds of apostolic works.

Counter-Reformation: The period of approximately 100 years following the Council of Trent, which witnessed a reform within the Church to stimulate genuine Catholic life and to counteract effects of the Reformation.

Covenant: A bond of relationship between parties pledged to each other. God-initiated covenants in the Old Testament included those with Abraham, Noah, Moses, Levi, David. The Mosaic (Sinai) covenant made Israel God's Chosen People on terms of fidelity to true faith, true worship, and righteous conduct according to the Decalogue. The New Testament covenant, prefigured in the Old Testament, is the bond persons have with God through Christ. All persons are called to be parties to this perfect and everlasting covenant, which was mediated and ratified by Christ. The marriage covenant seals the closest possible relationship between a man and a woman.

Creation: The production by God of something out of nothing. The biblical account of creation is contained in the first two chapters of Genesis.

Creator: God, the supreme, self-existing Being, the absolute and infinite First Cause of all things.

Creature: Everything in the realm of being is a creature, except God.

Cremation: The reduction of a human corpse to ashes by means of fire. Cremation is not in line with Catholic tradition and practice, even though it is not opposed to any article of faith. The Congregation for the Doctrine of the Faith, under date of May 8, 1963, circulated among bishops an instruction which upheld the traditional practices of Christian burial but modified anti-cremation legislation. Cremation may be permitted for serious reasons, of a private as well as public nature, provided it does not involve any contempt of the Church or of religion, or any attempt to deny, question, or belittle the doctrine of the resurrection of the body. The person may receive the last rites and be given ecclesiastical burial. A priest may say prayers for the deceased at the crematorium, but full liturgical ceremonies may not take place there. The principal reason behind an earlier prohibition against cremation was the fact that, historically, the practice had represented an attempt to deny the doctrine of the resurrection of the body. (See Burial, Ecclesiastical.)

Crib: A devotional representation of the birth of Jesus. The custom of erecting cribs is generally attributed to St. Francis of Assisi who in 1223 obtained from Pope Honorius III permission to use a crib and figures of the Christ Child, Mary, St. Joseph, and others, to represent the mystery of the Nativity.

Crosier: The bishop's staff, symbolic of his pastoral office, responsibility and authority.

Crypt: An underground or partly underground chamber; e.g., the lower part of a church used for worship and/or burial.

Cura Animarum: A Latin phrase, meaning care of souls, designating the pastoral ministry and responsibility of bishops and priests.

Curia: The personnel and offices through which (1) the pope administers the affairs of the universal Church, the Roman Curia (see separate entry), or (2) a bishop the affairs of a diocese, diocesan curia. The principal officials of a diocesan curia are the vicar general of the diocese, the chancellor, officials of the diocesan tribunal or court, examiners, consultors, auditors, notaries.

Custos: A religious superior who presides over a number of convents collectively called a custody. In some institutes of consecrated life a custos may be the deputy of a higher superior.

D

Deaconess: A woman officially appointed and charged by the Church to carry out service-like functions. Phoebe apparently was one (Rom. 16:1-2); a second probable reference to the office is in 1 Tm. 3:11. The office — for assistance at the baptism of women, for pastoral service to women and for works of charity — had considerable development in the third and also in the fourth century when the actual term came into use (in place of such designations as *diacona, vidua, virgo canonica*). Its importance declined subsequently with the substitution of infusion in place of immersion as the common method of baptism in the West, and with the increase of the practice of infant baptism. There is no record of the ministry of deaconess in the West after the beginning of the 11th century. The office continued, however, for a longer time in the East. The Vatican's Theological Commission, in a paper prepared in 1971, noted that there had been in the past a form of diaconal ordination for women. With a rite and purpose distinctive to women, it differed essentially from the ordination of deacons, which had sacramental effects. Several Christian churches have had revivals of the office of deaconess since the 1830s. There is a contemporary movement in support of such a revival among some Catholics.

Dean: (1) A priest with supervisory responsibility over a section of a diocese known as a deanery. The post-Vatican II counterpart of a dean is an episcopal vicar. (2) The senior or ranking member of a group.

Dean of the Sacred College: The president of the College of Cardinals (the ranking cardinal bishop).

Decision: A judgment or pronouncement on a cause or suit, given by a church tribunal or official with judicial authority. A decision has the force of law for concerned parties.

Declaration: (1) An ecclesiastical document which presents an interpretation of an existing law. (2) A position paper on a specific subject; e.g., the three declarations issued by the Second Vatican Council on religious freedom, non-Christian religions, and Christian education.

Decree: An edict or ordinance issued by a pope and/or by an ecumenical council, with binding force in the whole Church; by a department of the Roman Curia, with binding force for concerned parties; by a territorial body of bishops, with binding force for persons in the area; by individual bishops, with binding force for concerned parties until revocation or the death of the bishop. The nine decrees issued by the Second Vatican Council were combinations of doctrinal and pastoral statements with executive orders for action and movement toward renewal and reform in the Church.

Dedication of a Church: The ceremony whereby a church is solemnly set apart for the worship of God. The custom of dedicating churches had an antecedent in Old Testament ceremonies for the dedication of the Temple, as in the times of Solomon and the Maccabees. The earliest extant record of the dedication of a Christian church dates from early in the fourth century, when it was done simply by the celebration of Mass. Other ceremonies developed later. A church can be dedicated by a simple blessing or a solemn consecration. The rite of consecration is generally performed by a bishop.

Deism: A system of natural religion which acknowledges the existence of God but regards him as so transcendent and remote from man and the universe that divine revelation and the supernatural order of things are irrelevant and unacceptable. It developed from rationalistic principles in England in the 17th and 18th centuries, and had Voltaire, Rousseau and the Encyclopedists among its advocates in France.

Despair: Abandonment of hope for salvation arising from the conviction that God will not provide the necessary means for attaining it, that following God's way of life for salvation is impossible, or that one's sins are unforgivable; a serious sin against the Holy Spirit and the theological virtues of hope and faith, involving distrust in the mercy and goodness of God and a denial of the truths that God wills the salvation of all persons and provides sufficient grace for it. Real despair is distinguished from unreasonable fear with respect to the difficulties of attaining salvation, from morbid anxiety over the demands of divine justice, and from feelings of despair.

Detachment: Control of affection for creatures by two principles: (1) supreme love and devotion belong to God; (2) love and service of creatures should be an expression of love for God.

Detraction: Revelation of true but hidden faults of a person without sufficient and justifying reason; a violation of requirements of justice and charity, involving the obligation to make restitution when this is possible without doing more harm to the good name of the offended party. In some cases, e.g., to prevent evil, secret faults may and should be disclosed.

Devil: (1) Lucifer, Satan, chief of the fallen angels who sinned and were banished from heaven. Still possessing angelic powers, he can cause such diabolical phenomena as possession and obsession, and can tempt men to sin. (2) Any fallen angel.

Devotion: (1) Religious fervor, piety; dedication. (2) The consolation experienced at times during prayer; a reverent manner of praying.

Devotions: Pious practices of members of the Church include not only participation in various acts of the liturgy but also in other acts of worship generally called popular or private devotions. Concerning these, the Second Vatican Council said in the *Constitution on the Sacred Liturgy* (No. 13): "Popular devotions of the Christian people are warmly commended, provided they accord with the laws and norms of the Church. Such is especially the case with devotions called for by the Apostolic See. Devotions proper to the individual churches also have a special dignity. . . . These devotions should be so drawn up that they harmonize with the liturgical seasons, accord with the sacred liturgy, are in some fashion derived from it, and lead the people to it, since the liturgy by its very nature far surpasses any of them." Devotions of a liturgical type are Exposition of the Blessed Sacrament, recitation of Evening Prayer and Night Prayer of the Liturgy of the Hours. Examples of paraliturgical devotion are a Bible Service or Vigil, and the Angelus, Rosary and Stations of the Cross, which have a strong scriptural basis.

Diocese: A particular church, a fully organized ecclesiastical jurisdiction under the pastoral direction of a bishop as local Ordinary.

Discalced: Of Latin derivation and meaning without shoes, the word is applied to religious orders or congregations whose members go barefoot or wear sandals.

Disciple: A term used sometimes in reference to the Apostles but more often to a larger number of followers (70 or 72) of Christ mentioned in Lk. 10:1.

Disciplina Arcani: A Latin phrase, meaning discipline of the secret and referring to a practice of the early Church, especially during the Roman persecutions, to: (1) conceal Christian truths from those who, it was feared, would misinterpret, ridicule and profane the teachings, and persecute Christians for believing them; (2) instruct catechumens in a gradual manner, withholding the teaching of certain doctrines until the catechumens proved themselves of good faith and sufficient understanding.

Dispensation: The relaxation of a law in a particular case. Laws made for the common good sometimes work undue hardship in particular cases. In such cases, where sufficient reasons are present, dispensations may be granted by proper authorities. Bishops, religious superiors and others may dispense from certain laws; the pope can dispense from all ecclesiastical laws. No one has authority to dispense from obligations of the divine law.

Divination: Attempting to foretell future or hidden things by means of things like dreams, necromancy, spiritism, examination of entrails, astrology, augury, omens, palmistry, drawing straws, dice, cards, etc. Practices like these attribute to creatural things a power which belongs to God alone and are violations of the First Commandment.

Divine Praises: Fourteen praises recited or sung at Benediction of the Blessed Sacrament in reparation for sins of sacrilege, blasphemy and profanity. Some of these praises date from the end of the 18th century: Blessed be God. / Blessed be his holy Name. / Blessed be Jesus Christ, true God and true Man. / Blessed be the Name of Jesus. / Blessed be his most Sacred Heart. / Blessed be his most Precious Blood. / Blessed be Jesus in the most holy Sacrament of the Altar. / Blessed be the Holy Spirit, the Paraclete. / Blessed be the great Mother of God, Mary most holy. / Blessed be her holy and Immaculate Conception. / Blessed be her glorious Assumption. / Blessed be the name of Mary, Virgin and Mother. / Blessed be St. Joseph, her most chaste Spouse. / Blessed be God in his Angels and in his Saints.

Double Effect Principle: Actions sometimes have two effects closely related to each other, one good and the other bad, and a difficult moral question can arise: Is it permissible to place an action from which two such results follow? It is permissible to place the action, if: the action is good in itself and is directly productive of the good effect; the circumstances are good; the intention of the person is good; the reason for placing the action is proportionately serious to the seriousness of the indirect bad effect. For example: Is it morally permissible for a pregnant woman to undergo medical or surgical treatment for a pathological condition if the indirect and secondary effect of the treatment will be the loss of the child? The reply is affirmative, for these reasons: The action, i.e., the treatment, is good in itself, cannot be deferred until a later time without very serious consequences, and is ordered directly to the cure of critically grave pathology. By means of the treatment, the woman intends to save her life, which she has a right to do. The loss of the child is not directly sought as a means for the cure of the mother but results indirectly and in a secondary manner from the placing of the action, i.e., the treatment, which is good in itself. The double effect principle does not support the principle that the end justifies the means.

Doxology: (1) The lesser doxology, or ascription of glory to the Trinity, is the Glory be to the Father. The first part dates back to the third or fourth century, and came from the form of baptism. The concluding words, As it was in the beginning, etc., are of later origin. (2) The greater doxology, Glory to God in the highest, begins with the words of angelic praise at the birth of Christ recounted in the Infancy Narrative (Lk. 2:14). It is often recited at Mass. Of early Eastern origin, it is found in the *Apostolic Constitutions* in a form much like the present. (3) The formula of praise at the end of the Eucharistic Prayer at Mass, sung or said by the celebrant while he holds aloft the paten containing the consecrated host in one hand and the chalice containing the consecrated wine in the other.

Dulia: A Greek term meaning the veneration or homage, different in nature and degree from that given to God, paid to the saints. It includes honoring the saints and seeking their intercession with God.

Duty: A moral obligation deriving from the binding force of law, the exigencies of one's state in life, and other sources.

E

Easter Controversy: A three-phase controversy over the time for the celebration of Easter. Some early Christians in the Near East, called Quartodecimans, favored the observance of Easter on the 14th day of Nisan, the spring month of the Hebrew calendar, whenever it occurred. Against this practice, Pope St. Victor I, about 190, ordered a Sunday observance of the feast. The Council of Nicaea, in line with usages of the Church at Rome and Alexandria, decreed in 325 that Easter should be observed on the first Sunday following the first full moon of spring. Uniformity of practice in the West was not achieved until several centuries later, when the British Isles, in delayed compliance with measures enacted by the Synod of Whitby in 664, accepted the Roman date of observance. Unrelated to the controversy is the fact that some Eastern Christians, in accordance with traditional calendar practices, celebrate Easter at a different time than the Roman and Eastern-Rite churches.

Easter Duty, Season: The serious obligation binding Catholics of Roman Rite, to receive the Eucharist during the Easter season (in the U.S., from the first Sunday of Lent to Trinity Sunday).

Easter Water: Holy water blessed with special ceremonies and distributed on the Easter Vigil; used during Easter Week for blessing the faithful and homes.

Ecclesiology: Study of the nature, constitution, members, mission, functions, etc., of the Church.

Ecstasy: An extraordinary state of mystical experience in which a person is so absorbed in God that the activity of the exterior senses is suspended.

Ecumenism: The movement of Christians and their churches toward the unity willed by Christ. The Second Vatican Council called the movement "those activities and enterprises which, according to various needs of the Church and opportune occasions, are started and organized for the fostering of unity among Christians" (*Decree on Ecumenism,* No. 4). Spiritual ecumenism, i.e., mutual prayer for unity, is the heart of the movement. The movement also involves scholarly and pew-level efforts for the development of mutual understanding and better interfaith relations in general, and collaboration by the churches and their members in the social area.

Elevation: The raising of the host after consecration at Mass for adoration by the faithful. The custom was introduced in the Diocese of Paris about the close of the 12th century to offset an erroneous teaching of the time which held that transubstantiation of the bread did not take place until after the consecration of the wine in the chalice. The elevation of the chalice following the consecration of the wine was introduced in the 15th century.

End Justifies the Means: An unacceptable ethical principle which states that evil means may be used to produce good effects.

Envy: Sadness over another's good fortune because it is considered a loss to oneself or a detraction from one's own excellence; one of the seven capital sins, a violation of the obligations of charity.

Epikeia: A Greek word meaning reasonableness and designating a moral theory and practice, a mild interpretation of the mind of a legislator who is prudently considered not to wish positive law to bind in certain circumstances. Use of the principle is justified in practice when the lawgiver himself cannot be appealed to and when it can be prudently assumed that in particular cases, e.g., because of special hardship, he would not wish the law to be applied in a strict manner. Epikeia may not be applied with respect to acts that are intrinsically wrong or those covered by laws which automatically make them invalid.

Episcopate: (1) The office, dignity and sacramental powers bestowed upon a bishop at his ordination. (2) The body of bishops collectively.

Equivocation: (1) The use of words, phrases, or gestures having more than one meaning in order to conceal information which a questioner has no strict right to know. It is permissible to equivocate (have a broad mental reservation) in some circumstances. (2) A lie, i.e., a statement of untruth. Lying is intrinsically wrong. A lie told in joking, evident as such, is not wrong.

Eschatology: Doctrine concerning the last things: death, judgment, heaven and hell, and the final state of perfection of the people and kingdom of God at the end of time.

Eternity: The interminable, perfect possession of life in its totality without beginning or end; an attribute of God, who has no past or future but always is. Man's existence has a beginning but no end and is, accordingly, called immortal.

Ethics: Moral philosophy, the science of the morality of human acts deriving from natural law, the natural end of man, and the powers of human reason. It includes all the spheres of human activity — personal, social, economic, political, etc. Ethics is distinct from but can be related to moral theology, whose primary principles are drawn from divine revelation.

Eucharistic Congresses: Public demonstrations of faith in the Holy Eucharist. Combining liturgical services, other public ceremonies, subsidiary meetings, different kinds of instructional and inspirational elements, they are unified by central themes and serve to increase understanding of and devotion to Christ in the Eucharist, and to relate this liturgy of worship and witness to life. The first international congress developed from a proposal by Marie Marthe Tamisier of Touraine, organizing efforts of Msgr. Louis Gaston de Segur, and backing by industrialist Philibert Vrau. It was held with the approval of Pope Leo XIII at the University of Lille, France, and was attended by some 800 persons from France, Belgium, Holland, England, Spain and Switzerland. International congresses are planned and held under the auspices of a permanent committee for international Eucharistic congresses. Participants include clergy, religious and lay persons from many countries, and representatives of national and international Catholic organizations. Forty-three international congresses were held from 1881 to 1985: Lille (1881), Avignon (1882), Liege (1883), Freiburg (1885), Toulouse (1886), Paris (1888), Antwerp (1890), Jerusalem (1893), Rheims (1894), Paray-le-Monial (1897), Brussels (1898), Lourdes (1899), Angers (1901), Namur (1902), Angouleme (1904), Rome (1905), Tournai (1906), Metz (1907), London (1908), Cologne (1909), Montreal (1910), Madrid (1911), Vienna (1912), Malta (1913), Lourdes (1914), Rome (1922), Amsterdam (1924), Chicago (1926), Sydney (1928), Carthage (1930), Dublin (1932), Buenos Aires (1934), Manila (1937), Budapest (1938), Barcelona (1952), Rio de Janeiro (1955), Munich, Germany (1960), Bombay, India (1964), Bogota, Colombia (1968), Melbourne, Australia (1973), Philadelphia (1976), Lourdes (1981), Nairobi, Kenya

(1985). The 44th international congress will be held in 1989 in Seoul, South Korea.

Eugenics: The science of heredity and environment for the physical and mental improvement of offspring. Extreme eugenics is untenable in practice because it advocates immoral means, such as compulsory breeding of the select, sterilization of persons said to be unfit, abortion, and unacceptable methods of birth regulation.

Euthanasia: Mercy killing, the direct causing of death for the purpose of ending human suffering. Euthanasia is murder and is totally illicit, for the natural law forbids the direct taking of one's own life or that of an innocent person. The use of drugs to relieve suffering in serious cases, even when this results in a shortening of life as an indirect and secondary effect, is permissible under conditions of the double effect principle. It is also permissible for a seriously ill person to refuse to follow — or for other responsible persons to refuse to permit — extraordinary medical procedures even though the refusal might entail shortening of life.

Evolution: Scientific theory concerning the development of the physical universe from unorganized matter (inorganic evolution) and, especially, the development of existing forms of vegetable, animal and human life from earlier and more primitive organisms (organic evolution). Various ideas about evolution were advanced for some centuries before scientific evidence in support of the main-line theory of organic evolution, which has several formulations, was discovered and verified in the second half of the 19th century and afterwards. This evidence — from the findings of comparative anatomy and other sciences — confirmed evolution within species and cleared the way to further investigation of questions regarding the processes of its accomplishment. While a number of such questions remain open with respect to human evolution, a point of doctrine not open to question is the immediate creation of the human soul by God. For some time, theologians regarded the theory with hostility, considering it to be in opposition to the account of creation in the early chapters of Genesis and subversive of belief in such doctrines as creation, the early state of man in grace, and the fall of man from grace. This state of affairs and the tension it generated led to considerable controversy regarding an alleged conflict between religion and science. Gradually, however, the tension was diminished with the development of biblical studies from the latter part of the 19th century onwards, with clarification of the distinctive features of religious truth and scientific truth, and with the refinement of evolutionary concepts. So far as the Genesis account of creation is concerned, the Catholic view is that the writer(s) did not write as a scientist but as the communicator of religious truth in a manner adapted to the understanding of the people of his time. He used anthropomorphic language, the figure of days and other literary devices to state the salvation truths of creation, the fall of man from grace, and the promise of redemption. It was beyond the competency and purpose of the writer(s) to describe creation and related events in a scientific manner.

Excommunication: A penalty or censure by which a baptized person is excluded from the communion of the faithful, for committing and remaining obstinate in certain serious offenses specified in canon law. As by baptism a person is made a member of the Church in which there is a communication of spiritual goods, so by excommunication he is deprived of the same spiritual goods until he repents and receives absolution. Even though excommunicated, a person is still responsible for fulfillment of the normal obligations of a Catholic. (See Censures.)

Existentialism: A philosophy with radical concern for the problems of individual existence and identity viewed in particular here-and-now patterns of thought which presuppose irrationality and absurdity in human life and the whole universe. It is preoccupied with questions about freedom, moral decision and responsibility against a background of denial of objective truth and universal norms of conduct; is characterized by prevailing anguish, dread, fear, pessimism, despair; is generally atheistic, although its modern originator, Soren Kierkegaard (d. 1855), and Gabriel Marcel (d. 1973) attempted to give it a Christian orientation. Pius XII called it "the new erroneous philosophy which, opposing itself to idealism, immanentism and pragmatism, has assumed the name of existentialism, since it concerns itself only with the existence of individual things and neglects all consideration of their immutable essences" (Encyclical *Humani Generis,* Aug. 12, 1950).

Exorcism: (1) Driving out evil spirits; a rite in which evil spirits are charged and commanded on the authority of God and with the prayer of the Church to depart from a person or to cease causing harm to a person suffering from diabolical possession or obsession. The sacramental is officially administered by a priest delegated for the purpose by the bishop of the place. Elements of the rite include the Litany of Saints; recitation of the Our Father, one or more creeds, and other prayers; specific prayers of exorcism; the reading of Gospel passages and use of the Sign of the Cross. (2) Exorcisms which do not imply the conditions of either diabolical possession or obsession form part of the ceremony of baptism, and are also included in formulas for various blessings; e.g., of water.

Exposition of the Blessed Sacrament: "In churches where the Eucharist is regularly reserved, it is recommended that solemn exposition of the Blessed Sacrament for an extended period of time should take place once a year, even though the period is not strictly continuous. . . . Shorter expositions of the Eucharist (**Benediction**) are to be arranged in such a way that the blessing with the Eucharist is preceded by a reasonable time for readings of the word of God, songs, prayers and a period for silent prayer." So stated Vatican directives issued in 1973.

F

Faculties: Grants of jurisdiction or authority by the law of the Church or superiors (pope, bishop, religious superior) for exercise of the powers of holy orders; e.g., priests are given faculties to hear confessions, officiate at weddings; bishops are given faculties to grant dispensations, etc.

Faith: In religion, faith has several aspects. Catholic doctrine calls faith the assent of the mind to truths revealed by God, the assent being made with the help of grace and by command of the will on account of the authority and trustworthiness of God revealing. The term faith also refers to the truths that are believed (content of faith) and to the way in which a person, in response to Christ, gives witness to and expresses belief in daily life (living faith). All of these elements, and more, are included in the following statement: " 'The obedience of faith' (Rom. 16:26; 1:5; 2 Cor. 10:5-6) must be given to God who reveals, an obedience by which man entrusts his whole self freely to God, offering 'the full submission of intellect and will to God who reveals' (First Vatican Council, *Dogmatic Constitution on the Catholic Faith,* Chap. 3), and freely assenting to the truth revealed by him. If this faith is to be shown, the grace of God and the interior help of the Holy Spirit must precede and assist, moving the heart and turning it to God, opening the eyes of the mind, and giving 'joy and ease to everyone in assenting to the truth and believing it' " (Second Council of Orange, Canon 7) (Second Vatican Council, *Constitution on Revelation,* No. 5). Faith is necessary for salvation.

Faith, Rule of: The norm or standard of religious belief. The Catholic doctrine is that belief must be professed in the divinely revealed truths in the Bible and tradition as interpreted and proposed by the infallible teaching authority of the Church.

Fast, Eucharistic: Abstinence from food and drink, except water and medicine, is required for one hour before the reception of the Eucharist. Persons who are advanced in age or suffer from infirmity or illness, together with those who care for them, can receive Holy Communion even if they have not abstained from food and drink for an hour. A priest celebrating two or three Masses on the same day can eat and drink something before the second or third Mass without regard for the hour limit.

Father: A title of priests, who are regarded as spiritual fathers because they are the ordinary ministers of baptism, by which persons are born to supernatural life, and because of their pastoral service to people.

Fear: A mental state caused by the apprehension of present or future danger. Grave fear does not necessarily remove moral responsibility for an act, but may lessen it.

First Friday: A devotion consisting of the reception of Holy Communion on the first Friday of nine consecutive months in honor of the Sacred Heart of Jesus and in reparation for sin. (See Sacred Heart, Promises.)

First Saturday: A devotion tracing its origin to the apparitions of the Blessed Virgin Mary at Fatima in 1917. Those practicing the devotion go to confession and, on the first Saturday of five consecutive months, receive Holy Communion, recite five decades of the Rosary, and meditate on the mysteries for 15 minutes.

Fisherman's Ring: A signet ring engraved with the image of St. Peter fishing from a boat, and encircled with the name of the reigning pope. It is not worn by the pope. It is used to seal briefs, and is destroyed after each pope's death.

Forgiveness of Sin: Catholics believe that sins are forgiven by God through the mediation of Christ in view of the repentance of the sinner and by means of the sacrament of penance. (See Penance, Contrition).

Fortitude: Courage to face dangers or hardships for the sake of what is good; one of the four cardinal virtues and one of the seven gifts of the Holy Spirit.

Fortune Telling: Attempting to predict the future or the occult by means of cards, palm reading, etc.; a form of divination, prohibited by the First Commandment.

Forty Hours Devotion: A Eucharistic observance consisting of solemn exposition of the Blessed Sacrament coupled with special Masses and forms of prayer, for the purposes of making reparation for sin and praying for God's blessings of grace and peace. The devotion was instituted in 1534 in Milan. St. John Neumann of Philadelphia was the first bishop in the U.S. to prescribe its observance in his diocese. For many years in this country, the observance was held annually on a rotating basis in all parishes of a diocese. Simplified and abbreviated Eucharistic observances have taken the place of the devotion in some places.

Forum: The sphere in which ecclesiastical authority or jurisdiction is exercised. (1) External: Authority is exercised in the external forum to deal with matters affecting the public welfare of the Church and its members. Those who have such authority because of their office (e.g., diocesan bishops) are called ordinaries. (2) Internal: Authority is exercised in the internal forum to deal with matters affecting the private spiritual good of individuals. The sacramental forum is the sphere in which the sacrament of penance is administered; other exercises of jurisdiction in the internal forum take place in the non-sacramental forum.

Franciscan Crown: A seven-decade rosary used to commemorate the seven Joys of the Blessed Virgin: the Annunciation, the Visitation, the Nativity of Our Lord, the Adoration of the Magi, the Finding of the Child Jesus in the Temple, the Apparition of the Risen Christ to his Mother, the Assumption and Coronation of the Blessed Virgin. Introduced in 1422, the Crown originally consisted only of seven Our Fathers and 70 Hail Marys. Two Hail Marys were added to complete the number 72 (thought to be the number of years of Mary's life), and one Our Father, Hail Mary and Glory be to the Father are said for the intention of the pope.

Freedom, Religious: The Second Vatican Council declared that the right to religious freedom in civil society "means that all men are to be immune from coercion on the part of individuals or of social groups and of any human power, in such wise that in matters religious no one is to be forced to act in a manner contrary to his own beliefs. Nor is anyone to be restrained from acting in accordance with his own beliefs, whether privately or publicly, whether alone or in association with others, within due limits" of requirements for the common good. The foundation of this right in civil society is the "very dignity of the human person" (*Declaration on Religious Freedom,* No. 2). The conciliar statement did not deal with the subject of freedom within the Church. It noted the responsibility of the faithful "carefully to attend to the sacred and certain doctrine of the Church" (No. 14).

Freemasons: A fraternal order which originated in London in 1717 with the formation of the first Grand Lodge of Freemasons. From England, the order spread to Europe and elsewhere. Its principles and basic rituals embody a naturalistic religion, active participation in which is incompatible with Christian faith and practice. Grand Orient Freemasonry, developed in Latin countries, is atheistic, irreligious and anticlerical. In some places, Freemasonry has been regarded as subversive of the state; in Catholic quarters, it has been considered hostile to the Church and its doctrine. In the United States, Freemasonry has been widely regarded as a fraternal and philanthropic order. For serious doctrinal and pastoral reasons, Catholics were forbidden to join the Freemasons under penalty of excommunication, according to church law before 1983. Eight different popes in 17 different pronouncements, and at least six different local councils, condemned Freemasonry. The first condemnation was made by Clement XII in 1738. Eastern Orthodox and many Protestant bodies have also opposed the order. In the U.S., there was some easing of the ban against Masonic membership by Catholics in view of a letter written in 1974 by Cardinal Franjo Seper, prefect of the Congregation for the Doctrine of the Faith. The letter was interpreted to mean that Catholics might join Masonic lodges which were not anti-Catholic. This was called erroneous in a declaration issued by the Doctrinal Congregation Feb. 17, 1981. The prohibition against Masonic membership was restated in a declaration issued by the Doctrinal Congregation Nov. 26, 1983, with the approval of Pope John Paul II, as follows. "The Church's negative position on Masonic associations . . . remains unaltered, since their principles have always been regarded as irreconcilable with the Church's doctrine. Hence, joining them remains prohibited by the Church. Catholics enrolled in Masonic associations are involved in serious sin and may not approach Holy Communion. Local ecclesiastical authorities do not have the faculty to pronounce a judgment on the nature of Masonic associations which might include a diminution of the above-mentioned judgment." This latest declaration, like the revised Code of Canon Law, does not include a penalty of excommunication for Catholics who join the Masons. Local bishops are not authorized to grant dispensations from the prohibition. The foregoing strictures against Masonic membership by Catholics were reiterated in a re-

port by the Committee for Pastoral Research and Practice, National Conference of Catholic Bishops, released through NC News Service June 7, 1985.

Free Will: The faculty or capability of making a reasonable choice among several alternatives. Freedom of will underlies the possibility and fact of moral responsibility.

Friar: Term applied to members of mendicant orders to distinguish them from members of monastic orders. (See Mendicants.)

Fruits of the Holy Spirit: Charity, joy, peace, patience, benignity, goodness, long-animity, mildness, faith, modesty, continence, chastity.

G

Gambling: The backing of an issue with a sum of money or other valuables, which is permissible if the object is honest, if the two parties have the free disposal of their stakes without prejudice to the rights of others, if the terms are thoroughly understood by both parties, and if the outcome is not known beforehand. Gambling often falls into disrepute and may be forbidden by civil law, as well as by divine law, because of cheating, fraud and other accompanying evils.

Gehenna: Greek form of a Jewish name, *Gehinnom,* for a valley near Jerusalem, the site of Moloch worship; used as a synonym for hell.

Genuflection: Bending of the knee, a natural sign of adoration or reverence, as when persons genuflect with the right knee in passing before the tabernacle to acknowledge the Eucharistic presence of Christ.

Gethsemani: A Hebrew word meaning oil press, designating the place on the Mount of Olives where Christ prayed and suffered in agony the night before he died.

Gifts of the Holy Spirit: Supernatural habits disposing a person to respond promptly to the inspiration of grace; promised by Christ and communicated through the Holy Spirit, especially in the sacrament of confirmation. They are: wisdom, understanding, counsel, fortitude, knowledge, piety, fear of the Lord.

Gluttony: An unreasonable appetite for food and drink; one of the seven capital sins.

God: The infinitely perfect Supreme Being, uncaused and absolutely self-sufficient, eternal, the Creator and final end of all things. The one God subsists in three equal Persons, the Father and the Son and the Holy Spirit. God, although transcendent and distinct from the universe, is present and active in the world in realization of his plan for the salvation of men, principally through Revelation, the operations of the Holy Spirit, the life and ministry of Christ, and the continuation of Christ's ministry in the Church. The existence of God is an article of faith, clearly communicated in divine Revelation. Even without this Revelation, however, the Church teaches, in a declaration by the First Vatican Council, that men can acquire certain knowledge of the existence of God and some of his attributes. This can be done on the bases of principles of reason and reflection on human experience. Non-revealed arguments or demonstrations for the existence of God have been developed from the principle of causality; the contingency of man and the universe; the existence of design, change and movement in the universe; human awareness of moral responsibility; widespread human testimony to the existence of God.

Grace: A free gift of God to men (and angels), grace is a created sharing or participation in the life of God. It is given to men through the merits of Christ and is communicated by the Holy Spirit. It is necessary for salvation. The principal means of grace are the sacraments (especially the Eucharist), prayer and good works. (1) Sanctifying or habitual grace makes men holy and pleasing to God, adopted children of God, members of Christ, temples of the Holy Spirit, heirs of heaven capable of supernaturally meritorious acts. With grace, God gives men the supernatural virtues and gifts of the Holy Spirit. The sacraments of baptism and penance were instituted to give grace to those who do not have it; the other sacraments, to increase it in those already in the state of grace. The means for growth in holiness, or the increase of grace, are prayer, the sacraments, and good works. Sanctifying grace is lost by the commission of serious sin. Each sacrament confers sanctifying grace for the special purpose of the sacrament; in this context, grace is called sacramental grace. (2) Actual grace is a supernatural help of God which enlightens and strengthens a person to do good and to avoid evil. It is not a permanent quality, like sanctifying grace. It is necessary for the performance of supernatural acts. It can be resisted and refused. Persons in the state of serious sin are given actual grace to lead them to repentance.

Grace at Meals: Prayers said before meals, asking a blessing of God, and after meals, giving thanks to God. In addition to traditional prayers for these purposes, many variations suitable for different occasions are possible, at personal option.

H

Habit: (1) A disposition to do things easily, given with grace (and therefore supernatural) and/or acquired by repetition of similar acts. (2) The garb worn by Religious.

Hagiography: Writings or documents about saints and other holy persons.

Hail Mary: A prayer addressed to the Blessed Virgin Mary; also called the *Ave Maria* (Latin equivalent of Hail Mary) and the Angelic Salutation. In three parts, it consists of the words addressed to Mary by the Archangel Gabriel on the occasion of the Annunciation, in the Infancy Narrative (Hail full of grace, the Lord is with you, blessed are you among women.); the words addressed to Mary by her cousin Elizabeth on the occasion of the Visitation (Blessed is the fruit of your womb.); a concluding petition (Holy Mary, Mother of God, pray for us sinners now and at the hour of our death. Amen.). The first two salutations were joined in Eastern Rite formulas by the sixth century, and were similarly used at Rome in the seventh century. Insertion of the name of Jesus at the conclusion of the salutations was probably

made by Urban IV about 1262. The present form of the petition was incorporated into the breviary in 1514.

Heaven: The state of those who, having achieved salvation, are in glory with God and enjoy the beatific vision. The phrase, kingdom of heaven, refers to the order or kingdom of God, grace, salvation.

Hell: The state of punishment of the damned — i.e., those who die in mortal sin, in a condition of self-alienation from God and of opposition to the divine plan of salvation. The punishment of hell begins immediately after death and lasts forever.

Hermit: See Anchorite.

Heroic Act of Charity: The completely unselfish offering to God of one's good works and merits for the benefit of the souls in purgatory rather than for oneself. Thus a person may offer to God for the souls in purgatory all the good works he performs during life, all the indulgences he gains, and all the prayers and indulgences that will be offered for him after his death. The act is revocable at will, and is not a vow. Its actual ratification depends on the will of God.

Heterodoxy: False doctrine, teaching or belief; a departure from truth.

Holy See: (1) The diocese of the pope, Rome. (2) The pope himself and/or the various officials and bodies of the Church's central administration at Vatican City — the Roman Curia — which act in the name and by authority of the pope.

Holy Spirit: God the Holy Spirit, third Person of the Holy Trinity, who proceeds from the Father and the Son and with whom he is equal in every respect; inspirer of the prophets and writers of sacred Scripture; promised by Christ to the Apostles as their advocate and strengthener; appeared in the form of a dove at the baptism of Christ and as tongues of fire at his descent upon the Apostles; soul of the Church and guarantor, by his abiding presence and action, of truth in doctrine; communicator of grace to men, for which reason he is called the sanctifier.

Holy Water: Water blessed by the Church and used as a sacramental, a practice which originated in apostolic times.

Holy Year: A year during which the pope grants the plenary Jubilee Indulgence to the faithful who fulfill certain conditions. For those who make a pilgrimage to Rome during the year, the conditions are reception of the sacraments of penance and the Eucharist, visits and prayer for the intention of the pope in the basilicas of St. Peter, St. John Lateran, St. Paul and St. Mary Major. For those who do not make a pilgrimage to Rome, the conditions are reception of the sacraments and prayer for the pope during a visit or community celebration in a church designated by the bishop of the locality. Holy Year observances have biblical counterparts in the Years of Jubilee observed at 50-year intervals by the pre-exilic Israelites — when debts were pardoned and slaves freed (Lv. 25:25-54) — and in sabbatical years observed from the end of the Exile to 70 A.D. — in which debts to fellow Jews were remitted. The practice of Christians from early times to go on pilgrimage to the

Holy Land, the shrines of martyrs and the tombs of the Apostles in Rome influenced the institution of Holy Years. There was also a prevailing belief among the people that every 100th year was a year of "Great Pardon." Accordingly, even before Boniface VIII formally proclaimed the first Holy Year Feb. 22, 1300, scores of thousands of pilgrims were already on the way to or in Rome. Medieval popes embodied in the observance of Holy Years the practice of good works (reception of the sacraments of penance and the Eucharist, pilgrimages and/or visits to the tombs of the Apostles, and related actions) and spiritual benefits (particularly, special indulgences for the souls in purgatory). These and related practices, with suitable changes for celebrations in local churches, remain staple features of Holy Year observances. The first three Holy Years were observed in 1300, 1350 and 1390. Subsequent ones were celebrated at 25-year intervals except in 1800 and 1850 when, respectively, the French invasion of Italy and political turmoil made observance impossible. Pope Paul II (1464-1471) set the 25-year timetable. In 1500, Pope Alexander VI prescribed the start and finish ceremonies — the opening and closing of the Holy Doors in the major basilicas on successive Christmas Eves. All but a few of the earlier Holy Years were classified as ordinary. Several — like those of 1933 and 1983-84 to commemorate the 1900th and 1950th anniversaries of the death and resurrection of Christ — were in the extraordinary category.

Homosexuality: The condition of a person whose sexual orientation is toward persons of the same rather than the opposite sex. The condition, usually discovered during adolescence rather than deliberately caused, is not normal but is not sinful in itself. Homosexual acts are seriously sinful in themselves; subjective responsibility for such acts, however, may be conditioned and diminished by compulsion and related factors.

Hope: One of the three theological virtues, by which one firmly trusts that God wills his salvation and will give him the means to attain it.

Hosanna: A Hebrew word, meaning O Lord, save, we pray.

Host, The Sacred: The bread under whose appearances Christ is and remains present in a unique manner after the consecration which takes place during Mass. (See Transubstantiation.)

Humility: A virtue which induces a person to evaluate himself at his true worth, to recognize his dependence on God, and to give glory to God for the good he has and can do.

Hyperdulia: The special veneration accorded the Blessed Virgin Mary because of her unique role in the mystery of Redemption, her exceptional gifts of grace from God, and her preeminence among the saints. Hyperdulia is not adoration; only God is adored.

Hypnosis: A mental state resembling sleep, induced by suggestion, in which the subject does the bidding of the hypnotist. Hypnotism is permissible under certain conditions: the existence of a serious reason, e.g., for anesthetic or therapeutic purposes, and the competence and integrity of the hypnotist. Hypnotism may not be practiced for the sake of amusement. Experiments indicate that, contrary to popular opinion, hypnotized subjects may be induced to perform immoral acts which, normally, they would not do.

Hypostatic Union: The union of the human and divine natures in the one divine Person of Christ.

I

Icons: Byzantine-style paintings or representations of Christ, the Blessed Virgin and other saints, venerated in the Eastern Churches where they take the place of statues.

Idolatry: Worship of any but the true God; a violation of the First Commandment.

IHS: In Greek, the first three letters of the name of Jesus — Iota, Eta, Sigma.

Immortality: The survival and continuing existence of the human soul after death.

Impurity: Unlawful indulgence in sexual pleasure. (See Chastity.)

Incardination: The affiliation of a priest to his diocese. Every secular priest must belong to a certain diocese. Similarly, every priest of a religious community must belong to some jurisdiction of his community; this affiliation, however, is not called incardination.

Incarnation: (1) The coming-into-flesh or taking of human nature by the Second Person of the Trinity. He became human as the Son of Mary, being miraculously conceived by the power of the Holy Spirit, without ceasing to be divine. His divine Person hypostatically unites his divine and human natures. (2) The supernatural mystery coextensive with Christ from the moment of his human conception and continuing through his life on earth; his sufferings and death; his resurrection from the dead and ascension to glory with the Father; his sending, with the Father, of the Holy Spirit upon the Apostles and the Church; and his unending mediation with the Father for the salvation of men.

Incense: A granulated substance which, when burnt, emits an aromatic smoke. It symbolizes the zeal with which the faithful should be consumed, the good odor of Christian virtue, the ascent of prayer to God.

Incest: Sexual intercourse with relatives by blood or marriage; a sin of impurity and also a grave violation of the natural reverence due to relatives. Other sins of impurity (desire, etc.) concerning relatives have the nature of incest.

Inculturation: This was one of the subjects of an address delivered by Pope John Paul II Feb. 15, 1982, at a meeting in Lagos with the bishops of Nigeria. "An important aspect of your own evangelizing role is the whole dimension of the inculturation of the Gospel into the lives of your people. . . . The Church truly respects the culture of each people. In offering the Gospel message, the Church does not intend to destroy or to abolish what is good and beautiful. In fact, she recognizes many cultural values and, through the power of the Gospel, purifies and takes into Christian worship certain elements of a people's customs. The Church comes to bring Christ; she does not come to bring the culture of another race. Evangelization aims at penetrating and elevating culture by the power of the Gospel. . . . It is through the Providence of God that the divine message is made incarnate and is communicated through the culture of each people. It is forever true that the path of culture is the path of man, and it is on this path that man encounters the one who embodies the values of all cultures and fully reveals the man of each culture to himself. The Gospel of Christ, the Incarnate Word, finds its home along the path of culture, and from this path it continues to offer its message of salvation and eternal life."

Index of Prohibited Books: A list of books which Catholics were formerly forbidden to read, possess or sell, under penalty of excommunication. The books were banned by the Holy See after publication because their treatment of matters of faith and morals and related subjects were judged to be erroneous or serious occasions of doctrinal error. Some books were listed in the Index by name; others were covered under general norms. The Congregation for the Doctrine of the Faith declared June 14, 1966, that the Index and its related penalties of excommunication no longer had the force of law in the Church. Persons are still obliged, however, to take normal precautions against occasions of doctrinal error.

Indifferentism: A theory that any one religion is as true and good — or false — as any other religion, and that it makes no difference, objectively, what religion one professes, if any. The theory is completely subjective, finding its justification entirely in personal choice without reference to or respect for objective validity. It is also self-contradictory, since it regards as equally acceptable — or unacceptable — the beliefs of all religions, which in fact are not only not all the same but are in some cases opposed to each other.

Indulgence: According to *The Doctrine and Practice of Indulgences,* an apostolic constitution issued by Paul VI Jan. 1, 1967, an indulgence is the remission before God of the temporal punishment due for sins already forgiven as far as their guilt is concerned, which a follower of Christ — with the proper dispositions and under certain determined conditions — acquires through the intervention of the Church. The Church grants indulgences in accordance with doctrine concerning the superabundant merits of Christ and the saints, the Power of the Keys, and the sharing of spiritual goods in the communion of saints. An indulgence is partial or plenary, depending on whether it does away with either part or all of the temporal punishment due for sin. Both types of indulgences can always be applied to the dead by way of suffrage; the actual disposition of indulgences applied to the dead rests with God. (1) Partial indulgence: Properly disposed faithful who perform an action to which a partial indulgence is attached obtain, in addition to the remission of temporal punishment acquired by the action itself, an equal remission of punishment through the intervention of the Church. (This grant was formerly designated in terms of days and years.) The proper dispositions for gaining a partial indulgence are sorrow for sin and freedom from serious sin, performance of the required good work, and the intention (which can

be general or immediate) to gain the indulgence. In addition to customary prayers and other good works to which partial indulgences are attached, there are general grants of partial indulgences to the faithful who: (a) with some kind of prayer, raise their minds to God with humble confidence while carrying out their duties and bearing the difficulties of everyday life; (b) motivated by the spirit of faith and compassion, give of themselves or their goods for the service of persons in need; (c) in a spirit of penance, spontaneously refrain from the enjoyment of things which are lawful and pleasing to them. (2) Plenary indulgence: To gain a plenary indulgence, it is necessary for a person to be free of all attachment to sin, to perform the work to which the indulgence is attached, and to fulfill the three conditions of sacramental confession, Eucharistic Communion, and prayer for the intention of the pope. The three conditions may be fulfilled several days before or after the performance of the prescribed work, but it is fitting that Communion be received and prayers for the intentions of the pope be offered on the same day the work is performed. The condition of praying for the pope's intention is fully satisfied by praying one Our Father and one Hail Mary, and sometimes the Creed, but persons are free to choose other prayers. Four of the several devotional practices for which a plenary indulgence is granted are: (a) adoration of the Blessed Sacrament for at least one-half hour; (b) devout reading of sacred Scripture for at least one-half hour; (c) the Way of the Cross; (d) recitation of the Rosary in a church, public oratory or private chapel, or in a family group, a religious community or pious association. Only one plenary indulgence can be gained in a single day. The Apostolic Penitentiary issued a decree Dec. 14, 1985, granting diocesan bishops the right to impart — three times a year on solemn feasts of their choice — the papal blessing with a plenary indulgence to those who cannot be physically present but who follow the sacred rites at which the blessing is imparted by radio or television transmission. In July, 1986, publication was announced of a new and simplified *Enchiridion Indulgentiarum,* in accord with provisions of the revised Code of Canon Law.

Indult: A favor or privilege granted by competent ecclesiastical authority, giving permission to do something not allowed by the common law of the Church.

Infant Jesus of Prague: An 18-inch-high wooden statue of the Child Jesus which has figured in a form of devotion to the Holy Childhood and Kingship of Christ since the 17th century. Of uncertain origin, the statue was presented by Princess Polixena to the Carmelites of Our Lady of Victory Church, Prague, in 1628.

Infused Virtues: The theological virtues of faith, hope, and charity; principles or capabilities of supernatural action, they are given with sanctifying grace by God rather than acquired by repeated acts of a person. They can be increased by practice; they are lost by contrary acts. Natural-acquired moral virtues, like the cardinal virtues of prudence, justice, temperance, and fortitude, can be considered infused in a person whose state of grace gives them supernatural orientation.

Inquisition: A tribunal for dealing with heretics, authorized by Gregory IX in 1231 to search them out, hear and judge them, sentence them to various forms of punishment, and in some cases to hand them over to civil authorities for punishment. The Inquisition was a creature of its time when crimes against faith, which threatened the good of the Christian community, were regarded also as crimes against the state, and when heretical doctrines of such extremists as the Cathari and Albigensians threatened the very fabric of society. The institution, which was responsible for many excesses, was most active in the second half of the 13th century.

Inquisition, Spanish: An institution peculiar to Spain and the colonies in Spanish America. In 1478, at the urging of King Ferdinand, Pope Sixtus IV approved the establishment of the Inquisition for trying charges of heresy brought against Jewish (Marranos) and Moorish (Moriscos) converts. It acquired jurisdiction over other cases as well, however, and fell into disrepute because of irregularities in its functions, cruelty in its sentences, and the manner in which it served the interests of the Spanish crown more than the accused persons and the good of the Church. Protests by the Holy See failed to curb excesses of the Inquisition, which lingered in Spanish history until early in the 19th century.

I N R I: The first letters of words in the Latin inscription atop the cross on which Christ was crucified: (I)esus (N)azaraenus, (R)ex (J)udaeorum — Jesus of Nazareth, King of the Jews.

Insemination, Artificial: The implanting of human semen by some means other than consummation of natural marital intercourse. In view of the principle that procreation should result only from marital intercourse, donor insemination is not permissible. The use of legitimate artificial means to further the fruitfulness of marital intercourse is permissible.

In Sin: The condition of a person called spiritually dead because he does not possess sanctifying grace, the principle of supernatural life, action and merit. Such grace can be regained through repentance.

Instruction: A document containing doctrinal explanations, directive norms, rules, recommendations, admonitions, issued by the pope, a department of the Roman Curia or other competent authority in the Church. To the extent that they so prescribe, instructions have the force of law.

Intercommunion: The common celebration and reception of the Eucharist by members of different Christian churches; a pivotal issue in ecumenical theory and practice. Catholic participation and intercommunion in the Eucharistic liturgy of another church without a valid priesthood and with a variant Eucharistic belief is out of order. Under certain conditions, other Christians may receive the Eucharist in the Catholic Church (see additional Intercommunion entry). Intercom-

munion is acceptable to some Protestant churches and unacceptable to others.

Interdict: A censure imposed on persons for certain violations of church law. Interdicted persons may not take part in certain liturgical services, administer or receive certain sacraments.

Interregnum: The period of time between the death of a pope and the election of his successor. Another term applied to the period is *Sede vacante*, meaning the See (of Rome) being vacant. The main concerns during an interregnum are matters connected with the death and burial of the pope, the election of his successor, and the maintenance of ordinary routine for the proper functioning of the Roman Curia and the Diocese of Rome. Interregnum procedures follow norms contained in the apostolic constitution *Romano Pontifici Eligendo* issued by Paul VI Oct. 1, 1975. "During the vacancy of the Apostolic See," the constitution states, "the government of the Church is entrusted to the Sacred College of Cardinals for the sole dispatch of ordinary business and of matters which cannot be postponed, and for the preparation of everything necessary for the election of the new pope." The general congregation of the whole college, presided over by the dean, sub-dean or senior cardinal, has responsibility for major decisions during an interregnum. Other decisions of a routine nature are left to a particular congregation consisting of the chamberlain of the Holy Roman Church and three assistant cardinals. The chamberlain of the Holy Roman Church and the dean of the college are the key officials, with directive responsibilities before and during the electoral conclave. The chamberlain is in general charge of ordinary administration. He — or the dean prior to a chamberlain's election by the cardinals — certifies the death of the pope; orders the destruction of the Fisherman's Ring and personal seals of the pope; and sets in motion procedures, carried out in collaboration with the dean, for informing the world about the pope's death, for funeral preparations, and for summoning and supervising the conclave for the election of a new pope. Cardinals in charge of departments of the Roman Curia relinquish their offices at the death of the pope. Remaining in office, however, are the vicar of Rome, for ordinary jurisdiction over the diocese, and the major penitentiary. The substitute secretary of state or papal secretariat maintains the secretariat in a status quo. Papal representatives, such as nuncios and apostolic delegates, remain in office. The congregations, offices and tribunals of the Curia retain ordinary jurisdiction for routine affairs but may not initiate new business during an interregnum. If the pope should die during sessions of an ecumenical council or the Synod of Bishops, they would automatically be suspended. The deceased pope is buried in St. Peter's Basilica, following prescribed ceremonies and traditional customs during a mourning period of nine days. The conclave for the election of a new pope begins no sooner than 15 and no later than 20 days after the death of his predecessor. On the election of the new pope, the interregnum comes to an end.

Intinction: A method of administering Holy Communion under the dual appearances of bread and wine, in which the consecrated host is dipped in the consecrated wine before being given to the communicant. The administering of Holy Communion in this manner, which has been traditional in Eastern-Rite liturgies, was authorized in the Roman Rite for various occasions by the *Constitution on the Sacred Liturgy* promulgated by the Second Vatican Council.

Irenicism: Peace-seeking, conciliation, as opposed to polemics; an important element in ecumenism, provided it furthers pursuit of the Christian unity willed by Christ without degenerating into a peace-at-any-price disregard for religious truth.

Irregularity: An impediment to the lawful reception or exercise of holy orders. The Church instituted irregularities — which include apostasy, heresy, homicide, attempted suicide — out of reverence for the dignity of the sacraments.

Itinerarium: Prayers for a spiritually profitable journey.

J

Jansenism: Opinions developed and proposed by Cornelius Jansenius (1585-1638). He held that: human nature was radically and intrinsically corrupted by original sin; some men are predestined to heaven and others to hell; Christ died only for those predestined to heaven; for those who are predestined, the operations of grace are irresistible. Jansenism also advocated an extremely rigorous code of morals and asceticism. The errors were proscribed by Urban VIII in 1642, by Innocent X in 1653, by Clement XI in 1713, and by other popes. Despite these condemnations, the rigoristic spirit of Jansenism lingered for a long time afterwards, particularly in France.

Jehovah's Witnesses: The Witnesses, together with the Watchtower and Bible Tract Society, trace their beginnings to a Bible class organized by Charles Taze Russell in 1872 at· Allegheny, Pa. They take their name from a passage in Isaiah (43:12): " 'You are my witnesses,' says Jehovah." They are generally fundamentalist and revivalist with respect to the Bible, and believe that Christ is God's Son but is inferior to God. They place great emphasis on the Battle of Armageddon (as a decisive confrontation of good and evil) that is depicted vividly in Revelation, believing that God will then destroy the existing system of things and that, with the establishment of Jehovah's Kingdom, a small band of 144,000 spiritual sons of God will go to heaven, rule with Christ, and share in some way their happiness with some others. Each Witness is considered by the society to be an ordained minister charged with the duty of spreading the message of Jehovah, which is accomplished through publications, house-to-house visitations, and other methods. The Witnesses refuse to salute the flag of any nation, regarding this as a form of idolatry, or to sanction blood transfusions even for the saving of life. There are approximately one million Witnesses in more than 22,000 congregations in some 80 countries. The freedom and activi-ties of Witnesses are restricted in some places.

Jesus: The name of Jesus, meaning Savior in Christian usage, derived from the Aramaic and Hebrew *Yeshua* and *Joshua*, meaning *Yahweh* is salvation.

Jesus Prayer: A form of prayer dating back to the fifth century, "Lord Jesus Christ, Son of God, have mercy on me (a sinner)."

Judgment: (1) Last or final judgment: Final judgment by Christ, at the end of the world and the general resurrection. (2) Particular judgment: The judgment that takes place immediately after a person's death, followed by entrance into heaven, hell or purgatory.

Jurisdiction: Right, power, authority to rule. Jurisdiction in the Church is of divine institution; has pastoral service for its purpose; includes legislative, judicial and executive authority; can be exercised only by persons with the power of orders. (1) Ordinary jurisdiction is attached to ecclesiastical offices by law; the officeholders, called Ordinaries, have authority over those who are subject to them. (2) Delegated jurisdiction is that which is granted to persons rather than attached to offices. Its extent depends on the terms of the delegation.

Justice: One of the four cardinal virtues by which a person gives to others what is due to them as a matter of right. (See Cardinal Virtues.)

Justification: The act by which God makes a person just, and the consequent change in the spiritual status of a person, from sin to grace; the remission of sin and the infusion of sanctifying grace through the merits of Christ and the action of the Holy Spirit.

K

Kerygma: Proclaiming the word of God, in the manner of the Apostles, as here and now effective for salvation. This method of preaching or instruction, centered on Christ and geared to the facts and themes of salvation history, is designed to dispose people to faith in Christ and or to intensify the experience and practice of that faith in those who have it.

Keys, Power of the: Spiritual authority and jurisdiction in the Church, symbolized by the keys of the kingdom of heaven. Christ promised the keys to St. Peter, as head-to-be of the Church (Mt. 16:19), and commissioned him with full pastoral responsibility to feed his lambs and sheep (Jn. 21:15-17), The pope, as the successor of St. Peter, has this power in a primary and supreme manner. The bishops of the Church also have the power, in union with and subordinate to the pope. Priests share in it through holy orders and the delegation of authority. Examples of the application of the Power of the Keys are the exercise of teaching and pastoral authority by the pope and bishops, the absolving of sins in the sacrament of penance, the granting of indulgences, the imposing of spiritual penalties on persons who commit certain serious sins.

L

Laicization: The process by which a man ordained to holy orders is relieved of the obligations of orders and the ministry and is returned to the status of a lay person.

Languages of the Church: The first language in church use, for divine worship and the conduct of ecclesiastical affairs, was Aramaic, the language of the first Christians in and around Jerusalem. As the Church spread westward, Greek was adopted and prevailed until the third century when it was supplanted by Latin for official use in the West. According to traditions established very early in churches of the Eastern Rites, many different languages were adopted for use in divine worship and for the conduct of ecclesiastical affairs. The practice was, and still is, to use the vernacular or a language closely related to the common tongue of the people. In the Western Church, Latin prevailed as the general official language until the promulgation on Dec. 4, 1963, of the *Constitution on the Sacred Liturgy* by the second session of the Second Vatican Council. Since that time, vernacular languages have come into use in the Mass, administration of the sacraments, and the Liturgy of the Hours. The change was introduced in order to make the prayers and ceremonies of divine worship more informative and meaningful to all. Latin, however, remains the official language for documents of the Holy See, administrative and procedural matters.

Law: An ordinance or rule governing the activity of things. (1) Natural law: Moral norms corresponding to man's nature by which he orders his conduct toward God, neighbor, society and himself. This law, which is rooted in human nature, is of divine origin, can be known by the use of reason, and binds all men having the use of reason. The Ten Commandments are declarations and amplifications of natural law. The primary precepts of natural law, to do good and to avoid evil, are universally recognized, despite differences with respect to understanding and application resulting from different philosophies of good and evil. (2) Divine positive law: That which has been revealed by God. Among its essentials are the twin precepts of love of God and love of neighbor, and the Ten Commandments. (3) Ecclesiastical law: That which is established by the Church for the spiritual welfare of the faithful and the orderly conduct of ecclesiastical affairs. (See Canon Law.) (4) Civil law: That which is established by a socio-political community for the common good.

Liberalism: A multiphased trend of thought and movement favoring liberty, independence and progress in moral, intellectual, religious, social, economic and political life. Traceable to the Renaissance, it developed through the Enlightenment, the rationalism of the 19th century, and modernist- and existentialist-related theories of the 20th century. Evaluations of various kinds of liberalism depend on the validity of their underlying principles. Extremist positions — regarding subjectivism, libertinarianism, naturalist denials of the supernatural, and the alienation of individuals and society from God and the Church were condemned by Gregory XVI in the 1830's, Pius IX in 1864, Leo XIII in 1899, and St. Pius X in 1907. There is, however, nothing objectionable about forms of liberalism patterned according to sound principles of Christian doctrine.

Life in Outer Space: Whether rational life exists on other bodies in the universe besides earth, is a question for scientific investigation to settle. The possibility can be granted, without prejudice to the body of revealed truth.

Limbo: The limbo of the fathers was the state of rest and natural happiness after death enjoyed by the just of pre-Christian times until they were admitted to heaven following the Ascension of Christ. Belief in this matter is stated in the Apostles' Creed. The existence of a limbo for unbaptized persons of infant status — a state of rest and natural happiness — has never been formally defined.

Litany: A prayer in the form of responsive petition; e.g., St. Joseph, pray for us, etc. Examples are the litanies of Loreto (Litany of the Blessed Mother), the Holy Name, All Saints, the Sacred Heart, the Precious Blood, St. Joseph, Litany for the Dying.

Loreto, House of: A Marian shrine in Loreto, Italy, consisting of the home of the Holy Family which, according to an old tradition, was transported in a miraculous manner from Nazareth to Dalmatia and finally to Loreto between 1291 and 1294. Investigations conducted shortly after the appearance of the structure in Loreto revealed that its dimensions matched those of the house of the Holy Family missing from its place of enshrinement in a basilica at Nazareth. Among the many popes who regarded it with high honor was John XXIII, who went there on pilgrimage Oct. 4, 1962. The house of the Holy Family is enshrined in the Basilica of Our Lady.

Lust: A disorderly desire for sexual pleasure; one of the seven capital sins.

M

Magi: In the Infancy Narrative of St. Matthew's Gospel (2:1-12), three wise men from the East whose visit and homage to the Child Jesus at Bethlehem indicated Christ's manifestation of himself to non-Jewish people. The narrative teaches the universality of salvation. The traditional names of the Magi are Caspar, Melchior and Balthasar.

Magnificat: The canticle or hymn of the Virgin Mary on the occasion of her visitation to her cousin Elizabeth (Lk. 1:46-55). It is an expression of praise, thanksgiving and acknowledgment of the great blessings given by God to Mary, the Mother of the Second Person of the Blessed Trinity made Man. The Magnificat is recited in the Liturgy of the Hours as part of the Evening Prayer.

Martyr: A Greek word, meaning witness, denoting one who voluntarily suffered death for the faith or some Christian virtue.

Martyrology: A catalogue of martyrs and other saints, arranged according to the calendar. The *Roman Martyrology* contains the official list of saints venerated by the Church. Additions to the list are made in beatification and canonization decrees of the Congregation for the Causes of Saints.

Mass for the People: On Sundays and certain

feasts throughout the year pastors are required to offer Mass for the faithful committed to their care. If they cannot offer the Mass on these days, they must do so at a later date or provide that another priest offer the Mass.

Master of Novices: The person in charge of the training and formation of candidates for an institute of consecrated life during novitiate.

Materialism: Theory which holds that matter is the only reality, and everything in existence is merely a manifestation of matter; there is no such thing as spirit, and the supernatural does not exist. Materialism is incompatible with Christian doctrine.

Meditation: Mental, as distinguished from vocal, prayer, in which thought, affections, and resolutions of the will predominate. There is a meditative element to all forms of prayer, which always involves the raising of the heart and mind to God.

Mendicants: A term derived from Latin and meaning beggars, applied to members of religious orders without property rights; the members, accordingly, worked or begged for their support. The original mendicants were Franciscans and Dominicans in the early 13th century; later, the Carmelites, Augustinians, Servites and others were given the mendicant title and privileges, with respect to exemption from episcopal jurisdiction and wide faculties for preaching and administering the sacrament of penance. The practice of begging is limited at the present time, although it is still allowed with the permission of competent superiors and bishops. Mendicants are supported by free will offerings and income received for spiritual services and other work.

Mercy, Divine: The love and goodness of God, manifested particularly in a time of need.

Merit: In religion, the right to a supernatural reward for good works freely done for a supernatural motive by a person in the state of and with the assistance of grace. The right to such reward is from God, who binds himself to give it. Accordingly, good works, as described above, are meritorious for salvation.

Metempsychosis: Theory of the passage or migration of the human soul after death from one body to another for the purpose of purification from guilt. The theory denies the unity of the soul and human personality, and the doctrine of individual moral responsibility.

Millennium: A thousand-year reign of Christ and the just upon earth before the end of the world. This belief of the Millenarians, Chiliasts, and some sects of modern times is based on an erroneous interpretation of Rv. 20.

Miracles: Observable events or effects in the physical or moral order of things, with reference to salvation, which cannot be explained by the ordinary operation of laws of nature and which, therefore, are attributed to the direct action of God. They make known, in an unusual way, the concern and intervention of God in human affairs for the salvation of men. The most striking examples are the miracles worked by Christ. Numbering about 35, they included his own Resurrection; the raising of three persons to life (Lazarus, the daughter of Jairus, the son of the widow of Naim); the healing of blind, leprous and other persons; nature miracles; and prophecies, or miracles of the intellectual order. The foregoing notion of miracles, which is based on the concept of a fixed order of nature, was not known by the writers of Sacred Scripture. In the Old Testament, particularly, they called some things miraculous which, according to the definition in contemporary use, may or may not have been miracles. Essentially, however, the occurrences so designated were regarded as exceptional manifestations of God's care and concern for the salvation of his people. The miracles of Christ were miracles in the full sense of the term. The Church believes it is reasonable to accept miracles as manifestations of divine power for purposes of salvation. God, who created the laws of nature, is their master; hence, without disturbing the ordinary course of things, he can — and has in the course of history before and after Christ — occasionally set aside these laws and has also produced effects beyond their power of operation. The Church does not call miraculous anything which does not admit of easy explanation; on the contrary, miracles are admitted only when the events have a bearing on the order of grace and every possible natural explanation has been tried and found wanting. (The transubstantiation — i.e., the conversion of the whole substance of bread and wine, their sensible appearances alone remaining, into the Body and Blood of Christ in the act of Consecration at Mass — is not an observable event. Traditionally, however, it has been called a miracle.)

Missal: A liturgical book of Roman Rite also called the *Sacramentary,* containing the celebrant's prayers of the Mass, along with general instructions and ceremonial directives. The Latin text of the new *Roman Missal,* replacing the one authorized by the Council of Trent in the 16th century, was published by the Vatican Polyglot Press in 1970. Its use in English was made mandatory in the U.S. from Dec. 1, 1974. Readings and scriptural responsories formerly in the missal are contained in the *Lectionary.*

Missiology: Study of the missionary nature, constitution and activity of the Church in all aspects: theological reasons for missionary activity, laws and instructions of the Holy See, history of the missions, social and cultural background, methods, norms for carrying on missionary work.

Mission: (1) Strictly, it means being sent to perform a certain work, such as the mission of Christ to redeem mankind, the mission of the Apostles and the Church and its members to perpetuate the prophetic, priestly and royal mission of Christ. (2) A place where: the Gospel has not been proclaimed; the Church has not been firmly established; the Church, although established, is weak. (3) An ecclesiastical territory with the simplest kind of canonical organization, under the jurisdiction of the Congregation for the Evangelization of Peoples. (4) A church or chapel without a resident priest. (5) A special course of sermons and spiritual exercises conducted in parishes for the purpose of renewing and deepening the spiritual life of the faithful and for the conversion of lapsed Catholics.

Modernism: The "synthesis of all heresies," which appeared near the beginning of the 20th century. It undermines the objective validity of religious beliefs and practices which, it contends, are products of the subconscious developed by mankind under the stimulus of a religious sense. It holds that the existence of a personal God cannot be demonstrated, the Bible is not inspired, Christ is not divine, nor did he establish the Church or institute the sacraments. A special danger lies in modernism, which is still influential, because it uses Catholic terms with perverted meanings. St. Pius X condemned 65 propositions of modernism in 1907 in the decree *Lamentabili* and issued the encyclical *Pascendi* to explain and analyze its errors.

Monastery: The dwelling place, as well as the community thereof, of monks belonging to the Benedictine and Benedictine-related orders like the Cistercians and Carthusians; also, the Augustinians and Canons Regular. Distinctive of monasteries are: their separation from the world; the enclosure or cloister; the permanence or stability of attachment characteristic of their members; autonomous government in accordance with a monastic rule, like that of St. Benedict in the West or of St. Basil in the East; the special dedication of its members to the community celebration of the liturgy as well as to work that is suitable to the surrounding area and the needs of its people. Monastic superiors of men have such titles as abbot and prior; of women, abbess and prioress. In most essentials, an abbey is the same as a monastery.

Monk: A member of a monastic order — e.g., the Benedictines, the Benedictine-related Cistercians and Carthusians, and the Basilians, who bind themselves by religious profession to stable attachment to a monastery, the contemplative life and the work of their community. In popular use, the title is wrongly applied to many men religious who really are not monks.

Monotheism: Belief in and worship of one God.

Morality: Conformity or difformity of behavior to standards of right conduct. (See Moral Obligations, Commandments of God, Precepts of the Church, Conscience, Law.)

Mormons: Members of the Church of Jesus Christ of Latter-Day Saints. The church was established by Joseph Smith (1805-1844) at Fayette, N.Y., three years after he said he had received from an angel golden tablets containing the *Book of the Prophet Mormon.* This book, the Bible, *Doctrine and Covenants,* and *The Pearl of Great Price,* are the basic doctrinal texts of the church. Characteristic of the Mormons are strong belief in the revelations of their leaders, among whom was Brigham Young; a strong community of religious-secular concern; a dual secular and spiritual priesthood, and vigorous missionary activity. The headquarters of the church are located at Salt Lake City, Utah, where the Mormons first settled in 1847.

Mortification: Acts of self-discipline, including prayer, hardship, austerities and penances undertaken for the sake of progress in virtue.

Motu Proprio: A Latin phrase designating a document issued by a pope on his own initiative. Documents of this kind often concern administrative matters.

Mysteries of Faith: Supernatural truths whose existence cannot be known without revelation by God and whose intrinsic truth, while not contrary to reason, can never be wholly understood even after revelation. These mysteries are above reason, not against reason. Among them are the divine mysteries of the Trinity, Incarnation and Eucharist. Some mysteries — e.g., concerning God's attributes — can be known by reason without revelation, although they cannot be fully understood.

N

Necromancy: Supposed communication with the dead; a form of divination.

Non-Expedit: A Latin expression. It is not expedient (fitting, proper), used to state a prohibition or refusal of permission.

Novena: A term designating public or private devotional practices over a period of nine consecutive days; or, by extension, over a period of nine weeks, in which one day a week is set aside for the devotions.

Novice: A man or woman preparing, in a formal period of trial and formation called a novitiate, for membership in an institute of consecrated life. The novitiate lasts a minimum of 12 and a maximum of 24 months; at its conclusion, the novice professes temporary vows of poverty, chastity and obedience. Norms require that certain periods of time be spent in the house of novitiate: the first three months, one solid period of six months, the final month before the profession of temporary commitment. Periods of apostolic work are also required, to acquaint the novice with the apostolate(s) of the institute. A novice is not bound by the obligations of the professed members of the institute, is free to leave at any time, and may be discharged at the discretion of competent superiors. The immediate superior of a novice is a master or mistress of novices.

Nun (1) Strictly, a member of a religious order of women with solemn vows (moniales). (2) In general, all women religious, even those in simple vows who are more properly called sisters.

Nunc Dimittis: The canticle or hymn of Simeon at the sight of Jesus at the Temple on the occasion of his presentation (Lk. 2:29-32). It is an expression of joy and thanksgiving for the blessing of having lived to see the Messiah. It is prescribed for use in the Night Prayer of the Liturgy of the Hours.

O

Oath: Calling upon God to witness the truth of a statement. Violating an oath, e.g., by perjury in court, or taking an oath without sufficient reason, is a violation of the honor due to God.

Obedience: Submission to one in authority. General obligations of obedience fall under the Fourth Commandment. The vow of obedience professed by religious is one of the evangelical counsels.

Obsession, Diabolical: The extraordinary state of one who is seriously molested by evil spirits in an external manner. Obsession is more than just temptation.

Occultism: Practices involving ceremonies, rituals, chants, incantations, other cult-related activities intended to affect the course of nature, the lives of practitioners and others, through esoteric powers of magic, diabolical or other forces; one of many forms of superstition.

Octave: A period of eight days given over to the celebration of a major feast such as Easter.

Oils, Holy: The oils consecrated by bishops on Holy Thursday or another suitable day, and by priests under certain conditions for use in certain sacraments and consecrations. (1) The oil of catechumens (olive or vegetable oil), used at baptism; also, poured with chrism into the baptismal water blessed in Easter Vigil ceremonies. (2) Chrism (olive or vegetable oil mixed with balm), used at baptism, in confirmation, at the ordination of a priest and bishop, in the dedication of churches and altars. (3) Oil of the sick (olive or vegetable oil) used in anointing the sick.

Old Catholics — Several sects, including: (1) the Church of Utrecht, which severed relations with Rome in 1724; (2) the National Polish Church in the U.S., which had its origin near the end of the 19th century; (3) German, Austrian and Swiss Old Catholics, who broke away from union with Rome following the First Vatican Council in 1870 because they objected to the dogma of papal infallibility. The formation of the Old Catholic communion of Germans, Austrians and Swiss began in 1870 at a public meeting held in Nuremberg under the leadership of A. Dollinger. Four years later episcopal succession was established with the ordination of an Old Catholic German bishop by a prelate of the Church of Utrecht. In line with the "Declaration of Utrecht" of 1889, they accept the first seven ecumenical councils and doctrine formulated before 1054, but reject communion with the pope and a number of other Catholic doctrines and practices. They have a valid priesthood and valid sacraments. *The Oxford Dictionary of the Christian Church* notes that they have recognized Anglican ordinations since 1925, that they have had full communion with the Church of England since 1932, and that their bishops, using their own formula, have taken part in the ordination of Anglican bishops. This communion does not recognize the "Old Catholic" status of several smaller sects calling themselves such. In turn, connection with it is disavowed by the Old Roman Catholic Church headquartered in Chicago, which contends that it has abandoned the traditions of the Church of Utrecht. The United States is the only English-speaking country with Old Catholic communities.

Opus Dei: Opus Dei was founded by Msgr. Josemaria Escriva de Balaguer in 1928 in Madrid with the aim of spreading throughout all sectors of society a profound awareness of the universal call to holiness and apostolate (of Christian witness and action) in the ordinary circumstances of life, and, more specifically, through one's professional work. The institution was fully approved by the Vatican as a secular institute in 1950. On Aug. 5, 1982, Pope John Paul II confirmed and ordered publication of a declaration concerning the erection of the then secular institute into the Prelature of the Holy Cross and Opus Dei. The 1986 edition of *Annuario Pontificio* reported that the prelature had 1,217 priests (56 newly ordained) and 352 major seminarians. Also, there were approximately 72,000 lay persons — men and women, married and single, of every class and social condition — of about 80 nationalities. In the United States, members of Opus Dei, along with non-member associates, conduct apostolic works corporately in major cities in the East and Midwest, Texas and on the West Coast. Elsewhere, members are engaged in universities, vocational institutes, training schools for farmers and numerous other apostolic initiatives. An information office is located at 330 Riverside Drive, New York, N.Y. 10025.

Oratory: A chapel.

Ordinariate: An ecclesiastical jurisdiction for special purposes and people. Examples are military ordinariates for armed services personnel (in accord with provisions of the apostolic constitution *Spirituali Militum Curae,* May 18, 1986) and Eastern-Rite ordinariates in places where Eastern-Rite dioceses do not exist.

Ordination: The consecration of sacred ministers for divine worship and the service of people in things pertaining to God. The power of ordination comes from Christ and the Church, and must be conferred by a minister capable of communicating it.

Organ Transplants: The transplanting of organs from one person to another is permissible provided it is done with the consent of the concerned parties and does not result in the death or essential mutilation of the donor. Advances in methods and technology have increased the range of transplant possibilities in recent years.

Original Sin: The sin of Adam (Gn. 2:8—3:24), personal to him and passed on to all persons as a state of privation of grace. Despite this privation and the related wounding of human nature and weakening of natural powers, original sin leaves unchanged all that man himself is by nature. The scriptural basis of the doctrine was stated especially by St. Paul in 1 Cor. 15:21, ff., and Romans 5:12-21. Original sin is remitted by baptism and incorporation in Christ, through whom grace is given to persons.

O Salutaris Hostia: The first three Latin words, O Saving Victim, of a Benediction hymn.

Ostpolitik: Policy adopted by Pope Paul VI in an attempt to improve the situation of Eastern European Catholics through diplomatic negotiations with their governments.

Oxford Movement: A movement in the Church of England from 1833 to about 1845 which had for its objective a threefold defense of the church as a divine institution, the apostolic succession of its bishops, and the Book of Common Prayer as the rule of faith. The movement took its name from Oxford University and involved a number of intellectuals who authored a series of influential *Tracts for Our Times.* Some of its leading figures — e.g., F. W. Faber, John Henry Newman and Henry Edward Manning — became converts to the Catholic Church. In the Church of England, the movement affected the liturgy, historical and theological scholarship, the status of the ministry, and other areas of ecclesiastical life.

P

Paganism: A term referring to non-revealed religions, i.e., religions other than Christianity, Judaism and Mohammedanism.

Palms: Blessed palms are a sacramental. They are blessed and distributed on the Sunday of the Passion in commemoration of the triumphant entrance of Christ into Jerusalem. Ashes of the burnt palms are used on Ash Wednesday.

Pange Lingua: First Latin words, Sing, my tongue, of a hymn in honor of the Holy Eucharist, used particularly on Holy Thursday and in Eucharistic processions.

Pantheism: Theory that all things are part of God, divine, in the sense that God realizes himself as the ultimate reality of matter or spirit through being and/or becoming all things that have been, are, and will be. The theory leads to hopeless confusion of the Creator and the created realm of being, identifies evil with good, and involves many inherent contradictions.

Papal Election: The pope is elected by members of the College of Cardinals in a secret conclave or meeting convened ordinarily in secluded quarters of the Vatican Palace between 15 and 20 days after the death of his predecessor. Cardinals under the age of 80, totaling no more than 120, are eligible to participate in a papal election. Following are some of the principal regulations decreed by Paul VI Oct. 1, 1975, in the apostolic constitution *Romano Pontifici Eligendo.* The ordinary manner of election is by scrutiny, with two votes each morning and afternoon in the Sistine Chapel until one of the candidates receives a two-thirds plus one vote majority. Alternative methods, which can be adopted by unanimous agreement of the cardinals in difficult cases, are provided for: (1) by delegation, in which the cardinals designate a limited number (nine to 15) to make the choice; (2) by changing the majority rule from two-thirds plus one vote to an absolute majority plus one; (3) by limiting final choice, if the procedure in force becomes protracted, to one between the two candidates who received the largest numbers of votes, but not a required majority, in the most recent balloting. An unusual manner of election is by acclamation or inspiration — that is, by spontaneous, unanimous choice without any need for normal voting procedure. The elected candidate is asked by the dean of the college if he accepts the election. If he does so and is already a bishop, he immediately becomes the bishop of Rome and pope, and signifies the name by which he will be called. The cardinals then pledge their obedience to him before the senior cardinal deacon proclaims his election to the world from the main balcony of the Vatican and the new pope imparts his blessing *Urbi et Orbi* (to

the City and the World). If the candidate is not a bishop, he is so ordained before receiving the pledge of obedience and being proclaimed pope. The subsequent coronation of the pope is a ceremonial recognition of the fact of his election. The pope is elected for life. If one should resign, a new pope would be elected in accordance with the foregoing regulations. Rigid rules govern the conclave — its personnel, freedom from internal and external influence and interference, absolute secrecy (with a ban on recording devices and a prohibition against any disclosures). Ordinarily, the first indication that a new pope has been elected is a plume of white smoke rising from the Vatican on burning of the last ballots. Early methods of electing a pope — with various degrees of participation by the clergy and people of Rome and others — were set aside by Pope Nicholas II, who decreed in 1059 that cardinal bishops would be the electors. Further modification of the process was decreed by the Lateran Council in 1179 (that election would take place by a two-thirds majority vote of the cardinals) and by Pope Gregory X in 1274 (regarding a secluded conclave arrangement for elections).

Paraclete: A title of the Holy Spirit meaning, in Greek, Advocate, Consoler.

Parental Duties: All duties related to the obligation of parents to provide for the welfare of their children. These obligations fall under the Fourth Commandment.

Parish: A community of the faithful served by a pastor charged with responsibility for providing them with full pastoral service. Most parishes are territorial, embracing all of the faithful in a certain area of a diocese; some are personal or national, for certain classes of people, without strict regard for their places of residence.

Parousia: The coming, or saving presence, of Christ which will mark the completion of salvation history and the coming to perfection of God's kingdom at the end of the world.

Paschal Candle: A large candle, symbolic of the risen Christ, blessed and lighted on the Easter Vigil and placed at the Gospel side of the altar until Ascension Day. It is ornamented with five large grains of incense, representing the wounds of Christ, inserted in the form of a cross; the Greek letters Alpha and Omega, symbolizing Christ the beginning and end of all things, at the top and bottom of the shaft of the cross; and the figures of the current year of salvation in the quadrants formed by the cross.

Paschal Precept: Church law requiring reception of the Eucharist in the Easter season (see separate entry) unless, for a just cause, once-a-year reception takes place at another time.

Passion of Christ: Sufferings of Christ, recorded in the four Gospels.

Pastor: An ordained minister charged with responsibility for the doctrinal, sacramental and related service of people committed to his care; e.g., a bishop for the people in his diocese, a priest for the people of his parish.

Pater Noster: The initial Latin words, Our Father, of the Lord's Prayer.

Peace, Sign of: A gesture of greeting — e.g., a

handshake — exchanged by the ministers and participants at Mass.

Pectoral Cross: A cross worn on a chain about the neck and over the breast by bishops and abbots as a mark of their office.

Penance or Penitence: (1) The spiritual change or conversion of mind and heart by which a person turns away from sin, and all that it implies, toward God, through a personal renewal under the influence of the Holy Spirit. In the apostolic constitution *Paenitemini*, Pope Paul VI called it "a religious, personal act which has as its aim love and surrender to God." Penance involves sorrow and contrition for sin, together with other internal and external acts of atonement. It serves the purposes of reestablishing in one's life the order of God's love and commandments, and of making satisfaction to God for sin. A divine precept states the necessity of penance for salvation: "Unless you do penance, you shall all likewise perish" (Lk. 13:3) . . . "Be converted and believe in the Gospel" (Mk. 1:15). In the penitential discipline of the Church, the various works of penance have been classified under the headings of prayer (interior), fasting and almsgiving (exterior). The Church has established minimum requirements for the common and social observance of the divine precept by Catholics — e.g., by requiring them to fast and/or abstain on certain days of the year. These observances, however, do not exhaust all the demands of the divine precept, whose fulfillment is a matter of personal responsibility; nor do they have any real value unless they proceed from the internal spirit and purpose of penance. Related to works of penance for sins actually committed are works of mortification. The purpose of the latter is to develop — through prayer, fasting, renunciations and similar actions — self-control and detachment from things which could otherwise become occasions of sin. (2) Penance is a virtue disposing a person to turn to God in sorrow for sin and to carry out works of amendment and atonement. (3) The sacrament of penance and sacramental penance.

Perjury: Taking a false oath, lying under oath, a violation of the honor due to God.

Persecution, Religious: A campaign waged against a church or other religious body by persons and governments intent on its destruction. The best known campaigns of this type against the Christian Church were the Roman persecutions which occurred intermittently from about 54 to the promulgation of the Edict of Milan in 313. The most extensive persecutions took place during the reigns of Nero, the first major Roman persecutor, Domitian, Trajan, Marcus Aurelius, and Diocletian. Besides the Roman persecutions, the Catholic Church has been subject to many others, including those of the 20th century in Communist-controlled countries.

Personal Prelature: A special-purpose jurisdiction — for particular pastoral and missionary work, etc., — consisting of secular priests and deacons and open to lay persons willing to dedicate themselves to its apostolic works. The prelate in charge is an Ordinary, with the authority of office; he can establish a national or international seminary, incardinate its students and promote them to holy orders under the title of service to the prelature. The prelature is constituted and governed according to statutes laid down by the Holy See. Statutes define its relationship and mode of operation with the bishops of territories in which members live and work. Opus Dei is a personal prelature.

Peter's Pence: A collection made each year among Catholics for the maintenance of the pope and his works of charity. It was originally a tax of a penny on each house, and was collected on St. Peter's day, whence the name. It originated in England in the eighth century.

Petition: One of the four purposes of prayer. In prayers of petition, persons ask of God the blessings they and others need.

Pharisees: Influential class among the Jews, referred to in the Gospels, noted for their self-righteousness, legalism, strict interpretation of the Law, acceptance of the traditions of the elders as well as the Law of Moses, and beliefs regarding angels and spirits, the resurrection of the dead and judgment. Most of them were laymen, and they were closely allied with the Scribes; their opposite numbers were the Sadducees. The Pharisaic and rabbinical traditions had a lasting influence on Judaism following the destruction of Jerusalem in 70 A.D.

Pious Fund: Property and money originally accumulated by the Jesuits to finance their missionary work in Lower California. When the Jesuits were expelled from the territory in 1767, the fund was appropriated by the Spanish Crown and used to support Dominican and Franciscan missionary work in Upper and Lower California. In 1842 the Mexican government took over administration of the fund, incorporated most of the revenue into the national treasury, and agreed to pay the Church interest of six per cent a year on the capital so incorporated. From 1848 to 1967 the fund was the subject of lengthy negotiations between the U.S. and Mexican governments because of the latter's failure to make payments as agreed. A lump-sum settlement was made in 1967 with payment by Mexico to the U.S. government of more than $700,000, to be turned over to the Archdiocese of San Francisco.

Polytheism: Belief in and worship of many gods or divinities, especially prevalent in pre-Christian religions.

Poor Box: Alms-box; found in churches from the earliest days of Christianity.

Pope Joan: Alleged name of a woman falsely said to have been pope from 855-858, the years of the reign of Benedict III. The myth was not heard of before the 13th century.

Portiuncula: (1) Meaning little portion (of land), the Portiuncula was the chapel of Our Lady of the Angels near Assisi, Italy, which the Benedictines gave to St. Francis early in the 13th century. He repaired the chapel and made it the first church of the Franciscan Order. It is now enshrined in the Basilica of St. Mary of the Angels in Assisi. (2) The Portiuncula Indulgence, or Pardon of Assisi, was authorized by Honorius III. Originally, it could be gained for the souls in purgatory only in the chapel of Our Lady of the Angels; by later concessions, it could be gained also in other Franciscan and parish churches. The Portiuncula Indulgence can be gained once from noon to midnight of Aug. 1 and once on Aug. 2, or on the following Sunday with permission of the bishop of the place. The conditions are, in addition to freedom from attachment to sin: reception of the sacraments of penance and the Eucharist on or near the day; a visit to a parish church on the day, during which the Our Father and Creed are offered for the intentions of the pope.

Possession, Diabolical: The extraordinary state of a person who is tormented from within by evil spirits who exercise strong influence over his powers of mind and body.

Postulant: One of several names used to designate a candidate for membership in a religious institute during the period before novitiate.

Poverty: (1) The quality or state of being poor, in actual destitution and need, or being poor in spirit. In the latter sense, poverty means the state of mind and disposition of persons who regard material things in proper perspective as gifts of God for the support of life and its reasonable enrichment, and for the service of others in need. It means freedom from unreasonable attachment to material things as ends in themselves, even though they may be possessed in small or large measure. (2) One of the evangelical counsels professed as a public vow by members of an institute of consecrated life. It involves the voluntary renunciation of rights of ownership and of independent use and disposal of material goods; or, the right of independent use and disposal, but not of the radical right of ownership. Religious institutes provide their members with necessary and useful goods and services from common resources. The manner in which goods are received and/or handled by religious is determined by poverty of spirit and the rule and constitutions of their institute.

Pragmatism: Theory that the truth of ideas, concepts and values depends on their utility or capacity to serve a useful purpose rather than on their conformity with objective standards; also called utilitarianism.

Prayer: The raising of the mind and heart to God in adoration, thanksgiving, reparation and petition. Prayer, which is always mental because it involves thought and love of God, may be vocal, meditative, private and personal, social, and official. The official prayer of the Church as a worshipping community is called the liturgy.

Precepts: Commands or orders given to individuals or communities in particular cases; they establish law for concerned parties. Preceptive documents are issued by the pope, departments of the Roman Curia and other competent authority in the Church.

Presence of God: A devotional practice of increasing one's awareness of the presence and action of God in daily life.

Presumption: A violation of the theological virtue of hope, by which a person striving for salvation either relies too much on his own capabilities

or expects God to do things which he cannot do, in keeping with his divine attributes, or does not will to do, according to his divine plan. Presumption is the opposite of despair.

Preternatural Gifts: Exceptional gifts, beyond the exigencies and powers of human nature, enjoyed by Adam in the state of original justice: immunity from suffering and death, superior knowledge, integrity or perfect control of the passions. These gifts were lost as the result of original sin; their loss, however, implied no impairment of the integrity of human nature.

Pride: Unreasonable self-esteem; one of the seven capital sins.

Prie-Dieu: A French phrase, meaning pray God, designating a kneeler or bench suitable for kneeling while at prayer.

Priesthood of the Laity: Lay persons share in the priesthood of Christ in virtue of the sacraments of baptism and confirmation. They are not only joined with Christ for a life of union with him but are also deputed by him for participation in his mission, now carried on by the Church, of worship, teaching, witness and apostolic works. St. Peter called Christians "a royal priesthood" (1 Pt. 2:9) in this connection. St. Thomas Aquinas declared: "The sacramental characters (of baptism and confirmation) are nothing else than certain sharings of the priesthood of Christ, derived from Christ himself." The priesthood of the laity differs from the official ministerial priesthood of ordained priests and bishops — who have the power of holy orders for celebrating the Eucharist, administering the other sacraments, and providing pastoral care. The ministerial priesthood, by divine commission, serves the universal priesthood. (See Role of Sacraments.)

Primary Option: The life-choice of a person for or against God which shapes the basic orientation of moral conduct. A primary option for God does not preclude the possibility of serious sin.

Prior: A superior or an assistant to an abbot in a monastery.

Privilege: A favor, an exemption from the obligation of a law. Privileges of various kinds, with respect to ecclesiastical laws, are granted by the pope, departments of the Roman Curia and other competent authority in the Church.

Probabilism: A moral system for use in cases of conscience which involve the obligation of doubtful laws. There is a general principle that a doubtful law does not bind. Probabilism, therefore, teaches that it is permissible to follow an opinion favoring liberty, provided the opinion is certainly and solidly probable. Probabilism may not be invoked when there is question of: a certain law or the certain obligation of a law; the certain right of another party; the validity of an action; something which is necessary for salvation.

Pro-Cathedral: A church used as a cathedral.

Promoter of the Faith: An official of the Congregation for the Causes of Saints, whose role in beatification and canonization procedures is to establish beyond reasonable doubt the validity of evidence regarding the holiness of prospective saints and miracles attributed to their intercession.

Prophecies of St. Malachy: These so-called prophecies, listing the designations of 102 popes and 10 antipopes, bear the name they have because they have been falsely attributed to St. Malachy, bishop of Armagh, who died in 1148. Actually, they are forgeries by an unknown author and came to light only in the last decade of the 16th century. The first 75 prophecies cover the 65 popes and 10 antipopes from Celestine II (1143-1144) to Gregory XIV (1590-91), and are exact with respect to names, coats of arms, birthplaces, and other identifying characteristics. This portion of the work, far from being prophetic, is the result of historical knowledge or hindsight. The 37 designations following that of Gregory are vague, fanciful, and subject to wide interpretation. According to the prophecies, John Paul II, from the Labor of the Sun, will have only two successors before the end of the world.

Prophecy: (1) The communication of divine revelation by inspired intermediaries, called prophets, between God and his people. Old Testament prophecy was unique in its origin and because of its ethical and religious content, which included disclosure of the saving will of Yahweh for the people, moral censures and warnings of divine punishment because of sin and violations of the Law and Covenant, in the form of promises, admonitions, reproaches and threats. Although Moses and other earlier figures are called prophets, the period of prophecy is generally dated from the early years of the monarchy to about 100 years after the Babylonian Exile. From that time on the written Law and its interpreters supplanted the prophets as guides of the people. Old Testament prophets are cited in the New Testament, with awareness that God spoke through them and that some of their oracles were fulfilled in Christ. John the Baptist is the outstanding prophetic figure in the New Testament. Christ never claimed the title of prophet for himself, although some people thought he was one. There were prophets in the early Church, and St. Paul mentioned the charism of prophecy in 1 Cor. 14:1-5. Prophecy disappeared after New Testament times. Revelation is classified as the prophetic book of the New Testament. (2) In contemporary non-scriptural usage, the term is applied to the witness given by persons to the relevance of their beliefs in everyday life and action.

Province: (1) A territory comprising one archdiocese called the metropolitan see and one or more dioceses called suffragan sees. The head of the archdiocese, an archbishop, has metropolitan rights and responsibilities over the province. (2) A division of a religious order under the jurisdiction of a provincial superior.

Prudence: Practical wisdom and judgment regarding the choice and use of the best ways and means of doing good; one of the four cardinal virtues.

Punishment Due for Sin: The punishment which is a consequence of sin. It is of two kinds: (1) Eternal punishment is the punishment of hell, to which one becomes subject by the commission of mortal sin. Such punishment is remitted when mortal sin is forgiven. (2) Temporal punishment is a consequence of venial sin and/or forgiven mortal sin; it is not everlasting and may be remitted in this life by means of penance. Temporal punishment unremitted during this life is remitted by suffering in purgatory.

Purgatory: The state or condition in which those who have died in the state of grace, but with some attachment to sin, suffer for a time before they are admitted to the glory and happiness of heaven. In this state and period of passive suffering, they are purified of unrepented venial sins, satisfy the demands of divine justice for temporal punishment due for sins, and are thus converted to a state of worthiness of the beatific vision.

R

Racism: A theory which holds that any one or several of the different races of the human family are inherently superior or inferior to any one or several of the others. The teaching denies the essential unity of the human race, the equality and dignity of all men because of their common possession of the same human nature, and the participation of all men in the divine plan of redemption. It is radically opposed to the virtue of justice and the precept of love of neighbor. Differences of superiority and inferiority which do exist are the result of accidental factors operating in a wide variety of circumstances, and are in no way due to essential defects in any one or several of the branches of the one human race. The theory of racism, together with practices related to it, is incompatible with Christian doctrine.

Rash Judgment: Attributing faults to another without sufficient reason; a violation of the obligations of justice and charity.

Rationalism: A theory which makes the mind the measure and arbiter of all things, including religious truth. A product of the Enlightenment, it rejects the supernatural, divine revelation, and authoritative teaching by any church.

Recollection: Meditation, attitude of concentration or awareness of spiritual matters and things pertaining to salvation and the accomplishment of God's will.

Relativism: Theory which holds that all truth, including religious truth, is relative, i.e., not absolute, certain or unchanging; a product of agnosticism, indifferentism, and an unwarranted extension of the notion of truth in positive science. Relativism is based on the tenet that certain knowledge of any and all truth is impossible. Therefore, no religion, philosophy or science can be said to possess the real truth; consequently, all religions, philosophies and sciences may be considered to have as much or as little of truth as any of the others.

Relics: The physical remains and effects of saints, which are considered worthy of veneration inasmuch as they are representative of persons in glory with God. Catholic doctrine proscribes the view that relics are not worthy of veneration. In line with norms laid down by the Council of Trent and subsequent enactments, discipline concerning relics is subject to control by the Congregation for the Causes of Saints.

Religion: The adoration and service of God as expressed in divine worship and in daily life. Religion is concerned with all of the relations existing between God and man, and between man and man because of the central significance of God. Objectively considered, religion consists of a body of truth which is believed, a code of morality for the guidance of conduct, and a form of divine worship. Subjectively, it is a person's total response, theoretically and practically, to the demands of faith; it is living faith, personal engagement, self-commitment to God. Thus, by creed, code and cult, a person orders and directs his life in reference to God and, through what the love and service of God implies, to his fellow men and all things.

Reliquary: A vessel for the preservation and exposition of a relic; sometimes made like a small monstrance.

Reparation: The making of amends to God for sin committed; one of the four ends of prayer and the purpose of penance.

Rescript: A written reply by an ecclesiastical superior regarding a question or request; its provisions bind concerned parties only. Papal dispensations are issued in the form of rescripts.

Reserved Case: A sin or censure, absolution from which is reserved to religious superiors, bishops, the pope, or confessors having special faculties. Reservations are made because of the serious nature and social effects of certain sins and censures.

Restitution: An act of reparation for an injury done to another. The injury may be caused by taking and/or retaining what belongs to another or by damaging either the property or reputation of another. The intention of making restitution, usually in kind, is required as a condition for the forgiveness of sins of injustice, even though actual restitution is not possible.

Ring: In the Church a ring is worn as part of the insignia of bishops, abbots, et al.; by sisters to denote their consecration to God and the Church. The wedding ring symbolizes the love and union of husband and wife.

Ritual: A book of prayers and ceremonies used in the administration of the sacraments and other ceremonial functions. In the Roman Rite, the standard book of this kind is the Roman Ritual.

Rogito: The official notarial act or document testifying to the burial of a pope.

Rosary: A form of mental and vocal prayer centered on mysteries or events in the lives of Jesus and Mary. Its essential elements are meditation on the mysteries and the recitation of a number of decades of Hail Marys, each beginning with the Lord's Prayer. Introductory prayers may include the Apostles' Creed, an initial Our Father, three Hail Marys and a Glory be to the Father; each decade is customarily concluded with a Glory be to the Father; at the end, it is customary to say the Hail, Holy Queen and a prayer from the liturgy for the feast of the Blessed Virgin Mary of the Rosary. The **Mysteries of the Rosary,** which are the subject of meditation, are: (1) Joyful — the Annuncia-

tion to Mary that she was to be the Mother of Christ, her visit to Elizabeth, the birth of Jesus, the presentation of Jesus in the Temple, the finding of Jesus in the Temple. (2) Sorrowful — Christ's agony in the Garden of Gethsemani, scourging at the pillar, crowning with thorns, carrying of the Cross to Calvary, and crucifixion. (3) Glorious — the Resurrection and Ascension of Christ, the descent of the Holy Spirit upon the Apostles, Mary's Assumption into heaven and her crowning as Queen of angels and men. The complete Rosary, called the Dominican Rosary, consists of 15 decades. In customary practice, only five decades are usually said at one time. Rosary beads are used to aid in counting the prayers without distraction. The Rosary originated through the coalescence of popular devotions to Jesus and Mary from the 12th century onward. Its present form dates from about the 15th century. Carthusians contributed greatly toward its development; Dominicans have been its greatest promoters.

S

Sabbath: The seventh day of the week, observed by Jews and Sabbatarians as the day for rest and religious observance.

Sacramentary: One of the first liturgical books, containing the celebrant's part of the Mass and rites for administration of the sacraments. The earliest book of this kind, the Leonine Sacramentary, dates from the middle or end of the sixth century. The *Sacramentary* in current use is the same as the *Roman Missal.*

Sacrarium: A basin with a drain leading directly into the ground; standard equipment of a sacristy.

Sacred Heart, Enthronement: An acknowledgment of the sovereignty of Jesus Christ over the Christian family, expressed by the installation of an image or picture of the Sacred Heart in a place of honor in the home, accompanied by an act of consecration.

Sacred Heart, Promises: Twelve promises to persons having devotion to the Sacred Heart of Jesus, which were communicated by Christ to St. Margaret Mary Alacoque in a private revelation in 1675: (1) I will give them all the graces necessary in their state in life. (2) I will establish peace in their homes. (3) I will comfort them in all their afflictions. (4) I will be their secure refuge during life and, above all, in death. (5) I will bestow abundant blessing upon all their undertakings. (6) Sinners shall find in my Heart the source and the infinite ocean of mercy. (7) By devotion to my Heart tepid souls shall grow fervent. (8) Fervent souls shall quickly mount to high perfection. (9) I will bless every place where a picture of my Heart shall be set up and honored. (10) I will give to priests the gift of touching the most hardened hearts. (11) Those who promote this devotion shall have their names written in my Heart, never to be blotted out. (12) I will grant the grace of final penitence to those who communicate (receive Holy Communion) on the first Friday of nine consecutive months.

Sacrilege: Violation of and irreverence toward a

person, place or thing that is sacred because of public dedication to God; a sin against the virtue of religion. Personal sacrilege is violence of some kind against a cleric or religious, or a violation of chastity with a cleric or religious. Local sacrilege is the desecration of sacred places. Real sacrilege is irreverence with respect to sacred things, such as the sacraments and sacred vessels.

Sacristy: A utility room where vestments, church furnishings and sacred vessels are kept and where the clergy vest for sacred functions.

Sadducees: The predominantly priestly party among the Jews in the time of Christ, noted for extreme conservatism, acceptance only of the Law of Moses, and rejection of the traditions of the elders. Their opposite numbers were the Pharisees.

Saints, Cult of: The veneration, called dulia, of holy persons who have died and are in glory with God in heaven; it includes honoring them and petitioning them for their intercession with God. Liturgical veneration is given only to saints officially recognized by the Church; private veneration may be given to anyone thought to be in heaven. The veneration of saints is essentially different from the adoration given to God alone; by its very nature, however, it terminates in the worship of God. According to the Second Vatican Council's *Dogmatic Constitution on the Church* (No. 50): "It is supremely fitting . . . that we love those friends and fellow heirs of Jesus Christ, who are also our brothers and extraordinary benefactors, that we render due thanks to God for them and 'suppliantly invoke them and have recourse to their prayers, their power and help in obtaining benefits from God through his Son, Jesus Christ, our Lord, who is our sole Redeemer and Savior.' For by its very nature every genuine testimony of love which we show to those in heaven tends toward and terminates in Christ, who is the 'crown of all saints.' Through him it tends toward and terminates in God, who is wonderful in his saints and is magnified in them."

Salvation: The liberation of persons from sin and its effects, reconciliation with God in and through Christ, the attainment of union with God forever in the glory of heaven as the supreme purpose of life and as the God-given reward for fulfillment of his will on earth. Salvation-in-process begins and continues in this life through union with Christ in faith professed and in action; its final term is union with God and the whole community of the saved in the ultimate perfection of God's kingdom. The Church teaches that: God wills the salvation of all men; men are saved in and through Christ; membership in the Church established by Christ, known and understood as the community of salvation, is necessary for salvation; men with this knowledge and understanding who deliberately reject this Church, cannot be saved. The Catholic Church is the Church founded by Christ. (See below, Salvation outside the Church.)

Salvation History: The facts and the record of God's relations with men, in the past, present and future, for the purpose of leading them to live in accordance with his will for the eventual attainment after death of salvation, or everlasting happiness with him in heaven. The essentials of salvation history are: God's love for all men and will for their salvation; his intervention and action in the world to express this love and bring about their salvation; the revelation he made of himself and the covenant he established with the Israelites in the Old Testament; the perfecting of this revelation and the new covenant of grace through Christ in the New Testament; the continuing action-for-salvation carried on in and through the Mystical Body of Christ, the Church; the communication of saving grace to men through the merits of Christ and the operations of the Holy Spirit in the here-and-now circumstances of daily life and with the cooperation of men themselves.

Salvation outside the Church: The Second Vatican Council covered this subject summarily in the following manner: "Those also can attain to everlasting salvation who through no fault of their own do not know the Gospel of Christ or his Church, yet sincerely seek God and, moved by grace, strive by their deeds to do his will as it is known to them through the dictates of conscience. Nor does divine Providence deny the help necessary for salvation to those who, without blame on their part, have not yet arrived at an explicit knowledge of God, but who strive to live a good life, thanks to his grace. Whatever good or truth is found among them is looked upon by the Church as a preparation for the Gospel. She regards such qualities as given by him who enlightens all men so that they may finally have life" *(Dogmatic Constitution on the Church,* No. 16).

Satanism: Worship of the devil, a blasphemous inversion of the order of worship which is due to God alone.

Scandal: Conduct which is the occasion of sin to another person.

Scapular: (1) A part of the habit of some religious orders like the Benedictines and Dominicans; a nearly shoulder-wide strip of cloth worn over the tunic and reaching almost to the feet in front and behind. Originally a kind of apron, it came to symbolize the cross and yoke of Christ. (2) Scapulars worn by lay persons as a sign of association with religious orders and for devotional purposes are an adaptation of monastic scapulars. Approved by the Church as sacramentals, they consist of two small squares of woolen cloth joined by strings and are worn about the neck. They are given for wearing in a ceremony of investiture or enrollment. There are nearly 20 scapulars for devotional use: the five principal ones are generally understood to include those of Our Lady of Mt. Carmel (the brown Carmelite Scapular), the Holy Trinity, Our Lady of the Seven Dolors, the Passion, the Immaculate Conception.

Scapular Medal: A medallion with a representation of the Sacred Heart on one side and of the Blessed Virgin Mary on the other. Authorized by St. Pius X in 1910, it may be worn or carried in place of a scapular by persons already invested with a scapular.

Scapular Promise: According to a legend of the Carmelite Order, the Blessed Virgin Mary appeared to St. Simon Stock in 1251 at Cambridge and declared that wearers of the brown Carmelite Scapular would be saved from hell and taken to heaven by her on the first Saturday after death. The validity of the legend has never been the subject of official decision by the Church. Essentially, it expresses belief in the intercession of Mary and the efficacy of sacramentals in the context of truly Christian life.

Schism: Derived from a Greek word meaning separation, the term designates formal and obstinate refusal by a baptized person, called a *schismatic*, to be in communion with the pope and the Church. The canonical penalty is excommunication. One of the most disastrous schisms in history resulted in the definitive separation of the Church in the East from union with Rome about 1054.

Scholasticism: The term usually applied to the Catholic theology and philosophy which developed in the Middle Ages.

Scribes: Hebrew intellectuals noted for their knowledge of the Law of Moses, influential from the time of the Exile to about 70 A.D. Many of them were Pharisees. They were the antecedents of rabbis and their traditions, as well as those of the Pharisees, had a lasting influence on Judaism following the destruction of Jerusalem in 70 A.D.

Scruple: A morbid, unreasonable fear and anxiety that one's actions are sinful when they are not, or more seriously sinful than they actually are. Compulsive scrupulosity is quite different from the transient scrupulosity of persons of tender or highly sensitive conscience, or of persons with faulty moral judgment.

Seal of Confession: The obligation of secrecy which must be observed regarding knowledge of things learned in connection with the confession of sin in the sacrament of penance. The seal covers matters whose revelation would make the sacrament burdensome. Confessors are prohibited, under penalty of excommunication, from making any direct revelation of confessional matter; this prohibition holds, outside of confession, even with respect to the person who made the confession unless the person releases the priest from the obligation. Persons other than confessors are obliged to maintain secrecy, but not under penalty of excommunication. General, non-specific discussion of confessional matter does not violate the seal.

Secularism: A school of thought, a spirit and manner of action which ignores and/or repudiates the validity or influence of supernatural religion with respect to individual and social life. In describing secularism in their annual statement in 1947, the bishops of the United States said in part: ". . . There are many men — and their number is daily increasing — who in practice live their lives without recognizing that this is God's world. For the most part they do not deny God. On formal occasions they may even mention his name. Not all of them would subscribe to the statement that all moral values derive from merely human conventions. But they fail to bring an awareness of their responsibility to God into their thought and action

as individuals and members of society. This, in essence, is what we mean by secularism."

See: Another name for diocese or archdiocese.

Seminary: A house of study and formation for men, called seminarians, preparing for the priesthood. Traditional seminaries date from the Council of Trent in the middle of the 16th century; before that time, candidates for the priesthood were variously trained in monastic schools, universities under church auspices, and in less formal ways. At the present time, seminaries are undergoing considerable change for the improvement of academic and formation programs and procedures.

Sermon on the Mount: A compilation of sayings of Our Lord in the form of an extended discourse in Matthew's Gospel (5:1 to 7:27) and, in a shorter discourse, in Luke (6:17-49). The passage in Matthew, called the "Constitution of the New Law," summarizes the living spirit of believers in Christ and members of the kingdom of God. Beginning with the Beatitudes and including the Lord's Prayer, it covers the perfect justice of the New Law, the fulfillment of the Old Law in the New Law of Christ, and the integrity of internal attitude and external conduct with respect to love of God and neighbor, justice, chastity, truth, trust and confidence in God.

Seven Last Words of Christ: Words of Christ on the Cross. (1) "Father, forgive them; for they do not know what they are doing." (2) To the penitent thief: "I assure you: today you will be with me in Paradise." (3) To Mary and his Apostle John: "Woman, there is your son . . . There is your mother." (4) "My God, my God, why have you forsaken me?" (5) "I am thirsty." (6) "Now it is finished." (7) "Father, into your hands I commend my spirit."

Shrine, Crowned: A shrine approved by the Holy See as a place of pilgrimage. The approval permits public devotion at the shrine and implies that at least one miracle has resulted from devotion at the shrine. Among the best known crowned shrines are those of the Virgin Mary at Lourdes and Fatima. Shrines with statues crowned by Pope John Paul in 1985 in South America were those of Our Lady of Coromoto, patroness of Venezuela, in Caracas, and Our Lady of Carmen of Paucartambo in Cuzco, Peru.

Shroud of Turin: A strip of brownish linen cloth, 14 feet, three inches in length and three feet, seven inches in width, bearing the front and back imprint of a human body. A tradition dating from the seventh century, which has not been verified beyond doubt, claims that the shroud is the fine linen in which the body of Christ was wrapped for burial. The early history of the shroud is obscure. It was enshrined at Lirey, France, in 1354 and was transferred in 1578 to Turin, Italy, where it has been kept in the cathedral down to the present time. Scientific investigation, which began in 1898, seems to indicate that the markings on the shroud are those of a human body. The shroud, for the first time since 1933, was placed on public view from Aug. 27 to Oct. 8, 1978, and was seen by an estimated 3.3 million people. Scientists conducted intensive studies of it for several days after the end of public viewing. The shroud, which had been the possession of the House of Savoy, was willed to Pope John Paul II in 1983.

Sick Calls: When a person is confined at home by illness or other cause and is unable to go to church for reception of the sacraments, a parish priest should be informed and arrangements made for him to visit the person at home. Such visitations are common in pastoral practice, both for special needs and for providing persons with regular opportunities for receiving the sacraments. If a priest cannot make the visitation, arrangements can be made for a deacon or Eucharistic minister to bring Holy Communion to the homebound or bedridden person.

Sign of the Cross: A sign, ceremonial gesture or movement in the form of a cross by which a person confesses faith in the Holy Trinity and Christ, and intercedes for the blessing of himself, other persons, and things. In Roman-Rite practice, a person making the sign touches the fingers of the right hand to his forehead, below the breast, left shoulder and right shoulder while saying: "In the name of the Father, and of the Son, and of the Holy Spirit." The sign is also made with the thumb on the forehead, the lips, and the breast. For the blessing of persons and objects, a large sign of the cross is made by movement of the right hand. In Eastern-Rite practice, the sign is made with the thumb and first two fingers of the right hand joined together and touching the forehead, below the breast, the right shoulder and the left shoulder; the formula generally used is the doxology, "O Holy God, O Holy Strong One, O Immortal One." The Eastern manner of making the sign was general until the first half of the 13th century; by the 17th century, Western practice involved the whole right hand and the reversal of direction from shoulder to shoulder.

Signs of the Times: Contemporary events, trends and features in culture and society, the needs and aspirations of people, all the factors that form the context in and through which the Church has to carry on its saving mission. The Second Vatican Council spoke on numerous occasions about these signs and the relationship between them and a kind of manifestation of God's will, positive or negative, and about subjecting them to judgment and action corresponding to the demands of divine revelation through Scripture, Christ, and the experience, tradition and teaching authority of the Church.

Simony: The deliberate intention and act of selling and/or buying spiritual goods or material things so connected with the spiritual that they cannot be separated therefrom; a violation of the virtue of religion, and a sacrilege, because it wrongfully puts a material price on spiritual things, which cannot be either sold or bought. In church law, actual sale or purchase is subject to censure in some cases. The term is derived from the name of Simon Magus, who attempted to buy from Sts. Peter and John the power to confirm people in the Holy Spirit (Acts 8:4-24).

Sin: (1) Actual sin is rejection of God man-ifested by free and deliberate violation of his law by thought, word or action. (a) Mortal sin — involving serious matter, sufficient reflection and full consent — results in total alienation from God, making a person dead to sanctifying grace, incapable of performing meritorious supernatural acts and subject to everlasting punishment. (b) Venial sin — involving less serious matter, reflection and consent — does not have such serious consequences. (2) Original sin is the sin of Adam, with consequences for all men. (See separate entry.)

Sins against the Holy Spirit: Despair of salvation, presumption of God's mercy, impugning the known truths of faith, envy at another's spiritual good, obstinacy in sin, final impenitence. Those guilty of such sins stubbornly resist the influence of grace and, as long as they do so, cannot be forgiven.

Sins, Occasions of: Circumstances (persons, places, things, etc.) which easily lead to sin. There is an obligation to avoid voluntary proximate occasions of sin, and to take precautions against the dangers of unavoidable occasions.

Sins That Cry to Heaven for Vengeance: Willful murder, sins against nature, oppression of the poor, widows and orphans, defrauding laborers of their wages.

Sister: Any woman religious, in popular speech; strictly, the title applies only to women Religious belonging to institutes whose members never professed solemn vows. Most of the institutes whose members are properly called Sisters were established during and since the 19th century. Women Religious with solemn vows, or belonging to institutes whose members formerly professed solemn vows, are properly called nuns.

Sisterhood: A generic term referring to the whole institution of the life of women religious in the Church, or to a particular institute of women religious.

Situation Ethics: A subjective, individualistic ethical theory which denies the binding force of ethical principles as universal laws and preceptive norms of moral conduct, and proposes that morality is determined only by situational conditions and considerations and the intention of the person. In an instruction issued on the subject in May, 1956, the Congregation for the Holy Office said: "It ignores the principles of objective ethics. This 'New Morality,' it is claimed, is not only the equal of objective morality, but is superior to it. The authors who follow this system state that the ultimate determining norm for activity is not the objective order as determined by the natural law and known with certainty from this law. It is instead some internal judgment and illumination of the mind of every individual by which the mind comes to know what is to be done in a concrete situation. This ultimate decision of man is, therefore, not the application of the objective law to a particular case after the particular circumstances of a 'situation' have been considered and weighed according to the rules of prudence, as the more important authors of objective ethics teach; but it is, according to them, immediate, internal illumination and judgment. With regard to its objective truth and correctness, this judgment, at least in many things, is not ultimately measured, is not to be measured or is not measurable by any objective norm found outside man and independent of his subjective persuasion, but it is fully sufficient in itself.... Much that is stated in this system of 'Situation Ethics' is contrary to the truth of reality and to the dictate of sound reason. It gives evidence of relativism and modernism, and deviates far from the Catholic teaching handed down through the ages."

Slander: Attributing to a person faults which he does not have; a violation of the obligations of justice and charity, for which restitution is due.

Sloth: One of the seven capital sins; spiritual laziness, involving distaste and disgust for spiritual things; spiritual boredom, which saps the vigor of spiritual life. Physical laziness is a counterpart of spiritual sloth.

Sorcery: A kind of black magic in which evil is invoked by means of diabolical intervention; a violation of the virtue of religion.

Soteriology: The division of theology which treats of the mission and work of Christ as Redeemer.

Species, Sacred: The appearances of bread and wine (color, taste, smell, etc.) which remain after the substance has been changed at the Consecration of the Mass into the Body and Blood of Christ. (See Transubstantiation.)

Spiritism: Attempts to communicate with spirits and departed souls by means of seances, table tapping, ouija boards, and other methods; a violation of the virtue of religion. Spiritualistic practices are noted for fakery.

Spiritual Works of Mercy: Works of spiritual assistance, motivated by love of God and neighbor, to persons in need: counseling the doubtful, instructing the ignorant, admonishing sinners, comforting the afflicted, forgiving offenses, bearing wrongs patiently, praying for the living and the dead.

Stational Churches, Days: Churches, especially in Rome, where the clergy and lay people were accustomed to gather with their bishop on certain days for the celebration of the liturgy. The 25 early titular or parish churches of Rome, plus other churches, each had their turn as the site of divine worship in practices which may have started in the third century. The observances were rather well developed toward the latter part of the fourth century, and by the fifth they included a Mass concelebrated by the pope and attendant priests. On some occasions, the stational liturgy was preceded by a procession from another church called a collecta. There were 42 Roman stational churches in the eighth century, and 89 stational services were scheduled annually in connection with the liturgical seasons. Stational observances fell into disuse toward the end of the Middle Ages. Some revival was begun by John XXIII in 1959 and continued by

Stations of the Cross: A series of meditations on the sufferings of Christ: his condemnation to death and taking up of the Cross; the first fall on the way

to Calvary; meeting his Mother; being assisted by Simon of Cyrene, and by Veronica who wiped his face; the second fall; meeting the women of Jerusalem; the third fall; being stripped and nailed to the Cross; his death; the removal of his body from the Cross and his burial. Depictions of these scenes are mounted in most churches, chapels and in some other places, beneath small crosses. A person making the Way of the Cross passes before these Stations, or stopping points, pausing at each for meditation. If the Stations are made by a group of people, only the leader has to pass from Station to Station. Prayer for the intentions of the pope is required for gaining the indulgence granted for the Stations. Those unable to make the Stations in the ordinary manner, because they are impeded from visiting a church or other place where the Stations are, can still practice the devotion by meditating on the sufferings of Christ; praying the Our Father, Hail Mary and Glory for each Station and five times in commemoration of the wounds of Christ; and praying for the intentions of the pope. This practice has involved the use of a Stations Crucifix. The Stations originated, remotely, from the practice of Holy Land pilgrims who visited the actual scenes of incidents in the Passion of Christ. Representations elsewhere of at least some of these scenes were known as early as the fifth century. Later, the Stations evolved in connection with and as a consequence of strong devotion to the Passion in the 12th and 13th centuries. Franciscans, who were given custody of the Holy Places in 1342, promoted the devotion widely; one of them, St. Leonard of Port Maurice, became known as the greatest preacher of the Way of the Cross in the 18th century. The general features of the devotion were fixed by Clement XII in 1731.

Statutes: Virtually the same as decrees (see separate entry), they almost always designate laws of a particular council or synod rather than pontifical laws.

Stigmata: Marks of the wounds suffered by Christ in his crucifixion, in hands and feet by nails, and side by the piercing of a lance. Some persons, called stigmatists, have been reported as recipients or sufferers of marks like these. The Church, however, has never issued any infallible declaration about their possession by anyone, even in the case of St. Francis of Assisi whose stigmata seem to be the best substantiated and may be commemorated in the Roman-Rite liturgy. Ninety percent of some 300 reputed stigmatists have been women. Judgment regarding the presence, significance, and manner of causation of stigmata would depend, among other things, on irrefutable experimental evidence.

Stipend, Mass: An offering given to a priest for applying the fruits of the Mass according to the intention of the donor. The offering is a contribution to the support of the priest. The disposition of the fruits of the sacrifice, in line with doctrine concerning the Mass in particular and prayer in general, is subject to the will of God. In the early Christian centuries, when Mass was not offered for the intentions of particular persons, the participants made offerings of bread and wine for the sacrifice and their own Holy Communion, and of other things useful for the support of the clergy and the poor. Some offerings may have been made as early as the fourth century for the celebration of Mass for particular intentions, and there are indications of the existence of this practice from the sixth century when private Masses began to be offered. The earliest certain proof of stipend practice, however, dates from the eighth century. By the 11th century, along with private Mass, it was established custom.

Stole Fee: An offering given on certain occasions; e.g., at a baptism, wedding, funeral, for the support of the clergy who administer the sacraments and perform other sacred rites.

Stoup: A vessel used to contain holy water.

Suffragan See: Any diocese, except the archdiocese, within a province.

Suicide: The taking of one's own life; a violation of God's dominion over human life. Ecclesiastical burial is denied to persons who deliberately commit suicide while in full possession of their faculties; it is permitted in cases of doubt.

Supererogation: Good and virtuous actions which go beyond the obligations of duty and the requirements enjoined by God's law as necessary for salvation. Examples of these works are the profession and observance of the evangelical counsels of poverty, chastity, and obedience, and efforts to practice charity to the highest degree.

Supernatural: Above the natural; that which exceeds and is not due or owed to the essence, exigencies, requirements, powers and merits of created nature. While man has no claim on supernatural things and does not need them in order to exist and act on a natural level, he does need them in order to exist and act in the higher order or economy of grace established by God for his salvation. God has freely given to man certain things which are beyond the powers and rights of his human nature. Examples of the supernatural are: grace, a kind of participation by man in the divine life, by which man becomes capable of performing acts meritorious for salvation; divine revelation by which God manifests himself to man and makes known truth that is inaccessible to human reason alone; faith, by which man believes divine truth because of the authority of God who reveals it through Sacred Scripture and tradition and the teaching of his Church.

Superstition: A violation of the virtue of religion, by which God is worshipped in an unworthy manner or creatures are given honor which belongs to God alone. False, vain, or futile worship involves elements which are incompatible with the honor and respect due to God, such as error, deception, and bizarre practices. Examples are: false and exaggerated devotions, chain prayers and allegedly unfailing prayers, the mixing of unbecoming practices in worship. The second kind of superstition attributes to persons and things powers and honor which belong to God alone. Examples are: idolatry, divination, magic, spiritism, necromancy.

Suspension: A censure by which a cleric is forbidden to exercise some or all of his powers of orders and jurisdiction, or to accept the financial support of his benefices.

Swearing: Taking an oath; calling upon God to witness the truth of a statement; a legitimate thing to do for serious reasons and under proper circumstances, as in a court of law. To swear without sufficient reason is to dishonor God's name; to swear falsely in a court of law is perjury.

Swedenborgianism: A doctrine developed in and from the writings of Emmanuel Swedenborg (1688-1772), who claimed that during a number of visions he had in 1745 Christ taught him the spiritual sense of Sacred Scripture and commissioned him to communicate it to others. He held that, just as Christianity succeeded Judaism, so his teaching supplemented Christianity. He rejected belief in the Trinity, original sin, the Resurrection, and all the sacraments except baptism and the Eucharist. His followers are members of the Church of the New Jerusalem or of the New Church.

Syllabus, The: (1) When not qualified, the term refers to the list of 80 errors accompanying Pope Pius IX's encyclical *Quanta Cura,* issued in 1864. (2) The *Syllabus* of St. Pius X in the decree *Lamentabili,* issued by the Holy Office July 4, 1907, condemning 65 heretical propositions of modernism. This schedule of errors was followed shortly by that pope's encyclical *Pascendi,* the principal ecclesiastical document against modernism, issued Sept. 8, 1907.

Synod, Diocesan: Meeting of representative persons of a diocese — priests, religious, lay persons — with the bishop, called by him for the purpose of considering and taking action on matters affecting the life and mission of the Church in the diocese. Persons taking part in a synod have consultative status; the bishop alone is the legislator, with power to authorize synodal decrees. According to canon law, every diocese should have a synod every 10 years.

T

Te Deum: The opening Latin words, Thee, God, of a hymn of praise and thanksgiving prescribed for use in the Office of Readings of the Liturgy of the Hours on many Sundays, solemnities and feasts.

Temperance: Moderation, one of the four cardinal virtues.

Temptation: Any enticement to sin, from any source: the strivings of one's own faculties, the action of the devil, other persons, circumstances of life, etc. Temptation itself is not sin. Temptation can be avoided and overcome with the use of prudence and the help of grace.

Thanksgiving: An expression of gratitude to God for his goodness and the blessings he grants; one of the four ends of prayer.

Theism: A philosophy which admits the existence of God and the possibility of divine revelation; it is generally monotheistic and acknowledges God as transcendent and also active in the world. Because it is a philosophy rather than a system of theology derived from revelation, it does not include specifically Christian doctrines, like those concerning the Trinity, the Incarnation and Redemption.

Theological Virtues: The virtues which have God for their direct object: faith, or belief in God's infallible teaching; hope, or confidence in divine assistance; charity, or love of God. They are given to a person with grace in the first instance, through baptism and incorporation in Christ.

Theology: Knowledge of God and religion, deriving from and based on the data of divine Revelation, organized and systematized according to some kind of scientific method. It involves systematic study and presentation of the truths of divine Revelation in Sacred Scripture, tradition, and the teaching of the Church. The Second Vatican Council made the following declaration about theology and its relation to divine Revelation: "Sacred theology rests on the written word of God, together with sacred tradition, as its primary and perpetual foundation. By scrutinizing in the light of faith all truth stored up in the mystery of Christ, theology is most powerfully strengthened and constantly rejuvenated by that word. For the sacred Scriptures contain the word of God and, since they are inspired, really are the word of God; and so the study of the sacred page is, as it were, the soul of sacred theology" *(Constitution on Revelation.* No. 24). Theology has been divided under various subject headings. Some of the major fields have been: dogma (systematic theology), moral, pastoral, ascetics (the practice of virtue and means of attaining holiness and perfection), mysticism (higher states of religious experience). Other subject headings include ecumenism (Christian unity, interfaith relations), ecclesiology (the nature and constitution of the Church), Mariology (doctrine concerning the Blessed Virgin Mary), the sacraments, etc.

Tithing: Contribution of a portion of one's income, originally one-tenth, for purposes of religion and charity. The practice is mentioned 46 times in the Bible. In early Christian times, tithing was adopted in continuance of Old Testament practices of the Jewish people, and the earliest positive church legislation on the subject was enacted in 567. Catholics are bound in conscience to contribute to the support of their church, but the manner in which they do so is not fixed by law. Tithing, which amounts to a pledged contribution of a portion of one's income, has aroused new attention in recent years in the United States.

Titular Sees: Dioceses where the Church once flourished but which later were overrun by pagans or Moslems and now exist only in name or title. Bishops without a territorial or residential diocese of their own; e.g., auxiliary bishops, are given titular sees.

Transfinalization, Transignification: Terms coined to express the sign value of consecrated bread and wine with respect to the presence and action of Christ in the Eucharistic sacrifice and the spiritually vivifying purpose of the Eucharistic banquet in Holy Communion. The theory behind the terms has strong undertones of existential and "sign" philosophy, and has been criticized for its openness to interpretations at variance with the doctrine of transubstantiation and the abiding presence of Christ under the appearances of bread and wine after the sacrifice of the Mass and Communion have been completed. The terms, if used as substitutes for transubstantiation, are unacceptable; if they presuppose transubstantiation, they are acceptable as clarifications of its meaning.

Transubstantiation: "The way Christ is made present in this sacrament (Holy Eucharist) is none other than by the change of the whole substance of the bread into his Body, and of the whole substance of the wine into his Blood (in the Consecration at Mass) . . . this unique and wonderful change the Catholic Church rightly calls transubstantiation" (encyclical *Mysterium Fidei* of Paul VI, Sept. 3, 1965). The first official use of the term was made by the Fourth Council of the Lateran in 1215. Authoritative teaching on the subject was issued by the Council of Trent.

Treasury of the Church: The superabundant merits of Christ and the saints from which the Church draws to confer spiritual benefits, such as indulgences.

Triduum: A three-day series of public or private devotions.

U-Z

Usury: Excessive interest charged for the loan and use of money; a violation of justice.

Veronica: A word resulting from the combination of a Latin word for true, *vera,* and a Greek word for image, *eikon,* designating a likeness of the face of Christ or the name of a woman said to have given him a cloth on which he caused an imprint of his face to appear. The veneration at Rome of a likeness depicted on cloth dates from about the end of the 10th century; it figured in a popular devotion during the Middle Ages, and in the Holy Face devotion practiced since the 19th century. A faint, indiscernible likeness said to be of this kind is preserved in St. Peter's Basilica. The origin of the likeness is uncertain, and the identity of the woman is unknown. Before the 14th century, there were no known artistic representations of an incident concerning a woman who wiped the face of Christ with a piece of cloth while He was carrying the Cross to Calvary.

Viaticum: Holy Communion given to those in danger of death. The word, derived from Latin, means provision for a journey through death to life hereafter.

Vicar General: A priest or bishop appointed by the bishop of a diocese to serve as his deputy, with ordinary executive power, in the administration of the diocese.

Virginity: Observance of perpetual sexual abstinence. The state of virginity, which is embraced for the love of God by religious with a public vow or by others with a private vow, was singled out for high praise by Christ (Mt. 19:10-12) and has always been so regarded by the Church. In the encyclical *Sacra Virginitas,* Pius XII stated: "Holy virginity and that perfect chastity which is consecrated to the service of God is without doubt among the most perfect treasures which the founder of the Church has left in heritage to the society which he established." Paul VI approved in 1970 a rite in which women can consecrate their virginity "to Christ and their brethren" without becoming members of a religious institute. The *Ordo Consecrationis Virginum*, a revision of a rite promulgated by Clement VII in 1596, is traceable to the Roman liturgy of about 500.

Virtue: A habit or established capability for performing good actions. Virtues are *natural* (acquired and increased by repeating good acts) and/or *supernatural* (given with grace by God).

Vocation: A call to a way of life. Generally, the term applies to the common call of all men, from God, to holiness and salvation. Specifically, it refers to particular states of life, each called a vocation, in which response is made to this universal call; viz., marriage, the religious life and/or priesthood, the single state freely chosen or accepted for the accomplishment of God's will. The term also applies to the various occupations in which persons make a living. The Church supports the freedom of each individual in choosing a particular vocation, and reserves the right to pass on the acceptability of candidates for the priesthood and religious life. Signs or indicators of particular vocations are many, including a person's talents and interests, circumstances and obligations, invitations of grace and willingness to respond thereto.

Vow: A promise made to God with sufficient knowledge and freedom, which has as its object a moral good that is possible and better than its voluntary omission. A person who professes a vow binds himself or herself by the virtue of religion to fulfill the promise. The best known examples of vows are those of poverty, chastity and obedience professed by religious (see Evangelical Counsels, individual entries). Public vows are made before a competent person, acting as an agent of the Church, who accepts the profession in the name of the Church, thereby giving public recognition to the person's dedication and consecration to God and divine worship. Vows of this kind are either solemn, rendering all contrary acts invalid as well as unlawful; or simple, rendering contrary acts unlawful. Solemn vows are for life; simple vows are for a definite period of time or for life. Vows professed without public recognition by the Church are called private vows. The Church, which has authority to accept and give public recognition to vows, also has authority to dispense persons from their obligations for serious reasons.

Week of Prayer for Christian Unity: Eight days of prayer, from Jan. 18 to 25, for the union of all men in the Church established by Christ. On the initiative of Father Paul James Francis, S.A., of Graymoor, N.Y., it originated in 1908 as the Chair of Unity Octave. In recent years, its observance on an interfaith basis has increased greatly.

Witness, Christian: Practical testimony or evidence given by Christians of their faith in all circumstances of life — by prayer and general conduct, through good example and good works, etc.; being and acting in accordance with Christian belief; actual practice of the Christian faith.

MARRIAGE ENCOUNTER

Marriage Encounter originated in Spain through the efforts of Father Gabriel Calvo who worked out its principal features between the early 1950s and 1962 with the collaboration of Diego and Fina Bartoneo and other parties interested in ministry to married couples. The first encounter was held with 28 couples in 1962 in Barcelona. Five years later the first encounter in the U.S. was conducted in conjunction with a convention of the Christian Family Movement at Notre Dame University. Marriage Encounter caught on from this beginning and went nationwide in 1969.

Marriage Encounter brings couples together for a weekend program of events directed by a team of several couples and a priest, for the purpose of developing their abilities to communicate with each other in their life together as husband and wife. This purpose is served by direction in techniques given by the team and by private dialogue of each couple.

Commentators insist that Marriage Encounter is not for troubled marriages and is not an exercise in group dynamics. Neither is it a retreat, although it has potential for spiritual development.

National Marriage Encounter of the U.S. follows the program initiated by Father Calvo. Deeply rooted in Roman Catholic tradition, it is open to members of other faiths in accordance with teachings of the Second Vatican Council.

The address of National Marriage Encounter is 4704 Jamerson Pl., Orlando, Fla. 32807.

The identifying logo or emblem of National Marriage Encounter consists of two wedding bands intertwined with the Greek letters Chi-Rho.

Worldwide Marriage Encounter is a weekend experience for married couples, priests and religious. The mission of the movement is renewal of the sacrament of matrimony in and for the sake of the Church; its intention is to join in the mission of the Church to change the world.

The movement was developed by Father Charles Gallagher and several couples after they experienced a weekend of events conducted under the leadership of Father Calvo at a conference of the Christian Family Movement at the University of Notre Dame in 1967. Since then, 12 other faith expressions of the movement have affiliated with WME.

The national office is located at 1025 W. 3rd Ave., Columbus, O. 43212.

Catholic Engaged Encounter is designed to prepare couples for marriage by focusing attention on its sacramental aspects and by increasing their potential for communication with each other. With appropriate modifications, it follows the pattern of the Marriage Encounter weekend and subsequent practice of dialogue.

Since 1975, Catholic Engaged Encounter has given new direction to marriage preparation programs in many dioceses of the United States. In 1977, it was incorporated as a national organization in the State of New Jersey.

(Principal sources for statistics: *Statistical Yearbook of the Church, 1983* (the most recent edition available at press time); *Annuario Pontificio, 1986.* Figures are as of Jan. 1, 1984, or Jan. 1 of the year indicated. For 1986 events, see Index entries for individual countries.)

Abbreviation code: archd. — archdiocese; dioc. — diocese; ap. ex. — apostolic exarchate; prel. — prelature; abb. — abbacy; v.a. — vicariate apostolic; p.a. — prefecture apostolic; a.a. — apostolic administration; mil. vic. — military vicariate; card. — cardinal; abp. — archbishops; nat. — native; bp. — bishops (diocesan and titular); priests (dioc. — diocesan or secular priests; rel. — those belonging to religious orders); p.d. — permanent deacons; sem. — major seminarians, diocesan and religious; bros. — brothers; srs. — sisters; bap. — baptisms; Caths. — Catholic population; tot. pop. — total population.

Afghanistan: People's Republic in south-central Asia; capital, Kabul. Christianity antedated Moslem conquest in the seventh century but was overcome by it. All inhabitants are subject to the law of Islam. Christian missionaries are prohibited. Population (est.), 15,540,000.

Albania: Communist people's republic in the Balkans, bordering the Adriatic Sea; capital, Tirana. Christianity was introduced before the middle of the fourth century. The Byzantine-Rite Church broke from unity with Rome following the schism of 1054. A large percentage of the population was forcibly Islamized following the invasion (15th century) and long centuries of occupation by the Ottoman Turks. At the time of the communist take-over in 1945, an estimated 68 per cent of the population was Moslem; 19 per cent, Orthodox and 13 per cent, Roman Catholic. The Catholic Church prevailed in the north. It fell victim, as did all religions, to systematic persecution by the government: non-Albanian missionaries were expelled; death, prison sentences and other repressive measures were enacted against church personnel and laity; Catholic schools and churches were closed and used for other purposes, and lines of communication with the Holy See were cut off. In 1967, the government, declaring it had eliminated all religion in the country, proclaimed itself the first atheist state in the world. Despite this, there are reports of a clandestine Catholic community in the country.

Archd., 2; dioc., 3; abb., 1; a.a. 1; bp., 3 (impeded). Tot. pop. (1982 est.), 2,800,000.

Algeria: Republic in northwest Africa: capital, Algiers. Christianity, introduced at an early date, succumbed to Vandal devastation in the fifth century and Moslem conquest in 709, but survived for centuries in small communities into the 12th century. Missionary work was unsuccessful except in service to traders, military personnel and captives along the coast. Church organization was established after the French gained control of the territory in the 1830s. A large number of Catholics were among the estimated million Europeans who left the country after it secured independence from France July 5, 1962. Islam is the state religion. Algeria maintains diplomatic relations with Vatican City.

Archd., 1; dioc., 3; card., 1; abp., 1; bp., 3 parishes, 82; priests, 179 (77 dioc., 102 rel.); p.d., 3; sem. 2; bros., 21; srs., 464; bap., 47; Caths., 62,710 (.3%); tot. pop., 21,000,000. (1985)

Andorra: Autonomous principality in the Pyrenees, under the rule of co-princes — the French head of state and the bishop of Urgel, Spain; capital, Andorra la Vella. Christianity was introduced at an early date. Catholicism is the state religion. The principality is under the ecclesiastical jurisdiction of the Spanish diocese of Urgel.

Parishes, 7; priests, 18 (13 dioc., 5 rel.); srs., 21; bap., 448; Caths., 38,000 (95%); tot. pop., 40,000.

Angola: People's Republic in West Africa; capital, Luanda. Evangelization by Catholic missionaries, dating from about 1570, reached high points in the 17th and 18th centuries. Independence from Portugal in 1975 left the Church with a heavy loss of personnel when about half of the foreign missionaries fled the country. Two ecclesiastical provinces were established in 1977; all but two of the hierarchy are Angolan; the first Angolan cardinal (Alexandre do Nascimento) was named in 1983. Angola has an apostolic delegate.

Archd., 3; dioc., 11; card., 1 (nat.); abp., 2 (nat.); bp., 11 (9 nat.); parishes, 231; priests, 292 (92 dioc., 200 rel.); p.d., 1; sem., 153; bros., 46; srs., 745; catechists, 9,553; bap., 78,658; Caths., 3,980,000 (47.7%); tot. pop., 8,340,000.

Anguilla: Self-governing British island territory in the Caribbean; capital, The Valley. Under ecclesiastical jurisdiction of St. John's-Basseterre diocese, Antigua. Statistics included in St. Christopher (St. Kitts)-Nevis.

Antigua and Barbuda: Independent (1981) Caribbean island nation; capital, St. John's, Antigua.

Dioc., 1; bp., 1; parishes, 2; priests, 5 (2 dioc., 3 rel.); sem., 1; bros., 6; srs., 7; bap., 70; Caths., 7,000 (8.7%); tot. pop., 80,000.

Arabian Peninsula: Christianity, introduced in various parts of the peninsula in early Christian centuries, succumbed to Islam in the seventh century. The native population is entirely Moslem. The only Christians are foreign workers mainly from the Philippines, India and Korea. Most of the peninsula is under the ecclesiastical jurisdiction of the Vicariate Apostolic of Arabia with its seat in Abu Dhabi, United Arab Emirates. The area has an apostolic delegate (to the Red Sea Region). See individual countries: Bahrain, Oman, Qatar, Saudi Arabia, United Arab Emirates, North Yemen, and South Yemen.

Argentina: Republic in southeast South America, bordering on the Atlantic; capital, Buenos Aires. Priests were with the Magellan exploration party and the first Mass in the country was celebrated Apr. 1, 1519. Missionary work began in the 1530s, diocesan organization in the late 1540s, and effective evangelization about 1570. Independence from Spain was proclaimed in 1816. Since its establishment in the country, the Church has been influenced by Spanish cultural and institutional forces, antagonistic liberalism, government interference and opposition; the latter reached a climax during the last five years of the first presidency of Juan Peron (1946-1955). Widespread human rights violations including the disappearance of thousands of people marked the period of military rule from 1976 to December, 1983, when an elected civilian government took over. The bishops' conference published in book form in September, 1983, communiques they had sent to the military government during those years concerning human right abuses. Catholicism is the state religion. Argentina maintains diplomatic relations with Vatican City.

Archd., 13; dioc., 45; prel., 3; ap. ex., 1 (for Armenians of Latin America); ord., 1; mil. vic.; card., 3; abp., 14; bp., 69; parishes, 2,234; priests, 5,496 (2,588 dioc., 2,908 rel.); p.d., 55; sem., 1,940; bros., 1,159; srs., 12,709; bap., 607,864; Caths., 27,507,000 (92.8%); tot. pop., 29,630,000

Australia: Commonwealth; island continent southeast of Asia; capital, Canberra. The first Catholics in the country were Irish under penal sentence, 1795-1804; the first public Mass was celebrated May 15, 1803. Official organization of the Church dates from 1820. The country was officially removed from mission status in March, 1976. Established diplomatic relations with Vatican City, 1973.

Archd., 7; dioc. (1986), 23; mil. vic.; card., 1; abp., 9; bp., 38; parishes, 1,423; priests, 3,843 (2,291 dioc., 1,552 rel.); p.d., 8; sem., 432; bros., 2,137; srs., 11,094; bap., 4,183,000; Caths., 4,183,000 (27.2%); tot. pop. 15,370,000.

Austria: Republic in central Europe; capital, Vienna. Christianity was introduced by the end of the third century, strengthened considerably by conversion of the Bavarians from about 600, and firmly established in the second half of the eighth century. Catholicism survived and grew stronger as the principal religion in the country in the post-Reformation period, but suffered from Josephinism in the 18th century. Although liberated from much government harassment in the aftermath of the Revolution of 1848, it came under pressure again some 20 years later in the Kulturkampf. During this time the Church became involved with a developing social movement. The Church faced strong opposition from Socialists after World War I and suffered persecution from 1938 to 1945 during the Nazi regime. Some Church-state matters are regulated by a concordat originally concluded in 1934. Austria maintains diplomatic relations with Vatican City.

Archd., 2; dioc., 7; abb., 1; ord., 1; mil.

vic.; card., 2; abp., 1; bp., 14; parishes, 3,069; priests, 5,820 (3,410 dioc., 2,410 rel.); p.d., 140; sem., 649; bros., 599; srs., 10,431; bap., 80,788; Caths., 6,569,000 (87%); tot. pop., 7,550,000.

Azores: North Atlantic island group 750 miles west of Portugal, of which it is part. Christianity was introduced in the second quarter of the 15th century. The diocese of Angra was established in 1534.

Dioc., 1 (suff. of Lisbon, Portugal), bp., 1; parishes, 181; priests, 199 (191 dioc., 8 rel.); sem., 37; bros., 15; srs., 258; bap., 5,761; Caths., 254,043; tot. pop., 255,432 (1985).

Bahamas: Independent (July 10, 1973) island group consisting of some 700 (30 inhabited) small islands southeast of Florida and north of Cuba; capital, Nassau. On Oct. 12, 1492, Columbus landed on one of these islands, where the first Mass was celebrated in the New World. Organization of the Catholic Church in the Bahamas dates from about the middle of the 19th century. Established diplomatic relations with Vatican City in 1979.

Dioc., 1; bp., 1; parishes, 29; priests, 45 (12 dioc., 33 rel.); p.d., 4; sem., 3; bros., 6; srs., 51; catechists, 218; bap., 1,542; Caths., 50,000 (22.7%); tot. pop., 220,000.

Bahrain: Island state in Persian Gulf; capital, Manama. Under ecclesiastical jurisdiction of Arabia vicariate apostolic.

Priests, 3 (rel); bap., 316; Caths., 9,000; tot. pop., 400,000.

Balearic Islands: Spanish province consisting of an island group in the western Mediterranean. Statistics are included in those for Spain.

Bangladesh: Formerly the eastern portion of Pakistan. Officially constituted as a separate nation Dec. 16, 1971; capital, Dacca (Dhaka). Islam is the principal religion; freedom of religion is granted. There were Jesuit, Dominican and Augustinian missionaries in the area in the 16th century. A vicariate apostolic (of Bengali) was established in 1834; the hierarchy was erected in 1950. Established diplomatic relations with Vatican City, 1972.

Archd., 1; dioc., 3; abp., 1 (nat.); bp., 3 (nat.); parishes, 53; priests, 179 (53 dioc., 126 rel.); sem., 129; bros., 50; srs., 633; catechists, 953; charit. inst., 172; bap., 5,256; Caths. (1985), 174,113 (.17%); tot. pop. 102,075,000.

Barbados: Parliamentary democracy (independent since 1966), easternmost of the Caribbean islands; capital, Bridgetown. About 70 per cent of the people are Anglicans. Established diplomatic relations with Vatican City in 1979.

Dioc., 1; bp., 1; parishes, 7; priests, 9 (2 dioc., 7 rel.); p.d., 2; sem., 4; bros., 5; srs., 27; bap., 233; Caths., 11,000 (4%); tot. pop., 250,000.

Belgium: Constitutional monarchy in northwestern Europe; capital, Brussels. Christianity was introduced about the first quarter of the fourth century and major evangelization was completed about 730. During the rest of the medieval period the Church had firm diocesan and parochial organization, generally vigorous monastic life, and influential monastic and cathedral schools. Lutherans and Calvinists made some gains during the Reformation period but there was a strong Catholic restoration in the first half of the 17th century, when the country was under Spanish rule. Jansenism disturbed the Church from about 1640 into the 18th century. Josephinism, imposed by an Austrian regime, hampered the Church late in the same century. Repressive and persecutory measures were enforced during the Napoleonic conquest. Freedom came with separation of Church and state in the wake of the Revolution of 1830, which ended the reign of William I. Thereafter, the Church encountered serious problems with philosophical liberalism and political socialism. Catholics have long been engaged in strong educational, social and political movements. Except for one five-year period (1880-1884), Belgium has maintained diplomatic relations with Vatican City since 1835.

Archd., 1; dioc., 7; mil. vic.; card., 3; priests, 12,027 (7,486 dioc., 4,541 rel.); p.d., 263; sem., 415; bros., 2,236; srs., 29,225; char-it. inst., 1,140; bap., 102,297; Caths., 8,991,000 (91.2%); tot. pop., 9,860,000.

Belize (formerly British Honduras): Independent (Sept. 21, 1981) republic on east coast of Central America; capital, Belmopan. Its history has points in common with Guatemala, where evangelization began in the 16th century. Established diplomatic relations with Vatican City, 1983.

Dioc., 1; bp., 1; parishes, 12; priests, 36 (13 dioc., 23 rel.); p.d., 1; sem., 2; bros., 10; srs., 85; catechists, 307; bap., 3,144; Caths., 99,528 (61.8%); tot. pop., 161,000 (1985).

Benin (formerly Dahomey): People's republic in west Africa, bordering on the Atlantic; capital, Porto Novo. Missionary work was very limited from the 16th to the 18th centuries. Effective evangelization dates from 1861. The hierarchy was established in 1955. The majority of Christians are Catholics. Benin maintains diplomatic relations with Vatican City.

Archd., 1; dioc., 5; card., 1 (nat.); abp., 2 (nat.); bp., 5 (nat.); parishes, 120; priests, 185 (99 dioc., 86 rel.); sem., 93; bros., 14; srs., 350; catechists, 1,861; bap., 15,047; Caths., 584,000 (15.7%); tot. pop., 3,720,000.

Bermuda: British dependency, consisting of 360 islands (20 of them inhabited) nearly 600 miles east of Cape Hatteras; capital, Hamilton. Catholics were not permitted until about 1800. Occasional pastoral care was provided the few Catholics there by visiting priests during the 19th century. Early in the 1900s priests from Halifax began serving the area. A prefecture apostolic was set up in 1953. The first bishop assumed jurisdiction in 1956 when it was made a vicariate apostolic; diocese established, 1967.

Dioc., 1; bp., 1; parishes, 7; priests, 8 (1 dioc., 7 rel.); p.d., 1; sem., 3; srs., 8; catechists, 98; bap., 157; Caths., 9,000 (15%); tot. pop., 60,000.

Bhutan: Kingdom in the Himalayas, northeast of India; capital, Thimphu. Most of the population

are Buddhists. Jesuits (1963) and Salesians (1965) were invited to country to direct schools. Salesians were expelled in February, 1982, on disputed charges of proselytism. Jesuits and some Sisters remained *(Fides)*. Ecclesiastical jurisdiction is under the Darjeeling diocese, India.

Parishes, 3; priests, 7 (2 dioc., 5 rel.); bro., 1; srs., 6; catechists, 3; bap., 13; Caths. (1982), 400; tot. pop., 1,360,000.

Bolivia: Republic in central South America; capital, Sucre; seat of government, La Paz. Catholicism, the official religion, was introduced in the 1530s and the first bishopric was established in 1552. Effective evangelization among the Indians, slow to start, reached high points in the middle of the 18th and the beginning of the 19th centuries and was resumed about 1840. Independence from Spain was proclaimed in 1825, at the end of a campaign that started in 1809. Church-state relations are regulated by a 1951 concordat with the Holy See. In recent years, human rights violations in conditions of political, economic and social turmoil have occasioned strong protests by members of the hierarchy and other people of the Church. Bolivia maintains diplomatic relations with Vatican City.

Archd., 4; dioc., 4; prel., 2; v.a., 6; mil. vic.; card., 1; abp., 7; bp., 20; parishes, 443; priests, 828 (213 dioc., 615 rel.); p.d., 25; sem., 176; bros., 200; srs., 1,732; catechists, 1,094; bap., 193,234; Caths., 5,752,000 (94.6%); tot. pop., 6,080,000.

Botswana: Republic (independent since 1966) in southern Africa; capital, Gaborone. Botswana has an apostolic delegate (to Southern Africa).

Dioc., 1; bp., 1 (nat.); priests, 33 (3 dioc., 30 rel.); p.d., 1; sem., 5; bros., 4; srs., 49; catechists, 57; bap., 3,098; Caths., 41,800 (4%); tot. pop., 1,038,000.

Brazil: Federal republic in northeast South America; capital, Brasilia. One of several priests with the discovery party celebrated the first Mass in the country Apr. 26, 1500. Evangelization began some years later and the first diocese was erected in 1551. During the colonial period, which lasted until 1822, evangelization made some notable progress — especially in the Amazon region between 1680 and 1750 — but was seriously hindered by government policy and the attitude of colonists regarding Amazon Indians the missionaries tried to protect from exploitation and slavery. The Jesuits were suppressed in 1782 and other missionaries expelled as well. Liberal anti-Church influence grew in strength. The government gave minimal support but exercised maximum control over the Church. After the proclamation of independence from Portugal in 1822 and throughout the regency, government control was tightened and the Church suffered greatly from dissident actions of ecclesiastical brotherhoods, Masonic anti-clericalism and general decline in religious life. Church and state were separated by the constitution of 1891, proclaimed two years after the end of the empire. The Church carried into the 20th century a load of inherited liabilities and problems amid increasingly difficult political, economic and social conditions affecting the majority of the population. A number of bishops, priests, religious and lay persons have been active in movements for social and religious reform. Brazil maintains diplomatic relations with Vatican City.

Archd., 36; dioc., 188; prel., 16; abb., 2; ord., 1; mil. vic.; card., 6; abp., 47; bp., 305; parishes, 6,872; priests, 13,367 (5,400 dioc., 7,967 rel.); p.d., 386; sem., 5,661; bros., 2,339; srs., 36,772; bap., 2,844,607; Caths., 116,824,000 (90.1%); tot. pop., 129,660,000.

Brunei: Independent state (1983) on the northern coast of Borneo; capital, Bandar Seri Begawan. Under ecclesiastical jurisdiction of Miri diocese, Malaysia.

Parishes, 3; priests, 5 (2 dioc., 3 rel.); srs., 4; catechists, 2; bap., 102; Caths., 5,000; tot. pop., 260,000.

Bulgaria: People's republic in southeastern Europe on the eastern part of the Balkan peninsula; capital, Sofia. Christianity was introduced before 343 but disappeared with the migration of Slavs into the territory. The baptism of Boris I about 865 ushered in a new period of Christianity which soon became involved in switches of loyalty between Constantinople and Rome. Through it all the Byzantine, and later Orthodox, element remained stronger and survived under the rule of Ottoman Turks into the 19th century. The few modern Latin Catholics in the country are traceable to 17th century converts from heresy. The Byzantines are products of a reunion movement of the 19th century. In 1947 the constitution of the new republic decreed the separation of Church and state. Catholic schools and institutions were abolished and foreign religious banished in 1948. A year later the apostolic delegate was expelled. Ivan Romanoff, vicar general of Plovdiv, died in prison in 1952. Bishop Eugene Bossilkoff, imprisoned in 1948, was sentenced to death in 1952; his fate remained unknown until 1975 when the Bulgarian government informed the Vatican that he had died in prison shortly after being sentenced. Roman and Bulgarian Rite vicars apostolic were permitted to attend the Second Vatican Council from 1962 to 1965. All church activity is under surveillance and/or control by the government, which professes to be atheistic. Pastoral and related activities are strictly limited. Most of the population is Orthodox. There was some improvement in Bulgarian-Vatican relations in 1975, following a visit of Bulgarian President Todor Zhivkov to Pope Paul VI June 19 and talks between Vatican and Bulgarian representatives at the Helsinki Conference in late July. The needs of the church in Bulgaria were outlined by Pope John Paul II in a private audience with the Bulgarian foreign minister in December, 1978. In 1979, the Sofia-Plovdiv vicariate apostolic was raised to a diocese and a bishop was appointed for the vacant see of Nicopoli.

Dioc., 2; ap. ex., 1; bp., 2. No statistics available. In 1968 there were approximately 65,000 Catholics. Tot. pop., 8,940,000.

Burkina Faso (Upper Volta): Republic inland in western Africa; capital, Ouagadougou. White Fathers (now known as Missionaries of Africa) started the first missions in 1900 and 1901. White Sisters began work in 1911. A minor and a major seminary were established in 1926 and 1942, respectively. The first native bishop in modern times from West Africa was ordained in 1956 and the first cardinal created in 1965. The hierarchy was established in 1955. Established diplomatic relations with Vatican City in 1973.

Archd., 1; dioc., 8; card., 1 (nat.); bp., 9 (nat.); parishes, 100; priests, 395 (171 dioc., 224 rel.); sem., 134; bros., 137; srs., 646; catechists, 3,578; bap., 27,813; Caths., 570,000 (8.6%); tot. pop., 6,610,000.

Burma: Union of Burma, a socialist republic in southeast Asia, on the Bay of Bengal; capital, Rangoon. Christianity was introduced about 1500. Small-scale evangelization had limited results from the middle of the 16th century until the 1850s when effective organization of the Church began. The hierarchy was established in 1955. Buddhism was declared the state religion in 1961, but the state is now officially secular. In 1965, church schools and hospitals were nationalized. In 1966, all foreign missionaries who had entered the country after 1948 for the first time were forced to leave when the government refused to renew their work permits. Despite these setbacks, the Church has shown some progress in recent years. Burma has an apostolic delegate (pro-nuncio to Bangladesh).

Archd., 2; dioc., 6; p.a., 1; abp., 2 (nat.); bp., 8 (7 nat.); parishes, 147; priests, 243 (219 dioc., 24 rel.); sem., 224; bros., 54; srs., 78; catechists, 1,859; bap., 20,213; Caths., 395,000 (1%); tot. pop., 37,550,000.

Burundi: Republic since 1966, near the equator in east-central Africa; capital, Bujumbura. The first permanent Catholic mission station was established late in the 19th century. Large numbers of persons were received into the Church following the ordination of the first Burundi priests in 1925. The first native bishop was appointed in 1959. Most education takes place in schools under Catholic auspices. In 1972-73, the country was torn by tribal warfare between the Tutsis, the ruling minority, and the Hutus. Since 1979, approximately 100 Catholic missionaries have been expelled. Burundi maintains diplomatic relations with Vatican City.

Archd., 1; dioc., 6; abp., 1 (nat.); bp., 6 (nat.); parishes, 110; priests, 348 (188 dioc., 160 rel.); sem., 110; bros., 146; srs., 742; catechists, 3,124; bap., 81,510; Caths., 2,532,000 (57.2%); tot. pop., 4,420,000.

Cambodia (Kampuchea): People's republic in southeast Asia, bordering on the Gulf of Siam, Thailand, Laos and Vietnam; capital Phnom Penh. Evangelization dating from the second half of the 16th century had limited results, more among Vietnamese than Khmers. Thousands of Catholics of Vietnamese origin were forced to flee in 1970 because of Khmer hostility. The status of the Church remained uncertain following the Khmer Rouge take-over in April, 1975. Foreign missionaries were expelled immediately. Local clergy and religious were sent to work the land; whether they would be able to minister to the faithful was not known. Buddhism is the state religion.

V.a., 1; p.a., 2. No statistics available. Catholics numbered 13,835 in 1973. Tot. pop. (est.), 6,890,000.

Cameroon: Republic in west Africa, bordering on the Gulf of Guinea; capital, Yaounde. Effective evangelization began in the 1890s, although Catholics had been in the country long before that time. In the 40-year period from 1920 to 1960, the number of Catholics increased from 60,000 to 700,000. The first native priests were ordained in 1935. Twenty years later the first native bishops were ordained and the hierarchy established. In 1982, three new ecclesiastical provinces and one diocese were established. Cameroon maintains diplomatic relations with Vatican City.

Archd., 4; dioc., 12; abp., 4 (nat.); bp., 13 (10 nat.); parishes, 396; priests, 836 (379 dioc., 457 rel.); p.d., 27; sem., 245; bros., 203; srs., 1,227; catechists, 10,254; bap., 118,671; Caths., 2,512,000 (27.4%); tot. pop., 9,160,000.

Canada: Independent federation comprising the northern half of North America; capital, Ottawa. Canada maintains diplomatic relations with Vatican City. (See Index for news events and pages 373-83 for the Church in Canada.)

Archd., 18; dioc., 54; abb., 1; ap. ex., 1; mil. vic., card., 5 (2 head archdioceses; 1 is Curia official; 2 are retired); abp., 25 (18 diocesan, 1 coadjutor, 6 retired); bp., 98 (52 diocesan, 20 auxiliary, 26 retired); parishes 5,981; priests, 11,835 (7,118 dioc., 4,717 rel.); p.d., 434; sem. (1984), 1,101; bros., 3,578; srs., 34,895; bap. (1984), 170,736; Caths., 10,999,964 (43.54%); tot. pop., 25,262,500. (Principal source: 1986 Directory of Canadian Conference of Catholic Bishops.)

Canary Islands: Two Spanish provinces, consisting of seven islands, off the northwest coast of Africa. Evangelization began about 1400. Almost all of the one million inhabitants are Catholics. Statistics are included in those for Spain.

Cape Verde: Independent (July 5, 1975) island group in the Atlantic 300 miles west of Senegal; formerly a Portuguese overseas province; capital, Praia, San Tiago Island. Evangelization began some years before the establishment of the first diocese in 1532. Established diplomatic relations with Vatican City in 1976.

Dioc., 1; bp., 1; parishes, 30; priests, 47 (12 dioc., 35 rel.); sem., 3; bros., 7; srs., 48; catechists, 3,711; bap., 7,949; Caths., 300,000; tot. pop., 311,000.

Carolines and Marshalls, The (Federated States of Micronesia): U.S. trust territory in the southwest Pacific; scheduled for independence. Effective evangelization began in the late 1880s.

Dioc., 1; bp., 1; parishes, 27; priests, 33 (rel.); p.d., 22; sem., 9; bros., 6; srs., 50; catechists, 274; bap., 2,130; Caths., 56,000; tot. pop., 125,000.

Cayman Islands: British colony in Caribbean; capital, George Town on Grand Cayman. Under ecclesiastical jurisdiction of Kingston diocese, Jamaica.

Srs., 3; catechists, 3; bap., 7; Caths. (1982), 300; tot. pop., 18,000.

Central African Republic: Former French colony (independent since 1960) in central Africa; capital, Bangui. Effective evangelization dates from 1894. The region was organized as a mission territory in 1909. The first native priest was ordained in 1938. The hierarchy was organized in 1955. Established diplomatic relations with Vatican City in 1975.

Archd., 1; dioc., 5; abp., 1 (nat.); bp., 4; parishes, 90; priests, 222 (46 dioc., 176 rel.); p.d., 3; sem., 68; bros., 50; srs., 285; catechists, 2,448; bap., 18,466; Caths., 413,000 (16.8%); tot. pop., 2,450,000.

Ceuta: Spanish possession (city) on the northern tip of Africa, south of Gibraltar. Statistics are included in those for Spain.

Chad: Republic (independent since 1960) in north-central Africa; former French possession; capital, N'Djamena. Evangelization began in 1929, leading to firm organization in 1947 and establishment of the hierarchy in 1955. Chad has an apostolic delegate (pro-nuncio, Central African Republic).

Archd., 1; dioc., 3; abp., 1; bp., 3; parishes, 88; priests, 140 (20 dioc., 120 rel.); sem., 42; bros., 47; srs., 215; catechists, 4,825; bap., 18,250; Caths., 266,000 (5.6%); tot. pop., 4,790,000.

Chile: Republic on the southwestern coast of South America; capital, Santiago. Priests were with the Spanish conquistadores on their entrance into the territory early in the 16th century. The first parish was established in 1547 and the first bishopric in 1561. Overall organization of the Church took place later in the century. By 1650 most of the peaceful Indians in the central and northern areas were evangelized. Missionary work was more difficult in the southern region. Church activity was hampered during the campaign for independence, 1810 to 1818, and through the first years of the new government, to 1830. Later gains were made, into this century, but hindering factors were shortages of native clergy and religious and attempts by the government to control church administration through the patronage system in force while the country was under Spanish control. Separation of Church and state were decreed in the constitution of 1925. Church-state relations were strained during the regime of Marxist president Salvator Allende Gossens (1970-73). He was overthrown in a bloody coup and was reported to have committed suicide Sept. 11, 1973. Conditions have remained unsettled under the military government which assumed control after the coup. The Chilean bishops have issued numerous statements strongly critical of the military government's human rights violations, urging the release of political prisoners and a return to civilian rule. Chile maintains diplomatic relations with Vatican City.

Archd., 5; dioc., 14; prel., 3; v.a., 2; mil. vic.; card., 2; abp., 4; bp., 29; parishes, 815; priests, 2,163 (814 dioc., 1,349 rel.); p.d., 192; sem., 999; bros., 446; srs., 4,994; catechists, 672; bap., 193,175; Caths., 9,929,000 (85%); tot. pop., 11,680,000.

China (*This article concerns mainland China which has been under Communist control since 1949*): People's Republic in eastern part of Asia; capital, Peking (Beijing), Christianity was introduced by Nestorians who had some influence on part of the area from 635 to 845 and again from the 11th century until 1368. John of Monte Corvino started a Franciscan mission in 1294; he was ordained an archbishop about 1307. Missionary activity involving more priests increased for a while thereafter but the Franciscan mission ended in 1368. The Jesuit Matteo Ricci initiated a remarkable period of activity in the 1580s. By 1700 the number of Catholics was reported to be 300,000. The Chinese Rites controversy, concerning the adaptation of rituals and other matters to Chinese traditions and practices, ran throughout the 17th century, ending in a negative decision by mission authorities in Rome. Bl. Francis de Capillas, the protomartyr of China, was killed in 1648. Persecution, a feature of Chinese history as recurrent as changes in dynasties, occurred several times in the 18th century and resulted in the departure of most missionaries from the country. The Chinese door swung open again in the 1840s and progress in evangelization increased with an extension of legal and social tolerance. At the turn of the 20th century, however, the Boxer Rebellion took one or the other kind of toll among an estimated 30,000 victims. Missionary work in the 1900s reached a new high in every respect before the disaster of persecution initiated by Communists before and especially since they established the republic in 1949. The Reds began a savage persecution as soon as they came into power. Among its results were the expulsion of over 5,000 foreign missionaries, 510 of whom were American priests, brothers and nuns; the arrest, imprisonment and harassment of all members of the native religious, clergy and hierarchy; the forced closing of 3,932 schools, 216 hospitals, 781 dispensaries, 254 orphanages, 29 printing presses and 55 periodicals; denial of the free exercise of religion to all the faithful; the detention of hundreds of priests, religious and lay persons in jail and their employment in slave labor; the proscription of the Legion of Mary and other Catholic Action groups for "counter-revolutionary activities" and "crimes against the new China"; complete outlawing of missionary work and pastoral activity. The government formally established a Patriotic Association of Chinese Catholics in July, 1957. Relatively few priests and lay persons joined the organization, which was condemned by Pius XII in 1958. The government formed the nucleus of what it hoped might become the hierarchy of a schismatic Chinese church in 1958 by "electing" 26 bishops and having them consecrated validly but illicitly between Apr. 13, 1958, and Nov. 15, 1959, without the permission or approval of the Holy See. By 1983, an estimated 60 bishops were consecrated in this manner. In March, 1960, Bishop James E. Walsh, M.M., the last American missionary in China, was sentenced and placed in custody for a period of 20 years. He was released in the summer of 1970. (He died in 1981.) Activity of the Patriotic Association and official policy of the government are in direct opposition to any connection between the Church in China and the Vatican. Bishop Ignatius Kung Pin-Mei, imprisoned for 30 years, was paroled in 1985.

Archd., 20; dioc., 92; p.a., 29. No Catholic statistics are available. In 1949 there were between 3,500,000-4,000,000 Catholics, about .7 per cent of the total population. Tot. pop. 1,020,877,000.

Colombia: Republic in northwest South America, with Atlantic and Pacific borders; capital, Bogota. Evangelization began in 1508. The first two dioceses were established in 1534. Vigorous development of the Church was reported by the middle of the 17th century despite obstacles posed by the multiplicity of Indian languages, government interference through patronage rights and otherwise, rivalry among religious orders and the small number of native priests among the predominantly Spanish clergy. Some persecution, including the confiscation of property, followed in the wake of the proclamation of independence from Spain in 1819. The Church was affected in many ways by the political and civil unrest of the nation through the 19th century and into the 20th. Various aspects of Church-state relations are regulated by a concordat with the Vatican signed July 12, 1973, and ratified July 2, 1975. The new concordat replaced one which had been in effect with some modifications since 1887. Guerrilla warfare aimed at Marxist-oriented radical social reform and redistribution of land has plagued the country since the 1960s, posing problems for the Church which backed reforms but rejected actions of radical groups. In 1984, a peace accord — calling for a cease-fire and peaceful implementation of reforms — was signed by Belisario Betancur, president of Colombia, and leaders of guerrilla factions. Colombia maintains diplomatic relations with Vatican City. (See Index for papal visit.)

Archd., 11; dioc. (1986), 33; prel., 2; v.a., 8; p.a., 7; mil. vic., card., 2; abp., 15; bp., 57; parishes, 2,367; priests, 5,355 (3,318 dioc., 2,037 rel.); p.d., 28; sem., 2,443; bros., 889; srs., 18,171; catechists, 2,360; bap., 761,959; Caths., 26,094,000 (94.8%); tot. pop., 27,520,000.

Comoros: Consists of main islands of Grande Comore, Anjouan and Moheli in Indian Ocean off southeast coast of Africa; capital, Moroni, Grande Comore Island. Former French territory; independent (July 6, 1975). The majority of the population is Moslem. An apostolic administration was established in 1975.

A.a., 1; parishes, 2; priests, 2 (rel.); srs., 7; bap., 5; Caths., 1,000 (.2%); tot. pop., 420,000.

Congo: People's republic (independent since 1960) in west central Africa; former French possession; capital, Brazzaville. Small-scale missionary work with little effect preceded modern evangelization dating from the 1880s. The work of the Church has been affected by political instability, Communist influence, tribalism and hostility to foreigners. The hierarchy was established in 1955. Established diplomatic relations with the Vatican in 1977.

Archd., 1; dioc., 4; abp., 1 (nat); bp., 4 (nat); parishes, 80; priests, 158 (52 dioc., 106 rel.); p.d., 2; sem., 75; bros., 39; srs., 208; catechists, 542; bap., 13,727; Caths., 740,000 (45.8%); tot. pop., 1,650,000.

Cook Islands: Self-governing territory of New Zealand, an archipelago of small islands in Oceania. Evangelization by Protestant missionaries started in 1821, resulting in a predominantly Protestant population. The first Catholic missionary work began in 1894. The hierarchy was established in 1966.

Dioc., 1; bp., 1; parishes, 11; priests, 14 (5 dioc., 9 rel.); sem., 4; bros., 3; srs., 10; catechists, 33; bap., 85; Caths., 3,000; tot. pop., 18,000.

Costa Rica: Republic in Central America; capital, San Jose. Evangelization began about 1520 and proceeded by degrees to real development and organization of the Church in the 17th and 18th centuries. The republic became independent in 1838. Twelve years later church jurisdiction also became independent with the establishment of a bishopric in the present capital. Costa Rica maintains diplomatic relations with Vatican City.

Archd., 1; dioc., 3; v.a., 1; abp., 2; bp., 5; parishes, 176; priests, 461 (274 dioc., 187 rel.); sem., 294; bros., 48; srs., 898; catechists, 662; bap., 67,287; Caths., 2,199,000 (92.3%); tot. pop., 2,380,000.

Cuba: Republic under Communist dictatorship, south of Florida; capital, Havana. Effective evangelization began about 1514, leading eventually to the predominance of Catholicism on the island. Native vocations to the priesthood and religious life were unusually numerous in the 18th century but declined in the 19th. The island became independent of Spain in 1902 following the Spanish-American War. Fidel Castro took control of the government Jan. 1, 1959. In 1961, after Cuba was officially declared a socialist state, the University of Villanueva was closed, 350 Catholic schools were nationalized and 136 priests expelled. A greater number of foreign priests and religious had already left the country. Freedom of worship and religious instruction are limited to church premises and no social action is permitted the Church, which survives under surveillance. A new constitution approved in 1976 guaranteed freedom of conscience but restricted its exercise. Cuba maintains diplomatic relations with Vatican City.

Archd., 2; dioc., 5; abp., 2; bp., 6; parishes, 231; priests, 205 (117 dioc., 88 rel.); sem., 47; bros., 25; srs., 240; bap., 21,871; Caths., 4,051,000 (41%); tot. pop., 9,880,000.

Cyprus: Republic in the eastern Mediterranean; capital, Nicosia. Christianity was preached on the island in apostolic times and has a continuous history from the fourth century. Latin and Eastern rites were established but the latter prevailed and became Orthodox after the schism of 1054. Roman and Orthodox Christians have suffered under many governments, particularly during the period of Turkish dominion from late in the 16th to late in the 19th centuries, and from differences between the 80 per cent Greek majority and the Turkish mi-

nority. About 80 per cent of the population are Orthodox. Cyprus established diplomatic relations with Vatican City in 1973. Maronite-Rite Catholics are under the jurisdiction of the archdiocese of Cyprus (of the Maronites), whose archbishop resides in Lebanon. Roman-Rite Catholics are under the jurisdiction of the Roman-Rite patriarchate of Jerusalem.

Archd., 1 (Maronite); abp., 1 (resides in Lebanon); parishes, 10; priests, 22 (6 dioc., 16 rel.); bros., 3; srs., 98; bap., 51; Caths., 7,000 (1.2%); tot. pop., 650,000.

Czechoslovakia: Federal socialist republic (since 1969) in Central Europe, consisting of the Czech Socialist Republic, capital Prague; and the Slovak Socialist Republic, capital Bratislava. The republics have local autonomy but are subordinate to the Federal Assembly at Prague made up of representatives from both regions. The Czech and Slovak regions of the country have separate religious and cultural backgrounds. Christianity was introduced in Slovakia in the 8th century by Irish and German missionaries and the area was under the jurisdiction of German bishops. In 863, at the invitation of the Slovak ruler Rastislav who wanted to preserve the cultural and liturgical heritage of the people, Sts. Cyril and Methodius began pastoral and missionary work in the region, ministering to the people in their own language. The saints introduced Old Slovak (Old Church Slavonic) into the liturgy and did so much to evangelize the territory that they are venerated as the apostles of Slovakia. A diocese established at Nitra in 880 had a continuous history except for a century ending in 1024. The Church in Slovakia was severely tested by the Reformation and political upheavals. After World War I, when it became part of the Republic of Czechoslovakia, it was 75 per cent Catholic. In the Czech lands, the martyrdom of Prince Wenceslaus in 929 triggered the spread of Christianity. Prague has had a continuous history as a diocese since 973. A parish system was organized about the 13th century in Bohemia and Moravia, the land of the Czechs. Mendicant orders strengthened relations with the Latin Rite in the 13th century. In the next century the teachings of John Hus in Bohemia brought trouble to the Church in the forms of schism and heresy, and initiated a series of religious wars which continued for decades following his death at the stake in 1415. Church property was confiscated, monastic communities were scattered and even murdered, ecclesiastical organization was shattered, and so many of the faithful joined the Bohemian Brethren that Catholics became a minority. The Reformation, with the way prepared by the Hussites and cleared by other factors, affected the Church seriously. A Counter Reformation got under way in the 1560s and led to a gradual restoration through the thickets of Josephinism, the Enlightenment, liberalism and troubled politics. In 1920, two years after the establishment of the Republic of Czechoslovakia, the schismatic Czechoslovak Church was proclaimed at Prague, resulting in numerous defections from the Catholic Church in the Czech region. In Ruthenia, 112,000 became Russian Orthodox between 1918 and 1930. Vigorous persecution of the church began in Slovakia before the end of World War II when Communists mounted a 1944 offensive against bishops, priests and religious. In 1945, church schools were nationalized, youth organizations were disbanded, the Catholic press was curtailed, the training of students for the priesthood was seriously impeded. Msgr. Josef Tiso, president of the Slovak Republic, was tried for "treason" in December, 1947, and was executed the following April. Between 1945 and 1949 approximately 10 per cent of the Slovak population spent some time in jail or a concentration camp. Persecution began later in the Czech part of the country, following the accession of the Gottwald regime to power early in 1948. Hospitals, schools and property were nationalized and Catholic organizations were liquidated. A puppet organization was formed in 1949 to infiltrate the Church and implement an unsuccessful plan for establishing a schismatic church. In the same year Archbishop Josef Beran of Prague was placed under house arrest. (He left the country in 1965, was made a cardinal, and died in 1969 in Rome.) A number of theatrical trials of bishops and priests were staged in 1950. All houses of religious were taken over between March, 1950, and the end of 1951. Pressure was applied on the clergy and faithful of the Eastern Rite in Slovakia to join the Orthodox Church. Diplomatic relations with Vatican City were terminated in 1950. About 3,000 priests were deprived of liberty in 1951 and attempts were made to force "peace priests" on the people. In 1958 it was reported that 450 to 500 priests were in jail; an undisclosed number of religious and Byzantine-Rite priests had been deported; two bishops released from prison in 1956 were under house arrest; one bishop was imprisoned at Leopoldov and two at the Mirov reformatory. In Bohemia, Moravia and Silesia, five of six dioceses were without ruling bishops; one archbishop and two bishops were active but subject to "supervision"; most of the clergy refused to join the "peace priests." In 1962 only three bishops were permitted to attend the first session of the Second Vatican Council. From January to October, 1968, Church-state relations improved to some extent under the Dubcek regime: a number of bishops were reinstated; some 3,000 priests were engaged in the pastoral ministry, although 1,500 were still barred from priestly work; the "peace priests" organization was disbanded; the Eastern-Rite Church, with 147 parishes, was reestablished. In 1969, an end was ordered to rehabilitation trials for priests and religious, but no wholesale restoration of priests and religious to their proper ways of life and work was in prospect. In 1972, the government ordered the removal of nuns from visible but limited apostolates to farms and mental hospitals where they would be out of sight. In 1973, the government allowed the ordination of four bishops — one in the Czech region and three in the Slovak region. Reports from Slovakia late in the same year stated that authorities there had placed severe restrictions on the education of seminarians and the functioning of priests. Government restrictions continued to hamper the

work of priests and nuns in recent years. Signatories of the human rights declaration called Charter 77 have been particular objects of government repression and retribution. In December, 1983, the Czechoslovakian foreign minister met with the Pope at Vatican City — the first meeting of a high Czech official with a pope since the country came under communist rule. In 1984, two Vatican officials visited Czechoslovakia. Despite the communication breakthrough, there was no indication of any change of policy toward the Church in the country.

Archd., 3; dioc., 10; card., 2 (1 heads archiepiscopal see, 1 is curia official); bp., 6 (2 head sees; 2 are apostolic administrators; 2 are impeded)); parishes, 4,444; priests, 3,662 (3,188 dioc., 474 rel.); sem., 356; bros., 60; srs., 5,030; bap., 104,873; Caths., 10,634,000 (68.9%); tot. pop., 15,420,000.

Denmark, including the Faroe Islands and Greenland: Constitutional monarchy in northwestern Europe, north of West Germany; capital, Copenhagen. Christianity was introduced in the ninth century and the first diocese for the area was established in 831. Intensive evangelization and full-scale organization of the Church occurred from the second half of the 10th century and ushered in a period of great development and influence in the 12th and 13th centuries. Decline followed, resulting in almost total loss to the Church during the Reformation when Lutheranism became the national religion. Catholics were considered foreigners until religious freedom was legally assured in 1849. Modern development of the Church dates from the second half of the 19th century. About 95 per cent of the population are Evangelical Lutherans. Established diplomatic relations with Vatican City in 1982.

Dioc., 1; bp., 1; parishes, 52; priests, 106 (38 dioc., 68 rel.); p.d., 1; sem., 5; bros., 6; srs., 438; bap., 343; Caths., 27,387 (.5%); tot. pop., 5,112,000 (1985).

Djibouti (formerly French Territory of Afars and Issas): Independent (1977) republic in east Africa, on the Gulf of Aden; capital, Djibouti. Christianity in the area, formerly part of Ethiopia, antedated but was overcome by the Arab invasion of 1200. Modern evangelization, begun in the latter part of the 19th century, had meager results. The hierarchy was established in 1955. The territory has an apostolic delegate (to the Red Sea Region).

Dioc., 1; bp., 1; parishes, 7; priests, 7 (1 dioc., 6 rel.); bros., 8; srs., 36; bap., 35; Caths., 8,500; tot. pop., 330,000 (1985).

Dominica: Independent (Nov. 3, 1978) state in Caribbean; capital, Roseau. Evangelization began in 1642. Established diplomatic relations with Vatican City in 1981.

Dioc., 1; bp., 1; parishes, 14; priests, 31 (4 dioc., 27 rel.); p.d., 1; sem., 5; bros., 5; srs., 34; catechists, 408; bap., 1,253; Caths., 65,000 (87.7%); tot. pop., 74,089 (1985).

Dominican Republic: Caribbean republic on the eastern two-thirds of the island of Hispaniola, bordering on Haiti; capital, Santo Domingo. Evangelization began shortly after discovery by Columbus in 1492 and church organization, the first in America, was established by 1510. Catholicism is the state religion. The Dominican Republic maintains diplomatic relations with Vatican City.

Archd., 1; dioc., 7; card., 1; abp., 1; bp., 9; parishes, 217; priests, 484 (133 dioc., 351 rel.); p.d., 33; sem., 263; bros., 84; srs., 1,322; bap., 88,511; Caths., 5,583,000 (93.7%); tot. pop., 5,960,000.

Ecuador (includes Galapagos Islands): Republic on the west coast of South America; capital, Quito. Evangelization began in the 1530s. The first diocese was established in 1545. A synod, one of the first in the Americas, was held in 1570 or 1594. Multiphased missionary work, spreading from the coastal and mountain regions into the Amazon, made the Church highly influential during the colonial period. The Church was practically enslaved by the constitution enacted in 1824, two years after Ecuador, as part of Colombia, gained independence from Spain. Some change for the better took place later in the century, but from 1891 until the 1930s the Church labored under serious liabilities imposed by liberal governments. The concordat of 1866 was violated; foreign missionaries were barred from the country for some time; the property of religious orders was confiscated; education was taken over by the state; traditional state support was refused; legal standing was denied; attempts to control church offices were made through insistence on rights of patronage. A period of harmony and independence for the Church began after agreement was reached on Church-state relations in 1937. Ecuador maintains diplomatic relations with Vatican City.

Archd., 3; dioc., 10; prel., 1; v.a., 7; p.a., 1; mil. vic., card., 1; abp., 3; bp., 24; parishes, 820; priests, 1,537 (660 dioc., 877 rel.); p.d., 14; sem., 293; bros., 329; srs., 4,112; catechists, 2,215; bap., 202,205; Caths., 8,518,000 (92%); tot. pop., 9,250,000.

Egypt, Arab Republic of: Republic in northeastern Africa, bordering on the Mediterranean; capital, Cairo. Alexandria was the influential hub of a Christian community established by the end of the second century; it became a patriarchate and the center of the Coptic Church, and had great influence on the spread of Christianity in various parts of Africa. Monasticism developed from desert communities of hermits in the third and fourth centuries. Arianism was first preached in Egypt in the 320s. In the fifth century, the Coptic church went Monophysite through failure to accept doctrine formulated by the Council of Chalcedon in 451 with respect to the two natures of Christ. The country was thoroughly Arabized after 640 and was under the rule of Ottoman Turks from 1517 to 1798. English influence was strong during the 19th century. A monarchy established in 1922 lasted about 30 years, ending with the proclamation of a republic in 1953-54. By that time Egypt had become the leader of pan-Arabism against Israel. It waged two unsuccessful wars against Israel in 1948-49 and 1967. Between 1958 and 1961 it was allied with Syria and Yemen, in the United Arab Republic. In 1979, following negotiations initiated by Pres. Anwar el-Sadat in 1977, Egypt and Israel signed a peace agreement. Islam, the religion of some 90 percent of the population, is the state religion. Egypt maintains diplomatic relations with Vatican City.

Patriarchate, 2 (Alexandria for the Copts and for the Melkites); dioc., 9; v.a., 3; card., 1; abp., 1; bp., 14; parishes, 207; priests, 347 (170 dioc., 177 rel.); p.d., 1; sem., 90; bros., 68; srs., 1,608; bap., 2,289; Caths., 171,000 (.4%); tot. pop., 44,530,000.

El Salvador: Republic in Central America; capital, San Salvador. Evangelization affecting the whole territory followed Spanish occupation in the 1520s. The country was administered by the captaincy general of Guatemala until 1821 when independence from Spain was declared and it was annexed to Mexico. El Salvador joined the Central American Federation in 1825, decreed its own independence in 1841 and became a republic formally in 1856. In recent years, Church efforts to achieve social justice have resulted in persecution of the Church. Archbishop Oscar Romero of San Salvador, peace advocate and outspoken champion of human rights, was murdered Mar. 24, 1980, while celebrating Mass. El Salvador maintains diplomatic relations with Vatican City. (See Index for coverage of late 1985 and 1986 events.)

Archd., 1; dioc. (1986), 5; mil. vic.; abp., 1; bp., 6; parishes, 230; priests, 391 (181 dioc., 210 rel.); sem., 129; bros., 60; srs., 890; bap., 83,474; Caths., 4,797,000 (91.7%); tot. pop., 5,230,000.

England: Center of the United Kingdom of Great Britain (England, Scotland, Wales) and Northern Ireland, off the northwestern coast of Europe; capital, London. The arrival of St. Augustine of Canterbury and a band of monks in 597 marked the beginning of evangelization. Real organization of the Church took place some years after the Synod of Whitby, held in 663. Heavy losses were sustained in the wake of the Danish invasion in the 780s, but recovery starting from the time of Alfred the Great and dating especially from the middle of the 10th century led to Christianization of the whole country and close Church-state relations. The Norman Conquest of 1066 opened the Church in England to European influence. The 13th century was climactic, but decline had already set in by 1300 when the country had an all-time high of 17,000 religious. In the 14th century, John Wycliff presaged the Protestant Reformation. Henry VIII, failing in 1529 to gain annulment of his marriage to Catherine of Aragon, refused to acknowledge papal authority over the Church in England, had himself proclaimed its head, suppressed all houses of religious, and persecuted persons — Sts. Thomas More and John Fisher, among others — for not subscribing to the Oath of Supremacy and Act of Succession. He held the line on other-than-papal doctrine, however, until his death in 1547. Doctrinal aberrations were introduced during the reign of Edward VI (1547-53), through the Order of Communion, two books of Common Prayer, and the Articles of the Established Church. Mary Tudor's attempted Catholic restoration (1553-58) was a disaster, resulting in the deaths of more than 300 Protestants. Elizabeth (1558-1603) firmed up the Established Church with formation of a hierarchy, legal enactments and multi-phased persecution. One hundred and 11 priests and 62 lay persons were among the casualties of persecution during the underground Catholic revival which followed the return to England of missionary priests from France and The Lowlands. Several periods of comparative toleration ensued after Elizabeth's death. The first of several apostolic vicariates was established in 1685; this form of church government was maintained until the restoration of the hierarchy and diocesan organization in 1850. The revolution of 1688 and subsequent developments to about 1781 subjected Catholics to a wide variety of penal laws and disabilities in religious, civic and social life. The situation began to improve in 1791, and from 1801 Parliament frequently considered proposals for the repeal of penal laws against Catholics. The Act of Emancipation restored citizenship rights to Catholics in 1829. Restrictions remained in force for some time afterwards, however, on public religious worship and activity. The hierarchy was restored in 1850. Since then the Catholic Church, existing side by side with the Established Churches of England and Scotland, has followed a general pattern of growth and development. Great Britain established diplomatic relations with Vatican City in 1982.

Archd., 4; dioc., 15; ap. ex., 1; mil. vic. (Great Britain); card., 1; abp., 3; bp., 31; parishes, 2,561; priests, 5,913 (3,904 dioc., 2,009 rel.); p.d., 111; sem., 516; bros., 758; srs., 10,633; bap., 73,531; Caths., 4,133,842 (8.9%); tot. pop., 46,625,000 (1985).

Equatorial Guinea: Republic on the west coast of Africa, consisting of Rio Muni on the mainland and the islands of Fernando Po and Annobon in the Gulf of Guinea: capital, Malabo (Santa Isabel). Evangelization began in 1841. The country became independent of Spain in 1968. The Church was severely repressed during the 11-year rule of Pres. Macias (Masie) Nguema. Developments since his overthrow (August 1979) indicated some measure of improvement. An ecclesiastical province was established in October, 1982. Established diplomatic relations with Vatican City in 1981.

Archd., 1; dioc., 2; abp., 1 (nat.); bp., 2 (nat.); parishes, 40; priests, 54 (21 dioc., 33 rel.); p.d. 1; sem., 22; bros., 21; srs., 147; catechists, 590; bap., 10,189; Caths., 327,000; tot. pop., 380,000.

Estonia: Baltic republic forcibly absorbed by the U.S.S.R. in 1941; capital Tallinn. Catholicism was introduced in the 11th and 12th centuries. Jurisdiction over the area was made directly subject to the Holy See in 1215. Lutheran penetration was general in the Reformation period and Russian Orthodox influence was strong from early in the 18th century until 1917 when independence was attained. The first of several apostolic administrators was appointed in 1924. The small Catholic community was hard hit during and since Russian occupation in 1941. The Russian take-over of Estonia has not been recognized by the Holy See or the United States.

Ethiopia: Socialist state in northeast Africa; capital, Addis Ababa. The country was evangelized by missionaries from Egypt in the fourth century and had a bishop by about 340. Following the lead of its parent body, the Egyptian (Coptic) Church, the Church in the area succumbed to the Monophysite heresy in the sixth century. Catholic influence was negligible for centuries. An ordinariate for the Ethiopian Rite was established in Eritrea in 1930. An apostolic delegation was set up in Addis Ababa in 1937 and several jurisdictions were organized, some under the Congregation for the Oriental Churches and others under the Congregation for the Evangelization of Peoples. Most of the Catholics in the country are in the former Italian colony of Eritrea. The first Ethiopian cardinal (Abp. Paulos Tzadua of Addis Ababa) was named in 1985. Ethiopia maintains diplomatic relations with Vatican City.

Archd., 1; dioc., 2; v.a., 5; p.a., 1; card., 1; abp., 1; bp., 6; parishes, 254; priests, 496 (142 dioc., 354 rel.); p.d., 5; sem., 119; bros., 180; srs., 1,014; catechists, 520; bap., 10,804; Caths., 245,000 (.7%); tot. pop., 33,680,000.

Falkland Islands: British colony off the southern tip of South America; capital, Port Stanley. The islands are called Islas Malvinas by Argentina which also claims sovereignty.

P.a., 1; priests, 2 (rel.); bap., 1; Caths., 200; tot. pop., 2,000 (1985).

Faroe Islands: Self-governing island group in North Atlantic; Danish possession. Under ecclesiastical jurisdiction of Copenhagen diocese.

Priest, 1 (rel.); srs., 12; Caths. (1982), 100; tot. pop., 42,000.

Fiji: Independent island group (100 inhabited) in the southwest Pacific; capital, Suva. Marist missionaries began work in 1844 after Methodism had been firmly established. A prefecture apostolic was organized in 1863. The hierarchy was established in 1966. Established diplomatic relations with Vatican City, 1978.

Archd., 1; abp., 1 (nat.); parishes, 23; priests, 90 (17 dioc., 73 rel.); sem., 45; bros., 54; srs., 311; catechists, 206; bap., 1,989; Caths., 57,000 (8.5%); tot. pop., 670,000.

Finland: Republic in northern Europe; capital, Helsinki. Swedes evangelized the country in the 12th century. The Reformation swept the country, resulting in the prohibition of Catholicism in 1595, general reorganization of ecclesiastical life and affairs, and dominance of the Evangelical Lutheran Church. Catholics were given religious liberty in 1781 but missionaries and conversions were forbidden by law. The first Finnish priest since the Reformation was ordained in 1903 in Paris. A vicariate apostolic for Finland was erected in 1920 (made a diocese in 1955). A law on religious liberty, enacted in 1923, banned the foundation of monasteries. Finland maintains diplomatic relations with Vatican City.

Dioc., 1; bp., 1; parishes, 5; priests, 18 (2 dioc., 16 rel.); p.d., 1; bros., 1; srs., 29; bap., 73; Caths., 4,000 (.08%); tot. pop., 4,860,000.

France: Republic in western Europe; capital, Paris. Christianity was known around Lyons by the middle of the second century. By 250 there were 30 bishoprics. The hierarchy reached a fair degree of organization by the end of the fourth century. Vandals and Franks subsequently invaded the territory and caused barbarian turmoil and doctrinal problems because of their Arianism. The Frankish nation was converted following the baptism of Clovis about 496. Christianization was complete by some time in the seventh century. From then on the Church, its leaders and people, figured in virtually every important development — religious, cultural, political and social — through the periods of the Carolingians, feudalism, the Middle Ages and monarchies to the end of the 18th century. The great University of Paris became one of the intellectual centers of the 13th century. Churchmen and secular rulers were involved with developments surrounding the Avignon residence of the popes and curia from 1309 until near the end of the 14th century and with the disastrous Western Schism that followed. Strong currents of Gallicanism and conciliarism ran through ecclesiastical and secular circles in France; the former was an ideology and movement to restrict papal control of the Church in the country, the latter sought to make the pope subservient to a general council. Calvinism invaded the country about the middle of the 16th century and won a strong body of converts. Jansenism with its rigorous spirit and other aberrations appeared in the next century, to be followed by the highly influential Enlightenment. The Revolution which started in 1789 and was succeeded by the Napoleonic period completely changed the status of the Church, taking a toll of numbers by persecution and defection and disenfranchising the Church in practically every way. Throughout the 19th century the Church was caught up in the whirl of imperial and republican developments and made the victim of official hostility, popular indifference and liberal opposition. In this century, the Church has struggled with problems involving the heritage of the Revolution and its aftermath, the alienation of intellectuals, liberalism, the estrangement of the working classes because of the Church's former identification with the ruling class, and the massive needs of contemporary society. France maintains diplomatic relations with Vatican City.

Archd., 18; dioc., 76; prel., 1; ap. ex., 1; ord., 1; mil. vic.; card., 9; abp., 33; bp., 160; parishes, 37,455; priests, 37,550 (29,421 dioc., 8,129 rel.); p.d., 207; sem., 1,439; bros., 5,200; srs., 78,996; bap., 507,710; Caths., 46,682,000 (85.4%); tot. pop., 54,650,000.

Gabon: Republic on the west coast of central Africa; capital, Libreville. Sporadic missionary effort took place before 1881 when effective evangelization began. The hierarchy was established in 1955. Gabon maintains diplomatic relations with Vatican City.

Archd., 1; dioc., 3; abp., 1 (nat.); bp., 3 (nat.); parishes, 59; priests, 105 (31 dioc., 74 rel.); sem., 9; bros., 35; srs., 153; catechists, 1,149; bap., 8,546; Caths., 575,000 (50.8%); tot. pop., 1,130,000.

Gambia, The: Republic (1970) on the north-western coast of Africa, smallest state in Africa; capital, Banjui. The country was under the jurisdiction of a vicariate apostolic until 1931. The hierarchy was established in 1957. Established diplomatic relations with Vatican City, 1978.

Dioc., 1; bp., 1; parishes, 12; priests, 20 (rel.); sem. 8; bros., 1; srs., 38; catechists, 33; bap., 378; Caths., 14,000 (2%); tot. pop., 686,000.

Germany: Country in northern Europe partitioned in 1949 into the Communist German Democratic Republic in the East (capital, East Berlin) and the German Federal Republic in the West (capital, Bonn). Christianity was introduced in the third century, if not earlier. Trier, which became a center for missionary activity, had a bishop by 400. Visigoth invaders introduced Arianism in the fifth century but were converted in the seventh century by the East Franks, Celtic and other missionaries. St. Boniface, the apostle of Germany, established real ecclesiastical organization in the eighth century. The Church had great influence during the Carolingian period. Bishops from that time onward began to act in dual roles as pastors and rulers, a state of affairs which led inevitably to confusion and conflict in Church-state relations and perplexing problems of investiture. The Church developed strength and vitality through the Middle Ages but succumbed to abuses which antedated and prepared the ground for the Reformation. Luther's actions from 1517 made Germany a confessional battleground. Religious strife continued until conclusion of the Peace of Westphalia at the end of the Thirty Years' War in 1648. Nearly a century earlier the Peace of Augsburg (1555) had been designed, without success, to assure a degree of tranquillity by recognizing the legitimacy of different religious confessions in different states, depending on the decisions of princes. The implicit principle that princes should control the churches emerged in practice into the absolutism and Josephinism of subsequent years. St. Peter Canisius and his fellow Jesuits spearheaded a Counter Reformation in the second half of the 16th century. Before the end of the century, however, 70 per cent of the population of north and central Germany were Lutheran. Calvinism also had established a strong presence. The Church gained internal strength in a defensive position. Through much of the 19th century, however, its influence was eclipsed by Protestant intellectuals and other influences. It suffered some impoverishment also as a result of shifting boundaries and the secularization of property shortly after 1800. It came under direct attack in the Kulturkampf of the 1870s but helped to generate the opposition which resulted in a dampening of the campaign of Bismarck against it. Despite action by Catholics on the social front and other developments, discrimination against the Church spilled over into the 20th century and lasted beyond World War I. Catholics in politics struggled with others to pull the country through numerous postwar crises. The dissolution of the Center Party, agreed to by the bishops in 1933 without awareness of the ultimate consequences, contributed negatively to the rise of

Hitler to supreme power. Church officials protested the Nazi anti-Church and anti-Semitic actions, but to no avail. After World War II Christian leadership had much to do with the recovery of Western Germany. East Germany, gone Communist under Russian auspices, initiated a program of control and repression of the Church in 1948 and 1949. With no prospect of success for measures designed to split bishops, priests, religious and lay persons, the regime has concentrated most of its attention on mind control, especially of the younger generation, by the elimination of religious schools, curtailment of freedom for religious instruction and formation, severe restriction of the religious press, and the substitution since the mid-50s of youth initiation and Communist ceremonies for the rites of baptism, confirmation, marriage, and funerals. Bishops are generally forbidden to travel outside the Republic. The number of priests is decreasing, partly because of reduced seminary enrollments ordered by the government since 1958. In 1973, the Vatican appointed three apostolic administrators and one auxiliary (all titular bishops) for the areas of three West German dioceses located in East Germany. West Germany maintains diplomatic relations with Vatican City.

West Germany: Archd., 5; dioc., 16 (also part of the Berlin diocese); ap., ex., 1; mil. vic.; card., 5; abp., 3; bp., 59; parishes, 11,893; priests, 22,175 (16,656 dioc., 5,519 rel.); p.d., 893; sem., 3,012; bros., 2,717; srs., 60,578; bap., 261,229; Caths., 28,487,000 (46.4%); tot. pop., 61,429,000.

East Germany: Dioc., 2 (Dresden-Meissen and Berlin, since most of its territory lies in East Germany); a.a., 1 (Gorlitz; there are also 3 territories with apostolic administrators); card., 1 (Joachim Meisner, bishop of Berlin); bps., 8; parishes, 903; priests, 1,396 (1,181 dioc., 215 rel.); p.d., 42; sem., 139; bros., 117; srs., 2,622; bap., 9,752; Caths., 1,339,000 (8%); tot. pop., 16,700,000.

Ghana: Republic on the western coast of Africa, bordering on the Gulf of Guinea; capital, Accra. Priests visited the country in 1482, 11 years after discovery by the Portuguese, but missionary effort — hindered by the slave trade and other factors — was slight until 1880 when systematic evangelization began. A prefecture apostolic was set up in 1879. The hierarchy was established in 1950. Ghana maintains diplomatic relations with Vatican City.

Archd., 2; dioc., 7; abp., 2 (nat.); bp., 7 (nat.); parishes, 162; priests, 490 (249 dioc., 241 rel.); sem., 279; bros., 145; srs., 510; catechists, 3,125; bap., 41,098; Caths., 1,538,000 (12%); tot. pop., 12,700,000.

Gibraltar: British dependency on the tip of the Spanish Peninsula on the Mediterranean. Evangelization took place after the Moors were driven out near the end of the 15th century. The Church was hindered by the British who acquired the colony in 1713. Most of the Catholics were, and are, Spanish and Italian immigrants and their descendants. A vicariate apostolic was organized in 1817. The diocese was erected in 1910.

Dioc., 1; bp., 1; parishes, 5; priests, 10 (9 dioc., 1 rel.); sem., 4; srs., 21; bap., 271; Caths., 20,000; tot. pop., 30,000.

Greece: Republic in southeastern Europe on the Balkan Peninsula; capital, Athens. St. Paul preached the Gospel at Athens and Corinth on his second missionary journey and visited the country again on his third tour. Other Apostles may have passed through also. Two bishops from Greece attended the First Council of Nicaea. After the division of the Roman Empire, the Church remained Eastern in rite and later broke ties with Rome as a result of the schism of 1054. A Latin-Rite jurisdiction was set up during the period of the Latin Empire of Constantinople, 1204-1261, but crumbled afterwards. Unity efforts of the Council of Florence had poor results. The country now has Greek Catholic and Latin jurisdictions. The Greek Orthodox Church is predominant. Established diplomatic relations with Vatican City in 1980.

Archd., 4; dioc., 4; v.a., 1; ap. ex., 1; ord., 1; abp., 3; bp., 2; parishes, 77; priests, 101 (56 dioc., 45 rel.); bros., 44; srs., 154; bap., 384; Caths., 50,000 (.5%); tot. pop., 9,850,000.

Greenland (Kalaalit Nunaat): Danish island province northeast of North America; granted self rule in 1979; capital, Nuuk (Godthaab). Catholicism was introduced about 1000. The first diocese was established in 1124 and a line of bishops dated from then until 1537. The first known churches in the western hemisphere, dating from about the 11th century, were on Greenland; the remains of 19 have been unearthed. The departure of Scandinavians and spread of the Reformation reduced the Church to nothing. The Moravian Brethren evangelized the Eskimos from the 1720s to 1901. By 1930 the Danish Church — Evangelical Lutheran — was in full possession. Since 1930 priests have been in Greenland, which is part of the Copenhagen diocese.

Priest, 1 (rel.); srs., 3; bap., 1; tot. pop., 50,000. No report on number of Catholics.

Grenada: Independent island state in the West Indies; capital, St. George's. Established diplomatic relations with Vatican City in 1979.

Dioc., 1; bp., 1; parishes, 20; priests, 20 (5 dioc., 15 rel.); p.d., 3; sem., 2; bros., 10; catechists, 56; bap., 1,089; Caths., 75,871; tot. pop., 115,481 (1985).

Guadeloupe: French overseas department in the Leeward Islands of the West Indies; capital, Basse-Terre. Catholicism was introduced in the islands in the 16th century.

Dioc., 1; bp., 1; parishes, 46; priests, 70 (46 dioc., 24 rel.); sem., 13; bros., 7; srs., 182; bap., 3,332; Caths., 260,000; tot. pop., 330,000 (1985).

Guam: Outlying area of U.S. in the southwest Pacific; capital, Agana. The first Mass was offered in the Mariana Islands in 1521. The islands were evangelized by the Jesuits, from 1668, and other missionaries. The first native Micronesian bishop was ordained in 1970. The Agana diocese, which had been a suffragan of San Francisco, was made a metropolitan see in 1984.

Archd., 1; archbp., 1 (nat.); parishes, 26;

priests, 47 *(15 dioc., 32 rel.); p.d., 7; sem., 20; bros., 5; srs., 138; catechists, 1,145; bap., 2,199; Caths., 103,000; tot. pop., 110,000.*

Guatemala: Republic in Central America; capital, Guatemala City. Evangelization dates from the beginning of Spanish occupation in 1524. The first diocese, for all Central American territories administered by the captaincy general of Guatemala, was established in 1534. The country became independent in 1839, following annexation to Mexico in 1821, secession in 1823 and membership in the Central American Federation from 1825. In 1870, a government installed by a liberal revolution repudiated the concordat of 1853 and took active measures against the Church. Separation of Church and state was decreed; religious orders were suppressed and their property seized; priests and religious were exiled; schools were secularized. Full freedom was subsequently granted. The country has been in a virtual state of civil war in recent years, with violence and repression directed at all segments of the population, including the Church which has been subjected to persecution. From 1980 to 1985 an estimated 60,000 people were reported killed or missing. The inauguration in January, 1986, of Vinicio Cerezo as president of the country's first civilian government in 20 years was greeted with the hope that he would promote a more just society.

Archd., 1; dioc., 8; prel., 2; v.a., 1; a.a., 1; bp., 15; parishes, 348; priests, 655 (192 dioc., 463 rel.); p.d., 2; sem., 310; bros., 127; srs., 1,094; bap., 178,739; Caths. 6,661,000 (84%); tot. pop. 7,930,000.

Guiana, French (Cayenne): French overseas department on the northeast coast of South America; capital, Cayenne. Catholicism was introduced in the 17th century. The Cayenne diocese was established in 1956.

Dioc., 1; bp., 1; parishes, 22; priests, 27 (5 dioc., 22 rel.); bros., 2; srs., 107; bap., 1,607; Caths., 59,000; tot. pop., 76,000.

Guinea: Republic on the west coast of Africa; capital, Conakry. Occasional missionary work followed exploration by the Portuguese about the middle of the 15th century; organized effort dates from 1877. The hierarchy was established in 1955. Following independence from France in 1958, Catholic schools were nationalized, youth organizations banned and missionaries restricted. Foreign missionaries were expelled in 1967. Archbishop Tchidimbo of Conakry, sentenced to life imprisonment in 1971 on a charge of conspiring to overthrow the government, was released in August, 1979; he resigned his see. Private schools, suppressed by the government for more than 20 years, were again authorized in 1984. Guinea established diplomatic relations with Vatican City in 1986.

Archd., 1; dioc., 1; p.a., 1; abp., 1 (nat.); bp., 1 (nat.); parishes, 28; priests, 22 (21 dioc., 1 rel.); sem., 25; bros., 3; srs., 24; catechists, 76; bap., 931; Caths., 49,000 (.9%); tot. pop., 5,180,000.

Guinea-Bissau (formerly Portuguese Guinea): Independent state on the west coast of Africa; capital, Bissau. Catholicism was introduced in the second half of the 15th century but limited missionary work, hampered by the slave trade, had meager results. Missionary work in this century dates from 1933. A prefecture apostolic was established in 1955 (made a diocese in 1977). Guinea-Bissau established diplomatic relations with Vatican City in 1986.

Dioc., 1; bp., 1; parishes, 22; priests, 47 (1 dioc., 46 rel.); p.d., 1; sem., 4; bros., 20; srs., 46; catechists, 154; bap., 1,231; Caths., 44,350; tot. pop., 900,000 (1985).

Guyana: Republic on the northern coast of South America; capital, Georgetown. In 1899 the Catholic Church and other churches were given equal status with the Church of England and the Church of Scotland, which had sole rights up to that time. Most of the Catholics are Portuguese. The Georgetown diocese was established in 1956, 10 years before Guyana became independent of England. The first native bishop was appointed in 1971. Schools were nationalized in 1976. Increased government interference was reported in 1980-81. The Catholic newspaper was forced to close and missionaries were denied access to certain areas. Government harassment of the Church increased in 1985-86 (see Index).

Dioc., 1; bp., 1; parishes, 27; priests, 45 (7 dioc., 38 rel.); sem., 4; bros., 6; srs., 40; catechists, 612; bap., 1,488; Caths., 94,000; tot. pop., 920,000.

Haiti: Caribbean republic on the western third of Hispaniola adjacent to the Dominican Republic; capital, Port-au-Prince. Evangelization followed discovery by Columbus in 1492. Capuchins and Jesuits did most of the missionary work in the 18th century. From 1804, when independence was declared, until 1860, the country was in schism. Relations were regularized by a concordat concluded in 1860, when an archdiocese and four dioceses were established. Factors hindering the development of the Church have been a shortage of native clergy, inadequate religious instruction and the prevalence of voodoo. Political upheavals in the 1960s had serious effects on the Church. In 1984, a new concordat was concluded replacing the one in effect since 1860. Haiti maintains diplomatic relations with Vatican City.

Archd., 1; dioc., 6; abp., 1; bp., 6; parishes, 190; priests, 427 (236 dioc., 191 rel.); p.d., 2; sem., 165; bros., 205; srs., 905; bap., 99,280; Caths., 4,582,000 (86%); tot. pop. 5,300,000.

Honduras: Republic in Central America; capital, Tegucigalpa. Evangelization preceded establishment of the first diocese in the 16th century. Under Spanish rule and after independence from 1823, the Church held a favored position until 1880 when equal legal status was given to all religions. Harassment of priests and nuns working among peasants and Salvadoran refugees was reported in recent years. Honduras maintains diplomatic relations with Vatican City.

Archd., 1; dioc., 4; prel., 1; abp., 1; bp., 7; parishes, 122; priests, 240 (64 dioc., 176 rel.); p.d., 4; sem., 46; bros., 12; srs., 308; cate-

chists, *1,364; bap., 92,586; Caths., 3,930,000 (96%); tot. pop., 4,090,000.*

Hong Kong: British crown colony at the mouth of the Canton River, adjacent to the southeast Chinese province of Kwangtung. Most of the territory, leased from China, is scheduled for return in 1997. A prefecture apostolic was established in 1841. Members of the Pontifical Institute for Foreign Missions began work there in 1858. The Hong Kong diocese was erected in 1946.

Dioc., 1; bp., 1; parishes, 53; priests, 354 (73 dioc., 281 rel.); sem., 27; bros., 77; srs., 785; catechists, 577; bap., 5,226; Caths., 270,000; tot. pop., 5,310,000.

Hungary: People's republic in east central Europe; capital, Budapest. The early origins of Christianity in the country, whose territory was subject to a great deal of change, is not known. Magyars accepted Christianity about the end of the 10th century. St. Stephen I (d. 1038) promoted its spread and helped to organize some of its historical dioceses. Bishops early became influential in politics as well as in the Church. For centuries the country served as a buffer for the Christian West against barbarians from the East, notably the Mongols in the 13th century. Religious orders, whose foundations started from the 1130s, provided the most effective missionaries, pastors and teachers. Outstanding for years were the Franciscans and Dominicans; the Jesuits were noted for their work in the Counter-Reformation from the second half of the 16th century onwards. Hussites and Waldensians prepared the way for the Reformation which struck at almost the same time as the Turks. The Reformation made considerable progress after 1526, resulting in the conversion of large numbers to Lutheranism and Calvinism by the end of the century. Most of them or their descendants returned to the Church later, but many Magyars remained staunch Calvinists. Turks repressed the churches, Protestant as well as Catholic, during a reign of 150 years but they managed to survive. Domination of the Church was one of the objectives of government policy during the reigns of Maria Theresa and Joseph II in the second half of the 18th century; their Josephinism affected Church-state relations until the first World War. More than 100,000 Eastern-Rite schismatics were reunited with Rome about the turn of the 18th century. Secularization increased in the second half of the 19th century, which also witnessed the birth of many new Catholic organizations and movements to influence life in the nation and the Church. Catholics were involved in the social chaos and anti-religious atmosphere of the years following World War I, struggling with their compatriots for religious as well as political survival. After World War II Communist strength, which had manifested itself with less intensity earlier in the century, was great long before it forced the legally elected president out of office in 1947 and imposed a Soviet type of constitution on the country in 1949. The campaign against the Church started with the disbanding of Catholic organizations in 1946. In 1948, "Caritas," the Catholic charitable organization, was taken over and all Catholic schools, colleges and institutions were suppressed. Interference in church administration and attempts to split the bishops preceded the arrest of Cardinal Mindszenty on Dec. 26, 1948, and his sentence to life imprisonment in 1949. (He was free for a few days during the unsuccessful uprising of 1956. He then took up residence at the U.S. Embassy in Budapest where he remained until September, 1971, when he was permitted to leave the country. He died in 1975 in Vienna.) In 1950, religious orders and congregations were suppressed and 10,000 religious were interned. At least 30 priests and monks were assassinated, jailed or deported. About 4,000 priests and religious were confined in jail or concentration camps. The government sponsored a national "Progressive Catholic" church and captive organizations for priests and "Catholic Action," which attracted only a small minority. Signs were clear in 1965 and 1966 that a 1964 agreement with the Holy See regarding episcopal appointments had settled nothing. Six bishops were appointed by the Holy See and some other posts were filled, but none of the prelates were free from government surveillance and harassment. Four new bishops were appointed by the Holy See in January and ordained in Budapest in February, 1969; three elderly prelates resigned their sees. Shortly thereafter, peace priests complained that the "too Roman" new bishops would not deal with them. Talks between Vatican and Hungarian representatives during the past several years have resulted in the appointment of diocesan bishops to fill long-vacant sees.

Archd., 3; dioc., 8; abb., 1; ap. ex., 1; abp., 4; bp., 14; parishes, 2,285; priests, 3,156 (3,020 dioc., 136 rel.); p.d., 3; sem., 309; bros., 54; srs., 75; bap., 70,574; Caths., 6,533,000 (61%); tot. pop., 10,690,000.

Iceland: Island republic between Norway and Greenland; capital, Reykjavik. Irish hermits were there in the eighth century. Missionaries subsequently evangelized the island and Christianity was officially accepted about 1000. The first bishop was ordained in 1056. The Black Death had dire effects and spiritual decline set in during the 15th century. Lutheranism was introduced from Denmark between 1537 and 1552 and made the official religion. Some Catholic missionary work was done in the 19th century. Religious freedom was granted to the few Catholics in 1874. A vicariate was erected in 1929 (made a diocese in 1968). Iceland maintains diplomatic relations with Vatican City.

Dioc., 1; bp., 1; parishes, 2; priests, 9 (5 dioc., 4 rel.); sem., 3; srs., 38; bap., 14; Caths., 2,000; tot. pop., 230,000.

India: Republic on the subcontinent of south central Asia; capital, New Delhi. Long-standing tradition credits the Apostle Thomas with the introduction of Christianity in the Kerala area. Evangelization followed the establishment of Portuguese posts and the conquest of Goa in 1510. Jesuits, Franciscans, Dominicans, Augustinians and members of other religious orders figured in the early missionary history. An archdiocese for Goa, with two suffragan sees, was set up in 1558. Five provincial councils were held between 1567 and 1606. The number of Catholics in 1572 was estimated to be 280,000. This figure rose to 800,000 in 1700 and declined to 500,000 in 1800. Missionaries had some difficulties with the British East India Co. which exercised virtual government control from 1757 to 1858. They also had trouble because of a conflict that developed between policies of the Portuguese government, which pressed its rights of patronage in episcopal and clerical appointments, and the Congregation for the Propagation of the Faith, which sought greater freedom of action in the same appointments. This struggle eventuated in the schism of Goa between 1838 and 1857. In 1886, when the number of Catholics was estimated to be one million, the hierarchy for India and Ceylon was restored. Jesuits contributed greatly to the development of Catholic education from the second half of the 19th century. A large percentage of the Catholic population is located around Goa and Kerala and farther south. The country is predominantly Hindu. So-called anti-conversion laws in effect in several states have had a restrictive effect on pastoral ministry and social service. India maintains diplomatic relations with Vatican City. (See Index for papal visit).

Patriarchate, 1 (titular of East Indies); archd., 19; dioc. (1986), 95; p.a., 1; card., 3; abp., 19; bp., 102; parishes, 5,558; priests, 12,662 (7,351 dioc., 5,311 rel.); p.d., 15; sem., 5,876; bros., 2,601; srs., 53,679; catechists, 28,508; Caths., 12,800,000 (1.7%); tot. pop. 746,740,000 (1985).

Indonesia: Republic southeast of Asia, consisting of some 3,000 islands including Kalimantan (most of Borneo), Sulawesi (Celebes), Java, the Lesser Sundas, Moluccas, Sumatra, Timor and West Irian (Irian Jaya, western part of New Guinea); capital, Jakarta. Evangelization by the Portuguese began about 1511. St. Francis Xavier, greatest of the modern missionaries, spent some 14 months in the area. Christianity was strongly rooted in some parts of the islands by 1600. Islam's rise to dominance began at this time. The Dutch East Indies Co., which gained effective control in the 17th century, banned evangelization by Catholic missionaries for some time but Dutch secular and religious priests managed to resume the work. A vicariate of Batavia for all the Dutch East Indies was set up in 1841. About 90 per cent of the population is Moslem. The hierarchy was established in 1961. Indonesia maintains diplomatic relations with Vatican City.

Archd., 7; dioc., 26; mil. vic.; card., 1; abp., 7; bps., 28; parishes, 617; priests, 1,742 (288 dioc., 1,454 rel.); p.d., 7; sem., 1,278; bros., 737; srs., 4,256; catechists, 12,267; bap., 164,694; Caths., 4,050,000 (2.5%); tot. pop., 159,430,000. (Statistics for former Portuguese Timor which was annexed by Indonesia in 1976 are listed separately; see Timor, Eastern.)

Iran: Islamic republic in southwestern Asia, between the Caspian Sea and the Persian Gulf; capital, Teheran. Some of the earliest Christian communities were established in this area outside the (then) Roman Empire. They suffered persecution in the fourth century and were then cut off from the outside world. Nestorianism was generally professed in the late fifth century. Islam became dominant after 640. Some later missionary work was attempted but without success. Religious liberty was granted in 1834, but Catholics were the victims of a massacre in 1918. Islam is the religion of perhaps 98 per cent of the population. In 1964 the country had 100,000 Monophysites, the largest group of Christians, and some 20,000 Nestorians. Catholics belong to the Latin, Armenian and Chaldean rites. Iran (Persia until 1935) maintains diplomatic relations with Vatican City.

Archd., 4; dioc., 2; abp., 3; bp., 1; parishes; 32; priests, 51 (9 dioc., 42 rel.); p.d., 10; bros., 12; srs., 42, bap., 244; Caths., 18,000 (.04%); tot. pop., 41,640,000.

Iraq: Republic in southwestern Asia, between Iran and Saudi Arabia; capital, Baghdad. Some of the earliest Christian communities were established in the area, whose history resembles that of Iran. Catholics belong to the Armenian, Chaldean, Latin and Syrian rites; Chaldeans are most numerous. Islam is the religion of some 90 per cent of the population. Iraq maintains diplomatic relations with Vatican City.

Patriarchate, 1; archd., 9; dioc., 5; patriarch, 1; abp., 9; bp., 4; parishes, 106; priests, 141 (105 dioc., 36 rel.); p.d., 2; sem., 15; bros., 12; srs., 241; bap., 5,270; Caths., 378,000 (2.5%); tot. pop., 14,650,000.

Ireland: Republic in the British Isles; capital, Dublin. St. Patrick, who is venerated as the apostle of Ireland, evangelized parts of the island for some years after the middle of the fifth century. Conversion of the island was not accomplished, however, until the seventh century or later. Celtic monks were the principal missionaries. The Church was organized along monastic lines at first, but a movement developed in the 11th century for the establishment of jurisdiction along episcopal lines. By that time many Roman usages had been adopted. The Church gathered strength during the period from the Norman Conquest of England to the reign of Henry VIII despite a wide variety of rivalries, wars, and other disturbances. Henry introduced an age of repression of the faith which continued for many years under several of his successors. The Irish suffered from proscription of the Catholic faith, economic and social disabilities, subjection to absentee landlords and a plantation system designed to keep them from owning property, and actual persecution which took an uncertain toll of lives up until about 1714. Most of those living in the northern part of Ireland became Anglican and Presbyterian in the 1600s but the south remained strong in faith. Some penal laws remained in force until emancipation in 1829. Nearly 100 years later Ireland was divided by two enactments which made Northern Ireland, consisting of six counties, part of the United Kindgom (1920) and gave dominion status to the Irish Free State, made up of the other 26 counties (1922). This state (Eire, in Gaelic) was proclaimed the Republic of Ireland in 1949. The Catholic Church predominates but religious freedom is guaranteed for all. Ireland maintains diplomatic relations with Vatican City.

Archd., 4; dioc., 22; card., 1; abp., 3; bp., 31; parishes, 1,333; priests, 6,420 (3,710 dioc., 2,710 rel.); p.d., 3; sem., 1,081; bros., 1,846; srs., 12,553; bap., 80,404 (preceding figures include Northern Ireland); Caths., (approx.), 3,286,600 (93%); tot. pop., 3,534,000.

Ireland, Northern: Part of the United Kingdom, it consists of six of the nine counties of Ulster in the northeast corner of Ireland; capital, Belfast. History is given under Ireland, above. For recent developments, see Index.

Tot. pop., 1,490,228, Catholics comprise about one third. (Other statistics are included in Ireland).

Israel: Parliamentary democracy in the Middle East, at the eastern end of the Mediterranean; capitals, Jerusalem and Tel Aviv (diplomatic). Israel was the birthplace of Christianity, the site of the first Christian communities. Some persecution was suffered in the early Christian era and again during the several hundred years of Roman control. Moslems conquered the territory in the seventh century and, except for the period of the Kingdom of Jerusalem established by Crusaders, remained in control most of the time up until World War I. The Church survived in the area, sometimes just barely, but it did not prosper greatly or show any notable increase in numbers. The British took over the protectorate of the area after World War I. Partition into Israel for the Jews and Palestine for the Arabs was approved by the United Nations in 1947. War broke out a year later with the proclamation of the Republic of Israel. The Israelis won the war and 50 percent more territory than they had originally been ceded. War broke out again for six days in June, 1967, and in October, 1973, resulting in a Middle East crisis which persists to the present time. Caught in the middle of the conflict are hundreds of thousands of dispossessed Palestinian refugees. Judaism is the faith professed by about 85 percent of the inhabitants; approximately one-third of them are considered observants. Most of the Arab minority are Moslems. The Akka archdiocese for Melkites is situated in Israel. Maronites are subject to the bishop of Tyr, Lebanon. Latins are under the jurisdiction of the Roman patriarchate of Jerusalem. Israel has an apostolic delegate. The *1983 Statistical Yearbook of the Church* reported a Catholic population of 131,000. The total population is 4,100,000.

Italy: Republic in southern Europe; capital, Rome. A Christian community was formed early at Rome, probably by the middle of the first century. St. Peter established his see there. He and St. Paul suffered death for the faith there in the 60s. The early Christians were persecuted at various times there, as in other parts of the empire, but the Church developed in numbers and influence, gradually spreading out from towns and cities in the center and south to rural areas and the north. Organization, in the process of formation in the second century, developed greatly between the

fifth and eighth centuries. By the latter date the Church had already come to grips with serious problems, including doctrinal and disciplinary disputes that threatened the unity of faith, barbarian invasions, and the need for the pope and bishops to take over civil responsibilities because of imperial default. The Church has been at the center of life on the peninsula throughout the centuries. It emerged from underground in 313, with the Edict of Milan, and rose to a position of prestige and lasting influence. It educated and converted the barbarians, preserved culture through the early Middle Ages and passed it on to later times, suffered periods of decline and gained strength through recurring reforms, engaged in military combat for political reasons and intellectual combat for the preservation and development of doctrine, saw and patronized the development of the arts, experienced all human strengths and weaknesses in its members, knew triumph and the humiliation of failure. For long centuries, from the fourth to the 19th, the Church was a temporal as well as spiritual power. This temporal aspect complicated its history in Italy. Since the 1870s, however, when the Papal States were annexed by the Kingdom of Italy, the history became simpler — but remained complicated — as the Church, shorn of temporal power, began to find new freedom for the fulfillment of its spiritual mission. In 1985, a new concordat was ratified between the Vatican and Italy, replacing one in effect since 1929. (See Index: Vatican-Italian Concordat.) Italy maintains diplomatic relations with Vatican City.

Patriarchate, 1; archd., 57; dioc., 208; prel., 4; abb., 7; mil. vic.; card., 34; abp., and bp., 451 (218 residential, 35 auxiliaries, remainder in other offices or retired); parishes, 28,691; priests, 61,670 (39,492 dioc., 22,178 rel.); p.d., 382; sem., 5,229; bros., 6,051; srs., 143,977; bap., 591,678; Caths., 55,703,000 (98%); tot. pop., 56,840,000.

Ivory Coast: Republic in western Africa; capital, Abidjan. The Holy Ghost Fathers began systematic evangelization in 1895. The first native priests from the area were ordained in 1934. The hierarchy was set up in 1955; the first native cardinal (Bernard Yago) was named in 1983. Ivory Coast maintains diplomatic relations with Vatican City.

Archd., 1; dioc., 9; card., 1 (nat.); bp., 10 (nat.); parishes, 186; priests, 413 (139 dioc., 274 rel.); sem., 75; bros., 74; srs., 522; catechists, 5,239; bap., 224,894; Caths., 972,000 (10.6%); tot. pop., 9,160,000.

Jamaica: Republic in the West Indies; capital, Kingston. Franciscans and Dominicans evangelized the island from about 1512 until 1655. Missionary work was interrupted after the English took possession but was resumed by Jesuits about the turn of the 19th century. A vicariate apostolic was organized in 1837. The hierarchy was established in 1967. Established diplomatic relations with Vatican City in 1979.

Archd., 1; dioc., 1; abp., 1; bp., 1; parishes, 65; priests, 80 (16 dioc., 64 rel.); p.d., 7; sem., 10; bros., 11; srs., 196; catechists, 372; bap.,

2,837; Caths., 220,000 (9.7%); tot. pop., 2,260,000.

Japan: Archipelago in the northwest Pacific; capital, Tokyo. Jesuits began evangelization in the middle of the 16th century and about 300,000 converts, most of them in Kyushu, were reported at the end of the century. The Nagasaki Martyrs were victims of persecution in 1597. Another persecution took some 4,000 lives between 1614 and 1651. Missionaries, banned for two centuries, returned about the middle of the 19th century and found Christian communities still surviving in Nagasaki and other places in Kyushu. A vicariate was organized in 1866. Religious freedom was guaranteed in 1889. The hierarchy was established in 1891. Japan maintains diplomatic relations with Vatican City.

Archd., 3; dioc., 13; p.a., 1; card., 1; abp., 2; bp., 15; parishes, 792; priests, 1,919 (530 dioc., 1,389 rel.); p.d., 3; sem., 215; bros., 397; srs., 7,164; catechists, 1,271; bap., 10,428; Caths., 416,000 (.34%); tot. pop., 119,260,000.

Jerusalem: The entire city, site of the first Christian community, has been under Israeli control since the Israeli-Arab war of June, 1967. There are two patriarchates in the city, Melkite and Latin. Jerusalem has an apostolic delegate.

Jordan: Constitutional monarchy in the Middle East; capital, Amman. Christianity there dates from apostolic times. Survival of the faith was threatened many times under the rule of Moslems from 636 and Ottoman Turks from 1517 to 1918, and in the Islamic Emirate of Trans-Jordan from 1918 to 1949. Since the creation of Israel, some 500,000 Palestinian refugees, some of them Christians, have been in Jordan. Islam is the state religion but religious freedom is guaranteed for all. The Greek Melkite-Rite Archdiocese of Petra and Philadelphia is located in Jordan. Latin (Roman)-Rite Catholics are under the jurisdiction of the Latin patriarchate of Jerusalem. Jordan has an apostolic delegate.

Archd., 1; abp., 1; parishes, 62; priests, 73 (51 dioc., 22 rel.); sem. 4; bros., 9; srs., 279; bap., 1,160; Caths., 99,000 (3%); tot. pop., 3,250,000.

Kenya: Republic in eastern Africa bordering on the Indian Ocean; capital, Nairobi. Systematic evangelization by the Holy Ghost Fathers began in 1892, nearly 40 years after the start of work by Protestant missionaries. The hierarchy was established in 1953. Kenya maintains diplomatic relations with Vatican City.

Archd., 1; dioc. (1986), 6; mil. vic., card., 1 (nat.); bp., 15 (10 nat.); parishes, 402; priests, 912 (291 dioc., 621 rel.); sem., 695; bros., 209; srs., 2,074; catechists, 5,252; bap., 224,894; Caths., 3,807,000 (20.2%); tot. pop., 17,780,000.

Kiribati (Gilbert Islands): Former British colony in Oceania; became independent July 12, 1979; capital Bairiki on Tarawa. French Missionaries of the Sacred Heart began work in the islands in 1888. A vicariate for the islands was organized in 1897. The hierarchy was established in 1966.

Dioc., 1; bp., 1; parishes, 24; priests, 16 (2 dioc., 14 rel.); sem., 6; bros., 5; srs., 56; bap., 2,070; Caths., 33,000 (60.7%); tot. pop., 65,000.

Korea: Peninsula in eastern Asia, east of China, divided into the (Communist) Democratic People's Republic in the North, formed May 1, 1948, with Pyongyang as its capital; and the Republic of Korea in the South, with Seoul as the capital. Some Catholics may have been in Korea before it became a "hermit kingdom" toward the end of the 16th century and closed its borders to foreigners. The real introduction to Catholicism came in 1784 through lay converts. A priest arriving in the country in 1794 found 4,000 Catholics there who had never seen a priest. A vicariate was erected in 1831 but was not manned for several years thereafter. There were 15,000 Catholics by 1857. Four persecutions in the 19th century took a terrible toll; several thousands died in the last one, 1866-69. (One-hundred and three martyrs of this period were canonized by Pope John Paul II during his 1984 apostolic visit to the country.) Freedom of religion was granted in 1883 when Korea opened its borders. Progress was made thereafter. The hierarchy was established in 1962. Since the war of 1950-1953, there have been no signs of Catholic life in the North, which has been blanketed by a news blackout. In July, 1972, both Koreas agreed to seek peaceful means of reunification. Bishop Tji of Won Ju, South Korea, convicted and sentenced to 15 years' imprisonment in 1974 on a charge of inciting to rebellion, was released in February, 1975. The South maintains diplomatic relations with Vatican City.

North Korea: Dioc., 2; abb., 1; bp., 1 (exiled); tot. pop., 19,190,000. No recent Catholic statistics available; there were an estimated 100,000 Catholics reported in 1969.

South Korea: Archd., 3; dioc., 11; mil. vic.; card., 1; abp., 2; bp., 14; parishes, 659; priests, 1,202 (895 dioc., 307 rel.); sem., 1,004; bros., 336; srs., 3,664; catechists, 5,503; bap., 137,784; Caths. 1,658,000 (4.1%); tot. pop., 39,950,000.

Kuwait: Constitutional monarchy (sultanate or sheikdom) in southwest Asia bordering on the Persian Gulf. Remote Christian origins probably date to apostolic times. Islam is the predominant and official religion. Kuwait maintains diplomatic relations with Vatican City.

V.a., 1; bp., 1; parishes, 4; priests, 8 (4 dioc., 4 rel.); srs., 29; bap., 828; Caths., 49,000; tot. pop., 1,670,000.

Laos: People's republic in southeast Asia, surrounded by China, Vietnam, Kampuchea, Thailand and Burma; capital, Vientiane. Systematic evangelization by French missionaries started about 1881; earlier efforts ended in 1688. The first mission was established in 1885 by Father Xavier Guégo. A vicariate apostolic was organized in 1899 when there were 8,000 Catholics and 2,000 catechumens in the country. Most of the foreign missionaries were expelled following the communist take-over in 1975. Buddhism is the state religion. Laos has an apostolic delegate.

V.a., 4; bp., 3; No statistics available.

Catholics numbered 35,000 (1% of the total population) in 1974. Tot. pop., 4,210,000.

Latvia: Baltic republic forcibly absorbed by the U.S.S.R. in the early 1940s; capital, Riga. Catholicism was introduced late in the 12th century. Lutheranism became the dominant religion after 1530. Catholics were free to practice their faith during the long period of Russian control and during independence from 1918 to 1940. The relatively small Catholic community has been repressed since the start of Soviet occupation. The Russian take-over of Latvia has not been recognized by the Holy See or the United States.

Archd., 1; dioc., 1; card., 1 (Julijans Vaivods, named in 1983); bp., 3 (titular, 1 is impeded); parishes, 179; priests, 104 (95 dioc., 9 rel.); sem., 54; bap., 5,003; Caths., 500,000; tot. pop. 2,500,000 (1986 Annuario Pontificio.)

Lebanon: Republic in the Middle East, north of Israel; capital, Beirut. Christianity, introduced in apostolic times, was firmly established by the end of the fourth century and has remained so despite heavy Moslem influence since early in the seventh century. The country is the center of the Maronite Rite. During the past 10 years the country has been torn by violence and often heavy fighting among rival political-religious factions drawn along Christian-Moslem lines. (See Index for 1986 developments.) Lebanon maintains diplomatic relations with Vatican City.

Archd. 11 (1 Armenian, 3 Maronite, 7 Greek Melkite); dioc., 6 (1 Chaldean, 5 Maronite); v.a., 1 (Latin); card., 1 (Patr. Antoine Khoraiche of Maronites); patriarchs, 3 (patriarchs of Antioch of the Maronites, a cardinal; Antioch of the Syrians and Cilicia of the Armenians who reside in Lebanon); abp. and bp., 19; parishes, 1,008; priests, 1,407 (660 dioc., 747 rel.); p.d., 1; sem., 282; bros., 116; srs., 3,415; bap., 15,010; Caths., 1,408,000; tot. pop., 2,640,000.

Lesotho: Constitutional monarchy, an enclave in the southeastern part of the Republic of South Africa; capital, Maseru. Oblates of Mary Immaculate, the first Catholic missionaries in the area, started evangelization in 1862. A prefecture apostolic was organized in 1894. The hierarchy was established in 1951. Lesotho maintains diplomatic relations with Vatican City.

Archd., 1; dioc., 3; abp., 1 (nat.); bp., 3 (nat.); parishes, 74; priests, 132 (22 dioc., 110 rel.); sem., 47; bros., 52; srs., 702; catechists, 2,044; bap., 287,228; Caths., 629,000 (14.4%); tot. pop., 1,440,000.

Liberia: Republic in western Africa, bordering on the Atlantic; capital, Monrovia. Missionary work and influence, dating interruptedly from the 16th century, were slight before the Society of African Missions undertook evangelization in 1906. The hierarchy was established in 1982. Liberia maintains diplomatic relations with Vatican City.

Archd., 1; dioc., 1; abp., 1 (nat.); bp., 1 (nat.); parishes, 47; priests, 53 (9 dioc., 44 rel.); p.d., 3; sem., 18; bros., 28; srs., 107; catechists, 192; bap. 1,908; Caths., 42,000 (2%); tot. pop., 2,060,000.

Libya: Arab state in northern Africa, on the Mediterranean between Egypt and Tunisia; capital, Tripoli. Christianity was probably preached in the area at an early date but was overcome by the spread of Islam from the 630s. Islamization was complete by 1067 and there has been no Christian influence since then. The Catholics in the country belong to the foreign colony. Islam is the state religion. Libya has an apostolic delegate.

V.a., 3; p.a., 1; bp., 2; parishes, 7; priests, 15 (rel.); bro., 1; srs., 120; bap., 210; Caths., 32,000 (.95%); tot. pop., 3,350,000.

Liechtenstein: Constitutional monarchy in central Europe, in the Alps and on the Rhine between Switzerland and Austria; capital, Vaduz. Christianity in the country dates from the fourth century; the area has been under the jurisdiction of Chur, Switzerland, since about that time. The Reformation had hardly any influence in the country. Catholicism is the state religion but religious freedom for all is guaranteed by law. Established diplomatic relations with Vatican City in 1985.

Parishes, 10; priests, 32 (18 dioc., 14 rel); bros., 9; srs., 102; bap., 350; Caths., 22,000; tot. pop., 30,000.

Lithuania: Baltic republic forcibly absorbed and under Soviet domination since 1945; capital, Vilna (Vilnius). Catholicism was introduced in 1251 and two dioceses were established by 1260. Effective evangelization took place between 1385 and 1417, when Catholicism became the state religion. Losses to Lutheranism in the 16th century were overcome. Efforts of czars to "russify" the Church between 1795 and 1918 were strongly resisted. Concordat relations with the Vatican were established in 1927, nine years after independence from Russia and 13 years before the start of another kind of Russian control with the following results, among others: all convents closed since 1940; four seminaries shut down; appointment to one seminary (Kaunas) only with government approval; priests restricted in pastoral ministry and subject to appointment by government officials; no religious services outside churches; no religious press; religious instruction banned; parish installations and activities controlled by directives enacted in 1976; two bishops — Vincentas Sladkevicius and Julijonas Steponavicius — forbidden to act as bishops and relegated to remote parishes in 1957 and 1961, respectively; arrest, imprisonment or detention in Siberia for four bishops, 185 priests, 275 lay persons between 1945 and 1955. Despite such developments and conditions, there remains a strong and vigorous underground Church in Lithuania, where the Soviet government finds its repressive potential limited by the solidarity of popular resistance. In July, 1982, two episcopal appointments were made: Rev. Antanas Vaicius was named titular bishop of Cubda and apostolic administrator of the Telsiai diocese and Klaipeda prelature; Bishop Vincentas Sladkevicius, titular bishop of Abora and auxiliary bishop of Kaisiadorys, was named apostolic administrator of that diocese. In 1983, four of the five bishops were allowed to go to Rome for their *ad limina* visit. The Soviet take-over of Lithuania is not recognized by the Holy See or the United States.

Archd., 2 (Kaunas and Vilna, which includes territory in political confines of Poland); dioc., 4; prel., 1; abp., 1 (titular); bp., 4 (none residential); parishes 631; priests, 700 (691 dioc., 9 rel.); sem., 101; bros., 19; srs., 245; Caths., 2,582,000 (79.9%); tot. pop., 3,228,000.

Luxembourg: Constitutional monarchy in western Europe, between Belgium, Germany and France; capital, Luxembourg. Christianity, introduced in the fifth and sixth centuries, was firmly established by the end of the eighth century. A full-scale parish system was in existence in the ninth century. Monastic influence was strong until the Reformation, which had minimal influence in the country. The Church experienced some adverse influence from the currents of the French Revolution. Luxembourg maintains diplomatic relations with Vatican City.

Dioc., 1; abp.-bp., 1; parishes, 274; priests, 419 (317 dioc., 102 rel.); p.d., 2; sem., 24; bros., 26; srs., 1,143; bap., 3,294; Caths. 360,386 (97%); tot. pop., 370,000.

Macau (Macao): Portuguese-administered territory in southeast Asia across the Pearl River estuary from Hong Kong. Christianity was introduced by the Jesuits in 1557. Diocese was established in 1576. Macau served as a base for missionary work in Japan and China.

Dioc., 1; bp., 1; parishes, 6; priests, 74 (44 dioc., 30 rel.); sem., 8; bros., 21; srs., 181; catechists, 137; bap., 522; Caths., 20,000; tot. pop., 336,000.

Madagascar (Malagasy Republic): Republic off the eastern coast of Africa; capital, Antananarivo. Missionary efforts were generally fruitless from early in the 16th century until the Jesuits were permitted to start open evangelization about 1845. A prefecture apostolic was set up in 1850 and a vicariate apostolic in the north was placed in charge of the Holy Ghost Fathers in 1898. There were 100,000 Catholics by 1900. The first native bishop was ordained in 1936. The hierarchy was established in 1955. Madagascar maintains diplomatic relations with Vatican City.

Archd., 3; dioc., 14; card., 1 (nat.); abp., 2 (nat.); bp., 16 (13 nat.); parishes, 235; priests, 671 (156 dioc., 515 rel.); p.d., 1; sem., 212; bros., 329; srs., 1,907; catechists, 7,614; bap., 72,996; Caths., 2,128,000 (22.6%); tot. pop. 9,400,000.

Madeira Islands: Portuguese province, an archipelago 340 miles west of the northwestern coast of Africa; capital, Funchal. Catholicism has had a continuous history since the first half of the 15th century. The diocese of Funchal was established in 1514. Statistics are included in those for Portugal.

Malawi: Republic in the interior of eastern Africa; capital, Lilongwe. Missionary work, begun by Jesuits in the late 16th and early 17th centuries, was generally ineffective until the end of the 19th century. The Missionaries of Africa (White Fathers) arrived in 1889 and later were joined by oth-

ers. A vicariate was set up in 1897. The hierarchy was established in 1959. Malawi maintains diplomatic relations with Vatican City.

Archd., 1; dioc., 6; abp., 1 (nat.); bp., 6 (4 nat.); parishes, 129; priests, 321 (115 dioc., 206 rel.); sem., 170; bros., 88; srs., 631; catechists, 3,880; bap., 47,870; Caths., 1,407,000 (21.8%); tot. pop., 6,430,000.

Malaysia: Parliamentary democracy in southeastern Asia; federation of former states of Malaya, Sabah (former Br. North Borneo), and Sarawak; capital, Kuala Lumpur. Christianity, introduced by Portuguese colonists about 1511, was confined almost exclusively to Malacca until late in the 18th century. The effectiveness of evangelization increased from then on because of the recruitment and training of native clergy. Singapore (see separate entry), founded in 1819, became a center for missionary work. Seventeen thousand Catholics were in the Malacca diocese in 1888. Effective evangelization in Sabah and Sarawak began in the second half of the 19th century. The hierarchy was established in 1973. Malaysia has an apostolic delegate.

Archd., 2; dioc., 4; abp., 2 (nat.); bp., 4 (nat.); parishes, 156; priests, 249 (160 dioc., 89 rel.); p.d., 3; sem., 39; bros., 103; srs., 530; catechists, 1,537; bap., 16,824; Caths., 447,000 (3%); tot. pop., 14,860,000.

Maldives: Republic, an archipelago 400 miles southwest of India and Ceylon; capital, Male. No serious attempt was ever made to evangelize the area, which is completely Moslem.

Tot. pop., 170,000.

Mali: Republic, inland in western Africa; capital, Bamako. Catholicism was introduced late in the second half of the 19th century. Missionary work made little progress in the midst of the predominantly Moslem population. A vicariate was set up in 1921. The hierarchy was established in 1955. Established diplomatic relations with Vatican City in 1979.

Archd., 1; dioc., 5; abp., 1 (nat.); bp., 5 (3 nat.); parishes, 37; priests, 136 (22 dioc., 114 rel.); sem., 27; bros., 24; srs., 170; catechists, 511; bap., 2,579; Caths., 68,000 (.9%); tot. pop., 7,350,000.

Malta: Republic 58 miles south of Sicily; capital, Valletta. Early catacombs and inscriptions are evidence of the early introduction of Christianity. St. Paul was shipwrecked on Malta in 60. Saracens controlled the island(s) from 870 to 1090, a period of difficulty for the Church. The line of bishops extends from 1090 to the present. Church-state conflict developed in recent years over passage of government-sponsored legislation affecting Catholic schools and church-owned property. An agreement reached in 1985 ended the dispute and established a joint commission to study other church-state problems. Malta maintains diplomatic relations with Vatican City.

Archd., 1; dioc., 1; abp., 1; bp., 1; parishes, 82; priests, 1,121 (653 dioc., 468 rel.); sem., 122; bros., 119; srs., 1,394; bap., 5,998; Caths., 373,000 (98%); tot. pop., 380,000.

Marianas, The (Northern): U.S. Trust territory

in Pacific (scheduled to become a U.S. commonwealth).

Dioc., 1; bp., 1; parishes, 9; priests, 7 (5 dioc., 2 rel.); p.d., 2; srs., 22; catechists, 149; bap., 507; Caths., 14,000; tot. pop., 20,000.

Martinique: French overseas department in the West Indies, about 130 miles south of Guadeloupe; capital, Fort-de-France. Catholicism was introduced in the 16th century. The hierarchy was established in 1967.

Archd., 1; abp., 1; parishes, 47; priests, 95 (41 dioc., 54 rel.); sem., 8; bros., 12; srs., 211; catechists, 2,000; bap., 3,888; Caths., 281,000; tot. pop., 310,000.

Mauritania: Islamic republic on the northwest coast of Africa; capital, Nouakchott. With few exceptions, the Catholics in the country are members of the foreign colony. Mauritania has an apostolic delegate.

Dioc., 1; bp., 1; parishes, 7; priests, 9 (2 dioc., 7 rel.); bros., 2; srs., 27; bap., 37; Caths., 4,000 (.2%); tot. pop., 1,780,000.

Mauritius: Self-governing island state 500 miles east of Madagascar; capital, Port Louis. Catholicism was introduced by Vincentians in 1722. Port Louis, made a vicariate in 1819 and a diocese in 1847, was a jumping-off point for missionaries to Australia, Madagascar and South Africa. Mauritius maintains diplomatic relations with Vatican City.

Dioc., 1; bp., 1; parishes, 43; priests, 95 (50 dioc., 45 rel.); sem., 6; bros., 30; srs., 283; bap., 6,260; Caths., 326,000 (32.7%); tot. pop., 995,000.

Mayotte: French overseas island territory, in Indian Ocean off southeast coast of Africa; formerly part of Comoros. Statistics included in Comoros.

Melilla: Spanish possession in northern Africa. Statistics are included in those for Spain.

Mexico (United States of Mexico): Republic in Middle America. Christianity was introduced early in the 16th century. Mexico City, made a diocese in 1530, became the missionary and cultural center of the whole country. Missionary work, started in 1524 and forwarded principally by Franciscans, Dominicans, Augustinians and Jesuits, resulted in the baptism of all persons in the central plateau by the end of the century. Progress there and in the rest of the country continued in the following century but tapered off and went into decline in the 18th century, for a variety of reasons ranging from diminishing government support to relaxations of Church discipline. The wars of independence, 1810-21, in which some Catholics participated, created serious problems of adjustment for the Church. Social problems, political unrest and government opposition climaxed in the constitution of 1917 which practically outlawed the Church. Persecution took serious tolls of life and kept the Church underground, under Calles, 1924-1928, again in 1931, and under Cardenas in 1934. President Camacho, 1940-1946, ended persecution and instituted a more lenient policy. The Church, however, still labors under legal and practical disabilities. Mexico has an apostolic delegate; the

Mexican president has a personal envoy to the Vatican.

Archd., 12; dioc., 55; prel., 7; v.a., 2; card., 2; abp., 10; bp., 75; parishes, 4,258; priests, 10,110 (7,208 dioc., 2,902 rel.); p.d., 60; sem., 4,217; bros., 1,423; srs., 24,207; catechists, 930; bap., 2,064,753; Caths., 72,095,000 (95%); tot. pop., 75,100,000.

Monaco: Constitutional monarchy, an enclave on the Mediterranean coast of France near the Italian border; capital, Monaco-Ville. Christianity was introduced before 1000. Catholicism is the official religion but freedom is guaranteed for all. Monaco has an ambassador at Vatican City.

Archd., 1; abp., 1; parishes, 5; priests, 32 (16 dioc., 16 rel.); p.d., 1; sem., 3; bros., 19; srs., 55; bap., 212; Caths., 25,000; tot. pop., 30,000.

Mongolia: People's republic in north central Asia; capital Ulaanbaatar. Christianity was introduced by Nestorians. Some Franciscans were in the country in the 13th and 14th centuries, en route to China. Limited evangelization efforts from the 18th century had little success among the Mongols in Outer Mongolia, where Buddhism was predominated for hundreds of years. No Christians were known to be there in 1953. There may be a few Catholics in Inner Mongolia. No foreign missionaries have been in the country since 1953.

Pop., 1,700,000.

Montserrat: British island possession in Caribbean; capital, Plymouth. Under ecclesiastical jurisdiction of St. John's-Basseterre diocese, Antigua.

Parish, 1; priests, 1 (rel.); p.d.; 1; srs., 4; catechists, 8; bap., 32; Caths., 1,000; tot. pop., 14,000.

Morocco: Constitutional monarchy in northwest Africa with Atlantic and Mediterranean coastlines; capital, Rabat. Christianity was known in the area by the end of the third century. Bishops from Morocco attended a council at Carthage in 484. Catholic life survived under Visigoth and, from 700, Arab rule; later it became subject to influence from the Spanish, Portuguese and French. Islam is the state religion. The hierarchy was established in 1955. Morocco maintains diplomatic relations with Vatican City.

Archd., 2; abp., 2; parishes, 56; priests, 98 (25 dioc., 73 rel.); bros., 11; srs., 392; catechists, 129; bap., 147; Caths., 64,000 (.28%); tot. pop., 22,110,000.

Mozambique: People's republic in southeast Africa, bordering on the Indian Ocean; former Portuguese territory (independent, 1975); capital, Maputo (formerly Lourenco Marques). Christianity was introduced by Portuguese Jesuits about the middle of the 16th century. Evangelization continued from then until the 18th century when it went into decline largely because of the Portuguese government's expulsion of the Jesuits. Conditions worsened in the 1830s, improved after 1881, but deteriorated again during the anticlerical period from 1910 to 1925. Conditions improved in 1940, the year Portugal concluded a new concordat with the Holy See and the hierarchy was established. Outspoken criticism by missionaries of Portuguese policies in Mozambique resulted in Church-state tensions in the years immediately preceding independence. Tension continues to be a factor, although to a smaller degree, in relations between the Church and the Marxist-oriented government in power since 1975. The first two native bishops were ordained March 9, 1975. Two ecclesiastical provinces were established in 1984. Mozambique has an apostolic delegate.

Archd., 3; dioc., 6; abp., 3 (2 nat.); bp., 6 (5 nat.); parishes, 259; priests, 281 (24 dioc., 257 rel.); sem., 25; bros., 74; srs., 500; catechists, 7,172; Caths., 1,756,000 (13.2%); tot. pop., 13,310,000.

Namibia (South West Africa): Territory in South Africa in dispute between the Republic of South Africa and the United Nations; capital, Windhoek. The area shares the history of South Africa. Namibia has an apostolic delegate (to Southern Africa).

V.a., 2; bp., 2 (1 nat); parishes, 53; priests, 64 (3 dioc., 61 rel.); p.d., 16; sem., 1; bros., 56; srs., 295; bap., 7,456; Caths., 195,690 (16%); tot. pop., 1,166,000 (1985).

Nauru: Independent republic in western Pacific; capital, Yaren. Forms part of the Tarawa and Nauru diocese (Kiribati).

Parish, 1; priest, 1 (rel.); bro., 1; srs., 16; Caths., 2,000; tot. pop., 7,000.

Nepal: Constitutional monarchy, the only Hindu kingdom in the world, in central Asia south of the Himalayas between India and Tibet; capital, Kathmandu. Little is known of the country before the 15th century. Some Jesuits passed through from 1628 and some sections were evangelized in the 18th century, with minimal results, before the country was closed to foreigners. Conversions from Hinduism, the state religion, are not recognized in law. Christian missionary work is not allowed. Nepal established diplomatic relations with Vatican City in 1983.

Mission "sui juris," 1; parishes, 3; priests, 29 (4 dioc.; 25 rel.); bros., 11; srs., 47; bap., 22; Caths., 976; tot. pop., 16,477,607. (1986 Annuario Pontificio; figures are for the Nepal mission "sui juris.")

Netherlands: Kingdom in northwestern Europe; capital, Amsterdam (seat of the government, The Hague). Evangelization, begun about the turn of the sixth century by Irish, Anglo-Saxon and Frankish missionaries, resulted in Christianization of the country by 800 and subsequent strong influence on The Lowlands. Invasion by French Calvinists in 1572 brought serious losses to the Catholic Church and made the Reformed Church dominant. Catholics suffered a practical persecution of official repression and social handicap in the 17th century. The schism of Utrecht occurred in 1724. Only one-third of the population was Catholic in 1726. The Church had only a skeleton organization from 1702 to 1853, when the hierarchy was reestablished. Despite this upturn, cultural isolation was the experience of Catholics until about 1914. From then on new vigor came into the life of the Church, and a whole new climate of interfaith relations began to develop. Before and for some years following the Second Vatican Council, the thrust and variety of thought and practice in the Dutch Church moved it to the vanguard position of "progressive" renewal. A particular synod of Dutch bishops held at the Vatican in January, 1980, and aimed at internal improvement of the Church in the Netherlands, had disappointing results, according to reports in 1981. The Netherlands maintains diplomatic relations with Vatican City.

Archd., 1; dioc., 6; mil vic.; card., 4; bp., 11; parishes, 1,790; priests 6,453 (2,488 dioc., 3,965 rel.); p.d., 38; sem., 283; bros., 2,582; srs., 21,012; bap., 52,957; Caths., 5,600,000 (39.9%); tot. pop., 14,360,000.

Netherlands Antilles: Autonomous part of the Kingdom of The Netherlands. Consists of two groups of islands in the Caribbean: Curacao, Aruba and Bonaire, off the northern coast of Venezuela; and St. Eustatius, Saba and the southern part of St. Martaan, southeast of Puerto Rico; capital, Willemstad on Curacao. Christianity was introduced in the 16th century. Apostolic delegation was established in 1975.

Dioc., 1; bp., 1; parishes, 47; priests, 59 (12 dioc., 47 rel.); bros., 50; srs., 131; catechists, 14; bap., 3,440; Caths., 236,000 (90%); tot. pop., 260,000.

New Caledonia: French territory consisting of several islands in Oceania east of Queensland, Australia; capital, Noumea. Catholicism was introduced in 1843, nine years after Protestant missionaries began evangelization. A vicariate was organized in 1847. The hierarchy was established in 1966.

Archd., 1; abp., 1; parishes, 36; priests, 65 (11 dioc., 54 rel.); sem., 5; bros., 62; srs., 192; catechists, 210; bap., 1,918; Caths., 94,000; tot. pop., 150,000.

New Zealand: Independent nation in Commonwealth, a group of islands in Oceania 1,200 miles southeast of Australia: capital, Wellington. Protestant missionaries were the first evangelizers. On North Island, Catholic missionaries started work before the establishment of two dioceses in 1848; their work among the Maoris was not organized until 1881. On South Island, whose first resident priest arrived in 1840, a diocese was established in 1869. These three jurisdictions were joined in a province in 1896. The Marists were the outstanding Catholic missionaries in the area. Established diplomatic relations with Vatican City, 1973.

Archd., 1; dioc., 5; mil. vic.; card., 1; bp., 8; parishes, 285; priests, 765 (419 dioc., 346 rel.); sem., 95; bros., 286; srs., 1,929; catechists, 85; bap., 8,886; Caths. 504,000 (15.7%); tot. pop., 3,200,000.

Nicaragua: Republic in Central America: capital, Managua. Evangelization began shortly after the Spanish conquest about 1524 and eight years later the first bishop took over jurisdiction of the Church in the country. Jesuits were leaders in missionary work during the colonial period, which lasted until the 1820s. Evangelization endeavor increased after establishment of the republic in 1838.

In this century it was extended to the Atlantic coastal area where Protestant missionaries had begun work about the middle of the 1900s. Many church leaders, clerical and lay, supported the aims but not necessarily all the methods of the revolution which forced the resignation and flight July 17, 1979, of Anastasio Somoza Debayle, whose family had controlled the government since the early 1930s. Nicaragua maintains diplomatic relations with Vatican City. (See Index for 1986 developments.)

Archd., 1; dioc., 4; prel., 2; v.a., 1; card., 1; bp., 9; parishes, 181; priests, 327 (116 dioc., 211 rel.); p.d., 29; sem., 46; bros., 61; srs., 651; catechists, 1,777; bap., 72,184; Caths., 2,658,000 (86.8%); 3,060,683.

Niger: Republic in west central Africa; capital, Niamey. The first mission was set up in 1831. A prefecture apostolic was organized in 1942 and the first diocese was established in 1961. The country is predominantly Moslem. Niger maintains diplomatic relations with Vatican City.

Dioc., 1; bp., 1; parishes, 16; priests, 34 (6 dioc., 28 rel.); sem., 1; bros., 6; srs., 66; bap., 210; Caths., 15,000 (.24%); tot. pop., 6,200,000 (1985).

Nigeria: Republic in western Africa; capital, Lagos. The Portuguese introduced Catholicism in the coastal region in the 15th century. Capuchins did some evangelization in the 17th century but systematic missionary work did not get under way along the coast until about 1840. A vicariate for this area was organized in 1870. A prefecture was set up in 1911 for missions in the northern part of the country where Islam was strongly entrenched. From 1967, when Biafra seceded, until early in 1970 the country was torn by civil war. The hierarchy was established in 1950. Nigeria maintains diplomatic relations with Vatican City.

Archd., 3; dioc., 28; mission "sui juris," 1; card., 2; abp., 3 (nat.); bp., 30 (24 nat.); parishes, 530; priests, 1,412 (878 dioc., 534 rel.); p.d., 6; sem., 1,553; bros., 353; srs., 1,438; catechists, 10,405; bap., 259,883; Caths., 6,044,000 (6.8%); tot. pop., 89,020,000.

Niue: New Zealand self-governing territory in South Pacific. Under ecclesiastical jurisdiction of Rarotonga diocese, Cook Islands.

Parish, 1; priest, 1 (rel.); srs., 2; bap. 16; Caths. (1982), 200; tot. pop., 3,000.

Norway: Constitutional monarchy in northern Europe, the western part of the Scandinavian peninsula; capital, Oslo. Evangelization begun in the ninth century by missionaries from England and Ireland put the Church on a firm footing about the turn of the 11th century. The first diocese was set up in 1153 and development of the Church progressed until the Black Death in 1349 inflicted losses from which it never recovered. Lutheranism, introduced from outside in 1537 and furthered cautiously, gained general acceptance by about 1600 and was made the state religion. Legal and other measures crippled the Church, forcing priests to flee the country and completely disrupting normal activity. Changes for the better came in the 19th century, with the granting of religious liberty in 1845 and the repeal of many legal disabilities in 1897. Norway was administered as a single apostolic vicariate from 1892 to 1932, when it was divided into three jurisdictions under the supervision of the Congregation for the Propagation of the Faith. Established diplomatic relations with Vatican City in 1982.

Dioc., 1; prel., 2; bp., 2; parishes, 28; priests, 56 (16 dioc., 40 rel.); sem., 6; bros., 13; srs., 353; bap., 277; Caths., 17,000; tot. pop., 4,130,000.

Oman: Independent monarchy in eastern corner of Arabian Peninsula; capital, Muscat. Under ecclesiastical jurisdiction of Arabia vicariate apostolic.

Parishes, 2; priests, 5 (1 dioc., 4 rel.); bros., 2; bap., 24; Caths., 8,000; tot. pop., 1,130,000.

Pakistan: Islamic republic in southwestern Asia; capital, Islamabad. (Formerly included East Pakistan which became the independent nation of Bangladesh in 1971.) Islam, firmly established in the eighth century, is the state religion. Christian evangelization of the native population began about the middle of the 19th century, years after earlier scattered attempts. The hierarchy was established in 1950. Pakistan maintains diplomatic relations with Vatican City.

Archd., 1; dioc., 5; card., 1 (nat.); bp., 6 (nat.); parishes, 53; priests, 228 (88 dioc., 140 rel.); p.d., 1; sem., 89; bros., 57; srs., 707; catechists, 402; bap., 20,547; Caths., 497,000 (.55%); tot. pop., 89,730,000.

Panama: Republic in Central America; capital, Panama City. Catholicism was introduced by Franciscan missionaries and evangelization started in 1514. The Panama diocese, oldest in the Americas, was set up at the same time. The Catholic Church has favored status and state aid for missions, charities and parochial schools, but religious freedom is guaranteed to all religions. Panama maintains diplomatic relations with Vatican City.

Archd., 1; dioc., 3; prel., 1; v.a., 1; abp., 1; bp., 6; parishes, 144; priests, 280 (76 dioc., 204 rel.); p.d., 7; sem., 130; bros., 39; srs., 454; catechists, 400; Caths., 1,842,000 (88.1%); tot. pop., 2,090,000.

Papua New Guinea: Independent (Sept. 16, 1975) republic (formerly under Australian administration) in southwest Pacific. Consists of the eastern half of the southwestern Pacific island of New Guinea and the Northern Solomon Islands; capital, Port Moresby. Marists began evangelization about 1844 but were handicapped by many factors, including "spheres of influence" laid out for Catholic and Protestant missionaries. A prefecture apostolic was set up in 1896 and placed in charge of the Divine Word Missionaries. The territory suffered greatly during World War II. Hierarchy was established for New Guinea and adjacent islands in 1966. Papua New Guinea established diplomatic relations with the Vatican in 1977.

Archd., 4; dioc., 14; abp., 4; bp., 16; parishes, 307; priests, 521 (64 dioc., 457 rel.);

p.d., 13; bros., 318; srs., 951; catechists, 2,413; bap., 35,698; Caths., 1,006,000 (31.5%); tot. pop., 3,190,000.

Paraguay: Republic in central South America; capital, Asuncion. Catholicism was introduced in 1542, evangelization began almost immediately. A diocese erected in 1547 was occupied for the first time in 1556. On many occasions thereafter dioceses in the country were left unoccupied because of political and other reasons. Jesuits who came into the country after 1609 devised the reductions system for evangelizing the Indians, teaching them agriculture, husbandry, trades and other useful arts, and giving them experience in property use and community life. The reductions were communes of Indians only, under the direction of the missionaries. About 50 of them were established in southern Brazil, Uruguay and northeastern Argentina as well as in Paraguay. They had an average population of three to four thousand. At their peak, some 30 reductions had a population of 100,000. Political officials regarded the reductions with disfavor because they did not control them and feared that the Indians trained in them might foment revolt and upset the established colonial system under Spanish control. The reductions lasted until about 1768 when their Jesuit founders and directors were expelled from Latin America. Church-state relations following independence from Spain in 1811 were tense as often as not because of government efforts to control the Church through continued exercise of Spanish patronage rights and by other means. The Church as well as the whole country suffered a great deal during the War of the Triple Alliance from 1865-70. After that time, the Church had the same kind of experience in Paraguay as in the rest of Latin America with forces of liberalism, anticlericalism, massive educational needs, poverty, a shortage of priests and other personnel. Most recently church leaders have been challenging the government to initiate long-needed economic and social reforms. Paraguay maintains diplomatic relations with Vatican City.

Archd., 1; dioc., 8; prel., 2; v.a., 2; mil. vic.; abp., 1; bp., 15; parishes, 282; priests, 536 (182 dioc., 354 rel.); p.d., 18; sem., 249; bros., 103; srs., 997; catechists, 119; bap., 101,032; Caths., 3,192,000 (91.9%); tot. pop., 3,470,000.

Peru: Republic on the western coast of South America; capital, Lima. An effective diocese became operational in 1537, five years after the Spanish conquest. Evangelization, already under way, developed for some time after 1570 but deteriorated before the end of the colonial period in the 1820s. The first native-born saint of the new world was a Peruvian, Rose of Lima, a Dominican tertiary who died in 1617 and was canonized in 1671. In the new republic founded after the wars of independence the Church experienced problems of adjustment and many of the difficulties that cropped up in other South American countries: government efforts to control it through continuation of the patronage rights of the Spanish crown; suppression of houses of religious and expropriation of church property; religious indifference and outright hostility. The Church was given special status but was not made the established religion. Repressive measures by the government against labor protests have been condemned by Church leaders in the past several years. Peru maintains diplomatic relations with Vatican City.

Archd., 7; dioc., 14; prel., 12; v.a., 8; mil. vic.; card., 1; abp., 6; bp., 44; parishes, 1,250; priests, 2,258 (966 dioc., 1,292 rel.); p.d., 39; sem., 895; bros., 461; srs., 4,910; catechists, 2,411; bap., 431,543; Caths., 17,296,000 (92.4%); tot. pop., 18,710,000.

Philippines: Republic, an archipelago of 7,000 islands off the southeast coast of Asia; capital, Quezon City. Systematic evangelization was begun in 1564 and resulted in firm establishment of the Church by the 19th century. During the period of Spanish rule, which lasted from the discovery of the islands by Magellan in 1521 to 1898, the Church experienced difficulties with the patronage system under which the Spanish crown tried to control ecclesiastical affairs through episcopal and other appointments. This system ended in 1898 when the United States gained possession of the islands and instituted a policy of separation of Church and state. Anticlericalism flared late in the 19th century. The Aglipayan schism, an attempt to set up a nationalist church, occurred a few years later, in 1902. The government of Ferdinand Marcos, under attack by people of the church for a number of years for violations of human rights, was replaced in 1986 (see Index). The republic maintains diplomatic relations with Vatican City.

Archd., 16; dioc., 46; prel., 5; v.a., 5; mil. vic.; card. (1985), 2; abp., 14; bp., 75; parishes, 2,129; priests, 5,039 (2,924 dioc., 2,115 rel.); p.d., 3; sem., 4,315; bros., 378; srs., 7,812; catechists, 1,299; bap., 1,383,140; Caths., 43,800,000 (84.1%); tot. pop., 52,060,000.

Poland: People's republic in eastern Europe; capital, Warsaw. The first traces of Christianity date from the second half of the ninth century. Its spread was accelerated by the union of the Slavs in the 10th century. The first bishopric was set up in 968. The Gniezno archdiocese, with suffragan sees and a mandate to evangelize the borderlands as well as Poland, was established in 1000. Steady growth continued thereafter, with religious orders and their schools playing a major role. Some tensions with the Orthodox were experienced. The Reformation, supported mainly by city dwellers and the upper classes, peaked from about the middle of the 16th century, resulting in numerous conversions to Lutheranism, the Reformed Church and the Bohemian Brethren. A successful Counter-Reformation, with the Jesuits in a position of leadership, was completed by about 1632. The movement served a nationalist as well as religious purpose; in restoring religious unity to a large degree, it united the country against potential invaders, the Swedes, Russians and Turks. The Counter-Reformation had bad side effects, leading to the repression of Protestants long after it was over and to prejudice against Orthodox who returned to allegiance with Rome in 1596 and later. The Church, in the same manner as the entire country, was adversely affected by the partitions of the 18th and 19th centuries. Russification hurt the Orthodox who had reunited with Rome and the Latins who were in the majority. Germans extended their Kulturkampf to the area they controlled. The Austrians exhibited some degree of tolerance. In the republic established after World War I the Church reorganized itself, continued to serve as a vital force in national life, and enjoyed generally harmonious relations with the state. Progressive growth was strong until 1939 when disaster struck in the form of invasion by German and Russian forces and six years of war. In 1945, seven years before the adoption of a Soviet-type of constitution, the Communist-controlled government initiated a policy that included a constant program of atheistic propaganda; a strong campaign against the hierarchy and clergy; the imprisonment in 1948 of 700 priests and even more religious; rigid limitation of the activities of religious; censorship and curtailment of the Catholic press and Catholic Action; interference with church administration and appointments of the clergy; the "deposition" of Cardinal Wyszynski in 1953 and the imprisonment of other members of the hierarchy; the suppression of "Caritas," the Catholic charitable organization; promotion of "Progressive Catholic" activities and a small minority of "patriotic priests." Establishment of the Gomulka regime, the freeing of Cardinal Wyszynski in October, 1956, and the signing of an agreement two months later by bishops and state officials, led to some improvement of conditions. The underlying fact, however, was that the regime conceded to Catholics only so much as was necessary to secure support of the government as a more tolerable evil than the harsh and real threat of a Russian-imposed puppet government like that in Hungary. This has been the controlling principle in Church-state relations. Auxiliary Bishop Ladislaw Rubin of Gniezno sketched the general state of affairs in March, 1968. He said that there was no sign that the government had any intention of releasing its oppressive grip on the Church. As evidence of the "climate of asphyxiation" in the country he cited: persistent questioning of priests by officials concerning their activities; the prohibition against Catholic schools, hospitals and charitable works; the financial burden of a 60 per cent tax on church income. Cardinal Wyszynski denounced "enforced atheism" in a Lenten pastoral in the same year. In May, 1969, the bishops drafted a list of grievances against the government which, they said, were "only some examples of difficulties which demonstrated the situation of the Church in our homeland." The grievances were: refusal of permits to build new churches and establish new parishes; refusal of permission "for the organization of new religion classes"; pressure on Catholics who attend religious ceremonies; censorship and the lack of an independent Catholic daily newspaper; lack of representation in public life; restriction of "freedom to conduct normal pastoral work" in the western portion of the country. There was a move toward improvement in Church-state relations in

1971-72. In 1973, the Polish bishops issued a pastoral letter urging Catholics to resist the official atheism imposed by the government. In 1974 the bishops expressed approval of renewed Vatican efforts at regularizing Church-state relations but insisted that they (the bishops) be consulted on every step of the negotiations. The bishops have continued their sharp criticism of anti-religious policies and human rights violations of the government. Regular contacts on a working level were initiated by the Vatican and Poland in 1974, but regular diplomatic relations have not been established. Cardinal Karol Wojtyla of Cracow was elected to the papacy in 1978. Church support was strong for the independent labor movement, Solidarity, which was recognized by the government in August, 1980, but outlawed in December, 1981, when martial law was imposed. The prevailing church-state condition is one of tension, affected by three principal internal factors: (1) the need of the government for social order, which is impossible to achieve without the moderating influence of the Church; (2) pressure by the Church for freedom from restraints on its pastoral, education, and social mission; (3) mutual resistance to Soviet intervention. (See entries in News Events.)

Archd., 7; dioc., 21; card., 5; abp., 3; bp., 81; parishes, 8,040; priests, 20,311 (15,718 dioc., 4,593 rel.); sem., 7,517; bros., 1,334; srs., 24,850; bap., 146,265; Caths., 34,460,000 (94.2%); tot. pop., 36,570,000.

Polynesia, French: French overseas territory in the southern Pacific, including Tahiti and the Marquesas Islands; capital, Papeete. The first phase of evangelization in the Marquesas Islands, begun in 1838, resulted in 216 baptisms in 10 years. A vicariate was organized in 1848 but real progress was not made until after the baptism of native rulers in 1853. Persecution caused missionaries to leave the islands several times. By the 1960s, more than 95 per cent of the population was Catholic. Isolated attempts to evangelize Tahiti were made in the 17th and 18th centuries. Two Picpus Fathers began missionary work in 1831. A vicariate was organized in 1848. By 1908, despite the hindrances of Protestant opposition, disease and other factors, the Church had firm roots.

Archd., 1; dioc., 1; abp., 1 (nat.); bp., 1; parishes, 78; priests, 35 (10 dioc., 25 rel.); p.d., 7; sem., 2; bros., 31; srs., 63; catechists, 158; bap., 1,644; Caths., 57,800; tot. pop., 166,000.

Portugal: Republic in the western part of the Iberian peninsula; capital, Lisbon. Christianity was introduced before the fourth century. From the fifth century to early in the eighth century the Church experienced difficulties from the physical invasion of barbarians and the intellectual invasion of doctrinal errors in the forms of Arianism, Priscillianism and Pelagianism. The Church survived under the rule of Arabs from about 711 and of the Moors until 1249. Ecclesiastical life was fairly vigorous from 1080 to 1185, and monastic influence became strong. A decline set in about 1450. Several decades later Portugal became the jumping-off place for many missionaries to newly discovered colonies. The Reformation had little effect in the country. Beginning about 1750, Pombal, minister of foreign affairs and prime minister, mounted a frontal attack on the Jesuits whom he succeeded in expelling from Portugal and the colonies. His anti-Jesuit campaign successful Pombal also attempted, and succeeded to some extent, in controlling the Church in Portugal until his fall from power about 1777. Liberal revolutionaries with anti-Church policies made the 19th century a difficult one for the Church. Similar policies prevailed in Church-state relations in this century until the accession of Salazar to power in 1928. In 1940 he concluded a concordat with the Holy See which regularized Church-state relations but still left the Church in a subservient condition. The prevailing spirit of church authorities in Portugal has been conservative. In 1971 several priests were tried for subversion for speaking out against colonialism and for taking part in guerrilla activities in Angola. A military coup of Apr. 25, 1974, triggered a succession of chaotic political developments which led to an attempt by Communists, after receiving only 18 per cent of the votes cast in a national election, to take over the government in the summer of 1975. Portugal maintains diplomatic relations with Vatican City.

Patriarchate, 1; archd., 2; dioc., 17; mil. vic.; card., 1; abp., 2; bp., 27; parishes, 4,316; priests, 4,771 (3,694 dioc., 1,077 rel.); p.d., 8; sem., 542; bros., 515; srs., 7,252; bap., 146,265; Caths., 9,537,000 (94.4%); tot. pop., 10,100,000.

Puerto Rico: A U.S. commonwealth, the smallest of the Greater Antilles, 885 miles southeast of the southern coast of Florida; capital, San Juan. Following its discovery by Columbus in 1493, the island was evangelized by Spanish missionaries and remained under Spanish ecclesiastical as well as political control until 1898 when it became a possession of the United States. The original diocese, San Juan, was erected in 1511. The present hierarchy was established in 1960. Puerto Rico has an apostolic delegate (nuncio to Dominican Republic).

Archd., 1; dioc., 4; card., 1; bp., 8; parishes, 269; priests, 724 (296 dioc., 428 rel.); p.d., 169; sem., 198; bros., 89; srs., 1,509; bap., 52,847; Caths., 2,735,000 (81.6%); tot. pop., 3,350,000.

Qatar: Independent state in the Persian Gulf; capital, Doha. Under ecclesiastical jurisdiction of Arabia vicariate apostolic.

Parish, 1; priest, 1 (rel.); bap., 51; Caths., 6,000; tot. pop., 280,000.

Reunion: French overseas department, 450 miles east of Madagascar; capital, Saint-Denis. Catholicism was introduced in 1667 and some intermittent missionary work was done through the rest of the century. A prefecture apostolic was organized in 1712. Vincentians began work there in 1817 and were joined later by Holy Ghost Fathers. Reunion has an apostolic delegate.

Dioc., 1; bp., 1; parishes, 71; priests, 107 (59 dioc., 48 rel.); sem., 16; bros., 41; srs., 440; catechists, 400; bap., 11,539; Caths., 468,000; tot. pop., 550,000.

Rhodes: Greek island in the Aegean Sea, 112 miles from the southwestern coast of Asia Minor. A diocese was established about the end of the third century. A bishop from Rhodes attended the Council of Nicaea in 325. Most of the Christians followed the Eastern Churches into schism in the 11th century and became Orthodox. Turks controlled the island from 1522 to 1912. The small Catholic population, for whom a diocese existed from 1328 to 1546, lived in crossfire between Turks and Orthodox. After 1719 Franciscans provided pastoral care for the Catholics, for whom an archdiocese was erected in 1928. Statistics are included in Greece.

Romania: Socialist republic in southeastern Europe; capital, Bucharest. Latin Christianity, introduced in the third century, all but disappeared during the barbarian invasions. The Byzantine Rite was introduced by the Bulgars about the beginning of the eighth century and established firm roots. It eventually became Orthodox, but a large number of its adherents returned later to union with Rome. Attempts to reintroduce the Latin Rite on any large scale have been unsuccessful. Communists took over the government following World War II, forced the abdication of Michael I in 1947, and enacted a Soviet type of constitution in 1952. By that time a campaign against religion was already in progress. In 1948 the government denounced a concordat concluded in 1929, nationalized all schools and passed a law on religions which resulted in the disorganization of Church administration. The 1.5 million-member Romanian Byzantine Rite Church, by government decree, was incorporated into the Romanian Orthodox Church, and the Orthodox bishops then seized the cathedrals of Roman Catholic bishops. Five of the six Latin Rite bishops were immediately disposed of by the government, and the last was sentenced to 18 years' imprisonment in 1951, when a great many arrests of priests and laymen were made. Religious orders were suppressed in 1949. Since 1948 more than 50 priests have been executed and 200 have died in prison. One hundred priests were reported in prison at the end of 1958. Some change for the better in Church-state relations was reported after the middle of the summer of 1964, although restrictions were still in effect. About 1,200 priests were engaged in parish work in August, 1965.

Archd., 2; dioc., 9; ord., 1; bp., 3 (one was ordained in 1984). Complete statistics are not available. The 1986 Annuario Pontificio reported the following statistics for 6 of the 12 jurisdictions: parishes, 657; priests, 932 (869 dioc., 63 rel.); sem., 230; bros., 13; srs., 160; bap., 20,353; Caths., 1,387,768; tot. pop., 22,683,000.

Rwanda: Republic in east central Africa; capital, Kigali. Catholicism was introduced about the turn of the 20th century. The hierarchy was established in 1959. Intertribal warfare between the ruling Hutus (90 per cent of the population) and the Tutsis (formerly the ruling aristocracy) plagued the country for a number of years. Rwanda maintains diplomatic relations with Vatican City.

Archd., 1; dioc., 7; abp., 1 (nat.); bp., 7 (6 nat.); parishes, 110; priests, 455 (252 dioc., 203 rel.); sem., 154; bros., 213; srs., 848; catechists, 1,584; bap., 95,804; Caths., 2,450,000 (43%); tot. pop., 5,700,000.

Saint Christopher (St. Kitts) and Nevis: Independent (Sept. 19, 1983) island states in West Indies; capital, Basseterre, on St. Christopher; Charlestown, on Nevis. Under ecclesiastical jurisdiction of St. John's-Basseterre diocese, Antigua.

Parishes, 4; priests, 8 (rel.); srs., 2; catechists, 14; bap., 85; Caths., 4,000; tot. pop., 66,000. Statistics include Anguilla.

Saint Lucia: Independent (Feb. 22, 1979) island state in West Indies; capital, Castries. Established diplomatic relations with Vatican City in 1984. (See Index for papal visit.)

Archd., 1; abp., 1; parishes, 22; priests, 33 (11 dioc., 22 rel.); p.d., 1; sem., 7; bros., 2; srs., 40; catechists, 260; bap., 3,274; Caths., 100,000; tot. pop., 124,000.

Saint Pierre and Miquelon: French overseas department, two groups of islands near the southwest coast of Newfoundland; capital, St. Pierre. Catholicism was introduced about 1689.

V.a., 1; bp., 1; parishes, 3; priests, 3 (rel.); srs., 13; bap., 89; Caths., 6,000; tot. pop., 6,350.

Saint Vincent and the Grenadines: Independent State (1979) in West Indies; capital, Kingstown. Under ecclesiastical jurisdiction of Bridgetown-Kingstown diocese, Barbados.

Parishes, 7; priests, 9 (2 dioc., 7 rel.); bros., 8; srs., 26; catechists, 32; bap., 211; Caths., 14,000; tot. pop., 100,000.

Samoa, American: Unincorporated U.S. territory in southwestern Pacific, consisting of six small islands; seat of government, Pago Pago on the Island of Tutuila. Samoa-Pago Pago diocese established in 1982.

Dioc., 1; bp., 1; parishes 5; priests, 7 (4 dioc., 3 rel.); sem., 3; bros., 7; srs., 13; catechists, 28; bap., 308; Caths., 7,500; tot. pop., 33,000.

Samoa, Western: Independent state in the southwestern Pacific; capital, Apia. Catholic missionary work began in 1845. Most of the missions now in operation were established by 1870 when the Catholic population numbered about 5,000. Additional progress was made in missionary work from 1896. The first Samoan priest was ordained in 1892. A diocese was established in 1966; elevated to a metropolitan see in 1982.

Archd., 1; card., 1; bp., 1; parishes, 19; priests, 51 (14 dioc., 37 rel.); sem., 32; bros., 36; srs., 114; catechists, 73; bap., 1,520; Caths., 31,000; tot. pop., 160,000.

San Marino: Republic, a 24-square-mile enclave in northeastern Italy; capital, San Marino. The date of initial evangelization is not known, but a diocese was established by the end of the third century. Ecclesiastically, it forms part of the diocese of San Marino-Montefeltro in Italy. San Marino is represented by an ambassador at Vatican City.

Parishes, 11; priests, 29 (15 dioc., 14 rel.); bro., 1; srs., 13; bap., 297; Caths., 22,000; tot. pop., 22,000.

Sao Tome and Principe: Independent republic (July 12, 1975), consisting of two islands off the western coast of Africa in the Gulf of Guinea; former Portuguese territory; capital Sao Tome. Evangelization was begun by the Portuguese who discovered the islands in 1471-72. The Sao Tome diocese was established in 1534. Established diplomatic relations with Vatican City in 1984.

Dioc., 1; bp., 1; parishes, 12; priests, 9 (rel.); bros., 3; srs., 15; catechists, 248; bap., 2,818; Caths., 81,000; tot. pop., 90,000.

Saudi Arabia: Monarchy occupying four-fifths of Arabian peninsula; capital, Riyadh. Under ecclesiastical jurisdiction of Arabia vicariate apostolic.

Parishes, 6; priests, 15 (1 dioc., 14 rel.); srs., 19; bap., 514; Caths., 426,000; tot. pop., 10,420,000.

Scotland: Part of the United Kingdom, in the northern British Isles; capital, Edinburgh. Christianity was introduced by the early years of the fifth century. The arrival of St. Columba and his monks in 563 inaugurated a new era of evangelization which reached into remote areas by the end of the sixth century. He was extremely influential in determining the character of the Celtic Church, which was tribal, monastic, and in union with Rome. Considerable disruption of church activity resulted from Scandinavian invasions in the late eighth and ninth centuries. By 1153 the Scottish Church took a turn away from its insularity and was drawn into closer contact with the European community. Anglo-Saxon religious and political relations, complicated by rivalries between princes and ecclesiastical superiors, were not always the happiest. Religious orders expanded greatly in the 12th century. From shortly after the Norman Conquest of England to 1560 the Church suffered adverse effects from the Hundred Years' War, the Black Death, the Western Schism and other developments. In 1560 parliament abrogated papal supremacy over the Church in Scotland and committed the country to Protestantism in 1567. The Catholic Church was proscribed, to remain that way for more than 200 years, and the hierarchy was disbanded. Defections made the Church a minority religion from that time on. Presbyterian church government was ratified in 1690. Priests launched the Scottish Mission in 1653, incorporating themselves as a mission body under a prefect apostolic and working underground to serve the faithful in much the same way their confreres did in England. About 100 heather priests, trained in clandestine places in the heather country, were ordained by the early 19th century. Catholics got some relief from legal disabilities in 1793 and more later. Many left the country about that time. Some of their numbers were filled subsequently by immigrants from Ireland. The hierarchy was restored in 1878. Scotland, though predominantly Protestant, has a better record for tolerance than Northern Ireland.

Archd., 2; dioc., 6; card., 1; abp., 2; bp., 9; parishes, 479; priests, 1,018 (787 dioc., 231 rel.); sem., 189; bros., 116; srs., 1,165; bap., 13,304; Caths., 812,482 (15.8%); tot. pop., 5,117,146 (1985).

Senegal: Republic in western Africa; capital, Dakar. The country had its first contact with Catholicism through the Portuguese some time after 1460. Some incidental missionary work was done by Jesuits and Capuchins in the 16th and 17th centuries. A vicariate for the area was placed in charge of the Holy Ghost Fathers in 1779. More effective evangelization efforts were accomplished after the Senegambia vicariate was established in 1955. Senegal maintains diplomatic relations with Vatican City.

Archd., 1; dioc., 4; p.a., 1; card., 1 (nat.); bp., 4 (nat.); parishes, 64; priests, 241 (84 dioc., 157 rel.); sem., 70; bros., 129; srs., 517; catechists, 1,300; bap., 10,062 Caths., 280,000 (4.4%); tot. pop., 6,320,000.

Seychelles: Independent (1976) group of 92 islands in the Indian Ocean 970 miles east of Kenya; capital, Victoria on Mahe. Catholicism was introduced in the 18th century. A vicariate apostolic was organized in 1852. All education in the islands was conducted under Catholic auspices until 1954. Seychelles established diplomatic relations with Vatican City in 1984.

Dioc., 1; bp., 1 (nat.); parishes, 17; priests, 21 (6 dioc., 15 rel.); sem., 2; bros., 10; srs., 58; catechists, 262; bap., 1,470; Caths., 59,000; tot. pop., 60,000.

Sierra Leone: Republic on the western coast of Africa; capital, Freetown. Catholicism was introduced in 1858. Members of the African Missions Society, the first Catholic missionaries in the area, were joined by Holy Ghost Fathers in 1864. Protestant missionaries were active in the area before their Catholic counterparts. Educational work had a major part in Catholic endeavor. The hierarchy was established in 1950. Sierra Leone has an apostolic delegate.

Archd., 1; dioc., 2; abp., 1; bp., 2; parishes, 31; priests, 116 (14 dioc., 102 rel.); sem., 36; bros., 12; srs., 96; catechists, 488; bap., 4,243; Caths., 68,000 (1.9%); tot. pop., 3,470,000.

Singapore: Independent island republic off the southern tip of the Malay Peninsula; capital, Singapore. Christianity was introduced in the area by Portuguese colonists about 1511. Singapore was founded in 1819; the first parish church was built in 1846. Established diplomatic relations with Vatican City, 1981.

Archd., 1; abp., 1 (nat.); parishes, 26; priests, 130 (71 dioc., 59 rel.); sem., 27; bros., 60; srs., 236; catechists, 640; bap., 3,171; Caths., 96,000 (3.8%); tot. pop., 2,500,000.

Solomon Islands: Independent (July 7, 1978) island group in Oceania; capital, Honiara, on Guadalcanal. Evangelization of the Southern Solomons, begun earlier but interrupted because of violence against them, was resumed by the Marists in 1898. A vicariate apostolic was organized in 1912. A similar jurisdiction was set up for the Western Solomons in 1959. World War II caused a great deal of damage to mission installa-tions. Established diplomatic relations with Vatican City in 1984.

Archd., 1; dioc., 2; abp., 1; bp., 2; parishes, 35; priests, 49 (12 dioc., 37 rel.); sem., 9; bros., 33; srs., 190; catechists, 325; bap., 2,173; Caths., 63,000; tot. pop., 260,000.

Somalia: Republic on the eastern coast of Africa; capital, Mogadishu. The country has been Moslem for centuries. Pastoral activity has been confined to immigrants. Schools and hospitals were nationalized in 1972, resulting in the departure of some foreign missionaries. Somalia has an apostolic delegate (to the Red Sea Region).

Dioc., 1; bp., 1; parishes, 2; priests, 5 (rel.); bros., 2; srs., 71; bap., 6; Caths., 2,000; tot. pop., 5,270,000.

South Africa: Republic in the southern part of Africa; capitals, Cape Town (legislative) and Pretoria (administrative). Christianity was introduced by the Portuguese who discovered the Cape of Good Hope in 1488. Boers, who founded Cape Town in 1652, expelled Catholics from the region. There was no Catholic missionary activity from that time until the 19th century. After a period of British opposition, a bishop established residence in 1837 and evangelization got under way thereafter among the Bantus and white immigrants. In recent years church authorities have strongly protested the white supremacy policy of apartheid which seriously infringes the human rights of the native Blacks and impedes the Church from carrying out its pastoral, educational and social service functions. The hierarchy was established in 1951. South Africa has an apostolic delegate.

Archd., 4; dioc., 19; abb., 1; p.a., 2; card., 1; abp., 3; bp., 21; parishes, 713; priests, 1,097 (269 dioc., 828 rel.); p.d., 90; sem., 192; bros., 336; srs., 3,524; catechists, 6,723; bap., 66,226; Caths., 2,237,000 (7.2%); tot. pop., 30,800,000.

Spain: Constitutional monarchy on the Iberian peninsula in southwestern Europe; capital, Madrid. Christians were on the peninsula by 200; some of them suffered martyrdom during persecutions of the third century. A council held in Elvira about 304/6 enacted the first legislation on clerical celibacy in the West. Vandals invaded the peninsula in the fifth century, bringing with them an Arian brand of Christianity which they retained until their conversion following the baptism of their king Reccared, in 589. One of the significant developments of the seventh century was the establishment of Toledo as the primatial see. The Visigoth kingdom lasted to the time of the Arab invasion, 711-14. The Church survived under Moslem rule but experienced some doctrinal and disciplinary irregularities as well as harassment. Reconquest of most of the peninsula was accomplished by 1248; unification was achieved during the reign of Ferdinand and Isabella. The discoveries of Columbus and other explorers ushered in an era of colonial expansion in which Spain became one of the greatest mission-sending countries in history. In 1492, in repetition of anti-Semitic actions of 694, the expulsion of unbaptized Jews was decreed, leading to mass baptisms but a questionable number of real conversions in 1502. (The Jewish minority numbered about 165,000.) Activity by the Inquisition followed. Spain was not seriously affected by the Reformation. Ecclesiastical decline set in about 1650. Anti-Church actions authorized by a constitution enacted in 1812 resulted in the suppression of religious and other encroachments on the leaders, people and goods of the Church. Political, religious and cultural turmoil recurred during the 19th century and into the 20th. A revolutionary republic was proclaimed in 1931, triggering a series of developments which led to civil war from 1936 to 1939. During the conflict, which pitted leftist Loyalists against the forces of Francisco Franco, 6,632 priests and religious and an unknown number of lay persons perished in addition to thousands of victims of combat. One-man, one-party rule, established after the civil war and with rigid control policies with respect to personal liberties and social and economic issues, continued for more than 35 years before giving way after the death of Franco to democratic reforms. The Catholic Church, long the established religion, was disestablished under a new constitution providing guarantees of freedom for other religions as well. Disestablishment was ratified with modifications of a 1976 revision of the earlier concordat of 1953. Spain maintains diplomatic relations with Vatican City.

Archd., 13; dioc., 52; mil. vic.; card., 5; abp., 11; bp., 68; parishes, 21,403; priests, 32,070 (21,274 dioc., 10,796 rel.); p.d., 68; sem., 3,344; bros., 7,157; srs., 78,450;. bap., 538,393; Caths., 37,465,000 (97.9%); tot. pop., 38,230,000.

Sri Lanka (formerly Ceylon): Independent socialist republic, island southeast of India; capital, Colombo. Effective evangelization began in 1543 and made great progress by the middle of the 17th century. The Church was seriously hampered during the Dutch period from about 1650 to 1795. Anti-Catholic laws were repealed by the British in 1806. The hierarchy was established in 1886. Leftist governments and other factors have worked against the Church since the country became independent in 1948. The high percentage of indigenous clergy and religious has been of great advantage to the Church. Sri Lanka maintains diplomatic relations with Vatican City.

Archd., 1; dioc., 8; card., 1 (nat.); abp., 1 (nat.); bp., 9 (nat.); parishes, 318; priests, 684 (379 dioc., 305 rel.); p.d., 2; sem., 219; srs., 2,352; catechists, 2,591; bap., 26,383; Caths., 1,093,000 (7%); tot. pop., 15,420,000.

Sudan: Republic in northeastern Africa, the largest country on the continent; capital, Khartoum. Christianity was introduced from Egypt and gained acceptance in the sixth century. Under Arab rule, it was eliminated in the northern region. No Christians were in the country in 1600. Evangelization attempts begun in the 19th century in the south yielded hard-won results. By 1931 there were nearly 40,000 Catholics there, and considerable progress was made by missionaries after that time. In 1957, a year after the republic was

established, Catholic schools were nationalized. An act restrictive of religious freedom went into effect in 1962, resulting in the harassment and expulsion of foreign missionaries. By 1964 all but a few Sudanese missionaries had been forced out of the southern region. The northern area, where Islam predominates, is impervious to Christian influence. Late in 1971 some missionaries were allowed to return to work in the South. Southern Sudan was granted regional autonomy within a unified country in March, 1972, thus ending often bitter fighting between the North and South dating back to 1955. The hierarchy was established in 1974. The imposition of Islamic penal codes in 1984 was a cause of concern to all Christian churches. Sudan maintains diplomatic relations with Vatican City.

Archd., 2; dioc. (1986), 7; abp., 2 (nat.); bp., 5 (nat.); parishes, 92; priests, 182 (40 dioc., 142 rel.); p.d., 1; sem., 49; bros., 48; srs., 236; catechists 1,285; bap., 16,152; Caths., 1,266,000 (6.2%); tot. pop., 20,360,000.

Suriname (formerly Dutch Guiana): Independent (Nov. 25, 1975) state in northern South America; capital, Paramaribo. Catholicism was introduced in 1683. Evangelization began in 1817.

Dioc., 1; bp., 1; parishes, 19; priests, 34 (3 dioc., 31 rel.); p.d., 1; sem., 3; bros., 27; srs., 88; catechists, 63; bap., 3,065; Caths., 78,000; tot. pop., 350,000.

Swaziland: Monarchy in southern Africa; almost totally surrounded by South Africa; capital, Mbabane. Missionary work was entrusted to the Servites in 1913. A prefecture apostolic was organized in 1923. The hierarchy was established in 1951. Swaziland has an apostolic delegate (to Southern Africa).

Dioc., 1; bp., 1 (nat.); priests, 37 (4 dioc., 33 rel.); sem., 2; bros., 8; srs., 115; catechists, 139; bap., 1,113; Caths., 37,000 (6%); tot. pop., 650,000.

Sweden: Kingdom in northwestern Europe; capital, Stockholm. Christianity was introduced by St. Ansgar, a Frankish monk, in 829/30. The Church became well established in the 12th century and was a major influence at the end of the Middle Ages. Political and other factors favored the introduction and spread of the Lutheran Church which became the state religion in 1560. The Augsburg Confession of 1530 was accepted by the government; all relations with Rome were severed; monasteries were suppressed; the very presence of Catholics in the country was forbidden in 1617. A decree of tolerance for foreign Catholics was issued about 1781. Two years later a vicariate apostolic was organized for the country. In 1873 Swedes were given the legal right to leave the Lutheran Church and join another Christian church. (Membership in the Lutheran Church is presumed by law unless notice is given of membership in another church.) In 1923 there were only 11 priests and five churches in the country. Since 1952 Catholics have enjoyed almost complete religious freedom. The hierarchy was reestablished in 1953. Hindrances to growth of the Church are the strongly entrenched established church, limited resources, a clergy shortage and the size of the country. Established diplomatic relations with Vatican City in 1982.

Dioc., 1; bp., 1; parishes, 33; priests, 88 (33 dioc., 55 rel.); p.d., 6; sem., 16; bros., 7; srs., 247; bap., 1,085; Caths., 114,000 (1.4%); tot. pop., 8,330,000.

Switzerland: Confederation in central Europe; capital, Bern. Christianity was introduced in the fourth century or earlier and was established on a firm footing before the barbarian invasions of the sixth century. Constance, established as a diocese in the seventh century, was a stronghold of the faith against the pagan Alamanni, in particular, who were not converted until some time in the ninth century. During this period of struggle with the barbarians, a number of monasteries of great influence were established. The Reformation in Switzerland was triggered by Zwingli in 1519 and furthered by him at Zurich until his death in battle against the Catholic cantons in 1531. Calvin set in motion the forces that made Geneva the international capital of the Reformation and transformed it into a theocracy. Catholics mobilized a Counter-Reformation in 1570, six years after Calvin's death. Struggle between Protestant and Catholic cantons was a fact of Swiss life for several hundred years. The Helvetic Constitution enacted at the turn of the 19th century embodied anti-Catholic measures and consequences, among them the dissolution of 130 monasteries. The Church was reorganized later in the century to meet the threats of liberalism, radicalism and the Kulturkampf. In the process, the Church, even though on the defensive, gained the strength and cohesion that characterizes it to the present time. The six dioceses in the country are immediately subject to the Holy See. In 1973, constitutional articles banning Jesuits from the country and prohibiting the establishment of convents and monasteries were repealed. There is a papal nuncio to Switzerland, but Switzerland does not have a diplomatic officer accredited to Vatican City.

Dioc., 6; abb., 2; bp., 8; parishes, 1,704; priests, 4,123 (2,452 dioc., 1,671 rel.); p.d., 21; sem., 217; bros., 361; srs., 9,779; bap., 34,898; Caths., 3,028,000 (46.7%); tot. pop., 6,480,000.

Syria: Arab republic in southwest Asia; capital, Damascus. Christian communities were formed in apostolic times. It is believed that St. Peter established a see at Antioch before going to Rome. Damascus became a center of influence. The area was the place of great men and great events in the early history of the Church. Monasticism developed there in the fourth century. So did the Monophysite and Monothelite heresies to which portions of the Church succumbed. Byzantine Syrians who remained in communion with Rome were given the name Melkites. Christians of various persuasions — Jacobites, Orthodox and Melkites — were subject to various degrees of harassment from the Arabs who took over in 638 and from the Ottoman Turks who isolated the country and remained in control from 1516 to the end of World War II. Syria maintains diplomatic relations with Vatican City.

Patriarchates, 3 (Antioch of Maronites, Greek Melkites and Syrians; patriarchs of Maronites and Syrians reside in Lebanon); Archd., 12 (1 Armenian, 2 Maronite, 5 Greek-Melkite, 4 Syrian); dioc., 3 (Armenian, Chaldean, Maronite); v.a., 1 (Latin); patr., 1; abp., 15; bp., 2; parishes, 188; priests, 212 (142 dioc., 70 rel.); p.d., 2; sem., 39; bros., 11; srs., 403; bap., 2,622; Caths., 257,000 (2.6%); tot. pop., 9,610,000.

Taiwan (Formosa): Location of the Nationalist Government of the Republic of China, an island 100 miles off the southern coast of mainland China; capital, Taipei. Attempts to introduce Christianity in the 17th century were unsuccessful. Evangelization in the 19th century resulted in some 1,300 converts in 1895. Missionary endeavor was hampered by the Japanese who occupied the island following the Sino-Japanese war of 1894-95. Nine thousand Catholics were reported in 1938. Great progress was made in missionary endeavor among the Chinese who emigrated to the island following the Communist take-over of the mainland in 1949. The hierarchy was established in 1952. Nationalist China maintains diplomatic relations with Vatican City.

Archd., 1; dioc., 6; abp., 1; bp., 8 (1 nat.); parishes, 442; priests, 735 (219 dioc., 516 rel.); sem., 93; bros., 88; srs., 1,151; catechists, 482; bap., 5,682; Caths., 291,000 (1.5%); tot. pop., 18,803,000.

Tanzania: Republic (consisting of former Tanganyika on the eastern coast of Africa and former Zanzibar, an island group off the eastern coast); capital, Dar es Salaam. The first Catholic mission in the former Tanganyikan portion of the republic was manned by Holy Ghost Fathers in 1868. The hierarchy was established there in 1953. Zanzibar was the landing place of Augustinians with the Portuguese in 1499. Some evangelization was attempted between then and 1698 when the Arabs expelled all priests from the territory. There was no Catholic missionary activity from then until the 1860s. The Holy Ghost Fathers arrived in 1863 and were entrusted with the mission in 1872. Zanzibar was important as a point of departure for missionaries to Tanganyika, Kenya and other places in East Africa. A vicariate for Zanzibar was set up in 1906. Tanzania maintains diplomatic relations with Vatican City.

Archd., 2; dioc., 25; card., 1 (nat.); abp., 1 (nat.); bp., 25 (24 nat.); parishes, 633; priests, 1,437 (814 dioc., 623 rel.); sem., 381; bros., 340; srs., 4,367; catechists, 8,567; bap., 171,967; Caths., 4,098,000 (20.1%); tot. pop., 20,380,000.

Thailand (Siam): Constitutional monarchy in southeastern Asia; capital, Bangkok. The first Christians in the region were Portuguese traders who arrived early in the 16th century. A number of missionaries began arriving in 1554 but pastoral care was confined mostly to the Portuguese until the 1660s. Evangelization of the natives got under way from about that time. A seminary was organized in 1665, a vicariate was set up four years later, and a point of departure was established for missionaries to Tonkin, Cochin China and China. Persecution and death for some of the missionaries ended evangelization efforts in 1688. It was resumed, however, and made progress from 1824 onwards. In 1881 missionaries were sent from Siam to neighboring Laos. The hierarchy was established in 1965. Abp., Michai Kitbunchu was named the first Thai cardinal in 1983. Thailand maintains diplomatic relations with Vatican City.

Archd., 2; dioc., 8; card., 1 (nat.); abp., 1 (nat.); bp., 8 (7 nat.); parishes, 267; priests, 420 (199 dioc., 221 rel.); sem., 184; bros., 150; srs., 1,184; catechists, 1,047; bap., 6,355; Caths., 207,000 (.4%); tot. pop., 49,460,000.

Timor, Eastern: Former Portuguese overseas province in the Malay archipelago; annexed by Indonesia in 1976.

Dioc., 1; parishes, 21; priests, 35 (18 dioc., 17 rel.); sem., 18; bros., 7; srs., 50; catechists, 912; bap., 20,936; Caths., 393,000; tot. pop., 620,000.

Togo: Republic on the western coast of Africa; capital, Lome. The first Catholic missionaries in the area, where slave raiders operated for nearly 200 years, were members of the African Missions Society who arrived in 1563. They were followed by Divine Word Missionaries in 1914, when a prefecture apostolic was organized. At that time the Catholic population numbered about 19,000. The African Missionaries returned after their German predecessors were deported following World War I. The first native priest was ordained in 1922. The hierarchy was established in 1955. Established diplomatic relations with Vatican City, 1981.

Archd., 1; dioc., 3; abp., 1 (nat.); bp., 3 (2 nat.); parishes, 73; priests, 195 (89 dioc., 106 rel.); sem., 102; bros., 63; srs., 281; catechists, 1,137; bap., 19,415; Caths., 606,000 (21.9%); tot. pop., 2,760,000.

Tokelau: Pacific islands administered by New Zealand. Forms part of Samoa-Apia and Tokelau archdiocese, Western Samoa.

Parish, 1; p.d., 1; srs., 2; catechist, 1; bap., 50; Caths., 1,000; tot. pop., 2,000.

Tonga: Polynesian monarchy in the southwestern Pacific, consisting of about 150 islands; capital Nuku'alofa. Marists started missionary work in 1842, some years after Protestants had begun evangelization. By 1880 the Catholic population numbered about 1,700. A vicariate was organized in 1937. The hierarchy was established in 1966.

Dioc., 1; bp., 1 (nat); parishes, 11; priests, 27; sem., 5; bros., 13; srs., 53; catechists, 54; bap., 606; Caths., 14,000 (14%); tot. pop., 100,000.

Trinidad and Tobago: Independent nation, consisting of two islands in the Caribbean; capital, Port-of-Spain. The first Catholic church in Trinidad was built in 1591, years after several missionary ventures had been launched and a number of missionaries killed. Capuchins were there from 1618 until about 1802. Missionary work continued after the British gained control early in the 19th century. Cordial relations have existed between the Church and state, both of which have manifested their desire for the development of native clergy. Established diplomatic relations with Vatican City in 1978.

Archd., 1; abp., 1; parishes, 58; priests, 129 (25 dioc., 104 rel.); sem., 33; bros., 27; srs., 181; catechists, 50; bap., 8,960; Caths., 386,000 (33.5%); tot. pop., 1,150,000.

Tunisia: Republic on the northern coast of Africa; capital, Tunis. There were few Christians in the territory until the 19th century. A prefecture apostolic was organized in 1843 and the Carthage archdiocese was established in 1884. The Catholic population in 1892 consisted of most of the approximately 50,000 Europeans in the country. When Tunis became a republic in 1956, most of the Europeans left the country. The Holy See and the Tunisian government concluded an agreement in 1964 which changed the Carthage archdiocese into a prelacy and handed over some ecclesiastical property to the republic. A considerable number of Moslem students are in Catholic schools, but the number of Moslem converts to the Church has been small. Tunisia maintains diplomatic relations with Vatican City.

Prel., 1; abp., 1; parishes, 17; priests, 51 (23 dioc., 28 rel.); p.d., 1; sem., 1; bros., 9; srs., 225; bap., 44; Caths., 20,000 (.3%); tot. pop., 6,890,000.

Turkey: Republic in Asia Minor and southeastern Europe, capital, Ankara. Christian communities were established in apostolic times, as attested in the Acts of the Apostles, some of the Letters of St. Paul, and Revelation. The territory was the scene of heresies and ecumenical councils, the place of residence of Fathers of the Church, the area in which ecclesiastical organization reached the dimensions of more than 450 sees in the middle of the seventh century. The region remained generally Byzantine except for the period of the Latin occupation of Constantinople from 1204 to 1261, but was conquered by the Ottoman Turks in 1453 and remained under their domination until establishment of the republic in 1923. Christians, always a minority, numbered more Orthodox than Latins; they were all under some restriction during the Ottoman period. They suffered persecution in the 19th and 20th centuries, the Armenians being the most numerous victims. Turkey is overwhelmingly Moslem. Catholics are tolerated to a degree. Turkey maintains diplomatic relations with Vatican City.

Patriarchate, 1 (Cilicia for the Armenians, the patriarch resides in Lebanon); archd., 3; dioc., 2; v.a., 2; mission "sui juris," 1; ap. ex., 1; abp., 3; bp., 1; parishes, 56; priests, 70 (15 dioc., 55 rel.); p.d., 2; sem., 4; bros., 29; srs., 142; bap., 183; Caths., 15,000; tot. pop., 47,280,000.

Turks and Caicos Islands: British possession in West Indies; capital, Grand Turk.

Mission "sui juris," 1; parish, 1; priest, 1 (rel.); Caths., 1,000; tot. pop., 8,000.

Tuvalu (formerly Ellice Islands): Independent state (1978) in Oceania, consisting of 9 islands (8 inhabited); capital, Funafuti.

Mission "sui juris," 1; *bp.,* 1; *Caths.,* 100; *tot. pop.,* 8,000.

Uganda: Republic in eastern Africa; capital, Kampala. The Missionaries of Africa (White Fathers) were the first Catholic missionaries, starting in 1879. Persecution broke out from 1885 to 1887, taking a toll of 22 Catholic martyrs, who were canonized in 1964, and a number of Anglican victims. (Pope Paul honored all those who died for the faith during a visit to Kampala in 1969.) By 1888, there were more than 8,000 Catholics. Evangelization was resumed in 1894, after being interrupted by war, and proceeded thereafter. The first native African bishop was ordained in 1939. The hierarchy was established in 1953. The Church was suppressed during the erratic regime of Pres. Idi-Amin, who was deposed in the spring of 1979. Uganda maintains diplomatic relations with Vatican City.

Archd., 1; *dioc.,* 13; *mil. vic., card.,* 1 *(nat.); bp.,* 13 *(12 nat.); parishes,* 318; *priests,* 938 *(625 dioc.,* 313 *rel.); p.d.,* 1; *sem.,* 596; *bros.,* 316; *srs.,* 2,028; *catechists,* 7,963; *bap.,* 207,540; *Caths.,* 5,914,000 (40.4%); *tot. pop.,* 14,630,000.

Union of Soviet Socialist Republics: Union of 15 Soviet Socialist Republics in northern Eurasia, from the Baltic Sea to the Pacific; Russian capital, Moscow. The Orthodox Church has been predominant in Russian history. It developed from the Byzantine Church before 1064. Some of its members subsequently established communion with Rome as the result of reunion movements but most of them remained Orthodox. The government has always retained some kind of general or particular control of this church. Latins, always a minority, had a little more freedom. From the beginning of the Communist government in 1917, all churches of whatever kind — including Jews and Moslems — became the targets of official campaigns designed to negate their influence on society and/or to eliminate them entirely. An accurate assessment of the situation of the Catholic Church in Russia is difficult to make. Its dimensions, however, can be gauged from the findings of a team of research specialists made public by the Judiciary Committee of the U.S. House of Representatives in 1964. It was reported: "The fate of the Catholic Church in the USSR and countries occupied by the Russians from 1917 to 1959 shows the following: (a) the number killed: 55 bishops; 12,800 priests and monks; 2.5 million Catholic believers; (b) imprisoned or deported: 199 bishops; 32,000 priests and 10 million believers; (c) 15,700 priests were forced to abandon their priesthood and accept other jobs; and (d) a large number of seminaries and religious communities were dissolved; 1,600 monasteries were nationalized, 31,779 churches were closed. 400 newspapers were prohibited, and all Catholic organizations were dissolved." Several Latin Rite churches are open; e.g., in Moscow, Leningrad, Odessa and Tiflis. An American chaplain is stationed in Moscow to serve Catholics at the U.S. embassy there. Recent reports indicate that, despite repression and attempts at Sovietization, the strongholds of Catholicism in the USSR

are Lithuania (incorporated in the USSR in 1940, together with Estonia and Latvia) and the Ukraine. No Catholic statistics are available for the USSR. See separate entries for Estonia, Latvia, Lithuania.

Tot. pop., 272,500,000.

United Arab Emirates: Independent state along Persian Gulf; capital, Abu Dhabi.

V.a., 1; *bp.,* 1; *parishes,* 4; *priests,* 11 *(3 dioc.,* 8 *rel.); sem.* 6; *bros.,* 4; *srs.,* 34; *bap.,* 880; *Caths.,* 48,000; *tot. pop.,* 1,210,000.

United States: See Catholic History in the United States, Statistics of the Church in the United States.

Uruguay: Republic (called the Eastern Republic of Uruguay) on the southeast coast of South America; capital, Montevideo. The Spanish established a settlement in 1624 and evangelization followed. Missionaries followed the reduction pattern to reach the Indians, form them in the faith and train them in agriculture, husbandry, other useful arts, and the experience of managing property and living in community. Montevideo was made a diocese in 1878. The constitution of 1830 made Catholicism the religion of the state and subsidized some of its activities, principally the missions to the Indians. Separation of Church and state was provided for in the constitution of 1917. Uruguay maintains diplomatic relations with Vatican City.

Archd., 1; *dioc.,* 9; *abp.,* 1; *bp.,* 11; *parishes,* 222; *priests,* 552 *(178 dioc.,* 374 *rel.); p.d.,* 24; *sem.,* 124; *bros.,* 148; *srs.,* 1,641; *bap.,* 40,221; *Caths.,* 2,347,000 (79%); *tot. pop.,* 2,970,000.

Vanuatu (New Hebrides): Independent (July 29, 1980) island group in the southwest Pacific, about 500 miles west of Fiji; formerly under joint British-French administration; capital, Vila. Effective, though slow, evangelization by Catholic missionaries began about 1887. A vicariate apostolic was set up in 1904. The hierarchy was established in 1966.

Dioc., 1; *bp.,* 1; *parishes,* 19; *priests,* 27 *(4 dioc.,* 23 *rel.); p.d.,* 1; *sem.,* 19; *bros.,* 17; *srs.,* 80; *catechists,* 143; *bap.,* 759; *Caths.,* 18,000 (15%); *tot. pop.,* 120,000.

Vatican City: See separate entry.

Venezuela: Republic in northern South America; capital, Caracas. Evangelization began in 1513-14 and involved members of a number of religious orders who worked in assigned territories, developing missions into pueblos or towns and villages of Indian converts. Nearly 350 towns originated as missions. Fifty-four missionaries met death by violence from the start of missionary work until 1817. Missionary work was seriously hindered during the wars of independence in the second decade of the 19th century and continued in decline through the rest of the century as dictator followed dictator in a period of political turbulence. Restoration of the missions got under way in 1922. The first diocese was established in 1531. Most of the bishops have been native Venezuelans. The first diocesan synod was held in 1574. Church-state relations are regulated by an agreement concluded with the Holy See in 1964. Venezuela maintains diplomatic relations with Vatican City.

Archd., 6; dioc., 18; v.a., 4; card., 2; abp., 4; bp., 33; parishes, 1,002; priests, 1,975 (895 dioc., 1,080 rel.); p.d., 23, sem., 496; bros., 234; srs., 3,862; catechists, 137; bap., 323,011; Caths., 14,859,000 (91%); tot. pop., 16,390,000.

Vietnam: Country in southeastern Asia, reunited officially July 2, 1976, as the Socialist Republic of Vietnam; capital, Hanoi. Previously, from 1954, partitioned into the Democratic Peoples' Republic of Vietnam in the North (capital, Hanoi) and the Republic of Vietnam in the South (capital, Saigon). Catholicism was introduced in 1533 but missionary work was intermittent until 1615 when Jesuits arrived to stay. One hundred thousand Catholics were reported in 1639. Two vicariates were organized in 1659. A seminary was set up in 1666 and two native priests were ordained two years later. A congregation of native women religious formed in 1670 is still active. Severe persecution broke out in 1698, three times in the 18th century, and again in the 19th. Between 100,000 and 300,000 persons suffered in some way from persecution during the 50 years before 1883 when the French moved in to secure religious liberty for the Catholics. Most of the 117 beatified Martyrs of Vietnam were killed during this 50-year period. After the French were forced out of Vietnam in 1954, the country was partitioned at the 17th parallel. The North went Communist and the Viet Cong, joined by North Vietnamese regular army troops in 1964, fought to gain control of the South. In 1954 there were approximately 1,114,000 Catholics in the North and 480,000 in the South. More than 650,000 fled to the South to avoid the government repression that silenced the Church in the North. In South Vietnam, the Church continued to develop during the war years. Fragmentary reports about the status of the Church since the end of the war in 1975 have been ominous. Freedom of religious belief, promised by the Revolutionary Government in May, 1975, shortly after its capture of Saigon (Ho Chi Min City), is denied in practice. Late in 1983, the government initiated support for a "patriotic" Catholic church analogous to the communist-sponsored church in China. The hierarchy was established in 1960. The apostolic delegation, formerly in Saigon, was transferred to Hanoi in 1976; it is presently vacant.

Archd., 3; dioc., 22; card., 1; abp., 2; bp., 35. No statistics are available. There were 2,749,475 Catholics (6.4% of the total population) in 1974. Pop., 57,180,000.

Virgin Islands: Organized unincorporated U.S. territory, about 34 miles east of Puerto Rico; capital, Charlotte Amalie on St. Thomas (one of the three principal islands). The islands were discovered by Columbus in 1493 and named for St. Ursula and her virgin companions. Missionaries began evangelization in the 16th century. A church on St. Croix dates from about 1660; another, on St. Thomas, from 1774. The Baltimore archdiocese had jurisdiction over the islands from 1804 to 1820 when it was passed on to the first of several places in the Caribbean area. Some trouble arose over a

pastoral appointment in the 19th century, resulting in a small schism. The Redemptorists took over pastoral care in 1858; normal conditions have prevailed since.

Dioc., 1 (St. Thomas, suffragan of Washington, D.C.); bp., 1; parishes, 6; priests, 15 (2 dioc., 13 rel.); sem., 2; bros., 3; srs., 17; bap., 692; Caths., 25,000; tot. pop., 100,000.

Virgin Islands, British: British possession in Caribbean; capital, Road Town.

Parish, 1; priest, 1 (rel.); sr., 1; catechists, 2; bap., 18; Caths. (1982), 300; tot. pop., 14,000.

Wales: Part of the United Kingdom, on the western part of the island of Great Britain. Celtic missionaries completed evangelization by the end of the sixth century, the climax of what has been called the age of saints. Welsh Christianity received its distinctive Celtic character at this time. Some conflict developed when attempts were made — and proved successful later — to place the Welsh Church under the jurisdiction of Canterbury; the Welsh opted for direct contact with Rome. The Church made progress despite the depredations of Norsemen in the eighth and ninth centuries. Norman infiltration occurred near the middle of the 12th century, resulting in a century-long effort to establish territorial dioceses and parishes to replace the Celtic organizational plan of monastic centers and satellite churches. The Western Schism produced split views and allegiances. Actions of Henry VIII in breaking away from Rome had serious repercussions. Proscription and penal laws crippled the Church, resulted in heavy defections and touched off a 150-year period of repression in which more than 91 persons died for the faith. Methodism prevailed by 1750. Modern Catholicism came to Wales with Irish immigrants in the 19th century, when the number of Welsh Catholics was negligible. Catholic emancipation was granted in 1829. The hierarchy was restored in 1850.

Archd., 1; dioc., 1; abp., 1; bp., 2; parishes, 169; priests, 303 (177 dioc., 126 rel.); p.d., 6; sem., 29; bros., 30; srs., 662; bap., 3,155; Caths., 151,302 (5.1%); tot. pop., 2,940,000 (1985).

Wallis and Futuna Islands: French overseas territory in the southwestern Pacific; capital Mata-Utu. Marists, who began evangelizing the islands in 1836-7, were the first Catholic missionaries. The entire populations of the two islands were baptized by the end of 1842 (Wallis) and 1843 (Futuna). The first missionary to the latter island was killed in 1841. Most of the priests on the islands are native Polynesians. The hierarchy was established in 1966.

Dioc., 1; bp., 1 (nat.); parishes, 5; priests, 19 (10 dioc., 9 rel.); sem., 3; bros., 7; srs., 47; bap., 423; Caths., 14,000 (almost the entire population).

Western Sahara: Former Spanish overseas province (Spanish Sahara) on the northwestern coast of Africa. Territory is under control of Morocco. Islam is the religion of non-Europeans. A prefecture apostolic was established in 1954 for the European Catholics there.

P.a., 1; parishes, 2; priests, 2 (rel.); bap., 2; Caths., 150 (1986 Annuario Pontificio); tot. pop., 150,000.

Yemen, North: Arab republic in southwestern Arabia; capital, Sanaa. Christians perished in the first quarter of the sixth century. Moslems have been in control since the seventh century. The state religion is Islam. In 1973, for the first time in 1,400 years, Catholic personnel — priests, religious, lay persons — were invited to work in the country as staff of a government hospital; they were not to engage in proselytizing. Under ecclesiastical jurisdiction of Arabia vicariate apostolic.

Parishes, 3; priests, 2 (rel.); bros., 31; bap., 15; Caths., 3,000; tot. pop., 6,230,000.

Yemen, South (People's Democratic Republic of Yemen): Republic in the southern part of the Arabian peninsula; capital, Aden. No Christian community has existed there since the Moslem conquest of the seventh century. Catholics are from other countries. Under ecclesiastical jurisdiction of Arabia vicariate apostolic.

Parish, 1; priest, 1 (rel); Caths., 1,000; tot. pop., 2,030,000.

Yugoslavia: Socialist republic in southeastern Europe; capital, Belgrade. Christianity was introduced from the seventh to ninth centuries in the regions which were combined to form the nation after World War I. Since these regions straddled the original line of demarcation for the Western and Eastern Empires (and churches), and since the Reformation had little lasting effect, the Christians are nearly all either Roman Catholics or Byzantines (some in communion with Rome, the majority Orthodox). Yugoslavia was proclaimed a Socialist republic in 1945. Repression of religion became government policy. Between May, 1945, and December, 1950, persecution took the following toll: almost two-thirds of 22 dioceses lost their bishops; about 348 priests were killed; 200 priests were under arrest and in prison; 12 of 18 seminaries were closed; the Catholic press was confiscated; religious instruction was suppressed in all schools; 300 religious houses and institutions were confiscated, and nuns and other religious driven out; all Church property was expropriated; the ministry of priests was severely restricted and subject to government interference; many thousands of the faithful shared the fate of priests and religious in death, imprisonment and slave labor. Cardinal Stepinac, arrested in 1946 and the symbol of the Church under persecution in Yugoslavia, died Feb. 10, 1960. In an agreement signed June 25, 1966, the government recognized the Holy See's spiritual jurisdiction over the Church in the country and guaranteed to bishops the possibility of maintaining contact with Rome in ecclesiastical and religious matters. The Holy See confirmed the principle that the activity of ecclesiastics, in the exercise of priestly functions, must take place within the religious and ecclesiastical sphere, and that abuse of these functions for political ends would be illegal. Less than two months after the

agreement was signed, a group of exiled Croatian priests issued a statement in which they accused the Yugoslav government of failing to abide by it. According to others, an improvement was noticeable. Yugoslavia maintains diplomatic relations with Vatican City.

Archd., 8; dioc., 14; a.a., 1, card., 1; abp., 7; bp., 23; parishes, 2,816; priests, 4,281 (2,764 dioc., 1,517 rel.); p.d., 3; sem., 770; bros., 270; srs., 6,207; catechists, 284; bap., 79,781; Caths., 7,243,000 (31.7%); tot. pop., 22,800,000.

Zaire (formerly the Congo): Republic in south central Africa; capital, Kinshasa. Christianity was introduced in 1484 and evangelization began about 1490. The first native bishop in black Africa was ordained in 1518. Subsequent missionary work was hindered by faulty methods of instruction and formation, inroads of the slave trade, wars among the tribes, and Portuguese policy based on the patronage system and having all the trappings of anticlericalism in the 18th and 19th centuries. Modern evangelization started in the second half of the 19th century. The hierarchy was established in 1959. In the civil disorders which followed independence in 1960, some missions and other church installations were abandoned, thousands of people reverted to tribal religions and many priests and religious were killed. Church-state tensions have developed in recent years because of the Church's criticism of the anti-Christian thrust of Pres. Mobutu's "Africanization" policies. Zaire maintains diplomatic relations with Vatican City.

Archd., 6; dioc., 41; card., 1 (nat.); abp., 5 (nat.); bp., 46 (43 nat.); parishes, 1,039; priests, 2,587 (834 dioc., 1,753 rel.); p.d., 13; sem., 2,186; bros., 879; srs., 4,636; catechists, 48,871; bap., 445,871; Caths., 13,596,000 (53.6%); tot. pop., 31,150,000.

Zambia: Republic in central Africa; capital, Lusaka. Portuguese priests did some evangelizing in the 16th and 17th centuries but no results of their work remained in the 19th century. Jesuits began work in the south in the 1880s and White Fathers in the north and east in 1895. Evangelization of the western region began for the first time in 1831. The number of Catholics doubled in the 20 years following World War II. Zambia maintains diplomatic relations with Vatican City.

Archd., 2; dioc., 7; abp., 2 (nat.); bp., 6 (4 nat.); parishes, 220; priests, 526 (113 dioc., 413 rel.); p.d., 2; sem., 151; bros., 171; srs., 774; catechists, 3,404; bap., 47,834; Caths., 1,772,000 (28.4%); tot. pop., 6,240,000.

Zimbabwe (formerly Rhodesia): Independent republic (Apr. 18, 1980) in south central Africa; capital, Harare (Salisbury). Earlier unsuccessful missionary ventures preceded the introduction of Catholicism in 1879. Missionaries began to make progress after 1893. The hierarchy was established in 1955; the first black bishop was ordained in 1973. In 1969, four years after the government of Ian Smith made a unilateral declaration of independence from England, a new constitution was enacted for the purpose of assuring continued white supremacy over the black majority. Catholic and

Protestant prelates in the country protested vigorously against the constitution and related enactments as opposed to human rights of the blacks and restrictive of the Church's freedom to carry out its pastoral, educational and social service functions. The Smith regime was ousted in 1979 after seven years of civil war in which at least 25,000 people were killed. Diplomatic relations with the Vatican were established in 1980.

Archd., 1; dioc., 5; abp., 1 (nat.); bp., 5 (3 nat.); parishes, 134; priests, 320 (70 dioc., 250 rel.); p.d., 7; sem., 40; bros., 107; srs., 957; catechists, 1,422; Caths., 660,000 (8.5%); tot. pop., 7,740,000.

CATHOLIC WORLD STATISTICS

(Principal sources: Statistical Yearbook of the Church, 1984, the latest edition; Annuario Pontificio, 1986. Figures are from Dec. 31, 1984, unless indicated otherwise.)

Patriarchates: 13. Eastern Rites, 8 (Africa, 2; Asia, 6). Roman Rite, 5 (Asia, 2; Europe, 2; West Indies, 1). The West Indies patriarchate has been vacant since 1963.

Archdioceses: 513 (Africa, 59; North and Middle America, 78; South America, 87; Asia, 124; Europe, 147; Oceania, 18).

Dioceses: 1,920 (Africa, 312; North and Middle America, 316; South America, 343; Asia, 366; Europe, 532; Oceania, 51).

Prelatures: 69 (Africa, 1; North and Middle America, 13; South America, 42; Asia, 5; Europe, 8).

Abbacies: 17 (Africa, 1; North and Middle America, 1; South America, 2; Asia, 1; Europe, 12).

Apostolic Exarchates, Ordinariates: 19 (North and Middle America, 2; South America, 3; Asia, 1; Europe, 13).

Vicariates Apostolic: 75 (Africa, 13; North and Middle America, 7; South America, 37; Asia, 17; Europe, 1).

Prefectures Apostolic: 52 (Africa, 8; South America, 9; Asia, 35).

Apostolic Administrations: 7 (Africa, 1; North and Middle America, 1; Asia, 1; Europe, 4).

Missions "Sui Juris": 6 (Africa, 1; Asia, 3; Middle America, 1; Oceania, 1).

Military Vicariates: 29 (Africa, 3; North and Middle America, 4; South America, 8; Asia, 3; Europe, 9; Oceania, 2).

Cardinals (as of Sept. 30, 1986): **146** (Africa, 16; North America, 18; Central and South America, 20; Asia, 13; Europe, 76; Oceania, 3).

Patriarchs: 6 (Asia, 5; Europe, 1).

Archbishops: 730 (Africa, 83; North and Middle America, 111; South America, 117; Asia, 138; Europe, 255; Oceania, 26).

Bishops: 3,102 (Africa, 385; North and Middle America, 644; South America, 629; Asia, 397; Europe, 972; Oceania, 75).

Figures for the hierarchy (cardinals, patriarchs, archbishops and bishops) include: 2,324 diocesan (heads of ecclesiastical territories); 627 coadjutors or auxiliaries; 172 who hold offices in the Roman Curia; 51 in other situations; 790 retired.

Priests, Total: 405,959 (Africa, 17,775; North and Middle America, 84,376; South America, 34,666; Asia, 28,266; Europe, 235,326; Oceania, 5,550).

• Diocesan Priests: **254,089** (Africa, 7,260; North and Middle America, 51,216; South America, 15,593; Asia, 14,709; Europe, 162,472; Oceania, 2,839).

• Religious Priests: **151,870** (Africa, 10,515; North and Middle America, 33,160; South America, 19,073; Asia, 13,557; Europe, 72,854; Oceania, 2,711).

Permanent Deacons: 11,733 (Africa, 188; North and Middle America, 8,042; South America, 898; Asia, 57; Europe, 2,480; Oceania, 68).

Brothers: 66,287 (Africa, 5,119; North and Middle America, 14,371; South America, 6,647; Asia, 5,629; Europe, 31,530; Oceania, 2,991).

Sisters: 926,335 (Africa, 37,346; North and Middle America, 191,621; South America, 89,823; Asia, 91,760; Europe, 500,961; Oceania, 14,824).

Major Seminarians: 80,302 (Africa, 8,894; North and Middle America, 14,679; South America, 13,768; Asia, 14,427; Europe, 27,616; Oceania, 918).

Lay Missionaries: 3,191 (Africa, 2,022; North and Middle America, 290; South America, 251; Asia, 423; Oceania, 205).

Catechists: 279,868 (Africa, 189,915; North and Middle America, 11,807; South America, 10,121; Asia, 61,709; Europe, 281; Oceania, 6,035).

Parishes, 211,156 (Africa, 8,059; North and Middle America, 32,020; South America, 16,619; Asia, 13,020; Europe, 139,095; Oceania, 2,343).

Elementary/Primary Schools and Students: 77,256 schools; **21,920,763** students. (Africa, 22,917 — 7,058,142; North and Middle America, 12,494 — 3,651,609; South America, 8,163 — 3,257,834; Asia, 11,227 — 3,859,963; Europe, 20,144 — 3,636,135; Oceania, 2,311 — 457,080).

Secondary Schools and Students: 30,268 schools; **11,833,790** students. (Africa, 3,561 — 995,759; North and Middle America, 3,610 — 1,520,048; South America, 4,861 — 1,991,946; Asia, 6,918 — 3,636,251; Europe, 10,643 — 3,396,548; Oceania, 675 — 293,238).

Students in Higher Institutes and Universities: 2,352,353 (Africa, 10,697; North and Middle America, 810,883; South America, 522,336; Asia, 767,573; Europe, 236,627; Oceania, 4,237).

Hospitals: 6,082 (Africa, 827; North and Middle America, 1,032; South America, 1,213; Asia, 1,053; Europe, 1,798; Oceania, 159).

Dispensaries: 12,394 (Africa, 3,472; North and Middle America, 1,425; South America, 2,229; Asia, 2,553; Europe, 2,474; Oceania, 241).

Leprosaria: 752 (Africa, 351; North and Middle America, 9; South America, 49; Asia, 333; Europe, 5; Oceania, 5).

Homes for Aged, Chronically Ill, Handicapped: 10,066 (Africa, 329; North and Middle America, 1,116; South America, 1,205; Asia, 613; Europe,

6,602; Oceania, 201).

Orphanages: 6,713 (Africa, 552; North and Middle America, 483; South America, 1,054; Asia, 1,902; Europe, 2,521; Oceania, 201).

Nurseries: 5,710(Africa, 619; North and Middle America, 339; South America, 1,262; Asia, 1,143; Europe, 2,325; Oceania, 22).

Baptisms: 17,745,248 (Africa, 2,365,242; North and Middle America, 4,021,819; South America 5,611,467; Asia, 2,183,490; Europe, 3,423,997; Oceania, 139,233). Includes 16,213,582 baptisms up to the age of seven and 1,531,666 over that age.

Marriages: 4,104,458 (Africa, 214,071: North and Middle America, 977,304; South America, 1,060,557; Asia, 407,370; Europe, 1,409,672; Oceania, 35,484). Includes 3,722,815 marriages between Catholics and 331,643 between Catholics and non-Catholics.

Catholic Population: 840,106,000 (17.7% of the total world population of 4,748,833,000).

• Africa — 69,104,000 (12.9%); tot. pop., 535,160,000.

• North America — 63,759,000 (24.3%); tot. pop., 261,926,000.

• Central America — 115,594,000 (87.3%); tot. pop., 132,316,000 (includes Mexico).

• South America — 236,730,000 (90.4%); tot. pop., 261,834,000.

• Asia — 70,652,000 (2.5%); tot. pop., 2,839,054,000.

• Europe — 277,827,000 (40%); tot. pop., 694,112,000.

• Oceania — 6,440,000 (26.3%); tot. pop., 24,431,000.

THE CHURCH IN TROUBLED AREAS IN 1986

These are some of the countries in which the Church and its members experienced troubles in 1986.

Czechoslovakia: The undergrounded publication *Information on the Church* reported that Communist authorities were concerned about the continuing influence of the Church in areas where it had strong traditional roots. In 1984: in Slovakia, 72 percent of newborns were baptized, 53 percent of weddings and 80 percent of funerals were performed in church ceremonies; in another republic, 31 percent of newborns were baptized, 16 percent of weddings and 51 percent of funerals took place with religious ceremonies. Meanwhile, religious life and parish activity remained restricted, and 10 of the nation's 13 dioceses were without resident bishops.

Lithuania: The underground *Chronicle of the Catholic Church in Lithuania* reported that the automobile accident in which Father Juozas Zdebskis was killed Feb. 5 was "a carefully planned and executed act of violence." He had been under surveillance by secret police for more than 20 years and had been repeatedly threatened during that time. He was the pastor of Holy Trinity Church in Rudamina and a founding member of the banned Catholic Committee for the Defense of Believers' Rights. He was imprisoned in 1971 to 1972 for teaching religion to children.

Nicaragua: As the Sandinista government celebrated July 19 the seventh anniversary of the overthrow of the regime of Gen. Anastasio Somoza, pressure against the Church was reported on the increase. It included the deportation of priests, the muzzling of church communications, efforts to alienate the people from the bishops, and the exiling of Msgr. Bismarck Carballo (in the U.S.) and Bishop Pablo Antonio Vega (in Honduras). The worst of the human toll of the revolution was the number of victims of continuing civil war — some 13,000 dead and other thousands wounded and injured.

The bishops were critical of the country's so-called "popular church," accusing activist priests and Religious of manipulating the Gospel "for their own ends." In a statement issued Apr. 7, they said: "A belligerent group of priests, religious workers and lay people of various nationalities, who say they belong to the Catholic Church, are in reality working actively to undermine the Church. . . . They manipulate the fundamental truths of our faith, taking upon themselves the right to reinterpret and even to rewrite the word of God, in order to make it fit their own ideology and use it for their own ends."

Paraguay: During Independence Day celebrations May 18, Archbishop Ismael Blas Rolon Silvero of Asuncion canceled a traditional Mass in his cathedral and spoke in criticism of violence by police and others, as well as of violations of human rights by the military regime of Gen. Alfredo Stroessner. The government announced July 3 that it had forbidden reentry to Spanish Franciscan Father Javier Arancon, director of Radio Charitas in Asuncion. Guillermo Yaluf, a spokesman for the station, said the staff believed the move against the priest stemmed from his criticism of the regime.

Vietnam: Despite government efforts to eliminate the Church, there was "terrific Mass attendance" along with conversions, according to Jesuit Father Henri Forest, undersecretary of the Pontifical Council Cor Unum. Available information indicated the government would like to "choke off the Church completely." Father Forest said the regime controlled the choice and education of candidates for the priesthood, and had established a controlled organization of patriotic Catholics analogous to a similar "church" to China.

Yugoslavia: An interfaith delegation that visited Yugoslavia in February reported it had found more religious freedom there than in other Communist countries of Eastern Europe. It was also reported that government authorities in Yugoslavia were appreciative of religion's positive contribution to social stability. At the same time, delegation members said the government continued to impose many restrictions on religion, and that believers could not expect to advance in professions or government leadership on an equal basis with Marxists.

EPISCOPAL CONFERENCES

(Principal source: *Annuario Pontificio.*)

Episcopal conferences, organized and operating under general norms and particular statutes approved by the Holy See, are official bodies in and through which the bishops of a given country or territory act together as pastors of the Church.

Listed below according to countries or regions are titles and addresses of conferences and names and sees of presidents (archbishops unless otherwise noted).

Africa, North: Conference Episcopale Regionale du Nord de l'Afrique (CERNA), 13 rue Khelifa-Boukhalfa, Algiers, Algeria. Henri Teissier (Coadjutor, Algiers).

Africa, South: Southern African Catholic Bishops' Conference (SACBC), P.O. Box 941, Pretoria 0001, S. Africa. Denis Eugene Hurley, O.M.I. (Durban).

Angola and Sao Tome: Conferencia Episcopal de Angola e Sao Tome (CEAST), C.P. 10, Huambo, Angola. Manuel F. da Costa (Huambo).

Antilles: Antilles Episcopal Conference, P.O. Box 43, 21 Hopefield Ave., Kingston 6, Jamaica. Samuel E. Carter, S.J. (Kingston in Jamaica).

Arab Countries: Conference des Eveques Latins dans les Regions Arabes (CELRA), Latin Patriarchate, P.O. Box 14152, Jerusalem (Old City). Patriarch Giacomo Beltritti (Jerusalem).

Argentina: Conferencia Episcopal Argentina (CEA), Calle Paraguay 1867, Buenos Aires. Card. Raul Francisco Primatesta (Cordoba).

Australia: Australian Episcopal Conference, P.O. Box 368, Canberra, A.C.T., 2601. Francis Roberts Rush (Brisbane).

Austria: Osterreichische Bischofskonferenz, Rotenturmstrasse 2, A1010 Vienna. Karl Berg (Salzburg).

Bangladesh: Catholic Bishops' Conference (CBCB), P.O. Box 3, Dhaka-2. Michael Rozario (Dhaka).

Belgium: Bisschoppenconferentie van Belgie — Conference Episcopale de Belgique, Aartsbidom, Wollemarkt 15, B-2800 Mechelen. Card. Godfried Danneels (Mechelen-Brussel).

Benin: Conference Episcopale du Benin, B.P. 491, Cotonou. Christophe Adimou (Cotonou).

Bolivia: Conferencia Episcopal de Bolivia (CEB), Casilla 2309, La Paz. Bp. Julio Terrazas Sandoval, C.SS.R. (Oruro).

Brazil: Conferencia Nacional dos Bispos do Brasil (CNBB), C.P. 13-2067, 70401 Brasilia, D.F. Bp. Jose Ivo Lorscheiter (Santa Maria).

Bulgaria: Ulitza Pashovi 10-B, Sofia VI. Bp. Metodio Dimitrow Stratiew, A.A. (Apostolic Exarch, Sofia).

Burkina Faso and Niger: Conference des Eveques de Bourkina Faso et du Niger, B.P. 1195, Ouagadougou, Burkina Faso. Bp. Anselme Titanma Sanon (Bobo-Dioulasso).

Burma: Burma Catholic Bishops' Conference (BCBC), 292 Prome Rd., Sanchaung P.O., Rangoon. Bp. Paul Zinghtung Grawng (Myitkyina).

Burundi: Conference Episcopale du Burundi, B. P. 1390, Bujumbura. Joachim Ruhuna (Gitega).

Cameroon: Conference Episcopale Nationale du Cameroun (CENC), P.O. Box 272, Garoua. Christian Wiyghan Tumi (Garoua).

Canada: See Canadian Conference of Catholic Bishops.

Central African Republic: Conference Episcopale Centrafricaine (CECA), B.P. 798, Bangui. Joachim N'Dayen (Bangui).

Chad: Conference Episcopale du Tchad, B.P. 456, N'Djamena. Charles Vandame, S.J. (N'Djamena).

Chile: Conferencia Episcopal de Chile (CECH), Casilla 13191, Correo 21, Santiago. Bernardino Piñero Carvallo (La Serena).

China (Republic of China, Taiwan): Regional Episcopal Conference of China, P.O. Box 36603, Taipeh 105, Taiwan. Stanislaus Lokuang (Taipeh, emeritus).

Colombia: Conferencia Episcopal de Colombia, Apartado 7448, Bogota D.E. Hector Rueda Hernandez (Bucamarango).

Congo: Conference Episcopale du Congo, B.P. 2301, Brazzaville. Bp. Georges Singha (Owanda).

Costa Rica: Conferencia Episcopal de Costa Rica (CECOR), Apartado 3187, San Jose. Roman Arrieta Villalobos (San Jose de Costa Rica).

Cuba: Conferencia Episcopal de Cuba (CEC), Apartado 594, Habana 152. Bp. Adolfo Rodriguez Herrera (Camaguey).

Dominican Republic: Conferencia del Episcopado Dominicano (CED), Apartado 186, Santo Domingo. Nicolas de Jesus Lopez Rodriguez (Santo Domingo).

Ecuador: Conferencia Episcopal Ecuatoriana, Apartado 1081, Quito. Bernardino Echeverria Ruiz, O.F.M. (Guayaquil).

El Salvador: Conferencia Episcopal de El Salvador (CEDES). Apartado Postal 1310, San Salvador. Bp. Marco Rene Revelo Contreras (Santa Ana).

Equatorial Guinea: Apartado 106, Malabo. Rafael Nze Abuy, C.M.F. (Malabo).

Ethiopia: Conferenza Episcopale di Etiopia, P.O. Box 21903, Addis Ababa. Card. Paulos Tzadua (Addis Ababa).

France: Conference Episcopale Francaise, 106 rue du Bac, 75341 Paris CEDEX 07. Bp. Jean Vilnet (Lille).

Gabon: Conference Episcopale du Gabon, B.P. 230, Franceville. Bp. Felicien-Patrice Makouaka (Franceville).

Gambia, Liberia and Sierra Leone: Inter-Territorial Episcopal Conference, P.O. Box 893, Freetown, Sierra Leone. Michael Kpakala Francis (Monrovia, Liberia).

Germany: Deutsche Bischofskonferenz, Kaiserstrasse 163, D-5300 Bonn. Card. Joseph Hoeffner (Cologne). Berliner Bischofskonferenz, Franzosische Strasse 34, DDR-1086 Berlin. Card. Joachim Meisner (Berlin, Bp.)

Ghana: Ghana Bishops' Conference, P.O. Box 42, Tamale. Peter Poreku Dery (Tamale).

Great Britain: Bishops' Conference of England and Wales, Archbishop's House, Westminster, London, SWIP IQJ. Card. George Basil Hume,

O.S.B. (Westminster). Bishops' Conference of Scotland, 18 Park Circus, Glasgow G3 6BE. Thomas Winning (Glasgow). Card. Gordon J. Gray (Saint Andrews and Edinburgh, emeritus).

Greece: Conferenza Episcopale di Grecia, Archeveche Catholique, Corfu. Antonio Varthalitis, A.A. (Corfu, Zante and Cefalonia.)

Guatemala: Conferencia Episcopal de Guatemala (CEG), 26 Calle 8-90, zona 12, Ciudad de Guatemala. Prospero Penados del Barrio (Guatemala).

Guinea: Conference Episcopale de la Guinee, B.P. 1006 Bis, Conakry. Robert Sarah (Conakry).

Haiti: Conference Episcopale de Haiti (CEH). C.P. 22, Cap Hatien, Haiti. Bp. Francois Gayot, S.M.M. (Cap Haitien).

Honduras: Conferencia Episcopal de Honduras (CEH), Arzobispado, Apartado 106, Tegucigalpa. Hector Enrique Santos Hernandez, S.D.B. (Tegucigalpa).

Hungary: Magyar Puspoki Kar Konferenciaja, Berenyi Zsigmond u. 2, Pf. 25, H-2500 Esztergom.

India: Catholic Bishops' Conference of India (CBCI), CBCI Centre, Goldakkhana, New Delhi-110001. Simon Ignatius Pimenta (Bombay).

Indonesia: General Conference of the Ordinaries of Indonesia (Majelis Agung Waligerija Indonesia — MAWI), Taman Cut Mutiah 10, Jakarta II/14. Bp. Francis Xavier Sudartanto Hadisumarta, O. Carm. (Malang).

Ireland: Episcopal Meetings, "Ara Coeli," Armagh. Card. Tomas O'Fiaich (Armagh).

Italy: Conferenza Episcopale Italiana (CEI), Circonvallazione Aurelia, 50, 00165 Roma. Card. Ugo Poletti (Vicar General, Rome).

Ivory Coast: Conference Episcopale de la Cote d'Ivoire, B.P. 1287, Abidjan. Card. Bernard Yago (Abidjan).

Japan: Japan Catholic Bishops' Conference, Catholic Center, 10-1 Rokubancho, Chiyoda-Ku, Tokyo 102. Peter Seiichi Shirayanagi (Tokyo).

Kenya: Kenya Episcopal Conference (KEC), P.O. Box 938, Nakuru. Bp. Raphael S. Ndingi Mwana's Nzeki (Nakuru).

Korea: Catholic Conference of Korea, Box 16, Seoul. Card. Stephen Sou Hwan Kim (Seoul).

Laos and Cambodia: Conference Episcopale du Laos et du Cambodge.

Latvia: Pils Jela, 2, Riga. Card. Julijans Vaivods (Ap. Admin., Riga and Liepaja).

Lesotho: Lesotho Catholic Bishops' Conference, P.O. Box 200, Maseru 100. Bp. Sebastian Koto Khoarai, O.M.I. (Mohale's Hoek).

Liberia: See Gambia, Liberia and Sierra Leone.

Lithuania: Vilniaus gatve 4, 233000 Kaunas. Bp. Liudas Povilonis (Ap. Admin., Kaunas and Vilkaviskis).

Madagascar: Conference Episcopale du Madagascar, 102 bis, Av. Marechal Joffre Antanimena, B. P 667, Antananarivo. Card. Victor Razafimahatratra, S.J. (Tananarive).

Malawi: Episcopal Conference of Malawi, Catholic Secretariat of Malawi, P.O. Box 30384, Lilongwe 3. James Chiona (Blantyre).

Malaysia-Singapore-Brunei: Catholic Bishops' Conference of Malaysia-Singapore-Brunei, (BCMSB),

Archbishop's House, 31 Victoria St., Singapore 0718. Gregory Yong Sooi Nghean (Singapore).

Mali: Conference Episcopale du Mali, B.P. 298, Bamako. Luc Auguste Sangare (Bamako).

Malta: Conferenza Episcopale Maltese, Archbishop's Curia, Floriana. Joseph Mercieca (Malta).

Mexico: Conferencia del Episcopado Mexicano (CEM), Apartado 118-055, 07050 Mexico D.F. Sergio Obeso Rivera (Jalapa).

Mozambique: Conferencia Episcopal de Mocambique (CEM), C.P. 286, Maputo. Jaime Pedro Goncalves (Beira).

Netherlands: Nederlandse Bisschoppenconferentie, Postbus 13049, NL-3507 LA, Utrecht. Card. Adrianus J. Simonis (Utrecht).

New Zealand: New Zealand Episcopal Conference, P.O. Box 198, Wellington. Card. Thomas Stafford Williams (Wellington).

Nicaragua: Conferencia Episcopal de Nicaragua, Apartado 2148, Managua. Card. Miguel Obando Bravo (Managua).

Niger: See Burkina Faso.

Nigeria: Catholic Bishops Conference of Nigeria, P.O. Box 951, Lagos. Bp. Gabriel Gonsum Ganaka (Jos).

Pacific: Conference des Eveques du Pacifique (CEPAC), P.O. Box 109, Suva (Fiji). Petero Mataca (Suva).

Pakistan: Pakistan Episcopal Conference, St. Patrick's Cathedral, Karachi 3. Card. Joseph Cordeiro (Karachi).

Panama: Conferencia Episcopal de Panama (CEP), Apartado 386, Panama 1. Marcos Gregorio McGrath, C.S.C. (Panama).

Papua New Guinea and Solomon Islands: Bishops' Conference of Papua New Guinea and Solomon Islands, Southern Highlands, P.O. Box 106, Kieta, North Solomons Province. Bp. Gregory Singkai (Bougainville).

Paraguay: Conferencia Episcopal Paraguaya (CEP), Calle Alberdi 782, Casilla Correo 1436, Asuncion. Ismael Blas Rolon Silvero, S.D.B. (Asuncion).

Peru: Conferencia Episcopal Peruana, Apartado 310, Lima 1. Card. Juan Landazuri Ricketts, O.F.M. (Lima).

Philippines: Catholic Bishops' Conference of the Philippines (CBCP), P.O. Box 1160, Manila. Card. Ricardo Vidal (Cebu).

Poland: Konferencja Episkopatu Polski, Skwer Kardynala Stefana Wyszynskiego 6, 01-015 Warsaw. Card. Jozef Glemp (Gniezno and Warsaw).

Portugal: Conferencia Episcopal Portuguesa, Campo dos martires de Patria, 43-1 Esq., 1198 Lisbon. Bp. Manuel de Almeida Trindade (Aveiro).

Puerto Rico: Conferencia Episcopal Puertorriquena (CEP), Apartado 205, Estacion 6, Ponce 00732. Bp. Juan Fremiot Torres Olivier (Ponce).

Rhodesia: See Zimbabwe.

Rumania: Vacant.

Rwanda: Conference Episcopale du Rwanda (C.Ep.R.), B.P. 357, Kigali. Bp. Joseph Ruzindana (Byumba).

Scandinavia: Conferentia Episcopalis Scandiae,

Akersvejen 5, P.B. 8270 Hammersborg, N-0129 Oslo 1, Norway. Bp. John W. Gran, O.C.S.O. (Oslo, Norway, emeritus).

Senegal-Mauritania: Conference Episcopale du Senegal-Mauritania, B.P. 5082, Dakar, Fann. Senegal. Card. Hyacinthe Thiandoum (Dakar).

Sierra Leone: See Gambia, Liberia and Sierra Leone.

Spain: Conferencia Episcopal Espanola, Calle Anastro 1, 28033 Madrid. Gabino Diaz Merchan (Oviedo).

Sri Lanka: Catholic Bishops' Conference of Sri Lanka, 19 Balcombe Place, Cotta Rd., Colombo 8. Bp. Frank Marcus Fernando (Chilaw).

Sudan: Sudan Episcopal Conference (SEC), P.O. Box 49, Khartoum. Gabriel Zubeir Wako (Khartoum).

Switzerland: Conference des Eveques Suisses, Secretariat, av. Moleson 30, CH-1700 Fribourg 1. Bp. Henri Schwery (Sion).

Tanzania: Tanzania Episcopal Conference (TEC), P.O. Box 2133, Dar-es-Salaam. Bp. Anthony Mayala (Musoma).

Thailand: Conference des Eveques de Thailand, 57 Oriental Ave., Praetham Bldg., Bangrak, Bangkok 10500. Card. Michael Michai Kitbunchu (Bangkok).

Togo: Conference Episcopale du Togo, B.P. 348, Lome. Robert Dosseh-Anyron (Lome).

Turkey: Conferenza Episcopale di Turchia, Olcek Sokak 83, Harbiye, Istanbul. Bp. Gauthier Pierre Dubois, O.F.M. Cap. (V.A., Istanbul).

Uganda: Uganda Episcopal Conference, P.O. Box 2886, Kampala. Bp. Barnabas Halem 'Imana (Kabale).

United States: See National Conference of Catholic Bishops.

Uruguay: Conferencia Episcopal Uruguaya (CEU), Avenida Uruguay 1319, Montevideo. Jose Gottardi Cristelli, S.D.B. (Montevideo).

Venezuela: Conferencia Episcopal de Venezuela (CEV), Apartado Postal 4897, Caracas 1010-A. Card. Jose Ali Lebrun Moratinos (Caracas).

Vietnam: Conference Episcopale du Vietnam, 40 Pho Nha Chung, Hanoi. Card. Joseph-Marie Trinh van-Can (Hanoi).

Yugoslavia: Biskupska Konferencija Jugoslavije, Kaptol 31, 41000, Zagreb. Card. Franjo Kuharic (Zagreb).

Zaire: Conference Episcopale du Zaire (CEZ), B.P. 3258, Kinshasa-Gombe. Bp. Monsengwo Pasinya (Kinsangani, auxiliary).

Zambia: Zambia Episcopal Conference, P.O. Box 31965, Lusaka. Bp. James Spaita (Mansa).

Zimbabwe: Zimbabwe Catholic Bishops' Conference (ZCBC), P.O. Box 8135, Causeway, Harare. Bp. Tobias Wunganayi Chiginya (Gweru).

Territorial Conferences

(Source: *Annuario Pontificio*.)

Territorial as well as national episcopal conferences have been established in some places. Some conferences of this kind are still in the planning stage.

Africa: Symposium of Episcopal Conferences of Africa and Madagascar (SECAM) (Symposium des Conferences Episcopales d'Afrique et de Madagascar, SCEAM): Card. Joseph Malula, Kinshasa, Zaire, president. Address: Secretariat, P.O. Box 7530, Accra North, Ghana.

Association of Member Episcopal Conferences in Eastern Africa (AMECEA): Represents Ethiopia, Kenya, Malawi, Sudan, Tanzania, Uganda and Zambia. The Seychelles was accepted as an affiliate member in 1979, Bp. Medard Joseph Mazombwe, Chipata, Zambia, president. Address: P.O. Box 21191, Nairobi, Kenya.

Regional Episcopal Conference of French-Speaking West Africa (Conference Episcopale Regionale de l'Afrique de l'Ouest Francophone, CERAO): Bp. Diedonne Yougbare, Koupela, Burkina Faso, president. Address: Secretariat General, B.P. 22, Abidjan 08, Ivory Coast.

Association of Episcopal Conferences of Anglophone West Africa (AECAWA): Abp. John Kodwo Amissah, Cape Coast, Ghana, president. Address: P.O. Box 297, Monrovia, Liberia.

Association of Episcopal Conferences of Congo, Central African Republic and Chad (ACECCT): Abp. Joachim N'Dayen, Bangui, Central African Republic, president. Address: Secretariat, B.P. 1518, Bangui, Central African Republic.

Inter-Regional Meeting of Bishops of Southern Africa (IMBISA): Abp. Jaime Pedro Gonclaves, Beira, Mozambique, president. Address: 4 Bayswater Rd., Highlands Harare, Zimbabwe.

Asia: Federation of Asian Bishops' Conferences (FABC): Represents 14 Asian episcopal conferences (excluding the Middle East). Headquarters, P.O. Box 2984, Hong Kong. Established in 1970; statutes approved experimentally Dec. 6, 1972. Abp. Henry Sebastian D'Souza, coadjutor Calcutta, India, secretary general.

Europe: Council of European Bishops' Conferences (Consilium Conferentiarum Episcopalium Europae, CCEE): Card. George Basil Hume, O.S.B., Westminster, England, president. Address of secretariat: Klosterhof 6b, CH-9000 St. Gallen, Switzerland.

Commission of the Episcopates of the European Community (Commissio Episcopatuum Communitatis Europaeae, COMECE): Established in 1980; represents episcopates of states which belong to European Community. Abp.-Bp. Jean Hengen, Luxembourg, president. Address of secretariat: 13 Avenue Pere Damien, 1150 Brussels, Belgium.

Central and South America: Latin American Bishops' Conference (Consejo Episcopal LatinoAmericano, CELAM): Established in 1956; statutes approved Nov. 9, 1974. Represents 22 Latin American national bishops' conferences. Abp. Antonio Quarracino, La Plata, Argentina, president. Address of the secretariat: Calle 78, no. 11-17, Apartado Aereo 5278, Bogota, Colombia.

Episcopal Secretariat of Central America and Panama (Secretariado Episcopal de America Central y Panama, SEDAC): Statutes approved experimentally Sept. 26, 1970. Abp. Arturo Rivera Damas, S.D.B., San Salvador, president. Address of secretariat: Calle S. Jose y Avenida Las Americas, Urbanizacion Isidro Menendez, San Salvador, El Salvador.

INTERNATIONAL CATHOLIC ORGANIZATIONS

(Principal sources: Conference of International Catholic Organizations; Pontifical Council for the Laity; Almanac survey.)

Guidelines

International organizations wanting to call themselves "Catholic" are required to meet standards set by the Vatican's Council for the Laity and to register with and get the approval of the Papal Secretariat of State, according to guidelines dated Dec. 3 and published in *Acta Apostolicae Sedis* under date of Dec. 23, 1971.

Among conditions for the right of organizations to "bear the name Catholic" are:

• leaders "will always be Catholics," and candidates for office will be approved by the Secretariat of State;

• adherence by the organization to the Catholic Church, its teaching authority and teachings of the Gospel;

• evidence that the organization is really international with a universal outlook and that it fulfills its mission through its own management, meetings and accomplishments.

The guidelines also stated that leaders of the organizations "will take care to maintain necessary reserve as regards taking a stand or engaging in public activity in the field of politics or trade unionism. Abstention in these fields will normally be the best attitude for them to adopt during their term of office."

The guidelines were in line with a provision stated by the Second Vatican Council in the *Decree on the Apostolate of the Laity*: "No project may claim the name 'Catholic' unless it has obtained the consent of the lawful church authority."

They made it clear that all organizations are not obliged to apply for recognition, but that the Church "reserves the right to recognize as linked with her mission and her aims those organizations or movements which see fit to ask for such recognition."

Conference

Conference of International Catholic Organizations: A permanent body for collaboration among various organizations which seek to promote the development of international life along the lines of Christian principles. Eleven international Catholic organizations participated in its foundation and first meeting in 1927 at Fribourg, Switzerland. In 1951, the conference established its general secretariat and adopted governing statutes which were approved by the Vatican Secretariat of State in 1953.

The permanent secretariat is located at 37-39 rue de Vermont, CH-1202 Geneva, Switzerland. Other office addresses are: 1 rue Varembe, CH-1211 Geneva 20, Switzerland (Information Center); 9, rue Cler, F-75007 Paris, France (International Catholic Center for UNESCO); ICO Information Center, 323 East 47th St., New York, N.Y. 10017.

International Organizations

International Catholic organizations are listed below. Information includes name, date and place of establishment (when available), address of general secretariat. An asterisk indicates that the organization is a member of the Conference of International Catholic Organizations. Approximately 30 of the organizations have consultative status with other international or regional non-governmental agencies.

Apostleship of Prayer (1849): Borgo Santo Spirito 5, I-00193 Rome, Italy. National secretariat in most countries. (See Index.)

Apostolatus Maris (Apostleship of the Sea) (1922, Glasgow, Scotland): Pontifical Commission for Migration and Tourism, Piazza San Calisto 16, 00153 Rome, Italy. (See Index.)

L'Arche Communities: B.P. 35, 60350 Cuise Lamotte, France.

Associationes Juventutis Salesianae (Associations of Salesian Youth) (1847): Via della Pisana, 1111, 00163 Rome, Italy.

Blue Army of Our Lady of Fatima: (See Index.)

Caritas Internationalis* (1951, Rome, Italy): Piazza San Calisto 16, I-00153, Rome, Italy. Coordinates and represents its 117 national member organizations (in 113 countries) operating in the fields of development, emergency aid, social action.

Catholic International Education Office* (1952): 60, rue des Eburons, B-1040 Brussels, Belgium.

Catholic International Federation for Physical and Sports Education (1911; present name, 1957): 5, rue Cernuschi, F-75017 Paris, France.

Catholic International Union for Social Service* (1925, Milan, Italy): rue de la Poste 111, B-1030 Brussels, Belgium (general secretariat).

Christian Fraternity of the Sick and Handicapped: 9, Avenue de la Gare, CH-1630, Bulle, Switzerland.

"Communione e Liberazione" Fraternity (1955, Milan, Italy): Via Marcello Malpighi 2, 00161 Rome, Italy. Catholic renewal movement.

European Forum of National Committees of the Laity: 12 Brookwood Lawn Artane, Dublin 5, Ireland.

"Focolare Movement" or "Work of Mary" (1943, Trent, Italy): Via di Frascati, 304, I-00040 Rocca di Papa (Rome), Italy. (See Index: Focolare Movement.)

Foi et Lumiere: 8 rue Serret, 75015 Paris, France.

Inter Cultural Association, formerly International Catholic Auxiliaries (1937, Belgium): 91, rue de la Servette, CH-1202 Geneva, Switzerland.

International Association of Charities of St. Vincent de Paul* (1617, Chatillon les Dombes, France): 38, rue d'Alsace-Lorraine, B-1050 Brussels, Belgium. (See Index: St. Vincent de Paul Society.)

International Association of Children of Mary (1847): 67 rue de Sèvres, F-75006 Paris, France.

International Catholic Association for Service

to Young Women* (1897): 37-39, rue de Vermont, CH-1202 Geneva, Switzerland. Welfare of Catholic girls living away from home.

International Catholic Child Bureau* (1948, in Paris): 65, rue de Lausanne, CH-1202 Geneva, Switzerland.

International Catholic Conference of Guiding* (1965): Rue Paul-Emile Janson, 35, B-1050 Brussels, Belgium. Founded by member bodies of interdenominational World Association of Guides and Girl Scouts.

International Catholic Conference of Scouting* (1948): 21, rue de Dublin, B-1050 Brussels, Belgium.

International Catholic Migration Commission* (1951): 37-39 rue de Vermont, C.P. 96, CH-1211 Geneva 20, Switzerland. Coordinates activities worldwide on behalf of refugees and migrants, both administering programs directly and supporting the efforts of national affiliated agencies.

International Catholic Organization for Cinema and Audiovisual* (1928, The Hague, The Netherlands): Rue de l'Orme, 8, B-1040 Brussels, Belgium (general secretariat). Federation of national Catholic film offices.

International Catholic Rural Association (1962, Rome): Piazza San Calisto, 00153 Rome, Italy. International body for agricultural and rural organizations.

International Catholic Union of Esperanto: Via Berni 9, 00185 Rome, Italy.

International Catholic Union of the Press*: 37-39 rue de Vermont, Case Postale 197 CH-1211 Geneva 20 CIC, Switzerland. Coordinates and represents at the international level the activities of Catholics and Catholic federations or associations in the field of press and information. Has five specialized branches: International Federation of Catholic Dailies and Periodicals (1928); International Federation of Catholic Journalists (1927); International Federation of Catholic Press Agencies (1950); International Catholic Association of Teachers and Scientific or Technical Research Workers on Information (1968); Federation of Church Press Associations (1974).

International Centre for Studies in Religious Education LUMEN VITAE* (1934-35, Louvain, Belgium, under name Catechetical Documentary Centre; present name, 1956): 184, rue Washington, B-1050 Brussels, Belgium. Also referred to as Lumen Vitae Centre; concerned with all aspects of religious formation.

International Committee of Catholic Nurses and Medical Social Workers* (1933): Piazza San Calisto 16, 00153 Rome, Italy.

International Cooperation for Socio-Economic Development (1965, Rome, Italy): Avenue des ARTS-1, 2, Boite 6, 1040 Brussels, Belgium.

International Federation of Catholic Medical Associations (1954): Palazzo San Calisto, I-00120 Vatican City.

International Federation of Catholic Men* (Unum Omnes) (1948): Piazza San Calisto 16, 00153 Rome, Italy.

International Federation of Catholic Parochial

Youth Communities* (1962, Rome, Italy): Kipdorp 30, B-2000 Antwerp, Belgium.

International Federation of Catholic Pharmacists* (1954): 59, Bergstrasse, B-4700 Eupen, Belgium.

International Federation of Catholic Rural Movements* (1964, Lisbon, Portugal): 92, rue Africaine, B-1050 Brussels, Belgium.

International Federation of Catholic Universities* (1949): 78A, rue de Sevres, F-75341 Paris Cedex 7, France.

International Federation of the Catholic Associations of the Blind: FIDACA, Chamblioux 18, CH-1700 Fribourg, Switzerland. Coordinates actions of Catholic groups and assciations for the blind and develops their apostolate.

International Military Apostolate (1967): Gablenzgasse 62, A-1160 Vienna, Austria. Comprised of organizations of military men.

International Movement of Apostolate of Children* (1929, France): 8, rue Duguay-Trouin, F-75006 Paris, France.

International Movement of Apostolate in Middle and Upper Classes* (1963): Piazza San Calisto 16, 00153 Rome, Italy. Evangelization of adults of the independent milieus (that part of population known as old or recent middle class, aristocracy, bourgeoisie or "white collar").

International Movement of Catholic Agricultural and Rural Youth* (1954, Annevoie, Belgium): Tiensevest 68, B-3000 Leuven, Belgium (permanent secretariat).

International Young Catholic Students* (1946, Fribourg, Switzerland; present name, 1954): 171 rue de Rennes, F-75006 Paris, France.

International Young Christian Workers* (1925, Belgium): 11, rue Plantin, B-1070 Brussels, Belgium.

Legion of Mary (1921, Dublin, Ireland): De Montfort House, North Brunswick St., Dublin, Ireland. (See Index.)

Medicus Mundi Internationalis: (1964. Bensberg. Germany FR): P.O. Box 1547, 6501 BM Nijmegen, Netherlands. Promote health and medico-social services, particularly in developing countries; recruit essential health and medical personnel for developing countries; contribute to training of medical and auxiliary personnel; undertake research in the field of health.

NOVALIS, Marriage Preparation Center: University of St. Paul, 1 rue Stewart, Ottawa 2, Ont. Canada.

Our Lady's Teams (Equipes Notre-Dame) (1937, France): 49, rue de la Glacière, F-75013 Paris, France. Movement for spiritual formation of couples.

Pax Christi International (1950): Kerkstraat, 150, B-2000 Antwerp, Belgium. (See Index.)

Pax Romana* (1921, Fribourg, Switzerland, divided into two movements, 1947):

  Pax Romana — IMCS* (International Movement of Catholic Students) (1921): 171, rue de Rennes, F-75006, Paris, France. For undergraduates.

  Pax Romana — ICMICA* (International Catholic Movement for Intellectual and Cultural

Affairs) (1947): 37-39 rue de Vermont, Case Postale n 85, CH-1211 Geneva 20 CIC, Switzerland. For Catholic intellectuals and professionals.

Pro Sanctity Movement: Piazza S. Andrea della Valle 3, 00166 Rome, Italy.

St. Joan's International Alliance (1911, in England, as Catholic Women's Suffrage Society): 15 London Rd., Canterbury, Kent CT2 8LR, England. Associate member of ICO.

Salesian Cooperators (1876): Don Bosco College, Newton, N.J. 07860. Third Salesian family founded by St. John Bosco. Members commit themselves to an apostolate at the service of the Church, giving particular attention to youth in the Salesian spirit and style.

Secular Franciscan Order (1221, first Rule approved): Via Piemonte, 70, 00187, Rome, Italy. (See Index.)

Secular Fraternity of Charles de Foucauld: Katharinenweg 4, B4700 Eupen, Belgium.

Serra International (1953, in U.S.): (See Index.)

Society of St. Vincent de Paul* (1833, Paris): 5, rue du Pré-aux-Clercs, F-75007 Paris, France.

The Grail (1921, Nijmegen, The Netherlands): Duisburgerstrasse 470, D-4330, Mulheim, West Germany. (See Index.)

Third Order of St. Dominic (1285): Convento Santa Sabina, Piazza Pietro d'Illiria, Aventino, I-00153 Rome, Italy. (See Index.)

Unda: International Catholic Association for Radio and Television* (1928, Cologne, Germany): rue de l'Orme, 12, B-1040 Brussels, Belgium. (See Index.)

Unio Internationalis Laicorum in Servitio Ecclesiae (1965, Aachen, Germany): Postfach 990125, Am Kielshof 2, 5000 Cologne, Germany 91. Consists of national and diocesan associations of persons who give professional services to the Church.

Union of Adorers of the Blessed Sacrament (1937): Largo dei Monti Parioli 3, I-00197, Rome, Italy.

World Catholic Federation for the Biblical Apostolate (1969, Rome): Mittelstrasse, 12, P.O. Box 601, D-7000, Stuttgart 1, Germany.

World Federation of Christian Life Communities* (1953): 8, Borgo Santo Spirito, 00193 Rome, Italy. First Sodality of Our Lady founded in 1563.

World Movement of Christian Workers* (1961): 90, rue des Palais, 1210 Brussels, Belgium.

World Organization of Former Students of Catholic Schools (1967, Rome): Largo Nazareno 25, I-00187 Rome, Italy.

World Union of Catholic Philosophical Societies (1948, Amsterdam, The Netherlands): The Catholic University of America, Washington, D.C. 20064.

World Union of Catholic Teachers* (1951): Piazza San Calisto 16, 00153 Rome, Italy.

World Union of Catholic Women's Organizations* (1910): 20, rue Notre Dame des Champs, F-75006 Paris, France.

Regional Organizations

European Federation for Catholic Adult Education (1963, Lucerne, Switzerland): Kapuzinerstrasse 84, A-4020 Linz, Austria.

European Forum of National Committees of the Laity (1968): 12, Brookwood Lawn Artane, Dublin 5, Ireland.

Movimiento Familiar Cristiano (1949-50, Montevideo and Buenos Aires): Carrera 17 n. 4671, Bogota, D.E., Colombia. Christian Family Movement of Latin America.

CANADIAN SHRINES

Our Lady of the Cape (Cap de la Madeleine), Queen of the Most Holy Rosary: The Three Rivers, Quebec, parish church, built of fieldstone in 1714 and considered the oldest stone church on the North American continent preserved in its original state, was rededicated June 22, 1888, as a shrine of the Queen of the Most Holy Rosary. Thereafter, the site increased in importance as a pilgrimage and devotional center, and in 1904 St. Pius X decreed the crowning of a statue of the Blessed Virgin which had been donated 50 years earlier to commemorate the dogma of the Immaculate Conception. In 1909, the First Plenary Council of Quebec declared the church a shrine of national pilgrimage. In 1964, the church at the shrine was given the status and title of minor basilica.

St. Anne de Beaupre: The devotional history of this shrine in Quebec, began with the reported cure of a cripple, Louis Guimont, on Mar. 16, 1658, the starting date of construction work on a small chapel of St. Anne. The original building was successively enlarged and replaced by a stone church which was given the rank of minor basilica in 1888. The present structure, a Romanesque-Gothic basilica, houses the shrine proper in its north transept. The centers of attraction are an eight-foot-high oaken statue and the great relic of St. Anne, a portion of her forearm.

St. Joseph's Oratory: The massive oratory basilica standing on the western side of Mount Royal and overlooking the city of Montreal had its origin in a primitive chapel erected there by Blessed Andre Bessette, C.S.C., in 1904. Eleven years later, a large crypt was built to accommodate an increasing number of pilgrims, and in 1924 construction work was begun on the large church. A belfry, housing a 60-bell carillon and standing on the site of the original chapel, was dedicated May 15, 1955, as the first major event of the jubilee year observed after the oratory was given the rank of minor basilica.

Martyrs' Shrine: A shrine commemorating several of the Jesuit Martyrs of North America who were killed between 1642 and 1649 in the Ontario and northern New York area is located on the former site of old Fort Sainte Marie. Before its location was fixed near Midland, Ont., in 1925, a small chapel had been erected in 1907 at old Mission St. Ignace to mark the martyrdom of Fathers Jean de Brebeuf and Gabriel Lalemant. This sanctuary has a U.S. counterpart in the Shrine of the North American Martyrs near Auriesville, N.Y.

THE CATHOLIC CHURCH IN CANADA

The first date in the remote background of the Catholic history of Canada was July 7, 1534, when a priest in the exploration company of Jacques Cartier celebrated Mass on the Gaspe Peninsula.

Successful colonization and the significant beginnings of the Catholic history of the country date from the foundation of Quebec in 1608 by Samuel de Champlain and French settlers. Montreal was established in 1642.

The earliest missionaries were Franciscan Recollects and Jesuits who arrived in 1615 and 1625, respectively. They provided some pastoral care for the settlers but worked mainly among the 100,000 Indians — Algonquins, Hurons and Iroquois — in the interior and in the Lake Ontario region. Eight of the Jesuit missionaries, killed in the 1640s, were canonized in 1930. (See Index: Jesuit North American Martyrs.) Sulpician Fathers, who arrived in Canada late in the 1640s, played a part in the great missionary period which ended about 1700.

Kateri Tekakwitha, "Lily of the Mohawks," who was baptized in 1676 and died in 1680, was declared "Blessed" June 22, 1980.

The communities of women religious with the longest histories in Canada are the Canonesses of St. Augustine, since 1637; the Ursulines, since 1639; and the Hospitallers of St. Joseph, since 1642. Communities of Canadian origin are the Congregation of Notre Dame, founded by St. Marguerite Bourgeoys in 1658, and the Grey Nuns, formed by Bl. Marie Marguerite d'Youville in 1738.

Mother Marie (Guyard) of the Incarnation, an Ursuline nun, was one of the first three women missionaries to New France; called "Mother of the Church in Canada," she was declared "Blessed" June 22, 1980.

Start of Church Organization

Ecclesiastical organization began with the appointment in 1658 of Francois De Montmorency-Laval, "Father of the Church in Canada," as vicar apostolic of New France. He was the first bishop of Quebec from 1674 to 1688, with jurisdiction over all French-claimed territory in North America. He was declared "Blessed" June 22, 1980.

In 1713, the French Canadian population numbered 18,000. In the same year, the Treaty of Utrecht ceded Acadia, Newfoundland and the Hudson Bay Territory to England. The Acadians were scattered among the American Colonies in 1755.

The English acquired possession of Canada and its 70,000 French-speaking inhabitants in virtue of the Treaty of Paris in 1763. Anglo-French and Anglican-Catholic differences and tensions developed. The pro-British government at first refused to recognize the titles of church officials, hindered the clergy in their work and tried to install a non-Catholic educational system. Laws were passed which guaranteed religious liberties to Catholics (Quebec Act of 1774, Constitutional Act of 1791, legislation approved by Queen Victoria

in 1851), but it took some time before actual respect for these liberties matched the legal enactments. The initial moderation of government antipathy toward the Church was caused partly by the loyalty of Catholics to the Crown during the American Revolution and the War of 1812.

Growth

The 15 years following the passage in 1840 of the Act of Union, which joined Upper and Lower Canada, were significant. New communities of men and women religious joined those already in the country. The Oblates of Mary Immaculate, missionaries par excellence in Canada, advanced the penetration of the West which had been started in 1818 by Abbe Provencher. New jurisdictions were established, and Quebec became a metropolitan see in 1844. The first Council of Quebec was held in 1851. The established Catholic school system enjoyed a period of growth.

Laval University was inaugurated in 1854 and canonically established in 1876.

Archbishop Elzear-Alexandre Taschereau of Quebec was named Canada's first cardinal in 1886.

The apostolic delegation to Canada was set up in 1899. It became a nunciature October 16, 1969, with the establishment of diplomatic relations with the Vatican.

Early in this century, Canada had eight ecclesiastical provinces, 23 dioceses, three vicariates apostolic, 3,500 priests, 2.4 million Catholics, about 30 communities of men religious, and 70 or more communities of women religious. The Church in Canada was phased out of mission status and removed from the jurisdiction of the Congregation for the Propagation of the Faith in 1908.

Diverse Population

The greatest concentration of Catholics is in the eastern portion of the country. In the northern and western portions, outside metropolitan centers, there are some of the most difficult parish and mission areas in the world. Bilingual (English-French) differences in the general population are reflected in the Church; for example, in the parallel structures of the Canadian Conference of Catholic Bishops, which was established in 1943. Quebec is the center of French cultural influence. Many language groups are represented among Catholics, who include about 211,265 members of Eastern Rite in a metropolitan see, six eparchies and an apostolic exarchate.

Education, a past source of friction between the Church and the government, is administered by the civil provinces in a variety of arrangements authorized by the Canadian Constitution. Denominational schools have tax support in one way in Quebec and Newfoundland, and in another way in Alberta, Ontario and Saskatchewan. Several provinces provide tax support only for public schools, making private financing necessary for separate church-related schools.

ECCLESIASTICAL JURISDICTIONS OF CANADA

Provinces

Names of ecclesiastical provinces and metropolitan sees in bold face: suffragan sees in parentheses.

Edmonton (Calgary, St. Paul).

Grouard-McLennan (Mackenzie-Ft. Smith, Prince George, Whitehorse).

Halifax (Antigonish, Charlottetown, Yarmouth).

Keewatin-LePas (Churchill-Hudson Bay, Labrador-Schefferville, Moosonee).

Kingston (Alexandria-Cornwall, Peterborough, Sault Ste. Marie).

Moncton (Bathurst, Edmundston, St. John).

Montreal (Joliette, St. Jean-Longueuil, St. Jerome, Valleyfield).

Ottawa (Gatineau-Hull, Hearst, Mont-Laurier, Pembroke, Rouyn-Noranda, Timmins).

Quebec (Amos, Chicoutimi, Ste.-Anne-de-la-Pocatiere, Trois Rivieres).

Regina (Gravelbourg, Prince Albert, Saskatoon, Abbey of St. Peter).

Rimouski (Gaspe, Hauterive).

St. Boniface (no suffragans).

St. John's (Grand Falls, St. George).

Sherbrooke (Nicolet, St. Hyacinthe).

Toronto (Hamilton, London, St. Catharines, Thunder Bay).

Vancouver (Kamloops, Nelson, Victoria).

Winnipeg — Ukrainian (Edmonton, New Westminster, Saskatoon, Toronto).

Jurisdictions immediately subject to the Holy See: Roman-Rite Archdiocese of Winnipeg, Byzantine-Rite Eparchy of Sts. Cyril and Methodius for Slovaks, Byzantine-Rite Eparchy of St. Sauveur de Montreal for Greek Melkites; Antiochene-Rite Eparchy of St. Maron of Montreal for Maronites.

Archdioceses, Archbishops

Edmonton, Alta. (St. Albert, 1871; archdiocese, transferred Edmonton, 1912): Joseph N. MacNeil, archbishop, 1973.

Grouard-McLennan, Alta. (v.a. Athabaska-Mackenzie, 1862; Grouard, 1927; archdiocese Grouard-McLennan, 1967); Henri Legare, O.M.I., archbishop, 1972.

Halifax, N.S. (1842; archdiocese, 1852): James M. Hayes, archbishop, 1967.

Keewatin-Le Pas, Man. (v.a., 1910; archdiocese, 1967): Paul Dumouchel, O.M.I., archbishop, 1967. Peter Sutton, O.M.I., coadjutor.

Kingston, Ont. (1826; archdiocese, 1889): Francis J. Spence, archbishop, 1982.

Moncton, N.B. (1936): Donat Chiasson, archbishop, 1972.

Montreal, Que. (1836; archdiocese, 1886): Paul Gregoire, archbishop, 1968. Andre Cimichella, O.S.M., Gerard Tremblay, P.S.S., Jude Saint-Antoine, Jean-Claude Turcotte, Leonard Crowley, auxiliaries.

Ottawa, Ont. (Bytown, 1847, name changed, 1854; archdiocese, 1886): Joseph Aurele Plourde, archbishop, 1967. John Beahen, Gilles Belisle, auxiliaries.

Quebec, Que. (v.a., 1658; diocese, 1674; archdiocese, 1819; metropolitan, 1844; primatial see, 1956): Cardinal Louis-Albert Vachon, archbishop, 1981. Jean-Paul Labrie, Maurice Couture, Marc Leclerc, auxiliaries.

Regina, Sask. (1910; archdiocese, 1915): Charles A. Halpin, archbishop, 1973.

Rimouski, Que. (1867; archdiocese, 1946): Gilles Ouellet, P.M.E., archbishop, 1973.

St. Boniface, Man. (1847; archdiocese, 1871): Antoine Hacault, archbishop, 1974.

St. John's, Nfld. (p.a., 1784; v.a., 1796; diocese, 1847; archdiocese, 1904): Alphonsus Penney, archbishop, 1979.

Sherbrooke, Que. (1874; archdiocese, 1951); J.-M. Fortier, archbishop, 1968.

Toronto, Ont. (1841; archdiocese, 1870): Cardinal G. Emmett Carter, archbishop, 1978. Aloysius M. Ambrozic, coadjutor. Michael Pearse Lacey, Robert B. Clune, Leonard J. Wall, auxiliaries.

Vancouver, B. C. (v.a. British Columbia, 1863; diocese New Westminster, 1890; archdiocese Vancouver, 1908): James F. Carney, archbishop, 1969.

Winnipeg, Man. (1915): Adam Exner, O.M.I., archbishop, 1982.

Winnipeg, Man. (Ukrainian Byzantine Rite) (Ordinariate of Canada, 1912; ap. ex. Central Canada, 1948; ap. ex. Manitoba, 1951; archdiocese Winnipeg, 1956): Maxim Hermaniuk, C.SS.R., archbishop, 1956. Myron Daciuk, O.S.B.M., auxiliary.

Dioceses, Bishops

Alexandria-Cornwall, Ont. (1890): Eugene Philippe LaRocque, bishop, 1974.

Amos, Que. (1938): Gerard Drainville, bishop, 1978.

Antigonish, N.S. (Arichat, 1844; transferred, 1886): William E. Power, bishop, 1960.

Bathurst, N.B. (Chatham, 1860; transferred, 1938): Arsène Richard, bishop, 1986.

Calgary, Alta. (1912): Paul J. O'Byrne, bishop, 1968.

Charlottetown, P.E.I. (1829): James H. MacDonald, C.S.C., bishop, 1982.

Chicoutimi, Que. (1878): Jean-Guy Couture, bishop, 1979. Roch Pedneault, auxiliary.

Churchill-Hudson Bay, Man. (p.a., 1925; v.a. Hudson Bay, 1931; diocese Churchill, 1967; Churchill-Hudson Bay, 1968): Omer Robidoux, O.M.I., bishop, 1970.

Edmonton, Alta. (Ukrainian Byzantine Rite) (ap. ex., 1948; diocese, 1956): Martin Greschuk, bishop, 1986.

Edmundston, N.B. (1944): Gerard Dionne, bishop, 1983.

Gaspe, Que. (1922): Bertrand Blanchet, bishop, 1973.

Gatineau-Hull, Que. (1963 as Hull; name changed, 1982); Adolphe E. Proulx, bishop, 1974.

Grand Falls, Nfld. (Harbour Grace, 1856; present title, 1964): Joseph Faber MacDonald, bishop, 1980.

Gravelbourg, Sask. (1930): Noel Delaquis, bishop, 1974.

Hamilton, Ont. (1856): Anthony Tonnos, bishop, 1984. Matthew Ustrzycki, auxiliary.

Hauterive, Que. (p.a., 1882; v.a., 1905; diocese Gulf of St. Lawrence, 1945; name changed, 1960): Roger Ebacher, bishop, 1979.

Hearst, Ont. (p.a., 1918; v.a., 1920; diocese, 1938): Roger Despatie, bishop, 1973.

Joliette, Que. (1904): Rene Audet, bishop, 1968.

Kamloops, B.C. (1945): Lawrence Sabatini, C.S., bishop, 1982.

Labrador (Nfld.)-Schefferville, Que. (v.a. Labrador, 1945; diocese, 1967): Vacant as of Aug. 1, 1986.

London, Ont. (1855; transferred Sandwich, 1859; London, 1869): John Sherlock, bishop, 1978. Frederick Henry, auxiliary.

Mackenzie-Fort Smith, N.W.T. (v.a. Mackenzie, 1901; diocese Mackenzie-Fort Smith, 1967): Denis Croteau, bishop, 1986.

Mont-Laurier, Que. (1913): Jean Gratton, bishop, 1978.

Moosonee, Ont. (v.a. James Bay, 1938; diocese Moosonee, 1967): Jules LeGuerrier, O.M.I., bishop, 1967.

Nelson, B.C. (1936): Wilfred Emmett Doyle, bishop, 1958.

New Westminster, B.C. (Ukrainian Byzantine Rite) (1974): Jerome Chimy, O.S.B.M., bishop, 1974.

Nicolet, Que. (1885): Albertus Martin, bishop, 1950.

Pembroke, Ont. (v.a. 1882; diocese, 1898): Joseph R. Windle, bishop, 1971.

Peterborough, Ont. (1882): James L. Doyle, bishop, 1976.

Prince Albert, Sask. (v.a., 1890; diocese, 1907): Blaise Morand, bishop, 1983.

Prince George, B.C. (p.a., 1908; v.a. Yukon and Prince Rupert, 1944; diocese Prince George, 1967): Hubert P. O'Connor, bishop, 1986.

Rouyn-Noranda, Que. (1973): Jean-Guy Hamelin, bishop, 1974.

St. Catharines, Ont. (1958): Thomas B. Fulton, bishop, 1978.

St. George's, Nfld. (p.a., 1870; v.a., 1890; diocese, 1904): Raymond J. Lahey, bishop, 1986.

St. Hyacinthe, Que. (1852): Louis-de-Gonzague Langevin, bishop, 1979.

Saint-Jean-Longueuil, Que. (1933 as St.-Jean-de-Quebec; named changed, 1982): Bernard Hubert, bishop, 1978.

St. Jerome, Que. (1951): Charles Valois, bishop, 1977. Raymond Saint-Gelais, auxiliary.

Saint John, N.B. (1842): J. Edward Troy, bishop, 1986.

St. Maron of Montreal (Maronites) (1982): Elias Shaheen, archeparch-eparch, 1982.

St. Paul in Alberta (1948): Raymond Roy, bishop, 1972.

St. Sauveur de Montreal (Greek Melkites) (ap. ex. 1980; eparchy, 1984): Archbishop Michel Hakim, B.S., eparch, 1980.

Sts. Cyril and Methodius, Toronto, Ont. (Slovakian Byzantine Rite) (1980): Michael Rusnak, C.Ss.R., bishop, 1981.

Sainte-Anne-de-la-Pocatiere, Que. (1951): Rev. Andre Gaumond, bishop, 1985.

Saskatoon, Sask. (1933): James P. Mahoney, bishop, 1967.

Saskatoon, Sask. (Ukrainian Byzantine Rite) (ap. ex., 1951; diocese, 1956): Basil (Wasyl) Filevich, bishop, 1984.

Sault Ste. Marie, Ont. (1904): Marcel Gervais, bishop, 1985. Bernard F. Pappin, auxiliary.

Thunder Bay, Ont. (Ft. William, 1952; transferred, 1970): John A. O'Mara, bishop, 1976.

Timmins, Ont. (v.a. Temiskaming, 1908; diocese Haileybury, 1915; present title, 1938): Jacques Landriault, bishop, 1971.

Toronto, Ont. (Ukrainian Byzantine Rite) (ap. ex., 1948; diocese, 1956): Isidore Borecky, bishop, 1948.

Trois-Rivieres, Que. (1852): Laurent Noel, bishop, 1975.

Valleyfield, Que. (1892): Robert Lebel, bishop, 1976.

Victoria, B.C. (diocese Vancouver Is., 1846; archdiocese, 1903; diocese Victoria, 1908): Remi J. De Roo, bishop, 1962.

Whitehorse, Y.T. (v.a., 1944; diocese 1967): Vacant as of Aug. 1, 1986.

Yarmouth, N.S. (1953): Austin-Emile Burke, bishop, 1968.

Military Vicariate of Canada (1951): Archbishop Francis J. Spence, military vicar.

Abbacy of St. Peter, Muenster, Sask. (1921): Jerome Weber, O.S.B. (blessed, 1960).

An **Apostolic Exarchate for Armenian-Rite Catholics in Canada and the United States** was established in July, 1981, with headquarters in New York City. Nerses Mikail Setian, exarch.

Dioceses with Interprovincial Lines

The following dioceses, indicated by + in the table, have interprovincial lines.

Churchill-Hudson Bay includes part of Northwest Territories.

Keewatin-Le Pas includes part of Manitoba and Saskatchewan provinces.

Labrador-Schefferville includes the Labrador region of Newfoundland and the northern part of Quebec province.

MacKenzie-Fort Smith, Northwest Territories, includes part of Alberta and Saskatchewan provinces.

Moosonee, Ont., includes part of Quebec province.

Pembroke, Ont., includes one county of Quebec province.

Whitehorse, Y.T., includes part of British Columbia.

The Pastoral Team of the Canadian Bishops' Conference was established in 1974 to further pastoral planning. Its tasks include preparation of the agenda for the plenary assembly of the conference and other meetings of the bishops, along with various other study and action projects assigned by the conference. The team is composed of six bishops, the two general secretaries of the conference and a multidisciplinary staff of six persons.

STATISTICS OF THE CATHOLIC CHURCH IN CANADA

(Principal source: *1986 Directory of the Canadian Conference of Catholic Bishops*. Permanent deacon statistics are from the *1986 Annuario Pontificio*. Archdioceses are indicated by an asterisk. For dioceses marked +, see Canadian Dioceses with Interprovincial Lines.)

Canada's 10 civil provinces and two territories are divided into 17 ecclesiastical provinces consisting of 17 metropolitan sees (archdioceses) and 52 suffragan sees (51 dioceses and one territorial abbacy); there are also one archdiocese, and three eparchies immediately subject to the Holy See. (See listing of Ecclesiastical Provinces elsewhere in this section.)

This table presents a regional breakdown of Catholic statistics. In some cases, the totals are approximate because diocesan boundaries fall within several civil provinces.

Civil Province Diocese	Cath. Pop.	Dioc. Priests	Rel. Priests	Total Priests	Perm. Deacs.	Bros.	Srs.	Par- ishes
Newfoundland	205,116	121	31	152	—	69	478	220
*St. John's	120,720	58	19	77	—	45	316	93
Grand Falls	32,378	30	—	30	—	12	68	45
Labrador- Schefferville+	13,455	3	11	14	—	5	36	22
St. George's	38,563	30	1	31	—	7	58	60
Prince Edward Island Charlottetown	60,598	77	2	79	1	—	249	57
Nova Scotia	284,995	274	61	335	18	12	1,033	221
*Halifax	120,000	68	30	98	17	2	457	52
Antigonish	126,995	183	10	193	—	6	508	127
Yarmouth	38,000	23	21	44	1	4	68	42
New Brunswick	362,676	308	96	404	2	43	1,171	263
*Moncton	83,142	82	42	124	—	23	434	64
Bathurst	115,694	85	23	108	—	11	321	70
Edmundston	53,840	53	17	70	—	7	181	37
St. John	110,000	88	14	102	2	2	235	92
Quebec	5,729,199	4,047	2,436	6,483	166	2,884	23,573	1,895
*Montreal	1,506,220	737	964	1,701	43	864	7,622	281
*Quebec	979,204	771	481	1,252	51	565	5,534	274
*Rimouski	167,748	209	59	268	—	41	964	119
*Sherbrooke	253,623	291	120	411	6	59	1,375	144
Amos	109,734	88	27	115	—	23	249	78
Chicoutimi	273,474	276	67	343	6	102	884	95
Gaspe	104,209	105	16	121	—	8	237	63
Gatineau-Hull	187,000	82	58	140	2	18	368	62
Hauterive	101,335	58	28	86	5	29	227	50
Joliette	159,000	142	59	201	1	140	560	57
Mont Laurier	71,530	65	18	83	—	46	206	59
Nicolet	170,552	225	40	265	12	127	1,010	85
Rouyn-Noranda	53,625	35	19	54	—	11	146	43
Ste.-Anne-de- la-Pocatiere	91,858	181	5	186	1	15	369	54
St. Hyacinthe	318,426	228	110	338	21	280	1,461	115
St. Jean-Longueuil	490,000	154	102	256	—	111	633	89
St. Jerome	267,405	108	123	231	5	132	316	66
Trois Rivieres	251,500	189	91	280	10	228	1,080	96
Valleyfield	172,756	103	49	152	3	85	332	65
Ontario	2,751,158	1,316	1,204	2,520	179	370	5,231	1,134
*Kingston	70,770	73	8	81	—	—	253	69
*Ottawa	302,629	157	226	383	10	109	1,479	115
*Toronto	1,100,000	238	526	764	90	155	964	197
Alexandria-Cornwall	45,624	46	10	56	5	11	116	34
Hamilton	304,562	148	153	301	1	36	561	120
Hearst	33,074	26	3	29	—	—	57	37
London	350,876	251	106	357	4	18	673	174
Moosonee+	2,900	2	12	14	1	6	9	8

Civil Province Diocese	Cath. Pop.	Dioc. Priests	Rel. Priests	Total Priests	Perm. Deacs.	Bros.	Srs.	Par- ishes
Ontario								
Pembroke+	60,025	58	13	71	2	1	280	72
Peterborough	63,078	79	5	84	1	2	171	77
St. Catharines	105,000	63	34	97	—	3	80	49
Sault Ste. Marie	175,000	121	65	186	59	14	425	100
Thunder Bay	80,000	27	35	62	—	3	79	49
Timmins	57,620	27	8	35	6	12	84	33
Manitoba	**208,150**	**143**	**189**	**332**	**28**	**62**	**924**	**335**
*Keewatin-LePas+	22,500	1	32	33	1	8	48	55
*St. Boniface	82,000	99	73	172	9	37	541	112
*Winnipeg	97,500	43	68	111	18	14	325	152
Churchill-Hudson Bay+	6,150	—	16	16	—	3	10	16
Saskatchewan	**211,560**	**191**	**137**	**328**	**3**	**24**	**732**	**403**
*Regina	91,500	82	35	117	—	3	235	196
Gravelbourg	13,293	26	4	30	—	—	87	43
Prince Albert	47,767	42	23	65	—	4	141	83
Saskatoon	47,000	41	50	91	3	1	171	58
St. Peter-Muenster (Abb.)	12,000	—	25	25	—	16	98	23
Alberta	**394,125**	**228**	**236**	**464**	**2**	**29**	**746**	**461**
*Edmonton	186,000	100	119	219	—	18	426	186
*Grouard-McLennan	35,000	5	40	45	—	3	60	77
Calgary	130,000	97	70	167	1	8	185	126
St. Paul	43,125	26	7	33	1	—	75	72
British Columbia	**327,268**	**169**	**173**	**342**	**1**	**45**	**584**	**344**
*Vancouver	175,000	92	107	199	—	25	312	90
Kamloops	38,000	13	14	27	1	6	39	79
Nelson..................	40,045	28	12	40	—	1	51	58
Prince George	30,223	4	23	27	—	8	47	59
Victoria	44,000	32	17	49	—	5	135	58
Yukon Territory								
Whitehorse+	6,823	1	18	19	—	1	9	24
Northwest Territories								
MacKenzie-Ft. Smith+	18,000	1	32	33	—	28	26	35
Eastern Rite (Ukrainians) ...	**205,365**	**176**	**66**	**242**	**34**	**11**	**129**	**496**
*Winnipeg	49,000	41	15	56	11	1	30	166
Edmonton	41,065	29	14	43	6	6	28	92
New Westminster	7,000	14	4	18	2	—	5	23
Saskatoon	25,100	19	17	36	—	2	41	128
Toronto	83,200	73	16	89	15	2	25	87
Other Eastern Rites								
St. Maron of Montreal (Maronites)	100,000	3	9	12	—	—	—	12
St. Sauveur-Montreal (Greek Melkites)	33,000	2	7	9	—	—	—	9
Sts. Cyril and Methodius- Toronto (Slovaks)	15,000	7	2	9	—	—	—	12
Armenian Exarchate	7,000	2	—	2	—	—	4	—
Military Vicariate	**79,931**	**52**	**18**	**70**	**—**	**—**	**6**	**60**
TOTALS 1986	**10,999,964**	**7,118**	**4,717**	**11,835**	**434**	**3,578**	**34,895**	**5,981**
Totals 1985	**10,881,950**	**7,214**	**4,737**	**11,951**	**392**	**3,564**	**35,999**	**5,976**

The bishops of Canada, in addition to meeting together at the national level, meet also in four regional conferences: The Atlantic Episcopal Assembly, The Assemblee des eveques du Quebec, The Ontario Conference of Catholic Bishops and the Western Catholic Conference. These conferences enable the bishops to deal directly with pastoral concerns in their respective regions.

CANADIAN CONFERENCE OF CATHOLIC BISHOPS

The Canadian Conference of Catholic Bishops was established Oct. 12, 1943, as a permanent voluntary association of the bishops of Canada, was given official approval by the Holy See in 1948, and acquired the status of an episcopal conference after the Second Vatican Council.

The CCCB acts in two ways: (1) as a strictly ecclesiastical body through which the bishops act together with pastoral authority and responsibility for the Church throughout the country; (2) as an operational secretariat through which the bishops act on a wider scale for the good of the Church and society.

At the top of the CCCB organizational table are the president, an executive committee, an administrative board and a plenary assembly. The membership consists of all the bishops of Canada.

Departments and Offices

The CCCB's work is planned and co-ordinated by a Pastoral Team of 14 members — six bishops and six staff members (lay and clergy) and the two general secretaries.

The CCCB's nine episcopal commissions undertake study and projects in special areas of pastoral work. Six serve nationally (social affairs, canon law/inter-rite, ministries, missions, ecumenism, theology); three relate to French and English sectors (social communications, Christian education, liturgy).

The general secretariat consists of a French and an English general secretary and their assistants and directors of public relations.

Administrative services for purchasing, archives and library, accounting, personnel, publications, printing and distribution are supervised by directors who relate to the general secretaries.

Various advisory councils and committees with mixed memberships of lay persons, religious, priests and bishops also serve the CCCB on a variety of topics.

Operations

Meetings for the transaction of business are held at least once a year by the plenary assembly, six times a year by the executive committee, and four times a year by the administrative board.

Bishop Bernard Hubert of Saint-Jean-Longueuil, Que., is president of the CCCB; Archbishop James M. Hayes of Halifax, N.S., is vice-president.

Secretariat is located at 90 Parent Ave., Ottawa, K1N 7B1, Canada.

ORGANIZATIONS

The Catholic Church Extension Society of Canada supports home missions. Address: 67 Bond St., Toronto, Ontario M5B 1X5.

The Catholic Women's League of Canada, with a membership of more than 125,000. Address: 3081 Ness Ave., Winnipeg, Man. R2Y 2G3.

PERCENTAGE OF CATHOLICS

Catholic population statistics are from the *1986 Directory of the Canadian Conference of Catholic Bishops;* total population figures are 1985 estimates.

The table presents a regional breakdown of Catholic percentage in total population. In some cases, the Catholic totals are approximate because diocesan boundaries fall within several civil provinces. See Index: Canadian Dioceses with Interprovincial Lines.

Civil Province Territory	Cath. Pop.	Total Pop.	Cath. Pct.
Alberta	394,125	2,337,500	16.9
British Columbia	327,268	2,883,000	11.3
Manitoba	208,150	1,065,000	19.5
New Brunswick	362,676	717,200	50.6
Newfoundland	205,116	578,900	35.4
Nova Scotia	284,995	878,300	32.4
Ontario	2,751,158	9,023,900	30.4
Prince Edward Is.	60,598	126,800	47.8
Quebec	5,729,199	6,562,200	87.3
Saskatchewan	211,560	1,016,400	20.8
Yukon	6,823	22,800	29.9
Northwest Territories	18,000	50,500	35.6
Eastern Rites	360,365	—	—
Military Vicariate	79,931	—	—
TOTALS 1986	**10,999,964**	**25,262,500**	**43.54**
Totals 1985	10,881,950	25,015,800	43.50

BIOGRAPHIES OF CANADIAN BISHOPS

(Sources: Almanac survey; *1986 Directory of Canadian Conference of Catholic Bishops; Annuario Pontificio.* Data as of July 15, 1986.)

Ambrozic, Aloysius M.: b. Jan. 27, 1930; ord. priest June 4, 1955; ord. titular bishop of Valabria and auxiliary bishop of Toronto, May 27, 1976; coadjutor archbishop of Toronto, May 28, 1986.

Audet, Lionel: b. May 22, 1908, Ste. Marie de Beauce, Que.; ord. priest July 8, 1934; ord. titular bishop of Tibari and auxiliary bishop of Quebec, May 1, 1952; retired Mar. 26, 1983.

Audet, Rene: b. Jan. 18, 1920, Montreal, Que.; ord. priest May 30, 1948; ord. titular bishop of Chonochora and auxiliary bishop of Ottawa, July 31, 1963; bishop of Joliette, Jan. 3, 1968.

Baudoux, Maurice: b. July 10, 1902, Louviere, Belgium; ord. priest July 17, 1929; ord. bishop of St. Paul in Alberta, Oct. 28, 1948; titular archbishop of Preslavus and coadjutor archbishop of St. Boniface, Mar. 4, 1952; archbishop of St. Boniface, Sept. 14, 1955; retired Sept. 7, 1974.

Beahen, John: b. Feb. 14, 1922, Ottawa, Ont.; ord. priest June 15, 1946; ord. titular bishop of Ploaghe and auxiliary bishop of Ottawa, June 21, 1977.

Belisle, Gilles: b. Oct. 7, 1923, Clarence Creek, Ont.; ord. priest Feb. 2, 1950; ord. titular bishop of Uccula and auxiliary bishop of Ottawa, June 21, 1977.

Blais, Leo: b. Apr. 28, 1904, Dollar Bay, Mich.;

ord. priest June 14, 1930; ord. bishop of Prince Albert, Aug. 28, 1952; titular bishop of Geron and auxiliary bishop of Montreal, 1959; retired 1964.

Blanchet, Bertrand: b. Sept. 19, 1932, Saint Thomas de Montmagny, Que.; ord. priest May 20, 1956; ord. bishop of Gaspe, Dec. 8, 1973.

Borecky, Isidore: b. Oct. 1, 1911, Ostrovec, Ukraine; ord. priest July 17, 1938; ord. titular bishop of Amathus in Cypro and exarch of Toronto, May 27, 1948; bishop of Toronto (Ukrainians), Nov. 3, 1956.

Burke, Austin-Emile: b. Jan. 11, 1922, Sluice Point, N.S.; ord. priest Mar. 25, 1950; ord. bishop of Yarmouth, May 14, 1968.

Carew, William A.: b. Oct. 23, 1922, St. John's, Nfld., ord. priest June 15, 1947; ord. titular archbishop of Telde, Jan. 4, 1970; nuncio to Rwanda and Burundi, 1970-74; apostolic delegate to Jerusalem and Palestine and pro-nuncio to Cyprus, 1974-83; pro-nuncio to Japan, Aug. 30, 1983.

Carney, James F.: b. June 28, 1915, Vancouver, B.C.; ord. priest Mar. 21, 1942; ord. titular bishop of Obori and auxiliary bishop of Vancouver, Feb. 11, 1966; archbishop of Vancouver, Jan. 8, 1969.

Carter, Alexander: b. Apr. 16, 1909, Montreal, Que.; ord. priest June 6, 1936; ord. titular bishop of Sita and coadjutor bishop of Sault Ste. Marie, Feb. 2, 1957; bishop of Sault Ste. Marie, Nov. 22, 1958; retired May 8, 1985.

Carter, G. Emmett: (See Cardinals, Biographies.)

Charbonneau, Paul E.: b. May 4, 1922, Ste. Therese de Blainville, Que.; ord. priest May 31, 1947; ord. titular bishop of Thapsus and auxiliary bishop of Ottawa, Jan. 18, 1961; first bishop of Hull, May 21, 1963; retired Apr. 12, 1973, because of ill health.

Chiasson, Donat: b. Jan. 2, 1930, Paquetville, N.B.; ord. priest May 6, 1956; ord. archbishop of Moncton, June 1, 1972.

Chimy, Jerome I., O.S.B.M.: b. Mar. 12, 1919, Radway, Alta.; ord. priest, June 29, 1944; ord. first bishop of New Westminster, B.C., for the Ukrainians, Sept. 5, 1974.

Cimichella, Andre, O.S.M.: b. Feb. 21, 1921, Grotte Santo Stefano, Italy; ord. priest May 26, 1945; ord. titular bishop of Quiza and auxiliary of Montreal, July 16, 1964.

Clune, Robert B.: b. Sept. 18, 1920, Toronto, Ont.; ord. priest May 26, 1945; ord. titular bishop of Lacubaza and auxiliary bishop of Toronto, June 21, 1979.

Coderre, Gerard Marie: b. Dec. 19, 1904, St. Jacques de Montcalm, Que.; ord. priest May 30, 1931; ord. titular bishop of Aegae and coadjutor bishop of St.-Jean-de-Quebec, Sept. 12, 1951; bishop of St.-Jean-de-Quebec, (now Saint-Jean-Longueuil); Feb. 3, 1955; retired May 3, 1978.

Couture, Jean-Guy: b. May 6, 1929, St.-Jean-Baptiste de Quebec, Que.; ord. priest May 30, 1953; ord. bishop of Hauterive, Que., Aug. 15, 1975; bishop of Chicoutimi, Apr. 5, 1979.

Couture, Maurice, R.S.V.: b. Nov. 3, 1926, Saint-Pierre-de-Broughton, Que.; ord. priest June 17, 1951; ord. titular bishop of Talaptula and auxiliary bishop of Quebec, Oct. 22, 1982.

Couturier, Gerard: b. Jan. 12, 1913, St. Louis du Ha Ha, Que; ord. priest Mar. 25, 1938; ord. bishop of Hauterive, Feb. 28, 1957; resigned see Sept. 7, 1974.

Croteau, Denis, O.M.I: b. Oct. 23, 1932, Thetford Mines, Que., ord. priest Aug. 31, 1958; ord. bishop of MacKenzie-Fort Smith, 1986.

Crowley, Leonard: b. Dec. 28, 1921, Montreal, Que.; ord. priest May 31, 1947; ord. titular bishop of Mons and auxiliary bishop of Montreal, Mar. 24, 1971.

Daciuk, Myron, O.S.B.M.: b. Nov. 16, 1919, Mundare, Alta; ord. priest June 10, 1945; ord. titular bishop of Thyatira and auxiliary bishop of Winnipeg (Ukrainians), Oct. 14, 1982.

Decosse, Aime: b. June 21, 1903, Somerset, Man.; ord. priest July 4, 1926; ord. bishop of Gravelbourg, Jan. 20, 1954; retired May 12, 1973.

Delaquis, Noel: b. Dec. 25, 1934, Notre-Dame-de-Lourdes, Man.; ord. priest June 5, 1958; ord. bishop of Gravelbourg, Feb. 19, 1974.

De Roo, Remi J.: b. Feb. 24, 1924, Swan Lake, Man.; ord. priest June 8, 1950; ord. bishop of Victoria, Dec. 14, 1962.

Despatie, Roger: b. Apr. 12, 1927, Sudbury, Ont.; ord. priest Apr. 12, 1952; ord. titular bishop of Usinaza and auxiliary bishop of Sault Ste. Marie, June 28, 1968; bishop of Hearst, Feb. 8, 1973.

Dionne, Gerard: b. June 19, 1919, Saint-Basile, N.B.; ord. priest May 1, 1948; ord. titular bishop of Garba and auxiliary bishop of Sault Ste. Marie, Apr. 8, 1975; bishop of Edmundston, Nov. 17, 1983.

Douville, Arthur: b. July 22, 1894, St. Casimir de Portneuf, Que.; ord. priest May 25, 1919; ord. titular bishop of Vita and auxiliary bishop of St. Hyacinthe, Jan. 29, 1940; coadjutor bishop of St. Hyacinthe, Mar. 21, 1942; bishop of St. Hyacinthe, Nov. 27, 1942; retired June 13, 1967.

Doyle, James L.: b. June 20, 1929, Chatham, Ont.; ord. priest June 12, 1954; ord. bishop of Peterborough June 28, 1976.

Doyle, W. Emmett: b. Feb. 18, 1913, Calgary, Alta.: ord. priest June 5, 1938; ord. bishop of Nelson, Dec. 3, 1958.

Drainville, Gerard: b. May 20, 1930, L'Isle-du-Pas, Que.; ord. priest May 30, 1953; ord. bishop of Amos, June 12, 1978.

Dumouchel, Paul, O.M.I.: b. Sept. 19, 1911, St. Boniface, Man.; ord. priest June 24, 1936; ord. titular bishop of Sufes and vicar apostolic of Keewatin, May 24, 1955; archbishop of Keewatin-Le Pas, July 13, 1967.

Ebacher, Roger: b. Oct. 6, 1936, Amos, Que.; ord. priest May 27, 1961; ord. bishop of Hauterive, July 31, 1979.

Exner, Adam, O.M.I.: b. Dec. 24, 1928, Killaly, Sask.; ord. priest July 7, 1957; ord. bishop of Kamloops, B.C., Mar. 12, 1974; archbishop of Winnipeg, April, 1982.

Filevich, Basil (Wasyl): b. Jan. 13, 1918; ord. priest Apr. 17, 1942; ord. bishop of Ukrainian eparchy of Saskatoon Feb. 27, 1984.

Flahiff, George F.: (See Cardinals Biographies.)

Fortier, Jean-Marie: b. July 1, 1920, Quebec, Que.; ord. priest June 16, 1944; ord. titular bishop of Pomaria and auxiliary bishop of Ste. Anne-de-la-Pocatiere, Jan. 23, 1961; bishop of Gaspe, Jan. 19, 1965; archbishop of Sherbrooke, Apr. 20, 1968.

Fulton, Thomas B.: b. Jan. 13, 1918, St. Catharines, Ont.; ord. priest June 7, 1941; ord. titular bishop of Cursola and auxiliary bishop of Toronto, Jan. 6, 1969; bishop of St. Catharines, July 7, 1978.

Gagnon, Edouard, P.S.S.: (See Cardinals, Biographies.)

Gaumond, Andre: b. June 3, 1936, St. Thomas de Montmagny, Que.; ord. priest May 27, 1961; ord. bishop of Ste. Anne-de-la-Pocatiere, Aug. 15, 1985.

Gervais, Marcel A.: b. Sept. 21, 1931, Elie, Man.; ord. priest May 31, 1958; ord. titular bishop of Rosmarkaeum and auxiliary bishop of London, Ont., June 11, 1980; bishop of Sault Ste. Marie, May 8, 1985.

Gilbert, Arthur J.: b. Oct. 26, 1915, Oromocto, N.B.; ord. priest June 3, 1943; ord. bishop of St. John, N.B., June 19, 1974; retired Apr. 2, 1986.

Gratton, Jean: b. Dec. 4, 1924, Wendover, Ont.; ord. priest Apr. 27, 1952; ord. bishop of Mont Laurier, June 29, 1978.

Gregoire, Paul: b. Oct. 24, 1911, Verdun, Que.; ord. priest May 22, 1937; ord. titular bishop of Curubis and auxiliary bishop of Montreal, Dec. 27, 1961; archbishop of Montreal, Apr. 20, 1968.

Greschuk, Martin: b. Nov. 7, 1923, Innisfree, Alta.; ord. priest June 11, 1950; ord. titular bishop of Nazianus and auxiliary bishop of Edmonton of the Ukrainians, Oct. 3, 1974; apostolic administrator "sede plena" of Edmonton, Apr. 14, 1984; bishop of Edmonton, May 7, 1986.

Hacault, Antoine: b. Jan. 17, 1926, Bruxelles, Man.; ord. priest May 20, 1951; ord. titular bishop of Media and coadjutor of St. Boniface, Sept. 8, 1964; archbishop of St. Boniface, Sept. 7, 1974.

Hains, Gaston: b. Sept. 10, 1921, Drummondville, Que.; ord. priest June 15, 1946; ord. titular bishop of Belesana and auxiliary bishop of St. Hyacinthe, Oct. 10, 1964; coadjutor bishop of Amos, 1967; bishop of Amos, Oct. 31, 1968; retired 1978.

Hakim, Michel: b. Apr. 21, 1921, Magdouche, South Lebanon; ord. priest Nov. 10, 1947; ord. archbishop of Saida of Greek Melkites, Sept. 10, 1977; app. titular archbishop of Caesarea in Cappadocia and apostolic exarch of Greek Melkite Catholics in Canada, Oct. 13, 1980; first eparch (with personal title of archbishop), Sept. 1, 1984, when exarchate was raised to eparchy with title St. Sauveur de Montreal.

Halpin, Charles A.: b. Aug. 30, 1930, St. Eustache, Man.; ord. priest May 27, 1956; ord. archbishop of Regina, Nov. 26, 1973.

Hamelin, Jean-Guy: b. Oct. 8, 1925, St. Severin-de-Proulxville, Que.; ord. priest June 11, 1949; ord. first bishop of Rouyn-Noranda, Que., Feb. 9, 1974.

Hayes, James M.: b. May 27, 1924, Halifax, N.S.; ord. priest June 15, 1947; ord. titular bishop of Reperi and apostolic administrator of Halifax, Apr. 20, 1965; archbishop of Halifax, June 22, 1967.

Henry, Frederick: Appointed titular bishop of Carinola and auxiliary bishop of London, Ont., Apr. 23, 1986.

Hermaniuk, Maxim, C.Ss.R.: b. Oct. 30, 1911, Nove Selo, Ukraine; ord. priest Sept. 4, 1938; ord. titular bishop of Sinna and exarch of Manitoba (Ukrainians), June 29, 1951; archbishop of Winnipeg (Ukrainians), Nov. 3, 1956.

Hubert, Bernard: b. June 1, 1929, Beloeil, Que.; ord. priest May 30, 1953; ord. bishop of St. Jerome, Sept. 12, 1971; coadjutor bishop of Saint-Jean-de-Quebec, 1977; succeeded as bishop of Saint-Jean-de-Quebec, May 3, 1978; title of see changed to Saint-Jean-Longueuil, 1982. President of Canadian Conference of Catholic Bishops, 1985-.

Jette, Edouard: b. Aug. 9, 1898, St. Jacques, Que.; ord. priest May 31, 1923; ord. titular bishop of Tabe and auxiliary of Joliette, Apr. 14, 1948; retired 1968.

Labrie, Jean-Paul: b. Nov. 4, 1922, Laurieville, Que.; ord. priest May 20, 1951; ord. titular bishop of Urci and auxiliary bishop of Quebec, May 14, 1977.

Lacey, Michael Pearse: b. Nov. 27, 1916, Toronto, Ont.; ord. priest May 23, 1943; ord. titular bishop of Diana and auxiliary bishop of Toronto, June 21, 1979.

Lacroix, Fernand, C.J.M.: b. Oct. 16, 1919, Quebec; ord. priest Feb. 10, 1946; ord. bishop of Edmundston, Oct. 20, 1970; retired May 31, 1983.

Lahey, Raymond: Appointed bishop of St. George's, Nfld., July 14, 1986.

Landriault, Jacques: b. Sept. 23, 1921, Alfred, Ont.; ord. priest Feb. 9, 1947; ord. titular bishop of Cadi and auxiliary bishop of Alexandria, July 25, 1962; bishop of Hearst, May 27, 1964; app. bishop of Timmins, Mar. 24, 1971.

Langevin, Louis-de-Gonzague, P.B.: b. Oct. 31, 1921, Oka, Que.; ord. priest Feb. 2, 1950; ord. titular bishop of Rosemarkie and auxiliary of St. Hyacinthe Sept. 23, 1974; bishop of St. Hyacinthe, July 18, 1979.

LaRocque, Eugene Philippe: b. Mar. 27, 1927, Windsor, Ont.; ord. priest June 7, 1952; ord. bishop of Alexandria, Ont., Sept. 3, 1974; title of see changed to Alexandria-Cornwall, 1976.

Lebel, Robert: b. Nov. 8, 1924, Trois-Pistoles, Que.; ord. priest June 18, 1950; ord. titular bishop of Alinda and auxiliary of St. Jean de Quebec, May 12, 1974; bishop of Valleyfield, Mar. 26, 1976.

Le Blanc, Camille A.: b. Aug. 25, 1898, Barachois, N.B.; ord. priest Apr. 5, 1924; ord. bishop of Bathurst, Sept. 8, 1942; retired Jan. 8, 1969.

Leclerc, Marc: b. Jan. 9, 1933, Saint-Gregoire de Montmorency, Que; ord. priest, May 31, 1958; ord. titular bishop of Eguga and auxiliary bishop of Quebec, Oct. 22, 1982.

Legare, Henri, O.M.I.: b. Feb. 20, 1918, Willow Bunch, Sask.; ord. priest June 29, 1943; ord. first bishop of Labrador-Schefferville, Sept. 9, 1967; archbishop of Grouard-McLennan, Nov. 21, 1972.

President of Canadian Conference of Catholic Bishops, 1981-83.

Leger, Paul-Emile: (See Cardinals, Biographies).

Leguerrier, Jules, O.M.I.: b. Feb. 18, 1915, Clarence Creek, Ont.; ord. priest June 19, 1943; ord. titular bishop of Bavagaliana and vicar apostolic of James Bay, June 29, 1964; first bishop of Moosonee, July 13, 1967.

Lemieux, Marie Joseph, O.P.: b. May 10, 1902, Quebec, Que.; ord. priest Apr. 15, 1928; ord. bishop of Sendai, Japan, June 29, 1936; titular bishop of Calydon, 1941; apostolic administrator of Gravelbourg, 1942; bishop of Gravelbourg, Apr. 15, 1944; archbishop of Ottawa, 1953-66; titular archbishop of Salde, Nov. 16, 1966, apostolic nuncio. Retired. Archbishop emeritus of Ottawa.

Levesque, Louis: b. May 27, 1908, Amqui, Que.; ord. priest June 26, 1932; ord. bishop of Hearst, Aug. 15, 1952; titular archbishop of Egnatia and coadjutor of Rimouski, Apr. 13, 1964; archbishop of Rimouski, Feb. 25, 1967; retired May 14, 1973.

Lussier, Philippe, C.Ss.R.: b. Oct. 3, 1911, Weedon, Que.; ord. priest Sept. 18, 1937; ord. bishop of St. Paul in Alberta, Aug. 17, 1952; retired Aug. 17, 1968.

McCarthy, Thomas J.: b. Oct. 4, 1905, Goderich, Ont.; ord. priest May 25, 1929; ord. bishop of Nelson, Aug. 1, 1955; bishop of St. Catharines, Nov. 9, 1958; retired July 7, 1978.

MacDonald, James H., C.S.C.: b. Apr. 28, 1925, Wycogama, N.S.; ord. priest June 28, 1953; ord. titular bishop of Gibba and auxiliary bishop of Hamilton April 17, 1978; app. bishop of Charlottetown, Aug. 12, 1982.

MacDonald, Joseph Faber: b. Jan. 20, 1932, Little Pond, P.E.I.; ord. priest Mar. 9, 1963; ord. bishop of Grand Falls, Mar. 19, 1980.

McGrath, Richard T.: b. June 17, 1912, Oderin, Placentia Bay, Nfld.; ord. priest June 24, 1936; ord. bishop of St. George's, Nfld., July 22, 1970; retired June 5, 1985.

MacNeil, Joseph N.: b. Apr. 15, 1924, Sydney, N.S.; ord. priest May 23, 1948; ord. bishop of St. John, N.B., June 24, 1969; archbishop of Edmonton, July 6, 1973. President Canadian Conference of Catholic Bishops, 1979-81.

Mahoney, James P.: b. Dec. 7, 1927, Saskatoon, Sask.; ord. priest June 7, 1952; ord. bishop of Saskatoon, Dec. 13, 1967.

Martin, Albertus: b. Oct. 4, 1913, Southbridge, Mass.; ord. priest May 18, 1939; ord. titular bishop of Bassiana and coadjutor bishop of Nicolet, Oct. 7, 1950; bishop of Nicolet, Nov. 8, 1950.

Morand, Blaise E.: b. Sept. 12, 1932, Tecumseh, Ont.; ord. priest Mar. 22, 1958; ord. coadjutor bishop of Prince Albert, June 29, 1981; bishop of Prince Albert, Apr. 9, 1983.

Morin, Laurent: b. Feb. 14, 1908, Montreal, Que.; ord. priest May 27, 1934; ord. titular bishop of Arsamosata and auxiliary bishop of Montreal, Oct. 30, 1955; bishop of Prince Albert, Feb. 28, 1959; retired Apr. 9, 1983.

Noel, Laurent: b. Mar. 19, 1920, Saint-Just-de-Bretenieres, Que.; ord. priest June 16, 1944; ord.

titular bishop of Agathopolis and auxiliary bishop of Quebec, Aug. 29, 1963; bishop of Trois Rivieres, Nov. 5, 1975.

O'Byrne, Paul J.: b. Dec. 21, 1922, Calgary, Alta.; ord. priest Feb. 21, 1948; ord. bishop of Calgary, Aug. 22, 1968.

O'Connor, Hubert P., O.M.I.: b. Feb. 17, 1928, Huntingdon, Que.; ord. priest June 5, 1955; ord. bishop of Whitehorse, Dec. 8, 1971; bishop of Prince George, June, 1986.

O'Grady, John Fergus, O.M.I.: b. July 27, 1908, Macton, Ont.; ord. priest June 29, 1934; ord. titular bishop of Aspendus and vicar apostolic of Prince Rupert, Mar. 7, 1956; first bishop of Prince George, July 13, 1967; retired June, 1986.

O'Mara, John A.: b. Nov. 17, 1924, Buffalo, N.Y.; ord. priest June 1, 1951; ord. bishop of Thunder Bay, June 29, 1976.

Ouellet, Gilles, P.M.E.: b. Aug. 14, 1922, Bromptonville, Que.; ord. priest June 30, 1946; ord. bishop of Gaspe, June 23, 1968; app. archbishop of Rimouski, Apr. 27, 1973. President Canadian Conference of Catholic Bishops, 1977-79.

Ouellette, Andre: b. Feb. 4, 1913, Salem, Mass.; ord. priest June 11, 1938; ord. titular bishop of Carre and auxiliary bishop of Mont-Laurier, Feb. 25, 1957; bishop of Mont-Laurier, Mar. 27, 1965; retired Feb. 15. 1978.

Pappin, Bernard F.: b. July 10, 1928, Westmeath, Ont.; ord. priest May 27, 1954; ord. titular bishop of Aradi and auxiliary bishop of Sault Ste. Marie, Apr. 11, 1975.

Pare, Marius: b. May 22, 1903, Montmagny, Que.; ord. priest July 3, 1927; ord. titular bishop of Aegae and auxiliary bishop of Chicoutimi, May 1, 1956; bishop of Chicoutimi, Feb. 18, 1961; retired Apr. 5, 1979.

Pedneault, Roch: b. Apr. 10, 1927, Saint Joseph d'Alma, Que.; ord. priest Feb. 8, 1953; ord. titular bishop of Aggersel and auxiliary of Chicoutimi, Que., June 29, 1974.

Pelletier, Georges Leon: b. Aug. 19, 1904, Saint-Epiphane, Que.; ord. priest June 24, 1931; ord. titular bishop of Hephaestus and auxiliary bishop of Quebec, Feb. 24, 1943; bishop of Trois Rivieres, July 26, 1947; retired Oct. 31, 1975.

Penney, Alphonsus L.: b. Sept. 17, 1924, St. John's, Nfld.; ord. priest June 29, 1949; ord. bishop of Grand Falls, Jan. 18, 1973; archbishop of St. John's, Nfld., Apr. 5, 1979.

Piche, Paul, O.M.I.: b. Sept. 14, 1909, Gravelbourg, Sask.; ord. priest Dec. 23, 1934; ord. titular bishop of Orcistus and vicar apostolic of Mackenzie, June 11, 1959; first bishop of Mackenzie-Fort Smith, July 13, 1967; retired Feb. 6, 1986.

Plourde, Joseph Aurele: b. Jan. 12, 1915, St. Francois de Madawaska, N.B.; ord. priest May 7, 1944; ord. titular bishop of Lapda and auxiliary bishop of Alexandria, Aug. 26, 1964; archbishop of Ottawa, Jan. 2, 1967.

Power, William E.: b. Sept. 27, 1915; Montreal, Que.; ord. priest June 7, 1941; ord. bishop of Antigonish, July 20, 1960; president Canadian Conference of Catholic Bishops, 1971-73.

Proulx, Adolphe J.: b. Dec. 12, 1927, Hanmer, Ont., Canada; ord. priest Apr. 17, 1954; ord. titular bishop of Missua and auxiliary bishop of Sault Ste. Marie, Feb. 24, 1965; bishop of Alexandria, Apr. 28, 1967; bishop of Hull, Feb. 13, 1974; title of see changed to Gatineau-Hull, 1982.

Richard, Arsène: b. May 9, 1935, St-Louis-de-Kent, N.B.; ord. priest June 11, 1960; ord. bishop of Bathurst Nov. 20, 1985.

Robidoux, Omer, O.M.I.: b. Nov. 19, 1913, Saint-Pierre-Jolys, Man.; ord. priest June 29, 1939; ord. bishop of Churchill-Hudson Bay, May 20, 1970.

Routhier, Henri, O.M.I.: b. Feb. 28, 1900, Pincher Creek, Alta.; ord. priest Sept. 7, 1924; ord. titular bishop of Naissus and coadjutor vicar apostolic of Grouard, Sept. 8, 1945; vicar apostolic of Grouard, 1953; archbishop of Grouard-McLennan, July 13, 1967; retired Nov. 21, 1972.

Roy, Raymond: b. May 3, 1919, St. Boniface, Man.; ord. priest May 31, 1947; ord. bishop of St. Paul in Alberta, July 18, 1972.

Rusnak, Michael, C.Ss.R.: b. Aug. 21, 1921, Beaverdale, Pa.; ord. priest July 3, 1949; ord. titular bishop of Tzernicus and auxiliary bishop of Toronto eparchy and apostolic visitator to Slovak Catholics of Byzantine rite in Canada, Jan. 2, 1965; first bishop of Sts Cyril and Methoduis Eparchy for Slovaks of Byzantine Rite, Feb. 28, 1981.

Ryan, Joseph F.: b. Mar. 1, 1897, Dundas, Ont.; ord. priest May 21, 1921; ord. bishop of Hamilton, Oct. 19, 1937; retired Mar. 27, 1973.

Sabatini, Lawrence, C.S.: b. May 15, 1930, Chicago, Ill.; ord. priest Mar. 19, 1957; ord. titular bishop of Nasai and auxiliary bishop of Vancouver, Sept. 21, 1978; bishop of Kamloops, Sept. 30, 1982.

Saint-Antoine, Jude: b. Oct. 29, 1930, Montreal, Que.; ord. priest May 31, 1956; ord. titular bishop of Scardona and auxiliary bishop of Montreal, May 22, 1981. Episcopal vicar of west central region.

Saint-Gelais, Raymond: b. Mar. 23, 1936, Baie St. Paul, Que.; ord. priest June 12, 1960; ord. titular bishop of Diana and auxiliary bishop of St. Jerome, July 31, 1980.

Sanschagrin, Albert, O.M.I.: b. Aug. 5, 1911, Saint-Tite, Que.; ord. priest May 24, 1936; ord. titular bishop of Bagi and coadjutor bishop of Amos Sept. 14, 1957; bishop of Saint-Hyacinthe, June 13, 1967; retired July 18, 1979.

Setian, Nerses Mikail: Apostolic Exarch of Armenian Catholics in Canada and the U.S. (see Index).

Shaheen, Elias: b. July 20, 1914, Ebrine, Patriarchate of Antioch of Maronites; ord. priest Mar. 25, 1939; ord. first eparch of St. Maron of Montreal for the Maronites, Nov. 7, 1982; personal title of archbishop, 1985.

Sherlock, John M.: b. Jan. 20, 1926, Regina, Sask.; ord. priest June 3, 1950; ord. titular bishop of Macriana and auxiliary of London, Ont., Aug. 28, 1974; bishop of London, July 7, 1978. President of the Canadian Conference of Catholic Bishops, 1983-85.

Skinner, Patrick J., C.J.M.: b. Mar. 9, 1904, St. John's, Nfld.; ord. priest May 30, 1929; ord. titular bishop of Zenobia and auxiliary bishop of St. John's, Mar. 17, 1950; archbishop of St. John's, Mar. 23, 1951; retired Apr. 5, 1979.

Smith, William J.: b. Jan. 2, 1897, Greenfield, Ont.; ord. priest June 16, 1927; ord. bishop of Pembroke, July 25, 1945; retired Feb. 8, 1971.

Spence, Francis J.: b. June 3, 1926, Perth, Ont.; ord. priest Apr. 16, 1950; ord. titular bishop of Nova and auxiliary bishop of the military vicariate, June 15, 1967; bishop of Charlottetown, Aug. 15, 1970; military vicar of Canada, March 1982; archbishop of Kingston, May, 1982.

Sutton, Peter A., O.M.I.: b. Oct. 18, 1934, Chandler, Que.; ord. priest Oct. 22, 1960; ord. bishop of Labrador-Schefferville, July 18, 1974; coadjutor archbishop of Keewatin-Le Pas, Feb. 5, 1986.

Tessier, Maxime: b. Oct. 9, 1906, St. Sebastien, Que.; ord. priest June 14, 1930; ord. titular bishop of Christopolis and auxiliary bishop of Ottawa, Aug. 2, 1951; coadjutor bishop of Timmins, 1953; bishop of Timmins, May 8, 1955; retired Mar. 24, 1971.

Tonnos, Anthony: b. Aug. 1, 1935, Port Colborne, Ont.; ord. priest May 27, 1961; ord. titular bishop of Naziona and auxiliary bishop of Hamilton, July 12, 1983; app. bishop of Hamilton, May 5, 1984.

Tremblay, Gerard, P.S.S.: b. Oct. 27, 1918, Montreal, Que.; ord. priest June 16, 1946; ord. titular bishop of Trisipa and auxiliary bishop of Montreal, May 22, 1981.

Troy, J. Edward: b. Sept. 3, 1931, Chatham, N.B.; ord. priest May 28, 1959; ord. coadjutor bishop of St. John, N.B., May 22, 1984; bishop of St. John, N.B., Apr. 2, 1986.

Turcotte, Jean-Claude: b. June 26, 1936, Montreal, Que.; ord. priest May 24, 1959; ord. titular bishop of Suas and auxiliary bishop of Montreal, June 29, 1982.

Ustrzycki, Matthew: b. Mar. 25, 1932, Saint Catharines, Ont.; ord. priest May 30, 1959; ord. titular bishop of Nationa and auxiliary of Hamilton, July 3, 1985.

Vachon, Louis-Albert: (See Cardinals, Biographies.)

Valois, Charles: b. Apr. 24, 1924, Montreal, Que.; ord. priest June 3, 1950; ord. bishop of St. Jerome, June 29, 1977.

Wall, Leonard J.: b. Sept. 27, 1924, Windsor, Ont.; ord. priest June 11, 1949; ord. titular bishop of Leptiminus and auxiliary bishop of Toronto, June 21, 1979.

Weber, Jerome, O.S.B.: b. Sept. 14, 1915, Muenster, Sask., Canada; ord. priest June 8, 1941; app. abbot-ordinary of St. Peter Muenster, Apr. 6, 1960; abbatial blessing, Aug. 24, 1960.

Wilhelm, Joseph L.: b. Nov. 16, 1909, Walkerton, Ont.; ord. priest June 9, 1934; ord. titular bishop of Saccaea and auxiliary bishop of Calgary, Aug. 22, 1963; archbishop of Kingston, Dec. 14, 1966; retired Mar. 12, 1982.

Windle, Joseph R.: b. Aug. 28, 1917, Ashdad, Ont.; ord. priest May 16, 1943; ord. titular bishop of Uzita and auxiliary bishop of Ottawa, Jan. 18, 1961; coadjutor bishop of Pembroke, 1969; bishop of Pembroke, Feb. 15, 1971.

CONFERENCE OF RELIGIOUS

The Canadian Religious Conference, founded in 1954, is a union of major superiors of men and women in Canada. Offices are located at 324 E. Laurier Ave., Ottawa, Ont. K1N 6P6.

CANADIAN CATHOLIC PUBLICATIONS

(Sources: *Catholic Press Directory,* Canadian Conference of Catholic Bishops.)

Newspapers

British Columbia Catholic, The, w; 150 Robson St., Vancouver, B.C. V6B 2A7.

Catholic New Times (national), biweekly; 80 Sackville St., Toronto, Ont. M5A 3E5.

Catholic Register, The (national), w; 67 Bond St., Toronto, Ont. M5B 1X6. Lay edited.

Catholic Times, The, 10 times a year; 2005 St. Marc St., Montreal, Que. H3H 2G8.

Diocesan News, m; P.O. Box 1689, Charlottetown, P.E.I. C1A 7N4.

Diocesan Review, The, m; 16 Hammond Dr., Corner Brook, Nfld. A2H 2W2.

Hamilton Diocesan News, 3 times a year; 700 King St. West, Hamilton, Ont. L8P 1C7.

L'Informateur, semimonthly; 1915 Est-Boulevard Gouin, Montreal, Que. H2B 1W7.

Monitor, The, m; P.O. Box 986, St. John's, Nfld. A1C 5M3.

New Freeman, The, w; 1 Bayard Dr., St. John, N.B. E2L 4C3.

Our Diocese, bm; P.O. Box 397, Grand Falls, Nfld. A2A 2J8.

Pastoral Reporter, The, 4 times a year; 1916 Second St. S.W., Calgary. Alta: T2S 1S3.

Prairie Messenger, w; Box 190, Muenster, Sask. S0K 2Y0.

Teviskes, Ziburiai (Lithuanian), w; 2185 Stavebank Rd., Mississauga, Ont. L5C 1T3.

Western Catholic Reporter, w; 10562 109th St., Edmonton, Alta. T5H 3B2.

Magazines

Annals of St. Anne de Beaupre, m; Box 1000, St. Anne de Beaupre, Que. G0A 3C0; Basilica of St. Anne.

Apostolat, bm; 460 Primiere Rue, Richelieu, Que. J3L 4B5, Oblates of Mary Immaculate.

Bread of Life, The, 6 times a year; Box 4068, Sta. D, Hamilton, Ont. L8V 4L5.

Bulletin (French-English), q; 324 E. Laurier St., Ottawa, Ont. K1N 6P6. Canadian Religious Conference.

Canadian Catholic Review, 11 times a year; 1437 College Dr., Saskatoon, Saskatchewan S7N 0W6.

Canadian League, The, 4 times a year; 3081 Ness Ave., Winnipeg, Man. R2Y 2G3. Catholic Women's League of Canada.

Casket, The, w; 88 College St., Antigonish, N.S. B2G 2L7.

Chesterton Review, q; 1437 College Dr., Saskatoon, Sask. S7N 0W6.

Companion of St. Francis and St. Anthony, m; P.O. Box 535, Sta. F., Toronto, Ont. M4Y 2L8; Conventual Franciscan Fathers.

Fatima Crusader, The, 4 times a year, P.O. Box 602, Fort Erie, Ont. L2A 5X3.

Global Village Voice, The, 4 times a year; 3028 Danforth Ave., Toronto, Ont. M4C 1N2. Canadian Catholic Organization for Development and Peace.

Grail: An Ecumenical Journal, q; Univ. of St. Jerome's College, Waterloo, Ont. N2L 3G3.

Home Missions, q; 67 Bond St., Toronto, Ont. M5B 1X5.

Indian Record, 4 times a year; 503-480 Aulneau, Winnipeg, Man. R2H 2V2.

Kateri (English-French), q; P.O. Box 70, Caughnawaga, Que. J0L 1B0.

Martyrs' Shrine Message, q; Midland, Ont. L4R 4K5.

Messager de Saint Antoine, Le, 10 times a year; Lac-Bouchette, Que. G0W 1V0.

Messenger of the Sacred Heart, m; 661 Greenwood Ave., Toronto, Ont. M4J 4B3.

Missions Etrangeres, 6 times a year; 180 Place Juge-Desnoyers, Laval, Que. H7G 1A4.

Oratory, 6 times a year; 3800 Ch. Reine-Marie, Montreal, Que. H3V 1H6.

Our Family, m; P.O. Box 249, Battleford, Sask.; S0M 0E0; Oblates of Mary Immaculate.

Prete et Pasteur, m; 4450 St. Hubert St., Montreal, Que. H2J 2W9.

Redeemer's Voice (Ukrainian-English), m; 165 Catherine St., P.O. Box 220, Yorkton, Sask. S3N 2V7.

Regard de Foi, 6 times a year; 5875 Est. rue Sherbrooke, Montreal, Que. H1N 1B6.

Relations, m; 8100 Blvd. Saint-Laurent, Montreal Que. H2P 2L9; Jesuit Fathers.

Restoration, 10 times a year; Madonna House, Combermere, Ont., K0J 1L0.

Sainte Anne de Beaupre, m; Basilica of St. Anne, Que. G0A 3C0.

Scarboro Missions, m; 2685 Kingston Rd., Scarboro, Ont. M1M 1M4.

Spiritan Missionary News, 4 times a year; 1440 McQueen Rd., Edmonton, Alta. T5N 3L2.

Unity, bm; 308 Young St., Montreal, Que. H3C 2G2.

Vox Benedictina, q; 409 Garrison Crescent, Saskatoon, Saskatchewan S7H 2Z9.

Historic Churches in Canada include the following: In Quebec City — the Basilica of Notre Dame, dating from 1650, once the cathedral of a diocese extending from Canada to Mexico; Notre Dame des Victoires, on the waterfront, dedicated in 1690; the Ursuline Convent, built in 1720, on du Parloir St. In Montreal — Notre Dame Basilica, constructed in 1829 on the pattern of Notre Dame in Paris.

MISSIONARIES TO THE AMERICAS

Allouez, Claude Jean (1622-1689): French Jesuit; missionary in Canada and midwestern U.S.; preached to 20 different tribes of Indians and baptized over 10,000; vicar general of Northwest.

Altham, John (1589-1640): English Jesuit; missionary among Indians in Maryland.

Anchieta, Jose de, Bl. (1534-1597): Portuguese Jesuit, b. Canary Islands; missionary in Brazil; writer; beatified 1980; feast, June 9.

Andreis, Felix de (1778-1820): Italian Vincentian; missionary and educator in western U.S.

Aparicio, Sebastian, Bl. (1502-1600): Franciscan brother, born Spain; settled in Mexico, c. 1533; worked as road builder and farmer before becoming Franciscan at about the age of 70; beatified, 1787; feast, Feb. 25.

Badin, Stephen T. (1768-1853): French missioner; came to U.S., 1792, when Sulpician seminary in Paris was closed; ordained, 1793, Baltimore, the first priest ordained in U.S.; missionary in Kentucky, Ohio and Michigan; bought land on which Notre Dame University now stands; buried on its campus.

Baraga, Frederic (1797-1868): Slovenian missionary bishop in U.S.; studied at Ljubljana and Vienna, ordained, 1823; came to U.S., 1830; missionary to Indians of Upper Michigan; first bishop of Marquette, 1857-1868; wrote Chippewa grammar, dictionary, prayer book and other works.

Bertran, Louis, St. (1526-1581): Spanish Dominican; missionary in Colombia and Caribbean, 1562-69; canonized, 1671; feast, Oct. 9.

Betancur, Pedro de San Jose, Bl. (1626-1667): Secular Franciscan, b. Canary Islands; arrived in Guatemala, 1651; established hospital, school and homes for poor; beatified 1980; feast, Apr. 25.

Bourgeoys, Marguerite, St. (1620-1700): French foundress, missionary; settled in Canada, 1653; founded Congregation of Notre Dame de Montreal, 1658; beatified, 1950; canonized 1982; feast, Jan. 19.

Brebeuf, John de, St. (1593-1649): French Jesuit; missionary among Huron Indians in Canada; martyred by Iroquois, Mar. 16, 1649; canonized, 1930; one of Jesuit North American martyrs; feast, Oct. 19.

Cancer de Barbastro, Louis (1500-1549): Spanish Dominican; began missionary work in Middle America, 1533; killed at Tampa Bay, Fla.

Castillo, John de, Bl. (1596-1628): Spanish Jesuit; worked in Paraguay Indian mission settlements (reductions); martyred; beatified, 1934; feast, Nov. 17.

Catala, Magin (1761-1830): Spanish Franciscan; worked in California mission of Santa Clara for 36 years.

Chabanel, Noel, St. (1613-1649): French Jesuit; missionary among Huron Indians in Canada; murdered by renegade Huron, Dec. 8, 1649; canonized, 1930; one of Jesuit North American martyrs; feast, Oct. 19.

Chaumonot, Pierre Joseph (1611-1693): French Jesuit; missionary among Indians in Canada.

Claver, Peter, St. (1581-1654): Spanish Jesuit;

missionary among Negroes of South America and West Indies; canonized, 1888; patron of Catholic missions among black people; feast, Sept. 9.

Daniel, Anthony, St. (1601-1648): French Jesuit; missionary among Huron Indians in Canada; martyred by Iroquois, July 4, 1648; canonized, 1930; one of Jesuit North American martyrs; feast, Oct. 19.

De Smet, Pierre Jean (1801-1873): Belgian-born Jesuit; missionary among Indians of northwestern U.S.; served as intermediary between Indians and U.S. government; wrote on Indian culture.

Duchesne, Rose Philippine, Bl. (1769-1852): French nun; educator and missionary in the U.S.; established first convent of the Society of the Sacred Heart in the U.S., at St. Charles, Mo. (later Florissant); founded schools for girls; did missionary work among Indians; beatified, 1940; feast, Nov. 17.

Farmer, Ferdinand (family name, Steinmeyer) (1720-1786): German Jesuit; missionary in Philadelphia, where he died; one of the first missionaries in New Jersey.

Flaget, Benedict J. (1763-1850): French Sulpician bishop; came to U.S., 1792; missionary and educator in U.S.; first bishop of Bardstown, Ky. (now Louisville), 1810-32; 1833-50.

Gallitzin, Demetrius (1770-1840): Russian prince, born The Hague; convert, 1787; ordained priest at Baltimore, 1795; frontier missionary, known as Father Smith; Gallitzin, Pa., named for him.

Garnier, Charles, St. (c. 1606-1649): French Jesuit; missionary among Hurons in Canada; martyred by Iroquois, Dec. 7, 1649; canonized, 1930; one of Jesuit North American martyrs; feast, Oct. 19.

Gibault, Pierre (1737-1804): Canadian missionary in Illinois and Indiana; aided in securing states of Ohio, Indiana, Illinois, Michigan and Wisconsin for the Americans during Revolution.

Gonzalez, Roch, Bl. (1576-1628): Paraguayan Jesuit; worked in Paraguay Indian mission settlements (reductions); martyred; beatified, 1934; feast, Nov. 17.

Goupil, Rene, St. (1607-1642): French lay missionary; had studied surgery at Orleans, France; missionary companion of St. Isaac Jogues among the Hurons; martyred, Sept. 29, 1642; canonized, 1930; one of Jesuit North American martyrs; feast, Oct. 19.

Gravier, Jacques (1651-1708): French Jesuit; missionary among Indians of Canada and midwestern U.S.

Hennepin, Louis (d. c. 1701): Belgian-born Franciscan missionary and explorer of Great Lakes region and Upper Mississippi, 1675-81, when he returned to Europe; first European to see and describe Niagara Falls.

Jesuit North American Martyrs: Isaac Jogues, Anthony Daniel, John de Brebeuf, Gabriel Lalemant, Charles Garnier, Noel Chabanel (Jesuit priests), and Rene Goupil and John Lalande (lay missionaries) who were martyred between Sept.

29, 1642, and Dec. 9, 1649, in the missions of New France; canonized June 29, 1930; feast, Oct. 19. See separate entries.

Jogues, Isaac, St. (1607-1646): French Jesuit; missionary among Indians in Canada; martyred near present site of Auriesville, N.Y., by Mohawks, Oct. 18, 1646; canonized, 1930; one of Jesuit North American martyrs; feast, Oct. 19.

Kino, Eusebio (1645-1711): Italian Jesuit; missionary and explorer in U.S.; arrived Southwest, 1681; established 25 Indian missions, took part in 14 exploring expeditions in northern Mexico, Arizona and southern California; helped develop livestock raising and farming in the area. He was selected in 1965 to represent Arizona in Statuary Hall.

Lalande, John, St. (d. 1646): French lay missionary, companion of Isaac Jogues; martyred by Mohawks at Auriesville, N.Y., Oct. 19, 1646; canonized, 1930; one of Jesuit North American martyrs; feast, Oct. 19.

Lalemant, Gabriel, St. (1610-1649): French Jesuit; missionary among the Hurons in Canada; martyred by the Iroquois, Mar. 17, 1649; canonized, 1930; one of Jesuit North American martyrs; feast, Oct. 19.

Lamy, Jean Baptiste (1814-1888): French prelate; came to U.S., 1839; missionary in Ohio and Kentucky; bishop in Southwest from 1850; first bishop (later archbishop) of Santa Fe, 1850-1885. He was nominated in 1951 to represent New Mexico in Statuary Hall.

Las Casas, Bartolome (1474-1566): Spanish Dominican; missionary in Haiti, Jamaica and Venezuela; reformer of abuses against Indians and black people; bishop of Chalapas, Mexico, 1544-47; historian.

Laval, Francoise de Montmorency, Bl. (1623-1708): French-born missionary bishop in Canada; named vicar apostolic of Canada, 1658; first bishop of Quebec, 1674; jurisdiction extended over all French-claimed territory in New World; beatified 1980; feast, May 6.

Manogue, Patrick (1831-1895): Missionary bishop in U.S., b. Ireland; migrated to U.S.; miner in California; studied for priesthood at St. Mary's of the Lake, Chicago, and St. Sulpice, Paris; ordained, 1861; missionary among Indians of California and Nevada; coadjutor bishop, 1881-84, and bishop, 1884-86, of Grass Valley; first bishop of Sacramento, 1886-1895, when see was transferred there.

Margil, Antonio (1657-1726): Spanish Franciscan; missionary in Middle America; apostle of Guatemala; established missions in Texas.

Marie of the Incarnation, Bl. (Marie Guyard Martin) (1599-1672): French widow; joined Ursuline Nuns; arrived in Canada, 1639; first superior of Ursulines in Quebec; missionary to Indians; writer; beatified 1980; feast, Apr. 30.

Marquette, Jacques (1637-1675): French Jesuit; missionary and explorer in America; sent to New France, 1666; began missionary work among Ottawa Indians on Lake Superior, 1668; accompanied Joliet down the Mississippi to mouth of the Arkansas, 1673, and returned to Lake Michigan by way of Illinois River; made a second trip over the same route; his diary and map are of historical significance. He was selected in 1895 to represent Wisconsin in Statuary Hall.

Massias (Macias), John de, St. (1585-1645); Dominican brother, a native of Spain; entered Dominican Friary at Lima, Peru, 1622; served as doorkeeper until his death; beatified, 1837; canonized 1975; feast, Sept. 16.

Mazzuchelli, Samuel C. (1806-1864): Italian Dominican; missionary in midwestern U.S.; called builder of the West; writer.

Membre, Zenobius (1645-1687): French Franciscan; missionary among Indians of Illinois; accompanied LaSalle expedition down the Mississippi (1681-1682) and Louisiana colonizing expedition (1684) which landed in Texas; murdered by Indians.

Nerinckx, Charles (1761-1824): Belgian priest; missionary in Kentucky; founded Sisters of Loretto at the Foot of the Cross.

Nobrega, Manoel (1517-1570): Portuguese Jesuit; leader of first Jesuit missionaries to Brazil, 1549.

Padilla, Juan de (d. 1542): Spanish Franciscan; missionary among Indians of Mexico and southwestern U.S.; killed by Indians in Kansas; protomartyr of the U.S.

Palou, Francisco (c. 1722-1789): Spanish Franciscan; accompanied Junipero Serra to Mexico, 1749; founded Mission Dolores in San Francisco; wrote history of the Franciscans in California.

Pariseau, Mother Mary Joseph (1833-1902): Canadian Sister of Charity of Providence; missionary in state of Washington from 1856; founded first hospitals in northwest territory; artisan and architect. Represents Washington in National Statuary Hall.

Peter of Ghent (d. 1572): Belgian Franciscan brother; missionary in Mexico for 49 years.

Porres, Martin de, St. (1579-1639): Peruvian Dominican oblate; his father was a Spanish soldier and his mother a black freedwoman from Panama; called wonder worker of Peru; beatified, 1837; canonized, 1962; feast, Nov. 3.

Quiroga, Vasco de (1470-1565): Spanish missionary in Mexico; founded hospitals; bishop of Michoacan, 1537.

Ravalli, Antonio (1811-1884): Italian Jesuit; missionary in far-western United States, mostly Montana, for 40 years.

Raymbaut, Charles (1602-1643): French Jesuit; missionary among Indians of Canada and northern U.S..

Richard, Gabriel (1767-1832): French Sulpician; missionary in Illinois and Michigan; a founder of University of Michigan; elected delegate to Congress from Michigan, 1823; first priest to hold seat in the House of Representatives.

Rodriguez, Alonso, Bl. (1598-1628): Spanish Jesuit; missionary in Paraguay; martyred; beatified, 1934; feast, Nov. 17.

Rosati, Joseph (1789-1843): Italian Vincentian; missionary bishop in U.S. (vicar apostolic of Mississippi and Alabama, 1822; coadjutor of Louisiana and the Two Floridas, 1823-26; administrator of

New Orleans, 1826-29; first bishop of St. Louis, 1826-1843).

Sahagun, Bernardino de (c. 1500-1590): Spanish Franciscan; missionary in Mexico for over 60 years; expert on Aztec archaeology.

Seelos, Francis X. (1819-1867): Redemptorist missionary, born Bavaria; ordained, 1844, at Baltimore; missionary in Pittsburgh and New Orleans.

Serra, Junipero (1713-1784): Spanish Franciscan, b. Majorca; missionary in America; arrived Mexico, 1749, where he did missionary work for 20 years; began work in Upper California in 1769 and established nine of the 21 Franciscan missions along the Pacific coast; baptized some 6,000 Indians and confirmed almost 5,000; a cultural pioneer of California. Represents California in Statuary Hall. He was declared venerable May 9, 1985, by Pope John Paul II.

Seghers, Charles J. (1839-1886): Belgian missionary bishop in North America; Apostle of Alaska; archbishop of Oregon City (now Portland), 1880-1884; murdered by berserk companion while on missionary journey.

Solanus, St. Francis (1549-1610): Spanish Franciscan; missionary in Paraguay, Argentina and Peru; wonder worker of the New World; canonized, 1726; feast, July 14.

Sorin, Edward F. (1814-1893): French priest; member of Congregation of Holy Cross; sent to U.S. in 1841; founder and first president of the University of Notre Dame; missionary in Indiana and Michigan.

Todadilla, Anthony de (1704-1746): Spanish Capuchin; missionary to Indians of Venezuela; killed by Motilones.

Turibius de Mogrovejo, St. (1538-1606): Spanish archbishop of Lima, Peru, c. 1580-1606; canonized 1726; feast, Mar. 23.

Twelve Apostles of Mexico (early 16th century): Franciscan priests; arrived in Mexico, 1524: Fathers Martin de Valencia (leader), Francisco de Soto, Martin de la Coruna, Juan Suares, Antonio de Ciudad Rodrigo, Toribio de Benevente, Garcia de Cisneros, Luis de Fuensalida, Juan de Ribas, Francisco Ximenes; Brothers Andres de Coroboda, Juan de Palos.

Valdivia, Luis de (1561-1641): Spanish Jesuit; defender of Indians in Peru and Chile.

Vasques de Espinosa, Antonio (early 17th century): Spanish Carmelite; missionary and explorer in Mexico, Panama and western coast of South America.

Vieira, Antonio (1608-1687): Portuguese Jesuit; preacher; missionary in Peru and Chile; protector of Indians against exploitation by slave owners and traders; considered foremost prose writer of 17th-century Portugal.

White, Andrew (1579-1656): English Jesuit; missionary among Indians in Maryland.

Wimmer, Boniface (1809-1887): German Benedictine; missionary among German immigrants in the U.S..

Youville, Marie Marguerite d', Bl. (1701-1771): Canadian widow; foundress of Sisters of Charity (Grey Nuns), 1738, at Montreal: beatified, 1959; feast, Dec. 23.

Zumarraga, Juan de (1468-1548): Spanish Franciscan; missionary; first bishop of Mexico; introduced first printing press in New World, published first book in America, a catechism for Aztec Indians; extended missions in Mexico and Central America; vigorous opponent of exploitation of Indians; approved of devotions at Guadalupe; leading figure in early church history in Mexico.

FRANCISCAN MISSIONS

The 21 Franciscan missions of Upper California were established during the 54-year period from 1769 to 1822. Located along the old El Camino Real, or King's Highway, they extended from San Diego to San Francisco and were the centers of Indian civilization, Christianity and industry in the early history of the state.

Fray Junipero Serra was the great pioneer of the missions of Upper California. He and his successor as superior of the work, Fray Fermin Lasuen, each directed the establishment of nine missions. One hundred and 46 priests of the Order of Friars Minor, most of them Spaniards, labored in the region from 1769 to 1845; 67 of them died at their posts, two as martyrs. The regular time of mission service was 10 years.

The missions were secularized by the Mexican government in the 1830's but were subsequently restored to the Church by the U.S. government. They are now variously used as the sites of parish churches, a university, houses of study and museums.

The names of the missions and the order of their establishment were as follows:

San Diego de Alcala, San Carlos Borromeo (El Carmelo), San Antonio de Padua, San Gabriel Arcangel, San Luis Obispo de Tolosa, San Francisco de Asis (Dolores), San Juan Capistrano;

Santa Clara de Asis, San Buenaventura, Santa Barbara, La Purisima Concepcion de Maria Santisima, Santa Cruz, Nuestra Senora de la Soledad, San Jose de Guadalupe;

San Juan Bautista, San Miguel Arcangel, San Fernando Rey de Espana, San Luis Rey de Francia, Santa Ines, San Rafael Arcangel, San Francisco Solano de Sonoma (Sonoma).

AGRIMISSIO

Agrimissio is a service office established for the purpose of assisting missionaries in rural development work in agriculture. Founded in 1970 by Msgr. Luigi Ligutti, late honorary president, it is sponsored by the Union of Superiors General (of male religious), the International Union of Superiors General (of female religious). It promotes cooperation among missionaries, the Rome headquarters of religious orders, governmental and non-governmental organizations, especially the international Food and Agriculture Organization.

Headquarters are located at the Palazzo S. Calisto, 00120, Vatican City.

THE CATHOLIC CHURCH IN THE UNITED STATES

The starting point of the mainstream of Catholic history in the United States was Baltimore at the end of the Revolutionary War, although before that time Catholic explorers had traversed much of the country and missionaries had done considerable work among the Indians in the Southeast, Northeast and Southwest. (See Index: Chronology of Church in U.S.)

Beginning of Organization

Father John Carroll's appointment as superior of the American missions on June 9, 1784, was the first step toward organization of the Church in this country.

At that time, according to a report he made to Rome in 1785, there were approximately 25,000 Catholics in the general population of four million. Many of them had been in the Colonies for several generations. Among them were such outstanding figures as Charles Carroll, a member of the Continental Congress and signer of the Declaration of Independence; Thomas FitzSimons of Philadelphia and Oliver Pollock, the Virginia agent, who raised funds for the militia; Commander John Barry, father of the American Navy, and numerous high-ranking army officers. For the most part, however, Catholics were an unknown minority laboring under legal and social handicaps.

Father Carroll, the cousin of Charles Carroll, was named the first American bishop in 1789 and placed in charge of the Diocese of Baltimore, whose boundaries were coextensive with those of the United States. He was ordained in England Aug. 15, 1790, and installed in his see the following Dec. 12.

Ten years later, Father Leonard Neale became his coadjutor and the first bishop ordained in the United States. Bishop Carroll became an archbishop in 1808 when Baltimore was designated a metropolitan see and the new dioceses of Boston, New York, Philadelphia and Bardstown were established. These jurisdictions were later subdivided, and by 1840 there were, in addition to Baltimore, 15 dioceses, 500 priests and 663,000 Catholics in the general population of 17 million.

Priests and First Seminaries

The original number of 24 priests noted in Bishop Carroll's 1785 report was gradually augmented with the arrival of others from France, after the Civil Constitution on the Clergy went into effect there, and other countries. Among the earliest arrivals were several Sulpicians who established the first seminary in the U.S., St. Mary's, Baltimore, in 1791. By 1815, 30 alumni of the school had been ordained to the priesthood. By that time, two additional seminaries were in operation: Mt. St. Mary's, established in 1809 at Emmitsburg, Md., and St. Thomas, founded two years later, at Bardstown, Ky. These and similar institutions founded later played key roles in the development and growth of the American clergy.

Early Schools

Early educational enterprises included the establishment in 1791 of a school at Georgetown which later became the first Catholic university in the U.S.; the opening of a secondary school for girls, conducted by Visitation Nuns, in 1799 at Georgetown; and the start of a similar school in the first decade of the 19th century at Emmitsburg, Md., by Saint Elizabeth Ann Seton and the Sisters of Charity of St. Joseph, the first religious community of American foundation.

By the 1840s, which saw the beginnings of the present public school system, more than 200 Catholic elementary schools, half of them west of the Alleghenies, were in operation. From this start, the Church subsequently built the greatest private system of education in the world.

Trusteeism

The initial lack of organization in ecclesiastical affairs, nationalistic feeling among Catholics and the independent action of some priests were factors involved in several early crises.

In Philadelphia, some German Catholics, with the reluctant consent of Bishop Carroll, founded Holy Trinity, the first national parish in the U.S. They refused to accept the pastor appointed by the bishop and elected their own. This and other abuses led to formal schism in 1796, a condition which existed until 1802 when they returned to canonical jurisdiction. Philadelphia was also the scene of the Hogan Schism, which developed in the 1820s when Father William Hogan, with the aid of lay trustees, seized control of St. Mary's Cathedral. His movement, for churches and parishes controlled by other than canonical procedures and run in extralegal ways, was nullified by a decision of the Pennsylvania Supreme Court in 1822.

Similar troubles seriously disturbed the peace of the Church in other places, principally New York, Baltimore, Buffalo, Charleston and New Orleans.

Dangers arising from the exploitation of lay control were gradually diminished with the extension and enforcement of canonical procedures and with changes in civil law about the middle of the century.

Bigotry

Bigotry against Catholics waxed and waned during the 19th century and into the 20th. The first major campaign of this kind, which developed in the wake of the panic of 1819 and lasted for about 25 years, was mounted in 1830 when the number of Catholic immigrants began to increase to a noticeable degree. Nativist anti-Catholicism generated a great deal of violence, represented by climaxes in loss of life and property in Charlestown, Mass., in 1834, and in Philadelphia 10 years later. Later bigotry was fomented by the Know-Nothings, in the 1850s; the Ku Klux Klan, from 1866; the American Protective Association, from 1887, and the Guardians of Liberty. Perhaps the last eruption of virulently overt anti-Catholicism occurred during the campaign of Alfred E. Smith for the presidency in 1928. Observers feel the issue was muted to a considerable extent in the political area with the election of John F. Kennedy to the presidency in 1960.

Growth and Immigration

Between 1830 and 1900, the combined factors of natural increase, immigration and conversion raised the Catholic population to 12 million. A large percentage of the growth figure represented immigrants: some 2.7 million, largely from Ireland, Germany and France, between 1830 and 1880; and another 1.25 million during the 1880s when Eastern and Southern Europeans came in increasing numbers. By the 1860s the Catholic Church, with most of its members concentrated in urban areas, was one of the largest religious bodies in the country.

The efforts of progressive bishops to hasten the acculturation of Catholic immigrants occasioned a number of controversies, which generally centered around questions concerning national or foreign-language parishes. One of them, called Cahenslyism, arose from complaints that German Catholic immigrants were not being given adequate pastoral care.

Immigration continued after the turn of the century, but its impact was more easily cushioned through the application of lessons learned earlier in dealing with problems of nationality and language.

Councils of Baltimore

The bishops of the growing U.S. dioceses met at Baltimore for seven provincial councils between 1829 and 1849.

In 1846, they proclaimed the Blessed Virgin Mary patroness of the United States under the title of the Immaculate Conception, eight years before the dogma was proclaimed.

After the establishment of the Archdiocese of Oregon City in 1846 and the elevation to metropolitan status of St. Louis, New Orleans, Cincinnati and New York, the first of the three plenary councils of Baltimore was held.

The first plenary assembly was convoked on May 9, 1852, with Archbishop Francis P. Kenrick of Baltimore as papal legate. The bishops drew up regulations concerning parochial life, matters of church ritual and ceremonies, the administration of church funds and the teaching of Christian doctrine.

The second plenary council, meeting from Oct. 7 to 21, 1866, under the presidency of Archbishop Martin J. Spalding, formulated a condemnation of several current doctrinal errors and established norms affecting the organization of dioceses, the education and conduct of the clergy, the management of ecclesiastical property, parochial duties and general education.

Archbishop (later Cardinal) James Gibbons called into session the third plenary council which lasted from Nov. 9 to Dec. 7, 1884. Among highly significant results of actions taken by this as-

sembly were the preparation of the line of Baltimore catechisms which became a basic means of religious instruction in this country; legislation which fixed the pattern of Catholic education by requiring the building of elementary schools in all parishes; the establishment of the Catholic University of America in Washington, D.C., in 1889; and the determination of six holy days of obligation for observance in this country.

The enactments of the three plenary councils have had the force of particular law for the Church in the United States.

The Holy See established the Apostolic Delegation in Washington, D.C., on Jan. 24, 1893.

Slavery

In the Civil War period, as before, Catholics reflected attitudes of the general population with respect to the issue of slavery. Some supported it, some opposed it, but none were prominent in the Abolition Movement. Gregory XVI had condemned the slave trade in 1839, but no contemporary pope or American bishop published an official document on slavery itself. The issue did not split Catholics in schism as it did Baptists, Methodists and Presbyterians.

Catholics fought on both sides in the Civil War. Five hundred members of 20 or more sisterhoods served the wounded of both sides.

One hundred thousand of the four million slaves emancipated in 1863 were Catholics; the highest concentrations were in Louisiana, about 60,000, and Maryland, 16,000. Three years later, their pastoral care was one of the subjects covered in nine decrees issued by the Second Plenary Council of Baltimore. The measures had little practical effect with respect to integration of the total Catholic community, predicated as they were on the proposition that individual bishops should handle questions regarding segregation in churches and related matters as best they could in the pattern of local customs.

Long entrenched segregation practices continued in force through the rest of the 19th century and well into the 20th. The first effective efforts to alter them were initiated by Cardinal Joseph Ritter of St. Louis in 1947, Cardinal (then Archbishop) Patrick O'Boyle of Washington in 1948, and Bishop Vincent Waters of Raleigh in 1953.

Friend of Labor

The Church became known during the 19th century as a friend and ally of labor in seeking justice for the working man. Cardinal Gibbons journeyed to Rome in 1887, for example, to defend and prevent a condemnation of the Knights of Labor by Leo XIII. The encyclical *Rerum Novarum* was hailed by many American bishops as a confirmation, if not vindication, of their own theories. Catholics have always formed a large percentage of union membership, and some have served unions in positions of leadership.

The American Heresy

Near the end of the century some controversy developed over what was characterized as Americanism or the phantom heresy. It was alleged that Americans were discounting the importance of contemplative virtues, exalting the practical virtues, and watering down the purity of Catholic doctrine for the sake of facilitating convert work.

The French translation of Father Walter Elliott's *Life of Isaac Hecker,* which fired the controversy, was one of many factors that led to the issuance of Leo XIII's *Testem Benevolentiae* in January, 1899, in an attempt to end the matter. It was the first time the orthodoxy of the Church in the U.S. was called into question.

Schism

In the 1890s, serious friction developed between Poles and Irish in Scranton, Buffalo and Chicago, resulting in schism and the establishment of the Polish National Church. A central figure in the affair was Father Francis Hodur, who was excommunicated by Bishop William O'Hara of Scranton in 1898. Nine years later, his ordination by an Old Catholic Archbishop of Utrecht gave the new church its first bishop.

Another schism of the period led to formation of the American Carpatho-Russian Orthodox Greek Catholic Church.

Coming of Age

In 1900, there were 12 million Catholics in the total U.S. population of 76 million, 82 dioceses in 14 provinces, and 12,000 priests and members of about 40 communities of men Religious. Many sisterhoods, most of them of European origin and some of American foundation, were engaged in Catholic educational and hospital work, two of their traditional apostolates.

The Church in the United States was removed from mission status with promulgation of the apostolic constitution *Sapienti Consilio* by Pope St. Pius X on June 29, 1908.

Before that time, and even into the early 1920s, the Church in this country received financial assistance from mission-aid societies in France, Bavaria and Austria. Already, however, it was making increasing contributions of its own. At the present time, it is one of the major national contributors to the worldwide Society for the Propagation of the Faith.

American foreign missionary personnel increased from 14 or less in 1906 to an all-time high in 1968 of 9,655 priests, brothers, sisters, seminarians, and lay persons. The first missionary seminary in the U.S. was in operation at Techny, Ill., in 1909, under the auspices of the Society of the Divine Word. Maryknoll, the first American missionary society, was established in 1911 and sent its first priests to China in 1918. Despite these contributions, the Church in the U.S. has not matched the missionary commitment of some other nations.

Bishops' Conference

A highly important apparatus for mobilizing the Church's resources was established in 1917 under the title of the National Catholic War Council. Its name was changed to National Catholic Welfare Conference several years later, but its objectives remained the same: to serve as an advisory and coordinating agency of the American bishops for advancing works of the Church in fields of social significance and impact — education, communications, immigration, social action, legislation, youth and lay organizations.

The forward thrust of the bishops' social thinking was evidenced in a program of social reconstruction they recommended in 1919. By 1945, all but one of their twelve points had been enacted into legislation.

The NCWC was renamed the United States Catholic Conference (USCC) in November, 1966, when the hierarchy also organized itself as a territorial conference with pastoral-juridical authority under the title, National Conference of Catholic Bishops. The USCC is carrying on the functions of the former NCWC.

Pastoral Concerns

The potential for growth of the Church in this country by immigration was sharply reduced but not entirely curtailed after 1921 with the passage of restrictive federal legislation. As a result, the Catholic population became more stabilized and, to a certain extent and for many reasons, began to acquire an identity of its own.

Some increase from outside has taken place in the past 50 years, however; from Canada, from Central and Eastern European countries, and from Puerto Rico and Latin American countries since World War II. This influx, while not as great as that of the 19th century and early 20th, has enriched the Church here with a sizable body of Eastern-Rite Catholics for whom eight ecclesiastical jurisdictions were established between 1924 and 1969. It has also created a challenge for pastoral care of millions of Hispanics in urban centers and in agricultural areas where migrant workers are employed.

The Church continues to grapple with serious pastoral problems in rural areas, where about 600 counties are no-priest land. The National Catholic Rural Life Conference was established in 1922 in an attempt to make the Catholic presence felt on the land, and the Glenmary Society since its foundation in 1939 has devoted itself to this single apostolate. Religious communities and diocesan priests are similarly engaged.

Other challenges lie in the cities and suburbs where 75 percent of the Catholic population lives. Conditions peculiar to each segment of the metropolitan area have developed in recent years as the flight to the suburbs has not only altered some traditional aspects of parish life but has also, in combination with many other factors, left behind a complex of special problems in inner city areas.

Contemporary Factors

The Church in the U.S. is in a stage of transition from a relatively stable and long established order of life and action to a new order of things. Some of the phenomena of this period are:

• differences in trends and emphasis in theology, and in interpretation and implementation of directives of the Second Vatican Council, resulting in situations of conflict;

• the changing spiritual formation, professional education, style of life and ministry of priests and Religious (men and women), which are altering influential patterns of pastoral and specialized service;

• vocations to the priesthood and religious life, which are generally in decline;

• departures from the priesthood and religious life which, while small percentage-wise, are numerous enough to be a matter of serious concern;

• decline of traditional devotional practices, along with the emergence of new ones.

• exercise of authority along the lines of collegiality and subsidiarity;

• structure and administration, marked by a trend toward greater participation in the life and work of the Church by its members on all levels, from the parish on up;

• alienation from the Church, leading some persons into the catacombs of an underground church, "anonymous Christianity" and religious indifferentism;

• education, undergoing crisis and change in Catholic schools and seeking new ways of reaching out to the young not in Catholic schools and to adults;

• social witness in ministry to the world, which is being shaped by the form of contemporary needs — e.g., race relations, poverty, the peace movement, the Third World;

• ecumenism, involving the Church in interfaith relations on a wider scale than before.

BACKGROUND DATES IN U.S. CATHOLIC CHRONOLOGY

Dates in this section refer mostly to earlier "firsts" and developments in the background of Catholic history in the United States. For other dates, see various sections of the Almanac.

Alabama

1540: Priests crossed the territory with De Soto's expedition.

1560: Five Dominicans in charge of mission at Santa Cruz des Nanipacna.

1682: La Salle claimed territory for France.

1704: First parish church established at Fort Louis de la Mobile under the care of diocesan priests.

1829: Mobile diocese established (redesignated Mobile-Birmingham, 1954-69).

1830: Spring Hill College, Mobile, established.

1834: Visitation Nuns established an academy at Summerville.

1969: Birmingham diocese established.

1980: Mobile made metropolitan see.

Alaska

1779: Mass celebrated for first time on shore of Port Santa Cruz on lower Bucareli Bay on May 13 by Franciscan Juan Riobo.

1868: Alaska placed under jurisdiction of Vancouver Island.

1879: Father John Althoff became first resident missionary.

1886: Archbishop Charles J. Seghers, "Apostle of Alaska," murdered by a guide; had surveyed southern and northwest Alaska in 1873 and 1877, respectively.

Sisters of St. Ann first nuns in Alaska.

1887: Jesuits enter Alaska territory.

1894: Alaska made prefecture apostolic.

1902: Sisters of Providence opened hospital at Nome.

1916: Alaska made vicariate apostolic.

1917: In first ordination in territory, Rev. G. Edgar Gallant raised to priesthood.

1951: Juneau diocese established.

1962: Fairbanks diocese established.

1966: Anchorage archdiocese established.

Arizona

1539: Franciscan Marcos de Niza explored the state.

1540: Franciscans Juan de Padilla and Marcos de Niza accompanied Coronado expedition through the territory.

1629: Spanish Franciscans began work among Moqui Indians.

1632: Franciscan Martin de Arvide killed by Indians.

1680: Franciscans Jose de Espeleta, Augustin de Santa Maria, Jose de Figueroa and Jose de Trujillo killed in Pueblo Revolt.

1700: Jesuit Eusebio Kino, who first visited the area in 1692, established mission at San Xavier del Bac, near Tucson. In 1783, under Franciscan administration, construction was begun of the Mission Church of San Xavier del Bac near the site of the original mission; it is still in use as a parish church.

1767: Jesuits expelled; Franciscans took over 10 missions.

1828: Spanish missionaries expelled by Mexican government.

1863: Jesuits returned to San Xavier del Bac briefly.

1869: Sisters of Loretto arrived to conduct schools at Bisbee and Douglas.

1897: Tucson diocese established.

1969: Phoenix diocese established.

Arkansas

1541: Priests accompanied De Soto expedition through the territory.

1673: Marquette visited Indians in east.

1686: Henri de Tonti established trading post, first white settlement in territory.

1700-1702: Fr. Nicholas Foucault working among Indians.

1805: Bishop Carroll of Baltimore appointed Administrator Apostolic of Arkansas.

1838: Sisters of Loretto opened first Catholic school.

1843: Little Rock diocese established. There were about 700 Catholics in state, two churches, one priest.

1851: Sisters of Mercy founded St. Mary's Convent in Little Rock.

California

1542: Cabrillo discovered Upper (Alta) California; name of priest accompanying expedition unknown.

1602: On Nov. 12 Carmelite Andres de la Ascencion offered first recorded Mass in California on shore of San Diego Bay.

1697: Missionary work in Lower and Upper Californias entrusted to Jesuits.

1767: Jesuits expelled from territory. Spanish Crown confiscated their property, including the Pious Fund for Missions. Upper California missions entrusted to Franciscans.

1769: Franciscan Junipero Serra began establishment of Franciscan missions in California, in present San Diego.

1775: Franciscan Luis Jayme killed by Indians at San Diego Mission.

1779: Diocese of Sonora, Mexico, which included Upper California, established.

1781: On Sept. 4 an expedition from San Gabriel Mission founded present city of Los Angeles — Pueblo "de Nuestra Senora de los Angeles."

Franciscans Francisco Hermenegildo Garces, Juan Antonio Barreneche, Juan Marcello Diaz and Jose Matias Moreno killed by Indians.

1812: Franciscan Andres Quintana killed at Santa Cruz Mission.

1822: Dedication on Dec. 8 of Old Plaza Church, "Assistant Mission of Our Lady of the Angels."

1833: Missions secularized, finally confiscated.

1840: Pope Gregory XVI established Diocese of Both Californias.

1846: Peter H. Burnett, who became first governor of California in 1849, received into Catholic Church.

1848: Mexico ceded California to the United States.

1850: Monterey diocese erected; title changed to Monterey-Los Angeles, 1859; and to Los Angeles-San Diego, 1922.

1851: University of Santa Clara chartered.

Sisters of Notre Dame de Namur opened women's College of Notre Dame at San Jose; chartered in 1868; moved to Belmont, 1923.

1852: Baja California detached from Monterey diocese.

1853: San Francisco archdiocese established.

1855: Negotiations inaugurated to restore confiscated California missions to Church.

1868: Grass Valley diocese established; transferred to Sacramento in 1886.

1922: Monterey-Fresno diocese established; became separate dioceses, 1967.

1934: Sesquicentennial of Serra's death observed; Serra Year officially declared by Legislature and Aug. 24 observed as Serra Day.

1936: Los Angeles made archdiocese. San Diego diocese established.

1952: Law exempting non-profit, religious-sponsored elementary and secondary schools from taxation upheld in referendum, Nov. 4.

1953: Archbishop James Francis McIntyre of Los Angeles made cardinal by Pius XII.

1962: Oakland, Santa Rosa and Stockton dioceses established.

1973: Archbishop Timothy Manning of Los Angeles made cardinal by Pope Paul VI.

1976: Orange diocese established.

1978: San Bernardino diocese established.

1981: San Jose diocese established.

Byzantine-Rite eparchy of Van Nuys established.

Colorado

1858: First parish in Colorado established.

1864: Sisters of Loretto at the Foot of the Cross, first nuns in the state, established academy at Denver.

1868: Vicariate Apostolic of Colorado and Utah established.

1887: Denver diocese established.

1888: Regis College founded.

1941: Denver made archdiocese.

Pueblo diocese established.

1983: Colorado Springs diocese established.

Connecticut

1651: Probably first priest to enter state was Jesuit Gabriel Druillettes; ambassador of Governor of Canada, he participated in a New England Colonial Council at New Haven.

1756: Catholic Acadians, expelled from Nova Scotia, settled in the state.

1791: Rev. John Thayer, first native New England priest, offered Mass at the Hartford home of Noah Webster, his Yale classmate.

1808: Connecticut became part of Boston diocese.

1818: Religious freedom established by new constitution, although the Congregational Church remained, in practice, the state church.

1829: Father Bernard O'Cavanaugh became first resident priest in state.

Catholic Press of Hartford established.

1830: First Catholic church in state dedicated at Hartford.

Father James Fitton (1805-81), New England missionary, was assigned to Hartford for six years. He ministered to Catholics throughout the state.

1843: Hartford diocese established.

1882: Knights of Columbus founded by Father Michael J. McGivney.

1942: Fairfield University founded.

1953: Norwich and Bridgeport dioceses established. Hartford made archdiocese.

1956: Byzantine Rite Exarchate of Stamford established; made eparchy, 1958.

Delaware

1730: Mount Cuba, New Castle County, the scene of Catholic services.

1750: Jesuit mission at Apoquiniminck administered from Maryland.

1772: First permanent parish established at Coffee Run.

1792: French Catholics from Santo Domingo settled near Wilmington.

1816: St. Peter's Church, later the cathedral of the diocese, erected at Wilmington.

1830: Daughters of Charity opened school and orphanage at Wilmington.

1868: Wilmington diocese established.

1869: Visitation Nuns established residence in Wilmington.

District of Columbia

1641: Jesuit Andrew White evangelized Anacosta Indians.

1774: Father John Carroll ministered to Catholics.

1789: Georgetown, first Catholic college in U.S., established.

1791: Pierre Charles L'Enfant designed the Federal City of Washington. His plans were not fully implemented until the early 1900s.

1792: James Hoban designed the White House.

1794: Father Anthony Caffrey began St. Patrick's Church, first parish church in the new Federal City.

1801: Poor Clares opened school for girls in Georgetown; first school established by nuns in U.S..

1802: First mayor of Washington, appointed by President Jefferson, was Judge Robert Brent.

1889: Catholic University of America founded.

1893: Apostolic Delegation established; became an Apostolic Nunciature in 1984 with the establishment of full diplomatic relations between the U.S. and the Vatican.

1919: National Catholic Welfare Conference (now the United States Catholic Conference) organized by American hierarchy to succeed National Catholic War Council.

1920: Cornerstone of National Shrine of Immaculate Conception laid.

1939: Washington made archdiocese of equal rank with Baltimore, under direction of same archbishop.

1947: Washington archdiocese received its own archbishop, was separated from Baltimore; became a metropolitan see in 1965.

1967: Archbishop Patrick A. O'Boyle of Washington made cardinal by Pope Paul VI.

1976: Archbishop William Baum of Washington made a cardinal by Pope Paul VI; transferred to Roman Curia in 1980 as prefect of Sacred Congregation for Catholic Education.

Florida

1513: Ponce de Leon discovered Florida.

1521: Missionaries accompanying Ponce de Leon and other explorers probably said first Masses within present limits of U.S..

1528: Franciscans landed on western shore.

1539: Twelve missionaries landed with De Soto at Tampa Bay.

1549: Dominican Luis Cancer de Barbastro and two companions slain by Indians near Tampa Bay.

1565: City of St. Augustine, oldest in U.S., founded by Pedro Menendez de Aviles, who was accompanied by four secular priests.

America's oldest mission, Nombre de Dios, was established.

Father Martin Francisco Lopez de Mendoza Grajales became the first parish priest of St. Augustine, where the first parish in the U.S. was established.

1572: St. Francis Borgia, general of the Society, withdrew Jesuits from Florida.

1606: Bishop Juan de las Cabeyas de Altamirano, O.P., conducted the first episcopal visitation in the U.S..

1620: The chapel of Nombre de Dios was dedicated to Nuestra Senora de la Leche y Buen Parto (Our Nursing Mother of the Happy Delivery); oldest shrine to the Blessed Mother in the U.S..

1704: Destruction of Florida's northern missions by English and Indian troops led by Governor James Moore of South Carolina. Franciscans Juan de Parga, Dominic Criodo, Tiburcio de Osorio, Augustine Ponze de Leon, Marcos Delgado and two Indians, Anthony Enixa and Amador Cuipa Feliciano, were slain by the invaders.

1735: Bishop Francis Martinez de Tejadu Diaz de Velasco, auxiliary of Santiago, was the first bishop to take up residence in U.S., at St. Augustine.

1793: Florida and Louisiana were included in Diocese of New Orleans.

1857: Eastern Florida made a vicariate apostolic.

1870: St. Augustine diocese established.

1917: Convent Inspection Bill passed; repealed 1935.

1958: Miami diocese established.

1968: Miami made metropolitan see; Orlando and St. Petersburg dioceses established.

1976: Pensacola-Tallahassee diocese established.

1984: Palm Beach and Venice dioceses established.

Georgia

1540: First priests to enter were chaplains with De Soto. They celebrated first Mass within territory of 13 original colonies.

1566: Pedro Martinez, first Jesuit martyr of the New World, was slain by Indians on Cumberland Island.

1569: Jesuit mission was opened at Guale Island by Father Antonio Sedeno.

1572: Jesuits withdrawn from area.

1595: Five Franciscans assigned to Province of Guale.

1597: Five Franciscan missionaries (Fathers Pedro de Corpa, Blas de Rodriguez, Miguel de Anon, Francisco de Berascolo and Brother Antonio de Badajoz) killed in coastal missions. Their cause for beatification was formally opened in 1984.

1606: Bishop Altamirano, O.P., conducted visitation of the Georgia area.

1612: First Franciscan province in U.S. erected under title of Santa Elena; it included Georgia, South Carolina and Florida.

1655: Franciscans had nine flourishing missions among Indians.

1742: Spanish missions ended as result of English conquest at Battle of Bloody Marsh.

1796: Augustinian Father Le Mercier was first post-colonial missionary to Georgia.

1798: Catholics granted right of refuge.

1800: First church erected in Savannah on lot given by city council.

1810: First church erected in Augusta on lot given by State Legislature.

1850: Savannah diocese established; became Savannah-Atlanta, 1937; divided into two separate sees, 1956.

1864: Father Emmeran Bliemel, of the Benedictine community of Latrobe, Pa., was killed at the battle of Jonesboro while serving as chaplain of the Confederate 10th Tennessee Artillery.

1962: Atlanta made metropolitan see.

Hawaii

1825: Pope Leo XII entrusted missionary efforts in Islands to Sacred Hearts Fathers.

1827: The first Catholic missionaries arrived — Fathers Alexis Bachelot, Abraham Armand and Patrick Short, along with three lay brothers. After three years of persecution, the priests were forcibly exiled.

1836: Father Arsenius Walsh, SS. CC., a British subject, was allowed to remain in Islands but was not permitted to proselytize or conduct missions.

1839: Hawaiian government signed treaty with France granting Catholics freedom of worship and same privileges as Protestants.

1844: Vicariate Apostolic of Sandwich Islands (Hawaii) erected.

1873: Father Damien de Veuster of the Sacred Hearts Fathers arrived in Molokai and spent the remainder of his life working among lepers.

1941: Honolulu diocese established, made a suffragan of San Francisco.

Idaho

1840: Jesuit Pierre de Smet preached to the Flathead and Pend d'Oreille Indians; probably offered first Mass in state.

1842: Jesuit Nicholas Point opened a mission among Coeur d'Alene Indians near St. Maries.

1863: Secular priests sent from Oregon City to administer to incoming miners.

1867: Sisters of Holy Names of Jesus and Mary opened first Catholic school at Idaho City.

1868: Idaho made a vicariate apostolic.

1870: First church in Boise established.

Church lost most of missions among Indians of Northwest Territory when Commission on Indian Affairs appointed Protestant missionaries to take over.

1893: Boise diocese established.

Illinois

1673: Jesuit Jacques Marquette, accompanying Joliet, preached to Indians.

1674: Father Marquette set up a cabin for saying Mass in what later became City of Chicago.

1675: Father Marquette established Mission of the Immaculate Conception among Kaskaskia Indians, near present site of Utica; transferred to Kaskaskia, 1703.

1679: La Salle brought with him Franciscans Louis Hennepin, Gabriel de la Ribourde, and Zenobius Membre.

1680: Father Ribourde was killed by Kickapoo Indians.

1689: Jesuit Claude Allouez died after 32 years of missionary activity among Indians of Midwest; he had evangelized Indians of 20 different tribes. Jesuit Jacques Gravier succeeded Allouez as vicar general of Illinois.

1699: Mission established at Cahokia, first permanent settlement in state.

1730: Father Gaston, a diocesan priest, was killed at the Cahokia Mission.

1763: Jesuits were banished from the territory.

1778: Father Pierre Gibault championed Colonial cause in the Revolution and aided greatly in securing states of Ohio, Indiana, Illinois, Michigan and Wisconsin for Americans.

1827: The present St. Patrick's Parish at Ruma, oldest English-speaking Catholic congregation in state, was founded.

1833: Visitation Nuns established residence in Kaskaskia.

1843: Chicago diocese established.

1853: Quincy diocese established; transferred to Alton, 1857; Springfield, 1923.

1860: Quincy College founded.

1877: Peoria diocese established.

1880: Chicago made archdiocese.

1887: Belleville diocese established.

1894: Franciscan Sisters of Bl. Kunegunda (now the Franciscan Sisters of Chicago) founded by Mother Marie Therese (Josephine Dudzik).

1908: Rockford diocese established.

First American Missionary Congress held in Chicago.

1924: Archbishop Mundelein of Chicago made cardinal by Pope Pius XI.

1926: The 28th International Eucharistic Congress, first held in U.S., convened in Chicago.

1946: Blessed Frances Xavier Cabrini, former resident of Chicago, was canonized; first U.S. citizen raised to dignity of altar.

Archbishop Samuel A. Stritch of Chicago made cardinal by Pope Pius XII.

1948: Joliet diocese established.

1958: Cardinal Stritch appointed Pro-Prefect of the Sacred Congregation for the Propagation of the Faith — the first U.S.-born prelate to be named to the Roman Curia.

1959: Archbishop Albert G. Meyer of Chicago made cardinal by Pope John XXIII.

1961: Eparchy of St. Nicholas of the Ukrainians established at Chicago.

1967: Archbishop John P. Cody of Chicago made cardinal by Pope Paul VI.

1983: Archbishop Joseph L. Bernardin of Chicago made cardinal by Pope John Paul II.

Indiana

1679: Recollects Louis Hennepin and Gabriel de la Ribourde passed through state.

1686: Land near present Notre Dame University at South Bend given by French government to Jesuits for mission.

1749: Beginning of the records of St. Francis Xavier Church, Vincennes. These records continue with minor interruptions to the present.

1778: Father Gibault aided George Rogers Clark in campaign against British in conquest of Northwest Territory.

1824: Sisters of Charity of Nazareth, Ky., opened St. Clare's Academy in Vincennes.

1825: Laying of cornerstone of third church of St. Francis Xavier, which later (from 1834-98) was the cathedral of the Vincennes diocese. The church was designated a minor basilica in 1970 and is still in use as a parish church.

1834: Vincennes diocese established with Simon Gabriel Brute as bishop; title changed to Indianapolis, 1898.

1840: Sisters of Providence founded St. Mary-of-the-Woods College for women.

1842: University of Notre Dame founded by Holy Cross Father Edward Sorin and Brothers of St. Joseph on land given the diocese of Vincennes by Father Stephen Badin.

1853: First Benedictine community established in state at St. Meinrad. It became an abbey in 1870 and an archabbey in 1954.

1857: Fort Wayne diocese established; changed to Fort Wayne-South Bend, 1960.

1944: Indianapolis made archdiocese. Lafayette and Evansville dioceses established.

1957: Gary diocese established.

Iowa

1673: A Peoria village on Mississippi was visited by Father Marquette.

1679: Fathers Louis Hennepin and Gabriel de la Ribourde visited Indian villages.

1836: First permanent church, St. Raphael's, founded at Dubuque by Dominican Samuel Mazzuchelli.

1837: Dubuque diocese established.

1838: St. Joseph's Mission founded at Council Bluffs by Jesuit Father De Smet.

1843: Sisters of Charity of the Blessed Virgin Mary were first sisterhood in state.

Sisters of Charity opened Clarke College, Dubuque.

1850: First Trappist Monastery in state, Our Lady of New Melleray, was begun.

1881: Davenport diocese established.

1882: St. Ambrose College, Davenport, established.

1893: Dubuque made archdiocese.

1902: Sioux City diocese established.

1911: Des Moines diocese established.

Kansas

1542: Franciscan Juan de Padilla, first martyr of the United States, was killed in central Kansas.

1858: St. Benedict's College founded.

1863: Sisters of Charity opened orphanage at Leavenworth, and St. John's Hospital in following year.

1877: Leavenworth diocese established; transferred to Kansas City in 1947.

1887: Dioceses of Concordia (transferred to Salina in 1944) and Wichita established.

1888: Oblate Sisters of Providence opened an orphanage for Negro boys at Leavenworth, first west of Mississippi.

1951: Dodge City diocese established.

1952: Kansas City made archdiocese.

Kentucky

1775: First Catholic settlers came to Kentucky.

1787: Father Charles Maurice Whelan, first resident priest, ministered to settlers in the Bardstown district.

1793: Father Stephen T. Badin began missionary work in Kentucky.

1806: Dominican Fathers built Priory at St. Rose of Lima.

1808: Bardstown diocese established with Benedict Flaget as its first bishop; transferred to Louisville, 1841.

1811: Rev. Guy I. Chabrat first priest ordained west of the Allegheny Mountains.

St. Thomas Seminary founded.

1812: Sisters of Loretto founded by Rev. Charles Nerinckx; first religious community in the United States without foreign affiliation.

Sisters of Charity of Nazareth founded, the second native community of women founded in the West.

1814: Nazareth College for women established.

1816: Cornerstone of St. Joseph's Cathedral, Bardstown, laid.

1836: Hon. Benedict J. Webb founded *Catholic Advocate* first Catholic weekly newspaper in Kentucky.

1848: Trappist monks took up residence in Gethsemani.

1849: Cornerstone of Cathedral of the Assumption laid at Louisville.

1852: Know-Nothing troubles in state.

1853: Covington diocese established.

1937: Louisville made archdiocese. Owensboro diocese established.

Louisiana

1682: La Salle's expedition, accompanied by two priests, completed discoveries of De Soto at mouth of Mississippi. LaSalle named territory Louisiana.

1699: French Catholics founded colony of Louisiana.

First recorded Mass offered Mar. 3, by Franciscan Father Anastase Douay.

1706: Father John Francis Buisson de St. Cosme was killed near Donaldsonville.

1717: Franciscan Anthony Margil established first Spanish mission in north central Louisiana.

1718: City of New Orleans founded by Jean Baptiste Le Moyne de Bienville.

1720: First resident priest in New Orleans was the French Recollect Prothais Boyer.

1725: Capuchin Fathers opened school for boys.

1727: Ursuline Nuns founded convent in New Orleans, oldest convent in what is now U.S.; they conducted a school, hospital and orphan asylum.

1793: New Orleans diocese established.

1850: New Orleans made archdiocese.

1853: Natchitoches diocese established; transferred to Alexandria in 1910; became Alexandria-Shreveport in 1977; redesignated Alexandria, 1986.

1892: Sisters of Holy Family, a black congregation, established at New Orleans.

1912: Loyola University of South established.

1918: Lafayette diocese established.

1925: Xavier University established in New Orleans.

1961: Baton Rouge diocese established.

1962: Catholic schools on all levels desegregated in New Orleans archdiocese.

1977: Houma-Thibodaux diocese established.

1980: Lake Charles diocese established.

1986: Shreveport diocese established.

Maine

1604: First Mass in territory celebrated by Father Nicholas Aubry, accompanying De Monts' expedition which was authorized by King of France to begin colonizing region.

1605: Colony founded on St. Croix Island; two secular priests served as chaplains.

1613: Four Jesuits attempted to establish permanent French settlement near mouth of Kennebec River.

1619: French Franciscans began work among settlers and Indians; driven out by English in 1628.

1630: New England made a prefecture apostolic in charge of French Capuchins.

1633: Capuchin Fathers founded missions on Penobscot River.

1646: Jesuits established Assumption Mission on Kennebec River.

1688: Church of St. Anne, oldest in New England, built at Oldtown.

1704: English soldiers destroyed French missions.

1724: English forces again attacked French settlements, killed Jesuit Sebastian Rale.

1853: Portland diocese established.

1854: Know-Nothing uprising resulted in burning of church in Bath.

1856: Anti-Catholic feeling continued; church at Ellsworth burned.

1864: Sisters of Congregation of Notre Dame from Montreal opened academy at Portland.

1875: James A. Healy, first bishop of Negro blood consecrated in U.S., became second Bishop of Portland.

Maryland

1634: Maryland established by Lord Calvert. Two Jesuits among first colonists.

First Mass offered on Island of St. Clement in Lower Potomac by Jesuit Father Andrew White. St. Mary's founded by English and Irish Catholics.

1641: St. Ignatius Parish founded by English Jesuits at Chapel Point, near Port Tobacco.

1649: Religious Toleration Act passed by Maryland Assembly. It was repealed in 1654 by Puritan-controlled government.

1651: Cecil Calvert, second Lord Baltimore, gave Jesuits 10,000 acres for use as Indian mission.

1658: Lord Baltimore restored Toleration Act.

1672: Franciscans came to Maryland under leadership of Father Massius Massey.

1688: Maryland became royal colony as a result of the Revolution in England; Anglican Church became the official religion (1692); Toleration Act repealed; Catholics disenfranchised and persecuted until 1776.

1704: Jesuits founded St. Francis Xavier Mission, Old Bohemia, to serve Catholics of Delaware, Maryland and southeastern Pennsylvania; its Bohemia Academy established in the 1740s was attended by sons of prominent Catholics in the area.

1784: Father John Carroll appointed prefect apostolic for the territory embraced by new Republic.

1789: Baltimore became first diocese established in U.S., with John Carroll as first bishop.

1790: Carmelite Nuns founded convent at Port Tobacco, the first in the English-speaking Colonies.

1791: First Synod of Baltimore held.

St. Mary's Seminary, first seminary in U.S., established.

1793: Rev. Stephen T. Badin first priest ordained by Bishop Carroll.

1800: Jesuit Leonard Neale became first bishop consecrated in present limits of U.S..

1806: Cornerstone of Assumption Cathedral, Baltimore, was laid.

1808: Baltimore made archdiocese.

1809: St. Joseph's College, first women's college in U.S., founded.

Sisters of Charity of St. Joseph founded by St. Elizabeth Ann Seton; first native American sisterhood.

1821: Assumption Cathedral, Baltimore, formally opened.

1829: Oblate Sisters of Providence, a Negro congregation, established at Baltimore.

First Provincial Council of Baltimore held; six others followed, in 1833, 1837, 1840, 1843, 1846 and 1849.

1836: Roger B. Taney appointed Chief Justice of Supreme Court by President Jackson.

1852: First of the three Plenary Councils of Baltimore convened. Subsequent councils were held in 1866 and 1884.

1855: German Catholic Central Verein founded.

1886: Archbishop James Gibbons of Baltimore made cardinal by Pope Leo XIII.

1965: Archbishop Lawrence Shehan of Baltimore made cardinal by Pope Paul VI.

Massachusetts

1630: New England made a prefecture apostolic in charge of French Capuchins.

1647: Massachusetts Bay Company enacted an anti-priest law.

1732: Although Catholics were not legally admitted to colony, a few Irish families were in Boston; a priest was reported working among them.

1755-56: Acadians landing in Boston were denied services of a Catholic priest.

1775: General Washington discouraged Guy Fawkes Day procession in which pope was carried in effigy, and expressed surprise that there were men in his army "so void of common sense as to insult the religious feelings of the Canadians with whom friendship and an alliance are being sought."

1780: The Massachusetts State Constitution granted religious liberty, but required a religious test to hold public office and provided for tax to support Protestant teachers of piety, religion and morality.

1788: First public Mass said in Boston on Nov. 2 by Abbe de la Poterie, first resident priest.

1803: Church of Holy Cross erected in Boston with financial aid given by Protestants headed by John Adams.

1808: Boston diocese established.

1831: Irish Catholic immigration increased.

1832: St. Vincent's Orphan Asylum, oldest charitable institution in Boston, opened by Sisters of Mercy.

1834: Ursuline Convent in Charlestown burned by a Nativist mob.

1843: Holy Cross College founded.

1855: Catholic militia companies disbanded; nunneries' inspection bill passed.

1859: St. Mary's, first parochial school in Boston, opened.

1860: Portuguese Catholics from Azores settled in New Bedford.

1870: Springfield diocese established.

1875: Boston made archdiocese.

1904: Fall River diocese established.

1911: Archbishop O'Connell of Boston made cardinal by Pope Pius X.

1950: Worcester diocese established.

1958: Archbishop Richard J. Cushing of Boston made cardinal by Pope John XXIII.

1966: Apostolic Exarchate for Melkites in the U.S. established, with headquarters in Boston; made an eparchy (Newton) in 1976.

1973: Archbishop Humberto S. Medeiros of Boston made cardinal by Pope Paul VI.

1985: Archbishop Bernard F. Law of Boston made a cardinal by Pope John Paul II.

Michigan

1641: Jesuits Isaac Jogues and Charles Raymbaut preached to Chippewas; named the rapids Sault Sainte Marie.

1660: Jesuit Rene Menard opened first regular mission in Lake Superior region.

1668: Father Marquette founded Sainte Marie Mission at Sault Sainte Marie.

1671: Father Marquette founded St. Ignace Mission at Michilimackinac.

1701: Fort Pontchartrain founded on present site of Detroit and placed in command of Antoine de la Mothe Cadillac. The Chapel of Sainte-Anne-de-Detroit founded.

1706: Franciscan Father Delhalle killed by Indians at Detroit.

1823: Father Gabriel Richard elected delegate to Congress from Michigan territory; he was the first priest chosen for the House of Representatives.

1833: Father Frederic Baraga celebrated first Mass in present Grand Rapids.
Detroit diocese established, embracing whole Northwest Territory.

1843: *Western Catholic Register* founded at Detroit.

1845: St. Vincent's Hospital, Detroit, opened by Sisters of Charity.

1848: Cathedral of Sts. Peter and Paul, Detroit, consecrated.

1853: Vicariate Apostolic of Upper Michigan established.

1857: Sault Ste. Marie diocese established; later transferred to Marquette.

1877: University of Detroit founded.

1882: Grand Rapids diocese established.

1897: Nazareth College for women founded.

1937: Detroit made archdiocese. Lansing diocese established.

1938: Saginaw diocese established.

1946: Archbishop Edward Mooney of Detroit created cardinal by Pope Pius XII.

1949: Opening of St. John's Theological (major) Seminary at Plymouth; this was first seminary in U.S. serving an entire ecclesiastical province (Detroit).

1966: Apostolic Exarchate for Maronites in the United States established, with headquarters in Detroit; made an eparchy in 1972; transferred to Brooklyn, 1977.

1969: Archbishop John Dearden of Detroit made cardinal by Pope Paul VI.

1971: Gaylord and Kalamazoo dioceses established.

1982: Apostolic Exarchate for Chaldean-Rite Catholics in United States established. Detroit designated see city; made an eparchy, 1985, under title St. Thomas Apostle of Detroit.

Minnesota

1680: Falls of St. Anthony discovered by Franciscan Louis Hennepin.

1727: First chapel, St. Michael the Archangel, erected near town of Frontenac and placed in charge of French Jesuits.

1732: Fort St. Charles built; Jesuits ministered to settlers.

1736: Jesuit Jean Pierre Aulneau killed by Indians.

1839: Swiss Catholics from Canada settled near Fort Snelling; Bishop Loras of Dubuque, accompanied by Father Pellamourgues, visited the Fort and administered sacraments.

1841: Father Lucian Galtier built Church of St. Paul, thus forming nucleus of modern city of same name.

1850: St. Paul diocese established.

1851: Sisters of St. Joseph arrived in state.

1857: St. John's University founded.

1888: St. Paul made archdiocese; name changed to St. Paul and Minneapolis in 1966.

1889: Duluth, St. Cloud and Winona dioceses established.

1909: Crookston diocese established.

1957: New Ulm diocese established.

Mississippi

1540: Chaplains with De Soto expedition entered territory.

1682: Franciscans Zenobius Membre and Anastase Douay preached to Taensa and Natchez Indians. Father Membre offered first recorded Mass in the state on Mar. 29, Easter Sunday.

1698: Priests of Quebec Seminary founded missions near Natchez and Fort Adams.

1702: Father Nicholas Foucault murdered by Indians near Fort Adams.

1721: Missions practically abandoned, with only Father Juif working among Yazoos.

1725: Jesuit Mathurin de Petit carried on mission work in northern Mississippi.

1729: Indians tomahawked Jesuit Paul du Poisson near Fort Rosalie; Father Jean Souel shot by Yazoos.

1736: Jesuit Antoine Senat burned at stake by Chickasaws.

1822: Vicariate Apostolic of Mississippi and Alabama established.

1825: Mississippi made a separate vicariate apostolic.

1837: Natchez diocese established; became Natchez-Jackson in 1956; transferred to Jackson in 1977.

1848: Sisters of Charity opened orphan asylum and school in Natchez.

1977: Biloxi diocese established.

Missouri

1700: Jesuit Gabriel Marest established a mission among Kaskaskia Indians near St. Louis.

1734: French Catholic miners and traders settled Old Mines and Sainte Genevieve.

1750: Jesuits visited French settlers.

1762: Mission established at St. Charles.

1767: Carondelet mission established.

1770: First church founded at St. Louis.

1811: Jesuits established Indian mission school at Florissant.

1818: Bishop Dubourg arrived at St. Louis, with Vincentians Joseph Rosati and Felix de Andreis. St. Louis University, the diocesan (Kenrick) seminary and the Vincentian Seminary in Perryville trace their origins to them.

1826: St. Louis diocese established.

1828: Sisters of Charity opened first hospital west of the Mississippi, at St. Louis.

1832: *The Shepherd of the Valley,* first Catholic paper west of the Mississippi.

1845: First conference of Society of St. Vincent de Paul in U.S. founded at St. Louis.

1847: St. Louis made archdiocese.

1865: A Test Oath Law passed by State Legislature (called Drake Convention) to crush Catholicism in Missouri. Law declared unconstitutional by Supreme Court in 1866.

1867: College of St. Teresa for women founded at Kansas City.

1868: St. Joseph diocese established.

1880: Kansas City diocese established.

1946: Archbishop John J. Glennon of St. Louis made cardinal by Pope Pius XII.

1956: Kansas City and St. Joseph dioceses combined into one see. Jefferson City and Springfield-Cape Girardeau dioceses established.

1961: Archbishop Joseph E. Ritter of St. Louis made cardinal by Pope John XXIII.

1969: Archbishop John J. Carberry of St. Louis made cardinal by Pope Paul VI.

Montana

1743: Pierre and Francois Verendrye, accompanied by Jesuit Father Coquart, may have explored territory.

1833: Indian missions handed over to care of Jesuits by Second Provincial Council of Baltimore.

1840: Jesuit Pierre De Smet began missionary work among Flathead and Pend d'Oreille Indians.

1841: St. Mary's Mission established by Father De Smet and two companions on the Bitter Root River in present Stevensville.

1845: Jesuit Antonio Ravalli arrived at St. Mary's Mission; Ravalli County named in his honor.

1859: Fathers Point and Hoecken established St. Peter's Mission near the Great Falls.

1869: Sisters of Charity founded a hospital and school in Helena.

1884: Helena diocese established.

1904: Great Falls diocese established; redesignated Great Falls-Billings in 1980.

1910: Carroll College founded.

1935: Rev. Joseph M. Gilmore became first Montana priest elevated to hierarchy.

Nebraska

1541: Coronado expedition, accompanied by Franciscan Juan de Padilla, reached the Platte River.

1673: Father Marquette visited Nebraska Indians.

1720: Franciscan Juan Miguel killed by Indians near Columbus.

1855: Father J. F. Tracy administered to Catholic settlement of St. Patrick and to Catholics in Omaha.

1856: Land was donated by Governor Alfred Cumming for a church in Omaha.

1857: Nebraska vicariate apostolic established.

1878: Creighton University established.

1881: Poor Clares, first contemplative group in state, arrived in Omaha.

Duchesne College established.

1885: Omaha diocese established.

1887: Lincoln diocese established.

1912: Kearney diocese established; name changed to Grand Island, 1917.

1917: Father Edward Flanagan founded Boy's Town for homeless boys, an institution which gained national and international recognition in subsequent years.

1945: Omaha made archdiocese.

Nevada

1774: Franciscan missionaries passed through Nevada on way to California missions.

1860: First parish, serving Genoa, Carson City and Virginia City, established.

1862: Rev. Patrick Manogue appointed pastor of Virginia City. He established a school for boys and girls, an orphanage and hospital.

1871: Church erected at Reno.

1931: Reno diocese established; name changed to Reno-Las Vegas, 1977.

New Hampshire

1630: Territory made part of a prefecture apostolic embracing all of New England.

1784: State Constitution included a religious test which barred Catholics from public office; local support was provided for public Protestant teachers of religion.

1818: The Barber family of Claremont was visited by their son Virgil (converted to Catholicism in 1816) accompanied by Father Charles Ffrench, O.P. The visit led to the conversion of the entire Barber family.

1823: Father Virgil Barber, minister who became a Jesuit priest, built first Catholic church and school at Claremont.

1830: Church of St. Aloysius dedicated at Dover.

1853: New Hampshire made part of the Portland diocese.

1858: Sisters of Mercy began to teach school at St. Anne's, Manchester.

1877: Catholics obtained full civil liberty and rights.

1884: Manchester diocese established.

1893: St. Anselm's College opened; St. Anselm's Abbey canonically erected.

1937: Francis P. Murphy became first Catholic governor of New Hampshire.

New Jersey

1668: William Douglass of Bergen was refused a seat in General Assembly because he was a Catholic.

1672: Fathers Harvey and Gage visited Catholics in Woodbridge and Elizabethtown.

1701: Tolerance granted to all but "papists."

1744: Jesuit Theodore Schneider of Pennsylvania visited German Catholics of New Jersey.

1762: Fathers Ferdinand Farmer and Robert Harding working among Catholics in state.

1765: First Catholic community organized in New Jersey at Macopin in Passaic County.

1776: State Constitution tacitly excluded Catholics from office.

1799: Foundation of first Catholic school in state, St. John's at Trenton.

1814: First church in Trenton erected.

1820: Father Richard Bulger, of St. John's, Paterson, first resident pastor in state.

1844: Catholics obtained full civil liberty and rights.

1853: Newark diocese established.

1856: Seton Hall University established.

1878: John P. Holland, teacher at St. John's School, Paterson, invented first workable submarine.

1881: Trenton diocese established.

1937: Newark made archdiocese. Paterson and Camden dioceses established.

1947: U.S. Supreme Court ruled on N.J. bus case, permitting children attending non-public schools to ride on buses and be given other health services provided for those in public schools.

1957: Seton Hall College of Medicine and Dentistry established: the first medical school in state; it was run by Seton Hall until 1965.

1963: Byzantine Eparchy of Passaic established.

1981: Metuchen diocese established.

New Mexico

1539: Territory explored by Franciscan Marcos de Niza.

1581: Franciscans Agustin Rodriguez, Juan de Santa Maria and Francisco Lopez named the region "New Mexico"; they later died at hands of Indians.

1598: Juan de Onate founded a colony at Chamita, where first chapel in state was built.

1609-10: Santa Fe founded.

1631: Franciscan Pedro de Miranda was killed by Indians.

1632: Franciscan Francisco Letrado was killed by Indians.

1672: Franciscan Pedro de Avila y Ayala was killed by Indians.

1675: Franciscan Alonso Gil de Avila was killed by Indians.

1680: Pueblo Indian revolt; 21 Franciscan missionaries massacred; missions destroyed.

1692: Franciscan missions refounded and expanded.

1696: Indians rebelled, five more Franciscan missionaries killed.

1850: Jean Baptiste Lamy appointed head of newly established Vicariate Apostolic of New Mexico.

1852: Sisters of Loretto arrived in Santa Fe.

1853: Santa Fe diocese established.

1859: Christian Brothers arrived, established first school for boys in New Mexico (later St. Michael's College).

1865: Sisters of Charity started first orphanage and hospital in Santa Fe. It was closed in 1966.

1875: Santa Fe made archdiocese.

1939: Gallup diocese established.

1982: Las Cruces diocese established.

New York

1524: Giovanni da Verrazano was first white man to enter New York Bay.

1642: Jesuits Isaac Jogues and Rene Goupil were mutilated by Mohawks; Rene Goupil was killed by them shortly afterwards. Dutch Calvinists rescued Father Jogues.

1646: Jesuit Isaac Jogues and John Lalande were martyred by Iroquois at Ossernenon, now Auriesville.

1654: The Onondagas were visited by Jesuits from Canada.

1655: First permanent mission established near Syracuse.

1656: Church of St. Mary erected on Onondaga Lake, in first French settlement within state.

Kateri Tekakwitha, "Lily of the Mohawks," was born at Ossernenon, now Auriesville (d. in Canada, 1680). She was beatified in 1980.

1658: Indian uprisings destroyed missions among Cayugas, Senecas and Oneidas.

1664: English took New Amsterdam. Freedom of conscience allowed by the Duke of York, the new Lord Proprietor.

1667: Missions were restored under protection of Garaconthie, Onondaga chief.

1678: Franciscan Louis Hennepin, first white man to describe Niagara Falls, celebrated Mass there.

1682: Thomas Dongan appointed governor by Duke of York.

1683: English Jesuits came to New York, later opened a school.

1700: Although Assembly enacted a bill calling for religious toleration of all Christians in 1683, other penal laws were now enforced against Catholics; all priests were ordered out of the province.

1709: French Jesuit missionaries obliged to give up their central New York missions.

1741: Because of an alleged popish plot to burn city of New York, four whites were hanged and 11 blacks burned at stake.

1774: Elizabeth Bayley Seton, foundress of the American Sisters of Charity, was born in New York City on Aug. 28. She was canonized in 1975.

1777: State Constitution gave religious liberty, but the naturalization law required an oath to renounce allegiance to any foreign ruler, ecclesiastical as well as civil.

1785: Cornerstone was laid for St. Peter's Church, New York City, first permanent structure of Catholic worship in state.

Trusteeism began to cause trouble at New York.

1806: Anti-Catholic 1777 Test Oath for naturalization repealed.

1808: New York diocese established.

1828: New York State Legislature enacted a law upholding sanctity of seal of confession.

1834: First native New Yorker to become a secular priest, Rev. John McCloskey, was ordained.

1836: John Nepomucene Neumann arrived from Bohemia and was ordained a priest in Old St. Patrick's Cathedral, New York City. He was canonized in 1977.

1841: Fordham University and Manhattanville College established.

1847: Albany and Buffalo dioceses established.

1850: New York made archdiocese.

1853: Brooklyn diocese established.

1856: Present St. Bonaventure University and Christ the King Seminary founded at Allegany.

1858: Cornerstone was laid of second (present) St. Patrick's Cathedral, New York City. The cathedral was completed in 1879.

1868: Rochester diocese established.

1872: Ogdensburg diocese established.

1875: Archbishop John McCloskey of New York made first American cardinal by Pope Pius IX.

1878: Franciscan Sisters of Allegany were first native American community to send members to foreign missions.

1880: William R. Grace was first Catholic mayor of New York City.

1886: Syracuse diocese established.

1889: Mother Frances Xavier Cabrini arrived in New York City to begin work among Italian immigrants. She was canonized in 1946.

1911: Archbishop John M. Farley of New York made cardinal by Pope Pius X.

Catholic Foreign Mission Society of America (Maryknoll) opened a seminary for foreign missions, the first of its kind in U.S. The Maryknollers were also unique as the first U.S.-established foreign mission society.

1917: Military Ordinariate established with headquarters at New York; transferred to Washington, D.C., in 1985.

1919: Alfred E. Smith became first elected Catholic governor.

1924: Archbishop Patrick Hayes of New York made cardinal by Pope Pius XI.

1930: Jesuit Martyrs of New York and Canada were canonized on June 29.

1946: Archbishop Francis J. Spellman of New York made cardinal by Pope Pius XII.

1957: Rockville Centre diocese established.

1969: Archbishop Terence Cooke of New York made cardinal by Pope Paul VI.

1981: Apostolic Exarchate for Armenian-Rite Catholics in the United States and Canada established. New York designated see city.

1985: Archbishop John J. O'Connor of New York made cardinal by Pope John Paul II.

North Carolina

1526: The Ayllon expedition attempted to establish a settlement on Carolina coast.

1540: De Soto expedition, accompanied by chaplains, entered state.

1776: State Constitution denied office to "those who denied the truths of the Protestant religion."

1805: The few Catholics in state were served by visiting missionaries.

1821: Bishop John England of Charleston celebrated Mass in the ballroom of the home of William Gaston at New Bern, marking the start of organization of the first parish, St. Paul's, in the state.

1835: William Gaston, State Supreme Court Justice, succeeded in having the article denying religious freedom repealed.

1852: First Catholic church erected in Charlotte.

1868: North Carolina vicariate apostolic established.

Catholics obtained full civil liberty and rights.

1874: Sisters of Mercy arrived, opened an academy, several schools, hospitals and an orphanage.

1876: Benedictine priory and school (later Belmont Abbey College) founded at Belmont; priory designated an abbey in 1884.

1910: Belmont Abbey established as an abbacy nullius; abbacy nullius status suppressed in 1977.

1924: Raleigh diocese established.

1971: Charlotte diocese established.

North Dakota

1742: Pierre and Francois Verendrye, accompanied by Jesuit Father Coquart, explored territory.

1818: Canadian priests ministered to Catholics in area.

1840: Jesuit Father De Smet made first of several trips among Mandan and Gros Ventre Indians.

1848: Father George Belcourt, first American resident priest in territory, reestablished Pembina Mission.

1874: Grey Nuns arrived at Fort Totten to conduct a school.

1889: Jamestown diocese established; transferred to Fargo in 1897.

1893: Benedictines founded St. Gall Monastery at Devil's Lake. (It was moved to Richardton in 1899 and became an abbey in 1903.)

1909: Bismarck diocese established.

1959: Archbishop Aloysius J. Muench, bishop of Fargo, made cardinal by Pope John XXIII.

Ohio

1749: Jesuits in expedition of Céleron de Blainville preached to Indians.

First religious services were held within present limits of Ohio. Jesuit Joseph de Bonnecamps celebrated Mass at mouth of Little Miami River and in other places.

1751: First Catholic settlement founded among Huron Indians near Sandusky by Jesuit Father de la Richardie.

1790: Benedictine Pierre Didier ministered to French immigrants.

1812: Bishop Flaget of Bardstown visited and baptized Catholics of Lancaster and Somerset Counties.

1818: Dominican Father Edward Fenwick (later first bishop of Cincinnati) built St. Joseph's Church and established first Dominican convent in Ohio.

1821: Cincinnati diocese established.

1831: Xavier University founded.

1843: Members of Congregation of Most Precious Blood arrived in Cincinnati from Switzerland.

1845: Cornerstone laid for St. Peter's Cathedral, Cincinnati.

1847: Cleveland diocese established.

1850: Cincinnati made archdiocese.

Marianists opened St. Mary's Institute, now University of Dayton.

1865: Sisters of Charity opened hospital in Cleveland, first institution of its kind in city.

1868: Columbus diocese established.

1871: Ursuline College for women opened at Cleveland.

1910: Toledo diocese established.

1935: Archbishop John T. McNicholas, O.P., founded the Institutum Divi Thomae in Cincinnati for fundamental research in natural sciences.

1943: Youngstown diocese established.

1944: Steubenville diocese established.

1969: Byzantine Rite Eparchy of Parma (for Ruthenians) established.

1982: Apostolic Exarchate for Romanian Byzantine-Rite Catholics in the United States established. Canton designated see city.

1983: Byzantine Rite Eparchy of Saint Josaphat in Parma (for Ukrainians) established.

Oklahoma

1540: De Soto expedition, accompanied by chaplains, explored territory.

1541: Coronado expedition, accompanied by Franciscan Juan de Padilla, explored state.

1630: Spanish Franciscan Juan de Salas labored among Indians.

1700: Scattered Catholic families were visited by priests from Kansas and Arkansas.

1874: First Catholic church built by Father Smyth at Atoka.

1876: Prefecture Apostolic of Indian Territory established with Benedictine Isidore Robot as its head.

1886: First Catholic day school for Choctaw and white children opened by Sisters of Mercy at Krebs.

1891: Vicariate Apostolic of Oklahoma and Indian Territory established.

1905: Oklahoma diocese established; title changed to Oklahoma City and Tulsa, 1930.

1917: Benedictine Heights College for women founded.

Carmelite Sisters of St. Theresa of the Infant Jesus founded at Oklahoma City.

1972: Oklahoma City made archdiocese. Tulsa diocese established.

Oregon

1603: Vizcaino explored northern Oregon coast.

1774: Franciscan missionaries accompanied Juan Perez on his expedition to coast, and Heceta a year later.

1811: Catholic Canadian trappers and traders with John J. Astor expedition founded first American settlement — Astoria.

1834: Indian missions in Northwest entrusted to Jesuits by Holy See.

1838: Abbe Blanchet appointed vicar general to Bishop of Quebec with jurisdiction over area which included Oregon Territory.

1839: First Mass celebrated at present site of St. Paul.

1843: Oregon vicariate apostolic established.

St. Joseph's College for boys opened.

1844: Jesuit Pierre de Smet established Mission of St. Francis Xavier near St. Paul.

Sisters of Notre Dame de Namur, first to enter Oregon, opened an academy for girls.

1846: Vicariate made an ecclesiastical province with Bishop Blanchet as first Archbishop of Oregon City (now Portland).

Walla Walla diocese established; suppressed in 1853.

1847: First priest was ordained in Oregon.

1848: First Provincial Council of Oregon.

1857: Death of Dr. John McLoughlin, "Father of Oregon."

1865: Rev. H. H. Spalding, a Protestant missionary, published the Whitman Myth to hinder work of Catholic missionaries.

1874: Catholic Indian Mission Bureau established.

1875: St. Vincent's Hospital, first in state, opened at Portland.

1903: Baker diocese established.

1922: Anti-private school bill sponsored by Scottish Rite Masons was passed by popular vote, 115,506 to 103,685.

1925: U.S. Supreme Court declared Oregon anti-private school bill unconstitutional.

1953: First Trappist monastery on West Coast established in Willamette Valley north of Lafayette.

Pennsylvania

1673: Priests from Maryland ministered to Catholics in the Colony.

1682: Religious toleration was extended to members of all faiths.

1729: Jesuit Joseph Greaton became first resident missionary of Philadelphia.

1734: St. Joseph's Church, first Catholic church in Philadelphia, was opened by Father Greaton.

1741: Jesuit Fathers Schneider and Wappeler ministered to German immigrants.

Conewego Chapel, a combination chapel and dwelling, was built by Father William Wappeler, S.J., a priest sent to minister to the German Catholic immigrants who settled in the area in the 1730's.

1782: St. Mary's Parochial School opened at Philadelphia.

1788: Holy Trinity Church, Philadelphia, was incorporated; first exclusively national church organized in U.S.

1797: Augustinian Matthew Carr founded St. Augustine parish, Philadelphia.

1799: Prince Demetrius Gallitzin (Father Augustine Smith) built church in western Pennsylvania, at Loretto.

1808: Philadelphia diocese established.

1814: St. Joseph's Orphanage was opened at Philadelphia; first Catholic institution for children in U.S.

1842: University of Villanova founded by Augustinians.

1843: Pittsburgh diocese established.

1844: Thirteen persons killed, two churches and a school burned in Know-Nothing riots at Philadelphia.

1846: First Benedictine Abbey in New World founded near Latrobe by Father Boniface Wimmer.

1852: Redemptorist John Nepomucene Neumann became fourth bishop of Philadelphia. He was beatified in 1963 and canonized in 1977.

1853: Erie diocese established.

1868: Scranton and Harrisburg dioceses established.

1871: Chestnut Hill College, first for women in state, founded.

1875: Philadelphia made archdiocese.

1901: Altoona-Johnstown diocese established.

1913: Byzantine Rite Apostolic Exarchate of Philadelphia established; became metropolitan see, 1958.

1921: Archbishop Dennis Dougherty made cardinal by Pope Benedict XV.

1924: Byzantine Rite Apostolic Exarchate of Pittsburgh established; made an eparchy in 1963; raised to metropolitan status and transferred to Munhall, 1969; transferred back to Pittsburgh in 1977.

1951: Greensburg diocese established.

1958: Archbishop John O'Hara, C.S.C., of Philadelphia made cardinal by Pope John.

1961: Allentown diocese established.

1967: Archbishop John J. Krol of Philadelphia made cardinal by Pope Paul VI.

1969: Bishop John J. Wright of Pittsburgh made cardinal by Pope Paul VI and transferred to Curia post.

1976: The 41st International Eucharistic Congress, the second held in the U.S., convened in Philadelphia, August 1-8.

1985: Major Archbishop Myroslav Lubachivsky of the Ukrainians, former metropolitan of Byzantine-rite Philadelphia archeparchy (1979-80), made cardinal by Pope John Paul II.

Rhode Island

1663: Colonial Charter granted freedom of conscience.

1719: Laws denied Catholics the right to hold public office.

1829: St. Mary's Church, Pawtucket, was first Catholic church in state.

1837: Parochial schools inaugurated in state.

First Catholic church in Providence was built.

1851: Sisters of Mercy began work in Rhode Island.

1872: Providence diocese established.

1900: Trappists took up residence in state.

1917: Providence College founded.

South Carolina

1569: Jesuit Juan Rogel was the first resident priest in the territory.

1573: First Franciscans arrived in southeastern section.

1606: Bishop Altamirano conducted visitation of area.

1655: Franciscans had two missions among Indians; later destroyed by English.

1697: Religious liberty granted to all except "papists."

1790: Catholics given right to vote.

1820: Charleston diocese established.

1822: Bishop England founded *U.S. Catholic Miscellany,* first Catholic paper of a strictly religious nature in U.S.

1830: Sisters of Our Lady of Mercy, first in state, took up residence at Charleston.

1847: Cornerstone of Cathedral of St. John the Baptist, Charleston, was laid.

1861: Cathedral and many institutions destroyed in Charleston fire.

South Dakota

1842: Father Augustine Ravoux began ministrations to French and Indians at Fort Pierre, Vermilion and Prairie du Chien; printed devotional book in Sioux language the following year.

1867: Parish organized among the French at Jefferson.

1878: Benedictines opened school for Sioux children at Fort Yates.

1889: Sioux Falls diocese established.

1902: Lead diocese established; transferred to Rapid City, 1930.

1950: Mount Marty College for women founded.

1952: Blue Cloud Abbey, first Benedictine foundation in state, was dedicated.

Tennessee

1541: Cross planted on shore of Mississippi by De Soto; accompanying the expedition were Fathers John de Gallegos and Louis De Soto.

1682: Franciscan Fathers Membre and Douay accompanied La Salle to present site of Memphis; may have offered the first Masses in the territory.

1800: Catholics were served by priests from Bardstown, Ky.

1822: Non-Catholics assisted in building church in Nashville.

1837: Nashville diocese established.

1843: Sisters of Charity opened a school for girls in Nashville.

1921: Sisters of St. Dominic opened Siena College for women at Memphis; closed in 1971.

1940: Christian Brothers College founded at Memphis.

1970: Memphis diocese established.

Texas

1541: Missionaries with Coronado expedition probably entered territory.

1553: Dominicans Diego de la Cruz, Hernando Mendez, Juan Ferrer, Brother Juan de Mina killed by Indians.

1675: Bosque-Larios missionary expedition entered region; Father Juan Larios offered first recorded high Mass.

1682: Mission Corpus Christi de Isleta (Ysleta) founded by Franciscans near El Paso, first mission in present-day Texas.

1690: Mission San Francisco de los Tejas founded in east Texas.

1703: Mission San Francisco de Solano founded on Rio Grande; rebuilt in 1718 as San Antonio de Valero or the Alamo.

1717: Franciscan Antonio Margil founded six missions in northeast.

1720: San Jose y San Miguel de Aguayo Mission founded by Fray Antonio Margil de Jesus.

1721: Franciscan Brother Jose Pita killed by Indians at Carnezeria.

1728: Site of San Antonio settled.

1738: Construction of San Fernando Cathedral at San Antonio.

1744: Mission church of the Alamo built.

1750: Franciscan Francisco Xavier was killed by Indians; so were Jose Ganzabal in 1752, and Alonzo Ferrares and Jose San Esteban in 1758.

1793: Mexico secularized missions.

1825: Governments of Cohuila and Texas secularized all Indian missions.

1838-39: Irish priests ministered to settlements of Refugio and San Patricio.

1841: Vicariate of Texas established.

1847: Ursuline Sisters established their first academy in territory at Galveston.

Galveston diocese established.

1852: Oblate Fathers and Franciscans arrived in Galveston to care for new influx of German Catholics.

St. Mary's College founded at San Antonio.

1854: Know-Nothing Party began to stir up hatred against Catholics.

1858: Texas Legislature passed law entitling all schools granting free scholarships and meeting state requirements to share in school fund.

1874: San Antonio diocese established.

Vicariate of Brownsville established.

1881: St. Edward's College founded: became first chartered college in state in 1889.

Sisters of Charity founded Incarnate Word College at San Antonio.

1890: Dallas diocese established; changed to Dallas-Ft. Worth, 1953; made two separate dioceses, 1969.

1912: Corpus Christi diocese established.

1914: El Paso diocese established.

1926: San Antonio made archdiocese. Amarillo diocese established.

1947: Austin diocese established.

1959: Galveston diocese redesignated Galveston-Houston.

1961: San Angelo diocese established.

1965: Brownsville diocese established.

1966: Beaumont diocese established.

1982: Victoria diocese established.

1983: Lubbock diocese established.

Utah

1776: Franciscans Silvestre de Escalante and Atanasio Dominguez reached Utah (Salt) Lake; first white men known to enter the territory.

1858: Jesuit Father De Smet accompanied General Harney as chaplain on expedition sent to settle troubles between Mormons and U.S. Government.

1866: On June 29 Father Edward Kelly offered first Mass in Salt Lake City in Mormon Assembly Hall.

1886: Utah vicariate apostolic established.

1891: Salt Lake City diocese established.

1926: College of St. Mary-of-the-Wasatch for women was founded.

Vermont

1609: Champlain expedition passed through territory.

1666: Captain La Motte built fort and shrine of St.

Anne on Isle La Motte; Sulpician Father Dollier de Casson celebrated first Mass.

1668: Bishop Laval of Quebec (beatified in 1980), administered confirmation in region; this was the first area in northeastern U.S. to receive an episcopal visit.

1710: Jesuits ministered to Indians near Lake Champlain.

1793: Discriminatory measures against Catholics were repealed.

1830: Father Jeremiah O'Callaghan became first resident priest in state.

1853: Burlington diocese established.

1854: Sisters of Charity of Providence arrived to conduct St. Joseph's Orphanage at Burlington.

1904: St. Michael's College founded.

1951: First Carthusian foundation in America established at Whitingham.

Virginia

1526: Dominican Antonio de Montesinos offered first Mass on Virginia soil.

1561: Dominicans visited the coast.

1571: Father John Baptist de Segura and seven Jesuit companions killed by Indians.

1642: Priests outlawed and Catholics denied right to vote.

1689: Capuchin Christopher Plunket was captured and exiled to a coastal island where he died in 1697.

1776: Religious freedom granted.

1791: Father Jean Dubois arrived at Richmond with letters from Lafayette. The House of Delegates was placed at his disposal for celebration of Mass.

1796: A church was built at Alexandria.

1820: Richmond diocese established.

1822: Trusteeism created serious problems in diocese; Bishop Kelly resigned the see.

1848: Sisters of Charity opened an orphan asylum at Norfolk.

1866: School Sisters of Notre Dame and Sisters of Charity opened academies for girls at Richmond.

1974: Arlington diocese established.

Washington

1774: Spaniards explored the region.

1838: Fathers Blanchet and Demers, "Apostles of the Northwest," were sent to territory by archbishop of Quebec.

1840: Cross erected on Whidby Island, Puget Sound.

1843: Vicariate Apostolic of Oregon, including Washington, was established.

1844: Mission of St. Paul founded at Colville. Six Sisters of Notre Dame de Namur began work in area.

1850: Nesqually diocese established; transferred to Seattle, 1907.

1856: Providence Academy, the first permanent Catholic school in the Northwest, was built at Fort Vancouver by Mother Joseph Pariseau of the Sisters of Charity of Providence.

1887: Gonzaga University founded.

1913: Spokane diocese established.

1951: Seattle made archdiocese. Yakima diocese established.

West Virginia

1749: Father Joseph de Bonnecamps, accompanying the Bienville expedition, may have offered first Mass in the territory.

1821: First Catholic church in Wheeling.

1838: Sisters of Charity founded school at Martinsburg.

1848: Visitation Nuns established academy for girls in Wheeling.

1850: Wheeling diocese established; name changed to Wheeling-Charleston, 1974. Wheeling Hospital incorporated, the oldest Catholic charitable institution in territory.

1955: Wheeling College established.

Wisconsin

1661: Jesuit Rene Menard, first known missionary in the territory, was killed or lost in the Black River district.

1665: Jesuit Claude Allouez founded Mission of the Holy Ghost at La Pointe Chegoimegon, now Bayfield; was the first permanent mission in region.

1673: Father Marquette and Louis Joliet traveled from Green Bay down the Wisconsin and Mississippi rivers.

1762: Suppression of Jesuits in French Colonies closed many missions for 30 years.

1843: Milwaukee diocese established.

1853: St. John's Cathedral, Milwaukee, was built.

1864: State charter granted for establishment of Marquette University. First students admitted, 1881.

1868: Green Bay and La Crosse dioceses established.

1875: Milwaukee made archdiocese.

1905: Superior diocese established.

1946: Madison diocese established.

Wyoming

1840: Jesuit Pierre de Smet offered first Mass near Green River.

1851: Father De Smet held peace conference with Indians near Fort Laramie.

1867: Father William Kelly, first resident priest, arrived in Cheyenne and built first church a year later.

1873: Father Eugene Cusson became first resident pastor in Laramie.

1875: Sisters of Charity of Leavenworth opened school and orphanage at Laramie.

1884: Jesuits took over pastoral care of Shoshone and Arapaho Indians.

1887: Cheyenne diocese established.

1949: Weston Memorial Hospital opened near Newcastle.

Puerto Rico

1493: Island discovered by Columbus on his second voyage; he named it San Juan de Borinquen (the Indian name for Puerto Rico).

1509: Juan Ponce de Leon, searching for gold, colonized the island and became its first governor; present population descended mainly from early Spanish settlers.

1511: Diocese of Puerto Rico established as suffragan of Seville, Spain; Bishop Alonso, Manso, sailing from Spain in 1512, became first bishop to take up residence in New World.

1645: Synod held in Puerto Rico to regulate frequency of Masses according to distances people had to walk.

1898: Puerto Rico ceded to U.S. (became self-governing Commonwealth in 1952); inhabitants granted U.S. citizenship in 1917.

1924: Diocese of Puerto Rico renamed San Juan de Puerto Rico and made immediately subject to the Holy See; Ponce diocese established.

1948: Catholic University of Puerto Rico founded at Ponce through efforts of Bishop James E. McManus, C.SS.R., 1947-63.

1960: San Juan made metropolitan see. Arecibo diocese established.

1964: Caguas diocese established.

1973: Archbishop Luis Aponte Martinez of San Juan made first native Puerto Rican cardinal by Pope Paul VI.

1976: Mayaguez diocese established.

Virgin of Providence officially approved as Patroness of Puerto Rico by Pope Paul VI.

CATHOLICS IN PRESIDENTS' CABINETS

Roger B. Taney, Attorney General 1831-33, Secretary of Treasury 1833-34; app. by Andrew Jackson.

James Campbell, Postmaster General 1853-57; app. by Franklin Pierce.

John B. Floyd, Secretary of War 1857-61; app. by James Buchanan.

Joseph McKenna, Attorney General 1897-98; app. by William McKinley.

Robert J. Wynne, Postmaster General 1904-05; app. by Theodore Roosevelt.

Charles Bonaparte, Secretary of Navy 1905-06, Attorney General 1906-09; app. by Theodore Roosevelt.

James A. Farley, Postmaster General 1933-40; app. by Franklin D. Roosevelt.

Frank Murphy, Attorney General 1939-40; app. by Franklin D. Roosevelt.

Frank C. Walker, Postmaster General 1940-45; app. by Franklin D. Roosevelt.

Robert E. Hannegan, Postmaster General 1945-47; app. by Harry S. Truman.

J. Howard McGrath, Attorney General 1949-52; app. by Harry S. Truman.

Maurice J. Tobin, Secretary of Labor; 1949-53; app. by Harry S. Truman.

James P. McGranery, Attorney General 1952-53; app. by Harry S. Truman.

Martin P. Durkin, Secretary of Labor 1953; app. by Dwight D. Eisenhower.

James P. Mitchell, Secretary of Labor 1953-61; app. by Dwight D. Eisenhower.

Robert F. Kennedy, Attorney General 1961-65; app. by John F. Kennedy, reapp. by Lyndon B. Johnson.

Anthony Celebrezze, Secretary of Health, Education and Welfare 1962-65; app. by John F. Kennedy, reapp. by Lyndon B. Johnson.

John S. Gronouski, Postmaster General 1963-65; app. by John F. Kennedy, reapp. by Lyndon B. Johnson.

John T. Connor, Secretary of Commerce 1965-67; app. by Lyndon B. Johnson.

Lawrence O'Brien, Postmaster General 1965-68; app. by Lyndon B. Johnson.

Walter J. Hickel, Secretary of Interior 1969-71; app. by Richard M. Nixon.

John A. Volpe, Secretary of Transportation 1969-72; app. by Richard M. Nixon.

Maurice H. Stans, Secretary of Commerce, 1969-72; app. by Richard M. Nixon.

Peter J. Brennan, Secretary of Labor, 1973-75; app. by Richard M. Nixon, reapp. by Gerald R. Ford.

William E. Simon, Secretary of Treasury, 1974-76; app. by Richard M. Nixon, reapp. by Gerald R. Ford.

Joseph A. Califano, Jr., Secretary of Health, Education and Welfare, 1977-79; app. by Jimmy Carter.

Benjamin Civiletti, Attorney General, 1979-81; app. by Jimmy Carter.

Moon Landrieu, Secretary of Housing and Urban Development, 1979-81; app. by Jimmy Carter.

Edmund S. Muskie, Secretary of State, 1980-81; app. by Jimmy Carter.

Alexander M. Haig, Secretary of State, 1981-82; app. by Ronald Reagan.

Raymond J. Donovan, Secretary of Labor, 1981-84; app. by Ronald Reagan.

Margaret M. Heckler, Secretary of Health and Human Services, 1983-85; app. by Ronald Reagan.

William J. Bennett, Secretary of Education, 1985-; app. by Ronald Reagan.

Men who became Catholics after leaving Cabinet posts: Thomas Ewing, Secretary of Treasury under William A. Harrison, and Secretary of Interior under Zachary Taylor; Luke E. Wright, Secretary of War under Theodore Roosevelt; Albert B. Fall, Secretary of Interior under Warren G. Harding.

CATHOLICS IN STATUARY HALL

Statues of 13 Catholics deemed worthy of national commemoration by the donating states are among those enshrined in National Statuary Hall and other places in the U.S. Capitol. The Hall, formerly the chamber of the House of Representatives, was erected by Act of Congress July 2, 1864.

Donating states, names and years of placement are listed. An asterisk indicates placement of a statue in the Hall itself.

Arizona: Rev. Eusebio Kino, S. J., missionary, 1965.

California: Rev. Junipero Serra, O. F. M.* missionary, 1931.

Hawaii: Father Damien, missionary, 1969.

Illinois: Gen. James Shields, statesman, 1893.

Louisiana: Edward D. White, Justice of the U.S. Supreme Court (1894-1921), 1955.

Maryland: Charles Carroll,* statesman, 1901.

Nevada: Patrick A. McCarran,* statesman, 1960.

New Mexico: Dennis Chavez, statesman, 1966.

(Archbishop Jean B. Lamy, pioneer prelate of Santa Fe, was nominated for Hall honor in 1951.)

North Dakota: John Burke,* U.S. treasurer, 1963.

Oregon: Dr. John McLoughlin, pioneer, 1953.

Washington: Mother Mary Joseph Pariseau, pioneer missionary and humanitarian.

West Virginia: John E. Kenna, statesman, 1901.

Wisconsin: Rev. Jacques Marquette, S.J., missionary, explorer, 1895.

CATHOLIC SUPREME COURT JUSTICES

Roger B. Taney, Chief Justice 1836-64; app. by Andrew Jackson.

Edward D. White, Associate Justice 1894-1910, app. by Grover Cleveland; Chief Justice 1910-21, app. by William H. Taft.

Joseph McKenna, Associate Justice 1898-1925; app. by William McKinley.

Pierce Butler, Associate Justice 1923-39; app. by Warren G. Harding.

Frank Murphy, Associate Justice 1940-49; app. by Franklin D. Roosevelt.

William Brennan, Associate Justice 1956-; app. by Dwight D. Eisenhower.

Antonin Scalia, Associate Justice 1986-; app. by Ronald Reagan.

Fifty-year-old Scalia was nominated June 17, 1986, to take the place of Associate Justice William Rehnquist who was named to succeed retiring Chief Justice Warren Burger. On the completion of required hearings, both nominees were approved by the Senate in September. Scalia, a judge of the U.S. Circuit of Appeals for the District of Columbia since 1982, had been a professor of law at the University of Chicago. He is a graduate of Georgetown University.

Sherman Minton, Associate Justice from 1949 to 1956, became a Catholic several years before his death in 1965.

CHURCH-STATE DECISIONS OF THE SUPREME COURT

(Among sources of this listing of U.S. Supreme Court decisions was *The Supreme Court on Church and State,* Joseph Tussman, editor; Oxford University Press, New York, 1962.)

Terrett v. Taylor, 9 Cranch 43 (1815): The Court declared unconstitutional an act of the Virginia Legislature which denied property rights to Protestant Episcopal churches in the state. Religious corporations, like other corporations, have rights to their property.

Vidal v. Girard's Executors, 2 Howard 205 (1844): The Court upheld the will of Stephen Girard, which barred ministers of any religion from serving as faculty members or visitors in a school he established for orphans.

Watson v. Jones, 13 Wallace 679 (1872): The Court declared that a member of a religious organization may not appeal to secular courts against a decision made by a church tribunal within the area of its competence.

Reynolds v. United States, 98 US 145 (1879): The Court declared, in reference to the Mormon practice of polygamy, that one may not knowingly violate by external practices the law of the land on religious grounds, since such conduct would make the professed doctrines of belief superior to federal or state law. One must keep the external practice of religion within the framework of laws enacted for the common welfare. This was the first decision rendered on the Free Exercise Clause of the First Amendment.

Davis v. Beason, 133 US 333 (1890): The Court upheld the denial of the right of Mormons to vote in Idaho if they refused to sign a registration oath stating that they were not bigamists or polygamists and would not encourage or preach bigamy or polygamy.

Church of Latter-Day Saints v. United States, 136 US 1 (1890): The Court upheld an Act of Congress which annulled the charter of the Corporation of the Church of Jesus Christ of Latter-Day Saints, and declared "forfeited to the government all its real estate except a small portion used exclusively for public worship" (Tussman, *op. cit.,* p. 33). The Court held that the Corporation continually used its power to violate US laws prohibiting polygamy.

Church of the Holy Trinity v. United States, 143 US 457 (1892): The Court declared it is not "a misdemeanor for a church of this country to contract for the services of a Christian minister residing in another nation" (from the text of the decision).

Bradfield v. Roberts, 175 US 291 (1899): The Court denied that an appropriation of government funds for an institution (Providence Hospital, Washington, D.C.) run by Roman Catholic sisters violated the No Establishment Clause of the First Amendment.

Pierce v. Society of Sisters, 268 US 510 (1925): The Court denied that a state can require children to attend public schools only. The Court held that the liberty of the Constitution forbids standardization by such compulsion, and that the parochial schools involved had claims to protection under the Fourteenth Amendment.

Cochran v. Board of Education, 281 US 370 (1930): The Court upheld a Louisiana statute providing textbooks at public expense for children attending public or parochial schools. The Court held that the children and state were beneficiaries of the appropriations, with incidental secondary benefit going to the schools.

United States v. MacIntosh, 283 US 605 (1931): The Court denied that anyone can place allegiance to the will of God above his allegiance to the government, since such a person could make his own interpretation of God's will the decisive test as to whether he would or would not obey the nation's law. The Court stated that the nation, which has a duty to survive, can require citizens to bear arms in its defense.

Hamilton v. Regents of University of California, 293 US 245 (1934): The Court rejected a "claim to exemption from R.O.T.C. based on conscientious objection to war" (Tussman *op. cit.,* p. 64). If such an exemption were allowed, the liberties of the objector might be extended to the point of refusal to pay taxes in furtherance of a war or any other end condemned by his conscience. This would be an undue exaltation of the right of private judgment.

Cantwell v. Connecticut, 310 US 296 (1940): The Court declared that the right to religious freedom is violated by a statute requiring a person to secure a permit from a government official before soliciting money for alleged religious purposes from someone not of his or her sect. Such a practice would constitute censorship of religion.

Minersville School District v. Gobitis, 310 US 586 (1940): The Court upheld the right of a state to require the salute to the national flag from school children, even from those who refused to do so for sincere religious reasons.

Jones v. City of Opelika, 316 US 584 (1942): The court upheld licensing ordinances in three municipalities against "the claim by Jehovah's Witnesses that they interfere with the free exercise of religion" (Tussman, *op. cit.*, p. 91).

Murdock v. Commonwealth of Pennsylvania, 319 US 105 (1943): In a reversal of the decision handed down in Jones v. City of Opelika, the Court declared the licensing unconstitutional since it violated a freedom guaranteed under the First Amendment. The selling of religious literature by traveling preachers does not make evangelism the equivalent of a commercial enterprise taxable by the State.

Jones v. City of Opelika, 316 US 584 105 (1943): The Court declared that the Constitution denies a city the right to control the expression of men's minds and denies also the right of men to win others to their views through a program of taxes levied against such activity.

Douglas v. City of Jeannette, 319 US 157 (1943): The Court again upheld the proselytizing rights of Jehovah's Witnesses, ruling unconstitutional the action of any public authority in regulating or taxing such activity.

West Virginia State Board of Education v. Barnette, 319 US 624 (1943): In a reversal of the decision handed down in Minersville School District v. Gobitis, the Court declared unconstitutional a state statute requiring of all children a salute to the national flag and a pledge of allegiance which a child may consider contrary to sincere religious beliefs.

Prince v. Commonwealth of Massachusetts, 321 US 158 (1944): The Court upheld a "child-labor regulation against the claim that it prevents a child from performing her religious duty" (Tussman, *op. cit.*, p. 170). The Court asserted a general principle that the state has a wide range of power for limiting parental freedom and authority in things affecting the child's welfare.

United States v. Ballard, 322 US 78 (1944): The Court upheld the general principle that "the truth of religious claims is not for secular authority to determine" (Tussman, *op. cit.*, p. 181).

In Re Summers, 325 US 561 (1945): The Court upheld "the denial, to an otherwise qualified applicant, of admission to the bar on the basis of the applicant's religiously motivated 'conscientious scruples against participation in war' " (Tussman, *op. cit.*, p. 192). The petitioner was barred because he could not in good faith take the prescribed oath to support the Constitution of Illinois which required service in the state militia in times of necessity.

Girouard v. United States, 328 US 61 (1946): In a ruling related to that handed down in United States v. MacIntosh, the Court affirmed the opinion that the refusal of an alien to bear arms does not deny him citizenship.

Everson v. Board of Education, 330 US 1 (1947): The Court upheld the constitutionality of a New Jersey statute authorizing free school bus transportation for parochial as well as public school students. The Court expressed the opinion that the benefits of public welfare legislation, included under such bus transportation, do not run contrary to the concept of separation of Church and State.

McCollum v. Board of Education, 333 US 203 (1948): The Court declared unconstitutional a program for releasing children, with parental consent, from public school classes so they could receive religious instruction on public school premises from representatives of their own faiths.

Zorach v. Clauson, 343 US 306 (1952): The Court upheld the constitutionality of a New York statute permitting, on a voluntary basis, the release during school time of students from public school classes for religious instruction given off public school premises.

Kedroff v. St. Nicholas Cathedral, 344 US 94 (1952): The Court ruled against an action of New York in taking "control of St. Nicholas Cathedral away from the Moscow hierarchy" (Tussman, *op. cit.*, p. 292), on the ground that the controversy involved a matter of church government.

Fowler v. Rhode Island, 345 US 67 (1953): The Court upheld the right of a Jehovah's Witness to preach in a public park against a city ordinance which forbade such preaching. The Court held that the ordinance, as construed and applied, discriminated against the Witness and therefore amounted to preferment by the state of other religious groups.

Torcaso v. Watkins, 367 US 488 (1961): The Court declared unconstitutional a Maryland requirement that one must make a declaration of belief in the existence of God as part of the oath of office for notaries public.

McGowan v. Maryland, 81 Sp Ct 1101; **Two Guys from Harrison v. McGinley,** 81 Sp Ct 1135; **Gallagher v. Crown Kosher Super Market,** 81 Sp Ct 1128; **Braunfield v. Brown,** 81 Sp Ct 1144 (1961): The Court ruled that Sunday closing laws do not violate the No Establishment of Religion Clause of the First Amendment, even though the laws were religious in their inception and still have some religious overtones. The Court held that, "as presently written and administered, most of them, at least, are of a secular rather than of a religious character, and that presently they bear no relationship to establishment of religion as those words are used in the Constitution of the United States."

Engel v. Vitale, 370 US 42 (1962): The Court declared that the voluntary recitation in public schools of a prayer composed by the New York

State Board of Regents is unconstitutional on the ground that it violates the No Establishment of Religion Clause of the First Amendment.

Abington Township School District v. Schempp and **Murray v. Curlett,** 83 Sp Ct 1560 (1963): The Court ruled that Bible reading and recitation of the Lord's Prayer in public schools, with voluntary participation by students, are unconstitutional on the ground that they violate the No Establishment of Religion Clause of the First Amendment.

Sherbert v. Verner, 83 A Sp Ct 1790 (1963): The Court ruled that individuals of any religious faith may not, because of their faith or lack of it, be deprived of the benefits of public welfare legislation.

Chamberlin v. Dade County, 83 Sp Ct 1864 (1964): The Court reversed a decision of the Florida Supreme Court concerning the constitutionality of prayer and devotional Bible reading in public schools during the school day, as sanctioned by a state statute which specifically related the practices to a sound public purpose.

Board of Education v. Allen, No. 660 (1968): The Court declared constitutional the New York school book loan law which requires local school boards to purchase books with state funds and lend them to parochial and private school students.

Flast v. Cohen, No. 416 (1968): The Court held that individual taxpayers can bring suits to challenge federal expenditures on grounds that they violate the principle of separation of Church and State even though generally taxpayers cannot challenge federal expenditures in court.

Walz v. Tax Commission of New York (1970): The Court upheld the constitutionality of a New York statute exempting church-owned property from taxation.

Earle v. DiCenso, Robinson v. DiCenso, Lemon v. Kurtzman, Tilton v. Richardson (1971): In Earle v. DiCenso and Robinson v. DiCenso, the Court ruled unconstitutional a 1969 Rhode Island statute which provided salary supplements to teachers of secular subjects in parochial schools; in Lemon v. Kurtzman, the Court ruled unconstitutional a 1968 Pennsylvania statute which authorized the state to purchase services for the teaching of secular subjects in nonpublic schools. The principal argument against constitutionality in these cases was that the statutes and programs at issue entailed excessive entanglement of government with religion. In Tilton v. Richardson, the Court held that this argument did not apply to a prohibitive degree with respect to federal grants, under the Higher Education Facilities Act of 1963, for the construction of facilities for nonreligious purposes by four church-related institutions of higher learning, three of which were Catholic, in Connecticut.

Amish Decision (1972): In a case appealed on behalf of Yoder, Miller and Yutzy, the Court ruled that Amish parents were exempt from a Wisconsin statute requiring them to send their children to school until the age of 16. The Court said in its decision that secondary schooling exposed Amish children to attitudes, goals and values contrary to their beliefs, and substantially hindered "the religious development of the Amish child and his integration into the way of life of the Amish faith-community at the crucial adolescent state of development."

Committee for Public Education and Religious Liberty, et al., v. Nyquist, et al., No. 72-694 (1973): The Court ruled that provisions of a 1972 New York statute were unconstitutional on the grounds that they were violative of the No Establishment Clause of the First Amendment and had the "impermissible effect" of advancing the sectarian activities of church-affiliated schools. The programs ruled unconstitutional concerned: (1) maintenance and repair grants, for facilities and equipment, to ensure the health, welfare and safety of students in nonpublic, non-profit elementary and secondary schools serving a high concentration of students from low income families; (2) tuition reimbursement ($50 per grade school child, $100 per high school student) for parents (with income less than $5,000) of children attending nonpublic elementary or secondary schools; tax deduction from adjusted gross income for parents failing to qualify under the above reimbursement plan, for each child attending a nonpublic school.

Sloan, Treasurer of Pennsylvania, et al., v. Lemon, et al., No. 72-459 (1973): The Court ruled unconstitutional a Pennsylvania Parent Reimbursement Act for Nonpublic Education which provided funds to reimburse parents (to a maximum of $150) for a portion of tuition expenses incurred in sending their children to nonpublic schools. The Court held that there was no significant difference between this and the New York tuition reimbursement program (above), and declared that the Equal Protection Clause of the Fourteenth Amendment cannot be relied upon to sustain a program held to be violative of the No Establishment Clause.

Levitt, et al., v. Committee for Public Education and Religious Liberty, et al., No. 72-269 (1973): The Court ruled unconstitutional the Mandated Services Act of 1970 under which New York provided $28 million ($27 per pupil from first to seventh grade, $45 per pupil from seventh to 12th grade) to reimburse nonpublic schools for testing, recording and reporting services required by the state. The Court declared that the act provided "impermissible aid" to religion in contravention of the No Establishment Clause.

In related decisions handed down June 25, 1973, the Court: (1) affirmed a lower court decision against the constitutionality of an Ohio tax credit law benefiting parents with children in nonpublic schools; (2) reinstated an injunction against a parent reimbursement program in New Jersey; (3) affirmed South Carolina's right to grant construction loans to church-affiliated colleges, and dismissed an appeal contesting its right to provide loans to students attending church-affiliated colleges (**Hunt v. McNair, Durham v. McLeod**).

Wheeler v. Barrera (1974): The Court ruled that nonpublic school students in Missouri must share in federal funds for educationally deprived students on a comparable basis with public school students under Title I of the Elementary and Secondary Education Act of 1965.

Norwood v. Harrison (93 S. Ct. 2804): The Court ruled that public assistance which avoids the prohibitions of the "effect" and "entanglement" tests (and which therefore does not substantially promote the religious mission of sectarian schools) may be confined to the secular functions of such schools.

Wiest v. Mt. Lebanon School District (1974): The Court upheld a lower court ruling that invocation and benediction prayers at public high school commencement ceremonies do not violate the principle of separation of Church and state.

Meek v. Pittenger (1975): The Court ruled unconstitutional portions of a Pennsylvania law providing auxiliary services for students of nonpublic schools; at the same time, it ruled in favor of provisions of the law permitting textbook loans to students of such schools. In denying the constitutionality of auxiliary services, the Court held that they had the "primary effect of establishing religion" and involved "excessive entanglement" of Church and state officials with respect to supervision; objection was also made against providing such services only on the premises of non-public schools and only at the request of such schools.

Roemer v. Board of Public Works of Maryland, 96 S. Ct. 2337 (1976): The Court ruled that a Maryland statute which authorized state funds to any private institution meeting certain minimal criteria was constitutional. The Court said the statute met the test previously outlined in Lemon v. Kurtzman because the colleges were not pervasively sectarian and the aid was in fact intended only for secular purposes.

Serbian Eastern Orthodox Diocese v. Milivojevich, 96 S. Ct. 2372 (1976): The Court held unconstitutional the decision of the Illinois Supreme Court that the Serbian Orthodox Church had arbitrarily removed one of its bishops and that its reorganization of the diocese was beyond the power of the church. The Court declared that the First Amendment does not permit civil courts to make ecclesiastical decisions.

TWA, Inc., v. Hardison, 75-1126; **International Association of Machinists and Aero Space Workers v. Hardison,** 75-1385 (1977): The Court ruled that federal civil rights legislation does not require employers to make more than minimal efforts to accommodate employees who want a particular working day off as their religion's Sabbath Day, and that an employer cannot accommodate such an employee by violating seniority systems determined by a union collective bargaining agreement. The Court noted that its ruling was not a constitutional judgment but an interpretation of existing law.

Wolman v. Walter (1977): The Court ruled constitutional portions of an Ohio statute providing tax-paid textbook loans and some auxiliary services (standardized and diagnostic testing, therapeutic and remedial services, off school premises) for nonpublic school students. It decided that other portions of the law, providing state funds for nonpublic school field trips and instructional materials (audio-visual equipment, maps, tape recorders), were unconstitutional.

Clergymen (1978): The Court struck down the last state ban against the holding of public office by clergymen, nullifying the 182-year-old provision of the Tennessee constitution which held that involvement in politics might affect the clergy's "dedication to God and the care of souls."

Lay Teachers (1979): The Court ruled that lay teachers in church-related schools are not covered by the National Labor Relations Act. The decision was based, not on church-state grounds, but on the lack of any affirmative decision of the Congress to include such teachers in coverage of the law.

Church Property (1979): The Court ruled, in Jones v. Wolf, that civil courts are not always bound to yield to decisions of church courts in settling local church property disputes.

Parochiaid (1979): The Court decided, in Byrne v. Public Funds for Public Schools, against the constitutionality of a 1976 New Jersey law providing state income tax deductions for tuition paid by parents of students attending parochial and other private schools.

Religious Belief v. Union (1979): The Court supported the claim of a San Diego man that his right to religious freedom was violated when he was fired from his job because his Seventh Day Adventist beliefs prevented him from belonging to a union.

Student Bus Transportation (1979): The Court upheld a Pennsylvania law providing bus transportation at public expense for students to non-public schools up to 10 miles away from the boundaries of the public school districts in which they lived.

Reimbursement (1980): The Court upheld the constitutionality of a 1974 New York law providing direct cash payment to non-public schools for the costs of state-mandated testing and record-keeping.

Solicitation of Funds (1980): The Court struck down a Schaumburg, Ill., ordinance permitting the solicitation of funds only by groups spending a specific percentage of their funds for charitable purposes.

Remedial Teaching (1980): The Court refused to hear an appeal from a lower court ruling in support of a New York law permitting the use of federal funds to pay for remedial teaching in non-public schools.

Ten Commandments (1980): The Court struck down a 1978 Kentucky law requiring the posting of the Ten Commandments in public school classrooms in the state.

Christmas Carols (1980): The Court refused to hear an appeal from a lower court ruling permitting the singing of Christmas carols in public school holiday programs in Sioux City, S.D.

Highway Prayer (1981): The Court ruled that North Carolina could not publish a prayer for highway safety on official state maps.

Unemployment Benefits (1981): The Court decided, in Thomas v. Review Board, that a worker who, for religious reasons, quits his job rather than help to produce armaments cannot be denied state unemployment benefits.

Unemployment Taxes (1981): The Court ruled, in St. Martin Evangelical Lutheran Church v. South Dakota, that church-run schools do not have to pay state unemployment compensation taxes for their employees, because the relevant 1976 law did not "reveal any clear intent to repeal" their tax-exempt status.

Campus Worship (1981): The Court ruled, in Widmar v. Vincent, that the University of Missouri at Kansas City could not deny student religious groups the use of campus facilities for worship services. The Court also, in Brandon v. Board of Education of Guilderland Schools, declined without comment to hear an appeal for reversal of lower court decisions denying a group of New York high school students the right to meet for prayer on public school property before the beginning of the school day.

Americans United (1982): The Court ruled that Americans United for the Separation of Church and State did not have legal standing to challenge in court the transfer of government property to a Protestant college in Pennsylvania.

Social Security Taxes (1982): The Court ruled that Amish businessmen must pay Social Security taxes for their employees even if such payments violate their religious beliefs.

Unification Church (1982): The Court struck down a Minnesota law, aimed at the Unification Church, which required detailed financial reports from religious groups which raise more than half of their funds from non-members.

No Meeting on Public School Property (1983): By refusing to hear an appeal in Lubbock v. Lubbock Civil Liberties Union, the Court upheld a lower court ruling against a public policy of permitting student religious groups to meet on public school property before and after school hours.

Tuition Tax Deduction (1983): In Mueller v. Allen, the Court upheld a Minnesota law allowing parents of students in public and non-public (including parochial) schools to take a tax deduction for the expenses of tuition, textbooks and transportation. Maximum allowable deductions were $500 per child in elementary school and $700 per child in grades seven through 12.

Pay for Chaplain (1983): The Court ruled in Marsh v. Chambers that it was not against the Constitution for the Nebraska Legislature to pay a chaplain to open each day's session with a prayer.

Christmas Nativity Scene (1984): The Court ruled 5-to-4 in Lynch v. Donnelly that the First Amendment does not mandate "complete separation of church and state," and that, therefore, the sponsorship of a Christmas nativity scene by the City of Pawtucket, R.I., was not unconstitutional. The case involved a scene included in a display of Christmas symbols sponsored by the city in a park owned by a non-profit group. The majority opinion said "the Constitution (does not) require complete separation of church and state; it affirmatively mandates accommodation, not merely tolerance, of all religions and forbids hostility toward any. Anything less" would entail callous indifference not intended by the Constitution. Moreover, "such hostility would bring us into 'war with our national

tradition as embodied in the First Amendment's guaranty of the free exercise of religion.' " (The additional quotation was from the 1948 decision in McCollum v. Board of Education.)

Christmas Nativity Scene (1985): The Court upheld a lower court ruling that the Village of Scarsdale, N.Y., must make public space available for the display of privately sponsored nativity scenes.

Wallace v. Jaffree, No. 83-812 (1985): The Court ruled against the constitutionality of a 1981 Alabama law calling for a public-school moment of silence that specifically included optional prayer.

Thornton v. Caldor, No. 83-1158 (1985): The Court ruled against the validity of a Connecticut law providing employees an unqualified right not to work on the Sabbath of their choice.

Grand Rapids v. Ball, No. 83-990, and **Aguilar v. Felton**, No. 84-237 (1985): The Court ruled against the constitutionality of programs in Grand Rapids and New York City allowing public school teachers to teach remedial entitlement subjects (under the Elementary and Secondary Education Act of 1965) in private schools, many of which were Catholic.

Alamo Foundation v. Secretary of Labor, No. 83-1935 (1985): The Court ruled that religious organizations running commercial businesses must pay employees the minimum wage.

CHURCH TAX EXEMPTION

The exemption of church-owned property was ruled constitutional by the U.S. Supreme Court May 4, 1970, in the case of Walz v. The Tax Commission of New York.

Suit in the case was brought by Frederick Walz, who purchsed in June, 1967, a 22-by-29-foot plot of ground in Staten Island valued at $100 and taxable at $5.24 a year. Shortly after making the purchase, Walz instituted a suit in New York State, contending that the exemption of church property from taxation authorized by state law increased his own tax rate and forced him indirectly to support churches in violation of his constitutional right to freedom of religion under the First Amendment. Three New York courts dismissed the suit, which had been instituted by mail. The Supreme Court, judging that it had probable jurisdiction, then took the case.

In a 7-1 decison affecting church-state relations in every state in the nation, the Court upheld the New York law under challenge.

FOR AND AGAINST

Chief Justice Warren E. Burger, who wrote the majority opinion, said that Congress from its earliest days had viewed the religion clauses of the Constitution as authorizing statutory real estate tax exemption to religious bodies. He declared: "Nothing in this national attitude toward religious tolerance and two centuries of uninterrupted freedom from taxation has given the remotest sign of leading to an established church or religion, and on the contrary it has operated affirmatively to help guarantee the free exercise of all forms of religious beliefs."

Justice William O. Douglas wrote in dissent

that the involvement of government in religion as typified in tax exemption may seem inconsequential but: "It is, I fear, a long step down the establishment path. . . . Perhaps I have been misinformed. But, as I read the Constitution and the philosophy, I gathered that independence was the price of liberty."

Burger rejected Douglas' "establishment" fears. If tax exemption is the first step toward establishment, he said, "the second step has been long in coming."

The basic issue centered on the following question: Is there a contradiction between federal constitutional provisions against the establishment of religion, or the use of public funds for religious purposes, and state statutes exempting church property from taxation?

In the Walz' decision, the Supreme Court ruled that there is no contradiction.

Legal Background

The U.S. Constitution makes no reference to tax exemption.

There was no discussion of the issue in the Constitutional Convention nor in debates on the Bill of Rights.

In the Colonial and post-Revolutionary years, some churches had established status and were state-supported. This state of affairs changed with enactment of the First Amendment, which laid down no-establishment as the federal norm. This norm was adopted by the states which, however, exempted churches from tax liabilities.

No establishment, no hindrance, was the early American view of Church-state relationships.

This view, reflected in custom law, was not generally formulated in statute law until the second half of the 19th century, although specific tax exemption was provided for churches in Maryland in 1798, in Virginia in 1800, and in North Carolina in 1806.

The first major challenge to church property exemption was initiated by the Liberal League in the 1870s. It reached the point that President Grant included the recommendation in a State of the Union address in 1875, stating that church property should bear its own proportion of taxes. The plea fell on deaf ears in Congress, but there was some support for the idea at state levels. The exemption, however, continued to survive various challenges.

About 36 state constitutions contain either mandatory or permissive provisions for exemption.

THE WALL OF SEPARATION

Thomas Jefferson, in a letter written to the Danbury (Conn.) Baptist Association Jan. 1, 1802, coined the metaphor, "a wall of separation between Church and State," to express a theory concerning interpretation of the religion clauses of the First Amendment: "Congress shall make no law respecting an establishment of religion or prohibiting the free exercise thereof."

The metaphor was cited for the first time in judicial proceedings in 1879, in the opinion by Chief Justice Waite in Reynolds v. United States. It did not, however, figure substantially in the decision.

In 1947 the wall of separation gained acceptance as a constitutional rule, in the decision handed down in Everson v. Board of Education. Associate Justice Black, in describing the principles involved in the No Establishment Clause, wrote:

"Neither a state nor the Federal Government can set up a church. Neither can pass laws which aid one religion, aid all religions, or prefer one religion over another. Neither can force nor influence a person to go to or to remain away from church against his will or force him to profess a belief or disbelief in any religion. No person can be punished for entertaining or professing religious beliefs or disbeliefs, for church attendance or nonattendance. No tax in any amount, large or small, can be levied to support any religious activities or institutions, whatever they may be called, or whatever form they may adopt to teach or practice religion. Neither a state nor the Federal Government can, openly or secretly, participate in the affairs of any religious organizations or groups and vice versa. In the words of Jefferson, the clause against establishment of religion by law was intended to erect 'a wall of separation between Church and State.' "

Mr. Black's associates agreed with his statement of principles, which were framed without reference to the Freedom of Exercise Clause. They disagreed, however, with respect to application of the principles, as the split decision in the case indicated. Five members of the Court held that the benefits of public welfare legislation — in this case, free bus transportation to school for parochial as well as public school students — did not run contrary to the concept of separation of Church and State embodied in the First Amendment.

Inside and outside the legal profession, opinion is divided concerning the wall of separation and the balance of the religion clauses of the First Amendment.

The view of absolute separationists, carried to the extreme, would make government the adversary of religion. The bishops of the United States, following the McCollum decision in 1948, said that the wall metaphor had become for some persons the "shibboleth of doctrinaire secularism."

Proponents of governmental neutrality toward religion are of the opinion that such neutrality should not be so interpreted as to prohibit incidental aid to religious institutions providing secular services.

1986 DECISIONS

Bender v. Williamsport Area School District (1986): Ruling on a procedural question that avoided a First Amendment dispute, the Court let stand a federal court decision allowing a public high school student Bible study group the same "equal access" to school facilities as other extracurricular clubs.

Witters v. Washington, No. 84-1070 (1986): The Court ruled that the First Amendment does not necessarily forbid the use of state vocational rehabilitation money to finance religious studies by a partially blind student at a Christian college.

The organizational structure of the Catholic Church in the United States consists of 33 provinces with as many archdioceses (metropolitan sees); 147 suffragan sees (dioceses); three Eastern-Rite jurisdictions immediately subject to the Holy See — the eparchies of St. Maron (Maronites), Newton (Melkites) and St. Thomas Apostle of Detroit (Chaldeans); one apostolic exarchate (for Romanians of Byzantine Rite) and the Military Archdiocese. An Armenian-Rite apostolic exarchate for the United States and Canada has its seat in New York. Each of these jurisdictions is under the direction of an archbishop or bishop, called an ordinary, who has apostolic responsibility and authority for the pastoral service of the people in his care.

The structure includes the territorial episcopal conference known as the National Conference of Catholic Bishops. In and through this body, which is strictly ecclesiastical and has defined juridical authority, the bishops exercise their collegiate pastorate over the Church in the entire country (see Index).

Related to the NCCB is the United States Catholic Conference, a civil corporation and operational secretariat through which the bishops, in cooperation with other members of the Church, act on a wider-than-ecclesiastical scale for the good of the Church and society in the United States (see Index).

The representative of the Holy See to the Church in this country is an Apostolic Pro-Nuncio.

ECCLESIASTICAL PROVINCES

(Sources: *The Official Catholic Directory,* NC News Service.)

The 33 ecclesiastical provinces bear the names of archdioceses, i.e., of metropolitan sees.

Anchorage: Archdiocese of Anchorage and suffragan sees of Fairbanks, Juneau. Geographical area: Alaska.

Atlanta: Archdiocese of Atlanta (Ga.) and suffragan sees of Savannah (Ga.), Charlotte and Raleigh (N.C.), Charleston (S.C.). Geographical area: Georgia, North Carolina, South Carolina.

Baltimore: Archdiocese of Baltimore (Md.) and suffragan sees of Wilmington (Del.), Arlington and Richmond (Va.), Wheeling-Charleston (W. Va.). Geographical area: Maryland (except five counties), Delaware, Virginia, West Virginia.

Boston: Archdiocese of Boston (Mass.) and suffragan sees of Fall River, Springfield and Worcester (Mass.), Portland (Me.), Manchester (N.H.), Burlington (Vt.). Geographical area: Massachusetts, Maine, New Hampshire, Vermont.

Chicago: Archdiocese of Chicago and suffragan sees of Belleville, Joliet, Peoria, Rockford, Springfield. Geographical area: Illinois.

Cincinnati: Archdiocese of Cincinnati and suffragan sees of Cleveland, Columbus, Steubenville, Toledo, Youngstown. Geographical area: Ohio.

Denver: Archdiocese of Denver (Colo.) and suffragan sees of Colorado Springs and Pueblo (Colo.), Cheyenne (Wyo.). Geographical area: Colorado, Wyoming.

Detroit: Archdiocese of Detroit and suffragan sees of Gaylord, Grand Rapids, Kalamazoo, Lansing, Marquette, Saginaw. Geographical area: Michigan.

Dubuque: Archdiocese of Dubuque and suffragan sees of Davenport, Des Moines, Sioux City. Geographical area: Iowa.

Hartford: Archdiocese of Hartford (Conn.) and suffragan sees of Bridgeport and Norwich (Conn.), Providence (R.I.). Geographical area: Connecticut, Rhode Island.

Indianapolis: Archdiocese of Indianapolis and suffragan sees of Evansville, Fort Wayne-South

Bend, Gary, Lafayette. Geographical area: Indiana.

Kansas City (Kans.): Archdiocese of Kansas City and suffragan sees of Dodge City, Salina, Wichita. Geographical area: Kansas.

Los Angeles: Archdiocese of Los Angeles and suffragan sees of Fresno, Monterey, Orange, San Bernardino, San Diego. Geographical area: Southern and Central California.

Louisville: Archdiocese of Louisville (Ky.) and suffragan sees of Covington and Owensboro (Ky.), Memphis and Nashville (Tenn.). Geographical area: Kentucky, Tennessee.

Miami: Archdiocese of Miami and suffragan sees of Orlando, Palm Beach, Pensacola-Tallahassee, St. Augustine, St. Petersburg, Venice. Geographical area: Florida.

Milwaukee: Archdiocese of Milwaukee and suffragan sees of Green Bay, La Crosse, Madison, Superior. Geographical area: Wisconsin.

Mobile: Archdiocese of Mobile, Ala., and suffragan sees of Birmingham (Ala.) and Biloxi and Jackson (Miss.). Geographical area: Alabama, Mississippi.

Newark: Archdiocese of Newark and suffragan sees of Camden, Metuchen, Paterson, Trenton. Geographical area: New Jersey.

New Orleans: Archdiocese of New Orleans and suffragan sees of Alexandria, Baton Rouge, Houma-Thibodaux, Lafayette, Lake Charles and Shreveport. Geographical area: Louisiana.

New York: Archdiocese of New York and suffragan sees of Albany, Brooklyn, Buffalo, Ogdensburg, Rochester, Rockville Centre, Syracuse. Geographical area: New York.

Oklahoma City: Archdiocese of Oklahoma City (Okla.) and suffragan sees of Tulsa (Okla.) and Little Rock (Ark.). Geographical area: Oklahoma, Arkansas.

Omaha: Archdiocese of Omaha and suffragan sees of Grand Island, Lincoln. Geographical area: Nebraska.

Philadelphia: Archdiocese of Philadelphia and suffragan sees of Allentown, Altoona-Johnstown,

Erie, Greensburg, Harrisburg, Pittsburgh, Scranton. Geographical area: Pennsylvania.

Philadelphia (Byzantine Rite, Ukrainians): Metropolitan See of Philadelphia (Byzantine Rite) and Eparchies of St. Josaphat in Parma, St. Nicholas of the Ukrainians in Chicago and Stamford, Conn. The jurisdiction extends to all Ukrainian Catholics in the U.S. from the ecclesiastical province of Galicia in the Ukraine.

Pittsburgh (Byzantine Rite, Ruthenians): Metropolitan See of Pittsburgh, Pa. and Eparchies of Passaic (N.J.), Parma (Ohio), Van Nuys (Calif.).

Portland: Archdiocese of Portland (Ore.) and suffragan sees of Baker (Ore.), Boise (Ida.), Great Falls-Billings and Helena (Mont.). Geographical area: Oregon, Idaho, Montana.

St. Louis: Archdiocese of St. Louis and suffragan sees of Jefferson City, Kansas City-St. Joseph, Springfield-Cape Girardeau. Geographical area: Missouri.

St. Paul and Minneapolis: Archdiocese of St. Paul and Minneapolis (Minn.) and suffragan sees of Crookston, Duluth, New Ulm, St. Cloud and Winona (Minn.), Bismarck and Fargo (N.D.),

Rapid City and Sioux Falls (S.D.). Geographical area: Minnesota, North Dakota, South Dakota.

San Antonio: Archdiocese of San Antonio (Tex.) and suffragan sees of Amarillo, Austin, Beaumont, Brownsville, Corpus Christi, Dallas, El Paso, Fort Worth, Galveston-Houston, Lubbock, San Angelo and Victoria (Tex.). Geographical area: Texas.

San Francisco: Archdiocese of San Francisco (Calif.) and suffragan sees of Oakland, Sacramento, San Jose, Santa Rosa and Stockton (Calif.), Honolulu (Hawaii), Reno-Las Vegas (Nev.), Salt Lake City (Utah). Geographical area: Northern California, Nevada, Utah, Hawaii.

Santa Fe: Archdiocese of Santa Fe (N.M.) and suffragan sees of Gallup and Las Cruces (N.M.), Phoenix and Tucson (Ariz.). Geographical area: New Mexico, Arizona.

Seattle: Archdiocese of Seattle and suffragan sees of Spokane, Yakima. Geographical area: Washington.

Washington: Archdiocese of Washington, D.C., and suffragan see of St. Thomas (Virgin Islands). Geographical area: District of Columbia, five counties of Maryland, Virgin Islands.

ARCHDIOCESES, DIOCESES, ARCHBISHOPS, BISHOPS

(Sources: *The Official Catholic Directory;* NC News Service. As of Aug. 15, 1985.)

Information includes name of diocese, year of foundation (as it appears on the official document erecting the see), present ordinaries and auxiliaries (for biographies, see Index), former ordinaries.

Archdioceses are indicated by an asterisk.

Albany, N.Y. (1847): Howard J. Hubbard, bishop, 1977.

Former bishops: John McCloskey, 1847-64; John J. Conroy, 1865-77; Francis McNeirny, 1877-94; Thomas M. Burke, 1894-1915; Thomas F. Cusack, 1915-18; Edmund F. Gibbons, 1919-54; William A. Scully, 1954-69; Edwin B. Broderick, 1969-76.

Alexandria, La. (1853): John C. Favalora, bishop, 1986.

Established at Natchitoches, transferred to Alexandria 1910; title changed to Alexandria-Shreveport, 1977; redesignated Alexandria, 1986, when Shreveport was made a diocese.

Former bishops: Augustus M. Martin, 1853-75; Francis X. Leray, 1877-79, administrator, 1879-83; Anthony Durier, 1885-1904; Cornelius Van de Ven, 1904-32; Daniel F. Desmond, 1933-45; Charles P. Greco, 1946-73; Lawrence P. Graves, 1973-82; William B. Friend, 1983-86.

Allentown, Pa. (1961): Thomas J. Welsh, bishop, 1983.

Former bishop: Joseph McShea, 1961-83.

Altoona-Johnstown, Pa. (1901): James J. Hogan, bishop, 1966.

Established as Altoona, name changed, 1957.

Former bishops: Eugene A. Garvey, 1901-20; John J. McCort, 1920-36; Richard T. Guilfoyle, 1936-57; Howard J. Carroll, 1958-60; J. Carroll McCormick, 1960-66.

Amarillo, Tex. (1926): Leroy T. Matthiesen, bishop, 1980.

Former bishops; Rudolph A. Gerken, 1927-33;

Robert E. Lucey, 1934-41; Laurence J. Fitzsimon, 1941-58; John L. Morkovsky, 1958-63; Lawrence M. De Falco, 1963-79.

Anchorage,* Alaska (1966): Francis T. Hurley, archbishop, 1976.

Former archbishop: Joseph T. Ryan, 1966-75.

Arlington, Va. (1974): John R. Keating, bishop, 1983.

Former bishop: Thomas J. Welsh, 1974-83.

Atlanta,* Ga. (1956; archdiocese, 1962): Thomas A. Donnellan, archbishop, 1968.

Former ordinaries: Francis E. Hyland, 1956-61; Paul J. Hallinan, first archbishop, 1962-68.

Austin, Tex. (1947): John E. McCarthy, bishop, 1986.

Former bishop: Louis J. Reicher, 1947-71; Vincent M. Harris, 1971-86.

Baker, Ore. (1903): Thomas J. Connolly, bishop, 1971.

Established as Baker City, name changed, 1952.

Former bishops: Charles J. O'Reilly, 1903-18; Joseph F. McGrath, 1919-50; Francis P. Leipzig, 1950-71.

Baltimore,* Md. (1789; archdiocese, 1808): William D. Borders, archbishop, 1974. P. Francis Murphy, William C. Newman, John H. Ricard, S.S.J. auxiliaries.

Former ordinaries: John Carroll, 1789-1815, first archbishop; Leonard Neale, 1815-17; Ambrose Marechal, S.S., 1817-28; James Whitfield, 1828-34; Samuel Eccleston, S.S., 1834-51; Francis P. Kenrick, 1851-63; Martin J. Spalding, 1864-72; James R. Bayley, 1872-77; Cardinal James Gibbons, 1877-1921; Michael J. Curley, 1921-47; Francis P. Keough, 1947-61; Cardinal Lawrence J. Shehan, 1961-74.

Baton Rouge, La. (1961): Stanley J. Ott, bishop, 1983.

Former bishops: Robert E. Tracy, 1961-74; Joseph V. Sullivan, 1974-82.

Beaumont, Tex. (1966): Bernard J. Ganter, bishop, 1977.

Former bishops: Vincent M. Harris, 1966-71; Warren L. Boudreaux, 1971-77.

Belleville, Ill. (1887): James P. Keleher, bishop, 1984.

Former bishops: John Janssen, 1888-1913; Henry Althoff, 1914-47; Albert R. Zuroweste, 1948-76; William M. Cosgrove, 1976-81; John N. Wurm, 1981-84.

Biloxi, Miss. (1977): Joseph Lawson Howze, bishop, 1977.

Birmingham, Ala. (1969): Joseph G. Vath, bishop, 1969.

Bismarck, N. Dak. (1909): John F. Kinney, bishop, 1982.

Former bishops: Vincent Wehrle, O.S.B., 1910-39; Vincent J. Ryan, 1940-51; Lambert A. Hoch, 1952-56; Hilary B. Hacker, 1957-82.

Boise, Ida. (1893): Sylvester Treinen, bishop, 1962.

Former bishops: Alphonse J. Glorieux, 1893-1917; Daniel M. Gorman, 1918-27; Edward J. Kelly, 1928-56; James J. Byrne, 1956-62.

Boston,* Mass. (1808; archdiocese, 1875): Cardinal Bernard F. Law, archbishop, 1984. Lawrence J. Riley, John J. Mulcahy, Daniel A. Hart, Alfred C. Hughes, Robert J. Banks, auxiliaries.

Former ordinaries: John L. de Cheverus, 1810-23; Benedict J. Fenwick, S.J., 1825-46; John B. Fitzpatrick, 1846-66; John J. Williams, 1866-1907, first archbishop; Cardinal William O'Connell, 1907-44; Cardinal Richard Cushing, 1944-70; Cardinal Humberto Medeiros, 1970-83.

Bridgeport, Conn. (1953): Walter W. Curtis, bishop, 1961.

Former bishop: Lawrence J. Shehan, 1953-61.

Brooklyn, N.Y. (1853): Francis J. Mugavero, bishop, 1968. Joseph M. Sullivan, Rene A. Valero, auxiliaries.

Former bishops: John Loughlin, 1853-91; Charles E. McDonnell, 1892-1921; Thomas E. Molloy, 1921-56; Bryan J. McEntegart, 1957-68.

Brownsville, Tex. (1965): John J. Fitzpatrick, bishop, 1971.

Former bishops: Adolph Marx, 1965; Humberto S. Medeiros, 1966-70.

Buffalo, N.Y. (1847): Edward D. Head, bishop, 1973. Bernard J. McLaughlin, Donald W. Trautman, auxiliaries.

Former bishops: John Timon, C.M., 1847-67; Stephen V. Ryan, C.M., 1868-96; James E. Quigley, 1897-1903; Charles H. Colton, 1903-15; Dennis J. Dougherty, 1915-18; William Turner, 1919-36; John A. Duffy, 1937-44; John F. O'Hara, C.S.C., 1945-51; Joseph A. Burke, 1952-60; James McNulty, 1963-72.

Burlington, Vt. (1853): John A. Marshall, bishop, 1972.

Former bishops: Louis De Goesbriand, 1853-99; John S. Michaud, 1899-1908; Joseph J. Rice, 1910-38; Matthew F. Brady, 1938-44; Edward F. Ryan, 1945-56; Robert F. Joyce, 1957-71.

Camden, N.J. (1937): George H. Guilfoyle, bishop, 1968. James L. Schad, auxiliary.

Former bishops: Bartholomew J. Eustace, 1938-56; Justin J. McCarthy, 1957-59; Celestine J. Damiano, 1960-67.

Charleston, S.C. (1820): Ernest L. Unterkoefler, bishop, 1964.

Former bishops: John England, 1820-42; Ignatius W. Reynolds, 1844-55; Patrick N. Lynch, 1858-82; Henry P. Northrop, 1883-1916; William T. Russell, 1917-27; Emmet M. Walsh, 1927-49; John J. Russell, 1950-58; Paul J. Hallinan, 1958-62; Francis F. Reh, 1962-64.

Charlotte, N.C. (1971): John F. Donoghue, bishop, 1984.

Former bishop: Michael J. Begley, 1972-84.

Cheyenne, Wyo. (1887): Joseph Hart, bishop, 1978.

Former bishops: Maurice F. Burke, 1887-93; Thomas M. Lenihan, 1897-1901; James J. Keane, 1902-11; Patrick A. McGovern, 1912-51; Hubert M. Newell, 1951-78.

Chicago,* Ill. (1843; archdiocese, 1880): Cardinal Joseph L. Bernardin, archbishop, 1982. Alfred L. Abramowicz, Nevin W. Hayes, O. Carm., Placido Rodriguez, C.M.F., Timothy J. Lyne, John G. Vlazny, Wilton D. Gregory, auxiliaries.

Former ordinaries: William Quarter, 1844-48; James O. Van de Velde, S.J., 1849-53; Anthony O'Regan, 1854-58; James Duggan, 1859-70; Thomas P. Foley, administrator, 1870-79; Patrick A. Feehan, 1880-1902, first archbishop; James E. Quigley, 1903-15; Cardinal George Mundelein, 1915-39; Cardinal Samuel Stritch, 1939-58; Cardinal Albert Meyer, 1958-65; Cardinal John Cody, 1965-82.

Cincinnati,* Ohio (1821; archdiocese, 1850): Daniel E. Pilarczyk, archbishop, 1982. James H. Garland, auxiliary.

Former ordinaries: Edward D. Fenwick, O.P., 1822-32; John B. Purcell, 1833-83, first archbishop; William H. Elder, 1883-1904; Henry Moeller, 1904-1925; John T. McNicholas, O.P., 1925-50; Karl J. Alter, 1950-69; Paul F. Leibold, 1969-72; Joseph L. Bernardin, 1972-82.

Cleveland, Ohio (1847): Anthony M. Pilla, bishop, 1980. Gilbert I. Sheldon, James P. Lyke, O.F.M., A. Edward Pevec, A. James Quinn, auxiliaries.

Former bishops: L. Amadeus Rappe, 1847-70; Richard Gilmour, 1872-91; Ignatius F. Horstmann, 1892-1908; John P. Farrelly, 1909-21; Joseph Schrembs, 1921-45; Edward F. Hoban, 1945-66; Clarence G. Issenmann, 1966-74; James A. Hickey, 1974-80.

Colorado Springs, Colo. (1983): Richard C. Hanifen, bishop, 1984.

Columbus, Ohio (1868): James A. Griffin, bishop, 1983.

Former bishops: Sylvester H. Rosecrans, 1868-78; John A. Watterson, 1880-99; Henry Moeller, 1900-03; James J. Hartley, 1904-44; Michael J. Ready, 1944-57; Clarence Issenmann, 1957-64; John J. Carberry, 1965-68; Clarence E. Elwell, 1968-73; Edward J. Herrmann, 1973-82.

Corpus Christi, Tex. (1912): Rene H. Gracida, bishop, 1983.

Former bishops: Paul J. Nussbaum, C.P., 1913-20; Emmanuel B. Ledvina, 1921-49; Mariano S. Garriga, 1949-65; Thomas J. Drury, 1965-83.

Covington, Ky. (1853): William A. Hughes, bishop. 1979. James Kendrick Williams, auxiliary.

Former bishops: George A. Carrell, S.J., 1853-68; Augustus M. Toebbe, 1870-84; Camillus P. Maes. 1885-1914; Ferdinand Brossart, 1916-23; Francis W. Howard, 1923-44; William T. Mulloy, 1945-59; Richard Ackerman, C.S.Sp., 1960-78.

Crookston, Minn. (1909): Victor Balke, bishop, 1976.

Former bishops: Timothy Corbett, 1910-38; John H. Peschges, 1938-44; Francis J. Schenk, 1945-60; Laurence A. Glenn, 1960-70; Kenneth J. Povish, 1970-75.

Dallas, Tex. (1890): Thomas Tschoepe, bishop, 1969.

Established 1890, as Dallas, title changed to Dallas-Ft. Worth 1953; redesignated Dallas, 1969, when Ft. Worth was made diocese.

Former bishops: Thomas F. Brennan, 1891-92; Edward J. Dunne, 1893-1910; Joseph P. Lynch, 1911-54; Thomas K. Gorman, 1954-69.

Davenport, Ia. (1881): Gerald F. O'Keefe, bishop, 1966.

Former bishops: John McMullen, 1881-83; Henry Cosgrove, 1884-1906; James Davis, 1906-26; Henry P. Rohlman, 1927-44; Ralph L. Hayes, 1944-66.

Denver,* Colo. (1887; archdiocese, 1941): J. Francis Stafford, archbishop, 1986.

Former ordinaries: Joseph P. Machebeuf, 1887-89; Nicholas C. Matz, 1889-1917; J. Henry Tihen, 1917-31; Urban J. Vehr, 1931-67, first archbishop; James V. Casey, 1967-86.

Des Moines, Ia. (1911): Maurice J. Dingman, bishop, 1968.

Former bishops: Austin Dowling, 1912-19; Thomas W. Drumm, 1919-33; Gerald T. Bergan, 1934-48; Edward C. Daly, O.P., 1948-64; George J. Biskup, 1965-67.

Detroit,* Mich. (1833; archdiocese, 1937): Edmund C. Szoka, archbishop, 1981. Thomas J. Gumbleton, Walter J. Schoenherr, Moses B. Anderson, S.S.E., Patrick R. Cooney, Dale J. Melczek, auxiliaries.

Former ordinaries: Frederic Rese, 1833-71; Peter P. Lefevere, administrator, 1841-69; Caspar H. Borgess, 1871-88; John S. Foley, 1888-1918; Michael J. Gallagher, 1918-37; Cardinal Edward Mooney, 1937-58, first archbishop; Cardinal John F. Dearden, 1958-80.

Dodge City, Kans. (1951): Stanley G. Schlarman, bishop, 1983.

Former bishops: John B. Franz, 1951-59; Marion F. Forst, 1960-76; Eugene J. Gerber, 1976-82.

Dubuque,* Iowa (1837; archdiocese, 1893): Daniel W. Kucera, O.S.B., archbishop, 1984. Francis J. Dunn, auxiliary.

Former ordinaries: Mathias Loras, 1837-58; Clement Smyth, O.C.S.O., 1858-65; John Hennessy, 1866-1900, first archbishop; John J. Keane, 1900-11; James J. Keane, 1911-29; Francis J. Beckman, 1930-46; Henry P. Rohlman, 1946-54; Leo Binz, 1954-61; James J. Byrne, 1962-83.

Duluth, Minn. (1889): Robert H. Brom, bishop, 1983.

Former bishops: James McGolrick, 1889-1918; John T. McNicholas, O.P., 1918-25; Thomas A.

Welch, 1926-59; Francis J. Schenk, 1960-69; Paul F. Anderson, 1969-82.

El Paso, Tex. (1914): Raymundo J. Pena, bishop, 1980.

Former bishops: Anthony J. Schuler, S.J., 1915-42; Sidney M. Metzger, 1942-78. Patrick F. Flores, 1978-79.

Erie, Pa. (1853): Michael J. Murphy, bishop, 1982.

Former bishops: Michael O'Connor, 1853-54; Josue M. Young, 1854-66; Tobias Mullen, 1868-99; John E. Fitzmaurice, 1899-1920; John M. Gannon, 1920-66; John F. Whealon, 1966-69; Alfred M. Watson, 1969-82.

Evansville, Ind. (1944): Francis Raymond Shea, bishop, 1970.

Former bishops: Henry J. Grimmelsman, 1944-65; Paul F. Leibold, 1966-69.

Fairbanks, Alaska (1962): Michael J. Kaniecki, S.J., bishop, 1985.

Former bishops: Francis D. Gleeson, S.J., 1962-68; Robert L. Whelan, S.J., 1968-85.

Fall River, Mass. (1904): Daniel A. Cronin, bishop, 1970.

Former bishops: William Stang, 1904-07; Daniel F. Feehan, 1907-34; James E. Cassidy, 1934-51; James L. Connolly, 1951-70.

Fargo, N. Dak. (1889): James S. Sullivan, bishop, 1985.

Established at Jamestown, transferred, 1897.

Former bishops: John Shanley, 1889-1909; James O'Reilly, 1910-34; Aloysius J. Muench, 1935-59; Leo F. Dworschak, 1960-70; Justin A. Driscoll, 1970-84.

Fort Wayne-South Bend, Ind. (1857): John M. D'Arcy, bishop, 1985. Joseph R. Crowley, auxiliary.

Established as Fort Wayne, name changed, 1960.

Former bishops: John H. Luers, 1858-71; Joseph Dwenger, C.Pp. S., 1872-93; Joseph Rademacher, 1893-1900; Herman J. Alerding, 1900-24; John F. Noll, 1925-56; Leo A. Pursley, 1957-76; William E. McManus, 1976-85.

Fort Worth, Tex. (1969): Joseph P. Delaney, bishop, 1981.

Former bishop: John J. Cassata, 1969-80.

Fresno, Calif. (1967): Joseph J. Madera, M.Sp.S., bishop, 1980.

Formerly Monterey-Fresno, 1922.

Former bishops (Monterey-Fresno): John J. Cantwell, administrator, 1922-24; John B. MacGinley, first bishop, 1924-32; Philip G. Sher, 1933-53; Aloysius J. Willinger, 1953-67.

Former bishops (Fresno): Timothy Manning, 1967-69; Hugh A. Donohoe, 1969-80.

Gallup, N. Mex. (1939): Jerome J. Hastrich, bishop, 1969. Donald Pelotte, S.S.S., coadjutor.

Former bishop: Bernard T. Espelage, O.F.M., 1940-69.

Galveston-Houston, Tex. (1847): Joseph A. Fiorenza, bishop, 1985. Enrique San Pedro, S.J., auxiliary.

Established as Galveston, name changed, 1959.

Former bishops: John M. Odin, C.M., 1847-61; Claude M. Dubuis, 1862-92; Nicholas A. Gallagher, 1892-1918; Christopher E. Byrne, 1918-50; Wendelin J. Nold, 1950-75; John L. Morkovsky, 1975-84.

Gary, Ind. (1956): Norbert F. Gaughan, bishop, 1984.

Former bishop: Andrew G. Grutka, 1957-84.

Gaylord, Mich. (1971): Robert J. Rose, bishop, 1981.

Former bishop: Edmund C. Szoka, 1971-81.

Grand Island, Neb. (1912): Lawrence McNamara, bishop, 1978.

Established at Kearney, transferred, 1917.

Former bishops: James A. Duffy, 1913-31; Stanislaus V. Bona, 1932-44; Edward J. Hunkeler, 1945-51; John L. Paschang, 1951-72; John J. Sullivan, 1972-77.

Grand Rapids, Mich. (1882): Joseph M. Breitenbeck, bishop, 1969. Joseph C. McKinney, auxiliary.

Former bishops: Henry J. Richter, 1883-1916; Michael J. Gallagher, 1916-18; Edward D. Kelly, 1919-26; Joseph G. Pinten, 1926-40; Joseph C. Plagens, 1941-43; Francis J. Haas, 1943-53; Allen J. Babcock, 1954-69.

Great Falls-Billings, Mont. (1904): Thomas J. Murphy, bishop, 1978.

Established as Great Falls; name changed, 1980.

Former bishops: Mathias C. Lenihan, 1904-30; Edwin V. O'Hara, 1930-39; William J. Condon, 1939-67; Eldon B. Schuster, 1968-77.

Green Bay, Wis. (1868): Adam J. Maida, bishop, 1984. Robert F. Morneau, auxiliary.

Former bishops: Joseph Melcher, 1868-73; Francis X. Krautbauer, 1875-85; Frederick X. Katzer, 1886-91; Sebastian G. Messmer, 1892-1903; Joseph J. Fox, 1904-14; Paul P. Rhode, 1915-45; Stanislaus V. Bona, 1945-67; Aloysius J. Wycislo, 1968-83.

Greensburg, Pa. (1951): William G. Connare, bishop, 1960.

Former bishop: Hugh L. Lamb, 1951-59.

Harrisburg, Pa. (1868): William H. Keeler, bishop, 1984.

Former bishops: Jeremiah F. Shanahan, 1868-86; Thomas McGovern, 1888-98; John W. Shanahan,1899-1916; Philip R. McDevitt, 1916-35; George L. Leech, 1935-71; Joseph T. Daley, 1971-83.

Hartford,* Conn. (1843; archdiocese, 1953): John F. Whealon, archbishop, 1969. John F. Hackett, Peter A. Rosazza, auxiliaries.

Former ordinaries: William Tyler, 1844-49; Bernard O'Reilly, 1850-56; F. P. MacFarland, 1858-74; Thomas Galberry, O.S.A., 1876-78; Lawrence S. McMahon, 1879-93; Michael Tierney, 1894-1908; John J. Nilan, 1910-34; Maurice F. McAuliffe, 1934-44; Henry J. O'Brien, 1945-68, first archbishop.

Helena, Mont. (1884): Elden F. Curtiss, bishop, 1976.

Former bishops: John B. Brondel, 1884-1903; John P. Carroll, 1904-25; George J. Finnigan, C.S.C., 1927-32; Ralph L. Hayes, 1933-35; Joseph M. Gilmore, 1936-62; Raymond Hunthausen, 1962-75.

Honolulu, Hawaii (1941): Joseph A. Ferrario, bishop, 1982.

Former bishops: James J. Sweeney, 1941-68; John J. Scanlan, 1968-81.

Houma-Thibodaux, La. (1977): Warren L. Boudreaux, bishop, 1977.

Indianapolis,* Ind. (1834; archdiocese, 1944): Edward T. O'Meara, archbishop, 1980.

Established at Vincennes, transferred, 1898.

Former ordinaries: Simon G. Bruté, 1834-39; Celestine de la Hailandiere, 1839-47; John S. Bazin, 1847-48; Maurice de St. Palais, 1849-77; Francis S. Chatard, 1878-1918; Joseph Chartrand, 1918-33; Joseph E. Ritter, 1934-46, first archbishop; Paul C. Schulte, 1946-70; George J. Biskup, 1970-79.

Jackson, Miss. (1837): William R. Houck, bishop, 1984.

Established at Natchez; title changed to Natchez-Jackson, 1956; transferred to Jackson, 1977 (Natchez made titular see).

Former bishops: John J. Chanche, S.S., 1841-52; James Van de Velde, S.J., 1853-55; William H. Elder, 1857-80; Francis A. Jansens, 1881-88; Thomas Heslin, 1889-1911; John E. Gunn, S.M., 1911-24; Richard O. Gerow, 1924-67; Joseph B. Brunini, 1968-84.

Jefferson City, Mo. (1956): Michael F. McAuliffe, bishop, 1969.

Former bishop: Joseph Marling, C.Pp.S., 1956-69.

Joliet, Ill. (1948): Joseph I. Imesch, bishop, 1979. Raymond J. Vonesh, Roger L. Kaffer, auxiliaries.

Former bishop: Martin D. McNamara, 1949-66. Romeo Blanchette, 1966-79.

Juneau, Alaska (1951): Michael H. Kenny, bishop, 1979.

Former bishops: Dermot O'Flanagan, 1951-68; Joseph T. Ryan, administrator, 1968-71; Francis T. Hurley, 1971-76, administrator, 1976-79.

Kalamazoo, Mich. (1971): Paul V. Donovan, bishop, 1971.

Kansas City,* Kans. (1877; archdiocese, 1952): Ignatius J. Strecker, archbishop, 1969. Marion F. Forst, auxiliary.

Established as vicariate apostolic, 1850, became Diocese of Leavenworth, 1877, transferred to Kansas City 1947.

Former ordinaries: J. B. Miege, vicar apostolic, 1851-74; Louis M. Fink, O.S.B., vicar apostolic, 1874-77, first bishop, 1877-1904; Thomas F. Lillis, 1904-10; John Ward, 1910-29; Francis Johannes, 1929-37; Paul C. Schulte, 1937-46; George J. Donnelly, 1946-50; Edward Hunkeler, 1951-69, first archbishop.

Kansas City-St. Joseph, Mo. (Kansas City, 1880; St. Joseph, 1868; united 1956): John J. Sullivan, bishop, 1977.

Former bishops: John J. Hogan, 1880-1913; Thomas F. Lillis, 1913-38; Edwin V. O'Hara, 1939-56; John P. Cody, 1956-61; Charles H. Helmsing, 1962-77.

Former bishops (St. Joseph): John J. Hogan, 1868-80, administrator, 1880-93; Maurice F. Burke, 1893-1923; Francis Gilfillan, 1923-33; Charles H. Le Blond, 1933-56.

La Crosse, Wis. (1868): John J. Paul, bishop, 1983.

Former bishops: Michael Heiss, 1868-80; Kilian C. Flasch, 1881-91; James Schwebach, 1892-1921; Alexander J. McGavick, 1921-48; John P. Treacy, 1948-64; Frederick W. Freking, 1965-83.

Lafayette, Ind. (1944): William L. Higi, bishop, 1984.

Former bishops: John G. Bennett, 1944-57; John

J. Carberry, 1957-65; Raymond J. Gallagher, 1965-82; George A. Fulcher, 1983-84.

Lafayette, La. (1918): Gerard L. Frey, bishop, 1973. Harry J. Flynn, coadjutor.

Former bishops: Jules B. Jeanmard, 1918-56; Maurice Schexnayder, 1956-72.

Lake Charles, La. (1980): Jude Speyrer, bishop, 1980.

Lansing, Mich. (1937): Kenneth J. Povish, bishop, 1975.

Former bishops: Joseph H. Albers, 1937-65; Alexander Zaleski, 1965-75.

Las Cruces, N. Mex. (1982): Ricardo Ramirez, C.S.B., bishop, 1982.

Lincoln, Neb. (1887): Glennon P. Flavin, bishop, 1967.

Former bishops: Thomas Bonacum, 1887-1911; J. Henry Tihen, 1911-17; Charles J. O'Reilly, 1918-23; Francis J. Beckman, 1924-30; Louis B. Kucera, 1930-57; James V. Casey, 1957-67.

Little Rock, Ark. (1843): Andrew J. McDonald, bishop, 1972.

Former bishops: Andrew Byrne, 1844-62; Edward Fitzgerald, 1867-1907; John Morris, 1907-46; Albert L. Fletcher, 1946-72.

Los Angeles,* Calif. (1840; archdiocese, 1936): Roger M. Mahony, archbishop, 1985. John J. Ward, Juan A. Arzube, auxiliaries.

Founded as diocese of Two Californias, 1840; became Monterey diocese, 1850; Baja California detached from Monterey diocese, 1852; title changed to Monterey-Los Angeles, 1859; Los Angeles-San Diego, 1922; became archdiocese under present title, 1936 (San Diego became separate see).

Former ordinaries: Francisco Garcia Diego y Moreno, O.F.M., 1840-46; Joseph S. Alemany, O.P., 1850-53; Thaddeus Amat, C.M., 1854-78; Francis Mora, 1878-96; George T. Montgomery, 1896-1903; Thomas J. Conaty, 1903-15; John J. Cantwell, 1917-47, first archbishop; Cardinal James McIntyre, 1948-70; Cardinal Timothy Manning, 1970-85.

Louisville,* Ky. (1808; archdiocese, 1937): Thomas C. Kelly, O.P., archbishop, 1982. Charles G. Maloney, auxiliary.

Established at Bardstown, transferred, 1841.

Former ordinaries: Benedict J. Flaget, S.S. 1810-32; John B. David, S.S., 1832-33; Benedict J. Flaget, S.S., 1833-50; Martin J. Spalding, 1850-64; Peter J. Lavialle, 1865-67; William G. McCloskey, 1868-1909; Denis O'Donaghue, 1910-24; John A. Floersh, 1924-67, first archbishop; Thomas J. McDonough, 1967-81.

Lubbock, Tex. (1983): Michael J. Sheehan, bishop, 1983.

Madison, Wis. (1946): Cletus F. O'Donnell, bishop, 1967. George O. Wirz, auxiliary.

Former bishop: William P. O'Connor, 1946-67.

Manchester, N.H. (1884): Odore J. Gendron, bishop, 1975. Joseph Gerry, O.S.B., auxiliary.

Former bishops: Denis M. Bradley, 1884-1903; John B. Delany, 1904-06; George A. Guertin, 1907-32; John B. Peterson, 1932-44; Matthew F. Brady, 1944-59; Ernest J. Primeau, 1960-74.

Marquette, Mich. (1857): Mark F. Schmitt, bishop, 1978.

Former bishops: Frederic Baraga, 1857-68; Ignatius Mrak, 1869-78; John Vertin, 1879-99; Frederick Eis, 1899-1922; Paul J. Nussbaum, C.P., 1922-35; Joseph C. Plagens, 1935-40; Francis Magner, 1941-47; Thomas L. Noa, 1947-68; Charles A. Salatka, 1968-77.

Memphis, Tenn. (1970): Vacant as of Aug. 15, 1986.

Former bishops: Carroll T. Dozier, 1971-82; J. Francis Stafford, 1982-86.

Metuchen, N.J. (1981): Vacant as of Aug. 15, 1986.

Former bishop: Theodore E. McCarrick, 1981-86.

Miami,* Fla. (1958; archdiocese, 1968): Edward A. McCarthy, archbishop, 1977. Agustin A. Roman, Norbert M. Dorsey, C.P., auxiliaries.

Former ordinary: Coleman F. Carroll, 1958-77, first archbishop.

Milwaukee,* Wis. (1843; archdiocese, 1875): Rembert G. Weakland, O.S.B., archbishop, 1977. Leo J. Brust, Richard J. Sklba, auxiliaries.

Former ordinaries: John M. Henni, 1844-81, first archbishop; Michael Heiss, 1881-90; Frederick X. Katzer, 1891-1903; Sebastian G. Messmer, 1903-30; Samuel A. Stritch, 1930-39; Moses E. Kiley, 1940-53; Albert G. Meyer, 1953-58; William E. Cousins, 1959-77.

Mobile,* Ala. (1829; archdiocese, 1980): Oscar H. Lipscomb, first archbishop, 1980.

Founded as Mobile, 1829; title changed to Mobile-Birmingham, 1954; redesignated Mobile, 1969.

Former bishops: Michael Portier, 1829-59; John Quinlan, 1859-83; Dominic Manucy, 1884; Jeremiah O'Sullivan, 1885-96; Edward P. Allen, 1897-1926; Thomas J. Toolen, 1927-69; John L. May, 1969-80.

Monterey in California (1967): Thaddeus A. Shubsda, bishop, 1982.

Formerly Monterey-Fresno, 1922. (Originally established in 1850, see Los Angeles listing.)

Former bishops (Monterey-Fresno): John J. Cantwell, administrator, 1922-24; John B. MacGinley, first bishop, 1924-32; Philip G. Scher, 1933-53; Aloysius J. Willinger, 1953-67.

Former bishop (Monterey): Harry A. Clinch, 1967-82.

Nashville, Tenn. (1837): James D. Niedergeses, bishop, 1975.

Former bishops: Richard P. Miles, O.P., 1838-60; James Whelan, O.P., 1860-64; Patrick A. Feehan, 1865-80; Joseph Rademacher, 1883-93; Thomas S. Byrne, 1894-1923; Alphonse J. Smith, 1924-35; William L. Adrian, 1936-69; Joseph A. Durick, 1969-75.

Newark,* N.J. (1853; archdiocese, 1937): Theodore E. McCarrick, archbishop, 1986. Jerome Pechillo, T.O.R., Robert F. Garner, Joseph A. Francis, S.V.D., Dominic A. Marconi, David Arias, O.A.R., auxiliaries.

Former ordinaries: James R. Bayley, 1853-72; Michael A. Corrigan, 1873-80; Winand M. Wigger, 1881-1901; John J. O'Connor, 1901-27; Thomas J. Walsh, 1928-52, first archbishop; Thomas A. Boland, 1953-74; Peter L. Gerety, 1974-86.

New Orleans,* La. (1793; archdiocese, 1850):

Philip M. Hannan, archbishop, 1965. Harold R. Perry, S. V. D., auxiliary.

Former ordinaries: Luis Penalver y Cardenas, 1793-1801; John Carroll, administrator, 1809-15; W. Louis Dubourg, S.S., 1815-25; Joseph Rosati, C.M., administrator, 1826-29; Leo De Neckere, C.M., 1829-33; Anthony Blanc, 1835-60, first archbishop; Jean Marie Odin, C.M., 1861-70; Napoleon J. Perche, 1870-83; Francis X. Leray, 1883-87; Francis A. Janssens, 1888-97; Placide L. Chapelle, 1897-1905; James H. Blenk, S.M., 1906-17; John W. Shaw, 1918-34; Joseph F. Rummel, 1935-64; John P. Cody, 1964-65.

Newton, Mass. (Melkite Rite) (1966; eparchy, 1976): Archbishop Joseph Tawil, exarch, 1969, first eparch, 1976. John A. Elya, auxiliary.

Former ordinary: Justin Najmy, 1966-68.

New Ulm, Minn. (1957): Raymond A. Lucker, bishop, 1975.

Former bishop: Alphonse J. Schladweiler, 1958-75.

New York,* N.Y. (1808; archdiocese, 1850): Cardinal John J. O'Connor, archbishop, 1984. Patrick V. Ahern, James P. Mahoney, Anthony F. Mestice, Austin B. Vaughan, Francisco Garmendia, Joseph T. O'Keefe, Emerson J. Moore, Edward M. Egan, auxiliaries.

Former ordinaries: Richard L. Concanen, O.P., 1808-10; John Connolly, O.P., 1814-25; John Dubois, S.S., 1826-42; John J. Hughes, 1842-64, first archbishop; Cardinal John McCloskey, 1864-85; Michael A. Corrigan, 1885-1902; Cardinal John Farley, 1902-18; Cardinal Patrick Hayes, 1919-38; Cardinal Francis Spellman, 1939-67; Cardinal Terence J. Cooke, 1968-83.

Norwich, Conn. (1953): Daniel P. Reilly, bishop, 1975.

Former bishops: Bernard J. Flanagan, 1953-59; Vincent J. Hines, 1960-75.

Oakland, Calif. (1962): John S. Cummins, bishop, 1977.

Former bishop: Floyd L. Begin, 1962-77.

Ogdensburg, N.Y. (1872): Stanislaus J. Brzana, bishop, 1968.

Former bishops: Edgar P. Wadhams, 1872-91; Henry Gabriels, 1892-1921; Joseph H. Conroy, 1921-39; Francis J. Monaghan, 1939-42; Bryan J. McEntegart, 1943-53; Walter P. Kellenberg, 1954-57; James J. Navagh, 1957-63; Leo R. Smith, 1963; Thomas A. Donnellan, 1964-68.

Oklahoma City,* Okla. (1905; archdiocese, 1972): Charles A. Salatka, archbishop, 1977.

Former ordinaries: Theophile Meerschaert, 1905-24; Francis C. Kelley, 1924-48; Eugene J. McGuinness, 1948-57; Victor J. Reed, 1958-71; John R. Quinn, 1971-77, first archbishop.

Omaha,* Nebr. (1885; archdiocese, 1945): Daniel E. Sheehan, archbishop, 1969. Anthony Milone, auxiliary.

Former ordinaries: James O'Gorman, O.C.S.O., 1859-74, vicar apostolic; James O'Connor, vicar apostolic, 1876-85, first bishop, 1885-90; Richard Scannell, 1891-1916; Jeremiah J. Harty, 1916-27; Francis Beckman, administrator, 1926-28; Joseph F. Rummel, 1928-35; James H. Ryan, 1935-47, first archbishop; Gerald T. Bergan, 1948-69.

Orange, Calif. (1976): Vacant as of Aug. 15, 1986. John T. Steinbock, auxiliary.

Former bishop: William R. Johnson, 1976-86.

Orlando, Fla. (1968): Thomas J. Grady, bishop, 1974.

Former bishop: William Borders, 1968-74.

Owensboro, Ky. (1937): John J. McRaith, bishop, 1982.

Former bishops: Francis R. Cotton, 1938-60, Henry J. Soenneker, 1961-82.

Palm Beach, Fla. (1984): Thomas V. Dailey, bishop, 1984.

Parma, Ohio (Byzantine Rite) (1969): Andrew Pataki, eparch, 1984.

Former bishop: Emil Mihalik, 1969-84.

Passaic, N.J. (Byzantine Rite) (1963): Michael J. Dudick, eparch, 1968.

Former bishop: Stephen Kocisko, 1963-68.

Paterson, N.J. (1937): Frank J. Rodimer, bishop, 1978.

Former bishops: Thomas H. McLaughlin, 1937-47; Thomas A. Boland, 1947-52; James A. McNulty, 1953-63; James J. Navagh, 1963-65; Lawrence B. Casey, 1966-77.

Pensacola-Tallahassee, Fla. (1975): J. Keith Symons, bishop, 1983.

Former bishop: Rene H. Gracida, 1975-83.

Peoria, Ill. (1877): Edward W. O'Rourke, bishop, 1971.

Former bishops: John L. Spalding, 1877-1908; Edmund M. Dunne, 1909-29; Joseph H. Schlarman, 1930-51; William E. Cousins, 1952-58; John B. Franz, 1959-71.

Philadelphia,* Pa. (1808; archdiocese, 1875): Cardinal John Krol, Archbishop, 1961. John J. Graham, Martin J. Lohmuller, Edward T. Hughes, Louis A. De Simone, auxiliaries.

Former ordinaries: Michael Egan, O.F.M., 1810-14; Henry Conwell, 1820-42; Francis P. Kenrick, 1842-51; John N. Neumann, C.SS.R., 1852-60; James F. Wood, 1860-83, first archbishop; Patrick J. Ryan, 1884-1911; Edmond F. Prendergast, 1911-18; Cardinal Dennis Dougherty, 1918-51; Cardinal John O'Hara, C.S.C., 1951-60.

Philadelphia,* Pa. (Byzantine Rite, Ukrainians) (1924; metropolitan, 1958): Stephen Sulyk, archbishop, 1981.

Former ordinaries: Stephen Ortynsky, O.S.B.M., 1907-16; Constantine Bohachevsky, 1924-61; Ambrose Senyshyn, O.S.B.M., 1961-76; Joseph Schmondiuk, 1977-78; Myroslav J. Lubachivsky, 1979-80, apostolic administrator, 1980-81.

Phoenix, Ariz. (1969): Thomas J. O'Brien, bishop, 1982.

Former bishops: Edward A. McCarthy, 1969-76; James S. Rausch, 1977-81.

Pittsburgh,* Pa. (Byzantine Rite, Ruthenians) (1924; metropolitan, 1969): Stephen J. Kocisko, eparch, 1968, first metropolitan, 1969. John M. Bilock, auxiliary.

Former ordinaries: Basil Takach 1924-48; Daniel Ivancho, 1948-54; Nicholas T. Elko, 1955-67.

Pittsburgh, Pa. (1843): Anthony J. Bevilacqua, bishop, 1983. John B. McDowell, Anthony G. Bosco, auxiliaries.

Former bishops: Michael O'Connor, 1843-53, 1854-60; Michael Domenec, C.M., 1860-76; J. Tuigg, 1876-89; Richard Phelan, 1889-1904; J.F. Regis Canevin, 1904-20; Hugh C. Boyle, 1921-55; John F. Dearden, 1950-58; John J. Wright, 1959-69; Vincent M. Leonard, 1969-83.

Portland, Me. (1853): Edward C. O'Leary, bishop, 1974. Amedee W. Proulx, auxiliary.

Former bishops: David W. Bacon, 1855-74; James A. Healy, 1875-1900; William H. O'Connell, 1901-06; Louis S. Walsh, 1906-24; John G. Murray, 1925-31; Joseph E. McCarthy, 1932-55; Daniel J. Feeney, 1955-69; Peter L. Gerety, 1969-74.

Portland,* Ore. (1846): William J. Levada, archbishop, 1986. Paul E. Waldschmidt, C.S.C., Kenneth D. Steiner, auxiliaries.

Established as Oregon City, name changed, 1928.

Former ordinaries: Francis N. Blanchet, 1846-80 vicar apostolic, first archbishop; Charles J. Seghers, 1880-84; William H. Gross, C.SS.R., 1885-98; Alexander Christie, 1899-1925; Edward D. Howard, 1926-66; Robert J. Dwyer, 1966-74; Cornelius M. Power, 1974-86.

Providence, R.I. (1872): Louis E. Gelineau, bishop, 1972. Kenneth A. Angell, auxiliary.

Former bishops: Thomas F. Hendricken, 1872-86; Matthew Harkins, 1887-1921; William A. Hickey, 1921-33; Francis P. Keough, 1934-47; Russell J. McVinney, 1948-71.

Pueblo, Colo. (1941): Arthur J. Tafoya, bishop, 1980.

Former bishops: Joseph C. Willging, 1942-59; Charles A. Buswell, 1959-79.

Raleigh, N.C. (1924): F. Joseph Gossman, bishop, 1975.

Former bishops: William J. Hafey, 1925-37; Eugene J. McGuinness, 1937-44; Vincent S. Waters, 1945-75.

Rapid City, S. Dak. (1902): Harold J. Dimmerling, bishop, 1969.

Established at Lead, transferred, 1930.

Former bishops: John Stariha, 1902-09; Joseph F. Busch, 1910-15; John J. Lawler, 1916-48; William T. McCarty, C.SS.R., 1948-69.

Reno-Las Vegas, Nev. (1931): Norman F. McFarland, bishop, 1976.

Established at Reno; title changed to Reno-Las Vegas, 1976.

Former bishops: Thomas K. Gorman, 1931-52; Robert J. Dwyer, 1952-66; Joseph Green, 1967-74.

Richmond, Va. (1820): Walter F. Sullivan, bishop, 1974. David E. Foley, auxiliary.

Former bishops: Patrick Kelly, 1820-22; Richard V. Whelan, 1841-50; John McGill, 1850-72; James Gibbons, 1872-77; John J. Keane, 1878-88; Augustine Van de Vyver, 1889-1911; Denis J. O'Connell, 1912-26; Andrew J. Brennan, 1926-45; Peter L. Ireton, 1945-58; John J. Russell, 1958-73.

Rochester, N.Y. (1868): Matthew H. Clark, bishop, 1979. Dennis W. Hickey, auxiliary.

Former bishops: Bernard J. McQuaid, 1868-1909; Thomas F. Hickey, 1909-28; John F. O'Hern, 1929-33; Edward F. Mooney, 1933-37; James E. Kearney, 1937-66; Fulton J. Sheen, 1966-69; Joseph L. Hogan, 1969-78.

Rockford, Ill. (1908): Arthur J. O'Neill, bishop, 1968.

Former bishops: Peter J. Muldoon, 1908-27; Edward F. Hoban, 1928-42; John J. Boylan, 1943-53; Raymond P. Hillinger, 1953-56; Loras T. Lane, 1956-68.

Rockville Centre, N.Y. (1957): John R. McGann, bishop, 1976. James Daly, Alfred R. Markiewicz, auxiliaries.

Former bishop: Walter P. Kellenberg, 1957-76.

Sacramento, Calif. (1886): Francis A. Quinn, bishop, 1979. Alphonse Gallegos, O.A.R., auxiliary.

Former bishops: Patrick Manogue, 1886-95; Thomas Grace, 1896-1921; Patrick J. Keane, 1922-28; Robert J. Armstrong, 1929-57; Joseph T. McGucken, 1957-62; Alden J. Bell, 1962-79.

Saginaw, Mich. (1938): Kenneth E. Untener, bishop, 1980.

Former bishops: William F. Murphy, 1938-50; Stephen S. Woznicki, 1950-68; Francis F. Reh, 1969-80.

St. Augustine, Fla. (1870): John J. Snyder, bishop, 1979.

Former bishops: Augustin Verot, S.S., 1870-76; John Moore, 1877-1901; William J. Kenny, 1902-13; Michael J. Curley, 1914-21; Patrick J. Barry, 1922-40; Joseph P. Hurley, 1940-67; Paul F. Tanner, 1968-79,

St. Cloud, Minn. (1889): George H. Speltz, bishop, 1968.

Former bishops: Otto Zardetti, 1889-94; Martin Marty, O.S.B., 1895-96; James Trobec, 1897-1914; Joseph F. Busch, 1915-53; Peter Bartholome, 1953-68.

St. Josaphat in Parma, Ohio (Byzantine Rite, Ukrainians) (1983): Robert M. Moskal, bishop, 1984.

St. Louis,* Mo. (1826; archdiocese, 1847): John L. May, archbishop, 1980. George J. Gottwald, Charles R. Koester, Edward J. O'Donnell, J. Terry Steib, auxiliaries.

Former ordinaries: Joseph Rosati, C.M., 1827-43; Peter R. Kenrick, 1843-95, first archbishop; John J. Kain, 1895-1903; Cardinal John Glennon, 1903-46; Cardinal Joseph Ritter, 1946-67; Cardinal John J. Carberry, 1968-79.

St. Maron, Brooklyn, N.Y. (Maronite Rite) (1966; diocese, 1971): Francis Zayek (titular archbishop), exarch, 1966, first eparch, 1972. John Chedid, auxiliary.

Established at Detroit; transferred to Brooklyn, 1977.

St. Nicholas in Chicago (Byzantine Rite Eparchy of St. Nicholas of the Ukrainians) (1961): Innocent H. Lotocky, O.S.B.M., bishop, 1981.

Former bishop: Jaroslav Gabro, 1961-80.

St. Paul and Minneapolis,* Minn. (1850; archdiocese, 1888): John R. Roach, archbishop, 1975. William H. Bullock, J. Richard Ham, M.M., Robert J. Carlson, auxiliaries.

Former ordinaries: Joseph Cretin, 1851-57; Thomas L. Grace, O.P., 1859-84; John Ireland, 1884-1918, first archbishop; Austin Dowling, 1919-30; John G. Murray, 1931-56; William O. Brady, 1956-61; Leo Binz, 1962-75.

St. Petersburg, Fla. (1968): W. Thomas Larkin, bishop, 1979.

Former bishop: Charles McLaughlin, 1968-78.

St. Thomas the Apostle of Detroit (Chaldean Rite) (1982; eparchy, 1985): Ibrahim Ibrahim, ex-arch, 1982; first eparch, 1985.

Salina, Kans. (1887): George K. Fitzsimons, bishop, 1984.

Established at Concordia, transferred, 1944.

Former bishops: Richard Scannell, 1887-91; John J. Hennessy, administrator, 1891-98; John F. Cunningham, 1898-1919; Francis J. Tief, 1921-38; Frank A. Thill, 1938-57; Frederick W. Freking, 1957-64; Cyril J. Vogel, 1965-79; Daniel W. Kucera, O.S.B., 1980-84.

Salt Lake City, Utah (1891): William K. Weigand, bishop, 1980.

Former bishops: Lawrence Scanlan, 1891-1915; Joseph S. Glass, C.M., 1915-26; John J. Mitty, 1926-32; James E. Kearney, 1932-37; Duane G. Hunt, 1937-60; J. Lennox Federal, 1960-80.

San Angelo, Tex. (1961): Michael Pfeifer, O.M.I., bishop, 1985.

Former bishops: Thomas J. Drury, 1962-65; Thomas Tschoepe, 1966-69; Stephen A. Leven, 1969-79; Joseph A. Fiorenza, 1979-84.

San Antonio,* Tex. (1874; archdiocese, 1926): Patrick F. Flores, archbishop, 1979. Bernard Popp, auxiliary.

Former ordinaries: Anthony D. Pellicer, 1874-80; John C. Neraz, 1881-94; John A. Forest, 1895-1911; John W. Shaw, 1911-18; Arthur Jerome Drossaerts, 1918-40, first archbishop; Robert E. Lucey, 1941-69; Francis Furey, 1969-79.

San Bernardino, Calif. (1978): Phillip F. Straling, bishop, 1978.

San Diego, Calif. (1936): Leo T. Maher, bishop, 1969. Gilbert Espinoza Chavez, auxiliary.

Former bishops: Charles F. Buddy, 1936-66; Francis J. Furey, 1966-69.

San Francisco,* Calif. (1853): John R. Quinn, archbishop, 1977. Daniel F. Walsh, auxiliary.

Former ordinaries: Joseph S. Alemany, O.P., 1853-84; Patrick W. Riordan, 1884-1914; Edward J. Hanna, 1915-35; John Mitty, 1935-61; Joseph T. McGucken, 1962-77.

San Jose, Calif. (1981): R. Pierre DuMaine, first bishop, 1981.

Santa Fe,* N. Mex. (1850; archdiocese, 1875): Robert Sanchez, archbishop, 1974.

Former ordinaries: John B. Lamy, 1850-85, first archbishop; John B. Salpointe, 1885-94; Placide L. Chapelle, 1894-97; Peter Bourgade, 1899-1908; John B. Pitaval, 1909-18; Albert T. Daeger, O.F.M., 1919-32; Rudolph A. Gerken, 1933-43; Edwin V. Byrne, 1943-63; James P. Davis, 1964-74.

Santa Rosa, Calif. (1962): Vacant as of Aug. 14, 1986.

Former bishops: Leo T. Maher, 1962-69; Mark J. Hurley, 1969-86.

Savannah, Ga. (1850): Raymond W. Lessard, bishop, 1973.

Former bishops: Francis X. Gartland, 1850-54; John Barry, 1857-59; Augustin Verot, S.S., 1861-70; Ignatius Persico, O.F.M. Cap., 1870-72; William H. Gross, C.SS.R., 1873-85; Thomas A. Becker,

1886-99; Benjamin J. Keiley, 1900-22; Michael Keyes, S.M., 1922-35; Gerald P. O'Hara, 1935-59; Thomas J. McDonough, 1960-67; Gerard L. Frey, 1967-72.

Scranton, Pa. (1868): James C. Timlin, bishop, 1984.

Former bishops: William O'Hara, 1868-99; Michael J. Hoban, 1899-1926; Thomas C. O'Reilly, 1928-38; William J. Hafey, 1938-54; Jerome D. Hannan, 1954-65; J. Carroll McCormick, 1966-83; John J. O'Connor, 1983-84.

Seattle,* Wash. (1850; archdiocese, 1951): Raymond G. Hunthausen, archbishop, 1975. Donald Wuerl, auxiliary.

Established as Nesqually, name changed, 1907.

Former ordinaries; Augustin M. Blanchet, 1850-79; Aegidius Junger, 1879-95; Edward J. O'Dea, 1896-1932; Gerald Shaughnessy, S.M., 1933-50; Thomas A. Connolly, first archbishop, 1950-75.

Shreveport, La. (1986): William B. Friend, bishop, 1986.

Sioux City, Ia. (1902): Lawrence D. Soens, bishop, 1983.

Former bishops: Philip J. Garrigan, 1902-19; Edmond Heelan, 1919-48; Joseph M. Mueller, 1948-70; Frank H. Greteman, 1970-83.

Sioux Falls, S. Dak. (1889): Paul V. Dudley, bishop, 1978. Paul F. Anderson, auxiliary.

Former bishops: Martin Marty, O.S.B., 1889-94; Thomas O'Gorman, 1896-1921; Bernard J. Mahoney, 1922-39; William O. Brady, 1939-56; Lambert A. Hoch, 1956-78.

Spokane, Wash. (1913): Lawrence H. Welsh, bishop, 1978.

Former bishops: Augustine F. Schinner, 1914-25; Charles D. White, 1927-55; Bernard J. Topel, 1955-78.

Springfield, Ill. (1853): Daniel L. Ryan, bishop, 1984.

Established at Quincy, transferred to Alton 1857; transferred to Springfield 1923.

Former bishops: Henry D. Juncker, 1857-68; Peter J. Baltes, 1870-86; James Ryan, 1888-1923; James A. Griffin, 1924-48; William A. O'Connor, 1949-75; Joseph A. McNicholas, 1975-83.

Springfield, Mass. (1870): Joseph F. Maguire, bishop, 1977. Leo E. O'Neil, auxiliary.

Former bishops: Patrick T. O'Reilly, 1870-92; Thomas D. Beaven, 1892-1920; Thomas M. O'Leary, 1921-49; Christopher J. Weldon, 1950-77.

Springfield-Cape Girardeau, Mo. (1956): John J. Leibrecht, bishop, 1984.

Former bishops: Charles Helmsing, 1956-62; Ignatius J. Strecker, 1962-69; William Baum, 1970-73; Bernard F. Law, 1973-84.

Stamford, Conn. (Byzantine Rite, Ukrainians) (1956); Basil Losten, eparch, 1977.

Former eparchs: Ambrose Senyshyn, O.S.B.M., 1956-61; Joseph Schmondiuk, 1961-77.

Steubenville, Ohio (1944): Albert H. Ottenweller, bishop, 1977.

Former bishop: John K. Mussio, 1945-77.

Stockton, Calif. (1962): Donald W. Montrose, bishop, 1986.

Former bishops: Hugh A. Donohoe, 1962-69;

Merlin J. Guilfoyle, 1969-79; Roger M. Mahony, 1980-85.

Superior, Wis. (1905): Raphael M. Fliss, bishop, 1985.

Former bishops: Augustine F. Schinner, 1905-13; Joseph M. Koudelka, 1913-21; Joseph G. Pinten, 1922-26; Theodore M. Reverman, 1926-41; William P. O'Connor, 1942-46; Albert G. Meyer, 1946-53; Joseph Annabring, 1954-59; George A. Hammes, 1960-85.

Syracuse, N.Y. (1886): Frank J. Harrison, bishop, 1976. Thomas J. Costello, auxiliary.

Former bishops: Patrick A. Ludden, 1887-1912; John Grimes, 1912-22; Daniel J. Curley, 1923-32; John A. Duffy, 1933-37; Walter A. Foery, 1937-70; David F. Cunningham, 1970-76.

Toledo, Ohio (1910): James R. Hoffman, bishop, 1980. Robert Donnelly, auxiliary.

Former bishops: Joseph Schrembs, 1911-21; Samuel A. Stritch, 1921-30; Karl J. Alter, 1931-50; George J. Rehring, 1950-67; John A. Donovan, 1967-80.

Trenton, N.J. (1881): John C. Reiss, bishop, 1980. Edward U. Kmiec, auxiliary.

Former bishops: Michael J. O'Farrell, 1881-94; James A. McFaul, 1894-1917; Thomas J. Walsh, 1918-28; John J. McMahon, 1928-32; Moses E. Kiley, 1934-40; William A. Griffin, 1940-50; George W. Ahr, 1950-79.

Tucson, Ariz. (1897): Manuel D. Moreno, bishop, 1982.

Former bishops: Peter Bourgade, 1897-99; Henry Granjon, 1900-22; Daniel J. Gercke, 1923-60; Francis J. Green, 1960-81.

Tulsa, Okla. (1972): Eusebius J. Beltran, bishop, 1978.

Former bishop: Bernard J. Ganter, 1973-77.

Van Nuys, Calif. (Byzantine Rite, Ruthenians) (1981): Thomas Dolinay, bishop, 1982.

Venice, Fla. (1984): John J. Nevins, bishop, 1984.

Victoria, Tex. (1982): Charles Grahmann, bishop, 1982.

Washington,* D.C. (1939): James A. Hickey, archbishop, 1980. Thomas W. Lyons, Eugene A. Marino, S.S.J., Alvaro Corrada del Rio, S.J., auxiliaries.

Former ordinaries: Michael J. Curley, 1939-47; Cardinal Patrick O'Boyle, 1948-73; Cardinal William Baum, 1973-80.

Wheeling-Charleston, W. Va. (1850): Francis B. Schulte, bishop, 1985. James E. Michaels, S.S.C., auxiliary.

Established as Wheeling; name changed, 1974.

Former bishops: Richard V. Whelan, 1850-74; John J. Kain, 1875-93; Patrick J. Donahue, 1894-1922; John J. Swint, 1922-62; Joseph H. Hodges, 1962-85.

Wichita, Kans. (1887): Eugene J. Gerber, bishop, 1982.

Former bishops: John J. Hennessy, 1888-1920; Augustus J. Schwertner, 1921-39; Christian H. Winkelmann, 1940-46; Mark K. Carroll, 1947-67; David M. Maloney, 1967-82.

Wilmington, Del. (1868): Robert E. Mulvee, bishop, 1985.

Former bishops: Thomas A. Becker, 1868-86;

Alfred A. Curtis, 1886-96; John J. Monaghan, 1897-1925; Edmond Fitzmaurice, 1925-60; Michael Hyle, 1960-67; Thomas J. Mardaga, 1968-84.

Winona, Minn. (1889): Loras J. Watters, bishop, 1969.

Former bishops: Joseph B. Cotter, 1889-1909; Patrick R. Heffron, 1910-27; Francis M. Kelly, 1928-49; Edward A. Fitzgerald, 1949-69.

Worcester, Mass. (1950): Timothy J. Harrington, bishop, 1983.

Former bishops: John J. Wright, 1950-59; Bernard J. Flanagan, 1959-83.

Yakima, Wash. (1951): William Skylstad, bishop, 1977.

Former bishops: Joseph P. Dougherty, 1951-69; Cornelius M. Power, 1969-74; Nicholas E. Walsh, 1974-76.

Youngstown, Ohio (1943): James W. Malone, bishop, 1968. Benedict C. Franzetta, auxiliary.

Former bishops: James A. McFadden, 1943-52; Emmet M. Walsh, 1952-68.

Apostolic Exarchate for Armenian-Rite Catholics in the United States and Canada, New York, N.Y. (1981); Nerses Mikail Setian, exarch, 1981.

Apostolic Exarchate for Romanians of Byzantine Rite in the United States, Canton, O. (1982): Louis Puscas, exarch, 1983.

Archdiocese for the Military Services, U.S.A., Washington, D.C. (1957; restructured, 1985): Archbishop Joseph T. Ryan, military vicar, 1985. Lawrence J. Kenney, Francis Roque, Joseph T. Dimino, Angelo T. Acerro, O.S.B., auxiliaries.

Military vicar appointed, 1917; canonically established, 1957, as U.S. Military Vicariate under jurisdiction of New York archbishop; name changed, restructured as independent jurisdiction, 1985.

Former military vicars: Cardinal Patrick Hayes, 1917-38; Cardinal Francis Spellman, 1939-67; Cardinal Terence J. Cooke, 1968-83; Cardinal John J. O'Connor, apostolic administrator, 1984-85.

MISSIONARY BISHOPS

Africa

Namibia (South West Africa): Keetmanshoop (vicariate apostolic), Edward F. Schlotterback, O.S.F.S.

South Africa: De Aar (diocese), Joseph A. De Palma, S.C.J.

  Keimos-Upington (diocese), John Minder, O.S.F.S.

Tanzania: Arusha (diocese), Dennis V. Durning, C.S.Sp.

Asia

India: Bhagalpur (diocese), Urban McGarry, T.O.R.

Indonesia: Agats (diocese), Alphonse A. Sowada, O.S.C.

Iraq: Mossul (Chaldean-rite archdiocese), George Garmo.

Korea: Inchon (diocese), William J. McNaughton, M.M.

Philippines: Cotabato (archdiocese), Philip F. Smith, O.M.I.

  Jolo (vicariate apostolic), Georges Dion, O.M.I.

Taiwan: Taichung (diocese), William F. Kupfer, M.M.

Central America, West Indies

Dominican Republic: San Juan de la Maguana (diocese), Ronald G. Connors, C.SS.R.
Honduras: Comayagua (diocese), Gerald Scarpone, O.F.M.
Nicaragua: Bluefields (vicariate apostolic), Salvator Schlaefer Berg, O.F.M.Cap., vicar apostolic; Paul Schmitz, O.F.M. Cap., auxiliary.
Virgin Islands: St. Thomas (diocese), Sean O'Malley, O.F.M. Cap.

North America

Mexico: Mexico City (archdiocese), Ricardo Watty Urquidi, M.Sp.S., auxiliary.

Oceania

American Samoa: Samoa-Pago Pago (diocese), John Quinn Weitzel, M.M.
Caroline and Marshall Islands: Carolines-Marshalls (diocese), Martin J. Neylon, S.J.
Papua New Guinea: Goroko (diocese), Raymond R. Caesar, S.V.D.
Madang (archdiocese), Leo Arkfeld, S.V.D.
Mendi (diocese), Firmin Schmidt, O.F.M.Cap.

Mount Hagen (archdiocese), George Bernarding, S.V.D.
Wewak (diocese), Raymond P. Kalisz, S.V.D.
Vanuatu (New Hebrides): Port Vila (diocese), Francis Lambert, S.M.

South America

Bolivia: Coroico (diocese), Thomas R. Manning, O.F.M.
La Paz (archdiocese), Luis Morgan Casey, auxiliary.
Pando (vicariate), Andrew B. Schierhoff.
Santa Cruz (archdiocese), Charles A. Brown, M.M., auxiliary.
Brazil: Abaetetuba (diocese), Angelo Frosi, S.X.
Belem do Para (archdiocese), Jude Prost, O.F.M., auxiliary.
Borba (prelacy), Adrian J. M. Veigle, T.O.R.
Cristalandia (prelacy), James A. Schuck, O.F.M.
Jatai (diocese), Benedict D. Coscia, O.F.M., bishop; Michael P. Mundo, auxiliary.
Paranagua (diocese), Bernard Nolker, C.SS.R.
Rui Barbosa (diocese), Mathias Schmidt, O.S.B.
Sao Paulo (archdiocese), Alfred Novak, C.SS.R., auxiliary.
Sao Salvador da Bahia (archdiocese), Thomas W. Murphy, C.SS.R., auxiliary.
Peru: Chulucanas (prelacy), John McNabb, O.S.A.

CATHOLIC POPULATION OF THE UNITED STATES

(Source: *The Official Catholic Directory, 1986;* figures as of Jan. 1, 1986. Archdioceses are indicated by an asterisk; for dioceses marked +, see Dioceses with Interstate Lines. Figures for the Chaldean rite diocese of St. Thomas Apostle of Detroit are from the *Annuario Pontificio, 1986*)

Section, State Diocese	Catholics	Dioc. Priests	Rel. Priests	Total Priests	Perm. Deacons	Bros.	Sisters	Parishes
NEW ENGLAND	5,645,963	3,944	2,596	6,540	687	803	12,044	1,709
Maine, Portland	280,057	212	117	329	—	38	733	145
New Hampshire, Manchester	296,032	276	106	382	18	73	1,027	130
Vermont, Burlington	154,512	157	74	231	28	19	352	100
Massachusetts	2,942,348	1,908	1,831	3,739	237	420	6,309	785
*Boston	1,918,715	1,114	1,338	2,452	132	270	4,047	408
Fall River	340,000	205	195	400	23	28	681	113
Springfield	348,495	258	135	393	28	22	890	136
Worcester	335,138	331	163	494	54	100	691	128
Rhode Island, Providence	617,872	376	195	571	76	162	1,080	159
Connecticut	1,355,142	1,015	273	1,288	328	91	2,543	390
*Hartford	817,794	540	111	651	246	60	1,384	223
Bridgeport	333,213	321	85	406	43	5	810	91
Norwich+	204,135	154	77	231	39	26	349	76
MIDDLE ATLANTIC	13,374,832	9,444	5,278	14,722	1,486	1,811	31,827	3,901
New York	6,650,882	4,325	2,897	7,222	736	1,169	14,319	1,711
*New York	1,808,879	985	1,442	2,427	228	400	5,018	410
Albany	408,648	385	192	577	60	88	1,240	201
Brooklyn	1,414,889	872	467	1,339	125	270	2,050	221
Buffalo	808,119	568	336	904	62	64	2,088	295
Ogdensburg	169,845	193	37	230	42	32	321	122
Rochester	379,200	347	195	542	49	163	1,017	161
Rockville Centre	1,320,167	586	127	713	131	130	1,903	129
Syracuse	341,135	389	101	490	39	22	682	172

Section, State Diocese	Catholics	Dioc. Priests	Rel. Priests	Total Priests	Perm. Deacons	Bros.	Sisters	Par- ishes
New Jersey	**3,085,832**	**1,999**	**942**	**2,941**	**595**	**308**	**5,108**	**707**
*Newark	1,338,500	787	490	1,277	229	170	2,190	242
Camden	366,538	493	60	553	65	22	523	127
Metuchen	456,646	156	87	243	72	39	634	108
Paterson	376,783	291	206	497	82	36	1,119	107
Trenton	547,365	272	99	371	147	41	642	123
Pennsylvania	**3,638,118**	**3,120**	**1,439**	**4,559**	**155**	**334**	**12,400**	**1,483**
*Philadelphia	1,353,004	916	602	1,518	27	219	5,206	301
Allentown	253,481	311	97	408	32	20	852	153
Altoona-Johnstown	147,357	182	95	277	5	19	169	122
Erie	214,558	285	38	323	1	4	705	128
Greensburg	215,743	188	125	313	—	8	427	115
Harrisburg	208,726	179	81	260	64	12	798	110
Pittsburgh	887,798	603	270	873	25	43	3,058	315
Scranton	357,451	456	131	587	1	9	1,185	239
SOUTH ATLANTIC	**3,140,279**	**2,404**	**2,179**	**4,583**	**681**	**558**	**6,269**	**1,352**
Delaware, Wilmington+	**128,997**	**122**	**111**	**233**	**18**	**37**	**372**	**56**
Maryland, *Baltimore	**436,447**	**345**	**404**	**749**	**130**	**104**	**1,678**	**153**
District of Columbia								
*Washington+	**384,356**	**357**	**663**	**1,020**	**135**	**175**	**951**	**133**
Virginia	**329,165**	**280**	**152**	**432**	**69**	**28**	**647**	**170**
Arlington	205,148	94	109	203	61	20	279	58
Richmond	124,017	186	43	229	8	8	368	112
West Virginia								
Wheeling-Charleston	**106,941**	**131**	**66**	**197**	**27**	**10**	**441**	**128**
North Carolina	**123,769**	**142**	**87**	**229**	**22**	**15**	**315**	**125**
Charlotte	63,212	73	61	134	20	9	208	63
Raleigh	60,557	69	26	95	2	6	107	62
South Carolina, Charleston	**72,449**	**77**	**57**	**134**	**26**	**28**	**250**	**83**
Georgia	**194,060**	**169**	**150**	**319**	**55**	**37**	**370**	**111**
*Atlanta	132,482	101	112	213	19	27	158	63
Savannah	61,578	68	38	106	36	10	212	48
Florida	**1,364,095**	**781**	**489**	**1,270**	**199**	**124**	**1,245**	**393**
*Miami	528,600	281	157	438	61	60	440	104
Orlando	186,000	112	46	158	36	—	68	61
Palm Beach	117,120	67	51	118	18	5	191	38
Pensacola-Tallahassee	48,038	74	14	88	49	—	72	46
St. Augustine	81,294	82	19	101	5	3	116	46
St. Petersburg	269,884	104	155	259	15	50	248	58
Venice	133,159	61	47	108	15	6	110	40
EAST NORTH CENTRAL	**10,413,298**	**7,549**	**4,376**	**11,925**	**1,678**	**1,654**	**27,434**	**4,242**
Ohio	**2,278,916**	**1,959**	**887**	**2,846**	**394**	**403**	**6,433**	**965**
*Cincinnati	532,790	440	380	820	85	223	1,974	256
Cleveland	865,635	624	256	880	80	104	2,230	245
Columbus	194,392	224	59	283	49	5	547	108
Steubenville	54,684	151	16	167	—	8	111	77
Toledo	348,971	263	118	381	147	20	1,152	165
Youngstown	282,444	257	58	315	33	43	419	114
Indiana	**706,659**	**718**	**489**	**1,207**	**102**	**240**	**2,619**	**445**
*Indianapolis	200,549	202	166	368	—	82	990	142
Evansville	87,390	123	19	142	21	2	401	67
Ft. Wayne-South Bend	141,953	131	198	329	36	115	948	89
Gary	187,037	143	67	210	40	29	247	83
Lafayette	89,730	119	39	158	5	12	33	64
Illinois	**3,586,728**	**2,172**	**1,651**	**3,823**	**729**	**629**	**8,647**	**1,104**
*Chicago	2,362,162	1,201	1,159	2,360	485	432	5,339	446
Belleville	122,419	156	44	200	31	16	302	130
Joliet	425,000	216	166	382	92	125	1,015	113
Peoria	247,068	245	101	346	49	11	540	170
Rockford	243,224	167	84	251	72	22	531	100
Springfield	186,855	187	97	284	—	23	920	145

Section, State Diocese	Catholics	Dioc. Priests	Rel. Priests	Total Priests	Perm. Deacons	Bros.	Sisters	Par- ishes
Michigan	**2,271,716**	**1,281**	**613**	**1,894**	**246**	**166**	**4,252**	**833**
*Detroit	1,466,106	588	422	1,010	149	132	2,500	331
Gaylord	90,383	67	18	85	4	4	128	85
Grand Rapids	152,169	147	44	191	14	4	464	90
Kalamazoo	96,461	59	23	82	19	7	286	47
Lansing	227,156	151	53	204	31	16	547	89
Marquette	81,316	126	19	145	3	—	121	86
Saginaw	158,125	143	34	177	26	3	206	105
Wisconsin	**1,569,279**	**1,419**	**736**	**2,155**	**207**	**216**	**5,483**	**895**
*Milwaukee	662,348	590	471	1,061	137	126	3,189	268
Green Bay	355,546	278	177	455	59	58	858	211
La Crosse	235,410	249	31	280	11	13	631	192
Madison	231,211	206	32	238	—	16	605	138
Superior	84,764	96	25	121	—	3	200	86
EAST SOUTH CENTRAL	**721,829**	**981**	**404**	**1,385**	**249**	**290**	**3,618**	**671**
Kentucky	**371,693**	**505**	**156**	**661**	**102**	**128**	**2,450**	**290**
*Louisville	211,403	237	99	336	86	108	1,353	130
Covington	106,380	188	31	219	16	9	775	87
Owensboro	53,910	80	26	106	—	11	322	73
Tennessee	**130,272**	**173**	**53**	**226**	**95**	**70**	**340**	**123**
Memphis	50,308	75	20	95	34	56	158	39
Nashville	79,964	98	33	131	61	14	182	84
Alabama	**123,105**	**162**	**130**	**292**	**34**	**30**	**452**	**139**
*Mobile	66,623	92	71	163	21	17	274	78
Birmingham	56,482	70	59	129	13	13	178	61
Mississippi	**96,759**	**141**	**65**	**206**	**18**	**62**	**376**	**119**
Biloxi	54,375	64	30	94	6	46	81	44
Jackson	42,384	77	35	112	12	16	295	75
WEST NORTH CENTRAL	**3,405,886**	**3,911**	**1,794**	**5,705**	**659**	**699**	**13,832**	**2,824**
Minnesota	**1,049,258**	**941**	**415**	**1,356**	**130**	**164**	**3,756**	**718**
*St. Paul and Minneapolis	565,195	379	197	576	94	76	1,706	220
Crookston	43,083	53	18	71	1	3	292	44
Duluth	87,222	93	26	119	12	—	222	100
New Ulm	70,262	103	10	113	2	—	129	93
St. Cloud	146,647	157	149	306	21	66	735	137
Winona	136,849	156	15	171	—	19	672	124
Iowa	**521,681**	**840**	**103**	**943**	**126**	**40**	**2,154**	**552**
*Dubuque	218,734	343	62	405	42	23	1,343	232
Davenport	108,351	179	22	201	28	14	374	116
Des Moines	86,353	122	9	131	28	—	197	85
Sioux City	108,243	196	10	206	28	3	240	119
Missouri	**834,065**	**925**	**742**	**1,667**	**212**	**364**	**3,957**	**497**
*St. Louis	553,993	555	484	1,039	95	216	3,121	245
Jefferson City	85,655	136	27	163	44	14	140	95
Kansas City-St. Joseph	147,006	155	168	323	71	59	491	93
Springfield- Cape Girardeau	47,411	79	63	142	2	75	205	64
North Dakota	**178,534**	**205**	**70**	**275**	**48**	**30**	**533**	**185**
Bismarck	78,716	76	44	120	22	25	233	70
Fargo	99,818	129	26	155	26	5	300	115
South Dakota	**139,035**	**185**	**88**	**273**	**30**	**32**	**657**	**204**
Rapid City	35,465	43	46	89	18	13	91	82
Sioux Falls	103,570	142	42	184	12	19	566	122
Nebraska	**337,855**	**426**	**211**	**637**	**105**	**44**	**797**	**276**
*Omaha	207,200	213	191	404	105	44	667	138
Grand Island	56,654	89	2	91	—	—	130	51
Lincoln	74,001	124	18	142	—	—	—	87
Kansas	**345,458**	**389**	**165**	**554**	**8**	**25**	**1,978**	**392**
*Kansas	153,150	124	89	213	—	20	1,043	122
Dodge City	39,121	59	12	71	7	—	170	59
Salina	56,846	70	36	106	—	5	306	98
Wichita	96,341	136	28	164	1	—	459	113

Section, State Diocese	Catholics	Dioc. Priests	Rel. Priests	Total Priests	Perm. Deacons	Bros.	Sisters	Par-ishes
WEST SOUTH CENTRAL	**4,513,025**	**2,152**	**1,620**	**3,772**	**1,024**	**604**	**6,187**	**1,618**
Arkansas, Little Rock	**60,048**	**100**	**60**	**160**	**29**	**56**	**398**	**89**
Louisiana	**1,364,704**	**727**	**505**	**1,232**	**232**	**272**	**1,815**	**491**
*New Orleans	535,156	257	297	554	113	200	1,160	143
Alexandria-Shreveport	85,894	114	38	152	3	10	192	83
Baton Rouge	192,345	92	54	146	21	17	140	72
Houma-Thibodaux	124,930	52	11	63	24	12	46	37
Lafayette	336,534	169	74	243	46	31	237	120
Lake Charles	89,845	43	31	74	25	2	40	36
Oklahoma	**145,095**	**178**	**64**	**242**	**61**	**30**	**389**	**129**
*Oklahoma City	90,595	109	24	133	35	23	175	72
Tulsa	54,500	69	40	109	26	7	214	57
Texas	**2,943,178**	**1,147**	**991**	**2,138**	**702**	**246**	**3,585**	**909**
*San Antonio	566,805	161	248	409	124	135	1,203	135
Amarillo	32,129	39	15	54	26	1	145	27
Austin	138,640	103	59	162	36	35	131	86
Beaumont	88,335	58	29	87	20	1	125	44
Brownsville	427,044	51	77	128	48	9	162	61
Corpus Christi	320,479	89	78	167	32	20	326	80
Dallas	208,982	119	92	211	104	3	274	70
El Paso+	187,530	100	47	147	32	9	264	51
Fort Worth	122,764	62	60	122	27	12	141	81
Galveston-Houston	611,477	225	225	450	166	20	613	147
Lubbock	48,365	29	14	43	30	—	—	33
San Angelo	75,628	58	30	88	52	—	42	48
Victoria	115,000	53	17	70	5	1	159	46
MOUNTAIN	**1,905,857**	**1,233**	**830**	**2,063**	**420**	**254**	**2,863**	**864**
Montana	**136,413**	**207**	**52**	**259**	**15**	**6**	**251**	**133**
Great Falls-Billings	66,092	91	29	120	3	2	170	74
Helena	70,321	116	23	139	12	4	81	59
Idaho, Boise	**70,724**	**97**	**23**	**120**	**27**	**3**	**115**	**73**
Wyoming, Cheyenne+	**63,000**	**56**	**7**	**63**	**2**	**4**	**69**	**39**
Colorado	**481,783**	**283**	**262**	**545**	**100**	**47**	**984**	**196**
*Denver	330,270	161	195	356	85	29	592	112
Colorado Springs	65,000	29	17	46	12	4	230	25
Pueblo	86,513	93	50	143	3	14	162	59
New Mexico	**415,364**	**211**	**185**	**396**	**92**	**116**	**609**	**189**
*Santa Fe	248,317	130	101	231	60	90	339	88
Gallup+	42,047	54	41	95	9	21	184	58
Las Cruces	125,000	27	43	70	23	5	86	43
Arizona	**529,801**	**274**	**202**	**476**	**153**	**47**	**595**	**144**
Phoenix	292,000	136	120	256	89	32	275	85
Tucson	237,801	138	82	220	64	15	320	59
Utah, Salt Lake City	**64,772**	**56**	**55**	**111**	**28**	**20**	**126**	**43**
Nevada, Reno-Las Vegas	**144,000**	**49**	**44**	**93**	**3**	**11**	**114**	**47**
PACIFIC	**6,885,805**	**2,950**	**2,837**	**5,787**	**629**	**746**	**9,202**	**1,592**
Washington	**428,889**	**377**	**325**	**702**	**122**	**44**	**1,241**	**249**
*Seattle	290,731	226	224	450	80	36	749	132
Spokane	81,260	94	89	183	34	8	441	77
Yakima	56,898	57	12	69	8	—	51	40
Oregon	**328,254**	**212**	**254**	**466**	**6**	**80**	**805**	**159**
*Portland	298,259	170	243	413	5	78	744	127
Baker	29,995	42	11	53	1	2	61	32
California	**5,862,260**	**2,259**	**2,104**	**4,363**	**436**	**557**	**6,731**	**1,058**
*Los Angeles	2,650,000	633	768	1,401	141	141	2,543	284
*San Francisco	375,000	239	297	536	13	40	1,071	103
Fresno	295,249	120	49	169	2	11	209	86
Monterey	144,700	78	27	105	1	36	285	45
Oakland	424,234	168	296	464	41	110	538	87
Orange	417,590	155	88	243	41	15	441	52
Sacramento	289,147	180	79	259	50	54	292	94
San Bernardino	318,672	148	72	220	48	16	195	89

Section, State Diocese	Catholics	Dioc. Priests	Rel. Priests	Total Priests	Perm. Deacons	Bros.	Sisters	Par- ishes
California								
San Diego	381,747	260	100	360	64	22	488	98
San Jose	324,135	139	274	413	18	72	488	49
Santa Rosa	98,673	90	23	113	6	35	116	40
Stockton	143,113	49	31	80	11	5	65	31
Alaska	49,402	50	51	101	48	13	104	62
*Anchorage	26,647	25	21	46	11	8	49	19
Fairbanks	15,604	10	28	38	29	5	42	34
Juneau	7,151	15	2	17	8	—	13	9
Hawaii, Honolulu	217,000	52	103	155	17	52	321	64
EASTERN RITES								
*Philadelphia	80,588	79	10	89	1	—	107	76
St. Nicholas	20,000	31	12	43	6	—	14	34
Stamford	44,099	61	23	84	3	1	49	51
St. Josaphat (Parma)	11,987	36	3	39	1	—	7	35
*Pittsburgh	152,237	79	8	87	—	5	142	84
Parma	27,548	46	5	51	—	—	19	40
Passaic	93,140	100	21	121	10	—	15	93
Van Nuys	8,524	23	2	25	6	—	2	14
St. Maron (Maronites)	50,893	70	2	72	5	—	5	52
Newton (Melkites)	24,218	43	20	63	15	4	4	35
St. Thomas Apostle of Detroit (Chaldean)	42,000	12	—	12	40	—	9	9
Armenian (Ap. Ex.)	31,500	6	8	14	—	—	18	10
Romanians (Ap. Ex.)	3,400	13	—	13	2	—	—	16
MILITARY ARCHDIOCESE	2,100,000	—	—	—	—	—	—	—
TOTALS 1986	52,654,908	35,155	22,028	57,183	7,562	7,429	113,658	19,313
Totals 1985	52,286,043	35,052	22,265	57,317	7,204	7,544	115,386	19,244
Totals 1976	48,881,872	36,175	22,672	58,847	—	8,563	130,995	18,531

Dioceses with Interstate Lines

Diocesan lines usually fall within a single state and in some cases include a whole state.

The following dioceses, with their statistics as reported in tables throughout the Almanac, are exceptions.

Norwich, Conn., includes Fisher's Island, N.Y.

Wilmington, Del., includes all of Delaware and nine counties of Maryland.

Washington, D.C., includes five counties of Maryland.

Gallup, N.M., has jurisdiction over several counties of Arizona.

Cheyenne, Wyo., includes all of Yellowstone National Park.

PERCENTAGE OF CATHOLICS IN U.S. POPULATION

(Source: *The Official Catholic Directory, 1986;* figures are as of Jan. 1, 1986. Total general population figures at the end of the table are U.S. Census Bureau estimates for Jan. 1 of the respective years. Archdioceses are indicated by an asterisk; for dioceses marked +, see Dioceses with Interstate Lines.)

Section, State Diocese	Catholic Pop.	Total Pop.	Cath. Pct.	Section, State Diocese	Catholic Pop.	Total Pop.	Cath. Pct.
NEW ENGLAND	**5,645,963**	**12,376,023**	**45.62**	Connecticut Bridgeport	333,213	832,360	40.03
				Norwich+	204,135	590,930	34.54
Maine, Portland	280,057	1,124,660	24.90	**MIDDLE ATLANTIC**	**13,374,832**	**37,263,559**	**35.89**
New Hampshire Manchester	296,032	977,000	30.30	New York	6,650,882	17,928,720	37.09
Vermont, Burlington	154,512	535,000	28.88	*New York	1,808,879	5,007,307	36.12
Massachusetts	2,942,348	5,599,539	52.54	Albany	408,648	1,472,684	27.74
*Boston	1,918,715	3,634,846	52.78	Brooklyn	1,414,889	4,165,100	33.97
Fall River	340,000	530,000	64.15	Buffalo	808,119	1,628,300	49.62
Springfield	348,495	790,725	44.07	Ogdensburg	169,845	395,563	42.93
Worcester	335,138	643,968	52.04	Rochester	379,200	1,432,000	26.48
Rhode Island, Providence	617,872	947,154	65.23	Rockville Centre	1,320,167	2,620,203	50.38
Connecticut	1,355,142	3,192,670	42.44	Syracuse	341,135	1,207,563	28.24
*Hartford	817,794	1,769,380	46.21				

Section, State Diocese	Catholic Pop.	Total Pop.	Cath. Pct.
New Jersey	3,085,832	7,419,616	41.59
*Newark	1,338,500	2,741,500	48.82
Camden	366,538	1,165,800	31.44
Metuchen	456,646	1,005,000	45.43
Paterson	376,783	987,700	38.14
Trenton	547,365	1,519,616	36.01
Pennsylvania	3,638,118	11,915,223	30.53
*Philadelphia	1,353,004	3,676,411	36.80
Allentown	253,481	1,027,302	24.67
Altoona-Johnstown	147,357	654,338	22.52
Erie	214,558	902,529	23.77
Greensburg	215,743	718,511	30.02
Harrisburg	208,726	1,800,000	11.59
Pittsburgh	887,798	2,165,361	40.99
Scranton	357,451	970,771	36.82
SOUTH ATLANTIC	**3,140,279**	**40,100,171**	**7.83**
Delaware, Wilmington+	128,997	814,300	15.84
Maryland, *Baltimore	436,447	2,508,947	17.39
District of Columbia			
*Washington+	384,356	2,107,000	18.24
Virginia	329,165	6,044,207	5.44
Arlington	205,148	2,000,000	10.25
Richmond	124,017	4,044,207	3.06
West Virginia			
Wheeling-Charleston	106,941	1,949,644	5.48
North Carolina	123,769	5,879,518	2.10
Charlotte	63,212	3,101,207	2.03
Raleigh	60,557	2,778,311	2.17
South Carolina			
Charleston	72,449	3,347,000	2.16
Georgia	194,060	6,374,617	3.04
*Atlanta	132,482	4,450,067	2.97
Savannah	61,578	1,924,550	3.19
Florida	1,364,095	11,074,938	12.31
*Miami	528,600	2,940,000	17.97
Orlando	186,000	2,135,000	8.71
Palm Beach	117,120	1,017,669	11.50
Pensacola-Tallahassee	48,038	952,159	5.04
St. Augustine	81,294	1,115,000	7.29
St. Petersburg	269,884	1,925,642	14.01
Venice	133,159	989,468	13.45
EAST NORTH CENTRAL	**10,413,298**	**41,425,460**	**25.13**
Ohio	2,278,916	10,764,047	21.17
*Cincinnati	532,790	2,716,191	19.61
Cleveland	865,635	2,816,000	30.73
Columbus	194,392	1,940,333	10.01
Steubenville	54,684	541,093	10.10
Toledo	348,971	1,486,614	23.47
Youngstown	282,444	1,263,816	22.34
Indiana	706,659	5,389,675	13.11
*Indianapolis	200,549	2,127,915	9.42
Evansville	87,390	466,821	18.72
Ft. Wayne-S. Bend	141,953	1,044,602	13.58
Gary	187,037	685,237	27.29
Lafayette	89,730	1,065,100	8.42
Illinois	3,586,728	11,502,223	31.18
*Chicago	2,362,162	5,707,300	41.38
Belleville	122,419	861,986	14.20
Joliet	425,000	1,270,000	33.46

Section, State Diocese	Catholic Pop.	Total Pop.	Cath. Pct.
Illinois			
Peoria	247,068	1,501,917	16.45
Rockford	243,224	1,027,342	23.67
Springfield	186,855	1,133,678	16.48
Michigan	2,271,716	8,958,973	25.35
*Detroit	1,466,106	4,215,108	34.78
Gaylord	90,383	391,843	23.06
Grand Rapids	152,169	906,483	16.78
Kalamazoo	96,461	863,911	11.16
Lansing	227,156	1,556,180	14.59
Marquette	81,316	312,028	26.06
Saginaw	158,125	713,420	22.16
Wisconsin	1,569,279	4,810,542	32.62
*Milwaukee	662,348	2,029,553	32.63
Green Bay	355,546	796,204	44.65
La Crosse	235,410	751,203	31.33
Madison	231,211	924,844	25.00
Superior	84,764	308,738	27.45
EAST SOUTH CENTRAL	**721,829**	**14,732,163**	**4.89**
Kentucky	371,693	3,657,774	10.16
*Louisville	211,403	1,301,024	16.24
Covington	106,380	1,591,000	6.68
Owensboro	53,910	765,750	7.04
Tennessee	130,272	4,604,469	2.82
Memphis	50,308	1,326,000	3.79
Nashville	79,964	3,278,469	2.43
Alabama	123,105	3,922,670	3.13
*Mobile	66,623	1,422,835	4.68
Birmingham	56,482	2,499,835	2.25
Mississippi	96,759	2,547,250	3.79
Biloxi	54,375	637,250	8.53
Jackson	42,384	1,910,000	2.21
WEST NORTH CENTRAL	**3,405,886**	**17,264,264**	**19.72**
Minnesota	1,049,258	4,072,371	25.76
*St. Paul and			
Minneapolis	565,195	2,173,572	26.00
Crookston	43,083	239,045	18.02
Duluth	87,222	425,987	20.47
New Ulm	70,262	291,014	24.14
St. Cloud	146,647	409,791	35.78
Winona	136,849	532,962	25.67
Iowa	521,681	2,909,826	17.92
*Dubuque	218,734	995,648	21.96
Davenport	108,351	733,591	14.76
Des Moines	86,353	667,726	12.93
Sioux City	108,243	512,861	21.10
Missouri	834,065	4,925,242	16.93
*St. Louis	553,993	1,940,387	28.55
Jefferson City	85,655	727,080	11.78
Kansas City-St. Joseph	147,006	1,260,051	11.66
Springfield-			
Cape Girardeau	47,411	997,724	4.75
North Dakota	178,534	652,633	27.35
Bismarck	78,716	269,310	29.22
Fargo	99,818	383,323	26.04
South Dakota	139,035	689,316	20.16
Rapid City	35,465	202,816	17.48
Sioux Falls	103,570	486,500	21.28

Section, State Diocese	Catholic Pop.	Total Pop.	Cath. Pct.
Nebraska	337,855	1,567,902	21.54
*Omaha	207,200	750,259	27.61
Grand Island	56,654	306,000	18.51
Lincoln	74,001	511,643	14.46
Kansas	345,458	2,446,974	14.11
*Kansas City	153,150	952,000	16.08
Dodge City	39,121	224,680	17.41
Salina	56,846	348,953	16.29
Wichita	96,341	921,341	10.45
WEST SOUTH CENTRAL	**4,513,025**	**24,695,601**	**18.27**
Arkansas, Little Rock	60,048	2,328,000	2.57
Louisiana	1,364,704	4,254,144	32.07
*New Orleans	535,156	1,433,355	37.33
Alexandria-Shreveport	85,894	1,083,132	7.93
Baton Rouge	192,345	745,000	25.81
Houma-Thibodaux	124,930	202,000	61.84
Lafayette	336,534	563,812	59.68
Lake Charles	89,845	226,845	39.60
Oklahoma	145,095	3,125,740	4.64
*Oklahoma City	90,595	1,869,140	4.84
Tulsa	54,500	1,256,600	4.33
Texas	2,943,178	14,987,717	19.63
*San Antonio	566,805	1,180,510	48.01
Amarillo	32,129	360,500	8.91
Austin	138,640	1,335,464	10.38
Beaumont	88,335	676,746	13.05
Brownsville	427,044	537,607	79.43
Corpus Christi	320,479	596,393	53.73
Dallas	208,982	3,104,700	6.73
El Paso	187,530	640,578	29.27
Fort Worth	122,764	1,789,600	6.85
Galveston-Houston	611,477	3,486,231	17.53
Lubbock	48,365	451,330	10.71
San Angelo	75,628	604,958	12.50
Victoria	115,000	223,100	51.54
MOUNTAIN	**1,905,857**	**12,305,474**	**15.48**
Montana	136,413	766,553	17.79
Great Falls-Billings	66,092	351,858	18.78
Helena	70,321	414,695	16.95
Idaho, Boise	70,724	1,049,894	6.73
Wyoming, Cheyenne+	63,000	461,000	13.66
Colorado	481,783	2,898,072	16.62
*Denver	330,270	2,036,806	16.21
Colorado			
Colorado Springs	65,000	391,266	16.61
Pueblo	86,513	470,000	18.40
New Mexico	415,364	1,567,340	26.50
*Santa Fe	248,317	800,000	31.03
Gallup+	42,047	355,340	11.83
Las Cruces	125,000	412,000	30.34
Arizona	529,801	2,975,000	17.80
Phoenix	292,000	2,040,000	14.31
Tucson	237,801	935,000	25.43
Utah, Salt Lake City	64,772	1,643,000	3.94
Nevada, Reno-Las Vegas	144,000	944,615	15.24
PACIFIC	**6,885,805**	**34,423,923**	**20.00**
Washington	428,889	4,297,523	9.97
*Seattle	290,731	3,331,000	8.72
Spokane	81,260	574,023	14.15
Yakima	56,898	392,500	14.49
Oregon	328,254	2,655,100	12.36
*Portland	298,259	2,301,000	12.96
Baker	29,995	354,100	8.47
California	5,862,260	25,838,779	22.68
*Los Angeles	2,650,000	9,027,775	29.35
*San Francisco	375,000	1,548,600	24.21
Fresno	295,249	1,463,878	20.16
Monterey	144,700	723,500	20.00
Oakland	424,234	1,878,171	22.58
Orange	417,590	2,088,350	19.99
Sacramento	289,147	2,244,776	12.88
San Bernardino	318,672	1,814,628	17.56
San Diego	381,747	2,257,800	16.90
San Jose	324,510	1,380,100	23.48
Santa Rosa	98,673	628,371	15.70
Stockton	143,113	782,830	18.28
Alaska	49,402	491,921	10.04
*Anchorage	26,647	300,000	8.88
Fairbanks	15,604	125,000	12.48
Juneau	7,151	66,921	10.68
Hawaii, Honolulu	217,000	1,140,600	19.02
EASTERN RITES	**548,134**	—	—
MILITARY ARCHDIOCESE	**2,100,000**	—	—
TOTALS 1986	**52,654,908**	**239,999,874**	**21.99**
Totals 1985	**52,286,043**	**237,232,946**	**22.04**
Totals 1976	**48,881,872**	**214,529,000**	**22.78**

INFANT BAPTISMS AND CONVERTS IN THE UNITED STATES

(Source: *The Official Catholic Directory, 1986;* figures as of Jan. 1, 1986. Archdioceses are indicated by an asterisk; for dioceses marked +, see Dioceses with Interstate Lines.)

Section, State Diocese	Infant Baptisms	Converts
NEW ENGLAND	**86,869**	**3,455**
Maine, Portland	4,287	526
New Hampshire, Manchester	5,393	229
Vermont, Burlington	2,450	187
Massachusetts	47,019	1,382
*Boston	31,398	790
Fall River	5,497	128
Massachusetts		
Springfield	4,769	240
Worcester	5,355	224
Rhode Island, Providence	7,350	214
Connecticut	20,370	907
*Hartford	12,161	559
Bridgeport	5,020	165
Norwich+	3,189	183

Section, State Diocese	Infant Baptisms	Converts
MIDDLE ATLANTIC	**211,481**	**11,268**
New York	108,729	4,400
*New York	32,075	1,321
Albany	7,091	—
Brooklyn	24,629	770
Buffalo	9,169	495
Ogdensburg	2,732	333
Rochester	6,632	329
Rockville Centre	19,267	635
Syracuse	7,134	517
New Jersey	47,834	1,806
*Newark	18,022	491
Camden	7,343	302
Metuchen	6,199	190
Paterson	7,142	322
Trenton	9,128	501
Pennsylvania	54,918	5,062
*Philadelphia	21,032	1,855
Allentown	3,918	184
Altoona-Johnstown	2,285	345
Erie	3,788	405
Greensburg	2,852	303
Harrisburg	3,904	836
Pittsburgh	11,534	830
Scranton	5,605	304
SOUTH ATLANTIC	**64,579**	**9,543**
Delaware, Wilmington+	2,749	147
Maryland, *Baltimore	8,246	1,118
District of Columbia, *Washington+	7,169	1,006
Virginia	7,377	1,602
Arlington	4,461	428
Richmond	2,916	1,174
West Virginia, Wheeling-Charleston	1,570	653
North Carolina	2,650	682
Charlotte	1,359	353
Raleigh	1,291	329
South Carolina, Charleston	1,691	367
Georgia	4,015	1,115
*Atlanta	2,694	686
Savannah	1,321	429
Florida	29,112	2,853
*Miami	13,853	690
Orlando	4,016	610
Palm Beach	2,810	309
Pensacola-Tallahassee	1,145	182
St. Augustine	1,472	275
St. Petersburg	3,742	546
Venice	2,074	241
EAST NORTH CENTRAL	**167,554**	**22,763**
Ohio	36,106	6,886
*Cincinnati	9,080	1,925
Cleveland	12,456	2,127
Columbus	3,908	975
Steubenville	940	473
Toledo	5,625	822
Youngstown	4,097	564
Indiana	13,340	2,730
*Indianapolis	4,383	1,087
Evansville	1,852	346

Section, State Diocese	Infant Baptisms	Converts
Indiana		
Ft. Wayne-South Bend	2,696	412
Gary	2,824	404
Lafayette	1,585	481
Illinois	58,952	6,843
*Chicago	35,573	3,393
Belleville	2,039	824
Joliet	8,323	552
Peoria	5,197	887
Rockford	4,418	486
Springfield	3,402	701
Michigan	32,325	4,308
*Detroit	17,403	1,733
Gaylord	1,439	210
Grand Rapids	3,298	561
Kalamazoo	1,668	353
Lansing	4,101	914
Marquette	1,582	171
Saginaw	2,834	366
Wisconsin	26,831	1,996
*Milwaukee	11,546	782
Green Bay	5,158	312
La Crosse	4,470	355
Madison	3,742	356
Superior	1,915	191
EAST SOUTH CENTRAL	**13,564**	**3,961**
Kentucky	7,018	1,437
*Louisville	3,647	692
Covington	2,249	462
Owensboro	1,122	283
Tennessee	2,503	1,098
Memphis	980	414
Nashville	1,523	684
Alabama	2,032	746
*Mobile	1,097	387
Birmingham	935	359
Mississippi	2,011	680
Biloxi	1,188	304
Jackson	823	376
WEST NORTH CENTRAL	**71,854**	**10,909**
Minnesota	22,453	2,255
*St. Paul and Minneapolis	12,181	1,249
Crookston	1,011	101
Duluth	1,553	134
New Ulm	1,601	140
St. Cloud	3,507	155
Winona	2,600	476
Iowa	11,124	1,838
*Dubuque	4,434	617
Davenport	2,501	576
Des Moines	1,782	386
Sioux City	2,407	259
Missouri	14,752	3,003
*St. Louis	9,572	1,439
Jefferson City	1,683	366
Kansas City-St. Joseph	2,586	841
Springfield-Cape Girardeau	911	357
North Dakota	4,049	399
Bismarck	1,892	160
Fargo	2,157	239

Section, State Diocese	Catholic Pop.	Total Pop.	Cath. Pct.
South Dakota		3,767	560
Rapid City		1,432	192
Sioux Falls		2,335	368
Nebraska		7,429	1,275
*Omaha		4,687	622
Grand Island		1,237	249
Lincoln		1,505	404
Kansas		8,280	1,579
*Kansas City		3,315	640
Dodge City		968	120
Salina		1,382	263
Wichita		2,615	556
WEST SOUTH CENTRAL	**106,871**	**8,336**	
Arkansas, Little Rock		1,303	424
Louisiana		26,914	2,035
*New Orleans		9,858	704
Alexandria-Shreveport		1,719	363
Baton Rouge		3,702	439
Houma-Thibodaux		2,454	108
Lafayette		7,253	213
Lake Charles		1,928	208
Oklahoma		3,246	925
*Oklahoma City		2,162	576
Tulsa		1,084	349
Texas		75,408	4,952
*San Antonio		14,847	502
Amarillo		1,235	130
Austin		4,074	436
Beaumont		1,798	331
Brownsville		7,002	122
Corpus Christi		7,221	190
Dallas		6,265	913
El Paso		7,052	84
Fort Worth		3,915	488
Galveston-Houston		14,763	1,398
Lubbock		2,406	87
San Angelo		2,877	167
Victoria		1,953	104
MOUNTAIN	**48,118**	**4,297**	
Montana		3,007	713
Great Falls-Billings		1,611	287
Helena		1,396	426
Idaho, Boise		2,061	410
Wyoming, Cheyenne+		1,375	215
Colorado		12,279	1,089
*Denver		8,786	824
Colorado Springs		1,203	92
Pueblo		2,290	173
New Mexico		12,134	490
*Santa Fe		7,088	265
Gallup+		1,182	128
Las Cruces		3,864	97
Arizona		12,916	775
Phoenix		7,766	540
Tucson		5,150	235
Utah, Salt Lake City		1,801	285
Nevada, Reno-Las Vegas		2,545	320
PACIFIC	**167,486**	**11,061**	
Washington		9,261	1,756
*Seattle		5,864	1,245
Spokane		1,679	375
Yakima		1,718	136
Oregon		4,352	970
*Portland		3,666	820
Baker		686	150
California		148,617	7,860
*Los Angeles		68,937	2,301
*San Francisco		7,492	503
Fresno		11,511	463
Monterey		4,022	262
Oakland		7,122	601
Orange		10,685	700
Sacramento		6,447	590
San Bernardino		9,538	654
San Diego		9,812	786
San Jose		7,640	534
Santa Rosa		2,117	198
Stockton		3,294	268
Alaska		1,339	159
*Anchorage		741	101
Fairbanks		465	32
Juneau		133	26
Hawaii, Honolulu		3,917	316
EASTERN RITES			
*Philadelphia		440	18
St. Nicholas		304	7
Stamford		319	6
St. Josaphat (Parma)		203	3
*Pittsburgh		514	106
Parma		257	40
Passaic		582	35
Van Nuys		69	13
St. Maron (Maronites)		543	96
Newton (Melkites)		246	42
St. Thomas Apostle of Detroit (Chaldeans)		768	7
Armenians (Ap. Ex.)		180	—
Romanians (Ap. Ex.)		28	7
MILITARY ARCHDIOCESE	**11,262**	**2,040**	
TOTALS 1986		**953,323**	**87,996**
Totals 1985		**947,668**	**91,750**
Totals 1976		**894,992**	**80,035**

BIRTHRIGHT

Birthright is an interdenominational guidance and referral service organization offering pregnant women alternatives to abortion, in line with the motto, "It is the right of every pregnant woman to give birth and the right of every child to be born." Started by Mrs. Louise Summerhill of Toronto, Canada, in 1968, it has chapters in Canada, the United States, the United Kingdom, Ireland, New Zealand, Australia, Hong Kong and South Africa. The executive director of Birthright, U.S.A., is Mrs. D. Cocciolone, 686 N. Broad St., Woodbury, N.J. 08096. Birthright is independent and interdenominational. Birthright operates a national 800 number.

STATISTICAL SUMMARY OF THE CHURCH IN THE U.S.

(Principal source: *The Official Catholic Directory, 1986*. Comparisons are with figures reported in the previous edition.)

Catholic Population: 52,654,908; increase, 368,865. Percent of total population, 21.99.

Jurisdictions: 34 archdioceses (includes Military Archdiocese), 150 dioceses, 2 apostolic exarchates (includes New York-based Armenian exarchate for U.S. and Canada).

Cardinals: 10 (4 head archiepiscopal sees in U.S., 1, in Europe; 1 is a Roman Curia official; 4 are retired). As of Sept. 1, 1986.

Archbishops: 61. Diocesan, in U.S., 34 (includes 4 cardinals and the Military Vicar); retired, 18 (includes 4 cardinals); outside U.S., 9 (includes 1 cardinal). As of Sept. 1, 1986.

Bishops: 388. Diocesan, in U.S., 147 (2 are titular archbishops); coadjutors, 2; exarchs, 2; auxiliaries, 109; retired, 91; serving outside U.S., 37. As of Sept. 1, 1986.

Priests: 57,183; decrease, 134. Diocesan, 35,155 (increase, 103); religious order priests, 22,028 (decrease, 237).

Permanent Deacons: 7,562; increase, 358.

Brothers: 7,429; decrease, 115.

Sisters: 113,658; decrease, 1,728.

Seminarians: 10,440; decrease, 588. Diocesan seminarians, 7,018 (decrease, 259); religious order seminarians, 3,422 (decrease, 329).

Infant Baptisms: 953,323; increase, 5,655.

Converts: 87,996; decrease, 3,754.

Marriages: 348,300; increase, 2,547.

Deaths: 446,822; increase, 8,791.

Parishes: 19,313; increase, 69.

Seminaries, Diocesan: 90; no change.

Religious Seminaries, Novitiates, Scholasticates: 229; increase, 1.

Colleges and Universities: 243; increase, 1. Students, 545,461; decrease, 4,479.

High Schools: 1,418; decrease, 7. Students, 766,744; decrease, 27,284.

Elementary Schools: 7,865; decrease, 92. Students, 2,099,379; decrease, 63,576.

Teachers: 170,683; decrease, 1,476. Priests, 4,236 (decrease, 364); brothers, 2,491 (decrease, 187); scholastics, 161 (increase, 23); sisters, 27,638 (decrease, 2,585); laity, 136,157 (increase, 1,637).

Public School students in Religious Instruction Programs: 3,934,846; decrease, 117,330. High school students, 831,131 (decrease, 64,037); elementary school students, 3,103,715 (decrease, 53,293).

Hospitals: 737; increase, 6. Patients treated, 37,181,154; decrease 188,294.

Nurses' Schools: 114; decrease, 15. Students, 20,090; decrease, 2,207.

Homes for Aged: 615; increase, 8. Residents, 76,900; increase, 3,056.

Orphanages: 168; resident children, 12,484. Children in foster homes, 9,248.

CATHEDRALS IN THE UNITED STATES

A cathedral is the principal church in a diocese, the one in which the bishop has his seat (*cathedra*). He is the actual rector, although many functions of the church, which usually serves a parish, are the responsibility of a priest serving as the administrator. Because of the dignity of a cathedral, the dates of its dedication and its patronal feast are observed throughout a diocese.

The pope's cathedral, the Basilica of St. John Lateran, is the highest-ranking church in the world.

(Archdioceses are indicated by asterisk.)

Albany, N.Y.: Immaculate Conception.
Alexandria, La.: St. Francis Xavier.
Allentown, Pa.: St. Catherine of Siena.
Altoona-Johnstown, Pa.: Blessed Sacrament (Altoona); St. John Gualbert (Johnstown Co-Cathedral).
Amarillo, Tex.: St. Laurence.
Anchorage,* Alaska: Holy Family.
Arlington, Va: St. Thomas More.
Atlanta,* Ga.: Christ the King.
Austin, Tex.: St. Mary (Immaculate Conception).
Baker, Ore.: St. Francis de Sales.
Baltimore,* Md.: Mary Our Queen; Basilica of the Assumption of the Blessed Virgin Mary (Co-Cathedral).
Baton Rouge, La.: St. Joseph.
Beaumont, Tex.: St. Anthony (of Padua).
Belleville, Ill.: St. Peter.
Biloxi, Miss.: Nativity of the Blessed Virgin Mary.

Birmingham, Ala.: St. Paul.
Bismarck, N.D.: Holy Spirit.
Boise, Ida.: St. John the Evangelist.
Boston,* Mass.: Holy Cross.
Bridgeport, Conn.: St. Augustine.
Brooklyn, N.Y.: St. James (Minor Basilica).
Brownsville, Tex.: Immaculate Conception.
Buffalo, N.Y.: St. Joseph.
Burlington, Vt.: Immaculate Conception.
Camden, N.J.: Immaculate Conception.
Charleston, S.C.: St. John the Baptist.
Charlotte, N.C.: St. Patrick.
Cheyenne, Wyo.: St. Mary.
Chicago,* Ill.: Holy Name (of Jesus).
Cincinnati,* Ohio: St. Peter in Chains.
Cleveland, Ohio: St. John the Evangelist.
Colorado Springs, Colo: St. Mary.
Columbus, Ohio: St. Joseph.
Corpus Christi, Tex.: Corpus Christi.
Covington, Ky.: Basilica of the Assumption.
Crookston, Minn.: Immaculate Conception.
Dallas, Tex.: Cathedral-Santuario de Guadalupe.
Davenport, Ia.: Sacred Heart.
Denver,* Colo.: Immaculate Conception (Minor Basilica).
Des Moines, Ia.: St. Ambrose.
Detroit,* Mich.: Most Blessed Sacrament.
Dodge City, Kans.: Sacred Heart.
Dubuque,* Ia.: St. Raphael.
Duluth, Minn.: Our Lady of the Rosary.
El Paso, Tex.: St. Patrick.

Erie, Pa.: St. Peter.

Evansville, Ind.: Most Holy Trinity (Pro-Cathedral).

Fairbanks, Alaska: Sacred Heart.

Fall River, Mass.: St. Mary of the Assumption.

Fargo, N.D.: St. Mary.

Fort Wayne-S. Bend, Ind.: Immaculate Conception (Fort Wayne); St. Matthew (South Bend Co-Cathedral).

Fort Worth, Tex.: St. Patrick.

Fresno, Calif.: St. John the Baptist.

Gallup, N.M.: Sacred Heart.

Galveston-Houston, Tex.: St. Mary (Minor Basilica, Galveston); Sacred Heart (Houston Co-Cathedral).

Gary, Ind.: Holy Angels.

Gaylord, Mich.: St. Mary, Our Lady of Mt. Carmel.

Grand Island, Nebr.: Nativity of Blessed Virgin Mary.

Grand Rapids, Mich.: St. Andrew.

Great Falls-Billings, Mont.: St. Ann (Great Falls); St. Patrick (Billings Co-Cathedral).

Green Bay, Wis.: St. Francis Xavier.

Greensburg, Pa.: Blessed Sacrament.

Harrisburg, Pa.: St. Patrick.

Hartford,* Conn.: St. Joseph.

Helena, Mont.: St. Helena.

Honolulu, Hawaii: Our Lady of Peace; St. Theresa of the Child Jesus (Co-Cathedral).

Houma-Thibodaux, La.: St. Francis de Sales (Houma); St. Joseph (Thibodaux Co-Cathedral).

Indianapolis,* Ind.: Sts. Peter and Paul.

Jackson, Miss.: St. Peter.

Jefferson City, Mo.: St. Joseph.

Joliet, Ill.: St. Raymond Nonnatus.

Juneau, Alaska: Nativity of the Blessed Virgin Mary.

Kalamazoo, Mich.: St. Augustine.

Kansas City,* Kans.: St. Peter the Apostle.

Kansas City-St. Joseph, Mo.: Immaculate Conception (Kansas City); St. Joseph (St. Joseph Co-Cathedral).

La Crosse, Wis.: St. Joseph.

Lafayette, Ind.: St. Mary.

Lafayette, La.: St. John the Evangelist.

Lake Charles, La.: Immaculate Conception.

Lansing, Mich.: St. Mary.

Las Cruces, N. Mex.: Immaculate Heart of Mary.

Lincoln, Nebr.: Cathedral of the Risen Christ.

Little Rock, Ark.: St. Andrew.

Los Angeles,* Calif.: St. Vibiana.

Louisville,* Ky.: Assumption.

Lubbock, Tex.: Christ the King.

Madison, Wis.: St. Raphael.

Manchester, N.H.: St. Joseph.

Marquette, Mich.: St. Peter.

Memphis, Tenn.: Immaculate Conception.

Metuchen, N.J.: St. Francis (of Assisi).

Miami,* Fla.: St. Mary (Immaculate Conception).

Milwaukee,* Wis.: St. John.

Mobile,* Ala.: Immaculate Conception (Minor Basilica).

Monterey, Calif.: San Carlos Borromeo.

Nashville, Tenn.: Incarnation.

Newark,* N.J.: Sacred Heart.

New Orleans,* La.: Cathedral (Basilica) of St. Louis.

Newton, Mass. (Melkite Rite): Our Lady of the Annunciation (Boston).

New Ulm, Minn.: Holy Trinity.

New York,* N.Y.: St. Patrick.

Norwich, Conn.: St. Patrick.

Oakland, Calif.: St. Francis de Sales.

Ogdensburg, N.Y.: St. Mary (Immaculate Conception).

Oklahoma City,* Okla.: Our Lady of Perpetual Help.

Omaha,* Nebr.: St. Cecilia.

Orange, Calif.: Holy Family.

Orlando, Fla.: St. James.

Owensboro, Ky.: St. Stephen.

Palm Beach, Fla.: St. Ignatius Loyola, Palm Beach Gardens.

Parma, Ohio (Byzantine Rite): St. John the Baptist.

Passaic, N.J. (Byzantine Rite): St. Michael.

Paterson, N.J.: St. John the Baptist.

Pensacola-Tallahassee, Fla.: Sacred Heart (Pensacola); St. Thomas More (Tallahassee Co-Cathedral).

Peoria, Ill.: St. Mary.

Philadelphia,* Pa.: Sts. Peter and Paul (Minor Basilica).

Philadelphia,* Pa. (Byzantine Rite): Immaculate Conception.

Phoenix, Ariz.: Sts. Simon and Jude.

Pittsburgh,* Pa. (Byzantine Rite): St. John the Baptist, Munhall.

Pittsburgh, Pa.: St. Paul.

Portland, Me.: Immaculate Conception.

Portland,* Ore.: Immaculate Conception.

Providence, R.I.: Sts. Peter and Paul.

Pueblo, Colo.: Sacred Heart.

Raleigh, N.C.: Sacred Heart.

Rapid City, S.D.: Our Lady of Perpetual Help.

Reno-Las Vegas, Nev.: St. Thomas Aquinas (Reno), Guardian Angel (Las Vegas Co-Cathedral).

Richmond, Va.: Sacred Heart.

Rochester, N.Y.: Sacred Heart.

Rockford, Ill.: St. Peter.

Rockville Centre, N.Y.: St. Agnes.

Sacramento, Calif.: Blessed Sacrament.

Saginaw, Mich.: St. Mary.

St. Augustine, Fla.: St. Augustine (Minor Basilica).

St. Cloud, Minn.: St. Mary.

St. Josaphat in Parma, Ohio (Byzantine Rite): St. Josaphat.

St. Louis,* Mo.: St. Louis.

St. Maron, Brooklyn, N.Y. (Maronite Rite): Our Lady of Lebanon.

St. Nicholas in Chicago (Byzantine Rite): St. Nicholas.

St. Paul and Minneapolis,* Minn.: St. Paul (St. Paul); Basilica of St. Mary (Minneapolis Co-Cathedral).

St. Petersburg, Fla.: St. Jude the Apostle.

St. Thomas the Apostle of Detroit (Chaldean

Rite): Our Lady of Chaldeans Cathedral (Mother of God Church), Southfield, Mich.
Salina, Kans.: Sacred Heart.
Salt Lake City, Utah: The Madeleine.
San Angelo, Tex.: Sacred Heart.
San Antonio,* Tex.: San Fernando.
San Bernardino, Calif: Our Lady of the Rosary.
San Diego, Calif.: St. Joseph.
San Francisco,* Calif.: St. Mary (Assumption).
San Jose, Calif.: St. Patrick (to be replaced by St. Joseph Church when renovations are completed).
Santa Fe,* N.M.: San Francisco de Asis.
Santa Rosa, Calif.: St. Eugene.
Savannah, Ga.: St. John the Baptist.
Scranton, Pa.: St. Peter.
Seattle,* Wash.: St. James.
Shreveport, La.: St. John Berchmans.
Sioux City, Ia.: Epiphany.
Sioux Falls, S.D.: St. Joseph.
Spokane, Wash.: Our Lady of Lourdes.
Springfield, Ill.: Immaculate Conception.
Springfield, Mass.: St. Michael.
Springfield-Cape Girardeau, Mo.: St. Agnes (Springfield): St. Mary (Cape Girardeau Co-Cathedral).
Stamford, Conn. (Byzantine Rite): St. Vladimir.
Steubenville, Ohio: Holy Name.
Stockton, Calif: Annunciation.
Superior, Wis.: Christ the King.
Syracuse, N.Y.: Immaculate Conception.
Toledo, Ohio: Queen of the Most Holy Rosary.
Trenton, N.J.: St. Mary (Assumption).
Tucson, Ariz.: St. Augustine.
Tulsa, Okla.: Holy Family.
Van Nuys, Calif. (Byzantine Rite). St. Mary.
Venice, Fla: Epiphany.
Victoria, Tex.: Our Lady of Victory.
Washington,* D.C.: St. Matthew.
Wheeling-Charleston, W. Va.: St. Joseph (Wheeling); Sacred Heart (Charleston Co-Cathedral).
Wichita, Kans.: Immaculate Conception.
Wilmington, Del.: St. Peter.
Winona, Minn.: Sacred Heart.
Worcester, Mass.: St. Paul.
Yakima, Wash.: St. Paul.
Youngstown, Ohio: St. Columba.
Apostolic Exarchate for Romanian Catholics of Byzantine Rite in U.S.: St. George, Canton, O. (Pro-Cathedral).
Apostolic Exarchate for Armenian-Rite Catholics in the U.S. and Canada: St. Ann (110 E. 12th St., New York, N.Y. 10003).

BASILICAS IN U.S. AND CANADA

Basilica is a title assigned to certain churches because of their antiquity, dignity, historical importance or significance as centers of worship. Major basilicas have the papal altar and holy door, which is opened at the beginning of a Jubilee Year; minor basilicas enjoy certain ceremonial privileges.

Among the major basilicas are the patriarchal basilicas of St. John Lateran, St. Peter, St. Paul Outside the Walls and St. Mary Major in Rome; St. Francis and St. Mary of the Angels in Assisi, Italy.

The patriarchal basilica of St. Lawrence, Rome, is a minor basilica.

The dates in the listings below indicate when the churches were designated as basilicas.

Minor Basilicas in U.S., Puerto Rico, Guam

Alabama: Mobile, Cathedral of the Immaculate Conception (Mar. 10, 1962).

Arizona: Phoenix, St. Mary's (Immaculate Conception) (Sept. 11, 1985).

California: San Francisco, Mission Dolores (Feb. 8, 1952); Carmel, Old Mission of San Carlos (Feb. 5, 1960); Alameda, St. Joseph (Jan. 21, 1972); San Diego, Mission San Diego de Alcala (Nov. 17, 1975).

Colorado: Denver, Cathedral of the Immaculate Conception (Nov. 3, 1979).

Florida: St. Augustine, Cathedral of St. Augustine (Dec. 4, 1976).

Illinois: Chicago, Our Lady of Sorrows (May 4, 1956), Queen of All Saints (Mar. 26, 1962).

Indiana: Vincennes, Old Cathedral (Mar. 14, 1970).

Iowa: Dyersville, St. Francis Xavier (May 11, 1956).

Kentucky: Trappist, Our Lady of Gethsemani (May 3, 1949); Covington, Cathedral of Assumption (Dec. 8, 1953).

Louisiana: New Orleans, St. Louis King of France (Dec. 9, 1964).

Maryland: Baltimore, Assumption of the Blessed Virgin Mary (Sept. 1, 1937).

Massachusetts: Roxbury, Perpetual Help ("Mission Church") (Sept. 8, 1954).

Michigan: Grand Rapids, St. Adalbert (Aug. 22, 1979).

Minnesota: Minneapolis. St. Mary (Feb. 1, 1926).

Missouri: Conception, Basilica of Immaculate Conception (Sept. 14, 1940); St. Louis, St. Louis King of France (Jan. 27, 1961).

New York: Brooklyn, Our Lady of Perpetual Help (Sept. 5, 1969), Cathedral-Basilica of St. James (June 22, 1982); Lackawanna, Our Lady of Victory (1926); Youngstown, Blessed Virgin Mary of the Rosary of Fatima (Oct. 7, 1975).

Ohio: Carey, Shrine of Our Lady of Consolation (Oct. 21, 1971).

Pennsylvania: Latrobe, St. Vincent Basilica, Benedictine Archabbey (Aug. 22, 1955); Conewago, Basilica of the Sacred Heart (June 30, 1962); Philadelphia, Sts. Peter and Paul (Sept. 27, 1976).

Texas: Galveston, St. Mary Cathedral (Aug. 11, 1979).

Wisconsin: Milwaukee, St. Josaphat (Mar. 10, 1929).

Puerto Rico: San Juan, Cathedral of San Juan (Jan. 25, 1978).

Guam: Agana, Cathedral of Dulce Nombre de Maria (Sweet Name of Mary) (1985).

Minor Basilicas in Canada

Alberta: Edmonton, Cathedral Basilica of St. Joseph (Mar. 15, 1984).

Manitoba: St. Boniface, Cathedral Basilica of St. Boniface (June 10, 1949).

Newfoundland: St. John's, Cathedral Basilica of St. John the Baptist.

Nova Scotia: Halifax, St. Mary's Basilica (June 14, 1950).

Ontario: Ottawa, Basilica of Notre Dame; London, St. Peter's Cathedral (Dec. 13, 1961).

Prince Edward Island: Charlottetown, Basilica of St. Dunstan.

Quebec: Sherbrooke, Cathedral Basilica of St. Michael (July 31, 1959). Montreal, Cathedral Basilica of Our Lady Queen of the World; St. Joseph of Mount Royal; Basilica of Notre Dame (Feb. 15, 1982). Cap-de-la-Madeleine, Basilica of Our Lady of the Cape (Aug. 15, 1964). Quebec, Basilica of Notre Dame; St. Anne de Beaupre, Basilica of St. Anne.

CHANCERY OFFICES OF U.S. ARCHDIOCESES AND DIOCESES

A chancery office, under this or another title, is the central administrative office of an archdiocese or diocese.

(Archdioceses are indicated by asterisk.)

Albany, N.Y.: 465 State St., Box 6297, Quail Station. 12206.

Alexandria, La.: 4400 Gardner Hwy., P.O. Box 7417, Alexandria. 71306.

Allentown, Pa.: 202 N. 17th St., P.O. Box F. 18105.

Altoona-Johnstown, Pa.: Box 126, Logan Blvd., Hollidaysburg, Pa. 16648.

Amarillo, Tex.: 1800 N. Spring St., P.O. Box 5644. 79117.

Anchorage,* Alaska: P.O. Box 2239. 99510.

Arlington, Va.: 200 N. Glebe Rd. 22203.

Atlanta,* Ga.: Catholic Center, 680 W. Peachtree St. N.W. 30308.

Austin, Tex.: N. Congress and 16th, P.O. Box 13327. Capitol Sta. 78711.

Baker, Ore.: Baker and First Sts., P.O. Box 826, 97814.

Baltimore,* Md.: 320 Cathedral St. 21201.

Baton Rouge, La.: P.O. Box 2028. 70821.

Beaumont, Tex.: 703 Archie St., P.O. Box 3948. 77704.

Belleville, Ill.: 222 S. Third St., 62220.

Biloxi, Miss.: P.O. Box 1189. 39533.

Birmingham, Ala.: P.O. Box 2086. 35201.

Bismarck, N.D.: 420 Raymond St., Box 1575. 58502.

Boise, Ida.: Box 769. 83701.

Boston,* Mass.: 2121 Commonwealth Ave., Brighton, Mass. 02135.

Bridgeport, Conn.: The Catholic Center, 238 Jewett Ave. 06606.

Brooklyn, N.Y.: 75 Greene Ave., P.O. Box C. 11202.

Brownsville, Tex.: P.O. Box 2279. 78522.

Buffalo, N.Y.: 795 Main St. 14203.

Burlington, Vt.: 351 North Ave. 05401.

Camden, N.J.: 1845 Haddon Ave., P.O. Box 709, 01801.

Charleston, S.C.: 119 Broad St., P.O. Box 818. 29402.

Charlotte, N.C.: P.O. Box 36776. 28236.

Cheyenne, Wyo.: Box 426. 82003.

Chicago,* Ill,: 155 E. Superior St., P.O. Box 1979. 60690.

Cincinnati,* O.: 100 E. 8th St. 45202.

Cleveland, O.: Chancery Bldg., 1027 Superior Ave. 44114.

Colorado Springs, Colo.: 29 W. Kiowa. 80903.

Columbus, O.: 198 E. Broad St. 43215.

Corpus Christi, Tex.: 620 Lipan St. 78401.

Covington, Ky.: 1140 Madison Ave., P.O. Box 192. 41012.

Crookston, Minn.: 1200 Memorial Dr., P.O. Box 610. 56716.

Dallas, Tex.: 3915 Lemmon Ave., P.O. Box 190507. 75219.

Davenport, Ia.: St. Vincent Center, 2706 Gaines St. 52804.

Denver,* Colo.: 200 Josephine St. 80206.

Des Moines, Ia.: P.O. Box 1816. 50306.

Detroit,* Mich.: 1234 Washington Blvd. 48226.

Dodge City, Kans.: 910 Central Ave., P.O. Box 849. 67801.

Dubuque,* Ia.: 1229 Mt. Loretta Ave. 52001.

Duluth, Minn.: 215 W. 4th St. 55806.

El Paso, Tex.: 499 St. Matthews St. 79907.

Erie, Pa.: 205 W. 9th St. 16501.

Evansville, Ind.: P.O. Box 4169. 47711.

Fairbanks, Alaska: 1316 Peger Rd. 99709.

Fall River, Mass.: 47 Underwood St., Box 2577. 02722.

Fargo, N.D.: 1310 Broadway, Box 1750. 58107.

Fort Wayne-South Bend, Ind.: P.O. Box 390, Fort Wayne. 46801.

Fort Worth, Tex.: 800 W. Loop, 820 South. 76108.

Fresno, Calif.: P.O. Box 1668, 1550 N. Fresno St. 93717.

Gallup, N. Mex.: 711 S. Puerco Dr., P.O. Box 1338. 87301.

Galveston-Houston, Tex.: 1700 San Jacinto St., Houston. 77002.

Gary, Ind.: 9292 Broadway, Merrillville. 46410.

Gaylord, Mich.: P.O. Box 1020. 49735.

Grand Island, Nebr.: 311 W. 17th St., P.O. Box 996. 68802.

Grand Rapids, Mich.: 660 Burton St., S.E. 49507.

Great Falls-Billings, Mont.: P.O. Box 1399, Great Falls. 59403.

Green Bay, Wis.: Box 66. 54305.

Greensburg, Pa.: 723 E. Pittsburgh St. 15601.

Harrisburg, Pa.: P.O. Box 2153. 17105.

Hartford,* Conn.: 134 Farmington Ave. 06105.

Helena, Mont.: 515 North Ewing, P.O. Box 1729. 59624.

Honolulu, Hawaii: 1184 Bishop St. 96813.

Houma-Thibodaux, La.: 1220 Aycock St., P.O. Box 9077, Houma, La. 70361.

Indianapolis,* Ind.: 1400 N. Meridian St., P.O. Box 1410, 46206.

Jackson, Miss.: 237 E. Amite St., P.O. Box 2248. 39225.

Jefferson City, Mo.: 605 Clark Ave. P.O. Box 417. 65101.

Joliet, Ill.: 425 Summit St. 60435.

Juneau, Alaska: 419 6th St. 99801.

Kalamazoo, Mich.: 215 N. Westnedge Ave., P.O. Box 949, 49005.

Kansas City,* Kans.: 2220 Central Ave., P.O. Box 2328. 66110.

Kansas City-St. Joseph, Mo.: P.O. Box 1037, Kansas City. 64141.

La Crosse, Wis.: 3710 East Ave., Box 4004. 54602.

Lafayette in Indiana: P.O. Box 260, 47902.

Lafayette, La.: P.O. Drawer 3387. 70502.

Lake Charles, La.: P.O. Box 3223. 70602.

Lansing, Mich.: 300 W. Ottawa. 48933.

Las Cruces, N. Mex.: P.O. Box 16318. 88004.

Lincoln, Nebr.: 3400 Sheridan Blvd., P.O. Box 80328. 68501.

Little Rock, Ark.: 2415 N. Tyler St. 72217.

Los Angeles,* Calif.: 1531 W. 9th St. 90015.

Louisville,* Ky.: 212 E. College St., P.O. Box 1073. 40201.

Lubbock, Tex.: P.O. Box 98700. 79499.

Madison, Wis.: 15 E. Wilson St., P.O. Box 111. 53701.

Manchester, N. H.: 153 Ash St., P.O. Box 310. 03105.

Marquette, Mich.: 444 S. Fourth St., P.O. Box 550. 49855.

Memphis, Tenn.: 1325 Jefferson Ave., 38104.

Metuchen, N.J.: P.O. Box 191. 08840.

Miami,* Fla.: 9401 Biscayne Blvd., Miami Shores. 33138.

Milwaukee,* Wis.: P.O. Box 2018. 53201.

Mobile,* Ala.: 400 Government St., P.O. Box 1966. 36633.

Monterey, Calif.: P.O. Box 2048. 93940.

Nashville, Tenn.: 2400 21st Ave. S. 37212.

Newark,* N.J.: 31 Mulberry St. 07102.

New Orleans,* La.: 7887 Walmsley Ave. 70125.

Newton, Mass. (Melkite Rite): 19 Dartmouth St., W. Newton, Mass. 02165.

New Ulm, Minn.: 1400 Chancery Drive. 56073.

New York,* N.Y.: 1011 First Ave. 10022.

Norwich, Conn.: 201 Broadway, P.O. Box 587. 06360.

Oakland, Calif.: 2900 Lakeshore Ave. 94610.

Ogdensburg, N.Y.: 622 Washington St. 13669.

Oklahoma City,* Okla.: P.O. Box 32180. 73123.

Omaha,* Nebr.: 100 N. 62nd St. 68132.

Orange, Calif.: 2811 E. Villa Real Dr. 92667.

Orlando, Fla.: P.O. Box 1800. 32802.

Owensboro, Ky.: 4005 Frederica St. 42301.

Palm Beach, Fla.: 8895 N. Military Trail, Palm Beach Gardens 33410.

Parma, Ohio (Byzantine Rite): 1900 Carlton Rd. 44134.

Passaic, N.J. (Byzantine Rite): 101 Market St. 07055.

Paterson, N.J.: 777 Valley Rd., Clifton. 07013.

Pensacola-Tallahassee, Fla.: P.O. Drawer 17329, Pensacola. 32522.

Peoria, Ill.: 607 N.E. Madison Ave., P.O. Box 1406. 61655.

Philadelphia,* Pa.: 222 N. 17th St. 19103.

Philadelphia,* Pa. (Byzantine Rite): 827 N. Franklin St. 19123.

Phoenix, Ariz.: 400 E. Monroe St. 85004.

Pittsburgh,* Pa. (Byzantine Rite): 54 Riverview Ave. 15214.

Pittsburgh, Pa.: 111 Blvd. of the Allies. 15222.

Portland, Me.: 510 Ocean Ave., Woodfords P.O. Box 6750. 04103.

Portland in Oregon*: 2838 E. Burnside St. 97214.

Providence, R.I.: One Cathedral Sq. 02903.

Pueblo, Colo.: 1001 N. Grand Ave., 81003.

Raleigh, N.C.: 300 Cardinal Gibbons Dr. 27606.

Rapid City, S.D.: 606 Cathedral Dr., P.O. Box 678. 57709.

Reno-Las Vegas, Nev.: P.O. Box 1211, Reno. 89504.

Richmond, Va.: 811 Cathedral Pl., Suite C. 23220.

Rochester, N.Y.: 1150 Buffalo Rd. 14624.

Rockford, Ill.: 1245 N. Court St. 61103.

Rockville Centre, N.Y.: 50 N. Park Ave. 11570.

Sacramento, Calif.: 1119 K St., P.O. Box 1706. 95808.

Saginaw, Mich.: 5800 Weiss St. 48603.

St. Augustine, Fla.: P.O. Box 24000, Jacksonville, Fla. 32241.

St. Cloud, Minn.: P.O. Box 1248. 56302.

St. Josaphat in Parma, Ohio (Byzantine Rite): P.O. Box 347180, Parma 44134.

St. Louis,* Mo.: 4445 Lindell Blvd. 63108.

St. Maron (Maronite Rite), Brooklyn, N.Y.: 8120 15th Ave., Brooklyn. 11228.

St. Nicholas in Chicago (Byzantine Rite): 2245 W. Rice St. 60622.

St. Paul and Minneapolis,* Minn.: 226 Summit Ave., St. Paul. 55102.

St. Petersburg, Fla.: P.O. Box 40200. 33743.

St. Thomas the Apostle of Detroit (Chaldean Rite): 25585 Berg Rd., Southfield, Mich. 48034.

Salina, Kans.: P.O. Box 980. 67402.

Salt Lake City, Utah: 27 C St., 84103.

San Angelo, Tex.: 116 S. Oakes. Box 1829. 76902.

San Antonio,* Tex.: P.O. Box 28410. 78228.

San Bernardino, Calif.: 1450 North D St. 92405.

San Diego, Calif.: P.O. Box 80428. 92138.

San Francisco,* Calif.: 445 Church St. 94114.

San Jose, Calif.: 7600 St. Joseph Ave., Los Altos 94022.

Santa Fe,* N. Mex.: 202 Morningside Dr. S.E., Albuquerque. 87108.

Santa Rosa, Calif.: P.O. Box 1297. 95402.

Savannah, Ga.: P.O. Box 8789. 31412.

Scranton, Pa.: 300 Wyoming Ave. 18503.

Seattle,* Wash.: 910 Marion St. 98104.

Shreveport, La.: 939 Jordan St. 71101 (address of cathedral).

Sioux City, Ia.: P.O. Box 3379. 51102.

Sioux Falls, S.D.: Box 5033. 57117.

Spokane, Wash.: 1023 W. Riverside Ave. 99201.

Springfield, Illinois: P.O. Box 1667. 62705.

Springfield, Mass.: P.O. Box 1730, 01101.

Springfield-Cape Girardeau, Mo.: P.O. Box 1957, SSS, Springfield. 65805.

Stamford, Conn. (Byzantine Rite): 161 Glenbrook Rd. 06902.

Steubenville, Ohio: P.O. Box 969. 43952.

Stockton, Calif.: P.O. Box 4237. 95204.

Superior, Wis.: Box 969, 54880.

Syracuse, N.Y.: P.O. Box 511. 13201.

Toledo, Ohio: 2544 Parkwood Ave. 43610.

Trenton, N.J.: P.O. Box 5309. 08638.

Tucson, Ariz.: 192 S. Stone Ave., Box 31, 85702.

Tulsa, Okla.: P.O. Box 2009. 74101.

Van Nuys, Calif. (Byzantine Rite): 5335 Sepulveda Blvd. 91411.

Venice, Fla.: P.O. Box 2006. 34284.

Victoria, Tex.: P.O. Box 4708. 77903.

Washington,* D.C.: P.O. Box 29260. 20017.

Wheeling-Charleston, W. Va.: 1300 Byron St., Wheeling. 26003.

Wichita, Kans.: 424 N. Broadway. 67202.

Wilmington, Del.: P.O. Box 2030. 19899.

Winona, Minn.: P.O. Box 588. 55987.

Worcester, Mass.: 49 Elm St. 01609.

Yakima, Wash.: P.O. Box 505. 98907.

Youngstown, Ohio: 144 W. Wood St. 44503.

Military Vicariate: 832 Varnum St. N.E., Washington, D.C. 20017.

Armenian-Rite Catholic Apostolic Exarchate for the United States and Canada: 110 E. 12th St., New York, N.Y. 10003.

Romanian Catholic Apostolic Exarchate for the United States (Byzantine Rite): 1121 44th St. N.E., Canton, O. 44714.

Byelorussian Catholics outside Byelorussia: 3117 W. Fullerton Ave., Chicago, Ill. 60647.

NATIONAL CATHOLIC CONFERENCES

The two conferences described below are related in membership and directive control but distinct in nature, purpose and function.

The National Conference of Catholic Bishops (NCCB) is a strictly ecclesiastical body in and through which the bishops of the United States act together, officially and with authority as pastors of the Church. It is the sponsoring organization of the United States Catholic Conference.

The United States Catholic Conference (USCC) is a civil corporation and operational secretariat in and through which the bishops, together with other members of the Church, act on a wider scale for the good of the Church and society. It is sponsored by the National Conference of Catholic Bishops.

The principal officers of both conferences are: Bishop James W. Malone, president; Archbishop John L. May, vice president; Bishop John R. McGann, treasurer; Bishop Eugene A. Marino, S.S.J., secretary.

The membership of the Administrative Committee of the NCCB and the Administrative Board of the USCC is identical.

Headquarters of both conferences are located at 1312 Massachusetts Ave. N.W., Washington, D.C. 20005.

NCCB

The National Conference of Catholic Bishops, established by action of the U.S. hierarchy Nov. 14, 1966, is a strictly ecclesiastical body with defined juridical authority over the Church in this country. It was set up with the approval of the Holy See and in line with directives from the Second Vatican Council. Its constitution was formally ratified during the November, 1967, meeting of the U.S. hierarchy.

The NCCB is a development from the Annual Meeting of the Bishops of the United States, whose pastoral character was originally approved by Pope Benedict XV Apr. 10, 1919.

The address of the Conference is 1312 Massachusetts Ave. N.W., Washington, D.C. 20005. Rev. Msgr. Daniel F. Hoye is general secretary.

Pastoral Council

The conference, one of many similar territorial conferences envisioned in the conciliar *Decree on the Pastoral Office of Bishops in the Church* (No. 38), is "a council in which the bishops of a given nation or territory (in this case, the United States) jointly exercise their pastoral office to promote the greater good which the Church offers mankind, especially through the forms and methods of the apostolate fittingly adapted to the circumstances of the age."

Its decisions, "provided they have been approved legitimately and by the votes of at least two-thirds of the prelates who have a deliberative vote in the conference, and have been recognized by the Apostolic See, are to have juridically binding force only in those cases prescribed by the common law or determined by a special mandate of the Apostolic See, given either spontaneously or in response to a petition of the conference itself."

All bishops who serve the Church in the U.S., its territories and possessions, have membership and voting rights in the NCCB.

Officers, Committees

The conference operates through a number of bishops' committees with functions in specific areas of work and concern. Their basic assignments are to prepare materials on the basis of which the bishops, assembled as a conference, make decisions, and to put suitable action plans into effect.

The principal officers are: Bishop James W. Malone, president; Archbishop John L. May, vice president; Bishop John R. McGann, treasurer; Bishop Eugene A. Marino, S.S.J., secretary.

These officers, with several other bishops, hold positions on executive-level committees — Executive Committee, the Committee on Budget and Finance, the Committee on Personnel and Administrative Services, and the Committee on Priorities and Plans. They also, with other bishops, serve on the NCCB Administrative Board.

The standing committees and their chairmen (Archbishops and Bishops) are as follows.

American Board of Catholic Missions, Thomas V. Daily.

Bishops' Welfare Emergency Relief, James W. Malone.

Boundaries of Dioceses and Provinces, James W. Malone.

Canonical Affairs, Adam J. Maida.

Church in Latin America, Ricardo Ramirez, C.S.B.

Doctrine, Raymond W. Lessard.

Ecumenical and Interreligious Affairs, William H. Keeler.

Human Values, James A. Hickey.

Laity, Stanley J. Ott.

Liaison with Priests, Religious and Laity, Andrew J. McDonald.

Liturgy, Daniel E. Pilarczyk.
Men Religious, Joseph A. Francis, S.V.D.
Missions, Joseph A. Fiorenza.
American College, Louvain, Eusebius J. Beltran.
North American College, Rome, James A. Griffin.
Pastoral Research and Practices, Cardinal Bernard F. Law.
Permanent Diaconate, John F. Kinney.
Priestly Formation, John R. Roach.
Priestly Life and Ministry, Thomas J. Murphy.
Selection of Bishops, James W. Malone.
Vocations, Lawrence H. Welsh.
Women Religious, Daniel W. Kucera, O.S.B.
Ad hoc committees and their chairmen are as follows.
Bicentennial of Establishment of U.S. Hierarchy, William D. Borders.
Campaign for Human Development, Arthur N. Tafoya.
Catholic Charismatic Renewal, Joseph McKinney.
Catholic Social Teaching and the U.S. Economy, Rembert G. Weakland, O.S.B.
Economic Concerns of the Holy See, Edward T. O'Meara.
Evangelization, William R. Houck.
Farm Labor, Roger M. Mahony.
Hispanic Affairs, Robert F. Sanchez.
Inter-Rite, William G. Connare.
Liaison with National Office for Black Catholics, Eugene A. Marino, S.S.J.
Migration and Tourism, Anthony J. Bevilacqua.
Nomination of Conference Offices, Warren L. Boudreaux.
Pro-Life Activities, Cardinal Joseph Bernardin.
Sapientia Christiana, Paul E. Waldschmidt, C.S.C.
Women in Society and Church, Joseph L. Imesch.

USCC

The United States Catholic Conference, Inc. (USCC), is the operational secretariat and service agency of the National Conference of Catholic Bishops for carrying out the civic-religious work of the Church in this country. It is a civil corporation related to the NCCB in membership and directive control but distinct from it in purpose and function.

The address of the Conference is 1312 Massachusetts Ave. N.W., Washington, D.C. 20005. Rev. Msgr. Daniel F. Hoye is general secretary.

Service Secretariat

The USCC, as of Jan. 1, 1967, took over the general organization and operations of the former National Catholic Welfare Conference, Inc., whose origins dated back to the National Catholic War Council of 1917. The council underwent some change after World War I and was established on a permanent basis Sept. 24, 1919, as the National Catholic Welfare Council to serve as a central agency for organizing and coordinating the efforts of U.S. Catholics in carrying out the social mission of the Church in this country. In 1923, its name was changed to National Catholic Welfare Conference, Inc., and clarification was made of its nature as a service agency of the bishops and the Church rather than as a conference of bishops with real juridical authority in ecclesiastical affairs.

The Official Catholic Directory states that the USCC assists "the bishops in their service to the Church in this country by uniting the people of God where voluntary collective action on a broad interdiocesan level is needed. The USCC provides an organizational structure and the resources needed to insure coordination, cooperation, and assistance in the public, educational and social concerns of the Church at the national or interdiocesan level."

Officers, Departments

The principal officers of the USCC are Bishop James W. Malone, president; Archbishop John L. May, vice president; Bishop John R. McGann, treasurer; Bishop Eugene A. Marino, S.S.J., secretary. These officers, with several other bishops, hold positions on executive-level committees — the Executive Committee; the Committee on Priorities and Plans; the Committee on Budget and Finance; the Committee on Personnel and Administrative Services. They also serve on the Administrative Board.

The Executive Committee, organized in 1969, is authorized to handle matters of urgency between meetings of the Administrative Board and the general conference, to coordinate items for the agenda of general meetings, and to speak in the name of the USCC.

The major departments and their chairmen (Archbishops and Bishops) are: Communications, Anthony A. Bosco; Education, William A. Hughes, Committee of Bishops and Catholic College and University Presidents, William A. Hughes; Social Development and World Peace, Cardinal John J. O'Connor. Each department is supervised by a committee composed of an equal number of episcopal and non-episcopal members, including lay persons.

A national Advisory Council of bishops, priests, men and women religious, lay men and women advises the Administrative Board on overall plans and operations of the USCC.

The administrative general secretariat, in addition to other duties, supervises staff-service offices of Finance and Administration, General Counsel, Government Liaison, and Priorities and Plans.

Most of the organizations and associations affiliated with the USCC are covered in separate Almanac entries.

GROUNDBREAKING

Formal groundbreaking ceremonies were held Aug. 18, 1986, for a five-story building that will serve as the new headquarters of the National Conference of Catholic Bishops and the U.S. Catholic Conference. The new building, near The Catholic University in Washington, will replace the one at 1312 Massachusetts Ave. N.W. Completion and relocation of staff is expected in 1988.

The $20 million relocation project is being financed through donations and sale of the former headquarters. The Catholic Daughters of America have pledged $1 million for the project.

1985 MEETING OF THE U.S. BISHOPS

Approximately 300 bishops attended the annual meeting of the National Conference of Catholic Bishops and the U.S. Catholic Conference Nov. 11 to 15, 1985, in Washington, D.C.

Introductory Addresses

In his presidential address, Bishop James W. Malone spoke about the Second Vatican Council, trends and developments since the Council, and his views regarding likely subjects for consideration during the soon-to-be-held extraordinary assembly of the Synod of Bishops.

He noted that the Synod was called by Pope John Paul to evaluate implementation of the work and directives of the Council. Subjects of particular significance, he thought, were collegiality, the role and authority of episcopal conferences, ecumenism and social ministry.

Archbishop Pio Laghi, papal nuncio to the U.S., spoke about episcopal collegiality in service to particular churches and to the "universal unity" of the Church. He also reminded the bishops, in the words of Pope John Paul, "that 'a precise duty falls to today's shepherds . . . to defend the authenticity of the Gospel teaching from all that contaminates and distorts it.' "

Items of Business

Black Catholics: A statement by the 10 black bishops in the U.S. hierarchy called for: efforts to eradicate racism in the Church; leadership opportunities and placement for blacks (bishops, priests, deacons, Religious, lay persons); special evangelizing outreach to blacks; recommitment of Catholic schools to the education of blacks and members of other minorities; establishment of a national office of black affairs.

Budget: A 1986 budget of $26.9 million was approved for the operation of both conferences.

Campus Ministry: "Empowered by the Spirit; Campus Ministry Faces the Future" was approved at the meeting and ratified in January, 1986, by a vote of 237 to 4.

Catechetics: Several suggestions were recommended for consideration by various committees. Among them were: a pastoral letter on Catholic schools; formation of a national bishops' committee on catechetics; development of a national catechism or of short catechisms of essential elements to be taught at each age level; national guidelines to help assure the access of mentally retarded persons to the sacraments.

Catholic Relief Services: A committee report cleared the overseas aid agency of charges against its operations for the relief of famine in Ethiopia. Relief contributions reported were $50 million for Ethiopian aid, from October. 1984, and $4.6 million for aid to victims of Sept. 19 and 20, 1985, earthquakes in Mexico.

Committees: Authorization was approved for the formation of an ad hoc committee to study and monitor the nuclear deterrence policy of the United States, in the light of the pastoral letter, "The Challenge of Peace: God's Promise and Our Response," issued by the bishops in 1983.

• Two ad hoc committees were made standing committees: Pro-Life Activities and Women in Society and Church.

• The Conciliation and Arbitration Committee was terminated, to be replaced with another agency.

Economics: A revised draft of the pastoral letter, "Catholic Social Teaching and the U.S. Economy," was discussed. Voting on the final version of the letter was scheduled to take place in November, 1986.

Evangelization: An approved statement, entitled "A Vision of Evangelization," linked preaching of the Gospel with ministry for social justice.

Farms: Approved was a statement in support of emergency and long-term federal legislation in favor of mid-sized and family farms, with special reference to: a just return for farmers and a just wage for farmworkers; incentives for regenerative agriculture through soil conservation and other means; support for more rather than fewer owner-operator farms.

Funeral Rites: The bishops voted 208 to 15 to seek Vatican approval of their endorsement of a revision of the 1969 English translation of rites for funerals.

Headquarters: The cost of new headquarters of the conferences was estimated at $20 million, for the building and furnishings.

Hispanics: A report was received on proceedings of the 1985 Third National Hispanic Pastoral Encuentro; one of its major accomplishments was the development of background information for the forthcoming preparation of a pastoral plan for ministry to Hispanics.

Hostages: A resolution was passed expressing "deep concern" over the plight of Father Lawrence M. Jenco, an official of Catholic Relief Services, and several other hostages held in Beirut.

Immigration: A resolution was adopted in favor of immigration reform, with a measure of legalization for undocumented aliens; also cited was the need for specialized ministry to immigrants.

Legal: The bishops urged "sustained protest" against the "blatant injustice" of the U.S. Supreme Court's ruling in Felton v. Aguilar, in which the Court declared it unconstitutional for public school teachers to provide remedial educational services on the premises of church-related schools. They said the decision deprived students of such schools of aid funded under Chapter I of the Education Consolidation and Improvement Act.

Lithuania: A resolution was adopted urging the U.S.S.R. to respect religious freedom in the country.

Missions: "To the Ends of the Earth" was the title of a statement on foreign missions released during the meeting but not scheduled for action until November, 1986.

Priest Exchange: Agreement was reached with bishops of the Philippines governing work by Filipino priests in the United States.

Pro-Life Activities: Approval was voted of a revised pastoral plan in line with a "seamless garment" range of respect-for-life concerns.

Property Disposal: Regulations governing the disposal of church property, approved during the meeting, were ratified in January, 1986, by a vote of 236 to 3; the norms were referred to the Vatican for approval.

Women: A committee recommendation called for study of the employment practices of church agencies.

1986 COLLEGEVILLE MEETING

Two hundred and 59 bishops attended a retreat-discussion-reflection type of meeting June 9 to 16, 1986, at St. John's University, Collegeville, Minn. Vocations were the subject of concern.

At the conclusion of the meeting, the bishops were in general agreement that:

• The Church in the U.S. is in the midst of a crisis with respect to vocations to the priesthood and the religious life.

• Solutions to the crisis do not include a married priesthood or women priests.

• The crisis in vocations to the priesthood and religious life exists alongside an "explosion" of lay ministries.

Bishops who expressed views made public after the meeting included the following.

Various Views

Cardinal Bernard F. Law of Boston: The vocation crisis is "a crisis of faith, a crisis of our call to holiness."

Bishop Raymond Lucker of New Ulm: In the first place, the vocation of lay persons is "to change the society in which they live and work. After that, they can be called to ecclesial ministries." We have mistakenly reversed the order of their calling, tending to call them first to ministries within the church community. "Where we have not done so well is in recognizing, affirming, encouraging and supporting people in ministries affecting the transformation of society, which is essentially the ministry of the laity."

Archbishop Daniel Pilarczyk of Cincinnati: Confusion over the nature and purpose of the priesthood and the value of celibacy have contributed to the decline of vocations. He noted the real distinction between the ordained priesthood and the common priesthood of the faithful.

Cardinal Joseph L. Bernardin of Chicago: The church community should be one "in which all members, in virtue of their incorporation into Christ through baptism and confirmation, witness to his saving deeds before the entire world. . . . It is a community whose designated ministers — whether ordained or lay — understand and accept their uniquely different but complementary roles, working together for the good of all."

NCCB-USCC REGIONS

I. Maine, Vermont, New Hampshire, Massachusetts, Rhode Island, Connecticut.

II. New York. III. New Jersey, Pennsylvania.

IV. Delaware, District of Columbia, Florida, Georgia, Maryland, North Carolina, South Carolina, Virgin Islands, Virginia, West Virginia.

V. Alabama, Kentucky, Louisiana, Mississippi, Tennessee.

VI. Michigan, Ohio.

VII. Illinois, Indiana, Wisconsin.

VIII. Minnesota, North Dakota, South Dakota.

IX. Iowa, Kansas, Missouri, Nebraska.

X. Arkansas, Oklahoma, Texas.

XI. California, Hawaii, Nevada. XII. Idaho, Montana, Alaska, Washington, Oregon.

XIII. Utah, Arizona, New Mexico, Colorado, Wyo.

STATE CATHOLIC CONFERENCES

These conferences are agencies of bishops and dioceses in the various states. Their general purposes are to develop and sponsor cooperative programs designed to cope with pastoral and common-welfare needs, and to represent the dioceses before governmental bodies, the public, and in private sectors. Their membership consists of representatives from the dioceses in the states — bishops, clergy and lay persons in various capacities.

The **National Association of State Catholic Conference Directors** maintains liaison with the general secretariat of the United States Catholic Conference.

Arizona Catholic Conference, 400 E. Monroe St., Phoenix, Ariz. 85004; exec. dir., Rev. Edward J. Ryle.

California Catholic Conference, Cathedral Square, 1010 11th St., Suite 200, Sacramento, Calif. 95814; exec. dir., Rev. William J. Wood, S.J.

Colorado Catholic Conference, 200 Josephine St., Denver, Colo. 80206; exec. dir., Sr. Loretto Anne Madden, S.L.

Connecticut Catholic Conference, 134 Farmington Ave., Hartford, Conn. 06105; exec. dir., William Wholean.

Florida Catholic Conference, P.O. Box 1571, Tallahassee, Fla. 32302; exec. dir., Thomas A. Horkan, Jr.

Georgia Catholic Conference, Suite 2129, First Atlanta Tower, Atlanta, Ga. 30383; exec. dir., Cheatham E. Hodges, Jr.

Illinois, Catholic Conference of, One East Superior St., Chicago, Ill. 60611; 300 E. Monroe St., Springfield, Ill. 62701; exec. dir., Jimmy M. Lago.

Indiana Catholic Conference, 1400 N. Meridian St., P.O. Box 1410, Indianapolis, Ind. 46206; exec. dir., M. Desmond Ryan.

Iowa Catholic Conference, 818 Insurance Exchange Building, Des Moines, Iowa 50309; exec. dir., Timothy McCarthy.

Kansas Catholic Conference, 702 Commercial National Bank Bldg., Kansas City, Kan. 66101; exec. dir., Robert Runnels, Jr.

Kentucky Catholic Conference, P.O. Box 590, Louisville, Ky. 40201; exec. dir., Ken Dupre.

Louisiana Catholic Conference, P.O. Box 52948, New Orleans, La. 70152; exec. dir., Emile Comar.

Maryland Catholic Conference, 309 Cathedral St., Baltimore, Md. 21201; exec. dir., Richard J. Dowling.

Massachusetts Catholic Conference, 60 School St., Boston, Mass. 02107; exec. dir., Gerald D. D'Avolio, Esq.

Michigan Catholic Conference, 505 N. Capitol Ave., Lansing, Mich. 48933; exec. dir., Sr. Monica Kostielney.

Minnesota Catholic Conference, 296 Chester St., St. Paul, Minn. 55107; exec. dir., Rev. Msgr. James D. Habiger.

Missouri Catholic Conference, P.O. Box 1022, 600 Clark Ave., Jefferson City, Mo. 65102; exec. dir., Louis C. DeFeo, Jr.

Montana Catholic Conference, P.O. Box 1708, Helena, Mont. 59624; exec. dir., John L. Ortwein.

Nebraska Catholic Conference, 521 S. 14th St., Lincoln, Nebr. 68508; exec. dir., James R. Cunningham.

New Jersey Catholic Conference, 211 N. Warren St., Trenton, N.J. 08618; exec. dir., William F. Bolan, Jr.

New York State Catholic Conference, 119 Washington Ave., Albany, N.Y. 12210; exec. dir., J. Alan Davitt.

North Dakota Catholic Conference, 227 West Broadway Suite No. 2, Bismarck, N. Dak. 58501; exec. dir., Mrs. Corinne Engelstad.

Ohio, Catholic Conference of, 35 E. Gay St., Suite 502, Columbus, Ohio 43215; exec. dir., Nelson N. Harper.

Oregon Catholic Conference, 2838 E. Burnside, Portland, Ore. 97214; exec. dir., Robert J. Castagna.

Pennsylvania Catholic Conference, 223 North St., Box 2835, Harrisburg, Pa. 17105; exec. dir., Howard J. Fetterhoff.

Texas Catholic Conference, 3001 S. Congress Ave., Austin, Tex. 78704; exec. dir., Bro. Richard Daly, C.S.C.

Washington State Catholic Conference, 1402 3rd Ave., Suite 618, Seattle, Wash. 98101; exec. dir. Rev. D. Harvey McIntyre.

Wisconsin Catholic Conference, 30 W. Mifflin St., Suite 910, Madison, Wis. 53703; exec. dir., Charles M. Phillips.

BIOGRAPHIES OF AMERICAN BISHOPS

(Sources: Almanac survey, *The Official Catholic Directory,* NC News Service. As of Aug. 1, 1986.)

Information includes: date and place of birth; educational institutions attended; date of ordination to the priesthood with, where applicable, name of archdiocese (*) or diocese in parentheses; date of episcopal ordination; episcopal appointments; date of resignation.

A

Abramowicz, Alfred L.: b. Jan. 27, 1919, Chicago, Ill.; educ. St. Mary of the Lake Seminary (Mundelein, Ill.), Gregorian Univ. (Rome); ord. priest (Chicago*) May 1, 1943; ord. titular bishop of Paestum and auxiliary bishop of Chicago, June 13, 1968.

Acerra, Angelo Thomas, O.S.B.: b. Nov. 7, 1925, Memphis, Tenn.; educ. St. Benedict's (Atchison, Kans.), Catholic Univ. (Washington, D.C.), St. Mary's Univ. (San Antonio, Tex.), Univ. of Northern Colorado (Greeley, Colo.), Angelicum (Rome); ord. priest May 20, 1950; ord. titular bishop of Lete and auxiliary bishop of the Military Vicariate, Nov. 29, 1983; vicar for the Far East.

Ackerman, Richard Henry, C.S.Sp.: b. Aug. 30, 1903, Pittsburgh, Pa.; educ. Duquesne Univ. (Pittsburgh, Pa.), St. Mary's Scholasticate (Norwalk, Conn.), Univ. of Fribourg (Switzerland); ord. priest Aug. 28, 1926; ord. titular bishop of Lares and auxiliary bishop of San Diego, May 22, 1956; app. bishop of Covington, Apr. 4, 1960; resigned Nov. 28, 1978.

Ahern, Patrick V.: b. Mar. 8, 1919, New York, N.Y.; educ. Manhattan College and Cathedral College (New York City), St. Joseph's Seminary (Yonkers, N.Y.), St. Louis Univ. (St. Louis, Mo.), Notre Dame Univ. (Notre Dame, Ind.); ord. priest (New York*) Jan. 27, 1945; ord. titular bishop of Naiera and auxiliary bishop of New York, Mar. 19, 1970.

Ahr, George William: b. June 23, 1904, Newark, N.J.; educ. St. Vincent College (Latrobe, Pa.), Seton Hall College (S. Orange, N.J.), North American College (Rome); ord. priest (Newark*) July 29, 1928; ord. bishop of Trenton, Mar. 20, 1950; resigned June 23, 1979.

Anderson, Moses B., S.S.E.: b. Sept. 9, 1928, Selma, Ala.; educ. St. Michael's College (Winooski, Vt.), St. Edmund Seminary (Burlington, Vt.), Univ. of Legon (Ghana); ord. priest May 30, 1958; ord. titular bishop of Vatarba and auxiliary bishop of Detroit, Jan. 27, 1983.

Anderson, Paul F.: b. Apr. 20, 1917, Roslindale, Mass.; educ. Boston College (Chestnut Hill, Mass.), St. John's Seminary (Brighton, Mass.); ord. priest (Boston*) Jan. 6, 1943; ord. titular bishop of Polignano and coadjutor bishop of Duluth, Oct. 17, 1968; bishop of Duluth, Apr. 30, 1969; resigned Aug. 17, 1982; app. auxiliary bishop of Sioux Falls.

Angell, Kenneth A.: b. Aug. 3, 1930, Providence, R.I.; educ. St. Mary's Seminary (Baltimore, Md.); ord. priest (Providence) May 26, 1956; ord. titular bishop of Septimunicia and auxiliary bishop of Providence, R.I., Oct. 7, 1974.

Apuron, Anthony Sablan, O.F.M. Cap.: b. Nov. 1, 1945, Agana, Guam; educ. St. Anthony College and Capuchin Seminary (Hudson, N.H.), Capuchin Seminary (Garrison, N.Y.), Maryknoll Seminary (New York), Notre Dame Univ. (Notre Dame, Ind.); ord. priest Aug. 26, 1972, in Guam; ord.

titular bishop of Muzuca in Proconsulari and auxiliary bishop of Agana, Guam (U.S. Trust Territory), Feb. 19, 1984; archbishop of Agana, 1986.

Arias, David, O.A.R.: b. July 22, 1929, Leon, Spain; educ. St. Rita's College (San Sebastian, Spain), Our Lady of Good Counsel Theologate (Granada, Spain), Teresianum Institute (Rome, Italy); ord. priest May 31, 1952; ord. titular bishop of Badie and auxiliary bishop of Newark, Apr. 7, 1983; episcopal vicar for Hispanic affairs.

Arkfeld, Leo, S.V.D.: b. Feb. 4, 1912, Butte, Nebr.; educ. Divine Word Seminary (Techny, Ill.), Sacred Heart College (Girard, Pa.); ord. priest Aug. 15, 1943; ord. titular bishop of Bucellus and vicar apostolic of Central New Guinea, Nov. 30, 1948; name of vicariate changed to Wewak, May 15, 1952; first bishop of Wewak, Nov. 15, 1966; app. archbishop of Madang, Papua New Guinea, Dec. 19, 1975.

Arliss, Reginald, C.P.: b. Sept. 8, 1906, East Orange, N.J.; educ. Immaculate Conception Seminary (Jamaica, N.Y.) and other Passionist houses of study; ord. priest Apr. 28, 1934; missionary in China for 16 years, expelled 1951; missionary in Philippines; rector of the Pontifical Philippine College Seminary in Rome, 1961-69; ord. titular bishop of Cerbali and prelate of Marbel, Philippines (now a diocese), Jan. 30, 1970; resigned from titular see and prelature, Oct. 1, 1981.

Arzube, Juan A.: b. June 1, 1918, Guayaquil, Ecuador; educ. Rensselaer Polytechnic Institute (Troy, N.Y.), St. John's Seminary (Camarillo, Calif.); ord. priest (Los Angeles*) May 5, 1954; ord. titular bishop of Civitate and auxiliary bishop of Los Angeles, Mar. 25, 1971.

B

Balke, Victor: b. Sept. 29, 1931, Meppen, Ill.; educ. St. Mary of the Lake Seminary (Mundelein, Ill.), St. Louis Univ. (St. Louis, Mo.); ord. priest (Springfield, Ill.) May 24, 1958; ord. bishop of Crookston, Sept. 2, 1976.

Baltakis, Paul Antanas, O.F.M.: b. Jan. 1, 1925, Troskunai, Lithuania; educ. seminaries of the Franciscan Province of St. Joseph (Belgium); ord. priest Aug. 24, 1952, in Belgium; served in U.S. as director of Lithuanian Cultural Center, New York, and among Lithuanian youth; head of U.S. Lithuanian Franciscan Vicariate, Kennebunkport, Maine, from 1979; ord. titular bishop of Egara, Sept. 24, 1984; assigned to pastoral assistance to Lithuanian Catholics living outside Lithuania.

Banks, Robert J.: b. Feb. 26, 1928, Winthrop, Mass.; educ. St. John's Seminary (Brighton, Mass.), Gregorian Univ., Lateran Univ. (Rome); ord. priest (Boston*) Dec. 20, 1952, in Rome; rector of St. John's Seminary, Brighton, Mass., 1971-81; vicar general of Boston archdiocese, 1984; ord. titular bishop of Taraqua and auxiliary bishop of Boston, Sept. 19, 1985.

Baum, William W.: (See Cardinals, Biographies.)

Begley, Michael J.: b. Mar. 12, 1909, Mattineague, Mass.; educ. Mt. St. Mary Seminary (Emmitsburg, Md.); ord. priest (Raleigh) May 26,

1934; ord. first bishop of Charlotte, N.C., Jan. 12, 1972; retired May 29, 1984.

Beltran, Eusebius J.: b. Aug. 31, 1934, Ashley, Pa.; educ. St. Charles Seminary (Philadelphia, Pa.); ord. priest (Atlanta*) May 14, 1960; ord. bishop of Tulsa, Apr. 20, 1978.

Bernardin, Joseph L.: (See Cardinals, Biographies.)

Bernarding, George, S.V.D.: b. Feb. 15, 1912, Carrick, Pa.; educ. Divine Word Seminary (Girard, Pa.); ord. priest Aug. 13, 1939; ord. titular bishop of Belabitene and first vicar apostolic of Mount Hagen, New Guinea, Apr. 21, 1960; first bishop of Mount Hagen, Nov. 15, 1966; app. first archbishop Mar. 29, 1982, when see was elevated to metropolitan rank.

Bevilacqua, Anthony J.: b. June 17, 1923, Brooklyn, N.Y.; educ. Cathedral College (Brooklyn, N.Y.), Immaculate Conception Seminary (Huntington, N.Y.), Gregorian Univ. (Rome), Columbia Univ. and St. John's Univ. (New York); ord. priest (Brooklyn) June 11, 1949; ord. titular bishop of Aquae Albae in Byzacena and auxiliary bishop of Brooklyn, Nov. 24, 1980; app. bishop of Pittsburgh Oct. 7, 1983, installed Dec. 11, 1983.

Bilock, John M.: b. June 20, 1916, McAdoo, Pa.; educ. St. Procopius College and Seminary (Lisle, Ill.); ord. priest (Pittsburgh,* Byzantine Rite) Feb. 3, 1946; vicar general of Byzantine archdiocese of Munhall, 1969; ord. titular bishop of Pergamum and auxiliary bishop of Munhall, May 15, 1973; title of see changed to Pittsburgh, 1977.

Boccella, John H., T.O.R.: b. June 25, 1912, Castelfranci, Italy; came to U.S. at the age of two; educ. St. Francis College and Seminary (Loretto, Pa.), Angelicum Univ. (Rome), Catholic Univ. (Washington, D.C.); ord. priest Mar. 29, 1941; minister general of Third Order Regular, 1947-65; ord. archbishop of Izmir, Turkey, Apr. 17, 1968; transferred to titular see of Ephesus, Dec. 7, 1978 (resides in Rome).

Boland, Ernest B., O.P.: b. July 10, 1925, Providence, R.I.; educ. Providence College (Rhode Island), Dominican Houses of Study (Somerset, Ohio; Washington, D.C.); ord. priest June 9, 1955; ord. bishop of Multan, Pakistan, July 25, 1966; resigned Oct. 20, 1984.

Borders, William D.: b. Oct. 9, 1913, Washington, Ind.; educ. St. Meinrad Seminary (St. Meinrad, Ind.), Notre Dame Seminary (New Orleans, La.), Notre Dame Univ. (Notre Dame, Ind.); ord. priest (New Orleans*) May 18, 1940; ord. first bishop of Orlando, June 14, 1968; app. archbishop of Baltimore, Apr. 2, 1974, installed June 26, 1974.

Bosco, Anthony G.: b. Aug. 1, 1927, New Castle, Pa.; educ. St. Vincent Seminary (Latrobe, Pa.), Lateran Univ. (Rome); ord. priest (Pittsburgh) June 7, 1952; ord. titular bishop of Labicum and auxiliary of Pittsburgh, June 30, 1970.

Boudreaux, Warren L.: b. Jan. 25, 1918, Berwick, La.; educ. St. Joseph's Seminary (St. Benedict, La.), St. Sulpice Seminary (Paris, France), Notre Dame Seminary (New Orleans, La.), Catholic Univ. (Washington, D.C.); ord.

priest (Lafayette, La.) May 30, 1942; ord. titular bishop of Calynda and auxiliary bishop of Lafayette, La., July 25, 1962; app. bishop of Beaumont, June 5, 1971; app. first bishop of Houma-Thibodaux, installed June 5, 1977.

Breitenbeck, Joseph M.: b. Aug. 3, 1914, Detroit, Mich.; educ. University of Detroit, Sacred Heart Seminary (Detroit, Mich.), North American College and Lateran Univ. (Rome), Catholic Univ. (Washington, D.C.); ord. priest (Detroit*) May 30, 1942; ord. titular bishop of Tepelta and auxiliary bishop of Detroit, Dec. 20, 1965; app. bishop of Grand Rapids, Oct. 15, 1969, installed Dec. 2, 1969.

Brizgys, Vincas: b. Nov. 10, 1903, Plyniai, Lithuania; ord. priest June 5, 1927; ord. titular bishop of Bosano and auxiliary bishop of Kaunas, Lithuania, May 10, 1940; taken into custody and deported to Germany, 1944; liberated by Americans, 1945; U.S. citizen, 1958.

Broderick, Edwin B.: b. Jan. 16, 1917, New York, N.Y.; educ. Cathedral College (New York City), St. Joseph's Seminary (Yonkers, N.Y.), Fordham Univ. (New York City); ord. priest (New York*) May 30, 1942; ord. titular bishop of Tizica and auxiliary of New York, Apr. 21, 1967; bishop of Albany, 1969-76; executive director of Catholic Relief Services, 1976-82. Bishop emeritus of Albany.

Brom, Robert H.: b. Sept. 18, 1938, Arcadia, Wis.; educ. St. Mary's College (Winona, Minn.), Gregorian Univ. (Rome); ord. priest (Winona) Dec. 18, 1963, in Rome; ord. bishop of Duluth, May 23, 1983.

Brown, Charles A., M.M.: b. Aug. 20, 1919, New York, N.Y.; educ. Cathedral College (New York City), Maryknoll Seminary (Maryknoll, N.Y.); ord. priest June 9, 1946; ord. titular bishop of Vallis and auxiliary bishop of Santa Cruz, Bolivia, Mar. 27, 1957.

Brunini, Joseph B.: b. July 24, 1909, Vicksburg, Miss.; educ. Georgetown Univ. (Washington, D.C.), North American College (Rome), Catholic Univ. (Washington, D.C.); ord. priest (Jackson) Dec. 5, 1933; ord. titular bishop of Axomis and auxiliary bishop of Natchez-Jackson, Jan. 29, 1957; apostolic administrator of Natchez-Jackson, 1966; app. bishop of Natchez-Jackson, Dec. 2, 1967, installed Jan. 29, 1968; title of see changed to Jackson, 1977; retired Jan. 24, 1984.

Brust, Leo J.: b. Jan. 7, 1916, St. Francis, Wis.; educ. St. Francis Seminary (Milwaukee, Wis.), Canisianum (Innsbruck, Austria), Catholic Univ. (Washington, D.C.); ord. priest (Milwaukee*) May 30, 1942; ord. titular bishop of Suelli and auxiliary bishop of Milwaukee. Oct. 16, 1969.

Brzana, Stanislaus J.: b. July 1, 1917, Buffalo, N.Y.; educ. Christ the King Seminary (St. Bonaventure, N.Y.), Gregorian Univ. (Rome); ord. priest (Buffalo) June 7, 1941; ord, titular bishop of Cufruta and auxiliary bishop of Buffalo, June 29, 1964; bishop of Ogdensburg, Oct. 22, 1968.

Bullock, William H.: b. Apr. 13, 1927, Maple Lake, Minn.; educ. St. Thomas College and St. Paul Seminary (St. Paul, Minn.), Notre Dame Univ. (Notre Dame, Ind.); ord. priest (St. Paul-Minneapolis*) June 7, 1952; ord. titular bishop of

Natchez and auxiliary bishop of St. Paul and Minneapolis, Aug. 12, 1980.

Burke, James C., O.P.: b. Nov. 30, 1926, Philadelphia, Pa.; educ. King's College (Wilkes-Barre, Pa.), Providence College (R.I.); ord. priest June 8, 1956; ord. titular bishop of Lamiggiga and prelate of Chimbote, Peru, May 25, 1967, resigned from prelature (now a diocese), June 8, 1978. Titular bishop of Lamiggiga. Vicar for urban affairs, Wilmington, Del., diocese Aug. 31, 1978.

Buswell, Charles A.: b. Oct. 15, 1913, Homestead, Okla.; educ. St. Louis Preparatory Seminary (St. Louis, Mo.), Kenrick Seminary (Webster Groves, Mo.), American College, Univ. of Louvain (Belgium); ord. priest (Oklahoma City*) July 9, 1939; ord. bishop of Pueblo, Sept. 30, 1959; resigned Sept. 18, 1979.

Byrne, James J.: b. July 28, 1908, St. Paul, Minn.; educ. Nazareth Hall Preparatory Seminary and St. Paul Seminary (St. Paul, Minn.), Univ. of Minnesota (Minneapolis, Minn.); Louvain Univ. (Belgium); ord. priest (St. Paul-Minneapolis*) June 3, 1933; ord. titular bishop of Etenna and auxiliary bishop of St. Paul, July 2, 1947; app. bishop of Boise, June 16, 1956; app. archbishop of Dubuque, Mar. 19, 1962, installed May 8, 1962; retired Aug. 23, 1983.

C

Caesar, Raymond R., S.V.D.: b. Feb. 14, 1932, Eunice, La.; educ. Divine Word Seminary (Bay St. Louis, Miss.); Catholic Univ. (Washington, D.C.); ord. priest June 4, 1961; missionary in New Guinea from 1962; ord. coadjutor bishop of Goroka, Papua New Guinea, Oct. 25, 1978; bishop of Goroko, Aug. 30, 1980.

Camacho, Tomas Aguon: b. Sept. 18, 1933, Chalon Kanoa, Saipan; educ. St. Patrick's Seminary (Menlo Park, Calif.); ord. priest June 14, 1961; ord. first bishop of Chalon Kanoa, Northern Marianas (U.S. Trust Territory), Jan. 13, 1985.

Carberry, John J.: (See Cardinals, Biographies.)

Carlson, Robert J.: b. June 30, 1944, Minneapolis, Minn.; educ. Nazareth Hall and St. Paul Seminary (St. Paul, Minn.), Catholic Univ. (Washington, D.C.): ord. priest (St. Paul-Minneapolis*) May 23, 1970; ord. titular bishop of Avioccala and auxiliary bishop of St. Paul and Minneapolis, Jan. 11, 1984; vicar of eastern vicariate.

Casey, Luis Morgan: b. June 23, 1935, Portageville, Mo.; ord. priest (St. Louis*) Apr. 7, 1962; missionary in Bolivia from 1965; ord. titular bishop of Mibiarca and auxiliary of La Paz, Jan. 28, 1984.

Cassata, John J.: b. Nov. 8, 1908, Galveston, Tex.; educ. St. Mary's Seminary (La Porte, Tex.), North American College, Urban Univ. and Gregorian Univ. (Rome); ord. priest (Galveston-Houston) Dec. 8, 1932; ord. titular bishop of Bida and auxiliary bishop of Dallas-Fort Worth, June 5, 1968; app. bishop of Fort Worth, Aug. 27, 1969, installed Oct. 21, 1969; retired Sept. 16, 1980.

Chavez, Gilbert Espinoza: b. May 9, 1932, Ontario, Calif.; educ. St. Francis Seminary (El Cajon, Calif.), Immaculate Heart Seminary (San Diego), Univ. of California; ord. priest (San Diego)

Mar. 19, 1960; ord. titular bishop of Magarmel and auxiliary of San Diego, June 21, 1974.

Chedid, John: b. July 4, 1923, Eddid, Lebanon; educ. seminaries in Lebanon and Pontifical Urban College (Rome); ord. priest Dec. 21, 1951, in Rome; ord. titular bishop of Callinico and auxiliary bishop of St. Maron of Brooklyn for the Maronites, Jan. 25, 1981.

Clark, Matthew H.: b. July 15, 1937, Troy, N.Y.; educ. St. Bernard's Seminary (Rochester, N.Y.), Gregorian Univ. (Rome); ord. priest (Albany) Dec. 19, 1962; ord. bishop of Rochester, May 27, 1979; installed June 26, 1979.

Clinch, Harry A.: b. Oct. 27, 1908, San Anselmo, Calif.; educ. St. Joseph's College (Mountain View, Calif.), St. Patrick's Seminary (Menlo Park, Calif.); ord. priest (Monterey-Fresno) June 6, 1936; ord. titular bishop of Badiae and auxiliary bishop of Monterey-Fresno, Feb. 27, 1957; app. first bishop of Monterey in California, installed Dec. 14, 1967; resigned Jan. 19, 1982.

Cohill, John Edward, S.V.D.: b. Dec. 13, 1907, Elizabeth, N.J.; educ. Divine Word Seminary (Techny, Ill.); ord. priest Mar. 20, 1936; ord. first bishop of Goroko, Papua New Guinea, Mar. 11, 1967; resigned Aug. 30, 1980.

Comber, John W., M.M.: b. Mar. 12, 1906, Lawrence, Mass.; educ. St. John's Preparatory College (Danvers, Mass.), Boston College (Boston, Mass.), Maryknoll Seminary (Maryknoll, N.Y.); ord. priest Feb. 1, 1931; superior general of Maryknoll, 1956-66; ord. titular bishop of Foratiana, Apr. 9, 1959.

Connare, William G.: b. Dec. 11, 1911, Pittsburgh, Pa.; educ. Duquesne Univ. (Pittsburgh, Pa.), St. Vincent Seminary (Latrobe, Pa.); ord. priest (Pittsburgh) June 14, 1936; ord. bishop of Greensburg, May 4, 1960.

Connolly, James L.: b. Nov. 15, 1894, Fall River, Mass.; educ. St. Charles College (Catonsville, Md.), St. Mary's Seminary (Baltimore, Md.), Catholic Univ. (Washington, D.C.), Louvain Univ. (Belgium); ord. priest (Fall River) Dec. 21, 1923; rector of St. Paul (Minn.) minor seminary 1940-43; major seminary 1943-45; ord. titular bishop of Mylasa and coadjutor of Fall River, May 24, 1945; bishop of Fall River, May 17, 1951; resigned Oct. 30, 1970.

Connolly, Thomas Arthur: b. Oct. 5, 1899, San Francisco, Calif.; educ. St. Patrick's Seminary (Menlo Park, Calif.), Catholic Univ. (Washington, D.C.); ord. priest (San Francisco*) June 11, 1926; ord. titular bishop of Sila and auxiliary bishop of San Francisco, Aug. 24, 1939; app. coadjutor bishop of Seattle, Feb. 28, 1948; succeeded as bishop of Seattle, May 18, 1950; first archbishop of Seattle, June 23, 1951; retired Feb. 25, 1975.

Connolly, Thomas J.: b. July 18, 1922, Tonopah, Nev.; educ. St. Patrick's Seminary (Menlo Park, Calif.), Catholic Univ. (Washington, D.C.), Lateran Univ. (Rome); ord. priest (Reno-Las Vegas) Apr. 8, 1947; ord. bishop of Baker, June 30, 1971.

Connors, Ronald G., C.SS.R.: b. Nov. 1, 1915, Brooklyn, N.Y.; ord. priest June 22, 1941; ord. titular bishop of Equizetum and coadjutor bishop of San Juan de la Maguana, Dominican Republic, July 20, 1976; succeeded as bishop of San Juan de la Maguana, July 20, 1977.

Cooney, Patrick R.: b. Mar. 10, 1934, Detroit, Mich.; educ. Sacred Heart Seminary (Detroit), Gregorian Univ. (Rome), Notre Dame Univ. (Notre Dame, Ind.); ord. priest (Detroit*) Dec. 20, 1959; ord. titular bishop of Hodelm and auxiliary bishop of Detroit, Jan. 27, 1983.

Corrada del Rio, Alvaro, S.J.: b. May 13, 1942, Santurce, Puerto Rico; entered Society of Jesus, 1960, at novitiate of St. Andrew-on-Hudson (Poughkeepsie, N.Y.); educ. Jesuit seminaries, Fordham Univ. (New York), Institut Catholique (Paris); ord. priest July 6, 1974, in Puerto Rico; pastoral coordinator of Northeast Catholic Hispanic Center, New York, 1982-85; ord. titular bishop of Rusticiana and auxiliary bishop of Washington, D.C., Aug. 4, 1985.

Coscia, Benedict Dominic, O.F.M.: b. Aug. 10, 1922, Brooklyn, N.Y.; educ. St. Francis College (Brooklyn, N.Y.), Holy Name College (Washington, D.C.); ord. priest June 11, 1949; ord. bishop of Jatai, Brazil, Sept. 21, 1961.

Cosgrove, William M.: b. Nov. 26, 1916, Canton, Ohio; educ. John Carroll Univ. (Cleveland, O.); ord. priest (Cleveland) Dec. 18, 1943; ord. titular bishop of Trisipa and auxiliary bishop of Cleveland, Sept. 3, 1968; app. bishop of Belleville, installed Oct. 28, 1976; retired May 19, 1981.

Costello, Thomas J.: b. Feb. 23, 1929, Camden, N.Y.; educ. Niagara Univ. (Niagara Falls, N.Y.), St. Bernard's Seminary (Rochester, N.Y.), Catholic Univ. (Washington, D.C.); ord. priest (Syracuse) June 5, 1954; ord. titular bishop of Perdices and auxiliary bishop of Syracuse Mar. 13, 1978.

Cotey, Arnold R., S.D.S.: b. June 15, 1921, Milwaukee, Wis.; educ. Divine Savior Seminary (Lanham, Md.), Marquette Univ. (Milwaukee, Wis.); ord. priest June 7, 1949; ord. first bishop of Nachingwea, Tanzania, Oct. 20, 1963; retired Nov. 11, 1983.

Cousins, William E.: b. Aug. 20, 1902, Chicago, Ill.; educ. Quigley Seminary (Chicago, Ill.), St. Mary of the Lake Seminary (Mundelein, Ill.); ord. priest (Chicago*) Apr. 23, 1927; ord. titular bishop of Forma and auxiliary bishop of Chicago, Mar. 7, 1949; app. bishop of Peoria, May 21, 1952; archbishop of Milwaukee, Jan. 27, 1959; retired Jan. 17, 1977.

Cronin, Daniel A.: b. Nov. 14, 1927, Newton, Mass.; educ. St. John's Seminary (Boston, Mass.), North American College and Gregorian Univ. (Rome); ord. priest (Boston*) Dec. 20, 1952; attaché apostolic nunciature (Addis Ababa), 1957-61; served in papal Secretariat of State, 1961-68; ord. titular bishop of Egnatia and auxiliary bishop of Boston, Sept. 12, 1968; bishop of Fall River, Dec. 16, 1970.

Crowley, Joseph R.: b. Jan. 12, 1915, Fort Wayne, Ind.; educ. St. Mary's College (St. Mary, Ky.), St. Meinrad Seminary (St. Meinrad, Ind.); served in US Air Force, 1942-46; ord. priest (Ft. Wayne-S. Bend) May 1, 1953; editor of *Our Sunday Visitor* 1958-67; ord. titular bishop of Maraguis and auxiliary bishop of Fort Wayne-South Bend, Aug. 24, 1971.

Cummins, John S.: b. Mar. 3, 1928, Oakland, Calif.; educ. St. Patrick's Seminary (Menlo Park, Calif.), Catholic Univ. (Washington, D.C.), Univ. of California; ord. priest (San Francisco*) Jan. 24, 1953; executive director of the California Catholic Conference 1971-76; ord. titular bishop of Lambaesis and auxiliary bishop of Sacramento, May 16, 1974; app. bishop of Oakland, installed June 30, 1977.

Curtis, Walter W.: b. May 3, 1913, Jersey City, N.J.; educ. Fordham Univ. (New York City), Seton Hall Univ. (South Orange, N.J.), Immaculate Conception Seminary (Darlington, N.J.), North American College and Gregorian Univ. (Rome), Catholic Univ. (Washington, D.C.); ord. priest (Newark*) Dec. 8, 1937; ord. titular bishop of Bisica and auxiliary bishop of Newark, Sept. 24, 1957; app. bishop of Bridgeport, 1961, installed Nov. 21, 1961.

Curtiss, Elden F.: b. June 16, 1932, Baker, Ore.; educ. St. Edward Seminary College and St. Thomas Seminary (Kenmore, Wash.); ord. priest (Baker) May 24, 1958; ord. bishop of Helena, Mont., Apr. 28, 1976.

D

Daily, Thomas V.: b. Sept. 23, 1927, Belmont, Mass.; educ. Boston College, St. John's Seminary (Brighton, Mass.); ord. priest (Boston*) Jan. 10, 1952; missionary in Peru for five years as a member of the Society of St. James the Apostle; ord. titular bishop of Bladia and auxiliary bishop of Boston, Feb. 11, 1975; app. first bishop of Palm Beach, Fla., July 17, 1984, installed Oct. 24, 1984.

Daly, James: b. Aug. 14, 1921, New York, N.Y.; educ. Cathedral College (Brooklyn, N.Y.), Immaculate Conception Seminary (Huntington, L.I.); ord. priest (Buffalo) May 22, 1948; ord. titular bishop of Castra Nova and auxiliary bishop of Rockville Centre, May 9, 1977.

Danglmayr, Augustine: b. Dec. 11, 1898, Muenster, Tex.; educ. Subiaco College (Arkansas), St. Mary's Seminary (La Porte, Tex.), Kenrick Seminary (St. Louis, Mo.); ord. priest (Dallas) June 10, 1922; ord. titular bishop of Olba, Oct. 7, 1942; auxiliary bishop of Dallas-Ft. Worth, 1942-69.

D'Antonio, Nicholas, O.F.M.: b. July 10, 1916, Rochester, N.Y.; educ. St. Anthony's Friary (Catskill, N.Y.); ord. priest June 7, 1942; ord. titular bishop of Giufi Salaria and prelate of Olancho, Honduras, July 25, 1966; resigned 1977; app. vicar general of New Orleans archdiocese and episcopal vicar for Spanish Speaking, August, 1977.

D'Arcy, John M.: b. Aug. 18, 1932, Brighton, Mass.; educ. St. John's Seminary (Brighton, Mass.), Angelicum Univ. (Rome); ord. priest (Boston*) Feb. 2, 1957; spiritual director of St. John's Seminary; ord. titular bishop of Mediana and auxiliary bishop of Boston, Feb. 11, 1975; app. bishop of Fort Wayne-South Bend, Feb. 26, 1985, installed May 1, 1985.

Davis, James Peter: b. June 9, 1904, Houghton, Mich.; educ. St. Joseph's College (Mountain View, Calif.), St. Patrick's Seminary (Menlo Park, Calif.); ord. priest (Tucson) May 19, 1929; ord. bishop of San Juan, Puerto Rico, Oct. 6, 1943; app. first archbishop of San Juan, July 30, 1960; app. archbishop of Santa Fe, installed Feb. 25, 1964; resigned June 4, 1974.

Dearden, John Francis: (See Cardinals, Biographies.)

Deksnys, Antanas L.: b. May 9, 1906, Buteniskiai, Lithuania; educ. Metropolitan Seminary and Theological and Philosophical Faculty at Vytautas the Great Univ. (all at Kaunas, Lithuania), Univ. of Fribourg (Switzerland); ord. priest May 30, 1931; served in U.S. parishes at Mt. Carmel, Pa., and East St. Louis, Ill.; ord. titular bishop of Lavellum, June 15, 1969; assigned to pastoral work among Lithuanians in Western Europe; retired June 5, 1984.

Delaney, Joseph P.: b. Aug. 29, 1934, Fall River, Mass.; educ. Cardinal O'Connell Seminary (Boston, Mass.), Theological College (Washington, D.C.), North American College (Rome), Rhode Island College (Providence, R.I.); ord. priest (Fall River) Dec. 18, 1960; ord. bishop of Fort Worth, Tex., Sept. 13, 1981.

Dempsey, Michael J., O.P.: b. Feb. 22, 1912, Providence, R.I.; entered Order of Preachers (Dominicans), Chicago province, 1935; ord. priest June 11, 1942; ord. bishop of Sokoto, Nigeria, Aug. 15, 1967; resigned Dec. 31, 1984.

Denning, Joseph P.: b. Jan. 4, 1907, Flushing, L.I.; educ. Cathedral College (Brooklyn, N.Y.), Immaculate Conception Seminary (Huntington, L.I.), St. Mary's Seminary (Baltimore, Md.); ord. priest (Brooklyn) May 21, 1932; ord. titular bishop of Mallus and auxiliary bishop of Brooklyn, Apr. 22, 1959; resigned Apr. 13, 1982.

De Palma, Joseph A., S.C.J.: b. Sept. 4, 1913, Walton, N.Y.; ord. priest May 20, 1944; superior general of Congregation of Priests of the Sacred Heart, 1959-67; ord. first bishop of De Aar, South Africa, July 19, 1967.

De Paoli, Ambrose: b. Aug. 19, 1934, Jeannette, Pa., moved to Miami at age of nine; educ. St. Joseph Seminary (Bloomfield, Conn.), St. Mary of the West Seminary (Cincinnati, O.), North American College and Lateran Univ. (Rome); ord. priest (Miami*) Dec. 18, 1960, in Rome; served in diplomatic posts in Canada, Turkey, Africa and Venezuela; ord. titular archbishop of Lares, Nov. 20, 1983, in Miami; apostolic pro-nuncio to Sri Lanka, 1983.

De Simone, Louis A.: b. Feb. 21, 1922, Philadelphia, Pa.; educ. Villanova Univ. (Villanova, Pa.), St. Charles Borromeo Seminary (Overbrook, Pa.); ord. priest (Philadelphia*) May 10, 1952; ord. titular bishop of Cillium and auxiliary bishop of Philadelphia, Aug. 12, 1981.

Dimino, Joseph T.: b. Jan. 7, 1923, New York, N.Y.; educ. Cathedral College (New York, N.Y.), St. Joseph's Seminary (Yonkers, N.Y.), Catholic Univ. (Washington, D.C.); ord. priest (New York*) June 4, 1949; ord. titular bishop of Carini and auxiliary bishop of the Military Archdiocese, May 10, 1983.

Dimmerling, Harold J.: b. Sept. 23, 1914, Braddock, Pa.; educ. St. Fidelis Preparatory Seminary (Herman, Pa.), St. Charles Seminary (Columbus, O.), St. Francis Seminary (Loretto, Pa.); ord. priest (St. Cloud) May 2, 1940; ord. bishop of Rapid City, Oct. 30, 1969.

Dingman, Maurice J.: b. Jan. 20, 1914, St. Paul, Ia.; educ. St. Ambrose College (Davenport, Ia.), North American College and Gregorian Univ. (Rome), Catholic Univ. (Washington, D.C.); ord. priest (Davenport) Dec. 8, 1939; ord. bishop of Des Moines, June 19, 1968.

Dion, Georges E., O.M.I.: b. Sept. 25, 1911, Central Falls, R.I.; educ. Holy Cross College (Worcester, Mass.), Oblate Juniorate (Colebrook, N.H.), Oblate Scholasticates (Natick, Mass., and Ottawa, Ont.); ord. priest June 24, 1936; ord. titular bishop of Arpaia and vicar apostolic of Jolo, Philippines Apr. 23, 1980.

Dolinay, Thomas V.: b. July 24, 1923, Uniontown, Pa.; educ. St. Procopius College (Lisle, Ill.); ord. priest (Pittsburgh*, Byzantine Rite) May 16, 1948; editor *Eastern Catholic Life,* 1966-82; ord. titular bishop of Tiatira and auxiliary bishop of Byzantine-Rite diocese of Passaic, Nov. 23, 1976; app. first bishop Byzantine-Rite diocese of Van Nuys, Calif., Dec. 3, 1981, installed Mar. 9, 1982.

Donaghy, Frederick Anthony, M.M.: b. Jan. 13, 1903, New Bedford, Mass.; educ. Holy Cross College (Worcester, Mass.), St. Mary's Seminary (Baltimore, Md.), Maryknoll Seminary (Maryknoll, N.Y.); ord. priest Jan. 29, 1929; ord. titular bishop of Setea and vicar apostolic of Wuchow, China, Sept. 21, 1939; title changed to bishop of Wuchow, Apr. 11, 1946; expelled by Communists; bishop emeritus of Wuchow.

Donnellan, Thomas A.: b. Jan. 24, 1914, New York, N.Y.; educ. Cathedral College and St. Joseph's Seminary (New York, N.Y.), Catholic Univ. (Washington, D.C.); ord. priest (New York*) June 3, 1939; ord. bishop of Ogdensburg, Apr. 9, 1964; app. archbishop of Atlanta, installed July 16, 1968.

Donnelly, Robert William: b. Mar. 22, 1931, Toledo, O.; educ. St. Meinrad Seminary College (St. Meinrad, Ind.), Mount St. Mary's in the West Seminary (Norwood, O.); ord. priest (Toledo) May 25, 1957; ord. titular bishop of Garba and auxiliary bishop of Toledo, May 3, 1984.

Donoghue, John F.: b. Aug. 9, 1928, Washington, D.C.; educ. St. Mary's Seminary (Baltimore, Md.); Catholic Univ. (Washington, D.C.); ord. priest (Washington*) June 4, 1955; chancellor and vicar general of Washington archdiocese, 1973-84; ord. bishop of Charlotte, N.C., Dec. 18, 1984.

Donohoe, Hugh A.: b. June 28, 1905, San Francisco, Calif.; educ. St. Patrick's Preparatory and Major Seminaries (Menlo Park, Calif.), Catholic Univ. (Washington, D.C.); ord. priest (San Francisco*) June 14, 1930; ord. titular bishop of Taium and auxiliary bishop of San Francisco, Oct. 7, 1947; app. first bishop of Stockton, Jan. 27, 1962; app. bishop of Fresno, Aug. 27, 1969, installed Oct. 7, 1969; retired July 1, 1980.

Donovan, John A.: b. Aug. 5, 1911, Chatham, Ont., Canada; educ. Sacred Heart Seminary (Detroit, Mich.), North American College and Gregorian Univ. (Rome); ord. priest (Detroit*) Dec. 8, 1935; ord. titular bishop of Rhasus and auxiliary bishop of Detroit, Oct. 26, 1954; app. bishop of Toledo, installed Apr. 18, 1967; retired July 29, 1980.

Donovan, Paul V.: b. Sept. 1, 1924, Bernard, Iowa; educ. St. Gregory's Seminary (Cincinnati, Ohio), Mt. St. Mary's Seminary (Norwood, Ohio), Lateran Univ. (Rome); ord. priest (Lansing) May 20, 1950; ord. first bishop of Kalamazoo, Mich., July 21, 1971.

Dorsey, Norbert M., C.P.: b. Dec. 14, 1929, Springfield, Mass.; educ. Passionist seminaries, Gregorian Univ. (Rome, Italy); ord priest Apr. 28, 1956; ord. titular bishop of Mectaris and auxiliary bishop of Miami, Mar. 19, 1986.

Drury, Thomas J.: b. Jan. 4, 1908, Co. Sligo, Ireland; educ. St. Benedict's College (Atchison, Kans.), Kenrick Seminary (St. Louis, Mo.); ord. priest (Amarillo) June 2, 1935; ord. first bishop of San Angelo, Tex., Jan. 24, 1962; app. bishop of Corpus Christi, installed Sept. 1, 1965; resigned May 24, 1983.

Dudick, Michael J.: b. Feb. 24, 1916, St. Clair, Pa.; educ. St. Procopius College and Seminary (Lisle, Ill.); ord. priest (Passaic, Byzantine Rite) Nov. 13, 1945; ord. bishop of Byzantine Rite Eparchy of Passaic, Oct. 24, 1968.

Dudley, Paul: b. Nov. 27, 1926, Northfield, Minn.; educ. Nazareth College and St. Paul Seminary (St. Paul, Minn.); ord. priest (St. Paul-Minneapolis*) June 2, 1951; ord. titular bishop of Ursona and auxiliary bishop of St. Paul and Minneapolis, Jan. 25, 1977; app. bishop of Sioux Falls, installed Dec. 13, 1978.

Duhart, Clarence James, C.SS.R.: b. Mar. 23, 1912, New Orleans, La.; ord. priest June 29, 1937; ord. bishop of Udon Thani, Thailand, Apr. 21, 1966; resigned Oct. 2, 1975.

DuMaine, (Roland) Pierre: b. Aug. 2, 1931, Paducah, Ky.; educ. St. Joseph's College (Mountain View, Calif.), St. Patrick's College and Seminary (Menlo Park, Calif.), Univ. of California (Berkeley), Catholic Univ. (Washington, D.C.); ord. priest (San Francisco*) June 15, 1957; ord. titular bishop of Sarda and auxiliary bishop of San Francisco, June 29, 1978; app. first bishop of San Jose, Jan. 27, 1981; installed Mar. 18, 1981.

Dunn, Francis J.: b. Mar. 22, 1922, Elkader, Ia.; educ. Loras College (Dubuque, Ia.), Kenrick Seminary (St. Louis, Mo.), Angelicum (Rome, Italy); ord. priest (Dubuque*) Jan. 11, 1948; chancellor of Dubuque, Aug. 27, 1960; ord. titular bishop of Turris Tamallani and auxiliary bishop of Dubuque, Aug. 27, 1969, app. vicar general, Aug. 28, 1969.

Durick, Joseph Aloysius: b. Oct. 13, 1914, Dayton, Tenn.; educ. St. Bernard Minor Seminary (St. Bernard, Ala.), St. Mary's Seminary (Baltimore, Md.), Urban Univ. (Rome); ord. priest (Mobile*) May 23, 1940; ord. titular bishop of Cerbal and auxiliary bishop of Mobile-Birmingham, Mar. 24, 1955; app. coadjutor bishop of Nashville, Tenn., installed Mar. 3, 1964; apostolic administrator, 1966; bishop of Nashville, Sept. 10, 1969; resigned Apr. 4, 1975, to work with inmates of Federal correctional institutions and their families.

Durning, Dennis V., C.S.Sp.: b. May 18, 1923, Germantown, Pa.; educ. St. Mary's Seminary (Ferndale, Conn.); ord. priest June 3, 1949; ord. first bishop of Arusha, Tanzania, May 28, 1963.

E

Egan, Edward M.: b. Apr. 2, 1932, Oak Park, Ill.; educ. Quigley Preparatory Seminary (Chicago, Ill.), St. Mary of the Lake Seminary (Mundelein, Ill.), Gregorian Univ. (Rome); ord. priest (Chicago*) Dec. 15, 1957, in Rome; judge of Roman Rota, 1972-85; ord. titular bishop of Allegheny and auxiliary bishop of New York, May 22, 1985.

Elko, Nicholas T.: b. Dec. 14, 1909, Donora, Pa.; educ. Duquesne Univ. (Pittsburgh, Pa.), Seminary of Uzhorod (Czechoslovakia), Louvain Univ. (Belgium); ord. priest (Pittsburgh*, Byzantine Rite) Sept. 30, 1934; ord. titular bishop of Apollonias and apostolic administrator of Byzantine-Rite exarchy of Pittsburgh, Mar. 6, 1955; succeeded as exarch of Pittsburgh, Sept. 5, 1955; became eparch when Pittsburgh was raised to eparchy, July, 1963; app. titular archbishop of Dara, 1967, and ordaining prelate for Byzantine Rite in Rome; head of Oriental liturgical commission; app. auxiliary bishop of Cincinnati, Aug. 10, 1971; resigned Apr. 16, 1985.

Elya, John A., B.S.O.: b. 1929, Maghdouche, Lebanon; educ. diocesan monastery (Sidon, Lebanon), Gregorian Univ. (Rome, Italy), Boston College (Boston, Mass.); professed as member of Basilian Salvatorian Order, 1949; ord. priest 1952, in Rome; came to U.S., 1958; app. titular bishop of Abila Lysaniae and auxiliary bishop of Melkite-Rite diocese of Newton, Mass., Apr. 5, 1986.

F

Favalora, John C.: b. Dec. 5, 1935, New Orleans, La.; educ. St. Joseph Seminary (St. Benedict, La.), Notre Dame Seminary (New Orleans, La.), Gregorian Univ. (Rome), Catholic Univ. of America (Washington, D.C.), Xavier Univ. and Tulane Univ. (New Orleans); ord. priest (New Orleans*) Dec. 20, 1961; ord. bishop of Alexandria, La., July 29, 1986.

Federal, Joseph Lennox: b. Jan. 13, 1910, Greensboro, N.C.; educ. Belmont Abbey College (Belmont Abbey, N.C.), Niagara Univ. (Niagara Falls, N.Y.), Univ. of Fribourg (Switzerland), North American College and Gregorian Univ. (Rome); ord. priest (Raleigh) Dec. 8, 1934; ord. titular bishop of Appiaria and auxiliary bishop of Salt Lake City, Apr. 11, 1951; app. coadjutor with right of succession, May, 1958; bishop of Salt Lake City, Mar. 31, 1960; retired Apr. 22, 1980.

Ferrario, Joseph A.: b. Mar. 3, 1926, Scranton, Pa.; educ. St. Charles College (Catonsville, Md.), St. Mary's Seminary (Baltimore, Md.), Catholic Univ. (Washington, D.C.); Univ. of Scranton; ord. priest (Honolulu) May 19, 1951; ord. titular bishop of Cuse and auxiliary bishop of Honolulu Jan. 13, 1978; bishop of Honolulu, May 13, 1982.

Fiorenza, Joseph A.: b. Jan. 25, 1931, Beaumont, Tex.; educ. St. Mary's Seminary (LaPorte, Tex.); ord. priest (Galveston-Houston) May 29, 1954; ord. bishop of San Angelo, Oct. 25, 1979; app. bishop of Galveston-Houston, Dec. 18, 1984, installed Feb. 18, 1985.

Fitzpatrick, John J.: b. Oct. 12, 1918, Trenton, Ont., Canada; educ. Urban Univ. (Rome), Our Lady of the Angels Seminary (Niagara Falls, N.Y.); ord. priest (Buffalo) Dec. 13, 1942; ord. titular bishop of Cenae and auxiliary bishop of Miami, Aug. 28, 1968; bishop of Brownsville, Tex., May 28, 1971.

Fitzsimons, George K.: b. Sept. 4, 1928, Kansas City, Mo.; educ. Rockhurst College (Kansas City, Mo.), Immaculate Conception Seminary (Conception, Mo.); ord. priest (Kansas City-St. Joseph) Mar. 18, 1961; ord. titular bishop of Pertusa and auxiliary bishop of Kansas City-St. Joseph, July 3, 1975; app. bishop of Salina, Apr. 3, 1984.

Flanagan, Bernard Joseph: b. Mar. 31, 1908, Proctor, Vt.; educ. Holy Cross College (Worcester, Mass.), North American College (Rome), Catholic Univ. (Washington, D.C.); ord. priest (Hartford*) Dec. 8, 1931; ord. first bishop of Norwich, Nov. 30, 1953; app. bishop of Worcester, installed, Sept. 24, 1959; resigned Apr. 12, 1983.

Flavin, Glennon P.: b. Mar. 2, 1916, St. Louis, Mo.; educ. Kenrick Seminary (St. Louis, Mo.); ord. priest (St. Louis*) Dec. 20, 1941; ord. titular bishop of Joannina and auxiliary bishop of St. Louis, May 30, 1957; app. bishop of Lincoln, installed Aug. 17, 1967.

Fliss, Raphael M.: b. Oct. 25, 1930, Milwaukee, Wis.; educ. St. Francis Seminary (Milwaukee, Wis.), Catholic University (Washington, D.C.), Pontifical Lateran Univ. (Rome); ord. priest (Milwaukee*) May 26, 1956; ord. coadjutor bishop of Superior with right of succession, Dec. 20, 1979; bishop of Superior, June 27, 1985.

Flores, Patrick F.: b. July 26, 1929, Ganado, Tex.; educ. St. Mary's Seminary (Houston, Tex.); ord. priest (Galveston-Houston) May 26, 1956; ord. titular bishop of Itolica and auxiliary bishop of San Antonio, May 5, 1970 (first Mexican-American bishop); app. bishop of El Paso, Apr. 4, 1978, installed May 29, 1978; app. archbishop of San Antonio 1979; installed Oct. 13, 1979.

Flynn, Harry J.: b. May 2, 1933, Schenectady, N.Y.; educ. Siena College (Loudonville, N.Y.), Mt. St. Mary's College (Emmitsburg, Md.); ord. priest (Albany) May 28, 1960; ord. coadjutor bishop of Lafayette, La., June 24, 1986.

Foley, David E.: b. Feb. 3, 1930, Worcester, Mass.; educ. St. Charles College (Catonsville, Md.), St. Mary's Seminary (Baltimore, Md.); ord. priest (Washington*) May 26, 1952; ord. titular bishop of Octaba and auxiliary bishop of Richmond, June 27, 1986.

Foley, John Patrick: b. Nov. 11, 1935, Sharon Hill, Pa.; educ. St. Joseph's Preparatory School (Philadelphia, Pa.), St. Joseph's College (now University) (Philadelphia, Pa.), St. Charles Borromeo Seminary (Overbrook, Pa.), St. Thomas Univ. (Rome), Columbia School of Journalism (New York); ord. priest (Philadelphia*) May 19, 1962; assistant editor (1967-70) and editor (1970-84) of *The Catholic Standard and Times,* Philadelphia archdiocesan paper; ord. titular archbishop of Neapolis in Proconsulari, May 8, 1984, in Philadelphia; app. to five-year term as president of the Pontifical Commission for Social Communications, Apr. 5, 1984; is also president of the council of administration of the Vatican Television Center.

Forst, Marion F.: b. Sept. 3, 1910, St. Louis, Mo.; educ. St. Louis Preparatory Seminary (St. Louis, Mo.), Kenrick Seminary (Webster Groves, Mo.); ord. priest (St. Louis*) June 10, 1934; ord. bishop of Dodge City, Mar. 24, 1960; app. titular bishop of Scala and auxiliary bishop of Kansas City, Kans. Oct. 16, 1976.

Francis, Joseph A., S.V.D.: b. Sept. 30, 1923, Lafayette, La.; educ. St. Augustine Seminary (Bay St. Louis, Miss.), St. Mary Seminary (Techny, Ill.), Catholic Univ. (Washington, D.C.); ord. priest Oct. 7, 1950; president Conference of Major Superiors of Men, 1974-76, and the National Black Catholic Clergy Caucus; ord. titular bishop of Valliposita and auxiliary bishop of Newark, June 25, 1976.

Franz, John B.: b. Oct. 29, 1896, Springfield, Ill.; educ. Quincy College (Quincy, Ill.), Kenrick Seminary (Webster Groves, Mo.), Catholic Univ. (Washington, D.C.); ord. priest (Springfield, Ill.) June 13, 1920; ord. first bishop of Dodge City, Aug. 29, 1951; app. bishop of Peoria, installed Nov. 4, 1959; resigned May 24, 1971.

Franzetta, Benedict C.: b. Aug. 1, 1921, East Liverpool, O.; educ. St. Charles College (Catonsville, Md.), St. Mary Seminary (Cleveland, O.); ord. priest (Youngstown) Apr. 29, 1950; ord. titular bishop of Oderzo and auxiliary bishop of Youngstown, Sept. 4, 1980.

Freking, Frederick W.: b. Aug. 11, 1913, Heron Lake, Minn.; educ. St. Mary's College (Winona, Minn.), North American College and Gregorian Univ. (Rome), Catholic Univ. (Washington, D.C.); ord. priest (Winona) July 31, 1938; ord. bishop of Salina, Nov. 30, 1957; app. bishop of La Crosse, Dec. 30, 1964, installed Feb. 24, 1965; resigned May 10, 1983.

Frey, Gerard L.: b. May 10, 1914, New Orleans, La.; educ. Notre Dame Seminary (New Orleans, La.); ord. priest (New Orleans*) Apr. 2, 1938; ord. bishop of Savannah, Aug. 8, 1967; app. bishop of Lafayette, La., Nov. 7, 1972, installed Jan, 7, 1973.

Friend, William B.: b. Oct. 22, 1931, Miami, Fla.; educ. St. Mary's College (St. Mary, Ky.), Mt. St. Mary Seminary (Emmitsburg, Md.), Catholic Univ. (Washington, D.C.), Notre Dame Univ. (Notre Dame, Ind.); ord. priest (Mobile*) May 7, 1959; ord. titular bishop of Pomaria and auxiliary bishop of Alexandria-Shreveport, La., Oct. 30, 1979; app. bishop of Alexandria-Shreveport, Nov. 17, 1982, installed Jan 11, 1983; app. first bishop of Shreveport, June, 1986; installed July 30, 1986.

Frosi, Angelo, S. X.: b. Jan. 31, 1924, Baffano Cremona, Italy; ord. priest May 6, 1948; U.S. citizen; ord. titular bishop of Magneto, May 1, 1970, and prelate of Abaete do Tocantins, Brazil; app. first bishop of Abaetetuba, Brazil, Sept. 17, 1981.

Furlong, Philip J.: b. Dec. 8, 1892, New York, N.Y.; educ. Cathedral College (New York, N.Y.), St. Joseph's Seminary (Yonkers, N.Y.); ord. priest (New York*) May 18, 1918; ord. titular bish-

op of Araxa and auxiliary to military vicar, Jan. 25, 1956. Retired 1971.

G

Gallagher, Raymond J.: b. Nov. 19, 1912, Cleveland, Ohio; educ. John Carroll Univ. and Our Lady of the Lake Seminary (Cleveland, O.); ord. priest (Cleveland) Mar. 25, 1939; secretary of the National Conference of Catholic Charities 1961-65; ord. bishop of Lafayette in Indiana, Aug. 11, 1965; resigned Oct. 26, 1982.

Gallegos, Alphonse, O.A.R.: b. Feb. 20, 1931, Albuquerque, N. Mex., ord. priest May 24, 1958; ord. titular bishop of Sasabe and auxiliary bishop of Sacramento, Nov. 4, 1981.

Ganter, Bernard J.: b. July 17,1928, Galveston, Tex.; educ. Texas A & M Univ. (College Sta., Tex.), St. Mary's Seminary (La Porte, Tex.), Catholic Univ. (Washington, D.C.); ord. priest (Galveston-Houston) May 22, 1952; chancellor of Galveston-Houston diocese, 1966-73; ord. first bishop of Tulsa, Feb. 7, 1973; app. bishop of Beaumont, Tex., Oct. 18, 1977, installed Dec. 13, 1977.

Garland, James H.: b. Dec. 13, 1931, Wilmington, Ohio; educ. Wilmington College (Ohio), Ohio State Univ. (Columbus, O.); Mt. St. Mary's Seminary (Cincinnati, O.), Catholic Univ. (Washington, D.C.); ord. priest (Cincinnati*) Aug. 15, 1959; ord. titular bishop of Garriana and auxiliary bishop of Cincinnati, July 25, 1984; director of department of social services.

Garmendia, Francisco: b. Nov. 6, 1924, Lozcano, Spain; ord. priest June 29, 1947, in Spain; came to New York in 1964; became naturalized citizen; ord. titular bishop of Limisa and auxiliary bishop of New York, June 29, 1977. Vicar for Spanish pastoral development in New York archdiocese.

Garmo, George: b. Dec. 8, 1921, Telkaif, Iraq; educ. St. Peter Chaldean Patriarchal Seminary (Mossul, Iraq), Pontifical Urban Univ. (Rome); ord. priest Dec. 8, 1945; pastor of Chaldean parish in Detroit archdiocese, 1960-64, 1966-80; ord. archbishop of Chaldean-Rite archdiocese of Mossul, Iraq, Sept. 14, 1980.

Garner, Robert F.: b. Apr. 27, 1920, Jersey City, N.J.; educ. Seton Hall Univ. (S. Orange, N.J.), Immaculate Conception Seminary (Darlington, N.J.); ord. priest (Newark*) June 15, 1946; ord. titular bishop of Blera and auxiliary bishop of Newark, June 25, 1976.

Gaughan, Norbert F.: b. May 30, 1921, Pittsburgh, Pa.; educ. St. Vincent College (Latrobe, Pa.), Univ. of Pittsburgh; ord. priest (Pittsburgh) Nov. 4, 1945; ord. titular bishop of Taraqua and auxiliary bishop of Greensburg, June 26, 1975; app. bishop of Gary, July 24, 1984, installed Oct. 1, 1984.

Gelineau, Louis E.: b. May 3, 1928, Burlington, Vt.; educ. St. Michael's College (Winooski, Vt.), St. Paul's Univ. Seminary (Ottawa, Ont.), Catholic Univ. (Washington, D.C.); ord. priest (Hartford*) June 5, 1954; ord. bishop of Providence, R.I., Jan. 26, 1972.

Gendron, Odore: b. Sept. 13, 1921, Manchester, N.H.; educ. St. Charles Borromeo Seminary (Sherbrooke, Que., Canada), Univ. of Ottawa, St. Paul Univ. Seminary (Ottawa, Ont., Canada); ord.

priest (Manchester) May 31, 1947; ord. bishop of Manchester, Feb. 3, 1975.

Gerber, Eugene J.: b. Apr. 30, 1931, Kingman, Kans.; educ. St. Thomas Seminary (Denver, Colo.), Wichita State Univ.; Catholic Univ. (Washington, D.C.), Angelicum (Rome); ord. priest (Wichita) May 19, 1959; ord. bishop of Dodge City, Dec. 14, 1976; app. bishop of Wichita, Nov. 17, 1982.

Gerbermann, Hugo, M.M.: b. Sept. 11, 1913, Nada, Tex.; educ. St. John's Minor and Major Seminary (San Antonio, Tex.), Maryknoll Seminary (Maryknoll, N.Y.); ord. priest Feb. 7, 1943; missionary work in Ecuador and Guatemala; ord. titular bishop of Amathus and prelate of Huehuetenango, Guatemala, July 22, 1962; first bishop of Huehuetenango, Dec. 23, 1967; app. titular bishop of Pinkel and auxiliary bishop of San Antonio, July 24, 1975; resigned June 30, 1982.

Gerety, Peter L.: b. July 19, 1912, Shelton, Conn.; educ. Sulpician Seminary (Paris, France); ord. priest (Hartford*) June 29, 1939; ord. titular bishop of Crepedula and coadjutor bishop of Portland, Me., with right of succession, June 1, 1966; app. apostolic administrator of Portland, 1967; bishop of Portland, Me., Sept. 15, 1969; app. archbishop of Newark, Apr. 2, 1974; installed June 28, 1974; retired June 3, 1986.

Gerrard, James J.: b. June 9, 1897, New Bedford, Mass.; educ. St. Laurent College (Montreal, Que.), St. Bernard's Seminary (Rochester, N.Y.); ord. priest (Fall River) May 26, 1923; ord. titular bishop of Forma and auxiliary bishop of Fall River, Mar. 19, 1959. Retired January, 1976.

Gerry, Joseph, O.S.B.: b. Sept. 12, 1928, Millinocket, Me.; educ. St. Anselm Abbey Seminary (Manchester, N.H.), Univ. of Toronto (Canada), Fordham Univ. (New York); ord. priest June 12, 1954; abbot of St. Anselm Abbey, Manchester, N.H., 1972; ord. titular bishop of Praecausa and auxiliary of Manchester, Apr. 21, 1986.

Glennie, Ignatius T., S.J.: b. Feb. 5, 1907, Mexico City; educ. Mt. St. Michael's Scholasticate (Spokane, Wash.), Pontifical Seminary (Kandy, Ceylon), St. Mary's College (Kurdeong, India); entered Society of Jesus, 1924; ord. priest Nov. 21, 1938; ord. bishop of Trincomalee, Ceylon, Sept. 21, 1947; title of see changed to Trincomalee-Batticaloa (Sri Lanka), 1967; resigned Feb. 15, 1974.

Gossman, F. Joseph: b. Apr. 1, 1930, Baltimore, Md.; educ. St. Charles College (Catonsville, Md.), St. Mary's Seminary (Baltimore, Md.), North American College (Rome), Catholic Univ. (Washington, D.C.); ord. priest (Baltimore*) Dec. 17, 1955; ord. titular bishop of Agunto and auxiliary bishop of Baltimore, Sept. 11, 1968; named urban vicar, June 13, 1970; app. bishop of Raleigh April 8, 1975.

Gottwald, George J.: b. May 12, 1914, St. Louis, Mo.; educ. Kenrick Seminary (Webster Groves, Mo.); ord. priest (St. Louis*) June 9, 1940; ord. titular bishop of Cedamusa and auxiliary bishop of St. Louis, Aug. 8, 1961.

Gracida, Rene H.: b. June 9, 1923, New Orleans, La.; educ. Rice Univ. and Univ. of Houston (Houston, Tex.), Univ. of Fribourg (Switzerland); ord. priest (Miami*) May 23, 1959; ord. titular bishop of

Masuccaba and auxiliary bishop of Miami, Jan. 25, 1972; app. first bishop of Pensacola-Tallahassee, Oct. 1, 1975, installed Nov. 6, 1975; app. bishop of Corpus Christi, May 24, 1983, installed July 11, 1983.

Grady, Thomas J.: b. Oct. 9, 1914, Chicago, Ill.; educ. St. Mary of the Lake Seminary (Mundelein, Ill.), Gregorian Univ. (Rome), Loyola Univ. (Chicago, Ill.); ord. priest (Chicago*) Apr. 23, 1938; ord. titular bishop of Vamalla and auxiliary bishop of Chicago, Aug. 24, 1967; app. bishop of Orlando, Fla., Nov. 11, 1974, installed Dec. 16, 1974.

Graham, John J.: b. Sept. 11, 1913, Philadelphia, Pa.; educ. St. Charles Borromeo Seminary (Philadelphia, Pa.), Pontifical Roman Seminary (Rome, Italy); ord. priest (Philadelphia*) Feb. 26, 1938; ord. titular bishop of Sabrata and auxiliary bishop of Philadelphia, Jan. 7, 1964.

Grahmann, Charles V.: b. July 15, 1931, Halletsville, Tex.; educ. The Assumption-St. John's Seminary (San Antonio, Tex.); ord. priest (San Antonio*) Mar. 17, 1956; ord. titular bishop of Equilium and auxiliary bishop of San Antonio, Aug. 20, 1981; app. first bishop of Victoria, Tex., Apr. 13, 1982.

Graves, Lawrence P.: b. May 4, 1916, Texarkana, Ark.; educ. St. John's Seminary (Little Rock, Ark.), North American College (Rome), Catholic Univ. (Washington, D.C.); ord. priest (Little Rock) June 11, 1942; ord. titular bishop of Vina and auxiliary bishop of Little Rock, Apr. 25, 1969; app. bishop of Alexandria, May 22, 1973, installed Sept. 18, 1973; title of see changed to Alexandria-Shreveport, Jan. 12, 1977; resigned July 20, 1982.

Graziano, Lawrence, O.F.M.: b. Apr. 5, 1921, Mt. Vernon, N.Y.; educ. Mt. Alvernia Seminary (Wappingers Falls, N.Y.); ord. priest Jan. 26, 1947; ord. titular bishop of Limata and auxiliary bishop of Santa Ana, El Salvador, Sept. 21, 1961; app. coadjutor bishop of San Miguel, El Salvador, with right of succession, 1965; bishop of San Miguel, Jan. 10, 1968; resigned June 27, 1969.

Greco, Charles Paschal: b. Oct. 29, 1894, Rodney, Miss.; educ. St. Joseph's Seminary (St. Benedict, La.), Louvain Univ. (Belgium), Dominican Univ. (Fribourg, Switzerland); ord. priest (New Orleans*) July 25, 1918; ord. bishop of Alexandria, Feb. 25, 1946; retired May 22, 1973.

Green, Francis J.: b. July 7, 1906, Corning, N.Y.; educ. St. Patrick's Seminary (Menlo Park, Calif.); ord. priest (Tucson) May 15, 1932; ord. titular bishop of Serra and auxiliary bishop of Tucson, Sept. 17, 1953; named coadjutor of Tucson with right of succession, May 11, 1960; bishop of Tucson, Oct. 26, 1960; retired July 27, 1981.

Gregory, Wilton D.: b. Dec. 7, 1947, Chicago, Ill.; educ. Quigley Preparatory Seminary South, Niles College of Loyola Univ. (Chicago, Ill.), St. Mary of the Lake Seminary (Mundelein, Ill.), Pontifical Liturgical Institute, Sant'Anselmo (Rome); ord. priest (Chicago*) May 9, 1973; ord. titular bishop of Oliva and auxiliary bishop of Chicago, Dec. 13, 1983.

Greteman, Frank H.: b. Dec. 25, 1907, Willey, Ia.; educ. Loras Academy and Loras College (Dubuque, Ia.), North American College (Rome),

Catholic Univ. (Washington, D.C.); ord. priest (Sioux City) Dec. 8, 1932; ord. titular bishop of Vissalsa and auxiliary bishop of Sioux City, May 26, 1965; bishop of Sioux City, Dec. 9, 1970; resigned Jan. 23, 1983.

Griffin, James A.: b. June 13, 1934, Fairview Park, O.; educ. St. Charles College (Baltimore, Md.), Borromeo College (Wicklife, O.); St. Mary Seminary (Cleveland, O.); Lateran Univ. (Rome); Cleveland State Univ.; ord. priest (Cleveland) May 28, 1960; ord. titular bishop of Holar and auxiliary bishop of Cleveland, Aug. 1, 1979; app. bishop of Columbus, Feb. 8, 1983.

Grutka, Andrew G.: b. Nov. 17, 1908, Joliet, Ill.; educ. St. Procopius College and Seminary (Lisle, Ill.), Urban Univ. and Gregorian Univ. (Rome); ord. priest (Ft. Wayne-S. Bend) Dec. 5, 1933; app. moderator of lay activities in Gary diocese, 1955; ord. first bishop of Gary, Feb. 25, 1957; app. member of Pontifical Marian Academy, Jan. 5, 1970; retired July 24, 1984.

Guilfoyle, George H.: b. Nov. 13, 1913, New York, N.Y.; educ. Georgetown Univ. (Washington, D.C.), Fordham Univ. (New York City), St. Joseph's Seminary (Dunwoodie, N.Y.), Columbia Univ. Law School (New York City); ord. priest (New York*) Mar. 25, 1944; ord. titular bishop of Marazane and auxiliary bishop of New York, Nov. 30, 1964; app. bishop of Camden, installed Mar. 4, 1968.

Gumbleton, Thomas J.: b. Jan. 26, 1930, Detroit, Mich.; educ. St. John Provincial Seminary (Detroit, Mich.), Pontifical Lateran Univ. (Rome); ord. priest (Detroit*) June 2, 1956; ord. titular bishop of Ululi and auxiliary bishop of Detroit, May 1, 1968.

H

Hacker, Hilary B.: b. Jan. 10, 1913, New Ulm, Minn.; educ. St. Paul Seminary (St. Paul, Minn.), Gregorian Univ. (Rome); ord. priest (St. Paul-Minneapolis*) June 4, 1938; ord. bishop of Bismarck, N. Dak., Feb. 27, 1957; resigned June 30, 1982.

Hackett, John F.: b. Dec. 7, 1911, New Haven, Conn.; educ. St. Thomas Seminary (Bloomfield, Conn.), Seminaire Ste. Sulpice (Paris); ord. priest (Hartford*) June 29, 1936; ord. titular bishop of Helenopolis in Palaestina and auxiliary bishop of Hartford, Mar. 19, 1953.

Ham, J. Richard, M.M.: b. July 11, 1921, Chicago, Ill.; educ. Maryknoll Seminary (New York); ord. priest June 12, 1948; missionary to Guatemala, 1958; ord. titular bishop of Puzia di Numidia and auxiliary bishop of Guatemala, Jan. 6, 1968; resigned see 1979; app. vicar for Hispanic ministry in St. Paul and Minneapolis archdiocese, January, 1980; auxiliary bishop of St. Paul and Minneapolis, October, 1980.

Hammes, George A.: b. Sept. 11, 1911, St. Joseph Ridge, Wis.; educ. St. Lawrence Seminary (Mt. Calvary. Wis.), St. Louis Preparatory Seminary (St. Louis, Mo.), Kenrick Seminary (Webster Groves, Mo.), Sulpician Seminary, Catholic Univ. (Washington, D.C.); ord. priest (LaCrosse) May

22, 1937; ord. bishop of Superior, May 24, 1960; resigned June 29, 1985.

Hanifen, Richard C.: b. June 15, 1931, Denver, Colo,; educ. Regis College and St. Thomas Seminary (Denver, Colo.), Catholic Univ. (Washington, D.C.), Lateran Univ. (Rome); ord. priest (Denver*) June 6, 1959; ord. titular bishop of Abercorn and auxiliary bishop of Denver, Sept. 20, 1974; app. first bishop of Colorado Springs, 1983; installed Jan. 30, 1984.

Hannan, Philip M.: b. May 20, 1913, Washington, D.C.; educ. St. Charles College (Catonsville, Md.), Catholic Univ. (Washington, D.C.), North American College (Rome); ord. priest (Washington*) Dec. 8, 1939; ord. titular bishop of Hieropolis and auxiliary bishop of Washington, D.C., Aug. 28, 1956; app. archbishop of New Orleans, installed Oct. 13, 1965.

Harper, Edward, C.SS.R.: b. July 23, 1910, Brooklyn, N.Y.; educ. Redemptorist Houses of Study; ord. priest June 18, 1939; ord. titular bishop of Heraclea Pontica and first prelate of Virgin Islands, Oct. 6, 1960; became first bishop, 1977, when prelacy was made diocese of St. Thomas; retired Oct. 16, 1985.

Harrington, Timothy J.: b. Dec. 19, 1918, Holyoke, Mass.; educ. Holy Cross College (Worcester, Mass.), Grand Seminary (Montreal, Que.), Boston College School of Social Work; ord. priest (Springfield, Mass.*) Jan. 19, 1946; ord. titular bishop of Rusuca and auxiliary bishop of Worcester, Mass., July 2, 1968; app. bishop of Worcester, Sept. 1, 1983, installed Oct. 13, 1983.

Harris, Vincent M.: b. Oct. 14, 1913, Conroe, Tex.; educ. St. Mary's Seminary (La Porte, Tex.), North American College and Gregorian Univ. (Rome), Catholic Univ. (Washington, D.C.); ord. priest (Galveston-Houston) Mar. 19, 1938; ord. first bishop of Beaumont, Tex., Sept. 28, 1966; app. titular bishop of Rotaria and coadjutor bishop of Austin, Apr. 27, 1971; bishop of Austin, Nov. 16, 1971; retired Dec. 19, 1985.

Harrison, Frank J.: b. Aug. 12, 1912; Syracuse, N.Y.; educ. Notre Dame Univ. (Notre Dame, Ind.), St. Bernard's Seminary (Rochester, N.Y.), ord. priest (Syracuse) June 4, 1937; ord. titular bishop of Aquae in Numidia and auxiliary bishop of Syracuse, Apr. 22, 1971; app. bishop of Syracuse, Nov. 9, 1976, installed Feb. 6, 1977.

Hart, Daniel A.: b. Aug. 24, 1927, Lawrence, Mass.; educ. St. John's Seminary (Brighton, Mass.); ord. priest (Boston*) Feb. 2, 1953; ord. titular bishop of Tepelta and auxiliary bishop of Boston, Oct. 18, 1976.

Hart, Joseph: b. Sept. 26, 1931, Kansas City, Missouri; educ. St. John Seminary (Kansas City, Mo.), St. Meinrad Seminary (Indianapolis, Ind.); ord. priest (Kansas City-St. Joseph) May 1, 1956; ord. titular bishop of Thimida Regia and auxiliary bishop of Cheyenne, Wyo., Aug. 31, 1976; app. bishop of Cheyenne, installed June 12, 1978.

Hastrich, Jerome J.: b. Nov. 13, 1914, Milwaukee, Wis.; educ. Marquette Univ., St. Francis Seminary (Milwaukee, Wis.); ord. priest (Milwaukee*) Feb. 9, 1941; ord. titular bishop of Gurza and auxiliary bishop of Madison, Sept. 3, 1963; app. bishop of Gallup, N.Mex., Sept. 3, 1969.

Hayes, Nevin W., O.Carm: b. Feb. 17, 1922, Chicago, Ill.; entered Carmelite novitiate Aug. 15, 1939; educ. Mt. Carmel College (Niagara Falls, Canada), Whitefriars Hall and Catholic Univ. (Washington, D.C.); ord. priest June 8, 1946; prelate nullius of Sicuani, Peru, 1959; ord. titular bishop of Nova Sinna and prelate of Sicuani, Aug. 5, 1965; resigned November 1970; app. auxiliary bishop of Chicago, Feb. 2, 1971.

Head, Edward D.: b. Aug. 5, 1919, White Plains, N.Y.; educ. Cathedral College, St. Joseph's Seminary, Columbia Univ. (New York City); ord. priest (New York*) Jan. 27, 1945; director of New York Catholic Charities; ord. titular bishop of Ardsratha and auxiliary bishop of New York, Mar. 19, 1970; app. bishop of Buffalo, Jan. 23, 1973, installed Mar. 19, 1973.

Helmsing, Charles H.: b. Mar. 23, 1908, Shrewsbury, Mo.; educ. St. Louis Preparatory Seminary (St. Louis, Mo.), Kenrick Seminary (Webster Groves, Mo.); ord. priest (St. Louis*) June 10, 1933; ord. titular bishop of Axomis and auxiliary bishop of St. Louis, Apr. 19, 1949; first bishop of Springfield-Cape Girardeau, Aug. 24, 1956; bishop of Kansas City-St. Joseph, 1962, installed Apr. 3, 1962; resigned June 25, 1977.

Herrmann, Edward J.: b. Nov. 6, 1913, Baltimore, Md.; educ. Mt. St. Mary's Seminary (Emmitsburg, Md.), Catholic Univ. (Washington, D.C.); ord. priest (Washington*) June 12, 1947; ord. titular bishop of Lamzella and auxiliary bishop of Washington, D.C., Apr. 26, 1966; app. bishop of Columbus, June 26, 1973; resigned Sept. 18, 1982.

Hettinger, Edward Gerhard: b. Oct. 14, 1902, Lancaster, O.; educ. St. Vincent's College (Beatty, Pa.); ord. priest (Columbus) June 2, 1928; ord. titular bishop of Teos and auxiliary bishop of Columbus, Feb. 24, 1942; retired Oct. 18, 1977.

Hickey, Dennis W.: b. Oct. 28, 1914, Dansville, N.Y.; educ. Colgate Univ. and St. Bernard's Seminary (Rochester, N.Y.); ord. priest (Rochester) June 7, 1941; ord. titular bishop of Rusuccuru and auxiliary bishop of Rochester, N.Y., Mar. 14, 1968.

Hickey, James A.: b. Oct. 11, 1920, Midland, Mich.; educ. Sacred Heart Seminary (Detroit, Mich.), Catholic Univ. (Washington, D.C.), Lateran Univ. and Angelicum (Rome), Michigan State Univ.; ord. priest (Saginaw) June 15, 1946; ord. titular bishop of Taraqua and auxiliary bishop of Saginaw, Apr. 14, 1967; rector of North American College, Rome, 1969-74; app. bishop of Cleveland, June 5, 1974; installed July 16, 1974; app. archbishop of Washington, D.C., installed Aug. 5, 1980.

Higi, William L.: b. Aug. 29, 1933, Anderson, Ind.; educ. Our Lady of the Lakes Preparatory Seminary (Wawasee, Ind.), Mt. St. Mary of the West Seminary and Xavier Univ. (Cincinnati, O.); ord. priest (Lafayette, Ind.) May 30, 1959; ord. bishop of Lafayette, Ind., June 6, 1984.

Hines, Vincent J.: b. Sept. 14, 1912, New Haven, Conn.; educ. St. Thomas Seminary (Bloomfield, Conn.), St. Sulpice Seminary (Paris), Lateran Univ. (Rome); ord. priest (Hartford*) May 2, 1937; ord. bishop of Norwich, Conn., Mar. 17, 1960; retired June 17, 1975.

Hoch, Lambert A.: b. Feb. 6, 1903, Elkton, S.D.; educ. Creighton Univ. (Omaha, Nebr.), St. Paul Seminary (St. Paul, Minn.); ord. priest (Sioux Falls) May 30, 1928; ord. bishop of Bismarck, Mar. 25, 1952; app. bishop of Sioux Falls Dec. 5, 1956; retired June 13, 1978.

Hodapp, Robert L., S.J.: b. Oct. 1, 1910. Mankato, Minn.; educ. St. Stanislaus Seminary (Florissant, Mo.), St. Louis Univ. (St. Louis, Mo.); ord. priest June 18, 1941; ord. bishop of Belize (now Belize City-Belmopan), June 26, 1958; retired Nov. 11, 1983.

Hoffman, James R.: b. June 12, 1932, Fremont, O.; educ. Our Lady of the Lake Minor Seminary (Wawasee, Ind.), St. Meinrad College (St. Meinrad, Ind.); Mt. St. Mary Seminary (Norwood, O.); Catholic Univ. (Washington, D.C.); ord. priest (Toledo) July 28, 1957; ord. titular bishop of Italica and auxiliary bishop of Toledo, June 23, 1978; bishop of Toledo, Dec. 16, 1980.

Hogan, James J.: b. Oct. 17, 1911, Philadelphia, Pa.; educ. St. Charles College (Catonsville, Md.), St. Mary's Seminary (Baltimore), Gregorian Univ. (Rome), Catholic Univ. (Washington, D.C.); ord. priest (Trenton) Dec. 8, 1937; ord. titular bishop of Philomelium and auxiliary bishop of Trenton, Feb. 25, 1960; app. bishop of Altoona-Johnstown, installed July 6, 1966.

Hogan, Joseph L.: b. Mar. 11, 1916, Lima, N.Y.; educ. St. Bernard's Seminary (Rochester, N.Y.), Canisius College (Buffalo, N.Y.), Angelicum (Rome); ord. priest (Rochester) June 6, 1942; ord. bishop of Rochester, Nov. 28, 1969; resigned Nov. 28, 1978.

Houck, William Russell: b. June 26, 1926, Mobile Ala.; educ. St. Bernard Junior College (Cullman, Ala.), St. Mary's Seminary College and St. Mary's Seminary (Baltimore, Md.), Catholic Univ. (Washington, D.C.); ord. priest (Mobile*) May 19, 1951; ord. titular bishop of Alessano and auxiliary bishop of Jackson, Miss., May 27, 1979, by Pope John Paul II; app. bishop of Jackson, Apr. 11, 1984, installed June 5, 1984.

Howze, Joseph Lawson E.: b. Aug. 30, 1923, Daphne, Ala.; convert to Catholicism, 1948; educ. St. Bonaventure Univ. (St. Bonaventure, N.Y.); ord. priest (Raleigh) May 7, 1959; ord. titular bishop of Massita and auxiliary bishop of Natchez-Jackson, Jan. 28, 1973; app. first bishop of Biloxi, Miss., Mar. 8, 1977; installed June 6, 1977.

Hubbard, Howard J.: b. Oct. 31, 1938, Troy, N.Y.; educ. St. Joseph's Seminary (Dunwoodie, N.Y.); North American College and Gregorian Univ. (Rome), Catholic Univ. (Washington, D.C.); ord. priest (Albany) Dec. 18, 1963; ord. bishop of Albany, Mar. 27, 1977.

Hughes, Alfred C.: b. Dec. 2, 1932, Boston, Mass.; educ. St. John Seminary (Brighton, Mass), Gregorian Univ. (Rome); ord. priest (Boston*) Dec. 15, 1957, in Rome; ord. titular bishop of Maximiana in Byzacena and auxiliary bishop of Boston, Sept. 14, 1981.

Hughes, Edward T.: b. Nov. 13, 1920, Lansdowne, Pa.; educ. St. Charles Seminary,

Univ. of Pennsylvania (Philadelphia); ord. priest (Philadelphia*) May 31, 1947; ord. titular bishop of Segia and auxiliary bishop of Philadelphia, July 21, 1976.

Hughes, William A.: b. Sept. 23, 1921, Youngstown, O.; educ. St. Charles College (Catonsville, Md.), St. Mary's Seminary (Cleveland, O.) Notre Dame Univ. (Notre Dame, Ind.); ord. priest (Youngstown) Apr. 6, 1946; ord. titular bishop of Inis Cathaig and auxiliary bishop of Youngstown, Sept. 12, 1974; app. bishop of Covington, installed May 8, 1979.

Hunthausen, Raymond G.: b. Aug. 21, 1921, Anaconda, Mont.; educ. Carroll College (Helena, Mont.), St. Edward's Seminary (Kenmore, Wash.), St. Louis Univ. (St. Louis, Mo.), Catholic Univ. (Washington, D.C.), Fordham Univ. (New York City), Notre Dame Univ. (Notre Dame, Ind.); ord. priest (Helena) June 1, 1946; ord. bishop of Helena, Aug. 30, 1962; app. archbishop of Seattle, Feb. 25, 1975.

Hurley, Francis T.: b. Jan. 12, 1927, San Francisco, Calif.; educ. St. Patrick's Seminary (Menlo Park, Calif.), Catholic Univ. (Washington, D.C.); ord. priest (San Francisco*) June 16, 1951; assigned to NCWC in Washington, D.C., 1957; assistant (1958) and later (1968) associate secretary of NCCB and USCC; ord. titular bishop of Daimlaig and auxiliary bishop of Juneau, Alaska, Mar. 19, 1970; app. bishop of Juneau, July 20, 1971, installed Sept. 8, 1971; app. archbishop of Anchorage, May 4, 1976, installed July 8, 1976.

Hurley, Mark J.: b. Dec. 13, 1919, San Francisco, Calif.; educ. St. Patrick's Seminary (Menlo Park, Calif.), Univ. of California (Berkeley), Catholic Univ. (Washington, D.C.), Lateran Univ. (Rome), Univ. of Portland (Portland, Ore.); ord. priest (San Francisco*) Sept. 23, 1944; ord. titular bishop of Thunusuda and auxiliary bishop of San Francisco, Jan. 4, 1968; app. bishop of Santa Rosa, Nov. 19, 1969; resigned Apr. 15, 1986.

I-J

Ibrahim, Ibrahim N.: b. Oct. 1, 1937, Telkaif, Mosul, Iraq; educ. Patriarchal Seminary (Mosul, Iraq), St. Sulpice Seminary (Paris, France); ord. priest Dec. 30, 1962, in Baghdad, Iraq; ord. titular bishop of Anbar and apostolic exarch for Chaldean-Rite Catholics in the United States, Mar. 8, 1982, in Baghdad; installed in Detroit, Apr. 18, 1982.

Imesch, Joseph L.: b. June 21, 1931, Detroit, Mich.; educ. Sacred Heart Seminary (Detroit, Mich.), North American College, Gregorian Univ. (Rome); ord. priest (Detroit*) Dec. 16, 1956; ord. titular bishop of Pomaria and auxiliary bishop of Detroit, Apr. 3, 1973; app. bishop of Joliet, June 30, 1979.

Iranyi, Ladislaus A., Sch.P.: b. Apr. 9, 1923, Szeged, Hungary; educ. Pazmany Univ. (Budapest, Hungary), Angelicum and Gregorian Univ. (Rome); ord. priest Mar. 13, 1948, in Rome; became U.S. citizen, 1958; ord. titular bishop of Castel Mediano, July 27, 1983; responsible for spiritual care of Hungarian Catholics living outside Hungary.

Joyce, Robert F.: b. Oct. 7, 1896, Proctor, Vt.; educ. Univ. of Vermont (Burlington, Vt.), Grand Seminary (Montreal, Canada); ord. priest (Hartford*) May 26, 1923; ord. titular bishop of Citium and auxiliary bishop of Burlington, Oct. 28, 1954; installed as bishop of Burlington, Feb. 26, 1957; resigned Dec. 14, 1971.

K

Kaffer, Roger L.: b. Aug. 14, 1927, Joliet, Ill.; educ. Quigley Preparatory Seminary (Chicago, Ill.), St. Mary of the Lake Seminary (Mundelein, Ill.), Gregorian Univ. (Rome); ord. priest (Joliet) May 1, 1954; ord. titular bishop of Dusa and auxiliary bishop of Joliet, June 26, 1985.

Kalisz, Raymond P., S.V.D.: b. Sept. 25, 1927, Melvindale, Mich.; educ. St. Mary's Seminary (Techny, Ill.); ord. priest Aug. 15, 1954; ord. bishop of Wewak, Papua New Guinea, August 15, 1980.

Kaniecki, Michael Joseph, S.J.: b. Apr. 13, 1935, Detroit Mich.; joined Jesuits 1953; educ. Xavier Univ. (Milford, O.), Mt. St. Michael's Seminary (Spokane, Wash.), Regis College (Willowdale, Ont.); ord. priest June 5, 1965; ord. coadjutor bishop of Fairbanks, May 1, 1984; bishop of Fairbanks, June 1, 1985.

Keating, John Richard: b. July 20, 1934, Chicago, Ill.; educ. Quigley Preparatory Seminary (Chicago, Ill.), St. Mary of the Lake Seminary (Mundelein, Ill.), Gregorian Univ. (Rome); ord. priest (Chicago*) Dec. 20, 1958; ord. bishop of Arlington, Aug. 4, 1983.

Keeler, William Henry: b. Mar. 4, 1931, San Antonio, Tex.; educ. St. Charles Seminary (Overbrook, Pa.), North American College, Pontifical Gregorian Univ. (Rome); ord. priest (Harrisburg) July 17, 1955; ord. titular bishop of Ulcinium and auxiliary bishop of Harrisburg, Sept. 21, 1979; app. bishop of Harrisburg, Nov. 15, 1983; installed Jan. 4, 1984.

Keleher, James P.: b. July 31, 1931, Chicago, Ill.; educ. Quigley Preparatory Seminary (Chicago, Ill.), St. Mary of the Lake Seminary (Mundelein, Ill.); ord. priest (Chicago*) Apr. 12, 1958; ord. bishop of Belleville, Dec. 11, 1984.

Kelly, Thomas C., O.P.: b. July 14, 1931, Rochester, N.Y.; educ. Providence College (Providence, R.I.), Immaculate Conception College (Washington, D.C.), Angelicum (Rome); professed in Dominicans, Aug. 26, 1952; secretary, apostolic delegation, Washington, D.C., 1965-71; associate general secretary, 1971-77, and general secretary, 1977-81, NCCB/USCC; ord. titular bishop of Tusurus and auxiliary bishop of Washington, D.C., Aug. 15, 1977; app. archbishop of Louisville, Dec. 28, 1981, installed Feb. 18, 1982.

Kenney, Lawrence J.: b. Aug. 30, 1930, New Rochelle, N.Y.; educ. Cathedral College (New York, N.Y.), St. Joseph's Seminary (Yonkers, N.Y.), Iona College (New Rochelle, N.Y.); ord. priest (New York*) June 2, 1956; ord. titular bishop of Holar and auxiliary bishop of the Military Archdiocese, May 10, 1983.

Kenny, Michael H.: b. June 26, 1937, Hollywood, Calif.; educ. St. Joseph College (Mountain View, Calif.), St. Patrick's Seminary (Menlo Park, Calif.), Catholic Univ. (Washington, D.C.); ord.

priest (Santa Rosa) Mar. 30, 1963; ord. bishop of Juneau, May 27, 1979.

Kinney, John F.: b. June 11, 1937, Oelwein, Iowa; educ. Nazareth Hall and St. Paul Seminaries (St. Paul, Minn.); Pontifical Lateran University (Rome); ord. priest (St. Paul-Minneapolis*) Feb. 2, 1963; ord. titular bishop of Caorle and auxiliary bishop of St. Paul and Minneapolis, Jan. 25, 1977; app. bishop of Bismarck June 30, 1982.

Kmiec, Edward U.: b. June 4, 1936, Trenton, N.J.; educ. St. Charles College (Catonsville, Md.), St. Mary's Seminary (Baltimore, Md.), Gregorian Univ. (Rome); ord. priest (Trenton) Dec. 20, 1961; ord. titular bishop of Simidicca and auxiliary bishop of Trenton, Nov. 3, 1982.

Kocisko, Stephen: b. June 11, 1915, Minneapolis, Minn.; educ. Nazareth Hall Minor Seminary (St. Paul, Minn.), Pontifical Ruthenian College, Urban Univ. (Rome); ord. priest (Pittsburgh*, Byzantine Rite) Mar. 30, 1941; ord. titular bishop of Teveste and auxiliary bishop of apostolic exarchate of Pittsburgh, Oct. 23, 1956; installed as first eparch of the eparchy of Passaic, Sept. 10, 1963; app. eparch of Byzantine-Rite diocese of Pittsburgh, installed Mar. 5, 1968; app. first metropolitan of Munhall, installed June 11, 1969; title of see changed to Pittsburgh, 1977.

Koester, Charles R.: b. Sept. 16, 1915, Jefferson City, Mo.; educ. Conception Academy (Conception, Mo.), St. Louis Preparatory Seminary and Kenrick Seminary (St. Louis, Mo.), North American College (Rome); ord. priest (St. Louis*) Dec. 20, 1941; ord. titular bishop of Suacia and auxiliary bishop of St. Louis, Feb. 11, 1971.

Krawczak, Arthur H.: b. Feb. 2, 1913, Detroit, Mich.; educ. Sacred Heart Seminary, Sts. Cyril and Methodius Seminary (Orchard Lake, Mich.), Catholic Univ. (Washington, D.C.); ord. priest (Detroit*) May 18, 1940; ord. titular bishop of Subbar and auxiliary bishop of Detroit, Apr. 3, 1973; retired Aug. 17, 1982.

Krol, John J.: (See Cardinals, Biographies.)

Kucera, Daniel, O.S.B.: b. May 7, 1923, Chicago, Ill.; educ. St. Procopius College (Lisle, Ill.), Catholic Univ. (Washington, D.C.); professed in Order of St. Benedict, June 16, 1944; ord. priest May 26, 1949; abbot, St. Procopius Abbey, 1964-71; pres. Illinois Benedictine College, 1959-65 and 1971-76; ord. titular bishop of Natchez and auxiliary bishop of Joliet, July 21, 1977; app. bishop of Salina, Mar. 5, 1980, installed May 7, 1980; app. archbishop of Dubuque, installed Feb. 23, 1984.

Kupfer, William F., M.M.: b. Jan. 28, 1909, Brooklyn, N.Y.; educ. Cathedral College (Brooklyn, N.Y.), Maryknoll Seminary (Maryknoll, N.Y.); ord. priest June 11, 1933; missionary in China; app. prefect apostolic of Taichung, Taiwan, 1951; ord. first bishop of Taichung, July 25, 1962.

L

Lambert, Francis, S.M.: b. Feb. 7, 1921, Lawrence, Mass.; educ. Marist Seminary (Framingham, Mass.); ord. priest, June 29, 1946; served in Marist missions in Oceania; provincial of Marist Oceania province, 1971; ord. bishop of Port Vila, Vanuatu (New Hebrides), Mar. 20, 1977.

Larkin, W. Thomas: b. Mar. 31, 1923, Mt. Morris, N.Y.; educ. St. Andrew Seminary and St. Bernard Seminary (Rochester, N.Y.); Angelicum Univ. (Rome); ord. priest (St. Augustine) May 15, 1947; ord. bishop of St. Petersburg, May 27, 1979.

Law, Bernard F.: (See Cardinals, Biographies.)

Leibrecht, John J.: b. Aug. 30, 1930, Overland, Mo.; educ. Catholic Univ. (Washington, D.C.); ord. priest (St. Louis*) Mar. 17, 1956; superintendent of schools of St. Louis archdiocese, 1962-1981; ord. bishop of Springfield-Cape Girardeau, Mo., Dec. 12, 1984.

Leonard, Vincent M.: b. Dec. 11, 1908, Pittsburgh, Pa.; educ. Duquesne Univ. (Pittsburgh, Pa.), St. Vincent Seminary (Latrobe, Pa.); ord. priest (Pittsburgh) June 16, 1935; ord. titular bishop of Arsacal and auxiliary bishop of Pittsburgh, Apr. 21, 1964; app. bishop of Pittsburgh, installed July 2, 1969; resigned June 30, 1983.

Lessard, Raymond W.: b. Dec. 21, 1930, Grafton, N.D.; educ. St. Paul Seminary (St. Paul, Minn.), North American College (Rome); ord. priest (Fargo) Dec. 16, 1956; served on staff of the Congregation for Bishops in the Roman Curia, 1964-73; ord. bishop of Savannah, Apr. 27, 1973.

Levada, William J.: b. June 15, 1936, Long Beach, Calif.; educ. St. John's College (Camarillo, Calif.), Gregorian Univ. (Rome); ord. priest (Los Angeles*) Dec. 20, 1961; ord. titular bishop of Capri and auxiliary bishop of Los Angeles, May 12, 1983; app. archbishop of Portland, Ore., July 3, 1986.

Lipscomb, Oscar H.: b. Sept. 21, 1931, Mobile, Ala.; educ. McGill Institute, St. Bernard College (Cullman, Ala.), North American College and Gregorian Univ. (Rome), Catholic Univ. (Washington, D.C.); ord. priest (Mobile*) July 15, 1956; ord. first archbishop of Mobile, Nov. 16, 1980.

Lohmuller, Martin J.: b. Aug. 21, 1919, Philadelphia, Pa.; educ. St. Charles Borromeo Seminary (Philadelphia, Pa.), Catholic Univ. (Washington, D.C.); ord. priest (Philadelphia*) June 3, 1944; ord. titular bishop of Ramsbury and auxiliary bishop of Philadelphia, Apr. 2, 1970.

Losten, Basil: b. May 11, 1930, Chesapeake City, Md.; educ. St. Basil's College (Stamford, Conn.), Catholic University (Washington, D.C.); ord. priest (Philadelphia*, Byzantine Rite) June 10, 1957; ord. titular bishop of Arcadiopolis in Asia and auxiliary bishop of Ukrainian archeparchy of Philadelphia, May 25, 1971; app. apostolic administrator of archeparchy, 1976; app. bishop of Ukrainian eparchy of Stamford, Sept. 20, 1977.

Lotocky, Innocent Hilarius, O.S.B.M.: b. Nov. 3, 1915, Petlykiwci, Ukraine; educ. seminaries in Ukraine, Czechoslovakia and Austria; ord. priest Nov. 24, 1940; ord. bishop of St. Nicholas of Chicago for the Ukrainians, Mar. 1, 1981.

Lubachivsky, Myroslav I.: (See Cardinals, Biographies.)

Lucker, Raymond A.: b. Feb. 24, 1927, St. Paul, Minn.; educ. St. Paul Seminary (St. Paul, Minn.); University of Minnesota (Minneapolis), Angelicum (Rome); ord. priest (St. Paul-Minneapolis*)

June 7, 1952; director of USCC department of education, 1968-71; ord. titular bishop of Meta and auxiliary bishop of St. Paul and Minneapolis, Sept. 8, 1971; app. bishop of New Ulm, Dec. 23, 1975, installed Feb. 19, 1976.

Lyke, James Patterson, O.F.M.: b. Feb. 18, 1939, Chicago, Ill.; educ. Quincy College (Quincy, Ill.), Antonianum (Rome), Union Graduate School (Cincinnati, O.); professed in Order of Friars Minor, June 21, 1963; ord. priest June 24, 1966; president of National Black Catholic Clergy Caucus; ord. titular bishop of Furnos Maior and auxiliary bishop of Cleveland, Aug. 1, 1979.

Lynch, George E.: b. Mar. 4, 1917, New York, N.Y.; educ. Fordham Univ. (New York), Mt. St. Mary's Seminary (Emmitsburg, Md.), Catholic Univ. (Washington, D.C.); ord. priest (Raleigh) May 29, 1943; ord. titular bishop of Satafi and auxiliary of Raleigh Jan. 6, 1970; retired Apr. 16, 1985.

Lyne, Timothy J.: b. Mar. 21, 1919, Chicago, Ill.; educ. Quigley Preparatory Seminary, St. Mary of the Lake Seminary (Mundelein, Ill.); ord. priest (Chicago*) May 1, 1943; ord. titular bishop of Vamalla and auxiliary bishop of Chicago, Dec. 13, 1983.

Lyons, Thomas W.: b. Sept. 26, 1923, Washington, D.C.; educ. St. Charles College (Catonsville, Md.), St. Mary's Seminary (Baltimore, Md.); ord. priest (Washington*) May 22, 1948; ord. titular bishop of Mortlach and auxiliary bishop of Washington, D.C., Sept. 12, 1974.

M

McAuliffe, Michael F.: b. Nov. 22, 1920, Kansas City, Mo.; educ. St. Louis Preparatory Seminary (St. Louis, Mo.), Catholic Univ. (Washington, D.C.): ord. priest (Kansas City-St. Joseph) May 31, 1945; ord. bishop of Jefferson City, Aug. 18, 1969.

McCarrick, Theodore E.: b. July 7, 1930, New York, N.Y.; educ. Fordham Univ. (Bronx, N.Y.), St. Joseph's Seminary (Dunwoodie, N.Y.), Catholic Univ. (Washington, D.C.); ord. priest (New York*) May 31, 1958; dean of students Catholic Univ. of America, 1961-63; pres., Catholic Univ. of Puerto Rico, 1965-69; secretary to Cardinal Cooke, 1970; ord. titular bishop of Rusubisir and auxiliary bishop of New York, June 29, 1977; app. first bishop of Metuchen, N.J., Nov. 19, 1981, installed Jan. 31, 1982; app. archbishop of Newark, June 3, 1986, installed July 25, 1986.

McCarthy, Edward A.: b. Apr. 10, 1918, Cincinnati, O.; educ. Mt. St. Mary Seminary (Norwood, O.), Catholic Univ. (Washington, D.C.), Lateran and Angelicum (Rome); ord. priest (Cincinnati*) May 29, 1943; ord. titular bishop of Tamascani and auxiliary bishop of Cincinnati, June 15, 1965; first bishop of Phoenix, Ariz., Dec. 2, 1969; app. coadjutor archbishop of Miami, Fla., July 7, 1976; succeeded as archbishop of Miami, July 26, 1977.

McCarthy, John E., b. June 21, 1930, Houston, Tex.; educ. Univ. of St. Thomas (Houston, Tex.); ord. priest (Galveston-Houston) May 26, 1956; assistant director Social Action Dept. USCC, 1967-69; executive director Texas Catholic Conference; ord. titular bishop of Pedena and auxiliary bishop

of Galveston-Houston, Mar. 14, 1979; app. bishop of Austin, Dec. 19, 1985, installed Feb. 25, 1986.

McCormick, J. Carroll: b. Dec. 15, 1907, Philadelphia, Pa.; educ. College Ste. Marie (Montreal), St. Charles Seminary (Overbrook, Pa.), Minor and Major Roman Seminary (Rome); ord. priest (Philadelphia*) July 10, 1932; ord. titular bishop of Ruspae and auxiliary bishop of Philadelphia, Apr. 23, 1947; app. bishop of Altoona-Johnstown, installed Sept. 21, 1960; app. bishop of Scranton, installed May 25, 1966; resigned Feb. 15, 1983.

McDonald, Andrew J.: b. Oct. 24, 1923, Savannah, Ga.; educ. St. Mary's Seminary (Baltimore, Md.), Catholic Univ. (Washington, D.C.), Lateran Univ. (Rome); ord. priest (Savannah) May 8, 1948; ord. bishop of Little Rock, Sept. 5, 1972.

McDonald, William J.: b. June 17, 1904, Mooncoin, Ireland; educ. St. Kieran's College and Seminary (Kilkenny, Ireland), Catholic Univ. (Washington, D.C.); ord. priest (San Francisco*) June 10, 1928; rector of Catholic Univ. of America, 1957-67; ord. titular bishop of Aquae Regiae and auxiliary bishop of Washington, May 19, 1964; app. auxiliary bishop of San Francisco, July 26, 1967; retired June 5, 1979.

McDonough, Thomas J.: b. Dec. 5, 1911, Philadelphia, Pa.; educ. St. Charles Seminary (Overbrook, Pa.), Catholic Univ. (Washington, D.C.); ord. priest (Philadelphia*) May 26, 1938; ord. titular bishop of Thenae and auxiliary bishop of St. Augustine, Apr. 30, 1947; app. auxiliary bishop of Savannah, Jan. 2, 1957; named bishop of Savannah, installed Apr. 27, 1960; app. archbishop of Louisville, installed May 2, 1967; resigned Sept. 29, 1981.

McDowell, John B.: b. July 17, 1921, New Castle, Pa.; educ. St. Vincent College, St. Vincent Theological Seminary (Latrobe, Pa.), Catholic Univ. (Washington, D.C.); ord. priest (Pittsburgh) Nov. 4, 1945; superintendent of schools, Pittsburgh diocese, 1955-70; ord. titular bishop of Tamazuca, and auxiliary bishop of Pittsburgh, Sept. 8, 1966.

McEleney, John J., S.J.: b. Nov. 13, 1895, Woburn, Mass.; educ. Boston College (Boston, Mass.), Jesuit Scholasticate (New England Province); entered Society of Jesus, 1918; ord. priest June 18, 1930; app. provincial of New England Province, 1944; ord. titular bishop of Zeugma and vicar apostolic of Jamaica, Apr. 15, 1950; title changed to bishop of Kingston, Feb. 29, 1956; archbishop of Kingston, Sept. 14, 1967; retired Sept. 1, 1970.

McFarland, Norman F.: b. Feb. 21, 1922, Martinez, Calif.; educ. St. Patrick's Seminary (Menlo Park, Calif.), Catholic Univ. (Washington, D.C.); ord. priest (San Francisco*) June 15, 1946; ord. titular bishop of Bida and auxiliary bishop of San Francisco, Sept. 8, 1970; apostolic administrator of Reno, 1974; app. bishop of Reno, Feb. 10, 1976, installed Mar. 31, 1976; title of see changed to Reno-Las Vegas.

McGann, John R.: b. Dec. 2, 1924, Brooklyn, N.Y.; educ. Cathedral College (Brooklyn, N.Y.), Immaculate Conception Seminary (Huntington, L.I.); ord. priest (Rockville Centre) June 3, 1950; ord. titular bishop of Morosbisdus and auxiliary bishop of Rockville Centre, Jan. 7, 1971; vicar general and episcopal vicar; app. bishop of Rockville Centre May 3, 1976, installed June 24, 1976.

McGarry, Urban, T.O.R.: b. Nov. 11, 1911, Warren, Pa.; ord. priest Oct. 3, 1942, in India; prefect apostolic of Bhagalpur, Aug. 7, 1956; ord. first bishop of Bhagalpur, India, May 10, 1965.

McKinney, Joseph C.: b. Sept. 10, 1928, Grand Rapids, Mich.; educ. St. Joseph's Seminary (Grand Rapids, Mich.), Seminaire de Philosophie (Montreal, Canada), Urban Univ. (Rome, Italy); ord. priest (Grand Rapids) Dec. 20, 1953; ord. titular bishop of Lentini and auxiliary bishop of Grand Rapids, Sept. 26, 1968.

McLaughlin, Bernard J.: b. Nov. 19, 1912, Buffalo, N.Y.; educ. Urban Univ. (Rome, Italy); ord. priest (Buffalo) Dec. 21, 1935, at Rome; ord. titular bishop of Mottola and auxiliary bishop of Buffalo, Jan. 6, 1969.

McManus, William E.: b. Jan. 27, 1914, Chicago, Ill.; educ. St. Mary of the Lake Seminary (Mundelein, Ill.), Catholic Univ. (Washington, D.C.); ord. priest (Chicago*) Apr. 15, 1939; ord. titular bishop of Mesarfelta and auxiliary bishop of Chicago, Aug. 24, 1967; app. bishop of Fort Wayne-South Bend, Aug. 31, 1976, installed Oct. 19, 1976; retired Feb. 26, 1985.

McNabb, John C., O.S.A.: b. Dec. 11, 1925, Beloit, Wis.; educ. Villanova Univ. (Villanova, Pa.), Augustinian College and Catholic Univ. (Washington, D.C.), De Paul Univ. (Chicago, Ill.); ord. priest May 24, 1952; ord. titular bishop of Saia Maggiore, June 17, 1967 (resigned titular see, Dec. 27, 1977); prelate of Chulucanas, Peru, 1967.

McNamara, Lawrence J.: b. Aug. 5, 1928, Chicago, Ill.; educ. St. Paul Seminary (St. Paul, Minn.), Catholic Univ. (Washington, D.C.); ord. priest (Kansas City-St. Joseph) May 30, 1953; executive director of Campaign for Human Development 1973-77; ord. bishop of Grand Island, Nebr., Mar. 28, 1978.

McNaughton, William J., M.M.: b. Dec. 7, 1926, Lawrence, Mass.; educ. Maryknoll Seminary (Maryknoll, N.Y.); ord. priest June 13, 1953; ord. titular bishop of Thuburbo Minus and vicar apostolic of Inchon, Korea, Aug. 24, 1961; title changed to bishop of Inchon, Mar. 10, 1962.

McRaith, John Jeremiah: b. Dec. 6, 1934, Hutchinson, Minn.; educ. St. John Preparatory School (Collegeville, Minn.), Loras College, St. Bernard Seminary (Dubuque, Ia); ord. priest (New Ulm) Feb. 21, 1960; exec. dir. of Catholic Rural Life Conference, 1971-78; ord. bishop of Owensboro, Ky., Dec. 15, 1982.

McShea, Joseph M.: b. Feb. 22, 1907, Latimer, Pa.; educ. St. Charles Seminary (Philadelphia, Pa.), Major Pontifical Roman Seminary (Rome); ord. priest (Philadelphia*) Dec. 6, 1931; ord. titular bishop of Mina and auxiliary bishop of Philadelphia, Mar. 19, 1952; app. first bishop of Allentown, installed Apr. 11, 1961; resigned Feb. 8, 1983.

Madera, Joseph J., M.Sp.S.: b. Nov. 27, 1927, San Francisco, Calif.; educ. Domus Studiorum of the Missionaries of the Holy Spirit (Coyoacan, D.F. Mexico); ord. priest June 15, 1957; ord. coadjutor

bishop of Fresno, Mar. 4, 1980; bishop of Fresno, July 1, 1980.

Maguire, John J.: b. Dec. 11, 1904, New York, N.Y.; educ. Cathedral College (New York City), St. Joseph's Seminary (Dunwoodie, N.Y.), North American College (Rome); ord. priest (New York*) Dec. 22, 1928; ord. titular bishop of Antiphrae and auxiliary bishop of New York, June 29, 1959; app. titular archbishop of Tabalta and coadjutor archbishop of New York, Sept. 15, 1965; retired Jan. 8, 1980.

Maguire, Joseph F.: b. Sept. 4, 1919, Boston, Mass.; educ. Boston College, St. John's Seminary (Boston, Mass.); ord. priest (Boston*) June 29, 1945; ord. titular bishop of Macteris and auxiliary bishop of Boston, Feb. 2, 1972; app. coadjutor bishop of Springfield, Mass., Apr. 13, 1976; succeeded as bishop of Springfield, Mass., Oct. 15, 1977.

Maher, Leo T.: b. July 1, 1915, Mount Union, Ia.; educ. St. Joseph's College (Mountain View, Calif.); St. Patrick's Seminary (Menlo Park, Calif.); ord. priest (San Francisco*) Dec. 18, 1943; ord. first bishop of Santa Rosa, April 5, 1962; bishop of San Diego, Oct. 4, 1969.

Mahoney, James P.: b. Aug. 16, 1925, Kingston, N.Y.; educ. St. Joseph's Seminary (Dunwoodie, N.Y.); ord. priest (New York*) May 19, 1951; ord. titular bishop of Ipagro and auxiliary bishop of New York, Sept. 15, 1972.

Mahony, Roger M.: b. Feb. 27, 1936, Hollywood, Calif.; educ. St. John's Seminary (Camarillo, Calif.), National Catholic School of Social Service (Catholic Univ., Washington, D.C.); ord. priest (Fresno) May 1, 1962; ord. titular bishop of Tamascani and auxiliary bishop of Fresno, Mar. 19, 1975; app. bishop of Stockton, installed Apr. 25, 1980; archbishop of Los Angeles, July 16, 1985, installed Sept. 5, 1985.

Maida, Adam J.: b. Mar. 18, 1930, East Vandergrift, Pa.; educ. St. Vincent College (Latrobe, Pa.). St. Mary Univ. (Baltimore, Md.), Lateran Univ. (Rome), Duquesne Univ. (Pittsburgh, Pa.); ord. priest (Pittsburgh) May 26, 1956; ord. bishop of Green Bay, Jan. 25, 1984.

Malone, James W.: b. Mar. 8, 1920, Youngstown, O.; educ. St. Charles Preparatory Seminary (Catonsville, Md.), St. Mary's Seminary (Cleveland, O.), Catholic Univ. (Washington, D.C.); ord. priest (Youngstown) May 26, 1945; ord. titular bishop of Alabanda and auxiliary bishop of Youngstown, Mar. 24, 1960; apostolic administrator, 1966; bishop of Youngstown, installed June 20, 1968; president of NCCB/USCC, 1983-.

Maloney, Charles G.: b. Sept. 9, 1912, Louisville, Ky.; educ. St. Joseph's College (Rensselaer, Ind.), North American College (Rome); ord. priest (Louisville*) Dec. 8, 1937; ord. titular bishop of Capsa and auxiliary bishop of Louisville, Feb. 2, 1955.

Maloney, David M.: b. Mar. 15, 1912, Littleton, Colo.; educ. St. Thomas Seminary (Denver, Colo.), Gregorian Univ. and Apollinare Univ. (Rome); ord. priest (Denver*) Dec. 8, 1936; ord. titular bishop of Ruspe and auxiliary bishop of Denver, Jan. 4, 1961; app. bishop of Wichita, Kans., Dec. 6, 1967; resigned July 16, 1982.

Manning, Thomas R., O.F.M.: b. Aug. 29, 1922, Baltimore. Md.; educ. Duns Scotus College (Southfield. Mich.), Holy Name College (Washington, D.C.); ord. priest June 5, 1948; ord. titular bishop of Arsamosata, July 14, 1959 (resigned titular see Dec. 30, 1977); prelate of Coroico, Bolivia, July 14, 1959; became first bishop, 1983, when prelature was raised to diocese.

Manning, Timothy: (See Cardinals, Biographies.)

Marcinkus, Paul C.: b. Jan. 15, 1922, Cicero, Ill.; ord. priest (Chicago*) May 3, 1947; served in Vatican secretariat from 1952; ord. titular bishop of Orta, Jan. 6, 1969; secretary (1968-71) and president (1971-) of Institute for Works of Religion (Vatican Bank); titular archbishop, Sept. 26, 1981; pro-president of Pontifical Commission for the State of Vatican City.

Marconi, Dominic A.: b. Mar. 13, 1927, Newark, N.J.; educ. Seton Hall Univ. (S. Orange, N.J.), Immaculate Conception Seminary (Darlington, N.J.), Catholic Univ. (Washington, D.C.); ord. priest (Newark*) May 30, 1953; ord. titular bishop of Bure and auxiliary bishop of Newark, June 25, 1976.

Marino, Eugene A., S.S.J.: b. May 29, 1934, Biloxi, Miss.; educ. Epiphany Apostolic College and Mary Immaculate Novitiate (Newburgh, N.Y.), St. Joseph's Seminary (Washington, D.C.), Catholic Univ. (Washington, D.C.), Loyola Univ. (New Orleans, La.), Fordham Univ. (New York City); ord. priest June 9, 1962; ord. titular bishop of Walla Walla and auxiliary bishop of Washington, D.C., Sept. 12, 1974.

Markiewicz, Alfred J.: b. May 17, 1928, Brooklyn, N.Y.; educ. St. Francis College (Brooklyn, N.Y.), Immaculate Conception Seminary (Huntington, N.Y.); ord. priest (Brooklyn) June 6, 1953; ord. titular bishop of Afufenia and auxiliary bishop of Rockville Centre, Sept. 17, 1986. Vicar for Nassau.

Marshall, John A.: b. Apr. 26, 1928, Worcester, Mass.; educ. Holy Cross College (Worcester, Mass.), Sulpician Seminary (Montreal), North American College and Gregorian Univ. (Rome), Assumption College (Worcester); ord. priest (Worcester) Dec. 19, 1953; ord. bishop of Burlington, Jan. 25, 1972.

Matthiesen, Leroy Theodore: b. June 11, 1921, Olfen, Tex.; educ. Josephinum College (Columbus, O.), Catholic Univ. (Washington, D.C.), Register School of Journalism; ord. priest (Amarillo) Mar. 10, 1946; ord. bishop of Amarillo, May 30, 1980.

May, John L.: b. Mar. 31, 1922, Evanston, Ill.; educ. St. Mary of the Lake Seminary (Mundelein, Ill.); ord. priest (Chicago*) May 3, 1947; general secretary and vice-president of the Catholic Church Extension Society, 1959; ord. titular bishop of Tagarbala and auxiliary bishop of Chicago, Aug. 24, 1967; bishop of Mobile, Ala., Sept. 29, 1969; app. archbishop of St. Louis, installed Mar. 25, 1980.

Melczek, Dale J.: b. Nov. 9, 1938, Detroit, Mich.; educ. St. Mary's College (Orchard Lake, Mich.), St. John's Provincial Seminary (Plymouth, Mich.), Univ. of Detroit; ord. priest (Detroit*) June 6, 1964; ord. titular bishop of Trau

and auxiliary bishop of Detroit, Jan. 27, 1983; vicar general; regional bishop of northwest region of Detroit archdiocese.

Mendez, Alfred, C.S.C.: b. June 3, 1907, Chicago, Ill.; educ. Notre Dame Univ. (Notre Dame, Ind.), Institute of Holy Cross (Washington, D.C.); ord. priest June 24, 1935; ord. first bishop of Arecibo, Puerto Rico, Oct. 28, 1960; resigned Jan. 24, 1974.

Mestice, Anthony F.: b. Dec. 6, 1923, New York, N.Y.; educ. St. Joseph Seminary (Yonkers, N.Y.); ord. priest (New York*) June 4, 1949; ord. titular bishop of Villa Nova and auxiliary bishop of New York, Apr. 27, 1973.

Michaels, James E., S.S.C.: b. May 30, 1926, Chicago, Ill.; educ. Columban Seminary (St. Columban, Neb.), Gregorian Univ. (Rome); ord. priest Dec. 21, 1951; ord. titular bishop of Verbe and auxiliary bishop of Kwang Ju, Korea, Apr. 14, 1966; app. auxiliary bishop of Wheeling, Apr. 3, 1973; title of see changed to Wheeling-Charleston, 1974.

Milone, Anthony: b. Sept. 24, 1932, Omaha, Nebr.; educ. North American College (Rome); ord. priest (Omaha*) Dec. 15, 1957, in Rome; ord. titular bishop of Plestia and auxiliary bishop of Omaha, Jan. 6, 1982.

Minder, John, O.S.F.S.: b. Nov. 1, 1923, Philadelphia, Pa.; educ. Catholic Univ. (Washington, D.C.); ord. priest June 3, 1950; ord. bishop of Keimos (renamed Keimos-Upington, 1985), South Africa, Jan. 10, 1968.

Montrose, Donald: b. May 13, 1923, Denver, Colo.; educ. St. John's Seminary (Camarillo, Calif.); ord. priest (Los Angeles*) May 7, 1949; ord. titular bishop of Forum Novum and auxiliary bishop of Los Angeles, May 12, 1983; app. bishop of Stockton, Dec. 17, 1985.

Moore, Emerson John: b. May 16, 1938, New York, N.Y.; educ. Cathedral College (New York City), St. Joseph's Seminary (Yonkers, N.Y.); New York University, Columbia Univ. School of Social Work (New York City); ord. priest (New York*) May 30, 1964; ord. auxiliary bishop of Curubi and auxiliary bishop of New York, Sept. 8, 1982.

Moran, William J.: b. Jan. 15, 1906, San Francisco, Calif.; educ. St. Patrick's Seminary (Menlo Park, Calif.); ord. priest (San Francisco*) June 20, 1931; Army chaplain, 1933; ord. titular bishop of Centuria and auxiliary to the military vicar, Dec. 13, 1965; retired Jan. 15, 1981.

Moreno, Manuel D.: b. Nov. 27, 1930, Placentia, Calif.; educ. Univ. of California (Los Angeles), Our Lady Queen of Angels (San Fernando, Calif.), St. John's Seminary (Camarillo, Calif.); ord. priest (Los Angeles*) Apr. 25, 1961; ord. titular bishop of Tanagra and auxiliary bishop of Los Angeles, Feb. 19, 1977; bishop of Tucson, Jan. 12, 1982, installed Mar. 11, 1982.

Morkovsky, John Louis: b. Aug. 16, 1909, Praha, Tex.; educ. St. John's Seminary (San Antonio, Tex.), North American College, Urban Univ. and Gregorian Univ. (Rome), Catholic Univ. (Washington, D.C.); ord. priest (San Antonio*) Dec. 5, 1933; ord titular bishop of Hieron and auxiliary bishop of Amarillo, Feb. 22, 1956; app. bishop of

Amarillo, Aug. 27, 1958; titular bishop of Tigava and coadjutor bishop of Galveston-Houston with right of succession, June 11, 1963; apostolic administrator; president Texas Conference of Churches, 1970-72; bishop of Galveston-Houston, Apr. 22, 1975; retired Aug. 21, 1984.

Morneau, Robert F.: b. Sept. 10, 1938, New London, Wis.; educ. St. Norbert's College (De Pere, Wis.); Sacred Heart Seminary (Oneida, Wis.), Catholic Univ. (Washington, D.C.); ord. priest (Green Bay) May 28, 1966; ord. titular bishop of Massa Lubrense and auxiliary bishop of Green Bay, Feb. 22, 1979.

Morrow, Louis La Ravoire, S.D.B.: b. Dec. 24, 1892, Weatherford, Tex.; educ. Salesian School and Palafox (Puebla, Mexico); professed in Salesians of St. John Bosco, Sept. 29, 1912; ord. priest May 21, 1921; ord. bishop of Krishnagar, India, Oct. 29, 1939; resigned Oct. 31, 1969.

Moskal, Robert M.: b. Oct. 24, 1937, Carnegie, Pa.; educ. St. Basil Minor Seminary (Stamford, Conn.), St. Josaphat Seminary and Catholic Univ. (Washington, D.C.); ord. priest (Philadelphia*, Byzantine Rite) Mar. 25, 1963; ord. titular bishop of Agatopoli and auxiliary bishop of the Ukrainian-Rite archeparchy of Philadelphia, Oct. 13, 1981; app. first bishop of St. Josaphat in Parma, Dec. 5, 1983.

Mugavero, Francis John: b. June 8, 1914, Brooklyn, N.Y.; educ. Cathedral College (Brooklyn, N.Y.), Immaculate Conception Seminary (Huntington, N.Y.), Fordham Univ. (New York City); ord. priest (Brooklyn) May 18, 1940; ord. bishop of Brooklyn, Sept. 12, 1968.

Mulcahy, John J.: b. June 26, 1922, Dorchester, Mass.; educ. St. John's Seminary (Brighton, Mass.); ord. priest (Boston*) May 1, 1947; rector Pope John XXIII Seminary for Delayed Vocations, 1969-73; ord. titular bishop of Penafiel and auxiliary bishop of Boston, Feb. 11, 1975.

Mulrooney, Charles R.: b. Jan. 13, 1906, Brooklyn, N.Y.; educ. Cathedral College (Brooklyn, N.Y.), St. Mary's Seminary (Baltimore, Md.), Sulpician Seminary (Washington, D.C.); ord. priest (Brooklyn) June 10, 1930; ord. titular bishop of Valentiniana and auxiliary bishop of Brooklyn, Apr. 22, 1959; retired Jan. 13, 1981.

Mulvee, Robert E.: b. Feb. 15, 1930, Boston, Mass.; educ. St. Thomas Seminary (Bloomfield, Conn.), University Seminary (Ottawa, Ont., Canada), American College (Louvain, Belgium), Lateran Univ. (Rome); ord. priest (Manchester) June 30, 1957; ord. titular bishop of Summa and auxiliary bishop of Manchester, N.H., Apr. 14, 1977; app. bishop of Wilmington, Del., Feb. 19, 1985.

Mundo, Michael P.: b. July 25, 1937, New York, N.Y.; educ. Fordham Univ. (Bronx, N.Y.), St. Jerome's College (Kitchener, Ont., Canada), St. Francis Seminary (Loretto, Pa.); ord. priest (Camden) May 19, 1962; missionary in Brazil from 1963; ord. titular bishop of Blanda Julia and auxiliary bishop of Jatai, Brazil, June 2, 1978.

Murphy, Michael J.: b. July 1, 1915, Cleveland, O.; educ. Niagara Univ. (Niagara Falls, N.Y.); North American College (Rome), Catholic Univ. (Washington, D.C.); ord. priest (Cleveland) Feb. 28, 1942; ord. titular bishop of Ariendela and auxiliary bishop of Cleveland, June 11, 1976; app. coadjutor bishop of Erie, Nov. 20, 1978; bishop of Erie, July 16, 1982.

Murphy, Philip Francis: b. Mar. 25, 1933, Cumberland, Md.; educ. St. Mary Seminary (Baltimore, Md.), North American College (Rome); ord. priest (Baltimore*) Dec. 20, 1958; ord. titular bishop of Tacarata and auxiliary bishop of Baltimore, Feb. 29, 1976.

Murphy, T. Austin: b. May 11, 1911, Baltimore, Md.; educ. St. Charles College (Catonsville, Md.), St. Mary's Seminary (Baltimore, Md.); ord. priest (Baltimore*) June 10, 1937; ord. titular bishop of Appiaria and auxiliary bishop of Baltimore, July 3, 1962; retired May 29, 1984.

Murphy, Thomas J.: b. Oct. 3, 1932, Chicago, Ill.; educ. Quigley Preparatory Seminary (Chicago, Ill.), St. Mary of the Lake Seminary (Mundelein, Ill.); ord. priest (Chicago*) Apr. 12, 1958; ord. bishop of Great Falls, Mont. Aug. 21, 1978; title of see changed to Great Falls-Billings, 1980.

Murphy, Thomas W.; C.SS.R.: b. Dec. 17, 1917, Omaha, Nebr.; educ. St. Joseph's College (Kirkwood, Mo.); ord. priest June 29, 1943; ord. first bishop of Juazeiro, Brazil, Jan. 2, 1963; resigned Dec. 29, 1973; app. titular bishop of Sululos and auxiliary bishop of Sao Salvador da Bahia, Brazil, Jan. 31, 1974.

N

Nelson, Knute Ansgar, O.S.B.: b. Oct. 1, 1906, Copenhagen, Denmark; educ. Abbey of Maria Laach (Germany), Brown Univ. (Providence, R.I.); professed in the Order of St. Benedict, May 30, 1932; ord. priest May 22, 1937; became an American citizen, Mar. 4, 1941; ord. titular bishop of Bilta and coadjutor bishop of Stockholm, Sweden, Sept. 8, 1947; succeeded as bishop of Stockholm, Oct. 1, 1957; retired; titular bishop of Dura. 1962.

Nevins, John J.: b. Jan. 19, 1932, New Rochelle, N.Y.; educ. Iona College (New Rochelle, N.Y.), Catholic Univ. (Washington, D.C.); ord. priest (Miami*) June 6, 1959; ord. titular bishop of Rusticana and auxiliary bishop of Miami, Mar. 24, 1979; app. first bishop of Venice, Fla., July 17, 1984; installed Oct. 25, 1984.

Newell, Hubert M.: b. Feb. 16, 1904, Denver, Colo.; educ. Regis College and St. Thomas Seminary (Denver, Colo.), Catholic Univ. (Washington, D.C.); ord. priest (Denver*) June 15, 1930; ord. titular bishop of Zapara and coadjutor bishop of Cheyenne, Sept. 24, 1947; bishop of Cheyenne, Nov. 10, 1951; retired Jan. 3, 1978.

Newman, William C.: b. Aug. 16, 1928, Baltimore, Md.; educ. St. Mary Seminary (Baltimore, Md.). Catholic Univ. (Washington, D.C.), Loyola College (Baltimore, Md.); ord. priest (Baltimore*) May 29, 1954; ord. titular bishop of Numluli and auxiliary bishop of Baltimore, July 2, 1984.

Neylon, Martin J., S.J.: b. Feb. 13, 1920, Buffalo, N.Y.; ord. priest June 18, 1950; ord. titular bishop of Libertina and coadjutor vicar apostolic of the

Caroline and Marshall Islands, Feb. 2, 1970; vicar apostolic of Caroline and Marshall Is., Sept. 20, 1971; first bishop of Carolines-Marshalls when vicarate apostolic was raised to diocese, 1979.

Niedergeses, James D.: b. Feb. 2, 1917, Lawrenceburg, Tenn.; educ. St. Bernard College (St. Bernard, Ala.), St. Ambrose College (Davenport, Ia.), Mt. St. Mary Seminary of the West and Athenaeum (Cincinnati, Ohio); ord. priest (Nashville) May 20, 1944; ord. bishop of Nashville May 20, 1975.

Nolker, Bernard, C.SS.R.: b. Sept. 25, 1912, Baltimore, Md.; educ. St. Mary's College (North East, Pa.), St. Mary's College (Ilchester, Md.), Mt. St. Alphonsus Seminary (Esopus, N.Y.); ord. priest June 18, 1939; ord. first bishop of Paranagua, Brazil, Apr. 25, 1963.

Novak, Alfred, C.SS.R.: b. June 2, 1930, Dwight, Nebr.; educ. Immaculate Conception Seminary (Oconomowoc, Wis.); ord. priest July 2, 1956; ord. titular bishop of Vardimissa and auxiliary bishop of Sao Paulo, Brazil, May 25, 1979.

O

O'Boyle, Patrick A.: (See Cardinals, Biographies.)

O'Brien, Thomas Joseph: b. Nov. 29, 1935, Indianapolis, Ind.; educ. St. Meinrad High School Seminary, St. Meinrad College Seminary (St. Meinrad, Ind.); ord. priest (Tucson) May 7, 1961; ord. bishop of Phoenix, Jan. 6, 1982.

O'Connor, John J.: (See Cardinals, Biographies.)

O'Connor, Martin J.: b. May 18, 1900, Scranton, Pa.; educ. St. Thomas College (Scranton, Pa.), St. Mary's Seminary (Baltimore, Md.), North American College, Urban Univ. and Apollinaris (Rome); ord. priest (Scranton) Mar. 15, 1924; ord. titular bishop of Thespia and auxiliary bishop of Scranton, Jan. 27, 1943; rector of North American College 1946-1964; app. titular archbishop of Laodicea in Syria, Sept. 5, 1959; apostolic nuncio to Malta, 1965-69; president emeritus Pontifical Commission for Social Communications.

O'Donnell, Cletus F.: b. Aug. 22, 1917, Waukon, Ia.; educ. St. Mary Seminary (Mundelein, Ill.), Catholic Univ. (Washington, D.C.); ord. priest (Chicago*) May 3, 1941; ord. titular bishop of Abritto and auxiliary bishop of Chicago, Dec. 21, 1960; app. bishop of Madison, Feb. 22, 1967, installed Apr. 25, 1967.

O'Donnell, Edward J.: b. July 4, 1931, St. Louis, Mo.; educ. St. Louis Preparatory Seminary and Kenrick Seminary (St. Louis, Mo.); ord. priest (St. Louis*) Apr. 6, 1957; ord. titular bishop of Britania and auxiliary bishop of St. Louis, Feb. 10, 1984.

O'Keefe, Gerald F.: b. Mar. 30, 1918, St. Paul, Minn.; educ. College of St. Thomas, St. Paul Seminary (St. Paul, Minn.); ord. priest (St. Paul-Minneapolis*) Jan. 29, 1944; ord. titular bishop of Candyba and auxiliary bishop of St. Paul July 2, 1961; bishop of Davenport, Oct. 20, 1966, installed Jan. 4, 1967.

O'Keefe, Joseph Thomas: b. Mar. 12, 1919, New York, N.Y.; educ. Cathedral College (New York City), St. Joseph's Seminary (Yonkers, N.Y.),

Catholic Univ. (Washington, D.C.); ord. priest (New York*) Apr. 17, 1948; ord. titular bishop of Tre Taverne and auxiliary bishop of New York, Sept. 8, 1982.

O'Leary, Edward C.: b. Aug. 21, 1920, Bangor, Me.; educ. Holy Cross College (Worcester, Mass.), St. Paul's Seminary (Ottawa, Canada); ord. priest (Portland, Me.) June 15, 1946; ord. titular bishop of Moglena and auxiliary bishop of Portland, Me., Jan. 25, 1971; app. bishop of Portland, installed Dec. 18, 1974.

O'Malley, Sean, O.F.M. Cap.: b. June 29, 1944, Lakewood, O.; educ. St. Fidelis Seminary (Herman, Pa.), Capuchin College and Catholic Univ. (Washington, D.C.); ord. priest Aug. 29, 1970; episcopal vicar of priests serving Spanish speaking in Washington archdiocese, 1978-84; executive director of Spanish Catholic Center, Washington, from 1973; ord. coadjutor bishop of St. Thomas, Virgin Islands, Aug. 2, 1984; bishop of St. Thomas, Oct. 16, 1985.

O'Meara, Edward T.: b. Aug. 3, 1921, St. Louis, Mo.; educ. Cardinal Glennon College and Kenrick Seminary (St. Louis, Mo.), Angelicum (Rome); ord. priest (St. Louis*) Dec. 21, 1946; app. national director of Society for the Propagation of the Faith, 1967; ord. titular bishop of Thisiduo and auxiliary bishop of St. Louis, Feb. 13, 1972; app. archbishop of Indianapolis, installed Jan. 10, 1980.

O'Neil, Leo E.: b. Jan. 31, 1928, Holyoke, Mass.; educ. Maryknoll Seminary (Maryknoll, N.Y.), St. Anselm's College (Manchester, N.H.), Grand Seminary (Montreal, Canada); ord. priest (Springfield, Mass.) June 4, 1955; ord. titular bishop of Bencenna and auxiliary bishop of Springfield, Mass., Aug. 22, 1980.

O'Neill, Arthur J.: b. Dec. 14, 1917, East Dubuque, Ill.; educ. Loras College (Dubuque, Ia.), St. Mary's Seminary (Baltimore, Md.); ord. priest (Rockford) Mar. 27, 1943; ord. bishop of Rockford, Oct. 11, 1968.

O'Rourke, Edward W.: b. Oct. 31, 1917, Downs, Ill.; educ. St. Mary's Seminary (Mundelein, Ill.), Aquinas Institute of Philosophy and Theology (River Forest, Ill.); ord. priest (Peoria) May 28, 1944; exec. dir. National Catholic Rural Life Conference, 1960-71; ord. bishop of Peoria, July 15, 1971.

Ott, Stanley J.: b. June 29, 1927, Gretna, La.; educ. Notre Dame Seminary (New Orleans, La.), North American College and Gregorian Univ. (Rome); ord. priest (New Orleans*) Dec. 8, 1951; ord. titular bishop of Nicives and auxiliary bishop of New Orleans, June 29, 1976; app. bishop of Baton Rouge, Jan 17, 1983, installed Mar. 24, 1983.

Ottenweller, Albert H.: b. Apr. 5, 1916, Stanford, Mont.; educ. St. Joseph's Seminary (Rensselaer, Ind.), Catholic Univ. (Washington, D.C.); ord. priest (Toledo) June 19, 1943; ord. titular bishop of Perdices and auxiliary bishop of Toledo, May 29, 1974; app. bishop of Steubenville, Oct. 11, 1977, installed Nov. 22, 1977.

P

Paschang, John L.: b. Oct. 5, 1895, Hemingford, Nebr.; educ. Conception College (Conception,

Mo.), St. John Seminary (Collegeville, Minn.), Catholic Univ. (Washington, D.C.); ord. priest (Omaha*) June 12, 1921; ord. bishop of Grand Island, Oct. 9, 1951; resigned July 25, 1972.

Pataki, Andrew: b. Aug. 30, 1927, Palmerton, Pa.; educ. St. Vincent College (Latrobe, Pa.), St. Procopius College, St. Procopius Seminary (Lisle, Ill.), Sts. Cyril and Methodius Byzantine Catholic Seminary (Pittsburgh, Pa.), Gregorian Univ. and Oriental Pontifical Institute (Rome, Italy); ord. priest (Pittsburgh,* Byzantine Rite) Feb. 24, 1952; ord. titular bishop of Telmisso and auxiliary bishop of Byzantine diocese of Passaic, Aug. 23, 1983; vicar general; episcopal vicar of Pennsylvania; app. bishop of Ruthenian Byzantine diocese of Parma, July 3, 1984.

Paul, John J.: b. Aug. 17, 1918, La Crosse, Wis.; educ. Loras College (Dubuque, Iowa), St. Mary's Seminary (Baltimore, Md.), Marquette Univ. (Milwaukee, Wis.), ord. priest (Lincoln) Jan. 24, 1943; ord. titular bishop of Lambaesis and auxiliary bishop of La Crosse, Aug. 4, 1977; app. bishop of La Crosse, Oct. 18, 1983, installed Dec. 5, 1983.

Pearce, George H., S.M.: b. Jan. 9, 1921, Brighton, Mass.; educ. Marist College and Seminary (Framington, Mass.); ord. priest Feb. 2, 1947; ord. titular bishop of Attalea in Pamphylia and vicar apostolic of the Samoa and Tokelau Islands, June 29, 1956; title changed to bishop of Apia, June 21, 1966; app. archbishop of Suva, Fiji Islands, June 22, 1967; resigned Apr. 10, 1976.

Pechillo, Jerome, T.O.R.: b. May 16, 1919, Brooklyn, N.Y.; educ. Catholic Univ. (Washington, D.C.); ord. priest June 10, 1947; ord. titular bishop of Novasparsa and prelate of Coronel Oviedo, Paraguay, Jan. 25, 1966; app. auxiliary bishop of Newark, N.J., Mar. 6, 1976.

Pelotte, Donald E., S.S.S.: b. Apr. 13, 1945, Waterville, Me.; educ. Eymard Seminary and Junior College (Hyde Park, N.Y.), John Carroll Univ. (Cleveland, O.), Fordham Univ. (Bronx, N.Y.); ord. priest Sept. 2, 1972; ord. coadjutor bishop of Gallup, May 6, 1986. First priest of Native American ancestry to be named U.S. bishop.

Pena, Raymundo J.: b. Feb. 19, 1934, Robstown, Tex.; educ. Assumption Seminary (San Antonio, Tex.); ord. priest (Corpus Christi) May 25, 1957; ord. titular bishop of Trisipa and auxiliary bishop of San Antonio, Dec. 13, 1976; app. bishop of El Paso, Apr. 29, 1980.

Perry, Harold R., S.V.D.: b. Oct. 9, 1916, Lake Charles, La.; educ. St. Augustine Seminary (Bay St. Louis, Miss.), St. Mary's Seminary (Techny, Ill.); ord. priest Jan. 6, 1944; app. provincial of southern province of Society of the Divine Word, 1964; ord. titular bishop of Mons in Mauretania and auxiliary bishop of New Orleans, Jan. 6, 1966.

Pevec, A. Edward: b. Apr. 16, 1925, Cleveland, O.; educ. St. Mary's Seminary, John Carroll Univ. (Cleveland, O.); ord. priest (Cleveland) Apr. 29, 1950; ord. titular bishop of Mercia and auxiliary bishop of Cleveland, July 2, 1982.

Pfeifer, Michael, O.M.I.: b. May 18, 1937, Alamo, Tex.; educ. Oblate school of theology (San Antonio, Tex.); ord. priest Dec. 21, 1964; provincial of southern province of Oblates of Mary Immaculate, 1981; ord. bishop of San Angelo, July 26, 1985.

Pilarczyk, Daniel E.: b. Aug. 12, 1934, Dayton, Ohio; educ. St. Gregory's Seminary (Cincinnati, O.), Urban Univ. (Rome), Xavier Univ. and Univ. of Cincinnati (Cincinnati, O.); ord. priest (Cincinnati*) Dec. 20, 1959; ord. titular bishop of Hodelm and auxiliary bishop of Cincinnati, Dec. 20, 1974; app. archbishop of Cincinnati, Oct. 30, 1982; installed Dec. 2, 1982.

Pilla, Anthony M.: b. Nov. 12, 1932, Cleveland, O.; educ. St. Gregory College Seminary (Cincinnati, O.), Borromeo College Seminary (Wickliffe, O.), St. Mary Seminary and John Carroll Univ. (Cleveland, O.); ord. priest (Cleveland) May 23, 1959; ord. titular bishop of Scardona and auxiliary bishop of Cleveland, Aug. 1, 1979; app. apostolic administrator of Cleveland, 1980; bishop of Cleveland, Nov. 13, 1980.

Pinger, Henry A., O.F.M.: b. Aug. 16, 1897, Lindsay, Nebr.; educ. Our Lady of Angels Seminary (Cleveland, O.), St. Anthony's Seminary (St. Louis, Mo.); professed in the Order of Friars Minor, June 18, 1918; ord. priest June 27, 1924; ord. titular bishop of Capitolias and vicar apostolic of Chowtsun, China, Sept. 21, 1937; title changed to bishop of Chowtsun, Apr. 11, 1946; imprisoned by Reds in 1951, released in 1956; expelled; bishop emeritus of Chowtsun.

Popp, Bernard F.: b. Dec. 6, 1917, Nada, Tex.; educ. St. John's Seminary and St. Mary's Univ. (San Antonio, Tex.); ord. priest (San Antonio*) Feb. 24, 1943; ord. titular bishop of Capsus and auxiliary bishop of San Antonio, July 25, 1983.

Povish, Kenneth J.: b. Apr. 19, 1924, Alpena, Mich.; educ. St. Joseph's Seminary (Grand Rapids, Mich.), Sacred Heart Seminary (Detroit, Mich.), Catholic Univ. (Washington, D.C.); ord. priest (Saginaw) June 3, 1950; ord. bishop of Crookston, Sept. 29, 1970; app. bishop of Lansing, Oct. 8, 1975, installed Dec. 11, 1975.

Power, Cornelius M.: b. Dec. 18, 1913, Seattle, Wash.; educ. St. Patrick's College (Menlo Park, Calif.), St. Edward's Seminary (Kenmore, Wash.), Catholic Univ. (Washington, D.C.); priest (Seattle*) June 3, 1939; ord. bishop of Yakima, May 1, 1969, installed May 20, 1969; app. archbishop of Portland, Ore., Jan. 22, 1974, installed Apr. 17, 1974; retired 1986.

Primeau, Ernest J.: b. Sept. 17, 1909, Chicago, Ill.; educ. Loyola Univ. (Chicago, Ill.), St. Mary of the Lake Seminary (Mundelein, Ill.), Lateran Univ. (Rome); ord. priest (Chicago*) Apr. 7, 1934; ord. bishop of Manchester, Feb. 25, 1960; resigned Jan. 30, 1974; director of Villa Stritch, Rome, 1974-79.

Prost, Jude, O.F.M.: b. Dec. 6, 1915, Chicago, Ill.; educ. Our Lady of the Angels Seminary (Cleveland, O.), St. Joseph's Seminary (Teutopolis, Ill.); ord. priest June 24, 1942; ord. titular bishop of Fronta and auxiliary bishop of Belem do Para, Brazil, Nov. 1, 1962.

Proulx, Amedee W.: b. Aug. 31, 1932, Sanford, Me.; educ. St. Hyacinthe Seminary (Quebec), St. Paul Univ. Seminary (Ottawa), Catholic Univ.

(Washington, D.C.); ord. priest (Portland, Me.) May 31, 1958; ord. titular bishop of Clipia and auxiliary bishop of Portland, Me., Nov. 12, 1975.

Pursley, Leo A.: b. Mar. 12, 1902, Hartford City, Ind.; educ. Mt. St. Mary's Seminary (Cincinnati, O.); ord. priest (Ft. Wayne-S. Bend) June 11, 1927; ord. titular bishop of Hadrianapolis in Pisidia and auxiliary bishop of Fort Wayne, Sept. 19, 1950; app. apostolic administrator of Fort Wayne, Mar. 9, 1955; installed as bishop of Fort Wayne, Feb. 26, 1957; title of see changed to Fort Wayne-South Bend, 1960; resigned Aug. 31, 1976.

Puscas, Louis: b. Sept. 13, 1915, Aurora, Ill.; educ. Quigley Preparatory Seminary (Chicago, Ill.), seminary in Oradea-Mare (Romania), Propaganda Fide Seminary (Rome), Illinois Benedictine College (Lisle, Ill.); ord. priest (Erie) May 14, 1942; ord. titular bishop of Leuce and first exarch of apostolic exarchate for Romanians of the Byzantine Rite in the U.S., June 26, 1983 (seat of the exarchate is Canton, Ohio).

Q

Quinn, Alexander James: b. Apr. 8, 1932, Cleveland, O.; educ. St. Charles College (Catonsville, Md.), St. Mary Seminary (Cleveland, O.), Lateran Univ. (Rome), Cleveland State Univ.; ord. priest (Cincinnati*) May 24, 1958; ord. titular bishop of Socia and auxiliary bishop of Cleveland, Dec. 5, 1983; vicar of western region of Cleveland diocese.

Quinn, Francis A.: b. Sept. 11, 1921, Los Angeles, Calif.; educ. St. Joseph's College (Mountain View, Calif.), St. Patrick's Seminary (Menlo Park, Calif.), Catholic Univ. (Washington, D.C.); Univ. of California (Berkley); ord. priest (San Francisco*) June 15, 1946; ord. titular bishop of Numana and auxiliary bishop of San Francisco, June 29, 1978; app. bishop of Sacramento Dec. 18, 1979.

Quinn, John R.: b. Mar. 28, 1929, Riverside, Calif.; educ. St. Francis Seminary (El Cajon, Calif.), North American College (Rome); ord. priest (San Diego) July 19, 1953; ord. titular bishop of Thisiduo and auxiliary bishop of San Diego, Dec. 12, 1967; bishop of Oklahoma City and Tulsa, Nov. 30, 1971; first archbishop of Oklahoma City, Dec. 19, 1972; app. archbishop of San Francisco Feb. 22, 1977, installed Apr. 26, 1977; president NCCB, USCC, 1977-80.

R

Ramirez, Ricardo, C.S.B.: b. Sept. 12, 1936, Bay City, Tex.; educ. Univ. of St. Thomas (Houston, Tex.), Univ. of Detroit (Detroit, Mich.), St. Basil's Seminary (Toronto, Ont.); Seminario Concilium (Mexico City, Mexico), East Asian Pastoral Institute (Manila, Philippines); ord. priest Dec. 10, 1966; ord titular bishop of Vatarba and auxiliary of San Antonio, Dec. 6, 1981; app. first bishop of Las Cruces, N. Mex., Aug. 17, 1982; installed Oct. 18, 1982.

Raya, Joseph M.: b. July 20, 1917, Zahle, Lebanon; educ. St. Louis College (Paris, France), St. Anne's Seminary (Jerusalem); ord. priest July 20, 1941; came to U.S., 1949, became U.S. citizen; ord. archbishop of Acre, Israel, of the Melkites, Oct. 20,

1968; resigned Aug. 20, 1974; assigned titular metropolitan see of Scytopolis.

Regan, Joseph W., M.M.: b. Apr. 5, 1905, Boston, Mass.; educ. Boston College (Boston, Mass.), St. Bernard's Seminary (Rochester, N.Y.), Maryknoll Seminary (Maryknoll, N.Y.); ord. priest Jan. 27, 1929; missionary in China 15 years; in Philippines since 1952; ord. titular bishop of Isinda and prelate of Tagum, Philippine Islands, Apr. 25, 1962; resigned May 16, 1980.

Reh, Francis F.: b. Jan. 9, 1911, New York, N.Y.; educ. St. Joseph's Seminary (Dunwoodie, N.Y.), North American College and Gregorian Univ. (Rome); ord. priest (New York*) Dec. 8, 1935; ord. bishop of Charleston, S.C., June 29, 1962; named titular bishop of Macriana in Mauretania, 1964; rector of North American College, 1964-68; bishop of Saginaw, installed Feb. 26, 1969; resigned Apr. 28, 1980.

Reilly, Daniel P.: b. May 12, 1928, Providence, R.I.; educ. Our Lady of Providence Seminary (Warwick, R.I.), St. Brieuc Major Seminary (Cotes du Nord, France); ord. priest (Providence) May 30, 1953; ord. bishop of Norwich, Aug. 6, 1975.

Reilly, Thomas F., C.SS.R.: b. Dec. 20, 1908, Boston, Mass.; educ. Mt. St. Alphonsus Seminary (Esopus, N.Y.), Catholic Univ. (Washington, D.C.); ord. priest June 10, 1933; ord. titular bishop of Themisonium and prelate of San Juan de la Maguana, Dominican Republic, Nov. 30, 1956; first bishop of San Juan de la Maguana, Nov. 21, 1969; retired July 20, 1977.

Reiss, John C.: b. May 13, 1922, Red Bank, N.J.; educ. Catholic Univ. (Washington, D.C.), Immaculate Conception Seminary (Darlington, N.J.); ord. priest (Trenton) May 31, 1947; ord. titular bishop of Simidicca and auxiliary bishop of Trenton, Dec. 12, 1967; app. bishop of Trenton, Mar. 11, 1980.

Ricard, John H., S.S.J.: b. Feb. 29, 1940, Baton Rouge, La.; educ. St. Joseph's Seminary (Washington, D.C.), Tulane Univ. (New Orleans, La.); ord. priest May 25, 1968; ord. titular bishop of Rucuma and auxiliary of Baltimore, July 2, 1984; urban vicar, Baltimore.

Rigali, Justin: b. Apr. 19, 1935, Los Angeles, Calif.; educ. St. John's Seminary (Camarillo, Calif.); ord. priest (Los Angeles*) Apr. 25, 1961; in Vatican diplomatic service from 1964; ord. titular archbishop of Bolsena, Sept. 14, 1985, by Pope John Paul II; president of the Pontifical Ecclesiastical Academy.

Riley, Lawrence J.: b. Sept. 6, 1914; Boston, Mass.; educ. Boston College and St. John's Seminary (Boston, Mass.), North American College and Gregorian Univ. (Rome), Catholic Univ. (Washington, D.C.); ord. priest (Boston*) Sept. 21 1940; ord. titular bishop of Daimlaig and auxiliary bishop of Boston, Feb. 2, 1972.

Roach, John R.: b. July 31, 1921, Prior Lake, Minn.; educ. St. Paul Seminary (St. Paul, Minn.), Univ. of Minnesota (Minneapolis); ord. priest (St. Paul and Minneapolis*) June 18, 1946; ord. titular bishop of Cenae and auxiliary bishop of St. Paul and Minneapolis, Sept. 8, 1971; app. archbishop of St. Paul and Minneapolis, May 28, 1975; vice-president NCCB/USCC, 1977-80; president, 1980-83.

Rodimer, Frank J.: b. Oct. 25, 1927, Rockaway, N.J.; educ. Seton Hall Prep (South Orange, N.J.), St. Charles College (Catonsville, Md.), St. Mary's Seminary (Baltimore, Md.), Immaculate Conception Seminary (Darlington, N.J.), Catholic Univ. (Washington, D.C.); ord. priest (Paterson) May 19, 1951; ord. bishop of Paterson, Feb. 28, 1978.

Rodriguez, Migúel, C.SS.R.: b. Apr. 18, 1931, Mayaguez, P.R.; educ. St. Mary's Minor Seminary (North East, Pa.), Mt. St. Alphonsus Major Seminary (Esopus, N.Y.); ord. priest June 22, 1958; ord. bishop of Arecibo, P.R., Mar. 23, 1974.

Rodriguez, Placido, C.M.F.: b. Oct. 11, 1940, Celaya, Guanajuato, Mexico; educ. Claretian Novitate (Los Angeles, Calif.), Claretville Seminary College (Calabasas, Calif.), Catholic Univ. (Washington, D.C.), Loyola Univ. (Chicago, Ill.); ord. priest May 23, 1968; ord. titular bishop of Fuerteventura and auxiliary bishop of Chicago, Dec. 13, 1983.

Roman, Agustin A.: b. May 5, 1928, San Antonio de los Banos, Havana, Cuba; educ. San Alberto Magno Seminary (Matanzas, Cuba), Missions Etrangeres (Montreal, Canada), Barry College (Miami, Fla.); ord. priest July 5, 1959, Cuba; vicar for Spanish speaking in Miami archdiocese, 1976; ord. titular bishop of Sertei and auxiliary bishop of Miami, Mar. 24, 1979.

Roque, Francis: b. Oct. 9, 1928, Providence R.I.; educ. St. John's Seminary (Brighton, Mass.); ord. priest (Providence) Sept. 19, 1953; became chaplain in U.S. Army 1961; ord. titular bishop of Bagai and auxiliary bishop of Military Archdiocese, May 10, 1983.

Rosazza, Peter Anthony: b. Feb. 13, 1935, New Haven, Conn.; educ. St. Thomas Seminary (Bloomfield, Conn.), Dartmouth College (Hanover, N.H.), St. Bernard's Seminary (Rochester, N.Y.), St. Sulpice (Issy, France); ord. priest (Hartford*) June 29, 1961; ord. titular bishop of Oppido Nuovo and auxiliary bishop of Hartford, June 24, 1978.

Rose, Robert John: b. Feb. 28, 1930, Grand Rapids, Mich.; educ. St. Joseph's Seminary (Grand Rapids, Mich.), Seminaire de Philosophie (Montreal, Canada), Pontifical Urban University (Rome), Univ. of Michigan (Ann Arbor, Mich.); ord. priest (Grand Rapids) Dec. 21, 1955; ord. bishop of Gaylord, Dec. 6, 1981.

Rudin, John J., M.M.: b. Nov. 27, 1916, Pittsfield, Mass.; educ. Maryknoll Seminary (Maryknoll, N.Y.), Gregorian Univ. (Rome); ord. priest June 11, 1944; ord. first bishop of Musoma, Tanzania, Oct. 3, 1957; retired Jan. 12, 1979.

Russell, John J.: b. Dec. 1, 1897, Baltimore, Md.; educ. St. Charles College (Catonsville, Md.), St. Mary's Seminary (Baltimore, Md.), North American College (Rome); ord. priest (Baltimore*) July 8, 1923; ord. bishop of Charleston, Mar. 14, 1950; bishop of Richmond, July 3, 1958; retired Apr. 30, 1973.

Ryan, Daniel L.: b. Sept. 28, 1930, Mankato, Minn.; educ. St. Procopius Seminary (Lisle, Ill.), Lateran Univ. (Rome); ord. priest (Joliet) May 3, 1956; ord. titular bishop of Surista and auxiliary bishop of Joliet, Sept. 30, 1981; app. bishop of Springfield, Ill., Nov. 22, 1983, installed Jan. 18, 1984.

Ryan, James C., O.F.M.: b. Nov. 17, 1912, Chicago, Ill.; educ. St. Joseph's Seraphic Seminary (Westmont, Ill.), Our Lady of the Angels Seminary (Cleveland, O.); ord. priest June 24, 1938; ord. titular bishop of Margo and prelate of Santarem, Brazil, April 9, 1958; first bishop of Santarem, Dec. 4, 1979; retired Nov. 27, 1985.

Ryan, Joseph T.: b. Nov. 1, 1913, Albany, N.Y.; educ. Manhattan College (New York City); ord. priest (Albany) June 3, 1939; national secretary of Catholic Near East Welfare Assn. 1960-65; ord. first archbishop of Anchorage, Alaska, Mar. 25, 1966; app. titular archbishop of Gabi and coadjutor archbishop of the military ordinariate, Oct. 24, 1975, installed Dec. 13, 1975; app. military vicar of U.S. military archdiocese, Mar. 16, 1985, installed Apr. 30, 1985, at National Shrine of the Immaculate Conception, Washington, D.C.

S

Salatka, Charles A.: b. Feb. 26, 1918, Grand Rapids, Mich.; educ. St. Joseph's Seminary (Grand Rapids, Mich.), Catholic Univ. (Washington, D.C.), Lateran Univ. (Rome); ord. priest (Grand Rapids) Feb. 24, 1945; ord. titular bishop of Cariana and auxiliary bishop of Grand Rapids, Mich., Mar. 6, 1962; app. bishop of Marquette, installed Mar. 25, 1968; app. archbishop of Oklahoma City, Sept. 27, 1977; installed Dec. 15, 1977.

Sanchez, Robert: b. Mar. 20, 1934, Socorro, N.M.; educ. Immaculate Heart Seminary (Santa Fe, N.M.), Gregorian Univ. (Rome), Catholic Univ. (Washington, D.C.); ord. priest (Santa Fe*) Dec. 20, 1959; ord. archbishop of Santa Fe, N.M., July 25, 1974.

San Pedro, Enrique, S.J.: b. Mar. 9, 1926, Havana, Cuba; educ. Spain, Philippines, Pontifical Biblical Institute (Rome), Leopold-Franzens Univ. (Innsbruck, Austria); ord. priest Mar. 18, 1957; taught Scripture and did missionary work in Vietnam, 1965-75, when he was expelled; visiting Scripture professor at St. Vincent de Paul Regional Seminary, Florida, from 1981; ord. titular bishop of Siccessi and auxiliary bishop of Galveston-Houston, June 29, 1986.

Scanlan, John J.: b. May 24, 1906, County Cork, Ireland; educ. National Univ. of Ireland (Dublin), All Hallows College (Dublin); ord. priest (San Francisco*) June 22, 1930; U.S. citizen 1938; ord. titular bishop of Cenae and auxiliary bishop of Honolulu, Sept. 21, 1954; bishop of Honolulu, installed May 1, 1968; retired June 30, 1981.

Scarpone, Gerald, O.F.M.: b. Oct. 1, 1928, Watertown, Mass.; ord. priest June 24, 1956; ord. coadjutor bishop of Comayagua, Honduras, Feb. 21, 1979; succeeded as bishop of Comayagua, May 30, 1979.

Schad, James L.: b. July 20, 1917, Philadelphia, Pa.; educ. St. Mary's Seminary (Baltimore, Md.); ord. priest (Camden) Apr. 10, 1943; ord. titular bishop of Panatoria and auxiliary bishop of Camden, Dec. 8, 1966.

Schierhoff, Andrew B.: b. Feb. 10, 1922, St. Louis, Mo.; ord. priest (St. Louis) Apr. 14, 1948;

missionary in Bolivia from 1956; ord. titular bishop of Cerenza and auxiliary of La Paz, Bolivia, Jan. 6, 1969; app. vicar apostolic of Pando, Bolivia, Dec. 17, 1982.

Schladweiler, Alphonse: b. July 18, 1902, Milwaukee, Wis.; educ. St. Joseph College (Teutopolis, Ill.), St. Paul's Seminary (St. Paul, Minn.), Univ. of Minnesota (Minneapolis, Minn.); ord. priest (St. Paul and Minneapolis*) June 9, 1929; ord. first bishop of New Ulm, Jan. 29, 1958; retired Dec. 23, 1975.

Schlaefer Berg, Salvator, O.F.M. Cap.: b. June 27, 1920, Campbellsport, Wis.; ord. priest June 5, 1946; missionary in Bluefields, Nicaragua from 1947; ord. titular bishop of Fiumepiscense and vicar apostolic of Bluefields, Nicaragua, Aug. 12, 1970.

Schlarman, Stanley Gerard: b. July 27, 1933, Belleville, Ill.; educ. St. Henry Prep Seminary (Belleville, Ill.), Gregorian Univ. (Rome), St. Louis Univ. (St. Louis, Mo.); ord. priest (Belleville) July 13, 1958, Rome; ord. titular bishop of Capri and auxiliary bishop of Belleville, May 14, 1979; app. bishop of Dodge City, Mar. 1, 1983.

Schlotterback, Edward F., O.S.F.S.: b. Mar. 2, 1912, Philadelphia, Pa.; educ. Catholic Univ. (Washington, D.C.); ord. priest Dec. 17, 1938; ord. titular bishop of Balanea and vicar apostolic of Keetmanshoop, Namibia, June 11, 1956.

Schmidt, Firmin M., O.F.M.Cap.: b. Oct. 12, 1918, Catherine, Kans.; educ. Catholic Univ. (Washington, D.C.); ord. priest June 2, 1946; app. prefect apostolic of Mendi, Papua New Guinea, Apr. 3, 1959; ord. titular bishop of Conana and first vicar apostolic of Mendi, Dec. 15, 1965; became first bishop of Mendi when vicariate apostolic was raised to a diocese, Nov. 15, 1966.

Schmidt, Mathias, O.S.B.: b. Apr. 21, 1931, Wortonville, Kans.; ord. priest May 30, 1957; missionary in Brazil; ord. titular bishop of Mutugenna and auxiliary bishop of Jatai, Brazil, Sept. 10, 1972; bishop of Rui Barbosa, Brazil, May 14, 1976.

Schmitt, Mark: b. Feb. 14, 1923, Algoma, Wis., educ. Salvatorian Seminary (St. Nazianz, Wis.), St. John's Seminary (Collegeville, Minn.); ord. priest (Green Bay) May 22, 1948; ord. titular bishop of Ceanannus Mor and auxiliary bishop of Green Bay, June 24, 1970; app. bishop of Marquette, Mar. 21, 1978, installed May 8, 1978.

Schmitz, Paul, O.F.M. Cap.: b. Dec. 4, 1943, Fond du Lac, Wis.; ord. priest Sept. 3, 1970; missionary in Nicaragua from 1970; superior of vice province of Capuchins in Central America (headquartered in Managua), 1982-84; ord. titular bishop of Elepla and auxiliary bishop of the vicariate apostolic of Bluefields, Nicaragua, Sept. 17, 1984.

Schoenherr, Walter J.: b. Feb. 28, 1920, Detroit, Mich.; educ. Sacred Heart Seminary (Detroit, Mich.), Mt. St. Mary Seminary (Norwood, O.); ord. priest (Detroit*) Oct. 27, 1945; ord. titular bishop of Timidana and auxiliary bishop of Detroit, May 1, 1968.

Schuck, James A., O.F.M.: b. Jan. 17, 1913, Treverton, Pa.; educ. St. Joseph's Seminary (Callicoon, N.Y.), St. Bonaventure's University (St. Bonaventure, N.Y.). Holy Name College

(Washington, D.C.); ord. priest June 11, 1940; ord. titular bishop of Avissa, Feb. 24, 1959 (resigned titular see May 26, 1978); prelate of Cristalandia, Brazil, 1959.

Schulte, Francis B.: b. Dec. 23, 1926, Philadelphia, Pa.; educ. St. Charles Borromeo Seminary (Overbrook, Pa.): ord. priest (Philadelphia*) May 10, 1952; ord. titular bishop of Afufenia and auxiliary bishop of Philadelphia, Aug. 12, 1981; app. bishop of Wheeling-Charleston, June 4, 1985.

Schuster, Eldon B.: b. Mar. 10, 1911, Calio, N. Dak.; educ. Loras College (Dubuque, Ia.), Catholic Univ. (Washington, D.C.), Oxford Univ. (England), St. Louis Univ. (St. Louis, Mo.); ord. priest (Great Falls) May 27, 1937; ord. titular bishop of Ambladaand auxiliary bishop of Great Falls, Mont., Dec. 21, 1961; app. bishop of Great Falls, Dec. 2, 1967, installed Jan. 23, 1968; resigned Dec. 28, 1977.

Setian, Nerses Mikail: b. Oct. 18,1918, Sebaste, Turkey; educ. Armenian Pontifical College and Gregorian Univ. (Rome); ord. priest Apr. 13, 1941, in Rome; ord. titular bishop of Ancira of the Armenians and first exarch of the apostolic exarchate for Armenian-Rite Catholics in Canada and the United States (see city New York), Dec. 5, 1981.

Shea, Francis R.: b. Dec. 4, 1913, Knoxville, Tenn.;˚ educ. St. Mary's Seminary (Baltimore, Md.), North American College (Rome), Peabody College (Nashville, Tenn.); ord. priest (Nashville) Mar. 19, 1939; ord. bishop of Evansville, Ind., Feb. 3, 1970.

Sheehan, Daniel E.: b. May 14, 1917, Emerson, Nebr.; educ. Creighton Univ. (Omaha, Nebr.), Kenrick Seminary (Webster Groves, Mo.), Catholic Univ. (Washington, D.C.): ord. priest (Omaha*) May 23, 1942; ord. titular bishop of Capsus and auxiliary bishop of Omaha, Mar. 19, 1964; app. archbishop of Omaha, installed Aug. 11, 1969.

Sheehan, Michael J.: b. July 9, 1939, Wichita, Kans.; educ. Assumption Seminary (San Antonio, Tex.), Gregorian Univ. and Lateran Univ. (Rome); ord. priest (Dallas) July 12, 1964; ord. first bishop of Lubbock, Tex., June 17, 1983.

Sheldon, Gilbert I.: b. Sept. 20, 1926, Cleveland, O.; educ. John Carroll Univ. and St. Mary Seminary (Cleveland, O.); ord. priest (Cleveland) Feb. 28, 1953; ord. titular bishop of Taparura and auxiliary bishop of Cleveland, June 11, 1976.

Shubsda, Thaddeus A.: b. Apr. 2, 1925, Los Angeles, Calif.; educ. St. John's Seminary (Camarillo, Calif.); ord. priest (Los Angeles*) Apr. 26, 1950; ord. titular bishop of Trau and auxiliary bishop of Los Angeles, Feb. 19, 1977; app. bishop of Monterey, June 1, 1982.

Sklba, Richard J.: b. Sept. 11, 1935, Racine, Wis.; educ. Old St. Francis Minor Seminary (Milwaukee, Wis.), North American College, Gregorian Univ., Pontifical Biblical Institute, Angelicum (Rome); ord. priest (Milwaukee*) Dec. 20, 1959; ord. titular bishop of Castra and auxiliary bishop of Milwaukee, Dec. 19, 1979.

Skylstad, William: b. Mar. 2, 1934, Omak, Wash.; educ. Pontifical College Josephinum (Worthington, Ohio), Washington State Univ. (Pullman, Wash.), Gonzaga Univ. (Spokane, Wash.); ord. priest (Spokane) May 21, 1960; ord. bishop of Yakima, May 12, 1977.

Smith, Philip F., O.M.I.: b. Oct. 16, 1924, Lowell, Mass.; ord. priest Oct. 29, 1950; ord. titular bishop of Lamfua and vicar apostolic of Jolo, Philippine Islands, Sept. 8, 1972; app. coadjutor archbishop of Cotabato, Philippines, April 11, 1979; archbishop of Cotabato, Mar. 14, 1980.

Snyder, John J.: b. Oct. 25, 1925, New York, N.Y.; educ. Cathedral College (Brooklyn, N.Y.), Immaculate Conception Seminary (Huntington, N.Y.); ord. priest (Brooklyn) June 9, 1951; ord. titular bishop of Forlimpopli and auxiliary bishop of Brooklyn, Feb. 2, 1973; app. bishop of St. Augustine, installed Dec. 5, 1979.

Soenneker, Henry J.: b. May 27, 1907, Melrose, Minn.; educ. Pontifical Josephinum College (Worthington, O.), Catholic Univ. (Washington, D.C.); ord. priest (St. Cloud) May 26, 1934; ord. bishop of Owensboro, Apr. 26, 1961; resigned June 30, 1982.

Soens, Lawrence D.: b. Aug. 26, 1926, Iowa City, Ia.; educ. Loras College (Dubuque, Ia.), St. Ambrose College (Davenport, Ia.), Kenrick Seminary (St. Louis, Mo.), Univ. of Iowa; ord. priest (Davenport) May 6, 1950; ord. bishop of Sioux City, Aug. 17, 1983.

Sowada, Alphonse A., O.S.C.: b. June 23, 1933, Avon, Minn.; educ. Holy Cross Scholasticate (Fort Wayne, Ind.), Catholic Univ. (Washington, D.C.), ord. priest May 31, 1958; missionary in Indonesia from 1958; ord. bishop of Agats, Indonesia, Nov. 23, 1969.

Speltz, George H.: b. May 29, 1912, Altura, Minn.; educ. St. Mary's College, St. Paul's Seminary (St. Paul, Minn.), Catholic Univ. (Washington, D.C.); ord. priest (St. Cloud) June 2, 1940; ord. titular bishop of Claneus and auxiliary bishop of Winona, Mar. 25, 1963; app. coadjutor bishop of St. Cloud, Apr. 4, 1966; bishop of St. Cloud, Jan. 31, 1968.

Speyrer, Jude: b. Apr. 14, 1929, Leonville, La.; educ. St. Joseph Seminary (Covington, La.), Notre Dame Seminary (New Orleans, La.), Gregorian Univ. (Rome), Univ. of Fribourg (Switzerland); ord. priest (Lafayette, La.) July 25, 1953; ord. first bishop of Lake Charles, La., Apr. 25, 1980.

Stafford, James Francis: b. July 26, 1932, Baltimore, Md.; educ. St. Mary's Seminary (Baltimore, Md.), North American College and Gregorian Univ. (Rome); ord. priest (Baltimore*) Dec. 15, 1957; ord. titular bishop of Respecta and auxiliary bishop of Baltimore, Feb. 29, 1976; app. bishop of Memphis, Nov. 17, 1982; app. archbishop of Denver, June 3, 1986, installed July 30, 1986.

Steib, J. (James) Terry, S.V.D.: b. May 17, 1940, Vacherie, La.; educ. Divine Word seminaries (Bay St. Louis, Miss., Conesus, N.Y., Techny, Ill.), Xavier Univ. (New Orleans, La.); ord. priest Jan. 6, 1967; ord. titular bishop of Fallaba and auxiliary bishop of St. Louis, Feb. 10, 1984.

Steinbock, John T.: b. July 16, 1937, Los Angeles, Calif.; educ. Los Angeles archdiocesan seminaries; ord. priest (Los Angeles*) May 1, 1963;

ord. titular bishop of Midila and auxiliary bishop of Orange, Calif., July 14, 1984.

Steiner, Kenneth Donald: b. Nov. 25, 1936, David City, Nebr.; educ. Mt. Angel Seminary (St. Benedict, Ore.), St. Thomas Seminary (Seattle, Wash.); ord. priest (Portland,* Ore.) May 19, 1962; ord. titular bishop of Avensa and auxiliary bishop of Portland, Ore., Mar. 2, 1978.

Straling, Phillip F.: b. Apr. 25, 1933, San Bernardino, Calif.; educ. Immaculate Heart Seminary, St. Francis Seminary, Univ. of San Diego and San Diego State University (San Diego, Calif.), North American College (Rome); ord. priest (San Diego) Mar. 19, 1959; ord. first bishop of San Bernardino, Nov. 6, 1978.

Strecker, Ignatius J.: b. Nov. 23, 1917, Spearville, Kans.; educ. St. Benedict's College (Atchison, Kans.), Kenrick Seminary (Webster Groves, Mo.), Catholic Univ. (Washington, D.C.); ord. priest (Wichita) Dec. 19, 1942; ord. bishop of Springfield-Cape Girardeau, Mo., June 20, 1962; archbishop of Kansas City, Kans., Oct. 28, 1969.

Sullivan, James S.: b. July 23, 1929, Kalamazoo, Mich.; educ. Sacred Heart Seminary (Detroit, Mich.), St. John Provincial Seminary (Plymouth, Mich.); ord. priest (Lansing) June 4, 1955; ord. titular bishop of Siccessi and auxiliary bishop of Lansing, Sept. 21, 1972; app. bishop of Fargo, Apr. 2, 1985; installed May 30, 1985.

Sullivan, John J.: b. July 5, 1920, Horton, Kans.; educ. Kenrick Seminary (St. Louis, Mo.); ord. priest (Oklahoma City*) Sept. 23, 1944; vice-president of Catholic Church Extension Society and national director of Extension Lay Volunteers, 1961-68; ord. bishop of Grand Island, Sept. 19, 1972; app. bishop of Kansas City-St. Joseph, June 27, 1977, installed Aug. 17, 1977.

Sullivan, Joseph M.: b. Mar. 23, 1930, Brooklyn, N.Y.; educ. Immaculate Conception Seminary (Huntington, N.Y.), Fordham Univ. (New York); ord. priest (Brooklyn) June 2, 1956; ord. titular bishop of Suliana and auxiliary bishop of Brooklyn, Nov. 24, 1980.

Sullivan, Walter F.: b. June 10, 1928, Washington, D.C.; educ. St. Mary's Seminary (Baltimore, Md.), Catholic Univ. (Washington, D.C.); ord. priest (Richmond) May 9, 1953; ord. titular bishop of Selsea and auxiliary bishop of Richmond, Va., Dec. 1, 1970; app. bishop of Richmond, June 4, 1974.

Sulyk, Stephen: b. Oct. 2, 1924, Balnycia, Western Ukraine; migrated to U.S. 1948; educ. Ukrainian Catholic Seminary of the Holy Spirit (Hirschberg, Germany), St. Josaphat's Seminary and Catholic Univ. (Washington, D.C.); ord. priest (Philadelphia,* Byzantine Rite) June 14, 1952; ord. archbishop of the Ukrainian-Rite archeparcy of Philadelphia, Mar. 1, 1981.

Symons, J. Keith: b. Oct. 14, 1932, Champion, Mich.; educ. St. Thomas Seminary (Bloomfield, Conn.), St. Mary Seminary (Baltimore, Md.); ord. priest (St. Augustine) May 18, 1958; ord. titular bishop of Sigus and auxiliary bishop of St. Petersburg, Mar. 19, 1981; app. bishop of Pensacola-Tallahassee, Oct. 4, 1983, installed Nov. 8, 1983.

Szoka, Edmund C.: b. Sept. 14, 1927, Grand

Rapids, Mich.; educ. Sacred Heart Seminary (Detroit, Mich.), St. John's Provincial Seminary (Plymouth, Mich.), Lateran Univ. (Rome); ord. priest (Marquette) June 5, 1954; ord. first bishop of Gaylord, Mich., July 20, 1971; app. archbishop of Detroit, Mar. 28, 1981, installed May 17, 1981.

T

Tafoya, Arthur N.: b. Mar. 2, 1933, Alameda, N.M.; educ. St. Thomas Seminary (Denver, Colo.), Conception Seminary (Conception, Mo.); ord. priest (Santa Fe*) May 12, 1962; ord. bishop of Pueblo, Sept. 10, 1980.

Tanner, Paul F.: b. Jan. 15, 1905, Peoria, Ill.; educ. Marquette Univ. (Milwaukee, Wis.), Kenrick Seminary (Webster Groves, Mo.), St. Francis Seminary (Milwaukee, Wis.), Catholic Univ. (Washington, D.C.): ord. priest (Milwaukee*) May 30, 1931; assistant director NCWC Youth Department 1940-45; assistant general secretary of NCWC 1945-58; general secretary of NCWC (now USCC) 1958-68; ord. titular bishop of Lamasba, Dec. 21, 1965; bishop of St. Augustine, Mar. 27, 1968; resigned Apr. 21, 1979.

Tawil, Joseph: b. Dec. 25, 1913, Damascus, Syria; ord. priest July 20, 1936; ord. titular archbishop of Mira and patriarchal vicar for eparchy of Damascus of the Patriarchate of Antioch for the Melkites, Jan. 1, 1960; apostolic exarch for faithful of the Melkite rite in the U.S., Oct. 31, 1969; app. first eparch with personal title of archbishop when exarchate was raised to eparchy, July 15, 1976; title of see changed to Newton, 1977.

Timlin, James C.: b. Aug. 5, 1927, Scranton, Pa.; educ. St. Charles College (Catonsville, Md.), St. Mary's Seminary (Baltimore, Md.), North American College (Rome); ord. priest (Scranton) July 16, 1951; ord. titular bishop of Gunugo and auxiliary bishop of Scranton, Sept. 21, 1976; app. bishop of Scranton, Apr. 24, 1984.

Topel, Bernard J.: b. May 31, 1903, Bozeman, Mont.; educ. Carroll College (Helena, Mont.), Grand Seminary (Montreal), Catholic Univ. (Washington, D.C.), Harvard Univ. (Cambridge, Mass.), Notre Dame Univ. (Notre Dame, Ind.); ord. priest (Helena) June 7, 1927; ord. titular bishop of Binda and coadjutor bishop of Spokane, Sept. 21, 1955; bishop of Spokane, Sept. 25, 1955; retired Apr. 11, 1978.

Trautman, Donald W.: b. June 24, 1936, Buffalo, N.Y.; educ. Our Lady of Angels Seminary (Niagara Falls, N.Y.), Theology Faculty (Innsbruck, Austria), Pontifical Biblical Institute (Rome), Catholic Univ. (Washington, D.C.); ord. priest (Buffalo) 1962, in Innsbruck; ord. titular bishop of Sassura and auxiliary of Buffalo, 1985.

Treinen, Sylvester: b. Nov. 19, 1917, Donnelly, Minn.; educ. Crosier Seminary (Onamia, Minn.), St. Paul Seminary (St. Paul, Minn.); ord. priest (Bismarck) June 11, 1946; ord. bishop of Boise, July 25, 1962.

Tschoepe, Thomas: b. Dec. 17, 1915, Pilot Point, Tex.; educ. Pontifical College Josephinum (Worthington, O.); ord. priest (Dallas) May 30, 1943; ord. bishop of San Angelo, Tex., Mar. 9, 1966; app. bishop of Dallas, Tex., Aug. 27, 1969.

U-V

Untener, Kenneth E.: b. Aug. 3, 1937, Detroit, Mich.; educ. Sacred Heart Seminary (Detroit, Mich.), St. John's Provincial Seminary (Plymouth, Mich.), Gregorian Univ. (Rome); ord. priest (Detroit*) June 1, 1963; ord. bishop of Saginaw, Nov. 24, 1980.

Unterkoefler, Ernest L.: b. Aug. 17, 1917, Philadelphia, Pa.; educ. Catholic Univ. (Washington, D.C.); ord. priest (Richmond) May 18, 1944; ord. titular bishop of Latopolis and auxiliary bishop of Richmond, Va., Feb. 22, 1962; app. bishop of Charleston, Dec. 12, 1964, installed Feb. 22, 1965.

Valero, René A.: b. Aug. 15, 1930, New York, N.Y.; educ. Cathedral College, Immaculate Conception Seminary (Huntington, N.Y.), Fordham Univ. (New York); ord. priest (Brooklyn) June 2, 1956; ord. titular bishop of Turris Vicus and auxiliary bishop of Brooklyn, Nov. 24, 1980.

Vath, Joseph G.: b. Mar. 12, 1918, New Orleans, La.; educ. Notre Dame Seminary (New Orleans, La.), Catholic Univ. (Washington, D.C.); ord. priest (New Orleans*) June 7, 1941; ord. titular bishop of Novaliciana and auxiliary bishop of Mobile-Birmingham, May 26, 1966; app. first bishop of Birmingham, Oct. 8, 1969.

Vaughan, Austin B.: b. Sept. 27, 1927, New York, N.Y.; educ. North American College and Gregorian Univ. (Rome), ord. priest (New York*) Dec. 8, 1951; pres. Catholic Theological Society of America, 1967; rector of St. Joseph's Seminary (Dunwoodie, N.Y.), 1973; ord. titular bishop of Cluain Iraird and auxiliary bishop of New York, June 29, 1977.

Veigle, Adrian J.M., T.O.R.: b. Sept. 15, 1912, Lilly, Pa.; educ. St. Francis College (Loretto, Pa.), Pennsylvania State College; ord. priest May 22, 1937; ord. titular bishop of Gigthi June 9, 1966 (resigned titular see May 26, 1978); prelate of Borba, Brazil, 1966.

Vlazny, John G.: b. Feb. 22, 1937, Chicago, Ill.; educ. Quigley Preparatory Seminary (Chicago, Ill.), St. Mary of the Lake Seminary (Mundelein, Ill.), Gregorian Univ. (Rome), Univ. of Michigan, Loyola Univ. (Chicago, Ill.); ord. priest (Chicago*) Dec. 20, 1961; ord. titular bishop of Stagno and auxiliary bishop of Chicago, Dec. 13, 1983; episcopal vicar.

Vonesh, Raymond J.: b. Jan. 25, 1916, Chicago, Ill.; educ. St. Mary of the Lake Seminary (Mundelein, Ill.). Gregorian Univ. (Rome); ord. priest (Chicago*) May 3, 1941; ord. titular bishop of Vanariona and auxiliary bishop of Joliet, Ill., Apr. 3, 1968.

W

Waldschmidt, Paul E., C.S.C.: b. Jan. 7, 1920, Evansville, Ind.; educ. Notre Dame Univ. (Notre Dame, Ind.), Holy Cross College (Washington, D.C.), Laval Univ. (Quebec), Angelicum (Rome), Louvain (Belgium), Sorbonne (Paris), ord. priest June 24, 1946; president University of Portland, 1962-77; ord. titular bishop of Citium and auxiliary bishop of Portland, Ore., Mar. 2, 1978.

Walsh, Daniel Francis: b. Oct. 2, 1937, San Francisco, Calif.; educ. St. Joseph Seminary (Mountain View, Calif.), St. Patrick Seminary (Menlo Park, Calif.) Catholic Univ. (Washington, D.C.); ord. priest (San Francisco*) Mar. 30, 1963; ord.titular bishop of Tigia and auxiliary bishop of San Francisco, Sept. 24, 1981.

Walsh, Nicolas E.: b. Oct. 20, 1916, Burnsville, Minn.; educ. St. Paul Seminary (St. Paul, Minn.), Catholic Univ. (Washington, D.C.), Pontifical Palafoxianum Seminary (Puebla, Mexico), Register College of Journalism (Denver, Colo.); ord. priest (Boise) June 6, 1942; first editor of *Idaho Register;* diocesan vicar for Mexican Americans; ord. bishop of Yakima, Oct. 28, 1974; app. titular bishop of Bolsena and auxiliary bishop of Seattle, Aug. 10, 1976; retired Sept. 6, 1983. Bishop emeritus of Yakima.

Ward, John J.: b. Sept. 28, 1920, Los Angeles, Calif.; educ. St. John's Seminary (Camarillo, Calif.), Catholic Univ. (Washington, D.C.); ord. priest (Los Angeles*) May 4, 1946; ord. titular bishop of Bria and auxiliary of Los Angeles, Dec. 12, 1963.

Watson, Alfred M.: b. July 11, 1907, Erie, Pa.; educ. St. Mary's Seminary (Baltimore, Md.), Catholic Univ. (Washington, D.C.); ord. priest (Erie) May 10, 1934; ord. titular bishop of Nationa and auxiliary bishop of Erie, June 29, 1965; app. bishop of Erie, 1969, installed May 13, 1969; resigned July 16, 1982.

Watters, Loras J.: b. Oct. 14, 1915, Dubuque, Ia.; educ. Loras College (Dubuque, Ia.), Gregorian Univ. (Rome), Catholic Univ. (Washington, D.C.); ord. priest (Dubuque*) June 7, 1941; ord. titular bishop of Fidoloma and auxiliary bishop of Dubuque, Aug. 26, 1965; bishop of Winona, installed Mar. 13, 1969.

Watty Urquidi, Ricardo, M.Sp.S.: b. July 16, 1938, San Diego, Calif.; ord. priest June 8, 1968; ord. titular bishop of Macomedes and auxiliary bishop of Mexico City, July 19, 1980.

Weakland, Rembert G., O.S.B.: b. Apr. 2, 1927, Patton, Pa.; joined Benedictines, 1945; ord. priest June 24, 1951; abbot-primate of Benedictine Confederation, 1967-77; ord. archbishop of Milwaukee, Nov. 8, 1977.

Weigand, William K.: b. May 23, 1937, Bend, Ore.; educ. Mt. Angel Seminary (St. Benedict, Ore.), St. Edward's Seminary and St. Thomas Seminary (Kenmore, Wash.); ord. priest (Boise) May 25, 1963; ord. bishop of Salt Lake City, Nov. 17, 1980.

Weitzel, John Quinn, M.M.: b. 1928, Chicago, Ill.; ord. priest 1955; app. bishop of Samoa-Pago Pago, American Samoa, July 15, 1986.

Welsh, Lawrence H.: b. Feb. 1, 1935, Winton, Wyo.; educ. Univ. of Wyoming (Laramie, Wyo.), St. John's Seminary (Collegeville, Minn.), Catholic Univ. (Washington, D.C.); ord. priest (Rapid City) May 26, 1962; ord. bishop of Spokane, Dec. 14, 1978.

Welsh, Thomas J.: b. Dec. 20, 1921, Weatherly, Pa.; educ. St. Charles Borromeo Seminary (Philadelphia, Pa.), Catholic Univ. (Washington, D.C.); ord. priest (Philadelphia*) May 30, 1946; ord. titular bishop of Scattery Island and auxiliary bish-

op of Philadelphia, Apr. 2, 1970; app. first bishop of Arlington, Va., June 4, 1974, installed Aug. 13, 1974; app. bishop of Allentown, Feb. 8, 1983, installed Mar. 21, 1983.

Whealon, John F.: b. Jan. 15, 1921, Barberton, O.; educ. St. Charles College (Catonsville, Md.), St. Mary's Seminary (Cleveland, O.); ord. priest (Cleveland) May 26, 1945; ord. titular bishop of Andrapa and auxiliary bishop of Cleveland, July 6, 1961; app. bishop of Erie, Dec. 9, 1966, installed Mar. 7, 1967; archbishop of Hartford, installed Mar. 19, 1969.

Whelan, Robert L., S.J.: b. Apr. 16, 1912, Wallace, Ida.; educ. St. Michael's College (Spokane, Wash.), Alma College (Alma, Calif.); ord. priest June 17, 1944; ord. titular bishop of Sicilibba and coadjutor bishop of Fairbanks, Alaska, with right of succession, Feb. 22, 1968; bishop of Fairbanks, Nov. 30, 1968; retired June 1, 1985.

Wildermuth, Augustine F., S.J.: b. Feb. 20, 1904, St. Louis, Mo.; educ. St. Stanislaus Seminary (Florissant, Mo.), St. Michael's Scholasticate (Spokane, Wash.), Sacred Heart College (Shembaganur, S. India), St. Mary's College (Kurseong, India), Gregorian Univ. (Rome); entered Society of Jesus, 1922; ord. priest July 25, 1935; ord. bishop of Patna, India, Oct. 28, 1947; retired Mar. 6, 1980.

Williams, James Kendrick: b. Sept. 5, 1936, Larue Co., Ky.; educ. St. Mary's College (St. Mary's, Ky.), St. Maur's School of Theology (South Union, Ky.); ord. priest (Louisville*) May 25, 1963; app. titular bishop of Catula and auxiliary bishop of Covington, Apr. 24, 1984.

Wirz, George O.: b. Jan. 17, 1929, Monroe, Wis.; educ. St. Francis Seminary and Marquette Univ. (Milwaukee, Wis.); Cath. Univ. (Washington, D.C.); ord. priest (Madison) May 31, 1952; ord. titular bishop of Municipa and auxiliary bishop of Madison, Mar. 9, 1978.

Wuerl, Donald: b. Nov. 12, 1940, Pittsburgh, Pa.; educ. Catholic Univ. of America (Washington, D.C.), North American College, Angelicum (Rome); ord. priest (Pittsburgh) Dec. 17, 1966, in Rome; ord. titular bishop of Rosemarkie and auxiliary bishop of Seattle, Jan. 6, 1986, in Rome.

Wycislo, Aloysius John: b. June 17, 1908, Chicago, Ill.; educ. St. Mary's Seminary (Mundelein, Ill.), Catholic Univ. (Washington, D.C.); ord. priest (Chicago*) Apr. 4, 1934; ord. titular bishop of Stadia and auxiliary bishop of Chicago, Dec. 21, 1960; app. bishop of Green Bay, installed Apr. 16, 1968; resigned May 10, 1983.

Z

Zayek, Francis: b. Oct. 18, 1920, Manzanillo, Cuba; ord. priest Mar. 17, 1946; ord. titular bishop of Callinicum and auxiliary bishop for Maronites in Brazil, Aug. 5, 1962; named apostolic exarch for Maronites in U.S., with headquarters in Detroit; installed June 11, 1966; first eparch of St. Maron of Detroit, Mar. 25, 1972; see transferred to Brooklyn, June 27, 1977; given personal title of archbishop, Dec. 22, 1982.

Zuroweste, Albert R.: b. Apr. 26, 1901, East St. Louis, Ill.; educ. St. Francis College (Quincy, Ill.), Kenrick Seminary (Webster Groves, Mo.), Catholic Univ. (Washington, D.C.); ord. priest (Belleville) June 8, 1924; ord. bishop of Belleville, Jan. 29, 1948; retired Oct. 29, 1976.

U.S. BISHOPS OVERSEAS

Cardinal William W. Baum, prefect of the Congregation for Catholic Education; Cardinal Myroslav Ivan Lubachivsky, archbishop of Lwow and major archbishop of Ukrainians; Archbishop Ambrose De Paoli, apostolic pro-nuncio to Sri Lanka; Archbishop John P. Foley, president of the Pontifical Commission for Social Communications; Bishop Ladislaus Iranyi, Sch. P., pastoral care of Hungarian Catholics living outside of Hungary; Archbishop Paul C. Marcinkus, president of Institute for Works of Religion (Vatican Bank) and pro-president of Pontifical Commission for the State of Vatian City; Archbishop Justin Rigali, president of Pontifical Ecclesiastical Academy.

(See also Missionary Bishops.)

BISHOP-BROTHERS

(The asterisk indicates brothers who were bishops at the same time.)

There have been nine pairs of brother-bishops in the history of the U.S. hierarchy.

Living: Francis T. Hurley,* archbishop of Anchorage and Mark J. Hurley,* bishop emeritus of Santa Rosa.

Deceased: Francis Blanchet* of Oregon City (Portland) and Augustin Blanchet* of Walla Walla; John S. Foley of Detroit and Thomas P. Foley of Chicago; Francis P. Kenrick,* apostolic administrator of Philadelphia, bishop of Philadelphia and Baltimore, and Peter R. Kenrick* of St. Louis; Matthias C. Lenihan of Great Falls and Thomas M. Lenihan of Cheyenne; James O'Connor, vicar apostolic of Nebraska and bishop of Omaha, and Michael O'Connor of Pittsburgh and Erie; Jeremiah F. and John W. Shanahan, both of Harrisburg; Sylvester J. Espelage, O.F.M.,* of Wuchang, China, who died 10 days after the ordination of his brother, Bernard T. Espelage,* O.F.M., of Gallup; Coleman F. Carroll* of Miami and Howard Carroll* of Altoona-Johnstown.

RETIRED U.S. PRELATES

Information, as of Aug. 15, 1986, includes name of the prelate and see held at the time of retirement or resignation; archbishops are indicated by an asterisk. Most of the prelates listed below resigned their sees because of age in accordance with church law. See Index: Biographies of American Bishops.

Forms of address of retired residential prelates (unless they have a titular see): *Archbishop or Bishop Emeritus of* (last see held); *Former Archbishop or Bishop of* (last see held).

Richard H. Ackerman, C.S.Sp. (Covington), George W. Ahr (Trenton), Reginald Arliss, C.P. (Marbel, Philippines, prelate), Michael J. Begley (Charlotte), John H. Boccella, T.O.R.* (Izmir, Turkey), Ernest B. Boland, O.P. (Multan, Pakistan), Edwin B. Broderick (Albany), Joseph Brunini (Jackson), James C. Burke, O.P. (Chim-

bote, Peru, prelate), Charles A. Buswell (Pueblo), James J. Byrne* (Dubuque), Cardinal John Carberry* (St. Louis), John J. Cassata (Fort Worth), Harry A. Clinch (Monterey), John E. Cohill, S.V.D. (Goroka, Papua New Guinea), James L. Connolly (Fall River), Thomas Connolly* (Seattle), William M. Cosgrove (Belleville), Arnold R. Cotey, S.D.S. (Nachingwea, Tanzania), William E. Cousins* (Milwaukee), Augustine Danglmayr (Ft. Worth, auxiliary), Nicholas D'Antonio, O.F.M. (Olancho, Honduras).

James P. Davis* (Santa Fè), Cardinal John F. Dearden* (Detroit), Antanas L. Deksnys (Lavellum, titular see), Michael J. Dempsey, O.P. (Sokoto, Nigeria), Joseph P. Denning (Brooklyn, auxiliary), Frederick A. Donaghy, M.M. (Wuchow, China), Hugh A. Donohoe (Fresno), John A. Donovan (Toledo), Thomas J. Drury (Corpus Christi), Clarence J. Duhart, C.SS.R. (Udon Thani, Thailand), Joseph A. Durick (Nashville), Nicholas T. Elko* (Cincinnati, auxiliary), J. Lennox Federal (Salt Lake City), Bernard J. Flanagan (Worcester), John B. Franz (Peoria), Frederick W. Freking (La Crosse), Philip J. Furlong (Military Vicariate, auxiliary).

Raymond J. Gallagher (Lafayette, Ind.), Hugo Gerbermann, M.M. (San Antonio, auxiliary), Peter L. Gerety* (Newark), James J. Gerrard (Fall River, auxiliary), Ignatius T. Glennie, S.J. (Trincomalee-Batticaloa, Sri Lanka), Lawrence P. Graves (Alexandria-Shreveport), Lawrence Graziano, O.F.M. (San Miguel, El Salvador), Charles P. Greco (Alexandria), Francis J. Green (Tucson), Frank J. Greteman (Sioux City), Andrew G. Grutka (Gary).

Hilary B. Hacker (Bismarck), George A. Hammes (Superior), Edward Harper, C.SS.R. (St. Thomas, V.I.), Vincent M. Harris (Austin), Charles H. Helmsing (Kansas City-St. Joseph), Edward J. Herrmann (Columbus), Edward G. Hettinger (Columbus, auxiliary), Vincent J. Hines (Norwich), Lambert A. Hoch (Sioux Falls), Robert L. Hodapp, S.J. (Belize), Joseph L. Hogan (Rochester), Mark J. Hurley (Santa Rosa), Robert F. Joyce (Burlington), Arthur H. Krawczak (Detroit, auxiliary), Vincent M. Leonard (Pittsburgh), George E. Lynch (Raleigh, auxiliary).

J. Carroll McCormick (Scranton), William McDonald (San Francisco, auxiliary), Thomas J. McDonough* (Louisville), John J. McEleney, S.J.* (Kingston, Jamaica), William E. McManus (Fort Wayne-South Bend), Joseph H. McShea (Allentown), John J. Maguire* (New York, coadjutor), David M. Maloney (Wichita), Cardinal Timothy Manning* (Los Angeles), Alfred Mendez, C.S.C. (Arecibo, P.R.), William J. Moran (Military Vicariate, delegate), John L. Morkovsky (Galveston-Houston).

Louis La Ravoire Morrow, S.D.B. (Krishnagar, India), Charles R. Mulrooney (Brooklyn, auxiliary), T. Austin Murphy (Baltimore, auxiliary), Knute Ansgar Nelson, O.S.B. (Stockholm, Sweden), Hubert M. Newell (Cheyenne), Cardinal Patrick O'Boyle* (Washington, D.C.).

Martin J. O'Connor* (Prefect Emeritus, Pontifical Commission for Social Communications),

John L. Paschang (Grand Island), George H. Pearce, S.M.* (Suva, Fiji Islands), Henry A. Pinger, O.F.M. (Chowtsun, China), Cornelius M. Power* (Portland, Ore.), Ernest J. Primeau (Manchester), Leo A. Pursley (Fort Wayne-South Bend), Joseph M. Raya* (Acre), Joseph W. Regan, M.M. (Tagum, P.I., Prelate), Francis F. Reh (Saginaw).

Thomas F. Reilly, C.SS.R. (San Juan de la Maguana, Dominican Republic), John J. Rudin, M.M. (Musoma, Tanzania), John J. Russell (Richmond), James C. Ryan, O.F.M. (Santarem, Brazil), John J. Scanlan (Honolulu), Alphonse Schladweiler (New Ulm), Eldon B. Schuster (Great Falls).

Henry J. Soenneker (Owensboro), Paul F. Tanner (St. Augustine), Bernard J. Topel (Spokane), Nicolas Walsh (Yakima), Alfred M. Watson (Erie), Robert L. Whelan (Fairbanks), Augustine Wildermuth, S.J. (Patna, India), Aloysius J. Wycislo (Green Bay), Albert R. Zuroweste (Belleville).

AMERICAN BISHOPS OF THE PAST

Information includes: dates; place of birth if outside the U.S.; date of ordination to the priesthood; titular see in parentheses of bishops who were not ordinaries; indication, where applicable, of date of resignation.

Abbreviation code: abp., archbishop; bp., bishop; v.a., vicar apostolic; aux., auxiliary bishop; coad., coadjutor; ord., ordained; res., resigned.

A

Adrian, William L. (1883-1972): ord. Apr. 15, 1911; bp. Nashville, 1936-69 (res.).

Albers, Joseph (1891-1965): ord. June 17, 1916; aux. Cincinnati (Lunda), 1929-37; first bp. Lansing, 1937-65.

Alemany, Joseph Sadoc, O.P. (1814-88): b. Spain; ord. Mar. 11, 1837; bp. Monterey, 1850-53; first abp. San Francisco, 1853-84 (res.).

Alencastre, Stephen P., SS.CC. (1876-1940): b. Madeira; ord. Apr. 5, 1902; coad. v.a. Sandwich Is. (Arabissus), 1924-36; v.a. Sandwich (Hawaiian) Is., 1936-40.

Alerding, Herman J. (1845-1924): b. Germany; ord. Sept. 22, 1869; bp. Fort Wayne, 1900-24.

Allen, Edward P. (1853-1926): ord. Dec. 17, 1881; bp. Mobile, 1897-1926.

Alter, Karl J. (1885-1977): ord. June 4, 1910; bp. Toledo, 1931-50; abp. Cincinnati, 1950-69 (res.).

Althoff, Henry (1873-1947): ord. July 26, 1902; bp. Belleville, 1914-47.

Amat, Thaddeus, C.M. (1811-78): b. Spain; ord. Dec. 23, 1837; bp. Monterey (title changed to Monterey-Los Angeles, 1859), 1854-78.

Anderson, Joseph (1865-1927): ord. May 20, 1892; aux. Boston (Myrina), 1909-27.

Anglim, Robert, C.SS.R. (1922-73): ord. Jan. 6, 1948; prelate Coari, Brazil (Gaguari), 1966-73.

Annabring, Joseph (1900-59): b. Hungary; ord. May 3, 1927; bp. Superior, 1954-59.

Appelhans, Stephen A., S.V.D. (1905-51): ord. May 5, 1932; v.a. East New Guinea (Catula), 1948-51.

Armstrong, Robert J. (1884-1957): ord. Dec. 10, 1910; bp. Sacramento, 1929-57.

Arnold, William R. (1881-1965): ord. June 13, 1908; delegate of U.S. military vicar (Phocaea), 1945-65.

Atkielski, Roman R. (1898-1969): ord. May 30, 1931; aux. Milwaukee (Stobi), 1947-69.

B

Babcock, Allen J. (1898-1969): ord. Mar. 7, 1925; aux. Detroit (Irenopolis), 1947-54; bp. Grand Rapids, 1954-69.

Bacon, David W. (1815-74): ord. Dec. 13, 1838; first bp. Portland, Me., 1855-74.

Baldwin, Vincent J. (1907-79): ord. July 26, 1931; aux. Rockville Centre (Bencenna), 1962-79.

Baltes, Peter J. (1827-86): b. Germany; ord. May 31, 1852; bp. Alton (now Springfield), Ill., 1870-86.

Baraga, Frederic: See Index.

Barron, Edward (1801-54): b. Ireland; ord. 1829; v.a. The Two Guineas (Constantina), 1842-44 (res.) missionary in U.S.

Barry, John (1799-1859): b. Ireland; ord. Sept. 24, 1825; bp. Savannah, 1857-59.

Barry, Patrick J. (1868-1940): b. Ireland; ord. June 9, 1895; bp. St. Augustine, 1922-40.

Bartholome, Peter W. (1893-1982): ord. June 12, 1917; coad. St. Cloud (Lete), 1942-53; bp. St. Cloud, 1953-68 (res.).

Baumgartner, Apollinaris, O.F.M. Cap. (1899-1970): ord. May 30, 1926; v.a. Guam (Joppa), 1945-65; first bp. Agana, Guam, 1965-70.

Bayley, James Roosevelt (1814-77): convert, 1842; ord. Mar. 2, 1843; first bp. Newark, 1853-72; abp. Baltimore, 1872-77.

Bazin John S. (1796-1848): b. France; ord. July 22, 1822; bp. Vincennes (now Indianapolis), 1847-48.

Beaven, Thomas D. (1851-1920): ord. Dec. 18, 1875; bp. Springfield, Mass., 1892-1920.

Becker, Thomas A. (1832-99): ord. June 18, 1859; first bp. Wilmington, 1868-86; bp. Savannah, 1886-99.

Beckman, Francis J. (1875-1948): ord. June 20, 1902; bp. Lincoln, 1924-30; abp. Dubuque, 1930-46 (res.).

Begin, Floyd L. (1902-77): ord, July 31, 1927; aux. Cleveland (Sala), 1947-62; first bp. Oakland, 1962-77.

Bell, Alden J. (1904-82): b. Canada; ord. May 14, 1932; aux. Los Angeles (Rhodopolis), 1956-62; bp. Sacramento, 1962-79 (res.).

Benincasa, Pius A. (1913-86): ord. Mar. 27, 1937; aux. Buffalo (Buruni), 1964-86.

Benjamin, Cletus J. (1909-61): ord. Dec. 8, 1935; aux. Philadelphia (Binda), 1960-61.

Bennett, John G. (1891-1957): ord. June 27, 1914; first bp. Lafayette, Ind. 1944-57.

Bergan, Gerald T. (1892-1972): ord. Oct. 28, 1915; bp. Des Moines, 1934-48; abp. Omaha, 1948-69 (res.).

Bidawid, Thomas M. (1910-71): b. Iraq; ord. May 15, 1935; U.S. citizen; first abp. Ahwaz, Iran

(Chaldean Rite), 1968-70; Chaldean patriarchal vicar for United Arab Republic, 1970-71.

Binz, Leo (1900-79): ord. Mar. 15, 1924; coad. bp., Winona (Pinara); coad. abp. Dubuque (Silyum), 1954-61; abp. Dubuque, 1949-54; abp. St. Paul and Minneapolis, 1962-75 (res.).

Biskup, George J. (1911-79): ord. Mar. 19, 1937; aux. Dubuque (Hemeria), 1957-65; bp. Des Moines, 1965-67; coad. abp. Indianapolis (Tamalluma), 1969-70; abp. Indianapolis, 1970-79 (res.).

Blanc, Anthony (1792-1860): b. France; ord. July 22, 1816; bp. New Orleans, 1835-50; first abp. New Orleans, 1850-60.

Blanchet (brothers): **Augustin M.** (1797-1887): b. Canada; ord. June 3, 1821; bp. Walla Walla, 1846-50; first bp. Nesqually (now Seattle), 1850-79 (res.). **Francis N.** (1795-1883): b. Canada; ord. July 19, 1819; v.a. Oregon Territory (Philadelphia, Adrasus), 1843-46; first abp. Oregon City (now Portland), 1846-80 (res.).

Blanchette, Romeo R. (1913-82): ord. Apr. 3, 1937; aux. Joliet (Maxita), 1965-66; bp. Joliet, 1966-79 (res.).

Blenk, James H., S.M. (1856-1917): b. Germany; ord. Aug. 16, 1885; bp. San Juan, 1899-1906; abp. New Orleans, 1906-17.

Boardman, John J. (1894-1978): ord. May 21, 1921; aux. Brooklyn (Gunela), 1952-77 (res.).

Boeynaems, Libert H., SS.CC. (1857-1926): b. Belgium; ord. Sept. 11, 1881; v.a. Sandwich (Hawaiian) Is. (Zeugma), 1903-26.

Bohachevsky, Constantine (1884-1961): b. Austrian Galicia; ord. Jan. 31, 1909; ap. ex. Ukrainian Byzantine Catholics in U.S. (Amisus), 1924-58; first metropolitan of Byzantine Rite archeparchy of Philadelphia, 1958-61.

Boileau, George, S.J. (1912-65): ord. June 13, 1948; coad. bp. Fairbanks (Ausuccura), 1964-65.

Bokenfohr, John, O.M.I. (1903-82): ord. July 11, 1927; bp. Kimberley, S. Africa, 1963-74 (res.).

Boland, Thomas A. (1896-1979): ord. Dec. 23, 1922; aux. Newark (Irina), 1940-47; bp. Paterson, 1947-52; abp. Newark, 1953-74 (res.).

Bona, Stanislaus (1888-1967): ord. Nov. 1, 1912; bp. Grand Island, 1932-44; coad. bp. Green Bay (Mela), 1944-45; bp. Green Bay, 1945-67.

Bonacum, Thomas (1847-1911): b. Ireland; ord. June 18, 1870; first bp. Lincoln, 1887-1911.

Borgess, Caspar H. (1826-90): b. Germany; ord. Dec. 8, 1848; coad. bp. and ap. admin. Detroit (Calydon), 1870-71; bp. Detroit, 1871-87 (res.).

Bourgade, Peter (1845-1908): b. France; ord. Nov. 30, 1869; v.a. Arizona (Thaumacus), 1885-97; first bp. Tucson, 1897-99; abp. Santa Fe, 1899-1908.

Boylan, John J. (1889-1953): ord. July 28, 1915; bp. Rockford, 1943-53.

Boyle, Hugh C. (1873-1950): ord. July 2, 1898; bp. Pittsburgh, 1921-50.

Bradley, Denis (1846-1903): b. Ireland; ord. June 3, 1871; first bp. Manchester, 1884-1903.

Brady, John (1842-1910): b. Ireland; ord. Dec. 4, 1864; aux. Boston (Alabanda), 1891-1910.

Brady, Matthew F. (1893-1959): ord. June 10, 1916; bp. Burlington, 1938-44; bp. Manchester, 1944-59.

Brady, William O. (1899-1961); ord. Dec. 21,

1923; bp. Sioux Falls, 1939-56; coad. abp. St. Paul (Selymbria), June-Oct. 1956; abp. St. Paul, 1956-61.

Brennan, Andrew J. (1877-1956): ord. Dec. 17, 1904; aux. Scranton (Thapsus), 1923-26; bp. Richmond, 1926-45 (res.).

Brennan, Francis J. (1894-1968): ord. Apr. 3, 1920; judge (1940-59) and dean (1959-67) of Roman Rota; ord. bp. 1967; cardinal 1967.

Brennan, Thomas F. (1853-1916): b. Ireland; ord. July 14, 1880; first bp. Dallas, 1981-93; aux. St. John's, Newfoundland (Usula), 1893-1905 (res.).

Broderick, Bonaventure (1868-1943): ord. July 26, 1896; aux. Havana, Cuba (Juliopolis), 1903-05 (res.).

Brondel, John B. (1842-1903): b. Belgium; ord. Dec. 17, 1864; bp. Vancouver Is., 1879-84; first bp. Helena, 1884-1903.

Brossart, Ferdinand (1849-1930): b. Germany; ord. Sept. 1, 1892; bp. Covington, 1916-23 (res.).

Brute, Simon G. (1779-1839): b. France; ord. June 11, 1808; first bp. Vincennes (now Indianapolis), 1834-39.

Buddy, Charles F. (1887-1966): ord. Sept. 19, 1914; first bp. San Diego, 1936-66.

Burke, Joseph A. (1886-1962): ord. Aug. 3, 1912; aux. Buffalo (Vita), 1943-52; bp. Buffalo, 1952-62.

Burke, Maurice F. (1845-1923): b. Ireland; ord. May 22, 1875; first bp. Cheyenne, 1887-93; bp. St. Joseph, 1893-1923.

Burke, Thomas M. (1840-1915): b. Ireland; ord. June 30, 1864; bp. Albany, 1894-1915.

Busch, Joseph F. (1866-1953): ord. July 28, 1889; bp. Lead (now Rapid City), 1910-15; bp. St. Cloud, 1915-53.

Byrne, Andrew (1802-62): b. Ireland; ord. Nov. 11, 1827; first bp. Little Rock, 1844-62.

Byrne, Christopher E. (1867-1950): ord. Sept. 23, 1891; bp. Galveston, 1918-50.

Byrne, Edwin V. (1891-1963): ord. May 22, 1915; first bp. Ponce, 1925-29; abp. San Juan, 1929-43; abp. Santa Fe, 1943-63.

Byrne, Leo C. (1908-74): ord. June 10, 1933; aux. St. Louis (Sabadia), 1954-61; coad. bp. Wichita, 1961-67; coad. abp. (Plestra) St. Paul and Minneapolis, 1967-74.

Byrne, Patrick J., M.M. (1888-1950): ord. June 23, 1915; apostolic delegate to Korea (Gazera), 1949-50.

Byrne, Thomas S. (1841-1923): ord. May 22, 1869; bp. Nashville, 1894-1923.

C

Caillouet, L. Abel (1900-84): ord. May 7, 1925; aux. New Orleans (Setea), 1947-76 (res.).

Canevin, J. F. Regis (1853-1927): ord. June 4, 1879; coad. bp. Pittsburgh (Sabrata), 1903-04; bp. Pittsburgh, 1904-21 (res.).

Cantwell, John J. (1874-1947): b. Ireland; ord. June 18, 1899; bp. Monterey-Los Angeles, 1917-22; bp. Los Angeles-San Diego, 1922-36; first abp. Los Angeles, 1936-47.

Carrell, George A., S.J. (1803-68): ord. Dec. 20, 1827; first bp. Covington, 1853-68.

Carroll (brothers) **Coleman F.** (1905-77): ord. June 15, 1930; aux. Pittsburgh (Pitanae), 1953-58; first bp. Miami, 1958-68 and first abp., 1968-77.

Howard J. (1902-60): ord. Apr. 2, 1927; bp. Altoona-Johnstown, 1958-60.

Carroll, James J. (1862-1913): ord. June 15, 1889; bp. Nueva Segovia, P.I., 1908-12 (res.).

Carroll, John (1735-1815): ord. Feb. 14, 1761; first bishop of the American hierarchy; first bp., 1789-1808, and first abp., 1808-15, of Baltimore.

Carroll, John P. (1864-1925): ord. July 7, 1886; bp. Helena, 1904-25.

Carroll, Mark K. (1896-1985): ord. June 10, 1922; bp. Wichita, 1947-67 (res.).

Cartwright, Hubert J. (1900-58): ord. June 11, 1927; coad. bp. Wilmington (Neve), 1956-58.

Caruana, George (1882-1951): b. Malta; ord. Oct. 28, 1905; bp. Puerto Rico (name changed to San Juan, 1924), 1921-25; ap. del. Mexico (Sebastea in Armenia), 1925-27; internuncio to Haiti, 1927-35; nuncio to Cuba, 1935-47 (res.).

Casey, James V. (1914-86): ord. Dec. 8, 1939; aux. Lincoln (Citium), Apr.-June, 1957; bp. Lincoln, 1957-67; abp. Denver 1967-86.

Casey, Lawrence B. (1905-77): ord. June 7, 1930; aux. Rochester (Cea), 1953-66; bp. Paterson, 1966-77.

Cassidy, James E. (1869-1951): ord. Sept. 8, 1898; aux. Fall River (Ibora), 1930-34; bp. Fall River, 1934-51.

Chabrat, Guy Ignatius, S.S. (1787-1868): b. France; ord. Dec. 21, 1811; coad. bp. Bardstown (Bolina), 1834-47 (res.).

Chanche, John J., S.S. (1795-1852): ord. June 5, 1819; bp. Natchez (now Jackson), 1841-52.

Chapelle, Placide L. (1842-1905): b. France; ord. June 28, 1865; coad. abp. Santa Fe (Arabissus), 1891-94; abp. Santa Fe, 1894-97; abp. New Orleans 1897-1905.

Chartrand, Joseph (1870-1933): ord. Sept. 24, 1892; coad. bp. Indianapolis (Flavias), 1910-18; bp. Indianapolis, 1918-33.

Chatard, Francis S. (1834-1918): ord. June 14, 1862; bp. Vincennes (now Indianapolis — title changed in 1898), 1878-1918.

Cheverus, John Lefebvre de (1768-1836): b. France; ord. Dec. 18, 1790; bp. Boston, 1810-23 (returned to France, made cardinal 1836).

Christie, Alexander (1848-1925): ord. Dec. 22, 1877; bp. Vancouver Is., 1898-99; abp. Oregon City (now Portland), 1899-1925.

Clancy, William (1802-47): b. Ireland; ord. May 24, 1823; coad. bp. Charleston (Oreus), 1834-37; v.a. British Guiana, 1837-43.

Cody, John P. (1907-82): ord. Dec. 8, 1931; aux. St. Louis (Apollonia), 1947-54; coad. bp. St. Joseph, Mo., 1954-55; bp. Kansas City-St. Joseph, 1956-61; coad. abp. 1961-62; ap. admin., 1962-64, and abp., 1964-65, New Orleans; abp. Chicago, 1965-82; cardinal, 1967.

Collins, John J., S.J. (1856-1934): ord. Aug. 29, 1891; v.a. Jamaica (Antiphellus), 1907-18 (res.).

Collins, Thomas P., M.M. (1915-73): ord. June 21, 1942; v.a. Pando, Bolivia (Sufetula), 1961-68 (res.).

Colton, Charles H. (1848-1915): ord. June 10, 1876; bp. Buffalo, 1903-15.

Conaty, Thomas J. (1847-1915): b. Ireland; ord. Dec. 21, 1872; rector of Catholic University, 1896-1903; tit. bp. Samos, 1901-03; bp. Monterey-Los Angeles (now Los Angeles), 1903-15.

Concanen, Richard L., O.P. (1747-1810): b. Ireland; ord. Dec. 22, 1770; first bp. New York, 1808-10 (detained in Italy, never reached his see).

Condon, William J. (1895-1967): ord. Oct. 14, 1917; bp. Great Falls, 1939-67.

Connolly, John, O.P. (1750-1825): b. Ireland; ord. Sept. 24, 1774; bp. New York, 1814-25.

Conroy, John J. (1819-95): b. Ireland; ord. May 21, 1842; bp. Albany, 1865-77 (res.).

Conroy, Joseph H. (1858-1939): ord. June 11, 1881; aux. Ogdensburg (Arindela), 1912-21; bp. Ogdensburg, 1921-39.

Conwell, Henry (1748-1842): b. Ireland; ord. 1776; bp. Philadelphia, 1820-42.

Cooke, Terence J. (1921-83): ord. Dec. 1, 1945; aux. New York (Summa), 1965-68; abp. New York, 1965-83; cardinal 1969.

Corbett, Timothy (1858-1939): ord. June 12, 1886; first bp. Crookston, 1910-38 (res.).

Corrigan, Joseph M. (1879-1942): ord. June 6, 1903; rector of Catholic University, 1936-42; tit. bp. Bilta, 1940-42.

Corrigan, Michael A. (1839-1902): ord. Sept. 19, 1863; bp. Newark, 1873-80; coad. abp. New York (Petra), 1880-85; abp. New York, 1885-1902.

Corrigan, Owen (1849-1929): ord. June 7, 1873; aux. Baltimore (Macri), 1908-29.

Cosgrove, Henry (1834-1906): ord. Aug. 27, 1857; bp. Davenport, 1884-1906.

Costello, Joseph A. (1915-78): ord. June 7, 1941; aux. Newark (Choma), 1963-78.

Cote, Philip, S.J. (1896-1970): ord. Aug. 14, 1927; v.a. Suchow, China (Polystylus), 1935-46; first bp. Suchow, 1946-70 (imprisoned by Chinese Communists, 1951; expelled from China, 1953; ap. admin. Islands of Quemoy and Matsu, 1969-70.

Cotter, Joseph B. (1844-1909): b. England; ord. May 3, 1871; first bp. Winona, 1889-1909.

Cotton, Francis R. (1895-1960): ord. June 17, 1920; first bp. Owensboro, 1938-60.

Cowley, Leonard P. (1913-73): ord. June 4, 1938; aux. St. Paul and Minneapolis (Pertusa), 1958-73.

Crane, Michael J. (1863-1928): ord. June 15, 1889; aux. Philadelphia (Curium), 1921-28.

Cretin, Joseph (1799-1857): b. France; ord. Dec. 20, 1823; bp. St. Paul, 1851-57.

Crimont, Joseph R., S.J. (1858-1945): b. France; ord. Aug. 26, 1888; v.a. Alaska (Ammaedara), 1917-45.

Crowley, Timothy J., C.S.C. (1880-1945): b. Ireland; ord. Aug. 2, 1906; coad. bp. Dacca (Epiphania), 1927-29; bp. Dacca, 1929-45.

Cunningham, David F. (1900-79): ord. June 12, 1926; aux., 1950-67, and coad. bp., 1967-79, Syracuse (Lampsacus); bp. Syracuse, 1970-76 (res.).

Cunningham, John F. (1842-1919): b. Ireland; ord. Aug. 8, 1865; bp. Concordia, 1898-1919.

Curley, Daniel J. (1869-1932): ord. May 19, 1894; bp. Syracuse, 1923-32.

Curley, Michael J. (1879-1947): b. Ireland; ord. Mar. 19, 1904; bp. St. Augustine, 1914-21; abp. Baltimore, 1921-39; title changed to abp. Baltimore and Washington, 1939-47.

Curtis, Alfred A. (1831-1908): convert, 1872; ord.

Dec. 19, 1874; bp. Wilmington, 1886-96 (res.).

Cusack, Thomas F. (1862-1918): ord. May 30, 1885; aux. New York (Temiscyra), 1904-15; bp. Albany, 1915-18.

Cushing, Richard J. (1895-1970): ord. May 26, 1921; aux. Boston (Mela), 1939-44; abp. Boston, 1944-70; cardinal 1958.

D

Daeger, Albert T., O.F.M. (1872-1932): ord. July 25, 1896; abp. Santa Fe, 1919-32.

Daley, Joseph T. (1915-83): ord. June 7, 1941; aux. Harrisburg (Barca), 1964-67; coad., 1967-71, and bp., 1971-83, Harrisburg.

Daly, Edward C., O.P. (1894-1964): ord. June 12, 1921; bp. Des Moines, 1948-64.

Damiano, Celestine (1911-67): ord. Dec. 21, 1935; apostolic delegate to South Africa (Nicopolis in Epiro), 1952-60; bp. Camden, 1960-67.

Danehy, Thomas J., M.M. (1914-59): ord. Sept. 17, 1939; ap. admin. v.a. Pando, Bolivia (Bita), 1953-59.

Dargin, Edward V. (1898-1981): ord. Sept. 23, 1922; aux. New York (Amphipolis), 1953-73 (res.).

David, John B., S.S. (1761-1841): b. France; ord. Sept. 24, 1785; coad. bp. Bardstown (Mauricastrum), 1819-32; bp. Bardstown (now Louisville), 1832-33 (res.).

Davis, James (1852-1926): b. Ireland; ord. June 21, 1878; coad. bp. Davenport (Milopotamus), 1904-06; bp. Davenport, 1906-26.

De Cheverus, John L.: See Cheverus, John

De Falco, Lawrence M. (1915-79): ord. June 11, 1942; bp. Amarillo, 1963-79 (res.).

De Goesbriand, Louis (1816-99): b. France; ord. July 13, 1840; first bp. Burlington, 1853-99.

De la Hailandiere, Celestine (1798-1882): b. France; ord. May 28, 1825; bp. Vincennes (now Indianapolis), 1839-47 (res.).

Delany, John B. (1864-1906): ord. May 23, 1891; bp. Manchester, 1904-06.

Demers, Modeste (1809-71): b. Canada; ord. Feb. 7, 1836; bp. Vancouver Is., 1846-71.

Dempsey, Michael R. (1918-74): ord. May 1, 1943; aux. Chicago (Truentum), 1968-74.

De Neckere, Leo, C.M. (1799-1833): b. Belgium; ord. Oct. 13, 1822; bp. New Orleans, 1829-33.

De Saint Palais, Maurice (1811-77): b. France; ord. May 28, 1836; bp. Vincennes (now Indianapolis), 1849-77.

Desmond, Daniel F. (1884-1945): ord. June 9, 1911; bp. Alexandria, 1933-45.

Dinand, Joseph N., S.J. (1869-1943): ord. June 25, 1903; v.a. Jamaica (Selinus), 1927-29 (res.).

Dobson, Robert (1867-1942): ord. May 23, 1891; aux. Liverpool, Eng. (Cynopolis), 1922-42.

Domenec, Michael, C.M. (1816-78): b. Spain; ord. June 30, 1839; bp. Pittsburgh, 1860-76; bp. Allegheny, 1876-77 (res.).

Donahue, Joseph P. (1870-1959): ord. June 8, 1895; aux. New York (Emmaus), 1945-59.

Donahue, Patrick J. (1849-1922): b. England; ord. Dec. 19, 1885; bp. Wheeling, 1894-1922.

Donahue, Stephen J. (1893-1982): ord. May 22, 1918; aux. New York (Medea), 1934-69 (res.).

Donnelly, George J. (1889-1950): ord. June 12, 1921; aux. St. Louis (Coela), 1940-46; bp. Leavenworth (now Kansas City — title changed in 1947), 1946-50.

Donnelly, Henry E. (1904-67): ord. Aug. 17, 1930; aux. Detroit (Tymbrias), 1954-67.

Donnelly, Joseph F. (1909-77): ord. June 29, 1934; aux. Hartford (Nabala), 1965-77.

Doran, Thomas F. (1856-1916): ord. July 4, 1880; aux. Providence (Halicarnassus), 1915-16.

Dougherty, Dennis (1865-1951): ord. May 31, 1890; bp. Nueva Segovia, P.I., 1903-08; bp. Jaro, P.I., 1908-15; bp. Buffalo, 1915-18; abp. Philadelphia, 1918-51; cardinal, 1921.

Dougherty, John J. (1907-86): ord. July 23, 1933; aux. Newark (Cotena), 1963-82 (res.).

Dougherty, Joseph P. (1905-70): ord. June 14, 1930; first bp. Yakima, 1951-69; aux. Los Angeles (Altino), 1969-70.

Dowling, Austin (1868-1930): ord. June 24, 1891; first bp. Des Moines, 1912-19; abp. St. Paul, 1919-30.

Dozier, Carroll T. (1911-85): ord. Mar. 19, 1937; first bp. Memphis, 1971-82 (res.).

Driscoll, Justin A. (1920-84): ord. July 28, 1945; bp. Fargo, 1970-84.

Drossaerts, Arthur J. (1862-1940): b. Holland; ord. June 15, 1889; bp. San Antonio 1918-26; first abp. San Antonio, 1926-40.

Drumm, Thomas W. (1871-1933): b. Ireland; ord. Dec. 21, 1901; bp. Des Moines, 1919-33.

Dubois, John, S.S. (1764-1842): b. France; ord. Sept. 28, 1787; bp. New York, 1826-42.

Dubourg, Louis William, S.S. (1766-1833): b. Santo Domingo; ord. 1788; bp. Louisiana and the Two Floridas (now New Orleans), 1815-25; returned to France; bp. Montauban, 1826-33; abp. Besancon 1833.

Dubuis, Claude M. (1817-1895): b. France; ord. June 1, 1844; bp. Galveston, 1862-92 (res.).

Dufal, Peter, C.S.C. (1822-98): b. France; ord. Sept. 29, 1852; v.a. Eastern Bengal (Delcon), 1860-78; coad. bp. Galveston, 1878-80 (res.).

Duffy, James A. (1873-1968): ord. May 27, 1899; bp. Kearney (see transferred to Grand Island, 1917), 1913-31 (res.).

Duffy, John A. (1884-1944): ord. June 13, 1908; bp. Syracuse, 1933-37; bp. Buffalo, 1937-44.

Duggan, James (1825-99): b. Ireland; ord. May 29, 1847; coad. bp. St. Louis (Gabala), 1857-59; bp. Chicago, 1859-80 (res.). Inactive from 1869 because of illness.

Dunn, John J. (1869-1933): ord. May 30, 1896; aux. New York (Camuliana), 1921-33.

Dunne, Edmund M. (1864-1929): ord. June 24, 1887; bp. Peoria, 1909-29.

Dunne, Edward (1848-1910): b. Ireland; ord. June 29, 1871; bp. Dallas, 1893-1910.

Durier, Anthony (1832-1904): b. France; ord. Oct. 28, 1856; bp. Natchitoches (now Alexandria), La., 1885-1904.

Dwenger, Joseph, C.Pp.S. (1837-93): ord. Sept. 4, 1859; bp. Fort Wayne, 1872-93.

Dworschak, Leo F. (1900-76): ord. May 29, 1926; coad. bp. Rapid City (Tium), 1946-47; aux. Fargo, 1947-60; bp. Fargo, 1960-70 (res.).

Dwyer, Robert J. (1908-76): ord. June 11, 1932;

bp. Reno, 1952-66; abp. Portland, Ore., 1966-74 (res.).

E

Eccleston, Samuel, S.S. (1801-51): ord. Apr. 24, 1825; coad. bp. Baltimore (Thermae), Sept.-Oct., 1834; abp. Baltimore, 1834-51.

Egan, Michael, O.F.M. (1761-1814): b. Ireland; first bp. Philadelphia, 1810-14.

Eis, Frederick (1843-1926): b. Germany; ord. Oct. 30, 1870; bp. Sault Ste. Marie and Marquette (now Marquette), 1899-1922 (res.).

Elder, William (1819-1904): ord. Mar. 29, 1846; bp. Natchez (now Jackson), 1857-80; coad. bp. Cincinnati (Avara), 1880-83; abp. Cincinnati, 1883-1904.

Elwell, Clarence E. (1904-73): ord. Mar. 17, 1929; aux. Cleveland (Cone) 1962-68; bp. Columbus, 1968-73.

Emmet, Thomas A., S.J. (1873-1950): ord. July 30, 1909; v.a. Jamaica (Tuscamia), 1930-49 (res.).

England, John (1786-1842): b. Ireland; ord. Oct. 11, 1808; first bp. Charleston, 1820-42.

Escalante, Alonso Manuel, M.M. (1906-67): b. Mexico; ord. Feb. 1, 1931; v.a. Pando, Bolivia (Sora), 1943-60 (res.).

Espelage (brothers): **Bernard T., O.F.M.** (1892-1971): ord. May 16, 1918; bp. Gallup, 1940-69 (res.). **Sylvester J., O.F.M.** (1877-1940): ord. Jan. 18, 1900; v.a. Wuchang, China (Oreus), 1930-40.

Etteldorf, Raymond P. (1911-86): ord. Dec. 8, 1937; apostolic delegate, 1969-73, and nuncio, 1973-74, to New Zealand (Tindari); pro-nuncio to Ethiopia, 1947-82.

Eustace, Bartholomew J. (1887-1956): ord. Nov. 1, 1914; bp. Camden, 1938-56.

Evans, George R. (1922-85): ord. May 31, 1947; aux. Denver (Tubyza), 1969-85.

F

Fahey, Leo F. (1898-1950): ord. May 29, 1926; coad. bp. Baker City (Ipsus), 1948-50.

Farley, John (1842-1918): b. Ireland; ord. June 11, 1870; aux. New York (Zeugma), 1895-1902; abp. New York, 1902-18; cardinal 1911.

Farrelly, John P. (1856-1921): ord. Mar. 22, 1880; bp. Cleveland, 1909-21.

Fearns, John M. (1897-1977): ord. Feb. 19, 1922; aux. New York (Geras), 1957-72 (res.).

Fedders, Edward L., M.M. (1913-73): ord. June 11, 1944; prelate Juli, Peru (Antiochia ad Meadrum), 1963-73.

Feehan, Daniel F. (1855-1934): ord. Dec. 29, 1879; bp. Fall River, 1907-34.

Feehan, Patrick A. (1829-1902): b. Ireland; ord. Nov. 1, 1852; bp. Nashville, 1865-80; first abp. Chicago, 1880-1902.

Feeney, Daniel J. (1894-1969): ord. May 21, 1921; aux. Portland, Me. (Sita), 1946-52; coad. bp. Portland, 1952-55; bp. Portland, 1955-69.

Feeney, Thomas J., S.J. (1894-1955): ord. June 23, 1927; v.a. Caroline and Marshall Is. (Agnus), 1951-55.

Fenwick, Benedict J., S.J. (1782-1846): ord. June 11, 1808; bp. Boston, 1825-46.

Fenwick, Edward D., O.P. (1768-1832): ord. Feb.

23, 1793; first bp. Cincinnati, 1822-32.

Fink, Michael, O.S.B. (1834-1904): b. Germany; ord. May 28, 1857; coad. v.a., 1871-74, and v.a., 1874-77, Kansas and Indian Territory (Eucarpia); first bp. Leavenworth (now Kansas City), 1877-1904.

Finnigan, George, C.S.C. (1885-1932): ord. June 13, 1915; bp. Helena, 1927-32.

Fitzgerald, Edward (1833-1907): b. Ireland; ord. Aug. 22, 1857; bp. Little Rock, 1867-1907.

Fitzgerald, Edward A. (1893-1972): ord. July 25, 1916; aux. Dubuque (Cantanus), 1946-49; bp. Winona, 1949-69 (res.).

Fitzgerald, Walter J., S.J. (1883-1947): ord. May 16, 1918; coad. v.a. Alaska (Tymbrias), 1939-45; v.a. Alaska, 1945-47.

Fitzmaurice, Edmond (1881-1962): b. Ireland; ord. May 28, 1904; bp. Wilmington, 1925-60 (res.).

Fitzmaurice, John E. (1837-1920): b. Ireland; ord. Dec. 21, 1862; coad. bp. Erie (Amisus), 1898-99; bp. Erie, 1899-1920.

Fitzpatrick, John B. (1812-66): ord. June 13, 1840; aux. Boston (Callipolis), 1843-46; bp. Boston, 1846-66.

Fitzsimon, Laurence J. (1895-1958): ord. May 17, 1921; bp. Amarillo, 1941-58.

Flaget, Benedict, S.S.: See Index.

Flaherty, J. Louis (1910-75): ord. Dec. 8, 1936; aux. Richmond (Tabudo), 1966-75.

Flannelly, Joseph F. (1894-1973): ord. Sept. 1, 1918; aux. New York (Metelis), 1948-70 (res.).

Flasch, Kilian C. (1831-91): b. Germany; ord. Dec. 16, 1859; bp. La Crosse, 1881-91.

Fletcher, Albert L. (1896-1979): ord. June 4, 1920; aux. Little Rock (Samos), 1940-46; bp. Little Rock, 1946-72 (res.).

Floersh, John (1886-1968): ord. June 10, 1911; coad. bp. Louisville (Lycopolis), 1923-24; bp. Louisville, 1924-37; first abp. Louisville, 1937-67 (res.).

Flores, Felixberto C. (1921-85): b. Gaum; ord. Apr. 30, 1949; ap. admin. Agana, Guam (Stonj), 1970-72; bp., 1977-84, and first abp. Agana, 1984-85.

Foery, Walter A. (1890-1978): ord. June 10, 1916; bp. Syracuse, 1937-70 (res.).

Foley (brothers): **John S.** (1833-1918): ord. Dec. 20, 1856; bp. Detroit, 1888-1918. **Thomas** (1822-79): ord. Aug. 16, 1846; coad. bp. and ap. admin. Chicago (Pergamum), 1870-79.

Foley, Maurice P. (1867-1919): ord. July 25, 1891; bp. Tuguegarao, P.I., 1910-16; bp. Jaro, P.I., 1916-19.

Ford, Francis X., M.M. (1892-1952): ord. Dec. 5, 1917; v.a. Kaying, China (Etenna), 1935-46; first bp. Kaying, 1946-52.

Forest, John A. (1838-1911): b. France; ord. Apr. 12, 1863; bp. San Antonio, 1895-1911.

Fox, Joseph J. (1855-1915): ord. June 7, 1879; bp. Green Bay, 1904-14 (res.).

Fulcher, George A. (1922-84): ord. Feb. 28, 1948; aux. Columbus (Morosbisdus), 1976-83; bp. Lafayette, 1983-84.

Furey, Francis J. (1905-79): ord. Mar. 15, 1930; aux. Philadelphia (Temnus), 1960-63; coad bp. San Diego, 1963-66; bp. San Diego, 1966-69; abp. San Antonio, 1969-79.

G

Gabriels, Henry (1838-1921): b. Belgium; ord. Sept. 21. 1861; bp. Ogdensburg, 1892-1921.

Gabro, Jaroslav (1919-80): ord. Sept. 27, 1945; bp. St. Nicholas of Chicago (Byzantine Rite, Ukrainians), 1961-80.

Galberry, Thomas, O.S.A. (1833-78): b. Ireland; ord. Dec. 20, 1856; bp. Hartford, 1876-78.

Gallagher, Michael J. (1866-1937): ord. Mar. 19, 1893; coad. bp. Grand Rapids (Tiposa in Mauretania), 1915-16; bp. Grand Rapids, 1916-18; bp. Detroit, 1918-37.

Gallagher, Nicholas (1846-1918): ord. Dec. 25, 1868; coad. bp. Galveston (Canopus), 1882-92; bp. Galveston, 1892-1918.

Gannon, John M. (1877-1968): ord. Dec. 21, 1901; aux. Erie (Nilopolis), 1918-20; bp. Erie, 1920-66 (res.).

Garcia Diego y Moreno, Francisco, O.F.M. (1785-1846): b. Mexico; ord. Nov. 14, 1808; bp. Two Californias (now Los Angeles), 1840-46.

Garriga, Mariano S. (1886-1965): ord. July 2, 1911; coad. bp. Corpus Christi (Syene), 1936-49; bp. Corpus Christi, 1949-65.

Garrigan, Philip (1840-1919): b. Ireland; ord. June 11, 1870; first bp. Sioux City, 1902-19.

Gartland, Francis X. (1808-54): b. Ireland; ord. Aug. 5, 1832; first bp. Savannah, 1850-54.

Garvey, Eugene A. (1845-1920): ord. Sept. 22, 1869; first bp. Altoona (now Altoona-Johnstown), 1901-20.

Gercke, Daniel J. (1874-1964): ord. June 1, 1901; bp. Tucson, 1923-60 (res.).

Gerken, Rudolph A. (1887-1943): ord. June 10, 1917; first bp. Amarillo, 1927-33; abp. Santa Fe, 1933-43.

Gerow, Richard O. (1885-1976): ord. June 5, 1909; bp. Natchez-Jackson (now Jackson), 1924-67 (res).

Gibbons, Edmund F. (1868-1964): ord. May 27, 1893; bp. Albany, 1919-54 (res.).

Gibbons, James (1834-1921): ord. June 30, 1861; v.a. North Carolina (Adramyttium), 1868-72; bp. Richmond, 1872-77; coad. Baltimore (Jonopolis), May-Oct., 1877; abp. Baltimore, 1877-1921; cardinal 1886.

Gilfillan, Francis (1872-1933): b. Ireland; ord. June 24, 1895; coad. bp. St. Joseph (Spiga), 1922-23; bp. St. Joseph, 1923-33.

Gill, Thomas E. (1908-73): ord. June 10, 1933; aux. Seattle (Lambesis) 1956-73.

Gilmore, Joseph M. (1893-1962): ord. July 25, 1915; bp. Helena, 1936-62.

Gilmour, Richard (1824-91): b. Scotland; ord. Aug. 30, 1852; bp. Cleveland, 1872-91.

Girouard, Paul J., M.S. (1898-1964): ord. July 26, 1927; first bp. Morondava, Madagascar, 1956-64.

Glass, Joseph S., C.M. (1874-1926): ord. Aug. 15, 1897; bp. Salt Lake City, 1915-26.

Gleeson, Francis D., S.J. (1895-1983): ord. July 29, 1926; v.a. Alaska (Cotenna), 1948-62; first bp. Fairbanks, 1962-68 (res.).

Glenn, Lawrence A. (1900-85): ord. June 11, 1927; aux. Duluth (Tuscamia), 1956-60; bp. Crookston, 1960-70 (res.).

Glennon, John J. (1862-1946): b. Ireland; ord. Dec. 20, 1884; coad. bp. Kansas City, Mo. (Pinara), 1896-1903; coad. St. Louis, April-Oct., 1903; abp. St. Louis, 1903-46; cardinal 1946.

Glorieux, Alphonse J. (1844-1917): b. Belgium; ord. Aug. 17, 1867; v.a. Idaho (Apollonia), 1885-93; bp. Boise, 1893-1917.

Gorman, Daniel (1861-1927): ord. June 24, 1893; bp. Boise, 1918-27.

Gorman, Thomas K. (1892-1980): ord. June 23, 1917; first bp. Reno, 1931-52; coad. bp. Dallas-Ft. Worth (Rhasus), 1952-54; bp. Dallas-Fort Worth (now Dallas), 1954-69 (res.).

Grace, Thomas (1841-1921): b. Ireland; ord. June 24, 1876; bp. Sacramento, 1896-1921.

Grace, Thomas L., O.P. (1814-97): ord. Dec. 21, 1839; bp. St. Paul, 1859-84 (res.).

Graner, Lawrence L., C.S.C. (1901-82): ord. June 24, 1928; bp. Dacca, 1947-50, and first abp., 1950-67 (res.).

Granjon, Henry (1863-1922): b. France; ord. Dec. 17, 1887; bp. Tucson, 1900-22.

Green, Joseph J. (1917-82): ord. July 14, 1946; aux. Lansing (Trisipa), 1962-67; bp. Reno 1967-74 (res.).

Grellinger, John B. (1899-1984): ord. priest July 14, 1929; aux. Green Bay (Syene), 1949-74 (res.).

Griffin, James A. (1883-1948): ord. July 4, 1909; bp. Springfield, Ill., 1924-48.

Griffin, William A. (1885-1950): ord. Aug. 15, 1910; aux. Newark (Sanavus), 1938-40; bp. Trenton, 1940-50.

Griffin, William R. (1883-1944): ord. May 25, 1907; aux. La Crosse (Lydda), 1935-44.

Griffiths, James H. (1903-64): ord. Mar. 12, 1927; aux. New York and delegate of U.S. military vicar (Gaza), 1950-64.

Grimes, John (1852-1922): b. Ireland; ord. Feb. 19, 1882; coad. bp. Syracuse (Hemeria), 1909-12; bp. Syracuse, 1912-22.

Grimmelsman, Henry J. (1890-1972); ord. Aug. 15, 1915; first bp. Evansville, 1945-65 (res.).

Gross, William H., C.SS.R. (1837-98): ord. Mar. 21, 1863; bp. Savannah, 1873-85; abp. Oregon City (now Portland), 1885-98.

Guertin, George A. (1869-1932): ord. Dec. 17, 1892; bp. Manchester, 1907-32.

Guilfoyle, Richard T. (1892-1957): ord. June 2, 1917; bp. Altoona (now Altoona-Johnstown), 1936-57.

Guilfoyle, Merlin J. (1908-81): ord. June 10, 1933; aux. San Francisco (Bulla), 1950-69; bp. Stockton, 1969-79 (res.).

Gunn, John E., S.M. (1863-1924): b. Ireland; ord. Feb. 2, 1890; bp. Natchez (now Jackson), 1911-24.

H

Haas, Francis J. (1889-1953): ord. June 11, 1913; bp. Grand Rapids, 1943-53.

Hafey, William (1888-1954): ord. June 16, 1914; first bp. Raleigh, 1925-37; coad. bp. Scranton (Appia), 1937-38; bp. Scranton, 1938-54.

Hagan, John R. (1890-1946): ord. Mar. 7, 1914; aux. Cleveland (Limata), 1946.

Hagarty, Paul L., O.S.B. (1909-84): ord. June 6,

1936; v.a. Bahamas (Arba), 1950-60; first bp. Nassau, Bahamas, 1960-81 (res.).

Haid, Leo M., O.S.B. (1849-1924): ord. Dec. 21, 1872; v.a. N. Carolina (Messene), 1888-1910; abbot Mary Help of Christians abbacy, 1910-24.

Hallinan, Paul J. (1911-68): ord. Feb. 20, 1937; bp. Charleston, 1958-62; first abp. Atlanta, 1962-68.

Hanna, Edward J. (1860-1944): ord. May 30, 1885; aux. San Francisco (Titiopolis). 1912-15; abp. San Francisco, 1915-35 (res.).

Hannan, Jerome D. (1896-1965): ord. May 22, 1921; bp. Scranton, 1954-65.

Harkins, Matthew (1845-1921): ord. May 22, 1869; bp. Providence, 1887-1921.

Hartley, James J. (1858-1944): ord. July 10, 1882; bp. Columbus, 1904-44.

Harty, Jeremiah J. (1853-1927): ord. Apr. 28, 1878; abp. Manila, 1903-16; abp. Omaha, 1916-27.

Hayes, James T., S.J. (1889-1980): ord. June 29, 1921; bp. of Cagayan, Philippines, 1933-51; first abp. Cagayan, 1951-70 (res.).

Hayes, Patrick J. (1867-1938): ord. Sept. 8, 1892; aux. New York (Thagaste), 1914-19; abp. New York, 1919-38; cardinal 1924.

Hayes, Ralph L. (1884-1970): ord. Sept. 19, 1909; bp. Helena 1933-35; rector North American College (Hieropolis) 1935-44; bp. Davenport, 1944-66 (res.).

Healy, James A. (1830-1900): ord. June 10, 1854; bp. Portland 1875-1900.

Heelan, Edmond (1868-1948): b. Ireland; ord. June 24, 1890; aux. Sioux City (Gerasa), 1919-20; bp. Sioux City, 1920-48.

Heffron, Patrick (1860-1927): ord. Dec. 22, 1884; bp. Winona, 1910-27.

Heiss, Michael (1818-90): b. Germany; ord. Oct. 18, 1840; bp. La Crosse, 1868-80; coad. abp. Milwaukee (Hadrianopolis), 1880-81; abp. Milwaukee, 1881-90.

Hendrick, Thomas A. (1849-1909): ord. June 7, 1873; bp. Cebu, P.I., 1904-09.

Hendricken, Thomas F. (1827-86): b. Ireland; ord. Apr. 25, 1853; bp. Providence, 1872-86.

Hennessy, John (1825-1900): b. Ireland; ord. Nov. 1, 1850; bp. Dubuque, 1866-93; first abp. Dubuque, 1893-1900.

Hennessy, John J. (1847-1920): b. Ireland; ord. Nov. 28, 1869; first bp. Wichita, 1888-1920; ap. admin. Concordia (now Salina), 1891-98.

Henni, John M. (1805-81): b. Switzerland; ord. Feb. 2, 1829; first bp. Milwaukee, 1844-75; first abp. Milwaukee, 1875-81.

Henry, Harold W., S.S.C. (1909-76): ord. Dec. 21, 1932; v.a. Kwang Ju, Korea (Coridala), 1957-62; first abp. Kwang Ju, 1962-71; ap. admin. p.a. Cheju-Do, Korea (Thubunae), 1971-76.

Heslin, Thomas (1845-1911): b. Ireland; ord. Sept. 8, 1869; bp. Natchez (now Jackson), 1889-1911.

Heston, Edward L. (1907-73): ord. Dec. 22, 1934; sec. Sacred Congregation for Religious and Secular Institutes, 1969-71; pres. Pontifical Commission for Social Communications, 1971-73; tit. abp. Numidea, 1972.

Hickey, David F., S.J. (1882-1973): ord. June 27, 1917; v.a. Belize, Br. Honduras (Bonitza), 1948-56;

first bp. Belize, 1956-57 (res.); tit. abp. Cabasa, 1957-73.

Hickey, Thomas F. (1861-1940): ord. Mar. 25, 1884; coad. bp. Rochester (Berenice), 1905-09; bp. Rochester, 1909-28 (res.).

Hickey, William A. (1869-1933): ord. Dec. 22, 1893; coad. bp. Providence (Claudiopolis), 1919-21; bp. Providence, 1921-33.

Hillinger, Raymond P. (1904-71): ord. Apr. 2, 1932; bp. Rockford, 1953-56; aux. Chicago (Derbe), 1956-71.

Hoban, Edward F. (1878-1966): ord. July 11, 1903; aux. Chicago (Colonia), 1921-28; bp. Rockford, 1928-42; coad. bp. Cleveland (Lystra), 1942-45; bp. Cleveland, 1945-66.

Hoban, Michael J. (1853-1926): ord. May 22, 1880; coad. bp. Scranton (Halius), 1896-99; bp. Scranton, 1899-1926.

Hodges, Joseph H. (1911-85): ord. Dec. 8, 1935; aux. Richmond (Rusadus), 1952-61; coad. Wheeling, 1961-62; bp. Wheeling (now Wheeling-Charleston), 1962-85.

Hogan, John J. (1829-1913): b. Ireland; ord. Apr. 10, 1852; first bp. St. Joseph, 1868-80; first bp. Kansas City, 1880-1913.

Horstmann, Ignatius (1840-1908): ord. June 10, 1865; bp. Cleveland, 1892-1908.

Howard, Edward D. (1877-1983): ord. June 12, 1906; aux. Davenport (Isauropolis), 1924-26; abp. Oregon City (title changed to Portland, 1928), 1926-66 (res.).

Howard, Francis W. (1867-1944): ord. June 16, 1891; bp. Covington, 1923-44.

Hughes, John J. (1797-1864): b. Ireland; ord. Oct. 15, 1826; coad. bp. New York (Basilinopolis), 1837-42; bp. New York, 1842-50, and first abp., 1850-64.

Hunkeler, Edward J. (1894-1970): ord. June 14, 1919; bp. Grand Island, 1945-51; bp. Kansas City, Kans. 1951-52; first abp. Kansas City, 1952-69 (res.).

Hunt, Duane G. (1884-1960): ord. June 27, 1920; bp. Salt Lake City, 1937-60.

Hurley, Joseph P. (1894-1967): ord. May 29, 1919; bp. St. Augustine, 1940-67.

Hyland, Francis E. (1901-68): ord. June 11, 1927; aux. Savannah-Atlanta (Gomphi), 1949-56; bp. Atlanta, 1956-61 (res.).

Hyle, Michael W. (1901-67): ord. Mar. 12, 1927; coad. bp. Wilmington, 1958-60; bp. Wilmington, 1960-67.

I

Ireland, John (1838-1918): b. Ireland; ord. Dec. 21, 1861; coad. bp. St. Paul (Marobea), 1875-84; bp. St. Paul, 1884-88, and first abp. St. Paul, 1888-1918.

Ireton, Peter L. (1882-1958): ord. June 20, 1906; coad. bp. Richmond (Cyme), 1935-45; bp. Richmond, 1945-58.

Issenmann, Clarence G. (1907-82): ord. June 29, 1932; aux. Cincinnati (Phytea), 1954-57; bp. Columbus, 1957-64; coad. bp. Cleveland (Filaca), 1964-66; bp. Cleveland, 1966-74 (res.).

J

Janssen, John (1835-1913): b. Germany; ord.

Nov. 19, 1858; first bp. Belleville, 1888-1913.

Janssens, Francis A. (1843-97): b. Holland; ord. Dec. 21, 1867; bp. Natchez (now Jackson) 1881-88; abp. New Orleans, 1888-97.

Jeanmard, Jules B. (1879-1957): ord. June 10, 1903; first bp. Lafayette, La., 1918-56 (res.).

Johannes, Francis (1874-1937): b. Germany; ord. Jan. 3, 1897; coad. bp. Leavenworth (Thasus), 1928-29; bp. Leavenworth (now Kansas City), 1929-37.

Johnson, William R. (1918-86): ord. May 28, 1944; aux. Los Angeles (Blera), 1971-76; first bp. Orange, 1976-86.

Jones, William A., O.S.A. (1865-1921): ord. Mar. 15, 1890; bp. San Juan, 1907-21.

Juncker, Henry D. (1809-68): b. Lorraine (France); ord. Mar. 16, 1834; first bp. Alton (now Springfield), Ill., 1857-68.

Junger, Aegidius (1833-95): b. Germany; ord. June 27, 1862; bp. Nesqually (now Seattle), 1879-95.

K

Kain, John J. (1841-1903): ord. July 2, 1866; bp. Wheeling, 1875-93; coad. abp. St. Louis (Oxyrynchus), 1893-95; abp. St. Louis, 1895-1903.

Katzer, Frederick X. (1844-1903): b. Austria; ord. Dec. 21, 1866; bp. Green Bay, 1886-91; abp. Milwaukee, 1891-1903.

Keane, James J. (1856-1929): ord. Dec. 23, 1882; bp. Cheyenne, 1902-11; abp. Dubuque, 1911-29.

Keane, John J. (1839-1918): b. Ireland; ord. July 2, 1866; bp. Richmond, 1878-88; rector of Catholic University, 1888-97; consultor of Congregation for Propagation of the Faith, 1897-1900; abp. Dubuque, 1900-11 (res.).

Keane, Patrick J. (1872-1928): b. Ireland; ord. June 20, 1895; aux. Sacramento (Samaria), 1920-22; bp. Sacramento, 1922-28.

Kearney, James E. (1884-1977): ord. Sept. 19, 1908; bp. Salt Lake City, 1932-37; bp. Rochester, 1937-66 (res.).

Kearney, Raymond A. (1902-56): ord. Mar. 12, 1927; aux. Brooklyn (Lysinia), 1935-56.

Keiley, Benjamin J. (1847-1925): ord. Dec. 31, 1873; bp. Savannah, 1900-22 (res.).

Kelleher, Louis F. (1889-1946): ord. Apr. 3, 1915; aux. Boston (Thenae), 1945-46.

Kellenberg, Walter P. (1901-86): ord. June 2, 1928; aux. New York (Joannina), 1953-54; bp. Ogdensburg, 1954-57; first bp. Rockville Centre, 1957-76 (res.).

Kelley, Francis C. (1870-1948): b. Canada; ord. Aug. 23, 1893; bp. Oklahoma, 1924-48.

Kelly, Edward D. (1860-1926): ord. June 16, 1886; aux. Detroit (Cestrus), 1911-19; bp. Grand Rapids, 1919-26.

Kelly, Edward J. (1890-1956): ord. June 2, 1917; bp. Boise, 1928-56.

Kelly, Francis M. (1886-1950): ord. Nov. 1, 1912; aux. Winona (Mylasa), 1926-28; bp. Winona, 1928-49 (res.).

Kelly, Patrick (1779-1829): b. Ireland; ord. July 18, 1802; first bp. Richmond, 1820-22 (returned to Ireland; bp. Waterford and Lismore, 1822-29).

Kennally, Vincent, S.J. (1895-1977): ord. June 20,

1928; v.a. Caroline and Marshall Islands (Sassura), 1957-71 (res.).

Kennedy, Thomas F. (1858-1917): ord. July 24, 1887; rector North American College, 1901-17; tit. bp. Hadrianapolis, 1907-15; tit. abp. Seleucia, 1915-17.

Kenny, William J. (1853-1913): ord. Jan. 15, 1879; bp. St. Augustine, 1902-13.

Kenrick (brothers): **Francis P.** (1796-1863): b. Ireland; ord. Apr. 7, 1821; coad. bp. Philadelphia (Aratha), 1830-42; bp. Philadelphia, 1842-51; abp. Baltimore, 1851-63. **Peter** (1806-96): b. Ireland; ord. Mar. 6, 1832; coad. bp. St. Louis (Adrasus), 1841-43; bp. 1843-47, and first abp. 1847-95, St. Louis (res.).

Keough, Francis P. (1890-1961): ord. June 10, 1916; bp. Providence, 1943-47; abp. Baltimore, 1947-61.

Keyes, Michael, S.M. (1876-1959): b. Ireland; ord. June 21, 1907; bp. Savannah, 1922-35 (res.).

Kiley, Moses E. (1876-1953): b. Nova Scotia; ord. June 10, 1911; bp. Trenton, 1934-40; abp. Milwaukee, 1940-53.

Killeen, James (1917-78): ord. May 30, 1942; aux. Military Vicariate (Valmalla), 1975-78.

Klonowski, Henry T. (1898-1977): ord. Aug. 8, 1920; aux. Scranton (Daldis), 1947-73 (res.).

Kogy, Lorenz S., O.M. (1895-1963): b. Georgia, Russia; ord. Nov. 15, 1917; U.S. citizen, 1944; patriarchal vicar for Armenian diocese of Beirut (Comana), 1951-63.

Koudelka, Joseph (1852-1921): b. Austria; ord. Oct. 8, 1875; aux. Cleveland (Germanicopolis), 1908-11; aux. Milwaukee, 1911-13; bp. Superior, 1913-21.

Kowalski, Rembert, O.F.M. (1884-1970): ord. June 22, 1911; v.a. Wuchang, China (Ipsus), 1942-46; first bp. Wuchang, 1946-70 (in exile from 1953).

Kozlowski, Edward (1860-1915): b. Poland; ord. June 29, 1887; aux. Milwaukee (Germia), 1914-15.

Krautbauer, Francix X. (1824-85): b. Germany; ord. July 16, 1850; bp. Green Bay, 1875-85.

Kucera, Louis B. (1888-1957): ord. June 8, 1915; bp. Lincoln, 1930-57.

L

Lamb, Hugh (1890-1959): ord. May 29, 1915; aux. Philadelphia (Helos), 1936-51; first bp. Greensburg, 1951-59.

Lamy, Jean B.: See Index.

Lane, Loras (1910-68): ord. Mar. 19, 1937; aux. Dubuque (Bencenna), 1951-56; bp. Rockford, 1956-68.

Lane, Raymond A., M.M. (1894-1974): ord. Feb. 8, 1920; v.a. Fushun, Manchukuo (Hypaepa), 1940-46; sup. gen. Maryknoll, 1946-56.

Lardone, Francesco (1887-1980): b. Italy; ord. June 29, 1910; U.S. citizen 1937; nuncio to various countries (tit. abp. Rhizaeum), 1949-66 (res.).

Laval, John M. (1854-1937): b. France; ord. Nov. 10, 1877; aux. New Orleans (Hierocaesarea), 1911-37.

Lavialle, Peter J. (1819-67): b. France; ord. Feb. 12, 1844; bp. Louisville, 1865-67.

Lawler, John J. (1862-1948): ord. Dec. 19, 1885;

aux. St. Paul (Hermopolis), 1910-16; bp. Lead (now Rapid City), 1916-48.

Le Blond, Charles H. (1883-1958): ord. June 29, 1909; bp. St. Joseph, 1933-56 (res.).

Ledvina, Emmanuel (1868-1952): ord. Mar. 18, 1893; bp. Corpus Christi, 1921-49 (res.).

Leech, George L. (1890-1985): ord. May 29, 1920; aux. Harrisburg (Mela), Oct.-Dec., 1935; bp. Harrisburg, 1935-71 (res.).

Lefevere, Peter P. (1804-69): b. Belgium; ord. Nov. 30, 1831; coad. bp. and admin. Detroit (Zela), 1841-69.

Leibold, Paul F. (1914-72): ord. May 18, 1940; aux. Cincinnati (Trebenna), 1958-66; bp. Evansville, 1966-69; abp. Cincinnati, 1969-72.

Leipzig, Francis P. (1895-1981): ord. Apr. 17, 1920; bp. Baker, 1950-71 (res.).

Lenihan (brothers): **Mathias C.** (1854-1943): ord. Dec. 20, 1879; first bp. Great Falls, 1904-30 (res.). **Thomas M.** (1844-1901): b. Ireland; ord. Nov. 19, 1868; bp. Cheyenne, 1897-1901.

Leray, Francis X. (1825-87): b. France; ord. Mar. 19, 1852; bp. Natchitoches (now Alexandria, La.), 1877-79; coad. bp. New Orleans and admin. of Natchitoches (Jonopolis), 1879-83; abp. New Orleans, 1883-87.

Leven, Stephen A. (1905-83): ord. June 10, 1928; aux. San Antonio (Bure), 1956-69; bp. San Angelo, 1969-79 (res.).

Ley, Felix, O.F.M. Cap. (1909-72): ord. June 14, 1936; ap. admin. Ryukyu Is. (Caporilla), 1968-72.

Lillis, Thomas F. (1861-1938): ord. Aug. 15, 1885; bp. Leavenworth (now Kansas City, Kans.), 1904-10; coad. bp. Kansas City, Mo. (Cibyra), 1910-13; bp. Kansas City, Mo., 1913-38.

Lootens, Louis (1827-98): b. Belgium; ord. June 14, 1851; v.a. Idaho and Montana (Castabala), 1868-75 (res.).

Loras, Mathias (1792-1858): b. France; ord. Nov. 12, 1815; first bp. Dubuque, 1837-58.

Loughlin, John (1817-91): b. Ireland; ord. Oct. 18, 1840; first bp. Brooklyn, 1853-91.

Lowney, Denis M. (1863-1918): b. Ireland; ord. Dec. 17, 1887; aux. Providence (Hadrianopolis), 1917-18.

Lucey, Robert E. (1891-1977): ord. May 14, 1916; bp. Amarillo, 1934-41; abp. San Antonio, 1941-69 (res.).

Ludden, Patrick A. (1838-1912): b. Ireland; ord. May 21, 1865; first bp. Syracuse, 1887-1912.

Luers, John (1819-71): b. Germany; ord. Nov. 11, 1846; first bp. Fort Wayne, 1858-71.

Lynch, Joseph P. (1872-1954): ord. June 9, 1900; bp. Dallas, 1911-54.

Lynch, Patrick N. (1817-82): b. Ireland; ord. Apr. 5, 1840; bp. Charleston, 1858-82.

M

McAuliffe, Maurice F. (1875-1944): ord. July 29, 1900; aux. Hartford (Dercos), 1923-34; bp. Hartford, 1934-44.

McCafferty, John E. (1920-80): ord. Mar. 17, 1945; aux. Rochester (Tanudaia), 1968-80.

McCarthy, Joseph E. (1876-1955): ord. July 4, 1903; bp. Portland, Me., 1932-55.

McCarthy, Justin J. (1900-59): ord. Apr. 16, 1927;

aux. Newark (Doberus), 1954-57; bp. Camden, 1957-59.

McCarty, William T., C.SS.R. (1889-1972): ord. June 10, 1915; military delegate (Anea), 1943-47; coad. bp. Rapid City, 1947-48; bp. Rapid City, 1948-69 (res.).

McCauley, Vincent J., C.S.C. (1906-82): ord. June 24, 1943; first bp. Fort Portal, Uganda, 1961-72 (res.).

McCloskey, James P. (1870-1945): ord. Dec. 17, 1898; bp. Zamboanga, P.I., 1917-20; bp. Jaro, P.I., 1920-45.

McCloskey, John (1810-85): ord. Jan. 12, 1834; coad. bp. New York (Axiere), 1843-47; first bp. Albany, 1847-64; abp. New York, 1864-85; first U.S. cardinal 1875.

McCloskey, William G. (1823-1909): ord. Oct. 6, 1852; bp. Louisville, 1868-1909.

McCormick, Patrick J. (1880-1953): ord. July 6, 1904; aux. Washington (Atenia), 1950-53.

McCort, John J. (1860-1936): ord. Oct. 14, 1883; aux. Philadelphia (Azotus), 1912-20; bp. Altoona, 1920-36.

McDevitt, Gerald V. (1917-80): ord. May 30, 1942; aux. Philadelphia (Tigias), 1962-80.

McDevitt, Philip R. (1858-1935): ord. July 14, 1885; bp. Harrisburg, 1916-35.

McDonnell, Charles E. (1854-1921): ord. May 19, 1878; bp. Brooklyn, 1892-1921.

McDonnell, Thomas J. (1894-1961): ord. Sept. 20, 1919; aux. New York (Sela), 1947-51; coad. bp. Wheeling, 1951-61.

McEntegart, Bryan (1893-1968): ord. Sept. 8, 1917; bp. Ogdensburg, 1943-53; rector Catholic University (Aradi), 1953-57; bp. Brooklyn, 1957-68.

McFadden, James A. (1880-1952): ord. June 17, 1905; aux. Cleveland (Bida), 1932-43; first bp. Youngstown, 1943-52.

MacFarland, Francis P. (1819-74): ord. May 1, 1845; bp. Hartford, 1858-74.

McFaul, James A. (1850-1917): b. Ireland; ord. May 26, 1877; bp. Trenton, 1894-1917.

McGavick, Alexander J. (1863-1948): ord. June 11, 1887; aux. Chicago (Marcopolis), 1899-1921; bp. La Crosse, 1921-48.

McGeough, Joseph F. (1903-70): ord. Dec. 20, 1930; internuncio Ethiopia, 1957-60; apostolic delegate (Hemesa) S. Africa, 1960-67; nuncio Ireland, 1967-69.

McGill, John (1809-72): ord. June 13, 1835; bp. Richmond, 1850-72.

MacGinley, John B. (1871-1969): b. Ireland; ord. June 8, 1895; bp. Nueva Caceres, 1910-24; first bp. Monterey-Fresno, 1924-32 (res.).

McGolrick, James (1841-1918): b. Ireland; ord. June 11, 1867; first bp. Duluth, 1889-1918.

McGovern, Patrick A. (1872-1951): ord. Aug. 18, 1895; bp. Cheyenne, 1912-51.

McGovern, Thomas (1832-98): b. Ireland; ord. Dec. 27, 1861; bp. Harrisburg, 1888-98.

McGrath, Joseph F. (1871-1950): b. Ireland; ord. Dec. 21, 1895; bp. Baker City (now Baker), 1919-50.

McGucken, Joseph T. (1902-84): ord. Jan. 15, 1928; aux. Los Angeles (Sanavus), 1940-55; coad. bp. Sacramento, 1957-62; abp. San Francisco, 1962-77 (res.).

McGuinness, Eugene (1889-1957): ord. May 22, 1915; bp. Raleigh, 1937-44; coad. bp. Oklahoma City and Tulsa (Ilium), 1944-48; bp. Oklahoma City and Tulsa, 1948-57.

McGurkin, Edward A., M.M. (1905-83): ord. Sept. 14, 1930; bp. Shinyanga, Tanzania, 1956-75 (res.).

McIntyre, James F. (1886-1979): ord. May 21, 1921; aux. New York (Cirene), 1941-46; coad. abp. New York (Palto), 1946-48; abp. Los Angeles, 1948-70 (res.); cardinal, 1953.

MacKenzie, Eric F. (1893-1969): ord. Oct. 20, 1918; aux. Boston (Alba), 1950-69.

McLaughlin, Charles B. (1913-78): ord. June 6, 1941; aux. Raleigh (Risinium), 1964-68; first bp. St. Petersburg, 1968-78.

McLaughlin, Thomas H. (1881-1947): ord. July 26, 1904; aux. Newark (Nisa), 1935-37; first bp. Paterson, 1937-47.

McMahon, John J. (1875-1932): ord. May 20, 1900; bp. Trenton, 1928-32.

McMahon, Lawrence S. (1835-93): ord. Mar. 24, 1860; bp. Hartford, 1879-93.

McManaman, Edward P. (1900-64): ord. Mar. 12, 1927; aux. Erie (Floriana), 1948-64.

McManus, James E., C.SS.R. (1900-76): ord. June 19, 1927; bp. Ponce, P.R., 1947-63; aux. New York (Banda), 1963-70 (res.).

McMullen, John (1832-83): b. Ireland; ord. June 20, 1858; first bp. Davenport, 1881-83.

McNamara, John M. (1878-1960): ord. June 21, 1902; aux. Baltimore (Eumenia), 1928-47; aux. Washington, 1947-60.

McNamara, Martin D. (1898-1966): ord. Dec. 23, 1922; first bp. Joliet, 1949-66.

McNeirny, Francis (1828-94): ord. Aug. 17, 1854; coad. bp. Albany (Rhesaina), 1872-77; bp. Albany, 1877-94.

McNicholas, John T., O.P. (1877-1950): b. Ireland; ord. Oct. 10, 1901; bp. Duluth, 1918-25; abp. Cincinnati, 1925-50.

McNicholas, Joseph A. (1923-83): ord. June 7, 1949; aux. St. Louis (Scala), 1969-75; bp. Springfield, Ill., 1975-83.

McNulty, James A. (1900-72): ord. July 12, 1925; aux. Newark (Methone), 1947-53; bp. Paterson, 1953-63; bp. Buffalo, 1963-72.

McQuaid, Bernard J. (1823-1909): ord. Jan. 16, 1848; first bp. Rochester, 1868-1909.

McSorley, Francis J., O.M.I. (1913-71): ord. May 30, 1939; v.a. Jolo, P.I. (Sozusa), 1958-71.

McVinney, Russell J. (1898-1971): ord. July 13, 1924; bp. Providence, 1948-71.

Machebeuf, Joseph P. (1812-89): b. France; ord. Dec. 17, 1836; v.a. Colorado and Utah (Epiphania), 1868-87; first bp. Denver, 1887-89.

Maes, Camillus P. (1846-1915): b. Belgium; ord. Dec. 19, 1868; bp. Covington, 1885-1915.

Maginn, Edward J. (1897-1984): b. Scotland; ord. June 10, 1922; aux. Albany (Curium), 1957-72 (res.).

Magner, Francis (1887-1947): ord. May 17, 1913; bp. Marquette, 1941-47.

Mahoney, Bernard (1875-1939): ord. Feb. 27, 1904; bp. Sioux Falls, 1922-39.

Maloney, Thomas F. (1903-62): ord. July 13, 1930; aux. Providence (Andropolis), 1960-62.

Manogue, Patrick: See Index.

Manucy, Dominic (1823-85): ord. Aug. 15, 1850; v.a. Brownsville (Dulma), 1874-84; bp. Mobile, Mar.-Sept., 1884 (res.); reappointed v.a. Brownsville (Maronea) (now diocese of Corpus Christi), 1884-85.

Mardaga, Thomas J. (1913-84): ord. May 14, 1940; aux. Baltimore (Mutugenna), 1967-68; bp. Wilmington, 1968-84.

Marechal, Ambrose, S.S. (1766-1828): b. France; ord. June 2, 1792; abp. Baltimore, 1817-28.

Markham, Thomas F. (1891-1952): ord. June 2, 1917; aux. Boston (Acalissus), 1950-52.

Marling, Joseph M., C.Pp.S. (1904-79): ord. Feb. 21, 1929; aux. Kansas City, Mo. (Thasus), 1947-56; first bp. Jefferson City, 1956-69 (res.).

Martin, Augustus M. (1803-75): b. France; ord. May 31, 1828; first bp. Natchitoches (now Alexandria), 1853-75.

Marty, Martin, O.S.B. (1834-96): b. Switzerland; ord. Sept. 14, 1856; v.a. Dakota (Tiberias), 1880-89; first bp. Sioux Falls, 1889-95; bp. St. Cloud, 1895-96.

Marx, Adolph (1915-65): b. Germany; ord. May 2, 1940; aux. Corpus Christi (Citrus), 1956-65; first bp. Brownsville, 1965.

Matz, Nicholas C. (1850-1917): b. France; ord. May 31, 1874; coad. bp. Denver (Telmissus), 1887-89; bp. Denver, 1889-1917.

Mazzarella, Bernardino N., O.F.M. (1904-79): ord. June 5, 1931; prelate Olancho, Honduras (Hadrianopolis in Pisidia), 1957-63; first bp. Comayagua, Honduras, 1963-79.

Medeiros, Humberto S. (1915-83): b. Azores; U.S. citizen, 1940; ord. June 15, 1946; bp. Brownsville, 1966-70; abp. Boston, 1970-83; cardinal 1973.

Meerschaert, Theophile (1847-1924): b. Belgium; ord. Dec. 23, 1871; v.a. Oklahoma and Indian Territory (Sidyma), 1891-1905; first bp. Oklahoma, 1905-24.

Melcher, Joseph (1806-73): b. Austria; ord. Mar. 27, 1830; first bp. Green Bay, 1868-73.

Messmer, Sebastian (1847-1930): b. Switzerland; ord. July 23, 1871; bp. Green Bay, 1892-1903; abp. Milwaukee, 1903-30.

Metzger, Sidney M. (1902-86): ord. Apr. 3, 1926; aux. Santa Fe (Birtha), 1940-41; coad. bp. El Paso, 1941-42; bp. El Paso, 1942-78 (res.).

Meyer, Albert (1903-65): ord. July 11, 1926; bp. Superior, 1946-53; abp. Milwaukee, 1953-58; abp. Chicago, 1958-65; cardinal, 1959.

Michaud, John S. (1843-1908): ord. June 7, 1873; coad. bp. Burlington (Modra), 1892-99; bp. Burlington, 1899-1908.

Miege, John B., S.J. (1815-84): b. France; ord. Sept. 12, 1844; v.a. Kansas and Indian Territory (now Kansas City) (Messene), 1851-74 (res.).

Mihalik, Emil J. (1920-84): ord. Sept. 21, 1945; first bp. Parma (Byzantine Rite, Ruthenians), 1969-84.

Miles, Richard P., O.P. (1791-1860): ord. Sept. 21, 1816; first bp. Nashville, 1838-60.

Minihan, Jeremiah F. (1903-73): ord. Dec. 21, 1929; aux. Boston (Paphus), 1954-73.

Misner, Paul B., C.M. (1891-1938): ord. Feb. 23, 1919; v.a. Yukiang, China (Myrica), 1935-38.

Mitty, John J. (1884-1961): ord. Dec. 22, 1906; bp. Salt Lake, 1926-32; coad. abp. San Francisco (Aegina), 1932-35; abp. San Francisco, 1935-61.

Moeller, Henry (1849-1925): ord. June 10, 1876; bp. Columbus, 1900-03; coad. abp. Cincinnati (Areopolis), 1903-04; abp. Cincinnati, 1904-25.

Molloy, Thomas E. (1884-1956): ord. Sept. 19, 1908; aux. Brooklyn (Lorea), 1920-21; bp. Brooklyn, 1921-56.

Monaghan, Francis J. (1890-1942): ord. May 29, 1915; coad. bp. Ogdensburg (Mela), 1936-39; bp. Ogdensburg, 1939-42.

Monaghan, John J. (1856-1935): ord. Dec. 18, 1880; bp. Wilmington, 1897-1925 (res.).

Montgomery, George T. (1847-1907): ord. Dec. 20, 1879; coad. bp. Monterey-Los Angeles (Thmuis), 1894-96; bp. Monterey-Los Angeles (now Los Angeles), 1896-1903; coad. abp. San Francisco (Auxum), 1903-07.

Mooney, Edward (1882-1958): ord. Apr. 10, 1909; ap. del. India (Irenopolis), 1926-31; ap. del. Japan, 1931-33; bp. Rochester, 1933-37; first abp. Detroit, 1937-58; cardinal, 1946.

Moore, John (1835-1901): b. Ireland; ord. Apr. 9, 1860; bp. St. Augustine, 1877-1901.

Mora, Francis (1827-1905): b. Spain; ord. Mar. 19, 1856; coad. bp. Monterey-Los Angeles (Mosynopolis), 1873-78; bp. Monterey-Los Angeles (now Los Angeles), 1878-96 (res.).

Morris, John (1866-1946): ord. June 11, 1892; coad. bp. Little Rock (Acmonia), 1906-07; bp. Little Rock, 1907-46.

Mrak, Ignatius (1810-1901): b. Austria; ord. July 31, 1837; bp. Sault Ste. Marie and Marquette (now Marquette), 1869-78 (res.).

Mueller, Joseph M. (1894-1981): ord. June 14, 1919; coad. bp. Sioux City (Sinda), 1947-48; bp. Sioux City, 1948-70 (res.).

Muench, Aloysius (1889-1962): ord. June 8, 1913; bp. Fargo, 1935-59 (res.); apostolic visitator to Germany, 1946; nuncio to Germany 1951-59; cardinal 1959.

Muldoon, Peter J. (1862-1927): ord. Dec. 18, 1886; aux. Chicago (Tamasus), 1901-08; first bp. Rockford, 1908-27.

Mullen, Tobias (1818-1900): b. Ireland; ord. Sept. 1, 1844; bp. Erie, 1868-99 (res.).

Mulloy, William T. (1892-1959): ord. June 7, 1916; bp. Covington, 1945-59.

Mundelein, George (1872-1939): ord. June 8, 1895; aux. Brooklyn (Loryma), 1909-15; abp. Chicago, 1915-39; cardinal, 1924.

Murphy, Joseph A., S.J. (1857-1939): b. Ireland; ord. Aug. 26, 1888; v.a. Belize, Br. Honduras (Birtha), 1923-39.

Murphy, William F. (1885-1950): ord. June 13, 1908; first bp. Saginaw, 1938-50.

Murray, John G. (1877-1956): ord. Apr. 14, 1900; aux. Hartford (Flavias), 1920-25; bp. Portland, 1925-31; abp. St. Paul, 1931-56.

Mussio, John K. (1902-78): ord. Aug. 15, 1935; bp. Steubenville, 1945-77 (res.).

N

Najmy, Justin, O.S.B.M. (1898-1968): b. Syria; ord. Dec. 25, 1926; ap. ex. Melkites (Augustopolis in Phrygia), 1966-68.

Navagh, James J. (1901-65): ord. Dec. 21, 1929; aux. Raleigh (Ombi), 1952-57; bp. Ogdensburg, 1957-63; bp. Paterson, 1963-65.

Neale, Leonard (1746-1817): ord. June 5, 1773; coad. bp. Baltimore (Gortyna), 1800-15; abp. Baltimore, 1815-17.

Neraz, John C. (1828-94): b. France; ord. Mar. 19, 1853; bp. San Antonio, 1881-1894.

Neumann, John, St.: See Index.

Newman, Thomas A., M.S. (1903-78): ord. June 29, 1929; first bp. Prome, Burma, 1961-75 (res.).

Niedhammer, Matthew A., O.F.M. Cap. (1901-70): ord. June 8, 1927; v.a. Bluefields, Nicaragua (Caloe), 1943-70.

Nilan, John J. (1855-1934): ord. Dec. 2, 1878; bp. Hartford, 1910-34.

Noa, Thomas L. (1892-1977): ord. Dec. 23, 1916; coad. bp. Sioux City (Salona), 1946-47; bp. Marquette, 1947-68 (res.).

Nold, Wendelin J. (1900-81): ord. Apr. 11, 1925; coad. bp. Galveston (Sasima), 1948-50; bp. Galveston-Houston, 1950-75 (res.).

Noll, John F. (1875-1956): ord. June 4, 1898; bp. Fort Wayne, 1925-56.

Northrop, Henry P. (1842-1916): ord. June 25, 1865; v.a. North Carolina (Rosalia), 1881-83; bp. Charleston, 1883-1916.

Noser, Adolph, S.V.D. (1900-81): ord. Sept. 27, 1925; v.a. Accra, British W. Africa (now Ghana) (Capitolias), 1947-50; bp. Accra, 1950-53; v.a. Alexishafen, New Guinea (Hierpiniana), 1953-66; abp. Madang, Papua New Guinea, 1966-75 (res.).

Nussbaum, Paul J., C.P. (1870-1935): ord. May 20, 1894; first bp. Corpus Christi, 1913-20 (res.); bp. Sault Ste. Marie and Marquette (now Marquette), 1922-35.

O

O'Brien, Henry J. (1896-1976): ord. July 8, 1923; aux. Hartford (Sita), 1940-45; bp. Hartford, 1945-53, and first abp. Hartford, 1953-68 (res.).

O'Brien, William D. (1878-1962): ord. July 11, 1903; aux. Chicago (Calynda), 1934-62.

O'Connell, Denis J. (1849-1927): b. Ireland; ord. May 26, 1877; aux. San Francisco (Sebaste), 1908-12; bp. Richmond, 1912-26 (res.).

O'Connell, Eugene (1815-91): b. Ireland; ord. May 21, 1842; v.a. Marysville (Flaviopolis), 1861-68; first bp. Grass Valley, 1868-84 (res.).

O'Connell, William H. (1859-1944): ord. June 7, 1884; bp. Portland, 1901-06; coad. bp. Boston (Constantia), 1906-07; abp. Boston, 1907-44; cardinal, 1911.

O'Connor (brothers), **James** (1823-90): b. Ireland; ord. Mar. 25, 1848; v.a. Nebraska (Dibon), 1876-85; first bp. Omaha, 1885-90. **Michael, S.J.** (1810-72): b. Ireland; ord. June 1, 1833; first bp. Pittsburgh, 1843-53; first bp. Erie, 1853-54; bp. Pittsburgh, 1854-60 (resigned, joined Jesuits).

O'Connor, John J. (1855-1927): ord. Dec. 22, 1877; bp. Newark, 1901-27.

O'Connor, William A. (1903-83): ord. Sept. 24, 1927; bp. Springfield, Ill., 1949-75 (res.).

O'Connor, William P. (1886-1973): ord. Mar. 10, 1912; bp. Superior, 1942-46; first bp. Madison, 1946-67 (res.).

O'Dea, Edward J. (1856-1932): ord. Dec. 23, 1882; bp. Nesqually (now Seattle — title changed in 1907), 1896-1932.

Odin, John M., C.M. (1800-70): b. France; ord. May 4, 1823; v.a. Texas (Claudiopolis), 1842-47; first bp. Galveston, 1847-61; abp. New Orleans, 1861-70.

O'Donaghue, Denis (1848-1925): ord. Sept. 6, 1874; aux. Indianapolis (Pomaria), 1900-10; bp. Louisville, 1910-24 (res.).

O'Dowd, James T. (1907-50): ord. June 4, 1932; aux. San Francisco (Cea), 1948-50.

O'Farrell, Michael J. (1832-94): b. Ireland; ord. Aug. 18, 1855; first bp. Trenton, 1881-94.

O'Flanagan, Dermot (1901-73): b. Ireland; ord. Aug. 27, 1929; first bp. Juneau, 1951-68 (res.).

O'Gara, Cuthbert, C.P. (1886-1968): b. Canada; ord. May 26, 1915; v.a. Yuanling, China (Elis), 1934-46; first bp. Yuanling, 1946-68 (imprisoned, 1951, and then expelled, 1953, by Chinese Communists).

O'Gorman, James, O.C.S.O. (1804-74): b. Ireland; ord. Dec. 23, 1843; v.a. Nebraska (now Omaha) (Raphanea), 1859-74.

O'Gorman, Thomas (1843-1921): ord. Nov. 5, 1865; bp. Sioux Falls, 1896-1921.

O'Hara, Edwin V. (1881-1956): ord. June 9, 1905; bp. Great Falls, 1930-39; bp. Kansas City, Mo., 1939-56 (title changed to Kansas City-St. Joseph, 1956).

O'Hara, Gerald P. (1888-1963): ord. Apr. 3, 1920; aux. Philadelphia (Heliopolis), 1929-35; bp. Savannah (title changed to Savannah-Atlanta in 1937), 1935-59 (res.); regent of Rumania nunciature, 1946-50 (expelled); nuncio to Ireland, 1951-54; ap. del. to Gret Britain, 1954-63; tit. abp. Pessinus, 1959-63.

O'Hara, John F., C.S.C. (1886-1960): ord. Sept. 9, 1916; delegate of U.S. military vicar (Mylasa), 1940-45; bp. Buffalo, 1945-51; abp. Philadelphia, 1951-60; cardinal, 1958.

O'Hara, William (1816-99): b. Ireland; ord. Dec. 21, 1842; first bp. Scranton, 1868-99.

O'Hare, William F., S.J. (1870-1926): ord. June 25, 1903; v.a. Jamaica (Maximianopolis), 1920-26.

O'Hern, John F. (1874-1933): ord. Feb. 17, 1901; bp. Rochester, 1929-33.

O'Leary, Thomas (1875-1949): ord. Dec. 18, 1897; bp. Springfield, Mass., 1921-49.

Olwell, Quentin, C.P. (1898-1972): ord. Feb. 4, 1923; prelate Marbel, P.I. (Thabraca), 1961-69 (res.).

O'Regan, Anthony (1809-66): b. Ireland; ord. Nov. 29, 1834; bp. Chicago, 1854-58 (res.).

O'Reilly, Bernard (1803-56): b. Ireland; ord. Oct. 16, 1831; bp. Hartford, 1850-56.

O'Reilly, Charles J. (1860-1923): b. Canada; ord. June 29, 1890; first bp. Baker City (now Baker), 1903-18; bp. Lincoln, 1918-23.

O'Reilly, James (1855-1934): b. Ireland; ord. June 24, 1880; bp. Fargo, 1910-34.

O'Reilly, Patrick T. (1833-92): b. Ireland; ord. Aug. 15, 1857; first bp. Springfield, Mass., 1870-92.

O'Reilly, Peter J. (1850-1924): b. Ireland; ord. June 24, 1877; aux. Peoria (Lebedus), 1900-24.

O'Reilly, Thomas C. (1873-1938): ord. June 4, 1898; bp. Scranton, 1928-38.

Ortynsky, Stephen, O.S.B.M. (1866-1916): b. Poland; ord. July 18, 1891; first Ukrainian Byzantine Rite bishop in U.S. (Daulia), 1907-16.

O'Shea, John A., C.M. (1887-1969): ord. May 30, 1914; v.a. Kanchow, China (Midila), 1928-46; first bp. Kanchow, 1949-69 (expelled by Chinese Communists, 1953).

O'Shea, William F., M.M. (1884-1945): ord. Dec. 5, 1917; v.a. Heijon, Japan (Naissusz), 1939-45; prisoner of Japanese 1941-42.

O'Sullivan, Jeremiah (1842-96): b. Ireland; ord. June 30, 1868; bp. Mobile, 1885-96.

P

Pardy, James V., M.M. (1898-1983): ord. Jan. 26, 1930; v.a. Cheong-Ju, Korea (Irenopolis), 1958-62; first bp. Cheong-Ju, 1962-69 (res.).

Paschang, Adolph J., M.M. (1895-1968): ord. May 21, 1921; v.a. Kong Moon, China (Sasima), 1937-46; first bp. Kong Moon, 1946-68 (expelled by Communists, 1951).

Pellicer, Anthony (1824-80): ord. Aug. 15, 1850; first bp. San Antonio, 1874-80.

Penalver y Cardenas, Luis (1749-1810): b. Cuba; ord. Apr. 4, 1772; first bp. Louisiana and the Two Floridas (now New Orleans), 1793-1801; abp. Guatemala, 1801-06 (res.).

Perche, Napoleon J. (1805-83): b. France; ord. Sept. 19, 1829; abp. New Orleans, 1870-83.

Pernicone, Joseph M. (1903-85): b. Sicily; ord. Dec. 18, 1926; aux. New York (Hadrianapolis) 1954-78 (res.).

Persico, Ignatius, O.F.M. Cap. (1823-95): b. Italy; ord. Jan. 24, 1846; bishop from 1854; bp. Savannah-Atlanta, 1870-72; cardinal, 1893.

Peschges, John H. (1881-1944): ord. Apr. 15, 1905; bp. Crookston, 1938-44.

Peterson, John B. (1871-1944): ord. Sept. 15, 1899; aux. Boston (Hippos), 1972-32; bp. Manchester, 1932-44.

Phelan, Richard (1828-1904): b. Ireland; ord. May 4, 1854; coad. bp. Pittsburgh (Cibyra), 1885-89; bp. Pittsburgh, 1889-1904.

Pinten, Joseph G. (1867-1945): ord. Nov. 1, 1890; bp. Superior, 1922-26; bp. Grand Rapids, 1926-40 (res.).

Pitaval, John B. (1858-1928): b. France; ord. Dec. 24, 1881; aux. Santa Fe (Sora), 1902-09; abp. Santa Fe, 1909-18 (res.).

Plagens, Joseph C. (1880-1943): b. Poland; ord. July 5, 1903; aux. Detroit (Rhodiapolis), 1924-35; bp. Sault Ste. Marie and Marquette (title changed to Marquette, 1937), 1935-40; bp. Grand Rapids, 1941-43.

Portier, Michael (1795-1859): b. France; ord. May 16, 1818; v.a. Two Floridas and Alabama (Olena), 1826-29; first bp. Mobile, 1829-59.

Prendergast, Edmond (1843-1918): b. Ireland; ord. Nov. 17, 1865; aux. Philadelphia (Scilium), 1897-1911; abp. Philadelphia, 1911-18.

Purcell, John B. (1800-83): b. Ireland; ord. May 20, 1826; bp., 1833-50, and first abp., 1850-83, Cincinnati.

Q

Quarter, William (1806-48): b. Ireland; ord. Sept. 19, 1829; first bp. Chicago, 1844-48.

Quigley, James F. (1855-1915): b. Canada; ord. Apr. 13, 1879; bp. Buffalo, 1897-1903; abp. Chicago, 1903-15.

Quinlan, John (1826-83): b. Ireland; ord. Aug. 30, 1852; bp. Mobile, 1859-83.

Quinn, William Charles, C.M. (1905-60): ord. Oct. 11, 1931; v.a. Yukiang, China (Halicarnassus), 1940-46; first bp. Yukiang, 1946-60 (expelled by Chinese Communists, 1951).

R

Rademacher, Joseph (1840-1900): ord. Aug. 2, 1863; bp. Nashville, 1883-93; bp. Fort Wayne, 1893-1900.

Rappe, Louis Amadeus (1801-77): b. France; ord. Mar. 14, 1829; first bp. Cleveland, 1847-70 (res.).

Rausch, James S. (1928-81): ord. June 2, 1956; aux. St. Cloud (Summa), 1973-77; bp. Phoenix, 1977-81.

Ready, Michael J. (1893-1957): ord. Sept. 14, 1918; bp. Columbus, 1944-57.

Reed, Victor J. (1905-71): ord. Dec. 21, 1929; aux. Oklahoma City and Tulsa (Limasa), 1957-58; bp. Oklahoma City and Tulsa, 1958-71.

Rehring, George J. (1890-1976): ord. Mar. 28, 1914; aux. Cincinnati (Lunda), 1937-50; bp. Toledo, 1950-67 (res.).

Reicher, Louis J. (1890-1984): ord. Dec. 6, 1918; first bp. Austin, 1948-71 (res.).

Reilly, Edmond J. (1897-1958): ord. Apr. 1, 1922; aux. Brooklyn (Nepte), 1955-58.

Rese, Frederic (1791-1871): b. Germany; ord. Mar. 15, 1823; first bp. Detroit, 1833-71. Inactive from 1841 because of ill health.

Reverman, Theodore (1877-1941): ord. July 26, 1901; bp. Superior, 1926-41.

Reynolds, Ignatius A. (1798-1855): ord. Oct. 24, 1823; bp. Charleston, 1844-55.

Rhode, Paul P. (1871-1945): b. Poland; ord. June 17, 1894; aux. Chicago (Barca), 1908-15; bp. Green Bay, 1915-45.

Rice, Joseph J. (1871-1938): ord. Sept. 29, 1894; bp. Burlington, 1910-38.

Rice, William A., S.J. (1891-1946): ord. Aug. 27, 1925; v.a. Belize, Br. Honduras (Rusicade), 1939-46.

Richter, Henry J. (1838-1916): b. Germany; ord. June 10, 1865; first bp. Grand Rapids, 1883-1916.

Riley, Thomas J. (1900-1977): ord. May 20, 1927; aux. Boston (Regiae), 1956-76 (res.).

Riordan, Patrick W. (1841-1914): b. Canada; ord. June 10, 1865; coad. abp. San Francisco (Cabasa), 1883-84; abp. San Francisco, 1884-1914.

Ritter, Joseph E. (1892-1967): ord. May 30, 1917; aux. Indianapolis (Hippos), 1933-34; bp., 1934-44, and first abp. Indianapolis, 1944-46; abp. St. Louis, 1946-67; cardinal 1961.

Robinson, Pascal C., O.F.M. (1870-1948): b. Ireland; ord. Dec. 21, 1901; ap. visitor to Palestine, Egypt, Syria and Cyprus (Tyana), 1927-29; ap. nuncio to Ireland, 1929-48.

Rohlman, Henry P. (1876-1957): b. Germany; ord. Dec. 21, 1901; bp. Davenport, 1927-44; coad. abp. Dubuque (Macra), 1944-46; abp. Dubuque, 1946-54 (res.).

Rooker, Fraderick Z. (1861-1907): ord. July 25, 1888; bp. Jaro, P.I., 1903-07.

Ropert, Gulstan F., SS.CC. (1839-1903): b. France; ord. May 26, 1866; v.a. Sandwich (now Hawaiian) Is. (Panopolis), 1892-1903.

Rosati, Joseph, C.M.: See Index.

Rosecrans, Sylvester (1827-78): ord. June 5, 1853; aux. Cincinnati (Pompeiopolis), 1862-68; first bp. Columbus, 1868-78.

Rouxel, Gustave A. (1840-1908): b. France, ord. Nov. 4, 1863; aux. New Orleans (Curium), 1899-1908.

Rummel, Joseph (1876-1964): b. Germany; ord. May 24, 1902; bp. Omaha, 1928-35; abp. New Orleans, 1935-64.

Ruocco, Joseph J. (1922-80): ord. May 6, 1948; aux. Boston (Polignano), 1975-80.

Russell, William T. (1863-1927): ord. June 21, 1889; bp. Charleston, 1917-27.

Ryan, Edward F. (1879-1956): ord. Aug. 10, 1905; bp. Burlington, 1945-56.

Ryan, Gerald J. (1923-85): ord. June 3, 1950; aux. Rockville Centre (Munatiana), 1977-85.

Ryan, James (1848-1923): b. Ireland; ord. Dec. 24, 1871; bp. Alton (now Springfield), Ill., 1888-1923.

Ryan, James H. (1886-1947): ord. June 5, 1909; rector Catholic University, 1928-35; tit. bp. Modra, 1933-35; bp., 1935-45, and first abp. Omaha, 1945-47.

Ryan, Patrick J. (1831-1911): b. Ireland; ord. Sept. 8, 1853; coad. bp. St. Louis (Tricomia), 1872-84; abp. Philadelphia, 1884-1911.

Ryan, Stephen, C.M. (1826-96): b. Canada; ord. June 24, 1849; bp. Buffalo, 1868-96.

Ryan, Vincent J. (1884-1951): ord. June 7, 1912; bp. Bismarck, 1940-41.

S

Salpointe, John B. (1825-98): b. France; ord. Dec. 20, 1851; v.a. Arizona (Dorylaeum), 1869-84; coad. abp. Santa Fe (Anazarbus), 1884-85; abp. Santa Fe, 1885-94 (res.).

Scanlan, Lawrence (1843-1915): b. Ireland; ord. June 28, 1868; v.a. Utah (Laranda), 1887-91; bp. Salt Lake (now Salt Lake City), 1891-1915.

Scannell, Richard (1845-1916): b. Ireland; ord. Feb. 26, 1871; first bp. Concordia (now Salina), 1887-91; bp. Omaha, 1891-1916.

Schenk, Francis J. (1901-69): ord. June 13, 1926; bp. Crookston, 1945-60; bp. Duluth, 1960-69.

Scher, Philip G. (1880-1953): ord. June 6, 1904; bp. Monterey-Fresno, 1933-53.

Schexnayder, Maurice (1895-1981): ord. Apr. 11, 1925; aux. Lafayette (Tuscamia), 1951-56; bp. Lafayette, La., 1956-72 (res.).

Schinner, Augustine (1863-1937): ord. Mar. 7, 1886; first bp. Superior, 1905-13; first bp. Spokane, 1914-25 (res.).

Schlarman, Joseph H. (1879-1951): ord. June 29, 1904; bp. Peoria, 1930-51.

Schmitt, Adolph G., C.M.M. (1905-76): b. Bavaria; U.S. citizen 1945; v.a. Bulawayo (Nasai), Rhodesia, 1951-55; first bp. Bulawayo, 1955-74 (res.). Murdered by terrorists.

Schmondiuk, Joseph (1912-1978): ord. Mar. 29, 1936; aux. Philadelphia exarchate (Zeugma in Syria), 1956-61; eparch Stamford, 1961-77; abp. Philadelphia, 1977-78.

Schott, Lawrence F. (1907-63): ord. July 15, 1935; aux. Harrisburg (Eluza), 1956-63.

Schrembs, Joseph (1866-1945): b. Germany; ord. June 29, 1889; aux. Grand Rapids (Sophene), 1911; first bp. Toledo, 1911-21; bp. Cleveland, 1921-45.

Schuler, Anthony J., S.J. (1869-1944): ord. June 27, 1901; first bp. El Paso, 1915-42 (res.).

Schulte, Paul (1890-1984): ord. June 11, 1915; bp. Leavenworth, 1937-46; abp. Indianapolis, 1946-70 (res.).

Schwebach, James (1847-1921): b. Luxembourg; ord. June 16, 1870; bp. La Crosse, 1892-1921.

Schwertner, August J. (1870-1939): ord. June 12, 1897; bp. Wichita, 1921-39.

Scully, William (1894-1969): ord. Sept. 20, 1919; coad. bp. Albany (Pharsalus), 1945-54; bp. Albany, 1954-69.

Sebastian, Jerome D. (1895-1960): ord. May 25, 1922; aux. Baltimore (Baris in Hellesponto), 1954-60.

Seghers, Charles J.: See Index.

Seidenbusch, Rupert, O.S.B. (1830-95): b. Germany; ord. June 22, 1853; v.a. Northern Minnesota (Halia), 1875-88 (res.).

Senyshyn, Ambrose, O.S.B.M. (1903-76): b. Galicia; ord. Aug. 23, 1931; aux. Ukrainian Catholic Diocese of U.S. (Maina), 1942-56; first bp. Stamford (Byzantine Rite), 1958-61; abp. Philadelphia (Byzantine Rite), 1961-76.

Seton, Robert J. (1839-1927): b. Italy, ord. Apr. 15, 1865; tit. abp. Heliopolis, 1903-27. Grandson of St. Elizabeth Seton.

Shahan, Thomas J. (1857-1932): ord. June 3, 1882; rector, Catholic University of America, 1909-27; tit. bp. Germanicopolis, 1914-32.

Shanahan (brothers): **Jeremiah F.** (1834-86): ord. July 3, 1859; first bp. Harrisburg, 1868-86. **John W.** (1846-1916): ord. Jan. 2, 1869; bp. Harrisburg, 1899-1916.

Shanley, John (1852-1909): ord. May 30, 1874; first bp. Jamestown (see transferred to Fargo in 1897), 1889-1909.

Shanley, Patrick H., O.C.D. (1896-1970): b. Ireland; ord. Dec. 21, 1930; U.S. citizen; prelate Infanta, P.I. (Sophene), 1953-60 (res.).

Shaughnessy, Gerald, S.M. (1887-1950): ord. June 20, 1920; bp. Seattle, 1933-50.

Shaw, John W. (1861-1934): ord. May 26, 1888; coad. bp. San Antonio (Castabala), 1910-11; bp. San Antonio, 1911-18; abp. New Orleans, 1918-34.

Sheehan, Edward T., C.M. (1888-1933): ord. June 7, 1916, v.a. Yukiang, China (Calydon), 1929-33.

Sheen, Fulton J. (1895-1979): ord. Sept. 20, 1919; aux. New York (Caesarina), 1951-66; bp. Rochester, 1966-69 (res.); tit. abp. Newport.

Shehan, Lawrence J. (1898-1984): ord. Dec. 23,

1922; aux. Baltimore and Washington (Lidda), 1945-53; bp. Bridgeport, 1953-61; coad. abp. Baltimore (Nicopolis ad Nestum), Sept.-Dec., 1961; abp. Baltimore, 1961-74 (res.); cardinal 1965.

Sheil, Bernard J. (1886-1969): ord. May 21, 1910; aux. bp. Chicago (Pegae), 1928-69; tit. abp. Selge, 1959-69.

Smith, Alphonse (1883-1935): ord. Apr. 18, 1908; bp. Nashville, 1924-35.

Smith, Eustace, O.F.M. (1908-75): ord. June 12, 1934; v.a. Beirut, Lebanon (Apamea Cibotus), 1958-73 (res.).

Smith, Leo R. (1905-63): ord. Dec. 21, 1929; aux. Buffalo (Marida), 1952-63; bp. Ogdensburg, 1963.

Smyth, Clement, O.C.S.O. (1810-65): b. Ireland; ord. May 29, 1841; coad. bp. Dubuque (Thennesus), 1857-58; bp. Dubuque, 1858-65.

Spalding, John F. (1840-1916): ord. Dec. 19, 1863, first bp. Peoria, 1876-1908 (res.).

Spalding, Martin J. (1810-72): ord. Aug. 13, 1834; aux. Louisville (Lengone), 1848-50; bp. Louisville, 1850-64; abp. Baltimore, 1864-72.

Spellman, Francis J. (1889-1967): ord. May 14, 1916; aux. Boston (Sila), 1932-39; abp. New York, 1939-67; cardinal 1946.

Spence, John S. (1909-73): ord. Dec. 5, 1933; aux. Washington (Aggersel), 1964-73.

Stang, William (1854-1907): b. Germany; ord. June 15, 1878; first bp. Fall River, 1904-07.

Stanton, Martin W. (1897-1977): ord. June 14, 1924; aux. Newark (Citium) 1957-72 (res.).

Stariha, John (1845-1915): b. Austria; ord. Sept. 19, 1869; first bp. Lead (now Rapid City), 1902-09 (res.).

Steck, Leo J. (1898-1950): ord. June 8, 1924; aux. Salt Lake City (Ilium), 1948-50.

Stemper, Alfred M., M.S.C. (1913-84): ord. June 26, 1940; v.a. Kavieng (Eleutheropolis), 1957-66; first bp. Kavieng, 1966-80 (res.).

Stock, John (1918-72): ord. Dec. 4, 1943; aux. Philadelphia (Ukrainian Rite) (Pergamum), 1971-72.

Stritch, Samuel (1887-1958): ord. May 21, 1909; bp. Toledo, 1921-30; abp. Milwaukee, 1930-39; abp. Chicago, 1939-58; cardinal 1946.

Sullivan, Bernard, S.J. (1889-1970): ord, June 26, 1921; bp. Patna, India, 1929-46 (res.).

Sullivan, Joseph V. (1919-82): ord. June 1, 1946; aux. Kansas City-St. Joseph (Tagamuta), 1964-74; bp. Baton Rouge, 1974-82.

Swanstrom, Edward E. (1903-85): ord. June 2, 1928; aux. New York (Arba), 1960-78 (res.).

Sweeney, James J. (1898-1968): ord. June 20, 1925; first bp. Honolulu, 1941-68.

Swint, John J. (1879-1962): ord. June 23, 1904; aux. Wheeling (Sura), 1922; bp. Wheeling, 1922-62.

T

Takach, Basil (1879-1948): b. Austria-Hungary; ord. Dec. 12, 1902; first ap. ex. Pittsburgh Byzantine Rite (Zela), 1924-48.

Tarasevitch, Vladimir L., O.S.B. (1921-86): b. Byelorussia (White Russia); ord. May 26, 1949; ap. visitator (with residence in Chicago) for Byelorussians outside Soviet Union (Mariamme), 1983-86.

Taylor, John E., O.M.I. (1914-76): ord. May 25, 1940; bp. Stockholm, Sweden, 1962-76.

Thill, Francis A. (1893-1957): ord. Feb. 28, 1920; bp. Concordia (title changed to Salina in 1944), 1938-57.

Tief, Francis J. (1881-1965): ord. June 11, 1908; bp. Concordia (now Salina), 1921-38 (res.).

Tierney, Michael (1839-1908): b. Ireland; ord. May 26, 1866; bp. Hartford, 1894-1908.

Tihen, J. Henry (1861-1940): ord. Apr. 26, 1886; bp. Lincoln, 1911-17; bp. Denver, 1917-31 (res.).

Timon, John, C.M. (1797-1867): ord. Sept. 23, 1826; first bp. Buffalo, 1847-67.

Toebbe, Augustus M. (1829-84): b. Germany; ord. Sept. 14, 1854; bp. Covington, 1870-84.

Toolen, Thomas J. (1886-1976): ord. Sept. 27, 1910; bp. (pers. tit. abp.), 1954), Mobile, 1927-69 (res.).

Tracy, Robert E. (1909-80): ord. June 12, 1932; aux. Lafayette, La. (Sergentiza), 1959-61; first bp. Baton Rouge, 1961-74 (res.).

Treacy, John P. (1890-1964): ord. Dec. 8, 1918; coad. bp. La Crosse (Metelis), 1945-48; bp. La Crosse, 1948-64.

Trobec, James (1838-1921): b. Austria; ord. Sept. 8, 1865; bp. St. Cloud, 1897-1914 (res.).

Tuigg, John (1820-89): b. Ireland; ord. May 14, 1850; bp. Pittsburgh, 1876-89.

Turner, William (1871-1936): b. Ireland; ord. Aug. 13, 1893; bp. Buffalo, 1919-36.

Tyler, William (1806-49): ord. June 3, 1829; first bp. Hartford, 1844-49.

V

Van de Velde, James O., S.J. (1795-1855): b. Belgium; ord. Sept. 16, 1827; bp. Chicago, 1849-53; bp. Natchez (now Jackson), 1853-55.

Van de Ven, Cornelius (1865-1932): b. Holland; ord. May 31, 1890; bp. Natchitoches (title changed to Alexandria, 1910), 1904-32.

Van de Vyver, Augustine (1844-1911): b. Belgium; ord. July 24, 1870; bp. Richmond, 1889-1911.

Vehr, Urban J. (1891-1973): ord. May 29, 1915; bp. 1931-41, and first abp. Denver, 1941-67 (res.).

Verdaguer, Peter (1835-1911): b. Spain; ord. Dec. 12, 1862; v.a. Brownsville (Aulon), 1890-1911.

Verot, Augustin, S.S. (1805-76): b. France; ord. Sept. 20, 1828; v.a. Florida (Danaba), 1856-61; bp. Savannah, 1961-70; bp. St. Augustine, 1870-76.

Vertin, John (1844-99): b. Austria; ord. Aug. 31, 1866; bp. Sault Ste. Marie and Marquette (now Marquette), 1879-99.

Vogel, Cyril J. (1905-79): ord. June 7, 1931; bp. Salina, 1965-79.

W

Wade, Thomas, S.M. (1893-1969): ord. June 15, 1922; v.a. Northern Solomons (Barbalissus), 1930-69.

Wadhams, Edgar (1817-91): convert, 1846; ord. Jan. 15, 1850; first bp. Ogdensburg, 1872-91.

Walsh, Emmet (1892-1968): ord. Jan. 15, 1916; bp. Charleston, 1927-49; coad. bp. Youngstown (Rhaedestus), 1949-52; bp. Youngstown, 1952-68.

Walsh, James A., M.M. (1867-1936): ord. May 20, 1892; co-founder (with Thomas F. Price) of Maryknoll, first U.S. established foreign mission society and first sponsor of a U.S. foreign mission seminary; superior of Maryknoll, 1911-36; tit. bp. Syene, 1933-36.

Walsh, James E., M.M. (1891-1981): ord. Dec. 7, 1915; v.a. Kongmoon, China (Sata), 1927-36; superior of Maryknoll, 1936-46; general secretary, Catholic Central Bureau, Shanghai, China, 1948; imprisoned by Chinese communists, 1958-70.

Walsh, Louis S. (1858-1924): ord. Dec. 23, 1882; bp. Portland, Me., 1906-24.

Walsh, Thomas J. (1873-1952): ord. Jan. 27, 1900; bp. Trenton, 1918-28; bp., 1928-37, and first abp. 1937-52, Newark.

Ward, John (1857-1929): ord. July 17, 1884; bp. Leavenworth (now Kansas City), 1910-29.

Waters, Vincent S. (1804-74): ord. Dec. 8, 1931; bp. Raleigh, 1945-74.

Watterson, John A. (1844-99): ord. Aug. 9, 1868; bp. Columbus, 1880-99.

Wehrle, Vincent, O.S.B. (1855-1941): b. Switzerland; ord. Apr. 23, 1882; first bp. Bismarck, 1910-39 (res.).

Welch, Thomas A. (1884-1959): ord. June 11, 1909; bp. Duluth, 1926-59.

Weldon, Christopher J. (1905-82): ord. Sept. 21, 1939; bp. Springfield, Mass., 1950-77 (res.).

Whelan, James O.P. (1822-78): b. Ireland; ord. Aug. 2, 1846; coad. bp. Nashville (Marcopolis), 1859-60; bp. Nashville, 1860-64 (res.).

Whelan, Richard V. (1809-74): ord. May 1, 1831; bp. Richmond, 1841-50; bp. Wheeling, 1850-74.

White, Charles (1879-1955): ord. Sept. 24, 1910; bp. Spokane, 1927-55.

Whitfield, James (1770-1834): b. England; ord. July 24, 1809; coad. bp. Baltimore (Apollonia), 1828; abp. Baltimore, 1828-34.

Wigger, Winand (1841-1901): ord. June 10, 1865; bp. Newark, 1881-1901.

Willging, Joseph C. (1884-1959): ord. June 20, 1908; first bp. Pueblo, 1942-59.

Williams, John J. (1822-1907): ord. May 17, 1845; bp., 1866-75, and first abp., 1875-1907, Boston.

Willinger, Aloysius J., C.SS.R. (1886-1973): ord. July 2, 1911; bp. Ponce, P.R., 1929-46; coad. bp. Monterey-Fresno, 1946-53; bp. Monterey-Fresno, 1953-67 (res.).

Winkelmann, Christian H. (1883-1946): ord. June 11, 1907; aux. St. Louis (Sita), 1933-39; bp. Wichita, 1939-46.

Wood, James F. (1813-83): convert, 1836; ord. Mar. 25, 1844; coad. bp. Philadelphia (Antigonea), 1857-60; bp., 1860-75, and first abp., 1875-83, Philadelphia.

Woznicki, Stephen (1894-1968): ord. Dec. 22, 1917; aux. Detroit (Peltae), 1938-50; bp. Saginaw, 1950-68.

Wright, John J. (1909-79): ord. Dec. 8, 1935; aux. Boston (Egee), 1947-50; bp. Worcester, 1950-59; bp. Pittsburgh, 1959-69; cardinal, 1969; prefect Congregation of the Clergy, 1969-79.

Wurm, John D. (1927-84): ord. Apr. 3, 1954; aux. St. Louis (Plestia), 1976-81; bp. Belleville, 1981-84.

Y-Z

Young, Josue (1808-66): ord. Apr. 1, 1838; bp. Erie, 1854-66.

Zaleski, Alexander, M. (1906-75): ord. July 12, 1931; aux. Detroit (Lybe), 1950-64; coad. bp. Lansing, 1964-65; bp. Lansing 1966-75.

Zardetti, Otto (1847-1902): b. Switzerland; ord. Aug. 21, 1870; first bp. St. Cloud, 1889-94; abp. Bucharest, Rumania, 1894-95 (res.).

BLACK CATHOLICS IN THE UNITED STATES

National Office

The National Office for Black Catholics, organized in July, 1970, is a central agency with the general purposes of promoting active and full participation by black Catholics in the Church and of making more effective the presence and ministry of the Church in the black community.

Its operations are in support of the aspirations and calls of black Catholics for a number of objectives, including the following:

• representation and voice for blacks among bishops and others with leadership and decision-making positions in the Church;

• promoting vocations to the priesthood and religious life;

• sponsoring programs of evangelization, pastoral ministry, education and liturgy on a national level;

• recognition of the black heritage in liturgy, community life, theology and education.

James McConduit is president of the NOBC.

The NOBC office is located at 810 Rhode Island Ave. N.E., Washington, D.C. 20018.

Clergy Caucus

The National Black Catholic Clergy Caucus, founded in 1968 in Detroit, is a fraternity of approximately 750 black priests, permanent deacons and brothers pledged to mutual support in their vocations and ministries.

The Caucus develops programs of spiritual, theological, educational and ministerial growth for its members, to counteract the effects of institutionalized racism within the Church and American society. A bimonthly newsletter is published.

Josephite Father William Norvel is president.

The NBCCC office is located at 1419 V St. N.W., Washington, D.C. 20009.

1986 Meetings

Members of the National Office for Black Catholics and the National Black Lay Caucus held a joint biennial conference during the month of August, 1986, in Philadelphia. A highlight of the meeting was an appeal by Father Edward K. Braxton to "provide a united Black Catholic front" in support of a request for the establishment of a permanent

TABLE

(Source: *Statistical Profile of Black Catholics, 1984,* published by the Josephite Pastoral Center, 1200 Varnum St. N.E., Washington, D.C. 20017.)

State	Black Cath. Population	Total Black Pop.	Cath. Pct. Black Pop.
Alabama	15,500	996,335	1.6
Alaska	350	13,643	2.6
Arizona	1,184	73,718	1.6
Arkansas	1,600	373,768	.4
California	102,895	1,819,281	5.7
Colorado	4,235	101,703	4.2
Connecticut	10,774	217,465	5.0
Delaware	2,000	154,086	1.3
District of Columbia	75,000	779,487	9.6
Florida	82,880	1,342,688	6.2
Georgia	12,000	1,465,181	.8
Hawaii	100	17,364	.6
Idaho	50	2,716	1.8
Illinois	113,550	1,675,398	6.8
Indiana	15,076	414,785	3.6
Iowa	956	41,700	2.3
Kansas	9,107	126,127	7.2
Kentucky	9,243	259,477	3.6
Louisiana	210,799	1,238,242	17.0
Maine	100	3,128	3.2
Maryland	25,074	569,328	4.4
Massachusetts	27,108	221,279	12.3
Michigan	62,785	1,199,023	5.2
Minnesota	6,230	53,344	11.7
Mississippi	9,731	887,206	1.1
Missouri	50,625	514,276	9.8
Montana	55	1,786	3.1
Nebraska	1,255	48,390	2.6
Nevada	1,800	50,999	3.5
New Hampshire	250	3,990	6.3
New Jersey	25,433	925,066	2.7
New Mexico	770	25,276	3.0
New York	205,500	2,401,974	8.6
North Carolina	4,684	1,318,857	.4
North Dakota	175	2,568	6.8
Ohio	20,754	1,076,748	1.9
Oklahoma	9,000	204,674	4.4
Oregon	3,025	37,060	8.2
Pennsylvania	49,717	1,046,810	4.7
Rhode Island	2,758	27,584	10.0
South Carolina	7,000	948,623	.7
South Dakota	120	2,144	5.6
Tennessee	10,000	725,942	1.4
Texas	71,397	1,710,175	4.2
Utah	200	9,225	2.2
Vermont	53	1,135	4.7
Virginia	10,500	1,008,668	1.0
Washington	4,812	105,574	4.6
West Virginia	700	65,051	1.1
Wisconsin	15,093	182,592	8.3
Wyoming	100	3,364	3.0
TOTALS 1984	**1,294,103**	**26,495,023**	**4.9**
Totals 1975	**916,854**	**22,549,815**	**4.0**

secretariat for Black Catholics within the structure of the National Conference of Catholic Bishops. The request for the secretariat was made by the nation's 10 Black Catholic bishops during the November, 1985, meeting of the U.S. bishops.

Members of the Black Catholic Office and the Lay Caucus — along with those belonging to the National Black Catholic Clergy Caucus, the National Black Sisters' Conference and the National Black Catholic Seminarians' Association — were involved in 1986 in planning and related preparations for a National Black Catholic Congress to be held May 21 to 24, 1987, at The Catholic University of America in Washington. Sponsors of the congress said its purpose would be the development of strategies for the evangelization of the black community. It was estimated that between six and 10 million Black Americans did not belong to any church.

Auxiliary Bishop John Ricard of Baltimore is chairman of the congress.

Bishops

There were ten black bishops in 1986: Bishop Joseph L. Howze, head of the Diocese of Biloxi, and Auxiliary Bishops Joseph A. Francis, S.V.D., of Newark, Eugene A. Marino, S.S.J., of Washington, Harold R. Perry, S.V.D., of New Orleans, James P. Lyke, O.F.M., of Cleveland, Emerson Moore of New York, Moses Anderson of Detroit, Wilton D. Gregory of Chicago, J. Terry Steib, S.V.D., of St. Louis and John H. Ricard, S.S.J., of Baltimore.

Josephite Pastoral Center

The Josephite Pastoral Center was established in September, 1968, as an educational and pastoral service agency for the Josephites in their mission work, specifically in the black community. St. Joseph's Society of the Sacred Heart, the sponsoring body, has about 185 priests and 20 brothers in 80 mostly southern parishes in 18 dioceses.

The staff of the center includes Father John G. Harfmann, S.S.J., director, and Maria M. Lannon, associate director. The center is located at St. Joseph Seminary, 1200 Varnum St. N.E., Washington, D.C. 20017.

Various dioceses have agencies like New York's Office of Black Ministry for pastoral and related service to the black community.

HISPANICS

U.S. Census Bureau figures indicate that there were 16,940,000 persons of Hispanic origin in the United States in 1985. (Not counted were undocumented Hispanic aliens estimated to number between three and six million in 1978; another estimate, as of 1984, placed the number between two and four million.)

Between 1970 and 1980, there was a nationwide increase of 5,037,440 persons.

Regional increases for the same period were: Northeast, 709,381 for a total of 2,604,261; North Central, 228,144 for a total of 1,276,405; South, 1,707,365 for a total of 4,473,172; West, 2,884,291 for a total of 6,252,045.

Most persons of Hispanic origin in the United States have been baptized in the Catholic Church and comprise, probably, between 25 and 30 per cent of the Catholic population.

In the U.S., as of September, 1986, there were 18 Hispanic bishops (eight heads of dioceses and 10 auxiliaries, all named since 1970).

Pastoral Patterns

Pastoral ministry to Hispanics varies, depending on differences among the people and the availability of personnel to carry it out.

The pattern in cities with large numbers of Spanish-speaking is built around special churches, centers or other agencies where pastoral and additional forms of service are provided in a manner suited to the needs, language and culture of the people. Services in some places are extensive and include legal advice, job placement, language instruction, recreational and social assistance, specialized counseling, replacement services. In many places, however, even where there are special ministries, the needs are generally greater than the means required to meet them.

Some of the urban dwellers have been absorbed into established parishes and routines of church life and activity. Many Spanish-speaking communities, especially those with migrants, remain in need of special ministries.

An itinerant form of ministry best meets the needs of the thousands of migrant workers who follow the crops.

Special ministries for the Spanish-speaking have been in operation for a long time in dioceses of the Southwest. The total number of dioceses with such ministries is more than 108.

Pastoral ministry to Hispanics was the central concern of three national meetings, *Encuentros,* held in 1972, 1977 and 1985. In line with recommendations emanating from these meetings, particular emphasis has since been focused on five general areas: evangelization, education, leadership development, youth ministry and social justice. (See separate entry, Tercer *Encuentro.*)

The U.S. bishops, at their annual meeting in November, 1983, approved and subsequently published a pastoral letter on Hispanic Ministry under the title, "The Hispanic Presence: Challenge and Commitment." (For text, see pp. 46-49 of the 1985 *Catholic Almanac.*)

Secretariat for Hispanic Affairs

The national secretariat was established by the U.S. Catholic Conference for service in promoting and coordinating pastoral ministry to the Spanish-speaking. Its basic orientation is toward integral evangelization, combining religious ministry with development efforts in programs geared to the culture and needs of Hispanics. Its concerns are urban and migrant Spanish-speaking people; communications and publications in line with secretariat purposes and the service of people; bilingual and bicultural religious and general education;

liaison for and representation of Hispanics with church, civic and governmental agencies.

The secretariat publishes a monthly newsletter, *En Marcha,* available on request to interested parties.

Paul Sedillo, Jr., is director of the national office at 1312 Massachusetts Ave. N.W., Wasington, D.C. 20005.

The secretariat has working relationships with regional offices in the Northeast, Southeast, Midwest, Southwest, Far West, Northwest and Mountain States. Each office shares the objectives of the secretariat. In addition, the Northeast, Southeast and Midwest offices have established pastoral institutes for formation, training and program development.

The Northeast regional office, officially the Northeast Catholic Pastoral Center for Hispanics, was established in 1976 and is supported by bishops in 14 states from Maine to Virginia. The office consists of professional staff members in the fields of pastoral work, communications, evangelization, research, development and publications. It has established the Conference of Diocesan Directors of the Hispanic Apostolate, Association of Hispanic Deacons, Regional Youth Task Force and a regional committee of Diocesan Coordinators of Religious Educators for the Hispanics. The executive director is Mario J. Paredes. The center is located at 1011 First Ave., New York, N.Y. 10022.

The Southeast regional office serves 24 dioceses in Tennessee, North and South Carolina, Florida, Georgia, Mississippi, Alabama and Louisiana. Its South East Pastoral Institute offers an academic degree in pastoral ministry, reaches out to communities throughout the region with its Evangelization Mobile Team and distributes audio-visual and print resources for Hispanic ministry. Father Mario Vizcaino, Sch. P., is director of the region and institute. The office is located at 2900 S.W. 87th Ave., Miami, Fla. 33165.

Five states of the Midwest (Ohio, Indiana, Illinois, Michigan, Wisconsin) are served by a Midwest Hispanic Catholic Commission. The executive director of the commission is Olga Villa Parra. The mailing address is P.O. Box 703 (Holy Cross Annex), Notre Dame, Ind. 46556.

In the Southwest, a reorganized regional office serving Arkansas, Oklahoma, and Texas was reopened Feb. 1, 1983. Sister Elisa Rodriguez is director of the office which is located at 3019 French Pl., San Antonio, Tex. 78228.

A regional office serving the Mountain States (Arizona, New Mexico, Utah, Colorado and Wyoming) is under the direction of Mr. Primitivo Romero, secretary of Hispanic Affairs, 400 E. Monroe, Phoenix, Ariz. 85004.

California and Nevada are served by the Far West office, which is a component of the California Catholic Conference. The regional director is Father Ricardo A. Chavez. The office is located at 1010 11th St., Suite 200, Sacramento Calif. 95814. A new component of the conference is the Catholic Hispanic Institute of California, with Father Ricardo A. Chavez and Sister Cecilia Calva as codirectors.

A regional office serving the northwestern corner of the U.S. is under the direction of Sister Dolorita Martinez, O.P. Its Mobile Pastoral Institute, under the direction of Sister Maria Loyola Maestas, O.P. and Mr. Alejandro Aguilera, has outreach to communities in Idaho, Montana, Oregon, Washington and Alaska. The office is located at 412 West Chestnut, Yakima, Wash. 98902.

PADRES

In the Southwest, 55 Mexican-American priests organized PADRES in February, 1970, to help the Church identify more closely with the pastoral, social, economic and educational needs of the Spanish-speaking. The present membership exceeds 500, mainly in California, Texas, New Mexico and on the East Coast. PADRES is an acronym for the Spanish title, "Padres Asociados para Derechos Religiosos, Educativos y Sociales."

Leadership development of Hispanos is one of the principal concerns of PADRES, now a national organization with membership open to priests, brothers and deacons working in Hispanic ministry. Seminarians and others interested in working with the Hispanic community are eligible for honorary membership. Father Ramon Gaitan, O.A.R., is the national president. The office is located at 2216 E. 108th St., Los Angeles, Calif. 90059.

(Two other organizations of priests are *La Asociacion de Sacerdotes Hispanos* in New York and Miami.)

Mexican American Cultural Center

This national center, specializing in pastoral studies and language education, was founded in 1972 to provide programs focused on ministry among Hispanics and personnel working with Hispanics in the U.S. and Latin America. Courses — developed according to the see-judge-act methodology — include culture, faith development, Scripture, theology, and praxis; some are offered in Spanish, others in English. Intensive language classes are offered in Spanish and English as second languages, with emphasis on pastoral usage.

The center also conducts workshops for the development of leadership skills. Faculty members serve as resource personnel for pastoral centers, dioceses and parishes throughout the U.S. The center offers master-degree programs in pastoral ministry in cooperation with Incarnate Word College, San Antonio, and Boston College. Participants attending summer study weeks can obtain a *Certificado de Pastoralista.*

A National Resource Center for Hispanic Ministry has information available on personnel and resources for the Hispanic apostolate, as well as a distribution center for the circulation of pastoral materials in the U.S. and Latin America.

Father Virgil Elizondo is president of the center located at 3019 W. French Place, San Antonio, Tex 78228.

One item on the agenda of the November, 1986 meeting of the National Conference of Catholic Bishops was a national pastoral plan for Hispanics, for discussion and vote.

Institutes of Consecrated Life

Religious orders and congregations are special societies in the Church — institutes of consecrated life — whose members, called Religious, commit themselves, by public vows to observance of the evangelical counsels of poverty, chastity and obedience in a community kind of life in accordance with rules and constitutions approved by church authority.

Secular institutes (covered in its own Almanac entry) are also institutes of consecrated life.

The particular goal of each institute and the means of realizing it in practice are stated in the rule and constitutions proper to the institute. Local bishops can give approval for rules and constitutions of institutes of diocesan rank. Pontifical rank belongs to institutes approved by the Holy See. General jurisdiction over all Religious is exercised by the Congregation for Religious and Secular Institutes. General legislation concerning Religious is contained in Canons 573 to 709 in Book II, Part III, of the Code of Canon Law.

All institutes of consecrated life are commonly called religious orders, despite the fact that there are differences between orders and congregations. The best known orders include the Benedictines, Trappists, Franciscans, Dominicans, Carmelites and Augustinians, for men; and the Carmelites, Benedictines, Poor Clares, Dominicans of the Second Order and Visitation Nuns, for women. The orders are older than the congregations, which did not appear until the 16th century.

Contemplative institutes are oriented to divine worship and service within the confines of their communities, by prayer, penitential practices, other spiritual activities and self-supporting work. Examples are the Trappists and Carthusians, the Carmelite and Poor Clare nuns. Active institutes are geared for pastoral ministry and various kinds of apostolic work. Mixed institutes combine elements of the contemplative and active ways of life. While most institutes of men and women can be classified as active, all of them have contemplative aspects.

Clerical communities of men are those whose membership is predominantly composed of priests.

Non-clerical or lay institutes of men are the various brotherhoods.

Societies of Apostolic Life

Some of the institutes of men listed below have a special kind of status because their members, while living a common life like that which is characteristic of Religious, do not profess the vows of Religious. Examples are the Maryknoll Fathers, the Oratorians of St. Philip Neri, the Paulists and Sulpicians. They are called societies of apostolic life and are the subject of Canons 731 to 746 in the Code of Canon Law.

RELIGIOUS INSTITUTES OF MEN IN THE UNITED STATES

(Sources: *Official Catholic Directory;* Catholic Almanac survey.)

Africa, Missionaries of (M. Afr.): Founded 1868 at Algiers by Cardinal Lavigerie; known as White Fathers until 1984. Generalate, Rome Italy; U.S. headquarters, 1624 21st St. N.W., Washington, D.C. 20009. Missionary work in Africa.

African Missions, Society of, S.M.A.: Founded 1856, at Lyons, France, by Bishop Melchior de Marion Brésillac. Generalate, Rome, Italy; American provincialate, 23 Bliss Ave., Tenafly, N.J. 07670. Missionary work.

Assumptionists (Augustinians of the Assumption), AA.: Founded 1845, at Nimes, France, by Rev. Emmanuel d'Alzon; in U.S., 1946. General house, Rome, Italy; U.S. province, 328 Adams St., Milton, Mass. 02186. Educational, parochial, ecumenical, retreat, foreign mission work.

Atonement, Franciscan Friars of the, S.A.: Founded as an Anglican Franciscan community in 1898 at Garrison, N.Y., by Rev. Paul Wattson. Community corporately received into the Catholic Church in 1909. Motherhouse, St. Paul Friary, Graymoor, Garrison N.Y. 10524. Ecumenical, mission, retreat and charitable works.

Augustinian Recollects, O.A.R.: Founded 1588: in U.S., 1944. General motherhouse, Rome, Italy. Missionary, parochial, education work.

St. Augustine Province (1944), 29 Ridgeway Ave., W. Orange, N.J. 07052.

St. Nicholas Province (Madrid): U.S. Delegate, 2800 Schurz Ave., Bronx, N.Y. 10465.

Augustinians (Order of St. Augustine), O.S.A.: Established canonically in 1256 by Pope Alexander IV; in U.S., 1796. General motherhouse, Rome, Italy.

St. Thomas of Villanova Province (1796), P.O. Box 338, Villanova, Pa. 19085.

Our Mother of Good Counsel Province (1941), Tolentine Center, 20300 Governors Hwy., Olympia Fields, Ill. 60461.

St. Augustine Province (1969), 1605 28th St., San Diego, Calif. 92102.

Good Counsel Vice-Province, St. Augustine Preparatory School, Richland, N.J. 08350.

U.S. Vicariate of Castile, Spain, Province, P.O. Box 190, Waxahachie, Tex. 75165.

Barnabites (Clerics Regular of St. Paul), C.R.S.P.: Founded 1530, in Milan, Italy, by St. Anthony M. Zaccaria. Generalate, Rome, Italy; American headquarters, 1023 Swann Rd., Youngstown, N.Y. 14174. Parochial, educational, mission work.

Basil the Great, Order of St. (Basilian Order of St. Josaphat), O.S.B.M.: General motherhouse, Rome, Italy; U.S. province, 31-12 30th St., Long Island City, N.Y. 11106. Parochial work among Byzantine Ukrainian Rite Catholics.

Basilian Fathers (Congregation of the Priests of

St. Basil), C.S.B.: Founded 1822, at Annonay, France. General motherhouse, 20 Humewood Dr., Toronto, Ont. M6C 2W2, Canada. Educational, parochial work.

Basilian Salvatorian Fathers: Founded 1684, at Saida, Lebanon, by Eftimios Saifi; in U.S., 1953. General motherhouse, Saida, Lebanon; American headquarters, 30 East St., Methuen, Mass. 01844. Educational, parochial work among Eastern Rite peoples.

Benedictine Monks (Order of St. Benedict), O.S.B.: Founded 529, in Italy, by St. Benedict of Nursia; in U.S., 1846.

• American Cassinese Federation (1855). Rt. Rev. John Eidenschink, O.S.B., pres., Church of Seven Dolors, Albany, Minn. 56307. Abbeys and Priories belonging to the federation:

St. Vincent Archabbey, Latrobe, Pa. 15650; St. John's Abbey, Collegeville, Minn. 56321; St. Benedict's Abbey, Atchison, Kans. 66002; St. Mary's Abbey, Delbarton, Morristown, N.J. 07960; Belmont Abbey, Belmont, N.C. 28012; St. Bernard Abbey, St. Bernard, Cullman, Ala. 35055; St. Procopius Abbey, 5601 College Rd., Lisle, Ill. 60532; St. Gregory's Abbey, Shawnee, Okla. 74801; St. Leo Abbey, St. Leo, Fla. 33574; Assumption Abbey, Richardton, N. Dak. 58652;

St. Bede Abbey, Peru, Ill. 61354; St. Martin's Abbey, Lacey, Wash. 98503; Holy Cross Abbey, P.O. Box 351, Canon City, Colo. 81212; St. Anselm's Abbey, Manchester, N.H. 03102; St. Andrew's Abbey, 2900 Martin Luther King Dr., Cleveland, O. 44104; Holy Trinity Priory, Butler, Pa. 16001; St. Maur Priory, 4615 N. Michigan Rd., Indianapolis, Ind. 46208; Newark Abbey, 528 Dr. Martin Luther King, Jr., Blvd., Newark, N.J. 07102; St. Mark's Priory, South Union, Ky. 42283; Benedictine Priory, 6502 Seawright Dr., Savannah, Ga. 31406; Woodside Priory, 302 Portola Rd., Portola Valley, Calif. 94025.

• Swiss-American Federation (1870), Rt. Rev. Jerome Hanus O.S.B., pres., Conception Abbey, Conception, Mo. 64433. Abbeys and priory belonging to the federation:

St. Meinrad Archabbey, St. Meinrad, Ind. 47577; Conception Abbey, Conception, Mo. 64433; Mt. Michael Abbey, Elkhorn, Nebr. 68022; New Subiaco Abbey, Subiaco, Ark. 72865; St. Joseph's Abbey, St. Benedict, La. 70457; Mt. Angel Abbey, St. Benedict, Ore. 97373; Marmion Abbey, Butterfield Rd., Aurora, Ill. 60504;

St. Benedict's Abbey, Benet Lake, Wis. 53102; Glastonbury Abbey, 16 Hull St., Hingham, Mass. 02043; Westminster Abbey, Mission, B.C., Canada; St. Pius X Abbey, Columbia, Mo. 65203; Blue Cloud Abbey, Marvin, S. Dak. 57251; Corpus Christi Abbey, HCR2, Box 6300, Sandia, Tex. 78383; Our Lady of Guadalupe Abbey, Pecos N. Mex. 87552; Prince of Peace Abbey, 650 Benet Hill Rd., Oceanside, Calif. 92054.

• English Benedictine Congregation: St. Anselm's Abbey, 4501 S. Dakota Ave. N.E., Washington, D.C. 20017; Abbey of St. Gregory, Cory's Lane, Portsmouth, R.I. 02871; Priory of St. Mary and St. Louis, 500 S. Mason Rd., St. Louis, Mo. 63141.

• Congregation of St. Ottilien for Foreign Missions, St. Paul's Abbey, Newton, N.J. 07860; Christ the King Priory, Schuyler, Neb. 68661.

• Congregation of the Annunciation, St. Andrew Priory, Valyermo, Calif. 93563.

• Houses not in Congregations: Mount Saviour Monastery, Pine City, N.Y. 14871; Conventual Priory of St. Gabriel the Archangel, Weston, Vt. 05161.

Benedictines, Olivetan, O.S.B.: General motherhouse, Siena, Italy. U.S. foundations, Our Lady of Mt. Olivet Priory, 4029 Ave. G, Lake Charles, La. 70601; Holy Trinity Monastery, P.O. Box 298, St. David, Ariz. 85630; Our Lady of Guadalupe Abbey, Pecos, N.M. 87552.

Benedictines, Sylvestrine, O.S.B.: Founded 1231, in Italy by Sylvester Gozzolini. General motherhouse, Rome, Italy; U.S. foundations: 17320 Rosemont Rd., Detroit, Mich. 48219; 2711 E. Drahner Rd., Oxford, Mich. 48051; 1697 State Highway 3, Clifton, N.J. 07012.

Bethlehem Missionaries, Society of, S.M.B.: Founded 1921, at Immensee, Switzerland, by Rt. Rev. Canon Peter Bondolfi. General motherhouse, Immensee, Switzerland; U.S. headquarters, 5630 E. 17th Ave., Denver, Colo. 80220. Foreign mission work.

Blessed Sacrament, Congregation of the, S.S.S.: Founded 1856, at Paris, France, by St. Pierre Julien Eymard; in U.S., 1900. General motherhouse, Rome, Italy; U.S. province, 5384 Wilson Mills Rd., Cleveland, O. 44143. Eucharistic apostolate.

Brigittine Monks (Order of the Most Holy Savior), O.Ss.S.: Monastery of the Most Holy Savior, 125 Northgate Dr., Woodside, Calif. 94062.

Camaldolese Congregation, Cam. O.S.B.: Founded 1012, at Camaldoli, near Arezzo, Italy, by St. Romuald; in U.S. 1958. General motherhouse, Arezzo, Italy; U.S. foundation, Immaculate Heart Hermitage, Big Sur, Calif. 93920.

Camaldolese Hermits of the Congregation of Monte Corona, Er. Cam.: Founded 1520, from Camaldoli, Italy, by Bl. Paul Giustiniani. General motherhouse, Frascati (Rome), Italy; U.S. foundation, Holy Family Hermitage, Rt. 2, Box 36, Bloomingdale, O. 43910.

Camillian Fathers and Brothers (Order of St. Camillus; Order of Ministers of the Sick), O.S.Cam.: Founded 1582, at Rome, by St. Camillus de Lellis; in U.S., 1923. General motherhouse, Rome, Italy; North American province, 10213 W. Wisconsin Ave., Wauwatosa, Wis. 53226.

Carmelites (Order of Our Lady of Mt. Carmel), O. Carm.: General motherhouse, Rome, Italy. Educational, charitable work.

Most Pure Heart of Mary Province (1864), 45 E. Dundee Rd., Barrington, Ill. 60010.

St. Elias Province (1931), Brandsma Hall, Box 127, Purchase, N.Y. 10577.

Mt. Carmel Hermitage, Pineland, R.D. 1, Box 36, New Florence, Pa. 15944 (immediately subject to Prior General.)

Carmelites, Order of Discalced, O.C.D.: Established 1562, a Reform Order of Our Lady of Mt.

Carmel; in U.S., 1924. Generalate, Rome, Italy. Spiritual direction, retreat, parochial work.

St. Therese of Oklahoma Province (1935), 1125 S. Walker St., P.O. Box 26127, Oklahoma City, Okla. 73126.

Immaculate Heart of Mary Province (1947), P.O. Box 67, Hubertus, Wis. 53033.

Central Office, Calif. (1924), St. Therese Church, 510 N. El Molino St., Alhambra, Calif. 91801.

Polish Province of the Holy Spirit, 1628 Ridge Rd., Munster, Ind. 46321.

Carthusians, Order of, O. Cart.: Founded 1084, in France, by St. Bruno; in U.S., 1951. General motherhouse, St. Pierre de Chartreuse, France; U.S. charterhouse, Arlington, Vt. 05250. Cloistered contemplatives; semi-eremitic.

Charity, Servants of, S.C.: Founded 1908, in Italy, by Bl. Luigi Guanella. General motherhouse, Rome, Italy; U.S. headquarters, Don Guanella Seminary, Sproul Rd., Springfield, Pa. 19064.

Christ, Society of, S.Ch.: Founded 1932, General Motherhouse, Poznan, Poland; U.S. address, 3000 Eighteen Mile Rd., Sterling Heights, Mich. 48078.

Cistercians, Order of, O. Cist.: Founded 1098, by St. Robert. Headquarters, Rome, Italy.

Our Lady of Spring Bank Abbey, Rt. 3, Box 159, Sparta, Wis. 54656.

Our Lady of Dallas Monastery, Cistercian Rd., Irving, Tex. 75039.

Cistercian Monastery of Our Lady of Fatima, Hainesport-Mt. Laurel Rd., Mt. Laurel, N.J. 08054.

Cistercian Conventual Priory, St. Mary's Priory, R.D. 1, Box 206, New Ringgold, Pa. 17960.

Cistercians of the Strict Observance, Order of (Trappists), O.C.S.O.: Founded 1098, in France, by St. Robert; in U.S., 1848. Generalate, Rome, Italy.

Our Lady of Gethsemani Abbey (1848), Trappist P.O., Ky. 40051.

Our Lady of New Melleray Abbey (1849), Dubuque, Iowa 52001.

St. Joseph's Abbey (1825), Spencer, Mass. 01562.

Holy Spirit Monastery (1944), Conyers, Ga. 30208.

Our Lady of Guadalupe Abbey (1947), Lafayette, Ore. 97127.

Our Lady of the Holy Trinity Abbey (1947), Huntsville, Utah 84317.

Abbey of the Genesee (1951), Piffard, N.Y. 14533.

Our Lady of Mepkin Abbey (1949), HC, Box 800, Moncks Corner, S. Car. 29461.

Our Lady of the Holy Cross Abbey (1950), Berryville, Va. 22611.

Our Lady of the Assumption Abbey (1950), Rt. 5, Box 193, Ava, Mo. 65608.

Abbey of New Clairvaux (1955), Vina, Calif. 96092.

St. Benedict's Monastery (1956), Snowmass, Colo. 81654.

Claretians (Missionary Sons of the Immaculate Heart of Mary), C.M.F.: Founded 1849, at Vich, Spain, by St. Anthony Mary Claret. General headquarters, Rome, Italy. Missionary, parochial, educational, retreat work.

Western Province, 1119 Westchester Pl., Los Angeles, Calif. 90019.

Eastern Province, 400 N. Euclid Ave. Oak Park, Ill. 60302.

Clerics Regular Minor (Adorno Fathers) C.R.M.: Founded 1588, at Naples, Italy, by Ven. Augustine Adorno and St. Francis Caracciolo. General motherhouse, Rome, Italy; U.S. address, 575 Darlington Ave., Ramsey, N.J. 07446.

Columban, Society of St. (St. Columban Foreign Mission Society, S.S.C.): Founded 1918. General headquarters, Dublin, Ireland. U.S. headquarters, St. Columbans, Nebr. 68056. Foreign mission work.

Comboni Missionaries of the Heart of Jesus (Verona Fathers), M.C.C.J.: Founded 1867, in Italy by Bp. Daniele Comboni. General motherhouse, Rome, Italy; North American headquarters, Comboni Mission Center, 8108 Beechmont Ave., Cincinnati, O. 45230. Mission work in Africa and the Americas.

Consolata Society for Foreign Missions, I.M.C.: Founded 1901, at Turin, Italy, by Father Joseph Allamano. General motherhouse, Rome, Italy; U.S. headquarters, P.O. Box C, Lincoln Hwy., Somerset, N.J. 08873.

Crosier Fathers (Canons Regular of the Order of the Holy Cross), O.S.C.: Founded 1210, in Belgium by Bl. Theodore De Celles. Generalate, Rome, Italy; U.S. province, 711 Lincoln Ave., St. Paul, Minn. 55105. Mission, retreat, educational work.

Cross, Priests of the Congregation of Holy, C.S.C.: Founded 1837, in France; in U.S., 1841. Generalate, Rome, Italy. Educational and pastoral work; home missions and retreats; foreign missions; social services and apostolate of the press.

Indiana Province (1841), 1304 E. Jefferson Blvd., South Bend, Ind. 46617.

Eastern Province (1952), 835 Clinton Ave., Bridgeport, Conn. 06604.

Southern Province (1968), 2111 Brackenridge St., Austin, Tex. 78704.

Divine Word, Society of the, S.V.D.: Founded 1875, in Holland, by Bl. Arnold Janssen. North American Province founded 1897 with headquarters in Techny, Ill. General motherhouse, Rome, Italy.

Province of Bl. Joseph Freinademetz (Chicago Province) (1985, from merger of Eastern and Northern provinces), 1985 Waukegan Rd., Techny, Ill. 60082.

St. Augustine's Province (Southern Province) (1940), 201 Ruella Ave., Bay St. Louis, Miss. 39520.

St. Therese Province (Western Province) (1964), 2737 Pleasant Ave., Riverside, Calif. 92507.

Dominicans (Order of Friars Preachers), O.P.: Founded early 13th century by St. Dominic de Guzman. General headquarters, Santa Sabina, Rome, Italy. Preaching, teaching, missions, research, parishes.

St. Joseph Province (1806), 141 E. 65th St., New York, N.Y. 10021.

Holy Name of Jesus Province (1912), 5877 Birch Ct., Oakland, Calif. 94618.

St. Albert the Great Province (1939), 1909 S. Ashland Ave., Chicago, Ill. 60608.

Southern Dominican Province (1979), 3407 Napoleon Ave., New Orleans, La. 70125.

St. Dominic Province (1873), 5353 Notre Dame de Grace Ave., Montreal, Que. H4A 1L2, Canada.

Spanish Province, U.S. foundation (1933), P.O. Box 279, San Diego, Tex. 78384.

Edmund, Society of St., S.S.E.: Founded 1843, in France, by Fr. Jean Baptiste Muard. General motherhouse, Edmundite Generalate, Fairholt, S. Prospect St., Burlington, Vt. 05401. Educational, missionary work.

Eudists (Congregation of Jesus and Mary), C.J.M.: Founded 1643, in France, by St. John Eudes. General motherhouse, Rome, Italy; North American province, 6125 Première Ave., Charlesbourg, Quebec G1H 2V9, Canada. Parochial, educational, pastoral, missionary work.

Francis, Third Order Regular of St., T.O.R.: Founded 1221, in Italy; in U.S., 1910. General motherhouse, Rome, Italy. Educational, parochial, missionary work.

Most Sacred Heart of Jesus Province (1910), 601 Pitcairn Pl., Pittsburgh, Pa. 15232.

Immaculate Conception Province (1925), 2006 Edgewater Parkway, Silver Springs, Md. 20903.

Commissariat of the Spanish Province (1924), 301 Jefferson Ave., Waco, Tex. 76702.

Francis de Sales, Oblates of St., O.S.F.S.: Founded 1871, by Fr. Louis Brisson. General motherhouse, Rome, Italy. Educational, missionary, parochial work.

Wilmington-Philadelphia Province (1906), 2200 Kentmere Parkway, Box 1452, Wilmington, Del. 19899.

Toledo-Detroit Province (1966), Box 4683, Toledo, Ohio 43620.

Franciscans (Order of Friars Minor), O.F.M.: A family of the First Order of St. Francis (of Assisi) founded in 1209 and established as a separate jurisdiction in 1517; in U.S., 1844. General headquarters, Rome, Italy. Preaching, missionary, educational, parochial, charitable work.

St. John the Baptist Province (1844), 1615 Vine St., Cincinnati, Ohio 45210.

Sacred Heart Province (1858), 3140 Meramec St., St. Louis, Mo. 63118.

Assumption of the Blessed Virgin Mary Province (1887), Pulaski, Wis. 54162.

Most Holy Name of Jesus Province (1901), 135 W. 31st St., New York, N.Y. 10001.

St. Barbara Province (1915), 1500 34th Ave., Oakland, Calif. 94601.

Immaculate Conception Province (1855), 147 Thompson St., New York, N.Y. 10012.

Our Lady of Guadalupe Province (1985), Box 12127, Albuquerque, N.M. 87105.

Holy Cross Custody (1912), 1400 Main St., P.O. Box 608, Lemont, Ill. 60439.

Most Holy Savior Custody, 232 S. Home Ave., Pittsburgh, Pa. 15202.

St. John Capistran Custody (1928), 1290 Hornberger Ave., Roebling, N.J. 08554.

St. Stephen Transylvanian Custody (1948), 517 S. Belle Vista Ave., Youngstown, Ohio 44509.

Holy Family Croatian Custody, (1927), 4848 S. Ellis Ave., Chicago, Ill. 60615.

St. Casimir Lithuanian Vicariate, Kennebunkport, Me. 04046.

Holy Gospel Province (Mexico), U.S. foundation, 2400 Marr St., El Paso, Tex. 79903.

Saints Francis and James Province (Jalisco, Mexico), U.S. foundation, 504 E. Santa Clara St., Hebbronville, Tex. 78361.

Commissariat of the Holy Land, Mt. St. Sepulchre, 1400 Quincy St. N.E., Washington, D.C. 20017.

St. Mary of the Angels Custody, Byzantine Slavonic Rite, P.O. Box 270, Sybertsville, Pa. 18251.

Academy of American Franciscan History, P.O. Box 34440, West Bethesda, Md. 20817.

Franciscans (Order of Friars Minor Capuchin), O.F.M. Cap.: A family of the First Order of St. Francis (of Assisi) founded in 1209 and established as a separate jurisdiction in 1528. General motherhouse, Rome, Italy. Missionary, parochial work, chaplaincies.

St. Joseph Province (1857), 1740 Mt. Elliott Ave., Detroit, Mich. 48207.

St. Augustine Province (1873), 220 37th St., Pittsburgh, Pa. 15201.

St. Mary Province (1952), 30 Gedney Park Dr., White Plains, N.Y. 10605.

Province of the Stigmata (1918), P.O. Box 6279, Hoboken, N.J. 07030.

Western American Capuchin Province, Our Lady of the Angels, 453 Miller Ave., S., San Francisco, Calif. 94080.

Sts. Adalbert and Stanislaus Province (Warsaw, Poland), Manor Dr., Oak Ridge, N.J. 07438.

Province of Mid-America (1977), St. Elizabeth Friary, 1060 St. Francis Way, Denver, Colo. 80204.

Texas Capuchin Fraternity (Province of Navarre, Spain), 5605 Bernal Dr., Dallas, Tex. 75212.

Franciscans (Order of Friars Minor Conventual), O.F.M. Conv.: A family of the First Order of St. Francis (of Assisi) founded in 1209 and established as a separate jurisdiction in 1517; first U.S. foundation, 1852. General curia, Rome, Italy. Missionary, educational, parochial work.

Immaculate Conception Province (1852), P.O. Box 830, Union City, N.J. 07087.

St. Anthony of Padua Province (1905), 1300 Dundalk Ave., Baltimore, Md. 21222.

St. Bonaventure Province (1939), 6107 Kenmore Ave., Chicago, Ill. 60660.

Our Lady of Consolation Province (1926), Mt. St. Francis, Ind. 47146.

Our Lady of Guadalupe Custody (vice-province), Holy Cross Friary, P.O. Box 158, Mesilla Park, N.M. 88047.

St. Joseph Cupertino Province (1981), P.O. Box 820, Arroyo Grande, Calif. 93420.

Glenmary Missioners (The Home Missioners of America): Founded 1939, in U.S. General headquarters, P.O. Box 46404, Cincinnati, Ohio 45246. Home mission work.

Holy Family, Congregation of the Missionaries of the, M.S.F.: Founded 1895, in Holland, by Rev. John P. Berthier. General motherhouse, Rome, Italy; U.S. provincial house, 10415 Midland Blvd., St.

Louis, Mo. 63114. Belated vocations for the missions.

Holy Family, Sons of the, S.F.: Founded 1864, at Barcelona, Spain, by Bl. Jose Mañanet y Vives; in U.S., 1920. General motherhouse, Barcelona, Spain; U.S. address, 401 Randolph Rd., Silver Spring, Md. 20904.

Holy Ghost Fathers, C.S.Sp.: Founded 1703, in Paris, by Claude Francois Poullart des Places; in U.S., 1872. Generalate, Rome, Italy. Missions, education.

Eastern Province (1872), 6230 Brush Run Rd., Bethel Park, Pa. 15102.

Western Province (1968), 919 Briarcliff, San Antonio, Tex. 78213.

Holy Ghost Fathers of Ireland (1971), U.S. delegates: 4849 37th St., Long Island City, N.Y. 11101 (East); St. Cecilia Church, 2555 17th Ave., San Francisco, Calif. 94116. (West); St. John Baptist Church, 1139 Dryades St., New Orleans, La. 70113.

Holy Spirit, Missionaries of the, M.Sp.S.: Founded 1914, at Mexico City, Mexico, by Felix Rougier. General motherhouse, Mexico City; U.S. headquarters, 1005 Colonia Rd., Oxnard, Calif. 93030. Missionary work.

Jesuits (Society of Jesus), S.J.: Founded 1534, in France, by St. Ignatius of Loyola; received papal approval, 1540; first U.S. province, 1833. Generalate, Rome, Italy; U.S. national office, Jesuit Conference, 1424 16th St. N.W., Suite 300, Washington, D.C. 20036. Missionary, educational, literary work.

Maryland Province (1833), 5704 Roland Ave., Baltimore, Md. 21210.

New York Province (1943), 501 E. Fordham Rd., Bronx, N.Y. 10458.

Missouri Province (1863), 4511 W. Pine Blvd., St. Louis, Mo. 63108.

New Orleans Province (1907), 500 S. Jefferson Davis Pkwy., New Orleans, La. 70119.

California Province (1909), 300 College Ave., P.O. Box 519, Los Gatos, Calif. 95031.

New England Province (1926), 761 Harrison Ave., Boston, Mass. 02118.

Chicago Province, 2050 N. Clark St., Chicago, Ill. 60614.

Oregon Province (1932), 2222 N.W. Hoyt, Portland, Ore. 97210.

Detroit Province (1955), 7303 W. Seven Mile Rd., Detroit, Mich. 48221.

Wisconsin Province (1955), 1434 W. State St., Milwaukee, Wis. 53233.

Province of the Antilles (1947), U.S. address, 720 N.E. 27th St., Miami, Fla. 33137.

Joseph, Congregation of St., C.S.J.: General motherhouse, Rome, Italy; U.S. vice province, 12021 Mayfield Rd., Cleveland, O. 44106. Parochial, missionary, educational work.

Joseph, Oblates of St., O.S.J.: Founded 1878, in Italy, by Bishop Joseph Marello. General motherhouse, Rome, Italy. Parochial, educational work.

Eastern Province, Route 315, Pittston, Pa. 18640.

Western Province, 544 W. Cliff Dr., Santa Cruz, Calif. 95060.

Josephite Fathers, C.J.: General motherhouse, Ghent, Belgium; U.S. foundation, 989 Brookside Ave., Santa Maria, Calif. 93454.

Josephites (St. Joseph's Society of the Sacred Heart), S.S.J.: Founded 1866, in England, by Cardinal Vaughan; in U.S., 1871. General motherhouse, 1130 N. Calvert St., Baltimore, Md. 21202. Work in black missions.

LaSalette, Missionaries of Our Lady of, M.S.: Founded 1852, by Msgr. de Bruillard; in U.S., 1892. Motherhouse, Rome, Italy.

Our Lady of Seven Dolors Province (1934), P.O. Box 6127, Hartford, Conn. 06106.

Immaculate Heart of Mary Province (1945), P.O. Box 538, Attleboro, Mass. 02703.

Mary Queen Province (1958), 4650 S. Broadway, St. Louis, Mo. 63111.

Mary Queen of Peace Vice Province (1967), P.O. Box 95, Georgetown, Ill. 61846.

Lateran, Canons Regular of the, C.R.L.: General house, Rome, Italy; U.S. address: 2317 Washington Ave., Bronx, N.Y. 10458.

Legionaries of Christ, L.C.: Founded 1941, in Mexico, by Rev. Marcial Maciel; in U.S., 1965. General headquarters, Rome, Italy; U.S. novitiate, 475 Oak Ave., Cheshire, Conn. 06410.

Marian Fathers and Brothers, M.I.C.: Founded 1673; U.S. foundation, 1913. General motherhouse, Rome, Italy. Educational, parochial, mission, publication work.

St. Casimir Province (1913), 6336 S. Kilbourn Ave., Chicago, Ill. 60629.

St. Stanislaus Kostka Province (1948), Eden Hill, Stockbridge, Mass. 01262.

Marianists (Society of Mary; Brothers of Mary), S.M.: Founded 1817, at Bordeaux, France, by Rev. William-Joseph Chaminade; in U.S., 1849. General motherhouse, Rome, Italy. Educational work.

Cincinnati Province (1849), 4435 E. Patterson Rd., Dayton, Ohio 45430.

St. Louis Province (1908), 4538 Maryland Ave., St. Louis, Mo. 63156.

Pacific Province (1948), 22825 San Juan Rd., Cupertino, Calif. 95015.

New York Province (1961), 4301 Roland Ave., Baltimore, Md. 21210.

Province of Meribah (1976), 240 Emory Rd., Mineola, N.Y. 11501.

Mariannhill, Congregation of the Missionaries of, C.M.M.: Trappist monastery, begun in 1882 by Abbot Francis Pfanner in Natal, South Africa, became an independent modern congregation in 1909; in U.S., 1920. Generalate, Rome, Italy; U.S.-Canadian province, St. Joseph Mission House, Route 1, Center Valley, Pa. 18034. Foreign mission work.

Marist Fathers (Society of Mary), S.M.: Founded 1816, at Lyons, France, by Jean Claude Colin; in U.S., 1863. General motherhouse, Rome, Italy. Educational, foreign mission, pastoral work.

Washington Province (1924), 815 Varnum St., N.E., Washington D.C. 20017.

Northeast Province (1924), 72 Beacon St., Chestnut Hill, Mass. 02167.

San Francisco Western Province (1961), 625 Pine St., San Francisco, Calif. 94108.

Maronite Hermits of St. Francis (of Assisi), **O.P.C.:** Most Holy Trinity Monastery, Dugway Rd., Petersham, Mass. 01366.

Mary Immaculate, Missionary Oblates of, O.M.I.: Founded 1816, in France, by Bl. Charles Joseph Eugene de Mazenod; in U.S., 1849. General house, Rome, Italy. U.S. consulate, 62 Kirkwood Rd., Brighton, Mass. 02135. Parochial, foreign mission, educational work; ministry to marginal.

Southern U.S. Province (1904), 334 W. Kings Hwy., San Antonio, Tex. 78212.

Our Lady of Hope, Eastern Province (1883), 350 Jamaicaway, Boston, Mass. 02130.

St. John the Baptist Province (1921), 45 Kenwood Ave., Worcester, Mass. 01605.

Central Province (1924), 267 E. 8th St., St. Paul, Minn. 55101.

Western Province (1953), 290 Lenox Ave., Oakland, Calif. 94610.

Italian Province, U.S. foundation, St. Nicholas Church, 442 Brinkerhoff Ave., Palisades Park, N.J. 07650.

Maryknoll (Catholic Foreign Mission Society of America), M.M.: Founded 1911, in U.S., by Frs. Thomas F. Price and James A. Walsh. General Center, Maryknoll, N.Y. 10545.

Mekhitarist Order of Vienna, C.M.Vd.: Established 1773. General headquarters, Vienna, Austria. U.S. address, Our Lady Queen of Martyrs Church, 1327 Pleasant Ave., Los Angeles, Calif. 90033. Work among Armenians in U.S..

Mercedarians (Order of Our Lady of Mercy), O. de M.: Founded 1218, in Spain, by St. Peter Nolasco. General motherhouse, Rome, Italy; U.S. headquarters, 8692 Lake St., LeRoy, N.Y. 14482.

Mercy, Congregation of Priests of (Fathers of Mercy), C.P.M.: Founded 1808, in France, by Rev. Jean Baptiste Rauzan; in U.S., 1839. General mission house, Cold Spring, N.Y. 10516. Mission work.

Mill Hill Missionaries (St. Joseph's Society for Foreign Missions), M.H.M.: Founded 1866, in England, by Cardinal Vaughan; in U.S., 1951. General motherhouse, London, England; American headquarters, 1377 Nepperhan Ave., Yonkers, N.Y. 10703.

Missionhurst — CICM (Congregation of the Immaculate Heart of Mary): Founded 1862, at Scheut, Brussels, Belgium, by Very Rev. Theophile Verbist. General motherhouse, Rome, Italy; U.S. province, 4651 N. 25th St., Arlington, Va. 22207. Home and foreign mission work.

Missionaries of St. Charles, Congregation of the, C.S.: Founded 1887, at Piacenza, Italy, by Bishop John Baptist Scalabrini. General motherhouse, Rome, Italy.

St. Charles Borromeo Province (1888), 27 Carmine St., New York, N.Y. 10014.

St. John Baptist Province (1903), 546 N. East Ave., Oak Park, Ill. 60302.

Missionaries of the Holy Apostles, M.Ss.A.: Founded 1962, Washington, D.C., by Eusebe M. Menard. North American headquarters, 33 Prospect Hill Rd., Cromwell, Conn. 06416.

Montfort Missionaries (Missionaries of the Company of Mary), S.M.M.: Founded 1715, by St. Louis Marie Grignon de Montfort; in U.S., 1948. General motherhouse, Rome, Italy; U.S. headquarters, 101-18 104th St., Ozone Park, N.Y. 11416. Mission work.

Mother Co-Redemptrix, Congregation of, C.M.C.: Founded 1953 at Lein-Thuy, Vietnam (North), by Fr. Dominic Mary Tran Dinh Thu; in U.S., 1975. General house, Hochiminhville, Vietnam; U.S. provincial house, 1900 Grand Ave., Carthage, Mo. 64836. Work among Vietnamese Catholics in U.S.

Oratorians (Congregation of the Oratory of St. Philip Neri), C.O.: Founded 1575, at Rome, by St. Philip Neri. A confederation of autonomous houses. U.S. addresses: P.O. Box 11586, Rock Hill, S.C. 29730; P.O. Box 1688, Monterey, Calif. 93940; 4040 Bigelow Blvd., Pittsburgh, Pa. 15213; P.O. Drawer J, Pharr, Tex. 78577.

Pallottines (Society of the Catholic Apostolate), S.A.C.: Founded 1835, at Rome, by St. Vincent Pallotti. Generalate, Rome, Italy. Charitable, educational, parochial, mission work.

Immaculate Conception Province (1953), P.O. Box 573, Pennsauken, N.J. 08110.

Mother of God Province (1946), 5424 W. Blue Mound Rd., Milwaukee, Wis. 53208.

Irish Province, U.S. address: 3352 4th St., Wyandotte, Mich. 48192.

Queen of Apostles Province (1909), 448 E. 116th St., New York, N.Y. 10029.

Christ the King Province, 3452 Niagara Falls, Blvd., N. Tonawanda, N.Y. 14120.

Paraclete, Servants of the, s.P.: Founded 1947, Santa Fe, N.M., archdiocese. General motherhouse, Rome, Italy; U.S. motherhouse, Via Coeli, Jemez Springs, N.M. 87025. Devoted to care of priests.

Paris Foreign Missions Society, M.E.P.: Founded 1662, at Paris, France. Headquarters, Paris, France; U.S. establishment, 930 Ashbury St., San Francisco, Calif. 94117. Mission work and training of native clergy.

Passionists (Congregation of the Passion), C.P.: Founded 1720, in Italy, by St. Paul of the Cross. General motherhouse, Rome, Italy.

St. Paul of the Cross Province (1852), 80 David St., South River, N.J. 08882.

Holy Cross Province (Western Province), 5700 N. Harlem Ave., Chicago, Ill. 60631.

Patrick's Missionary Society, St., S.P.S.: Founded 1932, at Wicklow, Ireland, by Msgr. Patrick Whitney; in U.S., 1953. International headquarters, Kiltegan Co., Wicklow, Ireland. U.S. foundations: 70 Edgewater Rd., Cliffside Park, N.J. 07010; 19536 Eric Dr., Saratoga, Calif. 95070; 1347 W. Granville Ave., Chicago, Ill. 60660.

Pauline Fathers (Order of St. Paul the First Hermit), O.S.P.: Founded 1215; established in U.S., 1955. General motherhouse, Czestochowa, Jasna Gora, Poland; U.S. headquarters, P.O. Box 151, Doylestown, Pa. 18901.

Pauline Fathers and Brothers (Society of St. Paul for the Apostolate of Communications), S.S.P.: Founded 1914, by Very Rev. James Alberione; in U.S., 1932. Motherhouse, Rome, Italy; American province, 6746 Lake Shore Rd., Derby, N.Y. 14047. Social communications work.

Paulists (Missionary Society of St. Paul the Apostle), C.S.P.: Founded 1858, in New York, by Fr. Isaac Thomas Hecker. General offices, 86

Dromore Rd., Scarsdale, N.Y. 10583. Missionary, ecumenical, pastoral work.

Piarists (Order of the Pious Schools), Sch.P.: Founded 1617, at Rome, Italy, by St. Joseph Calasanctius. General motherhouse, Rome, Italy. American province, 4605 Bayview Dr., Fort Lauderdale, Fla. 33308. New York-Puerto Rico vice-province (Calasanzian Fathers), 88 Convent Ave., New York, N.Y. 10027. California delegation, 3951 Rogers St., Los Angeles, Calif. 90063. Educational work.

Pontifical Institute for Foreign Missions, P.I.M.E.: Founded 1850, in Italy, at request of Pope Pius IX. General motherhouse, Rome, Italy; U.S. headquarters, 17330 Quincy Ave., Detroit, Mich. 48221. Foreign mission work.

Precious Blood, Society of, C.Pp.S.: Founded 1815, in Italy, by St. Gaspar del Bufalo. General motherhouse, Rome, Italy.

Cincinnati Province, 431 E. Second St., Dayton, O. 45402.

Kansas City Province, Ruth Ewing Rd., Liberty, Mo. 64068.

Pacific Province, 1850 Church Lane, San Pablo, Calif. 94806.

Atlantic Vicariate, 207 S. Garfield, E. Rochester, N.Y. 14445.

Premonstratensians (Order of the Canons Regular of Premontre; Norbertines), O. Praem.: Founded 1120, at Premontre, France, by St. Norbert. Generalate, Rome, Italy. Educational, parish work.

St. Norbert Abbey, 1016 N. Broadway, DePere, Wis. 54115.

Daylesford Abbey, 220 S. Valley Rd., Paoli, Pa. 19301.

St. Michael's Priory, 1042 Star Route, Orange, Calif. 92667.

Providence, Sons of Divine, F.D.P.: Founded 1893, at Tortona, Italy, by Bl. Luigi Orione; in U.S., 1933. General motherhouse, Rome, Italy; U.S. address, 111 Orient Ave., E. Boston, Mass. 02128.

Redemptorists (Congregation of the Most Holy Redeemer), C.SS.R.: Founded 1732, in Italy, by St. Alphonsus Mary Liguori. Generalate, Rome, Italy. Mission work.

Baltimore Province (1850), 7509 Shore Rd., Brooklyn, N.Y. 11209.

St. Louis Province (1875), Box 6, Glenview, Ill. 60025.

Oakland Province (1952), 3696 Clay St., San Francisco, Calif. 94118.

New Orleans Vice-Province, 1527 3rd St., New Orleans, La., 70130.

Resurrectionists (Congregation of the Resurrection), C.R.: Founded 1836, in France, under direction of Bogdan Janski. Motherhouse, Rome, Italy.

U.S. Province, 2250 N. Latrobe Ave., Chicago, Ill. 60639.

Ontario Kentucky Province, Resurrection College, Westmont Rd., N., Waterloo, Ont. N2L 3G7, Canada.

Rogationist Fathers, R.C.J.: Founded 1926. General motherhouse, Rome, Italy. U.S. addresses:

P.O. Box 248, Mendota, Calif. 93640; P.O. Box 335, Sanger, Calif. 93657.

Rosminians (Institute of Charity), I.C.: Founded 1828, in Italy, by Antonio Rosmini-Serbati. General motherhouse, Rome, Italy; U.S. address, 2327 W. Heading Ave., Peoria, Ill. 61604. Charitable work.

Sacerdotal Fraternity, Congregation of the, C.F.S.: Founded 1901, at Paris, France. General house, 500 Ave. Claremont, Montreal (Westmount), Que. H3Y 2N5 Canada. Care of priests.

Sacred Heart, Missionaries of the, M.S.C.: Founded 1854, by Rev. Jules Chevelier. General motherhouse, Rome, Italy; U.S. province, P.O. Box 270, Aurora, Ill. 60507.

Sacred Heart of Jesus, Congregation of the (Sacred Heart Fathers and Brothers), S.C.J.: Founded 1877, in France. General motherhouse, Rome, Italy; U.S. provincial office: P.O. Box 289, Hales Corners, Wis. 53130. Educational, preaching, mission work.

Sacred Hearts, Fathers of the (Picpus Fathers), SS.CC.: Founded 1805, in France, by Fr. Coudrin. General motherhouse, Rome, Italy. Mission, educational work.

Eastern Province (1946), 3 Adams St. (Box 111), Fairhaven, Mass. 02719.

Western Province (1970), 32481 Sage Rd., Hemet, Calif. 92343.

Hawaiian Province, Box 797, Kaneohe, Oahu, Hawaii 96744.

Sacred Hearts of Jesus and Mary, Missionaries of the, M.SS.CC.: Founded at Naples, Italy, by Ven. Cajetan Errico. General motherhouse, Rome, Italy; U.S. headquarters, 2249 Shore Rd., Linwood, N.J. 08221.

Salesians of St. John Bosco (Society of St. Francis de Sales), S.D.B.: Founded 1859, by St. John (Don) Bosco. Generalate, Rome, Italy.

St. Philip the Apostle Province (1902), 148 Main St., New Rochelle, N.Y. 10802.

San Francisco Province (1926), 1100 Franklin St., San Francisco, Calif. 94109.

Salvatorians (Society of the Divine Savior), S.D.S.: Founded 1881, in Rome, by Fr. Francis Jordan; in U.S., 1896. General headquarters, Rome, Italy; U.S. province, 1735 Hi-Mount Blvd., Milwaukee, Wis. 53208. Educational, parochial, mission work; campus ministries, chaplaincies.

Scalabrinians: See Missionaries of St. Charles, Congregation of the.

Servites (Order of Friar Servants of Mary), O.S.M.: Founded 1233, at Florence, Italy, by Seven Holy Founders. Generalate, Rome, Italy. General apostolic ministry.

Eastern Province (1967) 3401 S. Home Ave., Berwyn, Ill. 60402.

Western Province (1967), 5210 Somerset St., Buena Park, Calif. 90621.

Somascan Fathers, C.R.S.: Founded 1534, at Somasca, Italy, by St. Jerome Emiliani. General motherhouse, Rome, Italy; U.S. address, Pine Haven Boys Center, River Rd., P.O. 162, Suncook, N.H. 03275.

Sons of Mary Missionary Society (Sons of Mary, Health of the Sick), F.M.S.I.: Founded 1952, in the Boston archdiocese, by Rev. Edward F. Garesche,

S.J. Headquarters, 567 Salem End Rd., Framingham, Mass. 01701. Dedicated to health of the sick; medical, catechetical and social work in home and foreign missions.

Stigmatine Fathers and Brothers (Congregation of the Sacred Stigmata), C.S.S.: Founded 1816, by Bl. Gaspare Bertoni. General motherhouse, Rome, Italy; North American Province, 36 Fairmont Ave., Newton, Mass. 02158. Parish work.

Sulpicians (Society of Priests of St. Sulpice), S.S.: Founded 1641, at Paris, by Rev. Jean Jacques Olier. General motherhouse, Paris, France; U.S. province, 5408 Roland Ave., Baltimore, Md. 21210. Education of seminarians and priests.

Theatines (Congregation of Clerics Regular): C.R.: Founded 1524, at Rome, by St. Cajetan. General motherhouse, Rome, Italy; U.S. headquarters, 1050 S. Birch St., Denver, Colo. 80222.

Trappists: See Cistercians of the Strict Observance.

Trinitarians (Order of the Most Holy Trinity), O.SS.T.: Founded 1198, by St. John of Matha. General motherhouse, Rome, Italy; U.S. headquarters, P.O. Box 5719, Baltimore, Md. 21208.

Trinity Missions (Missionary Servants of the Most Holy Trinity), S.T.: Founded 1929, by Fr. Thomas Augustine Judge. Generalate, 1215 N. Scott St., Arlington, Va. 22209. Home mission work.

Viatorian Fathers (Clerics of St. Viator), C.S.V.: Founded 1831, in France, by Fr. Louis Joseph Querbes. General motherhouse, Rome, Italy; U.S. headquarters, 1212 E. Euclid St., Arlington Hts., Ill. 60004. Educational work.

Vincentians (Congregation of the Mission; Lazarists), C.M.: Founded 1625, in Paris, by St. Vincent de Paul; in U.S., 1818. General motherhouse, Rome, Italy. Educational work.

Eastern Province (1867), 500 E. Chelten Ave., Philadelphia, Pa. 19144.

Midwest Province (1888), 1723 Pennsylvania Ave., St. Louis, Mo. 63104.

New England Province (1975), 1109 Prospect Ave., W. Hartford, Conn. 06105.

American Italian Branch, Our Lady of Pompei Church, 3600 Claremont St., Baltimore, Md. 21224.

American Spanish Branch (Barcelona, Spain), 134 Vernon Ave., Brooklyn, N.Y. 11206.

American Spanish Branch (Zaragoza, Spain), Holy Agony Church, 1834 3rd Ave., New York, N.Y. 10029.

Western Province (1975), 649 W. 23rd St., Los Angeles, Calif. 90007.

Southern Province (1975), 1302 Kipling St., Houston, Tex. 77006.

Puerto Rico Province (1955), Box 8361, Santurce, P.R. 00910.

Vocationist Fathers (Society of Divine Vocations), S.D.V.: Founded 1920, in Italy; in U.S., 1962. General motherhouse, Naples, Italy; U.S. address, 170 Broad St., Newark, N.J. 07104.

Xaverian Missionary Fathers, S.X.: Founded 1895, by Archbishop Conforti, at Parma, Italy. General motherhouse, Rome, Italy; U.S. province, 12 Helene Ct., Wayne, N.J. 07470. Foreign mission work.

INSTITUTES OF BROTHERS

Alexian Brothers, C.F.A.: Founded 14th century in western Germany and Belgium during the Black Plague. Motherhouse, Aachen, Germany; generalate, Signal Mountain, Tenn. 37377. Hospital and general health work.

Bethany, Brothers of: Founded in 1984. Holy Trinity Monastery, Dunhamtown Rd., Palmer, Mass. 01069.

Charity, Brothers of, F.C.: Founded 1807, in Belgium, by Canon Peter J. Triest. General motherhouse, Rome, Italy: American District, 7720 Doe Lane, Philadelphia, Pa. 19118. Charitable, educational work.

Christian Brothers, Congregation of, C.F.C. (formerly Christian Brothers of Ireland): Founded 1802 at Waterford, Ireland, by Edmund Ignatius Rice. General motherhouse, Rome, Italy. Educational work.

American Province, Eastern U.S. (1916), 21 Pryer Terr., New Rochelle, N.Y. 10804. 354.

American Province, Western U.S. (1966), P.O. Box 85R, Romeoville, Ill. 60441.

Christian Instruction, Brothers of (La Mennais Brothers), F.I.C.: Founded 1817, at Ploermel, France, by Abbe Jean Marie de la Mennais and Abbe Gabriel Deshayes. General motherhouse, Rome, Italy; American province, Notre Dame Institute, Alfred, Me. 04002.

Christian Schools, Brothers of the (Christian Brothers), F.S.C.: Founded 1680, at Reims, France, by St. Jean Baptiste de la Salle. General motherhouse, Rome, Italy; U.S. Conference, 100 De La Salle Dr., Romeoville, Ill. 60441. Educational, charitable work.

Baltimore Province (1845), Box 29, Adamstown, Md. 21710.

Chicago Province (1966), 200 De La Salle Dr., Romeoville, Ill. 60441.

New York Province (1848), 820 Newman Springs Rd., Lincroft, N.J. 07738.

Long Island-New England Province (1957), Christian Brothers Center, 635 Ocean Ave., Narragansett, R.I. 02882.

St. Louis Province (1849), 2101 Rue de la Salle, Glencoe, Mo. 63038.

San Francisco Province (1868), P.O. Box A-D, Saint Mary's College, Moraga, Calif. 94575.

New Orleans-Santa Fe Province (1921), De La Salle Christian Brothers, 1522 Breaux Bridge Rd., Lafayette, La. 70501.

St. Paul-Minneapolis Province (1963), 807 Summit Ave., St. Paul, Minn. 55105.

Cross, Congregation of Holy, C.S.C.: Founded 1837, in France, by Rev. Basil Moreau; U.S. province, 1841. Generalate, Rome, Italy. Educational, social work; missions.

Midwest Province (1841), Box 460, Notre Dame, Ind. 46556.

Southwest Province (1956), St. Edward's University, Austin, Tex. 78704.

Eastern Province (1956), 85 Overlook Circle, New Rochelle, N.Y. 10804.

Francis, Brothers of Poor of St., C.F.P.: Founded 1857. Motherhouse, Aachen, Germany; U.S. province, 105 Valley St., Burlington, Ia. 52601. Educational work, especially with poor and emotionally disturbed youth.

Francis Xavier, Brothers of St. (Xaverian Brothers), C.F.X.: Founded 1839, in Belgium, by Theodore J. Ryken. Generalate, Rome, Italy. Educational work.

Sacred Heart Province, 10516 Summit Ave., Kensington, Md. 20895.

St. Joseph Province, 704 Brush Hill Rd., Milton, Mass. 02186.

Franciscan Brothers of Brooklyn, O.S.F.: Founded in Ireland; established at Brooklyn, 1858. Generalate, 135 Remsen St., Brooklyn, N.Y. 11201. Educational work.

Franciscan Brothers of Christ the King, O.S.F.: Founded 1961. General motherhouse, 1401 Central Ave., Bettendorf, Iowa 52722.

Franciscan Brothers of the Good News, O.S.F.: Founded 1970 in Archdiocese of New York. Central friary, Mount Road, Cummington, Mass. 01026. Combine volunteer works of mercy with contemplative life of prayer in hermitages.

Franciscan Brothers of the Holy Cross, F.F.S.C.: Founded 1862; in Germany. Generalate, Hausen, Linz Rhein, West Germany; U.S. region, R.R. 1, Springfield, Ill. 62707. Educational work.

Franciscan Missionary Brothers of the Sacred Heart of Jesus, O.S.F.: Founded 1927, in the St. Louis, Mo., archdiocese. Motherhouse, R.R. 3, Box 39, Eureka, Mo. 63025. Care of aged, infirm, homeless men and boys.

Good Shepherd, Society of Brothers of the, B.G.S.: Founded 1951, by Bro. Mathias Barrett. Motherhouse, P.O. Box 389, Albuquerque, N.M. 87102. Operate shelters and refuges for aged and homeless; homes for handicapped men and boys, alcoholic rehabilitation center.

Holy Eucharist, Brothers of the, F.S.E.: Founded in U.S., 1957. Generalate, P.O. Box 25, Plaucheville, La. 71362. Teaching, social, clerical, nursing work.

Immaculate Heart of Mary, Brothers of the, F.I.C.M.: Founded 1948, at Steubenville, Ohio, by Bishop John K. Mussio. Motherhouse, Villa Maria, 609 N. 7th St., Steubenville, Ohio 43952. Educational, charitable work.

John of God, Brothers of the Hospitaller Order of St., O.H.: Founded 1537, in Spain. General motherhouse, Rome, Italy; American province, 2425 S. Western Ave., Los Angeles, Calif. 90018; Irish Province of Immaculate Conception, 532 Delsea Dr., Westville Grove, N.J. 08093. Nursing work and related fields.

Little Brothers of Jesus: Generalate, London, England; U.S. foundation, 2833 Cochrane, Detroit, Mich. 48216.

Little Brothers of St. Francis, O.S.F.: Founded 1970 in Archdiocese of Boston. General fraternity, 785-789 Parker St., Roxbury (Boston), Mass. 02120. Combine contemplative life with evangelical street ministry

Marist Brothers, F.M.S.: Founded 1817, in France, by Bl. Marcellin Champagnat. General motherhouse, Rome, Italy. Educational, social, catechetical work.

Esopus Province, 1241 Kennedy Blvd., Bayonne, N.J. 07002 (office).

Poughkeepsie Province, 38 N. Clinton St., Poughkeepsie, N.Y. 12601.

Mercy, Brothers of, F.M.M.: Founded 1856, in Germany. General motherhouse, Montabaur, Germany. American headquarters, 4520 Ransom Rd., Clarence, N.Y. 14031. Hospital work.

Mercy, Brothers of Our Lady of, C.F.M.M.: Founded 1844, in The Netherlands by Abp. J. Zwijsen. Generalate, Tilburg, The Netherlands; U.S. region, 2336 South "C" St., Oxnard, Calif. 93030.

Patrician Brothers (Brothers of St. Patrick), F.S.P.: Founded 1808, in Ireland, by Bishop Daniel Delaney; U.S. novitiate, 7820 Bolsa Ave., Midway City, Calif. 92655. Educational work.

Pius X, Brothers of St.: Founded 1952, at La Crosse, Wis., by Bishop John P. Treacy. Motherhouse, 3710 East Ave. S., La Crosse, Wis. 54601. Education.

Presentation Brothers of Mary, F.P.M.: Founded 1802, at Waterford, Ireland, by Edmund Ignatius Rice. General motherhouse, Cork, Ireland. U.S. foundation (Canadian Province), 368 S. Ellsworth, Marshall, Mo. 65340.

Rosary, Brothers of the Holy, F.S.R.: Founded 1956, in U.S., Motherhouse and novitiate, 1725 S. McCarran Blvd., Reno, Nev. 89502.

Sacred Heart, Brothers of the, S.C.: Founded 1821, in France, by Rev. Andre Coindre. General motherhouse, Rome, Italy, Educational work.

New Orleans Province (1847), P.O. Box 89, Bay St. Louis, Miss. 39520.

New England Province (1945), Rt. 98, R.R. 1, Pascoag, R.I. 02859.

New York Province (1960), P.O. Box 68, Belvidere, N.J. 07823.

COMMUNISM

The substantive principles of modern Communism, a theory and system of economics and social organization, were stated about the middle of the 19th century by Karl Marx, author of *The Communist Manifesto* and, with Friedrich Engels, *Das Kapital*.

The elements of Communist ideology include: radical materialism; dialectical determinism; the inevitability of class struggle, which is to be furthered for the ultimate establishment of a worldwide, classless society; common ownership of productive and other goods; the subordination of all persons and institutions to the dictatorship of the collectivity; denial of the rights, dignity and liberty of persons; militant atheism and hostility to religion; utilitarian morality.

Communism in theory and practice has been the subject of many papal documents and statements. Pius IX condemned it in 1846. Leo XIII dealt with it at length in the encyclicals *Quod Apostolici Muneris* in 1878 and *Rerum Novarum* in 1891. Pius XI wrote on the same subject the encyclicals *Quadragesimo Anno* in 1931 and *Divini Redemptoris* in 1937. These writings were updated and developed in new directions by Pius XII, John XXIII, Paul VI and John Paul II.

MEMBERSHIP OF RELIGIOUS INSTITUTES OF MEN

(Principal source: *Annuario Pontificio*. Statistics as of Jan. 1, 1985, unless indicated otherwise.)

Listed below are world membership statistics of institutes of men of pontifical right with 500 or more members; the number of priests is in parentheses. Also listed are institutes with less than 500 members with houses in the United States.

Jesuits (18,534)	26,761
Franciscans (Friars Minor) (13,818)	20,295
Salesians (10,934)	17,146
Franciscans (Capuchins) (8,350)	11,890
Benedictines (5,819)	9,413
Brothers of Christian Schools	9,340
Dominicans (5,342)	7,042
Redemptorists (4,765)	6,463
Marist Brothers	6,427
Oblates of Mary Immaculate (4,326)	5,750
Society of the Divine Word (3,339)	5,409
Franciscans (Conventuals) (2,646)	4,118
Vincentians (3,503)	3,898
Holy Spirit, Congregation (2,882)	3,628
Discalced Carmelites (2,350)	3,482
Augustinians (2,617)	3,403
Claretians (1,922)	2,917
Trappists (1,390)	2,912
Passionists (2,227)	2,897
Missionaries of Africa (2,429)	2,797
Priests of the Sacred Heart (1,890)	2,697
Christian Brothers	2,586
Missionaries of the Sacred Heart of Jesus (1,785)	2,488
Pallottines (1,493)	2,245
Carmelites (Ancient Observance) (1,513)	2,013
Holy Cross, Congregation (915)	1,997
Marianists (605)	1,982
Combonian Missionaries of the Heart of Jesus (1,301)	1,885
Marists (1,508)	1,861
Brothers of the Sacred Heart (61)	1,783
Hospitallers of St. John of God (124)	1,655
Piarists (1,264)	1,604
Brothers of Christian Instruction (1)	1,522
Congregation of the Immaculate Heart of Mary (Scheut Missionaries) (1,213)	1,503
Carmelites of BVM (916)	1,474
Sacred Hearts, Congregation (Picpus) (1,167)	1,413
Cistercians (Common Observance) (833)	1,409
Premonstratensians (999)	1,328
Brothers of Christian Instruction of St. Gabriel (32)	1,314
Montfort Missionaries (996)	1,307
Society of African Missions (1,153)	1,296
Augustinians (Recollects) (975)	1,270
Salvatorians (829)	1,257
Servants of Mary (879)	1,161
Society of St. Paul (549)	1,148
Assumptionists (934)	1,148
Blessed Sacrament, Congr. of (767)	1,123
Missionaries of Holy Family (742)·	1,070
Viatorians (438)	1,068
Little Workers of Divine Providence (735)	1,063

Consolata Missionaries (797)	1,010
Ministers of Sick (Camillians) (644)	1,001
Mill Hill Missionaries (770)	952
LaSalette Missionaries (623)	917
Franciscans (Third Order Regular)(591)	883
Xaverian Missionaries (682)	883
Oblates of St. Francis de Sales (665)	873
Columbans (798)	868
Canons Regular of St. Augustine (674)	866
Legionaries of Christ (171)	865
Maryknollers (711)	835
Brothers of Charity	819
Mercedarians (519)	770
Scalabrinians (596)	756
Congregation of St. Joseph (559)	730
Missionaries of the Most Precious Blood (555)	706
Pontifical Institute for Foreign Missions (580)	639
Brothers of the Immaculate Conception (6)	614
Trinitarians (396)	592
Eudists (437)	573
Missionaries of St. Francis de Sales of Annecy (324)	570
Crosier Fathers and Brothers (417)	546
Brothers of Our Lady Mother of Mercy	540
Paris Foreign Mission Society (530)	533
Servants of Charity (370)	509
Sulpicians (486)	486
Barnabites (358)	482
Resurrection, Congregation of (341)	466
Somascan Fathers (307)	459
Society of Christ (269)	459
St. Patrick's Mission Society (393)	448
Congr. of St. Basil (Canada) (409)	444
Oratorians (332)	437
Mariannhill Missionaries (259)	437
Brothers of Our Lady of Lourdes	419
Oblates of St. Joseph (266)	418
Marian Fathers and Brothers (225)	411
Stigmatine Fathers and Brothers (335)	410
Order of St. Basil the Great (Basilians of St. Josaphat) (286)	407
Xaverian Brothers	405
Carthusians (206)	394
Rosminians (292)	391
Missionaries of the Holy Spirit (234)	359
Order of St. Paul the First Hermit (141)	332
Rogationists (186)	331
Bethlehem Missionaries (239)	305
Paulists (239)	285
Little Brothers of Jesus (75)	269
Brothers of St. Patrick	219
Vocationist Fathers (159)	203
Atonement Friars (126)	197
Josephites (St. Joseph's Society of the Sacred Heart—S.S.J.) (164)	193
Presentation Brothers	178
Missionary Servants of the Most Holy Trinity (121)	169
Alexian Brothers (1)	166

Josephites (C.J.) (112)	148
Theatines (106)	141
Basilian Salvatorian Fathers (1977) (84)	121
Bros. of Poor of St. Francis (3)	119
Glenmary Missioners (70)	107
Brothers of Mercy	104
Society of St. Edmund (83)	98
Brothers of the Good Shepherd	97
Camaldolese (29)	83
Congr. of Sacerdotal Fraternity (40)	83
Franciscan Bros. of Holy Cross (3)	78
Clerics Regular Minor (Adorno Fathers) (31)	40
Servants of Holy Paraclete (31)	37
Mekhitarist Order of Vienna (19)	22
Fathers of Mercy (7)	7

RELIGIOUS INSTITUTES OF WOMEN IN THE UNITED STATES

(Sources: *Official Catholic Directory;* Catholic Almanac survey.)

Africa, Missionary Sisters of Our Lady of (Sisters of Africa), S.A.: Founded 1869, at Algiers, Algeria, by Cardinal Lavigerie; in U.S., 1929. General motherhouse, Frascati, Italy; U.S. headquarters, 5335 16th St., N.W., Washington, D.C. 20011. Medical, educational, catechetical and social work in Africa.

Agnes, Sisters of St., C.S.A.: Founded 1858, in U.S., by Caspar Rehrl. General motherhouse, 475 Gillett St., Fond du Lac, Wis. 54935. Education, health care, social services.

Ann, Sisters of St., S.S.A.: Founded 1834, in Italy; in U.S., 1952. General motherhouse, Rome, Italy; U.S. headquarters, Mount St. Ann, Ebensburg, Pa. 15931.

Anne, Sisters of St., S.S.A.: Founded 1850, at Vaudreuil, Que., Canada; in U.S., 1866. General motherhouse, Lachine, Que., Canada; U.S. address, 720 Boston Post Rd., Marlboro, Mass. 01752. Retreat work, pastoral ministry, religious education.

Anthony, Missionary Servants of St., M.S.S.A.: Founded 1929, in U.S., by Rev. Peter Baque. General motherhouse, 100 Peter Baque Rd., San Antonio, Tex. 78209. Social work.

Apostolate, Sisters Auxiliaries of the, S.A.A.: Founded 1903, in Canada; in U.S., 1911. General motherhouse, 689 Maple Terr., Monongah, W. Va. 26554. Education, nursing.

Assumption, Little Sisters of the, L.S.A.: Founded 1865, in France; in U.S., 1891. General motherhouse, Paris, France; U.S. provincialate, 214 E. 30th St., New York, N.Y. 10016. Social work, nursing, family life education.

Assumption, Religious of the, R.A.: Founded 1839, in France; in U.S., 1919. Generalate, Paris, France; U.S. province, 227 N. Bowman Ave., Merion, Pa. 19066. Educational work.

Assumption of the Blessed Virgin, Sisters of the, S.A.S.V.: Founded 1853, in Canada; in U.S., 1891. General motherhouse, Nicolet, Que., Canada; U.S. province, North Main St., Box 128, Petersham, Mass. 01366. Education, mission, pastoral ministry.

Augustinian Cloistered Nuns, O.S.A.: Established in Spain in 13th century; U.S. foundation, Convent of Our Mother of Good Counsel, 4435 West Pine Blvd., St. Louis, Mo. 63108.

Augustinian Sisters, Servants of Jesus and Mary, Congregation of, As.S.J.M.: Generalate, Rome, Italy; U.S. foundation, St. John School, Brandenburg, Ky. 40108.

Basil the Great, Sisters of St. (Pittsburgh Byzantine Rite), O.S.B.M.: Founded fourth century, by

St. Basil the Great. Motherhouse, Mount St. Macrina. 500 W. Main St., Uniontown, Pa. 15401. Education, health care.

Basil the Great, Sisters of the Order of St. (Ukrainian Byzantine Rite), O.S.B.M.: Founded fourth century, in Cappadocia, by St. Basil the Great and his sister St. Macrina; in U.S., 1911. Generalate, Rome, Italy; U.S. motherhouse, 710 Fox Chase Rd., Philadelphia, Pa. 19111. Education.

Benedict, Sisters of the Order of St., O.S.B.: Our Lady of Mount Caritas Monastery (founded 1979, Ashford, Conn.), Seckar Rd., Ashford, Conn. 06278. Contemplative.

Benedict, Sisters of the Order of St. (of the Congregation of Solesmes), O.S.B.: U.S. establishment, 1981, in Burlington diocese. Monastery of the Immaculate Heart of Mary, Westfield, Vt. 05874. Cloistered, papal enclosure.

Benedictine Nuns of the Primitive Observance, O.S.B.; Founded c. 529, in Italy; in U.S., 1948. Abbey of Regina Laudis, Flanders Rd., Bethlehem, Conn. 06751. Cloistered.

Benedictine Sisters, O.S.B.: Founded c. 529, in Italy; in U.S., 1852. General motherhouse, Eichstatt, Bavaria, Germany. U.S. addresses: St. Vincent's Archabbey, Latrobe, Pa. 15650; St. Emma's Retreat House and Convent, 1001 Harvey St., Greensburg, Pa. 15601; St. Walburga Convent, 6717 S. Boulder Rd., Boulder, Colo. 80303.

Benedictine Sisters (Bedford, N.H.), **O.S.B.:** Founded 1627, in Lithuania as cloistered community; reformed 1918 as active community; established in U.S. 1957, by Mother M. Raphaela Simonis. Regina Pacis, 333 Wallace Rd., Bedford, N.H. 03102.

Benedictine Sisters, Missionary, O.S.B.: Founded 1885. Generalate, Rome, Italy; U.S. motherhouse, 300 N. 18th St., Norfolk, Nebr. 68701.

Benedictine Sisters, Olivetan, O.S.B.: Founded 1887, in U.S.. General motherhouse, Holy Angels Convent, P.O. Drawer 130, Jonesboro, Ark. 72401. Educational, hospital work.

Benedictine Sisters of Perpetual Adoration of Pontifical Jurisdiction, Congregation of the, O.S.B.: Founded in U.S., 1874, from Maria Rickenbach, Switzerland. General motherhouse, 8300 Morganford Rd., St. Louis, Mo. 63123.

Benedictine Sisters of Pontifical Jurisdiction, O.S.B.: Founded c. 529, in Italy. No general motherhouse in U.S.. Three federations.

• Federation of St. Scholastica (1922). Pres., Sister Johnette Putnam, O.S.B., St. Scholastica Priory, 238 Rio Vista, Jefferson, La. 70121. Motherhouses belonging to the federation:

Mt. St. Scholastica, Atchison, Kans. 66002;

Benedictine Sisters of Elk Co., St. Joseph's Convent. St. Mary's. Pa. 15857; Mt. St. Benedict Priory. 6101 E. Lake Rd., Erie, Pa. 16511; Benedictine Sisters of Chicago, St. Scholastica Priory, 7430 Ridge Blvd., Chicago, Ill. 60645; Sacred Heart Priory. 1910 Maple Ave., Lisle, Ill. 60532; Our Lady of Sorrows Convent, 5900 W. 147th St., Oak Forest, Ill. 60452; St. Walburga Priory, 851 N. Broad St., Elizabeth, N.J. 07208; Benedictine Sisters, Mt. St. Mary Priory, 4530 Perrysville Ave., Pittsburgh, Pa. 15229;

Red Plains Priory, P.O. Box 60165, Oklahoma City, Okla. 73146; St. Joseph's Convent, 2200 S. Lewis, Tulsa, Okla. 74114; St. Gertrude's Priory, Ridgely P.O., Md. 21660; St. Walburga Monastery, Villa Madonna, 2500 Amsterdam Rd., Covington, Ky. 41016; Sacred Heart Convent, Cullman, Ala. 35055; St. Scholastica Priory, Box 1118, Covington, La. 70434; Holy Family Priory, Benet Lake, Wis. 53102; St. Benedict's Convent, Bristow, Va. 22013; St. Scholastica Convent, P.O. Box 700, Boerne, Tex. 78006; St. Lucy's Priory, Glendora, Calif. 91740; Holy Name Priory, St. Leo, Fla. 33574; Benet Hill Priory, 2555 N. Chelton Rd., Colorado Springs, Colo. 80909; Queen of Heaven Convent (Byzantine Rite), 8640 Squires Lane N.E., Warren, O. 44484; Emmanuel Priory, 3812 Fifth St., Baltimore, Md. 21225.

• Federation of St. Gertrude the Great (1937). Pres., Sister Anselm Hammerling, O.S.B. Address: c/o Mount Saint Benedict, E. Summit Ave., Crookston, Minn. 56716. Motherhouses belonging to the federation:

Mother of God Priory, Watertown, S. Dak. 57201; Sacred Heart Convent, Yankton, S. Dak. 57078; Mt. St. Benedict Convent, E. Summit Ave., Crookston, Minn. 56716; Sacred Heart Priory, Richardton, N. Dak. 58652; Convent of St. Martin, R.R. 4, Box 1660, Rapid City, S. Dak. 57702; Convent of the Immaculate Conception, 802 E. 10th St., Ferdinand, Ind. 47532; Priory of St. Gertrude, Cottonwood, Ida. 83522;

St. Benedict Priory, Fox Bluff, Box 5070, Madison, Wis. 53705; Queen of Angels Priory, 840 S. Main St., Mt. Angel, Ore. 97362; St. Scholastica's Convent, Albert Pike and Rogers Ave., Fort Smith, Ark. 72913; Our Lady of Peace Convent, 1511 Wilson, Columbia, Mo. 65201; Queen of Peace Priory, Belcourt, N. Dak. 58316. Convent of Our Lady of Grace, Beech Grove, Ind. 46107; Holy Spirit Convent, 9725 Pigeon Pass Rd., Sunnymead, Calif. 92388.

• Federation of St. Benedict (1947). Pres., Sister Margaret Michaud, O.S.B., St. Bede Priory, P.O. Box 66, Eau Claire, Wis. 54702. Motherhouses belonging to the federation:

St. Benedict's Convent, St. Joseph, Minn. 56374; St. Scholastica Priory, Kenwood Ave., Duluth, Minn. 55811; St. Bede Priory, Priory Rd., Eau Claire, Wis. 54702; St. Mary Priory, Nauvoo, Ill. 62354; Annunciation Priory, Apple Creek Rd., Bismarck, N. Dak. 58501; St. Paul's Priory, 2675 Larpenteur Ave. E., St. Paul, Minn. 55109; St. Placid Priory, 320 College St. N.E., Lacey, Wash. 98506.

Bethany, Sisters of, C.V.D.: Founded 1928, in El Salvador; in U.S. 1949. General motherhouse, Santa Tecla, El Salvador. U.S. address: 850 N. Hobart Blvd., Los Angeles, Calif. 90029.

Bethlemita Sisters, Daughters of the Sacred Heart of Jesus, S.C.I.F.: Founded 1861, in Guatemala. Motherhouse, Bogota, Colombia; U.S. address, St. Joseph Residence, 330 W. Pembroke St., Dallas, Tex. 75208.

Blessed Virgin Mary, Institute of the (Loreto Sisters), I.B.V.M.: Founded 17th century in Belgium; in U.S., 1954. Motherhouse, Rathfarnham, Dublin, Ireland; U.S. addresses: 6351 N. 27th Ave., Phoenix, Ariz. 85017; 810 Patrick Lane, Prescott, Ariz. 86301; 202 S. Kendrick, Flagstaff, Ariz. 86001.

Blessed Virgin Mary, Institute of the (Loretto Sisters), I.B.V.M.: Founded 1609, in Belgium; in U.S., 1880. U.S. address, Loretto Convent, Box 508, Wheaton, Ill. 60187. Educational work.

Bon Secours, Sisters of, C.B.S.: Founded 1824, in France; in U.S., 1881. Generalate, Rome, Italy; U.S. provincial house, Marriottsville Rd., Marriottsville, Md. 21104. Hospital work.

Brigid, Congregation of St., C.S.B.: Founded 1807, in Ireland; in U.S., 1953. U.S. regional house, 5118 Loma Linda Dr., San Antonio, Tex. 78201.

Brigittine Sisters (Order of the Most Holy Savior), O.SS.S.: Founded 1344, at Vadstena, Sweden, by St. Bridget; in U.S., 1957. General motherhouse, Rome, Italy; U.S. address, Vikingsborg, Darien, Conn. 06820.

Carmel, Congregation of Our Lady of Mount, O. Carm.: Founded 1825, in France; in U.S., 1833. Generalate, P.O. Box 476, Lacombe, La. 70445. Education, social services, pastoral ministry, retreat work.

Carmel, Institute of Our Lady of Mount, O. Carm.: Founded 1854, in Italy; in U.S., 1947. General motherhouse, Rome, Italy; U.S. novitiate, 5 Wheatland St., Peabody, Mass. 01960. Apostolic work.

Carmel Community, C.C.: Founded 1975, Columbus, O. Address, 100 Noe-Bixby Rd., Columbus, O. 43213. Contemplative.

Carmelite Missionaries of St. Theresa, C.M.S.T.: Founded 1903, in Mexico. General motherhouse, Mexico City, Mexico; U.S. foundation, 9600 Deertrail Dr., Houston, Tex. 70038.

Carmelite Nuns, Byzantine: Holy Annunciation Monastery, R.D. 1, P.O. Box 245, Sugarloaf, Pa. 18249.

Carmelite Nuns, Discalced, O.C.D.: Founded 1562, Spain. First foundation in U.S. in 1790, at Charles County, Md.; this monastery was moved to Baltimore. Monasteries in U.S. are listed below, according to states.

Alabama: 716 Dauphin Island Pkwy., Mobile 36606. Arkansas: 7201 W. 32nd St., Little Rock 72204. California: 215 E. Alhambra Rd., Alhambra 91801; 27601 Highway 1, Carmel 93923; 68 Rincon Rd., Kensington 94707; 3361 E. Ocean Blvd., Long Beach 90803; 6981 Teresian Way, Georgetown 95634; 5158 Hawley Blvd., San Diego 92116; 721 Parker Ave., San Francisco 94118; 530 Blackstone

Dr., San Rafael 94903; 1000 Lincoln St., Santa Clara 95050.

Colorado: 6138 S. Gallup St., Littleton 80120. Georgia: Coffee Bluff, 11 W. Back St., Savannah 31419; Illinois: River Rd. and Central, Des Plaines 60016. Indiana: 2500 Cold Springs Rd., Indianapolis 46222; 63 Allendale Pl., Terre Haute 47802. Iowa: Carmelite Rd., Eldridge 52748; 2901 S. Cecilia St., Sioux City 51106. Kansas: 3535 Wood Ave., Kansas City, 66102. Kentucky: 1740 Newburg Rd., Louisville 40205. Louisiana: 1250 Carmel Ave., Lafayette 70507; 1611 Mirabeau Ave., New Orleans 70122.

Maryland: 1318 Dulaney Valley Rd., Towson, Baltimore 21204; R.R. 4, Box 4035A, LaPlata, Md. 20646. Massachusetts: 61 Mt. Pleasant Ave., Roxbury, Boston 02119; 15 Mt. Carmel Rd., Danvers 01923; Sol-E-Mar Rd., S. Dartmouth 02748. Michigan: 16630 Wyoming Ave., Detroit 48221; 1036 Valley Ave. N.W., Grand Rapids 49504; U.S. 2 Highway, P.O. Box 397, Iron Mountain 49801; 3501 Silver Lake Rd., Traverse City 49684. Minnesota: 8251 De Montreville Trail N., Lake Elmo 55042. Mississippi: 2155 Terry Rd., Jackson 39204.

Missouri: 2201 W. Main St., Jefferson City 65101; 9150 Clayton Rd., Ladue, St. Louis Co. 63124; 424 E. Republic Rd., Springfield 65807. Nevada: 1950 La Fond Dr., Reno 89509. New Hampshire: 275 Pleasant St., Concord, 03301. New Jersey: P.O. Box 785, Flemington 08822; 189 Madison Ave., Morristown 07960. New Mexico: Mt. Carmel Rd., Santa Fe 87501. New York: 745 St. John's Pl., Brooklyn 11216; 139 De Puyster Ave., Beacon 12508; 75 Carmel Rd., Buffalo 14214; 1931 W. Jefferson Rd., Pittsford 14534; 68 Franklin Ave., Saranac Lake 12983; 428 Duane Ave., Schenectady 12304.

Ohio: 3176 Fairmount Blvd., Cleveland Heights 44118. Oklahoma: 20,000 N. County Line Rd., Piedmont 73078. Oregon: 87609 Green Hill Rd., Eugene 97402. Pennsylvania: Elysburg 17824; 510 E. Gore Rd., Erie 16509; R.D. 6, Box 28, Center Dr., Latrobe 15650; P.O. Box 57, Loretto 15940; 66th Ave. and Old York Rd. (Oak Lane), Philadelphia 19126. Rhode Island: Watson Ave. at Nayatt Rd., Barrington 02806.

Texas: 600 South Flowers Ave., Dallas 75211; 5801 Mt. Carmel Dr., Arlington 76017; 1100 Parthenon Pl., Roman Forest, New Caney 77357. 6301 Culebra and St. Joseph Way, San Antonio 78238. Utah: 5714 Holladay Blvd., Salt Lake City 84121. Vermont: Beckley Hill, Barre, 05641. Washington: 2215 N.E. 147th St., Seattle 98155. Wisconsin: W267 N2517 Meadowbrook Rd., Pewaukee 53072.

Carmelite Nuns of the Ancient Observance (Calced Carmelites), O. Carm.: Founded 1452, in The Netherlands; in U.S., 1930, from Naples, Italy, convent (founded 1856). U.S. monasteries: Carmelite Monastery of St. Therese, R.D. 3, Box 551, Coopersburg, Pa. 18036; Carmel of Mary, Wahpeton, N.D. 58075; Carmel of the Sacred Heart, 430 Laurel Ave., Hudson, Wis. 54016. Papal enclosure.

Carmelite Sisters (Corpus Christi), O. Carm.: Founded 1908, in England; in U.S., 1920. General motherhouse, Tunapuna, Trinidad, W.I. U.S. addresses: Carmelite Retreat House, 21 Battery St.,

Newport, R.I. 02840; Mt. Carmel Home, 412 W. 18th St., Kearney, Nebr. 68847; Home and foreign mission work.

Carmelite Sisters for the Aged and Infirm, O. Carm.: Founded 1929, at New York, by Mother M. Angeline Teresa, O. Carm. Motherhouse, Avila-on-Hudson, Germantown, N.Y. 12526. Social work, nursing and educating in the field of gerontology.

Carmelite Sisters of Charity, C.a.Ch.: Founded 1826 at Vich, Spain, by St. Joaquina de Vedruna. General motherhouse, Rome, Italy; U.S. address, 4200 16th St. N.W., Washington, D.C. 20011.

Carmelite Sisters of St. Therese of the Infant Jesus, C.S.T.: Founded 1917, in U.S.. General motherhouse, 1300 Classen Dr., Oklahoma City, Okla. 73103. Educational work.

Carmelite Sisters of the Divine Heart of Jesus, D.C.J.: Founded 1891, in Germany; in U.S., 1912. General motherhouse, Sittard, Netherlands. U.S. provincial houses: 1230 Kavanaugh Pl., Milwaukee, Wis. 52313 (Northern Province); 10341 Manchester Rd., St. Louis, Mo. 63122 (Central Province); 8585 La Mesa Blvd., La Mesa, Calif. 92041 (South Western Province). Social services, mission work.

Carmelite Sisters of the Sacred Heart, O.C.D.: Founded 1904, in Mexico. General motherhouse, Guadalajara, Mexico; U.S. provincialate and novitiate, 920 E. Alhambra Rd., Alhambra, Calif. 91801. Social services, retreat and educational work.

Casimir, Sisters of St., S.S.C.: Founded 1907, in U.S. by Mother Maria Kaupas. General motherhouse, 2601 W. Marquette Rd., Chicago, Ill. 60629. Education, missions, social services.

Cenacle, Congregation of Our Lady of the Retreat in the, R.C.: Founded 1826, in France; in U.S., 1892. Generalate, Rome, Italy. Eastern Province: 154-27 Horace Harding Expressway, Flushing, N.Y. 11367; Midwestern Province, 513 Fullerton Pkwy., Chicago, Ill. 60614.

Charity, Daughters of Divine, F.D.C.: Founded 1868, at Vienna, Austria; in U.S., 1913. General motherhouse, Rome, Italy. U.S. provinces: 56 Meadowbrook Rd., White Plains, N.Y. 10605; 39 N. Portage Path, Akron, O. 44303; 1315 N. Woodward Ave., Bloomfield Hills, Mich. 48013. Education, social services.

Charity, Little Missionary Sisters of, P.M.C.: Founded 1915, in Italy; in U.S., 1949. General motherhouse, Rome, Italy; U.S. address, 120 Orient Ave., East Boston, Mass. 02128.

Charity, Missionaries of, M.C.: Founded 1950, in Calcutta, India, by Mother Teresa. General motherhouse, 54A Acharya Jagadish C. Bose Road, Calcutta 16, India. U.S. address, 335 E. 145th St., Bronx, N.Y. 10451. Service of the poor.

Charity, Religious Sisters of, R.S.C.: Founded 1815, in Ireland; in U.S., 1953. Motherhouse, Dublin, Ireland; U.S. headquarters, Marycrest Manor, 10664 St. James Dr., Culver City, Calif. 90230.

Charity, Sisters of (of Seton Hill), S.C.: Founded 1870, at Altoona, Pa., from Cincinnati foundation. Administrative Offices, De Paul Center, Mt. Thor Rd., Greensburg, Pa. 15601. Educational, hospital, social, foreign mission work.

Charity, Sisters of (Grey Nuns of Montreal), S.G.M.: Founded 1737, in Canada by Bl. Marie Marguerite d'Youville; in U.S., 1855. General administration, Montreal, Que. H2Y 2L7, Canada; U.S. provincial house, 10 Pelham Rd., Lexington, Mass. 02173.

Charity, Sisters of (of Leavenworth), S.C.L.: Founded 1858, in U.S.. Motherhouse, Leavenworth, Kans. 66048.

Charity, Sisters of (of Nazareth), S.C.N.: Founded 1812, in U.S.. General motherhouse, Nazareth P. O., Nelson Co., Ky. 40048.

Charity, Sisters of (of St. Augustine), C.S.A.: Founded 1851, at Cleveland, O. Motherhouse, 5232 Broadview Rd., Richfield, O. 44286.

Charity, Sisters of Christian, S.C.C.: Founded 1849, in Paderborn, Germany, by Bl. Pauline von Mallinckrodt; in U.S., 1873. General motherhouse, Rome, Italy. U.S. provinces: Mallinckrodt Convent, Mendham, N.J. 07945; Maria Immaculata Convent, 1041 Ridge Rd., Wilmette, Ill. 60091, Education, health services, other apostolic work.

Charity, Vincentian Sisters of, V.S.C.: Founded 1835, in Austria; in U.S., 1902. General motherhouse, 8200 McKnight Rd., Pittsburgh, Pa. 15237.

Charity, Vincentian Sisters of, V.S.C.: Founded 1928, at Bedford, O. General motherhouse, 1160 Broadway, Bedford, O. 44146.

Charity of Canossa, Daughters of, Canossian Sisters: Founded 1808 in Verona, Italy. General motherhouse, Rome, Italy; U.S. provincial house, 5625 Isleta Blvd. S.W., Albuquerque, N.M. 87105.

Charity of Cincinnati, Ohio, Sisters of, S.C.: Founded 1809; became independent community, 1852. General motherhouse, Mt. St. Joseph, Ohio 45051. Educational, hospital, social work.

Charity of Ottawa, Sisters of (Grey Nuns of the Cross), S.C.O.: Founded 1845, at Ottawa, Canada; in U.S., 1857. General motherhouse, Ottawa, Canada; U.S. provincial house, 975 Varnum Ave., Lowell, Mass. 01854. Educational, hospital work, extended health care.

Charity of Our Lady, Mother of Mercy, Sisters of, S.C.M.M.: Founded 1832, in Holland; in U.S., 1874. General motherhouse, Den Bosch, Netherlands; U.S. provincialate, 520 Thompson Ave., East Haven Conn. 06512.

Charity of Our Lady of Mercy, Sisters of, O.L.M.: Founded 1829, in Charleston, S.C. Generalate and motherhouse, 424 Fort Johnson Rd., James Island, Charleston, S.C. 29412. Education, campus ministry, social services.

Charity of Quebec, Sisters of (Grey Nuns), S.C.Q.: Founded 1849, at Quebec; in U.S., 1890. General motherhouse, 2655 rue Le Pelletier, Beauport, Quebec GIC 3X7, Canada. Social work.

Charity of St. Elizabeth, Sisters of (Convent, N.J.), S.C.: Founded 1859, at Newark, N. J. Generalate, Convent Station, N. J. 07961. Education, pastoral ministry, social services.

Charity of St. Hyacinthe, Sisters of (Grey Nuns), S.C.S.H.: Founded 1840, at St. Hyacinthe, Canada; in U.S., 1878. General motherhouse, 16470 Avenue Bourdages, SUD, St. Hyacinthe, Quebec J2T 4J8, Canada. Regional house, 98 Campus Ave., Lewiston Me. 04240.

Charity of St. Joan Antida, Sisters of, S.C.S.J.A.: Founded 1799, in France; in U.S., 1932. General motherhouse, Rome, Italy; U.S. provincial house, 8560 N. 76th Pl., Milwaukee, Wis. 53223.

Charity of St. Louis, Sisters of, S.C.S.L.: Founded 1803, in France; in U.S., 1910. Generalate, Rome, Italy; U.S. provincial house, 29 Casablanca Court, Clifton Park, N.Y. 12065.

Charity of St. Vincent de Paul, Daughters of, D.C.: Founded 1633, in France; in U.S. 1809, at Emmitsburg, Md., by St. Elizabeth Ann Seton. General motherhouse, Paris, France. U.S. provinces: Emmitsburg, Md. 21727; 7800 Natural Bridge Rd., St. Louis, Mo. 63121; 9400 New Harmony Rd., Evansville, Ind. 47712; 96 Menands Rd., Albany, N.Y. 12204; 26000 Altamont Rd., Los Altos Hills, Calif. 94022.

Charity of St. Vincent de Paul, Sisters of, S.V.Z.: Founded 1845, in Croatia; in U.S., 1955. General motherhouse, Zagreb, Yugoslavia; U.S. foundation, 171 Knox Ave., West Seneca, N.Y. 14224.

Charity of St. Vincent de Paul, Sisters of, Halifax, S.C.H.: Founded 1856, at Halifax, N. S., from Emmitsburg, Md., foundation. Generalate, Mt. St. Vincent, Halifax, N. S., Canada. U.S. addresses: Commonwealth of Massachusetts, 125 Oakland St., Wellesley Hills, Mass. 02181; Boston Province, 26 Phipps St., Quincy, Mass. 02169; New York Province, 410 Grant Ave., Brooklyn, N.Y. 11208. Educational, hospital, social work.

Charity of St. Vincent de Paul, Sisters of, New York, S.C.: Founded 1817, from Emmitsburg, Md. General motherhouse, Mt. St. Vincent on Hudson, New York, N.Y. 10471. Educational, hospital work.

Charity of the Blessed Virgin Mary, Sisters of, B.V.M.: Founded 1833, in U.S. by Mary Frances Clarke. General motherhouse, Mt. Carmel, 1100 Carmel Dr., Dubuque, Ia. 52001. Education, pastoral ministry, social services.

Charity of the Immaculate Conception of Ivrea, Sisters of, S.C.I.C.: General motherhouse, Rome, Italy; U.S. address, Immaculate Virgin of Miracles Convent, R.D. 2, Mt. Pleasant, Pa. 15666.

Charity of the Incarnate Word, Congregation of the Sisters of, C.C.V.I.: Founded 1869, at San Antonio, Tex., by Bishop C. M. Dubuis. Generalate, 4503 Broadway, San Antonio, Tex. 78209.

Charity of the Incarnate Word, Congregation of the Sisters of (Houston, Tex.), C.C.V.I.: Founded 1866, in U.S., by Bishop C. M. Dubuis. General motherhouse, 6510 Lawndale Ave., Houston, Tex. 77023. Educational, hospital, social work.

Charity of the Sacred Heart, Daughters of, F.C.S.C.J.: Founded 1823, at La Salle de Vihiers, France; in U.S., 1905. General motherhouse, La Salle de Vihiers, France; U.S. address, Sacred Heart Province, P.O. Box 642, Littleton, N.H. 03561.

Charles Borromeo, Missionary Sisters of St. (Scalabrini Srs.): Founded 1895, in Italy; in U.S., 1941. American novitiate, 1414 N. 37th Ave., Melrose Park, Ill. 60601.

Child Jesus, Sisters of the Poor, P.C.J.: Founded 1844, at Aix-la-Chapelle, Germany; in U.S., 1924. General motherhouse, Simpelveld, Netherlands,

Chretienne, Sisters of Ste., S.S.CH.: Founded 1807, in France; in U.S., 1903. General motherhouse, Metz, France; U.S. provincial house, 297 Arnold St., Wrentham, Mass. 02093. Educational, hospital, mission work.

Christ, Adorers of the Blood of, A.S.C.: Founded 1834, in Italy; in U.S., 1870. General motherhouse, Rome, Italy. U.S. provinces: Rt. 1, Box 115, Red Bud, Ill. 62278; 1400 South Sheridan, Wichita, Kans. 67213; Columbia, Pa. 17512. Education, retreats, social services, pastoral ministry.

Christ the King, Sister Servants of, S.S.C.K.: Founded 1936, in U.S. General motherhouse, Loretto Convent, Mt. Calvary, Wis. 53057. Social services.

Christian Doctrine, Sisters of Our Lady of, R.C.D.: Founded 1910, at New York. Central office, 23 Haskell Ave., Suffern, N.Y. 10901.

Christian Education, Religious of, R.C.E.: Founded 1817, in France; in U.S., 1905. General motherhouse, Farnborough, England; U.S. provincial residence, 36 Hillcrest Rd., Belmont, Mass. 02178.

Church, Daughters of the: Founded in Italy; U.S. foundation, 1965. General house, Rome; U.S. address, 1029 Arosa Ave., Charlotte, N.C. 28203. Parish work, Spanish apostolate, teaching.

Cistercian Nuns, O. Cist.: Headquarters, Rome, Italy; U.S. addresses, Valley of Our Lady Monastery, Rt. 1, Box 136, Prairie du Sac, Wis. 53578; Abbey of Our Lady of the Mississippi, R.R. 3, Dubuque, Ia. 52001.

Cistercian Nuns of the Strict Observance, Order of, O.C.S.O.: Founded 1125, in France, by St. Stephen Harding; in U.S., 1949. U.S. addresses: Mt. St. Mary's Abbey, Arnold St., Wrentham, Mass. 02093; Our Lady of the Santa Rita Abbey, HCR 929, Sonoita, Ariz. 85637; Our Lady of the Redwoods Abbey, Whitethorn, Calif. 95489.

Clare, Sisters of St.: General motherhouse, Dublin, Ireland; U.S. foundation 37 E. Emerson, Chula Vista, Calif. 92011.

Clergy, Congregation of Our Lady, Help of the, C.L.H.C.: Founded 1961, in U.S. Motherhouse, Maryvale Convent, Rt. 1, Box 164, Vale, N.C. 28168.

Clergy, Servants of Our Lady Queen of the, S.R.C.: Founded 1929, in Canada; in U.S., 1934. General motherhouse, St. Jean Rimouski, Que. G5L 1X1 Canada.

Colettines: See Franciscan Poor Clare Nuns.

Columban, Missionary Sisters of St., S.S.C.: Founded 1922, in Ireland; in U.S., 1930. General motherhouse, Wicklow, Ireland; U.S. region, 1250 W. Loyola Ave., Chicago, Ill. 60626.

Comboni Missionary Sisters (Missionary Sisters of Verona), C.M.S.: Founded 1872, in Italy; in U.S., 1950. U.S. address, 1307 S. Lakeside Ave., Richmond, Va. 23228.

Consolata Missionary Sisters, M.C.: Founded 1910, in Italy; in U.S., 1954. General motherhouse, Turin, Italy; U.S. headquarters, 6801 Belmont Rd., Belmont, Mich. 49306.

Cross, Daughters of the, D.C.: Founded 1640, in France; in U.S., 1855. General motherhouse, 1000 Fairview St., Shreveport, La. 71104. Educational work.

Cross, Daughters of, of Liege, F.C.: Founded 1833, in Liege, Belgium; in U.S., 1958. U.S. address, 165 W. Eaton Ave., Tracy, Calif. 95376.

Cross, Sisters, Lovers of the Holy (Phat Diem): Founded 1670, in Vietnam; in U.S. 1976. U.S. address, Holy Cross Convent, Mary Immaculate Seminary, Northampton, Pa. 18067.

Cross, Sisters of the Holy, C.S.C.: Founded 1841, at Le Mans, France, established 1847, in Canada; in U.S., 1881. General motherhouse, St. Laurent, Montreal, Que., Canada; U.S. provincial house, Fairview Rd., Pittsfield, N.H. 03263. Educational work.

Cross, Sisters of the Holy, Congregation of, C.S.C.: Founded 1841, at Le Mans, France; in U.S., 1843. General motherhouse, Saint Mary's, Notre Dame, Ind. 46556. Education, health care, social services, pastoral ministry.

Cross and Passion, Sisters of the (Passionist Sisters), C.P.: Founded 1852; in U.S., 1924. General motherhouse, Bolton, England; U.S. address: Holy Family Convent, One Wright Lane, N. Kingstown, R.I. 02852.

Cyril and Methodius, Sisters of Sts., SS.C.M.: Founded 1909, in U.S., by Rev. Matthew Jankola. General motherhouse, Danville, Pa. 17821. Education, care of aged.

Disciples of the Divine Master, Sister, P.D.D.M.: Founded 1924; in U.S., 1948. General motherhouse, Rome, Italy; U.S. headquarters, 60 Sunset Ave., Staten Island, N.Y. 10314.

Divine Compassion, Sisters of, R.D.C.: Founded 1886, in U.S. General motherhouse, 52 N. Broadway, White Plains, N.Y. 10603. Education, other ministries.

Divine Love, Oblates to, Sisters, R.O.D.A.: Founded 1923, in Italy; in U.S., 1947. General motherhouse, Rome, Italy; U.S. provincial house, St. Clare's Convent, 1925 Hone Ave., Bronx, N.Y. 10461.

Divine Spirit, Congregation of the, C.D.S.: Founded 1956, in U.S., by Archbishop John M. Gannon. Motherhouse, 409 W. 6th St., Erie, Pa. 16507. Education, social services.

Dominicans

Nuns of the Order of Preachers (Dominican Nuns), O.P.: Founded 1206 by St. Dominic at Prouille, France. Cloistered, contemplative. Two branches in the United States:

• Dominican Nuns having perpetual adoration. First monastery established 1880, in Newark, N.J., from Oullins, France, foundation (1868). Seven autonomous monasteries.

St. Dominic, 375 13th Ave., Newark, N.J. 07103; Corpus Christi, 1230 Lafayette Ave., Bronx, N.Y. 10474; Blessed Sacrament, 29575 Middlebelt Rd., Farmington Hills, Mich. 48018; Holy Name, 3020 Erie Ave., Cincinnati, O. 45208; Monastery of the Angels, 1977 Carmen Ave., Los Angeles, Calif. 90068; Corpus Christi, 215 Oak Grove Ave., Menlo Park, Calif. 94025; Infant Jesus, 1501 Lotus Lane, Lufkin, Tex. 75901.

• Dominican Nuns devoted to the perpetual Rosary. First monastery established 1891, in Union City, N.J., from Calais, France, foundation (1880). Twelve autonomous monasteries (some also observe perpetual adoration).

Dominican Nuns of Perpetual Rosary, 14th and West Sts., Union City, N.J. 07087; 217 N. 68th St., Milwaukee, Wis. 53213; Perpetual Rosary, 1500 Haddon Ave., Camden, N.J. 08103; Our Lady of the Rosary, 335 Doat St., Buffalo, N.Y. 14211; Our Lady of the Rosary, 543 Springfield Ave., Summit, N.J. 07901; Mother of God, 1430 Riverdale St., W. Springfield, Mass. 01089; Perpetual Rosary, 802 Court St., Syracuse, N.Y. 13208; Immaculate Heart of Mary, 1834 Lititz Pike, Lancaster, Pa. 17601; Mary the Queen, 1310 W. Church St., Elmira, N.Y. 14905; St. Jude, Marbury, Ala. 36051; Our Lady of Grace, North Guilford, Conn. 06437; St. Dominic, 4901 16th St. N.W., Washington, D.C. 20011.

Dominican Rural Missionaries, O.P.: Founded 1932, in France; in U.S., 1951, at Abbeville, La. General motherhouse, Luzarches, France; U.S. address, 1318 S. Henry St., Abbeville, La. 70510.

Dominican Sisters of Bethany, Congregation, O.P.: Founded 1866, in France. Motherhouse, France; U.S. novitiate, 204 Ridge St., Millis, Mass. 02054.

Dominican Sisters of Charity of the Presentation, O.P.: Founded 1684, in France; in U.S., 1906. General motherhouse, Tours, France; U.S. headquarters, 3012 Elm St., Dighton, Mass. 02715. Hospital work.

Dominican Sisters of Our Lady of the Rosary and of St. Catherine of Siena (Cabra): Founded 1644 in Ireland. General motherhouse, Cabra, Dublin, Ireland. U.S. regional house, Mater Dolorosa Convent, P.O. Box 380, Independence, La. 70443.

Dominican Sisters of the Roman Congregation of St. Dominic, O.P.: Founded 1621, in France; in U.S., 1904. General motherhouse, Rome, Italy; U.S. province, 2624 Fillmore St., Davenport, Ia. 52804. Educational work.

Eucharistic Missionaries of St. Dominic, O.P.: Founded 1927, in Louisiana. General motherhouse, 1101 Aline St., New Orleans, La. 70115. Parish work, social services .

Maryknoll Sisters of St. Dominic, M.M.: Founded 1912, in New York. Center, Maryknoll, N.Y. 10545.

Religious Missionaries of St. Dominic, O.P.: General motherhouse, Rome, Italy. U.S. foundations: 808 S. Wright St., Alice, Texas 78332; 445 W. Pleasant Valley Rd., Oxnard, Calif. 93033.

Sisters of St. Dominic, O.P.: Thirty congregations in the U.S. Educational, hospital work. Names of congregations are given below, followed by the date of foundation, and location of motherhouse.

St. Catharine of Siena, 1822. St. Catharine, Ky. 40061.

St. Mary of the Springs, 1830. Columbus Ohio 43219.

Most Holy Rosary, 1847. Sinsinawa, Wis. 53824.

Most Holy Name of Jesus, 1850. 1520 Grand Ave., San Rafael, Calif. 94901.

Holy Cross, 1853. Albany Ave., Amityville, N.Y. 11701.

Most Holy Rosary, 1859. Mt. St. Mary on Hudson, Newburgh, N.Y. 12550.

St. Cecilia, 1860. Eighth Ave. N. and Clay St., Nashville, Tenn. 37208.

St. Mary, 1860. 580 Broadway, New Orleans, La. 70118.

St. Catherine of Siena, 1862. 5635 Erie St., Racine, Wis. 53402.

Our Lady of the Sacred Heart, 1873. 1237 W. Monroe St., Springfield, Ill. 62704.

Our Lady of the Rosary, 1876. Sparkill, N.Y. 10976.

Queen of the Holy Rosary, 1876. Mission San Jose, Calif. 94539.

Most Holy Rosary, 1892. 1257 Siena Heights Dr., Adrian, Mich. 49221.

Our Lady of the Sacred Heart, 1877. 2025 E. Fulton St., Grand Rapids, Mich. 49503.

St. Dominic, 1878. Blauvelt, N.Y. 10913.

Immaculate Conception (Dominican Sisters of the Sick Poor), 1879. Ossining, N.Y. 10562. Social work.

St. Catherine de Ricci, 1880. 2850 N. Providence Rd., Media, Pa. 19063.

Sacred Heart of Jesus, 1881. Mt. St. Dominic, Caldwell, N.J. 07006.

Sacred Heart, 1882. 6501 Almeda Rd., Houston, Tex. 77021.

St. Thomas Aquinas, 1888. 423 E. 152nd St., Tacoma, Wash. 98445.

Holy Cross, 1890. P.O. Box 280, Edmonds, Wash. 98020.

St. Catherine of Siena, 1891. 37 Park St., Fall River, Mass. 02721.

St. Rose of Lima (Servants of Relief for Incurable Cancer), 1896. Hawthorne, N.Y. 10532.

Immaculate Conception, 1902. 3600 Broadway, Great Bend, Kans. 67530.

St. Catherine of Siena, 1911. 4600 93rd St., Kenosha, Wis. 53140.

St. Rose of Lima, 1923. 775 Drahner Rd., Oxford, Mich. 48051.

Immaculate Conception, 1929. 9000 W. 81st St., Justice, Ill. 60458.

Immaculate Heart of Mary, 1929. Our Lady of the Elms Convent, Akron, Ohio 44313.

Immaculate Heart of Mary Province (Dominican Sisters of Spokane). W. 3102 Fort George Wright Dr., Spokane, Wash. 99204.

Dominican Sisters of Oakford (St. Catherine of Siena), 1889. Motherhouse, Oakford, Natal, South Africa. U.S. regional house, 1965. Villa Siena, 1855 Miramonte Ave., Mountain View, Calif. 94040.

(End, Listing of Dominicans)

Dorothy, Institute of the Sisters of St., S.S.D.: Founded 1834, in Italy; by St. Paola Frassinetti; in U.S., 1911. General motherhouse, Rome, Italy; U.S. provincialate, Villa Fatima, Taunton, Mass. 02780.

Eucharist, Religious of the, R.E.: Founded 1857, in Belgium; in U.S., 1900. General motherhouse, Belgium; U.S. foundation, 2907 Ellicott Terr., N.W., Washington, D.C. 20008.

Eucharistic Missionary Sisters, E.M.S.: Founded 1943, in Mexico. Motherhouse, 943 S. Soto St., Los Angeles, Calif. 90023.

Family, Congregation of the Sisters of the Holy, S.S.F.: Founded 1842, in U.S. General motherhouse, 6901 Chef Menteur Hway., New Orleans, La. 70126. Educational, hospital work.

Family, Little Sisters of the Holy, P.S.S.F.: Founded 1880, in Canada; in U.S., 1900. General motherhouse, Sherbrooke, Que., Canada. U.S. novitiate, 285 Andover St., Lowell, Mass. 01852.

Family, Sisters of the Holy, S.H.F.: Founded 1872, in U.S. General motherhouse, P.O. Box 3248, Mission San Jose, Calif. 94539. Educational, social work.

Family of Nazareth, Sisters of the Holy, C.S.F.N.: Founded 1875, in Italy; in U.S., 1885. General motherhouse, Rome, Italy. U.S. provinces: 353 N. River Rd., Des Plaines, Ill. 60016; Grant and Torresdale Aves., Torresdale, Philadelphia, Pa. 19114; 285 Bellevue Rd., Pittsburgh, Pa. 15229; Marian Heights, 1428 Monroe Turnpike, Monroe, Conn. 06468; 1814 Egyptian Way, Box 757, Grand Prairie, Tex. 75050.

Filippini, Religious Teachers, M.P.F.: Founded 1692, in Italy; in U.S., 1910. General motherhouse, Rome, Italy; U.S. provinces: St. Lucy Filippini Province, Villa Walsh, Morristown, N.J. 07960; Queen of Apostles Province, 474 East Rd., Bristol, Conn. 06010. Educational work.

Francis de Sales, Oblate Sisters of St., O.S.F.S.: Founded 1866, in France; in U.S., 1951. General motherhouse, Troyes, France; U.S. headquarters, Villa Aviat Convent, Childs, Md. 21916. Educational, social work.

Franciscans

Bernardine Sisters of the Third Order of St. Francis, O.S.F.: Founded 1457, at Cracow, Poland; in U.S., 1894. Generalate, 647 Spring Mill Rd., Villanova, Pa. 19085. Educational, hospital, social work.

Capuchin Sisters of St. Clare (Madres Clarisas Capuchinas): U.S. establishment, 1981, Amarillo diocese. Convent of the Blessed Sacrament and Our Lady of Guadalupe, 4201 N.E. 18th St., Amarillo, Tex. 79107. Cloistered.

Congregation of the Servants of the Holy Infancy of Jesus, O.S.F.: Founded 1855, in Germany; in U.S., 1929. General motherhouse, Wuerzburg, Germany; American motherhouse, Villa Maria, P.O. Box 708, North Plainfield, N.J. 07061.

Congregation of the Third Order of St. Francis of Mary Immaculate, O.S.F.: Founded 1865, in U.S., by Fr. Pamphilus da Magliano, O.F.M. General motherhouse, 520 Plainfield Ave., Joliet, Ill. 60435. Educational and pastoral work.

Daughters of St. Francis of Assisi, D.S.F.: Founded 1890, in Austria-Hungary; in U.S., 1946. Provincial motherhouse, 507 N. Prairie St., Lacon, Ill. 61540. Nursing, CCD work.

Felician Sisters (Congregation of the Sisters of St. Felix), C.S.S.F.: Founded 1855, in Poland; in U.S., 1874. General motherhouse, Rome, Italy. U.S. provinces: 36800 Schoolcraft Rd., Livonia, Mich. 48150; 600 Doat St., Buffalo, N.Y. 14211; 3800 Peterson Ave., Chicago, Ill. 60659; 260 South Main St., Lodi, N.J. 07644; 1500 Woodcrest Ave., Coraopolis, Pa. 15108; 1315 Enfield St., Enfield, Conn. 06082; 4210 Meadowlark Lane, S.E., Rio Rancho, N. Mex. 87174.

Franciscan Handmaids of the Most Pure Heart of Mary, F.H.M.: Founded 1917, in U.S.. General motherhouse, 15 W. 124th St., New York, N.Y. 10027. Educational, social work.

Franciscan Hospitaller Sisters of the Immaculate Conception, F.H.I.C.: Founded 1876, in Portugal; in U.S., 1960. General motherhouse, Lisbon, Portugal; U.S. novitiate, 300 S. 17th St., San Jose, Calif. 95112.

Franciscan Missionaries of Mary, F.M.M.: Founded 1877, in India; in U.S., 1904. General motherhouse, Rome, Italy; U.S. provincialate, 225 E. 45th St., New York, N.Y. 10017. Mission work.

Franciscan Missionaries of Our Lady, O.S.F.: Founded 1854, at Calais, France; in U.S., 1913. General motherhouse, Desvres, France; U.S. provincial house, 4200 Essen Lane, Baton Rouge, La. 70809. Hospital work.

Franciscan Missionaries of St. Joseph (Mill Hill Sisters), F.M.S.J.: Founded 1883, at Rochdale, Lancashire, England; in U.S., 1952. General motherhouse, Eccleshall, Stafford, England; U.S. headquarters, Franciscan House, 1006 Madison Ave., Albany, N.Y. 12208.

Franciscan Missionary Sisters for Africa, O.S.F.: American foundation, 1953. Generalate, Ireland; U.S. headquarters, 172 Foster St., Brighton, Mass. 02135.

Franciscan Missionary Sisters of Assisi, F.M.S.A.: First foundation in U.S., 1961. General motherhouse, Assisi, Italy; U.S. address, St. Francis Convent, 1039 Northampton St., Holyoke, Mass. 01040.

Franciscan Missionary Sisters of Our Lady of Sorrows, O.S.F.: Founded 1937, in China, by Bishop R. Palazzi, O.F.M.; in U.S., 1949. U.S. address, 2385 Laurel Glen Rd., Santa Cruz, Calif. 95065. Educational, social, domestic, retreat and foreign mission work.

Franciscan Missionary Sisters of the Divine Child, F.M.D.C.: Founded 1927, at Buffalo, N.Y., by Bishop William Turner. General motherhouse, 6380 Main St., Williamsville, N.Y. 14221. Educational, social work.

Franciscan Missionary Sisters of the Immaculate Conception, O.S.F.: Founded 1874, in Mexico; in U.S., 1926. U.S. provincial house, 11306 Laurel Canyon Blvd., San Fernando, Calif. 91340.

Franciscan Missionary Sisters of the Immaculate Heart of Mary, F.M.I.H.M.: Founded at Cairo, Egypt by Bl. Catarino di S. Rosa (Costanzo Troiano). Generalate, Rome, Italy; U.S. address, Ave Maria House, 3501 Good Intent Rd., Deptford, N.J. 08096.

Franciscan Missionary Sisters of the Infant Jesus, F.M.I.S.: Generalate, Rome, Italy. U.S. provincialate, 1215 Kresson Rd., Cherry Hill, N.J. 08003.

Franciscan Missionary Sisters of the Sacred Heart, F.M.S.C.: Founded 1860, in Italy; in U.S., 1865. Generalate, Rome, Italy; U.S. provincialate,

250 South St., Peekskill, N.Y. 10566. Educational and social welfare apostolates and specialized services.

Franciscan Poor Clare Nuns (Poor Clares, Order of St. Clare, Poor Clares of St. Colette), P.C., O.S.C., P.C.C.: Founded 1212, at Assisi, Italy, by St. Francis of Assisi; in U.S., 1875. Proto-monastery, Assisi, Italy. Addresses of autonomous motherhouses in U.S. are listed below.

3626 N. 65th Ave., Omaha, Nebr. 68104; 720 Henry Clay Ave., New Orleans, La. 70118; 6825 Nurrenbern Rd., Evansville, Ind. 47712; 1310 Dellwood Ave., Memphis Tenn. 38127; 920 Centre St., Jamaica Plain, Mass. 02130; 201 Crosswicks St., Bordentown, N.J. 08505; 1271 Langhorne-Newton Rd., Langhorne, Pa. 19047; 4419 N. Hawthorne St., Spokane, Wash. 99205; 142 Hollywood Ave., Bronx, N.Y. 10465; 421 S. 4th St., Sauk Rapids, Minn. 56379; 8650 Russell Ave. S., Minneapolis, Minn. 55431; 3501 Rocky River Dr., Cleveland, O. 44111; 89th and Kean Ave., Hickory Hills, Ill. 60457; 280 State Park Dr., Aptos, Calif. 95003; 2111 S. Main St., Rockford, Ill. 61102; 215 E. Los Olivos St., Santa Barbara, Calif. 93105; 460 River Rd., W. Andover, Mass. 01810. 809 E. 19th St., Roswell, N. Mex. 88201; 28210 Natoma Rd., Los Altos Hills, Calif. 94022; 1916 N. Pleasantburg Dr., Greenville, S.C. 29609; 28 Harpersville Rd., Newport News, Va. 23601; 1175 N. County Rd. 300 W., Kokomo, Ind. 46901; 4000 Sherwood Blvd., Delray Beach, Fla. 33445; 200 Marycrest Dr., St. Louis, Mo. 63129.

Franciscan Sisters, Daughters of the Sacred Hearts of Jesus and Mary, O.S.F.: Founded 1860, in Germany; in U.S., 1872. Generalate, Rome, Italy; U.S. motherhouse, P.O. Box 667, Wheaton, Ill. 60189. Educational, hospital, foreign mission, social work.

Franciscan Sisters of Allegany, N.Y., O.S.F.: Founded 1859, at Allegany, N.Y., by Fr. Pamphilus da Magliano, O.F.M. General motherhouse Allegany, N.Y. 14706. Educational, hospital, foreign mission work.

Franciscan Sisters of Baltimore, O.S.F.: Founded 1868, in England; in U.S., 1881. General motherhouse, 3725 Ellerslie Ave., Baltimore, Md. 21218. Educational work; social services.

Franciscan Sisters of Chicago, O.S.F.: Founded 1894, in U.S., by Mother Mary Therese (Josephine Dudzik). General motherhouse, 1220 Main St., Lemont, Ill. 60439. Educational work, social services.

Franciscan Sisters of Christian Charity, O.S.F.: Founded 1869, in U.S. Holy Family Convent, 2409 S. Alverno Rd., Manitowoc, Wis. 54220. Educational, hospital work.

Franciscan Sisters of Little Falls, Minn., O.S.F.: Founded 1891, in U.S. General motherhouse, Little Falls, Minn. 56345. Health, education, social services, pastoral ministry, mission work.

Franciscan Sisters of Mary Immaculate of the Third Order of St. Francis of Assisi, F.M.I.: Founded 16th century, in Switzerland; in U.S., 1932. General motherhouse, Bogota, Colombia; U.S. provincial house, 4301 N.E. 18th Ave., Amarillo, Tex. 79107. Education.

Franciscan Sisters of Our Lady of Perpetual Help, O.S.F.: Founded 1901, in U.S., from Joliet,

Ill., foundation. General motherhouse, 201 Brotherton Lane, St. Louis, Mo. 63135. Educational, hospital work.

Franciscan Sisters of Ringwood, F.S.R.: Founded 1927, at Passaic, N.J. General motherhouse, Mt. St. Francis, Ringwood, N.J. 07456. Educational work.

Franciscan Sisters of St. Elizabeth, F.S.S.E.: Founded 1866, at Naples, Italy; in U.S., 1919. General motherhouse, Rome; U.S. novitiate, 449 Park Rd., Parsippany, N.J. 07054. Educational work, social services.

Franciscan Sisters of St. Joseph, F.S.S.J.: Founded 1897, in U.S. General motherhouse, 5286 S. Park Ave., Hamburg, N.Y. 14075. Educational, hospital work.

Franciscan Sisters of St. Joseph (of Mexico): U.S. foundation, St. Paul College, 3015 4th St., Washington, D.C. 20017.

Franciscan Sisters of the Atonement, Third Order Regular of St. Francis (Graymoor Sisters), S.A.: Founded 1898, in U.S., as Anglican community; entered Church, 1909. General motherhouse, Graymoor, Garrison P.O., N.Y. 10524. Mission work.

Franciscan Sisters of the Blessed Virgin Mary of the Holy Angels, O.S.F.: Founded 1863, at Neuwied, Germany; in U.S., 1923. General motherhouse, Rhine, Germany; U.S. motherhouse, 1388 Prior Ave. S., St. Paul, Minn. 55116. Educational, hospital, social work.

Franciscan Sisters of the Immaculate Conception, O.S.F.: Founded in Germany; in U.S., 1928. General motherhouse, Kloster, Bonlanden, Germany; U.S. province, 291 W. North St., Buffalo, N.Y. 14201.

Franciscan Sisters of the Immaculate Conception, O.S.F.: Founded 1901, in U.S. General motherhouse, 1000 30th St., Rock Island, Ill. 61201. Health care.

Franciscan Sisters of the Immaculate Conception, Missionary, O.S.F.: Founded 1873, in U.S. General motherhouse, Rome, Italy; U.S. address, 790 Centre St., Newton, Mass. 02158. Educational work.

Franciscan Sisters of the Immaculate Conception and St. Joseph for the Dying, O.S.F.: Founded 1919, in U.S. General motherhouse, 485 Church St., Monterey, Calif. 93940.

Franciscan Sisters of the Poor, S.F.P.: Founded 1845, at Aachen, Germany, by Bl. Frances Schervier; in U.S., 1858. Community service center, 191 Joralemon St., Brooklyn, N.Y. 11201. Hospital, social work and foreign missions.

Franciscan Sisters of the Sacred Heart, O.S.F.: Founded 1866, in Germany; in U.S., 1876. General motherhouse, St. Francis Woods, R.R. 4, Mokena, Ill. 60448. Education, health care, other service ministries.

Hospital Sisters of the Third Order of St. Francis, O.S.F.: Founded 1844, in Germany; in U.S., 1875. General motherhouse, Muenster, Germany; U.S. motherhouse, Box 42, Springfield, Ill. 62705. Hospital work.

Institute of the Franciscan Sisters of the Eucha-

rist, F.S.E.: Founded 1973. Motherhouse, 405 Allen Ave., Meriden, Conn. 06450.

Little Franciscan Sisters of Mary, P.F.M.: Founded 1889, in U.S. General motherhouse, Baie St. Paul, Que., Canada. U.S. region, 55 Moore Ave., Worcester, Mass. 01602. Educational, hospital, social work.

Missionaries of the Third Order of St. Francis of Our Lady of the Prairies, O.L.P.: Founded 1960, in U.S. General motherhouse, Powers Lake, N.D. 58773.

Missionary Sisters of the Immaculate Conception of the Mother of God, S.M.I.C.: Founded 1910, in Brazil; in U.S., 1922, U.S. provincialate, P.O. Box 3026, Paterson, N.J. 07509. Mission, educational, health work, social services.

Mothers of the Helpless, M.D.: Founded 1873, in Spain; in U.S., 1916. General motherhouse, Valencia, Spain; U.S. address, San Jose Day Nursery, 432 W. 20th St., New York, N.Y. 10011.

Philip Neri Missionary Teachers, Sisters of St., R.F.: Founded 1858, in Spain; in U.S., 1956. General house, Madrid, Spain; U.S. address: Sisters of St. Philip Neri, St. Albert's Convent, 1259 St. Alberts St., Reno, Nev. 89503.

Poor Clares of Perpetual Adoration, P.C.P.A.: Founded 1854, at Paris, France; in U.S., 1921, at Cleveland, Ohio. U.S. monasteries: 4200 N. Market Ave., Canton, O. 44714; 2311 Timlin Rd., Portsmouth, O. 45662; 4108 Euclid Ave., Cleveland, O. 44103; 3900 13th St. N.E., Washington, D.C. 20017; 5817 Old Leeds Rd., Birmingham, Ala. 35210. Contemplative, cloistered, perpetual adoration.

School Sisters of St. Francis, O.S.F.: Founded 1874, in U.S. General motherhouse, 1501 S. Layton Blvd., Milwaukee, Wis. 53215.

School Sisters of St. Francis (Bethlehem, Pa.), O.S.F.: Founded in Austria, 1843; in U.S., 1913. General motherhouse, Rome, Italy; U.S. province, 395 Bridle Path Rd., Bethlehem, Pa. 18017. Educational, mission work.

School Sisters of St. Francis, (Pittsburgh, Pa.), O.S.F.: Established 1913, in U.S. Motherhouse, Mt. Assisi Convent, 934 Forest Ave., Pittsburgh, Pa. 15202. Education, health care services and related ministries.

School Sisters of the Third Order of St. Francis (Panhandle, Tex.), O.S.F.: Founded 1845, in Austria; in U.S., 1942. General motherhouse, Vienna, Austria; U.S. center and novitiate, Sancta Maria Convent, Panhandle, Tex. 79068. Educational, social work.

Sisters of Charity of Our Lady, Mother of the Church, S.C.M.C.: Established 1970, in U.S. Motherhouse, Baltic, Conn. 06330. Teaching, nursing, care of aged, and dependent children.

Sisters of Mercy of the Holy Cross, S.C.S.C.: Founded 1856, in Switzerland; in U.S. 1912. General motherhouse, Ingenbohl, Switzerland; U.S. provincial house, 1500 O'Day St., Merrill, Wis. 54452.

Sisters of Our Lady of Mercy (Mercedarians), S.O.L.M.: General motherhouse, Rome, Italy; U.S. addresses: Most Precious Blood, 133 27th Ave., Brooklyn, N.Y. 11214; St. Edward School, Pine Hill, N.J. 08021.

Sisters of St. Elizabeth, S.S.E.: Founded 1931, at Milwaukee, Wis. General motherhouse, 745 N. Brookfield Rd., Brookfield, Wis. 53005.

Sisters of St. Francis (Clinton, Iowa), O.S.F.: Founded 1868, in U.S. General motherhouse, Bluff Blvd. and Springdale Dr., Clinton, Ia. 57232. Educational, hospital, social work.

Sisters of St. Francis (Maryville, Mo.), O.S.F.: Founded 1894, in U.S. Motherhouse, Mt. Alverno Convent, R.R. 3, Box 64, Maryville, Mo. 64468. Hospital work.

Sisters of St. Francis (Millvale, Pa.), O.S.F.: Founded 1865, Pittsburgh, Pa. General motherhouse, 146 Hawthorne Rd., Millvale P.O., Pittsburgh, Pa. 15209. Educational, hospital work.

Sisters of St. Francis (Hastings-on-Hudson), O.S.F.: Founded 1893, in New York. General motherhouse, Hastings-on-Hudson, N.Y. 10706. Education, parish ministry, social services.

Sisters of St. Francis of Christ the King, O.S.F.: Founded 1864, in Austria. General motherhouse, Rome, Italy; U.S. provincial house, 1600 Main St., Lemont, Ill. 60439. Educational work, home for aged.

Sisters of St. Francis of Penance and Christian Charity, O.S.F.: Founded 1835, in Holland; in U.S., 1874. General motherhouse, Rome, Italy. U.S. provinces: 4421 Lower River Rd., Stella Niagara, N.Y. 14144; 2851 W. 52nd Ave., Denver, Colo. 80221; 3910 Bret Harte Dr., P.O. Box 1028, Redwood City, Calif. 94064.

Sisters of St. Francis of Philadelphia, O.S.F.: Founded 1855, at Philadelphia, by Mother Mary Francis Bachmann and St. John N. Neumann. General motherhouse, Convent of Our Lady of the Angels, Aston, Pa. 19014. Education, health care, social services.

Sisters of St. Francis of Savannah, Mo., O.S.F.: Founded 1850, in Austria; in U.S., 1922. Provincial house, La Verna Heights, Savannah, Mo. 64485. Educational, hospital work.

Sisters of St. Francis of the Congregation of Our Lady of Lourdes, O.S.F.: Founded 1916, in U.S. General motherhouse, 6832 Convent Blvd., Sylvania, O. 43560. Education, health care, social services, pastoral ministry.

Sisters of St. Francis of the Holy Cross, O.S.F.: Founded 1881, in U.S., by Rev. Edward Daems, O.S.C. General motherhouse, 3025 Bay Settlement Rd., Green Bay, Wis. 54301. Educational, nursing work, pastoral ministry, foreign missions.

Sisters of St. Francis of the Holy Eucharist, O.S.F.: Founded 1378, in Switzerland; in U.S., 1893. General motherhouse, 2100 N. Noland Rd., Independence, Mo. 64050. Education, health care, social services, foreign missions.

Sisters of St. Francis of the Holy Family, O.S.F.: Founded 1875, in U.S. Motherhouse, Mt. St. Francis, 3390 Windsor Ave., Dubuque, Ia. 52001. Varied apostolates.

Sisters of St. Francis of the Immaculate Conception, O.S.F.: Founded 1890, in U.S. General motherhouse, 2408 W. Heading Ave., Peoria, Ill. 61604. Education, care of aging, pastoral ministry.

Sisters of St. Francis of the Immaculate Heart of Mary, O.S.F.: Founded 1241, in Bavaria; in U.S.,

1913. General motherhouse, Rome, Italy; U.S. motherhouse, Hankinson, N.D. 58041. Education, social services.

Sisters of St. Francis of the Martyr St. George, O.S.F.: Founded 1859, in Germany; in U.S., 1923. General motherhouse, Thuine, West Germany; U.S. provincial house, St. Francis Convent, 2120 Central Ave., Alton, Ill. 62002. Education, social services, foreign mission work.

Sisters of St. Francis of the Perpetual Adoration, O.S.F.: Founded 1863, in Germany; in U.S., 1875. General motherhouse, Olpe, Germany. U.S. provinces: Box 766, Mishawaka, Ind. 46544; P.O. Box 1060, Colorado Springs, Colo. 80901. Educational, hospital work.

Sisters of St. Francis of the Providence of God, O.S.F.: Founded 1922, in U.S., by Msgr. M. L. Krusas. General motherhouse, Grove and McRoberts Rds., Pittsburgh, Pa. 15234. Education, varied apostolates.

Sisters of St. Francis of the Third Order Regular, O.S.F.: Founded 1861, at Buffalo, N.Y., from Philadelphia foundation. General motherhouse, 400 Mill St., Williamsville, N.Y. 14221. Educational, hospital work.

Sisters of St. Joseph of the Third Order of St. Francis, S.S.J.: Founded 1901, in U.S. Administrative office, P.O. Box 688, South Bend, Ind. 46624. Education, health care, social services.

Sisters of St. Mary of the Third Order of St. Francis, S.S.M.: Founded 1872, in St. Louis, Mo. General motherhouse, 1100 Bellevue Ave., St. Louis, Mo. 63117. Health care, social services.

Sisters of the Infant Jesus, I.J.: Founded 1662, at Rouen, France; in U.S., 1950. Motherhouse, Paris, France. Generalate, Rome, Italy. U.S. addresses: 20 Reiner St., Colma, Calif. 94014; St. John the Baptist School, Healdsburg, Calif. 95448; 60 Bellevue Ave., Daly City, Calif. 94014.

Sisters of the Sorrowful Mother (Third Order of St. Francis), S.S.M.: Founded 1883, in Italy; in U.S., 1889. General motherhouse, Rome, Italy. U.S. provinces: 6618 N. Teutonia Ave., Milwaukee, Wis. 53209; 9 Pocono Rd., Denville, N.J. 07834; Tulsa Provincialate, 17600 E. 51st St. S., Broken Arrow, Okla. 74012. Educational, hospital work.

Sisters of the Third Franciscan Order, O.S.F.: Founded 1860, at Syracuse, N.Y. Generalate offices, 100 Michaels Ave., Syracuse, N.Y. 13208. Educational, hospital work.

Sisters of the Third Order of St. Francis, O.S.F.: Founded 1877, in U.S., by Bishop John L. Spalding. Motherhouse, Edgewood Hills, E. Peoria, Ill. 61611. Hospital work.

Sisters of the Third Order of St. Francis (Oldenburg, Ind.), O.S.F.: Founded 1851, in U.S. General motherhouse, Convent of the Immaculate Conception, Oldenburg, Ind. 47036. Education, social services, pastoral ministry, foreign missions.

Sisters of the Third Order of St. Francis of Assisi, O.S.F.: Founded 1849, in U.S. General motherhouse, 3221 S. Lake Dr., Milwaukee, Wis. 53207. Education, other ministries.

Sisters of the Third Order of St. Francis of Penance and Charity, O.S.F.: Founded 1869, in U.S., by Rev. Joseph Bihn. Motherhouse, St. Fran-

cis Convent, St. Francis Ave., Tiffin, O. 44883. Education, social services.

Sisters of the Third Order of St. Francis of the Perpetual Adoration, F.S.P.A.: Founded 1849, in U.S. Generalate, 912 Market St., La Crosse, Wis. 54601. Education, health care.

Sisters of the Third Order Regular of St. Francis of the Congregation of Our Lady of Lourdes, O.S.F.: Founded 1877, in U.S. General motherhouse, Assisi Heights, Rochester, Minn. 55901. Education, health care, social services.

(End, Listing of Franciscans)

Good Shepherd Sisters (Servants of the Immaculate Heart of Mary), S.C.I.M.: Founded 1850, in Canada; in U.S., 1882. General motherhouse, Quebec, Canada; Provincial House, Bay View, Saco, Maine 04072. Educational, social work.

Good Shepherd, Sisters of Our Lady of Charity of the, R.G.S.: Founded 1641, in France; in U.S., 1843. Generalate, Rome, Italy. U.S. provinces: 2849 Fischer Pl., Cincinnati, O. 45211; 82-31 Doncaster Pl., Jamaica, N.Y. 11432; 504 Hexton Hill Rd., Silver Spring, Md. 20904; 7654 Natural Bridge Rd., St. Louis, Mo. 63121; 5100 Hodgson Rd., St. Paul, Minn. 55112.

Graymoor Sisters: See Franciscan Sisters of the Atonement.

Grey Nuns of the Sacred Heart, G.N.S.H.: Founded 1921, in U.S. General motherhouse, 1750 Quarry Rd., Yardley, Pa. 19067.

Guadalupe, Sisters of, O.L.G.: Founded 1946, in Mexico City. General motherhouse, Mexico City, Mexico; U.S. address, St. Mary's College, Winona, Minn. 55987.

Guardian Angel, Sisters of the Holy, S.A.C.: Founded 1839, in France. General motherhouse, Madrid, Spain; U.S. foundation, 1245 S. Van Ness, Los Angeles, Calif. 90019.

Handmaids of Mary Immaculate, A.M.I.: Founded 1952 in Helena, Mont. Address: Ave Maria Institute, Washington, N.J. 07882.

Handmaids of the Precious Blood, Congregation of, H.P.B.: Founded 1947, at Jemez Springs, N.M. Motherhouse and novitiate, Cor Jesu Monastery, Jemez Springs, N.M. 87025.

Helpers, Society of, H.H.S.: Founded 1856, in France; in U.S., 1892. General motherhouse, Paris, France; American province, 303 W. Barry Ave., Chicago, Ill. 60657.

Hermanas Catequistas Guadalupanas, H.C.G.: Founded 1923, in Mexico; in U.S., 1950. General motherhouse, Mexico; U.S. foundation, 4110 S. Flores, San Antonio, Tex. 78214.

Hermanas Josefinas, H.J.: General motherhouse, Mexico; U.S. foundation, Assumption Seminary, 2600 W. Woodlawn Ave., P.O. Box 28240, San Antonio, Tex. 78284. Domestic work.

Hermit Sisters of Christ in Solitude: Hermitage of Christ the King, 6501 Orchard Station Road, Sebastopol, Calif. 95472.

Holy Child Jesus, Society of the, S.H.C.J.: Founded 1846, in England; in U.S., 1862. General motherhouse, Rome, Italy. U.S. province: 460 Shadeland Ave., Drexel Hill, Pa. 19026.

Holy Faith, Congregation of the Sisters of the,

C.H.F.: Founded 1856, in Ireland; in U.S., 1953. General motherhouse, Dublin, Ireland; U.S. regional superior, 1205 Corning St., Los Angeles, Calif. 90035.

Holy Heart of Mary, Servants of the, S.S.C.M.: Founded 1860, in France; in U.S., 1889. General motherhouse, Montreal, Que., Canada; U.S. province, 145 S. 4th Ave., Kankakee, Ill. 60901. Educational, hospital, social work.

Holy Names of Jesus and Mary, Sisters of the, S.N.J.M.: Founded 1843, in Canada; in U.S., 1859. General motherhouse, Pierrefonds H9K 1C6, P.Q., Canada. U.S. addresses: Oregon Province, Marylhurst, Ore. 97036; California Province, P.O. Box 907, Los Gatos, Calif. 95031; New York Province, 1061 New Scotland Rd., Albany, N.Y. 12208; Washington Province, W. 2911 Ft. Wright Dr., Spokane, Wash. 99204.

Holy Spirit, Community of the: Founded 1970 in San Diego, Calif. Address: 6680 Reservoir Lane, San Diego, Calif. 92115.

Holy Spirit, Daughters of the, D.H.S.: Founded 1706, in France; in U.S., 1902. Generalate, Bretagne, France; U.S. motherhouse, 72 Church St., Putnam, Conn. 06260. Educational work, district nursing; pastoral ministry.

Holy Spirit, Mission Sisters of the, M.SSp.: Founded 1932, at Cleveland, O. Motherhouse, 1030 N. River Rd., Saginaw, Mich. 48603.

Holy Spirit, Missionary Sisters, Servants of the: Founded 1889, in Holland; in U.S., 1901. Generalate, Rome, Italy; U.S. motherhouse, Convent of the Holy Spirit, Techny, Ill. 60082.

Holy Spirit, Sisters of the, C.SSp.: Founded 1890, in Rome, Italy; in U.S., 1929. General motherhouse, 10102 Granger Rd., Garfield Hts., Ohio 44125. Educational, social, nursing work.

Holy Spirit, Sisters of the, C.H.S.: Founded 1913, in U.S., by Most Rev. J. F. Regis Canevin. General motherhouse, 5246 Clarwin Ave., Ross Township, Pittsburgh, Pa. 15229. Educational, nursing work; care of aged.

Holy Spirit and Mary Immaculate, Sister Servants of, S.H.G.: Founded 1893, in U.S. Motherhouse, 301 Yucca St., San Antonio, Tex. 78203. Education, hospital work.

Holy Spirit of Perpetual Adoration, Sister Servants of the: Founded 1896, in Holland; in U.S., 1915. Generalate, West Germany; U.S. Province, 2212 Green St., Philadelphia, Pa. 19130.

Home Mission Sisters of America (Glenmary Sisters): Founded 1952, in U.S. Motherhouse, Morning Star, P.O. Box 39188, Cincinnati, O. 45239.

Home Visitors of Mary, Sisters, H.V.M.: Founded 1949, in Detroit, Mich. Motherhouse, 356 Arden Park, Detroit, Mich. 48202.

Humility of Mary, Congregation of, C.H.M.: Founded 1854, in France; in U.S., 1864. U.S. address, Humility of Mary Center, Davenport, Ia. 52804.

Humility of Mary, Sisters of the, H.M.: Founded 1854, in France; in U.S., 1864. U.S. address, Villa Maria, Pa. 16155.

Immaculate Conception, Little Servant Sisters of the: Founded 1850, in Poland; in U.S., 1926. General motherhouse, Poland; U.S. provincial house,

184 Amboy Ave., Woodbridge, N.J. 07095. Education, social services, African missions.

Immaculate Conception, Sisters of the, R.C.M.: Founded 1892, in Spain; in U.S., 1962. General motherhouse, Madrid, Spain; U.S. address, 2250 Franklin, San Francisco, Calif. 94109.

Immaculate Conception, Sisters of the, C.I.C.: Founded 1874, in U.S. General motherhouse, 4920 Kent Ave., Metairie, La. 70006.

Immaculate Conception of the Blessed Virgin Mary, Sisters of the (Lithuanian): Founded 1918, at Mariampole, Lithuania; in U.S., 1936. U.S. headquarters, Immaculate Conception Convent, Putnam, Conn. 06260.

Immaculate Heart of Mary, Missionary Sisters, I.C.M.: Founded 1897, in India; in U.S., 1919. Generalate, Rome, Italy; U.S. address, 1710 N. Glebe Rd., Arlington, Va. 22207. Educational social, foreign mission work.

Immaculate Heart of Mary, Sisters of the: Founded 1848, in Spain; in U.S., 1878. General motherhouse, Rome, Italy. U.S. province, 4100 Sabino Canyon Rd., Tucson, Ariz. 85715. Educational work.

Immaculate Heart of Mary, Sisters of the (California Institute of the Most Holy and Immaculate Heart of the B.V.M.), I.H.M.: Founded 1848, in Spain; in U.S., 1871. Generalate, 3431 Waverly Dr., Los Angeles, Calif. 90027.

Immaculate Heart of Mary, Sisters, Servants of the, I.H.M.: Founded 1845, at Monroe, Mich., by Rev. Louis Florent Gillet. Three independent branches: Generalate, 610 W. Elm St., Monroe, Mich. 48161; Villa Maria, Immaculata, Pa. 19345; Immaculate Heart of Mary Generalate, Marywood, Scranton, Pa. 18509.

Incarnate Word and Blessed Sacrament, Congregation of, V.I.: Founded 1625, in France; in U.S., 1853. Incarnate Word Convent, 3400 Bradford Pl., Houston, Tex. 77028.

Incarnate Word and Blessed Sacrament, Congregation of the, of the Archdiocese of San Antonio, I.W.B.S.: Motherhouses: 1101 Northeast Water St., Victoria, Tex. 77901; 2930 S. Alameda, Corpus Christi, Tex. 78404.

Incarnate Word and Blessed Sacrament, Sisters of the, S.I.W.: Founded 1625, in France; in U.S. 1853. Motherhouse, 6618 Pearl Rd., Parma Heights, Cleveland, O. 44130.

Infant Jesus, Congregation of the (Nursing Sisters of the Sick Poor), C.I.J.: Founded 1835, in France; in U.S., 1905. General motherhouse, 310 Prospect Park W., Brooklyn, N.Y. 11215.

Jeanne d'Arc, Sisters of Ste.: Founded 1914, in U.S., by Rev. Marie Clement Staub, A.A. General motherhouse, 1505, rue de l'Assomption Sillery, Que. G1S 4T3, Canada. U.S. novitiate, 2121 Commonwealth Ave., Brighton, Mass. 02135. Spiritual and temporal service of priests.

Jesus, Daughters of, F.I.: Founded 1871, in Spain; in U.S., 1950. General motherhouse, Rome, Italy; U.S. address, 410 Grand St., Apt. 24F, New York, N.Y.

Jesus, Daughters of (Filles de Jesus), F.J.: Founded 1834, in France; in U.S., 1904. General motherhouse, Kermaria, Locmine, France; U.S.

address, 4209 3rd Ave. S., Great Falls, Mont. 59405. Educational, hospital, parish and social work.

Jesus, Little Sisters of: Founded 1939, in Sahara; in U.S., 1952. General motherhouse, Rome, Italy; U.S. headquarters, 700 Irving St. N.E., Washington, D.C. 20017.

Jesus, Servants of, S.J.: Founded 1974, in U.S. Central Office, 9075 Big Lake Rd., P.O. Box 128, Clarkston, Mich. 48016.

Jesus, Society of the Sisters, Faithful Companions of, F.C.J.: Founded 1820, in France; in U.S., 1896. General motherhouse, Kent, England. U.S. convents: 20 Atkins St., Providence, R.I. 02908; St. Philomena Convent, Cory's Lane, Portsmouth, R.I. 02871.

Jesus Crucified, Congregation of: Founded 1930, in France; in U.S., 1955. General motherhouse, Brou, France; U.S. foundations: Regina Mundi Priory, Devon, Pa. 19333; St. Paul's Priory, 61 Narragansett, Newport, R.I. 02840.

Jesus Crucified and the Sorrowful Mother, Poor Sisters of, C.J.C.: Founded 1924, in U.S., by Rev. Alphonsus Maria, C.P. Motherhouse, 261 Thatcher St., Brockton, Mass. 02402. Education, nursing homes, catechetical centers.

Jesus-Mary, Religious of, R.J.M.: Founded 1818, at Lyons, France; in U.S., 1877. General motherhouse, Rome, Italy; U.S. province, 8908 Riggs Rd., Hyattsville, Md. 20783. Educational work.

Jesus, Mary and Joseph, Missionaries of, M.J.M.J.: Founded 1942, in Spain; in U.S., 1956. General motherhouse, Madrid, Spain; U.S. regional house, 12940 Up River Rd., Corpus Christi, Tex. 78410.

John the Baptist, Sisters of St., C.S.J.B.: Founded 1878, in Italy; in U.S., 1906. General motherhouse, Rome, Italy; U.S. provincialate, Anderson Hill Rd., Purchase, N.Y. 10577. Education, parish and retreat work; social services.

Joseph, Missionary Servants of St., M.S.S.J.: Founded 1874, in Spain; in U.S., 1957. General motherhouse, Salamanca, Spain; U.S. address, 203 N. Spring St., Falls Church, Va. 22046.

Joseph, Poor Sisters of St.: Founded 1880, in Argentina. General motherhouse, Muniz, Argentina; U.S. addresses, Casa Belen, 305 E. 4th St., Bethlehem, Pa. 78015; Casa Nazareth, 330 S. Spruce St., Reading, Pa. 19602; St. Gabriel Convent, 4319 Sano St., Alexandria, Va. 22312.

Joseph, Religious Daughters of St., F.S.J.: Founded 1875, in Spain. General motherhouse, Spain; U.S. foundation, 319 N. Humphreys Ave., Los Angeles, Calif. 90022.

Joseph, Religious Hospitallers of St., R.H.S.J.: Founded 1636, in France; in U.S., 1894. Generalate, 5621 Canterbury Ave., Montreal, Que., H3T 15B, Canada; U.S. address, 438 College St., Burlington, Vt. 05401. Hospital work.

Joseph, Sisters of St., C.S.J.: Founded 1650, in France; in U.S., 1836, at St. Louis. U.S. independent motherhouses:

637 Cambridge St., Brighton, Mass. 02135; 1515 W. Ogden Ave., La Grange Park, Ill., 60525; 480 S. Batavia St., Orange, Calif. 92668; Mt. St. Joseph Convent, Chestnut Hill, Philadelphia, Pa. 19118.

St. Joseph Convent, Brentwood, N.Y. 11717; 23 Agassiz Circle, Buffalo, N.Y. 14214; Avila Hall, Clement Rd., Rutland, Vt. 05701; 3430 Rocky River Dr., Cleveland, O. 44111; R.R. No. 3, Box 291A, Tipton, Ind. 46072; Motherhouse and novitiate, Nazareth, Mich. 49074; 1425 Washington St., Watertown, N.Y. 13601; Mt. Gallitzin Academy and Motherhouse, Baden, Pa. 15005; 819 W. 8th St., Erie, Pa. 16502.

4095 East Ave., Rochester, N.Y. 14610; 215 Court St., Concordia, Kans. 66901; Mont Marie, Holyoke, Mass. 01040; 1412 E. 2nd St., Superior, Wis. 54880; Pogue Run Rd., Wheeling, W. Va. 26003; 3700 E. Lincoln St., Wichita, Kans. 67218.

Joseph, Sisters of St. (Lyons, France), C.S.J.: Founded 1650, in France; in U.S., 1906. General motherhouse, Lyons, France; U.S. provincialate, 93 Halifax St., Winslow, Me. 04901. Educational, hospital work.

Joseph, Sisters of St., of Peace, C.S.J.: Founded 1884, in England. Generalate, 1225 Newton St. N.E., Washington, D.C. 20017. Educational, hospital, social service work.

Joseph of Carondelet, Sisters of St., C.S.J.: Founded 1650, in France; in U.S., 1836, at St. Louis, Mo. U.S. headquarters, 2307 S. Lindbergh Blvd., St. Louis, Mo. 63131.

Joseph of Chambery, Sisters of St.: Founded 1650, in France; in U.S., 1885. Generalate, Rome, Italy; U.S. provincial house, 27 Park Rd., West Hartford, Conn. 06119. Educational, hospital, social work.

Joseph of Cluny, Sisters of St., S.J.C.: Founded 1807, in France. Generalate, Paris, France; U.S. provincial house, Brenton Rd., Newport, R.I. 02840.

Joseph of Medaille, Sisters of, C.S.J.: Founded 1823, in France; in U.S., 1855. Became an American congregation Nov. 30, 1977. Central office, 5108 Reading Rd., Cincinnati, Ohio 45237.

Joseph of St. Augustine, Fla., Sisters of St., S.S.J.: General motherhouse, 241 St. George St., St. Augustine, Fla. 32084. Educational, hospital, pastoral, social work.

Joseph of St. Mark, Sisters of St., S.S.J.S.M.: Founded 1845, in France; in U.S., 1937. General motherhouse, 21800 Chardon Rd., Euclid, Cleveland, O. 44117. Nursing homes.

Joseph the Worker, Sisters of St., S.J.W.: General motherhouse, St. Joseph Convent, 143 S. Main St., Walton, Ky. 41094.

Lamb of God, Sisters of the, A.D.: Founded 1945, in France; in U.S., 1958. General motherhouse, France; U.S. address, Rt. 1, No. 260, Philpot, Ky 42366.

Living Word, Sisters of the, S.L.W.: Founded 1975, in U.S. Motherhouse, The Center, 7200 N. Osceola Ave., Chicago, Ill. 60648. Education, hospital, parish ministry work.

Loretto at the Foot of the Cross, Sisters of, S.L.: Founded 1812 in U.S., by Rev. Charles Nerinckx. General motherhouse, Nerinx, Ky. 40049. Educational work.

Louis, Congregation of Sisters of St., S.S.L.: Founded 1842, in France; in U.S., 1949. General motherhouse, Monaghan, Ireland; U.S. regional house, 22300 Mulholland Dr., Woodland Hills, Calif.

91364. Educational, medical, parish, foreign mission work.

Marian Sisters of the Diocese of Lincoln: Founded 1954. Motherhouse, Marycrest, R.R. 1, Box 108, Waverly, Nebr. 68462.

Marian Society of Dominican Catechists, O.P.: Founded 1954 in Louisiana. General motherhouse, P.O. Box 176, Boyce, La. 71409. Community of Alexandria-Shreveport, La., diocese.

Marianites of Holy Cross, Congregation of the Sisters, M.S.C.: Founded 1841, in France; in U.S., 1843. Motherhouse, Le Mans, Sarthe, France. U.S. provinces: 4123 Woodland Dr., New Orleans, La. 70114; Great Rd. and Drakes Corner, Princeton, N.J. 08540; 31 Cresci Blvd., Hazlet, N.J. 07730 (vice province).

Marist Sisters, Congregation of Mary, S.M.: Founded 1824, in France. General motherhouse, Rome, Italy; U.S. convents: St. Albert the Great, 4855 Parker, Dearborn Hts., Mich. 48125; St. Barnabas, 16103 Chesterfield, E. Detroit, Mich. 48021; Our Lady of the Snows, 4810 S. Leamington, Chicago, Ill. 60638.

Maronite Antonine Sisters: Established in U.S., 1966. U.S. address, 2961 N. Lipkey Rd., North Jackson, Ohio 44451.

Marthe, Sisters of Sainte (of St. Hyacinthe), S.M.S.H.: Founded 1883, in Canada; in U.S., 1929. General motherhouse 675 ouest, rue St.-Pierre, Hyacinthe, Que., J2T IN7 Canada.

Mary, Company of, O.D.N.: Founded 1607, in France; in U.S., 1926. General motherhouse, Rome, Italy; U.S. motherhouse, 16791 E. Main St., Tustin, Calif. 92680.

Mary, Daughters of the Heart of, D.H.M.: Founded 1790, in France; in U.S., 1851. Generalate, Paris, France; U.S. provincialate, 1339 Northampton St., Holyoke, Mass. 01040. Education retreat work.

Mary, Little Company of, Nursing Sisters, L.C.M.: Founded 1877, in England; in U.S., 1893. General motherhouse, Rome, Italy; U.S. provincial house, 9350 S. California Ave., Evergreen Park, Ill. 60642.

Mary, Missionary Sisters of the Society of (Marist Sisters), S.M.S.M.: Founded 1845, at St. Brieuc, France; in U.S., 1922. General motherhouse, Rome, Italy; U.S. provincial house, 357 Grove St., Waltham, Mass. 02154. Foreign missions.

Mary, Servants of, O.S.M.: Founded 13th century, in Italy; in U.S., 1893. Generalate, Rome, Italy; U.S. provincial motherhouse, 7400 Military Ave., Omaha, Nebr. 68134.

Mary, Servants of (Servite Sisters), O.S.M.: Founded 13th century, in Italy; in U.S., 1912. General motherhouse, Our Lady of Sorrows Convent, Ladysmith, Wis. 54848.

Mary, Servants of, of Blue Island (Mantellate Sisters), O.S.M.: Founded 1861, in Italy; in U.S., 1916. Generalate, Rome, Italy; U.S. motherhouse, 13811 S. Western Ave., Blue Island, Ill. 60406. Educational work.

Mary, Sisters of St., of Oregon, S.S.M.O.: Founded 1886, in Oregon, by Bishop William H. Gross, C.Ss.R. General motherhouse, 4440 S.W. 148th Ave., Beaverton, Ore. 97007. Educational, nursing work.

Mary, Sisters Servants of (Trained Nurses), S.M.: Founded 1851, at Madrid, Spain; in U.S., 1914. General motherhouse, Rome, Italy; U.S. motherhouse, 800 N. 18th St., Kansas City, Kans. 66102. Home nursing.

Mary and Joseph, Daughters of, D.M.J.: Founded 1817, in Belgium; in U.S., 1926. Generalate, Rome, Italy; American novitiate, 6037 W. 78th St., Los Angeles, Calif. 90045.

Mary Help of Christians, Daughters of (Salesian Sisters of St. John Bosco), F.M.A.: Founded 1872, in Italy, by St. John Bosco and St. Mary Dominic Mazzarello; in U.S., 1908. General motherhouse, Rome, Italy; U.S. provincial house, 655 Belmont Ave., Haledon, N.J. 07508. Education, youth work.

Mary Immaculate, Daughters of (Marianist Sisters), F.M.I.: Founded 1816, in France, by Very Rev. William-Joseph Chaminade. General motherhouse, Rome, Italy; U.S. foundation, 251 W. Ligustrum Dr., San Antonio, Tex. 78228. Educational work.

Mary Immaculate, Religious of, R.M.I.: Founded 1876, in Spain; in U.S., 1954. General motherhouse, Rome, Italy; U.S. foundation, 719 Augusta St., San Antonio, Tex. 78215.

Mary Immaculate, Sister Servants of, S.S.M.I.: Founded 1878 in Poland. General motherhouse, Mariowka, Poland; American provincialate, 1220 Tugwell Dr., Catonsville, Md. 21228.

Mary Immaculate, Sisters Servants of, S.S.M.I: Founded 1892, in Ukraine; in U.S., 1935. General motherhouse, Rome, Italy; U.S. province, Immaculate Conception Province, Table Rock, Sloatsburg, N.Y. 10974. Educational, hospital work.

Mary of Namur, Sisters of St., S.S.M.N.: Founded 1819, at Namur, Belgium; in U.S., 1863. General motherhouse, Namur, Belgium. U.S. provinces: 3756 Delaware Ave., Kenmore, N.Y. 14217; 3300 Hemphill St., Ft. Worth, Tex. 76110.

Mary of Providence, Daughters of St., D.S.M.P.: Founded 1872, at Como, Italy; in U.S., 1913. General motherhouse, Rome, Italy; U.S. provincial house, 4200 N. Austin Ave., Chicago, Ill. 60634. Special education for mentally handicapped.

Mary of the Immaculate Conception, Daughters of, D.M.: Founded 1904, in U.S., by Msgr. Lucian Bojnowski. General motherhouse, 314 Osgood Ave., New Britain, Conn. 06053. Educational, hospital work.

Mary Reparatrix, Society of, S.M.R.: Founded 1857, in France; in U.S., 1908. Generalate, Rome, Italy. U.S. province, 14 E. 29th St., New York, N.Y. 10016.

Medical Mission Sisters (Society of Catholic Medical Missionaries, Inc.), S.C.M.M.: Founded 1925, in U.S., by Mother Anna Dengel. Generalate, London, Eng.; U.S. headquarters, 8400 Pine Rd., Philadelphia, Pa. 19111. Medical work, health education, especially in mission areas.

Medical Missionaries of Mary, M.M.M.: Founded 1937, in Ireland, by Mother Mary Martin; in U.S., 1950. General motherhouse, Drogheda, Ireland; U.S. headquarters, 563 Minneford Ave., City

Island. Bronx, N.Y. 10464. Medical aid in missions.

Medical Sisters of St. Joseph, M.S.J.: Founded 1946, in India; first U.S. foundation, 1985. General motherhouse, Kerala, S. India; U.S. address, 3213 E. Grand, Wichita, Kans. 67218. Health care apostolate.

Mercedarian Missionaries of Berriz, M.M.B.: Founded 1930, in Spain; in U.S., 1946. General motherhouse, Rome, Italy. U.S. headquarters, 918 E. 9th St., Kansas City, Mo. 64106.

Mercy, Daughters of Our Lady of, D.M.: Founded 1837, in Italy, by St. Mary Joseph Rossello; in U.S., 1919. General motherhouse, Savona, Italy; U.S. motherhouse, Villa Rossello, Catawba Ave., Newfield, N.J. 08344. Educational, hospital work.

Mercy, Missionary Sisters of Our Lady of, M.O.M.: Founded 1938, in Brazil; in U.S., 1955. General motherhouse, Brazil; U.S. address, 388 Franklin St., Buffalo, N.Y. 14202.

Mercy, Sisters of, R.S.M.: Founded 1831, in Ireland, by Mother Mary Catherine McAuley. U.S. motherhouses:

634 New Scotland Ave., Albany, N.Y. 12208; 273 Willoughby Ave., Brooklyn, N.Y. 11205; S. 5245 Murphy Rd., Orchard Park, N.Y. 14127; 100 Mansfield Ave., Burlington, Vt. 05401; 1125 Prairie Dr., N.E., Cedar Rapids, Ia. 52402; 444 E. Grandview Blvd., Erie, Pa. 16504; 249 Steele Rd., W. Hartford, Conn. 06117.

21 Searles Rd., Windham, N.H. 03087; Sisters of Mercy, Merion, Pa. 10966; 3333 Fifth Ave., Pittsburgh, Pa. 15213; 605 Stevens Ave., Portland, Me. 04103; Sacred Heart Convent, Belmont, N. Car. 28012; 1437 Blossom Rd., Rochester, N.Y. 14610; 535 Sacramento St., Auburn, Calif. 95603.

2300 Adeline Dr., Burlingame, Calif. 94010; U.S. Route 22 at Terrill Rd., Plainfield, N.J. 07061; 101 Barry Rd., Worcester, Mass. 01609.

Mercy, Sisters of, of the Union in the United States of America, R.S.M.: Founded 1831 in Ireland, by Mother M. Catherine McAuley; union formed in 1929. Central headquarters, 1320 Fenwick Lane, Suite 610, Silver Spring, Md. 20910. U.S. provinces:

P.O. Box 11448, Baltimore, Md. 21239; 10024 S. Central Park Ave., Chicago, Ill. 60642; 2301 Grandview Ave., Cincinnati, Ohio 45206; 29000 Eleven Mile Rd., Farmington Hills, Mich. 48024; 541 Broadway, Dobbs Ferry, N.Y. 10522; 1801 S. 72nd St., Omaha, Nebr. 68124; R.D. 3, Cumberland, R.I. 02864; 2039 N. Geyer Rd., St. Louis, Mo. 63131; Dallas, Pa. 18612.

Mercy, Sisters of, Daughters of Christian Charity of St. Vincent de Paul, S.M.D.C.: Founded 1842, in Hungary; U.S. foundation, Rt. 1, Box 353, Hewitt, N.J. 07421.

Mercy of the Blessed Sacrament, Sisters of: Founded 1910 in Mexico. U.S. foundation, 555 E. Mountain View, Barstow, Calif. 92311.

Mill Hill Sisters; See Franciscan Missionaries of St. Joseph.

Minim Sisters of Mary Immaculate, C.F.M.M.: Founded 1886, in Mexico; in U.S. 1926. General motherhouse, Leon, Guanajuato, Mexico; U.S. ad-

dress, Our Lady of Lourdes Academy, Box 1856, Nogales, Ariz. 85621.

Misericordia Sisters, S.M.: Founded 1848, in Canada; in U.S., 1887. General motherhouse. 12435 Ave. Misericorde, Montreal H4J 2G3, Canada. Social work with unwed mothers and their children; hospital work.

Mission Helpers of the Sacred Heart, M.H.S.H.: Founded 1890, in U.S. General motherhouse, 1001 W. Joppa Rd., Baltimore, Md. 21204. Religious education, evangelization.

Missionary Catechists of the Sacred Hearts of Jesus and Mary (Violetas), M.C.: Founded 1918, in Mexico; in U.S., 1943. Motherhouse, Tlalpan, Mexico; U.S. address, 209 W. Murray St., Victoria, Tex. 77901.

Missionary Sisters of the Catholic Apostolate (Pallottine Missionary Sisters), S.A.C.: Founded in Rome, 1838; in U.S., 1912. Generalate, Rome, Italy; U.S. provincialate, Rt. 2, 15270 Old Halls Ferry Rd., Florissant, Mo. 63034.

Mother of God, Missionary Sisters of the, M.S.M.G.: Byzantine, Ukrainian Rite, Stamford. Motherhouse, 711-719 N. Franklin St., Philadelphia, Pa. 19123.

Mother of God, Sisters Poor Servants of the, S.M.G.: Founded 1869, in London, England; in U.S., 1947. General motherhouse, Maryfield, Roehampton, London. U.S. addresses: Maryfield Nursing Home, Greensboro Rd., High Point, N.C. 27260; St. Mary's Hospital, 916 Virginia Ave., Norton, Va. 24273; Holy Spirit School, 1800 Geary St., Philadelphia, Pa. 19145. Hospital, educational work.

Nazareth, Poor Sisters of: Founded in England; U.S. foundation, 1924. General motherhouse, Hammersmith, London, England; U.S. novitiate, 3333 Manning Ave., Los Angeles, Calif. 90064. Social services, education.

Notre Dame, School Sisters of, S.S.N.D.: Founded 1833, in Germany; in U.S., 1847. General motherhouse, Rome, Italy. U.S. motherhouse, 1233 N. Marshall St., Milwaukee, Wis. 53202. Provinces: 6401 N. Charles St., Baltimore, Md. 21212; 320 E. Ripa Ave., St. Louis, Mo. 63125; Good Counsel Hill, Mankato, Minn. 56001; 345 Belden Hill Rd., Wilton, Conn. 06897; 1451 E. Northgate, Irving, Tex. 75062; 1431 Euclid Ave., Berwyn, Ill. 60402.

Notre Dame, Sisters of, S.N.D.: Founded 1850 at Coesfeld, Germany; in U.S., 1874. General motherhouse, Rome, Italy. U.S. provinces: 1300 Auburn Rd., Chardon, O. 44024; 1601 Dixie Highway, Covington, Ky. 41011; 3837 Secor Rd., Toledo O. 43623; 1776 Hendrix Ave., Thousand Oaks, Calif. 91360.

Notre Dame, Sisters of the Congregation of C.N.D.: Founded 1653, in Canada; in U.S., 1860 General motherhouse, Montreal, Que., Canada U.S. province, 223 West Mountain Rd., Ridgefield Conn. 06877. Education.

Notre Dame de Namur, Sisters of, S.N.D. Founded 1803, in France; in U.S., 1840. General motherhouse, Rome, Italy. U.S. provinces: P.C Box 112, Boston, Mass. 02117; Jeffrey's Neck Rd.

Ipswich, Mass. 01938; 1561 N. Benson Rd., Fairfield, Conn. 06431; Landing Rd., Ilchester, Md. 21083; 701 E. Columbia Ave., Cincinnati, O. 45215; 14800 Bohlman Rd., Saratoga, Calif. 95070. Educational work.

Notre Dame de Sion, Congregation of, N.D.S.: Founded 1843, in France; in U.S., 1892. Generalate, Rome, Italy; U.S. provincial house, 3823 Locust St., Kansas City, Mo. 64109. Creation of better understanding and relations between Christians and Jews.

Notre Dame Sisters: Founded 1853, in Czechoslovakia; in U.S., 1910. General motherhouse, Javornik, Czechoslovakia; U.S. motherhouse, 3501 State St., Omaha, Nebr. 68112. Educational work.

Our Lady of Charity, North American Union of Sisters of, (Eudist Sisters (Sisters of Our Lady of Charity of the Refuge), O.L.C.: Founded 1641, in Caen, France, by St. John Eudes; in U.S., 1855. Autonomous houses were federated in 1944 and in May, 1978, the North American Union of the Sisters of Our Lady of Charity was established. General motherhouse and administrative center, Box 327, Wisconsin Dells, Wis. 53965. Primarily devoted to re-education and rehabilitation of women and girls in residential and non-residential settings.

Two independent monasteries; 1125 Malvern Ave., Hot Springs, Ark. 71901; 620 Roswell Rd. N.W., Carrollton, O. 44615.

Our Lady of Sorrows, Sisters of, O.L.S.: Founded 1839, in Italy; in U.S., 1947. General motherhouse, Rome, Italy; U.S. headquarters, 9494 Norris Ferry Rd., Shreveport, La. 71106.

Our Lady of the Garden, Sisters of, O.L.G.: Founded 1829, in Italy, by St. Anthony Mary Gianelli. Motherhouse, Rome, Italy; U.S. address, St. Brendan School, 445½ Whalley Ave., New Haven, Conn. 06511.

Our Lady of Victory Missionary Sisters, O.L.V.M.: Founded 1922, in U.S. Motherhouse, Victory Noll, Box 109, Huntington, Ind. 46750. Educational, social work.

Pallottine Sisters of the Catholic Apostolate, C.S.A.C.: Founded 1843, at Rome, Italy; in U.S., 1889. General motherhouse, Rome; U.S. motherhouse, St. Patrick's Villa, Harriman Heights, Harriman, N.Y. 10926. Educational work.

Parish Visitors of Mary Immaculate, P.V.M.I.: Founded 1920, in New York. General motherhouse, Box 658, Monroe, N.Y. 10950. Mission work.

Passion of Jesus Christ, Religious of (Passionist Nuns), C.P.: Founded 1771, in Italy, by St. Paul of the Cross; in U.S., 1910. U.S. convents: 2715 Churchview Ave., Pittsburgh, Pa. 15227; 631 Griffin Pond Rd., Clarks Summit, Pa. 18411; 1420 Benita Ave., Owensboro, Ky. 42301; 1151 Donaldson Hwy., Erlanger, Ky. 41018; 1032 Clayton Rd., Ellisville, Mo. 63011. Contemplatives.

Passionist Sisters: See Cross and Passion, Sisters of the.

Paul, Angelic Sisters of St.: Founded 1535, in Milan, Italy; U.S. address, Fatima Shrine, Swan Rd., Youngstown, N.Y. 14174.

Paul, Daughters of St. (Missionary Sisters of the Media of Communication), D.S.P.: Founded 1915,

at Alba, Piedmont, Italy; in U.S., 1932. General motherhouse, Rome, Italy; U.S. provincial house, 50 St. Paul's Ave., Jamaica Plain, Mass. 02130. Apostolate of the communications arts.

Paul of Chartres, Sisters of St., S.P.C.: Founded 1696, in France. General house, Rome, Italy; U.S. address, 492 County Rd., Box 165G, Marquette, Mich. 49855.

Peter Claver, Missionary Sisters of St., S.S.P.C.: Founded 1894; in U.S., 1914. General motherhouse, Rome, Italy; U.S. address, 667 Woods Mill Rd. S., Chesterfield, Mo. 63017.

Pious Schools, Sisters of, Sch. P.: Founded 1829 in Spain; in U.S., 1954. General motherhouse, Rome, Italy; U.S. headquarters, 9925 Mason Ave., Chatsworth, Calif. 91311.

Poor, Little Sisters of the, L.S.P.: Founded 1839, in France; in U.S., 1868. General motherhouse, St. Pern, France. U.S. provinces: 110-30 221st St., Queens Village, N.Y. 11429; 601 Maiden Choice Lane, Baltimore, Md. 21228; 2325 N. Lakewood Ave.; Chicago, Ill. 60614. Care of aged.

Poor Clare Missionary Sisters (Misioneras Clarisas), M.C.: Founded Mexico. General motherhouse, Rome, Italy; U.S. novitiate, 1019 N. Newhope, Santa Ana, Calif. 92703.

Poor Clare Nuns: See Franciscan Poor Clare Nuns.

Poor Handmaids of Jesus Christ (Ancilla Domini Sisters), P.H.J.C.: Founded 1851, in Germany; in U.S., 1868. General motherhouse, Dernbach, Westerwald, Germany; U.S. motherhouse, Ancilla Domini Convent, Donaldson, Ind. 46513. Educational, hospital work, social services.

Precious Blood, Daughters of Charity of the Most: Founded 1872, at Pagani, Italy; in U.S., 1908. General motherhouse, Rome, Italy; U.S. convent, 1482 North Ave., Bridgeport, Conn. 06604.

Precious Blood, Missionary Sisters of the, C.P.S.: Founded 1885, at Mariannhill, South Africa; in U.S., 1925. Generalate, Rome, Italy: U.S. novitiate, New Holland Ave., P.O. Box 97, Shillington, Pa. 19607. Home and foreign mission work.

Precious Blood, Sisters Adorers of the, A.P.B.: Founded 1861, in Canada; in U.S., 1890. General motherhouses, Canada. U.S. autonomous monasteries: 54th St. and Fort Hamilton Pkwy., Brooklyn, N.Y. 11219; 700 Bridge St., Manchester, N.H. 03104; 7408 S.E. Alder St., Portland, Ore. 97215; 166 State St., Portland, Me. 04101; 1106 State St., Lafayette, Ind. 47905; 400 Pratt St., Watertown, N.Y. 13601. Cloistered, contemplative.

Precious Blood, Sisters of the, C.Pp.S.: Founded 1834, in Switzerland; in U.S., 1844. Generalate, 4000 Denlinger Rd., Dayton, Ohio 45426. Education, health care, other ministries.

Precious Blood, Sisters of the Most, C.Pp.S.: Founded 1845, in Steinerberg, Switzerland; in U.S., 1870. General motherhouse, 204 N. Main St., O'Fallon, Mo. 63366. Education, other ministries.

Presentation, Sisters of Mary of the, S.M.P.: Founded 1829, in France; in U.S., 1903. General motherhouse, Broons, Cotes-du-Nord, France. U.S. address, Maryvale Novitiate, Valley City, N. Dak. 58072. Educational, hospital work.

Presentation of Mary, Sisters of the, P.M.: Founded 1796, in France; in U.S., 1873. General motherhouse, Castel Gandolfo, Italy. U.S. provincial houses: 495 Mammoth Rd., Manchester, N.H. 03104; 209 Lawrence St., Methuen, Mass. 01844.

Presentation of the B.V.M., Sisters of the, P.B.V.M.: Founded 1775, in Ireland; in U.S., 1854, in San Francisco. U.S. motherhouses: 2360 Carter Rd., Dubuque, Ia. 52001; R.D. 2, Box 33, Newburgh, N.Y. 12550; 8931 Callaghan Rd., San Antonio, Tex. 78230; 2340 Turk Blvd., San Francisco, Calif. 94118; St. Colman's Convent, Watervliet, N.Y. 12189.

1101 32nd Ave., S. Fargo, N. Dak. 58103; 250 S. Davis Dr., P.O. Box 1113, Warner Robbins, Ga. 31093; 1500 N. Main, Aberdeen, S. Dak. 57401; 1300 E. Cedar, Globe, Ariz. 85501; 1555 E. Dana, Mesa, Ariz. 85201; 366 South St., Fitchburg, Mass. 01420; 419 Woodrow Rd., Annadale, Staten Island, N.Y. 10312.

Presentation of the Blessed Virgin Mary, Sisters of, of Union: Founded in Ireland, 1775; union established in Ireland, 1976; first U.S. vice province, 1979. Generalate, Kildare, Ireland. U.S. addresses: 349 Oak Ave., San Bruno, Calif. 94066 (vice provincialate); Presentation Convent, 4410 Cleary Ave., Matairie, La. 70002 (Southeastern Region).

Providence, Daughters of Divine, F.D.P.: Founded 1832, Italy; in U.S., 1964. General motherhouse, Rome, Italy; U.S. address, 1625 Missouri St., Chalmette, La. 70043.

Providence, Missionary Catechists of Divine, M.C.D.P.: Founded 1930, as a filial society; adjunct branch of Sisters of Divine Providence (Helotes, Tex.). Administrative house, 4650 Eldridge Ave., San Antonio, Tex. 78237.

Providence, Oblate Sisters of, O.S.P.: Founded 1829, in U.S. General motherhouse, 701 Gun Rd., Baltimore, Md. 21227. Educational work.

Providence, Sisters of, S.P.: Founded 1861, in Canada; in U.S., 1873. General motherhouse, Our Lady of Victory Convent, Holyoke, Mass. 01040.

Providence, Sisters of, S.P.: Founded 1843, in Canada; in U.S., 1854. General motherhouse, Montreal, Canada. U.S. provinces: P.O. Box C-11038, Seattle, Wash. 98111; 9 E. 9th Ave., Spokane, Wash. 99202; 353 N. River Rd., Des Plaines, Ill. 60616.

Providence, Sisters of (of St. Mary-of-the-Woods), S.P.: Founded 1806, in France; in U.S., 1840. Generalate, St. Mary-of-the-Woods, Ind. 47876.

Providence, Sisters of Divine, C.D.P.: Founded 1762, in France; in U.S., 1866. Generalate, Box 197, Helotes, Tex. 78023. Educational, hospital work.

Providence, Sisters of Divine, C.D.P.: Founded 1851, in Germany; in U.S., 1876. Generalate, Rome, Italy. U.S. provinces: 9000 Babcock Blvd., Allison Park, Pa. 15101; 8351 Florissant Rd., St. Louis, Mo. 63121; Box 2, Rte. 80, Kingston, Mass. 02364. Educational, hospital work.

Providence, Sisters of Divine (of Kentucky), C.D.P.: Founded 1762, in France; in U.S., 1889. General motherhouse, Fenetrange, France; U.S.

province, Melbourne, Ky. 41059. Education, social services, other ministries.

Redeemer, Oblates of the Most Holy, O.SS.R.: Founded 1864, in Spain. General motherhouse, Spain; U.S. foundation, 60-80 Pond St., Jamaica Plain, Mass. 02130.

Redeemer, Order of the Most Holy, O.SS.R.: Founded 1731, by St. Alphonsus Liguori; in U.S., 1957. U.S. addresses: Mother of Perpetual Help Monastery, Esopus, N.Y. 12429; St. Alphonsus Monastery, Liguori, Mo. 63057.

Redeemer, Sisters of the Divine, S.D.R.: Founded 1849, in Niederbronn, France; in U.S., 1912. General motherhcuse, Rome, Italy; U.S. province, 999 Rock Run Road, Elizabeth, Pa. 15037. Educational, hospital work; care of the aged.

Redeemer, Sisters of the Holy, S.H.R.: Founded 1849, in Alsace; in U.S., 1924. General motherhouse, Wuerzburg, Germany; U.S. provincial house, Huntingdon Valley, Pa. 19006. Personalized medical care in hospitals, homes for aged, private homes; retreat work.

Reparation of the Congregation of Mary, Sisters of, S.R.C.M.: Founded 1903, in U.S. Motherhouse, St. Zita's Villa, Monsey, N.Y. 10952.

Resurrection, Sisters of the, C.R.: Founded 1891, in Italy; in U.S., 1900. General motherhouse, Rome, Italy. U.S. provinces: 7432 Talcott Ave., Chicago, Ill. 60631; Mt. St. Joseph, Castleton-on-Hudson, N.Y. 12033. Education, nursing.

Rita, Sisters of St., O.S.A.: General motherhouse, Wurzburg, Germany. U.S. foundation, St. Monica's Convent, 3920 Green Bay Rd., Racine, Wis. 53404.

Rosary, Congregation of Our Lady of the Holy, R.S.R.: Founded 1874, in Canada; in U.S., 1899. General motherhouse, C.P. 2020, Rimouski, Que., Canada. U.S. regional house, 20 Thomas St., Portland, Me. 04102. Educational work.

Rosary, Missionary Sisters of the Holy, M.S.H.R.: Founded 1924, in Ireland; in U.S., 1954. Motherhouse, Dublin, Ireland. U.S. regional address, P.O. Box 304, Bryn Mawr, Pa. 19010. African missions.

Sacrament, Missionary Sisters of the Most Blessed, M.SS.S.: General motherhouse, Madrid, Spain; U.S. foundation: 1111 Wordin Ave., Bridgeport, Conn. 06605.

Sacrament, Nuns of the Perpetual Adoration of the Blessed, A.P.: Founded 1807 in Rome, Italy; in U.S., 1925. U.S. monasteries: 145 N. Cotton Ave., El Paso, Tex. 79901; 771 Ashbury St., San Francisco, Calif. 94117.

Sacrament, Oblate Sisters of the Blessed, O.S.B.S.: Founded 1935, in U.S.; motherhouse, St. Sylvester Convent, Marty, S.D. 57361. Care of American Indians.

Sacrament, Religious Sisters of the Blessed, R.M.S.S.: Founded 1910, in Mexico; in U.S., 1926. General motherhouse, Mexico City, Mexico; U.S. convent, 222 W. Cevallos St., San Antonio, Tex. 78204.

Sacrament, Servants of the Blessed, S.S.S.: Founded 1858, in France, by St. Pierre Julien Eymard; in U.S., 1947. General motherhouse, Rome, Italy; American vice-provincial house, 101

Silver St., Waterville, Me. 04901. Contemplative.

Sacrament, Sisters of the Blessed, for Indians and Colored People, S.B.S.: Founded 1891, in U.S., by Katharine Drexel. General motherhouse, Bensalem, Pa. 19020.

Sacrament, Sisters of the Most Holy, M.H.S.: Founded 1851, in France; in U.S., 1872. Generalate, 409 W. St. Mary Blvd. (P.O. Box 30727), Lafayette, La. 70503.

Sacrament, Sisters Servants of the Blessed, S.S.B.S.: Founded 1904, in Mexico. General motherhouse, Guadalajara, Mexico. U.S. address, Our Lady of Guadalupe School, 536 Rockwood Ave., Calexico, Calif. 92231.

Sacramentine Nuns (Religious of the Order of the Blessed Sacrament and Our Lady), O.S.S.: Founded 1639, in France; in U.S., 1912. U.S. monasteries: 23 Park Ave., Yonkers, N.Y. 10703; US 31, Conway, Mich. 49722. Perpetual adoration of the Holy Eucharist.

Sacred Heart, Daughters of Our Lady of the: Founded 1882, in France; in U.S., 1955. General motherhouse, Rome, Italy; U.S. address, 424 E. Browning Rd., Bellmawr, N.J. 08031. Educational work.

Sacred Heart, Missionary Sisters of the (Cabrini Sisters), M.S.C.: Founded 1880, in Italy, by St. Frances Xavier Cabrini; in U.S., 1889. General motherhouse, Rome, Italy; U.S. provinces: 223 E. 19th St., New York, N.Y. 10003 (Eastern); 434 W. Deming Pl., Chicago, Ill. 60614 (Western). Educational, health, social and catechetical work.

Sacred Heart, Religious of the Apostolate of the, R.A.: General motherhouse, Madrid, Spain; U.S. address, 1120 6th St., Miami Beach, Fla., 33139.

Sacred Heart, Society Devoted to the, S.D.S.H.: Founded 1940, in Hungary; in U.S., 1956. U.S. motherhouse, 2121 W. Olive Dr., Burbank, Calif. 91506. Educational work.

Sacred Heart, Society of the, R.S.C.J.: Founded 1800, in France; in U.S., 1818. Generalate, Rome, Italy. U.S. provincial house, 4389 W. Pine Blvd., St. Louis, Mo. 63108. Educational work.

Sacred Heart of Jesus, Apostles of, A.S.C.J.: Founded 1894, in Italy; in U.S., 1902. General motherhouse, Rome, Italy; U.S. motherhouse, 265 Benham St., Hamden, Conn. 06514. Educational, social work.

Sacred Heart of Jesus, Handmaids of the, A.C.J.: Founded 1877, in Spain. General motherhouse, Rome, Italy; U.S. province, 616 Coopertown Rd., Haverford, Pa. 19041. Educational, retreat work.

Sacred Heart of Jesus, Missionary Sisters of the Most (Hiltrup), M.S.C.: Founded 1899, in Germany; in U.S., 1908. General motherhouse, Rome, Italy; U.S. province, Hyde Park, Reading, Pa. 19605. Education, health care, pastoral ministry.

Sacred Heart of Jesus, Oblate Sisters of the, O.S.H.J.: Founded 1894; in U.S., 1949. General motherhouse, Rome, Italy; U.S. headquarters, 50 Warner Rd., Hubbard, Ohio 44425. Educational, social work.

Sacred Heart of Jesus, Servants of the Most: Founded 1894, in Poland; in U.S., 1959. General motherhouse, Cracow, Poland; U.S. address, 231 Arch St., Cresson, Pa. 16630. Education, health care, social services.

Sacred Heart of Jesus, Sisters of the, S.S.C.J.: Founded 1816, in France; in U.S., 1903. General motherhouse, St. Jacut, Brittany, France; U.S. provincial house, 5922 Blanco Rd., San Antonio, Tex. 78216. Educational, hospital, domestic work.

Sacred Heart of Jesus and of the Poor, Servants of the (Mexican), S.S.H.J.P.: Founded 1885, in Mexico; in U.S., 1907. General motherhouse, Apartado 92, Puebla, Pue., Mexico; U.S. address, 237 Tobin Pl., El Paso, Tex. 79905.

Sacred Heart of Jesus for Reparation, Congregation of the Handmaids of the: Founded 1918, in Italy; in U.S., 1958. U.S. address, Sunshine Park, R.D. 3, Steubenville, Ohio 43952.

Sacred Heart of Mary, Religious of the, R.S.H.M.: Founded 1848, in France; in U.S., 1877. Generalate, Rome, Italy. U.S. provinces; 50 Wilson Park Dr., Tarrytown, N.Y. 10591; 8008 Loyola Blvd., Los Angeles, Calif. 90045.

Sacred Hearts, Religious of the Holy Union of the, S.U.S.C.: Founded 1826, in France; in U.S., 1886. Generalate, Rome, Italy. U.S. provinces: 550 Rock St., Fall River, Mass. 02720; Main St., Groton, Mass. 01450. Varied ministries.

Sacred Hearts and of Perpetual Adoration, Sisters of the, SS.CC.: Founded 1797, in France; in U.S., 1908. General motherhouse, Rome, Italy; U.S. provinces: 45-901A Wailele Rd., Kaneohe, Hawaii 96744 (Pacific); 3115 Queens Chapel Rd. (Apts. 301-302); Mt. Rainier, Md. 20822 (East Coast). Varied ministries.

Sacred Hearts of Jesus and Mary, Sisters of the, S.H.J.M.: Established 1953, in U.S. General motherhouse, Essex, England; U.S. address, 310 San Carlos Ave., El Cerrito, Calif. 94530.

Savior, Company of the, C.S.: Founded 1952, in Spain; in U.S., 1962. General motherhouse, Madrid, Spain; U.S. foundation, 820 Clinton Ave., Bridgeport, Conn. 06604.

Savior, Sisters of the Divine, S.D.S.: Founded 1888, in Italy; in U.S., 1895. General motherhouse, Rome, Italy; U.S. province, 4311 N. 100th St., Milwaukee, Wis. 53222. Educational, hospital work.

Social Service, Sisters of, S.S.S.: Founded in Hungary, 1923, by Sr. Margaret Slachta. U.S. address, 440 Linwood Ave., Buffalo, N.Y. 14209. Social work.

Social Service, Sisters of, of Los Angeles, S.S.S.: Founded 1908, in Hungary; in U.S., 1926. General motherhouse, 1120 Westchester Pl., Los Angeles, Calif. 90019.

Teresa of Jesus, Society of St., S.T.J.: Founded 1876, in Spain; in U.S., 1910. General motherhouse, Rome, Italy; U.S. provincial house, 154 Fair Ave., San Antonio, Tex. 78223.

Thomas of Villanova, Congregation of Sisters of St., S.S.T.V.: Founded 1661, in France; in U.S., 1948. General motherhouse, Neuilly-sur-Seine, France; U.S. foundation W. Rocks Rd., Norwalk, Conn. 06851.

Trinity, Missionary Servants of the Most Blessed, M.S.B.T.: Founded 1912, in U.S., by Very Rev. Thomas A. Judge. General motherhouse, 3501

Solly St.. Philadelphia, Pa. 19136. Educational, social work: health services.

Trinity, Sisters of the Most Holy, O.Ss.T.: Founded 1198, in Rome; in U.S., 1920. General motherhouse, Rome, Italy; U.S. address, Immaculate Conception Province, 21320 Euclid Ave., Euclid, Ohio 44117. Educational work.

Ursula of the Blessed Virgin, Society of the Sisters of St., S.U.: Founded 1606, in France; in U.S., 1902. General motherhouse, France; U.S. novitiate, Linwood Rd., Rhinebeck, N.Y. 12572. Educational work.

Ursuline Nuns (Roman Union), O.S.U.: Founded 1535, in Italy; in U.S., 1727. Generalate, Rome, Italy. U.S. provinces: 323 E. 198th St., Bronx, N.Y. 10458; Crystal Heights Rd., Crystal City, Mo. 63019; 639 Angela Dr., Santa Rosa, Calif. 95401; 71 Lowder St., Dedham, Mass. 02026,

Ursuline Nuns of the Congregation of Paris, O.S.U.: Founded 1535, in Italy; in U.S., 1727, in New Orleans. U.S. motherhouses: St. Martin, O. 45170; East and Miami Sts., Paola, Kans. 66071; 3115 Lexington Rd., Louisville, Ky. 40206; 2600 Lander Rd., Cleveland, O. 44124; Maple Mount, Ky. 42356; 436 W. Delaware, Toledo, O. 43610; 4250 Shields Rd., Canfield, O. 44406; 1339 E. McMillan St., Cincinnati, O. 45206.

Ursuline Nuns of the Congregation of Tildonk, Belgium, R.U.: Founded 1535, in Italy; in U.S., 1924. Generalate, Tildonk, Belgium; U.S. address, 81-15 Utopia Parkway, Jamaica, N.Y. 11432. Educational, foreign mission work.

Ursuline Sisters of Belleville, O.S.U.: Founded 1535, in Italy; in U.S., 1910; established as diocesan community, 1983. Central house, 1026 N. Douglas Ave., Belleville, Ill. 62221. Educational work.

Ursuline Sisters (Irish Ursuline Union), O.S.U.: General motherhouse, Blackrock, Cork, Ireland; U.S. address, 1973 Torch Hill Rd., Columbus, Ga. 31903.

Venerini Sisters, Religious, M.P.V.: Founded 1685, in Italy; in U.S., 1909. General motherhouse, Rome, Italy; U.S. provincialate; 23 Edward St., Worcester, Mass. 01605.

Vincent de Paul, Sisters: See Charity of St. Vincent de Paul, Sisters of.

Visitation Nuns, V.H.M.: Founded 1610, in France; in U.S. (Georgetown, D.C.), 1799. Contemplative, educational work. Two federations in U.S.

First Federation of North America. Major pontifical enclosure. Pres., Mother Mary Jozefa Kowalewski, Monastery of the Visitation, 2002 Bancroft Pkwy., Wilmington, Del. 19806. Addresses of monasteries belonging to the federation: 2300 Springhill Ave., Mobile, Ala. 36607; 2002 Bancroft Pkwy., Wilmington, Del. 19806; 2209 E. Grace St., Richmond, Va. 23223; 5820 City Ave., Philadelphia, Pa. 19131; 1745 Parkside Blvd., Toledo, O. 43607; 2055 Ridgedale Dr., Snellville, Ga. 30278.

Second Federation of North America. Constitutional enclosure. Pres., Rev. Mother Jeanne Charlotte Johnson, Visitation Monastery, 3200 S.W. Dash Point Rd., Federal Way, Wash. 98003. Addresses of monasteries belonging to the federation: 1500 35th St., Washington, D.C. 20007; 3020 N. Ballas Rd., St. Louis, Mo. 63131; 200 E. Second St., Frederick, Md. 21701; Mt. St. Chantal Monastery of the Visitation, Wheeling, W. Va. 26003; Ridge Blvd. and 89th St., Brooklyn, N.Y. 11209; 1600 Murdoch Ave., Parkersburg, W. Va. 26101; 2000 Sixteenth Ave., Rock Island, Ill. 61201; 2475 Dodd Rd., Mendota Heights, St. Paul, Minn. 55120; Visitation Monastery, Georgetown, Ky. 40324; 3200 S.W. Dash Point Rd., Federal Way, Wash. 98003.

Visitation of the Congregation of the Immaculate Heart of Mary, Sisters of the, S.V.M.: Founded 1952, in U.S. Motherhouse, 900 Alta Vista St., Dubuque, Ia. 52001. Educational work, parish ministry.

Vocationist Sisters (Sisters of the Divine Vocations): Founded 1921, in Italy. General motherhouse, Naples, Italy; U.S. foundation, Perpetual Help Nursery, 172 Broad St., Newark, N.J. 07104.

Wisdom, Daughters of, D.W.: Founded 1703, in France, by St. Louis Marie Grignion de Montfort; in U.S., 1904. General motherhouse, Vendee, France; U.S. province, 385 S. Ocean Ave., Islip, N.Y. Education, health care, parish ministry, social services.

Xaverian Missionary Society of Mary, Inc., X.M.M.: Founded 1945, in Italy; in U.S., 1954. General motherhouse, Parma, Italy; U.S. address, 242 Salisbury St., Worcester, Mass. 01609.

Xavier Mission Sisters (Catholic Mission Sisters of St. Francis Xavier), X.M.S.: Founded 1946, at Warren, Mich., by Cardinal Edward Mooney. General motherhouse, 37179 Moravian Dr., Mount Clemens, Mich. 48043. Educational, hospital, social work in missions.

ORGANIZATIONS OF RELIGIOUS

Conferences

Conferences of major superiors of religious institutes, dating from the 1950s and encouraged by the Code of Canon Law (canons 708, 709), have been established in 19 countries of Europe, 14 in North and Central America, 10 in South America, 26 in Africa and 20 in Asia and Oceania.

Listed below are U.S. and international conferences.

Conference of Major Superiors of Men: Founded in 1956; established officially Mar. 23, 1960, by decree of the Congregation for Religious and Secular Institutes. Its purposes are to promote the spiritual and apostolic welfare of men Religious, provide liaison opportunities among Religious and with church officials, and serve as a national voice for the corporate views of superiors. Membership, 263 major superiors representing institutes with a combined membership of approximately 30,000. President Rev. Stephen Tutas, S.M.; executive director, Rev. Roland J. Faley, T.O.R. National office: 8808 Cameron St., Silver Spring, Md. 20910.

Leadership Conference of Women Religious: Organized in the late 1950s as the Conference of Major Superiors of Women (name changed, 1971);

approved by the Congregation for Religious and Secular Institutes June 13, 1962. Its purpose is to promote the spiritual and apostolic calling and works of sisterhoods in the U.S. Membership, approximately 700. President, Sister Carol Quigley, I.H.M.; executive director, Sister Janet Roesener, C.S.J. National secretariat: 8808 Cameron St., Silver Spring, Md. 20910.

International Union of Superiors General (Women): Established in 1965; approved by the Congregation for Religious and Secular Institutes, 1967. President, Sister Helen McLaughlin, R.S.H.J. Address: Via Garibaldi 28, 00153, Rome, Italy.

Union of Superiors General (Men): Established in 1957; approved by the Congregation for Religious and Secular Institutes, 1967. President, Father John Vaughn, O.F.M. Address: Via dei Penitenzieri 19, 00193 Rome, Italy.

Latin American Confederation of Religious: Established in 1959, approved by the Congregation for Religious and Secular Institutes, 1967. President, Father Luis Ugalde Olalde, S.J. Address: Av. Berrizbeitia 14, el Paraiso, Qta. Santa Tecla, Caracas 1020-A Venezuela.

Union of European Conferences of Major Superiors: Established Dec. 25, 1983. President, Father Pier Giordano Cabra, F.N.; executive director, Father Leonhard Gregotsch, M.I. Address: Freyung 6/1-3, A-1010, Vienna, Austria.

World Conference of Secular Institutes: Established May 23, 1974. Address: Via deglia Ombrellari 40, 00193 Rome, Italy.

Other Organizations

Association of Contemplative Sisters (1969): Its principal purpose is development of the contemplative life-style for effective service to the Church. Membership, approximately 400. President, Sister Mary Lavin, O.C.D. Central office: 8650 Russell Ave. S., Minneapolis, Minn. 55431.

Consortium Perfectae Caritatis (Women) (1971): To encourage the development of religious life in line with Vatican II guidelines and related directives. President, Sister Mary Elise, S.N.D.; coordinator, Rev. James A. Viall. Mailing address: P.O. Box 1856, Middleburg, Va. 22117.

Institute on Religious Life (1974). To foster more effective understanding and implementation of teachings of the Church on religious life, promote vocations to religious life and the priesthood, and promote growth in sanctity of all the faithful according to their state in life. Executive director, Rev. James Downey. National office, 4200 N. Austin Ave., Chicago, Ill. 60634.

National Assembly of Religious Brothers (1972): To publicize the unique vocations of brothers, to further communication among brothers and provide liaison with various organizations of the Church. Executive director, Brother Brian Maloney, O.F.M. National office, 1307 S. Wabash Ave., Suite 201, Chicago, Ill. 60605.

National Black Sisters' Conference (1968): To determine priorities in service to Black people, promote Black vocations and the development of religious life in the unique Black life-style. Ex-

ecutive director, Sister Marie de Porres Taylor, S.N.J.M. Mailing address: 6226 Camden St., Oakland, Calif. 94605.

The National Catholic Vocation Council (1977): To give visible witness of the mutual collaboration of national vocation organizations and to service efforts of mutual concern and benefit in the recruitment and development of vocations to the priesthood, diaconate and vowed life. Member organizations are: National Conference of Catholic Bishops, Leadership Conference of Women Religious, Conference of Major Superiors of Men, Conference of Secular Institutes, National Sisters' Vocation Conference, National Conference of Diocesan Vocation Directors, National Conference of Religious Vocation Directors, Serra International, and the Knights of Columbus. Executive director, Sister Jacqueline Wetherholt, C.S.J. Address: 1307 S. Wabash Ave., Suite 350, Chicago, Ill. 60605

National Coalition of American Nuns (1969): To secure recognition and development of the role of women in the Church and society, along with advocacy for social activism. President, Sister Lillanna Kopp, S.F.C.C. Address: 1307 S. Wabash Ave., Chicago, Ill 60605.

National Conference of Vicars for Religious (1967): National organization of diocesan officials concerned with relations between their respective dioceses and religious communities engaged therein. President, Rev. Robert C. Nash, 1300 Byron St., P.O. Box 230, Wheeling, W. Va. 26003.

National Sisters' Vocation Conference (1970): To promote understanding of the role of women, especially Religious, in the Church through work in the vocation apostolate. Membership, approximately 1,000 women and men. Executive director, Sister Sarah Marie Sherman, R.S.M. National office: 1307 S. Wabash Ave., Chicago, Ill. 60605.

Religious Formation Conference (1953): Originally Sister Formation Conference; membership now includes men and persons belonging to non-canonical religious groups. Executive director, Sister Peggy Nichols, C.S.J. National office: 1234 Massachusetts Ave. N.W., Washington, D.C. 20005.

SECULAR INSTITUTES

(Sources: Almanac survey; United States Conference of Secular Institutes; *Annuario Pontificio.*)

Secular institutes are societies of men and women living in the world who dedicate themselves to observe the evangelical counsels and to carry on apostolic works suitable to their talents and opportunities in the areas of their everyday life.

"Secular institutes are not religious communities but they carry with them in the world a profession of evangelical counsels which is genuine and complete, and recognized as such by the Church. This profession confers a consecration on men and women, laity and clergy, who reside in the world. For this reason they should chiefly strive for total self-dedication to God, one inspired by perfect charity. These institutes should preserve their proper and particular character, a secular one, so that they may everywhere measure up successfully to that apostolate which they were designed to exercise, and which is both in the world and, in a sense, of the world" (*Decree on the Appropriate Renewal of Religious Life,* No. 11; Second Vatican Council).

Secular institutes are under the jurisdiction of the Congregation for Religious and Secular Institutes. General legislation concerning them is contained in Canons 710 to 730 of the Code of Canon Law.

A secular institute reaches maturity in several stages. It begins as an association of the faithful, technically called a pious union, with the approval of a local bishop. Once it has proved its viability, he can give it the status of an institute of diocesan right, in accordance with norms and permission emanating from the Congregation for Religious and Secular Institutes. On issuance of a separate decree from this congregation, an institute of diocesan right becomes an institute of pontifical right.

Secular institutes, which originated in the latter part of the 18th century, were given full recognition and approval by Pius XII Feb. 2, 1947, in the apostolic constitution *Provida Mater Ecclesia.* On Mar. 25 of the same year a special commission for secular institutes was set up within the Congregation for Religious. Institutes were commended and confirmed by Pius XII in a motu proprio of Mar. 12, 1948, and were the subject of a special instruction issued a week later, Mar. 19, 1948.

The **United States Conference of Secular Institutes (CSI)** was established in October, 1972, following the organization of the World Conference of Secular Institutes in Rome. Its membership is open to all canonically erected secular institutes with members living in the United States. The conference was organized to offer secular institutes an opportunity to exchange experiences, to do research in order to help the Church carry out its mission, and to search for ways and means to make known the existence of secular institutes in the U.S. Address: c/o Claudette Cyr, president, 121 Greenwood St., Watertown, Conn. 06795.

Institutes in the U.S.

Caritas Christi: Originated in Marseilles, 1937; for women. Established as a secular institute of pontifical right Mar. 19, 1955. Address: P.O. Box 162, River Forest, Ill. 60305.

Company of St. Paul: Originated in Milan, Italy, 1920; for lay people and priests. Approved as a secular institute of pontifical right June 30, 1950. Address: 52 Davis Ave., White Plains, N.Y. 10605.

Company of St. Ursula, Secular Institute of St. Angela Merici: Founded in Brescia, Italy, 1535; for women. Approved as a secular institute of pontifical right 1958. Addresses: Lina Moser, President, Via Rosmini 128, 38100 Trento, Italy; Juline Lamb, 2937 Hemphill St., Fort Worth, Tex. 76110. International membership of 3,000.

DeSales Secular Institute: Founded in Vienna, Austria, 1940; for women. Pontifical right, 1964. Address: Rev. John Conmy, O.S.F.S., National Assistant, 1120 Blue Ball Rd., Childs, Md. 21916.

Diocesan Laborer Priests: Approved as a secular institute of pontifical right, 1952. The specific aim of the institute is the promotion, sustenance and cultivation of apostolic, religious and priestly vocations. Address: c/o Rev. Ovid Percharroman, 3706 15th St. N.E., Washington, D.C. 20017.

Don Bosco Volunteers: Founded 1917; for women. Approved as a secular institute of pontifical right Aug. 5, 1978. Address: Don Bosco Volunteers, 202 Union Ave., Paterson, N.J. 07502. International membership of 900 in 25 countries.

Handmaids of Divine Mercy: Founded in Bari, Italy, 1951; for women. Approved as an institute of pontifical right 1972. Address: Mary I. DiFonzo, 2410 Hughes Ave., Bronx, N.Y. 10458. International membership of 980.

Institute of Secular Missionaries: Founded in Vitoria, Spain, 1939; for women. Approved as a secular institute, 1955. Address: 2710 Ruberg Ave., Cincinnati, O. 45211, Att. E. Dilger.

Institute of the Heart of Jesus: Originated in France Feb. 2, 1791; restored Oct. 29, 1918; for diocesan priests and lay people. Received final approval from the Holy See as a secular institute of pontifical right Feb. 2, 1952. Rev. Andre Loisel, superior general. Addresses: Central House, 202 Avenue du Maine, Paris 14me, France; U.S. address, Rev. Joseph O'Hara, Loras College, Dubuque, Ia. 52001. International membership of approximately 1,400.

Missionaries of the Kingship of Christ the King: Under this title are included three distinct and juridically separate institutes founded by Agostino Gemelli, O.F.M. (1878-1959).

(1) **Women Missionaries of the Kingship of Christ** — Founded in 1919, in Italy; definitively approved as an institute of pontifical rite 1953. Established in 15 countries. U.S. branch established 1950. Age at time of entrance, 21 to 40.

(2) **Men Missionaries of the Kingship of Christ** — Founded 1928, in Italy, as an institute of diocesan right. U.S. branch established 1962.

(3) **Priest Missionaries of the Kingship of Christ** — Established in U.S., 1954; approved as institute of pontifical right July 15, 1978. For diocesan priests.

Address: Rev. Stephen Hartdegen, O.F.M., 1650 St. Camillus Dr., Silver Spring, Md. 20903.

Oblate Missionaries of Mary Immaculate: Founded, 1952; approved as a secular institute of diocesan right Feb. 2, 1962, and of pontifical right Mar. 25, 1984; for women. Addresses: Oblate Missionaries of Mary Immaculate, 121 Greenwood St., Watertown, Conn. 06795; P.O. Box 303, Manville, R.I. 02838; 7535 Boulevard Parent, Trois Rivieres, P. Q. G9A 5E1, Canada. International membership.

Opus Spiritus Sancti: Originated in West Germany, 1952; for diocesan priests and unmarried deacons. Formally acknowledged by Rome in 1977. Address: Rev. Ronald J. Reicks, P.O. Box 337, Whittemore, Ia. 50598.

Rural Parish Workers of Christ the King: Originated in Cottleville, Mo., 1942; for women. An approved lay institute of apostolic action of the Archdiocese of St. Louis. Dedicated to the service of neighbor, especially in rural areas. Address: Box 300, Rt. 1, Cadet, Mo. 63630.

Schoenstatt Sisters of Mary: Originated in Schoenstatt, Germany, 1926; for women. Established as a secular institute of diocesan right May 20, 1948; of pontifical right Oct. 18, 1948. Addresses: Schoenstatt Sisters of Mary, W. 284 N. 404 Cherry Lane, Waukesha, Wis. 53188; House Schoenstatt, Star Rt. 1, Box 100, Rockport, Tex. 78382. International membership of more than 2,800.

Secular Institute of Pius X: Originated in Manchester, N.H., 1940; for priests and laymen. Approved as a secular institute, 1959 (first secular institute of diocesan right founded in the U.S. to be approved by the Holy See). Also admits married and unmarried men as associate members. Addresses: Lynchville Park, Goffstown, N.H. 03045. C.P. 1815, Quebec City, P.Q. G1K 7K7, Canada.

Servitium Christi Secular Institute of the Blessed Sacrament: Founded in Holland, 1952; for women. Approved as a secular institute of diocesan right May 8, 1963. Address: Miss Olympia Panagatos, 250 E. 77th St., Apt. 3B, New York, N.Y. 10021.

Society of Our Lady of the Way: Originated, 1936; for women. Approved as a secular institute of pontifical right Jan. 3, 1953. Addresses: 147 Dorado Terr., San Francisco, Calif. 94112; P.O. Box 412, Stamford, Conn. 06904; 2738 Noble Rd., No. 13B, Cleveland Heights, O. 44121. International membership, 300.

Teresian Institute: Founded in Spain 1911 by Pedro Poveda. Approved as an institute of pontifical right Jan. 11, 1924. Mailing Address: P.O. Box 14-3407, Coral Gables, Fla. 33114.

Voluntas Dei Institute: Originated in Canada, 1958; for secular priests, laymen and couples. Approved as a secular institute of diocesan right, May 6, 1965. Addresses: Institute Voluntas Dei, 6477 Lemay, Montreal, Que. H1T 2L6, Canada; U.S. delegate, Rev. Thomas Furlong. International membership of approximately 210.

The *Annuario Pontificio* lists the following secular institutes of pontifical right which are not established in the U.S.:

For men: Christ the King; Institute of Our Lady of Life; Institute of Prado; Priests of the Sacred Heart of Jesus.

For women: Alliance in Jesus through Mary; Apostles of the Sacred Heart; Catechists of Mary, Virgin and Mother; Catechists of the Sacred Heart of Jesus (Ukrainian); Cordimarian Filiation; Daughters of the Nativity of Mary; Daughters of the Queen of the Apostles; Daughters of the Sacred Heart; Evangelical Crusade; Faithful Servants of Jesus; Handmaids of Our Mother of Mercy; Institute of the Blessed Virgin Mary (della Strada); Institute of Notre Dame du Travail; Institute of Our Lady of Life; Institute of St. Boniface; Little Apostles of Charity;

Life and Peace in Christ Jesus; Missionaries of Royal Priesthood; Missionaries of the Sick; Oblates of Christ the King; Oblates of the Sacred Heart of Jesus; Servants of Jesus the Priest; Servite Secular Institute; Union of the Daughters of God; Workers of Divine Love; Workers of the Cross; Handmaids of Holy Church; Augustinian Auxiliary Missionaries; Heart of Jesus; Apostolic Missionaries of Charity; Combonian Secular Missionaries; Missionaries of the Gospel; Little Franciscan Family.

Associations

Caritas: Originated in New Orleans, 1950; for women. Follow guidelines of secular institutes. Small self-supporting groups who live and work among the poor and oppressed; work in Louisiana and Guatemala. Address: Box 308, Abita Springs, La. 70420.

Daughters of Our Lady of Fatima: Originated in Lansdowne, Pa., 1949; for women. Received diocesan approval, Jan., 1952. Address: Fatima House, Rolling Hills Rd., Ottsville, Pa. 18942.

Focolare Movement: Inaugurated in Trent, Italy, in 1943, by Chiara Lubich and a small group of companions; for men and women. Approved as an association of the faithful, 1962. It is not a secular institute by statute; however, vows are observed by its totally dedicated core membership of 4,000 who live in small communities called Focolare (Italian word for "hearth") centers. There are 16 resident centers in the U.S. and two in Canada. GEN (New Generation) is the youth organization of the movement. An estimated 70,000 are affiliated with the movement in the U.S. and Canada; 1,200,000, worldwide. Publications include *Living City,* monthly; *GEN II* and *GEN III* for young people and children. Five week-long summer conventions, called "Mariapolis" ("City of Mary"), are held annually. Address for information: P.O. Box 496, New York, N.Y. 10021 (indicate men's or women's branch).

Institute of Apostolic Oblates: Founded in Rome, Italy, 1947; for women. Address: 2125 W. Walnut Ave., Fullerton, Calif. 92633.

Jesus Caritas — Fraternity of Priests: An international association of priests who strive to live in the spirit of Charles de Foucauld, combining an active life with a contemplative calling. U.S. address: Rev. Michael Smith (National Responsible), P.O. Box 1471, Savannah, Ga. 31402.

Madonna House Apostolate: Originated in Toronto, Canada, 1930; for priests and lay persons. Diocesan pious union. Address: Madonna House, Combermere, Ontario, Canada K0J 1L0 — Jean Fox (women), Jim Guinan (men), Rev. Robert Pelton (priests). International membership and missions.

Pax Christi: Lay institute of men and women dedicated to witnessing to Christ, with special emphasis on service to the poor in Mississippi. Addresses: St. Francis Center, 708 Ave. I, Greenwood, Miss. 38930; LaVerna House, 2108 Altawoods Blvd., Jackson, Miss. 39204.

NFPC

The National Federation of Priests' Councils was organized by 233 delegates from 127 priests' organizations at a charter meeting held in Chicago May 20 and 21, 1968. Its stated purpose is to give priests' councils, a representative voice in matters of presbyteral, pastoral and ministerial concern to the U.S. and the universal Church.

SECULAR ORDERS

Secular orders (commonly called third orders) are societies of the faithful living in the world who seek to deepen their Christian life and apostolic commitment in association with and according to the spirit of various religious institutes. The orders are called "third" because their foundation followed the establishment of the first (for men) and second (for women) religious orders with which they are associated.

Augustine, Third Order Secular of St.: Founded, 13th century; approved Nov. 7, 1400.

Carmel (The Lay Carmelite Order) (Calced): Founded, 13th century; approved by Pope Nicholas V, Oct. 7, 1452. Revised rule approved November, 1977. Address: Aylesford, National Scapular Center, I-55 and Cass Ave. N. Darien, Ill. 60559. Approximately 16,500 members in U.S.

Carmelites, The Secular Order of Discalced (formerly the Third Order Secular of the Blessed Virgin Mary of Mt Carmel and of St. Teresa of Jesus): Rule based on the Carmelite reform established by St. Teresa and St. John of the Cross, 16th century; approved Mar. 23, 1594. Revised rule approved May 10, 1979. Office of National Secretariat, U.S.A.; P.O. Box 3079, San Jose, Calif. 95156. Approximately 22,245 throughout the world; 1,800 in U.S.

Dominican Laity: Founded in the 13th century. Addresses of provincial coordinators: 487 Michigan Ave. N.E., Washington, D.C. 20017; 1909 S.

Ashland Ave., Chicago, Ill. 60608; 374 N.E. Clarkamas St., Portland, Ore. 97232, 3407 Napoleon Ave., New Orleans, La. 70125.

Franciscan Order, Secular (SFO): Founded, 1209 by St. Francis of Assisi; approved Aug. 30, 1221. National minister, James David Lynch, 4143 "J" St., Juniata Park, Philadelphia, Pa. 19124. Approximately 780,000 throughout the world; 40,000 in U.S.

Mary, Third Order of: Founded, Dec. 8, 1850; rule approved by the Holy See, 1857. Addresses of provincial directors: 815 Varnum St. N.E., Washington, D.C. 20017; 7 Harvard St., P.O. Box 66, Charlestown, Mass. 02129; 566 Bush St., San Francisco, Calif. 94108. Approximately 14,000 in the world, 5,600 in U.S.

Mary, Secular Order of Servants of (Servite): Founded, 1233; approved, 1304. Revised rule approved 1986. Address: Assistant for Secular Order, 3401 S. Home Ave., Berwyn, Ill. 60402.

Mercy, Secular Third Order of Our Lady of (Mercedarian): Founded, 1219 by St. Peter Nolasco; approved the same year.

Norbert, Third Order of St.: Founded, 1122 by St. Norbert; approved by Pope Honorius II, 1126. Address: St. Norbert Abbey, De Pere, Wis. 54115.

Trinity, Third Order Secular of the Most Holy: Founded 1198; approved, 1219.

Oblates of St. Benedict are lay persons affiliated with a Benedictine abbey or monastery who strive to direct their lives, as circumstances permit, according to the spirit and Rule of St. Benedict.

MISSIONARY ACTIVITY OF THE CHURCH

UNITED STATES FOREIGN MISSIONARIES

Data on U.S. foreign missionary personnel in the following tables were gathered by, and are reproduced with permission of, the United States Catholic Mission Association, 1233 Lawrence St. N.E., Washington, D.C. 20017.

For additional information about the Church in mission areas, see News Events and other Almanac entries.

Field Distribution, 1986

Under this and following headings, Alaska, Hawaii, etc., are considered abroad because they are outside the 48 contiguous states.

Africa: 944 (469 men, 475 women). Largest numbers in Kenya, 193; Tanzania, 149; Ghana, 85; Zambia, 75; Liberia, 50.

Near East: 73 (52 men, 21 women). Largest numbers in Israel, 41; Egypt, 16; Lebanon, 5.

Far East: 1,356 (916 men, 440 women). Largest numbers in Philippines, 356; Japan, 303; Taiwan, 162; Korea, 125; India, 97; Hong Kong, 81.

Oceania: 631 (317 men, 314 women). Largest numbers in Hawaii, 210; Papua New Guinea, 200; Australia, 58; Caroline Islands, 48; Mariana Islands, 46; Samoa, 19.

Europe: 28 (16 men, 12 women). Largest numbers in Sweden, 10; Denmark, 7; Finland, 6.

North America: 306 (135 men, 171 women). Larg-

est numbers in Alaska, 175; Canada, 127.

Caribbean Islands: 495 (272 men, 223 women). Largest numbers in Puerto Rico, 208; Jamaica, 114; Bahamas, 44; Dominican Republic, 41; Haiti, 40.

Central America: 743 (426 men, 317 women). Largest numbers in Mexico, 235; Guatemala, 186.

South America: 1,461 (746 men, 715 women). Largest numbers in Peru, 444; Brazil, 421; Bolivia, 213; Chile, 166.

TOTAL: 6,037 (3,352 men, 2,685 women).

Men Religious, 1986

Ninety mission-sending groups had 3,035 priests and brothers in overseas assignments.

Jesuits: 513 in 42 countries; largest group, 84 in the Philippines.

Maryknoll Fathers: 504 in 25 countries; largest group, 51 in Tanzania.

Franciscans (O.F.M.): 202 in 27 countries; largest group, 54 in Brazil.

Divine Word Missionaries: 156 in 17 countries; largest group, 52 in Papua New Guinea.

Redemptorists: 141 in 7 countries; largest group, 54 in Brazil.

Oblates of Mary Immaculate: 139 in 17 countries; largest group, 26 in Brazil.

U.S. FOREIGN MISSIONARIES, 1960-1986

Year	Diocesan Priests	Religious Priests	Religious Brothers	Religious Sisters	Seminarians	Lay Persons	Total
1960	14	3018	575	2827	170	178	6782
1962	31	3172	720	2764	152	307	7146
1964	80	3438	782	3137	157	532	8126
1966	215	3731	901	3706	201	549	9303
1968	282	3727	869	4150	208	419	9655
1970	373	3117	666	3824	90	303	8373
1972+	246	3182	634	3121	97	376	7656
1973	237	3913*		3012		529	7691
1974	220	3084	639	2916	101	458	7418
1975	197	3023	669	2850	65	344	7148
1976	193	2961	691	2840	68	257	7010
1977	182	2882	630	2781	42	243	6760
1978	166	2830	610	2673	43	279	6601
1979	187	2800	592	2568	50	258	6455
1980	188	2750	592	2592	50	221	6393
1981	187	2702	584	2574	43	234	6324
1982	178	2668	578	2560	44	217	6245
1983	174	2668	569	2540	48	247	6246
1984	187	2603	549	2492	40	263	6134
1985	171	2500	558	2505	30	292	6056
1986	204	2473	532	2481	30	317	6037

+A corrected total for 1972 should read 7937, indicating losses of 436 from 1970 to 1972 and 246 from 1972 to 1973.
*Includes religious brothers and seminarians.

FIELD DISTRIBUTION BY AREAS, 1960-1986

Year	Africa	Far East	Near East	Oce- ania	Europe	N. Amer.	Carib. Is.	Cent. Amer.	S. Amer.	Total
1960	781	1959	111	986	203	337	991	433	981	6782
1962	901	2110	75	992	93	224	967	537	1247	7146
1964	1025	2332	122	846	69	220	1056	660	1796	8126
1966	1184	2453	142	953	38	211	1079	857	2386	9303
1968	1157	2470	128	1027	33	251	1198	936	2455	9655
1970	1141	2137	39	900	38	233	1067	738	2080	8373
1972	1107	1955	59	826	39	234	819	728	1889	7656
1973	1229	1962	54	811	40	253	796	763	1783	7691
1974	1121	1845	60	883	43	241	757	752	1716	7418
1975	1065	1814	71	808	37	252	698	734	1669	7148
1976	1042	1757	68	795	34	313	671	712	1618	7010
1977	1003	1659	62	784	34	296	629	702	1591	6760
1978	966	1601	57	769	34	339	593	705	1537	6601
1979	923	1562	65	743	37	332	562	686	1545	6455
1980	909	1576	65	711	35	294	548	699	1556	6393
1981	946	1529	70	696	36	315	511	693	1528	6324
1982	956	1501	62	673	32	319	522	669	1511	6245
1983	990	1468	68	640	34	346	517	650	1533	6246
1984	967	1420	84	644	29	329	513	650	1498	6134
1985	986	1366	78	650	31	312	500	692	1441	6056
1986	944	1356	73	631	28	306	495	743	1461	6037

Capuchins (O.F.M. Cap): 129 in 11 countries; largest group, 27 in Papua New Guinea.

Marianists: 106 in 13 countries; largest group, 28 in Hawaii.

Benedictines: 84 in 14 countries; largest group, 22 in Guatemala.

Columbans: 60 in 13 countries; largest group, 22 in the Philippines.

Conventual Franciscans (O.F.M. Conv): 59 in 9 countries; largest group, 14 in Canada.

Dominicans: 57 in 11 countries; largest groups, 14 each in Nigeria and Pakistan.

Brothers of the Christian Schools: 56 in 15 countries; largest group, 15 in the Philippines.

Holy Cross Fathers: 55 in 9 countries; largest group, 18 in Bangladesh.

Holy Ghost Fathers: 47 in 6 countries; largest group, 20 in Tanzania.

Holy Cross Brothers: 42 in 8 countries; largest group, 16 in Brazil.

Passionists: 41 in 7 countries; largest group, 19 in the Philippines.

La Salette Fathers: 40 in 7 countries; largest group, 14 in Argentina.

Vincentians: 38 in 6 countries; largest group, 19 in Panama.

Congregation of Christian Brothers: 32 in 5 countries; largest group, 16 in Peru.

Salesians: 28 in 10 countries; largest group, 9 in Canada.

Missionaries of the Sacred Heart: 27 in 4 countries; largest group, 19 in Papua New Guinea.

Marist Fathers: 27 in 7 countries; largest group, 9 in Hawaii.

Augustinians: 26 in 3 countries; largest group, 16 in Peru.

Missionaries of Africa: 21 in 9 countries; largest group, 5 in Ghana.

Marist Brothers: 21 in 5 countries; largest group, 10 in the Philippines.

Comboni Missionaries: 20 in 7 countries; largest group, 5 in Kenya.

Sixty-three other mission-sending institutes had 19 or less members in overseas assignments.

Diocesan Priests, 1986

Two hundred and four diocesan priests from 90 dioceses were in overseas assignments in 1986.

The largest groups were from Boston (17 in 4 countries) and St. Louis (9 in 2 countries).

Thirty-nine of the diocesan priests in overseas assignments were members of the Missionary Society of St. James the Apostle, founded by Cardinal Richard J. Cushing of Boston in 1958. Address: 24 Clark St., Boston, Mass. 02109.

Twenty-seven other diocesan priests in overseas assignments were working as priest associates with the Maryknoll Fathers, whose headquarters are in Maryknoll, New York 10545.

Sisters, 1986

Two hundred and 28 mission-sending groups had 2,481 sisters in overseas assignments.

Maryknoll Sisters: 373 in 25 countries; largest group, 50 in Hawaii.

School Sisters of Notre Dame: 110 in 18 countries; largest group, 15 in Guatemala.

Marist Sisters: 77 in 14 countries; largest group, 16 in Papua New Guinea.

Daughters of Charity: 60 in 11 countries; largest group, 26 in Bolivia.

Sisters of Notre Dame de Namur: 59 in 8 countries; largest group, 18 in Kenya.

Medical Mission Sisters: 53 in 13 countries; largest group, 15 in Ghana.

Sisters of St. Joseph (Carondelet): 52 in 4 countries; largest group, 23 in Hawaii.

Sisters, Servants of the Immaculate Heart of Mary (Philadelphia): 46 in 2 countries; larger group, 34 in Peru.

Benedictine Sisters: 42 in 11 countries: largest group, 10 in Colombia.

Sisters of the Holy Cross: 39 in 6 countries; largest group, 16 in Brazil.

Society of the Sacred Heart: 36 in 13 countries; largest group, 15 in Japan.

Ursulines of the Roman Union: 35 in 13 countries; largest group, 8 in Thailand.

Franciscan Missionaries of Mary: 31 in 17 countries; largest groups, 4 in Liberia.

Sisters of Mercy of the Union in the U.S.A.: 28 in 9 countries; largest group, 11 in Jamaica.

Sisters of the Holy Family of Nazareth: 28 in 5 countries; largest group, 16 in Australia.

Servants of the Holy Spirit: 27 in 7 countries; largest group, 8 in Ghana.

Sisters of the Third Franciscan Order, Minor Conventuals (Syracuse): 27 in 3 countries; largest group, 17 in Hawaii.

Sisters of St. Joseph (Brentwood): 23 in 3 countries; largest group, 20 in Puerto Rico.

Sisters of Notre Dame: 23 in 2 countries; larger group, 12 in Papua New Guinea.

Sisters of the Assumption B.V.M.: 22 in 3 countries; largest group, 19 in Canada.

Franciscan Sisters of Allegany: 22 in 2 countries; larger group, 17 in Jamaica.

Sisters of the Presentation B.V.M.: 22 in 7 countries; largest group, 6 in Mexico.

Sisters, Servants of the Immaculate Heart of Mary (Monroe): 21 in 7 countries; largest group, 5 in Puerto Rico.

Little Sisters of the Poor: 20 in 12 countries; largest group, 4 in India.

Two hundred and four other mission-sending institutes had 19 or less members in overseas assignments.

Lay Volunteers, 1986

Three hundred and 17 lay volunteers of 34 sponsoring organizations were in overseas assignments in 1986.

Maryknoll Lay Missioners: 89 in 18 countries; largest group, 21 in Venezuela.

Jesuit Volunteer Corps: 39 in Alaska.

Lay Mission Helpers: 26 in 8 countries; largest group, 9 in Papua New Guinea.

Jesuit International Volunteers: 22 in 3 countries; largest group, 12 in Belize.

Volunteer Missionary Movement: 18 in 6 countries; largest group, 5 in Uganda.

Holy Cross Associates: 13 in 3 countries; largest group, 10 in Chile.

Society of Our Lady of the Most Holy Trinity: 12 in 3 countries; largest group, 10 in Belize.

Frontier Apostolate: 10 in Canada.

Diocese of Davenport: 10 in 5 countries; largest group, 4 in Mexico.

Catholic Medical Mission Board: 8 in 3 countries; largest group, 4 in Papua New Guinea. (This figure represents those whose term of service was for at least one year. In addition, 36 short-term volunteers served in 7 countries during the year.)

The other twenty-four sponsoring organizations had 7 members or less in overseas assignments.

U.S. MISSION ASSOCIATION

The United States Catholic Mission Association, juridically established Sept. 1, 1981, continues the activities and functions of the former U.S. Catholic Mission Council.

According to existing bylaws approved by the general assembly May 25, 1982, the USCMA is "open to all those who seek to promote global mission in community with others. It is envisioned to be an experience of the renewed Church, in which all members are equal. The methods of decision-making, of financial support, and of committee service reflect the underlying ecclesiology." The purpose of the association is the "promotion of global mission. Its primary focus is cross-cultural mission, with special emphasis on international justice."

Typical activities of the association are educational efforts related to the Church's teaching about its missionary nature, sponsorship of conferences on theological and pastoral foundations of missionary endeavor, liaison and cooperation with missionary bodies of other Christian churches, training programs and refresher courses for departing and returning missionaries, and general mission animation. The USCMA is responsible for gathering and publishing annual statistical data on U.S. missionary personnel overseas. It publishes the data in the annual, *Mission Handbook.* Ten times a year, the association publishes *Mission Intercom,* a newsletter with brief information on the life and activities of the Church in the six continents.

The president of the association is Sister Mary Louise Lynch, S.C.M.M., and the executive director is Rev. Joseph R. Lang, M.M. The office is located at 1233 Lawrence St. N.E., Washington, D.C. 20017.

HOME MISSIONS

The expression "home missions" is applied to places in the U.S. where the local church does not have its own resources, human and otherwise, which are needed to begin or, if begun, to survive and grow. These areas share the name "missions" with their counterparts in foreign lands because they too need outside help to provide the personnel and means for making the Church present and active there in carrying out its mission for the salvation of people.

Dioceses in the Southeast, the Southwest, and the Far West are most urgently in need of outside help to carry on the work of the Church. Millions of persons live in counties in which there are no resident priests. Many others live in rural areas beyond the reach and influence of a Catholic center. According to recent statistics compiled by the Glenmary Research Center, there are approximately 545 priestless counties in the United States. Many states generally thought to be well off from a pastoral standpoint include areas in which the Catholic Church and the ministry of priests are virtually unknown.

About 20 per cent of the total U.S. population and less than three per cent of the Catholic population live within the boundaries of the 17 "most missionary" dioceses of the country. A "Survey of the Catholic Weakness" conducted by the National Catholic Rural Life Conference disclosed that the Catholic Church ranked near the bottom of about 40 religious bodies in percentage of rural membership.

Mission Workers

A number of forces are at work to meet the pastoral needs of these missionary areas and to establish permanent churches and operating institutions where they are required. In many dioceses, one or more missions and stations are attended from established parishes and are gradually growing to independent status. Priests, brothers and sisters belonging to scores of religious institutes are engaged full-time in the home missions. Lay persons, some of them in affiliation with special groups and movements, are also involved.

The Society for the Propagation of the Faith, which conducts an annual collection for mission support in all parishes of the U.S., allocates 40 per cent of this sum for disbursement to home missions through the American Board of Catholic Missions.

The Catholic Church Extension Society provides one million dollars or more a year for the building of mission installations and related needs.

Special mission support is the purpose of the Commission for the Catholic Missions among the Colored People and the Indians.

Various mission-aid societies frequently undertake projects in behalf of the home missions.

The **Glenmary Home Missioners,** founded by Father W. Howard Bishop in 1939, is the only home mission society established for the sole purpose of carrying out the pastoral ministry in small towns and rural districts of the United States. Glenmary serves in many areas where at least 20 per cent of the people live in poverty and less than one per cent are Catholic. With 69 priests and 24 professed brothers as of March, 1986, the Glenmary Missioners had 39 parishes and 39 missions in the archdioceses of Atlanta and Cincinnati, and in the dioceses of Birmingham, Charlotte, Covington, Dallas, Little Rock, Nashville, Jackson, Tulsa, Owensboro, Savannah, Richmond and Wheeling-Charleston. National headquarters are located at 4119 Glenmary Trace, Fairfield, O. The mailing address is P.O. Box 465618, Cincinnati, O. 45246.

Organizations

The Commission for Catholic Missions among the Colored People and the Indians: Organized officially in 1885 by decree of the Third Plenary Council of Baltimore; now also known as the Black and Indian Mission Office. Provides financial support for religious works among Blacks and Indians in 133 archdioceses and dioceses through funds raised by an annual collection in all parishes of the U.S. on the first Sunday of Lent, the designated Sunday. In 1985, over $5 million was raised. Cardinal John Krol is president of the board; Msgr. Paul A. Lenz is secretary. Headquarters: 2021 H St. N.W., Washington, D.C. 20006.

Bureau of Catholic Indian Missions: Established in 1874 as the representative of Catholic Indian missions before the federal government and the public; made permanent organization in 1884 by Third Plenary Council of Baltimore. After a remarkable history of rendering important services to the Indian people, the bureau continues to represent the Catholic Church in the U.S. in her apostolate to the American Indian. Concerns are evangelization. catechesis, liturgy, family life, education, advocacy. Cardinal John Krol is president of the board; Msgr. Paul A. Lenz is secretary. Address: 2021 H St., Washington, D.C. 20006.

Latest statistics of the bureau reported 285,354 Catholics (19 percent) in a total Indian population of 1,486,000. Among dioceses with the largest numbers of Catholic Indians: Santa Fe (archdiocese), 41,000; Gallup, N.M., 32,000; Tuscon, Ariz., 21,000; Santa Rosa, Calif., 16,000; Rapid City, S.D., 15,000; Great Falls-Billings, Mont., 14,000.

Catholic Negro-American Mission Board (1907): Support priests and sisters in southern states and provide monthly support to sisters and lay teachers in the poorest Black schools. In 1985, grants of nearly $250,000 were allocated to 27 needy schools. Cardinal John Krol is president of the board; Msgr. Paul A. Lenz is executive director; Patricia L. O'Rourke, administrator. Address: 2021 H St. N.W., Washington, D.C. 20005.

The Catholic Church Extension Society (1905): Established for the purpose of preserving and extending the Church in the U.S. and its dependencies principally through the collection and disbursement of funds for missions. Since the time of its founding, more than $100 million have been received and expended for this purpose. Disbursements in fiscal year 1985-86 were in excess of $11 million. Works of the society are supervised by a 12-member board of governors: Cardinal Joseph Bernardin, archbishop of Chicago, chancellor; Very Rev. Edward J. Slattery, president; five bishops, one sister and four laymen. Headquarters: 35 E. Wacker Drive, Chicago, Ill. 60601.

Rural Ministry Institute: The Edwin Vincent O'Hara Institute for Rural Ministry Education was founded in 1978 to provide training and other resource services for priests, seminarians religious and lay persons beginning or already involved in rural ministry. Brother David Andrews, C.S.C., is director. Address: 3700 Oakview Terr., N.E., Washington, D.C. 20017.

Tekakwitha Conference: Established in 1939, as a missionary priest advisory group in the Fargo, N.D., diocese. It became (1946-77) a missionary priest support group and, since 1977, a gathering of Catholic Native peoples together with men and women — clerical, Religious and lay — who minister with Native Catholic communities. The primary focus is evangelization, with specific emphasis on development of Native ministry and leadership. Other areas of priority include catechesis, liturgy, family life, social justice ministry, chemical dependency, youth ministry, spirituality and Native Catholic dialogue. The annual Conference serves as an opportunity for exchange of ideas, approaches, prayer and mutual support. Publications include a quarterly Newsletter. The conference has a nine-member board of directors the majority of whom are Native people. Most Rev. John F. Kinney of Bismarck is episcopal moderator; Rev. Gilbert F. Hemauer, O.F.M. Cap., is executive director; Rev. John Hascall O.F.M. Cap., is president. Address: P.O. Box 6759 Great Falls, Mont. 59405.

APPALACHIA COMMITTEE

The 600-member Catholic Committee of Appalachia consists of bishops, priests, religious and lay persons engaged in pastoral and social justice ministry in the 13-state region. Appalachia has been defined by Congress as including all of West Virginia and parts of Alabama, Georgia, Kentucky, Maryland, Mississippi, New York, North Carolina, Ohio, Pennsylvania, South Carolina, Tennessee and Virginia. The committee is the Catholic Caucus of the Commission on Religious in Appalachia, an interfaith group.

Address: P.O. Box 953, Whiteburg, Ky 41858.

Bishop William A. Hughes of Covington said May 18, 1985, that the 10th anniversary of a pastoral letter on powerlessness in Appalachia called for a "rededication" to the poor of the region.

EDUCATION

LEGAL STATUS OF CATHOLIC EDUCATION

The right of private schools to exist and operate in the United States is recognized in law. It was confirmed by the U.S. Supreme Court in 1925 when the tribunal ruled (Pierce v. Society of Sisters, see Church-State Decisions of the Supreme Court) that an Oregon state law requiring all children to attend public schools was unconstitutional.

Private schools are obliged to comply with the education laws in force in the various states regarding such matters as required basic curricula, periods of attendance, and standards for proper accreditation.

The special curricula and standards of private schools are determined by the schools themselves. Thus, in Catholic schools, the curricula include not only the subject matter required by state educational laws but also other fields of study, principally, education in the Catholic faith.

The Supreme Court has ruled that the First Amendment to the U.S. Constitution, in accordance with the No Establishment of Religion Clause of the First Amendment, prohibits direct federal and state aid from public funds to church-affiliated schools. (See several cases in Church-State Decisions of the Supreme Court.)

Public Aid

This prohibition does not extend to all child-benefit and public-purpose programs of aid to students of non-public elementary and secondary schools.

Statutes authorizing such programs have been ruled constitutional on the grounds that they:

• have a "secular legislative purpose";
• neither inhibit nor advance religion as a "principal or primary effect";

• do not foster "excessive government entanglement with religion."

Aid programs considered constitutional have provided bus transportation, textbook loans, school lunches and health services, and "secular, neutral or non-ideological services, facilities and materials provided in common to all school children," public and non-public.

The first major aid to education program in U.S. history containing provisions benefitting nonpublic school students was enacted by the 89th Congress and signed into law by President Lyndon B. Johnson Apr. 11, 1965. The Elementary and Secondary Education Act was designed to avoid the separation of Church and state impasse which had blocked all earlier aid proposals pertaining to nonpublic, and especially church-affiliated, schools. The objective of the program, under public control, is to serve the public purpose by aiding disadvantaged pupils in nonpublic as well as public schools.

In a highly significant 5-to-4 decision June 29, 1983, the U.S. Supreme Court upheld the constitutionality of a Minnesota tuition tax credit for the parents of students attending parochial, other private and public schools. The majority opinion rejected arguments that the law benefitted religion in an unconstitutional manner, and said that the program did not involve excessive church-state entanglement. Supporters of the measure called it sound tax policy.

With respect to college and university education in church-affiliated institutions, the Supreme Court has upheld the constitutionality of statutes providing student loans and, under the Federal Higher Education Facilities Act of 1963, construction loans and grants for secular-purpose facilities.

Catholic schools are exempt from real estate taxation in all of the states. Since Jan. 1, 1959, nonprofit parochial and private schools have also been exempt from several federal excise taxes.

Shared and Released Time

In a shared time program of education, students enrolled in Catholic or other church-related schools take some courses (e.g., religion, social studies, fine arts) in their own schools and others (e.g., science, mathematics, industrial arts) in public schools. Such a program has been given serious consideration in recent years by Catholic and other educators. Its constitutionality has not been seriously challenged, but practical problems — relating to teacher and student schedules, transportation, adjustment to new programs, and other factors — are knotty.

Several million children of elementary and high school age of all denominations have the opportunity of receiving religious instruction on released time. Under released time programs they are permitted to leave their public schools during school hours to attend religious instruction classes held off the public school premises. They are released at the request of their parents. Public school authorities merely provide for their dismissal, and take no part in the program.

CATHOLIC SCHOOLS AND STUDENTS IN THE UNITED STATES

(Source: *The Official Catholic Directory, 1986;* figures as of Jan. 1, 1986. Archdioceses are indicated by an asterisk.)

Section, State Diocese	Univs. Colleges	Students	High Schools	Students	Elem. Schools	Students
NEW ENGLAND	26	57,679	120	65,940	529	137,844
Maine, Portland	1	518	3	1,004	22	4,821
New Hampshire, Manchester	5	5,249	6	2,402	22	7,342
Vermont, Burlington	3	2,740	3	1,052	11	2,390
Massachusetts	9	29,579	65	34,858	242	68,994
*Boston	4	19,005	49	23,829	161	45,082
Fall River	1	2,800	4	3,400	24	6,710
Springfield	1	890	4	3,207	33	10,236
Worcester	3	6,884	8	4,422	24	6,966
Rhode Island, Providence	2	7,579	11	6,068	64	15,925
Connecticut	6	12,014	32	20,556	168	38,372
*Hartford	3	1,928	15	11,151	99	22,342
Bridgeport	2	9,936	10	6,200	48	11,822
Norwich	1	150	7	3,205	21	4,208
MIDDLE ATLANTIC	64	176,505	350	217,840	2,031	590,929
New York	30	96,969	151	96,678	876	266,126
*New York	12	52,136	63	34,290	271	84,631
Albany	4	6,600	13	4,406	55	12,939
Brooklyn	2	20,121	22	25,125	173	74,703
Buffalo	6	12,276	20	8,829	123	27,886
Ogdensburg	2	555	3	773	25	4,654
Rochester	—	—	8	5,909	79	18,608
Rockville Centre	2	3,038	14	13,849	88	31,103
Syracuse	2	2,243	8	3,497	62	11,602

Section, State Diocese	Univs. Colleges	Students	High Schools	Students	Elem. Schools	Students
New Jersey	8	16,331	85	48,207	440	118,160
*Newark	4	13,691	42	20,180	194	48,870
Camden	—	—	11	7,664	64	16,344
Metuchen	—	—	8	4,888	53	13,530
Paterson	3	1,032	13	5,442	65	16,088
Trenton	1	1,608	11	10,033	64	23,328
Pennsylvania	26	63,205	114	72,955	715	206,643
*Philadelphia	10	29,589	50	44,150	273	107,460
Allentown	2	1,956	10	4,557	64	13,902
Altoona-Johnstown	2	2,145	3	1,637	37	7,251
Erie	3	6,445	9	3,704	47	13,310
Greensburg	2	2,068	2	1,339	50	8,371
Harrisburg	—	—	10	4,474	50	11,734
Pittsburgh	3	9,525	19	8,284	137	32,924
Scranton	4	11,477	11	4,810	57	11,691
SOUTH ATLANTIC	14	40,937	126	61,044	544	149,345
Delaware, Wilmington	—	—	8	4,792	30	9,975
Maryland, *Baltimore	3	8,245	24	11,324	98	25,798
District of Columbia, *Washington	3	19,364	24	9,840	84	22,282
Virginia	2	2,334	15	6,023	55	16,026
Arlington	2	2,334	5	3,549	29	9,284
Richmond	—	—	10	2,474	26	6,742
West Virginia, Wheeling-Charleston	1	1,098	9	1,766	32	5,255
North Carolina	2	1,297	3	1,240	32	7,205
Charlotte	2	1,297	2	948	15	3,663
Raleigh	—	—	1	292	17	3,542
South Carolina, Charleston	—	—	4	1,418	28	5,092
Georgia	—	—	7	3,940	29	9,061
*Atlanta	—	—	2	1,791	13	4,427
Savannah	—	—	5	2,149	16	4,634
Florida	3	8,599	32	20,701	156	48,651
*Miami	2	7,478	13	9,678	53	19,321
Orlando	—	—	4	2,111	26	7,191
Palm Beach	—	—	4	2,852	14	4,346
Pensacola-Tallahassee	—	—	1	463	9	2,230
St. Augustine	—	—	2	1,368	16	4,658
St. Petersburg	1	1,121	5	2,997	30	8,623
Venice	—	—	3	1,232	8	2,282
EAST NORTH CENTRAL	56	128,152	298	183,914	2,078	552,750
Ohio	11	26,128	85	53,549	501	151,384
*Cincinnati	4	16,011	21	16,165	120	38,190
Cleveland	3	5,862	26	18,961	166	57,744
Columbus	1	1,247	14	5,631	52	13,611
Steubenville	1	1,010	3	913	16	2,756
Toledo	1	773	15	8,066	91	24,322
Youngstown	1	1,225	6	3,813	56	14,761
Indiana	9	17,336	24	12,953	204	44,714
*Indianapolis	2	1,770	9	4,998	71	14,930
Evansville	—	—	5	1,818	29	4,806
Ft. Wayne-South Bend	5	13,646	4	2,982	43	11,247
Gary	1	1,073	4	2,781	40	10,180
Lafayette	1	847	2	374	21	3,551
Illinois	19	44,812	96	69,855	637	189,391
*Chicago	13	35,982	58	49,713	358	124,886
Belleville	1	1,036	4	2,116	52	8,528
Joliet	3	5,998	9	7,092	61	17,986
Peoria	—	—	8	3,527	57	12,884
Rockford	—	—	8	4,128	45	11,762
Springfield	2	1,796	9	3,279	64	13,345

Section, State Diocese	Univs. Colleges	Students	High Schools	Students	Elem. Schools	Students
Michigan	8	18,804	62	31,879	333	88,902
*Detroit	5	14,024	42	23,121	158	53,036
Gaylord	—	—	5	779	20	3,528
Grand Rapids	1	2,724	4	2,590	46	9,283
Kalamazoo	1	856	3	981	21	4,556
Lansing	1	1,200	5	3,414	41	10,569
Marquette	—	—	—	—	12	2,291
Saginaw	—	—	3	994	35	5,639
Wisconsin	9	21,072	31	15,678	403	78,359
*Milwaukee	5	17,026	13	9,062	168	38,023
Green Bay	2	2,221	9	3,191	93	17,183
La Crosse	1	1,045	7	2,494	75	11,999
Madison	1	780	2	931	46	7,902
Superior	—	—	—	—	21	3,252
EAST SOUTH CENTRAL	8	8,809	51	23,912	275	62,437
Kentucky	5	6,015	26	12,336	150	34,395
*Louisville	3	4,071	10	7,226	76	18,531
Covington	1	1,200	12	3,624	50	10,736
Owensboro	1	744	4	1,486	24	5,128
Tennessee	2	1,852	10	4,590	40	9,209
Memphis	1	1,542	5	2,370	15	4,062
Nashville	1	310	5	2,220	25	5,147
Alabama	1	942	6	4,026	50	11,433
*Mobile	1	942	3	1,679	27	6,539
Birmingham	—	—	3	2,347	23	4,894
Mississippi	—	—	9	2,960	35	7,400
Biloxi	—	—	5	1,836	16	2,818
Jackson	—	—	4	1,124	19	4,582
WEST NORTH CENTRAL	34	56,522	153	61,898	901	190,399
Minnesota	9	17,044	23	11,470	225	47,805
*St. Paul and Minneapolis	3	9,939	14	8,620	111	29,026
Crookston	—	—	1	132	11	1,678
Duluth	1	1,449	—	—	14	1,582
New Ulm	—	—	3	529	26	3,799
St. Cloud	3	3,691	3	884	37	6,850
Winona	2	1,965	2	1,305	26	4,870
Iowa	7	9,703	29	10,367	151	30,387
*Dubuque	3	4,176	11	4,208	58	13,988
Davenport	3	4,210	7	1,482	38	4,969
Des Moines	—	—	2	1,823	19	4,043
Sioux City	1	1,317	9	2,854	36	7,387
Missouri	6	15,878	45	22,747	277	64,904
*St. Louis	4	11,484	32	17,401	178	45,696
Jefferson City	—	—	2	916	35	5,746
Kansas City-St. Joseph	2	4,394	8	3,787	42	10,874
Springfield-Cape Girardeau	—	—	3	643	22	2,588
North Dakota	2	1,358	1	1,860	33	5,072
Bismarck	1	1,193	—	1,386	18	2,502
Fargo	1	165	1	474	15	2,570
South Dakota	2	867	5	1,444	27	4,561
Rapid City	—	—	2	394	3	668
Sioux Falls	2	867	3	1,050	24	3,893
Nebraska	2	6,934	33	8,265	94	18,840
*Omaha	2	6,934	20	6,006	62	13,612
Grand Island	—	—	7	1,050	8	943
Lincoln	—	—	6	1,209	24	4,285
Kansas	6	4,738	17	5,745	94	18,830
*Kansas City	3	2,681	7	3,085	39	9,247
Dodge City	1	624	—	—	12	1,662
Salina	1	624	6	892	12	1,956
Wichita	1	809	4	1,768	31	5,965

Section, State Diocese	Univs. Colleges	Students	High Schools	Students	Elem. Schools	Students
WEST SOUTH CENTRAL	11	20,983	121	49,067	499	152,391
Arkansas, Little Rock	—	—	6	1,843	35	5,674
Louisiana	3	7,365	62	29,508	201	81,547
*New Orleans	3	7,365	27	17,795	95	41,723
Alexandria-Shreveport	—	—	7	2,021	23	5,897
Baton Rouge	—	—	10	4,264	28	15,195
Houma-Thibodaux	—	—	3	1,274	12	4,495
Lafayette	—	—	13	3,555	33	11,580
Lake Charles	—	—	2	599	10	2,657
Oklahoma	1	325	5	2,193	28	5,695
*Oklahoma City	1	325	2	970	16	3,000
Tulsa	—	—	3	1,223	12	2,695
Texas	7	13,293	48	15,523	235	59,475
*San Antonio	4	6,427	10	3,121	35	12,580
Amarillo	—	—	1	142	8	1,277
Austin	1	2,502	2	289	16	3,433
Beaumont	—	—	1	513	9	1,821
Brownsville	—	—	2	813	8	1,928
Corpus Christi	—	—	3	713	27	5,759
Dallas	1	2,553	9	3,073	35	9,687
El Paso	—	—	3	1,067	14	3,376
Fort Worth	—	—	4	1,460	15	4,084
Galveston-Houston	1	1,811	9	3,810	50	11,926
Lubbock	—	—	—	—	3	558
San Angelo	—	—	—	—	3	589
Victoria	—	—	4	522	12	2,457
MOUNTAIN	6	9,838	35	14,276	182	42,488
Montana	2	2,579	5	938	20	2,772
Great Falls-Billings	1	1,078	3	500	17	2,244
Helena	1	1,501	2	438	3	528
Idaho, Boise	1	48	1	424	13	1,800
Wyoming, Cheyenne	—	—	1	106	6	1,300
Colorado	1	5,111	9	3,160	50	11,734
*Denver	1	5,111	6	2,631	38	9,314
Colorado Springs	—	—	1	325	5	1,171
Pueblo	—	—	2	204	7	1,249
New Mexico	2	2,100	6	1,919	28	7,321
*Santa Fe	2	2,100	4	1,744	21	5,113
Gallup	—	—	2	175	1	1,558
Las Cruces	—	—	—	—	6	650
Arizona	—	—	9	5,076	46	12,357
Phoenix	—	—	6	3,639	25	7,530
Tucson	—	—	3	1,437	21	4,827
Utah, Salt Lake City	—	—	2	1,090	8	2,123
Nevada, Reno-Las Vegas	—	—	2	1,563	11	3,081
PACIFIC	22	45,600	159	88,179	780	214,429
Washington	3	8,002	11	6,806	81	18,118
*Seattle	2	4,885	8	5,594	58	13,316
Spokane	1	3,117	2	1,015	16	3,359
Yakima	—	—	1	197	7	1,443
Oregon	2	3,911	9	3,475	53	8,747
*Portland	2	3,911	8	3,364	49	8,011
Baker	—	—	1	111	4	736
California	16	32,649	129	74,223	613	177,986
*Los Angeles	5	8,850	60	35,377	237	72,555
*San Francisco	3	7,040	18	9,545	70	21,530
Fresno	—	—	2	1,290	25	5,786
Monterey	—	—	5	1,271	14	3,614
Oakland	4	3,770	10	6,317	56	15,216
Orange	1	100	5	4,118	36	13,404

Section, State Diocese	Univs. Colleges	Students	High Schools	Students	Elem. Schools	Students
California	—	—				
Sacramento	—	—·	8	3,697	43	10,667
San Bernardino	—	—	2	1,214	32	8,021
San Diego	1	5,265	5	3,241	44	12,485
San Jose	2	7,624	6	4,865	29	8,635
Santa Rosa	—	—	6	1,887	15	2,961
Stockton	—	—	2	1,401	12	3,112
Alaska	—	—	2	241	4	766
*Anchorage	—	—	—	—	2	271
Fairbanks	—	—	2	241	1	370
Juneau	—	—	—	—	1	125
Hawaii, Honolulu	1	1,038	8	3,434	29	8,812
EASTERN RITES	2	436	5	674	46	6,367
*Philadelphia	1	418	1	365	13	1,792
St. Nicholas (Chicago)	—	—	1	93	3	483
Stamford	1	18	3	216	8	669
St. Josaphat (Parma)	—	—	—	—	2	457
*Pittsburgh	—	—	—	—	6	1,014
Parma	—	—	—	—	4	654
Passaic	—	—	—	—	5	591
Van Nuys	—	—	—	—	—	—
St. Maron (Maronites)	—	—	—	—	—	—
Newton (Melkites)	—	—	—	—	—	—
St. Thomas Apostle of Detroit Chaldeans	—	—	—	—	—	—
Romanians (Ap. Ex.)	—	—	—	—	—	—
Armenians (Ap. Ex.)	—	—	—	—	5	707
MILITARY ARCHDIOCESE	**—**	**—**	**—**	**—**	**—**	**—**
TOTALS 1986	243	545,461	1,418	766,744	7,865	2,099,379
Totals 1985	242	549,940	1,425	794,028	7,957	2,162,955
Totals 1976	245	432,597	1,616	895,845	8,484	2,576,856

SCHOOL STATISTICS

The status of Catholic educational institutions and programs in the United States at the beginning of 1986, 1985 and 1976 was reflected in figures (as of Jan. 1) reported by "The Official Catholic Directory, 1986."

Colleges and Universities: 243 (+1, 1985; -2, 1976).
College and University Students: 545,461 (-4,479, 1985; +112,864, 1976).
High Schools: 1,418 (-7, 1985; -198, 1976).
High School Students: 766,744 (-27,284, 1985; -129,101, 1976).
Public High School Students Receiving Religious Instruction: 831,131 (-64,037, 1985; -182,067, 1976).

Elementary Schools: 7,865 (-92, 1985; -619, 1976).
Elementary School Students: 2,099,379 (-63,576, 1985; -477,477, 1976).
Public Elementary School Students Receiving Religious Instruction: 3,103,715 (-53,293, 1985; -788,742, 1976).

Teachers

Laity: 136,157 (+1,637, 1985; +27,655, 1976).
Sisters: 27,638 (-2,585, 1985; -25,319, 1976).
Priests (full time): 4,236 (-364, 1985; -2,138, 1976).
Brothers: 2,491 (-187, 1985; -1,113, 1976).
Scholastics: 161 (+23, 1985; -102, 1976).
TOTAL TEACHERS: 170,683 (-1,476, 1985; -1,017, 1976).

The National Catholic Educational Association, founded in 1904, is a voluntary organization of educational institutions and individuals concerned with Catholic education in the U.S. Its objectives are to promote and encourage the principles and ideals of Christian education and formation by suitable service and other activities.

The NCEA has 14,000 institutional and individual members. Its official publication is *Momentum.* Numerous service publications are issued to members.

Archbishop John Roach of St. Paul and Minne-apolis, is chairman of the association. Sister Catherine T. McNamee, C.S.J., is president.

Headquarters are located at: 1077 30th St. N.W., Washington, D.C. 20007.

National Association of Boards of Education, founded in 1971, was made a department of the National Catholic Educational Association in 1973, to develop and promote policy-making boards for the advancement of Catholic education. Has a national membership of diocesan and parish boards, councils and education committees. Office: 1077 30th St. N.W., Washington, D.C. 20007.

UNIVERSITIES AND COLLEGES IN THE UNITED STATES

(Sources: Almanac survey; *The Official Catholic Directory.*)

Listed below are institutions of higher learning established under Catholic auspices. Some of them are now independent.

Information includes: name of each institution; indication of male (m), female (w), coeducational (c) student body; name of founding group or group with which the institution is affiliated; year of foundation; number of students, in parentheses.

Albertus Magnus College (c): 700 Prospect St., New Haven, Conn. 06511. Dominican Sisters; 1925 (500).

Albuquerque, University of (c): St. Joseph Pl. N.W., Albuquerque, N.M. 87140. Sisters of St. Francis; 1920 (1,250).

Allentown College of St. Francis de Sales (c): Center Valley, Pa. 18034. Oblates of St. Francis de Sales; 1965 (1,200).

Alvernia College (c): Reading, Pa. 19607. Bernardine Sisters; 1958 (706).

Alverno College (w): 3401 S. 39th St. Milwaukee, Wis. 53215. School Sisters of St. Francis; 1887; independent (1,515).

Anna Maria College (c): Sunset Lane, Paxton, Mass. 01612. Sisters of St. Anne; 1946; independent (1,749).

Aquinas College (c): 1607 Robinson Rd. S.E., Grand Rapids, Mich. 49506. Sisters of St. Dominic; 1922 (2,724).

Assumption College (c): 500 Salisbury St., Worcester, Mass. 01609. Assumptionist Fathers; 1904 (2,685).

Avila College (c): 11901 Wornall Rd., Kansas City, Mo. 64145. Sisters of St. Joseph of Carondelet; 1916 (1,775).

Barat College (c): 700 Westleigh Rd., Lake Forest, Ill. 60045. Society of the Sacred Heart; 1919; independent (635).

Barry University (c): 11300 N.E. 2nd Ave., Miami, Fla. 33161. Dominican Sisters (Adrian, Mich.); 1940 (4,232).

Bellarmine College (c): Newburg Rd., Louisville, Ky. 40205; Louisville archdiocese, 1950 (2,710).

Belmont Abbey College (c): Belmont, N.C. 28012. Benedictine Fathers; 1876 (930).

Benedictine College (c): Atchison, Kans. 66002. Benedictines, 1971 (957).

Boston College (University Status) (c): Chestnut Hill, Mass. 02167. Jesuit Fathers; 1863 (14,476).

Brescia College (c): 120 W. 7th St., Owensboro, Ky. 42301. Ursuline Sisters; 1925 (850).

Briar Cliff College (c): 3303 Rebecca St., Sioux City, Ia. 51104. Sisters of St. Francis of the Holy Family; 1930 (1,300).

Cabrini College (c): Radnor, Pa. 19087. Missionary Srs. of Sacred Heart; 1957; private (900).

Caldwell College (w): Caldwell, N.J. 07006. Dominican Sisters; 1939 (690).

Calumet College (c): 2400 New York Ave., Whiting, Ind. 46394. Society of the Precious Blood, 1951 (1,073).

Canisius College (c): 2001 Main St., Buffalo, N.Y. 14208. Jesuit Fathers; 1870; independent (4,277).

Cardinal Stritch College (c): 6801 N. Yates Rd., Milwaukee, Wis. 53217. Sisters of St. Francis of Assisi; 1937; independent (2,107).

Carlow College (w): 3333 5th Ave., Pittsburgh, Pa. 15213. Sisters of Mercy; 1929 (1,246).

Carroll College (c): Helena, Mont. 59625. Diocesan; 1909 (1,533).

Catholic University of America, The (c): 620 Michigan Ave. N.E., Washington, D.C. 20064. Hierarchy of the Unied States; 1887. Pontifical University (7,057).

Catholic University of Puerto Rico (c): Ponce, P.R. Hierarchy of Puerto Rico; 1948; Pontifical University (13,308).

Chaminade University (c): 3140 Waialae Ave., Honolulu, Hawaii 96816. Marianists; 1955 (2,389).

Chestnut Hill College (w): Philadelphia, Pa. 19118. Sisters of St. Joseph; 1871 (976).

Christendom College (c): Rt. 3, Box 87, Front Royal, Va. 22630. Founded 1977 (125).

Christian Brothers College (c): 650 E. Parkway S., Memphis, Tenn. 38104. Brothers of the Christian Schools; 1871 (1,502).

Clarke College (c): 1550 Clarke Dr., Dubuque, Iowa 52001. Sisters of Charity, BVM; 1843 (922).

Creighton University (c): California St. at 24th, Omaha, Neb. 68178. Jesuit Fathers; 1878; independent (5,600).

Dallas, University of (c): 1845 E. Northgate, Irving, Tex. 75061. Dallas diocese; 1956; independent (2,553).

Dayton, University of (c): 300 College Park Ave., Dayton, Ohio 45409. Marianists; 1850 (10,700).

De Lourdes College (w): 353 N. River Rd., Des Plaines, Ill. 60016. Sisters of the Holy Family of Nazareth; 1927; independent (139).

DePaul University (c): 2323 N. Seminary Ave., Chicago, Ill. 60614. Vincentians; 1898 (12,447).

Detroit, University of (c): 4001 W. McNichols Rd. at Livernois, Detroit, Mich. 48221. Jesuit Fathers; 1877 (6,125).

Dominican College of Blauvelt (c): Orangeburg, N.Y. 10962. Dominican Sisters; 1952; independent (1,643).

Dominican College of San Rafael (c): 1520 Grand Ave.; San Rafael, Calif. 94901. Dominican Sisters; 1890; independent (710).

Duquesne University (c): 600 Forbes Ave., Pittsburgh, Pa. 15282. Congregation of the Holy Ghost; 1878 (6,300).

D'Youville College (c): One D'Youville Square, Buffalo, N.Y. 14201. Grey Nuns of the Sacred Heart; 1908; independent (1,400).

Edgewood College (c): 855 Woodrow St., Madison, Wis. 53711. Dominican Sisters; 1927 (809).

Emmanuel College (w): 400 The Fenway, Boston, Mass. 02115. Sisters of Notre Dame de Namur; independent (1,103).

Fairfield University (c): North Benson Rd., Fairfield, Conn. 06430. Jesuit Fathers; 1942 (5,104).

Felician College (w): S. Main St., Lodi, N.J. 07644. Felician Sisters; 1942 (631). Coed in nursing and evening programs.

Fontbonne College (c): 6800 Wydown Blvd., Clayton, Mo. 63105. Sisters of St. Joseph of Carondelet; 1917; independent (952).

Fordham University (c): Fordham Rd. and Third Ave., New York, N.Y. 10458. Society of Jesus (Jesuits); 1841; independent (13,110).

Gannon University (c): University Square, Erie, Pa. 16541. Diocese of Erie; 1933 (4,234).

Georgetown University (c): 37th and O Sts. N.W., Washington, D.C. 20007. Jesuit Fathers; 1789 (11,483).

Georgian Court College (w): Lakewood, N.J. 08701. Sisters of Mercy; 1908 (1,555). Coed in evening and graduate divisions.

Gonzaga University (c): Spokane, Wash. 99258. Jesuit Fathers; 1887 (3,209).

Great Falls, College of (c): 1301 20th St. S., Great Falls, Mont. 59405. Sisters of Providence; 1932 (1,200).

Gwynedd-Mercy College (c): Gwynedd Valley, Pa. 19437. Sisters of Mercy; 1948; independent (2,035).

Holy Cross, College of the (c): Worcester, Mass. 01610. Jesuit Fathers; 1843 (2,500).

Holy Family College (c): Grant and Frankford Aves., Philadelphia, Pa. 19114. Sisters of Holy Family of Nazareth; 1954 (1,528).

Holy Names College (c): 3500 Mountain Blvd., Oakland, Calif. 94619. Sisters of the Holy Names of Jesus and Mary; 1868 (645).

Illinois Benedictine College (c): Lisle, Ill. 60532. Benedictine Fathers of St. Procopius Abbey; 1887 (2,193).

Immaculata College (w): Immaculata, Pa. 19345. Sisters, Servants of the Immaculate Heart of Mary; 1920 (1,680).

Incarnate Word College (c): 4301 Broadway, San Antonio, Tex. 78209. Sisters of Charity of the Incarnate Word; 1881 (1,400).

Iona College (c): 715 North Ave., New Rochelle, N.Y. 10801. Congregation of Christian Brothers; 1940; independent (6,304).

John Carroll University (c): North Park and Miramar Blvds., Cleveland, Ohio. 44118. Jesuit Fathers; 1886 (3,583).

Kansas Newman College (formerly Sacred Heart College) (c): 3100 McCormick Ave., Wichita, Kans. 67213. Sisters Adorers of the Blood of Christ; 1933 (763).

King's College (c): Wilkes-Barre, Pa. 18711. Holy Cross Fathers; 1946 (2,306).

La Roche College (c): 9000 Babcock Blvd., Pittsburgh, Pa. 15237. Sisters of Divine Providence; 1963 (1,740)

La Salle University (c): 20th St. and Olney Ave., Philadelphia, Pa. 19141. Brothers of the Christian Schools; 1863 (7,000)

Le Moyne College (c): Syracuse, N.Y. 13214. Jesuit Fathers; 1946; independent (1,800).

Lewis University (c): Romeoville, Ill. 60441. Christian Brothers; 1932 (3,076).

Loras College (c): 1450 Alta Vista St., Dubuque, Ia. 52004. Archdiocese of Dubuque; 1839 (1,995).

Lourdes College (c): Sylvania, Ohio 43560. Franciscan Srs.; 1958 (842).

Loyola College (c): 4501 N. Charles St., Baltimore, Md. 21210, Jesuits; 1852; combined with Mt. St. Agnes College, 1971 (5,173).

Loyola Marymount University (c): Loyola Blvd. at W. 80th St., Los Angeles, Calif. 90045. Society of Jesus; Religious of Sacred Heart of Mary, Sisters of St. Joseph of Orange; 1911 (6,410).

Loyola University (c): 6363 St. Charles Ave., New Orleans, La. 70118. Jesuit Fathers; 1904 (4,873).

Loyola University of Chicago (c): 820 N. Michigan Ave., Chicago, Ill. 60611. Jesuit Fathers; 1870 (14,247).

Madonna College (c): 36600 Schoolcraft Rd., Livonia, Mich. 48150. Felician Sisters; 1947 (3,992).

Magdalen College (c): 270 D.W. Highway So., Bedford, N.H. 03102; Magdalen College Corporation; 1973 (70).

Mallinckrodt College (c): 1041 Ridge Rd., Wilmette, Ill. 60091. Sisters of Christian Charity 1918 (295).

Manhattan College (c): 4513 Manhattan College Pkwy., New York, N.Y. 10471. Brothers of the Christian Schools; 1853; independent (5,000). Cooperative program with College of Mt. St. Vincent.

Marian College (c): Fond du Lac, Wis. 54935. Sisters of St. Agnes; 1936 (450).

Marian College (c): 3200 Cold Spring Rd., Indianapolis, Ind. 46222. Sisters of St. Francis (Oldenburg, Ind.); 1851 (1,044).

Marist College (c): Poughkeepsie, N.Y. 12601. Marist Brothers of the Schools; 1946; independent (2,500).

Marquette University (c): 615 N. 11th St., Milwaukee, Wis. 53233. Jesuit Fathers; 1881; independent (12,000).

Mary, University of (c): P.O. Box 119, Bismarck, N.D. 58501. Benedictine Sisters; 1959 (1,180).

Marycrest College (c): 1607 W. 12th St., Davenport, Iowa 52804. Congregation of the Humility of Mary; 1939; independent (1,600).

Marygrove College (c): 8425 W. McNichols Rd., Detroit, Mich. 48221. Sisters, Servants of the Immaculate Heart of Mary; 1910 (1,237).

Marylhurst Education Center, College for Lifelong Learning (c): Marylhurst, Ore. 97036. Srs. of Holy Names of Jesus and Mary; 1893; independent (453).

Marymount College (w): Tarrytown, N.Y. 10591. Religious of the Sacred Heart of Mary; 1907; independent (1,271). Coed in weekend degree programs.

Marymount College of Kansas (c): Box 5050, Salina, Kans. 67401. Salina diocese; 1922 (651).

Marymount College of Virginia (w): 2807 N. Glebe Rd., Arlington, Va. 22007. Religious of the Sacred Heart of Mary; 1950; independent (2,210).

Marymount Manhattan College (w): 221 E. 71st St., New York, N.Y. 10021. Religious of the Sacred Heart of Mary; 1936; independent (2,214).

Maryville College (c): 13550 Conway Rd., St. Louis. Mo. 63141. Religious of the Sacred Heart; 1872; independent (2,052).

Marywood College (w): Scranton, Pa. 18509. Sisters. Servants of the Immaculate Heart of Mary; 1915 (3,158). Coed in graduate division.

Mater Dei College (c): Riverside Dr., Ogdensburg, N.Y. 13669. Sisters of St. Joseph; 1960; independent (614).

Mercy College of Detroit (c): 8200 W. Outer Dr., Detroit, Mich. 48219. Sisters of Mercy; 1941 (2,430).

Mercyhurst College (c): 501 E. 38th St., Erie, Pa. 16546. Sisters of Mercy; 1926 (1,750).

Merrimack College (c): North Andover, Mass. 01845. Augustinians; 1947 (2,300).

Misericordia (College Misericordia) (c): Dallas, Pa. 18612. Religious Sisters of Mercy of the Union; 1924 (1,292).

Molloy College (c): 1000 Hempstead Ave., Rockville Centre, N.Y. 11570. Dominican Sisters; 1955; independent (1,656).

Mount Marty College (c): Yankton, S.D. 57078. Benedictine Sisters; 1936 (631).

Mount Mary College (w): 2900 W. Menomonee River Pkwy., Milwaukee, Wis. 53222. School Sisters of Notre Dame; 1913 (1,290).

Mt. Mercy College (c): 1330 Elmhurst Dr. N.E., Cedar Rapids, Ia. 52402. Sisters of Mercy; 1928 (1,321).

Mt. St. Clare College (c): Bluff Blvd. and Springdale Dr., Clinton, Ia. 52732. Clinton Franciscans; 1928 (371).

Mt. St. Joseph on the Ohio, College of (c): Mt. St. Joseph, Ohio 45051. Sisters of Charity; 1920 (2,135).

Mt. St. Mary College (c): Newburgh, N.Y. 12550. Dominican Sisters; 1959; independent (1,078).

Mount St. Mary College (c): Emmitsburg, Md. 21727. Diocesan Clergy; 1808; independent (1,400).

Mount St. Mary's College (w): 12001 Chalon Rd., Los Angeles, Calif. 90049 and 10 Chester Pl., Los Angeles, Calif. 90007 (Doheny Campus). Sisters of St. Joseph of Carondelet; 1925 (1,200). Coed in music, nursing and graduate programs.

Mt. St. Vincent, College of (c): Mt. St. Vincent-on-Hudson, New York, N.Y. 10471. Sisters of Charity; 1847; independent (1,200). Cooperative program with Manhattan College.

Mundelein College (w): 6363 N. Sheridan Rd., Chicago, Ill. 60660. Sisters of Charity of the Blessed Virgin Mary; 1929 (1,282).

Nazareth College (c): 3333 Gull Rd., Kalamazoo, Mich. 49001. Sisters of St. Joseph; 1924; independent (790).

Nazareth College (c): East Ave., Rochester, N.Y. 14610. Sisters of St. Joseph of Rochester; 1924; independent (2,532).

Neumann College (formerly Our Lady of Angels) (c): Aston, Pa. 19014. Sisters of St. Francis; 1965 (1,006).

New Rochelle, College of (w): 29 Castle Pl., New Rochelle, N.Y. 10801 (main campus).

Ursuline Nuns; 1904; independent (5,521). Coed in nursing, graduate, new resources divisions.

Niagara University (c): Niagara Univ., N.Y. 14109. Vincentian Fathers; 1856 (4,305).

Notre Dame, College of (c): Belmont, Calif. 94002. Sisters of Notre Dame de Namur; 1868; independent (1,200).

Notre Dame, University of (c): Notre Dame, Ind. 46556. Congregation of Holy Cross; 1842 (9,050).

Notre Dame College (w): 4545 College Rd., Cleveland, Ohio 44121. Sisters of Notre Dame; 1922 (765).

Notre Dame College (w): Manchester, N.H. 03104. Sisters of the Holy Cross; 1950 (722).

Notre Dame of Maryland, College of (w): 4701 N. Charles St., Baltimore, Md. 21210. School Sisters of Notre Dame; 1873 (1,712).

Ohio Dominican College (c): Columbus, Ohio 43219. Dominican Sisters of St. Mary of the Springs; 1911 (1,129).

Our Lady of Holy Cross College (c): 4123 Woodland Dr., New Orleans, La. 70114. Congregation of Sisters Marianites of Holy Cross; 1916 (653).

Our Lady of the Elms, College of (w): Chicopee, Mass. 01013. Sisters of St. Joseph; 1928 (900).

Our Lady of the Lake University of San Antonio (c): 411 S.W. 24th St., San Antonio, Tex. 78285. Sisters of Divine Providence; 1911 (1,758).

Parks College of Saint Louis University (c): Cahokia, Ill. 62206. Jesuits; 1927; independent (1,051).

Portland, University of (c): 5000 N. Willamette Blvd., Portland, Ore. 97203. Holy Cross Fathers; 1901; independent (2,861).

Providence College (c): River Ave. and Eaton St., Providence, R.I. 02918. Dominican Friars; 1917 (3,700).

Quincy College (c): 1800 College Ave., Quincy, Ill. 62301. Franciscan Friars; 1859 (1,453).

Regis College (c): W. 50th Ave. and Lowell Blvd. Denver, Colo. 80221. Jesuit Fathers; 1887 (1,018).

Regis College (w): Weston, Mass. 02193. Sisters of St. Joseph; 1927; independent (1,126).

Rivier College (w): Nashua, N.H. 03060. Sisters of the Presentation of Mary; 1933; independent (2,257). Coed continuing education and graduate school.

Rockhurst College (c): 5225 Troost Ave., Kansas City, Mo. 64110. Jesuit Fathers; 1910 (3,163).

Rosary College (c): 7900 Division St., River Forest, Ill. 60305. Dominican Sisters; 1901 (1,608).

Rosemont College (w): Rosemont, Pa. 19010. Society of the Holy Child Jesus; 1921 (620).

Sacred Heart College (c): Belmont, N.C. 28012. Sisters of Mercy; 1935 (294).

Sacred Heart University (c): Fairfield (P.O. Bridgeport), Conn. 06606. Diocese of Bridgeport; 1963; independent (5,254).

St. Ambrose College (c): Davenport, Ia. 52803. Diocese of Davenport; 1882 (2,236).

Saint Anselm College (c): Manchester N.H 03102. Benedictine Monks; 1889 (1,800).

St. Basil's College (m): 195 Glenbrook Rd.

Stamford, Conn. 06902. Byzantine-Ukrainian Rite Diocese of Stamford; 1939 (20).

Saint Benedict, College of (w): St. Joseph, Minn. 56374. Benedictine Sisters; 1913 (1.779).

St. Bonaventure University (c): St. Bonaventure, N.Y. 14778. Franciscan Friars; 1856; independent (2,740).

St. Catherine, College of (w): 2004 Randolph St., St. Paul, Minn. 55105. Sisters of St. Joseph of Carondelet; 1905 (2,458).

St. Edward's University (c): 3001 S. Congress Ave., Austin, Tex. 78704. Holy Cross Brothers; 1885; independent (2,502).

St. Elizabeth, College of (w): Convent Station, N.J. 07961. Sisters of Charity; 1899; independent (932).

St. Francis, College of (c): 500 N. Wilcox St., Joliet, Ill. 60435. Sisters of St. Francis of Mary Immaculate; 1925; independent (1,020).

St. Francis College (c): 180 Remsen St., Brooklyn Heights, N.Y. 11201. Franciscan Brothers; 1884; private, independent in the Franciscsan tradition (2,400).

St. Francis College (c): 2701 Spring St., Fort Wayne, Ind. 46808. Sisters of St. Francis; 1890 (1,310).

St. Francis College (c): Loretto, Pa. 15940. Franciscan Fathers; 1847; independent (1,604).

St. John Fisher College (c): 3690 East Ave., Rochester, N.Y. 14618. Basilian Fathers; 1951; independent (1,600).

St. John's University (c): Grand Central and Utopia Pkwys., Jamaica, N.Y. 11439 (Queens Campus); 300 Howard Ave., Grymes Hill, Staten Island, N.Y. 10301 (Staten Island Campus). Vincentian Fathers; 1870 (19,248).

St. John's University (m): Collegeville, Minn. 56321. Benedictines; 1857 (2,024). Coed in graduate school.

Saint Joseph College (w): 1678 Asylum Ave., West Hartford, Conn. 06117. Sisters of Mercy; 1932 (1,465). Coed in graduate school.

Saint Joseph's College (c): N. Windham, Me. 04062. Sisters of Mercy; 1912 (500).

Saint Joseph's College (c): Rensselaer, Ind. 47978. Society of the Precious Blood; 1889 (950).

St. Joseph's College (c): 245 Clinton Ave., Brooklyn, N.Y. 11205 (403) and 155 Roe Blvd., Patchogue, N.Y. 11772 (1,445). Sisters of St. Joseph; 1916; independent.

St. Joseph's University (c): 5600 City Ave., Philadelphia, Pa. 19131. Jesuit Fathers; 1851 (6,006).

St. Joseph the Provider, College of (c): Clement Rd., Rutland, Vt. 05701. Sisters of St. Joseph; 1954; independent (387).

Saint Leo College (c): Saint Leo, Fla. 33574. Order of St. Benedict; 1889; independent (1,200).

St. Louis University (c): 221 N. Grand Blvd., St. Louis, Mo. 63103. Jesuit Fathers; 1818 (10,179).

Saint Martin's College (c): Lacey, Wash. 98503. Benedictine Monks; 1895 (612).

St. Mary, College of (w): 1901 S. 72nd St., Omaha, Neb. 68124. Sisters of Mercy; 1923; independent (1,055).

Saint Mary College (w): Leavenworth, Kans. 66048. Sisters of Charity of Leavenworth; 1923 (1,038).

St. Mary of the Plains College (c): Dodge City, Kans. 67801. Sisters of St. Joseph of Wichita; 1952 (705).

St.-Mary-of-the-Woods College (w): St. Mary-of-the-Woods, Ind. 47876. Sisters of Providence; 1840 (684).

St. Mary's College (w): Notre Dame, Ind. 46556. Sisters of the Holy Cross; 1844 (1,839).

St. Mary's College (c): Orchard Lake, Mich. 48033. Secular Clergy; 1885 (248).

St. Mary's College (c): Moraga, Calif. 94575. Brothers of the Christian Schools; 1863 (3,206).

St. Mary's College (c): Winona, Minn. 55987. Brothers of the Christian Schools; 1912 (1,480).

St. Mary's University (c): One Camino Santa Maria, San Antonio, Tex. 78284. Society of Mary (Marianists); 1852 (3,296).

St. Michael's College (c): Winooski, Vt. 05404. Society of St. Edmund; 1904 (2,050).

St. Norbert College (c): De Pere, Wis. 54115. Norbertine Fathers; 1898; independent (1,751).

St. Peter's College (c): 2641 Kennedy Blvd., Jersey City, N.J. 07306. Jesuit Fathers; independent; 1872 (4,217).

Saint Rose, College of (c): 432 Western Ave., Albany, N.Y. 12203. Sisters of St. Joseph of Carondelet; 1920; independent (2,886).

St. Scholastica, College of (c): 1200 Kenwood Ave., Duluth, Minn. 55811. Benedictine Sisters; 1912 (1,400).

Saint Teresa, College of (w): Winona, Minn. 55987. Sisters of St. Francis; 1907 (482).

St. Thomas, College of (c): St. Paul, Minn. 55105. Archdiocese of St. Paul; 1885 (6.435).

St. Thomas, University of (c): 3812 Montrose Blvd., Houston, Tex. 77006. Basilian Fathers; 1947 (1,811).

St. Thomas Aquinas College (c): Sparkill, N.Y. 10976. Dominican Sisters of Sparkill; 1952; independent, corporate board of trustees (2,000).

St. Thomas University (c): 16400 N.W. 32nd Ave., Miami, Fla. 33054. Augustinian Fathers; 1962 (3,100).

Saint Vincent College (c): Latrobe, Pa. 15650. Benedictine Fathers; 1846 (1,176).

St. Xavier College (c): 3700 W. 103rd St., Chicago, Ill. 60655. Sisters of Mercy; chartered 1847 (2,566).

Salve Regina — The Newport College (c): Ochre Point Ave., Newport, R.I. 02840. Sisters of Mercy; 1934 (2,065).

San Diego, University of (c): Alcala Park, San Diego, Calif. 92110. San Diego diocese and Religious of the Sacred Heart; 1949; independent (5,264).

San Francisco, University of (c): Ignation Heights, San Francisco, Calif. 94117. Jesuit Fathers; 1855 (7,000).

Santa Clara, University of (c): Santa Clara, Calif. 95053. Jesuit Fathers; 1851; independent (7,448).

Santa Fe, College of (c): Santa Fe, N. Mex. 87501. Brothers of the Christian Schools; 1947 (900).

Scranton, University of (c): Scranton, Pa. 18510. Society of Jesus; 1888 (4,685).

Seattle University (c): Broadway and East Madison, Seattle, Wash. 98122. Jesuit Fathers; 1891 (4,600).

Seton Hall University (c): South Orange, N.J. 07079. Diocesan Clergy; 1856 (9,193).

Seton Hill College (w): Greensburg, Pa. 15601. Sisters of Charity of Seton Hill; 1883 (886).

Siena College (c): Loudonville, N.Y. 12211. Franciscan Friars; 1937 (3,473).

Siena Heights College (c): Adrian, Mich. 49221. Dominican Sisters; 1919 (1,524).

Silver Lake College of Holy Family (c): 2406 S. Alverno Rd., Manitowoc, Wis. 54220. Franciscan Sisters of Christian Charity; 1935 (470).

Spalding University (c): 851 S. 4th Ave., Louisville, Ky. 40203. Sisters of Charity of Nazareth; 1814; independent (1,150).

Spring Hill College (c): Mobile, Ala. 36608. Jesuit Fathers; 1830 (940).

Steubenville, University of (c): Steubenville, Ohio 43952. Franciscan Fathers; 1946 (1,197).

Stonehill College (c): North Easton, Mass. 02357. Holy Cross Fathers; 1948; independent (2,710).

Thomas Aquinas College (c): 10000 N. Ojai Rd., Santa Paula, Calif. 93060.Founded 1971 (125).

Thomas More College (c): Crestview Hills, Covington, Ky. 41017. Diocese of Covington; 1921 (1,335).

Trinity College (w): Colchester Ave., Burlington, Vt. 05401. Sisters of Mercy; 1925 (932).

Trinity College (w): Michigan Ave. and Franklin St. N.E., Washington, D.C. 20017. Sisters of Notre Dame de Namur; 1897 (929). Coed in graduate school.

Ursuline College (w): 2550 Lander Rd., Cleveland, Ohio 44124. Ursuline Nuns; 1871 (1,514).

Villa Maria College (w): 2551 W. Lake Rd., Erie, Pa. 16505. Sisters of St. Joseph; 1925 (620).

Villanova University (c): Villanova, Pa. 19085. Order of St. Augustine; 1842 (11,665).

Viterbo College (c): La Crosse, Wis. 54601. Franciscan Sisters of Perpetual Adoration; 1890 (1,092).

Walsh College (c): 2020 Easton St. N.W., Canton, Ohio 44720. Brothers of Christian Instruction; 1958 (1,159).

Wheeling College (c): 316 Washington Ave., Wheeling, W. Va. 26003. Jesuit Fathers; 1954 (1,074).

Xavier University (c): 3800 Victory Pkwy., Cincinnati, Ohio 45207. Jesuit Fathers; 1831 (6,785).

Xavier University of Louisiana (c): 7325 Palmetto St., New Orleans, La. 70125. Sisters of Blessed Sacrament; 1925; lay-Religious administration board (2,070).

Catholic Junior Colleges

Ancilla College (c): Donaldson, Ind. 46513. Ancilla Domini Sisters; 1937 (420).

Aquinas Junior College (c): Harding Rd., Nashville, Tenn. 37205. Dominican Sisters; 1961 (361).

Assumption College for Sisters: Hilltop Rd.,

Mendham, N.J. 07945. Sisters of Christian Charity; 1953 (18).

Chatfield College (c): St. Martin, O. 45118. Ursulines; 1971 (200).

Donnelly College (c): 608 N. 18th St., Kansas City, Kans. 66102. Archdiocesan College; 1949 (800).

Don Bosco Technical Institute (m): 1151 San Gabriel Blvd., Rosemead, Calif. 91770. Salesians; 1969 (307).

Elizabeth Seton College (c): 1061 N. Broadway, Yonkers, N.Y. 10701. Sisters of Charity; 1960; independent (1,343).

Felician College (c): 3800 W. Peterson Ave., Chicago, Ill. 60659. Felician Sisters (325).

Hilbert College (c): 5200 S. Park Ave., Hamburg, N.Y. 14075. Franciscan Sisters of St. Joseph; 1957; independent (698).

Holy Cross Junior College (c): Notre Dame, Ind. 46556. Brothers of Holy Cross; 1966 (365).

Manor Junior College (w): Fox Chase Manor, Jenkintown, Pa. 19046. Sisters of St. Basil the Great; 1947 (450).

Maria College (c): 700 New Scotland Ave., Albany, N.Y. 12208. Sisters of Mercy; 1963 (911).

Maria Regina College (w): 1024 Court St., Syracuse, N.Y. 13208. Franciscan Sisters; 1963; independent (517).

Marymount Palos Verdes College (c): Rancho Palos Verdes, Calif. 90274. Religious of the Sacred Heart of Mary (755).

Mt. Aloysius Junior College (c): Cresson, Pa. 16630. Sisters of Mercy; 1939 (541).

Presentation College (c): Aberdeen, S.D. 57401. Sisters of the Presentation; 1951 (325).

St. Catharine College (c): St. Catharine, Ky. 40061. Dominican Sisters; 1931 (201).

St. Gertrude, College of (c): Cottonwood, Ida. 83522. Benedictine Sisters.

St. Gregory's College (c): Shawnee, Okla. 74801. Benedictine Monks; 1876 (325).

St. Mary's College of O'Fallon (c): 200 N. Main St., O'Fallon, Mo. 63366. Sisters of the Most Precious Blood; 1921 (674).

St. Mary's Junior College (c): 2500 S. 6th St., Minneapolis, Minn. 55454. Sisters of St. Joseph of Carondelet (824).

Springfield College in Illinois (c): 1500 N. Fifth St., Springfield, Ill. 62702. Ursuline Nuns; 1929 (567).

Trocaire College (c): 110 Red Jacket Pkwy., Buffalo, N.Y. 14220. Sisters of Mercy; 1958; independent (1,219).

Villa Julie College (c): Green Spring Valley Rd., Stevenson, Md. 21153. Sisters of Notre Dame de Namur; 1952; independent (1,083).

Villa Maria College of Buffalo (c): 240 Pine Ridge Rd., Buffalo, N.Y. 14225. Felician Srs.; 1960 (724).

National Forum of Catholic Parent Organizations: Founded in 1976 as a commission of the National Catholic Educational Association, to support and promote the role of parents as primary educators of their children. Has a national membership of diocesan and parish/private parent organizations. Office: 1077 30th St. N.W., Washington, D.C.

CAMPUS MINISTRY

"Campus ministry is a pastoral apostolate of service to the members of the entire university and college community through concern and care for persons, the proclamation of the Gospel, and the celebration of the liturgy," according to a set of guidelines drawn up by an eight-member commission of the National Catholic Educational Association. The general purpose of the ministry is to make the Church present and active in the academic community.

Ideally, according to the guidelines, elements of the ministry — carried on by teams of priests, men and women religious, and lay persons — include liturgical leadership; pastoral counseling; coordination of expressions and energies for religious life on campus; Christian witness on social and moral issues; objective and independent mediation between various groups on campus; participation in religious aspects of the work of the administration, faculty and students.

Status, Agencies

The dimensions and challenge of the campus ministry are evident from estimates that a large percentage of several million Catholics in colleges and universities are on non-Catholic public and private campuses. Serving them are about 1,200 full-time and 700 part-time campus ministry personnel.

The Desk of Campus and Young Adult Ministry, under the Department of Education of the U.S. Catholic Conference, has responsibility for continuing support of ministry in this field. The office is located at 1312 Massachusetts Ave. N.W., Washington, D.C. 20005.

The autonomous Catholic Campus Ministry Association, with a membership of 1,000, is headquartered at 300 College Park, Dayton, O. 45469. Donald R. McCrabb is executive director.

Pastoral Letter

A pastoral letter on campus ministry, entitled "Empowered by the Spirit: Campus Ministry Faces the Future," was approved by the U.S. bishops on a majority vote completed several weeks after their annual meeting in November, 1985. The letter explored the work of campus ministers, the relationship of the Church with the academic community, the spiritual needs and interests of students, as well as possible directions for religious education, attitudes on campus toward religion, education for justice and other subjects.

Special ministry on secular campuses began in 1893 with the first unit of the Newman movement.

DIOCESAN AND INTERDIOCESAN SEMINARIES

(Sources: Almanac survey; *Official Catholic Directory*; NC News Service.)

Information, according to states, includes names of archdioceses and dioceses, and names and addresses of seminaries. Types of seminaries, when not clear from titles, are indicated in most cases. Interdiocesan seminaries are generally conducted by religious orders for candidates for the priesthood from several dioceses. The list does not include houses of study reserved for members of religious communities. Archdioceses are indicated by an asterisk.

California: Los Angeles* — St. John's Seminary (major), 5012 E. Seminary Rd., Camarillo. 93010; St. John's College Seminary, 5118 E. Seminary Rd., Camarillo. 93010; Seminary of Our Lady, Queen of Angels (minor, high school), P.O. Box 1071, San Fernando, 91341.

San Diego — St. Francis Seminary (college residence), 1667 Santa Paula Dr., San Diego 92111.

San Francisco* — St. Patrick's Seminary (major), 320 Middlefield Rd., Menlo Park. 94025.

San Jose — St. Joseph's College, P.O. Box 7009, Mountain View 94039.

Colorado: Denver* — St. Thomas Theological Seminary (major), 1300 S. Steele St., Denver 80210.

Connecticut: Hartford* — St. Thomas Seminary (college formation program), 467 Bloomfield Ave., Bloomfield. 06002.

Norwich — Holy Apostles College and Seminary (delayed vocations), 33 Prospect Hill Rd., Cromwell 06416.

Stamford Byzantine Rite — Ukrainian Catholic Seminary: St. Basil College (minor), 195 Glenbrook Rd., Stamford 06902; St. Basil's Preparatory School (minor), 39 Clovelly Rd., Stamford 06902.

District of Columbia: Washington* — Theological College, The Catholic University of America, 401 Michigan Ave., N.E. 20017.

St. Josaphat's Seminary, 201 Taylor St. N.E., Washington 20017. (Major house of formation serving the four Ukrainian Byzantine-rite dioceses in the U.S.)

Florida: Miami*, Palm Beach, Pensacola-Tallahassee, St. Augustine, St. Petersburg, Venice — St. John Vianney College Seminary, 2900 S.W. 87th Ave., Miami 33165; St. Vincent de Paul Regional Seminary (major), 10701 S. Military Trail, Boynton Beach. 33436.

Illinois: Chicago* — Quigley Preparatory Seminary (North), 103 East Chestnut St., Chicago 60611; Quigley Preparatory Seminary (South), 7740 South Western Ave., Chicago 60620; Niles College of Loyola University, 7135 N. Harlem Ave., Chicago 60631; St. Mary of the Lake Seminary, Mundelein. 60060.

Indiana: Indianapolis* — St. Meinrad Seminary, College and School of Theology (interdiocesan), St. Meinrad. 47577.

Iowa: Davenport — St. Ambrose College Seminary, 518 W. Locust St., Davenport 52803.

Dubuque* — Seminary of St. Pius X, Loras College, Dubuque 52001.

Kansas: Kansas City* — Savior of the World Seminary (minor), 12601 Parallel Ave., Kansas City 66109.

Kentucky: Covington — Seminary of St. Pius X, 2799 Turkeyfoot Rd., Covington 41017.

Louisiana: New Orleans* — Notre Dame Seminary Graduate School of Theology, 2901 S. Carrollton Ave., New Orleans 70118; St. Joseph Seminary College (interdiocesan), St. Benedict 70457.

Maryland: Baltimore* — St. Mary's Seminary and University, 5400 Roland Ave., Baltimore 21210; Mt. St. Mary's Seminary, Emmitsburg. 21727.

Massachusetts: Boston* — St. John's Seminary School of Theology, 127 Lake St., Brighton. 02135; St. John's Seminary, College of Liberal Arts, 197 Foster St., Brighton 02135; Pope John XXIII National Seminary (for ages 30-60), 558 South Ave., Weston. 02193.

Melkite Eparchy of Newton — St. Gregory the Theologian Seminary, 233 Grant Ave., Newton 02159.

Michigan: Detroit* — Sacred Heart Seminary College, Inc., 2701 Chicago Blvd., Detroit 48206; The Orchard Lake Schools (Sts. Cyril and Methodius Seminary, St. Mary's College, St. Mary's Preparatory — graduate, undergraduate, secondary; independent, primarily serving Polish-American community), Orchard Lake 48033; St. John's Provincial Seminary (major, for dioceses in Detroit province), 44011 Five Mile Rd., Plymouth. 48170.

Grand Rapids — Christopher House, 2001 Robinson Rd., S.E., Grand Rapids 49506.

Minnesota: Seminary of the Diocese of St. Cloud, St. John's University, Collegeville. 56321.

St. Paul and Minneapolis* — St. Paul Seminary, 2260 Summit Ave., St. Paul. 55105; St. John Vianney College Seminary, 2115 Summit Ave., St. Paul. 55105.

Winona — Immaculate Heart of Mary Seminary, Terrace Heights, St. Mary's College, Winona 55987.

Missouri: Jefferson City — St. Thomas Aquinas Preparatory Seminary, 245 N. Levering Ave., P.O. Box 858, Hannibal. 63401.

St. Louis* — St. Louis Roman Catholic Theological Seminary (Kenrick Seminary), 7800 Kenrick Rd., St. Louis 63119; Cardinal Glennon College, 5200 Glennon Dr., St. Louis 63119; St. Louis Preparatory Seminary, 5200 Shrewsbury Ave., St. Louis 63119 (South), 3500 St. Catherine St., Florissant 63033 (North).

Montana: Helena — Borromeo Pre-Seminary Program, Carroll College, Helena 59625.

New Jersey: Newark* — Immaculate Conception Seminary (major), South Orange Ave., Newark 07079; Seton Hall University College Seminary, Seton Hall University, South Orange. 07079.

New Mexico: Gallup — Cristo Rey College and High School Seminary, 205 E. Wilson, Gallup 87301.

Santa Fe* — Immaculate Heart of Mary Seminary, Mt. Carmel Rd., Santa Fe 87501.

New York: Brooklyn — Cathedral Preparatory Seminary of the Immaculate Conception, 56-25 92nd St., Elmhurst. 11373; Cathedral College of the Immaculate Conception, 7200 Douglaston Parkway, Douglaston. 11362.

Buffalo — Christ the King Seminary (interdiocesan theologate), 711 Knox Rd., East Aurora. 14052.

U.S. SEMINARIES AND STUDENTS, 1962-1986

(Source: *The Official Catholic Directory.*)

Year	Dioc. Seminaries	Total Dioc. Students	Religious Seminaries Scholasticates	Total Rel. Students	Total Seminarians
1962	98	23,662	447	22,657	46,319
1963	107	25,247	454	22,327	47,574
1964	112	26,701	459	22,049	48,750
1965	117	26,762	479	22,230	48,992
1966	126	26,252	481	21,862	48,114
1967	123	24,293	452	21,086	45,379
1968	124	22,232	437	17,604	39,836
1969	122	19,573	407	14,417	33,990
1970	118	17,317	383	11,589	28,906
1971	110	14,987	340	10,723	25,710
1972	106	13,554	326	9,409	22,963
1973	107	12,925	304	8,855	21,780
1974	109	11,765	293	7,583	19,348
1975	104	11,223	269	6,579	17,802
1976	102	11,015	269	6,232	17,247
1977	100	10,344	287	5,599	15,943
1978	98	9,560	278	5,438	14,998
1979	92	8,694	258	5,266	13,960
1980	92	8,552	252	4,674	13,226
1981	88	7,954	240	4,514	12,468
1982	86	7,625	217	4,020	11,645
1983	86	8,046	234	4,008	12,054
1984	86	7,486	233	3,776	11,262
1985	90	7,277	228	3,751	11,028
1986	90	7,018	229	3,422	10,440

New York* — St. Joseph's Seminary (major), Dunwoodie, Yonkers. 10704; St. John Neumann Residence (college), 5655 Arlington Ave., Riverdale 10471. Cathedral Preparatory Seminary, 555 West End Ave., New York 10024.

Ogdensburg — Wadhams Hall Seminary College (interdiocesan), Riverside Dr., Ogdensburg 13669.

Rockville Centre — Seminary of the Immaculate Conception, Lloyd Harbor, Huntington, L.I. 11743.

St. Maron Diocese, Brooklyn — Our Lady of Lebanon Maronite Seminary, 7164 Alaska Ave. N.W., Washington, D.C. 20012.

Syracuse — Syracuse-Aquinas House, 702 Danforth St., Syracuse 13208.

North Dakota: Fargo — Cardinal Muench Seminary, 100 35th Ave. N.E., Fargo 58102.

Ohio: Cincinnati* — Mt. St. Mary's Seminary of the West, 6616 Beechmont Ave., Cincinnati. 45230 (division of the Athenaeum of Ohio).

Cleveland — St. Mary Seminary, 1227 Ansel Rd., Cleveland 44108; Borromeo College of Ohio, 28700 Euclid Ave. Wickliffe. 44092.

Columbus — Pontifical College Josephinum (national), theologate and college, Columbus. 43085.

Oregon: Portland* — Mt. Angel Seminary (college, pre-theology program, graduate school of theology), St. Benedict 97373.

Pennsylvania: Allentown — Mary Immaculate Seminary (interdiocesan; pre-theology program), Northampton 18067.

Erie — St. Mark's Seminary, 429 E. Grandview Blvd., Erie 16504.

Greensburg — St. Vincent Seminary School of Theology (interdiocesan), Latrobe 15650.

Philadelphia* — Theological Seminary of St. Charles Borromeo, Overbrook. 19151. (College,

pre-theology program, theologate, religious studies program.)

Pittsburgh Byzantine Rite (Ruthenians)* — Byzantine Catholic Seminary of Sts. Cyril and Methodius, 3605 Perrysville Ave., Pittsburgh. 15214.

Pittsburgh — St. Paul Seminary, 2900 Noblestown Rd. 15205.

Scranton — St. Pius X Seminary (college division), Dalton. 18414.

Rhode Island: Providence — House of Formation (college students), 485 Mount Pleasant Ave., Providence 02908.

Texas: Corpus Christi — Corpus Christi Academy (residential seminary program), Saratoga Blvd., P.O. Box 271490, Corpus Christi 78427.

Dallas — Holy Trinity Seminary (college), P.O. Box 160309, Irving. 75016.

El Paso — St. Charles Seminary High School and College, P.O. Box 17548, El Paso 79917.

Galveston-Houston — St. Mary's Seminary (major), 9845 Memorial Dr. Houston. 77024.

San Antonio* — The Assumption-St. John's Seminary (major), 2600 W. Woodlawn Ave., San Antonio 78284.

Washington: Spokane — Bishop White Seminary, E. 429 Sharp Ave., Spokane 99202.

West Virginia: Wheeling-Charleston — St. Joseph Preparatory Seminary (high school), Rt. 6, Vienna. 26101; Seminary House of Studies (college residence), 1252 National Rd., Wheeling. 26003.

Wisconsin: Madison — Holy Name Seminary (High School), 3577 High Point Rd., Madison 53711.

Milwaukee* — St. Francis Seminary, School of Pastoral Ministry, and St. Francis Seminary, College Formation Program, 3257 S. Lake Dr., Milwaukee 53207. Sacred Heart School of Theology (interdiocesan), P.O. Box 429, Hales Corner, Wis. 53130.

PONTIFICAL UNIVERSITIES

(Principal source: *Annuario Pontificio*.)

These universities, listed according to country of location, have been canonically erected and authorized by the Sacred Congregation for Catholic Education to award degrees in stated fields of study.

New laws and norms governing ecclesiastical universities and faculties were promulgated in the apostolic constitution *Sapientia Christiana,* issued Apr. 15, 1979.

Argentina: Pontifical Catholic University of S. Maria of Buenos Aires (June 16, 1960): Juncal 1912, 1116 Buenos Aires.

Belgium: Catholic University of Louvain (Dec. 9, 1425; 1834), with autonomous institutions for French- (Louvain) and Flemish- (Leuven) speaking: Place de l'Universite I, 1348 Louvain-La-Neuve (French); Naamsestraat 22B, 3000 Leuven (Flemish).

Brazil: Pontifical Catholic University of Rio de Janeiro (Jan. 20, 1947): Rua Marques de Sao Vicente 209, 20000 Rio de Janeiro, Est. de Guanabara.

Pontifical Catholic University of Minas Gerais (June 5, 1983): Av. Dom Jose Gaspar 500, C.P. 2686, 30000 Belo Horizonte MG.

Pontifical Catholic University of Parana (Aug. 6, 1985): Rua Imaculada Conceicao, 1155 — Prado Velho — 80000 Curitiba PA.

Pontifical Catholic University of Rio Grande do Sul (Nov. 1, 1950): Praca Dom. Sebastiao 2, Porto Alegre, RS.

Pontifical Catholic University of Sao Paulo (Jan. 25, 1947): Rua Monte Alegre 984, Sao Paulo.

Pontifical University of Campinas (Sept. 8, 1956): Rua Marechal Deodoro 1099, Campinas, Sao Paulo.

Canada: Laval University (Mar. 15, 1876): Case Postale 460, Quebec G1K 7P4.

St. Paul University (formerly University of Ottawa) (Feb. 5, 1889): 223, Rue Main, Ottawa, K1S 1C4, Ontario.

University of Sherbrooke (Nov. 21, 1957): Chemin Ste.-Catherine, Cite Universitaire, Sherbrooke, Que. J1K 2R1.

Chile: Pontifical Catholic University of Chile (June 21, 1888): Avenida Bernardo O'Higgins 340, Casilla 114D, Santiago.

Catholic University of Valparaiso (Nov. 1, 1961): Avenida Brasil 2950, Casilla 4059, Valparaiso.

Colombia: Bolivarian Pontifical Catholic University (Aug. 16, 1945): Calle 52, N. 43-53, Medellin.

Pontifical Xaverian University (July 31, 1937): Carrera 7, N. 40-76, Apartado 56710, Bogota D.E.

Cuba: Catholic University of St. Thomas of Villanueva (May 4, 1957): Avenida Quenta 16,660, Marianao, Havana. Taken over by the Castro government in May, 1961.

Ecuador: Pontifical Catholic University of Ecuador (July 16, 1954): Doce de Octubre, N. 1076, Apartado 2184, Quito.

Ethiopia: University of Asmara (Sept. 8, 1960): Via Menelik II, 45, Post Office Box 1220, Asmara.

France: Catholic University of Lille (Nov. 18, 1875): Boulevard Vauban 60, 59046 Lille.

Catholic Faculties of Lyon (Nov. 22, 1875): 25, Rue du Plat, 69288 Lyon.

Catholic Institute of Paris (Aug. 11, 1875): 21, Rue d'Assas, 75270 Paris.

Catholic Institute of Toulouse (Nov. 15,1877): Rue de la Fonderie 31, 31068 Toulouse.

Catholic University of the West (Sept. 16, 1875): 3, Place Andre Leroy, B.P. 808, 49005 Angers.

Germany: Eichstatt Catholic University (Apr. 1, 1980): Ostenstrasse 26-28, D-8078, Eichstatt.

Guatemala: Rafael Landivar University (Oct. 18, 1961): 17 Calle 8-64, Z 10 Guatemala.

Ireland: St. Patrick's College (Mar. 29, 1896): Maynooth, Co. Kildare.

Italy: Catholic University of the Sacred Heart (Dec. 25, 1920): Largo Gemelli 1, 20123 Milan.

Japan: *Jochi Daigaku* (Sophia University) (Mar. 29, 1913): Chiyoda-Ku, Kioi-cho 7, Tokyo.

Lebanon: St. Joseph University of Beirut (Mar. 25, 1881): Rue de l'Universite St.-Joseph, Boite Postale 293, Beyrouth.

Netherlands: Nijmegen Roman Catholic University (June 29, 1923): Wilhelminasingel 13, Nijmegen.

Panama: University of S. Maria La Antigua (May 27, 1965): Apartado 2143, Panama 1.

Paraguay: Catholic University of Our Lady of the Assumption (Feb. 2, 1965): Independencia Nacional y Comuneros, Casilla 1718, Asuncion.

Peru: Pontifical Catholic University of Peru (Sept. 30, 1942): Apartado 1761, Lima.

Philippine Islands: Pontifical University of Santo Tomas (Nov. 20, 1645): Espana Street, Manila.

Poland: Catholic University of Lublin (July 25, 1920): Aleje Raclawickie 14, Skr. Poczt. 279, 20-950, Lublin.

Pontifical Academy of Theology of Krakow (Dec. 8, 1981): Ul. Podzamcze 8, 31-003 Krakow.

Portugal: Portuguese Catholic University (Nov. 1, 1967): Palma de Cima, 1600 Lisbon.

Puerto Rico: Catholic University of Puerto Rico (Aug. 15, 1972): Ponce, Puerto Rico 00731.

Spain: Catholic University of Navarra (Aug. 6, 1960): Ciudad Universitaria, Pamplona.

Pontifical University "Comillas" (Mar. 29, 1904): Apartado Postal 3082, 28080 Madrid.

Pontifical University of Salamanca (Sept. 25, 1940): Apartado 541, 37080 Salamanca.

University of Deusto (Aug. 10, 1963): Avenida de las Universidades, 28, 48007 Bilbao.

Taiwan (China): Fu Jen Catholic University

(Nov. 15, 1923, at Peking; reconstituted at Taipeh, Sept. 8, 1961): Hsinchuang, Taipeh Hsien.

United States: Catholic University of America (Mar. 7, 1889): 620 Michigan Ave. N.E., Washington, D.C. 20064.

Georgetown University (Mar. 30, 1833): 37th and O Sts. N.W., Washington, D.C. 20057.

Niagara University (June 21, 1956): Niagara University, N.Y. 14109.

Uruguay: Catholic University of Uruguay "Damaso Antonio Larranaga" (Jan. 25, 1985): Avda. 8 de Octubre 2738, Montevideo.

Venezuela: Catholic University "Andres Bello" (Sept. 29, 1963): Esquina Jesuitas, Apartado 422, Caracas.

ECCLESIASTICAL FACULTIES
(Principal Source: *Annuario Pontificio*)

These faculties in Catholic seminaries and universities, listed according to country of location, have been canonically erected and authorized by the Sacred Congregation for Catholic Education to award degrees in stated fields of study. In addition to those listed here, there are other faculties of theology or philosophy in state universities and for members of certain religious orders only.

Argentina: Faculties of Philosophy and Theology, San Miguel (Sept. 8, 1932).

Australia: Institute of Theology, Sydney (Feb. 2, 1954).

Austria: Theological Faculty, Linz (Dec. 25, 1978).

Brazil: Ecclesiastical Faculty of Philosophy "John Paul II," Rio de Janeiro Aug. 6, 1981.

Philosophical and Theological Faculties of the Company of Jesus, Belo Horizonte (July 15, 1941 and Mar. 30, 1945).

Canada: Pontifical Institute of Medieval Studies, Toronto (Oct. 18, 1939).

Dominican Faculty of Theology of Canada, Ottawa (1965; Nov. 15, 1975).

Regis College — Toronto Section of the Jesuit Faculty of Theology in Canada, Toronto (Feb. 17, 1956; Dec. 25, 1977).

College of Immaculate Conception — Montreal Section of Jesuit Faculties in Canada (Sept. 8, 1932).

France: Centre Sevres — Faculties of Theology and Philosophy of the Jesuits, Paris (Sept. 8, 1932).

Germany: Theological Faculty, Paderborn (June 11, 1966).

Theological Faculty of the Major Episcopal Seminary, Trier (Sept. 8, 1955)

Philosophical Faculty, Munich (1932; Oct. 25, 1971).

Theological-Philosophical Faculty, Frankfurt (1932; June 7, 1971).

Theological Faculty, Fulda (Dec. 22, 1978).

Great Britain: Heythrop College, University of London, London (Nov. 1, 1964). Theology, philosophy.

India: "Jnana Deepa" (Pontifical Athenaeum), Institute of Philosophy and Religion, Poona (July 27, 1926).

Pontifical Institute of Theology and Philosophy, Alwaye, Kerala (Feb. 24, 1972).

"Vidyajyoti," Institute of Religious Studies, Faculty of Theology, Delhi (1932; Dec. 9, 1974).

Dharmaran Pontifical Institute of Theology and Philosophy, Bangalore (Jan. 6, 1976; Dec. 8, 1983).

Faculty of Theology, Ranchi (Aug. 15, 1982).

Pontifical Oriental Institute of Religious Studies, Kottayam (July 3, 1982).

St. Peter's Pontifical Institute of Theology, Bangalore (Jan. 6, 1976).

"Satya Nilayam," Institute of Philosophy and Culture. Faculty of Philosophy, Madras (Sept. 8, 1932; Dec. 15, 1976).

Indonesia: Wedabhakti Pontifical Faculty of Theology, Yogyakarta (Nov. 1, 1984).

Israel: French Biblical and Archeological School, Jerusalem (founded 1890; approved Sept. 17, 1892; canonically approved to confer Doctorate in Biblical Science, June 29, 1983).

Italy: Interregional Theological Faculty, Milan (Aug. 8, 1935; restructured 1969).

Pontifical Theological Faculty of the Most Sacred Heart of Jesus, Cagliari, of the Pontifical Regional Seminary of Sardinia (July 5, 1927).

Pontifical Ambrosian Institute of Sacred Music, Milan (Mar. 12, 1940).

Theological Faculty of Sicily, Palermo (Dec. 8, 1980).

Theological Faculty of Southern Italy, Naples. Two sections: St. Thomas Aquinas Capodimonte (Oct. 31, 1941) and St. Louis Posillipo (Mar. 16, 1918). Pastoral Ignatian Institute, Messina (July 31, 1972).

Faculty of Philosophy "Aloisianum," Gallarate (1937; Mar. 20, 1974).

Ivory Coast: Catholic Institute of West Africa, Abidjan (Aug. 12, 1975).

Japan: Faculty of Theology, Nagoya (May 25, 1984).

Lebanon: Faculty of Theology, University of the Holy Spirit, Kaslik (May 30, 1982).

Madagascar: Superior Institute of Theology, at the Regional Seminary of Antananarivo, Ambatoroka-Antananarivo (Apr. 21, 1960).

Malta: Faculty of Theology, Tal-Virtu (Nov. 22, 1769), with Institute of Philosophy and Human Studies (Sept. 8, 1984).

Mexico: Theological Faculty of Mexico, Mexico City (June 29, 1982).

Nigeria: Catholic Institute of West Africa, Port Harcourt (Nov. 30, 1981).

Peru: Pontifical and Civil Faculty of Theology, Lima (July 25, 1571).

Poland: Theological Faculty, Poznan (1969; pontifical designation, June 2, 1974).

Spain: Theological Faculty of Catalunya, (Mar. 7, 1968), with the Institute of Fundamental Theology (Dec. 28, 1984), Barcelona.

Theological Faculty, Granada (1940; July 31, 1973).

Theological Faculty of the North, of the Metropolitan Seminary of Burgos and the Diocesan Seminary of Vitoria (Feb. 6, 1967).

Theological Faculty "San Vicente Ferrer" (two sections), Valencia (Jan. 23, 1974).

Switzerland: Theological Faculty, Chur (Jan. 1, 1974).

Theological Faculty, Luzerne (Dec. 25, 1973).

United States: St. Mary's Seminary and University. School of Theology, Baltimore (May 1, 1822).

St. Mary of the Lake Faculty of Theology, Chicago (Sept. 30, 1929).

Weston School of Theology, Cambridge, Mass. (Oct. 18, 1932).

The Jesuit School of Theology, Berkeley, Calif. (Feb. 2, 1934, as "Alma College," Los Gatos, Calif.).

Faculty of Philosophy and Letters, St. Louis, Mo. (Feb. 2, 1934).

St. Michael's Institute, Jesuit School of Philosophy and Letters, Spokane, Wash. (Feb. 2, 1934).

Pontifical Faculty of Theology of the Immaculate Conception, Washington, D.C. (Nov. 15, 1941).

Vietnam: Theological Faculty of the Pontifical National Seminary of St. Pius X, Dalat (July 31, 1965). Activities suppressed.

The Pontifical College Josephinum (Theologate and College) at Columbus, Ohio, is a national pontifical seminary. Established Sept. 1, 1888, it is immediately subject to the Holy See.

PONTIFICAL UNIVERSITIES AND INSTITUTES IN ROME

(Source: *Annuario Pontificio.*)

Pontifical Gregorian University (1552): Piazza della Pilotta, 4, 00187 Rome. Associated with the university are:

The **Pontifical Biblical Institute** (May 7, 1909): Via della Pilotta, 25, 00187 Rome.

The **Pontifical Institute of Oriental Studies** (Oct. 15, 1917): Piazza S. Maria Maggiore, 7, 00185 Rome.

Pontifical Lateran University (1773). Piazza S. Giovanni in Laterano, 4, 00184 Rome.

Pontifical Urban University (1627): Via Urbano VIII, 16, 00165 Rome.

Pontifical University of St. Thomas Aquinas (Angelicum) (1580), of the Order of Preachers: Largo Angelicum, 1, 00184 Rome.

Pontifical University Salesianum (May 3, 1940; university designation May 24, 1973), of the Salesians of Don Bosco: Piazza dell' Ateneo Salesiano, 1, 00139 Rome. Associated with the university is the **Pontifical Institute of Higher Latin Studies,** known as the **Faculty of Christian and Classical Letters** (Feb. 22, 1964).

Pontifical Athenaeum of St. Anselm (1687), of the Benedictines: Piazza dei Cavalieri di Malta, 5, 00153 Rome.

Pontifical Athenaeum "Antonianum" (of St. Anthony) (May 17, 1933), of the Order of Friars Minor: Via Merulana, 124, 00185 Rome.

Pontifical Institute of Sacred Music (1911; May 24, 1931): Via di Torre Rossa, 21, 00165 Rome.

Pontifical Institute of Christian Archeology (Dec. 11, 1925): Via Napoleone III, 1, 00185 Rome.

Pontifical Theological Faculty "St. Bonaventure" (Dec. 18, 1587), of the Order of Friars Minor Conventual: Via del Serafico, 1, 00142 Rome.

Pontifical Theological Faculty, Pontifical Institute of Spirituality "Teresianum" (1935), of the

Discalced Carmelites: Piazza San Pancrazio, 5-A, 00152 Rome.

Pontifical Theological Faculty "Marianum" (1398), of the Servants of Mary: Viale Trente Aprile, 6, 00153 Rome.

Pontifical Institute of Arabic and Islamic Studies (1926), of the Missionaries of Africa: Piazza S.

Apollinare, 49, 00186 Rome.

Pontifical Faculty of Educational Science "Auxilium" (June 27, 1970), of the Daughters of Mary, Help of Christians: Via Cremolino, 141, 00166 Rome.

Pontifical Institute "Regina Mundi" (1954): Lungotevere Tor di Nona, 7, 00186 Rome.

PONTIFICAL ACADEMY OF SCIENCES

(Sources: *Annuario Pontificio,* NC News Service. Membership as of July 15, 1986.)

The Pontifical Academy of Sciences was constituted in its present form by Pius XI Oct. 28, 1936, in virtue of *In Multis Solaciis,* a document issued on his own initiative.

The academy is the only supranational body of its kind in the world, with a pope-selected, life-long membership of outstanding mathematicians and experimental scientists from many countries. The normal complement of 70 members was increased in 1986 by John Paul II who appointed 15 scientists to the Academy. There are additional honorary and supernumerary members. Non-Catholics as well as Catholics belong to the academy.

Purposes of the academy are to honor pure science and its practitioners, to promote the freedom of pure science and to foster research.

The academy traces its origin to the *Linceorum Academia* (Academy of the Lynxes — its symbol) founded in Rome Aug. 17, 1603. Pius IX reorganized this body and gave it a new name — *Pontificia Accademia dei Nuovi Lincei* — in 1847. It was taken over by the Italian state in 1870 and called the *Accademia Nazionale dei Lincei.* Leo XIII reconstituted it with a new charter in 1887. Pius XI designated the Vatican Gardens as the site of academy headquarters in 1922 and gave it its present title and status in 1936. In 1940, Pius XII gave the title of Excellency to its members; John XXIII extended the privilege to honorary members in 1961.

Members in U.S.

Scientists in the U.S. who presently hold membership in the Academy are listed below according to year of appointment.

1936 (Oct. 28): Franco Rasetti, professor emeritus of physics at Johns Hopkins University, Baltimore, Md.; George Speri-Sperti, president and director of the Institute Divi Thomae in the Athanaeum of Ohio.

1948 (May 29): Adelbert Doisy, professor emeritus of biochemistry at St. Louis University.

1964 (Sept. 24): William Wilson Morgan, professor emeritus of astronomy at the University of Chicago.

1970 (Apr. 10): Albert Szent-Gyorgyi, director of Institute for Muscle Research at the Marine Biological Laboratory, Woods Hole, Mass.

1974 (June 24): Rita Levi-Montalcini, professor emeritus of biology at Washington University, St. Louis, Mo.; Severo Ochoa, professor emeritus of the Roche Institute of Molecular Biology, Nutley, N.J.; Marshall Warren Nirenberg, professor of genetics and biochemistry at the National Institutes of Health, Bethesda, Md.

1975 (Dec. 2): George Palade, professor of cellular biology at Yale University, New Haven, Conn.; Victor Weisskopf, professor of physics at the Massachusetts Institute of Technology, Cambridge, Mass.

1978 (Apr. 17): David Baltimore, professor of biology, Har Gobind Khorana, professor of biochemistry, and Alexander Rich, professor of biophysics — all at the Massachusetts Institute of Technology, Cambridge, Mass.; Roger Walcott Sperry, professor of psychobiology, California Institute of Technology, Pasadena, Calif.

1981 (May 13): Christian Anfinsen, professor of biochemistry at Johns Hopkins University, Baltimore, Md.

1983 (Feb. 12): Charles Townes, professor of physics at the University of California at Berkeley.

1986 (Jan. 21): Carlo Rubbia, professor of physics at Harvard University and CERN, Geneva, Switzerland. (June 12): Beatrice Mintz, chief researcher, Cancer Research Institute of Philadelphia; Maxine Singer, director of biochemistry laboratory, Biologic and Diagnostic Division of National Cancer Institute, Bethesda, Md.

Deceased U.S. members of the Academy were: George D. Birkhoff, Alexis Carrel, Herbert Sidney Langfeld, Robert A. Millikan, Thomas H. Morgan, Theodore von Karman, Victor F. Hess, Peter Debye, Hugh Stott Taylor.

Members in Other Countries

Other members of the Academy are listed below according to country of location; dates of their selection are given in parentheses.

Argentina: Luis F. Leloir (Apr. 22, 1968).

Austria: Hans Tuppy (Apr. 10, 1970); Walter Thirring (June 12, 1986).

Belgium: Christian de Duve (Apr. 10, 1970).

Brazil: Carlos Chagas (Aug. 18, 1961); Johanna Dobereiner (Apr. 17, 1978); Crodowaldo Pavan (Apr. 17, 1978).

Canada: Gerhard Herzberg (Sept. 24, 1964); Karel Wiesner (Apr. 17, 1978); John Charles Polanyi (June 12, 1986).

Chile: Hector Croxatto Rezzio (Dec. 2, 1975).

Denmark: Bengt Georg Stromgren (Dec. 2, 1975); Aage Bohr (Apr. 17, 1978).

France: Louis de Broglie (Apr. 5, 1955); Pierre Raphael Lepine (Sept. 24, 1964); Louis Leprince-Ringuet (Aug. 18, 1961); Jerome Lejeune (June 24, 1974); Andre Blanc-LaPierre (Apr. 17, 1978), Anatole Abragam (May 13, 1981), Andre Lichnerowicz (May 13, 1981), Bernard Pullman (May 13, 1981); Paul Germain (June 12, 1986).

Germany: Rudolf L. Mossbauer (Apr. 10, 1970), Manfred Eigen (May 13, 1981).

Ghana: Daniel Azei Bekoe (Sept. 26, 1983).

Great Britain: Hermann Alexander Bruck (Apr. 5, 1955); Alan Lloyd Hodgkin (Apr. 22, 1968); Alfred R. Ubbelohde (Apr. 22, 1968); Percy C. C. Garnham (Apr. 10, 1970); George Porter (June 24, 1974); Max Ferdinand Perutz (May 13, 1981); Stanley Keith Runcorn (Sept. 13, 1981); Stephen William Hawking (Jan. 21, 1986).

Hungary: Janos Szentagothai (May 13, 1981).

India: Mambilliralathil Govind Kumar Menon (May 13, 1981).

Israel: Michael Sela (Dec. 2, 1975).

Italy: Giovanni Battista Marini-Bettolo (Apr. 22, 1968); Giuseppe Moruzzi (Apr. 17, 1978); Giampietro Puppi (Apr. 17, 1978), Ennio De Giorgi (May 13, 1981), Abdus Salam (May 13, 1981); Nicola Cabibbo (June 12, 1986).

Japan: Hamao Umezawa (Sept. 26, 1983); Kenichi Fukui (Jan. 21, 1986).

Kenya: Thomas R. Odhiambo (May 13, 1981).

Mexico: Marcos Moshinsky (June 12, 1986).

Netherlands: Jan Hendrik Oort (Aug. 18, 1961).

Pakistan: Salimuzzaman Siddiqui (Sept. 24, 1964).

Poland: Stanislaw Lojasiewicz (Feb. 12, 1983); Czeslaw Olech (June 12, 1986).

Spain: Manuel Lora Tamayo (Sept. 24, 1964).

Sweden: Sven Horstadius (Aug. 18, 1961); Sune Bergstrom (Jan. 21, 1986); Kai Siegbahn (Jan. 21, 1986).

Switzerland: John Carew Eccles (Apr. 8, 1961), Thomas Lambo (June 24, 1974), Werner Arber (May 13, 1981); Vladimir Prelog (Jan. 21, 1986); Albert Eschenmoser (June 12, 1986).

Venezuela: Marcel Roche (Apr. 10, 1970).

Zaire: Wa Kalengo Malu (Sept. 26, 1983).

Ex officio members: Rev. George V. Coyne, S.J., director of Vatican Observatory (Sept. 2, 1978); Very Rev. Leonard E. Boyle, O.P., prefect of the Vatican Library (May 24, 1984); Very Rev. Joseph Metzler, O.M.I., prefect of the Secret Vatican Archives (May 24, 1984).

Honorary member: Silvio Ranzi, professor emeritus of biology and zoology of the University of Milan (May 13, 1981).

President: Carlos Chagas (Nov. 9, 1972).

SOCIAL SERVICES

Catholic Charities USA (formerly National Conference of Catholic Charities): Established in 1910 to help advance and promote the charitable programs and activities of Catholic community and social service agencies in the United States. As the central and national organization for this purpose, it services member agencies and institutions by consultation, information and assistance in planning and evaluating social service programs under Catholic auspices.

The principal fields of service in which Catholic Charities agencies are engaged are family counseling, child welfare, services for unmarried mothers, community services, day care centers, neighborhood center programs, and care of the aged. Community organization, social action and parish social ministry are also functions of Catholic Charities.

The organization conducts research with respect to service to the aging, community self-help programs, the institutional care of children, and other social service projects. It represents the Catholic philosophy of social service to government agencies and personnel, and to professional organizations in the field. Its publications include *Charities USA*, a monthly membership magazine, and *Social Thought*, a scholarly quarterly co-sponsored with the National School of Social Service of the Catholic University of America.

Membership includes more than 900 local agencies and branches, 1,000 institutions and 3,000 individuals.

Rev. Thomas J. Harvey is executive director of the conference, with offices at 1319 F St. N.W., Washington, D.C. 20004.

The Society of St. Vincent de Paul, originally called the Conference of Charity: An association of Catholic laity devoted to personal service of the poor through the spiritual and corporal works of mercy. The first conference was formed at Paris in 1833 by Frederic Ozanam and his associates.

The first conference in the U.S. was organized in 1845 at St. Louis. There are now approximately 4,700 units of the society in this country, with a membership of about 36,000.

In the past 50 years, members of the society in this country have distributed among poor persons financial and other forms of assistance valued at approximately $400 million.

U.S. Vincentian councils and conferences participating in "twinning" programs assist their poorer counterparts abroad by sending them correspondence, information and financial aid on a continuing basis.

Under the society's revised regulations, women are being admitted to membership. Increasing emphasis is being given to stores and rehabilitation workshops of the society through which persons with marginal income can purchase refurbished goods at minimal cost. Handicapped persons are employed in renovating goods and store operations.

The office of the U.S. Superior Council is located at 4140 Lindell Blvd., St. Louis, Mo. 63108.

Catholic Health Association of the United States, formerly Catholic Hospital Association: Founded in 1915, is a service organization for more than 1,300 Catholic-sponsored health care organizations located throughout the United States.

The association is dedicated to the healing mission of the Church by promoting health of those who are sick or infirm because of age or disability; by respecting human dignity in the experience of sickness and death; and by fostering physical, psychological, emotional, spiritual and social well-being of people.

Membership in 1985 included 622 hospitals with 166,093 beds treating more than 39 million patients; 279 long-term care facilities with more than 37,000 beds; 278 religious congregations; 14 dioceses; 52 multi-institutional systems; 80 associate and 255 personal members.

John E. Curley, Jr., is president. Executive offices are located at 4455 Woodson Rd., St. Louis, Mo. 63134.

National Association of Catholic Chaplains: Founded in 1965. Membership is approximately 3,300.

Rev. Edward Dietrich is executive director. Address: 3257 S. Lake Dr., Milwaukee Wis. 53207.

FACILITIES FOR RETIRED AND AGED PERSONS

(Sources: Almanac survey, *The Official Catholic Directory.*)

This list covers residence, health care and other facilities for the retired and aged under Catholic auspices. Information includes name, type of facility if not evident from the title, address, and total capacity (in parentheses); unless noted otherwise, facilities are for both men and women. Many facilities for the aged offer intermediate nursing care.

Alabama: Allen Memorial Home (Skilled Nursing), 735 S. Washington Ave., Mobile 36603 (94).

Sacred Heart Residence Little Sisters of the Poor, 1655 McGill Ave., Mobile 36604 (120).

Villa Mercy (Skilled Nursing Facility, Hospice, Home Health Agency), P.O. Box 1090, Daphne 36526. Specialized hospital, not restricted to elderly.

Arizona: Villa Maria Geriatric Center (Skilled Nursing Facility and Apartments), 4310 E. Grant Rd., Tucson 85712 (93 beds, 50 apartments). Members of the Holy Cross health system.

Arkansas: Benedictine Manor (Retirement Home), 2nd and Grand Sts., Box 2249, Hot Springs 71914 (92).

California: Alexis Apartments of St. Patrick's Parish, 756 Mission St. 94103; 390 Clementina St., San Francisco 94103 (220).

Casa Manana Inn, 3700 N. Sutter St., Stockton 95204 (175).

Cathedral Plaza, 1551 Third Ave., San Diego 92101 (222 apartments).

Ellis Seniors Residence, 3263 First Ave., Sacramento 95817 (18).

Francis of Assisi Community, 145 Guerrero St., San Francisco 94103 (117). For elderly and handicapped.

Guadalupe Plaza, 4142 42nd St., San Diego 92105 (127 apartments).

Jeanne d'Arc Manor, 85 S. Fifth St., San Jose 95112 (91). For elderly and handicapped.

Little Flower Haven (Residential Care Facility for Retired), 8585 La Mesa Blvd., La Mesa 92041 (93).

Little Sisters of the Poor, 300 Lake St., San Francisco 94118 (120).

Little Sisters of the Poor, Jeanne Jugan Residence, 2100 South Western Ave., San Pedro, Calif. 90732 (120).

Madonna Residence (Retirement Home for Women 55 and over), 1055 Pine St., San Francisco 94109 (56).

Marian Residence (Retirement Home), 124 S. College Dr., Santa Maria 93454 (58).

Mercy Retirement and Care, 3431 Foothill Blvd., Oakland 94601 (130).

Mother Gertrude Balcazar Home for Senior Citizens, 11320 Laurel Canyon Blvd., San Fernando 91340 (114).

Nazareth House, 2121 N. 1st St., Fresno 93703 (91).

Nazareth House, 3333 Manning Ave., Los Angeles 90064 (138).

Nazareth House (Retirement Home), 245 Nova Albion Way, Terra Linda, San Rafael 94903 (145).

Nazareth House Retirement Home, 6333 Rancho Mission Rd., San Diego 92108 (122).

Our Lady of Fatima Villa (Skilled Nursing Facility, Women), 20400 Saratoga/Los Gatos Rd., Saratoga 95070 (85).

St. Francis Home (Elderly and Retired Women), 1718 W. 6th St., Santa Ana 92703 (83).

St. John of God Nursing Hospital and Residence, 2035 W. Adams Blvd., Los Angeles 90018.

St. John's Plaza, 8150 Broadway, Lemon Grove 92045 (100 apartments).

Villa Scalabrini (Retirement Center), 10631 Vinedale St., Sun Valley 91352 (130).

Villa Siena (Residence and Intermediate Care), 1855 Miramonte Ave., Mountain View 94040 (50, residence; 20, skilled nursing care).

Colorado: Little Sisters of the Poor, 3629 W. 29th Ave., Denver 80211 (105).

St. Elizabeth Center (Retirement Home), 2825 W. 32nd Ave., Denver 80211 (187).

Connecticut: Augustana Homes (Residence), Simeon Rd., Bethel 06801.

Carmel Ridge Estates, Gramco Management Co., 525 Palisade Ave., Bridgeport 06610 (36 units).

Matulaitis Nursing Home, Putnam 06260 (119).

Monsignor Bojnowski Manor, Inc. (Skilled Nursing Facility), 50 Pulaski St., New Britain 06053 (60).

Notre Dame Convalescent Home, 76 West Rocks Rd., Norwalk 06851 (60).

Regina Pacis Villa (Residence), RFD No. 1, Pomfret Center 06259 (16).

Roncalli Apartments, 430 Grant St., Bridgeport 06610.

St. Joseph Guest Home (Women, Employed and Retired), 311 Greene St., New Haven 06511 (80).

St. Joseph's Home for the Aged, 88 Jackson St., Willimantic 06226 (37).

St. Joseph's Manor, Carmelite Srs. for Aged and Infirm, 6448 Main St., Trumbull 06611 (294).

St. Joseph's Residence, Little Sisters of the Poor, 1365 Enfield St., Enfield, Conn. 06082 (94)

St. Lucian's Home for the Aged, 532 Burritt St., New Britain 06053 (54).

St. Mary's Home (Residence and Health Care

Facility), 291 Steele Rd., W. Hartford 06117 (177).

Teresian Towers, Carmelite Sisters for Aged and Infirm, 6454 Main St., Trumbull 06611 (50 units).

Villa Maria Rest Home for the Aged, West St., Thompson 06277 (24).

Delaware: The Antonian, 1701 W. 10th St., Wilmington 19805 (136).

Jeanne Jugan Residence, Little Sisters of the Poor, 185 Salem Church Rd., Newark 19713 (123).

Marydale, 135 Jeandell Dr., Newark 19713 (108 apartments).

St. Patrick's House, Inc., 14th and French Sts., Wilmington 19801 (14).

District of Columbia: Jeanne Jugan Residence — St. Joseph' Villa, Little Sisters of the Poor, 4200 Harewood Rd., N.E. Washington 20017 (117).

Florida: All Saints Home for the Aged, 2040 Riverside Ave., Jacksonville 32204 (60).

Carroll Manor (Retirement Apartments), 3667 S. Miami Ave., Miami 33133 (236 apartments).

Casa Calderon, Inc. (Retirement Apartments), 800 W. Virginia St., Tallahassee 32304 (111).

Cor Jesu Retirement Center, 4918 N. Habana Ave., Tampa 33614 (75).

Haven of Our Lady of Peace (Residence and Health Care Facility), 5203 N. 9th Ave., Pensacola 32504 (87).

Maria Manor Health Care Center, 10300 4th St. N., St. Petersburg 33702 (274).

Marian Towers, Inc. (Retirement Apartments), 17505 North Bay Rd., Miami Beach 33160.

Noreen McKeen Residence for Geriatric Care, 315 Flagler Dr. S., W. Palm Beach 33401.

Pennsylvania Retirement Residence, 208 Evernia St., W. Palm Beach 33401 (190).

St. Andrew Towers (Retirement Apartments), 2700 N.W. 99th Ave., Coral Springs 33065.

St. Dominic Gardens, 5849 N.W. 7th St., Miami 33126.

St. Elizabeth Gardens, Inc. (Retirement Apartments), 801 N.E. 33rd St., Pompano Beach 33064.

St. Joseph's Residence, 3485 N.W. 30th St., Ft. Lauderdale 33311.

Illinois: Addolorato Villa (Home for Aged), 555 McHenry Rd., Wheeling 60090 (98).

Alvernia Manor (Sheltered Care), 1598 Main St., Lemont 60439 (50).

Carlyle Healthcare Center, 501 Clinton St., Carlyle 62231 (124).

Carmelite Carefree Village, 8419 Bailey Rd., Darien 60559 (96 units, 150 residents).

Cortland Manor Retirement Home, 1900 N. Karlow, Chicago 68639. (52).

Holy Family Health Center, 2380 Dempster, Des Plaines 60016 (272).

Holy Family Villa (Intermediate Care Facility), Lemont 60439 (99).

Huber Memorial Home (Residence, Women), 1000 30th St., Rock Island 61201 (14).

Jugan Terrace, Little Sisters of the Poor, 2300 N. Racine, Chicago 60614 (50 apartments).

Little Sisters of the Poor Center for the Aging,

2325 N. Lakewood Ave., Chicago, Ill. 60614 (120).

Marian Heights Apartments (Elderly, Handicapped), 20 Oak St., Alton 62002 (141).

Marian Park, Inc., 2126 W. Roosevelt Rd., Wheaton 60187 (117 apartments).

Maryhaven, Inc. (Intermediate Care Facility), 1700 E. Lake Ave., Glenview 60025 (147).

Mayslake Village (Retirement Apartments), 1801 35th St., Oak Brook 60521 (630 apartments).

Meredith Memorial Home, 16 S. Illinois St., Belleville 62220 (90).

Merkle-Knipprath Nursing Home, Rt. 1, Franciscan Brothers. Clifton 60927 (100).

Mother Theresa Home (Sheltered and Intermediate Care), 1270 Main St., Lemont 60439 (57).

Nazarethville (Intermediate Care), 300 River Rd., Des Plaines 60016 (83).

Our Lady of Angels Retirement Home, 1201 Wyoming, Joliet 60435 (100).

Our Lady of the Snows Apartment Community (Retirement Apartment Community; Health Care Program), 9500 W. Ill., Rt. 15, Belleville 62223 (230).

Pope John Paul I Apartments (Elderly and Handicapped), 1 Pope John Paul Plaza, Springfield 62703 (160).

Resurrection Retirement Community, 7262 W. Peterson Ave., Chicago, 60631 (311 apartments).

Rosary Hill Home (Residence), 9000 W. 81st St., Justice 60458 (50).

St. Andrew Home for the Aged, 7000 N. Newark Ave., Niles 60648 (198).

St. Ann's Health Care Center, 770 State St., Chester 62233 (92).

St. Benedict Home, 6930 W. Touhy Ave., Niles 60648 (52).

St. Joseph's Home (Sheltered and Intermediate Care), 3306 S. 6th St. Rd., Springfield 62703 (133).

St. Joseph's Home (Sheltered and Intermediate Care), 2223 W. Heading Ave., Peoria 61604 (200).

St. Joseph's Home for the Aged, 649 E. Jefferson St., Freeport 61032 (106).

St. Joseph's Home for the Elderly, 80 W. Northwest Hwy., Palatine 60067 (137).

St. Joseph Home of Chicago, Inc., 2650 N. Ridgeway Ave., Chicago 60647 (173).

St. Patrick's Residence (Sheltered and Intermediate Care), 22 E. Clinton St., Joliet 60431 (197).

Villa Saint Cyril (Residence), 1111 St. John's Ave., Highland Park 60035 (80).

Villa Scalabrini (Sheltered, Intermediate and Skilled), 480 N. Wolf Rd., Northlake 60164 (265).

Indiana: Little Company of Mary Health Facility (Comprehensive Nursing), Route 421 San Pierre 46374 (180).

Providence Retirement Home, 703 E. Spring St., New Albany 47150 (95).

Regina Continuing Care Center (Skilled Nursing and Intermediate Care Facility), 3900 Washington Ave., Evansville 47715 (154).

Sacred Heart Home (Comprehensive Nursing), R.R. 2, Avilla 46710 (130). LaVerna Terrace, same address; independent living for senior citizens, handicapped and disabled (51 units).

St. Anne Home (Residence and Comprehensive Nursing), 1900 Randalia Dr., Ft. Wayne 46805 (205).

St. Anthony Medical Center and St. Anthony Home, Inc.; 201 Franciscan Rd., Crown Point 46307 (229).

St. Augustine Home for the Aged, Little Sisters of the Poor, 2345 W. 86th St., Indianapolis 46260 (120).

St. John's Home for the Aged, Little Sisters of the Poor, 1236 Lincoln Ave., Evansville 47714 (130).

St. Paul Hermitage, 501 N. 17th St., Beech Grove 46107 (105).

Iowa: The Alverno Health Care Facility (Intermediate Care), 849 13th Ave. N., Clinton 52732 (136).

Bishop Drumm Retirement Center, 5387 Winwood Dr., Johnston 50131 (120 beds; 87 apartments).

Hallmar-Mercy Hospital, 701 Tenth St. S.E., Cedar Rapids 52403 (64 residential; 12 skilled nursing facility).

Holy Spirit Retirement Home (Intermediate Care), 1701 W. 25th St., Sioux City 51103 (94).

Kahl Home for the Aged and Infirm (Intermediate Care Facility), 1101 W. 9th St., Davenport 52804 (125).

The Marian Home, 2400 6th Ave. North, Fort Dodge 50501 (Intermediate Care, 97) and Marian Village (Apartments), 2320 6th Ave. North, Fort Dodge 50501.

Mary of the Angels Home (Women, Employed and Retired), 605 Bluff St., Dubuque 52001 (85).

Padre Pio Health Care Center, Stonehill Care Center (Residence, Nursing Home), 3485 Windsor, Dubuque 52001 (250).

Ritter Home for Retired Women, 1837 Sunnyside Ave., Burlington 52601 (6).

St. Anthony Nursing Home (Intermediate Care), 406 E. Anthony St., Carroll 51401 (80).

St. Francis Continuation Care and Nursing Home Center, Burlington 52601 (29 skilled nursing; 59 intermediate care).

Kansas: Catholic Center for the Aging, 3411 E. Zimmerly, Wichita 67218 (150).

Mt. Joseph (Intermediate Care Facility), 1110 W. 11, R.R. 1, Concordia 66901 (100 nursing; 12 apartments).

St. John Rest Home (Intermediate Care Facility), 701 Seventh St., Victoria 67671 (60).

St. John's of Hays (Skilled Facility), 2403 Canterbury Rd., Hays 67601 (60 nursing; 12 apartments).

St. Joseph Home (Skilled Care Facility), 759 Vermont Ave., Kansas City 66101 (201 nursing; 36 apartments).

Villa Maria, Inc. (Intermediate Care Facility), 116 S. Central, Mulvane 67110 (66).

Kentucky: Carmel Home (Residence, Adult Day Care and Nursing Care), 2501 Old Hartford Rd., Owensboro 42301 (84).

Carmel Manor (Personal Care Home), Carmel Manor Rd., Ft. Thomas, 41075 (99).

The Knottsville Home, Rt. 1, Philpot 42366 (65).

Madonna Manor Intermediate Care Nursing Home, 2344 Amsterdam Rd., Covington 41016 (38). (Cottages for Senior Citizens: 9, with 48 apartments).

St. Charles Nursing Home, 500 Farrell Dr., Covington 41011 (147).

St. Margaret of Cortona Home (Women, Personal Care Home), 1310 Leestown Pike, Lexington 40508 (24).

Taylor Manor Nursing Home, Versailles 40383 (82).

Louisiana: Annunciation Inn, 1220 Spain St., New Orleans 70117 (106 residential units).

Bethany M.H.S. Health Care Center (Women), P.O. Box 2308, Lafayette 70502 (42).

Chateau de Notre Dame (Residence and Nursing Home), 2832 Burdette St., New Orleans 70125 (110 residential units, 180 nursing beds).

Christopher Inn Apartments, 2110 Royal St., New Orleans 70116 (144 residential units).

Consolata Home (Nursing Home), 2319 E. Main St., New Iberia 70560.

Lafon Nursing Home of the Holy Family, 6900 Chef Menteur Hwy., New Orleans 70126 (171).

Mary-Joseph Residence for the Elderly, 4201 Woodland Dr., New Orleans 70114 (122).

Metairie Manor, 4929 York St., Metairie 70001 (200 residential units).

Nazareth Inn, 9630 Haynes Blvd., New Orleans 70127 (270 apartments).

Ollie Steele Burden Manor (Nursing Home), 4200 Essen Lane, Baton Rouge 70809 (65).

Our Lady of Prompt Succor Home (Skilled Nursing Care), 751 E. Prudhomme Lane, Opelousas 70570.

Our Lady's Manor, Inc., 402 Monroe St., Alexandria 71301 (104 apartments).

Place Dubourg, 201 Rue Dubourg, LaPlace 70068 (115 residential units).

Rouquette Lodge, 4300 Hwy 22, Mandeville 70448 (119 residential units).

St. John Berchman's Manor, 3400 St. Anthony St., New Orleans 70122 (150 residential units).

St. Joseph's Home (Nursing Home), 2301 Sterlington Rd., Monroe 71201 (130).

St. Margaret's Daughters Nursing Home, (Women), 6220 Chartres St., New Orleans 70117 (112).

St. Martin Manor, 1501 N. Johnson St., New Orleans 70116 (140 residential units).

Villa St. Maurice, 500 St. Maurice Ave., New Orleans 70117. (110 residential units).

Wynhoven Apartments (Residence for Senior Citizens), 4600 - 10th St., Marrero 70072 (350).

Maine: Deering Pavilion (Apartments for Senior Citizens), 880 Forest Ave., Portland 04103 (200 units).

Marcotte Nursing Home-D'Youville Pavilion, 100 Campus Ave., Lewiston 04240 (280).

Mt. St. Joseph (Nursing Home), Highwood St., Waterville 04901 (77).

St. Andre Health Care Facility, Inc. (Nursing

Home), 407 Pool St., Biddeford 04005 (96).

St. Joseph's Manor (Nursing Home), 1133 Washington Ave., Portland 04103 (200).

Seton Village, Inc., 1 Carver St., Waterville 04901 (140 housing units.)

Villa Muir, Home for Women, Bay View, Saco 04072 (15).

Maryland: Cardinal Shehan Center for the Aging, Inc., 2300 Dulaney Valley Rd., Towson 21204. Services: 400-bed long-term care facility; Home Health Agency; 13 hospice care beds; 200 apartments for elderly; residence for elderly in urban area; outreach programs to elderly in homes; retirement residence for priests; rehabilitation services.

Carroll Manor (Residence and Nursing Home), 4922 La Salle Rd., Hyattsville 20782 (232).

Little Sisters of the Poor, St. Martin's Home (for the Aged), 601 Maiden Choice Lane, Baltimore 21228 (120).

Sacred Heart Home (Women), 5805 Queens Chapel Rd., Hyattsville 20782 (102).

St. Joseph Nursing Home, 1222 Tugwell Dr., Baltimore 21228 (40).

Villa Rosa (Nursing Home), 3800 Lottsford Vista Rd., Mitchellville 20716 (101).

Massachusetts: Beaven-Kelly Home for Men (Rest Home), 1245 Main St., Holyoke 01040 (55).

Catholic Memorial Home (Nursing Home), 2446 Highland Ave., Fall River 02720 (288).

Don Orione Nursing Home, 111 Orient Ave., East Boston 02128 (194). Adult day care center (30).

D'Youville Manor (Nursing Home), 981 Varnum Ave., Lowell 01854 (196). Day care program (20).

Jeanne Jugan Residence, Little Sisters of the Poor (Nursing Home), 186 Highland Ave., Somerville 02143 (120). Jeanne Jugan Pavilion, 190 Highland Ave., Somerville 02143 (apartments, 27; residents, 30).

Madonna Manor (Nursing Home), N. Washington St., N. Attleboro 02760 (121).

Marian Manor, for the Aged and Infirm (Nursing Home), 130 Dorchester St., S. Boston, 02127 (376).

Marian Manor of Taunton (Nursing Home), 33 Summer St., Taunton 02780 (83).

Maristhill Nursing Home, 66 Newton St., Waltham 02154 (120).

Mary Immaculate Nursing Home, Bennington St., Lawrence 01841 (250). Adult Day Health Care Center (30), Social Day Care (15).

Mt. St. Vincent Nursing Home, Holy Family Rd., Holyoke 01040 (121).

Our Lady's Haven (Nursing Home), 71 Center St., Fairhaven 02719 (110).

The Protectory, Inc., 189 Maple St., Lawrence 01841. (111 units). The Second Protectory, Inc., 191 Maple St., Lawrence (106 units). The Third Protectory, Inc., 193 Maple St., Lawrence 01841 (88 units). Congregate housing; apartments.

Sacred Heart Nursing Home, 359 Summer St., New Bedford 02740 (217).

St. Francis Home, 101 Plantation St., Worcester 01604 (140). Adult Day Health Care (40).

St. Joseph Manor Nursing Home, 215 Thatcher St., Brockton 02402 (120).

St. Joseph's Manor (Rest Home, Women), 321 Centre St., Dorchester, Boston 02122 (77).

St. Luke's Home (Rest Home, Women), 85 Spring St., Springfield 01105 (92).

St. Patrick's Manor (Nursing Home), 863 Central St., Framingham 01701 (292).

Michigan: Bishop Noa Home for Senior Citizens, Escanaba 49829 (109).

Burtha M. Fisher Home, Little Sisters of the Poor (Residence and Nursing Home), 17550 Southfield Rd., Detroit 48235 (130).

Casa Maria (Residence), 600 Maple Vista, Imlay City 48444 (96).

Kundig Center (Residence), 3300 Jefferies Freeway, Detroit 48208 (180). Rooms and apartments.

Lourdes Nursing Home (Skilled Facility), 2300 Watkins Lake Rd., Pontiac 48054 (108).

Madonna Villa Senior Residence, 17825 Fifteen Mile Rd., Fraser, 48026 (90).

Marian Hall (Residence), 529 Detroit St., Flint 48502 (124).

Marian-Oakland West, 29250 W. Ten Mile Rd., Farmington Hills 48024 (100). Rooms and apartments.

Marian Place (Residence), 408 W. Front St., Monroe 48161 (52).

Marycrest Manor (Skilled Nursing Facility), 15475 Middlebelt Rd., Livonia 48154 (55).

Marydale Center for Senior Citizens (Board and Apartments), 3147 Tenth Ave., Port Huron 48060 (74).

Maryhaven (Residence), 11350 Reeck Rd., Southgate 48195 (93).

St. Ann's Home, (Residence and Nursing Home), 2161 Leonard St. N.W., Grand Rapids 49504 (112).

St. Catherine Cooperative House for Elderly Women, 1641 Webb Ave., Detroit 48206 (12).

St. Elizabeth Briarbank (Women, Residence), 1315 N. Woodward Ave., Bloomfield Hills 48013 (54).

St. Francis Home (Nursing Home), 915 N. River Rd., Saginaw 48603 (100).

St. Joseph's Home for the Aged, 4800 Cadieux Rd., Detroit 48224 (104).

Stapleton Center (Residence), 9341 Agnes St., Detroit 48214 (65).

Villa Elizabeth (Nursing Home), 2100 Leonard St. N.E., Grand Rapids 49505 (136).

Villa Francesca (Residence, Women), 565 W. Long Lake Rd., Bloomfield Hills 48013 (18).

Villa Marie (Board and Apartments), 15131 Newburgh Rd., Livonia 48154 (100).

Minnesota: Alverna Apartments, 300 8th Ave. S.E., Little Falls 56345 (63).

Assumption Home, Cold Spring 56320 (95).

Benedictine Health Center, 935 Kenwood Ave., Duluth 55811 (120).

Bethany Home (Nursing Home), Onamia 56359 (80).

Divine Providence Community Home (Intermediate Care), 700 Third Ave. N.W., Sleepy Eye 56085 (58).

Divine Providence Home (Skilled Nursing Home), Ivanhoe 56142 (51).

John Paul Apartments, 200 8th Ave. N., Cold Spring 56320 (61). For elderly and handicapped.

Little Sisters of the Poor, Holy Family Residence (Skilled Nursing and Intermediate Care), 330 S. Exchange St., St. Paul 55102 (120).

Madonna Towers (Retirement Apartments and Nursing Home), 4001 19th Ave. N.W., Rochester 55901 (200).

Mary Rondorf Retirement Home, 222 N. 5th St., Staples 56479 (32).

Mother of Mercy Nursing Home, Albany 56307 (62).

Regina Nursing Home and Retirement Residence, Hastings 55033. Nursing home (61); retirement home (70); boarding care (16).

Sacred Heart Hospice (Skilled and Intermediate Nursing Care), 1200 Twelfth St. S.W., Austin 55912 (60 personal care units; 89 independent living apartments). Adult day care and home health nursing care.

St. Ann's Residence, 330 E. 3rd St., Duluth 55805 (200).

St. Anne Hospice, Inc. (Nursing Home), 1347 W. Broadway, Winona 55987 (121).

St. Benedict's Center (Nursing Home), 1810 Minnesota Blvd. S.E., St. Cloud 56301 (222). Skilled and intermediate nursing, adult day care, respite care. Benedict Village (Retirement Apartments), 2000 15th Ave. S.E., St. Cloud 56301.

St. Elizabeth's Hospital and Nursing Home, 1200-5th Grant Blvd., Wabasha 55981 (52).

St. Francis Home, 501 Oak St., Breckenridge 56520 (124).

St. Mary's Home (Nursing Home), 1925 Norfolk Ave., St. Paul 55116 (140).

St. Mary's Hospital and Nursing Home, Winsted 55395 (95).

St. Mary's Hospital and Nursing Home, Detroit Lakes 56501 (103).

St. Mary's Rehabilitation Center, 2512 S. 7th St., Minneapolis 55454 (139).

St. Mary's Villa (Nursing Home), Pierz 56364 (101).

St. Otto's Home (Nursing Home), Little Falls 56345 (159).

St. Therese Home (Residence and Health Care Facility) (302) and St. Therese Retirement Apartments (220), 8000 Bass Lake Rd., New Hope 55428.

St. William's Nursing Home, Parkers Prairie 56361 (70).

Villa of St. Francis Nursing Home, Morris 56267 (144).

Villa St. Vincent (Skilled Nursing Home and Residence), 516 Walsh St., Crookston 56716. Nursing home (80); residence (95).

Mississippi: Santa Maria Retirement Apartments, 305 E. Beach Blvd., Biloxi, 39530.

Villa Maria Retirement Apartments, 921 Porter Ave., Ocean Springs 39564.

Missouri: The Alverne (Retirement Home),

1014 Locust St., St. Louis 63101 (235).

Cathedral Square Towers, 444 W. 12th St., Kansas City 64105. Apartments for elderly and handicapped.

Chariton Apartments (Retirement Apartments), 4249 Michigan Ave., St. Louis 63111 (122 units; 143 residents).

DePaul Health Center — St. Anne's Division (Skilled Nursing), 12349 DePaul Dr., Bridgeton 63044 (100).

LaVerna Heights Retirement Home (Women), 104 E. Park Ave., Savannah 64485 (40).

LaVerna Village Apartments, 1000-1005 Hall Ave., Savannah 64485 (20).

LaVerna Village Nursing Home, 904 Hall Ave., Savannah 64485 (120).

Little Sisters of the Poor (Home for Aged), 3225 N. Florissant Ave., St. Louis 63107 (210).

Mary, Queen and Mother Center (Skilled-Intermediate Nursing Care), 7601 Watson Rd., St. Louis 63119 (220).

Mercy Villa (Nursing Home), Division of St. John's Regional Health Center, 1100 E. Montclair, Springfield 65807 (150).

Mother of Good Counsel Home (Skilled Nursing, Women), 6825 Natural Bridge Rd., Northwoods, 63121 (110).

Our Lady of Mercy Home (Residence and Nursing Home), 918-24 E. 9th St., Kansas City 64106 (153).

Our Lady of Mercy Country House, Box 451, R.R. No. 4, Liberty 64038 (39).

Price Memorial Skilled Nursing Facility Forby Rd., P.O. Box 476, Eureka 63025 (120).

St. Agnes Home for the Elderly, 10341 Manchester Rd., Kirkwood 63122 (130).

St. Joseph Hill Infirmary, Inc., (Nursing Care Facility, Men), St. Joseph Road, Eureka 63025 (130).

St. Joseph's Home, 723 First Capitol Dr., St. Charles 63301 (100).

St. Joseph's Home for the Aged, 1306 W. Main St., Jefferson City 65101 (75).

Nebraska: Madonna Professional Care Center, 2200 S. 52nd St., Lincoln 68506 (182).

Mercy Care Center (Health Care), 1870 S. 75th St., Omaha 68124 (250).

Mt. Carmel Home, Keens' Memorial (Nursing Home), 412 W. 18th St., Kearney 68847 (76).

New Cassel Retirement Center, 900 N. 90th St., Omaha 68114. (156).

St. Joseph's Home (Domiciliary Care), 320 E. Decatur St., West Point 68788 (48).

St. Joseph's Nursing Home, 401 N. 18th St., Norfolk 68701 (70).

St. Joseph's Villa, David City 68632. (65).

New Hampshire: Mount Carmel Nursing Home, 235 Myrtle St., Manchester 03104 (120).

St. Ann Home, 195 Dover Point Rd., Dover 03820 (53).

St. Francis Home (Nursing Home), Court St., Laconia 03246 (51).

St. Teresa Manor (Nursing Home), 519 Bridge St., Manchester 03104 (51).

St. Vincent de Paul Nursing Home, 29 Providence Ave., Berlin 03570 (80).

New Jersey: Holy Family Residence (Women), 44 Rifle Camp Rd., P.O. Box 536, W. Paterson 07424 (64).

Little Sisters of the Poor, St. Joseph Home, 140 Shepherd Lane, Totowa 07512 (183; also, 18 independent living units).

Mater Dei Nursing Home, RD 3, Box 164, Rt. 40, P.O. Newfield 08344 (64).

Morris Hall, Home for the Aged (Residence and Skilled Nursing Home), 2361 Lawrenceville Rd., Lawrenceville 08648 (115).

Mount St. Andrew Villa (Residence), 55 W. Midland Ave., Paramus 07652 (56).

Our Lady's Residence (Nursing Home), Glendale and Clematis Aves., Pleasantville 08232 (104).

St. Ann's Home for the Aged (Skilled Nursing Home, Women), 198 Old Bergen Rd., Jersey City 07305 (106). Adult Medical Day Care.

St. Joseph's Home (Women), 240 Longhouse Dr., Hewitt 07421.

St. Joseph's Rest Home for Aged Women, 46 Preakness Ave., Paterson 07522 (35).

St. Joseph's Senior Residence (Sheltered Care), 1 St. Joseph Terr., Woodbridge 07095 (60).

St. Mary's Catholic Home (Skilled Nursing Home), 1730 Kresson Rd., Cherry Hill 08003 (215).

St. Vincent's Nursing Home, 45 Elm St., Montclair 07042 (135).

Villa Maria (Residence and Infirmary, Women), 641 Somerset St., N. Plainfield 07061 (70).

New Mexico: Good Shepherd Manor (Residential Care for Aged Persons), Little Brothers of the Good Shepherd, P.O. Box 10248, Albuquerque 87114 (43).

New York: Bernardine Apartments, 417 Churchill Ave., Syracuse 13205.

Brothers of Mercy Sacred Heart Home (Residence) 4520 Ransom Rd., Clarence 14031 (82). Brothers of Mercy Nursing Home, 10570 Bergtold Rd., Clarence 14031 (240). Brothers of Mercy Housing Co., Inc. (Apartments), 10500 Bergtold Rd., Clarence 14031 (100 units).

Carmel Richmond Nursing Home, 88 Old Town Rd., Staten Island 10304 (300).

Consolation Residence, 111 Beach Dr., West Islip 11795 (250).

Ferncliff Nursing Home, P.O. Box 386, River Rd., Rhinebeck 12572 (320).

Frances Schervier Home and Hospital, 2975 Independence Ave., New York 10463 (364).

Good Samaritan Nursing Home (Skilled Nursing), 101 Elm St., Sayville, N.Y. 11782 (100).

Holy Family Home, 410 Mill St., Williamsville 14221 (87).

Kateri Residence (Skilled Nursing), 150 Riverside Dr., New York 10024 (520).

Little Sisters of the Poor, Jeanne Jugan Residence (Skilled Nursing and Health Related), 3200 Baychester Ave., Bronx 10475 (170).

Little Sisters of the Poor, Holy Family Home, 740-84th St., Brooklyn 11214 (146).

Little Sisters of the Poor, Queen of Peace Residence, 110-30 221st St., Queens Village 11429 (165).

Madonna Home of Mercy Hospital (Nursing Home and Extended Care Facility) (140), and Mercy Hospital Health Related Facility (Residence) (58), Watertown 13601.

Madonna Residence, Inc. (Skilled Nursing and Health Related), 1 Prospect Park W., Brooklyn, 11215 (290).

Mary Manning Walsh Home (Nursing Home), 1339 York Ave., New York 10021 (362).

Mercy Healthcare Center (Skilled Nursing Facility), Tupper Lake 12986 (54).

Mt. Loretto Nursing Home, (Skilled Nursing Facility), Sisters of the Resurrection, R.D., 3, Amsterdam 12010 (82).

Nazareth Nursing Home and Health Related Facility (Women), 291 W. North St., Buffalo 14201 (125).

Our Lady of Hope Residence (Home for the Aged), Little Sisters of the Poor, 1 Jeanne Jugan Lane, Latham 12210 (203).

Ozanam Hall of Queens Nursing Home, Inc. (Skilled Nursing and Health-Related Facilities), 42-41 201st St., Bayside 11361 (432).

Providence Rest, 3304 Waterbury Ave., Bronx 10465 (200).

Resurrection Rest Home (Nursing Home and Health Related Facility, Women), Castleton 12033 (48).

Sacred Heart Home (Skilled Nursing Facility), 8 Mickle St., Plattsburgh 12901 (89).

St. Ann's Home / The Heritage (Skilled Nursing), 1500 Portland Ave., Rochester 14621.

St. Clare Manor, 543 Locust St., Lockport 14094 (28).

St. Columban's on the Lake (Retirement Home), Silver Creek 14136 (50).

St. Elizabeth Home (Residence), 5539 Broadway, Lancaster 14086 (102).

St. Francis Home (Nursing and Health Related Facility), 147 Reist St., Williamsville 14221 (142).

St. Joseph Manor, W. State St., Olean 14760 (22).

St. Joseph's Guest Home, Missionary Sisters of St. Benedict,, 350 Cuba Hill Rd., Huntington 11743 (48).

St. Joseph's Home (Nursing Home), 420 Lafayette St., Ogdensburg 13669 (82).

St. Joseph's Nursing Home, 2535 Genesee St., Utica 13501 (120).

St. Joseph's Villa (Residence), 38 Prospect Ave., Catskill 12414 (60).

St. Luke Manor, 17 Wiard St., Batavia 14020 (20).

St. Mary's Manor, 515 Sixth St., Niagara Falls 14301 (119).

St. Patrick's Home for the Aged and Infirm, 66 Van Cortland Park S., Bronx 10463 (225).

St. Vincent's Home for the Aged, 319 Washington Ave., Dunkirk 14048 (36).

Terence Cardinal Cooke Health Care Center (Skilled Nursing), 1249 Fifth Ave., New York 10029 (237).

Teresian House, Washington Ave. Extension, Albany 12203 (300).

Uihlein Mercy Center (Nursing Home), Lake Placid 12946 (96).

North Carolina: Maryfield Nursing Home (115 beds) and Maryfield Acres (16 retirement homes), Greensboro Rd., High Point 27260.

North Dakota: Holy Family Guest Home (Nursing Home), Carrington 58421 (38).

Manor St. Joseph Home for Aged and Infirm; Edgeley 58433 (40).

Marillac Manor (Retirement Apartments), 1016 N. 28th St., Bismarck 58501 (42 apartments).

St. Anne's Guest Home (Retirement), 524 N. 17th St., Grand Forks 58201 (56) Apartments (30).

St. Vincent's Nursing Home, 1021 N. 26th St., Bismarck 58501 (98).

Ohio: Archbishop Leibold Home for the Aged, Little Sisters of the Poor, 476 Riddle Rd., Cincinnati 45220 (125).

Assumption Nursing Home, 550 W. Chalmers Ave., Youngstown 44511 (126).

Francesca Residence (Retirement), 39 N. Portage Path, Akron 44303 (45).

House of Loreto (Nursing Home), 2812 Harvard Ave. N.W., Canton 44709 (98).

Jennings Hall, Inc. (Intermediate Care Facility), 10204 Granger Rd., Garfield Heights 44125 (100).

Kirby Manor (Retirement Apartments), 11500 Detroit Ave., Cleveland 44102 (202 suites).

Little Sisters of the Poor, Sacred Heart Home, 4900 Navarre Ave., Oregon 43616 (126).

Little Sisters of the Poor, Sts. Joseph and Mary Home for Aged, 4291 Richmond Rd., Cleveland 44122 (140).

The Maria-Joseph Living Care Center, 4830 Salem Ave., Dayton 45416 (397).

Mount Alverna (Residence for Aged), 6765 State Rd., Cleveland 44134 (200).

Mt. St. Joseph (Skilled Nursing Facility, Dual Certified), 21800 Chardon Rd., Cleveland 44117 (100).

Nazareth Towers, 300 E. Rich St., Columbus 43215. Hi-rise apartments for independent living.

St. Augustine Manor (Nursing Home), 7800 Detroit Ave., Cleveland 44102 (194).

St. Clare Center, Inc. (Residence and Nursing Care), 80 Compton Rd., Cincinnati 45215 (90).

St. Edward Nursing Home, 3131 Smith Rd., Akron 44313 (100).

St. Francis Home, Inc. (Residence and Nursing Care), 182 St. Francis Ave., Tiffin 44883 (116).

St. Francis Rehabilitation Hospital and Nursing Home, 401 N. Broadway St., Green Springs 44836 (186).

St. Joseph's Hospice (Nursing Home), 2308 Reno Dr., Louisville 44641 (100).

St. Margaret Hall (Residence and Nursing Facility), 1960 Madison Rd., Cincinnati 45206 (145).

St. Raphael Home (Nursing Home), 1550 Roxbury Rd., Columbus 43212 (80).

St. Rita's Home (Skilled Nursing Home), 880 Greenlawn Ave., Columbus 43223 (100).

St. Theresa Home for the Aged, 6760 Belkenton Pl., Cincinnati 45236 (100).

Schroder Manor (Residence and Skilled Nursing Care), Franciscan Sisters of the Poor, 1302

Millville Ave., Hamilton 45013 (85). Independent living units are under construction.

The Siena Home (Skilled Nursing Home), 235 W. Orchard Spring Dr., Dayton 45415 (99).

The Villa Sancta Anna Home for the Aged, Inc. 25000 Chagrin Blvd., Beachwood 44122 (68).

Oklahoma: Franciscan Villa, 17110 E. 51st St. S., Broken Arrow 74012. Intermediate nursing car (60); apartments (66).

St. Ann's Nursing Home, 3825 N.W. 19th St. Oklahoma City 73107 (82).

Oregon: Benedictine Nursing Center and Hom Health Agency, S. Main St., Mt. Angel 97362 (127).

Evergreen Court Retirement Apartments, 395 Sheridan Ave., North Bend 97459.

Maryville Nursing Home, 14645 S.W. Farm ington, Beaverton 97007 (132).

Mt. St. Joseph's Residence and Extended Car Center, 3060 S.E. Stark St., Portland 97214 (325).

St. Catherine's Residence and Nursing Center 3959 Sheridan Ave., North Bend 97459 (166).

St. Elizabeth's Nursing Home, 2365 4th St., Bak er 97814 (93).

Pennsylvania: Ascension Manor I (Senior Ci izen Housing), 911 N. Franklin St., Philadelphi 19123 (140 units).

Ascension Manor II (Senior Citizen Housing) 970 N. 7th St., Philadelphia 19123 (140 units).

Benetwood Apartments for Elderly and Handi capped, 640 Troupe Rd., Erie 16421 (75).

Bethlehem Retirement Village, 100 W Wissahickon Ave., Flourtown 19031. Apartment for well elderly. (100).

Christ the King Manor, 1100 W. Long Ave., D Bois 15801 (160).

Corpus Christi Residence, 7165 Churchland St. Pittsburgh 15206 (27).

Drueding Infirmary (Intermediate Nursing), 4 W. Master St., Philadelphia 19122 (52).

Garvey Manor (Nursing Home), Logan Blvd Hollidaysburg, 16648 (150).

Holy Family Home, Little Sisters of the Poo 5300 Chester Ave., Philadelphia 19143 (130).

Holy Family Manor (Skilled Nursing Facility 1200 Spring St., Bethlehem 18018 (200).

Holy Family Residence, 217 Spring Garden St Easton 18042 (14).

Immaculate Mary Home, (Skilled and Ir termediate Nursing Care), Holme Circle an Welsh Rd., Philadelphia 19136 (296).

John XXIII Home, 2250 Shenango Freewa Hermitage 16148 (119).

Little Flower Manor Nursing Home (Skille Nursing), 1201 Springfield Rd., Darby 19023 (122).

Little Flower Manor of Diocese of Scranto (Long-Term Skilled Nursing Care Facility), 200 S Meade St., Wilkes-Barre 18702 (133).

Little Sisters of the Poor, 1028 Benton Ave. N.S Pittsburgh 15212 (124).

Little Sisters of the Poor, Holy Family Res dence, 2500 Adams Ave., Scranton 18509 (82).

Maria Joseph Manor, Danville 17821 (94).

Marian Manor (Intermediate Care), 26

Winchester Dr., Pittsburgh 15220 (170).

Mount Macrina Manor (Skilled Nursing Facility), 520 W. Main St., Uniontown 15401 (54).

Redeemer Village (Senior Citizen Housing), Huntingdon Pike, Huntingdon Valley 19006 (250 apartments).

Sacred Heart Manor (Nursing Home), 6445 Germantown Ave., Philadelphia 19119 (142).

St. Anne Home (Skilled, Intermediate and Personal Care; Independent Living), R.D. 2, Columbia 17512 (120).

St. Anne Home for the Elderly (Nursing Facility), 685 Angela Dr., Greensburg 15601 (125).

St. Basil's Home for Aged Women (Residential), Box 878, Uniontown 15401 (14).

St. Ignatius Nursing Home, 4401 Haverford Ave., Philadelphia 19104 (176).

St. John Neumann Nursing Home, 10400 Roosevelt Blvd. Philadelphia 19116 (218).

St. Joseph Home for the Aged (Residential and Skilled Nursing Facility), 1182 Holland Rd., Holland 18966 (96).

St. Joseph Nursing and Health Care Center (Skilled Nursing Facility), 5324 Penn Ave., Pittsburgh 15224 (161).

St. Joseph's House of Hospitality (Low Income Senior Citizen Residence for Men and Women), 1635 Bedford Ave., Pittsburgh 15219 (65).

St. Joseph Manor (Skilled Nursing Facility), 1616 Huntingdon Pike, Meadowbrook 19046 (250).

St. Joseph's Residence, 1111 S. Cascade St., New Castle 16101.

St. Leonard's Guest Home, 601 N. Montgomery St., Hollidaysburg 16648 (21).

St. Mary's Home of Erie, 607 E. 26th St., Erie 16504. Residential facility (110); geriatric nursing facility (196).

Saint Mary's Manor, 701 Lansdale Ave., Lansdale 19446 (160).

St. Mary's Villa (Nursing Home), Elmhurst 18416 (121).

Villa de Marillac Nursing Home, 5300 Stanton Ave., Pittsburgh 15206 (50).

Villa St. Teresa (Residence, Women), 1215 Springfield Rd., Darby 19023 (53).

Villa Teresa (Nursing Home), 1051 Avila Rd., Harrisburg 17109 (184).

Vincentian Home for the Chronically Ill., Perrymont Rd., Pittsburgh 15237 (219).

Rhode Island: Jeanne Jugan Residence of the Little Sisters of the Poor, 964 Main St., Pawtucket 02860 (120).

L'Hospice St. Antoine (Home for Aged), 400 Mendon Rd., North Smithfield 02895 (244).

St. Clare Home, 309 Spring St., Newport 02840 (44).

Scalabrini Villa (Convalescent, Rest — Nursing Home). 860 N. Quidnessett Rd., North Kingstown 02852 (70).

South Carolina: Carter-May Home, 1660 Ingram Rd., Charleston 29407 (12). Personal care home for elderly ladies.

South Dakota: Brady Memorial Home (Skilled Nursing Facility), 500 S. Ohlman St., Mitchell 57301 (60). Independent living units (9).

Maryhouse, Inc. (Skilled Nursing Facility), 717 E. Dakota, Pierre 57501 (105).

Mother Joseph Manor (Intermediate Care and Skilled Nursing Facility), 1002 North Jay St., Aberdeen 57401 (30 intermediate; 50 skilled). Apartment units (7). Adult day care program. Respite nursing care.

St. William's Home for the Aged (Intermediate Care, 60), and Angela Hall (Supervised Living, 15), 901 E. Virgil, Box 432, Milbank 57252.

Tekakwitha Nursing Home (Skilled and Intermediate Care). Sisseton 57262 (101). Tekakwitha Housing Corp. (Independent Living), same address (24 units).

Tennessee: Alexian Village of Tennessee (Retired Men and Women), Signal Mountain 37377 (150) and Health Care Center (124).

Ave Maria Home, 2805 Charles Bryan Rd., Memphis 38134 (73).

St. Mary Manor, 1771 Highway 45 Bypass, Jackson 38305.

St. Peter Manor, 108 N. Aubrundale, Memphis 38104.

St. Peter Villa (Nursing Home), 141 N. McLean, Memphis 38104.

Texas: Casa Apartment Complex for Elderly and Handicapped, 3201 Sondra Dr., Fort Worth 76107.

Casa Brendan and Casa II Housing for the Elderly and Handicapped, 1302 Hyman St., Stephenville 76401.

Home for Aged Women-Men, 920 S. Oregon St., El Paso 79901 (24).

John Paul II Nursing Home (Home for Aged and Convalescents), 215 Tilden St., Kenedy 78219.

Laboure Care Center, 1950 Record Crossing Rd., Dallas 75235.

Mother of Perpetual Help Home (Intermediate Care Facility), 519 E. Madison Ave., Brownsville 78520 (37).

Mt. Carmel Home (Personal Care Home), 4130 S. Alameda St., Corpus Christi 78411 (92).

The Regis Retirement Home and St. Elizabeth Nursing Home, 400 Austin Ave., Waco 76701 (420).

The Retirement Residence, Inc., The Whitestone, 2819 Rio Grande, Austin 78705 (100).

St. Ann's Home (Skilled Nursing Facility), P.O. Box 1179, Panhandle 79068 (52).

St. Anthony Center (Skilled Nursing, Rehabilitation, Geriatric), 6301 Almeda Rd., Houston 77021 (372).

St. Dominic Nursing Home, 6502 Grand Ave., Houston 77021 (120).

St. Dominic Residence Hall, 2401 E. Holcombe Blvd., Houston 77021 (80).

St. Francis Nursing Home (Home for Aged and Convalescents), 2717 N. Flores St., San Antonio 78212 (143).

St. Francis Village, Inc. (Retired and Elderly), 1 Chapel Plaza, Crowley 76036 (415).

St. Joseph Residence, 330 W. Pembroke St., Dallas 75208 (49).

San Juan Nursing Home, Inc. (Skilled and Intermediate Care Facility), 300 N. Nebraska Ave., P.O. Box 1238, San Juan 78589 (120).

Utah: St. Joseph Villa (Skilled and Intermediate Care Facility), 475 Ramona Ave., Salt Lake City 84115 (175).

Vermont: Loretto Home for Aged, 59 Meadow St., Rutland 05701 (54).
Michaud Memorial Manor (Home for Aged), Derby Line 05830 (24).
St. Joseph's Home for Aged, 243 N. Prospect St., Burlington 05401 (53).

Virginia: Madonna Home, 814 W. 37th St., Norfolk 23508 (15).
Russell House, 900 First Colonial Rd., Virginia Beach 23454 (127).
St. Francis Home, 2511 Wise St., Richmond 23225 (25).
St. Joseph's Home for the Aged, Little Sisters of the Poor, 1503 Michael Rd., Richmond 23229 (126).

Washington: Cathedral Plaza Apartments (Retirement Apartments), W. 1120 Sprague Ave., Spokane 99204 (150).
The Delaney, W. 242 Riverside Ave., Spokane 99201 (84).
The De Paul Retirement Apartments, 4831 35th Ave. S.W., Seattle 98126 (118 units).
Fahy Garden Apartments, W. 1411 Dean Ave., Spokane 99201 (31).
Fahy West Apartments, W. 1523 Dean Ave., Spokane 99201 (55).
The Josephinum (Retirement Home), 1902 2nd Ave., Seattle 98101 (228).
Mt. St. Vincent Nursing Center, 4831 35th Ave., S.W., Seattle 98126 (198).
The O'Malley, E. 707 Mission, Spokane 99202 (100).
St. Joseph Nursing Home, 1006 North H St., Aberdeen 98520 (34).
St. Joseph Care Center (Skilled Long-Term Care), West 20 — 90th Ave., Spokane 99204 (103).

West Virginia: Knights of St. George Home, Wellsburg 26070 (44).
Welty Home for the Aged (Women), 21 Washington Ave., Wheeling 26003 (44).

Wisconsin: Alexian Village of Milwaukee (Retirement Community/Skilled Nursing Home), 7979 W. Glenbrook Rd., Milwaukee 53223 (331 apartments; 61 skilled nursing).
Bethany-St. Joseph Health Care Center, 2507 Shelby Rd., La Crosse 54601 (226).
Clement Manor (Retirement Community and Skilled Nursing), 3939 S. 92nd St., Greenfield 53228 (164 skilled nursing; 99 apartments). Senior day care.
Divine Savior Nursing Home, 715 W. Pleasant St., Portage 53901 (128).
Franciscan Villa (Skilled Nursing Home), 3601 S. Chicago Ave., S. Milwaukee 53172 (150).
Hope Nursing Home, 438 Ashford Ave., Lomira 53048 (40).

McCormick Memorial Home for the Aged, 212 Iroquois St., Green Bay 54301 (72).
Marian Catholic Home, 3333 W. Highland Blvd., Milwaukee 53208 (360).
Maryhill Manor Nursing and Retirement Home, 973 Main St., Niagara 54151 (45).
Milwaukee Catholic Home, Inc., 2462 N. Prospect Ave., Milwaukee 53211 (200).

Nazareth House (Skilled Nursing Facility), Stoughton 53589 (100).

St. Ann Rest Home (Intermediate Care Facility, Women), 2020 S. Muskego Ave., Milwaukee 53204 (54).
St. Anne's Home for the Elderly (Aged Poor), 3800 N. 92nd St., Milwaukee 53222 (144).
St. Camillus Health Center (Skilled Nursing Home), 10100 W. Bluemound Rd., Wauwatosa 53226 (188).
St. Catherine Infirmary (Nursing Home), 5635 Erie St., Racine 53402 (40).
St. Elizabeth Nursing Home, 502 St. Lawrence Ave., Janesville 53545 (43).
St. Elizabeth's Nursing Home (Intermediate Care; Women), 745 N. Brookfield Rd., Brookfield 53005 (16).
St. Francis Home, 620 S. 11th St., La Crosse 54601 (95).
St. Francis Home (Skilled Nursing Facility), 1800 New York Ave., Superior 54880 (192).
St. Francis Home (Skilled Nursing), 365 Gillett St., Fond du Lac 54935 (70).
St. Francis Manor (Retirement Residence), 3553 S. 41st St., Milwaukee 53221 (125).
St. Joan Antida Home (Women), 6640 W. Beloit Rd., W. Allis 53219 (76).
St. Joseph's Home, 705 Clyman St., Watertown 53094 (28).
St. Joseph's Home, 9244 29th Ave., Kenosha 53140 (93).
St. Joseph's Home, 5301 W. Lincoln Ave., W. Allis 53219 (124).
St. Joseph's Nursing Home, 464 S. St. Joseph Ave., Arcadia 54612 (75).
St. Joseph's Nursing Home, 2902 East Ave. S., La Crosse 54601 (80).
St. Joseph's Nursing Home, 400 Water Ave., Hillsboro 54634 (65).
St. Joseph Residence, Inc. (Nursing Home), 1925 Division St., New London 54961 (107).
St. Mary's Home for the Aged (Residence and Nursing Care), 2005 Division St., Manitowoc 54220 (256).
St. Mary's Nursing Home, 3516 W. Center St., Milwaukee 53210 (130).
St. Monica's Senior Citizens Home, 3920 N. Green Bay Rd., Racine 53404 (90).
St. Paul Home (Intermediate and Skilled Nursing Home), 509 W. Wisconsin Ave., Kaukauna 54130 (52). St. Paul Manor, same address (8). For well elderly.

Villa Clement (Nursing and Convalescent Center), 9047 W. Greenfield Ave., W. Allis 53214 (190).
Villa Loretto Nursing Home, Mount Calvary 53057 (52).

FACILITIES FOR HANDICAPPED CHILDREN AND ADULTS

Sources: Almanac survey; *Directory of Catholic Special Facilities and Programs for Handicapped Children and Adults,* published by the National Catholic Educational Association; *Official Catholic Directory.*

This listing covers facilities and programs with educational and training orientation. Information about other services for the handicapped can generally be obtained from the Catholic Charities Office or its equivalent (c/o Chancery Office) in any diocese. (See Index for listing of addresses of chancery offices in the U.S.)

Abbreviation code: b, boys; c, coeducational; d, day; g, girls; r, residential. Other information includes chronological age for admission. The number in parentheses at the end of an entry indicates total capacity or enrollment.

Deaf and Hard of Hearing

California: St. Joseph's Center for Deaf and Hard of Hearing, 37588 Fremont Blvd., Fremont 94536.

Illinois: Holy Trinity Day Classes for the Deaf (c; 3-14 yrs.) 1910 Taylor, Chicago 60612 (45).

Louisiana: Chinchuba Institute (d,c; parent-infant through 16 yrs.), 1131 Barataria Blvd., Marrero. 70072 (101).

Massachusetts: Boston School for the Deaf (r,d,c; 3-21 yrs.), 800 N. Main St., Randolph. 02368 (236). Psycho-Education Center (PEC) for emotionally disturbed deaf children (r, d; 3-10 yrs.).

Missouri: St. Joseph Institute for the Deaf (r,d,c; birth to 15 yrs.), 1483 82nd Blvd., St. Louis 63132 (150).

New York: Cleary School for the Deaf (d,c; infancy through high school), 301 Smithtown Blvd., Lake Ronkonkoma, L.I. 11779 (105).

St. Francis de Sales School for the Deaf (d,c; parent-infant programs through age 14), 260 Eastern Parkway, Brooklyn 11225.

St. Joseph's School for the Deaf (d,c; birth-13 yrs.), 1000 Hutchinson River Pkwy, Bronx. 10465 (180).

St. Mary's School for the Deaf (r,d,c; birth to 21 yrs.), 2253 Main St., Buffalo. 14214 (220).

Ohio: St. Rita School for the Deaf (r,d,c; 4-21 yrs.), 1720 Glendale-Milford Rd., Cincinnati. 45215 (120).

Pennsylvania: Abp. Ryan Memorial Institute for Deaf (d,c; parent-infant programs through 8th grade), 3509 Spring Garden St., Philadelphia. 19104 (62).

De Paul Institute (d,c; birth-21 yrs.), Castlegate Ave., Pittsburgh. 15226 (132).

Emotionally And/Or Socially Maladjusted

This listing includes facilities for abused, abandoned and neglected as well as emotionally disturbed children and youth.

California: Hanna Boys Center (r; 9-14 yrs. at intake; school goes to 10th grade), Box 100, Sonoma. 95476 (72).

Rancho San Antonio (r,b; 12-16 yrs.), 21000 Plummer St., Chatsworth. 91311 (118).

Stanford Lathrop Memorial Home and Group Homes, Sisters of Social Service, 800 N. Street, Sacramento 95814. Conduct five homes for boys and girls.

Colorado: Mt. St. Vincent Home (r,c; 5-13 yrs.), 4159 Lowell Blvd., Denver. 80211 (45).

Connecticut: Highland Heights — St. Francis Home for Children (r,d,c; 6-17 yrs.), 651 Prospect St., New Haven. 06505 (64).

Mt. St. John (r,b; 11-16 yrs.), Kirtland St., Deep River. 06417 (75).

Delaware: Our Lady of Grace Home for Children (r,c; 6-12 yrs.), 487 Chestnut Hill Rd., Newark 19713 (16).

Georgia: Village of St. Joseph (r,d,c; 6-16 yrs.), 2969 Butner Rd. S.W., Atlanta 30331 (39 r; 48 d). Residential treatment center and therapeutic special school for children with emotional problems, behavior disorders, learning disabilities.

Illinois: Charles I. Doyle, S.J., Center and Day School of Loyola University (d, c; pre-school to 12 yrs.), 1043 Loyola Ave., Chicago 60626 (25 in day school, unlimited in guidance center).

Guardian Angel (r,d,c; 5-17 yrs.), Plainfield at Theodore St., Joliet 60435 (20 r, 40 d).

St. Joseph Carondelet Child Center (r,b; 5-16 yrs. and d,c; 5-15 yrs.); 739 E. 35th St., Chicago 60616 (32 r, 20 d).

Indiana: Gibault School for Boys (r; 10-16 yrs.), 5901 Dixie Bee Rd., Terre Haute. 47802 (104).

Hoosier Boys Town (r; 9-18 yrs.), Schererville. 46375 (65).

Kentucky: Boys' Haven (r; 13-18 yrs.), 3201 Bardstown Rd., Louisville. 40205 (51).

Maryhurst School (r,g; 13-17 yrs.), 1015 Dorsey Lane, Louisville 40223 (42).

Louisiana: Hope Haven — Madonna Manor Residential Treatment Center (r,b; 5-18 yrs.), 1101 Barataria Blvd., Marrero 70072 (162).

Maison Marie Group Home (r,g; 13-18 yrs.), 3020 Independence St., Metairie 70002 (12).

Maryland: Good Shepherd Center (r,d,g; 14-18 yrs.), 4100 Maple Ave., Baltimore. 21227 (90r, 15d).

Massachusetts: McAuley Nazareth Home for Boys (r; 6-14 yrs.), 77 Mulberry St., Leicester. 01524 (27).

Nazareth Child Care Center (r,d,c; 5-14 yrs.), 420 Pond St., Jamaica Plain, Mass. 02130 (56).

Our Lady of Providence Children's Center (r,d,c; 5-15 yrs.), 2112 Riverdale St., W. Springfield. 01089 (50). Diagnostic treatment program also.

St. Vincent Home (r,c 6-18 yrs.), 2425 Highland Ave., Fall River 02720 (61 b; 14 g). Residential treatment center.

Michigan: Barat House, Barat Human Services, League of Catholic Women (r,g; 13-17 yrs.), 5250 John R. St., Detroit. 48202 (24).

Boysville of Michigan, Inc. (r; 13-18 yrs.), 8744 Clinton-Macon Rd., Clinton. 49236 (180).

Don Bosco Hall (r,b; 13-17 years.), 10001 Petoskey Ave., Detroit. 48204 (38).

St. John's Home (r,c; 9-16 yrs.), 385 E. Leonard N.E., Grand Rapids 49503 (40).

St. Vincent Home for Children (r,c; 10-16 yrs.), 2800 W. Willow St., Lansing 48917 (30).

Vista Maria (r,d, g; 13-17 yrs.), 20651 W. Warren Ave., Dearborn Heights. 48127 (129 r; 10 d).

Minnesota: Home of the Good Shepherd, (r.g; 12-17 yrs.), 5100 Hodgson Rd., St. Paul. 55112 (48).

St. Cloud Children's Home (r,c; 8-17 yrs.), 1726 7th Ave. S., St. Cloud. 56301 (72).

St. James Children's Home (r,c), Woodland Hills, Duluth 55803 (60).

Tiffany House Group Home (c), 374 4th Ave. S., St. Cloud 56301 (11).

Missouri: Child Center of Our Lady (r,c; 4-12 yrs. — d,c; 4-17 yrs.), 7900 Natural Bridge Rd., St. Louis. 63121 (79).

Marillac Center for Children (r,d,c; 4-14 yrs.), 310 W. 106th St., Kansas City. 64114 (28 r; 60 d).

Marygrove (r,c; 6-18 yrs.), 2705 Mullanphy Lane, Florissant. 63031 (80).

Nebraska: Father Flanagan's Boys' Home (r; 10-18 yrs.), Boys Town, Nebr. 68010 (410).

Nevada: Home of Good Shepherd (r,g; 13-17 yrs.), 7000 North Jones Blvd., Las Vegas, 89131 (56).

New Jersey: Christopher House (c; 18 and over), 55 N. Clinton Ave., Trenton 08607 (90). Psychiatric day treatment.

Collier Group Home (r,g; 14-18 yrs.), 47 Reckless Pl., Red Bank 07701 (10).

Collier School (d,c; 13-18 yrs.), Wickatunk 07765.

Guidance Clinic of Catholic Welfare Bureau (c), 39 N. Clinton Ave., Trenton 08607. Psychiatric counseling for children and adults.

Mt. St. Joseph Children's Center (r,d,c; 6-12 yrs.), Shepherd Lane, Totowa 07512 (32).

New Jersey's Boystown (r; adolescents), 499 Belgrove Dr., Kearney 07032.

New York: The Astor Home for Children (r,d,c; 5-12 yrs.), 36 Mill St., Rhinebeck 12572 (75). Group Homes (7-18 yrs.), 1967 Turnbull Ave., Bronx 10473 (52). Child Guidance Clinics/Day Treatment (Rhinebeck, Poughkeepsie, Beacon, Bronx). Head start — Day Care (Poughkeepsie, Beacon, Hyde Park, Dover, Millerton).

Baker Hall (r,d,b; 10-18 yrs.), 150 Martin Rd., Lackawanna. 14218 (250). Special services, institution, group homes, foster homes, preventive services, special education school.

LaSalle School (r,d,b; 12-18 yrs.), 391 Western Ave., Albany. 12203 (145). Also conducts a group home and prevention programs.

Madonna Heights Services (r,d,g; 11-17 yrs.), Burrs Lane, Huntington. 11743 (110). Also conducts group homes on Long Island and outpatient programs.

Saint Anne Institute (r,d,g; 12-18 yrs.), 160 N. Main Ave., Albany. 12206 (140). Critical level, preventive services, group home. Sex abuse prevention programs.

St. Helena's Residence (r,g; 12-17 yrs.), 120 W. 60th St., New York. 10023 (20).

St. John's of Rockaway Beach (r,b; 10-18 yrs.),

144 Beach 111th St., Rockaway Park. 11694 (112). Also conducts group homes in Far Rockaway and Richmond Hill.

North Dakota: Home on the Range for Boys (r; 12-18 yrs.), Box 41, Sentinel Butte. 58654 (46).

Ohio: Diocesan Child Guidance Center, Inc. (d,c; preschool) Outpatient counseling program (c; 2-18 yrs.), 840 W. State St., Columbus 43222.

Marycrest (r,g; 13-18 yrs.), 7800 Brookside Rd., Independence. 44131 (70).

Parmadale/St. Anthony's Youth Services Village (r,c; 7-21 yrs.), 6753 State Rd., Parma 44134.

Rosemont (r,g;d,c; 12-18 yrs.), 2440 Dawnlight Ave., Columbus 43211 (150).

Oregon: St. Mary's Home for Boys (r; 9-17 yrs.), 16535 S.W. Tualatin Valley Highway, Beaverton 97006 (43).

Pennsylvania: De LaSalle in Towne (d,b; 12-17 yrs.), 25 S. Van Pelt St., Philadelphia 19103 (110).

De LaSalle Vocational Day Treatment (b; 15-17 yrs.), P.O. Box 344 — Street Rd. and Bristol Pike, Bensalem 19020 (120).

Gannondale School for Girls (r; 12-17 yrs.), 4635 E. Lake Rd., Erie 16511 (57).

Harborcreek School for Boys (r; 10-17 yrs.), 5712 Iroquois Ave., Harborcreek 16421 (135). Also conducts group homes.

Lourdesmont Good Shepherd Youth and Family Services (r,g;d,c; 13-17 yrs.), 537 Venard Rd., Clarks Summit 18411 (100).

Pauline Auberle Foundation, The Auberle Home for Boys (r,b; 13-18 yrs.), 1101 Hartman St., McKeesport 15132 (50).

St. Gabriel Hall (r,b; 12-17 yrs.), P.O. Box 13, Audobon 19407 (220). Also conducts group homes.

St. Michael's School for Boys (r,b; d,c; 12-17 yrs.), Hoban Heights, Tunkhannock 18657 (120). Also conducts group homes, day treatment program.

Tennessee: DeNeuville Heights School for Girls (r; 12-18 yrs.), 3060 Baskin St., Memphis 38127 (52).

Texas: St. Joseph Youth Center (r,c; 13-17 yrs.), 901 S. Madison St., Dallas 75208 (48).

Washington: Morning Star Boys Ranch (Spokane Boys' Ranch, Inc.), (r,b; 9-18 yrs.), Box 8087 Manito Station, Spokane 99203 (30).

Wisconsin: Eudes Corporation at Our Lady of Charity Center (r,c; 10-17 yrs.), 2640 West Point Rd., Green Bay 54303 (50).

St. Aemilian Child Care Center, Inc. (r,b; 5-14 yrs.), 8901 W. Capitol Dr., Milwaukee 53222 (60).

St. Charles Boys Home (r; 12-18 yrs.), 151 S. 84th St., Milwaukee 53214 (63).

Wyoming: St. Joseph's Children's Home (r,c; 6-18 yrs.), P.O. Box 1117, Torrington 82240 (38). Also conducts group home.

Developmentally Handicapped

This listing includes facilities for children, youth and adults with learning disabilities and/or mental retardation.

Alabama: Father Walter Memorial Child Care Center (r,c; birth-12 yrs.), 2815 Forbes Dr., Montgomery 36199 (44). Skilled nursing facility.

California: Catholic Charities Services to Developmentally Disabled Persons, 433 Jefferson St., Oakland 94607.

Child Study Center (d,c; birth-18 yrs.), 1339 - 20th St., Santa Monica. 90404 (80). Also conducts a developmental nursery (birth-3 yrs.) and a private school program for children (3-9 yrs.).

Helpers of the Mentally Retarded, Inc., 2626 Fulton St., San Francisco 94118. Conducts three homes: Helpers Home for Girls (18 years and older), 2608 Fulton St. and 2626 Fulton St., San Francisco 94118; Helpers Home for Men (18 years and older), 2750 Fulton St., San Francisco 94118.

St. Madeleine Sophie's Training Center (d,c; 18 yrs. and older), 2111 E. Madison Ave., El Cajon 92021 (110).

St. Vincent's (r,d,c; 8-21 yrs.), P.O. Drawer V, 4200 Calle Real, Santa Barbara 93102 (116).

Tierra del Sol (d,c; 18 yrs. and older), 9919 Sunland Blvd., Sunland 91040 (160).

Connecticut: Gengras Center (d,c; 8-21 yrs.), St. Joseph College, 1678 Asylum Ave., W. Hartford 06117 (70).

Special Education Department, Diocese of Bridgeport, 238 Jewett Ave., Bridgeport 06606.

Villa Maria Education Center (d,c), 159 Sky Meadow Dr., Stamford 06903 (31). For children with learning disabilities.

District of Columbia: Lt. Joseph P. Kennedy Jr. Institute (d,c; 5-85 yrs.), 801 Buchanan St. N.E., Washington 20017 (400). Also conducts group homes, continuing education and life skills training programs, contract employment and job placement.

St. Gertrude's School of Arts and Crafts (r,d,g; 6-19 yrs.), 4801 Sargent Rd. N.E., Washington 20017 (40).

Florida: Marian Center Services for Developmentally Handicapped and Mentally Retarded (r,d,c), 15701 Northwest 37th Ave., Opa Locka 33054. Offers variety of services.

Marian School for Exceptional Children (d,c; 2-5 yrs.), 326 Pine Terr., W. Palm Beach 33401.

Morning Star School (d,c; 4-12 yrs.), 725 Mickler Rd., Jacksonville 32211 (100). For children with learning disabilities.

Morning Star School (d,c; 3-12 yrs.), 954 Leigh Ave., Orlando 32804 (45).

Morning Star School (d,c; 6-13 yrs.), 4661 - 80th Ave., N., Pinellas Park 33565 (50). For children with learning disabilities and other learning handicaps.

Morning Star School (d,c; 6-13 yrs.), 210 E. Linebaugh Ave., Tampa 33612. (88). For children with learning disabilities.

Illinois: Bartlett Learning Center (r,d,c; 3-21 yrs.), 801 W. Bartlett Rd., Bartlett 60103 (112).

Good Shepherd Manor (permanent home for men; 18 yrs. and older), Little Brothers of the Good Shepherd, P.O. Box 260, Momence. 60954 (120).

Lt. Joseph P. Kennedy, Jr., School (r,d,c; 6-21 yrs.) and Job Training Center (c; 16 yrs. and older), 123rd and Wolf Rd., Palos Park. 60464 (101).

Misericordia Home South (r,c; 1 mo.-6 yrs.), 2916 W. 47th St., Chicago 60632 (119).

Misericordia Home North (r,c; 4-21 yrs.), 6300 North Ridge, Chicago 60660 (82).

Mt. St. Joseph (mentally handicapped women; 20-45 yrs.), 24955 N. Highway 12, Lake Zurich 60047 (160).

St. Francis School for Exceptional Children (r,c; 2-12 yrs.), 1209 S. Walnut Ave., Freeport 61032 (36).

St. Jude Special Education Center (d,c), 2nd and Spring Ave., Aviston 62216.

St. Mary of Providence (r,d,g; 4-21 yrs.), 4200 N. Austin Ave., Chicago 60634 (190).

St. Rose Day School (d,c; 3-21 yrs.), 4911 S. Hoyne Ave., Chicago 60609 (60). For mentally handicapped children.

St. Vincent Residential School (c; 10-21 yrs.) (25), and St. Vincent Community Living Facility (adults, over 18 yrs.) (20), and St. Vincent Supported Living Arrangement (adults, over 18 yrs.), 659 E. Jefferson St., Freeport 61032.

Special Education Program of the East St. Louis Deanery (d,c; 5-16 yrs.), 8213 Church Lane, East St. Louis 62203 (60).

Indiana: Marian Day Program (d,c; 6-16 yrs.), 700 Herndon Dr., Evansville 47711 (35).

Providence House (r, men; 18 yrs. and up), 520 W. 9th St., Jasper 47546 (66).

St. Bavo Special Class (d,c; 6-15 yrs.), 512 W. 8th St., Mishawaka 46544 (12).

St. Mary Child Center School (d,c; 3-16 yrs.), 311 N. New Jersey St., Indianapolis 46204 (32). Developmentally Disabled.

Kansas: Holy Family Center (d,c; 6-21 yrs.), 619 S. Maize Rd., Wichita 67209 (65).

Lakemary Center, Inc. (r,d,c; 3-16 yrs.), 100 Lakemary Dr., Paola 66071 (72r,35d).

Kentucky: Ursuline-Pitt School (d,c), 2117 Payne St., Louisville 40206 (75).

Ursuline Speech Clinic (d,c; 3 yrs.-adult), 3105 Lexington Rd., Louisville 40206 (105).

Louisiana: Department of Special Education, Archdiocese of New Orleans, St. Michael Special School, 1522 Chippewa St., New Orleans 70130.

Holy Angels School (r,c; teen-age, 14 yrs. and older; nursery, 2 mo. to kindergarten age), 10450 Ellerbe Rd., Shreveport 71106 (200).

Our Lady of Fatima School (d,c; 6-18 yrs.), 2315 Johnston St., Lafayette 70503 (50).

Padua House (r,c; birth-21 yrs.), 200 Beta St., Belle Chase 70037 (44).

Regina Caeli Center (d,c; 6-16 yrs.), P.O. Box 5950, Drew Station, Lake Charles. 70606 (50).

St. Agnes Vocational Evaluation and Training Center (d,c), P.O. Box 53326, 715 East Blvd., Baton Rouge 70802 (140).

St. Mary's Training School (r,c; 3-22 yrs.), P.O. Drawer 7768, Alexandria 71306 (152).

Maryland: The Benedictine School for Exceptional Children (r,c; 6-21 yrs.), Ridgely 21660 (100). Also conducts Habilitation Center (r,c; 17 yrs. and older) (50) and 5 community-based homes (21 yrs. and older).

Francis X. Gallagher Center (r), 2520 Pot Spring Rd., Timonium 21093 (92). Adult day activity programs.

St. Elizabeth School and Habilitation Center

(d,c; 12-21 yrs.), 801 Argonne Dr., Baltimore 21218 (125).

St. Francis School for Special Education (d,c; 3-13 yrs.), 2226 Maryland Ave., Baltimore 21218 (60).

Massachusetts: Cardinal Cushing School and Training Center (r,d,c; 10-22 yrs.), Hanover 02339 (130 r; 65 d).

Mercy Centre for Developmental Disabilities (d,c; 3-22 yrs. and over), 25 West Chester St., Worcester 01605 (160).

Nazareth Hall (d,c; 7-22 yrs.), 887 Highland Ave., Fall River, 02720 (45).

St. Coletta Day School (d,c; 6-20 yrs., admission age), 85 Washington St., Braintree 02184 (132).

Michigan: Our Lady of Providence Center (r,d,g; 5-17 yrs., child caring; 18-26, adult foster care), 16115 Beck Rd., Northville. 48167 (100).

St. Louis Center and School (r,d,b; 6-18 yrs. child care; 18-26 yrs. adult foster care), 16195 Old U.S. 12, Chelsea 48118 (68).

Minnesota: Mother Teresa Home (r,c; 18 yrs. and older), 101-10th Ave. N., Cold Spring 56320 (14).

St. Elizabeth Home (r,c; 18 yrs. and older), 306 15th Ave. N., St. Cloud 56301 (14).

St. Francis Home (r,c; 9-12 yrs.) 25-2nd St. N., Waite Park 56387 (6).

Missouri: Department of Special Education, Archdiocese of St. Louis, 4472 Lindell Blvd., St. Louis. 63108. Conducts 43 special day classes (c; 5-16 yrs.).

Good Shepherd Manor (residential for developmentally disabled men; 16 yrs. and up), Little Brothers of the Good Shepherd, 3220 E. 23rd St., Kansas City 64127 (43).

Mt. Carmel Group Home (r,c; 16-21 yrs.), 8757 Annetta Ave., St. Louis 63147.

St. Casimir Group Home (r; young women, 16-21 yrs.), 10735 Verhof Dr., St. Louis 63136.

St. Joseph's Vocational Center (d,c; 15-21 yrs.), 5341 Emerson Ave., St. Louis 63120 (150).

St. Mary's Special School (r,c; 5-16 yrs.), 5341 Emerson Ave., St. Louis 63120 (135).

Universal Sheltered Workshop (c, adults), 6912 W. Florissant Ave., St. Louis 63136. Sheltered employment (80).

Vogelweid Special Education School (d,c; 5-21 yrs.), 314 W. High St., Jefferson City 65101 (30).

Nebraska: Madonna School for Exceptional Children (d,c; 5-21 yrs.), 2537 N. 62nd St., Omaha 68104 (65).

Villa Marie School (r,d,c; 7-16 yrs.), P. O. Box 80328, Lincoln 68501 (17).

New Jersey: Alhambra Child Study Center (d,c; 5-12 yrs.), 31 Centre St., Newark 07102 (35).

Archbishop Boland Rehabilitation Center (d,c; 16-60 yrs.), 450 Market St. Newark 07105 (350).

Archbishop Damiano School (d,c; 5-21 yrs.), 532 Delsea Ave., Westville Grove 08093.

Catholic Communities Services, Archdiocese of Newark, 17 Mulberry St., Newark 07102. Services include: Alhambra Child Study Center, Archbishop Boland Rehabilitation Center, Mt. Carmel Guild, St. Anthony's and St. Patrick's Special Education Schools (see separate entries).

Department of Special Education, Diocese of Camden, 1845 Haddon Ave., Camden 08108. Services include: Archbishop Damiano School (above), and full time programs at 6 Catholic Schools; adult evening classes (18-65 yrs.); religious education programs.

Department of Special Education, Diocese of Paterson. Murray House (r; adults), 389 Main St., Paterson 07501. Also conducts four other adult group homes and one adult opportunity center.

Felician School for Exceptional Children (r,d,c; 2½-14 yrs.), 260 S. Main St., Lodi 07644 (120).

McAuley School for Exceptional Children (d,c; 5-9 yrs.), 1633 Rt. 22 at Terrill Rd., Plainfield-Watchung 07060 (40).

Mt. Carmel Guild Special Education School (d,c; 6-15 yrs.), 189 Brunswick St., Jersey City 07302 (30).

Mt. Carmel Guild Special Education School (d,c; 6-12 yrs.), 550 E. Broad St., Westfield 07079 (35).

St. Anthony's Special Education School (d,c; 10-20 yrs.), 25 N. 7th St., Belleville 07109 (40).

Sr. Georgine Learning Center (d,c; 6-17 yrs.), 544 Chestnut Ave., Trenton 08611 (30).

St. John of God Community Services (d,c; birth to adults), 532 Delsea Dr., Westville Grove 05093.

St. Patrick's Special Education School (d,c; 6-17 yrs.), 72 Central Ave., Newark 07102 (50).

New Mexico: St. Joseph's Manor (r,b; 18-35 yrs.), P.O. Box 610, Bernalillo 87004. Little Brothers of the Good Shepherd, P.O. Box 610, Bernalillo 87004. Twenty-four-hour adult care center for mentally retarded men.

New York: Cantalician Center for Learning (d,c; birth-21 yrs.), 3233 Main St., Buffalo 14214 (300).

Cantalician Center Workshop (d,c; 18 yrs. and older), 129A Central Park Plaza, Buffalo 14214 (150). Also conducts a vocational evaluation and rehabilitation training program.

Catholic Charities, Diocese of Rockville Centre — Services for Retarded Adults, 50 N. Park Ave., Box X, Rockville Centre 11570. Conducts four residences for retarded adults (Christopher Residence; Neumann Residence for Deaf Retarded; Alhambra House; Seton Residence — r,c; 21 yrs. and up).

Cobb Memorial School (r,d,c; 6-10 yrs.), Altamont 12009 (40).

Friends of L'Arche of Greater Syracuse, Inc. (r, adults), 1701 James St., Syracuse 13206 (12). Long-term facility for mentally retarded adults following philosophy of Jean Vanier and L'Arche movement.

Maryhaven Center of Hope (r,d,c; pre-school to adult), Myrtle Ave., Port Jefferson 11777. Offers variety of services.

Mercy Home for Children (r,c), 273 Willoughby Ave., Brooklyn 11205.

Office for Disabled Persons, Diocese of Brooklyn, 191 Joralemon St., Brooklyn 11201. Services include day care center and community residences for retarded adults.

Office of the Handicapped, Archdiocese of New York, 1011 First Ave., New York 10022.

St. Catherine Center for Children (r,c; birth to 12 yrs. and d,c; 3-12 yrs.), 30 N. Main St., Albany 12203 (150). Also conducts group home and specialized foster care programs.

St. Joseph School for Exceptional Children (r,d,c; 5-21 yrs.), 10807 Bennett Rd., Dunkirk 14048 (26 r, 14 d). Residents must return home weekends and vacations.

School of the Holy Childhood (d,c; 5-21 yrs.), 100 Groton Parkway, Rochester 14623 (94). Adult program, 18-50 yrs.

North Carolina: Holy Angels Nursery (r,c; birth to 18 yrs.), Belmont 28012 (66).

Ohio: Good Shepherd Manor (permanent care of men 18 years and older), Little Brothers of the Good Shepherd, P.O. Box 387, Wakefield 45687 (104).

Julie Billiart School, (d,c; 6-12 yrs.), 4982 Clubside Rd., Lyndhurst 44124. (135). Non-graded school for children with learning problems.

Mary Immaculate School (d,c; 7-14 yrs.), 3837 Secor Rd., Toledo 43623 (60). For children with learning disabilities.

Mt. Aloysius (r, men; 21 yrs. and over), Little Brothers of the Good Shepherd, P.O. Box 598, New Lexington 43764 (100).

Our Lady of Angels Special School (d,c; 6-16 yrs.), 3570 Rocky River Dr., Cleveland 44111 (30).

Our Lady of the Elms Special School (d,c; 6-15 yrs.), 1230 W. Market St., Akron 44313 (61).

Rose Mary, The Johanna Graselli Rehabilitation and Education Center (r,c; 3-12 yrs.), 19350 Euclid Ave., Cleveland 44117 (40).

St. John's Villa (r,c,b, 6-14 yrs; g, 6-18 yrs., continued care, g, 18 yrs. and over), 620 Roswell Rd. N.W., Carrollton 44615 (182).

St. Joseph Center (d,c; 6-16 yrs.), 2346 W. 14th St., Cleveland 44113 (60).

Oregon: Emily School for Multi-Handicapped Children (d,c; 2½-5 yrs.), 830 N.E. 47th Ave., Portland 97213 (12).

Providence Children's Nursing Center (r, c; nursing care), 830 N. E. 47th Ave., Portland 97213 (54).

Pennsylvania: Clelian Heights School for Exceptional Children (r,d,c; 5-21 yrs.), R.D. 9, Box 607, Greensburg 15601 (140). Also conducts re-socialization program (r,d,c; young adults).

Divine Providence Village (r, women), 686 Old Marple Rd., Springfield 19064 (96).

Don Guanella School (r,d,b; 6-21 yrs.) and C. K. Center (r,c; adults, post-school age), 1797 S. Sproul Rd., Springfield 19064.

McGuire Memorial (r,d,c; infancy to 7 yrs.), 2119 Mercer Rd., New Brighton 15066 (99).

Mercy Day School: Center for Special Learning (d,c; 2-21 yrs. and infant stimulation), 830 S. Woodward St., Allentown 18103 (82).

Our Lady of Confidence Day School (d,c; 4½-21 yrs.), 10th and Lycoming Sts., Philadelphia 19140 (140).

St. Anthony School for Exceptional Children (r,d,c; 5-21 yrs.), 13th St. and Hulton Rd., Oakmont 15139 (135).

St. Joseph Center for Special Learning (d,c;

4,7-21 yrs.), 619 Mahantongo St., Pottsville 17901 (40).

St. Joseph's Center (r,c; birth-17 yrs.), 2010 Adams Ave., Scranton 18509 (93).

St. Katherine School (d,c; 4-21 yrs.), William Rd. and Bowman Ave., Philadelphia 19151 (150)

Tennessee: Madonna Day School for Retarded Children (d,c; 5-16 yrs.), 4189 Leroy, Memphis 38108 (52).

St. Bernard School for Exceptional Children, (c; 4-8 yrs.), 2021 21st Ave. S., Nashville 37212 (25).

Texas: Notre Dame of Dallas Special School (d,c; 3-16 yrs.), 1451 E. Northgate Dr., Irving 75062. (115). Notre Dame Vocational Center (d,c; 16 yrs. and over), same address, provides workstudy program for exceptional people over 16 (60).

Virginia: St. Coletta School (d,c; 3-25 yrs.), 1305 N. Jackson St., Arlington 22201 (45). For developmentally disabled.

St. Mary's Infant Home (r,c; 3 days-9 yrs.), 317 Chapel St., Norfolk 23504 (50).

Wisconsin: St. Coletta School (r,c), Jefferson 53549 (372). Offers the following programs:

a complete program of special education from kindergarten through elementary and advanced levels (r,d,c);

a work training center in preparation for job placement (r,c; 18-25 yrs.);

a residential care center (r,c; 45-85 yrs.);

a half-way house to give guidance and assist with problems (r; 18-24 yrs.);

sheltered workshop employment for the mentally retarded in a homelike environment (r,c; 25-45 yrs.).

St. Coletta Day School (c; 8-16 yrs.), 1725 N. 54th St., Milwaukee. 53208 (12).

Orthopedically Handicapped

Alabama: Father Purcell Memorial (r,c; birth to 14 yrs.), 2048 W. Fairview Ave., Montgomery 36108 (52). Skilled nursing home.

Pennsylvania: St. Edmond's Home for Crippled Children (r,c; birth-16 yrs.)., 320 S. Roberts Rd., Rosemont 19010 (40).

Visually Handicapped

Illinois: Vision Services (d,c), Catholic Charities, 721 N. LaSalle Dr., Chicago 60610. Itinerant education services for visually impaired students attending regular Catholic elementary and high schools in Chicago archdiocese (30).

Maine: Visually Handicapped Services: 87 High St., Portland 04101; 15 Vaughn St., Caribou 04736; 382 Sabattus St., Lewiston 04240; 95 Main St., Orono 04472; 224 Main St., Waterville. Itinerant teacher and other services.

New Jersey: St. Joseph's School for the Multiple Handicapped Blind (r,d,c; 3-21 yrs.), 253 Baldwin Ave., Jersey City 07306 (27).

New York: Catholic Charities Services for Visually Impaired Persons (c), 272 Merrick Rd., Lynbrook 11563. All ages, differing programs.

Lavelle School for the Blind (d,c; 3-21 yrs.), 221st St. and Paulding Ave., Bronx 10469 (120).

Pennsylvania: St. Lucy Day School (d,c; 3½-14 yrs.), 929 S. Farragut St., Philadelphia. 19143.

ORGANIZATIONS

(See separate article for a listing of facilities for the handicapped.)

Blind

The Carroll Center for the Blind (formerly the Catholic Guild for All the Blind): Located at 770 Centre St., Newton. Mass. 02158, the center conducts diagnostic evaluation and rehabilitation programs for blind people over 16 years of age, and maintains programs in community services for all ages, volunteer and special services, computer access training, low-vision training and professional training. It offers a large range of services for blind people who are not in residence, and maintains an office of public education and information. *AAR Review* is the quarterly publication of the center. The executive director is Rachel Rosenbaum.

Xavier Society for the Blind: The Society is located at 154 E. 23rd St., New York, 10010. Founded in 1900 by Rev. Joseph Stadelman, S.J., it is a center for publications for the blind and partially sighted and for the deaf blind and maintains a circulating library of approximately 7,000 volumes in Braille, large type and on tape. Its many publications include *The Catholic Review,* a monthly selection of articles of current interest from the Catholic press presented for the visually handicapped in Braille, on tape, and in large print. All services provided for the visually impaired are free. The director of Xavier is Rev. Anthony F. La Bau, S.J.

The Deaf

According to the National Catholic Office for the Deaf, there are approximately 95,000 Catholics among the total deaf population of 410,522. (The deaf were defined by the 1974 National Census of the Deaf Population as "those persons who could not hear and understand speech and who had lost — or never had — that ability prior to 19 years of age.) Reported statistics indicated: Students in Catholic schools for the deaf, 1,969; teachers, 570 (147 were religious). Personnel involved in out-of-school pastoral ministry to the deaf included: priests, 87 (35 full-time, 52 part-time); permanent deacons, 8 (2 full-time, 6 part-time); sisters, 65 (41 full-time, 24 part-time); brothers, 4 (2 full-time, 2 part-time); lay people, 61 (20 full-time, 41 part-time).

Organizations involved in work for the deaf include the following.

International Catholic Deaf Association: Established by deaf adults in Toronto, Canada, in 1949, the association has more than 3,000 members in 121 chapters, mostly in the U.S. It is the only international lay association founded and controlled by deaf Catholic adults. It is affiliated with the World Federation of the Deaf. Home office address: 814 Thayer Ave., Silver Spring, Md. 20910. The ICDA publishes *The Deaf Catholic,* a bimonthly, and sponsors regional conferences, workshops and an annual convention.

National Catholic Office for the Deaf: Formally established in 1976, at Washington, D.C., to provide pastoral service to those who teach deaf children and adults, to the parents of deaf children, to pastors of deaf persons, and to organizations of the deaf. The office develops liturgical and religious education materials; organizes workshops, pastoral weeks, community weeks, leadership programs, cursillos; and serves as a clearinghouse for information concerning ministry to the deaf. It publishes *Listening,* a pastoral service for the hearing impaired, five times a year. The executive director is Sister Alverna Hollis, O.P. Address: 814 Thayer Ave., Silver Spring, Md. 20910.

Mentally Retarded

National Apostolate with Mentally Retarded Persons: Established in 1968 to promote the full participation in the Church by persons who are mentally retarded. It publishes the quarterly *NAMRP Journal* and a monthly newsletter, and has available a bibliography on religious education for mentally retarded persons. Sister Gabrielle Kowalski is president of the apostolate; the executive director is Charles M. Luce, P.O. Box 4711, Columbia, S.C. 29240.

Service Agencies

National Catholic Office for Persons with Disabilities: Established in 1982 to assist dioceses in developing pastoral services with handicapped persons. The executive director is Sister Rita Baum, S.S.J. Address: P.O. Box 29113, Washington, D.C. 20017.

Special Education Department, National Catholic Educational Association: Established in 1954 to coordinate under one agency information and service functions for all areas of special education under Catholic auspices. The executive director is Sr. Suzanne Hall, S.N.D. de N. Address: 1077 30th St. N.W., Washington, D.C. 20007.

OTHER SOCIAL SERVICES

Cancer Hospitals or Homes: The following homes or hospitals specialize in the care of cancer patients. They are listed according to state.

Our Lady of Perpetual Help Home, Servants of Relief for Incurable Cancer, 760 Washington St., S.W., Atlanta, Ga. 30315 (54).

Rose Hawthorne Lathrop Home, Servants of Relief for Incurable Cancer, 1600 Bay St., Fall River, Mass. 02724 (35).

Our Lady of Good Counsel Free Cancer Home, Servants of Relief for Incurable Cancer, 2076 St. Anthony Ave., St. Paul, Minn. 55104 (40).

Calvary Hospital, Inc., 1740 Eastchester Rd., Bronx, N.Y. 10461 (200). Sponsored by Catholic Charities, Department of Health and Hospitals, Archdiocese of New York.

St. Rose's Free Home for Incurable Cancer, Servants of Relief for Incurable Cancer, 71 Jackson St., New York, N.Y. 10002 (45).

Rosary Hill Home, Servants of Relief for Incurable Cancer, Hawthorne, N.Y. 10532 (72).

Holy Family Home, Servants of Relief for Incurable Cancer, 6707 State Rd., Parma, O. 44134 (50).

Sacred Heart Free Home for Incurable Cancer, Servants of Relief for Incurable Cancer, 1315 W. Hunting Park Ave., Philadelphia, Pa. 19140 (59).

Drug Abuse: Rehabilitation centers and outpatient clinics have been established in several dioceses. Facilities include:

Alpha House for Drug Rehabilitation (women) and Dismas House for Drug Rehabilitation (men), 396 Straight St., Paterson, N.J. 07501 (residential rehabilitation programs). Cedar Outpatient Clinic and Cedar Day Care Center, 101-105 Cedar St., Paterson, N.J. 07501 (outpatient services). Straight and Narrow Hospital for Detoxification (20 beds).

Daytop Village, Inc., 54 W. 40th St., New York, N.Y. 10018. Msgr. William B. O'Brien. Five residential facilities and six outreach centers in New York.

New Hope Manor (live in therapeutic community for rehabilitation of female drug addicts), Graymoor, Barryville, N.Y. 12719.

St. Joseph's Hospital, L. E. Phillips Center for the Chemically Dependent, 2661 County Trunk I, Chippewa Falls, Wis. 54729 (46). Residential and outpatient. Adult and adolescent programs. Hospital Sisters of the Third Order of St. Francis.

St. Luke's Center/Bethesda Manor, 2693 Biscayne Blvd., Miami, Fla. 33137. Residential and outpatient detoxification programs for drug abusers; day care services for children of addicts in treatment. Miami DARE, same address, trains parents, youth, priests and teachers as prevention volunteers in the area of substance abuse.

Transitus House for Chemically Dependent Women. 1830 Wheaton St., Chippewa Falls, Wis. 54729 (21). Six month residential transitional living after primary treatment. Hospital Sisters of the Third Order of St. Francis.

Alcoholics: Some priests and religious throughout the U.S. are committed in a special way to the personal rehabilitation and pastoral care of alcoholics through participation in Alcoholics Anonymous and other programs. Facilities for the rehabilitation of alcoholics include:

Matt Talbot Inn, 2270 Professor St., Cleveland, Ohio 44113 (capacity 23 men; Halfway House; residential treatment for male alcoholics).

Straight and Narrow Hospital for Alcoholism (20 beds), and Straight and Narrow Rehabilitation Center for Male Alcoholics (35 beds), 396 Straight St., Paterson, N.J. 07501. McNulty House for Male Alcoholics (10 beds), 101 Cedar St., Paterson, N.J. 07501. Straight and Narrow Alcohol Abuse Services (outpatient services), 896 E. 19th St., Paterson, N.J. 07501. Intoxicated Drivers Resource Center, 184 First St., Passaic, N.J. 07055.

Sacred Heart Rehabilitation Center, Inc., 569 E. Elizabeth St., Detroit, Mich. 48201 (9 beds, detoxification; 60 beds, early treatment); 400 Stoddard Rd., Memphis, Mich. 48041 (75 beds, advance treatment). Both facilities serve male and female live-in clients.

The National Clergy Conference on Alcoholism and Related Drug Problems, 1200 Varnum St., N.E., Washington, D.C. 20017, offers educational material to those involved in pastoral ministry on ways of dealing with problems related to alcohol-

ism and medication dependency.

Convicts: Priests serve as full- or part-time chaplains in penal and correctional institutions throughout the country. Limited efforts have been made to assist in the rehabilitation of released prisoners in Halfway House establishments.

Dining Rooms; Facilities for Homeless: Representative of places where meals are provided, and in some cases lodging and other services as well, are:

St. Anthony's Dining Room, 121 Golden Gate Ave., San Francisco, Calif. 94102. Founded in 1950. Over 2,000 complete meals served free daily; more than 17 million since its founding. Clothing, temporary shelter and basic medical care also provided. Rehabilitation program (farm and rural). Director, Rev. Floyd A. Lotito, O.F.M.

St. Vincent de Paul Free Dining Room, 675 23rd St., Oakland, Calif. 94604. Administered by Daughters of Charity of St. Vincent de Paul, under sponsorship of St. Vincent de Paul Society. Hot meals served at lunch time 7 days a week; clothing, lodging provided those in need.

St. Vincent's Dining Room, 505 W. 3rd St., Reno, Nev. 89503.

St. Vincent Dining Room, 1501 Las Vegas Blvd. N. Las Vegas, Nev. 89101. Hot meal every day at noon.

Good Shepherd Refuge, Little Brothers of the Good Shepherd, 601 2nd St. S.W., Albuquerque, N.M. 87102.

Holy Name Centre for Homeless Men, Inc., 18 Bleeker St., New York, N.Y. 10012. A day shelter for alcoholic, homeless men. Provides social services and aid to transients and those in need. Affiliated with New York Catholic Charities.

St. Francis Inn, P.O. Box 3746, 2441 Kensington Ave., Philadelphia, Pa. 19125. Serves hot meals. Temporary shelter for men and women. Two thrift shops.

St. John's Hospice for Men, staffed by Little Brothers of the Good Shepherd, 1221 Race St., Philadelphia, Pa. 19107. Founded in 1963. Hot breakfast and dinner served to all in need; accommodations for 35 men for night shelter; clothing distributed daily to needy.

Camillus House, Little Brothers of the Good Shepherd, 726 N.E. First Ave., Miami, Fla. 33132. Breakfast and dinner served to all in need; accommodations for 65 men for night lodging; clothing distributed daily.

Temporary Shelters: Facilities for runaways, the abused, exploited and homeless include:

Anthony House, under sponsorship of St. Anthony's Guild (see Index). Four locations: 246 2nd St., Jersey City, N.J. 07302 (for homeless women and children); 38 E. Roosevelt Ave., Roosevelt, N.Y. 11575 (with St. Vincent de Paul Society — for homeless men); P.O. Box 880, Zellwood, Fla. 32798 (for migrant workers and their families); 2130 N. Hancock St., Philadelphia, Pa. 19122 (for homeless youth).

Covenant House, 460 W. 41st St., New York, N.Y. 10036. Non-sectarian. President, Rev. Bruce Ritter, O.F.M. Conv. Provides shelter and services for homeless, runaway and exploited youth under the age of 21, in New York, Houston, Toronto (Canada) and Antigua (Guatemala).

Crescent House, Associated Catholic Charities, 1231 Prytania St., New Orleans, La. 70130. Provides temporary shelter, counseling and advocacy for battered women and their children.

The Dwelling Place, 409 W. 40th St., New York, N.Y. 10018. For homeless women.

The Good Shepherd Shelter, 1126 W. Grace St., Chicago, Ill. 60613. For abused women with children.

Good Shepherd Shelter, 2561 Venice Blvd., Los Angeles, Calif. 90019. For battered women with children.

Gracenter, Convent of the Good Shepherd, 503 Cambridge, San Francisco, Calif. 94134. Residence for women in need.

Mercy Hospice, Sisters of Mercy, 334 S. 13th St., Philadelphia, Pa. 19107. Temporary shelter and relocation assistance for homeless women and children.

Mt. Carmel House, Carmelite Sisters, 471 G Pl., N.W., Washington, D.C. 20001. For homeless women.

Ozanam Inn, Little Brothers of the Good Shepherd, 843 Camp St., New Orleans, La. 70130. Under sponsorship of the St. Vincent de Paul Society.

Hospice for homeless men.

St. Christopher Inn, Graymoor, Garrison, N.Y. 10524. Temporary shelter for homeless and needy men.

Siena/Francis House, Inc. P.O. Box 217 D.T.S., Omaha, Nebr. 68102. Two facilities: Siena House, 804 N. 19th St., Omaha, Nebr. 68102 (for homeless and abused women or women with children; provides 24-hour assistance and advocacy services); Francis House, 1902 Cuming St., Omaha, Nebr. 68102 (temporary shelter for homeless men).

Unwed Mothers: Residential and care services for unwed mothers are available in many dioceses.

CATHOLIC RIGHTS LEAGUE

The Catholic League for Religious and Civil Rights, founded in 1973, serves the Catholic community as an anti-defamation and civil-rights agency. Father Virgil C. Blum, S.J., is president and founder of the league, which is headquartered at 1100 W. Wells St., Milwaukee, Wis. 53233. The league also has 15 local chapters across the country.

The Catholic League serves the Church in safeguarding Catholic beliefs, values and practices, and defending the religious freedom rights of Catholics and others.

RETREATS, SPIRITUAL RENEWAL PROGRAMS

There is great variety in retreat and renewal programs, with orientations ranging from the traditional to teen encounters. Central to all of them are celebration of the liturgy and deepening of a person's commitment to faith and witness in life.

Features of many of the forms are as follows.

Traditional Retreats: Centered around conferences and the direction of a retreat master; oriented to the personal needs of the retreatants; including such standard practices as participation in Mass, reception of the sacraments, private and group prayer, silence and meditation, discussions.

Team Retreat: Conducted by a team of several leaders or directors (priests, religious, lay persons) with division of subject matter and activities according to their special skills and the nature and needs of the group.

Closed Retreat: Involving withdrawal for a period of time — overnight, several days, a weekend — from everyday occupations and activities.

Open Retreat: Made without total disengagement from everyday involvements, on a part-time basis.

Private Retreat: By one person, on a kind of do-it-yourself basis with the one-to-one assistance of a director.

Special Groups: With formats and activities geared to particular groups; e.g., members of Alcoholics Anonymous, vocational groups and apostolic groups.

Marriage Encounters: Usually weekend periods of husband-wife reflection and dialogue; introduced into the U.S. from Spain in 1967.

Charismatic Renewal: Featuring elements of the movement of the same name; "Spirit-oriented"; communitarian and flexible, with spontaneous and shared prayer, personal testimonies of faith and witness.

Christian Community: Characterized by strong community thrust.

Teens Encounter Christ (TEC), SEARCH: Formats adapted to the mentality and needs of youth, involving experience of Christian faith and commitment in a community setting.

Christian Maturity Seminars: Similar to teen encounters in basic concept but different to suit persons of greater maturity.

Cursillo: see separate entry.

Movement for a Better World: see separate entry.

Conference

Retreats International Inc.: The first organization for promoting retreats in the U.S. was started in 1904 in New York. Its initial efforts and the gradual growth of the movement led to the formation in 1927 of the National Catholic Laymen's Retreat Conference, the forerunner of the men's division of Retreats International. The women's division developed from the National Laywomen's Retreat Movement which was founded in Chicago in 1936. The men's and women's divisions merged July 9, 1977. The services of the organization include an annual summer institute for retreat and pastoral ministry, regional conferences for retreat center leadership and area meetings of directors and key leadership in the retreat movement. The officers are: Auxiliary Bishop Robert Morneau of Green Bay, episcopal advisor; Mr. John Van den Wymelenberg, president; Rev. Thomas W. Gedeon, S.J., executive director. National office: Box 1067, Notre Dame, Ind. 46556.

HOUSES OF RETREAT AND RENEWAL

(Principal sources: Almanac survey; *Retreats International; The Official Catholic Directory.*)

Abbreviation code: m, men; w, women; mc, married couples; y, youth. Houses and centers without code generally offer facilities to most groups. An asterisk after an abbreviation indicates that the facility is primarily for the group designated but that special groups are also accommodated. Houses furnish information concerning the types of programs they offer.

Alabama: Blessed Trinity Shrine Retreat, Holy Trinity 36859.

Visitation Sacred Heart Retreat House, 2300 Spring Hill Ave., Mobile 36607.

Alaska: Holy Spirit Retreat House, 10980 Hillside Dr., Anchorage 99516.

Arizona: Franciscan Renewal Center, 5802 E. Lincoln Dr., Box 220, Scottsdale 85252.

Mount Claret Cursillo Center, 4633 N. 54th St., Phoenix 85018.

Picture Rocks Retreat — A Christian Renewal Center and Desert House of Prayer, 7101 W. Picture Rocks Rd., Tucson 85743.

Arkansas: Coury Retreat House, Subiaco 72865.

Little Portion Franciscan Hermitage, Rt. 3, Box 608, Eureka Springs 72632.

California: Angela Center, 535 Angela Dr., Santa Rosa 95401.

Camp Mariastella (y*, families, ecumenical), Wrightwood 92397. Office, 1120 Westchester Pl., Los Angeles 90019.

Christ the King Retreat Center, 6520 Van Maren Lane, Citrus Heights 95621.

Christian Brothers Retreat House (y*), 2233 Sulphur Springs Ave., St. Helena 94574.

Claretian Retreat Center, 1119 Westchester Pl., Los Angeles 90019.

El Carmelo Retreat House, P.O. Box 446, Redlands 92373.

Heart of Jesus Retreat Center, 2927 S. Greenville St., Santa Ana 92704.

Holy Spirit Retreat Center, 4316 Lanai Rd., Encino 91436.

Immaculate Heart Retreat House, 3431 Waverly Dr., Los Angeles 90027. (Days of Recollection only.)

Jesuit Retreat House, P.O. Box 128, Los Altos 94022.

La Casa de Maria, 800 El Bosque Rd., Santa Barbara 93108.

Manresa Retreat House, P.O. Box K, Azusa 91702.

Mary and Joseph Retreat Center, 5300 Crest Rd., Rancho Palos Verdes 90274.

Mater Dolorosa Retreat House (m*), 700 N. Sunnyside Ave., Sierra Madre 91024.

Mercy Center (m, w, engaged encounter), 2300 Adeline Dr., Burlingame 94010.

Mother of Mercy Convent, 10210 Oakdale Ave., Chatsworth 91311.

Mount Mary Immaculate Center for Spiritual Growth, 3254 Gloria Terr., Lafayette 94549.

Mt. Tabor Monastery, 17001 Tomki Rd., Redwood Valley 95470.

New Camaldoli Immaculate Heart Hermitage Big Sur 93920.

Old Mission Retreat, P.O. Box 409, San Luis Rey 92068.

Our Lady of Trust Spirituality Center, 205 Pine St., Fullerton 92633.

Poverello of Assisi Retreat House, 1519 Woodworth St., San Fernando 91340.

Presentation Education and Retreat Center, 19480 Bear Creek Rd., Los Gatos 95030.

Prince of Peace Abbey, 650 Benet Hill Rd., Oceanside 92054.

Sacred Heart Retreat House (w*), 920 E. Alhambra Rd., Alhambra 91801.

St. Andrew's Priory Retreat House, Valyermo 93563.

St. Anthony's Retreat House, P.O. Box 249, Three Rivers 93271.

St. Clare's Retreat, 2381 Laurel Glen Rd. Soquel 95073.

St. Francis Retreat, P.O. Box 1070, San Juan Bautista 95045.

St. Francis Salesian Retreat House (y), 2400 E. Lake Ave., Watsonville 95076.

St. Joseph's Salesian Youth Center (St. Dominic Savio Retreat House) (y), 8301 Arroyo Dr., Rosemead 91770.

St. Mary's Center and Retreat House, 1964 Las Conoas Rd., Santa Barbara 93105.

San Damiano Retreat, P.O. Box 767, Danville 94526.

San Miguel Retreat House, P.O. Box 69, San Miguel 93451.

Santa Sabina Center, 1520 Grand Ave., San Rafael 94901.

Serra Retreat, 3401 S. Serra Rd., Box 127, Malibu 90265.

Starcross Monastery, House of Prayer, Annapolis, Calif. 95412.

Vallombrosa Center, 250 Oak Grove Ave., Menlo Park 94025.

Villa Maria del Mar, Santa Cruz. Mailing address, 2-198 E. Cliff Dr., Santa Cruz 95062.

Villa Maria — House of Prayer (w), 1252 N. Citrus Dr., La Habra 90631.

Colorado: Benet Hill Center, 2577 N. Chelton Rd., Colorado Springs 80909. Primarily day center.

Bethlehem Center, W. 128th Ave. at Zuni, Broomfield 80020.

Convent of St. Walburga, 6717 S. Boulder Rd., Boulder 80303.

Julie Penrose Center (formerly El Pomar), 1661 Mesa Ave., Colorado Springs 80906.

Sacred Heart Retreat House, Box 185, Sedalia 80135.

Spiritual Life Institute (individuals only), Nada Hermitage, Crestone 81131.

Connecticut: Archdiocesan Spiritual Life Center, 467 Bloomfield Ave., Bloomfield 06002.

Cenacle Center for Meditation and Spiritual Renewal, Wadsworth St., P.O. Box 550,Middletown 06457.

Edmundite Apostolate and Conference Center, Enders Island, Mystic 06355.

Emmaus Spiritual Life Center, 24 Maple Ave., Uncasville 06382.

Holy Family Retreat (m, mc*), 303 Tunxis Rd., West Hartford 06107.

Immaculata Retreat House, Windham Rd., Willimantic 06226.

Mercy Center, P.O. Box 191, 167 Neck Rd., Madison 06443.

Montfort Missionaries Retreat Center, P.O. Box 667, Litchfield 06759.

My Father's House, Box 22, North Moodus Rd., Moodus 06469.

Our Lady of Calvary Retreat (w*), 31 Colton St., Farmington 06032.

Trinita Ecumenical Retreat Center, Town Hill Rd., New Hartford 06057.

Villa Maria Retreat House, 159 Sky Meadow Dr., Stamford 06903.

Delaware: St. Francis Renewal Center, 1901 Prior Rd., Wilmington 19809.

District of Columbia: Washington Retreat House (w*), 4000 Harewood Rd. N.E., Washington 20017.

Florida: Cenacle Spiritual Life Center, 1400 S. Dixie Highway, Lantana 33462.

Dominican Retreat House, Inc., 7275 S.W. 124th St., Miami 33156.

Franciscan Center, 3010 Perry Ave., Tampa 33603.

Holy Name Priory, P.O. Drawer H, St. Leo 33574.

Our Lady of Florida Monastery Retreat, 1300 US Hwy. No. 1, North Palm Beach 33408.

Pilgrim Center of St. Leo Abbey, P.O. Drawer "L," St. Leo 33574.

Saint John Neumann Renewal Center, 685 Miccosukee Rd., Tallahassee 32303.

Georgia: Ignatius House, 6700 Riverside Dr. N.W., Atlanta 30328.

Idaho: Nazareth, 4450 N. Five Mile Rd., Boise 83704.

Illinois: Aylesford Carmelite Spiritual Center, I-55 at Cass Ave. N., Darien 60559.

Bellarmine Hall (m*), Box 268, Barrington 60010.

Bishop Lane Retreat House, R.R. 2, Box 214 A, Rockford 61102.

Cabrini Retreat Center (m, w, y), 9430 Golf Rd., Des Plaines 60016.

Cenacle Retreat House, 513 Fullerton Parkway, Chicago 60614.

Cenacle Retreat and Conference Center, P.O. Box 340, Warrenville 60555.

Childerley Retreat House, 506 McHenry Rd., Wheeling 60090.

Christian Life Center, 1515 W. Ogden Ave., La Grange Park 60525.

Divine Word International, 2001 Waukegan Rd., Techny 60082.

Franciscan Apostolic Center, P.O. Box 42, Sangamon Ave., Springfield 62705.

King's House, N. 66th St., Belleville 62223.

King's House of Retreats, Box 165, Henry 61537.

La Salle Manor, Christian Brothers Retreat House, Plano 60545.

National Shrine of Our Lady of the Snows, 9500 W. Illinois Route 15, Belleville 62223.

Sacred Heart Center, 3000 Central Rd., Rolling Meadows 60008.

St. Francis Retreat, House at Mayslake, 1717 31st St., Oak Brook 60521.

St. Joseph Retreat Center, 353 N. River Rd., Des Plaines 60016.

St. Mary's Retreat House, P.O. Box 608, 1400 Main St., Lemont 60439.

Tolentine Center, 20300 Governors Highway, Olympia Fields 60461.

Villa Desiderata Retreat House, 3015 N. Bayview Lane, McHenry 60050.

Villa Center for Renewal, 35 W. 076 Villa Maria Rd., St. Charles 60174.

Villa Redeemer, Redeemer Center, Box 6, Glenview 60025.

Indiana: Alverna Center, 8140 Spring Mill Rd., Indianapolis 46260.

Beech Grove Benedictine Center, 1402 Southern Ave., Beech Grove 46107.

Franciscan Retreat House (m*), Box 500, Cedar Lake 46303.

John XXIII Center, 407 W. McDonald St., Hartford City 47348.

Kordes Enrichment Center, R.R. 3, Box 200, Ferdinand 47532.

Mount Saint Francis Retreat Center, Mount Saint Francis 47146.

Our Lady of Fatima Retreat Center, Notre Dame 46556.

Our Lady of Fatima Retreat House, 5353 E. 56th St., Indianapolis 46226.

St. Jude Guest House, St. Meinrad 47577.

Saint Maur Hospitality Center, 4545 Northwestern Ave., Indianapolis 46208.

Sarto Retreat House, 4200 N. Kentucky Ave., Evansville 47711.

Solitude of St. Joseph, Notre Dame, Ind. 46556.

Iowa: American Martyrs Retreat House, 2209 N. Union Rd., Cedar Falls 50613.

Colette Renewal Center, 3380 Windsor Ave., Dubuque 52001.

Colfax Interfaith Spiritual Center, Box 37, Colfax, 50054.

Emmanuel House of Prayer and Retreat Center 925 Kirkwood Ave., Iowa City 52240.

Kansas: St. Augustine Retreat Center, A 330 Parallel Parkway, Kansas City 66104.

Villa Christi Retreat House, 3033 W. Second St., Wichita 67203.

Kentucky: Catherine Spalding Center, P.O. Box 24, Nazareth 40048.

Marydale Retreat Center, 945 Donaldson Hwy., Erlanger 41018.

Our Lady of Gethsemani (m, private), The Guestmaster, Abbey of Gethsemani, Trappist 40051.

Saint Thomas Center, 170 Crabbs Lane, Louisville 40206.

Louisiana: Abbey Christian Life Center, St. Joseph's Abbey, St. Benedict 70457.

Ave Maria Retreat House, Route 1, Box 0368 AB, Marrero 70072.

Cenacle Retreat House (w*), 5500 St. Mary St., P.O. Box 8115, Metairie 70011.

Jesuit Spirituality Center, P.O. Box C, Grand Coteau 70541.

Manresa House of Retreats (m), P.O. Box 89, Convent 70723.

Maryhill Renewal Center, 600 Maryhill Rd., Pineville 71360.

Our Lady of the Oaks Retreat House, P.O. Drawer D, Grand Coteau 70541.

Maine: Marie Joseph Spiritual Center, RFD 2, Biddeford 04005.

St. Paul's Center, Oblate Fathers Retreat House (French-English), 136 State St., Augusta 04330.

Maryland: Bon Secours Spiritual Center, Marriottsville 21104.

CYO Retreat Center, 5625 Edson Lane, Rockville 20852.

Christian Brothers Spiritual Center, 2535 Buckeyestown Pike, Adamstown 21710.

Loyola Retreat House-on-Potomac, Faulkner 20632.

Manresa Retreat House, P.O. Box 9, Annapolis 21404.

Monsignor Clare J. O'Dwyer Youth Retreat House, 15523 York Rd., Sparks 21152.

Villa Cortona, 7007 Bradley Blvd., Bethesda 20817.

Massachusetts: Calvary Retreat Center, Passionist Community, 59 South St., Shrewsbury 01545.

Campion Renewal Center, 319 Concord Rd., Weston 02193.

Cenacle Retreat House, 200 Lake St., Brighton, Boston 02135.

Eastern Point Retreat Center, Gonzaga Hall, Gloucester 01930.

Espousal Center, 554 Lexington St., Waltham 02154.

Esther House of Spiritual Renewal, Sisters of St. Anne, 1015 Pleasant St., Worcester 01602.

Genesis Spiritual Life Center, 53 Mill St., Westfield 01085.

Glastonbury Abbey (Benedictine Monks), 16 Hull St., Hingham 02043.

Holy Cross Fathers Retreat House, 490 Washington St., N. Easton 02356.

Jesuit Center, Sullivan Square, Charlestown, Boston 02129.

Julie Center of Spirituality, Jeffrey's Neck Rd., Ipswich 01938.

La Salette Center for Christian Living, 947 Park St., Attleboro 02703.

Marian Center (w*), 1365 Northampton St., Holyoke 01040. Day and evening programs only.

Mater Dei Retreat House (boys), Old Groveland Rd., Bradford 01830.

Miramar Retreat House, Duxbury, 02331.

Mother of Sorrows Retreat House, 110 Monastery Ave., W. Springfield 01089.

Mt. Carmel Christian Life Center, Oblong Rd., Box 613, Williamstown 01267.

Sacred Heart Retreat House, Salesians of St. John Bosco, P.O. Box 271, Ipswich 01938.

St. Benedict Priory, Box 67, Still River (Harvard) 01467. Self-directed.

St. Joseph's Abbey Retreat House (m) (Trappist Monks), Spencer 01562.

St. Stephen Priory (Dominican), 20 Glen St., Box 370, Dover, Mass. 02030.

Michigan: Blessed Sacrament Retreat House, Sacramentine Sisters, Conway 49722.

Capuchin Retreat, Box 188, Washington 48094.

Colombiere Retreat/Conference Center, Box 139, 9075 Big Lake Rd., Clarkston 48016.

Manresa Jesuit Retreat House, 1390 Quarton Rd., Bloomfield Hills 48013.

Marygrove Center, Garden 49835.

Portiuncula in the Pines, 703 E. Main St., De Witt 48820.

Queen of Angels Retreat, Box 2026, 3400 S. Washington Blvd., Saginaw 48605.

Retreat Center (w*), Sisters of Mary Reparatrix, 13600 Virgil Ave., Detroit 48223.

St. Basil's Center, 3990 Giddings Rd., Pontiac 48055.

St. Clare Capuchin Retreat (y*), 1975 N. River Rd., St. Clair 48079.

St. Lazare Retreat House, 18600 W. Spring Lake Rd., Spring Lake 49456.

St. Mary's Retreat House (w*), 775 W. Drahner Rd., Oxford 48051.

St. Paul of the Cross Retreat Center, 23333 Schoolcraft, Detroit 48223.

Minnesota: Assisi Heights Christian Community Center, Box 4900, Rochester 55903.

Benedictine Center, St. Paul's Priory, 2675 E. Larpenteur Ave., St. Paul 55109.

The Cenacle, 1221 Wayzata Blvd., Wayzata 55391.

Center for Spiritual Development, Box 538, 211 Tenth St., Bird Island 55310.

Christian Brothers Retreat Center, 15525 St. Croix Trail North, Marine-on-St. Croix 55047.

The Dwelling Place, 116 S.E. Eighth Ave., Little Falls 56345.

Franciscan Retreats, Conventual Franciscan Friars, 16385 St. Francis Lane, rior Lake 55372.

Jesuit Retreat House, 8243 De Montreville Trail North, Lake Elmo 55042.

King's House of Retreats, 621 First Ave. S., Buffalo 55313.

Maryhill Retreat Center, Society of Daughters of the Heart of Mary, 260 Summit Ave., St. Paul 55102.

Minneapolis Catholic Youth Center (y, mc), 2120 Park Ave. S., Minneapolis 55404.

Villa Maria Center, Ursuline Sisters, Frontenac 55026.

Welch Center, 605 N. Central Ave., Duluth 55807.

Missouri: Cenacle Retreat House, 900 S. Spoede Rd., St. Louis 63131.

Christina House Hermitages, Abbey Lane, P.O. Box 619, Pevely 63070.

La Salle Retreat Center, 1886 Rue De La Salle, Glencoe 63038.

Maria Fonte Solitude (private; individual hermitages), P.O. Box 322, High Ridge 63049.

Marianist Apostolic Center, P.O. Box 127, Glencoe 63038.

Our Lady of Assumption Abbey (m, w), Trappists, Rt. 5, Box 193, Ava 65608.

Our Lady's Retreat House, Passionist Community, 3036 Bellerive Dr., St. Louis 63121.

Pallottine Renewal Center, 15270 Old Halls Ferry Rd., Florissant 63034.

Queen of Heaven Solitude (private, individual hermitages), Rt. 1, Box 107A, Marionville 65705.

Retreat and Conference Center, Conception Seminary College, Conception 64433.

The White House Retreat (m), 7400 Christopher Dr., St. Louis 63129.

Montana: Emmaus Retreat House, Box 407, Havre 59501.

Ursuline Retreat Center, 2300 Central Ave., Great Falls 59401.

Nebraska: Crosier Renewal Center, 223 E. 14th St., P.O. Box 789, Hastings 68901.

Good Counsel, R.R. 1, Box 110, Waverly 68462.

St. Columban's Conference Center, St. Columbans 68056.

New Hampshire: The Common - St. Joseph Monastery, Discalced Carmelite Friars, Peterborough 03458.

La Salette Conference and Retreat Center, Enfield 03748.

New Hampshire Monastery, Hundred Acres, New Boston 03070.

Oblates of Mary Immaculate Retreat House, Hudson 03051.

St. Francis Friary and Retreat House, 860 Central Rd., Rye Beach 03871.

New Jersey: Bethlehem Hermitage, Pleasant Hill Rd., Box 315, Chester 07930.

Blackwood Center, St. Pius X House, Box 216, Blackwood 08012.

Carmel Retreat House, 1071 Ramapo Valley Rd., Mahwah 07430.

Cenacle Retreat House, 411 River Rd., Highland Park 08904.

Felician Retreat House, Windemere Ave., Mt. Arlington 07856.

Good Shepherd Center, 74 Kahdena Rd., Morristown 07960.

Loyola House of Retreats, 161 James St., Morristown 07960.

Marianist Christian Family Living Center (families), Cape and Yale Ave., Cape May Point 08212.

Maris Stella, P.O. Box 335, Harvey Cedars 08008.

Mt. St. Francis Retreat House, Sloatsburg Rd., Ringwood 07456. Facilities only.

Queen of Peace Retreat House, St. Paul's Abbey, P.O. Box 7, Newton 07860.

St. Joseph's Villa (w, guest and retreat house), Srs. of St. John the Baptist, Peapack 07977.

San Alfonso Retreat House, 755 Ocean Ave., Long Branch 07740.

Sanctuary of Mary, R.R. 1, Box 106, Branchville 07826. Days of Recollection.

Stella Maris Retreat House, 981 Ocean Ave., Elberon 07740.

Villa Pauline Retreat and Guest House (w*), Hilltop Rd., Mendham 07945.

Xavier Center, Convent Station 07961.

New Mexico: Dominican Retreat House, 5825 Coors Rd. S.W., Albuquerque 87105.

Holy Cross Retreat House, P.O. Box 158, Mesilla Park 88047.

Our Lady of Guadalupe Monastery, Pecos 87552.

New York: At Home Retreats, 310 Cenacle Rd., Lake Ronkonkoma 11779.

Bethany Retreat House, County Road 105, Highland Mills 10930.

Bethlehem Retreat House (m*), Abbey of the Genesee, Piffard 14533.

Bishop Molloy Retreat House, 178th St. and Wexford Terr., Jamaica, L.I. 11432.

Cabrini-on-the-Hudson, West Park, N.Y. 12493.

Cardinal Spellman Retreat House, Passionist Fathers, 5801 Palisade Ave., Bronx (Riverdale) 10471.

Cenacle Center for Spiritual Renewal, 310 Cenacle Rd., Lake Ronkonkoma 11779.

The Cenacle: Center for Spiritual Renewal, 693 East Ave., Rochester 14607.

Cenacle Retreat House, State Rd., P.O. Box 467, Bedford Village 10506.

Christ the King Retreat House, 500 Brookford Rd., Syracuse 13224.

Cormaria Retreat House, Sag Harbor, L.I. 11963.

Diocesan Cursillo Center (Spanish), 118 Congress St., Brooklyn 11201.

Dominican Retreat House, 1945 Union St., Schenectady 12309.

Don Bosco Retreat Center, Filor's Lane, West Haverstraw 10993.

Graymoor Christian Unity Center, Graymoor, Garrison 10524.

Island Retreat (June-Sept.), Bluff Island, Tupper Lake 12986.

Jesuit Retreat House, North American Martyrs Shrine, Auriesville 12016.

Little Portion, 292 E. 151st St., Bronx 10451.

Mary Reparatrix Retreat Center, 14 E. 29th St., New York 10016.

Monastery of the Precious Blood (w), Ft. Hamilton Parkway and 54th St., Brooklyn 11219.

Mount Alvernia Retreat House, Box 858, Wappingers Falls 12590.

Mount Manresa Retreat House, 239 Fingerboard Rd., Staten Island 10305.

Notre Dame Retreat House (m*), Box 342, Foster Rd., Canandaigua 14424.

Our Lady of Hope Center, 434 River Rd., Newburgh 12550.

Regina Maria Retreat House, 77 Brinkerhoff St., Plattsburgh 12901.

St. Albert's Spiritual Life Center, Carmelite Fathers, Box 868, Middletown 10940.

St. Andrew's House, 89 A St. Andrew's Rd., Walden 12586.

St. Columban's Center, 6892 Lake Shore Rd., P.O. Box 816, Derby 14047.

St. Gabriel Retreat House, 64 Burns Rd., P.O. Box P, Shelter Island 11965.

St. Ignatius Renewal Center, Diocese of Buffalo, 6969 Strickler Rd., Clarence Center 14032. Poustinia available.

St. Ignatius Retreat House, Searington Rd., Manhasset, L.I. 11030.

St. Josaphat's Retreat House, Basilian Monastery, East Beach Rd., Glen Cove 11542.

St. Joseph Center (Spanish Center), 523 W. 142nd St., New York 10031.

St. Mary's Villa, Sloatsburg 10974.

St. Ursula Center, Middle Rd. and Blue Point Ave., Blue Point 11715.

Stella Maris Retreat House and Center for Renewal, 130 E. Genesee St., Skaneateles 13152.

Stella Niagara Center of Renewal, 4421 Lower River Rd., Stella Niagara 14144.

Tagaste Monastery Retreat House (m, y), Suffern 10901.

North Carolina: Avila Retreat Center, 711 Mason Rd., Durham 27712.

Living Waters Catholic Reflection Center, Rt. 1, Box 476, Maggie Valley 28751.

Maryhurst Retreat House, P.O. Box 38, Pinehurst 28374.

North Dakota: Queen of Peace Retreat, Redemptorist Fathers, 1310 N. Broadway, Fargo 58102.

Ohio: Bergamo Conference Center, 4435 E. Patterson Rd., Dayton 45430.

Brunnerdale Center, 4001 Brunnerdale Ave. N.W., Canton 44718.

Friarhurst Retreat House, 8136 Wooster Pike, Cincinnati 45227.

Jesuit Renewal Center, 5361 S. Milford Rd., Milford 45150.

Jesuit Retreat House, 5629 State Rd., Cleveland 44134.

Loyola of the Lake, 700 Killinger Rd., Clinton 44216.

Maria Stein Center, 2365 St. Johns Rd., Maria Stein 45860.

Men of Milford Retreat House, Box 348, Milford 45150.

MSC Center, Rt. 4, Shelby 44875.

Our Lady of Consolation Renewal Center, 320 West St., Carey 43316.

Our Lady of the Pines, 1250 Tiffin St., Fremont 43420.

Sacred Heart, 3128 Logan Ave., Box 6074, Youngstown 44501.

St. Anthony Pilgrim House, 321 Clay St., Carey 43316. (Facilities only.)

St. Joseph Christian Life Center, 18485 Lake Shore Blvd., Cleveland 44119.

Shrine Center for Renewal, Diocese of Columbus, 5277 E. Broad St., Columbus 43213.

Oklahoma: St. Gregory's Abbey, Shawnee 74801.

Oregon: Franciscan Retreat Center, 0858 S.W. Palatine Hill Rd., Portland 97219.

Loyola Retreat House (Jesuit Center for Spiritual Renewal), 3220 S.E. 43rd St., Portland 97206.

Mt. Angel Abbey Guest-Retreat Center, St. Benedict 97373.

Our Lady of Peace Retreat (m, w); 3600 S. W. 170th Ave., Beaverton 97006.

Shalom Prayer Center, Benedictine Sisters, Mt. Angel 97362.

Trappist Abbey Retreat (private), P.O. Box 97, Lafayette 97127.

Pennsylvania: Byzantine Catholic Seminary (m), 3605 Perrysville Ave., Pittsburgh 15214.

Cenacle Retreat House, 4721 Fifth Ave., Pittsburgh 15213.

Dominican Retreat House, Ashbourne Rd. and Juniper Ave., Elkins Park 19117.

Family Life Center, P.O. Box 306, Route 219 North, Ebensburg 15931.

Fatima House, Rolling Hills Rd., Ottsville 18942.

Gilmary Diocesan Center, Flaugherty Run Rd., Coraopolis 15108.

Jesuit Center for Spiritual Growth, Box 223, Church Rd., Wernersville 19565.

Maria Wald Retreat House, Convent of the Precious Blood, Box 97, New Holland Ave., Shillington 19607.

Marian Hall, St. Joseph Convent/Academy, RD 2, Columbia 17512.

Mercy Center, Box 370, Dallas 18612.

Mount St. Macrina Retreat Center, Mt. St. Macrina, Box 878, Uniontown 15401.

Our Lady of Fatima Center, Griffin Rd., Box 163, Elmhurst 18416.

St. Alphonsus Retreat House (m*), Box 218, Tobyhanna 18466 (1,200).

St. Emma Retreat House, 1001 Harvey St., Greensburg 15601.

St. Fidelis Retreat Center, Herman 16039.

St. Francis Retreat House, 3918 Chipman Rd., Easton 18042.

St. Francis Retreat House (w), Monocacy Manor, 395 Bridle Path Rd., Bethlehem 18017.

St. Gabriel's Retreat House (w), 631 Griffin Pond Rd., Clarks Summit 18411.

St. Joseph's in the Hills (m), 313 Warren Ave., Malvern 19355.

St. Paul of the Cross Retreat House, 148 Monastery Ave., Pittsburgh 15203.

Saint Raphaela Mary Retreat House, 616 Coopertown Rd., Haverford 19041.

St. Vincent Archabbey (m*, summer), Latrobe 15650.

Trinity Spiritual Center, 3609 Simpson Ferry Rd., Camp Hill 17011.

Villa Maria Retreat Center, Box 208, Wernersville 19565.

Villa of Our Lady Retreat Center (w, mc, y), HCR No. 1, Box 41, Mt. Pocono 18344.

Rhode Island: Carmel Renewal Center, 21 Battery St., Newport 02840.

Ephpheta House — A Center for Renewal, 10 Manville Hill Rd; mailing address, P.O. Box 1, Manville 02838.

Father Marot CYO Center (y), 53 Federal St., Woonsocket 02895.

Our Lady of Peace Spiritual Life Center, Ocean Rd., Narragansett 02882.

St. Dominic Savio Youth Center (y*), Broad Rock Rd., Box 67, Peace Dale 02883.

South Carolina: The Oratory, 434 Charlotte Ave., Box 11586, Rock Hill 29730.

Springbank Christian Center, Dominican Retreat House, Kingstree 29556.

South Dakota: St. Martin's Community Center, R.R. 4, Box 1660, Rapid City 57702.

Sioux Spiritual Center (for Native Americans), Diocese of Rapid City, Howes Star Route Box 271, Plainview 57748.

Tennessee: House of the Lord, 1306 Dellwood Ave., Memphis 38127.

Texas: Bishop DeFalco Retreat Center, 2100 N. Spring, Amarillo 79107.

Catholic Renewal Center of North Texas, 4503 Bridge St., Ft. Worth 76103.

Cenacle Retreat House, 420 N. Kirkwood, Houston 77079.

Christian Holiday House and Renewal Center, Oblate Fathers, P.O. Box 635, Dickinson 77539.

Holy Family, Retreat Center, 9920 N. Major Dr., Beaumont 77706.

Holy Name Retreat Center (m*), 430 Bunker Hill Rd., Houston 77024.

Montserrat Jesuit Retreat House, P.O. Box 398, Lake Dallas 75065.

Mount Tabor Retreat House, 12940 Up River Rd., Corpus Christi 78410.

Our Lady of the Pillar Marianist Retreat Center, 2507 N.W. 36th St., San Antonio 78228.

Saint Joseph Retreat House (Casa San Jose), 127 Oblate Dr., San Antonio 78216.

San Juan Retreat House, Diocese of Brownsville, P.O. Box 998, San Juan 78589.

Utah: Our Lady of the Holy Trinity Retreat House (m), Huntsville 84317.

Our Lady of the Mountains, 1794 Lake St., Ogden 84401.

Virginia: Dominican Retreat, 7103 Old Dominion Dr., McLean 22101.

The Franciscan Center, Rt. 642, Box 825, Winchester 22601.

Holy Family Retreat House, Redemptorist Fathers, 1414 N. Mallory St., Hampton 23663.

Missionhurst CICM Mission Center, 4651 N. 25th St., Arlington 22207.

Spiritual Renewal Center (Genesis House), Rt. 2, Box 388 B, Richmond 23233.

Washington: Camp Field Retreat Center, P.O. Box 128, Leavenworth 98826.

Immaculate Heart Retreat House, Route 3, Box 653, Spokane 99203.

Redemptorist Palisades Retreat, P.O. Box 3739, Federal Way 98063.

St. Peter the Apostle Diocesan Retreat Center, Route 1, Box 86, Cowiche 98923.

St. Thomas Center, 14500 Juanita Dr. N.E., Bothell 98011.

Visitation Retreat Center (w), 3200 S.W. Dash Point Rd., Federal Way 98023.

West Virginia: Bishop Hodges Pastoral Center, P.O. Box 60, Huttonsville, 26273.

Cenacle Retreat House, 1114 Virginia St. E., Charleston 25301.

John XXIII Pastoral Center, 100 Hodges Rd., Charleston, W. Va. 25314.

Paul VI Pastoral Center, 667 Stone and Shannon Rd., Wheeling 26003.

Priest Field Pastoral Center, Rt. 1, Box 133, Kearneysville 25430.

Wisconsin: Archdiocesan Retreat Center, 3501 S. Lake Dr., P.O. Box 2018, Milwaukee 53201.

Cardoner Jesuit Retreat Center, 1501 S. Layton Blvd., Milwaukee 53215.

Chapel House of Prayer, Route 1, New Franken, Wis. 54229.

Holy Cross Center for Spiritual Growth, 503 S. Center Ave., Merrill 54452.

Holy Name Retreat House, Chambers Island; mailing address, 1825 Riverside Drive, P.O. Box 1825, Green Bay 54305.

Jesuit Retreat House, 4800 Fahrnwald Rd., Oshkosh 54901.

Marynook — House of the Lord (ecumenical retreat and conference center), 500 S. 12th St., P.O. Box 9, Galesville 54630.

Monte Alverno Retreat Center, 1000 N. Ballard Rd., Appleton 54911.

Perpetual Help Retreat Center, 1800 N. Timber Trail Lane, Oconomowoc 53066.

St. Anthony Retreat Center, Marathon 54448.

St. Benedict Center (ecumenical retreat and conference center), Fox Bluff, P.O. Box 5070, Madison 53705.

St. Francis Friary and Retreat Center, 503 S. Browns Lake Dr., Burlington 53105.

St. Joseph's Retreat Center, Bailey's Harbor 54202.

St. Vincent Pallotti Center, Rt. 3, Box 61, Elkhorn 53121.

Schoenstatt Center, W. 284 N. 698 Cherry Lane, Waukesha 53186.

LAY PERSONS AND THEIR APOSTOLATE

SPECIAL AGENCIES

Some of the following agencies are engaged in carrying out programs of the United States Catholic Conference. Additional agencies are reported in other Almanac entries.

Religious Education/Catechesis/CCD (Confraternity of Christian Doctrine): Its objective is the catechesis of persons from early childhood through adult life.

The modern expansion of catechesis dates from publication of the encyclical letter *Acerbo Nimis* by Pope St. Pius X in 1905. His directive, that CCD programs be established in every parish, was incorporated in the 1917 Code of Canon Law, reaffirmed by the Second Vatican Council in the *Decree on the Bishops' Pastoral Office in the Church*, and given direction by the publication of the *National Catechetical Directory* in 1971.

Programs for catechesis are parish-based. Policies are developed by parish boards or commissions, and responsibility for administering programs rests ideally with a coordinator or director who is a trained professional.

On the diocesan level, religious education is coordinated by a director with a staff operating under the title of an office of religious education or a similar title. The diocesan office coordinates and acts as consultant to the work of local parish and regional programs; it conducts teacher-training courses, issues guidelines for unified programs, provides overall in-service aid and resources for local staffs and programs.

On the national level, Religious Education/Catechetical Ministry/CCD (formerly called the National Center for the Confraternity of Christian Doctrine, and since 1969 under the Department of Education, U.S. Catholic Conference) provides representation and service for local diocesan staffs and programs. On the international level, it participates in programs which find their roots with the Vatican congregations that deal with religious education or catechesis. Publications include *The Living Light,* Catechetical Sunday material and other related programs.

Offices are located at 1312 Massachusetts Ave. N.W., Washington, D.C. 20005.

National Council of Catholic Men: A federation of Catholic organizations through which Catholic men may be heard nationally on matters of common interest. NCCM is a constituent of the National Council of Catholic Laity.

Offices are located at 4712 Randolph Dr., Annandale, Va. 22003.

National Council of Catholic Women: A federation of some 10,000 organizations of Catholic women in the U.S.; founded in 1920. NCCW unites Catholic organizations and individual Catholic women of the U.S., develops their leadership potential, assists them to act upon current issues in the Church and society, provides a medium through which Catholic women may speak and act upon matters of common interest, and relates to

other national and international organizations in the solution of present-day problems. It is an affiliate of the World Union of Catholic Women's Organizations.

The official publication is *Catholic Woman,* issued 6 times a year.

National office: 1312 Massachusetts Ave. N.W., Washington, D.C. 20005.

National Council of Catholic Laity: Formed in 1971 by the National Council of Catholic Men and the National Council of Catholic Women to provide direction and guidance to existing and new lay organizations. It sponsors conferences and is a contact agency for information about specialized groups in the Church.

The mailing address is P.O. Box 14525, Cincinnati, Ohio 45214.

National Catholic Rural Life Conference: Founded in 1923 through the efforts of Bishop Edwin V. O'Hara for the purpose of promoting the general welfare of rural people by a program of extensive services, publications and rural-related activities. Publications include a newsletter and *Catholic Rural Life.*

The conference has approximately 2,000 members among rural pastors, farmers, teachers, sociologists, economists, agricultural agents and officials. There are 114 officially appointed diocesan rural life directors.

Most Rev. Ignatius J. Strecker, archbishop of Kansas City, Kans., is president. Mr. Gregory Cusack is executive director.

National headquarters are located at 4625 N.W. Beaver Dr., Des Moines, Ia. 50310.

Catholic Relief Services — USCC: The official overseas aid and development agency of American Catholics; it is a separately incorporated organization of the U.S. Catholic Conference.

CRS was founded in 1943 by the bishops of the United States to help civilians in Europe and North Africa caught in the disruption and devastation of World War II.

Initially, CRS collected, purchased and shipped to war-torn countries huge quantities of food, clothing, medicines and other relief supplies which were distributed to hundreds of thousands of displaced persons, prisoners of war, bombed-out families, widows, orphans and other war victims.

As conditions in Europe improved in the late 1940s and early 1950s, the works conducted by CRS spread to other continents and areas — Asia, Africa and Latin America.

CRS has programs or projects in 63 countries, representatives in another 30 countries. The agency works with local counterpart organizations to provide humanitarian assistance and emergency relief. Help is given strictly in response to need; race, creed, color and political affiliation are no consideration.

Although best known for its record of disaster response, compassionate aid to refugees and commitment to reconstruction and rehabilitation, CRS places primary focus on long-term development projects designed to help people to help themselves and to determine their own future.

Administrative funding for CRS comes from an annual collection, the Catholic Relief Services Annual Appeal (known variously as Bishops' Relief or American Catholic Overseas Aid Appeal), held during Lent in most of the 18,000 Catholic parishes of the U.S.

Major support is derived from private, individual donors through direct contributions and through a program of sacrificial giving called Operation Rice Bowl. Funds are also received from philanthropic foundations and humanitarian organizations in the U.S. and Europe. Clothing is collected each year, generally at Thanksgiving, for distribution overseas. More than 8 million pounds of used clothing, blankets and bolt goods are contributed annually through Catholic churches.

Assistance is received from the U.S. Government in several forms: foodstuffs available under Title II of Public Law 480, ocean-freight subsidies for government food and other privately generated relief supplies, and grants for both emergency programs and community development projects.

In 1985, the CRS global program in 63 countries employed 1,100 people and was valued at $499 million.

Lawrence Pezzullo is executive director.

CRS headquarters are located at 1011 First Ave., New York, N.Y. 10022.

SPECIAL APOSTOLATES AND GROUPS

Apostleship of the Sea: An international Catholic organization for the moral, social and spiritual welfare of seafarers and those involved in the maritime industry. It was founded in 1920 in Glasgow, Scotland, and formally approved by the Holy See in 1922. It is promoted and directed by the Pontifical Commission for Migrants and Tourism, Piazza San Calisto 16, Rome, Italy 00153. The U.S. unit is the Apostleship of the Sea in the United States, an affiliate of the NCCB-USCC, established in 1947. It serves 70 port chaplains in 58 U.S. ports on the seacoasts and the Great Lakes. Operations include a hospitality and welcoming program as well as counseling and spiritual services carried on by individual port chaplains through Catholic maritime clubs in Alabama (Mobile); California (Oakland, San Francisco, Wilmington); Florida (Miami, Port Everglades, Jacksonville, Pensacola); New Jersey (Newark), New York (Brooklyn); Washington (Seattle); and interfaith clubs located in Alaska (Ketchikan); Florida (Pensacola); Georgia (Savannah); New Jersey (Newark, Port Elizabeth); Texas (Corpus Christi, Galveston, Houston); Washington (Tacoma); Wisconsin (Milwaukee). Recent developments have emphasized the interfaith cooperation on the port level in seamen's ministry. The episcopal promoter of the conference is Most Rev. Rene Gracida, 620 Lipan St., Corpus Christi, Tex. 78401. Rev. Raymond F. Rau is national director. Address of the national office is P.O. Box 4787, Corpus Christi, Tex. 78469. Also affiliated with the Apostleship of the Sea in the United States is the **National Catholic Conference for Seafarers.** The president is Rev. Mario Balbi, S.D.B., 222 E. Harris, P.O. Box 8307, Savannah, Ga. 31412.

Augustinian Volunteers (1983): Founded by Rev. Patrick H. O'Neill, O.S.A., to promote values of social justice by direct service to those who do not have access to educational, cultural, social and economic resources throughout the State of Florida. Volunteers, 21 years of age and older, serve for a one-year period. There are currently seven volunteers serving in urban and rural settings. Address: P.O. Box 702, Goldenrod, Fla. 32733.

Auxiliaries of Our Lady of the Cenacle (1878, France): An association of Catholic laywomen, under the direction of the Congregation of Our Lady of the Cenacle, who serve God through their own professions and life styles by means of vows. Members live a fully secular life consecrated according to the spirituality of the Cenacle and pursue individual apostolates. They number approximately 150 throughout the world. U.S. regional director: Sister Barbara Whittemore, r.c., 310 Cenacle Rd., Lake Ronkonkoma, N.Y. 11779.

Catholic Central Union of America (1855): One of the oldest Catholic lay organizations in the U.S., the Union is devoted to the development and vigor of Christian principles in personal, social, cultural, economic and civic life. It was the first society ever given an official mandate for Catholic Action by a committee of the American bishops, in 1936. The Central Bureau in St. Louis is the center for the separate but coordinated direction of the National Catholic Women's Union. The headquarters is also a publishing house (*Social Justice Review,* other publications), a library of German-Americana and Catholic Americana, a clearinghouse for information, and a center for works of charity. Aid is given to the missions, and maintenance and direction are provided for St. Elizabeth's Center in St. Louis. Union membership is approximately 8,100. Address: 3835 Westminster Place, St. Louis, Mo. 63108.

Catholic Medical Mission Board (1928): Founded by Dr. Paluel Flagg and the Rev. Edward Garesche, S.J. Its purposes are to gather and ship medical supplies for the sick poor in mission lands, and to recruit and assign medical and paramedical personnel to overseas mission hospitals and dispensaries. Since its foundation, it has shipped approximately 50 million pounds of supplies. In 1985, more than $13.8 million in medicines were shipped to 2,898 mission distribution centers in 54 countries. Also in 1985, 41 medical volunteers were placed in 8 countries. Rev. Joseph J. Walter, S.J., is the director. Office: 10 W. 17th Street, New York, N.Y. 10011.

Center for Applied Research in the Apostolate (CARA): A research and development agency in the field of the Church's worldwide religious and social mission. Its purpose is to gather information for the use of decision-makers in evaluating the present status of the Church's mission of service and in planning programs of development toward greater effectiveness of its multiphased ministry in the future. CARA has research and planning programs focused on: church personnel (recruitment, selection training, utilization, effectiveness), diocesan planning, religious life, and other subjects. CARA was incorporated as a non-profit corporation in the District of Columbia Aug. 5, 1964. William P. Clark is president. Offices are located at 3700 Oakview Terrace, N.E., Washington, D.C. 20017.

Christian Family Movement (CFM) (1947): Originating in Chicago and having a membership of married couples and individuals, its purpose is to Christianize family life and create communities conducive to Christian family life. Since 1968, CFM in the U.S. has included couples from all Christian churches. The International Confederation of Christian Family Movements embraces a worldwide membership. Executive directors, Gary and Kay Aitchison, Box 272, Ames, Iowa 50010.

Christian Life Communities: Formerly known as Sodalities of Our Lady, they are groups of men and women, adults and youth, joined with other people involved in living their full Christian vocation and commitment in the world. The governing principles and operating norms of Sodalities, revised in the spirit of documents of the Second Vatican Council, were promulgated and approved by Pope Paul VI in 1971. The Spiritual Exercises of St. Ignatius remain a specific source and characteristic of the spirituality of the movement. Christian Life Communities are located in more than 60 countries; the U.S. Federation is comprised of approximately 150 communities. National office: 3721 Westminster Blvd., St. Louis, Mo. 63108. The World Federation office is located in Rome.

Cursillo Movement: An instrument of Christian renewal designed to form and stimulate persons to engage in apostolic action individually and in the organized apostolate, in accordance with the mission which individuals have to transform the environments in which they live into Christian environments. The movement originated in Spain, where the first cursillo was held near Palma, Mallorca, in 1949. It was introduced in the U.S. in 1957 and is functioning in more than 160 dioceses. The method of the movement involves a three-day weekend called a cursillo and a follow-up program known as the post-cursillo.

The weekend is an intensive experience in Christian community living centered on Christ and built around 15 talks (10 by laymen, five by priests), active participation in discussions and related activities, the celebration of the liturgy. The follow-up program focuses on small weekly reunions of three to five persons and larger group reunions, called ultreyas, in which participants share experiences and insights derived from their prayer life, study and apostolic action. The movement operates within the framework of diocesan and parish pastoral plans, and functions autonomously in each diocese under the direction of the bishop. Responsibility for growth and effectiveness rests with a diocesan leaders' school, a diocesan secretariat, or both. Bishop James S. Sullivan of Fargo, N. Dak., is episcopal advisor to the movement.

Gerald P. Hughes is executive director of the National Cursillo Center, P.O. Box 210226, Dallas, Tex. 75211.

Frontier Apostolate (1956): Volunteers for a minimum of two years' service in their professional line (teachers, secretaries, houseparents, etc.) in the Diocese of Prince George, British Columbia, Canada. More than 2,600 have served since the start of the corps by Bishop Fergus O'Grady. There are about 150 men and women from 8 different countries actively engaged in works throughout the diocese. Address: Bishop O'Grady, College Rd., P.O. Box 7000, Prince George, B.C., Canada V2N 3Z2.

Grail, The (1921): An international movement of women concerned about the full development of all peoples, working in education, religious, social and cultural areas. Founded by Rev. Jacques van Ginneken, S.J., in The Netherlands, it was introduced in the U.S. in 1940. The Grail is at work in: Australia, Brazil, Canada, Costa Rica, Egypt, France, Germany, India, Italy, Kenya, The Netherlands, Nigeria, Philippines, Portugal, South Africa. Tanzania, Uganda, United States. U.S. headquarters: Grailville, Loveland, Ohio 45140. International Secretariat: Duisburger Strasse 470, 4330 Mulheim, West Germany.

International Liaison, Inc. (1963): The U.S. Catholic Coordinating Center for Lay Missioners, an affiliate of the U.S. Catholic Conference, acts as a clearinghouse for promotion, recruitment and referral of lay missioners who serve interdenominationally in church missions and public and private volunteer agencies throughout the world. The organization also assists mission agencies to facilitate participation by lay persons in ministries of the Church. Publications include *The Response,* an annual directory of lay mission opportunities, and a quarterly newsletter. David J. Suley is the executive director. National office: 810 Rhode Island Ave. N.E., Washington, D.C. 20018.

Jesuit Volunteer Corps (1956): Established by the Oregon Province of the Jesuits, for service to the poor and oppressed throughout the U.S. Men and women volunteers must be 21 years of age and older. A minimum one-year commitment is requested. JVC emphasizes Christian service, community and simple lifestyle. Address for information: JVC/Northwest, P.O. Box 3928, Portland Ore. 97208.

Lay Mission-Helpers Association (1955): It trains and assigns men and women for work in overseas apostolates for periods of three years. Approximately 600 members of the association have served in overseas assignments since 1955. The Rev. Msgr. Joseph Alzugaray is director of the association. Headquarters: 1531 West Ninth St., Los Angeles, Calif. 90015.

The **Mission Doctors Association** recruits, trains and sends Catholic physicians and their families to mission hospitals and clinics throughout the world for tours of two to three years. Address: 1531 W. Ninth St., Los Angeles, Calif. 90015.

Legion of Mary (1921): Founded in Dublin, its purposes are the sanctification of its members and service to others. It is one of the largest lay organizations in the Church. U.S. address for information: The Legion of Mary, St. Louis Regional Senatus, Box 1313, St. Louis, Mo. 63188. The supreme governing body has offices at De Montfort House, North Brunswick St., Dublin 7, Ireland.

Movement for a Better World (1952): An international movement founded by Rev. Riccardo Lombardi, S.J. The U.S. promoting group, like its counterparts in other countries, conducts various types of renewal programs with a distinctive communitarian thrust for the purpose of motivating Christian witness and action for making a better world in accordance with the plan of God. Address for information: Sr. Mary Byrnes, 78 Grand St., Jersey City, N.J. 07302. The movement is a nongovernmental organization with the United Nations.

Movimiento Familiar Cristiano — USA (MFC) (1969): Movement of Catholic Hispanic families united in their efforts to promote the human and Christian virtues of the family so that it may become a force that forms persons, transmits the faith and contributes to the total development of the community. National president couple, Rey and Alma Enriquez. National office, 1041 Wyatt Dr., El Paso, Tex. 79907. Rev. Rafael Miranda is national spiritual director.

Pax Christi (1948): International Catholic peace movement. Originated in Lourdes, France, as a union of French and German Catholics to symbolize a mutual effort to heal wounds inflicted by World War II, spread to Poland and Italy, and acquired its international title when it merged with the English organization Pax. A general secretar-

iat is located at Antwerp, Belgium. **Pax Christi USA,** was founded in 1973 to establish peacemaking as a priority for the American Catholic Church, to work for disarmament, primacy of conscience, a just world order, education for peace and alternatives to violence. A newsletter is published quarterly; membership, 10,000. Sr. Mary Lou Kownacki, O.S.B., is national coordinator. Address: 348 E. 10th St., Erie, Pa. 16503.

Pax Romana — Catholic Movement for Intellectual and Cultural Affairs: The U.S. affiliate of Pax Romana, (see Catholic International Organizations). The president is Edward J. Kirchner, 31 Chesterfield Rd., Stamford, Conn 06902. The Pax Romana representative to the United Nations is Professor W. Hilary Lee, Stevens Institute of Technology, Hoboken, N.J. 07030.

Regis College Lay Apostolate (1950): Founded by Sister Mary John Sullivan, C.S.J., it enlists college graduates for a year of teaching service in home and overseas missions. More than 250 lay apostles from Regis College and more than 400 from other colleges have served since the beginning of the program. Headquarters: Regis College, Weston, Mass. 02193

Southwest Volunteer Apostolate (1970): Places volunteers for work among the Indians and Spanish-speaking of the Diocese of Gallup. Mailing address: P. O. Box 626, Gallup, N.M. 87301.

Center of Concern (1971): An independent public-interest group engaged in analysis, education and advocacy relating to issues of global concern. Address: 3700 13th St. N.E., Washington D.C. 20017.

CATHOLIC YOUTH ORGANIZATIONS

Boy Scouts in the Catholic Church: The National Catholic Committee on Scouting works with the Boy Scouts of America in developing the character and spiritual life of 600,000 members in units chartered to Catholic and non-Catholic organizations. *Boy's Life.* Committee Chairman, Marvin L. Smith, 4416 Basswood Lane, Bellaire, Tex. 77401.

Camp Fire, Inc. (1910): 4601 Madison Ave., Kansas City, Mo. 64112. The National Catholic Committee for Girl Scouts and Camp Fire, a standing committee of the National Federation for Catholic Youth Ministry, cooperates with Camp Fire. To help young people learn and grow in their individual ways through participation in enjoyable activities. Open to youth up to 21 years of age. Membership: approximately 500,000 (no exact statistics available on number of Catholics participating).

Catholic Forester Youth Program, Catholic Order of Foresters: 425 W. Shuman Blvd., Naperville, Ill. 60566. To develop Christian leadership and promote the moral, intellectual, social and physical growth of its youth members. *Catholic Forester.* Membership: youth up to 16 years of age — about 20,000 in 805 local courts in U.S. the High Chief Ranger is John A. Gorski.

Catholic Youth Organization (CYO): Name of parish-centered diocesan Catholic youth programs throughout the country. CYO promotes a program of spiritual, social and physical activities. The

original CYO was organized by Bishop Bernard Sheil of Chicago in 1930.

Columbian Squires (1925): One Columbus Plaza, New Haven, Conn. 06507. Junior organization of the Knights of Columbus. To train and develop leadership through active participation in a well-organized program of activities. Membership: Catholic young men, 12-18 years old. More than 22,000 in over 900 circles (local units) active in the U.S., Canada, Puerto Rico, Mexico, Guam and the Philippines. *Squires Newsletter,* monthly.

Girl Scouts of the U.S.A.: 830 Third Ave., New York, N.Y. 10022. Girls from archdioceses and dioceses in the U.S. and its possessions participate in Girl Scouting. The National Catholic Committee for Girl Scouts and Camp Fire, a standing committee of the National Federation for Catholic Youth Ministry, cooperates with Girl Scouts of the U.S.A. *Girl Scout Leader.* Membership: approximately three million (no exact statistics available on number of Catholic girls participating).

Holy Childhood Association (Pontifical Association of the Holy Childhood) (1843): 1720 Massachusetts Ave. N.W., Washington, D.C. 20036. The official children's mission-aid society of the Church; provides financial assistance to children in 94 developing countries. Produces mission and global education material for teachers and students in Catholic schools and religious education programs. *It's Our World,* four times a year in three editions. National Director, Rev. Francis W. Wright, C.S.Sp.

Junior Catholic Daughters of the Americas: 10 W. 71st St., New York, N.Y. 10023. A major department of the Catholic Daughters of the Americas. To promote development of the whole person, service to others, spiritual growth. Membership: Juniors (11 to 18 years old); Juniorettes (6 to 10 years old).

Knights of the Altar (1938): P.O. Drawer 5476, Lakeland, Fla. 33807 (national office). Society for altar boys. *Young Heralds,* 6 times a year. Membership: 3,000 units in the U.S. and foreign countries.

National Catholic Forensic League (1952): To develop articulate Catholic leaders through an inter-diocesan program of speech and debate activities. *Newsletter,* quarterly. Membership: 600 schools; membership open to Catholic, private and public schools through the local diocesan league. Secretary-Treasurer, Richard Gaudette, 21 Nancy Rd., Milford, Mass. 01757.

National Catholic Young Adult Ministry Association (1982): 3900-A Harewood Rd. N.E., Washington, D.C. 20017. To strengthen the professional competence of those engaged in young adult ministry. President, Ms. Brigid O'Donnell.

National Christ Child Society Inc. (1887): 5100 Wisconsin Ave. N.W., Washington, D.C. 20016. Founder, Mary V. Merrick. A non-profit association of Catholic volunteers dedicated to the service of needy children and youth regardless of race or creed. The service has been expanded to include underprivileged adults. Membership: approximately 8,000 adult and junior members in 34 cities in U.S. President, Mrs. James H. Kavanagh.

National Federation for Catholic Youth Ministry (1982): 3900-A Harewood Rd. N.E., Washington, D.C. 20017. To foster the development of youth ministry in the United States through CYO and other expressions of ministry to, with, by and for youth. *Catholic Teen,* monthly. Executive Director, Mrs. Maggie Brown.

St. Dominic Savio Club (1950): Marian Shrine, Filor's Lane, West Haverstraw, N.Y. 10993. A character-building, leadership and public service program conducted in Catholic schools, CCD classes and home/neighborhood units. *Savio Notes,* six times a year. Membership: students in grades three through twelve — more than 1,500,000 since its founding. Director, Rev. Peter Malloy, S.D.B. members in U.S., Canada and nine foreign countries.

Young Christian Students: 7436 W. Harrison, Forest Park, Ill. 60130. A student movement for Christian personal and social change. Membership: 500 in high schools and parishes.

COLLEGE SOCIETIES

Alpha Sigma Nu (1915): Marquette Univ., 1324 W. Wisconsin Ave., Milwaukee, Wis. 53233 (national headquarters). National honor society of the 28 Jesuit colleges and universities of the U.S.; members chosen on the basis of scholarship, loyalty and service; 1,400 student and 25,000 alumni members. Member, Association of College Honor Societies. Gamma Pi Epsilon (1924) merged with Alpha Sigma Nu in 1973 to form society open to men and women.

Delta Epsilon Sigma (1939): Barry University, Miami Shores, Fla. 33161. National scholastic honor society for students, faculty and alumni of colleges and universities with a Catholic tradition. Membership: 28,500 in 100 chapters. Secretary, Dr. J. Patrick Lee.

Kappa Gamma Pi (1926): A national Catholic college women's honor society for graduates who, in addition to academic excellence, have shown outstanding leadership in extra-curricular activities. *Kappa Gamma Pi News,* quarterly. Membership: approximately 16,000 in 123 colleges; 40 alumnae chapters in metropolitan areas. President, Dr. Sally Ann Vonderbrink, 5747 Colerain Ave., Cincinnati, O. 45239.

Phi Kappa Theta: 3901 W. 86th St., Indianapolis, Ind. 46268. National social fraternity with a Catholic heritage. Merger (1959) of Phi Kappa Fraternity, founded at Brown Univ. in 1889, and Theta Kappa Phi Fraternity, founded at Lehigh Univ. in 1919. *The Temple Magazine* quarterly, and newsletter, *The Sun.* Membership: 2,500 undergraduate and 40,000 alumni in 50 collegiate and 15 alumni chapters. Acting Executive Director, Douglas D. Dilling.

ASSOCIATIONS, MOVEMENTS, SOCIETIES IN THE U.S.

(Principal source: Almanac survey.)

See Index for other associations, movements and societies covered elsewhere.

A

Academy of American Franciscan History (1944), Box 34440, Bethesda, Md. 20817. Dir., Rev. James McManamon, O.F.M.

Albanian Catholic Information Center (1972), P.O. Box 1217 (University), Santa Clara, Calif. 95053; 1,500 in North and South America, Europe, Australia, Japan and New Zealand; *Albanian Catholic Bulletin,* annually. To encourage and restore religious freedom in Albania and to promote Albania's religious and cultural heritage. Director, Rev. Leo C. Neal, O.F.M. Conv.

American Benedictine Academy (1947), Scholarly Benedictine society. Pres., Sr. Ruth Fox, O.S.B., Sacred Heart Priory, Richardton, N.D. 58652.

American Catholic Correctional Chaplains Association (1952), 350 in 475 institutions. Pres., Rev. John Noe; Sec., Rev. Dismas Boeff, O.S.B., 2900 King Dr., Cleveland, O. 44104.

American Catholic Historical Association (1919), Catholic University of America, Washington, D.C. 20064. *The Catholic Historical Review,* quarterly. Sec.-Treas., Rev. Robert Trisco.

American Catholic Philosophical Association (1926), Catholic University of America, Washington, D.C. 20064. *New Scholasticism,* quarterly, *Proceedings,* annually.

American Committee on Italian Migration (1952), 352 W. 44th St., New York, N.Y. 10036; 6,000. *ACIM Newsletter* and *ACIM Nuova Via,* 6 times a year. Sec., Rev. Joseph A. Cogo, C.S.

American Friends of the Vatican Library (1981), 157 Lakeshore Rd., Grosse Point Farms, Mich. 48236. Sponsored by the Catholic Library Association. To assist in supporting the Vatican Library: *AMICI,* newsletter.

Ancient Order of Hibernians in America, Inc. (1836); 120,000. *National Hibernian Digest,* bimonthly. Nat. Pres., Joseph A. Roche, 13002 Fork Rd., Baldwin, Md. 21013.

Apostleship of Prayer (1844-France; 1861-U.S.): 3 Stephen Ave., New Hyde Park, N.Y. 11040. Promotes Daily Offering and Sacred Heart devotion.

Apostolate for Family Consecration (1975), St. Joseph Center, 6305 Third Ave., P.O. Box 220, Kenosha, Wis. 53141; 26,000 members. Family reinforcement by transforming neighborhoods into God-centered communities Pres., Jerome F. Coniker.

Archconfraternity of Christian Mothers (Christian Mothers) (1881), 220 37th St., Pittsburgh, Pa. 15201; over 3,900 branches. Dir., Rev. Bertin Roll, O.F.M. Cap.

Archconfraternity of Our Lady of Perpetual Help and St. Alphonsus (1871), 526 59th St., Brooklyn, N.Y. 11220.

Archconfraternity of the Holy Ghost (1912), Holy Ghost Fathers, Bensalem, Pa. 19020 (U.S. headquarters). Nat. Dir., Rev. Henry J. Brown, C.S.Sp.

Association for Religious and Value Issues in Counseling (1962), division of American Association for Counseling and Development. *Counseling and Values,* 2 times a year. Address, 5999 Stevenson Ave., Alexandria, Va. 22304.

Association for Social Economics (formerly the Catholic Economic Association) (1941), De Paul University, 25 E. Jackson Blvd., Chicago, Ill. 60604; 1,300. *Review of Social Economy,* triannually.

Association of Catholic Diocesan Archivists (1983), c/o Archives, Archdiocese of Boston, 2121 Commonwealth Ave., Brighton, Mass. 02135; 125 members. To work for establishment of an archival program in every American diocese. Pres., Rev. Leonard P. Blair, Archdiocese of Detroit.

Association of Catholic Trade Unionists (1937), 12 Holly Hills Dr., Woodstock, N.Y. 12498. Exec. Sec., John C. Donohue.

Association of Marian Helpers (1946), Stockbridge, Mass. 01263; 1,100,000, mostly in U.S. *The Marian Helpers Bulletin,* quarterly.

Association of Romanian Catholics of America (1948), 4309 Olcott Ave., E. Chicago, Ind. 46312.

B

Blue Army (World Apostolate of Fatima) (1946), Washington, N.J. 07882; worldwide membership. *Soul,* bimonthly. U.S. Pres., Most Rev. Jerome Hastrich, bishop of Gallup, N. Mex.

C

Calix Society (1947), 7601 Wayzata Blvd., Minne-

apolis, Minn. 55426; 2,000 members in U.S. and Canada; *Chalice,* bimonthly. Association of Catholic alcoholics maintaining their sobriety through affiliation with and participation in Alcoholics Anonymous. Dir., R. D. Dickinson.

Canon Law Society of America (1939), Catholic University, Washington, D.C. 20064. To further research and study in canon law; 1,600. Exec. Coord., Rev. Edward G. Pfnausch.

Cardinal Mindszenty Foundation (CMF) (1958), P.O. Box 11321, St. Louis, Mo. 63105. To combat communism with knowledge and facts. Exec. Dir., Eleanor Schlafly.

Catholic Aid Association (1878), 49 W. Ninth St., St. Paul, Minn. 55102; 80,000. *Catholic Aid News,* monthly. Fraternal life insurance society. Pres., F. L. Spanier.

Catholic Alumni Clubs International (1957), To advance social, cultural and spiritual well-being of members. Membership limited to single Catholics with professional education; 10,000 in 47 clubs in U.S. International Chaplain, Rev. William C. Parker, 3650 Victory Parkway, Toledo, O. 43607.

Catholic Biblical Association of America (1936), Catholic University of America, Washington, D.C. 20064; 1,080. *The Catholic Biblical Quarterly.*

Catholic Commission on Intellectual and Cultural Affairs (CCICA) (1946), P.O. Box 21, Notre Dame, Ind. 46556; 246. Exec. Dir., Dr. Konrad Schaum.

Catholic Daughters of the Americas (1903), 10 W. 71st St., New York, N.Y. 10023; 170,000. *Share Magazine.* Nat. Regent, Miss Loretta J. Knebel.

Catholic Family Life Insurance (1868), 1572 E. Capitol Dr., Milwaukee, Wis. 53211; 41,000. *The Family Friend,* quarterly. Pres., David L. Springob.

Catholic Golden Age: National Headquarters, Scranton, Pa. 18503; 800,000. *CGA World Magazine,* quarterly. For Catholics over 50 years of age. Pres., Thomas D. Hinton.

Catholic Guardian Society (1913), 1011 First Ave., New York, N.Y. 10022. Exec. Dir., James P. O'Neill.

Catholic Home Bureau for Dependent Children (1898), 1011 First Ave., New York, N.Y. 10022. Exec. Dir., Sr. Una McCormack.

Catholic Interracial Council of New York, Inc. (1934), 16 W. 36th St., New York, N.Y. 10018. Exec. Dir., John J. Gara.

Catholic Knights of America (1877), 1850 Dalton St., Cincinnati, O. 45214; 10,200. *Catholic Knights of America Journal,* monthly. Fraternal insurance society.

Catholic Knights of Ohio (1891): 16010 Detroit Ave., Lakewood, O. 44107; 12,000 in Ohio and Kentucky. *The Messenger,* monthly. Fraternal insurance society. Pres., Victor D. Huss.

Catholic Kolping Society of America (1923), 22515 Masonic Blvd., St. Clair Shores, Mich. 48082. *Kolping Banner,* monthly. International society concerned with spiritual, educational and physical development of members.

Catholic Lawyers' Guild. Organization usually on a diocesan basis, under different titles.

Catholic League (1943), 1200 N. Ashland Ave.,

Chicago, Ill. 60622. Exec. Dir., Most Rev. Alfred Abramowicz.

Catholic Library Association (1921), 461 W. Lancaster Avenue, Haverford, Pa., 19041; 3,162. *Catholic Library World,* bimonthly; *Catholic Periodical and Literature Index.* Pres., Mary A. Grant; Exec. Dir., Matthew R. Wilt.

Catholic Near East Welfare Association (Near East Missions) (1926), 1011 First Ave., New York, N.Y. 10022. *Near East Missions,* weekly column in 132 diocesan and four national newspapers. Aids missionary activity in 18 countries (under jurisdiction of the Sacred Congregation for the Oriental Church) in Europe, Africa and Asia, including the Holy Land. Nat. Sec., Rev. Msgr. John G. Nolan; Assoc. Sec., Rev. Msgr. Edward C. Foster.

Catholic One Parent Organization (COPO): To give widows and widowers an opportunity to meet others in the same situation, blending social and spiritual programs. Organized in various dioceses.

Catholic Order of Foresters (1883), 425 W. Shuman Blvd., Naperville, Ill. 60566; 150,000. *The Catholic Forester,* bimonthly. Fraternal insurance society. High Chief Ranger, John A. Gorski.

Catholic Pamphlet Society (1938), 888 Delaware Ave., Buffalo, N.Y. 14209. Parish pamphlet rack distributors. Dir., Rev. Walter O. Kern.

Catholic Peace Fellowship (1964), 339 Lafayette St., New York, N.Y. 10012; 6,500, *CPF Bulletin.* Peace education and direct action projects, development of the nonviolent tradition within the Catholic Church; draft counseling. Nat. Sec., Thomas C. Cornell.

Catholic Press Association of the U.S., Inc. (1911), 119 N. Park Ave., Rockville Centre, N.Y. 11570. *The Catholic Journalist* monthly; *Catholic Press Directory,* annually. Pres., Albina Aspell; Exec. Dir., James A. Doyle.

Catholic Theological Society of America (1946), Office of Secretary, Loyola University, Chicago, Ill. 60626; 1,200. *Proceedings,* annually. Pres. (1986-87), Monika Hellwig.

Catholic War Veterans (1935), 2 Massachusetts Ave. N.W., Washington, D.C. 20001; 500 posts, *Catholic War Veteran,* bimonthly.

Catholic Worker Movement (1933), 36 E. First St., New York, N.Y. 10003. *The Catholic Worker,* 8 times a year. Lay apostolate founded by Peter Maurin and Dorothy Day; has Houses of Hospitality in over 60 U.S. cities and several communal farms in various parts of the country. Promotes pacifism, personalism, voluntary poverty and anarchism in that it is decentralist, and believes in what the popes have termed the principle of subsidiarity, urging decentralization in the school system, community control, and in the economic field credit unions, cooperatives and unions of workers and mutual aid.

Catholic Workman (Katolicky Delnik) (1891), P.O. Box 47, New Prague, Minn. 56071; 16,967. *Catholic Workman,* monthly. Fraternal and insurance society.

Catholics United for Spiritual Action, Inc. (CUSA) (1947), 63 Wall St., New York, N.Y. 10005 (legal office); 1,200. An apostolate for the disabled. Admin. Leader, Miss Anna Marie Sopko, 176 W. 8th St., Bayonne, N.J. 07002 (national central office).

Catholics United for the Faith (1968), 45 Union Ave., New Rochelle, N.Y. 10801; 15,000 worldwide, *Lay Witness,* monthly. Lay apostolate founded in response to Vatican II's call to the laity. Pres., Donald G. McLane.

Central Association of the Miraculous Medal (1915), 475 E. Chelten Ave., Philadelphia, Pa. 19144. *Miraculous Medal,* quarterly. Dir., Rev. Robert P. Cawley, C.M.

Chaplains' Aid Association, Inc. (1917), 962 Wayne Ave., Silver Spring, Md. 20910. Pres., Most Rev. Joseph T. Ryan.

Christopher Movement (1945), 12 E. 48th St., New York, N.Y. 10017. Without formal organization or meetings, the movement stimulates personal initiative and responsible action in line with Christian principles, particularly in the fields of education, government, industrial relations and communications. Christopher radio and TV programs are broadcast by more than 1,500 radio and TV stations; 750,000 copies of *Christopher News Notes* are distributed seven times a year without subscription fee; 152 weekly and 14 daily newspapers carry Christopher columns. Dir., Rev. John Catoir.

Citizens for Educational Freedom (1959): Nonsectarian group concerned with parents' right to educational choice by means of tuition tax credits and vouchers. Exec. dir., Sr. Renee Oliver, O.S.U., 1611 N. Kent St., Arlington, Va. 22209.

Confraternity of Catholic Clergy (1976), 21-72 43rd St., Astoria, N.Y. 11105 (national office). Association of priests pledged to pursuit of personal holiness, loyalty to the Pope, theological study and adherence to authentic teachings of the Catholic faith. Pres., Rev. Msgr. Nelson Logal.

Confraternity of the Immaculate Conception of Our Lady of Lourdes (1874), Box 561, Notre Dame, Ind. 46556. Distributors of Lourdes water.

Confraternity of the Most Holy Rosary: See Rosary Altar Society.

Convert Movement Our Apostolate (CMOA) (1945), formerly Convert Makers of America, c/o Our Lady of Grace Rectory, 430 Avenue W, Brooklyn, N.Y. 11223. *Bulletin* quarterly. To train and assist lay persons on a parish level to discuss and present the Faith to interested persons on a one-to-one basis. Dir., Msgr. Erwin A. Juraschek.

Czech Catholic Union of Texas (K.J.T.) (1889), 214 Colorado St., La Grange, Tex. 78945; 17,500. *Nasinec,* weekly, and *K. J. T. News,* monthly. Fraternal and insurance society. Pres., Amos Pavlik.

D

Damien-Dutton Society for Leprosy Aid, Inc. (1944), 616 Bedford Ave., Bellmore, N.Y. 11710; 25,000. *Damien Dutton Call,* quarterly. Provides medicine, rehabilitation and research for conquest of leprosy. Pres., Howard E. Crouch, Dir., Sr. Mary Augustine, S.M.S.M.

Daughters of Isabella (1897), P.O. Box 9585, New Haven, Conn. 06535; 120,000.

E

Edith Stein Guild, Inc. (1955), Our Lady of Victory Church. 60 William St., New York, N.Y. 10005; quarterly newsletter. Promotes Judaeo-Christian understanding, extends friendship to Catholics of Jewish background, spreads knowledge of life and writings of Edith Stein (Sister Benedicta of the Cross).

Enthronement of the Sacred Heart in the Home (1907), 3 Adams St., Fairhaven, Mass. 02719; over 2,500,000.

Eucharistic Guard for Nocturnal Adoration (1938), 800 North Country Club Rd., Tucson, Ariz. 85716.

Eymard League (1948), 194 E. 76 St., New York, N.Y. 10021; approximately 24,000.

F

Families for Christ (1977), 6026 W. Harwood Ave., Orlando, Fla., 32811; 8,000. Promote social reign of Christ. Pres., Albert Barone.

Families for Prayer (1982), 775 Madison Ave., Albany, N.Y. 12208. Dir., Rev. John J. Gurley, C.S.C.

Family Rosary, Inc., The (1942), Executive Park Drive, Albany, N.Y. 12203. Pres., Rev. Patrick Peyton, C.S.C.

Federation of Diocesan Liturgical Commissions (FDLC) (1969), P.O. Box 29039, Washington, D.C. 20017. Voluntary association of personnel from diocesan liturgical commissions of the U.S. The main purpose is promotion of the liturgy as the heart of Christian life, especially in the parish community. Exec. Sec., Mr. Lawrence J. Johnson.

Fellowship of Catholic Scholars (1977), Msgr. George A. Kelly, president, St. John's University, Jamaica, N.Y. 11439; 600 members. Interdisciplinary research and publications of Catholic scholars in accord with the magisterium of the Catholic Church.

First Catholic Slovak Ladies' Association, USA (1892), 24950 Chagrin Blvd., Beachwood, Ohio 44122; 102,000. *Fraternally Yours,* monthly. Fraternal insurance society. Pres., Anna S. Granchay.

First Catholic Slovak Union (Jednota) (1890), 3289 E. 55th St., Cleveland, Ohio 44127; 96,206. *Jednota,* weekly. Exec. Sec., Joseph R. Vehec.

Friendship House (1938), 1746 W. Division, Chicago, Ill. 60622. Apostolate in the inner city.

G

Gabriel Richard Institute (1949), 2315 Orleans Ave., Detroit, Mich. 48207. Conducts Christopher leadership courses in 18 dioceses.

Gelasian Guild (1976), Association of Catholic attorneys working with the USCC; concerned with scholarly study of legal questions affecting Church-state relations. Pres., Rev. Charles Whelan, S.J., 106 W. 56th St., New York, N.Y. 10019.

Guard of Honor of the Immaculate Heart of Mary (1932), 135 West 31st St., New York, N.Y. 10001. An archconfraternity approved by the Holy See whose members cultivate devotion to the Blessed Virgin Mary, particularly through a daily Guard Hour of Prayer.

Guild of Our Lady of Ransom (1948), c/o St. Timothy's Rectory, 650 Nichols St., Norwood, Mass. 02062. Boston archdiocesan ministry for spiritual aid and rehabilitation of inmates of penal institutions. Exec. Dir. and Treas., Rev. Dr. Joseph P. McDermott.

Guild of St. Paul (1937), 230 Waller Ave., Lexington, Ky. 40503; For converts. Nat. Spir. Dir., Rev. Msgr. Leonard Nienaber.

H

Holy Name Society: Founded in 1274 by Blessed John Vercelli, master general of the Dominicans, to promote reverence for the Holy Name of Jesus; this is still the principal purpose of the society, which also develops lay apostolic programs in line with directives of the Second Vatican Council. Introduced in the U.S. by Dominican Father Charles H. McKenna in 1870-71, the society has about 5 million members on diocesan and parochial levels. With approval of the local bishop and pastor, women as well as men may be members.

Holy Name Society, National Association (NAHNS) (1970), 516 N. Front St., Minersville, Pa. 17954 (supply office). *Holy Name Newsletter,* monthly. Association of diocesan and parochial Holy Name Societies. Pres., Kenneth J. Livaudais.

Hungarian Catholic League of America, Inc. (1945), 30 E. 30th St., New York, N.Y. 10016. Member of the National Catholic Resettlement Council. *Catholic Hungarian Sunday,* weekly. Pres., Rev. Msgr. John S. Sabo.

I

International Institute of the Heart of Jesus (1972), 7700 Blue Mound Rd., Milwaukee Wis. 53213 (corporate headquarters); Delegacion Latino-americana, IIHJ, Apartado Aereo 3047, Transv. 28 No. 35A-25, Bogota 1, Colombia (executive offices). Promote awareness and appreciation of the mystery of the Heart of Christ and establish an international forum for the apostolate. Pres., Rev. Roger Vekemans, S.J.

Italian Catholic Federation of California, Central Council (1924), 1801 Van Ness Ave., San Francisco, Calif. 94109; 30,000; *Bollettino,* monthly.

J

John Carroll Society, The (1951), 4844B South 28th St., Arlington, Va. 22206. Pres., James J. Bierbower, Esq.

Judean Society, Inc., The (1966), 1075 Space Park Way No. 336, Mt. View, Calif. 94043; over 800. International organization for divorced Catholic women. Self-help, mutual-help counseling groups. Foundress/Internatl., Dir., Frances A. Miller.

K

Knights of Peter Claver (1909), 554 Palmetto St., P.O. Box 204, Mobile, Ala. 36601; 17,000. *The Claverite,* biannually. Fraternal and aid society.

Knights of St. John, Supreme Commandery (1886), 6517 Charles Ave., Parma, O. 44129; Sup Sec., Brig. Gen. Salvatore La Bianca.

Knights of the Immaculata (Militia Im

maculatae, M.I.) (1917), National Center, 1600 W. Park Ave., Libertyville, Ill. 60048; canonically established with international headquarters in Rome. A pious association for evangelization and catechesis beginning with members' own inner renewal, through the intercession of the Blessed Virgin Mary.

L

Ladies of Charity of the United States, Association of (1960), 7806 Natural Bridge Rd., P.O. Box 5730, St. Louis, Mo. 63121; 40,000 in U.S. International Association founded by St. Vincent de Paul in 1617.

Las Hermanas (1971): A national organization of Hispanic women and non-Hispanic associates concerned with being "actively present to the ever-changing needs" of Hispanics in the U.S.

Latin Liturgy Association (1975), Office of Chairman, Prof. Anthony Lo Bello, Box 29, Dept. of Mathematics, Allegheny College, Meadville, Pa. 16335; 1,300. To promote the use of the Latin language and music in the approved rites of the Church.

Lithuanian Groups: Ateitininkai, members of Lithuanian Catholic Federation Ateitis (1910), 7235 Sacramento Ave., Chicago, Ill. 60629; to promote Catholic action and uphold Lithuanian heritage among youth; *Ateitis,* bimonthly; Pres., Juozas Polikaitis. Knights of Lithuania (1913), educational-fraternal organization; *Vytis,* monthly; Pres., Loretta T. Stukas, 234 Sunlit Dr., Watchung, N.J. 07060. Lithuanian Catholic Alliance (1886), 73 S. Washington St., Wilkes-Barre, Pa. 18701; 118 branches; *Garsas,* monthly; fraternal insurance organization; Pres., Thomas E. Mack. Lithuanian Roman Catholic Federation of America (1906), umbrella organization for Lithuanian parishes and organizations; *The Observer,* monthly; Pres., Saulius Kuprys, 4545 W. 63rd St., Chicago, Ill. 60629. Lithuanian Roman Catholic Priests' League (1909): religious-professional association, Pres., Albert Contons, 50 Orton-Marotta Way, Boston, Mass. 02127. Lithuanian Catholic Religious Aid, Inc. (1961); 351 Highland Blvd., Brooklyn, N.Y. 11207; to assist persecuted Catholics in Lithuania; Pres., Most Rev. Vincent Brizgys; Exec. Dir., Rev. Casimir Pugevicius.

Little Flower Mission League (1957), P.O. Box 25, Plaucheville, La. 71362. Sponsored by the Brothers of the Holy Eucharist.

Little Flower Society (1923), 1313 Frontage Rd.; Darien, Ill. 60559; 200,000 Nat. Dir., Rev. Terrence L. Sempowski, O. Carm.

Liturgical Conference, The, 806 Rhode Island Ave. N.E., Washington, D.C. 20018. *Liturgy, Accent on Worship, Homily Service.* Education, research and publication programs for renewing and enriching Christian liturgical life. Ecumenical. Exec. Dir., Rachel Reeder.

Loyal Christian Benefit Association (1890), P.O. Box 13005, Erie, Pa. 16514; 56,623. *The Fraternal Leader,* bimonthly.

M

Marian Movement of Priests, Nat. Dir., Rev.

Albert G. Roux, P.O. Box 8, St. Francis, Me. 04774.

Mariological Society of America (1949), Sec., Rev. Theodore A. Koehler, S.M., Marian Library, University of Dayton, Dayton, O. 45469; 300. *Marian Studies,* annually. Founded by Rev. Juniper B. Carol, O.F.M., and other priest-scholars to promote greater appreciation of and scientific research in Marian theology.

Maryheart Crusaders, The (1964), 22 Button St., Meriden, Conn. 06450; 3,000. *The Maryheart Crusader,* 4 times a year. To reunite fallen-away Catholics and promote religious education for adults. Pres., Louise D'Angelo.

Men of the Sacred Hearts (1964), Shrine of the Sacred Heart, Harleigh, Pa. 18225. Promote enthronement of Sacred Heart.

Missionary Association of Catholic Women (1916), 3521 W. National Ave., Milwaukee, Wis. 53215. Pres., Mrs. Elizabeth Schneider.

Missionary Cenacle Apostolate (MCA) (1909), General Office, Holy Trinity, Ala. 36859; 600. To foster spiritual and apostolic life of the laity through prayer, instruction, example and service.

Missionary Vehicle Association, Inc. (MIVA America) (1971), 1326 Perry St., N.E., Washington, D.C. 20017. To raise funds and distribute them annually as grants to missionaries working with the poor in Third World countries. Nat. Dir., Rev. Philip De Rea, M.S.C.

Morality in Media, Inc. (1962), 475 Riverside Dr., New York, N.Y. 10115; 50,000 members. Newsletter, 8 times a year; *The Obscenity Law Bulletin,* bimonthly. To stop traffic in pornography constitutionally and effectively, and promote principles of love, truth and taste in the media. A major project is the National Obscenity Law Center which provides legal information for prosecutors and other attorneys. Pres., Rev. Paul J. Murphy, S.J.

N

National Assembly of Religious Women (NARW): Founded as the National Assembly of Women Religious, 1970; title changed, 1980. A movement of feminist religious and lay women committed to prophetic tasks of giving witness, raising awareness and engaging in public action and advocacy for justice. Address: 1307 S. Wabash Ave., Chicago, Ill. 60605.

National Association of Church Personnel Administrators (1973), 100 E. 8th St., Cincinnati, O. 45202. Pres., Rev. Eugene Hackbarth, O. Praem.; Exec. Dir., Sr. Christine Matthews, O.P.

National Association of Diocesan Ecumenical Officers, Pres., Rev. John H. McDonnell, P.O. Box 230, Wheeling, W. Va. 26003.

National Association of Pastoral Musicians (1976), 225 Sheridan St., N.W., Washington, D.C. 20011; 7,000. *Pastoral Music,* six times a year. For clergy and musicians. Pres. and Exec. Dir., Rev. Virgil C. Funk.

National Association of Priest Pilots (1964), Pres., Rev. John Hemann, 510 First Ave. N.W., Cedar Rapids, Ia. 52405.

National Catholic Bandmasters' Association (1953), Box 1023, Notre Dame University, Notre

Dame, Ind. 46556. *The School Musician Magazine.*

National Catholic Cemetery Conference (1949), 710 N. River Rd., Des Plaines, Ill. 60016. *The Catholic Cemetery,* monthly. Pres., Rev. Msgr. Paul T. Dotson.

National Catholic Conference for Interracial Justice (NCCIJ) (1960), 1200 Varnum St. N.E., Washington, D.C. 20017. Stresses moral dimension of civil rights, intercultural cooperation and interracial justice programming in each diocese/organization. Exec. Dir. Mr. Jerome B. Ernst.

National Catholic Development Conference (1968), 86 Front St., Hempstead, N.Y. 11550. Professional association of organizations and individuals engaged in raising funds for Catholic charitable activities. Pres., Msgr. Robert C. Wurtz; Exec. Dir., George T. Holloway.

National Catholic Disaster Relief Committee, 1319 F St. N.W., Washington, D.C. 20036.

National Catholic Pharmacists Guild of the United States (1962), 400 members; *The Catholic Pharmacist.* Exec. Dir., John P. Winkelmann, 1012 Surrey Hills Dr., St. Louis, Mo. 63117.

National Catholic Society of Foresters (1891), 446 E. Ontario St., Chicago, Ill. 60611; 70,951; *National Catholic Forester,* quarterly. A fraternal insurance society. Pres., Miss Rosemary Trettin.

National Catholic Stewardship Council (1962), 1 Columbia Place, Albany, N.Y. 12207. To promote the concept of Christian stewardship. Exec. Dir., Amato A. Semenza.

National Catholic Women's Union (1916), 3835 Westminster Pl., St. Louis, Mo. 63108; 10,500.

National Center for the Laity (1977), 14 E. Chestnut St., Chicago, Ill. 60611. *Initiatives,* six times a year. To promote and implement the vision of Vatican II: That the laity are the Church in the modern world as they attend to their occupational, family and neighborhood responsibilities. Pres., Gregory Pierce.

National Center for Urban Ethnic Affairs (1971): P.O. Box 33279, Washington, D.C. 20033. Research and action related to the Church's concern for cultural pluralism and urban neighborhoods. An affiliate of the USCC. Pres., Dr. John A. Kromkowski.

National Clergy Conference on Alcoholism and Related Drug Problems, 1200 Varnum St. N.E., Washington, D.C. 20017. Exec. Dir., Rev. John F. X. O'Neill.

National Conference of Diocesan Directors of Religious Education: 3021 4th St. N.E., Washington, D.C. 20017.

National Conference of Diocesan Vocation Directors (NCDVD) (1961), 1307 S. Wabash, Suite 350, Chicago, Ill. 60605. To provide diocesan vocation personnel with information and services regarding: awareness and discernment of vocations to the diocesan or religious priesthood and the religious life for both men and women; formation of diocesan priesthood candidates. Exec. Dir., Rev. Henry Mancuso.

National Conference of Religious Vocation Directors (NCRVD), 1307 S. Wabash Ave., Suite 350, Chicago, Ill. 60605. *Call to Growth/Ministry,* *NCRVD Newsletter,* quarterlies. Service organization for men and women assigned to vocation ministry for religious orders.

National Federation of Catholic Physicians' Guilds (1927), 850 Elm Grove, Suite 11, Elm Grove, Wis. 53122; 5,500 in 81 autonomous guilds in U.S. and Canada, *Linacre Quarterly.* Pres., William White, M.D.; Andrew Peters, M.D., pres.-elect.

National Federation of Spiritual Directors (1972). Pres., Rev. Michael A. Becker, Pontifical College Josephinum, 7625 N. High St., Columbus, O. 43085.

National Guild of Catholic Psychiatrists, Inc. (1949). Integration of psychiatry and Roman Catholic theology. *The Bulletin.* Pres. (1984-1985), Louis M. Vuksinick, M.D. Mailing address: Exec. Sec., 120 Hill St., Whitinsville, Mass. 01588.

National Organization for Continuing Education of Roman Catholic Clergy, Inc. (1973). Membership, 150 dioceses, 82 religious provinces, 53 affiliated institutions. Pres., Rev. David Brinkmoeller, 100 E. 8th St., Cincinnati, O. 45202. Exec. Dir., Rev. Jerome Thompson, Catholic Theological Union, 5401 S. Cornell, Chicago, Ill. 60615 (national office).

Network (1971), 806 Rhode Island Ave. N.E., Washington, D.C. 20018. A Catholic social justice lobby.

Nocturnal Adoration Society of the United States (1882), 1335 W. Harrison St., Chicago, Ill. 60607. 57,000. Nat. Dir., Rev. Thomas E. Waldie, S.S.S.

North American Academy of Liturgy, c/o Dr. David Truemper, Valparaiso Univ., Valparaiso, Ind. 46383. *Proceedings,* annually. Foster liturgical research, publication and dialogue on a scholarly level. Pres., Dr. John Barry Ryan.

O

Order of the Alhambra (1904), 4200 Leeds Ave., Baltimore, Md. 21229. 11,000 in U.S. and Canada. Fraternal society dedicated to assisting retarded children. Supreme Commander, Louis P. Alcamo, Sr.

P

Paulist League (1924), 997 Macarthur Blvd., Mahwah, N.J. 07430; 25,000. Exec. Dir., Rev. John E. Hurley, C.S.P.

Paulist National Catholic Evangelization Association (1977), 3031 Fourth St., N.E., Washington, D.C. 20017; 165,000, *Share the Word,* bimonthly. To work with unchurched and alienated Catholics; to develop, test and document contemporary ways in which Catholic parishes and dioceses can evangelize unchurched and inactive. Pres., Rev. Alvin A. Illig, C.S.P.

Philangeli (Friends of the Angels) (1949 in England; 1956 in U.S.), Viatorian Fathers, 1115 E. Euclid St., Arlington Heights, Ill. 60004; approximately 750,000 in 60 countries. To encourage devotion to the angels.

Pious Union of Prayer (1898), St. Joseph's Home, P.O. Box 288, Jersey City, N.J. 07303; 35,000. *St. Joseph's Messenger and Advocate of the Blind,* quarterly.

Pious Union of the Holy Spirit (1900), 30 Gedney Park Dr., White Plains, N.Y. 10605. Pres., Rev. Jerome McHugh, O.F.M. Cap.

Pontifical Mission for Palestine (1949), c/o Catholic Near East Welfare Association, 1011 First Ave., New York, N.Y. 10022. Field offices in Rome, Italy, Beirut, Lebanon, Jerusalem, and Amman, Jordan. The papal relief agency for 1.8 million Palestinian refugees in Lebanon, Syria, Jordan, and the Gaza Strip. Distributes food, clothing, other essentials; maintains medical clinics, orphanages, libraries, refugee camp schools and chapels, the Pontifical Mission Center for the Blind (Gaza), the Pontifical Mission Libraries (Jerusalem, Bethlehem, Nazareth, Amman), the Epheta Institute for Deaf-Mutes (Bethlehem). Pres., Rev. Msgr. John G. Nolan, Exec. Vice-Pres., Rev. Msgr. Edward C. Foster.

Pontifical Missionary Union (1916), 366 Fifth Ave., New York, N.Y. 10001. To promote mission awareness among clergy, religious, candidates to priestly and religious life, and others engaged in pastoral ministry of the Church. Nat. Dir., Rev. Msgr. William J. McCormack; Nat. Sec., Rev. Roman R. Vanasse, O. Praem.

Priests' Eucharistic League (1887), 184 E. 76th St., New York, N.Y. 10021; 17,500. *Emmanuel*, 10 issues a year. Nat. Dir., Rev. Eugene La Verdiere, S.S.S.

Pro Ecclesia Foundation (1970), 663 Fifth Ave., New York, N.Y. 10022. *Pro Ecclesia, Talks of Pope John Paul II, Common Good;* Manhattan Cable-TV program. To answer attacks against Church and promote Church teachings. Pres., Dr. Timothy A. Mitchell.

Pro Maria Committee (1952), 22 Second Ave., Lowell, Mass. 01854. Promote devotion to Our Lady of Beauraing (See Index).

Pro Sanctity Movement. A worldwide force of laity organized to spread God's call of all persons to holiness. Addresses: 205 S. Pine Dr., Fullerton, Calif. 92633; 730 E. 87th St., Brooklyn, N.Y. 11236; 5310 S. 52nd St., Omaha, Nebr. 68117.

The Providence Association of the Ukrainian Catholics in America (Ukrainian Catholic Fraternal Benefit Society) (1912), 817 N. Franklin St., Philadelphia, Pa. 19123. *America* (Ukrainian-English).

R

Raskob Foundation for Catholic Activities, Inc. (1945), Kennett Pike and Montchanin Rd., P.O. Box 4019, Wilmington, Del. 19807. Pres., Gerard S. Garey.

Reparation Society of the Immaculate Heart of Mary, Inc. (1946), 100 E. 20th St., Baltimore, Md. 21218. *Fatima Findings,* monthly. Dir. Rev. John Ryan, S.J.

Rosary Altar Society (Confraternity of the Most Holy Rosary) (1891, in U.S.), 141 E. 65th St., New York, N.Y. 10021; 3,000,000.

Rosary League (1901), Franciscan Sisters of the Atonement, Graymoor, Garrison, N.Y. 10524.

S

Sacred Heart League, Walls, Miss. 38686;

700,000. Promote devotion to the Sacred Heart. Its program services include the Sacred Heart Auto League for careful, prayerful driving and the Apostolate of the Printed Word. Pres., Rev. Robert Hess, S.C.J.

St. Ansgar's Scandinavian Catholic League (1910), 40 W. 13th St., New York, N.Y. 10011; 1,000. *St. Ansgar's Bulletin,* annually.

St. Anthony's Guild (1924), Paterson, N.J. 07509. *Anthonian,* quarterly. Dir., Rev. Salvator Fink, O.F.M.

St. Jude League (1929), 221 W. Madison St., Chicago, Ill. 60606. *St. Jude Journal,* bi-monthly. Dir., Rev. Mark J. Brummel, C.M.F.

St. Margaret of Scotland Guild, Inc. (1938), Graymoor, Garrison, N.Y. 10524; 1,000. Moderator, Bro. Pius MacIsaac, S.A.

St. Martin de Porres Guild (1935), 141 E. 65th St., New York, N.Y. 10021. Dir., Rev. John A. Farren, O.P.

St. Thomas Aquinas Foundation of the Dominican Fathers of the United States (STAF). Mod., Very Rev. Thomas H. McBrien, O.P., Providence College, Providence, R.I. 02918

Serra International (1938), 22 W. Monroe St., Chicago, Ill. 60603; 15,200 members in 490 clubs in 31 countries. *Serran,* bimonthly. Fosters vocations to the priesthood, and religious life, trains Catholic lay leadership. Formally aggregated to the Pontifical Society for Priestly Vocations, 1951. Pres., John A. Gennaro.

Slovak Catholic Federation (1911): Founded by Rev. Joseph Murgas to promote and coordinate religious activities among Slovak Catholic fraternal societies, religious communities and Slovak ethnic parishes in their effort to address themselves to the special needs of Slovak Catholics in the U.S. and Canada. Pres., Rev. Msgr. Joseph V. Adamec, 4735 W. Michigan Ave., Saginaw, Mich. 48603; Sec., Mr. John Mizenko, 32283 Sedgefield Oval, Solon, Ohio 44139.

Slovak Catholic Sokol (1905), 205 Madison St., Passaic, N.J. 07055; 48,500. *Katolicky Sokol (Catholic Falcon),* weekly. Pres., Stephen J. Hruska.

Society for the Propagation of the Faith (1822), 366 Fifth Ave., New York, N.Y. 10001; established in 171 dioceses. Church's principal instrument for promoting mission awareness and generating financial support for the missions. General fund for ordinary and extraordinary subsidies for all mission dioceses. *Mission,* 4 times a year; *Director's Newsletter.* Is subject to Sacred Congregation for the Evangelization of Peoples. Nat. Dir., Rev. Msgr. William J. McCormack.

Society of St. Peter the Apostle (1889), 366 Fifth Ave., New York, N.Y. 10001; 171 dioceses. Church's central fund for support of seminaries, seminarians and novices in all mission dioceses. Nat. Dir., Rev. Msgr. William J. McCormack.

Spiritual Life Institute of America (1960), Box 119, Crestone, Colo. 81131. *Desert Call,* seasonal. An eremetical movement to foster the contemplative spirit in America. Founder, Rev. William McNamara, O.C.D. Second foundation: Primitive

Wilderness Hermitage, Kemptville, Nova Scotia, Canada B0W 1Y0.

T

Theresians of the United States (1961), 5326 E. Pershing Ave., Scottsdale, Ariz. 85254; 5,000. Spiritual, educational and ministerial organization of Christian women. Exec. Dir., Patricia Mullen, S.F.C.C.

U

United Societies of U.S.A. (1903), 613 Sinclair St., McKeesport, Pa. 15132; 3,500 members. *Prosvita-Enlightenment,* monthly newspaper.

United States Catholic Historical Society (1884). 500. *Journal,* quarterly; and *Monograph Series,* annually. Address: 77 Sacamore Rd., Bronxville, N.Y. 10708.

W-Y

Western Catholic Union (1877), W.C.U. Bldg., 506-510 Maine St., Quincy, Ill. 62301; 25,025 members. *Western Catholic Union Record,* bimonthly.

Women for Faith and Family (1984), P.O. Box 8326, St. Louis, Mo. 63132. *Voices,* seasonal. To provide Catholic women with a means of expressing unity with the teachings of the Catholic Church through the "Affirmation for Catholic Women" (35,000 signers worldwide).

Word of God Institute (1972), 487 Michigan Ave. N.E., Washington, D.C. 20017. For renewed biblical preaching, Bible sharing and evangelization. Dir., Rev. John Burke, O.P.

Young Ladies' Institute (1887), P.O. Box 64087, San Francisco, Calif. 94164. Grand Sec. Miss Loretto O'Rourke.

Young Men's Institute (1883), 50 Oak St., San Francisco, Calif. 94102; 4,500. *Institute Journal,* bimonthly. Grand Sec., R. A. Bettencourt.

Knights of Columbus

The Knights of Columbus, which originated as a fraternal benefit society of Catholic men, was founded by Father Michael J. McGivney and chartered by the General Assembly of Connecticut Mar. 29, 1882.

In line with their general purpose to be of service to the Church, the Knights are active in many apostolic works and community programs.

Since January, 1947, the Knights have sponsored a program of Catholic advertising in secular publications with national circulation. This has brought some 7.5 million inquiries and led to more than 800,000 enrollments in courses in the Catholic faith. In more recent years the Knights have broadened this program to include other media for spreading Christian and religious ideals. In 1975 the Knights also undertook funding of the up-link costs for telecasting papal ceremonies throughout the world via satellite.

K. of C. scholarship funds — two at the Catholic University of America, another for disbursement at other Catholic colleges in the U.S., one at Canadian colleges and others for the Philippines, Mexico and Puerto Rico — have provided college educations for about 1,700 students since 1914.

The order promotes youth activity through sponsorship of the Columbian Squires and through cooperation with other organized youth groups.

Recent programs undertaken by the Knights include: promotion of vocations to the priesthood and religious life; promotion of rosary devotion with free distribution of more than 100,000 rosaries a year; securing aid for private schools; efforts to halt the increased killing of the unborn; assistance to the retarded and other disadvantaged people.

The Knights have formed an association with the Bishops in the United States, Canada and Mexico to help protect the lives of the unborn and to disseminate information on responsible family planning. Assistance also has been provided to the Eternal Word Television Network to help spread positive values over the airwaves and to Morality in Media to assist that organization in its battle to contain the spread of pornography.

In 1985, local units of the Knights contributed more than $66 million to charitable and benevolent causes, and gave more than 23.1 million hours of community service.

K. of C. membership, as of Apr. 1, 1986, was 1,429,969 in 8,386 councils in the U.S., Canada, the Philippines, Cuba, Mexico, Puerto Rico, Panama, Guatemala, Guam, the Dominican Republic and the Virgin Islands. Assets, as of Dec. 31, 1985, amounted to $1,714,947,151 and total insurance in force, $10,369,435,095.

The Knights' publication, *Columbia,* has the largest circulation (over 1.4 million) of any Catholic monthly in North America.

Virgil C. Dechant is Supreme Knight.

International headquarters are located at One Columbus Plaza, New Haven, Conn. 06507.

PLENARY INDULGENCE GRANT

Pope John Paul in a decree dated Dec. 14, 1985, gave bishops permission to grant a plenary indulgence three times a year during religious services broadcast by radio and television to persons in their jurisdictions who "for a reasonable cause cannot be present at sacred rites" at which a plenary indulgence is granted. "The decree would allow a bishop to grant a plenary indulgence through radio or television on a major local feast day or other special liturgical observance that would have widespread coverge," said Archbishop John P. Foley, president of the Pontifical Commission for Social Communications. The primary beneficiaries of the grant would be elderly and sick people unable to travel to church services. Conditions for gaining such an indulgence are freedom from all attachment to sin, reception of the sacraments of penance and the Eucharist, and prayer for the intentions of the pope. A new Manual of Indulgences, which are also the subject of Canons 992 to 997 of the Code of Canon Law, was published in 1986. The doctrine and practice of indulgences are related to, among other things, church teaching on the power of the keys and the communion of saints.

COMMUNICATIONS

CATHOLIC PRESS STATISTICS

The 1986 *Catholic Press Directory,* published by the Catholic Press Association, reported a total of 609 periodicals in North America with a circulation of 27,834,760. The figures included 179 English-language newspapers with a circulation of 5,590,828; 387 English-language magazines with a circulation of 21,546,782; and 43 other-language periodicals (newspapers and magazines) with a circulation of 697,150.

Newspapers in the U.S.

There were 163 English-language newspapers (circulation 5,356,523); 9 Spanish-language (circulation, 105,881); and 10 in other languages (circulation, approximately 103,000). Nine of these had national circulation; 157 English-language (including 4 editions of *Our Sunday Visitor*) and 9 in other languages were diocesan newspapers. Listed below, according to circulation figures are the national weekly newspapers and diocesan newspapers with large circulations.

National: *Our Sunday Visitor,* 235,793; *National Catholic Register,* 57,225; *Catholic Twin Circle,* 50,301; *National Catholic Reporter,* 48,837; *Jednota* (Slovak and English), 36,491; *The Wanderer,* 36,273; *The Catholic Mentor* (first issue scheduled for publication, October, 1986), 35,000 (projected); *El Visitante Dominical* (Spanish), 31,000. *Katolicky Sokol — Catholic Falcon* (Slovak and English), 10,000.

Diocesan (weeklies, unless indicated otherwise): *Long Island Catholic* (Rockville Centre), 138,384; *Catholic New York* (New York), 129,137; *Pittsburgh Catholic,* 117,317; *Western New York Catholic* (monthly, Buffalo), 99,000; *Chicago Catholic,* 98,279; *St. Louis Review,* 94,986; *The Tablet* (Brooklyn, N.Y.), 90,325; *Catholic Standard and Times* (Philadelphia), 87,534; *Catholic Voice* (biweekly, Oakland), 86,823; *Catholic Sun* (biweekly, Phoenix), 80,804; *Denver Catholic Register,* 76,860; *Clarion Herald* (New Orleans), 72,204; *The Evangelist* (Albany), 66,500; *Catholic Universe Bulletin* (biweekly, Cleveland), 61,581; *The Record* (Louisville), 60,989;

Catholic Voice (Omaha), 58,684; *Catholic Review* (Baltimore), 54,543; *Catholic Witness* (biweekly, Harrisburg), 54,289; *Catholic Accent* (Greensburg), 53,299; *Catholic Bulletin* (St. Paul and Minneapolis), 53,021; *Catholic Light* (biweekly, Scranton), 52,597; *The Pilot* (Boston), 52,141; *Catholic Standard* (Washington, D.C.), 52,039; *The Monitor* (Trenton and Metuchen), 51,668; *The Criterion* (Indianapolis), 49,366; *Courier Journal* (Rochester), 49,109; *The Voice* (biweekly, Miami), 47,000; *Catholic Sun* (Syracuse), 45,700; *Catholic Commentator* (Baton Rouge), 45,151; *The Tidings* (Los Angeles), 45,100.

The oldest Catholic newspaper in the United States is *The Pilot* of Boston, established in 1829 (under a different title).

Magazines in U.S.

The *Catholic Press Directory* reported more than 375 English- and other-language magazines in the U.S. with a circulation of more than 21,000,000.

America (circulation, 32,985) and *Commonweal* (circulation, 19,000), are the only weekly and biweekly magazines, respectively, of general interest.

The monthly magazine with the largest circulation is *Columbia* (1,381,844), the official organ of the Knights of Columbus.

General-interest monthly magazines with large circulations include: *Catholic Digest* (618,067); *Liguorian* (500,000); *St. Anthony's Messenger* (421,782); *U.S. Catholic* (95,003).

CATHOLIC NEWSPAPERS AND MAGAZINES IN THE U.S.

(Sources: *Catholic Press Directory, 1986;* Almanac survey; NC News Service.)

Abbreviation code: a, annual; bm, bimonthly; m, monthly; q, quarterly; w, weekly.

Circulation figures for some of these newspapers and magazines are given in the article, Catholic Press Statistics.

Newspapers

Acadiana Catholic (formerly The Morning Star), biweekly; P.O. Box 3223, Lafayette, La. 70502; Lafayette diocese.

Advocate, The, w; 37 Evergreen Pl., E. Orange, N.J. 07018; Newark archdiocese.

Alaskan Shepherd, 6 times a year; 1312 Peger Rd., Fairbanks, Alaska 99701; Fairbanks diocese.

America (Ukrainian-English), daily; 817 N. Franklin St., Philadelphia, Pa. 19123.

Anchor, The w; P.O. Box 7, Fall River, Mass. 02722; Fall River diocese.

Arkansas Catholic, w; P.O. Box 7417, Little Rock, Ark. 72217.

Arlington Catholic Herald, w; 200 N. Glebe Rd., Suite 614, Arlington, Va. 22203; Arlington diocese.

Bayou Catholic, The, w; P.O. Box 9077, Houma, La. 70361; Houma-Thibodaux diocese.

Beacon, The, w; P.O. Box 1887, Clifton, N.J. 07015. Paterson diocese.

Bishop's Bulletin, m; P.O. Box 665, Yankton, S. Dak. 57078.

Bolletino, m; 1801 Van Ness Ave., San Francisco, Calif. 94109; Central Council of Italian Catholic Federation.

Byzantine Catholic World, biweekly; 3643 Perrysville Ave., Pittsburgh, Pa. 15214; Pittsburgh Byzantine archdiocese.

Catholic Accent, w; P.O. Box 850, Greensburg, Pa. 15601; Greensburg diocese.

Catholic Advance, The, w; 424 N. Broadway, Wichita, Kans. 67202; Wichita diocese.

Catholic Banner, w; P.O. Box 818, Charleston, S.C. 29402; Charleston diocese.

Catholic Bulletin, w; 244 Dayton Ave., St. Paul, Minn. 55102; St. Paul and Minneapolis archdiocese.

Catholic Calendar, bm; 834 Ryan St., Lake Charles, La. 70601; one page in local newspaper; Lake Charles diocese.

Catholic Chronicle, biweekly; P.O. Box 1866, Toledo, O. 43603; Toledo diocese.

Catholic Commentary, w; P.O. Box 2239, Anchorage, Alaska 99510; one-page supplement in local newspaper; Anchorage archdiocese.

Catholic Commentator, The, biweekly; P.O. Box 14746, Baton Rouge, La. 70898; Baton Rouge diocese.

Catholic Crosswinds, semimonthly; 1001 N. Grand Ave., Pueblo, Colo. 81003; Pueblo diocese.

Catholic Exponent, biweekly; 25 East Boardman St., Room 330, Youngstown, O. 44503; Youngstown diocese.

Catholic Free Press, w; 47 Elm St., Worcester, Mass. 01609; Worcester diocese.

Catholic Herald, The, m; 514 El Paso Blvd., Manitou Springs, Colo. 80829; Colorado Springs diocese.

Catholic Herald, w; P.O. Box 1572, Milwaukee, Wis. 53201; Milwaukee archdiocese.

Catholic Herald — Madison Edition, w; P.O. Box 5913, Madison, Wis. 53705.

Catholic Herald — Superior Edition, w; P.O. Box 969, Superior, Wis. 54880.

Catholic Herald, w; 5890 Newman Ct., Sacramento, Calif. 95819; Sacramento diocese.

Catholic Hungarian's Sunday, w; 1739 Mahoning Ave., Youngstown, O. 44509.

Catholic Key, The, w; P.O. Box 1037, Kansas City, Mo. 64141; Kansas City-St. Joseph diocese.

Catholic Lantern, m; P.O. Box 4237, Stockton, Calif. 95204; Stockton diocese.

Catholic Light, biweekly; P.O. Box 708, Scranton, Pa. 18501; Scranton diocese.

Catholic Messenger, w; P.O. Box 460, Davenport, Ia. 52805; Davenport diocese.

Catholic Missourian, w; P.O. Box 1107, Jefferson City, Mo. 65102; Jefferson City diocese.

Catholic New York, w; P.O. Box 5133, New York, N.Y. 10150; New York archdiocese.

Catholic Observer, biweekly; Box 1570, Springfield, Mass. 01101; Springfield diocese.

Catholic Outlook, m; 215 W. 4th St., Duluth, Minn. 55806; Duluth diocese.

Catholic Post, The, w; P.O. Box 1722, Peoria, Ill. 61656; Peoria diocese.

Catholic Register, biweekly; Box 126-C, Logan Blvd., Hollidaysburg, Pa. 16648; Altoona-Johnstown diocese.

Catholic Review, w; P.O. Box 777, Baltimore, Md. 21203; Baltimore archdiocese.

Catholic Sentinel, w; 5536 N.E. Hassalo St., Portland, Ore. 97213; Portland archdiocese, Baker diocese.

Catholic Spirit, The, m; P.O. Box 13327, Capitol Sta., Austin, Tex. 78711; Austin diocese.

Catholic Spirit, The, w; P.O. Box 951, Wheeling, W. Va. 26003; Wheeling-Charleston diocese.

Catholic Standard, w; P.O. Box 4464, Washington, D.C. 20017; Washington archdiocese.

Catholic Standard and Times, w; 222 N. 17th St., Philadelphia, Pa. 19103; Philadelphia archdiocese; Allentown diocese.

Catholic Star Herald, w; 1845 Haddon Ave., Camden, N.J. 08101; Camden diocese.

Catholic Sun, The, biweekly; 400 E. Monroe, Phoenix, Ariz. 85004; Phoenix diocese.

Catholic Sun, The, w; 257 E. Onondaga St., Syracuse, N.Y. 13202; Syracuse diocese.

Catholic Telegraph, w; 100 E. 8th St., Cincinnati, O. 45202; Cincinnati archdiocese.

Catholic Times, w; P.O. Box 636, Columbus, O. 43216; Columbus diocese.

Catholic Times, w; 514 E. Lawrence St., Springfield, Ill. 62703; Springfield diocese.

Catholic Transcript, w; 785 Asylum Ave., Hartford, Conn. 06105; Hartford archdiocese, Bridgeport and Norwich dioceses.

Catholic Twin Circle, w; 6404 Wilshire Blvd., Suite 900, Los Angeles, Calif. 90048.

Catholic Universe Bulletin, biweekly; 1027 Superior Ave. N.E., Cleveland, O. 44114; Cleveland diocese.

Catholic Virginian, biweekly; 14 N. Laurel St., Box 26843, Richmond, Va. 23261; Richmond diocese.

Catholic Voice, The, biweekly; 2918 Lakeshore Ave., Oakland, Calif. 94610; Oakland diocese.

Catholic Voice, The, w; P.O. Box 4010, Omaha, Nebr. 68104; Omaha archdiocese.

Catholic Week, w; P.O. Box 349, Mobile, Ala. 36601; Mobile archdiocese.

Catholic Weekly, The, w; P.O. Box 1405, Saginaw, Mich. 48605; Saginaw and Gaylord dioceses.

Catholic Weekly, The, w; P.O. Box 167, Flint, Mich. 48501; Lansing diocese.

Catholic Witness, The, w; P.O. Box 2555, Harrisburg, Pa. 17105; Harrisburg diocese.

Central Washington Catholic, m; P.O. Box 505, Yakima, Wash. 98907. Yakima diocese.

Challenge, The, semimonthly; P.O. Box 14278, Jefferson Sta., Detroit, Mich. 48214. St. Maron diocese.

Chicago Catholic, The w; P.O. Box 11181, Chicago, Ill. 60611; Chicago archdiocese.

Chicago Catolico, El, m; P.O. Box 11181, Chicago, Ill. 60611.

Church Today, every 3 weeks; P.O. Box 7417, Alexandria, La. 71306; Alexandria diocese.

Church World, w; Industry Rd., Brunswick, Me. 04011; Portland diocese.

Clarion Herald, w; 523 Natchez St., New Orleans, La. 70130; New Orleans archdiocese.

Common Sense, w; 1325 Jefferson Ave., Memphis, Tenn. 38104; Memphis diocese.

Community, w; P.O. Box 24000, Jacksonville, Fla. 32241; one-page weekly in Sunday editions of two daily newspapers; St. Augustine diocese.

Compass, The, w; Box 1825, Green Bay, Wis. 54305; Green Bay diocese.

Courier, The, m; P.O. Box 949, Winona, Minn. 55987; Winona diocese.

Courier-Journal, w; 1150 Buffalo Rd., Rochester, N.Y. 14624; Rochester diocese.

Criterion, The, w; P.O. Box 1410, Indianapolis, Ind. 46206; Indianapolis archdiocese.

Dakota Catholic Action, 9 times a year; P.O. Box 1137, Bismarck, N.D. 58502; Bismarck diocese.

Darbininkas (The Worker) (Lithuanian), w; 341 Highland Blvd., Brooklyn, N.Y. 11207; Lithuanian Franciscan Fathers.

Denver Catholic Register, w; P.O. Box 1620, Denver, Colo. 80201; Denver archdiocese.

Dialog, The, w; 1925 Delaware Ave., Wilmington, Del. 19806; Wilmington diocese.

Diocese of Orange Bulletin, m; 2811 E. Villa Real Dr., Orange, Calif. 92667.

Diocese of Van Nuys Newsletter, bm; 5335 Sepulveda Blvd., Van Nuys, Calif. 91411; Van Nuys Byzantine-Rite diocese.

Draugas (Lithuanian), daily; 4545 W. 63rd St., Chicago, Ill. 60629; Lithuanian Catholic Press Society.

East Texas Catholic, The, biweekly; P.O. Box 3948, Beaumont, Tex. 77704; Beaumont diocese.

Eastern Catholic Life, w; 101 Market St., Passaic, N.J. 07055; Passaic Byzantine eparchy.

Eastern Oklahoma Catholic, biweekly; Box 520, Tulsa, Okla. 74101; Tulsa diocese.

Evangelist, The, w; 39 Philip St., Albany, N.Y. 12207; Albany diocese.

Fairfield County Catholic, m; 238 Jewett Ave., Bridgeport, Conn. 06606; Bridgeport diocese.

Florida Catholic, The, w; P.O. Box 3551, Orlando, Fla. 32802; Orlando diocese. Publishes editions for Palm Beach, Pensacola-Tallahassee, St. Petersburg and Venice dioceses.

Gary Sunday Visitor, w; 9292 Broadway, Merrillville, Ind. 46410; Gary diocese.

Georgia Bulletin, w; 680 W. Peachtree St. N.W., Atlanta, Ga. 30308; Atlanta archdiocese.

Glasilo KSK Jednote (Amerikanski Slovenec) (Slovenian), semimonthly; 2439 Glenwood Ave., Joliet, Ill. 60435; American Slovenian Catholic Union.

Globe, The, w; 1825 Jackson St., Sioux City, Ia. 51105; Sioux City diocese.

Gulf Pine Catholic, w; P.O. Box 1189, Biloxi, Miss. 39533; Biloxi diocese.

Hawaii Catholic Herald, w; 1184 Bishop St., Honolulu, H.I. 96813; Honolulu diocese.

Heraldo Catolico, El (Spanish), bm; P.O. Box 19312, Sacramento, Calif. 95819; Sacramento and Stockton dioceses.

Hlas Naroda (Voice of the Nation) (Czech-English), w; 2657-59 S. Lawndale Ave., Chicago. 60623.

Horizons, semimonthly; 1900 Carlton Rd., Parma, O. 44134; Parma diocese.

Idaho Register, w; P.O. Box 2835, Boise, Idaho 83701; Boise diocese.

Inland Catholic, w; P.O. Box 2788, San Bernardino, Calif. 92406. San Bernardino diocese.

Inland Register, every 3 weeks; P.O. Box 48, Spokane, Wash. 99210; Spokane diocese.

Inside Passage, biweekly; 419 6th St., Juneau, Alaska 99801; Juneau diocese.

Intermountain Catholic, The, w; P.O. Box 2489, Salt Lake City, Utah 84110; Salt Lake City diocese.

Jednota (Slovak-Eng.), w; Jednota and Rosedale Aves., Middletown, Pa. 17057; First Catholic Slovak Union.

Joliet Catholic Explorer, w; St. Charles Borromeo Pastoral Center, Rt. 53 and Airport Rd., Romeoville, Ill. 60441. Joliet diocese.

Katolicky Sokol (Catholic Falcon) (Slovak-English), biweekly; 205 Madison St., Passaic, N.J. 07055; Slovak Catholic Sokol.

Lafayette Sunday Visitor, w; P.O. Box 1603, Lafayette, Ind. 47902; Lafayette diocese.

Lake Shore Visitor, w; P.O. Box 4047, Erie, Pa. 16512; Erie diocese.

Leaven, The, w; 2220 Central, P.O. Box 2329, Kansas City, Kans. 66110; Kansas City archdiocese.

Long Island Catholic, The, w; P.O. Box 700, Hempstead, N.Y. 11551; Rockville Centre diocese.

Mensajero Catolico, El (Spanish), m; P.O. Box 1572, Milwaukee, Wis. 53201; Milwaukee archdiocese.

Message, The, w; P.O. Box 4169, Evansville, Ind. 47711; Evansville diocese.

Messenger, The, w; P.O. Box 327, Belleville, Ill. 62222; Belleville diocese.

Messenger, The, w; P.O. Box 268, Covington, Ky. 41012; Covington diocese.

Michigan Catholic, The, w; 2701 Chicago Blvd., Detroit, Mich. 48206; Detroit archdiocese.

Mirror, The, w; M.P.O. Box 847, Springfield, Mo. 65801; Springfield-Cape Girardeau diocese.

Mississippi Today, w; P.O. Box 2130, Jackson, Miss. 39225; Jackson diocese.

Monitor, The, w; P.O. Box 3095, Trenton, N.J. 08619; Trenton and Metuchen dioceses.

Montana Catholic, The, biweekly; P.O. Box 1729, Helena, Mont. 59624; Helena diocese.

Narod Polski (Polish Nation) (Polish-Eng.) semimonthly; 984 Milwaukee Ave., Chicago, Ill. 60622.

National Catholic Register, w; 6404 Wilshire Blvd., Suite 900, Los Angeles, Calif. 90048.

National Catholic Reporter, The, w; P.O. Box 419281, Kansas City, Mo. 64141.

New Earth, The, m (Oct-June); P.O. Box 1750, Fargo, N.D. 58107; Fargo diocese.

New Star, The, biweekly; 2208 W. Chicago Ave., Chicago, Ill. 60622; St. Nicholas of Chicago Ukrainian diocese.

Newsletter, The, m; 215 N. Westnedge, Kalamazoo, Mich. 49001; Kalamazoo diocese.

North Carolina Catholic, w; 300 Cardinal Gibbons Dr., Raleigh, N.C. 27606 and 1524 E.

Morehead St., Charlotte, N.C. 28207; Raleigh and Charlotte dioceses.

North Country Catholic, w; Box 326, Ogdensburg, N.Y. 13669; Ogdensburg diocese.

North Texas Catholic, w; 800 West Loop 820 South, Fort Worth, Tex. 76108; Fort Worth diocese.

Northwestern Kansas Register, w; P.O. Box 1038, Salina, Kans. 67402; Salina diocese.

Nuevo Amanecer, m; P.O. Box 155, Brooklyn, N.Y. 11243; for Hispanic Catholic community of Brooklyn diocese.

Observer, The, biweekly; P.O. Box 2079, Monterey, Calif. 93942; Monterey diocese.

Observer, The, biweekly; 921 W. State St., Rockford, Ill. 61102; Rockford diocese.

One Voice, w; P.O. Box 10822, Birmingham, Ala. 35202; Birmingham diocese.

Our Northland Diocese, 22 issues annually; P.O. Box 610, Crookston, Minn. 56716; Crookston diocese.

Our Sunday Visitor, w; 200 Noll Plaza, Huntington, Ind. 46750; national edition and official publication for 4 dioceses.

People of God, m; 1800 Martha N.E., Albuquerque, N. Mex. 87112; Santa Fe archdiocese.

Pilot, The, w; 49 Franklin St., Boston, Mass. 02110; Boston archdiocese.

Pittsburgh Catholic, The, w; 100 Wood St., Suite 500, Pittsburgh, Pa. 15222; Pittsburgh diocese.

Polish American Journal, m; 774 Fillmore Ave., Buffalo, N.Y. 14212.

Pregonero, El (Spanish), w; P.O. Box 4464; Washington, D.C. 20017.

Progress, The, w; 910 Marion St., Seattle, Wash. 98104; Seattle archdiocese.

Providence Visitor, The, w; 184 Broad St., Providence, R.I. 02903. Providence diocese.

Pueblo de Dios (Spanish), biweekly; 37 Evergreen Pl., E. Orange N.J. 07018; Newark archdiocese.

Pueblo de Dios (Spanish), biweekly; Box 1887, Clifton, N.J. 07015; Paterson diocese.

Record, The, w; 701 W. Jefferson St., Louisville, Ky. 40202; Louisville archdiocese.

Redwood Crozier, The, biweekly, 547 B St., Santa Rosa, Calif. 95401; Santa Rosa diocese.

Register, The, biweekly; P.O. Box 1668, Fresno, Calif. 93717; Fresno diocese.

St. Cloud Visitor, w; P. O. Box 1068, St. Cloud, Minn. 56302; St. Cloud diocese.

St. Louis Review, w; 462 N. Taylor Ave., St. Louis, Mo. 63108; St. Louis archdiocese.

San Francisco Catholic, m; 441 Church St., San Francisco, Calif. 94114; San Francisco archdiocese.

Shlakh — The Way, (Ukrainian-Eng.), w; 827 N. Franklin St., Philadelphia, Pa. 19123; Philadelphia archeparchy.

Sooner Catholic, The, biweekly; P.O. Box 32180, Oklahoma City, Okla. 73123; Oklahoma City archdiocese.

South Plains Catholic, biweekly; 5802 22nd St., Lubbock, Tex. 79407; Lubbock diocese.

South Texas Catholic, w; 1200 Lantana St., Corpus Christi, Tex. 78407; Corpus Christi diocese.

Southern Cross, The, w; P.O. Box 81869, San Diego, Calif. 92138; San Diego diocese.

Southern Cross, The, w; 601 E. 6th St., Waynesboro, Ga. 30830; Savannah diocese.

Southern Nebraska Register, w; P.O. Box 80329, Lincoln, Nebr. 68501; Lincoln diocese.

Southwest Kansas Register, w; P.O. Box 1317, Dodge City, Kans. 67801; Dodge City diocese.

Sower, biweekly; 161 Glenbrook Rd., Stamford, Conn. 06902. Stamford Ukrainian diocese.

Steubenville Register, w; P.O. Box 160, Steubenville, O. 43952; Steubenville diocese.

Tablet, w; 1 Hanson Pl., Brooklyn, N.Y. 11243; Brooklyn diocese.

Tennessee Register, The, w; 2400 21st Ave. S., Nashville, Tenn. 37212; Nashville diocese.

Texas Catholic, w; 3915 Lemmon Ave., P.O. Box 190347, Dallas, Tex. 75219; Dallas diocese.

Texas Catholic Herald, The, semi-monthly; 1700 San Jacinto St., Houston, Tex. 77002; Galveston-Houston diocese.

Tidings, The, w; 1530 W. 9th St., Los Angeles, Calif. 90015; Los Angeles archdiocese.

Times Review, The, w; P.O. Box 4004, La Crosse, Wis. 54602; La Crosse diocese.

Today's Catholic (Edition O.S.V.), w; Cathedral Center, P.O. Box 11169, Fort Wayne, Ind. 46856; Fort Wayne-S. Bend diocese.

Today's Catholic, biweekly; P.O. Box 28410, San Antonio, Tex. 78228; San Antonio archdiocese.

Upper Peninsula Catholic, biweekly; P.O. Box 548, Marquette, Mich. 49855; Marquette diocese.

Valley Catholic, m; 7600 Y St. Joseph Ave., Los Altos, Calif. 94022; San Jose diocese.

Vermont Catholic Tribune, biweekly; 351 North Ave., Burlington, Vt. 05401; Burlington diocese.

Visitante Dominical, El (Spanish), w; P.O. Box 96, San Antonio, Tex. 78291; Southern Province of Society of Oblates.

Voice, The, biweekly; 9401 Biscayne Blvd., P.O. Box 38-1059, Miami, Fla. 33138; Miami archdiocese.

Voice of the Southwest, w; P.O. Box 1338, Gallup, N. Mex. 87301; Gallup diocese.

Voz, La (Spanish); biweekly; 9401 Biscayne Blvd., Miami, Fla. 33138; Miami archdiocese.

Wanderer, The, w; 201 Ohio St., St. Paul, Minn. 55107.

West Nebraska Register, w; P.O. Box 608, Grand Island, Nebr. 68802; Grand Island diocese.

West River Catholic, m; P.O. Box 678, Rapid City, S. Dak. 57709; Rapid City diocese.

West Texas Angelus, biweekly; 116 S. Oakes, San Angelo, Tex. 76903; San Angelo diocese.

West Texas Catholic, every 3 weeks; P.O. Box 5644, Amarillo, Tex. 79117; Amarillo diocese.

Western Kentucky Catholic, m; 4005 Frederica St., Owensboro, Ky. 42301.

Western Michigan Catholic, w; 650 Burton

S.E., Grand Rapids, Mich. 49507; Grand Rapids diocese.

Western New York Catholic, m; The Catholic Center, 795 Main St., Buffalo, N.Y. 14203; Buffalo diocese.

Witness, The, w; 1229 Mt. Loretta, P.O. Box 917, Dubuque, Ia. 52004; Dubuque archdiocese.

Wyoming Catholic Register, m; P.O. Box 4279, Caspar, Wyo. 82604; Cheyenne diocese.

Magazines, Other Periodicals

Act, 10 times a year; R.D. 9, Box 512, Greensburg, Pa. 15601; Christian Family Movement.

ADRIS Newsletter, q; Department of Theology, Fordham University, Bronx, N.Y. 10458. Association for the Development of Religious Information Services.

AIM (Aids in Ministry), q; P.O. Box 2703, Schiller Park, Ill. 60176.

Albanian Catholic Bulletin (Buletini Katholik Shqiptar), a; P.O. Box 1217, (University), Santa Clara, Calif. 95053; Albanian Catholic Information Center.

America, w; 106 W. 56th St., New York, N.Y. 10019.

American Benedictine Review, q; Assumption Abbey, Richardton, N.D. 58652.

American Midland Naturalist, q; Notre Dame, Ind. 46556.

Americas, The, q; Box 34440, W. Bethesda, Md. 20817; Academy of American Franciscan History.

Angel Guardian Home Quarterly, The, q; 6301 12th Ave., Brooklyn, N.Y. 11219.

Anthonian, The, q; Paterson, N.J. 07509; St. Anthony's Guild.

Anthropological Quarterly, q; 620 Michigan Ave. N.E., Washington, D.C. 20064.

Apostolate of Our Lady, m; 315 Clay St., Carey, O. 43316; Our Lady of Consolation National Shrine.

Apostolate of the Little Flower, bm; P.O. Box 5280, San Antonio, Tex. 78201; Discalced Carmelite Fathers.

Archeparchal Bulletin, m; 827 N. Franklin St., Philadelphia, Pa. 19123; Philadelphia archeparchy.

Atchison Benedictine Community News, q; Mount St. Scholastica Convent, 801 S. 8th St., Atchison, Kans. 66002.

Ateitis (The Future) (Lithuanian), bm; 7235 S. Sacramento Ave., Chicago, Ill. 60629; for youth.

Ave Maria (Polish), 6 times a year; 600 Doat St., Buffalo, N.Y. 14211; Felician Srs.

Aylesford Carmelite Newsletter, q; P.O. Box 65, Darien, Ill. 60559.

Benedictine Orient, bm; 2400 Maple Ave., Lisle, Ill. 60532.

Benedictines, semiannually; Mt. St. Scholastica, Atchison, Kans. 66002.

Best Sellers, m; Univ. of Scranton, Scranton, Pa. 18510.

Bible Today, The, bm; Liturgical Press, Collegeville, Minn. 56321.

Biblical Theology Bulletin, q; St. John's Univ., Theology Dept., Jamaica, N.Y. 11439.

BLUEPRINT for Social Justice, 10 times a year; Institute of Human Relations, Loyola University, New Orleans, La. 70118.

Bringing Religion Home, m; 221 W. Madison St., Chicago, Ill. 60606.

Brothers, bm; 555 Cardinal Dr., Thibodaux, La. 70301; National Assembly of Religious Brothers.

Call Board, The, 5 times a year; 1501 Broadway, Suite 2400, New York, N.Y. 10036; Catholic Actors' Guild.

Camillian: Journal of the National Association of Catholic Chaplains, bm; 3257 S. Lake Dr., Milwaukee, Wis. 53207.

Caring Community, The, m; 115 E. Armour Blvd., Kansas City, Mo. 64111.

Carmelite Review, The, m; 29 N. Broadway, Joliet, Ill. 60435; Canadian-American Province of Carmelite Order.

Catechist, The, 8 times a year; 2451 E. River Rd., Dayton, O. 45439.

Catechist's Connection, The, 10 times a year; 115 E. Armour Blvd., Kansas City, Mo. 64111.

Catholic Aid News, m; 49 W. 9th St., St. Paul, Minn. 55102.

Catholic Biblical Quarterly, q; Catholic University of America, Washington, D.C. 20064; Catholic Biblical Assn.

Catholic Cemetery, The, m; 710 N. River Rd., Des Plaines, Ill. 60016; National Catholic Cemetery Conference.

Catholic Communicator, The, q; 9 Loudoun St. S.E., Leesburg, Va. 22075; Catholic Home Study Institute.

Catholic Digest, The, m; P.O. Box 64090, St. Paul, Minn. 55164.

Catholic Family, The, q; P.O. Box 331389, Fort Worth, Tex. 76163.

Catholic Forester Magazine, bm; 425 W. Shuman Blvd., Naperville, Ill. 60566; Catholic Order of Foresters.

CGA World, q; National Headquarters, 400 Lackawanna Ave., Scranton, Pa. 18503. Catholic Golden Age.

Catholic Health World, semimonthly; 4455 Woodson Rd., St. Louis, Mo. 63134.

Catholic Historical Review, q; 620 Michigan Ave. N.E., Washington, D.C. 20064; American Catholic Historical Assn.

Catholic Journalist, The, m; 119 N. Park Ave., Rockville Centre, N.Y. 11570; Catholic Press Association.

C.K. of A. Journal, m; 1850 Dalton St., Cincinnati, O. 45214; Catholic Knights of America.

Catholic Lawyer, q; St. John's University, Jamaica, N.Y. 11439; St. Thomas More Institute for Legal Research.

Catholic League Newsletter, m; 1100 W. Wells St., Milwaukee, Wis. 53233; Catholic League for Religious and Civil Rights.

Catholic Library World, 6 times a year; 461 W. Lancaster Ave., Haverford, Pa. 19041; Catholic Library Association.

Catholic Life Magazine, m (exc. July-Aug.); 35750 Moravian Dr., Fraser, Mich. 48026; PIME Missionaries.

Catholic Near East Magazine, q; 1011 First

Ave., New York, N.Y. 10022; Catholic Near East Welfare Assn.

Catholic Periodical and Literature Index, bm; 461 W. Lancaster Ave., Haverford, Pa. 19041; Catholic Library Association.

Catholic Pharmacist, a; 1012 Surrey Hills Dr., St. Louis, Mo. 63117; National Catholic Pharmacists Guild.

Catholic Press Directory, a; 119 N. Park Ave. Rockville Centre, N.Y. 11570; Catholic Press Assn.

Catholic Quote, m; Valparaiso, Nebr. 68065; Rev. Jerome Pokorny.

CRS News, q; 1011 First Ave., New York, N.Y. 10022. Catholic Relief Services.

Catholic Review (Braille), m; 154 E. 23rd St., New York, N.Y. 10010; Xavier Society for the Blind.

Catholic Rural Life, 5 times a year; 4625 N.W. Beaver Dr., Des Moines, Ia. 50310; National Catholic Rural Life Conference.

Catholic Singles Magazine, bm; 8408 S. Muskegon, Chicago, Ill. 60617.

Catholic Teen Magazine, m (Sept.-June); 3900-A Harewood Rd. N.E., Washington, D.C.; National Federation for Catholic Youth Ministry.

Catholic Trends, biweekly; 1312 Massachusetts Ave. N.W., Washington, D.C. 20005; NC News Service.

Catholic University of America Law Review, q; Washington, D.C. 20064.

Catholic Update, m; 1615 Republic St., Cincinnati, O. 45210.

Catholic War Veteran, bm; 2 Massachusetts Ave. N.W., Washington, D.C. 20001.

Catholic Woman, bm; 1312 Massachusetts Ave. N.W., Washington, D.C. 20005. National Council of Catholic Women.

Catholic Worker, 8 times a year; 36 E. First St., New York, N.Y. 10003.

Catholic Workman, m; 111 W. Main, P.O. Box 47, New Prague, Minn. 56071.

Catholic Youth Ministry, q; P.O. Box 215, Weston, Vt. 05161.

Catholicism in Crisis, m; P.O. Box 1006, Notre Dame, Ind. 46556.

Celebration, m; 11211 Monticello Ave., Silver Spring, Md. 20902; National Catholic Reporter Publishing Co.

Center Journal, q; P.O. Box A, Notre Dame, Ind. 46556; Center for Christian Studies.

Charism; q; 4435 E. Patterson Rd., Dayton, O. 45430; Society of Mary.

Charicenter USA Newsletter, 10 times a year; P.O. Box 1065, Notre Dame, Ind. 46556.

Charities USA, m; 1319 F St. N.W., Washington, D.C. 20004.

Chicago Studies, 3 times a year; P.O. Box 665, Mundelein, Ill. 60060; Civitas Dei Foundation.

Children's Friend, The (Priatel Dietok) (Eng.-Slovak), P.O. Box 899, Passaic, N.J. 07055; Slovak Catholic Sokol.

CFC Newsletter, 6 times a year; 13001 Wornall Rd., Kansas City, Mo. 64145. Christian Foundation for Children.

Christian Renewal News, P.O. Box 467, La Puente, Calif. 91747. Apostolate of Christian Renewal.

Christopher News Notes, 7 times a year; 12 E. 48th St., New York, N.Y. 10017; The Christophers, Inc.

Chronicle of Catholic Church in Lithuania, 6 times a year; 351 Highland Blvd., Brooklyn, N.Y. 11207; Lithuanian Catholic Religious Aid.

Church, q; 299 Elizabeth St., New York, N.Y. 10012; National Pastoral Life Center.

Cistercian Studies, q; Abbey of Gethsemani, Trappist, Ky. 40051; international review dedicated to monastic and contemplative spirituality.

Clarion, The, 5 times a year; Brothers Residence, 133B Granite St., Worcester, Mass. 01604; Brothers of Christian Instruction.

Columban Mission, m (exc. June, Aug.); St. Columbans, Nebr. 68056; Columban Fathers.

Columbia, m; One Columbus Plaza, P.O. Drawer 1670, New Haven, Conn. 06507; Knights of Columbus.

Columbian, The, biweekly; 188 W. Randolph St., Chicago, Ill. 60601.

Comboni Mission Newsletter, q; 8108 Beechmont Ave., Cincinnati, O. 45230.

Commitment, q; 1200 Varnum St. N.E., Washington, D.C. 20017; National Catholic Conference for Interracial Justice.

Commonweal, biweekly; 15 Dutch St., New York, N.Y. 10038.

Communio — International Catholic Review, q; P.O. Box 1046, Notre Dame, Ind. 46556.

Company, q; 3441 N. Ashland Ave., Chicago, Ill. 60657. National Jesuit Magazine.

Compassion, q; 526 Monastery Pl., Union City, N.J. 07087.

Consecrated Life, semi-annually; 4200 N. Austin Ave., Chicago, Ill. 60634; Institute on Religious Life. English edition of *Informationes,* official publication of Congregation for Religious and Secular Institutes.

Consolata Missionaries, bm; P.O. Box C, Somerset, N.J. 08873.

Contact, q; 555 Albany Ave., Amityville, N.Y. 11701; Sisters of St. Dominic.

Context, 22 issues a year; 221 W. Madison St., Chicago, Ill. 60606.

Cord, The, m; P.O. Drawer F, St. Bonaventure, N.Y. 14778.

Counseling and Values, 2 times a year; College of Education, Univ. of Iowa, Iowa City, Ia. 52242.

Crescat, 3 times a year; Belmont Abbey, Belmont, N.C. 28012; Benedictine Monks.

Critic, The, 4 times a year; 223 W. Erie, Chicago, Ill. 60610. Thomas More Assn.

Cross Currents, q; Mercy College, 555 Broadway, Dobbs Ferry, N.Y. 10522.

Crusader's Almanac, The, biannually; 1400 Quincy St. N.E., Washington, D.C. 20017; Commissariat of the Holy Land.

CRUX of the News, w; 75 Champlain St., Albany, N.Y. 12204.

Damien-Dutton Call, q; 616 Bedford Ave., Bellmore, N.Y. 11710.

Deaf Blind Weekly, The (Braille), w; 154 E.

23rd St., New York, N.Y. 10010; Xavier Society for the Blind.

Desert Call, q; Box 260, Crestone, Colo. 81131; Spiritual Life Institute of America.

Diaconate, bm; 1937 Tenth Ave. N., P.O. Box 9501, Lake Worth, Fla. 33466.

Dimensions, m; 86 Front St., Hempstead, N.Y. 11550; National Catholic Development Conference.

Divine Love, q; P.O. Box 24, Fresno, Calif. 93707.

Divine Word Missionaries, q; Techny, Ill. 60082.

Ecumenical Trends, m (exc. Aug.); 475 Riverside Dr., Room 528, New York, N.Y. 10115. Friars of the Atonement.

Ecumenist, The, 6 times a year; Paulist Press, 997 MacArthur Blvd., Mahwah, N.J. 07430.

Educating in Faith, q; 2021 H St. N.W., Washington, D.C. 20006. Catholic Negro-American Mission Board.

Eglute (The Little Fir Tree) (Lithuanian), m; Putnam, Conn. 06260; Srs. of Immaculate Conception. For children ages 5-10.

Emmanuel, m (bm July-Aug.); 184 E. 76th St., New York, N.Y. 10021; Blessed Sacrament Fathers.

Envoy, q; Office of Public Affairs, Catholic University of America, Washington, D.C. 20064.

Eucharistic Minister, m; 115 E. Armour, Kansas City, Mo. 64111.

Evangelization and Initiation, 6 times a year; 3031 Fourth St. N.E., Washington, D.C. 20017.

Extension, m; 35 E. Wacker Dr., Suite 400, Chicago, Ill. 60601; Catholic Church Extension Society.

Faith and Reason, q. Route 3, Box 87, Front Royal, Va. 22630; Christendom College.

Family, m; 50 St. Paul's Ave., Boston, Mass. 02130; Daughters of St. Paul.

Family Festivals, bm; 160 E. Virginia St., San Jose, Calif. 95112.

Family Friend, q; P.O. Box 11563, Milwaukee, Wis. 53211; Catholic Family Life Insurance.

Family Spirit, q; 409 Big Bayou Rd., Warrington, Fla. 32507. Worldwide Marriage Encounter.

Fatima Findings, m; 100 E. 20th St., Baltimore, Md. 21218; Reparation Society of the Immaculate Heart of Mary.

Fellowship of Catholic Scholars Newsletter, q; St. John's University, Jamaica, N.Y. 11439.

Fidelity, m; 206 Marquette Ave., South Bend, Ind. 46617.

Flame, The, m; Barry Univ., 11300 N.E. 2nd Ave., Miami Shores, Fla. 33161.

Fonda Tekakwitha News, q; P.O. Box 627, Fonda, N.Y. 12068.

Franciscan Herald, m; 1434 W. 51st St., Chicago, Ill. 60609.

F.M.A. Focus, q; 274-280 W. Lincoln Ave., Mt. Vernon, N.Y. 10550; Franciscan Mission Associates.

Franciscan Reporter, q; 3140 Meramec St., St. Louis, Mo. 63118.

Franciscan Studies, a; St. Bonaventure, N.Y. 14778; Franciscan Institute.

Fraternal Leader, bm; P.O. Box 6196, Erie, Pa.

16512; Loyal Christian Benefit Association.

Fraternally Yours (Zenska Jednota) (Eng.-Slovak), m; 24950 Chagrin Blvd., Beachwood, O. 44122; First Catholic Slovak Ladies Assn.

Frontline Report, bm; 23 Bliss Ave., Tenafly, N.J. 07670.

Fund Raising Forum, m; 86 Front St., Hempstead, N.Y. 11550; National Catholic Development Conference.

Garsas (The Sound) (Lithuanian-English), m; 341 Highland Blvd., Brooklyn, N.Y. 11207; Lithuanian Roman Catholic Alliance of America.

Generation, m; 221 Madison St., Chicago, Ill. 60606.

Glenmary Challenge, The, q; P.O. Box 465618, Cincinnati, O. 45246; Glenmary Home Missioners.

God's Anchor, 4 times a year; 264 Elm St., Holyoke, Mass. 01040.

God's Word Today, m; Box 40664, St. Petersburg, Fla. 33743.

Good News, m; P.. Box 9501; Lake Worth, Fla. 33466; Sunday Publications, Inc.

Good News for Children, 24 times during school year; 2451 E. River Rd., Dayton, Ohio 45439.

Good Shepherd (Dobry Pastier) (Slovak and English), a; 2260 Adams, Gary, Ind. 46407; Slovak Catholic Federation of America.

Goose Corn, 10 issues a year; 221 W. Madison St., Chicago, Ill. 60606.

Guadalupe Missioners Newsletter, m; 4714 W. 8th St., Los Angeles, Calif. 90005.

Guide to Religious Ministries, A, a; 210 Main St., New Rochelle, N.Y. 10801.

Happiness, q; 567 Salem End Rd., Framingham, Mass. 01701; Sons of Mary, Health of the Sick.

Harmony, 3 times a year; 8300 Morganford Rd., St. Louis, Mo. 63123; Benedictine Srs. of Perpetual Adoration.

Health Progress, m; 4455 Woodson Rd., St. Louis, Mo. 63134; Catholic Health Association.

Holy Name Newsletter, m (exc. July and Dec.); P.O. Box 7244, Rocky Mount, N.C. 27801; National Association of the Holy Name Society.

Homiletic and Pastoral Review, m; 86 Riverside Dr., New York, N.Y. 10024.

Horizons, biannual; Villanova University, Villanova, Pa. 19085. College Theology Society.

Human Development, q; Jesuit Educational Center, 53 Park Pl., New York, N.Y. 10007.

Human Life Issues, q; University of Steubenville, Steubenville, O. 43952.

IDEA Ink, q; P.O. Box 4010, Madison, Wis. 53711.

Image, q; 4121 Harewood Rd., Washington, D.C. 20017. Queen of the Americas Guild.

In a Word, m; Bay Saint Louis, Miss. 39520; Society of the Divine Word.

In-Formation, 8 times a year; 1234 Massachusetts Ave., N.W., Washington, D.C. 20005; Religious Formation Conference.

Institute Journal, bm; 50 Oak St., San Francisco, Calif. 94102; Young Men's Institute.

International Philosophical Quarterly; Fordham University, Bronx, N.Y. 10458.

International Review — Natural Family Planning, q; St. John's University, Collegeville, Minn. 56321.

It's Our World, 4 times a year; 1720 Massachusetts Ave. N.W., Washington, D.C. 20036. Holy Childhood Association.

Jesuit Blackrobe, semiannually; 3601 W. Fond du Lac Ave., Milwaukee, Wis. 53216.

Jesuit Bulletin, 4 times a year; 4511 W. Pine Blvd., St. Louis, Mo. 63108; Jesuit Seminary Aid Association.

Josephite Harvest, The, q; 1130 N. Calvert St., Baltimore, Md. 21202; Josephite Missionaries.

Jurist, The, semiannually; Catholic University of America, Washington, D.C. 20064; School of Canon Law.

Kinship, q; P.O. Box 39188, Cincinnati, O. 45239; Glenmary Sisters.

Knights of St. John, q; 6517 Charles Ave., Cleveland, O. 44129.

Kolping Banner, m; 115-14 227th St., Cambria Heights., N.Y. 11411; Catholic Kolping Society.

Laivas (Lithuanian), bm; 4545 W. 63rd St., Chicago, Ill. 60629.

Land of Cotton, q; 2048 W. Fairview Ave., Montgomery, Ala. 39196; City of St. Jude.

Law Briefs, m; 1312 Massachusetts Ave. N.W., Washington, D.C. 20005; Office of General Counsel, USCC.

Law Reports, m; 4455 Woodson Rd., St. Louis, Mo. 63134.

Laywitness, m; 45 Union Ave., New Rochelle, N.Y. 10801; Catholics United for the Faith.

Leaven, q; Convent of the Holy Spirit, Techny, Ill. 60082.

Leaves, bm; 23715 Ann Arbor Trail, Dearborn Heights, Mich. 48127; Mariannhill Mission Society.

Let's Pray Together, w; 775 Madison Ave., Albany, N.Y. 12208; Families for Prayer.

Liguorian, m; 1 Liguori Rd., Liguori, Mo. 63057; Redemptorists.

Linacre Quarterly, q; 850 Elm Grove Rd., Elm Grove, Wis. 53122; Federation of Catholic Physicians Guilds.

Link, The, 6 times a year; Teleport One, The Teleport Staten Island, N.Y. 10314; Catholic Telecommunications Network of America.

Listening, 5 times a year; 814 Thayer Ave., Silver Spring, Md. 20910. National Catholic Office for the Deaf.

Liturgy, q; 806 Rhode Island Ave. N.E. Washington, D.C. 20018.

Living City, m; P.O. Box 496, New York, N.Y. 10021; Focolare Movement.

Living Light, The, q; 1312 Massachusetts Ave. N.W., Washington, D.C. 20005; Department of Education, USCC.

Living Prayer, bm; Beckley Hill, Barre, Vt. 05641; Assn. of Contemplative Sisters.

Marian Helpers Bulletin, q; Stockbridge, Mass.

01262; Association of Marian Helpers and of the Congregation of Marian Fathers.

Marriage and Family Living, m; Abbey Press St. Meinrad, Ind. 47577.

Marriage Encounter, m; 955 Lake Dr., St. Paul Minn. 55120; International Marriage Encounter.

Maryknoll, m; Maryknoll, N.Y. 10545; Catholic Foreign Mission Society.

Mary's Shrine, q; Michigan Ave. and 4th St N.E., Washington, D.C. 20017.

Medical Mission News, bm; 10 W. 17th St., New York, N.Y. 10011; Catholic Medical Mission Board Inc.

Medical Mission Sisters News, 4 times a year 8400 Pine Road, Philadelphia, Pa. 19111.

Men of Malvern, bm; Malvern, Pa. 19355; Laymen's Retreat League of Philadelphia.

Messenger of St. Joseph's Union, The, 3 times a year; 108 Bedell St., Staten Island, N.Y. 10309.

Mid-America, 3 times a year; Loyola University, Chicago, Ill. 60626.

Miesiecznik Franciszkanski (Polish), m; 165 E Pulaski St., Pulaski, Wis. 54162; Franciscan Fathers.

Migration Today, 5 times a year; 209 Flagg Pl. Staten Island, N.Y. 10304; Center for Migration Studies.

Miraculous Medal, The, q; 475 E. Chelten Ave. Philadelphia, Pa. 19144; Central Association of the Miraculous Medal.

Mission, 4 times a year; 366 Fifth Ave., New York, N.Y. 10001; Society for Propagation of the Faith.

Mission, q; 1663 Bristol Pike, Bensalem, Pa 19020; Sisters of the Blessed Sacrament.

Mission Handbook, a; 1233 Lawrence St. N.E. Washington, D.C. 20017. United States Catholic Mission Association.

Mission Helper, The, q; 1001 W. Joppa Rd., Baltimore, Md. 21204; Mission Helpers of the Sacred Heart.

Missionhurst, 6 times a year; 4651 N. 25th St. Arlington, Va. 22207; Immaculate Heart of Mary Mission Society, Inc.

Mission Intercom, 10 times a year; 1233 Lawrence St., N.E., Washington, D.C. 20017; U.S Catholic Mission Association.

Mission of the Immaculata, The, biweekly; 160 W. Park Ave., Libertyville, Ill. 60048; Conventual Franciscan Friars.

Missionaries of Africa Report, bm; 1622 21st St N.W., Washington, D.C. 20009; Society of Missionaries of Africa (White Fathers).

Modern Liturgy, 9 times a year; Resource Publications, 160 E. Virginia St., San Jose, Calif. 95112

Modern Schoolman, The, q; 3700 W. Pine Blvd., St. Louis, Mo. 63108; St. Louis University.

Momentum, 4 times a year; Suite 100, 1077 30th St., N.W., Washington, D.C. 20007; National Catholic Educational Association.

Mountain Spirit, The, 6 times a year; 322 Crab Orchard Rd., Lancaster, Ky. 40446; ecumenical Christian Appalachian Project.

Mustard Seed, m; 1615 Vine St., Cincinnati, O 45210; Franciscans.

My Daily Visitor, bm; 200 Noll Plaza, Huntington

ton, Ind. 46750; Our Sunday Visitor, Inc.

My Friend, 10 times a year; 50 St. Paul's Ave., Jamaica Plain, Boston, Mass. 02130; for children.

National Catholic Forester, q; 35 E. Wacker Dr., Chicago, Ill. 60601.

NCSC News, bm; 1 Columbia Pl., Albany, N.Y. 12207. National Catholic Stewardship Council.

National Directory of Catholic Higher Education, a; 210 Main St., New Rochelle, N.Y. 10801.

National Jesuit News, m; St. Joseph's University, Philadelphia, Pa. 19131.

Network, bm; 806 Rhode Island Ave. N.E., Washington, D.C. 20018; Network.

Nevada Catholic Newsletter, m; P.O. Box 1211, Reno, Nev. 89504; Reno-Las Vegas diocese.

New Catholic World, bm; 997 Macarthur Blvd., Mahwah, N.J. 07430.

New Covenant, m; P.O. Box 400, Steubenville, O. 43952; Catholic Charismatic Renewal.

New Heaven/New Earth, m; 107 S. Greenlawn Ave., South Bend, Ind. 46617.

New Oxford Review, 10 issues a year; 1069 Kains Ave., Berkeley, Calif. 94706.

New Scholasticism, q; 715 Memorial Library, Notre Dame, Ind. 46556. American Catholic Philosophical Association.

News/Views, 5 times a year; 1307 S. Wabash Ave., Chicago, Ill. 60605; National Sisters Vocation Conference.

News and Views, q; 3900 Westminster Pl.; St. Louis, Mo. 63108; Sacred Heart Program.

Newsletter of the Bureau of Catholic Indian Missions, 10 times a year; 2021 H St. N.W., Washington, D.C. 20006.

North American Voice of Fatima, m; 1023 Swann Rd., Youngstown, N.Y. 14174.

Notre Dame Magazine, 5 times a year; Notre Dame Univ., Notre Dame, Ind. 46556.

Oblate World and Voice of Hope, bm; 350 Jamaica Way, Boston, Mass. 02130; Oblates of Mary Immaculate.

Oblates, bm; 15 S. 59th St., Belleville, Ill. 62222; Oblate Fathers.

Observer, The, m; 4545 W. 63rd St., Chicago, Ill. 60629; Lithuanian Roman Catholic Federation of America.

Old Testament Abstracts, 3 times a year; Catholic University of America, Washington, D.C. 20064.

Origins, 48 times a year; 1312 Massachusetts Ave., N.W., Washington, D.C. 20005; NC News Service.

Our Lady's Digest, q; Box 777, Twin Lakes, Wis. 53181; La Salette Fathers.

Overview, m; 223 W. Erie St., Chicago, Ill. 60610; Thomas More Assn.

Pacer, bm; 500 17th Ave., Seattle, Wash. 98124; Providence Medical Center.

Padres' Trail, 4 times a year; St. Michael's Mission, St. Michael, Ariz. 86511; Franciscan Fathers.

Paraclete, 2 times a year; 11411 Amhurst Ave., Wheaton, Md. 20902; Holy Ghost Fathers.

Parish Communication, 10 times a year, P.O. Box 215, Weston, Vt. 05161.

Parish Family Digest, bm; 200 Noll Plaza, Huntington, Ind. 46750.

Passionist Series, m; 1089 Elm St., W. Springfield, Mass. 01089.

Pastoral Life, m; Route 224, Canfield, Ohio 44406; Society of St. Paul.

Pastoral Music, 6 times a year; 225 Sheridan St., N.W. Washington, D.C. 20011; National Association of Pastoral Musicians.

Paulist, q; 997 Macarthur Blvd., Mahwah, N.J. 07430.

Philosophy Today, q; Carthagena Station, Celina, Ohio 45822.

Piarist Newsletter, 2 times a year; 363 N. Valley Forge Rd., Devon, Pa. 19333.

Pilgrim, q; Jesuit Fathers, Auriesville, N.Y. 12016; Shrine of North American Martyrs.

Pope Speaks, The, q; Our Sunday Visitor, Inc., 200 Noll Plaza, Huntington, Ind. 46750.

Praying, 6 times a year; 115 E. Armour Blvd., Kansas City, Mo. 64111.

Priest, The, 11 times a year; 200 Noll Plaza, Huntington, Ind. 46750; Our Sunday Visitor, Inc.

Probe, bm (Sept.-June); 1307 S. Wabash Ave., Chicago, Ill. 60605; NARW.

Professional Placement Newsnotes, bm; 10 W. 17th St., New York, N.Y. 10011; Catholic Medical Mission Board, Inc.

Program Supplement, 18 times a year; Columbus Plaza, New Haven, Conn. 06507; Knights of Columbus.

Quarterly, The, 2021 H St. N.W., Washington, D.C. 20006; Commission for Catholic Missions Among the Colored People and the Indians.

Queen; bm; 26 S. Saxon Ave., Bay Shore, N.Y. 11706; Montfort Fathers.

Reign of the Sacred Heart, m; Hales Corners, Wis. 53130.

Religion Teacher's Journal, m (Sept.-May); P.O. Box 180, Mystic, Conn. 06355.

Religious Life, m (bm, May-Aug.); 4200 N. Austin Ave., Chicago, Ill. 60634; Institute on Religious Life.

RSCJ Newsletter, bm; 801 S. Spoede Rd., St. Louis, Mo. 63131; Religious of Sacred Heart.

Renascence, q; Marquette University, Milwaukee, Wis. 53233.

Respect Life Report, m; 1312 Massachusetts Ave. N.W., Washington, D.C. 20005; Committee for Pro-Life Activities, NCCB.

Response, The, biannual; 810 Rhode Island Ave. N.E., Washington, D.C. 20018; International Liaison.

Review for Religious, bm; Room 428, 3601 Lindell Blvd., St. Louis, Mo. 63108.

Review of Politics, q; Box B, Notre Dame, Ind. 46556.

Review of Social Economy, 3 times a year; 25 E. Jackson Blvd., Chicago, Ill. 60604; Association for Social Economics.

Revista Maryknoll (Spanish-English), m; Maryknoll, N.Y. 10545; Catholic Foreign Mission Society of America.

Roze Maryi (Polish), m; Eden Hill, Stockbridge, Mass. 01262; Marian Fathers.

SCJ News, 9 times a year; P.O. Box 289, Hales Corners, Wis. 53130; Sacred Heart Fathers and Brothers.

Sacred Music, q; 548 Lafond Ave., St. Paul, Minn. 55103.

St. Anthony Messenger, m; 1615 Republic St., Cincinnati, O. 45210; Franciscan Fathers.

St. Anthony's Newsletter, m; Mt. St. Francis, Ind. 47146.

St. Joseph's Messenger and Advocate of the Blind, q; St. Joseph Home, P.O. Box 288, Jersey City, N.J. 07303.

St. Paul's Children's Magazine, q; P.O. Box 772, Ft. Scott, Kans. 66701.

Salesian Bulletin, bm; 148 Main St., New Rochelle, N.Y. 10802; Salesian Fathers.

Salesian Missions, q; 148 Main St., New Rochelle, N.Y. 10802; Salesians of St. John Bosco.

Salt, m; 221 W. Madison St., Chicago, Ill. 60606; Claretians.

Salvatorian Newsletter, The, q; 1303 Milwaukee Dr., Salvatorian Center, Wis. 53062.

Savio Notes, bm; Filors Lane, W. Haverstraw, N.Y. 10993; St. Dominic Savio Clubs International.

Scalabrinians, 3 times a year; 25 Carmine St., New York, N.Y. 10014.

School Guide, a; 210 Main St., New Rochelle, N.Y. 10801.

School Sister, The, 3 times a year; 1233 N. Marshall St., Milwaukee, Wis. 53202; Sisters of Notre Dame.

SCRC Vision, The, m; 2810 Artesia Blvd., Redondo Beach, Calif. 90278; Southern California Renewal Communities.

Scripture in Church, 4 times a year; P.O. Box 9, Northport, N.Y. 11768.

Senior Update, m; 1615 Republic St., Cincinnati, O. 45210.

Serenity, q; 601 Maiden Choice Lane, Baltimore, Md. 21228; Little Sisters of the Poor.

Serran, The, bm; 22 W. Monroe St., Chicago, Ill. 60603; Serra International.

Share the Word, bm; 3031 Fourth St. N.E., Washington, D.C. 20017; Paulist Catholic Evangelist Center.

Shepherd's Call, The, q; P.O. Box 7775, Albuquerque, N.M. 87194; Brothers of Good Shepherd.

Silent Advocate, q; St. Rita School for the Deaf, 1720 Glendale-Milford Rd., Cincinnati, O. 45215.

Sister Miriam Teresa League of Prayer Bulletin, q; League Headquarters, Convent Station, N.J. 07961.

SC News, 10 times a year; 2208 Dixie Highway, Louisville, Ky. 40210; Sisters of Charity of Nazareth.

SSM Network, q; 1100 Bellevue Ave., St. Louis, Mo. 63117. Sisters of St. Mary.

Sisters Today, m (exc. July-Aug.); Liturgical Press, Collegeville, Minn. 56321.

Social Justice Review, bm; 3835 Westminster Pl., St. Louis, Mo. 63108; Catholic Central Union of America.

Social Thought, q; 1319 F St. N.W., Washington, D.C. 20004; Catholic Charities USA.

Sophia, bm; P.O. Box 265, Newton Center, Mass. 02159; Newton Melkite eparchy.

Soul, bm; Mountain View Rd., Washington, N.J. 07882; Blue Army.

Spectrum, q; 1011 First Ave., New York, N.Y. 10022; Catholic Relief Services.

Spinnaker, q; 610 W. Elm, Monroe, Mich. 48161; IHM Sisters.

Spirit, biannually; Seton Hall University, South Orange, N.J. 07079; poetry magazine.

Spirit and Life, 6 times a year; 8300 Morganford Rd., St. Louis, Mo. 63123; Benedictine Srs. of Perpetual Adoration.

Spiritual Book News, 8 times a year; Notre Dame, Ind. 46556.

Spiritual Life, q; 2131 Lincoln Rd. N.E., Washington, D.C. 20002; Discalced Carmelites.

Spirituality Today (formerly Cross and Crown), q; 7200 W. Division, River Forest, Ill. 60605; Dominican Fathers.

Squires Newsletter, m; Columbus Plaza, New Haven, Conn. 06507; Columbian Squires.

Star, 10 times a year; 16 W. Bijou, Colorado Springs, Colo. 80903.

Strain Forward, 11 times a year; 50 St. Paul's Avenue, Jamaica Plain, Boston, Mass. 02130; Daughters of St. Paul.

Studies in Formative Spirituality, 3 times a year; Institute of Formative Spirituality, Duquesne Univ., Pittsburgh, Pa. 15282.

Studies in the Spirituality of Jesuits, 5 times a year; 3700 W. Pine Blvd., St. Louis, Mo. 63108.

Tekakwitha Conference Newsletter, q; P.O. Box 6759, Great Falls, Mont. 59406.

Theological Studies, q; Georgetown Univ., 37th and O Sts., N.W., Washington, D.C. 20057.

Theology Digest, q; 3634 Lindell Blvd., St. Louis, Mo. 63108.

Theresian, The, 4 times a year; 5326 E. Pershing Ave., Scottsdale, Ariz. 85254.

Thirsting for Justice, q; 1312 Massachusetts Ave. N.W. Washington, D.C. 20005, Campaign for Human Development.

This Week, w; 135 W. 31st St., New York, N.Y. 10001; Franciscan Communications Office, Holy Name Province.

Thomist, The, q; 487 Michigan Ave. N.E., Washington, D.C. 20017; Dominican Fathers.

Thought, q; Fordham University Press, Box L, Bronx, N.Y. 10458; Fordham University.

Today's Catholic Teacher, m (Sept.-May); 2451 E. River Rd., Suite 200, Dayton, O. 45439.

Today's Parish, m (Sept.-May); P.O. Box 180, Mystic, Conn. 06355.

Topic, semiannually; 38 Michigan Ave., Lynn, Mass. 01902. Third Order Province of Immaculate Conception.

Touchstone, 4 times a year; 1307 S. Wabash Ave., Chicago, Ill. 60605; National Federation of Priests' Councils.

Tracings, q; Gamelin St., Holyoke, Mass. 01040; Sisters of Mercy.

Trinity Missions Magazine, q; 9001 New Hampshire Ave., Silver Springs, Md. 20903.

Trinity Review, bm; 3606 Coolcrest Dr., P.O. Box 169, Jefferson, Md. 21755.

Ultreya Magazine, m; 4500 W. Davis St., Dallas, Tex. 75211. Cursillo Movement.

Unda USA Newsletter, 6 times a year; Univ. of Dayton, Dayton, O. 45469.

L'Union (French), bm; 1 Social St., Woonsocket, R.I. 02895.

UNIREA, The Union (Romanian and English), m; 4309 Olcott Ave., East Chicago, Ind. 46312.

Universitas, q; 221 N. Grand, Room 303, St. Louis, Mo. 63103; St. Louis University.

U.S. Catholic, m; 221 W. Madison St., Chicago, Ill. 60606; Claretian Fathers and Brothers.

U.S. Catholic Historian, q; P.O. Box 16229, Baltimore, Md. 21210.

U.S. Dominican, q; 1909 S. Ashland Ave., Chicago, Ill. 60608.

U.S. Parish, m; 221 W. Madison St., Chicago, Ill. 60606.

Venture, 26 times during school year; 2451 E. River Rd., Dayton, O. 45439, Intermediate grades.

Vision, 3 times a year; P.O. Box 28185, San Antonio, Tex. 78228. Mexican American Cultural Center.

Visions, 24 times during school year; 2451 E. River Rd., Dayton, O. 45439.

Vocation News, q; 26 Brentford Ct., Camarillo, Calif. 93010.

Voices, seasonal; P.O. Box 8326, St. Louis, Mo. 63132; Women for Faith and Family.

Waif's Messenger, q; 1140 W. Jackson Blvd., Chicago, Ill. 60607; Mission of Our Lady of Mercy.

Washington Theological Union Newsletter, q; 9001 New Hampshire Ave., Silver Spring, Md 20903.

Way — of St. Francis, bm; 109 Golden Gate Ave., San Francisco, Calif. 94102; Franciscan Friars of California, Inc.

Wheeling College Chronicle, 4 times a year; 316 Washington Ave., Wheeling, W. Va. 26003.

World Lithuanian Catholic Directory, 351 Highland Blvd., Brooklyn, N.Y. 11207.

Word Among Us, The, m; P.O. Box 3646, Washington, D.C. 20037.

Word One, 5 times a year; 221 W. Madison St., Chicago, Ill. 60606; Claretians.

Word of God, w; 2187 Victory Blvd., Staten Island, N.Y. 10314; Society of St. Paul.

Worship, 6 times a year; St. John's Abbey, Collegeville, Minn. 56321.

Xaverian Missions Newsletter, bm; 101 Summer St., Holliston, Mass. 01746; Xaverian Missionary Fathers.

Your Edmundite Missions Newsletter, bm; 1428 Broad St., Selma, Ala. 36701; Southern Missions of Society of St. Edmund.

Youth Update, m; 1615 Republic St., Cincinnati, Ohio 45210.

Zeal Magazine, q; P.O. Box 86, Allegany, N.Y. 14706; Franciscan Sisters of Allegany.

BOOKS

The Official Catholic Directory, annual, P. J. Kenedy and Sons, 3004 Glenview Rd., Wilmette, Ill. 60091. First edition, 1817.

The Catholic Almanac, annual; Our Sunday Visitor, Inc., 200 Noll Plaza, Huntington, Ind. 46750, publisher; editorial offices, 620 Route 3, Clifton, N.J. 07014. First edition, 1904.

BOOK CLUBS

Catholic Book Club (1928), 106 W. 56th St., New York, N.Y. 10019. Sponsors the Campion Award.

Catholic Digest Book Club (1954), Catholic Digest Magazine, P.O. Box 64090, St. Paul, Minn. 55164.

Herald Book Club (1958), Franciscan Herald Press, 1434 W. 51st St., Chicago, Ill. 60609.

Thomas More Book Club (1939), Thomas More Association, 223 W. Erie St., Chicago, Ill. 60610.

FOREIGN CATHOLIC PERIODICALS

Principal source: Catholic Almanac survey. Included are English-language Catholic periodicals published outside the U.S.

African Ecclesial Review (AFER), bm; Gaba Publications, P.O. Box 908, Eldoret, Kenya.

Australasian Catholic Record, q; St. Patrick's Seminary, Manly, New South Wales, Australia.

Christ to the World, bm; Via di Propaganda 1-C, 00187, Rome, Italy.

Clergy Review, m; 48 Great Peter St., London, SW1P 2HB, England.

Doctrine and Life, m, and **Supplement to Doctrine and Life,** bm; Dominican Publications, St. Saviour's, Dublin 1, Ireland.

Downside Review, q; Downside Abbey, Stratton on Fosse, Bath, BA3 4RH, England.

East Asian Pastoral Review, q; East Asian Pastoral Institute, P.O. Box 1815, Manila, Philippines.

Eastern Churches Review, semi-annual; 9 Alfred St., Oxford, England.

Faith Today, 10 times a year; Dominican Publications, St. Saviour's, Dublin 1, Ireland.

Furrow, m; St. Patrick's College, Maynooth, Ireland.

Heythrop Journal q; Heythrop College, 11 Cavendish Sq., London W1M, OAN, England (Editorial Office).

Irish Biblical Studies, q; Union Theological College, Belfast BT7 1JT, N. Ireland.

Irish Theological Quarterly, q; St. Patrick's College, Maynooth, Ireland.

L'Osservatore Romano, w; Vatican City. (See Index.)

Louvain Studies, 4 times a year; St. Michielsstraat 2 B-3000, Leuven, Belgium.

Lumen Vitae (English and French editions), q; International Center for Studies in Religious Education, 186, rue Washington, 1050 Brussels, Belgium.

Maynooth Review, q; St. Patrick's College, Maynooth, Ireland.

Mediaeval Studies, annual; Pontifical Institute of Mediaeval Studies, 59 Queen's Park Crescent East, Toronto, Ont., Canada M5S 2C4.

Month, m; 114 Mount St., London, WIY, 6AH, England.

Music and Liturgy, q; Bamsthorn, Ockham Rd., North. West Horsley, Leatherhead, Surrey, T24 6PE, England.

New Blackfriars, m; edited by English Dominicans. Blackfriars, Oxford, England.

One in Christ, q; Edited at: Turvey Abbey, Turvey, Beds. MK43 8DE, England.

Recusant History, biannual; Catholic Record Society, 12 Melbourne Pl., Walsingham, Durham DL13 3EH, England.

Social Studies, q; St. Patrick's College, Maynooth, Ireland.

Spearhead, 5 times a year; Gaba Publications, P.O. Box 908, Eldoret, Kenya.

Studies in Religion/Sciences Religieuses (bilingual), q; Wilfrid Laurier University Press, Waterloo, Ont., Canada N2L 3C5.

Tablet, The w; 48 Great Peter St., London, SW1P 2HB, England.

Teilhard Review, The, 3 times a year; The Teilhard Centre for the Future of Man, 23 Kensington Square, London W8 5 HN, England.

Theology, bm; S.P.C.K. Holy Trinity Church, Marylebone Rd., London, NW1 4DU, England.

Way, The, q; and **Supplements to The Way,** triannual: 39 Fitzjohn's Ave., London NW3 5JT, England.

CATHOLIC NEWS AGENCIES

(Sources: International Catholic Union of the Press, Geneva; Catholic Press Association, U.S.)

Argentina: Agencia Informativa Catolica Argentina (AICA), av. Rivadavia, 413,4° Casilla de Correo Central 2886, 1020 Buenos Aires.

Austria: Katholische Presse-Agentur (Kathpress), Singerstrasse 6.2, 1010 Vienna 1.

Belgium: Centre d'Information de Presse (CIP), 1 Bd. Charlemagne, 1041 Bruxelles (Brussels).

Germany: Katholische Nachrichten Agentur (KNA), Adenauer Allee 134, 5300 Bonn 1.

Great Britain: Catholic Information Office of England and Wales (CIOEW), 38/40 Eccleston Square, London SW1V 1PD.

Greece: Agence TYPOS Rue Acharnon 246, Athenes 815.

Hong Kong: UCA-News, P.O. Box 69.626, Kwun Tong (Hong Kong).

Hungary: Magyar Kurir, Karolyi w 4-8, Postafiok 41, Budapest V.

India: South Asia Religious News (SAR-News), P.O. Box 4228, New Delhi 110.048.

Italy: Servizio Informazioni Settimanali (SIS-

Roma) 1, via della Conciliazione, I-00193 Roma. Centrum Informationis Catolicae (CIC-Roma), via Domenico Silveri, 30, I-00165 Roma.

Switzerland: Katholische Internationale Presse-Agentur (KIPA), Case Postale 1054 CH 1701, Fribourg.

Centre International de Reportages et d'Information Culturelle (CIRIC), 10, av. de la Gare-des-Eaux Vives, CH-1207 Geneva.

United States of America: NC News Service (NC), 1312 Massachusetts Ave. N.W., Washington, D.C. 20005.

Yugoslavia: Aktusinosti Krscanska Sadasnjost (AKSA), Marulicev TRG 14, Zagreb p.p. 02-748.

Zaire: Documentation et Information Africaine (DIA), B.P. 2598, Kinshasa I.

Missions: Agenzia Internationale Fides (AIF), Palazzo di Propagande Fide, Via di Propaganda I-c, 00187 Rome, Italy.

U.S. PRESS SERVICES

National Catholic News Service (NC), established in 1920, provides a worldwide daily news report by wire throughout the U.S. and into several foreign countries, and by mail to other clients, serving Catholic periodicals and broadcasters including Vatican Radio in about 40 countries. NC also provides feature and photo services and a weekly religious education tabloid insert, "Faith Today." It publishes "Origins," a weekly documentary service, and "Catholic Trends," a fortnightly newsletter. NC maintains a full-time bureau in Rome. It is a division of the United States Catholic Conference, with offices at 1312 Massachusetts Ave. N.W., Washington, D.C. 20005. The director and editor-in-chief is Richard W. Daw.

Religious News Service (RNS) provides domestic and foreign religious news in daily photos and features; RNS was inaugurated in 1933 by the National Conference of Christians and Jews as an independent news agency. In 1983, it was taken over by the United Methodist Reporter, a chain of newspapers with headquarters in Dallas, Tex. Its offices are located at 106 W. 56th St., New York, N.Y. 10019.

Eastern Rite Information Service (ER), for Eastern Church news; 2208 W. Chicago Ave., Chicago, Ill. 60622.

Spanish-Language Service: A weekly news summary provided by NC News Service is used by a number of diocesan newspapers. Some papers carry features of their own in Spanish.

CATHOLIC WRITERS' MARKET

(Source: Almanac survey.)

Editors call the following suggestions to the attention of writers:

Manuscripts should be typewritten, double-spaced, on one side of the page.

Writers should know the editorial policy, purpose and style of the publication to which they submit manuscripts. Sample copies may easily be obtained, often for the mere cost of postage. Some editors suggest that writers send outlines of proposed material, in order to facilitate editorial decision and direction. "Timely" copy should be sub-

mitted considerably in advance of the date of proposed publication; some editors advise a period of three months. Authors are urged to avoid sermonizing. Writers should not expect extensive criticism of their work, although they should profit from advice and direction when these are given. Editors are not required to state their reasons for rejecting manuscripts. Replies regarding the acceptance or rejection of copy are usually made within a few weeks.

All writers should send to editors stamped, self-addressed envelopes for the return of material.

Those who write to Canadian editors may use international reply coupons, not U.S. stamps.

Payment is made on acceptance or publication. Rates are sometimes variable because of the reputation of the writer, the quality and length of the manuscript, the amount of editorial work required for its final preparation.

America: 106 W. 56th St., New York, N.Y. 10019. Ed., Rev. George W. Hunt, S.J. Weekly, circulation 33,000; $25 per year.

ARTICLES on important public issues evaluated scientifically and morally; serious and authenticated articles on family life, education, religion, and social and political issues with ethical or religious implications; occasionally, "thought" pieces; 1,000-2,000 words — 6¢ a word. VERSE, short and modern, befitting a Catholic publication but not necessarily religious—$7.50 and up. No fiction.

Annals of St. Anne de Beaupre, The: P.O. Box 1000, St. Anne de Beaupre, Que., Canada G0A 3C0. Ed., Rev. Roch Achard, C.Ss.R. Monthly, circulation 55,000; $6.50 per year.

FICTION: Stories of general Catholic interest, preferably with slant on devotion to St. Anne; 700-1,200 words — 2-4¢ a word. ARTICLES of solid general interest to Catholics: on aspects of devotion to St. Anne, relative to history of the devotion in North America or elsewhere; on educational or social problems, or situations that should be of concern to all — especially Christians: 700-1,200 words — 2-4¢ a word, Payment on acceptance.

BLUEPRINT for Social Justice: Institute of Human Relations, Loyola University, Box 12, New Orleans, La. 70118. Ed., Robert Udick. Ten times a year, circulation 6,200; sent free on request.

ARTICLES analyzing current justice issues in economics, labor, peace and human rights; length, 3,200 words.

Catechist: 2451 E. River Rd., Dayton, O. 45439. Ed., Patricia Fischer. Monthly August through April (exc. Dec.), circulation 45,620; $15.95 per year.

ARTICLES of interest to teachers of religion in parochial schools and CCD programs: 1,200-1,800 words — rate varies. PHOTOGRAPHS, black and white — rate varies. Payment on publication.

Catholic Digest: P.O. Box 64090, St. Paul, Minn. 55164. Ed., Henry Lexau. Monthly, circulation 637,000; $10.97 per year.

ARTICLES of close-to-home interest for average Catholic — rates vary; most frequent payments are $200 for originals, $100 for reprints; payment on acceptance. FILLERS, short features and jokes — rates vary; payment on publication. Cover pictures — $150. No fiction or verse. No queries necessary.

Columban Mission: St. Columbans, Nebr. 68056. Ed., Rev. Richard Steinhilber. Monthly (exc. June, Aug.); circulation 228,975; $5 per year.

ARTICLES mostly from missions or staff written: occasionally accept feature or factual articles on social and religious aspects of Asian and Latin American life: 2,000 words — $100 and up. PHOTOGRAPHS of Asian and Latin American subjects and photo stories — $10 each.

Columbia: Columbus Plaza, New Haven, Conn. 06507. Ed., Elmer Von Feldt. Monthly, circulation 1,399,332; $6 per year. Official organ of the Knights of Columbus.

ARTICLES on K of C councils dealing with current events, social problems, Catholic apostolic activities: 2,500-3,500 words (must be accompanied by color glossy photos or transparencies) — $600 to $750. SATIRE: 1,000 words — $200. CARTOONS, pungent, wordless humor — $50. COVERS — $1,000. No fiction.

Commonweal: 15 Dutch St., New York, N.Y. 10038. Ed., Peter Steinfels. Biweekly, circulation 18,500; $28 per year.

ARTICLES, political, religious and literary subjects: 1,000-3,000 words — 3¢ a word. VERSE, serious poetry of high literary merit — about 50¢ a line.

Crusader's Almanac: Franciscan Monastery, 1400 Quincy St. N.E., Washington, D.C. 20017. Ed., Rev. Kevin Treston, O.F.M. Biannually, circulation 85,000; free.

ARTICLES about the Holy Land, Bible and Crusades given preference — 1¢ a word.

Emmanuel: 184 E. 76th Street, New York, N.Y. 10021. Editor-in-Chief, Rev. Eugene La Verdiere, S.S.S. Monthly (combined Jan.-Feb., July-Aug. issues), circulation 7,000; $18 per year.

ARTICLES, spirituality for those in Church ministry, Eucharistic, pastoral, theological, Scriptural: 2,000-3,000 words — $50.

Extension: 35 E. Wacker Dr., Chicago, Ill. 60601. Ed., Brad Collins. Ten times a year, circulation, 90,000; free.

ARTICLES featuring U.S. home missioners, their work and the cultures and issues of the people they serve in poor, rural and remote parts of the U.S. Also, short catechetical and inspirational articles; 800-2,000 words — rate varies. Queries required before submitting material. PHOTOGRAPHS — black-and-white and color related to U.S. home missions — rate varies.

Franciscan Herald: 1434 W. 51st St., Chicago, Ill. 60609. Monthly, circulation 8,000; $11 per year.

ARTICLES concerning St. Francis of Assisi and related subjects; application of Gospel principles to living Catholicism today; 2,000 words — $35. BOOK REVIEWS related to Franciscan topics — $10.

Health Progress: 4455 Woodson Rd., St. Louis, Mo. 63134. Ten issues per year. Circulation 12,613; $30 per year (U.S. and Canada); $35 (foreign).

Official journal of the Catholic Health Association of the United States.

ARTICLES, health-care oriented; administrative procedures and theories; hospital departmental services: 1,500-3,000 words — payment by agreement. BOOK REVIEWS, hospital oriented — payment by agreement.

Liguorian: One Liguori Dr., Liguori, Mo. 63057. Ed., Norman J. Muckerman, C.SS.R. Monthly, circulation over 500,000; $12 per year.

STORIES with a Christian influence yet without maudlin sentimentality; 1,500-2,000 words — 7-10¢ a word. ARTICLES on family, Scripture, liturgy; material for older readers and those under 21 needed; 1,500-2,000 words — 7-10¢ a word. POETRY, $25. ILLUSTRATIONS and BOOK REVIEWS on assignment only.

Marriage and Family Living: St. Meinrad, Ind. 47577. Man. Ed., Kass Dotterweich. Monthly, circulation 45,000; $12.50 per year.

ARTICLES: (1) aimed at enriching the husband-wife and parent-child relationships by expanding religious and psychological insights or sensitivity: (2) informative, aimed at helping couples cope, in practical ways, with problems of modern living; (3) personal essays relating amusing and/or heart-warming incidents that point up the human side of marriage and family life: maximum 2,500 words — 7¢ a word. POETRY: any style and length — $15. PHOTOS: b & w glossies (8 x 10), color transparencies or 35mm slides. 4-color cover or center-spread photo — $250. Photos of couples especially desired. Model releases required.

Maryknoll: Maryknoll, N.Y. 10545. Ed., Moises Sandoval. Monthly, circulation more than 1,000,000; $1 per year.

ARTICLES must apply in some way to the hopes and aspirations, the culture, the problems and challenges of peoples in Asia, Africa and Latin America: 1,000-1,500 words — average payment, $100. Outline wanted before submission of material. PHOTOS: More interested in photo stories than in individual black and whites and color transparencies. Photo stories — up to $150, black and white; up to $200, color. Individual photos — $20, black and white; $35, color. Transparencies returned after use. Query before sending photos.

Messenger of the Sacred Heart, The: 661 Greenwood Ave., Toronto, Ont., Canada, M4J 4B3. Ed., Rev. F. J. Power, S.J. Monthly, circulation 15,000; $5 per year.

FICTION: stories which appeal to men, written with humor—good family reading: maximum, 1,800 words — 2¢ a word. ARTICLES of Catholic interest: 1,500 words — 2¢ a word. Payment upon acceptance.

Miraculous Medal, The: 475 E. Chelten Ave., Philadelphia, Pa. 19144. Ed., Rev. Robert P. Cawley, C.M. Quarterly, circulation 85,000.

FICTION, of general interest. Catholic in principle: 1,500-2,000 words — 2¢ a word and up. VERSE, religious in theme or turn; preferably about Our Lady: maximum 20 lines — 50¢ a line and up. Payment on acceptance. No articles.

Modern Liturgy: 160 E. Virginia St., No. 290, San Jose, Calif. 95112. Ed. Kenneth Guentert. Nine issues a year, circulation, 15,000; $36 per year.

FICTION: parables, fantasy, fables; 1,000 words. ARTICLES: how-to, sample services, skills for liturgical artists; 1,200 words — 3¢ a word. POETRY, up to 50 lines — $10. BOOK REVIEWS appropriate for liturgy or religious education. Pays first time in sample copies and subscriptions.

My Daily Visitor: 200 Noll Plaza, Huntington, Ind. 46750. Ed., Jacquelyn M. Murphy. Bimonthly, circulation 30,000; $6.75 per year.

A pocket-sized booklet of reflections for each day of the month.

MATERIAL: Daily reflections based on readings from the Mass, spiritual meditation, the feast of the day or the liturgical season: maximum 165 words per page (each day's reflection is printed on a separate page) — $100 for series of reflections.

New Catholic World: 997 Macarthur Blvd., Mahwah, N.J. 07430. Mng. Ed., Laurie Felknor. Bimonthly, circulation 14,000; $10 per year. Thematic issues.

ARTICLES, related to themes of issue (query editor): about 1,800-2,000 words. Rates of payment supplied.

Our Family: Box 249,Dept. C, Battleford, Sask., Canada SOM OEO. Ed., Rev. Albert Lalonde, O.M.I. Monthly, circulation 14,265; $13.98 per year; $17.48 in U.S.

FICTION, adult only; stories that reflect lives, problems and concerns of audience; anything true to human nature; no sentimentality or blatant moralizing; stories with "woven in" Christian message: 1,000-3,000 words — 7¢ to 10¢ a word. ARTICLES related to family living; religion, education, social, biographical, marriage, courtship, domestic, institutional: 1,000-3,000 words — 7¢ to 10¢ a word. POETRY, in the market for many more poems; should deal with man in search for himself, for God, for others, for love, for meaning in life, for commitment: 8-30 lines — 75¢-$1.00 per line. PHOTOS — purchased with manuscript as package (extra payment for photos); also in search of individual photos for editorial use. FILLERS — anecdotes of inspirational value, straight exposition, short humor.

Our Sunday Visitor Magazine: 200 Noll Plaza, Huntington, Ind. 46750. Ed., Robert P. Lockwood. Weekly, circulation 290,000; $20 per year.

ARTICLES, no limitation on subjects other than those imposed by good taste and orthodoxy. Picture and text stories, profiles of individuals and organizations; articles that reflect moral, cultural, historical, social, economic and certain political concerns about the U.S. and the world; articles on current problems. Practical, factual and anecdotal material is sought: 750-1,000 words — $75-$100, usual payment. Queries are preferred to unsolicited completed manuscripts. PHOTOGRAPHS, picture stories preferred rather than individual photos. Picture stories (color) — $100 and up. No fiction or poetry.

Parish Family Digest: 200 Noll Plaza, Huntington, Ind. 46750. Ed., Louis F. Jacquet. Bimonthly, circulation 150,000.

ARTICLES of timely interest to the young and growing Catholic family as a unit of the Catholic parish — personality profiles, interviews, social concerns, education, humor, inspiration and family and parish-family interrelationships; 1,000 words or less — 5¢ a word. REPRINTS — 2½¢ a word. CARTOONS — $10 each for exclusives. FILLERS — $5 each for exclusives based on personal experience. No poetry.

Pastoral Music: 225 Sheridan St. N.W., Washington, D.C. 20011. Ed. Daniel Connors. Bimonthly, circulation 8,000; $18 per year.

FICTION and ARTICLES — 4¢ a word.

Priest, The: 200 Noll Plaza, Huntington, Ind.

46750. Ed., Rev. Vincent J. Giese. Eleven issues a year, circulation 12,388; $16.50 per year.

ARTICLES of benefit to priests and seminarians in any of the following areas: priestly spirituality, contemporary theology, liturgy, apostolate and ministry, pastoral notes, Scripture. Controversial subject matter acceptable provided it does not go beyond the realm of orthodoxy or respect for authority or demands of fraternal charity: 6-15 double-spaced pages — $25 to $100 (about $6 per manuscript page).

Queen of All Hearts: 26 S. Saxon Ave., Bay Shore, N.Y. 11706. Ed., Rev. James McMillan, S.M.M.; Mng. Ed., Rev. Roger M. Charest S.M.M. Bimonthly; circulation 6,000; $10 per year (U.S.), $11 (Canada and foreign).

FICTION: short stories, preferably with a Marian theme: 1,000-2,000 words. ARTICLES that bring out the importance of devotion to Mary. Payment varies. VERSE with Marian theme — payment, two years' subscription. No artwork or fillers.

Religion Teacher's Journal: Twenty-Third Publications, P.O. Box 180, Mystic, Conn. 06355. Ed., Gwen Costello. Seven issues a year, circulation 40,000; $14 per year.

ARTICLES on catechesis, methods, theology, sample programs, how-to ideas, etc.; maximum length, 6 typewritten, double-spaced pages — $100 maximum. ILLUSTRATIONS, black and white — $20 each; covers/color slides — $50.

Review for Religious: Room 428, 3601 Lindell Blvd., St. Louis, Mo. 63108. Ed., D.F.X. Meenan, S.J. Bimonthly, circulation 17,579; $11 per year.

ARTICLES, of interest to religious: 3,000-6,000 words — $6 per printed page.

St. Anthony Messenger: 1615 Republic St., Cincinnati, O. 45210. Ed., Rev. Norman Perry, O.F.M. Monthly, circulation 424,000; $12 per year.

FICTION: Written out of a totally Christian background, illuminating the truth of human nature for adults. No preachiness, sentimentality. FACT ARTICLES: 3,000-3,500 words. Outstanding personalities (must be based on personal interview). Information and comment on major movements in the Church: application of Christian faith to daily life; real-life solutions in the areas of a) family life, education; b) personal living (labor, leisure, art, psychology, spirituality). Human interest narrative. Humor. Photos and picture stories. Query letters welcome.

St. Joseph's Messenger and Advocate of the Blind: St. Joseph's Home, P.O. Box 288, Jersey City, N.J. 07303. Ed., Sr. Ursula Maphet, C.S.J. Quarterly, circulation 35,000; $4 per year.

FICTION, and ARTICLES, contemporary, mainstream themes, 500-1,500 words — 1¢ to 3¢ a word.

Salesian Missions: 148 Main St., New Rochelle, New York 10802. Ed., Rev. Edward J. Cappelletti, S.D.B. Quarterly, circulation 1,000,000; $1 per year.

ARTICLES: mission interest; pertaining to Salesian Society, life, spirit and educational system of St. John Bosco; adolescent interest and education — 5¢ a word and up. PHOTOGRAPHS — $6. Suggest queries before submitting material. Payment on acceptance. Early report.

Social Justice Review: 3835 Westminster Pl., St. Louis, Mo. 63108. Bimonthly, circulation 1,050; $12 per year.

ARTICLES: research, editorial and review: 2,000-4,000 words — $6 per column. No fiction.

Spiritual Life: 2131 Lincoln Rd., N.E., Washington, D.C. 20002. Eds., Revs. Steven Payne, O.C.D. and Christopher Latimer, O.C.D. Quarterly, circulation 18,000; $9 per year.

ARTICLES, must follow scope of magazine: 3,000-5,000 words — rate varies. Sample copy and instructions for writers sent upon request.

Spirituality Today: 1909 S. Ashland Ave., Chicago, Ill. 60608. Ed., Rev. Richard John Woods, O.P. Quarterly, circulation 5,000; $11 per year.

ARTICLES concerning any phase of the spiritual life: minimum 3,000-4,000 words — 1¢ a word. No fiction or poetry.

Today's Catholic Teacher: 2451 E. River Rd., Suite 200, Dayton, O. 45439. Monthly Sept. through May (exc. Dec.), circulation 65,000; $14.95 per year.

ARTICLES of professional and personal interest to teachers, administrators, pastors, parish councils and school board members concerning Catholic schools and CCD programs: 900-1,200 words, 1,500-3,000 words — $15-$75. Premium payment for superior content and writing presentation. Black and white photos helpful. Payment on publication.

Today's Parish: Twenty-Third Publications, P.O. Box 180, Mystic, Conn. 06355. Ed., Mary Carol Kendzia. Seven issues a year, circulation 22,000; $15 per year.

ARTICLES related to all aspects of parish life and ministry; minimum 1,200-1,500 words — $60 to $100. PHOTOS — $20; four-color cover photos $50.

Worship: St. John's Abbey, Collegeville, Minn. 56321. Ed., Rev. Aelred Tegels, O.S.B. Bimonthly, circulation 7,000; $17 per year; $18, foreign.

ARTICLES related to the engagement of the magazine in ongoing study of both the theoretical and pastoral dimensions of liturgy; examines historical traditions of worship in their doctrinal context, the experience of worship in Christian churches, the findings of contemporary theology, psychology, communications, cultural anthropology, and sociology insofar as they have a bearing on public worship: 5,000-8,000 words. No fiction or poetry.

FATHER THURSTON DAVIS, S.J.

Jesuit Father Thurston Davis, 72, died Sept. 16, 1986 of an apparent heart attack. He was the editor of *America* magazine from 1955 to 1968, founder — and leader until his death — of the John LaFarge Institute and the John Courtney Murray Forum, a consultant to the general secretary of the U.S. Catholic Conference from 1970 to 1978, dean of Fordham University, and a member of the board of Georgetown University. Because of his great service to men and women of the Catholic press, he was awarded the St. Francis de Sales Award of the Catholic Press Association in 1980.

RADIO, TELEVISION, THEATRE

Radio and Television

Christopher Radio Program: 15-minute interview-discussion series, "Christopher Closeup," weekly, on 236 stations; a one-minute "Christopher Thought for Today," daily, on 1,500 stations. Address: 12 E. 48th St., New York, N.Y. 10017.

Christopher TV Series, "Christopher Closeup": Originated in 1951. Half-hour and quarter-hour interviews in color, weekly, on 52 commercial stations, American Forces Network outlets, CBN and PTL syndicate stations and 41 cable systems, Address; 12 E. 48th St., New York, N.Y. 10017.

Crossroads (Radio): Originated in 1954 as the Hour of the Crucified, produced by the Passionist Priests and Brothers. Weekly, on nearly 129 stations. Address: 1089 Elm St., West Springfield, Mass. 01089.

Directions (TV): Premiered as a quarterly special in June, 1984. This one-hour program is a news-oriented approach to reporting the moral and religious issues reflected in the national and international community. The NCCB/USCC Department of Communication consults with ABC News in the production of this program and in the seasonal liturgical programs broadcast each year. Broadcast on approximately 100 stations. (ABC-TV).

For Our Times (TV): Originated in April 1979, this weekly half-hour series produced by CBS in a unique joint cooperative consultation with the Department of Communication, NCCB/USCC, the National Council of Churches and the New York Board of Rabbis focuses on the ethical and social challenges confronting American society today. Format: documentary and studio discussion (CBS-TV).

Guideline (Radio): Produced in cooperation with the Department of Communication, NCCB/USCC. Weekly program designed to set forth the teachings of the Catholic Church and to discuss issues the Church faces in the contemporary world; heard on approximately 65 stations (NBC).

On This Rock (Radio): Originated in 1941, produced in cooperation with the Department of Communication, NCCB/USCC. A 15-minute weekly program currently employing a youth-oriented music and commentary format; heard on more than 950 stations (ABC).

Sacred Heart Program (Radio, TV): Originated in 1939, operated by the Jesuits. Produces and syndicates nationally one TV program and nine radio programs each week on approximately 1,800 stations. Address: 3900 Westminster Place, St. Louis, Mo. 63108.

Religious Specials (TV): The NCCB/USCC Department of Communication consults in the production of four one-hour Catholic specials a year and additional seasonal liturgical services. The specials use a variety of formats and are broadcast on 100 stations (NBC-TV).

Communications Services

Eternal Word Television Network, Inc., 5817 Old Leeds Rd., Birmingham, Ala. 35210. Mother M. Angelica, P.C.P.A., foundress. More than 10 million viewers.

Father Justin Rosary Hour: Station F — Box 217, Buffalo, N.Y. 14212. Rev. Cornelian Dende, O.F.M. Conv., director.

Father Peyton's Family Theater Productions: Films for TV, for sale and rental. Address: 7201 Sunset Blvd., Hollywood, Calif. 90046.

Franciscan Advertising and Media Enterprises (F.A.M.E.): Produces and distributes media and advertising programs for religious education and evangelization. Address: 620 Route 3, Clifton, N.J. 07014.

Franciscan Communications: An award-winning religious producer of quality films, videos, filmstrips, media kits, phonograph records, audio cassettes and print materials for catechetical use in parishes and schools worldwide, distributed under the trade name TeleKETICS. Also produces TeleSPOTS and AudioSPOTS — public service messages for radio and TV. Address: 1229 South Santee St., Los Angeles, Calif. 90015.

Hispanic Telecommunications Network, Inc. (HTN): Produces *Nuestra Familia,* a national weekly Spanish-language TV series. Address: 130 Lewis, San Antonio, Tex. 78212.

Mary Productions: Originated in 1950. Offers royalty-free scripts for stage, film, radio and tape production. Audio and video tapes of lives of the saints and historical characters. Address: Mary Productions, Tomaso Pl., Apt. 212, Oakdale Dr., Middletown, N.J. 07748.

Oblate Media Images: 5901 West Main, Suite A, Belleville, Ill. 62223.

Passionist Communications, Inc.: Present Sunday Mass on TV seen in U.S. and available to dioceses and channels; publish "TV Prayer Guide," semi-annually. Address: 117 Harmon Ave., P.O. Box 440, Pelham, N.Y. 10803.

Paulist Communications: Contracts with dioceses and parishes to provide public service programs and spot series free to radio stations and scripts to priest-broadcasters; contacts stations for dioceses. Address: 2257 Barry Ave., Los Angeles, Calif. 90064.

Paulist Productions: Producers and distributor of the INSIGHT Film Series (available for TV and educational film series. Purchase and rental information available. Address: P.O. Box 1057 Pacific Palisades, Calif. 90272.

Real to Reel: 850 Sligo Ave., Suite 602, Silver Spring, Md. 20910.

St. Francis Association for Catholic Evangelism (F.A.C.E.): Founded in 1981. Produces "The Glory of God," a weekly evangelistic Catholic TV series aired in 5,000 cities in the U.S. and other countries and "Let Me Sow Love," a weekly and daily radio program aired on 50 commercial radio stations and the CTNA Radio Services. The programs are hosted by Father John Patrick Bertolucci, S.F.O.

The association also produces audio and video cassette tapes. Address: P.O. Box 8000, Steubenville, O. 43952.

That's the Spirit Productions, Inc.: Produces "That's the Spirit," a family show, in cooperation with Passionist Fathers. Available to dioceses, organizations or channels. Address: P.O. Box 440, Pelham, N.Y. 10803.

Catholic Telecommunications Network of America (CTNA): Satellite communications network of the Church in U.S. Address: Teleport One, The Teleport, Staten Island, N.Y. 10314.

Catholic Television Network (CTN): Instructional TV operations have been established in the following archdioceses and dioceses. Archdioceses are indicated by an asterisk.

Boston,* Mass.: Ms. Marianne Mazer, Director, 55 Chapel, Box 56, Newton 02160.

Brooklyn, N.Y.: Rev. Msgr. Michael J. Dempsey, Director, 1712 10th Ave., 11215.

Chicago,* Ill.: Mr. Kenneth P. Murr, Director, 2001 W. Devon Ave. 60659.

Detroit,* Mich.: Rev. Robert Humitz, Director, 305 Michigan Ave., Detroit, Mich. 48226.

Los Angeles,* Calif.: Mr. Steven J. Gorski, 1520 W. Ninth St. 90015.

New York,* N.Y.: Sr. M. Irene Fugazy, Director, Seminary Ave., Yonkers, N.Y. 10704.

Orange, Calif.: Rev. Jerome Henson, Director, 2811 E. Villa Real Dr., Orange, Calif. 92667.

Rockville Centre, N.Y.: Rev. Msgr. Thomas Hartman, Director, 1345 Admiral Lane, Uniondale, N.Y. 11553.

San Bernardino, Calif.: Ms. Clare Colella, Director, 1450 N. D St., San Bernardino, Calif. 92405.

San Francisco,* Calif. (Bay Area): Mr. Thomas A. Combellick, 324 Middlefield Rd., Menlo Park, Calif. 94025.

Unda-USA: A national professional Catholic association for broadcasters and allied communicators organized in 1972. It succeeded the Catholic Broadcasters Association of America which in 1948 had replaced the Catholic Forum of the Air organized in 1938. It is a member of the international Catholic association for radio and television known as Unda (the Latin word for "wave," symbolic of air waves of communication). Subgroups include Catholic Television Network, the Association of Catholic Radio and Television Syndicators, and the Association of Diocesan Directors. Unda-USA publishes a newsletter six times a year for members, produces "Real to Reel," a Catholic TV magazine, sponsors an annual general assembly and presents the Gabriel Awards annually for excellence in broadcasting. President, Dr. Maury R. Sheridan. National office: 850 Sligo Ave., Suite 602, Silver Spring, Md. 20910.

The Catholic Communications Foundation (CCF) was established by the Catholic Fraternal Benefit Societies in 1966 to lend support and assistance to development of the communications apostolate of the Church. The CCF, promotes the development of diocesan communications capabilities and funds a scholarship program at the Annual Institute for Religious Communications. CCF officers include Bishop Anthony G. Bosco, chairman of the board. Address: Suite 198, Box 9000, Carlsbad, Calif. 92008.

Theatre

Catholic University Drama Department: Established in 1937. Offers degree courses in theatre arts, produces five plays a year in The Hartke Theatre. Affiliated with National Players and Olney Theatre. Chairman of the department, William H. Graham. Address: Catholic University of America, Washington, D.C. 20064.

National Players: An operation of University Players, a non-profit organization affiliated with the Drama Department of the Catholic University. It originated in 1949 and is the oldest classical touring company in the U.S.

Olney Theatre Corporation: A non-profit organization affiliated with the Drama Department of Catholic University. It operates Olney Theatre, Olney, Md., an Equity theatre designated the State Summer Theatre of Maryland in 1978.

Catholic Actors' Guild of America, Inc.: Established in 1914 to provide material and spiritual assistance to people in the theatre. Has more than 500 members; publishes *The Call Board* bimonthly. Address: 1501 Broadway, Suite 2400, New York, N.Y. 10036.

DIOCESAN COMMUNICATIONS OFFICES, DIRECTORS

(Sources: *1986 Directory of Catholic Communications Personnel,* published by the Office of Public Affairs, USCC; *Official Catholic Directory;* NC News Service. Archdioceses are designated by an asterisk.)

Alabama: Birmingham — Rev. Martin Muller (Communications), Box 6147, Birmingham 35209.

Mobile* — Director of Communications, 400 Government St., Box 349, Mobile 36601.

Alaska: Anchorage* — Bro. Charles P. McBride, C.S.C. (Communications), 225 Cordova, Bldg. A, Anchorage 99501.

Fairbanks — c/o Catholic Bishop of North Alaska, 1316 Peger Rd., Fairbanks 99701. Rev. James Poole, S.J. (Radio-TV), Box 988, Nome 99762.

Juneau — Christine Rielley, (Ed., *Inside Passage*), 419 Sixth St., Room 230, Juneau 99801.

Arizona: Phoenix — Ms. Marge Injasoulian (Communications), 400 E. Monroe St., Phoenix 85004.

Tucson — Mr. Robert Nordmeyer (Communications), 1855 N. 6th Ave., Tucson 85705.

Arkansas: Little Rock — Director of Communications, 2500 N. Tyler St., Box 7417, Little Rock 72217.

California: Fresno — Mr. Joseph Jasmin (Information), Box 1668, Fresno 93717.

Los Angeles* — Rev. Joseph Battaglia (Communications), Sr. Gail Tenney, O.S.F., Mr. Steven Gorski (ETV), 1530 W. 9th St., Los Angeles 90015.

Monterey — Theodore Elisee (Communications Commission), P.O. Box 2079, Monterey 93942.

Oakland — Director of Public Relations, 2918 Lakeshore Ave., Dan Morris (Ed., *The Catholic*

Voice), 2900 Lakeshore Ave., Oakland 94610.

Orange — Mr. Thomas A. Fuentes (Communications), Box 2590, Newport Beach 92663.

Sacramento — Jose Ramirez (Communications), P.O. Box 19312, Sacramento 95819.

San Bernardino — Dan E. Pitre (Ed., *Inland Catholic*), Box 2788, San Bernardino 92405. Clare M. Colella (Electronic Communications), 1550 North "D" St., San Bernardino 92405.

San Diego — Rev. Stephen P. McCall (Communications), Box 80428, San Diego 92138.

San Francisco* — Rev. Miles O'Brien Riley (Communications), 441 Church St., San Francisco 94114.

San Jose — Rev. Eugene J. Boyle (Interreligious and Public Affairs), 7600 St. Joseph Ave., Los Altos 94022.

Santa Rosa — Rev. Anthony Di Russo (Communications), P.O. Box 1297, Santa Rosa 95402.

Stockton — Charles Goodman (Communications), Box 4237, Stockton 95204.

Colorado: Colorado Springs — Most Rev. Richard C. Hanifen, 29 W. Kiowa St., Colorado Springs 80903.

Denver* — Rev. C. B. Woodrich (Communications), 200 Josephine St., Box 1620, Denver 80206.

Pueblo — Ms. Geraldine Carrigan (Communications; Ed., *Catholic Crosswinds*), 1001 N. Grand Ave., Pueblo 81003.

Connecticut: Bridgeport — Rev. Nicholas V. Grieco (Communications), 238 Jewett Ave., Bridgeport 06606; Rev. Alfred J. Sienkiewicz (Radio-TV), 385 Scofieldtown Rd., Stamford 06903.

Hartford* — Rev. Edmund O'Brien (Communications), 785 Asylum Ave., Hartford 06105.

Norwich — Jacqueline M. Keller (Communications), 201 Hickory St., Norwich 06360.

Stamford (Ukrainian Diocese) — Rev. Lew Lubynsky, 303 Eddy Glover Blvd., New Britain 06053.

Delaware: Wilmington — Mr. F. Eugene Donnelly (Secretary, Communications), Box 2030, Wilmington 19899.

District of Columbia: Washington* — Rev. Raymond J. Boland (Delegate, Communications), Mr. Barrett McGurn (Director), Box 29260, Washington 20017.

Florida: Miami* — George Lezcano (Communications), Marjorie Donohue (Public Information), Rev. Jose P. Nickse (Radio-TV), 9401 Biscayne Blvd., Miami 33138.

Orlando — Mr. George Fournier (Communications), Box 2728, Orlando 32802.

Palm Beach — Rev. Leo F. Armbrust (Communications), 47 Southeast First Ave., Boca Raton 33432.

Pensacola-Tallahassee — Rev. Michael Mooney (Communications), P.O. Drawer 17329, Pensacola 32522.

St. Augustine — Sr. Carol Stovall, S.S.J. (Communications), Box 24000, Jacksonville 32241. Msgr. R. Joseph James (Chairman, Communications Commission), Rt. 3, Box 50, Williston 32696.

St. Petersburg — David MacNamara (Communications), Jeff Rago (Radio), Miss Jeanine Jacob (Catholic Media Center), Box 18081, Tampa 33679.

Venice — Sr. Luke Crawford, S.P. (Communications), P.O. Box 2006, Venice 34284.

Georgia: Atlanta* — Msgr. Noel C. Burtenshaw (Communications), 680 W. Peachtree St. N.W., Atlanta 30308.

Savannah — Rev. Joseph Stranc (Communications), 12 W. Jones Ave., Statesboro 30458. Mrs. Gillian Brown (Information), P.O. Box 8789, Savannah 31412.

Hawaii: Honolulu — Rev. James Drew (Communications), 1184 Bishop St., Honolulu 96813.

Idaho: Boise — Rev. David L. Riffle (Communications Center), 6003 Overland, Boise 83709.

Illinois: Belleville — Vicar General, The Catholic Center, 220 W. Lincoln St., Belleville 62221.

Chicago* — Sr. Joy Clough (Media Coordinator), Rev. Alphonse Spilly, C.PP.S. (Communications), 155 E. Superior St., Chicago 60611. Mr. Kenneth Murr (Catholic Television Center), 2011 W. Devon Ave., Chicago 60659. Miss Anne McCarthy (Radio-TV), 25 W. Chicago Ave., Chicago 60610.

Joliet — Rev. William F. Irwin (Communications), St. Charles Borromeo Pastoral Center, Rt. 53 and Airport Rd., Romeoville 60441.

Peoria — Mr. Robert England (Communications), 1301 N.E. Glendale,, Peoria 61603.

Rockford — Rev. David D. Kagan (Communications), 850 N. Church St., Rockford 61103.

St. Nicholas in Chicago for Ukrainians — Msgr. Jaroslav Swyschuk (Eastern Rite Information Bureau), 2208 W. Chicago Ave., Chicago 60622.

Springfield — Office for Communications, 514 E. Lawrence, Springfield 62703.

Indiana: Evansville — Rev. Joseph L. Ziliak (Information), P.O. Box 4169, Evansville 47711.

Fort Wayne-South Bend — Box 11169, Fort Wayne 46856.

Gary — Mr. Brian T. Olszewski (Communications), 9292 Broadway, Merrillville, Ind. 46410.

Indianapolis* — Mr. Charles J. Schisla (Communications), Box 1410, Indianapolis 46206.

Lafayette — P.O. Box 1603, Lafayette 47902.

Iowa: Davenport — Rev. Francis C. Henricksen (Communications), P.O. Box 460, Davenport 52805. Sr. Hillary Mullany, O.S.F. (Television), 2706 Gaines St., Davenport 52804.

Des Moines — Sr. Mira Mosle, B.V.M. (Communications), 818 Fifth Ave., Box 1816, Des Moines 50306.

Dubuque* — Sr. Carol Hoverman (Communications), 1229 Mt. Loretta Ave., Box 479, Dubuque 52001.

Sioux City — Mr. Joe Maher (Communications), 1825 Jackson St., P.O. Box 5079, Sioux City 51102.

Kansas: Dodge City — Communications Office, Box 849, Dodge City 67801.

Kansas City* — Rev. William Maher (Ed., *The Leaven*), Box 2329, Kansas City 66110.

Salina — Msgr. James Hake (Chancellor), Box 980, Salina 67402.

Wichita — Rev. Arthur A. Busch (Communications), 424 N. Broadway, Wichita 67202.

Kentucky: Covington — Sr. Colleen Winston, O.S.B. (Communications), Box 192, Covington 41012.

Louisville* — Rev. George N. Rice (Communications), 1951 Bishop Lane, Suite 407, Louisville 40218.

Owensboro — Mel Howard (Communications), 4005 Frederica St., Owensboro 42301.

Louisiana: Alexandria-Shreveport — Msgr. Frederick J. Lyons (Public Affairs), Mr. Al Nassif (Information), Mr. Ronald Hines (Electronic Media), Box 7417, Alexandria 71306.

Baton Rouge — Mr. Bob Furlow (Communications), P.O. Box 2028, Baton Rouge 70821.

Houma-Thibodaux — Mr. Louis Aguirre (Communications, Ed., *The Bayou Catholic*), Box 9077, Houma 70361.

Lafayette — Robert R. Breaux (Communications), Box 3223, Lafayette 70502.

Lake Charles — Mr. Truman Stacey (Diocesan News), 834 Ryan St., Lake Charles 70601.

New Orleans* — Mr. Thomas M. Finney (Public Relations), 7887 Walmsley Ave., New Orleans 70125. Mr. Jerry Romig (TV), 2929 S. Carrollton Ave., New Orleans 70118.

Maine: Portland — Mr. Marc R. Mutty (Communications), 510 Ocean Ave., Portland 04103.

Maryland: Baltimore* — Director of Communications, 320 Cathedral St., Baltimore 21201.

Massachusetts: Boston* — Rev. Peter V. Conley (Communications), 49 Franklin St., Boston 02110; Rev. Francis T. McFarland (Radio-TV), 55 Chapel St., Box 56, Newton 02160.

Fall River — Rev. John F. Moore (Communications), 410 Highland Ave., Fall River 02722; Rev. John F. Hogan, (TV), 494 Slocum Rd., N. Dartmouth 02747.

Springfield — Michael Graziano (Communications), 1089 Elm St., W. Springfield 01089.

Worcester — Rev. John W. Barrett (Communications), 49 Elm St., Worcester 01609.

Melkite Eparchy of Newton — Rev. Albert Gorayeb (Media Communications), 1244 McBride Ave., W. Paterson, N.J. 07424.

Michigan: Detroit* — Mr. Jay M. Berman (Communications), 305 Michigan Ave., Detroit 48226.

Gaylord — Betty J. Ballou (Communications), Box 1020, Gaylord 49735.

Grand Rapids — Michael G. Ghering (Communications), 660 Burton St. S.E., Grand Rapids 49507.

Kalamazoo — Office of Communications, 215 N. Westnedge Ave., Box 949, Kalamazoo 49005.

Lansing — Rev. Donald L. Eder (Communications), 300 W. Ottawa St., Lansing 48933.

Marquette — Gregory B. Bell (Communications), Box 548, 347 Rock St., Marquette 49855.

Saginaw — Rev. David Parsch (Communications), 5800 Weiss St., Saginaw 48603.

Minnesota: Crookston — Rev. Michael Patnode (Information), Rev. Gerald Noesen (Radio-TV), Box 610, Crookston 56716.

Duluth — Mr. Keith O. Bower (Information), 215 W. 4th St., Duluth 55806.

New Ulm — Paula Marti (Communications), 400 Chancery Dr., New Ulm 56073.

St. Cloud — Ms. Rosemary Borgert (Communications), 305 7th Ave. N., Suite 207, St. Cloud 56301.

St. Paul and Minneapolis* — Ms. Joan Bernet (Communications), 226 Summit Ave., St. Paul 55102.

Winona — Ivan Kubista (Communications), 55 West Sanborn, Winona 55987.

Mississippi: Biloxi — Rev. James Russell (Communications), P.O. Box 1189, Biloxi 39533.

Jackson — Director of Communications, Box 2248, Jackson 39225.

Missouri: Jefferson City — Mr. Mark Saucier (Communications), Box 417, 613 Clark St., Jefferson City 65102.

Kansas City-St. Joseph — Rev. John C. Weiss (Communications), 1357 N.E. 42nd Terr., Kansas City 64116.

St. Louis* — Rev. Edward J. Sudekum (Ed., *St. Louis Review*), 462 N. Tyler, St. Louis 63108; Rev. Joseph M. O'Brien (Radio-TV), 9229 Lackland Rd., St. Louis 63114.

Springfield-Cape Girardeau — Mrs. Marilyn Vydra (Communications), P.O. Box 1957 SSS, Springfield 65806.

Montana: Great Falls-Billings — Kenneth V. Egan (Communications), Box 1399, Great Falls 59403.

Helena — Rev. John W. Robertson (Chancellor, Communications), Box 1729, Helena 59624.

Nebraska: Grand Island — Rev. Robert E. Wiest (Communications), P.O. Box 37, Wood River 68883.

Lincoln — Rev. James D. Dawson (Information), Box 80328, Lincoln 68501.

Omaha* — Rev. Mel Rempe (Communications), 100 N. 62nd St., Omaha 68132.

Nevada: Reno-Las Vegas — Rev. Gilbert J. Canuel, Jr., Chancellor, Box 1211, Reno 89504.

New Hampshire: Manchester — Richard B. Carozza (Communications), 153 Ash St., Manchester 03105.

New Jersey: Camden — Rev. Roger E. McGrath (Communications), Box 709, Camden 08101.

Metuchen — Rev. Michael J. Corona, P.O. Box 191, Metuchen 08840.

Newark* — Director, Information Services and Public Affairs, 31 Mulberry St., Newark 07102.

Passaic (Byzantine Rite Eparchy) — Msgr. Robert G. Moneta (*Eastern Catholic Life*), 101 Market St., Passaic 07055.

Paterson — Tim Manning (Communications), Box 1595, Clifton, N.J. 07015.

Trenton — Rev. Joseph C. Glass (Communications), 315 Lowell Ave., P.O. Box 3095, Trenton 08619.

New Mexico: Gallup — Rev. Cormac Antram, O.F.M. (Communications, Radio-TV), P.O. Box 517, Kayenta 86033.

Las Cruces — Rev. Robert Power (Communications), P.O. Box 16318, Las Cruces 88004.

Santa Fe* — Rev. Jack Oster, S.J. (Communications-Media), 7208 Arvada N.E., Albuquerque 87110.

New York: Albany — Rev. Michael Farano (Information), P. O. Box 6297, Quail Sta., Albany 12206. Rev. Walter J. Laskos, O.F.M. (Media Operations), 40 N. Main Ave., Albany 12203.

Brooklyn — Mr. Frank DeRosa (Information), Box C, Brooklyn 11202.

Buffalo — Rev. David M. Lee (Communications), 100 S. Elmwood Dr., Buffalo 14202.

New York* — Rev. Peter G. Finn (Communications), Tony Dora (Hispanic Communications), 1011 First Ave., New York, N.Y. 10022. Sr. Irene Fugazy (Instructional TV), Seminary Ave., Yonkers, 10704.

Ogdensburg — Rev. Msgr. David W. Stinebrickner (Information), 622 Washington St., Ogdensburg 13669; Rev. Bruce T. Favreau (Radio-TV), St. Mary's Church, 521 James St., Clayton 13624.

Rochester — Rev. George Norton (Information), 1150 Buffalo Rd., Rochester 14624.

Rockville Centre — Rev. Msgr. Francis J. Maniscalco (Communications, Information), Box 700, Hempstead 11551; Rev. Msgr. Thomas J. Hartman (Radio-TV), 1345 Admiral Lane, Uniondale 11553.

St. Maron Diocese (Maronite Rite) — Rev. Richard Saad, 836 8th St. S., Birmingham, Ala. 35256.

Syracuse — Mr. Ronald D. Smith (Communications), P.O. Box 511, Syracuse 13201.

North Carolina: Charlotte — Director of Communications, 1524 E. Moorehead St., Charlotte 28207.

Raleigh — Rev. Joseph G. Vetter (Communications), 300 Cardinal Gibbons Dr., Raleigh 27606.

North Dakota: Bismarck — Rev. John J. Owens (Communications), P.O. Box 1137, Bismarck 58502.

Fargo — Box 1750, Fargo 58107.

Ohio: Cincinnati* — Rev. Theodore Kosse (Acting Dir., Communications; Radio-TV), 100 E. 8th St., Cincinnati 45202.

Cleveland — Rev. Michael G. Dimengo (Communications), Mr. J. Jerome Lackamp (Radio-TV), Mr. Patrick DiSalvatore (Catholic Communications Center), 1027 Superior Ave., Cleveland 44114.

Columbus — Rev. James P. Hanley (Vicar, Communications), Fr. Thomas Holahan, C.S.P. (Director), Susan Linebaugh (Public Relations, Information), 197 E. Gay St., Columbus 43215.

Parma (Byzantine Rite Eparchy) — Rev. Michael Hayduk (Communications), 5390 W. 220th St., Fairview Park 44126.

St. Josaphat in Parma (Ukrainian) — Most Rev. Robert M. Moskal, P.O. Box 347180, Parma 44134.

Steubenville — Rev. Gerald E. Calovini, Box 969, Steubenville 43952.

Toledo — Mr. Jim Richards (Communications), 2544 Parkwood Ave., Toledo 43610.

Youngstown — Rev. Bernard Bonnot (Communications), Miss Jean M. Nero (Public/Media Relations), 144 W. Wood St., Youngstown 44503. Mitch Stanley (Telecommunications Center), Box 430, Canfield 44406.

Oklahoma: Oklahoma City* — Rev. David F. Monahan (Communications), Box 32180, Oklahoma City 73123.

Tulsa — Mr. Tom J. Smith (Communications), Box 2009, Tulsa 74101.

Oregon: Baker — Rev. Joseph B. Hayes, Sacred Heart Church, 815 High St., Klamath Falls 97601.

Portland* — Robert Riler (Communications), 2838 E. Burnside St., Portland 97214.

Pennsylvania: Allentown — Rev. Stanley T. Sosnowski (Information), 202 N. 17th St., Box F, Allentown 18105. Rev. Joseph T. Whalen (Radio-TV), 22 S. Catawissa St., Mahanoy City 17948.

Altoona-Johnstown — Msgr. Philip Saylor (Information), Box 413 Logan Blvd., Hollidaysburg 16648.

Erie — Rev. Henry A. Kriegel (Communications), 515 State St., Erie 16512. Rev. Thomas McSweeney (TV), Gannon University, 703 Peach St. Erie 16541.

Greensburg — Mrs. Alice Laurich (Communications), Box 850, Greensburg 15601.

Harrisburg — Joseph G. Aponick (Communications), 4800 Union Deposit Rd., Box 3557, Harrisburg 17105.

Philadelphia* — Rev. John J. Sibel (Communications), 222 North 17th St., Philadelphia 19103.

Philadelphia* (Ukrainian) — Rev. Ronald Popivchak, Box 126, Bridgeport 19405.

Pittsburgh* (Byzantine Rite) — Msgr. Edward V. Rosack (Information), 624 Park Rd., Ambridge 15003.

Pittsburgh — Rev. Ronald P. Lengwin (Communications), 111 Boulevard of the Allies, Pittsburgh 15222.

Scranton — Maria Orzel (Communications), 400 Wyoming Ave., Scranton 18503.

Rhode Island: Providence — Marianne Postiglione, R.S.M. (Communications), Gilles D. Dery (Media Center), One Cathedral Square, Providence 02903.

South Carolina: Charleston — Dr. Paul C. Beach (Communications), Box 818, Charleston 29402.

South Dakota: Rapid City — Bette Traill, Box 678, Rapid City 57709.

Sioux Falls — Paul Sadek (Communications), 3100 W. 41st St., Suite 205, Sioux Falls 57105.

Tennessee: Memphis — Gary Honnert (Communications), 1325 Jefferson Ave., Memphis 38104.

Nashville — Mr. Joseph A. Sweat (Communications, Public Relations), 2400 21st Ave. S., Nashville 37212.

Texas: Amarillo — Rev. Michael Wood (Communications), P.O. Box 28, Stratford 79084.

Austin — Ms. Bertha Lopez Paskos (Information Services), Box 13327, Austin 78711.

Beaumont — Rev. James Vanderholt (Communications), P.O. Box 3948, Beaumont 77704.

Brownsville — Sarah E. Rodriguez (Telecommunication-Information) P.O. Box 2147, Harlingen 78551.

Corpus Christi — Rev. Robert E. Freeman (Communications), Sr. Janie Barrera (Radio-TV) 1200 Lantana St., Corpus Christi 78407.

Dallas — Steve Landregan (Communications) Patricia Martin (ETV), P.O. Box 190507, Dallas 75219.

El Paso — Mr. Andrew Sparke (Parochial Schools TV), 1101 Birch St., El Paso 79930.

Fort Worth — Rev. Reynold Matus (Communications), 3508 Maurice Ave., Fort Worth 76111.

Galveston-Houston — Msgr. John L. Fos, 170

San Jacinto St., Box 1878, Houston 77002; Rev. Bert Akers, S.J. (Radio-TV), Box 907, Houston 77001.

Lubbock — Mr. Leroy Behnke (Communications), Box 98700, Lubbock 79499.

San Angelo — Rev. Maurice J. Voity (Communications, Public Relations), Box 1829, San Angelo 76902.

San Antonio* — Richard J. Hemberger (Television), 2718 W. Woodlawn Ave., San Antonio 78228.

Victoria — Msgr. Thomas C. McLaughlin (Acting Dir., Communications), P.O. Box 4708, Victoria 77903.

Utah: Salt Lake City — Sr. Margaret Stechschulte, O.P. (Communications Media), 27C St., Salt Lake City 84103.

Vermont: Burlington — Rev. Joseph T. Sullivan (Communications), 351 North Ave., Burlington 05401.

Virginia: Arlington — Ellen McCloskey (Communications), 200 N. Glebe Rd., Arlington 22203.

Richmond — Mr. Bob Edwards (Communications), 811 Cathedral Pl., Richmond 23220.

Washington: Seattle* — Dr. Maury Sheridan, 910 Marion St., Seattle 98104.

Spokane — Rev. Michael J. Savelesky (Communications), Box 1453, Spokane 99210.

Yakima — Rev. P. J. Auve, Pastoral Office, Box 505, Yakima 98907.

West Virginia: Wheeling-Charleston — Mr. Mark W. Welsh, 1300 Byron St., Box 230, Wheeling 26003.

Wisconsin: Green Bay — Mr. Tony Kuick (Communications), Box 1825, Green Bay 54305.

La Crosse — Rev. Bernard McGarty (Communications), Box 4004, La Crosse 54602.

Madison — Maureen Quinn (Communications), 3577 High Point Rd., Rt. 2, Madison 53719.

Milwaukee* — Sr. Mary Luke Baldwin, S.S.N.D. (Communications), Box 2018, Milwaukee 53201.

Superior — Rev. Robert Urban (Information), 1512 N. 12th St., Superior 54880.

Wyoming: Cheyenne — Sally Michalov (Information), P.O. Box 4279, Casper 82604

Archdiocese for Military Services: Most Rev. Joseph T. Dimino (Communications), 962 Wayne Ave., Silver Spring, Md. 20910.

Delaware Valley Catholic Office for Television and Radio: Interdiocesan agency of the Archdiocese of Philadelphia, the dioceses of Camden and Trenton, N.J. and Wilmington, Del. Address: 222 North 17th St., Philadelphia, Pa. 19103.

Other Communications Offices

International Mission Radio Association: Rev. Jude Bradley, O.S.B., treasurer-administrator, St. Paul's Abbey, Newton, N.J. 07860.

Jesuits in Communication (JESCOM): Rev. Joseph J. McHugh, S.J., executive secretary, Suite 300, 1424 16th St. N.W., Washington, D.C. 20036.

Maryknoll Media Relations: Rev. Donald Doherty, M.M., director, Maryknoll Fathers and Brothers, Maryknoll, N.Y. 10545.

National Franciscan Communications Conference: Rev. James J. Gardiner, S.A., president, St. Joseph's Church, 371 Sixth Ave., New York, N.Y. 10014.

National Office

The National Catholic Office for Information (NCOI), successor to the NCWC Bureau of Information, serves as the official spokesman for both the United States Catholic Conference and the National Conference of Catholic Bishops in relating to the news media. The NCOI is part of the NCCB USCC Office for Public Affairs, directed by Russell Shaw.

The office prepares and distributes news releases; handles inquiries from the press; arranges news media coverage of bishops' meetings; offers public information and public relations counsel on a day-to-day basis to the office of the general secretary of the USCC and the NCCB, and to other agencies and staff members; performs a number of special research and writing functions on behalf of the conferences and their staffs.

The office also provides services and coordination for diocesan information offices.

William Ryan is director of the office, which is located at 1312 Massachusetts Ave. N.W., Washington, D.C. 20005.

PUBLISHERS

(Principal source: *Catholic Press Directory*, 1986.)

Abbey Press, St. Meinrad, Ind. 47577.

ACTA Foundation, 4848 N. Clark St., Chicago, Ill. 60640.

Affirmation Books, 109 Woodland St., Natick, Mass. 02215.

Alba House, 2187 Victory Blvd., Staten Island, N.Y. 10314.

Alleluia Press, 672 Franklin Turnpike, Allendale, N.J. 07401.

American Catholic Press, 1223 Rossell Ave., Oak Park, Ill. 60302.

Ave Maria Press, Notre Dame, Ind. 46556.

Benziger Publishing Co., 17337 Ventura Blvd., Encino, Calif. 91316.

Wm. C. Brown Company Publishers, 2460 Kerper Blvd., Dubuque, Ia. 52001.

Catholic Book Publishing, 257 W. 17th St., New York, N.Y. 10011.

Catholic Home Study Institute, 9 Loudoun St. S.E., Leesburg, Va. 22075.

Catholic University of America Press, 620 Michigan Ave. N.E., Washington, D.C. 20064.

Christian Classics, Inc., 73 West Main St., P.O. Box 30, Westminster, Md. 21157.

Claretian Publications, 221 W. Madison St., Chicago, Ill. 60606.

Costello Publishing Co., Box 9, Northport, N.Y. 11768.

Crossroad Publishing Co., 370 Lexington Ave., New York, N.Y. 10017.

Daughters of St. Paul, 50 St. Paul's Ave., Jamaica Plain, Boston, Mass. 02130.

Dimension Books, Inc., 1 Summit St., Rockaway, N.J. 07866.

Don Bosco Multimedia, 475 North Ave., Box T, New Rochelle, N.Y. 10802.

Doubleday and Co., Inc., 245 Park Ave., New York, N.Y. 10167.

Fordham University Press, University Box L, Bronx, N.Y. 10458.

Franciscan Herald Press, 1434 W. 51st St. Chicago, Ill. 60609.

Georgetown University Press, Georgetown Univ., Washington, D.C. 20057.

The K.S. Giniger Co., Inc., 1133 Broadway, Suite 1301, New York, N.Y. 10010.

Michael Glazier, Inc., 1935 Fourth St., Wilmington, Del. 19805.

Ignatius Press, P.O. Box 18990, San Francisco, Calif. 94118.

Kosmos Publishing Co., Inc. 3700 Oakview Terr. N.E., Washington, D.C. 20017.

Liguori Publications, One Liguori Dr., Liguori, Mo. 63057.

The Liturgical Press, St. John's Abbey, Collegeville, Minn. 56321.

Living Flame Press, 123 Birch Hill Rd., Locust Valley, N.Y. 11560.

Loyola University Press, 3441 N. Ashland Ave., Chicago, Ill. 60657.

Lumen Christi Press, 2229 Pech Rd., Houston, Tex. 77055.

McGrath Publishing Co., 6231 Leesburg Pike, Suite 404, Falls Church, Va. 22044.

Marquette University Press, 1324 W. Wisconsin Ave., Milwaukee, Wis. 53233.

New City Press, 206 Skillman Ave., Brooklyn, N.Y. 11211.

Orbis Books, Maryknoll, N.Y. 10545.

Our Sunday Visitor, Inc., 200 Noll Plaza, Huntington, Ind. 46750.

Paulist Press, 997 Macarthur Blvd., Mahwah, N.J. 07430.

Peter Li, Inc. (Pflaum Press Imprint), 2451 East River Rd., Dayton, O. 45439.

Pope John XXIII Medical-Moral Research and Education Center, 186 Forbes Rd., Braintree, Mass. 02184.

Pueblo Publishing Co., 100 W. 32nd St., New York, N.Y. 10001.

Resource Publications, Inc., 160 E. Virginia St., No. 290, San Jose, Calif. 95112.

William H. Sadlier, Inc., 11 Park Place, New York, N.Y. 10007.

St. Anthony Messenger Press, 1615 Republic St., Cincinnati, O. 45210.

St. Bede's Publications, P.O. Box 545, Petersham, Mass. 01366.

Saint Mary's Press, Terrace Heights, Winona, Minn. 55987.

Scepter Press, 481 Main St., Suite 401, New Rochelle, N.Y. 10801.

Servant Publications, Box 8617, Ann Arbor, Mich. 48107.

Silver Burdett Company, 250 James St. CN-1918, Morristown, N.J. 07960.

Templegate Publishers, 302 E. Adams St., Springfield, Ill. 62705.

Thomas More Association, 223 W. Erie St., Chicago, Ill. 60610.

Thomas Nelson Publishers (Catholic Bible Press imprint), P.O. Box 141000, Nashville, Tenn. 37214.

Twenty-Third Publications, 185 Willow St., Mystic, Conn. 06355.

USCC Office of Publishing Services, 1312 Massachusetts Ave. N.W., Washington, D.C. 20005.

University of Notre Dame Press, P.O. Box L, Notre Dame, Ind. 46556.

Winston-Derek Publishers, Inc., P.O. Box 90883, Nashville, Tenn. 37209.

Winston Press, Inc., 600 First Ave. N., Suite 800, Minneapolis, Minn. 55403.

SHRINES AND PLACES OF HISTORIC INTEREST IN THE UNITED STATES

(Principal source: Catholic Almanac Survey.)

Listed below, according to state, are shrines, other centers of devotion and some places of historic interest with special significance for Catholics. The list is necessarily incomplete because of space limitations.

Information includes: name and location of shrine or place of interest, date of foundation, sponsoring agency or group, and address for more information.

Alabama: St. Jude Church of the City of St. Jude, Montgomery (1934; dedicated, 1938); Mobile Archdiocese. Address: 2048 W. Fairview Ave., Montgomery, Ala. 36196.

• Shrine of the Most Blessed Trinity, Holy Trinity (1924); Missionary Servants of the Most Blessed Trinity. Address: Holy Trinity, Ala. 36859.

Arizona: Chapel of the Holy Cross, in Oak Creek Canyon, Sedona (1956); Phoenix Diocese: P.O. Box 1043, Sedona, Ariz. 86336.

• Mission San Francis Xavier del Bac, near Tucson (1700); National Historic Landmark;

Franciscan Friars and Tucson Diocese; Address: Route 11, Box 645, Tucson, Ariz. 85746.

• Shrine of St. Joseph of the Mountains, Yarnell (1939); Catholic Action League of Arizona. Address: P.O. Box 98, Yarnell, Ariz. 65362.

California: Mission San Diego del Alcala (July 16, 1769); first of the 21 Franciscan missions of Upper California; Minor Basilica; National Historic Landmark; San Diego Diocese. Address: 1018 San Diego Mission Rd., San Diego 92108.

• Carmel Mission (Mission San Carlos Borromeo del Rio Carmelo), Carmel by the Sea (June 3, 1770); Monterey Diocese. Address: 3080 Rio Rd., Carmel, Calif. 93923.

• Old Mission San Luis Obispo de Tolosa, San Luis Obispo (Sept. 1, 1772); Monterey Diocese (Parish Church). Address: P.O. Box 1483, San Luis Obispo, Calif. 93402.

• San Gabriel Mission, San Gabriel (Sept. 8, 1771); Los Angeles Archdiocese (Parish Church, staffed by Claretians). Address: 537 W. Mission, San Gabriel, Calif. 91776.

• Mission San Francisco de Asis (Oct. 9, 1776) and Mission Dolores Basilica (1860s); San Francisco Archdiocese. Address: 3321 Sixteenth St., San Francisco, Calif. 94114.

• Mission San Juan Capistrano, San Juan Capistrano (Nov. 1, 1776); Orange Diocese. Address: 31882 Camino Capistrano, Suite 218, San Juan Capistrano, Calif. 92675.

• Old Mission Santa Barbara, Santa Barbara (Dec. 4, 1786); National Historic Landmark; Franciscan Friars. Address: 2201 Laguna St., Santa Barbara, Calif. 93105.

• Old Mission San Juan Bautista, San Juan Bautista (June 24, 1797); Monterey Diocese (Parish Church). Address: P.O. Box 410, San Juan Bautista, Calif. 95045.

• Mission San Miguel, San Miguel (July 25, 1797); Franciscan Friars. Address: P.O. Box 69, San Miguel, Calif. 93451.

• Old Mission Santa Ines, Solvang (1804); Los Angeles Archdiocese (Parish Church). Address: P.O. Box 408, Solvang, Calif. 93463.

Franciscan Friars founded 21 missions in California. Ten are listed above; for the others, see p. 386.

• Shrine of Our Lady of Sorrows, Colusa (1883): Sacramento Diocese. Address: c/o Our Lady of Lourdes Church, 745 Ware Ave., Colusa, Calif. 95932.

Connecticut: Lourdes in Litchfield (Shrine Grotto of Our Lady of Lourdes), Litchfield (1958); Montfort Missionaries. Address: P.O. Box 667, Litchfield, Conn. 06759.

• Shrine of the Infant of Prague, New Haven (1945); Dominican Friars. Address: P.O. Box 1202, 5 Hillhouse Ave., New Haven, Conn. 06505.

District of Columbia: Mount St. Sepulchre, Franciscan Monastery of the Holy Land (1897; church dedicated, 1899); Order of Friars Minor. Address: 1400 Quincy St. N.E., Washington, D.C. 20017.

• National Shrine of the Immaculate Conception. See Index for separate entry.

Florida: Our Lady of La Leche Shrine and Mission of Nombre de Dios, Saint Augustine (1565); St. Augustine Diocese. Address: P.O. Box 3845, St. Augustine, Fla. 32084.

• Our Lady of Guadalupe, Patroness of Unborn, Miami (1981; dedicated, 1984); Respect Life Apostolate, Miami Archdiocese. Address: P.O. Box 3235, Miami, Fla. 33169.

Illinois: Holy Family Log Church, Cahokia (1799); Belleville Diocese (Parish Church). Address: 116 Church St., Cahokia, Ill. 62206.

• National Shrine of Our Lady of the Snows, Belleville (1958); Missionary Oblates of Mary Immaculate. Address: 9500 W. Illinois, Rt. 15, Belleville, Ill. 62223.

• National Shrine of St. Jude, Chicago (1929); located in Our Lady of Guadalupe Church, founded and staffed by Claretians. Address: 221 W. Madison St., Chicago, Ill. 60606.

• Shrine of St. Jude Thaddeus, Chicago (1929) located in St. Pius V Church, staffed by Dominicans,

Central Province. Address: 1909 S. Ashland Ave., Chicago, Ill. 60608.

Indiana: Our Lady of Monte Cassino Shrine, St. Meinrad (1870); Benedictines. Address: St. Meinrad Archabbey, St. Meinrad, Ind. 47577.

• Old Cathedral (Basilica of St. Francis Xavier), Vincennes (1826, parish records go back to 1749); Evansville Diocese. Minor Basilica, 1970. Address: 205 Church St., Vincennes, Ind. 47591.

Iowa: Grotto of the Redemption, West Bend (1912); Sts. Peter and Paul Church, Sioux City Diocese. Mailing address: P.O. Box 376, West Bend, Iowa 50597.

Louisiana: National Shrine of Our Lady of Prompt Succor, New Orleans (1810); located in the Chapel of the Ursuline Convent (a National Historic Landmark). Address: 2635 State St., New Orleans, La. 70118.

• Shrine of St. Roch, New Orleans (1876); located in St. Roch's *Campo Santo* (Cemetery); New Orleans Archdiocese. Address: 1725 St. Roch Ave., New Orleans, La. 70117.

Maryland: National Shrine of St. Elizabeth Ann Seton, Emmitsburg (1975); Daughters of Charity of St. Vincent de Paul. Address: 333 South Seton Ave., Emmitsburg, Md. 21727.

• St. Francis Xavier Shrine, "Old Bohemia", near Warwick (1704), located in Wilmington, Del., Diocese; restoration under auspices of Old Bohemia Historical Society, Inc. Address: P.O. Box 61, Warwick, Md. 21912.

• St. Anthony Shrine, Emmitsburg (1893); attached to St. Anthony Parish, Baltimore Archdiocese. Address: 16150 St. Anthony Rd., Emmitsburg, Md. 21727.

Massachusetts: National Shrine of Our Lady of La Salette, Ipswich (1945); Missionaries of Our Lady of La Salette. Address: 315 Topsfield Rd., Ipswich, Mass. 01938.

• Our Lady of Fatima Shrine, Holliston (1950); Xaverian Missionaries. Address: 101 Summer St. Holliston, Mass. 01746.

• St. Anthony Shrine, Boston (1947); downtown Service Church with shrine; Boston Archdiocese and Franciscans of Holy Name Province. Address: 100 Arch St., Boston, Mass. 02107.

• Saint Clement's Eucharistic Shrine, Boston (1945); Boston Archdiocese, staffed by Oblates of Virgin Mary. Address: 1105 Boylston St., Boston, Mass. 02215.

Missouri: National Shrine of Our Lady of the Miraculous Medal, Perryville; located in St. Mary of the Barrens Church (1837); Vincentians. Address: 1811 W. St. Joseph St., Perryville, Mo. 63775.

• Shrine of Our Lady of Sorrows, Starkenburg (1887; shrine building, 1910); Jefferson City Diocese. Address: c/o Risen Savior Parish, Rhineland, Mo. 65069.

New Hampshire: Our Lady of Grace, Colebrook (1948); Oblates of Mary Immaculate. Address: R.R. 1, Box 521, Colebrook, N.H. 03576.

• Shrine to Our Lady of La Salette, Enfield

(1951); Missionaries of Our Lady of La Salette. Address: Rt. 4A, P.O. Box 420, Enfield, N.H. 03748.

New Jersey: National Blue Army Shrine of Immaculate Heart of Mary, Washington (1978); World Apostolate of Fatima (The Blue Army). Address: Washington, N.J. 07882.

• Shrine of St. Joseph, Stirling (1924); Missionary Servants of the Most Blessed Trinity. Address: 1050 Long Hill Rd., Stirling, N.J. 07980.

New Mexico: St. Augustine Mission, Isleta (1613); Santa Fe Archdiocese. Address: P.O. Box 463, Isleta, N. Mex. 87022.

• San Miguel Chapel, Santa Fe (1610); Private Chapel; Brothers of the Christian Schools. Address: c/o 100 Diringo Rd., Santa Fe, N. Mex. 87501.

New York: National Shrine of Bl. Kateri Tekakwitha, Fonda (1938); Order of Friars Minor Conventual. Address: P.O. Box 627, Fonda, N.Y. 12068.

• Infant Jesus Shrine, North Tonawanda (1958); Society of the Catholic Apostolate. Address: 3452 Niagara Falls Blvd., N. Tonawanda, N.Y. 14120.

• Marian Shrine (National Shrine of Mary Help of Christians), West Haverstraw (1953); Salesians of St. John Bosco. Address: Filor's Lane, W. Haverstraw, N.Y. 10993.

• National Shrine of St. Frances Xavier Cabrini, New York (1938); Missionary Sisters of the Sacred Heart. Address: 701 Fort Washington Ave., New York, N.Y. 10040.

• Original Shrine of St. Ann in New York City (1892); located in St. Jean Baptiste Church; Blessed Sacrament Fathers. Address: 184 E. 76th St., New York, N.Y. 10021.

• Our Lady of Fatima Shrine, Youngstown (1954); Barnabite Fathers. Address: 1023 Swan Rd., Youngstown, N.Y. 14174.

• Our Lady of Victory National Shrine, Lackawanna (1926); Minor Basilica; Our Lady of Victory Homes of Charity. Address: 767 Ridge Rd., Lackawanna, N.Y. 14218.

• Shrine Church of Our Lady of Mt. Carmel, Brooklyn (1888); Brooklyn Diocese (Parish Church). Address: 275 N. 8th St., Brooklyn, N.Y. 11218.

• Shrine of Our Lady of Martyrs, Auriesville (1885); Society of Jesus. Address: Auriesville, N.Y. 12016.

• Shrine of Our Lady of the Island, Eastport (1975); Montfort Missionaries. Address: Box 31, Eastport, L.I., 11941.

Ohio: Basilica and National Shrine of Our Lady of Consolation, Carey (1867); Minor Basilica; Toledo Diocese; staffed by Conventual Franciscan Fathers. Address: 315 Clay St., Carey, O. 43316.

• National Shrine of Our Lady of Lebanon, North Jackson (1965); St. Maron diocese (Brooklyn). Address: 2759 N. Lipkey Rd., N. Jackson, O. 44451.

• Our Lady of Czestochowa, Garfield Heights (1939); Sisters of St. Joseph, Third Order of St. Francis. Address: 12215 Granger Rd., Garfield Hts., O. 44125.

• Our Lady of Fatima, Ironton (1954); Watterson Council of Knights of Columbus. Address: P.O. Box, 112, Ironton, O. 45638.

• Our Lady Queen of the Most Holy Rosary, Parma Heights (1936); Sisters of the Incarnate Word. Address: 6618 Pearl Rd., Parma Hts., O. 44130.

• St. Anthony Shrine, Cincinnati (1888); Franciscan Friars, St. John Baptist Province. Address: 5000 Colerain Ave., Cincinnati, O. 45223.

• Shrine of the Holy Relics, Maria Stein (1892); Sisters of the Precious Blood. Address: 2291 St. John's Rd., Maria Stein, O. 45860.

• Sorrowful Mother Shrine, Bellevue (1850); Society of the Precious Blood. Address: 4106 State Rt. 269, Bellevue, O. 44811.

Oklahoma: National Shrine of the Infant Jesus of Prague, Prague (1949); Oklahoma City Archdiocese. Address: P.O. Box 488, Prague, Okla. 74864.

Oregon: The Grotto (National Sanctuary of Our Sorrowful Mother), Portland (1924); Servite Friars. Address: P.O. Box 20008, Portland, Ore. 97220.

Pennsylvania: Basilica of the Sacred Heart of Jesus (1741; present church, 1787); Minor Basilica; Harrisburg Diocese. Address: 30 Basilica Dr., Hanover, Pa. 17331.

• National Shrine Center of Our Lady of Guadalupe, Mother of the Americas, Allentown (1974); located in Immaculate Conception Church; Allentown Diocese. Address: 501 Ridge Ave., Allentown, Pa. 18102.

• National Shrine of Our Lady of Czestochowa (1955); Order of St. Paul the Hermit (Pauline Fathers). Address: P.O. Box 151, Doylestown, Pa. 18901.

• National Shrine of St. John Neumann, Philadelphia (1860); Redemptorist Fathers, St. Peter's Church. Address: 1019 N. 5th St., Philadelphia, Pa. 19123.

• National Shrine of the Sacred Heart, Harleigh (1975); Scranton Diocese. Address: P.O. Box 500, Harleigh, Pa. 18225.

• Old St. Joseph's National Shrine, a unit of the Independence National Historical Park, Philadelphia (1733); Philadelphia Archdiocese (Parish Church). Address: 321 Willings Alley, Philadelphia, Pa. 19106.

• St. Ann's Monastery Shrine, Scranton (1902); Passionist Community. Address: 1230 St. Ann's St., Scranton, Pa. 18504.

• St. Anthony's Chapel, Pittsburgh (1883); Pittsburgh Diocese; St. Anthony's Chapel Committee. Address: 1700 Harpster St., Pittsburgh, Pa. 15212.

• Shrine of St. Walburga, Greensburg (1974); Sisters of St. Benedict. Address: 1001 Harvey Ave., Greensburg, Pa. 15601.

Texas: Virgen de San Juan del Valle Shrine, San Juan (1949); Brownsville Diocese; staffed by Oblates of Mary Immaculate. Address: P.O. Box 747, San Juan, Tex. 78589.

Vermont: St. Anne's Shrine, Isle La Motte (1666); Burlington Diocese, conducted by Edmundites. Address: West Shore Rd., Isle La Motte, Vt. 05463.

Wisconsin: Holy Hill — Shrine of Mary, Help of Christians (1857); Discalced Carmelite Fathers. Address: 1525 Carmel Rd., Hubertus, Wis. 53033.

• National Shrine of St. Joseph, De Pere (1889); Norbertine Fathers. Address: 1016 N. Broadway, De Pere, Wis. 54115.

HONORS AND AWARDS

PONTIFICAL ORDERS

The Pontifical Orders of Knighthood are secular orders of merit whose membership depends directly on the pope. Details regarding the various orders are handled by a special agency in the Secretariat of Briefs, an office in the Papal Secretariat of State.

Supreme Order of Christ (Militia of Our Lord Jesus Christ): The highest of the five pontifical orders of knighthood, the Supreme Order of Christ was approved Mar. 14, 1319, by John XXII as a continuation in Portugal of the suppressed Order of Templars. Members were religious with vows and a rule of life until the order lost its religious character toward the end of the 15th century. Since that time it has existed as an order of merit. Paul VI, in 1966, restricted awards of the order to Christian heads of state.

Order of the Golden Spur (Golden Militia): Although the original founder is not certainly known, this order is one of the oldest knighthoods. Indiscriminate bestowal and inheritance diminished its prestige, however, and in 1841 Gregory XVI replaced it with the Order of St. Sylvester and gave it the title of Golden Militia. In 1905 St. Pius X restored the Order of the Golden Spur in its own right, separating it from the Order of St. Sylvester. Paul VI, in 1966, restricted awards of the order to Christian heads of state.

Order of Pius IX: Founded by Pius IX June 17, 1847, the order is awarded for outstanding services for the Church and society, and may be given to non-Catholics as well as Catholics. The title to nobility formerly attached to membership was abolished by Pius XII in 1939. In 1957 Pius XII instituted the Class of the Grand Collar as the highest category of the order; in 1966, Paul VI restricted this award to heads of state "in solemn circumstances." The other three classes are of Knights of the Grand Cross, Knight Commanders with and without emblem, and Knights. The new class was created to avoid difficulties in presenting papal honors to Christian or non-Christian leaders of high merit.

Order of St. Gregory the Great: First established by Gregory XVI in 1831 to honor citizens of the Papal States, the order is conferred on persons who are distinguished for personal character and reputation, and for notable accomplishment. The order has civil and military divisions, and three classes of knights.

Order of St. Sylvester: Instituted Oct. 31, 1841, by Gregory XVI to absorb the Order of the Golden Spur, this order was divided into two by St. Pius X in 1905, one retaining the name of St. Sylvester and the other assuming the title of Golden Militia. Membership consists of three degrees: Knights of the Grand Cross, Knight Commanders with and without emblem, and Knights.

ECCLESIASTICAL ORDER

Equestrian Order of the Holy Sepulchre of Jerusalem: The order traces its origin to Godfrey of Bouillon who instituted it in 1099. It took its name from the Basilica of the Holy Sepulchre where its members were knighted. After the fall of the Latin Kingdom of Jerusalem and the consequent departure of the knights from the Holy Land, national divisions were established in various countries.

The order was reorganized by Pius IX in 1847 when he reestablished the Latin Patriarchate of Jerusalem and placed the order under the jurisdiction of its patriarch. In 1888, Leo XIII confirmed permission to admit women — Ladies of the Holy Sepulchre — to all degrees of rank. Pius X reserved the office of grand master to himself in 1907; Pius XII gave the order a cardinal patron in 1940 and, in 1949, transferred the office of grand master from the pope to the cardinal patron. Pope John XXIII approved updated constitutions in 1962; the latest statutes were approved by Paul VI in 1977.

The purposes of the order are strictly religious and charitable. Members are committed to sustain and aid the charitable, cultural and social works of the Catholic Church in the Holy Land, particularly in the Latin Patriarchate of Jerusalem.

The order is composed of knights and ladies grouped in three classes: class of Knights of the Collar and Ladies of the Collar; Class of Knights (in four grades); Class of Ladies (in four grades). Members are appointed by the cardinal grand master according to procedures outlined in the constitution.

Under the present constitution, the order is divided into national lieutenancies, largely autonomous, with international headquarters in Rome. Cardinal Maximilien de Furstenberg is the grand master of the order; the official church in Rome, given to the order in 1945 by Pius XII, is S. Onofrio on the Janiculum Hill.

There are five lieutenancies of the order in the United States and one in Puerto Rico.

ORDER OF MALTA

The Sovereign Military Hospitaller Order of St. John of Jerusalem of Rhodes and of Malta traces its origin to a group of men who maintained a Christian hospital in the Holy Land in the 11th century. The group was approved as a religious order — the Hospitallers of St. John — by Paschal II in 1113.

The order, while continuing its service to the poor, principally in hospital work, assumed military duties in the twelfth century and included knights, chaplains and sergeants-at-arms among its members. All the knights were professed monks with the vows of poverty, chastity and obedience. Headquarters were located in the Holy Land until the last decade of the 13th century and on Rhodes after 1308 (whence the title, Knights of Rhodes).

After establishing itself on Rhodes, the order became a sovereign power like the sea republics of Italy and the Hanseatic cities of Germany, flying its own flag, coining its own money, floating its own navy, and maintaining diplomatic relations with many nations.

The order was forced to abandon Rhodes in 1522 after the third siege of the island by the Turks under Sultan Suliman I. Eight years later, the Knights were given the island of Malta, where they remained as a bastion of Christianity until near the end of the 18th century. Headquarters have been located in Rome since 1834.

The title of Grand Master of the Order, in abeyance for some time, was restored by Leo XIII in 1879. A more precise definition of both the religious and the sovereign status of the order was embodied in a new constitution of 1961 and a code issued in 1966.

Religious aspects of the order are subject to regulation by the Holy See. At the same time the sovereignty of the order, which is based on international law, is recognized by the Holy See and by 43 countries with which full diplomatic relations are maintained.

The four main classifications of members are: Knights of Justice, who are religious with the vows of poverty, chastity and obedience; Knights of Obedience, who make a solemn promise to strive for Christian perfection; Knights of Honor and Devotion and of Grace and Devotion — all of noble lineage; and Knights of Magistral Grace. There are also chaplains, Dames and Donats of the order.

The order, with five grand priories, three sub-priories and 38 national associations, is devoted to hospital and charitable work of all kinds in some 77 countries.

The Grand Master, who is the head of the order, has the title of Most Eminent Highness with the rank of Cardinal. He must be of noble lineage and under solemn vows for a minimum period of 10 years, if under 50.

The present Grand Master is Fra' Angelo de Mojana di Cologna, a lawyer of Milan, who was elected for life May 8, 1962, by the Council of State.

The address of headquarters of the order is Via Condotti, 68, Palazzo Malta, 00187 Roma, Italia.

PAPAL MEDALS

Pro Ecclesia et Pontifice: This decoration ("For the Church and the Pontiff") had its origin in 1888 as a token of the golden sacerdotal jubilee of Leo XIII; he bestowed it on those who had assisted in the observance of his jubilee and on persons responsible for the success of the Vatican Exposition. The medal, cruciform in shape, bears the likenesses of Sts. Peter and Paul, the tiara and the papal keys, the words *Pro Ecclesia et Pontifice,* and the name of the present pontiff, all on the same side; it is attached to a ribbon of yellow and white, the papal colors. Originally, the medal was issued in gold, silver or bronze. It is awarded in recognition of service to the Church and the papacy.

Benemerenti: Several medals ("To a well-deserving person") have been conferred by popes for exceptional accomplishment and service. The medals, which are made of gold, silver or bronze, bear the likeness and name of the reigning pope on one side; on the other, a laurel crown and the letter "B."

These two medals may be given by the pope to both men and women. Their bestowal does not convey any title or honor of knighthood.

AMERICAN CATHOLIC AWARDS

Aquinas Medal, by the American Catholic Philosophical Association for outstanding contributions to the field of Catholic philosophy. Jean T. Oesterle (1984).

Bellarmine Medal (1955), by Bellarmine College (Louisville, Ky.), to persons in national or international affairs who, in controversial matters, exemplify the characteristics of St. Robert Bellarmine in charity, justice and temperateness. Ambassador Philip C. Habib (1984).

Berakah Award (1976), by the North American Academy of the Liturgy, to recognize distinguished contribution to the professional work of liturgy by a liturgist or person of an allied vocation. Gerard S. Sloyan (1986).

Borromeo Award (1960), by Carroll College (Helena, Mont.), for zeal, courage and devotion in the spirit of St. Charles Borromeo. Sisters of Charity of Leavenworth (1984).

Brent Award (1976), by the Diocese of Arlington, Va., for distinguished service to fellowman. Ambassador Edward L. Rowny (1986).

Campion Award (1955), by the Catholic Book Club for distinguished service in Catholic letters. Walker Percy (1986).

Cardinal Gibbons Medal (1949) by the Alumni Association of The Catholic University of America for distinguished and meritorious service to the Church, the United States or The Catholic University of America. Mildred Jefferson (1985).

Cardinal Spellman Award (1947), by the Catholic Theological Society for outstanding achievement in the field of theology. Raymond E. Brown, S.S. (1971). See John Courtney Murray Award.

Cardinal Wright Award (1979), by the Fellowship of Catholic Scholars to a Catholic adjudged to have done an outstanding service for the Church. Herbert Ratner, M.D. (1985).

The Catholic University of America Patronal Medal (1974), by the University in cooperation with the National Shrine of the Immaculate Conception for outstanding contributions to the Catholic Church and in promoting interest and devotion to Mary, patroness of the University. Rev. Joseph A. Fitzmyer, S.J. (1985).

Cecilia Medal (1952), by the Music Department

of Boys Town (Nebr.) for outstanding work in liturgical music. Evelyn Letter (1980).

Christian Culture Award (1941), by Assumption University (Canada) to outstanding lay exponents of Christian ideals. Douglas Roche (1986).

College of New Rochelle Pope John XXIII Award (1963), by College of New Rochelle (N.Y.) to those whose lives are witnesses "to the centrality of human dignity in the creation of peace." Sisters Mary Collins, O.S.B., M. Patrice Murphy, S.C., Marie Augusta Neal, S.N.D. deN., Elaine Roulet, C.S.J., Mary Luke Tobin, S.L. (1985).

Collegian Award (1949), by "The Collegian," weekly student newspaper of La Salle College (Phila.), for public service in the field of communications. Lawrence M. O'Rourke (1978).

Compostela Award, The (1982), by the Cathedral-Basilica of St. James (Diocese of Brooklyn) to men and women whose lives represent the noblest ideals of the cathedral tradition of fidelity to justice, truth, beauty and peace. Jacques D'Amboise, Dr. Helen Caldicott, Bishop Thomas Gumbleton, Louise Nevelson (1986).

Damien-Dutton Award (1953), by the Damien-Dutton Society for service toward conquest of leprosy or for the promotion of better understanding of social problems connected with the disease. Samuel Butcher (1986).

Edith Stein Award (1955), by the Edith Stein Guild for service toward better understanding between Christians and Jews. Dr. Eugene Fisher (1983).

Emmanuel D'Alzon Medal (1954), by Assumptionists to persons exemplifying the ideals of their founder. Mother Helene-Marie Bories, S.A., and Cardinal Johannes Willebrands (1980).

Father McKenna Award (1950), by the national headquarters of the Holy Name Society, for outstanding service to the society's ideals. Rev. John Morley (1981).

Fidelitas Medal (1949), by Orchard Lake Schools (Sts. Cyril and Methodius Seminary, St. Mary's College, St. Mary's Preparatory), to an outstanding American Catholic of Polish descent for fidelity in serving God and country. Congressman Dan Rostenkowski (1986).

Franciscan International Award (1958), by the Conventual Franciscans (Prior Lake, Minn.) for outstanding contributions to the development of life. Wilko B. Schoenbohm (1986).

George M. Cohan Award (1970), by the Catholic Actors Guild of America, Inc., for outstanding contribution to Church and the arts. Dina Merrill and Cliff Robertson (1985).

Good Samaritan Award (1968), by the National Catholic Development Conference to recognize the concern for one's fellowman exemplified by the Good Samaritan. Rev. Marvin A. Mottet (1985).

Hoey Awards (1942), by the Catholic Interracial Council of New York, to persons who have worked to promote social and interracial justice. Thomas W. Gleason, Sr., Rosetta LeNoire, Joseph Papp, Edwin R. Werner (1985).

Honor et Veritas Award (1959), by the Catholic War Veterans to outstanding Americans. Congressman Joseph G. Minish (1984).

Howard R. Marraro Prize (1973), by the American Catholic Historical Association for a book on Italian history or Italo-American history or relations. David Herlihy and Christiane Klapisch-Zuber (1985).

Insignis Medal (1951), by Fordham University for extraordinary distinction in the service of God and humanity. Harold Mulqueen, S.J., Jack F. Haggerty, Esq. (1984).

John Courtney Murray Award (1972), by the Catholic Theological Society for distinguished achievement in theology. Originated in 1947 as the Cardinal Spellman Award. Gregory Baum (1986).

John Gilmary Shea Prize (1944), by the American Catholic Historical Association for scholarly works on the history of the Catholic Church broadly considered. Eugene Franklin Rice, Jr. (1985).

John La Farge Memorial Award for Interracial Justice (1965), by the Catholic Interracial Council of New York. Presented annually to leading citizens of the community regardless of race, color or creed for promoting social and interracial justice. Stanley Hill, Bruce Ritter, O.F.M. Conv., Vincent Tese (1986).

King Award (1971), by the U.S. Catholic Historical Society for significant contribution in the study of the history of the Catholic Church in the U.S. Elisa A. Carrillo (1976).

Laetare Medal (1883), by the University of Notre Dame for distinguished accomplishment for Church or nation by an American Catholic. Thomas and Mary Elizabeth Carney (1986).

Lumen Christi Award (1978) by the Catholic Church Extension Society to persons making an outstanding contribution in service to the American home missions. Ethel J. Williams (1986).

The Manhattan College De La Salle Medal, by Manhattan College, for significant contribution to the moral, cultural and educational life of the nation. J. Richard Munro (1986).

Marianist Award (1949), by the University of Dayton for outstanding service in America to the Mother of God (until 1966); for outstanding contributions to mankind (from 1967); for outstanding scholarship by a Roman Catholic (from 1986). Msgr. John Tracy Ellis (1986).

Marian Library Medal (1953), by the Marian Library of the University of Dayton. Awarded annually (until 1967) to encourage books in English on the Blessed Virgin Mary. Awarded every four years (from 1971), at the time of an International Mariological Congress, to a scholar for Mariological studies. Stefano De Fiores, S.M.M. (1983).

Mater et Magistra Award (1963), by the College of Mt. St. Joseph on the Ohio to women for social action in the pattern and spirit of the encyclical *Mater et Magistra.* Mother Teresa (1974).

Mendel Medal (1928), by Villanova University for scientists. Dr. Alfred M. Bongiovanni (1968).

Msgr. John P. Monaghan Social Action Award by the Assn. of Catholic Trade Unionists; originally (1948), the Quadragesimo Anno Medal. Vincent McDonnell (1970).

The O'Neil D'Amour Award (1976), by the National Association of Boards of Education/NCEA,

for outstanding contribution of statewide, regional. national or international significance to the
Catholic board movement. Mary Angela Harper
(1986).

O'Reilly-Conway Medal (1979), by *The Pilot*,
Boston archdiocesan newspaper, for distinctive
contributions to journalism. Timothy Johnson,
M.D. (1985).

Paulist Award for Lay Evangelization (1979), by
the Paulist Fathers to Catholic laity for significant
contribution in ministry of evangelizing inactive
Catholics and the unchurched in the U.S. Gertrude
Morris (1986).

Pax Christi Award (1963), by St. John's University (Collegeville, Minn.), to honor persons of
strong faith whose lives exemplify the importance
of spiritual values and concern for the welfare of
others. Sr. Emmanuel Renner, O.S.B. (1986).

Peace Award (1950), by the Secular Franciscan
Order. Pres. Anwar Sadat (1980).

Peter Guilday Prize (1972), by the American
Catholic Historical Association for articles accepted by the editors of the *Catholic Historical Review* which are the first scholarly publications of
their authors. Vincent J. McNally (1980).

Pius XII Marian Award (1955), by the Montfort
Missionaries for promotion of the devotion of consecration to the Immaculate Heart of Mary. Mr.
and Mrs. Thomas F. Larkin, Jr. (1973).

Poverello Medal (1949), by The University of
Steubenville (Ohio), "in recognition of great bene-
factions to humanity, exemplifying in our age the
Christ-like spirit of charity which filled the life of
St. Francis of Assisi." James D. Lynch, S.F.O.
(1986).

Regina Medal (1959), by the Catholic Library
Association for outstanding contributions to children's literature. Lloyd Alexander (1986).

Role of Law Award (1973), by the Canon Law Society of America, to recognize a canon lawyer who
embodies a pastoral attitude and is committed to
research and study. Rev. John E. Lynch, C.S.P.
(1984).

**St. Bonaventure University Justice and Peace
Medal** (1981), by St. Bonaventure University (St.
Bonaventure, N.Y.). Sister Joan Malone, O.S.F.
(1983).

St. Francis de Sales Award (1958), by the Catholic Press Association for distinguished contribution to Catholic journalism. Moises Sandoval
(1986).

St. Francis Xavier Medal (1954), by Xavier University (Cincinnati) to persons exemplifying the
spirit of St. Francis Xavier. Msgr. John Tracy Ellis (1984).

St. Vincent de Paul Medal (1948), by St. John's
University (Jamaica, N.Y.), for outstanding service to Catholic charities. Joseph Sciame (1984).

Serra Award of the Americas (1947), by the
Academy of American Franciscan History for ser-
vice to Inter-American good will. Miguel Leon-
Portilla (1978).

Signum Fidei Medal (1942), by the Alumni Association of La Salle University (Phila.) for noteworthy contributions to the advancement of hu-

manitarian principles in keeping with Christian
tradition. Linda O'Donnell (1986).

Soteriological Award (1967), by the Confraternity of the Passion (Third Order of the Passionists,
Corpus Christi Residence, 80 David St., South River, N.J. 08882), for outstanding exemplification of
sharing in the Passion of Christ in contemporary
society. Doris Froelich (1984), Rev. Jude Meade,
C.P. (1985).

Sword of Loyola (1964), by Loyola University of
Chicago to person or persons exemplifying Ig-
natius of Loyola's courage, dedication and service.
Danny Thomas (1985).

U.S. Catholic Award (1978), by editors of *U.S.
Catholic* magazine for furthering the cause of
women in the Church. Sister Mary Luke Tobin,
S.L. (1986).

Vercelli Medal (1947), by the Holy Name Society for distinguished service to ideals of the society.
J. Earl Knott, Jr. (1980).

1986 CPA AWARDS

Catholic Press Association Awards for material
published in 1985 were presented during the 75th
anniversary CPA convention held June 4-7, 1986, in
Columbus, Ohio. Some of the awards are listed
below.

Newspapers — General Excellence

National Newspapers: *National Catholic Reporter* (first place); *Our Sunday Visitor* (second place); *National Catholic Register* (third
place).

Diocesan Newspapers, to 17,000 circulation:
Catholic Spirit, Austin, Tex. (first place);
Horizons, Parma, O. (second); *The Catholic
Observer,* Springfield, Mass. (third).

Diocesan Newspapers, 17,001 to 40,000 circula-
tion: *The Catholic Free Press,* Worcester,
Mass. (first place), *The Florida Catholic,* Orlan-
do, Fla. (second), *The Compass,* Green Bay,
Wis., and *The Sooner Catholic,* Oklahoma City,
Okla. (third, tie).

Diocesan Newspapers, 40,001 and over:
Courier-Journal, Rochester, N.Y. (first place);
The Voice, Miami, Fla. (second); *Catholic Tel-
egraph,* Cincinnati, O. (third).

First, second and third place awards were presented in 18 other categories.

Magazines — General Excellence

General Interest: *U.S. Catholic* (first place);
America (second); *Liguorian* (third).

Mission: *Company* (first place); *Columban
Mission* (second); *Catholic Near East* (third).

Religious Order: *National Jesuit News* (first
place); *The Carmelite Review* (second).

Professional and Special Interest: *U.S. Catholic Historian* (first place); *Catholic Rural Life*
and *Church* (second, tie).

Magazines for Clergy and Religious: *Chicago
Studies* (first place); *The Priest* (second).

Scholarly: *Thought* (first place); *Horizons*
(second).

Devotional/Inspirational: *Spiritual Life* (first

place); *Queen* (second); *Spirit and Life* and *God's Word Today* (third, tie).

Newsletters, General Interest: *U.S. Parish* (first place), *Catholic Update* (second); *Youth Update* (third).

Newsletters, Special Interest: *Origins* (first place); *Medical Mission Sisters News* (second); *Missionaries of Africa Report* (third).

First, second and third place awards were presented in 14 other categories.

Spanish-Language Awards

General Excellence: *La Voz*, Miami, Fla. (first place); *El Mensajero Catolico*, Milwaukee, Wis., *Revista Maryknoll*, Maryknoll, N.Y., and *Ecos Cristoforos*, New York, N.Y. (second, tie); *Nuevo Amanecer*, Brooklyn, N.Y. (third).

Books — First Place Awards

Children (up to age 12): Winston-Derek Publishers, Nashville, Tenn., *Back-Back and Lima Bear*, by Thomas L. Weck.

Youth (age 12 and over): First place tie: Paulist Press, Mahwah, N.J., *Hang Toughf*, by Matthew Lancaster, and Catholic Bulletin Press, Milwaukee, Wis., *Going All Out: An Invitation to Belong*, by Bishop Robert J. Carlson.

Adult: Orbis Books, Maryknoll, N.Y., *Spirituality and Justice*, by Donal Dorr.

Professional and Educational: Paulist Press, Mahwah, N.J., *The Code of Canon Law*, edited by James A. Coriden, Thomas H. Green, Donald E. Heintschel.

Quality of Design and Production: Loyola University Press, Chicago, Ill.; *The Art of G.K. Chesterton*, by Alzina Stone Dale.

1986 CHRISTOPHER AWARDS

Christopher Awards are given each year to recognize the creative writers, producers and directors who have achieved artistic excellence in films, books and television specials affirming the highest values of the human spirit.

The 1986 awards were presented Feb. 27, 1986, in New York.

Books for Adults: *The City of Joy*, by Dominique Lapierre, tr. Kathryn Spink. *Healing from the War: Trauma and Transformation after Vietnam*, by Arthur Egendorf; *My Quest for Beauty*, by Rollo May; *Pope John XXIII: Shepherd of the Modern World*, by Peter Hebblethwaite; *Such a Vision of the Street: Mother Teresa — The Spirit and the Work*, by Eileen Egan.

Books for Young People: *The Patchwork Quilt*, by Valerie Flournoy; *Sara, Plain and Tall*, by Patricia MacLachlan; *Promise Not to Tell*, by Carolyn Polese; *Underdog*, by Marilyn Sachs; *The Mount Rushmore Story*, by Judith St. George.

Films: Producers, directors and writers of: "The Color Purple" (Warner Bros.); "Marie" (MGM); "The Official Story" (Almi Pictures, Inc.); "Shoah" (New Yorker Films).

Television Specials: Producers, directors and writers of: "The Fire Unleashed" (ABC News Closeup); "Do You Remember Love?" (CBS); "The Living Planet — A Portrait of the Earth" (BBC/Time-Life/ PBS/WGBH); "Love Is Never Silent" (NBC); "A Time to Live" (NBC); "Out of the Darkness" (CBS); "Wallenberg — A Hero's Story" (NBC).

Special Award: "We Are the World," the best-selling recording that helped bring world hunger into focus.

DEATHS SEPTEMBER 1985 TO SEPTEMBER 1986

Benincasa, Bishop Pius A., 73, Aug. 12, 1986, Buffalo, N.Y.; auxiliary bishop of Buffalo from 1964; served (1954-64) in the Vatican Secretariat of State.

Boyle, Sister Cornelia, O.S.B., 72, Feb. 26, 1986, Elizabeth, N.J.; educator, prioress.

Cagney, James, 86, Mar. 30, 1986, Dutchess County, N.Y.; Academy Award-winning film star.

Casey, Archbishop James V., 71, Mar. 14, 1986, Denver, Colo.; archbishop of Denver from 1967.

Clinchy, Everett R., 89, Jan. 22, 1986, Guilford, Conn.; Presbyterian minister, a founder and former president of the National Conference of Christians and Jews.

Confalonieri, Cardinal Carlo, 93, Aug. 1, 1986, Rome, Italy; dean of the College of Cardinals; headed the Congregation for Bishops, 1965 to 1973.

Connolly, Bishop James L., 91, Sept. 12, 1986, Fall River, Mass.; retired (1970) bishop of Fall River.

Crowley, Jim, 83, Jan. 15, 1986, Scranton, Pa.; last of the famed Four Horsemen of Notre Dame football of the 1920s.

Dazzi, Bernard, O.F.M., 67, Dec. 31, 1985, Mount

Vernon, N.Y.; founder of the Franciscan Mission Associates a mission aid association.

Doherty, Catherine de Hueck, 89, Dec. 18, 1985. Combermere, Ont., Canada; Russian-born foundress of Friendship Houses for interracial justice and Madonna Houses for social service; author.

Donoghue, John D., 77, July 29, 1986, Burlington, Vt.; journalist, music critic.

Dougherty, Bishop John J., 78, Mar. 20, 1986, Teaneck, N.J.; retired (1982) auxiliary bishop of Newark.

Downey, Morton, 83, Oct. 25, 1985, Palm Beach, Fla.; popular Irish tenor, composer.

Dozier, Bishop Carroll T., 74, Dec. 7, 1985, Memphis, Tenn.; retired (1982) first bishop of Memphis.

Etteldorf, Archbishop Raymond P., 74, Mar. 15, 1986, Dubuque, Ia.; retired (1985) longtime Vatican diplomat.

Fabian, Bishop Arpad, 59, May 15, 1986, Szombathely, Hungary; bishop of Szombathely from 1975.

Flores, Archbishop Felixberto C., 64, Oct. 25, 1985, San Francisco, Calif.; archbishop of Agana,

Guam; first native of Micronesia ordained a bishop (1970).

Florit, Cardinal Ermenegildo, 84, Dec. 8, 1985, Florence, Italy; doctrinal expert at the Second Vatican Council; retired archbishop of Florence.

Groppi, James E., 54, Nov. 4, 1985, Milwaukee, Wis.; former priest; gained national attention in the 1960s as an inner city priest-leader of protest marches for civil rights causes.

Handschiegel, Bro. Arsenius, C.M.M., 87, Feb. 16, 1986, Dearborn Heights, Mich.; spent almost 50 years on the road as a promoter of *Leaves,* the magazine of the Mariannhill Missionaries.

Hartke, Gilbert V., O.P., 79, Feb. 21, 1986, Washington, D.C.; founder and chairman (for almost 40 years) of the drama department of The Catholic University.

Hill, Morton A., S.J., 68, Nov. 4, 1985, New York, N.Y.; anti-pornography crusader; founder (1968) of Morality in Media, a national anti-obscenity campaign.

Hofstee, Leo Anthony, O.P., 82, Apr. 26, 1986, Philippines; missionary among lepers of the Tala Leprosarium outside Manila from 1947.

Hugo, Father John J., 74, Oct. 1, 1985, Pittsburgh, Pa.; widely known in the 1940s for his promotion of silent retreats and support groups for priests; author.

Johnson, Harvey J., 61, Feb. 7, 1986, St. Louis, Mo.; editor of the *Social Justice Review* from 1962.

Johnson, Bishop William R., 67, July 28, 1986, Orange, Calif.; first bishop of Orange, from 1976.

Kashmitter, William A., M.M., 87, Aug. 6, 1986, North Tarrytown, N.Y.; former missionary in the Far East; a founder of the Research Center for International Justice at Louvain, Belgium.

Kellenberg, Bishop Walter P., 74, Jan. 11, 1986, Rockville Centre, N.Y.; retired (1974) first bishop of Rockville Centre.

Koenigsknecht, Msgr. Albert I., M.M., 68, Peru; missionary; apostolic administrator (from 1973) of Juli prelature, Peru.

Lekai, Cardinal Laszlo, 76, June 30, 1986, Esztergom, Hungary; archbishop of Esztergom and primate of Hungary; named cardinal in 1976.

Lavery, Charles J., C.S.B., 70, Dec. 3, 1985, Rochester, N.Y.; president of St. John Fisher College, Rochester, 1958-80.

Lavery, Emmet, 84, Jan. 1, 1986, Tarzana, Calif.; screen writer, playwright.

Little, Msgr. Thomas F., 74, Aug. 3, 1986, San Diego, Calif.; headed the Catholic film-rating office (known as the Legion of Decency in its earlier years), 1943-66.

Maris, Roger E., 51, Dec. 14, 1985, Houston, Tex.; baseball player; his 61 home runs in the 1961 season with the New York Yankees broke Babe Ruth's record.

Marquard, Philip, O.F.M., 73, Apr. 20, 1986, Chicago, Ill.; former director of the Franciscan Herald Press; longtime spiritual assistant and promoter of the Secular Franciscan Order.

Mary Aquinas, Sister, O.S.F., 91, Oct. 20, 1985, Manitowoc, Wis.; famed as a pilot and aero-

nautical instructor; subject of a TV play (1951); inspiration for "The Flying Nun" TV series.

Metzger, Bishop Sidney M., 83, Apr. 12, 1986, El Paso, Tex.; retired (1978) bishop of El Paso; supporter of the rights of farm and factory workers.

Miranda y Gomez, Cardinal Miguel Dario, 90, Mar. 15, 1986, Mexico City, Mexico; retired (1977) archbishop of Mexico City; named cardinal, 1969.

Moran, Patrick R., 60, Jan. 28, 1986, Huntington, Ind.; editor, staff member of *Our Sunday Visitor* for 34 years.

Nevin, John ("Jake"), 75, Dec. 9, 1985, Bryn Mawr, Pa.; athletic trainer of Villanova Univ. for more than 50 years.

O'Donnell, Edward J., S.J., 77, June 30, 1986, Milwaukee, Wis.; former president of Marquette University.

Poma, Cardinal Antonio, 75, Sept. 25, 1985, Bologna, Italy; retired (1983) archbishop of Bologna.

Ring, William, 82, Sept. 21, 1985, Silver Spring, Md.; former news editor of NC News Service.

Red Elk, Steven, 68, Feb. 21, 1986, Manderson, S.D.; first Native American ordained a permanent deacon in U.S.

Romaniello, Msgr. John, M.M., 85, Oct. 22, 1985, Maryknoll, N.Y.; missionary; relief worker; known as the "Noodle Priest" because of noodle factories he built in Hong Kong and Mississippi.

Roy, Cardinal Maurice, 80, Oct. 24, 1985, Quebec, Canada; retired (1971) archbishop and primate of Canada; headed the Justice and Peace Commission and the Laity Council of the Roman Curia.

Schroeder, William, Aug. 6, 1986, Louisville, Ky.; world's second permanent artificial heart recipient; survived 620 days.

Smith, Kathryn (Kate), 79, June 17, 1986, Raleigh, N.C.; popular radio-TV singer; "God Bless America," her trademark; became a Catholic in 1965.

Tarasevitch, Bishop Vladimir, O.S.B., 64, Jan. 2, 1986, Chicago, Ill.; apostolic visitator for Byelorussian Catholics outside the U.S.S.R.

Tuite, Sister Marjorie, O.P., 63, June 28, 1986, New York, N.Y.; social justice activist; advocate of women's rights.

Veeck, William (Bill), 71, Jan. 2, 1986, Chicago, Ill.; baseball owner; promoter; became a Catholic in 1949.

Welch, Msgr. David P., 60, June 17, 1986, Springfield, Mass.; editor of the Springfield diocesan paper from 1969.

Welzbacher, Robert, 70, Mar. 10, 1986, Belleville, Ill.; former managing editor of the Belleville diocesan paper.

Wynne, Gerard R., 55, Mar. 29, 1986, Washington, D.C.; director of the U.S.C.C. Migration and Refugee Program Office.

Yuan, Paul, S.V.D., 75, Jan. 14, 1985, in prison in China (news of his death reached his order in November, 1985); Chinese priest; had spent 24 years in prison.

Zdebskis, Father Juozas, 56, Feb. 6, 1986, Lithuania, in an automobile accident; Lithuanian religious rights activist.